THE SIXTEENTH MENTAL
MEASUREMENTS YEARBOOK

EARLIER PUBLICATIONS IN THIS SERIES

THE SIXTEENTH MENTAL MEASUREMENTS YEARBOOK

ROBERT A. SPIES

and

BARBARA S. PLAKE

Editors

LINDA L. MURPHY
Managing Editor

The Buros Institute of Mental Measurements
The University of Nebraska-Lincoln
Lincoln, Nebraska

2005
Distributed by The University of Nebraska Press

LC 39-3422
ISBN 910674-58-2

Manufactured in the United States of America.

The paper used in this publication meets the minimum requirements of American National Standard for Information Sciences—Permanence of Paper for Printed Library Materials, ANSI Z39.48-1984.

Note to Users

TABLE OF CONTENTS

Page

111845

INTRODUCTION

Over 65 years ago, Oscar K. Buros (1905-1978) created the *Mental Measurements Yearbook* series in the belief that tests, like any consumer product, should be subject to critical evaluation and independent review. In order to assist in the monumental effort of evaluating large numbers of new and revised tests, Buros turned to a growing community of professionals and scholars skilled in test evaluation. Recognizing the historic importance of this effort to improve the quality of overall testing, many accomplished individuals came forward to share their expertise in *The 1938 Mental Measurements Yearbook*.

The willingness to make a professional contribution within the field of testing and to serve a larger public interest continues to this day. During the past 20 years, the Buros Institute has published over 5,000 test reviews from skilled analysts of many different interests, backgrounds, and professional training programs. The consideration shown by these individuals in service to the long-standing goal of improving the science and practice of testing is very much appreciated.

Based on the recommendations of our National Advisory Committee, the Buros Institute will begin recognizing many of the long-standing reviewers to the MMY series. Individuals who have contributed to six or more publications, beginning in 1985 with *The Ninth Mental Measurements Yearbook*, will be designated as "Distinguished Reviewers" for their enduring service to the field of testing and measurement. A listing of these reviewers is referenced on page 1199 of this edition.

THE SIXTEENTH MENTAL MEASUREMENTS YEARBOOK

The *16th MMY* contains reviews of tests that are new or significantly revised since the publication of the *15th MMY* in 2003. Reviews, descriptions, and references associated with many older tests can be located in other Buros publications: previous *MMY*s and *Tests in Print VI*. Criteria for inclusion in this edition of the MMY remain that a test be (a) new or substantively revised since it was last reviewed in the MMY series, (b) commercially available from its publishers, (c) available in the English language, and (d) published with adequate developmental and technical documentation.

Content. The contents of the *16th MMY* include: (a) a bibliography of 283 commercially available tests, new or revised, published as separates for use with English-speaking individuals; (b) 525 critical test reviews from specialists selected by the editors on the basis of their expertise in measurement and, often, the content of the test being reviewed; (c) a test title index with appropriate cross-references; (d) a classified subject index; (e) a publishers directory and index, including publisher addresses and other contact information with test listings by publisher; (f) a name index including the names of authors of all tests, reviews, or references included in this MMY; (g) an index of acronyms for easy reference when only a test acronym is known; and (h) a score index to identify for users test scores of potential interest.

Appendix. Three separate listings appear in the *16th MMY* for users requiring additional information when a specific test cannot be otherwise located in the *Mental Measurements Yearbook* series. Beginning with the *14th MMY* (2001), a test qualifying for review must provide an adequate developmental history and sufficient evidence describing the instrument's technical properties. Not all tests submitted for evaluation meet these two criteria for review in the MMY series. A listing of tests received (but not reviewed) is included to make users aware of the availability of these tests, albeit without supporting documentation or reviews. The Appendix also provides a list of tests that meet review criteria but were received too late for review in this volume. These tests (plus additional tests received in following months) will be reviewed in *The Seventeenth Mental Measurements Yearbook*. Test reviews that are completed prior to publication of the *17th MMY* are available electronically for a small fee on our web-based service Test Reviews Online (http://www.unl.edu/buros). A third list in the Appendix includes titles of tests requested from publishers but not yet received as of this volume's publication. This listing includes tests for which publishers refuse to allow their tests to be reviewed as well as those who routinely make their instruments available for review but who have failed at this point to provide a new or revised test for evaluation.

Organization. The current MMY series is organized like an encyclopedia, with tests being ordered alphabetically by title. If the title of a test is known, the reader can locate the test immediately without having to consult the Index of Titles.

The page headings reflect the encyclopedic organization. The page heading of the left-hand page cites the number and title of the first test listed on that page, and the page heading of the right-hand page cites the number and title of the last test listed on that page. All numbers presented in the various indexes are test numbers, not page numbers. Page

TABLE 1
TESTS BY MAJOR CLASSIFICATIONS

Classification	Number	Percentage
Personality	45	15.9
Vocations	42	14.8
Intelligence and General Aptitude	31	11.0
Behavior Assessment	25	8.8
Reading	22	7.8
English and Language	18	6.4
Mathematics	15	5.3
Neuropsychological	15	5.3
Miscellaneous	14	4.9
Speech and Hearing	13	4.6
Developmental	12	4.2
Achievement	11	3.9
Sensory-Motor	8	2.8
Education	7	2.5
Fine Arts	2	.7
Foreign Languages	2	.7
Science	1	.4
Social Studies	0	.0
Total	283	100.0

TABLE 2
NEW AND REVISED OR SUPPLEMENTED TESTS BY MAJOR CLASSIFICATION

Classification	Number of Tests	Percentage New	Revised
Achievement	11	36.4	63.6
Behavior Assessment	25	52.0	48.0
Developmental	12	66.7	33.3
Education	7	85.7	14.3
English and Language	18	77.8	22.2
Fine Arts	2	50.0	5.0
Foreign Languages	2	100.0	0.0
Intelligence and General Aptitude	31	51.6	48.4
Mathematics	15	80.0	20.0
Miscellaneous	14	85.7	14.3
Neuropsychological	15	93.3	6.7
Personality	45	73.3	26.7
Reading	22	72.7	27.3
Science	1	100.0	0.0
Sensory-Motor	8	62.5	37.5
Social Studies	0	0.0	0.0
Speech and Hearing	13	46.2	53.8
Vocations	42	83.3	16.7
Total	283	70.0	30.0

numbers are important only for the Table of Contents and are located at the bottom of each page.

TESTS AND REVIEWS

The *16th MMY* contains descriptive information on 283 tests as well as test reviews by 336 different authors. Statistics on the number and percentage of tests in each of 18 major classifications are contained in Table 1.

The percentage of new and revised or supplemented tests according to major classifications is contained in Table 2. Overall, 198 of the tests included in the *16th MMY* are new and have not been listed in a previous MMY although some descriptions may have been included in *Tests in Print VI* (TIP VI; 2002). The Index of Titles may be consulted to determine if a test is new or revised.

Test Selection. A new policy for selecting tests for review became effective with the *14th MMY* (2001). This new policy for selecting tests for review requires at least minimal information be available regarding test development. The requirement that tests have such minimal information does not assure the quality of the test; it simply provides reviewers with a minimum basis for critically evaluating the quality of the test. We select our reviewers carefully and let them and well-informed readers decide for themselves about the essential features needed to assure the appropriate use of a test. Some new or revised tests are not included because they were received too late to undergo the review process and still permit timely publication, or because some reviewers did not meet their commitment to review the test. A list of these tests is included in the Appendix and every effort will be made to have them reviewed for *The Seventeenth Mental Measurements Yearbook*, and included before then through our web-based service Test Reviews Online (TROL).

There are some new or revised tests for which there will be no reviews although these tests are described in *Tests in Print VI*. The absence of reviews occurred for a variety of reasons including: We could not identify qualified reviewers, the test materials were incomplete so reviews were not possible, the tests were sufficiently obscure that reviews were deemed unnecessary, the publisher advised us the test is now out-of-print before reviews were completed, or the test did not meet our criterion for documentation. Descriptions of all these tests still in print were published in *TIP VI* and are included in the Test Reviews Online database.

Reviewer Selection. The selection of reviewers was done with great care. The objective was to secure measurement and subject specialists who would be independent and represent a variety of different viewpoints. It was also important to find individuals who would write critical reviews competently, judiciously, fairly, and in a timely manner. Reviewers were identified by means of extensive searches of the professional literature, attendance at professional meetings, and recommendations from leaders in various professional fields. Perusal of reviews in this volume will also reveal that reviewers work in and represent a cross-section of the places in which testing is taught and tests are used: universities, public schools, businesses, and community agencies. These reviewers represent an outstanding array of professional talent, and their contributions are obviously of primary importance in making this Yearbook a valuable resource. A list of the individuals reviewing in this volume is included at the beginning of the Index section.

Readers of test reviews in the *16th MMY* are encouraged to exercise an active, analytical, and evaluative perspective in reading the reviews. Just as one would evaluate a test, the readers should evaluate critically the reviewer's comments about the test. The reviewers selected are competent professionals in their respective fields, but it is inevitable that their reviews also reflect their individual perspectives. The *Mental Measurements Yearbook* series was developed to stimulate critical thinking and assist in the selection of the best available test for a given purpose, not to promote the passive acceptance of reviewer judgment. Active, evaluative reading is the key to the most effective use of the professional expertise offered in each of the reviews.

INDEXES

As mentioned above, the *16th MMY* includes six indexes invaluable as aids to effective use: (a) Index of Titles, (b) Index of Acronyms, (c) Classified Subject Index, (d) Publishers Directory and Index, (e) Index of Names, and (f) Score Index. Additional comment on these indexes is presented below.

Index of Titles. Because the organization of the *16th MMY* is encyclopedic in nature, with the tests ordered alphabetically by title throughout the volume, the test title index does not have to be consulted to find a test if the title is known. However, the title index has some features that make it useful beyond its function as a complete title listing. First, it includes cross-reference information useful for tests with superseded or alternative titles or tests commonly (and sometimes inaccurately) known by multiple titles. Second, it identifies tests that are new or revised. Third, it may cue the user to other tests with similar titles that may be useful. Titles for the 35 tests not reviewed because of insufficient technical documentation are included in the Index of Titles. It is important to keep in mind that the numbers in this index, like those for all MMY indexes, are test numbers and not page numbers.

Because no MMY includes reviews of all tests currently in print, a particular test of interest may not be reviewed in this volume. To learn if a commercially published test has been reviewed in this or an earlier volume of the MMY, users may access the Buros page on the World Wide Web (www.unl.edu/buros). A search on Test Reviews Online (TROL) will indicate if a test has been reviewed and will also indicate the MMY in which the review can be found. TROL also provides electronic access to reviews provided in recent MMYs (most current reviews only) and test reviews that have been finalized since the publication of the most recent MMY. Therefore, TROL provides ready access, for a small fee, to the majority of tests that have been reviewed in *The Mental Measurements Yearbook* series. As an alternative, *Tests in Print VI* can be consulted. This volume provides a cross-reference to reviews of still-in-print tests in the MMY series.

Index of Acronyms. Some tests seem to be better known by their acronyms than by their full titles. The Index of Acronyms can help in these instances; it refers the reader to the full title of the test and to the relevant descriptive information and reviews.

Classified Subject Index. The Classified Subject Index classifies all tests listed in the *16th MMY* into 17 of 18 major categories: Achievement, Behavior Assessment, Developmental, Education, English and Language, Fine Arts, Foreign Languages, Intelligence and General Aptitude, Mathematics, Miscellaneous, Neuropsychological, Personality, Reading, Science, Sensory-Motor, Social Studies, Speech and Hearing, and Vocations. (No tests in the Social Studies category are reviewed in the *16th MMY.*) Each test entry in this index includes test title, population for which the test is intended, and test number. The Classified Subject Index is of great help to readers who seek a listing of tests in given subject areas. The Classified Subject Index represents a starting point for readers who know their area of interest but do not know how to further focus that interest in order to identify the best test(s) for their particular purposes.

Publishers Directory and Index. The Publishers Directory and Index includes the names and addresses of the publishers of all tests included in the *16th MMY* plus a listing of test numbers for each individual publisher. Also included are the telephone, FAX numbers, email, and Web addresses for those publishers who responded to our request for this information. This index can be particularly useful in obtaining addresses for specimen sets or catalogs after the test reviews have been read and evaluated. It can also be useful when a reader knows the publisher of a certain test but is uncertain about the test title, or when a reader is interested in the range of tests published by a given publisher.

Index of Names. The Index of Names provides a comprehensive list of names, indicating authorship of a test, test review, or reviewer's reference.

Score Index. The Score Index is a listing of the scored parts of all tests reviewed in the *16th MMY.* Test titles are sometimes misleading or ambiguous, and test content may be difficult to define with precision. In contrast, test scores often represent operational definitions of the variables the test author is trying to measure, and as such they can define test purpose and content more adequately than other descriptive information. A search for a particular test is most often a search for a test that measures some specific variable(s). Test scores and their associated labels can often be the best definitions of the variable(s) of interest. The Score Index is a detailed subject index based on the most critical operational features of any test—the scores and their associated labels.

HOW TO USE THIS YEARBOOK

A reference work like *The Sixteenth Mental Measurements Yearbook* can be of far greater benefit to a reader if some time is taken to become familiar with what it has to offer and how it might be used most effectively to obtain the information wanted.

Step 1: Read the Introduction to the *16th MMY* in its entirety.

Step 2: Become familiar with the six indexes and particularly with the instructions preceding each index listing.

Step 3: Use the book by looking up needed information. This step is simple if one keeps the following procedures in mind:

1. Go directly to the test entry using the alphabetical page headings if you know the title of the test.

2. Consult the Index of Titles for possible variants of the title or consult the appropriate subject area of the Classified Subject Index for other possible leads or for similar or related tests in the same area, if you do not know, cannot find, or are unsure of the title of a test. (Other uses for both of these indexes were described above.)

3. Consult the Index of Names if you know the author of a test but not the title or publisher. Look up the author's titles until you find the test you want.

4. Consult the Publishers Directory and Index if you know the test publisher but not the title or author. Look up the publisher's titles until you find the test you want.

5. Consult the Score Index and locate the test or tests that include the score variable of interest if you are looking for a test that yields a particular kind of test score.

6. If after following the above steps you are not able to find a review of the test you want, consult the Appendix for a list of tests that are not reviewed. Reasons tests are not reviewed include (a) they did not meet our selection criteria, (b) the reviews were not completed in time for publication in this volume, or (c) the publisher failed to respond in a timely manner to our request for testing materials. You also can look in TIP VI or visit the Buros web page (www.unl.edu/buros) and use the Test Reviews Online service (TROL) to identify the MMY that contains the description and any available reviews for a test of interest.

7. Once you have found the test or tests you are looking for, read the descriptive entries for these tests carefully so that you can take advantage of the information provided. A description of the information in these test entries is presented later in this section.

8. Read the test reviews carefully and analytically, as suggested above. The information and evaluations contained in these reviews are meant to assist test consumers in making well-informed decisions about the choice and applications of tests.

9. Once you have read the descriptive information and test reviews, you may want to contact the publisher to order a specimen set for a particular test so that you can examine it firsthand. The Publishers Directory and Index has the address information needed to obtain specimen sets or catalogs.

Making Effective Use of the Test Entries. The test entries include extensive information. For each test, descriptive information is presented in the following order:

a) TITLES. Test titles are printed in bold-face type. Secondary or series titles are set off from main titles by a colon.

b) PURPOSE. For each test there is a brief, clear statement describing the purpose of the test. Often these statements are quotations from the test manual.

c) POPULATION. This describes the groups for which the test is intended. The grade, chronological age, semester range, or employment category is usually given. For example, "Grades 1.5–2.5, 2–3, 4–12, 13–17" means that there are four

test booklets: a booklet for the middle of first grade through the middle of the second grade, a booklet for the beginning of the second grade through the end of third grade, a booklet for grades 4 through 12 inclusive, and a booklet for undergraduate and graduate students in colleges and universities.

d) PUBLICATION DATE. The inclusive range of publication dates for the various forms, accessories, and editions of a test is reported.

e) ACRONYM. When a test is often referred to by an acronym, the acronym is given in the test entry.

f) SCORES. The number of part scores is presented along with their titles or descriptions of what they are intended to represent or measure.

g) ADMINISTRATION. Individual or group administration is indicated. A test is considered a group test unless it may be administered only individually.

h) FORMS, PARTS, AND LEVELS. All available forms, parts, and levels are listed.

i) MANUAL. Notation is made if no manual is available. All other manual information is included under Price Data.

j) RESTRICTED DISTRIBUTION. This is noted only for tests that are made available to a special market by the publisher. Educational and psychological restrictions are not noted (unless a special training course is required for use).

k) PRICE DATA. Price information is reported for test packages (usually 20 to 35 tests), answer sheets, all other accessories, and specimen sets. The statement "$17.50 per 35 tests" means that all accessories are included unless otherwise indicated by the reporting of separate prices for accessories. The statement also means 35 tests of one level, one edition, or one part unless stated otherwise. Because test prices can change very quickly, the year that the listed test prices were obtained is also given. Foreign currency is assigned the appropriate symbol. When prices are given in foreign dollars, a qualifying symbol is added (e.g., A$16.50 refers to 16 dollars and 50 cents in Australian currency). Along with cost, the publication date and number of pages on which print occurs is reported for manuals and technical reports (e.g., 1999, 102 pages). All types of machine-scorable answer sheets available for use with a specific test are also reported in the descriptive entry. Scoring and reporting services provided by publishers are reported along with information on costs. In a few cases, special computerized scoring and interpretation services are noted at the end of the price information.

l) FOREIGN LANGUAGE AND OTHER SPECIAL EDITIONS. This section concerns foreign language editions published by the same publisher who sells the English-language edition. It also indicates special editions (e.g., Braille, large type) available from the same or a different publisher.

m) TIME. The number of minutes of actual working time allowed examinees and the approximate length of time needed for administering a test are reported whenever obtainable. The latter figure is always enclosed in parentheses. Thus, "50(60) minutes" indicates that the examinees are allowed 50 minutes of working time and that a total of 60 minutes is needed to administer the test. A time of "40–50 minutes" indicates an untimed test that takes approximately 45 minutes to administer, or—in a few instances—a test so timed that working time and administration time are very difficult to disentangle. When the time necessary to administer a test is not reported or suggested in the test materials but has been obtained from a catalog or through correspondence with the test publisher or author, the time is enclosed in brackets.

n) COMMENTS. Some entries contain special notations, such as: "for research use only"; "revision of the ABC Test"; "tests administered monthly at centers throughout the United States"; "subtests available as separates"; and "verbal creativity." A statement such as "verbal creativity" is intended to further describe what the test claims to measure. Some of the test entries include factual statements that imply criticism of the test, such as "1999 test identical with test copyrighted 1980."

o) AUTHOR. For most tests, all authors are reported. In the case of tests that appear in a new form each year, only authors of the most recent forms are listed. Names are reported exactly as printed on test booklets. Names of editors generally are not reported.

p) PUBLISHER. The name of the publisher or distributor is reported for each test. Foreign publishers are identified by listing the country in brackets immediately following the name of the publisher. The Publishers Directory and Index must be consulted for a publisher's address and other contact information.

q) FOREIGN ADAPTATIONS. Revisions and adaptations of tests for foreign use are listed in a separate paragraph following the original edition.

r) SUBLISTINGS. Levels, editions, subtests, or parts of a test available in separate booklets are sometimes presented as sublistings with titles set in small capitals. Sub-sublistings are indented and titles are set in italic type.

s) CROSS REFERENCES. For tests that have been listed previously in a Buros Institute of Mental Measurements publication, a test entry includes—if relevant—a final item containing cross references to the reviews, excerpts, and references for that test in those volumes. In the cross references, "T6:467" refers to test 467 in *Tests in Print VI*, "14:121" refers to test 121 in *The Fourteenth Mental Measurements Yearbook*, "8:1023" refers to test 1023 in *The Eighth Mental Measurements Yearbook*, "T3:144" refers to test 144 in *Tests in Print III*, "7:637" refers to test 637 in *The Seventh Mental Measurements Yearbook*, "P:262" refers to test 262 in *Personality Tests and Reviews*, "2:1427" refers to test 1427 in *The 1940 Yearbook*, and "1:1110" refers to test 1110 in *The 1938 Yearbook*. In the case of batteries and programs, the paragraph also includes cross references—from the battery to the separately listed subtests and vice versa—to entries in this volume and to entries and reviews in earlier Yearbooks. Test numbers not preceded by a colon refer to tests in this Yearbook; for example, "see 45" refers to test 45 in this Yearbook.

ACKNOWLEDGMENTS

The publication of *The Sixteenth Mental Measurements Yearbook* has required the concerted effort and the contributions of many individuals without whom this edition would not have been possible. The editors gratefully acknowledge the talent, expertise, and dedication of all individuals who have assisted in the publication process.

Linda Murphy, Managing Editor, has long been a critical factor to the publication of each new edition of the MMY series. Her attention to detail, good humor, and long-standing commitment to the production of this series makes our job as editors much more agreeable than would otherwise be possible. The wise counsel and historical insights she provides keep us alert to the many errors that might otherwise be made if not for her thoughtful presence. Nor would the publication of this volume be possible without the substantive efforts of our Assistant Editor, Gary Anderson, who balances his ongoing support as webmaster for the Buros Institute's website with his good-natured communications to all of our reviewers. Rosemary Sieck, Clerical Assistant, and Rasma Strautkalns, Institute Secretary, also must be recognized for their important contributions to the success of our efforts. In addition, we would like to cite other members of the Buros Center for Testing, our parent organization, for their support and encouragement during the publication of this edition of the MMY. Former editor James C. Impara, as well as Chad W. Buckendahl, Teresa J. Eckhout, Susan L. Davis, and Janice Nelsen have all made generous contributions to discussions of our current and future directions. We appreciate the efforts of all permanent staff, each of whom contributes more than their share to the development and production of products from the Buros Institute of Mental Measurements.

This volume would not exist without the substantial efforts of test reviewers. We are very grateful to the many reviewers (and especially to those Distinguished Reviewers recognized in this edition) who have prepared test reviews for the Buros Institute of Mental Measurements. Their willingness to take time from busy professional schedules and to share their expertise in the form of thoughtful test reviews is very much appreciated. *The Mental Measurements Yearbook* series would not exist were it not for their efforts.

The work of many graduate students helps make possible the quality of this volume. Their efforts have included writing test descriptions, fact checking reviews, verifying test references, and innumerable other tasks. We thank Brad Merker, M.

Kelly Haack, Alejandro Morales, Anja Roemhild, and Rhonda Turner for their assistance.

Appreciation is also extended to the members of our National Advisory Committee for their willingness to assist in the operation of the Buros Institute of Mental Measurements and for their thought-provoking suggestions for improving the MMY series and other publications of the Institute. During the period in which this volume was prepared the National Advisory Committee has included Jane Close Conoley, Gail Latta, Lawrence Rudner, Milton Hakel, and Jeffrey Smith.

The Buros Institute of Mental Measurements is part of the Department of Educational Psychology of the University of Nebraska-Lincoln. We have benefited from the many departmental colleagues who have contributed to this work. We are also grateful for the contribution of the University of Nebraska Press, which provides expert consultation and serves as distributor of the MMY series.

SUMMARY

The MMY series is an essential resource for individuals seeking information for the evaluation, selection, and use of specific testing instruments. This current edition contains 525 test reviews of 283 different tests. Now available in an electronic version at many university and research libraries and directly from the Buros Institute (www.unl.edu/buros) on a modest fee per review basis, this series has worked to support both knowledgeable professionals and an informed public since 1938.

Our hope is that with the publication of the *16th MMY,* test authors and publishers will consider carefully the comments made by these reviewers and continue to refine and perfect their assessment products.

Robert A. Spies
Barbara S. Plake
June 2005

Tests and Reviews

[1]

Academic Competence Evaluation Scales.

Purpose: "Measures academic skills (reading/language arts, mathematics, critical thinking) as well as academic enablers (motivation, study skills, engagement, interpersonal skills)."

Population: Grades K–12, Grades 6–12, 2- or 4-year college.

Publication Date: 2000.

Acronym: ACES.

Scores, 9: Academic Skills (Reading/Language Arts, Mathematics, Critical Thinking, Total), Academic Enablers (Interpersonal Skills, Motivation, Study Skills, Engagement, Total).

Administration: Group.

Forms, 3: Teacher (Grades K–12), Student (Grades 6–12), College (2- or 4-year college).

Price Data, 2001: $119 per K–12 basic kit including manual, 25 each of student and teacher record forms, boxed; $195 per K–12 complete kit including manual (154 pages), 25 each of student and teacher record forms, scoring assistant (disk or CD-ROM version); $165 per college complete kit including manual, 25 college record forms, scoring assistant (disk or CD-ROM version); $65 per K–12 manual or college manual; $34 per 25 record forms (specify Student, Teacher, or College), quantity discounts available; $91 per scoring assistant software (disk or CD-ROM version).

Time: (10–15) minutes.

Comments: Standardized; indicates confidence intervals for each subscale; allows ranking of scale and subscale scores into one of three competence levels (developing, competent, advanced); Assistant software (version 2.0) scores, monitors change in scores over time, graphs data, generates descriptive reports; system requirements: Windows 95/98/2000/NT 4.0/ME, 32 MB RAM, 100 MHz processor or higher, CD-ROM and 3.5-inch floppy diskette drive (CD-ROM version) or 3.5-diskette drive only (diskette version), 2 MB video card, 800 x 600 resolution, 256 colors, 25 MB free disk space.

Authors: James C. DiPerna and Stephen N. Elliott.

Publisher: PsychCorp, A brand of Harcourt Assessment, Inc.

Review of the Academic Competence Evaluation Scales by RONALD K. HAMBLETON, Distinguished University Professor, School of Education, University of Massachusetts at Amherst, Amherst, MA:

DESCRIPTION. The Academic Competence Evaluation Scales (ACES) was designed (a) to assess the academic functioning of students in Grades K to 12 and college, and (b) to assist in the planning and evaluating of classroom-based interventions for students having academic difficulty. Three forms of the ACES are available-one for teachers, one for Grades 6 to 12 students, and one for college students. The teacher form is designed for use with students in Grades K to 12. For students in Grades 6 to 12, information is collected from a self-report form and from their teachers. For college students, only the self-report form is used.

According to the authors, their intention is to measure the skills, attitudes, and behaviors that have often been identified in the research literature as important for academic success. The authors also describe how the ACES can be used in a five-step problem-solving process with the ACES being the key source of information. First, the teacher completes the ACES. Then, parents become involved in the decision-making process, and for students in Grades 6 to 12, they complete the student form of the ACES. What follows in practice are steps to plan the intervention, implement the intervention, and monitor student progress. Finally, the teacher completes the ACES again and the intervention is evaluated.

The ACES reports a number of scores including three Academic Skills scores (Reading/Language Arts, Mathematics, and Critical Thinking) and a total Academic Skills score, and four Academic Enablers scores (Motivation, Engagement, Interpersonal Skills, and Study Skills) and a total Academic Enablers score. Because of the nature of the teacher rating scale, criterion-referenced information is available and should prove useful in coming up with intervention strategies for students with identified problems. One of the strengths of the ACES is the availability of a full chapter of the technical manual (24 pages) describing the correct interpretation of scores in the context of a very useful example.

The authors provide a good caution about the use of the instrument: You must know the students, and you must have observed the behaviors. These are eminently sensible rules. The readability level of the student form is pitched to the fourth grade, and so teachers are discouraged from administering the form to students in Grades 6 to 12 who are functioning below the fourth grade reading level. Scoring of teacher and student ratings is easy to do by hand. No scales need to be "flipped" or complicated calculations made. Omitted responses are discouraged, but the instructions are clear for handling them. Some step-by-step examples are offered to do the scoring. It is a very straightforward process. One very handy feature is the availability of something called the "ACES Scoring Assistant" software for record keeping and monitoring student progress. Graphics are also available.

Score interpretations are viewed at three levels. First, the focus is on the academic and academic enabling scales. Next, focus turns to the subscales, and finally, to the item level ratings. At the two highest levels, scores are interpreted in a criterion-referenced way: developing (i.e., below grade level), competent, (i.e., at or slightly above grade level), and advanced (i.e., well above grade level). Score interpretations begin to get more complicated when the emphasis shifts to the five-step identification process involving other instruments. To the authors' credit, the user is not left with some scores and wondering what to do next. The authors offer some very specific examples for developing plans.

DEVELOPMENT. The theory underlying the ACES is straightforward-academic competence is viewed as the key to student success in school. In their theory, the authors view academic competence as consisting of clusters of skills, attitudes, and behaviors: Academic Enablers (Motivation, Engagement, Interpersonal Skills, Study Skills), and Academic Skills (consisting of Reading, Mathematics, and Critical Thinking). They argue, and offer research studies to show, that the four Academic Enabling Skills often interact with classroom instruction to help students develop and use their Academic Skills.

The instrument itself includes approximately 70 items (73 items on the Grades 3 to 12 teacher form, 66 items on the Grades K to 2 teacher form, and 68 items on the Grades 6 to 12 and college student form). The instrument can be completed by teachers and students in less than 20 minutes. Roughly 30 of the items measure Academic Skills (about 10 items per academic skill) and the remaining 40 items measure the Academic Enablers (about 10 items per academic enabler). Teachers respond to the Academic Skills items (e.g., understanding of spatial relationships) using a 5-point rating scale: far below, below, grade level, above, and far above. They also rate each item in terms of its importance: Not important, important, and critical. Teachers respond to the items on the academic enablers portion of the instrument (e.g., "follows classroom rules") using a 5-point frequency rating scale: never, seldom, sometimes, often, and almost always. Also, they judge the importance of each item on a 3-point scale: Not important, important, and critical. Students respond to each item (e.g., "I read at a steady pace") using the same 5-point frequency rating scale: never, seldom, sometimes, often, almost always.

The instrument itself was developed over a number of years (probably dating back to 1986) as the underlying theory was developed and field-tested. Development of the teacher and student forms of the ACES went through the usual steps: development of the theory and modifications, drafts and reviews of items for the rating forms, field-testing, identification of poor items and redundancies, further clarifications, etc. After standardization in 1999, further items were dropped, and the teacher and student forms of the ACES were finalized. All of the development steps seemed reasonable and appropriately handled.

TECHNICAL. Score reliability (as estimated by coefficient alpha) is very high (over .90) for all reported scores (nine main scores). Standard errors of measurement for each score are correspondingly low, though a bit higher, generally, for the academic enabling scores. A small test-retest study was carried out, and revealed reliabilities in excess of .88. I was very pleased to see score bands being emphasized in score reporting. What was not clear to me was why both 90% and 95% confidence bands were being offered as options to users. I wondered whether the choice between the two was meaningful, and if choices were to be made, I wondered about the merit of choices being rather different such as 68% and 90% or 68% and 95% confidence bands.

Both teacher (N = 188) and student (N = 37) test-retest reliability is reported for the nine scale and subscale scores. For teacher ratings, reliabilities over 2 to 3 weeks were in the range .88 to .97. For student ratings, reliabilities over a month of time dropped to a range of .68 to .84. Two points are noteworthy: 37 students is too small a sample, and some of these reliability estimates seem problematic. At the same time, the authors argued that these levels are acceptable for screening purposes and I think I would agree. Test-retest reliability values for the ACES are important and should be carried out on substantially larger samples, and an investigation might be carried out to see if the reliabilities could be raised by using clearer directions, more practice ratings, and possibly clearer items.

A considerable amount of construct validity evidence is offered. First, a factor analysis (actually a principal components analysis) reveals two factors—the Academic Skills and the Academic Enablers. Follow-up investigations revealed, as hypothesized, that the factor structure of the academic items involves three factors—Reading, Mathematics, and Critical Thinking. The Academic Enabler items produced a four-factor solution: Interpersonal Skills, Engagement, Motivation, and Study Skills. The highest factor loading of each item was on the intended factor. The factor structure of the instrument was exactly as hypothesized.

The authors also report correlations between the Academic Skills score and the Iowa Test of Basic Skills in the range of .55 to .76. These seem to be very appropriate. They also compiled some contrasting groups evidence. Here, students were independently classified as general education or at-risk or with disabilities and it was found that about 86% of the students could be correctly classified based on scores from the ACES. This study was replicated several times. It was helpful, also, to see that the use of teacher ratings in predicting academic achievement is validated by high correlations between their ratings on the ACES and academic achievement scores for students based on standardized achievement tests.

Norms for the ACES were developed in 1999 in conjunction with the norming of the Wechsler Individual Achievement Test—Second Edition. In total, 1,000 students were judged by their teachers across four grade clusters: K–2, 3–5, 6–8, and 9–12, or 250 students per cluster. In addition, 302 students distributed across Grades 6 to 12 were administered the student form. Detailed demographics for students rated by teachers, and the students providing self-ratings, are provided in the technical manual. Students are sorted by sex, ethnicity, region of the country, educational status (general education, learning disabled, and at-risk), and SES, and the match of the norming sample on these demographic variables to the 1998 U.S. Census is excellent.

COMMENTARY. I like very much many of the characteristics about the ACES and have only a few minor criticisms. The sample of students used in norming was small-only 302 students spread over 7 years of schooling. This was a pretty skimpy sample to prepare two sets of norms. To their credit, the authors report scores in deciles, which addresses both the imprecision in the norms themselves, and measurement error, but I would still like to have norms based on a larger sample. Importantly too, though the authors suggest the ACES can be used with college students, norms are not available, and only limited validity data are available on this sample. This shortcoming seriously limits the merits of the ACES with college students.

Score interpretations of the Academic Skills are criterion-referenced because of the nature of the rating scale. Score interpretations of the Academic Enabler Skills out of necessity needed to be norm-referenced. The authors were disappointed that they could not provide criterion-referenced benchmarks for these Academic Enabler Skills but, as they point out, often these skills are interpreted in a normative way in practice anyway and so I see little problem. It would be helpful if it could be determined sometime in the future if the arbitrary rules for interpreting these normative scores could be confirmed in validity studies.

SUMMARY. I was impressed with the ACES and the technical documentation. The instrument itself is based upon an understandable theory about the academic accomplishments of students. This gives rise to an instrument that assesses both Academic Skills and Academic Enabling Skills. These skills appear to be assessed in ways that result in both reliable and valid scores, with substantial technical evidence available to support both. I commented on some of the validity evidence in an earlier section but substantially more evidence is provided in the technical manual including evidence about content, criterion-related, convergent, and divergent validity. On the other hand, little documentation is available to support the use of the instrument in college student samples.

Review of the Academic Competence Evaluation Scales by DARRELL L. SABERS, Professor and Head of Educational Psychology, and SARAH BONNER, Doctoral Student, University of Arizona, Tucson, AZ:

DESCRIPTION. The Academic Competence Evaluation Scales (ACES) uses rating scales to assess the academic functioning of students in Grades K–12. The basic kit consists of a K–12 manual and student and teacher record forms. The teacher form has 73 items (66 for Grades K–2). For Academic Skills, there are 33 (or 26) items for the teacher to rate both a student's academic skill in comparison with the grade-level expectations in the school—from far below to far above—and how important each skill is for academic success in the classroom. For the 40 Academic Enabler items the teacher rates how frequently the student exhibits desired behavior and how important that behavior is in the classroom. The student form is for Grades 6–12 only, and is titled "About My Learning." It has 30 items for the student self-rating of Academic Skills and 38 items for self-rating of Academic Enablers. All student items are rated on a five-category scale from *never* to *almost always*, the same scale teachers use to rate the Academic Enablers.

ACES is intended as the start of a five-step problem-solving process to design and implement an intervention for improving a student's academic competence. As part of this process, the Academic Intervention Monitoring System (AIMS)—a companion intervention guidebook to the ACES—is recommended but not referenced in the ACES K–12 manual, and is not part of the basic kit for ACES.

Scores can be reported as deciles or as competence levels of Developing, Competent, or Advanced for all Academic Skills and Enablers. The developers encourage users to employ Goal Attainment Scaling (GAS) methods to develop and evaluate interventions to improve academic competence. If some monitoring system is not to be implemented, there is probably no reason for the teacher to rate how important each academic skill is for success in the classroom.

DEVELOPMENT. ACES is an extension of the work on "teachers as tests" where academic competence is judged by the classroom teacher rather than by a standardized test. Previous measures have been as simple as a single item for each measure of competence with little emphasis on the reliability of the instruments. ACES is based on an extended description of the intended construct of academic competence and more evidence of reliability and validity. It is easy to use the forms and to understand the directions for scoring. The manual has no information on administration except to address the importance of having an adult available to answer student questions. One potential area for confusion is that the student form includes instructions on scoring and the scoring summary on the same page where the student makes comments about "yourself and how you learn best."

The discussion of user qualifications demonstrates that the developers are current in their understanding of the responsibility of the users to determine whether there is evidence supporting the decision to use any instrument for the users' purpose. This instrument is probably still in development given that 25 items were deleted from the form used to obtain standardization data. The developers acted responsibly when they deleted items that were not supported by the results of their analyses; however, the data now reported are for an instrument that is different from the one that was standardized.

TECHNICAL. Given the difficulty of norming an instrument where so much depends on volunteers agreeing to participate, the user will likely be satisfied with the extensive norms of the teacher form and the description of the standardization where 1,000 teachers rated students. Less satisfying is that only 302 students provided ratings for the student form. Also, it is unfortunate that the students who completed the student form are not the same students for whom the teachers completed the ratings, but that difference is expected as a result of the difficulty of obtaining permission for testing students. The inadequacy of the data for the student form has led the reviewers to concentrate on the teacher form in this review.

One questionable aspect of the intended population is the attempt to target 20% as "at risk" plus 10% as being LD, which includes SLI or MR. That total of 30% may seem strange when the label of Developing (below competent) intended for the lowest scoring students may include from 16% of an age group to nearly half. The developers of the ACES discuss the varying criteria for the use of the competency labels, but that discussion is spread over the pages of the manual. It is reasonable to expect some variability in the percentages of students in the categories as explained in the manual. The developers are to be commended for the extensive discussion of the rationale for their sampling.

The section on validity evidence demonstrates current thinking in measurement. The evidence presented is substantial and thorough, including evidence on consequences of testing. It is reasonable to expect fewer negative consequences with ACES than with testing programs imposed on teachers, because the "teachers are tests" with ACES.

The section on evidence based on test content includes a demonstration that the "No Opportunity to Observe" category was used in developing the final scales, and this demonstration should convince the users that they should take that category seriously. Content on the student form is very similar to that on the teacher form although the response categories differ by necessity. Certain items may be criticized; for example, the student form asks if a student sounds out each letter separately in reading unfamiliar words. The factor analysis data support the criticism of that item. Another item asks if the student *measures* area accurately—but does one measure area, or calculate it? The potential user should verify the content relevance and representativeness of the ACES for local use, but the developers have provided a good amount of other important data to support its use.

The section on evidence based on internal structure shows that each item loads on the factor it is intended to represent. No loadings on any factor other than the intended target are reported. This section is presented in an easy-to-read format that indicates the order of the loadings on each factor, and would facilitate choosing one particular item or a smaller set to represent each factor should a shorter form of the instrument be desired.

The evidence based on relationships with other variables and with test-criterion relationships is compelling and thorough. Although one might find cases to disagree with the conclusion that these data are highly supportive of the validity of the instrument, those cases are few. For example, the ITBS and WIAT-II Math both correlate higher with ACES-Teacher Reading than with ACES-Teacher Math. Also, evidence presented as supporting discriminant validity is based on negative correlations between problem behaviors and desired behaviors, not the kind of evidence that Messick (1989) has suggested should be presented to discount the redundancy in rival constructs. But there is much more to praise than to condemn in the validity presentation. There is little doubt that the teachers' ratings of student competence correlate well with standardized test scores.

The section on test-criterion relationships demonstrates that teachers can differentiate between the general education students and those labeled "at risk" and "LD." However, as has been suggested in the literature, teachers in the classroom already know which students are given those labels and would not present unbiased ratings because of that knowledge. That same criticism likely applies to all ratings by classroom teachers, and thus might be one reason why some critics would not support the use of ACES.

The section on reliability is not as praiseworthy as the validity section. The statement that "three methods were used to estimate the reliability of the ACES" (manual, p. 77) suggests that there is one reliability and different ways to estimate it. It would be preferable to admit that there are different reliabilities for different data sets and different methods. Interrater agreement is difficult to estimate for the teacher instrument because there is usually only one classroom teacher who knows the child's abilities in all the relevant dimensions. Test-retest correlations for the teacher's ratings (2–3 weeks apart) for the same students are consistently above .90—but those high correlations are expected by those who believe that the teacher is biased. The student test-retest correlations are near .8 but are based on only 37 students. These test-retest correlations are not intrarater coefficients even if rated by the same teacher because of some expected change over time in the student competency—the change that is the object of the intervention teachers refer to as teaching.

The internal consistency coefficients for the teacher scales are very high, with the median for an age group at .97 or .98. For the student scales, the median is near .90.

These high correlations could result from two factors contributing to an increased variability of student scores—great differences among students tested with the 30% targeted lower-scoring students, and the greater spread of talent found in a national sample than expected in a school where the instrument is to be used. Because these internal consistency coefficients were the basis for calculating the standard errors of measurement, the values in the manual would underestimate the actual measurement errors obtained in estimating individual scores for the students.

COMMENTARY. A problem with the internal consistency reliabilities for the teacher's scales is that one wonders why there is a need for such a high reliability. An instrument half as long would still be very reliable, and would save the teacher time in marking the instrument. These obtained high reliabilities suggest redundancy, and led one school psychologist interviewed to suggest that there is no need for more than one item per scale. The suggestion was that ACES was using "teachers as items" rather than "teachers as tests." Gresham, Reschly, and Carey (1987) provide evidence of the validity of the Teacher Rating of Academic Performance (TRAP) that uses a single item per facet measured.

SUMMARY. A very impressive aspect of the ACES is the extensive description of how to link assessment results to intervention. The problem-solving process is described thoroughly, and the individualized criterion-referenced GAS demonstrates a credible and commendable approach to intervention. The description demonstrates the developers' reasons for including the "student as

test" in the process, and encourages careful thinking and communication among participants. Any shortcomings in the instrument are small compared to the positive contributions of the manual. Although the reviewers might prefer an instrument with a single item per facet as in the TRAP, the intervention program supported by the ACES is worthy of consideration.

REVIEWERS' REFERENCES
Gresham, F. M., Reschly, D. J., & Carey, M. P. (1987). Teachers as "tests": Classification accuracy and concurrent validation in the identification of learning disabled children. *School Psychology Review, 16*, 543-553.
Messick, S. (1989). Validity. *Educational Measurement*, (3rd ed., pp. 13-103). Washington, DC: The American Council on Education and the National Council on Measurement in Education.

[2]
Accountant Staff Selector.

Purpose: Designed "to evaluate the administrative, intellectual and analytical skills necessary for successful performance as an accountant."
Population: Adult applicants for accounting positions.
Publication Dates: 1982–2002.
Scores, 7: Numerical Skills, Attention to Detail, Problem Solving Ability, Reading Comprehension, Spreadsheet Simulation, Verbal Fluency, Bookkeeping Skills.
Administration: Individual or group.
Price Data: Available from publisher.
Foreign Language Edition: French edition available.
Time: (66) minutes.
Comments: Scoring available by mail, courier service, fax, or telephone.
Author: Walden Personnel Testing and Consulting, Inc.
Publisher: Walden Personnel Performance, Inc. [Canada].

Review of the Accountant Selector Test by JoELLEN V. CARLSON, Carlson Consulting, Indian Rocks Beach, FL:

DESCRIPTION. The Accountant Selector Test is intended for companies to use in the selection of candidates for accounting positions. The publisher claims that the instrument is appropriate for two positions: Junior Accountant and Accountant.

The test consists of six basic sections and a seventh optional, section (Bookkeeping Skills). Each section is administered separately and timed. The test can be administered individually or to a group and does not require specialized knowledge or skill to administer.

The Numerical Skills section consists of 60 computation items to be completed in 5 minutes. Most of the items require two operations, though some require only one. Attention to Detail comprises 45 items, each requiring identification of which of four sets of symbols match; 5 minutes is allotted. Problem Solving consists of 30 items to be completed in 5 minutes; these items require determining the fifth entry in a series of letters, numerals, or letter-numeral combinations. Reading Comprehension consists of 7 items of mixed types (e.g., cloze, short passage-main idea, sentence ordering, statement paraphrase), to be completed in 5 minutes. Some items include questionable content, some of which could open an employer to a sexual harassment charge. The Spreadsheet Simulation task is quite unlike the use of an actual spreadsheet program, as it is a paper-and-pencil attempt to simulate spreadsheet use. It contains technically inaccurate language and seems overly complicated by the testing mode. Twenty minutes are allotted for this section. Verbal Fluency, a 6-minute section, consists of three stimuli, each requiring the candidate to write as many words as possible that begin and/or end with specified letter combination(s). The final section, Bookkeeping Skills, which is optional, seems to test few skills, including instead multiple-choice questions of knowledge.

Before beginning the test, the candidate must sign a disclaimer/release form and consent to the "procedure whereby the organization administering this test will receive the evaluation report derived therefrom" (test form, p. 2) but not to the use of the results. It appears that the candidate for a position at a company using the test must grant the *publisher* permission to provide a copy of the evaluation report to other clients of the publisher to whom the candidate may apply for a position in the future; none of the materials describes how this would work.

Along with the test booklet, a test manual and a document entitled "Content Validation Study" are provided. The test manual provides brief, general administration directions, time limits, and a few sample questions without examples of the directions for the questions or answers. Two pages are devoted to a sample score report, and more than half a page to the options for receiving score reports (e.g., mail, courier, fax, collect call).

The test manual includes an evaluation table (Evaluation Guide) listing score bands (range of percents), an evaluative word associated with each score band (i.e., superior, good, moderate, low), and a prediction (which the publisher calls a "recommendation") associated with each (e.g., "Candidate only moderately displays the skills needed to be successful as an Accountant.").

Though responses all can be scored objectively, no scoring key is provided. The user must return each test booklet to the publisher for scoring.

DEVELOPMENT. The publisher provides absolutely *no information* on the development of the instrument, either in the print materials provided for this review or on the publisher's website.

TECHNICAL. The publisher provides *no* acceptable data on psychometric characteristics of the instrument—from the most basic reliability estimates for these "sections" to evidence of content, concurrent, or predictive validity. There is no discussion of how the content basis for the sections or their content was identified. There is no discussion of how the score bands and their accompanying evaluations and "recommendations" were derived.

Accompanying the test and the test manual is a document entitled "Content Validation Study." Rather than provide actual evidence of content validity, this document appears to be a hypothetical case exemplifying what a company would receive if it purchased the "validation study" at a "moderate cost," as advertised in the test manual. Its statements are broad and sketchy at best (e.g., "Each of the identified tasks was ranked (weighted) in order of importance to the Accountant position by ABC Corp. Financial, Inc. personnel"). Further, the conclusions represent overgeneralizations, such as "the test represents a content valid evaluation device for those job functions."

Apparently, this "validation" service includes cross-referencing the description of each position for which a company wishes to use this instrument with what the publisher calls the "job criteria measured" by the test. The results then indicate the percentage of "essential traits" for a position covered by the test. Interestingly, the identical percentage of correspondence between "essential skills tested" and essential skills identified (58.8%) is cited in the hardcopy document dated August 2001 and on the website dated August 1998. These descriptions correspond exactly throughout, including a second indicator, called overlap of the "weighted" importance of the task, which is cited as 63.9% in both instances.

COMMENTARY. Though the publisher indicates that the purpose of this instrument is "to evaluate the administrative, intellectual and analytical skills necessary for successful performance as an Accountant" (test manual, p. 1), there is no evidence of its acceptability or utility for this purpose. It remains the responsibility of the publisher to provide or point to basic evidence of the utility and defensibility of the instrument and the interpretations to be made of the scores derived from it. This is true regardless of the publisher's desire to sell the service of conducting a study of validity specific to a company that is considering use of the instrument.

SUMMARY. This reviewer cannot recommend the use of this test for any purpose without some evidence of the background of its development and its psychometric properties. Further, if the "Content Validation Study" sample submitted for review is indicative of the procedures that would be followed in conducting such a study for a specific company and the validity claims that would be made, it is questionable whether such service would contribute to its defensibility.

[3]

Achenbach System of Empirically Based Assessment.

Purpose: "An integrated ... [approach] designed to provide standardized descriptions of ... competencies, adaptive functioning, and problems."

Population: Ages 18 months to 90+ years.

Publication Dates: 1980–2003.

Acronym: ASEBA.

Administration: Individual or group.

Levels, 3: Preschool, School-Age, Young Adult.

Price Data, 2004: $150 per Preschool hand-scoring starter kit including 50 each of CBCL/1 1/2–5 & LDS forms, C-TRF forms, CBCL/1 1/2–5 hand-scoring profiles, C-TRF hand-scoring profiles, LDS hand-scoring forms, CBCL/1 1/2–5 and C-TRF templates, and manual for the Preschool Forms & Profiles (2000, 189 pages); $230 per Preschool computer-scoring starter kit including 50 CBCL/1 1/2–5 & LDS forms, 50 C-TRF forms, Ages 1 1/2–5 entry scoring module, manual for the Preschool Forms & Profiles; $325 per School-Age computer-scoring starter kit including 50 CBCL forms, 50 TRF forms, 50 YSR forms, Ages 6–18 entry scoring module, and manual for the School-Age Forms & Profiles (2001, 238 pages); $35 per manual for the Preschool Forms and Profiles,

manual for the School-Age Forms and profiles, or manual for the SCICA (2001, 164 pages); $35 per manual for the ASEBA Adult forms and profiles (2003, 216 pages); $10 per Mental Health Practitioners' Guide for the ASEBA (2004, 42 pages), School-Based Practitioners' Guide for the ASEBA (2004, 48 pages), Child and Family Service Workers' Guide for the ASEBA (2003, 37 pages), or Medical Practitioners' Guide for the ASEBA (2003, 33 pages); $595 per full set of ADM Software Modules including Ages 1 1/2–5, 6–18, 18–59, SCICA, and Test Observation Form (TOF); $170 per ADM Software Modules for ages 1 1/2–5, 18–5/9, SCICA, or TOF; $250 per ADM Software Modules for Ages 6–18; $220 per Scanning Module or Client Entry Module for CBCL/6–18, TRF/6–18, and YSR/11–18; $220 per ASEBA Web-Link (following purchase of any ADM Module) including E-package of 100 E-units; $25 per 50 CBCL/1 1/2–5 & LDS, C-TRF, CBCL/16–18, TRF/6–18, YSR, DOF, ASR, SCICA, or ABCL forms; $25 per 50 Profiles for hand scoring profiles for any of CBCL/1 1/2–5, C-TRF, CBCL/6–18 (specify gender), TRF (specify gender), YSR, DOF, SCICA, ASR, or ABCL; $25 per 50 forms for hand-scoring LDS; $25 per 50 Combined SCICA Observation and Self-Report scoring forms; $25 per 50 CBCL, TRF, YSR, or SCICA DSM-Oriented Profiles for Boys & Girls; $7 per reusable templates for hand scoring CBCL/1 1/2–5, C-TRF, CBCL/6–18, TRF, YSR, ASR, or ABCL Profiles.

Foreign Language Editions: One or more forms have been translated into 69 languages, check website (www.ASEBA.org) for availability.

Comments: Revised version of the Child Behavior Checklist; includes both empirically based syndrome scales and DSM-oriented scales for scoring consistent with DSM-IV categories; designed to be usable in diverse contexts, including schools, mental health, medical, child and family service, and other settings; all forms except DOF and SCICA are parallel, facilitating comparisons across informants; hand- or computer-scorable; reusable hand-scoring templates available; data processed by Assessment Data Manager (ADM); cross-informant bar graphs; minimum system requirements Windows 95/98/NT/2000, 64 MB RAM, 65 MB free hard disk space, Pentium recommended; can be completed using paper forms (hand- or machine-readable), by direct client-entry on computer, or via Web-Link; LDS, Preschool and School-Age manuals.

Authors: Thomas M. Achenbach (all forms and manuals), Leslie A. Rescorla (all forms and Mental Health Practitioners' Guide for the ASEBA), Stephanie H. McConaughy (SCICA, SCICA manual, and School-Based Practitioners' Guide for the ASEBA), Peter J. Pecora and Kathleen M. Wetherbee (Child and Family Service Workers' Guide for the ASEBA), and Thomas

M. Ruffle (Medical Practitioners' Guide for the ASEBA).

Publisher: Research Center for Children, Youth, and Families at the University of Vermont.

a) PRESCHOOL FORMS AND PROFILES.

Purpose: To provide "systematic assessment of maladaptive behavior among preschoolers."

Comments: DSM-Oriented Scales rated as very consistent with the following DSM-IV categories: Affective Problems consistent with Dysthymia, Major Depressive Disorder; Anxiety Problems consistent with Generalized Anxiety Disorder, Separation Anxiety Disorder, Specific Phobia; Pervasive Developmental Problems consistent with Asperger's Disorder and Autistic Disorder; Attention Deficit/Hyperactivity Problems consistent with Hyperactive-Impulsive and Inattentive types of ADHD.

1) *Child Behavior Checklist for Ages 1 1/2–5.*

Population: Ages 18 months to 5 years.

Publication Dates: 1988–2000.

Acronym: CBCL/1 1/2–5.

Scores: 7 Syndrome scales (Emotionally Reactive, Anxious/Depressed, Somatic Complaints, Withdrawn, Sleep Problems, Attention Problems, Aggressive Behavior), plus Internalizing, Externalizing, Total Problems; Language Development Survey (LDS) scored (for children age 18–35 months); 5 DSM-Oriented scales (Affective Problems, Anxiety Problems, Pervasive Developmental Problems, Attention Deficit/Hyperactivity Problems, Oppositional Defiant Problems).

Time: (10) minutes.

Comments: Designed to be completed by parents and others who see children in home-like settings; includes the Language Development Survey (LDS) for evaluating language delays in children under age 3 as well as those over age 3 suspected of having language delays.

2) *Caregiver-Teacher Report Form for Ages 1 1/2–5.*

Population: Ages 18 months to 5 years.

Publication Dates: 1997–2000.

Acronym: C-TRF.

Scores: 6 Syndrome scales (Emotionally Reactive, Anxious/Depressed, Somatic Complaints, Withdrawn, Attention Problems, Aggressive Behavior), plus Internalizing, Externalizing, Total Problems.

Time: (10) minutes.

Comments: Designed to be completed by daycare providers and preschool teachers who have known a child in daycare, preschool, or similar settings for at least 2 months.

b) SCHOOL-AGE FORMS AND PROFILES.

Comments: DSM-Oriented Scales rated as very consistent with the following DSM-IV categories: Affective Problems consistent with Dysthymia, Major Depressive Disorder; Anxiety Problems consistent with Generalized Anxiety Disorder, Separation Anxiety Disorder, Specific Phobia; Attention Deficit/Hyperactivity Problems consistent with Hyperactive-Impulsive and Inattentive types of ADHD; Somatic Problems consistent with Somatization Disorder and Somatoform Disorder.

1) *Child Behavior Checklist for Ages 6–18.*

Population: Ages 6–18.

Publication Dates: 1981–2001.

Acronym: CBCL/6–18.

Scores: 4 Competence scales (Activities, Social, School, Total Competence); 8 Syndrome scales (Anxious/Depressed, Withdrawn/Depressed, Somatic Complaints, Social Problems, Thought Problems, Attention Problems, Rule-Breaking Behavior, Aggressive Behavior), plus Internalizing, Externalizing, Total Problems; 6 DSM-Oriented scales (Affective Problems, Anxiety Problems, Somatic Problems, Attention Deficit/Hyperactivity Problems, Oppositional Defiant Problems, Conduct Problems).

Time: (15–20) minutes.

2) *Teacher's Report Form for Ages 6–18.*

Purpose: "Quickly obtain[s] a picture of children's functioning in school, as seen by teachers and other personnel."

Population: Teachers of children ages 6–18.

Publication Dates: 1981–2001.

Acronym: TRF.

Scores: 6 Adaptive Functioning scales (Academic Performance, Working Hard, Behaving Appropriately, Learning, Happy, Total); same Syndrome and DSM-Oriented scales as CBCL/6–18; yields separate scores for Inattention and Hyperactivity-Impulsivity.

Time: (15–20) minutes.

3) *Youth Self-Report for Ages 11–18.*

Purpose: To obtain youths' reports of their own problems and competencies in a standardized format.

Population: Ages 11–18.

Publication Dates: 1981–2001.

Acronym: YSR.

Scores: 2 Competence scales (Activities, Social) plus Total Competence; same Syndrome and DSM-Oriented scales as CBCL/6–18.

4) *Direct Observation Form for Ages 5–14.*

Purpose: "Used to record and rate behavior in group settings."

Publication Dates: 1983–1986.

Acronym: DOF.

Comments: Used to obtain 10-minute samples of children's behavior in classrooms and other group settings; enables users to compare an observed child with 2 control children for on-task, Internalizing, Externalizing, and Total Problems, averaged for up to 6 observation sessions; 6 syndrome scales available (computer-scored profiles only).

5) *Semistructured Clinical Interview for Children and Adolescents.*

Purpose: "Used to record and rate children's behavior and self-reports during an interview."

Population: Ages 6–18.

Publication Dates: 1989–2001.

Acronym: SCICA.

Scores: 8 Syndrome scales (Anxious, Anxious/Depressed, Withdrawn/Depressed, Language/Motor Problems, Aggressive/Rule-Breaking Behavior, Attention Problems, Self-Control Problems, Somatic Complaints (ages 12–18 only), plus Internalizing, Externalizing, Total Problems; same DSM-Oriented scales as CBCL/6–18.

Time: (60–90) minutes.

Comments: Designed for use by experienced clinical interviewers; protocol form includes topic questions and activities, such as kinetic family drawing and tasks for screening fine and gross motor functioning; observation and self-report form for rating what a child does and says during interview.

c) ADULT FORMS AND PROFILES.

Publication Dates: 1997–2003.

1) *Adult Self-Report for Ages 18–59.*

Population: Ages 18–30.

Acronym: YASR.

Scores: 5 Adaptive Functioning scales (Education, Friends, Job, Family, Spouse or Partner), 3 Substance Use scales (Tobacco, Alcohol, Drugs) plus Mean Substance Use score, same Syndrome scales as CBCL/6–18 plus Intrusive, Internalizing, Externalizing, Total Problems.

Time: (15–20) minutes.

Comments: Upward extension of YASR.

2) *Adult Behavior Checklist for Ages 18–59.*

Population: Ages 18–59.

Acronym: ABCL.

Time: (10–15) minutes.

Comments: Ratings by parents, surrogates, friends, and spouses of adults.

Cross References: See T5:451 (292 references); for reviews by Beth Doll and by Michael J. Furlong and Michelle Wood of an earlier edition, see 13:55 (556 references); see also T4:433 (135 references); for reviews by Sandra L. Christenson and by Stephen N. Elliott and R. T. Busse of the Teacher's Report Form and the Youth Self-Report, see 11:64 (216 references); for additional information and reviews by B. J. Freeman and Mary Lou Kelley, see 9:213 (5 references).

Review of the Achenbach System of Empirically Based Assessment by ROSEMARY FLANAGAN, Assistant Professor/Director, Masters Program in School Psychology, Adelphi University, Garden City, NY:

DESCRIPTION. The Achenbach System of Empirically Based Assessment (ASEBA) available in two versions for children (ages 1.5–5 and 6–18), is a multiple-rater system used to assess the behavior and personality of youth. Compared to the previous editions (Achenbach, 1991; Achenbach, 1992), the beginning age for the preschool version has been extended downward, and the beginning age for the school-age form has increased. Parents complete the Child Behavior Checklist (CBCL/1 1/2–5, CBCL/6–18), those working in school or care settings complete the Teacher Report Form (TRF/6–18) or the Caregiver-Teacher Report (C-TRF), and youngsters aged 11-18 complete the Youth Self-Report (YSR). The version for school age youth contains 113 items and the version for preschoolers contains 100 items. Subscales for the YSR and CBCL/6–18 are subsumed under groupings called Competence, Syndrome, and DSM-Oriented, the latter of which is based on the *Diagnostic and Statistical Manual of Mental Disorders, 4th Edition* (DSM-IV; American Psychiatric Association, 1994). The TRF/6–18 yields 20 scales categorized as Adaptive, Syndrome, and DSM-Oriented. The CBCL/1 1/2–5 and C-TRF yields 8 Syndrome and 6 DSM-Oriented scales. The Language Development Survey (LDS; Rescorla, 1989) is part of the CBCL/1 1/2–5; it is composed of questions about the child's birth history, ear infections, and speech problems within the family. Parents are also asked to report the child's best multiword phrases and indicate whether their child knows words commonly known by preschoolers. Although not a substitute for a more established speech-language screening, it is helpful given the comorbidity of delays in language development with psychopathology.

Practical applications for these forms are in an array of settings serving children that include schools, mental health settings, medical settings, forensic settings, and child and family service settings. The manual provides case studies to illustrate the application and interpretation of the data. Summary manuals are available to guide professionals who are consumers of the data (but not necessarily direct test users) in several settings as to the nature of the scales and their usage.

The authors recommend using the computer-scoring program, but scoring can also be accomplished by hand, by laboriously transferring item ratings to a profile sheet that groups the items by scales; clerical errors seem likely. Cross-informant comparisons can be made readily with the computer-scoring program only.

DEVELOPMENT. The revision of the scales includes an updating of the norms and refinement of the scales; the procedures used to accomplish this were thorough. Competence scales were derived by comparing the responses of referred versus nonreferred youth, with items having been retained from the CBCL/4–18, TRF, and YSR; some refinement in scoring has been incorporated. Extensive procedures were followed to scientifically obtain a nationally representative nonreferred/nontreated sample. The norming samples contain 1,753, 1,057, and 2,319 individuals for the CBCL/6–18, YSR, and TRF, respectively. The sample for the TRF initially derived from the norming sample for the CBCL/6–18 was small. Given that the 1989 sample did not score differently from the 2001 sample, the data from the two cohorts were combined to have a larger normative sample. Normalized T-scores were assigned to the raw scores for each gender at two age levels: 6–11 and 12–18 years. Particular attention was given to areas of the score distribution that were skewed, as it was thought desirable to make these more sensitive to differences in functioning.

The Syndrome scales were developed to produce information about patterns of problems. In addition to the sample used to norm the Competence scales, additional children who received inpatient and outpatient treatment were included. This resulted in sample sizes for the CBCL/6–18, TRF, and YSR of 4,994, 4,437, and 2,551, respectively. Sample sizes for the CBCL/1 1/2–5 and the C-TRF are 1,728 and 1,113 youth, respectively. Some items from the 1991 versions of the CBCL, TRF, and YSR were eliminated because these were endorsed by considerably less than 5% of the respondents; the net result was that six items were replaced in the CBCL/6–18 and YSR; three items were replaced in the TRF. Similarly, two items were replaced in the CBCL/1 1/2–5 and C-TRF. Principal components analysis yielded an eight-factor solution, for the CBCL/6–18 and the YSR, which also proved to demonstrate the best fit upon confirmatory factor analysis. A seven-factor solution was realized for the TRF. A subsequent factor analysis grouped the Syndromes according to Total Problems, Internalizing Problems, and Externalizing Problems. The names of two Syndrome scales were changed from the 1991 versions; *Withdrawn* is now *Withdrawn/Depressed*, and *Delinquent Behavior* is *Rule Breaking Behavior*. Factor analysis of the TRF scales indicates that the Attention Problems Scale is composed of items that may be categorized as Inattentive and Hyperactive-Impulsive, parallel to DSM-IV (American Psychiatric Association, 1994). Normalizing the data at points on the distributions that were skewed was done to derive T-scores. Segments of scales that correspond to those individuals making an appropriate adjustment were truncated. Thus, the statistical treatment focuses on the portions of the scales that potentially yield the greatest amount of diagnostic and classification data. To limit false negatives, the borderline clinical range was extended downward, now beginning at $T = 65$, which is consistent with other commonly used rating forms. T-scores of 70 and above are clearly in the clinical range. The Syndrome scales for the CBCL/1 1/2–5 were similarly developed, using a norming sample of 700 individuals. Norms for the LDS are based on the mean length of utterance and vocabulary development by 5-month intervals.

The DSM-Oriented scales for the CBCL/1 1/2–5 and the CBCL/6–18 were developed by psychologists and psychiatrists indicating the degree of consistency of each item with nine DSM categories. Only items that were rated as very consistent with a particular diagnosis were retained.

TECHNICAL. Psychometric properties are generally strong. For the CBCL/6–18, internal consistency reliability (coefficient alpha) ranged from .55–.90 for Competence and Adaptive scales, from .71–.97 for the Syndrome scales, and from .67–.94 for the DSM-Oriented scales. Mean stability for the CBCL/6–18 at 12 months is .65, .51 for the YSR at 7 months, and .65 for the TRF at

2 months. Mean test-retest reliability ranged from .88–.90, .79–.88, and .85–.90 for 8- or 16-day intervals for CBCL/6–18, YSR, and TRF, respectively. The CBCL/1 1/2–5 similarly demonstrates strong internal consistency, with coefficient alpha ranging from .66–.96 for the Syndrome scales, and .from .63–.93 for the DSM-Oriented scales. Test-retest reliability for an 8-day interval ranged from .68–.92 for the Syndrome scales and from .57–.87 for the DSM-Oriented scales. The mean stability for the CBCL/1 1/2–5 at a 12-month interval is .61, and is .59 for the C-TRF at a 3-month interval.

Mean cross-informant agreement for the CBCL/1 1/2–5 and the C-TRF are .61 and .65, respectively. For the Competence and Adaptive scales of the CBCL/6–18 and the TRF, the mean cross-informant agreement values are .69 and .49, respectively. For the Syndrome scales, these values are .76 and .60 for the CBCL/6–18 and the TRF, respectively. For the DSM-Oriented scales, the mean cross-informant agreement for the CBCL/6–18 is .73, for the TRF it is .58. These values are substantial.

Validity evidence is extensive, with analysis of the scores on scales as well as items that document the successfulness of the scale in youth scoring differently, based on referral status. For some scales and items at shorter item intervals, the test-retest score relationship may be attenuated. Evidence substantiating content validity is based on prior research with the scales. Items that failed to differentiate between referred and nonreferred children were excluded from the scales. Evidence of criterion–related validity of the CBCL/6–18, YSR, and TRF is based on multiple regression analyses and indicates that 2–33% of the variance on individual scales is accounted for by referral status. Additional evidence is based on classification accuracy by referral status using discriminant analysis procedures (79–85%). Information is in the manual that will assist practitioners interpreting the data for youth who are not clearly in the clinical range, but may be exhibiting behavior or affect of concern; this is of considerable importance to school-based practitioners. Construct validity was evaluated on the basis of correlations with similar instruments, in particular the BASC (Reynolds & Kamphaus, 1992), the Conners' Rating Scales—Revised (Conners, 1997), and the DSM-IV Checklist (Hudziak, 1998). Correla-

tions with the Conners' Rating Scales and the DSM-IV Checklist are moderate; correlations with the BASC are more substantial.

Similarly, the content validity for the CBCL/ 1 1/2–5 was examined based on prior research with the scales. Content validity of the LDS was evaluated by repeated correlational studies using other measures of language development. Evidence of criterion-related validity is based on multiple regression analyses of the CBCL/1 1/2–5 and C-TRF that yielded percentages of explained variance accounted for by referral status ranging from 2–25% for the individual scales. Moreover, classification accuracy according to referral status was documented using discriminant analysis at 84.2%. Criterion validity of the LDS is demonstrated through a series of studies that report correlations with cognitive and language measures; these correlations range from .56–.87, with most values exceeding .70. Evidence of construct validity of the CBCL/1 1/2–5 and C-TRF is based on correlations with measures not common to clinical practice. The correlations for series of studies range from .46–.72. Construct validity evidence for scores from the LDS includes correlations that predict language scores at age 13, ranging from .38–.55.

COMMENTARY. Compared to the previous editions, the new ASEBA is improved and refined. The manuals are clear, providing technical information in a format understandable to practitioners. Extensive covariance analyses are reported in the manuals, substantiating that each item retained on the scales effectively differentiates youth based on referral status. The computer-scoring program is more effective. Important to practitioners, in particular, is that the borderline clinical range was made broader to limit the false negatives and aid in the identification of youth who might need attention. The Competence scales were made more sensitive, having expanded the possible score range. These features bring the ASEBA more in line with its main competitor, the BASC. A companion semistructured clinical interview and a direct observation form are available. The LDS of the ASEBA is an important feature that does not appear on the BASC. Nevertheless, the BASC continues to be easier to score and interpretation is less complicated. The CBCL/ 1 1/2–5 and CBCL/6–18 scales are substantially correlated across age levels. Thus, the manner in which the components of these assessment systems are related differs. The BASC forms may be easier for respondents to complete, as the items are in one format. One reason to use the ASEBA over the BASC for researchers is to take advantage of the lengthier research history as compared to the BASC.

SUMMARY. The new ASEBA (CBCL/1 1/2–5, C-TRF, CBCL/6–18, TRF, YSR) is composed of multiple-respondent rating forms and companion scales that may be used in any combination to rate the behavior and affect of youth aged 1 1/2–5, or 6–18. Procedures to develop the scales and examine their psychometric properties are exemplary. Although the psychometric properties are stronger for the school-aged versions than for the preschool versions, this may reflect the inherent variability of preschoolers. The scales are supported by a solid research base and are technically sound, both from test development and psychometric perspectives. Applicability in various settings serving children is apparent. Practitioners and researchers alike should expect the new versions to be useful as were their predecessors.

REVIEWER'S REFERENCES

Achenbach, T. M. (1991). Child Behavior Checklist for Ages 4–18. Burlington, VT: University of Vermont Department of Psychiatry.
Achenbach, T. M. (1992). *Manual for the Child Behavior Checklist/2–3 and 1992 profile.* Burlington, VT: University of Vermont Department of Psychiatry.
American Psychiatric Association. (1994). *Diagnostic and statistical manual of mental disorders (4th ed.).* Washington, DC: Author.
Conners, C. K. (1990). *Manual for the Conners' Rating Scales.* North Tonawanda, NY: Multi-Health Systems.
Hudziak, J. J. (1998). DSM-IV Checklist for Childhood Disorders. Burlington, VT: University of Vermont, Research Center for Children, Youth.
Rescorla, L. (1989). The Language Development Survey: A screening tool for delayed language in toddlers. *Journal of Speech and Hearing Disorders, 54,* 587-599.
Reynolds, C. R., & Kamphaus, R. W. (1992). The Behavior Assessment System for Children. Circle Pines, MN: AGS Publishing.
Salvia, J., & Ysseldyke, J. E. (2000). *Assessment* (8th ed.). Boston: Houghton-Mifflin.

Review of the Achenbach System of Empirically Based Assessment by T. STEUART WATSON, Professor and Chair of Educational Psychology, Miami University, Oxford, OH:

GENERAL DESCRIPTION. The Achenbach System of Empirically Based Assessment (ASEBA) is a revision of the popular Achenbach scales of 1991 and 1992. The ASEBA is a set of integrated instruments designed to assess children's problems and competencies and includes the Child Behavior Checklist for ages 1 1/2–5 and 6–18 (CBCL), the Teacher Report Form (TRF) for Ages 6–18, the Youth Self Report (YSR) for Ages 11–18, and the Semistructured Clinical Interview for Children and Adolescents (SCICA). The ASEBA is

designed for assessment, intervention planning, and outcome evaluation in a number of settings and is one of the most widely researched and used behavioral rating scales.

The 21st Century edition of the CBCL for ages 6–18 is a revision of the 1991 version for children ages 4–18 (Parent Report Form; PRF) and ages 5–18 (TRF). The CBCL 1 1/2–5 is a revision of the CBCL/2–3. Although there is a high degree of consistency between the previous and current versions of the CBCL, some items have been removed or reworded in order to more accurately discriminate between referred and nonreferred children. There is also a Language Development Survey (LDS) that is part of the CBCL 1 1/2–5. It is intended for parents of all children under the age of 3 and children over the age of 3 who are suspected of having language delays. After answering some basic questions on the front page, parents are instructed to circle any of 310 words that their child spontaneously emits. Two percentile rank scores are provided—one based on the child's age and number of words circled and another based on the average length of phrases emitted by the child. Scores below the 15th and 20th percentiles, respectively, are considered delayed. The LDS is a valuable addition to the ASEBA and allows the clinician to assess the impact of language on other problems noted by parents and teachers.

The parent and teacher versions of the CBCL can be completed in about 15–20 minutes. The parent version may be completed by a parent, caregiver, or anyone else who has experience with the child in a residential setting. The teacher version may be completed by any of the children's teachers or school personnel who are familiar with the child. The first two pages ask for demographic information, children's competencies at home or school, and either activities or academic information. As with previous editions, this information is more descriptive of incompetence than competence and is not particularly useful for intervention planning or diagnostic purposes. The remaining two pages contain 120 items that are rated: 0 = *not true (as far as you know)*; 1 = *somewhat or sometimes true*; or 2 = *very true or often true.* Although the authors contend that a wider gradient of ratings would add little in the way of increased discriminative power, some respondents may find it difficult to accurately rate behaviors that have differing rates of occurrence that meet the descriptors of the numerical scale. For instance, Item 57 "Physically attacks people" may require only 1 or 2 instances in the past 6 months to warrant a 2 whereas Item 109 "Whining" may require several incidents per day over 6 months to warrant a rating of 2.

There are separate scoring profiles for boys and girls ages 6 to 11 and 12 to 18. Raw scores, *T* scores, and percentiles for Total Competence, three Competence scales (Activities, Social, and School), eight Syndrome scales, six DSM-Oriented scales, Internalizing Problems, Externalizing Problems, and Total Problems are provided. The Syndrome scales include Anxious/Depressed, Withdrawn/ Depressed, Somatic Complaints, Social Problems, Thought Problems, Attention Problems, Rule-Breaking Behavior, and Aggressive Behavior. The DSM-Oriented scales include Affective Problems, Anxiety Problems, Somatic Problems, Attention Deficit/Hyperactivity Problems, Oppositional Defiant Problems, and Conduct Problems. The Internalizing scale is the sum of scores for the Anxious/Depressed, Withdrawn/Depressed, and Somatic Complaints syndromes. The Externalizing scale is the sum of scores from the Rule-Breaking Behavior and Aggressive Behavior syndromes. The Total Problem score is the sum of scores on all 120 items. The Syndrome and DSM-Oriented scales are similar across the PRF, TRF, and YSR.

A number of different scores are available to assist in the interpretation of the CBCL. *T* scores and percentile rank scores allow for comparisons to the normative sample to determine if a child's competencies and problems differ from what is considered typical of a child that age and gender. On the Activities, Social, and School scales, *T* scores of 31 to 35 are in the borderline range and *T* scores below 31 fall in the clinical range. On Total Competence, *T* scores of 37 to 40 are borderline range, whereas *T* scores below 37 are considered to fall in the clinical range. *T* scores of 65–69 on the Syndrome and DSM-Oriented scales are considered borderline whereas *T* scores above 69 are in the clinical range. *T* scores of 60 to 63 on the Total Problems, Internalizing, and Externalizing scales are borderline and *T* scores above 63 fall within the clinical range.

The scoring profile for the CBCL/6–18 was normed on a sample of 1,753 children ages 6 to 18 who had not been referred for professional help for behavioral or emotional problems within the preceding 12 months. All 48 contiguous states were represented in the sample and were stratified by socioeconomic status, ethnicity, region, and urban-suburban-rural residence. Separate norms are provided for boys and girls ages 6 to 11 and 12 to 18.

The YSR is for children ages 11 to 18 and is very similar to the 1991 edition. Four pages in length, it requires fifth grade reading skills to accurately complete the form, which takes about 20 minutes. For children with reading difficulties, items may be read aloud and respondents indicate the score orally. It is similar in format to the CBCL, thus there is a high degree of consistency among the items. As with the CBCL, most users will probably find the first two pages of information to be useless. The real meat of the instrument is the two pages with problem items. Each item is rated for how true it is for them in the past 6 months: 0 = *not true (as far as you know)*; 1 = *somewhat or sometimes true*; 2 = *very true or often true*. Scores and scales on the YSR are identical to those on the CBCL. Rule-Breaking Behavior is on this edition, which replaces the Delinquent Behavior Scale from the 1991 version.

The YSR scoring profile was normed on a sample of 1,057 children ages 11 to 18 from the contiguous 48 states and was stratified by ethnicity, geographic region, and SES. Separate norms are provided for boys and girls. The *T* scores and percentile ranks allow the clinician to compare a child's score with children of the same age and gender to determine if they are exhibiting more problems than is typical for someone of similar age and gender.

Although responses on the CBCL, YSR, and TRF may be hand scored, which takes experienced examiners about 15 minutes per instrument, computerized scoring is much simpler, is far less likely to result in errors than the hand-scoring option, and yields several different types of reports. The computer scoring is in a Windows format called the Assessment Data Manager (ADM).

One type of report generated by the ADM is cross-informant comparisons. This printout allows comparisons for up to eight informants for the 93 items that are similar across the YSR, TRF, and PRF Syndrome scales and the 45 items that are similar on the DSM-Oriented scales. Other comparisons include the T scores for the eight Syndrome scales, the six DSM-Oriented scales, and the three Problems scales (Internalizing, Externalizing, and Total). This is a particularly useful feature, especially when there are multiple informants and the clinician is attempting to identify patterns within an individual. An additional feature based on cross-informant data is Q correlations that indicate whether the agreement between pairs of informants is average, above average, or below average. Having agreement information readily available is particularly helpful in clinical situations by providing areas for probing regarding disagreements.

A second type of report compiled by the ADM is a narrative report. This report summarizes results for the Competence and Problems scales. A noted improvement over earlier versions of the Achenbach is the recognition of critical items from the PRF, TRF, and YSR that are important for further assessment and intervention. The narrative report also lists the scores for each of these items.

SEMISTRUCTURED CLINICAL INTERVIEW FOR CHILDREN AND ADOLESCENTS (SCICA). The SCICA is a standardized interview for children ages 6 to 18 and includes interview questions, tasks, and standardized rating forms for scoring observations and self-reported problems. Only experienced clinicians should use the SCICA, which takes about 60–90 minutes. Nine areas are covered by the SCICA and include Activities, Friends, Family Relations, Fantasies, Self-Perception, Parent/Teacher Reported Problems, Achievement tests (optional), for ages 6–11, a screen for fine and gross motor problems (optional), and for ages 12–18, somatic complaints, alcohol, drugs, and legal trouble. Children aged 6–11 are also asked to make a drawing of their family doing something, which can provide information for further questioning. The protocol is extremely user-friendly as it contains instructions, open-ended questions, and interviewing tasks. There is also ample space to record and make notations regarding the child's behavior during the interview.

For children ages 6 to 11, interviewers may administer other tests in order to gather a more complete picture of the child's functioning. Suggestions for additional testing include brief forms of standardized achievement tests, writing samples,

and assessing gross motor functioning. For children ages 12 to 18, the SCICA includes more structured questions to assess somatic complaints, alcohol and drug use, and legal difficulties. After completing the SCICA, the interviewer scores both the SCICA Observation and Self-Report Forms. The Observation Form contains 96 problem items, many of which are similar to the problem items from the YSR, TRF, and PRF. The Self-Report Form contains 114 items for ages 6 to 18 and several additional items for ages 13 to 18. As with the observation form, many of the items on the SCICA self-report are similar to those on the CBCL/6–18 PRF and TRF. All items from the SCICA observation and self-report forms are scored on a 4-point scale: 0 = *no occurrence*; 1 = *very slight or ambiguous occurrence*; 2 = *definite occurrence with mild to moderate intensity and less than 3 minutes duration*; 3 = *definite occurrence with severe intensity or 3 or more minutes duration*. For the additional self-report items for ages 12 to 18, a 4-point scale is used with varying time lines for reports of somatic complaints, alcohol and drug use, and legal trouble.

The current version of the SCICA provides separate scores for children ages 6 to 11 and 12 to 18. This represents an improvement over the 1994 version, which only provided scores for children ages 6 to 12. Raw scores, T scores, and percentile ranks are provided for Total Observation, Total Self-Report, Externalizing Problems, Internalizing Problems, the eight Syndrome scales, and the six DSM scales. Of the eight Syndrome scales, five are derived based on interview observations (Anxious, Withdrawn/Depressed, Language/Motor Problems, Attention Problems, and Self-Control Problems) and three are derived from the child's self-report during the interview (Anxious/Depressed, Aggressive/Rule-Breaking, and Somatic Complaints). The Somatic Complaints scale is scored only for children ages 12–18. For children ages 12 to 18, items on the Aggressive/Rule-Breaking syndrome are scored on separate Aggressive and Rule-Breaking scales.

DEVELOPMENT. The Syndrome scales for the PRF were derived by analyzing data from 4,994 children referred for mental health services whose parents completed the CBCL. The Syndrome scales for the TRF were developed by statistically analyzing data from TRFs completed by teachers from 4,437 children referred for mental health or special education services. The DSM-Oriented scales for the PRF, TRF, and YSR were derived from the ratings of psychiatrists and psychologists who rated items from the three versions of the CBCL. The items were rated as being *not consistent, somewhat consistent,* or *very consistent* with the diagnostic criteria of the *Diagnostic and Statistical Manual of Mental Disorders* (DSM-IV; American Psychiatric Association, 1994). To be included on the DSM scale, items had to be rated as very consistent with diagnostic criteria by at least 14 of the 22 raters. High scores on the DSM-Oriented scales can assist clinicians in determining whether a DSM-IV diagnosis is appropriate for a particular child. As is true with any assessment situation, clinicians should not rely solely on the results of the CBCL to make a diagnosis.

The Syndrome scales of the SCICA were developed by statistically analyzing interviewers' ratings of 381 children ages 6 to 11 and 305 children ages 12 to 18. All of the children in the samples had been referred for either mental health or special education services. Items endorsed for fewer than 5% of the samples in each age group were excluded from further analysis.

TECHNICAL. The ASEBA is a well-researched instrument with exceptionally strong reliability and validity data. The scales from the parent version of the CBCL/1 1/2–5 with the lowest test-retest reliabilities are Anxious/Depressed and ADHD Problems. Those from the Caregiver-Teacher Report Form (C-TRF) were the Anxiety Problems and Anxious/Depressed. This is not surprising given the difficult nature of identifying these types of behaviors in young children. In fact, one may reasonably question the clinical validity of attempting to identify ADHD behaviors in such a young sample. Internal consistency coefficients were acceptable with the possible exceptions of Anxiety Problems and Somatic Problems from the DSM-Oriented scales. Cross-informant correlations ranged from extremely low to extremely high. As might be expected, correlations between the YSR and TRF were uniformly low whereas mother and father correlations on the PRF were the highest.

Given the purposes of the ASEBA, perhaps the most important psychometric aspect is criterion-related validity. In this case, do the scores on the instrument(s) differentiate referred from nonreferred children? Without going into undue detail, it is accurate to say that all 120 items from the PRF, YSR, and TRF significantly discriminated at $p<.01$. A number of other computations are provided in the manual that demonstrate criterion-related and other types of validity of scores from the ASEBA. Overall, the ASEBA is a psychometrically sound instrument with weaknesses on some of the scales, particularly at the younger age ranges and with some of the more ubiquitous scales (e.g., Anxiety, Thought Problems).

MANUALS. A number of manuals and guides are included as part of the ASEBA package: (a) Manual for the ASEBA Preschool Forms & Profiles including the CBCL for ages 1 1/2–5, Language Development Survey, and Caregiver-Teacher Report Form; (b) Manual for the ASEBA School-Age Forms & Profiles including the CBCL for Ages 6–18, Teacher's Report Form, and Youth Self-Report Form; (c) Mental Health Practitioner's Guide for the ASEBA; (d) School-Based Practitioner's Guide for the ASEBA; (e) Child and Family Service Worker's Guide for the ASEBA; and (f) Medical Practitioner's Guide for the ASEBA. The first two are comprehensive in scope and contain far more information than the average practitioner requires to use the scales. The guides are clearly directed at practitioners who will find them more useful than the technical manuals. Although there are four separate guides, the distinction between them is minor but is an excellent marketing strategy to reach a wider audience of users. Although it may simply be a matter of personal preference, this reviewer would find it helpful to have a "Users Manual" for all the instruments and a "Technical Manual" for all the instruments. Dividing the manuals in such a manner would make it easier for both practitioners and researchers to easily access desired information without having to wade through two information-dense manuals.

SUMMARY. Overall, the ASEBA is a well-researched, empirically derived battery of instruments that allows a clinician to assess a wide range of behaviors across a variety of settings and informants. There are some minor drawbacks, but none that render the ASEBA unusable or seriously questioned. The standardization and psychometric qualities are more than adequate and the manuals contain far more information than is required by most test consumers. There are some components that are not particularly useful, such as the first two pages of the PRF, TRF, and YSR, but these do not interfere with the quality of information obtained on other parts of the instruments.

REVIEWER'S REFERENCE

American Psychiatric Association. (1994). *Diagnostic and statistical manual of mental disorders* (4th ed.). Washington, DC: Author.

[4]

Adaptive Behavior Assessment System®—Second Edition.

Purpose: Designed to provide a comprehensive norm-referenced assessment of adaptive skills.
Population: Birth to 89 years.
Publication Dates: 2002–2003.
Acronym: ABAS-Second Edition.
Scores, 14: 10 skill areas, 3 adaptive domains, 1 overall score: Conceptual (Communication, Functional Academics, Self-Direction, Composite), Social (Leisure, Social, Composite), Practical (Community Use, Home Living, Health and Safety, Self-Care, Work, Composite), Motor, General Adaptive Composite.
Administration: Individual.
Forms, 5: Parent/Primary Caregiver Form (Ages Birth–5), Parent Form (Ages 5–21), Teacher/Daycare Provider Form (Ages 2–5), Teacher Form (Ages 5–21), Adult Form (Ages 16–89).
Price Data, 2004: $165 per Examination kit including manual, 5 Parent/Primary Caregiver Forms (Ages 0–5), 5 Teacher/Daycare Provider Forms (Ages 2–5), 5 Parent Forms (Ages 5–21), 5 Teacher Forms (Ages 5–21), and 5 Adult Forms; $110 per manual; $55 per 25 Forms (specify respondent and age); $165 per Infant and Preschool kit including manual, 25 Parent/Primary Caregiver Forms, and 25 Teacher/Daycare Provider Forms; $165 per School kit including manual, 25 Parent Forms, and 25 Teacher Forms; $165 per Adult kit including manual and 25 Adult Forms; $160 per Scoring Assistant CD-ROM version or disk version; $55 per 25 e-record form™ credits.
Time: (20) minutes.
Comments: Personal Computer and Personal Digital Assistant scoring software available; incorporates current AAMR and DSM-IV diagnostic guidelines.
Authors: Patti Harrison and Thomas Oakland.
Publisher: PsychCorp, A brand of Harcourt Assessment, Inc.
Cross References: For a review by James K. Benish of the original edition, see 15:6.

Review of the Adaptive Behavior Assessment System®—Second Edition by MATTHEW K. BURNS, Associate Professor of Educational Psychology, University of Minnesota, Minneapolis, MN:

DESCRIPTION. The second edition of the Adaptive Behavior Assessment System (ABAS-II) is a revision of a respected norm-referenced measure of adaptive behavior. Scales are provided for parents, teacher/daycare providers, and adult self-report to rate individuals from infancy to age 89. The Infant and Preschool forms (ages 0 to 5 years) are new to the second edition. Each scale provides a General Adaptive Composite (GAC) score along with three domain scores (Conceptual, Social, and Practical), and scores for nine skill areas. Each skill area contains at least 20 items.

The format of the ABAS-II closely follows that of typical measures of adaptive behavior in that the respondent rates the behavioral frequency of various skills, using a 4-point rubric (*not able, never, sometimes,* and *always*), grouped together into skill areas and domains. In addition, respondents are provided an option of marking the item as guessed and can provide additional comments as desired. The number of items marked as guessed is then compared to a normative sample to aid in the interpretation of the results. Scales in which too many items were guessed at, as determined by exceeding the mean number of guessed items for the norm group, result in questionable data and it is recommended that a different respondent complete the scale.

DEVELOPMENT. A pilot study was conducted in which 92 parents, 63 teachers, and 273 other adults participated. Next, a national tryout study was conducted with 1,045 parents, 980 teachers, and 1,406 other adults. The results of these studies were used to identify and refine items for standardization. Having said that, the extent of the two studies exceeded that of most test development efforts and was impressive.

The manual reported that the ABAS-II was based on definitions of mental retardation delineated by the American Association on Mental Retardation (AAMR, 2002) and the *Diagnostic and Statistical Manual of Mental Disorders—Fourth Edition: Text Revision* (DSM-IV-TR; American Psychiatric Association, 2000). Thus, the scale is theoretically grounded while providing data useful for most diagnostic criteria.

TECHNICAL.

Standardization. Extensive data were provided regarding the standardization sample. The number of participants ranged from 750 (Teacher/Daycare Provider Form of the Infant-Preschool Form) to 1,690 (Teacher Form of the School-Age Forms), and nearly every age grouping included at least 100 participants. Representativeness of the sample seemed to closely match United States Census data in regard to age, gender, race/ethnicity, and education. Further, the sample seemed to be geographically representative as well. Percentage of children diagnosed with various disabilities included in the normative samples were provided and ranged from 2.93% (Teacher/Daycare Provider Form) to 8.46% (Adult Self-Report Form). Given that estimates of total school-aged population with disabilities are approximately 11% (U.S. Department of Education, 2001), these numbers seem somewhat low.

Due to the simple and well-defined administration procedures, standardization of administration seems easily achieved. Perhaps the only area of concern is when the age of the individual being rated overlaps with more than one form. For example, the Infant and Preschool Forms are for children ages 0 to 5 years and the School-Aged Forms are for children ages 5 to 21 years. Further, the Adult forms are for individuals ages 16 to 89 years. Thus, there is more than one appropriate form for individuals who are 5 years old, or who are 16 to 21 years old. The manual provides only limited criteria with which to decide the appropriate form. More specific decision-making procedures and data are needed.

Reliability and validity. The ABAS-II manual provides extensive reliability and validity data that are impressive in both scope and quality. Estimates of reliability are provided for internal consistency, test-retest, interrater, and cross-form consistency. Coefficients are provided according to the different forms and for each age grouping. Further, estimates were also provided for levels of performance such as average and below average. Generally speaking, coefficients for the GAC exceeded .90, except for children less than 1 year old, and the domain scores were also near, at, or exceeded .90. Thus, those scores can be used with confidence. Some variance in coefficients occurred for the individual skill areas, which implied that interpretation of those scores should be done cautiously. Interrater reliability estimates were lower, but generally exceeded .80, and cross-respondent coefficients generally exceeded .70. Although these scores are lower than desired standards, they still considerably exceed similar estimates with other scales.

The content validity of the ABAS-II was adequately argued through expert ratings of items, respondent comments on ease of completing the scales, and consistency with AAMR and DSM-IV-TR definitions. Expected differences between age groups were also demonstrated and supported the validity of the data. Skill, domain, and GAC scores were intercorrelated and resulted in corrected coefficients that ranged from .47 to .93. Further, confirmatory factor analyses supported the current factor structure. These two analyses suggested adequate support for the theoretical structure of the ABAS-II.

Scores from the ABAS-II were correlated with other measures of adaptive behavior and resulted in coefficients that suggested moderate to strong relationships. Data were also correlated with the Behavior Assessment System for Children (BASC) and resulted in negative correlations with Externalizing Problems, Internalizing Problems, and Behavior Symptoms Index, but a correlation coefficient of .80 was noted between the GAC and the BASC Adaptive Skill Composite. These data suggested adequate divergent and convergent properties of the data. Finally, scores were correlated with various measures of achievement and intelligence and resulted in mostly moderate relationships.

The authors should be commended for thoroughly discussing the uses of ABAS-II data. Diagnostic utility was examined with several studies that compared scores of individuals diagnosed with various disorders including mental retardation, developmental delays, known biological risk factors, physical impairments, language disorders, pervasive developmental disorder not otherwise specified, autism, and attention deficit/hyperactivity disorder to a matched group. Significant differences and moderate to strong effects were found. It would be difficult to find a measure of adaptive behavior with more convincing data regarding clinical validity.

Arguably as important as diagnostic utility could be providing data useful for intervention design and progress monitoring. The ABAS-II provides specific steps for developing programs and progress monitoring, and presents five case studies of various uses of the data. Although additional data are needed to fully determine the program planning and progress monitoring uses of ABAS-II scores, the case studies are an acceptable start.

COMMENTARY AND SUMMARY. The ABAS-II was developed from sound theory and empirical methodology, and provides a norm group that is sufficiently representative and large. Scores from the GAC are adequately reliable to make eligibility and entitlement decisions, and domain scores are stable enough for clinical and intervention utility. Skill area scores should be interpreted cautiously. Data to support the tool's reliability and validity are impressive and the authors should be commended for exploring the usefulness of the data for intervention planning and progress monitoring. Although the assessment of adaptive behavior should not be limited to norm-referenced testing, the ABAS-II provides data that could strengthen most comprehensive assessments of adaptive behavior and/or mental retardation in general. Further, many commercially prepared norm-referenced measures already exist, and at first glance the ABAS-II does not significantly differ from the usual approach. However, the ABAS-II appears technically superior to most of its competitors and it is recommended for use with few reservations.

REVIEWER'S REFERENCES

American Association on Mental Retardation. (2002). *Mental retardation: Definition, classification, and systems of support.* Washington, DC: Author.
American Psychiatric Association. (2000). *Diagnostic and statistical manual of mental disorders* (4th ed., text revision). Washington, DC: Author.
U.S. Department of Education. (2001). *To assure the free appropriate public education of all children with disabilities: Twenty-third annual report to Congress on the implementation of the Individuals with Disabilities Act.* Washington, DC: U.S. Government Printing Office.

Review of the Adaptive Behavior Assessment System®—Second Edition by JOYCE MEIKAMP, Professor of Special Education, Marshall University, South Charleston, WV, and CAROLYN H. SUPPA, Associate Professor of Counseling, Marshall University, South Charleston, WV:

DESCRIPTION. The Adaptive Behavior Assessment System®—Second Edition (ABAS-II) is an assessment of overall adaptive functioning as well as an assessment of 10 adaptive skill areas for individuals ages birth to 89 years. The ABAS-II comprises five separate rating forms relevant to various age ranges and environmental settings including home, school, community, and work. This is an expanded version of the first edition, which did not include parent/primary caregiver forms for ages 0 to 5 or teacher/daycare forms for ages 2–5. Information obtained regarding an individual's ability to function effectively and independently historically has been integral to diagnosis, classification, treatment planning, documentation, and monitoring of individuals with various

disorders and disabilities. The ABAS-II has incorporated the most recent definitions of adaptive skills presented by both the *Diagnostic and Statistical Manual of Mental Disorders-Fourth Edition-Text Revision* (DSM-TR; APA, 2000) and the American Association on Mental Retardation (AAMR, 2002) in terms of classification criteria for diagnosis of mental retardation. Also it is consistent with the Individuals with Disabilities Education Act (IDEA; 1997) classification system for special education and disability. Clinical validity studies were conducted to present information on the comparison of the ABAS-II performances of a wide range of different clinical samples to control groups.

Each of the five rating forms can be completed in approximately 20 minutes and handscored in 5–10 minutes. A computerized Windows CD-ROM Scoring Assistant is available that produces a technical report including composite scores, a plotted Skills Area profile, and an analysis of strengths and weaknesses. The School-Aged Parent Form, the Teacher/Daycare Provider Form, and the Parent/Primary Caregiver Form are available in Spanish.

Respondents can be any adult individual, including the one to be evaluated, adequately familiar with the daily adaptive skills being rated. The form may be read aloud to the respondent if necessary. Multiple ratings from various settings are recommended to provide a comprehensive assessment. Scoring involves rating an individual on how often a behavior is performed without help when the behavior needs to be displayed. Responses include 0 for "Is Not Able," 1 for "Never or Almost Never When Needed," 2 for "Sometimes When Needed," or 3 for "Always or Almost Always When Needed." The rater is instructed to evaluate whether the behavior has been observed or if the rating was a guess about the frequency of the occurrence. For each skill area, the total number of guesses is recorded. The manual states if there are four or more guessed responses in a skill area, the respondent should be interviewed to evaluate the reason for the amount of guessing and whether or not scoring should continue. A professional user should be responsible for supervision of the administration and scoring as well as for the use of the scores.

ABAS-II scores result not only in an overall composite score (General Adaptive Composite—

GAC) but also scores, if age appropriate, on each of the 10 DSM-TR adaptive skill areas (Communication, Community Use, Functional Academics, Home/School Living, Health and Safety, Leisure, Self-Care, Self-Direction, Social, and Work) and for the three adaptive domains identified by AAMR (Conceptual, Social, and Practical) into which the 10 skills are grouped. Normative scores are provided for the composite score, the skill areas, and the adaptive domains. Raw scores on each of the skill areas are converted to scaled scores that then are used to derive standard scores for the adaptive domains and the GAC. Tables of age-based percentile ranks and test-age equivalents are provided. A supplemental analysis of strengths and weaknesses can be performed based on tables of confidence intervals provided in the manual. These data provide a normative comparison between the adaptive skills of the individual being rated to those of typically developing individuals of the same age in the standardization sample. New to the ABAS-II are extended validity studies allowing for evaluating the relationship between adaptive skills and intelligence and ability as measured by other adaptive behavior scales and intelligence tests.

DEVELOPMENT. The ABAS-II was written on average at the fifth-grade level with all rating forms reviewed by an independent consultant. One pilot study and one national tryout study provided support for the psychometric properties of the scales. Normative information for the national standardization samples is based on demographics from 1999 and 2000 U.S. Census data purported to be representative of the English-speaking U.S. population from age birth to 89. Samples were stratified by sex, race/ethnicity, and educational parameters and were selected from four geographical regions considered to be proportionate to the population percentages in each region. The ABAS-II manual provides comprehensive tables regarding all aspects of the standardization sample as well as other research conducted for the ABAS-II that represent a well-developed approach to test development.

TECHNICAL. Data from analyses of internal consistency, test-retest reliability, interrater reliability, and cross-form consistency are provided along with standard errors of measurement. The reliability coefficients for the GAC averaged from .97–.99 across the six standardization samples whereas the adaptive domains ranged from .91–.98 and the skill areas were typically in the .90s, ranging from .80 to .97. When possible, tables provide the internal consistency reliability by level of performance and by clinical groups. The reliability data reflect an overall high degree of internal consistency for the skill areas, adaptive domains, and GAC scaled scores and suggest that the ABAS-II is reliable for assessing individuals with different levels of functioning and with different clinical diagnoses. Test-retest reliability using the Pearson product moment correlation coefficient yielded estimates in the .90s for most GAC samples; the adaptive domain coefficients were generally in the .80s; and, as expected, the skill area estimates were slightly lower ranging from the .70s to .90s depending on skill area and age group. Interrater reliability, estimated by the Pearson product moment correlation coefficient, was evaluated using five samples and ranged from .82 to .93 depending on the form. Cross-form consistency correlations between the ratings of teacher and parent ratings for children and between self-report and other respondent ratings for adults were estimated using the Pearson product moment correlation on relatively small samples. The correlations between the parents' and teachers' ratings of children suggest potential differences whereas the ratings within the adult samples suggest consistency. Detailed standard error of measurement tables are provided for all forms in all score areas.

The ABAS-II manual discusses various forms of validity evidence including test content, response process, internal structure, internal consistency, age group differences, clinical validity, and the consequences of testing. Tables display results from comparison studies of the ABAS-II and other instruments measuring adaptive skills or intelligence or achievement. Relatively high correlations of convergent validity were reported in relationships between the ABAS-II and the Vineland Adaptive Behavior Scale, another comprehensive measure of adaptive behavior. However, lower correlations were found with brief behavior rating scales (generally less than the .50s) as well as with measures of problem behavior, intelligence, and achievement. The authors encourage users to examine all validity evidence in relation to users' individual needs and practices. The manual also recognizes the ongoing need for additional data on the validity of the ABAS-II regarding use in various settings and purposes.

COMMENTARY. The ABAS-II provides a well-researched and developed alternative to other comprehensive adaptive behavior scales. Its advantages over other instruments include (a) assessment areas compliant with the new AAMR domains, (b) the ability to use multiple respondents in multiple settings including an option for adult self-report, (c) the opportunity to guess about a behavior, and (d) the ability for the respondent to answer each question directly without an interviewer who must be trained in an indirect interview strategy. The second edition includes an expanded structure to incorporate current practice standards, a downward extension of norms, and an extension of validity studies. Considering the amount of research conducted on other areas of this system, the standardization sample seems relatively small. Further research is indicated to support generalizability of results. Because correlations show some discrepancy between parent and teacher ratings of children, it is important to consider results from multiple settings.

The manual is well-written and helpful, particularly regarding basic statistical and measurement information and guidelines for interpretation and intervention. Results of all evidence are provided in detailed, well-organized tables throughout the manual.

SUMMARY. The ABAS-II offers a system for assessing adaptive behavior skills based on current construct definitions for individuals from ages 0 to 89 in a variety of settings. It shows high convergent validity with the Vineland Adaptive Behavior Scale—Classroom Edition, another comprehensive adaptive behavior scale. However, the ABAS-II yields not only a composite score (General Adaptive Score) but also scores on the three AAMR domains and the 10 DSM-TR skills. It allows guessing about a skill level and employs direct questioning instead of an indirect interview process. A supplemental analysis can be performed to identify areas of strength and weakness. Helpful guidelines are provided for the use of the ABAS-II within a comprehensive assessment. Detailed and well-organized research results support a high level of reliability throughout the system and present substantial validity evidence. The ability to use direct questioning of multiple respondents in multiple settings and adult self-rating to yield assessments of adaptive skills within the context of the AAMR domains and the DSM-TR definitions, as well as the comparison studies with other tests and diagnoses other that MR, makes the ABAS-II an asset in a comprehensive assessment in a variety of clinical settings. Increasing the size of the standardization sample is the major recommendation.

REVIEWERS' REFERENCES

American Association on Mental Retardation. (2002). *Mental retardation: Definition, classification, and systems of support.* Washington, DC: Author.
American Psychiatric Association. (2000). *Diagnostic and statistical manual of mental disorders* (4th ed., text revision). Washington, DC: Author.
Individuals with Disabilities Act of 1997, Final Regulations, 34 C.F.R. Pt. 3000 and 303, *Assistance to States for the Education of Children with Disabilities and the Early Intervention Program for Infants and Toddlers with Disabilities.* (Fed. Reg. 64, 1999).

[5]

Adolescent/Adult Sensory Profile.

Purpose: Designed "to promote self-evaluation of behavioral responses to everyday sensory experiences."

Population: Ages 11–65+.

Publication Date: 2002.

Scores, 4: Low Registration, Sensation Seeking, Sensory Sensitivity, Sensation Avoiding.

Administration: Individual.

Price Data, 2003: $85 per complete kit including user's manual (144 pages) and 25 self-questionnaire/ summary reports; $65 per user's manual; $27 per 25 self-questionnaire/summary reports.

Time: (10–15) minutes.

Comments: Self-report inventory based on the Sensory Profile (220), a measure developed for children.

Authors: Catana E. Brown and Winnie Dunn.

Publisher: PsychCorp, A brand of Harcourt Assessment, Inc.

Review of the Adolescent/Adult Sensory Profile by CORINE FITZPATRICK, Director of the Master's Program in Counseling, Manhattan College, Riverdale, NY:

DESCRIPTION. The Adolescent/Adult Sensory Profile is a 60-item self-report questionnaire. It is designed to enable self-evaluation of behavioral responses to everyday sensory experiences. An individual completes the form by indicating the frequency of a response (almost never, seldom, occasionally, frequently, almost always) to various sensory experiences. The profile takes approximately 15 minutes to administer.

The profile is summarized for interpretation into quadrant scores: Low Registration, Sensation Seeking, Sensory Sensitivity, and Sensation Avoiding. The quadrant scores derived from the profile represent patterns of sensory processing as described in Dunn's (1997) Model of Sensory Processing based on the intersection of two continua (neurological threshold and behavioral response/ self-regulation). The model describes quadrants identified as Low Registration, Sensation Seeking, Sensory Sensitivity, and Sensation Avoiding. There are cut off scores for each of the quadrant raw score totals on the summary score sheet. The classification system describes the individual's likelihood for behaviors in the sensory processing quadrant as: much less than most people, less than most people, similar to most people, more than most people, and much more than most people. Scores are described according to a continuum based on a normal distribution of scores, allowing for a description of an individual's placement on this continuum rather than an indication of an area of concern.

The Adolescent/Adult Sensory Profile provides a standard method for professionals and individuals to measure and to profile the effect of sensory processing on functional performance. There are two purposes for the profile. It can provide information to help in understanding an individual's sensory processing. It results in an increased awareness of an individual's preferences in processing. The second principal purpose is to address intervention planning related to one's needs.

DEVELOPMENT. The profile is based on the Sensory Profile (Dunn, 1999; 220), a measure developed for children 3–10 years of age. Items from that profile were modified for this measure and for use as a self-report. The scoring was modified to enable a higher score to represent more of an attribute. For example, a 5 is a high score and reflects more of an attribute. The manual provides a brief description of Dunn's theory and sufficient exploration of the research done both on the Dunn model and on sensory processing. The rationale for evaluating sensory processing in daily life is particularly thorough. Much discussion is focused on the "principles and features of the neurological threshold continuum," yet this construct is not scored on the test, but rather is provided minimally in an appendix. Considering how interrelated the measures of processing and this neurological continuum are according to the authors, there should be some easy way to compare them. The rationale in the manual for how these scales fit together needs to be more explicitly

explained and the Appendix B material not placed in an appendix.

TECHNICAL. Although the development of test items is described in detail for this profile, items were drawn primarily from the other profile and modified. Information regarding how those initial items were developed is lacking. Additionally, the expert panel of judges, although seemingly qualified, was from the same University and affiliated Medical Center. Their exposure to the Dunn model was noted, but exposure or understanding of any other models or work in this area were not specified.

Descriptions of the scales are fairly clear. The connection to the quadrants, as described in the Dunn model is less clear and less well documented. Factor analysis results, although mentioned in the manual, were not shown. A four factor model was chosen, according to the authors, because it was consistent with the Dunn model. The decision here seems to have been a priori, based on the hypothesis of the model rather than using the analysis to look at goodness of fit with the model. The report of a goodness of fit test would have enhanced this discussion. Also, although the authors say that "generally" the four factor model was supportive, the data should have been in the manual for the user to make that determination. Two of the scales, Sensory Sensitivity and Sensation Avoiding, overlapped. As the authors point out, however, these scales are both viewed as low-threshold questions.

Internal consistency reliability was the only reliability used in the development of items for each quadrant. The internal consistency reliability was .82 for Low Registration, .79 for Sensation Seeking, .81 for Sensory Sensitivity, and .66 for Sensation Avoiding. Eleven items from the Sensation Avoiding quadrant correlated more strongly with Sensory Sensitivity. Other reliability estimates to support this instrument are lacking.

Evidence to support validity is limited. As described above, experts were drawn from people connected to the University and who were most familiar with the Dunn model. These experts were then asked to sort cards with items from the earlier survey (Sensory Profile) into the quadrants. A description of how the original items were determined would have added credence to the validity here. No other related studies or comparisons to other measures are mentioned. As such, the authors may well be charting new territory, but it might help to know what else has been done in this area. It should be noted that the manual does describe a relationship between the four quadrant categories of the Dunn model to a model of temperament. Also, they provide a strong rationale for evaluating sensory processing. Ultimately, some more explicit description of what others in this field are doing would have enhanced the knowledge of the reader.

COMMENTARY. The rationale for the use of some self-report measure of sensory processing that relates to activities in every day life is a strong one. In clinical practice, expensive physiological approaches are often used to measure processing. The self-reporting not only is simpler, but the relevance of the items to everyday life increases the understanding and utility of the measure for the individual. In this regard, it is a needed addition to the field. Explanation of how the measure could be used in treatment planning and intervention, although mentioned, should be more clearly articulated and explicit; such enhanced description would add to the value of the instrument. Chapter 5 makes a good attempt to show types of strategies that would be effective in intervention, but the critical link to why these behaviors might be more problematic is less clear. The connection to various forms of processing (e.g., visual, touch) is good. The variety of case studies is excellent and would have been even better had the interpretation section utilized more of the exact strategies listed in the intervention list.

As stated above, however, there are some psychometric concerns. Included in those concerns are the lack of any other reliability than internal consistency, limited validity, and related information from the original instrument that was used as the basis for this one (Sensory Profile). The data regarding the factor analysis should have been given in the manual.

SUMMARY. The developers of this instrument are attempting to develop a means, through self-report, to assess sensory processing. It would appear that there is a need to gain this kind of information for clients who are seeking help in functional performance. The practicality of the measure, its noticeable focus on everyday life, and its potential application in a variety of counseling settings (as indicated in the sample case studies) is compelling. Also, the wide age span that is included with both measures enables, for example, parents to gain perspective of their own processing preferences, those of their children, and to better develop strategies that would be effective in working with their children.

This instrument, although meritorious in its practical application, needs to address the reliability and validity issues, and to offer more research studies that have focused on this area, so that those who use the instrument have a better understanding of the work of others in the area.

REVIEWER'S REFERENCES

Dunn, W. (1997). The impact of sensory processing abilities in the daily lives of young children and their families: A conceptual model. *Infants and Young Children, 9*, 23–35.
Dunn, W. (1999). *Sensory Profile: User's manual.* San Antonio, TX: The Psychological Corporation.

Review of the Adolescent/Adult Sensory Profile by JANET V. SMITH, Assistant Professor, Department of Psychology and Counseling, Pittsburg State University, Pittsburg, KS:

DESCRIPTION. The Adolescent/Adult Sensory Profile is a 60-item self-report measure of sensory processing. It is designed as a trait measure to promote increased awareness of enduring sensory processing preferences of an individual. This understanding may then be utilized in intervention planning in a variety of settings, including school and employment, to enable an individual to "optimize his or her sensory environment to support daily life" (user's manual, p. 3). The manual lists numerous possible interventions associated with scores obtained on the measure.

Respondents are asked to rate the frequency of a variety of behaviors pertaining to sensory experiences on a 5-point Likert scale. These experiences are grouped into six major areas: Taste/Smell Processing, Movement Processing, Visual Processing, Touch Processing, Activity Level, and Auditory Processing. Item raw scores are transferred to a summary score sheet and totaled in four different quadrants or aspects of sensory functioning. Raw scores are compared to normative data to produce descriptors for each separate quadrant, ranging from *Much Less than Most People* to *Much More than Most People*, with descriptors based on a normal distribution of raw scores. The accompanying quadrant profile allows a visual display of test scores. The four quadrants are: Low Registration, a measure of passive behavioral responses associated with high neurological thresholds; Sensation Seeking, a measure of active behavioral responses associated with high neurological thresholds; Sensory Sensitivity, a measure of passive behavioral responses associated with low neurological thresholds; and Sensation Avoiding, a measure of active behavioral responses associated with high neurological thresholds.

DEVELOPMENT. The underlying theory of the measure is Dunn's (1997) model of sensory processing. The model generates a 2 x 2 matrix based on the dimensions of neurological threshold and behavioral response/self-regulation. Neurological threshold addresses ease of activation of an individual's nervous system. Behavioral response/self-regulation involves a continuum of behaviors ranging from passively acting in accordance with neurological thresholds to actively responding to counteract neurological thresholds and control sensory input. This results in the four quadrants of Low Registration, Sensation Seeking, Sensory Sensitivity, and Sensation Avoiding.

The Adolescent/Adult Sensory Profile is based on the Sensory Profile for children ages 3 to 10. Initial development of the Adolescent/Adult Sensory Profile involved selecting items from the original Sensory Profile that were applicable to adults, rewriting these items in a self-report format, and adding new items to ensure that all quadrants were adequately represented. Items were reviewed by an expert panel as well as subjected to pilot study. Test items were revised on the basis of initial pilot data, and finally item wording was revised on the basis of pilot testing with a small group of adolescents.

TECHNICAL. The standardization sample consisted of 193 adolescents, 496 adults aged 18–64, and 261 adults aged 65 and older. The manual reports that approximately 92% of the sample was white and predominantly from the Mid-west. Individuals with psychiatric diagnoses were excluded from the sample. Evidence of reliability is provided by coefficient alphas for each quadrant score, separately for each age group. Coefficient alpha values ranged from .639 to .775. Content validity was examined through an expert panel review, and the manual notes that members of the panel were able to sort test items accurately into the four quadrants. In addition, evidence of convergent and divergent validity was examined in a study of 207 adults who completed both the Adolescent/Adult Sensory Profile and the New York Longitudinal Scales Adult Temperament Questionnaire.

Although the two instruments measure different constructs, the manual outlines common theoretical underpinnings, and correlations between the two measures generally are in the predicted directions. Further evidence of validity was presented in the form of a study of 20 undergraduate students whose scores on the Adolescent/Adult Sensory Profile were compared to their skin conductance rates. Again, results were consistent with predictions made on the basis of underlying test theory. Finally, the scores of 29 mentally healthy individuals were compared with the scores of 27 individuals with schizophrenia and a control group of 30 individuals with bipolar disorder. Data mostly supported the hypothesized differences in sensory processing in individuals with schizophrenia.

COMMENTARY. The manual is well-written and very easy to follow. The self-report questionnaire is easy to complete, and scoring and interpretation are very straightforward. Several case examples are provided to illustrate potential use of the instrument. Interventions based on test scores are very specific, practical, and easy to implement, although it should be kept in mind that the interventions appear theory-based rather than empirically supported. The main limitations of the test lie in some of the psychometric properties. Specifically, the norm sample was not representative of the U.S. population in terms of race and geographic region, and no information was collected on socioeconomic status. Although the manual acknowledges this problem, it poses a serious concern for interpretation of test scores. In addition, reliability coefficients are moderate at best and no information is provided on test-retest reliability. Given that the test is designed as a trait measure, it would have been helpful to see evidence of temporal stability of scores. There is reasonable validity evidence presented for use of the test with an adult population, but no evidence is presented addressing validity of use with adolescent respondents.

SUMMARY. The Adolescent/Adult Sensory Profile is a very straightforward, easy-to-use measure of sensory processing. Traditionally, sensory processing measures have focused on a younger age group and the Adolescent/Adult Sensory Profile is one of the few measures of sensory processing available for adults. The test is solidly grounded in theory and offers direct practical interventions associated with test scores. Provided that the psychometric limitations are taken into consideration, the test provides a useful vehicle for exploring sensory processing in individuals as well as generating specific ideas to maximize a person's environment based on their sensory characteristics.

REVIEWER'S REFERENCE

Dunn, W. (1997). The impact of sensory processing abilities on the daily lives of young children and their families: A conceptual model. *Infants and Young Children, 9,* 23–35.

[6]

Adolescent American Drug and Alcohol Survey with Prevention Planning Survey.

Purpose: Designed to survey youth "about their experiences with alcohol, tobacco and twenty-five illicit drugs."
Population: Grades 6–12.
Publication Date: 1999.
Acronym: ADAS.
Scores: Not scored.
Administration: Group.
Price Data, 2003: $1.90 per booklet with Prevention Planning Survey (volume discount available for orders of 1,000 booklets or more); $250 per detailed report.
Time: (20–30) minutes.
Comments: For information about the Children's ADAS, see T6:147.
Authors: Ruth Edwards, Fred Beauvais, and Eugene R. Oetting.
Publisher: Rocky Mountain Behavioral Science Institute, Inc.

Review of the Adolescent American Drug and Alcohol Survey and the Prevention Planning Survey by JODY L. KULSTAD, Assistant Professor of Professional Psychology and Family Therapy, Seton Hall University, South Orange, NJ:

DESCRIPTION. The Adolescent American Drug and Alcohol Survey (A-ADAS) is a 55-item survey designed to provide objective data on substance use by youth in communities or community settings. Unlike the nationally based Monitoring the Future study or the National Household Survey of Drug Abuse, the A-ADAS provides comprehensive information *unique* to the community in which the survey is conducted. The A-ADAS surveys use and characteristics of use of over 22 drugs and also assesses contextual factors related to drug use. This wealth of hard data is intended for use in developing or strengthening prevention and intervention efforts. Strengthening the prevention focus is the inclusion of the Prevention Planning Survey (PPS), a 57-item measure of contextual (family, school, peer) dimensions of youth substance use, specifically risk and protective factors derived by the interaction between family, school, and peer contexts that can directly be channeled into prevention or intervention efforts.

The A-ADAS with PPS is available for 8th to 12th graders. Before undertaking this survey project, many steps must take place. Decisions must be made about who to sample, how many to sample, when to survey, and what reports to order. Also, securing school board approval and parental consent is necessary. Due to the widescale nature of the survey administration, a coordinator (or coordinators) is typically identified and that individual serves as the liaison between the persons administering the survey and Rocky Mountain Behavioral Science Institute, Incorporated (RMBSI), the survey organization. Survey materials include A-ADAS PPS forms, test booklets, checklists for tracking survey completion, and instructions for the coordinator, teachers who are administering the survey, and the students. Administration is typically done in a group format by the teacher during class and should take approximately 45–55 minutes to complete. Student instructions are read aloud, verbatim, to ensure all students receive the same guidance. Because completion time varies, RMBSI recommends preparing a quiet, alternate activity for students to do while the class is completing the survey. Completed forms are treated as confidential and are not viewed by anyone in the school. The forms are then sent to RMBSI for analysis to ensure single survey validity. RMBSI evaluates each survey for exaggeration and inconsistency before including it in the results. Typically 30, but no more than 45 days later, two bound survey report volumes are returned along with materials to help organize presentations. The latter includes either overheads of key results or a PowerPoint presentation on disk. The A-ADAS report includes an executive summary along with a detailed report. The report is approximately 55 pages long and includes both text and comparison tables organized into three sections: overview of drug use, experiences and attitudes regarding drugs and alcohol, and use of individual drugs in alcohol. National comparison data are included. The PPS report is approximately 50 pages long and includes text and tables/charts regarding substance use and specific risk and protective factors. Sections of this report include social and personal characteristics of drug use and violence, comparing drug-using students with non-drug-using students, drug use and problems in school, drug use and family influences, personal characteristics and drug use, drug use and prevention, violence, and prevention of violence.

The A-ADAS is composed of approximately 27 separate scales addressing Individual/Peer and Alcohol, Tobacco, and Other Drug Use. Items address age at first use, frequency, peer influence on use, peer use, problems related to use, attempts to get the substance, perceptions of harm, and use characteristics. Item response formats include both dichotomous yes/no and Likert scale. There are also two items asking about style of responding to the survey (e.g., honestly, overexaggerated, underreported). The PPS is organized into approximately 24 scales addressing Individual/Peer, Family, and School/Institutional Factors. Items address peer and family relationships; the individual's school attitude, performance, and fit; parental involvement in school and attitudes toward school, peer attitudes toward school, school performance, and behavior at school; violence behaviors (both as perpetrator and victim) and perception of safety; psychological and emotional issues; parental expectations and discipline, and family environment and attitudes toward substance use. As with the A-ADAS, response format is both dichotomous and likert scale.

DEVELOPMENT. The A-ADAS was developed from a Small Business Innovative Research grant from the National Institute on Drug Abuse from 1983–1986. Items were developed based on the authors' many studies in the alcohol and drug use field. Further refinements, and on-going instrument development (e.g., the PPS), are the result of these ongoing research endeavors. Specific information about item development and scale construction was not available.

TECHNICAL. Psychometric information is based on the ADAS, which addresses use in Grades 6–12 as opposed to the A-ADAS, which is used for Grades 8 through 12.

Reliability. The ADAS PPS has evidenced good reliability and validity in general and across sex and ethnic groups. Internal consistency estimates (coefficient alpha) range from .72 to .94 across drug use scales, with most in the .80 to .90 range, considered exceptionally high for a large

survey. Internal consistency estimates for the PPS range from .60 to .91 for the PPS scales, though only one scale fell below .70 and above .90 with all others in the .70 to high .80 range, suggesting acceptable to good reliability.

Validity. The ADAS evidences good concurrent validity. Comparisons between the ADAS and the University of Michigan National Monitoring the Future study yield similar overall drug use results over several decades, including downturns in use as well as increases. Construct validity, convergent and discriminant, is shown through comparison of the ADAS scales and several measures within the ADAS and PPS. Using cluster analysis, the scales showed unique clusters from other drug use measures indicating that although they may be measuring a similar construct, they are clustering uniquely. Convergent validity was shown through strong correlations with characteristics and risk factors associated with drug use (e.g., peer substance use, delinquency) as well as relationships between risk and use level of use. Furthermore, the authors cite use of the ADAS in over 45 refereed studies as providing evidence for construct validity. The PPS has also been used in several studies that support its validity.

COMMENTARY. The A-ADAS with PPS is an excellent survey that is both practical and useful in what it offers to schools and communities. It is a full service package, complete with analyses and report and presentation materials. RMBSI takes the guesswork out of some of the processes associated with conducting a survey, but to a very little extent this comes at a cost. There is no user manual, and as a result specific information on test development, scale information, and scoring procedures is not easily obtained, which leads to less control by those conducting the survey. That being said, for the population this survey serves, this may well be less of an issue. Also, there is a wealth of information on the ADAS, the general version of the survey, and less available on the A-ADAS and even less for the PPS. Although it appears that ADAS information is used interchangeably with that of A-ADAS, materials do not clearly note the actual differences that may exist, if any, which limits full understanding of the psychometric information.

SUMMARY. The A-ADAS with PPS is a thorough, reliable, and valid survey of drug use behaviors and risk and protective factors supporting or limiting drug use. A key strength of the A-ADAS PPS is that it can be used by lay people to answer hard questions that lead to constructive solutions. Survey users are able to undertake a widescale survey and, within a relatively short period of time, have data that are professionally presented and easily understood. For school or other community entities, this ease of administration and rapid information return allow for addressing problems and concerns in a more expedient manner, with the tools necessary to garner support from officials to fund such prevention and intervention efforts.

Review of the Adolescent American Drug and Alcohol Survey with Prevention Planning Survey by NATHANIEL J. PALLONE, *University Distinguished Professor (Psychology), Center of Alcohol Studies, Rutgers—The State University, New Brunswick, NJ, and* JAMES J. HENNESSY, *Professor (Educational Psychology), Graduate School of Education, Fordham University, New York, NY:*

DESCRIPTION. The Adolescent American Drug and Alcohol Survey (ADAS) is a self-report instrument consisting of 55 items that deal with frequency and pattern of use of alcohol and/or several varieties of what are, in the main, "controlled dangerous substances," but including pharmaceutical preparations (barbiturates, amphetamines) and such everyday substances as gasoline and model airplane glue. Said by its publisher (Rocky Mountain Behavioral Science Institute, or RMBSI) to be usable by respondents in Grades 6–12, the instrument asks questions about drug use not only by the respondent but also by his or her friends—but prudently, given the character of privacy legislation at both federal and state levels, the instrument does not inquire into substance use or abuse among siblings or other family members. Some items contain several subparts (e.g., How much do you think people harm themselves [physically or otherwise] if they ... [a] use alcohol 1 or two times; [b] use alcohol regularly; [c] get drunk 1 or 2 times; [d] get drunk regularly?). Although technically untimed, it is estimated that most students in Grades 6–12 will require 20–30 minutes to complete the ADAS. (There are two companion instruments available from RMBSI to supplement the ADAS: The American Tobacco Survey, containing 32 items similar to those of the ADAS but focused on tobacco use, and the Pre-

vention Planning Survey, comprising 57 items—with, again, several containing subparts—covering a range of topics related to school interest and achievement; family interaction, especially around school events; victimization in violent or coercive behavior in school and community; generalized and specific feelings of fear or safety; and inclination toward, and experience with, firearms.)

Self-report responses are entered anonymously by examinees on machine-scorable answer sheets that are to be returned to RMBSI; there are, apparently, no hand-scoring keys presently available to end users. Responses available to examinees primarily concern frequency on an attitude or a behavior. The structure of the instrument's items poses vexing questions about lack of objectified anchors and about equal-appearing intervals.

Because responses are made anonymously and because scoring is available only through RMBSI, the instrument cannot be used to gather information about a particular respondent's involvement, or lack of involvement, with substance use/abuse. Instead, according to its publishers, the overarching goal of the ADAS is to assess the extent of drug or alcohol use, and attitudes favorable or unfavorable thereto, within the entire student population of a school or perhaps school district. Results are conveyed in a document (the sample report supplied by RMBSI prints to 61 single-sided pages, handsomely spiral-bound) that details frequency of response on each of the 30 "scales" of the ADAS.

That responses to the 55 items on the ADAS combine (one must presume, in various permutations) to yield scores on 30 scales suggests a feat of unusual psychometric legerdemain. Some "scales" are derived from responses to a single item, whereas others combine responses to as many as 4 items. Unfortunately, the manner in which items are parsed to yield these scales is specified neither in the manual distributed by RMBSI, in the sample report, nor on the website (www.rmbsi.com) to which the manual directs the user for updated technical information: Is the "score" associated with a single item scale merely a reflection of the numeric value (perhaps arbitrarily, given the issue of equal-appearing intervals without objectified anchors) associated with each category of response on whatever nonuniform continuum is invoked in that item? If so, why? Similarly, the prospective user searches those sources in vain for terms like "factor loadings" or "cluster analysis." Nor is a description provided of the process by which cumulative scores are available for scales that rest on responses to more than one item: Are frequency counts predicated on nonuniform but perhaps equal-appearing intervals simply added? If so, on the basis of what rationale?

DEVELOPMENT. The same three sources (manual, sample report, RMBSI website) are also remarkably silent on how the ADAS was developed, its origins and pilot versions, the construction and discarding of items, etc. Instead, the prospective user is told that the instrument has been administered to something over 108,000 respondents in Grades 6–12, an aggregate that "includes a substantial (though not precisely representative) proportion of students from each major ethnic group" (manual, p. 1). No further information concerning demographics or even geographics is offered, so that one cannot be sure of what universe those 108,000 respondents (in what is at least implicitly a standardization sample) is held to be representative. When added to nonuniformity in weight in response category, equal-appearing intervals, and what appears to be the derivation of scales on the basis of strictly nominal criteria, the gaps in information on how this instrument was constructed widen appreciably. Those lacunae render interpretation problematic at best.

TECHNICAL. Reliability for each of the 30 scales was estimated through Cronbach's alpha and range from .72 to .94, with the majority in the high .80 to .90 range. Validity is another matter. After admitting that "Establishing validity is not as straight forward as reliability and usually requires evidence from several sources" (manual, p. 3), the publisher then weakly asserts that "Concurrent validity ... has been established by demonstrating that similar results are obtained when ADAS results are compared with the findings from other well-designed and established surveys over time" (manual, p. 3). But neither is what those "other surveys" might be nor how concurrent validity was in fact measured specified in RMBSI's information material. Instead, the black-box aura that hovers over the scoring process rises once more, calling into question whether the essential character of public verifiability and, therefore, of replicability that are the cornerstones of scientific test construction can properly be attributed to this

instrument, at least on the basis of the information provided to end users by its publisher.

Had an instrument such as this been constructed for clinical (individual) use, one could have assayed validity of responses against such admittedly gross external criteria as DUI or DWI stops, emergency room admissions for detoxification, health records held by school nurses, and/or even absences from school; that process, of course, could not have progressed anonymously. To predicate validity for the ADAS on whether, in a global sense, "results" (such as they are) are or are not congruent with those of unspecified "other surveys" begs the question of the veracity, no less than the accuracy, of responses given by junior and senior high school students *both* to the ADAS *and* to those "other surveys." Accuracy hinges on whether the respondent in fact knows the answer to a question; veracity hinges on whether he or she is willing to share accurate knowledge. There are a number of studies that suggest that how students respond to self-report inquiry is highly colored by social desirability variables, including most pertinently what the respondent understands the purpose of the inquiry to be, particularly when what amounts to self-accusation in formally criminal behavior (ranging from underage drinking to possession and use of street drugs) is implicated (Inciardi, 1982; McGlothlin, 1985; Dent et al., 1993). RMSBI's information materials highlight only one sort of assault on veracity: "Exaggerated drug use could be a very critical problem ... that could lead to skepticism about the survey results." To remedy that situation, "we have a fake drug on the survey"; when a student asserts that he or she has used that nonexistent drug, "we would suspect there might be exaggeration on the use of other drugs as well" (Reliability and Validity flyer, p. 2). Yet minimization that is at least as likely in respect of self-reporting formal criminal behavior to which aversive sanctions attach is not addressed.

COMMENTARY. Although raised only tangentially in the instrument's manual and other printed information materials, the RMBSI website wisely contains a lengthy, downloadable memorandum on the thorny issues of privacy rights and parental consent engaged whenever school officials administer any but standardized achievement tests related to subject content mastery. Opinion both in the professional community and in the courts remains divided on whether anonymous survey instruments are subject to a priori review under prevailing human subjects legislation (Harris, 2001; Noll, Zeller, Vannatta, Bukowski, & Davies, 1997; O'Donnell et al., 1997; Pear, 2004). In respect of "knowing, informed, and voluntary" consent, as of this writing, it appears to be the case that a minor child may *volunteer* to respond to an *anonymous* questionnaire without prior notice to his or her parents and thus in the absence of parental consent; obversely, a minor child may not be *compelled* to do so—or at least so case law seems to say until higher courts decide otherwise. But it is not apparent that a student in a junior or senior high school who is told that he or she has the right to decide not to participate *but* who nonetheless inadequately distinguishes self-report from self-accusation *and* who may wish to conceal "guilty knowledge" is likely, on the face of those circumstances, to experience any strong inner compulsion toward veracity.

SUMMARY. The Adolescent American Drug and Alcohol Survey (ADAS) is a 55-item self-report questionnaire intended to survey the extent of, and attitudes toward, drug and alcohol use among groups of junior and senior high school students; it is not designed as a clinical instrument to be used in individual cases (e.g., as an alternate to the MacAndrews Alcoholism Scale, the Michigan Alcoholism Screening Test, or the Miller-Marlatt instruments). Results are reported for groups of examinees in relation to comparison groups of indeterminate demographic, socioeconomic, and ethnic dimensions. Reliability for each of the 30 scales derived from these 55 items, as determined by Cronbach's alpha, is acceptable, but there is little evidence of validity beyond obscure references to "findings from other well-designed and established surveys" (Reliability and Validity flyer, p. 3). Because the issue of parental consent in advance of student participation in self-report surveys of attitude and behavior such as the ADAS remains problematic, the end user might want to exercise unusual prudence before wide distribution of the press release that accompanies each RMBSI report. Alternately, in situations in which there are external (non-self-report, whether by psychometric instrument or through self-revelation to health service or psychological service professionals) indicators of substance use/abuse in a student body of proportions greater than odd or isolated cases, the ADAS may prove beneficial in assessing whether systemic or clinical remedies should more appropriately be mobilized—especially by attending differentially to those items (and scales) that relate to behaviors and those that relate to attitudes on the other, either supportive or tolerant of formally proscribed behaviors.

REVIEWERS' REFERENCES

Dent, C., Galaif, J., Sussman, S., Stacy, A., Burton, D., & Flay, B. (1993). Demographic, psychosocial and behavioral differences in samples of actively and passively consented adolescents. *Addictive Behaviors, 18,* 51–56.
Harris, D. (2001). Discomfort triumphed in a student survey. *New York Times,* March 4, NJW-19.
Inciardi, J. 1982. The production and detection of fraud in street studies of crime and drugs. *Journal of Drug Issues, 12,* 241–250.
McGlothlin, W. (1985). Distinguishing effects from concomitants of drug use: The case of crime. In L. Robins (ed.), *Studying drug abuse* (pp. 153–172). New Brunswick, NJ: Rutgers University Press.
Noll, R., Zeller, M., Vannatta, K., Bukowski, W., & Davies, W. (1997). Potential bias in classroom research: Comparison of children with permission and those who do not receive permission to participate. *Journal of Clinical Child Psychology, 26*(1), 36–42.
O'Donnell, L., Duran, R., Sandoval, A., Breslin, M., Juhn., G., & Stueve, A. (1997). Obtaining written parent permission for school-based health surveys of urban young adolescents. *Journal of Adolescent Health, 21,* 376–383.
Pear, R. (2004). Survey finds U.S. agencies engaged in "data mining." *New York Times,* May 17, A-24.

[7]

The Adult Manifest Anxiety Scale.

Purpose: Used to evaluate the level of anxiety experienced by individuals across the age spectrum from early adulthood to elderly.

Publication Date: 2003.

Administration: Group.

Levels, 3: AMAS-A, AMAS-C, AMAS-E.

Price Data, 2003: $84 per kit including 30 AutoScore™ answer forms (10 for each subtest) and manual (44 pages); $32.50 per 20 AutoScore™ answer forms; $39.95 per manual.

Time: (10–15) minutes.

Comments: All three scales together represent an upward extension of the Revised Children's Manifest Anxiety Scale (T6:2106); the original CMAS was a downward extension of the Taylor Manifest Anxiety Scale.

Authors: Cecil R. Reynolds, Bert O. Richmond, and Patricia A. Lowe.

Publisher: Western Psychological Services.

a) AMAS-A.

Population: Ages 19–59.

Acronym: AMAS-A.

Scores, 5: Worry/Oversensitivity, Physiological Anxiety, Social Concerns/Stress, Lie, Worry.

b) AMAS-C.

Population: College students.

Acronym: AMAS-C.

Scores, 6: Worry/Oversensitivity, Physiological Anxiety, Social Concerns/Stress, Test Anxiety, Lie, Total.

c) AMAS-E.

Population: Ages 60 and over.

Acronym: AMAS-E.
Scores, 5: Worry/Oversensitivity, Physiological Anxiety, Fear of Aging, Lie, Total.

Review of the Adult Manifest Anxiety Scale by ASHRAF KAGEE, Professor of Psychology, University of Stellenbosch, Matieland, South Africa:

DESCRIPTION. The Adult Manifest Anxiety Scale (AMAS) is a paper-and-pencil test for which the purpose is to evaluate the level of anxiety experienced by individuals across the age spectrum from early adulthood to elderly. The AMAS consists of three different instruments: the AMAS-A (for adults), the AMAS-C (for college students), and the AMAS-E (for the elderly).

The AMAS-A has 36 items and is intended for use in evaluating the level of anxiety experienced by individuals in the general adult population. It has three anxiety scales (Worry/Oversensitivity, Physiological Anxiety, and Social Concerns/Stress) and a validity scale. The AMAS-C has 49 items and is geared toward screening and evaluating college students for anxiety, including test anxiety. It has four anxiety scales (Worry/Oversensitivity, Social Concerns/Stress, Physiological Manifestations of Anxiety, and Test Anxiety) and a validity scale. The AMAS-E has 44 items and has been designed for use in evaluating anxiety among individuals aged 60 and above. It has three anxiety scales (Worry/Oversensitivity, Physiological Manifestations of Anxiety, and Fear of Aging) and a validity scale.

The AMAS in its various versions is appropriate for use in general clinic practices, college counseling centers, hospices, and geriatric centers. No practice effects of responding to the measure have been observed. Thus the instrument may be used to track changes over time by means of repeated administrations. The subscales of the AMAS are helpful in identifying individuals with clinically significant levels of anxiety.

Test takers are provided with a WPS Autoscore Form for the relevant version of the AMAS. The items for all the versions of the AMAS require forced choice (yes/no) responses, which the test taker is asked to circle. The test may be administered in either a group or individual format.

DEVELOPMENT. The materials furnished by the developers provide useful information concerning how the instrument was developed. For example, they indicate that items for all three versions of the AMAS were derived from the Revised Children's Manifest Anxiety Scale (RCMAS) whereas several additional items were added to reflect age-appropriate concerns of test-takers for each version. The original trial version of the RCMAS, which consisted of more than 100 items, was used as a model for generating items for the AMAS. The developers state that the construction of items related to test anxiety (for the AMAS-C) and fear of aging (for the AMAS-E) were informed by their clinical experience and reviewing the relevant literature. Appropriately, items were reviewed by measurement experts for readability and clarity of presentation, as well as for congruity with the construct of anxiety.

The constructs underlying the various subscales appear to be appropriately discrete from one another. The definitions offered to describe each subscale are useful in indicating the concerns relevant to individuals for whom the three versions of the instrument are intended. The manual makes a convincing argument for the way in which the scales fit together to measure an overarching construct of manifest anxiety. It would be very helpful if the developers cited references to current research in the area of manifest anxiety.

TECHNICAL. Information describing the standardization process is provided in detail for all three versions of the instrument. Large samples were recruited in the standardization process (1,419 for the adult version, 818 for the college version, and 636 for the elderly version). Considerable efforts have been made to ensure that the groups on which the instruments have been standardized are representative of the American population. On the other hand, normative data for non–American countries and cultures are absent, representing limitations to the use of these data in such contexts.

There does not seem to be obvious overlap of items, although all items appear to be directly linked in an obvious way to the context of the subscales. Most of the items are phrased in the direction of psychological disturbance and responding "yes" to an item suggests the existence of a problem and the need for treatment. Despite the inclusion of the validity scale, the apparent face validity of the items may limit the extent to which the test is able to elicit honest responses from test-takers. The manual does not refer to any means by which test results may be "truth-corrected" based on the scores on the validity scale.

The reliability coefficients as measured by Cronbach's alpha for the various subscales on all versions of the instrument all fall above .70, which is considered sufficient for most measures of psychological variables. Test-retest reliability estimates range from .67 to .90 across an interval of 1 week.

The indices of construct validity for the three versions of the instrument are generally good. Intercorrelations between the subscales are of a magnitude consistent with adequate construct validity. These correlation coefficients are statistically significant but modest, indicating that they measure a conceptually unified domain but are not redundant with one another. The test manual provides limited data regarding the convergent and divergent validity of the instrument. Comparisons with the Multiscore Depression Inventory (MDI) and the California Psychological Inventory (CPI) are presented. The subscales of the AMAS show appropriately modest correlations with subscales of the MDI, in keeping with evidence of a modest relationship between depression and anxiety. These intercorrelations demonstrate that the AMAS shares substantial variance with the MDI and indicate that the constructs of anxiety and depression are related to each other but are not redundant. In addition, the negative correlations between subscales on the AMAS-A and relevant indices on the CPI that measure positive affect suggest that the AMAS-A is an adequate measure of negative affect.

COMMENTARY. The AMAS-C and AMAS-E are useful adjuncts to existing measures of anxiety such as the Beck Anxiety Inventory (T6:272) and the Spielberger State-Trait Anxiety Inventory (T6:2372), as these versions of the AMAS are tailored to assess the unique concerns of college students and the elderly, respectively. It is unclear how the AMAS-A offers additional value to already existing and well-established self-report instruments that measure anxiety, as no motivation for this is made in the manual. Moreover, additional and more robust studies that assess divergent and convergent validity are necessary to support the construct validity of all versions of the AMAS. The items on the WPS Autoscore Form are easy to read for most people. However, for elderly persons the font size may present some difficulties. This is a potentially serious issue as it may affect the validity of the data yielded by the instrument in both clinical and research settings with this population. On the whole, however, the instrument is easy to administer and score. The norms provided in the appendix of the manual were obtained from American samples. If this instrument is to gain widespread usage in other parts of the world, additional culture-specific norms will need to be developed accordingly.

SUMMARY. The developers have made a concerted effort to develop an instrument to measure anxiety in specific populations, namely, college students and elderly persons. The strength of the test lies in its application to these specific contexts. Thus, the AMAS-C and AMAS-E are especially welcome instruments that psychologists and counselors may find useful in their work. As several other and more established measures of anxiety for the general adult population already exist, the need for an additional instrument of this nature such as the AMAS-A is questionable.

[8]

Ages & Stages Questionnaires: A Parent-Completed, Child-Monitoring System, Second Edition.

Purpose: Designed to screen "infants and young children for developmental delays."

Population: Ages 4–60 months.

Publication Dates: 1995–1999.

Acronym: ASQ.

Scores, 5: Communication, Gross Motor, Fine Motor, Problem Solving, Personal-Social.

Administration: Individual.

Levels, 19: 4, 6, 8, 10, 12, 14, 16, 18, 20, 22, 24, 27, 30, 33, 36, 42, 48, 54, and 60 months.

Price Data, 2005: $190 per complete kit including user's guide (1999, 195 pages) and set of 19 master questionnaires for photocopying; $165 per set of 19 master questionnaires; $45 per user's guide; $44 per The Ages & Stages Questionnaires on a Home Visit (VHS video); $49.95 per ASQ Scoring and Referral (video).

Foreign Language Editions: Spanish, French, and Korean editions available; contact publisher for availability in additional languages.

Time: (10–20) minutes.

Comments: Parent-completed questionnaire.

Authors: Diane Bricker and Jane Squires, with assistance from Linda Mounts, LaWanda Potter, Robert Nickel, Elizabeth Twombly, and Jane Farrell.

Publisher: Brookes Publishing Co., Inc.
Cross References: For reviews by Dorothy M. Singleton and Rhonda H. Solomon of the original edition, see 14:14.

Review of the Ages & Stages Questionnaires: A Parent-Completed, Child-Monitoring System, Second Edition by B. ANN BOYCE, Associate Professor, Curry School of Education, University of Virginia, Charlottesville, VA:

DESCRIPTION.

Overview and purposes. The Ages & Stages Questionnaires (ASQ): A Parent-Completed, Child-Monitoring System, Second Edition is a first-level screening program designed to identify infants and young children who may be at-risk for developmental delays or disorders. According to the authors of the ASQ, the requirements of a first-level comprehensive screening program are: (a) ability to test large numbers of children, (b) easy to use, (c) low in cost, and (d) suitable for use with diverse populations. This parent- or primary caregiver-administered screening test purports to identify accurately young children who may need further evaluation to determine their eligibility for early intervention services. In addition to the first purpose of the ASQ as a screening program, the ASQ can also be used to monitor a child's developmental progress, especially for those who are at-risk for developmental delays or disabilities resulting from medical (e.g., low birth weight) or environmental (e.g., low socioeconomic status) factors.

The ASQ is composed of 19 questionnaires used in 2-, 3-, and 6-month intervals starting at 4 months of age and continuing through 60 months of age. Each of the 19 questionnaires is composed of 30 items/questions that are grouped by five developmental areas: (a) Communication, (b) Gross Motor, (c) Fine Motor, (d) Problem Solving, and (e) Personal-Social. In addition, there is a section on each questionnaire for parental/caregiver concerns. The ASQ materials consist of: (a) 19 reproducible master questionnaires; (b) 19 reproducible, age-appropriate scoring and data summary sheets available in print or CD-ROM; and (c) a user's guide. In the user's guide, it is stated that the ASQ master questionnaires are available in French and Spanish translations, and in addition, within the ASQ packet, it is noted that the ASQ questionnaires are also available in Korean.

The ASQ can be completed by the parent or caregiver in a home setting with the results mailed to a central location for scoring or delivered to a clinic for evaluation and discussion during a "well-child" visit. Each ASQ can be completed in approximately 10–20 minutes with scoring taking as little as 5 minutes. Each test item uses a rating scale format where parents/caregivers observe a specific behavior and record whether that behavior is present. Item scores are recorded in one of three ways (yes, sometimes, or not yet). These three responses are then converted to point values, and a summary score (consisting of items belonging to each area) is calculated for each of the five areas (e.g., Communication, Fine Motor, etc.). These scores are then compared to empirically derived cutoff scores for each area. If a child falls below a given cutoff score then further diagnostic testing is recommended.

DEVELOPMENT. The original impetus for the development of the ASQ was based on three information sources. First was the belief that early detection of developmental problems was critical to successful intervention. Second, the research supported the notion that biological or medical indicators are not good predictors of subsequent infant/child outcomes. Instead, socioeconomic factors were thought to better predict developmental delays or disorders (Blackman, 1986; Werner & Smith, 1992). Third was the prevalent use of the multidisciplinary team, which relies heavily on professional judgment and does not usually collect data on the child's behavior. This type of team often evaluates a child only once or at widely spaced intervals thus creating a possibility for a missed opportunity to identify a child who may be in need of early intervention. In addition, due to the sporadic testing, proper monitoring of the child's progress is lacking.

The Infant/Child Monitoring Questionnaire (I/CMQ), developed in 1980, was the predecessor of the ASQ. The work of Hilda Knobloch and her associates (Knobloch, Stevens, Malone, Ellison, & Risemburg, 1979) served as a catalyst for the development of the I/CMQ and ASQ. The ASQ has more than 20 years of study and numerous research grants that focused on the following research questions: (a) comparing parent/caregiver test results with a trained examiner; (b) examining the areas of overreferrals, underreferrals, and test sensitivity; (c) calculating test-retest reliability and interrater reliability; (d) investigating the validity of the ASQ compared to other standardized, professionally administered classification assessments; (e) evaluating the cost of the questionnaire; and (f) discerning whether parents/caregivers from low SES backgrounds with limited education can successfully administer the ASQ. In general, the findings have been positive with agreement between the results of trained evaluators and parents/caregivers when administering the questionnaires. The amount of over- and underreferral varies depending on which study's findings are considered but these findings are promising and the test's sensitivity was acceptable. The test-retest reliability (2-week interval) exceeded 90% agreement and the interrater reliability was also high. The agreement related to other classification assessment instruments was high with an overall correlation of .83. The cost was modest and acceptable and is kept low by providing copyright for local reproduction of the questionnaires. Results of the ASQ's use with diverse populations revealed that with some training, low SES individuals can successfully give this instrument but because of the limited sample size used in this particular study caution must be exercised when interpreting these data.

Based on the results of these studies the first edition of the ASQ was released for publication in 1995. Since that time, the researchers have continued to collect data on the efficacy of this instrument and the revision process has been ongoing. For example, the second edition of the ASQ published in 1999 contains an expansion of questionnaires that monitor and identify developmental delays for infants as young as 4 months of age through 60 months of age.

TECHNICAL.

Test administration. The ASQ system was developed to screen and monitor infants and young children who may be at-risk for developmental delays during the first 5 years of life. Several options are available for administering the ASQ: (a) parent/caregiver completes ASQ at home, (b) parent/ caregiver completes ASQ at home during a home visit by a service care provider, or (c) parent/ caregiver or service provider completes ASQ at clinic or child care center. Scoring of the ASQ can also be accomplished by: (a) mailing completed ASQ to a support staff member, (b) scoring by a service care provider during a home visit or visit to a clinic or child care center, or (c) scoring by a parent/caretaker.

The reading level for the ASQ was set at fourth to sixth grade. This level was established to account for the diversity of the population that may complete this instrument. There are two commercially available training tapes.

The questionnaire packet consists of 6 to 8 pages depending on the interval (4 months of age or 12 months of age). Overall, the directions are clear and concise. The packet consists of three parts: (a) general instructions, (b) ASQ questionnaire, and (c) summary sheet. Each of the age intervals is color coded for easy identification by age of the child. Cutoff scores, shaded in gray, are identified on the summary sheet for each of the five developmental areas. These cutoff scores are used as markers to identify infants/young children who should receive further evaluation.

Scoring and interpretation. The ASQ is composed of 19 questionnaires given in 2–6 month intervals starting at 4 months of age and continuing through 60 months of age. Each of the 19 questionnaires is composed of 30 items/questions that are grouped by the five developmental areas of: (a) Communication, (b) Gross Motor, (c) Fine Motor, (d) Problem Solving, and (e) Personal-Social. As previously stated, each test item uses a rating scale format where parents/caregivers observe a specific behavior and record whether that behavior is present. Item scores are recorded in one of three ways (yes, sometimes, or not yet). These three responses are then converted to point values. A "yes" response receives 10 points, a "sometimes" response receives 5 points, and a "not yet" response scores 0 points. A summary score (consisting of items belonging to each developmental area) is computed and compared to empirically derived cutoff scores for each area. If a child falls below a given cutoff score then further diagnostic testing is recommended. The cutoff scores, shaded in gray on each questionnaire's summary sheet, are estimated by using 2 standard deviations below the mean for most of the developmental areas. This adjusted cutoff procedure was found to produce the best results regarding over- and underreferral. However, this is not a flawless procedure and children may not be correctly identified, which is why the authors strongly recommend multiple testing at different age intervals (2- to 6-month intervals).

The large normative data base aided in the establishment of the generation of the means and ultimately the cutoff scores. The population size was sufficient to develop norms for each of the 2- to 6-month intervals.

COMMENTARY. The ASQ is recommended by the American Academy of Pediatrics, the Child Neurology Society, and Healthy Start. The second edition of the ASQ is a comprehensive guide that includes: (a) introduction to the ASQ, (b) implementation instructions, (c) procedures for administering and scoring, (d) methodology options and alternatives, (e) selection criteria for participants, (f) cultural and language adaptations, (g) guidelines for referral criteria, and (h) systems for monitoring and evaluating infants and young children.

At some age intervals the ASQ has a high rate of false positives and false negatives. Certain age levels produce false negatives as high as 48.98% and false positives as high as 18.67%. When one considers that parental/caregiver involvement is at the center of the ASQ with these individuals representative of a wide range of SES and educational levels this is not really surprising. However, because the ASQ is a first-level screening and monitoring system that provides parents/caregivers with evidence for further evaluation, it seems that the ASQ is sufficient to accomplish its goal as a first-level system.

There are some inconsistencies within the user's guide that need editorial attention. For example, Blackman was not published in 1996 but in 1986. And the reference for Blackman should be found at the end of the Preface section of the user's guide. Further, there were a few areas where the user's guide and the actual questionnaire were not consistent. For example, the inclusion of the Korean language information was present in the questionnaire information and excluded in the user's guide.

SUMMARY. The ASQ (2nd ed.) appears to be a low cost, parent- or caregiver-centered screening and monitoring system that can identify infants and young children with developmental delays. It is important to note that it is not a diagnostic tool to be used to determine if a child is gifted or developmentally challenged. Instead the ASQ is a first-level system and once a child is identified then the involvement of trained professionals is needed.

REVIEWER'S REFERENCES

Blackman, J. (1986). *Warning signals: Basic criteria for tracking at-risk infants and toddlers.* Washington, DC: National Centers for Clinical Infant Programs.
Knobloch, H., Stevens, F., Malone, A. F., Ellison, P., & Risemburg, H. (1979). The validity of parental reporting of infant development. *Pediatrics, 63,* 872—879.
Werner, E. E., & Smith, R. S. (1992). *Overcoming the odds: High risk children from birth to adulthood.* Ithaca, NY: Cornell University Press.

Review of the Ages & Stages Questionnaires: A Parent-Completed, Child-Monitoring System, Second Edition by G. MICHAEL POTEAT, Director of Institutional Effectiveness, East Carolina University, Glenville, NC:

DESCRIPTION AND DEVELOPMENT. The Ages & Stages Questionnaires (ASQ): A Parent-Completed, Child-Monitoring System, Second Edition is described by the authors as a comprehensive, first-level screening instrument for the identification of infants and young children with developmental delays or disorders. The ASQ consists of questionnaires, which are completed by either parents or primary caregivers. There are 19 separate questionnaires for children at ages 4, 6, 8, 10, 12, 14, 16, 18, 20, 22, 24, 27, 30, 33, 36, 42, 48, 54, and 60 months. Each questionnaire is described as being valid for administration for 1 month before and 1 month after the interval age. For example, a 22-month questionnaire could be used with children from 21 to 23 months of age. Each questionnaire has 30 developmental items that are completed by the parents/caregivers using the responses "Yes," "Sometimes," and "Not Yet." The questionnaires, scoring, and data summary sheets are reproducible and may be photocopied. Both Spanish and French translations are available. A Korean translation is also available for some ages.

Although the ASQ is described as being useful for monitoring children's progress while in developmental programs, its greatest utility would be for identifying children at risk for developmental delays and especially children who have delays that are relatively moderate and consequently not obvious to the casual or untrained observer. This function is evidenced by the amount of coverage in the manual (almost 80 pages) devoted to developing a screening and monitoring program for identifying children who are "at risk." This section of the user's guide has information on many different issues and tasks, ranging from possible risk factors used to select populations to obtaining informed consent. The guidelines are very comprehensive and would be useful for those professionals developing an infant screening program even if they were not using the ASQ.

Because funding for early childhood intervention programs varies both across location and with time, there are a number of different methods for administering the ASQ. These range from one-time mailings of the ASQ to families identified as having children who are at-risk for developmental disorders to the monitoring of children's development from birth to kindergarten. Again, the user's guide contains detailed instructions for almost all conceivable scenarios.

Regardless of how it is employed, the basic method for administering the ASQ is to ask the parents or primary caregovers to rate the child's development on 30 items. The items (examples are from the 12-month questionnaire) are equally divided among Communication (e.g., Does your baby shake his head when he means "no" or "yes"?); Gross Motor (e.g., walking holding furniture); Fine Motor (e.g., throwing a small ball); Problem Solving (e.g., looking for hidden objects); and Personal-Social (e.g., playing with stuffed animals). Again, each item is rated Yes (scored as 10 points), Sometimes (5 points), and Not Yet (0 points). Parents are encouraged to elicit behaviors when they are uncertain, and a list of materials that are related to the behaviors rated is included in an appendix. However, most of the materials would be found in almost every home and there is not a test kit per se. Professionals can also complete the ASQ after completing a home visit where they have had an opportunity to observe the child.

The reading level of the ASQ is described as approximately the fourth to sixth grade level and many items have simple illustrations. Illiterate or poorly educated parents may have difficulty with the items but the questionnaires are not complicated. Children are identified as requiring further observation or assessment if they obtain a score two standard deviations or more below the mean in one or more developmental areas.

TECHNICAL. More than 20 pages of technical data are presented in a technical report section of the ASQ user's guide. The normative sample is based on the questionnaires completed by parents of 2,008 children between 4 and 36 months of age with additional data collected on 320 children at 48 and 60 months of age. Characteristics of the sample are presented but the data are incomplete (e.g., ethnicity is reported for only 1,287 families and the occupational level of the father for only 801 cases).

The limited amount of data makes it difficult to reach conclusions about the adequacy of the normative sample. Nonetheless, it appears that Caucasians and African Americans were sampled representatively, making up 65% and 13.5% of the sample, respectively. Native Americans were overrepresented (14.6%) and Latino/Hispanic families (4.0%) were underrepresented. In terms of occupational status and education, the available data suggest that the sample consisted primarily of families where the parents worked as laborers, clerks, or in lower level administrative positions. About 30% of fathers and 20% of mothers had completed college.

A number of psychometric characteristics of the ASQ are presented in detail. The reliability evidence of the instrument is limited but acceptable. Coefficient alphas for the developmental areas are typically in the .60 to .70 ranges. Alphas increase with the age interval and are typically lower for the Personal-Social area. Given the small number of items in each area and the age range of the sample, these coefficients indicate reasonable internal consistency. Test-retest and interobserver reliability were assessed by comparing assessments completed by parents over a time interval of 2 weeks and by comparing the assessments completed by parents with those completed by professionals. In both cases, reliability was calculated based on the percentage of agreement in classification. Test-retest reliability calculated over 2 weeks for a sample of 175 parents was 94%. Interobserver reliability calculated on the basis of agreement between 112 parents when compared to two examiners was also 94%. The reliabilities were based on "classification" but unfortunately no other details of the calculations are provided.

Evidence for the validity of the ASQ was obtained by comparing classifications based on the ASQ with classifications obtained using standardized measures of development (e.g., Bayley Scales of Infant Development, Stanford-Binet Intelligence Scale). Two basic measures of validity were calculated: (a) *sensitivity*, which is defined as the proportion of the children who were classified as having developmental delays on both the ASQ and the comparison instrument and (b) *specificity*, which refers to the proportion of children classified as not having a developmental disability by both the ASQ and the comparison instrument (e.g., the Stanford-Binet). Overall, concurrent sensitivity was 72% and specificity was 86%. The positive predictive validity, the probability of a child identified by the ASQ as being at risk having a need for intervention, was approximately 44%. The positive predictive validity was obtained by dividing the number of children identified as having developmental delays on the ASQ and the comparison instrument (e.g., the Stanford-Binet) by the total number of children identified as having developmental delays on the ASQ. In a sample of 1,644 children, a total of 362 were classified as being at risk on the ASQ but only 161 children also had standardized developmental scores that classified them as having developmental delays (161/362 = 44.47%).

SUMMARY. The ASQ has limitations in terms of the normative sample. Also, the evidence for reliability is limited because of the failure to define what is meant by classification, but my assumption is that classification refers to developing typically or at-risk, which are very broad definitions for reliability. Finally, the evidence for validity is moderate because more than 50% of children identified at-risk were not found to have developmental delays using standardized assessment. Nevertheless, I would still recommend the ASQ for consideration as a screening instrument. The assessment of infants and young children is notoriously difficult, and the ASQ offers an economical method of screening for children. Also, in the validity study, only 63 children were identified as having developmental delays on a standardized instrument and were not identified as being at-risk by the ASQ. When all factors are considered, the ASQ offers an inexpensive method for screening large numbers of children whose developmental problems might otherwise go undetected until they enter preschool or kindergarten programs. I would suggest that the authors provide more information on reliability and that the manual be revised and reorganized. Information on the psychometric properties of the ASQ is scattered throughout the manual with definitions in a glossary contained near the middle of the manual and the technical data in an appendix. Overall, the ASQ should prove to be a useful screening instrument for use by professionals who work with infants and young children and who are charged with identifying children with risks for developmental delays.

[9]

Ages & Stages Questionnaires: Social-Emotional: A Parent-Completed, Child-Monitoring System for Social-Emotional Behaviors.

Purpose: Designed to assess "children's social-emotional development."
Population: Ages 3–66 months.
Publication Dates: 2002–2003.
Acronym: ASQ:SE.
Scores, 7: Self-Regulation, Compliance, Communication, Adaptive Functioning, Autonomy, Affect, Interaction with People.
Administration: Individual.
Levels, 8: 6, 12, 18, 24, 30, 36, 48, and 60 months questionnaires.
Price Data, 2003: $125 per complete kit including user's guide (2003, 192 pages), and a boxed set of 8 photocopiable master questionnaires and corresponding scoring sheets; $100 per boxed set of 8 photocopiable master questionnaires and corresponding scoring sheets; $40 per user's guide.
Foreign Language Edition: Questionnaires available in Spanish.
Time: (10–15) minutes.
Comments: Parent-completed questionnaires.
Authors: Jane Squires, Diane Bricker, Elizabeth Twombly, Suzanne Yockelson, Maura Schoen Davis, and Younghee Kim.
Publisher: Brookes Publishing Co., Inc.

Review of the Ages & Stages Questionnaires: Social-Emotional: A Parent-Completed, Child-Monitoring System for Social-Emotional Behaviors by JOHN J. VACCA, Assistant Professor of Individual and Family Studies, Developmental School Psychologist, University of Delaware, Middletown, DE:

DESCRIPTION. The Ages & Stages Questionnaires: Social-Emotional (ASQ:SE) was developed to accompany the Ages & Stages Questionnaires (ASQ; 8) and to provide a mechanism for assessing the social and emotional competence of infants, toddlers, and preschoolers (ages 3 to 66 months). The Ages & Stages Questionnaires is a set of 19 questionnaires designed for infants and young children (ages 4 to 60 months) as a screening measure to identify children who have developmental problems. The tool is judgment-based, and it is completed by primary caregivers.

The completion time for the ASQ:SE is approximately 10-15 minutes. The items are grouped together around the following seven behavioral areas: Self-Regulation, Compliance, Communication, Adaptive Functioning, Autonomy, Affect, and Interaction with People. Caregivers are provided with three choices for their response: *most of the time, sometimes,* or *never or rarely.* Additionally, they are provided with the opportunity to identify which behaviors are of concern for them. Point values 0, 5, and 10 are assigned to each response, depending on the response (e.g., 10 = *most of the time; 5 = sometimes; 0 = never*). Scores that are significantly high are suggestive of children with potential developmental problems. Total scores are then compared against specific cutoff scores (depending on the age of the child) indicating whether the child is at-risk or okay.

DEVELOPMENT. The ASQ:SE grew out of the growing concern among early care and education professionals about the social and emotional needs of very young children. Further, increased attention as seen in legislation such as Public Law 105-17 (Amendments to the Individuals with Disabilities Education Act-IDEA) draws attention to the critical need to attend to children's early emotional needs. Assessment of social and emotional development in very young children is cumbersome, however, and it is often a source of debates about whether deviance seen in early childhood is reflective of normal development or if such deviance is reflective of pathology identified in its early stage.

The authors of the ASQ:SE do an excellent job providing the reader with a clear perspective on the topic of early childhood social and emotional development. Additionally, they integrate information from related literature to present the theoretical foundations for the development of their instrument. Of primary influence is the work done by Raver and Zigler. The authors cite their work and its importance in shaping the way we regard early social and emotional competence in young children.

The conceptual framework for the ASQ:SE is based largely on social learning theory, which highlights the reciprocal relationship between an individual and the world around them. The authors also include the contributions of Cicchetti's developmental organizational theory (1993, as cited in ASQ:SE manual) and Dishion, French, and Patterson's marginal deviation model (1995, as cited in ASQ:SE manual). In combination, these two theories highlight the difficulties children and older individuals can have later as a result of unmet needs in their social environment.

Development of the ASQ:SE centered on the following key variables: Setting/Time (Where, when, and under what conditions does the behavior occur?), Development (What is the child's developmental level?), Health (What is the child's health status?), and Family/Culture (What family/cultural factors are potentially associated with the behavior?). The authors specifically state that the ASQ:SE is not designed to be used as a diagnostic tool, but rather as a screening tool to identify children who may need more in-depth evaluation and intervention.

The normative sample used for the development of the instrument approximated the 2000 U.S. Census data for income, level of education, and ethnicity. The authors specified that a minimum of 175 cases at each age level were included. The original version of the tool (Behavior-Ages and Stages Questionnaires; B-ASQ) was field tested in 1996. An expert review of the items was conducted by a variety of professionals from mental health, medicine, and education. Additionally, certain early care and education programs also participated in the field testing activities. The programs served mainly families in Head Start, Migrant Head Start, or Healthy Start in the states of California, Hawaii, Oregon, Ohio, Utah, Arizona, and Washington. Utility questionnaires were completed by the practitioners and families from these programs to provide feedback on the tool. Following review of this process, the final version was completed. A Spanish version of the tool was also developed following the completion of the final edition of the ASQ:SE.

TECHNICAL. The authors went to extensive lengths, especially with examination of validity, to demonstrate the psychometric properties of the ASQ:SE. The data were based on the participation of 3,014 individuals who completed the questionnaires. Validity studies included the participation of 1,041 children. Detailed information both in narrative and table form is well documented in the user manual.

Concurrent validity was investigated comparing the ASQ:SE with the Vineland Social Emotional Early Childhood Scale (SEEC; 1998, as cited in manual) and the Achenbach Child Behavior Checklist (CBCL; 1991, 1992, as cited in manual). The reported values ranged from .81 to .95, with an overall agreement of .93. Values for Sensitivity (the ability to identify those children with social-emotional difficulties) ranged from .71 to .85, with an overall value of .78. Values for Specificity (the ability of a tool to identify those children without social-emotional difficulties) were significantly higher from .90 to .98, with an overall value of .95. Overall, the ability of the tool to identify children with genuine social and emotional difficulties was lower across intervals, whereas the ability to identify children whose social and emotional development was within normal limits was higher.

Values for overall utility, as acknowledged by parents who had completed the tool, reflected that 96% of parents reported that the tool was easy to understand and complete. An impressive extension of the validity studies carried out for this instrument is the comparison between genders. Two procedures were used: Box plots and nonparametric Kruskal-Wallis Test. Review of the Box plot data reveals more variability between males and females as they get older, especially beyond 30 months. Results from the Kruskal-Wallis Test also support this finding, yet a sufficient number of females were not available at the time of this procedure, and, therefore, conclusive data are not reported. Admirably, the authors recognize this limitation and they indicate that as data are collected, information about gender differences will be reported further.

With respect to reliability, measures for internal consistency (using Cronbach's coefficient alpha) ranged from .67 to .91. This provides support for a moderate to strong relationship between the items of the tool and the behavioral area under which it is grouped. Test-retest reliability was achieved by having parents complete the instrument on two separate occasions (i.e., 1- to 3-week intervals). The reported value was .94. Earlier in the manual, the authors mention that interrater reliability was also examined for professionals. They briefly mention that two professionals completed the tool on two occasions and that the reliability coefficient was .95.

COMMENTARY. It seems that almost every other issue of given periodicals in early childhood contains manuscripts related to infant-toddler mental health, early childhood wellness, or social-emotional development and behavior. Such topics are also beginning to emerge in legislation and state initiatives across the country, given the growing concern among our society to protect and preserve the well-being of our youngest citizens. With the advent of the No Child Left Behind Act and similar pieces of related legislation, numerous initiatives are being undertaken to monitor how schools and programs provide for their population and foster positive self-esteem and autonomous learning.

The authors of the ASQ:SE are to be commended for providing the pediatric community with a useful tool to accompany the other tools they routinely use to provide a comprehensive picture of the child's strengths, needs, learning styles, and social-emotional competence. The layout of the tool itself is simple and easy to follow. The inclusion of a Spanish version helps with the utility of the tool with families from diverse backgrounds.

SUMMARY. The ASQ:SE represents an innovative approach in gathering information about social-emotional development in early childhood. Ongoing research should continue with the ASQ:SE and other similar tools to provide information about generalizability across gender, race, and ethnicity and to document how the social-emotional development of individuals changes and adapts across the lifespan. Finally, as with other data that are generated from the assessment process, the information one receives is only as good as it allows for the development of appropriate services and training of qualified professionals to carry out such services with children and families. Presently, although social and emotional development is recognized under federal law as a key area needing provision in educating young children, oftentimes, providers do not feel adequately prepared to manage behavioral and emotional difficulties especially those that pose significant challenges to traditional forms of teaching. Therefore, it is hoped that with the development of tools like the ASQ:SE equal attention will go to personnel training and curriculum development with a special focus on social-emotional development so that providers will find the data generated from assessment tools useful for helping children and planning for groups of children.

[10]
Alzheimer's Disease Caregiver's Questionnaire.

Purpose: Designed to "evaluate the likelihood that a specific individual has a dementia suggestive of Alzheimer's Disease."

Population: Ages 40 and over.

Publication Dates: 1998–2002.

Acronym: ADCQ.

Scores, 7: Likelihood of a Dementia Consistent with or Suggestive of Alzheimer's Disease (Memory, Confusion and Disorientation, Geographic Disorientation, Behavior, Reasoning and Judgment, Language Abilities, Total).

Administration: Individual.

Price Data, 2003: $299 per introductory kit on a 3.5-inch disk including 25 paper-and-pencil versions, software program, on-screen user's manual, installation guide, and 25 caregiver's report generations; $350 per 50 record forms with 50-use key disk.

Time: (5–10) minutes.

Comments: Symptom checklist completed by caregiver; can be administered on-line, on desk-top computer, or in paper-and-pencil format; software requires Windows 95/98/ME/NT/2000/XP and standard 3.5-inch, 1.44 MB disk.

Authors: Paul R. Solomon and Cynthia A. Murphy (manual).

Publisher: Psychological Assessment Resources, Inc.

Review of the Alzheimer's Disease Caregiver's Questionnaire by MARK A. ALBANESE, Professor of Population Health Sciences, University of Wisconsin, Madison, WI:

DESCRIPTION. The Alzheimer's Disease Caregiver's Questionnaire (ADCQ) is an 18-item symptom checklist that is completed by the caregiver (i.e., family member, spouse, or companion) or someone else who has knowledge of a patient or individual to determine whether it is likely or unlikely that the rated individual has a dementia characteristic of Alzheimer's disease. The ADCQ was designed to be used to rate individuals 40 years of age or older and the authors give specific prohibitions for use with younger individuals. The ADCQ takes between 5 and 10 minutes to complete; requires no participation from office staff, a physician, or health care professional; and it requires no cooperation, or even participation, from the patient. However, clinicians should determine that the individual who is providing the ratings has had sufficient contact with the patient to make a reasonable observation.

The ADCQ can be completed using the paper-and-pencil version of the questionnaire or it can be completed via a computerized on-screen administration using the ADCQ software. It can be completed in the course of an interview with the caregiver, or the caregiver can complete it in the waiting room, at home by mail, or over the Internet (www.ADCQ.net). The results of the ADCQ are presented in the ADCQ Caregiver's Report. This report is a brief (e.g., 4- to 6-page) document that summarizes the caregiver's item endorsements on the ADCQ, documents whether it is likely or unlikely that the rated individual has a dementia characteristic of Alzheimer's disease, and provides recommendations that the caregiver can use to obtain a comprehensive evaluation for the rated individual. The ADCQ Caregiver's Report was developed to be given directly to caregivers. However, the clinician administering the ADCQ should be prepared to answer questions pertaining to issues such as limitations of the ADCQ (e.g., the instrument is not intended to diagnose Alzheimer's disease) and Alzheimer's disease (AD).

DEVELOPMENT. The initial development efforts began with the compilation of a list of attributes describing AD patients. This was accomplished through two steps. First, current instruments were reviewed. Next, a number of experts were consulted regarding appropriate item selection. This initial list consisted of 56 items that could be answered "Yes" or "No." To determine whether the questions were understandable for the patients to respond "Yes" or "No" appropriately to each item, a group of caregivers of AD patients was given the list to review. Many items were revised and a response alternative of "N/A" was added. Based upon analysis of data obtained for validation purposes, the 3 most discriminating symptom items were identified in each of six commonly identified AD problem areas: Memory, Confusion and Disorientation, Geographic Disorientation, Reasoning and Judgment, Language Abilities, and Behavior. This led to the creation of the final 18-item pool that has 3 items assessing each of the six different problem areas.

TECHNICAL.

Scoring. To obtain an ADCQ total score, the mean for each of the six problem areas is calculated and the sum of all of the means is used as the ADCQ total score. "Yes" responses are coded as 1 and "No" responses as 0. "N/A" responses are coded as "0." Thus, scores range from 0 to 6. A score of 1.5 or greater is interpreted as likely that the person rated has a dementia characteristic of AD.

Standardization. In the initial validation study, caregivers for patients who were successively admitted to an outpatient memory clinic completed the ADCQ before the patients were seen by a clinician. Data were also collected about an age- and education-matched sample of community-dwelling individuals whose companions completed the ADCQ. All participants then received a neuropsychological evaluation to verify their cognitive status. The evaluation included the Mini-Mental State Examination (MMSE) along with nine additional tests. The final sample consisted of 141 caregivers of patients with successive admissions to an outpatient memory clinic who were subsequently diagnosed with probable Alzheimer's disease using NINCDS-ADRDA criteria and 93 cognitively intact individuals. The sample of patients with probable Alzheimer's disease was all Caucasian and had a mean age of 77 years (*SD* = 6.4 years), with women comprising 66% of the sample. Members of the control sample who were rated with the ADCQ were also all Caucasian with a mean age of 73 years (*SD* = 6.8 years), with women comprising 67% of the sample.

Reliability. The internal consistency reliability (coefficient alpha) estimates of the ADCQ total score for ratings of a combined sample of 141 AD patients and 93 normal controls is reported to be .87. Test-retest reliability was examined in a new sample of caregivers (*N* = 19) of AD patients who completed the ADCQ on two different occasions (average was 17.5 days apart, with a range from 6 to 40 days). These individuals were not part of the initial sample used to validate the instrument. The sample of individuals who were rated was all Caucasian, 63% were male, and the average age was 80 years (*SD* = 6 years). The test-retest correlation of the ADCQ scores was .71.

Validity. A Receiver Operator Characteristic analysis (ROC) was used on the total sample in order to identify a cutoff score for the ADCQ. The ROC analyses were calculated using the ADCQ total score (i.e., ADCQ total score = the sum of the means for each item grouping). The ROC was significant ($p < .001$), with an Area Under the Curve (A) value of .97 (95% confidence interval ranging from .95 to .99). A series of cutoff scores were evaluated and the cutoff score of 1.5 was selected because it had the best balance of sensitivity (.92) and specificity (.86).

The level of agreement between the two administrations for the categorical classification of Likely AD or Unlikely AD using the total score cutoff established with the ROC analysis was evaluated with the sample used for the test-retest analysis (*N* = 19). Time 1 and Time 2 ADCQ classifications produced a phi coefficient = .67, with 89% of the sample being classified consistently across different test administrations.

The relationship between the ADCQ and the MMSE was also examined. ADCQ total scores were significantly associated with MMSE total scores ($r = -.29$, $p < .01$), with higher ADCQ scores being linked to lower MMSE scores. The relatively small magnitude of the correlation suggested that the two instruments may be assessing different aspects of functioning. The percentages of patients who were suspected of having AD (*N* = 141) and who were identified as cognitively impaired with the MMSE (i.e., MMSE total score < 23) were compared to the patients who were identified as having a likely diagnosis of AD based on the ADCQ rating provided by a caregiver. Sixty percent of the AD sample had MMSE scores of 23 or lower whereas 92% of the AD sample had ADCQ scores above the cutoff of 1.5. Moreover, of the approximately 40% of AD patients who had MMSE scores above the cutoff for cognitive impairment (i.e., MMSE total scores > 24), 90% were rated on the ADCQ as Likely for having a dementia characteristic of AD. The ADCQ authors state that these results are preliminary, but suggest that the ADCQ might have more validity for identifying suspected AD than the MMSE.

COMMENTARY. The ADCQ manual lists a number of competing screening instruments for AD; however, these instruments must be administered directly to the patient. The real advantage of the ADCQ is that it can be completed by the people who have observed behaviors in a person and are concerned about their welfare. These are usually family members or friends who want information that can help them make a decision about whether to have their loved one more formally assessed. This can be of benefit to physicians in their counseling of families of AD patients. The other factor to consider is that AD is underdiagnosed; by some estimates, fewer than half of all individuals with AD have been diagnosed. The technical manual indicates that underdiagnosis is a problem because the four medications currently available to treat AD are most effective when administered early in the course of the disease. Also, implementation of social support systems can be most beneficial when initiated early in the course of a progressive disease. Thus, having a screening instrument available that is inexpensive and easy to administer can make a real difference in the lives of both AD patients and those who care for them. The ADCQ seems to possess these qualities.

The main problems with the ADCQ as it currently exists are that the data to support its use with non-Caucasian patient populations and the reliability and validity of the cutscore are limited. Even though the technical manual reports data from an initial validation study, it is preliminary and has not been published in the peer-reviewed literature. Also, none of the patients evaluated in any of the instrument development phases appear to be from non-Caucasian populations. Based upon this limited study, a number of different statistical procedures were used to demonstrate that the instrument successfully discriminates between individuals who have a clear diagnosis of AD and those who are lacking any demonstrable mental deficiencies. However, it is unclear how the ADCQ will work with those who fall between these extremes. There also is a lot of information lacking about the instrument development process. For example, at some point, 56 initial items were reduced to the final 18. This was a critical step and it is not clear what patient population this was based upon. Another problem is that in the validation study, the ADCQ was administered along with 10 other instruments, the MMSE being one of those. In the validity analysis section of the technical manual, only results from the MMSE are reported. A more complete reporting of the validity data with the other instruments is needed.

A final concern has to do with the need for further psychometric analysis of the results. The operational score is a single value (1.5), at or above which the person being rated is suspected of AD. However, the reliability reported in the technical manual does not reflect the reliability about a cutpoint. Perhaps more perplexing is the fact that the initial analysis included a series of elegant statistical analyses (e.g., logistic regression) performed on randomly selected 65% of the samples with the remaining 35% serving as holdouts for validation purposes. The random sampling and holdout process was replicated 99 times. These analyses would seem to be the method of choice for determining cutscores that would be maximally stable and discriminating for the data in hand. However, the cutscore was selected by a receiver-operator curve (ROC) computed for the entire sample. Although the ROC approach enables one to weigh the relative value of sensitivity and specificity in the choice of a cutscore, it may not be stable.

SUMMARY. The ADCQ is an 18-item symptom checklist that is completed by the caregiver (i.e., family member, spouse, or companion) or someone else who has knowledge of a patient or individual to determine whether it is likely or unlikely that the rated individual has a dementia characteristic of Alzheimer's disease. The ADCQ was designed to be used to rate individuals 40 years of age or older and the authors give specific prohibitions for use with younger individuals. The ADCQ takes between 5 and 10 minutes to complete; requires no participation from office staff, a physician, or health care professional; and it requires no cooperation, or even participation, from the patient. The ADCQ has the potential to be extremely valuable for its use in helping patients with concerns about a friend or loved one and to aid early identification and intervention for patients with AD. Although preliminary data indicate that the ADCQ can effectively discriminate between patients with a clear diagnosis of AD and those who are clearly without AD symptoms, its use with patients who are in between is unclear. Further, the methods used in developing the final 18-item instrument need better documentation and the normative data and reliability and validity estimates are currently inadequate.

Review of Alzheimer's Disease Caregiver's Questionnaire by MATTHEW E. LAMBERT, Assistant Clinical Professor of Neuropsychiatry, Texas Tech University Health Sciences Center, Lubbock, TX:

DESCRIPTION. The Alzheimer's Disease Caregiver's Questionnaire (ADCQ) is an 18-item checklist designed to be completed by caregivers of patients, aged 40 and older, suspected of suffering an Alzheimer's type dementia. It is to be completed in approximately 5 to 10 minutes and independent of any professional in a paper-and-pencil format, although it can be administered by a professional with responses entered directly into the scoring program. The ADCQ items address problem areas of Memory, Confusion and Disorientation, Geographic Disorientation, Reasoning and Judgment, Language Abilities, and Behavior with 3 items representing each area. Responses are Yes, No, or N/A related to specific problems the patient has had in the past 6 months. Information related to soundness of the caregivers' responses is obtained by determining how many times per week the caregiver sees the patient or talks to him or her on the phone.

ADCQ responses are entered into a software scoring program that uses an algorithm to yield a "Likely" or "Unlikely" classification that the patient has a dementia suggestive of Alzheimer's disease. A five-page report is then printed that interprets the results of the ADCQ, provides recommendations for further follow-up and resource outlets, and includes a listing of the items and responses. The software is required for scoring the ADCQ and includes an internal counter with an initial 25 reports included. Additional reports must be purchased from the publisher.

The test manual is included as a file on the software installation disk. It is a 49-page double-spaced manual. Approximately 10 pages of the manual are dedicated to the technical development and psychometric properties of the instrument. The remainder is dedicated to software installation and utilization, upgrade policy, technical support, return policy, warranty, and references.

DEVELOPMENT. According to the manual, the ADCQ items were initially developed by compiling a list of attributes that are typical of individuals suffering Alzheimer's disease. Items were generated by surveying other screening instruments and through expert consultation. The initial list of 56 items was then shown to a group of caregivers to determine if they were understandable and could be answered "Yes" or "No." Items

were then revised as necessary, and a response of "N/A" was added.

The items were then presented to a group of caregivers who accompanied patients to an outpatient memory disorders clinic. The responses for a group of 141 caregivers of patients with probable Alzheimer's were then drawn from the initial caregiver group and compared to 93 caregivers for cognitively intact patients. There is little description, however, of what medical problems the patients from the comparison caregivers group were suffering. Using the caregiver responses, a statistical model was created to select the three most discriminating items from the initial item pool for each of six problem areas typically associated with Alzheimer's disease: Memory, Confusion and Disorientation, Geographic Disorientation, Reasoning and Judgment, Language Abilities, and Behavior.

TECHNICAL. Internal consistency reliability was estimated by calculating a coefficient alpha of .87 for the combined pool of Alzheimer's and cognitively intact caregivers' responses with a mean interitem correlation result of .54. Test-retest reliability was assessed with a new 19-person pool of Alzheimer's caregivers administered on an average of 17.5 days apart and produced a reliability coefficient of .71.

Various methodologies were then used to identify algorithms that would classify patients as either "Likely" or "Unlikely" to be suffering a dementia suggestive of Alzheimer's Disease. The statistical analyses included correlation and regression tree analysis (CART), logistic regression, and stepwise regression using 90 of the 141 Alzheimer's patients and 60 of the 93 cognitively intact patients. Cross-validation of the classification rates was conducted using the remaining caregiver pools. The manual then states:

> This process was repeated 99 times, each time using a different random sample of approximately 65% of the patients and 65% of the controls for the initial analysis, and then using the remaining participants for the cross validation. The results indicated that the CART techniques had optimal classification rates (mean sensitivity = .88; mean specificity = .93), whereas the logistic regression (mean sensitivity = .85; mean specificity = .87) and stepwise logistic regression (mean sensitivity = .88; mean specificity = .88) had slightly lower classification rates. (pp. 8 and 10)

Following this, a Receiver Operator Characteristic analysis was conducted to produce a cutoff score based on the ADCQ algorithm. A cutoff score of 1.5 was established based on a total score that was the sum of the means for each item group. The process of establishing the cutoff score is described. The cutoff score was found to have a sensitivity of .92 and a specificity of .86. A level of agreement analysis for the two categorical classifications of "Likely" versus "Unlikely" Alzheimer's disease was conducted using the test-retest reliability sample and yielding 89% of the sample being classified consistently.

Further validity analyses were conducted by comparing ADCQ scores to Folstein Mini Mental State Examination (MMSE) scores. Higher ADCQ scores were weakly associated with lower MMSE score ($r = -.29$, $p < .01$) suggesting they measured different constructs. Further analysis compared the categorical classification of "Likely" versus "Unlikely" Alzheimer's disease with those patients identified as cognitively impaired based on MMSE scores. The results were interpreted as suggesting the ADCQ may be a better screen for suspected Alzheimer's disease than the MMSE.

COMMENTARY. Even though the ADCQ authors tout the instrument for the screening of Alzheimer's disease, it unfortunately suffers a number of difficulties that make it less than what it is supposed to be. Foremost, the authors seem to have stacked the deck in its development. A quite small and highly selective sample was utilized for development, reliability analyses, and validation and then compared to an equally small and poorly described population whose relevance for comparison is uncertain at best. Without any description of the comparison population it can only be assumed that the populations were selected so as to magnify the ADCQ's discriminant ability. The validation analyses, in this respect, only served to re-identify the two comparison groups. It would have been much more important to compare a variety of groups suffering suspected dementing illnesses (e.g., vascular dementia, Parkinson's dementia) with relevant comparison groups such as those suffering depression along with unimpaired controls. A larger and broader set of reliability and validity studies would significantly improve the validity evidence for the ADCQ. In this same vein, the test authors fail to account for the significant overlap in symptoms common to dementing illnesses and depression, increasing the chance for errant classification of patients.

Several additional studies need to be completed before the ADCQ can be considered to have the base reliability and validity necessary for its general usage. Should those studies be completed then they also need to be described fully in the technical manual. The manual included on the ADCQ diskette is primarily devoted to the installation and usage of the ADCQ software and generation of reports. Information that would be needed to replicate the developmental process and analyses—construction of statistical models, means by which analyses are conducted (including equations), and discussions of limitations—is absent from the manual.

With these problems, the ADCQ seems to be an instrument that was rushed to publication. This perspective is underscored by there being no rationale for routine Alzheimer's disease screening or ADCQ usage as no health care policies exist for routine Alzheimer's screening. It is much more likely to be the case that caregivers or concerned others will present to health care professionals with complaints about patients that include those problems screened for in the ADCQ.

Moreover, the necessity of purchasing scoring software and reports to make sense of ADCQ responses adds another cost layer to the overall health care costs facing patients. If the authors really wanted to make the ADCQ useful for consumers then hand scoring and interpretation guidelines could be included in the manual.

SUMMARY. The ADCQ is an 18-item caregivers questionnaire to identify patients suffering from likely Alzheimer's disease. Although numerous complicated statistical procedures were utilized in its development and validation it suffers from significant limitations due to the small and highly restricted population upon which it is based. Moreover, there is no current indication for the routine screening of patients for Alzheimer's disease or other dementing illnesses, which makes its clinical utility questionable.

[11]

Alzheimer's Quick Test: Assessment of Parietal Function.

Purpose: Designed to "screen adolescents and adults for parietal lobe dysfunctions indicative of mild cognitive impairments, acquired neurogenic disorders of language and communication ... or degenerative neurological disorders such as Alzheimer's or Parkinson's disease."

Population: Adolescents and adults.
Publication Date: 2002.
Acronym: AQT.
Scores, 5: Color-Form, Color-Number, Color-Letter, Color-Animal, Color-Object.
Administration: Individual.
Price Data, 2004: $249 per complete kit including examiner's manual (88 pages), stimulus manual, and 25 record forms; $75 per examiner's manual; $150 per stimulus manual; $50 per 25 record forms.
Foreign Language Edition: Spanish and French-Canadian directions included in examiner's manual.
Time: [3–5] minutes.
Comments: "Criterion-referenced."
Authors: Elisabeth H. Wiig, Niels Peter Nielsen, Lennart Minthon, and Siegbert Warkentin.
Publisher: PsychCorp, A brand of Harcourt Assessment, Inc.

Review of the Alzheimer's Quick Test: Assessment of Parietal Function by SHAWN K. ACHESON, Associate Professor of Neuropsychology, Western Carolina University, Cullowhee, NC:

DESCRIPTION. The Alzheimer's Quick Test (AQT) is a short screening instrument that can purportedly be used to detect parietal lobe dysfunction in adolescents and adults associated with a variety of disorders including aphasia and other language disorders, TBI, ADHD, learning disabilities, neurodegenerative disorders, and various psychopathologies. The AQT includes five parallel naming tasks (Color-Form, Color-Number, Color-Letter, Color-Animal, and Color-Object naming). The first three tasks are considered the primary tasks and the remaining two are considered alternates. Each of the tasks consists of an untimed trial and three timed tests (for example, Task A includes Color naming, Form naming and Color-Form naming). Performance is assessed by calculating time to complete each test within each task as well as the number (and type) of errors.

The record form provides a space for recording time, number and type of errors, and time and error performance classification (normal, slower-than-normal or more-errors-than-normal, non-normal). Standard scores such as *t*-scores or percentile ranks are not used. The record form also provides a place to plot Color-Form Naming time against Color-Number Naming time and Color-Form Naming time against Color-Letter Naming time. However, the value of such a graph is never explained. Moreover, the manual indicates that the alternate Color-Animal and Color-Object Naming times, if administered, may be plotted on these graphs. However, one must be cautious because the cutoff scores for these latter tasks differ from the other tasks and therefore the graph may be inaccurate.

DEVELOPMENT. The AQT is a variation on a theme—rapid, continuous, automatic naming of familiar stimuli. Although similar to tasks such as the Stroop Color-Word task or the Controlled Oral Word Association (COWA) task it is unique in several respects. Unlike the Stroop, the AQT requires less executive control and does not require the participant to read, which makes it more appropriate for aphasic clients. The AQT is also less dependent on the participant's acquired lexicon than the COWA.

At least two preliminary studies are reported in the manual. Both appear to be unpublished and the details of each are scant. The pilot study demonstrates a significant effect of age on 6 of the 9 dependent variables (time scores from each of the three tests for the first three tasks—Color-Form, Color-Number, and Color-Letter). However, the authors appear to make no provision for such differences in establishing cutoff scores. Subsequent to this latter pilot study, the authors added the Color-Animal and Color-Object naming tasks (Tasks 4 and 5, respectively) to provide alternates for Tasks 1–3 in the event that one of these tasks were invalidated.

TECHNICAL.
Standardization. The standardization sample should be considered inadequate, both in terms of numbers and ethnic representation. Only 135 adolescents and adults (ages 15 to 72 years) were used. There appears to have been no attempt to match ethnicity to recent census figures. The standardization sample consisted of Caucasians (58%), Hispanics (21%), African Americans (17%), and Asian Americans (4%). There is no Native American representation.

More importantly, there is little information provided concerning the establishment of cutoff scores for each of the tasks. The authors indicate that "scatter plots and descriptive distributive information were used to guide the development of criterion cut scores (normal, slower-than-normal, non-normal/pathological) for the combination-naming times of all task sets" (examiner's manual, p. 34). Although the authors report that a criterion of 1.5 standard deviations above the mean was used in one of the initial studies, there is no reference to a specific criterion in the standardization study.

Reliability. Test-retest reliability was assessed with a 1- to 2-week delay in 30 participants selected from the standardization sample. All test-retest correlations ranged from .84 to .94 for single-dimension naming (i.e., Tests 1 and 2 from each of the five tasks) and from .88 to .96 for dual-dimension naming (i.e., Test 3 from each of the five tasks).

Validity. Validity of the AQT either as a measure of parietal lobe function or in the diagnosis of Alzheimer's disease is not presented clearly, coherently, or convincingly. Chapter 5 of the examiner's manual (p. 45) begins, "Significant cortical activation of the parietal lobes and reduced activation of the prefrontal cortex occur in normal adults while they are performing the AQT Color-Form combination-naming test (Task A, Test 3)." There is no reference listed to substantiate this statement and there are no details provided to support the data that purport to demonstrate decreased prefrontal activity and concurrent increased parietal activity associated with AQT performance.

The authors go on to claim that "this pattern—prefrontal deactivation associated with accentuated parietal lobe activation—has been designated to be a hallmark of the involvement of working memory and selective attention during visual decoding tasks" (examiner's manual, p. 47) and cite articles in support of this statement (Downing, 2000; Fockert, 2001; Fockert, Rees, Rith, & Lavie, 2001; Furey, Pietrini, & Haxby, 2001; and Robbins, Mehta, & Sahakian, 2000). Please note that Fockert (2001) is not listed in the reference list of the examiner's manual and does not appear in PubMed or in PsychInfo. In addition, Robbins et al. (2000) is only a summary of the Furey et al. (2001) paper appearing in the same volume and Downing's (2000) paper is a purely behavioral study and makes no reference to differential activation of prefrontal and parietal cortices.

Moreover, careful review of the remaining two articles (Fockert et al., 2001; and Furey et al., 2001) suggests that there is no "designated hallmark." Fockert et al., (2001) demonstrate increased inferior, middle, and medial prefrontal activity as working memory load increases, not decreased. Furey et al. (2001) investigate the effects of increased cholinergic activity on a visual working memory task and associated cortical activity. As such, it is not really relevant to discussions of the normal association between working memory and visual selective attention. Even if it were relevant, these investigators found increased activity in extrastriate, ventral extrastriate, and inferior prefrontal cortex; decreased activity in dorsal prefrontal cortex; and no change in activity in the intraparietal sulcus, hardly the "designated hallmark" indicated by the AQT authors.

The authors of the AQT make a similarly inadequate case for a connection between Alzheimer's disease (AD) and parietal lobe function. Although there is clear evidence throughout the literature for a connection between the two, the test authors make vague reference in the examiner's manual to a study of 135 AD patients demonstrating reduced Regional Cerebral Blood Flow (rCBF) in parietal areas and increased flow in dorsal prefrontal and occipital areas relative to normal controls at rest. They also provide rCBF data from 2 AD patients and another 11 patients with suspected AD during administration of the AQT. They provide no citation for any of these studies or sufficient detail to properly evaluate these findings.

One final shortcoming is the lack of concurrent validity evidence. No information is provided about correlations between the AQT and other AD diagnostic instruments.

COMMENTARY. The AQT is easy to administer, easy to score, and easy to interpret. Unfortunately, given the limited validity of the underlying theory and evidence, there is not much to interpret. There is no doubt that the parietal lobes play an important role in attention and that attention is modulated by executive control. However, there remain many questions concerning the extent to which AQT performance activates the parietal lobes and/or serves as a good screening of AD or parietal lobe dysfunction.

SUMMARY. At this point, the AQT should be considered a measure with considerable potential but one that currently lacks sufficient validity or theoretical foundation. The AQT is in need of significant further study before it is used on a large scale to screen for AD or parietal lobe dysfunction. It should also be used cautiously in minority populations due to inadequate normative information, especially among Native Americans.

REVIEWER'S REFERENCES

Downing, P. E. (2000). Interactions between working memory and selective attention. *Psychological Science, 11*, 467–473.

Fockert, J. W., Rees, G., Rith, C. D., & Lavie, N. (2001). The role of working memory in visual selective attention. *Science, 291*, 1803–1806.

Furey, M. L., Pietrini, P., & Haxby, J. V. (2000). Cholinergic enhancement and increased selectivity of perceptual processing during working memory. *Science, 290*, 2315–2319.

Robbins, T. W., Mehta, M. A., & Sahakian, B. J. (2000). Boosting working memory. *Science, 290*, 2275–2276.

Review of the Alzheimer's Quick Test: Assessment of Parietal Function by JOAN C. BALLARD, Clinical Neuropsychologist, Associate Professor of Psychology, State University of New York College at Geneseo, Geneseo, NY:

DESCRIPTION. The Alzheimer's Quick Test (AQT) is described as a brief test of parietal function. The manual describes the uses and purposes of the test, administration procedures, examiner qualifications, and requirements for training paraprofessionals to administer the test. Most of the manual is somewhat disorganized, with information about administration, scoring, and interpreting results scattered throughout.

The test includes five task sets, two of which serve as replacements or supplements. The procedures and rationale for selecting task sets for a given patient are not clearly explained. In each task set, the patient must first name a sequence of colors, then a sequence of single-dimension items (forms, numbers, letters, animals, or household objects), and finally a sequence of dual-dimension items (e.g., Color-Form, Color-Number). The dual-dimension naming tasks are considered the essential measures. Each sequence is presented on a separate page of a spiral-bound booklet. The stimulus pages look very much like those of the Stroop task (Stroop, 1935). However, instead of identifying the colors of competing color-names, the patient states both characteristics of dual-dimension stimuli (e.g., "red square"). No printed words are used as stimuli, and dual-dimension stimuli do not include inherently competing characteristics.

Directions for each sequence are printed on facing pages. An appendix includes translations of stimulus names for English, French, German, Portuguese, Spanish, Danish, Norwegian, and Swedish. However, separate sets of stimuli and directions are provided only for Spanish and French-Canadian languages. Short practice trials precede each stimulus set. The examiner reads the directions and then folds the directions page under. It is unclear why printed directions are shown to the patient, particularly considering that one purpose of the test is its use with aphasic patients. An easel presentation might be more appropriate. Obtained scores include total time, errors, and self-corrections for each stimulus page. A response form is provided, but with limited space for tallying errors. Time scores of the dual dimension sequences are plotted against each other on a scatterplot diagram, which includes cutoff lines for determining normal, slower-than-normal, or nonnormal performance. The reason for using these plots is unclear. They seem to provide little information beyond that of simply comparing time scores on each stimulus set to norms or cutoff values.

DEVELOPMENT. The authors provide background information primarily for the presumed cognitive substrates of performance on the Stroop task and the F-A-S Verbal Fluency task. They state that the original goal of the Color-Form portion of the AQT was to eliminate the need for reading (as in the Stroop) and to test for rapid identification of visually presented stimuli, rather than rapid search and retrieval from the stored lexicon (as in the F-A-S). The original Color-Form test was included in the Clinical Evaluation of Language Fundamentals (CELF and CELF-3) on which Wiig was second author. The AQT manual includes references but no other information about the initial development of the Color-Form naming task. Development of the AQT included pilot studies for the Color-Form, Color-Number, and Color-Letter versions, standardization samples for all stimulus sets, and Regional Cerebral Blood Flow (rCBF) studies of cortical activation during task performance. Case studies of patients are included in the manual.

TECHNICAL.

Standardization. Initial studies of Color-Form and Color-Number tests in 20 normal English-speaking adults yielded preliminary cutoff scores. In a subsequent pilot study of 60 individuals (equal number of males and females within younger and older groups; no information on nationality), the Color-Letter task was added (no rationale given). In this pilot study, age differences were found on at least some of the single- and dual-dimension tasks. However, such differences either were not explored in the standardization sample or were not reported. The standardization sample included 135 male and female Euro-, Hispanic-, African-, and Asian-Americans, with an age range of 15 to 72. The manual provides gender and ethnicity total numbers, but neither the distribution of participants' ages, nor the gender and age ratios within ethnic groups are stated. Means and standard deviations of naming times and self-corrections are provided, but these apparently were not used explicitly to develop norms. Instead, scatterplots for the correlations of each pair of dual-dimension tasks were used for the identification of cutoff scores, apparently through visual inspection of the plots and descriptive information. The reason for this procedure is unclear. Although the distributions for each variable were skewed, a straightforward use of percentiles seems more appropriate. In scoring, the same scatterplots, minus the original data points, are used to plot an examinee's performance. However, performance in the "nonnormal" range is identified by scores above the cutoff on *either* stimulus set. Consequently, comparison of each score to cutoffs seems sufficient, without plotting scores on a chart that essentially provides no additional useful information.

The authors cite a previous study of the Color-Form naming task, which yielded significantly more self-corrections by bilingual (English-Spanish) children and adolescents than by monolingual children. However, such differences apparently were not explored in the standardization sample.

Reliability. In the standardization sample, correlations among five administrations of the Color Naming stimuli (which is presented once before each of the dual dimension tasks) were strong (.88 to .93). Retesting of a subgroup of 30 participants yielded strong (.84 to .96) 1- to 2-week reliability estimates. The authors describe repeated-trials scores on the Color-Form stimulus set for six Scandinavian examinees.

Validity. Comparisons of means for 30 Scandinavian and 30 American-English participants revealed significant differences only on the Form task, suggesting that task administration may be valid for Germanic languages. Intertest correlations among all single- and dual-dimension tasks were relatively but not extremely high, suggesting that each stimulus set may measure somewhat different constructs.

In cortical activation studies (rCBF) in a sample of normal adults ($n = 14$), parietal areas were more active and prefrontal areas were less active during performance of the Color-Form sequence of the AQT compared to rest and to F-A-S Verbal Fluency. In contrast, two Alzheimer's Disease (AD) patients showed the opposite pattern, with more prefrontal and less parietal activation during task performance. Although a similar reversal of activation is also seen in AD patients at rest, the data on these two patients suggest that measures during task performance illustrate the parietal deactivation more clearly.

COMMENTARY. As noted above, the AQT response sheet is not particularly useful, and the manual is poorly organized. Norms are based on a relatively small sample of normal subjects ($n = 135$), whose characteristics are not well-described. Cutoff scores are apparently based on visual inspection of scatterplots showing the correlations between pairs of dual-dimension scores. No clear rationale is given for this procedure.

A strength of the AQT is its brevity. Another strength is that it can be administered during rCBF studies, and presumably during other functional imaging and cortical activation procedures. Results from AD-diagnosed patients, as well as from 14 normal individuals, are provided. These suggest that patterns of abnormal regional activity can be demonstrated during task performance.

The most serious concern is the interpretation of test results. The title of the test implies that poor performance suggests a diagnosis of Alzheimer's Disease. The authors concede that many other patient groups can show abnormal parietal functioning, but they deemphasize these possibilities. They note that the patient's history must be taken into account in diagnosis, but this would be the case in any screening. Unfortunately, in their case studies of patients with poor test performance, the history occasionally seems to be selectively interpreted to support an AD diagnosis. Finally, suggestions about follow-up for abnormal performance, which are scattered throughout the manual, primarily focus on obtaining CT images. Additional testing is mentioned only once, and no suggestions for ruling out other sources of parietal dysfunction are provided.

SUMMARY. The Alzheimer's Quick Test (AQT) may be useful as a brief screening tool for parietal dysfunction. The stimuli are well-constructed and easy to use. However, the title of the test is potentially misleading, given the variety of patient groups who demonstrate parietal deficits. Inappropriate use of the test may lead to overdiagnosis of Alzheimer's, at the expense of determining evidence of other disorders. The manual needs revision for clarity and completeness. Interpretative guidelines are very limited, both in terms of norms for score interpretation and in terms of suggested follow-up for nonnormal scores.

REVIEWER'S REFERENCE

Stroop, J. R. (1935). Studies of interference in serial verbal reactions. *Psychological Monographs, 50,* 38–48.

[12]

Am I Musical? Music Audiation Games.

Purpose: Designed to objectively reveal a general estimate of the extent of music potential a child or adult possess.
Population: Ages 7–12, 13–adult.
Publication Date: 2003.
Scores: Total score only.
Administration: Group.
Levels, 2: Youth Game, Adult Game.
Price Data: Available from publisher.
Time: (12) minutes.
Comments: Test administered via CD; CD player needed; self-administered, self-scored.
Author: Edwin E. Gordon.
Publisher: GIA Publications, Inc.

Review of Am I Musical? Music Audiation Games by CHRISTOPHER M. JOHNSON, Professor of Music Education and Music Therapy, University of Kansas, Lawrence, KS:

DESCRIPTION. The Am I Musical? Music Audiation Games is a 40-item test administered by playing an audio compact disk and completing an answer sheet. The test comes in an attractive booklet, which contains a series of water-color prints and inspirational quotes about music, followed by a purpose statement and printed instructions for the "game." There is then information on scoring the results, interpreting the results, item analysis information, a key, and test sheets that the user is given permission to copy. On the back cover is the compact disk. Two tests are contained in the booklet. Test 1 is for children ages 12 and under. The adult game is designed for individuals 13 and older. However, the test booklet does mention that if one game is too easy or difficult,

he or she can take the alternative game. The youth instructions are on Track 1 of the CD, the game is on Track 2. The adult instructions are on Track 3, and the game is on Track 4.

The items on the test for the youth version give a model and then either replay the model, or play something similar but not the same as the model, and the child is to answer that the targeted piece is either the same or different than the model. On the adult test the task is generally the same except the test taker is to add one further level of discrimination by describing the nature of difference as either a change in melody, rhythm, or harmony.

No training is required to administer the test. It is feasible that anyone could administer and grade the test. The test is a paper-and-pencil format and the answer sheets must be hand graded. The instructions take approximately 4 minutes, and the testing portion lasts just over 7.5 minutes.

DEVELOPMENT. The specifics of the test development are not presented with the testing materials, and although there are some references to the Musical Aptitude Profile, they are not very closely related.

TECHNICAL. An item analysis chart is provided, but there is no reference to how many tests were factored into this analysis. There is also a scale by which one can compare results to find out their musicality level (i.e., for the adult game: 10–14 = Fair, 15–19 = Below Average, 20–30 = Average, 31–35 = Very Good, 36–40 = Excellent), but there is no information about how this scale was derived other than to say the scale was "based on statistical analyses of the results of thousands of participants of varied ages and backgrounds in the United States" (manual, p. 25). The reliability estimates provided with the item analysis information are .91 and .92 for the youth and adult tests, respectively. No information is given as to how these estimates were calculated.

COMMENTARY. The Am I Musical? game is marketed as just that, a game. There are very limited validity claims or statements. It does not contain much more information than a test one might find in a magazine, and because it is a "Music Audiation Game" should not require such. At the same time, the item analysis included in the booklet gives it the appearance of something much more substantive and weighty. It also does not sound like, or have the light-hearted feel of a game. In every manner except the packaging, it is a test. It is a test wherein the people who purchase it are looking for a quick answer to a burning question, and will try to find out if they have the musical genetic makeup to be a potential musician. As a published test, it should adhere to a higher standard.

SUMMARY. This is a test in game clothing that has not gone through the rigors of scientific verification, therefore it does not carry the recommendation that other musical aptitude tests do.

Review of Am I Musical? Music Audiation Games by JAMES W. SHERBON, Professor Emeritus of Music, School of Music, Unversity of North Carolina at Greensboro, Greensboro, NC:

DESCRIPTION. The purpose of Am I Musical more commonly known as Music Audiation Games (MAGS) is to determine the extent of music potential that children and adults possess and, for the adult, provide additional indicators of strengths and weaknesses in melodic, rhythm, and harmonic audiation and potential. In contrast to Gordon's other tests, the MAGS "manual" sparingly refers to audiation—the ability to hear and to comprehend music for which the sound is not physically present—while emphasizing the term music "potential," audiation being the basis of music potential. Gordon states: "To understand the extent of that potential is to be well informed, particularly about the appropriate way to learn music in accord with ... [a] child's individual musical needs and differences" (test booklet, p. 17).

Although the content of the MAGS obviously is couched in traditional "Gordon theory," the game approach in this instrument is clearly a departure from Gordon's tradition in testing and use of terminology. Further, the term "manual," as associate with testing, can, in this case, be more appropriately referenced as a "booklet" without implication of degrading content quality.

The Music Audiation Games are presented in a light, informal, attractive, and affable context in which general populations of individuals, with or without music exposure or formal study, can participate and benefit. Of special mention is the presence of numerous illustrations throughout the initial pages of the booklet. This artwork by Yolanda Duran, accompanied by light philosophical quotations, contributes in many aesthetic, attractive, and tasteful ways to the global flavor of the booklet while extending an invitational, compatible, and appealing communication to potential consumers.

The test booklet of 40 pages is self-contained and includes supportive information, narrative about the purpose, descriptions of the games, and comparative details. Instructions also are provided regarding administration, scoring, and interpreting the scores. Answer keys and answer sheets also are printed in the booklet with instructions to reproduce the latter, as needed, for simultaneous or repeated administration. In addition, a high quality compact disk containing spoken directions and test stimuli is attached to the back cover.

The games are structured so they may be played individually or simultaneously among children and adults; administration is accomplished with a high quality compact disk player, the compact disk, answer sheet, and pencil. Composed in two parts, the Music Audiation Games consist of a "Youth Game" designed for children ages 12 and under, and an "Adult Game" for persons ages 13 and over, each requiring about 12 minutes to complete. The games contain 40 questions that are identical for both youth and adults. Procedures for completing the game involve presentations of a short model song (unchanged throughout) compared with "other" short songs of the same duration. The participant is asked to mark the answer sheet indicating whether the other song sounds the same as the model or not the same-changes, if any, may occur in melody, rhythm, or harmony. The model is provided periodically throughout the game. Although stimuli are identical, the answer sheet for the youth game allows responses of "Same" or "Not Same" whereas the adult game answer sheet contains four possible response options: "Same" or differing by "Melody," "Rhythm," or "Harmony." Musical examples of melody, rhythm, and harmony are presented in the recorded directions—thus, introducing and explaining the terms associated with the three respective musical elements.

DEVELOPMENT. Development of the Music Audiation Games is rooted in Gordon's research in music aptitude and evaluative approaches, distributed across age ranges, venues, media, and socioeconomic strata. Gordon's extensive research, experience, field testing, and knowledge obviously permeate the development of the Music Audiation Games. Appropriately, however, with the booklet written for the novice and not containing a bibliography, Gordon cites many of his other works by title and publisher should supplementary administration of standardized tests of music aptitude be desired-all being foundational to the development of the Music Audiation Games (see Gordon, 1998, 2001, 2003).

Gordon has developed a score interpretation table for youths and adults, indicating the estimated extent of musical potential one may expect from obtained scores. These estimates, printed in the booklet, are classified by five levels of score intervals ranging from Excellent to Fair. The intervals are based on means derived from administration of the Music Audiation Games to youth ($N > 3,000$) and adults ($N > 1,800$), the subject pool consisting of varied ages and backgrounds in the United States. In addition, a table is provided serving the adult in identifying strengths and weaknesses in melody, rhythm, and harmony. Norms are not included in the booklet and, according to Gordon, the obtained means sufficiently provide classificatory information by which participants can determine individual music potential by consulting the respective tables. Of importance when considering the development of the Music Audiation Games is the relative stability of the means regardless of age for the youth game and the same for the adult game. This phenomenon is supported by the reported correlations of scores with age. The correlations between the ages of both the youth, ages 7 through 12, and the scores on the Music Audiation Games (correlation = .16) and those of the adult, ages 13 and beyond, and the Music Audiation Games (correlation = -.08) are close to zero.

TECHNICAL. Of special technical significance in the development and evaluation of the Music Audiation Games is a current study investigating the objective validity of music audiation games, published in monograph form (Gordon, 2004). For purposes of understanding the technical and underlying theories and research explaining and solidifying the rationale and empirical development of the Music Audiation Games, this objective and comprehensive report is a "must" for individuals beyond the novice stage who seek additional technical detail and research results regarding validity associated with audiation games.

Although this monograph is thorough and comprehensive in content, beginning with historical aspects of the study of music aptitude, the principal interest herein deals with congruent validity, described by Gordon as the correlation of scores on a new music aptitude test with scores on an established music aptitude test shown to possess longitudinal predictive validity. To examine congruent validity for the Music Audiation Games, Gordon employed four tests possessing longitudinal predictive validity: the Primary Measures of Music Audiation (PMMA; Gordon, 1979) and the Intermediate Measures of Music Audiation (IMMA; Gordon, 1982) considered as developmental music aptitude tests (innate music potential and music environment continuously interacting and contributing to a student's level of music aptitude at any specific time from a pre-postnatal period to about age 9) and the Musical Aptitude Profile (MAP; Gordon, 1995) and the Advanced Measures of Music Audiation (AMMA; Gordon, 1989) representing stabilized music aptitude tests (music environmental influences not affecting students' level of music aptitude and commencing around age 9, extending throughout life). Gordon provides rationale supporting the claim that the Music Audiation Games comprises elements of both developmental and stabilized music aptitude tests.

The investigation designed for purposes of examining congruent validity of the Music Audiation Games was conducted from September to December 2003. Gordon obtained a group of volunteer music educators who agreed to administer the games to students in elementary, middle, high school, and college locations while also drawing from sectors of private students and church choirs. Geographically, the test participants primarily were from a cross section of schools in Midwestern states. Although the exact number of participants comprising the 12 groupings listed below varies considerably between these groupings, the total number of individuals participating in the validation process ($N = 3,480$) is impressive and meaningful. In addition to the Music Audiation Games, the administrators independently selected tests from the four established tests of music aptitude listed above and administered them in their respective environments. This quasi-random procedure of administration produced 12 groups of completed answer sheets dispersed across a respectable distribution of grades (1 through 6 and adults), games (youth = 9 groupings, adult = 3 groupings), and companion tests (PMMA = 6, IMMA = 4, MAP = 1, and AMMA = 1).

Results of the congruent validity investigation are thoroughly reported in the monograph and interpreted by Gordon for each group, plus presented in tabular form showing comparative and representative means, standard deviations, and combinations of congruent validity coefficients. Gordon's discussions, explanations, and interpretations of the results are accurate, unbiased, and presented so the reader recognizes that Gordon's intent is to present both the strengths and weaknesses of the comprehensive investigation. Although global generalizations should not be made under the current conditions in which so many variables are thrust together, one cannot ignore the observation that the congruent validity coefficients are impressively strong.

COMMENTARY. Gordon's Am I Musical? is marketed toward the general public and provides a welcome breath of fresh air to the traditional academic and scholarly arena encompassing the evaluation of music potential. The Music Audiation Games contains an unobtrusive foundation of research and theory in a context that precludes an overtly sophisticated, research-based, or academic forum—often visibly associated with his other music tests. When composing the Music Audiation Games, however, Gordon obviously has applied experience, objectivity, empirical knowledge, and research-supported findings to ensure quality and applicability in a game format. In the Music Audiation Games, he has created a unique, viable, and "user friendly" instrument for evaluating music potential—thus, providing an opportunity for broad populations of individuals to gain a personal awareness of the extent of that potential, subsequently motivating sensitivity toward educational pursuits and musical participation within the realms of basic human needs.

Thorough review, analysis, and study of all aspects of this new and different work by Gordon reveal a unique contribution to ways of evaluating music potential, audiation, and music aptitude, supporting an infrastructure that may pilot music philosophies, methods, instruction, and people toward musical achievement and participation in the 21st century. The time has arrived for extending evaluative approaches beyond the world of academia and into the hands of the general population; the Music Audiation Games serves this opportunity.

SUMMARY. Gordon exhibited perceptiveness when associating "games" with the title of Am I Musical? Although in traditional thinking, even though the Music Audiation Games may not be considered a game per se, the connotation implied therein has merit and attractiveness to those for whom it is intended. The Music Audiation Games are a beacon, perhaps signaling an emergence of new trends and techniques in music aptitude evaluation as well as reaching expanded and diverse populations of individuals who may have long been seeking opportunities to learn about individual potentialities in music. The game approach introduces an innovative way of reaching outward toward populations of individuals generally disassociated with formal musical experiences—thus, leading them toward the importance of identifying and pursuing experiences in music learning, listening, and performing. Creative efforts toward the identification of music potential and productivity as exhibited in Gordon's Music Audiation Games may awaken dormant interests or reveal unidentified musical opportunities among broad populations.

REVIEWER'S REFERENCES
Gordon, E. E. (1979). Primary Measures of Music Audiation. Chicago: GIA Publications.
Gordon, E. E. (1982). Intermediate Measures of Music Audiation. Chicago: GIA Publications.
Gordon, E. E. (1989). Advanced Measures of Music Audiation. Chicago: GIA Publications.
Gordon, E. E. (1995). Musical Aptitude Profile. Chicago: GIA Publications.
Gordon, E. E. (1998). Introduction to research and the psychology of music. Chicago: GIA Publications.
Gordon, E. E. (2001). Preparatory audiation, audiation, and music learning theory. Chicago: GIA Publications.
Gordon, E. E. (2003). Learning sequences in music: Skill, content, and patterns. Chicago: GIA Publications.
Gordon, E. E. (2004). An investigation of the objective validity of music audiation games. Chicago: GIA Publications.

[13]

Antisocial Process Screening Device.

Purpose: Designed to assess personality processes related to antisocial behavior in young populations.
Population: Ages 6–13.
Publication Date: 2001.
Acronym: APSD.
Scores, 4: Callous/Unemotional, Impulsivity, Narcissism, Total.
Administration: Individual.
Price Data, 2001: $105 per complete kit including technical manual (84 pages), 25 parent forms, 25 teacher forms, and 25 Quikscore forms; $37 per technical manual; $27 per 25 Quikscore forms; $45 per specimen

set including technical manual, 1 parent form, 1 teacher form, and 1 Quikscore form.

Time: 10 minutes per rater for Parent and Teacher forms.

Comments: Individual Parent and Teacher ratings.

Authors: Paul J. Frick and Robert D. Hare.

Publisher: Multi-Health Systems, Inc.

Review of the Antisocial Process Screening Device by ARTHUR S. ELLEN, Senior Psychometrician, National League of Nursing, New York, NY:

DESCRIPTION. The Antisocial Process Screening Device (APSD) is a 20-item informant-completed behavior rating scale for children 6 to 13 years old. It is intended for research into the psychopathology of conduct disorders, for careful clinical use as part of a comprehensive psychological evaluation, and potentially for the screening of severely conduct-disordered youth. A parent and/or teacher rates the child using a 3-point rating scale (0 = *not at all true*, 1 = *sometimes true*, and 2 = *definitely true*). The instrument's QuikScore carbon-like forms facilitate reverse scoring of 5 items, obtaining T-scores (mean of 50, standard deviation of 10) for boys or girls, and transferring parent and teacher ratings onto a combined form. When both a parent and a teacher rate a child, the APSD uses the higher of each item's rating to form a composite score. This results in Total scores for the parent (20 items), teacher (19 items), and a combined rating (19 items)—one item on the teacher form is not used in scoring. Additionally, the APSD has three dimensions: Callous/Unemotional (6 items), Narcissism (7 items), and Impulsivity (5 items).

The technical manual identifies challenges in the clinical use of the APSD scales. The clinician needs to consider the consistency of parent and teacher ratings, the influence of social desirability and level of rapport, and the consequences of either overendorsing or underendorsing items. Two cases illustrate these clinical strategies. In addition to this clinical advice, the manual emphasizes current limits in the use of the APSD as a screen. Clearly considerable clinical judgment is required for use. Prudently, the publisher requires the highest level of clearance to purchase the test.

DEVELOPMENT. The APSD, the renamed Psychopathy Screening Device (Frick, O'Brian, Wootton, & McBurnett, 1994), is a downward extension of the Hare Psychopathy Checklist—Revised (PCL-R; Hare, 1991; T6:1122). The

PCL-R is a 20-item scale completed by a trained clinician for the assessment of adult psychopathy. It employs extensive scoring criteria to evaluate a file review and a clinical interview. PCL-R content and principles guided the development of the APSD. PCL-R items and item descriptors were carefully rewritten, slightly modified, or not used. Items difficult to endorse because they exhibited socially undesirable traits were reverse keyed. To create an age-relevant scale for use by teachers and parents, it was necessary to remove some items from the PCL-R's Factor 2-chronically unstable, antisocial, and socially deviant lifestyle. In lieu of these adult items, the authors included more items from Factor 1-selfish, callous, and remorseless use of others. Although the manual does not provide a direct mapping of the APSD to the PCL-R, such a link and a more extensive discussion of why items were selected would provide an enhanced conception of the scale.

TECHNICAL. Test norms are based upon a community sample of 1,120 children from the third, fourth, sixth, and seventh grades from two southeast school districts. The data guided the current choice of the scale's dimensions, enabled an examination of score profiles, and provided comparisons by demographic characteristics. Due to missing data, actual sample sizes for various analyses fluctuated.

Based upon a previous factor analysis with a sample of clinic-referred children, Frick et al. (1994) found support for 10-item Impulsivity/Conduct Problems (I/CP) and 6-item Callous-Unemotional (CU) factors. However, the current empirical justification for the three APSD dimensions is based upon factor analyses from the community and clinic-referred samples (Frick, Bodin, & Barry, 2000), correlations with alternate criteria of psychopathology, and confirmatory factor analyses across gender and raters. The changes from the 1994 scale to the current version result from splitting the I/CP factor into the Narcissism and Impulsivity dimensions, the use of some items that were not previously assigned to a factor, and several items having loaded on different factors.

The manual provides several reliability indices. Cronbach's alpha estimates of internal consistency for each dimension and total score are evaluated by gender and rater. Total score values were above .85 whereas values for the three dimensions ranged from .64 to .89. There were moderate correlations between parent and teacher ratings (.43 for the total scale). Ratings between a teacher and a teacher aid demonstrated high correlations. With a community sample and the earlier version of the scale, 1-week test-retest reliabilities for the I/CP and CU factors were .87 and .73, respectively. Nonetheless, having estimates, perhaps longer than 1 week, of test-retest reliability for the current version of the scale in both a community and referred sample is merited. The authors provide a table of standard errors of measurement for the total score and dimensions, usefully reported across parent and teacher raters.

Analyses using demographic variables found that boys had significantly higher scores than girls, there were some differences based upon minority status, and an index of SES was unrelated to test scores. The categories of gender, race, and informant were used to report the instrument's descriptive statistics, which included the 75th, 90th, and 95th percentiles. Although these useful score reference points are certainly not suggested as clinical cut scores, several studies have employed similar scores to create extreme groups. Though not included with these other descriptive statistics, summary data from Frick et al.'s (2000) clinic-referred sample would have enabled a functional clinical comparison.

The authors summarized numerous concurrent validity studies, employing diverse methods including ratings by the child, parent, and teacher; intelligence tests; laboratory; and developmental tasks. These studies reveal a pattern of relationships to many aspects of adult psychopathy that may well characterize children. Some of these include the inability to learn from past experience, sensation seeking, lack of fear, and potential cruelty.

One study exemplifies the increased understanding that may emerge when using the APSD to identify homogenous groups of conduct-disordered children. Christian, Frick, Hill, Tyler, and Frazer (1997) used the I/CP and CU factors in conjunction with the number of conduct-disorder symptoms to cluster analyze a sample of clinic-referred children. They identified a group of children with high CU traits along with elevations on other variables, characterizing them as a severe group of conduct-disordered youth. Most importantly, when using parent-reported police contacts and school suspensions, the authors found higher proportions of these reports for this high-risk group. The results from the cluster analysis of the community sample identified a group of children with high scores on the three APSD dimensions. This group also had elevated ratings for the DSM-IV categories of Oppositional Defiant Disorder, Conduct Disorder, and Attention Deficit Hyperactivity Disorder. Together these results underscore the importance of finding both high overall APSD ratings and high ratings on the CU dimension in the possible diagnosis of childhood psychopathy.

COMMENTARY. A crucial assumption in the development of the APSD is that aspects of adult psychopathy based upon the PCL-R can be extended downward to preadolescent children. Hence, long-term predictive validity studies inevitably must compare the APSD to either adolescent or adult measures of psychopathy. When dichotomous decisions are made based upon the APSD, such complexities as the low base rate of adult psychopaths (Hare, 1991, p. 92) and the choice of a cut score will impact predictive utility. Meanwhile, criticisms that APSD traits can be confused with traits of normal preadolescent children and thus inflate the rate of false positives (Seagrave & Grisso, 2002) seem theoretical.

Almost a corollary to the above assumption is that among the heterogeneous group of conduct-disordered children there is a subtype who mature into adult psychopaths and who currently exhibit characteristics similar to adult psychopaths. This proposition is supported by much of the concurrent validity research reported in the manual, which relies upon the CU dimension to differentiate conduct-disordered children. A recent one-year prospective validity study extended the results of these concurrent validity studies. Frick, Cornell, Barry, Bodin, and Dane (2003) found high proportions of self-rated delinquency for a group of children from the community sample who had exhibited a high number of conduct problems and an elevated CU dimension.

Additional empirical support for the instrument's construction comes from the Fast Track project data—a 10-year collaborative study on the prevention of conduct disorders. Doyle and McCarty (2000) corroborated the APSD three-factor structure and the reliability of the scale's dimensions. Moreover, when they compared a normal and a high-risk control group, they noted significant differences for the scale's dimensions.

SUMMARY. The APSD, a careful modification of the PCL-R, provides in one place a set of useful questions to be asked of the parents and teachers of children who are suspected of severe conduct disorder. Mounting research has indicated the scale's potential in measuring possible precursors to adult psychopathy and current aspects of severe conduct disorder. The authors are aware of the possibilities of pejorative, premature, and potentially erroneous labeling of children. In the face of this, the manual earnestly delineates the instrument's current limits and provides direction for crucial future research. As the scale achieves wider use, it is hoped that professionals will rely upon sound judgment, professional self-restraint, and the guidance provided in the manual to refrain from making unreasonable inferences in the use of the APSD.

REVIEWER'S REFERENCES

Doyle, S. R., & McCarty, C. A. (2000). *Psychopathy Screening Device* (Technical Report) [On-line]. Available: http://www.fasttrackproject.org

Christian, R. E., Frick, P. J., Hill, N. L., Tyler, L., & Frazer, D. R. (1997). Psychopathy and conduct problems in children: II. Implications for subtyping children with conduct problems. *Journal of the American Academy of Child and Adolescent Psychiatry, 36,* 233–241.

Frick, P. J., Bodin, S. D., & Barry, C. T. (2000). Psychopathic traits and conduct problems in community and clinic-referred samples of children: Further development of the Psychopathy Screening Device. *Psychological Assessment, 12,* 382–393.

Frick, P. J., Cornell, A. H., Barry, C. T., Bodin, S. D., & Dane, H. E. (2003). Callous-unemotional traits and conduct problems in the prediction of conduct problem severity, aggression, and self-report of delinquency. *Journal of Abnormal Child Psychology, 31,* 457–470.

Frick, P. J., O'Brien, B. S., Wootton, J. M., & McBurnett, K. (1994). Psychopathy and conduct problems in children. *Journal of Abnormal Psychology, 103,* 700–707.

Hare, R. D. (1991). *Manual for the Hare Psychopathy Checklist—Revised.* Toronto, Ontario, Canada: Multi-Health Systems.

Seagrave, D., & Grisso, T. (2002). Adolescent development and the measurement of juvenile psychopathy. *Law and Human Behavior, 26,* 219–239.

Review of the Antisocial Process Screening Device by MARY LOU KELLEY, Professor of Psychology, Louisiana State University, Baton Rouge, LA:

DESCRIPTION. The Antisocial Process Screening Device (APSD) is a 20-item rating scale with parent, teacher, and combined versions of the scale. The APSD consists of multiple subscales: Callous-Unemotional, Narcissism, Impulsivity, and Total. These content areas have been associated with psychopathy in adults, greater recidivism in adults, and a tendency to be prone to violence. The scale is intended to measure early manifestations of psychopathy in children ages 6–13. A self-report version is not commercially available. An important rationale for developing the instrument is to provide researchers with a scale that may measure a subgroup of children and adolescents for whom more intensive intervention is required due to higher violent behavior and recidivism.

The APSD is administered in paper-pencil format using the MHS QuikScore forms. Respondents rate the degree to which each item is characteristic of the child using three categories: *Not At All True, Sometimes True,* or *Definitely True.* The scale can be completed in about 10 minutes. It is a very straightforward and clear instrument with simple language.

The Callous/Unemotional dimension consists of six items, the Narcissism scale consists of seven items, and the Impulsivity dimension contains five items. The majority of evidence supporting the rationale for instrument development is based on the relationship between high scores on the Callous/Unemotional factor and greater violence and recidivism. Items on this scale are: (a) does not show emotions, and the following reverse scored items: (b) keeps promises, (c) feels bad or guilty when he/she does something wrong, (d) concerned about school work, (e) concerned about feelings of others, and (f) keeps the same friends. However, the other scales have been shown to be related to psychopathy in adults.

Scoring of the APSD is similar to other commercially available instruments using the QuikScore forms. Item ratings are recorded and summed for each of the three scale dimensions and the total scale. Scores for each dimension are plotted easily on profile sheets for parents, teacher, and combined informants. The plotted scores correspond to standard scores and, thus, scores are easily interpreted.

When both teacher and parent rating are available, the authors recommend that the combined informant scores be calculated based on the highest rating for each item. The combined informant scores are plotted in the same manner as the other scores on a profile form.

DEVELOPMENT. The authors provide a comprehensive description of the theoretical and clinical rationales for developing the APSD. The authors make a good case for subtyping conduct disordered individuals on the basis of psychopathy. The authors provide theoretical rationales for the three dimensions measured by the scale. For example, the Callous-Unemotional factor is associated with greater psychopathy in forensic populations.

The APSD is somewhat of a downward extension of the Psychopathy Checklist—Revised (PCL-R; Hare, 1991; T6:1122). The item contents are the same although there are major differences in the two instruments. The APSD was designed to assess precursors to psychopathy and avoids using the term "psychopathy" altogether given that pre-adolescents are evaluated. Also, the APSD uses a rating scale format instead of a semistructured interview format. Finally, items were modified or eliminated given their irrelevance to children.

TECHNICAL. Information on the normative sample is clear. Although the sample was diverse with regard to ethnicity, gender, and socioeconomic status, the sample was based on two southeastern school systems demographically. Studies on the factor structure of the APSD indicate either a two-factor or three-factor scale. The two-factor structure combines the Narcissism and the Impulsivity items. The authors indicate additional studies are needed.

Studies support the reliability and preliminary validity of the APSD. The internal consistency of the dimensions and Total score are generally above .70 with the lowest Cronbach alpha coefficients obtained on the Impulsive dimension items and the highest on the Total score items. Interrater reliability between teachers and parents was low to moderate, which is not surprising given reliability scores obtained on other scales using the same informants.

Validity studies indicate that APSD scores are moderately correlated positively with DSM-IV symptoms of conduct problems, higher rate of police contacts, and increased school suspensions.

COMMENTARY AND SUMMARY. The authors appropriately caution using the APSD diagnostically. Further, use of cutoff scores is discouraged and not reported. The authors also appropriately caution against considering the APSD as a measure of psychopathy in children. The measure is theoretically embedded within a larger research context conducted with adults and adolescents. Although the instrument may be useful as a clinical tool used with other sources of data, it may be best to consider the instrument most useful in research until additional data are collected in support of the clinical utility of the instrument. However, the results obtained thus far are promising.

REVIEWER'S REFERENCE

Hare, R. D. (1991). *Manual for the Hare Psychopathy Checklist—Revised.* Toronto: Multi-Health Systems.

[14]

Arabic Proficiency Test.

Purpose: "Designed to measure the general proficiency in listening and reading attained by English-speaking learners of Arabic."
Population: Postsecondary to adult.
Publication Date: 1994.
Acronym: APT.
Scores, 2: Listening Comprehension, Reading Comprehension.
Administration: Group.
Price Data, 2002: $25 per test; quantity discounts available.
Time: (125) minutes.
Comments: Multiple-choice, machine-scorable test.
Authors: University of Michigan and Center for Applied Linguistics.
Publisher: Center for Applied Linguistics.

Review of the Arabic Proficiency Test by JAMES D. BROWN, Professor of Second Language Studies, and ATIQA HACHIMI, Lecturer & Coordinator of Arabic, University of Hawaii at Manoa, Honolulu, HI:

DESCRIPTION. The Arabic Proficiency Test (APT) is a four-option multiple-choice test with 100 items in each of two forms (A & B). Each form has two sections: Listening Comprehension (50 items) and Reading Comprehension (50 items). The APT includes a 23-page test interpretation manual, two 24-page test booklets, two cassette tapes, and answer sheets.

The APT is designed to test "Modern Standard Arabic" for examinees in the Novice High to Superior proficiency levels in the *ACTFL Arabic Proficiency Guidelines* (see Allen, 1985; *Foreign Language Annals*, 1989). "The primary focus of the APT is on assessing the examinee's ability to understand spoken and written Arabic encountered in contemporary, real-life language-use contexts" (test interpretation manual, p. 2). According to the test designers, the APT can be used to objectively measure general Arabic proficiency for admissions to Arabic programs, placement within such programs, exemption from Arabic study, scholarship applications, certification of Arabic proficiency, and evaluation of Arabic language programs.

The Listening Materials are presented on a cassette tape with segments based on both dialogues and single-speaker monologues. The segments are authentic samples of recorded real-world sources (including advertisements, commentaries, interviews, lectures, proverbs and jokes, poetry readings, radio and television news reports, radio announcements, recorded conversations, and television announcements), and consequently, the pacing and intonation is always natural. The Reading passages are similarly drawn from the real world (including advertisements, biography, bulletins, editorials, instructions, letters, magazine articles, newspaper articles, popular novels, reports, and signs).

The test interpretation manual is made up of six sections: *General Information* briefly discusses the history of the test, as well as its content and format; *Uses of the APT* covers the various uses mentioned above, but also explains ways score users can consult with the test developers; *Test Administration Procedures* discusses test registration, ordering the test, score reporting, billing, and test fees; *Interpretation of Test Scores* explains the meaning of the APT scores, describes the norm group, clarifies how to use the tables (of quintile distributions, means, and medians) for decision making, and describes how institutional interpretations of test scores can be obtained from the test developers; and *Statistical Characteristics of the Test* discusses reliability, score precision, and validity.

DEVELOPMENT. The APT was developed in 1992 at the University of Michigan and published in 1994 by the Center for Applied Linguistics in Washington, DC. The items were developed to assess three types of comprehension: understanding main ideas, understanding facts or supporting details, and understanding inferences. According to the manual, the items cover 21 topic areas, 16 language functions, and 22 different types of authentic language.

TECHNICAL. Standardization of the APT was based on the 206 students in the norm group, which was a subset of the 429 examinees who took either Form A or B. It appears that this norm group sample was selected because they had taken both forms, but the selection criteria are not clear. This sample is described in terms of their level of Arabic language study, gender, other background in Arabic, and dialects of Arabic to which they had been exposed.

The scores are standardized with a mean of 100 and a standard deviation of 20. The results are described statistically in two tables: one that breaks the results down for ranges of scores in each of five quintile groups for four different levels of study (first, second, third, higher years), separately for the Listening and Reading sections; and a second that shows means and medians separately for the different levels of study for the Listening and Reading sections.

In terms of reliability, the "Rasch equivalent of the KR-20 reliability" (test interpretation manual, p. 9) is reported (Form A Listening = .77 and Reading = .86, and Form B Listening = .82 and Reading = .83). Confusingly, this "Rasch equivalent" reliability would seem to imply a one-parameter (Rasch) model instead of the three-parameter model mentioned above. Standard errors of measurement (Form A Listening = 10 and Reading = 7, and Form A Listening = 10 and Reading = 8) are also reported. In addition, standard errors of estimate are given separately for Listening and Reading on each form for each possible standardized score.

Validity is defended in terms of content and construct validities. Nothing is mentioned about consequential validity or values implications (e.g., what should test users do with "heritage" speakers of Arabic, who may be strong in listening, but weak in reading?).

Content validity is discussed in terms of the following general content domains (with more specific descriptors also given separately for Listening and Reading):

1. Intermediate level—Survival including "simple daily tasks such as shopping for food, clothes, and incidental necessities."

2. Advanced level—Tourist resident in Arab society where "the learner can understand social conversation on everyday topics and can read short, descriptive narrations."

3. Superior level—Foreign professional in Arab society where "the learner can comprehend oral and written language on virtually any matter of general interest to educated native speakers in authentic situations."

The manual also points out that the use of authentic sources for the Listening segments and

Reading passages supports the content validity of the test.

Construct validity is defended in two ways. First, the manual makes the argument that IRT analyses indicated that "none of the listening items in Form A and three of the listening items in Form B were misfitting. In the reading section, five of the Form A items and one of the Form B items were misfitting.... This high degree of fit provides evidence for the construct validity of both Form A and Form B of the APT" (p. 13). Second, the manual discusses the correlations between Listening and Reading for Form A (.72) and Form B (.75) (but oddly, it does not discuss the correlation between forms for each skill).

COMMENTARY. We noted above a number of problems with the reporting of statistic analyses. In addition, the taped material was unclear for some of the items because of static, especially for items taken from the radio. Sometimes in dialog items, the voices of the speakers are almost identical, making it hard to answer questions about what Speaker A or Speaker B meant (e.g., Items 10 and 12 on Form A). Moreover, a number of inference items appear to test knowledge of math rather than knowledge of Arabic. Such items could lead to situations in which a student does understand the Arabic but does not have time to do the necessary calculations (e.g., Item 28 on Form A).

The APT also has a number of positive features in the statistical explanations: Seven helpful examples are provided to illustrate the statistical concepts; the descriptive statistics are clearly explained along with how to use them for sound decision making; the norm group sample is adequately described; reliability is clearly explained and includes standard errors of measurement and estimate; and adequate content validity arguments are provided.

In addition, both the Listening and Reading items are based on authentic and interesting materials. The Listening items (a) include a diversity of accents in Standard Arabic pronunciation throughout the Gulf region, the Levant, Egypt, and North Africa; (b) reflect the full range of emotions in the taped voices so that listeners can better understand the intended meanings; and (c) tap into a good mixture of cultural expressions and proverbs to test knowledge of cultural appropriateness.

SUMMARY. All in all, the APT is a challenging test of overall Arabic language proficiency. Although it has some problems in terms of the explanations of the statistical analyses and a few problems of item quality, on balance, it provides a practical external objective assessment tool that can usefully be used to evaluate Arabic language students and Arabic programs. In addition, the APT can provide a good index for students and teachers of Arabic to gauge where they are relative to the *ACTFL Arabic Proficiency Guidelines.* As such, it can provide curricular direction, especially for newly founded Arabic programs, and will allow for comparisons among Arabic programs nationwide.

REVIEWERS' REFERENCES

Allen, R. M. A. (1985). Arabic proficiency guidelines. *Al-Arabiyya, 18*(1-2), 45–70.

Foreign Language Annals. (1989). ACTFL Arabic proficiency guidelines. *Foreign Language Annals, 22*(4), 373–392.

Review of the Arabic Proficiency Test by ANTONY JOHN KUNNAN, *Professor, TESOL Program, Charter College of Education, California State University—Los Angeles, Los Angeles, CA:*

DESCRIPTION. The Arabic Proficiency Test (APT) consists of a total of 100 four-option multiple-choice items in two sections, Listening Comprehension and Reading Comprehension, each with 50 items.

The Listening Comprehension section is in three parts, to be completed in 50 minutes: Part one consists of 15 short, spoken Arabic utterances; each utterance is followed by a spoken question or statement about it in English. Part two consists of 20 items based on a variety of short spoken passages in Arabic including radio and TV news items, commercials, simple announcements, brief conversations, and short descriptions and narratives. Part three consists of 15 items based on a variety of passages including radio and TV commentaries, parts of lectures, poetry readings, jokes, proverbs, and interviews. Test takers have a few seconds after listening to the recorded items to choose the correct response from the options printed in English. The Arabic voices on the audiotape are native speakers of Arabic speaking Modern Standard Arabic in a natural pacing and intonation. All the listening materials are authentic although some of the passages are recorded for clarity and others are taken directly from radio broadcasts.

The Reading Comprehension section is in three parts to be completed in 60 minutes: Part one consists of 15 short common printed texts including street signs, messages, invitations, and advertisements. Part two consists of 20 passages of varying length featuring news items, announcements, biography, correspondence, narration, and description. Each statement or passage in these two sections is followed by a statement or question in English along with four choices in English. Part three consists of 15 challenging passages featuring discussion, argumentation, and supported opinion. Each passage is followed by questions and four choices in Arabic.

DEVELOPMENT. The Arabic Proficiency Test (APT) was developed in 1992 by the University of Michigan and the Center for Applied Linguistics (CAL) and is part of the CAL's Arabic language testing program that includes the Arabic Speaking Test and the Arabic Writing Test. The APT is designed to measure the ability to understand spoken and written standard Arabic by American and other English-speaking learners of Arabic. The major focus of the test is on assessing the test takers' ability to function in typical real-life language-use situations. The test is intended for test takers at proficiency levels from Novice High to Superior according to the ACTFL Arabic Proficiency Guidelines developed by a team of professors of Arabic in 1989. Test developers classified each item in the Listening Comprehension and Reading Comprehension sections as to the type of comprehension task required to answer the item correctly. Three broad areas were used: understanding the main idea, understanding a fact or detail, or understanding an inference.

The APT may be used for the following purposes: admission, placement, or exemption to/from an Arabic study program; application for a scholarship or an appointment; competency testing upon exit from an Arabic program; certification of Arabic language proficiency for occupational purposes; and evaluation of an Arabic instructional program. Two forms, Forms A and B, are currently available.

TECHNICAL. According to the APT test interpretation manual (herein referred to as the manual) developed by CAL, test takers receive scale scores for each section of the test in addition to raw scores based on the number of correct answers. The APT scale score more accurately reflects a test taker's proficiency than the number of correct answers for three reasons: first, scale scores can be compared across the two forms of the test; second, scaled scores are based on the proficiency shown by the test taker in terms of the difficulty of the items the test taker answers correctly; and finally, the scale is interpreted in a normative manner based on a norming sample of 206 North American test takers studying Arabic at the college level.

In terms of the validity of APT score interpretations, the manual reports on evidence from content, concurrent, and construct validity studies. In terms of content validity, the content and functional domains can be grouped into three categories based on the ACTFL Guidelines: Intermediate Level—Survival includes simple daily tasks such as shopping for food, clothes, and incidental necessities. The Advanced Level—Tourist Resident in Arab society includes understanding social conversation on everyday topics and reading short, descriptive narrations. The highest level, the Superior Level—Foreign Professional in Arab Society, includes oral and written language on matters that are of general interest to educated native speakers in authentic situations. However, although the authenticity of the content and function domains in the APT is commendable, the complete dependence on the multiple-choice response format diminishes the overall authenticity of the APT.

In terms of concurrent validity, the manual reports a study ($N = 429$) in which the reported level of Arabic study was used as an external criterion. Average and median APT scores increase as amount of study increases. This provides evidence for the concurrent validity of the APT as a measure of proficiency in Modern Standard Arabic.

In terms of evidence from construct validity, the manual reports the use of the Item Response Theory (IRT) model to develop and score the APT. The fit statistics provided by the IRT analysis offer evidence of the extent to which unidimensionality exists. The infit mean square is one of the most useful statistics in a test like the APT that has a wide range of proficiency. This statistic has an expected value of 1.00 and items with +1.20 and above and .80 are considered misfitting the model. Using this criterion, in the Listening section, none of the items in Form A and three in

Form B were misfitting; in the Reading section, five items in Form A and one in Form B were misfitting. This shows that a high number of items fit the IRT model providing evidence for the construct validity of both Form A and Form B of the APT.

In terms of reliability, the IRT equivalent of the KR-20 reliability is provided for each section of each form of the APT. The reliability estimates are: Form A Listening section .77; Reading section .86 and Form B Listening section .82 and Reading section .83. These estimates suggest that the APT has high internal consistency reliability. In terms of the precision of measurement of the APT, this is estimated by the standard error of measurement (*SEM*). The *SEM* estimates (rounded to the nearest whole) are: Form A Listening section 10, Reading section 7; and Form B Listening section 10 , Reading section 8. These estimates are used in constructing confidence intervals such as that the "true score" of a test taker lies, with a 67% certainty within +1 or -1 standard error of the given score. So, if a given score is 95 on Form A of the APT reading, the true score could lie between 88 and 102 (95 minus 7 and 95 plus 7).

COMMENTARY. The value of the APT as an instrument to measure the general proficiency in listening and reading attained by English-speaking learners of Arabic is well established through authentic content and function domain tasks and reports of studies that provide evidence for the validity and reliability of the APT test score interpretation. However, a few additional measures could have strengthened the case for the APT. These are (a) incorporating alternative response formats such as true-false, matching, and gap-filling so that task authenticity is enhanced and any bias due to the multiple-choice format is minimized; (b) conducting a content review of test items for test bias and test performance analysis for differential item/test functioning (DIF/DTF) for salient test-taking groups such as gender and academic major (for subject matter) as suggested in the fairness chapter in the *Standards for Educational and Psychological Testing* (AERA, APA, & NCME, 1999); and (c) reporting on studies with test accommodations such as extended time for test takers with disabilities as required of testing agencies by the Americans with Disabilities Act of 1990.

SUMMARY. The APT is a well-designed test for its purpose and the reported validity and reliability studies should give test users confidence regarding the usefulness of this instrument. The APT test interpretation manual is an additional tool that test users can consult prior to purchasing and administering the test. However, there are two important concerns to which the test developers of the APT should pay attention: the complete dependence on the multiple-choice response format both in terms of lack of authenticity as well as any bias created by it and the lack of studies on test fairness specifically in terms of test bias and DIF/DTF.

REVIEWER'S REFERENCE

American Educational Research Association, American Psychological Association, & National Council on Measurement in Education. (1999). *Standards for educational and psychological testing*. Washington, DC: AERA.

[15]
Arizona Articulation Proficiency Scale, Third Revision.

Purpose: An "assessment measure of articulatory proficiency in children, adolescents, and adults."
Population: Ages 1-6 through 18-11 years.
Publication Dates: 1963–2000.
Acronym: Arizona-3.
Scores: Total score only.
Administration: Individual.
Price Data, 2002: $124 per kit including 42 picture cards, 25 test booklets, and manual (2000, 60 pages); $62.50 per picture cards; $19.95 per 25 test booklets, quantity discounts available; $45 per manual.
Time: (3) minutes.
Comments: Replaces the Arizona Articulation Proficiency Scale, Second Edition (AAPS); has updated picture cards, new gender-specific norms.
Author: Janet Barker Fudala.
Publisher: Western Psychological Services.
Cross References: See T5:175 (12 references) and T4:191 (4 references); for reviews by Penelope K. Hall and Charles Wm. Martin of a previous edition, see 11:17 (12 references); see also T3:200 (8 references); for reviews by Raphael M. Haller and Ronald K. Sommers, and an excerpted review by Barton B. Proger, see 8:954 (6 references); see also T2:2065 (2 references), 7:948 (2 references), and 6:307a (2 references).

Review of the Arizona Articulation Proficiency Scale, Third Revision by STEVEN LONG, Assistant Professor, Speech Pathology and Audiology, Marquette University, Milwaukee, WI:

DESCRIPTION. The Arizona Articulation Proficiency Scale, Third Revision (Arizona-3) is a norm-referenced test of Standard American English consonant and vowel articulation that can be administered to individuals 1:6–18:11 years of age. In addition to the single-word articulation test, the Arizona-3 includes materials for conducting a Language Screening and gathering a Continuous Speech Language Sample. Only the articulation test, however, is norm referenced. Administration time for the articulation test is estimated at 3 minutes or less for "most children" (manual, p. 1). The Language Screening and Continuous Speech Language Sample would require additional time.

Test scoring calls upon the examiner to judge the accuracy of production of target vowels and consonants. The author recommends that errors be phonetically transcribed; however, the total score for the Arizona-3 is based on correct/incorrect judgments alone, for which skill in phonetic transcription is not needed. By comparing the total score to the normative data, one can derive a standard score, percentile rank, or developmental age score.

DEVELOPMENT. The Arizona-3 is the third revision of a test originally published in 1963. The new version includes some updating of stimuli and a reduction in the number of picture cards from 48 to 42. The age range of the norms has been expanded upward to 18:11 and the standardization sample was recruited to reflect population characteristics of the 1998 U.S. Census.

For the sake of time efficiency, the test samples more than one vowel or consonant phoneme in most target words. The picture stimuli are black-and-white line drawings, with color used only to elicit the target words "red," "yellow," and "green." The most distinctive design feature of the Arizona-3 is its method of scoring, which weights each error according to the frequency of the target sound in American speech. The reference data on sound frequency are dated (French, Carter, & Koenig, 1930), though one would not expect the statistical properties of English to change markedly over this period of time. Comparison of the test's weightings for consonants to more recent phoneme frequency data (Shriberg, 1986) yielded a correlation of .86, indicating that the Arizona-3 scoring system is a reasonable representation of phoneme frequency.

The Arizona-3 uses a syllable model of phonological structure. Thus, any target consonant that does not occur in the final position of a word is designated as "initial" and no sounds are analyzed as "medial" or "intervocalic." With only 42 (mostly monosyllabic) target words, the test sample is limited in a number of respects. Each target phoneme is sampled only once and only in initial and final position. Only eight consonant blends (clusters) are targeted, representing a mixture of manner classes and sound positions (pl-, -ld, tr-, gr-, st-, -st, -ts, -ks). Only one word in the test ("television") is more than two syllables in length and its shortened, bisyllabic form ("TV") is considered an acceptable response. Consequently, the Arizona-3 yields little information about a child's mastery of strong and weak syllables in longer words. Furthermore, it contains no words with an iambic (initial weak syllable) stress pattern such as "banana" or "giraffe."

TECHNICAL. The test manual describes the procedures by which testing sites were identified and operated in order to obtain the Arizona-3 standardization sample. Although data contributions from the 32 sites were uneven—one site contributed nearly 10% of the data—the final sample appears to be adequately representative. A table indicates how the standardization sample was distributed by age, gender, geographic region, ethnic group, and parents' educational level, and how that distribution compared to 1998 U.S. Census figures. Although the sample was stratified by region and ethnicity, no attempt was made to ascertain the use of dialect by the speakers tested. It is therefore unknown, for example, how many of the African American children in the sample were speakers of African American English. More importantly, the norms themselves are not tabulated by ethnicity or region, making it impossible to compare a dialect speaker to his or her most likely linguistic peers. Thus, the test remains biased against such speakers because no allowance is made in scoring for pronunciations that are acceptable dialectal variations.

The standardization data for the Arizona-3 were gathered by both students and credentialed professionals practicing at a variety of sites. It is not stated whether examiners were required to demonstrate proficiency in judging the accuracy of children's speech. Though one would like to assume that anyone working as a speech pathologist must possess such skill, previous normative research has not found this to be the case (Smit, Hand, Freilinger, Bernthal, & Bird, 1991). Thus, the validity of the norms is open to question.

The Arizona-3 shows very high internal consistency across test items. Cronbach's alpha values are .92 or higher for all but the three oldest age groups. By age 11, nearly all children have normalized their speech and the resulting ceiling effect on articulation test scores reduces score variability, which in turn lowers internal consistency.

Studies pertaining to interexaminer, intraexaminer, and test-retest reliability are reported in the Arizona-3 manual. Although the reported percentages and coefficients show good reliability estimates, ranging from .82 to .99, only the data on test-retest reliability were obtained on the third revision of the Arizona. Studies of interexaminer and intraexaminer reliability were conducted using previous versions of the test and are dated; the latest publication was in 1979. Even accepting the reliability data at face value, several cautions are warranted about interpretation. First, the examiners who participated in the reliability studies are not identified and therefore cannot be evaluated for how well they represent the typical Arizona-3 user. Second, in judging the Arizona-3's reliability evidence and its relationship to test interpretation, it is important to remember that the reliability estimates are only for presence of error, not type of error. Thus, any interpretation of test results that relies on information from the phonetic transcription (e.g., the ratio of omissions to substitutions and distortions) rather than the mere notation of error cannot be assumed as reliable. Finally, the author of the Arizona-3 does not report the severity of the samples compared for reliability purposes. As the data from the standardization sample indicate, the average number of errors produced on the test falls dramatically after age 4. The majority of the reliability samples reported in the manual were taken from school-aged children. What is important to know is how reliably the Arizona-3 can be administered with children who produce numerous errors, that is, preschool children or ones with severe phonological disorders. The reliability of perceptual judgments is greatly inflated when the sample(s) to be judged contain mostly normal behaviors (Kearns & Simmons, 1988).

To administer a single-word articulation test validly, the examinee must say all the words on the test and the examiner must record whether the target phonemes are accurately produced. The only major problems that can occur are if a child does not recognize the picture stimulus for a word or if his production cannot be heard well enough to be evaluated. The picture stimuli for the Arizona-3 are potentially problematic. Several stimulus items (ball, television, cake, table, trees) might not be recognized because of their old-fashioned appearance, the line drawing rendering, or their depiction in isolation, separate from a familiar context. Although it may not affect picture recognition, the claim that this version of the Arizona depicts "more current clothing styles and activities" and "include[s] more ethnic diversity" seems far-fetched. The people shown are distinctly Caucasian in appearance and the clothing and hairstyles appear decades old.

Once a word is spoken, it must be evaluated by the examiner, but the Arizona-3 manual has no discussion of whether it violates the test protocol for examiners to record productions for later listening and scoring. This is a widespread practice among clinicians, and was used in some of the Arizona-3 reliability studies, but it goes unmentioned in the discussion of administration and standardization procedures.

The Language Screening and Continuous Speech Language Sample components of the Arizona-3 seem to have been added as an afterthought, as they have no relationship to the articulation test. It is unlikely that a sample representative of all phonemes would be obtained by following the author's recommendation of "no more than about 100 words" (manual, p. 11). The test form contains no worksheet to analyze a connected speech sample or facilitate a comparison to the single word results. Space is provided for an orthographic transcription and calculation of mean length of utterance (MLU). However, the calculation examples in the manual are incorrect (they count only words, not morphemes) and the normative data fail to meet any of the usual psychometric expectations for sample selection, size, or reliability of measurement.

The Language Screening of the Arizona-3 consists of an additional prompt on 32 of the 42 stimulus cards that assesses the child's ability to produce developmentally significant words (colors, body parts, etc.), imitate complex phrases ("have eaten"), comprehend bound morphemes ("bigger"), and so on. The screening is not norm-referenced and is criterion-referenced only in that a child's failure or success on each item can be compared to an unreferenced list of expressive language milestones.

COMMENTARY. The Arizona-3 has been designed to be time efficient and to yield a total score that correlates well with clinical judgments of speaker intelligibility. These are important aims that the test in large measure achieves. At the same time, there are flaws in its design that should be known to anyone using the instrument.

In the Arizona-3, speech intelligibility is associated solely with the frequency of occurrence of target phonemes produced in error. As a construct, this ignores many other factors that can alter the intelligibility of connected speech: the effect of errors on nontarget phonemes; the existence of "acceptable" errors due to dialect or casual speech; the effect of syllable structure changes; the impact of error type whereby omission errors tend to reduce intelligibility the most and distortion errors the least; the effect of prosodic disturbances of rate, rhythm, intonation, and voice quality; and the effect on intelligibility of problems in other language domains, such as immature syntax or mistakes in vocabulary selection.

The Arizona-3 is not designed to help in the identification of a child's strengths and weaknesses that can be used as the basis for intervention planning. The sample it gathers is small (42 words) and the test form offers little help in identifying even basic patterns of error such as constraints operating on particular manner classes or places of articulation. For any interpretation of Arizona-3 results in terms of phonetic inventories, word shapes, metrical patterns, or phonological processes, one must be prepared to transfer the transcription data to other worksheets designed for this purpose or to software that can perform the desired analyses.

SUMMARY. The Arizona-3 is best used as a time-efficient, norm-referenced instrument to document the existence of an articulation impairment, to qualify the examinee for clinical services, and to help quantify a problem of intelligibility. It has little value for the screening of language. It is poorly designed for the identification of phonological patterns that could be applied in treatment

planning, especially with individuals who demonstrate severe articulation disorders. Other samples and methods of phonological analysis must be employed for this purpose.

REVIEWER'S REFERENCES

French, N. R., Carter, C. W., & Koenig, W., Jr. (1930). The words and sounds of telephone conversations. *Journal of Acoustical Society of America, 35,* 892–904.

Kearns, K. P. & Simmons, N. N. (1988). Interobserver reliability and perceptual ratings: More than meets the ear. *Journal of Speech and Hearing Research, 31,* 131–136.

Shriberg, L. D. (1986). *Programs to examine phonetic and phonologic evaluation records. Version 4.0. User's manual.* Madison, WI: Department of Communicative Disorders and Waisman Center on Mental Retardation and Human Development.

Smit, A. B., Hand, L., Freilinger, J., Bernthal, J., & Bird, A. (1991). The Iowa articulation norms project and its Nebraska replication. *Journal of Speech and Hearing Disorders, 55,* 779–799.

Review of the Arizona Articulation Proficiency Scale, Third Revision by ROGER L. TOWNE, Associate Professor and Head, Department of Communication Disorders, Northern Michigan University, Marquette, MI:

DESCRIPTION. As its name notes, the Arizona Articulation Proficiency Scale, Third Revision (Arizona-3), is the third revision of the original test and comes some 14 years after the second revision in 1986. The Arizona-3 retains much of the familiar format of the previous edition including the use of simple picture stimuli, the use of "Total Score" to scale a child's successful speech productions, and the broad sampling of major speech sounds in various word contexts. This third edition contains updated picture stimuli, test booklet and manual, and a restandardization of the test on a representative sample of 5,500 individuals.

The Arizona-3 is designed primarily to test the articulation skills of children ages 18 months through 18 years. The author notes, however, that the test can also be a useful measure in the speech assessment of unintelligible adults. Optional features include a printed stimulus word list that can be read by older children, pictures used to stimulate continuous speech, and items that allow for informal language screening. According to the author, common applications of the Arizona-3 included (a) identification of misarticulations and total articulation proficiency; (b) identification and selection of children for therapy; (c) determination of speech therapy progress; (d) providing a frame of reference for discussing speech development, therapy needs, and progress; (e) identification of children in need of more in-depth assessment; and (f) facilitation of research.

Test administration requires only the spiral-bound picture cards consisting of 42 individual black line drawings, and the test booklet used for recording and scoring a child's responses. Each picture is presented to the child with the general instruction to "please tell me what it is." Older children can simply read the target words from a list. Many pictures also have associated questions about the picture that can be asked if a larger language sample is also being acquired. As the child proceeds, the examiner completes the test booklet by indicating only erred responses and the type of error committed (i.e., substitution, omission, or distortion). There is also space to record any additional behavioral observations relative to each response.

Scoring the Arizona-3 is quite simple and involves only a two-step process. First, a "Total Score" is obtained that is calculated by adding up all the given sound values for the speech sounds that were accurately produced. Sound values are weighted values between .5 and 6.0 that reflect how frequently a particular sound occurs in American speech. A child who makes no speech errors on the 67 sounds tested would have a total score of 100. To simplify this process, space is provided to find the sum of the sound values for erred initial and final consonants and vowels and subtract this number from 100. The total score can then be compared to that of other individuals of the same age (and gender in younger children). This comparison can be made by recording standard score, Z-score, normal curve equivalent, and percentile rank from tables found in the manual. The total score is also used to indicate the child's overall level of articulation impairment (i.e., normal, mild, moderate, or severe) from a table provided on the first page of the test booklet. Finally, the test booklet provides space to record future retesting results and a comparison to the original test performance.

DEVELOPMENT. The Arizona-3 was developed by making modest improvements in test format and in restandardizing the test on a more current representation of children in the country. The author notes improved features to include updated picture stimuli that reflect current children's dress and activities, more ethnic diversity, and the removal of possible objectionable pictures (e.g., a gun). Improvements also were made to the test booklet, and to the text of the manual, including its tables and appendices to make them easier to use and more informative. The picture stimuli were also reduced to 42 and reorganized to test for 67 sound/position items. In addition, a list of stimulus words was added so that older children could be tested through reading rather than picture naming, and language screening prompts were added.

TECHNICAL. Perhaps the most significant improvement to the Arizona-3 has been its restandardization to more closely represent current census data relative to geographic region, ethnicity, and socioeconomic status. The standardization sample was collected by enlisting the help of speech-language pathologists in a variety of clinical settings throughout the country. The Arizona-3 was restandardized on 5,500 individuals between the ages of 18 months through 18 years representing an equal number of males and females. Approximately 300 individuals were tested in each of 11 age groups between 1-6 and 6-11 years with each group representing a 6-month interval, and 7 age groups representing 12-month intervals between 7-0 and 18-11 years of age. Individual ethnic identity proportions also generally reflected U.S. Census figures for Asians, Blacks, and Native Americans, whereas they were slightly lower for Hispanic and slightly higher for White. Likewise, geographic proportions generally reflected Census data reflecting the percentage of people living in the East, Midwest, South, and West. Finally, parent's education level, used as a standard index for socioeconomic status in educational research, also generally reflected Census data for the country.

Development of the norms for the Arizona-3 was preceded by looking at the relationship between obtained total scores and age and gender. This was accomplished using an analysis of variance procedure where total score was the dependent variable and age group and gender were the independent factors. It was found that the effects for age and gender were very strong ($p < .001$), providing evidence of test validity relative to established developmental relationships between articulation, age, and gender. Norms were then calculated based on the normative sample and sample groupings (age and gender). As previously noted, norms developed include standard scores, z-scores, normal curve equivalents, and percentile ranks all based on a child's total score on the test.

Articulatory impairment ratings were also developed using specific cutoff scores relative to standard deviation, standard score, and percentile rank for each age group, thus categorizing a child's articulation as being normal, mildly impaired, moderately impaired, or severely impaired. According to the author, this categorization allows for a summary of test results and a clear guide to clinical interpretation.

Reliability of the Arizona-3 was measured by evaluating internal consistency, rater reliability, and test-retest reliability. Tests for internal consistency, as a measure of test item intercorrelation and ordered difficulty, resulted in alpha estimates ranging from .78 to .96 (median .925) and quite similar to those for previous editions of the test. As the Arizona-3's testing procedures are essentially the same as previous editions no new interrater reliability measures were done. Results from previous studies of the Arizona's interrater reliability have demonstrated interrater reliability to be .90 or higher, suggesting similarly predictable results across examiners. Test-retest reliability on the previous edition of the Arizona had an overall coefficient of .96 (with a 1-week interval) whereas results of test-retest reliability done on the Arizona-3 demonstrated an overall coefficient of .97 thus confirming that the latest edition is as reliable on repeated administrations as in the past.

Validity of the Arizona has been demonstrated over the years in several studies that have looked at its content and concurrent validity. Test performance has been shown to correlate highly with clinical evaluations of articulation problems. In the past, the Arizona has been shown to correlate highly with other well known articulation tests including the Photo Articulation Test (r = .82), the Goldman-Fristoe Test of Articulation (r = .84), and the Templin-Darley Screening and Diagnostic Tests of Articulation (r = .89). New correlations between the Arizona-3 and the Goldman-Fristoe and Photo Articulation Test also resulted in high test correlations of .88 and .91, respectively. These data would suggest a strong concurrent validity relative to articulation measures. Weaker correlations were found between the Arizona-3 and measures of cognitive ability including the Wechsler Intelligence Scale for Children III and the Wechsler Preschool and Primary Scale of Intelligence-Revised.

COMMENTARY. The Arizona-3 represents an updating of a long-used measure of articulation performance in children. Like its predecessors, the Arizona-3 uses the standard format of picture presentation to elicit targeted words from which specific sound articulation performance is measured. Like other articulation tests, the Arizona-3 is easy to administer, easy to score, and does not require a lot of time. One of its unique features is that a child's articulation performance is measured by the number of speech sounds the child produces correctly rather than on the speech sound errors they make. This focus more easily facilitates the separation of normal articulation from disordered articulation as well as knowing when a child has reached normalcy following therapy.

As with all articulation measures, the Arizona-3 measures articulation competency only from a small sample of a child's speech and, therefore, one must use caution and professional judgment in reaching conclusions regarding a child's overall articulation proficiency. Additional testing of a child's articulation skills in a variety of contexts and settings is necessary before a sufficient sample is acquired from which sound clinical judgments can be made. No single test of articulation, including the Arizona-3, is comprehensive enough to provide sufficient data regarding a child's overall articulation competency.

SUMMARY. The Arizona series is well known and has been a widely used measure of articulation proficiency in children for a number of years. Its latest edition, the Arizona-3, has retained the familiar format to which clinicians are accustomed while making modest changes in its stimulus pictures and examiner's manual. Its restandardization to be more representative of current demographics is a significant and important update. Although the Arizona-3 is not a unique articulation assessment instrument, for those clinicians who have had the previous edition of the Arizona as part of their articulation assessment repertoire, the Arizona-3 should be a welcomed updating. The Arizona-3 should also be considered by those who have not used previous editions but are looking for a valid and reliable measure of children's articulation performance.

[16]

Assessment of Comprehension and Expression 6–11.

Purpose: Designed to "assess language development."
Population: Ages 6-0 to 11-11.
Publication Date: 2002.
Acronym: ACE 6–11.
Administration: Individual.
Price Data: Available from publisher.
Comments: Subtests may be administered individually although it is recommended that a minimum of three subtests be employed.
Authors: Catherine Adams, Rosanne Cooke, Alison Crutchley, Anne Hesketh, and David Reeves.
Publisher: NFER-Nelson Publishing Co., Ltd. [England].

a) MAIN TEST.
Scores, 6: Sentence Completion, Inferential Comprehension, Naming, Syntactic Formulation, Semantic Decisions, Total.
Time: (26–32) minutes.
b) EXTENDED TEST.
Scores, 10: Same as *a* above with the addition of Non-Literal Comprehension, Narrative Propositions, Narrative Syntax/Discourse, Total.
Time: (46–59) minutes.

Review of the Assessment of Comprehension and Expression 6–11 by CLEBORNE D. MADDUX, Foundation Professor of Counseling and Educational Psychology, University of Nevada—Reno, Reno, NV:

DESCRIPTION. The Assessment of Comprehension and Expression 6–11 (ACE 6-11) is an individually administered group of five to seven subtests designed to assess language development in children between the ages of 6 and 11 years. The intended use of the test is to identify children with language deficits or delay. The test consists of two versions—the Main Test and the Extended Test. The Main Test requires approximately 26 minutes to administer and consists of five subtests including Sentence Comprehension, Inferential Comprehension, Naming, Syntactic Formulation, and Semantic Decisions. The Extended Test requires about 42 minutes to administer and consists of seven subtests: the five subtests of the Main Test plus a Non-Literal Comprehension subtest and a Narrative subtest. Although the Extended Test is recommended by the developers, the Main Test can be used when time is short. A reduced number of subtests may be administered in place of the entire Main Test or Extended Test, although the manual cautions that the subtest reliabilities are too low to make it advisable to administer fewer than three subtests to any child.

Standard scores with 80% and 95% confidence intervals and percentile ranks are provided for all subtests as well as for the total Main and Extended Tests. Standard score means and standard deviations are 10 and 3 respectively for subtests and 100 and 15 for both total Main and Extended Tests.

The record booklet includes a provision for recording of all scores and the profiling of subtest scores including confidence intervals, with the recommendation that scores of any two subtests be considered statistically different only if the confidence intervals are nonoverlapping. Although the test developers state that no hard and fast ACE 6-11 cutoff points should be used for diagnosing a child as language impaired, they suggest that a reasonable criterion might be scores between one and two standard deviations below the mean.

DEVELOPMENT. The ACE 6-11 was developed at the University of Manchester and a preliminary version was piloted by speech and language therapists who used it with children with and without language impairments. The developers state that test development was conducted with the intention of assessing "language as it is likely to be used in the everyday environments" (manual, p. 3) of children ages 6 through 11, while keeping the test interesting and engaging. Research is cited to justify the selection of skills chosen in each of the subtests.

TECHNICAL.

Normative data. The ACE 6-11 was standardized in 2000 and 2001 with 790 children ages 6 to 11 in the United Kingdom and Republic of Ireland. The standardization sample also included an additional clinical sample of 45 male and 21 female children who had previously been diagnosed with developmental language impairments and who were receiving speech and language therapy in language classes in the northwest of England. These were students with normal IQs, no hearing loss, and whose first language was English. The test was administered by students at the University of Manchester studying speech and language therapy. The students were trained by the test developers and all scoring was checked and validated by another, specially trained team.

The original 790 children in the standardization sample were selected by first obtaining a stratified sample of 105 primary schools restricted to "areas of the country to which fieldworkers could reasonably travel" (manual, p. 93). Stratification was by country, region, school size, and type of Local Education Authority (LEA). No private or special schools were included. Eighty-six schools were eventually selected and invited to participate, and 42 primary and 8 secondary schools were used. Each school sent parental permission forms for 5 male and 5 female children whose birthdays fell on the 14th, 15th, 16th, or 17th of any month and whose language development was thought to be normal. Twenty-four hundred consent forms were distributed and 1,137 were returned with approval. Nine hundred of these were randomly selected and 790 from 50 schools completed the test and made up the final standardization sample.

The standardization of the instrument is adequate for use in countries from which the sample was drawn (the United Kingdom and Republic of Ireland). However, many items require knowledge of culture-specific vocabulary, making the norms of unknown accuracy for use outside these countries. Curiously, the Sentence Comprehension subtest contains several items that require the child to be able to tell time by looking at a picture of an analog clock face.

The manual states that whenever possible, there were equal numbers of boys and girls in each age group. Gender differences were investigated by testing the total language raw scores of both Main and Extended Tests for statistical differences by gender at each age group. No significant gender differences or gender-by-age interactions were found and the average effect sizes of gender across all ages were -.02 and -.05 for Main and Extended Tests. The standardization sample was primarily White, and was a good match with the ethnic makeup of the population of England and Wales.

Standard errors of measurement for subtests at all ages are acceptably small. All but two are less than 2 points (mean = 10, standard deviation = 3). For the total scores on Main and Extended Tests, the standard errors of measurement for all age groups range from 3.91 to 5.71, with the average across all ages 5.26 points for the Main Test and 4.36 on the Extended Test (mean = 100, standard deviation = 15).

Reliability. Internal reliability was investigated by calculating Cronbach's alpha (1951) for each of seven age groups for all subtests and for total scores of the Main and Extended Tests. Four of the subtests have average coefficients across age groups between .70 and .78 (Semantic Decisions, Narrative Propositions, Syntactic Formulation, and Naming), three subtests have average coefficients between .61 and .69 (Non-Literal Comprehension, Sentence Comprehension, and Narrative Syntax), and the Inferential Comprehension subtest has an average coefficient of .48. This latter subtest has coefficients that range from .41 to .59 across age groups. Coefficients for total Main and Extended Tests are all above .85 for each age group, with the average across all ages reported as .88 for the Main Test and .92 for the Extended Test.

A test-retest reliability study was conducted with 47 seven-year-olds and 44 ten-year-olds from the standardization sample. Test-retest correlation coefficients (2-week interval) are reported for each subtest and total scores of the Main and Extended Tests for all 91 students combined. The subtest correlations range from .47 to .84, with only two exceeding .70 (Semantic Decisions and Naming) and one as low as .47 (Inferential Comprehension). Test-retest correlations for Main and Extended Tests were .80 and .83, respectively.

Validity. Face validity was addressed by presenting pictures and stimuli to expert speech and language therapists. No details of the procedures used were given. Construct validity is addressed by pointing out the moderate positive correlations among the subtests and by presenting the results of an investigation of concurrent validity. Total scores on both the Main Test and the Extended Test and the British Picture Vocabulary Scale Second Edition (Dunn, Dunn, & Whetton, 1997), and the Test for Reception of Grammar (Bishop, 1982) were calculated and compared. This study was conducted with a subset of 163 children from the standardization sample. A minimum of 24 children were from each of the test's six age groups (the younger two age groups were combined into a single group). The mean standard scores across the four tests ranged from 102 to 104. Correlations between the two tests and the Main and Extended Tests of the ACE 6-11 were moderate, ranging from .49 to .66.

Analysis of scores of the 66 children in the clinical sample of children previously diagnosed with language disorders or delays provided evidence that these children had group mean scores across subtests of the ACE 6-11 that ranged from 5.8 to 7.2.

COMMENTARY. The ACE 6-11 is a relatively quick, individually administered test that could be useful as one tool in the identification of young children with delayed language development. The test materials are interesting and attractive, and the manual is well-written and informative. Standardization is adequate, but because all children in the standardization sample were in schools in the U.K. and the Irish Republic, and because many items employ culturally specific vocabulary and concepts, the test must be considered of unknown value for use outside the U.K. and the Irish Republic. Furthermore, individual subtest reliability coefficients are too low to justify their use to diagnose specific language deficits. Test-retest reliabilities for the total scores of both Main and Extended Tests are adequate, but even for these global scores, coefficients fall a little short of .90, the level often regarded as necessary for tests to be used for critical decisions such as placement in special education.

SUMMARY. Total scores of the ACE 6-11 Main and Extended Tests could be useful in the U.K. and Ireland to help identify children for further investigation for language deficits or delays. The instrument can be administered in well under an hour and is easy to give and to score. Restandardization with students in other English-speaking countries would be necessary before the test could be recommended for use outside Great Britain, and further psychometric refinement should be undertaken to document the usefulness of the individual subtest scores.

REVIEWER'S REFERENCES

Bishop, D. V. M. (1982). Test for Reception of Grammar (Second Edition). University of Manchester: Age and Cognitive Performance Research Centre.
Cronbach, L. J. (1951). Coefficient alpha and the internal structure of tests. *Psychometrika, 16*, 297-334.
Dunn, L. M., Dunn, L. M., & Whetton, C. (1997). The British Picture Vocabulary Scale (Second Edition). Windsor: NFER-NELSON.

Review of the Assessment of Comprehension and Expression 6–11 by SHEILA PRATT, Associate Professor, Communication Science and Disorders Department, University of Pittsburgh, Pittsburgh, PA:

OVERVIEW. The Assessment of Comprehension and Expression 6–11 (ACE 6–11) is a broadly focused test developed to assess oral language understanding and use in school-aged children. Its primary application is the diagnosis of language delay and disorder. The test consists of seven subtests of varying lengths that pertain to specific language skills, namely Sentence Completion, Inferential Comprehension, Naming, Syntactic Formulation, Semantic Decisions, Non-Literal Comprehension, and Narrative Production. The ACE 6–11 is administered individually by professionals trained in speech-language development and disorders. The test is administered with visual plates that include verbal cues and instructions for the tester on the backside. The ACE 6–11 is handscored, and includes norm-referencing and an option for cross-subtest profiling.

CONSTRUCTION. The language skills sampled by the ACE 6–11 were selected in response to the research literature on language development and disorders in school-aged children. As such, the ACE 6–11 has theoretical and empirical support. The test is organized with subtests dedicated to each of the targeted skills. The first five subtests are considered the main test whereas the Non-Literal and Narrative Production subtests are considered the extension subtests. When all of the subtests are given, it is referred to as the Extended Test. The ACE 6–11 also is organized so that word, sentence, and beyond-sentence-level processing is assessed across the test. Pictures and text are used to provide visual support and context, but the impact of memory and other related cognitive functions is not otherwise controlled. On a number of items, comprehension of the visual context may dictate performance rather than comprehension of the verbal stimuli.

Initial items and materials were obtained and reviewed by a number of sources. Two forms were constructed and after preliminary testing, items from both forms were extracted to construct a 148-item test. The 148-item test was then administered to a sample of typically developing children (aged 6 through 11 years) who represented 50 schools from across the United Kingdom and the Republic of Ireland. The demographic properties of the children tested suggested that they were reasonably consistent with those of the target population. The final ACE 6-11 was constituted with 120 of the 148 items.

TECHNICAL.

Normative Data. Normative data were derived from 790 children who provided complete results on the 148-item test. The published 120-item version of the ACE 6–11 was not administered to a normative sample for additional standardization. The raw scores obtained from the 790 children were used to develop standard scores per subtest per age level. Composite standard scores for the Main and Extended Test also were established. The standard scores were associated with 80% and 95% confidence intervals, percentile ranks, and descriptive language-skill intervals.

Psychometric Properties. The test manual provides internal consistency and reliability results for the subtests, and the Main and Extended forms of the test. Internal consistency values are modest at the subtest level (.81–.41) and variable across the age levels. The Inferential Comprehension subtest is the least consistent, which may be a function of the limited number of items comprising the subtest. In contrast, internal consistency values for the Main Test vary from .86 to .90 across the age levels, whereas values for the Extended Test range from .90 to .93.

Similarly, test-retest reliability coefficients are modest at the subtest level but reasonably good at the composite-test level, with correlation coefficients of .80 for the Main Test and .83 for the Extended Test. Validity is adequately documented in the test manual and suggests that the test's construction and performance is consistent with its intended use. However, data associated with its application with children previously diagnosed with language disorder are limited. Furthermore, the reliability and validity results indicate that the test appears to perform best in the extended form.

COMMENTARY AND SUMMARY. The ACE 6–11 is a reasonably well-constructed, norm-referenced test of language skills. It targets language skills that often are not mature in children ages 6–11 and are known to be problematic for children with language disorders. The reliability and validity evidence of the composite versions of the test is good but many of the individual subtests lack sufficient reliability evidence and should not be administered in isolation or even within a subset. Some of the weaknesses of the individual subtests might relate to the number of items, the age of the children being tested, and the complexity of the linguistic constructs. One weakness of

the test is that the manual provides only limited data on its sensitivity and informativeness with regard to the diagnosis of language disorder. Some information is provided on a relatively small group of children with language impairment, but the data are applicable only to the validity of score interpretation for the test, and do little to guide the use of the test for differential diagnosis and treatment. Users of the test also should keep in mind that the test was standardized on children in the United Kingdom and the Republic of Ireland and, although it appears to represent well the demographic properties of that population, it would not be applicable to other English-speaking populations.

[17]
Auditory Processing Abilities Test.

Purpose: Designed to assess auditory processing.
Population: Ages 5.0–12.11.
Publication Date: 2004.
Acronym: APAT.
Scores, 20: Phonemic Awareness, Word Sequences, Semantic Relationships, Sentence Memory, Cued Recall, Content Memory, Complex Sentences, Sentence Absurdities, Following Directions, Passage Comprehension, Global Index, Auditory Memory Index, Linguistic Processing Index, Auditory Discrimination Index (optional), Auditory Sequencing Index (optional), Auditory Cohesion Index (optional), Immediate Recall Index (optional), Delayed Recall Index (optional), Sequential Recall Index (optional), Cued Recall Index (optional).
Administration: Individual.
Price Data, 2003: $112 per complete kit including examiner's manual (95 pages), 25 Test booklets, 25 summary sheets in portfolio; $42 per manual; $45 per 25 test booklets; $25 per 20 summary sheets.
Time: (30–45) minutes.
Authors: Deborah Ross-Swain and Nancy Long.
Publisher: Academic Therapy Publications.

Review of the Auditory Processing Abilities Test by JEFFERY P. BRADEN, Professor of Psychology, North Carolina State University, Raleigh, NC, and KELLY M. LAUGLE, Graduate Student in Psychology, North Carolina State University, Raleigh, NC:

DESCRIPTION. The Auditory Processing Abilities Test (APAT) is designed to evaluate auditory processing skills that range from listening for specific sounds in nonwords to comprehending entire paragraphs of spoken language. It is an individually administered test appropriate for use with children ages 5 years 0 months through 12 years 11 months. The APAT is intended to assess children at risk for or presently experiencing auditory processing disorder (APD), to identify specific strengths and weaknesses in auditory processing skills, to measure progress in response to intervention, and to facilitate research. Appropriate cautions regarding the need to establish children's hearing and attention skills, and examiners' articulation skills, are included in the manual.

The 10 APAT subtests are divided into scales. The first scale, Linguistic Processing, includes seven subtests that measure: (a) phonemic awareness, (b) semantic relationships between words, (c) repetition of sentences, (d) repetition of word pairs with no linguistic similarities, (e) comprehension of complex sentences, (f) recognition of absurdities within sentences, and (g) comprehension of passages. The second scale, Auditory Memory, includes three subtests that measure the child's ability to: (a) sequence words of increasing length, (b) recall information from a brief story, and (c) follow oral instructions. The APAT yields standard scaled scores for individual subtests (M = 10, SD = 3), and three composite indices representing performance on each scale (Linguistic Processing and Auditory Memory) and the entire battery (M = 100, SD = 15). Seven optional indices are also provided (M = 100, SD = 15), which are intended to reflect three skills contributing to linguistic processing and four skills contributing to auditory memory.

DEVELOPMENT. The APAT was standardized on 1,087 U.S. children drawn from public, private, and parochial schools, and from speech clinics. The normative sample was well matched to the 2002 U.S. Census parameters for region, race/ethnicity, gender, and disability status. A pilot test of the APAT was conducted on 154 students whose ages ranged from 2 through 18. Classical Test Theory and Item Response Theory analyses were conducted to eliminate items and determine item order for the standardization edition. Item bias contrasts were made between groups based on gender and race using the Mantel-Haenzel procedure for analyzing differential item functioning. The manual reported no evidence of bias in any of the APAT items for the contrasted groups; however, sample sizes

were not reported, so we cannot determine whether the procedures were likely to have sufficient power to detect group differences.

TECHNICAL. Internal consistency estimates for subtests and scales (using Cronbach's alpha and Spearman-Brown split-half coefficients) were relatively high (.60–.96) for all ages. Test-retest stability, with an average duration of less than 7 days between administrations, for 226 examinees was excellent (r = .99). Average Standard Errors of Measurement for all subtests at each age level ranged from .79 to 1.51.

Validity evidence was provided with respect to content and construct validity (see commentary below). Test content was clearly linked to a defined and well-articulated theoretical structure. Construct validity evidence was presented in two major forms: internal structure and relations to other tests. Exploratory factor analyses supported the assignment of subtests to two correlated scales (Linguistic Processing and Auditory Memory). Test developers reported using confirmatory factor analyses to justify the creation and structure of optional indices, but specific data for these analyses (e.g., model permutations, residual mean square values) are not provided. Where data are presented, the information is not congruent with the text. For example, a highly unusual (p < .0001) chi-square statistic for a goodness of fit test is presented as evidence that the optional index factor structure fits the data well, rather than as evidence of mismatch between the data and structure.

The relationship between APAT scores and other tests is limited to correlations with the Lindamood Auditory Conceptualization Test (LACT; Lindamood & Lindamood, 1979). These correlations are low to moderate, indicating little overlap between the tests. Furthermore, the sample on which data are based is not described, although the available evidence suggests the sample may be too small (n = 18) to provide reliable estimates of overlap.

COMMENTARY. The APAT has some significant strengths. The content of the test is well aligned with its theoretical grounding, and has strong intuitive appeal for use by speech/language clinicians. The standardization sample is reasonable and closely resembles U.S. Census data with respect to gender, ethnicity, and geographic factors. Internal consistency is moderate to excellent, and factor analytic evidence is largely consistent with the primary organization of subtests into two (Auditory Memory and Linguistic Processing) scales. The importance of auditory processing for academic success and literacy is high; the intent of the APAT is laudable and potentially quite relevant for linguistic, educational, and psychological assessment.

However, a number of weaknesses were identified, mostly relating to omissions from the test manual and materials. First, there is no explicit acknowledgement that APAT items presume examinees' native exposure to spoken English, and some items require prior knowledge (e.g., knowing that one cannot drive to Hawaii from North America). These assumptions should be explicit, as should cautions about making inferences about scores for examinees who have atypical schooling experiences or who are not exclusively native English speakers.

Second, a number of important details are omitted. Some technical information is missing (e.g., SES, parental education, language background data for the normative sample) or described too briefly to allow the reader to evaluate the test (e.g., the manual reports that confirmatory factor and item bias analyses were performed, but provides no specific data on sample sizes, models, etc.). Also, the correct answers for test items are not provided in the record form or the manual; some examiners may find explicit statements of correct answers helpful in test administration and scoring.

Third, the validity section uses an outdated framework to present information. Rather than using the current *Standards* (AERA, APA, & NCME, 1999), which identify five forms of validity evidence, the manual presents the "holy trinity" of content, construct, and criterion validity used in previous versions of the *Standards*. Even within the old framework, evidence is quite limited. Although age differences, correlations among scales, and factor analyses are generally supportive, the only relationship to another test (the LACT) yields surprisingly low correlations and appears to be based on an unacceptably small and undefined sample.

Fourth, the complete absence of evidence showing that APAT results are useful for diagnosis of disorder, identifying relative strengths and weaknesses in auditory processing, and for progress

monitoring is surprising. We expected studies comparing APAT scores for children with and without auditory processing disorder, evidence that test scores are useful for planning interventions (e.g., showing APAT-generated interventions produce better outcomes than randomly selected interventions), and proof that APAT can reliably detect improvements in auditory processing skills (e.g., improved scores following treatment vs. no change in untreated students). Additional information (e.g., correlations with other tests of auditory processing or oral language) would be helpful for examiners to understand what skills are tested by the APAT and how they relate to other constructs and tests used to measure those constructs.

On a practical note, the APAT could provide an audio recording (e.g., tape or CD) to improve standardized administration of items, such as is available for auditory processing tests of the Woodcock-Johnson Third Edition (WJ-III; 15:281). Other competitors to the APAT include subtests of the WJ-III and Lindamood Auditory Conceptualization Test (T6:1433), which may offer less breadth of coverage than the APAT, but may also offer stronger evidence to support their validity for assessing auditory processing abilities.

SUMMARY. The APAT purports to measure a wide range of auditory processing abilities that would be of particular value for linguistic, educational, and psychological assessment purposes. The efficiency, breadth, and reliability of the APAT are strong, but do not compensate for limited evidence to support its claims of diagnosing strengths/weaknesses, disorders, and response to treatment. Therefore, we view the APAT as a promising but as yet unproven tool for assessing auditory processing disorders.

REVIEWERS' REFERENCES

American Educational Research Association, American Psychological Association, & National Council on Measurement in Education. (1999). *Standards for educational and psychological testing*. Washington, DC: American Educational Research Association.
Lindamood, C. H., & Lindamood, P. C. (1979). The Lindamood Auditory Conceptualization Test—Revised. Itasca, IL: Riverside.

Review of the Auditory Processing Abilities Test by CHRISTOPHER A. SINK, Professor and Chair, School Counseling and Psychology, Seattle Pacific University, Seattle, WA, and RICK EIGENBROOD, Associate Professor, Education and Director of Doctoral Studies, Seattle Pacific University, Seattle, WA:

DESCRIPTION. The Auditory Processing Abilities Test (APAT) is a norm-referenced test battery for use with children ages 5 years, 0 months through 12 years, 11 months. The battery is fairly long for young children, with 10 subtests, including Phonemic Awareness (18 items), Word Sequences (10 items), Semantic Relationships (12 items), Sentence Memory (15 items), Cued Recall (15 items), Content Memory (immediate and delayed recall-1 paragraph), Complex Sentences (10 items), Sentence Absurdities (13 items), Following Directions (12 items), and Passage Comprehension (18 items). In addition, the APAT has four general indices: Auditory Memory Index (AMI; sum of scaled scores for 4 subtests), Linguistic Processing Index (LPI; sum of scaled scores for 7 subtests), and Global Index (GI; sum of scaled scores for 10 subtests). Optional analyses produce three linguistic processing indices (Auditory Discrimination Index, Auditory Sequencing Index, and Auditory Cohesion Index) and five memory indices (Immediate Recall Index, Delayed Recall Index, Sequential Recall Index, and Cued Recall Index).

According to the APAT manual, the battery is primarily to be used to identify children who may experience an auditory processing disorder (APD) as well as to discriminate their specific auditory processing skill strengths and deficits. Test items are individually administered to children who, in turn, respond verbally or by performing a task. The 10 raw subtest scores are then converted to scaled scores ($M = 10$, $SD = 3$) and percentile ranks, whereas the broader Index scores can be reported as standard scores ($M = 100$, $SD = 15$), percentile ranks, and/or age-equivalents. The authors contend that the APAT requires 30–45 minutes to administer and 10 minutes to score. Instructions for item administration and scoring are clearly explained.

The test manual is somewhat confusing about which professionals should administer the instrument. Initially, the authors specify that the APAT should be utilized by speech-language pathologists but may also be employed by appropriately trained professionals (e.g., learning disability specialists, psychologists, resource specialists) who are interested in appraising children's auditory processing skills. Conversely, the manual states that according to the American Speech-Language Hearing Association, the diagnosis of auditory processing disorder (APD) is the responsibility of a certified audiologist. If this is the case, qualified audiologists should primarily use the instrument.

DEVELOPMENT. The APAT's development is briefly summarized in the manual and is largely limited to item development and selection. To determine the item's psychometric properties, a pilot study was conducted with 154 students (ages 2–18) in five California schools. Further demographic characteristics were not specified. The manual states that both classical test theory and item response theory were deployed to eliminate items and determine item order. No ethnicity or gender item bias was found in the pilot sample.

As to the theoretical grounding for the instrument's underlying construct(s) and subtests, the manual includes an overview of the APAT test model. The instrument's theoretical and practical utility is based on the assumption that it is possible to reliably detect APDs in children that lead to difficulties in learning, understanding speech, and language development. Regrettably, however, much of the supportive evidence for the authors' model and this assumption is garnered from a small literature base.

TECHNICAL. General information about the norming process was adequate. The APAT manual presents specific demographic information for the 1,087 children used as the standardization sample. The sample was comparable to that of the U.S. population for gender, race/ethnicity, and geographic region. However, stratification data indicate the sample was not entirely representative across age levels for these variables, resulting in percentages that were either higher or lower then the general population. For example, the sample's race/ethnicity proportion for age 11 included approximately 85.4% White children (U.S. 69.8%), 3.3% Black children (U.S. 11.9%), 1% Asian respondents (U.S. 3.6%), and 4.9% for the children in the "other" category (U.S. 2.6%). Although the standardization sample was composed of children at each age level (5 through 12), for the purposes of norming a diagnostic test, the number of children included at each level was inconsistent and insufficient. Sample size per age level ranged from 95 children in the 12-year-old group to 162 respondents in the age 6 and age 8 groups. Data on the sample's disability status were also reported in the manual, generally reflecting the proportions found in the U.S. population.

APAT subscale internal consistency and stability reliability coefficients were computed for each age level and ranged from the "unacceptable" (.89 or below) to the "acceptable" range (.90 or higher) for diagnostic instruments. Specifically, Cronbach alpha coefficients ranged from .60 for the Complex Sentences subtest at age 11 to .93 for the Following Directions subtest at age 9. For all subtests across each age group, 5 out of a possible 88 alphas computed were .90 or higher. Nearly 40 of the alpha coefficients were below .80 and 10 alphas failed to reach .70. All of the coefficients above .90 were associated with either the Following Directions or Passage Comprehension subtests. Similar findings were reported in the test manual for the Spearman-Brown corrected split-half reliability coefficients. If the APAT is to be used as a tool for the diagnosis of APDs, as the authors recommend, then the derived reliability coefficients generally fail to reach the appropriate threshold suggested by experts in special education diagnosis (e.g., Salvia & Ysseldyke, 2004).

The test-retest reliability was assessed to document temporal stability using 226 respondents from the original standardization sample. A very high stability coefficient (r = .99) was reported in the manual. The average duration between testing sessions was oddly described as "less than 7 days" (examiner's manual, p. 68). However, no background information was presented on those children in the retest group.

Evidence to support the validity of the APAT is sparse. First, the authors vaguely discuss the instrument's content validity in terms of item discrimination and item bias studies. Median item difficulty correlations were tabled in the test manual, some of which were low, especially for the younger ages (e.g., 7 of the 11 subtests produced median item correlations of less than .30 for age 5), whereas others exceeded .80. Median biserial correlations measuring item discrimination were satisfactory. There was no discussion in the manual of whether the items were submitted for external expert analysis. In brief, the evidence for the APAT's content validity is limited.

The manual fails to demonstrate the APAT's criterion-related validity. Even though concurrent validity between the APAT and Lindamood Auditory Conceptualization (LAC) test was reported at the moderate level ("hovering around .50," examiner's manual, p. 73), the authors omitted essential background information discussed in Salvia and Ysseldyke (2004). For instance, the criterion measure (LAC) was not well described and the rationale for its selection was not made explicit. The manual does not provide a thorough accounting of the statistical analyses used or a description of the sample examined. Finally, the LAC's generalizibility, especially because it appears to be normed in 1974, was not documented.

Construct validity is summarized in terms of four areas. First, the authors suggested that because the children's auditory processing abilities, as measured by the APAT, increased with age, these developmental differences show the soundness of the underlying construct. Second, similarities in auditory processing abilities scores between the APAT and the LAC provide additional evidence for the construct. Third, according to the test manual, moderate to high subtest intercorrelations indicate that these scales tap various elements of the same construct.

Finally, the appropriateness for the APAT model, or its construct validity, is discussed primarily through use of factor analyses on the subtest scores. Without going into detail here, the limited results presented in the manual were, in part, confusing and erroneous. A two-factor solution supporting the presence of two underlying APAT dimensions (Linguistic Processes and Auditory Memory) was reported both for the principal component and maximum likelihood (ML) procedures; however, the ML produced a significant chi square (a goodness-of-fit index [GFI]), suggesting an *inadequate* fit, rather than a "robust" fit, as the authors posited (see Thompson, 2004, for details on ML and appropriate interpretation of GFIs). No other psychometric research is described in the manual to support the APAT model. In short, the evidence provided in the manual to establish the battery's construct validity is, at best, insufficient.

COMMENTARY. The relationship between APD and significant learning problems remains a controversial area in special education. Research supporting the association between one specific modality (e.g., auditory processing) has yet to be established (Cacace & McFarland, 1998), though Kavale and Forness (2000) did find some evidence for a connection between reading and perceptual skills when visual and auditory processes were considered together. However, even if the research is able to establish a clear link between auditory processing skills and learning (especially reading) most experts question the ability to assess the central APDs directly (Kavale & Forness; Keith, 2001). These key concerns are not addressed in the development of the APAT.

The usefulness of APAT scores to estimate accurately deficiencies in auditory processing skills as well as potential APDs must be downgraded for several reasons. First, the validity of this causal assumption remains equivocal in the research literature. The authors make no effort to demonstrate that the skills assessed by the APAT are, in fact, directly related to any specific academic skill deficit. Second, the measure's underlying construct(s) and its subcomponents (i.e., the APAT model) were not established in the research documented in the test manual nor by a solid corpus of previous empirical studies. Third, there were multiple areas of the test manual that were unclear, especially the more technical elements of the standardization process and the APAT's psychometric properties.

Another major concern about the utility of the APAT involves score interpretation. The manual recommends that qualified examiners can use the children's subtest performances as a window to their auditory processing strengths and weaknesses. This recommendation is suspect given the brief overviews of subtests provided in the manual and the lack of comprehensible guidelines on what weak or low scores actually mean. Moreover, the authors indicate that auditory processing deficits can be translated into functional categories ("mild," "moderate," or "severe") depending on the respondents' scaled or standard scores. These functional labels went unsubstantiated and underexplained in the test manual.

SUMMARY. Despite the fact that the APAT authors have developed an instrument that can be administered and scored in a relatively efficient manner, the major concerns outlined above compromise its value to speech and language clinicians. Evidence for the validity of score interpretations of the APAT falls far short of accepted professional and technical standards. Without adequate construct validity, we cannot recommend its use as a diagnostic tool. With further research, it may become a helpful screening device for children with auditory processing deficits.

REVIEWERS' REFERENCES

Cacace, A. T., & McFarland, D. J. (1998). Central auditory processing disorder in school-aged children: A critical review. *Journal of Speech, Language, & Hearing Research, 41,* 355–373.
Kavale, K. A., & Forness, S. R. (2000). Auditory and visual perception processes and reading ability: A quantitative reanalysis and historical reinterpretation. *Learning Disability Quarterly, 23,* 253–270.
Keith, R. W. (2001). Clinical issues in central auditory processing disorders. *Language, Speech, and Hearing Services in Schools, 30,* 339–344.
Salvia, J., & Ysseldyke, J. A. (2004). *Assessment: In special and inclusive education* (9th ed.). Boston: Houghton Mifflin.
Thompson, B. (2004). *Exploratory and confirmatory factor analysis.* Washington, DC: American Psychological Association.

[18]
Balanced Assessment in Mathematics.

Purpose: Designed to improve the teaching and learning of mathematics in schools by introducing goals and curricula based on national and international standards.
Population: Grades 3–10.
Publication Dates: 2002–2003.
Scores: Total score only.
Administration: Group.
Levels, 8: 3, 4, 5, 6, 7, 8, 9, 10.
Forms, 2: A, B.
Price Data: Available from publisher.
Foreign Language Edition: Spanish edition available.
Time: (40) minutes per form.
Comments: Two forms per grade each year (practice and secure tests) are published; scoring is done locally; performance is reported at four levels and cut scores are determined each year; no norms.
Author: Mathematics Assessment Resource Service.
Publisher: CTB/McGraw-Hill.

Review of the Balanced Assessment in Mathematics by MATTHEW K. BURNS, Associate Professor of Educational Psychology, University of Minnesota, Minneapolis, MN:

DESCRIPTION. The Balanced Assessment in Mathematics (BAM) is a performance-based group-administered test of mathematical skills published in collaboration between CTB/McGraw-Hill and the Mathematics Assessment Resource Service (MARS). Two forms (A and B) and two practice tests are provided for Grades 3 through 10, which require a reported 40 minutes each to complete. Test forms are revised on an annual basis to allow for continuous use between years with assured test security. The BAM is a criterion-referenced test that groups data into one of four scores using predetermined cut scores. Data are purportedly useful for better understanding student knowledge and understanding of mathematical content based on national standards to identify student strengths and areas of difficulty.

Emphasis of the assessments reportedly addresses reasoning within practical applications.

DEVELOPMENT. The BAM provides five problem areas for each grade with tasks that vary in number and difficulty. Students complete items that may involve concrete and exact answers, or those that are more subjective such as explaining reasoning or how answers were derived. The manual that accompanied the BAM provided adequate detail in comparing test items with standards developed by the National Council of Teachers of Mathematics (NCTM). Test developers should be commended both for the adherence to current standards and the use of various item formats. Given that the goal of the assessment is a balanced measurement of both computational and reasoning mathematical skills, the combined item formats seem especially relevant. Few commercially prepared assessments of mathematical achievement blend the objective measurement of computation (product) with the breadth of information obtained from process assessments as well as the BAM. However, no information was provided about how the problems were derived, written, or tested beyond stating that the test was developed by a panel of international experts and is consistent with NCTM standards. Clearly, matching items with current standards is an essential component of test item development, and a strength of the BAM, but more information is needed including empirical analyses. No information was provided regarding item development for the practice tests either, but this appeared to be a less-critical omission.

Given that the BAM is a criterion-referenced test, cutoff scores for the different levels of performance are essential for data interpretation. The BAM provided cutoff scores for the tests at each grade level, but again no information was provided about how the cutoff scores were derived and data supporting their validity were lacking.

It was interesting to note how the test developers discussed use of the BAM's two forms. The manual suggested that Form A could be used to present a balanced assessment in districts that currently rely on multiple-choice formats for mathematics assessment. Districts that do not use assessments other than the BAM could use both Forms A and B to achieve the balanced assessment. Could the two forms be used instead to assess mathematics progress? This question was

never addressed in the manual and adding additional forms for this purpose might strengthen the overall utility of the tool. Of course, delayed alternate-form reliability data would be needed before this application could be implemented.

TECHNICAL.

Standardization. Testing directions are straightforward and seem easy to follow. Administration procedures are presumably easily standardized given the group administration format. The only potential breach of standardization could be that although administrations are timed, no predetermined time limit is used. Although this may be beneficial to assess a wider range of student skill, it does make comparisons between students and student groups (e.g., classrooms and cohorts) difficult. Although the test manual primarily discussed instructional uses of the data, it also eluded to uses for accountability purposes. This lack of standardization in timing makes use of data for any accountability function questionable.

Reliability and validity. As stated earlier, BAM items are composed of both objective and subjective items. Thus, consistency in scoring is important to assure standardization. The manual correctly stated that clear rubrics improve the scoring consistency of performance assessments and assist in improving the reliability of the data, but no information was provided about the rubrics. Moreover, examples were provided to assist in scoring, but the examples did not seem sufficient to cover the large range of grades covered by the test. Therefore, although rubrics were provided to enhance consistency, they did not seem adequate to assure reliable scoring.

The test manual stated that high interrater reliability could be achieved if scorers were trained, but no data were provided to support this claim. Moreover, the manual asserted that the most prevalent sources of test error are generally not linked to scoring, but are due to testing students on a too narrow range of tasks. This was a seemingly confined view of test error and subsequent reliability. No reliability data were reported anywhere within the test manual, which makes use of the results questionable. The BAM was purportedly developed for instructional decisions, which suggested a relatively lower minimum standard for reliability coefficients than for data used for entitlement decisions. It is quite likely that the BAM would demonstrate sufficient reliability for instructional decision making, but these data are needed. Further, use of BAM data for decisions regarding individual students with important decisions such as entitlement to programs is inappropriate.

Given the lack of reliability data, it was not surprising that empirical investigations to evaluate the valid use of BAM results were also almost absent. The test manual reported correlation coefficients between the BAM and Stanford Achievement Test (9th ed.) of .65. This suggested comparable results, but the coefficients were not so large as to suggest measurements of the same construct. In other words, test developers claimed that this moderate coefficient suggested that the variance between the two sets of scores could be attributed to different formats of assessment, which supported the balance between objective and process items within the BAM. This interpretation could be better supported had divergent validity coefficients been presented as well, especially given that correlations between intelligence and academic achievement generally fall in the same range as reported here. Moreover, the coefficient of .65 was not interpretable because no information about this study was provided (e.g., number, grade, gender, and cultural background of participants).

No other data besides the correlation between the BAM and SAT-9 were reported to support the valid use of test results. Test developers made a strong case regarding the consistency of test items with NCTM standards, which could provide an adequate source of validity inference if coupled with even minimal data. Perhaps even simply describing more adequately the study that compared results to SAT-9 scores would provide sufficient data with which validity could be evaluated.

COMMENTARY. It has been several years since the NCTM standards changed how mathematics is viewed and taught, but standards-based revisions in assessment have lagged behind changes in instructional practice. The BAM is a solid step toward assessing what is taught within the NCTM standards. However, psychometric data and descriptions of development are lacking. This lack of data is especially disappointing given the low sophistication of necessary studies and the focus on instructional implications suggested that basic standards would probably be met. There is an accompanying manual that is easy to read and quite user-friendly, but it appeared to be more of a marketing tool, complete with testimonials, than a technical report. A detailed description of technical data is needed before use of the BAM can be recommended.

SUMMARY. The Balanced Assessment of Mathematics was developed to provide a performance-based assessment of student understanding of mathematical content based on NCTM standards. It is perhaps the assessment tool that is most closely aligned with current standards regarding mathematics instruction. Thus, it is a considerable step in the right direction, but only cautious use of data can be recommended given the lack of psychometric and development information. However, with fairly minimal additional research, the BAM could be a tool useful for instructional decision making and would, therefore, represent a significant contribution to mathematics assessment.

Review of the Balanced Assessment in Mathematics by JOSEPH C. CIECHALSKI, Professor, East Carolina University, Greenville, NC:

DESCRIPTION. The Balanced Assessment in Mathematics (BAM) tests consist of two alternate forms (A & B) for Grades 3 through 10. New versions of the BAM are published yearly by CTB/McGraw-Hill. A Spanish version of the BAM is also available.

All test items present problems called tasks. These tasks are performance based and developed to enable students to show that they understand and can apply mathematical standards at their grade level. For each grade level (3–10), the tasks assess objectives sampled from the following five areas: (a) Numbers and Operations, (b) Algebra, (c) Geometry, (d) Measurement, and (e) Data Analysis and Probability.

Directions for administering the BAM are contained in a separate booklet. The BAM is easy to administer and is designed to take 40 minutes. It is interesting to note that the administrator may allow more time for students who work slowly. Students are required to use a Number 2 pencil and to show all their work in the test booklet. In addition, students are allowed to use a calculator and for the Grade 9 test they are allowed to use a compass.

The tests are scored using rubrics that are based on a point system. Points are assigned based on the time (in minutes) it takes the typical successful student to complete it. The BAM may be scored locally. To help in the scoring, sample items for training in scoring are provided in the manual. This enables the scorers to apply the rubrics in a standard way. Scoring services are not available at this time from CTB.

No percentile ranks or standard scores are reported. Rather, performance on the BAM is reported using cut scores. Each year, the Mathematics Board develops a report that presents the cut scores. The report includes the cut scores for each grade level and provides a description of performance based on four levels (1–4) with four being the highest.

Material furnished by the publishers included: separate test booklets (Form A) for Grades 3–10, an administration manual, and a CD-ROM containing the test manual.

DEVELOPMENT. The Balanced Assessment in Mathematics (BAM) tests were developed by the Mathematics Assessment Resource Service (MARS) in 2001. This review is based on the 2003 version of the BAM (Form A). Tests are published yearly by CTB/McGraw-Hill under the direction of the Mathematics Board. The Mathematics Board includes math teachers and other math experts.

The items or tasks on the BAM are based on the mathematics principles and standards developed by the National Council of Teachers of Mathematics (NCTM). For each grade level test, the manual includes detailed descriptions of the objectives for each of the five goal areas: Number and Operations, Algebra, Geometry, Measurement, and Data Analysis and Probability.

Tables indicating the alignment of the BAM with the content and process standards for the 2 previous years are included in the manual. These tables are easy to understand. In addition, task descriptions are included for all grade level tests (Forms A & B) for the 2002 version of the BAM. Unfortunately, very little information on how the individual tasks were developed is given in the manual. However, according to the manual, professional development support is available on the MARS web site.

TECHNICAL. There are no norms reported for the BAM. Thus, scores are not reported as percentile ranks, grade equivalents, or as standard scores. Rather, minimum or cut scores, as determined by the Mathematics Board, are re-

ported based on four performance levels. General descriptions of the kind of performance required at each of the four levels are provided on a yearly basis. The cut scores for the 2003 version of the BAM tests are presented for each grade level of Form A. Information on how these cut scores were determined is not included in the manual.

Comprehensive learning objectives for each grade level are presented in the manual. The items or tasks are not multiple-choice but are open-ended and based on the standards developed by the NCTM. All work must be shown and students are required to explain how they arrived at their solution. Thus, the emphasis is on the higher learning objectives that focus on application and evaluation of mathematics.

Although two forms of the test are available, alternate form reliability is not reported nor is test-retest reliability. Interrater reliability is not reported and this is surprising. Considering the training that is available in scoring the test using the rubrics, I believe that interrater reliability could easily be derived. The authors state that human scoring is reliable, "provided the scorers are appropriately trained in using the scoring rubrics, interrater consistency is excellent" (p. 3).

The authors state that, "The emphasis in Balanced Assessment in Mathematics is on this key issue—the *validity* of the task set, and the scoring rubrics" (p. 3). The BAM definitely has face validity. Concurrent validity between the BAM and the SAT9 was reported as .65. No other information on how this coefficient was derived is given. The authors do a fine job of describing how the BAM is aligned with the standards developed by NCTM; however, evidence of content validity is not substantiated in the manual. Although it may be difficult to report on the technical quality of an instrument that is new every year, this information can be derived from the data collected from the previous year's administration. According to the *Standards for Educational and Psychological Testing* (AERA, APA, & NCME, 1999), "The process of validation involves accumulating evidence to provide a sound scientific basis for the proposed score interpretations" (p. 9).

COMMENTARY. The BAM is designed to assess higher order thinking skills in mathematics. Students must solve problems by showing how they arrived at their answers. The BAM accomplishes this rather well.

The manual contains extensive information on the principles and standards assessed for Grades 3 to 10. For each grade level, the objectives are clearly stated. In addition, the manual contains practice tasks for all grade levels.

Unfortunately, very little technical information is provided in the manual. No norms are provided. Evidence of the technical quality of the BAM is implied but not reported.

Scoring the test is time-consuming. Although examples of scored papers are provided in the manual, scorers may need to be formally trained and this can be costly.

SUMMARY. The BAM is easy to administer and time-consuming to score. Scoring requires practice and training that, if required, can be costly. Information on the development of the items is needed. Likewise, evidence of the technical quality of the test is lacking. If these technical issues can be resolved, then the use of the BAM in the schools may be worthwhile.

REVIEWER'S REFERENCE

American Educational Research Association, American Psychological Association, & National Council on Measurement in Education. (1999). *Standards for educational and psychological testing.* Washington: DC: AERA.

[19]

Ball Aptitude Battery, Form M.

Purpose: Designed to measure "various aptitudes needed for successful performance in a wide variety of educational and work settings."
Population: Grades 8–adult.
Publication Dates: 1981–2002.
Acronym: BAB, Form M.
Scores, 12: Clerical, Analytical Reasoning, Inductive Reasoning, Vocabulary, Numerical Computation, Numerical Reasoning, Paper Folding, Writing Speed, Associative Memory, Auditory Memory Span, Idea Generation, Word Association.
Administration: Group.
Levels, 2: Level 1 and Level 2.
Price Data: Available from publisher.
Time: 130(135) minutes.
Comments: Scoring is done by publisher and reports/counselor feedback are provided in the form of the Ball Career System.
Author: The Ball Foundation.
Publisher: The Ball Foundation.
Cross References: See T5:239 (1 reference) and T4:238 (5 references); for reviews by Philip G. Benson and Wilbur L. Layton of an earlier edition, see 9:106 (5 references).

[Editor's Note: The publisher advised in March 2005 that this test is now out of print.]

Review of the Ball Aptitude Battery, Form M by KARL N. KELLEY, Professor of Psychology, North Central College, Naperville, IL:

DESCRIPTION. The Ball Aptitude Battery (BAB) is the assessment portion of the Ball Career System designed to be used by high school students (Grades 8 to 12) for educational and career planning. The primary goal of this test is to assess an individual's aptitude (potential) in a variety of skill areas and provide them with career options that match their intellectual strengths. A total of 404 content items are organized into 12 occupational clusters—Clerical, Vocabulary, Numerical/Computation, Numerical Reasoning, Paper Folding, Inductive Reasoning, Analytical Reasoning, Word Association, Writing Speed, Idea Generation, Associative Memory, and Auditory Memory Span. These 12 subtests are organized into seven categories: Speed & Accuracy, Memory, Reasoning, Academic, Spatial, Creativity, and Orientation. The occupational cluster scores are then explained using four work families (Physical, Artistic, Information, and Social) based on the U.S. Department of Labor's Guide for Occupational Exploration (GOE).

There are two levels for this test. Level 1 is designed for 8th, 9th, and 10th graders whereas Level 2 is for 11th and 12th graders.

The total test time is estimated to be 2 hours and 10 minutes. After completion of the test, responses are returned to the Ball Foundation for scoring and three reports are generated for each individual. These reports include a profile (scores of the different tests), narrative (explanation of the test results), and an Aptitude Pattern Indicator (API—suggesting areas for career exploration). The profile presents raw and percentile scores for each of the 12 occupational cluster scores and the accompanying narrative explains each occupational cluster test and what the examinee's test score means in detail. The Aptitude Pattern Indicator is organized using the four work families and describes the participant's aptitude as high, medium, or low for various jobs within each group.

DEVELOPMENT. The original (or classic) BAB was developed in the late 1970s and used until the mid 1980s. This test went though revisions in 1986–1988 (Forms A & B), 1993 (Form

E), 1996 (Forms 8910SE and 1112SA), and 1997 (Form M—Levels 1 & 2). The national norming study was completed and published in 1998.

The technical manual accompanying this test is reasonably comprehensive and presents research supporting the development and use of this test. The test developers utilized a process called neural networks modeling to produce API recommendations for this test. A thorough discussion of this three phase process (taking about 5 years to complete) is presented in the manual. The results of this modeling supported the overall usefulness of this test.

TECHNICAL. The BAB Level 1 was nationally normed in 1998 using a stratified sampling procedure addressing geographic location, setting (urban or rural), type of school (public or private), sex, and ethnicity. In general, the proportions in the large normative sample (n = 2,688) are close to the population characteristics, with the exceptions of fewer individuals who are African American and fewer males in the sample. The BAB Level 2 norms are based on the classic BAB norms established in 1978.

Internal consistency for this test is strong with KR-20 reliability estimates for scales ranging from .52 to .88 with a median KR-20 of .80. The technical manual provides detailed information of these scores for all grade levels. Short-term test-retest reliabilities ranging from 2 to 6 weeks time periods are generally very good with correlations ranging from .50 to .94 with a median correlation of .75. Long term reliabilities have not been documented for this test.

In terms of validity, other forms of the test have yielded appropriate discriminant and convergent validity indices. Scale scores are moderately correlated with each other. Both exploratory factor analysis and structured equation modeling support the overall validity of this test.

Construct validity for the BAB has been documented by examining the relationship between BAB scores and other multiple aptitude batteries such as the Comprehensive Ability Battery (CAB), the Differential Aptitude Tests (DAT), General Aptitude Test Battery (GATB), and the Armed Services Vocational Aptitude Battery (ASVAB). The median correlation between the BAB and these tests is .63. Additional detailed information is presented in the technical manual and references are provided for more information.

Criteria validity was examined by comparing BAB scores with student grades, standardized tests, and occupation-related criteria. In terms of academic performance, Analytical Reasoning, Numerical Computation, Numerical Reasoning, and Vocabulary yielded the strongest relationships whereas the Word Association subtest was not related to academic performance. Correlations between BAB subtests and PSAT, PLAN, and ACT tests ranged from .02 to .80. These results should be interpreted with caution because the samples were small. The technical manual refers to studies using the BAB to predict success in various training programs and other occupational criteria, but does not present any specific information.

COMMENTARY. This test differs from many other popular career tests by assessing a student's performance as opposed to self-reported interests. The measure of potential will likely be more stable over time than interests thus providing more reliable recommendations.

The technical manual and supporting materials provide a clear and organized theoretical structure for understanding and using this test. The theory is supported by strong empirical evidence, including peer reviewed work in academic journals. The technical manual is well organized and sufficiently detailed. Tables and appendices address major psychometric issues including reliability and validity and also standard errors, item difficulty, and item discrimination indices. Overall, the technical manual provides a strong case for using the BAB. Supporting material is tempered with reasonable cautions for interpreting test scores.

The test administration protocol is detailed and clear, ensuring consistency among administrations. The test itself has strong face validity—it is well designed and easy to understand. Students taking this test should be sufficiently engaged to complete it and they should be motivated because it is helping them to find their strengths (and a career) as opposed to purely evaluative tests they are likely to take in school.

SUMMARY. The Ball Aptitude Battery (as the core of the Ball Career System) provides a sound basis for assisting high school students in addressing career development. Because this test is based on student performance rather than interests, it may give students a different perspective on their career goals. The reports presented to the students are clear and engaging. Although there is a lot of material presented in the three reports, it is organized and easy to follow.

It is clear that one test alone is not sufficient to make a career decision, thus the Ball Career System suggests that these aptitudes be considered within a framework involving motivation (including interests and values) and opportunity (understanding employment conditions and personal situations). Overall, this test conveys useful information and when considered with other relevant information, provides students with a good foundation to begin exploring their career options.

Review of the Ball Aptitude Battery, Form M by JUDITH A. REIN, Adjunct Assistant Professor, Department of Educational Psychology, University of Arizona, Tucson, AZ:

DESCRIPTION. Form M of the Ball Aptitude Battery (BAB) is a set of 12 multiple-aptitude tests designed to help individuals from eighth grade through adulthood increase their knowledge of their own aptitudes, both their strengths and weaknesses, and then use that information for career planning and to maximize their success and satisfaction in work and educational settings. Form M, specifically designed for group settings, takes 2 hours 10 minutes, with no scheduled breaks, to be administered. There are 12 subtests: Clerical (CL), Analytical Reasoning (AR), Inductive Reasoning (IR), Vocabulary (VO), Numerical Computation (NC), Numerical Reasoning (NR), Paper Folding (PF), Writing Speed (WS), Associative Memory (AM), Auditory Memory Span (AU), Idea Generation (IG), and Word Association (WA).

Form M is composed of approximately (e.g., in 2 subtests the item is repeated but counted as only 1 item) 404 items across 12 subtests with 240 items in the CL subtest, 50 items in the WA subtest, and the remaining 114 items distributed more evenly across the remaining 10 subtests. Level 1 is targeted to 8th to 10th grade students. Level 2 is for 11th grade through continuing education and adult students. The difference between Level 1 and Level 2 items is the inclusion of a small number of easier items in some Level 1 subtests.

The Form M three-tiered feedback system is extensive and detailed. First, the Ball Aptitude Battery Profile is reported in a graphical display that contains the subtest descriptions, percentile ranks, and raw scores on each subtest and permits individuals to see their pattern of scores—their aptitude profile. Percentile ranks (PRs) with a scoreband of +/- 1 standard error of measurement are used. Second, the Narrative Report summarizes and interprets the profile report. Percentile ranks are collapsed into three categories—High, Mid-Range, or Low. Third, the Ball Aptitude Pattern Indicator (API) report suggests career areas the individual should explore.

The API report is conceptually based on the relationship of its four occupational clusters (i.e., Physical, Artistic, Information, Social) to the United States Employment Service (USES) occupational aptitude patterns (OAP) as modified by Gottfredson in 1986 into an OAP map that also provides a conceptual crosswalk to Holland's six vocational personality types. In this report only, feedback is given for the occupational clusters and their associated U.S. Department of Labor Guide for Occupational Exploration (GOE) work groups. Two fit ratings, Minimum Aptitude Fit and Best Aptitude Fit, are reported. To obtain the Minimum Aptitude Fit Rating, scores on the Classic BAB are used in regression equations to predict the individual's score on the USES General Aptitude Test Battery (GATB). The predicted GATB score is then compared to grade-appropriate scores developed by the U.S. Department of Labor and modified by the Ball Foundation and the scores/ratings are classified as H (High), M (Moderate), or L (Low). A rating of H, for example, indicates that an individual's score exceeds or equals the score of workers who are judged satisfactory in a particular GOE work group's jobs. Best Aptitude Fit Ratings indicate API occupational clusters that best fit an individual's aptitude profile and from which the individual would start career exploration. The ratings were developed in a three-phase process using probabilistic neural networks (PNN), a form of artificial intelligence often used for classification purposes. Ball Foundation career counselors' recommendations based on an individual's Aptitude Battery Profile Report (i.e., the 12 subtest percentile scores) of how well a particular BAB profile fits an occupational cluster provided the training for the PNN statistical software. In essence, the software was trained to make cluster assignments comparable to those made by the counselors. Unfortunately, based on technical manual evidence, all counselors were from the Ball Foundation.

DEVELOPMENT. The BAB tests are rooted in the work sample tests developed by Johnson O'Connor in the 1920s. From 1975 to 1985, 25 ability tests, most based on O'Connor's work, were created or modified, researched, and psychometrically revised. This work resulted in the creation of the original or Classic BAB, a series of 18 aptitude tests that included some individually administered apparatus tests. Form M was developed from those Classic BAB subtests. Development was completed in 1997. Form M is shorter and easier to administer in group settings than the classic BAB is.

Classic BAB subtest items were used to develop Form M items. Three BAB subtests (CL, WS, AM) were not changed; the others were either shortened, had testing time reduced, or had nonscored items eliminated. Changes were based on the results from several studies ($Ns = 1,225$, $1,467$, $1,627$). Items selected had item difficulty levels ranging from .35 to .73 and item-subtest total correlations from .33 to .65. A validation sample of 112 university students was administered both the Classic BAB and Form M Level 2, with a testing interval of 3 weeks. Correlations between the Form M Level 2 subtests and Classic BAB subtests ranged from .63 (AR) and .64 (IR) to .89 (VO). An additional validation sample of 99 students was used for the IG subtest; acceptable internal consistency (.63 to .84) and test-retest with 3-week interval (.63 to .89) estimates were found. Item-level data analysis on the Form M Level 1 test found correlations in the mid .90s between the VO, NC, and NR subtests from the Classic BAB compared to Form M.

TECHNICAL. New norms for Form M Level 1 were completed in 1998. The norming sample ($N = 2,688$) was representative of the U.S. population based on geographic region, urban and rural area, public and private school, and 9th and 10th grade educational levels. Gender and ethnicity were not representative, but results from other analyses "suggest that Form M measures aptitude in comparable ways for members of different gender and ethnic groups" (technical manual, p. 15). Eighth grade norms were obtained using linear extrapolation and validated using a convenience sample ($N = 191$) of 8th grade students.

Norms for Form M Level 2 are not current. The norms are from the Classic BAB administered in 1977–1978 to a sample ($N = 836$) of high school seniors from Illinois and Texas. Four new subtests (i.e., NC, NR, AM, AU) were added to Form M Level 2 since the original standardization. The means and standard deviations for these subtests were calibrated using a sample of high school seniors who took the Classic BAB in 1981–1982 and the four new subtests in 1984-1985.

Adequate internal consistency (i.e., KR-20) estimates were obtained with sample sizes ranging from 191 to 300 students for the seven dichotomously scored subtests (i.e., AR, IR, NC, NR, PF, VO, WA). For six grade levels, 8th grade through college freshman, the range was .52 to .88, with a median of .80. Similar estimates were found based on ethnic groups. Adequate test-retest reliability estimates with intervals from 2 to 6 weeks were obtained from 9th grade, 10th grade, and college students, with sample sizes ranging from 75 to 104. For Form M Level 1, the range was .50 to .94, with a median of .75. For Level 2, the range was .64 to .89, with a median of .79. Form M long-term stability has not been examined.

Direct validation evidence is inadequate for Form M Level 1 and nonexistent, based on the technical manual validity information, for Level 2. For Level 1 there is adequate documentation of the battery's internal structure based on structural equation modeling and confirmatory factor analyses. Using the entire Classic BAB norming sample, a six-factor model (i.e., General Cognitive Ability, Perceptual/Motor, Spatial/Reasoning, Verbal, Numerical Ability, Memory) was posited and fit the data. The same sample was used to validate the structure across gender and ethnic groups. The resulting equivalence was cited as proof that the same constructs were being measured. Although relationships between the Classic BAB and several aptitude batteries have been studied, only one study was cited that focused on Form M Level 1. This 1999 correlational study based on 175 ninth and tenth grade students from five midwest high schools found that the median cross correlations between Form M subtests and GATB aptitudes was .49. This was offered as evidence that the Form M Level 1-GATB relationship is similar to earlier studies of the Classic BAB-GATB relationship. Form M Level 1 subtests' scores are related to some academic performance measures.

In a 3-year longitudinal study (1998, $N = 173$), for example, the relationship of Form M scores to overall and subject-specific high school grade-point averages was addressed. All subtest scores were statistically significant predictors with the exception of Word Association—a test of orientation, not of aptitude.

Evidence of differential item functioning (DIF) was found. Possible DIF based on gender and on race of 133 items from seven nonspeeded subtests was investigated using a sample of 9th ($N = 550$) and 10th graders ($N = 450$) drawn from the standardization sample for Form M Level 1 and analyzed separately. For race, three 9th grade items and four 10th grade items displayed DIF. For gender, there were seven 9th grade items and four 10th grade items. Due to a lack of readily available subject experts, the identified items were not investigated further.

COMMENTARY. Weaknesses of Form M Levels 1 and 2 balance their strengths at this time. Strong points include (a) the ease of test administration, (b) clarity of training materials, (c) numerous cautions against overinterpreting scores, (d) adequate internal consistency and test-retest reliability estimates, (e) the strongly suggested though not quite adequately demonstrated relationship between Form M scores and other BAB scores, (f) the connection with BAB scores to the GOE work groups, and (g) the rigor with which items were selected for Form M. The three tiered feedback system is a strength, but to fully interpret the feedback, the assistance and resources (i.e., *Dictionary of Occupational Titles, Occupational Outlook Handbook, Guide for Occupational Exploration*) of a counselor, as suggested by The Ball Foundation, are necessary.

One weakness is that the definition of reliability, "reliability is a property of the test administration, as well as the testing instrument" (examiner's manual, p. 24), does not meet established psychometric standards that reliability is a function of the test scores, not the test. It is unacceptable to state, for example, that "the reliability of test X is .90" (AERA, APA, & NCME, 1999, p. 32). Inconsistencies also exist between information reported in the examiner's manual compared to the technical manual. For example, the examiner's manual states that Form M Level 1 norms were generated from a weighted sample. Yet, in the technical manual, final Form M Level 1 norms were based on unweighted samples. The

technical manual was confusing because validation studies for the classic BAB were consistently intertwined with studies for Form M.

There are, however, weaknesses of more concern. Validity evidence is scant for Level 1 and essentially absent for Level 2. Validation of the internal structure of Level 1 across the entire norming sample was convincing, but the same sample was used to cross-validate the structure across gender and ethnicity. This reviewer does not accept that cross-validation as sufficient evidence that the same construct is measured across gender and ethnicity and would prefer that the cross-validation be across a new sample or hold-out sample. Criterion-related validation evidence is critical for aptitude batteries. Yet, for Form M, which focuses on occupational aptitudes, there are no criterion-related (i.e., occupation-related) studies using Form M data only. Another major concern is the use of 1978 norms for Level 2. Additionally, some DIF was found when Level 1 was renormed, but none of the identified items were examined. Finally, validation of the PNN classification was by Ball Foundation counselors only. A comment from a previous review in *The Ninth Mental Measurements Yearbook* is germane, because validation is needed "by individuals not affiliated with the Ball Foundation" (Benson, 1985, p. 123).

SUMMARY. Form M is intended to be easier to administer in group settings and succeeds. If the user can accept the impressive body of research conducted using the Classic BAB as evidence for the validity of Form M, then Level 1 for 8th to 10th grades should be considered. Level 2 for 11th grade through adults is not recommended. Both Form M levels would merit consideration for career and educational counseling when criterion-related validity evidence is gathered for both Form M Levels 1 and 2 and new norms for Level 2 are developed.

REVIEWER'S REFERENCES

American Educational Research Association, American Psychological Association, & National Council of Measurement in Education. (1999). *Standards for educational and psychological testing.* Washington, DC: American Educational Research Association.

Benson, P. (1985). [Review of the Ball Aptitude Battery.] In J. V. Mitchell, Jr. (Ed.), *The ninth mental measurements yearbook* (p. 123). Lincoln, NE: The Buros Institute of Mental Measurements.

[20]

BarOn Emotional Quotient Inventory: Short Development Edition.

Purpose: Designed to measure emotionally intelligent behavior in situations where a more detailed assessment is not possible or required.

Population: Age 16 and older.
Publication Date: 2002.
Acronym: BarOn EQ-i:S.
Scores, 8: Intrapersonal, Interpersonal, Adaptability, Stress Management, General Mood, Positive Impression, Inconsistency Index, Total EQ.
Administration: Group or individual.
Price Data: Available from publisher.
Time: 10–15 minutes.
Comments: Self-report.
Author: Reuven Bar-On.
Publisher: Multi-Health Systems, Inc.

Review of the BarOn Emotional Quotient Inventory: Short Development Edition by R. AN-THONY DOGGETT, Assistant Professor of Educational Psychology, and CARL J. SHEPERIS, Assistant Professor of Counselor Education, Mississippi State University, Starkville, MS:

DESCRIPTION. The BarOn Emotional Quotient Inventory: Short Development Edition (BarOn EQ-i:S) is a 51-item self-report rating scale designed to measure emotional intelligence across eight scales (i.e., Inconsistency Index, Positive Impression Scale, Total EQ, Intrapersonal EQ, Interpersonal EQ, Stress Management EQ, Adaptability EQ, and General Mood EQ). Published in 2002, the BarOn EQ-i:S is a shortened form of the BarOn Emotional Quotient Inventory (T6:244). Both forms of the instrument are based on the BarOn model of emotional intelligence. Users of the BarOn EQ-i:S rate items on a 5-point Likert scale (i.e., *very seldom or not true of me, seldom true of me, sometimes true of me, often true of me,* and *very often true of me*). Higher scores on the BarOn EQ-i:S "indicate higher emotionally intelligent behavior, positive mood, and positive impression" (technical manual, p. 1).

Qualified users of the BarOn EQ-i:S should have formal training in the use of psychological instruments. However, individuals without formal training can complete a certification program through Multi-Health Systems, Inc. Although nonclinical staff (e.g., research assistants and support staff) can administer the instrument, a qualified user should score and interpret the data. The BarOn EQ-i:S can be administered individually, in groups, or remotely (i.e., by phone or independent of a testing professional). However, it should be noted that remote testing was not part of the standardization process for this instrument and results should be interpreted with caution.

Scoring the BarOn EQ-i:S is a relatively quick and simple process (approximately 5 minutes). The instrument is printed on a quick score form and individual responses are automatically transferred to the scoring page. Raw scores for each of the eight scales are calculated and subsequently converted to standard scores with a mean of 100 and standard deviation of 15. Scores are converted according to gender norms contained in the Complete Assessment Set booklet. The Inconsistency Index score provides test users with a method for determining validity of the profile through an examination of consistency in response patterns. The Positive Impression scale is also used to evaluate validity of a profile. High scores on this scale indicate a person's attempt to create an exaggerated positive impression (i.e., PI>130) whereas low scores (i.e., PI<70) may indicate malingering.

According to the author of the technical manual, interpretation of the BarOn EQ-i:S should include an evaluation of individual item responses in order to identify strengths and underdeveloped areas in an individual's life. Scale scores are interpreted using emotional intelligence theory and are compared to the instrument's normative sample. In general, high standard scores (e.g., 130+) are indicative of a well-adjusted individual with high social and emotional capacity. In contrast, low standard scores (e.g., under 70) are indicative of an individual who has a marked impairment with regard to social and emotional capacity.

DEVELOPMENT. The original BarOn Emotional Quotient Inventory (BarOn EQ-i) is a 133-item self-report measure with 15 subscales. The short form of this instrument (i.e., BarOn EQ-i:S) was developed through a series of exploratory factor analyses aimed at identifying five scales that would match scales on the BarOn EQ-i. The sample for the initial development of the short form consisted of 1,020 females and 980 males ranging in age from 16 to 83 years. A principal-axis factor analysis with varimax rotation was performed on a four-factor model (i.e., Intrapersonal, Interpersonal, Stress Management, and Adaptability). Items that loaded solely on one factor and loaded higher than .30 were retained for further evaluation (35 items). According to BarOn, "The four-factor model accounted for 44% of the variance" (technical manual, p. 33). Although the rationale was not clearly stated in the manual, General Mood items were evaluated separately. This scale was evaluated using confirmatory factor analysis on a one-factor model.

TECHNICAL. The BarOn EQ-i:S was tested on a normative sample of 3,174 adults (1,543 males and 1,631 females) across the United States and Canada. However, the majority of data collection sites for the normative sample were located in the Northeastern United States. Data related to the psychometric properties of the instrument are organized in the manual by gender and according to four broad age groups (i.e., 16 to 29 years, 30 to 39 years, 40 to 49 years, and 50 years and older). Caucasians were the largest group of participants in the normative sample (79%). Asian (8.1%), Black (7.1%), Hispanic (2.8%), Native American (.7%), and other racial designations (2.3%) made up the remainder of the participants. A majority of participants attained educational levels ranging between a high school diploma and a college degree (73.9%). The test developer performed two-way ANOVAs in order to examine age and gender effects as well as their interaction. Evident in the results was the notion that individuals between 16 and 29 years of age score significantly lower on all factors of the BarOn EQ-i:S. A main effect was discovered for age on each of the seven factors (i.e., Positive Impression, Total EQ, Intrapersonal, Interpersonal, Stress Management, Adaptability, and General Mood scales). Significant main effects for gender were discovered on the Intrapersonal, Interpersonal, and General Mood scales. Males tended to score higher on the Intrapersonal and General Mood scales whereas females scored higher on the Interpersonal scale. With regard to ethnic differences, Black respondents were found to score significantly higher than Hispanic or Caucasian respondents on the Positive Impression scale.

Internal reliability coefficients for each of the BarOn EQ-i:S scales were examined by age and gender. The Cronbach's alpha for each of the scales ranged between .51 for females on the Positive Impression Scale to .93 for males on the Total EQ Scale. Overall, the instrument has acceptable internal consistency reliability with most values in the .70–.80 range. High internal reliability scores for each of the scales suggest that items within those scales are consistently measuring the same construct. The test developer includes additional reliability evidence in the form of mean interitem correlations by age and gender groups. Although still supportive of the scale's overall reliability, greater fluctuation was evidenced with regard to interitem correlations. Likewise, stability of the instrument was examined with test-retest procedures at an interval of 6 months. Test-retest reliability estimates ranged between .46 and .80 for each of the scales by gender. Although several studies have been conducted on the longer parent instrument, a search of the EBSCO database did not reveal any independent studies supporting estimates reported by the author. Independent evaluations of the EQ-i have generally supported item homogeneity and internal consistency (Dawda & Fraser, 2000).

As is the case with reliability, independent evidence to support the validity of the BarOn EQ-i:S is severely limited. Limited factorial validity, construct validity, and predictive validity evidence is presented in the technical manual. However, none of the studies cited have been published in peer-reviewed journals. Because the author found correlations ranging from .73 to .97 between the BarOn EQ-i:S and the 133-item BarOn EQ-i, he contends that studies related to the validity of the full scale instrument support the validity of the short form. Although significant correlations between the long and short version of the EQ-I may provide some hypotheses about the validity of the short form, independent analyses are necessary to make sound judgment. A particularly confusing aspect of the few studies reported using the BarOn EQ-i:S is that they predate publication of the instrument by several years. Thus, it is unclear as to the actual dates the instrument was normed, raising questions about the representativeness of the sample with regard to the current North American population.

COMMENTARY. One of the main criticisms of most self-report instruments with a Likert scale response format is that use of numbers (e.g., 1–5) as part of the rating system gives the illusion of mathematical precision in measuring a construct. Using letter abbreviations for Likert scale names (e.g., ST for sometimes true) is a more accurate representation of the measurement process. A more specific comment about the weakness of the BarOn EQ-i:S is relative to the construct of emotional intelligence (Cox, 2001). Although the manual indicates that the inventory can be used in a variety of educational, clinical, business, or research settings, clinical utility in the diagnostic process is questionable (Cox, 2001). To the author's credit, it is recommended that the instrument be part of a comprehensive assessment process and not be used in isolation. The instrument may prove useful as a means for identifying therapeutic gains with regard to anxiety, depression, and overall behavioral change. In general, it appears that the BarOn EQ-i:S would prove useful with individuals who are relatively stable and insight-oriented but seek clinical services (Guion, 2001). A true benefit of this instrument would be its ability to highlight individual client strengths.

SUMMARY. The BarOn EQ-i:S is a low-cost, easy-to-score measure of emotional intelligence that has been carefully developed over a long period of time. Although more independent, peer-reviewed research is needed to support the validity and reliability of the instrument, the author's research agenda shows promise for the future of the BarOn EQ-i:S. Because emotional intelligence is a relatively new concept in the assessment arena, very few instruments exist to measure the construct. The BarOn EQ-i:S appears to reliably measure the various facets of emotional intelligence and shows promise for utility in a variety of settings. Technical characteristics of the BarOn EQ-i:S appear to be generally adequate. Normative procedures, psychometric properties, scoring, and interpretation information are well represented in the technical manual.

REVIEWERS' REFERENCES

Cox, A. A. (2001). [Review of the BarOn Emotional Quotient Inventory.] In B. S. Plake & J. C. Impara (Eds.), *The fourteenth mental measurements yearbook* (pp. 106-108). Lincoln, NE: Buros Institute of Mental Measurements.

Dawda, D., & Fraser, S. (2000). Assessing emotional intelligence: Reliability and validity of the Bar-On Emotional Quotient Inventory (EQ-i) in university students. *Personality & Individual Differences, 28*, 797-812.

Guion, R. M. (2001). [Review of the BarOn Emotional Quotient Inventory.] In B. S. Plake & J. C. Impara (Eds.), *The fourteenth mental measurements yearbook* (pp. 108-109). Lincoln, NE: Buros Institute of Mental Measurements.

Review of the BarOn Emotional Quotient Inventory: Short Development Edition by JOHN T. WILLSE, Assistant Professor of Educational Research Methodology, University of North Carolina at Greensboro, Greensboro, NC:

DESCRIPTION. The BarOn Emotional Quotient Inventory: Short (BarOn EQ-i:S) is a 51-item self-report instrument designed to measure the emotional, personal, and social dimensions of general intelligence. On each item, respondents indicate their level of agreement with statements using a 5-point Likert-type scale rang-

ing from "very seldom or not true of me" to "very often true of me or true of me." The 51 items are distributed across eight scales: (a) Inconsistency Index, (b) Positive Impression Scale, (c) Total EQ, (d) Intrapersonal EQ, (e) Interpersonal EQ, (f) Stress Management EQ, (g) Adaptability EQ, and (h) General Mood EQ. The first two scales provide validity checks by indexing inconsistent or random responding and overly positive self-reports. The remaining six scales, one of which is an overall score, address dimensions of emotional intelligence. The author of the instrument suggests the information provided by this form could be useful in business (e.g., for use by human resources officers), educational, medical, or research settings. An included assessment booklet is focused on how to interpret results and on suggestions for how to use results to provide formative feedback for respondents.

Administration of the BarOn EQ-i:S is straightforward and could be performed by research assistants or support staff; however, the technical manual does warn that ultimate responsibility for proper administration and use should reside with a person with a background in psychometrics. The technical manual further suggests that "any person whose only exposure to BarOn EQ-i assessment is gained from this manual is neither appropriate nor qualified as a user of this instrument" (p. 3). Completion of the form should take 10–15 minutes. Respondents' answers are automatically transferred to a quick scoring sheet through carbonized paper. Directions for the scoring process are clear and easy to follow.

DEVELOPMENT. The BarOn EQ-i:S is the fifth emotional intelligence instrument produced by this author and publisher. The BarOn EQ-i:S is a short form of the original BarOn EQ-i (released in 1997). The short form's items were culled from the 133-item long form. A combination of exploratory and confirmatory factor analyses was used to identify the best items for inclusion on the short form. This approach provides a strong empirical basis for claiming that the five defined subscales of emotional intelligence are independent factors. Low to moderate correlations between the subscales provide additional support for the distinctiveness of the subscales. The manual lacks specific details about the connection of the instrument design to relevant aspects of theory or the rationale for asserting that overall emotional intelligence is a linear composite of these five subscales.

TECHNICAL. Normative data for the BarOn EQ-i:S are based on over 3,000 adults. Normative data for the BarOn EQ-i:S are provided across four age ranges—persons 17 and under should be assessed with the youth version, BarOn EQ-i: Youth Version—and by gender. Separate conversions from raw scores to scale scores are provided for each of these age and gender categories. These separate norms are provided to ameliorate age and gender effects present for some of the subscale raw scores. Because these adjustments are made to offset differences across norm groups, it seems most appropriate to interpret scale scores as providing a respondent's relative ranking compared to other respondents of the same gender and of similar age.

Internal consistency reliability evidence for the BarOn EQ-i:S is quite good. The large coefficient alphas are to be expected given the rigorous methodology employed to select items for inclusion on the form. The suggested applications of the BarOn EQ-i:S as a tool for evaluating employees or as a guide for professional, educational, or psychological counseling require that the measure be able to provide consistent information about emotional intelligence across testing occasions. As such, test-retest reliability is an important criterion for evaluating the form. The manual asserts that test-retest reliability for the BarOn EQ-i:S is "excellent" (p. 41). This evaluation may overstate the case. The stability coefficients reported for a test-retest period of 6 months result in standard errors of prediction large enough to hinder clear interpretation of an individual's score (see elaboration below).

Given the standard errors of prediction reported in the manual, a 95% confidence interval around a respondent's score will almost always encompass nearly the entire range of scores that the publisher has labeled as "effective functioning" on the scoring profiles (first and last page of the assessment booklet). For instance, a 95% confidence interval for a female between 30 and 39 years of age (the norm group with the *smallest* standard error) would range plus or minus 4.44 raw score units around her original score for the total EQ. The resultant 8.88 unit range for the confidence interval is wider than the 7-point (33 to 40) effective functioning range listed on the

scoring profile. The implication is that a person scoring in the middle of the effective functioning range could score in either the "enhanced skills" (i.e., above average) or "area for enrichment" (i.e., below average) categories if tested again. In interpreting results of the BarOn EQ-i:S, the manual suggests that "test administrators should employ additional assessment methods and review findings from collateral sources of information whenever possible" (p. 16). This advice should be closely followed whenever the assessment is being used to make judgments about an individual.

The BarOn EQ-i:S is a well-documented tool in terms of validity. As already mentioned, confirmatory factor analysis and other correlational studies support the use of separate subscales. Correlation matrices displayed for each age-based norm group provide evidence that the BarOn EQ-i:S functions similarly across respondents of different ages. Some validity evidence for the BarOn EQ-i:S is borrowed from the full length BarOn EQ-i. With high correlations between the two forms, this use is appropriate. Although, at times it is difficult to determinine whether validity studies presented in the manual represent a study of the BarOn EQ-i:S, the full BarOn EQ-i, or a reanalysis of the full BarOn EQ-i to produce results as if the shorter BarOn EQ-i:S had been administered.

Evidence of construct validity is documented in several ways. Results of studies with positive implications for convergent and divergent validity are presented. Several studies support use of the BarOn EQ-i:S in varied settings. Most of the conclusions asserted in the manual follow clearly from the results tables presented. One exception is in the area of divergent validity. The manual indicates that results from presented studies show it would be incorrect to classify the BarOn EQ-i:S as a personality test. Significant correlations between the BarOn EQ-i:S subscales and personality measures, which the manual dismisses as not indicative of overlapping constructs, are of similar magnitude to correlations presented elsewhere as confirming relationships between BarOn EQ-i:S subscales and other related constructs.

COMMENTARY. The BarOn EQ-i:S is a well-researched instrument. The manual provides a clear introduction to the instrument and technical details about the functioning of the measure. Directions for use, scoring, and interpretation of results are clear. As such the provided materials are in line with the *Standards for Educational and Psychological Testing* (AERA, APA, & NCME, 1999).

The most serious concern with this instrument is in regard to whether the test-retest reliability of the instrument tempers its utility for applications with individuals. As described above, standard errors of prediction are large enough that confidence intervals around individual scores will encompass large parts of the scale. Although all information needed to understand this limitation is presented in the manual and the author clearly indicates that an understanding of psychometrics is required of users, there is potential for an uninformed user to overlook the possibility that scores could vary widely across administrations.

Evidence for the validity of scores interpretations for the BarOn EQ-i:S is thorough and clearly presented. There is support for interpreting results from the overall score as a measure of emotional intelligence and for conceptualizing the subscales as distinct factors. The evidence distinguishing this measure from general personality measures is not as strong, but may be of little concern to most users. Predictive validity of the measure in specific settings was documented.

SUMMARY. Used appropriately, the BarOn EQ-i:S could be a useful tool for research or for assessing the emotional intelligence of individuals. If used for assessing individuals, the inventory's results should be only one part of a set of related information. Placing a great deal of weight on one administration of this instrument would not be advisable (e.g., in hiring decisions). The manual presents needed information but is not always explicit about the implications of some findings (i.e., test-retest reliability). Other forms of the BarOn EQ-i:S, available from this author and publisher, could be considered as alternatives depending on the user's needs.

REVIEWER'S REFERENCE

American Educational Research Association, American Psychological Association, & National Council on Measurement in Education. (1999). *Standards for educational and psychological testing*. Washington, DC: American Educational Research Association.

[21]

BarOn Emotional Quotient-360.

Purpose: Designed to provide a "multiperspective view of [an] individual's emotional functioning."
Population: Ages 16 and over.
Publication Date: 2003.
Acronym: EQ-360.

Scores, 21: Intrapersonal (Self-Regard, Emotional Self-Awareness, Assertiveness, Independence, Self-Actualization, Total), Interpersonal (Empathy, Social Responsibility, Interpersonal Relationship, Total), Stress Management (Stress Tolerance, Impulse Control, Total), Adaptability (Reality Testing, Flexibility, Problem Solving, Total), General Mood (Optimism, Happiness, Total), Total.
Administration: Individual.
Price Data: Available from publisher.
Time: (30) minutes.
Comments: Designed for use in conjunction with the BarOn EQ-i (T6:244); multi-informant rating scale available for paper-and-pencil or on-line administration.
Authors: Reuven Bar-On and Rich Handley.
Publisher: Multi-Health Systems, Inc.

Review of the BarOn Emotional Quotient-360 by DEBORAH L. BANDALOS, Professor of Educational Psychology, University of Georgia, Athens, GA:

DESCRIPTION. The BarOn Emotional Quotient-360 (EQ-360) is an 88-item measure of emotional and social intelligence, which the authors define as "a cross-section of inter-related emotional and social competencies that determine how effectively we understand and express ourselves and relate with others, as well as cope with daily demands and pressures" (technical manual, p. 2). Developed in the manner of the "360 degree" assessments popular in business and other settings, the EQ-360 is based on 5-point Likert scale ratings obtained from managers, coworkers, subordinates, clients, family members, and friends of the individual being rated. These ratings can be averaged across raters within each rater group and compared with the ratee's self-ratings obtained from a companion instrument, the BarOn EQ-i (T6:244).

Both paper-and-pencil and computerized versions of the EQ-360 are available. The latter format allows raters to complete the instrument from their home or workstation. This is an especially attractive feature for an instrument such as the EQ-360 that requires several different individuals, who may be in different settings, to provide ratings. Raters are assigned passwords to assure anonymity, and a report manager can access scores and order reports online using the detailed instructions provided by the publisher. The manual reports a Dale-Chall derived fourth grade reading level for the instrument, which should make the instrument accessible to most rater groups.

The EQ-360 was designed to be used in conjunction with the BarOn EQ-i, a self-report instrument designed to measure the same components of emotional and social intelligence. Use of both instruments allows for the comparison of self- and other-ratings, which should be useful to both employers and clinicians. However, the degree to which items on the two instruments are actually parallel is not entirely clear. Although the EQ-i consists of 133 items, the EQ-360 has only 88, so it appears that some items were dropped in the construction of the latter instrument. Unfortunately, the degree of overlap between the two instruments is not addressed in the manual. This makes it difficult to know how much concordance one should expect between the two scales. A related problem is that the two instruments were normed on different samples. Although this is unavoidable given that the instruments are designed to be used by different populations (raters and ratees), the scores obtained from the EQ-360 rater norm group were not based on ratings of those in the EQ-i ratee norm group. Instead, the two sets of norms are entirely separate. Although this is not necessarily problematic, it appears that the norm group for the EQ-360 is much more diverse in terms of nationality and possibly other characteristics than the EQ-i norm group. Because of this, what appear to be differences in self- and other-ratings may be due in part to differences in the norm groups to which the two groups are compared. However, given the data available it is not possible to know the extent to which this affects comparisons.

The EQ-360 measures the same five composite and 15 subscales as the EQ-i: Intrapersonal, including Self-Regard, Emotional Self-Awareness, Assertiveness, Independence, and Self-Actualization; Interpersonal, comprising subscales labeled Empathy, Social Responsibility, and Interpersonal Relationship; Stress Management, which consists of Stress Tolerance and Impulse Control; Adaptability, including Reality Testing, Flexibility, and Problem Solving; and General Mood, made up of the Optimism and Happiness subscales. Raw scores on each scale are converted to standard scores with a mean of 100 and standard deviation of 15. The manual states that scores for which more than 2% of the responses are missing are considered to be invalid. Although this may be reasonable, no evidence is provided to indicate how this number was determined. In the same vein, although scores based on omitted items are "adjusted" by the scoring program, the type of adjustment used is not specified.

Completed instruments must be sent to the publisher for scoring; hand scoring is not available. However, an administrator from the organization using the instruments can manage administration, scoring, and report generation online using a simple point-and-click interface. Detailed instructions for administration of the instrument and interpretation of the score reports are included in the manual, including an entire score report with interpretative comments by the authors. The information on administration and interpretation and the ease of administration and report management are, in my view, among the strong points of this instrument.

Several possible uses of the EQ-360, in conjunction with the EQ-i, are suggested by the authors. These include employee evaluations, leadership development, and team building. The authors appropriately stress that these instruments should be used in conjunction with other available information rather than in isolation. However, the fact that the manual provides no information concerning the efficacy of the EQ instruments in these situations is problematic.

DEVELOPMENT. As noted previously, the EQ-360 was derived from the EQ-i. However, only the development of the former instrument is discussed in the EQ-360 manual. The current version represents a substantial revision of an earlier pilot version of the instrument, including the addition of 42 items. The first author also reworded items to obtain the "closest match possible with original EQ-i items" (manual, p. 27). Although the manual makes reference to examination of data, the analyses that were conducted and the results of these are not specified. More information on the specific analyses conducted, as well as on the comparability of EQ-360 and EQ-i items would be a useful addition to the manual.

TECHNICAL. The standardization sample consists of 1,900 raters of 745 ratees representing several types of businesses including architecture, finance, healthcare, and education. This sample is drawn from several different countries (Australia, Canada, Mexico, the Netherlands, South Africa, Sweden, the U.K., and the U.S.A.) but no information is given regarding the number of participants from different countries or businesses. Norms are provided for each rater group (manager, peer, subordinate, and "other") but are not broken down by country or by type of business. This is unfortunate as it seems possible that there may be cross-cultural and even cross-disciplinary differences in definitions and/or perceptions of emotional intelligence. Because norms are reported only across the entire group, and this group includes several countries and business types, it is difficult to judge the degree to which one's sample of interest is comparable to the norm group. The authors do report information on average score differences across age and gender groups. Few statistically significant differences were found, and those that were found appear to be fairly small. On the basis of this information, the authors elected not to provide separate gender or age norms, a decision that appears to be justified based on my inspection of the data.

Although the EQ-360 was designed to be used in conjunction with the EQ-i, and comparisons of scores from the two instruments are provided as part of the EQ-360 score report, users of this instrument should be cognizant of the fact that the two instruments were normed on two different samples, as noted previously. It is not clear how much this affects the validity of score interpretations for EQ-360/EQ-i comparisons, but at best it would seem that such comparisons should be interpreted cautiously. Provision of more information on comparability of the norm groups for the two instruments should be a priority for the authors of this instrument.

Values of coefficient alpha based on the entire norm group are reported for each subscale as well as for the composite and total scores. For subscales these values range from .77 to .91; values for composite scales range from .91 to .95, and the value for the total scale is .98. Given that subscales consist of only five to seven items each, these values are quite good for internal consistency. Because the EQ-360 consists of ratings done by multiple raters, information on interrater reliability would also be important for this instrument. Although this information is not reported in the manual, each score report provided by the publisher does include tables of response frequencies of ratings for each item. Those using the instrument could use this information to determine interrater reliability for their own raters either within or across rater groups.

The paucity of validity evidence provided is a notable weak point of this instrument. Tables of correlations among subscales and composite scales based on the total normative sample and correlations of the EQ-360 and EQ-i based on much smaller samples constitute the only information that could conceivably fall into this category. The correlations between EQ-360 and EQ-i scales are based on samples ranging in size from 106 to 185 but no descriptive information on these samples is given, making interpretation of the values difficult. Like the EQ-i, the EQ-360 is based on a hypothesized hierarchical structure with a total score made up of five composite scores that are in turn based on subscale scores. Evidence for the existence of such a structure is typically provided by a higher order factor analysis. However, no factor analytic results are mentioned in the manual, nor is any evidence relevant to the efficacy of the proposed uses of the instrument provided. Although factor analytic evidence is available for the EQ-i, the EQ-360, although related, is a separate instrument and must be validated separately. As stated in the *Standards for Educational and Psychological Testing* (AERA, APA, & NCME, 1999), "If a test is used in a way that has not been validated, it is incumbent on the user to justify the new use, collecting new evidence if necessary" (Standard 1.4; p. 18). The EQ-360 represents not just a new use of the EQ-i but a new instrument, so it is incumbent on the authors to provide validity evidence for its use.

SUMMARY. Use of the BarOn-360 in conjunction with the BarOn-i has the potential to provide a wealth of information on social and emotional functioning that could be useful in personnel evaluation and feedback, employee development, and treatment programs designed to improve functioning in these areas. However, the current lack of validity evidence for the EQ-360 prevents this potential from being realized. This is exacerbated by the fact that the two instruments have been normed on samples that do not appear to represent comparable populations, which may introduce more differences between scores than is warranted. At present, although I applaud the intent and promise of the EQ-360, particularly in combination with the EQ-i, I find it difficult to recommend its use in such high-stakes situations as personnel evaluations. The detailed and helpful information on administration and interpretation are strong points of this instrument, as is the user-friendly computer interface and availability of online reporting and data management capabilities. The authors of this instrument appear to be committed to offering quality assessments and I urge them to continue the development of this instrument with a focus on obtaining validity evidence and clarifying the degree of similarity between the EQ-360 and EQ-i norm groups.

REVIEWER'S REFERENCE

American Educational Research Association, American Psychological Association, & National Council on Measurement in Education. (1999). *Standards for educational and psychological testing.* Washington, DC: AERA.

Review of the BarOn Emotional Quotient—360 by RIC BROWN, Vice President for Academic Affairs, California State University—Sacramento, Sacramento, CA:

DESCRIPTION. The BarOn Emotional Quotient—360 (EQ-360) is a multirater measure of emotional intelligence intended to provide a full range (thus the 360 reference), three dimensional overview of a person's present emotional and social functioning. It is intended to be used in conjunction with the individual based BarOn EQ-i (T6:244).

To better understand what is being measured by the EQ-360, two terms must be defined: emotional quotient (EQ) and emotional intelligence (EI). Just as IQ refers to the degree of cognitive intelligence, EQ is defined by one of the test's authors (BarOn) as the degree of emotional and social intelligence. Similar to the standard IQ test, the EQ scale has a converted standard score with a mean of 100 and a standard deviation of 15. Scores close to 100 are interpreted to represent effective emotional and social functioning (although no quantitative basis for such a claim is given).

Emotional intelligence is defined by the following factors: (a) the ability to be aware of and express emotions; (b) empathy and the ability for establishing personal relationships; (c) management and control of emotions; (d) coping and problem solving with respect to interpersonal situations; and (e) being sufficiently self-motivated. All of these constructs are said to be measured by the BarOn EQ-360.

The current version of the BarOn EQ-360 consists of 88 statements that are rated by several raters (30 minutes to complete) pertaining to a client. The manual recommends that at least three raters provide scores for the client (ratee). Rating is done on a 5 point Likert scale from 1 - *very seldom or not true* to 5 - *very often true or true.* Examples of statements include: "This person sets achievable goals"; "This person smiles easily"; "This person is patient."

In addition to an overall EQ score, there are five (5) composite scores, each with subscales: Intrapersonal (Self-Regard, Emotional Self-Awareness, Assertiveness, Independence and Self-Actualization); Interpersonal (Empathy, Social Responsibility, Interpersonal Relationship); Stress Management (Stress Tolerance, Impulse Control); Adaptability (Reality Testing, Flexibility, Problem Solving); General Mood (Optimism, Happiness).

Administration can be completed by paper/pencil or on the web on ratees over the age of 16. The manual suggests applications in settings such as corporate, clinical, medical or research.

DEVELOPMENT. The BarOn EQ-360 was developed based on the BarOn EQ-i (a self-report measure of emotional intelligence also developed by BarOn). An initial version of the BarOn EQ-360 consisted of 46 items and was piloted on over 1,000 raters (managers, spouses, co-workers, etc.). Recommendations from that study led to the current 88-item version. An additional 3,000 raters piloted the new version leading the authors to conclude that the instrument produced the psychometric properties required for publication. As well, two appendices provide competencies assessed by the related scales and a lengthy sample report showing how the EQ-i and EQ-360 can be used for interpretation.

TECHNICAL. The test manual presents extensive data analysis on a sample of 1,900 raters who rated 745 ratees. Descriptive statistics of the raters are presented for all 15 scales, and total EQ scores. Cronbach's alpha coefficients for the 15 subscales ranged from .77 to .91 and .98 on the total EQ. Several measures of validity are reported including comparisons of self-rating (modified instrument to include "I" statements rather than "This person ..." and raters, yielding Pearson correlations of .21 to .52 for the scale and total score; interscale correlations (most in the .6 to .8 range) and analyses of rater gender and age difference (female raters scored significantly higher than males for managers, peers, and others, and older raters scored higher for direct report).

Although the authors point out that the current scale (providing correlation coefficients across all scales between the two instruments) is based on the BarOn EQ-i, which is acknowledged to be a technically sound measure of emotional intelligence (see reviews in *The Fourteenth Mental Measurements Yearbook*), no data are presented for relationships of the BarOn EQ-360 scales with other similar measures of the constructs, nor are data presented with respect to any application in the corporate, clinical, medical, or research settings.

COMMENTARY. The authors present a theoretical rationale for the measurement of emotional intelligence and provide a modest level of technical support for the current instrument. As noted above, the testing manual also presents a reasonably detailed section for interpretation of the scale for use in conjunction with the BarOn EQ-i. Conspicuously missing are any data regarding applicability in the settings suggested. For example, the manual suggests the BarOn EQ-360 might be utilized for employee evaluation (with other measures) but offers no information that employees so evaluated are good, bad, productive, malcontents, etc. Although there is a "case study" of a 35-year-old sales supervisor (not clear if this is a real person or fictitious to make the point), the outcome of the application of the EQ-360 and the EQ-i was that the sales supervisor received "a great deal of insight" (technical manual, p. 26) and was convinced to engage in a development program. In the clinical setting, the manual suggests use to assess emotional functioning, again with no data to substantiate the validity of such assessment. Without any data, decision making in any setting would not be appropriate.

SUMMARY. At this point in its development, the BarOn EQ-360 might be best utilized in research in attempts to validate its usefulness in the settings for which it was developed. Clearly, the concept of self-awareness combined with how others perceive the individual has appeal.

[22]

Barrier to Employment Success Inventory, Second Edition.

Purpose: Designed to help identify personal barriers to getting or keeping a job.
Population: Adult and teenage job seekers and career planners.
Publication Date: 2002.

Acronym: BESI.
Scores, 5: Personal and Financial, Emotional and Physical, Career Decision-Making and Planning, Job Seeking Knowledge, Training and Education.
Administration: Group or individual.
Price Data, 2003: $39.95 per 25 inventories including copy of instructor's guide (12 pages).
Time: (10–15) minutes.
Comments: Self-administered and self-scored; revised version features simplified language, and color-coded response and scoring tables.
Author: John J. Liptak.
Publisher: JIST Publishing, Inc.

Review of the Barrier to Employment Success Inventory, Second Edition by WAYNE J. CAMARA, Vice President of Research and Psychometrics, The College Board, New York, NY:

DESCRIPTION. The Barrier to Employment Success Inventory (BESI) is a self-scored and self-interpreted inventory to assist those who are unemployed (or unable to keep a job), and vocational counselors who work with such populations, to identify major obstacles to employment success. The inventory is based on barriers to employment, found in a group-based needs assessment program designed to assist unemployed adults in making informed decisions about the types of assistance required to reconnect with the labor market. The program, Starting Points, identified a number of statements that were considered critical barriers to employment from focus groups with unemployed adults and counselors; however, no validation of these constructs or categories was ever conducted (Borgen, 1999). The administrator's guide explains that five such BESI categories were chosen based on this study:

1. Education and training (chosen by 30% of the respondents as an area in which they needed the most assistance) correlates with the Training and Education scale on the BESI.

2. Career exploration and testing (22% of the respondents) and career information (19% of the respondents) correlate with the Career Decision Making and Planning scale of the BESI.

3. Job search skills and opportunities (19% of the respondents) correlates with the Job-Seeking Knowledge scale of the BESI.

4. Issues related to financial assistance, transportation, and day care (12% of the respondents) correlate with the Personal and Financial scale on the BESI.

5. Psychological problems (10% of respondents) correlate with the Emotional and Physical scale on the BESI.

Each of these five scales contains 10 items that are scored from 1 to 4 based on "how much of a concern" each of the 50 very short statements are to them (i.e., none, little, some, great). Respondents complete a three-page colored, fold-out form and then complete the self-scoring by summing the number of points for each of the scales. The test form notes "high scores are not necessarily better or worse than low scores. They are simply measures of how you answered in Step 1." Scores of 31 to 40 indicate "more barriers in this category than most adults," scores of 20 to 30 indicate "the same level of barriers in this category as most adults," and scores below that indicate "fewer barriers in this category than most adults." However, there is no indication how such scaling was developed. It is assumed that a sample of 150 unemployed adults participating in government-sponsored job training programs who were used for other technical analyses were also used for determining cut scores for each scale.

After the test taker sums his or her score for each scale, he or she then plots them on a profile. The next step in the scoring requires the test taker to again transfer the scale scores to the back sheet and advises them to check examples in each scale that are particularly important to them. For example, in the Training and Education scale, possible barriers may be lack of high school diploma or needed technical school training. The final step asks the test taker to consider several possible strategies to overcome these barriers. The overall instructions, scoring, profiles, and self-interpretation guide for this inventory are similar to those of hundreds of other self-selection instruments. However, unlike many such instruments, there is little available documentation of the test development, norming sample, and validation evidence for this inventory.

The 12-page administrator's guide devotes 5 pages to describing changes in the workplace that range from the increased role of technology, globalization, changing demographics, to employment barriers, to special populations. Administration is straightforward and generally quite simple, requiring 20 minutes for administration, scoring, and self-interpretation. The web page (http://www.jist.com/productDetail.asp?AID=79&ID=85&type=sum) indicates that there is an online version available although there is no information on this format in published materials. The available materials do not meet the requirements for technical documentation noted in the *Standards for Educational and Psychological Testing* (AERA, APA, & NCME, 1999).

DEVELOPMENT. A national-empirical method of test construction is cited, which uses a content-based approach to develop scales that are designed to measure constructs identified as barriers to the unemployed in research studies. The author notes that statements were designed to be realistic and were based on an initial pool of 100 statements found in literature and input from employment and career counselors. The items on each scale do appear to be generally related to the domain.

Counselors then placed the statements into one of the five categories (scales) and the author then discarded statements that did not represent the barriers to employment, reducing statements from 100 to 75. There is no explanation of how the 75 statements were then reduced to the final set of 50 statements or items. Brief definitions of each scale are available in the administration's manual. For example, the description of one scale reads, "Emotional and Physical: The E scale measures barriers stemming from feelings of insecurity, low self-esteem, and physical problems. Respondents scoring high on this scale are concerned with maintaining their health or a positive attitude. In addition, they may be concerned about dealing with the anger and depression associated with unemployment or underemployment" (administrator's manual, p. 7).

TECHNICAL. Internal consistency (alpha coefficients) of each scale is quite high ranging from .87 to .95 with a sample of 135 unemployed adults participating in government-sponsored job training programs. Test-retest reliability was conducted with the same sample of individuals 6 months after the initial testing and ranged from .79 to .90 with 95 of the adults who repeated testing. Split-half reliability was .90.

Interscale correlation values were moderate, ranging from .45 to .69, suggesting there is only modest independence among the scales (e.g., the Emotional and Physical scale correlates at .6 to .7 with all other scales). Means for four of the five scales are 25–27 (scores range from 10 to 40) with standard deviations of about 7 to 8. The mean on the Training and Education scale was slightly lower (23.41). Means and standard deviations for males and females are reported separately and vary little across gender groups. The manual implies that the single study with unemployed adults was used to compute item level statistics, develop a final form of the instrument (reducing items from 75 to 50), compute interscale correlations and test reliability, and provide evidence of scale independence. However, it is not clear how one study could accomplish all of these technical requirements. A second set of means and standard deviations is also reported for a sample of 642 test takers described as "long-term unemployed, offenders and ex-offenders, students and welfare-to-work clients" (administrator's manual, p. 10). There is no description of how these data were collected or characteristics of the sample. Generally, the same pattern of data is found across scales for the two samples.

COMMENTARY. The BESI scales and items were developed to reflect some of the concerns and barriers to finding and maintaining employment primarily for less educated adults in a handful of studies. Generally, traditional methods were used in test development; however, the absence of detailed description about these methods and the sample prevent a test user from evaluating the test development and test quality. Much of the basic descriptive data required for any new test is reported in the administrator's manual; however, the lack of information on data collection, sample composition, administrative conditions, and characteristics of the respondents makes the data much less useful to the test user. Available documentation is inadequate.

All data used in developing the inventory and providing evidence of its validity and reliability appear to be based on a single sample of 85 to 150 unemployed adults participating in government-sponsored job training programs. The sample is not described in sufficient detail to determine its representativeness in areas such as age, educational training, geographic region, language proficiency, or ethnicity and race. Such demographic factors are clearly relevant to employment success, and the absence of such data is a major concern. It would also be helpful to understand how long these adults had been employed and whether adults in such government-sponsored training programs

differ in meaningful ways from other unemployed adults. In addition, it is likely that many of the scales used on this instrument are designed for less educated and nonprofessional workers, although such cautions or restrictions are absent in the testing materials.

The inventory appears relatively easy and efficient to complete, score, and interpret; however, interpretation may be problematic for some of the adults this instrument is designed to assist. At best, the inventory appears most useful as a structured interview or intake tool for vocational counselors who may desire to have some information about clients before beginning training or providing services. Test takers are instructed on how to compute and plot scores for each scale and are then provided with some prompts to help them identify specific obstacles and ways to address them. Some data are reported about the reliability and consistency of scores attained from a sample of adults in one government-sponsored training program. However, there is insufficient information about the data collection, characteristics of the sample, data analysis methods, and test development procedures to permit test users to determine the usefulness of this inventory with specific individuals and groups. There is no predictive validation evidence and minimal construct-related evidence reported for this instrument. Finally, although the inventory may be useful as an intact or structured interview tool for vocational counselors with experience in this field and who are knowledgeable about the limitations of assessment, independent use by unemployed workers could be potentially harmful because there is no evidence to help determine generalizability across unemployed workers with different levels of education, training, and other special characteristics.

SUMMARY. The Barrier to Employment Success Inventory (BESI) is a self-scored and self-interpreted inventory designed to assist unemployed workers and vocational counselors who work with such populations to identify major obstacles to employment success. The inventory was developed to reflect barriers or problems encountered by adults in seeking and maintaining employment from a single intervention program, Starting Points. The inventory is relatively quick to complete and contains 50 items, evenly divided among five scales that reflect different types of barriers: Training and Education; Job Seeking

Knowledge; Career Decision-Making and Planning; Personal and Financial; and Emotional and Physical.

REVIEWER'S REFERENCES

American Educational Research Association, American Psychological Association, & National Council on Measurement in Education. (1999). *Standards for educational and psychological testing.* Washington, DC: American Educational Research Association.

Borgen, W. A. (1999). Implementing "starting points": A follow-up study. *Journal of Employment Counseling, 36*(3), 98—114.

JIST Publishing. (n.d.). Retrieved March 31, 2004, from http://www.jist.com/ product Detail.asp?AID=79&ID=85&type=sum

Review of the Barrier to Employment Success Inventory, Second Edition by KATHY E. GREEN, Professor of Quantitative Research Methods, University of Denver, Denver, CO:

DESCRIPTION. The Barriers to Employment Success Inventory (BESI) is intended to help individuals identify their major barriers to getting a job or succeeding in a job. It is meant for use as a career counseling tool to open a discussion of employment barriers and how they might be addressed. Scores are obtained for barriers in five categories: Personal and Financial, Emotional and Physical, Career Decision-Making and Planning, Job-Seeking Knowledge, and Training and Education. The BESI is a 50-item paper-and-pencil or online assessment designed to be self-administered, self-scored, and self-interpreted. It can be used individually or in groups and takes about 10–15 minutes. It is appropriate for teenagers and adults with at least an eighth grade reading level. Items are rated on a 4-point (*of no concern* to *of great concern*) scale directly on the inventory booklet and responses are summed for items within a category, higher scores indicating more concern with barriers. Color coding is used to indicate which item response scores are to be summed. The color coding is carried through from item response to scoring to score interpretation. Because it is self-scored, immediate results are available. The publisher suggests this will be especially useful for people preparing to look for a job, who have not found a job, or who are unable to keep a job. The publisher also notes that counselors will increasingly need the ability to assess the special needs and barriers of groups such as women, immigrants, and racial and ethnic minorities as the workplace, society, and jobs change. Examples relevant to core categories are listed, as are suggestions for overcoming barriers in each category.

DEVELOPMENT. The publisher cites research by Miller and Oetting (1977) that led to development of the BESI. Miller and Oetting generated a list of 37 barriers to employment that clustered into four groups plus 3 single-item barriers; they identified barriers from a review of the literature plus consultation with disadvantaged clients. The author of the BESI developed 100 items based on Miller and Oetting's work, a literature review, and consultation with employment and career counselors. Case studies, interviews with unemployed adults, and the literature on job search programs were reviewed to develop inventory items. Professional counselors reviewed the 100 items for appropriateness, clarity, and category placement, reducing the item pool to approximately 75 items. It is unclear how the 75 items were reduced to the 50 items comprising the BESI.

TECHNICAL. Internal consistency and test-retest reliability were assessed for each score category in the development study, with values ranging from .87 to .92 for coefficient alpha ($n = 135$) and from .79 to .90 for stability ($n = 95$, 6 months between tests). The participants were over 150 unemployed adults participating in government-sponsored job training programs. Although it seems that the 10 items comprising each scale category were the basis for calculating internal consistency, this was not clear. Also reported is a split-half reliability coefficient (.90), which is inappropriate because no total score is calculated, nor should it be. Internal consistency is high. Especially impressive are the high test-retest correlations, although the interpretation of those correlations for individuals participating in job training is unclear. It would be useful to have the pre- and posttraining scale means. A second, larger sample is noted in the administrator's manual, but reliability coefficients were not provided for that sample.

The author cites low scale intercorrelations as evidence of concurrent validity. Scale correlations range from .45 to .70, in a moderate to high rather than low range. Scale intercorrelations would be evidence of validity if they were predictable from theory or from the proposed inventory factor structure. Neither theory nor statements about inventory structure were available, thus scale intercorrelations are not evidence of validity. When a sufficient number of cases is available, the inventory could be factor analyzed to see if the five-category structure is upheld. Concurrent validity would hold if scale scores were correlated at a moderate to high level with another measure of barriers to employment success, which was not done. The only support provided for validity aside from face validity comes from professional counselors' review of inventory items, which is a content validity approach.

The sample used to estimate reliability was described as adults in job training. A more complete description of the sample with the distribution by gender, race, ethnicity, age, educational level, and marital status is needed.

After users calculate category scores, they place scores on a profile graph, which has boundaries for fewer, average, and more barriers than most adults. No explanation is provided of how these boundaries were determined. The administrator's manual lists category means for the development sample and for another larger sample, and it seems the boundaries were roughly determined by adding and subtracting one standard deviation from the category mean. However, the means differ across categories by up to about 4 points and standard deviations differ as well, but the boundaries for low, average, and high are shown as the same. This profile would likely be interpreted as normative but normed data are not provided. Also, the reference group in the profile is listed as "most adults," which is misleading because the data referenced are a sample of unemployed adults participating in job training who may not be representative of most adults.

COMMENTARY. The BESI is attractively packaged and easy to use and to understand. Reliability is quite high but empirical validity evidence is lacking. Evidence of criterion-related validity would greatly strengthen the inventory's utility. Evidence of effects of job training on category scores would also be desirable. Although a profile with normative implication is included, its development was not explained. Only one small scale study was conducted to assess psychometric quality, though additional data were available at the time of publication. Although five category scores are provided, there is no evidence to support the structure of the measure. But, as a tool to encourage people to start thinking about what keeps them from finding employment, the tool has face and content validity, is inexpensive, and provides immediate results. Suggestions for overcoming barriers are listed; however, these suggestions are simplistic and possibly impractical to implement without the assistance of a counselor.

SUMMARY. The inventory has face validity, support for content validity, and strong reliability, and is inexpensive, attractively presented, and easy to use. Lack of criterion-related, factorial, concurrent, and convergent validity limit its use to being a tool to promote discussion rather than a predictor of employment and job training outcomes. The normative information is not supported and suggestions for overcoming barriers are simplistic. However, the stated purpose is to help individuals identify major barriers to employment and the inventory seems useful for this purpose.

REVIEWER'S REFERENCE

Miller, C. D., & Oetting, G. (1977). Barriers to employment and the disadvantaged. *Personnel and Guidance Journal, 56*, 89–93.

[23]

Basic Early Assessment of Reading.

Purpose: Designed "to assess young students' acquisition of the essential components of reading—phonemic awareness, phonics, vocabulary, comprehension, and oral reading fluency."

Population: Grades K–3.

Publication Date: 2002.

Acronym: BEAR.

Levels, 4: K, 1, 2, 3.

Price Data, 2005: $280.75 per complete kit (specify Levels K and 1 or Levels 2 and 3) including 25 Initial-Skills Analysis student booklets for each level, 1 Initial-Skills Analysis administration and scoring guide for each level, 1 Specific-Skill Analysis—Reading Basics black line master for each level, 1 Specific-Skill Analysis—Language Arts black line master for each level, 1 Specific-Skill Analysis—Comprehension black line master for each level, 1 Specific-Skill Analysis administration and scoring guide for each level, 13 Oral Reading Fluency Assessment Passage Sheets for Levels K–3, 1 Oral Reading Fluency Assessment administration and scoring guide for Levels K–3, 25 Summative Assessment—Reading Basics student booklets for each level, 25 Summative Assessment—Language Arts student booklets for each level, 25 Summative Assessment—Comprehension student booklets for each level, 1 Summative Assessment administration guide for each level, 1 Summative Assessment scoring guide for each level, and Scoring and Reporting Software; $25 per 25 Initial-Skills Analysis test booklets (specify level); $74.50 per set of 3 Specific-Skill Analysis black line masters (specify Levels K and 1, or 2 and 3); $34.25 per 13 Oral Reading Fluency Assessment Passage sheets; $19.50 per 25

Summative Assessment test booklets (specify level and content area); $5.75 per administration and scoring guide—Initial-Skills Analysis (specify level); $5.75 per administration scoring guide—Specific-Skill Analysis (specify Levels K and 1 or 2 and 3); $28.50 per administration and scoring guide—Oral Reading fluency Assessment; $5.75 per administration guide—Summative Assessment (specify level); $17.25 per scoring guide—Summative Assessment (specify level); $31.75 per technical manual; $86.25 per scoring and reporting software.

Comments: Criterion-referenced testing program with modules designed for use in conjunction with classroom activities; computer-scoring and reporting available for PC.

Author: Riverside Publishing.

Publisher: Riverside Publishing.

a) INITIAL-SKILLS ANALYSIS.

Purpose: Designed to provide a quick overview of students' reading and language arts skills.

Scores, 4: Reading Basics, Comprehension, Language Arts, Total.

Administration: Individual or group.

Time: (45–60) minutes.

b) SPECIFIC-SKILL ANALYSIS.

Purpose: Designed to provide diagnostic information about students' Specific-Skill in Reading Basics, Comprehension, or Language Arts.

Scores, 4: Reading Basics, Comprehension, Language Arts, Total.

Administration: Individual or group.

Forms: 3.

Time: (30–40) minutes per content area.

c) ORAL READING FLUENCY ASSESSMENT.

Purpose: Designed to provide information about students' reading skills, accuracy, ability to retell what was read, and oral reading rate (for Levels 1–3).

Scores, 4: Letter Recognition, Informational, Narrative, Total.

Administration: Individual.

Forms: 6 (8 at Level K).

Time: (15–30) minutes per passage or list.

d) SUMMATIVE ASSESSMENT.

Purpose: Designed to assess early reading and language arts skills for placement and instructional planning.

Scores, 4: Reading Basics, Comprehension, Language Arts, Total.

Administration: Individual or group.

Forms: 3.

Time: (30–40) minutes per content area.

Review of the Basic Early Assessment of Reading by ZANDRA S. GRATZ, Professor of Psychology, Kean University, Union, NJ:

DESCRIPTION. The Basic Early Assessment of Reading (BEAR) is a criterion-referenced assessment system designed to measure reading and language arts skills of kindergarten through third grade youngsters. At each grade level, four assessment components are available.

The Initial-Skills component is designed to be administered at the start of the school year. Subtest areas of Reading Basics, Comprehension, and Language Arts may be administered in a separate session, each requiring approximately 20 minutes and generating number and percent correct scores. Total Initial-Skills component scores may be categorized as either indicating Emerging (on grade level) or Limited (below grade level) performance levels.

The Specific-Skill component is a skill-specific diagnostic tool for which the subtests parallel those of the Initial-Skills component. In particular, the Reading Basics subtest measures concepts and conventions of print, phonological/phonemic awareness, decoding, structural analysis and vocabulary, and concept development standards. The Comprehension subtest includes listening and reading passages written for the BEAR. The Language Arts subtest measures penmanship, sentence structure and construction, grammar and usage, punctuation and capitalization, and spelling standards. Each subtest may be administered in a separate session requiring 30–40 minutes. Scoring directions allow for the computation of number and percent correct scores for each subtest and skill area.

Similar to the Initial-Skills and Specific-Skill components, the Summative component measures Reading Basics, Comprehension and Language Arts. It is designed as a progress check to be administered at the end of the school year. Each subtest may be administered separately and requires 30–40 minutes to administer. Scoring directions allow for the computation of total and specific skill scores (number and percent correct). In addition, each subtest total score may be categorized as suggesting either Developed, Developing, or Not Developed skill levels.

The Oral Reading Fluency component is designed as an authentic, individually administered assessment measuring four areas: Accuracy, Retelling, Oral Reading Skills and Reading Rate. With the exception of Reading Rate, a 4-point rubric (ranging from no points to 3) is provided to support scoring. Administration times vary between 15 and 30 minutes and the assessment may be administered up to three times per year.

With the exception of the Oral Reading Fluency component, software is available to enable computer administration and scoring of the BEAR. Test score maintenance software is available as are worksheets to support scoring and test score organization.

DEVELOPMENT. The BEAR was developed as a measure of skills that would enable youngsters to meet nationwide reading and language arts standards. To accomplish this, BEAR developers reportedly analyzed content standards nationwide as well as research in reading and language arts.

Test blueprints and item prototypes were generated to guide item writing and scoring rubrics. Items were examined for grade level appropriateness, match to standards, bias, sensitivity, clarity, and relevance. Each component was field tested; in addition to analyses of item difficulty and discrimination, statistical analyses of bias were generated using the Mantel-Haenszel dichotomous and generalized differential item functioning indices. Instructional-level descriptors for the Initial-Skills and Summative components were based on consensus about what youngsters at each grade level and point in the school year should be able to perform. The Hofstee method was used to combine the judgments of 50 educators per grade to create cut scores. With regard to Oral Fluency, difficulty of passages and letter recognition cards were examined via graded word lists and readability formulas (Dale-Chall, Fry, and Spache).

Initial-Skills, Specific—Skill, and Summative components were converted into a computer-administered version of the BEAR. Where possible, items remained the same; the exception to this was the Summative component where free response items were revised to a multiple-choice format. Warm-up items are available to allow youngsters to practice responding on the computer; audio instructions are provided via headphones. To deter copying, the computer version varies the order of item presentation within subtest per examinee. Cutoffs for instructional-level descriptors were developed for the computer version in a manner parallel to that of the paper-and-pencil version.

TECHNICAL. Reliability analyses of the paper-and-pencil version of the BEAR were conducted during 2001–2002 using students from 37 schools nationwide. Initial-Skills (total test) coefficient alphas ranged from .83 to .88. A 4-week test-retest study of the Initial-Skills component, using large and small group test administration settings yielded reliability estimates ranging from .70 to .77. Coefficient alpha reliability estimates for each subtest (Reading Basics, Comprehension, and Language Arts) of the Specific-Skill component ranged from .68 to .92, with most falling between .72 and .78. Summative Assessment subtest coefficient alpha estimates ranged from .71 to .89. A small study was reported regarding the intrarater reliability of the Oral Reading Fluency Assessment. Reported percent agreement ranged from 67 to 100 for Accuracy and 67 to 83 for Oral Reading Skills. No information was reported for specific skill areas measured within each subtest of the Summative and Specific-Skill components.

Reliability data are presented for the Computer Administered Initial-Skills and Summative components based on studies using students from 18 schools in the Spring of 2002 (Summative) and 21 schools in the Fall of 2002 (Initial-Skills). Initial-Skills coefficient alphas ranged from .82 to .85, whereas that of the Summative component ranged from .75 to .91. A study comparing computer- and paper-and-pencil administered Initial-Skills components yielded correlations ranging from .71 to .82 and mean differences ranging from 1.57 to 2.66. No reliability information is provided for the computer-administered Specific-Skill component.

Content validity was built into each component of the BEAR. That is, Initial-Skills, Specific-Skill, and Summative component items were written to reflect each content standard identified by the publishers of the BEAR. Content standards are also linked to those reported in the *National Reading Panel Teaching Children to Read: An Evidence-Based Assessment of the Scientific Research Literature on Reading and its Implications for Reading Instruction* (National Institute of Child Health & Human Development, 2000). Results of readability analyses confirm grade range appropriateness of passages.

Predictive validity evidence offered in the manual depicts the relationship between Initial-Skills component scores and that of both Specific-Skill and Summative Assessment components. In kindergarten and Grade 1, these correlations range between .38 and .61. For Grades 2 and 3, correlations ranged from .55 to .75. It should also be noted that the correlations among subtest scores within the Specific-Skill component ranged from a low of .34 (kindergarten) to .68 (Grade 2). A similar pattern, ranging from .30 (kindergarten) to .78 (Grade 2), was observed across subtest scores within the Summative component.

COMMENTARY. Although the levels of internal consistency reported for the BEAR are acceptable, the lack of reported reliability estimates for Specific-Skill measured within Summative and Specific-Skill components is a concern. Although the advantage of criterion-referenced assessment is the skill level, diagnostic information traditionally offered, lack of skill level reliability estimates preclude this application. Lack of test-retest reliability estimates for Specific-Skill and Summative components also serves as a caution.

Correlations between the Initial-Skills component computer and paper/pencil versions range from .71 for Grade 1 to .82 for Grade 3. Descriptive data presented for the Initial-Skills component suggest that the computer-administered version is somewhat more difficult than the paper-and-pencil version. Given the score differences, the computation of instructional skill level cutoffs specifically for each format are appropriate. It may prove useful to explore further plausible explanations for the score difference (e.g., familiarity/experience with computers). Beyond this, additional comparative studies between computer and paper-pencil versions of BEAR Summative and Specific-Skill components may prove informative.

Although intrarater percent agreement data are presented for the accuracy and fluency scores of the Oral Reading component, no information regarding interrater reliability is provided. Beyond this, the relatively high percent agreement among scores by the same rater is neither surprising nor convincing given the limited score range.

High intercorrelations among subtest scores within components call into question the extent to which distinct skills and abilities are being assessed by each subtest. For example, the correlations between the subtests of the Specific-Skill component ranged from .60 and .68 for Grade 2; these coefficients approach that of the coefficient alpha estimates of reliability, which ranged from .72 to .77 for each Grade 2 subtest. Beyond this,

although the manual indicates "confirmatory factor analysis supported the construct and measurement equivalence of computerized and paper-pencil formats" (technical manual, p. 54), results of factor analyses are not provided nor is any mention made as to the extent to which factor analyses confirm the structure of the BEAR.

The manual suggests that youngsters demonstrating a "Limited" instructional level on the Initial-Skills component should be further assessed via the Specific-Skill component, which "allows the teacher to focus on a student's specific areas of weakness in order to guide instruction" (Specific-Skill manual, p. 1). Although the manual suggests testing be stopped if the youngster appears frustrated, it offers no guidance about out-of-level use of the Specific-Skill component based on Initial-Skills performance. Beyond this, concerns relative to the uniqueness and reliability of the Specific-Skill component notwithstanding, the time required for the Initial-Skills may best be spent having all youngsters take the Specific-Skill component. Also, no linkages are made between BEAR assessment scores and instructional materials and activities as found in other assessments (e.g., Learning Accomplishment Profile Diagnostic Edition, 2002, Kaplan Early Learning Company).

The lack of connections between components, across and within grade levels, may limit the usefulness of the Summative component. Although described as a "progress check of students' development toward grade-appropriate skills" (Summative Assessment scoring guide, p. 2), without a means for measuring growth, or linking scores to grade level norms, the Summative component may not be able to fulfill its reported role. More broadly, the absence of scale scores to facilitate tracking student progress over time may be a liability and require yet another test be administered. Other measures, such as the Group Reading Assessment and Diagnostic Evaluation (15:113) or the Gray Oral Reading Tests (15:111) provide diagnostic information regarding student strengths and weaknesses as well as standard scores to allow for comparisons over time and across students.

SUMMARY. The BEAR makes considerable effort to provide an instruction-relevant assessment tool. Detailed information is provided about the nature of the skills students are likely to exhibit relative to BEAR instructional classification. However, limited psychometric properties such as skill level reliability estimates and standard scores that link components across and within grades may limit the efficacy of the BEAR to fulfill its mission.

REVIEWER'S REFERENCE

National Institute of Child Health & Human Development. (2000). *National Reading Panel Teaching Children to Read: An evidence-based assessment of the scientific research literature on reading and its implications for reading instruction.* Retrieved from: http://www.nichd.nih.gov/publications/nrp/smallbook.htm.

Review of the Basic Early Assessment of Reading by ANNITA MARIE WARD, Associate Professor of Education and TESL, Salem International University, Salem, WV:

DESCRIPTION. The Basic Early Assessment of Reading (BEAR) is a criterion-referenced testing program that can be administered with paper and pencil or on the computer. It is appropriate for use with students in kindergarten through third grade. Scoring of the test is done at the place of administration. Scoring and reporting software is available for the paper-and-pencil test, whereas the computer-administered test is scored automatically.

The test is divided into several modules. These include Initial-Skills Analysis, given to students at the beginning of the school year or when they first enter a school; Specific-Skill Analysis, given after the Initial-Skills Analysis to determine in-depth information about students' reading and language arts skills; Oral Reading Fluency Assessment, which can be given three times a year and which is designed to measure a student's oral reading skills; and the Summative Assessment administered at the end of the school year to determine students' overall achievements in reading and language arts.

Once each module is scored, the administrator can use information from the Basic Early Assessment of Reading (BEAR) technical manual. Total scores achieved on the Initial-Skills Analysis and scores for each content area on the Summative Assessment fall within instructional level descriptors. For the Initial-Skills Analysis these descriptors are "emerging" and "limited." For the Summative Assessment these descriptors are "not developed," "developing," and "developed."

DEVELOPMENT. The BEAR is designed to measure students' proficiency in reading skills and language arts that have been identified as essential to content standards across the United States. To identify these skills, test developers at the Riverside Publishing Company did in-depth analyses of K–3 reading and language arts standards across the United States. They also analyzed current research studies to find important factors of reading and language arts proficiency. The technical manual identifies which skills the test developers pinpointed as key to effective language arts and reading instruction.

After test developers had identified important factors in reading and language arts instruction, they developed an Initial-Skills Analysis and a Summative Assessment and field tested them together. The Specific-Skill Analysis was then developed based on research conducted during the development and administration of the first two sections of the test.

Item prototypes for multiple-choice and open-ended questions were developed for the Specific-Skill Analysis and Summative Assessment and were pilot tested and presented to focus groups between December 1999 and June 2000. Item prototypes that were accepted were used as models for test items, and twice as many test items as were needed were developed.

In developing listening and reading comprehension sections, test developers used some passages from published sources and wrote some original ones for the test. Original judgments about grade-level appropriateness were based on readability formulas and professional knowledge, and final judgments were based on actual students' performances during field testing.

Approximately 10,000 students participated in the Fall 2000 and Spring 2001 field testing for the paper-and-pencil BEAR—82 schools in the fall and 150 in the spring. Rubrics were developed for scoring the open-ended questions and were based on the item prototypes. Consistent application of rubrics was achieved by having experienced scorers participate in scoring sessions.

In order to choose final items for the test, p-values were calculated for all items field-tested as were point-biserial correlations. No-response items were also noted. When selecting items for the final tests, test developers made an attempt to select items with point-biserial correlations of .25 or greater. Items with point-biserial values below .25 were included only if needed to fulfill the original test plan. An attempt was made to use items with p-values of .35 to .90. Items that did not fall within this range were used only if they were needed to fulfill the original test plan.

A statistical analysis of test bias was performed on test items. A differential prediction study was done to ensure accurate equal prediction of results across gender and ethnicity. No significant prediction biases were found.

Instructional level descriptors for both reading and language arts were developed based on commonly accepted content standards for kindergarten through third grade. One-hundred-twenty-five educators participated in a Fall 2001 research study designed to establish cut scores for the instructional descriptor levels. Participants first of all familiarized themselves with descriptors, listed items that differentiate one descriptor level from another, and indicated a range of cut scores they would consider appropriate from one descriptor level to another.

TECHNICAL. A year-long research study of the paper-and-pencil test was done during 2001–2002. This study was conducted in 37 schools from various parts of the United States. An approximately equal number of males and females participated in the study and the schools reported that 29% of their overall populations were from minority groups.

Participating schools agreed to administer the BEAR paper-and-pencil test three times during the school year: the Initial-Skills Analysis at the beginning of the school year, the Specific-Skill Analysis in the winter, the Summative Assessment at the end of the school year. It was suggested that participant schools randomly choose six participants from each class to take the Oral Reading Fluency Assessment. Some schools chose only six students per grade and in some cases students were not retested because they had moved or were absent on days retesting was scheduled.

Descriptive statistics including means, standard deviations, reliability coefficients, and standard error of measurement were reported for Initial-Skills Analysis, Specific-Skill Analysis, and Summative Assessment for kindergarten through third grade. Reliability coefficients ranged from .68 to .92.

In order to examine predictive and concurrent validity, correlations were calculated among content areas of the modules of the test. Correlations ranged from a low of .23 to .74. Generally, correlations between test scores at Levels K and 1 were near or below .50. Of 52 correlations reported for these levels, only 3 were .60 or above.

Of 42 correlations reported for scores at Levels 2 and 3, 30 were above .60, but only 11 of these were above .70.

DEVELOPMENT OF COMPUTER-ADMINISTERED TEST. In order to capitalize on its paper-and-pencil test, Riverside Publishing developers, after meeting with focus groups in 2001, put together a computer-administered BEAR. The same items are on the computer-administered test as are on the paper-and-pencil test, but these items are offered in a random order within skill groups. The computer-assisted test offers a warm-up activity for students as well as an educators' module that helps school personnel prepare reports and track students.

TECHNICAL INFORMATION FOR COMPUTER-ADMINISTERED TEST. In the Spring of 2002, in order to provide reliability and validity data and item-level data for the computer-administered Summative Assessment of the BEAR, a research study was conducted in 18 schools across the United States.

In Fall 2002, a research study was done in 21 schools in order to compare students' scores on the paper-and-pencil Initial Skill Analysis to their scores on the same computer-administered assessment. All reliability coefficients for the Initial-Skills Analysis were reported as greater than .80 for all levels as were most reliability coefficients for the Summative Assessment.

COMMENTARY. The BEAR appears to be a comprehensive test of reading and language arts skills for kindergarten through third grade. The test developers report having made an attempt to analyze and determine which reading and language arts skills are needed for success at each of the grade levels as well as an attempt to sequence those skills appropriately within the BEAR. However, the technical manual simply does not offer enough information on how these skills were chosen to help the user to be sure that the test is assessing fundamental skills. Page 1 of the Basic Early Assessment of Reading (BEAR) technical manual does mention that the test measures skills identified as important by the National Reading Panel "and other reading experts," but no elaboration is given on this statement and within the manual little effort is made to help the test user understand who these "other reading experts" might be or how they themselves have pinpointed fundamental skills for reading and language arts instruction. The user is required to accept that the skills tested are those that have been recommended by vaguely referred to reading experts and that, in fact, these skills are those that are fundamental to good reading and language arts development in kindergarten through third grade. This sort of vague support is also used on page 6 of the manual with the suggestion that items for the test are appropriate because test developers at Riverside Publishing have extensive expertise in the development of a wide range of assessments. Additionally, the test user is given assurances about the rubric development by being told that "The rubrics were written and finalized by Riverside content-area test development specialists, who have a great deal of expertise in the development of rubrics for criterion-referenced tests" (technical manual, p. 9)

Absolutely no effort was made by the test developers to compare the BEAR to other well-known tests of reading and language arts skills. Absolutely no attempt was made by the test developers to validate that the criteria they have identified as essential to reading and language arts development at kindergarten through third grade are essential criteria. Users of the test are required to accept the test manual's statements that these skills are essential as recommended by various reading experts; however, few experts are identified and no effort is made to clarify in any in-depth manner exactly what reading experts actually did say about identified skills.

SUMMARY. The BEAR is a criterion-referenced reading and language arts assessment for kindergarten through third grade. The test is easily administered as a paper-and-pencil test or as a computer-assisted test. Vague information on test development and lack of research comparing this test to other tests of reading and language arts skills make it difficult for the user to know whether skills tested are those that are essential for reading and language arts development in the elementary school years.

[24]

Basic Number Screening Test [2001 Edition].

Purpose: "Quick assessment of a child's understanding of ... number concepts and number skills."
Population: Ages 7–12.
Publication Dates: 1976–2001.

Scores: No scores.
Administration: Group.
Forms, 2: A, B.
Price Data, 2002: £9.99 per 20 tests (Form A or B); £10.99 per manual; £11.99 per specimen set.
Time: (20–35) minutes.
Comments: May be orally administered.
Authors: Bill Gillham and Kenneth Heese.
Publisher: Hodder & Stoughton Educational [England].
Cross References: For reviews by John O. Anderson and Suzanna Lane of the 1996 edition, see 15:28; for reviews by Mary Montgomery Lindquist and Marilyn N. Suydam of an earlier edition, see 9:118.

Review of the Basic Number Screening Test [2001 Edition] by KEVIN D. CREHAN, Professor of Educational Psychology, University of Nevada—Las Vegas, Las Vegas, NV:

DESCRIPTION. The Basic Number Screening Test is intended as "a quick, *first stage* assessment of a child's grasp of the basic principles underlying the number system and the processes involved in calculation" (manual, p. 4) for ages 7—12 years. Test authors suggest the test results can be used for beginning year instructional planning and assessment of year-to-year progress. However, the main purpose of the test is for identification and differentiation among children with low levels of mathematics achievement. The two forms of the test are each commposed of 30 short answer items presented in 16 panels of 1 to 3 items on 4 pages. Presenting more than 1 item within a panel may cause children some confusion, especially when the items are of differing formats.

The test is not timed and administration time is estimated as 30 to 35 minutes for group testing and 20 minutes for individual administration. The test is administered orally using the script provided. Students are allowed to go back to skipped items but the instructions are not read a second time. Because instructions are necessary to answer about half the items, allowing additional time to return to skipped items without instructions is of questionable value. A 16-page manual provides information on test uses, development, administration, scoring, standardization, and norms. Some guidance is provided on percentile rank interpretation with progressively darker shading in the table for the 30th percentile rank and below. Children scoring in the progressively darker shaded areas are identified as needing intervention.

Scoring directions indicate that items are scored one or zero. Although near misses do not score, some allowance is suggested for answers that show obvious intention. Tables are provided for conversion of raw scores to number ages, percentile ranks, and quotients. The percentile rank and quotient conversion table is new to this revision. The 2001 revision of the test was prompted by Great Britain's National Numeracy Strategy (NNS) and involved minor revision to item format and ordering. The test is to be administered without calculations to support the NNS emphasis on mental operations.

DEVELOPMENT. The test content was determined by the authors' "understanding of the development of children's number concepts" and the "changing nature of mathematics in schools" (manual, p. 6). The items included in the test "are a fraction of those used during item try-outs in schools" (manual, p. 6). Final item selection was based largely on feedback from teachers and children. Items are mapped to the NNS *Framework for Teaching Mathematics* and the National Curriculum and are arranged to correspond to grade level instruction for Years 1 to 5. The alternate forms each have 15 number concept items (place value, series, grouping, conservation) and 15 number operations items that are said to test for understanding of calculation processes. However, the calculation items do not actually measure understanding of the calculation processes involved.

TECHNICAL. An earlier version of the test was standardized on a sample of 3,042 children ranging in age from 7-6 to 11-6. The sample was from the region of one city in England and the data were collected more than 25 years ago. Other than the age range, no other sample characteristics are provided. The authors did not believe it necessary to standardize the revised version of the test because the test content is essentially the same and because test users are familiar with the older norms. They suggest that the older norms provide a stable means for checking year-to-year progress. Norm tables provide raw score to number age, percentile rank, and quotient conversion. Percentile ranks above 10% have a 10% interval. The quotient scale has interval widths of from 3 to 6 points. Number age norms are at 3-month intervals from 7 years, 0 months to 11 years, 11 months. One additional item correct moves a child 3 months up the scale for 19 of the 21 age norms. The two remaining age norms require two additional correct items. The one top and one bottom age norms were determined by extrapolation. No grade level, gender, or ethnic norm data are provided. Means and standard deviations are also omitted.

Reliability is estimated by a Pearson correlation of .93 based on parallel forms administration with a 1-week interval. No information is given on sample characteristics or the number of children involved in determining this correlation and no other reliability estimates are provided.

Validity was not seen as a serious problem for the authors "since the test directly samples the attainment it is measuring" (manual, p. 16). The authors do report a Spearman's rho of .82 between test score and teacher's ratings of children (presumably on mathematics achievement) on a 7-point scale. These data were collected in one school and sample characteristics and sample size are not reported.

COMMENTARY. Earlier reviewers (9:118 and 15:28) expressed reservations about the usefulness of this test. The revised version adds little to satisfy the concerns expressed in these earlier reviews. The information presented on test development is very sketchy and informal. Although the items are clearly measuring elementary mathematics, the rationale for item selection and inclusion appears to be subjective. Although it is stated that the items are carefully mapped to Great Britain's NNS *Framework for Teaching Mathematics* and National Curriculum 2000, it is also stated that the content for the revison remains essentially the same as the first test edition. The authors state that "the test (was) revised to reflect as closely as possible the teaching progression, mathematical vocabulary and presentational formats recommended" (manual, p. 6) in the NNS Framework. If there was no need to revise the content of a test developed in 1967 to conform to a framework developed in 2000, the authors obviously had incredible foresight. There is no indication of any item analyses having been conducted. There is very limited evidence related to the reliability and validity of scores and what is presented is quite dated. The only evidence of reliability is a correlation of the parallel forms over a 1-week interval, which was presumably determined over 25 years ago. There are no test-retest correlations or indices of internal consistency. The only evidence of validity relates test scores to teacher ratings. Use of teacher rating is an interesting choice as the criterion for validity. Perhaps teacher rating could serve as well as test score to identify low-performing children. The original standardization sample from over 25 years ago was used to develop a table for raw score conversions to number ages for the first edition of the test. Added for the current revision are raw score conversions to broadly spaced percentile ranks and quotients. Although percentile ranks are considered useful for interpretation of performance, the difficulties in the interpretation of both quotients and age equivalents should be well known. A common error is to infer that a 7-year-old with an age equivalent of 11 would have mathematics achievment similar to the average 11-year-old. An inspection of the test's content would confirm that it does not contain many of mathematical skills an 11-year-old would be expected to master. A 7-year-old may have never been exposed to the mathematics skills expected of an 11-year-old. The *Standards* discouraged the use of age equivalent scores as early as 1974. It is unlikely that these norm tables are representative of children in general or even children in England for at least two important reasons. First, the standardization sample is somewhat dated having been observed in 1976. Second, the composition of the standardization sample is problematic because it was localized to the region of one city in England (Nottingham).

SUMMARY. The Basic Number Screening Test offers little to recommend it as a screening test for identifying children with low performance in mathematics. A teacher should be able to do as well after a few weeks' exposure to his or her class. However, if a teacher or a school is familiar with the test and the norms from usage over a number of years, perhaps it has value to them. On the other hand, if one is looking for an elementary level mathematics screening test, they would be advised to find a different measurement device.

Review of the Basic Number Screening Test [2001 Edition] by THANOS PATELIS, Executive Director, Psychometrics, Evaluation, and Data Reporting, The College Board, New York, NY:

DESCRIPTION. The Basic Number Screening Test is a 30-item norm-referenced test with two forms, A and B, that is administered in either a group setting or individually by paper-and-pencil with the directions read orally. Two practice questions are provided at the beginning of the testing session. In a group-administered setting, the testing time is 30 to 35 minutes. When the test is administered individually, the testing time is 20 minutes. In either case, however, these times are provided as estimates, because the test itself is untimed. The directions leave the speed of the administration to the judgment of the administrator—assumed to be a teacher. All responses are examinee-generated. A total raw score is obtained by applying a scoring key. The raw score is translated to a "Number Age" using a norm table. The Normal Age in the manual is defined as "the average performance of children at the various age levels" (p. 6). Percentile ranks and quotients are provided, as well.

The administration procedures are scripted clearly for each type of administration (i.e., group and individually administered). However, the lack of explicit time limits sacrifices standardization. The scoring for each form is described in pictorial format with some suggestions about how to score the constructed responses.

DEVELOPMENT. The description of the development of the test is lacking detail with only brief connections made to the constructs of number concept and number operations that seem to be fundamental to the basis of the test. References in the literature are not provided. The process of item development and evaluation is also not clear. The author states that only a fraction of the items from the pilot versions were selected based on feedback from teachers and students during item tryouts in schools. However, the details of the selection process, including statistical criteria of the items, were not provided. Thus, without the specifics associated with the procedure of the item tryouts and the qualifications of the test developers, an evaluation of the development of this test is not possible.

TECHNICAL. Similar to the specifics about the development process of this test, the manual lacks specifics about the technical aspects associated with the test. The manual indicates that the norms are based on the earlier version of the test, relying on an urban setting of 3,042 school-age children, who ranged in age from 7.5 to 11.5 years old. The exact distribution of these ages and more detailed relevant descriptive information (e.g., how the tests were administered, gender) were not provided. Finally, the rationale for not revising the norms was included. It was argued that (a) this revision of the original test measured the same thing and (b) test users want to have a comparable means of making assessments. Both arguments, however, are open questions needing answers. First, it must be verified that the revision and the original test measure the same thing. Second, the statistical linkage between the two tests (e.g., equating) must be established to ensure comparability of the inferences made.

Reliability information is reported in the form of alternate form reliability using a 1-week delayed procedure. The Pearson product-moment correlation coefficient is reported as .93. However, no additional descriptive information about the samples and specific procedures was provided.

The validity evidence provided, although not explicitly labeled as such, was concurrent validity evidence using teacher ratings in one school. The manual suggests that the teachers rated the children on their numeracy ability, but this is not made explicit. As indicated in the manual, the average correlation coefficient (using a Spearman's rho) between performance on this test and the teacher ratings was reported as .82. The descriptive statistics of the sample and the procedures utilized were not reported. Even though the correlation coefficient between test performance and teacher ratings was strong and positive, any meaningful inference about the concurrent validity evidence is difficult due to the lack of information. Finally, it was suggested that this test represents the content of the National Numeracy Strategy Framework for Teaching Mathematics and National Curriculum 2000. This statement, if true, may limit the utility of this test to schools that do not use these curriculum standards.

COMMENTARY. The Basic Number Screening Test, although packaged in a professional-looking format, lacks many of the recommendations in the *Standards for Educational and Psychological Testing* (American Educational Research Association, American Psychological Association, & National Council on Measurement in Education, 1999). The lack of information about the constructs that form the basis and the detailed characteristics of the norms, reliability, and validity evidence considerably weakens the utility of this test for its stated purpose to "identify, and differentiate amongst, those children whose attainment is below average" (manual, p. 4). The

indication that the use of this test is the first step in this identification and differentiation of children's numeracy is its strength. In light of the lack of empirical evidence, this test may only provide a teacher with a class activity that would lead to the collection of more information to determine numeracy deficiencies.

SUMMARY. The intent of the authors to build a quick screening tool for teachers to assess the numeracy of their students is commendable. Their goal to standardize this process and anchor it in a national curriculum is also a sound approach. Clear directions for both group and individual administrations were provided, even though strict time limits were not provided. The scoring is straightforward. However, there is a significant lack of information related to the constructs of numeracy, specific descriptive statistics associated with the norms, and detailed reliability and validity evidence. Thus, until more details are provided, the Basic Number Screening Test should be used as an activity in the classroom rather than a screening tool.

REVIEWER'S REFERENCE

American Educational Research Association, American Psychological Association, & National Council on Measurement in Education. (1999). *Standards for educational and psychological testing.* Washington, DC: American Educational Research Association.

[25]

BDI-FastScreen for Medical Patients.

Purpose: Designed to screen for depression in patients reporting somatic and behavioral symptoms that may be attributable to biological, medical, alcohol, and/or substance abuse problems.
Population: Ages 12–82.
Publication Date: 2000.
Acronym: BDI-FastScreen.
Scores: Total score only.
Administration: Group.
Price Data, 2003: $67 per complete kit including manual and 50 score forms; $39 per manual; $39 per 50 record forms; $43 per 50 scannable record forms; quantity discounts available.
Time: (5) minutes.
Comments: Formerly called Beck Depression Inventory for Primary Care; based upon Beck Depression Inventory—II (T6:273).
Authors: Aaron T. Beck, Robert A. Steer, and Gregory K. Brown.
Publisher: PsychCorp, A brand of Harcourt Assessment, Inc.

Review of the BDI—FastScreen for Medical Patients by JAMES J. HENNESSY, Professor (Edu-

cational Psychology), Graduate School of Education, Fordham University, New York, NY, and NATHANIEL J. PALLONE, University Distinguished Professor (Psychology), Center of Alcohol Studies, Rutgers—The State University, New Brunswick, NJ:

DESCRIPTION. The BDI-FastScreen for Medical Patients (BDI-FastScreen) is a seven-item self-report questionnaire intended to screen for symptoms of depression in adolescents and adults who are being evaluated by physicians for somatic and behavioral complaints that may be associated with biological, medical, or substance abuse problems. The seven items are rated on a 4-point scale (0–3) and assess frequency, over the past 2 weeks, of feelings of sadness, pessimism (hopelessness), sense of failure, and anhedonia or loss of a sense of pleasure, loss of self-confidence, self-blame, and suicidal thoughts or wishes. The questions were taken from the Beck Depression Inventory-II and its derivative, the Beck Depression Inventory-IA; the further shortened version reviewed here was constructed "to reduce the number of false positives for depression in patients with known medical or substance abuse [including alcohol] problems" (manual, p. 2).

The response form or answer sheet is a single page, on which a respondent's name, age, marital status, gender, occupation, and education are recorded. The seven items are presented in two columns that fill about two-thirds of the sheet, yielding a format that lends itself readily to attaching the questionnaire to a clipboard that can be presented to patients at the same time as other "clipboard" information is sought. A notice in the lower section of the answer sheet prudently advises users that the form is printed in green and black ink, and that any difference may indicate that it has been photocopied in violation of copyright laws.

The manual is generally clearly written, although clinical users who do not have adequate background in psychometrics may find technical details and terminology difficult. For example, in discussing the accuracy of the BDI-FastScreen, the words "specificity" and "sensitivity" are used without explaining their meanings in terms familiar to general medical practitioners, the intended "target group" of end-users. The manual contains detailed explanations of the procedures Beck and his colleagues used to identify the items selected for inclusion and to demonstrate their relationship to the longer instruments from which they were taken. Correlation between the 7-item total score and 21-item BDI-II total score was computed at .91 for samples of college students and outpatients in a local medical facility, a finding that indicates that the BDI-FastScreen score distribution is highly concordant with the distribution of scores on the longer form. The manual also contains several statements intended to caution users against relying on the BDI-FastScreen as the sole pivot for a diagnosis of major depressive disorders (MDD); interpretation should be undertaken only by those who have appropriate experience and training. Clinicians are advised to be especially attentive to non-zero responses to the pessimism and suicidal thoughts items.

The BDI-FastScreen may be administered as a self-report measure for patients able to read, or it may be read aloud (to nonreaders of English). Most patients complete the instrument in fewer than 5 minutes. Scores are obtained by summing numeric point values across the seven items, with 0–21 as the range of possible scores.

STANDARDIZATION. Interpretive guidelines reported in the manual suggest that scores in the range of 4–8 are indicative of a mild MDD; scores in the range of 9–12 are indicative of a moderate MDD; and scores of 13–21 are indicative of a severe MDD.

The authors present findings from a series of studies they and their colleagues and associates have conducted; these constitute the basis for the interpretive guidelines offered. Analyses reported in the manual, as well as in a more recent study (Scheinthal, Steer, Giffin, & Beck, 2001), found high sensitivity rates (correctly identifying MDD) in the range of 79% to 100%, and specificity rates (not diagnosing the MDD when it is not present) were also high, in the range of 83% to 99%. The probability of false positives and false negatives is acceptably low, especially when the cutoff score is set at 6 in most medical settings. The authors recommend a cutoff score of 4 in most settings, but the higher score may be more appropriate in settings where there is an increased likelihood of *not* diagnosing a major depressive disorder when it is present (i.e., where a false negative is more rather than less likely).

A persistent going concern with the predecessor BDI-II regarding the influence of response set and memory remains essentially unaddressed for the BDI-FastScreen. Reference is made in the manual to an early Beck study in which no significant response set effect was found, but that study was reported in 1967 and seems not sufficiently robust as the basis for a rather casual dismissal of concerns about this effect in the current version. The authors acknowledge that patients may more easily recall their responses to specific questions because the BDI-FastScreen contains only seven items; that no assessment of the effects of memory have been reported is a shortcoming for the measure (as it continues to be for the BDI-II).

RELIABILITY. Internal consistency estimates (alpha coefficients) are reported to be in the mid-.80 range. No test-retest analyses are reported; thus the extent to which responses are indicative of fluctuating mood states as contrasted with more enduring MDD remains indeterminate. The lack of test-retest studies is troublesome, especially in consequence of residual questions about response set and memory.

VALIDITY. Evidence of construct validity presented in the manual consists of correlations of the BDI-FastScreen with other measures that assess depressive symptoms. The BDI-FastScreen correlated highly ($r = .62$) with total scores on the Hospital Anxiety and Depression Scale Depression subscale, more highly with another Beck measure (the Beck Anxiety Inventory for Primary Care, or BAI-PC) at $r = .86$, and highly with the diagnosis of DSM-IV mood disorder ($r = .69$). The authors do not present sample sizes for two of these studies; in the third, the sample consisted of 50 inpatients admitted to a local hospital facility. The magnitude of the correlation between the BDI-FastScreen and the BAI-PC approaches the upper limit of the scale's possible correlations with other measures and suggests that the two measures are alternate methods for assessing the same underlying variable; whether that variable is appropriately construed as depression or as anxiety, however, is not entirely clear. Findings contrasting various samples of patients in medical settings, including those with and without a formal diagnosis of MDD, provide evidence of highly significant differences between mean cut scores of those so diagnosed and those not so diagnosed and thus buttress the recommended range of cutoff scores that maximize accuracy of classification.

The authors assert that the BDI-FastScreen builds on 40 years of "accumulated psychometric data and clinical experience" (manual, p. 24) with Beck-developed measures, but that foundation may not be quite so strong as the assertion suggests. Size and representativeness of samples described in the manual raise concerns. The combined sample of patients with "major depression" across four settings consisted of only 96 patients; the "no major depression" sample consisted of 268 people drawn from those same four settings. In the aggregate, the sample contained 50 adult inpatients, 100 adolescent outpatients in a pediatric clinic, and 120 outpatients in an internal medicine clinic, all at the same school of osteopathic medicine located in the greater Philadelphia metropolitan area, along with 94 patients "selected" from six family practice settings in that region (although the method of, and rationale for, selection is not further described). The samples used to estimate internal consistency are the same as those used to assess validity. Until findings from additional studies with more representative samples drawn from outside of the Philadelphia region are reported, questions regarding the validity of the scale cannot be answered definitively.

COMMENTARY. The BDI-FastScreen may represent the final point of distillation of the longer Beck scales and may more appropriately be described as a "scaled" checklist that a clinician can use much in the manner that the checklist format of DSM-IV diagnoses can used. Judgments made on the basis of scores represent categorical decisions rather than refined assessments of the degree of severity of depressive disorder. In that sense, the BDI-FastScreen accomplishes its intended purpose, which is to assess the likely presence or absence of depressive (and perhaps anxiety) symptoms. Its apparent ease of use may lead to overidentification of major depressive disorders, especially by general practitioners who may then be prone to prescribe treatment (likely pharmacological) for patients whose scores are 4 or higher. By focusing on the way patients have been feeling over the past 2 weeks, without further eliciting information about events that may have transpired over that time, false positive rates higher than those reported in the manual may be observed. For example, a person who was recently terminated from a job may admit to recent feelings of sadness, pessimism, anhedonia, and loss of confidence, feelings that may be entirely realistic and appropriate; a "normal reaction" to life's events cannot be differentiated from a depressive episode if results of the BDI-FastScreen are not interpreted within context. Decontextualized interpretation of scores should be more strongly discouraged by the authors and greater attention placed on the influence of situational factors on patient responses.

SUMMARY. The BDI-FastScreen is a short form of other Beck scales and is designed for use in medical settings as a screening index for symptoms of major depressive disorders. It is user-friendly, although perhaps too much so. The evidence presented to support its reliability and specific validities is based on small samples of patients admitted to a single hospital or receiving services at local practice settings affiliated with that hospital. Only one study supplementing those reported in the manual has been reported since the scale was published, and that study also was conducted by the Beck group. There is need for independent validation of the instrument using larger, more diverse, and more widely geographically distributed samples. The potential for overdiagnosis of a depressive disorder in general clinical practice may be high. Very high correlation between this measure of depression and a measure of anxiety suggests that the scale may screen for symptoms that occur in several disorders; its value as a first screen for depression may thus be overstated.

REVIEWERS' REFERENCE

Scheinthal, S. M., Steer, R. A., Giffin, L., & Beck, A. T. (2001). Evaluating geriatric medical patients with the Beck Depression Inventory-FastScreen for medical patients. *Aging & Mental Health, 5*(2), 143–148.

Review of the BDI-FastScreen for Medical Patients by SUSAN C. WHISTON, Professor, Counseling Psychology, Indiana University, Bloomington, IN, and KELLY EDER, Doctoral Student, Counseling Psychology, Indiana University, Bloomington, IN:

DESCRIPTION. The BDI-FastScreen for Medical Patients is a seven-item instrument designed for medical settings to screen for depression in adolescents and adults. The items were extracted from the Beck Depression Inventory-II (Beck, Steer, & Brown, 1996) and are designed to correspond to the criteria for diagnosing a Major Depressive Disorder (MDD) as defined in the *Diagnostic and Statistical Manual of Mental Disorders—Fourth Edition* (DSM-IV; American Psychiatric Association, 1994). The BDI-FastScreen can be self-administered, and most patients can complete it in less than 5 minutes. It focuses on

evaluating the somatic and behavioral symptoms of depression that may be attributable to biological, medical, and/or substance abuse problems and includes items related to sadness, pessimism, past failure, loss of pleasure, self-dislike, self-criticalness, and suicidal thoughts. Examinees respond based on how they have been feeling in the past 2 weeks, and each of the seven items has four responses that vary from (0) *not present* to (3) *severe.* The responses to all items are summed and a total score is interpreted with the suggested guidelines being: minimal (0–3), mild (4–8), moderate (9–12), and severe depression (13–21). The authors, however, stress cutoff scores for the BDI-FastScreen should be based upon both the context of the decision and the underlying prevalence of clinical depression in the sample being screened. The authors further caution that the BDI-FastScreen is not a substitute for the BDI-II, but is intended as a screening tool to be used by professionals.

DEVELOPMENT. The BDI-FastScreen for Medical Patients, formerly known as the Beck Depression Inventory for Primary Care (BDI-PC; Beck, Guth, Steer, & Ball, 1997) is an instrument that evolved from Aaron Beck and his associates' expertise in assessment and depression starting with the original version of the Beck Depression Inventory (BDI-I; Beck, Ward, Mendelson, Mock, & Erbaugh, 1961). Some clinicians, however, questioned whether the early versions of the BDI-I and BDI-II might yield spurious scores for patients with medical problems as many of the items were related to somatic and performance symptoms. For example, a number of medical conditions (e.g., diabetes, heart disease) often have overlapping symptoms with depression (tiredness, fatigue, sleep disturbance). Beck and Steer (1993) recommended using only the first 13 items in the BDI-I to assess depression in patients with known medical conditions, which they labeled the Cognitive-Affect subscale. After the BDI-II was published, Beck and his associates proposed that the 14 items related to psychological symptoms could probably be used when assessing depression with individuals with medical or substance abuse problems.

In developing a formal instrument that corresponded to medical personnel's desire for a quick screener for depression that excluded medical conditions, Beck and associates began by examining the 14 cognitive and affective items in the BDI-II.

They initially determined to retain the items related to sadness and loss of pleasure (anhedonia) as these symptoms must be present for the DSM-IV diagnosis of Major Depressive Disorder (MDD). Due to the importance and consequence of suicide, they also decided to retain an item related to suicidal thoughts or wishes. The four other items (pessimism, past failure, self-dislike, and self-criticism) were selected based on a principal factor loading analysis of the BDI-II items with a sample of 500 psychiatric outpatients and 120 college students. Hence, rather than using the 14 items of the Cognitive-Affect subscale, the BDI-FastScreen contains only 7 items.

In developing the scoring and interpretation, the authors determined cutoff scores using procedures similar to those used for establishing cutoff scores for the BDI-II. The two primary procedures were the receiver operating characteristic (ROC) and maximum information-gain analyses. ROC analysis is a mathematical technique that calculates the true positive rates and the false positive rates for various cutoff scores. In conducting ROC analyses, the authors used a sample of 23 individuals diagnosed with MDD and 71 who were diagnosed without MDD. The results from the ROC analyses were somewhat inconclusive as prevalence of MDD varies among samples. The maximum-information gain analyses also indicated that there was not a single optimal score for determining the presence of depression. In examining results from these analyses, the authors concluded that a score of 3 and above may be used as a general screening for depression and a score of 5 and above should be used if the goal is to decrease the probability of false negatives. The manual did not include research evidence related to the scoring differentials of mild (4–8), moderate (9–12), and severe depression (13–21), which indicates practitioners should be cautious in using these labels based solely on BDI-FastScreen results.

TECHNICAL. In developing psychometric information related to the BDI-FastScreen, the authors used four different medical samples. These samples are (a) 50 patients hospitalized for medical problems and then referred for psychiatric consultation and liaison (C&L); (b) 94 outpatients from family practice settings; (c) 100 pediatric patients (12 to 17 years old) scheduled to receive health-maintenance examinations; and (d) 120 internal medicine outpatients at a university medical facility. The coefficient alphas for the C&L, family practice, pediatric, and internal medicine patients were .86, .85, .88, and .86, respectively. No other sources of reliability evidence (e.g., test-retest coefficients) were provided in the manual.

In terms of content representation, the items were selected in consultation with the criteria for depressive disorders in the *DSM-IV*. Furthermore, the patients' BDI-FastScreen responses on all of the items significantly correlated with their total scores. In terms of convergent validity, Beck, Guth, et al. (1997) found the BDI-FastScreen correlated (r = .62) with the Depression subscale of the Hospital Anxiety and Depression Scale. Furthermore, Beck, Steer, Ball, Ciervo, and Kabat (1997) found the BDI-FastScreen was significantly correlated (r = .69) with a *DSM-IV* mood disorder diagnosis. Concerning divergent evidence, the BDI-FastScreen does not appear to correlate significantly with gender, ethnicity, age, or a number of medical disorders (e.g., cardiovascular disorders, neoplastic disorders).

The focus of the BDI-FastScreen is to distinguish between medical patients with clinical depression and those without; hence, its ability to discriminate among appropriate population is critical. Using the four samples described above, the authors investigated whether the BDI-FastScreen could differentiate between those diagnosed with a major depressive disorder and those diagnosed without using the Mode Module from the *Primary Evaluation of Mental Disorders* (PRIME-MD; Spitzer et al., 1995). They found that 26% of those diagnosed with MDD had BDI-FastScreen scores six times higher than 74% of those patients not diagnosed with MDD. Also related to diagnostic discrimination, the authors discussed a study by Cubic, Beck, and Levin (1998) who found that a modified version of the BDI-FastScreen had similar scores with the original version.

COMMENTARY. The BDI-FastScreen meets an important need as it is often difficult to discriminate among symptoms that are due to a medical condition and those associated with depression. The strength of the BDI-FastScreen is it has evolved from over 40 years of research related to assessing depression. However, if professionals base their analysis of the instrument solely on the manual of the BDI-FastScreen, the psychometric information provided is limited. Farmer (2001) also concluded that the manual for the BDI-II was too concise, and the authors of these instruments may want to consider expanding the psychometric information in both instruments' manuals in the future. Nevertheless, it would not be appropriate to evaluate the BDI-FastScreen based solely on the manual, particularly considering the history of the BDI-FastScreen and its close alignment with the BDI-II. In many ways, the positive reviews of the BDI-II (e.g., Arbisi, 2001; Dozois, Dobson, & Ahnberg, 1998; Farmer, 2001) apply to the BDI-FastScreen. For instance, Arbisi (2001) concluded that the BDI-II represented a highly successful revision of an acknowledged standard in the measurement of depression.

Although the BDI-FastScreen is based on a strong research-based foundation, there are still some concerns that should be considered when using it in clinical settings. The information regarding the cutoff scores related to the BDI-FastScreen is somewhat ambiguous and there is surprising little evidence in the manual regarding the categories of minimal (0–3), mild (4–8), moderate (9–12), and severe depression (13–21). There also is a need for additional research regarding the BDI-FastScreen's ability to differentiate among medical patients with MDD and those without. Moreover, the number of studies currently conducted exclusively with the BDI-FastScreen is limited, and the samples used in many of these studies are small and do not adequately represent the diverse population of individuals with medical and/or substance abuse problems. Given the extensive research on other instruments developed by Beck and his associates, it is anticipated that there will be numerous empirical investigations of the BDI-FastScreen in the near future.

SUMMARY. The BDI-FastScreen is a brief, seven-item instrument designed to screen for depression in adolescents and adults, with a particular focus on evaluating symptoms of depression in patients reporting somatic and behavioral symptoms that may be attributable to biological, medical, and/or substance abuse problems. The seven items in the BDI-FastScreen were extracted from the Beck Depression Inventory-II and address sadness, pessimism, past failure, loss of pleasure, self-dislike, self-criticalness, and suicidal thoughts. As the BDI-FastScreen is closely affiliated with the BDI-II, much of the validation evidence of the BDI-II also applies to the BDI-FastScreen; however, although the shortened version retains high reliability, additional evidence is needed related to its ability to differentiate among medical patients with a major depressive disorder and those without. Hence, practitioners using the BDI-FastScreen should attend to the authors' warning that it is not a substitute for the BDI-II. Furthermore, in making diagnostic decisions, the BDI-FastScreen may serve as a source of information, but it is not a substitute for a thorough evaluation conducted by a well-trained clinician.

REVIEWERS' REFERENCES

American Psychiatric Association. (1994). *Diagnostic and statistical manual of mental disorders* (4th ed). Washington, DC: Author.
Arbisi, P. A. (2001). [Review of the Beck Depression Inventory-II.] In B. S. Plake & J. C. Impara (Eds.), *The fourteenth mental measurements yearbook* (pp. 121–123). Lincoln, NE: Buros Institute of Mental Measurements.
Beck, A. T., Guth, D., Steer, R. A., & Ball, R. (1997). Screening for major depression disorders in medical inpatients with the Beck Depression Inventory for Primary Care. *Behavior Research & Therapy, 35*, 785–791.
Beck, A. T., & Steer, R. A. (1993). *Beck Depression Inventory manual.* San Antonio, TX: Psychological Corporation.
Beck, A. T., Steer, R. A., Ball, R., Ciervo, C. A., & Kabat, M. (1997). Use of the Beck Anxiety and Depression Inventories for primary care with medical outpatients. *Assessment, 4*, 211–219.
Beck, A. T., Steer, R. A., & Brown, G. K. (1996). Beck Depression Inventory-II. San Antonio, TX: Psychological Corporation.
Beck, A. T., Ward, C. H., Mendelson, M., Mock, J., & Erbaugh, J. (1961). An inventory for measuring depression. *Archives of General Psychiatry, 4*, 561–571.
Cubic, B. A., Beck, A.. T., & Levin, D. (1998). *Assessing the practical utility of the Beck Depression Inventory for Primary Care.* Unpublished manuscript, Department of Psychiatry and Behaviora Sciences, Eastern Virginia Medical School, Norfolk, VA.
Dozois, D. J. A., Dobson, K. S., & Ahnberg, J. L. (1998). A psychometric evaluation of the Beck Depression Inventory-II. *Psychological Assessment, 10*, 83–89.
Farmer, R. S. (2001). [Review of the Beck Depression Inventory-II.] In B. S. Plake & J. C. Impara (Eds.), *The fourteenth mental measurements yearbook* (pp. 123–126). Lincoln, NE: Buros Institute of Mental Measurements.
Spitzer, R. L., Williams, J. B. W., Kroenke, K., Linzer, M., deGruy, F. V., III, Hahn, S. R., & Brody, D. (1995). *Prime-MD instruction manual updated for DSM-IV.* New York: Biometrics Research Department, New York State Psychiatric Institute.

[26]

Behavior Disorders Identification Scale—Second Edition.

Purpose: "To document the existence of behaviors which meet the criteria for identifying the student as behaviorally disordered."

Population: Ages 4.5–21.

Publication Dates: 1988–2000.

Acronym: BDIS-2 SV (School Version); BDIS-2 HV (Home Version).

Scores, 5: Learning Problems, Interpersonal Relations, Inappropriate Behavior, Unhappiness/Depression, Physical Symptoms/Fears.

Administration: Individual.

Forms, 2: School Version, Home Version.

Price Data, 2005: $190 per complete kit including 50 Pre-Referral Behavior Checklists, 50 Intervention Strategies Documentation forms, 50 School Version Rating forms, 50 Home Version Rating forms, School Version Technical Manual, Home Version Technical Manual, and Teacher's Guide to Behavioral Interventions; $30 per 50 Pre-Referral Behavior Checklists; $30 per 50 Intervention Strategies Documentation forms; $15 per Technical Manual (School Version or Home Version); $35 per 50 rating forms (School Version, Home Version, or Home Version Spanish); $30 per Teacher's Guide to Behavioral Interventions; $35 per BDIS-2 Quick Score; $225 per Teacher's Guide to Behavioral Interventions computer version (Windows®). **Time:** [20] minutes for School Version; [15] minutes for Home Version.

Comments: Completed by adult observers; based on federal definitions of serious emotional disturbance (PL 94-142 and IDEA Amendments of 1997); available in paper or computer version; system requirements: IBM-compatible computer, 30 MB of drive space, 32–64 MB of free RAM, Windows 98 or newer, and a 2X CD-ROM drive, 580K memory; Quick Score computer scoring of school and Home Versions available, system requirements Windows 95 or newer, 8 MB RAM, 10 MB hard disk space, 2X CD-ROM drive; Quick Score provides individualized goals, objectives, interventions; Spanish language Home Version rating forms available.

Authors: Stephen B. McCarney and Tamara J. Arthaud (Technical Manuals, Home Version and School Version), and Kathy Cummins Wunderlich (Teacher's Guide to Behavioral Interventions).

Publisher: Hawthorne Educational Services, Inc.

Cross References: For reviews by Doreen Ward Fairbank and Harlan J. Stientjes of an earlier edition, see 12:46.

Review of the Behavior Disorders Identification Scale—Second Edition by JUDY OEHLER-STINNETT, Associate Professor, School of Applied Health and Educational Psychology, Oklahoma State University, Stillwater, OK:

DESCRIPTION. The Behavior Disorders Identification Scale (BDIS) is a behavior rating scale designed to identify and provide intervention recommendations for children and youth with behavioral and emotional problems. Because the instrument purports to be a sensitive diagnostic instrument for the identification of children having Serious Emotional Disturbance (SED) under the criteria set forth by IDEA, the test must be evaluated in terms of its validity to do so. The introduction to the scale suggests that it is offered as an alternative classification system to the DSM-IV, for which "subcategories are based on the clinical experiences of psychologists functioning outside of educational environments" (p. 5) and "may have little relevancy for definition and identification in the educational environment" (p. 5).

A definition of the constructs measured is: The BDIS was developed to provide scales congruent with the broad diagnostic criteria areas of IDEA for Serious Emotional Disturbance (learning, relationships, behavior or feelings, depression, and physical symptoms). A brief definition of each of the five SED constructs is provided, with example behaviors under each. However, a clear definition that would show the rational bases for item selection is not provided.

TEST DEVELOPMENT. Item selection and retention: Both Home (HV) and School (SV) versions of the test were developed. Items were selected to address the behavior and emotional problems "most indicative of serious emotional disturbance" (p. 6). The authors state that the items were developed by parents/guardians and educators as representing relevant descriptions of the most common characteristics of behavior disorders. Diagnosticians were also utilized. However, there is no direct reference to the empirical literature on components of child psychopathology, to items from similar instruments such as the Devereux (T6:799), or to professional psychologists or psychiatrists who do have school-based experience, as is commonly done to document content validity. A review of the items indicates that they certainly represent serious concerns presented by parents and teachers. Examining their construct and predictive validity beyond content validity is a necessary step to test development.

Items were reviewed by participants and reduced from an unnamed original number of items to 83. The BDIS manual also states that factor analytic techniques are important to scale development. Results are reported of a principal components analysis that addresses some of the differential diagnostic concerns, in that the item loadings yielded at least two factors within four of the five subscales. Many items cross-loaded on several factors, which could be the result of the items that are compound items containing several behaviors, or the forced five-factor solution. Only within-subscale analyses are reported, and differential diagnosis issues remain even within these. For example, items that are more associated with Attention Deficit Hyperactivity Disorder (ADHD) are contained throughout several factors and there is no mechanism for distinguishing SED from ADHD. Items that could also be indicative of a learning disability are included throughout the Learning Problems subscale and again differential diagnosis is not addressed. Despite the fact that the factor analysis did not confirm the five-subscale structure, the authors chose to retain the theoretical/rational scoring. Thus, the scale remains at this level and it cannot be stated that it is based on factor analysis. Reporting the full scale factor analysis, conducting a factor analysis based on the larger item pool, addressing problems with compound items and cross-loadings, and retaining scoring based on the statistical results with only minimal retention of items based on theory alone, would make the scale, in fact, factor based.

The authors further address item retention on scales through a presentation of item-subscale correlations, and they state that items had acceptable correlations with their subscale. The full correlation matrix is not presented, and the principal components results would suggest that many items might have had a higher loading on other subscales.

Standardization. The School and Home Versions were normed on a nationally representative sample (3,986 and 2,478, respectively). A relatively good balance was maintained across the age range (5–18) except for 16-year-olds for the School version, and across gender. However, norms are provided for 2-year intervals only, and norms are reported separately by gender only. Using gender-specific norms may lead to overidentification of girls and underidentification of boys as having SED. This caution regarding gender-specific norms is relevant to use of any rating scale. Additionally, minorities appear to be slightly underrepresented in the sample, and caution should be used when interpreting scores for such children. Almost 79% of the sample came from the Midwest and South for the SV and 70% for the HV, whereas the Northeast and West are underrepresented.

TECHNICAL.

Additional validity. For the SV and HV, concurrent validity is reported with the Behavior Evaluation Scale—Second Edition (T6:284) School Version and Home Version, respectively, by the same authors, and for the SV with the Devereux Behavior Rating Scale—School Form (T6:799), which has many of the same problems as the BDIS. There was congruence among similar subtests; unfortunately, the full correlation matrix was not reported, so discriminant validity of the subtests cannot be evaluated. Subtest specificity was not reported. Importantly, no broad-band rating scale that addresses areas such as ADHD was compared to the BDIS to further address discriminate validity. Internal consistency coefficients, which also address construct validity, are reported and range from .82 to .97 for the SV and from .75 to .94 for the HV, which are acceptable. Thus, although there are some data to support convergent validity, additional data are needed showing that each subscale measures what it purports to measure to document discriminant validity. The relationship of scale scores to actual observed behavior (performance-based criterion-related validity) or behavior at a later date (predictive validity) is not reported, nor are conditional probability analyses.

Clinical validity, or the ability to discriminate clinical from nonclinical children is reported. The manual states that because the test is able to discriminate between a normal group and a heterogeneous group of children identified as having SED, the test is diagnostically sensitive. Additional work needs to be done with clearly identified subgroups of children with specific disorders relevant to the diagnosis of SED, in addition to comparisons with groups of children with such disorders as ADHD and LD, to establish the diagnostic utility of the instrument. Other tests that do not claim to be able to diagnose SED, such as the Social Skills Rating System (T6: 2321), can also distinguish general clinical from normal groups. The data for the BDIS would need to clearly establish its diagnostic utility beyond that of other rating scales to be clearly valid for diagnosing such a serious disorder as SED.

The introduction to the manual states that the BDIS can be used for "measurement of behavior change over time as a result of program implementation" (p. 7). However, no treatment validity data are reported, and data regarding clinical groups do not indicate whether they were receiving treatment.

Reliability. Internal consistency, as noted, is adequate to good. Standard error of measurement at the 95% confidence level ranged from .84 to 5.32 for the subscales. Most were below the standard deviation, but for those that are not, consistency at the level needed for interpretation is problematic. Test-retest reliability was .91 (SV) and .82 (HV). Interrater reliability was within acceptable limits for the SV, with a coefficient of .57, and high for the HV, with a coefficient of .81. With use of multiple raters, overall reliability is good.

Despite these development limitations, the authors have paid careful attention to many other components for examining the psychometric properties of the scale.

ADMINISTRATION, SCORING AND INTERPRETATION.

User qualifications. There are no stated criteria for user qualifications as to scoring and interpretation, and there is no stated level of test protection, as is commonly reported for psychological measures for diagnosing emotional disturbance. The interpretation chapter states that teachers are making decisions about behavioral disorders and should be able to interpret the BDIS-2 SV. No statement that a psychologist is needed for an SED evaluation is noted. Implications and omissions regarding the school psychologist's role in SED assessments throughout the manual are problematic, as well as is omission of the role of the multidisciplinary team in making such decisions.

Administration. Directions for administration are included, and use of multiple raters is encouraged, which is good. There are clear instructions on how to complete the form and what each Likert unit means. Instructions for scoring are clear. It is not clear whether grouping the items for each scale together on the protocol influence respondent reporting.

Interpretation. Item interpretation is suggested by using the raw score for each item to determine severity. It would be nice to have conditional probability data to support this. Low standard scores indicate more severe problems, and the manual states that "If a student scores more than one standard deviation below the mean on any BDIS-2 SV subscale, the student is demonstrating significant behavior deviance in the educational environment and may be far more successful with a specialized support system ...[and] represents extreme behavior significant enough to qualify the student, along with documentation from other instruments, for special program services" (p. 27). No data regarding the statistical probability of having even ONE score only ONE standard deviation below the mean is presented. Most rating scales would indicate scores at the 1*SD* as at-risk and strongly caution that a diagnosis should not be made unless substantial data indicate a serious problem.

COMMENTARY. A much more thoughtful presentation and analysis for interpretation relevant to the seriousness of such decisions is needed. School diagnoses and labels have long-term consequences for children both in and out of school, and are not exempt from valid procedures for declaring that a child has a mental disorder.

Overall, although the authors' efforts are commendable, readers are strongly cautioned to avoid using this scale as a diagnostic instrument for classification of children as having an emotional disturbance, particularly using the interpretation guidelines in the manual. Other better-established instruments, such as the Behavior Assessment System for Children (BASC; T6:280) are recommended over the BDIS-2 for assessment of particular emotional and behavior problems. There continues to be a need for an instrument that is both empirically established and educationally useful, as the BASC has its own limitations in these areas. Readers are cautioned to consider results from any rating scale as only one small piece of information, and to use comprehensive assessment and response to intervention data to make eligibility decisions. The strength of the BDIS-2, the intervention manual, would be even greater with references that support the efficacy of treatments recommended. The items certainly represent behavioral concerns within the schools. Perhaps with substantially more psychometric work as outlined in this review, the test could live up to its promise.

SUMMARY. The Behavior Disorders Identification Scale—Second Edition, School and Home Versions, purport to measure the five major diagnostic categories for a classification of Serious Emotional Disturbance under the Individuals with Disabilities Education Act (IDEA). Each version has subscales for the areas of Learning Problems, Interpersonal Relations, Inappropriate Behavior, Unhappiness/Depression, and Physical Symptoms/Fears. Although substantial work was done in developing national norms for the test, items and subscales remain at the rational/theoretical level. Subscale principal component analyses indicate that the scale would better serve its purpose if these results had been used to develop scoring. Current subscales confound many important diagnostic issues, such as differential diagnosis of SED from other disorders such as LD and ADHD, and do not discriminate mental disorders that may respond to different treatment. Diagnostic recommendations are likely to overidentify children as having SED. The test is not recommended for eligibility determination. It, along with the intervention manual, may be used to pinpoint specific behaviors needing intervention, and as a screening tool to guide users to more appropriate broad and narrow band assessment techniques for a multifactored assessment.

Review of the Behavior Disorders Identification Scale—Second Edition by STEPHANIE STEIN, Professor of Psychology, and PHIL DIAZ, Assistant Professor of Psychology, Central Washington University, Ellensburg, WA:

DESCRIPTION. The Behavior Disorders Identification Scale, Second Edition (BDIS-2) is the current edition of two behavior rating scales, the School Version (BDIS-2-SV) and Home Version (BDIS-2-HV). The School Version consists of 83 items whereas the Home Version has 73. Each version is completed by someone who is familiar with the person to be rated and utilizes a 7-point scale. Each of the 7 points identifies the relative frequency with which the rater has observed the behavior. Descriptions ranging from "Not in my presence," "One time in several months," "Several times up to one time a month," "More than one time a month up to one time a week," "More than one time a week up to once a day," "More than once a day up to once an hour," and "More than once an hour" are represented as one through seven, respectively. Ratings are summed into five subscales and a total scale quotient. Subscales are titled Learning Problems, Interpersonal Relations, Inappropriate Behavior, Unhappiness/Depression, and Physical Symptoms/Fears.

Clinicians are to select raters carefully. Raters are to have developed "a measure of familiarity with the student," to be ranked (Home Version technical manual, p. 18). Rating and scoring takes approximately 20 minutes. Scores for the subscales are scale scores (mean = 10, SD = 3) and the total test quotient is a standard score (mean = 100, SD = 15) with available percentile ranks for the test quotient. The BDIS-2 is generally packaged with a teacher's guide to behavioral interventions that includes suggestions on how to develop behavioral objectives and intervene with 110 different student Behaviors.

DEVELOPMENT. The BDIS-2 is the latest version of the BDIS. The BDIS-2 is intended to identify children and youth, from 5 through 18 years of age, who may qualify under the Individuals with Disabilities Education Act (IDEA) as seriously emotionally disturbed, behaviorally disordered (SED/BD). The instrument was designed to address each of the five areas in Eli Bower's definition (1959), which form the basis for the IDEA criteria. The BDIS-2 is designed to document and quantify the existence of handicapping SED/BD criteria.

Materials provided by the publisher (two technical manuals and a companion guide entitled, Teacher's Guide to Behavioral Interventions) provide minimal information on the initial development of the BDIS and are silent regarding the differences between the BDIS and BDIS-2. Interpretation chapters in each of the technical manuals provide short descriptions of each of the five subscales and the total quotient.

TECHNICAL. The technical manuals do not address how cooperating school districts were recruited and selected to participate in norming the BDIS-2. Ratings were obtained on 2,478 individuals on the BDIS-2-HV (1,164 males, 1,314 females) and 3,986 individuals on the BDIS-2-SV (1,976 males, 2,010 females). Ratings spanned 14 ages with sample sizes ranging from 16 in the 18-year-old age range to 338 in the 8-year-old age range for the BDIS-2-HV and 194 (17- to 18-year-olds) to 1,180 (9- to 11-year-olds) on the BDIS-2-SV. Sampling is reported to reflect the 1998 U.S. census data as collected in 17 states for the BDIS-2-HV and 20 states for the BDIS-2-SV. Sampling underrepresents minorities, service and farm workers, and suburban sectors of the population as noted in 1998 Census.

The technical manuals also fail to describe the differences between the BDIS and the BDIS-2. Instead, the authors present the principal components factor analysis of the original BDIS as the development of the BDIS-2 and follows up with the principal components analysis of the BDIS-2. The authors present scree plots and rotated factor-loading tables with loadings above .30 reported as evidence of the BDIS-2's internal consistency and construct validity of the five-factor model. The scree plot for the BDIS-2-HV supports two factors and the scree plot for the BDIS-2-SV supports four factors. Factor loadings reveal a number of items that load equally well on multiple factors. The authors explain that five factors and items with multiple factor loadings are retained due to "theoretical purposes" (Home Version technical manual, p. 12). In this manner, the authors appear to be using exploratory factor analytic techniques for confirmatory purposes. No indices of fit are provided for the model, commonality coefficients are not provided, total percentage of variance accounted for by the model is not described, nor are the number of attempted iterations reported that produced the final factor loadings.

Content validity was reported as a product of a process in which the author generated a pool of possible items based upon review of the literature and suggestions from practicing professionals who work with students with SED/BD and parents of students with SED/BD. Those professionals and parents reviewed the final item pool for appropriateness and relevance; however, no pilot study was documented.

Concurrent validity was assessed utilizing a sample of 274 randomly selected individuals from the standardization sample who receive special education services in the area of SED/BD. These individuals were rated on the Behavior Evaluation Scale—Second Edition (McCarney, 1994; BES-2) and the Devereux Behavior Rating Scale—School Form (Naglieri, LeBuffe, & Pfeiffer, 1993; DBRS-SF). Significant correlations were noted with the DES-2 and ranged from .75 for Unhappiness/Depression to .98 on Physical Symptoms/Fears. The BDIS-2 significantly correlated with the DBRS-SF with correlations ranging from .65 on the Unhappiness/Depression subscale to .89 for the Interpersonal Relations and Physical Symptoms/Fears subscales.

The authors report "diagnostic validity" based on a randomly selected sample from the original BDIS norming group that numbered 284. Half the group were nonclinical and half were males who received special education services through the SED/BD category. The number of females in the clinical group was too few for comparison. The clinical group's mean scale scores were significantly lower than the nonclinical. No descriptions regarding controlling for various independent variables were noted. A similar study was not presented utilizing the BDIS-2.

Test-retest reliability analyses were accomplished on a randomly selected sample of the standardization sample consisting of 169 student records for the BDIS-2-SV and 77 for the BDIS-2-HV. These individuals were rated again at 30 days. Correlation coefficients for the total score quotient were .91 for the BDIS-2-SV and .82 for the BDIS-2-HV. Subscale coefficients ranged from .81 to .90 on the BDIS-2-SV and .72 to .86 on the BDIS-2-HV. Interrater reliability was examined by having two raters rate 84 individuals (168 behavior scales) on the BDIS-2-SV and 48 individuals (96 behavior scales) on the BDIS-2-HV. Correlations between raters were moderate, ranging from .57 to .81 for total score quotients on the BDIS-2-SV and BDIS-2-HV, respectively. Subscale coefficients were generally lower for the BDIS-2-SV (ranging from .33 to .64) and higher for the BDIS2-HV (.73 to .90). Internal consistency analysis resulted in alpha coefficients ranging from .82 to .90 on the BDIS-2-SV and .75 to .94 for the subscales on the BDIS-2-HV.

COMMENTARY. The primary value of the BDIS-2 is the attempt to quantify behaviors enabling educators and diagnosticians to systematically identify individuals with SED/BD. The BDIS-2 is designed to parallel the requirements of legislation resulting in the behavioral documentation required for qualification. Establishing normative data on the relative rates of behavior exhibited in nonclinical and clinical populations provides staffing teams with a means to compare relative rates of behavior objectively. To that end the authors suggest that anyone rated one standard deviation or more below the mean requires significant emotional or behavioral intervention. One standard deviation would identify approximately 16% of the student population, assuming school-aged students are normally distributed on these dimensions. Moreover, it does not require that a diagnostic classification be made.

Interpreting the total scale quotient as a measure of the student's overall behavioral functioning is helpful, but all items are phrased identifying difficulties in coping. This could produce a negative response bias, even though the rater is instructed to rate the relative number of times the behaviors have been observed. Many of the behaviors described are transparent. Should the rater want to make the student appear to have difficulties, the rater could easily inflate ratings. Interpreting the total scale quotient is also recommended based on the factor analysis. Item responses did not support a five-factor solution. Indeed, a four-factor solution appeared more appropriate for the BDIS-2-SV and a two-factor solution for the BDIS-2-HV. The authors support their decision to maintain the five factor structure and items that loaded heavily on more than one factor. Prudence suggests using the BDIS-2 primarily as a screening measure and only one of several data sources for making decisions. The authors agree that no decision should be made on the BDIS-2 alone. Additionally, the low numbers of students above 13 years of age in the standardization sample for the BDIS-2-HV make using this measure questionable for older students.

SUMMARY. The authors attempted to construct a rating scale that collects data from multiple sources to measure respondents' observations of relative rates of behavior efficiently and consistently. The items and subscales were designed to conform to the current definition codified in special education law. On balance, the authors' attempt is reasonable; however, the means they used to investigate the psychometric properties of the BDIS-2 did not confirm their theory. Despite this, the authors retained their a priori factor structure and multiple loading items and report single, small studies to provide evidence for reliability and validity of uses of the scores. No clear indication is given of how the BDIS-2 differs from the original BDIS, or if, in fact, there is a difference. The BDIS-2-SV and BDIS-2-HV can be used as screening measures; however, the reader is cautioned not to interpret the subscale scores. Readers seeking alternative tests to document the same areas may wish to examine the Behavior Assessment System for Children (Reynolds & Kamphaus, 1992) or the Devereux Behavior Rating Scale (Naglieri, LeBuffe, & Pfeiffer, 1993).

REVIEWERS' REFERENCES

Bower, E. (1959). The emotionally handicapped child and the school. *Exceptional Children, 26*, 6–11.
McCarney, S. B. (1994). *Behavior Evaluation Scale (2ⁿᵈ ed.): School Version technical manual.* Columbia, MO: Hawthorne Educational Services, Inc.
Naglieri, J. A., LeBuffe, P. A., & Pfeiffer, S. I. (1993). Devereux Behavior Rating Scale–School Form. San Antonio, TX: The Psychological Corporation.
Reynolds, C. R, & Kamphaus, R. W. (1992). Behavior Assessment System for Children. Circle Pines, MN: American Guidance Service, Inc.

[27]

Behavior Rating Inventory of Executive Function—Preschool Version.

Purpose: Designed to "assess executive function behaviors in the home and preschool environments."
Population: Ages 2-0 to 5-11.
Publication Dates: 1996–2003.

Acronym: BRIEF-P™.
Scores, 9: Inhibit, Shift, Emotional Control, Working Memory, Plan/Organize, Inhibitory Self-Control Index, Flexibility Index, Emergent Metacognition Index, Global Executive Composite.
Administration: Individual.
Price Data, 2005: $119 per introductory kit including manual (2003, 111 pages), 25 rating forms, and 25 scoring summary/profile forms; $54 per manual; $45 per 25 rating forms; $30 per 25 scoring summary/ profile forms.
Time: (10–15) minutes.
Comments: Behavior rating scale is completed by parent or teacher/child care worker who is familiar with the child.
Authors: Gerard A. Gioia, Kimberly Andrews Espy, and Peter K. Isquith.
Publisher: Psychological Assessment Resources, Inc.

Review of the Behavior Rating Inventory of Executive Function—Preschool Version by R. ANTHONY DOGGETT, Assistant Professor of Educational Psychology, and CARL J. SHEPERIS, Assistant Professor of Counselor Education, Mississippi State University, Starkville, MS:

DESCRIPTION AND DEVELOPMENT. "The Behavior Rating Inventory of Executive Function-Preschool Version (BRIEF-P) is a questionnaire for parents and teachers of preschool-aged children that enables professionals to assess executive function behaviors in the home and preschool environments" (professional manual, p. 1). The instrument is designed for a broad range of children between the ages of 2 years, 0 months and 5 years, 11 months including children with attentional disorders, emergent learning disabilities, language disorders, pervasive developmental disorders, traumatic brain injuries, lead exposure, and other potential developmental, neurological, medical, and psychiatric conditions. The BRIEF-P contains 63 items within five clinical scales (i.e., Inhibit, Shift, Emotional, Control, Working Memory, Plan/Organize) that measure different aspects of executive functioning. There are two validity scales (i.e., Inconsistency and Negativity) designed to measure inconsistent and/or excessively negative responses. The five clinical scales form three broader indexes (i.e., Inhibitory Self-Control, Flexibility, Emergent Metacognition) and an overall composite score labeled as the Global Executive Composite. The primary focus of the BRIEF-P is on executive functions that are "a collection of processes that are responsible for guiding, directing, and managing cognitive, emotional, and behavioral functions, particularly during novel problem solving" (professional manual, p. 1).

The original BRIEF (Gioia, Isquith, Guy, & Kenworthy, 2000; 15:32), designed for use with school-age children, served as the basis for the development of the BRIEF-P. The preschool version "was designed to address the need for measurement of executive function and early detection of self-regulatory difficulties in younger children" (professional manual, p. 37). Review of pertinent literature, consultation with colleagues experienced in research and clinical work with children, review of clinical cases, and examination of other empirically sound rating scales yielded an initial 97-item rating scale. After examination of the psychometric properties of the individual items and clarification of the scale structure through principal factor analysis procedures, a final 63-item scale remained.

The BRIEF-P takes approximately 10-15 minutes to administer. One version is administered to parents and/or school personnel (e.g., preschool teacher, teacher's aide/assistant, day care provider) who know the child well (i.e., for at least 1 month). Each informant rates how often specific behaviors have been *problematic* for the child over the past 6 months relative to other children of the same age. Items are rated on a Likert scale using *never* (N), *sometimes* (S), or *often* (O). These descriptors are translated into raw scores for each item where a rating of *never* receives a score of 1, a rating of *sometimes* yields a score of 2, and a rating of *often* yields a score of 3. Calculation of the raw scores for each of the five clinical scales and two validity scales is easily completed using the carbonless scoring sheet. *T*-scores and percentile ranks for the five clinical scales, three index scales, and global executive composite are obtained using normative tables in the appendices of the manual. Summary and profile forms are available to aid in the interpretation of the BRIEF-P.

The BRIEF-P is accompanied by a 105-page, well-written manual, complete with five chapters discussing the development, administration, scoring, interpretation, reliability, validity, and standardization of the instrument. Five case illustrations are included in the manual, which aid in the interpretation of the scores. The authors provided thorough discussions about the theoreti-cal and empirical basis for the inclusion of the items, development of the clinical scales and indexes, and normative and validation procedures.

TECHNICAL.

Norming-standardization procedures. A total of 460 parents and 302 teachers completed the BRIEF-P for children aged 2 to 5 years. Normative data samples were obtained through public and private school recruitment and pediatric well-child visits in urban, suburban, and rural settings across six states. A total of 20 preschool programs were sampled. As a result, samples approximated key demographic variables of the U.S. population.

Reliability. The manual reports internal consistency, interrater agreement, and test-retest stability for the BRIEF-P. Internal consistency reliability estimates were high, with alpha coefficients ranging from .80 to .95 across scales, indexes, and the composite score for the parent sample. Internal consistency ratings were slightly higher for teacher ratings with all scores falling at the .90 level and above. Interrater agreement ratings across the scales, indexes, and composite score were modest between the parent and teacher raters ranging from .06 to .28 with an overall mean correlation of .19. However, the authors appropriately point out that this finding is not entirely unexpected due to the fact that the expectations and opportunities for the performance of behaviors is not the same across home and school settings. For the parent sample, test-retest correlations across the clinical scales ranged from .78 to .90 with a mean of .86. Test-retest correlations for the three indexes and composite score ranged from .87 to .90. Stability of ratings was examined over a period of 1 to 9.5 weeks with an average interval of 4.5 weeks for the parent sample. For the teacher sample, test-retest correlations across the clinical scales ranged from .65 to .94, with a mean of .83. The test-retest correlations on the three indexes and composite score ranged from .77 to .92. The test-retest interval for the teacher sample ranged from 2.1 to 5.6 weeks, with an average of 4.2 weeks. Finally, the authors found that the *T*-scores remained stable over the test-retest interval across the groups, supporting "the repeat administration of the BRIEF-P with no significant degree of variability expected due to the instrument itself" (professional manual, p. 49). This finding makes the instrument useful for monitoring treatment effects.

Validity. The authors noted that valid interpretation of the BRIEF-P scores is based on "(a) the content of the items, (b) the convergence and divergence of BRIEF-P scores with those of other measures, and (c) the internal structure of the BRIEF-P" (professional manual, p. 49). Item content was developed through clinical interviews with parents and teachers as well as guidance from empirical literature and the expertise of pediatric neuropsychologists who have significant clinical experience with children in this age range who experience a variety of conditions that affect executive functioning. Using normative and clinically referred samples, convergent and divergent validity was addressed through correlational studies between the BRIEF-P and three other well-known behavioral rating scales: ADHD Rating Scale-IV, Preschool Version (ADHD-IV-P; McGoey, Bradley-Klug, Crone, Shelton, & Radcliffe, 2000); Child Behavior Checklist (CBCL/1 1/2-5; Achenbach & Rescorla, 2000); and Behavior Assessment System for Children (BASC; Reynolds & Kamphaus, 1992).

Significant correlations were obtained between the clinical scales and indexes on the BRIEF-P and the other measures across parent and teacher samples with regard to both internalizing and externalizing behaviors. Detailed information is presented in the manual with regard to divergent and convergent validity for the interested reader. Principal factor analysis with an oblique rotational procedure was used to evaluate the internal structure of the BRIEF-P across normative and clinical samples. Using the parent normative sample, parent clinical sample, and teacher normative sample, a three-factor model was retained as the best fitting model with Working Memory and Plan/Organize loading significantly on the first factor, Shift and Emotional Control loading on the second factor, and Inhibit and Emotional Control loading on the third factor. The three scales were moderately correlated with one another across the three analyses.

COMMENTARY. Strengths of the BRIEF-P include (a) easy administration and scoring, (b) user-friendly manual that is well organized and employs graphics to convey technical information, (c) summary and profile forms that aid in interpretation and explanation of results, (d) adequate standardization sample, (e) good reliability and validity evidence, and (f) sound theoretical basis.

Weaknesses include use of subjective ratings that are largely influenced by how well the rater knows the child.

SUMMARY. The BRIEF-P is a well-designed, useful measure for the assessment of executive function behaviors in preschool children across home and school environments. The instrument provides scores across five clinical subscales, three indexes, and a global executive composite. The instrument also contains inconsistency and negativity scales to assess appropriate responding from respondents. Although structured rating scales are often used by professionals because of their efficiency, the BRIEF-P will be best utilized as a component of a thorough assessment battery including clinical interviews, other behavioral rating scales, and direct observations. Finally, further investigation with populations and instruments other than those used by the authors of the BRIEF-P will continue to provide valuable information about the psychometric properties and clinical utility of the instrument.

REVIEWERS' REFERENCES

Achenbach, T. M., & Rescorla, L. A. (2000). *Manual for the ASEBA preschool forms and profiles.* Burlington: University of Vermont, Research Center for Children, Youth, and Families.
Gioia, G. A., Isquith, P. K., Guy, S. C., & Kenworthy, L. (2000). The Behavior Rating Inventory of Executive Function. Odessa, FL: Psychological Assessment Resources.
McGoey, K. E., Bradley-Klug, K., Crone, D., Shelton, T. L., & Radcliffe, J. (2000, April). *Normative data of the ADHD-Rating Scale IV-Preschool version.* Paper presented at the annual convention of the National Association of School Psychologists, New Orleans, LA.
Reynolds, C. R., & Kamphaus, R. W. (1992). Behavior Assessment System for Children. Circle Pines, MN: American Guidance Service.

Review of the Behavior Rating Inventory of Executive Function—Preschool Version by LEAH M. NELLIS, School Psychologist, RISE Special Services, Indianapolis, IN:

DESCRIPTION. The Behavior Rating Inventory of Executive Function—Preschool Version (BRIEF-P) is a questionnaire designed to be completed by parents and preschool teachers of children aged 2 years through 5 years, 11 months. The rating scale assesses the executive function processes and is organized into five clinical scales: Inhibit, Shift, Emotional Control, Working Memory, and Plan/Organize and four indexes: Inhibitory Self-Control, Flexibility, Emergent Metacognition, and the Global Executive Composite. Two validity scales, Inconsistency and Negativity, are also available.

Response to the 63 items of the BRIEF-P is on a 3-point Likert scale (*Never, Sometimes,* and *Often*) with regard to how often the behaviors have been problematic in the last 6 months. Test authors point out that all preschool children exhibit the item behaviors at some time, but that the rating reflects how problematic the behaviors have been, not how frequently they have occurred. The carbonless rating form can be scored by hand and produces T scores, percentile ranks, and confidence intervals for the scales and indexes. According to the manual, the BRIEF-P was designed for use by professionals in the assessment of young children with emerging learning disabilities, attentional disorders, pervasive developmental disorders, traumatic brain injury, and other medical and developmental conditions as well as in the design of treatment and intervention programming.

DEVELOPMENT. Theoretically, the BRIEF is based upon neuropsychological research and recognizes "executive functions" as a collective of cognitive processes that serve to direct and manage cognitive, emotional, and behavioral functions that are brain based and developmental in nature. The school-age version of the BRIEF served as the foundation for development of the BRIEF-P. The development process of the BRIEF-P began with literature reviews and clinical interviews with professionals in the field of neuropsychology that resulted in the development of items specific to preschool-aged children. These possible items were combined with the 86 items from the original BRIEF, which had been revised to reflect behaviors found in young children, to form a pool of 140 items. In addition, published behavior rating scales were also reviewed to ensure that the BRIEF-P provided a unique, focused assessment with limited overlap with more general behavior scales. The initial item pool was reduced to 97 items after addressing item redundancy, reading level, and overall clarity.

The 97-item tryout version was completed by 372 parents and 201 teachers from the Midwest, Mid-Atlantic, and Northeast regions of the United States. Data on children with identified disabilities or developmental delays were not included in the analysis.

Test authors reviewed statistical properties, such as high item means, frequency of missing responses, and dispersion indexes; item-total score correlations; and factor analysis results to select the items with the highest internal consistency and scale structure. This process resulted in a final version consisting of 63 items.

TECHNICAL. The manual states that the BRIEF-P was standardized with 460 parents and 302 teachers recruited through preschool and medical practices across six states (Maryland, Illinois, Vermont, New Hampshire, Florida, and Texas). Children ranged in age from 2 to 5 years with 67% of the girls being 3 and 4 years of age and 73% of the boys being 3 and 4 years. The sample consisted of approximately equal numbers of boys and girls, 246 and 214, respectively, for parent ratings and 164 and 138, respectively, for teacher ratings. Both parent and teacher samples were primarily white (73%, parent and 72%, teacher) in ethnicity with limited representation of African American (14%, teacher and 12%, parent) and Hispanic (5% parent and teacher) ethnicities. Seventy-four percent of the parent sample was from upper, upper-middle, middle-middle socioeconomic status with only 10% from low SES. The majority of the parent respondents were mothers (88.7%) although analyses indicated no significant differences between mother and father respondents. Additionally, parent educational level reportedly did not have a meaningful impact on ratings.

The manual reports high internal consistency reliability with coefficients ranging from a low of .80 (Plan/Organize scale on Parent rating) to a high of .97 (Plan/Organize and Global Composite on Teacher rating). For each scale, coefficients were higher on the teacher ratings than the parent ratings. Interrater agreement was addressed by examining correlation coefficients between parent and teacher ratings of the same child. Correlations were modest with an overall mean coefficient of .19. Ratings on the Inhibit, Shift, and Emotional Control scales were more strongly correlated (coefficients from .25 to .28) than those for the Working Memory ($r = .14$) and Plan/Organize scales ($r = .06$). Test-retest reliability was examined with a small group of parents ($n = 52$) and teachers ($n = 67$). Test-retest correlations for the parent subsample ranged from .78 to .90 for the clinical scales and .87 to .90 for the indexes, with an average interval of 4.5 weeks. For the teacher subsample, correlations ranged from .65 to .94 for the clinical scales and .77 to .92 for the indexes, with an average interval of 4.2 weeks. T-score differences were examined using the test-retest data with minimal changes reported (1.6 T-score points for the clinical scales and less than 2.0 for the indexes).

Evidence of construct and concurrent validity is based upon divergent and concurrent relationships and factor analysis. For both the parent and teacher samples, the relationship between the BRIEF-P and the ADHD Rating Scale-IV Preschool Version (ADHD-IV-P), the Child Behavior Checklist (CBCL), and the Behavior Assessment System for Children (BASC) was investigated. Test authors postulated that the BRIEF-P Working Memory scale would be highly related to scales of inattention on other measures and that the Inhibit scale would be highly related to scales of externalizing behaviors with lower correlations with theoretically unrelated constructs. Analyses using the ADHD-IV-P demonstrated the expected correlation patterns for both parents (n = 135) and teachers (n = 40). However, the expected relationship was not found in analyses using the CBCL (n = 137) or the BASC (n = 20).

Exploratory factor analyses were conducted using the normative samples. For both the parent and teacher respondents, a three-factor model was retained as the best fitting model. The Emotional Control scale loaded on the Inhibitory Self-Control factor (r = .63) and secondarily on the Flexibility factor (r = .37) but contributes to both indexes for scoring purposes. Similarly, the Inhibit scale loaded secondarily on the Emergent Metacognition factor but does not contribute to that index for scoring purposes. Thus, interpretation of the index scores should be done cautiously. Group differences were also investigated using clinical samples of children with identified ADHD (n = 17), prematurity (n = 34), language disorder (n = 21), and autism spectrum disorders (n = 16, mean age 6.7 years). These studies show preliminary evidence of the potential utility that the BRIEF-P has for discriminating between various diagnostic groups. Future research is needed to support the use of the BRIEF-P for such diagnostic purposes.

COMMENTARY. The BRIEF-P represents a valuable contribution to the assessment of young children. The importance of developing executive functioning is critical in evaluation and intervention planning and monitoring. The theoretical underpinnings of the instrument are a strength and are well explained by the test authors. Two areas of concern are noted for further consideration. First, the standardization sample was composed primarily of children between the ages of 3 to 4 years, which may limit utility with the broad age range for which the scale was developed. In addition, the sample was primarily white and from upper to middle income families. Because ratings reflect a parent's perception of how problematic a behavior has been, there is a potential for significant differences across socioeconomic, cultural, and ethnic backgrounds. These potential differences should be explored further. Second, the interpretation of the Index scores may be confounded by having some scales contribute to more than one Index score. More investigation into the factor structure may provide future recommendations.

SUMMARY. The BRIEF-P fills a critical void in the early childhood assessment repertoire. The conceptual foundation appears solid and well articulated and clearly has importance in identification of emerging learning and behavioral difficulties. In clinical practice, this reviewer has found the BRIEF-P to be user friendly for parents and easy to score and interpret. Of equal importance, the scale has provided a unique contribution to a comprehensive assessment and opened the door for discussion about numerous areas of strength and weakness that can be addressed through intervention and programming. Continued research in regard to the factor structure will be beneficial in expanding the understanding and interpretation of the results.

[28]

Behavior Rating Inventory of Executive Function—Self-Report Version.

Purpose: Designed to assess children's and adolescents' "views of their own executive functions, or self-regulation, in their everyday environment."

Population: Ages 11–18.

Publication Dates: 1996–2004.

Acronym: BRIEF-SR.

Scores, 15: Behavioral Regulation Index (Inhibit, Shift, Emotional Control, Monitor, Total), Metacognition Index (Working Memory, Plan/Organize, Organization of Materials, Task Completion, Total), Global Executive Composite, Behavioral Shift, Cognitive Shift, Inconsistency, Negativity.

Administration: Individual.

Price Data, 2005: $135 per introductory kit including professional manual (2004, 204 pages), 25 rating forms, and 50 scoring summary/profile forms; $55 per professional manual; $53 per 25 rating forms; $32 per 50 scoring summary/profile forms.

Time: (10–15) minutes.
Authors: Steven C. Guy, Peter K. Isquith, and Gerard A. Gioia.
Publisher: Psychological Assessment Resources, Inc.

Review of the Behavior Rating Inventory of Executive Function-Self-Report Version by STEPHEN L. BENTON, Professor of Educational Psychology, and SHERYL BENTON, Assistant Director of Counseling Services, Kansas State University, Manhattan, KS:

DESCRIPTION. The Behavior Rating Inventory of Executive Function-Self-Report (BRIEF-SR) is an 80-item standardized self-report inventory, administered by paper-and-pencil. It assesses self-regulation in children and adolescents, ages 11–18, who have at least a fifth-grade reading level. Respondents read a list of statements that describe young people's behaviors and then indicate whether they have had any "problems" with these behaviors over the past 6 months. All items are selection type (1 = *never* a problem, 2 = *sometimes* a problem, and 3 = *often* a problem). Derived scores are generated for eight clinical scales: Inhibit, Shift, Emotional Control, Monitor, Working Memory, Plan/Organize, Organization of Materials, and Task Completion. Scales are grouped into either a Behavioral Regulation Index (BRI) or a Metacognition Index (MI), which together form the Global Executive Composite (GEC). Behavioral Shift and Cognitive Shift are additional subscales that purportedly assess behavioral adaptiveness and cognitive flexibility, although their construct validity has not been established.

Nonclinical staff can administer and score the BRIEF-SR; however, interpretation requires relevant graduate education in psychological assessment. Hand scoring is done within several minutes. Age- and gender-specific *T*-scores, percentile ranks, and 90% confidence intervals are available. *T*-scores plotted on a Profile Form reveal the pattern of BRIEF-SR scales. An Inconsistency scale is determined by summing the absolute raw score differences between 10 sets of paired items. A Negativity scale is determined by counting the number of 10 negatively worded items that have raw scores of 3.

DEVELOPMENT. The BRIEF-SR was developed from the original BRIEF (Gioia, Isquith, Guy, & Kenworthy, 2000), created for parents and teachers to rate children, ages 5 to 18 years. The 86 items from the BRIEF were reworded into first

person (e.g., "Is impulsive" became "I am impulsive") and into language appropriate for adolescents (e.g., "My playroom is a mess" became "My desk/workspace is a mess"). The authors wrote additional items based on clinical experience. Responses from normative and clinical samples of adolescents led to the current 80-item scale. Several items contain clarifying parenthetical statements, which may indicate the initial item was worded poorly. For example, "I have a poor understanding of my own strengths and weaknesses (I try things that are too difficult or too easy for me)."

The professional manual provides information about the theory underlying the instrument and its development. The descriptions of clinical scales and subscales are fairly extensive, and citations of relevant research are helpful. However, the empirical evidence is not convincing enough to warrant valid interpretation of the clinical scales. The authors categorized items into scale subgroupings, based on the original BRIEF, prior to conducting the factor analysis on the BRIEF-SR. Because the authors assumed the factor structure among the items prior to investigation, the eight clinical scales are neither empirically derived nor confirmed. Similarly, the validity subscales—Inconsistency and Negativity—were created based on the authors' judgments about items they believed assessed those constructs. They were not derived from interitem correlations. The lack of standard scores on the validity scales also renders them less meaningful. Unfortunately, the authors failed to caution readers about the limitations of interpreting individual clinical scales.

TECHNICAL. The description of the norming sample and process is adequate. The claim that the normative sample represents U.S. Census Bureau demographics should have been supported with evidence. Separate gender norms are reported across two broad age groups: 11-to-14-year-olds and 15-to-18-year-olds. However, the authors failed to examine developmental differences within each broad age range. Ideally, separate gender norms should have been reported for ages 11 to 18.

Internal consistency reliability was estimated from the normative sample. Cronbach alpha coefficients for the eight clinical scales ranged from .72 to .87; those for the BRI (.93), MI (.95), and GEC (.96) were slightly higher. Stability was examined on a subsample of only 59 cases, inadequately described, over intervals ranging from approximately 2 to 10 weeks. Stability coefficients ranged from .59 to .85 on the clinical scales and from .84 to .89 for the two indices and the GEC. Alternate forms/interrater agreement was assessed in a combined clinical and normative sample of 243 adolescents who self-rated on the BRIEF-SR, and whose parents completed the BRIEF. Correlations between self- and parent-ratings on clinical scales, indices, and the GEC were moderate, ranging from .36 to .57. Self-ratings on the BRIEF-SR were paired with teacher ratings on the BRIEF in a normative and clinical sample of 148 adolescents. Correlations between self- and teacher-ratings were generally low, ranging from .20 to .41.

The authors did not report standard errors of measurement for all subscale and total scale raw scores and derived scores. In addition, reliability estimates were not reported for the separate gender and age groupings. Finally, confidence intervals should have accompanied all reliability estimates to remind test users that such estimates are subject to error (Fan & Thompson, 2003).

Validity evidence is mixed. The authors generated their initial set of items from interviews with parents, teachers, and adolescent clients. They also drew upon the expertise of several pediatric neuropsychologists who evaluated the test items. More information could have been provided about the level of agreement among consultants. Because no other self-report rating scale of executive function exists for adolescents, the authors correlated scores on the BRIEF-SR with other rating scales of attention and behavior. The descriptions of the samples used in assessing convergent validity are adequate, but the descriptions of the other rating scales are not. Although the authors proposed a few hypotheses about anticipated relationships between other rating scales and the BRIEF-SR, none is given in most cases. The authors wisely cautioned the reader to examine most closely the correlations between summary measures on each instrument and the GEC rather than the eight clinical scales. Overall, the BRIEF-SR GEC correlated moderately with the Child Behavior Checklist/Youth Self-Report *Total Problems* scale, and the Profile of Mood States-Short Form *Total Mood Disturbance* score.

Evidence to support construct validity is suspect. The authors performed factor analyses on the normative and clinical samples, using the hy-pothesized eight clinical scales as the unit of analysis. Because an exploratory rather than a confirmatory factor analysis was conducted, no goodness-of-fit indices were derived, making it difficult to assess the validity of the eight-scale model. Although the authors provided some evidence to support a two-factor solution, factor loadings for the eight scales are reported for only one of the two factors. Loadings on both factors should have been reported for all eight scales so that the reader could discern any ambiguities.

Discriminant evidence comes from studies comparing normative samples with clinical samples of adolescents with attention-deficit-hyperactivity disorder, autism spectrum disorders, emotional disorders, or insulin-dependent diabetes mellitus plus attentional learning and/or emotional disorders. Descriptions of the normative and clinical samples were adequate. Across all studies, adolescents in the normative samples scored lower, on average, on several subscales and the GEC than did those in the clinical samples.

COMMENTARY. The description of the clinical use of this test is a strong point. The authors appropriately advise readers to interpret the test results within the context of other test results and behavioral observations. The test provides two validity scales: The Inconsistency Scale, which purportedly indicates the extent to which respondents' answers are inconsistent relative to those in the combined normative and clinical samples, and a Negativity Scale, which purportedly indicates the extent to which respondents answered in an unusually negative manner. The parallel instruments for parents, teachers, and adolescents provide useful clinical material that would likely facilitate helpful discussions about the similarities and differences among each respondent's perception of problem areas. The breadth of coverage of the test scales adds to this clinical utility, although the questionable construct validity makes it difficult to feel confident about any conclusions drawn.

SUMMARY. The BRIEF-SR is an easily administered, scored, and interpreted instrument intended to assess self-regulation in children and adolescents through self-report. The instrument is designed to parallel the BRIEF, created for parents and teachers to rate children on self-regulation. Availability of parallel instruments is a particular strength because it likely enhances clinical utility and promotes helpful discussion among parents, teachers, and adolescents as to relative strengths and weaknesses. Given the questionable validity of the eight-scale model, users should limit their interpretations to the BRI, MI, and GEC.

REVIEWERS' REFERENCES

Fan, X., & Thompson, B. (2003). Confidence intervals about score reliability coefficients. In *Score reliability: Contemporary thinking on reliability issues* (pp. 69–84). Thousand Oaks, CA: Sage Publications.

Gioia, G. A., Isquith, P. K., Guy, S. C., & Kenworthy, L. (2000). *The Behavior Rating Inventory of Executive Function professional manual.* Odessa, FL: Psychological Assessment Resources.

Review of the Behavior Rating Inventory of Executive Function—Self-Report Version by MANUEL MARTINEZ-PONS, Professor of Education, Brooklyn College of the City University of New York, Belle Harbor, NY:

DESCRIPTION. The Behavior Rating Inventory of Executive Function—Self-Report Version (BRIEF-SR) is an 80-item inventory of personal processes that guide, direct, and manage cognitive, emotional, and behavioral functioning. The self-report instrument is designed for use with children and adolescents aged between 11 and 18 years, reading at a fifth-grade level or higher. It can be used with normal individuals as well as with individuals with various forms of developmental, neurological, psychiatric, and medical conditions.

The Brief-SR yields measures of eight executive functions that the authors term Inhibit, Shift, Emotional Control, Monitor, Working Memory, Plan/Organize, Organization of Materials, and Task Completion. Scores on these scales are combined in different ways to yield an overall Global Executive Composite Summary Score, a Behavioral Regulation Index, and a Metacognition Index. The test also contains inconsistency and negativity scales that help the user in ascertaining the degree to which the test taker has answered the items truthfully.

The authors developed the Brief-SR as part of an effort to overcome what they saw as a limitation in the traditional clinical assessment of executive function: the difficulty of pencil-and-paper tests in dealing with the function's dynamic nature, and the difficulty of performance assessment in tapping the function's integrated multidimensional nature.

DEVELOPMENT. The authors derived the Brief-SR's items from the BRIEF, a parent and teacher rating scale of children's executive func-

tion. In constructing the BRIEF, the authors, on the basis of clinical interviews, generated items that they sorted statistically and theoretically into the domains that eventually became the basis of the eight scales of the BRIEF-SR. From an original pool of 180 items the authors extracted 86 items for the BRIEF on the basis of item content analysis, item-score correlations, factor analysis, and internal consistency reliability findings. Following a review of the literature, the authors revised the 86 items of the BRIEF as self-statements for the BRIEF-SR, and they reviewed the revised items for age appropriateness. Further interviews with clinically and demographically diverse populations of children and adolescents yielded additional material for the BRIEF-SR item pool, and a review of standardized behavior scales enabled the authors to eliminate items that might reflect constructs not part of the conceptual basis of the BRIEF-SR. The authors tried out the resulting pool of 135 items with 197 normal adolescents and 230 clinical adolescents ranging in age between 11 and 18 years. On the bases of internal consistency reliability analysis, multivariate analysis of variance, and factor analysis outcomes, the authors reduced the test to 80 items for the final version of the BRIEF-SR.

TECHNICAL. The authors standardized the BRIEF-SR with over 1,000 adolescents aged between 11 and 18 years approximating ethnicity and gender proportions in the U.S. population according to Census Bureau data. No statistically significant effects of ethnicity emerged in the way in which the normative sample responded to the scale's items; SES proved to exhibit low negative correlations ranging between .10 and .13 with some of the subscales. For the age range of 15 through 18 years, boys tended to exhibit higher scores on all of the domains than did girls—except for Emotional Control, for which girls tended to score higher. The authors developed norms for the eight scales of the Brief-SR in the form of T scores and associated percentile ranks. They provide a table showing the means and standard deviations by gender and age group (11–14 years and 15–18 years) for the normative sample.

The authors report internal consistency Cronbach alpha reliabilities ranging between .72 for individual scales and .96 for the 80-item scale; and they report test-retest reliabilities ranging between .59 and .85 for the subscales, and .89 for the 80-item scale for administration intervals from 1–10 weeks. Interrater reliability estimates of BRIEF-SR ratings and BRIEF ratings by parents and teachers ranged between a low of .36 to a moderate .56 for parents, and .20 to .41 for teachers. The interrater reliabilities the authors report, and the interpretation they provide for these findings raise some issues concerning the validity of the test scores. These issues are discussed below in relation to the test's validity evidence.

One weak part of the authors' account of the BRIEF-SR involves the scale's validation. They report information regarding the scale's content, its convergent-discriminant properties, and its concurrent validity. Regarding content, the only decisive factor the authors report is that of whether in their judgment the scale's items reflect a number of ideas about executive functioning that they derived from clinical interviews and from input by a number of pediatric neurologists. But to simply say that they feel that their instrument reflects their thinking and let it go at that is self-referential and ignores a basic principle of scientific inquiry, which is *corroboration*. A true test of the BRIEF-SR's content validity would have involved assessment of the level of agreement between independent expert judges regarding the degree to which the scale's items and structure reflect the theory on which the scale is based.

A second problem with the validation of the BRIEF-SR involves the convergence-discriminant analyses the authors report. They performed exploratory factor analyses for the purpose, stipulating a two-factor model on the basis of speculation surrounding previous findings. Although the percentage of variance explained was substantial (70% for a normative sample and 74% for a clinical sample) the issue of corroboration applies in this case as well as it did in the case of the scales' content validation. The appropriate corroborative procedure to use to test the scale's convergent-discriminant properties would have been confirmatory factor analysis (CFA). CFA enables the investigator to test the stipulation of any number of factors by reference to the hypothesized model's fit of the data, as well as by the test of the statistical significance of the factor loadings. In the absence of this corroborative evidence, it is not legitimate to say that the items of the BRIEF-SR comprise the two-factor model stipulated by the authors.

Third, the criterion validation of the BRIEF-SR raises some questions concerning the ultimate ability of the scale to assess executive function. Noting the low correlations that emerged between BRIEF-SR and BRIEF ratings, the authors state, "In this case, adolescents are asked to reflect on their own self-regulatory capabilities. Theoretically, this requires a level of self-awareness that may not yet be adequately developed" (professional manual, p. 48). But if this is the case, does the fact not invalidate the very idea of asking adolescents, let alone children, to reflect on their executive functioning? Why not just use the adults' ratings and save the time and effort required to obtain what would be children's untrustworthy responses? In fact, the authors recommend that the Brief-SR be used in conjunction with the BRIEF, and state that differences between adults' and children's ratings on the two scales may be profitably interpreted as indicative of the children's lack of self-awareness. On the other hand, what if the two ratings agree as they must for the adult ratings to serve as criterion? The fact would still remain that, as the authors note, children have not developed neurologically to the point where their self-ratings can be trusted. But if their self-ratings cannot be trusted and they agree with those of adults, then it must be that the adults' ratings cannot be trusted. But if the adults' ratings cannot be trusted, how can they be used as the criterion against which to validate the children's self-rating?

The known-groups concurrent criterion tests the authors' report with normative groups, and groups experiencing ADHD and autism spectrum disorder do offer some evidence of the scale's ability to discriminate between normative and clinical populations. However, as the authors note, these tests were limited in their scope because the clinical samples were not experiencing problems on the exact BRIEF-SR domains on which the normative samples were tested.

Finally, what is possibly a minor point, all the items of the BRIEF-SR are presented in negative form. Although the authors feel this step was necessitated by their finding that positively stated items tended to be scored excessively high—constricting their variability—the possibility of a response set cannot be ruled out. One way around this issue might be to administer the scale with all items stated positively, and then reword in negative form items that do not exhibit an inflated response—although not enough items may survive this test to provide a balanced presentation.

COMMENTARY. The development of the Brief-SR—involving the generation of a large item pool based on clinical information, the pool's reduction through meticulous content and statistical analysis, the considerable effort that went into the scale's standardization, and extensive testing of the scale's internal consistency and stability—serves as a fine example of rigorous test development. However, its validation falls short of demonstrating the scale's ability to focus on the self-regulatory executive function of its intended population—even if used, as the authors recommend, in conjunction with the adult-administered BRIEF.

SUMMARY. Notwithstanding the rigorous development of the BRIEF-SR, the test's validation does not fully address the issue of whether the instrument addresses its intended target, and a potential user is left with the question, "If a child scores high on any part of the BRIEF-SR can I assume that he or she is truly experiencing a problem in this area? And if he or she scores low, can I assume that he or she is not experiencing a problem in this area?" Given the critical nature of decisions made on the basis of answers to questions such as these, it seems that much more validation of the BRIEF-SR is needed before the scale can be recommended for use for its intended purpose.

[29]

Behavioral and Emotional Rating Scale, Second Edition.

Purpose: Designed to "measure the personal strengths and competencies of children."
Population: Ages 5-0 to 18-11.
Publication Dates: 1998–2004.
Acronym: BERS-2.
Scores, 6: 5 subscales: Interpersonal Strength, Family Involvement, Intrapersonal Strength, School Functioning, Affective Strength, plus Strength Index.
Administration: Individual.
Price Data, 2004: $143 per complete kit including examiner's manual (2004, 112 pages), 25 teacher rating scales, 25 parent rating scales, 25 youth rating scales, and 50 summary forms; $51 per examiner's manual; $24 per 25 teacher rating scales; $25 per parent rating scales; $25 per youth rating scales; $25 per 50 summary forms.
Time: (10) minutes.

Comments: Revised edition adds Parent and Youth Rating Scales.
Author: Michael H. Epstein.
Publisher: PRO-ED.
Cross References: For reviews by Beth Doll and by D. Joe Olmi of an earlier edition, see 14:42.

Review of the Behavioral and Emotional Rating Scale—Second Edition by JOHN D. KING, Professor Emeritus, University of Texas at Austin, Licensed Psychologist, National Health Service Provider, Licensed Specialist in School Psychology, Austin, TX:

DESCRIPTION. The Behavioral and Emotional Rating Scale—Second Edition (BERS-2) is a battery of three rating scales, including the Teacher Rating Scale (TRS), the Parent Rating Scale (PRS), and the Youth Rating Scale (YRS). It is a standardized, norm-referenced instrument that is designed to assess children's emotional and behavioral strengths. The test can be used for children ages 5 to 18 years. Each of the three rating scales is made up of five core subscales: Interpersonal Strength, Family Involvement, Intrapersonal Strength, School Functioning, and Affective Strength. The PRS and YRS also contain a supplemental Career Strength subscale. Each rating scale yields a Strength Index, which is a composite score. Components of the BERS-2 include the examiner's manual, the TRS, PRS, YRS forms, and a Summary form. The TRS contains 52 items. The PRS and YRS each have 57 items. The Summary form can be used to record and compare scores from each rating scale. According to the manual, information should be obtained from all three sources for most children, but there may be circumstances when all three may not be relevant.

The purpose of assessment using the BERS-2 is to identify "child and family factors that may serve as protective factors for children at risk of poor life outcomes" (examiner's manual, p. 6). Primary uses reported in the manual are to identify children who have limited strengths, to set goals for Individual Education Plans or individual treatment plans, to identify strengths and weaknesses for intervention, to document progress made as a result of intervention services, and to measure emotional and behavioral strengths for research and program evaluation. No particular target population is specified. It appears that TRS and PRS can be used for the assessment of behavioral and emotional strengths of any child who is 5 to 18 years of age; however, the manual stipulates that the YRS should only be used for children ages 11 to 18 because adequate reading skills are required to complete the scale.

According to the manual, examiners should choose raters who have had contact with the child on a regular basis for at least several months and should be sure that raters understand how to complete the items. Directions for raters are provided on the forms. In order to complete the form, raters must read each item and circle the number that best describes the child. All test items are rated using a Likert-type scale. Raters then complete a number of open-ended questions to provide additional information on the child's strengths and resources. The test is not timed, but according to the manual, it typically takes approximately 10 minutes to complete. Typical raters for the TRS include the child's teachers or counselor, and for the PRS, the rater is usually a parent or guardian. As previously noted, children completing the YRS should be at least 11 years of age. The manual indicates that, if necessary, the examiner can read items to the child.

Instructions for scoring and examples of scoring procedures are clearly presented in the examiner's manual. Once the rater completes the form, the examiner calculates column subtotals and adds the column subtotals from both pages to obtain a total raw score for each of the subscales. Normative tables, which are included in the manual, are used to convert raw scores into scaled scores and percentile ranks. To find the Strength Index, the scaled scores from each of the five subscales are added together, and the appropriate table in the manual is used to find the standard score and percentile rank. Additional scoring procedures are required for dealing with omitted items and items with more than one response. The examiner estimates a score for those items by computing the average of the other items in the same subscale. For TRS, the examiner must also decide which set of norms to use. There is one set for students who have not been diagnosed with an emotional or behavioral disorder (EBD), and a second set for use with students who have a previous diagnosis of an EBD. In addition to scoring procedures, the manual includes information on the interpretation and presentation of test results.

DEVELOPMENT. This test is the second version of the BERS, which was originally developed in 1996. The original BERS included only one rating scale with 52 items. For the BERS-2, the original version was modified to create the TRS, and two new rating scales, the PRS and YRS, were created based on the BERS items. Open-ended questions were added, a Career Strength subscale was added to the PRS and YRS, and a Summary form was developed. According to the manual, the purpose, content, and format of the second edition is the same as the original. Scoring procedures are the same as well.

Development of the original BERS is described in detail in the manual. It was developed based on research in the areas of strength-based assessment, developmental psychology, resilience, and protective factors. Test developers also reviewed existing assessment tools relevant to the area. To form the subscales, test developers asked experts to contribute items. Using those items, item selection procedures were used to eliminate poor items. Item discrimination procedures and factor analysis were then used to reduce the number of items further. Five factors were produced, which correspond to the five BERS subscales. Items with a discrimination index less than .35 were eliminated, resulting in the final 52-item scale. For the TRS, PRS, and YRS of the BERS-2, test developers studied item discrimination using data from the norm sample. Item discrimination of all items included in those scales exceeded .35. Item bias studies were also conducted, which provided evidence that the test is not biased based on race or ethnicity.

TECHNICAL. The normative data used for the TRS were collected in 1996 for the original BERS. Two sets of norms were obtained. One group included children who were not identified as having emotional or behavioral disorders. There were 2,176 participants from 31 states ranging in age from 5 years to 18 years, 11 months. The second group was made up of individuals who had been diagnosed with an EBD. That group included 861 participants from 31 states who were 5 years to 18 years, 11 months of age. The norm samples for the PRS and YRS were collected between fall of 2001 and spring of 2002. The PRS sample included 927 children from 34 states, and the YRS sample included 1,301 children from 31 states. Age-specific norms are not provided. Evidence that the normative samples are representative of the population of the United States is provided in the manual.

Evidence of the reliability of the BERS-2 is provided. In order to obtain evidence for internal consistency, data from the norm sample were used to compute Cronbach's alpha for the subscales and the composite. For the five core subscales, average coefficients were .80 or above, with the exception of the YRS Career Strength subscale, which had an alpha of .79, and the average coefficient for the composite was .95. In addition, six studies were described that suggest that the BERS-2 is reliable over time. Evidence of interrater reliability is also reported. Based on the evidence presented, it appears that the BERS-2 is a reliable measure that can be used with confidence.

Three types of validity evidence including content, criterion-related, and construct validity are discussed. Evidence of content validity is provided in the description of test development. Items were developed based on expert opinion and were subject to adequate item discrimination and item bias analysis. In order to provide evidence of criterion-related validity, a number of studies comparing the TRS, PRS, and YRS to similar measures were reported. When the TRS was compared to similar measures, moderate to large positive correlations were found, as expected. In studies comparing the PRS and the YRS to similar measures, as expected, large positive correlations were found. The measures used for the comparisons were commonly used and up to date. As for evidence of construct validity, studies showed that the BERS-2 differentiated between individuals with emotional or behavioral disturbances and those without and between individuals with learning disabilities and those with emotional or behavioral disturbances. In addition, factor analysis was used to confirm the relationship of the subscales to the construct, and a study of items indicated that each item is highly correlated with its total subscale score. It does not appear that differential validity of the test across gender or culture groups was examined. Overall, the BERS-2 seems to be a valid measure of emotional and behavioral strengths.

COMMENTARY. The BERS-2 provides a valid measure of the construct of emotional and behavioral strength. It also appears that it can be used reliably for individuals ages 5 to 18 years from different racial and ethnic backgrounds. In addition, the test provides information from multiple informants and includes a summary form to facilitate comparisons between those informants. A limitation of the BERS-2 is that no age-specific norms are provided. As a result, children's emotional and behavioral competencies cannot be specifically compared to those of other children in their age group. This would be useful due to the fact that children's emotional and behavioral competencies typically change as they get older.

SUMMARY. The BERS-2 is easy to administer and score, and it appears to provide valid, reliable information about the emotional and behavioral strengths of children. It is likely to be a useful tool for examining strengths and protective factors present for children and for planning of educational and therapeutic interventions and measurement of progress over time following an intervention.

Review of the Behavioral and Emotional Rating Scale, Second Edition by MARK E. SWERDLIK, Professor of Psychology, and W. JOEL SCHNEIDER, Assistant Professor of Psychology, Illinois State University, Normal, IL:

DESCRIPTION. The Behavioral and Emotional Rating Scale, Second Edition (BERS-2) represents an expansion of the strength-based assessment model by incorporating a more systematic consideration of multiple perspectives. The BERS-2, developed for children and adolescents ages 5–18, includes the original 52-item BERS scale and the eight open-ended questions focusing on strengths such as in academic and community settings.

The BERS-2 includes separate rating forms for teachers or nonteaching personnel such as a counselor (Teacher Rating Scale, TRS); for a parent, guardian, or other caregiver (Parent Rating Scale, PRS); and a self-report form (Youth Rating Scale, YRS) for ages 11–18. Raters must have at least a fifth grade reading level. The TRS and the PRS items may be read to the informant but no data are presented on the impact that reading items has on reliability or validity. These three rating scales are composed of identical questions except a supplemental five-item Career Strength subscale has been added to the PRS and YRS but no guidelines are provided for appropriate ages for use and the YRS has items reworded in the first person.

For all three ratings scales, items are organized into five scales including Interpersonal Strength, Family Involvement, Intrapersonal

Strength, School Functioning, and Affective Strength with the five summed to yield a Strength Index Score. The Career Strength supplemental scale does not enter into the Strength Index Score.

Items are rated based on observations within the last 3 months from 0–3 ranging from "not at all like the youth" to "very much like." Although the scales are untimed, each can be completed within approximately 10 minutes, with no data provided to support this estimate. Directions are clearly printed on each of the rating forms. Scoring is simple and consists of summing the ratings for each item to compute raw scores for each subscale and the sum of the Scaled Scores for the Strength Index. Tables (for each separate rating scale and norm group if available) provide corresponding percentile ranks, and Scaled scores with a mean of 10 and a standard deviation of 3 for the subscale scores and a mean of 100 and standard deviation of 15 for the Strength Index. The eight open-ended questions are, according to the author, useful for developing key questions for follow-up interviews and treatment planning purposes but are not scored. Clear directions are provided in the manual for the number of items that may be omitted or for which there is more than one response before rendering the scale or composite unusable as are procedures for the pro-rating of scores. However, an explanation on how these numbers were derived is lacking. Larger scores correspond to greater strengths. Related to interpretation of scores (e.g., below 70), guidelines are given but no empirical support is provided for the meaning of these specific cutoffs.

The BERS-2 is attractively produced and is intended to be used by a variety of appropriately trained and experienced professionals, including classroom teachers, psychologists, and social workers who work in a variety of settings including schools, mental health clinics, and various social service agencies. The BERS-2 has several uses including as part of a comprehensive assessment for identification of children with limited strengths; for developing target goals for Individual Education Plans (IEP) or treatment plans; to identify strengths and weaknesses for intervention planning; for progress monitoring; and for research.

The manual is comprehensive and generally clearly written. Materials are attractively produced with separate printed forms for the TRS, PRS, YRS, and the Summary Form with a space for notes on interpretation and recommendations and to graph all scores.

DEVELOPMENT. Under the assumption that children can be motivated to make greater progress if parents, teachers and other caregivers focus on their strengths rather then their weaknesses, the BERS-2 was developed based upon a unique strength-based model of assessment rather than a behavioral deficits model. The goal of this model is to assess the child and family factors that may serve as protective factors for youth at risk for negative outcomes. These protective factors include skills and characteristics such as a sense of personal accomplishment; satisfying relationships with peers, family members, and adults; and the ability to deal with stress and adversity.

TECHNICAL. The norms for the TRS have not been updated for the second edition but continue to use those collected in 1995–1996. TRS norms were based on 2,176 children and adolescents from the general population and 861 youth with Emotional Behavioral Disorders (EBD). Somewhat smaller (927 and 1,301) and weighted (for race, Hispanic ethnicity, and geographic region) norm samples are provided for the PRS and YRS. The demographic characteristics of the standardization sample are generally equivalent to the most recent 2001 U.S. Census data except Hispanics and females were undersampled, and some family income levels were oversampled. The groups were weighted to ensure that their contributions to the norms were in proportion to the general U.S. population. Separate gender norms are provided for all rating forms. Separate norms are not provided by age and no data or rationale are presented to support why age differences would not be expected. For the EBD norms, no description is provided as to how these children were classified and how similar or different they might be considering that different criteria are used by states for classification purposes.

Internal consistency coefficients for the TRS, PRS, and YRS subscales were generally adequate, if not excellent (average coefficient alphas range from .79 to .96). Like all composite scores, the Strength Index from the TRS, PRS, and YRS is more reliable than its component subscales (average coefficient alphas range from .95 to .98). Satisfactory internal consistency reliability coefficients are equally reliable (and reflect little or no bias) for the subgroups of gender, race, and students with EBD. Several peer-reviewed studies support satisfactory test-retest reliability for short-term (2 weeks) with averages ranging from .82 to .99 for the subscales and from .87 to .99 for the Strength Index of the TRS, PRS, and YRS. Lower long-term stability (6 months) is reported only for the TRS (.53 to .79). No long-term stability reliability data are reported for the PRS or TRS. Three different studies suggest that the interrater reliability is generally satisfactory. Specifically, the interrater reliability is higher when the two raters are teachers (ranging from .85 to .96 for the subscales and .98 for the Strength Index) than parent-child interrater reliability (ranging from .50 to .63 for the subscales and .54 for the Strength Index). Parent-teacher interrater reliability ranged from .20 to .67 for the subscales. No data are provided for multiple parent raters (e.g., both parents). Reliability data are also not presented by age and, as previously noted, no data are provided to support the lack of significant age-based differences in scores. Reliability studies presented in the manual represent a beginning point but are limited in terms of age, sample size, and geographical and racial/ethnic representativeness.

Satisfactory qualitative and quantitative evidence is presented for Content-Description Validity for the TRS. Qualitative evidence included a review of the literature and existing checklists with items confirmed by surveying 250 professionals for their opinions and suggestions for additional items. Items were then subjected to item discrimination and factor analysis including their ability to discriminate between youth with and without serious emotional disturbance (SED) but again, no information is provided for how these students with SED (arguably a highly subjective classification) were diagnosed. A factor analysis was then conducted. As the items for the PRS and YRS are identical to or represent slight rewording of TRS items, no additional qualitative content-description validity evidence was collected for these two scales other than the Career Strength Subscale, which followed a plan similar to the one for the TRS. Item analyses of the TRS, PRS, and YRS norm samples ensured that no item had an item-total correlation lower than .35 with its respective subscale. Results of differential item functioning analyses suggest that the BERS-2 has little bias in regard to race or ethnicity. No item bias analyses for gender or different age groups were reported.

Criterion-related validity evidence is presented and includes correlating the three BERS-2 rating scales with other published behavioral scales such as the Social Skills Rating System, Achenbach Child Behavior Checklist, Teacher Report Form, and Youth Self-Report. A number of these studies have been published in peer-reviewed journals and all suggest satisfactory concurrent criterion-related validity. Construct-identification validity evidence included group differentiation (e.g., differentiating between groups of people identified with EBD and those who are not identified), subscale interrelationships, and confirmatory and exploratory factor analyses which all support the five-factor structure of the BERS-2. Additional validity evidence is needed to document that the BERS-2 adds information beyond that which can typically be obtained in an interview (incremental validity), or that findings can be used for the purposes suggested by the author. For example, it is not yet clear to what degree the ratings relate to such important outcomes as the ability to deal with stress and adversity, how sensitive are the ratings to change for use in progress monitoring, and how the ratings lead to the development of more effective Individual Education Plans (IEP) or treatment plans.

COMMENTARY. The BERS-2 remains a unique rating scale system in that it is based on a strength-based assessment model that is clearly articulated in the manual. However, as was noted by Doll (2001) in her review of the first edition, the degree to which the scale represents a comprehensive set of emotional and behavioral strengths has not been documented. Without this critical support, users have to rely on a content analysis interpretation of the subscale labels and item content for score interpretation. Norms are generally representative but no rationale or data are provided as to why separate age norms are not needed. Reliability evidence, including internal consistency, test-retest, and interrater, are generally satisfactory. Validity evidence that is presented relating to content-description, criterion-prediction, and construct-identification is satisfactory but limited for the latter two categories. A notable strength is that various analyses suggest that the BERS-2 is not statistically biased with respect to major racial or ethnic groups. The strength-based model is intuitively appealing to mental health professionals who value protective factors and the wisdom of building on strengths. However, important evidence is lacking related to validity of the strength-based model (e.g., how strengths are functionally related to diagnosis and important outcomes), treatment validity (how results improve the development of IEPs), and incremental validity (i.e., how much more is gained from an interview). Further, although interpretive guidelines are provided with cutoff scores, no validity data to support their use are provided. Further, the manual would benefit from better articulated interpretive guidelines including more extensive case material to illustrate the various uses of the BERS-2.

SUMMARY. Although the BERS-2 represents a unique approach to assessment and the author cautions that it should be only part of a comprehensive assessment that includes ratings that assess deficits, it remains unclear how much the BERS-2 adds to an assessment to justify its use in terms of expense and rater's time. More frequently used scales, which are primarily deficit oriented but also include strength-based subscales, such as the Achenbach (Achenbach, 1991a, 1991b, & 1991c) and Behavior Assessment System for Children-II (Reynolds & Kamphaus, 2004), are recommended at this time until more convincing validity evidence for the BERS-2 becomes available.

REVIEWERS' REFERENCES

Achenbach, T. M. (1991a). *Manual for the Child Behavior Checklist/4–18 and 1991 Profile.* Burlington: University of Vermont, Department of Psychiatry.
Achenbach, T. M. (1991b). *Manual for the Youth Self-Report and 1991 Profile.* Burlington: University of Vermont, Department of Psychiatry.
Achenbach, T. M. (1991c). Teacher Report Form. Burlington: University of Vermont, Department of Psychiatry.
Doll, B. (2001). [Review of the Behavioral and Emotional Rating Scale.] In B. S. Plake & J. C. Impara (Eds.), *The fourteenth mental measurements yearbook* (p. 142). Lincoln, NE: Buros Institute of Mental Measurements.
Reynolds, C. R., & Kamphaus, R. W. (2004). Behavior Assessment System for Children-II. Circle Pines, MN: American Guidance Service.

[30]

Bender Visual-Motor Gestalt Test, Second Edition.

Purpose: Designed to measure visual-motor integration skills in children and adults.
Population: Ages 4–85+.
Publication Dates: 1938–2003.
Acronym: Bender-Gestalt II.
Scores, 4: Copy Score, Recall Score, Motor Test Score, Perception Test Score.
Administration: Individual.
Price Data, 2005: $124.50 per complete kit.
Time: Administration time not reported.
Comments: Revision of the Visual Motor Gestalt Test [Bender-Gestalt Test].
Authors: Gary G. Brannigan and Scott L. Decker.
Publisher: Riverside Publishing.

Cross References: See T5:301 (61 references) and T4:291 (34 references); for reviews by Jack A. Naglieri and by John E. Obrzut and Carol A. Boliek of an earlier edition, see 11:40 (92 references) for reviews by Kenneth W. Howell and Jerome M. Sattler, see 9:139 (65 references); see also T3:280 (159 references), 8:506 (253 references), and T2:1447 (144 references); for a review by Phillip M. Kitay, see 7:161 (192 references); see also P:415 (170 references); for a review by C. B. Blakemore and an excerpted review by Fred Y. Billingslea, see 6:203 (99 references); see also 5:172 (118 references); for reviews by Arthur L. Benton and Howard R. White, see 4:144 (34 references); see also 3:108 (8 references.

Review of the Bender Visual-Motor Gestalt Test, Second Edition by D. JOE OLMI, Associate Professor and Clinic Director, School Psychology Program, Department of Psychology, The University of Southern Mississippi, Hattiesburg, MS:

DESCRIPTION. The Bender Visual-Motor Gestalt Test, Second Edition (Bender-Gestalt II) is designed to "measure visual-motor integration skills in children and adults from 4 to 85+ years of age" (examiner's manual, p. 1). The kit contains the examiner's manual (containing test development, administration, normative, and psychometric data), the 16 stimulus cards, the observation forms, the Motor Test record forms, and the Perception Test record forms. The stimulus cards have been manufactured in plastic for durability. Required materials for administration include two pencils with erasers, a timing device or stopwatch, and multiple sheets of paper.

The Bender-Gestalt II is significantly different from the original Bender in several respects. Although the new edition still contains the original design templates, seven new design templates have been added to increase the range of assessment. There are four specific designs for use at lower ages (4 years to 7 years, 11 months), whereas there are three new designs for use at the upper range of administration (8 years to 85+ years of age). For the lower ages, Plates 1–13 are used, whereas Plates 5–16 are used for the upper age range. The new edition also includes a behavioral observation form for use during administration to record information pertaining to "Physical Observation," "Test-Taking Observations," space for commenting on "Copy Observations," "Recall," and a "Summary" section for recording results of performance. Additionally, two new tests were added (i.e., Perception and Motor). Stratified normative data were collected that are reflective of the U.S. 2000 Census, as well as data from other special groups.

Administration of the Bender-Gestalt II appears fairly straightforward and is accomplished in two stages or phases, the Copy phase and the Recall phase. As mentioned previously, there are 16 stimulus cards, with certain designs administered to individuals dependent on age. In the Copy phase, the examinee is asked to copy the appropriate design onto a blank sheet of paper; in the Recall phase the examinee is asked to recall as many of the presented designs as possible. There is no time limit for the administration. Information pertinent to examinee behaviors observed by the examiner is recorded on the observation form. The instructions detailing how that form is used during the administration process is simple and straightforward, as are the instructions for general administration. It is important to note that a stopwatch of some sort is necessary for timing both portions of the administration.

The Perception and Motor tests are administered following the Recall phase of the administration and are intended as brief screeners for motor and/or perceptual difficulties. Four minutes are allowed for both test administrations. Again, administration and scoring procedures are simple and easy to follow.

Scoring of the Bender-Gestalt II Copy and Recall phases is easy as well. The "Global Scoring System" is a 5-point system with scores ranging from 0–4 (0 = no resemblance; 1 = slight, vague resemblance; 2 = some, moderate resemblance; 3 = strong resemblance; and 4 = nearly perfect). Raw scores by age group are then converted to standard scores using tables in the examiner's manual. Scoring criteria and examples are also provided in order to minimize subjectivity. Interpretative information that is easily understood is provided in the manual.

DEVELOPMENT AND TECHNICAL. In the examiner's manual, the authors note three primary goals for the Bender-Gestalt II including (a) extending the age range of the instrument, (b) renorming the instrument with a larger, more representative sample across a larger age span, and (c) retaining the original designs if possible. Using appropriate item development, norming, and statistical analysis procedures, it certainly appears to

this reviewer that all three goals were adequately accomplished.

Standardization procedures were based on "a carefully designed, stratified, random sampling plan that closely matched the U.S. 2000 census" (examiner's manual, p. 23). Data were collected on 4,000 participants between 2001–2002. Additional sample participants from specified groups, for example ADHD, autism, and learning disabilities, were examined for validity studies. Information provided in the examiner's manual suggested a comprehensive, detailed, and prescribed approach to the norming and standardization process.

Reliability and validity studies of the Bender-Gestalt II were based on the standard scores generated from the Global Scoring System pertaining to the Copy and Recall phases of the test. For the Copy phase, interrater consistency estimates ranged from .83 to .94 with a mean of .90; for the Recall phase, the range was .94 to .97 with a mean of .96. Split-half reliability coefficients across age levels ranged from .86 to .95. Mean test-retest coefficients (with a 2–3 week time period) for the Copy phase were .85 and .83 for the Recall phase. Validity studies suggested that the Bender-Gestalt II served as a valid measure of visual-motor integration, especially for the Copy portion of the instrument. Validity data for the Recall portion of the test suggested a similar, yet different construct. Although the authors assert that the Bender-Gestalt II "is significantly related to many areas of academic achievement" (examiner's manual, p. 53), this reviewer would not make such an assertion based on the review of the validity data. Similar statements were made relative to correlations with measures of intelligence.

COMMENTARY AND SUMMARY. In summary, the Bender-Gestalt II is a welcomed revision of a measure of visual motor integration that has been around for many years and has served as the gold standard. It is easily administered and scored, is sound psychometrically, and the authors/publishers engaged in a well-thought-out norming and standardization plan. Its use as a screening procedure or an initial assessment procedure in a comprehensive battery for determining visual motor integration functioning is appropriate. It may also be coupled with other technically sound measures in a comprehensive assessment protocol to arrive at assessment-based decisions involving executive functioning.

Review of the Bender Visual-Motor Gestalt Test, Second Edition by DARRELL L. SABERS, Professor and Head of Educational Psychology, and SARAH BONNER, Doctoral Student, University of Arizona, Tucson, AZ:

DESCRIPTION. The Bender Visual-Motor Gestalt Test, Second Edition (Bender-Gestalt II) is a revision of an old and very popular test, the Bender Visual Motor Gestalt Test (Bender, 1938). This edition includes seven new items; a standardized procedure for assessing recall of designs; forms for recording test-taking behaviors; new, more extensive norms; an objective scoring system; and additional tests for ruling out motor and perceptual problems.

The Bender-Gestalt II is targeted at individuals aged 4 and up in educational, psychological, and neuropsychological settings. The previous edition of the Bender and its numerous scoring systems have been applied to diverse purposes: as a screening for brain dysfunction, an index of developmental delay, and a projective test for personality assessment. The developer of the current edition sanctions these uses and more, as long as they are within the test user's range of expertise or qualifications. The developer also recommends the use of the test as an aid in differentiating learning, psychological, and neurological problems.

The basic test has two phases. The Copy Phase consists of simple line drawings that individuals are asked to copy following brief oral instructions. There are 13 items for ages 4 to 7, and 12 items for ages 8 and older. The Recall Phase asks examinees to draw all the designs they can remember from the Copy Phase. The test is not timed, but average times for the standardization sample range from 9 to 14 minutes (Copy) and 2 to 4 minutes (Recall). Each item is scored on a 5-point rubric with descriptors ranging from no resemblance to the original to nearly perfect reproduction. Point values in each item's rubric are accompanied by several drawings illustrating that level of skill.

DEVELOPMENT. Lauretta Bender developed her original test in 1938 to study the Gestalt function, held to be a biological process that determined the pattern of motor responses of an organism to a "constellation" of visual stimuli. The test has attained immense popularity over the last 75 years. The *Handbook of Psychological Assessment*

(Groth-Marnat, 2003) ranks it as "one of the five or six most frequently used tests." However, the original test had few easy items to measure examinees at very low skill levels and few difficult items to measure adult examinees. To address this problem, the Bender-Gestalt II adds seven new items to the original nine, extending the measurement scale in both directions. Following development of a large pool of potential new items, a subset was selected for pilot testing based on judgments of expert raters. The piloted items were placed on the same measurement scale as the original items, which had been calibrated using the Rasch model. Items that best met the desired objective of extending the measurement scale were selected for the new edition.

TECHNICAL. The Bender-Gestalt II includes expanded norms intended to represent a broad general population. The standardization sample of 4,000 individuals aged 4–85+ was based on a stratified random sampling plan matched to the 2000 U.S. Census. The test manual provides charts comparing demographic characteristics of the norm group to 2000 U.S. Census data. The evidence appears credible that the Bender norms adequately represent the general U.S. population. However, some of the norms lack precision at those points of the score ranges that are probably most interesting to the clinician; for instance, for 8-year-olds, a raw score of 9 on the Motor Test is placed in a range somewhere between the 26th and the 50th percentile.

Studies of interrater consistency are important in a subjectively scored assessment. For the Bender-Gestalt II, interrater agreement averaged .90 for the Copy Phase and .96 for the Recall Phase among experienced scorers. To their credit, the developers also examined interrater agreement among scorers whose training was based solely on the test manual, and found correlations of .85 (Copy) and .92 (Recall). This indicates that extensive training is not a major requirement for administering the Bender-Gestalt II, an attraction for clinicians. An internal consistency study (Copy Phase only) using the split-half method on the standardization sample yielded a reliability estimate of .91. It is unknown how well this coefficient will estimate the reliability of scores in applied settings, where the clinical population is likely to be a distinct subset of the population represented in the standardization sample. A test-retest reliability study based on a sample of 213 examinees in four age groups averaged .85 for the Copy Phase and .83 for Recall and for an administration interval of 2–3 weeks. Information is not given about the examinees who participated in the test-retest study. It would have been desirable for the test publishers to provide information about internal consistency and test-retest reliability for clinical examinees.

Validity studies showing moderate positive correlations between scores on Bender-Gestalt II and other tests of visual-motor integration, academic skills, and cognitive ability are reported. Whether these results are intended to demonstrate convergent validity, or usefulness for prediction, or something else entirely is not stated.

Users should also note errors in reporting results of some of the statistical tests: Tables 5-14 and 5-15 (examiner's manual, p. 63) contain the same means, standard deviations, and *t* values with different degrees of freedom for tests based on different groups. [Editor's Note: The publisher advises that a corrected Table 5-14 is now available on their website.]

Several pages at the end of the manual are devoted to ways clinicians can use observations of test-taking behaviors to gain clinical insights and for making differential diagnoses. However, no evidence is provided by the test developers for the empirical accuracy of such insights/diagnoses.

COMMENTARY. When one of the reviewers reached the Recall Phase of the Bender-Gestalt II while administering the test to a 12-year-old, the child complained forcefully that he had not been told to try to remember. Standard 8.2 of the *Standards for Educational and Psychological Testing* (AERA, APA, & NCME, 1999) states that test takers should be provided in advance with as much information about the testing process as is consistent with obtaining valid responses. If valid measurement of the visual-motor integration construct requires that test takers be left in the dark about the recall process, this requirement should be explicitly argued by the developers. If prior knowledge of the expectation to recall the designs would not contaminate the interpretation of test scores, then there is no compelling reason to subject test takers to any anxiety that may result from being inadequately informed about the testing process.

A validity argument about the nature of the construct and the meaning of the demonstrated interrelationships among test scores is lacking in the manual. As a reviewer of the original Bender in the *Mental Measurements Yearbook* suggested (Blakemore, 1965), the real weakness of this test is its poor argument for construct validity. Exactly what is the nature of "visual-motor integration skill," and how is it hypothesized to relate to other psychological functions? Is it a construct distinct from simple drawing skill or general intelligence? Are motivation, fatigue, and poor attention to instructions sources of construct-irrelevant variance? To the extent that the test assesses the ability of examinees to copy and recall simple figures, evidence should be shown that there is some value for researchers or clinicians in knowing how well individuals copy and recall figures. No such evidence is given. To the extent that the test purports to measure an underlying trait, a coherent argument that such a construct is measured should be made, drawing on both convergent and discriminant validity evidence. No such argument is presented.

In the absence of construct validity the developers try to show that, anyway, the test "works." The predictive validity of the Bender-Gestalt II is demonstrated through studies that find significant differences between nonclinical and clinical or exceptional samples. Unfortunately, there is considerable overlap between the normal and clinical groups in Bender-Gestalt II scores. For instance, a slightly below-average nonclinical examinee would be expected to attain the same score in copying as an average examinee with a learning disability in reading. Scores for above average mentally retarded examinees (+1 *SD*) and below average normal examinees (-1 *SD*) are nearly the same. With these broad overlaps, only extreme scores will be useful in discriminating between normal and nonnormal populations. Furthermore, if an individual scores very low on the Bender-Gestalt II, the clinician will still have no information about the type of abnormality that generated the test score. The test does not help the user distinguish the mentally retarded from the autistic, for example.

The test developers argue that, even if results from the Bender-Gestalt II are never conclusive on their own, they make an important contribution to a complete psychological assessment. Using multiple methods, however, is only valuable when test scores are meaningful. Tests that do not contribute unique and valid information for measurement of important attributes may do more harm than good by encouraging users to draw unwarranted conclusions from shaky evidence. It is the test developer's responsibility to provide evidence that recommended uses of the test are valid, not to leave it up to the test user's range of expertise or qualifications.

SUMMARY. Overall, the Bender-Gestalt II is quick, easy to administer, easy to score, and probably not intimidating to most test takers. The new scoring system appears to have good interrater agreement, and the norms allow interpretations referenced to the general U.S. population, although not to a clinical population. However, these qualities are not useful if the test does not measure an underlying attribute of clinical or research importance, or if use of the test cannot help clinicians discriminate between normal and nonnormal populations with reasonable precision, or distinguish between diagnostic groups.

REVIEWERS' REFERENCES

American Educational Research Association, American Psychological Association, and National Council on Measurement in Education. (1999). *Standards for educational and psychological testing*. Washington, DC: American Educational Research Association.

Bender, L. (1938). *A visual motor gestalt test and its clinical use*. American Orthopsychiatric Association, Research Monographs (No. 3). New York: American Orthopsychiatric Association.

Blakemore, C. B. (1965). [Review of the Bender-Gestalt Test.] In O. K. Buros (Ed.), *The sixth mental measurements yearbook* (pp. 414-415). Highland Park, NJ: Gryphon Press.

Groth-Marnat, G. (2003). *Handbook of psychological assessment*. Hoboken, NJ: Wiley.

[31]

Bennett Mechanical Comprehension Test, Second Edition.

Purpose: "Designed to measure the ability to perceive and understand the relationship of physical forces and mechanical elements in practical situations."

Population: Industrial employees and high school and adult applicants for mechanical positions or engineering schools.

Publication Dates: 1940–1994.

Acronym: BMCT.

Scores: Total score only.

Administration: Group.

Forms, 2: S, T (equivalent forms).

Price Data, 2005: $250 per complete starter kit including 10 forms test booklet, 50 answer booklets for both forms, and manual (1994, 89 pages); $185 per 25 test booklets; $50 per hand-scoring keys; $45 per manual; $135 per taped recordings of test questions.

Time: (30) minutes.

Comments: Tape recordings of test questions read aloud are available for use with examinees who have limited reading abilities; Spanish version available.

Author: George K. Bennett.

Publisher: Harcourt Assessment, Inc.

Cross References: See T5:302 (4 references) and T4:292 (2 references); for a review by Hilda Wing of an earlier edition, see 11:41 (3 references); see also T3:282 (7 references) and T2:2239 (9 references); for reviews by Harold P. Bechtoldt and A. Oscar H. Roberts, and an excerpted review by Ronald K. Hambleton of the first edition, see 7:1049 (22 references); see also 6:1094 (15 references) and 5:889 (46 references); for a review by N. W. Morton of earlier forms, see 4:766 (28 references); for reviews by Charles M. Harsh, Lloyd G. Humphreys, and George A. Satter, see 3:683 (19 references).

Review of the Bennett Mechanical Comprehension Test by JOSEPH C. CIECHALSKI, Professor, East Carolina University, Greenville, NC:

DESCRIPTION. The Bennett Mechanical Comprehension Test (BMCT) is designed to assess an individual's understanding of mechanical relationships and physical laws found in everyday life situations. It has been used for over 60 years to select individuals for a wide variety of civilian and military occupations as well as training programs requiring mechanical aptitudes and abilities.

The BMCT is a 68 item test available in two equivalent forms (S and T). Items consist of pictures and questions concerning some mechanical principle and the examinee must select the best answer from among three alternatives. For example, a sample item shows two people carrying a weighted object on a plank and the question asks, "Which man carries more weight?" (If equal, mark C). The reading level of the items is at or below the sixth-grade level.

Directions for administering the BMCT are contained in the test manual. Chapter 2 presents the directions for the regular administration of the BMCT and Appendix C contains the directions for the oral administration of the BMCT. The BMCT can be administered using a tape recording of the directions and test. Examinees who have limited reading ability or other types of disabilities would take the recorded version. Each examinee needs a test booklet, answer sheet, and two Number 2 pencils, plus a tape recorder for those who will be tested orally. The BMCT has a 30-minute time limit. According to the test manual, no special training is needed to administer the BMCT; however, it states, "To ensure accurate and reliable results, the administrator must become thoroughly familiar with the Directions for Administering and the test materials before attempting to administer the test" (p. 15).

The answer sheet may be scored either by hand or machine. A separate scoring key for each form of the test is available. Scores are reported as percentile ranks.

DEVELOPMENT. The BMCT was first published in 1940 as Form AA, a second version (BB) followed in 1941, and Form W1 in 1942. During WWII, restricted versions were developed under a military contract. In 1966, a complete revision was undertaken that included four objectives. These objectives included: (a) to develop a pair of alternate forms to replace Forms AA, BB, and W1; (b) to increase the range of item difficulty and maintain test reliability; (c) to replace dated illustrations with current ones; and (d) to simplify scoring by eliminating the correction for guessing.

After reviewing the items of Forms AA, BB, and W1, 95 items were retained, 43 items were revised, and 42 new items were developed. These items were administered to over 700 male students in Grades 11 and 12. Out of the 180 items analyzed, 136 items were found to be acceptable. Two equivalent forms (S and T) of 68 items each were developed based on item difficulty and discrimination indices. To determine the equivalence of Forms S and T, a study was conducted in 1969 using 302 applicants from skilled trade jobs at an auto company. The two forms were determined to be equivalent.

TECHNICAL. The norming process for the BMCT is described in the 1994 BMCT manual. Two tables present combined group norms for males and females, and for whites and minorities based on data collected from 8,992 adults. These two tables present raw score to percentile rank conversions for a variety of occupations (utilities and manufacturing), vocational rehabilitation clients, and employees in bindery, press, and maintenance jobs to mention a few. The 1994 manual informs users of the BMCT that these tables are presented for research purposes and caution needs to be used in employee selection decisions. Considering the long history of the BMCT (over 60 years), separate norming data for males, females, and minorities need to be developed and reported.

Evidence of the equivalence among Form AA, Form BB, and Forms S and T of the BMCT was examined based on information from the 1969 BMCT manual. To show that the Mechanical Reasoning Test (Form T) of the Differential Aptitude Test (DAT) (also published by Harcourt Assessment, Inc.) and the BMCT are equivalent, the tests were administered to 175 employees of an oil company. Half the group completed the DAT first and the other half completed the BMCT first. The resulting correlations were .80 and .83 and were reported originally in the 1980 BMCT supplement. Two new forms of the DAT (Forms C & D) were developed in 1991 with norming tables available in separate booklets. There are separate norming group tables reported for students (Grades 7–12) and adults (college and employment). Perhaps a correlation between this version of the DAT and the BMCT could be conducted with the results published in a revised manual.

The reliability estimates for Forms S and T were reported by the split-half method using the Spearman-Brown formula. Reliability coefficients and standard errors of measurement (*SEM*) are reported. This information is presented not only on Forms S and T, but also for older versions of the BMCT. The reliability coefficients range from .75 to .93 for different groups and are based on the data reported in the 1969 BMCT manual. Considering all of the correlation derived from the various forms of the BMCT, I am surprised that no test-retest reliability coefficients were reported for Forms S and T.

Evidence of criterion-related validity for the BMCT is also presented. This information is based on nearly 60 correlations derived from the evaluations of people employed in jobs or training for employment. Forty-two correlations were at or above .30 with the highest being .69. These data were compiled from the 1969 BMCT manual, the 1980 manual supplement, and literature reviews from users of the BMCT in 1993 and 1994.

Construct validity is described in the manual and evidence is presented based on studies conducted in the 1980s. In addition, over 100 correlations are presented for the BMCT with other tests that claim to measure the same or similar constructs. Over 80 correlations had a coefficient of .30 or higher.

COMMENTARY. From its inception in 1940 until 1969, a number of forms of the BMCT have been available. In 1969, the most recent revision of the BMCT (Forms S and T) was published and was reviewed by Wing in 1992. What changes have been made since Wing's (1992) review?

In her review of the BMCT, Wing's (1992) most critical remarks concerned the appearance of the test, "It just looks old" (p. 106). Although the items in Forms S and T were unchanged, the publisher has now redesigned the covers of the test booklets. The answer sheet accommodates both forms of the test and may be scored either by hand or computer. In addition, directions for scoring the test are included on the scoring keys.

The second edition of the BMCT manual (1994) is well organized and based on information from the 1969 manual and the 1980 supplement. Separate chapters covering administering, scoring, normative data, reliability, and validity are easy to read and understand.

My two concerns of the BMCT include the test items and the normative data. First, the point made by Wing (1992) in her review, "Of the 68 test items in Form S, 5 had male figures while 3 had female figures" (p. 106), still holds true because the test items have not been revised. Second, although the normative data presented are very comprehensive and detailed, I believe that separate norming data for males, females, and minorities are needed.

SUMMARY. The BMCT is a well-designed mechanical aptitude test. A considerable number of research studies have been reported in support of the technical quality of this instrument. The manual is well organized and easy to read. However, some of the test items need to be revised and separate norms are needed for gender and race. In spite of these concerns, the BMCT is a useful measure of mechanical aptitude.

REVIEWER'S REFERENCE

Wing, H. (1992). [Review of the Bennett Mechanical Comprehension Test.] In J. J. Kramer & J. C. Conoley (Eds.), *The eleventh mental measurements yearbook* (pp. 106–107). Lincoln, NE: Buros Institute of Mental Measurements.

Review of the Bennett Mechanical Comprehension Test, Second Edition by MICHAEL SPANGLER, Dean of Business & Technology, Highland Community College, Freeport, IL:

DESCRIPTION. The Bennett Mechanical Comprehension Test (BMCT) is an aptitude test designed to measure a complex set of abilities that include: mechanical information, spatial perception, and mechanical reasoning or understanding. The test is employed to predict performance in technical training programs and to select employees for mechanical, industrial, or engineering related occupations. The focus is on cognitive abilities and an individual's capacity for future learning

of mechanical principles. The conclusions are drawn from mechanical reasoning problems that involve inferring the motion of components of a mechanical system from a static diagram (Hegarty & Kozhevnikov, 1999). This test is not intended to measure achievement, physical dexterity, or psychomotor skills.

The test administration requires no special training and can be conducted by competent staff. The test contains 68 selection type items. Although the test is not intended as a speeded test, a 30-minute administration time is required.

The answer sheet, used for both forms (S and T) may be hand or machine scored using keys provided by the publisher. Maximum raw score is 68 and the percentile score is determined after identifying a norm group. The publishers attest that the raw scores are useful only to rank examinees' performance and few other inferences from the raw scores are of value. Adopters of this instrument are advised that local norming is most useful. One must examine the appropriateness of the norm groups provided by the developers and remain cautious of the relationship between those supplied in the manual and norms constructed from the local population. Given this interpretive requirement, a final scoring decision process should be developed by skilled personnel.

DEVELOPMENT. The materials provided by the publisher include both test forms, a sample answer sheet, and the second edition manual. The most recent editions of the test (Forms S and T) were published in 1969 after a major revision of the original 1940s instrument. The most recent changes in the test forms include newly designed test booklet covers and scannable answer sheet. Additions to the test manual include updated normative information with 18 new norm groups based on 1993 and 1994 studies.

The test manual (copyright 1994) includes considerable information on the nature of mechanical comprehension, and history of the instrument as well as its components, update, and development processes. The publishers provide an extensive overview of the use of the BMCT in human resource functions.

The manual addresses a considerable body of research on construct validity of the instrument. A table of item categories identifies the breadth of content addressed in the test. Additionally, the user is provided with an extensive table of correlations with other tests. Notably missing from this table is any correlation with the Armed Services Vocational Aptitude Battery (ASVAB; T6:185).

TECHNICAL. Form equivalence is well supported by data in the manual as are indices of item difficulty and discrimination. Item design is a presentation of questions of varying difficulty with illustrations representing mechanical relationships and understanding of physical principles. Typical item construction involves a brief stem question with reference to the illustration and a choice of three alternatives. Item reading levels and vocabulary distribution are well presented and established at a sixth grade equivalence for greater than 98% of all words in the items and directions.

Normative data are provided as combined group norms. Typically, the norm group tables display combined data for males and females, and for whites and minorities. Of particular note are the differences in test scores by gender. In a study of the DAT Mechanical Reasoning Test, a statistically equivalent form of the BMCT, females scored significantly lower than did males. Quoting the test manual, "The differences were not only statistically significant, but of such size as to have practical meaning" (p. 30). The differences increased as grade level (8–12) increased. No data were presented on gender differences among adult populations.

The test developers reasonably state that due to the wide variety of content areas the reliability "is lower than is usually the case with numerical or verbal items" (manual, p. 33), yet creditably, the split-half coefficients remain consistently in the .80s to lower .90s. It is noted that BMCT scores are resistant to improvement through training and practice, thus, lending stability to scoring interpretation.

Evidence to support the validity of the BMCT is presented in a sizeable table of criterion-related validity coefficients. However, it is noteworthy that the age and population characteristics of these data are problematic. The only study reported within the last two decades yielded $r = .12$ with a nearly homogenous population (93.5% male, 75.7% white). Similar age and homogeneity concerns exist in the tables presented in evidence of construct validity. In this instance, the only correlations developed within the last two decades are from a group of 149 female college students with no ethnicity data given.

COMMENTARY. Mechanical comprehension is a necessary but not conclusive trait for success in technical occupations. However, assessing mechanical comprehension to predict potential for success in training is of considerable benefit. The Bennett Mechanical Comprehension Test is an appropriate initial tool for personnel selection in certain circumstances, specifically, selection for training. Evidence for its job relatedness has been offered in the form of correlations with training tests, job performance ratings, and work samples. Although the evidence is not entirely clear about the validity of this test across genders or ethnicities, this test's content is clearly appropriate in many industries or occupations. The developers noted that explanations for group differences range from biological/societal to interactions of the two. Human action and development as well as organizational, cultural, and societal adaptation can affect the nature of the workforce (National Science and Technology Council, 2001). New validity studies with attention to age, gender, and ethnicity of the subjects would strengthen the conclusions expressed by the developers. Item-characteristic curves may be useful in further supporting test validity.

This reviewer is concerned with the appearance of the instrument. Both forms of the test (S and T) sport a new cover page intended to improve face validity, yet that which is truly critical, the illustrations in the items themselves, are woefully out of date. There are serious questions about ability of a young examinee to find a meaningful frame of reference for some of the items illustrated. Other face validity concerns in the illustrations include the choices of units (English/metric), the predominance of Caucasian figures, and the proportion of active/passive gender representations. Many of these points were expressed in prior reviews (Wing, 1992). It is possible that investment in improved graphics for this test could facilitate not only improved test validity but marketability and alternative delivery methods such as a web-based product.

The test manual is very useful. It provides articulate explanations of the concepts (reliability, validity, norms) and an ample glossary of terms to facilitate adoption and use by human resource professionals. In addition, the test administration components (testing conditions, materials, and proctor instructions) are clear and concise. The test is readily available from the publisher via the Harcourt web site. Easy acquisition, administration, and scoring makes the test a reasonable investment for interested business users.

SUMMARY. The constructs assessed by the Bennett Mechanical Comprehension Test have a well-established history of measuring mechanical reasoning, The test has proven valuable in decisions about an individual's ability to understand the relationships between physical principles and the work environment. Although the BMCT is a very useful tool, the results from this assessment are only part of a complete personnel evaluation. Other factors, including experience, education, and job history, are not evaluated by this test and warrant consideration along with the BMCT results in making a final evaluation of an individual's likelihood for success in the workplace. An organization in need of an easily administered, well-recognized, and reasonably priced test would find the BMCT quite worthwhile.

REVIEWER'S REFERENCES

Hegarty, M., & Kozhevnikov, M. (1999). Spatial abilities, working memory, and mechanical reasoning. In J. Gero & B. Tversky (Eds.), *Visual and spatial reasoning in design.* Sydney, Australia: Key Centre for Design and Cognition.
National Science and Technology Council. (2001). *Information technology: The 21st century revolution.* Washington, DC: U.S. Government Printing Office.
Wing, H. (1992). Test review of the Bennett Mechanical Comprehension Test. From J. J. Kramer & J. C. Conoley (Eds.), *The eleventh mental measurements yearbook* [Electronic version]. Retrieved December 7, 2004, from the Buros Institute's Test Reviews Online website: http://www.unl.edu/buros

[32]

The Benziger Thinking Styles Assessment.

Purpose: Designed to "help individuals increase their general effectiveness, collaborative skills and overall well-being through enhanced self-awareness and understanding."

Population: Working adults, aged 18 or older.

Publication Dates: 1988–2004.

Acronym: BTSA, E-BTSA.

Scores: Frontal Left, Basal Left, Basal Right, Frontal Right, Introversion/Extraversion.

Administration: Individual or group.

Restricted Distribution: Administrators must be persons (licensees) who have completed the publisher's training course.

Price Data, 2004: $100 per E-BTSA (electronic version); $25 per book *Thriving in Mind* (2003, 326 pages); North American and European licensee prices: $45 per BTSA and book *Thriving in Mind;* $15 per workbook, Thriving in Mind: The Workbook (specify English or Spanish); $75 per hour telephone feedback from author; price information for other countries available from publisher.

Time: (30–45) minutes.

Comments: Not intended as a psychometric measure; paper and electronic versions available.

Author: Katherine Benziger.

Publisher: KBA, LLC.

Review of The Benziger Thinking Styles Assessment by RICHARD E. HARDING, Director of Research, Kenexa Technology, Lincoln, NE:

DESCRIPTION. The Benziger Thinking Styles Assessment (BTSA) is a paper-and-pencil tool composed of 58 questions. The booklet that respondents fill out is eight pages in length. According to the manual, the questions cover a wide range of situations from adolescent to adulthood experiences, from work to leisure time. According to the author, the length of time it takes most people to complete the assessment is in the 30- to 45-minute range. Associated with most of the questions are four possible responses in which the respondent is asked to rank each possible response from "most like me" to "least like me." According to the author, this repeated rank ordering of four options resulted in a statistical verification of Jung's fundamental premise that was never statistically verified by Jung or Myers-Briggs.

The author indicates that "the purpose of the BTSA is to help individuals increase their general effectiveness, collaborative skills and overall well-being through enhanced self-awareness and understanding" (user manual, p. 7). Another purpose, according to the author, was that the original BTSA was developed between 1985 and 1987 to identify the presence or absence of falsification of type in a person's life. Falsification of type or adaptation is thought to result when an individual is using one or more of their nonpreferences (weaknesses) as their leading style.

This assessment was designed to use with working adults over the age of 18 who possess at least a ninth grade reading level. Additionally, people who are in a job transition can also benefit by using the BTSA.

The results of an individual's assessment are presented in a 22-page feedback report that analyzes and interprets the individual's data. The user's manual has a copyright date of 1994; the BTSA has been utilized in both Spanish and Japanese. Other cross-cultural usages alluded to in the manual, but not documented, include African American, Hispanic, Native American, and Scandinavian populations. No data are presented on any cross-cultural use.

Within the tool, corresponding to Jung's four functions of Thinking, Feeling, Sensing, and Intuition, the Frontal Right and Frontal Left modes correspond to the Frontal Right and Frontal Left lobes of the brain. The Basal Right and Basal Left modes correspond to the Right Posterior Convexity and Left Posterior convexity. The Frontal Left, if used as a strength, indicates a person who is "logical, mathematical, quantitative, analytical" (p. 32); Basal Left yields people who are "procedural, thorough, predictable, dependable, reliable, and efficient in performing sequential routine tasks" (p. 33); Basal Right includes people who are "sensitive, soothing, spiritual, and accommodating" (p. 34); and finally, Frontal Right, is characterized as "imaginative, metaphoric, visionary, creative, risk-taking, and spatial" (p. 35). Additional combinations of profiles are given when the Introversion/Extraversion scales are utilized. The author claims to be able to measure adaptation or falsification of type. Falsification of type according to the author was a strong impetus for the development of the BTSA. Throughout the manual, references are made to Jung and his theories about psychological types.

According to the author, the uses of the BTSA are widespread and quite varied. They include career counseling; Organizational Development (OD) and management consulting; counseling for individuals, couples, and families; assistance in overcoming depression and addictions; and use in education.

The scoring algorithms were not available for review due to the proprietary nature of the tool. They exist in a 300-page licensee's manual that may be accessed only by individuals licensed to use the BTSA. Therefore, how the scores are derived in each of the modes for the final report is unknown at this point. The scores for each mode can range from 0 to 140 with range descriptors. The higher the score, the more the person uses the mode or the higher it is developed.

DEVELOPMENT. The purpose of this review is not to evaluate Jung's theory of psychological types but rather to recognize that the BTSA is a derivative of Jung and according to the author both confirms and extends Jung's theories. The manual indicates that children are born with a tendency to move in one direction over another and to use one function over the other three. A person can be either inward focused, which is introverted, or outward focused, which is extraverted and either a sensor, feeler, thinker, or an intuitive type person. The manual presents research indicating that those four functions each exist in one of the four areas of the brain. These are then coupled with introversion or extraversion. Falsification of type occurs when one is not using their natural preference in terms of the four functions in his or her life but has been forced through one means or another to use another function to adapt to the environment or a situation more than they are using their preference. Jung's theories and physiology of the brain are well stated and well known.

ITEM DEVELOPMENT. There is a limited discussion of how the items were developed and chosen for the final tool but no statistical evidence was presented. According to the author, items were chosen based on (a) "their significance as indicators of the respondent's underlying preferences" and (b) "the insight they could provide on the full range or ways in which our dominances affect our life" (user manual, p. 60). The questions themselves deal with adolescent experience as well as experiences in adulthood. In fact, one part of the report analyzes the similarities and differences between the way the individual adapts as an adult and the way they adapted as an adolescent. Items are also based on the work of Hans Eysenck. This involves the categorization of a person as extraverted, balanced, or introverted. No developmental statistics are presented either at the item level or scale level.

TECHNICAL.

Reliability. According to the manual, the "reliability of the BTSA was established in the traditional manner" (p. 67). This seems like a rather broad statement and one must read further in the reliability section to determine that a test-retest reliability was used over a 7-year period. Working adults were tested up to three times; according to the manual, the mean interval between testing was 2.2 years. The sample size for this was 77 paired sets of data. The stability over time of the relative strength of each of the four key modes of thinking was being tested. According to the author, the stability of the BTSA mode scores was anywhere from 85.5% to 93.5%. Stability in the most used mode was 93.5%. Apparently, this means that over an average time of 2.2 years, 93.5% of the sample had identified the most used mode as the same over the two testing times. Very few additional data were presented on the reliability of the tool. Rather the authors are relying on anecdotal information on a case-by-case basis. With regard to the reliability of the Extraversion/Introversion scale, 63.3% of the sample showed stability in their level of extraversion. As near as can be determined, the author explains this: "under chronic anxiety people move towards increased introversion due to the sustained heightened sense of arousal" (user manual, p. 73). Another issue identified by the author is that as a person's life is stable over a period of years, so will be their extraversion data. From this the author concludes that the "BTSA has an acceptable level of reliability" (user manual, p. 76). This reviewer would take exception to that. Very little information was presented on the reliability of the process, the tables were difficult to read and understand, and the explanation around the tables was not as it should be in a tool that claims to measure thinking styles with this degree of accuracy. [Editor's note: Test author has improved the presentation of the tables in a newly edited edition of the user manual.]

Validity. The author states, "The validity of the BTSA was established in the traditional manner" (user manual, p. 77). Once again, this reviewer is not absolutely certain what the traditional manner of validity really means. Reading further in the manual, the author presents data on 1,321 respondents. It also appears that an earlier study on 132 working adults was conducted. For these 132 working adults, the correlation coefficients between the BTSA and the Myers—Briggs Type Indicator (MBTI) range between .35 BTSA Frontal Left to Thinking MBTI, .96 BTSA Basal Left to Sensing MBTI, .63 BTSA Basal Right to Feeling MBTI, and .59 BTSA Frontal Right to Intuition MBTI. In comparing BTSA and MBTI Extraversion/Introversion scores, it appears that a sample of 125 was used. Further, the author indicates that BTSA and MBTI for Introversion/Extraversion compared at a 74.4% rate of agreement.

On the sample of 1,328 individuals, data are presented on the mean scores on the BTSA for the entire sample, males, and females. This sample was composed of health care professionals, heavy manufacturing, educators, light manufacturing, sales and service, people in therapy, human resource professionals, banking, utilities, legal, cre-

ative directors, interior designers, and software designers. According to the number of persons in each of these groups, the sample size added up to 1,393. Heavy reliance on what the author calls face validity is used in the validity section. Liberal use of phrases such as "everyone knows" are used to provide evidence supporting the validity of the process. For example, "everyone knows that people who succeed in business enough to be promoted to, or hired as top executives in medium sized corporations excel at using logic to identify and evaluate options" (user manual, p. 83). Thus, the argument is made that the BTSA is valid because it upholds our stereotypical views of various professions and the differences between males and females in those professions. This is not the type of validity evidence one would expect.

COMMENTARY. It would be expected that the tables and research presented in both the reliability and validity sections would be well laid out, easy to follow, and with adequate explanations provided; this was not the case. There were few attempts to identify the actual sample demographics; different sample sizes were interjected into the tables with no explanation as to why. For example, in one table, the means and standard deviations were presented for one sample whereas for another sample in the same table only the means were presented. Accordingly, concerns exist about the actual reliability and validity work reported. The use of statements that begin with "everyone knows," use of face validity, and presenting evidence that the BTSA correlates to the MBTI, do not inspire confidence in this tool. In fact, the MBTI was reviewed in the *Fourteenth Mental Measurements Yearbook* (Plake & Impara, 2001; 14:251). Both reviewers in their summaries had some concerns about the use of the MBTI as it exists with regard to Form M.

SUMMARY. The theory on which the BTSA was developed regarding Jungian concepts was sound, well researched, and is generally accepted. The author has put a lot of effort and work into the BTSA. It is very likely that this tool does have utility for some of its intended uses. However, the user manual is a disappointment in that it seems to be a long sales pitch and this detracts from what may be a useful tool. More specifics in the studies are needed, not anecdotal, *n* of 1 testimonials. More research is needed or at least the existing research needs to be better reported. Furthermore, to be licensed to use the BTSA, one does not appear to have to be trained in counseling or psychology. Rather, according to the manual, one must participate in a 4-day seminar conducted by the author where he or she learns how to use the BTSA and other BTSA products. Finally, with a publication date of 1994, one wonders why no update or additional research has been incorporated in the 10 years since the manual was published. The BTSA may be a marvelous tool but deficiencies in the user manual make it difficult to endorse without great reservations.

REVIEWER'S REFERENCE

Plake, B. S., & Impara, J. C. (Eds.). (2001). *The fourteenth mental measurements yearbook.* Lincoln, NE: Buros Institute of Mental Measurements.

Review of The Benziger Thinking Styles Assessment by MARK L. POPE, Associate Professor, Division of Counseling and Family Therapy, University of Missouri—St. Louis, St. Louis, MO:

DESCRIPTION AND DEVELOPMENT. The Benziger Thinking Styles Assessment (BTSA) is an inventory to assess an individual's thinking style. The BTSA was designed to "help individuals increase their general effectiveness, collaborative skills and overall well-being through enhanced self-awareness and understanding" (user manual, p. 7). It is based on the work of Carl Jung and the author, Katherine Benziger. In this way it is similar to the Gray-Wheelrights' Jungian Type Survey (T6:1306), Myers-Briggs Type Indicator (MBTI; T6:1678), Singer-Loomis Type Deployment Inventory (T6:2285), Keirsey Temperament Sorter (125), Type Differentiation Indicator, DISC/Performax, Personality Type Inventory, Jung Type Indicator, and other commercially available inventories that have been developed to assess Jungian personality types. It was developed between 1985 and 1987 to identify the issue of "falsification of type," which refers to a developed nonnatural (learned) behavioral pattern of habitually choosing and using a Jungian function (Sensing, Intuition, Thinking, Feeling) other than the person's own natural lead (or dominant) function.

The BTSA is available as an eight-page, single use, combined item and response booklet or through a software program that allows for data entry only, not scoring. It is scored only electronically and available only through a network of trained and licensed consultants who have attended a 4-day workshop presented by the author

at various times and various places. The booklet is printed in black ink on sheets of ivory-colored, heavy-weight 11-inch by 17-inch paper that is then folded and staple-stitched into an 8 1/2-inch by 11-inch format. The BTSA consists of 58 items in a variety of formats that are preceded by a 10-item demographic section (Part 1). Almost all of Parts 2–5 use a four-option, rank order format where 1 is "least like you" and 4 is "most like you." Items are grouped into a section where the respondent is asked about their youth, their adult working life, their leisure and home life, and their overall self-perception. The final part consists of 6 items on the respondent's emotional state of being. No item-specific data are presented regarding the development of the four mode or Jungian function scales. There are some statements in the user manual that would lead this reviewer to believe that items were rationally derived, but without any data this is conjecture.

The results are returned in two parts: a 22–24-page narrative report that provides a substantial amount of analysis and a 4-page profile report that provides an item-by-item listing of the test taker's responses along with a full-page figure that graphically displays a comparison between the reported adolescent and adult personality profiles.

There are four modes or subscales on the BTSA: Frontal Left, Frontal Right, Basal Left, and Basal Right as well as a measure of Extraversion/Introversion. Scores on each of the four modes can range from 0–140 with scores in the range 0–40 labeled low, 41–80 labeled moderate, 81–100 is strong, and 101–140 is very strong or committed. The level of Extraversion/Introversion is reported as a ratio of Extraversion to Introversion from 12:0 to 0:12 with 12:0 to 8:4 considered extraverted, 7:5 to 5:7 balanced, and 4:8 to 0:12 introverted. There are, however, no data presented in the user manual on the development of the scores (either mode/function subscales or attitude/extraversion-introversion subscale) or the kind of scores (standardized, transformed, or raw) that are reported. Along with the profile and narrative reports, the results also include a book written by the author, *Thriving in Mind*, and individual feedback on the results by a trained and licensed consultant.

TECHNICAL. Evidence of reliability and validity along with cross-cultural usage is presented in the user manual. Validity data were composed of evidence of construct-related convergent validity. These data included comparisons of the BTSA with MBTI (N = 132 working adults) and an analysis using the extant BTSA data (N = 1,321) of the foundational Jungian concept that, when one function is dominant, the opposite function will be the weakest. For example, if Sensing is strongest, then Intuition will be the weakest of the four Jungian functions.

Data in the first study (N = 132) measured the statistical relationships between the four BTSA subscales (Basal Left, Frontal Right, Frontal Left, and Basal Right) with the four Jungian functions subscales as measured by the Myers-Briggs Type Indicator. The four BTSA subscales had strong positive relationships with three of the MBTI subscales (r = .96 to .59). Only a moderate relationship was found between the BTSA Frontal Left scale and the MBTI Thinking scale (r = .35). This is certainly sufficient. Data in the second study (N = 1,321) were also strongly supportive of the construct validity of the BTSA.

Evidence of the stability of the subscales over time was also presented in the user manual (N = 77). Test-retest reliability data are usually reported as correlation coefficients, which gives a more accurate test of scores reported as numbers. Stability in Jungian type measures and some career interest measures that report typologies is many times reported as stability in identifying the order of such categories and the percentage of agreement between the two testings. No specific reliability studies were conducted over a standard time period (e.g., 6 months). Instead, the author reported retests of individuals from the BTSA scoring database. Only 77 paired respondents were reported with intervals from 3 months to 7 years with a mean of 2.2 years. This method of collecting reliability data is highly suspect and it is recommended that a more traditional method be employed.

Regarding the cross-cultural use of the instrument, the author addresses this in the user manual. Statements, however, such as "Black, Hispanic, Native American, and Scandinavian workers and professionals have also taken the English version of the BTSA and reported positive experiences" (p. 15) are not a substitute for research and more quantifiable data. There were also reports of Spanish and Japanese translations, but with no report of resultant studies on their validity and reliability.

COMMENTARY. Other materials made available for this review included a 108-page "user manual"; a 94-page booklet titled "Falsification of Type: Its Jungian and Physiological Foundations and Mental, Emotional, and Physiological Costs" written by the author; a 62-page booklet titled "Physiological & Psychophysiological Bases for Jungian Concepts: An Annotated Bibliography" written by the author; four sample profile/narrative reports; and a 57-page packet titled "Articles about the BTSA and Benziger Breakthroughs." Throughout the materials there are substantial numbers of typographic errors and this detracts from the perception that this instrument was carefully constructed. [Editor's note: The test author has provided a 2004 revision of the manual with the typographical errors corrected.]

The BTSA was developed in 1987 to measure the "falsification of type" by individuals. The term "falsification" carries with it negative connotations of individual responsibility, of actively lying, but this is not the meaning that Jung nor Benziger attribute to it. They both refer to falsification as having a developmental aspect—that as one matures, falsification of type occurs naturally over a person's lifetime (i.e., we begin to work on our opposite preferences and, therefore, develop some competencies in those opposites). That competence sometimes masks our natural leads or dominant preferences allowing us to report our false types as our dominant ones on certain inventories. This is a concept that is reported in various places in the Jungian literature (Grutter, 1996; Holmes, 1982; Myers & McCaulley, 1985; Yabroff, 1996).

According to the author, the item format used is what makes the BTSA different from all the other Jungian type inventories. For example, the MBTI uses generally a forced-choice, two-option item format; it's either this or it's that. Such a format seems theoretically appropriate for such an inventory, as Jungian types are generally referred to in the literature as dichotomous and discrete concepts. This format, however, does not easily allow for the measurement of the more complicated issue of "falsification of type." The BTSA item format of rank ordering the four presented options allows the individual to respond directly to the four Jungian functions and provide a more nuanced type measurement. This format certainly allows the BTSA to more effectively measure what it says it is trying to measure (i.e., the falsification of type). And, although this format is a better one for a discrete Jungian function measure, it still does not exactly get at the *degree* of difference between the rank-ordered options.

This instrument and the theory/model developed by Dr. Benziger is based on the assumption that thinking styles are tied to specific parts of the brain; however, there appear to be no definitive data that support that assumption. The author does cite some theoretical writings and states that the neurophysiological claims are based on a:

> Premise recommended to us by Karl Pribram, M.D., Ph.D., that the thinking function is housed in the Left Frontal Lobe, intuition in the Right Frontal Lobe, sensation in the Left Posterior Cortical Convexity and Feeling (i.e. the feeling function, not the emotions seated in the limbic structures) in the Right Posterior Cortical Convexity; and ... Hans Eysenck's work linking extraversion and introversion to differing innate arousal levels. (author, "Rethinking stress, depression and midlife crisis," pp. 5–14, in the packet titled "Articles about the BTSA and Benziger Breakthroughs")

Unfortunately for all of us, there remains much about brain physiology and function that is unknown. The question must be asked: Where are the data that tie the thinking styles to specific parts of the brain? Dr. Benziger argues forcefully for this relationship, but does it through analogy not with specific data nor specific journal articles directed to this specific question. Dr. Benziger may indeed be correct in her arguments as they are logical, persuasive, and based in the current neurophysiological literature. The heart of her entire typology, however, lies in the relationship of thinking styles to brain physiology and there is as yet no definitive data that speak directly to that. Further, it is not enough then to rely solely on Eysenck, for his work speaks only to the existence and direction of the energy not to the physiological basis of the four Jungian functions.

The author recommended that individuals be retested periodically in a subsection of the user's manual titled "Repeated Profiling of Individuals." This recommendation flies in the face of personality research that has been done over the last 100 years that reports substantial stability in such constructs. It would also seem to go against the test-retest reliability data reported by the author. Repeated administrations of this measure could be costly and this could be an issue for some individuals or companies.

SUMMARY. The BTSA has substantial reasons to recommend its use. It is the only Jungian type assessment instrument that is designed to address issues of falsifying type with a unique item format (for similar Jungian-based inventories) that is specifically designed to assess this construct. Also, the profile and narrative reports are useful and absorbing, providing rich insights into the individual. The validity data are strong, but a better method of studying the reliability of the scores is needed. More attention needs to be paid to the errors in the text in all documents. It appears from the materials that the author is currently the only person studying this instrument and there are no studies utilizing the BTSA reported in any refereed professional journals. Finally, although the author makes a strong and persuasive argument for the relationship between brain physiology and Jungian functions, there are no definitive studies on this—yet.

REVIEWER'S REFERENCES

Grutter, J. (1998). *Making it in today's organizations: Using the Strong and the MBTI—career advancement.* Palo Alto, CA: Consulting Psychologists Press.

Holmes, J. M. (1982). *Normal neuropsychological development.* Providence, RI: The Healing Dove.

Myers, I. B., & McCaulley, M. H. (1985). *Manual: A guide to the development of the Myers-Briggs Type Indicator.* Palo Alto, CA: Consulting Psychologists Press.

Yabroff, W. (1990). *The inner image: A resource for type development.* Palo Alto, CA: Consulting Psychologists Press.

[33]

Beta III.

Purpose: "Provides a quick ... measure of nonverbal intellectual ability."

Population: Ages 16–89.

Publication Dates: 1934–1999.

Scores, 6: Coding, Picture Completion, Clerical Checking, Picture Absurdities, Matrix Reasoning, IQ Score.

Administration: Group or individual.

Price Data, 2002: $145 per complete kit including manual (1999, 58 pages), 25 response booklets, and scoring key; $42 per manual; $104 per 25 response booklets; $299 per 100 response booklets; quantity discounts available; $16 per scoring key.

Time: 15(25–30) minutes including 10–15 minutes of instruction and practice.

Comments: Revision of the Revised Beta Examination, Second Edition.

Authors: C. E. Kellogg and N. W. Morton.

Publisher: PsychCorp, A brand of Harcourt Assessment, Inc.

Cross References: For information regarding the previous edition, see T5:2212 (3 references) and T4:2255

(4 references); see also T2:447 (29 references); for a review by Bert A. Goldman, see 6:494 (13 references); see also 5:375 (14 references); for reviews by Raleigh M. Drake and Walter C. Shipley, see 3:259 (5 references); for reviews by S. D. Porteus and David Wechsler, see 2:1419 (4 references).

Review of the Beta III by C. G. BELLAH, Director of Special Services, Parker College, Dallas, TX:
DESCRIPTION. The Beta III is the current revision of the Beta II and is a test of nonverbal intellectual ability. The Beta III is designed to assess various facets of nonverbal intelligence, such as: spatial reasoning, processing speed, and visual information processing. Historically, earlier editions of the Beta III were used to estimate general intelligence in an adult population, particularly adults for whom verbal tests of intelligence are inappropriate, such as the poorly educated, illiterate, or non-English speakers. Contemporaneously, the Beta III is often used for this purpose in our nation's prisons and by industrial organizations that hire unskilled workers.

The Beta III may be administered either individually or in groups and is available in both English and Spanish versions. The authors indicate the Beta III may be administered by paraprofessionals with appropriate training in psychological assessment. Test administration is expected to require between 25–30 minutes, which includes 10-15 minutes for instruction/practice and approximately 14 minutes for test taking.

In its current form, the Beta III consists of five subtests, including: Coding, Picture Completion, Clerical Checking, Picture Absurdities, and Matrix Reasoning. The Coding subtest is noticeably similar to the Wechsler Adult Intelligence Scale—Third Edition (WAIS-III; T6: 2691) Coding subtest and involves writing the number that is associated with a hieroglyphic-like symbol. Each correct response on the Coding subtest items is scored as 1 point, with a possible range of scores spanning between 3 and 140. The Picture Completion subtest is also similar to its WAIS-III counterpart and requires the test taker to examine a series of illustrations and draw the missing components that would complete the pictures. Each correct response is scored as 1 point, with a maximum score of 24.

The Clerical Checking subtest requires the test taker to indicate (by circling the equal sign or the does not equal sign) whether pairs of pictures,

symbols, or numbers are the same or different. Scoring of the Clerical Checking subtest requires the test administrator to compare examinee's responses to a scoring key, and test administrators are instructed to indicate correct responses with a "+" and incorrect responses with a "-." In deriving the raw scores, test administrators are directed to subtract the number of minus signs from the number of plus signs, with a maximum total raw score of 55.

The Picture Absurdities subtest requires the test taker to select one of four pictures that illustrates something wrong or foolish by placing an "X" on the identified picture. Examinee responses are compared to a scoring key. Correct answers are scored 1 point each, with a maximum score of 24. Finally, the Matrix Reasoning is also similar to its WAIS-III counterpart and requires the test taker to select the missing symbol or picture that best completes the set of four. Correct answers are scored 1 point with 25 points possible. After deriving raw scores for each of the five scales, the raw scores are then converted to age-corrected scaled scores and a summative IQ equivalent scaled score.

DEVELOPMENT. The Beta III is the product of a long and rich history in research and psychometric development. Its original version, the Group Beta Examination, was developed by the United States Army during WWI and was used to estimate the intellectual ability of uneducated military recruits. The test was revised in 1934 for use with a civilian population and was published as the Revised Beta Examination (Beta I). The Beta I was subsequently restandardized in 1946 using methods that were patterned after those used by Wechsler in standardizing the Wechsler—Bellevue Intelligence Scale. The test was modernized and restandardized once again in 1978 using stratified sampling techniques and was published as the Beta II.

Finally, the Beta III was published in 1999 and boasts a number of improvements to the Beta II, including: improved illustrations; replacement of outdated or potentially biased items; replacement of the Paper Form Board subtest with Matrix Reasoning, which negates drawing ability as a confound; modernized norms; and improved utility in a broader range of applied settings.

Unfortunately, the test manual does not present any item-level analyses or information regarding derivation of individual items. Regarding scale-level analyses, the manual presents the results of one exploratory factor analysis, in which two second-order factors were retained for rotation (oblique) using a principal components extraction. Regrettably, the manual provides no information regarding the sample that was used in these analyses. Moreover, the second factor ("Processing Speed") was specified to have only two manifest indicators, which is fewer than the minimum of three that is required for factor stability (Kline, 1998). Therefore, generalization of the results of these analyses is not recommended.

Secondly, the authors present results of one confirmatory factor analysis in estimation of the two-factor structure identified in exploratory work. Again, it is unfortunate that the manual does not provide the reader with any clear report of the sample characteristics used in these analyses, although it is possible that the standardization sample (discussed below) may have been used. Nevertheless, available results indicate low to moderate correspondence between predicted and observed scores. Overall, there appears to be little empirical evidence in support of the proposed factor solution.

TECHNICAL. Standardization of the Beta III is based on a sample of 1,260 participants that was stratified by sex, age, ethnicity, education level, and geographic region of residence according to findings from the 1997 U.S. Census. The normative data were collected between January 1997 and November 1998 by 113 examiners in 82 cities in the United States. Like the WAIS-III, standard scores for the Beta III are derived by converting raw scores for each subtest to scaled scores that were normed using a mean of 10 and a standard deviation of 3.

Also like the WAIS-III, a sum of scaled scores is used to estimate IQ and is normed using a mean of 100 and a standard deviation of 15. The authors note that individual subtest scores are not to be interpreted, given that only the summative scale has sufficient psychometric properties (i.e., validity, reliability) for clinical interpretation.

Evidence of the reliability of the Beta III is very limited. The authors argue that measures of internal consistency such as split-half and coefficient alpha are inappropriate for use due to overestimation, so reliability of the Beta III is limited to test-retest estimates (2- to 12-week interval) derived from a single sample of 204 participants. Unfortunately, reliability estimates are only provided for the summative scaled scores stratified across three age groups. Overall, estimated test-retest reliability for the Beta III is reported to be .87 (SE_M = 4.50), with an estimate of .91 when allowances are given due to a restriction in range.

Regarding content validity, the authors of the Beta III argue the Beta III scales represent the scope of interest in measuring nonverbal intellectual ability as indicated by their structural similarities to the performance scales of the WAIS-III. Additionally, construct validity of the Beta III is evidenced by several correlational studies with other measures of nonverbal intelligence, including: WAIS-III, Beta II, and the Standard Progressive Matrices.

In sum, available evidence reflects moderate correlations between Beta III summative scaled scores and the full-scale scores of other tests of nonverbal intelligence. Unfortunately, although the degree of construct validity is fairly well established, the content validity of the Beta III remains largely unsubstantiated, and there remains a dearth of information regarding the criterion and discriminant validity as well. Likewise, any treatment of differential item functioning is not apparent in the test manual.

COMMENTARY AND SUMMARY. The Beta III boasts a number of positive attributes. The test may be administered in either English or Spanish, and normative data are available for both the general and correctional populations. Also, administration of the Beta III is relatively quick, requiring approximately 30 minutes to complete. It is also advantageous that the Beta III may be administered by paraprofessionals, and the correspondence between its IQ estimate and that of the WAIS-III is convenient for clinical interpretation.

However, despite its long and distinguished developmental history, there is very little information available to the reader of the test manual that supports the psychometric properties of the Beta III. Although a preponderance of the research in development of the Beta III has apparently focused on standardization of the instrument and establishing its relation to other assessments of nonverbal intelligence, a great deal remains lacking in its psychometric investigation.

First, the reported factor analytic examinations of the structural model are largely inadequate by modern standards, and the reliability of the Beta III remains largely unsubstantiated as well. Likewise, readers of the test manual are left wanting for evidence of some basic test attributes, particularly criterion and discriminant validity, and differential item functioning. In sum, despite its inception during World War I, evidentiary presentation of the psychometric properties of the Beta III suggests that it remains in the early stages of development. It is recommended that the interested reader consider using the Wechsler Abbreviated Scale of Intelligence (WASI; T6:2690) or the performance scales of the WAIS-III as alternatives to the Beta-III in estimating nonverbal intellectual ability.

REVIEWER'S REFERENCE

Kline, R. B. (1998). *Principles and practice of structural equation modeling.* New York: The Guilford Press.

Review of the Beta III by LOUISE M. SOARES, Professor of Educational Psychology, University of New Haven, West Haven, CT:

DESCRIPTION. The Beta III is a group-administered test of nonverbal intellectual ability, designed for individuals in the general population from ages 16 to 89 and for those who are illiterate or non-English-speaking, or who have language difficulties. It contains five sections: (a) *Coding*—with instructions to write numbers that correspond to hieroglyphic-like symbols; (b) *Picture Completion*—for drawing what is missing to complete a picture; (c) *Clerical Checking*—for determining whether pairs of pictures, symbols, or numbers are the same or different by circling the equal sign (=) for the "same" or nonequal sign (≠) if they are not; (d) *Picture Absurdities*—placing an X on the one picture out of four that illustrates something wrong or foolish; and (e) *Matrix Reasoning*—choosing the missing symbol or picture that best completes a set of four symbols or pictures.

The total administration time is between 25 and 30 minutes, with 10–15 minutes for instruction and practice and 14.5 minutes for actual testing. A different set of instructions is provided for each of the five sections of the test. The administration directions are available in English and Spanish.

For all but the third section, Clerical Checking, each correct response receives one point. The maximum raw scores are as follows: Coding, 140; Picture Completion, 24; Picture Absurdities, 24; Matrix Reasoning, 25. For the section on Clerical Checking, a plus sign (+) is recorded when matched correctly against the scoring key, and a minus sign

(-) for incorrect matches. The raw score is obtained by subtracting the number of items with a minus sign from the number of items with a plus sign. The maximum raw score is 55, but it is also possible to obtain a negative total raw score on this third set of items.

The raw scores from each of the five sections are then converted to age-corrected scaled scores. The range of the scaled scores is 1 to 19 for each section of the test, although most of the raw scores do not have scaled-score equivalents above 15 for Picture Absurdities and Matrix Reasoning. The authors compensate for this in their final conversion to IQ scores. The five scaled scores from the five test sections are summed and then converted to IQ scores, ranging from 48 (for the sum of the scaled scores of 5) to 155 (for the sum of the scaled scores of 84 to 95).

DEVELOPMENT. The Beta III constitutes a revision of the Revised Beta Examination—Second Edition (1978). It was nationally standardized "using a large representative sample stratified by age, education level, sex, race/ethnicity, and geographic region" (manual, p. 1), according to the 1997 U.S. Census data (manual, p. 1). It was designed to assess forms of nonverbal intelligence including visual information processing, processing speed, spatial and nonverbal reasoning, and aspects of fluid intelligence.

According to the manual (pp. 2 and 3), specific changes were undertaken: (a) discontinuation of two sections, Mazes and Paper Form Board; (b) improved the quality of the testing materials; (c) replaced outdated or potentially biased items; (d) replaced Paper Form Board with Matrix Reasoning; (e) extended the age range from 64 years to 89 years; (f) improved clinical utility and validity; (g) improved ceiling to an IQ of 155 points; updated the norms, re-anchored at 100. These changes were made, and they may be considered improvements. However, the scoring template is cumbersome and cannot be readily aligned in all cases with the answers in the response booklet, possibly leading to incorrect scoring.

TECHNICAL. The standardization data were collected between January 1997 and November 1998 by 113 independent examiners in 82 U.S. cities (manual, p. 7). Recruitment of participants included random telephone calls, newspaper advertisements, and flyers placed in schools, senior centers, churches, and various community organizations. Potential participants were medically and psychiatrically screened through interviews and self-report questionnaires. The list of exclusionary criteria included such factors as uncorrected visual impairment, current treatment for addiction, and specific conditions that could affect cognitive functioning, such as epilepsy, meningitis, or brain surgery. The norms were established from the sums of the scale scores—age-corrected—and then converted to IQs and percentile equivalents, along with the confidence intervals at the 90% and 95% levels. No norms were established for gender, ethnicity, geographical region, or education.

The reliability of scores from the Beta III was assessed by the test-retest method. The sample consisted of 204 participants, tested between 2 and 12 weeks. The coefficients were displayed in three age-bands: 16–24, 25–54, 55–89. The resulting coefficients were .87, .82, and .90, respectively, for the three age bands. When corrected for restriction of range, the coefficients were .91, .90, and .91, respectively. Without knowing how many participants were retested within 2 weeks, we are left wondering about the impact of memory and practice effects.

Intercorrelations among the five sections of the Beta III range from .40 to .61, suggesting that each subtest does not measure independent factors. The manual states that Beta III measures two different domains of nonverbal intellectual ability. Matrix Reasoning, Picture Completion, and Picture Absurdities reflect "fluid reasoning"; Coding and Clerical Checking related to "processing speed." These assertions of construct validity are supported with the goodness-of-fit analysis. The manual does not suggest how these results confirm the Beta III's mission for measuring general intelligence.

In other analyses of validity, the manual indicates coefficients (all corrected for variability of the Beta III standardization sample) with Beta-II (.71 and .87, two separate samples), WAIS-III (.67 for VFQ, .80 for PIQ, and .77 for FSIQ), Raven's Standard Progressive Matrices (.75), Revised Minnesota Paper Form Board Test (.73), Personnel Tests for Industry—Oral Tests (.74), Bennett Mechanical Comprehension Test (.46), and The Adult Basic Learning Examination—Screening Battery (.39/.40 and .56/.57 for two separate samples). None of these comparisons provides solid support for validity of the Beta III. In the comparison of earlier forms of the WAIS with the Revised Beta Examination, the validity coefficient between these two tests was .92 (see reviews of Test 259 in the *Third Mental Measurements Yearbook* and Test 494 in the *Sixth Mental Measurements Yearbook*).

COMMENTARY. As indicated in previous reviews, cited above, a nonverbal test cannot readily substitute for a verbal test of intelligence. The Beta III does not measure general intelligence or provide a comprehensive evaluation of any individual's intellectual functioning. It does assess certain attributes of nonverbal intellectual ability, but these are not necessarily related to other measures of intelligence or generalizable to a larger population with a wide range of ages, development, and experiences.

SUMMARY. Generally, the Beta III seems to have been improved; necessary changes were undertaken. However, work should be continued on the Beta III by conducting item analyses, discriminant analyses, and the derivation of IQ scores for separate groups (e.g., females, nonprison populations, race/ethnicity). The additional comparisons of results for individuals identified with mental retardation or attention-deficit/hyperactivity disorder are welcome and should be expanded to include other disabilities or handicaps. Although the definition of intelligence remains in debate, the Beta III can be interpreted as providing a rough approximation to measured intellectual ability commonly known as IQ. Its usefulness is consistent with its original purpose—measuring the intellectual ability of non-English-speaking individuals, illiterates, and poor readers.

[34]

Boehm Test of Basic Concepts—Third Edition.

Purpose: Designed to "assess ... [school] readiness or [to] identify students who may be at risk for learning difficulty."

Population: Grades K–2.

Publication Dates: 1967–2001.

Acronym: Boehm-3.

Scores: Total score only.

Administration: Group or individual.

Forms, 2: E, F.

Price Data, 2004: $62 per examination set including examiner's manual (2001, 145 pages), 1 Form E booklet, 1 Form F booklet, 1 Form E class key, 1 Form F class key, and 1 directions for administration (Forms E and F, English and Spanish); $83 per testing kit

(Form E or F) including directions for administration (English and Spanish), 1 package of 25 booklets, and 1 class key; $57 per examiner's manual (Fall norms manual); $7 per class key (Form E or F); $18 per directions for administration (English and Spanish).

Foreign Language Edition: Directions for administering in Spanish are available for both forms.

Time: 30(45) minutes if administered in one session; 45(60) minutes if administered in two test sessions.

Comments: Revision of the Boehm Test of Basic Concepts—Revised; yields raw scores, percent correct, performance range, and percentiles by grade.

Author: Ann E. Boehm.

Publisher: PsychCorp, A brand of Harcourt Assessment, Inc.

Cross References: For information regarding previous editions, see T5:324 (12 references) and T4:314 (5 references); for reviews by Robert L. Linn and by Colleen Fitzmaurice and Joseph C. Witt, see 10:32 (16 references); see also T3:302 (18 references); for an excerpted review by Theodore A. Dahl, see 8:178 (22 references); se also T2:344 (1 reference); for reviews by Boyd R. McCandless and Charles D. Smock, and excerpted reviews by Frank S. Freeman, George Lawlor, Victor H. Noll, and Barton B. Proger, see 7:335 (1 reference).

Review of the Boehm Test of Basic Concepts–3 by SHERRY K. BAIN, Associate Professor, Department of Educational Psychology & Counseling, and JAMES HAWKINS, Doctoral Student in School Psychology, University of Tennessee, Knoxville, TN:

DESCRIPTION. The Boehm Test of Basic Concepts—Third Edition (Boehm-3) is designed for assessing students' understanding of concepts related to school success. Boehm defines basic concepts as words that describe qualities of people or objects, spatial relationships, time, and quantity. The connection between understanding basic concepts and success in school-related activities, such as following teacher's instructions, remains a primary concern during preschool, kindergarten, and the early elementary grades, lending strong credibility to the usefulness of this test. The Boehm-3 is recommended by its author for use in designing instruction based on discrete weaknesses, collecting normative information about a child's performance, as part of a test battery for identifying at-risk students, providing pre- and postintervention information about student progress, and for use in research. Two parallel forms of the test are provided, Forms E and F, and each test includes both an English and Spanish edition.

Originally published in 1971 and revised in 1986, goals of the current edition included updating normative information, providing four response choices instead of three, modifying and updating illustrations, increasing diversity in persons depicted, introducing observation forms and parent report forms, developing a Spanish edition, enhancing transition between levels of testing (e.g., between the Boehm-3 and the Boehm-3 Preschool; Boehm, 2001), and improving user-friendliness. In addition to addressing these concerns, Boehm rearranged test items, interspersing easy items with more difficult items, rather than arranging items from easy to difficult, as in earlier editions.

The Boehm-3 can be administered to groups of children, or individually. Test administration can take up to 45 minutes in a single session, or about 30 minutes per session, if divided into two sessions. Fifty items are administered in either Form E or F, with 3 additional practice items preceding the first test item, and 3 practice items embedded at midpoint, in case the test is administered in two sessions. For the Spanish edition, alternate vocabulary words are offered to adjust for geographically related differences in Spanish usage.

Individual administration of the Boehm-3 is generally straightforward and simple. Class-wide administration may require additional adults to monitor students. The test's stimulus pictures are interesting and colorful, and can easily maintain a child's attention. Specific administration instructions are easy to follow, with administrator's comments in bold.

A class record form is provided to compare student's skills across the classroom, giving a quick visual reference of the classwide range of skills. Test results are easily derived in the form of raw scores, percent correct, performance range, and percentile ranks. Incorrect answers may be broken down for analysis, indicating whether students chose the antonym, circled more than one response, or other miscellaneous responses. Scoring information also provides the difficulty level for each concept by grade, and the percent of students passing each item by grade level. Boehm recommends that the test be used by "knowledgeable professionals who have experience in test administration and interpretation" (examiner's manual, p. 8). Recommendations are also provided for modifying and adapting the test when assessing older students with special needs.

DEVELOPMENT. In developing this revision, the test author relied on reviews of recent curriculum changes in early reading and mathematics programs, a review of verbal instructions and directions in standardized tests to identify consistently used concepts, and feedback from user surveys. Items from the Boehm Test of Basic Concepts—Revised (Boehm-R, Boehm, 1986) were reviewed by experts for bias issues, including gender, ethnic, socioeconomic class, cultural, and regional biases. Item changes for the Boehm-3 were the result of these various sources of information. Five new items were added to the tryout version of the Boehm-3. Test directions were also modified to minimize language complexity.

In the manual, Boehm provides fairly detailed descriptions of the development, standardization, and collection of evidence for reliability and validity for this revision of the test. In developing the two parallel forms, attention was paid to the number and location of foils, the picture orientation, and item content across forms. A tryout version for the English edition was carried out with a demographically representative group of over 5,000 children, with an oversampling of minority groups to examine bias.

For standardization of the English edition, a sample of more than 6,000 students were included in the fall testing session; over 4,000 were included in the spring session. Participants represented stratified samples across demographic characteristics based on U.S. Census information. The manual includes specific information on demographic variables for both the try-out and standardization groups, including percentages of gender, racial/ethnic groups, socioeconomic level, and geographic representation. Following examination of *p* values, item difficulty, and bias, 5 items were deleted from the standardization version, bringing the total items for Forms E and F to 50 each.

The Spanish edition, based upon item translations from the English edition, was not administered at the try-out level, only at the standardization level. Participants in standardization of the Spanish edition included over 800 students for the fall testing and nearly 300 for spring. Boehm reports that geographic sampling was poor in the northeast region of the United States. Modest-sized samples represent the south and west regions. Following data collection, data analyses similar to those carried out for the English edition

were completed, and five items corresponding to those excluded from the standardization version of the English edition were deleted, leaving somewhat equivalent and parallel concepts for both editions. Differences between difficulty levels for items from the Spanish and English editions are discussed in the manual.

TECHNICAL INFORMATION. The Boehm-3 English edition reports reliability evidence in the form of internal consistency, standard error of measurement, test-retest, and alternate form reliability. Internal consistency coefficients ranged from .80 to .91 across grades, forms, and testing times. Standard errors of measurement ranged from 1.14 to 2.43 across the same variables.

Test-retest reliability estimates for the English edition, based upon a sample of 313 children across grade levels, with testing intervals averaging 1 week, ranged from .70 to .89 across forms and grades. Alternate form reliability, based upon 216 first graders, produced a reliability coefficient of .83.

Internal consistency estimates for the Spanish edition ranged from .79 to .88 across forms, grade levels, and administration times. Test-retest reliability for the Spanish edition was based upon 106 students across grade levels, tested at approximately 1-week intervals, producing reliability coefficients ranging from .78 to .80. The standard errors of measurement across forms, grades, and administration times ranged from 2.02 to 2.90, slightly larger than standard errors for the English edition.

Evidence of several types of validity are presented in the manual for the English edition of the Boehm-3. Content validity for this revised edition was reexamined by reviewing the frequency of test item concepts in reading vocabularies and curricula for the grade levels of interest. Current mathematics curricula were not reexamined in this manner. However, random samplings of words in five major reading and math series, respectively, confirmed the use of tested concepts across grades K through 2. Finally, examination of teachers' verbal directions produced evidence of Boehm-3 concepts in classroom instructions.

Concurrent validity for the English edition was based upon comparisons with the Boehm-R, the Metropolitan Achievement Tests, Metropolitan Readiness Test, and the Otis-Lennon School Ability Test, with correlations ranging from .48 to .96 depending upon the comparison test.

Evidence of construct validity for the Spanish edition was based upon comparison with the Naglieri Nonverbal Ability Test, a group-administered test measuring reasoning and problem-solving. Correlations from this comparison ranged from .32 to .59. Further evidence of construct validity is not reported in the manual for the Spanish edition.

Studies of predictive validity, based upon the Boehm-3, are not reported. However, studies predicting school achievement based upon the Boehm Test of Basic Concepts (BTBC; Boehm, 1976) and the Boehm-R (Boehm, 1998) are cited and summarized. Additionally, studies providing evidence of successful instructional activities based upon test results are cited.

COMMENTARY AND SUMMARY. In its third edition, the Boehm-3 continues to be carefully researched, incorporating needed changes and adaptations for the English edition, and adding a Spanish version. The standardization sample for the English edition is adequate and representative of the U.S. population. Evidence of reliability and validity presented in the manual is thoroughly detailed and gives confidence in the use of the English edition. Probably because it is newly developed, the Spanish edition lacks the breadth and depth of reliability and validity evidence that supports the English edition. In addition, the standardization sample is much smaller, and by the author's admission, lacks adequate representation for one geographic region.

The Boehm-3 seems particularly useful as an indicator of strengths and weaknesses in concept acquisition across individuals in a classroom. Alternate forms allow teachers to measure growth in concept knowledge across instruction time. For its identified purposes, the Boehm-3 English edition is highly recommended, and could prove an asset in classes including young children who are at risk for school failure. The temptation of professionals to include the Boehm-3 in diagnostic batteries, particularly for language problems, may be strong. However, the manual offers no information on discriminant or diagnostic validity. The Spanish edition might best be used for ipsative comparisons of English and Spanish skills regarding basic concepts, and for much needed research with children for whom English is a second language.

REVIEWERS' REFERENCES
Boehm, A. E. (1986). Boehm Test of Basic Concepts-Revised. San Antonio, TX: The Psychological Corporation.
Boehm, A. E. (2001). Boehm-3 Preschool. San Antonio, TX: The Psychological Corporation.

Review of the Boehm Test of Basic Concepts, Third Edition by HAROLD R. KELLER, Professor and Chair, Department of Psychological and Social Foundations, University of South Florida, Tampa, FL:

DESCRIPTION. The Boehm Test of Basic Concepts, Third Edition (Boehm-3) is a 50-item measure designed to assess children's (K–2) understanding of 50 relational concepts, considered important for school success. There are two parallel forms and, for each, an English and Spanish version. The Boehm-3 is designed to identify students who might be targeted for instruction on the key concepts, students at-risk for learning difficulties, student readiness for school learning, and may be used to measure student progress from instruction (pre-post assessment with parallel forms) and for research. The author defined basic concepts as words that describe qualities of people/objects, spatial relationships, time, and quantity. Relationship concepts defined by the test include size (medium-sized), direction (away), position in space (top), quantity (as many), time (first), classification (all), and general (other).

The norm-referenced measure is administered individually or in a group to children in kindergarten through second grades. Children are presented with a booklet of 50 pictorial items and 6 practice items (3 at the beginning and 3 after 25 items). Items are read to the children, and they are to circle the picture (from among four alternatives) described in the item. Administration may be done in one session of about 45 minutes, or two sessions of about 30 minutes each. Scores are presented in terms of raw scores, percent correct, performance range (1—student knows the basic concepts needed for grade level; 2—student knows most of the basic concepts but lacks understanding of some; 3—student's knowledge of basic concepts is extremely low for grade level), and percentile rank. There is also an optional error analysis, a teacher observation form to record generalized use of basic concepts across curriculum areas, and a parent report form to communicate results and suggestions for working with their children in the home environment. The manual provides good suggestions for intervention and for involvement of parents in the intervention. Teachers and/or clinicians would need to work with parents and teachers, as the teacher observation and parent report forms are insufficient by themselves for many recipients of the forms.

The Boehm-3 is a revision of two prior versions (Boehm, 1971, 1986). The revision updated the norms, added a fourth response choice for each item, modified the illustrations to enhance student appeal with color, increased the diversity of people pictured, developed and standardized a Spanish edition along with the English edition, and developed the teacher observation form and the parent report. Spanish vocabulary used in the Spanish version is typical of the vocabulary used in the Southwestern United States. Alternatives are provided for some words in the administration manual. Administrators of the Spanish version are encouraged to familiarize themselves with the directions and 50 words, so that they will appropriately modify and present the words and items specific to the child/children being assessed.

DEVELOPMENT. For the English version, revised items were selected and created from prior versions and two parallel forms of the items were administered to a national tryout sample ($n >$ 5,000), varying by grade, gender, race/ethnicity, region, and socioeconomic status. Outside experts reviewed the items, and teachers were surveyed. For each item the two closest versions in terms of quantitatively determined difficulty level were selected for the parallel forms to be standardized. Teacher and outside expert qualitative judgments relating to appeal, understandability, and diversity of pictures were used to eliminate or modify some items. The resulting 50 concepts were presented in the same order (randomized by difficulty level) on each parallel form, with different pictorial contexts, for the standardization testing.

More than 6,000 students were tested in the Fall and more than 4,000 students in the Spring. There was a gender disparity in the Fall (41.2% females for Form E), and a good match with U.S. population data for race/ethnicity. The Northeast region was underrepresented in the Fall with the North Central and West overrepresented for Form E. Children from low socioeconomic status were overrepresented in the Fall and underrepresented in the Spring. Children from urban settings were more highly represented in the Fall (25%) than in

the Spring (3%), as were children from rural settings (30% vs. 24%); whereas children from suburban settings showed the reverse pattern (30% in Fall vs. 57% in Spring). These demographic disparities, along with possible growth in acquisition of basic concepts over the course of an academic year, may have accounted for the lower score variability in the Spring.

The development and standardization of the Spanish version did not include a tryout with Spanish-speaking children. The translation was reviewed by Spanish-speaking experts. The standardization sample included more than 800 Spanish-speaking children (K–2) in the Fall and more than 400 similar children in the Spring. Females were disproportionately overrepresented (56%) in the Spring testing for Form F. No comparison data with regard to U.S. Census data were presented, but children from the Northeast region were dramatically underrepresented. Not surprisingly, a number of items did not follow the expected grade progression (i.e., increasing percentage correct across grade). Translation of concepts resulted in more complex presentations of some items (e.g., multiple words in Spanish vs. a single word in English, multiple meanings for some words), probably accounting for the above results.

TECHNICAL. Mean raw scores for the English version increased by grade, and variance decreased by grade and from Fall to Spring. Internal consistency estimates ranged from .80 to .91, lower with increasing grade and with decreasing variance. The standard error of measurement ranged from 1.14 to 2.43, decreasing with grade and from Fall to Spring. A separate study of test-retest reliability was conducted with 313 children in the standardization sample repeating the test after a 2–14-day interval (average 7 days), yielding coefficients ranging for .80 to .84 for Form E and .70 to .89 for Form F. A separate study ($n = 216$) of the relationship between alternate forms resulted in a coefficient of .83.

Content validity evidence appears satisfactory through reported examination of frequency of usage of basic concepts in reading and math curricula, print material in basal reading series, and examination of teacher verbal instructions. Separate concurrent validity studies in which Boehm-3 performance was correlated with performance on earlier versions or achievement/readiness tests consistently revealed higher coefficients for Form

E than Form F. Coefficients for first graders taking the Boehm-3 and Boehm-R were .89 and .96 for Form E, and .77 and .61 for Form F. Similarly, for kindergarten and first graders taking the Boehm-3 and Metropolitan Achievement Tests, Eighth Edition (Harcourt Educational Measurement, 1999), coefficients were .79 and .88 (Form E) vs. .58 and .59 (Form F). For kindergartners taking the Boehm-3 and Metropolitan Readiness Test, Sixth Edition (Nurss & McGauvran, 1995), the coefficients were .63 vs. .48 for Forms E and F, respectively. In a study correlating performance of children in Grades K–2 on the Boehm-3 with the Otis-Lennon School Ability Test, Seventh Edition (Otis & Lennon, 1996), the coefficients were comparable across forms ranging from .45 to .68, with expected decreases with increasing grade level. A longitudinal study with kindergartners from Fall to Spring with each form revealed identical coefficients of .78. The author presented the results of a variety of predictive validity studies for predecessors of the Boehm-3 (BTBC and Boehm-R). The reported results were positive, but they are not directly germane to the Boehm-3 and its modified items and format.

Mean raw scores for the Spanish version increased with grade, and variance decreased with grade. Internal consistency coefficients were comparable across forms and across Fall and Spring testing, ranging from .79 to .88. Standard error of measurement ranged from 2.02 to 2.90, decreasing with grade and from Fall to Spring. Test-retest reliability (2–14-day interval; average interval of 1 week), with a combined K–2 sample of 106 children was comparable across forms, .80 and .78. One validity study was conducted with 338 children (K–2), correlating performance on the Boehm-3 with the Naglieri Nonverbal Ability Test (Naglieri, 1996). Form E coefficients varied across grade level, .48, .54, .32, for Grades K, 1, and 2, respectively; while comparable Form F coefficients were .59, .55, and .43.

COMMENTARY. The Boehm-3 is a well-developed measure that may be useful as part of a readiness screening program for English- and Spanish-speaking children. The concepts assessed are certainly high frequency concepts in early elementary school. Information derived from the measure might heighten awareness of teachers and clinicians with difficulties children might have with various instructions in class or as part of other tests. The results could inform teachers and clinicians of the need to instruct children directly in these and other basic concepts.

SUMMARY. The Boehm-3 appears to be a psychometrically sound screening measure of basic concepts among children in Grades K–2. The measure can serve as part of a comprehensive screening approach in the schools. Results can inform instruction in basic concepts to ensure that children will benefit from other instruction, and to help ensure that other measures are assessing the intended performance rather than children's understanding of concepts embedded in the instructions.

REVIEWER'S REFERENCES

Boehm, A. E. (1971). Boehm Test of Basic Concepts. New York: Psychological Corporation.
Boehm, A. E. (1986). Boehm Test of Basic Concepts—Revised. New York: Psychological Corporation.
Harcourt Educational Measurement (1999). Metropolitan Achievement Tests (8th ed.). San Antonio, TX: Author.
Naglieri, J. A. (1996). Naglieri Nonverbal Ability Test—Multilevel Form. San Antonio, TX: Psychological Corporation.
Nurss, J. R., & McGauvran, M. E. (1995). Metropolitan Readiness Tests (6th ed.). San Antonio, TX: Harcourt Educational Measurement.
Otis, A. S. & Lennon, R. T. (1996). Otis-Lennon School Ability Test (7th ed.). San Antonio, TX: Harcourt Educational Measurement.

[35]

Boehm Test of Basic Concepts—3 Preschool.

Purpose: "Designed to assess young children's understanding of the basic relational concepts" ("quality, spatial, temporal, quantity") "important for language and cognitive development."

Population: Ages 3-0 to 5-11.

Publication Dates: 1986–2001.

Acronym: Boehm-3 Preschool.

Scores: Total score only.

Administration: Individual.

Price Data, 2001: $129 per complete kit including examiner's manual (2001, 111 pages), picture manual, and 25 record forms; $41 per examiner's manual; $85 per picture manual; $27 per 25 record forms.

Foreign Language Edition: Spanish version available.

Time: (15–20) minutes.

Comments: Revision of Boehm Test of Basic Concepts—Preschool Version; norms extended upward; provides Parent Report Form, Ongoing Observation and Intervention Planning Form (Spanish versions included); includes directions for Spanish administration and scoring; both English and Spanish norms available.

Author: Ann E. Boehm.

Publisher: PsychCorp, A brand of Harcourt Assessment, Inc.

Cross References: See T5:323 (1 reference) and T4:313 (1 reference); for reviews by Judy Oehler-Stinnett and Stephanie Stein of an earlier edition, see 11:46 (1 reference).

Review of the Boehm Test of Basic Concepts—3 Preschool by THERESA GRAHAM, Adjunct Faculty, Educational Psychology, University of Nebraska—Lincoln, Lincoln, NE:

DESCRIPTION. The Boehm Test of Basic Concepts—3 Preschool (Boehm-3 Preschool) is a norm-referenced test used to assess "young children's understanding of the basic relational concepts important for language and cognitive development, as well as for later success in school" (examiner's manual, p. 1). The Boehm-3 Preschool is intended for children ages 3 years 0 months to 5 years 11 months and is a downward extension of the Boehm Test of Basic Concepts (34), which assesses relational knowledge in children in kindergarten through second grade. The Boehm-3 Preschool covers 26 relational concepts in total assessed in two contexts. Some of the basic relational concepts assessed are size (tallest), direction (in front), position in space (nearest), time (before), quantity (some, but not many), classification (all), and general (another). These relational concepts are said to be important for children's understanding of the relationship between objects, for development of emergent literacy, and for following directions. The current revision of the Boehm-3 Preschool updated the previous version in the following ways: to provide updated normative information and to extend the norms through age 5 years and 11 months, to add a fourth response choice to reduce the occurrence of guessing, to overlap easy items with those included on the Boehm-3 (13 items overlap with the Boehm-3), to alter the illustrations used to increase the diversity of individuals depicted in the test manual, and to develop and standardize a Spanish version.

The test has two starting points: one for 3-year-olds and one for 4- and 5-year-olds. There are a total of 76 items. Three-year-olds begin on Item 1 and proceed to Item 52; 4-year-olds begin on Item 25 and proceed to Item 76. Thus, there are 14 items that overlap both age groups. The assessment takes about 15–20 minutes to complete and is administered individually. Information on calculating chronological age and test administration and protocol are described fully in the examiner's manual. Both suggested prompts and directions on what not to do in administering the test are provided to help ensure uniformity in test administration. The flip-top picture manual simplifies administration by providing the verbal prompts for the examiner on one side and the pictures for the children on the other. Children indicate their answer by pointing to the picture.

Scoring is recorded on the record form by noting a "1" by the item for each item that the child correctly answers and noting a "0" or blank for items answered incorrectly. Because each relational concept was tested in two questions, a concept score is calculated by adding the correct responses for both questions. Concept scores range from 0 to 2. A total raw score is calculated by adding up the concept scores. The child's raw score can be used to calculate the percent correct, the performance range, and the percentile rank for the child's specific age range. Tables for each of these scores are provided in the examiner's manual.

In addition to the report form, two other evaluation forms are provided: Parent Report Form and the Test Summary and Ongoing Observation and Intervention Planning Form. The Parent Report Form is intended to help explain the results of the test. On each form, the concepts are listed and briefly described. Incorrect answers are circled. Suggestions for activities to do at home to facilitate learning the relational concepts are provided. A Spanish version is also available.

The Test Summary and Ongoing Observation and Intervention Planning Form provides a form for recording the goals and development of a child's acquisition of particular relational concepts. The relational concepts are divided into three categories: concepts needed for following direction, concepts needed for math, and concepts needed for reading. Space is provided for noting when the child understands a concept receptively, when the child has used the concept expressively, and specific examples.

DEVELOPMENT AND STANDARDIZATION OF THE ENGLISH VERSION. The development of the current version of the Boehm-3 Preschool occurred in three phases. In Phase 1, research literature on relational concepts was examined to assure that the concepts being assessed were up to date, and a survey was administered to Boehm Preschool users. Although the total number of surveys solicited or received is not recorded, the surveys indicated that a new version needed more difficult items, updated pictures in the picture manual, and a Spanish version. In addition, a bias review of the Boehm Preschool was conducted by soliciting the review of experts in the field. Results of this review indicated that there was little ethnic diversity in the version and that there existed a gender bias in the pictures.

In Phase 2, information gathered in the survey and research literature was used to create the Boehm-3 Preschool Try-Out version. In this version, 88 items were used: 52 items were revisions of Boehm Preschool items, and 36 were new items. The try-out sample consisted of 300 children, generally representing the U.S. population in gender, race and ethnicity, region, and parents' education. In addition, examiners were given surveys to complete regarding the clarity of test items, concepts, and illustrations. Few specific results of the surveys and try-out testing were provided. The author notes that generally examiners liked the test items and that "items that presented problems were either modified or not included in the standardization edition" (examiner's manual, p. 50).

In the third phase of the test development, items were selected from the Try-Out version for standardization based on *p*-values and item difficulties. Items with poor correlations were omitted. In addition, items were reviewed by a second panel of bias reviewers. Bias was evaluated in terms of reviewers' comments and analyzed using the Mantel-Haenszel procedure.

The standardization sample included 660 children representing the U.S. population in terms of gender, race/ethnicity, region, and parental education. In addition, equal numbers of children were sampled at 6-month intervals from 3-0 to 5-11 years of age.

The data gathered from the standardization data were used to generate the percent of children who passed each item according to 6-month age intervals. In addition, tables provide the percent correct for the raw scores received by the children in the standardization sample according to 6-month age intervals. As expected, the mean raw scores increase across the age intervals. Moreover, the standard deviations for the mean raw scores decrease across the age intervals indicating decline in the variability in scores as children's understanding of relational concepts increase.

The performance range is another way the author chose to represent a child's performance. The author suggests a three-tier range: upper third (1), middle third (2), and lower third (3). Ranges of raw scores are provided that correspond with each performance range score (1, 2, or 3) for each 6-month age interval. According to the examiner's manual, a performance range of 1 means that a child knows most of the basic concepts. A performance range of 2 means that a child knows most concepts, but does not know certain key concepts. A performance range of 3 means that the child lacks understanding of the basic relational concepts. It does not seem to be based on empirical data gathered from the standardization sample.

Finally, percentile ranks are provided in tables for each of the 6-month age intervals. Because variability in scores is low for the older children, missing 1 or 2 questions can greatly affect the percentile rank received. For example, if one child age 5 years and 6 months receives a raw score of 48 out of a total of 52, he or she would be in the 54th percentile. Another child of the same age with a score of 47 out of 52 would be in the 40th percentile.

Reliability was assessed in terms of internal consistency, standard error of measurement, and test-retest reliability. Using Cronbach's coefficient alpha, Boehm-3 Preschool ranged from .85 to .92 across the different 6-month age intervals in terms of internal consistency. Moreover, standard error of measurement ranged from 2.08 to 2.88 indicating low variability. Finally, a test-retest was conducted with 98 children ages 4-0 to 5-11. The retest occurred anywhere between 2 and 21 days with the average retest time being 1 week. The test-retest reliability coefficients ranged from .90 to .94. Given the narrowness of raw score range for the older children, it is especially important that the test-retest reliability of this age sample was high. Yet, test-retest reliability would have been important for the 3-year-old children, especially because the standard error of measurement was higher.

Content validity was examined by considering the frequency of 38 concepts in printed materials, reading and mathematics curricula, and teachers' verbal instructions. Research literature in this area supports the inclusion of the relational concepts tested in the Boehm-3 Preschool. In addition, the author notes that other measures include similar concepts (although no specific measures are mentioned).

In addition, concurrent validity was examined by two studies in which children's performance on the Boehm-3 Preschool was compared to their performance on other measures. In the first study, 59 children between the ages of 4-0 and 4-11 were given the Boehm-3 Preschool and the Boehm Preschool. The correlation between the two assessments was .84. In a second study, 33 children between the ages of 3-0 and 3-11 and 29 children between the ages of 5-0 and 5-11 were given the Boehm-3 Preschool and the Bracken Basic Concept Scale—Revised. A correlation between the two tests was .80 for the 3-year-olds and .73 for the 5-year-olds.

Finally, 290 children between the ages of 3-0 and 5-11 were given the Boehm-3 Preschool to assess whether the results of the Boehm-3 Preschool could accurately distinguish between children diagnosed with a receptive language disorder and those without a receptive language disorder. The study found a significant difference in the mean raw scores for the two groups of children. However, the author cautions that the intent of the Boehm-3 Preschool is not to identify disability but rather to be used as a tool for intervention planning for children who have already been diagnosed with a language disorder.

DEVELOPMENT AND STANDARDIZATION OF THE SPANISH VERSION. The development of the Spanish version coincided with the development of the English version. A professional Spanish translator translated the English try-out version. Each item in the Spanish version was reviewed by experts in Spanish language and multicultural assessment.

To participate in the standardization study of the Spanish version, bilingual examiners needed to complete a Spanish proficiency check. Three-hundred Spanish-speaking children between the ages of 3-0 and 5-11 participated in the initial standardization version with an equal number of children in 6-month age groups. No information is given regarding whether the children were bilingual speakers or sole Spanish speakers. As in the English version, tables are presented that give the percent of children passing each item according to the 6-month age intervals. In addition, tables with raw total scores, performance ranges, and percentile ranks are also provided.

Reliability was assessed in terms of internal consistency, standard error of measurement, and test-retest reliability. The internal consistency coefficient alphas ranged from .80 to .91 and *SEM* ranged from 2.43 to 3.25. Test-retest reliability (average administration time equaled 1-week) was determined with a study of 125 children ages 3-0

to 5-11. The correlation ranged from .76 to .88. Reliability in all areas was somewhat lower for the Spanish version than for the English version.

Content validity was not discussed for the Spanish version. The author refers to the content validity of the English version. Although assessment of the content validity for the Spanish version would be difficult if not elusive to ascertain, it is not clear that the content validity of the English version is evidence for content validity for the Spanish version, especially given that the average raw scores obtained on the Spanish version are lower than the average raw scores obtained on the English version.

The only validity information provided is a study examining whether the Spanish version of the Boehm-3 Preschool could differentiate between children identified with receptive language disorder. In this study, participants were 120 children ranging in age from 3-0 to 5-11, 60 with a receptive language disorder, and 60 without a receptive language disorder. Although the results indicate that the children who have a receptive language disorder score significantly lower on the Boehm-3 Preschool than children without a receptive language disorder, the author cautions against using the Boehm-3 Preschool as a diagnostic tool.

SUMMARY. In general, the Boehm-3 Preschool succeeds in addressing many of the issues raised in the goals of the revision. Most notably, it provides updated normative data, increases diversity in the people depicted in the illustrations, and includes items that overlap with the Boehm-3. However, the revision falls short in a few areas. From the technical data, it seems that the Boehm-3 Preschool may suffer from a ceiling effect as children near the end of their fifth year. Missing one question greatly affects their percentile rank. In addition, although a Spanish version is definitely needed, it is not clear that the content validity has been met given the lower average raw scores of the Spanish-speaking children. It may be that there are issues with the translation, or it may be that a larger population of Spanish-speaking children needed to be included in the standardization given the potential significant diversity in language background of the Spanish-speaking children (e.g., what is their home language environment, exposure to English). The issue of the impact of the degree of bilingualism on relational concept development seems critical but not addressed by the author. Yet, given these limitations, the Boehm-3 Preschool is still a useful tool for therapists and teachers in examining children's understanding of relational concepts and providing suggestions for enhancing that development through planning and intervention.

Review of the Boehm Test of Basic Concepts—3 Preschool by KORESSA KUTSICK MALCOLM, School Psychologist, Augusta County Public Schools, Fishersville, VA and Adjunct Faculty Member, Mary Baldwin College, Staunton, VA:

DESCRIPTION. The Boehm Test of Basic Concepts—3 Preschool (Boehm-3 Preschool) was designed to provide a measure of a young child's understanding of basic relational concepts. The concepts presented in this test are those believed to be necessary for successful negotiation of learning activities in early childhood educational experiences. The test is composed of a series of picture response choices that are arranged in an ascending order of developmental difficulty. These concepts attempt to describe common qualities of people and objects, as well as those of relationships of time, space, quantity, and quality. English and Spanish versions of this test are available. The test also provides a Parent Report form that summarizes a child's test performance.

Administration and scoring of the Boehm-3 Preschool is simple and straightforward. Examiners present a page of picture cues to a child and ask the child to point to one picture that depicts the meaning of the presented concept word. Administration time is 10 to 15 minutes. Scoring is based on a correct/incorrect format. A few code letters can be used to help examiners identify items where the child may have randomly guessed at a response, pointed to all of the possible choices, did not respond to the item, or responded with an antonym of the targeted concept. These codes can help examiners analyze error patterns for later instructional use. A tally of correct responses produces a raw score for the test. The raw score is then translated into three scores: Percent of correct items, a performance range, and a percentile rank. These scores provide an index of a child's status in relationship to the standardization sample, as well as to expected levels of understanding for their age.

DEVELOPMENT. The Boehm-3 Preschool is a revision of the Boehm Test of Basic Concepts (1971) and the Boehm Test of Basic Concepts—Preschool (1986). The revision work for the Boehm-3 Preschool focused on creating a user- and child-friendly assessment tool that addressed recent trends in preschool assessment. The new edition extended the normative data through age 5 years, 11 months.

The developmental history of the Boehm-3 Preschool is one of its positive features. The author reviewed the theoretical and pragmatic foundations for the test. Tryout items were written to reflect identified concepts found in preschool literature, instructional activities, and on early childhood assessment instruments. Structured reviews and analyses of items on the previous Boehm tests were also considered in the item selection process for the Boehm-3 Preschool. Items for the final version were selected based on results of technical data as well as on such information as consumer feedback and expert reviews. Extensive discussion was provided regarding the selection of items for the Spanish Edition. Much of this discussion focused on identifying items that minimized translation difficulties of presented concepts. Many systematic efforts were used to generate items that were culturally fair and unbiased for both the English and Spanish versions of the test.

TECHNICAL. The standardization of the Boehm-3 Preschool English and Spanish Editions was based on a national sample of over 1,600 children who were representative of U.S. demographic features of gender, race/ethnicity, geographic region of residence, and parent education levels. Children with disabilities were included in the sample, as well as in subsequent reliability and validity studies.

Reliability information available for the Boehm-3 Preschool was presented as results of internal consistency, standard error of measurement, and test-retest studies. Although none of the studies presented in the manual were extensive, the results were promising. Coefficient alphas for the Boehm-3 Preschool for internal consistency ranged from .85 to .92. The standard error of measurement was low across all age levels for the standardization sample (ranging from 1.98 to 2.88). Only one test-retest reliability study was reported (average administration interval equaled 1 week), which was obtained during the standardization phase of the test. When the Boehm-3 Preschool was re-administered to a group of 98 children ages 4 to 5 years, 11 months from the standardization sample, test-retest reliability coefficients ranged from .90 to .94.

Validity information for the Boehm-3 Preschool was presented in the manual and these data were consistent with previous studies done on earlier versions of the test. The test item selection process lent support for the content validity of the Boehm-3 Preschool. Concurrent validity studies of the Boehm-3 Preschool that compared its scores with those of previous editions of the test yielded a Pearson correlation coefficient of .84. When the Boehm-3 Preschool scores were compared to scores children also obtained on the Bracken Basic Concept Scale—Revised, resulting coefficients ranged from .73 to .80. Although a clear discussion of these studies was not presented, it was indicated that predictive validity of the Boehm-3 Preschool was supported when it was determined that children who did not score well on the Boehm-3 Preschool had already been identified as having developmental delays through other assessment procedures.

COMMENTARY. There are many positive features of the Boehm-3 Preschool. One is the existence of a Spanish edition of the test. There are a growing number of children in the United States whose primary language is Spanish. These students can present many assessment challenges when educators are trying to discern if a child's learning weaknesses are a result of limited English proficiency or a true learning difficulty. With a Spanish version of the Boehm-3 Preschool, children whose primary language has been Spanish can be given both forms of the test to help define developmental strengths and needs.

Another positive feature of the Boehm-3 Preschool is the available Parent Report. By completing this report, examiners can provide parents specific feedback regarding the concepts their child did or did not know. This report also provides ideas for parents to follow to help foster the development of these concepts in their children.

The easy test administration process is an additional positive feature of the Boehm-3 Preschool. Examiners need no extra materials besides the record booklet and the stimulus book. This is a nice feature for itinerate examiners who must carry their test kits with them. The colorful and large picture cues, and the flow of item presentation, help to keep young children focused on the testing task.

SUMMARY. The Boehm-3 Preschool is a well-designed test of basic concepts in young children. This test could be used as a part of a battery of tests selected to identify children at-risk for developmental delays and/or future academic difficulties. The Boehm-3 Preschool is easy to administer, score, and translate into educational activities. As with most preschool tests, further statistical analysis would help to increase the application base of the test. Examiners who are searching for tests of basic concepts for preschool populations might want to also examine the Bracken Basic Concept Scale—Revised (Bracken, 1998; T6:330).

REVIEWER'S REFERENCES
Bracken, B. A. (1998). Bracken Test of Basic Concepts—Revised. San Antonio, TX: The Psychological Corporation.
Boehm, A. E. (1971). Boehm Test of Basic Concepts. New York: The Psychological Corporation.
Boehm, A. E. (1986). Boehm Test of Basic Concepts—Preschool Edition. San Antonio, TX: The Psychological Corporation.

[36]

Bracken School Readiness Assessment.

Purpose: Designed to "assess academic readiness by evaluating a child's understanding of 88 important fundamental concepts in the categories of Colors, Letters, Numbers/Counting, Sizes, Comparisons and Shapes."

Population: Ages 2:6 to 7:11.

Publication Date: 2002.

Acronym: BSRA.

Scores, 7: Colors, Letters, Numbers/Counting, Sizes, Comparisons, Shapes, School Readiness Composite.

Administration: Individual.

Price Data, 2003: $119 per complete kit including administration manual (104 pages), stimulus manual, and 25 record forms (specify English or Spanish); $39 per administration manual; $89 per stimulus manual; $25 per 25 record forms (specify English or Spanish).

Foreign Language Edition: Spanish edition available.

Time: (10–15) minutes.

Comments: The subtests in this test are the first 6 of 11 subtests of the Bracken Basic Concept Scale—Revised (T6:330); national norms not available for Spanish edition.

Author: Bruce A. Bracken.

Publisher: PsychCorp, A brand of Harcourt Assessment, Inc.

Review of the Bracken School Readiness Assessment by THOMAS McKNIGHT, Psychologist, Private Practice, Spokane, WA:

DESCRIPTION. According to the manual, "the Bracken School Readiness Assessment (BSRA) is used to assess academic readiness by evaluating a child's understanding of 88 important foundational concepts in the categories of Colors, Letters, Numbers/Counting, Sizes, Comparisons, and Shapes" (p. 1). The test is individually administered and, according to the author, is appropriate for children 2 years, 6 months to 7 years, 11 months old. Concepts are presented orally in complete sentences and visually in a multiple-choice format; answers can include pointing or short verbal responses.

Test material includes a stimulus manual, English and Spanish record forms, and an administration manual. The author notes that administration time is 10–15 minutes, in English or Spanish. Subtest performance is recorded in raw scores and percent mastery, and total test performance is recorded as a raw score, a standard score (mean = 100, SD = 15), a percentile rank, and an "interpretive label for a child's location within the normative population" (very delayed to very advanced). The author notes the instrument can be administered by classroom teachers, school psychologists, educational diagnosticians, speech-language pathologists, special education teachers, and teacher aides who have "appropriate supervision."

DEVELOPMENT. This instrument is "composed of the first six of the 11 subtests" of the revised Bracken Basic Concept Scale (manual, p. 5). The English standardization process included a "tryout sample" with 399 children and follow-up study of 1,100 children (2 years, 6 months old to 8 years, 0 months old), stratified by age, gender, ethnicity, region, and parent education, with 50 children at specified age levels within each year. Research with the Spanish version used 193 children, ranging in number from 16 children at age 2 to 40 children at age 7.

TECHNICAL ASPECTS. According to the author, split-half reliability (Spearman-Brown) ranged from .78 to .97 and test-retest reliability was .88, reasonably good findings. Internal consistency for the Spanish version ranged from .72 to .95 for the 193 children in the study. Content validity is discussed in the manual. As expected, concurrent validity with the revised Bracken Basic Concepts Scale is high (corrected r of .81). Correlation coefficients, using the Wechsler Preschool and Primary Scale of Intelligence—Revised (WPPSI-R) ranged from .76 to .88 and .69 to .79 using the Differential Ability Scales. The author reports a correct classification of 82% to 90% for 71 children, when identifying students nominated for retention. Less impressive were correlations with scores on the Peabody Picture Vocabulary test (3rd edition), revised Boehm Test of Basic Concepts, or Preschool Language Scale-3. However, correlations were higher when the preschool edition of the Boehm Test of Basic Concepts-3 was used. There were no validity studies, using Spanish children, reported in the manual.

COMMENTARY. Directions for administering and scoring this instrument, English and Spanish, are clear. Findings related to reliability and validity are adequate for the English version but reliability evidence using Spanish children is limited and there were no reports of validity studies with Spanish children. The manual reports an accuracy rate of 82% to 90% using the BSRA to predict which of 71 kindergarten children were recommended for retention, a reasonably good preliminary finding. The explanation of the process of translating the instrument from English to Spanish seems reasonable.

SUMMARY. The Bracken School Readiness Assessment is a reasonably good choice for assessing the preschool needs of children. It also has value, as part of a more involved assessment, when looking at children who might be considered for early school entrance. Drawings are well done, colorful, and expected to appeal to children. Technical information about the English version is adequate but additional studies, with more children, across geographical areas, reporting false positives and false negatives, are always needed with these instruments. Reliability and validity studies of the Spanish version are minimal or absent and should be the focus of research prior to releasing a revised edition of this instrument.

Review of the Bracken School Readiness Assessment by GENE SCHWARTING, Associate Professor, Education Department, Fontbonne University, St. Louis, MO:

DESCRIPTION. The stated purpose of the Bracken School Readiness Assessment (BSRA) is to measure the academic readiness of children age

2 years 6 months through 7 years 11 months, by assessing their understanding of basic concepts in the following six areas: Colors, Letters, Numbers/Counting, Sizes, Comparisons, and Shapes. This individually administered instrument is also presented as a pre-post measure useful for assessing school readiness, as a preschool screener, as a tool for kindergarten round-up, and for designing instructional interventions. The 88 items may be administered by classroom teachers, school psychologists, educational diagnosticians, speech-language pathologists, or teacher aides under supervision. The BSRA consists of an easily used administration/technical manual, a stimulus manual with color artwork, and record forms. These forms are available in both English and Spanish versions, although there are not national norms for Spanish administration. Both forms require only pointing or short verbal responses from the child.

DEVELOPMENT. The BSRA is not a new instrument, but has been in existence since 1998 as the first six subtests (School Readiness Composite) of the Bracken Basic Concept Scale—Revised (BBCS-R). The BBCS-R was reviewed in the *Fourteenth Mental Measurements Yearbook* by Leah M. Nellis and Rhonda H. Solomon (14:48). Their comments, therefore, also apply to the BSRA. As part of the BBCS-R the items in the BSRA received a tryout with 399 children in 1996, with subsequent evaluation by psychologists and speech-language pathologists to verify age-appropriateness and freedom from bias.

TECHNICAL. Standardization in 1997 involved a sample of 1,100 children representative of the 1995 U.S. Census, including small groups of individuals with disabilities (4%) and gifts/talents (1.7%). A total raw score for the six subtests is converted with norms tables at 3-month age intervals to z-scores, percentile ranks, and standard scores with a mean of 100 and a standard deviation of 15. Confidence intervals of 90% and 95% are provided, as well as classification into five categories based on the relationship of the score obtained to the mean. Cutoff scores for identifying children as at-risk for educational failure in local schools are not provided, but directions for developing them based on local norms are noted.

The Spanish version (also from the BBCS-R) contains items that were adapted or modified, rather than being translated, by representatives of a number of Spanish-speaking countries. Field studies involved a small, nonstratified sample of children (n = 193), with national norms not developed for this population. Rather, the development of local norms is encouraged.

Internal consistency reliability estimates for the BSRA range from .78 for 7-year-olds to .97 for 5-year-olds, with an overall average of .91; test-retest (7 to 14 days) reliability results in an overall coefficient of .88. Standard errors of measurement vary from 2.6 for 5-year-olds to 7.0 for 7-year-olds.

Concurrent validity for the BSRA is based on the normative data from the BBCS-R, and as a result involves comparison to the Wechsler Preschool and Primary Scale of Intelligence-Revised, the Differential Abilities Scale, the Preschool Language Scale-3, the Boehm Test of Basic Concepts—Revised, and the Boehm Test of Basic Concepts-3—Preschool Edition. The relationships established were adequate, reflecting the presence of language as a common factor; however, a number of these instruments are outdated and have now been replaced with newer versions.

COMMENTARY. Concern exists as to how the BSRA, like any early childhood screening instrument, might be used. The information obtained could be employed in a positive manner to make decisions about the needs of young children and provide interventions. Or, the results could be used in a negative manner to label children, make long-term predictions, or keep children out of programs.

SUMMARY. In conclusion, the BSRA is a well-developed screening instrument derived from the Bracken Basic Concept Scale—Revised. The items are appropriate, the protocols and manual user-friendly, and the alternative Spanish format could be quite useful despite the absence of norms. It would be best employed with younger children, as there appears to be an insufficient ceiling, lower reliability, and a larger standard error of measurement when used with 7-year-old children. In addition, the BSRA should be regarded as an instrument developed and normed in 1997, making it less current than the 2002 publication date would indicate.

[37]

British Ability Scales: Second Edition.

Purpose: Designed as a battery to assess "cognitive abilities and educational achievement."
Population: Ages 2.6 to 17.11.
Publication Dates: 1977–1997.

Acronym: BAS II.

Scores: Early Years Core Scales (Block Building, Verbal Comprehension, Picture Similarities, Naming Vocabulary, Pattern Construction, Early Number Concepts, Copying), School Age Core Scales (Recall of Designs, Word Definitions, Pattern Construction, Matrices, Verbal Similarities, Quantitative Reasoning), Diagnostic Scales (Speed of Information Processing, Recall of Digits Forward, Recall of Objects—Immediate, Recall of Objects—Delayed, Matching Letter-Like Forms, Recognition of Pictures, Recall of Digits Backward), Achievement Scales (Number Skills, Spelling, Word Reading).

Administration: Individual.

Forms, 2: Early Years, School Age.

Price Data, 2005: £810 per full age range complete set including stimulus books, 10 relevant record forms and consumable booklets; £575 per early years complete set including stimulus books, 10 record forms and consumable booklets; £495 per school age complete set including stimulus books, 10 record forms and consumable booklets; £40.50 per 25 early years record booklets; £52.50 per 25 school age record booklets; £10.90 per 25 achievement scales record forms; £12 per 10 Speed of Information Processing booklets A, B, or C; £12 per 10 Quantitative Reasoning booklets set A; £6 per 100 sheets copying paper; £6 per 100 recall of designs sheets; £17.50 per 25 number skills/spelling worksheets; £8.75 per 25 number skills worksheets; £8.75 per 25 spelling worksheets; £87.25 per administration and scoring manual (1996, 544 pages); £70 per technical manual (1997, 341 pages); £168.80 per BAS II Scoring and Reporting Software.

Time: Administration time varies.

Comments: Considerations for testing special populations detailed in manual.

Authors: Colin D. Elliott with Pauline Smith and Kay McCulloch.

Publisher: NFER-Nelson Publishing Co., Ltd. [England].

Cross References: See T5:349 (39 references) and T4:336 (25 references); for reviews by Susan Embretson (Whitely), Benjamin D. Wright, and Mark H. Stone of an earlier edition, see 9:172 (5 references); for reviews by Steve Graham and William D. Schafer of an earlier edition of the British Ability Scales: Spelling Scale, see 12:55.

Review of the British Ability Scales: Second Edition by COLIN COOPER, Senior Lecturer, School of Psychology, The Queen's University, Belfast, United Kingdom:

DESCRIPTION. The British Ability Scales: Second Edition (BAS II) is designed to assess a wide range of cognitive abilities in British children aged between 2 years 6 months (2:6) and 17 years 11 months (17:11). It is based on the first edition of the test, and on the American Differential Ability Scales (Elliott, 1990) and comprises 22 subtests, which form two overlapping batteries. Between four and seven subtests are suitable for children between 2:6 and 5:11 (the "early years" core scales). Six are designed for children aged between 6:0 and 17:11 (the "school age" core scales) and there are another seven diagnostic scales (four measuring memory) plus three measures of school achievement.

The test is well presented, with drawings and other materials that are attractive and apparently robust. The administration manual is a model of clarity, and though the test administrator needs to remember a considerable amount of detail (responses to questions, prompts for ambiguous answers, etc.), the test booklets provide as many prompts as possible, and make deriving scores on the test remarkably straightforward.

The authors claim (technical manual, p. 10) that the BAS assesses some of the main primary abilities (subtest scores) and second-order cognitive abilities (cluster scores) that constitute the hierarchical model of abilities identified by Carroll (1993), Gustafsson (1984) and others. Thus, the content of this test is less arbitrary than some. However, these claims are apparently based on face validity alone, and attempts to produce Guilford-style cognitive flexibility scales previously proved unsuccessful, and a memory cluster also failed to emerge (technical manual pp. 33, 20). Factor analyses (technical manual, p. 228) suggest that the test measures fluid intelligence, crystallized intelligence, and spatial ability in the school-aged sample—three of the seven main second-order factors identified by Carroll (1993).

The norms allow scores to be interpreted at three levels of generality. First, it is possible to obtain norm-related scores for each of the individual subtests. Second, it is possible to aggregate some of the individual subtests to give "cluster scores" for each battery—Verbal, Spatial, and Pictorial Reasoning scores for the Early Years battery, and Verbal, Spatial, and Non-Verbal Reasoning for the school age battery. Finally, it is possible to derive a measure of general intelligence, which the authors term "General Conceptual Ability" (GCA). Most other test batteries base the IQ score on all of the tests in the battery, including those that show only modest loadings on the *g*-factor. This is problematic, because including tests with substantial specific variance or large loadings on group factors means that the nature of the *g* factor will vary from test to test. The BAS II estimates GCA from only those subtests that show very substantial loadings on the general factor. In the case of the school age battery, these are the six subtests that define the crystallized, fluid, and spatial ability clusters. The authors assume that these should be averaged to give a measure of general ability, although the work of Gustafsson (Gustafsson, 1984) and others suggests that general ability is essentially the same as fluid ability. Hierarchical modelling based on grounded second-order factors would be useful to test this assumption.

Some of the subtests (e.g., pattern construction, recognition of pictures) span an extremely broad age range. For each scale in the BAS II the items are divided into sections, with suggested starting points for children of varying ages and detailed instructions for shifting to an easier section should a child find the items too difficult. This system of "starting points," "decision points," and "alternative stopping points" for each scale ensures that the child is presented with items of appropriate difficulty.

DEVELOPMENT. A distinctive feature of the BAS II is that all scales were constructed using Rasch scaling. Thus, if the test items fit the Rasch model, it is possible to equate the scores of children who saw different samples of items, as described above. Scoring the BAS II scales therefore involves one more step than is usual. Scores on the blocks of items taken by a child are transformed into an arbitrarily scaled "ability score" using tables developed using Rasch scaling. This represents the child's ability, irrespective of which blocks of items he or she has taken. For example, if a child is given Items 1–14 of Matrices and scores 11 correct, a table shows that their ability is equivalent to a child who scores 9 out of 24 when administered Items 5–33. These ability scores may be translated into *T*-scores using age-related norms, and/or combined with other ability scores to yield *T*-scores for the group factors or GCA. Although the technical manual mentions that it is essential to ensure that the items fit the model (and the test-construction process eliminated the worst-fitting items) the manuals do not report goodness-of-fit statistics. Thus, it is not possible to comment on the appropriateness of the Rasch model

for these data. As the same sample appears to have been used to develop the test and standardize it, the cross-sample stability of item difficulties (which reflects their fit to the Rasch model) is unknown.

TECHNICAL. Assessing the reliability of a test such as the BAS is no easy matter, as different participants will have been administered different items. Rasch scaling was used to estimate participants' ability on the odd- and even-numbered items of each subtest, and the Spearman-Brown correction was applied to estimate the split-half reliability. A second Spearman-Brown correction was then applied to take into account that children at different ages will have taken different numbers of items.

The treatment of bias is exemplary. Item content was scrutinized and Mantel-Haenszel analyses explored differential item functioning with respect to gender and ethnicity (white vs. black and Pakistani/Bangladeshi) within modest samples of inner-city children. These analyses informed the item-selection procedure. Rather few items showed differential functioning, although there is an obvious caveat about using the Verbal scales with children who are new to the U.K. or for whom English is their second language. External bias was assessed by regressing scores onto a standard test of reading comprehension; it showed that the same regression line fitted the data for all groups.

Validity information consists mainly of factor analytic studies and correlations with other tests. Though generally impressive, these correlations are not as high as one might perhaps expect given the reported reliability estimates of the tests. For example, the correlation of the BAS II and WISC-III Verbal Ability scores is .69. Correcting for reliability, this becomes .75, suggesting that the two tests only share about 56% of true-score variance. Either the tests measure rather different traits or there are issues with the norming process.

The normative samples are modest (between 56 and 127 children per 12-month age band) and so sophisticated techniques are used to estimate the distribution of scores for each age band, drawing on information from adjacent age bands. The amount of error involved in applying sophisticated scaling techniques to these very small samples is unknown.

COMMENTARY. The BAS II is a psychometrically sophisticated test, which makes strong assumptions about the relationship between ability and performance on test items. An imperfectly fitting Rasch model, errors in equating scores of children who saw different samples of items, the use of the same sample for both developing and standardizing the test, and the use of small normative samples all introduce unknown amounts of measurement error, and some authors (Rust & Golombok, 1999) have questioned whether it is appropriate to develop commercial tests by such means. There is certainly a need for some old-fashioned cross-validation to demonstrate that the item-fit (and hence item-difficulties) is adequate in other samples and that the norms are appropriate for each age-group.

SUMMARY. The BAS II is an attractive, well-designed test suitable for a very wide age range. The choice of subtests has been guided by modern research into the structure of human abilities, and Rasch scaling permits the scores of children who have taken different subsets of items to be compared. However, the psychometric sophistication of the test makes the adequacy of the norms difficult to evaluate without additional data.

REVIEWER'S REFERENCES

Carroll, J. B. (1993). *Human cognitive abilities: A survey of factor-analytic studies.* Cambridge: Cambridge University Press.
Elliott, C. D. (1990). *Differential Ability Scales administration and scoring manual.* San Antonio, TX: The Psychological Corporation.
Gustafsson, J. E. (1984). A unifying model for the structure of intellectual abilities. *Intelligence, 8,* 179–203.
Rust, J., & Golombok, S. (1999). *Modern psychometrics: The science of psychological assessment* (2nd ed.). London: Routledge.

Review of the British Ability Scales: Second Edition by ROBERT W. HILTONSMITH, Professor of Psychology, Radford University, Radford, VA:

DESCRIPTION. The British Ability Scales: Second Edition (BAS II) is an individually administered, comprehensive battery of cognitive ability and educational achievement tests. It is targeted at children from 2 years 6 months to 17 years 11 months of age. The BAS II is a major revision and update of the original British Ability Scales (BAS; Elliott, Murray, & Pearson, 1979) and the British Ability Scales—Revised (BAS-R; Elliott, 1983). The Differential Ability Scales (DAS; Elliott, 1990) is a revision and adaptation of the BAS and BAS-R for the United States (Kamphaus, 2001).

According to the administration and scoring manual, the purpose of the BAS II is to "facilitate the psychological assessment of this age range by educational and clinical psychologists for a wide range of purposes, as well as providing researchers with a valuable research tool" (p. 1). The author

adds that the cognitive portion of the BAS II focuses on general conceptual and reasoning abilities, the application of these abilities to specific kinds of information, and a diversity of very specific cognitive abilities. The achievement portion "provides standardized measures of basic literacy and numeracy [numerical] skills" (administration and scoring manual, p. 1). The organization of the cognitive scales reflects a three-level hierarchy of abilities consisting of an overall General Conceptual Ability (GCA) score for general cognitive ability ("g"); three clusters of scales that provide measures of verbal, spatial, and reasoning ability (only for children ages 3 years 6 months to 17 years 11 months); and individual scale [subtest] scores. There is also a Nonverbal Composite and between two and six Diagnostic scales, depending on the child's age. The GCA, Nonverbal Composite, and Cluster scores are based on a mean of 100 and standard deviation (*SD*) of 15, whereas the individual ability scales consist of normalized *T*-scores (mean = 50, *SD* of 15).

The administration and scoring manual notes clearly that "those who administer, score and interpret the BAS II should have a relevant psychology background, with formal training in the individual administration and interpretation of cognitive test batteries for children and adolescents of the age range covered by this test" (p. 14). The procedures for administering and scoring the 22 different scales that comprise the BAS II are explained clearly and in great detail in the 534-page administration and scoring manual and no attempt will be made to summarize them here. Administration times vary greatly according to the child's age and number of scales administered, ranging from 35 minutes for children between 2.5 and 3.5 years of age to 90 minutes for school-age children who are administered both the cognitive and achievement sections.

DEVELOPMENT. The development of the BAS II was guided by several explicit assumptions. First, human cognitive abilities cannot be explained solely in terms of a single cognitive factor ("g"). Second, a variety of theoretical frameworks can explain human intelligence (though the BAS II is clearly based on a hierarchical model). Third, in line with Carroll's (1993) work, human abilities are multidimensional and can be reliably measured and related to how children learn, achieve, and solve problems. Finally, these human abilities are linked in complex ways that have correlates in both information processing and neuropsychological theory. Thus, the BAS II, like the DAS, places the center of interpretive analysis squarely at the level of specific cognitive abilities rather than the overall GCA score. In doing so, the BAS II makes it clear that not only is there much to gain by looking beyond the overall GCA score, but that a fine-grained analysis of the child's performance on the various clusters and scales [subtests] can provide information that is "critical to our understanding of a child's learning styles and characteristics" (technical manual, p. 7).

The BAS II was developed over a 3-year period starting in 1993. The measure was adapted from the BAS-R and the DAS, particularly the latter measure. Both project review and user groups were involved in the revision of DAS items and the drafting of new items. Readers of this review should consult Chapter 6 of the technical manual for extensive and clearly presented information on the development of the BAS II.

TECHNICAL.

Standardization. Standardization on a representative, stratified sample in England and Wales was completed in 1995, after extensive trialing [tryout] of preliminary test items. The overall standardization sample included 1,689 children. Chapter 6 of the BAS II technical manual provides detailed information on the standardization and concludes that the standardization sample is representative of all ages encompassed by the test except for 2-year-olds and 17-year-olds, for whom the evidence is "more equivocal but is not strong enough to indicate that the score ranges from these groups will be misleadingly skewed" (technical manual, p. 146).

Reliability. The technical manual presents an in-depth theoretical discussion of issues related to the reliability and accuracy of test scores, with emphasis on tests like the BAS II, which use item response theory to estimate ability levels on the various scales. Internal reliabilities for the scores on each BAS II scale and composite were estimated using a modified split-half correlation, adjusted for the number of items likely to be given to each child. These estimates show ample evidence for the reliability of the BAS II. For example, the reliability of the overall GCA score averages .92 for preschool-aged children and .95 for school-aged children. The cluster scores have reliabilities

averaging between .85 and .92. Test-retest reliabilities for the school-age section of the BAS II were determined by retesting a randomly selected subsample of 40 children from the standardization sample after a period of between 2 and 6 weeks. For this group, test-retest reliabilities were very good, ranging from .77 for Nonverbal Reasoning Ability to .96 for Verbal Ability. For preschoolers, only data from test-retest studies involving the DAS are reported.

Validity. The BAS II technical manual presents ample evidence for both the internal and external validity of the scale. Internal validity data include intercorrelations of scales and composite scores for three ages (young preschoolers, older preschoolers, and school-aged children) as well as series exploratory and confirmatory factor analysis studies. In general, these factor analyses support a one-factor model for the BAS II for children ages 2:6 to 3:5, a three-factor model (Verbal Ability, Pictorial Reasoning Ability, and Spatial Ability) for children ages 3:6 to 5:11, and a three-factor model (Verbal Ability, Nonverbal Reasoning Ability, and Spatial Ability) for children ages 6 through 17. Concurrent validity data, although extensive, are somewhat limited by the fact that the two major studies cited by the author used the Wechsler Preschool and Primary Scale of Intelligence—Revised (WPPSI-R) and the Wechsler Intelligence Scale for Children—Third Edition (WISC-III), whereas there are now newer versions of both measures. The technical manual also refers to concurrent validity studies using the essentially similar DAS with earlier versions of the WISC and the Stanford-Binet Intelligence Scales. Because all these instruments are now dated, their applicability for judging the validity of the BAS II is limited.

The author notes that because both the DAS and BAS II emphasize cognitive processing and high subtest specificity, they appear "well-suited to the identification of children with specific learning difficulties" (technical manual, p. 249). Evidence is provided regarding the usefulness of the DAS in identifying children with reading difficulties and children with specific learning difficulties. Because the BAS II and DAS are so similar in structure and content, the author presumes that these studies with the DAS will apply to the BAS II as well.

COMMENTARY. The BAS II is an exceedingly well-constructed test that, like its American cousin the DAS, provides a wealth of information for both practitioners and researchers. As others (e.g., Kamphaus, 2001) have noted about the DAS, the BAS II is not an easy test to master, but once this is done, the payoff appears to be substantial. The various scales provide a comprehensive picture of cognitive functioning, and the use of item sets would appear to help examinees feel less failure during the administration. Whether or not individual scales (subtests) should be given as much emphasis as they are in interpretation is debatable, however, as many in the field (e.g., Flanagan & Kaufman, 2004) have recently moved away from unplanned a posteriori subtest analyses.

SUMMARY. The British Ability Scales: Second Edition (BAS II) is an individually administered, comprehensive battery of cognitive ability and educational achievement tests. It is targeted at children from 2 years 6 months to 17 years 11 months of age. The theoretical basis of the test is eclectic and is based on a three-level hierarchy of cognitive abilities. Although the test focuses on distinct abilities, an overall measure of cognitive ability is available. The test is meticulously constructed and normed. Both the administration and scoring manual and the technical manual are exemplary in their clarity and thoroughness, and the test materials are engaging and well-constructed.

REVIEWER'S REFERENCES

Carroll, J. B. (1993). *Human cognitive abilities: A survey of factor-analytic studies.* Cambridge, England: Cambridge University Press.
Elliott, C. D. (1983). The British Ability Scales: Revised. Windsor, England: National Foundation for Educational Research.
Elliott, C. D. (1990). Differential Ability Scales. San Antonio, TX: The Psychological Corporation.
Elliott, C. D., Murray, D. J., & Pearson, L. S. (1979). British Ability Scales. Slough, England: National Foundation for Educational Research.
Flanagan, D. P., & Kaufman, A. S. (2004). *Essentials of WISC-IV assessment.* Hoboken, NJ: John Wiley & Sons.
Kamphaus, R. W. (2001). *Clinical assessment of child and adolescent intelligence* (2ⁿᵈ ed.). Boston: Allyn & Bacon.

[38]

The British Picture Vocabulary Scale, Second Edition.

Purpose: Designed to serve as a "norm referenced wide-range test of hearing vocabulary for Standard English."
Population: Ages 3.0 to 15.8.
Publication Dates: 1982–1997.
Acronym: BPVS-II.
Scores: Total score only.
Administration: Individual.
Price Data: Available from publisher.
Time: (5–8) minutes.

Comments: Manual is incorporated in the easeled test book.
Authors: Lloyd M. Dunn, Leota M. Dunn, Chris Whetton, and Juliet Burley.
Publisher: NFER-Nelson Publishing Co., Ltd. [England].
Cross References: For information regarding the original edition, see T5:350 (53 references) and T4:338 (16 references).

Review of The British Picture Vocabulary Scale, Second Edition by ALFRED P. LONGO, Instructor in Education, Social Science Department, Ocean County College, Toms River, NJ:

DESCRIPTION. The British Picture Vocabulary Scale (BPVS) is the most widely used standardized picture-based test of receptive vocabulary in the U.K. Quickly and easily administered, it does not require the test taker to do any reading, speaking, or writing, only to offer simple responses to picture cards.

The instrument is appropriate for speech and language therapists, educational psychologists, and teachers. It measures the extent of children's acquisition of English vocabulary.

The latest version, BPVS-II, is directly linked with the Peabody Picture Vocabulary Test, Third Edition (PPVT-III). The original edition of the BPVS was based on the second edition of the PPVT. The updated version of the BPVS, the BPVS-II, is, in good part, based upon the PPVT-III.

Many aspects of the initial edition of the BPVS have been retained in the latest version. Some of these include: age range assessed (ages 3 to 15); the ability to both administer (5 to 8 minutes) and score in a short time span; the flexibility of individual administration; the lack of a requirement for verbal recognition, written response, or reading; and norm-referenced interpretation of scores.

The BPVS-II has undergone several modifications. These include: more focused directions for administration and scoring, reorganization of test items, an increase of 10% in the number of test items, the elimination of an alternate form, and an updating of both illustrations and technical data.

Like its predecessor, the BPVS-II measures a child's hearing, or receptive vocabulary. In essence it is an achievement test and, as such, reflects the scope of the individual's verbal ability. Although limited, when utilized with individuals who have been immersed in the English language both in school and at home, the BPVS-II has relevance as a determinant of overall intelligence. It also has utility as an initial screening device to identify high and low ability or language difficulties in an individual and to establish an initial baseline from which reading progress may be measured. Where individual educational program decisions are to be made, however, results from the BPVS-II need to be reviewed in the light of more comprehensive assessments of intelligence (Beech, 1991). The score is obtained by subtracting errors from the total ceiling score, which is based on a "critical range" designation (age) of the student.

DEVELOPMENT. The BPVS-II contains new test items and items from the previous edition. The pool used to construct the BPVS-II was composed of 182 items from the BPVS and 480 items from the PPVT-III. From this pool, 250 items were selected. Selection of items was based on difficulty, variety, and cultural balance of word types. Words and illustrations that were outdated or deemed unsuitable were removed from the pool or new artwork was commissioned.

The 250 "select" items were field tested on over 1,100 individuals in 108 schools in England and Wales. Classroom teachers conducted the testing with a mixture of individual and group testing. Older students were tested in group administrations.

Item analysis of results incorporated tests of facility, discrimination, distraction analysis, and internal consistency. Anecdotal commentary in the form of a survey of teachers who had administered the BPVS-II was also used for analysis of items and administration. From this review, 168 test items were selected, organized by difficulty and then placed in 14 sets of 12.

Standardization procedures were comprehensive in breadth. A stratified sample was taken from The National Foundation for Educational Research (NFER) Register of Schools. Twenty-five hundred and seventy-one students from 152 schools were represented in the sample. To assure stratification, weighting procedures were used to compensate where it was felt that certain groups were under- or overrepresented.

Standardization data received the same type of item analysis (facility, discrimination, and internal reliability) that was completed for item selection. A distinct focus was placed on the results in the light of the nature of the administration (group versus individual). The correlation between these

scores was .75. The developers used a correction factor in the calculation of norms in order to reconcile any discrepancies created by virtue of the variation in the type of administration.

A statistical program developed by Schagen (1990) was used for the transformation of raw scores into standardized scores. The results of this procedure are reflected in the published mean (100) and the standard deviation (15).

TECHNICAL. Internal consistency of the BPVS-II was measured by using Cronbach's alpha and a split-half method comparing student responses on odd versus even items. Reliability has increased from the BPVS. The internal consistency of the BPVS-II items as calculated by Cronbach's alpha was .93. Split-half procedures yielded a mean of .86. The authors believe that the corrected split-half values are the "best single overall measure of the reliability of the BPVS-II" (manual, p. 33).

Predictive validity is based upon a comparison to the PPVT because of the similarity of the instruments and because the research relating to the PPVT is far more numerous. Correlations between the original BPVS and other reading tests range from .43 with the Salford Sentence Reading Test (Bookbinder, 1976) to .72 for the Expressive One-Word Picture Vocabulary Test (Gardner, 1979).

The developers support the content and construct validity of the BPVS-II on the basis that raw scores increase with the age of the subjects. Studies assessing validity were also conducted with groups of English as an Additional Language (EAL) learners and with adults.

The developers are realistic and straightforward with reference to reliability and validity issues. They have made sincere attempts to reconcile statistical differences between age groups, male and female subjects, and adults and second language learners; they have also properly placed the BPVS-II in the context of the measurement of more global intelligence. Based on the various correlations presented, the BPVS-II is technically sound.

COMMENTARY AND SUMMARY. This is the second edition of a highly successful vocabulary test. The previous edition included 150 items. The revision contains 168.

The current edition has been extensively field-tested. Hundreds of stimulus words were tried out on thousands of individuals to arrive at the item pool for this edition. Content, artwork, and test procedures have been greatly improved. Organization of test items and norming has been improved. The developers are fully professional in their approach to the technical information. They are quick to point out any areas where correction factors were used. Additionally, they are also realistic about the scope of test results and their utility in making educational program judgments.

Desirable features from the previous edition, such as quick administration, fast and reliable scoring, and precise line drawings were retained. Artwork has been redone and attention paid to gender/racial balance and second language learners. A comprehensive manual is part of the testing package. Guidelines for administration are clear; standardization and technical properties are well presented.

The BPVS-II is recommended for use as a screening measure in primary grades. It has application as an indication of the verbal aptitude of students who have been immersed in the English Language in the home, students who have learning difficulties, and students who are learning English as a second language and, in a clinical setting, for the assessment of those with severe cognitive disorders.

The BPVS-II is an instrument that although limited in scope presents in a short time an analysis of receptive vocabulary development. The authors suggest a link with overall intelligence because of the importance of language in that regard. They are properly cautious, however, when it comes to using this test as a foundation for assessing broad intelligence.

REVIEWER'S REFERENCES

Beech, J. R. (1991). [Review of British Picture Vocabulary Scale (BPVS)]. In L. M. Harding & J. R. Beech (Eds.), Educational assessment of the primary school child (pp. 171-172). Windsor, U.K.: NFER-Nelson.

Bookbinder, G. E. (1976). Salford Sentence Reading Test. Sevenoaks: Hodder and Stoughton.

Gardner, M. (1979). Expressive One-Word Picture Vocabulary Test. Los Angeles, CA: Western Psychological Services.

Schagen, I. P. (1990). A method for the age standardization of test scores. Applied Psychological Measurement, 14, 387–93.

Review of The British Picture Vocabulary Scale, Second Edition by DOLORES KLUPPEL VETTER, Professor Emerita, University of Wisconsin-Madison, Madison, WI:

DESCRIPTION. The British Picture Vocabulary Scale, Second Edition (BPVS-II) was designed to assess the receptive (hearing) vocabulary for Standard English of British children 3:00 to 15:08 years. The manual states that it may also be used as a screening test of scholastic aptitude or as part of an assessment evaluating cognitive processes when English is the primary language of the home, community, and school. Finally, a parallel study of children aged 3:00 to 8:05 years for whom English is an Additional Language (EAL) was conducted.

The BPVS-II is an individually administered multiple-choice test containing 168 test items ordered into 14 sets of test items (and their distractors). Each set of 12 test items is more difficult than its predecessor. Four black-and-white drawings (one test item and three distractors) are arranged on a single plate; the location of the test item on the plate varies. After the examiner verbally names the test item, several types of responses are acceptable: The child can point to the picture of the item, can provide a number that has been associated with the picture, or can nod "yes" or "no" as the examiner points to each picture on the plate. This allows children with different capacities for responding to be assessed for their receptive vocabulary of Standard English.

Although formal training in tests and measurements is not required, the examiner must be thoroughly familiar with the specific procedures used for administering the BPVS-II. Interpretation of scores, however, requires familiarity with the types and meanings of the normative information provided in the manual (e.g., errors of measurements, standard scores). The authors state that with training and experience most professionals who work with children (e.g., school teachers, speech therapists, or learning specialists) should be able to administer and interpret the data from the BPVS-II. The manual provides explicit instructions for administration of the test, recording and scoring responses, establishing a basal and ceiling set, and calculating the chronological age and the raw score of the child. Additionally, it has summaries of important information.

DEVELOPMENT. The British Picture Vocabulary Scale, Second Edition (BPVS-II) is the result of a substantial revision of the BPVS, originally published in 1982. The BPVS was itself based on the second edition of the Peabody Picture Vocabulary Test (PPVT-R), a test with a history of use in the United States (starting in 1959) for determining the receptive vocabulary of children.

The authors maintained certain features of the BPVS in the new edition: brevity and ease of administration of the test; nature of the stimuli and their presentation; and the acceptable responses and age range of the children. The purpose of the revision was to develop a more comprehensive set of test items and updated illustrations to increase the test's technical properties. After the revision was accomplished, standardization data and norms based on the new materials were required. A supplemental set of norms was developed for children for whom English is an additional language (EAL).

An initial pool of items (662) taken from the BPVS and the PPVT-III was reviewed for appropriateness for British children, functional value in everyday communication, and the ability to be depicted with black-and-white line drawings. Two hundred and fifty items with a range of difficulty and word types representing 20 semantic categories (e.g., actions, household items, emotions, and social expression) resulted. Items were arranged in sets, assigned appropriate distractor pictures, and roughly ordered in difficulty. Field testing was conducted on 1,142 children from schools in England and Wales, grouped by year in school from Preschool: Age 3–5 years to Year 10: Age 14–15 years. Item difficulty and discrimination ability, effectiveness of the distractors, and the internal consistency of the test were determined, as was a one-parameter item response theory (IRT) analysis for each set of items.

A final selection yielded 168 items for standardization. They were chosen based on difficulty at a given age and discrimination (in the context of distractors items) as age progressed. Items were arranged in 14 sets of 12 test items; difficulty level of items within a set was similar and the sets became progressively more difficult from Set 1 through Set 14. Responses from a small sample of volunteer adults were used to ascertain finer degrees of difficulty at the upper end of the scale.

TECHNICAL. For standardization of the BPVS-II, a stratified sample of schools was chosen using the National Foundation for Educational Research (NFER) Register of Schools in England and Wales. The authors state that the sample was reflective of the population at large given that geographical considerations, and school size and type were taken into account. Instructions for randomly selecting children and the method of test administration (individual or group) were provided to the schools; testing was done by teachers.

A total of 2,571 children from 152 schools took part in the standardization. No demographic factors were specified other than age and gender.

Comparisons of adjusted raw scores for gender at each age bracket indicated a significant difference at only one age (Year 5: 9–10 years). The authors argue that given there is a general increase in raw scores over age and that mean differences between genders change direction from one year to the next, there is no reason to conclude that there are overall differences between genders.

Although the BPVS-II is designed to be administered individually, children from Year 6: 10–11 years and Year 7: 11–12 years received group administration of the test with a small subsample (approximately 12%) also tested individually. When a comparison of individual and group administrations was made, scores were significantly greater for the individual administration. Therefore, a correction factor was devised and applied to the raw scores obtained through group administration to equate them with those obtained from the individual administration of the test. Scores for individual administration and the corrected raw scores for group administration were transformed into standardized scores with a mean of 100 and a standard deviation of 15.

The standardization data were subjected to several types of item analyses. When the results were studied, a few items were apparently not at the appropriate difficulty level; therefore, items in Set 5 and upwards were reorganized for difficulty level and new sets, based on standardization IRT data, were constructed. For Sets 13 and 14 the adult sample's data were used to assure that the final set (Set 14) was the most difficult.

The manual provides Cronbach's alpha and split-half reliability coefficients presented by school year/age group. The authors note that the BPVS-II employs basal and ceiling scores, thus elevating Cronbach's alpha (i.e., median Cronbach's alpha = .93, range .86–.97). Split-half reliabilities, corrected using the Spearman-Brown formula, ranged from .81 to .95 with a median of .86. Standard errors of measurement are reported for the 68% level of confidence, and there is a discussion of how the 90% and the 95% levels of confidence may be determined.

The rationale for content validity is based upon the extensive procedure used to choose items relevant to British children, with the caveat that the items had to be able to be depicted in line drawings. Construct validity was not deemed necessary if the BPVS-II is being used to determine the receptive vocabulary of a child. If the BPVS-II is used to predict intelligence or cognitive ability, the examiner should be aware of extensive discussions in the literature relevant to the use of vocabulary as a predictor of overall cognition.

BPVS-II for pupils with English as an Additional Language (EAL). A second standardization study of children with English as an Additional Language (EAL) took place in parallel with the standardization of the new materials. Three groups of children (Preschool, Year 1, and Year 3) for whom English was an additional language, drawn from schools from primarily metropolitan areas where large immigrant populations were served, were tested individually. There was a roughly comparable number of boys and girls at each age for a total of 410. The ethnic composition of the sample is not described. The norms provided are similar to those for the parent test: Standardized scores with mean = 100, *sd* = 15, age equivalents, and 68% confidence bands. The manual also compares these scores with those obtained in the main standardization study. Numerous cautions emphasize the importance of specifying that these are EAL age equivalent scores.

COMMENTARY. The BPVS-II is a rapidly administered test of receptive oral vocabulary for use with children, including those with limited response capabilities and with English as an Additional Language. The authors described the statistical procedures they used, their interpretations, and the various corrections that were employed (e.g., item difficulty, test administration, gender differences) in detail. Unfortunately, the level of detail in the manual made it difficult to follow some arguments presented. At the same time the explanations of statistics are excellent and could provide the training that the authors state is needed for appropriate interpretation of scores on the BPVS-II.

A major deficit in the standardization study is the lack of information on the ethnic makeup and first language of the children in either the main or the EAL study. Demographic information on age and gender is valuable, but given the ethnic diversity in the U.K., it is likely that ethnic background and first language of the children is contributing to the error variance in the scores. This would be of particular importance to the EAL study because scores might be more interpretable (i.e., valid) with first language taken into account.

The design of the Performance Record is excellent, and the Graphic Display of Test Results contained in it should assist examiners with relatively little psychometric experience to accurately interpret scores obtained on the BPVS-II.

SUMMARY. The BPVS-II is a rapidly administered instrument useful in assessing the receptive vocabulary of children 3:00 to 15:08 years old in England and Wales. Because it permits several types of responses, it can be used with children who have limited or no oral language abilities. The manual provides tables for scores to be converted to standardized scores, age equivalent scores, and 68% confidence limits. Supplemental norms with comparable scores are provided for children 3:00 to 8:05 years for whom English is an Additional Language.

[39]
British Spelling Test Series.

Purpose: Developed to serve as a "comprehensive screening test that delivers detailed information about the spelling ability of groups or individuals."
Population: Ages 5–adult.
Publication Date: 1997.
Acronym: BSTS.
Scores: Total score only.
Administration: Individual or group.
Levels, 5: 1, 2, 3, 4, 5.
Forms, 2: X and Y, alternate forms.
Price Data: Available from publisher.
Time: (30–40) minutes.
Authors: Denis Vincent and Mary Crumpler.
Publisher: NFER-Nelson Publishing Co., Ltd. [England].

Review of the British Spelling Test Series by TIMOTHY Z. KEITH, Professor of Educational Psychology, The University of Texas—Austin, Austin, TX:

DESCRIPTION. The British Spelling Test Series (BSTS) is a set of 10 short group tests designed to assess the spelling skills of children and adults in the United Kingdom. There are five overlapping age levels of the test (5 to 8-11, 7 to 11-11, 9-11 to 15-1, 12-6 to 17-5, and 15-6 to 24+ years), with two forms at each age level. Examiners are encouraged to consider the characteristics and estimated spelling level of examinees when choosing from overlapping tests. According to the authors, the BSTS may be used to assess individuals and groups, and is appropriate "whenever it is important to know how well an individual can spell, or to know the levels of spelling ability within a particular group" (Level 5X/Y manual, p. 2). The authors recommend the test for "screening, monitoring, grouping and educational guidance" (Level 5X/Y manual, p. 2), and as a part of diagnostic testing for learning concerns.

Each BST includes single word spelling items (like a traditional spelling test), dictation, and proofreading. For young children the dictation items involve specific words within sentences (cloze items) as well as short passages. Specific words in each passage are scored as correct or incorrect. For the proofreading items, examinees must circle misspelled words and provide the correct spelling of those words.

The total number of words spelled correctly is converted into a standard score ($M = 100$, $SD = 15$) and percentile rank. Scoring is simple, and the norms are finely grained. For several of the tests the floors and ceilings are restricted for the younger and older ages within a test; thus users should choose the appropriate test level with care. It is also possible to convert raw scores to age equivalents. For all but the youngest age level, scores may also be converted into an "ability scale score," a scaled score designed to provide a continuous, equal interval score across all forms of the test. The ability scale score may be used, for example, to evaluate progress from one testing to another when two different forms of the test are used. The ability scale score has an overall mean of 100. This statistical equating of the tests across ages was accomplished through a 16-item reference test administered following the main test. The description of the ability scale scores is somewhat vague; it is unclear, for example, how they are derived.

The tests are untimed, but generally require 30–40 minutes for completion. Each test includes a manual and a set of record forms. Materials are attractive and easy to use.

DEVELOPMENT. According to the manual, the BSTS treats spelling as a unitary skill, an educational outcome, rather than attempting to break spelling into its component psychological processes. The initial process of selecting words for inclusion in the test is not well described in the manuals. For example, for Test 1 (ages 5 to 8-11), words "were selected by a) examining common misspellings in a large number of samples of children's writing and b) consulting Word for Word (Reid, 1989) which lists the words most frequently used by 7-year-olds in their writing" (Level 1X/Y manual, p. 31). For Test 5 (the oldest age level), words were selected from national newspapers available in London and a list previously developed for literacy research by the authors. The initial sample of words was used in trial versions of the tests and normal item analysis procedures used to select the final words and dictation passages.

TECHNICAL. Each test was standardized on a large sample of students in the U.K. (England, Wales, Scotland, and Northern Ireland) in 1995 and 1996; sample sizes ranged from 1,725 (Test 5, Form X) to 4,843 (Test 2, Form X). According to the manuals, these were national standardization samples from "a range of schools and colleges" (Level 1X/Y manual, p. 31). Additional details (e.g., sex, ethnic background, country or region, SES) of the standardization sample are not provided.

For Test 5 (ages 15-6 and above), the standardization sample included secondary school students, post secondary students, and "students on a cross section of vocational and academic courses" (Level 5X/Y manual, p. 34).

Internal consistency reliability estimates (KR20) are provided for each test and each form. These are uniformly high, and are all above .95. It is unclear whether these estimates are based on raw or standard scores. Alternate form reliability estimates are not reported. The manuals include a conceptually appealing explanation of standard errors of measurement and confidence intervals. Each manual also reports the correlation of the BSTS with another test of spelling; these, too, are generally high (.84 and higher), and support the concurrent validity of the tests. The authors also note that the activities included in the tests have obvious "face validity," presumably meaning that they correspond well with normal educational and practical applications of spelling.

SUMMARY. The BSTS appears to be a well-developed, comprehensive group measure of overall spelling skill, appropriate for children and young adults in the U.K. The tests should be useful for assessment of groups (e.g., classes) as well as individuals with spelling difficulties. Subsequent editions of the manuals should provide additional detail on the development of the tests, the normative groups, and reliability and validity.

Review of the British Spelling Test Series by S. KATHLEEN KRACH, School Psychologist, Henry County Schools, McDonough, GA:

DESCRIPTION. The British Spelling Test Series (BSTS) was designed to test the spelling skills of British children between the ages of 5 years and adult, using 10 group tests of ability. These 10 group tests consist of two versions each across five overlapping ability levels. For example, both the X and Y versions of the Level 1 test kit (BSTS 1X/Y) measure age 5 years through age 8 years, 11 months. BSTS 2X/Y measures age 7 years through age 11 years, 11 months. The administrator decides which version to use for examinees whose ages fall in the overlapping range.

The BSTS provides an overall standard score, confidence interval for the standard score, percentile rank, and spelling age equivalent. No subtest scores are calculated. The purposes of the BSTS as described by the manual are to determine spelling ability for use in "screening, monitoring, grouping, and educational guidance" (p. 2). Two versions of each test (X and Y) were created to gather any further information needed or to measure spelling growth across time.

Each level and each version of the BSTS is administered the same way. The examinees are given a worksheet and the administrator reads the directions aloud. The examinees are then asked to write their answers on the worksheet; however, if there is some reason examinees cannot write the answers themselves, the manual allows for them to dictate (letter by letter) the answers to someone else. All test items are administered to all examinees.

The BSTS contains several types of subtests, a few of which are found across all versions. One is a single-word dictation subtest administered as follows: The administrator reads one word at a time, reads a sentence using the word, and finally reads the word again. The examinees are asked to write the word. Another subtest is a passage dictation, administered by reading a short passage aloud, reading it again slowly enough for examinees to copy it, then reading it a third time so examinees may check their work. Finally, all examinees are shown written items with spelling errors, which they must identify and correct.

Some subtests are specific to certain versions. In Version BSTS 1X/Y, examinees must write the initial letter for a word read aloud. Also, in BSTS 1X/Y, examinees must write two- to three-word phrases that are read aloud. In Versions BSTS 1X/Y, BSTS 2X/Y, BSTS 3X/Y, and BSTS 4X/Y, examinees must fill in blanks with correctly spelled words. In all subtests, grammar and punctuation are not scored; however, if the handwriting is illegible, the item is scored as incorrect.

DEVELOPMENT. The test developers indicate that the BSTS was designed to assess progress in spelling, a major curriculum component for schools in the United Kingdom. To this end, they wanted to devise an easy-to-use test that would measure several aspects of spelling and be interesting to the examinee. Also, they wanted a measure that features items commonly known to students at each age level.

All test items were selected because they are considered commonly used words that are frequently misspelled. A list of 203 words for the BSTS 1X/Y were selected by examining children's work samples and by consulting a text that lists commonly used words for 7-year-olds. Curriculum materials and samples of students' writing supplied the original pool of 297 words for the BSTS 2X/Y and 325 words for the BSTS 3X/Y. Items on the BSTS 4X/Y were selected from 357 words found in the General Certificate of Secondary Education (GCSE) scripts, and suggested by GCSE examiners. An original pool of 538 words for the BSTS 5X/Y was selected from words found in national daily newspapers found in London. Items included in the final two versions (X and Y) were determined by administering word-pools from the BSTS 2, BSTS 3, and BSTS 5 in six trials, and word-pools from the BSTS 1 and the BSTS 4 in three trials, to approximately 300 students. Conventional item analysis was used to choose the best items. No statistical data from this item analysis were provided in the manual.

TECHNICAL. The standardization sample was developed by administering the BSTS 1X and BSTS 1Y to approximately 2,900 students each. The BSTS 2X and the BSTS 2Y were administered to approximately 4,700 students each. The BSTS 3X and the BSTS 3Y were administered to approximately 3,900 students each. The BSTS 4X was administered to approximately 3,400 students, and the BSTS 4Y to approximately 4,600 students. The BSTS 5X was administered to approximately 1,700 students, and the BSTS 5Y to approximately 2,200 students. Students in the standardization sample were selected from a range of schools and higher education institutions across the United Kingdom.

Reliability data were calculated through internal consistency measures. The KR20 coefficient data from all versions of the BSTS fell at or above .96, suggesting good internal reliability. Although there were two versions of this test (X and Y) available for each level, no reliability data were reported in the manual across the parallel forms.

All of the tests of the BSTS were described as having "high 'face' validity" (BSTS 1X/Y manual, p. 32). However, the developers expressed concern that although the BSTS is good for discriminating very good or very poor spellers, it may not be as strong at determining and interpreting the fine differences between midrange spellers.

Concurrent validity correlation studies were done on all versions of the BSTS at each level. For the BSTS 1X/Y and BSTS 2X/Y, the spelling test from the British Ability Scales was administered as a comparison measure. For the BSTS 3X/Y, BSTS 4X/Y, and the BSTS 5X/Y, the Schonell's Graded Word Spelling Tests were administered as the comparative measure. Each comparative test was given to approximately 30 people from each standardization sample for the 10 versions of the test. Correlation data between each version of the test and the comparative measure fell between .84 and .93, suggesting good concurrent validity.

COMMENTARY. The BSTS is an extremely thorough test of spelling ability. It uses varied subtests to engage the examinee and allows for students to demonstrate spelling skills outside of simple word lists. However, although the test uses many subtests to form the overall composite score, no individual subtest scores were available. This is a shortfall of the measure, as the data from the individual subtests may have been useful when diagnosing different types of spelling difficulties.

The original pool of words was pulled from British materials that are commonly used or read by those living in the United Kingdom, so they should be familiar to the examinees. This makes it a more valid measure of assessing spelling for each

level; however, given the difference between English spelling rules and normative group differences across countries, this test should be considered valid only for examinees in the United Kingdom.

Another strength of the BSTS is that developers made two parallel versions. This allows test users to examine spelling growth along with the impact of various spelling programs. However, it is likely the developers could have provided more information about these parallel forms. No reliability data were reported using the two forms, nor is there any statistical report of how useful the scores are when compared to one another.

Finally, there were problems in the standardization sample. All people in the sample were students in some type of training program. However, the manual states that the test is useful for all adults (even those who did not attend further training). Also, although the test is described as accurate for all adults, the manual does not indicate any information that examinees over the age of 24 were included in the normative sample. Finally, the highest spelling ages available for each version (for the BSTS 5X, 27 years, 1 month; for the BSTS 5Y, 25 years, 6 months) are too low to be meaningful to older examinees. For example, if a 40-year-old takes the BSTS 5X and gets every point available, their spelling age will still be calculated at only 27 years.

SUMMARY. The BSTS appears to be a good, comprehensive measure of spelling for students from the United Kingdom. Although it contains varied subtest types that are easy to administer and score, it provides normative data on only the overall test and not the individual subtest raw scores. Given the nature of the item selection, the strict British scoring criteria, and the population in the standardization sample, the normative data from this test should be considered accurate only when administered to students from the United Kingdom.

Reliability and validity data presented in the manual suggest this is a sound test for its designed purposes and population. However, reliability data reflect only a measure of internal consistency (although an alternate form was available for more data). With the data available at this time, it appears the BSTS is a useful measure when one needs a comprehensive assessment of spelling skills for British students.

[40]

Business Analyst Skills Evaluation [One-Hour].

Purpose: Measures practical and analytical skills for the position of Business Systems Analyst.

Population: Candidates for Business Analyst positions.

Publication Dates: 1984–1998.

Acronym: BUSAN.

Scores: Total Score, Narrative Evaluation, Ranking, Recommendation.

Administration: Group.

Price Data, 2001: $225 per candidate, quantity discounts available.

Foreign Language Edition: Available in French.

Time: (60) minutes.

Comments: Available in booklet and Internet formats; scored by publisher; must be proctored.

Author: Bruce A. Winrow.

Publisher: Walden Personnel Performance, Inc. [Canada].

Review of the Business Analyst Skills Evaluation [One-Hour] by CHARLES K. PARSONS, Professor of Management, Georgia Institute of Technology, Atlanta, GA:

DESCRIPTION. The Business Analyst Skills Evaluation [One-Hour] is a paper-and-pencil test that contains a small number of problems that will require a variety of skills and abilities to analyze and correctly solve. Scores are generated for the following skills: (a) Analysis of Procedures; (b) Mathematical, Logic, and Analytical; (c) Problem Solving; and (d) Business Analysis and Error Detection. The test is intended for use with job titles such as business analyst, procedures analyst, liaison officer, and business systems officer. The common role these jobs would tend to have is that they are at the interface of an organization's information technology department and user departments. However, the test does not require information technology knowledge.

According to the test manual, administering the test requires that the candidate be given the test booklet and told that all instructions are in the booklet. Language options are English and French. The room should be quiet without distractions such as ringing phones. All work should be done in the booklet without scrap paper. Scoring can be done by mailing the completed booklet to the publisher (either regular mail or courier). In addition, fax service and real-time telephone scoring

are available for an additional cost. Results will be presented as scores on the four skills mentioned above as well as an overall recommendation on hiring. The client company can then incorporate these results with other facets of the employee selection process in reaching a decision.

DEVELOPMENT. The Business Analyst Skills Evaluation [One-Hour] is a shorter version of a test of about the same name (called the 2 Hour version). The formats of the 1- and 2-hour versions look much the same. There is little information on initial test development. The sample problem given in the test manual looks like it might have come from a "critical incident" methodology. The test author spent many years working in information technology jobs and has probably been exposed to many jobs like those using competencies being assessed. The 1-hour version focuses on skills and abilities rather than personality. The test manual gives brief descriptions of the skills and abilities as well as their presumed linkages to test problems.

TECHNICAL. There is no information on the development of test norms. Scores are interpreted on intuitive scales that are anchored with labels of below average, average, and above average. No information was given about the sample used to create these scales or the distribution of scores. Additionally, there are no data to substantiate the nonequal intervals associated with the various recommendations. For example, scores of 80% to 100% lead to the "strongly recommended" outcome with the advice that the individual has the potential for a successful career as a Business Analyst. The score range of 65%–79% yields a "recommended" outcome with the advice that the individual is recommended for the career (not just having the potential), provided further supervision is provided. Does this imply that individuals who score at or above 80% do not need supervised training? The score range of 58%–64% yields a "Recommended for Limited Use" outcome with advice that one should be hired only if there is intensive training and the individual is highly motivated. The advice given for all three categories could be better understood by a test user if there was some underlying rationale as to the factors that ultimately go into successful performance on this job.

In addition, no reliability estimates were provided in the test manual. Test-retest reliability would be an important statistic that would help users gauge the test's usefulness for their setting. The psychometric data given are derived from two sources. In one source, the publisher describes a content validation study of the 1-hour version. In the other source, the publisher describes a predictive validation study of the 2-hour version.

The purpose of the content validation study was to demonstrate the domain overlap between the knowledge, skills, and abilities (KSAs) required in the job and the knowledge, skills, and abilities assessed in the test. Although content validation is a legitimate approach to establishing validity, it is most relevant for a specific job, as opposed to a more generic job family such as the listing of jobs for which this test is recommended. In the study presented, the authors took the existing test and tried to demonstrate domain overlap with the Business Analyst position in a specific company. There was an extensive job analysis that listed eight essential job functions and the essential KSAs required to perform these tasks. Then there was a judgment as to whether each of these KSAs was assessed by the Business Analyst Test. This yielded an unweighted overlap of 58%. Finally, when the tasks were weighted by importance, the weighted overlap statistic was 77.3%.

Not much information was given about the methods used in making the judgments about everything from task importance to whether or not the test taps the requisite skill. We do know that corporate personnel provided an initial job description as well as ratings of task importance. We do not know if these personnel were job incumbents, supervisors, or trained job analysts. Nor do we know whether or not there were multiple raters or the level of agreement between raters. It would also be helpful to know the source of the judgments about the correspondence between the test and the KSAs. Were these representatives of the publisher or impartial job analysts? All of this information would help both the reviewer and user better interpret the meaningfulness of the content validity statistics.

The other validation results came from a predictive validity study conducted on the 2-hour version. In the report, *Validation Study,* the authors describe a test (2-hour version) that taps both traditional KSAs and also personality traits such as drive, maturity, and dominance. Thus, any results here would have to be interpreted with caution when projecting them onto the 1-hour version. The authors describe a predictive validity coefficient of .49 ($p < .01$) for 30 applicants who took the test, were hired into a business analyst position by one company, and were evaluated by their supervisors after 1 year. Test scores and supervisory ratings are included in the report.

COMMENTARY. The value of a job-specific aptitude test to a wider range of employers and other test users will ultimately depend on the relevance of the underlying skills assessed by the tests to similar jobs in other settings. Within the U.S. Department of Labor's Occupational Listings, the key word, "Business Analyst," generates three job titles (Management Analyst, Computer Systems Analyst, and Accountant), each of which generates lists of KSAs that have some overlap with those associated with the Business Analyst Test. However, the test authors have not gone far enough to provide the research necessary to support the assertion that this test is a good measure of these skills. Rather they have provided evidence from a content-validation study for a single employer.

In addition, the much preferred approach is that of criterion-related validation followed by validity generalization studies. A series of employer-specific predictive studies would allow both a computation of a weighted average validity coefficient (corrected for attenuation, range restriction and sample size limits) and a test for the situational specificity.

In general, the publisher should provide further reliability and validity evidence for this test. Test-retest data should be easily obtained. The content validity approach is inappropriate for tests of this type that are being used in many different settings. Instead the publisher should work on predictive validity, construct validity, and validity generalization studies. A stronger case could be made for the assumed abilities and skills underlying this test if the publisher was able to show convergent and discriminate validities with alternative measures of such abilities and skills. Especially useful would be evidence of the overlap with a test of general cognitive ability.

More data could also be provided on the derivation of the cut scores associated with the four levels of "Likelihood for Success." The overall aggregate score is divided into nonequal intervals with some suggestions on whether or not to hire the individual and additional advice for managing an individual in the score category. The substantive suggestions might be useful guidance, but the authors should better explain the rationale behind the advice.

SUMMARY. The developers have created a test that is targeted toward an important job in many organizations. The author of the test has worked in the occupation and has been involved in the development of other tests related to information technology jobs. The publisher has provided quick scoring through fax or telephone as well as discount pricing for volume users. It seems that the potential is there for this test to be technically sound as well as commercially successful, but users should be cautioned about the nature of the validity evidence provided.

Review of the Business Analyst Skills Evaluation [One-Hour] by MICHAEL SPANGLER, Dean of Business & Technology, Highland Community College, Freeport, IL:

DESCRIPTION. The Business Analyst Skills Evaluation [One-Hour] (BUSAN) is intended to evaluate the aptitude of a job candidate for a position as a business systems analyst, procedures analyst, or IT liaison. The publisher states that the test may be employed in hiring, promotion, or training of business analysts. The constructs intended to be assessed are logic, interpretation of specifications, attention to detail, accuracy, symbolic problem solving, organizational relationships, understanding of business procedures, and error recognition. No personality traits are measured in this version of the test.

The BUSAN form is presented as either a paper booklet or internet-based document containing four problems. Each problem may have from three to six subordinate items.

Test administration is straightforward and easily accomplished by any competent proctor. The test is timed at 60 minutes with adequate instructions for the proctor and examinee as well as time estimates for each problem.

Scoring and reporting is accomplished by the publisher. The test manual states that a three-page report is provided to the client. A one-page sample report is included in the manual. The four evaluative criteria reported include: Analyze procedures; Mathematical, Logic, & Analytical Skills; Problem Solving; and Business Analysis & Error Detection. Results in each of the criteria are presented as a number of points out of the number possible. Those data are translated to a horizontal bar graph scaled by stanines. A "Recommendation" section with an overall weighted aggregate score is reported along with an explanatory statement derived from irregularly scaled intervals of that aggregate score. The explanatory statements range from "Strongly Recommended" through "Not Recommended" for the position.

DEVELOPMENT. Information from the publisher about the test development is scant. The items selected for use in this test appear to have been drawn from an earlier developed longer version, which was reviewed in the 10th edition of the *Mental Measurements Yearbook*. There is no provenance to the test items. They may be the original product of the test author (Harmon, 1989).

No information is presented on the underlying assumptions or theory guiding the development of the test items. One case study of the BASE test, a predecessor, identified 16 primary and 41 secondary traits to be measured using the test. No evidence of construct validity is present and no explanation of the source of the traits is provided. How these traits relate to the nature of the profession is unknown (Cronbach & Meehl, 1955).

TECHNICAL. No normative information is included in the manual or any accompanying materials. No item analyses or information on test scaling are present. No reliability data or references to reliability studies are provided.

The publisher furnished two case studies of the earlier test version (BASE) in evidence of the content and concurrent validity of the test. The studies reported a coefficient generated $r = .29$. Although significant, the strength of the correlation is moderate at best. Cronbach (1970) characterized validity coefficients of .30 or better as having "definite practical value."

Differential validity evidence for the BUSAN test across gender, racial, ethic, or cultural groups is not provided. The publisher does provide in one of the case studies of the earlier BASE test some data (Mean and *SD*) on performance by race and by gender.

COMMENTARY. The value of the BUSAN as a predictive tool for identifying potential business analysts is difficult to establish. The evidence for any informed decision is not provided, leaving serious gaps in the knowledge base. This reviewer has several reservations about the underlying constructs ostensibly addressed by this test. There is presented no clear descriptive or inferential evidence that connects the target constructs with the intended occupations.

The scoring of the test items except for one is objective. The four test report criteria: Analyze Procedures; Mathematical, Logic, & Analytical Skills; Problem Solving; and Business Analysis & Error Detection appear to be the product of scores from multiple items. The manual does not explain how any report scores are derived. Nor does the manual explain how the overall weighted aggregate score is computed. There is no mention in the manual as to why the test is timed at 60 minutes or why timing should be required (AERA, APA, & NCME, 1999).

SUMMARY. The critical and volatile nature of the business systems analyst occupation demands tools for assessing members or potential members of the profession. A cursory examination shows few competing products. The publishers of the Business Analyst Skills Evaluation [One-Hour] (BUSAN) should pursue improvement of this instrument and construct a more informative manual. A beginning might be to conduct meaningful studies to properly construct norms, document reliability, and confirm validity.

In her 1989 review of the BASE for the *Tenth Mental Measurements Yearbook*, Harmon stated, "In addition to the fact that the manual presents no evidence as to how the test was scaled or normed, or how it is scored, or whether it is reliable, there is no evidence that it is useful as a 'hiring, promotion, or training tool,' as claimed" (p. 120). In the intervening 15 years that condition appears to have remained largely unchanged. Again quoting Harmon (1989), "There seems to be no plausible reason to use this evaluation as currently presented" (p. 120). In regard to the BUSAN, this reviewer concurs.

REVIEWER'S REFERENCES

American Educational Research Association, American Psychological Association, & National Council on Measurement in Education. (1999). *Standards for educational and psychological testing*. Washington, DC: American Educational Research Association.
Cronbach, L. J. (1970). *Essentials of psychological testing*. New York: Harper & Row.
Cronbach, L. J., & Meehl, P. E. (1955). Construct validity in psychological tests. *Psychological Bulletin, 52*, 281–302.
Harmon, L. (1989). [Review of the Business Analyst Skills Evaluation.] From J. C. Conoley & J. J. Kramer (Eds.), *The tenth mental measurements yearbook* [Electronic version]. Retrieved December 7, 2004 from the Buros Institute's *Test Reviews Online* website: http://www.unl.edu/buros

[41]

California Verbal Learning Test, Second Edition, Adult Version.

Purpose: To "obtain a detailed and comprehensive assessment of verbal learning and memory."

Population: 16–89 years.
Publication Dates: 1983–2000.
Acronym: CVLT-II (Standard); CVLT-II SF (Short Form).
Scores: Immediate Recall (Trial 1, Trials 2–5, Trials 1–5 Total), Learning Slope, Semantic Clustering, Serial Clustering, Subjective Clustering, Primacy/Recency Recall, Percentage of Recall Consistency, List B Trial, Proactive Interference, Short-Delay Free Recall, Retroactive Interference, Short-Delay Cued Recall, Long-Delay Free Recall, Long-Delay Free Recall Retention, Long-Delay Cued Recall, Repetition Errors, Synonym/Subordinate Intrusions, Across-List Intrusions, Categorical Intrusions, Non-Categorical Intrusions, Yes/No Recognition Testing, False-Positive Errors, Total Recognition Discriminability, Source Recognition Discriminability, Semantic Recognition Discriminability, Novel Recognition Discriminability, Response Bias, Critical Item Analysis, Forced-Choice Recognition [optional].
Administration: Individual.
Forms, 3: Standard Form, Alternate Form, Short Form.
Price Data, 2005: $499 per complete kit including software package (CD-ROM or diskette version), manual (2000, 287 pages), 25 Standard Record Forms, 1 Alternate Record Form, and 25 Short Record Forms; $96 per manual; $45 per 25 Standard or Alternate Record Forms (quantity discounts available); $33 per 25 Short Record Forms (quantity discounts available).
Time: (30) minutes plus 30 minutes of delay for Standard and Alternate Forms; (15) minutes plus 15 minutes of delay for Short Form.
Comments: Comprehensive Scoring System software generates Core Report (generates 27 scores), Expanded Report (generates 66 scores), Research Report (generates over 260 scores); computer system requirements: Windows 95/98/NT 4.0, 100 MHz processor, 32 MB RAM, CD-ROM and 3.5-inch floppy diskette drive (CD-ROM version) or 3.5-inch diskette drive (diskette version), 2 MB video card with 800 x 600 resolution (256 colors), and 25 MB free disk space.
Authors: Dean C. Delis, Joel H. Kramer, Edith Kaplan, and Beth A. Ober.
Publisher: PsychCorp, A brand of Harcourt Assessment, Inc.
Cross References: See T5:376 (35 references); for a review by Ray Fenton of the previous edition, see 13:42 (57 references); see also T4:364 (12 references).

Review of the California Verbal Learning Test, Second Edition, Adult Version by ANITA M. HUBLEY, Associate Professor of Measurement, Evaluation, and Research Methodology, University of British Columbia, Vancouver, British Columbia, Canada:

DESCRIPTION. The California Verbal Learning Test, Second Edition, Adult Version (CVLT-II) is an individually administered measure of strategies and processes involved in learning and remembering verbal information. It can be used with examinees aged 16 to 89 years. There are three forms of the CVLT-II. The standard and alternate forms each contain two word lists composed of 16 words each from four categories. List A is the primary list whereas List B serves only as an interference task. These two forms of the CVLT-II consist of five immediate free recall trials of List A, an immediate free recall trial of List B, short delay free and cued recall trials of List A, long delay free and cued recall trials of List A, long delay yes/no recognition trial of List A, and an optional long delay forced-choice recognition trial of List A. The short form version contains 9 words from three categories, uses four immediate free recall trials for List A, uses a counting backwards task rather than a second list to provide interference, uses shorter delay intervals, and does not include a short delay cued recall trial for List A. The CVLT-II short form can be used with examinees with more severe cognitive dysfunction or as a screening measure.

The administration instructions are clear, easy to find, and well described. The reading rate for presenting the word lists is just over 1 second per word (i.e., 18–20 seconds to read 16 words), which would seem to be a difficult reading rate to both train and maintain. Based on the national standardization sample, total administration time for the standard and alternate forms of the test, including two delay intervals of approximately 20 and 10 minutes each, ranged from about 47 to 54 minutes, on average, for nonclinical and clinical examinees, but could take as long as 90 minutes. It is not clear how long the short form version takes to administer.

The record form is easy to follow. The manual provides a good summary of available scoring and report options as well as excellent instructions, figures, and examples to assist the examiner in scoring the CVLT-II by hand. Attention has also been paid to the scoring of particular responses (e.g., plurals, short forms of words) or nonresponses. There are clear benefits to scoring the CVLT-II using the computerized scoring as not all scores are easily obtained by hand. Moreover, it takes 10–15 minutes to obtain scores for all variables using the computerized scoring but, by hand, it takes 10–15 minutes to calculate scores for 18 key variables and at least 60 minutes to calculate scores for all variables.

DEVELOPMENT. The CVLT-II is, in many respects, a new test. Although the original CVLT research edition consisted of two word lists (each with 16 words from four categories), in revising the test, the authors decided not to present the lists as shopping lists because this restricted their ability to develop alternate and short forms of the test. They also changed both the categories and words used in the lists. Mean word frequency ratings for the standard and alternate CVLT-II versions were significantly higher than for the CVLT.

Another difference with the CVLT-II is the considerable number of scores that can be obtained. Raw and standardized scores are provided for 27 commonly used CVLT-II measures in the Core Report, for 66 measures (51 measures for the short form) in the Expanded Report, and for over 260 variables in the Research Report. In addition to adding new measures, the authors have incorporated new approaches to computing some scores (e.g., cluster scores). The number of scores and amount of information provided is overwhelming but, to the authors' credit, they also provided considerable interpretive information for each measure and incorporated much of the published literature related to the CVLT and these scores.

TECHNICAL. A major criticism of the CVLT involved the relatively small, nonrepresentative, and highly educated standardization sample (e.g., Elwood, 1995). The standardization sample for the CVLT-II, which consists of 1,087 adults (565 females, 522 males) ages 16–89 who were matched to the March 1999 U.S. Census in terms of race/ethnicity, educational level, and geographic region, represents a substantial improvement. Normative data for most scores are provided separately for males and females within seven age groups. The alternate and short forms were equated to the standard form of the CVLT-II using linear and equipercentile equating, respectively. Few details, however, are provided on the two samples used in these equating studies.

Given the particular features of memory tests (e.g., item interdependence within and between trials, practice or recall effects), it is very difficult to obtain meaningful estimates of reliability using standard approaches. As a result, the authors have used several innovative, but imperfect, approaches to estimate internal consistency that must be viewed with caution. Using these approaches, internal consistency estimates based on the overall standardization sample and other clinical samples are quite good and usually higher than .80, but the estimates for individual age and gender groups from the standardization sample are often unacceptably low.

Stability estimates are provided for 20 CVLT-II scores. However, these values provide little meaningful information about score stability and are difficult to interpret because (a) the examinees have received extensive exposure to the test, and (b) the retest interval ranged widely from 9 to 49 days. Alternate forms reliability estimates for 22 scores on the CVLT-II Standard and Alternate forms do not support the authors' claim that the two forms yield a "high degree of alternate-form reliability" (manual, p. 85). Correlations between the scores on the two forms varied widely with the highest correlation being only .79. Another problem with these estimates is that the interval between administration of the standard and alternate forms ranged widely from 0 to 77 days, which makes it difficult to interpret these results.

Contrary to statements made by the authors, the presence of significant correlations between the CVLT and CVLT-II do not suggest that the latter "maintains a similar level of construct validity as that of the first edition of the instrument" (manual, p. 87); rather, validity evidence for inferences made from the CVLT-II scores must be reestablished. In the manual, validity evidence provided for the CVLT-II included factor structures with both nonclinical and mixed clinical samples, fairly high correlations with the CVLT, expected gender effects, and expected correlations with age, education, and IQ scores. An extensive summary of literature using the CVLT from 1987 to 1999 was provided using 15 headings, including older versus younger nonclinical adults, males versus females, Alzheimer's Disease, head injury, schizophrenia, and insufficient effort. This summary is very useful, but further construct validation studies using the CVLT-II are essential.

COMMENTARY. At present, there are several different verbal learning and memory tests using word lists available in the literature, although each offers something a little different to the test user. The key strength of the CVLT-II is the extent to which one can explore the strategies and processes involved in learning and remembering a word list that incorporates the use of categories. These strategies and processes include clustering, primacy and recency effects, proactive and retroactive interference, cuing and recognition, intrusion errors, response bias, and test-taking effort, to name but a few. Other strengths include greatly improved norms for men and women aged 16–89 years, alternate and short-form versions of the test, detailed information for the various CVLT-II scores, relative ease of administration, and a user-friendly computer-scoring system.

The strengths and weaknesses of the CVLT-II are closely connected, however. The authors provide an extensive number of scores as well as several report options that will delight some test users and completely overwhelm others. Given the number of scores available, it would be beneficial to provide more than one report writing example so one can better understand how the various scores may be implemented in the assessment process. Considerable information is provided in the manual about the use and interpretation of CVLT scores with various disease processes. However, the extensive revisions made to the test also mean that this information cannot be directly applied to the CVLT-II without further validation studies. Finally, although it is recognized that it is difficult to evaluate the reliability of memory test scores, the estimates provided are not as strong as suggested and no attention is paid to standard error of measurement.

SUMMARY. If one is interested in assessing the strategies and processes involved in learning and remembering verbal information such as word lists, then there probably is not a better measure for adults than the CVLT-II. The authors are to be commended for addressing previous criticisms of the CVLT, incorporating new developments in the CVLT-II, and providing a well-organized and detailed manual. Test administration is straightforward but purchase of the computer scoring system should be considered essential. Some test users may find the number of scores and report options available to be overwhelming and the lack of several report writing examples to be frustrating. Finally, caution must be exercised in applying validity evidence and research findings obtained with the CVLT to the CVLT-II given the extensive revisions that have been made to this test.

REVIEWER'S REFERENCE

Elwood, R. W. (1995). The California Verbal Learning Test: Psychometric characteristics and clinical application. *Neuropsychology Review, 5,* 173-201.

Review of the California Verbal Learning Test, Second Edition, Adult Version by CEDERICK O. LINDSKOG, Professor, Pittsburg State University, Pittsburg, KS:

DESCRIPTION. The California Verbal Learning Test, Second Edition, Adult Version (CVLT-II) is intended to provide "a short, individually administered assessment of the strategies and processes involved in learning and remembering verbal information" (manual, p. 1). Notable updates from the original form include revised word lists, a large normative database, new scoring intended to distinguish among types of memory profiles, a short form for screening, and software for computer scoring. The scoring software, which provides scaled scores for over 50 variables, is recommended. Hand scoring is somewhat limited in the range of analyses available due to formula complexity. An Alternate Form and a Short Form of the CVLT-II are also included. The test should be administered in one session. The manual reports average administration time of 47 minutes for individuals aged up to 60 years, and 51 minutes for those 61 and above. These average times include both the 20- and 10-minute delay intervals.

The authors provide references for the instrument's uses in distinguishing memory profiles for depression, Alzheimer's, predicting which nonclinical elderly might eventually fall victim to Alzheimer's, detection of residual brain damage in cases of head trauma, alcoholism/drug abuse, and neurotoxic exposure, differentiating memory profiles among schizophrenia, depression, other psychiatric disorders, detecting malingerers, and assessing the degree to which a person might return to work.

DEVELOPMENT. The CVLT-II is a 2000 update of the CVLT 1983–1997 Research Edition-Adult Version. It is similar to the Rey Auditory Verbal Learning Test (RAVLT; Rey, 1964), with notable improvements including semantic categories. Administration involves presenting a word list to the examinee in both immediate and delayed recall conditions. Word List A has 16 words, 4 words in each of four semantic categories (Furniture, Vegetables, Ways of Traveling, and Animals). The list of 16 words is presented by the examiner, who reads the words at a rate of just over 1 second each. The task is to measure how many words the examinee can recall following each of five presentation trials. Then an interference task (List B) of 16 different words is presented, followed by Short-Delay Free Recall and Short-Delay Cued Recall trials for the original words from List A. Following a 20-minute delay during which any nonverbal testing takes place, the examinee will again recall words from List A in Long-Delay Free-Recall, Long-Delay Cued-Recall. An optional Long-Delay Forced-Choice Recognition trial may be administered following another 10-minute delay period.

Errors are organized by two broad types, Repetitions and Intrusions. Repetition error is the repeating of a target word, and Intrusions (Category and Non-Category) are when a word is given that is not on the current target list. Category Intrusions are words similar to the target list word (e.g., ship/boat), and Non-Category Intrusions are words unrelated to any on the list. Category Intrusions are further broken down into Synonym or Subordinate; Synonym is self-explanatory, and Subordinate is exemplified by the participant giving a word from a subgroup (e.g., substituting "red beet" for "beet").

With one exception (List A Total Trials 1–5 Recall is reported as a T-score), raw scores are converted to z-scores. The manual provides a rationale and interpretation for each score and comparison, and includes a sample case report, albeit with more detail than would usually be used.

TECHNICAL. The CVLT-II underwent national standardization using 1,087 individuals (565 females and 522 males) well matched to the most recent U.S. Census in race/ethnicity, education level, and geographic region. Norms are provided for seven age groups ages 16 to 89, and because there were gender differences in total recall, separate norms are provided for males and females.

Reliability for this instrument was reported using three different forms of split-half reliability, citing difficulties in other approaches due to item interdependence within trials, and between trials (manual, p. 80). The first used an odd-even combination across trials (Trials 1+3 versus 2+4, and Trials 2+4 versus 3+5) using Spearman-Brown correction. The reliability estimates within age groups were generally above .90, and were for the whole population ($r = .94$), with no significant differences between genders. The same method was then applied to test reliability estimates at the lower, middle, and upper aged populations in this sample. The reliabilities for these three subsets were $r = .87$, $r = 88$, and $r = .89$, respectively. The third study using this methodology involved a sample of 124 neuropsychiatric patients. The split-half reliability estimate in this group was $r = .96$.

The second form of internal consistency was designed in which participants' performance in the four categories of words in List A were examined across the five immediate-recall trials. The researchers treated each of the categories across trials as an item, and coefficient alphas were calculated. The coefficient alpha for the whole group was $r = .82$, and for the mixed clinical group, $r = .83$.

Another approach was a modified split-half, which compared total items recalled on two categories across five trials to total items on the other two categories across the five trials. The reliability estimate for the total sample was $r = .83$, and for the clinical sample, $r = .84$.

A test-retest study ($N = 78$) yielded $r = .82$ uncorrected. The median interval was 21 days, with participants recalling approximately eight more words across the five trials. In one other reliability study, a counterbalanced administration of the Alternate Form of the CVLT-II was administered to a population of 288 nonclinical adults. All correlation coefficients were statistically significant ($p<.001$, r ranged between .72–.79). Results support use of the key recall and recognition.

Validity of the CVLT-II is grounded in its relationship to the original CVLT, which has accumulated considerable research support. The manual cites over 150 published research studies involving neurologically normal and clinical populations.

Correlations between the CVLT and the CVLT-II in a study of 62 nonclinical adults (disproportionately female) ranged from .63 to .86. The original and revised forms have nearly equivalent means of common raw scores. The CVLT-II correlates very well with the CVLT, and the raw score differences are minor. The CVLT-II seems to retain the construct validity of the original.

Factor analytic studies of several populations fit a six-factor model. The authors point out that these studies are not an indication of learning and memory constructs as they are summaries of "the interrelationships of the test's multiple variables in non-clinical individuals and in a heterogeneous patient group" (manual, p. 88). The manual also provides additional data on demographic variables, in particular gender differences, and studies relating the CVLT-II to IQ.

The authors include a section in the manual relating CVLT-II profiles to different common clinical disorders such as Alzheimer's, Korsakoff Syndrome, Parkinson's, Huntington's, Schizophrenia, and Depression. These profiles are described in terms of CVLT profiles, and referenced with relevant research publications.

The Short Form of the CVLT-II (CVLT-II SF) is intended to be used for those who cannot tolerate a longer exam, as well as for screening purposes. The scoring uses the same procedures, except that the CVLT-II SF has fewer measures, because it only has nine word items across four trials, three instead of four semantic categories, and no List B.

COMMENTARY. In publishing the CVLT-II, the authors have improved a valuable clinical tool designed to measure learning and retention of verbal material in neurologically intact and disordered adults. The amount of interpretable information gained from a relatively simple task of multiple repetition of a word list (with an interference task and time delays) is impressive. The test is easy to administer, and the computerized scoring program accompanying test materials is invaluable. This test will deserve attention from both practitioners and researchers who wish to differentiate among different types of verbal learning and memory impairment, as well as to better discriminate those who are malingering or "faking bad." This instrument builds upon the clinical utility of the CVLT, which boasts over 200 published research articles differentiating profiles for a range of neurological disorders including schizophrenia, neurological trauma, substance abuse, and depression. There is an Alternate Form and a Short Form.

The authors cite extensive reliability statistics, which indicate adequate reliability for internal consistency and test-retest. Validity for the instrument is in part demonstrated by its similarity to the CVLT, which boasts a significant research base with regard to differentiating among learning and memory profiles of clinical populations. The only possible addition to expand this instrument might be inclusion of nonverbal memory measures.

SUMMARY. The CVLT-II was published in 2000 as a revision of the well-researched CVLT Research Edition, Adult Version. The standardization group of adults was broken into seven age groups ranging from 16 to 89 years of age. The test consists of a list of 16 words (List A) read aloud to the participant, who is to recall those exact words. That measure is repeated multiple times, and data are kept regarding the slope of retention across tasks. The participant is then presented an interference task (List B), and repeats those new words.

Next, the participant is asked to recall words from the original list. Following that, the participant is asked to recall the original words according to semantic category (e.g., furniture, vegetables), and finally asked to identify which words read one at a time were on the list. Nested within these "subtests" are two time delays, one for 20 minutes, and the other for 10 minutes. From these data, a set of z-scores are derived, which may be interpreted, some in relation to other scores, to provide clinical indicators and diagnostic information. The test manual is well written and easy to use, and the computer scoring is recommended for full use of this instrument. Testing procedures are well outlined in the manual, and are easy to follow. The authors cite suitable reliability and validity statistics to support use of the CVLT-II. This instrument appears to be a valuable upgrade of an established measure of adult learning and memory.

REVIEWER'S REFERENCE

Rey, A. (1964). L'examineer clinic en psychologie. (The Clinical Exam in Psychology). Paris: Presses Universitaires de France.

[42]

Call Center Skills Test.

Purpose: Measures practical and intellectual skills for call center positions.
Population: Candidates for call center positions.
Publication Date: 2001.
Acronym: CCTR.
Scores: Total Score, Narrative Evaluation, Ranking, Recommendation.
Administration: Group.
Price Data, 2001: $150 per candidate; quantity discounts available.
Foreign Language Edition: Available in French.
Time: (60) minutes.
Comments: Available in booklet and Internet versions; scored by publisher; must be proctored.
Author: Bruce A. Winrow.
Publisher: Walden Personnel Performance, Inc. [Canada].

Review of the Call Center Skills Test by THEODORE L. HAYES, *Research Director, The Gallup Organization, Washington, DC:*

DESCRIPTION. The Call Center Skills Test (CCST) is a paper/pencil self-report measure designed for applicants for call center representative or nontechnical help desk positions. There are five test sections that are inexplicably referred to in the manual as "Problem 1" through "Problem 5." The first section "evaluates telephone etiquette and the ability to respond professionally to clients on the telephone" (test manual, p. 1). The second section evaluates "the candidate's ability to use proper grammar" (manual, p. 1). The third section evaluates "vocabulary skills relevant to a call center position" (manual, p. 1). The fourth section evaluates "telephone knowledge and ability to handle various customer situations" (manual, p. 1). The final section evaluates "basic math, logic, analytical and telephone problem solving skills" (manual, p. 1). There are 83 test items in all with a total test time of 60 minutes. For some reason, the test itself seems to indicate that there are fewer test items than there actually are. The various sections have suggested time limits but there is no penalty for finishing more slowly than indicated in the manual. There is no special training required for test administration. The test is meant to be scored by sending the answer sheet to the publisher via any of several means (including "Super-Fast Service— This service provides 2-hour turnaround," manual, p. 5). All test materials are written in English, although the publisher does not provide an indication of reading level. A "content validation study" is included with the test materials. It seems that the publisher expects to test applicants for more than one client, and the applicant is thus expected to sign a waiver granting the test publisher rights to provide test results to other client companies.

DEVELOPMENT. The CCST seems to be the result of a job analysis study conducted in February 2001, in one call center of a small plastics manufacturing and supply company.

TECHNICAL. One cannot dispute that a sound, thorough job analysis is necessary to document the evidence of content validation. Also, one would not dispute that the test publisher has documented that a job analysis was conducted that incorporated, in some manner, the opinion of subject matter experts. However, simply conducting a job analysis that establishes that traits are important for tasks does not mean that the resulting test of those traits is "content valid." In short, the CCST falls short in several regards.

Although content validation is an entirely valid approach to develop a call center test, content validation universally focuses on observable behaviors, or at least on observable work products, in a particular work setting—not traits. The test should have either a sample of work behavior, or produce a sample of work product based on behavior. However, in this case, the test publisher is actually conducting a construct validation study. As documented in the report accompanying the CCST, this job analysis study started with 12 given functions and then attempted to substantiate the psychological constructs that girded these functions. Furthermore, several somewhat obvious call center functions identified by the study—"Ability to communicate orally," "Ability to interact with a computer terminal"—are not measured at all. The fact that a "content valid" call center operator test has no telephone component should give one pause immediately. Finally, some knowledge areas identified in the job analysis that one would expect to be trained—"Knowledge of accepted procedure for handling client calls"—are part of the test.

The CCST itself is essentially a measure of general mental ability. The first section includes a mixture of situational reasoning items (of the type "What would you do if ...?") and general knowledge items (of the type "If it's this time in this city, what time is it in this other city?"), for a total of 12 items. Again, from a content validity perspective, one could ask: Why 12 items? How do these items reflect the content of the job without giving incumbents an unintentional advantage? How were the response options generated? And so on. The second section is a group of 24 grammar items. At least two of these items have more than one correct answer. The third section presents 22 synonym items, but the publisher provides the answer for two of these items (without changing the item numbers). The fourth section includes 15 items that mirror in type and almost in content the items in the first section. The difference is that this set

includes "knowledge of" items—which could easily be trained rather than tested—and the applicant is supposed to indicate whether the item presents true or false information. The first and fourth item sets at least are worded to reflect telephone work, but the synonyms and grammar items have no obvious relation to phone work. The final section has four question parts. The first part has one quantitative reasoning item; the second part has six number/letter series-type items; the third part has four vocabulary items; and the final part is a logical series of events item framed in a call center environment. The publisher states that a score of 80%–100% is "superior," 70%–79% is "good," 60%–69% is "moderate," and 0%–59% is "low." No technical discussion is provided to substantiate these levels.

The publisher presents no psychometric data regarding the test. Apparently, the publisher's argument that this is a "content valid" test is meant to deflect any responsibility for collecting or providing those data. Instead of test metrics, the publisher provides several practitioner-oriented journal articles that support the publisher's job analysis/test content "validation." These articles simply highlight the limitations of the CCST rather than buttress it. Calling something "content valid" does not excuse the test developer from needing to examine that the test has adequate psychometric properties. A complete content validation study would demonstrate that the domain sampling reflected in the items was appropriate, not that (as in this case) a majority of the subbehavior trait domain was measured by at least one item. Furthermore, it is clear that the content of the vocabulary, grammar, and reasoning items are unrelated in any obvious way to call center work, especially in the situation studied in the job analysis report.

COMMENTARY. One could develop a meaningful test of call center work from a variety of perspectives, such as personality, cognitive ability, behavior, content knowledge, etc. The Call Center Skills Test in its current form is inadequate from any of these perspectives.

SUMMARY. The CCST presents some content-based validity evidence regarding call center performance. It is inadequate as a stand-alone measure in its current form. Finally, potential users should consider that content validation is highly situationally specific, which may limit this test's utility in a setting meaningfully different from the one used for test development.

Review of the Call Center Skills Test by JUDITH A. REIN, Adjunct Assistant Professor, Department of Educational Psychology, University of Arizona, Tucson, AZ:

DESCRIPTION. The Call Center Skills Test purportedly evaluates the aptitudes and abilities required for successful performance as a call center or a nontechnical help desk representative. Using the test's confusing terminology, there are five problems each with varying numbers of multiple-choice or true-false items. The problems are (a) Telephone Skills, 12 multiple-choice items; (b) English Grammar Skills, 24 multiple-choice items; (c) Vocabulary Skills, 20 multiple-choice items; (d) Telephone Knowledge and Customer Situations, 15 true-false items; and (e) Math, Logic, Analytical Reasoning, and Telephone Problem Solving, 4 multiple-choice items. Three scores are reported. First, a raw score is reported for each problem. Second, an unnamed score with a range from 1 to 9 is reported for each problem with scores from 1–3 classified as below average, 4–6 average, and 7–9 above average. Derivation and meaning of the unnamed scores are not discussed in any testing materials. Third, the overall rating is a percentage correct score, apparently across all items, and evaluated as Superior (80–100), Good (70–79), Moderate (60–69), or Low (59 or lower). Test administration procedures are simple: (a) Hand out the test, (b) explain that all instructions are in the test booklet, (c) test applicant in a relatively quiet room preferably without a telephone, (d) tell applicant not to communicate with anyone, (e) instruct applicant to use a pencil and complete all work in the test booklet, (f) provide no scrap paper, and (g) do not give the applicant the opportunity to photocopy the test. Because these procedures are inadequate to maintain comparable testing environments across potential employees, they jeopardize the validity of the scores. Testing time is 1 hour with suggested, but not enforced, time limits for each problem area.

DEVELOPMENT. A job analysis of a call center agent's job was conducted. This analysis indicated five essential job function areas; their relative importance; the 53 primary knowledge, skills, and abilities (KSAs) required; the method

of evaluation (e.g., paper-and-pencil test, scanning resumes, previous job training) required; and the secondary KSAs (e.g., ability to persevere, perform repetitive tasks) described as nice to have but not essential. Some of the primary KSAs are measured by one item. For example, the ability to analyze data is allegedly measured by an item that requires following instructions and performing basic math. However, four KSAs—the ability to read, to work under pressure, to follow instructions, and to work independently—are allegedly measured by all items. Other than an implied correspondence between the problems and the KSAs, there is no evidence that the problems measure the intended KSAs.

TECHNICAL. Of great concern is the lack of technical information for the test. There is no standardization evidence, no reliability estimates, and meager content validity evidence. The job analysis is the sole proof of content validity. No studies are cited.

COMMENTARY AND SUMMARY. Weaknesses proliferate, five will be highlighted. First, basic item writing guidelines should be followed. Many of the true-false Telephone Knowledge and Customer Situations items are poorly written, using, for example, absolute terms in the stem (e.g., always, never). At least one true-false item is ambiguous and based on opinion. For some multiple-choice items, the longer answer tends to be correct. Some items contain grammatical mistakes including comma and colon misuse. Second, all testing materials need to be proofread. For example, the applicant must sign an agreement with this statement: "Your company may provide a copy of the evaluation report to other of your clients to whom I may apply for a position in the future" (Call Center Skills Test, p. 2). Third, approximately 40% of the Content Validation Study's manual is not pertinent (e.g., articles pertaining to other tests, other articles by the test author) to the Call Center Skills test. Fourth, there is no item analysis and development information. Fifth, standardization, reliability, and robust validation evidence are absent. This test is not recommended.

[43]
Canadian Achievement Tests, Third Edition.

Purpose: Designed to measure achievement in the basic skills of reading, language, spelling, mathematics, and writing.

Population: Grades 1.6–postsecondary.
Publication Dates: 1981–2002.
Acronym: CAT-3.
Administration: Group.
Parts, 3: Basic Battery, Supplemental Tests, Constructed-Response Tests.
Levels, 10: 11 (Grades 1.6–2.5), 12 (Grades 2.6–3.5), 13 (Grades 3.6–4.5), 14 (Grades 4.6–5.5), 15 (Grades 5.6–6.5), 16 (Grades 6.6–7.5), 17 (Grades 7.6–8.5), 18 (Grades 8.6–9.5), 19 (Grades 9.6–11.5), 20 (Grades 11.6–postsecondary).
Price Data, 2002: C$205 per Teacher Resource Kit including 3 Student Books at each of Levels 11–13, 1 Student Book at each of Levels 14–19/20, 1 Test Directions for Teachers for each level, 3 Practice Tests for each level, 3 U-Score answer sheets each (Levels 14–19/20), 3 Student Diagnostic Profiles for each level, 9 each of Locator Tests 1 and 2, 1 Locator Test Directions, 18 Locator Test answer sheets, 1 scoring key at each of Levels 11–13, 1 scoring mask at each of Levels 14–18, 1 Norms Book (2001, 101 pages), 1 Teacher Resource Manual for CAT-3 (2002, 242 pages), 1 Parents' Guide to Understanding CAT Results, and 1 carrying bag; $105 per 30 Basic Battery Plus test books (Levels 11–13, specify level); $120 per 30 Basic Battery Plus test books (Levels 14–19/20, specify level); $90 per 30 Basic Battery test books (Levels 12, 13, specify level); $65 per 50 machine-scorable answer sheets (Levels 14–19/20, specify level); $42 per 30 hand-scorable answer sheets (Levels 14–19/20, specify level); $1 per machine-scoring Directions for Test Coordinators; $8 per Test Directions for Teachers (Levels 11–18) or Administering Directions (Levels 19/20), specify level; $40 per Norms Book; $48 per Technical Manual (2002, 156 pages); $35 per Teacher Resource Manual for CAT-3; $1.50 per Parents' Guide to CAT Results; $15 per 30 Student Diagnostic Profiles (Levels 11–19/20, specify level); $12 per 30 Practice Tests (Levels 11–19/20, specify level); $1.50 per scoring key (Levels 11–19/20, specify level); $21 per Locator Test 1 or 2 (specify Test 1 or 2) including directions and 35 answer sheets; $8 per additional directions for Locator Tests 1–2; $21 per 50 additional answer sheets for Locator Tests 1–2; $1.50 per Constructed Response Dictation Worksheet Photocopy Master (Levels 14–16, specify level); $22.50 per Constructed Response Writing Directions including 30 Student Worksheets Narrative Prompts (Levels 12–16), Informational Prompts (Levels 14–16), Letter Prompts (Levels 17–19/20), or Persuasive Prompts (Levels 17–19/20), specify level and prompt; $22.50 per Constructed Response Mathematics directions including 30 Student Worksheets (Levels 11–18), specify level and task; $50 per scoring binder for Constructed-Response Writing or Mathematics including blackline masters for scoring manual, rubrics, and anchor papers

(Levels 12–19/20, specify level); $.44 per Administrator's Summary/Graphic Frequency Distribution (per student); $2.90 per Class Record Sheet (per student, Level 11); $4 per Class Record Sheet (per student, Levels 12–13, specify level), $2.10 per Class Record Sheet (per student, Levels 14–19/20, specify level); $.61 per Objective Competency Report (per student); $.91 per Parent Report or Student Test Record (per student); additional price information available from publisher.
Time: Varies by level; (85–115) minutes for Basic Battery, (55–75) minutes for Supplemental Tests, (40–230) minutes for Constructed Response Test.
Comments: Revision of the CAT/2; hand- or machine-scored by the Canadian Test Centre; machine-scoring recommended when testing 30 or more students; Supplemental and Constructed Response Tests optional.
Author: Canadian Test Centre, Educational Assessment Services.
Publisher: Canadian Test Centre, Educational Assessment Services [Canada].

a) LOCATOR TESTS.
Population: Grades 2–12.
Scores, 2: Vocabulary, Mathematics.
Levels, 2: 1 (Grades 2–6), 2 (Grades 6–12).
Time: (10) minutes.

b) LEVEL 11.
Population: Grades 1.6–2.5.
Scores, 6: 2 Basic Battery Tests (Reading/Language, Mathematics), 3 Supplemental Tests (Word Analysis, Vocabulary, Computation), 1 Constructed Response Test (Mathematics).
Time: (85) minutes for Basic Battery, (55) minutes for Supplemental Tests, (40) minutes for Constructed Response Test.

c) LEVEL 12.
Population: Grades 2.6–3.5.
Scores, 9: 2 Basic Battery Tests (Reading/Language, Mathematics), 4 Supplemental Tests (Word Analysis, Vocabulary, Language/Writing, Computation), 3 Constructed Response Tests (Dictation, Mathematics, Writing-Narrative).
Time: (115) minutes for Basic Battery, (70) minutes for Supplemental Tests, (110) minutes for Constructed Response Test.

d) LEVEL 13.
Population: Grades 3.6–4.5.
Scores, 9: 2 Basic Battery Tests (Reading/Language, Mathematics), 4 Supplemental Tests (Word Analysis, Vocabulary, Language/Writing, Computation), 3 Constructed Response Tests (Dictation, Mathematics, Writing-Narrative).
Time: (110) minutes for Basic Battery, (70) minutes for Supplemental Tests, (110) minutes for Constructed Response Test.

e) LEVEL 14.
Population: Grades 4.6–5.5.

Scores, 10: 2 Basic Battery Tests (Reading/Language, Mathematics), 4 Supplemental Tests (Vocabulary, Spelling, Language/Writing, Computation), 4 Constructed Response Tests (Dictation, Mathematics, Writing-Narrative, Writing-Informational).
Time: (110) minutes for Basic Battery, (75) minutes for Supplemental Tests, (230) minutes for Constructed Response Test.
f) LEVEL 15.
Population: Grades 5.6–6.5.
Scores, 10: 2 Basic Battery Tests (Reading/Language, Mathematics), 4 Supplemental Tests (Vocabulary, Spelling, Language/Writing, Computation), 4 Constructed Response Tests (Dictation, Mathematics, Writing-Narrative, Writing-Informational).
Time: (110) minutes for Basic Battery, (75) minutes for Supplemental Tests, (220) minutes for Constructed Response Test.
g) LEVEL 16.
Population: Grades 6.6–7.5.
Scores, 10: 2 Basic Battery Tests (Reading/Language, Mathematics), 4 Supplemental Tests (Vocabulary, Spelling, Language/Writing, Computation), 4 Constructed Response Tests (Dictation, Mathematics, Writing-Narrative, Writing-Informational).
Time: (110) minutes for Basic Battery, (75) minutes for Supplemental Tests, (220) minutes for Constructed Response Test.
h) LEVEL 17.
Population: Grades 7.6–8.5.
Scores, 10: 2 Basic Battery Tests (Reading/Language, Mathematics), 4 Supplemental Tests (Vocabulary, Spelling, Language/Writing, Computation), 3 Constructed Response Tests (Mathematics, Writing-Letter, Writing-Persuasive).
Time: (110) minutes for Basic Battery, (75) minutes for Supplemental Tests, (220) minutes for Constructed Response Test.
i) LEVEL 18.
Population: Grades 8.6–9.5.
Scores, 10: 2 Basic Battery Tests (Reading/Language, Mathematics), 4 Supplemental Tests (Vocabulary, Spelling, Language/Writing, Computation), 3 Constructed Response Tests (Mathematics, Writing-Letter, Writing-Persuasive).
Time: (110) minutes for Basic Battery, (75) minutes for Supplemental Tests, (220) minutes for Constructed Response Test.
j) LEVEL 19.
Population: Grades 9.6–11.5.
Scores, 10: 2 Basic Battery Tests (Reading/Language, Mathematics), 4 Supplemental Tests (Vocabulary, Spelling, Language/Writing, Computation), 2 Constructed Response Tests (Writing-Letter, Writing-Persuasive).
Time: (110) minutes for Basic Battery, (75) minutes for Supplemental Tests, (180) minutes for Constructed Response Test.
k) LEVEL 20.
Population: Grades 11.6-postsecondary.
Scores, 10: 2 Basic Battery Tests (Reading/Language, Mathematics), 4 Supplemental Tests (Vocabulary, Spelling, Language/Writing, Computation), 2 Constructed Response Tests (Writing-Letter, Writing-Persuasive).
Time: (110) minutes for Basic Battery, (75) minutes for Supplemental Tests, (180) minutes for Constructed Response Test.
Cross References: See T5:384; for reviews by John Hattie and Leslie Eastman Lukin of the second edition, see 13:44 (2 references); see also T4:371 (3 references); for a review by L. A. Whyte of an earlier edition, see 9:187.

Review of the Canadian Achievement Tests, Third Edition by JOHN O. ANDERSON, Professor and Chair, Department of Educational Psychology, University of Victoria, Victoria, British Columbia, Canada:

DESCRIPTION. The Canadian Achievement Tests (CAT) are a multilevel battery of standardized tests of student achievement in the basic academic areas of reading, language usage, vocabulary, mathematics, and computation. The tests are designed for students aged from 11 to 20 years—there are eight separate test booklets designated as Levels 11, 12, 13, 14, 15, 16, 17, 18, and 19/20. The tests consist mainly of multiple-choice items and some constructed-response items.

The test booklets are single documents containing all of the test items for that level. Each section of each booklet begins with several sample items to allow students to familiarize themselves with the specific item format of the subsequent section of the test. The test booklets for Level 11, 12, and 13 are between 40 and 52 pages in length, and are designed so that students enter their item responses into the test booklet. The time required for students to complete the tests ranges from about 140 minutes to about 210 minutes. The booklets for the older students vary in length from 56 to 61 pages and are designed so that students enter their responses on a separate answer sheet. The test booklets or answer sheets can be scored by the teacher using answer keys provided, or sent to the publisher for scanning and generation via printer of student, class, and school reports.

The tests consist of the Basic Battery (Reading/Language, and Mathematics), Supplemental Tests (Word Analysis, Vocabulary, Spelling, Language, and Computation), and Constructed-Response (Dictation, Mathematics, and Writing). Scores are generated for each section of the test the student completes in the form of scale scores, national percentiles, stanines, and grade equivalent scores. In addition, test results can also be reported as scores on test objectives that are further subdivisions of the items sets. The CAT is accompanied by short locator tests that help select the appropriate level of test for those students for whom age may not be the best index of level of achievement.

The tests are accompanied by a number of supporting documents. The *Test Directions for Teachers* provides a brief overview of the test and materials required for classroom administration, and a script for administering the tests to students. The *Norms Book* provides tables to convert raw scores to scale scores to national percentiles and grade equivalent scores. The *Technical Manual* provides a comprehensive description of the test structure, the development procedures, the sampling design, and the summary statistics at both test, objective, and item levels. The *Teacher Resource Manual* provides suggested instructional activities related to the objectives on which the tests are based. There is a *Parent Guide* pamphlet that could be distributed to parents to help them better understand test results for their child and offers suggestions of activities parents could do with their child to help improve test performance. Another resource for test users is a website (www.Canadiantestcentre.com) that provides descriptions of the tests, order information, and a contact e-mail address to ask specific questions.

DEVELOPMENT. The test battery is the third edition of the Canadian Achievement Tests that were initially derived from the California Achievement Tests. For this third edition the test developers involved a number of educators in creating test specifications that would be representative of the reading and mathematics curricula common in Canadian schools. From this procedure 84 testing objectives were derived and defined, and from these objectives the test items were developed and field-tested. Each item was

assigned to a particular objective and test level. Each item was responded to by at least 100 students in the field test. Items were selected for the final test batteries on the basis of their fit to the test specifications, evaluative comments by participating teachers, and the statistical properties of the items (p-values centered at .62 and discrimination indices above .30). The readability of all passages in the tests was evaluated by teachers participating in the field studies and, in addition, readability indices were used to identify age-appropriate passages for the final tests. National norming was conducted using a well-described plan resulting in a final sample of over 44,000 students from 211 schools throughout Canada. As part of the norming process teachers participated in a standard setting procedure in which items were rated in terms of *Low*, *Competent*, and *Proficient* students. This led to creation of cutscores for each testing objective—for each objective a student can be classified as *low*, *competent*, or *proficient* on the basis of these national cutscores.

To evaluate the CAT, item and test summary statistics were reviewed and reported in the technical manual, factor analyses were conducted to investigate test structure, comparison of scores one age group to another were made, and gender bias was evaluated using differential item functioning approaches. The tests had limited gender bias (2.5% of the items) but no comment was made in regard to modifying or removing the biased items.

TECHNICAL. The technical manual for the CAT is one of the most comprehensive reports of the development and statistical characteristics of a commercial standardized test. The information provided allows a test user to make better judgments regarding the use of test results in making decisions about students and programs.

The considerations of validity of the CAT were based on content and structural characteristics of the tests. Content validity evidence was based on the development of test items that matched to the test specifications created by educators that describe the major common features of reading, language, and mathematics in Canadian schools. The structure of the test was evaluated by means of factor analysis and the results, which are reported in the technical manual, support the structure upon which subtest scores are reported. A further study related to validity was to assess the discriminating ability of tests scores in regard to adjacent age groups—this indicated that appropriate discriminations were made by the CAT. The studies of differential item functioning evaluating male/female bias in the items suggests a relatively unbiased instrument. It would be expected that future editions will further reduce any bias.

The reliability was reported as KR20 internal consistency estimates, ranging from .72 to .92. Most of the coefficients (83%) exceeded .80, yet only 9% of the tests in the battery had reliability coefficients over .90. These results are positive features of the CAT although they seem moderate given that the tests are primarily large sets of multiple-choice items.

The item level statistics are a welcome addition to technical manuals and the authors of the CAT should be commended for this. Two suggestions to enhance these data would be to include discrimination indices and also an indication of the omission rate. The omission rates would allow test users to evaluate the speededness of the tests.

COMMENTARY. The third edition of the CAT is an incremental improvement over a test that has a long history of use in Canadian schools. The technical manual is a marked improvement, in particular its attention to details that have utility to test users. This manual should promote better use of the test and its results. The detailed description of sampling for the norming of the test provides a base to evaluate the representativeness of the percentile scores reported. The description of the linkage of test items to learning objectives should enhance the instructional relevance of test results to students in classrooms.

Support resources for teachers and parents have a strong instructional focus including suggestions for learning activities associated with the learning objective on which the tests are based. This seems a worthwhile perspective for test resources to adopt. The locator tests and practice tests are useful resources for actual administration of the tests in an appropriate manner. Further, the website offers a good overview of the test and the opportunity to inquire about the CAT with company representatives.

One cautionary note: The CAT still provides results in the form of grade equivalent scores. Although there are cautions clearly stated in the manual about what these scores are and how they should and should not be used, there is a need for major test publishers to take a stand on the use and misuse of grade equivalent scores - and this stand should be to work for their elimination.

SUMMARY. The CAT provides a comprehensive battery of academically relevant standardized tests of basic skills appropriate for use with school-aged children. The CAT provides a practical range of test scoring and reporting, and support resources for test users—administrators, teachers, and parents. The tests offer a clear alternative to provincially mandated assessments of the basic skills, which are common throughout schools in Canada today.

Review of the Canadian Achievement Tests, Third Edition by LOUISE M. SOARES, Professor of Educational Psychology, University of New Haven, West Haven, CT:

DESCRIPTION. The Canadian Achievement Tests, Third Edition (CAT-3) is a standardized achievement test in Reading, Language, Spelling, Writing, and Mathematics for Grades 1 to 12, labeled Levels 11 through 20. Each level contains three categories of Basic Battery (multiple-choice format), Supplemental Tests (multiple-choice format), and Constructed Response. The Basic Battery has two sections: Reading/ Language integrated and calculator-based Mathematics. The time for administration of these tests ranges from 25 to 40 minutes. The Supplemental Tests offer more extensive testing of specific skills (i.e., Word Analysis, Vocabulary, Spelling, Language/Writing Conventions, and Computation). The administration time noted ranges from 15 to 25 minutes. The Constructed Response test contains Dictation (Levels 12–16), Mathematics (Levels 11–18), and four sections of Writing—specifically, Narrative (Levels 12–16), Informational (Levels 14–16), Letter (Levels 17–20), and Persuasive (Levels 17–20). Administration time for these sections varies according to the number of tasks assigned (e.g., 10 minutes per task for four tasks in Mathematics compared to 30 minutes per task for three tasks at Levels 17–20).

Two Locator tests are available for determining the appropriate levels of the Achievement Tests to administer to individual examinees. Locator 1 is given to students in Grades 3–6 and to adults with fewer than 6 years of formal schooling. Locator 2 is given to students in Grades 6–12 and to adults with 6 or more years of formal schooling. Each Locator Test consists of 20 vocabulary and

20 mathematics items, and takes approximately 23 minutes to administer.

The technical manual (published in 2002) contains most of the technical information—development, norming, standardized scores, validity, reliability, gender analysis, and student profiles in the field-testing process. Other documents and support materials include the Test Directions for Teachers (by level) and the CAT-3 Norms Book, which provides directions and tables required for converting number-correct scores to scale scores, national percentile ranks, national stanines, and grade equivalents. The Teacher Resource Manual is a revised and updated successor to the CAT-2 publication, Class Management Guide (1995). It is an instructional resource for assisting classroom teachers to help their students to improve their progress and achievement in learning. It provides activities useful for remedial, enrichment, and regular instruction. Practice Tests for Levels 11 to 17+ are included. The purpose of the Parents' Guide to CAT Results is to help parents interpret the test scores and track achievement over time. However, without the availability of equated alternate forms, reusing the same set of test items could produce correlated errors of measurement, inflated scores from subsequent testing within each grade level, or biased estimates of change. The technical manual does not contain any information about alternate forms or test scores that are produced by an adaptive testing system.

DEVELOPMENT. Specialists in language arts and mathematics were drawn from different regions of Canada to develop test specifications consistent with the four major curricula of Western Canada and the territories, Ontario, Quebec, and Atlantic Canada. Over a 3-year period of item construction, at least six items were matched to each objective. Four criteria guided this process: (a) Reading level for the language arts items would be at grade level; (b) one grade level below for mathematics; (c) test content would be free of racial, ethnic, gender, and social class stereotypes; (d) test content would reflect core Canadian values. Test development specialists reviewed, edited, and prepared the items for field-testing. Each test item was administered to between 100 and 200 students from 98 schools in the spring of 2000.

TECHNICAL. The sample was stratified by region, area (rural or nonrural), type (public, private, native), and grade range (elementary, secondary). At least one school was sampled for each of 119 cells, and 5,000 students were targeted in each grade. The final sample involved 44,519 students. Sociodemographic data were collected on the school population—retention rates, home language, family composition and size, labor force participation of parents, socioeconomic status (family income, parental education and occupation), and number of school computers available. Every province/territory was represented in the study—from mainly rural populations to highly urbanized student bodies. The authors concluded that the characteristics of the communities served corresponded to those of the national population. This sampling approach was similar to that of previous editions of the CAT, but no such reference was indicated.

The scoring procedures consist of the number of correct answers. They are converted to scale scores according to Thurstone's absolute scaling procedures of a single equal-interval scale. The norms book contains conversions of the number-correct scores to scale scores by level (11 to 19/20) and scale scores to grade-equivalents. It also provides conversions to national percentile ranks and stanines for testing in the Fall (beginning of Grades 2–12), Winter (middle of Grades 2–12), and Spring (end of Grades 1–12). The authors contend that "the validity of inferences from the scores depends partly on the relevance of CAT-3 to each provincial curriculum and the adequacy of the norming process and outcome" (technical manual, p. 23). Moreover, they acknowledge that educators in Canada do not rely solely on the CAT-3 scores as a measure of their students' achievement. More specifically, they are "usually considered one part of a multidimensional student profile. Many (but not all) curriculum expectations in language arts and mathematics are assessed by CAT-3" (technical manual, p. 23).

Analysis of the internal structure of the CAT-3 yielded two factors for Level 11 tests—language arts and mathematics. Levels 12 through 16 yielded a third factor, described as knowledge of specific rules and conventions (e.g., spelling). Levels 17 through 20 returned to a two-factor model of language arts and mathematics. The correlations between the language arts and the mathematics factors ranged between .80 and .87 for Levels 11 through 17, and between .73 and .77 for Levels 18 and 19/20. Based on this evidence and the process of placing the test scores on a common scale, the authors advanced the argument that the scale scores may be used "to measure a student's growth in achievement across the grades" (technical manual, p. 24). The possibility of the confounding of problem-solving ability in mathematics and ability in reading comprehension was dismissed because of the staff's attempt to minimize the impact of reading ability at all levels. In the analysis of possible gender bias, "none of the tests were biased in favor of females or in favor of males" (technical manual, p. 25).

In the measurement of reliability, tests with the larger numbers of test items tended to have larger KR-20 coefficients. They ranged from .69 (Language/Grade 2) to .92 (Dictation/Grade 4). The standard error of measurement was only briefly explained. The resulting *SEM*s in the norms book were quite varied, with no discernible pattern.

COMMENTARY. It appears that the CAT-3 is not simply a revision of CAT-2, but a new start in Canadian achievement testing. Except for the Locator Tests (dating from 1993), all the test forms and supportive materials are copyrighted between 2000 and 2002. The field-tested sample was again quite large and encompassed all the provinces/territories of Canada. The new tests continue the earlier traditions of providing support materials and information about the scores that are helpful to, and readily interpretable by, teachers and parents. The research staff responded to criticisms found in earlier reviews (9:187, 13:44) by providing validity studies of internal structure and degree of participation of sample students with special characteristics, ethnic background, and regional differences. A major advantage of the CAT-3 is the tracking of students' scores throughout their years in Canadian schools.

Work still needs to be done, of course. A single test form at each level is a major drawback, as noted above. The technical manual should then add information about reliability coefficients of parallel forms and stability. Many of the tests contain few items (e.g., six for Geometry and Spatial Sense [Mathematics/Level 17/Grade 7], six for Objective 9 [Level 14/Grade 4]). The authors depend upon educators in the different regions to determine whether the CAT-3 is relevant to each provincial curriculum. The staff should have aggregated the data, analyzed this information, and formally presented the comparisons.

SUMMARY. Like its predecessor, the CAT-3 appears to be a well-constructed measure of the basic academic skills in reading and mathematics. It includes a comprehensive spread of the content in these two areas. It provides a number of ancillary publications that help teachers and parents to track their students' achievement in order to inform instruction and progress. Whether it is actually connective to the curricula in the different regions of the country remains to be determined and documented.

[44]

CERAD Behavior Rating Scale for Dementia, Second Edition.

Purpose: Designed to "assess the behavioral problems and psychiatric symptoms of individuals with no history of mental retardation who have or are suspected to have acquired cognitive deficits."

Population: Adults who have, or are suspected to have, acquired cognitive deficits.

Publication Dates: 1991–2001.

Acronym: BRSD.

Scores, 7: Depressive Symptoms, Inertia, Vegetative Symptoms, Irritability/Aggression, Behavioral Dysregulation, Psychotic Symptoms, Total Weighted Score.

Administration: Individual.

Price Data, 2003: $85 per test kit including manual; $75 per training video.

Time: [20–40] minutes.

Comments: Informant report interview; short form available; may be administered via telephone.

Authors: James L. Mack and Marion Patterson.

Publisher: CERAD Administrative CORE, Duke University Medical Center.

Review of the CERAD Behavior Rating Scale for Dementia, Second Edition by PAMILLA RAMSDEN, Senior Lecturer, Bolton Institute, Bolton, Lancashire, England:

DESCRIPTION. The CERAD Behavior Rating Scale for Dementia, Second Edition (BRSD) was developed to assist the clinician in evaluating the behavioral problems and possible psychiatric symptoms of individuals who may be suffering from dementia. The BRSD was designed specifically for use with individuals with dementia but with no history of mental retardation and who demonstrate relatively stable behavior. It is not recommended for those individuals who are experiencing transitory changes in alertness such as those in delirium. The instrument interviews the primary caregiver or a person familiar with the subject/patient who indicates the presence or absence of symptoms/behavioral problems and the frequency and severity. The BRSD consists of a manual, standardized instructions to be read to the informant at the beginning of the interview (which may be in person or by telephone), a response form that is completed by the examiner during the interview, and a response card that lists the frequency levels with respect to the items that are being rated by an informant. In addition, a scoring form and scoring totals form are included. The instrument consists of 46 items, two total scores, and six 20–40 scores. Administration takes approximately 60–90 minutes dependent upon the response time of the informant. There is also a short form of the BRSD that is a 17-item instrument. Tables for converting the short version to an estimated full BRSD are provided.

The BRSD is to be administered to an informant and not directly to the patient. The manual contains specific guidelines concerning the selection of the informant and suggests the patient's primary caregiver. However, any person familiar with the individual can be an informant and the minimum suggested interaction is a "face-to-face" contact with him or her at least 2 days per week during the month prior to the interview. The instructions provided for the informant are relatively clear and standardized. Once the informant is acquainted with the materials, the informant then responds to the questions in reference to the response card that provides the informant with four alternatives in terms of frequency of the behavior (i.e., occurring on just 1 or 2 days, between 3 and 8, between 9 and 15, or more than 15 days). In addition to the frequency questions there are dichotomous yes/no questions and some "probing" questions that are used to indicate the severity of the behavior/symptoms.

Items on the BRSD have been chosen to examine discrete aspects of behavior not necessarily associated with dementia. Assessment questions on the BRSD "are concerned with either the presence or absence of a specific behavior or behaviors, regardless of whether they are associated with the onset or progression of dementia" (e.g., "difficulty" remaining asleep) (manual, p. 2). Interview questions are grouped into three basic

categories with some items indicating frequency, others absence/presence, and finally severity. Another method for measuring severity is that certain items are combined to generate a factor-based subscale score.

One aspect of the scoring that presents some reliability issues is that informants are asked to speculate rather than leave an item blank (and in fact are encouraged to provide an "educated guess"). If a behavior is reported as present, but the informant cannot be persuaded to estimate the frequency of the behavior, the manual suggests that the examiner propose to the informant that one or two times in the past might be the best guess. This type of prompting could encourage the informant to generate responses that may not be a true indication of the frequency of the behavior being displayed by the individual being rated. In addition, the amount of time spent with the individual by the informant could have a direct correlation to the accuracy of the report of the behavior as well as a halo effect with the informant wanting to present the individual in the best light.

Scoring for the BRSD is laborious as scores must be transferred from the response form to the scoring totals form and then totalled up. Before calculating total scores, the scorer must check the total number of ratings; if there are no more than six unrated items the scorer may continue to calculate the total scores. For any subscale, if one item is unrated the subscale score should not be calculated. Once total scores and subscores are calculated, these scores can be compared to the normative sample, which then can indicate gross psychopathology.

DEVELOPMENT. The CERAD Behavior Rating Scale for Dementia is an instrument developed by a work group from the Clinical Task Force of the Consortium to Establish a Registry for Alzheimer's Disease (CERAD) funded by the National Institute of Aging. The Consortium was interested in selecting or developing a scale to evaluate behavioral pathology in dementia. The work group evaluated several dementia instruments such as the BEHAVE-AD (Reisberg et al., 1987), The PGDRS (Wilkinson & Graham-White, 1980), and the RMBPC (Teri, Truax, Lodgson, Uomoto, & Zarit, 1992) and concluded that none of these assessment tools were appropriate for their objectives. The work group decided to create their own instrument utilizing modified items from the BEHAVE-AD, the CUSPAD (Devanand et al., 1992), and the Cornell Scale of Depression in Dementia (Alexopoulos, Abrams, Young, & Shamoian, 1988), as well as original items that were contributed by members of the work group. Following instrument design, a brief preliminary study was carried out in 1991 and was followed up by a full-scale multicenter pilot study in 1992 that produced a 48-item version of the Behavior Rating Scale for Dementia (BRSD). Following the release of the 1992 version of the BRSD, a study was conducted to develop a scoring system and normative data. A total of 555 individuals with Alzheimer's disease were drawn from three separate National Institute of Aging funded sources. This research led to the further development of the current BRSD and was revised to a 46-item version.

TECHNICAL. The norms for the BRSD were drawn from three separate National Institute of Aging funded clinical sources with the majority of the participants coming from multiple research projects that identified individuals with Alzheimer's disease. There were 555 participants (42% males and 58% females). These norms are not representative of the general U.S. population as they were predominately Caucasian adults with higher than average educational levels. Two additional rating scales were used to assess stage of dementia and level of cognitive functioning in this group, although few participants were administered both measures. These were the Mini-Mental State Exam (Folstein, Folstein, & McHugh, 1975; Cockrell & Folstein, 1988) which is a 30-item scale for the evaluation of gross cognitive functioning and the Clinical Dementia Rating (Hughes, Berg, Danziger, Coben, & Martin, 1982), which is a global rating used to stage severity of dementia. Correlations between individual item ratings and severity indicated that 26 out of the 45 items on the scale were significantly ($p<.05$) correlated with the amount of severity reported. Before the factor analysis was conducted, the missing scores were substituted with mean values for the missing items and then the norm table was generated. No further reliability/validity studies were included in the information made available to this reviewer. [Editor's Note: The publisher provided an article to support reliability/validity after the review was completed.]

COMMENTARY. The value of the BRSD is that it attempts to standardize a clinical interview system to evaluate behavioral pathology in Alzheimer's disease. However, there are many flaws inherent in the instrument that may contribute to the assessment tool either overcalculating or undercalculating problems and/or symptoms. Although there are guidelines in choosing the informant, the amount of time spent with the person being rated could directly influence the amount of information provided to the examiner. An informant who spends 2 days per week with the rated individual for 15 minutes per session may be less knowledgeable than an informant who spends 1 hour a day with the person. Also no provisions are made in distinguishing between those individuals who are cared for at home and those provided for within hospital/residential care facilities. The scoring is also problematic as a behavior that lasted only 30 seconds would be rated the same as if it had persisted for 24 hours within a given day. The normative group is based on a clinical sample of individuals with Alzheimer's disease that may not be representative of all patients with this condition. Although there are clear factors presented for the subscales, these lose their usefulness if one subscore is missing, as the subscale cannot then be calculated. Interpreting the results is difficult and the best information appears to come from individual item inspection that is dependent upon clinical judgment that in turn is influenced by clinical experience.

SUMMARY. The BRSD is an instrument designed to assess behavioral problems and psychiatric symptoms of individuals suspected of dementia, in particular, Alzheimer's disease. The test utilizes informants and does not access the subject/patient directly. The instrument appears to measure a wide spectrum of behavior, most of which is concerned with the presence or absence of specific behaviors regardless of their relationship to onset or progression of dementia. The normative sample is based exclusively on individuals with Alzheimer's disease, application to other dementias is unclear. In general, the BRSD does provide a more systematic way of interviewing and herein lies its utility to clinicians as an initial screening instrument for possible behavioral pathology in Alzheimer's patients.

REVIEWER'S REFERENCES

Alexopoulos, G. S., Abrams, R. C., Young, R. C., & Shamoian, C. A. (1988). Cornell Scale for Depression in Dementia. *Biological Psychiatry, 23,* 271–284.
Cockrell, J. R., & Folstein, M. F. (1988). Mini-Mental State Examination (MMSE). *Psychopharmacology Bulletin, 24,* 689–692.

Devanand, D. P., Miller, L., Richards, M., Marder, K., Bell, K., Mayeux, R., & Stern, Y. (1992). The Columbia University Scale for Psychpathology in Alzheimer's Disease. *Archives of Neurology, 49*, 371–376.

Folstein, M. F., Folstein, S. E., & McHugh, P. R. (1975). Mini-Mental State. *Journal of Psychiatric Research, 12*, 189–198.

Hughes, C. P., Berg, L., Denziger, W. L., Coben, L. A., & Martin, R. L. (1982). A new clinical scale for the staging of dementia. *British Journal of Psychiatry, 140*, 566–572.

Reisberg, B., Borenstein, J., Franssen, E., Salob, S. P., Steinberg, G., Shulman, E. et al. (1987). BEHAVE-AD: A clinical rating scale for the assessment of pharmacologically remedial behavioral symptomatology in Alzheimer's disease. In H. J. Altman (Ed.), *Alzheimer's disease*. New York: Plenum.

Teri, L., Truax, P., Lodgson, R., Uomoto, J., & Zarit, S. (1992). Assessment of behavioral problems in dementia: The Revised Memory and Behavior Problem Checklist. *Psychology and Aging, 7*, 622–631.

Wilkinson, I. M., & Graham-White, J. (1980). Psychogeriatric dependency rating scales (PGDRS): A method of assessment for use by nurses. *British Journal of Psychiatry, 137*, 558–565.

[45]
Chapin Social Insight Test.

Purpose: Designed to "assess the perceptiveness and accuracy with which an individual can appraise others and forecast what they might say and do."

Population: Ages 13 and over.

Publication Dates: 1967–1993.

Acronym: SCLT.

Scores: Total score only.

Administration: Group.

Price Data, 2004: $30 per sampler set including a sample of test booklet and manual; $120 per duplications set which grants permission to reproduce up to 150 copies of the test.

Time: (20–30) minutes.

Authors: F. Stuart Chapin (test) and Harrison G. Gough (manual).

Publisher: Mind Garden, Inc.

Cross References: See T3:384 (5 references); for reviews by Richard I. Lanyon and David B. Orr of an earlier edition, see 7:51; see also P:34 (3 references).

Review of the Chapin Social Insight Test by FRANK M. BERNT, Associate Professor, Health Services Department, Saint Joseph's University, Philadelphia, PA:

DESCRIPTION. The Chapin Social Insight Test (CSIT) was developed in order to "assess an individual's ability to appraise others, to sense what they feel and think, and to predict what they may say and do (manual, p. 3). Originally developed in 1942 by Dr. Stuart Chapin, it anticipated the more intensive efforts to measure aspects of emotional intelligence and social information processing that appeared more than 50 years later (Bar-On & Parker, 2000).

Consisting of 25 short descriptions of interpersonal "problem situations" involving a range of rather stereotypic hypothetical personalities, the CSIT instructs those taking the test to complete the statement at the end of each description by choosing from among four multiple-choice options, the response to which represents what is "most accurate" or "the wisest thing to do" in each situation (manual, p. 6). Each item is scored as correct or incorrect, according to an answer key provided.

The test is untimed. The manual states that most people can complete it in 30 minutes or less. The test contains very straightforward instructions, which can either be read by a proctor or by the individual taking the test (the manual indicates that self-administration is appropriate). According to the test manual, the CSIT is designed for use with "English-speaking and English-reading subjects of either gender, age 13-14 or over" (p. 4); however, nearly all of the validation work has been done with college-age people or adults, and there is no indication that the instrument was evaluated for readability.

DEVELOPMENT. The preliminary version of the test consisted of 45 items drawn from case histories, literary descriptions, and earlier instruments. It was administered to a group of 375 adults who were rated by their supervisors as either "above average" with respect to social insight or as not being so. Of the 375 adults, 65 were rated as above average. A point-biserial correlation of .21 indicated a significant though very modest relationship between supervisor ratings and individual CSIT scores.

Based upon results of this preliminary analysis, 25 items were selected for inclusion in the final version of the scale. Of the 25 items, correct responses for the 5 items showing the strongest differentiation are given a weight of 3; 6 items yielding moderate differentiation are given a weight of 2; and the remaining 14 items are given a weight of 1. Accordingly, the 25-item scale yields a score ranging from 0 to 41. Not surprisingly, this adjustment in scoring increased the correlation (from .21 to .36).

In 1993, the CSIT was revised to remove gender bias; however, the basic content of the original situations and responses was left intact.

TECHNICAL. Internal consistency estimates for the CSIT are adequate; measures for the 25-item scale range from .68–.78. No evidence of stability of scores over time is reported.

Efforts to examine criterion-related validity have yielded modestly suggestive results. The CSIT's median correlation with tests of cognitive ability is .34; correlations with social competence and wisdom prototype instruments developed by Sternberg (1989) were .43 and .46, respectively.

Correlations with other tests provide less-than-convincing evidence in support of the CSIT's criterion-related validity. Correlations with relevant subtests of the California Psychological Inventory were essentially zero. Significant but low correlations were found between the CSIT and the Femininity subscale of the Minnesota Multiphasic Personality Inventory ($r = .19$); with the Barron-Welsh Art Scales ($r = .19$); with the Welsh R scale ($r = .18$); and with the scales for aesthetic and social value preferences (positive correlations, not specified). The authors are careful to point out that such results are suggestive at best and beg further investigation.

COMMENTARY. Although efforts to examine the validity of scores from the CSIT deserve some credit, results are modest, not extensive, and less than convincing. A closer look at the phrasing and content of the 25 items raises questions about the face validity of the test. Revision to remove gender bias notwithstanding, examples used seem very dated, and correct answers in many cases are simplistic caricatures of textbook psychoanalytic and behaviorist dynamics; it is likely that high scores are more indicative of educated guessing and of exposure to psychological theory than of real social insight. More recent efforts have directly addressed the issue of "right answers" on such ability testing (Mayer, Caruso, & Salovey, 2000).

The manual's author urgently invites researchers to conduct studies using the revised CSIT, particularly focusing upon issues of gender and of cultural and ethnic diversity. This reviewer's impression is that, for whatever reason, research in this area has progressed substantially in the past 10 years while virtually ignoring the CSIT. A brief review of more recent instruments available for measuring a wide range of aspects of emotional and social intelligence indicates that the field has grown beyond the limited reach of Chapin's original scale. This places the potential user of the CSIT at a disadvantage, as it lacks a current body of literature within which one might see how the test behaves.

SUMMARY. Researchers interested in further exploring instruments and models relating to social insight or emotional intelligence are directed to Bar-On and Parker's (2000) collection of articles on the subject. Tests described therein that may represent more carefully developed and validated measures of the social insight construct include Mayer, Salovey, and Caruso's (1997) Emotional IQ test or their Multifactor Emotional Intelligence Scale (Mayer, Salovey, & Caruso, 2000).

Reading through Bar-On and Parker's (2000) book will leave one cautious about expecting too much even from the new scales. There is much debate and little consensus about the structure or even the existence of emotional intelligence in any of its forms. At the very least, however, the book provides a rich and deep understanding of the issues involved in measuring social insight, which was simply not available to the original author of the CSIT. New theories such as information-processing theory and social constructionism were not part of the vocabulary for most psychologists or sociologists in the 1950s; accordingly, it may well be that the CSIT is more of historical than of practical interest.

REVIEWER'S REFERENCES

Bar-On, R., & Parker, J. D. A. (Eds.). (2000). *The handbook of emotional intelligence: Theory, development, assessment, and application at home, school, and in the workplace.* San Francisco: Jossey-Bass.

Mayer, J. D., Caruso, D. R., & Salovey, P. (2000). Selecting a measure of emotional intelligence; The case for ability scales. In R. Bar-On & J. D. A. Parker (Eds.), *The handbook of emotional intelligence: theory, development, assessment, and application at home, school, and in the workplace* (pp. 320-342). San Francisco: Jossey-Bass.

Mayer, J. D., Salovey, P., & Caruso, D. (1997). Emotional IQ test [CD ROM]. Needham, MA: Virtual Knowledge.

Mayer, J. D., Salovey, P., & Caruso, D. (2000). Emotional intelligence. In R. J. Sternberg (Ed.), *Handbook of intelligence* (2nd ed., pp. 396-420). New York: Cambridge University Press.

Sternberg, R. J. (1989). Intelligence, wisdom, and creativity: Their natures and interrelationships. In R. L. Linn (Ed.), *Intelligence: Measurement, theory and public policy* (pp.119-146). Urbana, IL: University of Illinois Press.

Review of the Chapin Social Insight Test by COLLIE W. CONOLEY, *Professor, and* LINDA CASTILLO, *Assistant Professor of Educational Psychology, Texas A&M University, College Station, TX:*

DESCRIPTION. The Chapin Social Insight Test is a 25-item paper-and-pencil test that requires about 20–30 minutes to complete. The test was developed for English-speaking and English-reading populations ages 13 and older. The test measures a person's ability to evaluate and predict the behaviors of another. Social insight as measured by the test is said to be different from empathy, or emotional responsiveness. The manual states that social insight is a skill used by successful psychotherapists, politicians, managers, and social/religious leaders.

Each of the 25 items consists of a paragraph describing an individual followed by four possible alternatives that describe the individual. Only one of the options is deemed correct as determined by the developer. Five of the items are weighted as 3 points, 6 items are weighted as 2, and the remaining 14 items are weighted as 1 point. Summing the points yields the total score.

A sample item included in the manual describes a man criticizing another for spending too much money. The question is why would the critical man later perform the same act that he earlier criticized. Four choices are offered.

DEVELOPMENT. The Chapin Social Insight Test was developed in 1942 by Stuart Chapin. No definition of social insight other than Chapin's is referenced in defining the construct that guided the development of the test. The definition was:

We begin with the working hypothesis that social insight is the ability to recognize in principle in a given situation: (1) the existence and operation of specific substitute responses such as projection, rationalization, regression, sublimation, transference, etc.; and (2) the need of some specific stimulus to adjust group conflicts or tensions, such as a humorous remark to relax a dangerous intensity, a suggested compromise to attain temporary agreement, a face-saving remark to avoid embarrassment and to preserve status (to leave a loophole, a way out, etc.), or to discover the missing part required to complete a pattern of thought [Chapin, 1942, p. 214]. (as cited in the manual, p. 3)

The initial 45 items were derived from case histories, literary descriptions, and social-science literature. No information was provided on how the correct answer was determined and how answers were weighted. Only one score is derived from the measure so point-biserial correlations were used to select the retained items.

TECHNICAL. The original validity information was based upon the ability of the measure to reveal construct hypothesized differences in samples of social workers and clerical workers and the correlation between number of social organizations and the scores on the Chapin Social Insight Test.

A series of studies are presented in the test manual to enhance the validity information. Several of the studies indicate small correlations (around .27) between the Chapin Social Insight Test and measures of constructs such as quasi-

intelligence (e.g., general information, ability to evaluate ideas), and larger correlations (as large as .40) with measures of ability to supervise and demonstrate leadership. This is interpreted to mean that the measure is more than intelligence. The higher correlations with supervision and leadership abilities was interpreted as indicating that the Chapin Social Insight Test was associated with the interpersonal insight necessary in supervision and leadership.

Perhaps the most impressive validity evidence was a study involving the performance of doctoral psychology students. The Chapin Social Insight Test had a point-biserial correlation of .40 with 148 psychology students who completed a doctoral degree and 48 who dropped out. Gender or racial demographics of the sample in the study were not provided.

Reliability was reported as only moderate with an odd-even internal consistency correlation of .78. In the study of 191 men and 21 women, a .71 (men) and .68 (women) Guilford coefficient (based upon point-biserial correlations of items to total score and corrected for length) was found. Test-retest reliability information was not provided. There is no information about validity or reliability for racial/ethnic status.

COMMENTARY. The Chapin Social Insight Test appears to be related to a person's intellectual ability and to a greater degree a person's ability to work well with people. The latter indicator could be related to social perceptiveness or insight. The logic of the validity studies was reasonable in that the measures most relevant to social insight were most correlated with the Chapin Social Insight Test providing some discriminate validity.

The user should remember that the measure is clearly not independent of intellectual abilities or facility with the English language. The validity studies reveal around a .30 correlation with most measures of intellectual abilities. This issue is important when considering the use of the Chapin Social Insight Test with adolescents or nonprofessional populations. For example, the manual states that 13–14-year-old adolescents could use the test; however, their test scores appear to negatively interact with their intellectual development. The problem is evident in that the validity studies revealed a difference in mean scores from high school to college students. Another problem is that the cases are written at a 10th–12th-grade reading level. Furthermore, many of the case scenarios may be unfamiliar to adolescents. Thus, the age appropriateness of this measure for adolescents is questionable.

The confound of amount of English skills, intellectual ability gained from schooling, and social perceptiveness may also appear in using the Chapin Social Insight Test if the measure is used with a "blue collar" population. The amount of variance accounted for by high school achievement versus social perceptiveness would not be clear in testing 25-year-old high school graduates who apply for a store management job. Clearly, this scenario may be where the lack of norms for persons from a minority group or English as a second language would be at a disadvantage.

Culturally relevant behaviors are another potential confound of this measure. Many of the case scenarios are written from a European American perspective where culturally appropriate behaviors as defined by this culture are deemed as "social insight."

The most reasonable use of the Chapin Social Insight Test seems to be when the test should measure intellectual abilities and social perceptiveness of middle-class Caucasian populations. The confound now becomes helpful rather than a detriment. Still the problem of only differentiating middle-class Caucasian persons exists. There is no evidence for validity in using the test with other populations.

The Chapin Social Insight Test is simple to administer and score. The manual states that only persons qualified by the definitions of the American Psychological Association ethical standards should interpret the results.

SUMMARY. The Chapin Social Insight Test offers a potentially helpful measure when used within the confines of its limitations. The test scores appear to discriminate between levels of intellectual ability and social perceptiveness. The clarity of the construct of social perceptiveness or insight is probably not as clearly defined in the manual as the user may desire. The reliability and validity information suggests moderate confidence in the tests results for middle-class Caucasians. The administration and scoring is efficient using a paper-and-pencil format.

The major concerns of applying the results of the test are threefold. The first concern is the confound of intellectual abilities associated with formal schooling and the intended results of social perceptiveness or insight. A second potential confound is the culturally relevant meaning of social insight. The third concern is the absence of validity studies with racial/ethnic minorities. These three issues are critical when considering using the Chapin Social Insight Test.

Child Symptom Inventory-4 [2002 Update].

Purpose: Designed as a "screening instrument for the behavioral, affective, and cognitive symptoms" of childhood psychiatric disorders.

Population: Ages 5–12.

Publication Dates: 1994–2002.

Acronym: CSI-4.

Scores, 13: AD/HD Inattentive, AD/HD Hyper-Impulsive, AD/HD Combined, Oppositional Defiant Disorder, Conduct Disorder, Generalized Anxiety Disorder, Schizophrenia, Major Depressive Disorder, Dysthymic Disorder, Autistic Disorder, Asperger's Disorder, Social Phobia, Separation Anxiety Disorder.

Administration: Individual.

Forms, 2: Parent Checklist, Teacher Checklist.

Price Data, 2005: $98 per deluxe kit including screening and norms manual (2002, 179 pages), 25 parent checklists, 25 teacher checklists, 50 symptom count score sheets, and 50 symptom severity profile score sheets; $358 per deluxe kit also including scoring CD; $44 per screening and norms manual; $32 per 50 parent checklists; $60 per 100 parent checklists; $32 per 50 Spanish parent checklists; $32 per 50 teacher checklists; $13 per 50 profiles for parent or teacher checklists; $290 per computer scoring software.

Time: [10–15] minutes.

Comments: Instrument is designed to correspond to the DSM-IV classification system.

Authors: Kenneth D. Gadow and Joyce Sprafkin.

Publisher: Checkmate Plus Ltd.

Cross References: For reviews by James C. DiPerna and Robert J. Volpe and by Rosemary Flanagan based on an earlier edition of the manual for this test, see 15:47.

Review of the Child Symptom Inventory-4 [2002 Update] by KATHRYN E. HOFF, Assistant Professor of Psychology, and W. JOEL SCHNEIDER, Assistant Professor of Psychology, Illinois State University, Normal, IL:

DESCRIPTION. The Child Symptom Inventory-4 (CSI-4) is a rating scale that screens for the behavioral and affective symptoms of 13 major DSM-IV (American Psychiatric Association, 1994) childhood psychiatric disorders. Designed for use in clinical settings, the CSI-4 was developed as a time-efficient alternative to structured psychiatric interviews, to facilitate information gathering from parents and teachers about the symptoms of various childhood psychiatric disorders, and to systematize information exchange between the clinician and the school. Further, results on the CSI-4 can be used to determine whether a more in-depth evaluation by a qualified professional is warranted. The CSI-4 is appropriate for children 5 to 12 years old, and both parent (97 items) and teacher (77 items) versions are available.

The authors report each of the scales take between 10 and 15 minutes to complete. The test kit contains separate Parent and Teacher checklists, a screening and norms manual, and scoring guides. The manual is well organized, easy to understand, and information regarding administration and scoring is straightforward. The authors provide a useful overview of the diagnostic criteria for disorders that appear in the CSI-4, and include tables comparing item content with the DSM-IV criteria. A thorough description of the psychometric properties is presented, and a clinical applications section is included that assists in interpretation and application of scores.

Items are rated on a 4-point scale: (*never, sometimes, often,* and *very often*). The CSI-4 is scored using a Symptom Count (categorical) or a Symptom Severity (dimensional) method. A Symptom Count score is used to determine whether the child exhibits the minimum number of symptoms required to warrant a DSM diagnosis. Scoring is done on a 2-point scale where the score of a 0 ("no" category) is assigned if the behavior never or sometimes occurs, and the score of a 1 ("yes" category) is assigned if the behavior occurs often or very often. The child receives a screening cutoff score of "yes" for a particular disorder if his or her symptom count score is equal to or exceeds the minimum number of symptoms necessary for a DSM-IV diagnosis. The authors appropriately caution that a positive symptom count score does not immediately translate to a clinical diagnosis, especially because the symptom count score is based on the behavioral symptoms and other required diagnostic criteria (e.g., age of symptom onset, impairment of functioning) are not included in the scale. The Symptom Severity scoring procedure measures the degree of symptom severity compared with a gender-specific norm sample.

Scoring is accomplished by summing item scores within each symptom category, and converting these raw total scores to norm-referenced scores (*T*-scores and percentile ranks).

DEVELOPMENT. The CSI-4 was developed as a screening instrument for the major DSM-IV disorders. Initial versions of the scale began as a behavioral checklist for externalizing disorders in childhood (Sprafkin, Loney, und Gadow [SLUG] Checklist). Expanded symptom inventories were then created to correspond with the major diagnostic categories of the DSM, resulting in the Stony Brook Child Symptom Inventory-3 (CSI-3) and the Child Symptom Inventory 3-R (CSI 3-R). The CSI-4 was published in 1994, and like its predecessors, item content directly corresponds with DSM-IV behavioral symptom criteria. In 2002, the CSI-4 manual was published in an updated form with an expanded normative sample, although the item content did not change. Since publication of the 2002 updated manual, numerous studies on the CSI-4 have been reported in the professional literature.

TECHNICAL.

Standardization. The normative sample for the parent ratings are based on 551 children (272 males, 279 females) between 5 and 12 years old who attended public elementary schools. The sample was fairly evenly distributed across grade and gender. Children in the normative sample were excluded if they were receiving special education services; however, 3.6% of parents reported their child had received medication for an emotional or behavioral disorder such as AD/HD. The sample is limited in terms of ethnic diversity, with 89% Caucasian, 5% African American, 3% Hispanic American, and 2% Other. The sample is restricted in terms of geographical diversity; although the sample was drawn from seven states, 75% of participants were from New York. The normative sample for the Teacher Checklist was larger, consisting of 1,323 children (662 males, 661 females), but was even less diverse in its racial-ethnic composition (95.4% Caucasian) and geographic diversity (only three states sampled). Therefore, the standardization sample for the CSI-4 is not nationally representative of elementary school children. Normative data for children referred to an outpatient child psychiatry clinic are also available for the Parent Checklist (N = 590) and Teacher Checklist (N = 548).

Reliability. Test-retest reliability data for the parent form have been collected in at least four clinical samples, ranging from 2 weeks to 4 years. Test-retest reliability was generally in the acceptable to good range (.70–.87) in at least one sample for all scales except for Schizophrenia (.55), Conduct Disorder (.46), Generalized Anxiety Disorder (.67), and Dysthymic Disorder (.66). Test-retest reliabilities for the teacher form were collected from a sample of 74 elementary school children over a 2-week interval. Test-retest reliability was generally in the acceptable to good range, except for Compulsions (.47), Specific Phobia (.51), and Disturbing Events (.62). Internal consistency reliability coefficients were acceptable to good for all scales (range = .74–.94 parent and .70–.96 teacher). Interrater reliability evidence was based on parent and teacher ratings from a sample of 510 children with clinical diagnoses. Similar to results obtained from other cross-informant (i.e., teacher-parent) rating scales, a low to moderate degree of convergence was obtained for most categories.

Validity. Criterion validity was assessed by comparing CSI-4 parent and teacher ratings for an outpatient child psychiatric sample ($N = 101$) with psychiatric diagnoses. Results suggest moderate sensitivity and moderate to high specificity (.63–.95), particularly when parent and teacher ratings were considered together. Importantly, predictive validity could not be obtained for four of the categories (Schizophrenia, PTSD, OCD, Phobia), as there were too few children presented with that disorder. Convergent validity was assessed in multiple studies by correlating the CSI-4 parent and teacher scores with other commonly used taxonomies (Child Behavior Checklist, Achenbach, 1991a; Teacher Report Form, Achenbach, 1991b; IOWA Conners Teacher's Rating Scale, Loney & Milich, 1982). Results indicate satisfactory convergent validity and demonstrate the predicted patterns of relations. Published research on discriminant validity indicates that the CSI-4 can differentiate clinical versus nonclinical samples (e.g., Gadow et al., 2004; Mattison, Gadow, Sprafkin, & Nolan, 2002; Nolan, Gadow, & Sprafkin, 2001; Sprafkin, Gadow, Salisbury, Schneider, & Loney, 2002).

COMMENTARY. The CSI-4 appears to be a useful screening measure for the major childhood psychiatric disorders. The primary advantage of using the CSI-4 instead of other behavior rating scales is that questions are directly linked to DSM diagnostic criteria, thus facilitating a DSM-IV diagnosis reliably and efficiently. However, more reliable and well-established behavior rating scales based on empirically derived taxonomies should be used when a more theoretically based case conceptualization is needed. Reliability estimates are satisfactory for most subscales, and several research teams have provided evidence of content, criterion-related, and construct validity. The standardization sample was predominately Caucasian, thus generalizing results to individuals of ethnically diverse backgrounds is questionable. The authors cite communication with schools as an advantage of the CSI-4; however, the scale is not directly linked to the special education classification system used in schools.

SUMMARY. The CSI-4 is a DSM-IV referenced behavior rating scale that screens for the major emotional and behavioral disorders in childhood. The CSI-4 is easy to administer, score, and interpret, and the items are clear. The manual is user-friendly and provides detailed information for the examiner. Because items are linked to DSM, it can facilitate use in clinical practice and research. Reliability and validity data are encouraging but the standardization sample is limited. Although the CSI-4 succeeds in its practical ambition to operationalize DSM-IV constructs, its theoretical success depends entirely on the validity of the DSM-IV. The long-term prognosis of the CSI-4 is promising because of the willingness of multiple research teams to investigate its psychometric properties.

REVIEWERS' REFERENCES

Achenbach, T. M. (1991a). *Manual for the Child Behavior Checklist/4–18 and 1991 Profile.* Burlington, VT: University of Vermont, Department of Psychiatry.

Achenbach, T. M. (1991b). *Manual for the Teacher's Report Form and 1991 Profile.* Burlington, VT: University of Vermont, Department of Psychiatry.

American Psychiatric Association. (1994). *Diagnostic and statistical manual of mental disorders* (4th ed.). Washington, DC: Author.

Gadow, K. D., Drabick, D. A. G., Loney, J., Sprafkin, J., Salisbury, H., Azizian, A., & Schwartz, J. (2004). Comparison of ADHD symptom subtypes as source-specific syndromes. *Journal of Child Psychology and Psychiatry, 45,* 1135–1149.

Loney, J., & Milich, R. (1982). Hyperactivity, inattention, and aggression in clinical practice. In M. Wolraich & D. L. Routh (Eds.), *Advances in developmental and behavioral pediatrics* (Vol. 3, pp. 113–147). Greenwich, CT: JAI Press.

Mattison, R. E., Gadow, K. D., Sprafkin, J., & Nolan, E. E. (2002). Discriminant validity of a DSM-IV-based teacher checklist: Comparison of regular and special education students. *Behavioral Disorders, 27,* 304–316.

Nolan, E. E., Gadow, K. D., & Sprafkin, J. (2001). Teacher reports of DSM-IV ADHD, ODD, and CD symptoms in school children. *Journal of the American Academy of Child and Adolescent Psychiatry, 40,* 241–249.

Sprafkin, J., Gadow, K. D., Salisbury, H., Schneider, J., & Loney, J. (2002). Further evidence of reliability and validity of the Child Symptom Inventory-4: Parent Checklist in clinically referred boys. *Journal of Clinical Child and Adolescent Psychology, 31,* 513–524.

[47]

Children's Color Trails Test™.

Purpose: "Designed to provide an easily administered and objectively scored measure of alternating and sustained visual attention, sequencing, psychomotor speed, cognitive flexibility, and inhibition-disinhibition."

Population: Ages 8–16.

Publication Dates: 1989–2003.

Acronym: CCTT.

Scores, 6: Time Scores, Prompt Scores, Near-Miss Scores, Error Scores (Number Sequence Errors, Color Sequence Errors), Interference Index.

Subtests, 2: CCTT-1, CCTT-2.

Administration: Individual.

Forms, 4: K, X, Y, Z.

Price Data, 2004: $135 per introductory kit including professional manual (2003, 81 pages), 50 record forms, 50 copies of Form K, Parts 1 & 2; $215 per CTT/CCTT combination kit; $54 per professional manual; $32 per 50 record forms.

Time: (5–7) minutes.

Comments: Also called Kid's Color Trails, Kiddie Color Trails, K Color Trails; modeled after Color Trails Test.

Authors: Antolin M. Llorente, Jane Williams, Paul Satz, and Louis F. D'Elia.

Publisher: Psychological Assessment Resources, Inc.

Review of the Children's Color Trails Test by ANDREW S. DAVIS, Assistant Professor of Psychology, Ball State University, and W. HOLMES FINCH, Assistant Professor of Educational Psychology, Ball State University, Muncie, IN:

DESCRIPTION. Trail making tests have been a hallmark of neuropsychological assessment for more than 60 years, and trail making tests remain an integral part of the Halstead-Reitan Neuropsychological Test Battery (HRNB, Reitan & Wolfson, 1993; T6:1114), the most widely used standardized neuropsychological test battery (Guilmette & Faust, 1991). Trail making tests are thought to be one of the most sensitive tests to cerebral impairment, and are thought to measure mental flexibility, inhibition, processing speed, visual attention, and visual perception (Dean, 1985). The Children's Color Trails Test (CCTT) was developed to create a trail making test that would not be a downward extension of an adult trail making test, and to address concerns about the cultural and linguistic bias of other trail making tests. Historically, most trail making tests first require individuals to connect a series of circles using a pencil, drawing a line from circles with numbers inside them in ascending sequential order. Next, for the second task, the individual is required to draw a line from circle to circle, alternating between circles with numbers and letters in them in ascending sequential order. The test authors of the CCTT have replaced the letter recognition component with color recognition, which is fairer to children who either are not familiar with English language letters or children who struggle with linguistic tasks, such as children with learning disabilities. Additionally, the test authors point out that premorbidly high functioning children who present with mild to moderate brain injuries often complete the second part of traditional trail making tests within normal time limits due to the overlearned nature of the alphabet.

Designed for use by children aged 8 to 16, this paper-and-pencil test can be administered and scored with just a stopwatch, a pencil, and three pieces of paper, which includes the two-sided CCTT-1 and CCTT-2 and the record form, which has the administration instructions printed on the back. The test authors note that they are in the process of collecting normative data for children younger than 8. Children must be able to count to 15, use a pencil, and distinguish between pink and yellow in order to take the CCTT. Raw scores are obtained on several indices. The following indices are obtained for both the CCTT-1 and CCTT-2: Time (time to complete the task), Number Sequence Errors (the child fails to connect to the next highest number circle), Near-Misses (initiation of an incorrect response that is self-corrected), and Prompts (nonverbal pointing to the next circle after 10 seconds has elapsed). The CCTT also generates raw scores for Color Sequence Errors (the child consecutively connects two circles of the same color). Standard scores are available for the Time scores, and Percentile rank ranges are available for the Number Sequence Errors, Color Sequence Errors, and Prompts. Subtracting CCTT-1 from CCTT-2 and dividing by CCTT-1 calculates an Inference Index using the raw time scores. Alternative test forms are available to aid in longitudinal practice and research, although at this time, normative data exist only for the standard test form.

DEVELOPMENT. The CCTT was created based on the Color Trails Test (D'Elia, Satz, Uchiyama, & White, 1996), a trail making test for adults. The test authors cite concerns raised by the

World Health Organization (WHO, 1990) as one of the reasons the CCTT was created. The test authors also cite concerns about the sensitivity of other trail making tests to language impairment, cultural fairness, and the influence of developmental and cognitive factors. The authors provide an excellent discussion of the developmental, maturational, and psychometric considerations that underlie the construction of the CCTT. Background about the assessment of attention and executive functioning skills is also provided, which will aid clinicians in interpreting the CCTT. Unfortunately, the authors do not include detailed information about the development process of the CCTT, such as information about pilot studies or how the final structure of the CCTT-1 and CCTT-2 emerged.

TECHNICAL. The normative data for the CCTT were collected on a sample of 678 children aged 8 to 16. The sample is not representative of the U.S. population, as it was collected from one school district in Los Angeles. Yet the sample is about evenly split between males and females and contains a wide mix of ethnicity. It should be noted that with respect to ethnicity, African American children may be underrepresented, making up only 2% of the normative sample. The standardization sample consisted of healthy children with no known history of medical, psychiatric, or neurological problems. Nine normative tables, divided by age, are available to provide normative comparisons of children, and standard scores, T-Scores, and percentile ranks are available for Time scores for CCTT-1 and CCTT-2. Percentile ranks are available for Number Sequence Errors, Color Sequence Errors, and Prompts for age corrected norms. Interpretive ranges and base rates of occurrence are provided for a clinical sample of children with mild neurological difficulties.

The test authors report two reliability studies in the manual. A measure of alternate form reliability was reported by using an altered form of the CCTT with 12 children, 8 to 10 years of age, who were diagnosed with asymptomatic congenital cytomegalovirus (CMV). Correlations were good for CCTT-1 (.85) and CCTT-2 (.90). Another study using 63 children from ages 6 to 12 who were diagnosed with Attention Deficit Hyperactivity Disorder (ADHD) was conducted to examine test-retest reliability. Results were obtained by administering the CCTT at intervals of

2 and 4 months. Generally, results were lower than what would be hoped for, with correlation coefficients ranging from .45 to .68 for CCTT-1 and CCTT-2. However, the test authors point out, "Had the CCTT been administered at shorter test intervals (e.g., 2 weeks) as is customary when assessing test-retest reliability, it is highly likely that the reliability coefficients would have achieved greater magnitude" (professional manual, p. 40). Perhaps the test authors will themselves perform these studies in the future and report them in a revised or updated test manual.

Validity was assessed in a number of ways, including measures of construct, concurrent, and discriminant validity. Construct validity was examined through the relationship between age and time to completion of the CCTT. This relationship was presented using graphical tools, but no correlation coefficient was calculated. The construct validity of the instrument was also examined using factor analysis on three samples: the normative group, 366 children who had suffered head injuries, and 355 children with injuries other than to the head. In all three samples, three factors emerged, which the authors found to be consistent with theories underlying the CCTT.

The concurrent validity of the CCTT was investigated in two separate studies. The first of these used 223 children who were evaluated for learning, emotional, and behavioral difficulties at an outpatient center run by a school district. Members of this sample ranged in age from just under 6 years to nearly 17 years. The children were given both the CCTT and the Children's Trail Making Test A and B, widely accepted measures, and correlations between the two were calculated. These correlations ranged from .54 to .74, falling into the large effect size range based on Cohen's guidelines, and indicating that both instruments measure a similar construct. A second study was used to further establish the concurrent validity of the CCTT. In this case, 63 children diagnosed with ADHD were given the CCTT and the Test of Variables of Attention (TOVA; Greenberg & Kindschi, 1996). The authors found correlations from .27 to .55, generally in Cohen's moderate range. The authors note that given the very different methods of instrument administration (graphomotor versus computerized) and the relatively small size of the sample, these correlations are not terribly low.

Discriminant validity was ascertained in five separate studies. Nonclinical children from the normative sample were compared with individuals diagnosed with a neurological dysfunction on the CCTT using Analysis of Variance (ANOVA). Results show that the nonclinical sample had significantly faster performance times on both the CCTT-1 and CCTT-2. In the second study, groups of children with differing neurological disorders were compared with one another on CCTT performance, again using ANOVA. Significant differences were found between the CCTT-2, indicating that Learning Disabled (LD) children performed faster than those diagnosed as both ADHD and LD. A third study assessed the discriminant validity of the CCTT by comparing individuals with different clinical diagnoses to a sample of nonclinical individuals from the normative sample using t-tests. The authors used this approach rather than an ANOVA because two of the clinical groups (ADHD and ADHD/LD) were fairly small. They do not appear to have compensated for the number of tests conducted, using some correction such as Bonferroni to keep the Type I error from becoming inflated; therefore, their results must be interpreted with some caution. They did find statistically significant differences between the nonclinical sample and the LD and ADHD/LD samples, but not the ADHD only group. In all cases where significance was identified, the nonclinical group performed faster. In order to determine whether the CCTT was more sensitive to certain clinical conditions (LD or ADHD), T-Scores were compared to T-Scores on the Children's Trail Making Test using dependent samples t-tests. They found significant differences for the LD and ADHD/LD groups, with CCTT scores lower than those on the Trail Making Test. The authors suggest that these results indicate that the CCTT may be more sensitive at diagnosing these two conditions than the Trail Making instrument. The fourth study to be cited by the authors in support of discriminant validity compared CCTT scores 1-month post-injury for children who suffered from mild head injuries to a random part of the normative sample, another sample of healthy control children and a group of individuals who suffered a non-head injury. Results indicated the CCTT scores for the head injury group, although elevated in comparison to the noninjured children, were within normal limits and similar to scores obtained by the other injured group. The authors state that these null results further support the discriminant validity of the CCTT. The final discriminant validity study compared children with syndromal ADHD and a matched sample from the standardization cohort, and found, using t-tests, that the standardization sample had a lower mean (faster completion times) than the ADHD group.

A final examination of concurrent validity involved correlating performance on the CCTT with level of plasma phospholipids markers in the blood and monoamine metabolites in the urine. These biological markers are associated with brain functioning, and presumably should be related to performance on neurological assessments such as the CCTT. The absolute values of the correlations among these values ranged from .18 to .47, falling into the small to moderate effect size range as defined by Cohen.

COMMENTARY. The CCTT is a valuable addition to the universe of neuropsychological assessment instruments. By no means a new concept in the assessment of pediatric neuropsychological functioning, the CCTT does make a meaningful departure from the traditional use of numbers and letters by substituting color for letters. This should increase the utility of this very useful approach to assessing domains of cerebral impairment by easing the cultural and academic load that can interfere with traditional trail making tests. Additionally, the inclusion of several indexes allows the clinician to deeply assess test performance and speculate as to which neuropsychological functional system impairment led to poor test performance. The test will be further improved when the test authors finish collecting normative data for the alternative forms of the CCTT, which will enable the CCTT to be more effectively used longitudinally. Additionally, the authors indicate that they are collecting normative data for children under 8 years old. Younger children may benefit more from using colors as opposed to letters; and the benefits of the CCTT may be more salient with these younger children.

The size of the standardization sample is adequate, with almost 700 children with whom to compare performance. However, the limited area from which the sample was drawn, one school district with an ethnic makeup not consistent with that found in many other areas of the United

States, somewhat limits the external validity of the CCTT. Possibly normative samples from subsequent versions will be more representative of the U.S. census. The reliability studies presented in the manual provide adequate evidence of the reliability of the CCTT, though they are somewhat lacking. One study, which examines alternative form reliability, used only 12 children who were suffering with a medical disorder. Even though the reliability coefficients were very high, it is not clear if that would be maintained in a more diverse sample. The other study, which examined temporal reliability, had lower than expected reliability coefficients, which the authors attributed to the excessive length between administrations. The question must be asked why the test authors did not either administer the second CCTT earlier, or conduct another study prior to publication of the manual. It would also be useful if the authors supplied evidence of internal consistency reliability, such as Cronbach's alpha. This is particularly important given the very different conclusions regarding the instrument's reliability based on the two studies presented in the manual.

There is ample evidence supporting the validity of scores from the CCTT. The authors do an excellent job of describing a variety of studies that show evidence for the concurrent, construct, and discriminant validity of the instrument. There is a great deal of evidence to support the ability of the instrument to discriminate between the nonclinical population and individuals with ADHD, LD, and those who suffered a traumatic head injury. The factor analysis results show the clear presence of clean factors that correspond to meaningful, content-based constructs. Furthermore, these results were replicated in two different samples, both from the normative sample and from a clinical group. The authors rely a bit too much on the statistical significance of the correlations used to assess concurrent validity rather than commenting on the actual magnitude of these values. In some cases, they are large and appear to represent strong relationships between the CCTT and the concurrent instruments, but in others the relationships are not particularly strong. The authors do note that with respect to the TOVA, the restrictive nature of the sample may dampen the magnitude of the correlations, which then begs the question as to whether they will conduct further research with a more diverse group of people.

SUMMARY. The test authors have managed to produce what appears to be a worthy contribution to the field of neuropsychological testing. The development of nonverbal assessment instruments has lagged behind the rise in diversity (Athanasiou, 2000), and although the CCTT is not a nonverbal instrument, it does attempt to minimize the influences of cultural bias and linguistic requirements. The CCTT is very easy to administer and score, and can be quickly administered, yet it provides a wealth of information regarding the functioning of a child. Minimal materials are required to administer the CCTT. Multiple indices are supplied that provide more in-depth information than is commonly found on trail making tests. The CCTT is a new test, and in some ways it seems to be still in production, in that alterative forms and additional norms for children under 8 years old are being developed by the test authors, as reported in the test manual. Both of these additions will improve the utility of the CCTT.

The reliability information provided in the manual is somewhat disappointing in terms of extensive studies, wide samples, and high correlation coefficients, and clearly needs to be expanded. The validity evidence for the instrument seems to be solid, both in terms of measuring underlying constructs that are measured by other, similar, instruments, and in differentiating healthy children from those with some diagnosed dysfunction. Although more independent studies need to be done regarding the reliability and validity, the information provided in the test manual should leave the examiner comfortable in using this new measure. At this time, the CCTT seems to be a worthy, useful instrument that is recommended for use in neuropsychological assessments.

REVIEWERS' REFERENCES

Athanasiou, M. S. (2000). Current nonverbal assessment instruments: A comparison of psychometric integrity and fairness. *Journal of Psychoeducational Assessment, 18*, 211–229.
Dean, R. S. (1985). [Review of the Halstead-Reitan Neuropsychological Test Battery.] In J. V. Mitchell, Jr. (Ed.), *The ninth mental measurements yearbook* (pp. 644–646). Lincoln, NE: Buros Institute of Mental Measurements.
D'Elia, L. F., Satz, P., Uchiyama, C. L., & White, T. (1996). *Color Trails Test: Professional manual.* Odessa, FL: Psychological Assessment Resources.
Greenberg, L. M., & Kindschi, C. L. (1996). *T.O.V.A. clinical guide.* Los Alamitos, CA: Universal Attention Disorders.
Guilmette, T. J., & Faust, D. (1991). Characteristics of neuropsychologists who prefer the Halstead-Reitan or the Luria-Nebraska Neuropsychology Battery. *Professional Psychology: Research and Practice, 22*, 80–83.
Reitan, R. M., & Wolfson, D. (1993). *The Halstead-Reitan Neuropsychological Test Battery: Theory and clinical interpretation (2nd ed.).* Tucson, AZ: Neuropsychology Press.
World Health Organization. (1990). *Report of the second consultation on the neuropsychiatric aspects of HIV-1 infection.* Geneva, Switzerland: Author.

Review of the Children's Color Trails Test by SHAWN POWELL, *Associate Professor, and* MICHELLE A. BUTLER, *Associate Professor, Department of Behavioral Sciences and Leadership, United States Air Force Academy, USAF Academy, CO:*

DESCRIPTION. The Children's Color Trails Test (CCTT) is a standardized, paper-and-pencil, neuropsychological instrument intended to be individually administered to children 8 to 16 years of age. It was designed to provide an easily administered and objectively scored measure of alternating and sustained visual attention, sequencing, psychomotor speed, cognitive flexibility, and inhibition-disinhibition. Children being assessed with the CCTT must be able to recognize Arabic numbers 1 through 15 and to distinguish between the colors pink and yellow. Due to the colors used, the CCTT does not necessarily make color-blind individuals ineligible. Children should also possess sufficient eye-hand coordination to use a pencil for connecting stimuli circles.

The CCTT-1 is similar to the Trail Making Test A, with the exception that odd-numbered circles are printed against a pink background and even numbered circles are printed against a yellow background. A practice trial precedes the administration of the timed test trial. The child is instructed to draw a line rapidly through the circles numbered 1 through 15 in consecutive order. The incidental fact that the colors alternate with each succeeding number is not mentioned. The child is told to perform the task as quickly as possible without making errors. Information on errors, time, near-misses, and prompts is collected. Speed of completion (time raw score) is the variable of greatest clinical interest, although norms are included for research purposes for errors and prompts. No norms are provided for the near misses, but these may be used qualitatively.

For the CCTT-2, each number is printed twice, once in a pink colored circle and once in a yellow colored circle. Categorical shifts are based on color, not alternating letters and numbers such as those used in Children's Trail Making B. A practice trial precedes the timed test trial. The examiner instructs the child to rapidly draw a line through consecutively numbered circles, maintaining the sequence of numbers but alternating between pink and yellow colored circles. The child is required to draw a line from the Pink Circle 1 to the Yellow Circle 2, avoiding the distractor Pink Circle 2, and so on. Speed of completion (time raw score), near-misses, errors, and prompts are recorded as in the CCTT-1. Due to the dual nature of the test stimuli shifting categories (i.e., color and number), two types of errors (Number Sequence and Color Sequence) are recorded. A normed interference index is also derived which compares performance on CCTT-1 and CCTT-2 to determine the contribution of response shifting in CCTT-2.

DEVELOPMENT. The CCTT was modeled after the widely implemented and well established Trail Making Test A and B of the Halstead-Reitan Neuropsychological Test Battery (T6:1144). It is not an extension of the adult version of the Color Trails Test. The authors assert the CCTT has several advantages compared to the Trail Making Test including: Enhanced cross cultural assessments as it uses color shifting instead of alphabetical shifting; improved test administration with visual and nonverbal instruction; increased sensitivity to detect subtle neurological dysfunction due to the use of numbers compared to letters; and a theoretically sound design based on child development, maturation theory, developmental neuropsychology, child neurology, and pediatric psychopathology.

TECHNICAL. The CCTT normative sample involved 678 children, ages 8–16 from one school district in Los Angeles, California. The sample consisted of 306 (45%) boys and 372 (55%) girls whose average age was 12.3 years. Of the 678 children, 309 (46%) were Caucasian, 201 (30%) were Hispanic, 11 (2%) were African American/Black, and 105 (15%) were characterized as Other. The participants' average score on the Peabody Picture Vocabulary Test–Revised was 101.5 with a standard deviation of 16.6.

Because one of the reasons this test was created was to increase its applicability in a variety of cultures, it is appropriate that this sample is relatively diverse; however, the generalizability of the normative sample would be improved if participants from more than one area of the country had been included. Additionally, the sample is overrepresented in Hispanic participants and underrepresented in African American/Black participants. No significant differences across the ethnic groups were identified for the CCTT-1 Time raw scores.

Alternate form reliability and temporal stability reliability for the CCTT are reported. Alternate forms of the CCTT were created by spatially rotating, inverting or both rotating and inverting the original Form K. Both forms were administered to a group (N = 12) of 8–10-year-olds (M = 8.5 years; SD = 1.5 years) outpatient children of average intellect with a mean IQ of 95 (SD = 5.9) with asymptomatic congenital cytomegalovirus (CMV) infection. The alternate form reliability correlations ranged from .85 to .90.

Temporal stability was obtained by administering the CCTT to a group of outpatients (N = 63) ages 6–12 years who were part of a randomized, placebo-controlled, double masked investigation assessing the effectiveness of dietary supplementation to reduce ADHD symptomatology. The participants completed longitudinal assessment with the CCTT at baseline and at 2- and 4-months posttreatment. The reported temporal stability correlations ranged from .45 to .68 for CCTT-1 and CCTT-2.

Evidence of the CCTT's construct validity is presented through developmental comparisons and factor analysis studies. As children grow older it is reasonable to assume their CCTT scores reflect developmental changes. Increases in age were generally associated with decreases in CCTT completion times. Factor analysis was used to examine the internal structure of the CCTT. Scores from a portion of the standardization sample (N = 657) were entered into a principal components factor analysis resulting in a three factor solution accounting for 78.6% of total variance. The first factor (37.4% of the variance), purportedly measures "speed of perceptual tracking and interference" (professional manual, p. 42). The second (22.5% of the variance) purportedly measures "inattention and impulsivity" (professional manual, p. 42). The third (18.7% of the variance) purportedly measures "simple inattention" (professional manual, p. 41). The test's internal structure was also evaluated in a sample of 366 children with mild head injuries. A principal components factor analysis suggests the same three factors were operative in this sample as reported in the previous study. A third study (N = 355) of children with injuries other than head injury produce similar factor analysis results. These results suggest the CCTT has adequate construct validity as a measure of alternating and sustained visual attention, sequencing,

psychomotor speed, cognitive flexibility, and inhibition-disinhibition.

Concurrent validity is presented through correlations between the CCTT and the Children's Trail Making Test. Performance was compared on both measures in children (N = 223; 69 girls; 154 boys) who were evaluated for learning, emotional, or behavioral difficulties (M = 11.1 years; SD = 2.4 years). These correlations ranged from .54 to .74 suggesting both tests measure similar functional domains. A second study assessed the relationship between the Test of Variable Attention (TOVA) and the CCTT using a sample of children with ADHD. These correlations ranged from .27 to .55, suggesting that the TOVA and the CCTT measure different attributes of attention and information processing in children with ADHD.

The CCTT's discriminant validity is presented through comparisons between children in healthy control groups and children in various diagnostic groups (e.g., learning disabled, mild neurologically impaired, and learning disabled with ADHD). The children in the control group performed the CCTT faster than those in the diagnostic groups with a significant difference existing between the control group and the diagnostic groups' CCTT-1 and CCTT-2 time raw scores in one of the studies reported. These findings suggest the CCTT can be used to aid diagnosis, but more work needs to be done to clarify this area before cut scores are firmly established to differentiate children into various diagnostic categories on the basis of their CCTT scores.

COMMENTARY. The CCTT is an improvement on the Children's Trail Making Test as it is less culturally biased and can be used more effectively with a variety of special populations (e.g., illiterate children, those who use English as a second language, or individuals who have specific reading or language disorders). It is well designed using sound principles from the field of child development. Theoretically, it is meaningfully constructed. A broader sample of children reflective of the U.S. population collected across the country would improve the overall generalizability of the CCTT which is limited as its normative sample was collected from one school district in California. Until the supplement to the CCTT is published containing new norms, using Form K with children ages 8–16 and focusing on the "time raw score" measure for quantitative analysis is recommended as is using errors, prompts, and near misses for qualitative analysis/testing of limits. These recommendations apply to the use of special populations norms, which need further study. More work also needs to be collected on the reliability estimates, as the reported alternate form reliability is tentative due to limitations in design and the preliminary stimuli used. However, no difficulties are expected to be found given the methodology used to derive the alternate forms of the CCTT used in the reported reliability studies.

SUMMARY. The CCTT is a valuable addition to the tests available for the neuropsychological assessment of children. As intended, it appears to be less culturally biased and more versatile than the Children's Trail Making Test. The normative sample needs to be greatly expanded in terms of size, locations from which participants are drawn, and demographics. The reported reliability data suggest that data from different testing sessions are consistent, but more work needs to be done to make this statement more conclusive. Preliminary validity data are quite convincing, but more studies should also be conducted in this area. Comparisons of the CCTT to other assessments of planning and attention in children and adolescents such as the Das-Naglieri Cognitive Assessment System (T6:743) may be beneficial in this regard.

[48]
The Children's Test of Nonword Repetition.

Purpose: To assess short term memory in children.
Population: Ages 4–8.
Publication Date: 1996.
Acronym: CNRep.
Scores: Total score only.
Administration: Individual.
Price Data, 2005: £77.81 per complete set including scoring sheets, cassette tape, and manual (29 pages).
Time: [15] minutes.
Authors: Sue Gathercole and Alan Baddeley.
Publisher: Harcourt Assessment [England].

Review of The Children's Test of Nonword Repetition by PATRICK GREHAN, Assistant Professor, Derner Institute for Advanced Psychological Studies, Adelphi University, Garden City, NY:

DESCRIPTION. The Children's Test of Nonword Repetition (CNRep) is an individually administered test of short-term auditory memory normed on children aged 4 to 8 years attending "mainstream" schools. The authors recommend this test as a tool for identifying children during the early school years who are at risk of experiencing generalized delays in language development. They also recommend it for older children with language-related difficulties. The CNRep can be administered and scored rapidly. Standard scores and centile points are derived from a sample of 612 children attending primary schools in England. The CNRep has the advantage of being easily understood by children in preschool.

The test kit consists of a 23-page manual, audiocassette, and scoring sheets. The test consists of 40 nonwords presented on an audiocassette tape. Nonwords consist of unfamiliar spoken items two to five syllables in length such as "dopelate" and "woogalamic" that do not exist in the English language. The examiner gives short instructions followed by two practice items and the 40 test items presented on the audiocassette. The child listens to each word and then is required to repeat each nonword during a brief silent interval. The test administrator scores each response as either correct or incorrect. The test is relatively easy to administer requiring approximately 4 minutes. Use outside of England is complicated by differences with accents that may affect the familiarity with sound (phoneme) combinations in the nonwords presented on the cassette tape.

Examiners convert the total raw score into a standard score (mean = 100 and SD = 16) using a table consisting of five (1-year interval) age groups. Raw scores can also be converted into centile points, which are percentile ranks reported at the 10th, 25th, 50th, 75th, and 90th percentiles. Scores falling between these points are reported as falling within a range (e.g., 25–50th centile).

In addition, it is possible to sum the correct repetitions of nonwords for each syllable length on the syllable template portion of the scoring sheet. The manual indicates that children with language impairments show the greatest difficulty with accuracy at the longer syllable lengths. Mean syllable length repetition for the five age groups are reported. It is up to the examiner's judgment as to what constitutes a meaningful deficit. The manual indicates that children with problems learning to read tend to do poorly on tests of nonword repetition, but does not specify what scores would be meaningful in this regard.

The test does not specify potential users or their required qualifications. Given that the manual states that it could be used as a tool for identifying young children with potential language delays, this test would need to be administered by professionals with experience with standardized test administration, scoring, interpretation, and assessing young children (ages 4 through 8). This is particularly important given the limited information regarding test interpretation.

DEVELOPMENT. The manual describes the author's rationale for developing a test of nonword repetition. The authors cite observations that students with poor short-term auditory memory demonstrate delayed acquisition of language and literacy skills. They add that digit span tests are only moderately useful in identifying such children. The authors contend that the CNRep is a more powerful predictor of important language abilities such as vocabulary knowledge, reading, and language impairment than is digit span.

TECHNICAL.

Standardization. The test was standardized on 612 children in England. A minimum of 84 children were obtained in each of the five age intervals. The test was normed on students from urban, suburban, and rural areas from Cambridgeshire, Lancashire, and Cumbria. Reportedly "all available children in a particular class were given the test" (manual, p. 13). Children with known hearing problems or with a history of speech therapy were omitted from test standardization. Although the manual states that the test was normed on a "representative sample," there are few data given about the composition of the sample. There is no more specific information about gender, race, ethnicity, socioeconomic status, etc. Therefore, users should interpret the results obtained with this measure cautiously.

Reliability. The authors conducted two studies of test-retest reliability. The first was an independent study of 70 children with a mean age of 5 years 3 months. A test-retest coefficient of .77 was found across an interval of 4 weeks. A second sample of 83 children were given the CNRep on two occasions separated by a 14-month interval (4 years 1 month to 5 years 3 months.) The resulting correlation coefficient for scores was .72, showing good reliability and stability of test scores.

The authors also report data on split-half reliability determined by a sample of 57 children with a mean age of 4 years 9 months. Two list halves were constructed, each of which contained five nonwords at each of the four syllable lengths. Subscores for each half were computed. The split-half reliability coefficient was .66. Overall, reliability is acceptable given the instability of test scores typically found in young children.

Validity. The manual provides validity information for the CNRep by comparing it with measures of short-term memory, vocabulary knowledge, language comprehension, and reading ability. In addition, results with children with impaired language development are reported.

First, the authors cite evidence demonstrating nonword repetition as a valid measure of short-term memory. Results from five studies of concurrent validity between the CNRep and a measure of digit span exhibit moderate correlations ranging from .40 to .67.

Next, the authors report eight correlation coefficients between the CNRep and one of three established receptive vocabulary tests. Although the manual states that correlation coefficients "typically fall in the range of 0.4 to 0.7" (p. 14) the data in the table of the eight studies reveal coefficients ranging from a low of .28 to a high of .58. Furthermore, the authors report two studies demonstrating concurrent validity coefficients of .45 and .51 between the CNRep and an established measure of children's abilities to comprehend the syntax of spoken sentences.

The manual reports two lines of evidence examining the CNRep as a discriminator of children with reading difficulties. First, two studies indicate moderate correlations (.47 and .44) between the CNRep and a measure of single word reading in "unselected samples of children attending mainstream schools" (manual, p. 15). In addition, the authors cite a study of children with literacy difficulties .5 *SD* below their IQ scores, which revealed that students across age ranges demonstrated deficient CNRep scores (mean standard score = 85). Additionally, dyslexic children outside of the CNRep age norms did not show consistent improvements in raw scores as age increases. This is contrasted with normally achieving children who demonstrate near perfect performance on the CNRep at around 9 years of age.

The authors report two studies that indicate that children with specific language impairments demonstrate deficits on the CNRep on test items with longer syllable lengths (three and four syllables). In the first study, six 8-year-olds with language impairment demonstrated a 4-year lag in nonword repetition. The second study, using 53 children, indicated that CNRep deficits were consistent in both language-impaired and resolved-language-impaired groups. Subsequent research supports the strong link between language impairment and poor CNRep performance, especially with increased syllable length (e.g., Bishop, North, & Dolan, 1996).

COMMENTARY. The rationale for the CNRep is compelling, especially given the research demonstrating a strong link between low scores on the CNRep and language impairment. As such, the CNRep is a useful tool in the development of this line of research. However, there are several limitations that make it difficult to recommend for use as a screening measure for identifying children at risk for delays in language development.

First, the manual gives incomplete information on how to interpret scores. We only know that students with language impairments show poor performance on increased syllable length and students with reading difficulties score poorly on this test. It is left to the examiner's judgment as to what constitutes a meaningful deficit. Additionally, information about the composition of the normative sample is incomplete. It is unclear how representative the sampled communities are of England as a whole. Finally, if readers were to consider its use outside of England, they should note that the nonwords are pronounced with a distinct English accent that may cause difficulty for students unaccustomed to the accent.

SUMMARY. The CNRep is an easy-to-administer test of short-term auditory memory with good reliability data with a good deal of data demonstrating correlations between low scores on this measure with reading difficulties and specific language impairment. It has great potential as a screening measure for use in early childhood but requires examiners to use their own judgment regarding the meaningfulness of the scores. As a result it is most useful as a research measure. It may also be a useful measure for users in England who are adequately represented by the norm group; however, this may be difficult to ascertain from the manual. Users outside of England are unlikely to use it unless they read the nonwords aloud to the students and create local norms.

REVIEWER'S REFERENCE

Bishop, D. V. M., North, T., & Donlan, C. (1996). Nonword repetition as a behavioural marker for inherited language impairment: Evidence from a twin study. *Journal of Child Psychology and Psychiatry, 37,* 391–403.

Review of The Children's Test of Nonword Repetition by MANUEL MARTINEZ-PONS, Professor of Education, Brooklyn College of the City University of New York, Belle Harbor, NY:

DESCRIPTION. The Children's Test of Nonword Repetition (CNRep) is an individually administered 40-item test of short-term memory. The instrument is designed for use with children aged 4 to 9 years in mainstream classes, and with older children experiencing difficulties learning and processing language. The examinee listens to each of 40 nonwords (e.g., "glistow," "ballop," and "prindle") as recorded on a cassette tape, and then repeats the nonword. The scorer judges whether the child has pronounced the nonword in the same way that the speaker has pronounced it. The test yields raw, centile, and standardized scores for ages between 4 years and 8 years 11 months.

DEVELOPMENT. Although the authors refer to the widely used digit span short-term memory test as the precursor of the CNRep, they do not describe the manner in which they developed the CNRep. They state only that "In our work on children with both normal and impaired language development, we have developed a new method of testing short-term memory, which involves the child attempting to repeat single unfamiliar spoken items ('non-words') such as 'blonterstaping' or 'woogalamic'" (manual, p. 2), but do not describe the manner in which they chose these nonwords. This leaves the reader asking, was there a large item pool from which they selected those words that best differentiated between impaired and nonimpaired children—or from which they selected those that more highly correlated with criterion measures such as vocabulary knowledge or language comprehension than does the digit span test to which they offer the CNRep as an alternative? Because the authors provide no information concerning issues such as these, it is not possible to judge the adequacy of the test's development.

TECHNICAL. The CNRep was standardized with data collected from a representative sample of 612 children in three regions of Britain in suburban, urban, and rural areas: Cambridgeshire (5 schools), Lancashire (6 schools), and Cumbria (2 schools). All children available in particular classes within these schools were tested. Only those children not experiencing hearing problems nor with a history of speech therapy were used in the standardization sample. The standard CNRep scores have a mean of 100 and a standard deviation of 16 in each 1-year age band.

Regarding the validity of scores from the CNRep, the authors allude to a "a large body of evidence" (manual, p. 13). A problem occurs with the one study they cite in some detail: They state that correlations of the CNRep with "estimates of digit span" ranged between .40 and .70, but the values shown in the table range from .40 to .67. Although they state that the CNRep has been found to be a more powerful predictor of such language abilities as vocabulary knowledge, reading and oral comprehension than the digit span measure, they do not show the differences in prediction; instead they refer the reader to numerous other works for the evidence. It would have been better to summarize the correlational data involving the predictions in the technical manual. At any rate, regarding the relation of the CNRep with digit span tests, the reader is left with the question, if the CNRep is a more valid test of language-related difficulty than digit span, why refer to a correlation with digit span as evidence of the CNRep's validity?

The authors cite two studies regarding the test's test-retest (TR) reliability: one, with a 4-week interval, involving 70 children with a mean age of 5 years and 3 months ($r = .77$,); and one, with a 14-month interval, involving 83 children at a mean age of 4 years and 1 month, and later at a mean age of 5 years and 3 months ($r = .72$). Citing one study examining the CNRep's split-half (SH) reliability, they report a correlation of .66 for 57 children with a mean age of 4 years and 9 months.

Although the TR and SH reliability coefficients seem substantial, the report does not address a form of reliability particularly relevant to this form of test: interjudge reliability (IJR). IJR is particularly pertinent in the case of the CNRep because of the subjective nature of a rater's interpretation of an examinee's performance. Given the rating instructions provided for the CNRep, it would be important to know the degree to which more raters than one consistently interpret the accuracy of the repetition of each word. In the absence of this information, it is not possible to assess the accuracy of the rater's judgment of an examinee's performance.

COMMENTARY. A number of limitations prevent recommendation of the use of this test: the dearth of information regarding the test's development and the population on which the test has been standardized, the limited evidence presented concerning validity, and the absence of information concerning the CNRep's interjudge reliability. In addition, poor articulation and hearing impairments, cited by the authors as possible extraneous sources of poor test performance, make the use of additional testing to control for these possibilities particularly cumbersome. An even greater difficulty with the CNRep, especially for use in the U.S., involves regional accent, because a female speaker from the South of England recorded the test's nonwords. The authors recommend that for populations outside of the South of England, the user have a speaker with an accent more appropriate to the region record the words. But the use of the test outside of South England would require, in addition to the use of a new speaker, the normalization of the instrument with the new pronunciation and new population—tasks that would practically eliminate the convenience of the use of any standardized published test.

SUMMARY. The CNRep is based on the attractive premise that responses to stimuli involving word-like sounds more closely reflect a child's language-related difficulties than do responses to stimuli involving number-based digit span tests. However, limitations in the information provided about the test's development, the test's psychometric properties, and the population on which the CNRep was normed lead this reviewer to conclude that the authors have failed to demonstrate the test's preferability to the digit-span approach.

[49]
Clark-Beck Obsessive-Compulsive Inventory.

Purpose: Developed to "provide an efficient, yet comprehensive and precise self-report screening instrument for obsessive and compulsive symptoms."

Population: Adolescents and adults suspected of having Obsessive Compulsive Disorder.

Publication Date: 2002.

Acronym: CBOCI.

Scores, 3: Obsessions, Compulsions, Total.

Administration: Individual.

Price Data, 2003: $80 per complete kit including manual (68 pages) and 25 record forms; $55 per manual; $35 per 25 record forms; $133 per 100 record forms.

Time: (10–30) minutes.

Comments: Requires eighth grade reading level.

Authors: David A. Clark and Aaron T. Beck.

Publisher: PsychCorp, A brand of Harcourt Assessment, Inc.

Review of the Clark-Beck Obsessive-Compulsive Inventory by TONY CELLUCCI, Professor and Director of the Psychology Training Clinic, Idaho State University, Pocatello, ID:

DESCRIPTION. The Clark-Beck Obsessive-Compulsive Inventory (CBOCI) is a screening measure for obsessive and compulsive symptoms meant to complement existing Beck measures. It consists of 25 symptom items (14 Obsessions and 11 Compulsions) to which the respondent selects the statement best describing their experience over the last 2 weeks. The familiar 0–3 response format was used to facilitate comparison across Beck instruments. The items and wording reflect the DSM-IV diagnostic criteria as well as current cognitive-behavioral theory related to OCD. The authors argue that the format allows broader coverage of OCD content than traditional Likert scales. The inventory is divided into two sections, each preceded by a detailed definition and examples of obsessions and compulsions. An individual suspected of OCD is instructed to complete the questionnaire in reference to their primary obsession or compulsion. Administration time is estimated at 10–15 minutes for most individuals but may range to 30 minutes for OCD patients. The manual provides guidelines to assist administration to indecisive patients. Two subscale scores and a total score are calculated and interpreted in reference to clinical ranges (i.e., nonclinical, mild-moderate, or severe clinical). The accompanying manual is clear and detailed, including four case vignettes to illustrate potential uses of this measure (i.e., diagnosis, case formulation, treatment effectiveness, and OCD subtyping).

DEVELOPMENT. The development of the CBOCI was well considered, beginning with a review of strengths and weaknesses of existing instruments. Similarly, review of the diagnostic and assessment literature on OCD resulted in essentially a Table of Specifications outlining key features of obsessions and compulsions that were empirically supported and could be operationally defined. Experts from the Obsessive-Compulsive Cognitions Working Group rated initial items for suitability and suggested additions. The 27-item pilot version was administered to 94 outpatients (56 with primary OCD), 35 nonclinical community adults, and 403 university students. Pilot testing suggested good internal consistency. Extensive analyses were run on each item including testing for group differences, item-scale correlations, and item-option characteristic curves that evaluated how well response options were differentiated at increasing levels of OCD symptom severity. Several items (i.e., obsessional impulses and hoarding) were eliminated due to poor psychometric properties and 13 items were rewritten to improve assessment of symptom severity. The fourth option on some items was rarely endorsed and was therefore modified.

TECHNICAL.

Standardization sample and score interpretation. The CBOCI was administered to three clinical (OCD, Anxiety, and Depression) and two nonclinical (community adults and university student) samples. The OCD standardization group (St. Joseph's hospital, Hamilton, Ontario, Canada) was relatively small, consisting of 32 males and 51 female patients, with a mean age of 34 years (17-61 years). Eighty-three percent were white, with limited representation of other ethnic groups. Significantly, there was a high rate of diagnostic comorbidity; 82% met criteria for additional disorders such as depression and social phobia. The other clinical samples (43 Anxiety disorder not OCD, 32 Depressive disorder not OCD) were recruited from the University of Pennsylvania Psychiatry Department as well as the Hamilton site. The community group was a convenience sample of nonclinical Canadian adults recruited via multiple methods, and screened for any Axis I Disorders. Of those solicited, only 26 (7 males and 19 females) were retained, 88.5% were white, and lower educational levels were not represented. Finally, the student sample was from the University of New Brunswick, consisting of 110 males and 197 females with a mean age of 19.3 years. Ninety-six percent were single and 94% were white.

As indicated above, the authors provide recommended scoring ranges based on the frequency distribution of scores. The percentages of each sample scoring within the clinical ranges are listed in the manual. Twenty-eight percent of the OCD sample reported severe symptoms, and 65% mild-moderate. Forty-one percent of the anxious/depressed groups reported mild-moderate symptoms as opposed to no community adults and 26% of the students. The authors acknowledge that research examining the sensitivity and specificity of the interpretative guidelines has yet to be conducted. CBOCI scores were related to clinical ratings of distress and impairment among the OCD group. However, the findings suggest that patient scores within the mild-moderate range may be difficult to interpret. Students tended to score higher suggesting an age effect. There were few gender differences; one exception was female OCD patients scored higher than males on the Compulsion scale. Comorbidity was found to elevate CBOCI scores among patients with OCD.

Reliability. The CBOCI scales were shown to have acceptable internal consistency for the OCD (Obsessions = .90, Compulsions = .87, and Total scale = .93) and psychiatric sample (Obsessions = .90, Compulsions = .86, and Total scale = .92). However, item-total correlations for some individual items (e.g., religious/moral and cleaning) were still low. For community adults, Total scale was .85, Obsessions .81, and Compulsions only .69; Total scale was .86, Obsessions .77, and Compulsions .81 in the student sample. The authors explain that students in particular had high endorsement rates for certain items (i.e., 91% perfectionism, 85% doubting) suggesting caution in interpreting individual items and subscales in nonclinical samples. In these groups, item-total correlations were generally low. Stability data are limited to a sample of 55 students with a mean test-retest interval of 31.5 days (range 10–45 days). Reported test-retest correlations were: CBOCI total .77, Obsessions .69, and Compulsions .79.

All three scales showed modest declines (2–4 points) with retesting.

Validity. The CBOCI would appear to have good content validity based on the procedures described above. A factor analysis was performed on the combined OCD and psychiatric samples, which yielded two factors, accounting for 48.8% and 9.6% of the variance, respectively. The correlation between factors was .67. All of the Obsession items loaded on the first factor with the exception of dirt/contamination obsessions, which was more related to the Compulsions factor. Several Obsession items (i.e., religious/moral/sexual obsessions and aggression/harm) had low communality estimates. The Compulsion items all loaded on the second factor, although avoidance loaded on both. This two factor structure was replicated with the university sample but accounted for less variance; factor loadings and communality estimates were generally lower.

Criterion validity was examined by analysis of group differences. The OCD group scored significantly higher than all groups on CBOCI scales. The depression subgroup was higher than the remaining groups on the Obsessions scale, but the psychiatric patients and students did not differ on Compulsions. Nonclinical adults consistently scored the lowest. The CBOCI was also significantly correlated in the OCD sample with other self-report measures of obsessive and compulsive symptoms such as the Padua Inventory (.78) and the self-report version of the Yale-Brown Obsessive Compulsive Scale (YBOCS; .77). However, it also was highly correlated with measures of depression (BDI-II .72) and anxiety (BAI .61). The authors used partial correlations to indicate that although the CBOCI is sensitive to psychological distress reported by patients with OCD, it remains related to other measures of OCD after controlling for depression and anxiety. Overall, the CBOCI showed good convergent validity but weaker discriminant validity.

COMMENTARY. The CBOCI is a new instrument with a number of strengths. The development plan was well considered and the instrument would appear to have good content validity. The data presented above indicate diagnostic sensitivity and validity when used with individuals suspected of having OCD. Moreover, it is a relatively efficient assessment measure providing information regarding cognitive and behavioral aspects of the disorder that would be useful in case conceptualization and treatment planning.

Unfortunately, normative data are presently limited, especially for a general population. Virtually no information is available for ethnic groups and the instrument has not been examined for differential validity by sex. A curiosity is that the OCD sample took the CBOCI at home as part of a research packet, although the manual specifically advises against this practice. Further research is needed regarding validity within general population samples and the sensitivity/specificity of the proposed interpretative ranges. The limited discriminant validity from depression is consistent with other literature (Emmelkamp, Kraaijkamp, & van den Hout, 1999).

There are a large number of alternative measures for assessing OCD (Feske & Chambless, 2000; Taylor, Kyrios, Thordarson, Steketee, & Frost, 2002). A competing measure that apparently was developed concurrently is the Obsessive-Compulsive Inventory- Revised (Foa et al., 2002; Hajcak, Huppert, Simons, & Foa, 2004). Clinicians and researchers should consider their purpose and particular application in deciding what measure(s) to use. Also, some data suggest that self- and clinician-administered measures yield unique assessment information (Mataix-Cols, Fullana, Alonso, Menchon, & Vallejo, 2004).

SUMMARY. The CBOCI is a promising new measure to screen and assess for OCD symptoms. It complements other Beck inventories, has good internal consistency, a reasonable factor structure, and has strong validity evidence to identify individuals suspected of OCD. The manual is well written and clearly presents supporting data and limitations of the instrument. Generally, the data are consistent with OCD theory and prior research. More evidence is needed to support its use with general population samples and as a measure of treatment outcome.

REVIEWER'S REFERENCES

Emmelkamp, P. M., Kraaijkamp, H. J., & van den Hout, M. A. (1999). Assessment of obsessive-compulsive disorder. *Behavior Modification, 23*, 269–279.

Feske, U., & Chambless, D. L. (2000). A review of assessment measures for obsessive-compulsive disorder. In W. K. Goodman, M. V. Rudorfor, & J. D. Maser (Eds.), *Obsessive-compulsive disorder: Contemporary issues in treatment* (pp. 157–182). Mahwah, N.J.: Erlbaum.

Foa, E. B., Huppert, J. D., Leiberg, S., Langner, R., Kichic, R., Hajcak, G., & Salkovskis, P. M. (2002). The Obsessive-Compulsive Inventory: Development and validation of a short version. *Psychological Assessment, 14*, 485–495.

Hajcak, G., Huppert, J. D., Simons, R. F., & Foa, E. B. (2004). Psychometric properties of the OCI-R in a college sample. *Behaviour, Research & Therapy, 42*, 115–123.

Mataix-Cols, D., Fullana, M. A., Alonso, P., Menchon, J. P., & Vallejo, J. (2004). Convergent and discriminant validity of the Yale-Brown obsessive-compulsive scale symptom checklist. *Psychotherapy & Psychosomatics, 73*, 190–196.

Taylor, S., Kyrios, M., Thordarson, D., Steketee, G., & Frost, R. O. (2002). Development and validation of instruments for measuring intrusions and beliefs in obsessive compulsive disorder. In R. O. Frost & G. Steketee (Eds.), *Cognitive approaches to obsessions and compulsions: Theory assessment and treatment* (pp. 118–138). Amsterdam, Netherlands: Pergamon/Elsevier.

[50]

Clarke Sex History Questionnaire for Males—Revised.

Purpose: Designed "to evaluate a sex offender's sexual preference profile as well as evaluating their potential for sexually conventional behavior."

Population: Sex offenders.

Publication Dates: 1999–2002.

Acronym: SHQ-R.

Scores: 23 scales: Childhood and Adolescent Sexual Experiences and Sexual Abuse, Sexual Dysfunction, Female Adult Frequency, Female Pubescent Frequency, Female Child Frequency, Male Adult Frequency, Male Pubescent Frequency, Male Child Frequency, Child Identification, Fantasy Activities with Females, Fantasy Activities with Males, Exposure to Pornography, Transvestism, Fetishism, Feminine Gender Identity, Voyeurism, Exhibitionism Frequency, Exhibiting Behavior, Obscene Phone Calls, Toucheurism and Frotteurism, Sexual Aggression, Lie, Infrequency.

Administration: Individual.

Price Data, 2002: $50 per preview kit including technical manual (2002, 76 pages), 1 item booklet, and 1 summary report; $10 per 3 item booklets; $30 per 10 item booklets; $40 per technical manual; $10 per mail-in or fax-in individual summary report.

Time: (60–90) minutes.

Comments: Self-report paper-and-pencil inventory that is scored electronically by publisher.

Authors: Ron Langevin and Dan Paitch.

Publisher: Multi-Health Systems, Inc.

Review of the Clarke Sex History Questionnaire for Males—Revised by ROGER A. BOOTHROYD, Associate Professor, Department of Mental Health Law and Policy, Louis de la Parte Florida Mental Health Institute, University of South Florida, Tampa, FL:

DESCRIPTION. The Clarke Sex History Questionnaire for Males—Revised (SHQ-R) is a 508-item self-report measure used to examine a wide range of conventional and deviant sexual behaviors in an adult male population. The developers recommend that the SHQ-R be used with males over 18 years of age; however, they indicate it can be given to adolescents aged 14–17 as long as caution is used in interpreting the results, given that "many" of the items do not apply to this age group. The SHQ-R was specifically developed for the assessment of forensic psychiatric sex offenders. The SHQ-R is typically administered by paper-and-pencil although there is a computerized version available. The 508 items are categorized into six main categories containing 23 scales that include: Childhood and Adolescent Sexual Experiences (no subscales); Sexual Dysfunction (no subscales); Adult Age/Gender Sexual Outlets (Female Adult Frequency, Female Pubescent Frequency, Female Child Frequency, Male Adult Frequency, Male Pubescent Frequency, Male Child Frequency, Child Identification); Fantasy and Pornography (Fantasy Activities With Females, Fantasy Activities With Males, Exposure to Pornography); Transvestism, Fetishism, and Feminine Gender Identity (Transvestism, Fetishism, Feminine Gender Identity); Courtship Disorders (Voyeurism, Exhibitionism Frequency, Exhibiting Behavior, Obscene Phone Calls, Toucheurism and Frotteurism, Sexual Aggression); and Validity (Lie, Infrequency). There are additional sexual history items that are not associated with these scale scores.

ADMINISTRATION. The SHQ-R can be administered individually or in small groups. The measure is typically administered by paper-and-pencil although a computerized version is available. The test manual stipulates the measure "usually takes" 60–90 minutes to complete depending on the respondent's reading level and sexual history. The authors indicate that respondents with at least a seventh-grade reading level can complete the measure independently, although the SHQ-R can be read to respondents with lower reading levels. Given the sensitive nature of this measure, the test developers recommend it be administered to respondents in private settings. Trained professionals and paraprofessionals can administer the SHQ-R. Although there are no formal educational requirements for individuals administering the SHQ-R, the authors recommend that test administrators be familiar with issues related to measurement, informed consent procedures, confidentiality, avoiding bias, and that they adhere to the ethical guidelines of the American Psychological Association. It is also recommended that test administrators debrief respondents about what their answers mean and how they will be used. The manual does include steps to be followed when administering the SHQ-R that basically focus on ensuring the form is accurately and fully completed.

Scoring. Little detail is provided in the manual on the actual methods used to score the SHQ-R primarily because there is no hand-scoring option available. Scoring can be completed either through mail-in or faxed procedures purchased from Multi-Health Systems or through the purchase of a PC-based scoring option. If the computerized version of the SHQ-R is used or if the QuikEntry option has been purchased, the SHQ-R can be scored automatically and the results provided in various file formats.

Interpretation. The manual includes a detailed description of the 23 subscales along with six diverse case examples including SHQ-R profiles to assist users in interpreting SHQ-R responses. Although the SHQ-R can be administered by paraprofessionals, interpretation of results "must ultimately be assumed by a mental health professional with advanced training in psychological assessment" (technical manual, p. 5) who is knowledgeable about how to translate the findings into clinical practice as well as the limitations of psychosocial testing. The authors clearly state that the SHQ-R should not be the only source of information used when developing treatment plans and that the measure is not intended to be a substitute for a comprehensive clinical assessment.

DEVELOPMENT. The SHQ-R has nearly 40 years of developmental history. The SHQ-R is the fifth version of this assessment since the SHQ-1 was originally developed in the late 1960s. The SHQ-1 was initially developed based on the sexual behaviors reported by men assessed in forensic clinics. The scales in subsequent versions were expanded to include the broader range of sexual problems clinicians typically encounter as well as the changing knowledge of sexual disorders. The revisions to the SHQ are designed to examine the full range of behaviors exhibited by male sexual offenders rather than just classifying and diagnosing offenders based on presenting sexual behavior, as current theory suggests that sexual offenders are often "multiple deviants," tending to engage in more dangerous sexual outlets.

TECHNICAL.

Standardization. The normative samples of the SHQ vary across versions. They are of moderate size, ranging from 291 for the SHQ-2 to 482 for both the SHQ-1 and SHQ-3. Normative data were collected between the 1960s and 1990s. No normative data reported in the manual are based specifically on the administration of the SHQ-R. The characteristics of these normative samples have changed over time in two meaningful ways. First, the average age of these samples increased by over 10 years from 29.6 to 40.7 years old. Second, there has been a significant decline in the number of men who are single and never married from 59% to 32%. The authors suggest that these changing characteristics reflect changing social concerns, referral patterns, and diagnostics practices.

Reliability. The only form of evidence associated with the reliability for the SHQ-R is internal consistency. Additionally, the subscale internal consistencies were estimated using items from and respondents to the two previous versions of the SHQ. This makes it quite difficult to fully assess the scale reliabilities of the revised version as many of the subscale reliabilities are estimated on a reduced number of items with some subscales based on fewer than half of the items. For example, the Sexual Aggression scale contains 35 items, yet the reliability estimates for this scale are based on only 16 items. Although one might suppose that additional items would increase the internal consistency estimates reported, it would be advisable to examine the scale reliabilities based on the actual administration of the revised measure to a new sample of respondents.

This concern having been stated, the Cronbach's alphas reported in the manual on the 23 subscales are generally acceptable ranging from a low of .51 to .96. The median scale reliability estimate is .80. Three subscales have internal consistency estimated below .70 (i.e., Sexual Dysfunction, Female Gender Identity, and Toucheurism and Frotteurism). The manual also provides the Cronbach's alphas for each scale from the four previous versions of the SHQ. In general, the SHQ-R has similar or slightly improved scale reliabilities compared to the corresponding scales on its predecessor the SHQ-4.

Validity. Three forms of evidence are provided in the test manual supporting the SHQ-R's validity. These include: (a) evidence that the SHQ-R is free from bias of important confounding variables, (b) evidence of the truthfulness of respondents' answers to the SHQ-R, and (c) evidence documenting the SHQ-R's factor structure.

In response to concerns that SHQ-R scores may be biased because respondents would have literacy issues or low education attainment, the relationship of respondents' answers to the SHQ-R's items were compared with their educational levels and intelligence scores. In addition, because it was likely that older respondents would have more sexual experiences compared to younger men, the relationships between SHQ-R items and age were also examined. Over 96% of the item-to-education level correlations were in the .00 to .20 range, explaining less than 4% of the variability and suggesting that education level has little impact on individuals' SHQ-R responses. Similarly, the SHQ-R scale scores were correlated with education level and only the Exhibitionism Frequency scale (.202) resulted in a correlation above .069. Similarly, SHQ-R item-to-intelligence correlations resulted in 91% of the coefficients ranging between .00 and .20. Exceptions were the Exhibitionism Frequency scale (.303) and Female Adult Frequency scale (.219). These results suggest that intelligence is not a confounding variable.

Age was also not significantly related to respondents' SHQ-R item responses or scale scores. Nearly 99% of the item-to-age correlations ranged between .00 and .20 and none of the SHQ-R scale score-to-age correlations exceeded .153. SHQ-R responses were also examined in relation to respondents' marital status. These results were less supportive as 28.5% of the item-to-marital status correlations were significant as were five of the scale score-to-marital status correlations (i.e., Sexual Dysfunction, Female Adult Frequency, Male Adult Frequency, Male Pubescent Frequency, Male Child Frequency) suggesting that marital status should be taken into account when using the SHQ-R.

The validity of individuals' SHQ-R responses was examined against the MMPI-2's Lie (L scale), Faking Bad (F scale), and Social Desirability (K scale) scales. In excess of 90% of the item-to-scale correlations ranged between .00 and .20 on the Lie (91.9%), Faking Bad (90.9%), and Social Desirability (94.6%) scales, suggesting that response set is not a significant concern with the use of the SHQ-R. Additionally, correlations between SHQ-R scale scores and the MMPI-2's Lie, Faking Bad, and Social Desirability scales indicate that with the exception of the Exhibitionism Frequency scale, all correlations were less than .20, providing some evidence that SHQ-R scale scores are not associated with naïve lying, malingering, or social desirability. As the authors caution, however, there is some evidence that sex offenders may lie about their sexual behavior but respond more candidly about their personality traits (See Quinsey, Harris, Rice, & Cormier, 1998).

Correlations of the new SHQ-R scales with previous existing scales were also examined. Elevated scores on the SHQ-R Lie scale were negatively associated with Childhood and Adolescent Sexual Experiences (-.291), Female Adult Frequency (-.325), and Exhibiting Behavior (-.473), suggesting that respondents who lie underreported these sexual behaviors. None of the correlations with the Child Identification scale exceeded .20, suggesting relative independence of this scale from other SHQ-R scales. Higher scores on the Childhood and Adolescent Sexual Experiences scale were associated with increased sexual activity with males of all ages and to a lesser extent, with increased sexual activity with females of all ages. Feminine Gender Identity was significantly associated with increased scores on the Male Adult Frequency and Transvestism scale.

Finally, results are presented from factor analyses performed on the original SHQ-1 and SHQ-R scale items. Comparison of these solutions suggests that the two versions of the SHQ-R have similar dimensionality indicating the stability of the measures' factor structure over time. In addition, the factor structure of the SHQ-R comports reasonably well with the six functional domains the authors state that the SHQ-R was designed to assess.

COMMENTARY. The SHQ-R clearly has a substantial history as a clinical assessment tool used with male sexual offenders. However, the practical value of the measure for research purposes remains largely untested. There are gaps in available psychometric information on the SHQ-R. For example, there is no evidence presented supporting the SHQ-R's test-retest reliability or evidence substantiating the measure's convergent (e.g., agreement with other measures of sexual deviance) or discriminant validity (e.g., comparisons of offenders and nonoffenders). The length of the measure presents concerns for use as a standard research protocol. Some of the psychometric information provided is difficult to interpret given the use of responses to various versions of the SHQ administered to different normative samples over a 30-plus-year period. The lack of information regarding how the measure is scored

also raises some concerns. Given these concerns, it is recommended that investigators wishing to use the SHQ-R in research examine its psychometric characteristics within the research context. Additionally, following the authors' suggestion regarding the use of the SHQ-R in clinical assessment, researchers are advised to include other measures of sexual deviance in their research protocols against which SHQ-R results can be compared.

SUMMARY. The Clarke Sex History Questionnaire for Males—Revised is a self-report measure used to assess a wide range of sexual behaviors in adult men. The SHQ-R is the fifth version of a measure originally developed in the 1960s to assist in the clinical assessment of forensic psychiatric sex offenders. Although the SHQ-R has been frequently used in clinical assessments, its use in research is less well understood. Given that there are important gaps in the psychometric information available on the SHQ-R, researchers deciding to include the measure in research protocols are advised to closely examine its psychometric properties.

REVIEWER'S REFERENCE

Quinsey, V. L., Harris, G. T., Rice, M. E., & Cormier, C. A. (1998). *Violent offenders: Appraisal and managing risk.* Washington, DC: American Psychological Association Press.

Review of the Clarke Sex History Questionnaire for Males—Revised by DELORES D. WALCOTT, Associate Professor, Counseling and Testing Center, Western Michigan University, Kalamazoo, MI:

DESCRIPTION. The Clarke Sex History Questionnaire for Males—Revised (SHQ-R) is a self-report questionnaire developed specifically to examine a range of conventional and deviant sexual behaviors in adult males. The manual noted that the SHQ-R is especially useful in forensic and correctional settings, but can also be used in general clinical practice where sexual behavior is in question. The SHQ-R was designed to determine patterns of sexual preference. It examines a wide range of sexual disorders beyond what is criminal in a contemporary society. This tool also serves as a research instrument for data analysis.

The SHQ-R is a paper-and-pencil questionnaire that can be scored electronically by the publisher. It is a comprehensive questionnaire composed of 508 questions in a multiple-choice, Yes/No, and True/False response format. The SHQ-R is divided into 17 sections lettered "A" to "Q." The respondent is asked to follow the instructions for each section. The SHQ-R can be completed in 60 to 90 minutes depending on the respondents' reading level and sexual history. This 23-scale inventory measures six main sexual experiences: Childhood and Adolescent Sexual Experience and Sexual Abuse; Sexual Dysfunction; Adult Age/Gender Sexual Outlets; Fantasy and Pornography; Transvestism, Fetishism, Feminine Gender Identity; and Courtship Disorders. Each of these categories has various scales associated with them along with two validity scales. This version of the test has been expanded to include a sexual abuse history, a measure of fetishism, gender identity, childhood and adolescent sexual behavior, the use of pornographic or erotic materials, fantasy sexual dysfunction, items regarding the use of prostitutes and extramarital affairs, a measure of child identification, and two validity measures.

The questionnaire was targeted for adult males aged 18 years and older who have a seventh-grade reading ability. If the respondent has less than a seventh-grade reading level, the instrument can be read for the respondent. The manual did indicate that the SHQ-R can be administered to youths 14 –17, but caution should be taken when interpreting the results, as many of the items may not apply to this age group.

The manual is divided into seven chapters: Introduction, Administration and Scoring, Interpreting SHQ-R Results, Clinical Case Studies, Scale Development/Normative Sample/Reliability, Validity, and Concluding Comment. The technical manual outlines the purpose and application for which the test is recommended; it identifies qualifications required to administer and interpret the test and gives limited evidence of validity and reliability studies.

DEVELOPMENT. The SHQ-R is the fifth and current version, which includes the original SHQ-1 scales and is more broadly based to measure contemporary concerns, as the social climate has changed since the publication of the original test 35 years ago. The reporting laws, the rights of women, and social attention to protecting women and children from sexual predation have made the SHQ-R less candid. The first version of the SHQ-1 had 225 clinical items at that time, and was influenced by personality and marital difficulties. The second version, SHQ-R-2, had 417 items.

Instead of sexual desire and disgust, fantasy was examined, as this was of concern at the time. In SHQ-3, all the original scales in the first version remained. However, the third version had only 186 items and was examined on only 235 cases from 1986–1989. All the fantasy scales were excluded from this version and the labels on some of the scales were changed for clarity. The fourth version resembles most of the features of the SHQ-R. However, the validity scales were developed to address the respondent's tendency to be more circumspect and less candid, as later samples included all cases including nonadmitters, resulting in a drop in the alpha coefficient for some of the scales. Currently accused or convicted sex offenders are more defensive, which likely influences the internal consistency of tests. According to the manual, the reliability is high in the majority of sample cases, indicating that the SHQ-R scales are usable in clinical practice.

TECHNICAL. In earlier samples, which involved all admitters, reliability of the scales was high or very high. Reliability was estimated using Cronbach's alpha. The reliability of the SHQ-R is high in most cases (ranging from .51 to .96), suggesting that the SHQ-R scales are usable in clinical practice. The authors suggested that the alpha coefficients for the Pubescent and Child Frequency scales have dropped; adding that both the Heterosexual and Homosexual scales still have considerable reliability.

The mean age, education, IQ, marital status, test taking attitude, and composition of the samples were used as validation evidence. Validation of the SHQ-R described in the manual found the instrument to be relatively free from bias of age and education. The sample ages over the years have become increasingly older. The educational attainment of the sample has not changed significantly. However, verbal intelligence scores have declined. This decline might reflect changes in IQ tests over the years. There has been a significant drop in the number of men who are single and never married, indicating that it is relatively unrelated to the MMPI validity scales, and factor analyses showed that consistency of SHQ factors over time. Correlations with age and education are in the 0 to .20 ranges; none of the correlations were above .30, suggesting that age and education will have little impact on test results.

COMMENTARY. Overall, the chapters in the technical manual contained enough information for a qualified user or reviewer of a test to evaluate the appropriateness and purpose of the test. The nature and extent of the numerous revisions over the years was explicitly stated. However, the discussion on reliability and validity was limited for diagnostic usage. In the manual there is a large body of literature attesting to the validity of the original SHQ. However, additional research attesting to the validity of the current SHQ-R is warranted. Evidence of validity and reliability along with other relevant research data should have been more explicit. Therefore, future publication should include detail information on criterion-related validity, construct validity, and concurrent validity. As indicated in the manual, the SHQ-R examines a wide range of sexually deviant and conventional behaviors. It has a 30-year history of data collection, which was used to modify the SHQ-R to meet contemporary needs and expanding knowledge. Having such a history, this reviewer was expecting to read about extensive validity studies in the manual. One other challenge encountered, associated with the scoring of the SHQ-R, is that unless you have the SHQ-R software installed on your computer, you must risk faxing or mailing tests to the publisher and wait for turnaround time before integrating these data into a final report.

SUMMARY. The SHQ-R is a meaningful questionnaire for creating a sex offender's sexual profile as well as identifying their potential for sexually conventional behavior. This is particularly true for those working in the forensic field. However, it is a known fact that self-reporting is vulnerable to underreporting, inaccurate reporting, and denial. The trustworthiness of the results should be taken into consideration for this target population, as there are legal issues associated with outcomes of test results. Therefore, as with most self-reporting questionnaires, the SHQ-R should be used in conjunction with other sources to insure a comprehensive assessment.

[51]

Clerical Skills Test Series [Scored By Client].

Purpose: Measures 16 different clerical-administrative skills.
Population: Adults.
Publication Date: 1990.

Scores: 16 skills: Alphabetizing—Filing, Attention to Detail With Words & Numbers, Bookkeeping Skills, Coding, Grammar & Punctuation, Manual Dexterity, Mechanical Comprehension, Numerical Skills, Problem Solving, Proofreading Skills, Reading Comprehension, Receptionist Skills, Spatial Perception, Spelling, Verbal Fluency, English Vocabulary, plus Total Score.
Administration: Group.
Price Data, 2001: $300 per 20 of the same test; quantity discounts available.
Time: (4–10) minutes per subtest.
Comments: Scored by the client; includes scoring keys; must be proctored.
Author: Stephen Berke.
Publisher: Walden Personnel Performance, Inc. [Canada].

Review of the Clerical Skills Test Series [Scored by Client] by PHILLIP L. ACKERMAN, Professor of Psychology, Georgia Institute of Technology, Atlanta, GA:

DESCRIPTION. The Clerical Skills Test Series is made up of a set of 17 short tests that range in specificity from Attention to Detail and Alphabetizing and Filing to Verbal Fluency and Mechanical Comprehension. The tests are highly speeded—only two tests are longer than 6 minutes in test time.

DEVELOPMENT. The Test Series manual provides no information on the development of the tests. On the surface level, the scales appear to be relatively straightforward tests that appeal to "face validity," as they have format and content similar to existing tests in each of the named domains. There is no indication of how the scales should be selected for a particular application—the test manual indicates only that "The applicant should be given the appropriate test" (p. 10).

TECHNICAL.
Reliability/validity. There are no reliability data reported in the test manual, and no references to existing data on reliability. The only source of validity data comes from a concurrent validation sample of 47 clerical applicants who were hired and given an overall supervisory rating. Only 8 of the 17 scales were administered, so no validity data are provided for the other 9 scales.

Norms. There are no norms provided for any of the scales. The manual indicates scores that correspond to verbal descriptors (e.g., Below Average and Above Average) for each scale; however, this is no indication of how these descriptors were derived. For the single validity study of eight scales, only an overall "percent score" is provided for the norms—presumably across all eight scales, so it is impossible to ascertain what individual validity evidence applies to any of the scales.

Administration/interpretation. The administration instructions are minimal. The examinees are told to "work as quickly and as accurately as possible" (manual, p. 10). Aside from the verbal descriptors (e.g., Below Average) for each test, there is no information provided on interpretation of the test scores, or even how the scores across scales should be combined.

SUMMARY. The Clerical Skills Test Series is a set of tests that are purported to assess several different aspects of specific and general abilities associated to a greater (e.g., Spelling Ability) or lesser degree (Spatial Perception) to clerical jobs. The manual notes that the publisher "can perform a validation study of any test for a moderate cost" (p. 11). Given the lack of any substantive information on reliability or norms, and minimal validity information (e.g., no validity data for 9 of the 17 scales, only a single small study reporting validity for an aggregated score of the other 8 scales), it would be hard to justify any off-the-shelf use of these scales without completion of both norming and validity studies.

Review of the Clerical Skills Test Series [Scored by Client] by ELEANOR E. SANFORD, Vice-President of Research and Development, MetaMetrics, Inc., Durham, NC:

The Clerical Skills Test Series consists of a battery of tests designed to screen candidates for particular administrative and clerical skills. The battery consists of the following tests: Attention to Detail, Problem Solving Ability, Numerical Skills, Spelling Ability, Alphabetizing and Filing, Grammar and Punctuation, Vocabulary, Reading Comprehension, Receptionist Skills, Verbal Fluency, Ten Key Calculator, Bookkeeping, Coding, Proofreading Skills, Manual Dexterity, Mechanical Comprehension, and Spatial Perception.

ADMINISTRATION. Each test in the Clerical Skills Test Series is designed as a speed test where the examinee is requested to respond to as many of the items as possible in 3 to 5 minutes. The exception is the Bookkeeping Test, which is to be administered in 10 minutes (although, the directions on the test booklet say 20 minutes). The tests can be administered individually or in a group setting. Each test is self-administered and

self-scored. The scoring for each test is based on the Total Raw Score. For some tests, a correction for guessing is employed. A criterion-referenced interpretation is provided for each of the tests; scores are categorized into one of nine levels ranging from "Very Poor" to "Excellent."

DEVELOPMENT. No information is provided concerning the development of the Clerical Skills Test Series.

RELIABILITY. No information is provided concerning the reliability of the Clerical Skills Test Series.

VALIDITY. The test manual notes that validation studies can be conducted by the author, Walden Personnel Testing & Consulting, Inc., for the Clerical Skills Test Series. The manual describes one study conducted in 1994 at a large supermarket. The following tests were administered to 47 administrative office clerks: Numerical Skills, Attention to Detail, Problem Solving, Coding, Manual Dexterity, Alphabetizing and Filing, Spelling, and Reading Comprehension. Supervisory ratings (scale of 1 = *marginal* to 5 = *excellent*) were conducted 3 months after hiring or transferring candidates from the retail stores to the main office. The correlation between supervisory rating and an overall score (not described) on the Clerical Skills Test was .92 ($p = .01$). Based on this study, it was concluded that the Clerical Skills Test "appears to predict on-the-job success as measured by supervisory ratings for the clerical position" (p. 12). The summary of this study does not describe (a) how the relationship between the Clerical Skills Test and the skills required by job were determined, (b) the specific analyses that were conducted, or (c) the limitations of the inferences that can be made based upon the results.

SUMMARY. Although the Clerical Skills Test Series appears to have validity for the screening of applicants for administrative and clerical positions, no information is provided on the development of the assessments and the reliability. If decisions are to be made based upon the results from the test, adequate reliability needs to be ensured. Given today's office environments, some of the tests appear dated (e.g., Ten Key Calculator test). Finally, the Numerical Skills test requires examinees to do computations that are mathematically incorrect; the examinee is instructed to do the calculations from left to right, regardless of the correct order of operations.

[52]
Clinical Assessment of Behavior.

Purpose: "Developed to aid in the clinical assessment, diagnosis, and behavioral screening of, and treatment planning for, children and adolescents."

Population: Ages 2–18.

Publication Dates: 1996–2004.

Acronym: CAB.

Scores, 19: Internalizing Behaviors, Externalizing Behaviors, Critical Behaviors, Social Skills, Competence, Adaptive Behaviors, CAB Behavioral Index, Anxiety, Depression, Anger, Aggression, Bullying, Conduct Problems, Attention-Deficit/Hyperactivity, Autistic Spectrum Behaviors, Learning Disability, Mental Retardation, Executive Function, Gifted and Talented.

Administration: Individual.

Forms, 3: Parent Extended Rating Form, Parent Rating Form, Teacher Rating Form.

Price Data, 2005: $219 per introductory kit including scoring program with on-screen professional manual, installation guide, and professional manual (2004, 309 pages), 25 Parent Rating Forms, 25 Parent Extended Forms, and 25 Teacher Rating Forms.

Time: (10–30) minutes.

Comments: Informant-completed behavior rating scale.

Authors: Bruce A. Bracken and Lori K. Keith.

Publisher: Psychological Assessment Resources, Inc.

Review of the Clinical Assessment of Behavior by MIKE BONNER, Assistant Professor, Department of Psychology, University of Nebraska at Omaha, and METTA K. VOLKER-FRY, Graduate Student, School Psychology Program, University of Nebraska at Omaha, Omaha, NE:

DESCRIPTION. The Clinical Assessment of Behavior (CAB) is a broadband-behavior, informant-report rating scale for use in clinical, educational, and research settings for children ages 2 through 18 years. There are three rating forms: the Teacher Rating Form (CAB-T; 70 questions), Parent Rating Form (CAB-P; 70 questions), and Parent Extended Rating Form (CAB-PX; 170 questions). Completing the rating scales is appropriate for any adult with "a minimal literacy level" (professional manual, p. 9). All three scales require the respondent to rate the frequency of behaviors displayed "lately" using a 5-point Likert scale. Scoring must be done using the CAB Scoring Program (CAB-SP), compatible only with Windows systems. The CAB-SP generates a score report and profile for all three of the CAB Rating Forms, which includes raw scores, *T*-scores, percentile ranks, confidence intervals, qualitative classifications, and a graphical profile display. The manual provides raw score, *T*-score, percentile rank, and confidence interval data, although the CAB forms are not designed to be hand-scored. The CAB-SP will prorate raw scores when at least 90% of the items in a particular scale have appropriate completion.

Interpretation is organized using Clinical scales, Adaptive scales, and a CAB Behavioral Index (CBI), which combines both scales. The Clinical scales are composed of indices for Internalizing Behaviors, Externalizing Behaviors, and for the CAB-PX only, Critical Behaviors (CRI). The Internalizing Scale includes measures of Anxiety and Depression (called "clusters"). The Externalizing Scale clusters include Anger, Aggression, Bullying, and Conduct Problems. The Adaptive scale consists of measures for Social Skills, Competence, and for the CAB-PX only, Adaptive Behaviors.

DEVELOPMENT. Items were developed from a review of content and psychometric properties of existing behavior rating scales and, in a subsequent analysis, four preschool behavior rating scales for items that had high agreement between biological mothers' and fathers' ratings (Bracken, Keith, & Walker, 1994; Walker & Bracken, 1996). Their goal was to develop items with high interparent agreement and/or high internal consistency as well as items that had relevance for DSM-IV diagnosis. Using a process called "logical reanalysis for best fit," items were assigned to one of the six scales for the CAB-PX. From this, the abbreviated teacher and parent scales were developed so they would have matching items.

The CAB was normed and standardized over a 2-year period using two sampling procedures. The normative group is composed of 2,114 parents of children aged 2 to 18 and 1,689 teachers of 5- to 18-year-old students. The first method was a traditional direct solicitation for participation in standardization from schools, youth organizations, and mental health professionals. Data from this round were obtained in 17 states and made up 29% of the parent and 25% of the teacher normative samples. The remaining data were generated through an Internet survey research company. Parents (of children aged 2 to 18) and teachers (of children aged 5 to 18) who were members of the company's online survey panel were selected based on a stratified sampling plan designed to match the U.S. Bureau of the Census (2001) in terms of: age, gender, race/ethnicity, parental education, and geographic region. This method yielded respondents from 49 states.

Univariate analyses of variance were conducted controlling for the child's age, gender, grade, race/ethnicity, and urban/suburban/rural residency with results demonstrating that the two sampling methods were equivalent for mean CAB scale scores in the parent sample (accounting for up to 2.2% of the variance). The teacher sample demonstrated more variance due to the normative sampling method (between 9.1% and 12.2% of variance). The manual hypothesizes this difference is likely the result of a systematic orienting procedure for paper-pencil standardization (they were told to base ratings on a randomly selected student) and the Internet standardization (who could have selected the target student to rate based on unknown criteria).

The normative sample was matched to 2001 U.S. Census data for only age, gender and race/ethnicity, geographic region, and parent and teacher education level. There is a fair amount of discrepancy for some of the variables. For example, the CAB-T norms overrepresent males. There are small to moderate difference across race/ethnicity and age as well.

TECHNICAL.

Reliability. Internal consistency coefficients for the Clinical, Adaptive, and Behavioral Indices across the three forms are between .89 and .98. For the subscales (clusters), coefficients range from .88 to .97. There are some patterns of strength and weakness for internal consistency across forms and subscales for age and gender that need to be considered by potential users. Test-retest reliability (time intervals varied across forms but were on average about 18 days) was reported for a small (N = 102) sample with correlations between .75 and .93 for indices and subscales. Interrater reliability was evaluated for 368 children and adolescents. The Parent Forms were administered to 31 pairs of biological parents yielding a correlation of .82 on the CBI, and a range of .70 to .90 across the more specific subscales. Teacher and parent interrater reliability correlations across the scales and subscales ranged from .40 to .58, typical for

cross-context comparisons. The Standard Error of Measurement (*SEM*) is between 1.4 and 3.46 *T*-score points. Low *SEM*s, such as these, are indicators that the test has good evidence of reliability.

Validity. Evidence for content validity comes from the empirical approach used to derive items in the scale development. Criterion-related validity evidence is offered through comparisons with the Behavior Assessment System for Children (BASC; Reynolds & Kamphaus, 1998) and the Devereaux Scales of Mental Disorders (DSMD; Naglieri, LeBuffe, & Pfeiffer, 1994). The CAB and BASC correlations between theoretically equivalent scales and clusters ranged from .57 to .77. There are a few components of the CAB that do not correlate as would be expected with the BASC. In comparisons with the DSMD, the coefficients between similar scales and clusters ranged from .57 to .79. These findings give compelling evidence for criterion-referenced validity. Construct validity evidence was offered with correlations between specific clusters and the corresponding index, with a range between .71 to .95. Item-level factor analysis was conducted using the normative sample and provided support for four factors within the CAB-T and CAB-P and six factors within the CAB-PX.

COMMENTARY. The CAB was designed to aid in identification of individuals requiring behavioral, educational, or psychiatric assistance. Such a use seems reasonable, as long as the CAB is a component of multimethod assessment, not a stand-alone assessment, yet the qualitative classifications given by the Scoring Program may promote such use. Users of the CAB must be highly cautious when reviewing this classification, and may be best advised to use it as only a preliminary indicator or disregard it until additional assessment is included. The CAB is also purported to be appropriate to monitor the progress of children or adolescents during intervention. Use in this fashion is questionable, depending upon the evaluation methodology. The CAB was not standardized for use with teachers and parents who speak a native language other than English. Therefore, the CAB should not be used with people lacking a proficient understanding of English.

Although the CAB manual provides good preliminary reliability evidence through interrater, test-retest, and *SEM*, it did not include results of content sampling or split-half reliability tests. The collection of normative data through an Internet survey is novel, but this method is unexplored in research. The small sample size and underrepresentation of African American and Hispanic children in the investigations of reliability is also of concern. Interrater comparisons between teachers on the Teacher Form should have been included. Furthermore, the reliability coefficients for different subgroups of age, gender, and race/ethnicity were in some cases as low as .71. Bracken (1987) suggests cluster reliability should fall at or above the .80 criterion level; therefore, caution should be used when assessing an individual who falls into one of the subgroups with coefficients below the .80 level (as cited in the professional manual).

The evidence presented also provided preliminary support for the validity of the CAB. The manual claims the CAB connects well with the current child and adolescent psychopathology and behavioral disorder literature. The test authors and their colleagues reviewed the current literature surrounding rating scales to demonstrate content validity. Criterion-referenced validity was documented in that the CAB structure is similar to other parent and teacher rating scales. Internal consistency and item-level factor analysis coefficients were consistent with strong validity. Unfortunately, no differential item functioning analyses were used to show the absence of bias in the CAB items. No comparisons were made between responses for different gender or race/ethnic groups. With the exception of these questions, the CAB has strong psychometric properties.

SUMMARY. Given the strong psychometric development and preliminary technical properties, the CAB is likely to be a popular choice among child-focused mental health and educational professionals. The CAB was designed to more closely align with current diagnostic criteria and address concerns found with previous third party behavior rating scales (i.e., high interparent reliability and data on competence measures). However, more research is needed to support when and how the CAB can be used to contribute to diagnosis and intervention as well as success of these plans before absolute treatment utility could be claimed (Nelson-Gray, 2003; Messick, 1995).

REVIEWERS' REFERENCES

Bracken, B. A., Keith, L. K., & Walker, K. C. (1994). Assessment of preschool behavior and social-emotional functioning: A review of thirteen third-party instruments. *Journal of Psychoeducational Assessment, 16,* 153–169.

Messick, S. (1995). Validity of psychological assessment: Validation of inferences from persons' responses and performances as scientific inquiry into score meaning. *American Psychologist, 50,* 741–749.

Naglieri, J. A., LeBuffe, P. A., & Pfeiffer, S. I. (1994). Devereux Scales of Mental Disorder. San Antonio, TX: The Psychological Corporation.

Nelson-Gray, R. O. (2003). Treatment utility of psychological assessment. *Psychological Assessment, 15,* 521–531.

Reynolds, C. R., & Kamphaus, R. (1998). Behavior Assessment System for Children. Circle Pines, MN: American Guidance Service.

Walker, K. C., & Bracken, B. A. (1996). Inter-parent agreement on four preschool behavior rating scales: Effects of parent and child gender on inter-rater reliability. *Psychology in the Schools, 33,* 273–284.

Review of the Clinical Assessment of Behavior by JOHN HATTIE, Professor of Education, University of Aukland, Aukland, NZ:

DESCRIPTION. The Clinical Assessment of Behavior (CAB) aims to be a comprehensive, highly reliable instrument, based on a representative national sample, for use to provide a "balanced framework of competence-based and problematic or clinical scales, making it useful for strength-based evaluation of children and adolescents" (professional manual, p. 3). The CAB is applicable to 2–18-year-olds, and has three forms: a Parent Rating Form (70 items), a Parent Extended Rating Form (170 items), and a Teacher version (70 items). The responses to each item require choosing from a 5-point frequency scale (*Always* to *Never*).

The 12 subscales are grouped into three higher order domains: Clinical, Adaptive, and Educationally Related Clinical scales. The three Clinical scales include Internalizing Behaviors (Anxiety and Depression), Externalizing Behaviors (Anger, Aggression, Bullying, and Conduct Problems), and Critical Behaviors. The two higher order Adaptive scales relating to positive behavior orientations include Executive Functioning and Gifted and Talented. There are four Educationally Related Clinical clusters (Learning Disability, Mental Retardation, Autistic Spectrum Disorders, and Attention/Deficit Hyperactivity). All scales are transformed into *T*-scores (*Mn* = 50, *sd* = 10), and there are cut scores for each scale leading to classifying various degrees of (mal)adjustment, but no mention of the standard setting methods that led to these cut scores. Users are encouraged to use judgement, but it is a responsibility of test developers to defend their suggested criteria.

DEVELOPMENT. A content analysis reduced the initial 1,300 items to 528, which were then administered to a small sample (*N* = 276), and the best items chosen on the basis of interparent agreement. The final set of 70 items for the Parent and Teacher forms, and 170 for the Extended

Parent version were based on this small sample. These items were then administered to 2,114 parents and 1,689 teachers derived from direct solicitation and an internet survey. This led to a slightly more educated sample.

TECHNICAL. Although age and gender accounted for less than 5% of the variance of scores, extensive tables for age and sex are provided. A close inspection of these conversions shows nothing but trivial differences with a few exceptions. It is not clear why the conversions are so different for Mental Retardation for male and female adolescents (boys need higher raw scores to be at the 50th percentile), and for Gifted and Talented for male and female 2–6-year-olds (boys need lower raw scores to be classified gifted at the 50th percentile). This begs for a differential item analysis to detect if there is some bias in these items. Overall, however, it may have been more convincing to present tables not based on age and sex (for most scales), thus making the manual easier to use. At least it raises the question as to why there are no age and sex differences, when so many studies have made claims about age and sex differences in many of these attributes.

There is the usual sprinkling of coefficient alphas all in the .90s, which begs the question as to whether there is item redundancy. The standard errors are appropriately small. The indices of stability over time are high, which is not surprising given how "normal" the sample of children was in the norming sample. There is reasonable agreement between parents and teachers (.40 to .58 across the scales) although the differences may be more interesting and important than the agreements.

Validity is still considered a function of "the extent to which a test measures what it purports to measure" (professional manual, p. 79) as opposed to the new *Standards* relating more to the dependability of the interpretations that can be made from the test scores. There is a factor analysis, but the correlations are worrying—the average absolute intercorrelation is .75, with many correlations between scales exceeding .90, and over 40% exceeding .80. It is hard to defend, for example, a scale for Anxiety and another for Depression when the correlations between them are .97; and for Competence and Gifted with an intercorrelation of .96; Mental Retardation and Competence of -.95, but Bullying and Externalizing of .94 sug-

gest problems as these two dimensions are somewhat different. A major reason is that other than the first six scales, the items are scored on more than one scale—which introduces a higher dependency. In the case of Bullying and Externalizing, for example, 60% of the items are in common. There is no evidence to show the discrimination across the 16 scales.

COMMENTARY AND SUMMARY. The major problems with the CAB are the need for more justification for the interpretation of various scores, especially cut scores that lead to decisions about "clinical risk," the lack of discrimination across scales, and why a user would invest in this particular battery compared to the many alternatives. The major advantages of the CAB are that it has six overall scales that are well normed, highly reliable, and could be used in many research studies. The advantage of the CAB is its seeming comprehensiveness but its disadvantage is the lack of discrimination of many of the scales.

[53]

Clinical Evaluation of Language Fundamentals, Fourth Edition.

Purpose: Constructed as "a clinical tool for the identification, diagnosis and follow-up evaluation of language and communication disorders."

Population: Ages 5–21.

Publication Dates: 1980–2003.

Acronym: CELF-4.

Administration: Individual.

Price Data, 2005: $425 per complete kit including examiner's manual, 2 stimulus manuals, 10 record form1, 10 record form 2, 50 ORS record forms, and 1 luggage tag; $150 per examiner's manual; $215 per 2 stimulus manuals; $110 per stimulus manual 1; $110 per stimulus manual 2; $40 per 50 ORS record forms; $59 per 25 record form 1; $59 per 25 record form 2; $199 per Scoring Assistant; $550 per complete kit/Scoring Assistant Combo.

Time: (30-45) minutes.

Authors: Eleanor Semel, Elisabeth Wiig, and Wayne A. Secord.

Publisher: PsychCorp, A brand of Harcourt Assessment, Inc.

a) CELF-4, AGES 5–8.

Population: Ages 5–8.

Scores, 22: Core Language (Concepts and Following Directions, Word Structure, Recalling Sentences, Formulated Sentences), Receptive Language (Concepts and Following Directions, Word Classes 1 and 2-Receptive, Sentence Structure),

Expressive Language (Word Structure, Recalling Sentences, Formulated Sentences, Language Content (Concepts and Following Directions, Word Classes 1 and 2-Total, Expressive Vocabulary), Language Structure (Word Structure, Recalling Sentences, Formulated Sentences, Sentence Structure), Phonological Awareness, Word Associations, Rapid Automatic Naming, Number Repetition 1, Familiar Sequences 1.

b) CELF-4, AGES 9–12.

Population: Ages 9–12.

Scores, 21: Core Language (Concepts and Following Directions, Recalling Sentences, Formulated Sentences, Word Classes 2-Total) Receptive Language (Concepts and Following Directions, Word Classes 2-Receptive), Expressive Language (Recalling Sentences, Formulated Sentences, Word Classes 2-Expressive), Language Content (Word Classes 2-Total, Expressive Vocabulary [Age 9], Word Definitions [Ages 10–12], Understanding Spoken Paragraphs), Language Memory (Recalling Sentences, Concepts and Following Directions, Formulated Sentences), Phonological Awareness, Word Associations, Rapid Automatic Naming, Number Repetition 1, Familiar Sequences 1.

c) CELF-4, AGES 13–21.

Population: Ages 13–21.

Scores, 20: Core Language (Recalling Sentences, Formulated Sentences, Word Classes 2-Total, Word Definitions), Receptive Language (Word Classes 2-Receptive, Semantic Relationships, Understanding Spoken Paragraphs), Expressive Language (Recalling Sentences, Formulated Sentences, Word Classes 2-Expressive), Language Content (Word Definitions, Sentence Assembly, Understanding Spoken Paragraphs), Language Memory (Recalling Sentences, Formulated Sentences, Semantic Relationships), Word Associations, Rapid Automatic Naming, Number Repetition 1 and 2, Familiar Sequences 1 and 2.

Cross References: For reviews by Robert R. Haccoun and David P. Hurford of an earlier edition, see 14:76; see also T5:540 (26 references); for reviews by Ronald B. Gillam and John MacDonald of an earlier edition, see 13:68 (38 references); see also T4:521 (5 references); for reviews by Linda Crocker and David A. Shapiro of an earlier edition, see 11:72; for a review by Dixie D. Sanger of an earlier edition, see 9:233 (2 references); see also T3:474.

Review of the Clinical Evaluation of Language Fundamentals, Fourth Edition by AIMÉE LANGLOIS, Professor, Department of Child Development, Humboldt State University, Arcata, CA:

DESCRIPTION. The Clinical Evaluation of Language Fundamentals, Fourth Edition (CELF-4) was developed to identify, diagnose, and provide follow-up evaluation of language and communication disorders in children, adolescents, and young adults between 5 and 21 years of age. Like the CELF-3, the test assesses language content and form in both expressive and receptive language modalities; in addition, the CELF-4 includes a subtest for the assessment of pragmatics. The authors redesigned this fourth edition of the CELF based in part on feedback they received from professionals and on legislation that pertains to the education of students from 5 to 21 years of age. As such, the test is designed to help clinicians meet the Individuals with Disabilities Education Act mandate, assess a child's strengths and needs, and evaluate his or her parents' concerns. The CELF-4 consists of revised subtests from earlier versions of the test including provisions for "Extension Testing," as well as new subtests. As opposed to the CELF-3, it includes the Observation Rating Scales and adds a Pragmatics Profile. Depending on the age of the child, up to 18 subtests can be administered. A Core Language Score, as well as Receptive Language, Expressive Language, Language Content, Language Structure, and Working Memory Index scores can be obtained. In addition, criteria can be established for Phonological Awareness, Word Associations, Pragmatics Profile, and Rapid Automatic Naming.

Given the high number of subtests, the authors suggest a model of assessment that clinicians can follow to select what subtests to administer. This limits administration time along with clearer scoring instructions and the incorporation of both age-specific starting points and rules to discontinue testing. Like the CELF-3, the CELF-4 is relatively easy to learn because instructions, examples, and practice items are provided for each subtest. Overall, the colorful record forms and revised stimulus books are easy to use and appealing. A new feature of the CELF-4 is that clinicians can now simply enter raw scores in a computer with a "Scoring Assistant" CD that generates all the scaled and composite scores and charts found on the record form as well as a variety of reports. This feature of the CELF-4 not only minimizes the chance of scoring errors but also saves time, a valuable commodity for most clinicians.

The authors caution potential test users that they should have experience with standardized tests and testing children with diverse linguistic, cultural, and clinical backgrounds. They emphasize that examiners must not only become thoroughly familiar with each subtest they plan to administer but also maintain rapport, ensure that the room is comfortable, and allow breaks. The authors also encourage examiners to adapt test administration for children whose culture, dialect, ability level, and/or age require such. To that effect, an appendix in the examiner's manual provides examples of dialectal and Spanish-influenced variations for phonology, morphology, syntax, and word structure. The authors advise that clinicians who adapt the test should interpret results with caution and include comments about their modifications in their report.

DEVELOPMENT. The authors offer a sound rationale for the development of the CELF-4 and its use. They emphasize that, in addition to responding to feedback from test users, they developed this revised edition after conducting a "thorough review of the current literature" (examiner's manual, p. 199), pilot research, and national tryout testing prior to standardization. To that effect they describe how and why new subtests were introduced, existing ones modified, and items added to allow testing students in age groups not included in previous editions. They also report that after both the pilot and tryout research, a panel of experts reviewed the CELF-4 for "gender, racial/ethnic, socioeconomic status, and regional biases" (examiner's manual, p. 205). Items that were deemed biased were either modified or dropped from the final item set used for standardization.

TECHNICAL.

Standardization. The CELF-4 was standardized on 2,650 students; 5- to 17-year-olds included 200 examinees at each age level, 17- to 21-year-olds included 50 students for each age year. The sample represented the U.S. population with respect to age, gender, race/ethnicity, geographic region, and parent education level. In contrast to earlier versions of the test, which included only normally developing children, about 9% of children in the CELF-4 normative sample were receiving special services and 7% were diagnosed with speech and/or language disorders. These numbers are consistent with those reported by the National Dissemination Center for Children with Disabilities (2003) and the U.S. Office of Education Program (n.d.a, n.d.b) for children in special education.

Reliability. The authors evaluated the reliability of the CELF-4 with measures of test-retest, internal consistency, and interscorer reliability. Results of test-retest reliability with 320 students yielded high correlations for all age groups' composite scores (.90+). However, test-retest reliability coefficients for each subtest and each age group range from poor (.60) to excellent (.90+) with an average administration interval of 16 days.

Measures of internal consistency revealed higher reliability for the composite scores than for individual subtest scores. Reliability alpha coefficients range from .89 to .95 for the former and from .70 to .91 for the latter. As in the CELF-3, reliability for Understanding Spoken Paragraphs continues to be particularly low with a mean alpha coefficient of .69 and a range of .54 to .81. Split-half reliability coefficients are similar. The authors cogently explain possible reasons for these results and provide standard errors of measurement for all subtest and composite scores for each age level. This mitigates the impact of low reliability correlations by helping test users determine how much of a child's score on any subtest varies from his or her potential score. Examiners should therefore interpret results from subtests with low internal consistency by first consulting the standard error of measurement table in the manual and after having read sections of the manual that pertain both to possible reasons for low internal consistency and to score differences.

Interscorer reliability was examined by correlating the total raw scores given by two examiners for the seven subtests that require scoring judgment. Decision agreements ranged from .88 to .99, indicating that the CELF-4 has good to excellent interexaminer reliability. Clinicians can therefore feel confident that results obtained by colleagues and/or referral sources reflect a child's performance.

Validity. The authors attended to several types of validity in the development of the test: content, response process, internal structure, and relationships with other variables. The authors provide evidence of content validity by indicating that they conducted a thorough review of the literature on the development of language skills of 5- to 21-year-old students. As a result, the language skills sampled (e.g., morphology, syntax, semantics) reflect well-documented language constructs.

Another source of validity evidence comes from what is known as "response process," which entails showing that the task formats elicit responses in the desired manner, thus measuring the intended skills. The authors show that the verbal responses and behaviors required of the examinees to accomplish the tasks measured language skills by providing a sound rationale for the selection of subtest tasks in terms of language components and their rules (e.g., semantics, syntax), language modalities (receptive, expressive), and cognitive skills (e.g., working memory).

The internal structure of the test was assessed by factor analysis, which yielded high correlations between the Core Language score and the other language indexes. In addition, Expressive and Receptive Language were highly correlated at all age levels and their respective indexes showed moderate-to-high correlation with other indexes and composite scores. The authors discuss this aspect of validity at length and provide numerous tables to illustrate their findings, which leads to their conclusion that the factor analysis "studies strongly support the concept of a general language factor" (examiner's manual, p. 258).

The validity of use of the CELF-4 scores was also assessed by correlating it with CELF-3 results for a clinical and a nonclinical group, and by conducting group studies with children diagnosed with language disorders. The correlations between CELF-3 and CELF-4 are moderate, but this is not surprising in light of the CELF-4 revisions, which probably caused the much larger differences between the clinical and nonclinical samples than were seen for the CELF-3. Of note is the absence of, or marked decrease in, overlap between the two groups' subtest and composite scores for the CELF-4. Additional testing revealed that, as opposed to the CELF-3, the CELF-4 has high sensitivity and specificity, thus providing confidence for examiners that the test both accurately identifies children who have a language disability and can be used to rule out such a diagnosis.

COMMENTARY AND SUMMARY. The CELF-4, as a means to identify and diagnose language and communication disorders in students age 5 to 21, has many strengths. First and foremost, its standardization with a representative sample of the U.S. population and an appendix devoted to dialectal variations and cultural sensitivity indicate that the test can be used with students from multiple backgrounds. Second, the test reflects a well-established clinical decision-making process. In addition, the manual provides detailed administration, scoring, and interpretation instructions as well as comprehensive information about the revision of the test and its technical quality. The record forms are easy to follow with starting points and discontinuation rules that streamline test administration. The Scoring Assistant CD helps minimize scoring error and saves time with charting results, report writing, and record keeping.

However, the test also has some weaknesses that should not be ignored. Although each subtest is easy to administer, their sheer number may confuse inexperienced examiners. As prescribed by the authors, test users should have experience or training in using standardized tests with students whose characteristics are similar to those of the students they plan to assess with the CELF-4. As discussed above, examiners should also attend to concerns about reliability when interpreting results. However, the strengths of the CELF-4 override its weaknesses and should lead clinicians who assess and diagnose children with language disorders to consider it as a valuable addition to their test library.

REVIEWER'S REFERENCES

National Dissemination Center for Children and Youth with Disabilities. (2003). *Who are the children in special education?* Retrieved May 26, 2004, from http://www.nichcy.org/pubs/research/rb2.pdf

U.S. Office of Education Program. (n.d.a). *Percentage of children served under IDEA, Part B by age group during the 2001–02 school year.* Retrieved May 26, 2004, from http://www.ideadata.org/tables25th/ar_aa10.htm

U.S. Office of Education Program. (n.d.b). *Percentage of children served under IDEA, Part B by age group during the 2002–03 school year.* Retrieved May 26, 2004, from http://www.ideadata.org/tables26th/ar_aa10.htm

Review of the Clinical Evaluation of Language Fundamentals, Fourth Edition by VINCENT J. SAMAR, Associate Professor, Department of Research, National Technical Institute for the Deaf, Rochester Institute of Technology, Rochester, NY:

GENERAL DESCRIPTION. The Clinical Evaluation of Language Fundamentals, Fourth Edition (CELF-4) is a comprehensive clinical tool for identifying, diagnosing, and conducting follow-up evaluations of language and communication disorders in individuals in the age range of 5–21 years. The battery is supplied with a comprehensive manual, record forms for administering and scoring the battery, bound flip-style stimulus booklets, Windows-platform *Scoring Assistant* software on floppy disk and on CD-ROM, a booklet illustrating *Scoring Assistant* sample reports, and an Observational Rating Scale form for authentic assessment of communication and language behaviors in classroom and other situational contexts.

The scope of the battery, both in terms of its target age range and the range of skills and knowledge it tests, is substantially greater that that of its predecessor, the CELF-3. Notably, the instrument now includes a subtest for assessing phonological awareness, a critical precursor to literacy acquisition, as well as new tests for evaluating semantics, syntax, morphology, pragmatics, and memory. New measures are also included to provide authentic assessment of communication in academic environments and of context-specific social language skills. Finally, the CELF-4 is an improvement over previous versions because it has been explicitly redesigned to accord with state and federal regulations, as specified in the Individuals with Disabilities Education Act Amendment of 1997, and to facilitate the development of individualized education programs.

The flexibility and utility of the CELF-4 is supported by its four-level modular design, which permits the evaluator to customize the sequence of subtests to meet the individual goals of the assessment. The levels are sequenced so that an evaluator can make an initial determination of the presence of a language disability and the examinee's eligibility for services (Level 1), then proceed to a description of the nature of the disorder (Level 2), then evaluate the underlying clinical causes of the disorder (Level 3), and finally evaluate the examinee's authentic language and communication performance in classroom and other contexts (Level 4). Because of its modular organization, these levels can be applied independently for specialized purposes, without following the sequence.

The CELF-4 has two features that make it a particularly efficient measure for addressing the assessment needs of individual examinees. First, it has age-specific start points, allowing the evaluator to enter the testing protocol at the approximate level of the examinee's language skills. Second it has performance-based discontinue rules. This feature permits the evaluator to minimize test time by discontinuing testing at an appropriate point, based on the examinee's performance, without loss of the validity of test results.

MANUAL, FORMS, AND MATERIALS. In eight comprehensive chapters, the CELF-4 manual provides guidance for administering, interpreting, and scoring the sequence of subtests, describes in detail the purpose and process of the battery's development, and presents extensive evidence of the reliability and validity of the instrument. Appendix A presents scorer training materials. Appendix B deals explicitly and in welcome detail with the issue of dialectal variations and sensitivity to testing bias that can affect the scores of examinees from several American ethnic and linguistic subcultures. Appendices C–F provide the necessary scoring and conversion tables.

Chapter 1 provides a fairly clear statement of the design, test development goals, and flexibility of usage of the CELF-4. The use of graphics and large, clearly organized tables helps to illustrate the flexibility and overall organization of the battery.

Chapter 2 (Administration and Scoring Directions for Level 1 and Level 2 Assessments) begins with an excellent presentation of general testing guidelines, including well-stated caveats regarding handling validity issues associated with the many complex issues related to cultural diversity and to examinees with special needs. Most of the chapter is easy to follow.

Chapter 3 is an excellent guide to interpreting the results of Level 1 and Level 2 assessments. Chapter 4 describes the administration and interpretation of the subtests that provide an assessment of the key clinical behaviors and processes underlying an examinee's manifest language disorder, and of the authentic descriptive measures that relate these behaviors and processes to performance in the classroom and other social situations. A series of seven case studies that illustrate assessment at each level appear at the end of this chapter, providing the reader with a valuable orientation to the concrete and flexible application of the CELF-4.

The remaining chapters present details of the purpose and design, normative development, and reliability and validity evidence for scores from the CELF-4. Issues related to the information contained in these chapters are discussed below.

The record forms are well organized for easy use during administration. They contain a complete full-color replica of the stimulus materials that the examinee views in the bound stimulus books. This feature facilitates the examiner's ability to keep track of the items in sequence during the administration process.

The stimulus booklets stand on their own and have flipable pages with the stimulus printed on one side facing the examinee and the corresponding instructions and item statements appearing on the page facing the examiner. The examiner's booklet page also contains likely alternative responses for each item.

PURPOSE AND DESIGN. The CELF-4 was designed to be bigger and better than the CELF-3 along several significant dimensions. These include (a) an improved conceptual and psychometric link to current trends in education and in regulatory statutes; (b) reformatting the stimulus materials and report forms for faster, easier administration; (c) improving the psychometric properties of the instrument, across the board, including improvements in the control of test bias across diverse populations, the representativeness of the normative sample, and the instrument's reliability, validity, and diagnostic sensitivity; (d) shortening test administration time by increasing test efficiency psychometrically; (e) broadening the age range; and (f) linking clinical psychometric assessment results to authentic classroom and situational assessment. The addition of a phonological awareness subtest; a working memory index score; index scores for language content, structure, and memory; and index scores for receptive and expressive language has brought the CELF-4 into line with the most recent research and psychometric validation data in the areas of literacy acquisition, language learning disabilities, and psychoeducational assessment.

DEVELOPMENT, STANDARDIZATION, RELIABILITY, AND VALIDITY. The CELF-4 was revised through an extensive process that included obtaining feedback from a variety of evaluators and experts, conducting a current literature review, conducting pilot studies and a nationwide tryout, and completing a nationwide standardization. The standardization sample was well stratified over age, sex, race/ethnicity, geographic region, and parent education level, involving 4,500 children, adolescents, and young adults. Extensive tables identifying the demographic characteristics of the standardization sample are presented in Chapter 6.

Test-retest reliability was estimated by selecting a stratified subsample of examinees and re-administering the CELF-4 within a range of 7 to 35 days (mean of 16 days). Reliability coefficients across all ages and subtests ranged from adequate (in the .70s) to excellent (.90). These results indicate overall good time stability for CELF-4 assessment. The internal consistency reliability across all ages and subtests was generally good, as estimated by Cronbach's alpha (reliability coefficients ranging from .62–.96) and split-half reliability (reliability coefficients ranging from .53–.97). In addition, internal consistency reliability was computed separately for each of four clinical subgroups on most subtests, averaged over age. These coefficient ranges, combining the Cronbach's alpha and split-half coefficients, were generally good: Language Learning Disorder, .66–.96; Mental Retardation, .79–.99; Autism, .85–.98; and Hearing Impairment, .82–.97.

The validity evidence of scores from the the CELF-4 has been well documented, based on cumulative studies of the behavior of the entire CELF series as well as new evaluations in clinical settings. The appropriateness of the item content and the language and cognitive processes used by examinees to accomplish the instrument's tasks have been well documented, and are described in Chapter 8 of the CELF-4 manual. Furthermore, comprehensive intercorrelational and factor analytic analyses confirmed the basic construct validity of the instrument. A series of structural equation modeling studies on different age groups, reported in the manual, add new insight into the way different components of language function determine subtest performance at different developmental stages. Studies of children diagnosed with language disorders, autism, mental retardation, or hearing loss confirmed that the CELF-4 has robust clinical utility. In general, the validity studies confirmed that a strong general language factor and working memory capacity broadly affect performance across subtests for normally developing children, reflecting the coherent emergence of their language and cognitive function. At the same time, CELF-4 performance differentiates language and working memory weaknesses in specific clinical populations. Comparative studies indicate that the CELF-4 is substantially more sensitive to these weaknesses than the CELF-3.

COMMENTARY. A caution is in order regarding the application of the CELF-4 to special populations such as children with hearing losses. The CELF-4 manual is careful to point out in

Chapter 2 that accommodations for cultural and language diversity will invalidate the norm-referenced scores. However, the manual also reports validation data on children with hearing losses in Chapter 8, and suggests that performance results indicate that poor performance was not due to the inability of such children to hear the stimuli because they seemed to perform well as a group on number-processing subtests that "require the ability to hear auditory stimuli" (CELF-4 manual, p. 276). The manual claims, therefore, that the CELF-4 was sensitive to underlying difficulties processing language that may be secondary to children's hearing losses. However, this claim is unwarranted at this time. There was no control for individual differences in the children's ability to speech-read the examiner during the test. Therefore, the contribution of hearing loss versus speech reading to determining results on more linguistically complex subtests, which are likely to be more difficult to speech read than the number-related subtests, cannot be adequately assessed from these data. Furthermore, sign language was not used during test administration. Therefore, there is no assurance that all of the children tested fully understood the task requirements and materials. Furthermore, the limited data presented in the manual are based only on children with mild and moderate hearing losses up to 65 dB. Such data do not generalize to children with severe to profound hearing losses up to 120 dB, for whom linguistic and cultural issues are likely to have more prominent influences on test validity. In any case, the CELF-4 has never been comprehensively validated on children with hearing losses and no norms for that population are available. Great caution should be exercised in attempting to administer and interpret the results of the CELF-4 with children who have hearing losses, especially when the goal of the evaluation is to separate the intricate influences of deafness and other causes of underlying language disabilities, respectively, on language development.

SUMMARY. The CELF-4 is a significant improvement over previous versions in the series. It is a comprehensive, efficient, well-validated, and easily administered instrument. The CELF-4 generally satisfies the contemporary needs of speech-language pathologists, school psychologists, special educators, and diagnosticians to accurately evaluate a child's language and communication

skills and to satisfy the requirements for effective intervention and accommodation mandated by law.

[54]

CNS Vital Signs Screening Battery.

Purpose: Designed to "assess neurocognitive state."
Population: Children and adults.
Publication Date: 2003.
Scores, 5: Memory, Mental Speed, Reaction Time, Attention, Cognitive Flexibility.
Administration: Individual.
Price Data: Available from publisher.
Time: Administration time not reported.
Comments: Computer administered and scored; requires Windows 2000 or XP.
Author: CNS Vital Signs.
Publisher: CNS Vital Signs.

Review of the CNS Vital Signs Screening Battery by D. ASHLEY COHEN, Forensic Neuropsychologist, CogniMetrix, San Jose, CA:

DESCRIPTION. The CNS Vital Signs Screening Battery (CNSVS) is an individually administered, computer-based, neuropsychological screening instrument. The population for whom the test is intended is listed as "children and adults" but no age range is stated. The contents of the testing kit are: the manual, a computer disk, sample report, and printout of some computer screens of data. The examinee is administered the test on a computer, and enters responses by pressing certain keys. Only the numeric keys above the letter keys are supported, not a numeric keypad. Examinees must have sufficient vision to see the stimuli on screen, and the motor ability to execute keystrokes. The test is designed to be taken alone (i.e., without an administrator present).

The CNSVS yields five component scores: Memory, Mental Speed, Reaction Time, Attention, and Cognitive Flexibility. Individual tasks or tests are: Verbal Memory (recognition only), Visual Memory (recognition only), Finger Tapping, Symbol-Digit Coding, Stroop, Shifting Attention, and Continuous Performance. Raw scores are generated by the computer program, compared to means and standard deviations, then are assigned a rating of Above Average, Average, Below Average, or Well Below Average for each of the five areas listed above.

DEVELOPMENT. The CNSVS developers state that their test is meant to fill a niche between informal mental status exams and screens such as the Mini Mental Status on the one end and formal neuropsychological testing on the other. Current and potential applications are described as: detection of dementia; diagnosis of Attention Deficit Disorder; serial evaluations, such as in monitoring the effects of medications or treatments; following up on patient recovery, as from a CVA or head injury; and obtaining a cognitive baseline during a routine office visit. The test comprises several measures developed earlier by others, such as the Stroop test, finger tapping, and coding. How these particular tests were selected, and why these rather than some others, is unspecified. It is also unknown if the authors believe that each of these tests measures a normally distributed skill or attribute.

TECHNICAL. Standardization information as well as information regarding evidence of reliability and validity are not provided. The statements in the manual addressing this topic are as follows: "The tests in CNS Vital Signs are all venerable tests from clinical and experimental psychology, and have been used for many years. They are known to be reliable and valid; that is why we chose them for our battery" (p. 29), and "The tests in Vital Signs, like the tests they were derived from, are reliable and valid" (p. 30).

COMMENTARY. The disk sent as part of the test package loaded, but then reported that it had expired. The reviewer was unable to obtain another from the web site. Thus this review is based on the material available in the manual, which in all cases should suffice. Unfortunately, the test manual is highly deficient. It does not follow the conventions of published test manuals, with sections on the standardization sample, reliability and validity, and the like. The manual does an admirable job of describing many groups to which the test may be applicable, and discussing the particulars of working with each group.

When the program is started on a computer, there is first a legal agreement to which one must consent. In almost all similar cases, there is a provision for printing a hard copy of the agreement, but not so with this program. In this same document, one must agree never to administer the test outside of one's office. Why it would be seen as impermissible to take the laptop computer on which it is installed to another facility in order to test patients is completely unclear.

Very few references are offered in the manual to support statements made, nor are there references pertaining to the various tests of which their measure is composed. The citations that are in place in the text are not paired with a reference list in the back of the manual. The only published article on the test thus far is simply descriptive in nature. There are a few others mentioned, all recently submitted for possible publication, by the same two authors. An index in the manual would also be welcome.

The test yields a printed report, a sample of which was included with the manual. There appears to be discrepancy in patient category rankings between the sample report that was sent with the manual and data reported on the web site; these sometimes disagree with traditional rankings. For example, "Above Average" performance is described on the sample report sent to this reviewer as 69th percentile or above, which would be a standard score equivalent of 107, on the web site it is listed as 84th percentile or above, or 115 standard score, whereas traditionally it would be seen as 75th percentile or 110 and above. Some of the statements generated in the sample report are also overly simplistic, such as low scores on finger tapping "indicate motor slowing," but this may not be cerebral or even neurological, instead indicating inattention, low motivation, or even arthritis, and thus unwillingness to move the finger rapidly because of pain.

To its credit, the manual does offer a discussion of suboptimal test effort or frank malingering, and as the authors point out, this is of more concern when there is no examiner administering the test or at least observing the person taking the test (although the latter could be remedied if the examiner wished). However, the only check for malingering is a simplistic one, basically in the "forced-choice" paradigm. As many examiners who work in the forensic arena will know, coached or sophisticated dissimulators often know or intuit enough not to perform worse than chance. Thus if an examinee obtained a score of 16/30 incorrect, the CNSVS would conclude (almost certainly correctly) that the individual was taking the test in an insincere manner, but what to make of a score of 14/30 wrong? Most measures that employ this paradigm have gone to a more complex system of determining suboptimal effort, and that would improve this portion of the CNSVS as well. In addition to examinees' deliberate attempts to appear impaired, examiners must also address low motivation, lack of involvement with the testing process, depression or anxiety during testing, and wandering attention; there was no discussion of these topics. This is again more important with a test taken without the examiner's observations.

This reviewer has some difficulty with the memory portion of the test. It is only recognition memory that is being tested, both immediate and delayed. Recognition is the "easiest" of the memory tasks, and often even individuals with moderate dementia will score well on recognition tasks. Intrusions are a strong hallmark of dementing process, but there is no way for these to be generated using this measure. Knowing how to rate one's patient on memory performance is also somewhat vague. The manual gives a cutoff of 7 out of 15 or fewer for immediate memory, and 5 of 15 or fewer for delayed as indicating memory impairment. But then we are told if the patient has a college education "one might prefer to use" a +1 *SD* cutoff. No age correction is given. In the manual some tables are listed for "normal subjects age 50 or older" with means and standard deviations, but no *N* is given.

The test authors do not seem to believe that normative data are of great importance. There is a statement in the manual that the examiner should use normative data *only* if he or she is lacking patient data from earlier administration of the CNSVS. However, the test is also offered as a means of making decisions as to whether, for example, a patient is fit to drive, is becoming demented, or has ADHD, among others, and these types of decisions necessarily involve comparison to a normative group.

SUMMARY. The CNS Vital Signs Screening Battery is based on filling the need for a brief, repeatable assessment of cognitive deficits; it has a reasonable array of areas assessed, and states that it covers a wide array of possible populations. It would seem that individuals taking the test would not perceive it as objectionable, and may find it at least somewhat interesting. The manual is entirely deficient, containing no standardization, reliability, or validity data, and offering no reference list to support many of the statements made, or the few citations given. The instrument needs more development and a standard manual needs to be produced before the test is ready for professional dissemination and use.

Review of the CNS Vital Signs Screening Battery by KARL R. HANES, Director, Cognitive-Behavioural Treatment Centre, Victoria, Australia, and Editor, Vangard Publishing, Victoria, Australia:

DESCRIPTION. The CNS Vital Signs Screening Battery (CNSVS) is a brief computerized, multilingual screening instrument for cognitive impairment. It consists of seven individual tests, all based on established procedures for the assessment of Verbal and Visual Memory, Mental Speed and Coordination, Reaction Time, Attention, and Cognitive Flexibility. This self-directed measure requires a computer running Windows 2000 or XP, with approximately 3.3 mb of available disk space, and a properly functioning keyboard, to operate. Administration time is typically 20–30 minutes. Installation and administration are straightforward, requiring minimal knowledge of modern computer operations. The initial screen provides a "Help" feature, providing some brief details about the program, as well as a "CNSVS" popup screen that affords some fine tuning, including options to view an existing report, retest an individual, enter a password, and backup or alter the display resolution. There are options for entry of reference information, including demographic and diagnostic details, with subject reference and date of birth being compulsory fields. The administrator may choose to run all of the tests or an Attention Deficit Hyperactivity Disorder (ADHD) option, which features only the Stroop, Shifting Attention, Symbol Digit Coding, and Continuous Performance tests. At the commencement of each test, examinees are presented with instructions in bold, large type against a lightly colored background and, except in the case of the memory tests, a practice trial. The test phase is preceded by a 3-second countdown and examinees are reminded throughout that they will be evaluated according to their "Speed and Accuracy." A test session is not registered until all of the scheduled tests have been completed, useful in cases of interruptions to the program (e.g., computer malfunction).

Subtests. Verbal and Visual Memory Tests: A series of words and geometric shapes, respectively, are flashed on the screen, along with a permanent screen reminder to remember each of 15 target stimuli. The examinee is subsequently provided with 2 seconds to differentiate each of these stimuli from an equal number of distractors. Examinees are informed that these tests would later have to be repeated. The Finger Tapping Test: Requires examinees to use the index finger of each hand consecutively to tap the space bar "as quickly as possible" for 10 seconds across three trials. The Symbol Digit Coding Test: The examinee is asked to utilize the numeric keys 2–9 in order to match symbols and numbers on a "test grid" with those on an analogous "answer grid." The Stroop Test: The examinee is presented with the words Red, Blue, or Green and asked, in PHASE 1, where color neutral words are presented, to tap the space bar as soon as they see the word; in PHASE 2, to tap the space bar when the word matches the color (e.g., the word Red is colored red); and in PHASE 3, to tap the space bar when the word does not match the color (e.g., the word Blue is colored red or green). The Shifting Attention Test: Provides examinees with circles or squares colored either red or blue and requires use of the right and left Shift keys to match each stimulus according to either color or shape. The Continuous Performance Test: Requires examinees to press the space bar when a target letter is flashed on the screen and do nothing when other letters appear across a time span of 5 minutes. This is followed by the delay phase of the verbal and visual memory tests. Scoring criteria predominantly comprise accuracy and reaction time. The CNSVS needs to be completed in a single sitting.

The computer-generated "Initial Report" provides means and standard deviations for individual test scores and an integrated profile for Memory, Mental Speed, Reaction Time, Attention, and Cognitive Flexibility. The latter composite score is based on means and standard deviations on relevant measures, with ratings provided across four scales (above, average, below, and well-below). Presumably, the scoring profile could be extended to provide further detail, such as the precise location of failures on the various subtests, inconsistencies in performance, including intratest irregularities, or information suggesting confusion or distractibility.

The main target populations for the CNSVS are persons with dementia, ADHD, drug-induced cognitive impairment, and mild brain injury. It is also touted as an instrument to assist in the diagnosis and management of mild cognitive disorders, for monitoring disease progress, health and fitness, and medication effects, with other applications including the forensic, sports medicine, and fitness to drive fields.

DEVELOPMENT. The CNSVS is a recent innovation within the field of computerized cognitive testing (copyright 2003) and represents the automation of standard measurement protocols for processing speed, mnestic, attentional, and executive functions. The memory tests are analogs of the Auditory Verbal Learning Test (Rey, 1964) and Complex Figure Test (Rey, 1941; Osterreith, 1944); the Symbol Digit Coding Test is a variant of the Digit Symbol Substitution Test from the Wechsler Adult Intelligence Scale (WAIS; Wechsler, 1955) and the Stroop, Finger Tapping, and Continuous Performance tests are based on classic measures of manual dexterity, set-shifting, and vigilance (Stroop, 1935; Halstead, 1947). Although some cognitive testing professionals would favor a more comprehensive quantitative approach to these cognitive domains, with particular consideration to spontaneous as well as reactive forms of cognitive flexibility, the rationale for test selection in assessment of the main constructs is clear. Each of the subtests were selected based on previous research and established criteria for the assessment of conditions such as dementia, ADHD, and impairments arising from drug use.

There was no formal test manual available for the review process. The materials supplied by the developer include an evaluation copy CD, which can be upgraded to the latest working version via the internet, some introductory material on installation, and a useful "Clinical Applications" document, which details the background of testing for dementia, ADHD, drug-induced cognitive impairment, brain injury, and various other applications. These materials are supplemented by a website, providing additional supporting literature and information, including news and updates, clinical information, and purchase details. The evaluation copy includes five test sessions, with further sessions being available for purchase from the supplier. The program is based on the broad model of dementia screening and appears tailored to requirements for easy, inexpensive testing, ideally suited to health professionals not generally proficient in the administration of psychological or neurocognitive testing measures.

DEVELOPMENT AND TECHNICAL. There was little information available on the normative sample used in the construction of the CNSVS. The available supporting material does provide some norms for normal subjects on each of the subtests, divided into younger (mean age 24) and older (mean age 63) adults for those measures deemed to be age-sensitive, such as the Set Shifting and Continuous Performance tests. There are also norms provided for ADHD and unspecified brain injury populations. The provision of guidelines for deficit measurement in working with a number of groups, including cutoff score recommendations and heuristics for interpreting test scores, are helpful and demonstrate the developers' determination to ensure correct use of this program. Unfortunately, there were no reliability data provided for the review process and the available validity data consist mainly of norms comparing normal examinees with those from various target populations. One would expect potential users of this instrument to be interested in such information as correlations of individual test scores with other standardized measures and brain imaging results, intercorrelations of overlapping measures on the CNSVS, and in the longer term, reports of studies using this instrument in specialized settings. The supporting literature suggests that the program has been administered to over 2,500 patients (aged 8–89) in various testing centers. Also, the subtests are very close approximations of the proven measures on which they are based, suggesting likely corroboration of these computerized versions. Nonetheless, the absence of detailed validity and reliability information does limit a more comprehensive technical appraisal of this promising instrument.

COMMENTARY. It is important to recognize that traditional approaches, preferred by many cognitive testing professionals, do hold some advantages over computerized testing, with many excellent tests of the respective cognitive domains being readily available (Strub & Black, 1985; Lezak, 1995). Nonetheless, automated cognitive assessment tools such as this and more established measures such as the Cambridge Neuropsychological Test Automated Battery (CANTAB; Robbins et al., 1986/2004) and MicroCog (Powell et al., 1993), appear to be gaining acceptance as measures of precision and efficiency in some professional environments. Specialized, multiple-platform instruments for use in such fields as neuropsychology, pharmacology, and sports medicine are becoming more widely available, being particularly useful in time-limited and minimal supervision settings.

The CNSVS is a thoughtfully designed, modern instrument with potential for the evaluation of cognitive impairment in relevant areas of health practice, providing information pertinent to the assessment and management of a range of conditions. Test interpreters should note that it is not intended as a stand-alone diagnostic measure, but as a screening tool or to supplement a more comprehensive clinical evaluation. The program is not overly taxing to complete, relative to other screening measures (e.g., Folstein, Folstein, & McHugh, 1975), it contains reasonable security features, such as password protection, and the novelty value of this test presentation lends itself well to work with children as well as adults. There is overlap on some of the tests, although for such a brief test battery this redundancy is not without merit in the interests of robust assessment of the various cognitive domains. The provision for entry of reference information is adequate, though rendering most of the fields optional could limit the availability of important data (such as education, mood, keyboard facility, use of psychoactive substances, or disability), toward an estimate of an individual's expected level of performance. The refinement of the "Help" feature for this program, perhaps incorporating indexed information or frequently asked questions, for those with operational problems and perhaps minimal internet access, would be worthwhile. Scoring profile options could also be extended. Furthermore, if none were available to purchasers, the development of a dedicated test manual, with complete validity and reliability data, in accordance with the *Standards for Educational and Psychological Testing* (AERA, APA, & NCME, 1999) and, for those interested in technical specifications, a more detailed outline of program parameters, such as the composition of computer-generated profile scores, a neuroanatomical breakdown of specific functions measured by each of the subtests, the background of programming and content validation, and consideration of potential research applications, would further complement this package.

SUMMARY. This is an impressive, well-constructed instrument, in which the seven subtests are based on accepted methodologies for the assessment of memory, attention, reaction time, and cognitive flexibility. Although further enhancements of this working version are feasible, including the increased availability of technical information and elaboration of further scoring options, on the whole, it is very well-presented, providing clear instructions, and is easy to administer, score, and interpret. Subject to the availability of data supporting its utility in the various target populations, the CNSVS is a promising addition to the field of automated cognitive testing and, in what is becoming a competitive market, is likely to be of value in professional environments requiring a rapid, efficient assessment tool.

REVIEWER'S REFERENCES

American Educational Research Association, American Psychological Association, & National Council on Measurement in Education. (1999). *Standards for educational and psychological testing.* Washington, DC: American Educational Research Association.

Folstein, M. F., Folstein, R. E. & McHugh, P. R. (1975). Mini mental state: A practical method for grading the cognitive state of patients for the clinician. *Journal of Psychiatric Research, 12,* 189–198.

Halstead, W. C. (1947). *Brain and intelligence: A quantitative study of the frontal lobes.* Chicago: University of Chicago Press.

Lezak, M. D. (1995). *Neuropsychological assessment* (3rd ed,.). London: Oxford University Press.

Osterreith, P. A. (1944). Le test de copie d'une figure complexe. *Archives de Psychologie, 30,* 206–356.

Powell, D., Kaplan, E., Whitla, D., Weintraub, S., Catlin, R., & Funkenstein, H. (1993). *MicroCog: Assessment of Cognitive Functioning.* San Antonio: The Psychological Corporation.

Rey, A. (1941). L'examen psychologique dans les cas d'encephalopathie traumatique. *Archives de Psychologie, 28,* 215–285.

Rey, A. (1964). L'examen clinique en psychologie. Paris: Presses Universitaires de France.

Robbins, T. W. et al. (1986/2004). Cambridge Neuropsychological Test Automated Battery (CANTAB). Cambridge, U.K.: Cambridge Cognition Inc.

Stroop, J. R. (1935). Studies of interference in serial verbal reactions. *Journal of Experimental Psychology, 18,* 643–662.

Strub, R. L. & Black, F. W. (1985). *The mental status examination in neurology* (2nd ed.). Philadelphia: F. A. Davis Company.

Wechsler, D. (1955). *Wechsler Adult Intelligence Scale. Manual.* New York: The Psychological Corporation.

[55]

Cognitive Abilities Test, Form 6.

Purpose: Designed to "assess students' abilities in reasoning and problem solving using verbal, quantitative, and spatial (nonverbal) symbols."

Population: Grades K–12.

Publication Dates: 1954–2002.

Acronym: CogAT.

Scores, 4: Verbal Battery, Quantitative Battery, Nonverbal Battery, Composite.

Administration: Group.

Price Data, 2003: $18 per Interpretive Guide for Teachers and Counselors (2001, 174 pages); $18 per Interpretive Guide for School Administrators (2001, 140 pages); $52 per Research Handbook (2002, 112 pages); $46.50 per norms booklet; $22.25 per 25 practice tests (specify level); $95 per 25 machine-scorable test booklets (specify Level K, 1, or 2); $73.25 per 25 reusable test booklets (specify Level A through H); $13.75 per directions for administration (specify level); $37.75 per 50 answer sheets (specify level); $67.75 per 100 answer sheets (specify level); $9.75 per scoring key (specify Level K, 1, or 2); $18 per scoring key (Levels A—H).

Comments: Scoring service available from publisher.

Authors: David F. Lohman and Elizabeth P. Hagen.

Publisher: Riverside Publishing.

a) PRIMARY BATTERY.

Population: Grades K–3.

Subtests, 6: Verbal Reasoning, Oral Vocabulary, Relational Concepts, Quantitative Concepts, Figure Classification, Matrices.

Levels: 3 overlapping levels, K, 1, and 2.

Time: Untimed, approximately 140 minutes (Levels 1 and 2) to 170 minutes (Level K).

b) MULTILEVEL BATTERY.

Population: Grades 3–12.

Subtests, 9: Verbal Classification, Sentence Completion, Verbal Analogies, Quantitative Relations, Number Series, Equation Building, Figure Classification, Figure Analogies, Figure Analysis, Composite.

Levels: 8 overlapping Levels, A through H.

Time: Approximately 145 minutes.

Cross References: See T5:560 (4 references); for reviews by Bert A. Goldman and Stephen H. Ivens of an earlier edition, see 13:71 (23 references); see also T4:537 (19 references); for reviews by Anne Anastasi and Douglas Fuchs of an earlier edition, see 10:66 (13 references); for a review by Charles J. Ansorge of an earlier edition, see 9:240 (5 references); see also T3:483 (32 references); for reviews by Kenneth D. Hopkins and Robert C. Nichols, see 8:181 (12 references); for reviews by Marcel L. Goldschmid and Carol K. Tittle and an excerpted review by Richard C. Cox of the primary batteries, see 7:343.

Review of the Cognitive Abilities Test, Form 6 by JAMES C. DiPERNA, Assistant Professor, School Psycholoogy Program, Pennsylvania State University, University Park, PA:

DESCRIPTION. The Cognitive Abilities Test, Form 6 (CogAT-6) is a group-administered test of students' general reasoning abilities. The authors state that the purpose of the test is to appraise "the level and pattern of cognitive development of students from kindergarten through grade 12" (Interpretive Guide for Teachers and Counselors, p. 1). The authors identify three intended uses for scores from the CogAT-6. The first use is to guide instruction so it matches the cognitive abilities and needs of each student in a classroom. The second is to provide an "alternative" measure of cognitive development relative to more commonly used measures such as standardized achievement tests or grades. The third and final purpose is to identify achievement-ability discrepancies.

Like its immediate predecessor, the latest form of the CogAT is composed of two "editions"—the Primary Edition for students in kindergarten through 2nd grade and the Multilevel Edition for students in 3rd through 12th grade. The Primary Edition includes three test batteries (Verbal, Quantitative, Nonverbal), each composed of two tests. Three separate levels (K, 1, 2) are available for the Primary Edition, with items at each level becoming progressively more difficult. Teachers read both directions and items to the children in their classes, and the authors claim that studies have shown young children are capable of taking the tests (Directions for Administration—Level K, p. 10). They do not, however, provide (or reference) any studies to support this claim. The authors recommend distributing the testing across several sessions (six for Level K and three for Levels 1 and 2) and report that total time allocated to testing ranges from 124 to 169 minutes for the Primary Edition.

The Multilevel Edition also includes three test batteries (Verbal, Quantitative, and Nonverbal) with each battery including three separate tests. Eight levels (A—H) are available for the Multilevel Edition. Teachers read only the directions to students who are then expected to read individual items on their own. The authors report that each battery (three tests) requires approximately 45-50 minutes to complete yielding a total administration time of 135-150 minutes.

At all levels, the authors provide a list of the most frequent accommodations provided to students with disabilities (e.g., small group administration, items read aloud, assisted recording of student responses) or students who are English language learners (e.g., off-level testing, access to an English to native language dictionary). They also indicate that each of these accommodations can be used with the CogAT-6 for students with special needs. No data are provided, though, regarding the impact of any accommodation on validity of scores from the CogAT-6.

All forms of the CogAT-6 can be scored by hand, scoring software, or submitted for scoring by the publisher. Though possible, hand-scoring for all students in a classroom seems highly unlikely given the amount of time required to generate the variety of scores available for each student

in the classroom. Both editions of the CogAT-6 yield multiple scores for each of the three batteries (Verbal, Nonverbal, and Quantitative) as well as an overall composite. Norm-referenced scores include Standard Age Scores ($M = 100$, $SD = 16$), stanines, and percentile ranks, and each of these scores can be calculated based on age- or grade-based comparison groups. In addition to normative scores, the CogAT-6 yields a composite Universal Scale Score that provides a common metric for measuring performance across all levels of the test. This score can be used to assess change in cognitive skills over time and is useful for research purposes.

In addition to individual scores for each battery, the authors have developed a system for classifying profiles of cognitive skills across the three assessed domains. Although space precludes detailed discussion of these profiles, the authors assert that they can be useful for instructional planning and provide some guidelines regarding their use. A limited theoretical rationale for adapting instruction based on CogAT-6 profiles is provided in the Interpretive Guide for Teachers and Counselors; however, no data are provided to justify the claim that adapting instruction according to CogAT-6 profiles yields better learning outcomes for children.

DEVELOPMENT.

Theoretical framework. The authors cite Vernon's (1961) model of hierarchical abilities and Cattell's (1987) model of crystallized and fluid cognitive abilities as two theories that guided the development of earlier forms of the CogAT. In addition, they suggest that the model of cognitive abilities resulting from Carroll's (1993) seminal work provides support for the domains assessed by the CogAT-6. The authors note it would be difficult for any single test to measure all of the specific abilities identified in Carroll's model and conclude that the most important cognitive abilities to measure relative to school learning are general abstract reasoning and students' ability to apply this reasoning to verbal, quantitative, and nonverbal tasks.

Item development. Development of the items for the CogAT-6 included multiple phases. The first phase was comprised of generating items based on research regarding the validity of tasks as indices of abstract reasoning. After development of the initial item pool, the items were subjected to "extensive critical review" (Research Handbook, p.

35) to evaluate item clarity and appropriateness for the age/grade groups for which they were intended. The third phase of development featured a national item tryout including approximately 8,000 students from 22 states and the District of Columbia. In addition to developmental change across grades and discrimination, the authors used item difficulty to determine which items to retain for the final version of each form. They also used review by an expert panel and differential item functioning (DIF) analysis across known groups (race, gender) to ensure that items were fair, and they appear to have been successful in this task based on data reported in the Research Handbook. The items selected from the national tryout were then submitted for the national standardization phase.

TECHNICAL.

Standardization. The CogAT-6 was costandardized with the Iowa Test of Basic Skills (Grades K–8) and the Iowa Test of Educational Development (Grades 9–12). As a result, the standardization sample is large (180,538 students) and representative of the U.S. population (based on the 2000 Census data) with regard to school type (public, private, etc.), socioeconomic status, and geographic region. The Hispanic student population is slightly underrepresented in the sample even after weighting, but the authors hypothesize this may be due to a significant number of these students not demonstrating sufficient English language proficiency to participate in the testing with accommodations. English language learners comprised approximately 4–8% of the standardization sample across the elementary grades (K–5), with the percentage falling to .5–2.5% in the older grades. The percentage of these students receiving accommodations varied as well (6–44%). Students with disabilities were slightly under-represented in the standardization sample (3.4–8% across grades) and the percentage of these students receiving accommodations ranged from 7.1% to 39.1%.

Reliability evidence. Estimates of internal consistency were calculated for each battery and level of the CogAT-6 using the recommended grade(s) for each level. All estimates exceeded .90 with the exception of the Verbal Battery for Levels K–2, which exceeded .85. In addition to this internal consistency evidence, the authors offered two other forms of reliability evidence: short- (less than 3 weeks) and long-term (intervals of 3 and 6 years) stability. Unfortunately, the short-term es-

timates were based on one administration of the CogAT-6 and an administration of the CogAT-5, and the long-term correlations were based exclusively on CogAT-5 data collected with over 2,500 students in one Midwestern school district. Although the short-term correlations (.78–.95) indicate a strong relationship between the two forms of the test across batteries and composites, evidence based on a previous version of a test is insufficient to support the current version of the test.

In sum, internal consistency evidence is strong across the batteries and levels. Using these internal consistency estimates, the authors calculate various standard errors of measurement, which are useful for making decisions about the reliability of an individual student's score(s). Other forms of reliability evidence, however, remain to be explored with the current version of the CogAT. Short- and long-term stability are particularly important given that one of the stated purposes of the CogAT is to measure children's cognitive skill *development*. In addition, reliability evidence should be explored across known groups (race, disability status, English language learners) given they are included in the target population for the test.

Validity evidence. Overall, the tasks/items included in the various levels of the test appear to be appropriate indicators of the intended constructs. In addition, the item discrimination and floor/ceiling range appear to be appropriate to assess students at various points along the continuum of cognitive abilities. DIF analyses with the final item pool suggest that the items fairly assess ability across members of various known groups. Gender differences in performance across tests, batteries, and levels are minimal; however, no data are reported regarding differences across other known groups (according to race, disability status, etc.). (As noted previously, items were subjected to DIF analysis across these groups.)

Structural evidence was analyzed using confirmatory factor analysis. Although minimal information is provided about the confirmatory analyses, reported indices provide support for a three first-order factor model. Factor loadings for a hierarchical model featuring the three factors and a single second-order factor failed to indicate unique contributions of the Quantitative factor above and beyond the general factor for the Primary Edition. Similarly, small loadings on the Quantitative factor are noted in the Multilevel

Edition as well, though they do increase at the more advanced levels. In addition, the authors suggest that, based on other analyses not reported in the manual, the Verbal and Quantitative batteries could be combined in the Primary Edition. They rule out this approach based on "consequential validity" and refer the reader to a case study in the Interpretive Guide for Teachers and Counselors. They also assert that, from an interpretation standpoint, the most important consideration is whether or not the three factors are distinguishable from one another, rather than g.

Evidence for convergent validity of scores reported in the CogAT-6 Research Handbook demonstrates the same limitations as the stability evidence noted previously. That is, convergent validity evidence reported in the manual is based on relationships between scores from the CogAT-5 and two other tests of cognitive skills—the Stanford-Binet (edition not reported) and the Differential Aptitude Tests. Convergent evidence using the current form of the test is necessary, however, to document the validity of scores from this instrument. The authors noted that two such studies were in process at the time of publication, were subsequently published on the Internet, and are summarized in the Research Handbook. The first of these studies (Lohman, 2003a) explored relationships between CogAT-6 scores and the Wechsler Intelligence Scale for Children (3rd ed.) Results from this study demonstrated a strong relationship between latent constructs, but the analyses were conducted using a small sample (N = 91) from two schools. The second study (Lohman, 2003b) compared the CogAT-6 with the Woodcock-Johnson Tests of Cognitive Abilities (3rd ed.). This study demonstrated strong relationships between latent constructs and utilized a larger total sample (N = 178) across three grades, but each grade level subsample was small (less than 90).

Perhaps the strongest validity evidence for the CogAT-6 comes in the form of the concurrent evidence with scores on the two achievement tests with which it was co-standardized. Correlations between the CogAT-6 and the various tests of achievement at all grade levels fall in the moderate to high range as expected. High and stable predictive relationships were reported between CogAT-5 scores and future scores on achievement tests, but predictive studies with the CogAT-6 are necessary to provide predictive evidence for scores from this measure.

Similar to the reliability evidence, no data were reported exploring similarity/differences in validity evidence across known groups. Also, given the discussion of accommodations in the administration guidebooks, it was surprising that no validity studies are reported regarding the impact of accommodations on the validity of scores from the CogAT-6.

COMMENTARY AND SUMMARY. The CogAT-6 has several strengths including a large and nationally representative standardization sample, conorming with the Iowa Tests of Basic Skills and the Iowa Test of Educational Development, group administration, and a theoretical basis. In addition, the items demonstrate adequate technical characteristics including fairness across known groups. Scores from the batteries also have demonstrated strong internal consistency and concurrent validity, and, to a lesser extent, convergent validity.

Despite these strengths, there are some significant weaknesses in the reliability and validity evidence relative to the intended purposes of the tests. Most importantly, there is no empirical evidence presented in the test materials to support the use of test scores for instructional recommendations. Thus, it is not recommended to use the CogAT-6 for this purpose at this point in time. In addition, the lack of reliability (short- and long-term) and predictive validity evidence based on the current form of the CogAT precludes a strong endorsement of this measure for the other two stated purposes (measuring cognitive ability and predicting cognitive ability—achievement discrepancies) until such studies are completed. Additional convergent validity studies and exploration of psychometric properties across various groups (e.g., students with disabilities, race, English language learners) within the target population also should be explored in future studies.

REVIEWER'S REFERENCES

Carroll, J. B. (1993). *Human cognitive abilities: A survey of factor-analytic studies*. Cambridge, UK: Cambridge University Press.

Cattell, R. B. (1987). *Intelligence: Its structure, growth, and action*. Amsterdam: North-Holland.

Lohman, D. F. (2003a). *The Wechsler Intelligence Scale for Children III and the Cognitive Abilities Test (Form 6): Are the general factors the same?* Retrieved on January 15, 2005 from University of Iowa, College of Education website: http://faculty.education.uiowa.edu/dlohman/.

Lohman, D. F. (2003b). *The Woodcock-Johnson III and the Cognitive Abilities Test (Form 6): A concurrent validity study*. Retrieved on January 15, 2005 from University of Iowa, College of Education website: http://faculty.education.uiowa.edu/dlohman/.

Vernon, P. E. (1961). *The structure of human abilities* (2nd ed.). London: Methuen.

Review of the Cognitive Abilities Test, Form 6 by BRUCE G. ROGERS, Professor Emeritus of Education, University of Northern Iowa, Cedar Falls, IA:

DESCRIPTION. The Cognitive Abilities Test (CogAT), Form 6, measures reasoning abilities related to learning and problem solving for three basic purposes: (a) to help adapt instruction to the abilities of students, (b) to provide a measure of cognitive development as an alternative to achievement measures, and (c) to identify students whose ranking on aptitude is discrepant from their ranking on achievement. The CogAT reflects a strong theoretical tradition of P. E. Vernon and R. B. Cattell, and builds on it by attempting to incorporate current theoretical concepts from cognitive psychology.

CogAT, Form 6, consists of two separate sections, a Primary Battery (Grades K–2) and a Multilevel Battery (Grades 3–12). Each of these consists of three content Batteries, namely, Verbal, Quantitative and Non-Verbal.

Many innovations have been made for this new form. The three manuals, Interpretive Guide for Teachers, Interpretive Guide for School Administrators, and Research Handbook, have been updated and substantially expanded. The K Level is now administered in six sessions of about 30 minutes each, whereas all of the levels above that are administered in three sessions of about 40 to 50 minutes. Each of the three batteries at Grades K–2 contain two tests. At Grades 3–12 they each consist of three tests. (The names of these tests are listed in the descriptive information for this test.) The test booklets are professionally prepared, with clear pictures and print that is easily readable. The Instructions for Administration are complete and written clearly. The test administrators should carefully read these instructions in advance for proper preparation and to anticipate possible questions from the pupils.

In the Primary Battery, the test administrator reads the multiple-choice items orally and sets their own pace. At the K–2 level, the options are presented to the pupil as pictures. Because the test administrator is responsible for watching the pupils to see that they are responding according to the directions, teacher aids can be of vauable assistance.

All of the items in a particular subtest are arranged in ascending order of difficulty within modules and these modules are then combined to form the subtest for a given level. Thus, the test has Guttman scale ordered properties, similar to that of the Binet test. Because the test administrator must determine the level for the pupil, recommendations are given for selecting the suitable test level, including how to conduct "out of level" testing when appropriate.

DEVELOPMENT. In 1954, the Lorge-Thorndike Intelligence Tests by Irving Lorge and Robert Thorndike were first published. These tests were specifically designed to appraise those general abstract reasoning skills most likely to be used in educational settings. They reported only a verbal, a nonverbal, and a total score; and they were given to children in Grade 3 and above. In subsequent revisions, the following changes were made: a Primary test, with a single score, was added to extend the test down to kindergarten; the word "Intelligence" was deleted from the test title, to avoid the many misconceptions of that word; the quantitative items (in the verbal section) were extracted, to create a purer measure of verbal ability and to create a separate quantitative measure; and the name was changed to Cognitive Abilities Test to emphasize the cognitive theory. The separate reporting of a quantitative score can be questioned because the verbal and quantitative scores share over 70% variance in common. However, the authors chose to retain the quantitative score, because it is recognized as being distinct from the verbal scale both theoretically and practically in educational settings.

TECHNICAL.

Standardization. In the spring of 2000, Form 6 was standardized concurrently with the ITBS and ITED to generate both norms and predicted scores. The national norming process was carefully planned and executed. For the Public School sample, all public school districts in the nation were stratified into nine enrollment categories, four geographic regions, and five socioeconomic status (SES) strata. In each of the resulting 180 cells, districts were selected at random and invited to participate until one accepted. Catholic schools were sampled according to similar procedures, as were private schools.

After the districts were selected, school buildings were selected, but further details on participation rates were not made available. The CogAT was administered in each of the selected schools following the same procedures as prescribed in the manual. In the resulting data, the proportion of pupils in each stratification category was adjusted by appropriate weighting to approximate the national percentage. Separate norm tables were then produced for each of the three subtests. Age norms and grade norms are provided for all levels. Age norms are reported at 3-month intervals for ages 5 through 18. Grade norms are reported for fall, mid-year, and spring for Kindergarten through Grade 12. Local norms can be created by the publisher upon request.

The number of correct answers for a student constitutes the raw score, which is converted into a Universal Scale Score (USS), a developmental scale. The USS was developed using item response theory techniques. For each of the content batteries, the Rasch Model, a one-parameter (item difficulty) model, was used to create a continuous scale across all levels. USS scores from the three batteries were averaged to create the composite score.

The USS was then converted into the Standard Age Score (SAS), Percentile Rank (PR), and Stanine (S). The SAS scores are deviates on a normal curve with mean of 100 and standard deviation of 16. The authors write, "Sometimes SAS scores are mistakenly referred to as IQ scores. The term *IQ* should be used only for scores that are derived by dividing the mental age by chronological age" (Guide for Administrators, p. 48). Although this is technically correct (because SAS is a deviation score), it can be misleading to the reader, because SAS is a measure of intelligence. The Guide for Teachers states that "the Composite score on *CogAT* operationally defines *G* as the average scaled score on the three batteries" (p. 57). But the ratio IQ is also an operational definition of *G*. Basically, there are two operational definitions of *G*. Although the ratio IQ and the deviation IQ are operationally distinct, they are both estimates of the same parameter, *G*. If it were not so, there would be no need to involve the writings of Vernon, Cattell, and Carroll on the hypothetical construct *G*.

Item fairness. Several steps were taken to investigate the fairness of the test items in terms of ethnic and gender differences. Items were carefully reviewed by panels of classroom teachers and professional educators. In addition, the national tryout data were analyzed for differential item functioning (DIF), and the results are tallied in the Research Handbook. Overall, less than one-half of 1% of the items favored one group over another. The tests do appear to meet the conditions for fairness.

Reliability. To assess the internal consistency of scores for the CogAT, each subtest was analyzed with the Kuder Richardson formula 20 (KR20). Subtest reliabilities are quite high with a median value about .90 in the Primary Battery and about .94 in the Multilevel Battery. Stability coefficients are also shown, from data gathered within a time span of less than 21 days, for each level of each battery, with a median value of about .85. Because Form 6 has only been recently published, evidence for long-term stability was reported for Form 5, which had been given in Grades 3, 6, and 9 in a certain Midwestern school district. Median correlation values for 3-year intervals and 6-year intervals were about .80 and .75, respectively. It seems reasonable to expect similar results for Form 6. Estimates of the standard error of measurement (*SEM*) are also provided. These were used to calculate the confidence intervals, which are shown on the score reports, a useful feature.

Validity. In the discussion of content validity, a description of the construction of the items is given. This is appropriate; however, evidence is not provided that other experts had evaluated those procedures. In the future, such evidence would enhance the content validity of the test. Evidence for criterion-related validity is shown in the tables of correlations with ITBS and ITED. Mention is also made of ongoing studies of correlations with other intelligence tests. These data are all supportive of the criterion-related validity of scores from the CogAT.

Evidence for construct validity is the most extensive. A factor analysis of the Primary Battery shows a strong *G* factor and an interpretable verbal factor. For the Multilevel Battery, a strong *G* factor is shown and an interpretable factor associated with each of the batteries. These data support the claim that the CogAT measures an abstract hypothetical construct called cognitive ability and intelligence.

Predicted scores and discrepancies. One of the purposes of the CogAT is to provide an alternative measure of cognitive development when the scores are compared with achievement scores such as ITBS or ITED. Because there are strong correlations between the subtests of these, it is expected that percentile ranks would be comparable. When ITBS scores are regressed on CogAT scores, it is expected that the resulting predicted scores would be comparable to the actual scores. Unfortunately, the Guide for Teachers does not discuss this topic, but the Guide for Administrators does have a good discussion. About 40 years ago, Robert Thorndike wrote on what he called "overachievement" and "underachievement," and his explanations are reflected in the good discussions in the Interpretive Guide for Administrators and the Interpretive Guide for Teachers and Counselors.

Score profile interpretation. A strong feature of Form 6 is the development of what are called Score Profiles. On the score report, the three battery scores are plotted on a graph with confidence intervals around them. It is easy to see if there is overlap among the confidence intervals. Next to the graph is a Profile Narrative Report, which explains the interpretation of the graph. This report, which is written by the computer, is about 100 to 200 words in length. For each type of profile, the Guide for Teachers gives a discussion and suggestions for instructional adaptations. This feature is relatively new, so teachers are asked to try it and write their impression of its effectiveness. The authors have expended much effort to develop this new aspect and it has the potential of providing new contributions for the use of aptitude tests.

SUMMARY. The Cognitive Abilities Test, Form 6, is a major revision of a widely used group-administered aptitude measure, which has been in existence for about half of the twentieth century. The two distinguished authors have made important changes to further enhance its usefulness. It now contains three batteries, called Verbal, Quantitative, and Non-Verbal, which were developed to be compatible with two major theories of intelligence and cognitive ability. Three supporting manuals, written in clear, readable form for teachers and administrators, provide help and score interpretation, along with technical data to support it. The test booklets are attractive and the test content appears to meet high technical standards. We advise any serious user to read both the Guide for Administrators and the Guide for Teachers to gain the most from this valuable instrument. Because of its use in conjunction with the Iowa Tests of Basic Skills (ITBS) and the Iowa Tests of Educational Development (ITED), previous forms have been widely used in the schools, and this revision will likely continue, and perhaps increase, its acceptance by educators.

[56]
Cognitive Abilities Test 3 [British Edition].

Purpose: Designed to assess "an individual's ability to reason with and manipulate different types of material that play substantial roles in human thought—that is words, quantities and shapes."

Population: Ages 7:6-17 and older.

Publication Dates: 1973–2003.

Acronym: CAT3.

Scores, 12: Verbal (Verbal Classification, Sentence Completion, Verbal Analogies, Overall); Quantitative (Number Analogies, Number Series, Equation Building, Overall); Non-verbal (Figure Classification, Figure Analogies, Figure Analysis, Overall).

Administration: Group.

Levels: 8 overlapping levels: A, B, C, D, E, F, G, H.

Price Data, 2003: £27.50 per specimen set (specify Levels A–D, C–F, or G–H); £3.75 per pupil booklet (specify level); £4.25 per 10 answer sheets (specify level); £11.25 per set of 2 scoring overlays (specify level); £10 per administration manual (2003, 115 pages); £12.50 per technical manual (2001, 56 pages).

Time: 94(180) minutes.

Comments: On-line administration available.

Authors: David F. Lohman, Robert L. Thorndike, and Elizabeth P. Hagen, adapted by Pauline Smith, Cres Fernandes, and Steve Strand.

Publisher: NFER-Nelson Publishing Co., Ltd. [England].

Cross References: See T5:561 (2 references); for reviews by Bert A. Goldman and Stephen H. Ivens of the U.S. Edition, see 13:71 (23 references); see also T4:537 (19 references); for reviews by Anne Anastasi and Douglas Fuchs of an earlier U.S. edition, see 10:66 (13 references); for a review by Charles J. Ansorge of an earlier edition, see 9:240 (5 references); see also T3:483 (32 references),; for reviews by Kenneth D. Hopkins and Robert C. Nichols, see 8:181 (12 references); for reviews by Marcel L. Goldschmid and Carol K. Tittle and an excerpted review by Richard C. Cox of the primary batteries, see 7:343.

Review of the Cognitive Abilities Test 3 [British Edition] by MARK D. SHRIVER, Associate Professor, Pediatric Psychology, Munroe-Meyer Institute for Genetics and Rehabilitation, University of Nebraska Medical Center, Omaha, NE:

DESCRIPTION. The third edition of the United Kingdom version of the Cognitive Abilities Test (CAT3) was derived largely from the sixth edition of the Cognitive Abilities Test (CogAT6) used in the United States (55). The CAT3 was designed to assess cognitive abilities that have significant positive correlations with important societal and educational criteria in the United Kingdom. "CAT3 assesses general reasoning abilities and a pupil's capacity to apply these abilities to verbal, quantitative, and non-verbal tasks" (technical manual, p. 2). The CAT3 is a paper-and-pencil test administered in a group format and is intended for students from age 8 years [7.5 years according the publisher's website] through age 17 and above. There are multiple levels of the CAT3 that correspond with student grade levels based on the educational systems in England and Wales, Scotland, or Northern Ireland. Levels A through F were developed together and are intended for the last three levels of primary school and first three levels of secondary school. Levels G—H were developed separately after the development of Levels A through F and are intended for the later years of secondary school and beyond.

The CAT3 includes three batteries: Verbal, Quantitative, and Non-Verbal. At all levels, each battery consists of three subtests. The Verbal Battery includes subtests titled Verbal Classification, Sentence Completion, and Verbal Analogies. The Quantitative Battery includes subtests titled Number Analogies, Number Series, and Equation Building. The Non-Verbal Battery includes subtests titled Figure Classification, Figure Analogies, and Figure Analysis. Information is provided in the administration manual regarding scoring, score interpretation, using test results, and norms. Scoring can be completed by hand, but it is highly recommended that users take advantage of computer scoring available through the publisher. Given the number of test items and group administration format, this recommendation makes sense. Although the levels of the test correspond to grade levels (probably to ease test administration), the scores are reported in terms of standard age scores, percentile ranks corresponding to standard age scores, and stanines corresponding to standard age scores. Scores can be obtained for individual subtests, batteries, and an overall or total test mean score. For individual and most group interpretation purposes, the authors recommend analysis of the battery scores. The total test score is primarily used as a basis for predicting future performance on other assessments of academic related performance such as the General Certificate of Secondary Education (GCSE) public examination.

DEVELOPMENT. The theoretical foundation for the CAT3 is the same as for the CogAT6. The authors of the CAT3 write that the test is based on the model of cognitive abilities proposed by Vernon (1961) and the model of cognitive abilities described by Cattell and Horn (Cattell, 1987; Horn, 1985). The primary contribution of Vernon's theory appears to be largely structural in that Vernon proposes a three stratum theory of the structure of intelligence and the CAT3 has a three stratum hierarchy of structure. Essentially, the subtests are at the lowest level of the hierarchy and support the second level consisting of the three batteries. The three batteries contribute information about "g" or general cognitive ability of the student, the highest or top level of the hierarchy. All three batteries are proposed to include subtests that measure fluid analytic abilities as described by Cattell and Horn. The Verbal and Quantitative batteries also include subtests that measure crystallized abilities (e.g., achievement) as described by Cattell and Horn.

Although there is an earlier edition of the CAT3, namely the CAT2E developed in 1984, the CAT3 items were drawn from and developed directly based on the CogAT6 that was being developed in the United States in 1999. Information regarding how items and subtests were developed for the CogAT6 is not provided in the administration or technical manuals and users must refer to CogAT6 manuals directly or to reviews of the CogAT6 for this information. The CAT3 differs from the CogAT6 in that the Quantitative Relations subtest from the Quantitative Battery of the CogAT6 was replaced with the subtest Number Analogies. It is reported in the technical manual that, "This was because it was felt that Quantitative Relations necessarily relied too much on mathematical attainment rather than reasoning processes" (technical manual, p. 7). Empirical justification is not provided for this change. Information about how items were developed or identified for initial piloting of this new subtest is not provided. In addition, "a substantial number [of CogAT6 items] needed adaptation or replacement, particularly in the Verbal Battery" (technical manual, p. 7). Many items were replaced by items drawn from the CogAT5 or new items written by the CAT3 developers. One third to two thirds of the verbal items were anglicized. For example, a question about Ground Hog day was replaced by a question about Robin Hood.

For users familiar with the CAT2E, notable differences in the CAT3 include dropping the

Vocabulary subtest from the CAT2E, adding a Figural Analysis subtest in the Non-Verbal battery in place of the Figure Synthesis subtest, adding an instruction and practice section at the start of each subtest in place of the full length practice test administered with CAT2E, and creation of Levels G and H. Empirical information about item development, particularly how decisions were made regarding dropping items, subtests, including new items and subtests, and revising items is not provided. More empirical and logical rationale for item and subtest development would provide the user with important information regarding how the theoretical foundation, test purpose, and test development relate to each other. The empirical and logical linkages between these important variables are not presented in the technical or administration manuals.

Two forms of each subtest for the Years 4, 5, 7, and 9 (England) were developed. Schools were selected for trialing (piloting) and each school was administered one battery (three subtests). Between 216 and 312 students were included in each level (4, 5, 7, or 9). The parallel forms were administered in an alternative fashion within each class. It is unclear how many students took each subtest during the trial study. Analyses of item difficulty, discriminability, and gender differences were conducted. Items were ordered according to level of difficulty and six levels (A through F) were created.

Levels G and H were developed and piloted separately from Levels A—F. A single form was created based on items from Level F, new items, unused items from A—F, and a few CogAT items. Between 237 and 269 students in 24 schools were administered one of the batteries from the trial form. Analysis of item difficulty, discriminability, and gender differences were conducted and the two levels (G/H) were created. The piloting procedures in the development of the CAT3 are a clear strength. However, the empirical and theoretical basis for initial item development is unclear for Levels G and H as well as Levels A—F.

Differential item function (dif) analyses were conducted based on gender for all Levels of the CAT3. In addition, dif analyses were conducted based on students' ethnicity for all Levels of the CAT3. It is apparent that particular care was given to ensuring that test data did not reflect gender or ethnic specific variables. The technical manual is also clear in stating that children's backgrounds should be considered when interpreting low scores. The atten-

tion to gender, ethnicity, and background variables as variables that may affect test performance is a strength of the development of the CAT3.

TECHNICAL.

Standardization. The sample in the standardization of the CAT3 is very large and reflective of the wide spread use of the CAT2E in the United Kingdom. It appears that adequate attention was given to ensuring a representative sample. A total of 15,859 students were included in the initial standardization sample for Levels A—F and 3,623 students for Levels G—H.

Reliability. Internal consistency was analyzed using Kuder-Richardson (KR-20) reliability coefficients based on the entire initial standardization sample. With only two exceptions (.83 for Figure Analysis in the Non-Verbal Battery at Level F and .82 for Figure Analysis in the Non-Verbal Battery at Level E) the KR-20 coefficients were uniformly high (mid to high .80s and .90s) across subtests and batteries for Levels A—F. The KR-20 reliability coefficients were just a bit lower on average across subtests and batteries for Levels G—H with overall battery coefficients in the low to mid .90s and most subtest coefficients in the .80s.

No other reliability information is presented for the CAT3. At a minimum it would seem that information regarding the stability of the test data over time (test-retest) should be provided. In addition, Standard Error of Measurement (*SEM*) for scores would be helpful in judging the reliability of the test scores.

Validity. The manual describes two sources of validity evidence; analyses of the factoral structure of the CAT3 and correlations with other tests. Pearson correlations between subtests and exploratory factor analysis lend support for the structure of the test. Factor analysis was not conducted for Levels G—H. Intercorrelations between subtests for Levels G—H were all positive and the vast majority were above .50. A "vast majority" (technical manual, p. 28) of students in the standardization sample also were administered Teacher Assessments of National Curriculum levels in English, Mathematics, and Science. No other information regarding this sample of students is provided. Pearson correlations were computed between the CAT3 and the Teacher Assessments and indicated moderate correlations ranging from .45 to .77 for the mean CAT3 score and the different levels of the Teacher Assessments. Higher correlations with the Teacher Assessments are noted between the higher levels of the CAT3 (D—F) relative to the lower levels of the CAT3 (A—C).

Given the widespread use of the CAT2, correlations were also computed between the CAT2E and CAT3. A total of 10,240 students in 422 schools were administered both versions (CAT2E or CAT3) with the order of administration counter-balanced. Average correlations of battery raw scores adjusted for test unreliability were high (.80 for Non-Verbal, .91 for Quantitative, and .90 for Verbal Battery). Data from the equivalence study were used to compute score conversion tables for the CAT2E and CAT3 to allow for continuity of comparison of test performance across time.

Evidence regarding the predictive validity of the CAT3, one of the primary purposes for its use, can be found on the publisher's website. The publisher is continually collecting data from administrations of national tests given in England and Scotland. The publisher is clear that test users should consider that CAT3 scores predict a potential range of scores and that test users should use CAT3 scores as only one variable of many in analyzing current student performance. It would be helpful if the publisher would provide additional information about *SEM*s and confidence intervals in the technical manual to assist test users in evaluating the reliability of CAT3 scores.

COMMENTARY. The trialing and standardization of the CAT3 are strengths of this measure. Likewise the consideration of gender and ethnic variables in test performance and through dif analysis is a strong feature of the CAT3 test development. Internal reliability of scores is high. Factor analysis of the test structure and subtest correlations support the structure of the test, and lend some support to the construct validity of the test. Test users will find the publisher's website as well as the on-going collection of data to support the validity of the test for predicting performance on important educational indicators particularly useful.

There is a need for test developers to provide additional information that more clearly links the process of item and test development with the stated purposes of the test and with the purported theoretical foundation. There is also a need for empirical evidence for the stability of scores across

time. Similarly, evidence should be provided regarding the *SEM* for scores and confidence interval to facilitate interpretation of score reliability and predictability. Although predictive validity evidence (correlations with national education test indicators) can be found on the publisher's website, it seems that because this is a primary purpose of the test, more preliminary evidence for the predictive validity of the CAT3 scores should have been gathered and presented in the manual. In addition, empirical evidence supporting the purposes of the test for assessing general reasoning abilities and applying them to verbal, quantitative and nonverbal tasks is needed. This would involve demonstrating moderate to high positive correlations with other tests designed to measure similar constructs.

SUMMARY. With reason, the CAT2E appears to have enjoyed widespread use in the United Kingdom. Given the history of its predecessors, it may be expected that the CAT3 will also enjoy success as a useful measure for evaluating students' cognitive abilities, group differences, and predicting future achievement. The CAT3 will probably be most useful for standardized normative group comparisons. The analysis and progress monitoring of academic skills for individual students is probably most effectively accomplished through direct skills assessment in the student's curriculum (e.g., Shapiro, 2004).

REVIEWER'S REFERENCES

Cattell, R. B. (1987). *Intelligence: Its structure, growth and action*. Amsterdam: North Holland.

Horn, J. L. (1985). Remodeling old models of intelligence. In B. B. Wolman (ed.), *Handbook of intelligence: Theories, measurements and applications*. New York: Wiley.

Shapiro, E. S. (2004). *Academic skills problems: Direct assessment and intervention* (3rd ed.). New York: Guilford.

Vernon, P. E. (1961). *The structure of human abilities* (2nd ed.). London: Methuen.

Review of the Cognitive Abilities Test 3 [British Edition] by SUSANA URBINA, Professor of Psychology, University of North Florida, Jacksonville, FL:

DESCRIPTION. The Cognitive Abilities Test 3 (CAT3) is designed to assess reasoning ability by means of tasks that require the manipulation of verbal, quantitative, and spatial or figural materials and concepts. The CAT3 can be used to evaluate individual potential and learning styles as well as to provide the bases for a variety of decisions concerning the educational process. It consists of three batteries-Verbal, Quantitative, and Non-verbal-each of which in turn comprises three subtests: Verbal Classification, Sentence Completion, and Verbal Analogies, in the Verbal battery; Number Analogies, Number Series, and Equation Building, in the Quantitative battery; and Figure Classification, Figure Analogies, and Figure Analysis, in the Non-verbal battery. Thus, the CAT3 yields a total of 12 scores, 9 subtest scores plus an overall score for each battery.

The CAT3 is the British equivalent of the Cognitive Abilities Test—Form 6 (CogAT6), but it does not include tests comparable to those in the two lowest levels of the CogAT6. Its intended target population consists of students from England, Wales, Scotland, and Northern Ireland in the age range of 8 to 17+ years.

Administration of the timed subtests of the CAT3, which are arranged in an overlapping multilevel format, takes 94 minutes for Levels A–F (ages 8 to 15 years) and 91 minutes for Levels G and H (ages 14 to 17+ years). However, approximately twice that amount of time needs to be provided to accommodate all aspects of the testing, such as instructions and practice questions for each subtest and recommended break periods. Test materials include a separate test booklet and answer sheet for each level as well as a technical manual and an administration manual.

Scoring the CAT3 can be accomplished by hand with the use of a scoring overlay—in which case scores are recorded on a Group Record Sheet—or by computer. Raw scores for each subtest and battery can be converted to Standard Age Scores (SAS), percentile rank (PR) scores, and stanines. The computer scoring service also provides individual profiles for each student, graphs and reports on groups, as well as options to obtain additional indicators of projected performance on British national tests and examinations.

DEVELOPMENT. Like the CogAT, the CAT3 draws on Vernon's (1961) hierarchical model of human abilities and Cattell's (1987) model of fluid and crystallized abilities. Whereas all three of the CAT3 batteries assess the inductive and deductive reasoning skills that typify the fluid and analytic aspects of the general abilities continuum, the Verbal and Quantitative batteries necessarily rely more heavily on crystallized abilities that require the use of knowledge acquired through schooling. The average SAS on the three batteries may therefore be construed as a gauge of general cognitive ability or *g*.

Almost all the trial items for the CAT3 Levels A through F were drawn from the CogAT6,

with the exception of those that were deemed unsuitable for British children and had to be either replaced or adapted. In addition, the Quantitative Relations subtest of the CogAT6 was entirely discarded and replaced with a set of new items that comprise the Number Analogies subtest of the CAT3. Two parallel forms of each subtest were prepared and one or the other of these was administered to samples of children-stratified by school performance—from four age levels in 228 schools from throughout the British Isles. Levels G and H of the CAT3 were developed later, to provide a measure appropriate for the last 2 years of secondary schooling, through procedures similar to those used for Levels A through F.

Data from the trial items were analyzed for difficulty level, ability to discriminate between high and low scorers, as well as for differences in difficulty across sexes. These analyses were used to select and order items for the standardization version and to either eliminate or counterbalance those favoring one sex or the other. For Levels G and H, a single trial form with items from various sources was created and data from this form were analyzed and used in ways similar to the data from Levels A–F.

TECHNICAL. Standardization of Levels A–F of the CAT3 took place in schools from throughout England, Wales, Scotland, and Northern Ireland during the Fall of 2000; Levels G and H were standardized in the Spring of 2003. A total of 15,859 students participated in the standardization of Levels A–F and 3,623 were involved in this process for Levels G and H. These samples included approximately equal numbers of females and males at Levels A–F and a somewhat higher number of females (53%) at Levels G–H. Eighty-six percent of students in the A–F sample and 89% of those in the G–H sample were White and the rest were from a variety of ethnic groups originating from Africa, Asia, and the Caribbean. Data from these samples were weighted to ensure that norms would be representative of the ethnicities found in the British population. At some of the lower level (A–D) schools where the CAT Second Edition (CAT2E) was in use, students were given only one of the CAT3 batteries in the standardization process; students at every other school took all three batteries. In addition, studies aimed at equating CAT3 and CAT2E scores were conducted concurrently with the standardization of Levels A–F.

Means and standard deviations of the raw scores obtained by the standardization samples on every subtest and battery for all eight levels of the CAT3 are presented in the technical manual, along with the maximum raw scores possible and the mean raw scores expressed as percentages. Most of the figures indicate an appropriate range of difficulty for the subtests at each level. Tables for converting raw scores on the batteries to standard age scores (Mean = 100, SD = 15) and stanines are provided in the administration manuals for each age group from 7:06 to 17:00 or above, at intervals of 3 months. Tables for converting raw scores on subtests to stanines are also provided for all ages, at 6-month intervals.

Differential item functioning (DIF) analyses were carried out on the standardization data of the CAT3 to check for any remaining sex-related differences and to examine the extent and direction of differences across ethnic groups. These analyses suggest a good balance in the total number of items favoring females and males, with somewhat more items favoring females in the Verbal Battery and more favoring males in the Quantitative and Non-verbal batteries. Ethnically related DIF results reflect a larger number of items favoring the White ethnic majority group over the pooled non-White group (62 versus 51) in Levels A–F, but an equal number of items favoring each of these groups at Levels G–H. Mean scores for students in various ethnic categories are also presented and reveal some striking differences among these groups, such as a distinct tendency for Chinese students to excel in the Quantitative and Non-verbal battery scores, compared to White students and others, especially so in the two highest levels of the CAT3.

Reliability. Kuder-Richardson 20 (KR20) values were computed for all subtest and battery scores at every level of the CAT3. For Levels A–F, subtest reliabilities ranged from .82 to .95, with 27 out of 54 coefficients at or above .90; the KR20 values for scores on the three batteries at Levels A–F ranged from .94 to .97. For Levels G–H, subtest KR20 values were somewhat lower, ranging from .81 to .90, with 17 out of 27 coefficients at or above .85; comparable values for the three batteries at Levels G–H ranged from .93 to .95. In general, these figures suggest that the batteries and subtests sample relatively homogeneous and coherent sets of cognitive abilities.

The technical manual provides information useful for evaluating differences between scores on different subtests of the CAT3 or between scores on the same subtest taken on different occasions. This information includes the standard error of differences as well as tables showing percentages of students who obtain differences of certain magnitudes and direction across occasions and across batteries. Some guidance on judging the practical significance of obtained differences among scores is also provided.

Validity. Two sources of validity evidence are presented in the CAT3 technical manual. The first consists of tables displaying the intercorrelations of scores on the subtests and batteries along with results of exploratory factor analyses of those data for each level of the CAT3. The second source of evidence of validity stems from correlations between CAT3 scores and teacher assessments of educational progress.

Intercorrelations of within-battery subtests are highest for the Verbal Battery-ranging from .68 to .83—as would be predicted based on the language requirements common to the verbal subtests. With the exception of the correlations between Figure Classification and Figure Analogies, which are mostly in the .50s, the within-battery relationships across the Quantitative and Non-verbal subtests are in the .60s and .70s. The pattern of correlations between subtests from the three batteries is, on the whole, consonant with the nature of the underlying cognitive tasks. So, for example, the highest intercorrelations between subtests across batteries are those obtained for the Verbal, Numerical, and Figure Analogies subtests.

Factor analyses of the subtest data reveal a distinct patterning, with the three Verbal subtests showing their highest loadings on Factor 1, the three Quantitative subtests on Factor 2, and the three Non-verbal subtests on Factor 3. This three-factor solution, arrived at using oblique rotation, accounted for 80% of the variance. Intercorrelations among the factors ranged from .61 to .72, underscoring the fact that all of the CAT3 subtests assess reasoning processes.

Teacher Assessments (TAs) of National Curriculum levels in English, Mathematics, and Science were correlated with both the raw and standardized scores of the CAT3. As expected, the highest correlations (.50 to .71) were between the TAs in Mathematics and scores on the Quantitative Battery and between the TAs in English and scores on the Verbal Battery (.53 to .67). The lowest correlations obtained were those between the various TAs and the Non-verbal Battery (.37 to .64); this finding is explained by the fact that nonverbal abilities, as opposed to verbal or quantitative abilities, are typically not developed through direct instruction.

COMMENTARY AND SUMMARY. The CAT3 is a well-constructed, carefully developed, and thorough revision of an instrument for the assessment of reasoning abilities that is widely used in the United Kingdom. Prior to standardization, the CAT3 was subjected to extensive trials and fairness analyses; the scope and procedures of the standardization itself were exemplary. In addition, this revision incorporates changes that have resulted in streamlining the administration of the test and reducing the influence of confounding factors on test performance, as well as in a more effective targeting of difficulty levels.

Altogether, the CAT3 appears to be well suited for its stated purpose of measuring inductive and deductive reasoning abilities in the linguistic, quantitative, and figural or visual-spatial realms. The inclusion of a Non-verbal Battery provides an opportunity for students who are deficient in verbal and numerical skills to demonstrate their ability to reason through an additional avenue. Nevertheless, the CAT3 manual properly cautions users that the test may be inappropriate for children from disadvantaged or non-Western backgrounds who have had limited exposure to the kinds of activities common to school and home environments in the UK.

REVIEWER'S REFERENCES

Cattell, R. B. (1987). *Intelligence: Its structure, growth, and action.* Amsterdam: North Holland.
Vernon, P. E. (1961). *The structure of human abilities* (2nd ed.). London: Methuen.

[57]

College ADHD Response Evaluation.

Purpose: Designed to assess ADHD in postsecondary students.
Publication Date: 2002.
Acronym: CARE.
Administration: Individual.
Forms, 2: Student Response Inventory, Parent Response Inventory.
Price Data, 2003: $120 per complete kit including manual (144 pages), 25 each of student inventory, parent inventory, student profile, and parent profile;

$50 per manual; $49 per 25 inventories and 25 profiles (specify student or parent).
Time: 10–15 minutes.
Comments: Oral administration permitted.
Authors: Joseph Glutting, David Sheslow, and Wayne Adams.
Publisher: Psychological Assessment Resources, Inc.
a) STUDENT RESPONSE INVENTORY.
Population: College students.
Scores, 6: Inattention, Hyperactivity, Impulsivity, Total Score, DSM-IV Inattentive, DSM-IV Hyperactive/Impulsive.
b) PARENT RESPONSE INVENTORY.
Population: Parents of college students.
Scores, 5: Inattention, Hyperactivity, Total Score, DSM-IV Inattentive, DSM-IV Hyperactive/Impulsive.

Review of the College ADHD Response Evaluation by MARY "RINA" M. CHITTOORAN, Associate Professor of Educational Studies, Saint Louis University, St. Louis, MO:

DESCRIPTION. The College ADHD Response Evaluation (CARE) is an "assessment system" (manual, p. 1) designed to screen for symptoms of Attention Deficit Hyperactivity Disorder (ADHD) in a college-age population (between the ages of 17 and 23. The CARE consists of the 59-item Student Response Inventory (SRI), the 46-item Parent Response Inventory (PRI), and a comorbidity screener to identify concurrent deficits in psychological functioning. The SRI includes four empirical scales (Inattention, Hyperactivity, Impulsivity, and Total Score) and two clinical scales (DSM-IV Inattentive and DSM-IV Hyperactive-Impulsive) whereas the PRI includes three empirical scales, Inattention, Hyperactivity, and Total Score and the two DSM-IV clinical scales.

Ratings on the SRI and PRI may be completed in under 15 minutes by students and parents respectively, who have at least a sixth grade reading level. Responses on the carbon-backed rating form are automatically transferred to a scoring page. Results of the CARE may be interpreted according to two normative frameworks (the average college student and the general population), and two interpretive systems (empirical, factor scores; clinical, DSM-IV scores). Raw scores may be converted to T-scores (Mean = 50; SD = 10) using separate norms tables for the whole group, males, or females; however, percentile ranks are preferred for interpretive purposes. When the SRI or PRI college norms are used, a score between the 92nd and 96th percentiles on both factor and DSM-IV scales indicates that the student is At Risk for ADHD, and a score at or higher than the 97th percentile is considered High Risk. When a student's performance is compared with the general population, six or more questions with a score of 2 on either the DSM-I, DSM-HI scales, or both, may suggest a classification of ADHD Inattentive, ADHD Hyperactive-Impulsive, or ADHD-Combined. The CARE may be used by a variety of assessment personnel with minimal training in test administration; on the other hand, experience in test interpretation is highly desirable.

DEVELOPMENT. The initial pool of CARE items was generated on the basis of reviews of the literature on ADHD, clinical experience of the authors, and interviews with over 20 helping professionals. The item pool was reduced to 160 items subsequent to scrutiny by content experts. An item tryout was conducted using a sample of 680 students (mean age = 19.2 years) from 32 states; all students were enrolled at one Northeastern university, and all had SAT scores above the national average for same-age peers. Forty-two percent of the sample were male and the rest were female. With regard to race/ethnicity, 92.9% were Anglo, 6% African American, and the rest represented other backgrounds. Results of the item tryout revealed that ADHD was a multidimensional construct and that the CARE had superior internal consistency and predictive ability.

TECHNICAL. The CARE was standardized in 1999–2000 on a matched, weighted sample of 1,080 college freshmen between the ages of 17 and 23 (Mean = 18.7; SD = .7) and their parents. Of the students, 78.5% were Anglo, 10% were Black, 3.9% were Hispanic, 4.7% were Asian, and 2.9% were Other. Students in the sample represented 38 states in the Northeast, Mid-Atlantic, Northwest, and Southwest corridors of the United States and included 540 males and 540 females.

Exploratory factor analyses with the SRI revealed a three-factor structure—Inattention, Hyperactivity, and Impulsivity—that reflected the DSM-III-R, rather than the DSM-IV model of ADHD. Exploratory factor analyses with the PRI revealed a two-factor model, similar to that of the DSM-IV, that was supported by confirmatory factor analyses and replicated across genders. Generally, results of factor analyses indicated superior

construct validity, although the factor-based scores were more accurate than the DSM-IV scores in screening for ADHD.

The discriminant validity of the CARE was examined by comparing scores of 58 students with ADHD/their parents to those of 1,022 students without ADHD/their parents. The divergent validity of the CARE was explored by comparing 39 students with learning disabilities (LD) with 1,041 students without learning disabilities; results indicated that the CARE diagnosed constructs related to ADHD more consistently than constructs related to LD. Finally, convergent validity was documented by comparing the scores of 56 students on both the CARE and the Brown Attention-Deficit Disorder Scales.

Internal consistency was evaluated using Cronbach's alpha, with obtained coefficients for the SRI that ranged from a low of .63 for the DSM-IV Inattentive Scale to a high of .90 for the Total Score. For the PRI, coefficients ranged from .74 on the DSM-IV Hyperactive-Impulsive Scale to .89 for the Total Score. Results were consistent across males, females, and the Total Sample. Test-retest reliability was examined using data from 51 participants who were given the CARE twice during a period of 30–60 days. Coefficients ranged from a low of .77 for the Impulsivity scale to a high of .91 for the Combined Score.

COMMENTARY. The CARE was developed by individuals with considerable expertise in assessment and test development. It is unique in that it represents the first systematic effort to screen for ADHD in a college-age population and that it employs both parent and student perceptions of behavioral symptoms of ADHD. The technical manual is unusually complete; it includes detailed descriptions of important test constructs and simplified, but thorough discussions of various test development methods. Test materials are relatively inexpensive, directions for administration and scoring guidelines are simple and convenient, and interpretation of results is facilitated by the inclusion of sample protocols and profile forms. Test development and standardization appear to have been comprehensive, and the two sets of norms allow college students to be compared, both to other students like them, and to the general population. Further, the empirical and clinical scales are useful across a variety of populations and settings. Construct validity evidence is superior, at least as far as the factor scales are concerned, and discriminant and divergent validity evidence are adequate. The CARE exhibits superior internal consistency and test-retest reliability.

Despite its positive features, the CARE includes some features that are of some concern. Person-first terminology is not used consistently; for example, the manual refers to "post-secondary ADHD students" (p. 57) instead of "post-secondary students with ADHD." There appear to be inconsistencies in the manual that range from varying estimates of time needed for completion to different names for the individual scales. The DSM-IV scales seem to be less accurate than the factor scales in identifying ADHD; this, coupled with the fact that the DSM-IV is due for a revision, suggests a cautious interpretation of the clinical scales.

The item tryout sample was limited, given that it was based only on students from one Northeastern university and the manual does not specify whether the standardization sample included rural, urban, and suburban populations. Although the authors claim that the CARE claims is useful for students between the ages of 17 and 23, the standardization sample used only *freshmen* who were between these ages; it is possible that 17–23-year-old *nonfreshmen* could rate themselves differently than their freshman same-age peers because they might have learned to manage their behaviors. Convergent validity evidence from using the CARE and the Brown should be viewed with some caution, given that the two tests measure slightly different constructs in different age groups. Assessment of content validity and face validity appear to have been part of the original item tryout but are not mentioned in subsequent analyses. An additional measure of predictive validity might also have been useful. Test-retest reliability was not examined for the PRI because parents were unavailable for a second testing; however, this information is important and should be included. An examination of interrater reliability, with both parents rating their child, would have been helpful, especially as there is some research supporting differential parental ratings of the same behavior in children. Split-half reliability coefficients would also have been a desirable addition to the technical documentation for the CARE.

Use of the PRI may be problematic for a number of reasons. Confidentiality issues related to students who are no longer minors coupled with the historic difficulty of obtaining completed rating forms from parents who live at a distance from their children, may render the PRI difficult to administer. Further, the validity of parent reports is somewhat questionable, given that parents are asked to provide information, going back at least 10 years, about specific problem behaviors in their children. It may also be unrealistic to ask parents to comment on problem behaviors in their 5–8-year-olds that are common in *all* young children, regardless of whether or not they have ADHD; for example, all children this age are distracted by extraneous stimuli (Item 23), have difficulty with fidgeting and squirming (Item 42), and running around and climbing on things in stores or when visiting friends (Item 44). Finally, there are some ambiguous statements ("I am anxious ... most days"; SRI Item 7) and undesirable grammatical errors (e.g., "interrupted *peoples'* conversations or activities"; SRI Item 21).

SUMMARY. The CARE is a multi-informant, multidimensional measure of ADHD in a college-age population. Its strengths lie in the fact that it is the only measure of its kind presently available; that it is technically superior in many respects; that it is simple to administer, score, and interpret; and that student ratings may be confirmed by parent ratings of the same behavior. It may be very useful as a preliminary, screening measure of ADHD if the factor scales, rather than the clinical ones, are used. It should not, as the manual indicates, be used as a stand-alone measure of ADHD and must be followed up with a more comprehensive assessment of this complex condition.

Review of the College ADHD Response Evaluation by WILLIAM K. WILKINSON, Consulting Educational Psychologist, Boleybeg, Barna, Co. Galway, Republic of Ireland:

DESCRIPTION. The College ADHD Response Evaluation, or CARE, is designed to assess ADHD symptoms in the college population. The authors note the need for an assessment system specific to the college population because of the increasing awareness of the chronic nature of ADHD and how this disability relates to a growing number of university student requests related to said condition.

The CARE consists of two rating scales, one for student completion (Student Response Inventory—SRI) and one for parent completion

(Parent Response Inventory—PRI). The forms consist of 59 and 46 items, respectively. Rater responses are marked on a perforated scoring sheet that allows the scorer to add totals for the scales. Scale score totals can be transferred to Profile sheets for both the SRI and the PRI.

Raw scores are transformed to percentile ranks. For the SRI, the scale scores follow the traditional subtyping of ADHD as Inattentive, Impulsive, and/or Hyperactive. A total score is also available. If percentile rank scores are significantly elevated, the respondent is considered "At Risk" or "High Risk." The PRI follows a similar format, with the exception that factor analytic studies did not support an "Impulsivity" factor.

In addition, the CARE contains a DSM-IV interpretative system where items follow the core descriptions provided in the DSM-IV manual. This interpretative framework is available for both the SRI and PRI.

Finally, the CARE contains a Comorbidity Screener. Specifically, some of the items on the rating scales are relevant to the numerous and frequently coexisting conditions related to ADHD (e.g., depression, anxiety, substance use, disruptive behavior disorders). This is not a norm-referenced scale, but simply "alerts" the interpreter to possible areas in need of further consideration.

The manual accompanying the CARE is very detailed and thorough in most areas. In the manual, the authors include extensive discussions regarding AD/HD, the purpose of the test, the delimitations of their work, extensive technical information, and a clear rationale for most decisions made (e.g., establishing the cutscore for "At-Risk"). Also, the manual consists of clear guidelines regarding use and interpretation of the CARE.

DEVELOPMENT. The standardization sample consists of 1,080 college students (age 17 to 22, with a mean age of 18.7) and their parents, with the selection closely approximating the national average regarding race, gender, and ability. The sample was selected from four geographically distinct areas—Northwest, Southwest, Mid-Atlantic, and Northeast.

There is a brief discussion of item tryout and a reference to an empirical study related to it. Given the thoroughness of the manual, I am surprised that the authors did not include a more detailed discussion of how the initial item set was pared to the final totals on the scales.

TECHNICAL. Technical data/presentation is one of the strongest aspects of the CARE. The statistical development of the test is very thorough, especially the factor analytic support of the derived scales. In addition, there are convergent validity data regarding the CARE and the Brown Attention-Deficit Disorder Scales and these correlations are statistically significant in constructs that should converge (e.g., some correlations >.70). In general, there is ample evidence that the CARE is valid with regard to distinguishing a sample of ADHD college students from their non-ADHD counterparts.

Likewise, the reliability data for the test are more than adequate. There is no technical information regarding the Comorbidity Screener but this is consistent with the authors' desire that this information be used simply to orient the test user to other possible factors in the respondent's presentation. The Screener is not an empirically derived scale.

COMMENTARY. One of the most refreshing aspects of the CARE is the authors' extended discussion of the general construct being measured, such as its course, the need for the CARE, and appropriate cautions about it. For example, the authors note that the CARE is not a diagnostic tool by itself. Rather, it provides reliable and valid information about a student's self-perceptions of ADHD-type behavior and similar information from the student's parents.

The student population is very clearly defined and generally well sampled. The authors note that their intention was to detect ADHD in the beginning stages of a student's college experience when issues related to ADHD may come to fore. In this regard, the CARE should serve a very useful purpose as part of a multidimensional assessment.

The separate interpretive frameworks are very helpful for the assessing clinician. One can use the empirically derived factor scales where the respondent is compared with other college students. Alternatively, one can use the DSM-IV items that follow the DSM-IV manual and involve a comparison with the general population. It is understood that one can use either system, or both. I could not find a discussion in the manual about why one should adopt a particular approach, other than the basis for the different systems. Likewise, I did not see reference to possible differences in meeting cutoff criteria for the different interpretive approaches. Could one obtain discrepant results, within or across interpretive systems, using the gender or general norms? Inevitably, choice increases complexity.

SUMMARY. After reviewing the CARE materials, I concur with the authors that they have developed a technically sound assessment system related to the detection of AD/HD in the college student population. In this regard, CARE is a state-of-the-art instrument that should prove very useful to clinicians who predominately work with young adults in higher education.

The authors should be commended regarding the conceptual and technical development of the CARE. There is a great deal of information about the conceptual underpinnings of the CARE. Likewise, the authors go to great lengths to justify issues such as (a) the cutoff score adopted in determining "risk," (b) how to integrate discrepant results on student and parent ratings, and (c) how to interpret various outcomes (chapter 3 in the manual is devoted solely to interpretation, with several completed SRI and PRI forms as examples). It is in this chapter that the authors could clarify the questions raised in the "Commentary" section of this review.

[58]
College Student Experiences Questionnaire, Fourth Edition.

Purpose: Designed to measure (a) the quality of effort undergraduate students invest in using educational resources and opportunities provided for their learning and development, (b) the students' perceptions of how much the campus environment emphasizes a diverse set of educational priorities, and (c) how the students' efforts and perceptions relate to personal estimates of progress made toward a holistic set of learning outcomes.
Population: Undergraduate college students.
Publication Dates: 1979–2003.
Acronym: CSEQ.
Scores, 19: Background Information, College Activities Scales (Library, Computer and Information Technology, Course Learning, Writing Experiences, Experiences with Faculty, Art, Music and Theater, Campus Facilities, Clubs and Organizations, Personal Experiences, Student Acquaintances, Scientific and Quantitative Experiences, Conversations), Reading/Writing, Satisfaction, The College Environment, Estimate of Gains, Additional Questions.
Administration: Group.
Price Data, 2002: $.75 per questionnaire; $1.50 per questionnaire processing; $125 participation fee (including student responses, scores, and a summary

report of the results); $15 per Norms for the Fourth Edition (2003, 178 pages); $100 per hour for special additional analysis.
Time: (30–40) minutes.
Authors: C. Robert Pace and George D. Kuh.
Publisher: Indiana University Center for the Study of Postsecondary Research and Planning, Bloomington.
Cross References: See T5:620 (6 references) and T4:588 (4 references); for reviews by David A. Decoster and Susan McCammon of an earlier edition, see 10:67; for reviews by Robert D. Brown and John K. Miller, see 9:246 (1 reference).

Review of the College Student Experiences Questionnaire, Fourth Edition by KURT F. GEISINGER, Vice President of Academic Affairs, Professor of Psychology, The University of St. Thomas, Houston, TX:

DESCRIPTION AND DEVELOPMENT. Colleges and universities in a competitive environment continually seek to upgrade themselves, and primary among their goals of self-improvement are the attempts to enhance student learning. To do so, they must recognize that learning occurs both inside and outside the classroom, and hence, improve both instructional and campus environments to help engage their students in the active process of learning.

The College Student Experiences Questionnaires (CSEQ) was first developed by C. Robert Pace in 1979, and the fourth edition is the first not under the primary direction of Pace. The assessment program has moved to Indiana University—Bloomington, which has been active in the study of student engagement and other related topics under the direction of George D. Kuh, one of the foremost experts in higher education assessment. The third edition of the CSEQ was published in 1990 (Pace, 1990), and the present version was changed in relatively minor ways, although the modifications are all improvements; many of them are updates, bringing the measure into the 21st century. (For example, there are broader age ranges reflecting the larger numbers of older students; accommodations not only for students who live on and off campus, but also for those who live within walking distance of campus; more majors are provided; racial and ethnicity categories are now consistent with the U.S. Bureau of the Census; and the contents of the majority of the scales are changed to reflect the perceptions of experts in the field.) A number of items were deleted because they were redundant. Wording of other items was improved based upon data collected over the past decade.

The CSEQ is an eight-page machine-scorable questionnaire. The first page contains instructions to the respondents, who are intended to be undergraduate college students, and who respond anonymously. Pages 2–6 contain questions that students answer with a #2 lead pencil. Major categories include Background Information, College Activities, Conversations, Reading/Writing, Opinions About Your College or University, The College Environment, and Estimate of Gains. At the end of the survey, there is also a section where an individual institution may add up to 20 college-specific questions. The longest and potentially most important section of the survey is that related to College Activities, which is broken into 11 sections: Library; Computer and Information Technology; Course Learning; Writing Experiences; Experiences with Faculty; Art, Music, Theater; Campus Facilities; Clubs and Organizations; Personal Experiences; Student Acquaintances; and Scientific and Quantitative Experiences. This section is also known as the Quality of Effort section because items under each of the above areas are summed to estimate the amount of effort a student has made in that specific domain. The Conversations section asks students how often they have discussed various topics of intellectual interest with others outside of class and how these conversations may have changed them. Both of the Conversations scales are also considered as Quality of Effort scales; thus, 13 Quality of Effort scales are computed. The College Environment section is another critical one. It contains seven scales that ask respondents to reflect upon the growth areas they believe the institution has emphasized in them to develop (e.g., "academic, scholarly, and intellectual qualities"; "aesthetic, expressive, and creative qualities"; "critical, evaluative, and analytic qualities"; "understanding and appreciation of human diversity"). This section also includes three scales related to the relationships students have with other students, administrative personnel, and the faculty. Combined, there are 10 environmental items. Finally, the section on Estimate of Gains is another critical section. This section asks students to approximate to what extent they believe they have grown in each of a number of academic skills, knowledge, and habits (e.g., "writing clearly and effectively," "developing

your own values and ethical standards"). A few other indices are also available. These include student-faculty interaction, cooperation among students, active learning, capacity for life-long learning, and experiences with diversity. These computed indices reflect responses from items in a variety of the sections throughout the instrument. Clearly, the CSEQ provides a wealth of information on the student perceptions of an institution of higher learning. As such, it has great potential when used in formative evaluation by the faculty and administrative leaders at a college or university. The publisher will prepare institutional reports for such use.

The manual for the instrument (Gonyea, Kish, Kuh, Muthiah, & Thomas, 2003) provides an excellent overview for users of the instrument and it is accessible by those who are informed about higher education, but not necessarily psychometricians. The instrument is built upon the model that student learning is the goal, that student engagement greatly impacts student learning, and that institutions of higher education can control or improve campus aspects to increase student engagement. As the authors note, "The more effort students expend in using the resources and opportunities an institution provides for their learning and development, the more they benefit" (Gonyea et al., 2003, p. 4). As noted previously, many schools undoubtedly use the CSEQ because it helps them determine how students perceive the institution across a wide range of variables, all found in the literature to be important environmental and instructional concerns.

TECHNICAL. The measurement characteristics and psychometrics of the CSEQ have been frequently studied. As noted by the authors and others (DeCoster, 1989; Gonyea et al., 2003; McCammon, 1989), the items on the scale are clearly written. The wording appears appropriate for virtually any grouping of undergraduate students for whom English is the language of instruction. For each of their quality of effort scales the authors provide interitem correlations and coefficient alpha estimates of internal consistency reliability. These reliability estimates range from .70–.92, which is probably quite reasonable, especially for a measure that is not used in a high stakes manner and for which individual scores are far less likely to be critical than the means of students from a class year or institution. Some evidence of test-retest reliability would be useful.

Validation is primarily addressed through content and construct validity. That the authors and others using the instrument are at the forefront of the student engagement and higher education assessment literatures helps to insure that the coverage is good. It has been used in considerable research in higher education. That the instrument has emerged in a fourth edition with improvements with each edition is further indirect evidence of good coverage. That other experts in the field (Ewell, 1997; Ewell & Jones, 1994) have found the instrument appropriate, and have found the instrument useful in assessing critical dimensions of higher education is evidence of its content validity. One minor criticism that could be made about the instrument is that all of the items are written so that a high rating is most positive. Although this format is both logical and reasonable, it also could contribute to response styles from the student respondents, such as the "halo effect." Instructions to those completing the survey should emphasize the importance of carefully reading each item individually.

Among the sources of construct validation are factor-analytic and correlational data. Factor analyses suggest, for example, that the individual Quality of Effort scales are unifactorial, with the exception of the Campus Facilities factor (Gonyea et al., 2003). A number of results of the CSEQ measure have been consistent with the model of student engagement. The authors have looked to see if student responses fit hypothesized patterns. Expected differences have been found between residential and commuter students, for example, and differences among majors have also been in line with expectations (Gonyea et al., 2003; Kuh & Hu, 1999; Michael et al., 1983). As Pike (1995) has found, there are substantial correlations among self-reported gains and scholastic achievement test scores. Indeed, Michael, Nadson, and Michael (1983) found that predictions among CSEQ scales and achievement proved to be as high as would be expected between a measure of academic aptitude such as the SAT and subsequent academic achievement. For this reason, with the omnipresent requirement by accrediting bodies that schools work to improve themselves and document these improvements through outcomes assessment, many schools have used the CSEQ and other measures similar to it to document their successes and to develop plans to address relative weaknesses.

Factor analyses of the Environment and Gains factors have provided useful findings. Three Environmental factors have been noted: Scholarly & Intellectual Emphasis, Vocational & Practical Emphasis, and Quality of Personal Relations. Five Gains factors have been found: Personal Development, Vocational Preparation, Science & Technology, Intellectual Skills, and General Education. The manual also provides considerable evidence of the intercorrelations among the various scales.

One of the greatest contributions of the fourth edition of the CSEQ is the development of new norms tables. "Over 100,000 students have completed the College Student Experiences Questionnaire Fourth Edition since 1998" (Gonyea et al., 2003, p. 41). Norms are available in a manner in which students and schools are appropriately indexed in a matrix approach. That is, students are broken into freshmen, sophomore, junior, and senior classes. Schools are broken into Doctoral-Extensive, Doctoral-Intensive, Master's-Comprehensive, Baccalaureate-Liberal Arts, and Baccalaureate-General categories. The norms are most extensive, as expected, for Doctoral-Extensive and Master's Comprehensive universities, but there are almost 8,000 students represented in even the smallest of categories (Liberal Arts Colleges). Norms data are available for each of these categories for every item, for the various computed scales, factors, and indices. Thus, an institution can see not only how they have achieved in a raw numerical sense, but also with respect to appropriate comparisons. These norms provide considerable interpretive assistance to users of the CSEQ.

SUMMARY. In conclusion, there are a number of competitor measures for the CSEQ. The CSEQ is a comprehensive measure that can be used to provide formative feedback to an institution. This time-tested content appears quite comprehensive and the ability to add up to 20 additional items permits an institution to evaluate other components of the campus or education that they might wish to consider. The research basis for the instrument is extensive, the model supporting the measure impressive, and the psychometric quality, especially the extensive norms, is strong. Schools intending to improve, or facing accreditation visits are likely to find it very helpful.

REVIEWER'S REFERENCES

DeCoster, D. A. (1989). [Review of the College Student Experiences Questionnaire.] In J. C. Conoley & J. J. Kramer (Eds.), *The tenth mental measurements yearbook* (pp. 197–199). Lincoln, NE: Buros Institute of Mental Measurements.

Ewell, P. T. (1997). Identifying indicators of curricular quality. In G. Gaff & J. Ratcliff (Eds.), *Handbook of the undergraduate curriculum* (pp. 608–627). San Francisco: Jossey-Bass.

Ewell, P. T., & Jones, D. P. (1994). Data, indicators, and the national center for higher education management systems. *New Directions for Institutional Research, 82*.

Gonyea, R. M., Kish, K. A., Kuh, G. D., Muthiah, R. N., & Thomas, A. D. (2003). *College Student Experiences Questionnaire: Norms for the Fourth Edition.* Bloomington, IN: Indiana University Center for Postsecondary Research, Policy, and Planning.

Kuh, G. D., & Hu, S. (1999). Unraveling the complexity of the increase in college grades from the mid-1980s to the mid-1990s. *Educational Evaluation and Policy Analysis, 21*(3), 1–24.

McCammon, S. (1989). [Review of the College Student Experiences Questionnaire.] In J. C. Conoley & J. J. Kramer (Eds.), *The tenth mental measurements yearbook* (pp. 199–201). Lincoln, NE: Buros Institute of Mental Measurements.

Michael, J. J., Nadson, J. S., & Michael, W. B. (1983). Student background and quality of effort correlates of reported grades, opinions about college, and perceptions of magnitudes of cognitive and affective attainment by students in a public comprehensive university. *Educational and Psychological Measurement, 43*, 495–507.

Pace, C. R. (1990). College Student Experiences Questionnaire, Third edition. Los Angeles: University of California, Center for the Study of Evaluation.

Pike, G. R. (1995). The relationships between self reports of college experiences and achievement test scores. *Research in Higher Education, 36*, 1–22.

Review of the College Student Experiences Questionnaire, Fourth Edition by M. DAVID MILLER, Professor of Educational Psychology, and J. MONROE MILLER, Graduate Student, University of Florida, Gainesville, FL:

DESCRIPTION. The Fourth Edition of the College Student Experiences Questionnaire (CSEQ) consists of over 150 items primarily designed to assess college students' quality of effort (i.e., the relationship between efforts to use institutional resources/opportunities and their benefits). Additional scales include demographics, the college environment, estimates of gains, student-faculty interactions, active learning, cooperative learning, capacity for life-long learning, and experiences with diversity. Although primarily for summative assessment, the CSEQ is increasingly being used in formative assessments, especially when used in conjunction with the College Student Expectations Questionnaire (CSXQ).

The current edition can be administered using a paper-and-pencil version or online. Most response options use either a Likert scale or a semantic differential rating scale format. After administration, responses are scanned at the University of Indiana Center for Postsecondary Research and Planning. Reports include raw data for each student that can be imported into statistical software packages, an extensive SPSS output of descriptive and frequency data for the institution, and a codebook. Other options include additional item generation for the online version, the CSEQ

Norms for the Fourth Edition, and the student advising reports.

DEVELOPMENT. The First Edition, developed by Dr. C. Robert Pace, was introduced in 1979. The current edition is an update from the Third Edition in 1990. The CSEQ, originally designed at the University of California at Los Angeles, is now housed at the University of Indiana–Bloomington (www.iub.edu/~cseq). Changes from the Third Edition include scales targeting human diversity and information literacy added to the college environment section as well as items targeting presenting ideas/information and adapting to change added to the estimate of gains section. Overall, the number of items is about the same for the Third and Fourth Editions.

The CSEQ extends the typical examinations of the relationship between demographic variables and learning outcomes to include student experiences. Specifically, prompted by findings from the National Center of Educational Statistics in 1991, the CSEQ includes the interaction between the characteristics of the student and the environment of the campus as an indicator of "quality of effort." Borden (2001) reports the CSEQ as one of only a few assessments that inventory both learning processes and outcomes progress.

The items in the current edition of the CSEQ include those that target (a) demographics, (b) college activities, (c) college environment, and (d) estimates of gains. Additional scales target student-faculty interaction, active learning, cooperative learning, capacity for life-long learning, and experiences with diversity. Specifically, the items targeting college activities assess quality of effort through 13 scales (e.g., library experiences, course learning, campus facilities). Response options use a 4-point Likert scale measuring frequency of experiencing an event ranging from *Never* to *Very Often*. Responses to 10 scales with items targeting the college environment use a 7-point Likert scale indicating perceived strength of the college's emphasis on a particular topic (e.g., development of academic, scholarly, and intellectual qualities; being critical, evaluative, and analytical). Responses to 25 scales with items targeting estimates of gains use a 4-point Likert scale indicating perceived progress toward specific goals (e.g., using computers and other information technology; writing clearly and effectively) ranging from *Very Little* to *Very Much*.

TECHNICAL. Norming is based on a sample of approximately 87,000 students. The CSEQ Norms for the Fourth Edition provide 79 pages of norm tables for background items, individual items, and scales. Norms are presented as both frequencies and percentages; they are disaggregated by year in school and type of institution.

Evidence for statistical quality is provided through (a) adequacy of variance in responses, (b) acceptable examinations of distribution normality, and (c) minimal impact of missing data. The standard error of measurement for the scales ranged from .00 to .03. Skew ranged from −.7 to .8; kurtosis ranged from −.7 to .7. Missing data ranged from .1% to 3.4%.

Reliability was assessed using Cronbach's alpha for scales as well as reporting intercorrelations between items of individual scales. For quality of effort, the range of alpha coefficients was from .74 to .92. For college environment, the range of alpha coefficients was from .70 to .75. For gain estimates, the range of alpha coefficients was from .78 to .87. Most items were moderately correlated between .30 and .40.

Validity was assessed using multiple methods including a review of the content and multiple empirical procedures. Content representativeness and relevance was assessed through expert agreement. Experts also examined the loadings from a factor analysis. The analysis suggested that the campus facilities scale of the quality of effort section loads on two factors. All other scales loaded on a single factor. Overall, the factor analysis with oblique rotations of the principal factors was consistent with scale expectations. Construct validity was also assessed using blocked hierarchical regression suggesting convergence for theoretically related scales.

COMMENTARY AND SUMMARY. The CSEQ has a long history of development and use, and has changed consistent with growth in the theoretical understanding of college student learning processes and outcomes. Its major strengths are (a) administration history including over 30,000 students in the United States, (b) citation in over 250 sources, (c) extension to internet testing, (d) multiple methods of examining reliability and validity with reasonable results, and (e) revisions consistent with advancement in empirical and theoretical research. The CSEQ Norms for the Fourth Edition provide more comprehensive information

including respondent descriptive information, the norm tables, and bibliographic references as well as concise explanations for interpreting tables, computing effect sizes, and determining sampling error. The website, located at www.indiana.edu/~cse, provides additional information for the CSEQ and CSXQ as well as quarterly updates.

REVIEWERS' REFERENCE

Borden, V. M. H. (2001). *Measuring quality: Choosing among surveys and other assessments of college quality.* Washington, DC: American Council on Education.

[59]

College Student Inventory [part of the Retention Management System].

Purpose: Designed to assess "a variety of motives and background information related to college success," improved student retention, and enhancing student advising effectiveness.

Population: Candidates for college entrance.

Publication Date: 1988.

Acronym: CSI.

Scores: 4 Domains: Academic Motivation (Study Habits, Intellectual Interests, Academic Confidence, Desire to Finish College, Attitude Toward Educators), Social Motivation (Self-Reliance, Sociability, Leadership), General Coping Ability (Ease of Transition, Family Emotional Support, Openness, Career Planning, Sense of Financial Security), Receptivity to Support Services (Academic Assistance, Personal Counseling, Social Enhancement, Career Counseling).

Administration: Group.

Price Data: Available from publisher.

Time: (60) minutes.

Author: Michael L. Stratil.

Publisher: Noel-Levitz.

Review of the College Student Inventory [part of the Retention Management System] by MICHAEL H. CAMPBELL, Director of Residential Life and Food Service, New College of Florida, Sarasota, FL:

DESCRIPTION. The College Student Inventory (CSI) is a 194-item instrument used as the primary assessment tool for the Retention Management System (RMS), which seeks to improve retention of first-year college students. Most of the items are presented in a Likert format; the CSI also provides academic and personal background information useful to advisors. The comprehensive RMS seeks to "foster effective communication between students and their advisors" (coordinator's manual, p. 3). The manual uses a broad definition of advisor. Counselors, academic advisors, faculty members, or other trained staff may work with students to interpret results, identify resources for support, and make referrals.

The CSI itself provides scores on 19 separate subscales that comprise five main content areas: Academic Motivation, Social Motivation, General Coping Skills, Receptivity to Support Services, and Initial Impression. Reports present subscale scores as percentile ranks. A Summary of Academic Motivation section provides stanine scores for the following scales: Dropout-Proneness, Predicted Academic Difficulty, Educational Stress, and Receptivity to Institutional Help. Higher stanine scores suggest greater risk. The CSI also contains an internal validity measure designed to identify students who responded randomly to questions.

Noel-Levitz presents results in three targeted reports: The RMS Advisor/Counselor Report, the RMS Student Report, and the RMS College Summary and Planning Reports. The Student Report omits the Summary of Academic Motivation section and the Initial Impression score.

The manual provides very detailed recommendations for administration of the test. The most essential point is that administration should take place as early as possible during the term, because this allows timely intervention with at-risk students. Summer orientation is an ideal time for administration. The manual suggests allowing 1–1.5 hours to ensure that all students have sufficient time to finish. Noel-Levitz provides computerized scoring via postal mail within 7 days of receipt of completed questionnaires.

DEVELOPMENT. The instrument was first published as the Stratil Counseling Inventory (1971). The manual provides somewhat telegraphic detail on item development procedures other than a general statement of the goal "to identify the specific motivational variables that are most closely related to persistence and academic success in college" (p. 165). The author states that the subscales were not derived from factor analytic procedures; rather, it is stated that "great care was taken to ensure that the nuances in each item were appropriate to that intent" (p. 167). The manual states that the current (1998) version of the instrument incorporates changes based on field-testing, further statistical analyses, and expert input. Additionally, the manual states that the Dropout-Proneness scale was derived via multiple regression analyses from a 1987 national validity study (n = 3,048)

and that the Predicted Academic Difficulty scale was developed by correlating individual CSI items with first-term GPA.

TECHNICAL.

Standardization. The normative sample for the most recent (1988–1991) validity study included 4,915 students from 46 postsecondary institutions in the U.S.A. The manual provides a thorough summary of demographic characteristics of the institutions; unfortunately, the author does not report the demographic characteristics of the participants. Nonetheless, several characteristics of the institutional sample merit mention as potential limitations of the generalizability of the sample. First, 61% of the institutions are private. Second, the majority of institutions have enrollments of fewer than 5,000 students; only two institutions reported enrollments of more than 10,000 students. The majority of institutions reported average entering SAT and ACT scores below 930 and 18, respectively. No institutions reported average entering SAT scores above 1,100 or ACT scores above 26.

Reliability. The manual reports that the average Cronbach's alpha for the 19 subscales is .80. The author correctly notes that this compares favorably with the internal consistency of other well-known instruments; this is especially impressive given that the typical subscale length is only around 8 items. The author does not report reliability coefficients for each subscale, although doing so would provide useful information. The manual reports test-retest reliability coefficients in the same range. Overall, reliability estimates are acceptable.

Validity. The manual presents considerable documentation of content, construct, and criterion-related validity evidence. Evidence for content validity appears to be less well established. The CSI items were selected on a content-driven basis. In addition, Stratil employed a defensiveness scale to exclude items that tended to elicit favorable responses. However, the manual reports no additional empirical assessment of content validity.

Construct validity of the CSI is bolstered by high interscale correlations and the empirical documentation of a single-factor structure of the CSI as a whole. The manual asserts that the CSI taps a single construct termed "risk level" or "ability to succeed and persist in college" (p. 167). Additionally, the manual cites evidence that students who drop out have significantly higher risk scores on nine of the subscales than students who persist, even when controlling for high school GPA. Although the one-factor solution may support construct validity, this simultaneously presents problems with the discriminant validity of the individual scales. The essential issue is that, if all scales are reducible to a single factor, the distinctions among scales are not clearly relevant.

The manual reports criterion-related validity data based on national studies in 1987 and 1988–1991. The 1987 study demonstrated that students who dropped out differed significantly, regardless of college GPA, from those who persisted on z scores for the Desire to Finish College subscale. Additionally, academically successful students (i.e., those with a GPA > 2.0) differed significantly from others on the following subscales: Study Habits, Intellectual Interests, Academic Confidence, and Attitude Toward Educators. The 1987 study also demonstrated that first-semester GPA correlated significantly with Study Habits, Academic Confidence, Desire to Finish College, Attitude Toward Educators, and Openness Subscales.

The 1988–1991 study, which also provides the current normative data, demonstrated validity with regard to the criteria of college GPA and enrollment status at the beginning of second year. Parenthetically, the manual notes that second-year enrollment status is a conservative criterion, because it does not reflect persistence in later years.

The manual reports a correlation of .61 between "the various CSI scales" and first-year college GPA (p. 172). However, the presentation of these data is ambiguous. The manual does not indicate whether the correlation is an average across scales or a cumulative measure. Discriminant analyses demonstrated that the CSI subscales collectively classified 71.96% of students; however, this analytic strategy tended to overpredict persistence. Dropout-Proneness alone had a 58.84% hit rate but a much lower rate of false negatives. A subsequent discriminant analysis demonstrated that Dropout-Proneness, Family Emotional Support, Desire to Finish College, Study Habits, and Receptivity to Academic Assistance classified over 70% of students by GPA category; high school GPA correctly classified only 54%. Finally, an ANCOVA demonstrated that, when controlling for high school GPA, nine subscales were significantly associated with persistence.

COMMENTARY. The CSI is a simple and cost-effective method to identify at-risk first-year students for individual intervention and to inform macro-level policy change. The manual is a major strength. Although technical data could be more detailed in certain sections, the applied portions of the manual, especially those dealing with test administration, advisor training, and student counseling, are thorough and well written.

Neither the manual nor a preliminary literature review reveal a significant amount of peer-reviewed research on the CSI. McGrath and Braunstein (1997) are a notable exception; the authors found that the Initial Impression subscale and first-semester GPA accurately predicted retention in about 80% of cases. More external research would further substantiate the CSI's credibility.

The CSI's integration with the Retention Management System is a major advantage in applied settings. CSI scores are easily interpreted, and the prescriptive material for student advising and referral is well thought out, thorough, and excellently organized. One note of caution is that the CSI normative sample does not incorporate high-ability students or selective institutions. Although this limitation makes sense given the purpose of the test, the CSI does not have demonstrated utility for competitive colleges and universities.

SUMMARY. The CSI is a convenient, easily interpreted, and cost-effective instrument for identification of individual students who are at risk for attrition. Few competitors exist. The Retention Management System is a useful umbrella for counseling, referral, and larger scale policy change. Although the CSI would be bolstered by further independent research, the instrument is an excellent resource for colleges and universities seeking to promote retention of at-risk students.

REVIEWER'S REFERENCE

McGrath, M., & Braunstein, A. (1997). The prediction of freshmen attrition: An examination of the importance of certain demographic, academic, financial, and social factors. *College Student Journal, 31,* 396–408.

Review of the College Student Inventory [part of the Retention Management System] by THOMAS P. HOGAN, Professor of Psychology, University of Scranton, Scranton, PA:

DESCRIPTION. The College Student Inventory (CSI) is the central data collection instrument in the Noel-Levitz Retention Management System (RMS). The RMS consists of the reports, suggestions for use, and other supporting materials surrounding the CSI. Most of these supporting materials appear in a 229-page coordinator's manual (hereafter, the manual; Stratil, Schreiner, & Noel, 1993). The manual contains sections on administering the CSI, suggestions for interpretation, and a section labeled "technical guide" (to be distinguished from the guide mentioned below).

The CSI is a 194-item questionnaire. It has four parts. Part A contains simple identification information (name, age, etc.) not counted among the 194 items. Part B has 21 items on such matters as parents' education levels, self-report of admissions test scores, and highest degree sought. Part C has 158 simple statements answered on 7-point scales ranging from *not at all true* to *completely true*. Examples of the statements are "books have never gotten me very excited" and "I study hard for all my courses, even those I don't like." Part D consists of 15 items about initial impressions of the institution. Examples of questions are "the adequacy of financial aid" and "the faculty in general." Part D answers are on 7-point scales ranging from *very dissatisfied* to *very satisfied*. Embedded within Parts C and D is a type of validity-check item in which the student is simply asked to fill in a certain number for that item (e.g., "Enter a 3 for this question").

The CSI yields approximately 20 scores. We say approximately because the number of scales for which information is reported differs at various places in the manual and supporting materials. For example, the report for "Demonstration University" gives 23 scales, the sample Advisor/Counselor report gives 19 scales, and Appendix L: Brief Scale Descriptions gives 20 scales. Scales are generally organized into four major categories: Academic Motivation, Social Motivation, General Coping, and Receptivity to Support Services, each containing 3–5 scales. Examples of scales within each category are Study Habits, Sociability, Ease of Transition, and Career Counseling, respectively. The four major categories do not have total scores. There are also separate scores for Initial Impression (of the school) and Internal Validity. The RMS manual does not indicate which items go into each scale.

There is also a short form of the CSI, labeled Form B or CSI-B. It was apparently developed in the late 1990s; it is not mentioned in the 1993 manual. CSI-B has a copyright of 2000. With the appearance of CSI-B, the original CSI (long form) is now labeled CSI-A. Information about CSI-B is provided in The RMS Research and Technical Guide (hereafter, the guide; Stratil, 2001), an 87-page report providing more recent information on both Forms A and B. CSI-B has 100 items. According to the guide, CSI-B requires about 30 minutes to complete, whereas CSI-A requires about 60 minutes. Both forms are available in paper-and-pencil format; the guide notes that CSI-B is also available online. The major categories for reporting and the specific scales are similar but not identical in the two forms. The guide also mentions Canadian and Spanish versions, but these were not examined for this review. Although the guide provides new information about the CSI, there appears to be no updated version of the coordinator's manual relating the new information to actual use of the inventory.

The CSI yields three types of reports. One gives results for an individual student. Another summarizes results for an entire institution. A third type lists students in such categories as students with high dropout proneness, students needing academic assistance, and so on.

DEVELOPMENT. The original CSI was developed from the Stratil Counseling Inventory (Stratil, 1984). The coordinator's manual describes the CSI (long form) released in 1988. Both the RMS manual and the guide refer to goals of the various revision processes but do not adequately describe exactly how these goals were accomplished. For example, the documents refer to the desirability of having internally consistent scales but do not describe the procedures used to refine the scales. It is clear that CSI-B aims to be a shortened version of CSI-A, but the procedures for selecting items for CSI-B are presented only in general terms. The documents also refer to factor analyses of the respective item pools, but the results are not presented in sufficient detail to evaluate the outcomes. Thus, it is difficult to comment on the development procedures for the currently available forms. The publisher should undertake revision of the manuals to correct this deficiency.

TECHNICAL INFORMATION. The manual presents norms based on 4,915 students from 46 institutions, presumably from 1987. The manual gives minimal information about the nature of this group. However, it appears, based on information in the guide (p. 5), that the currently available norms are actually based on 14,999 students from 181 institutions for CSI-A in 1998; and 12,614 students from 62 institutions for CSI-B in 2000. No information is provided about the nature of these norm groups other than the number of students in 2-year, 4-year public, and 4-year private institutions. Further, the guide does not address the comparability of the groups for Forms A and B. Thus, the description of these norm groups is inadequate. It appears that the publisher assumes that the norms are comparable on the two forms. However, this assumption is not stated and no information is provided about the matter of comparability. The manual and the guide state that raw scores on the scales convert to percentile ranks and stanines. Conversion tables are not presented in either document. All reports examined by this reviewer employed percentile ranks as the reporting medium, although the manual refers to reports that use stanines. Interpretive materials did not refer to the problem of marked inequality of units at various points in the percentile scale.

Regarding reliability, the manual cites a median alpha coefficient of .80 for the scales and a median test-retest reliability of .80. It does not provide coefficients for the separate scales—a major deficiency in reporting. The guide does report alpha coefficients separately by scale. They range from .61–.90, with a mean of .80, for CSI-A; and from .62–.86, with a mean of .80, for CSI-B. The various interpretive materials seem oblivious to the fact that interpreting scores with reliabilities in the .60s is exceptionally hazardous. Reports for students and advisors examined by this reviewer never incorporate the concept of a standard error of measurement, which for some of these scales would be extremely wide, particularly in the central part of the percentile rank scale. The guide also cites a median test-retest reliability for CSI-A, again without giving data for separate scales. It appears that this paragraph in the guide was simply extracted from the earlier manual. It is not clear in either the manual or the guide what groups were used for the reliability reports.

The manual and the guide report a number of types of validity studies. There is also a separate Fall 2001 validity study, relating only to CSI-B (Noel-Levitz, undated). Factor analyses of the forms yielded results that accorded reasonably well but not exactly with the reporting categories actually used. Discussion of the results does not resolve the discrepancies between results of the analyses and the reporting categories. Several studies undertaken by the publisher as well as by other sources deal with the criterion-related validity of the instrument. Most of these studies use dropout status or general academic success (e.g., GPA) as the criterion. The results generally show that the CSI has some value for predicting both variables. The tendency to report "highly significant" results, with Ns in the thousands, is not helpful and is potentially misleading to the unwary. The guide does note that the absolute value of the prediction is not very high. The guide presents a number of very detailed reports on motivational styles of both men and women. Missing from the array of studies are any that relate to the stated purposes of improving communication between student and advisor.

COMMENTARY. To say the least, the overall configuration of the CSI and the array of publications supporting its use are confusing. The number of scales shifts unaccountably among various reports and parts of manuals. The relationship between the long form (CSI-A) and short form (CSI-B) is not always clear. Even the use of form designations is unfortunate because titles such as Form A and Form B usually denote equivalent forms, which these Forms A and B obviously are not. The exact purpose or purposes of the inventory are not clearly formulated. Some statements and analyses imply one or just a few specific purposes. The dominant purpose, as implied by the title Retention Management System, relates to dropout proneness. Other statements cast a much broader net. For example, the guide (p. 2) states that "The primary purpose of the RMS is to foster effective communication between students and their advisors." It also claims to "Assess students' individual academic and personal needs" and "Enable advisors to have effective and rewarding personal contact with students" (p. 2). These are exceptionally diverse goals for a single instrument. They call for a much broader program of validation than what is provided in the RMS publications. It appears that the CSI is pursuing too many different goals all at once. At the same time, it is shifting its structure and reports without allowing time for its published technical studies to catch up. The author and publisher should continue to pursue validation studies for the numerous stated purposes (or narrow the statement of purposes); greatly improve the description of the normative base and attend to the comparability of forms; and provide appropriate cautions about the reliability of the scales.

SUMMARY. The CSI is a promising source of information about new college students. It will certainly help to identify dropout-prone students. The supplementary reports, interpretive notes, and reference materials are appropriate and useful for retention-related uses. Additional work is needed to recommend the CSI for the multiplicity of other uses proposed for it. Although these other uses are plausible, the research base and its reporting for these other purposes should be coordinated and updated. The instrument, both its long form and short form, have more potential than what is realized in the currently published materials. The CSI has made some progress in providing the type of data needed for this type of instrument, especially in comparison with some of the homemade instruments circulating in the college entrance market. It can be made a better instrument.

REVIEWER'S REFERENCES

Noel-Levitz. (undated). *Fall 2001 validity study*. Littleton, CO: Noel-Levitz.
Stratil, M. L. (1984). *Stratil counseling inventory—College form*. Lumberton, NC: Psychological Configurations.
Stratil, M. L. (2001). *The RMS research and technical guide*. Iowa City, IA: USA Group Noel-Levitz.
Stratil, M. L., Schreiner, L. A., & Noel, P. (1993). *Retention management system coordinator's manual*. Iowa City, IA: USA Group Noel-Levitz.

[60]

Communication and Symbolic Behavior Scales Developmental Profile: First Normed Edition.

Purpose: Designed to "evaluate communication and symbolic abilities of children whose functional communication is between 6 months and 2 years."

Population: Ages 6–24 months.

Publication Dates: 1995–2002.

Acronym: CSBS DP.

Scores, 11: Social Composite (Emotion and Eye Gaze, Communication, Gestures, Total); Speech Composite (Sounds, Words, Total); Symbolic Composite (Understanding, Object Use, Total); Total.

Administration: Individual.

Levels, 3: Infant-Toddler Checklist, Caregiver Questionnaire, Behavior Sample.

Price Data, 2003: $399 per complete kit including manual (2002, 188 pages), 25 infant-toddler checklists, 25 caregiver questionnaires, 25 caregiver questionnaire scoring worksheets, 25 behavior sample scoring worksheets, 25 caregiver perception rating forms, 1 of each (Part 1 and Part 2) VHS sampling and scoring videos, and toy kit; $199.95 per test kit including manual, 25 infant-toddler checklists, 25 caregiver ques-

tionnaires, 25 caregiver questionnaire scoring worksheets, 25 behavior sample scoring worksheets, 25 caregiver perception rating forms, and 1 of each (Part 1 and Part 2) VHS sampling and scoring videos; $259.95 per toy kit; $65 per manual; $35 per 25 of each infant-toddler checklists, caregiver questionnaires, caregiver questionnaire scoring worksheets, behavior sample scoring worksheets, and caregiver perception rating forms; $25 per 50 caregiver questionnaires; $50 per VHS sampling and scoring video (specify Part 1 or Part 2).

Comments: May be used with children "up to 5–6 years if their developmental level of functioning is younger than 24 months."

Authors: Amy M. Wetherby and Barry M. Prizant.

Publisher: Brookes Publishing Co., Inc.

a) INFANT-TODDLER CHECKLIST.

Time: (5–10) minutes.

Comments: A screening tool completed by a caregiver; computer scoring available; may be administered independent of other components.

b) CAREGIVER QUESTIONNAIRE.

Time: (15–20) minutes.

Comments: Companion to the behavior sample completed by caregiver.

c) BEHAVIOR SAMPLE.

Time: (30) minutes.

Comments: A "face to face evaluation tool" conducted by professional evaluator with the caregiver present. The caregiver questionnaire is designed to "determine whether a child has a developmental delay or disability in the areas measured."

Cross References: See T5:630 (1 reference); for reviews by Steven H. Long and Dolores Kluppel Vetter of the original edition, see 13:76 (3 references).

Review of the Communication and Symbolic Behavior Scales Developmental Profile: First Normed Edition by KAREN T. CAREY, Professor, of Psychology, California State University,—Fresno, Fresno, CA:

DESCRIPTION. The Communication and Symbolic Behavior Scales Developmental Profile: First Normed Edition (CSBS DP) is a standardized instrument designed to assess communication and symbolic abilities of children with functional communication between 6 and 24 months of age. Children at ages 5 to 6 years can be assessed with the CSBS DP if their developmental age levels are below 24 months.

The CSBS DP measures social communication, expressive speech/language, and symbolic abilities through parent report and direct interaction with the child. The tool consists of three parts: An Infant-Toddler Checklist, a Caregiver

Questionnaire, and a 30-minute Behavior Sample of the child. All three parts take about 1 hour to administer. The examiner first uses the Infant Toddler Checklist to screen the child to determine if further assessment is necessary. If it is determined that further assessment is needed, the examiner administers the Caregiver Questionnaire and the Behavior Sample. The three parts measure seven cluster areas organized by three components: Social Composite, consisting of emotion and eye gaze, communication, and gestures; Speech Composite, including sounds and words; and the Symbolic Composite, composed of understanding and object use. The kit comes with two VHS sampling and scoring videos that can be used for learning to score the Behavior Sample portion of the scale.

DEVELOPMENT. The CSBS DP was adapted from the CSBS Caregiver Questionnaire and the MacArthur Communicative Development Inventories. Based on the authors' research of parent report information, a recognition format for the Caregiver Questionnaire was selected, in which the items are statements that the parent indicates he or she has observed. The Behavior Sample items were modified from the CSBS by reducing the number of scales and shortening the scoring system so that the examiner can assess the child quickly. The Behavior Sample consists of 20 scales: Emotion and Eye Gaze, which includes gaze shifts, shared positive affect, and gaze/point following; Communication, which includes rate of communicating, behavior regulation, social interaction, and joint attention; Gestures, which includes conventional gestures and distal gestures; Sounds, which includes syllables and consonants, and inventory of consonants; Words, which includes words, inventory of words, word combinations, and inventory of word combinations; Understanding, which includes language comprehension; and Object Use, which includes inventory of action schemes, action schemes toward one another, action schemes in sequence, and constructive play.

Sampling and scoring procedures were modified following studies with children who had or did not have communication problems. Using young children with these characteristics, the scale was developed over a period of time and scales that were less reliable or discriminating were eliminated from the CSBS DP. Of the 20 scales on the Behavior Sample, 19 were derived from the CSBS and the Gaze/Point scale was added based on a literature review.

TECHNICAL. Standardization consisted of 2,188 Infant Toddler Checklists, 790 Caregiver Questionnaires, and 337 Behavior Samples. The manual states that a parent or other caregiver completed the Infant Toddler Checklists and the Caregiver Questionnaires; however, no information on who other caregivers were or the numbers of other caregivers included in the sample are reported. Parents or caregivers were present when the Behavior Sample was conducted and each sample was videotaped. The videotapes were then scored by trained speech-language pathologists or graduate students in speech-language pathology.

Children included in the sample were primarily from the Tallahassee, Florida area for which the authors had knowledge, and children who were developmentally delayed or receiving early intervention services were excluded from the sample. Information related to race, parent age, and education is provided and although an attempt was made to equate the sample with the 2000 Census data, minority populations and parents with low education levels are not equally represented. The authors provide a caveat stating that the test should be used with caution with minority populations and with parents who have not completed high school. The CSBS DP is based on a mean of 100 and a standard deviation of 15 for the total scale with a mean of 10 and a standard deviation of 3 for the subtests.

Internal consistency was investigated using Cronbach's coefficient alpha. Results for the Infant Toddler Checklist ranged from .95 to .96 with an overall coefficient of .95; for the Caregiver Questionnaire, coefficients ranged from .95 to .97 with a total coefficient of .95; and for the Behavior Sample, coefficients ranged from .93 to .94 with a total coefficient of .92. (The values reported are the standardized coefficient alphas.) Standard errors of measurement for all clusters, composites, and total scores are reported in the manual along with confidence intervals.

Test-retest reliability was examined over one year of testing. On the Infant Toddler Checklist, 167 children were retested; on the Caregiver Questionnaire, retests were conducted with 128 children; and on the Behavior Sample, 76 children were retested. Coefficients on the total scores for each scale ranged from .86 to .93 and for the subtests from .65 to .93. These results are adequate for individual decision making.

Interrater reliability was investigated for the Behavior Sample as it is the only scale that requires judgment and the generalizability (g) or intraclass correlation coefficients between raters were calculated. Results revealed coefficients at .90 or above for composites and total.

Content, face, construct, criterion, concurrent, and predictive validity were all investigated and are described nicely in the manual. Content validity was supported through literature review and statistical findings; face validity was attributed to the naturalistic nature of the role of caregiver/parent as reporter and the use of behavioral observations. Four types of construct validity were evaluated: developmental progression of scores, intercorrelations, gender differences, and principal components analysis. Developmental progression was examined through an analysis of the growth and age differentiation of each skill. Intercorrelations were investigated by examining the item composites and clusters. Moderate correlations were found for most cluster scores when all ages were combined. Gender differences were analyzed by comparing two matched groups of males and females by race and age. Differences between the genders were noted on some scales, but the effect sizes were small. Principal components analysis was also conducted to examine the relationship between the 20 scales of the Behavior Sample. The three components of the Behavior Sample were supported as were the seven clusters.

As there are few similar scales, criterion validity could not be adequately documented. However, results of the concurrent and predictive validity studies indicated strong correlations between the three scales and good evidence of predictive validity across all three scales. In conclusion, the authors have done their homework with this scale and addressed the serious components of the *Standards for Educational and Psychological Testing* (AERA, APA, & NCME, 1999).

COMMENTARY. The authors of this test have developed a well-designed tool for use with young children. The primary problem with the CSBS DP is the lack of national norms. The limited sampling makes the use of the tool questionable for parts of the country other than the Florida area; however, the authors readily

acknowledge this problem as well as provide cautions for using the instrument with minority and low socioeconomic populations. The authors should be encouraged to conduct a national standardization of the instrument as it would be useful to many professionals working with young children. Furthermore, such a tool would be useful for the development of early intervention services for young children with communication delays.

SUMMARY. The CSBS DP is a well-designed instrument for use with young children; however, the lack of national norms makes its use somewhat limited. The needed reliability and validity evidence exists and meets the requirements of the *Standards for Educational and Psychological Testing* (AERA, APA, & NCME, 1999). Few tests of this type are available for use with infants and toddlers and it may be useful for those looking for a standardized measure for these populations.

REVIEWER'S REFERENCE

American Educational Research Association, American Psychological Association, & National Council on Measurement in Education. (1999). *Standards for Educational and Psychological Testing*. Washington, DC: American Educational Research Association.

[61]

Comprehensive Adult Student Assessment System—Third Edition.

Purpose: Designed to provide a measure to "place students in the appropriate program, level or test, diagnose student learning needs, monitor student progress and certify student proficiency levels."

Population: Adults.

Publication Dates: 1980-2004.

Acronym: CASAS.

Administration: Group.

Restricted Distribution: Agency training is required before test can be provided.

Price Data: Available from publisher.

Time: Administration times vary.

Comments: Third edition includes new technical manual; Computer scoring and individual and class score profiles available.

Author: CASAS.

Publisher: CASAS.

a) APPRAISAL TESTS.

1) *ESL Appraisal (English as a Second Language).*

Scores: 4 tests: Listening, Reading, Speaking, Writing.

Comments: Appraisal determines level of pretests of CASAS Life Skills Series to be administered.

2) *Life Skills Appraisal.*

Scores: 2 tests: Reading, Math.

Comments: Appraisal determines level of CASAS Life Skills Series Pre-Test to be administered.
3) *ECS Appraisal (Employability Competency System).*
Scores: 2 tests: Reading, Math.
Forms, 2: 120, 130.
Comments: Appraisal determines level of CASAS Basic Skills for Employability Pre-Test to be administered.
b) CASAS TESTS FOR MONITORING PROGRESS.
Comments: All test serve as pre/post tests.
1) *Employability Competency Series.*
   (a) Reading.
   Levels, 4: A, B, C, and D each with 2 forms.
   (b) Math.
   Levels, 4: A, B, C, and D each with 2 forms.
   (c) Listening.
   Levels, 3: A, B, and C each with 2 forms.
2) *Life Skills Series.*
   (a) Reading.
   Levels, 5: (Beginning Literacy, A, B, C, D), Beginning Literacy, Levels C and D each have 2 forms; Levels A and B have 3 forms.
   (b) Math.
   Levels, 4: A, B, C, and D each with 2 forms.
   (c) Listening.
   Levels, 3: A, B, and C each with 2 forms.
Cross References: See T5:645 (1 reference); for reviews by Ralph O. Mueller and Patricia K. Freitag and by William D. Schafer of a previous edition, see 13:78 (2 references).

Review of the Comprehensive Adult Student Assessment System—Third Edition by TERRI FLOWERDAY, Assistant Professor of Educational Psychology, University of New Mexico, Albuquerque, NM:

DESCRIPTION. The Comprehensive Adult Student Assessment System—Third Edition (CASAS) Employability Competency Series and Life Skills Series Tests is composed of a series of tests that can be used to evaluate student ability levels in Reading, Math and Listening. In addition, these tests can be used to monitor student progress toward learning goals and provide evidence of goal attainment through demonstrated competency. The emphasis is on functional life skill development in late adolescent and adult populations. The CASAS "provides learner-cen-

tered curriculum management, assessment, and evaluation" (technical manual, p. 1) for adult education and training programs. The CASAS can be used with all levels of adult basic education (ABE), English as a second language (ESL), adult secondary education such as GED programs, and employability and training programs for students functioning at or below high school level.

The system is used to assess competency in two primary areas: employability and life skills. The test items in the Life Skills series focus on basic abilities and applications that are considered necessary to function effectively in modern society. The Employability Competency items focus on the students' ability to perform tasks that are directly related to jobs and the workplace. "Either test series can be used in a pre- and post-test design to provide standardized information about learning gains" (technical manual, p. 71). Reading and Math tests in the Life Skills series are available for both native English speakers and English-as-a-second-language learners (ESL). Test packets are available at four levels of difficulty from "beginning literacy" through "high school." In addition, Listening Skills tests are available for ESL at three levels of difficulty. Tests in the Employability Competency Series are parallel to those described in the Life Skills Series.

In addition to the tests in the Life Skills Series and Employability Competency Series, CASAS provides two types of specialized tests: Appraisal Tests and Certification Tests. Appraisal Tests (Life Skills: Reading, Math; Employability: Reading, Math) are used to determine initial placement of native English speakers. Appraisal Tests for ESL students are available in Reading, Math, and Listening. Certification tests in Life Skills (Reading) and Employability (Reading and Math) can be used to verify learner ability levels upon completion of instruction. Most tests can be completed in 60 minutes.

CASAS provides test administration manuals for both the Life Skills series and Employability series. Manuals provide an overview of CASAS testing procedures from appraisal to certification, and include instructions for administering and scoring tests. In addition, interpretation of results and curriculum planning are discussed.

DEVELOPMENT. CASAS was developed after evaluations of Adult Basic Education Programs in California provided evidence for a lack of uniform standards, high attrition rates, use of traditional school curricular materials, and ineffective student assessment procedures. This prompted the review of program evaluation data and research on a national level. In 1980, a California Adult Student Assessment System (CASAS) consortium was formed. In 1984, CASAS "was nationally validated by the U.S. Department of Education, Joint Dissemination Review Panel" (administration manual, p. 2) and the name changed to reflect its new "comprehensive" status. Beginning in the 1970s, competency-based adult education became the topic of much study. The research literature in this area was rigorously reviewed, and skills and competencies necessary for adults to function in everyday life were identified. CASAS item bank development was based on these data.

In 1993, the Program Effectiveness Panel (PEP) of the U.S. Department of Education upheld the three claims made by CASAS. First, programs using CASAS demonstrate significant learning gains. Second, hours of student participation increase. Third, students experience increased goal attainment. These claims have been supported by data from national studies and multiple-agency studies in California, Oregon, and North Carolina. The findings of the PEP, and the aforementioned research studies, provide evidence supporting the validity of CASAS.

TECHNICAL. Test item development has been rigorously pursued and provides evidence to support claims of content validity. CASAS currently maintains a full-time team of "item and test development professionals and a cadre of field practitioners" (technical manual, p. 17) that is responsible for item construction. New items are piloted with ABE and ESL students, reviewed by experts in the content areas, field tested, and reviewed once again. The CASAS item bank has increased from 1,000 items to approximately 6,000 items. In addition, a series of studies was conducted to assess the validity of the CASAS competencies. Between 1995 and 1999, five validation studies in four states (Iowa, Indiana, Connecticut, California) surveyed more than 17,000 professionals who work in, or are stakeholders in, ABE. In all cases, a large majority of the competencies represented in CASAS were supported, and deemed important to ABE.

Evidence for criterion validity, the degree of precision with which test scores can predict performance in a competency, and at a specific level was also examined. The calibration process included input from expert instructors in each domain. CASAS Skill Level Descriptors evolved out of a series of collaborative studies in which GED and ABE programs worked with CASAS to develop common language to represent various levels of competency. Item response theory (IRT) procedures were used to assess the difficulty of individual items on instruments used by each of the 3 programs. A similar process was used to validate and calibrate the ESL items. CASAS scores were compared with scores on the Basic English Skills Test (BEST), and Mainstream English Language Training (MELT), and common student performance levels of difficulty were established.

Differential item functioning analyses were conducted to assess the performance of items with regard to gender and ethnicity (African American, Anglo American, Hispanic American). "Based on criteria developed by ETS" (technical manual, p. 189), items with delta values less than 1.0 were considered acceptable and retained. Items with values 1.0–1.5 were reviewed by content specialists, and items with delta values greater than 1.5 were reviewed and used only if no other item measuring the same content had performed better, and the content was considered critical. Test information function was analyzed to determine the degree of precision with which CASAS instruments estimate the test-taker's true ability level. The graphs of test information function for CASAS provide evidence for "acceptable precision/information across the ability range that each test was designed to measure" (technical manual, p. 191).

One criticism of the CASAS had been the lack of questions designed to assess higher order thought processes or critical thinking skill. After recalibration of CASAS items in 1985 and the addition of higher level questions, "thinking regarding the dimensionality of a single item bank assessing both math and reading skills was changed" (technical manual, p. 30). Two series of studies were conducted with more than 20,700 students. Data were analyzed using principal components analysis on Math and Reading data separately, and combined. In addition, confirmatory factor analysis supported a two-factor model composed of Math and Reading for both the Life Skills data and the Employability data.

No information was provided for test-retest reliability or split-half reliability. This seems odd because data could easily have been analyzed in this way.

COMMENTARY. The psychometric properties of CASAS have been subjected to rigorous analyses and evidence of validity is provided in many forms. There appears to be a high degree of content validity and criterion-validity built into item development. More evidence for reliability of the instrument could be provided in the manuals. This would make the CASAS more attractive. More information about validation sample characteristics is suggested, particularly with regard to socioeconomic status and English language competency and/or bilingualism. For example, data on ethnicity include African American, Anglo American, and Hispanic American (which could include Mexican American, Central American, and South American). Data for Asian Americans, and Native Americans should certainly be included. Also, immigrant status (years in the U.S.) and language proficiency or bilingualism should be noted. Reporting of these data would more clearly demonstrate that instrument analyses had been conducted with populations representative of the whole.

SUMMARY. The sheer size and complexity of the CASAS makes reporting (and review) of its many components a challenge. CASAS has improved its documentation over time and continues to conduct research to provide evidence for rigorous psychometric properties. Comment on all aspects of the Appraisal tests, the Certification tests, the Life Skills and Employability Competency tests, the ESL tests and the tests for developmentally disabled adults, is beyond the scope of this review. CASAS has been subjected to rigorous development and assessment procedures, as well as psychometric analyses. It has been validated with varied populations in several geographic areas. Practitioners involved in adult basic education can use these tests with a fair degree of confidence. Continued evaluation is encouraged, especially in the appropriateness of CASAS use with ESL and bilingual speakers. And studies should be conducted that include significant numbers of people who are Native American and Asian American. Results of reliability analyses need clarification. The CASAS should be tied more closely to a curriculum. Although Appendix A includes a section, "How to use the CASAS Competencies in curriculum, assessment, and instruction" (technical manual, p. 198), it provides less than extensive information. If additional information were available in the areas outlined above, the CASAS would be even more attractive.

Review of the Comprehensive Adult Student Assessment System—Third Edition by CAROL S. PARKE, Assistant Professor, School of Education, Duquesne University, Pittsburgh, PA:

DESCRIPTION. The Comprehensive Adult Student Assessment System—Third Edition (CASAS) consists of a series of assessments that measure the strengths and weaknesses of adults on more than 300 competencies representing life skills necessary to be successful members of communities, families, and the workforce. There are two major series of tests. The Life Skills Series measures competencies related to priority functional life-skills, and the Employability Competency System (ECS) Series focuses primarily on employment-related "basic skills necessary to get and to keep a job (technical manual, p. 71). Both series contain pre- and posttests in Reading, Mathematics, and Listening that can be used to: (a) identify learners' initial levels of competency, (b) diagnose learners' strengths and weaknesses on specific competencies, (c) monitor learning progress over time, and/or (d) certify learners. The assessments are integrated within a curriculum management system that provides resources and mechanisms linking the competencies, assessments, and instruction. Although the manuals provide much information about the competencies and assessments, details regarding the instructional aspect are rather scarce.

The CASAS is intended for use by agencies or programs serving learners in Adult Basic Education (ABE), English as a Second Language (ESL), and other education or employability training programs. Implementation training must be completed prior to using the CASAS. Training is offered at state, regional, and local levels or through distance courses. Complete and clear instructions for administering the tests and for providing appropriate accommodations are given in the manual. Reading and Math tests are not timed, although it is reported that most students finish within 60 minutes. Listening tests are administered by audiotape.

CASAS provides software for scoring tests, converting raw scores to scale scores, and creating reports for individuals and groups by each competency assessed. If scoring manually, easily understood charts and forms are available for converting scores and creating reports. When using CASAS to monitor progress, the Suggested Next Test charts allow test users to determine the appropriate level and form of the test that would most accurately reflect each examinee's ability level. The scale score range is divided into five skill levels. Descriptors at each level include general examples of the life-skill and job-related competencies that an examinee can be expected to accomplish. As indicated in the technical manual, descriptors are validated and updated annually by full-time staff as well as adult education field-based practitioners in government, education, and workforce development systems.

DEVELOPMENT. Competency-based and results-oriented education principles guide the development of the assessments. In order to evaluate the life-skill and workplace competencies, the CASAS item banks consist of more than 6,000 multiple-choice items. Each item is coded to represent the specific competency and content area assessed. Items are also classified into various task types. Examinees answer questions based on information contained in "(1) forms (2) charts, maps, consumer billings, matrices, graphs, tables (3) articles, paragraphs, sentences, directions, manuals (4) signs, price tags, advertisements, product labels (5) measurement scales diagrams (6) oral cue" (ECS Test Administration Manual, p. 6).

The initial creation of CASAS competencies, item taxonomy, item specifications, and item development in the early 1980s is discussed at great length. However, only minimal information related to ongoing test development and recent pilot- and field-testing was available in the materials examined by the reviewer. More specific details are needed, for example, on how the current cadre of item writers and field practitioners review items in terms of possible ethnic, gender, or other biases and how existing items are evaluated to ensure their appropriateness in measuring the current competencies. The Rasch model of Item Response Theory is identified as the underlying theoretical foundation of item development. The manual provides a thorough description of how the one-parameter model was used to calibrate items and link test forms.

TECHNICAL. Numerous studies were conducted to examine the validity and reliability of the CASAS. Based on 1996-2000 data, KR-20 reliability coefficients were computed. Coefficients ranged from .73 to .96 for the Reading, Math, and Listening forms in the Life Skills and ECS series. By item, point-biserial coefficients and item difficulties are available. For each test form and level, standard errors of the scale scores are also shown. For example, on Form 38, Level D of the Life Skills Reading test, standard errors ranged from 3.3 to 5.4 within the "accurate" scale score range of 212 to 259. Similar values occurred for the other forms and levels.

Initially, Reading and Math were thought to be unidimensional with a single latent variable underlying both content areas. Subsequent to 1985, this view of dimensionality changed. Math and Reading items were no longer included in the same item bank and calibration was done separately. Applying current research by Sireci, Rogers, Swaminathan, Meara, and Robin (2000), the dimensionality of the CASAS item banks was reexamined in 2002–2003. The sample for generating item response data included 20,738 examinees responding to 11 Reading and Math forms and 21,077 examinees responding to 5 Listening forms. A table displays the percentage of examinees by form for gender, ethnicity (white, Hispanic, black), and years of education (<6 and >6). The procedure for obtaining this sample was not stated and the dates of test administration were unclear. Information on other demographic variables, such as age, socioeconomic status, and geographic location, were not supplied. The technical manual states that "the two-factor model (reading and math) for both the Life Skills and ECS series provided a better fit than did the one-factor model without regard to the four fit statistics" (p. 49). Correlations between the Math and Reading raw scores ranged from .48 to .84, with a median correlation of .59. Although coefficient alphas were given for the Reading and Math forms combined (all were above .90), they were not available for Reading and Math separately.

Other studies evaluated the stability of item difficulties over time. For Forms 15 and 35 of the Math and Reading tests, correlations ranging from .76 to .89 were obtained between existing item bank difficulties and item difficulties generated from independent calibrations of items for tests administered between 1998 and 2002.

As pointed out in an earlier review of the CASAS (Mueller & Freitag, 1998), it does appear that a considerable amount of effort was put into ensuring content validity of the initial item bank. More recent studies, conducted from 1995 to 1999 in four states across the nation, briefly described validity evidence for the competencies. In addition, a 1996 study showed that the CASAS competencies closely parallel job skills competencies reported by the U.S. Department of Labor (1992). As for predictive validity, many studies are referenced. For example, a 2002 study comparing CASAS Reading and Math scores to GED Reading and Math scores showed a "clear monotonic increasing relationship" (technical manual, p. 63). Scoring high on the CASAS tended to relate to higher success on the GED. Samples in the four states were not described. Other research involving students enrolled in workforce literacy programs across eight states showed strong correlations between CASAS scores and ACT Work Keys levels (.71 for Reading and .70 for Math).

Differential item functioning was examined for gender and ethnicity. A clear explanation of DIF is provided for test users, including use of the Mantel-Haenszel procedure and criteria for identifying items. Items with deltas between |1| and |1.5| were subject to review, and items with values above |1.5| were used only if the item content was essential and no other item with a lower delta was available. Tables show the number of items within the delta ranges. In most cases, only a small proportion of items had deltas above |1.5|. For example, across five forms of the Life Skills Reading test, only 1 item was identified for gender DIF. On the other hand, 11 items across the four forms of the Life Skills Math test were identified for gender DIF. The implications of these DIF results were not discussed in the manual.

COMMENTARY. A strength of the CASAS is that it provides agencies and adult education programs with an assessment system that identifies skill levels of adults with respect to over 300 life skill and employability competencies. It also allows for monitoring progress and certifying skills in educational training programs. Since its inception in the early 1980s, CASAS has continually expanded its resources and services to accommodate new populations and new national and state initiatives including adult literacy, welfare reform, and the homeless. The CASAS National Consortium, representing a wide array of field-based practitioners across the nation, appears to play a major role in the expansion of the assessment and the development of competencies and items, thus lending credence to content and construct validity. In place for more than two decades, the CASAS remains current with new advancements in measurement theory research and uses them to guide further validation studies. Test users will also find helpful and easy-to-use charts for scoring, reporting, and identifying appropriate test levels for each examinee.

Although the general framework of the CASAS system was described thoroughly, an area of weakness was the lack of specific information regarding the link between the instruction and assessment aspects of the integrated system. Insufficient data were given for test users to evaluate the extent of alignment between instructional resources and the tests of Reading, Math, and Listening. If the claim is that "programs can use the CASAS Competencies in developing a standards-based curriculum that better meets learner, community, and program needs and helps fulfill federal, state, and local reporting requirements" (technical manual, p. 199), then rigorous research showing evidence of alignment among the aspects of the system is essential.

Secondly, certain sections of the manual were unclear with regard to the samples used for validation studies. Although a table of demographic information was provided for the calibration sample, the recent studies did not include descriptions of sample characteristics. In order to support the use of the CASAS tests with diverse and changing populations, the descriptions of samples used in validation are critical. As an example, the ECS test administration manual states that the assessments are "age-sensitive" (p. 8), but it was difficult to find evidence supporting this statement.

Finally, the CASAS is to be commended on their analyses of differential item functioning for gender and ethnicity. However, further information would be beneficial. For instance, only the absolute values of the deltas were given, thus it was impossible to determine which group was differentially favored. For instance, the number of DIF items that were differentially easier (or more difficult) for males versus females could not be determined. Moreover, potential test users would benefit from knowing the implication of the DIF results, the number of items retained or eliminated, and how the results impacted future item development.

SUMMARY. Overall, the CASAS provides sound empirical evidence to support its use. Test items are shown to closely match the critical skills addressed in national standards of job skill analysis, and the assessment system is said to meet the requirements of the Workforce Investment Act (WIA) of 1998. Clearer and more comprehensive information regarding characteristics of samples used in validity studies would strengthen the claim that the system is designed to serve diverse populations of adult learners. Potential test users would also benefit from a more explicit description of how the system can be customized to an agency's purpose and how instruction is linked to assessment. In an earlier review of CASAS, Schafer (1998) mentioned that documentation for extended-response and performance assessment item types was not available. Materials reviewed for this third edition of CASAS (test administration manuals, technical manual, test booklets, and answer sheets) did not contain information on item formats other than multiple-choice, although the LS test administration manual indicated that several supplements related to constructed response and performance assessments are currently under development.

REVIEWER'S REFERENCES

Mueller, R. O., & Freitag, P. K. (1998). [Review of the Comprehensive Adult Student Assessment System (CASAS)]. In J. C. Impara & B. S. Plake (Eds.), *The thirteenth mental measurements yearbook* (pp. 295–297). Lincoln, NE: Buros Institute of Mental Measurements.

Schafer, W. D. (1998). [Review of the Comprehensive Adult Student Assessment System (CASAS)]. In J. C. Impara & B. S. Plake (Eds.), *The thirteenth mental measurements yearbook* (pp. 298–299). Lincoln, NE: Buros Institute of Mental Measurements.

Sireci, S. G., Rogers, H. J., Swaminathan, H., Meara, K., & Robin, F. (2000). Appraising the dimensionality of the NAEP science assessment data. In *Grading the Nation's Report Card*. Washington, DC: National Academies Press.

[62]

Comprehensive Mathematical Abilities Test.

Purpose: Developed to "assess a broad spectrum of mathematical abilities in the areas of comprehension (reasoning), calculation and application."

Population: Ages 7:0 to 18:11.

Publication Date: 2003.

Acronym: CMAT.

Scores (10–18): General Mathematics (Basic Calculations, composed of Addition, Subtraction, Multiplication, Division, and Mathematical Reasoning, composed of Problem Solving, Charts/Tables/and Graphs); Advanced Calculations (Algebra, Geometry, Rational Numbers) [supplemental]; Practical Applications (Time, Money, Measurement) [supplemental]; Global Mathematics Ability.

Administration: Individual.

Price Data, 2002: $267 per complete kit including examiner's manual (199 pages), picture book, 25 profile/examiner record booklets, 25 student response booklet I, and 25 student response booklet II; $79 per examiner's manual; $64 per picture book.

Time: 45–60 minutes.

Comments: Computer scoring available.

Authors: Wayne P. Hresko, Paul L. Schlieve, Shelley R. Herron, Colleen Swain, and Rita J. Sherbenou.

Publisher: PRO-ED.

Review of the Comprehensive Mathematical Abilities Test by GEORGE ENGELHARD, JR., Professor of Educational Measurement and Policy, Emory University, Atlanta, GA:

DESCRIPTION. The Comprehensive Mathematical Abilities Test (CMAT) is an individually administered test developed to measure mathematical abilities in the areas of comprehension (reasoning), calculation, and application for students between the ages of 7-0 and 18-11. The CMAT includes 307 items classified in terms of 12 core subtests (number of items in parentheses): Addition (25); Subtraction (23); Multiplication (26); Division (25); Problem Solving (24); Charts, Tables, and Graphs (29); Algebra (25); Geometry (24); Rational Numbers (27); Time (25); Money (31); and Measurement (23). Scores are also reported based on various composites obtained from the 12 core subtests: General Mathematics, Basic Calculations, Mathematical Reasoning, Advanced Calculations, and Practical Applications. There is also a Global Mathematics Ability score based on the student performance on all of the items. Some of the subtests include items in a student response booklet, whereas other subtests require the students to view items included in a Picture Book. Although the CMAT is not a timed test, the authors estimate that administering the CMAT takes between 45 minutes and 1 hour depending upon a variety of contextual factors. Very detailed directions are provided for the examiner with clear and easy to understand scoring guidelines. The authors provide helpful advice on how to obtain fair and objective scores for each student. Because this is an individually administered and adaptive test, the authors provide easy to understand directions about the use of entry points, basals, and ceilings for each of the subtests.

According to the authors, the CMAT has four principal purposes: (a) to determine the strengths and weaknesses among developed mathematical abilities; (b) to identify students who are significantly below or above their peers in mathematical abilities; (c) to make predictions about students' future performance in mathematics; and (d) to serve as a measurement device in research studies investigating mathematics abilities.

DEVELOPMENT. The CMAT was developed to reflect the current mathematics curriculum taught in schools. The authors conducted extensive research on the content of existing mathematics curriculum materials, the National Council of Teachers of Mathematics standards, and expert opinions in order to create a test that reflects current theory and reform issues in mathematics education. A detailed description of the sources reviewed are listed in the examiner's manual. Of course, potential users should review the items and determine whether or not the CMAT matches the content within the local context.

TECHNICAL. The authors of the CMAT provide an examiner's manual that includes a very detailed description of the psychometric characteristics of the CMAT. Throughout the development process, the authors of the CMAT were guided by the *Standards for Educational and Psychological Testing* (AERA, APA, & NCME, 1999). As a result, the CMAT and supporting technical materials are of very high technical quality.

Normative information is provided for the CMAT. The norms are based on 1,625 students from a variety of settings. The authors have been very careful to construct a normative sample that is demographically representative of the school-age population in the United States based on census data (U.S. Census, 2000). Given the challenges of collecting this normative information for an individually administered test, the authors have done a good job. Detailed information is provided in the examiner's manual that allows potential users to see the close match of the normative sample to the school-age population. Because the CMAT covers a wide age range, the potential user needs to be reminded and cautioned about how few examinees actually were assessed within each grade or age group. The CMAT reports the following scores based on this normative sample: standard scores ($M = 10$, $SD = 3$), Composite Quotients ($M = 100$, $SD = 15$), percentile ranks, and age and grade equivalents. The authors provide descriptions for the user on how to interpret these standard scores. As with other aspects of the CMAT, a

great deal of time and effort went into teaching potential users about correct interpretations.

In the examiner's manual, the authors provide a nice description of test reliability, and potential sources of error variance in the CMAT related to content sampling, time sampling, and scorer differences. Coefficient alpha is reported for each of the core subtests and the composites. Coefficient alphas are between .83 and .90 for the core subtests, and .98 for the Global Composite. Coefficient alphas are also reported by age and subgroups; none of these fall below .80. Test-retest reliabilities range from .86 to .95 for the core subtests, and .99 for the Global Composite (administration interval = 2-3 weeks). Standard errors of measurement are also reported. A small study was conducted by the authors to examine scorer differences. Fifty completed protocols were scored by one of the authors of the CMAT and two graduate students. There were very high correlations between scorers ranging from .95 to .99 for all subtests, and .99 for the Global Composite. In the future, scorer agreement based on two examiners conducting the full assessment of children should be conducted. Overall, the reliability evidence of the CMAT is acceptable and within an acceptable range for individually administered tests.

The authors provide a nice description of the concept of validity that reflects the perspective that obtaining evidence of validity is an ongoing process, and that validity evidence is a function of the purposes and proposed uses of the CMAT. Evidence regarding the validity of the CMAT scores is presented related to item content, conventional item analyses, differential item functioning, criterion-prediction validity, construct-identification validity, age and group differentiation, subtest interrelationships, relationship of CMAT to other measures of school achievement and intelligence, and confirmatory factor analysis. As with other aspects of the development of the CMAT, the authors have been very thoughtful and careful in describing and presenting validity evidence for the CMAT. In particular, the authors have done an excellent job describing construct validity evidence in relationship to testable hypotheses regarding the constructs underlying the CMAT. Enough information is provided for potential users to determine whether or not the CMAT will be useful in making decisions and recommendations about their students.

COMMENTARY. The CMAT is a well-developed instrument that should be considered for use by practitioners who require an assessment of the mathematics ability of students. The authors are very careful to stress that this test is designed to measure developed abilities. The use of a Composite Quotient ($M = 100$, $SD = 15$) may have the potential to be misinterpreted as an IQ score, and users should be careful that parents and others are appropriately cautioned not to make this error. The examiner's manual provides very detailed descriptions regarding the appropriate uses of the CAMT, cautions about the limitations, and sufficient detail regarding the psychometric quality of the CMAT. The examiner's manual does not assume that the reader is an expert in psychometrics, and provides enough detail to teach the potential user about a variety of measurement issues.

Although the authors describe validity as related to test use, there are several places where the authors make broad blanket statements regarding validity, such as "one may conclude that the CMAT is a valid measure of mathematics ability" (examiner's manual, p. 94) and "we demonstrated that the CMAT was valid for these subgroups" (examiner's manual, p. 100). These statements can easily be misinterpreted to mean that the test is valid in and of itself instead of being valid for its intended purposes.

The potential user should carefully review the actual items included on the CMAT, and verify that the CMAT does indeed reflect the curriculum in their school. When a mathematics educator was asked to review the items, it was his view that the CMAT is primarily a measure of computational proficiency, and does not provide adequate coverage of the standards developed by the National Council of Teachers of Mathematics in areas related to communication, connections, real problem solving, mathematical reasoning, and probability.

SUMMARY. The CMAT is a good instrument that can be used by a skilled examiner to explore the mathematical abilities of students. The supporting materials are easy to use, and the psychometric characteristics of the CMAT are acceptable for this type of instrument. Users are provided with a very helpful examiner's manual that discusses proper uses of the CMAT. The authors repeatedly stress that the CMAT is a tool for examiners to help understand student strengths and weaknesses in mathematics, that these abilities are developed, and that individual diagnoses should not be based exclusively on the test results. Potential users should carefully consider the alignment between the mathematics curriculum in their schools and the content of the CMAT.

REVIEWER'S REFERENCES

American Educational Research Association, American Psychological Association, & National Council on Measurement in Education. (1999). *Standards for educational and psychological testing.* Washington, DC: American Educational Research Association.
U.S. Bureau of the Census. (2000). *Statistical abstract of the United States.* Washington, DC: Author.

Review of the Comprehensive Mathematical Abilities Test by SUZANNE LANE, Professor of Educational Measurement and Statistics, University of Pittsburgh, Pittsburgh, PA:

DESCRIPTION. The Comprehensive Mathematical Abilities Test (CMAT) was designed to assess "mathematical abilities in the areas of comprehension (reasoning), calculation, and application" (examiner's manual, p. 1). There are four purposes of the CMAT as indicated by the authors: "(1) to determine strengths and weaknesses among developed mathematical abilities; (2) to identify students who are significantly below or above their peers in mathematical abilities; (3) to make predictions about students' future performance in mathematics; and (4) to serve as a measurement device in research studies investigating mathematics ability" (examiner's manual, p. 6). The CMAT is an individually administered test and is designed for students between 7-0 years and 18-11 years. The amount of time to administer the CMAT General Mathematics subtests ranges from 45 minutes to 1 hour.

There are three core composites: General Mathematics, which is based on the scores of the Addition, Subtraction, Multiplication, Division, Problem Solving, and Charts, Tables, and Graphs subtests; Basic Calculations, which results in combining scores from the Addition, Subtraction, Multiplication, and Division subtests; and Mathematical Reasoning, which results in combining scores from the Problem Solving and the Charts, Tables, and Graphs subtests. There are two supplemental composites: Advanced Calculations and Practical Applications. The Advanced Calculations is formed by the Algebra, Geometry, and Rational Numbers subtests and the Practical Applications is formed by the Time, Money, and Measurement subtests. The Global Composite is obtained by combining the standard scores of all 12 subtests. All items in the subtests that form the

General Mathematics composite require students to produce a response, typically a numerical value. The majority of the items in the subtests that form either the Advanced Calculations or Practical Applications composites require students to produce a response, typically a numerical value, whereas approximately one-fifth are selected-response items.

The examiner's manual provides an introduction to the CMAT, a description of how to administer and score the test, information on how to complete the record booklet, a description of the norm-referenced scores and how to interpret them, and information on reliability and validity. The examiner's manual and the profile/examiner record booklet provide a very clear and complete description of how to administer the CMAT and how to complete the record booklet. The examples illustrating proper uses of basals and ceilings and those illustrating how to record information make the administration and scoring procedures very transparent. Also available is a software scoring program that calculates standard scores and percentile ranks once the raw scores are entered.

The authors indicate that those who administer, score, and interpret the CMAT should have some formal training in assessment. The administration of the test requires the use of entry points, basals and ceilings. On the profile/examiner record booklet the examiner records an individual's performance on the items and subtests, identifying information such as age and testing date, subtest scores, composite scores, and score interpretations and recommendations. The scores that can be obtained and recorded for the subtests include the raw score, age and grade equivalences, percentile ranks, and standard scores. The standard scores for the subtests have a mean of 10 and standard deviation of 3. The scores that can be obtained for the composites are standard scores, which have a mean of 100 and standard deviation of 15, and percentile ranks.

DEVELOPMENT. The authors indicate that the specification of the CMAT's content first involved a review of the existing research, commercial and noncommercial curriculum materials, existing tests, and standards developed by the National Council of Teachers of Mathematics (NCTM, 2000). These reviews took place between 1996 and 2000. The authors provide a list of publishers of the commercial materials and textbooks that they reviewed as well as the math-

ematics tests and the mathematics curriculum guides from states and school districts that they reviewed. The authors indicate that they examined the *NCTM Principles and Standards* (2000) to ensure that their items were in compliance. However, the authors provide no details on how this compliance process was implemented. They further state that the NCTM's Communication standard "does not lend itself to the standardized, individual administration format of the CMAT" (examiner's manual, p. 66) and therefore is not represented in the CMAT. It could be argued, however, that this format does lend itself to the assessment of the NCTM Communication standard, which would require students to describe their reasoning and problem solving. The authors state that they placed the items into the CMAT subtest based on their analysis of the research, curriculum materials, existing tests, and the *NCTM Principles and Standards*. The authors provide a matrix they developed illustrating the CMAT subtests that assess the NCTM Standards of Number and Operations, Algebra, Geometry, Measurement, Data Analysis and Probability, Problem Solving, Reasoning and Proof, Connections, and Representation. Although the CMAT does appear to assess some aspects of problem solving and reasoning, it is not as comprehensive in assessing these areas as the *NCTM Standards* suggest.

An expert panel consisting of a professor in mathematics education, a field editor from a major mathematics education publishing company, and two master's degree level mathematics teachers were asked to check the placement of items in subtests, to check the sequence of items in subtests, and to provide suggestions. The authors indicate that the agreement among the experts across subtests was .98 but the procedure used to obtain this agreement was not provided in the examiner's manual. The appropriateness of the vocabulary level for the items was checked against vocabulary lists that were provided in the manual and readability levels were calculated and appear reasonable.

Classical item difficulty (i.e., proportion correct) and item discrimination (i.e., item-total score Pearson correlation) statistics were used to identify satisfactory items for placement on the test in an easy-to-difficult order and to create the final version of the CMAT. Based on previous research, the authors indicate that discrimination indices of .35 or higher are acceptable and under certain circumstances indices as low as .20 are acceptable, but the authors do not indicate the criteria they used for selecting items. They also indicate that an average difficulty index should be .50 with a large dispersion, and that difficulty indices between .15 and .85 are generally considered acceptable. There was no mention of the agreement between the authors' ordering of items and the ordering based on item statistics. The range for the median item discriminations across 12 age intervals (i.e., 7 years to 18 years) is .30 to .69 and for median item difficulties it is .21 to .94. The lowest median difficulty, .21, is for the Division subtest for the 7-year age interval and the highest median difficulty, .94, is for the Charts, Tables, and Graphs subtest for the 16-year age interval. It should be noted that no other median difficulty value was higher than .84. The procedure used to determine which set of items should be placed in each age interval was not provided and the authors did not indicate the sample used to obtain these statistics.

TECHNICAL.

Standardization. The norming process was conducted between February 1999 and April 2000 using 1,625 students from public and private schools in 17 states. This sample was used to obtain standard scores, percentile ranks, and age and grade equivalents. Although a self-selected procedure was used for the obtainment of the normative sample, the percentage of students in the sample is comparable to the percentage of students in the nation for the categories used in the selection process (i.e., geographic region, gender, race, residence, ethnicity, family income, educational attainment of parents, and disability status). Although small discrepancies exist, most of the discrepancies are no larger than 4% with the exception of geographic region with the Midwest and South discrepancies at 11% and 10%, respectively.. The authors also stratified the demographic categories with age resulting in age samples that are fairly comparable to the nation for these categories.

Reliability. Internal consistency estimates, test-retest estimates, and interscorer estimates of reliability are provided. Cronbach's coefficient alpha was used to determine internal consistency estimates for the 12 age intervals using data from the entire normative sample. The internal consistency estimates ranged from .70 to .95 for the subtests and from .87 to .98 for the composites

across age intervals. The standard error of measurement (*SEM*) is 1 (rounded values) for most of the subtests across age intervals (standard score means and standard deviations are 10 and 3, respectively). The *SEM* for the composites range from 2 to 5 across age intervals (standard score means and standard deviations are 100 and 15, respectively). To ensure more appropriate score interpretations, the *SEM*s should have been rounded to at least the tenths place. Internal consistency estimates were also provided for several subgroups (males, females, European American, African American, Hispanic American, learning disabilities, and attention deficit) and appear to be comparable; however, they are not provided for age intervals. The sample sizes for the learning disabilities and attention deficit/hyperactivity disorder samples are relatively small, (n = 81 and n = 33, respectively). There is no indication of the ages of the students in these two samples.

Test-retest reliability estimates were obtained with two groups of students, one group composed of 30 "normally achieving students" from 7 to 12 years attending public schools in Idaho and the other group composed of 70 "normally achieving students" from 13 to 18 years attending public schools in South Dakota. The interval between the two test administrations was between 2 and 3 weeks. Although the samples were not representative of the nation, the test-retest correlation coefficients were relatively high ranging from .82 to .99 for the subtests and from .92 to .99 for the composites across the two groups.

Interscorer reliability estimates were obtained using 50 randomly drawn protocols from the normative sample. The correlation between the two scorers ranged from .95 to .99 across the subtests and the composites, indicating a high level of scorer relative agreement.

Validity. To provide validity evidence supporting the content of the CMAT, the authors indicate that they reviewed the existing research, commercial and noncommercial curriculum materials, existing tests, and *NCTM Standards* in addition to having experts review the items and ordering of items in the subtests as discussed in the Development section. In addition, differential item functioning was examined using logistic regression for all 307 items in the final form of the CMAT. The entire normative sample was used and the groups examined were male versus female,

European American versus non-European American, African American versus non-African American, and Hispanic American versus non-Hispanic American. A significant level of .001 was used because of the large number of items being examined. The criterion used to determine practical significance was an R^2 greater than .034. Out of 1,228 comparisons, 50 were significant at the .001 level and only 5 of the 50 effect sizes were greater than R^2 of .034. The items remained on the test after a content review of the 50 items because the authors were unable to detect any reasons for DIF.

In evaluating the relation of CMAT scores to a criterion, although not clearly stated, the authors imply that they chose a concurrent study in which the CMAT scores and the criterion information were obtained at the same time rather than a predictive study in which the criterion scores are obtained at a later time. There is no information provided about the test administration times or the samples used for these studies, making it difficult to evaluate the correlations obtained. The criterion scores were from individual and group achievement tests and diagnostic tests: Diagnostic Achievement Test for Adolescents—Second Edition, Woodcock-Johnson Psycho-Educational Battery—Revised, Stanford Achievement Test Series—Ninth Edition, and Metropolitan Achievement Test Series—Seventh Edition. The correlations among the CMAT General Mathematics Composite with the composites of the four criterion measures were .60, .83, .65, and .95, respectively. The correlations among the CMAT Basic Calculations with the calculation measures of the criterion tests were .80, .83, .64, and .39, respectively. The correlations among the CMAT Reasoning Composite with the reasoning/problem solving measures of the criterion tests were .60, .57, .62, and .89, respectively. Although the authors provide a rationale for choosing only the concurrent study and its results are informative, a predictive study should have also been conducted to provide evidence for one of their stated purposes of the CMAT, "to make predictions about students' future performance in mathematics" (examiner's manual, p. 6). The authors provided no direct validity evidence in support of this purpose.

Additional validity evidence was obtained through a series of studies to support a set of premises identified by the authors. First, the relationship between the CMAT scores and age is supported by an increase of mean scores from the lowest to the highest age level (7—18 years) and by correlations between age and subtest scores ranging from .56 (Problem Solving) to .74 (Charts, Tables, and Graphs). Second, the differential performance of groups was examined. As the authors predicted, the students with mathematics learning disabilities tended to score lower than the other groups and the African American and Hispanic American composite scores were lower but within 1 *SEM* of the European American composite scores.

Internal structure evidence was provided by intercorrelations among the standard scores for the normative sample. The intercorrelations among subtests range from .25 to .68. As might be expected, the intercorrelations among the four Basic Calculation subtests were the highest, ranging from .51 to .68, providing some support for the Basic Calculations Composite. The intercorrelation between the Problem Solving and the Charts, Tables, and Graphs subtests was .50, providing some support for the Mathematical Reasoning Composite. The intercorrelations among the six subtests that compose the General Mathematics Composite range from .30 to .68. The lowest intercorrelations are between the two subtests on the Mathematical Reasoning composite with the four subtests on the Calculation composite as would be expected and desired if, in fact, the Mathematical Reasoning subtests measure aspects of mathematical ability beyond calculations. Confirmatory factor analyses were also conducted to provide additional support for the internal structure of the CMAT. Three models were specified and estimated using maximum-likelihood procedures. The first model reflected one dimension in support of the Global Mathematics Ability Composite. The second model reflected three dimensions in support of the General Mathematics, Advanced Calculations, and Practical Application Composites. The third model reflected four dimensions in support of the Basic Calculations, Mathematical Reasoning, Advanced Calculations, and Practical Applications Composites. In general, the measures of fit indicated that all three models fit the data according to the indices and criteria specified by the authors.

Finally, the relationship of the CMAT to tests of intelligence was studied using the WISC-

III, Otis-Lennon School Ability Test—Seventh Edition, and Otis-Lennon School Ability Test—Sixth Edition. The correlations among the CMAT Core Composites (General Mathematics, Basic Calculations, Mathematical Reasoning) are moderate to high, ranging from .58 to .90; however, there is no information provided about the test administration times or the samples used for these studies.

COMMENTARY. The authors indicate that there are four major purposes for the CMAT so I will first comment on some of the evidence provided in support of each of these purposes. The first purpose proposed by the authors is "to determine strengths and weaknesses among developed mathematical abilities" (examiner's manual, p. 6). The internal consistency estimates for most of the subtest scores for most of the age intervals are moderate to high allowing for fairly reliable score interpretations at the subtest level. The intercorrelations among subtest scores vary from .25 to .68 suggesting that individual differences across some subtests may occur. The authors also provide a table of the difference scores that are needed for statistical significance as well as for practical significance or "clinical usefulness." Clear examples are included that illustrate the correct interpretation of difference scores. The second purpose identified by the author is "to identify students who are significantly below or above their peers in mathematical abilities" (examiner's manual, p. 6). The normative sample was well described and the percentages of students in the various subgroups are comparable to the percentages in the nation. The authors provide a table in Appendix C that clearly identifies the corresponding standard score and percentile rank as well as examples illustrating proper interpretation of percentile ranks. Internal consistency estimates for composites are relatively high allowing for reliable score interpretations. As mentioned previously, the authors do not provide direct validity evidence to support the third purpose: "to make predictions about students' future performance in mathematics" (examiner's manual, p. 6). With regard to the fourth purpose, "to serve as a measurement device in research studies investigating mathematics ability" (examiner's manual, p. 6), the authors provide ample evidence for researchers to review prior to adopting the CMAT for their research needs. For all four purposes, the potential user needs to ex-amine the subtests and items of the CMAT to ensure that it is measuring the mathematical skills and concepts that are aligned to the local purpose and use of the test. It should be noted that out of the six core subtests, four focus on calculations and the other two focus on problem solving and interpreting charts, tables, and graphs. If a user is interested in a mathematics test that has a heavy emphasis on problem solving and reasoning, the CMAT may not be appropriate.

In general, the section on the interpretation of scores is very informative. The authors clearly indicate that all scores reflect some degree of error as well as describe appropriate score interpretations and potential inappropriate score interpretations. However, there were some errors in this section. In an example illustrating how to interpret confidence bands, the authors state incorrectly that there is a 68% probability of a student's true score to lie between the observed score + and - 1 SEM. Also, I was surprised to see on page 26 the interpretation of a grade equivalent of 7.3 to mean "the student's performance is like that of students in the third month of the seventh grade" when on page 50 the authors indicate correctly that this type of interpretation is inaccurate. The authors provide a good description of percentile ranks, indicating that they represent interval data and describing how this affects their uses and interpretations. Validity, however, is discussed in terms of the "test's validity" rather than the validity of test score interpretations and the authors also use the traditional ways of dividing validity (i.e., content, criterion, and construct) rather than conceptualizing validity as a unified whole as expressed in the Standards for Educational and Psychological Testing (AERA, APA, & NCME, 1999).

SUMMARY. The CMAT is an individually administered test of mathematical concepts and skills that can be found in most mathematics curricula. In general, the examiner's manual is well-written and provides sound guidelines for administering, scoring, and interpreting the CMAT. The technical information available in the examiner's manual suggests that the authors were thoughtful in the design of the test although some shortcomings were noted as described above.

REVIEWER'S REFERENCES

American Educational Research Association, American Psychological Association, & National Council on Measurement in Education. (1999). Standards for educational and psychological testing. Washington, DC: AERA.
National Council of Teachers of Mathematics. (2000). Principles and standards of school mathematics. Reston, VA: Author.

[63]
Computer Career Assessment Test.

Purpose: Measures aptitude for work in the computer field.

Population: Any adult without prior computer experience.

Publication Date: 2000.

Acronym: CCAT.

Scores: Total Score, Narrative Evaluation, Ranking.

Administration: Group.

Price Data, 2001: $99 for industry; $65 for educational institutions; quantity discounts available.

Time: (60) minutes.

Comments: Available in booklet and internet versions; scored by publisher; must be proctored.

Author: Bruce A. Winrow.

Publisher: Walden Personnel Performance, Inc. [Canada].

Review of the Computer Career Assessment Test by MICHAEL B. BUNCH, Vice President, Measurement Incorporated, Durham, NC:

DESCRIPTION. The Computer Career Assessment Test consists of a test booklet and test manual. The publishers also provided a content validity study for review. The test consists of a set of five problems designed to assess the examinee's "abilities and aptitudes to aid in the decision on choosing a computer-related career" (test manual, p. 1). The five problems, each taking 15 to 20 minutes to complete (total time = 90 minutes), present hypothetical situations in which the examinee must apply programming logic and clerical accuracy to achieve correct solutions. For example, one problem requires the examinee to arrange a set of instructions or steps in a computer program to achieve a desired outcome. Another requires the examinee to answer a series of questions about the proper sequence of keystrokes to produce a given outcome.

DEVELOPMENT. The content validation study that accompanied the test materials described a process by which the five problems were developed or selected. This particular validation study was for the job title IT Computer Services Trainee. Presumably, the publishers would conduct a separate validation study for each application. Beyond showing the job analysis forms completed by content matter experts and summarizing the results (in terms of percent match between item content and job requirements), the publishers offer little information about item or test development. For example, there is no discussion of how these particular problems were chosen over other

possible problems, information about the number or nature of examinees on whom the problems were standardized, or any summary of performance data.

TECHNICAL. As noted above, the publishers offer no standardization data, nor do they offer any item statistics or test statistics. None of the materials provided by the publisher offered any technical data of any kind. Instead, the publishers offered 14 pages of job analysis survey results, a 2-page summary of the author's credentials, and several very old and poorly photocopied articles about personnel testing and related topics. Typical of this filler information is a 1977 article from *Personnel Journal.*

COMMENTARY. The test itself appears to be out of date. The problems are the sort that might have been useful 20 years ago but seem to have no place in today's information technology workplace. Even the stylized pictures of computers in the problems resemble the terminals of the 1980s far more than the computers of today. [Editor's Note: According to the publisher, this test is designed for use by a computer-illiterate population so these concerns about datedness may not be as salient.] The support materials provide no meaningful support. The guide to evaluation is typical: A score of 80—100% is labeled Superior; 70—79% is Good; 60—69% is Moderate, and 59% or less is Low. No support is offered for these ratings. There are no item analysis data; there is no report of performances of contrasting groups. There are no data at all. The prospective user is forced simply to take the author's word that these ratings are valid.

SUMMARY. There is no evidence that the Computer Career Assessment Test would be useful for selection or any other purpose. IT managers, others in need of IT employees, and individuals interested in finding out if they have an aptitude for the computer field are best advised to look elsewhere for assessment instruments.

Review of the Computer Career Assessment Test by THOMAS R. O'NEILL, Psychometrician, National Council of State Boards of Nursing, Chicago, IL:

DESCRIPTION. The Computer Career Assessment Test (CCAT) is a pencil-and-paper test that is designed to "evaluate an individual's abilities and aptitudes to aid in the decision on choosing a computer-related career" (manual, p. 1). The test is composed of five problems, which are treated as subtests. Problem 1 consists of 10 fill-in-the-blank questions in which the examinee is asked to identify a pattern and predict the next element in the series. Problem 2 consists of a description of a simple task and seven procedural steps (disordered) that when properly ordered will successfully accomplish the task described. Examinees are asked to order the steps. Problem 3 consists of four questions in which the examinee is asked to correct textual errors on a screen using a limited set of commands. This problem is intended to tap the examinee's ability to follow instructions, identify-correct errors, and manipulate characters. Problem 4 consists of four questions in which the examinee is given a restricted set of commands and asked to either generate the commands necessary to solve a simple math question or evaluate a set of these commands to produce a value. Problem 5 consists of four questions in which the examinee is presented with an illustration of a computer screen and asked to reproduce graphic elements on the screen using a restricted set of commands. The examinee has 90 minutes to complete the test. This evaluation of the CCAT is based upon three documents: CCAT Test Manual, a copy of the test, and a copy of the Content Validation Study.

DEVELOPMENT. The Content Validation Study submitted by the publishers appeared to be a "work for hire" performed for the XYZ National Bank's IT Computer Services Trainee position. As such, it addressed the larger issue of what did the XYZ National Bank need in a trainee. To address this, Subject Matter Experts (SMEs) from the XYZ National Bank identified 12 activities that trainees would be expected to perform. Next the knowledge, skills, and abilities (KSAs) required to perform those tasks were identified. Many of the KSAs were related to social skills (e.g., be tactful with people, show patience, keep an even temperament) or general work skills (e.g., work independently, work under pressure, sustain concentration). Interestingly, this study also identified how the different KSAs would be assessed and often the answer was on the job, via the interview, or by checking referrals. The problem this presents is that the study was designed for this trainee program, not for the CCAT. It is unclear whether selected KSAs from this study were used as the basis for the CCAT test specifications or if the CCAT already existed and the alignment of

KSAs from the study and the test occurred afterward. It seems likely that the latter is the case because there was no documentation that explained how the KSAs from the study were transformed into test plan specifications. Also, it would have been helpful to have some validation that the scope of activities described by the XYZ National Bank SMEs was applicable to a broader audience. However, inspection of the activities can reassure the reader that the traits being tapped are related to general IT activities. The items do not attempt to tap social skills and generic work traits, nor do they tap traits specific to working for XYZ National Bank.

With regard to developing the items, there is a nice description of the philosophy behind the process in Appendix B of the Content Validation Study. However, the problem with this description is that it is for the Program Analyst Aptitude Test (PAAT), which is a different test (by the same author and publisher) that measures a similar construct. Although the philosophy is probably the same, the sample item included is quite different from any item in the CCAT. Inspection of the test itself will reassure that the items are reasonably well crafted to test the aptitude for logical sequencing and the ability to combine very limited sets of commands to accomplish a task.

TECHNICAL. The technical information received from the publisher regarding this test was confusing. With regard to scoring, the documentation is sparse and requires the reader to infer the scoring process from the sample report. The test manual asserts there are 10 different "criteria" that are measured, yet the sample score report provides only five subscores. The subscores are reported as raw scores, percentage correct, and graphically represented with regard to being below average, average, or above average. Although these labels seem to imply a norming group, such a group is never described. The overall score is reported out as a percentage correct, which is classified as low, moderate, good, or superior. However, there was no documentation for how those categories were assigned to those percentage ranges. The range of raw scores appears to be 0-100 with each problem being worth between 19–21 points. The exact nature of how the responses are scored (several independent dichotomies within a problem, each problem as a hierarchical partial credit structure, etc.) is not explained. It also appears that there is only one form of this test. This is problematic because this test could be taken through different employers multiple times by the same candidate.

There is no documented evidence of construct validity, which is unfortunate because a glance at the items would suggest that the construct of logical analysis and procedure creation is probably there. The problem stems from the vague description of the purpose of the test and the construct. Although the publisher indicates that their company can perform validation studies for a moderate price, the user should know that these types of validity are not included in the price of the test. There is also no evidence that the test functioned in the same manner across gender and ethnicity groups. Similarly, there is no evidence of predictive validity. There is no description of either a norming sample nor a calibration sample. Likewise, there is no documented description of the internal consistency for any sample. Although this test has reasonable time limits, there is no discussion of whether speed is a salient aspect of the construct.

There is limited information in Appendix B of the Content Validity Study regarding the psychometric aspects of the PAAT, but this does not seem relevant to the CCAT. It is equally troubling that the PAAT psychometrics are not well presented. For example, the importance of a correlation of .45 between on-the-job performance ratings and test scores was described as being important because it was significant at the .01 level. Another example was that the mean score of the predictive validity sample was 82.2%. Yet, the mean scores for males and females were 86.2% and 83.2%, respectively. This cannot be, unless there were some very low scoring people who failed to report their gender.

COMMENTARY. Because both the construct and the purpose of this test are vaguely stated, the quality of the test is difficult to evaluate. All other aspects of a test's quality assume these two elements have been established. The lack of clarity on these two points substantially diminishes the utility of this test. The second major flaw with this test is the documentation. Although the test and the test manual are clearly for the CCAT, the information in the Content Validation Study refers to a work for hire regarding the XYZ National Bank and has an appendix that refers to the PAAT, a different test by the same author and publisher. I was disappointed that there really was no "technical specifications" manual that contained information specific to this test.

Although this test could be used to assist an examinee in deciding a career path, it should not be used to evaluate a person's ability to perform specific tasks or predict their ability to learn computer-related tasks unless the user is willing to take on the responsibility for justifying the interpretation of the test scores.

SUMMARY. The content is relevant to the activities of a computer operator in a general way and the test is easy to administer. The scoring has to be performed by Walden Personnel Performance so there is a little more administrative effort involved there. The intended construct is described in only a vague manner and never using a hierarchy of items or the meaning of correctly answering those items. There was no documentation to support the interpretation of the results and the psychometric data behind the instrument seem minimal, making the suggested interpretation of scores tenuous.

This instrument could be used for beginning a discussion regarding computer-related careers, but the stated purpose of the test was to "evaluate an individual's abilities and aptitudes to aid in the decision on choosing a computer-related career" (manual, p. 1). With regard to evaluating any aptitude or ability, this test falls short.

[64]

Conduct Disorder Scale.

Purpose: "To identify persons with Conduct Disorder by evaluating the characteristic behaviors that define this condition."

Population: Ages 5–22 years.

Publication Date: 2002.

Acronym: CDS.

Scores, 5: 4 subscales (Aggressive Conduct, Hostility, Deceitfulness/Theft, Rule Violations), Conduct Disorder Quotient.

Administration: Group or individual.

Price Data, 2002: $86 per complete kit including examiner's manual (41 pages), 50 summary/response forms, and storage box; $49 per examiner's manual; $39 per 50 summary/response forms.

Time: (5–10) minutes.

Comments: Based on the diagnostic criteria for conduct disorder specified by the Diagnostic and Statistical Manual of Mental Disorders—Fourth Edition—Text Revision (DSM-IV-TR); provides interpretation guide for classifying degree of severity of conduct disorder (severe, moderate, mild, not applicable).

Author: James E. Gilliam.

Publisher: PRO-ED.

Review of the Conduct Disorder Scale by MICHAEL J. FURLONG, Professor of Counseling/Clinical/School Psychology, and JENNE SIMENTAL, Doctoral Student, Counseling/Clinical/School Psychology, University of California—Santa Barbara, Santa Barbara, CA:

DESCRIPTION. The Conduct Disorder Scale (CDS) is an instrument designed to assess behaviors associated with the Conduct Disorder diagnostic category included in the *Diagnostic and Statistical Manual of the American Psychiatric Association-Fourth Edition Text Revision* (DSM-IV-TR; American Psychiatric Association, 2000). It has two main sections. The first section (Part V: Response Form) consists of 40 items that are organized into four norm-based subscales linked to the DSM-IV-TR categories (DSM category names in parentheses): Aggressive Conduct (Aggression to People and Animals), Hostility (no DSM parallel category), Deceitfulness and Theft (Destruction of Property and Deceitfulness of Theft), and Rule Violation (Serious Violations of Rules). These four subscales are summed to produce a Conduct Disorder Quotient (CDQ). Someone who has direct personal contact with the youth (teachers, parents, or siblings) can complete the CDS in 10–15 minutes. The second section (Part VI: Key Questions) has 13 items that are nearly identical to the DSM Conduct Disorder diagnostic symptoms. These offer the rater the opportunity to provide examples of behaviors that have been observed and when they occurred, but do not produce standardized ratings.

When completing the 40-item rating scale section of the CDS, the observer is asked to rate the child's "typical" behavior over a 6-hour period (if the rater is uncertain of how to complete certain items, the author suggests that observations be taken over a 6-hour period prior to rating the items). A behavioral frequency rating scale is used: 0 = *never observed*, 1 = *seldom observed* (1–2 times), 2 = *sometimes observed* (3–4 times), and 3 = *frequently observed* (5 or more times).

DEVELOPMENT. The CDS was developed specifically with the intent of developing an instrument that would help to differentiate conduct disorders from other behavioral/emotional conditions. The manual provides limited information about the generation of items for the core rating scale section. A total of 80 items were written based upon a review of the four DSM conduct disorder diagnostic categories, a review of the research literature, and an inspection of other instruments. It is stated that factor analysis procedures (unspecified) were completed and that this reduced the item pool to the final 40 used in the instrument. No specific information about the results of the factor analysis is provided other than it produced four subscales, which overlapped with, but did not match, the DSM diagnostic categories. The most notable difference is that the CDS includes a Hostility subscale, which is not among the DSM categories.

TECHNICAL CHARACTERISTICS. Among the four subscales, Aggressive Conduct (.94) and Hostility (.91) have better internal consistency coefficients than Deceitfulness/Theft (.79) and Rule Violation (.74). The derived Conduct Disorder Quotient shows strong reliability (.96). Stability and interrater reliability estimates are also presented, but the small sample sizes ($N = 15$) used in these analyses are inadequate to demonstrate the psychometric properties of the instrument. Concurrent validity studies are reported in the manual showing that the CDS has very high correlations with the Differential Test of Conduct and Emotional Problems and the Behavior Rating Profile—Second Edition (Teacher Rating Scale portion); however, these analyses use a small sample ($N = 26$) collected as part of an undergraduate student project. Validity analyses were completed and they show that youth with a formal Conduct Disorder diagnosis obtained significantly higher scores than youth without such a diagnosis and other groups of students in special education programs.

Norms. The primary normative sample consists of an opportunity sample of 644 students diagnosed with Conduct Disorder (376 non-conduct-disordered youth provided information for a validity study). These students range in age from 5 through 22, with 87% male and 13% female (only 84 females are included in the norm sample). The number of cases for ages 5–10 and 19–22 range from only 2 to 17, which is inadequate. The number of youth ages 13–17 (sample sizes of 63–127) is adequate, but the balance of cases in each age group for gender, ethnicity, and by geographic region are not provided. Another matter that is not addressed at all in the manual is that of the characteristics of the raters and the contexts in which they completed the ratings. Even more fundamentally, the manner in which the cases in the norm sample received formal DSM diagnoses is not presented. Consequently, the CDS norms should be used with extreme caution.

COMMENTARY. The CDS did not thoroughly attend to various research-based conduct disorder models in the generation of items. The extensive literature related to models of antisocial behavior (e.g., by Loeber, Moffit, Quay, and Chesney-Lind) is not discussed. The substantive importance of this is that the CDS uses the same norms across the entire 5–22-year age range. Well-founded research models indicate that there are various subtypes of conduct disorder (e.g., covert, authority, and overt, which may overlap) and that some forms of conduct disorder may manifest themselves first in early adolescence and be limited to that developmental stage. This distinguishes them from conduct disorders that are persistent across the age range. The CDS does not provide discussion of, or the mechanism to distinguish among, various forms of conduct disorder, as required by the DSM. Furthermore, the use of one set of norms raises questions because it implies that the same behaviors occurring at the same frequency for a 6-year-old, for example, is equivalent to the same behaviors for an 18-year-old.

Another particular matter with the CDS is that the response rating form is atypical of most rating scales. It uses a frequency count method that asks the rater to indicate how often a behavior occurred within a 6-hour period. This method raises at least three issues that are not adequately addressed in the manual. First a 6-hour observation period is specified; however, it is unclear how many 6-hour periods are required to obtain a stable rating. On the one hand, the manual indicates (p. 12) that a valid rating could be obtained in a single 6-hour period. On the other hand, the description of the 4-point rating rubric suggests that the rating need not be applied for a specific period, but could relate to an average of behavior over an unspecified period of time (e.g., "Seldom Observed—Person behaves in this manner 1–2 times per 6-hour period"). Thus, it appears that the CDS could be used in different ways by different raters with some ratings based on more extended observations than others. Second, there is no rationale given for the selection of the frequency ratings used, nor how each of the frequency ratings is equated across the 40 items. For example, less serious behaviors such as #6 "creates disturbances" and more serious behavior such as #11 "attempts to physically hurt others" are weighted equally, based solely on the frequency of behavior. Furthermore, it is difficult to imagine a setting in which an adult could observe for a 6-hour period to be one that would also allow physical fighting to occur at such a rate without intervention. Third, the manual does not provide adequate information about the contexts in which the normative rating were obtained nor the procedures on which to base the ratings. The administration and scoring guidelines merely suggest that the rater base their ratings on "typical behavior under ordinary circumstances (i.e., in most places, with people he or she is familiar with, and in usual daily activities)" (examiner's manual, p. 12). It is unclear how this procedure would be uniformly put into operation.

An additional issue involving the 6-hour rating time frame is that the CDS will often be used in school settings to explore differences between emotional disturbance and social maladjustment. As suggested by the author, it would be relatively difficult for a teacher to observe adolescent students for 6 hours. The authors make no mention of whether or not to hold off observations during lunch or recess or other school contexts.

SUMMARY. There is no doubting that a group of youths who were diagnosed as having a conduct disorder using DSM criteria would obtain higher scores on an instrument that contained the same set of criteria in a rating scale format. To the extent that such a scale formalizes that identification of conduct disorder, it may have some value as an aid to clinicians making such a diagnosis. The reviewers see some potential for the CDS as providing information about the level of severity of conduct disorder, as asked for in the DSM, but additional research is needed before it has acceptable sensitivity-specificity characteristics that would allow it to be used for any differential diagnosis purposes. Furthermore, the sample sizes used in the validity studies presented in the manual are too small to adequately assess the totality of its psychometric properties. More independent research with diverse samples is needed before the CDS can be considered a better measurement option than instruments such as the Quay Revised Behavior Checklist (T6:2104; Quay & Peterson, 1993).

REVIEWERS' REFERENCE

Quay, H. C., & Peterson, D. R. (1993). *The Revised Behavior Problem Checklist: Manual.* Odessa, FL: Psychological Assessment Resources, Inc.

Review of the Conduct Disorder Scale by STEVEN I. PFEIFFER, *Professor, Psychological Services in Education Program, Florida State University, Tallahassee, FL:*

DESCRIPTION. The Conduct Disorder Scale (CDS) is a 40-item rating scale composed of items grouped within four scales: Aggressive Conduct (13 items), Hostility (14 items), Deceitfulness/Theft (6 items), and Rule Violations (7 items). Items are rated on a 4-point Likert scale according to frequency of occurrence.

The CDS is designed to diagnose Conduct Disorder in persons ages 5 through 22. The examiner's manual states that the instrument can also be used to "assess persons referred for serious behavior problems, to document progress in the behavior problem areas as a consequence of special intervention programs, [and] to target goals for change and intervention on the student's behavioral plan" (p. 8).

The scale is completed by a "professional who is the most knowledgeable about the student, the most competent observer, and the most accurate in rating the behaviors" (examiner's manual, p. 11). In most instances this would be a teacher, although the rater can be an educational diagnostician, psychologist, or even a parent. Scoring is straightforward; raw scores are computed for each of the scales and then converted to percentile ranks and derived standard scores with a mean of 10 and standard deviation of 3. The sum of the four scale scores is converted into a total score, the Conduct Disorder Quotient (CDQ). The CDQ has a mean of 100 and a standard deviation of 15.

The record form includes, in addition to the 40 items, sections for identifying information; 13 yes/no items considered key diagnostic questions; a severity and CD probability rating; a profile to plot scores; space for recommendations; and a brief summary of the CDS highlights.

DEVELOPMENT. The CDS is "composed of items taken from the research literature and the *Diagnostic and Statistical Manual of Mental Disorders—Fourth Edition—Text Revision* (DSM-IV-TR; American Psychiatric Association, 2000)" (examiner's manual, p. 1). However, the manual provides no information on which research literature (or theory) guided test development, how items were developed, or how the 40 items were selected from a larger, initial pool. The manual does not report that experts were enlisted to help

guide test development nor that the scale underwent any item tryout or pilot.

The manual discusses the problem of differentiating students with Conduct Disorder (CD) and students with emotional/behavioral disorders (ED). The manual states that many instruments exist to identify students with ED but few are available to identify students with CD. However, the manual does not explain diagnostic or conceptual distinctions between CD and ED. It is unclear whether test development was guided exclusively by DSM-IV-TR criteria or considered distinctions between CD from ED. Compounding this issue, CD and ED are not absolutely distinct diagnoses. CD is a medical/psychiatric diagnosis and ED (or SED) is a special education classification; many youngsters meet the ED criteria (Individuals with Disabilities Education Act, 1997) during the school day and the CD criteria in the community.

TECHNICAL. A significant weakness is the norm sample. Norms are based on 644 participants, all ostensibly CD. For reasons unexplained in the manual, a normal, nonclinical national standardization sample was not used. As a result, scores can only be compared to scores for persons presumably with CD. The standardization procedure precludes knowing how normal individuals might score. There is no way of knowing whether a given score is atypical for a normal person. The use of a clinical sample as the primary norm group is *only* advisable if it is known that the signs or symptoms measured by the test items are always present in the clinical group and never present in the nonclinical group. This state of affairs, however, rarely exists for any psychiatric or special education disorder.

Two additional problems with the norms sample bear mentioning. First, too few of the age intervals include enough people to be considered representative. For example, six age groups (ages 5, 6, 7, 8, 20, and 22) consist of fewer than 10 individuals each, and only 5 of the 17 age groups include more than 50 individuals. The ability to make a diagnosis of Childhood-Onset Type CD becomes highly problematic with so few individuals included below age 10.

Second, the manual provides almost no information on the CD-norm sample. The manual states that "the test was standardized on 1,040 persons" (p. 2) consisting of a variety of diagnostic groups and that "norms were developed based on 644 representative subjects with Conduct Disorder" (p. 7). The "standardization group" consists of individuals from different diagnostic categories (e.g., ADHD, learning disability, mental retardation) and was not used for standardization but rather as contrast groups during validation studies. It is unclear exactly who constitute the "644 ... subjects with Conduct Disorder," the actual normative sample. The manual provides no information on how, when, or by whom the "644 subjects" were diagnosed. It is unclear if any were comorbid with other disorders, not unusual with a CD cohort. As a result, there is little confidence that the sample is representative of the clinical syndrome CD.

Internal consistency reliability evidence is adequate (.74 for Rule Violations; .79 for Deceitfulness/Theft) to very good (.96 CDQ; .94 for Aggressive Conduct; .91 Hostility). Test-retest (1–2-week administration interval) reliability evidence is adequate (.66 for Deceitfulness/Theft; .69 for Aggressive Conduct) to very good (.91 for Hostility; .80 for Rule Violations; .83 for CDQ) and interrater reliability extimates ranges from fair (.60 for Deceitfulness/Theft; .68 for Hostility), to adequate (.76 for Aggressive Conduct) to good (.89 for CDQ; .81 for Rule Violations). Only 15 participants were used to assess test-retest and interrater reliability; both studies would have benefited from larger samples.

The manual states that factor analytic procedures support the validity of the four scales; disappointingly, no factor analytic data are provided in the manual. The manual describes the use of an "item discrimination procedure" (p. 30) that purports to validate the items. However, without a nationally representative normative group, it is difficult to know how any item discriminates between normal individuals and persons with CD.

Criterion-related validity evidence consisted of correlating scores for 26 participants on the CDS with two rating scales, the Differential Test of Conduct and Emotional Problems (Kelly, 1990) and the Teacher Rating Scale from the Behavior Rating Profile–Second Edition (Brown & Hammill, 1990). Significant correlations were obtained for the CDS scale scores and total score. However, it is unclear why more widely used behavior rating scale such as the Behavior Assessment System for Children (BASC; Reynolds & Kamphaus, 1992), Child Behavior Checklist (CBCL; Achenbach, 1991), or Devereux Scales of Mental Disorders (DSMD, Naglieri, LeBuffe, & Pfeiffer, 1994) were not used as comparison measures. As mentioned above, the "standardization sample" consisted of a variety of diagnostic groups that were used as contrast groups during validation. The CD-norm sample differed significantly from the various clinical groups (e.g., ADHD, ED, learning disability, mental retardation) on the scale scores and CDQ (all differences significant at $p < .05$ and notably quite large). However, information was not provided on how the various clinical groups were diagnosed or whether some were comorbid with other diagnoses.

COMMENTARY. The value of the CDS as a clinical instrument is compromised for a number of reasons. The lack of a nationally representative normative sample precludes comparison with normal, nonclinical samples. The manual provides no information on how participants in the CD-norm group or clinical comparison groups were selected, and therefore, no assurance that they are representative of the groups that they are professed to represent. The small sample size of the CD-norm group, particularly in the 5–12-year age group, necessitates that the CDS should be used with great caution with children younger than 13. This precludes its use in diagnosing Childhood-Onset Type CD.

The manual states that the CDS can be used to target treatment goals and document treatment change. However, there is no evidence supporting either claim. Other than face validity, there are no data indicating that any items would be useful in treatment planning—at least not any more useful than treatment goals that a clinician would otherwise generate independent of the CDS. Before the CDS can be used to measure improvement, the manual has to provide formula or tables detailing exactly how much improvement is necessary for the change to be significant (or clinically meaningful). A 2- or even 3-point "improvement" on a number of items on the 4-point scale may simply prove to be an artifact of regression effects and/or less-than-perfect reliability.

SUMMARY. The CDS is a 40-item rating scale designed to identify persons with Conduct Disorder. It is easy to use and score. The record form is attractive and well designed. Persons familiar with DSM-IV-TR will recognize many of the items. The CDS falls short in meeting its stated goals of identifying persons with CD and differentiating CD and ED. Existing rating scales such as the BASC (Reynolds & Kamphaus, 1992), CBCL (Achenbach, 1991), and DSMD (Naglieri, LeBuffe, & Pfeiffer, 1994) include nationally representative normative samples, something missing in the CDS. Curry and Ilardi (2000), in a carefully designed study, found that the CBCL and DSMD accurately classify CD and other externalizing disorders, something the CDS has yet to demonstrate.

REVIEWER'S REFERENCES

Achenbach, T. M. (1991). *Manual for the Child Behavior Checklist: 4–18 and 1991 profile.* Burlington, VT: University of Vermont Department of Psychiatry.
American Psychiatric Association. (2000). *Diagnostic and statistical manual of mental disorders* (4th ed., text revision). Washington, DC: Author.
Brown, L., & Hammill, D. D. (1990). Behavior Rating Profile–Second Edition. Austin, TX: PRO-ED.
Curry, J. F., & Ilardi, S. S. (2000). Validity of the Devereux Scales of Mental Disorders with adolescent psychiatric inpatients. *Journal of Clinical Child Psychology, 29,* 578–588.
Individuals with Disabilities Education Act Amendments of 1997, Pub. L. No. 105–117. 20 USC Chapter 33, Sections 1400 *et seq.* (Statute).
Kelly, E. J. (1990). *Differential Test of Conduct and Emotional Problems.* East Aurora, NY: Slosson Educational Publications, Inc.
Naglieri, J. A., LeBuffe, P., & Pfeiffer, S. I. (1994). *Devereux Scales of Mental Disorders manual.* San Antonio, TX: The Psychological Corporation.
Reynolds, C., & Kamphaus, R. W. (1992). *Behavior Assessment System for Children.* Circle Pines, MN: American Guidance Service.

[65]

Conflict Analysis Battery.

Purpose: Designed to "assess a person's conflict resolution process, including relational pattern, energies, intertransformations, fixations of energies, etc...."
Population: Adults.
Publication Date: 1988.
Acronym: CAB.
Scores: 11 subtests: The Relational Modality Evaluation Scale, Transparent Mask Test, Balloon Portraits and Story, Conflictual Memories Test, Animal Metaphor Test, Fairy Tale Metaphor Test, Short Story Metaphor, Intensified Animal Metaphor Test, Dream Analysis, House-Tree-Person Metaphor Test, Scribble Metaphor.
Administration: Individual.
Price Data: Available from publisher.
Time: Administration time not reported.
Comments: Self-administered and self-interpreted projective test battery; developed for use with Conflict Analysis Training: A Program of Emotional Education.
Author: Albert J. Levis.
Publisher: The Institute of Conflict Analysis.

Review of the Conflict Analysis Battery by SUSAN M. BROOKHART, Coordinator of Assessment & Evaluation, School of Educationm, Duquesne University, Pittsburgh, PA:

DESCRIPTION. The Conflict Analysis Battery is described in its manual as the self-assessment portion of a program of "emotional educa-

tion" (Levis, 1988a). It is composed of a questionnaire and several projective tests. The Relational Modality Evaluation Scale is a 194-item questionnaire. The response to each item is on a 6-point Likert scale from *strongly disagree* (-3) to *strongly agree* (+3), with no zero point. The projective techniques include the following: Transparent Mask Test, Balloon Portraits and Story, Conflictual Memories Test, Metaphor Construction Tests (Animal, Fairy Tale, Short Story, and Intensified Animal Metaphor Tests), Dream Analysis, House-Tree-Person, and Scribble Test. The manual claims that "the pattern revealed in the metaphors is assessed by the testee. He or she is the sole recipient, interpreter, and beneficiary of the insights derived from the testing" (Levis, 1988a, p. 3).

DEVELOPMENT. The theoretical framework for the Conflict Analysis Battery is presented in a self-published textbook (Levis, 1988b). In describing the "six role Conflict Resolution Process," the text refers to things as disparate as the creation of the Universe through Adam and Eve, the rise of China and India and other historical events; mathematics, including trigonometric functions to describe the energy transformations in the psyche; natural science, including formulas about mass, force, and electromagnetism; anthropology; metaphysics; psychology; and philosophy, including claims that the theory also involves "moral alternatives." The author uses the Conflict Analysis Battery as part of his program of lectures, analysis, and training at his Manchester Institute of Conflict Analysis.

TECHNICAL. No standardization information was available. One empirical study of the reliability and validity of the questionnaire portion of the Conflict Analysis Battery was done (Karas, 1985). The study did not describe the sample. Karas (p. 2) listed split-half reliability coefficients ranging from .79 to .96 for six scales: Dominant Cooperative, Dominant Antagonistic, Antagonistic/Cooperative, Submissive Cooperative, Submissive Antagonistic, and Psychic Conflict Tension. The same study reported three kinds of evidence for validity: a concurrent and discriminant validity study using the Interpersonal Check List (Leary, 1957); a clinical study of test discrimination among clinical diagnosis groups; and a factor analysis.

When the scales were examined for whether they differentiated among four clinical diagnosis groups according to the conflict analysis theory used in the battery, three of the four clinical groups did not have as their highest mean the scale predicted by the theory. The factor analysis is described as "almost reproducing" the six scales, but no statistical results are presented. This empirical study referred to the use of information from the questionnaire in clinical practice, which appears to contradict the self-assessment purpose quoted from the manual.

Evidence for the validity of the projective portions of the test is presented as case studies of Dr. Levis's clients. Some of these are labeled as to the clinical diagnosis of the client (e.g., "suicidal"); some are not. There is no evidence from clients of any psychiatrists other than Dr. Levis, the battery's author.

COMMENTARY AND SUMMARY. The theoretical framework on which the Conflict Analysis Battery is based is self-published. One empirical study of the questionnaire portion of the battery was done in 1985 (at this writing, 20 years ago) and did not describe the sample. The clinical evidence for the usefulness of the projective portions of the battery comes from the author's own practice. Given these points, this reviewer does not recommend the use of the Conflict Analysis Battery for either the self-assessment purpose described by its manual or the clinical use inferred from its documentation.

REVIEWER'S REFERENCES
Karas, S. F. (1985, November). *Item analysis, reliability, and validity studies: Conflict Analysis Battery.* Unpublished report, Southern Connecticut State University.
Leary, T. (1957). *Interpersonal diagnosis of personality.* New York: Ronald Press.
Levis, A. J. (1988a). *Conflict Analysis Training: A program of emotional education.* Manchester Village, VT: Normative Publications.
Levis, A. J. (1988b). *Conflict Analysis: The formal theory of behavior.* Manchester Village, VT: Normative Publications.

Review of the Conflict Analysis Battery by CARL ISENHART, Coordinator, Addictive Disorders Section, VA Medical Center, Minneapolis, MN:

DESCRIPTION. The Conflict Analysis Battery (CAB) is an assessment process that is used as part of and is based on concepts from "Conflict Analysis Training." According to the author, Conflict Analysis "conceptually integrates mental processes and social transactions. Ideas, emotions, behaviors, and biological phenomena are redefined into part aspects of a formal and energetic continuum in which order abides by the laws of logic, mathematics, and physics" (Levis, 1988, p. 9a). Specifically, the CAB purports to: "identify both your relational modality, that is, your way of relating or communicating with others and the degree of psychic tension or intensity of conflict you currently experience" (p. 12).

The CAB consists of 11 subtests: the Relational Modality Evaluation Scale (RMES), the Transparent Mask Test, Balloon Portraits and Story, Conflictual Memories Test of Childhood, Animal Metaphor Test #1, Fairy Tale Metaphor Test, Short Story Metaphor, Intensified Animal Metaphor Test #2, Dream Analysis, House-Tree-Person Metaphor Test, and Scribble Metaphor.

There are brief instructions and information about the rationale of these subtests; however, the information and the theory on which these "instruments" are based is extremely abstract and difficult to follow.

DEVELOPMENT. There is little or no information about the process by which this "battery" was developed, other than how it evolved with the author's ideas about the Conflict Analysis Theory.

TECHNICAL. There is very little technical information regarding standardization, reliability, and validity. The information that is available comes in the form of a letter addressed "To Whom it may Concern" from a researcher trained in testing and measurement. In this letter there is a brief discussion about reliability and validity and description of some results; however, it is confusing in that the data do not relate back to the specific subtests, it does not provide a description of the samples, and it does not provide details of how the data were analyzed. [Editor's Note: The publisher advises that information regarding clinical and theoretical studies for this test are available at www.ArtToScience.org and TelionHolon.com.]

SUMMARY. All in all, there is nothing that impressed this reviewer about this "battery" that would justify its use in its current form. The theories and concepts on which it is based are difficult to follow and do not relate directly to the test itself, the battery lacks standardization for administration and interpretation, and there is a serious dearth of technical support.

REVIEWER'S REFERENCE
Levis, A. J. (1988). *Conflict analysis training: A program of emotional education.* Manchester Village, VT: Normative Publications.

[66]

Conners' Adult ADHD Diagnostic Interview for DSM-IV.

Purpose: Empirically based structured interview that assists the process of diagnosing ADHD.
Population: Age 18 and older.
Publication Date: 2001.
Acronym: CAADID.

Scores: Childhood and Adult ADHD Diagnosis (specifies Inattentive vs. Hyperactive Impulsive).
Administration: Individual.
Price Data, 2005: $102 per complete kit including technical manual (2001, 64 pages), 10 patient history forms, and 10 diagnostic criteria forms; $46 per specimen set including technical manual, 1 patient history form, and 1 diagnostic criteria form.
Time: (60–90) minutes for Interview; (30–60) minutes for Self-Report.
Comments: Interview format.
Authors: Jeff Epstein, Diane Johnson, and C. Keith Conners.
Publisher: Multi-Health Systems, Inc.

Review of the Conners' Adult ADHD Diagnostic Interview for DSM-IV by GEORGE J. DEMAKIS, Associate Professor, University of North Carolina at Charlotte, Charlotte, NC:

DESCRIPTION. The Conners' Adult ADHD Diagnostic Interview for DSM-IV (CAADID) is a structured interview of ADHD symptoms for adults based on DSM-IV criteria and is composed of two parts. Part 1 addresses a variety of background or history issues in both childhood and adulthood including demographic, academic, psychiatric, occupational, and health information. This section can be administered in interview format by the clinician or the patient can complete it independently. As a self-report measure, it should take about 30 to 60 minutes to complete, but if completed by a clinician in an interview format it may take 60 to 90 minutes. Part 2 addresses whether the patient meets the four DSM-IV criteria for ADHD including presence of symptoms (i.e., inattention or hyperactivity/impulsivity), age of onset, symptom pervasiveness, and severity of impairment. For the symptoms section, patients are queried whether they have the particular symptom currently as an adult and whether they had it as a child. Following each question across Part 2, items are scored as either present or not present. At the end of Part 2, a summary sheet and scoring algorithm concisely summarize the preceding responses and allow for a diagnosis to be made. Part 2 can only be administered by the clinician in interview-format and takes about 60 minutes.

DEVELOPMENT. The CAADID was designed to provide a categorical diagnosis of ADHD in adults in a structured interview format. Although such instruments exist for children and self-report dimensional measures exist for adults, this is apparently the first structured clinical interview of adult ADHD based on DSM-IV criteria that address both adult and childhood symptoms. Assessment of these is necessary to make such a diagnosis in adults. Authors state that they piloted the CAADID in their ADHD clinic and found it useful for making ADHD diagnoses in adults.

TECHNICAL. The user's manual provides no normative data of any sort nor does it provide any psychometric information, such as reliability and validity data. A review of the broader psychological and psychiatric literature via PsychInfo and Medline did not reveal other sources that may have included such information nor were any published studies located that used this measure to diagnose ADHD in adults.

COMMENTARY. Although the CAADID does address an important clinical need and provides clear administration and scoring instructions, there are two issues that limit its usefulness clinically. First, administration time is fairly lengthy—up to two hours of clinician time. It is difficult to imagine clinicians routinely using such a measure particularly when most ADHD evaluations include multiple sources of information, such as collateral interview as well as cognitive and personality testing. Moreover, the clinician may want to address issues that are not included in the structured clinical interview, thus increasing time. Perhaps like other structured interviews, this measure is more appropriate and more likely to be used for research purposes. Second, because the manual and wider literature are lacking in any normative or psychometric data, it is difficult to judge the quality of the CAADID. At a most basic level, authors should have provided at least some information on how diagnoses on this measure compare with other self-report or interview measures (concurrent validity), how diagnoses based on this measure hold up over time (test-retest reliability), and whether different raters agree on patient diagnosis using this measure (interrater reliability). Structured interviews routinely include such information and more, but this latter issue is particularly important.

SUMMARY. The CAADID is a structured interview for Adult ADHD that is composed of two parts: Part 1 extensively addresses background and historical information, whereas in Part 2 questions are asked about ADHD symptoms that are directly based on DSM-IV criteria. Part 1 can be completed in a self-report or clinician interview, whereas Part 2 is based only on clinician interview.

Total administration time can be as high as 2 to 2.5 hours. Although the interview forms are clearly laid out and easy to use, it seems unlikely that this measure would gain much of a following for clinical use given the lengthy administration time. Moreover, normative and technical information on this measure are totally lacking, precluding judgments about its psychometric properties. In total, before this measure can be recommended for clinical or research purposes, authors need to provide basic normative information and demonstrate empirically how the test actually works in clinical populations—issues expected to be addressed before such structured interviews are published.

Review of the Conners' Adult ADHD Diagnostic Interview for DSM-IV by TIMOTHY J. MAKATURA, Adjunct Professor of Psychology, Capella University, Minneapolis, MN:

The Conners' Adult ADHD Diagnostic Interview for DSM-IV (CAADID) was developed to assist clinicians in the evaluation of adults presenting with ADHD symptoms. The standard process to make the diagnosis of ADHD is to rely on the criteria found in the DSM-IV (American Psychiatric Association, 1994). However, the authors of the CAADID point out that these well-validated criteria are based on research with children and adolescents, and may not be appropriate for adults. The authors further comment that "ADHD was long thought to be a condition that generally subsided following puberty" (technical manual, p. 1). However, longitudinal studies conducted in the 1980s and 1990s revealed that ADHD may be a chronic condition as demonstrated by the fact 50–65% of children diagnosed with this disorder continue to demonstrate symptoms into adulthood (Barkley, 1995). The consequences of ADHD in adulthood can be quite significant and may be associated with lower levels of educational and occupational attainment, job instability, substance abuse, and antisocial behavior. Further, the authors present a rather extensive listing of specific symptoms of Adult ADHD that are adapted from a book by Sallee (1995).

The authors acknowledge that there is limited empirical research that defines adult ADHD and reports that using the existing DSM-IV criteria for adults may be questioned on a number of grounds including: limited information regarding age-related changes of ADHD symptoms and critical symptoms in adults, inappropriate wording of criteria, and unknown subtypes of ADHD in adults. The authors also conclude that there is no existing instrument that provides a viable alternative.

The CAADID appears to be a logical extension of the structured interview to assess for ADHD in children. To accommodate for adults, this instrument is designed to establish current and childhood symptoms of ADHD, screen for comorbid conditions, comprehensively screen for all current manifestations of ADHD, use language and format that is conducive to self-report, and provide a categorical diagnosis based on the DSM-IV.

DESCRIPTION. The CAADID is a screening instrument designed to systematically evaluate critical symptoms in the determination of the diagnosis of Attention Deficit Hyperactivity Disorder in adults. It is a two-part structured interview that consists of separate History and Diagnostic Criteria sections. The History section may be administered as a series of questions to the client or simply presented to the client as a paper-and-pencil task. Most items in this section require a yes/no answer but short answers are required including particulars related to family members, providers, medications, jobs, and schools. The Diagnostic Interview section is administered by a qualified clinician and involves a series of questions that address each specific criterion of the Attention Deficit Hyperactivity Disorder (ADHD) diagnosis from the *Diagnostic and Statistical Manual of Mental Disorders, Fourth Edition* (DSM-IV; American Psychiatric Association, 1994).

The History form is a 19-page questionnaire that solicits information from childhood to adulthood. Initial sections focus on childhood (birth through 18 years) and include questions regarding demographic data and information regarding risk factors for ADHD related to gestation, birth/delivery, temperament, development, environment, and medical history. This questionnaire proceeds through a detailed examination of academic performance from elementary through high school, questions regarding psychiatric history, and familial risk factors. This questionnaire then considers adulthood (age 18 and over) and solicits information regarding post secondary education, occupational history, social/interpersonal history, health history, and psychiatric history. The final section of the questionnaire considers information related to comorbidity of mental health symptoms and substance use.

The Diagnostic Criteria section also begins with questions regarding demographic data but then presents separate sections to consider Inattention Symptoms and Hyperactivity/Impulsive Symptoms. Each of the DSM-IV criteria is listed individually with separate subsections that address childhood and adulthood. The adulthood section is presented first and a primary question is presented that probes for the DSM-IV criterion and the examiner is provided with space to record comments or examples. Examples of critical behaviors are also provided. A secondary question is provided to determine if the symptom is clinically significant and space is again provided for the examiner to record comments or examples. From this information, the examiner determines if this particular symptom is present in adulthood. The examiner then follows the same procedure to determine if this symptom was present in childhood. This procedure continues for each of the criteria. This section for Inattention Symptoms concludes with questions regarding the age of onset, pervasiveness, and level of impairment. The section that considers Hyperactivity/Impulsive Symptoms follows the same format. A summary sheet is provided at the end of this section to total the number of symptoms, age of onset, symptoms of pervasiveness, level of impairment, and diagnosis. This scoring sheet provides side-by-side comparison of adulthood and childhood symptoms.

Regarding interpretation of the CAADID, the authors suggest the following six steps: Assess the validity of the responses, identify endorsed symptoms via the profile sheet, analyze for differential diagnoses, integrate results with all other information, and determine appropriate intervention or remediation strategy. Case studies are provided; however, these tend to demonstrate the efficiency of certain ADHD rating scales other than the CAADID.

TECHNICAL. There is very limited information presented to support the technical properties of this instrument. The authors allude to some general findings from a pilot study that was completed with the CAADID but they do not offer specific findings. From this pilot study, the authors report that clients did not have difficulty completing the History section and that they generally appreciated the savings in time and money. The Diagnostic Criteria section provides all of the DSM-IV criteria for ADHD and

there is certainly no question about the validity of this information. However, the specific questions that are asked and examples that are provided seem to extend beyond the specific criteria presented in the DSM-IV.

COMMENTARY AND SUMMARY. The CAADID is a relatively new instrument that seems to meet the need for a structured interview for critical symptoms of ADHD in adults. It certainly provides for a comprehensive collection of historical data and information relevant to the existence of ADHD symptoms in childhood and adulthood as well as a scoring sheet allows symptoms to be easily summarized. However, this instrument is based on the largely unsupported premise that the criteria for adult ADHD may be logically derived from the existing DSM-IV criteria for children and adolescents. Until the specific diagnostic criteria for adult ADHD are empirically established, the utility of the CAADID will remain in question. Caution is advised in the interpretation of the results of this instrument. Further research is strongly recommended.

REVIEWER'S REFERENCES

American Psychiatric Association. (1994). *Diagnostic and statistical manual of mental disorders* (4th ed.). Washington, DC: Author.
Barkley, R. A. (1995). *Taking charge of ADHD*. New York: Guilford.
Sallee, F. (1995). *Attention deficit/hyperactivity disorder in adults*. Champaign, IL: Grotelueschen Associates.

[67]

Conners' Kiddie Continuous Performance Test.

Purpose: Software program designed to identify attention problems and measure treatment effectiveness in very young children.

Population: Age 4–5.

Publication Date: 2001.

Acronym: K-CPT.

Scores: Omissions, Commissions, Hit RT, Hit RT Standard Error, Variability, Detectability (d'), Response Style, Perseverations, Hit RT Block Change, Hit SE Block Change, Hit RT ISI Change, Hit SE ISI Change, Confidence Index.

Administration: Individual.

Price Data, 2002: $200 per manual (156 pages) and PsychManager software kit; $45 per preview version.

Time: 7.5 minutes.

Comments: Self-completed; administered and scored on computer running Windows 95 or higher.

Authors: C. Keith Conners and Multi-Health Systems, Inc. staff.

Publisher: Multi-Health Systems, Inc.

Review of the Conners' Kiddie Continuous Performance Test by BRIAN F. FRENCH, Assistant Professor of Educational Psychology, Purdue University, West Lafayette, IN:

DESCRIPTION. The Conners' Kiddie Continuous Performance Test (K-CPT) is an individually administered computerized test that claims to assess attention difficulties in 4- and 5-year-old children. The K-CPT's primary use is as a quick screening tool to determine if further investigation of attention problems is warranted. Additional uses include research purposes and tracking children's behavior over time, especially related to changes in treatment (e.g., level of medication). The examinee's task for 7.5 minutes is to indicate when any black and white picture (e.g., car, house, bicycle) other than the nontarget picture (i.e., a ball) appears on a white screen by a click of the computer mouse or a press of the space bar on the keyboard. Target misses (Omissions) and nontarget hits (Commissions) are recorded. The administrator is present during testing and is to respond to questions from the examinee as quickly as possible with a standardized response (i.e., "I can answer that after you are finished. Please continue," p. 15), as time off task can influence performance.

The K-CPT is composed of five blocks, each containing two subblocks with 20 trials each. The pictures appear on the screen for 500 milliseconds and the Inter-Stimulus intervals (ISIs) are varied (i.e., 1.5 and 3.0 seconds) between subblocks. Measures include response times (i.e., speed and consistency of reactions) to the nearest millisecond and response errors (i.e., Omissions and Commissions). Scores in the form of T-scores and percentile ranks are given (a) in aggregate form, (b) by block to assess change in responses times as the test progresses, and (c) by ISIs to assess change in response times at the different levels of ISIs. Signal detection theory statistics (i.e., d prime and Beta) also are a component of the results. In addition, the Confidence Index is reported, which gives the level of confidence that an examinee's scores resulted in a correct classification.

Score reports, generated automatically, include (a) graphical summaries of performance; (b) profile graphs of T-scores; (c) tables of information regarding inattention, impulsivity, and vigilance; and (d) textual interpretation of the scores. The user can select examinee reports in comparison to ADHD or general population norms. The program provides a self-diagnostic check related to the validity of the administration. If an extreme percentage of omissions or perseverations occur, the program supplies a message about validity concerns of the results and the test must be administered again. Score interpretation information provided in the manual "will not alone be sufficient to correctly use and interpret the results" (p. 25). The information must be supplemented with additional reading and comprehension in the areas of CPT theory, signal detection theory, and statistical theory. Thus, the test should be administered, scored, and interpreted by a trained professional who (a) knows the standards specified in the *Standards for Educational and Psychological Testing* (AERA, APA, & NCME, 1999), (b) belongs to a professional organization that supports ethical use of psychological tests, and (c) in clinical settings, has an advanced degree (e.g., Ph.D., M.D.) in the behavioral or medical sciences.

DEVELOPMENT. The K-CPT is a downward extension of the Conners' Continuous Performance Test II (CPT II; Conners, 2000; 15:66). Specifically, the CPT II was customized to account for age-related differences in performance. The authors claim the CPT II "works well for 6 year olds and above but, for 4 and 5 year olds, the 14 minutes is clearly problematic" (p. 41). The program customization involved a change in (a) the administration time from 14 minutes to 7.5 minutes, (b) the stimuli from letters to pictures, (c) the stimuli display time from 250ms to 500ms, and (d) the ISIs from 1, 2, and 4 seconds to 1.5 and 3.0 seconds. This version is claimed to meet "the needs of this very specific population" (p. 41) because stimuli were selected to be most familiar to young children and time adjustments result in appropriate stimuli presentation time. Thus, the authors claim that confounded results that occur with the use of the CPT II with this age group are avoided. However, changes were based on observational data and no empirical evidence was presented to demonstrate that the CPT-II did not function well for this age group or to justify the levels of customization.

TECHNICAL. Normative data (N = 454) were provided for 4- and 5-year-old participants that included (a) general population (n = 314), (b) clinical-ADHD (n = 100), and (c) clinical-nonADHD (n = 40) samples. The samples were composed of participants drawn from 27 sites from 18 locations around the United States and 2 locations in Canada. Age and gender percentages are provided separately for each sample. Male and female representation was 47.7% and 52.3%, respectively, in the general population sample, 75% and 25%, respectively, in the clinical-ADHD sample, and 72.5% and 27.5%, respectively, in the clinical-nonADHD sample. Ethnic group information is provided in aggregate form for the general population and clinical-ADHD sample, with the majority of the sample being composed of White (76.3 %) and Black (10.5%) examinees. Ethnicity information by sample, not only in aggregate form, would be helpful. The general population sample was not prescreened for ADHD or other disabilities. Thus, this sample may contain participants with attention disorders at the rate that occurs in the population. Clinical-ADHD participants were identified with differing diagnostic procedures; however, all procedures met DSM-IV (American Psychiatric Association, 1994) criteria.

Split-half reliability estimates were provided for Hit Reaction Time, Standard Error, Omissions, and Commissions measures with a range of .72 to .88. These split-half reliability estimates were used in calculating the standard error of measurement and standard error of prediction for gender, age, and for two of the three norm samples (general population and clinical-ADHD) for the Hit Reaction Time, Standard Error, Omissions, and Commissions measures. The reliability data, especially for the Hit Reaction Time, did not meet recommended reliability standards (Nunnally & Bernstein, 1994). Reliability evidence to examine the stability of the scores across time (i.e., test-retest reliability) was not reported, which is of concern as a suggested use of the K-CPT is to track changes over time. The manual suggests that the standard errors of measurement and estimation should be used to obtain confidence intervals around the obtained scores. A more appropriate method is to construct the intervals around estimated true scores, as obtained scores are biased (Nunnally & Bernstein, 1994). Reliability coefficients should be reported by age and by sample, not only in aggregate form, as this would assist with interpretation of the standard error of measurement and estimation and be consistent with recommendations by the *Standards* (AERA, APA, & NCME, 1999).

Validity evidence consisted of contrasting groups, which demonstrated that there were sig-nificant differences on the measures between the clinical (ADHD and nonADHD) and general population samples. For instance, the clinical-ADHD sample had a higher percentage of omissions compared to the general population and the clinical-nonADHD clinical sample. Effect sizes for the multivariate and univariate tests and the standard deviations for each measure were not provided. Without the effect sizes, judging the magnitude of the differences among groups is difficult, if not impossible, without additional statistical information. A discriminant analysis was conducted to examine classification accuracy. Several measures (i.e., d prime, reaction time by block, Standard Error by ISI, and Hit Reaction Time) significantly contributed to discriminating between the clinical-ADHD and general population samples. False positives and false negatives were 27% and 9%, respectively. In the classification accuracy results, the number of general population participants used for this analysis ($n = 334$) is inconsistent with the number reported for the other analyses ($n = 314$) without explanation. Additional validity evidence (e.g., concurrent validity), would provide information concerning the extent to which the K-CPT provides information beyond what other screening measures (e.g., rating scales) provide.

COMMENTARY. The K-CPT appears to be a useful screening measure. However, a few concerns should be mentioned. First, the ADHD norms should not be used for interpretation, as this norm sample was limited and preliminary. The standard scores relative to the general population norms should be used. However, this sample also was somewhat limited. Second, reliability evidence did not meet recommended standards on all measures. Third, reliability evidence is insufficient in relation to suggestions for use of the scores over time. Fourth, the practicality of the K-CPT may be limited as a practitioner is required to have additional resources available in the areas of CPT theory, signal detection theory, and statistical theory for score use and interpretation. Fifth, the administrator answering examinee questions during this short and attention intensive test would appear to seriously influence the scores and lead to meaningless score interpretation. The authors appear to have somewhat addressed this concern with the program self-diagnostic validity check of the results. This check should help to guard against this concern but does not eliminate the threat.

SUMMARY. The K-CPT manual and online help files provide clear instructions and the computer software is easy to install and use. The K-CPT is a reasonable attempt to design a CPT to minimize bias associated with the use of longer CPTs with young children. Furthermore, the measure appears to be acceptable for screening purposes, the suggested primary use. However, the K-CPT scores do not have adequate reliability and validity evidence for diagnostic purposes. The K-CPT scores alone should not be used to make diagnostic decisions in the absence of additional valid evidence.

REVIEWER'S REFERENCES

American Educational Research Association, American Psychological Association, & National Council on Measurement in Education (1999). *Standards for educational and psychological testing.* Washington, DC: American Educational Research Association.
American Psychiatric Association. (1994). *Diagnostic and statistical manual of mental disorders* (4th ed.). Washington, DC: Author.
Conners, C. K. (2000). *Conners' Continuous Performance Test II technical guide and software manual.* Toronto, Ontario, Canada: Multi-Health Systems.
Nunnally, J. C., & Bernstein, I. H. (1994). *Psychometric theory.* New York: McGraw-Hill.

Review of the Conners' Kiddie Continuous Performance Test by SCOTT A. NAPOLITANO, Assistant Professor, Lincoln Pediatric Group, Lincoln, NE, and COURTNEY MILLER, Lecturer, Educational Psychology, University of Nebraska—Lincoln, Lincoln, NE:

DESCRIPTION. The Conners' Kiddie Continuous Performance Test (K-CPT) is a computerized instrument designed to assess attention disorders in 4- and 5-year-old children. The test kit includes computer software as well as a user manual and takes approximately 10 minutes to administer. This test can be administered individually for the purposes of initial screening as well as for progress monitoring. Respondents are asked to press the spacebar whenever any picture other than a soccer ball is presented on the computer screen. The K-CPT measures Omissions, Comissions, Hit Reaction Time, Hit Reaction Time Standard Error, Variability of Standard Errors, Attentiveness (d'), Perseverations, Hit Reaction Time Block Change, Hit Standard Error Block Change, Use of Block Change Statistics, Hit Reaction Time ISI Change, and Hit Standard Error ISI Change. Each of these measures is defined by the authors in the user manual, however, these definitions seem to assume prior knowledge of the Continuous Performance Test (CPT) on the part of the user. Upon completion of the test, individualized reports can be generated through the computer software, with results converted to *T*-scores and percentile ranks. The manual provides step-by-step technical instructions for installing and navigating the computer software.

DEVELOPMENT. The K-CPT was developed to meet the need of assessing attention difficulties in young children, utilizing similar procedures as the Conners' Continuous Performance Tests II (CPT-II; Conners, 2000) but tailoring the test to an appropriate development level. Although a theoretical background section on the CPT is included in the user's manual, it is at times difficult to understand and does not specifically address underlying assumptions for the K-CPT. The concepts of low arousal in hyperactivity, vigilance decrement, event rate, floor effect, and reaction time are mentioned in this section but are not always clearly defined. There is also limited empirical support provided for these concepts and an integration of the literature in terms of a theoretical foundation is lacking. Moreover, theories relative to attention problems such as behavioral inhibition, working memory, self-regulation, and motor control (Barkley, 1966), to name a few, are not included in this discussion.

In terms of development and normative data for the K-CPT, information reported in the manual is again vague; although a pilot version of the K-CPT was utilized, not much detail is provided in terms of stimuli selection or display time determinant. The K-CPT was administered to 454 four- and five-year-olds; however, only 100 of these children met criteria for ADHD. In determining clinical significance for ADHD, it appears no set protocol was followed; the authors allude to the use of the DSM-IV (APA, 1994) diagnostic criteria as well as a "recommended multimodal/multiple informant diagnostic approach" (technical guide and software manual, p. 44) but no further explanation is provided. Additionally, no information is provided in the manual with regard to the qualifications of the "site coordinators" for administering the K-CPT and gathering further information relative to attention problems with this specific population.

TECHNICAL. Reliability of the K-CPT is reported as split-half reliability and standard error. Split-half reliabilities are adequate and are as follows: Hit Reaction Time .72, Standard Error .78, Commissions .83, and Omissions .88. Standard error is calculated as standard error of measurement and standard error of prediction. Although tables for these standard errors are provided, limited explanation is given and overall interpretation of the results is left to the user. Because the primary purpose of the K-CPT is screening, the authors present validity evidence in terms of group differences and classification accuracy. Overall, the authors report significant differences between the general population, ADHD group, and other clinically impaired groups on the dependent measures. Classification accuracy for ADHD versus nonclinical was 73% for specificity with 27% false positives and 91% for sensitivity with 9% false negatives. In addition, the authors present overall age effects as another support for the K-CPT's validity. Although these effects for Hit Reaction Time, Standard Error, Commissions, and Omissions are visually represented and percentages given, no further statistical analyses are provided to support this conclusion.

COMMENTARY. As the authors justly note, the K-CPT is a screening instrument that is to be used in conjunction with other modalities to assess for attention difficulties. The K-CPT is not intended to be the sole determinant in diagnosing ADHD and the results of this test should be viewed as preliminary. Although the K-CPT is relatively easy to administer, the results always should be interpreted by a qualified professional as acknowledged by the authors. Users of this instrument are cautioned from drawing definite conclusions based solely on the K-CPT's report results. In addition, users should be wary of administering the K-CPT as a routine screener to avoid predisposed expectancies for behaviors. For example, the second case study given in the manual discusses a 4-year-old boy who was not experiencing any attentional difficulties but whose K-CPT scores were elevated and indicative of potential problems. Although monitoring of this behavior may be appropriate, the authors also suggested approaching the parents and potentially initiating a formal assessment.

SUMMARY. The K-CPT appears to have some utility as an initial assessment instrument for attention problems with 4- and 5-year-old children. Users with a solid knowledge base of continuous performance test paradigms may best be able to understand the constructs of this test and accurately interpret its results. Although the computerized report provides an "interpretive guide" printout that explains results in lay terms, users should exercise caution in drawing definite conclusions based on this alone. The K-CPT may be best viewed as one component of a comprehensive, multimodal method of assessment. Given the complexities of assessing ADHD in young children, the K-CPT may add a useful piece of information to help in the diagnostic process.

REVIEWERS' REFERENCES

American Psychiatric Association. (1994). *Diagnostic and statistical manual of mental disorders* (4th ed.). Washington, DC: Author.
Barkley, R. A. (1996). Attention-Deficit/Hyperactivity Disorder. In E. J. Mash & R. A. Barkley (Eds.), *Child psychopathology* (pp. 63–112). New York: Guilford Press.
Conners, C. K. (2000). *Conners' Continuous Performance Test II technical guide and software manual.* Toronto, ON: Multi-Health Systems.

[68]

Customer Service Skills Test.

Purpose: To evaluate technical and interpersonal skills of persons for the customer service position; available also to measure computer use skills.

Population: Candidates for customer service positions.

Publication Date: 1992.

Acronym: BASLCUS.

Scores: Total Score, Narrative Evaluation, Ranking, Recommendation.

Administration: Group.

Price Data, 2001: $150 per candidate; quantity discounts available.

Foreign Language Edition: Available in French.

Time: (70) minutes.

Comments: Scored by publisher; available in booklet and internet versions; must be proctored.

Author: Walden Personnel Performance, Inc.

Publisher: Walden Personnel Performance, Inc. [Canada].

Review of the Customer Service Skills Test by WAYNE J. CAMARA, Vice President of Research and Psychometrics, The College Board, New York, NY:

DESCRIPTION. The Customer Service Skills Test, available in paper and Internet versions, is designed to evaluate the suitability of applicants with all levels of experience for the position of Customer Service Representative, Non-Technical Help Desk positions, and Inside Sales or Order Desk positions. The two forms do not appear to be completely equivalent. Each form of the test measures seven skills, of which six are common across forms: Numerical Skills, Attention to Detail, Problem Solving Ability, Customer Service Skills, Customer Service Problem Solving, and Customer Service Logic. The paper form also includes a measure of Verbal Fluency, whereas the Internet form (http://www.waldentesting.com/salestests/custserv.html, 3/20/04) includes a measure of Reading Comprehension.

A six-page manual is available for the test that describes the test administration requirements, job criteria measured, skills measured by the test, scoring services, and provides sample items. The manual does not meet many of the requirements for a technical manual noted in the *Standards for Educational and Psychological Testing* (AERA, APA, & NCME, 1999). The test is 56 minutes in length, and although the manual states that only clerical supervision is required to administer the test, each section must be precisely timed—"it is important that the timed sections be timed to the second" (test manual, p. 2). Section timing ranges from 15 minutes for the Customer Service Logic section to 5 minutes for the Numerical Skills, Attention to Detail, and Problem Solving sections.

The seven subtests are divided into two parts of the test that are labeled Customer Service Related Skills (includes Customer Service Skills, Customer Service Problem Solving, and Customer Service Logic) and Administrative and Intellectual Skills (which is composed of the remaining subtests). The Customer Service Skills subtest requires the applicant to choose the most appropriate response to a specific customer inquiry from among four alternative actions, and the Customer Service Problem Solving subtest is actually a series of mathematical word problems. The Customer Service Logic subtest is the most unusual measure in the battery and measures procedural ability by asking a series of questions based on flow charts. Together, these three tests appear the most relevant to customer service occupations the test is designed to assess. The four subtests comprising the Administrative and Intellectual section include Verbal Fluency (thinking of words rapidly that have certain prefixes or suffixes), Reading Comprehension (Internet form only), Numerical Skills (one- and two-step computational problems), Attention to Detail (pattern recognition), and Problem Solving Ability (identify the next series of numbers or letters given a pattern). All subtests appear moderately speeded, which is understandable given the nature and requirements of many customer service positions.

Paper forms can be scored via regular mail, fax service, or telephone scoring. Two-hour fax scoring and telephone scoring require a substantial additional fee. Internet scoring is not described, but because most of the subtests require applicant-generated responses (not multiple-choice), scoring is most likely not immediate. The score report includes a narrative statement about each applicant's score for each subtest and a verbal description of its normative position, such as below average, above average, high average, superior. A sample statement reads, "This candidate achieved a score of 18 points, which demonstrates a high average numerical and computational skill. A superior score for numerical skills is 25 points or more" (test manual, p. 3). However, there is no indication of how the subscore is computed or the total number of points for the subscore. For example, the Numerical Skills subtest has 60 items, and if a Superior is 25, we do not know if completing just 25 of 60 items is adequate or if items are weighted to arrive at the score. Because each subtest appears to use a somewhat different scale range, it is difficult to compare performance across subtests with the Narrative Report. There is a summary report that reports each subtest score along a continuum ranging from Below Average to Average to Above Average, but there is a standardized score scale across subtests. Finally, weighted aggregate scores for the two areas and a total aggregate score are reported in percentile ranks (0 to 100%), along with a recommendation concerning hiring.

DEVELOPMENT. There is no information in the test manual, other print materials, or on the Internet that describes the development of the test, theoretical rationale, item development, or pilot testing. The test manual identifies seven job relevant criteria measured by the test that correspond to the seven subtests: Verbal Fluency, Numerical Skills and Reasoning, Attention to Administrative Detail, Logic and Problem Solving Ability, Ability to Deal with Situations Within a Customer Service Environment, Problem Solving Within a Customer Service Environment, and Procedural Ability Within a Customer Service Environment.

Tests such as the Customer Service Skills Test are generally developed to reflect job relevant skills and knowledge. In this instance, the skills measured on this test do appear logically and rationally related to the types of skills and problems associated with customer service positions. Of course, some of these skills may be more or less relevant depending on the specific environment and position requirements.

TECHNICAL. Information on the reliability of the test and internal consistency reliability for the individual scales are not reported. The correlations between scales are also omitted, which prevents test users from determining if seven scales are independent. One predictive study reports results by gender, yet sample sizes are too small to determine practical or statistical significance. No results for ethnic or racial groups are provided, and there is no indication of any analyses to examine item bias, test bias, or adverse impact.

Three technical studies are available for this test: predictive validity studies for the paper and Internet versions and a content validity study. The content validity study conducted in 1993 identified 48 traits, 32 of which are assessed by the test. Tasks and weights generally correspond to the measures on the test, but there is no explanation of the job analysis methodology or sample size in the study. In addition, there is no evidence provided demonstrating the generalizability of traits beyond this one organization.

A predictive validity study was conducted with 47 customer service candidates who were being hired for administrative offices of a utility company based in the Southeast United States. This study describes the sample as candidates, but because performance ratings were obtained, it appears that the sample included only applicants who were hired based on their test score. The correlation between scores on the Customer Service Skills Test and supervisory ratings (1–5) was .92. The standard deviation on the test was 1.57, which is quite small given the scale. In addition, the raw data on test scores and supervisory ratings show a near perfect linear relationship, and in no instance did a single applicant ever receive a test score that was higher than another applicant who received a higher supervisory rating (e.g., all applicants with ratings of 5 had higher scores than all applicants with ratings of 4). The Internet study illustrates positive and more traditional results with a correlation of .43 between the test and performance ratings for 33 existing employees (8 males). This study appears to be a concurrent validation effort with current employees although this is never explained. The standard deviation of test scores was 9.55, which again is much more typical than the standard deviation of 1.57 reported for the study of the paper test. The study states that these results are "well above the standards established by the American Psychological Association (APA)," which is a clear misinterpretation of the Testing Standards (AERA, APA, & NCME, 1985). The Testing Standards do not establish any such hard and fast rule for statistical significance of validity coefficients.

COMMENTARY. The authors state that the Customer Service Skills Test is designed to evaluate the suitability of candidates of all levels of experience for customer service representative positions. Unfortunately, one cannot verify these claims based on available materials and studies. There are major issues concerning the development of the test that are not addressed in the test manual, on the Internet site, or in any other published materials. These issues concern the original norming of the scales, test reliability, item development and item bias, the internal consistency of scales and interscale relationships, evidence contributing to the construct relevance of the test, and data on subgroup performance and fairness. The test manual and other materials do not presently meet the standards set forth in the Joint Testing Standards (AERA, APA, & NCME, 1999) or the *Principles for the Validation and Use of Personnel Selection Procedures* (SIOP, 2003). The predictive and content validation evidence presented is not described in sufficient detail to make inferences about the methods used and strength of reported relationships. The data in these studies are outdated, incomplete, and limited to one organization (in each study) with small samples that prevent generalizability to other organizational settings and samples.

SUMMARY. The Customer Service Skills Test is a paper or Internet administered test used in hiring customer service representatives (including nontechnical help desk positions). A total test score and two domain scores are reported: Administrative and Intellectual Skills and Customer Service Related Skills. Seven subtests comprise the total score: Numerical Skills, Attention to Detail, Problem Solving Ability, Customer Service Skills, Customer Service Problem Solving, Customer Service Logic, Verbal Fluency (paper only), and Reading Comprehension (Internet only) (http://www.waldentesting.com/salestests/custserv.html, 3/20/04). The score report includes a narrative statement about each applicant's score for each subtest and a verbal description of its normative position, such as below average, above average, high average, or superior. Aggregate scores for the two areas and a total aggregate score are reported in percentile ranks (0 to 100%), along with a recommendation concerning hiring.

The test requires 56 minutes to administer and is scored by mail, fax, or telephone. The manual notes that only clerical supervision is required for administration. Most subtests appear moderately to highly speeded although there is no mention of speededness in the test booklet, other than to note precise timing is required. The manual provides insufficient detail and technical documentation concerning test development, normative samples, and scoring. Validity information is outdated and limited to two studies with small samples. No evidence of reliability, comparability of Internet and paper forms, subgroup impact, or construct relevant evidence for the scales are provided. Many of the skills that the job analysis identified for customer service occupations are required for a much broader range of occupations. Readers seeking a pre-employment screening test for customer service representatives may be better served by considering broader based employment skills and temperament inventories that may measure the same types of skills and abilities with much stronger technical documentation and validation evidence.

REVIEWER'S REFERENCES

American Educational Research Association, American Psychological Association, & National Council on Measurement in Education. (1985). *Standards for educational and psychological testing.* Washington, DC: American Psychological Association.
American Educational Research Association, American Psychological Association, & National Council of Measurement in Education. (1999). *Standards for educational and psychological testing.* Washington, DC: American Educational Research Association.
Society for Industrial and Organizational Psychology. (2003). *Principles for the validation and use of personnel selection procedures.* Bowling Green, OH: Author.

Review of the Customer Service Skills Test by JEAN POWELL KIRNAN, *Professor of Psychology, The College of New Jersey, Ewing, NJ:*

The reviewer would like to thank Silvia Azevedo for her assistance on this review. Her hard work and insights contributed greatly to the critique.

DESCRIPTION. Introduced in 1994, the Customer Service Skills Test (CSST) is designed for use in the selection of individuals for jobs such as nontechnical help desk, order desk, and customer service representative. Through the use of seven separately timed subtests, the following skills

are measured: verbal communication skills, numerical skills, attention to detail, problem solving ability, customer service skills, customer service problem solving, and customer service logic.

The test has two versions, English and French; however, no information regarding the development of the French version was provided for this review. A clerical supervisor can administer the CSST to an individual or group in a quiet environment with strict time constraints. According to the manual, the testing time is 56 minutes. Timing for each section should be reexamined as some are easily completed in the allotted time, whereas others are not. It is unclear if this is purposeful (if only some sections are intended to be speed tests).

There is an issue with the face validity, as the items in some sections do not match the title of the subtest. The "attention to detail" section is a variation on the name and number comparison subtests seen in other clerical assessments. These are more accurately titled "clerical perception" than "attention to detail." The customer service skills section has many items for which the job desirable response is obvious, thus threatening the validity of this subtest. The items in the customer service problem-solving section are mathematical and not customer service oriented. The customer service logic uses dated instruments such as a rotary telephone. Additionally, this section uses flowcharts, a format that would not seem to be relevant to the job tasks.

The numerical skills section instructs candidates to complete the 60 problems from left to right even if the problem *ignores* previously learned mathematical concepts such as "order of operations." This could confuse candidates or penalize candidates with higher mathematical abilities. It appears that this section is not simply measuring math skills, but the ability to follow directions. The verbal communication skills are measured differently in the online versus the paper-and-pencil versions. The task for the paper-and-pencil version consists of generating words with specific prefixes and suffixes whereas the online version utilizes a reading comprehension section. There is no indication that these two sections have been equated, leaving one to assume that they measure different skills.

The test does not have a section that measures interpersonal skills, which would seem more important for a customer service position than some of the subtests provided. There are other tests, such as the Customer Service Skills Inventory (Martin & Fraser, 2002) and the PDI Employment Inventory and PDI Customer Service Inventory (Ward, 2001) that have sections similar to the CSST; however, these tests also measure interpersonal skills.

There are three options for obtaining the candidates' scores: mailing the completed tests, reading the respondents' answers over the phone, or faxing a separate answer sheet (it is unclear if the respondent answers directly on this form or if answers are transcribed). Both the phone and fax method hold the potential for introducing error.

Although a five-page sample score report is provided, its use is limited because there is no information as to whether the scores are criterion based (i.e., percent correct) or normative based (percentile rank). Points are reported for each of the seven skills along with a narrative indicating what a "superior" score would be and labeling the obtained scores as "above average," "high average," or "superior." "Average" and "below average," however, are not presented in this example, leaving the reader to ponder on the range of categories. Another page presents a continuum of "below average," "average," and "above average" for each of the seven skills. At a glance one can see the relative strengths and weaknesses of the candidate; however, it is unclear why this is a 3-point scale and the earlier labeling ranged up to "superior."

Weighted aggregate scores are also provided for "administrative and intellectual skills" (verbal communication, numerical, attention to detail, and problem solving), "customer service-related skills" (customer service, customer service problem solving, and customer service logic), and an "overall weighted aggregate score" (all seven subtests combined). It is not specified how the subtests are combined or if the aggregate scores, presented as percents, are norm or criterion-based. A chart is provided that places overall rating scores into intervals, labeling them as "excellent," "very good," "good," "acceptable," "marginal," or "unacceptable," and also provides a hiring recommendation. Again, how the intervals were determined and how the labels were assigned is not explained. Presumably, some normative group was utilized to assign these labels and the score. However, the size of that group, its demographic composition, date of data collection, and industry/job position are not reported.

DEVELOPMENT. There is no information on how the items were developed, who developed them, or if any item analysis techniques were utilized. A later content validity study was conducted at one company and included a job analysis. One would hope that job analyses had been conducted prior to writing the test items. Without an "upfront" job analysis there is no evidence to suggest that these seven skills are necessary for these job positions, and even if necessary, if they are measured properly.

TECHNICAL. Reliability is not reported for the test. A test-retest reliability study is recommended.

Although the test manual indicates that there is a major validation study in progress, it is unclear if that is one of the two reports described below or if there is an additional study yet to be completed.

A concurrent validity study was conducted, but only for the internet version of the test. Raw scores on the CSST were correlated with supervisor's ratings for a small sample of 33 customer service representatives of unknown job tenure and unknown industry. The resulting correlation of $r = .43$ is statistically significant and of good magnitude for use in personnel selection. Replication on a larger sample, a variety of industries, the paper-and-pencil test version, as well as the other job titles for which the test is recommended is needed.

A content validity study was conducted in 1993 at the request of a company that was considering using the CSST for selection of its customer service representatives. Several aspects of this study are unclear and thus cast doubt on its conclusions. Basically, the company provided task analysis data and ranked the various tasks for job importance. Next, a list of essential traits (such as working quickly under time constraints), skills, and knowledge required to perform those tasks were identified along with an indication as to whether CSST test questions could measure those traits.

Although 32 (67%) of the traits identified were reported as being measured by the CSST, those conclusions are not clear to this reader. For example, the report indicates that "ability to communicate orally" is measured by the "vocabulary" items on the CSST. How could a vocabulary item in an online or paper-and-pencil test measure oral communication? Further, 11 of the traits are measured by "16 PF," "NPF," or "CPF." There is no indication as to what subtest, if any, on the CSST these are referring. Evaluation by a neutral party and clearer connections between the traits and the subtests are needed.

Although companies often choose to conduct local validation studies, it is expected that a test publisher will provide basic psychometric information for an instrument. Although Walden offers to assist in local validation studies, these should be additional to the existing evidence of the test's worth and not the only evidence.

Fairness studies for protected groups should also be reported. In the concurrent validity study, separate correlations for males and females are presented although the male correlation is appropriately discounted given that the sample size is only 8.

COMMENTARY AND SUMMARY. Given that the CSST has been in existence for about 10 years, the lack of technical information and total absence of normative data is very disappointing. When one combines these psychometric shortcomings with the high cost, it is difficult to recommend this test for use. Added to these factors is the availability of numerous other customer service tests that measure more relevant customer service skills and provide more technical evidence. The PDI Employment Inventory and PDI Customer Service Inventory (Ward, 2001) have appropriate development procedures, as well as reliability and validity data. The PSI Basic Skills Tests for Business, Industry, and Government (Stahl, 1985) contain sections similar to those in the CSST, as well as normative and validation data. Users should review other tools before selecting the Customer Service Skills Test.

REVIEWER'S REFERENCES

Martin, L. A., & Fraser, S. L. (2002). Customer service orientation in managerial and non-managerial employees: An exploration study. *Journal of Business and Psychology, 16*, 477–484.

Stahl, M. J. (1985). [Review of the PSI Basic Skills Tests for Business, Industry, and Government.] In J. V. Mitchell, Jr. (Ed.), *The ninth mental measurements yearbook* (pp. 1238–1239). Lincoln, NE: Buros Institute of Mental Measurements.

Ward, A. W. (2001). [Review of the PDI Employment Inventory and PDI Customer Service Inventory.] In B. S. Plake & J. C. Impara (Eds.), *The fourteenth mental measurements yearbook* (pp. 902–904). Lincoln, NE: Buros Institute of Mental Measurements.

[69]

Degrees of Reading Power [Primary and Standard Test Forms J & K and Advanced Test Forms T & U].

Purpose: Designed to provide direct performance measures of reading comprehension.
Population: Grades 1–12 and over.
Publication Dates: 1979–2002.

Acronym: DRP.
Scores: Total score only.
Administration: Group.
Levels, 3: Primary, Standard, Advanced.
Price Data, 2003: $53 per Primary/Standard examination set including 1 copy of each J series test form, 5 answer sheets, 1 J & K tests handbook (2000, 124 pages), and 1 norms booklet; $18 per 25 answer sheets (Standard and Advanced tests); $5.50 per 3-year license to use answer sheets per package of test booklets ordered; $34 per J & K tests handbook; $30 per Primary/Standard norms booklet; $19 per 5 test administration procedures (specify Primary, Standard, or Advanced); $32 per Degrees of Reading Power Program technical manual; $17 per scoring key or scoring overlay per test form.
Time: (45) minutes.
Comments: Practice exercises provided; provides readability analysis of instructional material in print; computer or hand scored; group profiles, optional reports, services, and software also available.
Author: Touchstone Applied Science Associates (TASA), Inc.
Publisher: Touchstone Applied Science Associates (TASA), Inc.

a) PRIMARY.
Purpose: To provide a measure of how well students understand the meaning of text.
Population: Grades 1–3.
Forms, 2: J, K.
Levels, 2: 0, 9.
Price Data: $158 per Primary classroom set including 25 practice exercises, 25 test booklets, 25 answer sheets, test administration procedures, J & K tests handbook, norms booklet, and teacher class profile; $13 per 25 Primary practice exercises; $98 per 25 consumable Primary test booklets including 1 test administration procedures.

b) STANDARD.
Purpose: To provide a measure of how well students understand the meaning of text.
Population: Grades 3–12 and over.
Forms, 2: J, K.
Levels, 5: 8, 7, 6, 4, 2.
Price Data: $153 per Standard classroom set including 25 practice exercises, 25 test booklets, 25 answer sheets, test administration procedures, J & K tests handbook, norms booklet, and teacher class profile; $14 per 25 Standard practice exercises; $74 per reusable Standard test booklets including 1 test administration procedures.

c) ADVANCED.
Purpose: To assess how well students are able to reason with textual materials.
Population: Grades 6–12 and over.
Forms, 2: T, U.

Levels, 2: 4, 2.

Price Data: $45 per Advanced examination set including 1 T4 test booklet, 1 T2 test booklet, 5 answer sheets, and Advanced handbook (2002, 98 pages); $138 per Advanced classroom set including 25 practice exercises, 25 test booklets, 25 answer sheets, test administration procedures, and Advanced handbook; $16 per 25 Advanced practice exercises; $81 per 25 Advanced test booklets; $38 per Advanced handbook (T & U test forms).

Cross References: For reviews by Felice J. Green and Howard Margolis of a previous edition, see 14:111; see also T5:773 (5 references); for reviews by Darrell N. Caulley, Elaine Furniss, and Michael McNamara and by Lawrence Cross of an earlier edition, see 12:101 (9 references); see also T4:726 (14 references); for reviews by Roger Bruning and Gerald S. Hanna of an earlier edition, see 9:305 (1 reference).

Review of the Degrees of Reading Power [Primary and Standard Test Forms J & K and Advanced Test Forms T & U] by JEFFREY K. SMITH, Professor of Educational Psychology, Rutgers, the State University of New Jersey, New Brunswick, NJ:

DESCRIPTION. The Degrees of Reading Power (DRP) test series combines the cloze procedure of measuring reading achievement, readability analysis of text, and item response theory to provide a reading assessment program that ties student progress to the difficulty levels of the textbooks and the literature that children read in school and at home. The Primary (Grades 1–3) and the Standard (Grades 3–12) forms utilize the traditional cloze procedure of omitting a word from a text passage and providing four alternatives that the student must choose among. Each word will syntactically and semantically fit the sentence, but only one will be appropriate given the context of the passage. The authors argue that this approach measures "how well students understand the surface meaning of what they read" (Advanced DRP handbook, p. 2). The Advanced forms (T and U, recommended for Grade 6 and above) omit entire sentences at the end of various paragraphs in a passage and require the student to select, from among four alternatives, the sentence that best completes the paragraph. The authors contend that the Advanced forms measure "how well students are able to reason with textual materials" (Advanced DRP handbook, p. 4). The number of items on the Primary and Standard forms ranges from 28 for first and second grade students to 70

for students in Grades 4 and 5 and above. The Advanced forms have 24 items.

The DRP differs from other measures of reading comprehension in several ways. To begin, the cloze format used exclusively for the measure for the Primary and Standard forms of the DRP is not typically used on other standardized reading assessments, and is used in combination with other item formats when it is used. The advanced measure uses a format that is not found in other measures of reading comprehension. It might be considered to be a type of the cloze approach, although such an interpretation would be open for discussion. Use of the DRP necessitates a belief on the part of the user that the cloze procedure accurately and fairly assesses reading comprehension.

The second way in which the DRP differs from other approaches is that it attempts to directly tie reading performance on the part of students to difficulty estimates on the material that students read. This is done by using a readability formula on the passages that comprise the tests and linking performance on the cloze procedure to the readability estimates. For example, if a student's estimated ability level is 90% or better on material of a certain level of difficulty, the student is believed to be at an Independent Level of performance by the test authors, indicating that students can read material at that level of difficulty independently. The next level down is called an "Instructional Level," and below that is a "Frustration" level. The DRP program provides an extensive listing of readability ratings of popular books and textbooks tied to the DRP scale.

A third distinction between the DRP and other approaches to measuring reading is that the DRP attempts to measure reading holistically; that is, there is no notion here of measuring subskills associated with reading.

DEVELOPMENT. The DRP program was initially developed in the late 1970s and 1980s (Koslin, Zeno, & Koslin, 1987); the current forms of the DRP are the latest versions of the measures. The development of the original DRP is discussed in previous reviews in the *Mental Measurements Yearbook* (e.g., Cross, 1995; Hanna, 1985; Margolis, 2001); the current version is an extension of the approach and format of earlier versions of the DRP. Thus, the DRP has a long history in its current form. It should be mentioned, however, that the materials available for the DRP do not go into extensive discussion as to how the current form was developed in terms of the construction of the passages or the determination of which words to select for the cloze procedure.

TECHNICAL. The DRP program addresses issues of the technical quality of the measure in a fashion that is somewhat frustrating and difficult to interpret and use. In the "DRP Handbook, J & K Test Forms," strong reliabilities are reported for "calibration forms" for Form G, and for forms used in a Connecticut program, but not for Forms J and K, which are supposed to be the forms under consideration. The handbook also refers the reader to a technical manual published in 1987 for information that would speak to the reliability and validity of the measures (Koslin, Zeno, & Koslin, 1987). This manual is an exceptionally thorough and scholarly examination of the technical issues concerning the DRP program. However, the manual is almost 20 years old, and uses data that are even older and that were not generated by the current forms of the measures. The argument of the DRP program appears to be that the new forms of the program are extensions of the old forms, and that the technical analyses should apply to the new forms, as well. This is a tenuous argument to make, at best.

The Advanced DRP handbook reports reliabilities for earlier Forms R and S, but they are not particularly strong, ranging from .75 to .81 in samples across Grades 9–12. This is in all likelihood due to the fact that there are only 24 items on these forms. This leads to unacceptably large standard errors of measurement for assessment of individual levels of reading ability. This problem is exacerbated by the DRP program practice of not reporting standard errors along with estimates of reading ability in home or school reports. There is not a substantial amount of validity information provided on the advanced forms of the DRP.

The DRP program is criterion referenced in nature, and is perhaps one of the strongest examples of the criterion-referenced approach to measurement. The basic argument of the DRP approach is that the score that is provided on a student is directly related to how well a student might be able to read any given piece of writing. The 1987 handbook provides the results of the research of the developers to argue for that essential linkage. Since that publication, several researchers have questioned that linkage, as is discussed in the Cross (1995) review. There is fundamentally no advance in that research in one direction or the other since that publication.

COMMENTARY. The DRP program is based on the idea that item response theory, cloze procedure, and readability formulas can be used in combination to develop a powerful, criterion-referenced, and instructionally relevant assessment system in reading. The newest forms of that assessment program continue in this well-established approach to literacy assessment. The program provides an indicator of how well students can read that is tied to the readability level of basically any piece of written work. The original research on the DRP was quite strong, but that level of research simply has not been maintained or updated in the ensuing years. As a consequence, although it is probably the case that the DRP remains a high quality measure today, the technical backup simply is not sufficient to give an unqualified endorsement of the program.

SUMMARY. The new forms of the DRP assessment program continue in the program's tradition of the creative use of technical advances to provide reading assessments that allow for linking students' scores to instructional and leisure reading material. The program needs to revive its earlier strong research program to more firmly establish the asserted linkages and address concerns expressed in the research literature.

REVIEWER'S REFERENCES
Cross, L. H. (1995). [Review of the Degrees of Reading Power.] In J. C. Conoley & J. C. Impara (Eds.), *The twelfth mental measurements yearbook* (pp. 258–261). Lincoln, NE: Buros Institute of Mental Measurements.
Hanna, G. S. (1985). [Review of the Degrees of Reading Power.] In J. V. Mitchell, Jr. (Ed.), *The ninth mental measurements yearbook* (pp. 444–447). Lincoln, NE: Buros Institute of Mental Measurements.
Koslin, B. L., Zeno, S., & Koslin, S. (1987). *The DRP: An effectiveness measure in reading.* New York: College Entrance Examination Board.
Margolis, H. (2001). [Review of the Degrees of Reading Power.] In B. S. Plake & J. C. Impara (Eds.), *The fourteenth mental measurements yearbook* (pp. 375–378). Lincoln, NE: Buros Institute of Mental Measurements.

Review of the Degrees of Reading Power [Primary and Standard Test Forms J & K and Advanced Test Forms T & U] by KEITH F. WIDAMAN, Professor of Psychology, University of California, Davis, CA:

DESCRIPTION. The Degrees of Reading Power (DRP) tests are a set of assessment instruments, with multiple forms and levels, to measure or gauge reading comprehension and verbal reasoning. The company that developed the DRP—Touchstone Applied Science Associates (TASA), Inc.—also produces two additional tests that focus, respectively, on prereading skills and reading ability, and on English as a second language, bilingual, and limited English proficiency students. The set of assessment instruments developed by TASA is designed to inform instruction in the domain of reading and literacy development during primary and secondary school grades, to help monitor progress by students, and to yield outcome measures useful for school accountability.

The DRP Primary and Standard forms provide parallel test forms (J & K) for different grade levels. Different forms for a total of seven different grade levels (e.g., Grades 1–2 through Grades 9–12+) are available. Tests for the first three grade levels have 28, 42, and 56 items per form; tests for the last four grade levels have 70 items per form. Each item on DRP Primary and Standard test forms requires the test taker to select one of five alternative words to complete a sentence within a paragraph. Thus, these tests assess reading comprehension, or the ability to derive surface meaning from prose material.

The Advanced DRP test parallel forms (T & U) were developed for two grade levels (Grades 6–9 and Grades 9 and above). All test forms in this series comprise 24 items. Each item on these forms requires the test taker to select one of five alternative sentences that best or most accurately concludes a paragraph. The Advanced DRP tests therefore assess verbal reasoning, as opposed to reading comprehension.

Test takers are given as much time as they need to complete each form, so speededness is not a factor. Each DRP test form yields a single, overall test score. Raw scores on each form can be converted into scaled or standardized scores on a DRP score metric (range: -15 to 99+), which will be discussed in more detail below. Test scores may also be converted into percentile scores (median: 50; range: 1 to 99+), stanines (M = 5, SD = 2; range: 1 to 9), or normal curve equivalent scores (NCEs; M = 50, SD = 21.06).

DEVELOPMENT. The first edition of the DRP was published in 1979, and the current edition carries a 2000 copyright date. Little information in the DRP Handbook is given about the history of prior editions of the set of tests. However, because the DRP tests are used in "high stakes" testing by several states, the new revision of the tests is likely tied to the need to continually revise specific item information.

One very useful aspect of the DRP tests is the informative nature of the DRP score scale. In 1969, Bormuth developed a formula that characterized the readability of text across a very broad range of textual materials. The DRP scale is a transformation of Bormuth values that has ready benchmarks ranging from 31 (for *Green Eggs and Ham*) to 76 (for *Moll Flanders*). High school textbooks average around the low 60s in the DRP metric, whereas college texts would attain values at rather higher levels, in the 80s. In addition to rating textual material with regard to DRP value, student ability to deal with text is characterized at five levels that range from independent (or able to read text with 90% comprehension), through instructional (or able to read text with 75% comprehension), to frustration (or able to read text with 50% comprehension).

The utility of the DRP score scale is shown through the ready matching of student capability with text at different levels of difficulty. For example, a 10th grade student answering 37 items correct on Test Form J2 would have DRP scores of 51 for the independent level, 62 for the instructional level, and 73 for the frustration level. Thus, such a student would be able to attain 90% comprehension and therefore operate independently with text at a DRP readability level of 51, similar to that of *Charlotte's Web*; would be able to attain 75% comprehension and operate at the instructional level for text at a DRP level of 62, similar to high school textbooks or the novel *2001: A Space Odyssey*; and would be able to attain only 50% comprehension and operate at the frustration level with text at a DRP level of 73, such as the novel *The Adventures of Don Quixote*.

TECHNICAL. Little detailed information was provided regarding the standardization samples for the DRP tests. Certain data on reliability were provided for calibration test forms, based on responses by over 13,000 students in a mixed urban and suburban school district in the Pacific Northwest; other reliability data were based on a sample of 826 students from a city school district in New England; still other reliability data were based on responses by over 7,500 students from schools in Connecticut. Thus, although no formal representative selection of students was made, statistics are based on large, although nonrepresentative, samples of students from various regions of the U.S.

As for reliability, the K-R 20 reliability estimates on calibration and operational forms ranged between .94 and .97 for each grade between Grade 4 and Grade 12, and only slightly lower (.91 and .92) for Grades 2 and 3. The standard error of measurement (*SEM*) varied with the standard deviation (*SD*) of DRP scores, but tended to average about .25 *SD* units. This compares favorably with scores on IQ tests, which tend to have *SEM*s that average only slightly smaller, at .17 to .20 *SD* units. Alternate form reliabilities were reported for two large administrations of pilot and operational forms of DRP tests in Grades 4, 6, and 8. These alternate forms reliabilities ranged between .87 and .91.

Several forms of validity for the DRP tests were discussed, but little in the way of statistical information was provided. Construct validity was discussed in terms of the fit between DRP test scores and text that students could handle at different levels of success. However, no standard forms of construct validity—such as correlations with other instruments that purportedly assess the same underlying constructs—were provided. Content validity was covered in standard fashion, which is often based on evaluations by experts with regard to the fit between test questions and the domains to be assessed. Criterion validity was assessed in several ways. The manual cited one study in which DRP scores correlated .90 with scores on an unspecified criterion measure that required respondents to "produce semantically sensible responses for blanks in ordinary passages" (p. 62), which is different than the DRP approach that has respondents select one of five alternative responses to complete blanks in text. The manual also stated that DRP test scores tend to correlate between .75 and .80 with other tests of reading comprehension. But none of the other tests were described in sufficient detail to allow an informed evaluation of this evidence.

With regard to test fairness, the fit statistics from fitting the Rasch model to item responses indicated similar and very good fit of the model to data from different ethnic, gender, and SES groups. In addition, the correlations of Rasch item difficulties for different group comparisons (e.g., Black vs. White, male vs. female) ranged upward from .95, with most .97 or higher, providing some indication of lack of bias.

Norming tables were based on performance by over 48,000 respondents from across the U.S.,

so the norms are based on fairly representative samples. However, the relation between items correct and corresponding DRP and percentile scores reveals that the DRP tests have greatest precision in the middle of the distribution, with relatively lower levels of accuracy of scores near the tails of the distribution.

COMMENTARY. The DRP tests are well-formatted, simple-to-use tests of reading comprehension and verbal reasoning. Each form of a test can be administered easily in a single class period, and the DRP scores derived have ready interpretation in terms of the text that students can handle easily (e.g., with 90% comprehension) or at progressively more difficult levels.

My primary concern is the lack of detailed, psychometrically sophisticated evaluation of the validity of DRP scores. If the DRP is purportedly a measure of a single dimension of reading comprehension, then several forms of analysis should support this contention. For example, a factor analysis of item scores should exhibit essential unidimensionality, by revealing the presence of a single large factor. Correlations with other tests that assess the same reading comprehension construct should be discussed in sufficient detail to satisfy the test user that all instruments, including the DRP, assess a similar dimension of individual differences. Furthermore, certain types of group comparisons—such as comparing performance by students in gifted and talented programs with performance by students in typical curricula—might provide additional indications of validity. At present, the technical data on the DRP tests are heavy on reliability, but short on validity. Although the validity of DRP scores is likely good, little information documenting this validity has been presented.

SUMMARY. The developers of the DRP have produced measures of reading comprehension and verbal reasoning that can be administered and scored in an efficient manner. The scores derived from the DRP have rather strong psychometric properties and appear to be correlated highly with scores from comparable instruments. If a test yielding a single score for reading comprehension is wanted, the DRP is a worthy selection. Moreover, the DRP tests provide scores on the DRP scale, which has great utility with regard to the matching of student capability and text characteristics. If additional information were provided regarding the validity of DRP test scores, still firmer recommendations in favor of selection of the DRP tests could be made.

[70]

Developmental Test of Visual Perception—Adolescent and Adult.

Purpose: "To document the presence and degree of visual perceptual or visual-motor difficulties in individual adolescents and adults."

Population: Ages 11-0 to 74-11 years.

Publication Date: 2002.

Acronym: DTVP-A.

Scores, 9: Motor-Reduced Visual Perception (Figure-Ground, Visual Closure, Form Constancy, Motor-Reduced Visual Perception Index), Visual-Motor Integration (Copying, Visual-Motor Search, Visual-Motor Speed, Visual-Motor Integration Index), General Visual Perception Index.

Administration: Individual.

Price Data, 2002: $164 per complete kit including examiner's manual (135 pages), picture book, 25 profile/examiner record forms, 25 response booklets, and storage box; $59 per examiner's manual; $46 per picture book; $39 per 25 profiler/examiner record forms; $24 per 25 response booklets.

Time: (20–30) minutes.

Comments: Upward extension and redevelopment of the Developmental Test of Visual Perception, Second Edition (DTVP-2; T6:798); designed to identify candidates for referral to special education, cognitive rehabilitation, or occupational therapy; may be used to distinguish true visual-perception deficits from problems solely with complex eye-hand or perceptual-motor actions; may assist in differential diagnosis of various dementias.

Authors: Cecil R. Reynolds, Nils A. Pearson, and Judith K. Voress.

Publisher: PRO-ED.

Review of the Developmental Test of Visual Perception—Adolescent and Adult by JAMES M. HODGSON, Professor, Tennessee Center for the Study and Treatment of Dyslexia, Middle Tennessee State University, Murfreesboro, TN:

DESCRIPTION. The Developmental Test of Visual Perception—Adolescent and Adult (DTVP-A) provides a battery of six subtests intended to serve "four principal uses: (1) to document the presence and degree of visual perceptual or visual-motor difficulties in individual adolescents and adults; (2) to identify candidates for referral to special education, ... occupational therapy or cognitive rehabilitation; (3) to verify the effectiveness of these intervention programs; and (4) to serve as a research tool" (examiner's manual, p. 12). As this description suggests, the DTVP-A is intended for use in both educational and clinical settings to assess visual perceptual functioning in individuals ranging in age from 11-0 years to 74-11 years. The subtests are divided into two groups of three, providing the basis for two composite measures. The Visual Motor Integration Index (VMII) includes the Copying, Visual-Motor Search, and Visual-Motor Speed subtests. The Motor-Reduced Visual Perception Index (MRPI) includes Figure-Ground, Visual Closure, and Form Constancy tasks. Finally, a General Visual Perception Index (GVPI) is computed from the results of all six subtests.

The designs of the DTVP-A subtests will be quite familiar to any examiner experienced in assessing visual perceptual performance, in that they bear strong resemblances to commonly used test designs (e.g., Test of Visual-Perceptual Skills—Revised; Gardner, 1996). The Copying subtest, for example, is similar to the Developmental Test of Visual Motor Integration: 4th Ed. (Beery, 1997), in that the examinee is asked to copy a progressive series of two- and three-dimensional geometric figures as accurately as possible. The Visual-Motor Search task resembles the Trail-Making Test in having the examinee connect a series of sequentially numbered circles as quickly as possible. The Visual-Motor Speed subtest has much in common with speeded transcoding tasks like the Wechsler Digit Symbol or Coding subtests (e.g., Wechsler, 1991), with scoring being based on the number of correct inscriptions completed within a fixed time limit.

The three subtests included under the MRPI index also follow frequently encountered designs. The Figure-Ground subtest is an example of the Embedded- or Hidden-Figure test (e.g., Spreen & Benton, 1969). Examinees identify target figures that are "hidden" within an overlapping array of figures. The Visual Closure task presents the examinee with a completed figure, along with a series of similar drawings with significant portions of their outlines missing. The Form Constancy subtest assesses the ability to match a target stimulus to a second image of that item presented in a different size, orientation, or shading.

The DTVP-A manual provides clear, well laid-out instructions for administration. The profile/examiner record form is also well designed and includes brief instructions for administration and scoring for each of the subtests. The stimuli for the three motor-reduced subtests are provided in a robustly wire-bound picture book. Items for the three Motor-Enhanced subtests are provided in a consumable response booklet. Scoring is generally quite straightforward. Basals are not employed. On four subtests (Copying, Figure-Ground, Visual Closure, and Form Constancy), a simple ceiling of three consecutive scores of 0 is used to determine when to discontinue testing. The Motor-Reduced subtest items receive scores of 1 or 0. The timed tasks (Visual-Motor Search and Visual-Motor Speed) are scored for elapsed time (seconds) and number of correctly marked shapes, respectively. A scoring guide for the Copying task is provided in the manual. Drawings are rated on a scale of 0–3 points. Tables are provided for converting subtest raw scores to standard scores and percentile ranks and for converting sums of subtest standard scores to index scores and percentile ranks. The manual suggests that the test can be administered by professionally qualified staff "and others who are interested in examining the visual perceptual status and visual-motor integration skills" (p. 10).

DEVELOPMENT. The DTVP-A is described as "the latest version" (examiner's manual, p. 10) of the Marianne Frostig Developmental Test of Visual Perception (e.g., Frostig, Lefever, & Whittlesey, 1961). That test was also the basis of the DTVP-2 (Hammill, Pearson, & Voress, 1993; 12:112), which was normed for children between the ages of 4 and 10 years. The DTVP-A is presented as, in essence, an age extension of the DTVP-2 (examiner's manual, p. v). Both the constructs and the individual subtests remain close to those of the original test, strongly reflecting its mid-20th century roots. The manual's theoretical framework focuses on broad contrasts between sensation and perception, perception and cognition, and "pure" visual perception versus performance that includes a significant motor component. Importantly, the battery does not reflect the more modular constructs that have emerged in visual cognition over the last 25 years (e.g., Farah, 2004; Forde & Humphreys, 2002; Humphreys, 2001; McCloskey et al., 1995; Rapp, 2001). As noted below, this may account in part for the often noted limitations on the utility of the profiles obtained with this and similar assessment instruments (Hammill, Pearson, & Voress, 1993).

TECHNICAL.
Standardization. The manual cites a normative sample of 1,664 individuals residing in 19 states. Locations were selected to represent the four major U.S. geographic regions (Northeast, Midwest, South, and West). Assessors were recruited from the publisher's records of purchasers of the DTVP-2 in the targeted regions. The authors contend that the resulting sample was representative of the nation as a whole. Separate demographic breakdowns of the school-age and adult samples by region, gender, race, ethnicity, disability status, family income, and educational attainment are given. Age stratifications across four selected demographic factors are provided for the school-age and adult samples.

Reliability. The manual addresses test score reliability with respect to content sampling, time-sampling, and interscorer differences. For items in the untimed subtests, internal consistency reliability is addressed by reports of Cronbach's alpha. In the case of the timed subtests, estimates of test-retest reliability measure are used. Internal consistency measures for the three composite indexes were also derived. Coefficient alphas for individual subtests range from .70 to .92 across 14 age intervals. Coefficient alphas for the three composite indices within each of the 14 age groups ranged from .83 to .95. Thus, the reliability of item content scores appears to be good.

Reliability was also assessed separately for seven demographic groups: males, females, European Americans, African Americans, Hispanic Americans, right-hand-dominant individuals, and left-hand-dominant individuals. Coefficient alphas are provided for each subtest and composite index for each of these groups. These values range from .70 to .97 for subtests and from .86 to .96 for the three composite indexes.

Investigation of test-retest reliability was restricted to a sample of 30 adults, aged 20–57 years. This is a markedly more narrow age range than the 11-to-74-year range represented in the standardization sample, leaving room for doubt about the test-retest reliability for individuals at the lower and upper age ranges. No information is given about the other demographic attributes of this sample. These individuals were tested and retested within the span of 1 week. The resulting coefficients for the six subtests range from .70 to .84. The coefficients for the three composite indexes range from .81 to .84.

The approach taken in documenting interscorer reliability was also limited, but is consistent with common practice. Data were obtained by having two trained staff members independently score a set of 30 protocols. The manual suggests that the selected protocols were representative of age divisions of the sample, but no direct evidence on this is included. The manual reports interscorer coefficients ranging from .95 to .99 for subtests and .94 to .99 for composite indexes. Overall, the various sources of evidence reported in the manual indicate solid reliability for the DTVP-A.

Validity. The manual provides a variety of evidence, both qualitative and quantitative, bearing on the validity of the content and constructs of the DTVP-A. This includes sections addressing content-description validity, criterion-prediction validity, and construct-identification validity. The data that are offered in the manual provide a reasonable case for considering the overall validity of the battery to be adequately supported, but there may be other grounds for concern about validity in a broader construal of that notion. These concerns were raised independently by two reviewers of the DTVP-2 (12:112), citing comments made by the test authors, themselves. It appears that the authors have made efforts to respond to concerns of this kind in the DTVP-A manual's section on interpreting test results (pp. 13, 40–41), but those responses offer little of substance to address the sources of the difficulty or to offer test users useful ways of translating test results into interpretations that are helpful. Additional comments are offered below.

COMMENTARY. The DTVP-A provides a useful extension of the measures of visual performance available in the DTVP-2 and similar batteries (e.g., Gardner, 1996). Within its own frame of reference, the DTVP-A appears to be a well-designed, convenient instrument suitable to its purpose. The preservation of constructs and test designs across several decades has the virtue of preserving comparability and continuity of data. This continuity comes at a cost, however. As noted above, there have been enormous advances in the cognitive neurosciences in general, and in visual cognition in particular. There is very little evidence of these advances in the conceptual framework or the test designs employed in the DTVP-A, or other comparable assessment tools. In a review of the DTVP-2 in the *Twelfth Mental Measurements Yearbook*, Bologna (1995) comments, "Unfortunately, as the manual authors acknowledge, the diagnosis and treatment of visual-perceptual deficits have not always been found to be a useful adjunct to the treatment of educational difficulties" (p. 290).

In a second review of that test, Tindal (1995, p. 291) quotes the authors of the DTVP-2 as writing, "Students' performance on the DTVP-2 subtests has little to do with school skills as seen by their teachers" (Hammill, Pearson, & Voress, 1993, p. 42). He notes that "Such findings ... reflect the difficulty the authors eventually have in defining and establishing construct validity" (Tindal, 1995, p. 291).

These two factors—the practical usefulness of the results this battery provides, and the scientific datedness of its theoretical framework—may well be directly related. One suggestive example can be found in the complexity of impairments to written outputs (e.g., Ellis, 1988; Margolin & Goodman-Schulman, 1992). The simple three-level model detailed in the manual's first chapter, upon which the DTVP-A is based, is simply incapable of providing an account of these observations, or of many other well-attested phenomena in the domain of visual cognition and its specific impairments.

SUMMARY. The DTVP-A provides a convenient, compact, and well-designed assessment battery for evaluating visual and visual-motor performance in adolescents and adults. It derives directly from an extended family of assessment instruments stretching back a century. Although the conventional reliability and validity data for the battery appear solid with respect to the assumptions and constructs the authors adopt, there may be reason for concern about the practical utility of the interpretations that can be made based on the results obtained with these measures. Examiners thinking of employing this battery for purposes of guiding interventions or rehabilitation should acquaint themselves with those limits.

REVIEWER'S REFERENCES

Beery, K. (1997). Developmental Test of Visual-Motor Integration, Fourth Edition. Parsippany, NJ: Modern Curriculum Press.

Bologna, N. B. (1995). [Review of the Developmental Test of Visual Perception, Second Edition]. In J. C. Conoley & J. C. Impara (Eds.), *The twelfth mental measurements yearbook* (pp. 289–290). Lincoln, NE: Buros Institute of Mental Measurements.

Ellis, A. W. (1988). Normal writing processes and peripheral acquired dysgraphias. *Language and Cognitive Processes, 3*(2), 99–127.

Farah, M. J. (2004). *Visual agnosia* (2nd ed.). Cambridge, MA: MIT Press.

Forde, E. M. E., & Humphreys, G. W. (Eds.). (2002). *Category specificity in brain and mind.* Philadelphia: Psychology Press.

Frostig, M., Lefever, D. W., & Whittlesey, J. R. B. (1961). A developmental test of visual perception for evaluating normal and neurologically handicapped children. *Perceptual and Motor Skills, 12,* 383–389.

Gardner, M. F. (1996) Test of Visual-Perceptual Skills—Revised. San Francisco: Psychological and Educational Publications.

Hammill, D. D., Pearson, N. A., & Voress, J. K. (1993). Developmental Test of Visual Perception—Second Edition. Austin, TX: PRO-ED.

Humphreys, G. W. (Ed.). (2001). *Case studies in the neuropsychology of vision.* Philadelphia: Psychology Press.

Margolin, D. I., & Goodman-Schulman, R. (1992). Oral and written spelling impairments. In D. I. Margolin (Ed.), *Cognitive neuropsychology in clinical practice* (pp. 263–297). New York: Oxford University Press.

McCloskey, M., Rapp, B., Yantis, S., Rubin, G., Bacon, W. F., Dagnelie, G., Gordon, B., Aliminosa, D., Boatman, D. F., Badecker, W., Johnson, D. N., Tusa, R. J., & Palmer, E. (1995). A developmental deficit in localizing objects from vision. *Psychological Science, 6*(2), 112–117.

Rapp, B. (Ed.). (2001). *The handbook of cognitive neuropsychology: What deficits reveal about the human mind.* New York: Psychology Press.

Spreen, O., & Benton, A. L. (1969) Embedded Figures Test. Victoria, BC: Neuropsychological Laboratory, University of Victoria.

Tindal, G. (1995). [Review of the Developmental Test of Visual Perception, Second Edition]. In J. C. Conoley & J. C. Impara (Eds.), *The twelfth mental measurements yearbook* (pp. 290–292). Lincoln, NE: Buros Institute of Mental Measurements.

Wechsler, D. (1991). Wechsler Adult Intelligence Scale-III. San Antonio, TX: Psychological Corporation.

Review of the Developmental Test of Visual Perception—Adolescent and Adult by RALPH G. LEVERETT, Professor, Department of Education, Union University, Jackson, TN:

DESCRIPTION. The Developmental Test of Visual Perception—Adolescent and Adult (DTVP-A) is an upward extension of visual perception tests dating to Bender's initial work in the late 1930s. It is a direct successor to the Frostig tests popular in the 1960s and 1970s. This instrument is designed to measure visual perceptual skills in persons between the ages of 11-0 and 74-11. Its claim is, "To document the presence and degree of visual perceptual or visual-motor difficulties in individual adolescents and adults" (examiner's manual, p. 12). Of particular significance is the application of the test to persons who have experienced neurological insults or diseases. The six subtests are grouped equally into two categories. *Motor-Reduced* tasks are primarily visual perceptual. *Motor-Enhanced* tasks are visual motor. The thorough, straightforward examiner's manual provides an excellent review of the construct of visual perception and the application of the test to the target population. The stimulus materials for the DTVP-A are included in a picture booklet. The format is similar to previous editions of the DTVP and the Beery-Bucktenica Test of Visual Motor Integration (VMI). A profile/examiner record form provides a summary of an individual's performance. Explicit directions to the examiner are included in the summary form. These directions describe the examinee's task and measures that enable the examiner to correct misunderstanding on the part of the examinee. The DTVP-A is administered individually. It is designed to be completed in approximately 30 minutes. The response booklet is provided for Motor-Enhanced tasks. Subtests identified in this category include Copying, Visual-Motor Search, and Visual-Motor Speed. Materials needed for each of these subtests are noted in the profile/examiner record form. No directions are provided in the response booklet itself. Directions are given verbally with additional cues (pointing and gestures) for some subtests. Instructions are provided for correcting inappropriate responses on the Visual-Motor Search subtest. Several suggestions are provided to maximize the examinee's performance. The examiner is directed to exercise caution in interpreting test results. The developers of this test state clearly that no single measure can yield complete information regarding an individual's skills or rehabilitative needs. The DTVP-A should be considered as one element in a comprehensive test battery. This is especially true for examinees with significant neurological insult or disease. The test provides for percentile ranks and standard scores.

DEVELOPMENT. The developers of the DTVP-A have many years experience in the creation and revision of similar tests. A primary reason for the creation of this test is to provide useful information for persons who have a variety of neurological needs. This test provides a welcome alternative for the assessment and rehabilitation of adults who have experienced strokes, degenerative neurological diseases, and traumatic brain/head injury. The DTVP-A is an examiner-friendly test. Its format is simple, and scoring follows a pattern familiar to examiners who work with the target population. This test is based upon historic and recent research in the construct of visual perception.

TECHNICAL. The normative sample consisted of 1,664 persons from 19 states. This group represented four major geographic regions. Care was taken to ensure that the sample included the diverse groups represented within the United States. The developers have attempted to provide a format that allows the examiner to distinguish visual perceptual skills from those that are visual-motor in nature. Three types of reliability are described. The discussion of content sampling includes the following statement, "The subgroups represent a broad spectrum of identifiable groups within the U.S. population, embracing gender, ethnic, and hand dominance" (examiner's manual, p. 53). The latter group seems especially necessary given the nature of the visual-motor subtests. Another significant element of reliability addresses interscorer differences. Because subjectivity in the evaluation of an examinee's accuracy on visual-motor tasks is an issue, the developers have attempted to provide clear guidelines for administration, scoring, and practice scoring. The conclusion is that reliability is "consistently high across all three types of reliability" (examiner's manual, p. 58). The examiner's manual provides extensive discussion of validity. The issue of content validity, in particular, addresses some of the historic concerns of measuring visual perceptual skills. Items selected for the test have their roots in the Frostig tests of a previous generation. Overall, the test appears to have good evidence for validity.

COMMENTARY. The DTVP-A provides a format that is familiar and easy to administer and score. Although all issues related to the assessment of visual perceptual skills may never be completely addressed, this current test has profited from the discussion and criticism of similar tests over the years. The developers have addressed issues candidly. In particular, they caution the examiner to consider the results of the test as part of a more complete test battery. They are particularly cautious about the application of the test to remedial programs. Successful rehabilitation includes goals based upon the best formal tests available and the professional judgment that comes from direct intervention with the target population. One important area seems lacking in the extensive discussion of the assessment and interpretation of the test. Because the test targets a population with neurological deficits, some discussion of the language deficits that are common to this population would be welcome. For example, directions are given verbally and, for some subtests, with visual or gestural cues. Performance on this test could be affected as much by an inability to comprehend instructions accurately as by impairment in visual perceptual or visual-motor skills. Additionally, right hemisphere lesions frequently compromise spatial tasks. Future editions of this test might well include a discussion of the effect of lesions in either hemisphere.

SUMMARY. The DTVP-A is the most recent instrument based upon the work of Frostig. The developers are aware of the problems that

have been associated with the construct of visual perception. They have grounded this test in the most recent research related to this area. Examiners would do well to read the claims of the test and the extensive research that undergirds these claims. Cautious interpretation of the results should be beneficial in guiding rehabilitative goals.

[71]

Devereux Early Childhood Assessment—Clinical Form.

Purpose: Designed to evaluate "behaviors related to both social and emotional resilience as well as social and emotional concerns in preschool children."
Population: Ages 2:0–5:11.
Publication Dates: 2002–2003.
Acronym: DECA-C.
Scores, 9: Protective Factors (Initiative, Self-Control, Attachment, Total), Behavioral Concerns (Withdrawal/Depression, Emotional Control Problems, Attention Problems, Aggression, Total).
Administration: Individual.
Price Data: Prices for the manual, record forms, and norms reference card available from publisher.
Time: Administration time not reported.
Comments: Behavior rating scale may be completed by parent or family member or teacher.
Authors: Paul A. LeBuffe and Jack A. Naglieri.
Publisher: Kaplan Early Learning Company.

Review of the Devereux Early Childhood Assessment—Clinical Form by JOAN C. BALLARD, Clinical Neuropsychologist, Associate Professor of Psychology, State University of New York College at Geneseo, Geneseo, NY:

DESCRIPTION. The Devereux Early Childhood Assessment—Clinical Form (DECA-C) is the latest in a series of rating scales developed under the umbrella of the Devereux Foundation. Its stated purpose is to assess the behavior of children aged 2 to 5 years, with a focus on indicators of social and emotional resilience as well as behavioral concerns. The same 62-item instrument can be completed by parents, teachers, or others familiar with the child. Responses to 5-point rating scales indicate the frequency (from *never* to *very frequently*) of behaviors during the previous 4 weeks. Seven subscales, with 7 to 11 items each, are computed by adding scores. These subscale scores are added to compute two total scores: "Protective Factors" (Initiative, Self-control, and Attachment) and "Behavioral Concerns"

(Withdrawal/Depression, Emotional Control Problems, Attention Problems, and Aggression). Positively and negatively worded items are distributed throughout the instrument, which may help to reduce response set bias. Items refer to observable behavior only, which eliminates the need for inference on the part of the rater. Items on the scales describe behaviors that many young children exhibit. The rationale for assessing frequency is that the behaviors become problems (or strengths) when they occur more often than is normal. In addition to the normed scales, four "Increased Concerns" items assess behaviors that are very unusual for preschoolers (fire-setting, negative/critical self-appraisal, threats of self-harm, and animal abuse). The two major scales, as well as the Increased Concerns items, are intended to provide information about both risk and resiliency factors. A carbon-embedded answer sheet includes space for computing raw scores, converting them to standard scores, and constructing an Individual Child Profile. The profile includes shaded areas to indicate "strengths," "concerns," and "typical" ranges. Norms are reproduced on the answer sheet, as well as on a separate norm reference card. Separate norms for parent and teacher raters are provided. Age- and gender-specific norms are not provided.

DEVELOPMENT. The three Protective Factors scales of the DECA-C are identical to those of the Devereux Early Childhood Assessment (DECA; 15:81). The four Behavioral Concern Scales are new to the DECA-C, although many items were selected from the childhood version (for ages 5–12) of the Devereux Scales of Mental Disorders (DSMD; T6:801). The DSMD also was the source for the Behavioral Concerns scale on the original DECA. The DECA-C therefore seems to differ from the DECA only in the number of Behavioral Concerns items, and their grouping into subscales. Literature reviews and focus groups of parents and teachers also were used in item development. DECA and DECA-C were standardized simultaneously using two norm groups that closely matched U.S. population parameters, each of which was drawn from preschools and child care centers across the country. Of 2,000 children used to norm the DECA, 1,108 of them were assessed using the DECA-C version of the instrument. Roughly half of the assessments with each version were completed by parents and the other half by teachers. Results of all ratings for both norm groups were subjected to factor analysis to identify subscales within the Protective Factors and Behavioral Concerns scales. Items were deleted to improve the factor solution and to shorten the scales.

TECHNICAL.

Standardization. Following scale reduction, norms were computed for the remaining items using the original sample, rather than cross-validation samples. No age differences across the 2- to 5-year-old range were present; norms therefore are the same across all ages. However, the authors allude to gender differences, but provide a vague explanation for their decision not to provide separate norms for males and females. Different norms were computed for parent and teacher ratings. Such a division is logical given the different types of behaviors these raters have the opportunity to observe. Skewed distributions were normalized to allow conversion of raw scores to T-scores and percentiles.

Reliability. Internal reliability estimates were strong for the two total scores (.88 to .94), and good for the subscales (Protective Factors scales .76 to .90; Behavioral Concerns scales .66 to .90). The somewhat lower reliability estimates for the latter may be due in part to the smaller sample size. Teachers were somewhat more reliable than parents. The manual provides a table of standard errors of measurement (*SEM*) on T-scores for each scale and subscale. This information can be very helpful to the test user; however, no further discussion of the use of *SEM*s is included. On the profile form, T-scores are plotted as single points; procedures for marking the *SEM* range might help to avoid overinterpretation of results.

Test-retest reliability was assessed in small groups of parents ($n = 25$) and teachers ($n = 41$) across a 24- to 72-hour interval. Reliability estimates were adequate to good (most in the .80 to .90 range), with a low of .55 (parent rating of attachment) and a high of .94 (teacher total rating of Protective Factors). Reliability estimates across longer time intervals and with larger samples are needed, particularly given that one suggested use of the test is to examine pre- and postintervention scores. Interrater reliabilities were computed for pairs of teachers of small groups of children ($n = 80$ for Protective Factors scale; $n = 43$ for Behavioral Concerns scale). Reliability estimates, although significant, were in the low to moderate range (.32 to .77). Surprisingly, no interrater reliabilities were reported for parent-teacher pairs or for parent-parent pairs. The test developers chose to have each child rated by only a parent *or* a teacher, making such correlations unavailable. Nevertheless, their absence is a concern, given that guidelines are provided in the manual for comparing parent and teacher scores.

Validity. As with reliability, the authors present an array of validity information. They argue that content validity is demonstrated primarily by the method of selecting items. These items come largely from the DECA and the DSMD, which were developed based on "thorough review" of relevant literature, focus groups, and (for the Behavioral Concerns items) the DSM-IV (APA, 1994).

Criterion-referenced and construct validity were assessed in a series of studies. MANOVA comparison of a community sample ($n = 95$) to a sample of children with known emotional or behavioral problems ($n = 86$) yielded significant group differences on all subscales, with effect sizes ranging from $d = .42$ to 1.12. In the same sample, group membership was correctly identified for 69% of participants using the Protective Factors total score, and for 74% using the Behavioral Concerns total score. Prediction was based on cutoff T-scores of one SD above or below the mean. The ability of the scales to identify children with problems is important, but it must be noted that group differences were found for *all* scales. This finding raises the possibility that parent and teacher respondents may tend to give more extreme ratings for children they already perceive to have problems.

In the DECA-C manual, the authors indicate that construct validity information on the Protective Factors scale is presented in the original DECA manual. They state that "for both high risk and low risk children, high scores on the protective factor scales were associated with significantly fewer behavioral concerns than low scores on these scales" (manual, p. 42). The method of measuring risk or behavioral concern is unstated. If this information came from the same DECA rating scale as the protective factors, the correlation is hardly surprising.

Construct validity for the Behavioral Concerns scale was assessed in a new group of 123 children with psychiatric diagnoses. The authors argued that elevations on specific subscales should be seen for children with different diagnoses (ADHD, Oppositional-Defiant Disorder, and Depression). To some extent, expected differences are seen in group means and in percent of children with specific elevations. However, profiles were somewhat elevated on all subscales for all groups, and the authors report no statistical profile analysis. Given that diagnoses were not independently confirmed, and that raters were not blind to psychiatric diagnoses, rater bias also must be considered as a possible factor.

Finally, subscales were intercorrelated as expected, with positive correlations among subscales within each category (Protective Factors and Behavioral Concerns) and negative correlations among scales from different categories. The correlation of the total scales was not reported.

COMMENTARY. The DECA-C was developed concurrently with the DECA. In fact, the norms for the three Protective Factors scales on both tests were based on the same sample of 2,000 children. Although it is somewhat unclear in the manual, it appears that half these children were assessed with the DECA (which included a short Behavioral Concerns subscale), and that the other half were assessed with the DECA-C (with four such subscales). Both versions of the test included the same Protective Factors items, but it is not clear whether items were distributed differently on the two versions. There also is no mention of whether scores for the DECA and DECA-C samples were compared to determine differences that may have resulted from the use of a longer form or from the inclusion of more items about behavioral concerns. No information is provided on differences in reliability or validity of the Behavioral Concerns scales of the DECA-C compared to the shorter Behavioral Concern Screener of the DECA.

The manual includes a detailed chapter on interpretation of scores, with a clear description of steps in analysis, from the broad information provided by total scale scores, to the more fine-tuned information of subscale and item scores. Although the authors caution against making too much of an elevated score on a single item, they seem to encourage exactly that, by providing tables of scores that indicate when an item is "in the problem item range." They go on to suggest that such items can be used to develop intervention plans (e.g., a "problem" rating on "Asks other children to play" could become a specific treatment objective).

The manual also provides guidelines for determining the significance of differences between subscale scores, as well as between pre- and postintervention scores. However, given the absence of test-retest reliability data beyond 72 hours, any observed pretest-posttest differences cannot be attributed confidently to an intervention. Suggested comparisons between raters (parent-parent, parent-teacher) seem unwarranted given the lack of normative data on interrater reliability. Further evaluation of the DECA-C is warranted to determine longer term retest and interrater reliabilities, as well as to compare changes in scores for children who receive different (or no) interventions. Ideally, such evaluations should be completed by raters familiar with the child, but blind to the intervention. The connection between Protective Factors and positive outcomes in later childhood has yet to be demonstrated.

SUMMARY. The Devereux Early Childhood Assessment Clinical Form (DECA-C) is a brief rating scale for positive attributes and problem behaviors of children aged 2 to 5 years. It is based on a model of risk and resiliency in psychological development. As such, it is likely to prove a useful tool both in individual assessment and in treatment outcomes research. Psychometric data on the DECA-C indicate adequate internal consistency, short-term retest reliability, interrater reliability for teacher pairs, content validity, and predictable relationships of score profiles to diagnostic groups. Additional psychometric information is needed for interrater reliability of parent-teacher and parent-parent pairs, as well as for long-term retest reliability. In addition, further research is needed to examine the relationship between risk and resiliency factors, as measured by the DECA-C, and later childhood outcomes. The DECA-C was normed concurrently with the DECA. In fact, the three scales measuring resiliency (Protective Factors) are identical on the two instruments. A set of Behavioral Concerns scales on the DECA-C is expanded from the shorter version on the DECA. The DECA-C provides this extra information without being prohibitively lengthier than the DECA.

REVIEWER'S REFERENCE

American Psychiatric Association (APA). (1994). *Diagnostic and statistical manual* (4th ed.). Washington, DC: Author.

Review of the Devereux Early Childhood Assessment—Clinical Form by SANDRA A. LOEW, Associate Professor of Counselor Education, University of North Alabama, Florence, AL:

DESCRIPTION. The Devereux Early Childhood Assessment—Clinical Form (DECA-C) is a paper-and-pencil rating system used by parents and teachers to identify positive and negative behaviors in children of preschool age. The goal of the assessment is to categorize the positive behaviors or strengths into three areas: Initiative, Self-Control, and Attachment, and to categorize the negative behaviors or concerns into four areas: Attention Problems, Aggression, Emotional Control Problems, and Withdrawal/Depression. The first three areas comprise the Total Protective Factors Scale and the last four areas comprise the Total Behavioral Concerns Scale. Parents, teachers, or caregivers who have had regular contact with the child for at least 4 weeks fill out the 62-question test. A trained test scorer and interpreter charts the *T*-scores on a graph that is shaded gray, blue, or white, with the gray areas indicating strengths, blue areas indicating concerns, and the white areas indicating typical behavior. The resulting information can be used to create interventions that are based on increasing the strengths of young children and decreasing the behaviors that are causing concern.

DEVELOPMENT. The DECA-C was developed in conjunction with the Devereux Early Childhood Assessment (DECA). Although the DECA is designed to assist in the development of broad prevention programs and limited interventions for specific children, the DECA-C is designed to aid in the development of specific interventions for children showing behavioral difficulties. Therefore, the DECA-C has additional questions that are aimed at assessing behavioral problems.

Resilience theory underlies the DECA-C, which includes the idea that using positive approaches and promoting strengths is most effective at reducing problem behaviors. The idea of "Positive Psychology" challenges professionals to focus less on pathology and more on strengths and competencies that a person has (Seligman & Csikszentmihalyi, 2000). A discussion of positive psychology is beyond the scope of this review but it is sound theory on which to base an assessment instrument. An extensive literature review was done, and parent and teacher focus groups provided additional information. With a pool of items, the developers then did a pilot study of the instrument. This generated two forms: the DECA and the DECA-C. Although the scales that are used in the instrument such as Initiative, Self-Control, etc. are described in the manual, it is not clear how they emerged from the item pool, focus groups, or pilot study.

TECHNICAL. The normative group for the DECA-C was a stratified sample of preschool-aged children that is proportionally representative of the demographics of that population of the U.S. Because the DECA and the DECA-C were normed at the same time, the same 2,000 children were the sample for the Protective Factors, and an additional 1,108 children comprised the sample for the Behavioral Concerns portion of the DECA-C.

The internal consistency reliability coefficients using Cronbach's alpha range from .66 to .86 for parents' reports and .80 to .90 for teachers' reports. The lowest coefficient of .66 was for parents' reports on Withdrawal/Depression; it was also the teachers' lowest but at a more acceptable .80. Withdrawal/Depression is a difficult construct to evaluate in preschoolers and, because this is an assessment tool rather than a diagnostic tool, an awareness by the user of this shortcoming of the instrument should suffice.

The test-retest reliability coefficients ranged from .55 to .85 for parents' reports and .78 to .91 for teachers' reports over a 24- to 72-hour interval. Interrater reliability coefficients ranged from .32 to .77 for the various scales with the raters being teachers or teacher aides. The lowest coefficient was for the Withdrawal/Depression scale, which the developers explain as being "harder to reliably observe, presumably because of the subtle nature of the behaviors" (manual, p. 31). This is an area that, had the developers given more information on how they arrived at these scales in the development of the instrument, we might have more information about this shortcoming. They define the construct of Withdrawal/Depression as "behaviors related to emotional and social withdrawal in which the child is self-absorbed and often attends to his or her own thoughts or play rather than engaging in reciprocal interactions. This scale also includes feelings of sadness and the inability to enjoy activities and social interactions" (manual, p. 9). Even though this instrument is not to be used as a diagnostic tool, the user should be extremely careful in making decisions concerning a particular child based on scores in this subscale.

The evidence for content validity of the DECA-C is based on an extensive literature review, focus groups made up of parents and teachers, and the Devereux Scales of Mental Disorders. The criterion-related validity evidence was based on the results of giving the DECA-C to two groups of children: one, a community sample and the other, an identified sample of children who had observed behavioral difficulties. The two groups were matched for age, gender, and ethnicity, and there were found to be statistically significant differences between these groups for both Protective Factors and Behavioral Concerns. The developers explored the impact of the DECA-C on the scores of minority children and found there to be negligible differences.

Construct validity is suggested by the developers' study of the DECA that provided evidence that "high scores on the protective factor scales were associated with significantly fewer behavioral concerns than low scores on these scales" (manual, p. 42). Unfortunately, the developers did not present that study in the DECA-C manual so one cannot know if the results are applicable to this instrument. The construct validity of the Behavioral Concerns scales was examined by a study of 123 children with a psychiatric diagnosis. The children with the diagnoses received high scores on the DECA-C scales that would be appropriate given their disorder. The scales of the DECA-C showed positive correlation within Protective Factors and within Behavioral Concerns, and an inverse correlation between Protective Factors and Behavioral Concerns. This is suggested by the theory that Protective Factors are interrelated, as are the Behavioral Concerns, and the Protective Factors and Behavioral Concerns are inversely related.

COMMENTARY. The DECA-C is an instrument that provides users with a tool that identifies strengths and weaknesses that children of preschool age possess. It is well-developed based on resilience theory and has a place in any preschool environment. Its shortcomings have to do with the construct of Withdrawal/Depression. Possibly more research and pilot studies are needed to flesh out this construct so that it is more narrowly defined or the behaviors are more clearly indicative of the construct. Recognizing that this is not a diagnostic tool but an assessment to assist professionals in developing prevention and intervention programs is important for the user. Although the assessment gives valuable information about children's behavior, it is clear that it is part of a larger program (Devereux Early Childhood Interventions) that aims to provide prevention and intervention services in preschools and agencies serving young children. In a sense, this review takes the instrument out of context and examines it in isolation.

SUMMARY. The DECA-C is a useful assessment for professionals who want to implement prevention and intervention programs for preschoolers. The instrument is easy to use, score, and interpret. The resilience theory that underlies the DECA-C is sound and provides positive interventions that are most helpful to young children. The user of the DECA-C should be concerned about the Withdrawal/Depression scale and carefully consider other sources of information concerning a child before designing an intervention to address that issue. Overall, the DECA-C can provide valuable information, especially in the area of protective factors and can be used with other sources of information in developing prevention and intervention programs.

REVIEWER'S REFERENCE

Seligman, M. E., & Csikszentmihalyi, M. (2000). Positive psychology: An introduction. *American Psychologist, 55,* 5–14.

[72]
Diagnostic Evaluation of Language Variation™—Screening Test.

Purpose: Designed to "distinguish variations due to normal developmental language changes or to regional and cultural patterns of language difference from true markers of language disorder or delay."
Population: Ages 4-0 to 12-11.
Publication Dates: 2003.
Acronym: DELV—Screening Test.
Administration: Individual.
Parts, 2: Part I, Part II.
Price Data, 2005: $135 per complete test; $80 per examiner's manual (122 pages), $80 per stimulus manual; $59 per 25 record forms; $195 per 100 record forms.
Time: (15–20) minutes.
Comments: "Criterion-referenced."
Authors: Harry N. Seymour, Thomas W. Roeper, and Jill de Villiers with contributions by Peter A. de Villiers.
Publisher: PsychCorp, A brand of Harcourt Assessment, Inc.
a) PART I.
 Population: Ages 4-0 to 12-11.
 Scores: Language Variation Status.
b) PART II.
 Population: Ages 4-0 to 9-11.
 Scores: Diagnostic Risk Status.

Review of the Diagnostic Evaluation of Language Variation—Screening Test by AIMÉE LANGLOIS, Professor, Department of Child Development, Humboldt State University, Arcata, CA:

DESCRIPTION. The Diagnostic Evaluation of Language Variation—Screening Test (DELV—Screening Test) is designed to help clinicians differentiate between children who present language variations due to their linguistic and cultural backgrounds and children who are at risk for language disorders. To that effect the test includes two parts. Part I (Language Variation Status) helps identify children between the ages of 4 and 13 who speak Mainstream American English (MAE) and those who use variations of MAE. Part II (Diagnostic Risk Status) screens 4- to 10-year-old children who are at risk for language disorders. The test is thus intended to help identify children who demonstrate only language variations from MAE and thus do not need therapy services as well as children who need additional assessment of language for possible remediation.

The two parts of the test assess different components of language, although there is some overlap. In Part I, variations in phonology and morpho-syntactic skills are determined with a sentence completion format whereas in Part II, language disorder risk is assessed with additional morpho-syntactic items, responses to *wh*-questions, and repetition of nonword items. For Part I, the test form provides scoring criteria for each item as well as a list of responses that represent common MAE and non-MAE answers to the prompts under columns identified as A and B, respectively. Scoring for Part II is similar except that the responses listed represent those of children with normal language skills (Column A) and those with a language disorder (Column B). The examiner either encircles one of the provided responses or writes the child's own under the relevant category (MAE, non-MAE, error). There are also "Something Else" and "No Response" categories (Columns C and D) for responses that are deemed uncommon. An appendix in the examiner's manual provides additional examples of responses to help the examiner determine in what column (A, B, or C) a child's answers should be entered. For Part I, only the number of words encircled or entered in Columns A and B is computed to determine a child's language variationstatus. The entries in the "Something

Else" or "NR" categories are ignored in the final tally. For Part II, only the number of words circled or entered in Columns B, C, and D is computed to determine a child's diagnostic risk status. A child's scores are compared separately for each part of the test to a criterion score based on his or her age; this determines either the degree of variation from MAE that the child demonstrates (strong, some, MAE) or his or her diagnostic risk status for language disorder (lowest, low to medium, medium to high, highest).

The authors strongly caution potential test users to read the examiner's manual before administering the test. They emphasize that examiners must become familiar with the materials, follow the scripted procedures exactly without modifying them, and ensure that the test environment is comfortable. They also provide detailed instructions for administration, recording, and scoring. In addition, the manual includes a valuable interpretation section that includes case studies. However, during testing, the examiner must often consult both the manual and the score sheet simultaneously in order to administer the test according to the specified instructions. This can become unwieldy given that he or she must also handle a stimulus book and point to pictures while maintaining rapport with and encouraging the child.

The score sheet includes criterion scores for different ages and space to write information about the child's language use, his or her linguistic background, and teacher observations. At first glance, the test appears easy to administer given the specificity of the instructions; however, two factors mitigate against this. One, related to the logistics of handling the materials is discussed above; the other relates to the amount of information already printed on the score form, which can create confusion as the form includes scripts that users must read, instructions they must follow, common children's responses, and lines for writing additional information. Potential users should therefore heed the authors' admonition to "rehearse item administration" (p. 5) because they are cautioned to not modify test administration in any way.

DEVELOPMENT. The authors offer a sound rationale for the development of the DELV—Screening Test and its use. They point to, the longstanding issue of the misdiagnosis of language disorders in children whose language is simply, though at times markedly, different from MAE.

They convincingly argue that as a result of such misdiagnoses minority children are overrepresented in special education programs. The DELV—Screening Test was therefore developed to mitigate this problem, especially for African American children.

Item development. The authors provide quite a bit of information regarding item development for both parts of the test, but they do not mention why or how they selected the nonword repetition items for Part II. They also describe pilot studies that were conducted in terms of objectives, sites, subjects, results, and review by a panel of experts. It thus appears that the selection of the final set of items represents results of thorough research, except for the nonword repetition items. However, given the purpose of the test, the authors fail to discuss why items that pertain to the language domains of semantics and pragmatics were not included in the test. This is puzzling given that they present correlations between the DELV—Screening Test scores and the DELV—Criterion Referenced edition and given that this latter test includes items that assess semantics and pragmatics. The exclusion of these domains from the DELV—Screening Test is not discussed in the manual and thus might limit its usefulness becase all components of language are typically affected either by a variation or a disorder. Furthermore, the absence of any discussion about the selection of the nonword repetition items brings in question their validity.

TECHNICAL.

Standardization. In order to provide a sample representative of the United States population, the DELV—Screening Test was standardized on 1,258 MAE and African American English (AAE) speaking children from across the United States. They ranged in age from 4 to 13 years and were divided into "non-clinical" (i.e., typically developing children) and "clinical" (children with language disorders) groups of 861 and 397 children, respectively. The manual includes tables that specify the number of children in each group in terms of age, region, race/ethnicity, gender, and parent education level. A table identifies an additional number of 80 children in the sample who spoke a variety of American English that is not African American (e.g., Appalachian, Cajun, Southern, Spanish Influenced). However, given that age is the criterion for identifying target children with this test, the number of children at each age level is inadequate except for 4-, 5-, and 6-year-old AAE children in the nonclinical group. Of the 36 age groups (9 age levels * nonclinical and clinical * AAE and MAE) 33 had fewer than 100 children. The number of children in the subgroups ranged from 6 to 73, falling short of the mark of what is deemed adequate for test standardization (American Educational Research Association, American Psychological Association, & National Council on Measurement in Education, 1999). According to McCauley and Swisher (1984), subgroups should include at least 100 individuals to ensure that norms are stable.

Reliability. The authors provide evidence that interexaminer reliability testing was conducted to determine the decision consistency obtained from repeated test administration by African American and White examiners. Because the test places children into categories that suggest a clinical course of action, the authors deemed overall decision consistency between examiners as essential. To that effect they present tables that reflect the degree of decision consistency between five pairs of examiners who tested 25 children and provide a discussion to accompany the tables. These are difficult to decipher and the difficulty is compounded by the fact that the numbers included in the text discussion do not match those in the tables. Overall, it appears that both examiners placed only 72% of the children in the same categories for Part I, and 36% for Part II. The authors point out, however, that no child was "misclassified as being at the lowest risk for language disorder on one screening ... and at the highest risk ... on the other screening" (examiner's manual, p. 49). They state in the text that a correlation coefficient of .80 "between test scores" (p. 49) was obtained but provide no additional evidence in the form of a table to support this claim. It is also not clear whether .80 reflects test-retest or interexaminer reliability. It therefore appears that interexaminer reliability for the DELV—Screening Test is not high. Factors such as the complexity of test administration and the effect that examiners from different races may have on children cannot be discounted. Without such information it is unknown if and how the examiner affects the scores or the test takers and in what way, thus weakening the usefulness of the test results (AERA, APA, & NCME, 1999).

Validity. The authors attended to several types of validity in the development of the test: content, response process, evidence based on relationship to other variables, and evidence based on clinical studies. The section on item development supports content validity for syntax. How children responded during the pilot research (e.g., pointing, repeating) gives credence to the fact that the test measures the intended skill and thus supports response process validity. Evidence based on relationship to other variables was attempted by computing correlations between the test items on Part II of the DELV—Screening Test and the DELV—Criterion Referenced Domain Scores. Correlations range from .70 for syntax items to .23 for phonology items. Given that these are the domains of language assessed by the DELV—Screening Test, low correlations call into question the test's concurrent validity. Without such strong validity, tests fail to help assess whether an impairment exists or not (AERA, APA, & NCME, 1999; McCauley & Swisher, 1984; Rudner, 1994). Furthermore, the authors do not provide evidence based on relationship to other variables for Part I of the test, thus bringing into question whether it has concurrent validity. Absent this information, the usefulness of test results becomes compromised (AERA, APA, & NCME, 1999).

Finally, the authors provide evidence of validity based on clinical studies. They purport to have investigated "the agreement between performance [on the test] and the a priori classifications of the children" (examiner's manual, p. 51). To that effect 18 tables of means and standard deviations of scores for different ages and different speakers (MAE and AAE) are provided. However, the discussion of these tables does not specify what is meant by "a priori classification," how this concept is to be considered, and what the agreement entails. This section is particularly confusing and thus of limited value to the reader who must rely on the authors' assertion that "a good screener" (examiner's manual, p. 53) would classify children accurately in terms of language variation or MAE and "should miss a minimal number of children who have a language disorder (i.e., false negatives)" (examiner's manual, p. 56). However, data on false negative and false positive identifications are not provided. The authors do acknowledge that the agreement between test scores and a priori classification is less than perfect.

Qualifications of examiner. The manual specifies that "speech-language pathologists, psychologists, early childhood specialists, educational diagnosticians, and other professionals who have experience in training and assessment" (p. 4) can administer, score, and interpret the DELV—Screening Test. This varied group of individuals is likely to differ from the examiners who administered the test for its standardization, who were licensed and/or certified speech and language pathologists and who had to be approved, trained, and supervised to participate in the study. The contrast in training between this latter group and the group deemed qualified to administer the test is troubling. In light of the dubious interexaminer reliability, this issue cannot be overlooked.

COMMENTARY. The DELV—Screening Test, as a means to differentiate between children who speak a variation of MAE and children who may have language disorders, meets a need. The authors emphasize this point eloquently throughout the manual. In addition, the test does represent the assessment of a large nationwide sample of children, a complex task to say the least. Given that this represents a pioneering effort, there is ample truth in the authors' statements that the test is "an innovative instrument" (p. 56) and that "there is no gold standard against which to compare results" (examiner's manual, p. 56). It appears that the DELV—Screening Test's strength lies in its potential to facilitate the identification of non-MAE children who have language disorders that require "subtle probing" (examiner's manual, p. 56). As such the test appears to meet its purpose. Other strengths of the test lie not in the scores obtained but in the use of a child's own responses for the following purposes: (a) as a gauge to determine how his or her use of English compares to that used in instruction at his or her school, (b) as a departing point for selecting additional assessment procedures, (c) as an explanation for his or her performance on such assessment, and (d) as a guide to determine treatment goals when warranted.

However, several concerns about test administration, item selection, standardization sample, reliability, validity, and examiner qualifications discussed above weaken the usefulness of the test in terms of the accuracy of scores obtained. To allay these concerns, explanations must be provided regarding both the exclusion of semantics and pragmatics and the selection of the nonword repetition items; in addition, large samples of children must be assessed for most age groups and reliability research must be conducted with examiners from different backgrounds and levels of training. Finally, given that this is a screening test, information on its specificity, sensitivity, and false negatives/positives rates is needed.

SUMMARY. In spite of the fact that the DELV—Screening Test meets a need and that it was standardized on a representative sample of the U.S. population, it has limited usefulness. The exclusion of language domains is unexplained and dubious interexaminer reliability data fail to address potential sources of errors between examiners with different training. These factors undermine the DELV—Screening Test's usefulness as a means of comparing children to criterion scores. However, on the basis of their high content validity, the phonology and syntax items on the test form can be used as guidelines to decision making. Professionals with excellent listening skills who are well versed in language, its dialectal variations, and its pathologies in children are likely to find these items useful. Conversely, professionals who are not as familiar with language could misuse the test. Differentiating between children who speak dialectal variations of English and those who are at risk for language disorders is an essential undertaking that this test attempts to address. However, unless it is revised to include large groups and address the numerous concerns discussed above, its value is limited as a clinical tool.

REVIEWER'S REFERENCES

American Educational Research Association, American Psychological Association, & National Council on Measurement in Education. (1999). *Standards for educational and psychological testing.* Washington, DC: American Educational Research Association.

McCauley, R. J., & Swisher, L. (1984). Psychometric review of language and articulation tests for preschool children. *Journal of Speech and Hearing Disorders, 49*(1), 34–42.

Rudner, L. M. (1994, April). *Questions to ask when evaluating tests.* ERIC/AE Digest; Report No. TM024537) Washington, DC: ERIC Clearinghouse on Measurements and Evaluation (ERIC Document and Reproduction Services No. ED385607). Retrieved May 22, 2004, from http://www.ericfacility.net/databases/ERIC_Digests/ed385607.html

Review of the Diagnostic Evaluation of Language Variation—Screening Test by SHEILA PRATT, Associate Professor, Communication Science amd Disorders Department, University of Pittsburgh, Pittsburgh, PA:

DESCRIPTION. The Diagnostic Evaluation of Language Variation—Screening Test (DELV—Screening Test) is a two-part tool for screening language disorder in young children. The purpose of Part I of this screener is to identify children (ages 4 through 12) who use linguistic structures that are a variant from mainstream American English (e.g., African American English). The function of Part II is to identify children (ages 4 through 9) who are at-risk for language disorder independent of their dialect. The two parts of the screener are scored and interpreted separately.

The need for Part II of the screener is well documented in the manual and in the literature. Children with nonmainstream dialects are disproportionately referred for speech-language pathology testing and services, in part, because it is difficult to distinguish language disorder independent of dialect. However, the value of Part I is less clear. It could be argued that if a child is found to be at-risk for language disorder with a dialect-neutral measure, then identifying a dialect difference is somewhat irrelevant for screening purposes. Dialect might be an issue for diagnosis but not the screening of language disorder.

Part I of the DELV—Screening Test assesses dialect-sensitive sound production and morpho-syntactic use in sentences. It is composed of three types of tasks: sentence repetition, sentence completion, and question-answering tasks. The sentence completion and question-answering tasks are all preceded by sentence prompts and supported with pictures. All three tasks require a verbal response. Part II includes the same sentence completion and question-answering format used in Part I, but it also includes a nonword repetition task. The items in Part II assess wh-movement, the use of the verb "was," possessive pronoun use, and verbal working memory. The tasks are appropriate for the purposes of the screener except that some of the verbal prompts in Part II are lengthy, which may interfere with the goal of being dialect neutral.

For Part I the number of responses consistent with African American English is tabulated separately from the number of responses consistent with mainstream American English. Each score is referenced to a criterion score. Three possible results can emerge relative to the extent of variation from mainstream American English: strong, some, and no variation from mainstream American English. For Part II a total-error score is established and then referenced to four age-dependent risk categories: low, low-to-medium, medium-to-high, and highest risk for language disorder. Little rationale was provided for why a multicategory rather than a pass-fail classification

system was used given that the test was developed for screening purposes.

DEVELOPMENT. The items on both parts of the DELV—Screening Test were initially developed from a transcript database derived from a small number of 5- and 6-year-old children who used African American English. A set of over 175 test items resulted from the transcripts and was administered to children who spoke the two dialects of interest and to smaller numbers of children from other dialects. The items were then reduced to a total of 135 items, which were then administered to a sample of 1,258 children who represented nine age groups divided into two groups (normal language [nonclinical] and language impaired [clinical]) by two dialect groups (African American English dialect and Mainstream American English dialect). An additional group of 80 children who used other dialects also were tested but the application of their data was not clear. The overall number of participants per cell was low for standardization purposes. The participants were sampled according to the population distribution of African American children across the four major regions of the United States. They were predominately from lower socioeconomic levels, 63% used an African American English dialect, and only 32% were language impaired. This composition might limit the applicability of the DELV—Screening Test for other groups. For example, it may be an insensitive screening tool for language disorder in middle or upper SES children, or even groups that are mixed for race, ethnicity, and income.

From the 135-item pool, a subset of items sensitive to dialect were selected for Part I of the screening test based on item distribution. Items appearing to be discriminative for language disorder yet independent of dialect were selected for Part II based on frequency distributions and the relationship with overall performance on the DELV-Criterion Referenced Test (Seymour, Roeper, & de Villiers, 2003) or a test that was not yet in print (referred to as the DELV-African American Norm Referenced Edition). No additional item analyses or assessments of discriminative sensitivity were reported.

TECHNICAL. The final subset of 32 items constituted the published DELV—Screening Test but was not administered to a second group of children, making the final test criteria and categories suspect. The criteria and performance categories were based on the 135-item preliminary version, not the final 32-item version. As such, there were no data indicating that items or test performance was the same across both versions.

Reliability and sensitivity were inadequately documented for the DELV—Screening Test. Reliability was only estimated for examiner consistency between five black examiners and five white examiners who administered the screening test to a group of 25 black children. The authors argued that the inconsistencies between black and white examiners might have had to do with code switching by older children. For Part II, classification consistency was modest except when the four categories were collapsed into high-risk versus low-risk categories, which calls into question the validity of the multiple-risk categories. The authors did report a correlation of .80 between test administrations, but in the face of unstable categories the correlation has limited meaning.

Documentation of validity was weak. Although not clearly specified in the manual, it appears that validity was assessed with scores extrapolated for the 32 items of the screener when administered within the preliminary 135-item version of the test. These extrapolated scores were then compared to the children's performance on the DELV-Criterion Referenced Test, and to a priori dialect and clinical classifications. Agreement between the DELV-Criterion Referenced Test and the extrapolated scores for Part II was relatively poor with correlations ranging from -.15 to -.70. The authors compared screener classifications with dialect and clinical classifications only by showing percentage of cross-classification per age group. No measures of sensitivity and specificity were provided.

COMMENTARY. The score sheet and the instructions for administration and interpretation of the DELV—Screening Test are straightforward and easy to read, although it is likely that a nontrained individual would have difficulty administering it easily. The picture plates are clear and appropriate for the tasks. However, the manual is uneven with respect to the test's development and construction. The documentation of reliability and validity also was vague, and at times confusing.

SUMMARY. There is a documented need for a screening test of this type. The materials and organization of the test are appropriate and the rationale for the specific test items appears to be reasonable. Administration and scoring are straightforward although it requires some training and knowledge of speech and language development and dialect differences. However, the development and standardization of the DELV—Screening Test appear to be inadequate and incomplete. The documentation of its psychometric properties is limited, making it difficult to judge the quality of the test as a screening tool.

REVIEWER'S REFERENCE

Seymour, H. N., Roeper, T. W., & de Villiers, J. (2003). Diagnostic Evaluation of Language Variation-Criterion Referenced Test. San Antonio, TX: The Psychological Corporation.

[73]

DIBELS: Dynamic Indicators of Basic Early Literacy Skills, Sixth Edition.

Purpose: Designed to assess "growth and development of early literacy skills."

Population: Grades K–3.

Publication Dates: 2002–2003.

Acronym: DIBELS.

Scores, 7: Initial Sound Fluency, Letter Naming Fluency, Phoneme Segmentation Fluency, Nonsense Word Fluency, Oral Reading Fluency, Oral Retelling Fluency, Word Use Fluency.

Administration: Individual.

Levels, 4: K, 1, 2, 3.

Parts, 2: Benchmark Assessment, Progress Monitoring.

Price Data, 2003: $59 per classroom set (specify Grade); $79 per implementation video, "Catch Them Early, Watch them Grow! Using DIBELS in Your School"; $79 per implementation CD-ROM.

Time: (10–15) minutes.

Comments: Benchmark Assessments administered to whole class three times per year; progress monitoring components used with at-risk students on a week-to-week basis to determine progress.

Authors: Roland H. Good III, Ruth A. Kaminski, and Louisa C. Moats (overview only).

Publisher: Sopris West.

a) LETTER NAMING FLUENCY.

Population: Grades K–1.

Authors: Ruth A. Kaminski and Roland H. Good III.

b) INITIAL SOUND FLUENCY.

Population: Grade K.

Forms: 20 alternate forms.

Authors: Roland H. Good III, Deborah Laimon, Ruth A. Kaminski, and Sylvia Smith.

c) PHONEME SEGMENTATION FLUENCY.

Population: Grades K–1.

Forms: 20 alternate forms.

Authors: Roland H. Good III, Ruth A. Kaminski, and Sylvia Smith.

d) NONSENSE WORD FLUENCY.
Population: Grades K–2.
Forms: 20+ alternate forms.
Authors: Roland H. Good III and Ruth A. Kaminski.
e) ORAL READING FLUENCY.
Population: Grades 1–3.
Forms: 20 alternate forms.
Authors: Roland H. Good III, Ruth A. Kaminski, and Sheila Dill.
f) ORAL RETELLING FLUENCY.
Population: Grades 1–3.
Authors: Roland H. Good III, Ruth A. Kaminski, and Sheila Dill.
g) WORD USE FLUENCY.
Population: Grades K–3.
Authors: Roland H. Good III, Ruth A. Kaminski, and Sylvia Smith.

Review of the DIBELS: Dynamic Indicators of Basic Early Literacy Skills, Sixth Edition by BETHANY A. BRUNSMAN, Assessment Specialist, Lincoln Public Schools, Lincoln, NE:

DESCRIPTION. According to the administration and scoring guide, the Dynamic Indicators of Basic Early Literacy Skills (DIBELS) assessments were designed to measure "critical skills that underlie early reading success" (p. 1). Their purpose is to identify and monitor the progress of students who are unlikely to meet state reading standards in third grade. The administration and scoring guide asserts that "DIBELS scores are good predictors of performance on high-stakes, summative tests" of reading achievement (p. 2). They can be used to evaluate the effectiveness of reading instruction both for individual students and for groups of students (e.g., schoolwide). The DIBELS assessments were not meant to be used as the only diagnostic measures for students with reading disabilities (p. 17).

Students in kindergarten through Grade 3 complete three sets of benchmark tests each year. Students who are identified as "at risk" also complete progress-monitoring assessments throughout the school year. The following benchmark assessments are available: Letter Naming Fluency (kindergarten to Grade 1), Initial Sound Fluency (kindergarten), Phoneme Segmentation Fluency (kindergarten to Grade 1), Nonsense Word Fluency (kindergarten to Grade 2), Oral Reading Fluency and Oral Retelling Fluency (Grades 1 to 3), and Word Use Fluency (kindergarten to Grade 3). The progress-monitoring assessments include the same measures, with the exception of Letter Naming Fluency, which is included only in the benchmark assessments.

Letter Naming Fluency consists of a page of random upper- and lowercase letters. The student names as many letters as possible in 1 minute. For Initial Sound Fluency, the examiner reads four sets of four words (for a total of 16 items) and asks which word begins with a particular sound (e.g., /fl/). The student points to pictures representing the words to indicate the correct answers.Scores are reported as number of correct responses per minute. For Phoneme Segmentation Fluency, the examiner reads a word and then asks the student to say all of the individual sounds in the word. The maximum time allowed per sound is 3 seconds. The score is the number of correct sounds given in 1 minute. Nonsense Word Fluency consists of a page of two- and three-letter nonsense words (e.g., sig, rav, ov). The examiner scores the number of correctly pronounced sounds in 1 minute.For Oral Reading Fluency, the examiner listens while the student reads a fictional passage out loud and scores the number of correctly read words in 1 minute. Oral Retelling Fluency may be used with Oral Reading Fluency to check the relationship between oral fluency and comprehension. The examiner gives the student 1 minute to retell the details of the passage. The score for Oral Retelling Fluency is based on the number of words used by the student that indicate understanding of the passage. For Word Use Fluency the examiner says a word to the student and asks the student to "use" the word (p. 55). A response is correct if the word is used correctly in a phrase, expression, or sentence, or if the student gives the definition for the word (whether or not the word is included). The student's score is a count of words (all words, including the prompt word if used by the student) in correct responses in 1 minute.

The administration and scoring guide provides "instructional recommendations" for use with DIBELS scores (pp. 67-84). Decision rules are used to identify students who need intensive instructional support. Alternately, schools can create local norms. The administration and scoring guide provides specific instructional suggestions for students who score below the local percentile rank of 20 and between the 20th and 40th percentile ranks.

All of the assessments are individually administered by trained teachers or other professionals. The administration and scoring guide does not contain any information about the required training. A brochure on the DIBELS website (http://dibels.uoregon.edu) suggests that training for scorers requires 2 days. An additional 2 days of training allows teachers or other professionals to provide training to others. The training includes practice administering and scoring the DIBELS and instruction on how to use scores to track student progress. The administration and scoring of the DIBELS is quite complex. Examiners must time each DIBELS measure overall and follow guidelines for time limits on responses to individual prompts. Examiners must also interpret and record student responses during the assessment. The administration and scoring guide contains very specific instructions about whether and what parts of a student's responses should be counted as correct. Considerable judgment by examiners is required for scoring. Examiners must also make mathematical calculations and compare scores with the decision rules or locally developed percentile ranks. The developers suggest calculating an "aim line" for each student so that instruction can be adjusted if a student is not making sufficient progress toward the student's goal (p. 13). Although scoring must be done by hand by examiners, the administration and scoring guide suggests schools can (for a fee) enter student scores on the DIBELS website and produce score reports containing results for both individuals and groups of students.

DEVELOPMENT. No information about the development of the DIBELS assessments is included in the administration and scoring guide and no technical manual exists according to the publisher. Very minimal information about the research behind the DIBELS is provided in the administration and scoring guide. The introduction suggests that the DIBELS is based on "(a) research on the prediction of reading difficulty in young children; and (b) research on what is taking place in the minds of people who are learning to read" (p. 1).

Information that would allow a test user to evaluate the process used to develop the assessments might include a description of how the tables of specifications were developed, why particular item formats were chosen, who wrote the items/passages, the process for bias review, and pilot testing of assessments and related revision of items.

TECHNICAL. The administration and scoring guide contains a few indices related to reliability and validity, but the data provided are totally unusable because the developers do not describe the participants or methodologies used in the studies. The developers discuss indices related to alternate-form and internal consistency reliability, but do not mention interrater reliability. Three technical reports written by other authors are available on the DIBELS website and report concurrent correlations between the DIBELS and other measures. The developers have not described any studies investigating the predictive relationship of DIBELS scores to state assessments of reading standards.

No information is provided about how the decision rules (cut scores) were developed or why the developers suggest instructional intervention for students with local percentile ranks of 40 or less. The effects of such demographic factors as gender, ethnicity, and income level on scores or predictive relationships are not mentioned.

Information that would be helpful in evaluating the tests could include internal-consistency and alternate-forms reliability coefficients for scores on each assessment; interrater reliability estimates based on at least two trained examiners independently scoring the same student performance; decision-consistency reliability estimates for the decision rules; standard errors of measurement; comparisons of scores of males and females, students of different ethnicities and income levels, and students with varying levels of reading achievement; relationships among all of the assessments for the same group of students; relationships between the DIBELS measures and other related and unrelated measures; effectiveness of intensive reading instruction for students identified by the DIBELS as "at risk"; and predictive relationships between the DIBELS measures and state reading achievement tests at Grade 3. All of these data will only be meaningful with clear descriptions of the groups of students included and the methodologies used in the studies.

COMMENTARY. Documentation of reliability of scores and evidence of validity for the described purposes of the DIBELS is woefully inadequate. The *Standards for Educational and Psychological Testing* (AERA, APA, & NCME, 1999) state that "A rationale should be presented for each recommended interpretation and use of test scores, together with a comprehensive summary of the evidence and theory bearing on the intended use" (p. 17). The developers have provided neither a rationale nor evidence of validity of scores for the purposes they describe. If the goals are to predict success on high-stakes reading achievement tests and to evaluate reading instruction, it would seem appropriate to measure reading comprehension at some point, at least to establish a relationship with the DIBELS measures.

The lack of a rationale or data to support the decision rules is also a concern. From the information presented in the administration and scoring guide, the cut scores seem to be arbitrarily set.

To the credit of the developers, the administration and scoring guide does contain detailed information about how to score the assessments. The developers seem to have anticipated many different ways students might respond to the prompts and items. Also, the discussion of reliability of scores for individual students is helpful. Teachers are advised to conduct several assessments of students identified by DIBELS scores as "at risk" prior to developing an intervention plan. Because the scoring of the DIBELS is complicated, multiple assessments of students by different examiners might prevent making a wrong decision about instructional intervention. Test anxiety (related to stringent time limits) and lack of rapport with the examiner have the potential to negatively impact student scores.

SUMMARY. Although the DIBELS assessments are short, they require individual administration by trained examiners and scoring is complicated. The evidence of reliability and validity is insufficient to support the use of the DIBELS to identify students in need of instructional intervention in reading or to predict scores on high-stakes reading achievement tests. Users should be very cautious about using the DIBELS for the described purposes unless the developers make additional information available so that users can evaluate the validity of DIBELS scores for these purposes.

REVIEWER'S REFERENCE

American Educational Research Association, American Psychological Association, & National Council on Measurement in Education. (1999). *Standards for educational and psychological testing.* Washington, DC: American Educational Research Association.

Review of the DIBELS: Dynamic Indicators of Basic Early Literacy Skills, Sixth Edition by TIMOTHY SHANAHAN, Professor of Urban Education, University of Illinois at Chicago, Chicago, IL:

DESCRIPTION. The DIBELS is an individually administered battery of early literacy tests that measure phonemic awareness (K–1), letter knowledge (K–1), decoding skills (K–2), oral reading fluency (1–3), and vocabulary knowledge and expressive language (1–3). There is also a comprehension measure that requires students to retell what they have read aloud on the oral reading fluency test; however, this is used to ensure the validity of the fluency measure more than to arrive at an independent estimate of comprehension skills. These tests were designed for use as benchmark or monitoring assessments in regular and special education so that teachers could better emphasize instruction in needed skills. The benchmark versions are to be given three times per year to all primary grade students, and the progress-monitoring forms are to be used more frequently with children who are at risk of failure. This sounds like a lot of individual testing given those purposes, but these tests are quite brief—in fact, each can be administered to an individual child in 1 to 3 minutes. Most of the tests have 20 alternate forms allowing teachers to evaluate a struggling student frequently in a particular skill without danger of results contamination or without being tempted to teach the test items themselves.

Phonemic awareness is measured with two different subtests, one that evaluates the ability to identify which picture begins with a particular sound, and another that evaluates phoneme segmentation. The sound identification test (3 minutes) is for use in early kindergarten, and the phoneme segmentation test (2 minutes) can be used from late kindergarten through Grade 1. Letter naming (1 minute) evaluates knowledge of both upper and lower case letters. Decoding skills are evaluated using a nonsense word reading task (2 minutes) that focuses on common VC and CVC spelling patterns. In the oral reading fluency test, students are asked to read aloud three brief passages for 1 minute each and these are scored in terms of words correct per minute (speed and accuracy). Students are asked to retell the information from the passages and the number of words used in the retellings is used to index reading comprehension. The vocabulary measure (1 minute) asks students to provide an oral sentence using particular words.

There is a single administration and scoring guide for all levels, two or three booklets of test administration materials at each grade level, and multiple individual scoring booklets for recording the students' responses at each level. These materials can be purchased from Sopris West in an attractive easy-to-use format, or they can be downloaded for free use from the DIBELS website (http://dibels.uoregon.edu). For a small per child fee, schools can upload their data to the DIBELS website and receive reports that show how their students are doing on the various early literacy skills.

DEVELOPMENT. The development of the DIBELS has been complex and is still ongoing. At this point, entering scores into the online system allows a comparison with 300 school districts, 600 schools, and 32,000 children. The DIBELS also has recently published upper grade and Spanish-language versions (not reviewed here), and both of these can be obtained online. The DIBELS website currently lists 59 research studies concerning its development and use, and some of these are in downloadable form. This is a much more thorough documentation of development than is typically available for screening tests, but none of the documents is included in the Sopris package, and there are gaps in what is available in the downloadable technical reports.

TECHNICAL. The availability of technical information on the DIBELS is somewhat spotty. There is no technical manual for this test. Searching through the various online reports yielded some useful information about the reliability and validity of some of the tests, but not others. The test developers eventually provided this information, but it was more difficult to obtain that it should have been. The technical information that was available was highly encouraging, but it left some important questions. For example, the Initial Sound Fluency (ISF), Letter Name Fluency (LNF), Phonemic Segmentation Fluency (PSF), Word Use Fluency (WUF), Nonsense Word Fluency (NWF), and Oral Reading Fluency (ORF) measures all showed remarkable levels of reliability given the brief nature of these tests, their purposes, and the ages of the children. The WUF reliability was the lowest .64 (alternate form), and the LNF (alternate form: .87) and ORF (alternate form: .92, and test-retest: .92–.97) showed the most evidence of reliability. Similarly, these tests had strong predictive and concurrent validity evidence when compared to the Woodcock-Johnson Reading Tests and other measures. The average concurrent validity coefficients (correlations with other measures taken at the same time) were .80

for ORF, .58 for NWF, .44 for PSF, and .55 for ISF. The predictive validity coefficients were .47 for PSF, .53 for ISF, .66 for ORF, and .68 for NWF (there were no predictive validity data for WUF). No data were found concerning the retelling results on the oral reading fluency measure. DIBELS scores are used to categorize children so that teachers can respond to their learning needs more appropriately. No data were found concerning the reliability or validity of the instructional classifications that result from the DIBELS assessment.

COMMENTARY. The DIBELS tests are gaining wide use, probably due in part to the federal Reading First program. Reading First provides funding to low achieving schools and requires that benchmark and monitoring assessments be carried out in phonemic awareness, phonics, vocabulary, oral reading fluency, and comprehension and that these tests have sound psychometric properties including reliability and validity. DIBELS is tailor made for many of the Reading First requirements (not for reading comprehension, unfortunately). Additionally, its increasing poularity can be attributed to the fact that this test can be purchased inexpensively or even used without charge, that it has so many alternate forms and is so brief, and that the results have practical use in the classroom. I have been unable to locate any other reading test for children in this age group that provides as much sound information as inexpensively or quickly as this test and would not hesitate to use most subsections of it for screening and monitoring purposes.

The clever use of speed as a dimension of the DIBELS test design has made individual assessment practical for classroom purposes. For example, informal reading inventories have been used to estimate oral reading fluency. These tests, though useful, tend to be cumbersome and time-expensive, usually requiring 30–60 minutes per child to administer. Although such measures provide valuable information, teachers rarely use them because of the amount of testing required. DIBELS, instead of calculating percentage of word reading accuracy, adds a time component to this (numbers of words read correctly *per minute*), which allows key information to be derived in only a few minutes of individual testing without any evident loss in reliability. This makes it possible to test all children with such measures, and to retest along the way to determine progress. Few teachers would want to evaluate all of their children mid-year in oral reading if they knew it would require 15–30 hours of individual testing, but more would embrace the practice if this time could be reduced to 1 1/2 to 3 hours, which is what DIBELS has done.

The psychometric evidence for DIBELS is both highly encouraging and somewhat disappointing. These data suggest DIBELS to be an outstanding measure with higher reliabilities and concurrent and predictive validities than is typical of screeners. The sufficiency of validity and reliability for a measure depends upon the use of the measure. Given that the purpose of the DIBELS is to help teachers to prescribe individual instructional responses in targeted areas, the reliability and validity standards could be lower than for many educational tests that have higher stakes. If the DIBELS fails to identify a child who is struggling to learn letter names, then the teacher might fail to provide adequate support to help that child progress in that skill during ensuing weeks or months. Or, if the test indicated a problem that did not exist, then the child might get some additional help such as small group work, but the cost of these errors is small and the chance of correcting them through subsequent classroom observation is great. Despite the low stakes nature of DIBELS, the letter name and oral reading fluency measures have such strong pschometric properties they are more comparable to higher stakes individual assessments (such as the tests used to determine eligibility for special education).

The disappointment in DIBELS is due to the dearth of psychometric data and the lack of validation for the instructional decisions that result from DIBELS. Even with the data on the oddly designed vocabulary instrument, I would not use this one—at least not until there is a construct validation of this measure. It is not obviously a measure of word meaning knowledge, and there are various reasons why it might correlate well with other vocabulary measures even if it is not an adequate measure of vocabulary. It would be helpful also if all of the technical data were packaged in a single, well-organized document.

I find DIBELS to be useful for classroom and school decision making, but would consider it to be more trustworthy if it had information concerning the discriminant validity of the tests with regard to the instructional categories used. Given the lack of data, it is important to be cautious in the use of these educational groupings (at risk, some risk, low risk) and I would not hesitate to alter some placements depending upon other classroom observations. These categories are derived from the performance of 32,000 children. That sounds impressive, but this is not a traditional or necessarily representative norming sample. Participating schools enter their own data into this database and it seems likely that this would be rife with error. Because this process is ongoing, the participating volunteers continue to enter data and the benchmarks for these tests can change. Again, this should highlight their approximate nature.

SUMMARY. DIBELS represents an exciting development in classroom assessment. These measures, for the most part, evidence adequate or better psychometric properties and do a fine job of evaluating letter name knowledge, phonemic awareness, and oral reading fluency. The large numbers of alternative forms are valuable as they allow for frequent monitoring of the educational progress of younger children. That the tests can be used for free is a boon to cash-strapped schools.

However, DIBELS is not without problems. The lack of adequate measurement of readng comprehension and vocabulary knowlege are important gaps and schools that use DIBELS will need to supplement it with additional tests to evaluate these essential aspects of reading. Though most of the tests have sound psychometric evidence, this is difficult to find as it is scattered across several reports. Teachers need to treat the instructional recommendations derived from DIBELS as estimates—useful approximations—as there are no data supporting the validity of the instructional categories used. The tests generally are valid indicators of reading ability, but the ability of the test to correctly and accurately identify who would need additional help may or may not be sound, though they look sensible.

[74]

DiSC Classic.

Purpose: Designed to "help adults better understand themselves and others."
Population: Adults.
Publication Dates: 1996–2001.
Scores, 4: Dominance, Influence, Steadiness, Conscientiousness.
Administration: Individual or group.
Price Data: Available from publisher.

Time: (7–10) minutes.
Comments: Update of the Personal Profile System; self-report, self-scored instrument; related scripted seminar available from publisher.
Author: Inscape Publishing, Inc.
Publisher: Inscape Publishing, Inc.

Review of the DiSC Classic by COLLIE W. CONOLEY, Professor of Educational Psychology, and LINDA CASTILLO, Assistant Professor of Educational Psychology, Texas A&M University, College Station, TX:

DESCRIPTION. The DiSC Classic is a 28-item self-report, paper-and-pencil measure of a person's pattern of thinking and behavior for personal and professional development. The interpretation tables are designed to describe a person in the context of the work environment. The items are forced-choice responses. While thinking about a setting of their choice, the participant chooses the single best self-descriptor of four choices. The least likely self-descriptor is then chosen from among the remaining three choices. There are 28 groups of four single-word descriptors. The four core characteristics of the DiSC are computed by summing the most similar and least similar answers for each category then using the difference scores for each category to describe a person's thoughts and behaviors. The measure is based upon Marston's Model that hypothesized that people perceive the environment (favorable or unfavorable) and self (more or less powerful). These perceptions translate into consistent behaviors and thought patterns described as Dominance, Influence, Steadiness, or Conscientiousness (DiSC). The relative amount of these four characteristics provides a pattern that corresponds to the personal description.

The DiSC measure is designed for layperson use. Each participant receives a self-explanatory test booklet that contains a self-scoring chart and self-interpretation table. The facilitator's manual (which suffices for the test manual) describes the history of the Marston Model, the development of the measure, the psychometric data, and the interpretation guidelines.

DEVELOPMENT. The original scale was developed in 1972 on a sample of 1,000 business men and women, predominately in white-collar professions. In 1994, revisions to the Personal Profile System were made based on a sample of 3,000 respondents. The reliability data are based upon a sample of 812 employed individuals, 80% are Caucasian in predominately white-collar professions. The Facilitator's Manual, Volume 1 and a Personal Profile System 2800 formed the bases of the review. A request to the publisher did result in receiving more technical reports that were no more revealing than the manual. Although the publisher does link the DiSC to Marston's Model (1979), there appears to be no research that finds the DiSC predictive of the traits hypothesized in the model.

TECHNICAL. The manual presents incomplete information regarding the reliability and validity of the assessment. The information presented was based upon a 1996 study of 812 participants. The reliability of test scores is said to be internal consistency measures based upon Cronbach's alpha coefficient (personal communication, Mark Scullard, Inscape Publishing, December 19, 2003). The reliability of the forced—choice selection of "most-like-me" ranges from .72 to .85, and the "least-like-me" is .74 to .84. Cronbach's alpha coefficient values range from .85 to .92 (p. 17).

Validity data are based upon cluster analysis of the 812 participants. The presentation is vague, containing no detail. No coefficients that could be interpreted as goodness-of-fit were presented. The manual states that 100 clusters were found that could somehow be reduced to 15. The 15 clusters were said to represent the Classical Profile Patterns (Achiever, Agent, Appraiser, Counselor, Creative, Developer, Inspirational, Investigator, Overshift, Objective Thinker, Perfectionist, Persuader, Practitioner, Promoter, Result Oriented, Specialist, Tight, Undershift). Notice that there are 18 pattern types listed whereas the manual says that there were 15 clusters identified. The manual states that the patterns of "Overshift" and "Undershift" have never been observed. The pattern of Tight means the person should retake the assessment. The development of these three patterns was not described in the manual.

The Classic profile patterns are used in identifying the behavioral patterns of individuals. Each profile pattern describes an individual's behavioral responses in regard to eight categories: emotions, goal, judges others by, influences others by, value to the organization, overuses, under pressure, fears, and would increase effectiveness through.

The manual contains a section presenting summary statements about DiSC validity studies. The manual does not contain information about the number of participants, the characteristics of the participants, nor if there were statistical results. The summary reveals that the DiSC measures a different aspect of human behavior than the Myers-Briggs Type Indicator, the Personal Listening Profile, and the Team Dimensions Profile. Furthermore, the DiSC was not correlated with the Coping and Stress Profile. The paragraph describing the study comparing the DiSC and the Coping and Stress Profile did say that it was conducted in 1994 and had 215 professionals as a sample.

The authors interpreted the lack of relationship between the DiSC and the other measures as meaning that the DiSC offers unique information about people. There was no study that suggested what the unique information predicted. The substantiating evidence does not meet the criteria established in the *Standards for Educational and Psychological Testing* (AERA, APA, & NCME, 1999).

COMMENTARY. A user of the DiSC should be cautious. The reliability data for the items appear to be moderate at best. The use of test-retest reliability is recommended to the publishers if they wish to examine the reliability of the profiles. Additionally, there are no studies that specify what the DiSC predicts. The validity of the instrument is also questionable. Given the current reliability and validity information, it appears that the DiSC is limited to Caucasian professionals. Although the publishers claim that there are no differences in results between racial groups, the number of participants in each racial group, other than Caucasians, was too small to provide adequate data to substantiate this claim. Reliability and validity studies must be undertaken with a larger and more racially diverse population in order to obtain adequate information about the instrument's use with racial/ethnic minorities.

In addition, the DiSC appears be limited to white-collar professionals such as executives and management. Reliability and validity studies with participants in more service-oriented and blue-collar professions are also needed.

The developers claim that the DiSC has broad applicability within most organizations. However, this statement should be taken with caution. The developers list a variety of ways in which the DiSC can be helpful in areas such as communication skill development and conflict resolution. However, many of the statements are beyond the demonstrated applicability of the instrument.

The presentation and organization of the assessment does make it easy for the untrained administrator. Additionally, there is a statement directing the administrator to ask the user to cross out descriptors in the interpretation that do not seem to fit. This suggestion nicely softens the authoritative pattern descriptions.

SUMMARY. The DiSC Classic is an easy-to-use, well-organized self-assessment of behavior responses to work environments. On the surface level, it appears that the instrument is useful in personal or professional development. However, the test suffers from questionable reliability and unknown validity. The measure is also remiss in its lack of reliability and validity for diverse ethnic/racial populations and professional occupations. Therefore, the use of the DiSC is not recommended.

REVIEWERS' REFERENCES

American Educational Research Association, American Psychological Association, & National Council on Measurement in Education. (1999). *Standards for educational and psychological testing.* Washington, DC: American Educational Research Association.
Marston, W. (1979). *The emotions of normal people.* Minneapolis: Persona Press, Inc.

[75]

DiSC Indra.

Purpose: Provides "an in-depth understanding of relationship dynamics."
Population: Adults.
Publication Date: 2003.
Scores, 18: Convincing, Expressive, Sociable, Cheerful, Receptive, Cooperative, Patient, Modest, Careful, Private, Serious, Matter-of-Fact, Resolute, Demanding, Competitive, Pioneering, Control-Adapt, Affiliate-Detach.
Administration: Individual, dyad, or group.
Price Data: Available from publisher.
Time: Administration time not reported.
Comments: Self-report rating scale; computerized, on-line assessment.
Authors: Inscape Publishing, Inc. (test), Pamela Cole and Kathleen Tuzinski (research report).
Publisher: Inscape Publishing, Inc.

Review of the DiSC Indra by GYPSY M. DENZINE, Associate Professor of Educational Psychology, Northern Arizona University, Flagstaff, AZ:

DESCRIPTION. The developers of DiSC Indra claim the test offers an understanding of interpersonal behavior by mapping and measuring the relationships of people and providing feedback concerning relationship dynamics. Indra stands for IN-Depth Relationship Assessment. It is designed to measure the interrelatedness of people's DiSC styles and highlight the areas of compatibility and incompatibility. One of the major intended uses of DiSC Indra is to help individuals in any type of relationship reduce conflict, and increase effectiveness and understanding regarding their relationship dynamics.

Interpersonal style is described in terms of relationships at three levels: (a) the individual level in which feedback is presented about the person's interpersonal style, (b) the dyad level where information is about the interaction dynamics of two specific people, and (c) the group level where the styles of group members are expressed in terms of their impact on interpersonal behaviors in a specific group. In addition to providing feedback about one's interpersonal style at the three different levels, Profile Reports provide specific action steps for understanding relations in the work place and team dynamics. Although not explicitly stated in the technical manual, the target population for this scale appears to be a tool most appropriate for nonclinical adult populations.

Administration. DiSC Indra is an on-line, computerized, self-report rating scale. The assessment, scoring, and associated reports are available on-line and there is no paper version of the test. After logging on to a web site, individuals are prompted to answer several optional demographical questions (e.g., age, education, heritage, industrial classification). In order to receive the personal report, one must provide his or her name and gender. Respondents are presented with 150 words on a 5-point rating scale and are asked to rank how often the words apply to them. Six questions per screen appear in a list and a box at the bottom of each screen shows a bar graph of the percent of questions completed. Examples of the one-word descriptors used to measure one's interpersonal relationship style include: talkative, questioning, demanding, optimistic, animated, social, sociable. The process of logging on to the web site, reading the instructions, and completing the full scale takes approximately 15 minutes. The instructions state: "When responding, think about how you really are, rather than how you think you should be or you would like to be. This is not a test. It is an opportunity to learn more about how you relate to others. There are no right or wrong answers. You cannot pass or fail."

Scores from individuals are used to provide information for dyad and group interactions. However, a theoretical or empirical case is not made in support of the assumption that one's interpersonal style and related behaviors are consistent in dyad, small groups, and large groups.

Scoring and interpretation. Immediately following completion of the scale, respondents receive a personalized Profile Report. This report contains an individualized DiSC Indra Map, which is composed of three components: (a) Item Scores, (b) DiSC Contour, and (c) DiSC Vector. Using vector algebra, the 150 item scores are located on a unique Item Map for each person. These item scores are used to calculate a person's DiSC Contour and Vector. This map locates the items in relation to a two-axis bipolar interpersonal space, based on the dimensions of Control-Adapt and Affiliate-Detach. As noted in the technical manual, the map is actually a circumplex built from two orthogonal axes that together define a set of variables with a very specific ordering along the circumference (Browne, 1992; Guttman, 1954). The authors state the circumplex structure is believed to be superior to a simple two- or four-dimensional structure because it can demonstrate how the 16 distinct DiSC styles are related to each other in a continuous manner. The second level of scoring occurs as the octant level, which provides information about the octant pattern (i.e., contour or shape). There are eight octants, or DiSC scales, which are mathematically computed by summing neighboring items. The shape of the octant pattern is purported to indicate the "typicality" of the person's profile. In other words, it is meant to represent a measure of "goodness of fit" between the observed and expected pattern. The third type of score sums all of the item scores and, based on results from vector algebra, provides one DiSC vector. The location of this vector is said to characterize the individual into one of the 16 possible patterns around the circumplex, whereas, the length of the vector reveals the extent to which one's behavior is flexible.

Based on item responses, an individual's interpersonal style is described in terms of the following 16 specific DiSC Indra styles: Convincing, Expressive, Sociable, Cheerful, Receptive, Cooperative, Patient, Modest, Careful, Private, Serious, Matter-of-Fact, Resolute, Demanding, Competitive, and Pioneering. Two additional scores are provided for the styles of Control-Adapt and Affiliate-Detach. Profile reports also show a chart of 20 DiSC interpersonal behaviors. For example, one's interpersonal style is graphed in regard to behaviors one is most and least likely to exhibit such as: boisterous, conforming, direct, humble, outspoken, and pioneering. Information on a Relationship Fit Map is also contained in the report. Relationship Fit is described in terms of one's similarities, differences, effectiveness, and comfort of his or her relationships. Three categories of Relationship Fit are described based on one's expectations regarding other's style of Control and Affiliation.

DEVELOPMENT. DiSC Indra is one of the DiSC tests developed by researchers at Inscape Publishing. Although somewhat related, DiSC Indra is different from the DiSC Classic (initially called the Personal Profile System 2800), which was based on the Classical Patterns. According to the authors of the technical manual, the Classical Patterns were initially developed by Walter Clarke (1956) and later refined by John Cleaver (no references are cited in the manual). In contrast to the 15 DISC Classic Patterns identified by earlier researchers, which were based on extensive interviews with people, the DiSC Indra styles were conceptually developed from the work of William Marston (Marston, 1928). According to the Inscape Publisher's web site, the DiSC Classic measures how an individual sees themselves in relation to the environments, whereas DiSC Indra looks at the individual in their relationship with others (http://www.inscapepublishing.com).

Item development for this scale took place in three phases. In what the authors refer to as the "Pre-Alpha" phase, archival data from two previous DiSC-based scales (Personal Profile System® [PPS] and Points of View® [POV]) were analyzed. Although the samples were quite large ($N = 5,612$ for the POV data and $N = 23,286$ for the PPS), two major concerns are noted regarding this item development phase. First, the PPS is a forced-choice instrument, whereas the DiSC Indra employs a rating scale. Second, the authors do not describe in detail how they made their final selection for including specific items. In the second phase, the Alpha phase, 83 new items were written and added to the 112 PPS items to create the DiSC Indra. The purpose of this phase was to complete the item development phase "Through a highly iterative process of data analysis of the PPS, combined with a thorough examination of the extensive literature on statistical circumplex models, interpersonal theory, the lexical tradition, and the Five Factor Model of Personality, we gained the historical clarity that was necessary in order to proceed with item development" (Research Report, [technical manual], p. 13). However, the technical manual lacks details regarding the criteria the test developers used in their decision-making processes in terms of item and scale development. Of concern is the fact that no empirical investigations are cited on the relations between personality measures and DiSC Indra profiles. Overall, the technical manual provides incomplete and superficial treatment of important test development information. Moreover, I found no published articles on the psychometric properties of the DiSC Indra in any professional journals. Nor did my literature search reveal any empirical studies using this scale. However, an internet search reveals this scale is widely used in business and industry training.

The technical manual lacks information regarding who can administer and interpret the DiSC Indra, which conflicts with the *Standards for Educational and Psychological Testing* (AERA, APA, & NCME, 1999). The test distributor's web site offers information on numerous training sessions where people pay to complete the DiSC Indra Certificate training in order to become a facilitator. It appears anyone can obtain this training as no specific educational background or previous training is required to become a facilitator.

TECHNICAL. It may be the case that the technical manual was sacrificed of psychometric details due to the intended audience (laypersons). For example, the authors state items with low communality were removed. Yet, no cutoff value is provided to suggest what constituted a "low communality." In a similar manner, items with a "high reading level" were removed, but no further information about these criteria is provided in the manual. Overall, the manual lacks important information about the norming sample and test standardization procedures. Also missing is an in-depth discussion of the appropriateness of this scale for different gender or ethnic/culture groups.

Reliability data are provided in internal consistency form ($N = 811$; Cronbach's alpha ranging from .70 to .93 for the eight scales). No reliability data are provided in test-retest form. Of great concern is the fact that researchers using the DiSC Indra would not have the ability to compute reliability coefficients for their samples because the raw data are not available. Moreover, no information regarding which items comprise the subscales is provided.

Issues of validity were discussed in general terms including other researchers' conceptual and empirical support of circumplex models of interpersonal and personality theory (Kiesler, Schmidt, & Wagner, 1997; Wiggins, 1996; Wiggins, Steiger, & Gaelick, 1981).

Although the authors claim the DiSC Indra is to help individuals in any type of relationship to reduce conflict and increase effectiveness, and for understanding about their relationship dynamics, no studies providing evidence of predictive validity are reported.

There is also missing evidence of concurrent validity data with other measures of interpersonal behavior, communication style, and personality. Nor do the technical manual or professional literature contain studies providing evidence supporting the convergent, divergent, or criterion-related validity of the DiSC Indra.

COMMENTARY. Perhaps the greatest strength of this test is the ease of the administration and the availability of immediate results. All of the reports are user-friendly and provide for some interesting reflection. Although I found some merit in my own profile and the scale appears to have some practice evidence of face and content validity, the limitations of the technical manual cannot be ignored.

The potential user of the DiSC Indra should be aware of the conceptual and empirical limitations of this scale. There is minimal evidence that the theoretical model of interpersonal behavior is supported by the use of this test.

SUMMARY. Although the DiSC Indra is easy to administer, involves no scoring, and the reports are interesting and easy to interpret, there are several elements missing in the demonstration of a psychometrically sound measure of interpersonal style and people's interrelatedness. Given these limitations, there is a need for more sophisticated and ongoing research on the DiSC Indra before its use can be recommended.

REVIEWER'S REFERENCES

American Educational Research Association, American Psychological Association, & National Council on Measurement in Education. (1999). *Standards for educational and psychological testing.* Washington, DC: American Educational Research Association.
Browne, M. W. (1992). Circumplex models for correlation matrices. *Psychometrika, 57,* 46–197.
Clarke, W. V. (1956). The construction of an industrial selection personality test. *The Journal of Psychology, 41,* 379–394.
Guttman, L. (1954). A new approach to factor analysis: The radix. In P. F. Lazarsfeld (Ed.), *Mathematical thinking in the social sciences* (pp. 258–348) New York: The Free Press.
Kiesler, D. J., Schmidt, J. A., & Wagner, C. C. (1997). A circumplex inventory of impact messages: An operational bridge between emotion and interpersonal behavior. In R. Plutchik & H. Conte (Eds.), *Circumplex models of personality and emotions.* Washington, DC: American Psychological Association.
Marston, W. M. (1928). *The emotions of normal people.* New York: Harcourt Brace and Company.
Wiggins, J. S. (1996). An informal history of the interpersonal circumplex tradition. *Journal of Personality Assessment, 66,* 217–233.
Wiggins, J. S., Steiger, J. H., & Gaelick, L. (1981). Evaluating circumplexity in personality data. *Multivariate Behavioral Research, 16,* 263–289.

Review of DiSC Indra by FREDERICK T. L. LEONG, Professor of Psychology, University of Tennessee, Knoxville, TN:

DESCRIPTION. The DiSC Indra is a measure of interpersonal behavior that has a long history dating back to the work of William Moulton Marston in 1928 when he published a book entitled *Emotions of Normal People* and this model of behavior gives rise to the individual differences along dominance, inducement, submission, and compliance along a two-dimensional, two-axis space. In Marston's original disc model, the four dimensions of dominance, inducement, compliance, and submission that make up the model provide four separate quadrants along two dimensions. In the dimension of dominance and inducement, the individual views himself or herself as more powerful than the environment. In the dimension of compliance and submission, the individual views himself or herself as less powerful than the environment. So that particular axis has to do with self-perception in relation to the environment. Then along the east-west axis in terms of inducement and submission, the individual sees the environment as favorable. On the other hand, in terms of dominance and compliance, the individual sees the environment as unfavorable. This provides the four ends of the two axes in this model.

DEVELOPMENT. Building upon the work of Marston (1928), Walter Clarke (1956), an industrial psychologist, developed an instrument to measure the disc model and this was later developed into the Personal Profile System by John Geier, a faculty member at the University of Minnesota. The current instrument was developed based on the history of these three separate instruments: the disc model by Marston, the model developed by Walter Clarke, and more recently, in the 1970s the Personal Profile System developed by John Geier. So, the current DiSC Indra model is a measure of interpersonal behavior that is actually quite similar to Timothy Leary's (1957) work in terms of the well-known interpersonal circle. Leary's interpersonal circle is arrayed along two dimensions. The first dimension is the need for control and the two ends of that continuum can be a high need for control and a low need for control. The second dimension or axis is the need for affiliation with one end being a high need for affiliation and the other end being a low need for affiliation. Hence, the interpersonal behavior is organized in a circumplex fashion along these two orthogonal dimensions or axes. Hence, the DiSC Indra shares a great deal in common even though it appears to have been developed independently by Marston, Clarke, and Geier. It actually overlaps so much with the interpersonal circumplex that there are questions about whether there is a need for a separate instrument to measure these interpersonal dimensions.

TECHNICAL. The DiSC Indra actually is an extension of the Personal Profile System (PPS) of Geier and is able to provide a circular profile of an individual along those dimensions. The dimensions are organized along the four pure types, which are dominance, influence, steadiness, and conscientiousness, but there are also added dimensions that are in between these pure types.

The authors report a long history of research demonstrating the usefulness, reliability, and validity of the DiSC Indra. Based on research that was conducted on the Personal Profile System, which is a forced-choice instrument consisting of 112 items, the DiSC Indra consists of 150 items measuring those four pure dimensions as well as the dimensions in between. Using large samples, the authors were able to demonstrate good reliability and validity of the DiSC Indra. The sample on which the DiSC Indra was developed on was also quite appropriate in terms of the distribution of age, ethnicity, education, and employment.

Using the standard procedure of examining circumplex data, the authors present the correlations of a circular matrix that supports the idea that this Indra is indeed a circumplex model of interpersonal behavior similar to the Leary interpersonal circle. The authors report good reliability estimates for the scales ranging from .70 to .93 in terms of the Cronbach alphas for the four subscales and the scales in between. In addition in the beta

research part, the authors also report appropriate correlation matrices of the dimensions and the scales do array themselves in a circumplex structure as dictated by Marston's theory.

COMMENTARY/SUMMARY. Unfortunately, what is missing from the test manual is any research showing the predictive validity of the DiSC Indra in terms of actual behavior or even anything resembling the Campbell and Fiske (1959) multi-trait, multi-method (MTMM) approach. Furthermore, there is no attempt to demonstrate that the DiSC Indra provides any incremental validity above and beyond what can be measured by the various instruments developed for Leary's interpersonal circumplex. Hence, one is left with a very rich history for this instrument, but it does not provide any predictive validity data or any data suggesting how the DiSC Indra provides incremental validity or added usefulness above and beyond the measures of the interpersonal circumplex to which it is highly similar in theory and structure.

REVIEWER'S REFERENCES

Campbell, D. T., & Fiske, D. W. (1959). Convergent and discriminant validation by the multitrait-multimethod matrix. *Psychological Bulletin, 56*, 81–105.
Clarke, W. V. (1956). The construction of an industrial selection personality test. *The Journal of Psychology, 41*, 379–394.
Leary, T. (1957). *Interpersonal diagnosis of personality.* New York: Ronald Press.
Marston, W. M. (1928). *The emotions of normal people.* New York: Harcourt Brace and Company.

[76]

Drug Use Screening Inventory—Revised.

Purpose: Designed to quantify "severity of problems in multiple domains of health, behavior, and psychosocial development."

Population: Ages 10 to 16; 17 and over.

Publication Dates: 1990–1991.

Acronym: DUSI-R.

Scores: 12 Domains: Drug and Alcohol Use, Substance Use, Behavior Patterns, Health Status, Psychiatric Disorder, Social Competence, Family System, School Performance, Work Adjustment, Peer Relationships, Leisure/Recreation, Overall Problem Density Index.

Administration: Individual.

Levels, 2: Youth, Adult.

Forms, 3: Past Year, Past Month, Past Week.

Price Data, 2004: $199 per Computer System (specify Youth or Adult) including 3.5-inch diskette or CD-ROM; $50 per 25 paper version forms (specify Youth or Adult); $49 annual maintenance fee for software license; volume discounts available.

Foreign Language Edition: Spanish edition available for computer.

Time: [15] minutes.

Comments: Self-report behavior inventory.
Author: Ralph E. Tarter.
Publisher: Gordian Group.

Review of the Drug Use Screening Inventory—Revised by TONY CELLUCCI, Professor and Director of the Psychology Training Clinic, Idaho State University, Pocatello, ID:

DESCRIPTION. The Drug Use Screening Inventory—Revised (DUSI-R) is a revision of the earlier Drug Use Screening Inventory (Tarter & Hegedus, 1991; Tarter & Kirisci, 1997).

This measure is a 159-item (Yes/No) questionnaire that includes a 10-item Lie Scale. There are separate but parallel versions for youth (10–16 years) and adults (16 and older), and either version can be administered in one of three forms to provide information over the past week, past month, or past year. The DUSI-R serves as the first stage in a multistage screening and assessment process, efficiently identifying adolescents or adults suspected of having problems with alcohol or other drugs. The inventory provides information regarding severity of disturbance in 10 life domains. The life domains included are: Substance Use, Behavior Patterns, Health Status, Psychiatric Disorder, Social Competence, Family System, School Performance, Work Adjustment, Peer Relations, and Leisure/Recreation. Clinicians can use the DUSI-R and then obtain a more intensive diagnostic evaluation of indicated problem areas, providing an efficient but comprehensive assessment. The DUSI-R is said to require a fifth grade reading level, and takes approximately 20 minutes to complete.

The DUSI-R Inventory begins with a preliminary section questioning the respondent's frequency of use of 20 different substances (i.e., 0 times, 1–2 times, 3–9 times, 10–20 times, and more than 20 times). The inventory items follow, organized by domain with the exception that all the last items listed under each domain actually comprise the Lie Scale. Scoring is straightforward, simply involving summing the number of indicated (Yes) items for each domain to obtain raw scores. The Lie Scale is scored by summing the number of No items indicated out of the 10 items (e.g., ever told a lie, been angry). A score of 5 or higher on the Lie Scale is said to suggest possible invalidity. Interpretation is based on the individual's profile of scores translated to a common scale (0–100%). Two types of scores can be calculated and plotted: the absolute problem density profile (raw scores/# of items in domain x 100) and the relative problem density profile (raw scores/total YES items x 100). These percentage scores reflect graduations of severity of reported problems. There are no diagnostic cutoffs but an overall problem density score (# YES responses/149 items x 100) exceeding 15% is considered significant. There is apparently no manual for the DUSI-R; users are provided with a four-page handout describing the test. Possible stated uses of the DUSI-R include intake evaluation, intervention monitoring, outcome assessment, and program evaluation.

DEVELOPMENT. Limited information was available in the literature and materials provided as to how the DUSI items were selected. Tarter, Laird, Bukstein, and Kaminer (1992) indicate that items on the original adolescent version were "determined by two consensus panels consisting of experienced researchers, health service administrators, and practitioners" (p. 233). Tarter and Hegedus (1991) describe the content included in each of the domains. These authors make the statement that "to the extent possible, the items comprising the DUSI are free of cultural or ethnic bias" (p. 73). The DUSI-R items are slightly revised from the first edition. Specifically, many items were rewritten to reflect past tense (e.g., did you vs. do you), and perhaps of more importance, the qualifier "ever" was deleted from most items (e.g., ever had a craving, serious argument, problem remembering). The latter change would presumably increase specificity at the expense of sensitivity, albeit no explanation is provided. Although the items are certainly consistent with the past edition, it is presently unclear whether the available data (Kirisci, Tarter, & Hsu, 1994; Tarter & Kirisci, 1997) on the psychometric properties and sensitivity of the DUSI apply equally well to the DUSI-R. It might be mentioned here that there are also subtle wording differences (on about 20 items) between the adult and adolescent versions of the DUSI-R. The other noteworthy change to the new edition is the addition of the 10-item Lie Scale.

TECHNICAL.

Standardization sample and score interpretation. The nature of the DUSI-R as an individualized screening tool based on percentage of items endorsed does not necessarily suggest a normative reference group. The promotional materials state that norms are available but they were never provided. Overall means and standard deviations for the original adolescent DUSI domains are provided in Kirisci et al. (1994) for two samples: 846 12–18-year-olds and a subsample of 259 PSUD (Psychoactive Substance Use Disorders) youth. However, sex, as well as age, would be expected to be related to adolescent substance abuse and reported life problems.

Reliability. Prior research suggests that the DUSI domains are unidimensional (Kirisci et al., 1994; Tarter & Kirisci, 1997). Using an IRT analysis, marginal reliability estimates for the domains were found to be adequate. The domains with the lowest reliability estimates were Work Adjustment (.53), Health Status (.60), and Social Competence (.67). The handout provided with the DUSI-R reported traditional reliability estimates for a sample of 191 youth with alcohol and other drug problems. The assessment timeframe was unspecified. Average internal consistency (presumably Kuder-Richardson) coefficients across all domains were reported as .74 for males and .78 for females. The mean 1-week test-retest coefficients for a second sample (unknown size) were reported as .95 and .88 for males and females, respectively.

Validity. Given limited information about the theory and process governing item selection, it is difficult to evaluate the content validity of the DUSI-R. Sensitivity of the original adult DUSI for detecting PSUD cases was shown by Tarter and Kirisci (1997). A score of 4 or higher on the substance abuse domain correctly classified 80% of an adult PSUD group identified by a structured diagnostic interview. Mean group differences between male PSUD subjects and controls were found on all domains except School Adjustment; for females, group differences between PSUD and control subjects were found on all domains except Health Status.

Concurrent validity evidence for the adolescent DUSI-R was reportedly examined in relation to several measures. The K-SADS, a structured psychiatric interview for youth, was correlated with the Substance Use (.72) and Psychiatric (.65) domains. The Social Competence domain was negatively related (-.51) to an adolescent assertiveness measure. Finally, the Health domain was also related (.53) to a checklist of health problems. Unfortunately, the details of the studies involving the DUSI-R were unavailable. No data

on the revised version with adults were reported, and there is apparently no information regarding frequency of endorsement to Lie Scale items. Differential validity evidence for the DUSI-R across gender, racial, and ethnic groups has yet to be gathered. Consequently, use of the DUSI-R seems best supported with adolescents as an intake screening measure. No evidence (i.e., documented changes with treatment) has been presented that would support use of the DUSI-R in outcome assessment or program evaluation.

COMMENTARY. Current review of the DUSI-R is limited by lack of published research studies and the failure of the publisher to provide a detailed manual. The rationale for subtle wording differences between the adult and adolescent versions is unclear. The past week also appears to be an unreasonably short assessment interval. There is relevant literature on the earlier edition (DUSI) that suggests reasonable psychometric properties might be expected.

In particular, the use of Item Response Theory (IRT) is to be commended. However, clearly research is needed on the new edition. The promotional materials indicate that some research has been conducted with the revised adolescent version. A revised manual should more formally address issues related to item selection (i.e., content validity), and research should examine the DUSI-R for differential validity of items across ethnic groups. The number of items that must be endorsed for any particular domain to constitute a serious problem is presently a clinical judgment. Similarly, there is no basis to recommend interpretation of the Lie Scale. The use of the DUSI-R seems mainly validated for preliminary screening of adolescent substance abuse populations. Research is needed to recommend optimal cutoffs (e.g., two substance abuse items) for selecting PSUD adolescents in a general population.

SUMMARY. The most recent version of an established assessment tool, the DUSI-R is a viable screening measure for adolescents presenting with substance abuse issues. It is emphasized that findings from the DUSI-R should be considered the first step in a comprehensive assessment. The Problem Oriented Screening Instrument for Teenagers (POSIT) is an alternate measure in the public domain that has been used fairly extensively; a short form of the POSIT has recently been developed (Danseco & Marques, 2002).

REVIEWER'S REFERENCES

Danseco, E. R., & Marques, P. R. (2002). Development and validation of a POSIT-Short Form: Screening for problem behaviors among adolescents at risk for substance use. *Journal of Child and Adolescent Substance Abuse, 11*, 17–36.

Kirisci, L., Tarter, R. E., & Hsu, T. (1994). Fitting a two-parameter logistic item response model to clarify the psychometric properties of the Drug Use Screening Inventory for adolescent alcohol and drug abusers. *Alcoholism: Clinical and Experimental Research, 18*, 1335–1341.

Tarter, R. E., & Hegedus, A. M. (1991). The Drug Use Screening Inventory. *Alcohol Health & Research World, 15*, 65–75.

Tarter, R. E., & Kirisci, L. (1997). The Drug Use Screening Inventory for Adults: Psychometric structure and discriminative sensitivity. *American Journal of Drug and Alcohol Abuse, 23*, 207219.

Tarter, R.E., Laird, S. B., Bukstein, O., & Kaminer, Y. (1992). Validation of the Adolescent Drug Use Screening Inventory: Preliminary findings. *Psychology of Addictive Behaviors, 6*, 233–236.

[77]

Dynamic Assessment of Test Accommodations.

Purpose: "Designed to assist the teacher in determining the appropriate accommodations that will allow students with learning disabilities to demonstrate academic ability independent of their handicapping conditions."

Population: Students with special needs in Grades 2 to 7.

Publication Date: 2003.

Acronym: DATA.

Administration: Individual or group.

Levels, 3: Grades 2–3, Grades 4–5, Grades 6–7.

Price Data, 2003: $150 per complete kit including manual, and 3 test booklets (specify level); $5.50 per Reading Screener card; $14 per 25 Reading Screener score sheets; $5.50 per Workbook Symbols card; $65 per manual; $25 per 25 Math booklets (specify level); $45 per 25 Reading booklets (specify level).

Comments: Student must be capable of reading basic text at a rate of at least 10 words per minute before Reading Comprehension is assessed.

Authors: Lynn Fuchs, Douglas Fuchs, Susan Eaton, and Carol Hamlett.

Publisher: PsychCorp, A brand of Harcourt Assessment, Inc.

a) READING COMPREHENSION.

Scores, 4: Large Print Gain, Extended Time Gain, Read Aloud Gain, No Accommodation.

Time: 40(45) minutes.

b) MATH COMPUTATION.

Scores, 2: Extended Time Gain, No Accommodation.

Time: 24(29) minutes.

c) MATH APPLICATION.

Scores, 4: Extended Time Gain, Calculator Condition Gain, Reader Condition Gain, No Accommodation.

Time: (42) minutes.

Review of the Dynamic Assessment of Test Accommodations by MICHELLE ATHANASIOU,

Associate Professor of School Psychology, University of Northern Colorado, Greeley, CO:

DESCRIPTION. The Dynamic Assessment of Test Accommodations (DATA) is an instrument designed to identify students with disabilities in Grades 2 through 7 who might benefit from the use of common accommodations during classroom and district- or state-mandated achievement testing. The need for accommodations is measured for Reading Comprehension, Math Computation, and Math Application. The DATA assesses the gain in test performance when the following accommodations are made: Large Print, Extended Time, and Read Aloud (for Reading Comprehension); Extended Time (for Math Computation); Extended Time, Calculator, and Reader (for Math Application). In addition, a reading screener is included to ensure that students have the requisite reading fluency to complete the reading comprehension test. DATA components can be administered separately or aggregately. If all three areas are to be administered, a total of three to six sessions (depending on grade level) spread over a 3-week period, is required. With the exception of the Read Aloud accommodation for Reading Comprehension, the DATA can be group administered. The DATA produces gain scores for each of the accommodations; testing accommodations in the classroom are recommended for students whose gain scores exceed a cutoff determined by comparison to a normative sample of students without disabilities.

DEVELOPMENT. The DATA was developed to provide objective information on which to base decisions about the appropriateness of test accommodations. Federal law mandates appropriate accommodations for students with disabilities. According to the authors, test accommodations should not alter the underlying construct being measured by a test, and they should provide gains for students with disabilities that exceed those for students without disabilities. Decisions about accommodations made by teachers and IEP teams often err on the side of providing excessive accommodations, which in some instances may actually hinder student performance.

Items for the math tests were written after experts in math instruction selected a method for assessing the skills found in target grade curricula. Five teachers then reviewed the items, and nonspecified appropriate modifications were made based on their recommendations. The tests were then administered to samples of students to determine time limits and necessary modifications. Two alternate forms were developed for math computation (no accommodations and extended time), and four were developed for math application (no accommodations, extended time, calculator, reader).

For the Reading Comprehension test, graduate students wrote stories using a grade-appropriate reading level. Another group of student wrote multiple-choice questions corresponding to the stories. Graduate students then answered questions to ensure they could not be answered correctly without having read the story. Distractors that were obviously incorrect were removed, and excessively easy and hard questions were deleted. Finally, the stories were reviewed by a panel of editors and test developers for bias and sensitivity. Two stories for each accommodation condition (for each grade level) were selected for inclusion in the DATA.

TECHNICAL. The DATA was standardized on 300 students, 100 at each grade level. Students represented the Midwest, South, and West regions of the United States. Only students without diagnosed disabilities were included in the normative sample. The sample consisted of approximately equal numbers of males and females, and students representing minority and ethnic groups were included proportionately to 1998 U.S. Census Bureau data. Percentages of students from low SES families (as determined by eligibility for free or reduced lunch) are also presented in the manual; however, comparison data for children nationally are not, thereby making the figures difficult to interpret.

Reliability data on a tryout version of the DATA were collected from a sample of students in the Nashville, TN area. Additionally, reliability studies were conducted using students in the normative sample. The DATA appears to be internally consistent, with alpha coefficients for Reading Comprehension across grade levels and accommodation ranging from .64 to .91 ($Mdn = .82$); coefficients for Math Computation ranged from .83 to .95 ($Mdn = .91$); and coefficients for Math Application ranged from .82 to .90 ($Mdn = .86$).

Several validity studies were conducted with tryout and final versions of the DATA. One study using the tryout edition suggested that the DATA, as compared to teacher judgment, recommended accommodations for fewer students. Further, the

students selected by teachers for accommodations were disproportionately African American, had lower IQs and reading instructional levels, and were more likely to have been retained and eligible for free or reduced lunch. This research, according to the authors, highlights the need for more objective information, such as provided by the DATA, when making accommodation decisions. Although a description of the above research is presented in the manual, relevant statistics are not, leaving the reader to rely on the authors' interpretation of data.

Other evidence of validity is discussed with regard to correlations between DATA results and standardized achievement tests. DATA scores were correlated with the Iowa Tests of Basic Skills (Hoover, Hieronymus, Dunbar, & Frisbie, 1996), Comprehensive Tests of Basic Skills (CTB/McGraw-Hill, 1990), or the Stanford Achievement Test, Ninth Edition (Harcourt Educational Measurement, 1996). All correlations are positive and moderate to strong, suggesting the validity of the academic material tested by the DATA.

As previously mentioned, students' gain scores are compared to cut scores to determine whether accommodations are recommended. The authors use the 84th percentile as the cutoff point; however, no rationale for this decision is provided in the manual. Further, the manual includes no evidence of the consequential aspect of validity with regard to this cutoff. For example, what of the student whose gain score is at the 70th percentile? What is the rationale behind not recommending accommodations for that student? It is possible that the authors assume such a gain is too similar to that realized by students without disabilities (i.e., students in the normative sample), but neither specific information nor empirical support is provided in the manual.

COMMENTARY. The DATA is very user friendly, containing separate test booklets for each student that include space to record their results. All spoken directions required by the teacher are printed in bold in the manual, and the appendix contains a clear scoring key. Scoring the instrument is straightforward, and interpretation of scores is simple. Teachers using all the DATA tests need to be aware that the tests are administered over a 3-week period, and that the Read Aloud accommodation on the Reading Comprehension test needs to be individually administered. Therefore, advance planning is required. Based on the information provided in the manual, the DATA appears to have reliability and validity data to support it. Still, additional evidence is needed (e.g., stability, consistency across raters, and support for the cutoff point for accommodation decisions). In addition, information related to test fairness is needed. The standardization sample was small and did not include students from the Northeast, suggesting that caution should be used in interpreting DATA results with this population.

SUMMARY. The DATA should prove to be a very useful tool in educational systems. Given the legal mandates for appropriate testing accommodations for students with disabilities, it is imperative that educators and IEP team members have an objective method for making accommodation decisions. Using the DATA, educators have the opportunity to systematically test the usefulness of individual accommodations prior to using them on a large scale basis. Still, as should be the case with any assessment tool, outside information should be considered along with DATA results when making accommodation decisions.

REVIEWER'S REFERENCES

CTB/McGraw-Hill. (1990). Comprehensive Tests of Basic Skills. Monterey, CA: Author.
Harcourt Educational Measurement. (1996). Stanford Achievement Tests, Ninth Edition. San Antonio, TX: Author.
Hoover, H. D., Hieronymus, A. N., Dunbar, S. B., & Frisbie, D. A. (1996). Iowa Tests of Basic Skills®. Itasca, IL: Riverside Publishing.

Review of the Dynamic Assessment of Test Accommodations by BETHANY A. BRUNSMAN, Assessment Specialist, Lincoln Public Schools, Lincoln, NE:

DESCRIPTION. The Dynamic Assessment of Test Accommodations (DATA) was designed to be used by teachers and other educational professionals to determine what accommodations are appropriate for students with learning disabilities in Grades 2 through 7 for classroom and standardized (state and district) achievement tests. The DATA consists of a series of Short Reading Comprehension, Math Computation, and Math Application tests. Different tests are used for Grades 2–3, 4–5, and 6–7. Students complete one test without accommodations and a separate test for each accommodation. The tests may be group administered, with the exception of the Reading Comprehension test with the Read Aloud accommodation. A Reading Fluency screening test is used to determine if the Reading Comprehension test is appropriate for students.

The Reading Comprehension tests include two fiction passages with 16 accompanying multiple-choice items. There are 25 Math Computation and 18–24 Math Application fill-in-the-blank items on each test. The tested accommodations include Extended Time, Read Aloud (student), and Large Print for Reading Comprehension; Extended Time for Math Computation; and Extended Time, Teacher Reader, and Calculator for Math Application. All of the tests are timed, except the Math Application test with the Teacher Reader accommodation. The manual suggests the use of a timer that beeps or a stop watch. A suggested administration schedule for each grade level is also provided. The tests must be given in the prescribed order, but tests may be omitted if appropriate.

The teacher or education professional who administers the tests scores them by applying the provided answer keys and calculating a "gain" in raw score points for each accommodation over the score on the test without accommodations. Scores are calculated by hand, but the worksheets are relatively easy to use, except for the added complication of the correction for guessing on the Reading Comprehension tests. Teachers then compare the student's Gain score to Gain scores of students without disabilities in the norm group to determine if a particular accommodation should be recommended for the student for classroom and standardized tests of Reading Comprehension, Math Computation, or Math Application. An accommodation is recommended for a student if the student receives a Gain score with a percentile rank of 84 or higher for the reference group of students without disabilities.

DEVELOPMENT. According to the manual, the DATA was developed in response to legal mandates that appropriate accommodations be provided to students during testing. Research cited suggests that accommodations tend to be overused, which is costly to schools and may be detrimental to meaningful interpretations of student performance on achievement tests. The manual states that an accommodation is valid "if it significantly improves the test scores of students with disabilities more than it does the scores of students without disabilities" (p. 47). The accommodations chosen for inclusion are ones that are most commonly used on statewide assessments according to research cited in the manual.

Graduate students in Special Education wrote the reading passages and test items. Five curriculum "experts" at each grade level for each test provided feedback about the tables of specifications and sample item formats. The developers collected pilot data from a few students and calculated the Flesch-Kincaid readability index prior to finalizing passages and test items. The passages were "reviewed by a panel of editors and test developers for bias and sensitivity" (p. 53). No information is available about the qualifications of these bias reviewers, what training they received, or whether any changes were made to the passages based on their comments.

The developers then gave the tests to "tryout" samples of students that ranged in size from 373 to 710 (p. 55). No information is available about the tryout students. Some reading passages and items were eliminated after the tryouts, but no details are available in the manual about what criteria were used. No information is provided about measures used to ensure that the different tests within a content area are of equal difficulty.

To establish the time limits, the developers administered the tests to students "proficient" and "nonproficient" in math and reading (see manual, pp. 51 and 52). It is unclear if these students took the tests with accommodations.

TECHNICAL. The norm group consisted of 300 students without disabilities, 100 at each of the following grade level ranges: 2–3, 4–5, and 6–7, in 50 classrooms across the United States. Approximately equal numbers of males and females were included in the norm group. The sample mirrored relatively closely in terms of ethnicity the 1998 School Enrollment Supplement file data collected by the U.S. Census Bureau. The demographic information related to region of the U.S. and income level of students in the norm group are difficult to interpret as represented in the manual. No details are available about how the norm group was selected.

Alternate-form and coefficient alpha reliability indices were calculated for the scores of students in the tryouts. It is unclear from the manual what the developers actually mean by alternate-form reliability, given that there is only one form of each test. The reliability indices ranged from .73 to .96 and were generally lower for the Reading Comprehension and Math Application scores than for Math Computation scores.

Coefficient alpha reliability indices were also calculated for the scores of students in the norm group. These indices ranged from .64 to .91 for Reading Comprehension scores, .83 to .95 for Math Computation scores, and .82 to .90 for Math Application scores. These values are in the acceptable range, but no reliability indices were provided for scores of students with disabilities, the group for which the test was designed.

The developers provide two types of evidence related to validity. Two studies based on the tryout data are briefly summarized and correlations with other measures of student achievement are included. The studies mentioned in the manual found that students who received accommodations based on DATA scores performed better on the Iowa Test of Basic Skills (Hoover, Hieronymous, Dunbar, & Frisbie, 1996) than did students who received accommodations based only on teacher judgment. These studies are promising, but it is unclear what criteria the developers used to recommend accommodations from the DATA because there were no norm data at that time. The correlations with other achievement tests ranged from .55 to .93, but it is unclear who participated in these studies. No efforts to examine the decision-consistency reliability of recommendations for accommodations or to provide evidence of validity of the cut scores are included in the manual. No reliability or validity data are presented for scores of students in different demographic groups (e.g., gender, ethnicity, income level). More evidence to support the validity of recommended accommodations based on data scores is necessary.

COMMENTARY. This measure is an important addition to the literature because there are no others available like it. The developers' reasons for creating this instrument are sound. Teachers and schools need better guidance about what accommodations to provide for students during testing so that students with learning disabilities can demonstrate their achievement without compromising the validity of the test scores. The literature supports the use of gains in scores of students with disabilities over those of students without disabilities as a way to determine if accommodations are appropriate. More information about the development of the DATA and more evidence of the validity of recommendations for accommodations are necessary, however, to determine if the instrument is effective for its purpose. Questions about the use of the DATA for students in different ethnic and income groups also exist.

Some minor concerns also exist about the format, calculation of scores, recommendation related to extended time, and students' prior familiarity with the accommodations tested by the DATA. With respect to format, the font size for all of the tests, except the large print Reading Comprehension test, is too small for students in Grades 2 through 5 and there are too many items on a page with too little white space. No rationale is given for not allowing students to review the passages prior to answering the test items. Many achievement tests allow students to reread passages as necessary. Because the directions highlight the time limits, test anxiety could be a factor for some students that might potentially change across the tests.

The manual lacks an explanation of the rationale for using a correction for guessing on the reading comprehension tests. The directions do not inform students about this penalty. Moreover, this correction makes the scoring more complicated for teachers.

The manual recommends that students whose scores indicate that extended time is an appropriate accommodation receive one and a half times the regular amount of time on classroom and standardized achievement tests. This recommendation is inconsistent with the timing used on the DATA. The amount of time allowed for extended time on the DATA is twice the regular time limit for Reading Comprehension and five to six times the regular limit for the math tests. The developers provide neither a rationale for the recommendation of one and a half times the regular time limit nor any evidence that this amount of time is appropriate.

One of the important admonitions in both the literature and in legislative mandates is the importance of using accommodations on tests that students normally use in classroom instruction. The manual provides no guidance on this issue. Should students be given some practice using these accommodations before they take the DATA? Familiarity with the accommodations might have a significant impact on scores.

Finally, it would have been helpful to include the "read aloud" accommodation for the Math Application test. Unlike the Teacher Reader accommodation, some achievement test publishers do not consider allowing students to read items aloud to affect the interpretation of test scores.

SUMMARY. The DATA was designed to meet an important need in achievement testing: to provide data on which to base decisions about appropriate testing accommodations. The methodology of comparing gains in scores for students with learning disabilities with those of students without disabilities is sound. More reliability and validity evidence are necessary, however, to determine if the recommendations the developers have proposed based on scores are appropriate. Specifically, data should be collected for students with learning disabilities to show that the results of the DATA, including the provided cut scores, are associated with gains in student performance on achievement tests above those resulting for accommodations based only on teacher recommendations.

REVIEWER'S REFERENCE

Hoover, H. D., Hieronymous, A. N., Dunbar, S. B., & Frisbie, D. A. (1996). Iowa Test of Basic Skills®. Itasca, IL: Riverside Publishing.

[78]

Dyscalculia Screener.

Purpose: To screen pupil(s) to establish whether a pupil has low attainment because of a dyscalculic deficit.

Population: Ages 6–14.

Publication Date: 2003.

Scores: 4 tests: Dot Enumeration, Number Comparison (Numerical Stroop), Arithmetic Achievement, Simple Reaction Time.

Administration: Group.

Price Data, 2003: £150 for Annual License; £50 for License Renewal.

Time: (15–30) minutes.

Comments: Test administered via microcomputer conforming to the following specification: Pentium class system with at least 32 MB of RAM, 100 MB of free hard drive space, running Windows 98, 98SE, NT4, or 2000, with sound card.

Author: Brian Butterworth.

Publisher: NFER-Nelson Publishing Co., Ltd. [England].

Review of the Dyscalculia Screener by CLEBORNE D. MADDUX, Foundation Professor of Counseling and Educational Psychology, University of Nevada—Reno, Reno, NV:

DESCRIPTION. The Dyscalculia Screener is an individually administered, computer-based, response time test designed to identify children ages 6 to 14 who do not understand the concept of numerosity and who are unable to identify and use small numerosities. The manual regards these problems as dyscalculia and asserts that the test is intended "to screen a whole group of pupils to assess the number with dyscalculic tendencies" (manual, p. 19), to test a single child suspected to be at risk of dyscalculia, or for use in research. As a screening test with groups, the test is intended to guide resource planning, whereas use with a single child is intended to help in determining an individualized educational plan.

Speed of response to numerical items is what is measured by the Dyscalculia Screener. The test requires 15 to 30 minutes to administer and consists of an initial subtest of simple reaction time in milliseconds between presentation of a dot on the computer screen and the child's response of striking a key. Results of this subtest are then used to adjust the scores (reaction times of the child on all correctly answered items) that follow. The rest of the test is made up of the Dot Enumeration subtest, the Number Comparison subtest, and an Arithmetic Achievement subtest. The Dot Enumeration subtest involves counting dots on one side of the screen and indicating whether or not the numeral on the other side of the screen matches this count. The child indicates that there is a match by pressing one of a number of keys on the extreme right side of the keyboard, and indicates that there is not a match by pressing one of a number of keys on the extreme left side of the keyboard. The Number Comparison subtest involves selecting the larger of two numerals shown simultaneously on opposite sides of the screen—again with right- or left-side key presses. Some of these tasks involve Stroop effects, in that sometimes the lesser of the two numbers is presented in a larger or smaller type face than the greater of the two. (The manual never makes clear why these congruity and incongruity effects are incorporated in the subtest, other than to explain the known fact that when the lesser number appears in a larger type face, the item is more difficult, and when the lesser number appears in a smaller type face, the item is easier.) The Arithmetic Achievement subtest involves addition for children ages 6 to 9-11, and both addition and multiplication for children age 10 or older. In all addition or multiplication items, an equation is shown complete with an answer that is sometimes correct and sometimes incorrect. If correct, the child presses a right-side key, and if incorrect, a left-side key.

All subtests are administered via computer and instructions are presented orally via a female voice broadcast through the computer speakers. System requirements include a Pentium processor with a minimum of 32 MB of RAM (64 MB recommended), 100 MB of available space on the hard drive, a Windows 98 or newer Windows operating system, and a properly configured sound card and speaker system. The software must be installed on an individual computer rather than on a network, and the screen resolution should be set to 800 X 600 pixels. Installing the software requires the user to obtain a school name and a license key from the publisher. These codes can be obtained by telephone or by e-mail. Codes for the evaluation version described here were obtained by e-mail and required several days and repeated messages before they were furnished. After installation, the software works for one calendar year, after which new codes must be obtained in exchange for an additional fee.

The software works well, but some children with laterality problems may be confused by use of the words left and right. Then too, some teachers may be reluctant to expose children to many equations that have purposely been presented with incorrect answers. In the multiplication portion of the Arithmetic Achievement test, the term sum is used and could be confusing to students who have learned that the solution to a multiplication equation is a *product*.

The test yields only a computer-generated bar graph report that denotes the child's performance with four or five stanines—one each for the child's performance on the Simple Reaction Time subtest, the Dot Enumeration subtest, the Number Comparison subtest (called the Numerical Stroop on the profile), the Addition subtest, and, for students 10 years of age and older, the Multiplication subtest. The report also contains a short (one or two sentences), narrative interpretation of the main outcome pattern seen in the child's test performance. On the profile, low, medium, and high performance is demarcated by raising vertical lines at stanines 3.5 and 6.5. Low performance in Dot Enumeration, Numerical Stroop, and Multiplication and/or Addition is interpreted as evidence of dyscalculia. Normal (medium or better) performance in Dot Enumeration and Numerical Stroop and low performance in Multiplication and/or Addition is interpreted as failure in arithmetic not due to dyscalculia, but to other causes such as poor teaching, etc.

The manual mentions that the computer-generated profile of results may include a narrative diagnosis of dyscalculic tendencies or dyscalculic tendencies with compensatory aspects, but does not specify the details of how this latter diagnosis relates to the child's profile. The manual does not provide sufficient information related to the relationship between subtest performance and the narrative diagnoses produced by the computer.

DEVELOPMENT. The Dyscalculia Screener was conceived and developed by Brian Butterworth to be consistent with his conception of dyscalculia (i.e., that dyscalculia is a persistent, congenital deficit in understanding numerosity). The manual provides a summary of some research to establish the importance of numerosity in mathematical ability. The manual emphasizes that mathematical difficulty can be caused by problems other than dyscalculia, but then contradicts this statement by later claiming that the terms "mathematical disorder" and dyscalculia are interchangeable.

TECHNICAL.

Normative data. The Dyscalculia Screener was standardized in 2001 and 2002 on 549 children drawn from a pool of 1,497 children from 21 infant, primary, junior, and secondary schools in England. The manual states only that "the schools were chosen to be reasonably representative of schools in the UK according to type, size, and range of pupil ages" (manual, p. 53). No information is provided on gender, ethnicity, SES, or other demographics of the sample. The 549 children were selected from the initial pool of 1,497 children who were administered the Mental Mathematics Tests (National Foundation for Educational Research and nferNelson, 1999). The manual provides no information on how these 1,497 children were chosen. Neither does the manual provide details of how the smaller standardization sample of 549 students were chosen, other than to say that "the standardization sample was selected such that the distribution of Mental Mathematics test scores was skewed towards the lower performing pupils" (manual, p. 53), and that weighting was then used to restore the distribution to that observed nationally. The manual provides quartile graphs of reaction times for the standardization sample for all subtests. These graphs plot the lower quartile, median, and upper quartile performance curves with age in years on the abscissa and reaction times on the ordinate. Scores were calculated by first calculating the median reaction times for each pupil for those questions answered correctly on Dot Enumeration, Numerical Stroop, Addition, and/or Multiplication. Then, these reaction times were adjusted to take into account the simple reaction times by calculating the difference between the median reaction time of the test and the simple reaction time. These adjusted median reaction times were then divided by the proportion of questions that a child answered correctly in a test. Standard scores were then produced, adjusted for age with a mean of 100 and a standard deviation of 15. The standard scores were then converted to the stanine scales, which are the only scores shown on the profile. The original standard scores are not shown.

Reliability. The manual contains no discussion of internal or test-retest reliability.

Validity. No formal discussion of validity occurs in the manual. A matrix of intercorrelations of stanine scores for all subtests and for the Mental Mathematics (National Foundation for Educational Research and nferNelson, 1999) test is presented. These intercorrelations are small to moderate, ranging from .131 to .426. Correlations between the Dot Enumeration and Numerical Stroop subtests (the two subtests considered most diagnostic of dyscalculia) and the Mental Mathematics test are .369 and .332, respectively.

An appendix provides a helpful summary of research "leading to the definition of dyscalculia which is specific to the Dyscalculia Screener" (manual, p. 41). An in-press research study is cited in an earlier chapter in which 8-year-old children with deficits in numerosity were found to be poorest in arithmetic achievement and unhappiest when studying mathematics at school. The manual also mentions that a test similar to the Dyscalculia Screener was installed in a science museum in Bristol and was taken by 15,000 people of all ages. According to the manual, the patterns of results of these administrations replicated the patterns seen in the developers' research studies.

COMMENTARY AND SUMMARY. The Dyscalculia Screener is quick and easy to administer. The computer format is interesting and challenging to students,. although those with laterality problems may have difficulty remembering which set of keys are on the right and which on the left.

The manual is clear and well-written, and once installed, the software works well.

The instrument may be useful as one tool in identifying students with numerosity problems. The main difficulties with the instrument are the lack of extensive reliability and validity data. No reliability data were furnished. Test-retest data are particularly important, as response times on these items may be highly responsive to training. The idea of basing a screening test for deficits in an innate mathematically related skill on the measuring of response times to correctly answered items needs to be validated. Extensive validity data beyond related research needs to be presented, including data on predictive validity. Until the psychometric properties of the test are more fully addressed, it must be regarded as experimental and as possessing unknown levels of reliability and validity.

REVIEWER'S REFERENCE

National Foundation for Educational Research and nferNelson. (1999). Mental Mathematics 6–14. London: nferNelson.

Review of the Dyscalculia Screener by GRETCHEN OWENS, *Professor of Child Study, St. Joseph's College, Patchogue, NY:*

DESCRIPTION. The Dyscalculia Screener is an innovative approach to diagnosing dyscalculia, which the author describes as a persistent congenital condition with neurological underpinnings that primarily affects the most basic number concepts that underlie arithmetic (i.e., knowing that collections of things have a numerosity and that adding to or taking objects away from these sets changes their numerosity). He cites research showing that even infants under the age of 6 months are attuned to quantity and can differentiate between small sets of objects differing only in number. The goal of this instrument is to differentiate true dyscalculia from mathematical disabilities that are due to other factors, such as negative pupil attitudes, inappropriate teaching methods, or frequent absences.

The test differs considerably from traditional tests of mathematical abilities. It is presented via a computer program that explains each task in turn, presents the items, records answers, and calculates raw scores and stanines automatically. Students (ages 6–14) need only minimal keyboarding skills: They hit any key on the left side of the keyboard for *no* and on the right side for *yes*. The directions are clearly presented, and the screen images are clear, colorful, and nondistracting. The examination copy of the Screener loaded easily and the onscreen instructions were so easy to follow that consulting the manual was completely unnecessary (though the manual does provide step-by-step instructions for insecure computer users).

The Screener consists of four sections: Two are timed tests that focus on the basic capacity for grasping numerosity, a concept that serves as the foundation of arithmetic. The first of these tests involves counting dots to determine (as quickly as possible) whether the number of dots in the set on the left coincides with the numeral shown on the right. The second test requires the student to determine whether the numeral on the left or the numeral on the right is larger. The third group of items involves timed calculation tasks (one-digit addition, and for those over the age of 10, multiplication problems). Here, the student is shown a problem, such as $5 + 3 = 7$, and is asked to determine whether the given answer is correct or not. (The Screener is designed only to identify capacity for success in simple arithmetic, not in more advanced areas of mathematics).

The author notes that highly motivated students who have dyscalculia often manage to get the correct answers, but only by dint of great cognitive effort and considerable emotional strain. Therefore, he argues that the *time* required to solve a problem is a better indicator than the *accuracy* of the solution if one wishes to identify those who have a deficient capacity for identifying numerosities, ordering numbers by magnitude, and doing simple calculations. Because the speed of response to the various items is the critical factor, and people vary in their baseline speed of responding, one additional test precedes the others. It measures the person's basic reaction time to a dot that appears periodically anywhere on the monitor. The computer program subsequently adjusts the person's decision times during the Dot Enumeration, Number Comparison (also referred to at times as "Numerical Stroop"), and Arithmetic Achievement tests to take that individual's basic response time into account. The tasks are easy, and the expectation is that all pupils will get most of the answers right, so interstudent comparisons can focus on the critical factor of processing/response time. Thus the "efficiency measure" reflects the median reaction time of correct answers adjusted by the median simple reaction time, then divided by the proportion of correct answers.

An interesting component of the Number Comparison task is the incorporation of a Stroop-type effect. The two numerals to be compared are not always presented as the same size. Sometimes the numeral that represents the larger set is shown as physically larger than the numeral representing the smaller set (which facilities the comparison and leads to a shorter decision time), and sometimes just the reverse is shown (which interferes with processing and leads to a longer decision time). Again, the computer takes this into account.

As soon as the student finishes taking the test, the computer produces a pupil profile and diagnostic report. The profile presents the student's stanines on each of the tests. The user who would like to have a standard score must look in the manual for the normal curve (p. 34) that shows the range of standard scores ($M = 100$, $SD = 15$) that coincide with each stanine. The mean of the standard scores for that student is calculated but not revealed other than as a narrative interpretation of the outcome patterns, which are described as either (a) low performance on the two capacity tests, which is evidence of dyscalculia; (b) age-appropriate performance on both sets of tests and therefore the student is unlikely to have dyscalculia; or (c) age-appropriate performance on the two capacity tests, but low performance on the arithmetic achievement tests, which suggests the student is not failing in arithmetic because of dyscalculia.

The author recommends that the test be used for screening whole groups of pupils (a built-in class register stores results from all students) or for testing a single student believed to be at risk of dyscalculia. He suggests using it in conjunction with standardized mathematics achievement tests to determine *why* a student is performing poorly in math. The author says it "can be valuable for determining an individualised educational plan for the pupil ... [or] in a request to the Local Education Authority for a statement of special needs" (manual, p. 19). He also sees it as a research tool for studies of mathematical disabilities, and tells in the manual how to retrieve data files from the computer for this purpose.

The author also presents a brief chapter and an appendix containing suggestions for what to do if the Screener produces a diagnosis of dyscalculic tendencies, of dyscalculic tendencies with compensatory aspects, or of low achievement. Some represent basic pedagogical common sense, some are references to schools and organizations in England, and some are potentially useful software and websites available on the Worldwide Web.

DEVELOPMENT. The theoretical underpinnings for the Screener come from the author's work with students who have difficulty learning math. He notes that in some of these students, the normal inborn capacity for grasping that a set of things has a number, and that numerosities are ordered by size, is deficient. In research studies of various age groups from ages 6 to adult, he tested developmental changes and individual differences in the understanding of numerosity. He also carried out case studies of individuals who have serious difficulty with math and found that those who have the most difficulty and dislike math the most seem to lack the basic numerosity abilities. He confirmed this in a research study of 8-year-olds, after which he selected the tasks he found to be most effective at discriminating between pupils with true dyscalculia and those with other types of math difficulties. These tasks were the two timed tests that involved comparing numbers and counting dots, which he later put into the Dyscalculia Screener and called "capacity" tests. After developing a computerized version of his research instrument, he and his associates installed it in a science museum, where 15,000 people of all ages have taken the test.

TECHNICAL. The standardization sample was selected from among 1,497 students from infant, primary, junior, and secondary schools in England that were chosen to be "reasonably representative of schools in the UK according to type, size and range of pupil ages" (manual, p. 53). Students from Years 1, 2, 3, 5, 7, and 9 took tests from the Mental Mathematics series. (No students aged 9, 11, or 13 years were used in the studies; results for these age groups were estimated based on the results from the other age groups.) From this sample, 549 pupils (between 84 and 99 at each age level) were selected to take the Screener, with their selection "skewed towards the lower performing pupils" (manual, p. 53) so that the author would be certain of including enough dyscalculic students. The author notes that weighting was applied later to restore representativeness, but no specific information is given about how this was accomplished. No information is provided about the gender, race, place of residence, or socioeconomic level of the participants, and none is provided on the correspondence between the sample demographics and that of the larger population (via, for example, census data).

There is no chapter in the manual that deals with validity or reliability per se, and finding evidence of either requires a commitment to reading between the lines, preferably with a magnifying glass in hand. It is hoped that future editions of the manual will be more clearly laid out, with more explicit validity and reliability studies as they become available. For now, the user has only six pages of "Standardisation results" to decide whether the test is sufficiently documented to be appropriate for his or her purposes. In addition to showing that decision time decreases with age of pupil for all tests and that accuracy on the Numerical Stroop, Addition, and Multiplication tasks increase with age, the author looked at intercorrelations between the component tests and the Mental Mathematics achievement test used by the schools. These correlations range from .13–.43, with the strongest correlation between the two capacity tests, Dot Enumeration and Number Comparison. Surprisingly, the correlations between the two capacity tests and the Mental Mathematics achievement test scores were higher than the correlations between the achievement tests in the Screener (Addition and Multiplication) and the Mental Mathematics achievement test.

In addition, though the author does not explicitly identify it as validity, there is another section in which he argues indirectly for construct validity when he provides a review of research into developmental dyscalculia from 1978–2002, with the major focus placed on neuropsychological studies of processing and possible memory deficits in individuals with low performance in math, as well as studies of normally developing infants' sense of numerosity. His conclusion is that there is a specific numerical processing deficit in students with dyscalculia, which the Screener is designed to identify. No data on test reliability are presented. COMMENTARY AND SUMMARY. The Dyscalculia Screener is an intriguing new instrument designed to help identify students who have problems in grasping basic number concepts and learning number facts. The computerized format of the test presents a marked change from the usual standardized mathematics achievement test

and should be enjoyable for students to take. The manual appears to be written with an audience in mind of primarily classroom teachers who want an appealing instrument that may help them gain insight into their students' mathematical difficulties, and it provides some suggestions for intervention. Researchers will be interested in the literature review section with its theoretical rationale for viewing dyscalculia as a distinctive developmental processing disorder. The Screener appears appropriate at this time for informal use in the classroom and for research. However, with a lack of validity and reliability data and insufficient standardization information, it cannot be recommended for use as a major component in the battery of tests used for entitlement decisions, instructional planning, or progress evaluation of students with mathematics disabilities. Nonetheless, it appears promising and clearly warrants further research and documentation.

[79]

Dyslexia Adult Screening Test.

Purpose: To assess strengths and weaknesses often associated with dyslexia.

Population: 16 years 5 months to adult.

Publication Date: 1998.

Acronym: DAST.

Scores, 12: Rapid Naming, One Minute Reading, Postural Stability, Nonverbal Reasoning, Phonemic Segmentation, Two Minute Spelling, Backwards Span, Verbal Fluency, Semantic Fluency, Nonsense Passage Reading, One Minute Writing, Total.

Administration: Individual.

Price Data, 2005: £135 per complete kit.

Time: 30 minutes.

Authors: Angela J. Fawcett and Rod I. Nicholson.

Publisher: Harcourt Assessment [England].

Review of the Dyslexia Adult Screening Test by MANUELA H. HABICHT, Director of Psychology, Queensland Health, Toowoomba Health Service District, Senior Lecturer, University of Queensland, Medical School, Rural Clinical Division, Honorary Senior Lecturer, University of Southern Queensland, Department of Psychology, Queensland, Australia:

DESCRIPTION. The Dyslexia Adult Screening Test (DAST) is an instrument that includes 11 subtests, which are divided into tests of attainment (reading fluency, transcription, and spelling fluency) as well as diagnostic tests (speed of lexical access and articulation, balance, phonological skills, working memory, grapheme/phoneme translation fluency, nonverbal reasoning, verbal fluency, and semantic fluency) covering the range of skills known to be affected by dyslexia.

The authors point out that they can be used "stand-alone" and each "subject could then be given a percentile score in the test" (manual, p. 24). They then go on to justify the exclusion of percentile ranks because of the alleged difficulty to use and interpret a range of complex tables. The percentile scores are collapsed into five categories: very high at risk (1st–4th percentile), highly at risk (5th–11th percentile), at risk (12th–22nd percentile), normal performance (23rd–77th percentile), well above average (78th–100th percentile).

The manual describes and the record forms support the calculation of an "At Risk" score, by use of weighted mean of the individual "At Risk" indicators ignoring those scores that were not "At Risk." The inclusion of nondyslexia indices such as "Non-verbal Reasoning" and "Semantic Fluency" has not been statistically justified.

The DAST is an A-level instrument and only requires an individual to have advanced training in assessment and interpretation. There are no special qualifications to order or use the test.

DEVELOPMENT. The DAST is the latest version (copyright 1998) of a test that has been known as the Dyslexia Screening Test (DST, Fawcett & Nicholson, 1996; 80). The DST was designed for administration by "lightly trained school professionals" and normed on a sample of 800 British school children and validated on a panel of dyslexic children. It derived an overall quantitative "At Risk" index. The major difference between the tests is that the Bead Threading test from the DST has been replaced by the Nonverbal Reasoning test for the DAST. Some of the remaining subtests have been modified by increasing the difficulty or length.

Materials furnished by the developer include limited information regarding the initial test development. The manual fails to provide information on how the 15 dyslexic students have received their diagnosis of dyslexia. However, Nicholson and Fawcett (1997) indicate that The Adult Dyslexia Index (ADI) was used for diagnosis.

TECHNICAL. Information regarding the validity of the test points out that the DAST "made an excellent job of discriminating between clearly dyslexic and clearly non-dyslexic students (hit rate of 94%, false alarm rate of 0%)" (manual,

p. 18). It fails to point out that the analysis of false alarm rate among the students presenting for assessment is limited by the fact that most were identified as dyslexic. The rather small sample size (only 15 dyslexic students were included) is also a limiting factor. Although the 15 students with the diagnosis of dyslexia had an ADI score of at least 2.5, none of the 150 students in the control group were tested. They were solely allocated to the control group on the basis that they did not have problems in literacy or have any history of difficulties. However, they were not formally assessed.

Test-retest data are provided (approximate 1-week interval) with reliability evaluated as excellent on test of attainment. Reliabilities range from .64 (for Backwards Digit Span) to .92 (for Two Minute Spelling).

In Test 1, Rapid Naming, test instructions do not provide detailed instruction of which plausible errors should not be scored as a mistake.

In Test 3, Postural Stability, part of the verbatim test instruction is printed in green whereas there is no verbatim instruction when the assessor attempts a second push (with arms to the side or arms straight out in front).

In Test 4, Phonetic Segmentation, Spoonerisms are timed, but the participant's time is dependent on the administrator's speed of providing the names. There is no option for the participant to "pass" and there is no instruction for the test administrator to continue immediately after the participant provides an answer.

In Test 5, Two Minute Spelling, the verbatim test instructions in the procedure section are not printed in green and therefore are not easily identifiable. The test instruction also fails to give examples of good, average, and poor handwriting quality.

In Test 8, Nonverbal Reasoning, instructions fail to mention that following the Practice Card examples, the examiner should give the participant the test questions. For Test Questions 1 to 3, again verbatim instructions are not printed in green.

In Test 10, Verbal Fluency, it may be very difficult to record the words if the participant is very fluent. Another problem is the limited space on the record form. Although the authors acknowledge that it "may be difficult to score the words if the subject is very fluent" (manual, p. 72), they fail to make a suggestion such as recording the answers, instead they suggest "to do ticks." Although they note that repetitions are not counted and not penalized, it appears very difficult for the examiner to remember them without recording.

In Test 11, Semantic Fluency, the same problems as mentioned in Test 10 apply.

COMMENTARY. It should be further noticed that the numbering of subtests on the front page of the DAST Record Form is not congruent with the numbering in the interpretation of the section of the same page. This causes confusion for the first-time test user. The same mistake is visible on the reproduction of the DAST Record Form in the user manual. Although Subtest 8 is Nonverbal Reasoning, it is shown in the interpretation section together with One Minute Writing as Subtest 9.

However, the authors should be commended for chapter 4 of their manual, which informs the examiner about supports that are available for adults with dyslexia. Unfortunately, supports mentioned apart from books are solely based in the United Kingdom.

SUMMARY. The developers, to their credit, have produced a screening instrument that can be administered, scored, and interpreted in a relatively efficient and cost-effective manner. They have considered the limited time that is available and produced an instrument that does not require specific qualifications. On balance, however the DAST falls short of the mark. The validity evidence is influenced by the small sample size and the lack of percentile ranks to use subtests as a "stand alone." Further, the failure to screen the control group using the ADI must be seen as critical. Test instructions are on occasion not printed completely or cannot be easily identified because they are printed in black instead of green. Practical issues such as the use of a tape recorder for recording Tests 10 and 11 are not addressed. Unfortunately, readers seeking an alternative test for dyslexia screening do not have many options.

REVIEWER'S REFERENCE

Nicholson, R. I., & Fawcett, A. J. (1997). Development of objective procedures for screening and assessment of dyslexic students in higher education. *Journal of Research in Reading, 20,* 77–94.

Review of the Dyslexia Adult Screening Test by WILLIAM K. WILKINSON, *Consulting Educational Psychologist, Boleybeg, Barna, Co. Galway, Republic of Ireland:*

DESCRIPTION. The Dyslexia Adult Screening Test (DAST) is an upward age extension of its companion measure, the Dyslexia Screening Test (DST; age 6.6 to 16.5; 80). The age range of the DAST fills the adult void, as norms are developed for an age group between 16.6 and 55+.

The DAST draws on the authors' development of the DST, at least in terms of subtest development and interpretation. The specific need for the DAST is based on recent disability legislation in Britain related to training and higher education for persons with disabilities. Also, the authors report a survey of English professionals in adult literacy showing dissatisfaction with assessment and identification of adult dyslexia. This led them to extend the DST procedures to the adult population.

The DAST consists of 11 subtests roughly divided into three groups—attainment, "diagnostic," and nonverbal/verbal fluency/reasoning tests. In the attainment group, there is a core set of word reading, spelling, and writing subtests. One strength of the DAST is that these three core attainment tests are timed so that speed is a factor, as well as accuracy. Similarly, these three tests are easy to administer and score.

The next group consists of five "diagnostic" tests. The word "diagnostic" is used because these five tests are purported to explain why a person may have difficulty with the core attainment tests. For example, one could account for a person's poor performance on the word reading test as due to a similar low score on a diagnostic test like Phonemic Segmentation. The names of the other four diagnostic tests are Postural Stability, Rapid Naming, Backwards Digit Span, and Nonsense Passage Reading.

The name "diagnostic" may be apt within the context of this group of subtests, but in the broader picture, "diagnostic" could be misleading, given the test title and the authors' intended use of the DAST, which is frequently noted as "screening." Test users must keep in mind that the DAST is a first step in screening for dyslexia.

The "diagnostic" tests are also relatively easy to administer and score. However, scoring the nonsense reading passage may require "experiential training" as it is more subjective in nature (e.g., scoring a person's pronunciation of nonsense words as "close approximations" versus "less close approximations").

I question the inclusion of the Postural Stability subtest as a meaningful contributor to the overall battery. This subtest tends to have nonsignificant correlations with all other subtests. If one wishes, the test can be omitted, as the authors note that the "At-Risk Quotient" can be obtained with 10 rather than 11 subtests.

The final three subtests relate to verbal and nonverbal reasoning and fluency. These are the tests in which dyslexic adults may score relatively higher on compared to their performance on the attainment tests.

Raw scores for the 11 subtests are tallied on a record form. The "At-Risk Quotient" (ARQ) is obtained as follows. Raw scores for the 11 subtests are converted to a code of ---, --, -, 0, or +. These five divisions are based on stanines, so that a mark of --- corresponds to a stanine of 1, -- a stanine of 2, - a stanine of 3, 0 covers stanines 4 to 6, and + includes the stanines of 7, 8, and 9. The overall profile is considered "At-Risk" if the participant scores 4 or more --- or -- marks, or 7 or more ---, --, or -. The authors also note that one can get a quantitative ARQ by assigning a "3" to ---, "2" for --, and a "1" for -. These numbers are added and divided by 11. If the resultant ARQ is 1.0 or greater the individual is considered "At-Risk" for dyslexia.

The authors note that the intended users of the DAST are "employment or education professionals" (manual, p. xi). I would add that any professional undertaking the DAST should have experience in the assessment of adult literacy because some of the subtests require "informed analysis." To the authors' credit, the test materials come with practice items, verbatim administration instructions, and clear procedures for scoring and stopping subtests. For the most part, the test is "user friendly."

DEVELOPMENT. As noted earlier, the DAST was a logical extension of the DST and was developed to satisfy U.K. legislation and fill the gap in assessment instruments for adult dyslexia. The DAST tests originated from the existing DST format. As the authors note, there are several changes in the DAST to make it relevant to adults (e.g., increasing difficulty level). Also, the DST Beading subtest is replaced by the DAST Nonverbal Reading test. With other minor exceptions, the DST and DAST subtests are the same in name, administration, and scoring.

The DAST comes with separate age norms for "General Population" and for "Student Population." The general population (GP) norms use the same age divisions as the Wechsler Adult Intelligence Scale—Revised (U.K. Edition) and with similar gender and socioeconomic divisions (total n = 600). GP norms are divided into groups of 16.6 to 24, 25–34, 35–44, 45–54, and 55+. The student norms were developed on 550 students

from three British universities. The college norms are groups as 16.6 to 21 and 22–24. The authors provide a clear rationale for separate GP and college norms, as performance and expectations differ greatly based on academic skills related to the test and to the natural division between university-bound students and those who leave school.

The authors provide a rationale for the development and inclusion of each of the 11 DAST subtests. References to empirical and theoretical research papers are included in the manual for the interested reader.

TECHNICAL. The overall reliability and validity evidence for the DAST should be viewed in terms of the total "ARQ" score rather than on a subtest-by-subtest basis. The ARQ includes all 11 subtests and is the main purpose of the test. The ARQ is the "screen" for determining whether the individual should be further assessed. The authors note that the subtests can be useful for instructional planning (e.g., using strengths to remediate weaknesses), but the ARQ is the quintessential concept.

In this regard, the authors provide the incidence rates of different values of the ARQ for the "sample population." In terms of the ARQ critical value of 1.0 or greater, 14% of the standardization sample obtained a score of 1.0 or greater. This means that 14% of the normative sample are "At-Risk" for dyslexia (not that the individual is dyslexic). This outcome seems reasonable given the overall incidence of actual dyslexia in the adult population.

There is a single differential population validity outcome for a small sample of dyslexics (n = 15) compared with 150 control students with regard to selected subtest performance. As expected, the dyslexic sample had more difficulty with the attainment and word analysis subtests relative to the comparison group.

Subtest reliability (test-retest with a 1-week administration interval) data are adequate. Test-retest stability evidence for the ARQ was not given.

There is more that could be done regarding validity. I would be especially interested to see the intercorrelation matrix factor analyzed because the authors identify three possible factors in their grouping of the subtests.

Likewise, the authors do not present convergent or divergent validity data. This could be presented by assessing the close overlap age group (DST and DAST 16.0–16.11) on similarly constructed tests. Alternatively, the convergence/divergence of the DAST tests with their origin methods (e.g., Rapid Naming) could be empirically documented. Finally, the attainment tests could be correlated with performance on existing measure of adult reading/spelling. Perhaps such data will be forthcoming.

COMMENTARY. Keeping the general purpose of the DAST in mind, the authors fulfill the mission of providing a screening measure for adult dyslexia. The ARQ, if significantly elevated, does seem valid regarding referral of the assessed individual for further assessment. If the test user keeps in mind that the individual so assessed is "At-Risk" for dyslexia, then the DAST should be a useful assessment tool.

Of course, the DAST was developed in England so users in other regions should consult relevant legislation and resources related to adult literacy. Likewise, "local" norms may need to be established to determine if there are any significant performance differences.

Also, a close inspection of some subtests (e.g., Nonverbal Reasoning, Backwards Digit Span) reveals a restricted raw score range (e.g., 0 to 8) so that the assignment of stanines is less clear (e.g., for the Nonverbal Reasoning subtest, a raw score of 3 for the population of 16.6 to 24 could be a -- or a -). Although this is rarely an issue, it is unclear what the user is supposed to do when this happens.

Another advantage of the DAST is the inclusion of possible "strengths" in the selection of subtests, namely the verbal and nonverbal reasoning/fluency tests. Why the authors included two verbal fluency tests relative to the one nonverbal test is unclear.

SUMMARY. The authors of the DAST have logically extended the DST for the adult population. Professionals who screen for learning difficulties in higher education or employment should consider the DAST as a meaningful component to a screening battery, especially when the person has a previous history of dyslexia, or "self-diagnoses" of same. The test is well packaged and fairly easy to administer, score, and interpret (with a few provisos in mind).

[80]
Dyslexia Screening Test.

Purpose: "A screening instrument ... for profil[ing] the strengths and weaknesses often associated with dyslexia."
Population: Ages 6-6 to 16-5.
Publication Date: 1996.

Acronym: DST.
Scores, 11: 3 Tests of Attainment (One Minute Reading, Two Minute Spelling, One Minute Writing), 8 Diagnostic Tests (Rapid Naming, Bead Threading, Postural Stability, Phonemic Segmentation, Backwards Digit Span, Nonsense Passage Reading, Semantic Fluency, Verbal Fluency), At Risk Quotient.
Administration: Individual.
Price Data, 2004: $119 per complete kit including manual (1996, 63 pages), score keys, Backwards Digit Span audiocassette, and carrying case; $55 per 50 record forms.
Time: (30) minutes for entire battery.
Comments: Normed in the United Kingdom.
Authors: Angela J. Fawcett and Rod I. Nicolson.
Publisher: Harcourt Assessment [England].

Review of the Dyslexia Screening Test by KAREN T. CAREY, Professor of Psychology, California State University—Fresno, Fresno, CA:

DESCRIPTION. The Dyslexia Screening Test (DST) is designed as a screening instrument for use with children from 6 years 6 months to 16 years 5 months of age. Based on the World Federation of Neurology definition of 1968, dyslexia is "a disorder in children who despite conventional classroom experience, fail to attain the language skills of reading, writing, and spelling commensurate with their intellectual abilities" (manual, p. xi). The measure consists of 11 subtests including three Tests of Attainment (One Minute Reading, Two Minute Spelling, and One Minute Writing); eight Diagnostic Tests (Rapid Naming, Bead Threading, Postural Stability, Phonemic Segmentation, Backwards Digit Span, Nonsense Passage Reading, Semantic Fluency, and Verbal Fluency); and an At-Risk Quotient. Tests of Attainment include reading, writing, and spelling based on the definition from the World Federation of Neurology. The Diagnostic subtests are tests that the authors believe, based on their literature review, give "positive indicators of dyslexia" (manual, p. 3). The kit comes with an audiocassette tape for administering the Backwards Digit Span subtest and scoring keys. The test can be used by teachers and other school personnel and was normed in England on 1,000 children. It takes approximately 30 minutes to administer. In addition, the authors provide a list and brief description of programs available to assist children with dyslexia. This includes specific remedial academic program packages, books, information on associations, and journal references on dyslexia.

DEVELOPMENT. The authors' goal in developing the test was to "construct a quick, simple enjoyable test that could be used by school professionals and provided a simple 'at risk' index for dyslexia" (manual, p. 3). The United Kingdom Education Act of 1993 led to substantial changes in the country for meeting the needs of special education students and the tool was developed to be used as an objective measure to identify special needs children and assist in the development of intervention plans for such children. According to the authors, the tool was developed after several years of research and testing, although the specifics are not discussed in the manual.

The test format was selected and then norms were established for each of the subtests so that a child's performance on the test could be compared to what would be expected of a child of the same age. Each of the 11 subtests was developed in different ways based on a review of the literature. For example, the Phonemic Segmentation test was developed from the work of Rosner and Simon (1971) and Nonsense Passage Reading was selected and modified from work by Finucci, Guthrie, Childs, Abbey, and Childs (1976). One subtest, Postural Stability, was developed from work by Nicolson, Fawcett, and Dean (1995). The authors of the DST state that "dyslexic children show difficulties consistent with slight abnormalities in the cerebellum.... This test is based on clinical procedures for establishing cerebellar abnormalities" (manual, p. 46). A "balance tester" is included in the materials, which is a plastic device with a collar that slides back and forth. The examiner stands behind the child and holds the balance tester on the two vertebrae above the small of the child's back. This procedure seems quite dangerous as the examiner could potentially hurt the child.

Individual subtests were developed in this manner and pilot studies were conducted to ensure that children "enjoyed doing it" (manual, p. 9) and teachers were able to use the tool reliably. Several preliminary subtests were eliminated and others were modified due to poor reliabilities. The tests are the same for all age groups with four exceptions. The Nonsense Passage Reading, One Minute Writing Tests, the One Minute Reading, and the Two Minute Spelling Tests were modified for age differences, making the tests appropriate for children of different ages.

TECHNICAL. Children from selected schools in Sheffield, London, and Wales participated in the norming sample with at least 100 children at ages 6 years 6 months to 7 years 5 months, 7 years 6 months to 8 years 5 months, and then every 2 years (e.g., 8 years 6 months to 10 years 5 months). Norms were derived for each subtest for each age resulting in every score assigned a percentile point on average performance. The scores for each age group were ranked resulting in percentile ranks for each test. The actual percentile ranks used for scoring were developed through interpolation and smoothing for each age group.

The percentile scores are collapsed into five categories: very highly at risk, which the authors refer to as triple minus (---) (percentile ranks 1–4); highly at risk, double minus (--) (percentile ranks 5–11); at risk, single minus (-) (percentile ranks 12–22); normal performance, no minus (0) (percentile ranks from 23–77); and well above average performance, a + (percentile ranks 78–100). To obtain the At-Risk Quotient (ARQ), the mean of the at-risk scores (triple minus, double minus, single minus, and 0) was weighted; those individuals scoring not at-risk were not included. An ARQ of 1.0 or greater is considered "at-risk."

Construct validity was investigated through the administration of the DST to 17 children who had been diagnosed as dyslexic on other scales. Fifteen of the students ranging in age from 10 to 15 years had an ARQ of 1 or higher. Unfortunately, the sample for these studies is very small and must be interpreted with caution.

Test-retest reliability was estimated from 34 children, ages 6 years 6 months to 12 years, who were retested about 1 week apart. No information related to the ages of these children or whether they were at-risk is included in the manual. The correlations range from .72 to .99 on the subtests. A test-retest correlation for two forms of the One Minute Reading Test was .959. Interrater agreement for the postural stability subtest, which requires some judgment on the part of the examiner, was .98.

COMMENTARY. The DST needs to be further researched before it is widely used. The test has not been adequately evaluated for technical requirements including reliability and validity. In addition, the sample is limited to children in the United Kingdom, and as it has not been used in the United States or other countries, the norms must remain in question for use in countries other than the U.K. As the norms are limited and with the use of interpolation and smoothing of the norms to the degree done in this instrument, the DST does not appear appropriate for making individual decisions regarding students' with academic difficulties. Reliability and validity were not adequately assessed, resulting in questions regarding the consistency and accuracy of the tool.

In general, the academic subtests including Rapid Naming, One Minute Reading, Phonemic Segmentation, Two Minute Spelling, Nonsense Passage Reading, One Minute Writing, and Verbal and Semantic Fluency selected for inclusion in the test seem appropriate for this type of assessment. However, although the authors attempt to make cases for including Bead Memory, Postural Stability, and Backwards Digit Span, there is not enough evidence for including such subtests on a scale assessing dyslexia. In addition, the Postural Stability has the potential for harming children and would not be recommended for use in many school districts in the United States.

The scaling is difficult to understand with the minuses and plus and the development of these procedures. The resulting categories identified from the minuses and plus of *highly at risk* to *well above average* are not defined and the specifics of how the categories discriminate from one another are not explained. In addition, the authors do not address the potential problem for errors of measurement in their categorizations. In the final section of the manual, prior to the descriptions of the subtests, the authors do provide some information for users related to developing interventions for children identified as dyslexic. However, the material provided is simply a list of possible packages and readings for the examiner. Specific interventions for each subtest would be far more beneficial.

SUMMARY. The DST needs further evidence of technical adequacy before it can be used on a large scale basis. No information other than the ages of the norming sample are provided so it is unknown whether or not the test would be appropriate for boys and girls, children of different ethnic backgrounds, and children in different social economic classes. The reliability and validity evidence for the test is insufficient for individual decision making and although the authors state the test can be used to help develop interventions, it is unclear how this can be done. Overall, it appears more useful information could be obtained from conducting a thorough observation in the student's classroom.

REVIEWER'S REFERENCES

Finucci, J. M., Guthrie, J. T., Childs, A. L., Abbey, H., & Childs, B. (1976). The genetics of specific reading disability. *Annals of Human Genetics, 40,* 1–23.

Nicolson, R. I., Fawcett, A. J., & Dean, P. (1995). Time estimation deficits in developmental dyslexia: Evidence for cerebellar involvement. *Proceedings of the Royal Society: Biological Sciences, 259,* 43–47.

Rosner, J., & Simon, D. P. (1971). The auditory analysis test: An initial report. *Journal of Learning Disabilities, 4,* 384–392.

Review of the Dyslexia Screening Test by JAMES E. YSSELDYKE, *Associate Dean for Research, College of Education and Human Development, University of Minnesota—Twin Cities, Minneapolis, MN:*

DESCRIPTION. The Dyslexia Screening Test (DST) is an individually administered, norm-referenced test designed to provide an "at risk" dyslexia index for children ranging in age from 6-6 to 16-5. The DST was created to be a dyslexia screening instrument that could be administered by school professionals other than educational or clinical psychologists. The authors explain that the test can also be used (a) to derive a profile of a child's strengths and weaknesses in order to guide in-school supports, (b) as a basis from which to request formal assessment, and (c) to provide educational psychologists with an instrument that provides a valid index of dyslexia, thereby establishing a foundation for further assessment.

The DST test battery takes about 30 minutes to administer and includes 11 subtests: 3 Attainment tests and 8 Diagnostic tests. The purpose of the Attainment tests is to assess those areas in which dyslexic children typically demonstrate difficulties: Reading, Writing, and Spelling. The Diagnostic tests are designed to assess skills that the authors believe are affected by dyslexia, thereby providing a profile of a child's difficulties that is intended to inform (a) the causes of attainment difficulties, and (b) the skills that need to be targeted for intervention.

Raw scores for each individual subtest are converted into age-appropriate "at-risk index" scores, which are derived from the norm sample. Five "at-risk index" scores are possible for each subtest: triple minus (---; bottom 4%), double minus (--; bottom 5-11%), minus (- ; bottom 12-22%), zero (0 ; midrange, 23-77%), and plus (+ ; top 22%). The "at-risk quotient" (ARQ) is found by adding the individual subtest indices (triple minus = 3; double minus = 2; minus = 1; zero and plus = 0) and dividing that sum by 10. Although there are 11 subtests, Semantic Fluency is not included in this division because this is a supposed strength of dyslexic children. If the ARQ is 1 or greater, a child is considered "at-risk" for dyslexia.

DEVELOPMENT. Although the authors claim that test development "entailed a lengthy series of studies" (manual, p. 9), the manual provides little detail of the item development process. After reviewing the dyslexia literature, the authors originally developed 14 possible tests to be included in the DST. Through a series of studies, the authors established norms for performance on each test while also examining reliability, consistency of implementation, and student enjoyment of tasks. Following these studies, three tests were removed due to problems with reliability and/or test equipment, and other tests were modified to improve reliability and ease of use.

Attainment tests. The DST was developed under the assumption that dyslexic children typically demonstrate difficulties in reading, writing, and spelling, so the three attainment tests included in the DST specifically assess these areas. A description and the rationale or origin of each attainment test is included below.

One Minute Reading—This test measures how many words a child can read correctly from a one-page list in 60 seconds. The authors felt that a measure that assessed both accuracy *and* speed would more accurately estimate a child's reading skills than a measure that assessed only accuracy. It is based on the Dutch EMT test (Brus & Voeten, 1980, as cited in DST manual, p. 31).

Two Minute Spelling—During this test of spelling fluency, a child has 2 minutes to spell each word that the tester reads. (The tester reads the next word as soon as the child has completed the previous word.)

One Minute Writing—During this test, a child must copy text as quickly and accurately as possible in the 1-minute time limit. The authors describe this task as an indication of "pure" writing speed. One reason this test is included is to provide documented evidence for "slowness of writing" (manual, p. 32) so that children can apply to examination boards for extra time in taking tests.

Diagnostic tests. Because reading, writing, and spelling are all learned skills that can be at least partially alleviated through extensive instruction, the authors additionally included diagnostic tests to assess other difficulties typically associated with dyslexia (i.e., phonological skill, fluency, working memory, and balance). A description and

the rationale or origin of each diagnostic test is included below.

Rapid Naming—This test measures the amount of time it takes a child to name a series of familiar outline drawings (e.g., hat, ball). This test is based on the "Rapid Automatised Naming" test introduced by Martha Denckla in the 1970s. In explaining the inclusion of this activity, the authors claim there is evidence that dyslexic children are typically slower than normal when asked to name a series of pictures.

Bead Threading—This test measures how many beads a child can thread in 30 seconds. The authors explain that this activity is included because evidence suggests dyslexic children have difficulties in fine motor skill activities that involve hand-eye coordination.

Postural Stability—This test measures how well a child can balance following a slight push in the back. It is a clinical test of cerebellar abnormality and is included presumably because the authors have found evidence for cerebellar abnormality in dyslexia. Moreover, the authors claim this task successfully distinguishes between dyslexic children and nondyslexic poor readers (i.e., Unlike nondyslexic poor readers, dyslexic children face difficulties in balance).

Phonemic Segmentation—This test measures a child's ability to break down a word into its component sounds and then manipulate those sounds (e.g., say "grandma" without the "ma"). It is included because phonological difficulties are one of the most clearly established difficulties in dyslexia. The test is based on earlier measures developed by Jerome Rosner.

Backwards Digit Span—This test measures a child's ability to repeat a sequence of numbers in the opposite order in which they were verbally presented. It is a common measure of working memory found on many IQ tests. Dyslexic children typically perform poorly on this task.

Nonsense Passage Reading—This test assesses a child's ability to read a passage that is interspersed with nonsense words. This test is included based on evidence that dyslexic children continue to have difficulty with unfamiliar words even after they improve their scores on standard tests of reading.

Verbal Fluency and Semantic Fluency—In the Verbal Fluency test, children have 1 minute to name as many words as they can that begin with a specific letter (e.g., G—good, grape, golf, etc.).

In the Semantic Fluency test, children have 1 minute to name as many animals as they can. These tasks are included based on work by Frith and colleagues that suggests dyslexic children do well on tasks of semantic fluency but do poorly on tasks of verbal fluency.

In order to justify the inclusion of these diagnostic tests, the authors reference a study they conducted in which they distinguished dyslexic and nondyslexic children on the basis of an index that combined "indications of difficulties in phonological skills, balance and speed of processing" (manual, p. 4). Few details of this study are presented, making it difficult to examine the validity of the claim.

TECHNICAL. Information about the norm sample is vague. The authors explain that through a series of studies, "norms were derived for each test for each age" (manual, p. 9). The details included in the manual indicate that the DST was standardized on whole classes of children who attended school in Sheffield, London, and Wales. For the first 2 years (i.e., 6-6 to 7-5, and 7-6 to 8-5), at least 100 children represent each age group. At later ages, this number is spread over 2-year increments. No information is presented about procedures for ensuring the sample was representative of the population of children in the U.K., and no data are presented about how well the norm sample matches this population.

The authors present evidence for test-retest, interform, and interrater reliability, and argue that measures of internal consistency (another commonly reported reliability) are inappropriate for this test. For test-retest reliability, the authors report on a study in which 34 children aged 6-6 to 12 years were administered the test on two separate occasions (there was about 1 week between administrations). The majority of the test-retest reliabilities for each subtest exceed .80, with three subtests having reliabilities between .70 and .80 (i.e., Bead Threading, Postural Stability, and Semantic Fluency). The interform reliability for the One Minute Reading Test was found to be .96 in a study with 22 children. Postural stability was the only subtest for which interrater reliability was measured. It was measured by showing videotapes of 14 children participating in this test, and having three experimenters independently rate the task. Reliabilities ranged from .94–.98.

Evidence for validity is limited. The authors highlight the face validity of the DST by reiterating that reading, writing, and spelling are three areas in which dyslexic children typically struggle, and a poor performance in at least one of those areas is a prerequisite for a diagnosis of dyslexia. Moreover, they claim that evidence has shown that dyslexic children face difficulties with the remaining tests (except Semantic Fluency) as well. However, the reader is expected to take them at their word as no detailed evidence of these links is provided in the manual. The authors do reference a limited number of articles that might provide evidence regarding the inclusion of certain subtests. The only evidence for construct validity that is presented comes from a study in which DST was administered to 17 children ranging in age from 10–6 to 15–7 who had previously been diagnosed with dyslexia, and 20 children who showed no sign of dyslexia. All but 2 of the children diagnosed with dyslexia were identified as at-risk by their scores on the DST, whereas none of the children who showed no signs of dyslexia were identified as at-risk on the DST. Yet, no details are provided about the measures used initially to identify children as dyslexic. Moreover, no children below the age of 10-6 were included in the sample even though the test is supposedly valid for children as young as 6-6.

COMMENTARY. This is a strange mix of subtests that are to give the educator information that is predictive and diagnostic. The authors do not provide evidence of the validity of the test for the purposes they identify (see introductory paragraph). Those who use this test in a normative manner are comparing students to an unspecified population in the U.K.

SUMMARY. The DST is intended as a screener for dyslexia, a nebulous condition. It consists of a mixture of subtests that assess reading, writing, and spelling attainment, and measures of areas thought to be affected by dyslexia. The norm sample is vague, scores are reliable, yet evidence for validity is very limited.

[81]

Early Math Diagnostic Assessment.

Purpose: Designed to "screen and identify children at risk for math difficulties."

Population: Prekindergarten to Grade 3.

Publication Date: 2002.

Acronym: EMDA.

Scores: 2 subtests: Math Reasoning, Numerical Operations.

Administration: Individual.

Price Data, 2003: $110 per complete kit including examiner's manual (84 pages), stimulus book, 25 record forms, 25 response booklets, and 30 "Thumbs Up" worm stickers; $25 per examiner's manual; $75 per stimulus book; $50 per 25 record forms and response booklets.

Time: (20–30) minutes.

Comments: Items selected to "address mathematical domains identified by" the Principles and Standards for School Mathematics (2002) set forth by the National Council of Teachers of Mathematics.

Author: The Psychological Corporation.

Publisher: PsychCorp, A brand of Harcourt Assessment, Inc.

Review of the Early Math Diagnostic Assessment by MARK J. GIERL, Associate Professor of Educational Psychology, University of Alberta, Edmonton, Alberta, Canada, and XUAN TAN, Research Associate, Department of Educational Psychology, University of Alberta, Edmonton, Alberta, Canada:

DESCRIPTION. The Early Math Diagnostic Assessment (EMDA) is an individually administered, norm-referenced instrument that is derived from the Wechsler Individual Achievement Test—Second Edition (for reviews by Beth J. Doll and Gerald Tindal and Michelle Nutter of the WIAT-II, see 15:275). The EMDA is designed to measure select mathematics skills for students in PreKindergarten (PreK) to Grade 3. It is composed of two subtests. The first subtest is Math Reasoning, which measures skills such as counting, identifying shapes and patterns, and solving single- and multi-step problems related to time, money, measurement, and probability. This subtest is appropriate for students in PreK to Grade 3. The second subtest is Numerical Operations, which measures skills such as identifying and writing numbers, counting, and calculating. This subtest is appropriate for students in Kindergarten (K) to Grade 3. Results from EMDA subtests, when combined with "teacher observation, parent information, the student's cumulative school records, and the instructional environment and history" (examiner's manual, p. 3), help evaluate progress in mathematics, identify areas that may require additional instruction, and monitor skill attainment and intervention effectiveness.

Teachers and other school professionals can administer and score the EMDA. The examiner's manual provides detailed information about the administration and scoring procedures. It also provides information on interpreting EMDA scores. Start points (different across grades) and discontinue rules (stop after six consecutive errors) are clearly stated. Administration time varies according to the grade of the examinee and the number of subtests administered. Generally, however, the test can be administered within 20 to 30 minutes. Testing instructions for examinees with special needs are also provided.

The test administrator enters the student's answers and scores into the record form. A total raw score is calculated using number correct for each subtest. This raw score can also be converted to a percentile range that, in turn, yields a "category of achievement" and a standard score ($M = 100$, $SD = 15$). Students in PreK to K fall into three categories of achievement—Emerging, Basic, and Proficient—whereas students in Grades 2 to 3 fall into the categories Below Basic, Basic, and Proficient. These categories apply to scores on both the Math Reasoning and Numerical Operations subtests. "Emerging" students (i.e., PreK to K) and "Below Average" students (i.e., Grades 1 to 3) have raw scores that fall between the 1st and 29th percentile; "Basic" students have raw scores that fall between the 30th and 69th percentile; "Proficient" students have a raw scores that falls between the 70th and 99th percentile. Unfortunately, neither the rationale for these categories of achievement nor the score range is justified or substantiated empirically (using, for example, standard setting procedures; see Cizek, 2001).

DEVELOPMENT. The EMDA originated from the Math Reasoning and Numerical Operations subtests of the WIAT-II. Item development started in 1996 with an expert advisory panel consisting of educators, school psychologists, university professionals, and parents. The blueprint for the constructs measured by the EMDA was developed by incorporating the "recommendations of the advisory groups, review of state standards and curricula, and an extensive search of the literature" (examiner's manual, p. 35). The curriculum areas measured by the EMDA were based on the *Principles and Standards for School Mathematics* (National Council of Teachers of Mathematics, 2000), state standards, and recommendations from the expert advisory panel.

Once the item pool was developed, the EMDA was field tested. Unfortunately, the field test samples and procedures are vaguely described in the examiner's manual. Field testing was conducted in the Spring of 1997 with 100 students in K to Grade 2. Then, an additional 350 students in the "three targeted grades" were tested in the following year. Basic information about gender and ethnicity is provided for the K to Grade 2 sample but no information is provided about the characteristics for the 350-student sample. Sixty PreK "at risk" students were also included (these PreK students may have been in either the 100- or 350-student sample, but it is not clear from the description in the examiner's manual). Data from the pilot studies were then used for item analyses. The outcomes from these analyses, according to the examiner's manual, guided the item modification efforts and helped select the item administration order. The items retained from the field tests, based on their statistical characteristics and curriculum representativeness, were administered to the standardization sample.

TECHNICAL.

Standardization. Norms for the EMDA are based on the WIAT-II standardization sample. The standardization sample was collected between 1999 and 2001 from 1,374 school-aged children (i.e., 5 to 8 years old) from PreK to Grade 3. A stratified random sampling design was used to ensure the sample represented the 1998 Census of the United States for students in PreK to Grade 3. Grade, gender, race/ethnicity, geographic region, and parents' education level served as the stratification variables. The sample also included students from public and private schools; students with learning disabilities (including speech/language impairments, emotional disorders, mild mental impairment, attention deficit disorder, and physical impairment); and students from gifted and talented programs. However, it excluded students who could neither speak nor understand English.

To ensure the data from the standardization sample had integrity, two quality-control procedures were used. First, each primary examiner received training from the test publisher on the proper administration and scoring of the WIAT-II. Second, each protocol scored by a primary examiner was rescored by two independent examiners. The protocol scores were then compared across the examiners for consistency (the results from these comparisons are not reported in the examiner's manual).

Reliability. Reliability results for the EMDA consist of estimates for score precision, consistency, and stability. Split-half reliability, which measures score precision, ranged from .71 to .93 using data from the EMDA standardization sample. The standard error of measurement, which can be used to evaluate score consistency, ranged from 3.97 to 8.08 standard score units. Test-retest reliability, an index of score stability, ranged from .96 for Math Reasoning to .92 for Numerical Operations using a testing interval of 7 to 45 days ($M = 10$ days). It should be noted, however, that the test-retest reliability analyses were based on the data for 123 K to Grade 3 students drawn from the WIAT-II standardization sample. Although the gender and ethnicity proportions for the test-retest sample are presented, little additional information is provided that would allow the reader to compare the test-retest sample to the EMDA standardization sample or, more importantly, the 1998 census data. The mean testing interval of 10 days could also pose a threat to the accuracy of the information on score stability because this interval is relatively short. There is no information on score stability for the PreK students.

Validity. A contemporary view on test validation is provided where content, construct, and criterion-related evidence is described and presented. Content-based evidence is presented both in the Development and Validity sections in the examiner's manual. As we described earlier, results from the expert advisory panel and field test analyses guided item selection. Further, classical and modern item analyses were conducted using data from the standardization sample to ensure that items had appropriate psychometric characteristics. Unfortunately, the results from the item analyses are only described in the examiner's manual, not presented. For example, the authors state that the item-total correlations were inspected for each test and age level, and any item with a correlation less than .20 was considered for revision and replacement. But we are not told if the discrimination index is the biserial or point-biserial correlation; we are not shown the discrimination values for the items on the final form; and we are not told how the items were revised or if items with low discrimination were replaced. Another example: The authors claim that extensive item-bias studies were conducted using data from the field test and standardization samples, and any item noted as problematic according to empirical criteria was evaluated for deletion. Again, however, we are not told which groups were compared in the item bias study, which statistical and substantive methods were used to detect and interpret bias, what criteria constitute a problematic item, or whether problematic items were modified and/or deleted. In short, few empirical results are presented that would allow the reader to independently evaluate the content-related evidence; instead, the reader must rely on descriptive summaries from the test publisher.

A critical line of evidence to support the diagnostic value of the EMDA stems from information about the Math Reasoning and Numerical Operations constructs (Tate, 2002). To support the validity of the construct interpretation, the authors present results where the EMDA scores are correlated with other achievement constructs, including the other WIAT-II subtests, WIAT-II composites, and Wechsler intelligence scales (i.e., Wechsler Preschool and Primary Scale of Intelligence—Revised and Wechsler Intelligence Scale for Children—Third Edition) across five age groups (i.e., 5- to 9-year-olds). As expected, the EMDA scores were more highly correlated across all age groups with scales measuring mathematical constructs than with scales measuring nonmathematical constructs, such as reading. The correlations between the EMDA and Wechsler scales were variable, ranging from .25 to .81. Regrettably, the construct validity section does not include dimensionality results from either parametric (e.g., factor analysis) or nonparametric (e.g., DIMTEST, DETECT, or HCA/CCPROX; see Stout et al., 1996) procedures—a noteworthy omission in light of the fact that the EMDA is designed to measure two distinct constructs.

Criterion-related evidence is documented, in part, by correlating the EMDA scales with select achievement tests. Correlations between the EMDA and the Wechsler Individual Achievement Test (WIAT) math scales ranged from .78 to .82; correlations between the EMDA and the Wide Range Achievement Test—Third Edition (WRAT-3) arithmetic scale ranged from .67 to .77; and the correlation between the EMDA Numerical Operations scale and Differential Ability Scales (DAS) Basic Number Skills scale was .75. However, in all three studies the sample sizes are small, ranging from 27 to 70 examinees, and little

information is provided about the composition or characteristics of the samples. In fact, sample-related problems characterize all the studies presented in the criterion-related validity section of the examiner's manual. For instance, correlations between EMDA scores and teacher-assigned school grades are presented. The teacher-assigned mathematics grades correlated .35 with the EMDA Numerical Operations score and .51 with the EMDA Math Reasoning score. However, the student sample ranged in age from 6–18 years (M = 14 years) which is well beyond the age range in the EMDA standardization sample. Results from studies using special groups are also reported. The special groups included students who were gifted, mentally challenged, learning disabled, hearing impaired, or speech and/or language impaired. In almost every comparison, a matched control group performed differently than the special group in question. However, most of the special group samples, again, go beyond the age range for the EMDA standardization sample. For example, the gifted sample of 123 students ranged in age from 6 to 17 (M = 11) years; the mentally challenged sample of 39 students ranged in age from 7 to 14 (M = 10) years; the learning disabled sample of 81 students ranged in age from 7 to 18 (M = 12) years; and the hearing-impaired sample of 31 students ranged in age from 6–13 years, and included some 17-year-olds (M = 11 years). The speech- and/or language-impaired sample of 49 students ranged in age from 5–8 years (M = 7), which is comparable to the EMDA standardization sample, but there is no information on the sample composition making it impossible to compare the speech- and/or language-impaired group with the EMDA standardization sample.

COMMENTARY AND SUMMARY. The EMDA contains two subscales—Math Reasoning and Numerical Operations—derived from the WIAT-II. As such, the EMDA is not a new instrument but a set of subtests from an existing instrument, the WIAT-II. The EMDA has important strengths. For example, it is easy to administer and score; it can be used with young children who range from PreK to Grade 3; it is developed to reflect the *Principles and Standards for School Mathematics* based on consultation with a diverse expert advisory panel; and it is anchored to norms that represent the 1998 American Census for students in PreK to Grade 3. However, the

EMDA also has important weaknesses stemming, largely, from technical limitations and inadequacies. For instance, the "categories of achievement" (examiner's manual, p. 23) that are used to promote score interpretation are neither justified nor substantiated empirically; the samples used initially to develop the EMDA items and then validate the EMDA scales are relatively small and poorly described; and, most importantly, the evidence to support the Math Reasoning and Numerical Operations constructs is incomplete, as no dimensionality analyses are reported. These weaknesses should be addressed through additional validation studies designed to provide users with more information about the technical characteristics and quality of this test.

REVIEWERS' REFERENCES

Cizek, G. J. (2001). *Setting performance standards: Concepts, methods, and perspectives.* Mahwah, NJ: Erlbaum.
National Council of Teachers of Mathematics. (2000). *Principles and standards for school mathematics.* Reston, VA: Author.
Stout, W., Habing, B., Douglas, J., Kim, H. R., Roussos, L., & Zhang, J. (1996). Conditional covariance-based nonparametric multidimensionality assessment. *Applied Psychological Measurement, 20,* 331–354.
Tate, R. (2002). Test dimensionality. In J. Tindal & T. M. Haladyna (Eds.), *Large-scale assessment programs for all students: Validity, technical adequacy, and implementation* (pp. 181–211). Mahwah, NJ: Erlbaum.

Review of the Early Math Diagnostic Assessment by ARTURO OLIVAREZ, JR., Associate Professor of Educational Psychology, Texas Tech University, Lubbock, TX:

DESCRIPTION. The Early Math Diagnostic Assessment (EMDA) is an individually administered assessment intended to screen and identify children at risk for mathematics difficulties, proscribe areas of needed instruction, and monitor progress. According to its developers, the EMDA is closely aligned with the *Principles and Standards for School Mathematics* (2000) set forth by the National Council of Teachers of Mathematics. The EMDA package includes an examiner's manual, stimulus book, response booklets, and 30 "Thumbs Up" Worm Stickers. The EMDA is made up of two major subtests: The Math Reasoning test and the Numerical Operations test. The Math Reasoning test consists of a series of problems with both verbal and visual prompts that are designed to assess a student's ability to reason mathematically. The test includes counting, geometric shapes, and arithmetical operations with whole numbers. The Numerical Operations test consists primarily of basic arithmetical operations.

According to the test manual, test results from the EMDA may guide the instructional

decision-making process but they must always be interpreted in light of a child's background, personality, current emotional functioning, attention, and motivation levels. The EMDA was designed to be administered by classroom teachers, and the only qualification is that the administrator becomes familiar with the test instructions contained in the test manual. A set of standard procedures must be followed so that test results can be interpreted according to national norms. The administration time varies depending on the grade level of the student and the number of tests administered. Children in PreK are given only the Math Reasoning test; students in Grades K–3 have the option of being tested on both the Math Reasoning and Numerical Operations tests. The average assessment time for students taking both tests is between 20 and 30 minutes. The test manual provides detailed instruction about the materials needed, the physical setting, management of test materials, and establishing rapport with typical and with special needs students. In order to facilitate administration of the test, there are start points and discontinue rules for both tests. For example, students in PreK–1 start the Math Reasoning test (45 items) at Item 1 whereas every other grade starts at Item 16. For the Numerical Operations test (40 items), students in Grades K–1 start at Item 1 whereas students in Grades 2–3 start at Item 8. The PreK students are not required to take the Numerical Operations test. The discontinue rule (stop after six consecutive errors) is the same for both tests. A total raw score is generated for each test and then converted into percentile rank ranges. Each test score can be graphically illustrated by marking the corresponding percentile range. The EMDA provides three types of achievement categories. For PreK and K grades, the achievement categories are Emerging, Basic, or Proficient, whereas the categories for Grades 1–3 are Below Basic, Basic, and Proficient. The manual provides a clear discussion of assumptions and objectives for the appropriate interpretation of EMDA scores including suggestions and recommendations for conducting a skills analysis of a student's item responses and the importance that exists between assessment and intervention.

DEVELOPMENT. The developers of the EMDA were a team of researchers from the Psychological Corporation. These developers adapted the EMDA from subtests of the Wechsler Individual Achievement Test—Second edition (WIAT-II) published in 2001. The curriculum specifications for the EMDA's items are derived directly from the *Principles and Standards for School Mathematics* (NCTM, 2000), several state standards, and from recommendations made by several advisory groups. No specific underlying assumptions and theoretical underpinnings were presented except for the need to develop instruments that will assess mathematics achievement.

According to the manual, the items were developed in 1996 and reviewed by experts before the national tryout studies to ensure appropriate and relevant content coverage. Pilot testing was conducted in the spring of 1997, with approximately 100 children in each of the grade levels participating. During the 1998 school year, yet another large-scale tryout testing was conducted with approximately 350 students in each of the targeted grades. A stratified random sampling procedure using geographical regions was utilized to ensure student representation. The sample consisted of a balance in the representation of male and female students and a better than 6:4 ratio on the selection of race-majority and race-minority students was obtained. Item analyses used conventional percent-correct statistics, item-total correlations; grade-to-grade progressions in mean scores and internal-consistency reliability of scales were used to produce estimates that helped establish the order of item presentation. Biased items were identified and replaced based on close examination by a panel of reviewers and the use of item response theory (IRT) procedures to detect item bias. Once the final form of the test was obtained, the standardization process followed with the selection of 1,374 students in Grades PreK–3 with an even breakdown for gender and region and a 3 to 1 ratio on race/ethnicity for fall and spring semesters. Additionally, the standardization study was conducted in both public and private settings, as well as including students with learning or special disabilities (6%). The manual provides detailed information about the representativeness of the standardization sample and the quality control measures taken by the developers to ensure administration, scoring, and interpretation of the test results.

TECHNICAL. A variety of reliability measures were employed by the developers in their efforts to evaluate the consistency and stability of item functioning for both subtests. To measure internal consistency, split-half estimates, corrected by using the Spearman-Brown formula, were computed. Equivalent halves for each test, representing parallel forms with approximate equal variances were selected to perform this analysis. The reliability estimates and corresponding standard errors of measurement are presented for each grade level (PreK–3; for fall and spring semesters) for each individual subtest. No estimates were provided for the EMDA composite. Overall, the estimates were very high with the Numerical Operations subtest at Grade 1 in the fall semester yielding the lowest reliability estimate of .71 and the Math Reasoning subtest at Grade 3 in the fall semester producing the highest reliability estimate of .93. The reliability estimates tended to be higher for the Math Reasoning subtest than for the Numerical Operations subtest and there were higher reliabilities in the fall semester than in the spring.

Test-retest stability indexes were computed for a sample of 123 Grades K–3 students drawn from the standardization sample. The test-retest interval ranged from 7 to 45 days, with a mean of 10 days lag period. Overall means and standard deviations are reported for each subtest for each administration. Using a correction procedure suggested by Guilford and Fruchter (1978), the observed coefficient estimate for the Math Reasoning subtest was .96 whereas the observed coefficient estimate for the Numerical Operations subtest was .92.

The EMDA developers present clear evidence of their efforts to examine content-related and construct-related evidence of validity in the test manual. Analyses of the data by both classical and modern theories of measurement were conducted to document the degree to which individual items were empirically consistent with other items in the test. In terms of content-related validity evidence, item-total correlations were computed for each subtest and each grade level. Items with less than .20 point-biserial correlations were considered for revision and replacement. In terms of item difficulty information and item order, the developers used one-parameter IRT procedures to determine item-to-data fit. The manual does not explain how many items were in the original pool and how many items were deemed inadequate but results from these efforts appear to indicate that the subtests have a high degree of content homogeneity.

In terms of construct-related validity, the developers of the test claim that evidence of construct validity on the EMDA is inherited from the results observed on the standardization sample of the WIAT-II test, insisting that the EMDA scores are directly derived from the standardized scores of the WIAT-II. Given that this is the case, the intercorrelation results appear to confirm the expected relations between subtests and the specific domains they comprise. In other words, there are high correlation estimates between the Math Reasoning and Numerical Operations subtest (i.e., convergent validity evidence) whereas discriminant validity evidence is also observed by the expected low correlation estimates with other unrelated subtests in the WIAT-II (i.e., Oral Expression and Listening Comprehension). The series of tables in the manual's appendix present intercorrelation indexes between WIAT-II test scores and the Wechsler Intelligence Scale for Children—Third Edition (WISC-III) for ages 5 to 9 (Wechsler, 1991). Most of the intercorrelations among the Math Reasoning, Numerical Operations scores, and the Full Scale IQ scores ranged from .30 to .78, confirming the expectation that these subtests address mathematical curriculum content that requires a higher level of cognitive skill than other WIAT-II subtests. Again, the developers present another piece of evidence of the construct being measured by the EMDA through the use of data collected and analyzed for the WIAT-II test by using school grades in reading, spelling, English, and mathematics. The WIAT-II subscales of Math Reasoning and Numerical Operations with school mathematics grades yielded correlation estimates of .35 and .51, respectively. The lowest correlation indexes were observed between the WIAT-II subscales and grades in English/Language Arts.

The manual provides validity evidence of the EMDA by the use of group comparison performance. Individuals in these special groups were matched with a control (typical students) group of individuals in the standardization sample. These special groups include gifted students ($n = 123$), individuals with mental retardation ($n = 39$), individuals with learning disabilities not specific to reading ($n = 81$), individuals with hearing impairments ($n = 31$), and individuals with speech and/or language impairment. The computed comparative statistical analyses produced expected results for all 10 group comparisons. The gifted students outperformed the typical students and the typical students outperformed the special needs students with the exception of speech- and/or language-impaired special groups and the typical group. All in all, the developers made a serious effort to provide ample documentation about the important psychometric dimension aspects of the EMDA.

COMMENTARY. There are aspects that make the EMDA an important diagnostic assessment tool for use with children at risk for mathematics difficulties and make the tool attractive to teachers or school diagnosticians. First, the EMDA tests are clearly aligned to the *Principles and Standards for School Mathematics* and reliably and validly evaluate developmentally appropriate skills ranging from early numerical operations to quantitative and qualitative applications. Second, the EMDA can be administered and interpreted within 20 to 30 minutes. Third, the EMDA tests provide valid and reliable screening and diagnostic information for individualized instructional intervention. The tests allow teachers to determine each individual student's relative standing within the class or against the national norm. The EMDA appears to be a well thought out instrument; however, a couple of key observations are made with respect to its psychometric approach. Regarding internal consistency, an alternate and better approach to this step would have been the use of the Kuder-Richardson 20 formula, which deals with dichotomous data and is the lower-bound average of all the possible split-half estimates. Finally, the second major observation detected on the EMDA test resides within the weak efforts in attempting to indirectly infer the construct-related validity for the EMDA test. It would have been far more convincing if the actual items from each subtest had been used to collect this type of evidence rather than to infer it from the test items found in the WIAT-II standardization scores.

SUMMARY. Even with its current flaws, the EMDA serves an important role in assisting teachers to screen and identify children who may be at risk of developing mathematical deficiencies early in their school training. The efforts in producing a psychometrically sound measure are commendable; however, EMDA developers must provide a clear justification for their decision not to conduct construct-related validity studies given that the extant data from more than 1,300 students are available to them.

REVIEWER'S REFERENCES

Guilford, J. P., & Fruchter, B. (1978). *Fundamental statistics in psychology and education* (6th ed.). New York: McGraw-Hill.
National Council of Teachers of Mathematics. (2000). *Principles and standards for school mathematics.* Reston, VA: Author.
Wechsler, D. (1991). Wechsler Intelligence Scale for Children—Third Edition. San Antonio, TX: The Psychological Corporation.

[82]

Early Reading Diagnostic Assessment—Second Edition.

Purpose: Designed to evaluate "the essential components of reading defined by Reading First—phonemic awareness, phonics, fluency, vocabulary and comprehension."

Population: Grades K–3.

Publication Dates: 2002–2003.

Acronym: ERDA Second Edition.

Administration: Individual.

Levels, 4: Grades K, 1, 2, and 3.

Price Data: Available from publisher.

Author: The Psychological Corporation.

Publisher: PsychCorp, A brand of Harcourt Assessment, Inc.

a) GRADE K.

Population: Kindergarten.

Scores, 11: Letter Recognition, Story Retell, Phonological Awareness (Rhyming, Phonemes, Syllables, Composite), Vocabulary (Receptive, Expressive, Composite), Reading Comprehension, Passage Fluency.

Time: (65–75) minutes.

b) GRADE 1.

Population: Grade 1.

Scores, 14: Word Reading, Pseudoword Decoding, Letter Recognition, Listening Comprehension, Phonological Awareness (Phonemes, Rimes, Syllables, Composite), Reading Comprehension, Vocabulary (Receptive, Expressive, Word Opposites, Composite), Passage Fluency.

Time: (90–95) minutes.

c) GRADE 2.

Population: Grade 2.

Scores, 23: Brief Vocabulary (Receptive, Expressive, Composite), Reading Comprehension, Listening Comprehension, Phonological Awareness (Phonemes, Rimes, Syllables, Comprehension), Word Reading, Pseudoword Decoding, Rapid Automatic Naming (Letters, Words, Digits, Words and Digits, Composite), Full Vocabulary (Brief Vocabulary Composite, Synonyms, Word Definitions, Multiple Meanings, Composite), Passage Fluency (Narrative, Informational).

Time: (110) minutes.

d) GRADE 3.

Population: Grade 3.

Scores, 23: Same as Grade 2.

Time: (110) minutes.

Review of the Early Reading Diagnostic Assessment—Second Edition by MARIE MILLER-WHITEHEAD, Department of Education, University of North Alabama, Florence, AL:

DESCRIPTION. The Early Reading Diagnostic Assessment—Second Edition (ERDA) is a standardized norm-referenced individual assessment of preliteracy skills and early literacy appropriate for children in kindergarten to third grade. According to the publisher, the test is intended for use as (a) a norm-referenced assessment of student achievement levels, (b) a diagnostic assessment of student reading skills, (c) a guide for instructional planning, and (d) a means to link reading assessment results with intervention. This is an individual assessment that takes from 60 minutes to 110 minutes to administer, depending upon grade level. The assessment yields six composite scores: Brief and Full Vocabulary, Rapid Automatic Naming, Phonological Awareness, and Narrative and Informational Fluency. For instructional planning purposes, these categories are reported in five skill clusters. Raw scores may be converted to percentile ranges that correspond to literacy categories of Emerging (Below Basic), Basic, and Proficient.

The publisher provides two stimulus books, one for Grades K–1 and another for Grades 2–3, an administrator's manual, a technical manual, parent report forms, and student profile record forms. The administration manual provides ample directions for standardization procedures and scoring rubrics, recommendations for appropriate interventions and targeted instruction, and a bibliography of instructional resources. The technical manual includes discussions of tested skills, test psychometrics, directions for computing raw and percentile scores, and directions for score interpretation. The publishers provide an instructional tape and a timer because the scores of several sections require accurate timing.

DEVELOPMENT. The ERDA Second Edition was published by The Psychological Corporation in 2003. The ERDA test series began with the publication of the ERDA 2000, followed by the Early Reading Diagnostic Assessment-Revised (ERDA-R) in 2002. Each revision was based on enhanced content and new national norms designed to address requirements of Reading First legislation. Although the ERDA Second Edition is of relatively recent vintage, it has impressive antecedents, with subsection tests drawn from the

Wechsler Individual Achievement Test-Second Edition (WIAT-II, 2002), the Metropolitan Achievement Test (MAT6, 1985), the Test of Word Knowledge (TOWK, 1991), and the Process Assessment of the Learner: Test Battery for Reading and Writing (PAL-RW, 2001). Specifically, the Synonyms, Definitions, and Multiple Meanings subtests are drawn from selected items of the TOWK; the Reading Fluency subtest passages are from the MAT6; Pseudoword Decoding, Listening Comprehension, Listening Vocabulary, Letter Recognition, Reading Comprehension, and Word Reading are from the WIAT; and Phonological Awareness, Phonemes, Rimes, and Syllables subtests are from the PAL-RW.

TECHNICAL. The achievement skills are clustered for interpretation and intervention purposes as aggregate scores for Phonological Awareness, Phonics, Fluency, Vocabulary, and Comprehension. However, the kindergarten test yields 10 subtest scores, the Grade 1 test yields 14 subtest scores, and at Grades 2 and 3, there are 20 subtest scores, although at each level several of these are optional. The publisher provides demographic information for the norm population of 800 students by grade, gender, race/ethnicity, geographic region, and parent education level. The standardization sample was evenly divided at each grade level by gender, and was representative of populations by ethnicity and race. The sample excluded students who were receiving special education, ESL, bilingual education services, or those who were identified as Limited English Proficient. Where appropriate, the manuals specify discontinue rules so that students will not become frustrated in attempting material that is too difficult for them. Split-half reliability coefficients are provided; these range from .54 for the Vocabulary score to .98 for Fluency. Although not shown in the manuals, the publisher conducted IRT individual item analysis to assure absence of item bias. The technical manual also provides evidence of test validity from a variety of perspectives and correlations among the subtests. Look-up tables for conversion of raw scores to percentiles are provided for each grade level. Manuals include samples of completed student profiles and targeted instruction plans with narratives.

COMMENTARY. The ERDA Second Edition is an attractive package with adequate instructions for administering and scoring the various subtests, although an index would improve the usability of the manuals. Test administrators may wish to use their own timers if these are available. In any case, administrators should practice with the timers prior to testing, and should consider recording student responses on several of the sections in case of timer malfunction and to assure standardization, as slang, regionalisms, or articulation disorders are not penalized. There were large differences between the scores of children in Grades 2 and 3 diagnosed with reading disabilities and a matched control group, with the largest differences in the Phonics and Fluency subtests, and the smallest differences in Listening Comprehension. It is important to note that the Reading Fluency passages for Grades 2 and 3 are just that, and there are no comprehension questions on these reading passages. Thus, the publishers do not provide a readability index for the fluency passages.

Even though the standardization sample was disaggregated by subgroup, means and standard deviations for subgroups are not provided in the publisher's technical manual. Given that the test is relatively new, there are as yet few published studies that have used the ERDA Second Edition as a diagnostic, as a measure of student growth, or of group differences. Therefore, much of the psychometric data that result from published studies using the test as a measure are as yet unavailable.

It is a reality that tests may be administered under a wide range of conditions and it is unlikely that young children would complete the entire assessment at one time. However, according to the administration manual, subtests generally can be completed in 15 to 20 minutes. Although this is true for all tests, an additional issue of student performance on this test (and standardized conditions) is the extent to which children are tested for the same length of time at the same time of day.

SUMMARY. The ERDA Second Edition is predominantly a test of reading, listening, and speaking. Each of the skill sets are measured in multiple ways so that results may be interpreted for appropriate interventions, and the subtest correlations in the technical manual provide additional assistance in interpretation of results. Because the skills sets are complex, test administrators should receive appropriate training prior to use. However, those who have experience in working with children should have little difficulty in using this assessment after some practice. The completed student profile form can be used as a running record to document student progress in early literacy skills. Although other assessments are available that yield more depth of information in a specific skill set such as oral fluency (the GORT series, for example), the ERDA Second Edition provides the breadth that many schools expect and require of a single assessment instrument.

Review of the Early Reading Diagnostic Assessment—Second Edition by STEVEN R. SHAW, School Psychologist, The School District of Greenville County, Greenville, SC:

DESCRIPTION. The Early Reading Diagnostic Assessment—Second Edition (ERDA Second Edition) is a comprehensive diagnostic instrument that assesses five components of reading. The five components are: phonological awareness, phonics, vocabulary, comprehension, and fluency. The ERDA is also designed to be flexible enough so that teachers can customize aspects of the assessment based on their professional needs and correspondence with the curricula.

There are a number of subtests under each reading component: Phonemic and Phonological Awareness (Rhyming, Phonemes, Rimes, and Syllables); Phonics (Letter Recognition and Pseudoword Decoding); Fluency (Word Reading, Target Words in Context, Rapid Automatic Naming [RAN] of Digits, Letters, Words, and Words & Digits); Vocabulary (Word Opposites, Synonyms, Word Definitions, and Multiple Meanings); and Comprehension (Story Retell, Listening Comprehension, and Reading Comprehension).

In addition, six composite scores are also available: Brief Vocabulary Composite, Full Vocabulary Composite, RAN-Automaticity Composite, Phonological Awareness Composite, Narrative Passage Composite, and Information Passage Fluency Composite.

Scores. Scores are provided as percentile ranges. These percentile ranges correspond to categories of achievement, which are qualitative interpretations of performance. The classifications are: Proficient (70–99th percentile), Basic (30–69th percentile), and Below Basic (1–29th percentile). For Kindergarten only, the classification "Emerging" replaces "Below Basic."

DEVELOPMENT. The ERDA Second Edition was developed to assist in assessing the requirements of the *Reading First* Federal legislation (Title 1, Part B, Subpart 1 of the Elementary and Secondary Education Act as amended by the *No Child Left Behind Act* of 2001), which describes the five components of reading listed above. The intent is to use the ERDA as a diagnostic instrument and an outcome measure. The ERDA Second Edition is a content-enhanced and renormed revision of the ERDA-Revised (2002). Items from the ERDA Second Edition were adapted from four well-known and widely used reading tests: Wechsler Individual Achievement Test Second Edition, Process Assessment of the Learner: Test Battery for Reading and Writing, Test of Word Knowledge, and Metropolitan Achievement Test—Sixth Edition. There was some editing and addition of items to create new subtests.

TECHNICAL.

Standardization. The standardization sample was collected during the 2002–2003 academic year during the fall and spring. As such, norms are available for fall and spring administration. A total of 800 students were sampled. The sample was stratified on grade, gender, race/ethnicity, geographic region, and parent education. Students in the sample were from public and private schools. Students with learning disabilities, hearing or vision impairment, speech and language impairment, and students receiving services for English as a Second Language and Bilingual Education were excluded. However, data from students with learning disabilities were collected for validity studies. The standardization sample is remarkably close to the U.S. census data from 2000 on the stratified variables.

Reliability. Reliability was estimated via internal consistency and stability. Internal consistency was estimated via split-half correlations corrected with the Spearman-Brown formula the length of the test. The speeded tests (i.e., RAN and Passage Fluency) used test-retest correlations as reliability estimates. Overall, reliability is adequate for some diagnostic questions, but there are some relatively weak points. There are several subtests with reliability coefficients in the .60s and .70s. All of the subtests with fairly low reliability coefficients were subtests with 12 or less items. Listening comprehension (overall split-half reliability of .74) has only six items. Given that the ERDA is designed for teachers to administer to children 4 through 8 years of age, reduced testing time is a good trade for lower than usually accepted internal consistency.

Two of the subtests, Multiple Meanings and Word Definitions require a significant amount of clinical judgment. Interrater reliability was assessed on a sample of 199 student responses. For Word Definitions, the correlation coefficient for the two raters was .88. For Multiple Meanings, the correlation between the pair of scorers was .96.

In order to measure stability, a sample of 65 students was assessed twice with an interval between testings of 7 to 30 days. Most subtests showed minimal gain in items correct, possibly indicating that practice effects play a small role in repeated testings with the ERDA. Stability coefficients follow a pattern similar to that of the internal consistency coefficients. Most subtests have stability coefficients in the .80s to .90s. Some subtests have lower stabilities in the .70s and .60s. Overall, the ERDA is quite stable over time.

Validity. Validity information is divided into content, construct, and criterion-related validity. These data converge to create a case for the validity of the ERDA as a test of reading ability.

Content-related validity involved using the professional judgment of curriculum experts in reading, speech, and other language arts. These professionals matched the content of the items with the curriculum standards specified by the U.S. Department of Education standards known as *Reading First*. A major goal of the content examination process was to ensure that all curriculum areas were balanced. Efforts were also made to maintain subtest homogeneity. The experts examined items for ethnic and gender bias, and then removed offending items.

Construct validity consists of subtest intercorrelations for each grade (K–3) for fall and spring administrations. Throughout the six tables, there is consistent evidence of low to moderate positive subtest correlations. The general direction and magnitude of the correlations appear to be logical for the structure of the test. The fluency measures have the lowest correlations with other domains. RAN-Automaticity Composite is notable for having small or negative correlations with Vocabulary Composites. A simple exploratory factor analysis would have been helpful in describing the nature of the relationships among domains and subtests.

The case for criterion-related validity was developed by a study comparing performance on the ERDA of students diagnosed with learning disabilities in reading to a control group. The sample consisted of 47 second and third grade students (10 female and 37 male). These students received psychoeducational assessments through their local school districts and were found to be eligible for special education services. The eligibility criteria were not described. Certainly, there were significant differences in special education eligibility criteria across the different school districts. All had reading problems of a severe nature. Children receiving speech and language services; those who were hearing or vision impaired; and children receiving English as Second Language, Limited English Proficient, or Bilingual Services were not included in the study. There were statistically significant differences between the learning disabled and control group on all subtests and composite scores save for Word Definitions and Listening Comprehension for second grade students, and Brief Vocabulary Composite and Listening Comprehension for third grade students. There are certainly practical issues in identifying Kindergarten and first grade students with learning disabilities, yet there are no criterion-related validity data presented for these grades. Additional data correlating the ERDA with established diagnostic reading tests such as the Woodcock Reading Mastery Test would have been helpful additional information. Although rarely reported in manuals of diagnostic academic achievement tests and difficult to carry out, evidence that knowledge of strengths and weaknesses leads to improved instruction, such as aptitude x treatment interaction studies, would be compelling.

COMMENTARY. Technically, the ERDA is an adequate test. Unlike most new tests, the ERDA has the advantage of using well-established subtests and items. Therefore, this is a strong test that is consistent with the *Reading First* mandates from the U.S. Department of Education. Many educators and special educators will find the ERDA a useful tool.

There are several minor issues with the ERDA that did not become apparent until some of our staff members began using the ERDA on a regular basis. The administration of the ERDA can be confusing. In the effort to have maximum flexibility, it is unclear which subtests should be administered to which grades. In addition, the order of administration on the record form does not always match the order of appearance of items in the stimulus book. Scores are reported only as percentile ranges and categories of achievement.

There are no tables available for conversion to other scores. Given that most reading and academic achievement tests yield *t*-scores (mean of 50 and standard deviation of 10) or standard scores (mean of 100 and a standard deviation of 15), the ERDA is difficult to compare with other measures within a test battery. Although designed for teachers, school and clinical psychologists trying out the ERDA for the first time were frustrated and attempted to calculate *z*-scores and standard scores. This is not a good practices model for interpretation, but indicates the degree to which many will resist percentile ranges and categories of achievement as the sole scores reported. There were also many questions about whether test responses for some students (especially those with a history of grade retention or those young for grade) may not be best assessed with age norms versus grade norms. Although not severe flaws or severely problematic issues, these concerns can be tricky for the first time user.

SUMMARY. The ERDA is a quality measure of reading skills for students in Kindergarten through third grade. The ERDA is an amalgam of subtests from previously published reading tests. These tests are reorganized into the five basic requirements of reading as described by *Reading First* legislation: phonological awareness, phonics, fluency, vocabulary, and comprehension. In sum, the ERDA accomplishes what it sets out to do, which is to be a high quality diagnostic reading instrument for teacher use. It would have taken little additional effort to make the ERDA a detailed diagnostic assessment of reading for clinical psychology, school psychology, and developmental pediatrics as well. Nonetheless, the ERDA is a fine addition to the norm-referenced, diagnostic assessment of reading.

[83]

Emotional and Behavior Problem Scale— Second Edition.

Purpose: "Developed to contribute to the early identification and service delivery for students with behavior disorders/emotional disturbance."

Population: Ages 5–18.

Publication Dates: 1989–2001.

Acronym: EBPS-2.

Scores, 10: Theoretical (Learning Problems, Interpersonal Relations, Inappropriate Behavior, Unhappiness/Depression, Physical Symptoms/Fears), Empirical (Social Aggression/Conduct Disorder, Social-Emotional Withdrawal/Depression, Learning/Comprehension Disorder, Avoidance/Unresponsiveness, Aggressive/ Self-Destructive).

Administration: Individual.

Price Data, 2005: $125 per complete kit including technical manual (2001, 47 pages), 50 School Version rating forms, 50 Home Version rating forms, and IEP and intervention manual (2001, 205 pages); $15 per technical manual (specify Home or School); $35 per 50 rating forms; $25 per IEP and intervention manual; $35 per computerized quick score (Windows®); $225 per computerized IEP and intervention manual (Windows®).

Time: (15) minutes.

Comments: Ratings by teachers and/or parents/ guardians.

Authors: Stephen B. McCarney and Tamara J. Arthaud.

Publisher: Hawthorne Educational Services, Inc.

Cross References: For reviews by J. Jeffrey Grill and Robert C. Reinehr of the original edition, see 12:134.

Review of the Emotional and Behavior Problem Scale—Second Edition by ADRIENNE GARRO, Assistant Professor of Psychology, Kean University, Union, NJ:

DESCRIPTION. The Emotional and Behavior Problem Scale—Second Edition (EBPS-2) is a rating scale developed to help identify students ages 5–18 with behavior/emotional disorders. In addition, it can be utilized to specify areas of need for behavioral intervention and to measure behavior change over time as a result of service implementation. The instrument is also accompanied by a text, the Emotional and Behavior Problem Scale IEP and Intervention Manual, which enables the user to develop goals, objectives, and specific interventions for a student's IEP.

The EBPS-2 consists of two forms that can be used together or independently: the School Version containing 58 items (EBPS-2 SV) and the Home Version containing 53 items (EBPS-2 HV). The estimated time of completion for each version is 15–20 minutes. All of the items are statements of behavior problems that are rated using frequency quantifiers ranging from 1 (Not in my presence) to 7 (More than once an hour). These quantifiers allow the user to obtain detailed information but may be confusing for some raters. According to the test manuals, the EBPS-2 can be completed by a variety of individuals who have general knowledge of the child's or youth's behavior including educational personnel for the School Version (e.g., teachers, counselors, and/or paraprofessionals) and parents or guardians for the Home Version. The manuals do not specify who should interpret the EBPS-2 results.

The behaviors measured by the EBPS-2 represent a number of characteristics found in students with behavior/emotional disorders. Both versions of the instrument have a Theoretical interpretation and an Empirical interpretation. The Theoretical interpretation is based upon the federal definition of serious emotional disturbance (IDEA, 1997) and divides the items into five subscales: Learning Problems, Interpersonal Relations, Inappropriate Behavior, Unhappiness/Depression, and Physical Symptoms/Fears. The Empirical interpretation provides a more clinical framework for organizing the items and includes five subscales that approximate some diagnostic categories: Social Aggression/Conduct Disorder, Social-Emotional Withdrawal/ Depression, Learning/Comprehension Disorder, Avoidance/Unresponsiveness, and Aggressive/Self-Destructive.

Both the SV and HV yield subscale standard scores with a mean of 10 and an *SD* of 3 and quotient scores with a mean of 100 and an *SD* of 15. The quotient scores, which are described in the manuals as global measures of a student's overall behavioral problems, are obtained by separately summing the subscale scores for the Empirical and Theoretical interpretations. These scores have variable ranges depending upon the student's age and, in some cases, do not extend more than 1 *SD* above the mean. This is questionable given that the EBPS-2 is intended to be used as a norm-referenced instrument. Similarly, although the norm tables show a range of 0–20 for the subscale scores, the highest possible score is 13. To the developers' credit, standard errors of measurement are provided for the subscale and quotient scores. Also, there is a fairly thorough discussion of how to interpret results. Some of the information from this section should be considered cautiously, however, because it exaggerates the utility of the individual subscale scores.

DEVELOPMENT. Both versions of the EBPS-2 are shorter forms of the Behavior Disorders Identification Scale—Second Edition (BDIS-2). According to the test manuals, the initial item pool for both instruments was generated based upon careful review of the research literature and input from diagnosticians and educational personnel. Specifically, the authors asked for descriptions of behaviors and characteristics of children and youth with behavioral/emotional disorders seen in school or clinical settings. Following this input, specific items were developed. These were then sent to the same diagnosticians and educational personnel with instructions to remove, modify, and add items as needed to improve clarity. Subsequently, the developers conducted additional unspecified item analyses to produce the final shortened versions of the instrument.

To the developers' credit, both the Theoretical and Empirical subscales of the BDIS-2 are clearly and concisely defined in the test manuals. There are considerable intercorrelations among the subscales. The test manuals note that some overlap is to be expected because most students with behavior disorders show problems in multiple areas. The Theoretical subscales are based directly upon Bower's (1959) five-tenet definition of emotional disturbance, which in turn has been used to formulate the federal definition and special education legislation. This background is thoroughly described in the manuals. The foundation for the Empirical subscales, however, is not well explained. According to the developers, both the Theoretical and Empirical subscales are supported by factor analytic results. Although these results are discussed in detail in the manuals, the factor structures remain somewhat confusing and do not provide sufficient empirical support for the individual subscales.

TECHNICAL. The standardization sample and norming process for the EBPS-2 are adequately described, though dates for the norms are not clearly specified. The samples for the School and Home versions consisted of 3,986 and 2,473 students, respectively. It is unclear whether there was any overlap between these two samples. The students were described as a mix of regular education and behaviorally disordered students, but the specific percentages are not indicated in the standardization data. For both versions, the age range was 5–18 years. Based upon comparisons to U.S. Census data from 1998, the samples roughly approximated national demographic characteristics. For both the HV and SV, African American, Latino, and Asian/Pacific Islander students were underrepresented. Also, there was an overrepresentation of students from rural areas and an underrepresentation of students from the

Western region of the country. To the developers' credit, gender and age-specific norms are provided. An important note is that some of these are based upon small sample sizes and, thus, must be interpreted with caution. There are no norms specified by race/ethnicity and no separate norms for students with behavior/emotional disorders or other supplementary groups. The latter is disadvantageous if the intended use of the EBPS-2 is diagnosis or intervention planning for students with specific problems.

Internal consistency reliabilities were strong for the Empirical and Theoretical total scales and for a number of subscales. For a few subscales such as Physical Symptoms/Fears, these reliabilities were somewhat low with values in the .72–.75 range. There was only one set of studies for test-retest reliability and interrater reliability. These studies involved several shortcomings, and, thus, additional reliability evidence is needed. Specifically, the test-retest studies (30-day interval for SV; and HV) were conducted on relatively small samples of students. Reliabilities were adequate for the total scales of the SV ($r = .85$ and .86, respectively) but were somewhat lower for the HV ($r = .79$ and .79). The interrater reliability studies involved small samples for the SV, and relatively little information is provided about the raters. The coefficients from these studies indicated adequate reliabilities overall for the HV, with values ranging from .70–.90, but low reliabilities for several subscales of the SV including Aggressive/Self-Destructive ($r = .35$) and Physical Symptoms/Fears ($r = .25$).

Evidence supporting the validity of the EBPS-2 is mixed. As noted previously, the proposed factor structures are not adequately supported by empirical data. In addition, the separation of some of the items into distinct subscales is negated by relatively high intercorrelations among these subscales. Evidence of criterion-related validity is provided in the form of contrasted-groups research and concurrent studies, but this evidence is mitigated by several factors. In the former case, the EBPS-2 SV effectively discriminated between students with and without behavior disorders. However, because this study involved groups from the standardization sample, the results may not be generalizable to the general population. For the concurrent studies, the EBPS-2 HV and SV were correlated with the Behavior Evaluation Scale—Second Edition (BES-2). The SV was also correlated with the Devereux Behavior Rating Scales (DBRS). All of the above results indicated good correlations with most values falling in the range of .84–.98. However, some of these results are to be expected because the BES-2 uses the same frequency quantifiers as the EBPS-2 and contains identical subscales as the Theoretical scale of this instrument. Thus, more thorough criterion validity evidence could be provided by comparing the EBPS-2 to additional, more widely used behavior rating scales.

COMMENTARY. The value of the EBPS-2 depends upon its intended purpose as well as the user's choice of scores. The items are clearly linked to the federal definition of serious emotional disturbance and, thus, provide useful information that will aid in the identification of students with behavior/emotional disorders. However, the EBPS-2 user must be very careful in his or her interpretation and application of scores. For example, the manuals state that subscale scores falling more than one *SD* below the mean "constitute an area of serious behavior problems" (p. 35 of SV manual). This is an excessive statement that may lead to inappropriate diagnosis or classification because almost 16% of students can be expected to score in this range based upon the normal curve. In addition, due to lack of empirical support, the individual subscales should not be used for identification or diagnosis of students. These subscales would be more helpful in providing *supplementary* qualitative data. The frequency quantifiers of the EBPS-2 allow the user to obtain detailed information that is not available from most behavior rating scales. However, many users, especially those less experienced with behavior rating scales, will find these quantifiers cumbersome.

For the purpose of identifying students with more serious behavior problems, the quotient scores are the best choice. However, these must be interpreted very cautiously due to the restricted values for certain age ranges, as described above, as well as the limitations of the norm group, also noted previously. In addition, although the developers have addressed some of the validity and reliability deficits described in previous reviews (e.g., Grill, 1995), additional studies are clearly needed.

SUMMARY. As a behavior rating scale, the EBPS-2 has a distinct combination of features not generally found in other instruments including the use of specific frequency ratings and an intervention manual directly related to items and scores.

The most valuable quality of the EBPS-2 is its general content, which is directly linked to the federal definition of serious emotional disturbance and, thus, contributes to its utility. Despite the above strengths, from a psychometric standpoint, the EBPS-2 still demonstrates several shortcomings. Most notable are the lack of empirical support for its subscales/factors and minimal evidence of reliability and validity. Consequently, it is strongly recommended that the EBPS-2 only be used in combination with other forms of assessment to identify behavior disorders and never as the primary source of norm-referenced information. The quotient scores are acceptable as a *very general* indicator of behavior/emotional disorders in students ages 5–18.

REVIEWER'S REFERENCES

Bower, E. M. (1959). The emotionally handicapped child and the school. *Exceptional Children, 26,* 6–11.
Grill, J. J. (1995). [Review of the Emotional and Behavior Problem Scale.] In J. C. Conoley & J. C. Impara (Eds.), *The twelfth mental measurements yearbook* (pp. 342–343). Lincoln, NE: Buros Institute of Mental Measurements.
Individuals with Disabilities Education Act, PL 101-476, 104 STAT. 1103-1151.

Review of the Emotional and Behavior Problem Scale—Second Edition by JUDY OEHLER-STINNETT, Associate Professor, School of Applied Health and Educational Psychology, Oklahoma State University, Stillwater, OK:

DESCRIPTION. The Emotional and Behavior Problem Scale—Second Edition (EBPS-2) is a behavior rating scale with teacher (School; SV) and parent (Home; HV) versions designed to assess serious behaviors frequently noted by these informants. The scale has scoring for the five major criteria areas for a school-based classification of Serious Emotional Disturbance (SED) under the Individuals with Disabilities Educational Act (IDEA), as well as factor scoring for five areas of behavioral concern. Norms are provided for ages 5–18.

TEST DEVELOPMENT.

Definition of constructs of interest. The EBPS-2 authors developed the test to measure the five areas of SED, Learning Problems, Interpersonal Relations, Inappropriate Behavior or Feelings, Unhappiness or Depression, and Physical Symptoms and Fears. The empirically based subscales measure other categories, to be described below. However, the authors do not present clear operational definitions of these or describe the theoretical and/or empirical literature for their basis. The interpretation section does provide a brief descrip-

tion of each, but again does not tie their interpretations back to any classification system of emotional disturbance or mental disorders or operationally define the "cluster" of symptoms that the factor analysis was intended to validate. The authors do indicate some items were selected based on a literature review.

Item selection. Despite this weakness, the strength of item development of this scale was using teachers and others with direct observation of children with emotional disorders to generate items relevant to behaviors frequently encountered. Thus, several items appear on this scale that are not on other commonly used scales. Items appear to be modifications of items on the first author's 1988 Pre-Referral Behavior Checklist (13:236). Based on content validity analysis, the number of items were reduced to 83, and then based on an item analysis was reduced to 58, (unfortunately, before the reported factor analysis was conducted). The 58 items are described as a shorter version of the Behavior Disorders Identification Scale (BDIS-2; 26); however, that scale has only 73 items. There is no clear description of how item retention decisions were made or a rationale for the need for two separate tests. A comparison of items for the two tests does not reveal that the item elimination from the BDIS-2 to create the EBPS-2 increased content or discriminant validity of the new subscales.

The rational/theoretical scoring for items on the categories purported to cover the IDEA criteria is augmented by a factor analysis and additional scoring. However, the 58 items were retained on this scoring as well.

Factor analysis. The EBPS-2, unlike the BDIS-2, which was based only on rational scoring, was factor analyzed; factor as well as rational scoring are provided. Factor loadings for items from the rational scales, as well as the total scale factor analysis, are reported. A five-factor principal components solution was retained. Factor 1 was named Social Aggression/Conduct Disorder and is a relatively clean factor with few cross-loadings. The items do reflect socially inappropriate behavior. However, items more reflective of conduct disorder actually loaded on Factor 3, separate from Factor 1; self-harm items did as well even though these items should have loaded with depression items. This third factor was named Aggressive/Self-Destructive. Factor 4, Social-

Emotional Withdrawal/Depression contains appropriately loaded items except for two that did not load on the factor and should have been removed for scoring purposes. Factor 5 contained only two items relative to absences and tardies. This factor is not scored and these items were placed on another subscale; thus, the fifth "factor" scoring is not based on a factor at all. Factor 2 contains items relative to learning ability, avoidance, and motivational difficulties. Without explanation, this factor was split in two and is scored for Learning/Comprehension Disorder and for Avoidance/Unresponsiveness. From a content/theoretical basis, this separation represents a skill versus performance deficit, useful for interpretation, but it cannot be stated that these are separate factors. Thus, only the two aggression and the withdrawal factor subscales are actually factor-based. An examination of the scree test and eigen values indicate that a three-factor solution might have been most parsimonious, which most likely would have combined the aggression items and placed the two items from the actual Factor 5 on another factor.

Standardization. The School and Home Versions were normed on a nationally representative sample (3,986 and 2,473, respectively), likely the same sample as the BDIS-2. Intervals of 1 to 4 years are utilized for the norm tables, rather than the customary year or month intervals. Because there were gender differences, the norms are separated by gender, which may lead to overidentification of girls and underidentification of boys as having SED. Minorities are underrepresented in the sample, and caution should be used when interpreting scores for such children.

TECHNICAL.

Reliability. The overall alpha coefficient for the theoretical version was .97 (SV) and .96 (HV), and subtest coefficients are within acceptable limits. For the empirical version, the overall alpha was .97 (SV) and .95 (HV). Test-retest reliability (30-day interval) for the theoretical version was .85 (SV) and .79 (HV) and for the empirical version .86 (SV) and .79 (HV). Interrater reliability was within acceptable ranges for all versions, with a low of .25 for the Physical Symptoms/Fears on the theoretical SV to a high of .90 on Unhappiness/Depression on the theoretical HV and on Social-Emotional Withdrawal/Depression on the empirical HV. With use of multiple raters, overall reliability is good.

Validity. The discussion above regarding the factor analytic versus theoretical development of the test is relevant to construct validity. The scale does not have sufficient subtest specificity nor data to support differential diagnosis needed to support the claim that it can, in fact, diagnose emotional disturbance, even with the brief cautions relevant to using additional data to support the claim. For the SV and HV, concurrent validity is reported with the Behavior Evaluation Scale—Second Edition School and Home Version (T6:284), by the same authors, and for the SV with the Devereux Behavior Rating Scale School Form (T6:799), which has many of the same problems as the EBPS. There was congruence among similar subtests supporting the contention that they measure the same types of behaviors; unfortunately, the other correlations were not reported, so discriminant validity of the subtests cannot be evaluated. Further validity work comparing the scale to other broad and narrow-band scales to examine convergent and discriminant validity would add to the scale's ability to become a diagnostic instrument. Group differences from a 1989 study for males only are reported as evidence of the scale's ability to distinguish boys with behavior disorders from those in regular classrooms.

It is interesting that the empirical first factor shows much more severe problems for the SED students than the other factors or the rational scales, indicating that this factor does address the kinds of behaviors likely to be displayed by these students in school. Providing correlations between the scale and actual observed classroom behavior would add to the evidence of predictive validity of the scale. Although item interpretation is recommended, item predictive validity, particularly regarding critical items such as harm to self, is not reported. The effects of the students being in an educational or treatment program on the results are not noted. The manual states that the scale can be used to assess progress over time once a child receives services; no treatment outcomes studies are reported.

COMMENTARY. The EBPS-2 represents somewhat of an improvement over the BDIS-2 and is recommended in lieu of it. However, the EBPS-2 cannot be recommended as a true diagnostic instrument due to likely overidentification and lack of differential diagnosis. It can be useful in assisting teachers in operationalizing their behavior concerns in order to develop referral questions and interventions. The semi-factor-based scores for the constructs that are measured could be used in a limited fashion within the context of a multifactored assessment conducted by psychologists and psychiatrists trained to make diagnoses of mental disturbance, and are recommended over the theoretical interpretation of this scale. However, other better-established instruments, such as the Behavior Assessment System for Children (BASC-2), are recommended over the EBPS-2 for assessment of particular emotional and behavior problems. There continues to be a need for an instrument that is both empirically established and educationally useful, as the BASC-2 has its own limitations in these areas. The strength of the EBPS-2, the intervention manual, would be even greater with references that support the efficacy of treatments recommended. Demonstration that the EPBS-2 is sensitive to behavior changes based on the intervention manual would also strengthen the scale.

SUMMARY. The EBPS-2 is a school and home behavior rating scale with scoring for the rational scales of Learning Problems, Interpersonal Problems, Inappropriate Behavior, Unhappiness/Depression, and Physical Symptoms/Fears, as well as semi-factor-based scoring for Social Aggression/Conduct Disorder, Social Emotional Withdrawal/Depression, Learning/Comprehension Disorder, Avoidance/Unresponsiveness, and Aggressive/Self-Destructive. Although not currently recommended for diagnostic use as described in the manual, the scale has promise for screening and intervention development. With caution, the empirical scale scoring is recommended over the theoretical scoring and over the similar BDIS-2, and within the context of a comprehensive assessment conducted by psychologists and psychiatrists trained to diagnose mental disorders. The social aggression scale appears particularly sensitive to common behaviors exhibited in schools, the withdrawal scale minus two items does address internalizing behavior, and the aggressive/self-destructive scale might be useful in screening for externalizing behavior-disordered children at risk for suicide. The inclusion of the learning and avoidance subscales could be useful in assessing skill versus performance (motivational) problems in learning with further explanation of how these subscales were separated. However, additional scales must be utilized to conduct differential diagnosis of ED from LD and ADHD, and clini-

cal diagnosis of the particular mental disorder a child is exhibiting for treatment purposes.

[84]

Emotional Judgment Inventory.

Purpose: "Developed to assess emotional intelligence for use in employee selection and development in organizational contexts."

Population: Ages 16 and over.

Publication Date: 2003.

Acronym: EJI.

Scores, 8: Being Aware of Emotions, Identifying Own Emotions, Identifying Others' Emotions, Managing Own Emotions, Managing Others' Emotions, Using Emotions in Problem Solving, Expressing Emotions Adaptively, Impression Management.

Administration: Group.

Price Data, 2003: $41 per introductory kit (for 1 person only) including manual (56 pages), questionnaire, answer sheet, and prepaid Mail-In report; $38 per manual; $20 per 10 reusable test booklets; $18 per 25 answer sheets.

Time: (15) minutes.

Comments: Computer software available; online administration, mail-in scoring service.

Author: Scott Bedwell.

Publisher: Institute for Personality and Ability Testing, Inc. (IPAT).

Review of the Emotional Judgment Inventory by PHILLIP L. ACKERMAN, Professor of Psychology, Georgia Institute of Technology, Atlanta, GA:

DESCRIPTION. The Emotional Judgment Inventory (EJI) is an 80-item self-report inventory, where the respondent provides responses on a 7-point scale (from *I absolutely disagree* to *I absolutely agree*, with *Not sure* in the middle of the scale). From these 80 items, seven emotional intelligence scales are derived, along with an additional social desirability scale called Impression Management. The manual mentions that the EJI is "useful in predicting job performance" (p. 36) and that measures of emotional intelligence may be a useful addition to the organizational intervention toolbox, so the applications for the instrument appear to be intended for selection and for assessment of individual change, respectively.

DEVELOPMENT. The EJI is described by the author as an instantiation of the "initial theory of emotional intelligence by Salovey and Mayer" (manual, p. 4). It represents a refinement of this construct by including additional measures.

TECHNICAL.

Norms. Extensive norms are provided for the EJI. The norms show small, but significant, differences between age groups (over 40 or under 40), relatively smaller differences between racial/ethic groups, but more substantial differences between men and women (the largest difference had Cohen's $d = .65$). Presumably, these differences are reflected in the preparation of separate interpretive reports for men and women—but that is not entirely clear from the manual.

Reliability/validity. No overall score is reported for the EJI—each of the seven content scales are reported separately. As might be expected from scales composed of 9 to 11 items of relatively homogeneous content, internal consistency reliability estimates are adequate (averaging in the .80 range). However, test-retest reliability coefficients over a 4-week period are moderate for a sample of $N = 82$ (mean test-retest correlation is .76), and test-retest reliability estimates over an 8-week period are modest for a sample of $N = 69$ (mean test-retest correlation is .61, and the lowest test-retest correlation of .48). No test-retest reliability data are presented for the Impression Management scale. Such relatively low test-retest correlations bring into question whether the EJI is measuring relatively stable traits or less stable states. Validity information is provided along three lines: (a) interscale correlations and factor analyses of item parcels; (b) correlations with other measures; and (c) a narrative discussion of criterion related validity. The factor analysis of the interitem parcels appears to support a seven-factor representation (i.e., minus the Impression Management scale). For convergent validation purposes, the EJI scales were correlated with the Trait-Meta-Mood Scale (TMMS) and the Emotional Intelligence Scale (EIS). Significant and positive correlations were found across these scales. Substantial overlap was also found for the Own Emotions scales and the TMMS Clarity scale. EJI scales were also correlated with the Mayer-Salovey-Caruso Emotional Intelligence Test (MSCEIT) (which is a performance-based measure, rather than a self-report measure), the Wonderlic Personnel Test (a general intellectual ability measure), the Wechsler Abbreviated Scale of Intelligence, and the 16PF (a broad personality inventory). Correlations between the EJI scales and the MSCEIT were essentially all zero, as were nearly all of the correlations with the Wonderlic and the Wechsler tests (no correlation exceeded .22). In contrast, several correlations with the 16PF scales were significant and substantial (e.g., a correlation of .60 between Privateness on the 16PF and Expressing Emotions Adaptively, and .67 between Emotional Stability and Managing Own Emotions). This pattern of construct validity data suggests that the EJI has discriminant validity with intelligence and other performance tests, but in some cases either lacks discriminant validity or has convergent validity with personality traits (depending on one's perspective about whether emotional intelligence is separate from personality). Insufficient data were presented to allow for an evaluation of the criterion-related validity of the EJI scales. A narrative discussion was provided regarding leadership, sales performance, and health care, but the only quantitative information provided was that correlations between EJI scales and sales performance "ranged from 0 to .32" (manual, p. 34). Furthermore, no data were presented on the effects of organizational interventions on EJI scales.

Administration/interpretation. Administration is simple and straightforward—all of the instructions needed are provided in the examinee's test booklet or online. Scoring is not performed by the examiner, but rather the answer sheets must be returned to the publisher for scoring and preparation of an interpretive report. The interpretive report is designed only for use by a testing professional, and is not to be shared with the examinee. In fact, no feedback information is provided to the examinee. *T*-scores are provided, along with a confidence interval for each of the seven content scores, and a single statement is provided about the Impression Management score (as a validity index). A series of probabilistic statements are provided with each scale score, but these are represented as "hypotheses to be validated against additional information" (manual, p. 38). No additional interpretation information is provided to the examiner.

SUMMARY. The EJI is one of several self-report inventories that purport to measure aspects of emotional intelligence. Based on the limited information on criterion-related validity (minimal data for selection purposes and no data for the evaluation of organizational interventions), it seems premature to support the use of this measure in applied settings. There is still substantial controversy regarding the degree of construct overlap between emotional intelligence measures and personality traits. The EJI provides data supporting a lack of clean differentiation between these constructs for some of the scales. Finally, it is not clear that more than two separate content factors can be supported, and that greater integration among the scales might improve reliability, validity, and interpretive simplicity.

Review of the Emotional Judgment Inventory by DENIZ S. ONES, Hellervik Professor of Industrial Psychology, and STEPHAN DILCHERT, Doctoral Student, Department of Psychology, University of Minnesota, Minneapolis, MN:

DESCRIPTION. The Emotional Judgment Inventory (EJI) is a self-report measure, assessing seven dimensions of emotional intelligence. The test is based on the definition of emotional intelligence from Salovey and Mayer (1990) as "the ability to appraise one's own and others' emotions, manage one's own and others' emotions, and use one's emotions intelligently and adaptively in problem solving" (manual, p. 1). Seven EJI scales assess (a) being aware of emotions, (b) identifying own emotions, (c) identifying others' emotions, (d) managing own emotions, (e) managing others' emotions, (f) using emotions in problem solving, and (g) expressing emotions adaptively. An impression management scale assesses response distortion, "allowing you to spot potentially invalid test results" (promotional material), though the manual acknowledges potential true trait representation on this scale.

There are no time limits for administering the EJI. The test takes about 15 minutes to complete. There are 80 items requiring responses on a Likert-type scale ranging from 1 = *I absolutely disagree* to 7 = *I absolutely agree*. All items are phrased in work-related terms (e.g., "I use my feelings to improve my performance at work"). No overall "Emotional Intelligence" score is provided "because a total score would be difficult to interpret in any meaningful way" (manual, p. 5).

The main use of the EJI is in personnel selection and employee development. It appears that in using the test for selection purposes, organizations are free to combine scores from the scales in any manner they desire. The EJI can be administered individually or in group settings. Paper-and-pencil, computerized, and online administration formats are available. The psychometric equivalence of testing formats has not been examined for emotional intelligence constructs. Based on scale scores, a multiple-page, narrative interpretative EJI report focusing on work applications is generated for each respondent.

DEVELOPMENT. The theory that guided the development of the EJI was the conceptualization of emotional intelligence by Salovey and Mayer (1990). These authors regard the construct as a specific ability, to be distinguished from general cognitive ability, other dimensions of cognitive ability and personality traits. The manual indicates, "this personal characteristic is a relatively new construct hypothesized to account for systematic differences in human behavior beyond those explained by current measures of cognitive ability and personality" (p. 1).

Currently, there are two differing views on the nature of emotional intelligence. One school of thought suggests that emotional intelligence is a form of intelligence, positing the appropriateness of an ability model (Mayer, Salovey, & Caruso, 2000). The other suggests that emotional intelligence encompasses characteristics similar to those found in measures of personality (Bar-On, 1997; Goleman, 1995). Typically, the former conceptualizations are assessed using task-based procedures, whereas the latter rely on self-reports (Petrides & Furnham, 2000). Interestingly, task-based and self-report measures show small correlations (Van Rooy & Viswesvaran, in press).

The EJI was developed as a self-report measure to tap into the narrower ability-based conceptualization of emotional intelligence. Initially, based on theoretical considerations, a five-factor model was specified. However, data analyses (presumably factor analyses) suggested the appropriateness of a seven-factor model, which eventually constituted the seven scales. The technical manual lacks information on how items were generated, how large the initial item pool was, or how the initial item pool was refined to arrive at the 80 items used in the measure.

TECHNICAL. Norms are based on 1,736 individuals "representative of the U.S. population" (manual, p. 13). Although men and women are roughly equally represented (47.9% and 52.1%, respectively), the racial stratification of the standardization sample is somewhat less representative (73.7% Caucasian, 11.5% African American, .7%

American Indian, 6.3% Asian, 4.3% Hispanic, and 3.5% Other). Further, it is unsettling that 57.9% of the standardization sample is in the 18–24-year age group. An additional 23.3% of the sample is in the 25–44-year age group. The test manual does not indicate whether or not the standardization sample included working adults or job applicants. Given that one of the main uses of the EJI is personnel selection, it is important that the standardization sample be based on job applicants. Alternatively, empirical evidence is needed to support the inference that there are no differences in score distributions of individuals from the general population, working adults, and job applicants. Throughout the manual no such data are offered.

Commendably, the manual reports standardized mean group differences in scale scores for protected groups. The women's score is .65 standard deviations higher than that of the men on the Being Aware of Emotions scale. Higher scores for women are also evidenced on the Managing Others' Emotions, Using Emotions in Problem Solving, and Expressing Emotions Adaptively scales; though the magnitudes of these differences are somewhat smaller (*d*'s ranging from .22 to .47). Even smaller differences are reported among racial groups. On all EJI scales, older individuals score higher, but the magnitudes of these differences are small to moderate (*d*'s ranging from .16 to .46).

Internal consistency reliabilities are reported for three samples: an experimental calibration sample (*N* = 418), a validation sample (*N* = 852), and the norm sample. The reliabilities range between .73 and .90 for the seven EJI scales. Test-retest reliabilities have been examined for 4-week and 8-week time intervals. The sample for these investigations was a subset of the standardization sample (*N* = 82 and 69, respectively), though no further information is provided about subsample characteristics. Scale test-retest reliabilities range from .64 to .83 for the 4-week interval and from .48 to .69 for the 8-week interval. These temporal stability estimates are somewhat lower than means observed for personality scales (Viswesvaran & Ones, 2000).

Evidence aiming to support the validity of the EJI is multifaceted. An examination of correlations among inventory scales can be useful in assessing convergent and divergent validity. In the normative sample, we computed the mean correlation among the EJI scales to be .29 (*SD* = .18).

Some EJI scales are correlated over .50 (e.g., Being Aware of Emotions and Using Emotions in Problem Solving, Identifying Own Emotions and Managing Own Emotions). Nevertheless, exploratory and confirmatory factor analyses using bundles of items have recovered the hypothesized seven-factor structure of the EJI.

Convergent correlations for the EJI scales are reported with three emotional intelligence measures. First, scores on the EJI were correlated with scores on the self-report Trait-Meta-Mood Scale (TMMS; Salovey, Mayer, Goldman, Turvey, & Palfai, 1995), which assesses appraisal and management of emotions (*N* = 459 undergraduates). Overall, TMMS scores correlated on average .40 with the EJI scales. Second, correlations with the Emotional Intelligence Scale (EIS; Schutte et al., 1998) were reported for the same sample. The mean correlation with the EJI scales was also .40. Third, relationships with a task-based measure of emotional intelligence, the Mayer-Salovey-Caruso Emotional Intelligence Test (MSCEIT; Mayer, Salovey, & Caruso, 2002) were examined in a sample of 288 individuals (sample details not provided). In scoring the MSCEIT, the consensus scoring method was used. The total score from the MSCEIT correlated on average -.02 with the EJI scales. These results suggest that EJI displays adequate convergent validities with other self-report, ability-based conceptualizations of emotional intelligence; however, its convergence with a task-based measure of the same domain is poor. Two explanations can be offered for the low relationships with the task-based measure: differences in the scoring methods and/or differences in the cognitive loads of the two tests (manual, p. 28).

Divergent validities have been examined with cognitive and personality measures. Relationships with two cognitive ability measures are reported. In a sample of 189 working adults, the observed relationships between the Wonderlic Personnel Test, a test of general cognitive ability, and the EJI scales averaged .08. The highest correlation was between the Wonderlic Test score and Identifying Others' Emotions (*r* = .22). Correlations with the Wechsler Abbreviated Scale of Intelligence (WASI) were in the same range (mean observed *r* = .07, *N* = 142 undergraduates), though higher correlations were reported between the WASI full scale scores and Being Aware of Emotions (*r* = .20) and Using Emotions in Problem

Solving (r = .14). In general, it appears that most EJI scales do not carry heavy cognitive loads.

Relationships with personality scales were investigated using the 16PF and the International Personality Item Pool (IPIP) scales assessing the Big Five dimensions of personality (N = 634 and 459). Moderate to large correlations were reported between the EJI and 16PF Warmth, Emotional Stability, Social Boldness, Sensitivity, Vigilance, Privateness, Apprehension, Self-Reliance and Tension scales. Based on correlations with the IPIP scales, the most consistent correlate of EJI scales appears to be emotional stability. It would have been useful to report multiple correlations in predicting EJI scale scores from 16PF and IPIP scales. Although the test manual concludes that the constructs assessed by the EJI are mostly independent of personality traits, the data indicate some substantial relationships.

Three criterion-related validity studies are described for the EJI. The first study examined relations with the Multifactor Leadership Questionnaire (Bass & Avolio, 1997) and the Leadership Practices Inventory (Kouzes & Pozner, 1997) for executives participating in a development exercise. The manual reports neither sample sizes nor the correlations between the predictor and criterion scales in this study. Selected relationships are narratively described. In the second study, criterion-related validities were found to range between 0 and .32 for sales performance among job incumbents. Specific criterion-related validities and sample size for the study are not reported. Further, it is stated, "emotional intelligence demonstrated incremental validity in predicting sales performance beyond cognitive ability and personality" (manual, p. 34), yet no data supporting this important conclusion are offered. The third criterion-related validity study is reported for job incumbents in a health care setting. Again, sample size and specific correlations with supervisory ratings are not reported, though the narrative concludes that EJI scales were more strongly correlated with performance dimensions relating to interpersonal interactions. Additionally, it is declared, "emotional intelligence was predictive of job performance even after controlling for Neuroticism" (manual, p. 36), although data in support of this conclusion are not reported.

COMMENTARY. There are a number of strengths of the EJI. Foremost among these is its theoretical basis on the ability-based conceptualization of emotional intelligence from Salovey and Mayer (1990). Further, the seven scales of the EJI do appear to emerge in factor analytic investigations and appear to have acceptable scale score internal consistency reliabilities. Divergent relationships with cognitive ability tests are adequate. The weaknesses of the test include the apparent lack of job applicant norms, lack of independence from conventional personality traits, and poor reporting of criterion-related validity studies. Although response distortion among job applicants does not destroy criterion-related validity (Ones & Viswesvaran, 1998), applicant score inflation can render scores standardized on nonapplicants less informative. Future research will need to be conducted to support the test's use with job applicants. Divergent relationships with personality scales suggest significant, unintended overlap. Claims of incremental validity over personality, particularly over neuroticism, need to be supported by full data reporting from large sample studies. Further criterion-related validity studies using predictive validation designs are desirable.

SUMMARY. The EJI is aimed at satisfying the market demand for self-report measures of emotional intelligence for use in organizational settings, particularly in personnel selection. Many ability-based measures of emotional intelligence are available to users (see above). However, convergence of the EJI with task-based measures of the same domain is minimal. Small correlations with general mental ability and substantial relationships with personality variables suggest that the constructs tapped into by the EJI lie closer to the personality domain than the intelligence domain. The usefulness of the EJI for predicting job performance and other work behaviors above and beyond measures of cognitive ability and particularly personality will need to be documented by presentation of data.

REVIEWERS' REFERENCES

Bar-On, R. (1997). *Bar-On Emotional Quotient Inventory: User's manual.* Toronto, Ontario, Canada: Multi-Health Systems.

Bass, B. M., & Avolio, B. J. (1997). *Full range leadership development: Manual for the Multifactor Leadership Questionnaire.* Redwood, CA: Mind Garden, Inc.

Goleman, D. J. (1995). *Emotional intelligence.* New York: Bantam.

Kouzes, J. M., & Pozner, B. Z. (1995). *The leadership challenge.* San Francisco: Jossey-Bass.

Mayer, J. D., Salovey, P., & Caruso, D. (2000). Emotional intelligence as zeitgeist, as personality, and as a mental ability. In R. Bar-On & J. D. Parker (Eds.), *The handbook of emotional intelligence: theory, development, assessment and application at home, school and in the workplace.* San Francisco: Jossey-Bass.

Mayer, J. D., Salovey, P., & Caruso, D. R. (2002). *Mayer-Salovey-Caruso Emotional Intelligence Test (MSCEIT) user's manual.* Toronto, Ontario, Canada: Multi-Health Systems.

Ones, D. S., & Viswesvaran, C. (1998). The effects of social desirability and faking on personality and integrity assessment for personnel selection. *Human Performance, 11,* 245–271.

Petrides, K. V., & Furnham, A. (2000). On the dimensional structure of emotional intelligence. *Personality and Individual Differences, 29,* 313–320.

Salovey, P., & Mayer, J. (1990). Emotional intelligence. *Imagination, Cognition and Personality, 9,* 185–211.

Salovey, P., Mayer, J., Goldman, S. L., Turvey, C., & Palfai, T. P. (1995). Emotional attention, clarity and repair: Exploring emotional intelligence using the Trait Meta-Mood Scale. In J. W. Pennebaker (Ed.), *Emotion, disclosure, and health* (pp. 125–154). Washington, DC: American Psychological Association.

Schutte, N. S., Malouff, J. M., Hall, L. E., Haggerty, D. J., Cooper, J. T. Golden, C. J., & Dornheim, L. (1998). Development and validation of a measure of emotional intelligence. *Personality and Individual Differences, 25,* 167–177.

Van Rooy, D. L., & Viswesvaran, C. (in press). Emotional intelligence: A meta-analytic investigation of predictive validity and nomological net. *Journal of Vocational Behavior.*

Viswesvaran, C. & Ones, D. S. (2000). Measurement error in "big five factors" personality assessment: Reliability generalization across studies and measures, *Educational and Psychological Measurement, 60,* 224–235.

[85]
Emotional or Behavior Disorder Scale—Revised.

Purpose: "Designed to document those behaviors most indicative of emotional or behavioral disorders and the behavior problems which exceed the norms of any student in the environment."

Population: Ages 5–18.

Publication Dates: 1991–2003.

Acronym: EBDS-R.

Scores, 6: Behavioral Component (Academic Progress, Social Relationships, Personal Adjustment), Vocational Component (Work Related, Interpersonal Relations, Social/Community Expectations).

Administration: Individual.

Price Data, 2005: $80 per complete kit including technical manual (2003, 66 pages), 50 rating forms, and intervention manual (2003, 407 pages); $15 per technical manual; $35 per 50 rating forms; $30 per intervention manual; $35 per Quick Score; $225 per intervention manual (Windows®).

Time: Administration time not reported.

Comments: Behavior rating scale completed by observers familiar with the student; derived from the Emotional or Behavior Disorder Scale School Version and the Work Adjustment Scale (T6:2743); accompanied by Intervention manual; computer scoring software available.

Authors: Stephen B. McCarney (scale and manuals) and Tamara J. Arthaud (technical manual).

Publisher: Hawthorne Educational Services, Inc.

Cross References: For reviews by Patti L. Harrison and Steven W. Lee of the original edition, see 13:117.

Review of the Emotional or Behavior Disorder Scale—Revised by AMY M. REES, Assistant Professor of Counseling Psychology, Lewis & Clark College, Portland, OR:

DESCRIPTION. The Emotional or Behavior Disorder Scale—Revised was developed by packaging together two previously developed scales:

The Emotional or Behavior Disorder Scale School Version (EBDS SV; McCarney, 1992) and the Work Adjustment Scale (WAS; McCarney, 1991). The original instruments remain unchanged. The EBDS SV is now the EBDS-R: Behavioral component consisting of 64 items divided into three subscales: Academic Progress, Social Relationships, and Personal Adjustment. Students are rated on a Likert type scale ranging by frequency of behaviors (i.e., 3 = several times up to one time a month) with higher scores indicating more negative behaviors. The WAS is now the EBDS-R: Vocational component consisting of 54 items divided into three subscales: Work Related, Interpersonal Relations, and Social/Community Expectations. Students are rated on a Likert type scale rating demonstration of skills (i.e., 2 = Is developing the behavior or skill) with high scores indicating positive behaviors. Scores on both components are transformed into standard scores ($M = 10$, $SD = 3$). Although now housed on the same form, the Behavioral component is used for children aged 5 to 18, and the Vocational component is used for children aged 12-18. Given the complexity of reviewing an instrument consisting of two distinct measures, the following definitions for the review are offered. "Instrument" will refer to the EBDS-R as a whole, "component" will refer to the Behavioral and Vocational components of the scale, and "subscale" will refer to each of the six subscales within the instrument.

The EBDS-R is described as measuring the four areas of behavior identified in the National Mental Health and Special Education Coalition definition of emotional or behavioral disorder (U.S. Department of Education, February 10, 1993, p. 7938). The three subscales of the EBDS-R: Behavioral component are identified as corresponding to 3 of the definition areas: Academic, Social, and Personal skills. The three subscales of the EBDS-R: Vocational component are identified as a whole to correspond to the vocational area of the definition. The stated purpose of the instrument was to "develop an instrument based on an educational definition of emotional or behavioral disorder for the purpose of an educational diagnosis, and in order to provide educational service delivery" (technical manual, p. 7). Expected qualifications of the instrument user are not specified in the manual. A 399-page intervention manual with suggested interventions corresponding to each item on the instrument is included in the material package.

STANDARDIZATION. It is unclear whether the two components in the current instrument were normed on the same sample. The manual contains limited information on the initial development of the EBDS SV and WAS (currently the Behavior and Vocational components). The original standardization sample for the WAS was reviewed positively (Brown, 1998; Jeanrie, 1998). Reviewers of the original standardization sample for the EBDS SV raised serious concerns (Harrison, 1998; Lee, 1998). In general, the current samples for both components approach demographic characteristics of the 2000 U.S. Census data, but ethnic minorities are somewhat underrepresented. The Behavioral component was normed on 4,308 students "identified with behavioral disorders" and regular education students. The Vocational component was normed on 2,623 students in regular education and those identified with behavioral disorders. The number of students representing regular education versus those with "identified behavioral disorders" is not reported, nor is a clear definition offered to explain "identified with behavior disorders."

Furthermore, the age and sex groupings differ both within and between the components. For instance, the Behavioral component has categories for males aged 5–6 (n = 179) and females aged 5–7 (n = 268). The female age group 11–15 (n = 1,119) is spread across three age groups in the male sample. The Vocational component has categories for males aged 12—15 (n = 797), whereas the female sample for this age is spread across three age groups. These groupings correspond to the identified norm groups. On both components, the authors report that significant differences were found between ages and sexes, and therefore, they developed norm groups specific to age and sex. However, the data used to justify and determine these categories is not reported, and the categories raise significant problems with interpretation of the data including sex bias as outlined below. Also, given that it is unclear whether the components were normed on the same students, and there are different age groupings across components, comparisons between the components are problematic.

Subscale standard scores with a mean of 10 and standard deviation of 3, as well as percentile ranks and quotient scores are available. The Be-

havioral component has many of the same problems noted in the critique of the EBDS SV (Harrison, 1998) including a highly skewed distribution with directions to interpret the data as one would interpret a normally distributed sample. The authors recommend that obtained standard scores or quotients more than one standard deviation from the mean be interpreted as evidence of serious behavior problems. On the Personal Adjustment subscale, a raw score of 65 (a score more than one standard deviation above the reported general raw score subscale mean) for a 16-year-old, yields a standard score of 8 for a male student and a standard score of 3 for a female student. Given that the raw score is determined by recording how frequently behaviors occur, a female with the same reported behavior as her male counterpart would receive a standard score more than 2 standard deviations below the mean, whereas the male student's score places him in the average range.

RELIABILITY. Subsamples of the standardization sample were used to demonstrate test-retest reliability (range .78 to .87, n = 390, interval = 30 days) and interrater reliability (range .77 to .88, n = 289) on the Behavioral component subscales and total score. Cronbach's alpha ranged from .90 to .98. On the Vocational component, test-retest reliabilities range from .71 to .89; however, the authors do not indicate the number of students or the time frame used in the analysis. Cronbach's alpha for the Vocational component ranged from .95 to .99.

VALIDITY. Factor analysis of the Behavioral component is reported to support the construct validity, subscale structure, and item placement on the subscales; however, this interpretation of the factor analysis warrants reevaluation. One factor accounted for 43.04% of the total variance, with the second and third factors explaining 8.7% and 4.73% of the variance. All items from the Academic Progress scale clearly loaded on Factor 2. Items on the Social Relationships and Personal Adjustment scales do not appear to clearly load on any of the three identified factors. Furthermore, the subscale correlations ranged from .63 to .89, subscale to total score correlations ranged from .88 to .94, and item to subscale and item to total score correlations were very close for the majority of the items. The factor analysis may better be interpreted as supporting the instrument as measuring one construct rather than three. The Behavioral component is purported to measure three of the four components of the definition of emotional or behavioral disorders outlined by The National Mental Health and Special Education Coalition (U.S. Department of Education, February 10, 1993, p. 7938) and it is stated in the manual that subscale correlations "indicated that the students with behavioral problems in one area tend to also have problems in other areas" (technical manual, p. 14). A better interpretation of the data is that the subscales are not distinguishing between different types of behaviors.

Factor analysis of the Vocational Component revealed a similar pattern. One factor clearly emerged explaining 61.11% of the variance, subscales were intercorrelated ranging from .90 to .98, and item to subscale and item to total score correlations were very close or equal for a majority of the items. Despite these results the authors use the data to support the discriminant validity of the subscales.

Support for content validity is based on the literature review by the authors and assistance on item development from an unspecified number of "diagnosticians and educators" for the Behavioral component and "42 educational diagnosticians, guidance counselors, educational personnel, and employers" (technical manual, p. 27) for the Vocational component. Concurrent validity on the Behavioral component is supported by relatively high correlations of the subscales with subscales of the Behavior Evaluation Scale-2 School Version (McCarney, 1994) and the Devereux Behavior Rating Scale—School Form (Naglieri, LeBuffe, & Pfeiffer, 1993) for a subsample of 274 students identified as behavior disordered. Concurrent validity on the Vocational component is supported with subscale correlations from two instruments measuring adaptive behavior skills for a subsample of 40 students previously identified as behaviorally disordered. No demographic information was available for either subsample. Although the comparison measures are probably adequate, the small sample sizes, lack of demographic data, and lack of rationale for using only behavior disordered students in these studies are problematic. Also, given the lack of support for the subscale structures of the components, it may have been more appropriate to compare total scores on the components with other measures.

Criterion-related validity was not supported adequately. For the Behavioral component, an analysis of a subgroup of students with behavioral

disorders from the original EBDS SV is cited in support of criterion-related validity. However, the EBDS SV was normed on a more broad age group than the current standardization group for the Behavioral component, and the subsample compared only boys aged 4.5 to 15 with general education students aged 4.5 to 21. For the Vocational component, an analysis of a subgroup of students with and without behavioral disorders from the original WAS is cited in support of criterion-related validity. This sample contained only juniors and seniors in high school. No demographic information, including age, is reported.

No new information in support of predictive validity is offered in this revised packaging of previously developed instruments. Previous reviewers of the initial instruments found inadequate support for predictive validity, especially for the Vocational component (formerly WAS).

COMMENTARY AND SUMMARY. The Emotional or Behavior Disorder Scale—Revised provides no improvements over the original publishing of the separate measures (EBDS SV and WAS). The items appear to remain unchanged. The manual contains only part of the statistical analysis, with important basic information left out (i.e., full demographic information for subsamples used in analyses). A new standardization group was used with similar results in the psychometric properties of the instruments. The reliability evidence appears to be adequate. However, the factor structure of both of the EBDS-R components is not supported. Validity evidence is poor. The norms as developed with varying age and sex groupings provide problematic scoring and interpretation, and in some cases sex bias.

A large interventions manual is included with the testing materials. The manual is arranged to provide interventions for individual items contained on the EBDS-R. Portions of this manual could be helpful to teachers to assist them with writing in the specific language an IEP requires. However, as a manual to choose interventions it provides what appears to be a brainstorming approach to developing ideas without empirical support for the recommendations. Also, interventions are not listed in order of importance. For instance, Item 60 is: "Becomes pale, may throw up, or passes out when anxious or frightened." The first recommended intervention is "Reinforce the student for eating a nutritional lunch at school" (intervention manual, p. 194). Most pages contain items not necessarily specific to the identified problem, and miss important interventions that should be implemented. For instance, although such basic recommendations as "be a consistent authority figure" are offered, the section on "Threatens to hurt self or commit suicide" (intervention manual, p. 170) does not recommend risk assessment by a qualified professional.

REVIEWER'S REFERENCES

Brown, R. (1998) [Review of The Work Adjustment Scale]. In J. C. Impara & B. S. Plake (Eds.), *The thirteenth mental measurements yearbook* (pp. 1151–1152). Lincoln, NE: Buros Institute of Mental Measurements.

Harrison, P. L. (1998) [Review of The Emotional or Behavior Disorder Scale]. In J. C. Impara & B. S. Plake (Eds.), *The thirteenth mental measurements yearbook* (pp. 414–416). Lincoln, NE: Buros Institute of Mental Measurements.

Jeanrie, C. (1998) [Review of The Work Adjustment Scale]. In J. C. Impara & B. S. Plake (Eds.), *The thirteenth mental measurements yearbook* (pp. 1152–1153). Lincoln, NE: Buros Institute of Mental Measurements.

Lee, S. W. (1998) [Review of The Emotional or Behavior Disorder Scale]. In J. C. Impara & B. S. Plake (Eds.), *The thirteenth mental measurements yearbook* (pp. 416–417). Lincoln, NE: Buros Institute of Mental Measurements.

McCarney, S. B. (1994). *Behavior Evaluation Scale School Version: Second edition technical manual.* Columbia, MO: Hawthorne Educational Services, Inc.

McCarney, S. B. (1991). *Work Adjustment Scale technical manual.* Columbia, MO: Hawthorne Educational Services, Inc.

McCarney, S. B. (1992). *Emotional or Behavior Disorder Scale School Version technical manual.* Columbia, MO: Hawthorne Educational Services, Inc.

Naglieri, J. A., LeBuffe, P. A., & Pfeiffer, S. I. (1993). *Devereux Behavior Rating Scale—School Form.* San Antonio, TX: The Psychological Corporation.

U.S. Department of Education. (1993). "Notice of inquiry." *Federal Register* (February 10, p. 7938). Washington, DC: U.S. Government Printing Office.

Review of the Emotional or Behavior Disorder Scale—Revised by T. STEUART WATSON, Professor and Chair of Educational Psychology, Miami University, Oxford, OH:

GENERAL DESCRIPTION. The Emotional or Behavior Disorder Scale—Revised (EBDS-R) is a revision of the Emotional or Behavior Disorder Scale School Version (1992) and now includes a revision of the Work Adjustment Scale (1991). This instrument is designed to assist with the early identification of, and enhancement of service delivery to, students with emotional or behavior disorders. There are two broad components: Behavioral and Vocational.

The technical manual is very well organized, easy to read, and contains simple tables that facilitate understanding of the data. The instructions for administration and scoring are sufficiently detailed to allow even modestly experienced examiners to use the instrument appropriately. A sample protocol and profile sheet are also included that demonstrate the scoring procedures. There is also a brief chapter that describes how one should interpret the scores. There are separate scoring tables for males and females of various age ranges. These tables are easy to read and provide subscale standard scores and quotient and percentile scores for the total score.

Included in the kit of materials was a manual titled, "Emotional or Behavior Disorder Intervention Manual—Revised" with a subtitle of "Goals, Objectives, and Intervention Strategies for the Emotionally or Behaviorally Disordered Student." This essentially is a cookbook-style manual that lists the behaviors from both the Behavioral and Vocational components and offers goals, objectives, and a number of possible interventions to address that particular behavior. Quite simply, this manual is of little to no use for the practitioner. The suggested strategies are very generic, do not consider individual or contextual variations among students who exhibit or do not exhibit these behaviors, and completely ignore behavioral function.

DEVELOPMENT. The EBDS-R is based on the definition of emotional and behavioral disorders provided by the National Mental Health and Special Education Coalition. Four primary areas are assessed including academic, social, and personal skills (Behavioral component) and vocational skills (Vocational component). The Behavioral component is composed of 64 items that are observable and measurable by educational personnel. These items are intended to discriminate between students with and without emotional or behavioral disorders. The vocational component includes 54 items across three subscales: Work Related, Interpersonal Relations, and Social/Community Expectations. These items are also observed and measured by educational personnel and are designed to be predictive of behaviors outside of the school setting and more specifically, within the employment setting.

TECHNICAL. The Behavioral component of the EBDS-R was standardized on 2,122 males and 2,186 females ages 5-18 years of age. When compared with 2000 Census data, the standardization sample is underrepresentative of Blacks, Hispanics, and Asians, students in metropolitan areas, and students from the Northeast and West. Overrepresentation occurred for White students, students from nonmetropolitan areas, and students from the Midwest and South. Males younger than age 9 were not well represented nor were females younger than 8 and over the age of 15. The three-scale structure of the EBDS-R Behavioral component has moderate support from factor analyses. The first factor accounted for 43% of the variance and contained items related to aggression. The second factor was much less robust, accounting for only 9% of the variance, and contained items related to academically related behaviors. The third factor accounted for 5% of the variance and contained items dealing with avoidance or lack of social acceptance. In addition, there were moderate to high correlations among the three scales and with the total score, suggesting that each scale is measuring some central component related to either emotional or behavioral disorder. Given that many items loaded on more than one factor, one may question whether the scales are truly distinctive.

Test-retest coefficients at 30-day intervals were sufficiently high. Interrater reliability coefficients ranged from .77 to .88. Internal consistency reliability coefficients were well above what is considered sufficient. Concurrent validity of the scale was measured by correlating scores from the EBDS-R with the Behavior Evaluation Scale-2 School Version and the Devereux Behavior Rating Scale-School Form. The resulting correlations were sufficiently high. To demonstrate criterion-related validity, the author points out that the original instrument effectively discriminated between students with and without behavioral disorders and that the factor analyses of the current instrument support the three subscales of the EBDS-R. This is not a compelling argument for the criterion-related validity of this instrument. What is needed are data to show that the current version of this instrument effectively discriminates between students with and without emotional/behavioral disorders. Without such data, this instrument cannot be recommended as a diagnostic tool for identifying students with emotional or behavior disorders.

The Vocational component of the EBDS-R was standardized on 2,623 students ages 12–18 with approximately equal numbers of males and females. The standardization sample for the Vocational component more closely matched data from the 2000 Census than the Behavioral component with the exception of metropolitan and nonmetropolitan students. Factor analysis of the Vocational component indicates one very robust factor accounting for 61% of the overall variance. The other two factors did not account for substantial portions of variance (3.3% and 2.6%). Thus, although there are three subscales that purport to measure different vocation-related attributes, the factor analytic data suggest only one factor for this component. The one factor (subscale) solution is

supported by the extremely high correlations among the three subscales (i.e., .96 to .98). All of the reliability coefficients are moderate to high for the vocational component. Evidence of concurrent validity is insufficient as EBDS-R: VC scores for 40 students were correlated with scales of adaptive behavior. The author contends that this version of the Vocational component evidences criterion-related validity because the previous version did and because of the factor analytic data for the current version. These arguments are insufficient and do not demonstrate the criterion-related validity of the Vocational component.

COMMENTARY AND SUMMARY. The EBDS-R is a revised version of two related instruments, the EBDS School Version and the Work Adjustment Scale. Although the instrument has a high degree of face validity and intuitive appeal, the validity data do not support its use. There is questionable construct validity because of the lack of factor analytic support for the three subscale structure. Concurrent validity is demonstrated but relatively meaningless. Finally, criterion-related validity is virtually nonexistent as the author attempts to convince the reader that it exists because the previous version evidenced such validity and because of the factor structure of the current version. In addition, there is serious underrepresentation of certain students in the standardization sample that render the scale not applicable for a large number of students. Thus, use of this scale cannot be recommended in a clinical/diagnostic situation. It may be useful as a research instrument or as a gross screener for large numbers of students.

[86]
Employee Screening Questionnaire.

Purpose: "A personality-based selection measure designed to provide employers with a technique for identifying superior job candidates and to screen out dishonest and unproductive ones."

Population: Ages 16 and over.

Publication Dates: 2001–2002.

Acronym: ESQ.

Scores: 15 Performance Dimensions: Customer Service, Productivity, Accuracy, Commitment/Job Satisfaction, Promotability, Risk of Counter-Productive Behavior, Alcohol and Substance Abuse, Bogus Sick Days, Driving Delinquency, Lateness, Loafing, Sabotage of Employer's Production or Property, Safety Infractions, Theft, Overall Hiring Recommendation.

Administration: Individual or group.
Price Data, 2003: $17 per administration (1–99); volume discounts available.
Time: (20) minutes.
Comments: Internet administration or fax-in scoring service available through publisher; recommended by publisher for use in conjunction with the Personnel Assessment Form.
Author: Douglas N. Jackson.
Publisher: Sigma Assessment Systems, Inc.

Review of the Employee Screening Questionnaire by PAUL M. MUCHINSKY, Joseph M. Bryan Distinguished Professor of Business, University of North Carolina at Greensboro, Greensboro, NC:

DESCRIPTION. The Employee Screening Questionnaire (ESQ) is a personality-based selection measure designed to provide employers with a technique for identifying high quality job candidates and to screen out dishonest and unproductive ones. Previous research has revealed that personality measures are predictive of positive indices of job performance (Barrick & Mount, 1991). Similarly, personality-based integrity tests (Ones, Viswesvaran, & Schmidt, 1993) have been found to be moderately predictive of counterproductive job behavior (e.g., alcohol and substance abuse, bogus sick days, lateness, loafing). The development of the ESQ was guided by the desire to predict both types of behavior with one test. The prediction of positive job behavior is achieved by measurement of the Big Five personality factors (Extraversion, Agreeableness, Independence, Methodicalness, and Industriousness). The prediction of counterproductive job behavior is achieved by measurement of integrity through the development of a scale of Dependability. The 27 items are configured to yield assessments on 15 scales designed to predict various aspects of work behaviors (e.g., customer service, accuracy, promotability, safety infractions, theft).

The ESQ is composed of 27 forced-choice item tetrads that describe character, interests, and activities. Applicants indicate which of the four statements is most characteristic and which is least characteristic of himself or herself. Two methods of test administration are offered: a fax-in scoring system for paper-and-pencil assessment or online. The ESQ takes 15 minutes and the maximum cost per report is $17.

DEVELOPMENT. The theoretical basis of the ESQ is the Big Five theory of personality. The content of the ESQ was derived from the thousands of items comprising the original item pools of the Personality Research Form (Jackson, 1984), the Jackson Personality Inventory-Revised (Jackson, 1994), and the Six Factor Personality Questionnaire (Jackson, Paunonen, & Tremblay, 2000). The test requires a fifth grade reading level, thus it is deemed appropriate for a wide range of jobs across many occupations. Materials furnished by the publisher include a paper-and-pencil version of the test, a sample report form, and the test manual.

TECHNICAL. A long-standing problem with using personality-based assessments for personnel selection is the capacity of candidates to distort their responses to present themselves in an overly positive fashion (i.e., "fake good"). As such the developer of the ESQ used the forced-choice item format with the alternatives equated for desirability.

The ESQ is based upon extensive psychometric research conducted over several years to ultimately produce the current version of the test. Over 2,500 items were developed from which the final items were culled based on factor analysis and structural equation modeling. The manual describes in considerable detail the development of the faking-resistant forced-choice format of the ESQ. Internal consistency reliability estimates of the 15 scales range from .75 to .84 (median = .83). Only one correlation exceeds .50 in the interscale analysis of the six major personality dimensions (the Big Five and Dependability). Convergent validity coefficients are reported between the ESQ and the 16PF (Cattell, 1994). Some of these correlations strike me as markedly low, for example, a correlation of .25 between Independence (from the ESQ) and Self-Reliance (from the 16PF). However, the manual states, "In general correlations are consistent with expectations based on respective sets of scales" (p. 40).

The most difficult technical data to interpret pertain to criterion-related validity. The ESQ was based upon previous personality assessments developed by Jackson (e.g., Personality Research Form), and preliminary versions of the ESQ that did not use the forced-choice item format. Also, reference is made to validity generalized from personality-based tests to forecast various aspects of job behaviors. As such, it is difficult to disentangle the validity evidence from the 27-item forced-choice scale format version of the ESQ from the validity of its predecessors. Validational evidence is also presented on the superior validity of the forced-choice format versus the simple-stimulus format. The validational evidence for the current version of the ESQ is supportive but limited in volume. The degree of confidence one wishes to place on the predictive accuracy of the ESQ depends in large part on how much credibility is extended to the prior validational evidence conducted on precursors of the ESQ. No evidence is reported in the manual on the possible adverse impact of the ESQ, nor are any norms provided.

COMMENTARY. The ESQ tries to deliver on a very tall order: (a) a test predictive of positive work behaviors, (b) a test predictive of counterproductive work behaviors, (c) a test that does not produce adverse impact, (d) a test that is applicable to a very broad range of the working population, (e) a test that is supported (in one form or another) by over 20 years of previous research, (f) a personality test that is resistant to faking, (g) a test that takes 15 minutes to complete, and (h) a test that is very moderately priced. An unvarnished description of the ESQ is a test that follows from the legacy of other Jackson personality tests, one that is more resistant to faking in an employment context, and one that has evidenced moderate predictive accuracy. I believe the most distinguishing feature of this test is its capacity to diminish faking and thus (possibly) increase the predictive accuracy of personality tests used in an employment context. It is a matter of debate and future research as to whether 27 items, no matter how carefully developed and juxtaposed in a tetrad, can deliver on all that is proposed. My overall reaction to the ESQ is positive, based primarily on the quality of the research from which it was derived. The absence of data on possible adverse impact is disturbing from a practitioner perspective if nothing else. My biggest concern with the ESQ has nothing to do with its construction. By design the results of the ESQ are presented to the user as a tempting array of highly desirable pieces of information regarding a job applicant. I fear some users of the test might not be savvy enough to resist making definitive conclusions about job applicants based on a 15-minute assessment. Quite literally, for every one minute of testing time the user gets an assessment of one critical aspect of work behavior (15 scales in 15 minutes). It almost sounds too good to be true. Perhaps it is.

SUMMARY. The ESQ is one of a growing family of personality-based assessments intended for use with job applicants. Jackson has an esteemed professional reputation for his life-long research in personality assessment. Although I am skeptical as to whether this test can deliver on all that it proposes to do, I believe this test should be given serious consideration for operational use. However, in the hands of a novice user of psychological assessments in making employment-related personnel decisions, I believe the ESQ offers the possibility for misuse through overpromising what it can deliver.

REVIEWER'S REFERENCES

Barrick, M. R., & Mount, M. K. (1991). The Big Five personality dimensions and job performance: A meta-analysis. *Personnel Psychology, 44,* 1–26.

Cattell, R. B. (1994). Sixteen Personality Factor Questionnaire. Champaign, IL: IPAT.

Jackson, D. N. (1984). Personality Research Form. Port Huron, MI: Sigma Assessment Systems.

Jackson, D. N. (1994). *Jackson Personality Inventory—Revised manual.* Port Huron, MI: Sigma Assessment Systems.

Jackson, D. N., Paunonen, S. V., & Tremblay, P. F. (2000). *Six Factor Personality Questionnaire manual.* Port Huron, MI: Sigma Assessment Systems.

Ones, D. S., Viswesvaran, C., & Schmidt, F. L. (1993). Comprehensive meta-analysis of integrity test validities: Findings and implications for personnel selection and theories of job performance. *Journal of Applied Psychology, 78,* 679–703.

Review of the Employee Screening Questionnaire by FRANK SCHMIDT, Professor, Tippie College of Business, University of Iowa, Iowa City, IA:

DESCRIPTION. The Employee Screening Questionnaire (ESQ) is a personality-based integrity test intended for use in personnel selection and intended to predict both counterproductive behaviors (e.g., theft) and positive behaviors (e.g., customer service) on the job. The ESQ measures six basic dimensions (Dependability, Methodicalness, Industriousness, Extraversion, Agreeableness, and Independence); these basic scales and the items contained therein are combined in various ways to produce 14 work-related subscales (e.g., Customer Service, Alcohol and Substance Abuse) and a 15th scale that is an overall hiring recommendation. These latter scales are what is reported to users. A key feature of the ESQ is the use of a forced-choice format, which helps to prevent score inflation by job applicants seeking to convey positive impressions of themselves. The ESQ consists of 27 forced-choice blocks of statements with each block containing four statements. In each block, the test taker must select the statement that is most descriptive of himself or herself and the one that is least descriptive. According to the manual, the reading level of these statements is around the fifth grade level. The manual provides the needed information on instructions for standardized administration and proctoring. Completed ESQ questionnaires are forwarded to the publisher (by fax or the internet) where they are scored by a computer routine that provides candidate profiles in terms of the 15 work-related dimensions. Scores are presented in bar graph form as percentile ranks computed based on a large norm group. The report clarifies the meaning of each dimension by providing statements descriptive of high and low scoring candidates.

DEVELOPMENT. Except for the Dependability scale, all the basic scales measured by the ESQ are made up of personality statements from earlier personality inventories from this same publisher (The Jackson Personality Inventory–Revised, Personality Research Form, and the Six Factor Personality Questionnaire). Based on this item pool, fairly sophisticated item analysis and scale construction methods were used in development of the basic scales, parallel forms of each scale were developed, and studies were done to test the construct and criterion-related validity of the scales. Many of the statements in the "Integrity Facet" of the Dependability basic scale were selected because they were responded to differently by prison inmates and nonincarcerated employed people. The description in the manual of the construction of the "Responsibility and Risk Taking" facets of the Dependability scale is abbreviated and not very informative.

The manual describes the development of the forced-choice statement blocks. Each block of four statements is made of two pairs of statements. Within each pair, the two statements are matched on rated social desirability and frequency of choice by job applicants in past administrations of these statements in non-forced-choice format (a second index of social desirability). However, the two dyads are allowed to differ in their social desirability levels. In each block of four statements, the candidate must select the statement that is most descriptive of himself or herself—and presumably this statement is selected from the dyad with the higher social desirability level. Likewise, the candidate must select the statement that is least descriptive-and presumably he or she selects this statement from the dyad that has the less flattering statements (lower social desirability). However, this is not made clear in the manual. The manual states (p. 29) that this format ensures that candidates "are not *explicitly* [italics added] forced to choose between two equally undesirable items as characteristic of their behavior." This statement

appears to be disingenuous, because in fact this appears to be what actually does happen.

The manual presents criterion-related validity information for the ESQ basic scales (without the forced choice format) and for some of the work-related ESQ scales prior to introduction of the forced-choice format. These findings do show that scores are related to such employee behaviors as absenteeism, tardiness, alcohol abuse, and sabotage. But only one validity study is reported for an ESQ forced choice scale (and it is not clear what ESQ scales or scale this is for). This study shows that people "failing the ESQ" had higher rates of workplace delinquency than those passing it. The data presented on the forced-choice format scales are mostly devoted to showing that the mean score levels are lower with the forced-choice format than without it. This is interpreted as showing that the forced-choice format reduces applicant attempts to present themselves in an excessively positive light. But as noted above, the effect of these higher means on criterion-related validity may be small or nonexistent.

TECHNICAL. Although the ESQ manual presents more technical information than most manuals, there are many ways in which I found it to be unclear. Certainly the level of clarity is far below what is expected in a published journal article on scale development. Probably the most serious problem is the manual never explains how the test constructors went from the six basic scales to the 15 work-related scales. Chapter 3 of the manual ("Construction of the ESQ") has a section on the development of the five factor scales, another section on the construction of the separately developed Dependability basic scale, and a third section on the development of the forced choice response format. There is no discussion of how the six basic scales led to the 15 work-related scales. Nor is this to be found in the next chapter (chapter 4), on the reliability and criterion-related validity of the ESQ. In this chapter, we would expect to find validity evidence for the ESQ as marketed and used (i.e., for the 15 work-related ESQ scales in forced-choice format). Instead, as noted in the last section, most of the validity evidence is given for the ESQ basic scales in non-forced-choice format and for ESQ work-related scales in non-forced-choice format. Only one validity study is provided for the actual forced choice ESQ work-related scales.

Scale reliability estimates in an ipsative instrument cannot be determined independently-the reliability of any one scale depends on the reliability of the other scales (which is not true for non-ipsative scales). Even partial ipsativity can affect scale reliability estimates. The manual presents KR-20 reliability estimates for each of the 15 work-related scales (p. 31). Although these reliability figures are reasonably high (ranging from .75 to .84), they are not independent estimates for each scale, and this fact is not pointed out. Also, no alternate form or test-retest reliability estimates are presented. The ideal reliability estimate would be the correlation between alternate forms with a time interval intervening.

A number of additional things need to be improved in the manual. The manual opens with a discussion of the economic benefits (practical utility) of personnel selection testing that is correct in its overall thrust but which contains errors. For example, the Hunter and Hunter (1984) article did not report an average criterion validity of .38 for personality tests. Likewise, the information in Figure 1-2 in the test manual is incorrect. Also, Schmidt and Hunter (1983) did not say "a worker's salary will represent 40 percent of his or her contribution to the organization." They said that on any given job, 40% of salary is a conservative estimate of the standard deviation of the dollar value of job performance on that job across workers—a very different statement.

Another problem concerns much of the validity evidence presented in Chapter 4. In addition to mostly not being relevant to the forced-choice ESQ work-related scales, most of this evidence is presented in the wrong way. Put simply, what we need to know in connection with validity is the probability of performance given the test score—for example, the probability of being a top performer given that you have a high test score. This is the information we need, because we seek to know how well the test scores predict performance, not vice versa. Instead, what is typically presented is the probability of having a high test score given that you are a high performer. A typical graphic presented is the one showing that employees with no history of sabotage have higher average test scores than those who have engaged in sabotage (i.e., probability of a high test score given a history of sabotage). What is needed is the probability of sabotage given a low (or high) score.

These probabilities are very different and can lead to very different conclusions.

COMMENTARY. As noted earlier, the ESQ is a personality-based integrity test. There are many such instruments on the market today, and the research evidence indicates that they have criterion-related validity for both counterproductive behaviors and overall job performance (Ones, Viswesvaran, & Schmidt, 1993). The only thing really different about the ESQ is its use of the forced-choice response format. So a key question is whether this unusual format in any way compromises the empirical validity of the ESQ, especially in light of its partial ipsativity. As noted above, the manual presents one validity study that suggests that this is not the case.

Reviewing the ESQ was frustrating for me. On the one hand, the manual contains much more technical information than most and the author of the ESQ, the late Doug Jackson, was one of the foremost personality researchers of the 20th century. In addition, it is clear from the manual that the ESQ has a much more extensive research foundation that most of the competing instruments. Hence, there is reason to believe the ESQ is quite good. On the other hand, the manual omits key items of information, including any description of how the 15 work-related scales were developed from the six basic scales and any discussion of the ipsativity that could result from the use of the forced-choice format. In addition, there is only one validity study based on the forced-choice format ESQ scales.

SUMMARY. My best guess is that this is one of the better personality-based integrity tests on the market, but I cannot state this with certainty because of omissions in the ESQ manual. I believe that these omissions can be remedied and I encourage the publisher to do so.

REVIEWER'S REFERENCES

Hunter, J. E., & Hunter, R. F. (1984). Validity and utility of alternative predictors of job performance. *Psychological Bulletin, 96,* 72–98.

Ones, D. S., Viswesvaran, C., & Schmidt, F. L. (1993). Comprehensive meta-analysis of integrity test validities: Findings and implications for personnel selection and theories of job performance. *Journal of Applied Psychology, 78,* 679–703.

Schmidt, F. L., & Hunter, J. E. (1983). Individual differences in productivity: An empirical test of estimates derived from studies of selection procedure utility. *Journal of Applied Psychology, 68,* 407–414.

[87]

Evaluation of Competency to Stand Trial—Revised.

Purpose: "Designed for specialized forensic evaluations related to competency to stand trial."

Population: Ages 18 and over.
Publication Date: 2004.
Acronym: ECST-R.
Scores, 8: Competency Scales (Factual Understanding of Courtroom Proceedings, Rational Understanding of Courtroom Proceedings, Consult with Counsel), Atypical Presentation Scales (Realistic, Psychotic, Nonpsychotic Impairment, Both [Psychotic and Nonpsychotic combined]).
Administration: Individual.
Price Data, 2005: $205 per introductory kit including professional manual (2004, 176 pages), binder with interview booklet, 25 record forms, and 25 profile/summary forms in a soft-sided attaché case; $65 per professional manual; $60 per interview booklet; $60 per 25 record forms; $25 per 25 profile/summary forms; $15 per binder.
Time: Untimed.
Comments: Semistructured interview format.
Authors: Richard Rogers, Chad E. Tillbrook, and Kenneth W. Sewell.
Publisher: Psychological Assessment Resources, Inc.

Review of the Evaluation of Competency to Stand Trial—Revised by D. ASHLEY COHEN, Forensic Neuropsychologist, CogniMetrix, San Jose, CA:

DESCRIPTION. The Evaluation of Competency to Stand Trial—Revised [ECST-R] (pronounced: "x-ster") is an individually administered measure designed to assist a forensic clinician with conducting trial competency evaluations. It provides a semistructured interview format covering the domains deemed of importance for such assessments, namely: Factual Understanding of Courtroom Proceedings, Rational Understanding of Courtroom Proceedings, and Rational Ability to Consult With an Attorney. These domains were specified in the case of Dusky v. United States (1960), and affirmed by subsequent case law, including Supreme Court decisions. The ECST-R also was designed to meet the Daubert standard (Daubert v. Merrell Dow Pharmaceuticals, 1993), which established that evidentiary reliability will be based on scientific validity, and set out the criteria of: falsifiability, peer review and publication, known or potential error rate, and general acceptance. The ECST-R authors believe theirs is the only currently available competency measure that meets the Daubert standard.

Three Competency scales are derived from the examinee's responses to 18 queries. In addition, the ECST-R contains a 28-item scale assessing five atypical response styles. This scale is designed to serve as a screen for feigning of incompetency, and specifically targets both psychotic and nonpsychotic potential strategies.

The ECST-R is designed to use with defendants age 18 and above, and possibly with younger individuals involved with adult (as opposed to juvenile) criminal proceedings. Other than ability to hear the questions, and a minimal FSIQ of 60 or above, examinees need no specific abilities in order to take the test (e.g., neither vision nor intact motor skills are required). Separate norms are provided, when desired, for both genders and three ethnic groups (Caucasian, African American, and Hispanic). There are no competency measures currently available that are validated for use with non-English speakers using translators. The ECST-R may be used in such cases, but a caution should be noted in the report, and the screen for feigned incompetency is not recommended for administration via a translator because of possible mistranslation of idiomatic language. The authors make no mention of whether the test is usable for those employing sign language.

The test kit contains a manual, interview book, record form, and profile/summary form. Administering the test requires the first three, which is at times ungainly in the often cramped quarters in which in-custody interviewing can occur. Because of understandable concerns over test security under HIPPA, the record form corresponds to, but does not contain, the specific questions of the test, which are in the interview book. However, there are numerous qualifiers, suggestions, and follow-up inquiry questions contained in the manual, requiring memorization, pasting notes into the plastic-paged interview book, or shifting between the three while interviewing, none of which seems to be an elegant solution. There is space to write a verbatim response in the record form, and numerical ratings and scoring in the interview book, although again with many necessary explanations in the test manual.

The forensic clinician calculates Competency Scale scores by summing raw scores, and finding appropriate T-score conversions in the manual or on the Profile form; percentile ranks are also available. For scores found to be significantly elevated, one can establish four levels of impairment, and four levels of certitude for the Competency Scales. The Atypical Presentation (feigning) Scales [ATP scales] are in a structured format, and unlike the Competency Scales, do not permit follow-up or examiner-generated inquiries surrounding questions. The ATP Scales are scored similarly to the Competency Scales, with T-score conversions and percentile ranks.

DEVELOPMENT. The Evaluation of Competency to Stand Trial—Revised [ECST-R] was developed via definition and operationalization of the three prongs of the Dusky standard for competency to stand trial and based largely on a framework of construct validation. Richard Rogers initially developed the test items, then determined the relevance of these items for the various scales through prototypical analysis by five selected forensic experts with extensive work in the field of competency. ATP Scales items were developed through rational means, and validated by two methods, often used together in studies of malingering in other domains: known-group comparison and simulators. Discriminant validity distinguished those who were fabricating psychiatric impairment and incompetency from those who were genuinely incompetent due to a mental disorder. Pilot testing was conducted during the development of both Competency Scales and ATP Scales.

TECHNICAL.

Standardization. There were a total of 833 individuals of both genders (although men were overrepresented, as they are in the national criminal justice population). There was a mix of ethnic groups, with standardization data obtained separately for Caucasian, African American, and Hispanic. All of the participants were involved in the criminal justice system, some as detainees, some as pretrial defendants.

Reliability. As pointed out by the test authors, reliability is particularly of concern with tests such as the ECST-R in that many defendants have fluctuating symptoms secondary to their unstable psychiatric condition, affecting their level of competency from one time to another. The authors report data on internal consistency reliability, as well as interrater and test-retest reliability. Internal consistency reliability was high, with alpha coefficients from .83 to .89 for the Competency Scales, and .70 to .87 for the ATP Scales. Interrater reliability was even higher, ranging from .88 to 1.00 for the Competency Scales, and .98 for the ATP Scales. Test-retest reliability was somewhat constrained by the educational component of the test (if a defendant does not know a factual answer, the examiner is to instruct the defendant on the correct response) but greater than 90% of competency findings were identical between administrations of the test approximately 1 week apart.

Validity. Discussed briefly above, five forensic experts, along with trial judges, assisted with documenting content validity. Criterion-related validity was noted to be difficult as there is no completely independent standard for determining legal competency (e.g., the judge's ruling in a case cannot be used, as judges generally accept the recommendation of their consulting experts). The test authors used a bootstrap procedure employing expert clinicians' judgments as the criterion against which to measure ECST-R findings. They also obtained convergent and discriminant validity evidence against measures of related concepts. They made construct validity their major focus, using confirmatory factor analysis with models pertaining to the three prongs of the Dusky standard of competence.

COMMENTARY. As might be expected given such a measure and the complexity of the decision-making process for trial competency, over half of the main portion of the manual is devoted to interpretation of the testing findings—competency abilities, response styles, rational abilities, and case studies. Although this instrument is in no way designed to be used by novices in the field of forensics, the multiple examples and discussions of ways in which certain ranges of scores might be interpreted is very useful for those making the transition from another competency instrument, or those who have typically used no standardized measure in assessment of trial competency. Thorny issues are tackled in the manual, such as "Can a defendant feigning incompetency be genuinely incompetent?"—yes, and the ECST-R can assist in establishing this.

The test allows and encourages integration of the nomothetic data with case-specific information, and there is ample space to note the latter in the record form (e.g., examples of observed hallucinations, of impaired communication). Subtle concepts are elucidated, rarely seen in other competency discussions. Among these are discerning if a defendant has a self-defeating motivation or the ability to disagree with an attorney when necessary. The authors also discuss the idea that not all delusions impair trial competency abilities equally. The test is designed to be used in screenings, standard assessments, and comprehensive evaluations. The Appendices and the Profile/Summary form are clear and easy to understand, working well together to yield interpretive data for the forensic clinician to use in a report. Further examples are given of (legal) means of expressing findings in various ranges.

There are two minor comments for improvement of materials. In the ATP scales, Questions 9 and 19 are scored differently, and it would be a good reminder to examiners if these questions had a marking next to them in the record form and in the test book. There may be an error in the record form on Items 12b and 13a. Item 12b in the test booklet and manual pertains to psychotic reasoning processes that may emerge regarding a defendant's talking with a prosecutor, but is listed on the record form as "Self-Defeating Motivation." The next item, 13a, actually involves self-defeating motivation, per the test booklet and manual, but is not listed immediately following the question prompt in the record form.

SUMMARY. In the opinion of this reviewer, who performs forensic examinations routinely, there is no better single instrument than the ECST-R for assisting in determining trial competency. It appears this is the only published test addressing all aspects of the Dusky standard. It is readily understood by defendants, even those with lower intellectual functioning. Unlike some other competency instruments with vignettes in which the defendant must imagine what he or she would do in such a circumstance, the ECST-R elicits discussion of the relationship between a specific defendant and his or her particular attorney, and case. The advantages of the ECST-R are congruence with the Dusky standard of trial competency, admissibility under the Daubert standard, robust construct validity, and a means of systematically screening for feigned incompetency. It is likely to become the standard in many jurisdictions.

Review of the Evaluation of Competency to Stand Trial-Revised by ROBERT A. LEARK, Associate Professor, Forensic Psychology Program, Alliant International University, Alhambra, CA:

DESCRIPTION. The Evaluation of Competency to Stand Trial—Revised (ECST-R) is an 18-item semistructured interview with an additional 28 items that provide for a screen for feigned incompetency. The semistructured interview items

yield scores for three scales that formulate the basis of the decision as to whether the individual is competent to stand trial: Factual Understanding of the Courtroom Proceedings (FAC), Rational Understanding of the Courtroom Proceedings (RAC), Consult with Counsel (CWC) plus an Overall Rational Ability (Rational). The additional 28 items yield five additional scales measuring Atypical Presentation Response Style: Realistic (ATP-R), Psychotic (ATP-P), Nonpsychotic (ATP-N), Impairment (ATP-I), and Both Psychotic and Nonpsychotic (ATP-B).

The target population for the ECST-R is persons of age 18 and upward. The test is to be used by professionals who are licensed to practice independently within their state and who have specialized training in forensic evaluations. The test authors stress the necessity for the test user to have undergone supervised training in providing forensic evaluations. In addition the authors implore the user to remain current in the legal standards for the jurisdiction to which the evaluation will apply. Further, the ECST-R has not been validated for defendants with tested IQ scores of less than 60. Finally, the standardization of the ECST-R is with English-speaking defendants.

The administration and scoring of the ECST-R rests upon the information gleaned from the initial semistructured interview (18 items) and the responses for the structured interview format for the response style measures (28 items). For the initial competency scales there are specific questions posed by the evaluator. However, following this standardized question, the evaluator may ask further questions to inquire or clarify information. The CWC scale is composed of six scores based upon 15 ratings that involve the nature and quality of the attorney-client relationship. Each of the six test items has multiple rating questions. These rating questions utilize a Likert type rating format of 0 (not observed), 1 (questionable clinical significance), 2 (mild impairment, unrelated to competency), 3 (moderate impairment, peripherally related to competency—will affect but not impair competency), and 4 (severe impairment, directly related to competency—will substantially impair competency). The CWC scale score is the summation of the 15 specific ratings. The FAC scale uses six scores based upon 16 ratings that focus on the defendant's knowledge of the courtroom proceedings and the specific roles of the persons within the courtroom. The specific item ratings vary by question. The total FAC scale score is the summation of these ratings. The RAC scale comprises seven scores based on 11 ratings that measure the defendant's decision-making capacity on a variety of matters that could arise over the course of a trial. The total RAC score equals the summation of these ratings. The Rational score is found by adding the CWC plus the RAC.

The 28 response style items are scored either as 0 (no), 1 (sometimes, a qualified yes), or 2 (yes) for the ATP-R, APT-P, and the ATP-N direction. The ATP-I is scored either as 0 (nonimpaired) or 1 (impaired). The totals for the response style scores are simply the summation of those ratings.

Each of the summated scores is then plotted on the ECST-R profile form. The profile form converts the summated scores into linear T-score transformations. Each of the T-scores has four levels of impairment: Moderate: scores 60 to 69T, Severe: scores 70 to 79T, Extreme: scores 80 to 89T, and Very Extreme: scores 90T and higher. The Competency Scales can further be scored for four levels of certitude. These are: Preponderant (more likely than >50%), Probable (84.1% likelihood), Very Probable (95.0% likelihood), and Definite (98.0% likelihood). The linear T-score transformations can also be converted into percentile rankings if desired.

DEVELOPMENT. The ECST-R is based upon congruence with the Dusky standard articulated by the United States Supreme Court ruling (Dusky v. United States, 1960). This standard rests upon a single sentence: "The test must be whether he has sufficient present ability to consult with his lawyer with a reasonable degree of rational understanding—and whether he has a rational as well as factual understanding of the proceedings against him" (Dusky v. United States, 1960, p. 789). The initial version of the test, the ECST, was developed to meet the two-prong objectives of the Dusky standard plus provide a standardized format for this assessment (Rogers, 1995). An expert-based rating was used initially to score the original test items. The initial test items were derived from Rogers' review of appellate decisions and the forensic literature. This prototypical analysis allowed for a selection of items that are more consistent with the prongs of the Dusky standard. The authors then used a confirmatory factor analysis (CFA) to test for discrete abilities, domains,

and cognitive complexity (Rogers, Jackson, Sewell, Tillbrook, & Martin, 2003). The authors further tested their model using samples of competency cases, feigned incompetency cases, mentally disordered offenders, and jail detainees. The use of these samples permitted the refinement of the items as well as the analyses of the predictability of the scales. The final format of these analyses yielded the current revised version of the test.

TECHNICAL. The manual provides extant information concerning the standardization of the ECST-R. Following the derivation of the original test items and the initial analyses, the authors further refined the instrument. The standardized semistructured interview questions were then reformulated into simpler, easier to understand items. For example, the CWC questions have an average length of 7.73 words, the FAC average length is 7.22 words, and the RAC average length is 8.09 words. The items of the CWC were then reviewed to assure low face validity by keeping the items intentionally general. The FAC scale items assure the defendant could accurately identify the courtroom's personnel and their functions. The RAC items needed to assure that the questions would apply to most criminal cases and to develop potential trial outcome questions (Rogers, Tillbrook, & Sewell, 2004). The items comprising the feigning of incompetency were evaluated by using the known-groups comparison method (Rogers, 1997). The Structured Interview of Reported Symptoms (SIR; Rogers, Bagby, & Dickens, 1992) was used to classify the 87 participants into probable fake ($n = 22$) and a clinical group ($n = 65$). The participants were a consecutive referral sample from a jail mental health unit. The atypical presentation scales yielded overall classification hit rates of .67 (overall AP score), .63 (ATP-P), .62 (ATP-N), and .70 (ATP-I) (Rogers, Sewell, Grandjean, & Vitacco, 2002). The AP scales were further validated in a different study using participants from a competency restoration program ($n = 96$) with a clinical comparison group ($n = 56$) from a different prison mental health unit. An improved hit rate was reported: ATP-P (.77), ATP-N (.67), ATP-B (.77), and ATP-I (.86) (Rogers, Jackson, Sewell, & Harrison, 2004).

The manual provides tables of alpha reliability coefficients as follows: FAC (.87), RAC (.89), CWC (.83), Rational (.93), ATP-R (.63), ATP-P (.79), ATP-N (.70), ATP-I (.87), and ATP-B

(.86) based upon a sample of 411. Given that the instrument is a semistructured interview, interrater reliabilities are of critical importance. The manual reports the following interrater reliability coefficients for the ECST-R Scales: CWC (.91), FAC (.96), RAC (.91), Rational (.96), ATP-R (1.0), ATP-P (1.0), ATP-N (.98), ATP-I (1.0), and ATP-B (1.0) using a sample of 99. Average interrater reliability coefficients for the individual ECST-R items are also reported: CWC (.69), FAC (.90), RAC (.72) and rational (.77) using the same sample as above. Test-retest reliability poses a distinct issue concerning the nature of the construct being measured, namely current competency (or incompetency). Another issue is that of the estimates of reliability over any specific time period. The authors cite a limited sample of 29 detainees who were retested at a 1-week interval. A professional, blind to the fact that the detainee had been previously evaluated, did the second administration of the ECST-R. The overall concordance between evaluations was reported by the authors at: CWC (.98), FAC (.83), and RAC (.99) indicating seemingly stable estimates. The ATP items pose a separate matter as they distinctly measure the feigning of behavior. The concordance rates reported were: ATP-P (.84), ATP-N (.79), ATP-I (.86), and ATP-B (.79). Overall, the ECST-R scales demonstrate internal reliability, rather superior interrater reliability, and stable test-retest reliability.

The content validity of the ECST-R was initially documented by the use of test items gleaned from appellate reviews and forensic psychology literature. The use of the know-experts method of analyzing items further aided this process. Ancillary analysis using trial judges and forensic experts further increased the item content validity.

Construct validity is a more enduring task for most measurements, but more so for one that purports to measure behavior with a low incidence base rate (i.e., incompetency). To understand this, Rogers, Grandjean, Tillbrook, Vitacco, and Sewell (2001) used an exploratory factor analysis that yielded two factors. A second analysis using confirmatory factor analysis to test the ability of the items to fit into the three Dusky prongs was conducted. The authors note that using a three-factor discrete abilities model evidenced a good fit following a multivariate analysis. The authors also note that the factor loadings were "very robust (i.e., ≥ 60) with an overall mean loading of .72"

(Rogers, Tillbrook & Sewell, 2004, p. 136). Criterion-related validity was analyzed using the independent experts method that resulted in an overall mean hit rate of .82. In summary, the ECST-R has demonstrated evidence for construct and criterion-related validity.

COMMENTARY. The test authors have taken on a complex issue: the standardization of legal terms into traditional psychometrically sound instrumentation. In addition, the authors have attempted to assess a behavior that has a low base rate in the general population, namely incompetence. To this effort the authors must be applauded.

Because the ECST-R is designed to be used in a limited forensic arena to address specific legal issues, the normative data do not meet, and are not intended to meet, the expected sampling done on the majority of psychological tests. Specifically, the normative sample is of prison detainees who were either referred for competency reasons or other jail/correction referrals from offender samples that could be referred for competency evaluations. This yielded a total aggregate of 444 within the sample. Of these, 355 were males. The normative data used for the linear T-score transformations are a more restricted data sample. For these data, the sample was restricted to those offenders with "genuine impairment" (Rogers, Tillbrook & Sewell, 2004, p. 118). This restricted sample is of only 356 offenders. Thus, the test may be viewed by some as less than adequate in meeting the distribution according to a United States Census-based model of sampling. Given the rather specific nature of the instrument, this may not be so overwhelming of a problem.

SUMMARY. Overall, the authors have done a rather thorough job in creating test items that focus on key legal issues. They had added to this by developing the items into meaningful scales that address very specific (although still rather generalized legal terms) legal issues. Finally, the authors have attempted to develop this method into a test that meets standards of technical quality.

Users must be careful towards generalization of findings past the original intent of this instrument. It has limited range of use (i.e., specifically for competency-based issues) and its generalization towards other psychological constructs is not warranted. Further, it is clearly meant to be used on those individuals, primarily male, who have demonstrated IQ scores above 60.

REVIEWER'S REFERENCES

Dusky v. United States, 362 U.S. 402 (1960).

Rogers, R. (1995). Evaluation of Competency to Stand Trial (ECST). Unpublished test, University of North Texas, Denton.

Rogers, R. (Ed.). (1997). *Clinical assessment of malingering and deception* (2nd ed.). New York: Guilford.

Rogers, R., Bagby, R. M., & Dickens, S. E. (1992). Structured Interview of Reported Symptoms (SIRS). Odessa, FL: Psychological Assessment Resources.

Rogers, R., Grandjean, N. R., Tillbrook, C. E., Vitacco, M. J., & Sewell, K. W. (2001). Recent interview-based measures of competency to stand trial: A critical review augmented with research data. *Behavioral Sciences and the Law, 19,* 503–518.

Rogers, R., Sewell, K. W., Grandjean, N. R., & Vitacco, M. J. (2002). The detection of feigned mental disorders on specific competency measures. *Psychological Assessment, 14,* 177–183.

Rogers, R., Jackson, R. L., Sewell, K. W., Tillbrook, C. E., & Martin, M. A. (2003). Assessing dimensions of competency to stand trial: Construct validation of the ECST-R. *Assessment, 10*(4), 344–351.

Rogers, R., Tillbrook, C. E., & Sewell K. W. (2004). *Evaluation of Competency to Stand Trial—Revised professional manual.* Lutz, FL: Psychological Assessment Resources, Inc.

Rogers, R., Jackson, R. L., Sewell, K. W., & Harrison, K. S. (2004). An examination of the ECST-R as a screen for feigned incompetency to stand trial. *Psychological Assessment, 16*(2), 139–145.

[88]

Expressive One-Word Picture Vocabulary Test: Spanish-Bilingual Edition.

Purpose: Designed to "provide an assessment of an individual's combined Spanish and English vocabulary."

Population: Ages 4.0–12.11.

Publication Date: 2001.

Acronym: EOWPVT-SBE.

Scores: Total score only.

Administration: Individual.

Price Data, 2003: $140 per test kit including manual (108 pages), test plates, and 25 record forms in portfolio; $38 per Spanish-Bilingual Edition manual; $27 per Spanish-Bilingual record forms.

Time: (10–15) minutes.

Comments: Adaptation of the English edition of the Expressive One-Word Picture Vocabulary Test (15:95); shares norms with the Receptive One-Word Picture Vocabulary Test: Spanish-Bilingual Edition (209).

Author: Rick Brownell.

Publisher: Academic Therapy Publications.

Review of the Expressive One-Word Picture Vocabulary Test: Spanish-Bilingual Edition by JILL ANN JENKINS, Consultant Child & School Psychologist, Barcelona, Spain:

DESCRIPTION. The Expressive One-Word Picture Vocabulary Test: Spanish-Bilingual Edition (EOWPVT-SBE) is an individually administered test for children ages 4.0 years to 12.11 years of age. It is a norm-referenced test for use with bilingual children who speak Spanish and English, which has been adapted from the Expressive One-Word Picture Vocabulary Test (EOWPVT; 15:95) and which assesses children's English spoken vocabulary. The overall goal is for the examiner to acquire a meaningful evaluation of the examinee's total acquired vocabulary, in contrast to monolingual proficiency in either Spanish or English. Additionally, the test manual states that the EOWPVT-SBE can be used to assess cognitive ability (because vocabulary acquisition is related to the efficiency with which an individual learns), to diagnose reading difficulties (where students with restricted vocabularies have difficulty comprehending on-level reading materials), to compare bilingual language acquisition to monolingual language proficiency, to diagnose expressive aphasia (when used in conjunction with the Receptive One-Word Picture Vocabulary Test—SBE), as a screening tool for preschool and kindergarten children, to monitor growth, and for evaluating program effectiveness (e.g., for programs that are designed specifically to increase vocabulary).

Examinees being tested are asked to look at a series of colorful pictures that represent an object, action, or concept, which are presented in a spiral booklet with a fold-out easel. There are 170 test plates that are ordered in respect to difficulty. The examinee is then asked to name the illustration in their dominant language. If they are unable to respond, they are given the opportunity to do so in their second language. Testing time is between 15 and 20 minutes. Raw scores can be converted into standard scores, percentile ranks, and age equivalents.

National norms have been developed from a sample of Spanish-bilingual residents of the United States of America. The authors have additionally co-normed the EOWPVT-SBE with the Receptive One-Word Picture Vocabulary Test—Spanish-Bilingual Edition (ROWPVT-SBE; 209) to allow the examiner to easily view differences between receptive and expressive language functioning ranges.

The test form itself is easy to use and handle. The scoring system is easy to understand and to apply during testing. The EOWPVT-SBE comes with a helpful questionnaire on the third page of the test form to assist the examiner in determining primary language. The materials are easy to transport, being packaged in a light, clear plastic portfolio. The pictures themselves are engaging and colorful.

DEVELOPMENT. Development of the EOWPVT-SBE was initiated while the revision of the EOWPVT, which was published in 2000, was underway. While revising the EOWPVT, which is an English monolingual assessment of expressive language, a Spanish translation was created by a firm that specialized in the development of Spanish educational materials. Translators represented various Hispanic dialects.

Several of the items on the EOWPVT were determined by this group of translators to be difficult to translate accurately or consistently between dialects, and were therefore eliminated. All of the 170 test plates from the EOWPVT were left in the test plate booklet.

A form was created for the remaining 156 test items and four example items for the EOWPVT-SBE. Test plates not to be used during the EOWPVT-SBE were indicated as such on the test forms. The forms, test plates, and standardized instructions were reviewed by Spanish bilingual educators in four states that have large Hispanic populations. Comments regarding the translation and alternative responses were compiled and reviewed, with alterations made to the test where they were deemed appropriate.

The standardized edition was then administered to N = 1,050 individuals from January to December 2000. Item analysis was based on this sample's qualitative and quantitative feedback. Qualitatively, participants were asked to identify alternative responses that should have been counted as correct and to comment on any problematic items. After this information was compiled and reviewed items were rescored. Analyses based on Classical Test Theory, Item Response Theory, and a one parameter IRT analysis were conducted and resulted in six items being eliminated from the test.

The resulting 150-item test was then rescored using a basal of eight consecutive correct responses and a ceiling of six consecutive failures. The final form's item analysis statistics were calculated at both age group levels and for the total standardized sample.

The correlation of item difficulty to item order for the standardized sample was an impressive .95. Correlations for each age group based on range of items administered ranged, again impressively, from .92 to .97 with a median of .95. Additionally, an item discrimination index indicated that the level of discrimination of items typically administered to examinees in each age group is consistently high. Further analysis also indicated that the examination has relatively equal

sensitivity across age levels and that the range of item difficulties is sufficient for assessing individuals within the intended age range. Overall, the development of test items for the EOWPVT-SBE was impeccably and responsibly created, analyzed, reformulated, and researched.

TECHNICAL.

Standardization. The standardized edition of the EOWPBT-SBE was administered to 1,150 bilingual individuals from January to December 2000. From this overall subject pool 1,050 individuals were selected to meet the demographic criteria set by the test developers. Testing was conducted at 150 sites in 50 cities in 17 states across the United States of America. Testing sites included public, private, and parochial schools, as well as private practices. The majority of examiners were speech and language therapists; others included school psychologists, educational specialists, and graduate students supervised by an instructor. Test examiners were obtained by contacting individuals who had previously purchased Spanish record forms for the EOWPVT or the ROWPVT.

Examiners were requested to select students randomly from regular classrooms, in addition to students who represented a wide range of disability status. Demographic information was collected via parent or guardian and examiners provided information on class placement, disability status, Spanish dialect, and community size. All children were administered first the EOWPVE-SBE and then the ROWPVE-SBE.

The sample approximated the demographics of the U.S. Hispanic population. Individuals from the western region whose dialect was Mexican are overrepresented. Sample sizes for each age level ranged from n = 71 to n = 143, with the smallest representation for children age 4 and the largest for children aged 9. There was an even spread for gender, where n = 531 (50.6%) of the children were female and n = 519 (49.4%) were male. Approximately half of the participants' parents had education up to Grade 11 or less (n = 545; 51.8%). The majority of the participants were from an urban community (n = 877; 83.5%). The percentages represented are very close to those indicated by the U.S. Hispanic population parameters for region, origin, gender, parent education, and residence (according to the U.S. Census Bureau, March 2001).

The participants were further analyzed according to their language dominance, being divided into four groups: those who speak Spanish exclusively at home and at school with minimal knowledge of English, those who speak mostly Spanish but know some English, those who speak both Spanish and English with equal ease, and those who speak mostly English but also speak some Spanish. When comparing performance among the groups, the obtained variance indicated that no more than 3% of test score variance was due to language dominance group. Due to these findings, the test authors concluded that the EOWPVT-SBE performance between language dominance groups was equivalent enough that one set of test norms would suffice. Overall, the EOWPVT-SBE sample size, sample selection, demographics represented, and further analysis of sample specifics was very professionally executed and reported.

Reliability. The internal consistency of the test was examined by using coefficient alpha and split-half reliability coefficients (odd/even test items compared) computed by age group for all individuals participating in the standardization study. Results were very satisfying, with coefficient alphas ranging from .92 to .97, with a median of .95 and split half coefficients, corrected for the full length of the test, ranging from .93 to .98 (with a median of .96).

To examine the temporal stability (test-retest reliability), 32 examinees were re-examined by the same examiners approximately 20 days after the initial testing. Although a small amount of practice effect was observed (where a standard score gain of 3.32 was obtained between the first and second testing), the correlation was nonetheless highly acceptable at .91 (uncorrected .88).

Content validity. The EOWPVT-SBE is an adaptation of the EOWPVT (English monolingual test). The test items for the EOWPVT were selected from a variety of sources to represent words that examinees "at a given age level, regardless of gender or cultural background, would be expected to have equal likelihood of knowing" (manual, p. 32). The most basic words were obtained through parent interviews that asked parents to identify first words spoken by young children. The majority of the rest of the test items were selected depending on frequency of use in written material and the grade level at which they appeared in curriculum materials. According to the authors, some obscure words were also used to tap the highest level of vocabulary. Only words that could have an accompanying illustration were

used. The final version of the EOWPVT underwent item discrimination and item bias studies.

The EOWPVT-SBE adapted the items of the EOWPVT, eliminating items that could not be translated directly or consistently among Spanish dialects. After being administered, item discrimination and difficulty were analyzed via item analysis and qualitatively via feedback from participants. The resulting test had 150 of the original EOWPVT items. Content validity was obviously very responsibly considered and analyzed for the EOWPVT-SBE.

Criterion-related validity. Correlation between the EOWPVT-SBE and the ROWPVT-SBE was found to be .36 (n = 1,050) and between the EOWPVT-SBE and the SAT-9 was .57 (n = 36). Despite the subject sample being a good deal smaller for the validity study with SAT-9, the results are still convincing as to the tests' criterion-related validity.

Construct validity. The authors of this test, when analyzing construct validity, have observed the following constructs and proposed the following hypotheses: *Chronological Age*—As a child develops, so should his vocabulary, therefore, EOWPVE-SBE test scores should show a linear relationship to developmental age. *Cognitive Ability*—The relationship between vocabulary and cognitive ability is well documented, therefore, there should be a linear relationship between EOWPVE-SBE scores and cognitive functioning. *Academic Achievement*—Vocabulary and academic achievement are related, therefore, there should be a direct linear relationship between EOWPVE-SBE and academic achievement. *Expressive and Receptive Vocabulary*—Measures of receptive and expressive language, although related to each other will test unique other skills in language functioning. There should be a direct relationship with the EOWPVE-SBE, although unique variance will also be present. *Exceptional Group Differences*—Students who have academic challenges are more likely to show vocabulary difficulties; therefore, the EOWPVE-SBE should be lower with students having related disabilities. Empirical testing of the following constructs and their related hypothesis supported their validity: chronological age, cognitive ability, and academic achievement.

Empirical testing of the constructs of expressive and receptive language via comparison of the EOWPVE-SBE and its receptive partner test the ROWPVE-SBE, indicated a moderate correlation between standard scores of .43 (uncorrected). Eighteen percent of the variance in test performance was attributed to the same factor, and therefore, 82% of the variance is unique and related to other factors. Previous analysis of the English editions of this test (EOWPVE and ROWPVE) indicate a much higher correlation of .75 (uncorrected) and an estimated shared variance of 56%. Greater difference between receptive and expressive language in the Spanish-bilingual participants used for the EOWPVE-SBE may suggest that this is related to the characteristics of bilingualism. The authors suggest that the bilingual individual may have less morphological knowledge that they are able to call upon in selecting answers.

When empirically testing the constructs of exceptional group differences, the authors divided children with special needs into four distinct groups depending on their previous classifications: Mentally Retarded, Expressive/Receptive Language Disorder, Learning Disabled, and Articulation (disability). The differences between the mean and the mean of the standardization sample for all groups and their means, with the exception of the Articulation group, were statistically different. The Articulation group did not score significantly different from the mean, probably because their disorder was not one of language knowledge, but of language production. Overall the test developers were very thorough in evaluating the validity of the EOWPVT-SBE.

COMMENTARY. The EOWPVT-SBE has been developed by a highly responsible group of researchers. They have analyzed and described all aspects of the development of this test, and presented evidence for reliability and validity. Children used for the standardization represented rigorous demographic criteria set by the test developers. There was slight overrepresentation of Mexican-origin participants. Overall though, they have proven the test to be one of a very high quality.

There are some considerations for the potential examiner to keep in mind. First of all, there is a linguistic flaw in the test, where the language dominance survey is written in the formal tense of Spanish and the examination itself is in the informal tense. Additionally, the potential examiner must remember that this test was developed and standardized on a bilingual Hispanic culture in the United States of America. This population is unique from bilingual speakers in other regions. There may be dialect differences if using this test, for example, in Spain.

This reviewer disagrees with the test's claim that it could also be used to assess cognitive ability and to diagnose reading difficulties. Although there are linear correlations between expressive language, cognitive skills, and reading difficulties, neither of the latter could be "diagnosed" via this tool. To assess cognitive ability, a proper test of intelligence needs to be administered, such as the Wechsler Intelligence Scale for Children III (Wechsler, 2003) or the Stanford-Binet Intelligence Scale—Fifth Edition (Roid, 2003). Indeed the authors of the EOWPVT-SBE suggest that if used to diagnose cognitive ability, it should be done so "with caution." This examiner would recommend against it at all. To truly test for reading difficulties takes comparison of a well-established test of cognitive ability, such as those indicated above, and a well-established achievement test such as the Wechsler Individual Achievement Test-II (Psychological Corporation, 2001). Although the EOWPVT-SBE would help in profiling a child with reading challenges, it would need to be used in collaboration with these other tools.

SUMMARY. The EOWPVT-SBE is an excellent test to discover the total expressive language skills of bilingual Hispanic children in the USA. It has been well researched by the test developers, is easy to use, and engaging to students. This reviewer would have no doubts at all in using the EOWPVT-SBE specifically with the population for which it was normed and specifically to determine the students' overall expressive language skills. As the publishers suggest, this tool could also easily be used as a screening for preschool and kindergarten children, and as a way to monitor growth and program effectiveness for curriculum specifically geared towards developing expressive language skills. In addition, this test could be used to diagnose expressive aphasia (when used with the ROWPVT-SBE) and to compare bilingual language acquisition to monolingual proficiency.

REVIEWER'S REFERENCES

Psychological Corporation. (2001). The Wechsler Individual Achievement Test—Second Edition. San Antonio, TX: The Psychological Corporation.
Roid, G. (2003). Stanford-Binet Intelligence Scales, Fifth Edition. Itasca, IL: Riverside Publishing.
Wechsler, D. (2003). Wechsler Intelligence Scale for Children—Fourth Edition. San Antonio, TX: PsychCorp, A brand of Harcourt Assessment, Inc.

[89]
Extended Complex Figure Test.

Purpose: Designed to measure both perceptual organization and visual memory in persons with brain injury.
Population: Ages 19–85.
Publication Date: 2003.
Acronym: ECFT.
Scores, 14: Copy Total Correct, Copy Time, Immediate Recall Total Correct, Immediate Recall Time, Delayed Recall Total Correct, Delayed Recall Time, Recognition Total Correct, Recognition Global, Recognition Detail, Recognition Left Detail, Recognition Right Detail, Matching Total Correct, Matching Left Detail, Matching Right Detail.
Administration: Individual.
Price Data, 2003: $145 per kit including manual (94 pages), stimulus booklet, and administration scoring booklet; $62.50 per stimulus booklet; $42.50 per 25 administration and scoring booklets; $52.50 per manual.
Time: (15–20) minutes.
Author: Philip S. Fastenau.
Publisher: Western Psychological Services.

Review of the Extended Complex Figure Test by MARY "RINA" M. CHITTOORAN, Associate Professor of Educational Studies, Saint Louis University, St. Louis, MO:

DESCRIPTION. The Extended Complex Figure Test (ECFT), an extension of the Rey-Osterrieth Complex Figure Test (CFT), is a diagnostic neuropsychological measure that employs a series of complex drawing and memory tasks to assess perceptual-motor organization and visual memory in individuals between the ages of 19 and 85 years. The ECFT is intended to be used to (a) identify neurological damage subsequent to head injury, stroke, or other conditions; (b) help the examiner discriminate between various processes that affect the drawing task; and (c) assist in differential diagnosis (e.g., depression and dementia).

Detailed directions for administration are provided on the test protocol as well as in the manual. The examinee is first asked to copy a complex geometric figure on a blank sheet of paper using a series of colored pens; the target stimulus is removed and the examinee is immediately asked to reproduce the figure from memory, and again, after a delay of 15–60 minutes. The ECFT includes two additional tests that are not part of the CFT: Recognition, that assesses visual-spatial memory, and Matching, a test of recall that uses components of the target figure to assess visual-spatial perception. The entire test, excluding delay time, takes between 15 and 20 minutes.

Scoring can be accomplished using the Osterrieth scoring system and is facilitated by the inclusion of detailed scoring guidelines and a completed sample protocol in the manual. The ECFT results in 14 scores, including the number correct, the amount of time taken to complete each of the first three tasks, and the degree of detail recognized or matched on the last two tasks. Scores for the Matching Trial are treated categorically, with cutoff values based on age and education, that indicate varying degrees of impairment.

Norms are provided for nine age groups between the ages of 19 and 85; in addition, preliminary norms for 76 children, ages 6–18, are also provided. Raw scores may be converted to scaled scores (Mean = 10; SD = 3), by using the norms tables in the Appendix. The interpretation of scaled scores is as follows: 0 = moderate to severe impairment, 1 to 3 = mild impairment, 4 to 5 = marginal functioning, 6 to 14 = average functioning, 15 to 16 = superior functioning, and 17 to 19 = very superior functioning. The manual also offers various profiles that facilitate interpretation of test performance. Guidelines for qualitative analysis of drawings as well as ECFT score patterns for specific clinical conditions (e.g., schizophrenia) offer additional information about the examinee's functioning.

A shorter version of the ECFT, the ECFT-MI, is used to assess visual perception independent of motor functioning in cases where fatigue or limited motor strength is an issue. The ECFT-MI takes 10–15 minutes to administer, results in 8 of the 14 ECFT scores, and, according to the manual, may be interpreted using ECFT norms.

DEVELOPMENT. The initial set of ECFT items for the Recognition test was developed on the basis of reviews of the literature and examinees' test protocols. These 20 items were used in a pilot study with 42 healthy individuals, ranging in age from 18 to 55. Construct validity and internal consistency were deemed adequate for further test development, and content validity was examined through expert consultation. The final revision of the set included 30 Recognition items with 10 of those 30 items comprising the Matching test.

TECHNICAL. The ECFT was standardized using a sample of 239 adults, aged 19–85 years. The sample included healthy adults, 95% of whom were Caucasian, with no significant neurological impairments. Forty-four percent of the sample were male and 56% were female. The resulting norms for each score were stratified by age whereas the norms for the Matching Trial were stratified by age and education. The manual also addresses moderator variables that have an impact on test performance; for example, there was an inverse relationship between age and performance in adults, but there were no significant relationships between either education or gender and performance. Children between the ages of 6 and 18 also showed consistent age-related changes in performance. There were small gender-based differences favoring males, but educational level did not seem to have a differential impact on functioning. Finally, drawing time was studied; there were noticeable increases in time required for completion only among the oldest group (those over 80 years old).

The internal consistency of the ECFT was studied using Cronbach's alpha. Reliability coefficients for the Recognition Trial ranged from a low of .59 for Left Detail to a high of .84 for Total Correct. Coefficients for the Matching Trial ranged from a low of .08 for Right Detail to .58 for Total Correct. Test-retest reliability for the ECFT was expected to be low because of the nature of the test and was therefore not studied; instead, the manual reports on examinations of temporal stability for the ECFT-MI. One-week test-retest reliability for the ECFT-MI, in a sample of 34 adults, was reported to be .82 for the Total Correct score. Test-retest reliability for the Recognition subscale scores ranged from .48 to .75. Test-retest reliability coefficients for the Matching Total Correct score were very low ($r = .18$); further, this test did not differentiate between good and poor performance because of uniformly superior performance, regardless of actual ability.

Content validity of the ECFT was examined by submitting the measure to expert appraisal and stimulus analysis. Item-total correlations for the Recognition Trial were generally positive and significant and ranged from .18 to .60; on the Matching Trial, several item-total correlations ranged from .24 to .41. Convergent validity coefficients, examined by comparing test performance on the ECFT, the Wechsler Memory Scale—Revised, and the Judgment of Line Orientation tests, ranged from .65 to .90. Studies of discriminant validity indicated that the Recognition tests generally cor-

related better with other tests like it than with those unlike it (e.g., nonmemory tasks). Concurrent validity was demonstrated through the ability of the ECFT to discriminate between those with epilepsy and/or Alzheimer's and those without, as well as between individuals with left and right cortical stroke. The ECFT was also found to predict relief from seizures through the use of temporal lobe resection in 30 patients with temporal lobe epilepsy.

COMMENTARY. The ECFT extends the capabilities of the CFT and is therefore a welcome addition to the growing body of measures of neuropsychological functioning in adults. The inclusion of both a recall and recognition measure results in a test that has broader capabilities than one that assesses a single aspect of memory. Further, the inclusion of these tests serves to obviate some of the deficiencies and limited diagnostic utility of the CFT. Additionally, the ECFT-MI offers a useful way to assess visual-spatial abilities in individuals for whom motor control is a problem.

Test materials are simple and attractive, although an easel-backed stimulus booklet may have been a useful addition, both for the examiner and for the examinee. Training requirements for using the ECFT are significant and may be prohibitive for all but the most competent neuropsychologist; this is clearly not a measure for the novice examiner. On the other hand, scoring is facilitated by a completed sample protocol and illustrative cases. The manual also provides information about studies that examined the effect of changing test conditions, varying the order of administration, or excluding one test, so that examiners may vary administration procedures slightly, if warranted. Examiners should be warned that the ECFT is characterized by marked ceiling effects, particularly on the Matching Trial, that severely limit conclusions based on test performance. Chapter 3 of the manual provides important information regarding the clinical use and interpretation of the ECFT. The author warns against interpreting ECFT scores in isolation, and instead, encourages the examiner to interpret scores within the larger context of an examinee's typical neuropsychological functioning. Useful additions to the manual include score patterns for commonly occurring conditions such as schizophrenia and depression, a case example illustrating the use of the ECFT in an individual with epilepsy, and interpretive profiles based on ECFT score patterns (e.g., pathological forgetting). The ECFT is subject to the problems that occur with all tests that utilize a drawing format (i.e., the examiner's subjectivity in assessing examinee responses). Although provided guidelines make it easier to remain objective, there is still considerable room for error, and therefore, for erroneous conclusions based on test data.

The manual lacks critical information about the development and the standardization of the entire ECFT; instead, it focuses only on the Recognition and Matching Trials. Information about the rest of the CFT/ECFT would be desirable. Further, the description of the standardization sample seems to be incomplete; for example, it would be useful to know if the sample included diversity with regard to geographic areas, socioeconomic status, and a variety of other variables. The manual states that the norms may generalize to non-U.S. and non-English-speaking cultures because of the limited reliance of the ECFT on language; however, this recommendation should be followed sparingly, as with any measure for which norms have not been expressly developed for particular groups. Reliability and validity evidence ranges from excellent to poor for individual tests, thereby indicating a need for caution in interpreting performance on certain tests.

SUMMARY. The ECFT, an extension of the CFT, is a diagnostic neuropsychological measure that can be used as part of a comprehensive measure of neuropsychological functioning in adults over the age of 19. Although the ECFT suffers from the limitations of all drawing tasks, and is hindered somewhat by wide variations in reliability and validity evidence, it can provide very useful information regarding an individual's visual-spatial memory and perception, and can play an important role in program planning and implementation.

Review of the Extended Complex Figure Test by DANIEL C. MILLER, Professor of Psychology, Texas Woman's University, Denton, TX:

DESCRIPTION. The Extended Complex Figure Test (ECFT) is an extension of the well-known Rey-Osterrieth Complex Figure Test (CFT; Rey & Osterrieth, 1993). Both tests are neuropsychological instruments designed to measure perceptual organization and visual memory in adults with brain injuries. The ECFT (for ages 19–85) expands the clinical utility of the CFT by including recognition and matching components.

In order to administer the ECFT, an examiner will need the ECFT stimulus booklet, several blank 8.5 x 11-inch sheets of white paper, the ECFT administration and scoring booklet, and a stopwatch or timer. The examiner must provide the stopwatch/timer and the blank sheets of paper. The other materials are included in the ECFT test kit. The full-length administration of the ECFT is composed of five parts. The first two parts of the test are Copy and Immediate Recall. The last three parts of the test, Delayed Recall, Recognition, and Matching, are administered after a 30-minute delay from the Immediate Recall part of the test. A brief, motor-independent version of the test includes a Study trial of the test rather than the Copy trial, then it skips directly to the Recognition and Matching trials. The brief, motor-independent version of the test takes 10 to 15 minutes to administer; total testing time, excluding delay time, is 15–20 minutes.

The first part of the ECFT (Copy) requires the examinee to copy the complex geometric figures shown on the stimulus booklet onto a blank sheet of paper using different color pens. This portion of the test "provides a baseline measure of the examinee's visual-motor competence" (manual, p. 17). The total number of correctly drawn designs and the completion time across designs are recorded. The second part of the ECFT (Immediate Recall Trial) requires the examinee to recall from memory the designs and reproduce them on paper. The immediate recall trial "provides a baseline measure of visual memory" (manual, p. 17). As in the Copy trial, the total number of correctly drawn designs and the completion time across designs are recorded.

In the third part of the ECFT (Delayed Recall Trial), the examinee is asked to recall again from memory, but this time after a 30-minute delay, the designs and reproduce them on paper. The Delayed Recall Trial provides a measure of visual long-term memory. The scores for this trial, total correct and total time across designs, are the same as the previous two trials. The last two trials (Recognition and Matching) are unique to the ECFT. In the Recognition trial, the examinee is shown five pictures of complex figures and asked to identify the one that was previously displayed. The Recognition Trial provides "a measure of the adequacy of visual-spatial encoding processes as a foundation for visual-spatial memory performance" (manual, p. 17). The recognition stimuli vary from the original designs either globally, based on overall details, details on the left side of the design, or details on the right side of the design. Separate scores are generated for the Total Correct, Global Design, Total Details, Left Details, and Right Details.

In the fourth and final part of the ECFT (Matching), the examinee is shown a "target" complex figure drawing along with five pictures of complex figures. The Matching trial provides "a measure of whether an examinee is sufficiently well oriented and has the intactness of visual-perceptual function needed to actually perform the CFT task" (manual, p. 17). The examinee is asked to match the "target" complex figure drawing with one of the other five complex figures. Similar to the Recognition trial, the stimulus characteristics that facilitate the matching vary across designs based on left and right details within the drawings. The trial generates scores for the total number of correct matched items and total number of items matched based on either right or left details, respectively.

Test norms are provided for adults, ages 19 to 85, and preliminary norms are provided for children ages 6 to 18. For all of the measures across trials except Matching, raw scores are converted to scaled scores, with a mean of 10 and standard deviation of 3. The scaled scores are subdivided into three clinical categories: no apparent impairment, possible impairment, and impairment likely. Fastenau (the test author) cautions that the ECFT should be interpreted within the context of the results from a battery of neuropsychological tests. In addition to the major scores on the ECFT that can be interpreted, the examinee's performance within the test can be compared for signs of pathological forgetting, retrieval inefficiency, encoding deficiency, constructional deficit, perceptual deficit, and inattention. The ECFT manual provides evidence of how these within-test comparisons and clinical scores provide diagnostic evidence for "mild head injury, lateralized strokes, lateralized seizure foci, and exposure to neurotoxic substances, as well as medical conditions such as hippocampal sclerosis, Wernicke's encephalopathy, asymptomatic HIV-seropositive status, and AIDS" (manual, p. 3). Fastenau also reported "the ECFT is useful for differentiating between depression and dementia, for distinguishing demen-

tia-related memory deficits from the normal memory lapses associated with aging, and for identifying aspects of memory functioning relevant to rehabilitation planning" (manual, p. 3).

DEVELOPMENT. The ECFT manual reported a pilot study and a final revision process that was used in the development of the test. Twenty sample Recognition Trial items were constructed based upon the constructional elements and errors identified in the historical literature (as cited in the manual). A pilot study ($n = 42$) was conducted in 1996 to examine the psychometric properties of the new Recognition items (Fastenau, 1996; Fastenau & Manning, 1992). Some revisions were made to the Recognition items based on the pilot study, correlational data, and prior research. The author solicited expert appraisal of the initial instrument's content.

TECHNICAL.

Standardization. The ECFT norms for adults are based on the performance of 239 examinees aged 19 to 85. Data were aggregated across several studies. The sample was nearly equal in terms of male/female split, but there was an underrepresentation of minority groups in the sample. More than 95% of the sample was Caucasian and all were healthy adults with no known neurological conditions. Fastenau did provide some tentative norms (in the test manual) for using the ECFT with pediatric populations based on a sample of 76 children ages 6 to 18. No information about the geographic representativeness of the adult or child norms was included in the test manual.

Fastenau also reported several moderator variables on ECFT performance based on age, gender, and educational level. Rather than create norm tables to statistically account for these moderator variables, the author provided a reasonable rationale for basing the normative values for the test on an optimal reference group basis for age groups. For example, the performance of a 47-year-old was compared to a broader age range, 45- to 50-year-old group. The Matching Trial score did not convert to a scaled score but was rather classified into a category that indicated impairment levels if present.

Reliability. The ECFT Recognition Trial's total correct scale yielded split-half reliability coefficients of .81 and .78, respectively. Scale alphas ranged from moderate to high, largely as a function of the number of items on the scale. For the

Matching Trial's total correct scale the estimates of internal consistency were moderate. The restriction of range due to the inclusion of only healthy adults in the normative sample was the probable cause of the lower estimates of internal consistency for the Matching Trial's total correct scale.

Due to the nature of learning and delayed recall that takes place in the test, traditional test-retest reliabilities were not appropriate. However, the brief, motor-independent version of the test, not subject to the same limitations, yielded a correlation coefficient of .82 based on a 1-week delay between test and retest.

Validity. Evidence for content validity was provided in the test manual based on expert appraisal and stimulus analyses. Discrimination between levels of performance on the test was documented by correlating each item of the test with the Total Correct score. Evidence of construct validity was provided in the test manual based on correlations between the ECFT Recognition Total Correct scores with the ECFT Delayed Recall scores ($r = .81$) and with WMS-R Visual Reproductions ($r = .65$). The ECFT Matching Trial correlated with the visual-perceptual measure of Judgment of Line Orientation ($r = .68$), and with the perception-intensive Copy trials ($r = .74$).

The test's criterion-related validity was assessed using the ECFT with clinical samples such as patients with epilepsy, Alzheimer's disease, and left or right cortical stroke patients. The ECFT test results provided useful information to aid in the diagnosis of several neurological conditions.

COMMENTARY. The purpose of the ECFT was to add to the clinical utility of the existing Rey-Osterrieth Complex Figure Test (CFT), which has long been used in neuropsychological batteries to assess perceptual organization and visual memory. The author has succeeded in enhancing the CFT with the addition of the Recognition and Matching trials to the traditional ECFT and incorporated a higher level of a processing assessment approach to the administration and interpretation of the test. Further research needs to be conducted to gather validiity evidence for use of the test with other clinical populations and to verify the pediatric norms. Expansion of the standardization norms to ensure representativeness by ethnicity and geographic area would be useful.

SUMMARY. The ECFT appears to be a useful extension of the traditional Rey-Osterrieth Complex Figure Test (CFT). The added trials and the standardization of the qualitative aspects of the figures that facilitates or inhibits recall will be useful to a clinician.

REVIEWER'S REFERENCES

Fastenau, P. S. (1996). Development and preliminary standardization of the "Extended Complex Figure Test" (ECFT). *Journal of Clinical and Experimental Neuropsychology, 18,* 63–76.
Fastenau, P. S., & Manning, A. A. (1992). Development of a recognition task for the Complex Figure Test [Abstract]. *Journal of Clinical and Experimental Neuropsychology, 14,* 43.
Rey, A., & Osterrieth, P. A. (1993). Translations of excerpts from Andre Rey's "Psychological examination of traumatic encephalopathy" and P. A. Osterrieth's "The Complex Figure Copy Test" (J. Corwin & F. W. Bylsma, Trans.). *Clinical Neuropsychologist, 7,* 3–21. [Original works published 1941 and 1944, respectively.]

[90]

Fairy Tale Test.

Purpose: A projective test to help assess personality variables in children.

Population: Ages 7–12.

Publication Date: 2003.

Acronym: FTT.

Scores, 26: Ambivalence, Desire for Material Things, Desire for Superiority, Aggression as Dominance, Sense of Property or Ownership, Aggression as Retaliation, Aggression as Defense, Aggression as Envy, Aggression Type A, Fear of Aggression, Oral Aggression, Oral Needs, Desire to Help, Need for Affiliation, Anxiety, Depression, Need for Affection, Relationship with Mother, Relationship with Father, Adaptation to Fairy Tale Content, Repetitions, Self-Esteem, Need for Protection, Morality, Sexual Preoccupation, Bizarre Responses.

Administration: Individual.

Price Data, 2003: $115 per complete kit including manual (137 pages), picture cards, and 25 interview guides; $37 per manual, $19 set of 21 picture cards; $66 per 25 interview guides.

Time: (45) minutes.

Author: Carina Coulacoglou.

Publisher: Multi-Health Systems, Inc.

[Editor's Note: Multi-Health Systems, Inc. advised in June 2005 that they will no longer publish and distribute this test as of December 2005. The author advises that the test will then be withdrawn from the U.S. market for 2 years until American norms are developed. The test will be reviewed again at that time.]

Review of the Fairy Tale Test by FREDERIC J. MEDWAY, Professor of Psychology, University of South Carolina, Columbia, SC:

DESCRIPTION AND DEVELOPMENT. The Fairy Tale Test (FTT) is a projective test based upon story-telling methodology designed to assess a variety of personality variables and their interrelationships in children ages 7 to 12. The English version of the test was published in 2003 although the test's actual development, based on the author's dissertation, goes back at least to 1993. The rationale for developing the FTT is based heavily on the importance of fairy tales and folk lore within the psychoanalytic perspective. Fairy tales have certain characteristics that arguably lend themselves to projective use: The time and place often is not specified (they occur "once upon a time"), the characters' traits are stable throughout the story (usually good or evil, rich or poor, smart or naïve, etc.), the story ends happily, and nonhumans such as animals and ogres act like humans. This test is based on the notion that asking children about fairy tales and fairy tale characters will both engage them during the evaluation and elicit from them significant thematic content at conscious, preconscious, and unconscious levels through their identification with the scenes and characters.

The FTT incorporates primarily characters and events found in well-known fairy tales (e.g., "Snow White and the Seven Dwarfs," "Little Red Riding Hood"). Respondents are shown various picture cards and then asked a series of questions about them rather than simply making up a story. The primary card characters are a wolf, dwarfs, a (female) witch, a (male) giant, Little Red Riding Hood, and Snow White. The test was developed for both clinical and research purposes, was initially standardized on both normal and special population children in Greece, and yields both quantitative and qualitative scores. Administration time is reported to be 30–45 minutes, depending upon the number of picture cards administered. Scoring time is reported to be as little as 15 minutes or as long as an hour, depending on the familiarity of the examiner with the measure and scoring categories.

The FTT consists of 21 apperception cards, a 10-page interview guide (or test booklet), and a 123-page test manual. In addition, the author has a website that can be accessed at www.Fairytaletest.com. The website contains test updates and information on seminars. Besides English, the test has been translated into several languages. The manual reports that standardization has been completed in Brazil in addition to Greece, and is underway in Russia, India, and China. There is no standardization of the scale in any primarily English-speaking country.

The 21 stimulus cards are divided into seven sets of three cards and the drawings themselves vary on deliberately selected dimensions. The various illustrations represent the characters as they have appeared in both books and Disney-type films. Other characters are drawn in a unique manner to trigger novel responses in children. The drawings are both in black and white, and in color. Some characters look modern, realistic, and could be set in present time. Other characters are drawn fanciful and cartoon like. Little Red Riding Hood is drawn in color standing alone in a field, and also portrayed in black and white in the context of events from the fairy tale whereas Snow White is drawn only in black and white within the story context. These latter scenes show her encircled by the dwarfs, sitting on the floor by her father, and having the prince hold her hand.

Test administration as described in the interview guide requires the child to first tell the examiner the stories of Little Red Riding Hood and Snow White and the Seven Dwarfs *as the child remembers them*. The child also must know one fairy tale involving giants but is not asked to tell the story. Following this, the card sets are administered with the scene cards following the character cards. Children are asked what the characters think and feel (to elicit identification and projection) and up to four additional questions (e.g., which is the most wicked witch, which giant scares you the most?). They are asked to indicate which of the three scene cards ends the story.

The test manual has seven chapters. Chapter 1 provides the rationale for the test, a historical overview for the importance of folk and fairy tales in the lives of children, and describes test user qualifications. Chapter 2 describes the test stimulus characters and rationale for their selection. Chapter 3 covers test administration and scoring, and describes in depth the 26 quantitative scoring variables. In practice, however, 8–12 variables are most commonly derived: Ambivalence, Desire for Superiority, Oral Needs, Fear of Aggression, Anxiety, Aggression as Dominance, Aggression Type A, Aggression as Retaliation, Aggression as Envy, Depression, Relationship with Mother, and Adaptation to Fairy Tale Content. Thus, the FTT can suggest both internalizing and externalizing tendencies. Scoring of the variables is done by converting raw scores to T-scores ($M = 50$, $SD = 10$) using the standardization sample. Percentile ranks are not provided. Chapter 4 discusses test interpretation both in terms of the quantitative scores and more qualitative and subjective interpretation. Subjective analysis allows for the identification of children's defense mechanisms, personal conflicts, and atypical responses. Three sample case studies are presented. Chapter 6 demonstrates the application of the FTT to students with learning disabilities and mental retardation. Finally, two appendices present examples of scoring responses and normative data separately for boys and girls.

TECHNICAL. Normative data for the FTT are based on a sample of 803 children tested in Athens, Greece representing three age groups: 7–8 years ($n = 229$), 9–10 years ($n = 262$), and 11–12 years ($n = 312$). The sample represents different SES groups but it is not a normative sample and data for ethnicity are not presented. The standardization sample was also given the Rutter Behavior Questionnaires (parent and teacher versions) and Children's Personality Questionnaire for validation purposes. The latter scales were administered because they arguably measure constructs similar to the FTT. The test manual reports high interrater reliability indices for the scoring criteria (.47 to .97) and modest test-retest reliability coefficients after a 2-month period (.05 to .81). Factor analysis of test responses confirmed eight factors comprising the subscales with variance estimates ranging from 5.9 to 9.8%. The primary factors are Reality Contact and Mother Image, and these two factors are the ones found to primarily distinguish among clinical groups based on the CPQ and clinical judgment. Another factor, Depression, also significantly differentiates between disturbed and nondisturbed children using the Rutter Scales. Finally, throughout the test manual the author offers appropriate cautions for use in interpretation.

COMMENTARY. Great care and thought appears to have gone into the design and initial validation of the FTT. Children should find the test interesting and more so than the classic apperception scales such as the Thematic Apperception Test (T6:2593) and Children's Apperception Test (T6:456). Children are more likely to respond to direct questions than they would be if asked to simply make up a story about these stimuli. Compared to the Roberts Apperception Test for Children (T6:2129), which asks children to respond to common interpersonal scenes, the use of fairy tales may be less threatening for younger children; on the other hand, children also may be less likely to personally identify with the stimulus characters and project their own inner traits to their situations. A key limitation in FTT construction is the requirement that children know (or be told by an adult, not the examiner) the stories of "Little Red Riding Hood" and "Snow White and the Seven Dwarfs" prior to administration. How much story familiarization, factual memory, language skills, prior television and film viewing, and story descriptions, if needed, will impact test responses is unknown. It is unknown how many children from various cultural backgrounds will be unfamiliar with these fairy tales. It is unknown how much children's familiarity with other stories, including current literature (e.g., the "Harry Potter" series that includes giants and witches), will impact their responses. Because giants and witches more often than not act aggressively, some responding of this type may be expected even from nonaggressive respondents.

Although test administration is straightforward, test interpretation and scoring is relatively complex and examiners must ensure that their own biases do not affect test interpretation. Some test users may be uncomfortable with some of the psychodynamic assumptions underlying the test. Because there are no quantitative norms for English-speaking youth, psychologists in the United States and Canada cannot legitimately make normative comparisons at present and, for these countries, test use is not recommended, although the FTT might be used as an ice-breaker with children, to suggest hypotheses for further study, or used qualitatively by someone with advanced skills with projective instruments. Given that the Greek normative sample is small and the criterion-related validity of the FTT is not strong, even psychologists operating in countries where normative data exist should use the instrument with caution.

SUMMARY. In conclusion, the FTT is a novel and potentially useful tool in the measurement of children's personality. But considerable additional research and study, particularly validation and standardization, is needed before it can be recommended.

Review of the Fairy Tale Test by PETER ZACHAR, Associate Professor of Psychology, Auburn University Montgomery, Montgomery, AL:

DESCRIPTION AND DEVELOPMENT. The Fairy Tale Test (FTT), developed by Carina Coulacoglou, is a projective instrument designed to measure psychological traits, defenses, and interpersonal dynamics in children ages 7 to 12. Fairy tales are considered to be of continual fascination to children because they captivate their attention and symbolize universal themes that are endemic to development. The test provides a medium for children to articulate the roles these themes play in their own lives. It is appropriate for use by professionals trained in both projective assessment and psychometry. Administration time is approximately 45 minutes. Scoring time is variable and depends on the skill of the examiner.

The Fairy Tale Test begins by asking a child to narrate the stories of Little Red Riding Hood and Snow White and the Seven Dwarfs. The child also needs to know a story involving giants. If the child is not familiar with these stories, she or he is asked to learn them before taking the test.

The child is presented seven sets of pictures with three pictures in each set, and asked specific questions about each set of pictures. The questions serve to organize the test, and provide a kind of standardization that is absent in more open-ended projective instruments.

The first five sets of pictures are of Little Red Riding Hood, the Wolf, the Dwarf, the Witch, and the Giant, respectively. Each set contains three different variations on the character. All three pictures in a set are presented at once, and the child is asked to tell what each character thinks or feels. For example, the Wolf set contains drawings of an emaciated wolf, a well-groomed wolf with a blank expression, and a rapacious, villainous wolf. The child is asked which of the three characters in the set is the character in the story. Additional questions such as "Which wolf scares you the most?" and "Which Little Red Riding Hood would you have eaten had you been the wolf?" are also included— along with the question—"Why?" The sixth and seventh sets of pictures are called Scenes from Little Red Riding Hood and Scenes from Snow White and the Seven Dwarfs. These last two sets also contain three pictures each. The child is asked to describe each picture, pick which picture represents the end of the story and pick which picture he or she would like to represent the end of the story, and tell why. The child's answers are written on a preprinted answer sheet—called an Interview Guide.

Once the questions are answered, the person scoring the test engages in an analysis of the personality traits expressed in the answers. Only psychological traits attributed to the characters with which the child identifies are scored. The manual indicates which traits should be scored. Twenty-six traits are described and coded in the Interview Guide. The traits (or subscales) are a mix of Henry Murray's needs such as superiority, affiliation, and six kinds of aggression, plus various oedipally related traits involving sexual preoccupations, morality, and relationships with parents. There are also codings for more pathological kinds of characteristics that reflect possible problems with reality testing.

The theoretical framework for interpretation is psychodynamic, including an ego psychological focus on oedipal dynamics and an object relations perspective drawn from the work of Margaret Mahler and her colleagues. The description of the 26 characteristics is interesting and thought-provoking, but might be insufficient for someone lacking a background in psychodynamic theory.

TECHNICAL AND FURTHER COMMENTARY. Some people have a knack for making sense of these kinds of tests, others do not. The rules for thematic analysis can be very complicated, a disadvantage of projective assessment instruments in general. Learning to use them requires dedication. With respect to the FTT in particular, in addition to the problem of deciding whether or not a particular characteristic is present, the characteristics measured by the FTT are usually rated for intensity by assigning them 1, 2, or 3 points, but the rules for distinguishing between different intensity levels are not always clear.

Two kinds of interpretation strategies are used in the FTT—quantitative and qualitative. For the quantitative interpretation, each time one of the core traits appears in a set, it is tallied and then summed across all sets for a raw score. Raw scores are converted to T-scores for interpretation. There are separate norm tables for each subscale divided by both age and gender. For some reason, the tables for the subscales Ambivalence and Desire for Superiority have negative raw scores even though those subscales can be scored only from 0 to 3.

The normative group consists of 803 Greek children from Athens. It is unclear whether the raw score conversions can be used with children from other countries. The manual itself raises the possibility that a nation's history is an example of an environmental factor that might influence personality development, and no evidence that the norms collected in Greece can generalize to other populations is presented.

One of the problems with testing the personalities of children is that scores tend to be unstable, so even accurate measures will have somewhat lower reliabilities. It is difficult to decide if an inadequate coefficient reflects the test or reflects the nature of the construct as measured in children. The manual neither addresses this problem, nor predicts what variables are expected to be trait-like for children. For the FTT, the 2-month test-retest reliabilities of the subscales range from .05 to .81. Seventeen of the 26 subscales have test-retest reliabilities below .60. What the correlations indicate psychometrically is that most of the variance in these subscales is error variance. Whether better coefficients could be found with a sample larger than 52 is an open question.

Information allowing a reader to critically assess interrater reliability is absent. The author and four psychology graduate students were reported to collect the data, but no information was provided on who scored the tests. How many raters were there? How were they trained? How were disagreements between them resolved? Given the complicated nature of the scoring rules, detailed information about training raters should be provided. The manual also fails to indicate which kind of reliability coefficient was computed (it should be an intraclass correlation or Kappa coefficient), and exactly from which scores it was computed. No one reading the manual, as written, could replicate the assessment of interrater reliability.

The validity information presented in the manual is difficult to evaluate. A principal components analysis was computed, but not cross-replicated. This should have been easy to do with such a large sample. Cross-replication of an eight-factor solution is especially important when there is doubt about the reliability of the scales. Factor scores are mentioned, but directions for scoring the factors are not provided.

Criterion validity was reported, but the reader is left to interpret the results by reading a series of tables with incomplete information. One of the criteria, The Rutter Behavior Scales, is not likely to be familiar to readers. The Children's Personality Questionnaire (CPQ) is more likely to be familiar, but a correlation matrix between the FTT subscales and CPQ scales would have been more informative. Using an ANOVA/t-test strategy, they created various groups and looked for differences between those groups using the eight FTT factor scores. Most of the comparisons were nonsignificant. On the positive side, some of the factor scores showed age and gender differences. The manual also reports analyses of differences between learning disabled children versus normal children, and mentally retarded children versus normal children using the 26 subscales as dependent variables. These results are presented more succinctly, but their implications for test interpretation are not systematically explored.

The information presented in the validity section provides little guidance in helping users understand the meaning of the scores, and no help in distinguishing between low, average, high, or very high T-scores. Not providing this kind of guidance undermines the time-consuming process of scoring responses according to intensity level in the first place.

The qualitative analysis focuses on typical content analytic material. In addition to suggestions for coding defenses and lists of common conflicts that appear in each set of cards, a helpful summary of the common responses to each card is also provided. This summary helps the user quickly begin to identify the elaborations that tend to be psychologically meaningful. Although thematic analysis is inherently vague, this part of the manual reflects greater expertise than do the quantitative sections.

SUMMARY AND CONCLUSIONS. Projective instruments are intuitively appealing. The notion that test takers have to draw on their own internal psychological processes to make an ambiguous stimulus meaningful reaches back to the earliest days of scientific psychology. That this kind of "projection" occurs is not particularly controversial, but extracting the projected information in a reliable and valid way is difficult. Projective test developers have been attempting to justify their tests psychometrically for many years now, but the risk of attempting quantitative applications is that inadequate psychometric outcomes always reflect poorly on the test as a whole.

The Fairy Tale Test appears to have been an ambitious and clever project, but I do not believe that it was yet ready for publication. According to the reference list in the manual, none of the studies on the FTT have been published in peer-reviewed journals. Standards of reliability for using an instrument in research are lower than standards for using it in clinical practice, and a test that does not seem ready to produce journal-level research probably does not meet basic standards for clinical use. Once an adequate sample size is available, those subscales that cannot be shown to have adequate temporal stability should no longer be scored. Findings that cannot be replicated should not be used to guide interpretation. At present, the quantitative version of the test does not appear to be scientifically valid for either diagnostic evaluation or measuring change in personality, contrary to suggestions made in the manual.

As long as one is willing to accept thematic content analysis, the qualitative application of the test and the various themes it uncovers look fruitful. If diagnosis occurs according to an ego psychology framework involving an analysis of defense, the test offers some interesting options for assessing psychological processes in children. Those results, however, should be used only as interpretive hypotheses, and decisions about children should not be made unless those hypotheses are supported by independent evidence.

[91]
The Five P's (Parent/Professional Preschool Performance Profile) [2002 Update].

Purpose: Constructed to collect teacher and parent ratings of child's observed performance across all domains of development to create a comprehensive profile of child's current level of functioning, to link assessment to goal setting and remediation, to monitor change over time, and to promote home/school collaboration.
Population: Children with disabilities between the ages of 6 and 59 months.
Publication Dates: 1982–2004.
Scores: Standard Index and Percentile scores in six domains of development: Classroom Adjustment, Self Help (Toileting and Hygiene, Mealtime Behaviors, Dressing), Language Development (Communicative Competence, Receptive Language, Expressive Language), Social Development (Emerging Self, Relationships to Adults, Relationships to Children), Motor Development (Gross Motor/Balance/Coordination Skills, Perceptual/Fine Motor Skills), Cognitive Development.
Administration: Individual.
Price Data, 2004: $150 per materials for class of 10 children including 10 sets of scales, 1 user's manual, 10 Information and Directions, 10 graphic profiles, 1 copy

of The Five P's Preschool Annual Goals and Short-Term Instructional Objectives; $45 per training video (25 minutes); $10 per user manual; $25 per copy of The Five P's Preschool Annual Goals and Short-Term Instructional Objectives (bound copy); $45 per technical manual, which includes Index and Percentile Score Tables (2004, 132 pages); $85 per sample packet including assessment packet, training video, research papers and The Five P's Preschool Annual Goals and Short-Term Instructional Objectives.
Foreign Language Edition: Spanish edition available.
Time: (60) minutes.
Comments: Teacher and Parent Observer training protocol and training video available.
Authors: Judith Simon Bloch, John S. Hicks, and Janice L. Friedman.
Publisher: Variety Child Learning Center.
Cross References: For reviews by Annie W. Ward and Steven Zucker of an earlier edition, see 13:127; for a review by Barbara Perry-Sheldon, see 10:116.

Review of The Five P's (Parent/Professional Preschool Performance Profile) [2002 update] by KIMBERLY A. BLAIR, Assistant Professor of School Psychology, Duquesne University, Pittsburgh, PA:

DESCRIPTION. The Five P's System was initially developed by the Variety Pre-Schooler's Workshop (now the Variety Child Learning Center; VCLC) as a naturalistic, collaborative method of evaluating early development in children 2 to 5 years of age with learning, language, and behavior problems.

The Five P's is an observational tool. Parents and teachers are the informants, reporting on the observed performance of the child on 458 developmental skills and interfering behaviors at home and school, respectively. Functioning that falls between 6 months and 60 months is assessed across six domains: Language Development, Social Development, Motor Development, Cognitive Development, Classroom Adjustment, and Self Help Skills. The Developmental Skills on each scale are sequentially listed along age norms based on developmental milestones reported in research literature and VCLC clinical practice. The Interfering Behaviors for each scale contain atypical, problematic behaviors that may interfere with a child's learning.

The Five P's is described by the authors as easy to learn and use, does not require highly technical or costly training, and takes a relatively short time to complete. A training video is available to supplement a short training presentation to a group or individual.

The rating scales are completed independently by parents and teachers during a specified observational period (a 2-to-4-week period is recommended). The test items describe specific observed developmental skills and interfering behaviors that are rated as: *Yes* = always or usually true of their child, *Sometimes* = sometimes true of their child, and *No* = never or rarely true of their child. The child's demonstrated performance on the developmental skills and interfering behaviors is to be rated for all behaviors through his or her age level as well as for all interfering behaviors.

Raw scores for the Developmental Skills are converted to index scores and percentile ranks. The Five P's provides norm tables for children between 24 and 59 months of age. These norms can be used to calculate standard scores for both parent and teacher ratings. Raw scores for Interfering Behaviors are converted to one of three categories: Normal Range, At Risk, or Clinically Significant.

Three reports can be generated by the user or by the Variety Child Learning Center: The Share and Compare Report, The Graphic Profile, and a Goal Report. The Share and Compare provides a side-by-side comparison of the ratings of both informants regarding the child's skill achievement and interfering behavior across domains; this report facilitates selection of instructional goals and objectives and a means of monitoring the child's progress over time. The Graphic Profile is an item-by-item visual representation of the child's strengths or gaps in performance across all domains of development.

The Share and Compare Report and the Graphic Profile can then be used to develop a Goal Report. Interfering Behaviors and/or Developmental Skills may be designated as instructional objectives. A goal bank entitled The Five P's Preschool Annual Goals and Short-Term Instructional Objectives is available to assist the user in linking the results of The Five P's with appropriate instructional goals and objectives.

DEVELOPMENT. The development of The Five P's evolved over time while being used with the VCLC's student population and has been a result of ongoing research by the VCLC. The Developmental Skills and Interfering items on each scale are reported to be derived from VCLC clinical practice and developmental milestones re-

ported in research literature. Items are reported to have come from standardized tests, assessment scales, and source books in early child development. The specific resources used are referenced in the technical manual.

The idea of "judgment-based assessment," analogous to clinical judgment, is fundamental to The Five P's philosophy. The Five P's relies upon judgments of teachers and parents regarding the developmental skills displayed by the child at home and school. The Five P's was founded on the belief that evaluations of young children under 5 years of age are most valid when they include reports by familiar adults, based on observations about the child's behavior in their natural environment across time.

TECHNICAL. Several studies are reported that provide reliability, validity, and standardization information. Much of the psychometric data from the original version of The Five P's are reported to support reliability and validity of scores. The revised edition of The Five P's reports new standardization data that yield index and percentile rank scores. Norms were developed from the standardization of The Five P's on a national sample of over 1,000 typically developing children between 24 and 59 months of age.

Test-retest, internal reliability, and interrater reliability studies are reported to evaluate whether The Five P's is an adequately reliable measure for use in making educational decisions regarding placement and intervention planning. Reliability studies were conducted using a national, random sample of 370 diverse children with disabilities ranging in age from 20 months to 7 years. Test-retest reliability estimates for teachers on The Five P's subscales fell above +.90, with the exception of the Classroom Adjustment, which fell at +.87 (administration interval = 2–3 weeks). For parents, test-retest reliabilities ranged between the mid +.80s and the mid +.90s. For teachers and parents, Cronbach's alpha estimates for internal consistency reliability fell above +.90 for all domains, with the exception of teacher ratings for Classroom Adjustment, which fell in the mid +.80. A study of interrater reliability comparing 17 teachers and 25 assistant teachers found correlation coefficients between .92 and .96 across domains.

There is considerable evidence of validity provided for both teacher and parent ratings on The Five P's. To examine content validity, the content of The Five P's was generated using a variety of sources including established research, related tests and measures, and the professional observations and judgments; pilot studies were conducted in the early 1980s and with the assistance of several consultants, items were revised and refined. Concurrent validity was investigated in 1988/89 using a sample of 55 predominantly Caucasian children with disabilities. Coefficients for concurrent validity ranged from .40 to .70 when compared with ratings on similar measures. Extensive evidence of construct validity is reported from several factor analyses. For teacher ratings, the authors report that factors emerged for Motor Development and Self Help Skills, Language and Cognitive Development, and Social Development. For parent ratings, factors are reported for Language and Cognitive Development, Motor Development and Self Help Skills, followed by Social Development.

COMMENTARY. The appeal of The Five P's is a direct result of the theoretical basis on which it was developed. Fundamental to The Five P's philosophy is the idea of "judgment-based assessment" and the belief that evaluations of young children under 5 are most valid when they include reports by familiar adults and are based on observations about the child's behavior in their natural environment across time. This approach not only provides authentic information about a child's development, it facilitates a collaborative relationship between parents and teachers, as well as clinicians.

This revised edition includes many enhancements to the original version. For example, the available supplementary reports enhance the utility of this measure in developing Individual Education Plans and making placement decisions. Additional psychometric data are also provided, including a large, diverse normative sample of typically developing children. Using this sample, additional factor analyses are presented to further support the measure's construct validity.

SUMMARY. The Five P's provides a comprehensive, collaborative approach for evaluating young children with learning, language, and behavior problems. Parents and teachers are the informants, reporting on the child's observed developmental skills and interfering behaviors in their natural environment across time. Several supplementary reports are available that help to close the gap between assessment and intervention. It is clear that the authors have put forth much effort to improve both the technical and practical characteristics of this instrument. The result is an appealing, user-friendly, and psychometrically sound instrument that offers a wealth of valuable information needed in making important educational decisions.

Review of The Five P's (Parent/Professional Preschool Performance Profile) [2002 Update] by LISA F. SMITH, Associate Professor, Psychology Department, Kean University, Union, NJ:

DESCRIPTION. The Five P's (Parent/Professional Preschool Performance Profile) [2002 Update] is intended for use with children between the ages of 6 and 60 months who are at risk of learning, language, and behavior problems and for whom standardized testing is not sufficient. The assessment is based on independent, simultaneous observations by the child's parent and teacher. The data are meant to augment clinical evaluations, such as those made by an Individual Education Program (IEP) team, to help establish goals and interventions in school and at home.

The Five P's assesses six developmental domains, using 13 scales composed of 458 items. The six domains are: Classroom Adjustment, Self Help, Language Development, Social Development, Motor Development, and Cognitive Development. Only the teacher completes the Classroom Adjustment Scale; both the primary parent/caretaker and the teacher complete all scales in the remaining five domains. Within each scale, items are divided into Developmental Skills and Interfering Behaviors. The items for each of the Developmental Skills scales are grouped according to ages of 6–11, 12–23, 24–35, 36–47, and 48–60 months. Age groupings are not provided for the Interfering Behaviors; no rationale is provided for this. Items may be added as needed.

The Classroom Adjustment Scale measures skills necessary for making the transition from home to school and for success in a classroom. Sample items include, "Tolerates familiar transitions from one activity to another in the classroom" from the Developmental Skills and, "Cries a lot when in school" from the Interfering Behaviors.

The Self Help domain contains three subscales: Toileting and Hygiene, Mealtime Behaviors, and Dressing. Sample items include, "Feeds self with fingers" from the Developmental Skills and "Places nonedibles (e.g., dirt, paint) in mouth or eats them" from the Interfering Behaviors.

The Language Development domain contains three subscales: Communicative Competence, Receptive Language, and Expressive Language. The authors note that parental ratings in the Communicative Competence Scale may be higher than those of the teacher. Sample items include, "Uses words to engage others" from the Developmental Skills and "Does not respond to name" from the Interfering Behaviors. The Social Development domain contains three subscales: Emerging Self, Relationships to Adults (Primary Care Givers, Familiar Adults, and Unfamiliar Adults), and Relationships to Children. The authors note that parent/teacher discrepancies on the Relationships to Adults Scale are frequent and understandable. Sample items include, "Wants to do tasks by self" from the Developmental Skills and "Has frequent temper tantrums" from the Interfering Behaviors.

The Motor Development domain contains two subscales: Gross Motor/Balance/Coordination Skills and Perceptual/Fine Motor Skills. Sample items include, "Balances on one foot for 5 seconds" from the Developmental Skills and "Constantly touches objects or people" from the Interfering Behaviors.

On the Cognitive Development Scale sample items include, "Matches identical pictures" from the Developmental Skills and "Forgets or loses learned skills" from the Interfering Behaviors.

The user manual is easy to understand. Items are scored as Yes/No/Sometimes. One concern is whether the teacher of an older child can accurately rate early behaviors if there is no prior experience with the child. The user manual advises the teacher to rely on information from the parents in this situation, which may produce unwanted variability or even bias.

Data are compiled into two reports. The Share and Compare Report shows parent and teacher ratings side-by-side by item. The Graphic Profile uses colored bars to represent parent and teacher ratings for each Developmental Skills and Interfering Behaviors subscale. Results are used to complete an Annual Goals and Short-Term Instructional Objectives form.

DEVELOPMENT. The Five P's was initially designed by the Variety Child Learning Center (VCLC) for its student population. Its development dates to the 1970s/early 1980s. The authors

state that it meets federal standards for parental involvement as required under the Individuals with Disabilities Education Act.

TECHNICAL. The reliability studies are somewhat outdated; they were conducted during 1986 and 1988 on a sample of 63 teachers, 290 parents, and 370 children with disabilities from California, Florida, Illinois, Indiana, Maine, and New York. The authors assert that this sample represents the major geographic regions of the country. However, Florida may not be representative of the South. The sample was randomly selected from among those children whose parents gave consent for the studies. The authors acknowledge that the demographics of the sample may not be representative of the population of children with disabilities. The majority of the children were male (63%), Caucasian (65%), and spoke English as a first language (92%). No ethnicity data were available for 21% of the children and no family income data were available for 26% of the children. Parents' education levels were missing for a large portion of the sample, as well.

Test-retest reliabilities at 2 to 3 weeks were calculated for a random sample of approximately 37% of the children. Correlations are given by gender and for the total sample. For teacher ratings, coefficients range from a low of .85 for boys on the Classroom Adjustment Scale to low/mid .90s on all other scales. For parent ratings, coefficients range from .83 for boys on the Social Development Scale to .94 for girls on the Language Development Scale. Comparisons were calculated on subgroups tested during the fall or spring. Reliabilities on teacher ratings range from a low of .86 for the fall group on the Classroom Adjustment Scale to low/mid .90s on all other scales. For parent ratings, reliabilities are lower in the fall (.84, Motor Development to .90, Social Development); spring ratings range from .80 on the Social Development Scale to .95 on the Motor Development Scale. Cronbach's alphas for the scales show similar patterns for the teacher ratings. For parents, all ratings are in the low/mid .90s. Teacher ratings from an interrater reliability study conducted in 1994 on a random sample ($n = 59$, aged 26–59 months) from VCLC yielded coefficients in the .90s.

Adequate evidence of content validity is demonstrated through reports of input from parents, teachers, and experts leading to item development and refinement over time. Evidence of concurrent validity is based on a study completed in 1988/89 with a small sample (n = 44 males, n = 11 females). The Five P's and the Vineland Adaptive Behavior Scales (Sparrow, Balla, Cicchetti, & Harrison, 1984) were completed by the parents and teachers; the McCarthy Scales of Children's Abilities (McCarthy, 1972) and the Burks' Behavior Rating Scales (Burks, 1977) were completed by the school psychologists. Demographics of the sample and their parents may not be representative of the population. On the Developmental Skills Scales, parent and teacher correlations are reported as significant at alpha = .01. However, the lack of a Classroom Adjustment Scale corresponding to that on The Five P's prohibited comparison in that area. Future studies might correct this by using the AAMR Adaptive Behavior Scale—School, Second Edition (Lambert, Nihira, & Leland, 1993). For the Interfering Behaviors, The Five P's and the Burks' Behavior Rating Scales were compared. Of 40 possible comparisons, there were 17 significant correlations each for teacher and parent ratings in the areas of Coordination, Intellect, Attention, and Impulse Control.

Evidence of construct validity for the Developmental Scales is based on factor analyses using the 1986 sample. For teacher ratings, three factors account for 86.6% of the variance clustering around motor skills, language and cognition, and interpersonal skills. For parents, 83.7% of the variance is explained with a four factor solution; the fourth factor relates to self help. Factor analyses using larger and more recent samples (n = 1,018, 1990–2000; n = 495, 2000–2001) included the Interfering Behaviors and provide evidence that the Developmental Skills are distinct from the Interfering Behaviors.

The tables of norms are based on a standardization sample collected from 1990–2001. Data came from 210 classes in 80 schools in 21 states representing nine geographic regions. Conversion tables to obtain index and percentile scores for the Developmental Scales are easy to read. For the Interfering Behaviors Scales, raw scores are interpreted according to three categories: Normal Range, At Risk, or Clinically Significant.

COMMENTARY/SUMMARY. Overall, The Five P's appears to meet its objectives. Updated reliability studies with a representative sample are needed. The bibliography also needs to be updated. A Spanish version of The Five P's is available but is not part of this review. When used as part of an evaluation, The Five P's should add valuable information to an at-risk child's profile.

REVIEWER'S REFERENCES

Burks, H. F. (1977). Burks' Behavior Rating Scales: Preschool and Kindergarten. Los Angeles: Western Psychological Services.
Lambert, N., Nihira, K., & Leland, H. (1993). AAMR Adaptive Behavior Scale-School (2nd ed.) Austin, TX: PRO-ED.
McCarthy, D. (1972). McCarthy Scales of Children's Abilities. New York: The Psychological Corporation.
Sparrow, S. S., Balla, D. A., Cicchetti, D. V., & Harrison, P. L. (1984). Vineland Adaptive Behavior Scales. Circle Pines, MN: American Guidance Service.

[92]

Fox in a Box: An Adventure in Literacy.

Purpose: "A diagnostic classroom assessment ... measur[ing] literacy development as defined by specific, observable end-of-semester benchmarks ... to inform teachers' instructional planning."

Population: Grades K–2.

Publication Date: 1998.

Administration: Individual.

Levels, 6: 1 (midyear Kindergarten), 2 (end of Kindergarten), 3 (midyear Grade 1), 4 (end of Grade 1), 5 (midyear Grade 2), 6 (end of Grade 2).

Price Data, 2002: $295 per complete kit including 12 Leveled Readers, Individual Literacy Progress Reports and Student Folders, Teacher Tools and Child Cards, Teacher's Guide (48 pages), Training Video, Fox Puppet, and flip-top storage box; $25 per 25 Literacy Progress Reports; $25 per 25 Student Folders; $28.50 per Teacher's Guide; $32 per set of Child Cards; $32 per set of Teacher Tools; $108.10 per 12 Readers; $30 per Training Video; $28.50 per Fox Puppet.

Time: (35) minutes per child for individual activities; 80 minutes collectively for small group activities.

Comments: Test is administered over a 2–3 week period of time; includes individual and 3 group activities; online Fox in a Box e-Management and Reporting System reports, aggregates, and archives each student's literacy progress, allowing teachers to enter student data into a PC or Mac, or on a handheld PDA device and into a secure web-based environment; website manages data and generates multiple reports including class, grade, school, district, state, and individualized home reports.

Author: CTB/McGraw-Hill.

Publisher: CTB/McGraw-Hill.

a) LEVEL 1.

Scores, 6: Measures attainment of 6 benchmarks in 4 learning strands: Phonemic Awareness, Phonics (Alphabet Recognition, Alphabet Writing, Spelling), Reading and Oral Expression, Listening and Writing.

b) LEVEL 2.

Scores, 8: Measures attainment of 8 benchmarks in 4 learning strands: Phonemic Awareness,

Phonics (Alphabet Recognition, Alphabet Writing, Spelling, Decoding), Reading and Oral Expression (Sight Words, Reading), Listening and Writing.

c) LEVEL 3.

Scores, 5: Measures attainment of 5 benchmarks in 3 learning strands: Phonics (Spelling, Decoding), Reading and Oral Expression (Sight Words, Reading), Listening and Writing.

d) LEVELS 4–6.

Scores, 6: Measures attainment of 6 benchmarks in 3 learning strands: Phonics (Spelling, Decoding), Reading and Oral Expression (Sight Words, Reading, Reading Fluency), Listening and Writing.

Review of the Fox in a Box: An Adventure in Literacy by MILDRED MURRAY-WARD, Professor, Department of Advanced Studies, California Lutheran University, Thousand Oaks, CA:

DESCRIPTION. Fox in a Box: An Adventure in Literacy was designed as a teacher-administered individual diagnostic assessment of children's early literacy. The purpose of Fox in a Box is to inform teachers' instruction of children in kindergarten through Grade 2. During the test, the teacher uses a fox puppet to present tasks to the children. The Fox in a Box test is packaged in a kit containing the fox puppet, a training video, and five sets of materials: Overview of Activity Benchmarks and teacher's guide, Literacy Progress Records and student folders, child cards, teacher tools, and children's books.

The materials and tasks are organized in six levels, two for each grade (K–2). The teacher's guide presents the appropriate tasks by level within each grade. A total of 19 skills are organized in four strands: Phonemic Awareness, Phonics, Reading and Oral Expression, and Listening and Writing. Each strand has a set of assessment activities conducted in the early fall and spring in each grade. The activities are based on benchmarks to be mastered at the end of each year. For example, fall and spring tasks are based on end-of-year benchmarks. The authors define benchmarks as tasks to be mastered in order to benefit from the next level of instruction. Because of the use of benchmarks, and not normative performances, the test uses a criterion-referenced interpretation. Benchmarks were set with percentage of items correct being mastery. These mastery levels were set with the expectation that 75% to 80% of children could achieve that benchmark.

The teacher's guide provides detailed overviews of the strands and tasks. In addition, detailed directions on the process of assessment, procedures to be followed, and suggestions for managing the classroom during assessment are provided. The authors also developed a training video and strongly urge teachers to view it before test administrations.

Most of the test is administered individually to children and their responses are recorded on the Literacy Progress Record (LPR). The record may travel with students over several years and is organized to allow teachers to determine group and individual student needs.

The teacher's guide contains detailed information on the administration of each test. In addition, sample completed scoring sheets are included for two children with differing levels of literacy development. Each of the sample scoring sheets has completed student responses and notes concerning the quality of the student's performance and its interpretation. In addition, the teacher's guide contains copies of parent letters, blank forms, and grade-level benchmarks, as well as a glossary of terms.

DEVELOPMENT. The Fox in a Box tasks were generated from recommendations from the literature and standards developed for kindergarten through Grade 2 achievement. The authors clearly used those recommendations in developing benchmarks to design the tasks.

The test was field tested in 2000 with a sample of 1,616 children in fall and 1,341 in spring. Each sample included students in kindergarten through second grade, located in 140 classrooms in 21 states and the District of Columbia. The sample contained children of both genders who were from African American, Hispanic, Asian, and other ethnic origins. The children were from predominantly high SES, public schools. The authors did not indicate the degree of match of this sample to the latest U.S. Census.

The initial items and assessment procedures were previewed in an unspecified number of schools across the nation. Based on the feedback obtained from these studies, revisions were made. These included the addition of a training video and the correspondence of the correctness of administration and teachers' scoring. In addition, teachers completed questionnaires regarding administration and quality of the preview editions.

Finally, studies of potential bias were conducted in three ways. First, internal staff reviewed the materials at initial development. Second, final editions were reviewed by these same personnel. Finally, educational professionals representing different ethnic groups reviewed the final edition materials. However, the authors did not report findings from these reviews or changes made to the materials as a result of these reviews.

TECHNICAL. The test is based on the expectation that levels of literacy will increase over time. This expectation was observed in the mean increases in performances of students from fall to spring administrations in each of the three grade levels. Item difficulties also increased over time.

Validity was estimated through studies of the test's content and concurrent validity. Content validity was examined by choosing tasks related to the benchmarks created by the authors. The benchmark strands and activity content were generated by reviews of curricula and discussions with educational experts to determine common educational goals and the knowledge and skills found in early child curricula.

Concurrent validity was estimated by correlations of scores from Fox in a Box with scores from TerraNova. Correlation coefficients generally ranged from .3 to .6. However, the authors offered little discussion of the patterns of correlations found in the studies except to acknowledge differences in test format and note that the magnitudes of the correlations were as expected.

Reliability estimates were determined through internal consistency reliability coefficients (coefficient alpha) and interrater reliability for Listening Comprehension, Writing Development, and Writing Expression. The internal consistency reliability coefficient values were generally in the .70 to .95 range. The interrater reliability was examined through correlations of scores by teachers with a professional rater. The values ranged from .44 to 91.

COMMENTARY. The Fox in a Box test is an interesting teacher-administered assessment for young children. The materials and the use of the puppet provide a clever and eye-catching set of stimuli. The teacher's guide is easy to read and the directions are clear. The suggestions for managing the classrooms while completing these individual assessments are quite helpful.

The scoring is generally easy to complete and record. Achievement tasks are derived from commonly accepted educational goals and curricula. Each content area is justified through literature. Benchmark mastery scores were set for each level and semester, based on the criterion that 75-80% would achieve this performance level. However, the authors caution that these levels reflect curricula and expectations at the time of test development, and that these expectations could change over time.

The evidence provided to support content validity and reliability are acceptable. However, the concurrent validity study with the TerraNova raises some questions regarding the suitability of this test for concurrent validity studies. First, the two tests do not involve completely parallel sets of content. Second, the Fox in a Box is individually administered, whereas the TerraNova is a group achievement test. Finally, the Fox in a Box has a criterion-referenced interpretation; the TerraNova is a norm-referenced test.

SUMMARY. The Fox in a Box test is a well-designed individual student assessment of early literacy. It contains a well-documented set of content and acceptable criteria for task mastery. It will provide detailed information on children's early literacy skills and will support tracking of students' development over time. However, because it is criterion-based, with mastery levels set on curricula that can change over time or vary by state, teachers are cautioned to use the results with great care. Decisions about mastery of a literacy area should be evaluated in light of local and state curricular standards and the characteristics of the children being assessed.

Review of the Fox in a Box: An Adventure in Literacy by RAYNE A. SPERLING, Assistant Professor of Educational Psychology, and CYNTHIA R. BOCHNA, Doctoral Candidate in Educational Psychology, The Pennsylvania State University, University Park, PA:

DESCRIPTION. The Fox in a Box Literacy assessment is designed for use as a classroom-based diagnostic literacy assessment primarily for kindergarten through second-grade children. Fox in a Box is intended to assess individual literacy skills and to inform classroom curriculum. The assessment was designed by the content experts who developed the widely adopted literacy benchmarks that are the basis of the end of year accomplishments presented in the National Reading

Council (NRC) report *Preventing Reading Difficulties in Young Children* (Fox in a Box Technical Report 1, 2001). The assessment battery is directly administered by the primary classroom teacher and contains four strands composed of both individual- and group-administered measures. The assessment kit contains a fox puppet to model activities for the child, a training video, a chart of activity benchmarks, a teacher's guide, and child cards for administration that include alphabet cards, vocabulary cards, sight words, and passages for oral reading fluency. Additional teacher tools include spelling dictation cards, a marking reading accuracy card, and listening comprehension passages. Twelve books are also included as part of the assessment. The package contains literacy progress records to record assessment results and student folders to store these records and children's work samples and self-portraits. The provided teacher's guide includes master copies of a letter to parents, record sheets, spelling sheets, and writing sheets.

Fox in a Box assesses four literacy strands. Within each strand several skills are assessed. The Phonemic Awareness strand includes rhyme recognition and generation, syllable clapping, initial and final consonants, and blending and segmenting. The Phonics strand includes alphabet recognition and writing, spelling, and decoding. The Reading and Oral Language Expression strand includes sight words, concepts of print, emergent reading, reading accuracy, reading comprehension, oral expression, and reading fluency. The Listening and Writing strand includes listening comprehension, writing expression, and writing development.

Administration time for the Fox in a Box assessment entails approximately 30 minutes of individual administration and ranges, depending on age, from 65 to 90 minutes of group administration. The assessment system is designed for administration twice during each of the kindergarten through second grade academic years but may also be appropriate for older readers who are not at benchmark levels. Individual raw subscale scores are provided for each student, and teacher observation of performance is recorded at each administration time. Benchmarks are provided for each scored subscale.

DEVELOPMENT. The Fox in a Box assesses early literacy from a skill-based perspective. The strands assessed are those commonly identified as important for literacy success (e.g., Hoffman

et al., 2000) and the assessment methods used in the Fox in a Box assessment kit are similar to those commonly used in existing measures (e.g., Robertson & Salter, 1997). The assessment comprehensively covers known pertinent early literacy skills. The technical report (Fox in a Box Technical Report 1, 2001) notes that the publishers piloted preview editions of the assessment package in classrooms across the nation. No direct information is provided in the technical report, however, regarding pilot administration or item development and refinement procedures.

TECHNICAL. The separate technical report (Fox in a Box Technical Report 1, 2001) provides psychometric information regarding the assessment. The report indicates that approximately 3,000 students divided into three geographical zones, North, South, and West, in 21 states and the District of Columbia were included in two sample studies for reliability and validity analyses. Reasonable attempts were made to have a nationally representative sample. It is unclear, however, how the zones were developed and the representation across zones is discrepant. The sample also included a large proportion of both private school children and higher SES students. Although relevant, these limitations of the sample do not warrant substantial concern because existing research literature and practice includes items much like those presented in the Fox in a Box assessment and current accepted benchmarks suggest these types of items are appropriate for the grade levels given.

Internal consistency reliability was reported for the multi-item activities within each assessment strand. Across grade levels and across strands these reliability estimates are generally adequate for use in benchmarking or as components of a larger assessment context for individual readers. Where reliabilities were lower, such as with the Fall Kindergarten assessments in the Phonemic Assessment strand, or with reading and oral expression across the grades, these were expected. Interrater reliability estimates were provided for listening comprehension, writing expression, and writing development. These reliability values are of some concern. The majority of these were low (some less than $r = .50$) and these reliability estimates were also inconsistent from Fall to Spring.

Item difficulty levels and mastery percentages are also included in the technical report. These indicate areas where the activities and strands are relatively easy or difficult for learners as well as the percentage of students from the sample who were able to master particular tasks. These data are important for those administering and interpreting the assessment and illustrate the importance of the technical report data. The most current technical report data should be examined prior to administration and should be considered when interpreting findings.

Intercorrelation coefficients average in the moderate range and lend support that the assessment taps independent constructs within each strand. Some within-strand correlation coefficients are unexpectedly low. A subset of the sample was also administered components of the TerraNova standardized assessment to address construct validity. The technical report indicates that correlations between the TerraNova and the Fox in a Box assessment were as expected. Many of the correlations reported, however, are lower than expected by these reviewers.

Some administration strategies were built into the assessment package to address reliability and validity. These include very clear directions for administration including teacher administration scripts and a training video.

COMMENTARY. One of the primary strengths of the Fox in a Box is the breadth of the assessment. Educators can use the Fox in a Box to assess a comprehensive array of early literacy skills with one assessment. An additional strength of the assessment for practice is the ability for the assessment to follow learners through administrations in a single folder for 3 academic years. This allows teachers to access and share critical information regarding reader's skills.

In addition to some validity concerns, the format of two activities within the Phonemic Awareness strand may be problematic. First, the use of a single, very common, target word (i.e., cat) in the rhyme recognition activity is different than other common rhyme recognition tasks that employ multiple target words (e.g., Robertson & Salter, 1997). Second, the rhyme generation activity provides sentences that contain target words for which the learner must generate a rhyming word. The use of sentences confounds the generation task. Often rhyme generation tasks provide target words, without the context of a sentence, and learners generate a rhyming word or nonword response for each target word.

One drawback of the Fox in a Box assessment for standard classroom practice is the administration time. Although described as an informal assessment, Fox in a Box takes considerable instructional time and the teacher's administration and recording times are substantial. It is unlikely that the classroom teacher can provide this much assessment per child for an entire class. The assessment is appropriately designed for use for entire class or school populations. It could, however, easily be administered directly to those for whom additional early literacy information might be needed, such as those thought to be below or above benchmark level. In many school settings, with limited time and resources, this may be the most common use of the assessment.

SUMMARY. The Fox in a Box K-2 Literacy Assessment system provides a means for classroom teachers to test and document the pertinent early literacy skills known to be crucial for early reading success. The assessment is appropriate for administration to most learners and allows for modification, if necessary, to meet the individual needs of learners. When used in conjunction with other informal and formal assessments, Fox in a Box is recommended as a means to assess and track individual learners' literacy progress and for use to inform curriculum. It is not suggested for use as a means to make comparisons between groups of learners. The assessment is further not appropriate as a means to evaluate individual teachers or schools.

REVIEWERS' REFERENCES

Fox in a Box Technical Report 1. (2001). Monterey, CA: CTB-McGraw-Hill.
Hoffman, J. V., Baumann, J. F., Afflerbach, P., Duffy-Hester, A. M., McCarthey, S. J., & Ro, J. M. (Eds.). (2000). *Balancing principles for teaching elementary reading.* Mahwah, NJ: Lawrence Erlbaum Associates.
Robertson, C., & Salter, W. (1997). The Phonological Awareness Test. East Moline, IL: LinguiSystems, Inc.

[93]

Functional Assessment and Intervention System: Improving School Behavior.

Purpose: "Designed to enable interdisciplinary staff (school psychologists, teachers, counselors, and support staff) to systematically identify the intent or function of a student's challenging behaviors and gain a clear understanding of his or her needs."

Population: Early childhood through high school.

Publication Date: 2004.

Acronym: FAIS.

Scores: No scores.

Administration: Individual.

Forms, 2: Social Competence Performance Checklist, Classroom Competence Observation Form.

Price Data, 2004: $85 per complete kit including manual (177 pages) and 25 record forms.
Time: (10) minutes for Social Competence Performance Checklist; (15–30) minutes for observation and support plan development.
Comments: Components of the FAIS can be used with Outcomes: Planning, Monitoring, Evaluating (15:178) for planning interventions.
Author: Karen Callan Stoiber.
Publisher: PsychCorp, a brand of Harcourt Assessment, Inc.

Review of the Functional Assessment and Intervention System by ROBERT W. HILTONSMITH, Professor of Psychology, Radford University, Radford, VA:

DESCRIPTION. Functional behavioral assessments (FBAs) refer to a collection of methodologies for obtaining information about antecedents, behaviors, and consequences, with the intent of identifying the reason for the behavior and developing strategies that will support positive student performance while reducing the behaviors that interfere with the child's successful functioning (Witt, Daly, & Noell, 2000). Nelson, Roberts, and Smith (1998) note that the purpose of an FBA is to identify the functions of a student's behavior in relationship to various school, home, or community settings. The 1997 revisions of the Individuals with Disabilities Education Act (IDEA) specify that school assessment team members must conduct FBAs when a student has been suspended or placed in an alternative setting beyond 10 consecutive days, and when a student with a disability is being considered for certain disciplinary measures (Hardman, Drew, & Egan, 2004). The main purpose of the Functional Assessment and Intervention System (FAIS), according to the publisher, is "to enable interdisciplinary staff (school psychologists, teachers, counselors, and support staff) to systematically identify the intent or function of a student's (early childhood through high school age) challenging behaviors and gain a clear understanding of his or her needs" (manual, p. 1). In addition, the FAIS can assist in determining "contextual factors associated with a student's challenging behavior and social competence" (manual, p. 1), identifying potential events and conditions that should be modified to better fit the intervention to the student needs, designing and applying functionally derived interventions for challenging behavior

and social competence, monitoring the student's progress, and evaluating outcomes and planning future steps in working with the student.

The FAIS consists of the manual; five major assessment components or tools that are designed to assist in the development of the functional assessment, intervention planning, and outcomes evaluation process; as well as a Benchmark Planner and a procedural checklist that aid in the use of the FAIS. The main tool is the record form. This form may be completed by an individual consultant, such as a school psychologist, or collaboratively by a team, and provides the "organizational framework and operational structure for the functional assessment process" (manual, p. 6). The five-step functional assessment process is clearly delineated on the record form and includes: (a) Identify the concern, function of the behavior in question, and positive alternative behavior; (b) set meaningful goals and benchmarks; (c) develop a positive support plan; (d) implement the support plan and monitor progress; and (e) evaluate outcomes and plan next steps. In addition to the record form, the FAIS consists of a referral form, an Interview Guide, a Social Competence Performance Checklist, and a Classroom Competence Observation Form.

The manual notes that "numerous school professionals at multiple sites" (manual, p. 7) provided feedback about the time needed to complete the FAIS. The feedback indicated that this time varied widely based on a number of factors, but generally "all teams completed the functional assessment process in less time than it typically takes to conduct a traditional evaluation of a student's level of cognitive functioning and academic achievement" (manual, p. 7).

DEVELOPMENT. The FAIS manual clearly discusses the basic assumptions associated with functional assessment and how these assumptions guided development of the instrument. Focus groups involving over 200 educational professionals from a variety of disciplines were used to identify challenges in conducting effective functional behavior plans. These challenges were used to generate the main FAIS components and procedures. The manual then notes that "field-testing was conducted with students whose backgrounds and characteristics varied in ethnicity, culture, language, developmental age, social and economic conditions, and community setting" (p. 11), though no other information is given about this sample. The manual then mentions that additional field-testing and focus group feedback were used to refine the various components of the FAIS, resulting in a "comprehensive package that is empirically and theoretically sound, yet practical for planning and monitoring meaningful interventions" (p. 11). Because the record form is the linchpin of this system, the manual provides considerable detail about the assumptions and goals that informed the development of this component of the FAIS. The development and administration of all FAIS components, however, is articulated quite clearly in the manual.

TECHNICAL. Because the FAIS is a qualitative instrument that does not yield a score that distinguishes students who are in need of a functional assessment or special education, many of the components do not lend themselves to traditional approaches to determining reliability and validity. However, because the Social Competence Performance (SCP) Checklist is a behavioral rating scale (which the manual says can also be used independently), "evidence was gathered to support the use of the SCP Checklist in prioritizing concerns and monitoring progress" (manual, p. 22). To this end, data on internal consistency and interrater reliability for the SCP Checklist are presented, as well as evidence for content, criterion-related, and convergent validity. Internal consistency estimates were derived from a group of 298 educators and also from a limited sample of 30 parents. Estimates ranged from .82 to .97, with most estimates in the high .80s to mid-.90s. Likewise, interrater reliability estimates for a limited sample of 10 teacher dyads that rated 30 students ranged from .90 to .95. These estimates taken together provide evidence of good reliability for the SCP Checklist. In terms of content validity, items for the SCP Checklist were developed after an extensive literature review and within a multidimensional definition of social competence that emphasized "the presence of positive, prosocial competencies and the absence of problem behaviors" (manual, p. 23). The criterion-related validity of the SCP Checklist was investigated in a study of teachers of 300 students. The teachers were asked to group students into three academic/behavioral groupings (top third of class, middle, or bottom third). A series of discriminant function analyses found evidence to support the usefulness

of the SCP Checklist in sorting students with both positive behavior ratings and challenging behavior ratings from their teachers. Evidence for sorting students according to academic performance is lower, as expected, because the Checklist was developed primarily for students with social and behavioral difficulties.

The manual includes a section on the use of the SCP Checklist to monitor and document students' responses to intervention and to determine intervention effects. Although the sample sizes were small, change score data support the notion that "the students with challenging behavior who had functional assessments and positive support plans showed a significant increase in social competence based on teacher ratings at post-intervention" (manual, p. 28). The manual goes on to conclude that the SCP Checklist "is sensitive to change related to intervention effects and is a useful measure for monitoring progress" (p. 29).

Evidence of convergent validity for the SCP Checklist is also presented. SCP Checklist totals for Positive Behaviors and Challenging Behaviors of 42 children, rated by 18 teachers, were correlated with two corresponding indexes on the Behavioral Assessment System for Children (BASC; Reynolds & Kamphaus, 1992). All four intercorrelations were in the expected direction, and three of four were significant. In terms of academic functioning, SCP Checklist totals for 75 children were correlated with Academic Skills and Academic Enablers scores on the Academic Competence Evaluation Scales (ACES; DiPerna & Elliott, 2000). As expected, there was a significant correlation between positive behavior ratings on the SCP Checklist and academic competence on the ACES.

COMMENTARY. The FAIS appears to be a promising instrument for teachers, early childhood educators, school psychologists, counselors, and other professionals who must conduct functional assessments of children in a systematic and practical way. Through the use of focus groups, the instrument was constructed with the needs of practitioners firmly in mind. It addresses current IDEA mandates for functional behavioral assessment plans, and also helps practitioners develop and monitor interventions that are firmly rooted in evidence-based strategies.

SUMMARY. The Functional Assessment and Intervention System (FAIS) is a comprehensive set of assessment tools that enables a variety of school professionals to identify the intent or function of a student's challenging behaviors, both behavioral and academic, and develop, monitor, and evaluate interventions to help self-regulate challenging behaviors and enhance competencies. The instrument lends itself well to the multidisciplinary nature of most school-based teams as well as current mandates in education to develop interventions that are based on sound practice and are empirically verifiable.

REVIEWER'S REFERENCES

DiPerna, J. C., & Elliott, S. N. (2000). ACES: Academic Competence Evaluation Scales (K–12). San Antonio, TX: The Psychological Corporation.
Hardman, M. L., Drew, C. J., & Egan, M. W. (2004). Human exceptionality: School, community, and family (8th ed.). Boston: Allyn & Bacon.
Nelson, J. R., Roberts, M. L., & Smith, D. J. (1998). Conducting practical behavioral assessments: A practical guide. Longmont, CO: Sopris West.
Reynolds, C. R., & Kamphaus, R. W. (1992). Behavior Assessment System for Children. Circle Pines, MN: American Guidance Service.
Witt, J. C., Daly, E. M., & Noell, G. (2000). Functional assessments: A step-by-step guide to solving academic and behavioral problems. Longmont, CO: Sopris West.

Review of the Functional Assessment and Intervention System by DANIEL C. MILLER, Professor of Psychology, Texas Woman's University, Denton, TX:

DESCRIPTION. The Functional Assessment and Intervention System (FAIS) is a broad-based set of tools designed for educators to systematically identify a child's behaviors of concern, select meaningful goals and desired outcomes, develop a positive behavioral intervention plan, monitor the child's progress, and evaluate the child's needs based on the response to the intervention(s). The FAIS is designed for use with school-aged children, early childhood through high school.

The complete FAIS includes a 177-page manual, 25 record forms, and 25 Social Competence Performance Checklist forms. The manual includes a set of reproducible forms including a Referral Form, an Interview Guide, a Classroom Competence Observation Form, a Benchmark Planner, a Procedural Checklist, and a Manifestation Determination Form. The completion time for the FAIS varies based on the complexity of the behavioral concerns being addressed. The author reported that the FAIS record form, the Social Competence Performance Checklist, and the Classroom Competence Observation Form take approximately an hour to complete. The amount of time required to develop and monitor the targeted behaviors will vary from one child to another.

The FAIS incorporates a five-step process. The FAIS record form is the primary form used in the recording of the five steps; however, the supplemental forms in the manual may be used to gather additional information. The FAIS record form is typically completed by a school psychologist, educational professional, or collaboratively by a school-based team. Step 1 involves the identification of the primary concern(s) (the optional Interview Guide may be used), the context in which the behavior(s) occur (the optional Classroom Competence Observation Form may be used), the consequences or effects of the behavior(s), the functions of the behavior(s), identification of competencies and positive alternatives (the Social Competence Performance Checklist may be used), and the development of a summary statement. Step 2 involves setting meaningful goals and benchmarks toward the goals. Step 3 designs a positive support plan that encompasses environmental strategies, teaching strategies, and altered response strategies. Step 4 is the implementation of the strategies for the positive support plan and specifies the progress-monitoring procedures, the criteria for goal attainment, and a record sheet for progress-monitoring. Step 5 evaluates the outcomes of the positive behavioral intervention(s) that includes summarizing the student's progress towards the goal(s), analyzing the overall progress, planning the next steps, designing new strategies as warranted, specifying special education considerations if applicable, and a section for summarizing the final team recommendations.

DEVELOPMENT. The initial development of the FAIS began in the late 1990s by involving educators in focus groups. The goal of the FAIS author was to address the weaknesses to current approaches to functional behavioral assessment that were identified by the focus groups. The FAIS procedures and directions were clarified and modified as a result of the developmental focus groups. The FAIS is qualitative and descriptive in nature and it is theoretically driven. As a result, the FAIS does not generate traditional norm-referenced scores or technical data.

TECHNICAL.

Standardization. The FAIS was field-tested with approximately 200 professionals from 35 different interdisciplinary teams across urban, suburban, and rural settings.

Reliability. The FAIS manual does provide some technical data on the Social Competence Performance Checklist (SCP), a component part of the overall measure. Evidence for the internal consistency of the SCP was reported. The SCP Checklist coefficient alphas ranged from .94 to .97 on the Total Positive Behavior Ratings and the Challenging Behavior Ratings based on teacher ratings of a group of students in rural and urban schools (n = 298). The internal consistency reliability estimates ranged from .85 to .96 for the subscales as well. A very small sample of parents (n = 30) was used to evaluate the SCP Checklist for internal consistency and the coefficient alphas were similar to those obtained based on the teacher ratings.

Evidence of the interrater reliability of the SCP was also reported. Ten pairs of teachers each rated the behavior of 30 students at the same point in time. The interrater reliability coefficients on the SCP were .90 for the Positive Behavior Ratings, .93 for the Challenging Behavior Ratings, and .95 for the Total SCP Checklist Score.

Validity. Evidence for the content validity of the SCP Checklist, one component of the FAIS, was provided by the feedback of the focus groups during the course of development. The criterion-related validity was also examined. Teachers of 300 students were asked to group their students into three academic/behavioral groupings that fit into the categories of top third of their class, middle third of their class, or bottom third of their class. A series of discriminant functional analyses were conducted to validate the criterion relationships, the teacher ratings of class ranking, with the SCP Checklist ratings. The SCP Checklist ratings correctly classified 77% of the Appropriate Positive Behaviors and 83% of the Challenging Behaviors based on the rankings of the teachers. The SCP Checklist ratings correctly classified 70% of the Positive Academic Behaviors, and 67% of the Challenging Academic Behaviors. The SCP correctly identified only 55% of the bottom 1/3 of academic achievers. The author noted that the SCP Checklist was principally designed to measure students with behavioral and social difficulties, not necessarily academic difficulties, which may account for the lower discriminative power of the test for the challenging academic behaviors.

In the FAIS manual, the mean scores for the SCP Checklist for the same 300 students used in the discriminant validity study were reported based on referral type (either behavioral, academic, or both). The mean data for the different groups were used to provide support for the uniqueness of

the ratings of the behavioral competencies versus the academic competencies. A significant correlation of -.39 between the Positive Behavior Ratings and the Challenging Behavior Ratings provided support for the uniqueness between these two scales.

The FAIS manual reported a study that evaluated the effectiveness of the SCP for progress monitoring. A group of 12 kindergarten teachers each selected two children, one with challenging behaviors and one they considered typical, and rated them using the SCP. A positive behavioral intervention plan was implemented for 8 to 10 weeks for the group of students with behavioral concerns. The SCP was completed on all students at the end of the intervention period. Students with behavioral concerns and who received the targeted interventions showed significant increases in positive behaviors and significant decreases in challenging behaviors when compared to the students with no behavioral concerns and who received no targeted interventions.

Evidence of convergent validity for the SCP Checklist component of the FAIS was also provided in the FAIS manual. The SCP Checklist was correlated with the Behavior Assessment System for Children (BASC; Reynolds & Kamphaus, 1992) using a sample of 18 teachers rating 42 kindergarten children. Significant correlations were reported between the BASC Adaptability Index and the SCP Positive Behavior Scale Total (r = .37, p < .05), the BASC Adaptability Index and the Challenging Behavior Scale Total (r = -.54, p < .01), and the BASC Behavioral Symptoms Index and the Challenging Behavior Scale Total (r = .40, p < .05). The SCP Checklist was also correlated with the Academic Competency Evaluation Scales (ACES; DiPerna & Elliott, 2000) using a sample of 75 students. The SCP Positive Behavior Scale correlated with the ACES Academic Skills scale (r = .54, p < .01), and with the ACES Academic Enablers scale (r = .58, p < .01). The SCP Academic Performance Scale correlated with the ACES Academic Skills scale (r = .73, p < .01) and with the ACES Academic Enablers scale (r = .39, p < .01). The SCP Challenging Behaviors scale correlated with the Academic Enablers scale (r = -.32, p < .05).

The FAIS manual also included some convergent validity data that evaluated the relationship between the SCP scales and curriculum-based measures of median words read, median reading errors, and median math scores. The correlations indicated that students with positive behaviors as reported on the SCP had higher median reading scores, lower reading errors, and modestly higher math scores. Students with a higher number of challenging behaviors as reported on the SCP had lower median reading and math scores and higher reading errors. Students with high academic performance as reported on the SCP had higher median reading and math scores and fewer reading errors.

COMMENTARY. The FAIS is a comprehensive set of tools designed to facilitate a functional behavioral assessment and intervention planning for school-aged children. The record forms are well designed and easy to use. The administration manual provides clear instructions and case study examples on how to gather the functional behavioral assessment data, how to translate those data into positive behavioral intervention plans, and how to monitor the progress on the positive behavioral intervention plans. The FAIS is qualitative in design so traditional psychometric properties are difficult to apply. The Social Competence Performance (SCP) Checklist is an important component part of the FAIS and the psychometric properties of the SCP appear to be adequate. It would have been helpful to report the test-retest reliability estimates for scores from the SCP and the overall FAIS if possible.

SUMMARY. The Functional Assessment and Intervention System (FAIS) appears to be a well-designed set of data collection tools for conducting and monitoring functional behavioral assessments. Including test-retest reliability data for all of the FAIS components could strengthen the test. By design the Social Competence Performance (SCP) Checklist may be more useful for identifying and monitoring behavioral concerns rather than academic concerns.

REVIEWER'S REFERENCES

DiPerna, J. C., & Elliott, S. N. (2000). ACES: Academic Competence Evaluation Scales (K–12). San Antonio, TX: PsychCorp.
Reynolds, C. R., & Kamphaus, R. W. (1992). Behavior Assessment System for Children. Circle Pines, MN: American Guidance Service.

[94]

Gates-MacGinitie Reading Tests®, Fourth Edition, Forms S and T.

Purpose: Designed to assess students' "general level of reading achievement."

Population: Grades K.7–12 and adults.

Publication Dates: 1926–2000.

Acronym: GMRT®.

Scores, 11: Literacy Concepts, Oral Language Concepts, Letters and Letter/Sound Correspondences, Listening Comprehension, Initial Consonants and Consonant Clusters, Final Consonants and Consonant Clusters, Vowels, Basic Story Words, Word Decoding, Vocabulary/Word Knowledge, Comprehension.

Administration: Group.

Levels, 11: PR (Pre-Reading), BR (Beginning Reading), 1, 2, 3, 4, 5, 6, 7/9, 10/12, AR (Adult Reading).

Forms, 2: S, T.

Price Data, 2005: $78.75 per hand-scorable test booklet package (Levels PR–3) including 25 test booklets, one Directions for Administration, one Booklet Scoring Key, one Class Summary Record, and one Decoding Skills Analysis for (for Levels 1 and 2 only, specify level and form); $119.25 per machine-scorable test booklet package (Levels BR–3); $141.50 per Level PR machine-scorable test booklet package (scored by publisher for an additional fee) including 25 est booklets, one Directions for Administration, and materials needed for machine scoring (specify level and form); $78.75 per reusable test booklet package (Levels 4–10/12 and AR) including 25 test booklets, one Directions for Administration, one Booklet Scoring Key, and one Class Summary Record (specify level and form); $113.50 per machine-scorable answer sheet package (Levels 4–10/12 and AR; scored by publisher for an additional fee) including 100 answer sheets and materials for machine scoring (specify level); $42.75 per self-scored answer sheet package (Levels 4–10/12 and AR) including 25 answer sheets and one Class Summary Record (specify level); $380.75 per self-scored answer sheet package (Levels 4–10/12 and AR) including 250 answer sheets (specify level); $10.75 per extra copy of Directions for Administration (specify level); $21 per Manual for Scoring and Interpretation (specify level); $14.50 per Linking Testing to Teaching: A Classroom Resource for Reading Assessment and Instruction (specify level); $25.75 per Technical Report; $475 per Score Converting and Reporting Software (for PC only).

Time: (55–100) minutes.

Comments: Norms tables available on CD-ROM.

Authors: Walter H. MacGinitie, Ruth K. MacGinitie, Katherine Maria, and Lois G. Dreyer.

Publisher: Riverside Publishing.

Cross References: See T5:1072 (55 references) and T4:1022 (13 references); for a review by Mark E. Swerdlik of the third edition, see 11:146 (78 references); for reviews by Robert Calfee and William H. Rupley of an earlier edition, see 9:430 (15 references); see also T3:932 (77 references) and 8:726A (34 references); for reviews by Carolyn L. Burke and Byron H. Van Roekel and an excerpted review by William R. Powell of an earlier edition, see 7:689.

Review of the Gates-MacGinitie Reading Tests, Fourth Edition, Forms S and T by KATHLEEN M. JOHNSON, Psychologist, Lincoln Public Schools, Lincoln, NE:

DESCRIPTION. The Gates-MacGinitie Reading Tests, Fourth Edition, Forms S and T (GMRT-4) comprise the most recent version of this norm-referenced reading achievement test series. It includes subtests for assessing essential literacy skills based on current research (National Reading Panel, 2000). The test series was developed for group administration but can also be used with individual students. The main purpose of the series is to measure the general level of student reading achievement, according to the authors. They suggest that when complemented by other reading data, the test results are the basis for decisions such as: selecting students who need further diagnosis, instruction or advanced placement, planning an instructional emphasis or grouping, providing feedback to students, assessing new students in a school, evaluating instructional programs, and reporting reading results to parents and community. The authors recommend the GMRT-4 for use with individuals in kindergarten through early college/young adult.

The GMRT-4 is composed of specific subtests that vary somewhat across the grade levels based on the key skills that are being assessed. The subtests at the Pre-Reading (PR) Level include: Literacy Concepts (20 items), Oral Language Concepts (20 items), Letters and Letter/Sound Correspondence (30 items), and Listening (Story) Comprehension (20 items). At the Beginning Reading (BR) Level, the subtests are: Initial Consonants and Consonant Clusters (15 items), Final Consonants and Consonant Clusters (15 items), Vowels (15 items), and Basic Story Words (25 items). The Level 1 (first grade) subtests include: Word Decoding (43 items) and Comprehension (39 items). At Level 2, the subtests are Word Decoding (43 items), Word Knowledge (43 items), and Comprehension (39 items). The subtests for Levels 3, 4, 5, 6, 7/9, 10/12, and Adult Reading (AR) are Vocabulary (45 items) and Comprehension (48 items). Alternate forms (S and T) are provided for testing at Levels 2 through AR, whereas one form (S) is provided for PR, BR, and Level 1. The youngest norm group used was spring of kindergarten. For Levels BR through 10/12 the standardization testing occurred in the fall and spring. Quarter-month norm tables were created by interpolation to allow for testing at other times during a school year. The on-level norms allow for assessment of students with the "typical" range of grade level skills and the out-of-level norms allow for assessment of students with significantly more or less developed skills. For example, Level 7/9 is most appropriate for students in 7th, 8th, or 9th grade, but out-of-level scores are available for students in Grades 5 to 12 if such testing seems necessary.

Administration time for the GMRT-4 is specified for each subtest along with recommendations about the number of testing sessions needed for each level. Most levels require two sessions with a total of approximately 100 minutes including material distribution and verbal instructions. At the youngest levels, three sessions and 15–30 more minutes may be needed; there is no exact time limit and students may finish at various times.

For each level and form from PR through AR the test materials consist of: the test booklet, the Directions for Administration manual, the Manual for Scoring and Interpretation, and the Linking Testing to Teaching manual. In each Directions for Administration manual, a brief summary of the series is provided, as well as a detailed description of and rationale for each specific subtest at that particular level. The authors provided a clear description for the examiner/teacher about how to prepare for the testing (e.g., scheduling the sessions, space and supervision considerations, the materials needed) and general directions (e.g., how to use practice items, dealing with problems during testing, make-up testing for students who are absent). The specific test administration instructions are printed in dark, bold print and are easy to read and follow. The directions and all the items are read to the students at Levels PR and BR. At all other levels, the directions are read to the students and the students read the items on their own and work independently. The Manual for Scoring and Interpretation has a summary of the scoring procedures and a description of the types of scores and scoring options available for the test series.

The Linking Testing to Teaching manual provides at each level a detailed discussion of the rationale for each subtest and why students might score poorly on each subtest. Various instructional activities are also detailed to help address reading deficiencies. Additional materials available include:

the technical report for the entire Fourth Edition, norms tables on CD-ROM, score-converting and reporting software, and various kinds of test booklets and scoring keys. For Levels PR through 3, machine-scorable test booklets (which can be sent to Riverside for scoring or scanned locally with a license or softare purchase) and hand-scorable test booklets (for use with the booklet scoring key included) are available. For Levels 4 through AR, the GMRT-4 has a traditional answer sheet (which can be sent to Riverside, scanned locally, or scored with a transparent template) and a self-scorable answer sheet.

Five types of scores are provided for the test results: normal curve equivalent, percentile rank, stanine, grade equivalent, and extended scale score. These scores are available for each subtest and for total reading at each level except Pre-Reading and Beginning Reading. At these two lowest levels all five types of scores are available only for total reading; stanine scores are available for each subtest at the PR and BR levels. A variety of optional report plans and services are available through Riverside Publishing. Scores are based on the standardization testing that used the traditional fall and spring testing administrations although interpolated quarter-month norms have been developed for year-round testing use.

DEVELOPMENT. The GMRT-4 technical report describes the test development in detail; in addition, some details are referenced as available in the GMRT, Third Edition (MacGinitie & MacGinitie, 1989) material rather than provided in the current report. The development included pilot studies (particularly for the new subtests and for subtests containing new content and/or forms), field testing (with thousands of students for the equating studies), and the gathering of expert input (from test users, measurement specialists, curriculum specialists, and cultural specialists). Thorough efforts were made to address issues such as item selection, wrong answer selection, effective use of pictures/illustrations (e.g., at the earliest levels), and bias review. Differential item functioning (DIF) analysis along with cultural consultants provided the basis for item acceptance or elimination with regard to bias issues.

A specific blueprint was developed for each subtest and level so that essential variables would be represented in the item pools. The following are some examples: (a) vocabulary items were chosen to roughly approximate the proportions of similar parts of speech in the English language, (b) comprehension passages/items were newly selected for the Fourth Edition and not carried over from the Third Edition, (c) comprehension passages cover a wide range of content (e.g., fiction, science, humanities) and types of writing (e.g., narrative, expository, setting), and (d) the use of appropriate readability levels. The sampling procedures and the standardization sample are described in the technical report and indicated that a nationally representative sample was utilized. During 1998 and 1999, approximately 65,000 kindergarten through 12th grade students and approximately 2,800 adults (first year community college students) participated in the standardization process. Testing data were collected during both fall and spring each year. More than 30,000 students participated in the equating studies to examine the relationships between the adjacent test levels, the alternate forms and the Third and Fourth Editions of the GMRT. A description of the score derivation processes was also included in the technical report (e.g., interpretation and use of the extended scale scores, establishment of the quarter-month norms).

TECHNICAL. Test reliability data are presented in the technical report. The reliability estimates indicate strong total test and subtest internal consistency levels with coefficient values at or above .90 for the total tests and the subtests at all levels except AR (Adult Reading): Form S—Vocabulary .88 and Comprehension .89, Form T—Vocabulary .89 and Comprehension .89. Alternate form correlations for the total test scores were at or above .90 at all levels except for Grade 9 (.88) and Grade 11 (.81). Alternate form correlations for the subtests ranged from .74 to .92. Stability correlations were calculated for several thousand students who participated in testing with Form S for both fall and spring standardization administrations. The total test coefficient values were at or above .88 for all levels except Grade 12 (.71), BR (.77), and PR (.66). The authors note that at the youngest levels the lower stability values may have resulted from the significant variability in children's prior direct reading instruction.

Content validity was documented through the use of a thorough process of test development to identify the scope of the subtests and identify effective items within subtests (using conventional and item response methods). Item-bias studies were used to eliminate problematic items. Construct validity is supported by the strong intercorrelations between the subtests and their respective total test scores; however, no specific discussion of construct validity is included in the technical report. Similarly, no specific concurrent validity data were presented. The authors infer that the correlations between the Third and Fourth Editions of the GMRT-4 and the similarities between the two editions (in terms of design and development) provide the primary support for the validity of scores from the GMRT-4. They also state that correlations between the Third Edition and other reading tests, the PSAT, SAT, and course grades provide validity data for the GMRT-4 although no specific, current data were provided in the technical report.

COMMENTARY. The GMRT-4 is not only updated normatively but also improved as a reading achievement test series. The directions for administration and scoring procedures are effectively detailed in the materials and there are various scoring options available. The test developers have utilized a useful, picture-based format for the youngest students who may take the test; this allows the test administrator to guide/direct students who have few reading skills and make sure the students are on the item that is being read to them. Other improvements in this edition of the test include: new types of comprehension items included in the PR (Pre-Reading) and BR (Beginning Reading) levels, new post high school norms and detailed guidance as to how teachers can address various instructional needs in the Linking Testing to Teaching manuals. The technical report contains a wealth of psychometric data but could provide more thorough interpretation of some of the data. A definite limitation is that the authors infer adequate concurrent validity for the GMRT-4, but provide no actual data in the technical report; more information is needed in this area. The authors acknowledge that the GMRT-4 test data should not be used in isolation; the test results need to be combined with effective curriculum-based assessment if the overall goal is to provide specific instructional guidance (Good & Kaminski, 2002).

SUMMARY. The GMRT-4 is a well-developed and reliable norm-referenced reading achievement test series, the most recent in the long tradition of the Gates-MacGinitie. It includes subtests for assessing essential literacy skills based on current research from kindergarten through post high school levels (National Reading Panel, 2000). Although developed as a group test, individual administration is also an option. Commercial-scoring, hand-scoring and template-scoring options offer flexibility in its use. The most common uses of this instrument appear to be for measuring norm-referenced reading achievement levels and for reporting normative reading results to parents and community.

REVIEWER'S REFERENCES
Good, R. H., & Kaminski, R. A. (Eds.). (2002). Dynamic Indicators of Basic Early Literacy Skill (6th ed.). Eugene, OR: Institute for the Development of Educational Achievement.
MacGinitie, W. H., & MacGinitie, R. (1989). *Technical Report for the Third Edition of the Gates-MacGinitie Reading Tests.* Itasca, IL: Riverside Publishing.
National Reading Panel. (2000). *Report of the national reading panel: Teaching students to read: An evidence-based assessment of the scientific research literature on reading and its implications for reading instruction.* Bethesda, MD: National Institute of Child Health and Human Development, National Institute of Health.

Review of the Gates-MacGinitie Reading Tests, Fourth Edition, Forms S and T by PATRICK P. McCABE, Associate Professor, Graduate Literacy Program, St. John's University, Queens, NY:

DESCRIPTION. This Fourth Edition of the Gates-MacGinitie Reading Tests, Forms S and T (GMRT), assesses reading skills from Pre-Reading though Adult Reading. The battery is composed of four sets of materials. One set consists of grade level tests with accompanying directions for administration. (A useful "test content" summary table in the Directions for Administration at each level outlines the content of the entire battery from knowledge about "literacy concepts" in the Pre-Reading [PR] and Beginning Reading [BR] levels to vocabulary knowledge and comprehension skills appropriate for adult readers.) Second, the Manual for Scoring and Interpretation at each level provides percentile rankings, NCEs, stanines, extended scale scores (useful for tracking growth from level to level), and GEs for both on-level and out-of-level testing. Third, the technical report describes the battery's development, including field-testing, issues related to cultural diversity, a rationale for question selection and sequence, standardization procedures, test reliability and validity, item difficulties, and references supporting the test. Fourth, a Linking Testing to Teaching manual contains instructional suggestions. There is no time limit for Levels PR and BR, and Level 2 takes 75 minutes to administer. All other levels of this group test take 55 minutes to complete. Responses can be scored by hand or machine.

New to the Fourth Edition are the Listening (Story) Comprehension subtest and assessment of rhyming words in the Oral Language Concepts subtest in Level PR, and the entire Adult Reading (AR) level. According to the authors, the purpose of Level AR is to "provide community colleges and training programs with a reading test that, in concert with other assessment, can help locate students in need of improved reading skills" (technical report, p. 6). Selections averaged between Level 7/9 and 10/12 according to the authors.

DEVELOPMENT. The comprehension assessment of the GMRT grew from a constructivist perspective in which reader background information and author information interact during reading. The authors stated, "The aim must be to try to assess how well the student can apply reading skills and prior knowledge to construct an understanding of text" (technical report, p. 18). For the comprehension questions in Levels 3–12, one answer foil was constructed based on reader (likely) "prior knowledge"; a second answer foil, labeled "text-phrase wrong answers" by the authors, was constructed by including a "salient" word or phrase from the passage. Selections were all new to the Fourth Edition.

Vocabulary words for each level were also new to the Fourth Edition. The authors consulted published word lists to select words at each level to "supplement" authors' judgment of word difficulty. In the technical report, the authors reported the close parallel in frequency of parts of speech with the words they selected and other published master lists of frequency of parts of speech.

TECHNICAL.

Standardization. The rigorous standardization procedure included 65,000 students in a stratified random sample during fall 1998 and spring 1999, and adequate detail was presented in the technical report to support the development of the norms. National geographic region, school district enrollment, and socioeconomic status were the variables. The number of students at each grade from K through 10 for the spring standardization ranged from 1,634 (Grade 10) to 3,970 (Grade 2). Grades 11 and 12 had 872 and 941, respectively.

The authors noted their fall standardization sample did not correspond exactly to the national distribution of the variables. Therefore, they weighted the cell numbers to ensure the representativeness of the norms. (This is the usual correc-

tion procedure for such an exigency.) A glance at a distribution of the socioeconomic variable in the sample before the weighting revealed an overrepresentation in the fall standardization of students from high average SES category (48% of total sample) compared to the national percentage (25.6%). For a variety of reasons, school districts or schools may choose not to participate in standardization procedures, and the authors cannot be held responsible for this, especially given the careful procedure they reported for the development of this battery. However, a sentence or two or a technical note explaining the weighting procedure would have been useful. The profile of the spring 1999 sample appeared to align more closely with the U.S. population.

Pilot studies were conducted for the new subtests at the early reading levels (PR, BR, 1, and 2) to determine acceptability of format, content, and time needed. The authors stated, "Pilot studies of the new tests for Levels PR, 1, and 2 were conducted in April of 1995. Classes from all parts of the country participated in the studies" (technical report, p. 1). Although the authors did not present detailed information about the nature of the participating 65 classes in Grades K, 1, and 2 in the pilot testing, they did clearly describe their purpose in the pilot and changes that resulted.

Reliability. Convincing evidence for reliability rested upon three comparisons. Alternate form (S/T) correlations for total (Vocabulary plus Comprehension) scores ranged from .81 at Grade 11 to .95 at Grade 2. Internal consistency reliability for total scores for Form S ranged from .93 at Grade AR (the new test) to .97 at Grade 2. Correlations for total scores on the Third and Fourth Editions ranged from .82 at Grade 10 to .93, shared by Grades 1 and 9.

Table 20 in the technical report provided subtest correlations for Levels PR and BR. These were generally lower than those for Levels 1 and above, but good overall. Of interest was the strengthened intertest correlations from spring of grade K (PR) through spring of Grade 1 (BR). The subtest with the lowest (although still strong) correlation with total test score (.76) was the new Listening Comprehension test. The authors clearly explained (with supporting tables in the technical report) all reliability procedures.

Validity. The authors presented evidence for validity for the Fourth Edition. The major arguments are (a) the high score correlation with the Third Edition, (b) strong validity indicators on the Third Edition, (c) piloting, and (d) the careful procedures in developing the Fourth Edition, including input from teachers. The authors referred the reader to the technical report of the Third Edition for some of this information, a somewhat inconvenient task.

Validity evidence is particularly important, especially for the new tests and subtests included in the Fourth Edition. For this, the authors were careful to describe the development of the new subtests (Listening Comprehension in the PR and Basic Story Words in BR) and of Level AR. As I examined this test, I concur with their argument based on construct validity; however, an attempt to correlate the new sections of the Fourth Edition with other similar formal or informal tests or assessments would have augmented their case for validity.

COMMENTARY. The GMRT, Fourth Edition, is a well-designed reading test battery. Given its multiple-choice response paradigm, this test is an excellent measure of reading ability. Additionally, teachers may find it a useful complement to results of informal criterion- or curriculum-based assessments that include additional methods of assessing reading such as the use of constructed responses. The actual test selections appear to be appropriate for students at each level, the technical report is detailed and comprehensive, and the Linking Testing to Teaching manual is an excellent adjunct to this battery, giving the teacher meaningful direction.

I have some suggestions for a possible next edition of the GMRT. Although analysis of reader's decoding skills is desirable at Level 2, I found the directions for use of the decoding analysis chart for Level 2 to be somewhat confusing.

The comprehension part of Level 1, Form S, directs the child to read sections of a story and to respond to questions without reading the entire story first. I would direct the child to read the entire story before responding to questions about sections. In addition, an analysis chart, similar to the one at Level 2, charting students' comprehension responses in comparison to the question design noted above would add to the power of this test.

SUMMARY. I highly recommend the GMRT. It is an excellent test battery that can be especially useful to school districts to track students' progress, especially because out of level norms are included. This Fourth Edition builds on the work of the previous editions and results in a comprehensive, well-developed test that has value to teachers. The Linking Testing to Teaching manual is also an excellent resource that provides a variety of suggestions for those teachers who might flounder when teaching reading.

Of particular importance in this day of the No Child Left Behind legislation and the emphasis on early reading is the Levels PR, BR, 1, and 2 tests. Taken together, they provide detailed information regarding children's early progress toward proficiency in reading, including a listening test that, in part, measures student's knowledge of story structure. The combined 11 subtests at these levels measure the progression of skills from purposes for reading and writing to knowledge of basic sight words.

[95]
Gifted Rating Scales.

Purpose: Designed to "assess observable student behaviors indicating giftedness."
Publication Date: 2003.
Acronym: GRS.
Administration: Individual.
Price Data, 2003: $125 per complete kit including manual (86 pages), 25 Early Child record forms, and 25 School Age record forms; $75 per manual; $40 per 25 Early Child record forms; $40 per 25 School Age record forms.
Comments: Norm-referenced, teacher-completed rating scale.
Authors: Steven I. Pfeiffer and Tania Jarosewich.
Publisher: PsychCorp, A brand of Harcourt Assessment, Inc.
a) GIFTED RATING SCALE—PRESCHOOL AND KINDERGARTEN.
Population: Ages 4:0 to 6:11.
Acronym: GRS-P.
Scores, 5: Intellectual Ability, Academic Ability, Creativity, Artistic Talent, Motivation.
Time: (10) minutes.
b) GIFTED RATING SCALE—SCHOOL.
Population: Ages: 6:0 to 13:11.
Acronym: GRS-S.
Scores, 6: Same as *a* above with the addition of Leadership Ability.
Time: (15) minutes.

Review of the Gifted Rating Scales by SANDRA A. WARD, Professor of Education, The College of William & Mary, Williamsburg, VA:

DESCRIPTION. The Gifted Rating Scales are teacher-completed rating scales designed to assist in the identification of gifted students. The authors assert that the instrument can be used as a research tool, group screening measure, individual screening measure, or as part of a comprehensive battery to determine whether a student qualifies for placement in a gifted program. The scale consists of two forms. The School Form (GRS-S) is designed for students in Grades 1–8, ages 6:0–13:11. The Preschool/Kindergarten form (GRS-P) is designed for children in preschool and kindergarten, ages 4:0–6:11. Both forms include the following scales: (a) Intellectual Ability, (b) Academic Ability, (c) Creativity, (d) Artistic Talent, and (e) Motivation. The GRS-S includes a sixth scale, Leadership Ability. Each scale contains 12 items that are rated on a 9-point scale, where ratings of 1–3 correspond to below average, ratings of 4–6 correspond to average, and ratings of 7–9 correspond to above average. The manual states that raters should first determine whether the child's specific behavior falls in the below average, average, or above average range. Then, the rater determines whether the child's behavior is at the bottom, middle, or top of that range. The completion time for the GRS-P is 10 minutes or less, whereas the completion time for the GRS-S is 15 minutes or less.

The Gifted Rating Scales are intended to be user-friendly and require minimal training to use and interpret. Teachers who serve as raters must be familiar with the student. It is recommended that raters have 1 month of continuous contact with the student prior to completing the GRS. Specifically, raters should have at least 10 hours per week of contact with the student in order to use the GRS-P and at least 15 hours per week of contact with the student to use the GRS-S. The rating scales are to be completed based on direct observation of the student, and teacher ratings should be based on comparisons with typical students the same age in general education settings. Directions for the completion of the Gifted Rating Scales are clearly printed on the record form. They are straightforward and easily understood. Although the technical manual explains the 9-point scale rating scale and recommended application, this explanation is not included in the directions on the record form.

The GRS-P produces four scale scores (Intellectual Ability, Academic Ability, Creativity, and Artistic Talent) that indicate the likelihood that the child is gifted in one or more areas. The Motivation score is not considered an index of giftedness. Instead, it is a measure of the student's drive, persistence, and desire to succeed. The GRS-S produces five scale scores (the same four scale scores of the GRS-P plus Leadership), and a Motivation index. Raw scores for each scale are easily converted to T-scores with a mean of 50 and standard deviation of 10. Confidence intervals based on standard error of measurement are listed in the norms tables. The user can plot a profile of T-scores across scales on the front of the record form. Classifications are provided based on T-score ranges and cumulative percentages, relative to the average rating within a nationally stratified standardization sample. Scores above 70 correspond to a very high probability of gifted classification, scores between 60–69 correspond to a high probability of gifted classification, scores between 55–59 correspond to a moderate probability of gifted classification, and scores less than 55 correspond to a low probability of gifted classification. The Motivation scale is interpreted separately. Scores above 60 refer to above average motivation, scores between 40–59 refer to average motivation, and scores below 40 refer to below average motivation. The manual includes several case studies that are used to highlight interpretation of the Gifted Rating Scales. Overall, the instrument is easy to administer, score, and interpret. The manual is clearly written and easy to understand.

DEVELOPMENT. The authors are commended for their efforts in test development. The domains of giftedness for the GRS were selected based on the U.S. Department of Education Report, National Excellence: A Case of Developing America's talent (1993). Items for the GRS were developed through careful review and critique of other gifted scales, interviews with experts in the field, and a review of the literature on gifted and talented. A large pool of items was developed and subjected to review by 20 experts in areas of child development, education, school psychology, and gifted and talented development, including both academicians and practitioners. This review resulted in 80 items for the GRS-S and 65 items for the GRS-P. In a pilot study, five school psychologists with experience working with gifted students reviewed these items and assigned them to the most logical gifted category. Items without strong face validity were eliminated. In the first field test, 315 GRS-S and 88 GRS-P forms were completed across four states, including both urban and suburban areas. Items were discarded if their means were too high or if their standard deviations and/or item correlations were too low. In a second field test, 13 Texas school teachers provided input on the revised GRS-P and GRS-S forms. This qualitative feedback helped to eliminate or reword items. Finally, the GRS-S was administered to 250 students, and the GRS-P was administered to 150 students. Analysis of the factor structure, mean scores, bias, interrater reliability, and test-retest reliability resulted in the final item revision.

TECHNICAL. The standardization sample for the GRS-S included 600 children between ages 6:0–13:11. The sample for the GRS-P included 375 children between ages 4:0–6:11. The GRS-S sample was stratified within eight 12-month age bands, and the GRS-P sample was stratified within five 6-month age bands and one 12-month age band (6:0–6:11). Both samples were stratified to match the 2000 U.S. Census for race/ethnicity, parent educational level, and geographic region. Each age band was split by gender. The standardization samples for both the GRS-S and GRS-P closely match the U.S. Census data for race/ethnicity and parent education level. The sample for the GRS-S underrepresented the Northeast region at ages 6 and 13, and overrepresented the South region at age 13. The sample for the GRS-P overrepresented the North Central region and underrepresented the Northeast region at age 5:6–5:11. This sample overrepresented the Northeast region at age 4:0–4:5. All of the students in the standardization sample were in a general classroom setting, and they did not have any disability that prevented them from inclusion in a mainstream classroom. Additionally, the individuals in the sample had no formal classification as gifted. A total of 382 teachers completed ratings for the GRS-S standardization sample, and 90 teachers completed ratings for the GRS-P standardization sample. The teachers who completed the GRS-P and GRS-S for the standardization sample were trained and certified to teach at the grade level of the rated student, and they had opportunity to observe the rated student for a minimum of 1 month.

The internal consistency and test-retest reliability coefficients reported in the manual are sufficient for the intended purpose of the GRS.

Internal consistency coefficients were equal to or greater than .97 for each scale of the GRS-P and GRS-S by age. The standard errors of measurement were relatively small. Test-retest reliability for the GRS-P was computed on a sample of 124 students across age bands with a mean test-retest interval of 18 days. The correlations ranged from .91–.95 for the overall sample. Test-retest reliability for the GRS-S was based on a sample of 160 students with a median retest interval of 7 days. The correlations ranged from .83 (Artistic scale) to .97 (Academic scale) for the overall sample. Interrater reliability for the GRS-P ranged from .70–.84. Interrater reliability for the GRS-S ranged from .70–.79 for ages 6:0–9:11 and from .64–.75 for ages 10:0–13:11. The lowest coefficients were for Artistic Ability and Creativity as might be expected. These lower coefficients for interrater reliability raise some concerns about the consistency across different teachers' ratings of the same student.

Data are provided to support the instrument's validity. Support for the test's content validity is demonstrated in the purposeful and thorough approach to item development and selection. Furthermore, the moderate to high intercorrelations among the five GRS-P scales and among the six GRS-S scales suggest a consistent internal structure. The data supporting the validity of the GRS-S and GRS-P also reveal high intercorrelation between the Intellectual Ability scale and the Academic Ability scale. The authors state that previous item level factor analysis for both the GRS-P and GRS-S indicated that the items on both the Intellectual Ability scale and the Academic Ability scale loaded on one principal factor with all Intellectual Ability items loading consistently above the Academic Ability items. This indicates one, not two, factors. The results of this factor analysis are not reported in the manual. To support the interpretation of the separate scale scores, factor analysis confirming the existence of the separate factors should be performed and reported. Without a factor analysis, the support for the separate scales is unknown. The absence of a factor analysis warrants caution in the interpretation of individual scale scores.

The authors provide evidence to support the convergent and discriminant validity for the GRS-P and GRS-S. The individual scales of the GRS-P and GRS-S were correlated with accepted standardized measures of ability, achievement, creativity, artistic talent, motivation, and leadership (GRS-S only). The validity studies indicated that the scales of the GRS-P and GRS-S correlated significantly with the instruments in these domains. In most instances the appropriate scale of the GRS correlated highest with the instrument being used as the criterion. However, correlations between the test used as the criterion and other scales of the GRS also were significant and not much lower than the correlation with the appropriate scale used as a criterion. These results provide evidence for convergent validity, but they call into question the separateness of the individual scales of the GRS.

The results of several criterion group studies provide support for the criterion-related validity of the GRS-P and GRS-S. These studies compared the GRS-P and GRS-S scale scores of students identified as gifted with GRS-P and GRS-S scale scores of students similar in demographic characteristics who were not identified as gifted. In all three studies, the intellectually gifted group scored significantly higher on the GRS than the control group. It should be noted that the sample sizes for these studies were small, and the results may not be generalizable to the larger population without further research.

COMMENTARY. The Gifted Rating Scales is a useful instrument to assist in the identification of gifted students. The authors adhered to rigorous procedures and standards in the instrument's development. The GRS-P and GRS-S are well standardized. The data support the intended use of the instrument as a screening measure or as part of a comprehensive battery to determine whether a student qualifies for gifted programming. The lower interrater reliability coefficients suggest the need for explicit instructions for teachers who complete the scales to ensure consistency in their understanding of the rating scale. Although validity data for the GRS-S and GRS-P are generally adequate, a factor analysis confirming the existence of the separate scales would strengthen the instrument's validity. Furthermore, the correlations between the scales of the GRS-P and GRS-S with other criterion measures did not strongly support the separateness of the scales. Without confirmation of the separate scales, caution is warranted in their individual interpretation.

SUMMARY. The Gifted Rating Scales are user-friendly instruments that can be completed by teachers to assist in the identification of stu-dents who qualify for placement in a gifted program in Preschool–Grade 8. The rating scales are easy to administer and interpret. The technical adequacy of the instrument, including standardization and reliability, is robust. The content validity and convergent validity of the instrument is adequate. More evidence is needed to support the separate scale scores. Data presented in the manual suggest a considerable overlap of at least two scales. Additionally, correlations between the scales of the GRS and criterion measures do not support the separateness of the scales. A confirmatory factor analysis to support the existence of separate scales is recommended. The GRS can be used as a screening measure or used as part of a comprehensive assessment battery to determine whether a child qualifies for gifted programming. Individual scale scores from the GRS should not be the sole criterion for the identification of giftedness.

[96]
Gilliam Asperger's Disorder Scale [2003 Update].

Purpose: Designed to evaluate children with unique behavioral problems who may have Asperger's Disorder.
Population: Ages 3–22.
Publication Date: 2001.
Acronym: GADS.
Scores, 4: Social Interaction, Restricted Patterns of Behavior, Cognitive Patterns, Pragmatic Skills.
Administration: Individual.
Price Data, 2003: $92 per complete kit including examiner's manual (51 pages) and 25 summary/response booklets; $54 per examiner's manual; $40 per 25 summary/response booklets.
Time: (5–10) minutes.
Comments: 2003 second printing (provided free of charge to all who purchased initial printing) involves modifications to the Summary/Response booklets and examiner's manual including the deletion of the Early Development subscale and the addition of the Parent Interview Form.
Author: James E. Gilliam.
Publisher: PRO-ED.
Cross References: For reviews by Donald Oswald and Theresa Volpe-Johnstone of an earlier edition, see 15:108.

Review of the Gilliam Asperger's Disorder Scale [2003 Update] by CONNIE T. ENGLAND, Department Chair, Grad Counseling & Guidance, Lincoln Memorial University, Knoxville, TN:

DESCRIPTION. Gilliam Asperger's Disorder Scale [2003 Update] (GADS) is an individually administered 32-item behavior checklist designed to be used with persons ages 3 through 22. It is composed of four subscales: Social Interaction, Restricted Patterns, Cognitive Patterns, and Pragmatic Skills, and a Parent Interview Form. Nonclinical staff can administer and score the GADS. However, persons trained in test administration are required for interpretation.

This second printing of the GADS is a revision of the GADS 2001 version. The test developer provides a lengthy rationale for this second printing. Basically due to confusion arising from the earlier version of the "Early Development" standard (which was inversely related to the diagnosis of Asperger's Disorder), this subscale was replaced with the Parent Interview Form. The Parent Interview Form provides information on a child's language and cognitive development and age-appropriate self-help skills, adaptive behavior, and curiosity about the environment. Because children with Asperger's Disorder do not have clinically significant delays in these areas, this information is required for a diagnosis of AD.

Another change to the earlier printing of the GADS is in the criterion used for Asperger's Disorder identification. Previously a raw score of 121 was defined as being "very likely" an indication of Asperger's Disorder. This score was lowered to a raw score of 80 because, according to the GADS examiner manual, 92% of the normative sample had an Asperger Disorder Quotient at least that high. Therefore, it was deemed an appropriate cutoff measure for the "High/Probable" diagnosis of Asperger's Disorder.

The GADS consists of an examiner's manual and a set of 25 summary/response booklets. The manual contains information to administer, score, and interpret the GADS. The manual attempts to provide a consistent definition for Asperger's Disorder by listing both the DSM-IV-TR and the ICD-10 diagnostic criteria. Guidelines for differential diagnosis are also listed for Autism, Rett's Disorder, Childhood Disintegrative Disorder, Mental Retardation, Schizophrenia, Pervasive Developmental Disorder—Not Otherwise Specified, Hearing Impairment, Developmental Language Disorders, and Social Deprivation. The manual contains technical data pertaining to item analysis, demographics of the standardization sample, and reliability and validity information. A list of resources is provided for parents, teachers, and others concerned about persons with Asperger's Disorder.

The manual states that the GADS can be used to (a) identify persons with Asperger's Disorder, (b) assess persons referred for unique behavioral problems, (c) document progress in behavior management programs, (d) identify goals for individual education programs, and (e) measure Asperger's Disorder in research projects.

DEVELOPMENT. Item selection for the GADS was derived from three sources: the definitions for Asperger's Disorder from the *Diagnostic and Statistical Manual of Mental Disorders–Fourth Edition–Text Revision* (DSM-IV-TR; American Psychiatric Association, 2000), the *International Classification of Diseases and Related Health Problems–Tenth Edition* (ICD-10; World Health Organization, 1992), and a review of literature written about Asperger's Disorder. Behavioral characteristics associated with Asperger's Disorder were arranged into two categories: (a) qualitative impairment in social interaction and (b) restricted, repetitive, and stereotyped patterns of behavior. From an initial cadre of 70 items, 32 representing behavioral characteristics associated with Asperger's Disorder were selected.

The normative sample consisted of 371 individuals between the ages of 3 and 22. This admittedly small sample is reasoned to be adequate based on the low incidence prevalence of the exceptionality. Individuals in the normative sample were selected by having teachers, educational diagnosticians, psychologists, and other school district and treatment personnel complete the GADS on students diagnosed as having Asperger's Disorder. Demographic characteristics of the normative sample were based on the characteristics associated with the population of persons diagnosed with Asperger's Disorder and reportedly appear to be representative of that population except for statistics related to race and ethnicity.

TECHNICAL. According to the manual, the GADS produces reliable and valid scores for identification of students with Asperger's Disorder. The Asperger's Disorder Quotient has a mean of 100 and a standard deviation of 15. The subscales have a mean of 10 and a standard deviation of 3. Standard scores are derived from a cumulative frequency table containing raw scores received by the normative sample. The manual states that because no significant differences in frequency data were noted for age or gender, separate normative tables for age and gender were unnecessary. Percentile ranks are also derived from raw scores and indicate the percentage of scores in the normative group that fall at or below the score in question.

The manual stated that for the most part, the GADS demonstrated adequate internal consistency with a variety of diagnostic groups. For the four subscales, coefficient alphas were .70 or better. The only subscale with less than a .70 coefficient alpha was the Early Development subscale, which was replaced with the Parent Interview Form in the current printing. Moderate to strong alphas were reported for the Asperger's Disorder Quotient (ADQ), and based on this analysis, the GADS was deemed appropriate for use in most educational and clinical settings for the diagnosis of Asperger's Disorder.

Standard error of measurement (*SEM*) data calculated for each of the four subscales and for the ADQ revealed an *SEM* of 1 for each of the four subscales and 5 for the ADQ. Based on the test's reportedly strong reliability coefficients and small *SEM*, the GADS was deemed to have adequate internal consistency reliability.

Evidence of stability reliability (i.e., test-retest reliability) was based on a study of 10 students. The results of scores on two separate assessments made within a 2-week period were used to demonstrate adequate stability reliability for the GADS.

Interrater reliability was examined through a study of 16 participants—10 diagnosed with Asperger's Disorder, 4 diagnosed with autism, and 2 diagnosed with learning disabilities. Teachers and parents rated the participants and assessment results were correlated for each pair of ratings. Based on reportedly strong and statistically significant correlations, the test developer inferred adequate test reliability.

Three types of validity studies were reported in the manual: content description, criterion prediction, and construct identification. Content-description validation procedures were based on the process used to identify test items. As earlier discussed in the Development section, definitions for Asperger's Disorder were obtained through literature review of behavioral data associated with characteristics of the disorder and from definitions of the disorder listed in the DSM-IV-TR and the ICD-10. Domain-specific data were collected on all

cases from the normative sample and item analysis conducted. The following median item discrimination coefficients were obtained: .60 for Social Interaction, .56 for Restricted Patterns, .68 for Cognitive Patterns, and .61 for Pragmatic Skills.

Evidence of criterion-prediction validity was examined by demonstrating a relationship between the GADS and the Gilliam Autism Rating Scale (GARS; Gilliam, 1995). Sample data for 50 participants were used to demonstrate a significant positive relationship between GADS' subscales and GARS' subtests. The manual stated that although the magnitude of the hypothesized relationships of the two instruments was significant, the differences were not large enough to account for the majority of the variance. Based on these data, the developer deduced that the two instruments measure similar content, but that each contributed unique information about the individual assessed.

Concurrent criterion-prediction validity was examined via discriminative analyses of GADS scores of different diagnostic groups. On every subscale the Asperger's Disorder sample mean was significantly higher than that of the non-Asperger's Disorder sample. Results of discriminative validity analysis supported correct diagnosis of group membership 83% of the time.

COMMENTARY. The value of the GADS as an instrument for the differential diagnosis of Asperger's Disorder suffers several technical problems. For example, rather than actual event recording, which would provide an objective measure of each behavior's occurrence, the rater's impressions of how often the behavior occurs within a 6-hour period is used (i.e., *never observed*, *seldom observed* [1–2 times], *sometimes observed* [3–4 times], *frequently observed* [5+ times]). Such imprecise recording compromises the robustness of interscorer reliability data. Furthermore, general administration procedures suggest that a "classroom teacher, parent, or other caregiver who has had regular sustained contact with the subject for at least 2 weeks" (examiner's manual, p. 9) is an appropriate rater; that the rater may "accept reliable information from other professionals, parents, or others about items that the rater has not observed directly" (examiner's manual, p. 10); and, that if the examiner is not accustomed to behavior rating scales, he or she should read through the manual at least twice to familiarize himself or herself with both the behavior and frequency definitions. The level of experience with the test taker, the degree of familiarity with the instrument, and the rather imprecise measures of behavior rating all seem to compromise score reliability.

As stated in the *Standards for Educational and Psychological Testing* (AERA, APA, & NCME, 1999), "evolving conceptualizations of the concept of validity no longer speak of different types of validity but instead of different lines of validity evidence, all in service of providing information relevant to a specific intended interpretation of test scores" (p. 5). The *Standards* also emphasize that validity is a matter of degree and involves an evaluative judgment as to whether interpretations and uses of assessment results are justified.

Validity studies supporting content, criterion, and construct identification of the GADS are less than convincing. Although item analysis discrimination coefficients are reportedly acceptable, as previously noted, the procedures for administering and scoring the GADS jeopardize the developer's claim of adequate content validity. Moreover, evidence for criterion validity is based on establishing a relationship between the Gilliam Autism Rating Scale (GARS) and the Gilliam Asperger's Disorder Scale. Data from a sample of 50 participants, 42 diagnosed as having autism, 5 as having mental retardation, and 3 as having Asperger's Disorder were used to support the discriminative powers of the GADS. Based on such a small sample size it is unlikely that adequate data were available to support the GADS' discriminative powers. Clinical investigation used to support construct-identification validity of the GADS was based on small sample sizes, and may lack the discriminative power promised by the GADS' developer to discriminate persons with Asperger's Disorder from other people with behavior disorders.

SUMMARY. To the test developer's credit, consideration of examiners' queries and concerns over the earlier printing's test result interpretation has resulted in adjustments to both the summary/ response booklet and the test manual. Adjustments were also made of the criterion (from a raw score of 121 to a raw score of 80) used to differentiate those persons likely to have Asperger's Disorder from those who may have other conditions. Unfortunately, reliability and validity studies conducted to support the psychometric soundness of the GADS are limited. The utility of the GADS seems to be as a tool for developing Individual Education Plan (IEP) goals and for research purposes rather than for the differential diagnosis of Asperger's Disorder.

REVIEWER'S REFERENCES

American Educational Research Association, American Psychological Association, & National Council on Measurement in Education. (1999). *Standards for educational and psychological testing.* Washington, DC: Author.
American Psychiatric Association. (2000). *Diagnostic and Statistical Manual of mental disorders—Fourth edition—Text revision.* Washington, DC: Author.
Gilliam, J. E. (1995). Gilliam Autism Rating Scale. Austin, TX: PRO-ED.
World Health Organization. (1992). *International classification of diseases and related health problems* (10th ed.) Geneva, Switzerland: Author.

Review of the Gilliam Asperger's Disorder Scale [2003 Update] by CAROL M. McGREGOR, Associate Professor of Education, Brenau University, Gainesville, GA:

DESCRIPTION. The Gilliam Asperger's Disorder Scale (GADS) was developed as a standardized, norm-referenced rating scale of behaviors and characteristics that assist in the diagnosis of Asperger's Disorder (or Syndrome) and other severe behavioral disorders in individuals ages 3–22. The possible uses listed for this instrument include: identification of individuals with Asperger's Disorder, assessment of individuals referred for unique behavioral problems, documentation of progress due to intervention programs, development of goals and objectives for educational planning, and for research purposes.

This present update (2003) of the test that was published in 2001 is in response to users' concerns with the scoring and use of the Early Development subscale. The author states that the interpretation of this subscale was not included in the 2001 GADS manual and caused considerable confusion. Because of this the decision was made to eliminate the Early Development subscale and replace it with the Parent Interview Form, which includes questions addressing developmental issues. Several other changes were made, which will be discussed in later sections of this review.

The GADS has four subscales (Social Interaction, Restricted Patterns, Cognitive Patterns, and Pragmatic Skills) made up of 32 items that are based on the current definitions of Asperger's Disorder. The scales offer an Asperger's Disorder Quotient (ADQ) that is based on the sum of subscale standard scores. The Parent Interview Form replaces the supplemental Early Development subscale. It is made up of six questions with various subparts relating to Language Development, Cognitive Development, Self-Help Skills,

Adaptive Behavior, and Curiosity About the Environment. The purpose of this section is to give evidence that developmental delays were not present in the early childhood years because that is important in the diagnosis of Asperger's Disorder. The final section, Key Questions, is designed to summarize findings and check important assessment considerations. Materials include an examiner's manual and an eight-page summary/response booklet.

Standard scores, percentile ranks, and the ADQ are derived from raw scores. Subscale scores have a mean of 10 with a standard deviation of 3; the ADQ has a mean of 100 with a standard deviation of 15. The *SEM* for all subscales is reported to be 1; the *SEM* for the ADQ is reported to be 4.

Higher scores indicate a higher probability of the presence of Asperger's Disorder. An ADQ of ≤69 indicates Low/Not Probable, 70–79 indicates Borderline, and ≥80 indicates High/Probable probability of the presence of the disorder as indicated in the interpretation guide.

This instrument can be administered by anyone who knows the individual through direct and sustained contact, including parents and teachers. Siblings are mentioned as possible administrators of this scale, which seems to introduce unnecessary possibility of subjectivity and bias in scoring. (For the sake of efficacy, individuals administering and scoring the scale should be familiar with similar type tests.) It can be completed in 5 to 10 minutes.

DEVELOPMENT. The GADS is the second printing of the version of the test published in 2001. The original was modified in response to practitioners who found scoring of the Early Development supplemental subscale confusing with no interpretation of how to use it in the manual. Therefore, the information originally formatted in the Early Development Subscale is now sought through a more informal Parent Interview Form. This section does not produce numerical scores. There is no explanation as to how these questions were decided upon other than they represent important developmental skills in the areas of language and cognitive development, and age appropriate self-help skills, adaptive behavior, and curiosity about the environment.

The author states that item selection was based on the diagnostic criteria for Asperger's Disorder published in the *Diagnostic and Statistical Manual of Mental Disorders, Fourth Edition-Text Revision* (DSM-IV-TR; American Psychiatric Association, 2000); the *International Classification of Diseases and Related Health Problems—Tenth Edition* (ICD-10; World Health Organization, 1992); a review of literature written about Asperger's Disorder; and an inspection of instruments designed to assess the condition of Asperger's Disorder. The experimental version of this scale had 70 items and these were pared down to the remaining 32 items found in the test.

TECHNICAL. The author acknowledges that the sample size of 371 individuals between the ages of 3 and 22 is very small. Participants were sought from school psychologists and other educational staff as well as parents through email contact. There appears to be no verification of diagnosis. The rationale is used that the low incidence of the disorder along with lack of public awareness made data collection extremely difficult. Participants in the normative sample came from 46 states, the District of Columbia, Canada, Great Britain, Mexico, Australia and "other countries" (examiner's manual, p. 21). The ratio of male to female (3-4 to 1) was relatively well adhered to (85% male; 15% female) and racial representation was fair. A large majority of the norming sample was between the ages of 7 and 13, whereas very few samples were represented in ages 20-22.

Item selection was determined by a discrimination coefficient of .05 or above with a magnitude of .35 or above for those items found in the resources described above in DEVELOPMENT. For the subscales, median coefficients ranged from .56 to .68 and were all significant at the .01 level.

Internal consistency was investigated using Cronbach's coefficient alpha. Coefficient alphas were computed on the diagnostic groups listed as potential recipients of this scale (individuals with Asperger's Disorder, autistic disorder, other disabilities, and normal people). The GADS demonstrates a moderate to strong estimate of internal consistency for all groups. It is interesting that the internal consistency is higher in all other groups than in the individuals with Asperger's Disorder and the *SEM* is higher in the people with Asperger's Disorder. The number of people in each of the other groups is very small, which may affect these statistics. The examiner's manual refers to the Early Development subscale (examiner's manual,

p. 24), which has been deleted from the test and this may confuse some readers.

Test-retest reliability (referred to as stability reliability in the examiner's manual) was reported as .93 for the ADQ. The subscale correlational coefficients ranged from .71 to .77. This test was done on a very small group (*N* = 10) of participants with Asperger's Syndrome and the time interval was only 2 weeks.

Interrater reliability is important when using behavior rating scales. For this study, 16 participants (Asperger's Disorder = 10, autism = 4, and learning disabilities = 2) were rated by 6 teachers and 10 parents. For all subscales and the ADQ, the correlations were significant at the .01 level.

Several types of validity were provided. Criterion-prediction validity was examined by providing a relationship between the GADS and the Gilliam Autism Rating Scale (GARS; Gilliam, 1995), and concurrent criterion-prediction validity was examined by use of discriminative analyses of GADS scores of different diagnostic groups. The *N* for the non-Asperger's Disorder group was 78. Construct validity was evaluated by showing low coefficients of subscales across age. The results indicated a statistically significant score but low in magnitude (all coefficients were between -.08 and .21). A one-way ANOVA was conducted regarding differences due to gender. No difference was found so different norms tables were not required.

COMMENTARY. The author is to be commended for providing a standardized measure to assist professionals in the field in determining presence or absence of Asperger's Disorder. The decision to eliminate the Early Development Subscale also seems a wise move in that its presence seemed to add confusion rather than clarification of diagnostic criteria.

Although there are only 32 items in this scale, the author considers it a diagnostic tool. He also states that it should not be used in isolation, but that with so few items, it might better be considered a screening tool with a diagnostic workup to follow.

Reliability and validity studies support the instrument as representing the construct of Asperger's Disorder. The use of only 32 items to define a disorder across ages 3–22 seems a scant number of items. The author assumes that these items are valid for all age groups. However, in examining the items in the Pragmatics Skills Subscale, in particular, it is evident that the items are above the developmental level of even a normal 3- or 4-year-old. Also, there is no information on final item choice or item factor loadings that influenced the choices.

In that the language style of individuals with Asperger's is so unique, it would seem that evaluation of that component of the disorder would more appropriately be addressed in a subscale than in the informal Parent Interview.

SUMMARY. The GADS is a good beginning with strong research components in an effort to better define a controversial disorder. It is user friendly and does not require substantial time for administration and interpretation. As the author gains more returns for his research in this area, it will be strengthened by a larger *N* in the norming group. The newness of this present printing is an obvious drawback to research studies of its efficacy and overall usefulness by professionals.

REVIEWER'S REFERENCES

American Psychiatric Association. (2000). *Diagnostic and statistical manual of mental disorders-Fourth edition-Text revision.* Washington, DC: Author.
Gilliam, J. E. (1995). Gilliam Autism Rating Scale. Austin, TX: PRO-ED.
World Health Organization. (1992). *International classification of diseases and related health problems* (10th ed.). Geneva, Switzerland: Author.

[97]

Giotto.

Purpose: To provide a wide-ranging measure of personal integrity for use in staff selection.
Population: Adults.
Publication Dates: 1996–1997.
Scores: 7 scales: Prudence, Fortitude, Temperance, Justice, Faith, Charity, Hope.
Administration: Group or individual.
Price Data, 2002: $361.94 per complete set including answer booklet, scoring software, and manual (1997, 79 pages).
Time: (5–20) minutes.
Comments: Must be scored by computer on Giotto software using Windows 3.1 or Windows 95.
Author: John Rust.
Publisher: Harcourt Assessment [England].

Review of the Giotto by EUGENE V. AID-MAN, Senior Lecturer, University of Adelaide, Adelaide, Australia:

DESCRIPTION. Giotto is a 101-item self-report questionnaire designed to assess personality dimensions of work-related integrity. The instrument is based on the Prudentius model of personality and includes the following seven scales: Prudence, Fortitude, Temperance, Justice, Faith,

Charity, and Hope. According to the test developer, Giotto is intended for integrity assessment within a range of work settings, including selection, promotion, appraisal, and staff development. Administration is not timed, taking between 5 and 20 minutes to complete. Manual scoring is not available; the software requires manual data input from paper-and-pencil answer sheets and produces scoring and interpretive reports.

DEVELOPMENT. The instrument's development followed a personality-trait—based approach to integrity testing, with an ancient model of personality, attributed to Prudentius, used to underpin trait selection. The item bank was developed by generating adjective synonyms and antonyms to the model's basic constructs of Prudence, Fortitude, Temperance, Justice, Faith, Charity, and Hope. The test manual claims that the initial exhaustive item bank was "examined by a team of experts … to assess their suitability and relevance to work settings" (p. 49). However, no details of this evaluation procedure are presented (e.g., the size and composition of the expert team remains unknown). A pilot study was then conducted to refine item composition. Apart from its size (N = 43), no other details are known about the pilot sample. Given that item selection was based on an "item extremity score" (p. 50) derived from the pilot sample's endorsement rates, more information about the sample is clearly needed to afford meaningful evaluation of the pilot study.

The resulting item set contains two distinct sections. Part A includes 38 paired ipsative items covering 14 adjective groups (positive and negative poles for each of the seven scales). Each item in Part A consists of 4 adjectives, and the required response is to endorse one of these four that "applies most to you at work," plus to identify a second one "which least applies to you at work." Part B contains 63 unpaired items with a 5-point Likert-type response format ranging from *not in any way like me* to *very much like me*.

TECHNICAL. The psychometric properties of Giotto were evaluated simultaneously with its standardisation. This was complemented by a simulation study of over 7,000 simulated responses to evaluate the effects of Part A item ipsativity.

Reliability. Split-half reliability estimates are reported in the range from .71 for Fortitude to .76 for Hope. It is unclear, however, whether these estimates have been Spearman-Brown adjusted.

No other data on internal consistency are presented. Retest reliability is not reported either.

Validity. Intercorrelations between the seven Giotto scales range from .01 to .49 and, despite staying below the preset target of .5, clearly indicate a latent variable structure. The considerable variance overlap between some (but not all) of the seven Giotto scales raises doubts about their discriminant validity and calls for a multivariate (factor or principal components) analysis to resolve the issue. Content validity is almost self-evident as presented in the test manual. However, no empirical evidence is reported to support this. Correlations with another integrity test, Orpheus (Rust, 1996), are presented as evidence of concurrent validity. A construct validity interpretation for these data appears more appropriate, on two accounts at least. First, the test manual itself presents the low correlations with Orpheus's disclosure scale as evidence of Giotto scales' low social desirability contamination—a finding that clearly belongs to the discriminant validity domain. All other Orpheus scales correlate with their respective Giotto counterparts at between .40 and .61, thus indicating substantial agreement between alternative measures of the same (or similar) constructs—these data are clearly of a convergent validity type. Further evidence of construct validity is presented in a predictable pattern of correlations with the "Big Five" personality dimensions. Unfortunately, the description of validation samples is not always complete. Giotto scales were also correlated with a range of supervisor ratings (N = 432 within the same standardization study), providing some evidence of concurrent (criterion-related) validity.

Standardization. The standardisation sample (N = 701) is reasonably well described (age, gender, and occupational breakdown are presented) and asserted to be representative of the U.K. working population. Giotto standardized scale scores have a mean of 10 and standard deviation of 4. The software converts raw scores into the standard scale scores using linear conversion with the normative sample's mean and standard deviation assumed to represent the respective population parameters. Unfortunately, no evidence of normality in the standardization data is reported: the percentile equivalents are presented on the "assumption of a normal distribution" (p. 18)—but without actually examining it, which renders the percentile conversion table almost useless.

CONCLUSION. Overall, Giotto appears a novel and promising instrument, with a reasonable conceptual foundation and some initial empirical justification. However, evidence of its psychometric soundness, as currently documented, is not sufficient to recommend it for use as a proven instrument until more validation data become available for peer scrutiny (e.g., retest reliability, predictive validity, and empirically constructed normative tables).

REVIEWER'S REFERENCE

Rust, J. (1996). *Orpheus handbook.* London: The Psychological Corporation.

Review of the Giotto by DENIZ S. ONES, Hellervik Professor of Industrial Psychology, and STEPHAN DILCHERT, Doctoral Student, Department of Psychology, University of Minnesota, Minneapolis, MN:

DESCRIPTION. Giotto is a self-report, paper-and-pencil personality-based integrity test. The developers intended it to be used for selection, promotion, appraisal, and development purposes in work settings. Seven attributes asserted to tap into aspects of the overall integrity construct are measured: Prudence, Fortitude, Temperance, Justice, Faith, Charity, and Hope.

Giotto consists of 101 items. Thirty-eight items are composed of four adjectives each; the respondent is instructed to check the one most applicable and strike out the one least applicable. Thus, the first portion of Giotto is composed of ipsative items. The second part of the test presents 63 adjectives, to be endorsed on a Likert-type scale ranging from 1 = *Not in any way like me* to 5 = *Very much like me.*

There are no time limits for administering Giotto. The manual indicates that most individuals complete the test in 5 to 20 minutes. Responses are entered manually into a computer-based scoring program; the software is used to estimate missing data and to standardize responses to norm groups. Little guidance on software operation is given in the technical manual; however, the version reviewed (GIOTTO v1.1 NT Update) is simple and takes only a few minutes to produce scores and a report.

The seven Giotto scales assess different personality traits on a continuum. The Prudence scale assesses the competence versus carelessness aspect of conscientiousness. The Fortitude scale is intended to measure work orientation and industriousness. The traits assessed by the Temperance scale tap into a continuum ranging from self-controlled and nonviolent to hostile. The Justice scale aims to measure fair mindedness, ethicality versus suspiciousness, and resentfulness. The Faith scale evaluates loyalty, obedience, courtesy, trust versus infidelity, arrogance, and vanity. The Charity scale provides an appraisal of compassion, generosity, and benevolence versus envy and spite. The Hope scale assesses initiative, enthusiasm, and optimism.

DEVELOPMENT. The test was developed using a rationalist theory of integrity, based on the model of 4th Century AD philosopher Aurelius Prudentius Clementis. According to this model, within each person, "human nature [is] at war with itself" (manual, p. 35). The seven vices and virtues identified by Prudentius are described as representing bipolar personality traits. However, their links to the broader category of integrity tests in the literature are based on the rational judgment of Giotto's developer.

In developing items, a 234-item trait-relevant adjectival item bank was generated using thesaurus. For the pilot version, 168 items were chosen so that 12 would represent each polarity of every trait. Items were subsequently paired with same-polarity items from different traits. Each adjective pair was administered to 43 people who indicated which of the two best applied to them. Valence of each adjective was determined by computing an extremity score for each pair (i.e., proportion of participants selecting the first adjective *N*). Items were reassigned to pairs where extremity scores were "approximately balanced for desirability" (manual, p. 50). These pairs contributed toward the creation of ipsative tetrads (used for Part A), each representing four of the seven traits (and including two items from each polarity). For Part B, 84 adjectives with lower extremity scores were selected (6 positive and 6 negative items for each trait). Ten marker adjectives for each trait were also added. Overall, 84 ipsative adjective tetrads and 94 endorsement adjectives constituted the 178-item development version of the test.

This version was administered to 701 individuals in convenience samples (including insurance and accountancy personnel, teachers, security guards, firefighters, cashiers, drivers, managers, and clerical workers). Item analyses were used to refine the scales: Reliabilities had to be greater than .70, intercorrelations among scales less than

.50, and correlations with an external lie scale less than .30. Additional refinement resulted in 46 tetrads and 21 adjectives being deleted from the developmental version of the test; however, the technical manual does not provide clear information on how many of these items were excluded for what reasons.

TECHNICAL. The standardization sample of 701 individuals included 480 males and 206 females (mean age = 36.15 years, SD = 13.00). The standardization group generally sampled ethnic groups from the U.K. working population, including 12 Asians, 15 Blacks, and 9 undefined minority individuals.

It is not clear whether or not any of the groups included in the standardization sample were taking the test as job applicants. One of the major intended uses of Giotto is personnel selection. For personality measures, there is evidence that job applicants produce different normative data (Ones & Viswesvaran, 1998a) and hence job applicant norms are essential. Even though part of Giotto is ipsative, it is not obvious that this has actually served to reduce socially desirable responding in job applicant samples. No applicant data are provided, although the correlation with a social desirability scale was .31 among job incumbents.

The relations between Giotto scales and age, sex, and educational level document several correlations in the .20 range. Particularly, the Charity scale appears to correlate positively with sex and age (older individuals and women tend to score higher). Educational level is correlated with the Faith and Hope scales (rs = -.23 and .13, respectively).

The technical manual states "differences between ethnic groups, and between speakers of English as a second language, ... were examined for each Giotto scale using analysis of variance. No significant differences were found" (p. 57). However, statistical significance is a function of both effect size documenting any group differences (e.g., Cohen's d) and the sample sizes of the groups being compared. Considering the number of individuals from ethnic minorities included in the sample, nonsignificance of the group differences may be attributable to small sample sizes. This is not to suggest that large group differences exist on personality or integrity measures (cf., Hough, Oswald, & Ployhart, 2001; Ones & Viswesvaran, 1998b), but to encourage the test publisher to report actual effect sizes rather than a broad statement of nonsignificance.

Split-half reliabilities for the Giotto scales reported for the standardization sample were as follows: Prudence .72, Fortitude .71, Temperance .75, Justice .71, Faith .73, Charity .75, and Hope .76. These values are slightly lower than those reported for other personality inventories (Viswesvaran & Ones, 2000). However, the impact of partial ipsativity of the inventory on these reliabilities is unclear. As Tenopyr (1988) has demonstrated, interscale dependencies in ipsative measures can create spurious internal consistency reliabilities for some scales even when true reliabilities are low. No test-retest reliability estimates are provided.

Several lines of evidence have been offered for validity of Giotto scales. Adjectives with highest loadings on each scale have been presented as evidence for content validity. Construct validity has been examined by presenting convergent and divergent relations with one other personality measure, Orpheus. These analyses confirm the compound nature of most Giotto scales. Further, correlations between Giotto scales and individual items from Orpheus are reported.

The criterion-related validities were investigated in a concurrent study of 432 job incumbents (part of the standardization sample) predicting supervisory ratings of job performance. The observed correlations reported were small, with only the Hope scale producing validities in .10s with theoretically related single-item criteria. Correlations with overall job performance are not reported. It is important to keep in mind that these observed validities are attenuated by range restriction, though no corrections were possible as the standard deviations of Giotto scale scores in job applicant samples are not available. Future studies examining the predictive validities of Giotto scales are essential if the test's usefulness for selection purposes is to be demonstrated.

No data are presented examining differential validity for the test by age, gender, or racial group. However, the necessity of such investigations for personality measures is debatable because typically there do not appear to be large group mean differences on personality scales to trigger allegations of adverse impact in the first place.

COMMENTARY. Giotto is marketed as a psychometrically sound integrity test based on

Prudentius's theoretical model of integrity. Using virtues and vices in defining integrity is not novel, but using a particular depiction of these in creating an integrity test is. The validity and usefulness of such an approach needs to be demonstrated vis-à-vis existing integrity tests.

The author of Giotto provides post hoc linkages between the virtues/vices assessed by the inventory and work behaviors. However, data used to support these assertions are lacking. For example, although the Fortitude scale should theoretically be linked with long-term job commitment, or the Prudence score should theoretically be related to avoiding accidents, such relationships have not been examined. Also, criterion-related validities have not been examined for counterproductive behaviors in general (Ones & Viswesvaran, 2003).

Relationships with existing integrity tests also need to be offered as convergent validity evidence to fully place Giotto as an exemplar of the broad category of integrity tests. We have concerns that part ipsativity of the instrument may have had consequences on reliability, factor structure, and criterion-related validity of the instrument.

Although normative data for the instrument are based on working adults, norms for job applicants are lacking. Additional data are also required to establish the test's usefulness in non-U.K. settings (there are concerns with British English adjectives that may not carry the same meaning in American English).

Nevertheless, Giotto is a personality-based instrument that appears to assess multiple compound personality traits that may be of use in predicting and explaining work behaviors. The test's manual is especially noteworthy in its excellent summary of the integrity-testing literature and in offering substantial test administration advice.

The descriptions and adjectival markers for each scale suggest that the traits assessed can be mapped onto a personality taxonomy that distinguishes between the Big Five, facets of the Big Five, and compound traits (see Hough & Ones, 2001). The Prudence scale appears to assess the dependability facet of conscientiousness. The Fortitude scale evaluates the achievement facet of conscientiousness. The Temperance scale assesses violence potential by combining aspects of emotional stability, agreeableness, and conscientiousness (Ones & Viswesvaran, 2001). The Justice scale appears to measure aspects of both trust (emotional stability and agreeableness) and self control (emotional stability and conscientiousness. The Faith scale appears to assess lack of aggression (agreeableness and conscientiousness), wheras the Charity scale evaluates trust. The Hope scale appears to measure optimism (emotional stability and extraversion).

SUMMARY. Personality-based measures are increasingly being used in personnel selection and placement (Hough & Ones, 2001). There are over 40 integrity tests available to organizations (Ones & Viswesvaran, 1998c). The ideas behind Giotto are interesting. But if the measure is to be used as an integrity test in work settings, both linkages with existing integrity measures and criterion-related validity for counterproductive behavior need to be demonstrated. Particularly, future research will need to be conducted to support the test's use with job applicants.

REVIEWERS' REFERENCES
Hough, L. M., & Ones, D. S. (2001). The structure, measurement, validity, and use of personality variables in industrial, work, and organizational psychology. In N. Anderson, D. S. Ones, H. Sinangil, & C. Viswesvaran (Eds.), *Handbook of industrial, work, and organizational psychology: Vol. 1* (pp. 233–277). London: Sage.
Hough, L. M., Oswald, F. L., & Ployhart, R. E. (2001). Determinants, detection and amelioration of adverse impact in personnel selection procedures: Issues, evidence and lessons learned. *International Journal of Selection & Assessment, 9*, 152–194.
Ones, D. S., & Viswesvaran, C. (1998a). The effects of social desirability and faking on personality and integrity assessment for personnel selection. *Human Performance, 11*, 245–271.
Ones, D. S., & Viswesvaran, C. (1998b). Gender, age and race differences on overt integrity tests: Analyses across four large-scale applicant data sets. *Journal of Applied Psychology, 83*, 35–42.
Ones, D. S., & Viswesvaran, C. (1998c). Integrity testing in organizations. R. W. Griffin, A. O'Leary-Kelly, & J. M. Collins (Eds.), *Dysfunctional behavior in organizations: Vol. 2. Nonviolent behaviors in organizations* (pp. 243–276). Greenwich, CT: JAI Press.
Ones, D. S., & Viswesvaran, C. (2001). Personality at work: Criterion-focused occupational personality scales (COPS) used in personnel selection. In Roberts & R. T. Hogan (Eds.), *Personality psychology in the Workplace* (pp. 63–92). Washington, DC: American Psychological Association.
Ones, D. S., & Viswesvaran, C. (2003). Personality and counterproductive work behaviors. In M. Koslowsky, S. Stashevsky, & A. Sagie (Eds.), *Misbehavior and dysfunctional attitudes in organizations* (pp. 211–249). Palgrave/Macmillan.
Viswesvaran, C., & Ones, D. S. (2000). Measurement error in "big five factors" of personality assessment: Reliability generalization across studies and measures. *Educational and Psychological Measurement, 60*, 224–235.
Tenopyr, M. L. (1988). Artifactual reliability of forced-choice scales. *Journal of Applied Psychology, 73*, 749–751.

[98]

Group Reading Test II (6–14).

Purpose: Designed to monitor progress in reading and to screen and identify pupils who require further diagnostic assessment.

Population: Ages 6 years to 15 years 9 months.

Publication Dates: 1985–2000.

Acronym: GRT II(6–14).

Scores, 2: Sentence Completion, Context Comprehension.

Administration: Group.

Forms, 6: Forms A and B, Forms C and D, and Forms X and Y.

Price Data, 2004: Price data for teacher's guide (2000, 75 pages), At-a-Glance Guide, group record sheet, and record forms available from publisher.

Time: (30) minutes.

Comments: Computer and publisher scoring service available; originally published as Macmillan Group Reading Test.

Author: NFER-Nelson Publishing Co., Ltd.

Publisher: NFER-Nelson Publishing Co., Ltd. [England].

Cross References: For reviews by Koressa Kutsick and Gail E. Tompkins of the Macmillan Reading Test, see 10:179.

Review of the Group Reading Test II (6–14) by C. DALE CARPENTER, Professor of Special Education and Associate Dean, College of Education and Allied Professions, Western Carolina University, Cullowhee, NC:

DESCRIPTION. The Group Reading Test II (6–14) was designed as a short screening instrument for groups of children ages 6 through 15-3 in the area of reading. Although untimed, the manual states that most children finish the test in 30 minutes or less. GRT II (6–14) uses a multiple-choice format and has three different tests in two alternate forms.

Children ages 6 to 9 years can be administered Sentence Completion Forms A and B, two 48-item tests beginning with picture recognition questions and ending with multiple-choice sentence completion questions (example: The ___ bit the man).

Children ages 9 to 15 can be assessed using Sentence Completion Forms C and D or Context Comprehension Forms X and Y. Sentence Completion Forms C and D use the same format as Sentence Completion Forms A and B in the example above and consist of 45 items each. Context Comprehension Forms X and Y are tests where the students are presented with four prose passages with 40 missing words. Five choices are available from which to choose for each of the 40 blanks. Test users are advised to choose between the Sentence Completion Forms C and D or the Context Comprehension Forms X and Y. For test and retest purposes to monitor progress, users are told to use alternate forms of the same test rather than using Sentence Completion at one time and Context Comprehension at another time.

Children are tested in groups with instructions and sample items provided. After examples are completed, children work through the test at their own speed. The test requires children to mark answers by filling in a rectangle by the correct choice. No writing is required of students.

Computerized scoring is available from the publisher. However, manual scoring consists of using the key to count each correct answer. Raw scores are the sum of correct answers. Both reading age scores and standard scores are available using tables in the manual. Standard scores have a mean of 100 and standard deviation of 15. Tables do not show standard scores below 70 or above 130.

DEVELOPMENT. GRT II (6–14) is a revision and partial combination of two different tests. Sentence Completion Forms A and B of the current test were part of the Group Reading Test (6-12) originally published in 1985. Questions were revised to increase difficulty and discriminating ability and were piloted on 300 pupils in Years 4 and 7 in England and Wales. Sentence Completion Forms C and D and Context Comprehension Forms X and Y of the current test were part of the Group Reading Test 9-14 originally published in 1990. Items were updated and revised to increase discriminating ability and piloted on 300 pupils in Years 7 and 8 in England and Wales.

TECHNICAL. Standardization groups for all tests came from England, Wales, Scotland, and Northern Ireland. Schools were both metropolitan and nonmetropolitan. The manual shows the number of pupils with mean ages and number of schools taking each form of each test. The manual states that schools were randomly selected from national registers of schools. Other information on pupils is not provided including gender, race, socioeconomic status, presence of disabilities, or other factors that may affect achievement and would aid in interpreting the relevance of scores for potential users.

The number of students taking both forms of Sentence Completion Forms A and B was 3,524, whereas 2,315 were administered Sentence Completion Forms C and D, and 2,104 pupils participated in testing of Context Comprehension Forms X and Y. Testing for all groups took place in October and November of 1996.

Reliability estimates are provided for internal consistency and alternate form consistency. Internal consistency reliability coefficients range from .82 to .94. The sample used to estimate reliability is not described in the manual including the sample size. Alternate form reliability coefficients computed on unspecified samples between Forms A and B were .79 to .90. Alternate form reliability correlation coefficients for Forms C and D ranged from .87 to .88 and for Forms X and Y, correlation coefficients were .80 to .84. Alternate form reliability was calculated using a sample of 270 pupils in Years 6 and 7 who took Forms A and C yielding a correlation coefficient of .74.

Reliability results lack information about the samples used. Coefficients approach acceptable levels but users have no basis upon which to judge whether the pupils included were appropriate in number and representative of those prospective users might assess.

Validity information is provided in the form of content validity and concurrent validity evidence. Content validity is claimed rather than documented by stating that items on tests assess reading as provided in the National Curricula for England and Wales and for Northern Ireland as well as Scottish 5–14 Guidelines. No other content validity verification is provided including how items were selected and from what theory or domain they were chosen.

To address concurrent validity, mean scores on each of the forms are compared with teacher estimates of reading levels and with National Curricula Test Levels in tables showing the means of each. No coefficients are provided although sample sizes exceed 300 for each form of each test. A review of the tables indicates that higher teacher estimates of reading ability and higher National Curricula Test Levels correspond to higher mean raw scores for GRT II (6–14).

Additional concurrent validity is claimed through correlations of scores on the first editions of the tests with other available tests. These data are only minimally useful to prospective users of the current test because detailed information about the correlation of scores on the second test to scores on the first test is not provided.

COMMENTARY. The GRT II (6–14) compares favorably in format, length, and ease of use to other screening instruments. However, the manual does not state why the format was chosen and what reading factors are assessed. Given the complexity of the reading process, evidence that the GRT II (6–14) assesses reading in a useful way is lacking. Evidence that GRT II (6–14) scores correlate meaningfully with other measures of read-

ing, thus lending confidence and practicality to the results, is scant. The manual states that the GRT II (6–14) does not provide diagnostic information about a pupil's reading ability. Given the test scores and their reputed correlation with teacher estimates of reading ability, the test seems to offer no advantage to teacher judgment. The utility of the GRT II (6–14) for teachers in countries outside of the United Kingdom is not supported by the technical information. Close review of the items supports the conclusion that the test is inappropriate for students in the United States because of unfamiliar use and spelling of words (e.g., practise, flavours) and topics (e.g., ways Americans are different) included.

SUMMARY. The GRT II (6–14) offers alternate form utility for screening reading ability and progress in a group format for children ages 6 to 15 in the United Kingdom. It is not a comprehensive or detailed measure of reading, and technical information is inadequate to judge the utility or stability of scores, particularly for groups of pupils that may include demographic and learning ability diversity. In order for the GRT II (6–14) to be useful to teachers, users would need more information than is provided in the manual.

Review of the Group Reading Test II (6–14) by ALICE J. CORKILL, Associate Professor, Department of Counseling and Educational Psychology, University of Nevada, Las Vegas, Las Vegas, NV:

DESCRIPTION AND DEVELOPMENT. The Group Reading Test II (6–14) is a revised and restandardized version of the Group Reading Test that was published in the United Kingdom in 1985. The test is designed to give school teachers a quick and easy method for assessing the early reading skills of children and to monitor student reading progress up to age 14.

The Group Reading Test II consists of Sentence Completion Forms A and B, Sentence Completion Forms C and D, and Context Comprehension Forms X and Y. Sentence Completion Forms A and B are alternate forms of a test appropriate for use with children ages 6 to 9. Sentence Completion Forms C and D and Context Comprehension Forms X and Y are alternate forms of two tests appropriate for use with children ages 9 to 14.

Sentence Completion Forms A and B include five picture identification items and 43 sentence completion items. The picture identification items require the examinee to look at a picture and determine which of five provided words is the correct word. For example, the examinee sees a picture of a house and must select the word "house" from a list that includes "hall," "horse," "house," "show," and "mouse." The sentence completion items require the examinee to read a sentence in which a word is missing and to select the appropriate word to complete the sentence from five options. For example, the examinee reads the sentence, "The _____ bit the man." and must select the correct word to fill-in-the-blank from the following options: "log," "dog," "car," "bag," or "pen." The items in the sentence completion portion of the test appear to become progressively more difficult as the examinee moves through the test. The final item on Form A of the test, for example, is, "At the end of the performance the enthusiastic audience _____ loudly." The options from which the examinee has to choose are "left," "jeered," "applauded," "remained," and "restrained."

Sentence Completion Forms C and D are similar to Forms A and B except that Forms C and D do not include picture identification items. Sentence Completion Forms C and D include 45 items. Context Comprehension Forms X and Y are tests that require examinees to read a passage in which words are missing. The examinee is required to select the best word for each blank in the text from a set of five alternatives. For example, the examinee would read the following sentences, "Charlotte and Emma were sisters. One day they went to see _____ aunt Susan." The examinee is given the following selections for the blank in the above passage: "his," "her," "their," "them," and "both." Forms X and Y each include four such passages with 10 blanks per passage.

The Sentence Completion tests and Context Comprehension tests appear to be easy to administer and they may be scored by the classroom teacher as a scoring guide is provided in the teacher's guide that accompanies the test. Strictly speaking, the test is not timed, although the teacher's guide indicates that most examinees should be able to complete the test in 30 minutes at most.

The teacher's guide that accompanies the test is well constructed. It provides easy-to-understand information about administering, scoring, and interpreting all forms of the test. The teacher's guide also provides technical information about the test.

TECHNICAL. The Group Reading Test II, Forms A and B, was standardized using 3,524 students from England, Wales, Scotland, and Northern Ireland. The sample was taken from several regions and school types as well as from both metropolitan and nonmetropolitan areas. All students in the standardization sample took both Forms A and Form B, with half completing Form A first and half completing Form B first. Alternate forms reliability and internal consistency reliability (KR21) were calculated. KR21 reliability for Form A ranged from .89 to .95; KR21 reliability for Form B ranged from .90 to .96; and alternate forms reliability estimates ranged from .79 to .94.

The validity of Forms A and B was assessed by comparing: (a) test scores with teachers' estimates of student performance, (b) test scores with scores on other reading tests, and (c) the alignment of test items to National Curricula Guidelines. The comparison of teachers' estimates and comparisons to National Curricula Guidelines suggests that students show a reasonable progression in terms of test scores on the Group Reading Test II from one level to the next. Although the teacher's guide suggests that scores on the new version of the test have been compared to scores on other reading tests, the information reported is for the original version of the Group Reading Test.

The Group Reading Test II, Forms C and D, was standardized using 2,315 students from England, Wales, Scotland, and Northern Ireland. The sample was taken from several regions and school types as well as from both metropolitan and nonmetropolitan areas. All students in the standardization sample took both Form C and Form D. Alternate forms reliability and internal consistency reliability (KR21) were calculated. KR21 reliability for Form C ranged from .85 to .89; KR21 reliability for Form D ranged from .82 to .84; and alternate forms reliability estimates ranged from .87 to .89.

The validity of Forms X and Y was assessed by comparing: (a) test scores with teachers' estimates of student performance, (b) test scores with scores on other reading tests, and (c) the alignment of test items to National Curricula Guidelines. The comparison of teachers' estimates and comparisons to National Curricula Guidelines suggests that students show a reasonable progression in terms of test scores on the Group Reading Test II from one level to the next. Although the teacher's guide suggests that scores on the new version of the test have been compared to scores on other reading tests, no results were reported.

The Group Reading Test II, Forms X and Y, was standardized using 2,104 students from England, Wales, Scotland, and Northern Ireland. The sample was taken from several regions and school types as well as from both metropolitan and nonmetropolitan areas. All students in the standardization sample took both Form X and Form Y. Alternate forms reliability and internal consistency reliability (KR21) were calculated. KR21 reliability for Form X ranged from .86 to .88; KR21 reliability for Form Y ranged from .83 to .87; and alternate forms reliability estimates ranged from .80 to .85.

The validity of Forms C and D was assessed by comparing: (a) test scores with teachers' estimates of student performance, (b) test scores with scores on other reading tests, and (c) the alignment of test items to National Curricula Guidelines. The comparison of teachers' estimates and comparisons to National Curricula Guidelines suggests that students show a reasonable progression in terms of test scores on the Group Reading Test II from one level to the next. Although the teacher's guide suggests that scores on the new version of the test have been compared to scores on other reading tests, no results were reported.

COMMENTARY AND SUMMARY. The Group Reading Test II is a well-designed, easy-to-administer, easy-to-score test of reading ability for children ages 6 through 14. It demonstrates satisfactory reliability although the validity has not been demonstrated via comparisons with other standardized tests of reading. The classroom teacher would likely find this a suitable method of determining and monitoring reading ability in children ages 6 through 14. Classroom teachers would likely find the teacher's guide especially helpful as it clearly describes how to administer and score the test. In addition, it includes straightforward information related to using and interpreting standardized test scores.

[99]

Guide for Occupational Exploration Interest Inventory, Second Edition.

Purpose: Designed to help people identify their interests, then use this information to explore career, learning, and lifestyle alternatives.

Population: High school through adult.
Publication Date: 2002.
Acronym: GOEII.
Scores, 14: Arts/Entertainment/Media, Science/Math/Engineering, Plants and Animals, Law/Law Enforcement/Public Safety, Mechanics/Installers/Repairers, Construction/ Mining/Drilling, Transportation, Industrial Production, Business Detail, Sales and Marketing, Recreation/Travel/Other Personal Services, Education and Social Service, General Management and Support, Medical and Health Services.
Administration: Group or individual.
Price Data, 2003: $29.95 per 25 inventories including copy of administrator's guide (12 pages).
Time: Administration time not reported.
Comments: Self-administered and self-scored.
Author: J. Michael Farr.
Publisher: JIST Publishing, Inc.

Review of the Guide for Occupational Exploration Interest Inventory, Second Edition by M. DAVID MILLER, Professor of Educational Psychology, and JENNIFER M. BERGERON, Graduate Student, University of Florida, Gainesville, FL:

DESCRIPTION. The Guide for Occupational Exploration (GOE) Interest Inventory is a revision of the original GOE system that was based on research conducted by the U.S. Department of Labor and first appeared in the book *Guide for Occupational Exploration (GOE)*. The instrument consists of one large sheet of paper that is unfolded to reveal seven panels of information. It was developed to be self-scored and self-interpreted. In the first step, individuals rate their interests on a 3-point scale ranging from 0 for *low* or *no interest* to 2 for *high interest* for the 14 interest areas including: Arts/Entertainment/Media, Science/Math/Engineering, Plants and Animals, Law/Law Enforcement/Public Safety, Mechanics/Installers/Repairers, Construction/Mining/Drilling, Transportation, Industrial Production, Business Detail, Sales and Marketing, Recreation/Travel/Other Personal Services, Education and Social Service, General Management and Support, and Medical and Health Services. In the second step, individuals respond using the same 3-point scale to items focusing on six specialty areas for each of the 14 interest areas including Education, Previous Training, Work Experience, Leisure Activities, Home Activities, and Work Settings. The third and fourth steps include a self-scoring system to allow individuals to interpret their scores along with information about how they might explore their career interests. The fifth step is a career exploration worksheet that summarizes information gathered. The sixth step, a worksheet on researching career options, guides individuals in gathering additional information about the careers they have selected.

The instrument, developed to be self-administered and self-scored, can also be administered to a group. Administration time is not reported; however, the inventory can be completed in 30 to 45 minutes.

According to the manual, the intent of the GOE Interest Inventory is to help individuals identify their interests and use this information to explore career, learning, and lifestyle alternatives. Therefore, the information could be used for students who are trying to decide on a career or educational interest, an unemployed adult with work experience needing to find an alternative career, or someone changing jobs. The intended population for this instrument is high school and college students as well as adults.

DEVELOPMENT. The GOE is a revision of an instrument developed by the U.S. Department of Labor in 1979. Revisions were a result of new interest areas created to handle new technology-related jobs that did not exist when the old inventory was created. Modifications include (a) changes in format, (b) a simplified scoring system, and (c) new interest areas and information about O*NET job titles.

TECHNICAL. Documentation was not available on the technical characteristics of the modified instrument that is currently being used. Data are reported from the original instrument development in 1979. However, these data are limited. No reliability data are reported so psychometric properties are not known. Validity evidence of two types is provided in the form of content and construct validity. Evidence for item content is provided by a short narrative that notes that items were selected based on research initiated by the Functional Occupational Classification Project to design classification systems for jobs as well as based on expert review from national office personnel. Construct validity evidence for the original instrument was based on a principal components factor analysis and provided support for the original 12 interest areas. However, no attempt is made to integrate these results with the uses and interpretations of the instrument.

SUMMARY. The GOE Interest Inventory appears to have utility in helping individuals narrow their career options as well as learn more about how to approach the processes of making career decisions. Items appear to be appropriate for their intended target population; they are easy to read and interpret. Administration, scoring, and interpretation are simple and are facilitated by a four-step process with the addition of a list of contact information to aid in additional job exploration. However, despite these positive features, there is a lack of psychometric support so evidence is merely provided in the form of face value of individual items. The lack of reliability data is also a major concern. Although the test manual provides some information from validity studies, these are from the original 12-item instrument and the authors fail to integrate these results with the uses and interpretations of the instrument. The limited psychometric data make it clear that the instrument should only be used in low stakes, exploratory (as suggested in the title) situations, and in conjunction with other data to guide career decisions.

Review of the Guide for Occupational Exploration Interest Inventory, Second Edition by WILLIAM I. SAUSER, JR., Associate Dean and Professor, Business and Engineering Outreach, Auburn University, Auburn, AL:

DESCRIPTION. "Exploring career options is not easy for most people. How much education and training are you willing to get? What are you good at? What is important to you? The questions are complicated and the answers are often not very clear. And there seem to be too many options to consider them all." So states J. Michael Farr, a prolific writer in the field of job search and career planning, on the cover page of the Guide for Occupational Exploration Interest Inventory, Second Edition (GOEII). This instrument is designed to help literate adults work their way through these questions and navigate the terrain of the U.S. Department of Labor's *O*NET Dictionary of Occupational Titles, Occupational Outlook Handbook,* and other such resources for gathering information about the many vocational choices available today. The GOEII is not so much a test or inventory as it is a map for a self-guided tour of the world of work.

The GOEII "consists of one large [22 x 25.5-inch] sheet of paper that is unfolded to reveal

12 panels of information and activities. It is designed to be self-scored, self-contained, and self-interpreted" (administrator's guide, p. 2). The instrument instructs the job seeker to proceed in six logical steps: (a) Review the 14 interest areas, (b) complete the instrument, (c) score the interest profile, (d) use the "Interests to Careers Chart" to explore options, (e) complete the Career Exploration Worksheet, and then (f) research career options that interest you most. The first three steps are relatively simple. The 14 interest areas (by which the U.S. Department of Labor classifies jobs) are described straightforwardly, with good examples showing how each interest area can be met by jobs of varying skill levels and complexity. (The author is commended for making no implied value judgments about jobs; all examples are written to maintain the dignity of useful employment, no matter the socioeconomic status of the type of work being described.) In Step 1 the job seeker expresses overall interest in each of the 14 areas by marking them 0 (*low or no interest*), 1 (*some interest*), or 2 (*high interest*). In Step 2 the job seeker uses similar three-point rating scales to indicate the extent to which each interest area matches the respondent's (a) education and school subjects, (b) training, (c) work experience, (d) leisure activities, (e) home activities, and (f) preferred work settings. In Step 3 the ratings from Steps 1 and 2 are summed and graphed to establish "your interest profile." Completing these steps would likely take no more than 30 minutes for a literate adult. (Due to its complexity and reliance on verbal skills, this instrument does not appear suitable for use by those with poor language skills.)

Step 4 becomes far more complex and intimidating. At this point the entire poster-sized paper is unfolded to reveal a colorful yet highly detailed listing, for each of the 14 career interest areas, of "related major job titles," complete with coded information about required education and training, earnings, expected openings, and importance of math, English, science, and computer skills. What then follows on the chart is a listing of *all* the O*NET job titles that fit under each interest area found in the *Guide for Occupational Exploration*. The chart is complex and presented in very fine print, requiring keen eyesight or a magnifying glass to read. The author readily admits that the job seeker may be intimidated by seeing so much text, and suggests that the test

administrator assure the job seeker that "most users will be interested in only one or several of the interest areas and can quickly eliminate others" (administrator's guide, p. 5). Steps 5 and 6 then guide the job seeker in his or her effort to research in more depth the various career options available within the selected interest areas. The research outline presented is very pragmatic, action-oriented, and helpful. Also included on the back page of the instrument are publications and other sources of information the job seeker may wish to consult while completing this research. The "Interests to Careers Chart" itself, although visually intimidating, contains a wealth of useful information, making it indeed a helpful roadmap for exploring the myriad vocational choices available. States the author, "After the test-taker completes all the activities, he has narrowed down his career options as well as learned more about how to approach the process of making a career decision—and how to follow up with more research and action" (administrator's guide, p. 3).

Although the GOEII is designed to be a self-contained tool, the author does provide a number of excellent suggestions for professionals who might wish to incorporate the instrument into individual or group vocational counseling programs. The instrument is also helpful for identifying vocational options the job seeker may not have heretofore considered. "Specifically, counselees should be encouraged to think carefully about suitable occupational areas they may not have considered before because of lack of knowledge about the occupations, or because of misconceptions that the occupations were not open to members of the counselee's sex or ethnic group" (administrator's guide, p. 11).

DEVELOPMENT. The GOEII is not an independently developed instrument; it is rather more of an expanded index, chart, and workbook based on the U.S. Department of Labor's ongoing research related to job classification and description. The author gives proper credit to the U.S. Department of Labor, and expresses dependence on that agency's work: "The GOE system of organizing jobs within interest areas was developed as the result of research done by the U.S. Department of Labor. That research is the basis for the validity of the GOE structure as used for career exploration—and for the validity of the *GOE Interest Inventory*" (administrator's guide, p.

7). The manual contains a brief description of the initial research underlying the structure of the Department of Labor's classification plan, and provides references to those initial studies. Unfortunately, the most recent reference is to a study published in 1984. There has been considerable research in career planning and vocational interest over the intervening two decades, yet none of this research is cited. Instead, the author simply states, "Many changes have occurred since this [the first edition of the *Guide for Occupational Exploration*] was written, including the abandonment of the *Dictionary of Occupational Titles* as the primary system used by the U.S. Department of Labor ...; the introduction of a replacement occupational information database called the O*NET; and a major updating of the original GOE's structure" (administrator's guide, p. 7). Given so much fresh research and change, why does the manual still cling to dated research as the major claim to "validity" of the GOE Interest Inventory?

The administrator's guide (p. 4) does refer to various "major improvements" in the second edition, including a new format and design, simplified scoring, new interest areas and job groupings based on the revised GOE, and new O*NET job titles. Given so much change in the instrument, it is incumbent upon the author and publisher to update the section of the manual describing the research upon which it is based.

TECHNICAL. It is challenging to review the technical merits of the GOEII because no data on standardization, reliability, and validity are presented in the manual. There are no tables of norms, no justifications of the scoring procedure, no descriptions of studies of reliability and validity, and no discussions of pilot testing, fakability, or other issues related to administration and interpretation. The instrument is touted as "self-interpreted" (administrator's guide, p. 2), but there is no evidence provided to indicate that self-interpretations are accurate.

On the positive side, the GOEII is highly face valid, and the basic structure of the Department of Labor's classification approach does appear to possess construct validity. The content of the GOEII is drawn directly from the Department of Labor's publications, thus the instrument possesses content validity as a representation of that agency's considerable research and development work. Furthermore, the administrator's guide

(p. 10) illustrates the relationship between Holland's occupational categories and GOE interest areas as an indicator of construct validity.

COMMENTARY. As a psychometric instrument the GOEII has major weaknesses, as indicated above. It is based on dated research, there is no evidence of reliability or predictive validity for any of the scores it produces, interpretive guidance is lacking, and it assumes a relatively high level of maturity, motivation, worldliness, and self-understanding on the part of the job seeker. The GOEII "has been designed to keep the test-taker in control of the decision-making process. It teaches them to understand how to explore careers based on their interests and encourages them to make good decisions based on information and their own preferences" (administrator's guide, p. 3). This is all well and good if the job seeker possesses enough self-awareness and understanding to make informed choices, or enough knowledge of the world of work to evaluate various job demands and work site preferences. When this is not the case—as with many high school and college students seeking vocational counseling, and older adults seeking initial entry into the workplace—other instruments would likely prove more helpful. For example, the Kuder Occupational Interest Inventory Series (T6:1356), the Self-Directed Search (T6:2238), or the Strong Interest Inventory (15:248) would likely provide very helpful information to job seekers who are searching for career choices that fit their pattern of interests and abilities.

The GOEII does appear to have merit for mature, self-knowledgeable job-seekers, however; and this is the group for which the instrument will likely prove most useful. The self-directed, active format of the GOEII provides an excellent roadmap for individuals (a) possessing considerable self-awareness; (b) with enough knowledge about the world of work to make informed decisions about preferred tasks, worksites, and necessary skill levels; and (c) highly motivated to conduct a thorough investigation of the wide variety of job titles and occupational possibilities available to them. The GOEII is not an essential tool for this purpose, but it may prove valuable in eliminating a number of job possibilities that would not be suitable for the job seeker. This would save the job seeker considerable time and would help her or him to focus attention on researching realistic occupational choices aligned with interests and abilities.

SUMMARY. The GOEII is not a test or inventory in the traditional sense; it does not possess the characteristics of a sound psychometric instrument and would not be likely to prove useful as a basis for diagnosis or counseling with individuals who do not possess a high level of self-awareness and understanding, or a working knowledge of the world of work. The GOEII is more of a roadmap, summary index, or guide for exploring and evaluating the myriad occupational choices available in the modern world. For the self-directed, self-motivated, self-aware individual who desires focus and structure to guide his or her research into vocational choice, the GOEII could be a handy tool. It can sharpen one's focus on suitable jobs and guide the process of careful research before making a critical vocational choice. Though designed for self-administration, scoring, and interpretation, the GOEII would likely prove most beneficial when included as part of a vocational guidance program conducted by a qualified vocational counselor. A knowledgeable mentor could provide the "reality checks" necessary to assure the job seeker that he or she is pursuing a reasonable course of action while making difficult vocational choices.

[100]

Hall Occupational Orientation Inventory, Fourth Edition.

Purpose: Designed to help individuals understand their values, needs, interests, and preferred life-styles, and how these relate to career goals and future educational plans.

Population: Grades 3–7, 8–16 and adults, low-literate adults, junior high students–adults.

Publication Dates: 1968–2000.

Administration: Group or individual.

Price Data, 2005: $19.50 per Choosing: Your Way, a supplementary career reader (2000, 40 pages); $19.50 per Counselor/User's manual (2000, 59 pages); $16 per sample set including 1 inventory booklet, 1 interpretive manual, and 1 response sheet (specify Intermediate Form, Young Adult/College/Adult Form, or Adult Basic Forms); $24 per sample set with Choosing: Your Way; $24 per sample set with Counselor/User's Manual; $40.95 per sample set with both Choosing: Your Way and Counselor/User's manual; $19.50 per sample set (Form II); $26.50 per sample set with Professional Manual (Form II).

Time: (45–60) minutes.

Author: Lacy G. Hall.

Publisher: Scholastic Testing Service, Inc.

a) INTERMEDIATE FORM.

Population: Grades 3–7.

Publication Dates: 1968–1976.

Scores, 22: Free Choice, Chance Game, Effort to Learn, Belonging, Being Safe, Goals, Being Important, Being Yourself, Being Proud, Order, Working Alone, Working with Your Hands, Working with People, Places, Ready to Learn, Rewards, Physical Fitness, The World Around You, Others, Skills, Use of Time, Being on Guard.

Price Data: $34.90 per 20 inventory booklets; $25.30 per 20 interpretive folders; $25.30 per 20 response sheets.

b) YOUNG ADULT/COLLEGE/ADULT FORM.

Population: Grades 8–16 and adults.

Publication Dates: 1968–2000.

Scores, 29: Creativity-Independence, Information-Knowledge, Belongingness, Security, Aspiration, Esteem, Self-Actualization, Personal Satisfaction, Routine-Dependence, People-Social-Accommodating, Data-Information, Things-Physical, People-Business-Influencing, Ideas-Scientific, Aesthetics-Arts, Geographic Location, Abilities, Monetary-Compensation, Workplace, Coworkers, Time, Qualifications, Risk, Subjective External Authority, Objective External Authority, Subjective Internal Authority, Shaping/Autonomy/and Self-Empowerment, Interdependent, Procrastination.

Price Data: $38.75 per 20 inventory booklets; $27.50 per 20 self-interpretive folders; $26.25 per 20 response sheets.

c) ADULT BASIC FORM.

Population: Low-literate adults.

Publication Dates: 1968–2000.

Scores, 29: Same as for *b* above.

Price Data: $38.75 per 20 inventory booklets; $27.50 per 20 self-interpretive folders; $26.25 per 20 response sheets.

d) FORM II.

Population: Junior high students–adults.

Publication Dates: 1968–1989.

Scores, 15: Creativity-Independence, Information-Knowledge, Belongingness, Security, Aspiration, Esteem, Self-Actualization, Personal Satisfaction, Routine-Dependence, People-Social-Accommodating, Data-Information, Things-Physical, People-Business-Influencing, Ideas-Scientific, Aesthetics-Arts.

Price Data: $36.90 per 20 inventory booklets; $108.35 per 20 self-interpretive digests; $25.60 per 20 response sheets.

Cross References: For reviews by Gregory Schraw and Hilda Wing of an earlier edition, see 12:175 (1 reference); see T3:1051 (4 references); for reviews by Robert H. Dolliver and Austin C. Frank of an earlier edition, see 8:1003 (5 references); see also T2:2187 (3 references); for a review by Donald G. Zytowski of the original edition, see 7:104 (4 references).

Review of the Hall Occupational Orientation Inventory, Fourth Edition by JOHN S. GEISLER, Professor of Counselor Education and Counseling Psychology, Western Michigan University, Kalamazoo, MI:

DESCRIPTION. The Hall Occupational Orientation Inventory (HALL), Fourth Edition, is a 175-item, self-administered, self-scored, and self-interpreted instrument designed to assess personal factors deemed to be important in making career choices. The HALL (Young Adult/College/Adult and Adult Basic Forms) consists of 35 scales arranged into five scale categories: (a) Needs-Values (Creativity-Independence, Information-Knowledge, Belongingness, Security, Aspiration, Esteem, Self-Actualization, Personal Satisfaction, and Routine-Dependence); (b) Career Interest (People-Social-Accommodating, Data-Information, Things-Physical, People-Business-Influencing, Ideas-Scientific, and Aesthetic-Arts); (c) Job Characteristics (Geographic Location, Abilities, Monetary-Compensation, Workplace, Coworkers, Time, Qualifications, and Risk); (d) Choice Style (Subjective External Authority; Objective External Authority; Subjective Internal Authority, Shaping, Autonomy, and Self-Empowerment; Interdependent; and Procrastination); and (e) Ability (same scales as (b) above). No time limit is given for administration.

The answer sheet is arranged in four parts (for the five scales) and is self-scored. The scale scores are computed by summing the Likert-type responses that have been recorded on the second page of the answer sheet. The raw score summaries for each scale are then transferred to a self-interpreted profile sheet in a separate booklet, which contains the raw score profile and written interpretations for the 35 scales. There are 5 items per scale (reduced from 10 in earlier editions). A 40-page supplementary text (Choosing: Your Way) is available and describes the 35 scales and their meanings.

The Likert-type response score points for the scales are as follows: Needs-Values, Career Interest, and Job Characteristics scales: *Most Desirable* = 4, *Desirable* =3, *Not Important* = 2, *Undesirable* = 1, and *Very Undesirable* = 0; Choice Style scales: *Not Like Me* = 1, *Like Me* = 2, and *Very Much Like Me* = 4; and Ability scales: *Weak* = 1, *Average* = 2, *Above Average* = 3, and *Strong* = 4.

The Career Interest scales have their corollaries in the Ability scales for the purpose of matching perceived interests and perceived abilities on the same factors.

DEVELOPMENT. The purpose of the HALL is to initiate self-exploration and self-awareness in terms of psychological needs, personal values, career interests, perceived abilities, and choice-making styles. The original instrument was published in 1964 and was the outgrowth of a doctoral dissertation by the author, Lacy G. Hall. It is intended for career exploratory purposes only and takes into account important personal characteristics that can lead to careers/occupations/jobs that would be fulfilling, meaningful, and satisfying.

The six Career Interest scales were derived from the 1979 *Guide for Occupational Exploration* (U.S. Department of Labor) and its 12 Interest Areas and 66 Work Groups as well as the six major interest factors that resulted from research conducted by Guilford, Christensen, Bond, and Sutton (1954). These six scales also closely parallel the Holland model (Realistic, Investigative, Artistic, Social, Enterprising, and Conventional). Although these scales are now composed of five statements each, between 30 and 40 items were included in the original pool of items for each scale. The 5 items that are included in each scale had to have a minimum item/scale correlation coefficient of .55. The origins of the 9 Needs-Values Scales can be traced to Maslow's needs-based personality theory as well as Roe's theory of occupational choice. The Job Characteristics scales have their origins in the job characteristics as provided in the 1979 *Guide for Occupational Exploration*. One of the two new categories of scales incorporated into the HALL is the Choice Style scales (six scales). The model for these scales comes from the author's Hall Choice Model and was influenced by the theories and research of Piaget and Kohlberg. These scales "progress" on a dependent (external) to independent (internal) "locus of control" continuum. The six Ability scales were introduced into the fourth edition to complement the six Career Interest scales (same scale names) in order to assess self-perceived interests and abilities on the same dimensions.

TECHNICAL. By design, the HALL has no normative or predictive data, and little reliability or other validity data. The instrument's items were chosen by the author because they were "logically related to [the] scales" (counselor/user's manual, p. 5) that had been chosen, a priori. The concurrent validity of the Career Interest scales was examined by comparing the Career Interest scales to the Holland occupational categories. The intercorrelational coefficients among the scales ranged from .16 to .52. Holland's comparable correlation coefficients ranged from .11 to .68. The sample size for this research was not reported. Only one other validity study was reported in the HALL manual. For 288 people highest scale scores on the six Career Interest scales were identified and occupations were reported (e.g., Personal-Social-Accommodating [highest score]—School Counselor, Nurse, Bartender, Barber, etc.; People-Business-Influencing [highest score]—Lawyer, Editor, School Principal, Military Officer, etc.). The author said "With rare exception, their highest scores placed the workers in the career scales that one would expect" (counselor/user's manual, p. 37). No other validity studies were reported.

Limited reliability data are available. The author states that because the HALL is based on a theory that is dynamic and changing, traditional reliability research would not be appropriate and would, in fact, "provide a distortion" (counselor/user's manual, p. 38). However, he did include item/scale correlation coefficients for all 35 scales.

COMMENTARY. The HALL has limited value. Although it can be argued that traditional reliability studies may not be entirely appropriate for an instrument that is to be used only for exploratory purposes, the counterargument that there are appropriate reliability procedures that could be used to establish the consistency, dependability, and trustworthiness of the instrument holds sway. Although it is true that interests and values do change over time, nonetheless, having assurance that the obtained scale scores can be useful, are consistent, and are relatively free from measurement error would be most helpful, especially because the scale scores are based on five items/scale. The author also reports that the original, and subsequent, editions of the HALL had 10 items/scale. He states that correlational and factor analysis studies demonstrated that reducing items/scale from 10 to 5 did not affect the scores. However, no data were reported to justify this claim. The author also indicates that the item/scale correlation coefficients are demonstrable evidence of the instrument's reliability. The item/

scale correlation coefficients exceed the criterion of .55. Item/scale correlation coefficients are a type of validity and do not demonstrate that the scores are necessarily reliable.

Validity data are practically nonexistent. The reported study of 288 people who were already employed in careers has no data to support the conclusions that are reached. There is no information about how this sample was chosen, the number of persons in each career listed, the satisfaction with career choices, etc. The other "validity" reports in the manual have to do with opinions of very limited samples and have little to do with any type of empirical validity.

The value of the profile sheets is questionable. The respondents who are responsible for scoring their own answer sheets are then asked to transfer the score information to the profile sheets. The raw score points for three of the scales are arranged in categories: Low (0, 3, or 5), Average (7, 10, or 12), and High (15, 18, or 20). Scores of 1, 2, 4, 8, 9, 11, 16, 17, and 19 are to be interpolated. The score ranges for each scale are: Low (6), Average (6), and High (6) and yet there are a possible 21 points (0–20) for each scale. Scores 6, 13, and 14 lie between the categories. The weights assigned to the responses for the Needs-Values, Career Interest, and Job Characteristics scales are from 0 to 4 for each item. The weights for the Choice Style scales responses are: *Not Like Me* = 1, *Like Me* = 2, and *Very Much Like Me* = 4. It should be noted that two of the three response choices are on the "Like" side; only one response is on the "Not Like Me" side. And, the "Very Much Like Me" response is weighted four times the value of the only "Not Like Me" response. Profile scores using this weighted scoring system will be distorted. The "Weak" to "Strong" responses to the Ability scales items are weighted 1 to 4. The aggregate raw scores are categorized as either Low (5, 8, or 9), Average (10, 12, or 15), or High (16, 18, or 20). Scores of 6, 7, 11, 13, 14, 17, 19 are to be interpolated. There is no rationale provided as to the criteria for scores categorized as Low, Average, or High.

The research and foundational background for the instrument are dated. The basis for the Career Interest scales is the 1979 edition of the *Guide For Occupational Exploration*. The *Guide* is based on the job titles found in the 1977 *Dictionary Of Occupational Titles*. These six scales also have their foundation based on research reported in 1954. One of the citations supporting the development of the Job Characteristics scales was dated 1965. The Hall Choice Model, which was used to develop the Choice Style Scales has questionable rationale. The author also cites a study comparing the HALL with the Strong-Campbell Vocational Interest Blank (SVIB) and cites the 1971 SVIB Handbook in the reference list. The SVIB has not been in use for several years. It has been replaced by the Strong Interest Inventory (15:248). The reference list in the manual contains entries from 1954 to 1989. No recent citations are listed. There are two forms of the HALL: (a) Young Adult/College/Adult and (b) Adult Basic, with no explanation provided as to what the differences are.

SUMMARY. The HALL is a career interest inventory that has very limited utility. Reliability and validity data are very scarce and the quality of the data that are reported is questionable. The rationale, justification, and development of the scales are dated. Also, with the new technology now available, there is no need for respondents to self-score their own answer sheets and then be asked to transfer data to self-interpreting profile sheets. Self-scoring leads to possible recording errors. There appears to be little difference between the two HALL forms and no information is provided as to what the differences are. Both forms list "Adults" as potential clients. Although the author indicates that the instrument is to be used for exploratory purposes only, stronger and updated justification and rationale, new scoring procedures, and substantial reliability and validity research need to be provided before the instrument can be recommended for use. The supplementary text also needs to be revised and updated.

REVIEWER'S REFERENCE

Guilford, J. P., Christensen, P. R., Bond, N. A., & Sutton, M. A. (1954). A factor analysis study of human interests. *Psychological Monographs, 68*(4, Whole No. 375).

Review of the Hall Occupational Orientation Inventory, Fourth Edition by JOSEPH G. LAW, JR., Professor of Behavioral Studies, University of South Alabama, Mobile, AL:

DESCRIPTION. The Hall Occupational Orientation Inventory, Fourth Edition has an Adult Basic Form and a Young Adult/College/Adult Form. There is a 46-page counselor's manual and a 40-page supplementary career reader entitled *Choosing Your Way.* There is a 9-page reusable inventory booklet and a one-time self-scoring answer sheet. Both forms contain 175 items that are transformed into 35 scales. The accompanying self-interpretive folder describes the meaning of each scale and helps the user to fit himself or herself into the work force in a meaningful way. There are 9 Needs-Values scales: Creativity-Independence, Information-Knowledge, Belongingness, Security, Aspiration, Esteem, Self-Actualization, Personal Satisfaction, and Routine-Dependence. There are 6 Career Interest scales: People-Social-Accommodating, Data-Information, Things-Physical, People-Business-Influencing, Ideas-Scientific, and Aesthetic-Arts. These 15 scales have items that are weighted on a 5-point scale (0-*very undesirable,* 1-*undesirable,* 2-*not important,* 3-*desirable,* and 4-*most desirable*). The 8 Job Characteristics scales are Geographic Location, Abilities, Monetary-Compensation, Workplace, Coworkers, Time, Qualifications, and Risk. There are also 6 choice style scales: Subjective External Authority; Objective External Authority; Subjective Internal Authority; Shaping, Autonomy, and Self-Empowerment; Interdependent; and Procrastination. The 6 Ability scales have the same labels as the Career Interest Scales but ask the examinee to rate himself or herself on their ability in each area using a 4-point scale (*weak, average, above average, strong*). There are useful figures in the manual that illustrate the similarity of Hall's 6 interest scales to John Holland's Hexagonal model.

DEVELOPMENT. The manual contains a review of basic concepts, theoretical foundations, the six-level model of career choice, the relationship between interests and abilities, instructions for self-administration, scoring, and interpretation. The author explains in the introduction to the manual that the Hall, first published in 1968, is nonnormative and nonpredictive. The examinee who completes the Hall obtains raw scores on the 35 scales using the self-scoring answer sheet and transfers his or her score to a self-interpreting profile sheet, which is on the second and third pages of the self-interpretive folder. Raw scores are grouped on the profile sheet into three triads: Low, Average, and High. The examinee is then directed to an appropriate page in the folder for a brief description of the dimension covered by each scale.

TECHNICAL. There are no norms for group-based comparisons by age, gender, SES, level of education, or other characteristics because the Hall is nonnormative. Because interpretation is idiographic, the author did not provide normative data. This makes the usual kind of studies of reliability and validity difficult. Section VII of the 48-page manual for the 4th Edition contains 3 pages on validity and reliability and is followed by 1 page of references. The most recent reference is dated 1989, which is a serious lapse for a test manual dated in 2000. Many references are dated from 1954 to the early 1970s. Five are U.S. Department of Labor publications and many others are theoretical texts such as Kohlberg's study of moral development, and John Holland and Anne Roe's early works. There is no evidence of peer-reviewed research on the efficacy of the inventory. The author notes a survey of 2,200 individuals to illustrate the responsiveness of the items, but gives no data on the group's composition, characteristics, selection, or the date of the survey. There is no reference to any publication of the survey or the location of the data. Likewise, discussions of a survey of 225 college students (to demonstrate comprehensiveness), 75 professional counselors (showing acceptance of the inventory), a group of 160 first-year college students (illustrating developmental potency), and a group of college seniors (indicating relevancy) lack any mention of survey methodology, selection, characteristics, statistical results, or publication references. None of the reported validity studies are dated. The discussion of reliability is very brief. One table contains correlations between individual items and the scales under which they are grouped. Most items correlate above .55 with the respective scale. Unfortunately, the author does not give much data about the sample used to obtain these correlations. Most of the reliability section consists of the author's assertion that the traditional psychometric approach is more appropriate to static situations and not appropriate to dynamic areas such as interest assessment or career choice. There are no reported data in the manual on test-retest reliability and minimal discussion of factor analysis of the scales.

COMMENTARY. The Hall is one of those instruments that may be more like a projective test of the professional who uses it than of the client. The career counselor who prefers a humanistic approach and emphasis on hard-to-measure constructs such as self-actualization and self-esteem will enjoy the items, the supplementary career reader, and other materials associated with the Hall. It is a nonthreatening type of instrument,

user friendly, and the narrative discussion of career choices and values is very readable. In some ways, reading the interpretive folder and career reader could be a beneficial part of career education. The examinee is able to compare the strength of interests to perceived abilities in each interest area, thus enhancing self-assessment in determining strengths and weaknesses. Needs and values are inventoried in order to help the individual clarify what is and is not important in a job. The job characteristics scales enable the individual to rate more tangible variables such as time, risk, geographical location, and monetary compensation.

However, previous criticisms of the instrument's weaknesses are still relevant. There is little reported background on the normal developmental sequence of the six-level choice model proposed by the author, a bewildering number of scales for the examinee to interpret and try to fit into a decision-making matrix, and very limited reliability and validity data. Although the manual gives some examples and illustrations of individual and group use, an appendix with case studies would be very helpful. The lack of reported studies on the inventory in the past 20 years is a serious gap.

SUMMARY. The Hall Occupational Inventory is designed to be a comprehensive career assessment tool for individual self-exploration of interests, abilities, values, preferred job environments, and decision-making styles. The answer and profile sheets are designed for simple administration and scoring, with easy-to-read guides to self-interpretation. It should appeal to self-reflective, highly motivated high school students and young adults who wish to spend time thinking about their values, needs, interests, and abilities. Individuals who are more impulsive or less motivated to do the hard work of self-study will probably not find the Hall appealing. Involvement of a career counselor with individual and group sessions would be more appropriate for such individuals and the manual does provide some limited guidance in that direction. Career counselors working from a humanistic perspective will probably enjoy the Hall and those adhering to a trait factor model may find other instruments more to their liking. Construct validity data are weakly supported, there is no predictive validity and few reliability data. The Hall could be well utilized as part of a career education seminar, group-based approach to career counseling, or series of individual career counseling sessions.

Hare Psychopathy Checklist—Revised: 2nd Edition.

Purpose: Designed for "the assessment of psychopathy in research, clinical and forensic settings."
Population: Ages 18 and over.
Publication Dates: 1990–2003.
Acronym: PCL-R.
Scores, 7: Factor 1 (Interpersonal, Affective, Total), Factor 2 (Lifestyle, Antisocial, Total), Total.
Administration: Individual.
Forms, 2: Rating Booklet, Interview Guide.
Price Data, 2005: $268 per complete kit including technical manual (2003, 231 pages), 1 rating booklet, 25 QuikScore™ forms, and 25 interview guides; $94 per technical manual; $56 per rating booklet (reusable, hardcover); $63 per 25 QuikScore™ forms; $214 per 100 QuikScore™ forms; $103 per 25 interview guides; $350 per 100 interview guides.
Time: (90–120) minutes for interview; (60) minutes for collateral review.
Comments: Rating scale based on responses to semistructured interview and collateral information review. Expands previous edition for use with female and African-American offenders, substance abusers, and offenders in countries other than the U.S.
Author: Robert D. Hare.
Publisher: Multi-Health Systems, Inc.
Cross References: See T5:1174 (1 reference); for reviews by Solomon M. Fulero and Gerald L. Stone of a previous edition, see 12:177 (5 references); see also T4:1127 (3 references).

Review of the Hare Psychopathy Checklist— Revised: 2nd Edition by SHAWN K. ACHESON, Associate Professor of Neuropsychology, Department of Psychology, Western Carolina University, Cullowhee, NC, and by JOSHUA W. PAYNE, Doctoral Student, Department of Psychology, University of North Texas, Denton TX:

DESCRIPTION. The Hare Psychopathy Checklist—Revised: 2nd Edition (PCL-R) is among the most widely used measures of psychopathy. Each of the 20 items is scored based upon information obtained by a semistructured interview and review of available file and collateral information. Items of the checklist are scored in the following manner: 0 = "No," 1 = "Maybe," and 2 = "Yes." In addition to a Total score (the sum of all item scores), two broad factor scores and four corresponding facet scores (2 underlying each factor) can also be calculated. Principal components analysis as well as confirmatory factor analysis were performed on a very large and diverse data set (N = 9,016) and supported this two-factor/four-facet solution. Similar to the two-factor composition of prior PCL instruments, Factor 1 scores reflect a measure of interpersonal and affective traits and Factor 2 scores reflect a measure of social deviance. New to the PCL-R, however, is the availability of facet scores. Facet 1 scores reflect a measure of interpersonal traits, Facet 2 scores reflect a measure of affective traits, Facet 3 scores reflect a measure of lifestyle, and Facet 4 scores reflect a measure of antisocial behavior.

It should be emphasized that psychopathy and Antisocial Personality Disorder (APD), although similar, are not equivalent constructs. Psychopathy, according to Hare, is defined by the presence of specific interpersonal, affective, impulsive, and socially deviant characteristics. APD, on the other hand, is primarily defined by manifestations of social deviance and is strongly related to criminal behavior. For a more comprehensive review of the comparison between these similar but incongruent constructs refer to Hare (1996).

It is recommended that only licensed mental health clinicians, familiar with forensic populations (and specifically psychopathy), administer the PCL-R. These clinicians should have specific training in psychopathology, statistics, and psychometric theory. Moreover, it is expected that clinicians who use this instrument have specific training on its administration, scoring, and interpretation. These explicit and prominently emphasized recommendations are likely a result of the significant consequences of decisions made during a typical forensic evaluation utilizing the PCL-R. Recommended administration qualifications for individuals within research settings are less stringent.

DEVELOPMENT. Hare's conceptualization of psychopathy was influenced most notably by Cleckley's (1976) work "The Mask of Sanity" in which he idealized the prototypical psychopath to possess 16 specific traits. Unfortunately, a thorough history of the development of the original PCL and PCL-R is beyond the scope of this review. Developmentally, no revisions or alterations to checklist items, interview questions, administration, or scoring procedures of the PCL-R were performed in the latest revision, the Hare Psychopathy Checklist—Revised: 2nd Edition. Therefore, research of the PCL-R is appropriately generalizable to the 2nd Edition. The availability of facet level scoring appears to be a main developmental improvement upon the PCL-R. Readers are directed to the current PCL-R manual for a review of the scale development and item selection for the original PCL and PCL-R.

TECHNICAL. A well-written and thorough technical manual is provided for user reference. Larger normative samples (than those of the PCL-R) for North American male offenders ($N = 5,408$) and North American male forensic psychiatric patients ($N = 1,246$) are provided. Additionally, normative samples for North American female offenders ($N = 1,218$) and English male offenders ($N = 1,363$) are also provided, which are new to the 2nd Edition. Descriptive data regarding PCL-R scores and ethnicity are also provided and indicate that "PCL-R scores and their interpretation are not unduly influenced by ethnicity of the inmate or patient, at least with respect to White and African-American individuals" (technical manual, p. 51). A cursory review of the current investigations of the PCL-R's use among more specific populations of substance abusers, sexual offenders, as well as individuals at different age levels is also provided. The manual, however, does not provide descriptive data of these variables among the normative samples. Moreover, the instrument still provides limited normative information for diverse minority samples.

Overall, the psychometric properties of the PCL-R are beyond repute. Two types of intraclass correlations (interrater reliability for both single ratings and the mean of two independent ratings) as well as item-total correlations for all 20 items are provided for male offenders, male forensic psychiatric patients, and female offenders. All interrater reliabilities were acceptable or better. In addition, only 7 of the 60 item-total correlations (20 items x 3 samples) might be considered inadequate (below .3). Similar intraclass correlations and Cronbach's alpha coefficients are presented for item total scores, factor scores and facet scores using the same samples. Alpha coefficients for item total scores and the two factor scores are .73 or higher. However, alpha coefficients for individual facets in the female offender sample range from .6 to .69. In addition, alpha coefficients for Facets 3 and 4 in the male offender and male forensic psychiatric samples range from .61 to .67. These are considered to be at the low end of the generally accepted range of alpha values.

Over 40% of the manual's 211 pages are devoted to the topic of validity. This stands as small testament to the breadth and depth of the well-documented validity of this instrument throughout the literature. The modified factor structure of the PCL-R (the 2-factor, 4-facet model) is well documented from a factor analytic standpoint using both exploratory as well as confirmatory factor analyses. In the technical manual, Hare provides an excellent review of the various factor solutions and the strong evidence for the two-factor, four-facet approach selected for the PCL-R. Content-related, concurrent, convergent, and discriminant validity are all well documented for the Total, Factor 1, and Factor 2 scores. Unfortunately, there is far less validity evidence available for the new facet scores.

COMMENTARY. The PCL-R is an asset to any clinician performing psychological assessments within a forensic setting. It continues to be one of the most extensively studied forensic instruments available to clinicians. The availability of file information and lack of standardization outside of forensic settings, however, may limit the PCL-R's utility in nonforensic settings. The lack of response style/validity scales also appears to be a limitation of the PCL-R. A limited number of studies investigating the closely related PCL-SV and PCL-YV and their susceptibility to response styles have reported mixed results (Kropp & Rogers, 1991; Gacono, Meloy, Sheppard, Speth, & Roske, 1995; Rogers, Salekin, Sewell, Goldstein, & Leonard, 1998). Clinicians administering the PCL-R, especially clinicians with limited forensic experience, should be cognizant of patient response styles (i.e., malingering, positive impression management) during interviewing. The availability of facet level scoring, however, is a strength that previous PCL instruments did not possess. Clinical interpretation of PCL-R profiles is clearly enhanced by the addition of these descriptive facets.

SUMMARY. The PCL-R is a reliable and effective instrument for the measurement of psychopathy and is considered "the gold standard" for measurement of psychopathy. Presently, the PCL-R's impressive and ever-growing research base of empirical support is rivaled by no other psychopathy instrument. Therefore, the PCL-R should be strongly considered in any assessment of psychopathic/antisocial characteristics despite its limitations with regard to minority inclusion and evidence of facet validity.

REVIEWERS' REFERENCES

Cleckley, H. (1976). *The mask of sanity.* (5th ed.) St. Louis, MO: Mosby.

Gacono, C. B., Meloy, J. R., Sheppard, K., Speth, E., & Roske, A. (1995). A clinical investigation of malingering and psychopathy in hospitalized insanity acquittees. *Bulletin of the American Academy of Psychiatry and the Law, 23,* 387–397.

Hare, R. D. (1996). Psychopathy and antisocial personality disorder: A case of diagnostic confusion. *Psychiatric Times, 13,* 39–40.

Kropp, P. R., & Rogers, R. (1991, August). *Psychopathy and malingering.* Paper presented at the Meeting of the American Psychological Association, San Francisco, CA.

Rogers, R., Salekin, R. T., Sewell, K. W., Goldstein, A., & Leonard, K. (1998). A comparison of forensic and non-forensic malingerers: A prototypical analysis of explanatory models. *Law and Human Behavior, 22,* 353–367.

Review of the Hare Psychopathy Checklist— Revised: 2nd Edition by D. JOE OLMI, Associate Professor and Clinic Director, School Psychology Program, Department of Psychology, The University of Southern Mississippi, Hattiesburg, MS:

DESCRIPTION. The Hare Psychopathy Checklist—Revised: 2nd Edition (PCL-R), a 2003 revision of the 1991 edition, is "a 20-item scale for the assessment of psychopathy in research, clinical and forensic settings" (technical manual, p. 1). The PCL-R kit is composed of the technical manual, the rating booklet, the interview guide, and the QuikScore™ self-scoring item response forms, and is designed for use with individuals 18 years and older.

The PCL-R is designed for use in multiple settings (research, forensic, and clinical) for multiple purposes (research and clinical assessment), but the author makes the point that the PCL-R is intended for the clinical assessment of psychopathy only and no other psychological construct. The instrument is not intended for use as a measure of treatment outcome. Those who use the PCL-R should have appropriate training in the behavioral sciences, forensics, psychometrics, and psychopathology and possess appropriate credentials and advanced academic degrees. As noted by the author, the instrument is to be administered as designed. The items of the 1991 version of the PCL-R and their scoring criteria are unchanged for this edition and include, for example, grandiose sense of self-worth, pathological lying, poor behavioral controls, juvenile delinquency and criminal versatility.

The technical manual contains chapters pertinent to the design of the PCL-R as related to its predecessor, the administration procedures, item descriptions, technical adequacy, psychometric tables, and appendices related to development, sampling, and scoring. The rating booklet contains instructions and examples pertinent to administration, the assessment procedure, and scoring, including prorating. The latter portion of the

booklet details information describing the items and item scoring. The interview guide provides instructions for the semistructured interview process with 125 questions and additional "probes" provided in content areas including current status, school history, work experience, career goals, finances, health, family history, friends/intimate relationships, substance abuse/impulsive behaviors, anger control/emotions, antisocial behaviors, and general questions.

Responding to the QuikScore™ form is self-explanatory. The respondent is required to read each item description contained in the rating booklet when rating items pertaining to a target individual. Scoring options for each item include 0 (no; does not apply to the target individual, or the individual does not exhibit behaviors consistent with the item description), 1 (maybe; does not reach the level of a 2 response), 2 (yes; the individual exhibits behavior[s] consistent with the item description), and X (omit the item; no more than 5 items for the total score and 2 items for each factor).

Once responses are circled on the QuikScore™ form ratings are transferred to the scoring grid of the form where they are totaled for each of four facets (1 = Interpersonal; 2 = Affective; 3 = Lifestyle; and 4 = Antisocial), each of two factors (1 = Interpersonal/Affective and 2 = Social Deviance), and summed for a total score. Prorating tables are included in the QuikScore™ form, as well as profile forms for male offenders, female offenders, and male forensic patients. Raw score conversion tables (percentile ranks and T-scores) are available for the same populations previously mentioned. Scoring is relatively easy and well explained through the use of case examples. The author goes to great length to suggest to the reader that an absolute "cut score" is probably not advisable and "...will not be based on defensible psychometric grounds" (technical manual, p. 31). He does suggest scores and psychopathy descriptors that could possibly be used: PCL-R score of 33–40, Level 5, Very High; 25–32, Level 4, High; 17–24, Level 3, Moderate; 9–16, Level 2, Low; and 0–8, Level 1, Very Low.

The PCL-R assessment procedure as suggested by the author is composed of (a) the review of "collateral" sources of information to assist with determining the credibility of interview information, the social interactional style of the individual, and to provide data for scoring selected items (should take approximately 60 minutes to accomplish); (b) the semistructured interview (approximately 90–120 minutes in length); and (c) responding/scoring to the QuikScore™ form (no length of time was indicated by the author; this reviewer would estimate approximately 20 minutes). The assessment may be conducted based on file reviews alone, if the quality of the data are judged sufficient to do such, although it seems to not be recommended by the author.

DEVELOPMENT. The second edition of the PCL-R appears to merely be a technical update of the 1991 version. As indicated earlier in this review, the items of the PCL-R and their scoring criteria are unchanged for this edition. The primary changes appear to be the size and diversity of the standardization samples and the psychometric data offered for different groups (i.e., ethnicity and types of offenders). What is also new to this edition is the expansion of the two-factor model to include a two-facet per factor, or four-facet model of the PCL-R.

TECHNICAL. Second edition standardization data are based on 10,896 offenders and patients across North America (Canada and selected states in the U.S.) and Europe (Great Britain and Sweden) (standard assessment [interviews and review of file information]: 5,408 male offenders, 1,246 male forensic psychiatric patients, 1,218 female offenders; file reviews only: 2,622 male offenders and 402 male forensic psychiatric patients). The second edition sample includes the original sample from the 1991 edition. Although the sample in the second edition is an improvement over the original PCL-R sample, there appeared to be no particular sampling plan as part of the psychometric redesign which is certainly a psychometric weakness of the PCL-R.

Reliability estimates of total scores across pooled samples ranged from .87 for single ratings of sample participants (intraclass) to .93 for averaged ratings of sample participants who were rated on more than one occasion (delay between occasions not provided). Reliability coefficients were in this same range for each subgroup. As well, reliability estimates for factor and facet scores were within acceptable ranges. Descriptive and validity data are available in this edition for "male and female offenders, substance-abusers, sex offenders, African-American offenders, and forensic psychiatric patients, as well as with offenders in several other countries" (technical manual, p. 2). Data were considered to be adequate.

COMMENTARY AND SUMMARY. In conclusion, the PCL-R is easily administered with background training and practice, is fairly sound psychometrically, and could be a very important assessment component in a battery designed to assess psychopathy. Although there were minimal changes in the instrument itself, it is apparent that the author took a fairly "conservative" (technical manual, p. 1) approach to the revision, thereby not changing any items or the manner in which the items were scored. It is also unclear to this reviewer whether the sampling plan was prescribed before undergoing the revision. The PCL-R is widely used, and this reviewer anticipates that it will continue to be so.

[102]
Hare Psychopathy Checklist: Youth Version.

Purpose: Designed for "the assessment of psychopathic traits in adolescents."
Population: Ages 12–18.
Publication Date: 2003.
Acronym: PCL:YV.
Scores, 5: Interpersonal, Affective, Behavioral, Antisocial, Total.
Administration: Individual.
Forms, 2: Interview Guide, QuikScore™ Rating Form.
Price Data: Available from publisher.
Time: (120) minutes for interview.
Comments: Adapted from the Hare Psychopathy Checklist—Revised (101); expert-completed rating scale based on responses to semistructured interview and collateral information review.
Authors: Adelle E. Forth, David S. Kosson, and Robert D. Hare.
Publisher: Multi-Health Systems, Inc.

Review of the Hare Psychopathy Checklist: Youth Version by JOHN W. FLEENOR, Director of Knowledge Management, Center for Creative Leadership, Greensboro, NC:

DESCRIPTION. According to the manual, the purpose of the Hare Psychopathy Checklist: Youth Version (PCL:YV) is to help identify potential patterns of antisocial acts, such as fighting, bullying, and cheating, in adolescents ranging in age from 12 to 18 years. The PCL:YV measures interpersonal, affective, behavioral, and emotional traits related to the traditional concept of psychopathy. The early identification of these traits is believed to be critical to helping antisocial youths develop into responsible adults. The PCL:YV can also be used to help understand how adolescent antisocial behavior can lead to the development of adult psychopathy. It was adapted from the Hare Psychopathy Checklist-Revised (PCL-R; 101), a widely used measure of psychopathy in adults that uses a similar expert-rater format to capture multidomain and multisource information.

On the PCL:YV, experts provide ratings (no, maybe, yes, omit) on the following 20 items: impression management, grandiose sense of self worth; stimulation seeking; pathological lying; manipulation for personal gain; lack of remorse; shallow affect; callous/lack of empathy; parasitic orientation; poor anger control; impersonal sexual behavior; early behavior problems; lacks goals; impulsivity; irresponsibility; failure to accept responsibility; unstable interpersonal relationships; serious criminal behavior; serious violations of conditional release; and criminal versatility. These items are clustered on four factors: Interpersonal, Affective, Behavioral, and Antisocial.

Administration and scoring. The PCL:YV uses a semistructured interview with a 20-item rating scale to assess psychopathic traits in male and female adolescents. Also part of the assessment process is a review of collateral information, including court documents, school records, psychological assessments, and interviews with family members and peers.

The interview guide includes the interview questions with space for the interviewer to record his or her responses. The interview covers topics such as school adjustment, career goals, psychiatric history, health, family life, interpersonal relationships, drug use, attitudes toward self and others, and antisocial behavior.

The scoring form is used to record by hand the ratings on each of the 20 PCL:YV items. The rater then calculates scores for the PCL:YV factors (Interpersonal, Affective, Behavioral and Antisocial) and converts them into *T*-scores, using the tables on the scoring form. The rating booklet contains the rating criteria, which are discussed in detail in the manual. The rating book also includes a self-contained administration and rating guide.

Scoring is based on the degree to which an individual's personality traits match the rating booklet items. The PCL:YV also provides a total score that represents an overall assessment of psychopathy. The total score can be interpreted as the extent to which an individual is characterized by psychopathic traits.

The PCL:YV takes approximately 2 hours to complete. The interview section can be completed in 90 to 120 minutes, and the collateral review (the 20-item rating scale) takes approximately 60 minutes to complete. The interview may be spread over several sessions. The length of time required to administer the complete assessment depends on several factors, including the length of the interview, familiarity with the case, the amount of information to review, and whether collateral interviews need to be conducted.

DEVELOPMENT. Psychopathy is thought to be a stable dispositional factor that first manifests itself as a personality disorder in childhood. Although there is evidence of a heritable component to psychopathy, an adverse family environment may be just as important in its development. It is believed that psychopathy is related to difficulties in processing the emotional content of language; children with psychopathy appear to have difficulty learning the meaning of affective speech. Additionally, there is evidence that childhood psychopathic traits are related to the development of antisocial behavior in adults.

TECHNICAL.

Standardization sample. The sample consisted of 2,438 adolescents from Canada, the United States, and the United Kingdom. Data were collected from 19 different subsamples, including institutionalized offenders (detained in correctional or inpatient facilities); offenders on probation or in open custody or arrested youth referred for outpatient evaluation; and youth in the community (including conduct-disordered youth attending a treatment program).

Reliability. Mean interrater reliability estimates (intraclass correlations) of the 20 PCL:YV items across three settings (institutional, probation, and community) are generally acceptable. Most of these estimates are above .70. The internal consistency (Cronbach's alpha) estimates for the PCL:YV total score range from .85 to .94 across the settings. The mean interitem correlations for the instrument range from .23 to .43.

Validity. A great deal of validity information is presented in the manual. some of the reported validity studies were conducted with a modified version of the adult PCL where items were omitted that were inappropriate for youth. Convergent and discriminant validity studies report that the PCL:YV is related to several other measures associated with psychopathy in adolescents. A predictive validity study found that psychopathy as measured by the PCL:YV was relatively persistent into young adulthood, using criminal records as criteria. Additionally, a number of studies found evidence of predictive validity for the PCL:YV with recidivism as the criterion.

Exploratory and confirmatory factor analyses found that the PCL:YV items tended to load on the four factors: Interpersonal, Affective, Behavioral, and Antisocial. The factor structure of the PCL:YV appears to be similar to that of the PCL-R, indicating that there may be some continuity in the structure of psychopathy from adolescence to adulthood.

COMMENTARY AND SUMMARY. The ability to identify psychopathy during adolescence may be very important in the development of antisocial youth into adulthood. Although the PCL:YV appears to be very promising in this area, the extent to which personality disorders can be reliably measured in adolescents is unclear (Edens, Skeem, Cruise, & Cauffman, 2001). Traits such as irresponsibility and impulsivity, which are psychopathic in adults, may be developmentally appropriate for adolescents. [Editor's Note: The publisher advises that the PCL:YV does not rate youth on the normal presentation of traits such as impulsivity and irresponsibility. It rates them on extreme versions of these traits relative to other similarly aged youth.] Most of the psychometric studies of the PCL:YV employed classical test theory to estimate reliability and validity. Modern test theory techniques such as item response theory, however, may be more appropriate for evaluating the extent of measurement bias in its scores.

REVIEWER'S REFERENCE

Edens, J. F., Skeem, J. L., Cruise, K. R., & Cauffman, E. (2001). Assessment of juvenile psychopathy and its association with violence: A critical review. *Behavioral Sciences and the Law, 19*, 53–80.

[103]

The Harrington-O'Shea Career Decision-Making System—Revised, 2005 Update.

Purpose: An interest inventory that provides an assessment of career interests, job choices, school subjects, future plans, values, and abilities.
Population: Grade 7 and over.
Publication Dates: 1976-2005.
Acronym: CDM-R.
Administration: Individual or group.
Price Data, 2005: $399.95 per Career Exploration Classroom Set, Level 1, including CDM Level One, 25

workbooks, teacher's guide, and video set: $399.95 per Career Exploration Classroom Set, Level 2, including CDM Level 2, 25 workbooks, teacher's guide, and video set; $52.95 per 25 software scannable forms and interpretive folders; $52.95 per CDM Level 1 (English or Spanish), including 25 booklets, directions; $52.95 per CDM Level 2 (English or Spanish), including 25 booklets, interpretive folders, directions; $29.95 per manual (2000, 156 pages); $9.95 per sampler; $199.95 per set of career videos, "Tour of Your Tomorrow."
Foreign Language Editions: Available in Spanish.
Comments: Hand scored; updated every 2 years to reflect changes in occupational forecasts and titles; the reviewers had access to the 2003 update materials.
Authors: Thomas F. Harrington and Arthur J. O'Shea.
Publisher: AGS Publishing.
   a) LEVEL 1.
   Population: Middle school students, and other students and adults with reading difficulty.
   Publication Dates: 1992–2000.
   Scores: 6 Career Interest Areas: Crafts, Scientific, The Arts, Social, Business, Office Operations; 18 Career Clusters: Manual, Skilled Crafts, Technical, Math-Science, Medical-Dental, Literary, Art, Music, Entertainment, Customer Service, Personal Service, Social Service, Education, Sales, Management, Legal, Clerical, Data Analysis.
   Time: (20–25) minutes.
   b) LEVEL 2.
   Population: High school and college students and adults with average or better reading level.
   Publication Dates: 1976–2000.
   Scores: Same as *a* above and questions in 5 areas: Career Choices, School Subjects, Future Plans, Values, Abilities.
   Time: (30–45) minutes.
Cross References: See T5:1177 (2 references); for reviews by Debra Neubert and Marcia B. Shaffer of an earlier edition, see 12:179; see also T4:1128 (1 reference); for a review by Caroline Manuele-Adkins of an earlier edition, see 10:136 (1 reference); see also T3:1054 (3 references); for a review by Carl G. Willis of an earlier edition, see 8:1004.

Review of The Harrington-O'Shea Career Decision-Making System—Revised, 2005 Update by KEVIN R. KELLY, Head, Department of Educational Studies, Purdue University, West Lafayette, IN:

DESCRIPTION. The Career Decision-Making System—Revised, 2005 Update (CDM-R) is a career assessment and information package designed to provide step-by-step guidance through the career decision process. The CDM-R yields six interest scales paralleling Holland's (1997) interest model: Crafts (Realistic), Scientific (Investigative), The Arts (Artistic), Social (Social), Business (Enterprising), and Office Operations (Conventional). The Level 1 CDM-R is designed for "younger students or those clients who may be slow readers" (manual, p. 2) and consists of 96 interest items. The Level 2 CDM-R is designed for high school students and adults and consists of 120 interest items. The Level 1 test booklet provides comprehensive Job Charts that correspond to the six interest areas. These charts list typical jobs with education/training requirements and associated school subjects, work values, and abilities for each interest area. Level 1 test takers indicate their top Career Choices, School Subjects, Values, and Abilities after completing the interest questionnaire. The CDM-R Level 2 requires test-takers to designate their top Career Choices, School Subjects, Work Values, Abilities, and Future Plans before completing the 120-item interest assessment. The Level 2 CDM-R includes a separate Interpretive Folder that reports the typical jobs (with education and training requirements and associated school subjects, work values, abilities, and college major/training options) corresponding to the six interest areas.

Both the Level 1 and Level 2 CDM-R are available in Spanish. There is also a computer-scored (English only) CDM-R that produces a Client Interpretive Report, Interpretive Folder, and Summary Profile. Group summary reports for entire classes, groups, or schools can be generated with the computer-scored version. [Editor's Note: The publisher advises that the computer scoring software has been discontinued effective with the 2005 Update.]

DEVELOPMENT. The original CDM was developed in 1976. The authors significantly revised the CDM in 1991. The most important revisions were the development of a Level 1 CDM-R for middle school students and overall simplification of the reading level. The authors made four notable changes in the 2000 CDM-R revision. First, they redesigned the Job Charts and Interpretive Folder to "reflect a more contemporary image" (manual, p. 20). Second, they updated the job titles and school subjects in the Job Charts. Third, they included a "RIASEC Crosswalk" to enable test takers to match CDM-R interest scales with corresponding Holland interest types. Fourth, Feller and Vasos developed a Tour of Tomorrow videotape series to provide information about the six work environments.

TECHNICAL.

Reliability: Internal consistency. The following data are from the 1991 CDM-R standardization based on 1,961 students aged 11–20. For the Level 1 CDM-R, the median alpha coefficient was .89 for both girls and boys. The range was from .88 (Crafts, Social, Business) to .92 (Scientific) for girls and from .89 (Crafts, The Arts, Business) to .93 (Scientific) for boys. For the Level 2 CDM-R, the range of alpha coefficients for women was .90 (Social, Business) to .95 (Scientific); the range for men was .92 (The Arts) to .95 (Scientific). The median alpha coefficient for the Spanish CDM-R was .87. The CDM-R produces internally consistent interest scale scores.

Reliability: Temporal stability. For the original CDM interest scales, the median 30-day retest reliability coefficient for high school students was .85 for girls and .80 for boys. The median 30-day retest reliability coefficient for graduate students was .86 for women and .91 for men. The median 5-month retest reliability coefficient ranged from .75 (college women) to .82 (college men). For the Level 1 CDM-R, the 1-month retest reliability for unemployed adults was in the range of .74 (Social) to .87 (Office Operations) with a median of .79. The overall stability data were satisfactory. However, there is no evidence of the retest reliability for the Spanish CDM or for the Level 2 CDM-R. The temporal stability of these instruments remains to be demonstrated.

Reliability: Equivalence of forms. The authors administered Levels 1 and 2 of the CDM-R to a sample of 10th grade students. The correlations were in the range of .86 (Social) to .91 (Crafts, The Arts) with a median of .90. These results indicate that Levels 1 and 2 are equivalent forms of the CDM-R.

Reliability: Stability of self-reports. The authors assessed the stability of the Career Choice, School Subjects, Future Plans, Work Values, and Abilities self-reports over a period of 5 months for high school and first-year college students. The Career Choice and School Subject preferences of both college and high school students appeared to be highly stable over the 5-month period. The Abilities rankings of college students also appeared to be stable. However, the Abilities self-reports of high school students and the Future Plans of both high school and college students appeared to be subject to change. Counselors should be cautious in interpreting these client preferences.

VALIDITY.

Construct validity. Although the authors reported that they conducted a factor analysis in developing the 1991 CDM-R, they did not report the factor analysis results in the manual. Therefore, it is not possible to evaluate the adequacy of the six-interest scale structure chosen for the CDM-R.

The authors base the validity of the CDM-R interest scales on the correspondence of scale correlations to the pattern hypothesized in Holland's (1997) theory regarding the hexagonal ordering of interests. The authors compared the intercorrelations for four separate samples: Original CDM administered to 815 high school and college students, original CDM administered to 267 high school and junior college students, Level 2 CDM-R administered to 996 students in Grades 6–12, and reports of the Vocational Preference Inventory (VPI; Holland, 1997) scale correlations for 759 high school seniors taken from the VPI manual (Holland, 1985).

The results for the CDM-R Level 2 generally conformed to expectations. However, there were three notable exceptions. First, some correlations between adjacent interest scales were lower than expected. Second, correlations between adjacent CDM-R interest scales were consistently lower than those between adjacent VPI scales. Third, two of the three cross-hexagonal correlations were higher than expected; the Business-Scientific and The Arts-Office Operations correlations were .32 and .18, respectively.

Concurrent validity: Interest scales. The authors conducted three studies comparing three-letter CDM-R and Strong-Campbell Interest Inventory (SCII; Hansen & Campbell, 1985) interest codes. The first study included graduate students, the second included first-year college students, and the third included employed adults. In each study, the first three letters of the CDM-R and SCII were the same or the first two letters of each matched for 39%, 50%, and 18% of the members of each sample. The rate of agreement exceeded chance for each sample.

Concurrent validity: Self-report scales. The authors reported the School Subjects, Work Values, and Abilities preferences of students in 20 vocational-technical programs and 32 college majors and workers in 54 occupational groups. They used the *Guide for Occupational Exploration* (GOE; Harrington & O'Shea, 1984) to determine

"matches" between college majors/work settings and School Subjects, Values, and Abilities. The matches between School Subjects and GOE listings appear to be good.

The data for the Values self-reports raise serious questions about the validity of this measure. First, of the 14 Values, only 7 were listed as the top value for 99 of the 106 criterion groups. Second, the Good Salary value was listed as the top value for 46 of the criterion groups even some that provide relatively low income (e.g., Cosmetology, Flight Attendant, and Clerk). The Good Salary endorsement does not appear to be informative for either test takers or counselors. Third, there were several results that are simply difficult to explain: High Achievement was the top value for Ambulance Attendants; Independence was the top value for Secretaries; and Work with the Mind was the top value for Paralegals. Finally, the authors did not provide any concurrent validity data for the Values measures. The results for the Abilities findings were generally consistent with expectations.

Criterion-related validity. The authors administered the CDM to 53 occupational groups (overall *N* = 2,330) and 60 academic major groups (overall *N* = 3,313). They matched the modal CDM codes for each group with the interest codes from the Dictionary of Holland Occupational Codes (DOHC; Gottfredson & Holland, 1996) and used the Iachan index to quantify the quality of match. Of the 53 occupational groups, 55% had very close matches and 30% had reasonably close matches between the modal CDM interest code and the corresponding DOHC code. Of the 60 academic major groups, 45% had very close matches and 42% had reasonably close matches between CDM interest codes and DOHC codes. Overall, there is moderate to strong correspondence between CDM interests and occupational and academic major membership.

The authors reported the results of four predictive validity studies. In the first, Brown, Ware, and Brown (1985) studied the educational and occupational plans of high school seniors 3 years after they had been administered the CDM in ninth grade. Of those intending to directly enter the workforce, two-thirds expressed work goals that closely matched the CDM interest code. Of the students pursuing higher education, all had a close or reasonably close match to the CDM code.

The authors reported the results of a 5-year longitudinal follow-up of students who had completed the CDM in the 11th or 12th grade. The criterion was membership in a job or educational program matching the Career Cluster of the individual's highest two CDM codes. Overall, 56% of the students were in an occupation or academic major matching one of their top two CDM codes.

Cross-cultural validity. Harrington and O'Shea administered the CDM to English-speaking (N = 2,113) and French-speaking Canadian (N = 559) samples. They compared the hexagonal correlations among the CDM interest scales of the Canadian samples with those of the original CDM sample and the VPI (described previously in this review). The pattern of findings for the Canadian samples was generally parallel to those of the original CDM sample.

Harrington (1991) compared the mean CDM profiles for five culturally different samples of high school students: U.S. English speaking, U.S. Spanish speaking, Canadian English speaking, Canadian French speaking, and Australian. There were numerous differences in the mean CDM interest scale scores across the diverse samples. The author suggested that these results support the cross-cultural validity of the CDM, but it is not clear how this pattern of differences across cultures provides such support. In fact, the numerous differences across groups suggest that the CDM-R factor structure may differ across cultural groups.

Finally, the manual includes the results of a study in which a Norwegian translation of the CDM-R was administered to engineering, elementary teaching, business administration, and computer software development students. There were very close matches between the modal interest code for each academic group and the DHOC code for their academic specialty. Only the computer software development group did not match the DHOC code.

COMMENTARY. The CDM-R is a comprehensive interest assessment and career decision-making system. It has three principal assets. First, the CDM-R appears to have good predictive validity. CDM-R interests were demonstrated to have moderate associations with occupational fields and academic majors chosen 4 and 5 years following the initial assessment period. Second, the CDM-R is nicely packaged to provide students and decision-makers with extensive career information in a convenient package. The Level 2 Interpretive Folder is particularly informative and attractive. Third, the Tour of Tomorrow video package is an important resource for use in career guidance programs. The videos provide an effective narrative elaboration of the information provided in print format.

The CDM-R is not without its shortcomings. The biggest problem is the lack of convincing evidence to support the use of a six-factor career interest model. Although the authors reported the use of factor analyses, the results were not presented in the manual.

A second problem is the paucity of evidence regarding the relations of CDM-R scales to concurrent measures of the same constructs. It is common practice for interest test developers to use concurrent measures, such as the SDS or the SII.

The third major limitation of the CDM-R is the limited support for the self-report measures, particularly of Values and Abilities. The authors make the case for the usefulness of self-report measures in the manual. There is a general need for stronger validity data in support of the self-report measures.

The fourth concern is about the CDM interest scale labels. Although the CDM-R was designed to measure the Holland interest model, the authors do not use the Holland interest labels for five of the six interest scales. In the 2000 revision, the authors provided a "Crosswalk" for converting CDM labels to RIASEC terminology. One cannot help but wonder why the authors continue to use non-Holland labels for an instrument designed to measure the Holland interest model.

Finally, the authors did not provide evidence of the exploration or consequential validity of the CDM-R. Campbell and Raiff (2001) indicated that it is crucial to demonstrate that the CDM-R stimulates exploration of occupational and educational alternatives by test takers. The challenge remains to explore how the use and interpretation of the CDM-R is linked, if at all, to subsequent exploratory behaviors, personal growth, empowerment/discouragement, and choice.

SUMMARY. The CDM-R is a nicely formatted interest assessment and career information package. Its strength is the convenient link between interest testing and career exploration. CDM-R scales have been demonstrated to predict membership in occupational and academic major groups. These findings suggest that the CDM-R can be an effective career guidance tool. There is a need for a vigorous program of validity research to support the continued use of the CDM-R in the highly competitive market of career interest assessment.

REVIEWER'S REFERENCES

Brown, D., Ware, W. B., & Brown, S. T. (1985). A predictive validation of the Career Decision-Making System. *Measurement and Evaluation in Counseling and Development, 18,* 81–85.

Campbell, V. L., & Raiff, G. W. (2001). Harrington-O'Shea Career Decision-Making System, Revised (CDM). In J. T. Kapes & E. A. Whitfield (Eds.), *A counselor's guide to career assessment instruments* (pp. 228–234). Columbus, OH: National Career Development Association.

Gottfredson, G. D., & Holland, J. L. (1996). *Dictionary of Holland occupational codes* (3rd ed.). Odessa, FL: Psychological Assessment Resources.

Hansen, J. C., & Campbell, D. P. (1985). *Manual for the Strong-Campbell Interest Inventory* (4th ed.). Stanford, CA: Stanford University Press.

Harrington, T. F. (1991). The cross-cultural applicability of the Career Decision-Making System. *The Career Development Quarterly, 39,* 209–220.

Holland, J. L. (1985). *Manual for the Vocational Preference Inventory.* Odessa, FL: Psychological Assessment Resources.

Holland, J. L. (1997). *Making vocational choices* (3rd ed.). Odessa, FL: Psychological Assessment Resources, Inc.

U.S. Department of Labor. (1979). *Guide for occupational exploration.* Washington, DC: U.S. Government Printing Office.

Review of The Harrington-O'Shea Career Decision-Making System—Revised, 2005 Update by MARK L. POPE, *Associate Professor, Division of Counseling and Family Therapy, University of Missouri–St. Louis, St. Louis, MO:*

DESCRIPTION. The Harrington-O'Shea Career Decision-Making System—Revised, 2005 Update (CDM-R) was developed by Thomas F. Harrington and Arthur J. O'Shea in 1976 as a system rather than simply a classic interest inventory. From its inception, it has involved the student or client in a "number of steps that help in understanding self" (manual, p. 1), not just the measurement of career interest patterns. This is one way that it differs from the Strong Interest Inventory (15:248), Campbell Interest and Skills Survey (T6:380), or other such instruments. It is similar in its approach to the Self-Directed Search (T6: 2238). Although career interest measurement is an important part of the CDM-R, it is designed to assist the student or client in their career decisions by using measured patterns of interest along with self-estimates of work values and abilities as well as career information. The authors of the instrument describe the system as one where the clients/students "use interest survey scores and self-estimates to facilitate career planning, select college majors, choose training or retraining programs, and prepare for entering the job market" (manual, p. 7).

The version that was reviewed here is the 2000 revision and includes visual presentation changes; updating occupations, school subjects, and decision-making activities; and what the authors call a RIASEC crosswalk. The visual presentation changes include: a redesign of the materials adding color, a cleaner type font, an increase in the number of pages in the Level 2 booklet that allowed for more open space, and less dense listings in the Career Clusters Chart. Other revisions included adding more current jobs to the lists of typical cluster jobs (e.g. web site developer), adding occupations so that the job listings are representative of those that employ 90–95% of all workers in the U.S., and updating the terminology used to describe current curricular offerings in the schools. A new exercise was also added to aid in career decision-making. The final revision—a RIASEC crosswalk—was an important content addition as the authors have now included an explicit procedure for equating their subscale names with the more traditional RIASEC categories. This last revision is very useful as the new U.S. Department of Labor's O*NET program (the replacement for the *Dictionary of Occupational Titles* [DOT]) is organized around this typology.

The materials that are available for the 2000 revision of the CDM-R include: a 24-page Level 1 Booklet (U.S. English edition), a 2-page Level 1 "Directions for Administering" (U.S. English edition), a 16-page Level 2 Survey Booklet (hand-scored edition; U.S. English edition), a 17-inch x 22-inch folded Level 2 Interpretive Folder (U.S. English edition), a 24-page Level 1 Booklet (Spanish), a 16-page Level 2 Survey Booklet (hand-scored edition; Spanish), a 17-inch x 22-inch folded Level 2 Interpretive Folder (Spanish), an 8-page Level 2 Survey Booklet (computer-scored edition; U.S. English edition), a 16-page Level 2 Survey Booklet (Canadian English edition), a 17-inch x 22-inch folded Level 2 Interpretive Folder (Canadian English edition), a 16-page Level 2 Survey Booklet (Canadian French edition), a 17-inch x 22-inch folded Level 2 Interpretive Folder (Canadian French edition), a 144-page technical manual (copyright 2000), and a videotape series titled "Tour of Your Tomorrow."

In this review, I will restrict my descriptive and evaluative comments to the Level 1 and 2 materials including the technical manual.

The 24-page Level 1 booklet is hand-scored and it is a combined question booklet, answer sheet, and interpretative report booklet. It is "designed for many younger students and people of all ages with limited learning and reading ability" (manual, p. 7). It has a fourth-grade reading level with large print and lots of white space. The instructions are clear and simple. The process is direct. Sections include directions, a 96-item interest survey (using carbonless forms) (including answer sheet and scoring directions), finding your career areas, describing the career areas, learning to use the job charts, and six 2-page job charts with information on typical jobs.

The Level 2 materials include a survey booklet and an interpretive folder. These materials are for students and adults with stronger reading skills and have an eighth-grade reading level. The survey booklet uses strong ergonomic design principles (color, large print, direction lines) to assist the student or client in completing the questionnaire items. Sections include general directions, career choices, school subjects, work values, abilities, future plans, a 120-item interest survey, directions for scoring the interest survey, and directions for finding your career clusters.

The interpretive folder is a multicolored 17-inch x 22-inch, newspaper folded booklet. This a critical part of the CDM-R system. The instructions direct the student/client to transfer the results from the survey booklet to a "summary profile" in the interpretive folder. The student/client is then directed to follow a series of sequential sections that include your career interest areas, converting CDM interest areas to the RIASEC system, using the career clusters chart, interpreting and understanding your results, continuing your career exploration, and the next steps. Each section is clearly worded with the interpretive folder process conforming to effective professional career counseling practice.

The technical manual is very well done. It clearly presents the practical administration, scoring, and interpretation information along with the research bases for the development and refinement of the instrument. It also includes a chapter on gender fairness as well as extensive data on the use of the instrument with samples representing a diversity of ethnicities and races, genders, grade levels, and geographic regions. Issues of language and culture are also addressed as the data supporting the U.S. English, Spanish, Canadian English, and Canadian French editions are presented. It also has a new section that is an annotated bibliography of recently published research on the CDM-R.

It should be noted that this instrument has now been in continuous use for almost 30 years.

Further, the authors have consistently responded to the concerns of previous reviewers in their revisions (Manuele-Adkins, 1989; Neubert, 1995; Shaffer, 1995; Willis, 1978).

TECHNICAL. I have two concerns about the CDM-R: (a) equivalence of the forms of the instrument, and (b) the use of the instrument as a predictor of success and satisfaction in career choices.

I do have some concern with the equivalence between the original version of the interest inventory section and the two newest versions (Level 1 and 2). In the technical manual the authors detail the changes and present the data regarding the equivalence between the original version and Level 2 as well as between Level 1 and Level 2. Instead of a straightforward test of parallel forms reliability (same group, each taking the two forms) and then calculating a reliability coefficient, the authors test the equality of the covariance structures between the original CDM and the new CDM-R Level 2.

They do provide the straightforward parallel forms reliability data for one sample ($N = 230$) of 10th grade students and report a median reliability coefficient of .90 for the six scales. It should be noted that the parallel versions of the Social scale with the boys' sample had a reliability coefficient of only .81. This is somewhat problematic. Further, the reporting of a median instead of a mean is interesting. Finally, even a reliability coefficient of .90 is lower than what we would expect for acceptable equivalence. It would be better to have these coefficients in the mid to upper .90s. It would appear there is still work to be done in equating the two levels of the 2000 CDM-R. What this means for the practitioner is that some of the subscales may not be measuring exactly the same construct so care must be taken when choosing to use Level 1 or Level 2. The differences in length between the two versions or the differences in items that are detailed in the manual may also account for this.

COMMENTARY. The authors make a strong, reasoned, and data-driven argument about the differences between expressed interests and inventoried interests. This is not simply a theoretical difference. The CDM-R (and similar instruments like the Self-Directed Search) simply ask the student/client what their interests are (expressed), add them up, and because each subscale is composed of the same number of items, they can easily compare totals between each subscale. There are no criteria to be used for comparisons and, therefore, no norms. Interpretation is ipsative as the client is being compared with her/himself and the derived RIASEC codes are rank-ordered.

This stands in stark-contrast with the scale construction methods used in such inventories as the Strong Interest Inventory and the Campbell Interest and Skills Survey where specialized occupational criterion samples and general population samples provide comparison groups for a normative interpretation (inventoried interests).

The data used by the authors of the CDM-R to justify their method is based on expressed interests as better predictors of chosen college majors or actual career choices. Such data do not, however, address the issues of satisfaction, success, or happiness in career decisions, merely that expressed interests (what a person believes to be true about themselves) predict actual career choice. This seems obvious—what you believe to be true about yourself is the data that you use in your career decision-making that lead to a *certain* job choice. But what if you are unsure or confused? Or what if you do not know yourself very well? Will your expressed interests also be unsure or confused? The question that must be answered is: Does it lead to a "better" job choice?

With a more psychometrically sophisticated instrument that examines the item responses of criterion samples of satisfied and successful workers, will you have a better chance of making better predictions, especially for individuals who are unsure or confused or do not know themselves very well? Will the underlying interest patterns better emerge for such individuals through an expressed interest format or an inventoried interest format? The authors do not supply such information.

Further, ipsative interpretation strategies (rank-ordering subscales by total score) are important ways of making meaning of complicated inventory results; however, even if the scales have the same number of items, the question must be answered: How do we know that each item is similarly attractive? Just because the Social scale is #1 for this client, does it mean their interests are sufficiently strong to predict success or satisfaction in Social occupations? At a practical level for a particular client/student it is important self-knowledge that he or she prefers Social over Realistic interests, but is there any predictive validity (in terms of success or satisfaction) in that statement? For the CDM-R, we just do not know.

I was very impressed with the high quality of the instrument. From the production values to the quality of the content to the supporting research, the CDM-R is a very well-designed instrument. The issues raised in this review are relatively small and should not detract from the overall quality or the usefulness of the instrument itself as one instrument in a comprehensive battery of career assessment inventories.

SUMMARY. The CDM-R is the newest revision of the Harrington-O'Shea Career Decision-Making System. This review highlights important issues and concerns, but the issues and concerns that are raised do not override the utility of the CDM-R and its long history as an effective tool in a comprehensive career assessment battery. Because it is a self-scoring instrument that provides a useful interpretive system as part of its materials and because it is a well-researched and up-to-date instrument, it will likely be around for an even longer time.

REVIEWER'S REFERENCES

Manuele-Adkins, C. (1989). [Review of the Harrington O'Shea Career Decision-Making System.] In J. C. Conoley & J. J. Kramer (Eds.), *The tenth mental measurements yearbook* (pp. 344–345). Lincoln, NE: Buros Institute of Mental Measurements.

Neubert, D. (1995). [Review of the Harrington-O'Shea Career Decision-Making System—Revised.] In J. C. Conoley & J. C. Impara (Eds.), *The twelfth mental measurements yearbook* (pp. 456–457). Lincoln, NE: Buros Institute of Mental Measurements.

Shaffer, M. B. (1995). [Review of the Harrington-O'Shea Career Decision-Making System–Revised.] In J. C. Conoley & J. C. Impara (Eds.), The *twelfth mental measurements yearbook* (p. 457). Lincoln, NE: Buros Institute of Mental Measurements.

Willis, C. G. (1978). [Review of the Harrington-O'Shea System for Career Decision-Making.] In O. K. Buros (Ed.), *The eighth mental measurements yearbook* (pp. 1584–1585). Highland Park, NJ: Gryphon Press.

[**104**]

Health Dynamics Inventory.

Purpose: Developed to assess mental health status.
Population: Ages 3–18, 16–84.
Publication Date: 2003.
Acronym: HDI.
Scores, 13: Morale, Global Symptoms, Global Impairment, Depression, Anxiety, Attention Problems, Psychotic Thinking, Eating Disorders, Substance Abuse, Behavioral Problems, Occupational/Task Impairment, Relationship Impairment, Self-Care Impairment.
Administration: Group.
Forms, 2: Parent, Self.
Price Data, 2004: $210 per complete kit including technical manual (166 pages), 10 parent and 10 self item booklets, 25 parent and 10 self background information questionnaires, and 25 parent and 25 self response forms; $44 per technical manual; $16 per 10 item booklets (specify Parent or Self); $39 per 25 background information questionnaires (specify Parent or Self); $29 per 25 response forms (specify Parent or Self); $110 per 100 response forms (specify Parent or

Self); $50 per specimen set including technical manual, 1 Parent and 1 Self item booklets, 3 parent and 3 self background information questionnaires, and 3 parent and 3 self response forms.

Time: (15) minutes.

Comments: Parent form is completed for children ages 3–18 by parent.

Authors: Stephen M. Saunders and James V. Wojcik.

Publisher: Multi-Health Systems, Inc.

Review of the Health Dynamics Inventory by RIK CARL D'AMATO, *Assistant Dean and Director of the Center for Collaborative Research in Education, College of Education and Behavioral Sciences, M. Lucile Harrison Professor of Excellence, School of Professional Psychology, University of Northern Colorado, and* GREGORY C. WOCHOS, *Doctoral Student in School Psychology, Programs in School Psychology, University of Northern Colorado, Greeley, CO:*

DESCRIPTION. The Health Dynamics Inventory (HDI) is an individually administered instrument designed to quickly and accurately measure the current mental health status of individuals age 3 to 84. The HDI was developed to screen new patients for mental health problems and to measure treatment progress with continuing patients. Information is gathered using two sources, a background information questionnaire and either a self-report inventory and/or a parent-report inventory. The background information questionnaire indicates a patient's demographics, medical and psychiatric history, treatment experience, and a statement concerning why they are seeking treatment.

The HDI is available in two versions: the HDI-Self (HDI-S) and HDI-Parent (HDI-P). the HDI-S is a 50-item self-report inventory intended to be used with individuals ages 18 and above. The HDI-S can be administered out of age range to individuals as young as age 14; however, this is advocated only in conjunction with concurrent use of the parent form. The HDI-Parent (HDI-P) is a 49-item inventory completed by a parent or guardian for children under the age of 18. Three age profiles are compared on the HDI-P: 3–8-year-olds, 9–13-year-olds, and 14–18-year-olds. There is a discrepancy between the manual and the HDI-P Response Form regarding the first age profile, however. The manual reports the first age group profile as a 3- to 8-year-old range, whereas the HDI-P Response Form indicates a 4- to 8-year-old range. In addition, normal child and adolescent development varies substantially from year to year, therefore, comparing individuals grouped together in 5- or 6-year increments raises serious concerns regarding the developmental validity of the instrument.

The HDI operationalizes the tripartite model of mental health defined by the DSM-IV (American Psychiatric Association, 1994) via the Morale, Global Symptom, and Global Impairment scales. The Global Symptom scale consists of seven subscales found most frequently in mental health institutions: (a) Depression, (b) Anxiety, (c) Attention Problems, (d) Substance Abuse, (e) Psychotic Thinking, (f) Eating Disorders, and (g) Behavior Problems. These symptoms seem comprehensive and are based on previous research (Reynolds & Kamphaus, 2003). Critical items that relate to anger management, suicide, psychotic thinking, and substance abuse are also included. In addition, the Global Impairment scale addresses problems related to the responsibilities in one's life. Included in the Global Impairment scale are three subscales: (a) Occupational/Task Impairment, (b) Relationship Impairment, and (c) Self-Care Impairment. Although some components of the measure seem comprehensive, other important problem areas have not been addressed (e.g., child abuse).

Administration and scoring the HDI is fairly quick and easy, and can be done without the manual. Respondents begin by completing the Background Questionnaire, reading the item booklet, and then marking their answers with a pencil or pen on the corresponding response form. It is cumbersome to have respondents read from the item booklet and then mark their answers on a similar corresponding sheet. A clinician evaluation page is also located within the response form for noting additional information related to the patient (i.e., DSM diagnostic codes, general distress, psychological functioning). Raw scores are easily converted to *T*-scores and are graphically displayed on patient and nonpatient profiles for comparison.

DEVELOPMENT. The HDI was developed to provide a succinct assessment of psychological problems for a variety of mental health professionals. The HDI purportedly provides the documentation required by many insurance companies to initiate treatment. Readministration of the HDI can also document treatment progress that is required by many managed care organizations. In addition, the HDI was designed to be easily understandable for clinicians, patients, and their families. Because administration ease and efficiency was a primary goal, the authors deemed a questionnaire format most appropriate. Self-report instruments are widely used in mental health and medical arenas, and administration and scoring is usually easy to follow (D'Amato, Reynolds, & Fletcher-Janzen, in press).

Samples using nonpatient and patient groups were used for HDI development and testing. Although the authors did not elaborate on specific item development, they derived subscale items from patterns of symptoms defined by the DSM-IV diagnostic criteria. The HDI-P Global Symptoms scale contains 32 items encompassing the seven corresponding subscales. The Global Impairment Scale consists of 11 items for the three corresponding subscales. Conversely, the HDI-S contains 32 items covering its seven corresponding subscales and the Global Impairment Scale includes 12 items for the three corresponding subscales. On both versions of the HDI, the Morale scale is measured using 4 items related to the respondent's current mental health.

TECHNICAL. The normative sample used to develop the HDI was large. The HDI-P was administered to 1,030 nonpatients and 985 patients. Similarly, the HDI-S was administered to 2,161 patients and 1,574 nonpatients. The HDI-P norms are appropriately broken down in terms of gender, age, child's living situation, patient's marital status, school performance, child's mental health history, and whether the child was previously hospitalized for a mental or emotional condition. Similarly, the HDI-S contains age, gender, marital status, previous outpatient counseling, and hospitalization for emotional or psychiatric problems. The vast majority of respondents were recruited from Minnesota and Wisconsin, although some typical normative information is not included in the manual (level of SES, race, occupation). Thus, it is not clear that the sample is representative of the general population in the United States, although the authors did collect some participant date from eight other states.

The authors did an adequate job providing information about the reliability of scores from the HDI. Internal consistencies of the HDI scales and subscales were calculated using Cronbach's alpha coefficient and the split-half (Guttman) statistic. The full sample was used for the split-half calcu-

lation only. A coefficient alpha is used to calculate both the nonpatient sample and patient sample, as well as both samples grouped together. Because of the small number of items in some areas, the reliabilities were not calculated. There is a table displaying detailed internal reliability coefficients in the manual for each scale and subscale. Internal reliability coefficients for all scales and subscales on the HDI-S range from .70 to .95 for all participants combined, .70 to .95 for patients, and .69 to .94 for nonpatients. Internal reliability coefficients for all scales and subscales on the HDI-P range from .53 to .93 for all participants combined, .60 to .90 for patients, and .45 to .93 for nonpatients. Overall, it appears that reliability of the HDI-S is acceptable, and the HDI-P is marginally acceptable.

Validity of the HDI items, scales, and subscales was conducted using three sets of analyses. The authors did a fair job providing comprehensive validity information about the HDI. First, average scores from the items, scales, and subscales were compared between patients and nonpatients using independent t tests. For all but three items on the HDI-S and one item on the HDI-P, patient and nonpatient scores were significantly different, providing general support for the validity. Next, the validity of specific subscales was examined using the results of analyses of variance (ANOVA). Results support the authors' expected findings that patients with specific diagnosis would score higher on certain subscales than nondiagnosed patients and nonpatients. Finally, correlational analyses were conducted between clincian's rating of distress and impairment versus patient's reports. Overall, correlations on the HDI were acceptable.

COMMENTARY. The HDI appears to be a somewhat useful instrument for screening and measuring treatment progress of mental health problems in children and adults. The test is easy to administer and score and can be completed in a relatively short period of time. The HDI uses the tripartite model of mental health that closely matches the diagnostic symptoms outlined in the DSM-IV. Additionally, it measures symptoms commonly observed in mental health clinics. The HDI can be used by a variety of mental health professionals allowing application in various settings. One major flaw of the instrument relates to the normal developmental changes displayed in children, adolescents, and adults. Because of the large age ranges in each group, the content validity is clearly called into question. Because the HDI is such a brief instrument, it is not comprehensive in its evaluation of all mental health disorders. The HDI does not offer a lie scale to determine if the responder has answered honestly. Individuals can easily minimize or hide psychological symptoms on the HDI, and similarly, symptoms may be exaggerated.

SUMMARY. The test authors have produced a measure to aid in the assessment and treatment of an array of mental health problems found in adults and children. The HDI purports to identify and isolate treatment goals, screen for existing mental health conditions, and monitor treatment progress. It yields easily understandable information about the current mental health status of individuals ages 3 to 84, but serious concerns about content validity related to age group ranges are present. Until the HDI is revised to address these substantial issues, this inventory cannot be recommended for standardized use. However, it may have some informal clinical utility for individuals interested in qualitative information.

REVIEWERS' REFERENCES
American Psychiatric Association. (1994). *Diagnostic and statistical manual of mental disorders* (DSM-IV; 4th ed.). Washington, DC: American Psychiatric Association.
D'Amato, R. C., Reynolds, C. R., & Fletcher-Janzen, E. (Eds.). (in press). *The handbook of school neuropsychology.* New York: Wiley.
Reynolds, C. R., & Kamphaus, R. W. (Eds.). (2003). *Handbook of psychological and educational assessment of children: Personality, behavior, and context* (2nd ed.). New York: Guilford Press.

Review of the Health Dynamics Inventory by JEFFREY A. JENKINS, Assistant Professor, Roger Williams University, Bristol, RI:

DESCRIPTION AND DEVELOPMENT. The Health Dynamics Inventory (HDI) measures mental health conditions and problems for children, adolescents, and adults. It is intended for use by those who work in therapeutic settings as a screening instrument for evaluating the mental health of patients either at or before intake or to assess progress during therapy.

The HDI technical manual states that the authors relied on a tripartite model of mental health, which theorizes that mental health problems stem from (a) emotional or behavioral problems (symptoms), (b) emotional distress, and (c) inability to fulfill life roles (impairment) (see American Psychiatric Association, 1994, p. xxi; Howard, Lueger, Maling, & Martinovich, 1993). Thus, the HDI was designed to measure these three aspects of mental health. The emotional distress scale, labeled Morale (four items), is intended to reflect a patient's sense of well-being

and happiness. The Global Symptoms scale (33 items) includes the most common presenting problems in the population. These disorders comprise separate subscales of the Global Symptoms scale and include Depression (9 items), Anxiety (6 items), Attention Problems (2 items), Psychotic Thinking (4 items), Eating Disorders (6 items), Substance Abuse (4 items), and Behavior Problems (4 items). Finally, the Global Impairment scale consists of three subscales with 4 items within each: Occupational/Task Impairment, Relationship Impairment, and Self-Care Impairment.

The HDI was developed in two forms—an adult version (HDI-S) for those 18 years and older and a children's version (HDI-P) for those under 18. HDI-P is completed by the child's parent or guardian. HDI-S consists of 50 items (49 for HDI-P), along with a separate Background Information Questionnaire that gathers demographic, medical, and psychiatric history. Items in both forms are presented in Likert scale format. For example, in rating an item on the Morale scale, "In the past two weeks how much of the time have you felt content or satisfied with your life?" respondents use a 5-point rating scale from *None of the time* to *All of the time.* For each item in the Symptoms scale, respondents are asked to rate "How often have you been bothered by the following in the past two weeks?"; item prompts are then presented such as "Feeling anxious, agitated, or unable to relax" (Anxiety subscale). Similarly, the Impairment scale asks "Rate how much difficulty emotional or behavioral problems cause in your ability to do the following," and includes such items as "Concentrate on tasks" (Occupational/Task Impairment), and "Maintain good diet or health habits" (Self-Care Impairment).

Respondents mark their rating of each item on a carbonless answer sheet that is well-organized and easy to use; responses transfer to the multipart pages to facilitate scoring. Both forms of HDI are short and concise, requiring approximately 15 minutes to complete. The publisher estimates the reading level of the items to be sixth grade. Scoring is a simple matter of transferring and adding values for each item that appears in separate columns for each subscale on page 2 of the multipart scoring form. The third page of the multipart scoring form allows practitioners to create a profile of scale and subscale scores for normative comparison. In addition, the scoring form contains a clinical evaluation sheet that allows the clinician to rate the patient's degree of distress, occupational or task impairment, relationship impairment, and self-care impairment.

TECHNICAL. The norms for the HDI-S are derived from samples of both patients (n = 2,161) and nonpatients (n = 1,574); HDI-P norms are based on samples of 985 patients and 1,030 nonpatients. The technical manual provides useful tables of demographic and clinical characteristics for all samples, as well as scale and subscale means and standard deviations. For comparative purposes, the norm groups appear to be adequate, although the authors note that most of the nonpatient respondents were from Minnesota and Wisconsin, and the patient sample consisted of mental health patients at clinics operated by Human Services, Inc. Therefore, some caution is warranted in making normative interpretations.

The psychometric characteristics of both forms of the HDI are generally acceptable for clinical purposes, although some of the subscales of the HDI-P should not be used for individual diagnostic purposes (see below). Internal consistency reliability based on the norm sample yielded Cronbach's alpha estimates for the HDI-P scales of .82 (Morale), .90 (Global Symptoms), and .86 (Global Impairment) across all ages for patients. Subscale estimates of coefficient alpha for patients across all ages ranged from .60 to .87. When used with 3- to 8-year-old patients, some subscale scores should be interpreted cautiously because of their relatively low reliability (Eating Disorders, .51, Psychotic Thinking, .60). Likewise, low reliability estimates for some subscales warrant caution in their use with 9- to 13-year-old patients (Psychotic Thinking, .55, Eating Disorders, .61, and Relationship Impairment, .63).

For HDI-S, reliability estimates using coefficient alpha are somewhat higher than those for HDI-P. For patients, coefficient alpha for Morale was found to be .88, Global Symptoms was .95, and Global Impairment was .92. Subscale reliabilities ranged from .70 to .92. Thus, these reliability estimates support use of the HDI-S for individual diagnostic screening.

Validity of the HDI was assessed by taking a criterion-based approach that examined discriminant and convergent evidence of validity. This is appropriate given the diagnostic purpose of the instrument. Specifically, HDI scores for patients were compared to those for nonpatients, HDI scores for patients diagnosed with specific disorders were compared to patients without those disorders and to nonpatients, and correlations between patient HDI scores and their clinician's ratings of distress and impairment were computed. Thus, the goal was to determine whether the instrument could discriminate between those with and without various disorders, and to determine whether HDI scores for patients are consistent with independent psychological assessments of patients.

The validity of the HDI was supported in both respects. The mean scale and subscale scores differed significantly for patients and nonpatients. For each subscale, the mean HDI subscale score of patients diagnosed with the disorder measured by the subscale was significantly higher than that of patients without the disorder and was higher than that of nonpatients. Finally, correlations between patients' scale and subscale scores and clinicians' ratings of patients' distress, Occupational/Task Impairment, Relationship Impairment, and Self-Care Impairment were computed. This yielded validity coefficients ranging from .24 to .48 for the global scales, and ranging from .02 to .47 for the subscales. Most of the coefficients fall within an acceptable range for a mental health diagnostic tool, particularly given the potential unreliability of the clinical ratings. Although some of these coefficients are low for diagnostic purposes, when coupled with the evidence of discriminant validity reported, the HDI can be used with a fairly high degree of confidence for clinical mental health assessment.

SUMMARY. As a diagnostic tool for mental health problems, the HDI has many advantages. It has solid technical characteristics, is easy to administer and interpret, and provides considerable practical utility given the demands of clinical practice. The measurement of both psychological symptoms and the extent of impairment is a particular strength of the instrument. The technical manual is easy to read, reviews the purposes and background of the instrument's development, and offers clear directions for use and interpretation of responses. The manual also is thorough yet concise in reporting evidence of reliability, validity, and norming. The HDI can be used with considerable confidence by those requiring a mental health screening tool.

REVIEWER'S REFERENCES

American Psychiatric Association. (1994). *Diagnostic and statistical manual of mental disorders* (4th ed.). Washington, DC: Author.

Howard, K. I., Lueger, R. J., Maling, M. S., & Martinovich, Z. (1993). A phase model of psychotherapy outcome: Causal mediation of change. *Journal of Consulting and Clinical Psychology, 61,* 678–685.

[105]

Health Occupations Basic Entrance Test.

Purpose: "A diagnostic instrument [designed] to assist Health Occupation schools evaluate the academic and counseling skills of new applicants to their programs."

Population: Adult applicants to health occupation schools or programs.

Publication Dates: 2000–2001.

Acronym: HOBET.

Scores, 28: 7 Essential Math Skills scores (Whole Numbers, Number System Conversions, Algebra Equations, Percent Operations, Decimal Operations, Fractions Operations, Composite), 3 Reading Comprehension scores (Reading Rate, Reading Rate Placement, Composite), 3 Critical Thinking Appraisal scores (Main Idea of Passage, Inferential Reading, Predicting of Outcomes), Testtaking Skills score, 2 Social Interaction Profile scores (Passive, Aggressive), 5 Stress Level Profile scores (Family, Social, Money/Time, Academic, Work Place), 6 Learning Styles (Auditory Learner, Solitary Learner, Visual Learner, Social Learner, Oral Dependent Learner, Writing Dependent Learner), Composite Percentage.

Administration: Group.

Forms, 2: A, B.

Price Data, 2002: $17 per test by computer; $10.50 per test booklet (36 pages); $8 per answer sheet; $27.50 per Study Guide (150 pages); quantity discounts available.

Time: 150 minutes.

Comments: Generates a Diagnostic Report including Group Report and individual Student Reports; Group Report provides group-level mean percentages and normative comparisons for the 28 scores; optional Study Guide offers test-taking strategy tips and practice tests.

Author: Michael D. Frost.

Publisher: Educational Resources, Inc.

Review of the Health Occupations Basic Entrance Test by JAMES T. AUSTIN, Research Specialist 2, and ERICH C. FEIN, Senior Program Associate, Center on Education and Training for Employment, College of Education, The Ohio State University, Columbus, OH:

DESCRIPTION. The Health Occupations Basic Entrance Test (HOBET) was designed for Health Occupation schools to use in evaluating the academic and social skills of adult applicants. The HOBET provides a series of Math Skill scores for math operations deemed essential to success in health occupation programs. It also provides scores for Reading Comprehension of science-based text written at the 10th grade level. Individual scores for Math Skills and Reading Comprehension are combined into a Composite score. The HOBET also provides scores for the skills of Critical Thinking and Test Taking and provides profile data on Social Skills, Stress Level, and Learning Styles. This is a large number of scores from a single test. The test is divided into seven sections with the majority of test content devoted to the Math Skills and Reading Comprehension items. Most items are presented in a four-option, multiple-choice format. The HOBET is administered via both computer and paper-and-pencil methods. The test uses an electronic scoring option, which produces group profile reports as well as summary reports for individual students. Scores on these reports are compared to a 1993-1996 norming sample of 4,328 beginning students.

DEVELOPMENT. This test was constructed within a conceptual framework, thus satisfying one part of a key criterion of the *Standards for Educational and Psychological Testing* (AERA, APA, & NCME, 1999). Its stated purpose is to provide a set of scores that can be used in the selection of applicants for health occupations training programs. Panels of health occupations faculty served as content experts. Items were pilot tested using groups of health occupation students. However, the definitions offered for the constructs measured by most of the scales are limited. In addition, there is no rationale provided for including measures of test taking skills, social skills, stress level, and learning styles in a test developed to select applicants for admission into health occupation training programs.

TECHNICAL. We reviewed a technical manual of 25 pages by Frost, Jarvis, Lancaster, and Tuttle (2000) and the HOBET Form A testbook and a sample Diagnostic Report for test Form A.

Standardization. The manual provides two different numbers (2,155 and 1,872 students) for the "original standardization" of the HOBET. Therefore, the exact number of students in the standardization sample cannot be determined from the manual. Other than the claim that these students represent main geographical regions of the United States, no further information about the sample is provided. The HOBET was correlated with the ACT by comparing the projected HOBET composite scores of the students within this sample against the ACT composite for reading and math.

Reliability. Split-half reliability estimates are provided for HOBET subtests of Reading, Math, Social Interaction, Stress Level, and Learning Styles. These reliability coefficients ranged from .81–.98, with most estimates between .91–.98. Although these estimates fall within an appropriate range, the manual provides no other estimates of reliability (retest, internal consistency, parallel forms).

Validity. Content validity is supported through the use of judgments from the examination committee that guided the selection of test items. These judgments might be better documented. Criterion-related validity is supported through the correlation of HOBET composite scores with ACT composite scores. The resulting correlation was .81. The manual provides summaries of several other studies that found positive relationships between scores on the HOBET and variables of interest such as first-year course grades; however, important details of such analyses were omitted. For example, the manual reviews a criterion-related validation study by Abdur-Rahman, Femea, and Gains but fails to include tables referenced in the article that summarize correlational and regression analyses. In addition, the manual provides little or no validity evidence for the score categories of Critical Thinking, Test Taking Skills, Social Skills, Stress Level, and Learning Styles. This lack is particularly troublesome because many of the secondary scales measured by the HOBET, such as Social Skills and Test Taking Skills, are not well-established constructs. A highlight of the manual is a DIF analysis on a population of 1,060 examinees from various cultural groups and regions of the United States. Using the Mantel-Haenszel procedure, the author concluded that there is no culture bias in the HOBET.

COMMENTARY. The overall utility of the HOBET is somewhat compromised by the assessment of skills and profiles that are secondary to the intended purpose of the test. In fact, the manual claims that scores for the Test Taking Skills, Social Skills, Stress Level, and Learning Styles subtests are "more useful to an instructor than an administrator who is considering a student for possible enrollment" (p. 14). In addition, there

is virtually no validity evidence provided for these scores. The inclusion of such ancillary scales may induce decision makers to take these scores into account when selecting candidates, thus possibly contaminating the selection process. Overall, the strength of the test is in the production of numerous Math and Reading Comprehension Skill scores. The diagnostic report, which provides detailed and useful information about math and reading skills, is another strength of the HOBET. The HOBET's computer-based administration and electronic scoring are also useful options, and this functionality could be expanded via test delivery and scoring through the internet. It will be important going forward to develop information about comparability of administration formats (paper, computer).

SUMMARY. Based on the evidence available, it is possible to recommend the HOBET as a useful tool in the process of selecting applicants for admission into health occupation training programs. However, of the 28 scores produced by the HOBET, only 10—the essential Math Skills and Reading Comprehension scores—are likely to be useful in the selection of applicants. In addition, there is no evidence of the stability of these scores, as only split-half reliability estimates have been provided. The measurement of the remaining constructs such as Learning Styles and Test Taking Skills require the investment of time and energy from both organizations and examinees that may be better used elsewhere.

The HOBET would definitely benefit from expanded validity evidence to address the utility of scores other than essential Math Skills and Reading Comprehension. The manual mentions content validation judgments of learning style behaviors, and the inclusion of these data may be a good starting point for enhancing the validity evidence of the test. Furthermore, the issue of criterion-related validity should be addressed through comparing the HOBET with measures other than ACT scores. Other health occupation entrance assessments such as the Nurse Entrance Test (169), which provides seven math skills scores deemed essential to success in nursing, could provide useful comparison scores. The issue of divergent validity could be addressed through comparing HOBET scores to tests of nonverbal ability such as the Universal Nonverbal Intelligence Test (T6: 2636). However, in spite of gaps in validity evidence and the inclusion of scores that are questionable for selection purposes, there is enough evidence to suggest that the math and reading scores offered by the HOBET are free of bias and valid for the selection of applicants to health occupation training programs.

REVIEWERS' REFERENCE

American Educational Research Association, American Psychological Association, & National Council on Measurement in Education. (1999). *Standards for educational and psychological testing.* Washington, DC: American Educational Research Association.

Review of the Health Occupations Basic Entrance Test by NAMBURY S. RAJU, Distinguished Professor, Institute of Psychology, Illinois Institute of Technology, Chicago, IL:

DESCRIPTION. The Health Occupations Basic Entrance Test (HOBET) consists of six subtests: Essential Math Skills (60 items), Reading Comprehension for Science Textbooks (33 items), Social Interaction Profile (30 items), Stress Level Profile (50 items), Learning Style (45 items), and Test-Taking Skills (30 items). In addition to scores on these six subtests, a composite score based on scores from the math and reading comprehension subtests, a reading rate score, and over 30 different diagnostic scores are provided as part of the student diagnostic report. Some of the items in these subtests have a multiple-choice format and others have an agree/disagree or choose-one-of-two-options format.

The HOBET is intended as a diagnostic tool for use by Health Occupation schools in evaluating the academic and social skills of applicants to their programs. Student scores are reported as percentages; in addition, percentile scores are reported for math, reading comprehension, and the composite subtests. Also reported are various scores for use in admissions and in diagnosing strengths and weaknesses for individual students. There are two forms (Forms A and B) of the HOBET.

DEVELOPMENT. Results from a survey of a sample of health occupations program directors in the United States were used to define the content for the HOBET program in close consultation with professionals actively involved in both teaching and academic counseling in health occupations programs. Test items were written by individual health occupation faculty. These items were later pretested and evaluated for their psychometric quality. The HOBET technical and development manual contains only limited information about the item and test development process. Information about how many items were

initially written, the size and representativeness of the pretest sample, and which item statistics were computed and used in the final item selection would be very helpful in evaluating the overall psychometric quality of the HOBET.

TECHNICAL. The technical and development report offers information about reliability, validity, differential item functioning (DIF), and standardization of the HOBET. These psychometric data are reviewed and evaluated in this section.

Reliability. Reliability estimates are provided for only five subtests (Math, Reading Comprehension, Social Profile, Stress Profile, and Learning Styles). These are, according to the technical manual, parallel form estimates of reliability, ranging from .81 for the Math subtest to .98 for the Reading Comprehension test. These appear to be acceptable levels of reliability. There are no test-retest, internal consistency, or split-half estimates of reliability. Also not reported are reliability estimates for the Test-Taking Skills subtest and the various diagnostic skill scores.

Based on the information in the technical manual, it is difficult to determine the specific sample (or samples) used in the reliability investigation. It may have been the same sample used in the standardization of the HOBET, but the manual does not explicitly indicate that was the case. Additional information about the types of samples used and how they were obtained would help potential and current users of the HOBET better evaluate the psychometric quality of this instrument.

Validity. The technical manual considers three types of validity: content validity, criterion-related validity, and diagnostic validity. Review of health occupations programs in the United States and procedures used for defining test content and item development specifications were used as the basis for inferring the content validity of the HOBET. Although this may be considered an acceptable method for inferring content validity, additional details about the specifics involved would have been very helpful.

The criterion-related validity evidence of the HOBET was provided by correlating the Math and Reading Comprehension subtests with the American College Testing (ACT) Program subtests and the ACT composite. These correlations vary between .79 and .83, indicating a strong relationship between the HOBET academic subtests and the ACT subtests. No such information is presented for the other four subtests and the diagnostic scores.

Although the reported correlations with the ACT scores are high, one wonders whether these correlations are really a measure of the criterion-related validity of academic subtests of the HOBET. These high correlations appear to reflect more on the construct validity rather than on the criterion-related validity of these academic subtests. The fact that these subtests were equated to the ACT subtests for developing normative data (see below) for the HOBET academic subtests strongly suggests that the reported HOBET/ACT correlations are evidence more of construct validity rather than criterion-related validity.

Information about what is typically referred to as criterion-related validity is contained in a study, reproduced toward the end of the technical manual. This study, based on a sample of 128 cases, showed that the HOBET scores predicted the first semester grades of health occupation students quite well, in excess of 30% of common variance. Even though this study appears to have been well executed, two tables were missing from this report, which made it difficult to evaluate the claims about criterion-related validity.

DIF. Using the Mantel-Haenszel procedures, the test performance of four minority groups (African American, Native American, Hispanic, and Asian) was compared to the test performance of Caucasians. The sample sizes for the minority groups varied from a minimum of 152 (African American) to a maximum of 215 (Hispanic). The sample size for the Caucasian group was 353. Based on this analysis, it was concluded that there were no items with significant DIF across the four comparisons. It may be true, but it is difficult to evaluate this claim based on the reported data. In fact, the data shown in the technical and development manual are difficult to follow. Are these average alphas by subtest and comparison? How do these data relate to the significance or nonsignificance of item level DIF? There is a definite need for additional information before one can infer that there were no items with significant DIF across the six subtests and the four comparisons.

Standardization. There was no direct or typical standardization of the academic subtests of the HOBET, but percentiles for these subtests and the composite were derived by equating them to the appropriate subtests in the ACT. The equat-

ing sample consisted of over 2,000 participants, and the correlations between the HOBET and ACT subtests were in the .80s. It was not clear which equating method (an item response theory [IRT]-based method, equipercentile, or some other method) was used. Additional information about the equating method would be very helpful.

SUMMARY. The HOBET program was designed to meet an important need in the health occupations arena. It was designed for selection as well as for diagnosing the strengths and weaknesses of applicants to the health occupation schools. Although it may be accomplishing its objective, the lack of sufficient psychometric detail and information about the program makes it difficult to confirm it conclusively. There is a definite need for more information about the reliability of HOBET scores, especially the diagnostic scores, DIF, and the standardization. There is also a need for information about the size and representativeness of the various samples involved in the psychometric analysis. The authors may also want to consider using IRT methodology in developing future editions of the HOBET.

[106]
Healthcare Customer Service Test.

Purpose: Selects customer service oriented workers for hospitals and healthcare settings.
Population: Hospital employees (service, skilled, professional, nursing, administrative, physician, technicians, environmental services).
Publication Dates: 1996–1997.
Acronym: HCST.
Scores, 5: Collaborate, Accommodate, Respect, Engage, Total.
Administration: Group.
Price Data: Available from publisher.
Time: (25–35) minutes, untimed.
Comments: Used for selection; subtests can be used for interview probes.
Author: Healthcare Testing, Inc.
Publisher: Silverwood Enterprises, LLC.

Review of the Healthcare Customer Service Test by RONALD A. BERK, Professor of Biostatistics and Measurement, School of Nursing, The Johns Hopkins University, Baltimore, MD:

DESCRIPTION. The Healthcare Customer Service Test is a 27-item paper-and-pencil test designed to measure the customer service orientation of healthcare employees. All items are in multiple-choice format with five alternative courses of action. Each question presents a scenario involving a customer service situation for which the respondent picks the "Best" and "Worst" course of action. The scenarios represent a range of customer service behaviors for a wide variety of health care positions, including nurses, social workers, therapists, systems analysts, managers, supervisors, secretaries, and support staff (aides, orderlies, attendants).

The test can be administered to an individual or groups of job applicants. Standardized procedures are provided for administration along with detailed instructions for administrators. Scoring is conducted by a private company or by the institution administering the test. Raw scores and percentile ranks are reported for total test, best and worst alternatives, and four core dimensions of customer service (Collaborate, Accommodate, Respect, Engage). Norms and cutoff scores are given for high, average, and low performance for general jobs and support jobs. It is recommended that interviews of job applicants proceed in a logical order from the individual with the highest score to the one with the lowest.

DEVELOPMENT. This test is a shortened revision (copyright, 1996) of an earlier 35-item test. The administration and technical manuals do not indicate what changes were made in the items from the longer version or any evidence on the equivalence of the two tests. The technical manual information on the development of the test and the "validity" studies are based entirely on the original 35-item version. The original test was not provided for this review.

The domain of customer service situations was determined from two focus groups and the critical incidents technique. A total of 24 superior customer service employees from a large metropolitan hospital were asked to describe actual events that demonstrated good and poor customer service. These events were compiled into two lists: 19 behaviors identified as customer-service related and 34 common incidents that confront employees in a healthcare setting.

A job analysis survey of 65 employees in the same hospital provided additional information on (a) their frequency of contact with various customer groups, (b) the importance of the work behaviors, and (c) the frequency of the common incidents (work situations). The rankings from this survey and the 34 incidents were used to create the situationally based scenarios for the 34 test items. Although the rating scales and results were reported, there is no account of how the incidents were actually transformed into multiple-choice items.

TECHNICAL. The technical manual does not describe any norm sample. Reference is made to pilot data collected from 345 healthcare professionals, but there is no description of this group or specific scores derived from their performance. All other samples mentioned are defined in the context of validity studies: 24 superior employees for the focus group, 65 employees for the job analysis survey, and 103 volunteers for the criterion-related (predictive) validity study. Means and standard deviations are reported for these groups by general and support job categories.

In the test administration manual, the instructions for scoring and interpretation provide pages with Hospital General Norms for general and support jobs in terms of cutoff scores and ranges for "low," "average," and "high" performance. Another page indicates cutoff scores for the total test, best and worst scores, and the dimension subtests related to the 10th, 25th, 50th, and 75th percentile ranks. No explanations were given for how any of these cutoffs were determined or the sample upon which they were based.

Reliability was reported with one statement claiming high internal consistency reliability based on an alpha coefficient of .84 for the original 34-item test. The sample for this estimate was not identified nor was any coefficient computed for the "revised" 27-item test. No equivalence coefficient or any other information was reported on the relationship between the original and shortened tests.

Content validity evidence was presented as the results of the critical incidents technique with focus groups and the job analysis survey. They were used to develop the four core dimensions or CARE model of customer service, the list and definitions of behaviors under each dimension, and the 34-item (and 27-item) multiple-choice test. However, just how those results produced the job specifications and test items is unclear. There was also no systematic judgmental review of the relationship between the items (long or short version) and the specifications and the representativeness of the item sample.

Criterion-related validity evidence was based on a study of the relationship of the test to job performance ratings. A sample of 103 volunteer hospital employees (*n* = 82 general, *n* = 21 support) were rated by their supervisors on a 1 (low) to 7 (high) point scale on the four dimensions and overall customer service orientation. The composite dimension rating and overall rating correlated .33 and .23, respectively, with test performance. The inference from these statistically significant validity coefficients was that "the customer service test is highly predictive of job performance... [and it] is valid for use in selecting customer service oriented employees" (manual, p. 19). No regression analyses or standard errors of estimate were computed to support this predictive validity claim. The percentage of explained variance ranged from 5.3 to 11% and the standard errors of estimate were almost identical to the standard deviation of the test (criterion), indicating a high degree of inaccuracy in predicting job performance. About 89-95% of the variance in job performance is explained by factors other than the customer service test.

COMMENTARY. The latest version of the Healthcare Customer Service Test appears to be well-constructed and built on an explicitly defined domain of customer service behaviors. Focus groups and a comprehensive job analysis provided the foundation for both. Unfortunately, there are so many unexplained steps in developing the test that it is unclear what the relationship is among the foundation, the domain, and the test. The lack of any norm group questions the meaning of the test scores. Other weaknesses include small, unrepresentative employee samples from one hospital for the content validity and criterion-related validity studies, and an unidentified sample to estimate reliability. The results from these studies render the technical evidence inadequate to justify the use of the test scores for employee selection. The claims for the test's use far exceed the evidence reported, particularly for its predictive validity. Even the intent of the scoring system to differentiate customer-service-oriented employees from those who exhibit poor service on the job has no supportive evidence. No discriminant validity study was conducted to determine the accuracy with which the test could classify employees into those groups.

SUMMARY. On a superficial level, the test and the core dimensions upon which it is based seem content sound. However, a more thorough analysis of the procedures used to develop the original 34-item test and the failure to describe any process for creating the shorter 27-item version indicate serious problems. Despite the efforts to construct the tool according to job analysis specifications, the nondescriptive, unrepresentative convenience samples for that analysis as well as for the validity and reliability studies restrict the application of the test scores. Those samples limit localized, much less generalized use of the scores for furnishing meaningful information on the customer service orientation of healthcare employees. Systematically designed psychometric studies with appropriate samples of employees for each intended use of the test scores must be completed for the 27-item test to satisfy professional standards. Pending the outcomes of those studies, this Healthcare Customer Service Test might be worthy of recommendation.

[107]
Home & Community Social Behavior Scales.

Purpose: Provides rating of both social skills and antisocial behaviors.
Population: Ages 5–18.
Publication Date: 2002.
Acronym: HCSBS.
Scores, 6: Peer Relations, Self-Management/Compliance, Social Competence Total, Defiant/Disruptive, Antisocial/Aggressive, Antisocial Behavior Total.
Administration: Individual.
Price Data, 2002: $47 per user's guide (116 pages); $32 per 25 test forms.
Time: (5–10) minutes.
Comments: Rated by parent or other home-based rater.
Authors: Kenneth W. Merrell and Paul Caldarella.
Publisher: Assessment-Intervention Resources.

Review of the Home & Community Social Behavior Scales by THEODORE COLADARCI, Professor of Educational Psychology, University of Maine, Orono, ME:

DESCRIPTION. The Home & Community Social Behavior Scales (HCSBS) is a 64-item behavior rating scale that is completed by parents "and other home-based raters" of children and youth between ages 5 and 18. In contrast to the "highly clinical" nature of many child behavior rating instruments, the HCSBS is designed to emphasize "routine or commonly occurring social competencies and problems" (user's guide, p. 2).

The 103-page user's guide, although poorly edited, provides detailed information regarding development, administration, score interpretation and use (including illustrative case studies), and technical properties.

Taking only 8–10 minutes to complete, the HCSBS provides two total scores: Social Competence ("social skills and traits that are characteristic of well-adjusted and socially-skilled children and youth") and Antisocial Behavior ("socially-related problem behaviors that may impede socialization, be destructive or harmful to others, and produce negative social outcomes"). Each of these two scales in turn yields two subscale scores. For Social Competence, the subscales are Peer Relations ("behavioral characteristics important in making friends, being a positive and constructive member of a peer group, and being well-liked by other children or youth") and Self-Management/Compliance ("behaviors and characteristics that are important in responding to the social expectations of parents, teachers, and other influential adults"). For Antisocial Behavior, the two subscales are Defiant/Disruptive ("an oppositional, explosive, and 'in your face' pattern of behavior") and Antisocial/Aggressive ("coercive behavior, a lack of empathy, violation of family, community, and school rules, dishonesty, and threatening or menacing behavior").

For each item (e.g., "Argues or quarrels with peers"), the rater indicates on a 5-point scale the frequency with which the particular behavior was observed during the past 3 months ("never" to "frequently"). Curiously, a rating of "never" is given where the child does not exhibit a particular behavior as well as where the rater has had no opportunity to observe this behavior. This unnecessary conflating arguably compromises validity: A child may behave a certain way (e.g., "Demands help from peers") even though the rater had no opportunity to observe it. In any case, individual ratings are summed as subscale and total-scale raw scores, which, based on the authors' norms, are then converted to T-scores and percentile ranks. Scores also are expressed in terms of "Social Functioning Levels" (SFLs), which are labels for various percentile intervals. Each of the Social Competence scale and subscales has four SFLs: high functioning, average, at-risk, and high risk. Each of the Antisocial Behavior scale and subscales has three SFLs: average, at-risk, and high risk. T-

scores, percentile ranks, and SFLs are derived separately for ages 5–11 and 12–18.

The HCSBS is the companion instrument to the authors' School Social Behavior Scales (SSBS; 218), which is similar to the HCSBS except that the focus is on school settings and the ratings are provided by educators. Together, the two instruments provide a "cross-informant perspective of social and antisocial behavior of children and youth across settings and raters" (user's guide, p. 2). Such statements notwithstanding, the intended purpose of the HCSBS remains somewhat unclear. First, the HCSBS and SSBS often are discussed jointly, as is seen (oddly) in the section of the HCSBS user's guide entitled "Purpose." Second, and more problematic, the authors send mixed signals regarding the sufficiency of HCSBS results when used clinically. At times, they rightly echo the widely accepted injunction that, at best, such instruments should be used only to identify individuals for additional, more sensitive assessment. Elsewhere, however, their language encourages the prospective user to go directly from HCSBS scores to designing programs and interventions for the identified children.

DEVELOPMENT. By drawing on various sections of the user's guide, readers are able to piece together the process by which the HCSBS was developed. Because the HCSBS was adapted from, and closely parallels, the SSBS, the authors chose to emphasize SSBS, not HCSBS, in their description of instrument development.

SSBS items were developed after an extensive examination of the literature on social behavior, particularly research and conceptualizations reflecting a "behavioral dimensions approach" (versus "traditional medical models"). This resulted in the authors' focus on both positive (social competence) and negative (antisocial behavior) components of social behavior. Draft items were written, reviewed by a variety of individuals, revised, and, apparently without pilot testing, assembled as the 65-item SSBS: 32 Social Competence items and 33 (later reduced to 32) Antisocial Behavior items. The subsequent construction of the HCSBS entailed tweaking roughly one-third of the SSBS items in each scale to reflect the targeted context of home and community. Although the initial specification of these two scales was literature driven, the authors' decision to include two subscales for each was based on their exploratory factory analyses of norming-sample data (described below).

TECHNICAL. Insofar as the HCSBS and SSBS are packaged as companion instruments for cross-informant use, it is somewhat surprising that the instruments have different norming samples (rather than being conormed on a common sample). That said, the HCSBS norming sample comprises 1,562 cases, winnowed down from a larger pool of roughly 2,000 in order to achieve a more accurate representation of the general population. Although these 1,562 cases are from 12 communities in 10 states (or perhaps it is 13 and 9—there are inconsistencies in the user's guide), the adduced data suggest nonetheless that these youth are representative with respect to race and ethnicity, special education status, socioeconomic status, and gender. However, the authors depart from common practice by not providing separate norms for boys and girls—even though there is a "meaningful" gender difference on both scales. (Indeed, this difference is later used as part of the HCSBS validity argument.) However, separate age norms are reported for ages 5–11 and 12–18 (where a considerably more modest difference is observed). These age norms are similar to what is found in several widely used behavior-rating scales. As for regional representation, the norming sample overrepresents the West (46% of cases) and underrepresents the Northeast (5%). The authors acknowledge this; in any case, regional representation arguably is of questionable relevance to the validity of social behavior norms.

In short, HCSBS norms appear to be adequate (the absence of within-gender statistics notwithstanding) when one considers conventional dimensions of representation. But one also should consider the *raters* in the HCSBS norming sample. Mothers made up the lion's share—70%—with fathers constituting 10%. (About 3% of raters were grandparents or stepparents, and a full 17% were either "other" or declined to disclose a relation/role altogether.) The authors say very little about whether ratings from these different groups vary (e.g., mothers vs. fathers, parents vs. all others) and, if they do, what the possible implications are for HCSBS score interpretation.

As for reliability, the authors report internal-consistency, test-retest, and interrater indices. Internal-consistency reliability coefficients (alpha and split-half), which are reported for each scale

and subscale as well as within and across the two age ranges, are quite strong (.91 to .97). Test-retest reliability, estimated over a 2-week interval using a subset ($n = 137$) of the norming sample, is somewhat lower (as one would expect) and differs by scale: .82 to .84 for the Social Competence scale and subscales, and .89 to .91 for the Antisocial Behavior scale and subscales. Where HCSBS is used for screening or research, the magnitude of these reliability coefficients is adequate. However, if HCSBS results are to be used to identify individuals for interventions, these coefficients are low to marginal. All test-retest coefficients were estimated across the two age ranges, which may have inflated these values somewhat.

The authors estimated interrater reliability by correlating pairs of HCSBS scores for 83 children and youth ranging from 7 to 18 years of age. In most instances, the two raters were the child's parents, although there were "a handful of" exceptions. Interrater reliability ranges from .85 to .86 for the Social Competence scale and subscales, and .64 to .71 for the Antisocial Behavior scale and subscales. (As with test-retest reliability, interrater reliability was estimated across age.) Notwithstanding the authors' conclusion that "these data provide solid evidence of good to excellent interrater reliability" (user's guide, p. 53), the results for Antisocial Behavior are troubling. They are particularly troubling if users employ HCSBS scores to identify individuals for interventions rather than for screening or research. In any case, classification consistency arguably would be more informative than correlations between paired scores, given the authors' emphasis on Social Functioning Levels (at risk, high risk, etc.) when interpreting—and possibly acting on—HCSBS scores. Specifically, the authors should report, for each scale, the percentage of paired scores that placed the individual in the same SFL.

The authors present a laudably extensive validity argument. They begin by pointing to the face validity of their instrument. Although generally compelling, HCSBS face validity is lessened by at least two considerations. First, there are several references to the school context (e.g., "Behaves appropriately at school"), which, one would think, is more the province of the companion instrument. Second, some items are of questionable relevance to very young children (e.g., "Has good leadership skills"). Item-scale and item-subscale correlations constitute the second component of the authors' validity argument. Social Competence item-scale correlations range impressively from .62 to .79 and, for Antisocial Behavior, from .61 to .81. Item-subscale correlations for each scale are not dissimilar to that scale's item-scale correlations, which suggests considerable covariance between subscales.

As stated above, the authors' specification of two scales for HCSBS derived from their review of relevant literature. Although the aforementioned item-scale and item-subscale correlations are encouraging, they nevertheless are within-scale information. A confirmatory factor analysis of the complete instrument would be a more rigorous test of the internal structure of HCSBS. Do the two factors emerge and, if so, are factor loadings as expected? No such analysis was reported. Instead, the authors conducted exploratory factor analyses (with oblique rotation) on each scale separately. These analyses resulted in a two-factor solution for each scale, which provided the basis for the subscale structure of the HCSBS: Peer Relations and Self-Management/Compliance (Social Competence scale), and Defiant/Disruptive and Antisocial/Aggressive (Antisocial Behavior scale). For each scale, the two factors are highly correlated (.77 and .82, respectively). Not surprisingly, a higher order factor analysis—again on each scale separately—confirmed that a single construct underlies each scale. The authors consequently are correct to emphasize to HCSBS users that the two scales, not their respective subscales, should be the focus in clinical use of this instrument.

Correlational analyses involving scale and subscale scores echo some of these results as well as throw additional light on HCSBS properties. For example, the correlation between each pair of subscales echoes the high covariance between subscales: .84 for Social Competence subscales, and .89 for Antisocial Behavior subscales. Further, results confirm the reasonable expectation that social competence and antisocial behavior are inversely related: Correlations between Social Competence subscales and Antisocial Behavior subscales range from -.65 to -.82, and the correlation between the two total scores is -.77.

Finally, the authors report correlations between HCSBS and a vast assortment of criterion measures: Social Skills Rating System, Conners Parent Rating Scale-Revised, Child Behavior Checklist, Behavioral Assessment System for Children, ADHD Symptoms Rating Scale, and Psychopathy Screening Device. The magnitude and sign of these correlations adequately document the convergent and discriminant validity of the HCSBS. Evidence also is presented showing that scores from the HCSBS logically distinguish between various groups of youth (social-behavioral at-risk status, special-education status, ADHD clinical status, gender) and can be responsive to certain interventions designed to curb social-behavioral problems.

COMMENTARY. The HCSBS user's guide offers extensive and detailed information regarding the technical properties of this instrument as well as thoughtful discussion of HCSBS score interpretation and use. All in all, the authors are to be commended for the scope and depth of their document. However, this guide contains an embarrassing number of errors: missing words, extraneous words, typographical errors, incorrect punctuation, and errors in pagination. Further, there are many references to "teachers" (rather than "raters") and "students" (rather than "children" or "youth"), as if the authors lifted large blocks of text from the School Social Behavior Scale user's guide and then forgot to edit it. Paying customers deserve better.

SUMMARY. HCSBS reliability and validity evidence clearly supports the use of this instrument for research purposes or for screening individuals for further, more sensitive assessment. However, this instrument should not be used to identify individuals for interventions.

Review of the Home & Community Social Behavior Scales by STEPHANIE STEIN, Professor of Psychology, and PHIL DIAZ, Assistant Professor of Psychology, Central Washington University, Ellensburg, WA:

DESCRIPTION. The Home & Community Social Behavior Scales (HCSBS) was designed to assess the prosocial/adaptive behaviors and social behavior problems of children and adolescents, ages 5 to 18. The HCSBS is a behavioral rating scale that can be administered to parents or other individuals from the home setting (guardians, grandparents, group home supervisors, etc.). It is intended to be a companion instrument to the School Social Behavior Scales (SSBS; 218). Together, the two ratings scales constitute the Social

Behavior Scales, "a cross-informant rating system useful for screening and assessing social and anti-social behavior of children and youth" (user's guide, p. 2). The specific purposes of this scale (and the SSBS) are to (a) screen for children who are behaviorally at-risk; (b) determine eligibility for special services as part of a multimethod, multi-source, multisetting assessment; (c) develop appropriate interventions for skill deficiencies and/or antisocial behavior problems; (d) evaluate the effectiveness of an intervention as a measure of behavior change; and (e) study the social behavior of children and adolescents.

The HCSBS consists of 64 items distributed across two major scales, Social Competence and Antisocial Behavior, with 32 items in each scale. Within each major scale are two empirically derived subscales. The Peer Relations subscale (17 items) measures positive peer interactions and the Self-Management/Compliance subscale (15 items) measures the child's response to the social expectations of adults. Within the Antisocial scale are the Defiant/Disruptive subscale (15 items), measuring oppositional, irritating, and challenging behaviors and the Antisocial/Aggressive subscale (17 items), which measures dangerous, destructive, coercive, and rule-violating behaviors.

The parents or other home-based raters are asked to rate the frequency of specific prosocial and antisocial behaviors exhibited by the child or adolescent within the past 3 months. Ratings are provided on a 5-point scale, with 1 indicating *Never*, 3 indicating *Sometimes*, and 5 indicating *Frequently*. No specific descriptive anchors are given for ratings of 2 or 4 other than a comment in the directions that they also indicate *Sometimes*. Completion of the scale is estimated to take between 8 to 10 minutes.

The scores obtained from the HCSBS include raw scores, *T*-scores, and percentile ranks. Separate scores are given for each of the four subscales and the two main scales, with separate norms and conversion tables for children ages 5–11 and ages 12–18. The authors stress the use of three levels of score interpretation. The first level involves a normative comparison using the *T*-scores and percentile ranks. The second level of interpretation focuses on the general Social Functioning Level (SFL) associated with the scale and subscale scores. On the Social Competence scale and subscales, *High Functioning* refers to scores above the 80th percentile, *Average* for scores be-

tween the 20th and 80th percentile, *At-Risk* for scores between the 5th and 20th percentile, and *High Risk* for scores below the 5th percentile. Likewise, on the Antisocial Behavior scale and subscales, *Average* refers to scores below the 80th percentile, *At-Risk* for scores between the 80th and 95th percentile, and *High Risk* for scores above the 95th percentile. Though further descriptions of these functioning levels is provided in the manual, nowhere is there a discussion of how the score ranges for the SFLs were determined or their validity as indicators of risk. Finally, the third level of interpretation involves the qualitative examination of individual item responses for identifying specific behavioral concerns.

DEVELOPMENT. The manual accompanying the HCSBS provides detailed information about item development, the descriptions of the scales and subscales, and the theoretical basis for development of the instrument. The HCSBS was developed as a companion instrument to the SSBS to provide "cross-informant" ratings of social and antisocial behaviors in children and youth. The specific items on the HCSBS were modified from the items on the SSBS to be more appropriate for home and community settings. Twenty-one items from each of the SSBS scales were retained in the HCSBS and another 22 items were modified. The authors describe their approach to item development on both of these instruments as a combination of a "behavioral dimensions" (based on factor-analysis) as well as a "rationale-theoretical" approach (based on theoretical models of social and antisocial behavior).

Because of the similarity between the items on the HCSBS and the SSBS, the authors focused primarily on their item selection process for the SSBS. The development of the items for the SSBS was theory-driven, based on the assumption that children must adjust to social interactions with both adults and peers and that their social behaviors tend to be either prosocial or antisocial. Items consistent with theoretical perspective were compiled and reviewed by experts, parents, teachers, and graduate students for wording and content. The final compilation of items were subjected to a factor analysis, which supported a two subscale structure for both the Social Competence and Antisocial Behavior Scales of the HCSBS. The items were first pilot tested in a couple of small studies before the norming data were collected.

TECHNICAL. The HCSBS was normed on 1,562 children and adolescents representing all four major geographic regions (with heaviest sampling from the West and North Central), 10 different states, and a combination of urban, suburban, and rural communities. The raters completing the instrument were mostly mothers (70%), followed in frequency by "other" (foster parents, legal guardians, etc.), fathers, stepmothers, grandmothers, stepfathers, and grandfathers. The ethnic diversity of the sample closely paralleled the percentage of ethnic representation of the general U.S. population (based on the 2000 U.S. Census) regarding Caucasian, African American, and Hispanic populations, with Asian American and Native American participants moderately underrepresented in the standardization sample. Diversity in socioeconomic backgrounds was evident in the standardization sample, though there was a higher than typical percentage of parents employed in professional, paraprofessional, and technical occupations (32.6%). The percentage of participants in the various categories of special education represented in the standardization sample was very similar to that found in the general U.S. population.

The standardization sample consisted of 788 boys and 749 girls, with the remaining 25 unknown because gender data were not collected. An approximately equal percentage of boys and girls were in the younger (ages 5–11) and older (ages 12–18) norming samples. Though the small effect sizes were not substantial enough to justify dividing the norm group into two subgroups by age, the authors decided to do so anyway, presenting the weak rationale that many other behavioral rating instruments include age groupings.

The manual provides extensive data on the reliability of the HCSBS in the areas of internal consistency, test-retest reliability, and interrater reliability. Internal consistency alpha and split-half coefficients are quite high, ranging from 94–.97 for the two main scales. Similarly, the subscale coefficients range from .91 to .95. The test-retest reliability for a small subset ($n = 137$) was .82–.91 over a 2-week period. Though not as impressive as the internal consistency data, these coefficients are reasonably strong given that social-emotional variables are likely to be less stable than constructs such as intelligence. Finally, interrater reliability data were collected on a small subsample ($n = 83$) of predominantly Caucasian children and adolescents, based on ratings by both parents. The interrater coefficients ranged from .85 to .86 for the Social Competence scales and .64 to .73 for the Antisocial Behavior scales. Though the authors give several possible reasons for the lower interrater reliability coefficients, including "source bias" and the fact that these kinds of coefficients are frequently lower than those obtained through other methods, the lower coefficients on the Antisocial Behavior Scale in particular are troubling. This implies that a child's problem behavior ratings has a lot to do with who actually completes the instrument.

As with reliability, the validity data on the HCSBS described in the manual are quite thorough, addressing content, factorial, and criterion-related validity as well as identification of group differences and sensitivity to treatment outcomes. The discussion of content validity summarizes the development of the items described previously (review of literature, use of expert judges, and theory-driven). In addition, the obtained item-total correlations ranging from .62 to .79 for the Social Competence Scale and .60 to .80 for the Antisocial Behavior Scale provide support for the claim that the items within each scale are fairly homogenous and measure the same domain.

The oblique (promax) rotation factor analysis procedure conducted with the HCSBS revealed two factors in Social Competence that accounted for 58.6% of the variance. Items tended to load heavily on both factors, however, leading the authors to recommend "that the Social Competence scale is best considered as a unitary scale" (user's guide, p. 60). Similarly, though two factors in Antisocial Behavior Scale accounted for 58.5% of the variance, the authors suggested that this best be thought of as a unitary scale because most items loaded highly on both factors.

The largest body of validity data in the manual is criterion-related. Data in support of convergent and divergent validity were gathered though correlations of the scales on the HCSBS with the Social Skills Rating System (SSRS); the Conners Parent Rating Scale, Revised—Short Form (CPRS-R-S); the Child Behavior Checklist (CBCL) parent form; the Behavioral Assessment System for Children—Parent Rating Scale (BASC-PRS); and the ADHD Symptoms Rating Scale (ADHD-SRS). As expected, the Social Competence scale tended to correlate negatively with measures of problem behavior on the CPRS-R-S

(-.49 to -.77), CBCL (-.18 to -.67), BASC-PRS (-.60 to -.70 range), and the ADHD-SRS (-.41 to -.60). In contrast, the Antisocial Behavior Scale correlated positively with these same measures (.61 to .89 on the CPRS-R-S, .20 to .79 on the CBCL, .58 to .91 on the BASC-PRS, and .69 to .77 on the ADHD-SRS). Furthermore, the two scales of the HCSBS had weak to almost zero correlations with unrelated scales on the BASC-PRS, such as measures of anxiety and somatic problems.

The authors also provide evidence that the HCSBS can accurately differentiate between groups of children, including those considered "at-risk," special education versus regular education students and those with and without ADHD. In addition, two studies on the sensitivity to intervention indicated that the HCSBS can be used to measure changes in social behavior following a prevention program and one in anger-control training. Overall, the evidence for the validity of the HCSBS is quite solid.

COMMENTARY. One of the main strengths of the HCSBS appears to be its technical characteristics, as suggested by excellent evidence for reliability, satisfactory validity, and a reasonably diverse standardization sample. The only problematic psychometric characteristic is the relatively weak interrater reliability on the Antisocial Behavior Scale. The similarity of the HCSBS to the SSBS ensures that similar types of data on students can be gathered from both the home and school environments. The instrument has solid theoretical underpinnings, which are well-supported in the manual. The HCSBS has straightforward directions for administration and scoring and looks to be a quick and easy measure of prosocial and antisocial behaviors of children and youth in the home environment. The manual is very clear, detailed, and easy to use, providing a good overview of issues in the use of behavior rating scales, including their general characteristics, advantages, potential problems, and recommendations for best practices. One of the most unique positive aspects of this instrument is its focus on "typical" behaviors exhibited by children, rather than some of the atypical, low incidence and alarming behaviors addressed in similar behavior rating scales. It is likely that parents will not find the items on this instrument offensive or stigmatizing.

As for limitations, the presentation of the items separately by scale needlessly increases the risk of a response bias, as the first set of items all address desirable behaviors and the second set all focus on undesirable behaviors. No rationale is given for why these scales are presented separately, especially because there is no discussion in the manual regarding potential administration of just the Social Competence scale or the Antisocial Behavior Scale. In addition, the inclusion of the Social Functioning Level (SFL) is problematic because no information is provided on the development, reliability, or validity on the somewhat arbitrary risk levels. To complicate matters, there is no readily accessible scoring guideline for determining SFL other than what is embedded in the text. Furthermore, the manual uses inconsistent terminology, referring to Moderate Risk in one place and At-Risk in another (presumably the same SFL). Another weakness is the rationale for dividing the HCSBS into two age groups, as there is no reliable psychometric justification for this decision. Finally, the standardization sample somewhat underrepresents several ethnic groups and overrepresents families from professional and technical backgrounds.

SUMMARY. The HCSBS is a 64-item rating scale for parents and other home-based raters, designed to assess the social competence and antisocial behavior of children and adolescents, ages 5 to 18. Like its sibling instrument, the SSBS, the HCSBS appears to have satisfactory to superior psychometric properties and a well-organized and informative manual. The HCSBS has the potential to fill an important niche in the assessment of children's behavior in the home environment because of its focus on typical behaviors, as opposed to low-frequency, highly disturbing behaviors. Although some aspects of the HCSBS are problematic (the questionable use of the SFL, separate presentation of items reflecting desirable and undesirable behaviors, separate age scoring keys, and relatively weak interrater reliability of problem behavior ratings), these do not detract significantly from the value of this rating scale as a screening instrument for at-risk behavior, for determining eligibility for special services, for intervention planning and evaluation, or as a research tool.

[108]

Hopkins Verbal Learning Test—Revised.

Purpose: A "brief assessment of verbal learning and memory (immediate recall, delayed recall, delayed recognition)."

Population: Ages 16 years and older.
Publication Dates: 1991–2001.
Acronym: HVLT-R.
Scores, 4: Total Recall, Delayed Recall, Retention, Recognition Discrimination Index.
Administration: Individual.
Forms, 6: 1–6.
Price Data, 2004: $239 per introductory kit including professional manual (2001, 55 pages) and 25 each of 6 test booklets (Forms 1–6); $34 per 25 test booklets (any of Forms 1–6); $50 per professional manual.
Time: (5–10) minutes with a 25-minute delay.
Comments: Forms 1–6 are very similar psychometrically and can be used to eliminate practice effects on repeated administration.
Authors: Jason Brandt and Ralph H. B. Benedict.
Publisher: Psychological Assessment Resources, Inc.

Review of the Hopkins Verbal Learning Test— Revised by TIMOTHY Z. KEITH, Professor of Educational Psychology, The University of Texas—Austin, Austin, TX:

DESCRIPTION. The Hopkins Verbal Learning Test—Revised (HVLT-R) is one test with a set of six forms intended to measure verbal learning and memory in individuals ages 16 and older. It is "intended primarily for use with brain-disordered populations" (professional manual, p. 1), such as those with amnesia, Alzheimer's Disease, or brain injury.

The HVLT-R includes the test booklets (a different booklet for each form) and the manual. The six forms of the HVLT-R are designed to allow frequent, rapid retesting. Each test includes a list of 12 nouns; the examiner reads the list to the examinee, who repeats as many words as remembered, in any order. This process is repeated three times; 20–25 minutes later, examinees are asked again to recall as many words as possible; for the final task, the examiner reads a list of 24 words (including the 12 words from the list) and asks the examinee after each whether the word was on the list.

The HVLT-R produces several scores. The number of words correctly recalled in the first three learning trials is summed for the Total Recall score. The Delayed Recall portion produces both a Delayed Recall score and a Retention score (Delayed Recall divided by the higher score from the initial Learning Trials 2 or 3). The final section yields a Recognition Discrimination Index, the number of words recognized correctly minus the number of false positives, the words recalled that were not on the list. It is also possible

to examine semantically related versus unrelated false positives. All scores are converted to T-scores, by age level. With raw scores ranging from 0 to 12 for some scores (e.g., the Delayed Recall task), there are often large jumps between T scores for minor changes in raw scores.

DEVELOPMENT. The HVLT-R was standardized on a vaguely defined group of 1,179 people, without neurological or psychiatric problems, ages 16 to 92. Women made up 75% of the sample, and younger ages (16–19 years) were not well represented; close to 40% of the sample were females aged 70–79. The manual does not report when or where the standardization occurred.

TECHNICAL. Although a number of reliability studies are reported in the manual, detail is lacking for most of them. For example, given the six forms of the HVLT-R, alternate form reliability estimates are important. Although the manual reports three such studies of the HVLT and HVLT-R, no reliability estimates are reported; the reports focus on the presence or absence of statistically significant differences across forms rather than the degree of similarity. The use of alternate forms does appear to reduce or eliminate practice effects, however. Test-retest reliability estimates (mean interval of 6 weeks) for a small elderly sample ranged from .74 for Total Recall (the score with the most variability) to .39 for Retention.

More evidence is presented in the manual concerning the validity of the HVLT-R and the earlier HVLT. The evidence presented suggests that its scores correlate well with other scores on memory measures, and, more importantly, that low scores on the Total Recall scale can discriminate normal adults from those with Alzheimer's and mild dementia.

The HVLT-R manual also includes a section on interpretation that provides expectations for examinees with certain clinical disorders. The guidelines should be useful for those providing clinical assessments, although they do need to be verified via future research.

COMMENTARY AND SUMMARY. The HVLT-R is a short, individually administered test of verbal learning and memory with six forms. The test may indeed provide useful information for the diagnosis of memory problems, dementia, Alzheimer's, and other neurological problems, but more information and research is needed to evaluate this possibility. A careful and well-defined standardization is needed, with more even representation across the ages. Reliability and validity evidence need to be reported in more detail. The clinical guidelines suggested for interpretation need more complete investigation through research. Until such evidence is provided, users of the HVLT-R should be cautious in their use and interpretation of the instrument.

Review of the Hopkins Verbal Learning Test— Revised by WENDY J. STEINBERG, Assistant Professor of Psychology, Eastern University, St. Davids, PA:

DESCRIPTION. The Hopkins Verbal Learning Test—Revised (HVLT-R) is a neuropsychological test of memory pathology in the acquisition, retention, and retrieval of orally presented words. It is designed for use with brain-disordered populations. The manual states that it is appropriate for use with respondents 16–80+ years of age. The HVLT-R is a short test, consisting of only 12 words, 4 each from three different semantic categories (for example, animals, gems, and types of shelter). The revised test differs from the original Hopkins Verbal Learning Test (never reviewed in the *MMY* series) by the addition of a Delayed Recall trial and by the timing of administration of the Recognition trial (both discussed below).

There are six forms of the HVLT-R. The forms are parallel and can be used singly. They can also be used in a series over time to measure change in memory uncontaminated by practice effect for specific word lists.

The test consists primarily of repeated trials of the word list. The administrator reads the 12 words aloud, approximately 1 word every 2 seconds. At the completion of the list the respondent is asked to recall as many of the words as possible. Immediately thereafter, the test is repeated a second and third time, using the same word list. Each time, the respondent recalls as many words as possible. These are the three Learning Trials. Trial 4 takes place 20–25 minutes later, without having forewarned the respondent that another trial would follow. This is the Delayed Recall trial. Immediately thereafter is the Delayed Recognition Trial. This trial consists of 24 words: 12 are the original list words; 6 are words that did not appear on the original list but are semantically related to a word on the original list (for example, "dog" instead of "horse"); and 6 are words that did

not appear on the original list and are semantically unrelated to any word on the original list.

Administration is simple. The administrator reads the instructions verbatim, then reads the list of 12 words, then records the respondent's answers. On the first three trials, the administrator writes down the words as the respondent recalls them and counts the number of correctly recalled words, per trial and Total Recall. On the fourth trial the administrator writes down the words as the subject recalls them and counts the number of correct Delayed Recall words. On the fifth trial— recognition rather than recall—the respondent says "yes" or "no" as to whether or not he or she heard that word on the original list. The administrator then circles "y" or "n," counts the number of correct responses and number of incorrect responses, and computes a Retention Percentage.

DEVELOPMENT. Little is said about the development of the HVLT-R, probably because it is such a short and, frankly, simple test. From the manual, we know that all words are taken from Battig and Montague's (1969) collection of category exemplars. We also know that the authors used the two most common exemplars for each category as semantically related confusion words in the recognition trial, rather than placing them on the original list. The HVLT-R is shorter than its competitors in both list length and number of repeated trials.

TECHNICAL. The norm group consists of 300 men and 879 women ages 16–92, with a mean age of 59. Norm group members reported no signs of neurological or psychiatric disorder. Normal mental status of most norm group members was confirmed with the Mini Mental Status Examination (MMSE). Scores vary by age, so norms are reported for eight separate age groups, the first being 16–19 years and the last being 80+ years.

Although the manual states that the test is useful for young people as well as the elderly, the distribution of scores is very negatively skewed for younger persons. Thus, a perfect raw score converts to only an average standard score; that is, near perfection is expected. This very low ceiling negates the test's utility for younger persons; scores must therefore be interpreted with caution for this population, as only a couple of errors in recall will flag the respondent as neurologically impaired. If the test authors want the test to be useful for younger ages, more difficult forms would need to be developed, perhaps using less common exemplars or fewer semantic categories (two instead of three) per form, with more words per category.

Reliability data are weak. In the largest study group (N = 432, all college students) participants were each administered a different random form of the test a single time. Scores were similar across the forms, which the authors argue supports the comparability of the forms. However, this is neither a test-retest nor a parallel forms protocol, as different participants took different tests. Also, scores are so seriously skewed and so restricted in range for that age group (see discussion above) that it is difficult to know what "comparable" scores would look like. In another study, 18 students took the six forms of the test over a period of 6 weeks, one form per week. The design of this study is satisfactory, but the sample size is very small and the participants are again too young to generalize from their scores.

Based on these studies, the authors found slight score differences on the Delayed Recognition trial on Forms 1, 2 and 4 as opposed to Forms 3, 5, and 6, and so established slightly different scaling for the two sets of forms. I find this troubling because of the reasons cited above. Quite plausibly, the slight score differences on which scale differences were based were merely Type 1 errors.

Only one test-retest study is cited for the HVLT-R. Forty elderly participants took different forms of the test, and took the same test again after a 6-week interval. The author does not say how many participants took each form, only that the participants took different forms. Evenly dividing the 40 participants across the six forms, I am assuming that about 7 participants took each form (twice). This sample size is too small for reliability analysis.

Validity data are much better. This, of course, argues for the test's underlying reliability despite the lack of credible reliability data. Factor analysis of data from 126 neurologic and neuropsychiatric patients over age 55, as well as 302 elderly neuropsychiatric patients and normals supported the test's constructs, as well as supported the constructs' uniqueness from those measured by several other common neurocognitive tests. Although it could be argued that constructs across various neuropsychological tests ought to confirm rather than disconfirm each other, the authors argue convincingly for the additive rather than duplicative nature of the HVLT-R with these other tests. HVLT-R constructs were also supported by moderate correlations (.65 to .77) for scores for the 302 elderly neuropsychiatric patients and normals on subparts of the HVLT-R with similar subparts of the Weschler Memory Scale—Revised.

Evidence of predictive validity comes from the test's ability to correctly classify normals versus those who are memory impaired. A discriminant function analysis of 55 Alzheimer patients and 59 matched normals correctly classified 90% of participants. Another study of 34 patients with dementia and 37 normals correctly classified 85% of participants.

The test also distinguishes between various types of memory impairment. The manual cites evidence that scores differ by trials for patients with Amnestic Disorder, Huntington's Disease (HD), and Alzheimer's Disease (AD). For example, in HD free recall (Trials 1–3) and delayed recall (Trial 4) are impaired, but recognition (Trial 5) is intact. The pattern across trials is different for those with Amnestic Disorder, and different still for those with AD. The evidence cited, using clinic patients, is compelling.

SUMMARY. The Hopkins Verbal Learning Test—Revised is a short, easily administered test of neurocognitive impairment. Little is said about actual development of the test. Reliability evidence is surprisingly weak, and the authors would do well to increase sample sizes, diversify the age ranges of studied participants, and increase the difficulty of the test for younger individuals. Validity evidence, in contrast, is excellent. The HVLT-R's documented ability to distinguish between the memory impaired and normals, and between different types of memory impairment, makes it useful for diagnosis. Its brevity makes it ideal for patients having short attention spans. The multiple forms makes it useful for charting progress in degenerative or remitting disease. However, because of the low ceiling on young people's scores, the test's utility is limited to the middle-aged and elderly.

REVIEWER'S REFERENCE

Battig, W. F., & Montague, W. E. (1969). Category norms for verbal items in 56 categories: A replication and extension of the Connecticut category norms. *Journal of Experimental Psychology Monograph*, 80, 1–46.

[109]

I Can Do Maths.

Purpose: Designed "to inform teachers and parents about children's development in numeracy in the early years of schooling."

Population: Children in the first 3 years of Australian and New Zealand school systems.

Publication Date: 2000–2001.
Scores, 4: Number, Measurement, Space, Total.
Administration: Group.
Price Data, 2002: A$58.30 per specimen set including one Level A test booklet, one Level B test booklet, one Level A Ezi-guide, one Level B Ezi-guide, and teacher's guide (2001, 36 pages).
Time: (30–40) minutes.
Authors: Brian Doig and Marion de Lemos.
Publisher: Australian Council for Educational Research Ltd. [Australia].
a) LEVEL A.
Population: Children in the first 2 years of school.
Price Data: $27.50 per 10 Level A test booklets.
b) LEVEL B.
Population: Children in the second and third years of school.
Price Data: Same as Level A above.

Review of I Can Do Maths by THERESA GRAHAM, Adjunct Faculty, Educational Psychology, University of Nebraska-Lincoln, Lincoln, NE:

DESCRIPTION. The I Can Do Maths (herein referred to as "ICDM") was originally created as part of a research project entitled, "Curriculum and Organisation in the Early Years of Schooling," conducted by the Australian Council for Educational Research. The purpose of ICDM is to provide information to teachers and parents regarding children's understanding of numeracy in the first 3 years of schooling (kindergarten, first grade, second grade). Three main areas of numeracy are examined: general Number knowledge, Measurement, and Space (e.g., shapes). The instrument includes two forms (Level A and Level B). Level A is intended to assess math knowledge in children from kindergarten to the end of Year 1 (first grade). Level B is intended to assess math knowledge in children from the end of Year 1 to the end of Year 2 (second grade).

The testing packet includes a teacher's guide, Level A and Level B test booklets, and an "Ezi-guide" for each test form to use during test administration. The teacher's guide provides information regarding background of the instrument, test administration, scoring and interpretation of test results, and development of the instrument. Level A includes 30 questions; Level B includes 33 questions. Twenty-two questions are the same on both forms of the test.

Test administration is described in both the teacher's guide and in the Ezi-guide for administrators. Although no time limit is set, the test reportedly takes about 30–40 minutes to complete. The test is given orally and can be given either individually or in groups. Suggested group size is given in both the teacher's guide and Ezi-guide. Little information is given regarding providing feedback during the test except a brief statement indicating that responses to childrens questions should provide no additional help or prompting. Although the test is administered orally, children are instructed to indicate the correct response with a tick or a cross in the test booklet. The test booklet includes the complete question and space for the written response.

Answers are scored as either correct or incorrect using the answer key provided in the teacher's guide. Some questions are in a multiple-choice format and some are openended. Total scores can be recorded on the back of the test booklet. In addition, scores for each of the areas—Number, Measurement, and Spatial questions—can be summed. Next to each question in the test booklet is a symbol indicating whether a question is a Number, Measurement, or Spatial question. In addition, an assessment record is provided in the teacher's guide. The assessment guide provides spaces to indicate the correctness for each problem and spaces for total.

Three types of reports can be generated from the results: Individual Profile, Diagnostic Maps, and Descriptive Reports. The individual profile provides an overview of a child's performance and tables are provided that allow a normative comparison with other children at similar levels of schooling. Separate norms were created for the different educational systems because age of school entry and school structure differed across the different educational systems sampled in Australia. No information is provided regarding the relation of actual age of school entry and educational system. Nor is information provided regarding the different types of school structure that would result in creating separate norms.

Diagnostic Maps are provided in the teachers manual for both Test A and Test B. The maps are intended to provide a picture of what questions an individual child should have answered correctly based on total score. On the maps, the questions from the test are preprinted according to the different math areas and level of difficulty. Questions that are easier are placed lower on the map and more difficult questions are placed higher. No empirical or theoretical information was provided as to what determined the placement of different questions on the diagnostic map. Moreover, in this case only one map is provided for all of the different school systems. It is assumed that questions are of similar difficulty across the different school systems, but no information is given in support of this assumption. Finally, the diagnostic maps are premised on the fact that total score reflects similarly on knowledge within the three subareas. However, no justification for that premise was provided.

Finally, a Diagnostic Report is provided in the teachers manual. As in the Diagnostic Map, total score is used to make inferences regarding scores within the separate math areas. For example, if the total score is 10 on Test A, then the diagnostic report states that the child is typically able to count at least 10 objects, and understands "more" and "less." However, to confirm that the child actually answered those questions correctly, it is necessary to refer to the Diagnostic Map.

DEVELOPMENT. Items on the ICDM were based on "key learning objectives" (teacher's guide, p. 20) as described in various state and national mathematics curriculum documents. The 47 items across the two tests were selected from a larger pool of items that were piloted on 150 children. No information is given on how many total items were initially generated nor on how the pilot sample was recruited. Two tables are provided in the teachers manual that indicate the relationship between mathematics curriculum and the ICDM Test A and Test B questions, (i.e., whether a question was likely to occur in Grade 1 or Grade 2). No specific information was given on specific item difficulty.

TECHNICAL. The technical information includes information on the sample used to norm the study and the reliability and validity reported. The data reported in the teacher's guide were generated as part of the research project entitled, "Curriculum and Organisation in the Early Years of Schooling," conducted by the Australian Council for Educational Research. A total of 84 schools were randomly selected to represent different states and territories within Australia, resulting in over 800 children sampled at the pre-Year 1 (kindergarten) and over 1,000 children each at Year 1 (first grade) and Year 2 (second grade). No specific numbers were given. The number of schools varied from 6–15 schools within a participating state. The authors note that although "not proportionally representative" (teacher's guide, p. 20), the sample covers a range of schools. Little background information is given on the sample of children except to say that the study "included children drawn from different backgrounds throughout Australia" (teacher's guide, p. 20). No general demographic data were given. This seems critical because different means were found among the different regions sampled.

A reliability estimate of .91 was obtained using a Quest analysis. The Quest analysis was conducted on the entire sample. Internal consistency using KR-21 for the subgroups resulted in estimates ranging from .45 to .72. No test-retest data are provided.

Content validity evidence was based on the relationship between the questions on the test, mathematics curriculum, and objectives outlined in the national Profiles in Mathematics. The actual objectives are not stated nor is there any discussion about why the three areas—Number, Measurement, and Space—were selected. Finally, it is not clear whether the questions included completely cover the domains being assessed. From the description in the teacher's guide, the questions were not independently reviewed by other experts in the field to assess their content validity.

Evidence for construct validity is provided by assessing the change in mean score across the different school-level groups who took the test. Pre-Year 1 children scored lower than Year 1 and Year 2 children. No information is given on the subtests. Moreover, no other measure for construct validity is provided.

Criterion-related validity was evaluated by assessing the correlations between the scores on the ICDM and measures of early literacy and developmental level. Correlations between ICDM and teacher assessment of school progress at the end of the school year were also calculated. Correlations between early literacy and ICDM ranged from .30 and .61. Correlations between ICDM and teacher assessment ranged from .37 and .49. Both of these assessments of criterion-related validity are problematic. It is not clear what the relationship between literacy and math should be. Moreover, no information was given as to what criterion teachers used in their assessment of children's progress at school.

SUMMARY. In general, it is difficult to assess the utility of the ICDM beyond the Australian educational system. First, the results seem dependent upon age of school entry, but little explanation of the relation between age and scores on the ICDM was provided. Moreover, given that little specific information is provided on rationalization behind the development of the domains assessed and the lack of criterion-referenced validity, it is questionable whether the ICDM is a useful instrument for other groups. Future efforts to correlate the ICDM with other measures of early mathematical knowledge would greatly increase its potential value.

[110]
Illness Effects Questionnaire—Multi-Perspective.

Purpose: Designed to assess "the impact of a patient's illness from multiple perspectives."
Population: Ages 18 and over.
Publication Date: 2002.
Acronym: IEQ—MP.
Scores: Total score only.
Administration: Individual.
Forms, 4: Self-Report, Professional, Observer, Treatment.
Price Data, 2005: $220 per complete kit including user's manual (91 pages), 25 of each form, and 25 comparative and integrated profile forms; $51 per user's manual; $46 per 25 questionnaires (specify form); $147 per 100 questionnaires (specify form); $41 per 25 comprehensive and integrated profile forms; $140 per 100 comprehensive and integrated profile forms; $55 per specimen set including user's manual, 3 of each form, and 3 comparative and integrated profile forms.
Time: (10) minutes.
Authors: Glen D. Greenberg and Rolf A. Peterson.
Publisher: Multi-Health Systems, Inc.

Review of the Illness Effects Questionnaire—Multi-Perspective by ALAN C. BUGBEE, JR., Assistant Dean of Assessment/Associate Professor, School of Education, North Carolina Agricultural and Technical State University, Greensboro, NC:

DESCRIPTION. The Illness Effects Questionnaire—Multi-Perspective (IEQ-MP) is a set of summated rating scales to assess "the patient's perceptions (i.e., perspective, appraisal, attitude, belief, etc.) in relation to a disease or disability" (user's manual, p. 5). Unlike a single survey given to a patient, the IEQ-MP seeks to attain multiple points of view about the effects of illness upon the patient. There are four questionnaires: Self-Report (IEQ-S), Professional (IEQ-Pro), Observer (IEQ-O), and Treatment Effects (IEQ-Tx). Each form takes about 10 minutes to complete. The IEQ-S and IEQ-Tx forms are answered by the patient. The IEQ-Pro form is answered by a physician or nurse who has knowledge of the patient's medical condition. According to the test manual, if at all possible, the IEQ-S and IEQ-Pro should be administered simultaneously. If possible, the IEQ-O form is answered by a family member who lives with the patient. If this is not possible, a family member who is familiar with the patient's medical condition and daily activities may answer the questionnaire. A fifth form—Comparative and Integrative Profile (IEQ-CIP)—is used to combine the information from the four forms.

Each test form has two layers. The top layer has the questions and places for responses. The respondents circle their answers on the form. The second layer provides tables for converting the summed scores to a T-Score for the appropriate illness/medical condition.

All of the questionnaires have 20 questions. Forms IEQ-S, IEQ-O, and IEQ-Pro address the same 20 areas. Forms IEQ-O and IEQ-Pro are rewordings of the questions in Form IEQ-S. Form IEQ-Tx shares 13 areas with Form IEQ-S. The other questions were designed to assess treatment specific issues. Each of the questions is a Likert-type scale with eight options: *Disagree Strongly, Disagree Moderately, Disagree Somewhat, Disagree A Little, Agree A Little, Agree Somewhat, Agree Moderately,* and *Agree Strongly.* Each option has an assigned value from zero (*Disagree Strongly*) to seven (*Agree Strongly*). Each option is presented in the same order. The assigned values for each question are summed together. The summed value is compared to a chart, attached to each questionnaire, for seven types of illness/medical problems. These types include: Headache, Kidney, Arthritis, Cancer, Cardiac, Chronic Pain, and Infertile Women. The patient receives a T-score based upon the raw score and the specific illness/medical problem. There is also a General Medical category with T-score conversions. According to the test manual, this category should be used if the seven specific norms are not appropriate for the patient.

A Comparative and Integrative Profile (IEQ-CIP) is constructed from the T-scores for the four questionnaires. The IEQ-CIP shows the "Distress Level" of the patient from the four different perspectives. This form contains space for two different administrations of surveys given at different times. The Distress Level categories are Extreme (*T*-score of 68 to 88), Moderate (58 to 67), Average (46 to 57), Mild (34 to 45), and Minimal (10 to 33).

The outcomes of the IEQ-MP may be used for a number of different clinical and research purposes. According to the manual, the results can be used to provide a quality of life index or identify particular areas that require medical education and/or counseling. In addition, they may be used to evaluate treatment effectiveness or assess and/or track the progression of a disease or disability.

DEVELOPMENT. The IEQ-MP is a set of four Likert-type scales each with 20 questions ranging in response from *Strongly Disagree* to *Strongly Agree*. The Self-Report scale (IEQ-S) is the core of the set. All of the other forms are based on it. According to the manual, the statements used in the IEQ-S were selected through a survey of existent scales about patient behavior and attitudes towards illness. No information is provided about how the response choices were selected or why the scales have 20 questions. Indeed, information about the development of the scales is very limited. Interestingly enough, the information about development, norming, reliability, and validity is for the most part limited to the core scale only. This violates a number of requirements from the *Standards for Educational and Psychological Testing* (AERA, APA, & NCME, 1999), especially, 3.1, 3.2, 3.3, 3.11, 4.2, 6.3, and 6.15.

Normative samples are quite limited. The authors acknowledge that there are small samples in arthritis, cardiac, chronic pain, and infertile women. Because of these small samples, the authors recommend that "Users should refer to the general medical norm group, then make note of how their patients compare to other normative samples" (user's manual, p. 63). Unfortunately, the general medical sample consists of only 71 patients. No information is provided about the representativeness of these patients other than the distribution of diseases (16 different types) and average age (37.7, with a standard deviation of 12.7).

The largest sample (six different studies with a total of 507 patients) is from patients with kidney disease. It would seem that the authors did not wish to limit the use of the scales to kidney disease, so they opted for the broader category of general disease, even though the sample size was small and there is limited descriptive information.

The authors acknowledge the limitations of their samples and point out that other studies were ongoing at the time (2002) of the publication of the test. It is hoped that the next edition of the IEQ-MP will provide adequate and sufficient normative samples and details of the samples' representativeness. Much more explicit details about the rationale for the scale and how it was developed should be included about all of the scales.

TECHNICAL. As previously mentioned, the IEQ-MP limits itself to providing empirical information about only one scale, the Self-Report (IEQ-S). Because the test is intended to be used as a set of questionnaires, this is clearly inadequate.

Studies of the reliability for the single scale are quite limited, as is consistent with this test. Two internal consistency studies are reported, showing coefficient alpha of .93 for general medical patients (*n* = 71) and .88 for kidney dialysis patients (*n* = 62). Interestingly enough, the general medical patient study was conducted in 1986, 16 years before the commercial publication of the test. It seems odd that no other reliability studies were conducted on a larger sample during this period, given that the scale was apparently unchanged.

Two test-retest studies are also reported, although as the authors state, they are of such small sample size (*n* = 10 and *n* = 15) that their use is limited. Both of them show a very high reliability (.99 and .95, respectively). However, this, too, is limited because, in addition to the small sample size, the retesting was done over only 1 and 2 days, respectively. Because the diseases covered by this scale are long-term, it would be helpful if the test-retest reliability study covered a longer period between test administrations. Interestingly enough, the authors assert that "IEQ-MP can be re-administered safely without incurring testing effects" (user's manual, p. 9), but provide no information upon which to base this assertion.

The authors provide an interesting discussion on validity, including construct validity, correlational studies, regression, and factor analysis. The authors seem to limit their validity studies to the relationship of one scale (IEQ-MP) with other measures of patient attitudes about illness. However, the relatively small samples (*n* = 10 to 122) and lack of information about the samples and their representativeness of the populations of interest for this test call the effectiveness and meaning of these validity studies into question. The author's recommendations for future studies are quite necessary.

COMMENTARY. IEQ-MP is a group of four Likert scales used to assess the effects of illness on a medical patient from multiple perspectives. The intention of the scales is to see how the patient is affected by the illness. These scales acquire the information from three sources: the patient, a relative who lives with the patient, and a professional health care provider who is familiar with the patient's medical condition and treatment. The patient answers two forms: a self-report form (IEQ-S) and a treatment effects form (IEQ-Tx). The IEQ-MP is a combination of different perspectives on the illness or medical condition and its effects on the patient.

Unfortunately, only the self-report form (IEQ-S) is normed or has any validity evidence. In addition, the validity evidence is very minimal. In the manual and on the scale forms, the scales are presented as being applicable to patients with headaches, arthritis, cancer, cardiac disease, chronic pain, infertile women, and a general medical scale. From what is presented in the manual, however, it would seem that the actual normative and validation studies concentrated on patients with kidney disease. The manual does not present information about the adequacy or representativeness of the normative samples. To their credit, the authors recognize that the norms are limited and recommend that local norms be developed. Interestingly enough, despite the warnings about the small sample sizes in categories throughout the manual, the authors recommend using the norms upon which they are based for patients within these categories. This contradiction does not encourage use of this test.

Although the test is sold as a set of four scales, only the reliability and validity of one of the scales—Self-Report (IEQ-S)—has been seriously studied. Even here, there is a limit in adequacy and representativeness of the samples used. The concept behind this set of scales—effects of illness on the patient from different points of view—is a good idea. However, it is unclear about who would use it. The implication seems to be that the patient is receiving psychological treatment/counseling to help cope with illness effects. Because the set of scales has not been adequately evaluated, it does not provide necessary information for commercial use. More study is necessary for this. It is recommended that the authors and the publisher conduct sufficient normative and psychometric studies to establish this as a viable instrument in assessing the patient's well-being and the effects of an illness and its treatment on the patient. This test presents the possibility of useful information. It needs considerably more study to establish itself as a useful instrument.

SUMMARY. The Illness Effectiveness Questionnaire—Multi-Perspective (IEQ-MP) seems to be intended as a way of acquiring different views on the effects of the illness on a patient and how treatment is affecting the patient. The points of view are those of the patient, a health care professional, and a family member living with the patient. The intention appears to be to help patient cope with their illness and treatments, to monitor treatment effects, and to assess the outcomes of treatment(s). Unfortunately, the IEQ-MP is not adequately developed to justify its use in patient care or as a commercially available assessment instrument. It essentially limits its reliability and validity analysis to one of its scales (Self-Report, IEQ-S). It does not even provide sufficient information for these analyses. If the test user desires to utilize the IEQ-MP, the use should be limited to research or validation studies. It could be a very useful measure, but it needs considerably more work.

REVIEWER'S REFERENCE

American Educational Research Association, American Psychological Association, & National Council on Measurement in Education. (1999). *Standards for educational and psychological testing*. Washington, DC: American Educational Research Association.

Review of the Illness Effects Questionnaire— Multi-Perspective by BETH DOLL, Professor of Educational Psychology, University of Nebraska— Lincoln, Lincoln, NE:

DESCRIPTION. The Illness Effects Questionnaire—Multi-Perspective (IEQ-MP) is a measure of the biological, psychological, and social disruption that adults experience due to an illness. Parallel versions of the questionnaire are provided for the person's self-report (IEQ-S), that of a health professional who is working with them (IEQ-Pro), and that of a family member who is familiar with their illness experience (IEQ-O). In addition, the IEQ-MP incorporates a Treatment Effects (IEQ-TX) questionnaire that the person completes to describe their opinions regarding their treatment, and an integrative profile that aggregates all of the ratings on a single page. Using a norms table attached to each questionnaire, ratings are converted to *T* scores and subsequently interpreted as evidence of "minimal," "mild," "average," "moderate," or "extreme" distress.

The manual states that the IEQ-MP can be used with adults, aged 18 or older. However, the mean age of the participants in the principal norming study was 37.7 years, and it is impossible to tell how many adolescents or elderly adults were actually included in the norms. All four versions of the scale are 20 items long and use an 8-point Likert format, with ratings ranging from 0 (*disagree strongly*) to 7 (*agree strongly*). Particular care was taken to ensure the scales' readability: Items were written at the fifth grade reading level, are clearly stated, and were written to be applicable for adults having various medical conditions. All items are worded in the negative (i.e., "My condition makes sleeping difficult"), such that higher scores represent higher levels of illness-related distress. Scale totals are computed by summing the ratings across all 20 items, and converting the total IEQ raw score to a *t*-score with a mean of 50 and a standard deviation of 10. Total *t*-scores above 55 (approximately 30% of the standardization sample) are labeled "moderate distress" whereas those above 65 (approximately 7% of the standardization sample) are labeled "extreme distress." No clear rationale is given for assigning these labels. Finally, the manual describes a follow-up, qualitative interview that can be used to gather additional information about the difficulties a person is experiencing due to illness, and to make specific recommendations to alleviate the symptoms of distress. Unfortunately, the manual provides no evidence that this suggested interview procedure will result in accurate judgments or useful recommendations.

DEVELOPMENT. The IEQ-MP items were developed out of a cognitive behavioral perspective, in which the person's attitudes about their medical condition comprise their illness behaviors. Illness behaviors, in turn, can influence the degree to which an illness disrupts a person's life, the medical treatment decisions that they make, and their phenomenological experience of the illness. In particular, the authors contrast IEQ-MP items (that describe perceived and actual loss due to illness) with Activities of Daily Living scales (that assess the impact of an illness on a person's ability to perform daily tasks) and with Physical Symptom scales (that focus exclusively on the symptoms of a disease). They make a compelling case for the contributions that assessments of patient-perceived distress can make to the treatment of illness.

IEQ-MP items were initially written out of a review of existing illness behavior and attitude scales. Subsequently, these were piloted with a sample of patients in two hospitals, and then refined with feedback from patients and professionals. At least 12 different studies are cited that used the scales, although it is not clear whether all of these studies used the published version of the scale, and some of the studies are neither published nor peer reviewed.

TECHNICAL. Technical properties of the IEQ-MP are entirely inadequate for use in any applied setting. First, there is no true standardization provided for the IEQ-MP. Instead, norms attached to the questionnaires are derived from an aggregate of 12 separate studies, only 5 of which have been published in professional journals. The remaining studies were unpublished manuscripts or presentations at professional conferences. The studies were small, with only one sample size exceeding 100 participants. The manual omits critical information about study participants including their gender, ethnicity, and geographic distribution; the mean participant age is described for each study. Consequently, although it is very difficult to judge the quality of research from which the IEQ-MP norms were derived, it is clear that very little of this work has been held up to the scrutiny of peer review.

More importantly, participants' diagnoses ranged from chronic illnesses like arthritis or headaches to life-threatening illnesses such as cancer or kidney disease, with associated variations in the amount and nature of treatment required. Consequently, the norms tables provide separate norms for seven classes of illness: Headache, kidney, arthritis, cancer, cardiac, chronic pain, and infertile women. However, a small-print footnote at the bottom of the norms table recommends not using the last five classes of norms because they are too preliminary. Instead, the authors recommend relying principally on the general medical norms, which appear to be based on a single unpublished study of 71 participants with diverse illnesses.

Finally, the norms tables attached to all four questionnaires are identical; there are no separate norms provided for the alternative respondents (self, family, or healthcare professional) or for the alternative forms of the self-report (treatment effects or illness effects). Moreover, the manual never specifies whether participants in the norms studies were patients, family members, or professionals. Given the substantial evidence that scales have different properties with different classes of raters (Clark & Watson, 1998), it is irresponsible to endorse such "merged" norms even for preliminary use.

The manual describes strong test-retest reliability of .95 to .99 across 1–2-day intervals, but these results were derived from only 25 patients, participants in two different studies. There is somewhat stronger evidence of the scale's adequate internal consistency, because two studies are described with 62 and 71 participants, and reporting coefficient alphas of .88 and .93, respectively. Descriptions of the scales' validity is mixed because manual-reported correlations with similar scales are quite modest (below .5), correlations with related scales are often based on very small numbers of participants, and the adequacy of the research methodology was not often verified through peer review.

SUMMARY. The Illness Effects Questionnaire—Multi-Perspective (IEQ-MP) is an interesting collection of scales that have a clear purpose but are technically inadequate for use in practice. At the very least, the scales require norms that are based on a large and representative sample of adults, with separate norms for the four versions of the scale. Moreover, norms should only be combined across age groups and across illnesses when evidence demonstrates that the means and standard deviations are equivalent for the different groups. The standardization sample should be fully described in the manual, and evidence of the scale's reliability and validity must be held up to the scrutiny of peer review. Without these refinements, the IEQ-MP can only serve as a very preliminary research measure that cannot be used in actual practice.

REVIEWER'S REFERENCE

Clark, L. A., & Watson, D. (1995). Constructing validity: Basic issues in objective scale development. *Psychological Assessment, 7*, 309–319.

[111]
Individual Outlook Test.

Purpose: Designed to assess codependent orientation.

Population: Adults.
Publication Date: 1993.
Acronym: IOT.
Scores, 6: Codependent Orientation, Externally Derived Sense of Self Worth, Anxiety, Dysfunctional Family of Origin, Dependency within Relationships, Dysfunctional Relationships.
Administration: Group or individual.
Price Data: Available from publisher.
Time: (15–20) minutes.
Authors: Laurie A. Sim and Eugene E. Fox (test and manual); Michelle J. Worth and Donald Macnab (manual).
Publisher: Psychometrics Canada Ltd. [Canada].

Review of the Individual Outlook Test by JEFFREY A. ATLAS, Clinical Psychologist, St. Christopher-Ottilie Services for Children and Families, Queens, NY:

DESCRIPTION. The Individual Outlook Test (IOT) is a 60-item Likert-type self-report measure "designed to assess codependent orientation." Given the ambiguity of the codependence concept in the psychological literature and the relative paucity of empirical anchoring, this scale presents itself as a unique and potentially helpful addition to mental health practitioners. It should be noted, however, that the IOT, contrary to the field of study from which it originated, bears no necessary relation to actual evaluations of substance abuse in partners. Instead, the IOT presumes "codependence" to be a multidimensional interpersonal relationship construct composed of five behavioral factors. The authors' operational definition of codependency is that of "a persistent, self-defeating pattern of intra- and interpersonal relationships that arises out of a dysfunctional family system and is characterized by poor self-worth, dependency, disturbed emotional development, anxiety, and driven by an extreme external locus of control" (Alexander, 1992, p. 39 as quoted on p. 2 of IOT manual).

The IOT features a brief (28-page), mostly straightforward manual with a specimen question booklet/scoresheet and a summary profile for examiners. The IOT is primarily based on two unpublished master's theses from the early 1990s, one by the third author, as well as a cited but nonreferenced work by the first author, Michelle J. Worth. The resulting product carries the breadth and attention to detail of a university thesis, but the expectant small subject samples, scarcity of follow-up work, and poor availability of original source materials make this instrument's discriminative power difficult to evaluate.

The test is aimed at adults, assuming an estimated sixth-grade reading level, and is intended for use in planning appropriate therapeutic strategies, treatment plans, and interventions. The authors give as examples, depending upon significant subscale scores, use of relaxation techniques to address anxiety, or strategic use of a combination of group and individual therapy to mediate dependency in the therapeutic relationship.

Administration of the IOT may be individual or in group. Examinees are asked to endorse items on a 5-point scale from strongly disagree to strongly agree. The authors' estimation of 15–20 minutes for test completion and another 30 minutes for scoring and interpretation is reasonable. The test format is fairly easy for examinees to pick up and for examiners to score and summarize, comparing favorably to other self-report/hand-scorable instruments. Reverse scoring of six items is included to counter a fixed response set.

DEVELOPMENT. A review of the codependency literature for salient content yielded 117 descriptors, ranging from actual addictions and etiological intrafamilial factors, to an array of relational factors found to mediate self-defeating behaviors or "enable" others' chemical dependency. An inventory of potential factors in "codependency" thus might include a "physically abusive family system" (manual, p. 4), "need to be needed by others" (manual, p. 4), and becoming "involved in all aspects of lives of others" (manual, p. 5). As there is no predicted directionality or causal hypothesis related to the descriptor categories, one finds some anomalous descriptors (e.g., under Etiology the "existence of professionals who work with addictions") (manual, p. 4). Although some causal routes are ultimately "retrofitted" to the final scale, this atheoretical bent reverberates through different levels of the IOT.

Emerging from the descriptors were 100 items selected by subject-matter experts as having greatest face validity relative to the initial categories of codependency. Testing of a demographically representative sample of 178 individuals (110 females and 68 males) ranging in age from 19 to 67 years yielded a final item pool of 60 items. The items were described as having an item-total correlation of $r > .30$, and mean range on the 5-point Likert scale of 1.5 to 4.5 (standard deviation

between 1 and 1.5). Four reverse-scored items below the .3 correlation cutoff were reported to be included, but inspection of the appropriate data for the full normative sample reveals 9 other items, for a total of 13, missing this criterion. Factor analytic studies of the final 60-item scale yielded five subscales, which in aggregate yield the total IOT score.

TECHNICAL.

Standardization. One hundred and eighty-nine females and 111 males were selected "using a non-probability sample of convenience" (manual, p. 14) from urban and rural settings in Alberta, Canada. The authors acknowledge that the normative sample "over-represents married individuals and those between 20 and 30 years of age" (manual, p. 14), and also "comes from a restricted geographic area" (manual, p. 14). In addition, a "codependent Criterion Group" (N = 45), is introduced later in the manual, without reference to its origins. This sample greatly overrepresents females (r = 38) and separated individuals (r = 7). The nonrandom character of the normative group and skewed gender composition of the criterion group may limit the generalizability of the IOT.

Reliability. Cronbach alpha coefficients for the normative (r = .91) and criterion (r = .94) groups suggest good internal consistency of the items on the IOT. A very abbreviated evaluation of test-retest reliability with 13 graduate students in educational psychology yielded an r = .98 at a "three to four week interval" (manual, p. 15). Further studies are needed to determine if the high test-retest reliability holds across larger and more diverse samples.

Validity. Criterion-related validity for the IOT was assessed by comparing the Total score of the codependent group with that of a matched sample drawn from the normative group. The codependent group was found to have a significantly higher score. The criterion-related validity may be tempered by the fact that the codependent group earned an IOT score of 189.2, corresponding to a T-score of less than 61, or barely one standard deviation above the average score. Descriptively, this was near the basal score of the "Moderate Codependent Orientation" characterization. The normative group's IOT score of 153 corresponded to a T-value of 50, meriting a characterization of "Mild Dependent Orientation." Although this contrast represents a suggestive research finding, potential users of this scale would have to evaluate whether the difference between moderate and mild codependency warrants a difference that is noticeable enough to instill confidence in use of the IOT in its present form. The same caution applies more strongly to analyses of the scale's component categories.

Comparisons between the normative and criterion groups on the subscales Externally Derived Sense of Self-Worth and Anxiety, and Dysfunctional Family of Origin, Dysfunctional Relationships, and Dependency Within Relationships showed very significant to significant differences (with probability levels ranging from .0001 to .012). Inspection of the respective mean values, however, reveals that both groups were in virtually the same ("mild") range of responses. The Total IOT score demonstrates marginally greater validity psychometrically and descriptively than the authors' characterizations of codependency factors.

Subscale descriptions provided by the authors carry implications of causal pathways that are "retrofitted" without satisfactory supporting data. "Externally Derived Sense of Self-Worth" is said to arise "as a consequence of a dysfunctional family background," and "can result in anxiety" (manual, p. 13). A causal trajectory depicted by the authors goes from Dysfunctional Family of Origin, to Externally Derived Sense of Self-Worth, to Anxiety, to Dependency Within Relationships. Although this sequence appears broadly consistent with developmental psychopathology, one could make a case for Anxiety, for example, appearing earlier or later. Longitudinal study would be needed to strengthen the authors' suggestions of a typical sequencing of problems versus the more modest proposal that they are interrelated.

The validity of the subscale constructs was further examined by a factor analysis. The subscale "Externally Derived Sense of Self-Worth" appeared to encompass the greatest variance (17.6%), with the remaining four subscales showing ranges of 4.8% to 3.0% of the variance. This finding, considered in relation to significant correlations of the IOT to "other directedness" in the Self-Monitoring Scale (Snyder & Gangestad, 1986), further suggests that an "Externally Derived Sense of Self-Worth" is the strongest contributing factor in the scale. A correlational analysis of the codependent and matched groups also showed the first factor to have slightly higher intercorrelations (moderate to high) with the other subscales than each with each other.

Convergent validity of the IOT was assessed via a comparison with the Codependent Questionnaire (Potter-Efron & Potter-Efron, 1989) for a sample of 18 clients (17 female) clinically identified as "codependents" at an Alberta alcohol and drug abuse treatment center. The very high correlation of .89 (p < .05) between the two scales supports overlapping assessment of a viable psychological construct of codependency.

Tests of moderator variables that may have confounded the codependency construct showed that age, IQ, socioeconomic status, gender, and marital status did not correlate significantly with the IOT.

COMMENTARY. The IOT is a novel instrument to measure codependency, viewed as an assemblage of behavior patterns centered on the tendency to identify oneself with reference to another's (sometimes chemically dependent) need. Although based on restricted sampling and in need of standardization that might contribute to discriminative validity, the test shows promise as an overall estimate of codependent orientation. It is weaker in clinical identification and implied causal relations of codependency markers. The factor "Externally Derived Sense of Self-Worth" accounted for most of the variance of the test, and although there is evidence for correlation of the factors, there is not evidence for one being causative of another. Finally, the contrasts between a small codependent group and a matched sample yielded significant differences, but with virtually all values in the "mild" range.

SUMMARY. The Individual Outlook Test is an easily administered, hand-scorable measure of codependency. The standardization as it stands was completed on a restricted range of individuals limiting generalizability outside of the group of married individuals aged 20–30 living in Alberta, Canada. The truncated range of the subscale's descriptors (the codependent and matched samples falling near the "mild" range) limits further clinical utility, except through item analysis on a case-by-case basis. The IOT may be a useful screening measure in further research in family dynamics in chemical dependency, and in treatment of individuals in counseling contacts related to examination of relationship issues.

REVIEWER'S REFERENCES

Potter-Efron, R. T., & Potter-Efron, P. S. (1989). Assessment of codependency with individuals from alcoholic and chemically dependent families. *Alcoholism Treatment Quarterly, 6*(1), 37–57.

Snyder, M., & Gangestad, S. (1986). On the nature of self-monitoring: Matters of assessment; matters of validity. *Journal of Personality and Social Psychology, 51*, 125–139.

Review of the Individual Outlook Test by SUSAN C. WHISTON, *Professor, Counseling Psychology, Indiana University, Bloomington, IN, and* WENDI L. TAI, *Doctoral Student, Counseling Psychology, Indiana University, Bloomington, IN:*

DESCRIPTION. The Individual Outlook Test (IOT) is a self-report instrument designed to assess a codependent orientation in adults (i.e., individuals 18 years and older). It is intended to be used both as a screening device to assess the degree to which there is a codependent orientation and to monitor change in levels of codependency (e.g., during group therapy or individual counseling). The construction of the IOT is rooted in the belief that an individual with a clinically significant tendency toward a codependent orientation will experience a generalized sense of poor self-worth, anxiety and depression that is manifested in persistent self-defeating intrapersonal and interpersonal relationship patterns that are driven by an external locus of control. The IOT contains 60 items in which the examinee indicates whether they "strongly disagree," "disagree," "sometimes agree/ sometimes disagree," "agree," or "strongly agree" with the statement. In scoring, raw scores are converted to *T*-scores for five subscales and the Total IOT score. The five subscales are: (a) Externally Derived Sense of Self-Worth, (b) Anxiety, (c) Dysfunctional Family of Origin, (d) Dysfunctional Relationships, and (e) Dependency within Relationships. In addition, based on the normalized *T*-scores, the test authors of the IOT have assigned classifications that are designed to indicate degree of clinical significance of the five subscales and the Total IOT score. *T*-scores under 30 merit a classification of clinical alert and indicate the clinicians should interpret these scores in collaboration with other clinical data, whereas *T*-scores of 31 to 49 are classified of little clinical significance. A mild codependent orientation is associated with scores of 50–59, moderate codependent orientation with scores between 60–69, and severe codependent orientation with *T*-scores above 70.

DEVELOPMENT. The authors developed the IOT in order to measure a construct that has grown in popularity in both the professional and nonprofessional literature related to psychological and chemical dependency. The authors argued

that it is difficult to draw conclusions about the nature, symptomatology, and etiology of codependency because the research is not systematic and there is a lack of clarity in how the construct is both defined and measured. Adopted from Alexander (1992), the operational definition for the IOT is "a persistent, self-defeating pattern of intra- and interpersonal relationships that arise out of a dysfunctional family system and is characterized by poor self-worth, dependency, disturbed emotional development, anxiety, and driven by an extreme external locus of control" (manual, p. 2).

In developing the IOT, 117 descriptors were identified based on a review of the codependent literature, and subsequent analysis of these descriptors resulted in 14 categories. Initially, 174 items were developed to measure the 14 categories, but the items were refined and a 100-item IOT was field tested with a sample of 178. Item analysis was then conducted, with a focus on examining the correlations between the item and the total score, which resulted in 40 items being eliminated. The current 60-item instrument was subsequently administered to a normative sample of 300 Canadians.

TECHNICAL. The normative sample of the Individual Outlook Test was 300 adults (189 females and 111 males) from Alberta, Canada. The manual does not specify the procedures for recruiting this sample and the authors provided only limited information on the makeup of the sample, such as breakdowns according to gender, age, and marital status. The authors, however, included some limited documentation that the socioeconomic status of the sample is comparable to the city of Edmonton and an earlier study using the initial version of the IOT. The sample is predominantly married individuals who are between 30 to 39 years of age. Although it may be a typographical error, the manual indicates there were only 10 individuals in the norming group between the ages of 20 and 29, and all 10 of these were classified as codependent. Although presented as validation evidence, the authors supplied evidence that IOT scores are not significantly affected by age, gender, socioeconomic status, or marital status.

The internal consistency coefficients based on the normative sample were .91 for the Total IOT score and .65 to .85 for the five subscales. Test-retest coefficients are provided, but these estimates are based on a sample of 13. The manual includes information on standard error of measurement for the Total IOT score, but not for the five subscales.

In terms of validation evidence, the authors cited in the manual a study where the IOT discriminated between a codependent group ($n = 45$) and a matched sample drawn from the normative group ($n = 45$). Besides problems with the small sample size, the authors might also have been better served by using discriminant analysis as opposed to the repeated t-tests comparing the two groups' means on the five subscales and Total scores. Other validation evidence contained in the manual relates to the factor structure of the IOT and an examination of convergent and divergent validity. The manual cites three factor analytic studies that support the subscale structure of the IOT. In one of these studies, there were five factors with eigen values greater than 1.0 that accounted for 27% of the variance. A second study found five similar factors that accounted for 33% of the variance; however, in this analysis, many of the items loaded on more than one factor. The third study was generally supportive of the five subscales, but also found a sixth factor with items that reflected a concern for the welfare and feeling of others. Other validation efforts concerned convergent evidence, where Alexander (1992) found a significant relationship ($r = .89$) with the Codependency Questionnaire. Concerning divergent information, the manual includes information the IOT has a very small and inverse relationship ($r = -.14$) with a measure of intelligence.

COMMENTARY. There are a number of issues related to the IOT that warrant caution in using it, particularly in relationship to determining the degree to which an individual may have a codependent orientation. Even though the construct of codependency lacks a consistent definition, the authors have devised a sound operational definition; yet, they provide little documentation that the measure closely corresponds to that definition. For example, extreme external locus of control is embedded in the definition, but is not included as one of the five subscales. Furthermore, the validation evidence is scanty and lacks sufficient detail to assist the user in knowing when and how to use the instrument. The majority of the validation evidence concerns the factor structure of the instrument and there was only one study that examined convergent and divergent evidence. Although the factor analytic

studies provide some supporting evidence for the five subscales, there is concern about the number of items that loaded on multiple factors, and the possibility that five subscales may not capture the underlying structure of the items.

The labels of clinical alert, little clinical significance, mild codependent orientation, moderate codependent orientation, and severe codependent orientation appeared to be assigned simply based on a range of T-scores, and there was a significant lack of clinical data supporting these designations. These designations are particularly troubling, as they are based on T-scores that are presented as normalized when the sample is only 300 Canadians from one province. Furthermore, only one study was noted in the manual that examined differences between those with a codependent orientation and those without, and this study did not examine the classifications of clinical alert, little clinical significance, mild codependent orientation, moderate codependent orientation, and severe codependent orientation. Hence, clinicians would be advised to shy away from these labels and, at best, use the results of the IOT as tentative descriptive information that must be examined in conjunction with other clinical information.

SUMMARY. The Individual Outlook Test is a 60-item instrument designed to measure a codependent orientation in adults. It is a norm-referenced instrument with a norming sample of 300 Canadians. The scoring profile provides an indication of the degree of codependent orientation (i.e., clinical alert, little clinical significance, mild codependent orientation, moderate codependent orientation, and severe codependent orientation); however, there is very little empirical evidence in the manual supporting the use of these labels. The reliability evidence is primarily internal consistency coefficients, which were .91 for the Total IOT score and ranged .65 to .85 for the five subscales. Although some of the factor analyses results support the structure of the five subscales, professionals should be careful in using these subscales, as many of the items tend to load on different subscales than the authors intended. In conclusion, there are some questions about the content of the IOT and the validation evidence is sparse. Hence, additional research is needed before the IOT can be used by mental health practitioners or researchers to identify a codependent orientation.

REVIEWERS' REFERENCE

Alexander, D. (1992). *Measuring codependency: Construct validation for the individual outlook test.* Unpublished master's thesis, University of Alberta, Edmonton, Alberta.

[112]

Insight: Assessing and Developing Self-Esteem.

Purpose: Designed as a tool to "assess and, where required, improve a (child's) self-esteem."

Population: Ages 3 to 16.

Publication Date: 2002.

Scores, 4: Sense of Self, Sense of Belonging, Sense of Personal Power, Overall.

Administration: Individual or group.

Price Data: Available from publisher.

Time: (10) minutes.

Comments: Reproducible rating scale forms are titled "Self-Esteem Indicator."

Author: Elizabeth Morris.

Publisher: NFER-Nelson Publishing Co., Ltd. [England].

a) INSIGHT: PRE-SCHOOL.

Population: Ages 3 to 5.

Comments: Rating scale completed by adult observer.

b) INSIGHT: PRIMARY.

Population: Ages 5 to 11.

Comments: Rating scale can be completed by adult observer or by adult and student working together.

c) INSIGHT: SECONDARY.

Population: Ages 11 to 16.

Comments: Rating scale completed by adult observer or by adult and student working together.

Review of Insight: Assessing and Developing Self-Esteem by GERALD E. DeMAURO, Managing Assessment Education Scientist, American Institutes for Research, Washington, DC:

DESCRIPTION. The Self-Esteem Indicator has Preschool, Primary, and Secondary forms. Each takes about 10 minutes to administer, by an early years professional for a preschool child, the teacher or teacher and student for a primary school student, and the student for a secondary school student. It is an integral component of a test-intervene-retest system for building an environment that enhances self-esteem, including the self-esteem of the critical adults in the child's life, and for strengthening the self-esteem of the children. Specifically, the Indicator is most useful in providing information to validate the teacher's or other professional's own observations of the child, to stimulate the continued development of an intervention strategy, and to provide a focus of the intervention with objectives.

DEVELOPMENT. The three instruments have 24 (Preschool), 36 (Primary), and 30 (Secondary) statements that describe aspects of the child's self-esteem. Each is rated from 0 (*almost never*) to 3 (*most of the time*). About 21 statements are in common to the three instruments, although there are others that appear to differ only nominally.

Little information is presented concerning development of the scoring rubric. One concern is the nature of the scale it defines. Scores are awarded as: zero = *almost never*; 1 = *occasionally*; 2 = *quite often*; and 3 = *most of the time*. The subjective ordering of the 2- and 3-point values, in particular, as well as the psychophysical distance between the score points should be explored.

The instrument targets three components of self-esteem. The first, Sense of Self, involves knowing and being comfortable with oneself. The second, Sense of Belonging, refers to self-awareness and comfort in relationship to others. The third, Sense of Personal Power, refers to knowledge of one's capacity to influence their world. These components are each described as crucial to self-perception, interrelated, yet distinct. The total instruments appear to have the same number of statements devoted to each component. No information is provided about scales related to these components or the interpretation of totals other than that they should be compared to each other.

Each instrument was trial-tested over a 3-year period among 100 teaching professionals. Teachers' comments from most recent trials are cited. Details on the selection of the teacher sample are not reported, but the descriptions across the three Indicators are quite similar. Examinees were selected by teachers based on their judgments that the child had low self-esteem and was one with whom they wanted to work. The teachers were administered a "semi-structured" interview focusing on classroom behavior, social behaviors, emotional responses, and academic achievements. The assessment was administered, teachers selected esteem building intervention activities to implement regularly over a 6-week period, and a second interview and a retest on the Indicator was then administered. Among the students in the sample, 68% of the preschoolers and 56% of the primary students had a low sense of belonging at the outset. Among the secondary students, 75% had a low sense of personal power.

In response to teacher input, the Secondary Indicator was reduced from 36 to 30 statements and the Preschool Indicator was reduced from 29 to 24 statements. The Primary Indicator was expanded from 29 to 36 statements. This trial component seems to be central to the development of an instrument concerned with identifying intervention strategies. Empirical indices of internal consistency, test-retest reliability, correlations among subscales, and item difficulty and discriminability indices would assist interpretation of these results.

TECHNICAL.

Standardization. It is evident that the trial tests contributed to standardizing the instruments. Quartile ranges are reported that would yield Preschool, Primary, and Secondary instrument means of 42, 63, and 45, respectively, and standard deviations of 23.9, 34.3, and 19.4, respectively, assuming normal distributions. Percentile ranks are not reported. The degree of overlap among the three instruments raises the interesting prospect of common scaling and cross scale comparisons. There does not appear to be scaling within subtests.

Reliability. The argument for reliability rests heavily on the continued utility of the scales for intervention and their sensitivity to that intervention. Because the sample was chosen for its appearance of need for intervention, it is difficult to assess the extent to which the results of the intervention might be attributable to unreliability of the instrument at the outset. That is, measurement error contributing to low initial scores could confound estimates of improvement.

Validity. Validity evidence also rests heavily on the sensitivity of the Indicators to the initial status of the students and to the intervention selected to address that status. Improvements are reported by teacher interview in response to intervention on the four outcome variables: social behavior, emotional behavior, classroom behavior, and academic achievement. For the Secondary and Preschool groups the academic indicators were least likely to improve or last to improve. Operational definitions of these indicators might help explain differences in improvements. Data are not reported for subscales.

The test-intervene-retest model is a powerful tool in support of the consequential validity of the instruments. The intervention activities are related to six areas: creating a self-esteem building environ-ment, supporting the teaching (or other) professionals, developing a sense of self, developing a sense of belonging, developing a sense of personal power, and general activities. Guidelines for developing an intervention program and case studies referring to performance on the Indicators are provided.

Some attention could be given to whether the esteem components are state or trait variables. The issue is the extent to which change could be expected without intervention to gauge the magnitude of change with intervention. Of course, not intervening with children in need presents ethical problems. Providing test and retest information for students with all ranges of self-esteem might partially address this dilemma, but clear estimates of expected levels of improvement without intervention based on theory and normative information would greatly enhance score interpretation.

Finally, cut scores are provided based on the quartile information from trial testing. These are not related to expected behaviors at different levels of scoring. Such expectations would also enhance score interpretation, especially in relation to social behaviors, emotional behaviors, classroom behaviors, and academic achievement.

COMMENTARY. The three Indicators appear to have much promise for use to enhance student self-esteem, especially because the instruments are associated with intervention strategies. Some attention to the technical aspects of the Indicators would assist in score interpretation, and, therefore, improve their efficacy.

SUMMARY. The Self-Esteem Indicators are based on ratings of statements about the self-esteem of preschool, primary, and secondary school students. The instruments hold much promise for improving student self-esteem and consequent academic achievement, social behavior, emotional behavior, and classroom behavior. These improvements, in turn, are related to enhancing the lives of the children.

Review of Insight: Assessing and Developing Self-Esteem by GYPSY M. DENZINE, Associate Professor of Educational Psychology, Northern Arizona University, Flagstaff, AZ:

DESCRIPTION. According to the developer, Insight: Assessing and Developing Self-Esteem is designed to provide a practical tool for anyone involved in working with young people and enables them to assess and improve the self-esteem of students ages 3–16. Self-esteem is conceptualized as having three primary components—a Sense of Self, a Sense of Belonging, and a Sense of Personal Power.

Three different manuals are available from the publisher: Insight: Pre-School (ages 3–5), Insight: Primary (ages 5–11), and Insight: Secondary (ages 11–16). The rating scale for the Pre-School version is completed by an adult observer. The Insight Primary and Secondary rating scales can be completed by an adult observer or by an adult and student working together. Although not explicitly stated, this scale appears to be a tool most appropriate for a target population of nonclinical children and adolescents.

The three manuals contain a conceptual and theoretical overview of self-esteem, descriptions of the three self-esteem components, a scale for measuring self-esteem, a chapter on program interventions for improving self-esteem, and a section of activities for self-esteem interventions. Insight is based on theories of self-esteem developed by Coopersmith (1967), Rosenberg (1965), and Branden (1969). Although the manual contains a section on "Theories of self-esteem," the author includes only brief definitions of theorists' definitions of self-esteem. Nor does the manual provide an in-depth theoretical treatment of self-esteem or review of the empirical literature on self-esteem. The three components of self-esteem were identified by the author based on her 20 years of clinical experience and results from teaching self-esteem courses. Results from several studies are provided in the manuals. For example, it is noted in the Primary manual that 43% of the students assessed in a primary school had a vulnerable or low sense of self and 14% had a vulnerable or low sense of personal power. However, the manual does not provide any methodological information relative to the studies cited. The reader is left to question the sample size, testing procedures, school environment, and more.

Administration. For children under 9 years old, the author recommends that the rating scale be completed by an adult on behalf of the student. The tool was designed mostly for teachers, who can assess their students in a one-to-one or small group setting. In the Primary version, the adult photocopies the Indicator and rates each of the 36 items in turn by circling his or her chosen rating. Sample Primary rating items include: (a) Is this pupil co-operative if something needs to be done or achieved? (b) Do other pupils like him/her? (c) Does this pupil comfortably make social overtures to a new pupil? The four response categories are Most of the Time, Quite Often, Occasionally, and Almost Never. The Pre-School and Secondary versions contain 24 and 30 questions, respectively.

Scoring and interpretation. A total self-esteem score is obtained by summing the various items. The higher the score, the higher the level of self-esteem. Global self-esteem is presumed to fall into one of four classifications: very low, vulnerable, good, or high. The author does not discuss the conceptual or empirical rationale for using such cutoff scores for categorizing self-esteem scores into the different levels. A scoring overlay provided at the back of the manual is used for obtaining the three self-esteem component scores.

A significant amount of space in the manual is allocated to discussing how teachers and professionals can use children's Self-Esteem Indicator scores in their work. Short case studies serve as an instructional aid for adults who are interested in developing stronger self-esteem in children.

DEVELOPMENT. Other than the brief mention in the manual that the author developed the items based on 20 years of clinical experience, no information about the item or scale development for this tool is discussed. The technical manual lacks information regarding who can administer and interpret the scale. According to the manual, proficient facilitators of effective self-esteem-building programs need to have good counseling skills and be able to create a climate of warmth and trust.

TECHNICAL. A PsychInfo "all fields" search for "Insight scale," "Insight self-esteem," "Insight assessing and developing self-esteem," and "Insight Elizabeth Morris" yielded no publications. Nor are there any publications cited for Insight in the three versions of the manual.

Insight was developed as a practical tool and the manual is devoid of technical information. Overall, the manual lacks important information about the psychometric properties of the scale, which conflicts with the *Standards for Educational and Psychological Testing* (AERA, APA, & NCME, 1999). No information is provided about the norming sample and test standardization procedures. Also missing is an in-depth discussion of the appropriateness of this scale for different gender or ethnic/culture groups.

No reliability data are provided and issues of validity were not addressed in any of the three manuals (Pre-School, Primary, Secondary). Although the author claims the tool is to help teachers and professionals increase students' self-esteem by implementing specific strategies and activities, no studies providing evidence of predictive validity are reported. Absent in the technical manual, or professional literature, are studies providing any evidence supporting the face, content, construct, convergent, divergent, or criterion-related validity of the Insight: Assessing and Developing Self-Esteem.

COMMENTARY. Perhaps the greatest strength of this test is the ease of the administration and the availability of immediate results. The manual, rating sheet, scoring overlay, and photocopiable activities are all user-friendly. However, potential users of this tool should be aware of the conceptual and empirical limitations of this scale. There is minimal evidence that the theoretical model of self-esteem is supported by the use of this test. As one example, the Primary scale contains the item "Can this pupil read well for his/her age?" We are left with the question about how reading ability directly or indirectly relates to self-esteem? The user is also left with many questions about the structure of the construct. Noticeably missing is a literature review on the debate on the existence of a global measure of self-esteem. The author appears to have an extensive amount of practical experience and could possibly benefit from partnering with someone more interested in addressing the technical parts of this tool.

SUMMARY. Although this assessment tool is easy to administer, involves quick scoring, and the reports are easy to interpret, there are several important elements missing in the demonstration of a psychometrically sound measure of self-esteem. Given these limitations, there is a need for more sophisticated and ongoing research on the Insight: Assessing and Developing Self-Esteem scale before its use can be recommended.

REVIEWER'S REFERENCES

American Educational Research Association, American Psychological Association, & National Council on Measurement in Education. (1999). *Standards for educational and psychological testing.* Washington, DC: American Educational Research Association.
Branden, N. (1969). *The psychology of self-esteem: A new concept of man's psychological nature.* Los Angeles: Nash.
Coopersmith, S. (1967). *The antecedents of self-esteem.* San Francisco: W.H. Freeman and Company.
Rosenberg, M. (1965). *Society and the adolescent self-image.* Princeton, NJ: Princeton University Press.

[113]
Internalized Shame Scale.

Purpose: Developed to measure an individual's feelings of shame and the negative response patterns that result from internalized chance.
Population: Age 13 and older.
Publication Date: 2001.
Acronym: ISS.
Scores, 2: Shame, Self-Esteem.
Administration: Individual.
Price Data, 2002: $73 per complete kit including technical manual (128 pages), 25 Quikscore forms, and 25 brochure handouts; $36 per specimen set including technical manual, 3 Quikscore forms, and 3 brochure handouts; $32 per technical manual.
Time: 15 minutes.
Comments: Self-completed.
Author: David R. Cook.
Publisher: Multi-Health Systems, Inc.

Review of the Internalized Shame Scale by SEAN P. REILLEY, Assistant Professor of Psychology, Morehead State University, Morehead, KY:

DESCRIPTION. The Internalized Shame Scale (ISS) consists of 24 negatively worded items that measure intense affect and self-cognitions involving internalized shame. Six positively worded self-esteem items, adapted from the Rosenberg Self-Esteem Scale (Rosenberg, 1965), are included to discourage pervasive response sets. Tentative adolescent norms are available. However, the ISS has been primarily used with adults who possess at least a fourth grade reading level. The ISS can be used for research and clinical purposes, including screening and treatment monitoring, and can be completed in 15 minutes. Respondents use a 5-point Likert-type scale anchored *Never* to *Almost Always* to indicate the frequency of their cognitive-affective experiences. Raw responses are automatically transferred to an underlying QuikScore form that includes bolded values for strongly endorsed items. Appropriately trained staff can score the Shame subscale, the primary ISS indicant, as well as the Self-Esteem score in 5 minutes. Individuals with appropriate postgraduate training use raw Shame scores for interpretation. Tables for conversion to percentile ranks are provided for comparisons with other psychological inventories.

DEVELOPMENT. The ISS is an atheoretical inventory. However, Tomkin's affect theory (Tomkins, 1963) has increasingly been applied as a conceptual framework for interpreting scores. The 24 Shame items found on the current fifth edition share an intense emotional language involving self-experiences of inferiority, incompetence, defectiveness, and self-contempt. A majority of these items (18 of 24) derive from a pool of 114 statements developed by David Cook during the mid-1980s. Those frequently chosen as familiar and frequent experiences by inpatient alcoholics (n = 10) were piloted with a second alcoholic group (n = 35). The size of the pilot groups is insufficient by current test standards, and the specific choice of alcoholics appears to be one of clinical convention, rather than one based on strong theoretical grounds. Second and third revisions of the inventory contributed a total of 6 additional shame items to the current edition. These items were drawn in part from clinical work with shame-based clients and were selected following assessments of their item functioning with clinical and nonclinical samples. Positively worded, Self-Esteem items adapted from the Rosenberg Self-Esteem Scale were piloted on the fourth edition; six were retained on the current edition for response set detection. Although the efficacy of this procedure needs further validation, high scores on social desirability measures and on the Self-Esteem subscale have been significantly correlated.

TECHNICAL. Multiple, clinical (adults, n = 499; adolescents, n = 41) and nonclinical samples (adults, n = 1,130; adolescents, n = 200) were used to standardize the ISS. A minimum fourth grade reading level is suggested; however, no readability analyses are reported. The impact of gender and age on ISS scores yield conflicting results in different samples. This needs further investigation, especially in clinical samples. Similarly, a broader and more representative standardization sample is needed to improve the generalizability of the ISS for diverse populations.

Internal consistency estimates, including corrected item/total correlations (rs ranging from .52 to .82) and Cronbach alpha coefficients (alphas ranging from .87 to .96), are generally high for clinical (n = 370) and nonclinical samples (n = 645). No attempts to validate the factor structure of the current version are reported. Two correlated shame factors emerged on the proceeding edition. Because the statistical criteria for retention of a unitary shame factor were not reported, confirmatory factor analysis is needed to validate the latent factor structure of the ISS. Test-retest data are lacking. A small nonclinical sample (n = 44) yielded test-retest correlations ranging from adequate (Self-Esteem: .69) to good (Shame: .84) for a 7-week time frame. One subsequent study cited in the manual reports a higher Shame test-retest correlation (r = .94) for a 5-week time frame. No temporal stability estimates are reported for clinical groups, which the developer acknowledges is currently problematic.

Convergent and discriminant validity vis-à-vis questionnaire data are mixed. Moderate to strong (rs .49 to .86) trait shame correlations between the ISS and the Personal Feelings Questionnaire and the Dimensions of Shame Scale support its use as a trait shame measure. However, moderate correlations (rs ranging from .39 to .52) also emerge for a situation-based shame measure drawn from Tangney's Self-Conscious Affect and Attribution Inventory. Hence, the ISS currently provides some, albeit less than optimal, differentiation between state and trait shame. The ISS appears most distinct from situational guilt as evident by modest relations with a guilt subscale from the Tangney instrument (rs ranging from .07 to .10) and the Mosher Guilt Scale (rs ranging from .15 to .24). The one exception was a moderate correlation (r = .58) for morality guilt from the Mosher inventory. The ISS is least differentiated from trait guilt, as a strong relationship (r = .71) emerged with the Guilt Inventory of Kugler and Jones.

Finally, the ISS, as a trait shame measure, was hypothesized and found to generally correlate with a number of negative affective states, such as depression (rs ranging from from .32 to .75), anxiety (rs ranging from .42 to .91), anger (rs ranging from .22 to .57), and global poor self-esteem (rs ranging from .41 to .72). Significantly higher shame scores emerge for individuals diagnosed with Major Depressive Disorder, Alcohol/Drug Dependence, Post Traumatic Stress Disorder, and Eating Disorders relative to a nonclinical control group, thus supporting initial criterion validity. The sensitivity, specificity, and positive and negative predictive power of ISS cutting scores have not been clinically validated. In fact, due to a restricted clinical range, raw scores are currently recommended, which is problematic for clinical work. In subsequent standardization, the differential validity of ISS cutting scores should be clarified with respect to gender and diversity.

COMMENTARY. The ISS is a potentially valuable shame instrument, and one of the few designed specifically for clinical work. This being the case, several issues need to be addressed in future work with the ISS. First, more representative standardization and clinical samples are needed to evaluate the readability of individual items, to anchor the factor structure and temporal stability, and to address gender and diversity contributions to Shame scores. Second, additional studies are needed that permit tests of rival hypotheses for the ISS and measures of state and trait shame, state and trait guilt, and negative affectivity to increase differentiation among these constructs. Finally, the positive and negative predictive power of the ISS needs to be investigated, and standardized metrics are needed for classification and interpretive purposes.

SUMMARY. The developer, to his credit, has produced a potentially valuable trait shame instrument for clinical use. In order for this instrument to become a gold standard, more representative standardization and clinical samples are needed. Careful, continued validation work should solidify the factor structure and temporal stability of the ISS, as well as its clinical efficacy. Whether affect theory may provide a reliable theoretical base will need to be tested using hypotheses that can attempt to reliably differentiate the ISS from state shame, state and trait guilt, and general negative affectivity.

REVIEWER'S REFERENCES

Rosenberg, M. (1965). *Society and the adolescent self-image.* Princeton, NJ: Princeton University Press.
Tomkins, S. S. (1963). *Affect, imagery, consciousness, vol. 2: The negative affects.* New York: Springer.

Review of the Internalized Shame Scale by SUSAN M. SWEARER, Associate Professor of School Psychology, University of Nebraska–Lincoln, and KELLY BREY LOVE, Doctoral Student, University of Nebraska–Lincoln, Lincoln, NE:

DESCRIPTION. The Internalized Shame Scale (ISS) is a self-report measure of internal feelings of negative affect and the extent to which these negative response patterns become internalized in adolescents (over age 13) and adults. There is no known upper age limit for the ISS. The ISS is composed of 30 items, 24 that specifically measure shame and 6 items that measure self-esteem. The items measuring self-esteem were based on the Rosenberg Self-Esteem Scale (Rosenberg, 1965). The items measuring self-esteem are not included in the total Shame score. These questions may be totaled separately, deriving a measure of positive Self-Esteem. Responses to all 30 items are in the form of a 5-point Likert-type scale, ranging from 0 (*Never*) to 4 (*Almost Always*). Administra-

tion and scoring of the ISS are relatively simple. Administration takes approximately 10–15 minutes to complete, and approximately 5 minutes to score. The raw score is used to interpret the results. The ISS can be administered and scored by "untrained" individuals. However, the manual advises that a "mature professional" interpret the results.

There are two scores that can be derived from the ISS. They are the internalized Shame score, and the Self-Esteem score. The internalized Shame score ranges from 0–96, and the Self-Esteem score ranges from 0–24. The Self-Esteem subscale was included in an attempt to reduce respondent bias, as all the items in this subscale are positively worded (internalized Shame questions are negatively worded). The Self-Esteem subscale is not intended to be used as an independent measure of self-esteem; therefore, no norms are presented in the manual. Scores of 18 or higher are indicative of positive self-esteem, whereas scores below 18 likely indicate negative self-esteem. The manual states that normative cutoff scores for "problematic" levels of internalized Shame across a wide variety of clinical samples have not been created. The manual also reports that any raw Shame score above 50 likely indicates a relatively high incidence of internalized shame. It further states that a score above 60 might indicate depression, and scores above 70 very likely indicate depression and/or other emotional or behavioral problems. Analysis of individual highly scored items in the subscale is highly recommended by the authors of the scale. The ISS has a fourth grade, North American reading level. Therefore, limited reading ability, as well as limited English proficiency, could negatively impact the participant's understanding of the items.

DEVELOPMENT. The ISS was originally developed in 1984, and first released in 1989. The current version (publication date 2001) is the fifth revision of the ISS. The developers state that the initial scale was not based on any specific theory of shame. The developers also assert the current version has been supported by development of a theoretical framework regarding shame, as well as data published in recent research studies measuring shame. The five stages of development are described in the manual. The reliability coefficient from the first version was reported as .96, and the second as .95. The sample size used in the third version of the ISS was not reported.

TECHNICAL.

Standardization. Construct validity evidence (on subsequent versions of the scale) is presented at length in the manual. Normative adult (17–79) samples are limited to male and female nonclinical, male and female alcoholic, and a group titled "affective disorders." The affective disorders group is composed of a combined psychiatric sample, about half outpatient, most of whom were diagnosed with depression/dysthymia or an anxiety disorder. The adolescent sample (12–18) is composed of almost all Caucasian students in high school (nonclinical) and male students in a group home (clinical). Again, the extremely limited sample of both clinical and nonclinical participants is of concern.

Validity. The manual reports potential use of the ISS as a screener, treatment monitoring tool, research instrument, and a tool to provide clinical feedback. Discriminant validity is discussed by comparing measures of guilt and shame, and presented in table format in the manual. The ISS demonstrates modest, positive correlations between other measures of guilt and shame. Convergent validity of the ISS is demonstrated by correlations with the Tennessee Self-Concept Scale of -.66, with the Coopersmith Self-Esteem Inventories of -.52, the Janis-Field Feelings of Inadequacy Scale of -.77, the Low Self-Esteem Scale: Multiscore Depression Inventory of .68, the Ineffectiveness Scale: Eating Disorder Inventory of .79, the Rosenberg Self-Esteem Scale of -.74, the Multiscore Depression Inventory of .75, the Beck Depression Inventory total sample of .74, the Suicide Probability Scale (suicide probability) of .81, and the MCAACL-R of .69.

Reliability. Reliability estimates are provided in the manual. On the Shame items, item-total correlations for the nonclinical group ranged from .56–.73, with a median correlation of .63. The clinical group item-total correlations ranged from .52–.82, median correlation of .70. Internal consistency alpha is reported as .95 and .96. The reliability of the Self-Esteem scale was .90 for the nonclinical group, and .87 for the clinical group. Mean item-total correlation was reported as .73 (nonclinical) and .67 (clinical). Test-retest reliability was conducted with 44 nonclinical participants after an interval of 7 weeks. The test-retest correlation for the items on the Shame subscale was .84, and .69 for the Self-Esteem items. Individuals from the clinical group were not evaluated for test-retest reliability.

COMMENTARY. Initial construct validity for the ISS was low (the admitted absence of initial guiding theory). Some of the items are awkwardly worded and may be culturally/regionally specific (i.e., "I could beat myself over the head with a club when I make a mistake," and "Sometimes I feel no bigger than a pea"). There are many concerns regarding the normative sample. For example, the pilot nonclinical mean age was 24, using college undergraduate and graduate students. This is a relatively low median age for a scale that is intended to be used with adolescents through adults with no known age ceiling. Additionally, the education level of those sampled is higher than that of the general population. The manual reports that there are no significant differences based on age, gender, or ethnicity that would affect interpretation of the ISS; however, the norm sample utilized is too homogeneous to provide an accurate analysis of these potential differences. The nonclinical participants used in the norm group and validity sample are also very homogeneous (e.g., majority female, Caucasian, and highly educated).

Regarding analysis of validity, there is a significant age disparity between the clinical and nonclinical groups, with the majority of those in the clinical group several years older than those in the nonclinical group. The clinical sample is very limited; thus, generalizations and severity scores should also be interpreted with caution. Caution in interpretation of the six self-esteem items is advised, and this point is reiterated throughout the manual. Therefore, one might wonder about the reasons for inclusion of the Self-Esteem scale. The manual provides the rationale of the inclusion to circumvent response bias; however, this could also be achieved by reverse scoring of individual, random items on the Shame scale. Another rationale for inclusion of the Self-Esteem scale is to provide a type of internal reliability check regarding consistency of response. Again, this could be achieved through analysis of the items in the Shame scale (i.e., looking for patterns in response, individual items rated very high or very low).

SUMMARY. The Internalized Shame Scale is an instrument designed to measure the "extent to which negative affect of shame becomes magnified and internalized into one's sense of self" (technical manual, p. 1). Administration, scoring, and interpretation may be completed in a relatively short amount of time. The ISS appears to possess strong convergent validity with a number of reputable scales. Of concern is the extremely limited norm sample for both clinical and nonclinical individuals. The significant age disparity between clinical and nonclinical groups is also of concern, leading to a potential compromise of validity of score interpretations. Convincing rationale for the inclusion of the positive Self-Esteem scale appears to be lacking by the test developer. Given some of the psychometric concerns regarding scale development, the ISS appears to be best suited as a clinical tool for an initial assessment of shame and for monitoring patient progress.

REVIEWER'S REFERENCE

Rosenberg, M. (1965). *Society and the adolescent self-image.* Princeton, NJ: Princeton University Press.

[114]

InView.

Purpose: "A cognitive abilities test ... measur[ing] selected verbal, nonverbal, and quantitative reasoning abilities ... important for success in an educational program."

Population: Grades 2–12.

Publication Date: 2000.

Scores, 8: 5 subtest scores (Sequences, Analogies, Quantitative Reasoning, Verbal Reasoning—Words, Verbal Reasoning—Context); 3 composite scores (Verbal Composite, Nonverbal Composite, Total Test Scale Score).

Administration: Group.

Levels, 6: 1 (Grades 2–3), 2 (Grades 4–5), 3 (Grades 6–7), 4 (Grades 8–9), 5 (Grades 10–11), 6 (Grades 11–12).

Price Data, 2002: $84.80 per 25 InView-1 consumable test books; $66.25 per 25 InView 2–6 reusable test books (specify level); $28.60 per 50 InView 2–6 answer sheets; $1,115 per 2,500 InView continuous form answer sheets; $21.20 per InView 2–6 stencil set (specify level); $18 per examiner's manual, specify level); $31.80 per Teacher's Guide to InView, Technical Bulletin 1, Technical Report (CD-ROM version), or Norms Book (all levels); $2.10 per Class Record Sheet for Handscoring.

Time: 95 minutes.

Comments: Replaces the Test of Cognitive Skills, Second Edition (TCS/2); conormed with the Primary Test of Cognitive Skills (PTCS) (see T6:1978) and with TerraNova, The Second Edition (see 245); Level 1 students record answers in test books; Levels 2–6 students use separate answer sheets; variety of score report formats available; on-line feedback on test performance available, contact publisher for details.

Author: CTB/McGraw-Hill.

Publisher: CTB/McGraw-Hill.

Cross References: See T5:2677 for information on the Test of Cognitive Skills, Second Edition; for a review by Randy W. Kamphaus of an earlier edition, see 13:325 (8 references); see also T4:2745 (4 references); for reviews by Timothy Z. Keith and Robert J. Sternberg of an earlier edition, see 9:1248; for a review by Lynn H. Fox and an excerpted review by David M. Shoemaker of the Short Form Test of Academic Aptitude, see 8:202 (9 references).

Review of the InView by RUSSELL N. CARNEY, Professor of Psychology, Southwest Missouri State University, Springfield, MO:

DESCRIPTION. The InView replaces the Test of Cognitive Skills, Second Edition (TCS/2, 1992), and is described as a group-administered test of cognitive ability and anticipated academic achievement. It is available in both paper-and-pencil and online formats. The InView consists of five subtests—three tapping nonverbal abilities (Sequences, Analogies, Quantitative Reasoning), and two tapping verbal abilities (Verbal Reasoning—Words and Verbal Reasoning—Context). Based on this, the test yields five subtest scores, and three aggregate scores (Nonverbal, Verbal, and Total). The six levels of the InView span Grades 2 through 12. Types of scores provided include a Cognitive Skills Index (CSI) score, scale scores, grade mean equivalents, normal curve equivalents, national stanines, and national percentile ranks (and Anticipated Achievement Scores, when combined with TerraNova, The Second Edition). The CSI score has a mean of 100 and a standard deviation of 16, and serves as a measure of general cognitive ability. The maximum testing time is 105 minutes for Grades 2 and 3, and 95 minutes for Grades 4 through 12. This does not include instruction time for sample items. The InView was conormed with a group-administered achievement test, TerraNova, The Second Edition, in 2000.

DEVELOPMENT. Test blueprints provided guidance for professional item writers. Two to four times the number of needed items were written for each of the subtests, and all were screened for appropriate vocabulary level. The items were carefully reviewed for ethnic, racial, age, and gender bias. Tryout booklets were subsequently developed and administered. Additionally, selected anchor items (i.e., from the TCS/2 and TerraNova Mathematics) were included in the tryout booklets for each subtest. More than 17,000 students participated in the tryout, which involved a wide variety of students, including those with disabilities and those for whom English was a second language.

Traditional item analysis statistics (e.g., item difficulty and discrimination) were derived, and the items were scaled and calibrated using a three-parameter logistic IRT model. An analysis of differential item functioning (DIF) was used to minimize ethnic and gender bias. Item fit was also considered in item selection. Eventual item selection was done using the ITEMSYS software, which aided in the selection of the best statistical combination of test items.

TECHNICAL. Standardization took place in the spring of 2000, based on a national sample of over 100,000 students, Grades 2 through 12. Individual schools, rather than entire districts, were sampled to match detailed demographic criteria (e.g., to reflect specific minority and socioeconomic groups). Stratification variables included geographic region, community type, socioeconomic status, and special needs. As stated earlier, the InView was costandardized with TerraNova, The Second Edition, allowing for the calculation of anticipated achievement scores. According to the draft of the technical bulletin (2002), anticipated achievement scores "may be viewed as a special kind of norm that enables users to compare an individual's level of performance on TerraNova, The Second Edition with the performance of students of similar age, grade and cognitive ability" (p. 35).

The technical bulletin describes reliability as "an index of the consistency of test score results ... if the test were administered repeatedly" (p. 37). However, no estimate of test-retest reliability was provided.

The Kuder-Richardson Formula 20 (KR-20) was used to estimate internal consistency. On the subtests, and on the nonverbal and verbal composites, KR-20 values tended to run in the low- to mid-.80s across Grade Levels 2 through 12. For the total score, KR-20 values were consistently high (e.g., .95).

In defining validity, the authors cite the *Standards* definition: "Validity refers to the degree to which evidence and theory support the interpretations of test scores entailed by proposed users of tests. Validity is, therefore, the most fundamental consideration in developing and evaluating tests" (p. 10; AERA, APA, & NCME, 1999). In

a section dealing with content validity, the authors mention that the InView has evolved from earlier cognitive tests dating all the way back to 1936. Under this heading, the nature of the various nonverbal and verbal subtests are briefly described.

A more lengthy discussion of sources of construct validity evidence is provided. Intercorrelations among the subtests and correlations between the InView and TerraNova, The Second Edition, provide discriminant and convergent validity evidence. In addition, confirmatory factor analysis supported a single, general trait and nonverbal and verbal traits. This provides support for the provision of the three aggregate scores: Total, Nonverbal, and Verbal. Theoretically, these three scores are thought, to some extent, to represent Spearman's g, and Cattell's fluid (Gf) and crystallized intelligence (Gc), respectively.

COMMENTARY. Only a relatively short, 80-page draft of the InView technical bulletin (2002) was available at the time of this review. In contrast, TCS/2's technical report was 150 pages in length (Kamphaus, 1998). Thus, the issues raised in this commentary will likely be addressed in the final version of the technical bulletin.

Although reliability was defined as test consistency over repeated testings, the technical bulletin describes only KR-20 (internal consistency) reliability. No mention is made of test-retest studies. As indicated in the *Standards* (AERA, APA, & NCME, 1999), measures of internal consistency are not substitutes for test-retest reliability. This criticism does not mean that the test does not have good test-retest reliability—it just means that direct evidence was not available at the time of this review. Internal consistency reliability estimates for the total score across grade levels are certainly respectable.

Although some construct validity evidence was provided (e.g., factor analytic support for the Total, Nonverbal, and Verbal aggregate scores), no correlations were provided between the InView and either its predecessor, the TCS/2, or with other group or individually administered measures of cognitive ability/intelligence. Such consistency evidence is an important component of construct validity. Surely this is forthcoming.

On the positive side, the InView has a clearly written examiner's manual and test booklets. Like its predecessor, it should provide useful information in terms of students' cognitive abilities. Further, the authors have made a determined effort to include all students. Brochures titled "Guidelines for Using the Results of Standardized Tests Administered Under Nonstandard Conditions" and an "Assessment Accommodations Supplement" provide useful information. Further, the reports provided for InView conform to federal and state reporting requirements, such as Title I and the Individuals with Disabilities Education Act (IDEA).

SUMMARY. As in the case of the TCS/2 (Kamphaus, 1998), the developers of the InView used state-of-the-art techniques to produce what will likely prove to be a technically sound measure of general cognitive ability, and some of its components. Although not a substitute for an individually administered IQ test, the InView should serve the user well in situations where a group-administered test of cognitive ability is required.

REVIEWER'S REFERENCES

American Educational Research Association, American Psychological Association, & National Council on Measurement in Education. (1999). *Standards for educational and psychological testing.* Washington, DC: American Educational Research Association.
Kamphaus, R. W. (1998). [Review of the Test of Cognitive Skills, Second Edition.] In J. C. Impara & B. S. Plake, (Eds.), *The thirteenth mental measurements yearbook* (pp. 1026–1027). Lincoln, NE: Buros Institute of Mental Measurements.

Review of the InView by BRUCE THOMPSON, Professor and Distinguished Research Scholar, Texas A&M University, College Station, TX, and Adjunct Professor of Family and Community Medicine, Baylor College of Medicine (Houston), Houston, TX:

DESCRIPTION. InView is a comprehensive battery of cognitive abilities tests written at six levels: (a) Grades 2–3, (b) Grades 4–5, (c) Grades 6–7, (d) Grades 8–9, (e) Grades 10–11, and (f) Grades 11–12. InView at each level is composed of five subtests: (a) Sequences, (b) Analogies, (c) Quantitative Reasoning, (d) Verbal Reasoning—Words, and (e) Verbal Reasoning—Context. Several subtests (Sequences, Analaogies) are nonverbal measures of ability.

Not counting items on the practice test, there are 20 scored items in each of the five subtests at all six levels. Total administration times are 105 minutes for Level 1 and 95 minutes for the other five levels.

The full range of test components and ancillary materials are available, including test books, answer documents, examiner's manuals, practice tests, teacher's guide, and a norms book. InView can be administered standalone, or in conjunction with the academic achievement measure, TerraNova (245), also developed by the publisher. This second application yields anticipated academic achievement scores derived by comparing students of similar cognitive ability, age, and grade level.

InView can be administered online. In this application, items are presented one at a time, but students can move back and forth in the test, change answers, keep track of questions they have answered, and flag items for further attention.

DEVELOPMENT. InView is based on the publisher's previous cognitive skills test, the Test of Cognitive Skills, Second Edition. The new measure substitutes a Quantitative Reasoning subtest for a Memory subtest, and divides Verbal Reasoning into Words and Context subtests.

TECHNICAL. Final items were selected from the preliminary item pool using three-parameter item response theory, differential item functioning analyses, and other statistical tools. More than 17,000 students were involved in initial tryouts.

Item difficulty (p) values range from .30 to .95, with the majority of items at each level having p values from .5 to .7. A group-administered test must include an array of item difficulties, so that people at diverse ability levels may be tested fairly. Unlike computer adaptive testing, in a group-administered format some items will necessarily not fit the ability levels of a given test taker.

The KR-20 score reliability coefficients for subtests tend to be in the .80s, even at Grade 2. Total score reliability coefficients range from .95 to .96. Confidence intervals are not reported for these estimates (Fan & Thompson, 2001), but would be narrow given the large sample sizes and high coefficients.

Regarding validity evidence, concurrent validity correlations for subtests of InView with TerraNova scores largely are in the range of .4 to .7. The subtests that would be expected to be more highly related (e.g., InView and TerraNova Verbal scores) tend to have higher correlations.

Confirmatory factor analyses of one first-order and two second-order factor models suggest that all three models are reasonably plausible. Such results are not entirely unexpected. The fit of one model does not necessarily preclude the fit of rival models, and one can never "prove" a single model, notwithstanding common misconceptions to the contrary (Thompson, 2000). However, these analyses invoked item parceling, which is an analytic choice not universally accepted by all measurement specialists.

Scale scores are available. Vertical equating was accomplished at each of five grade levels with roughly 1,200 to 1,900 students in a given grade completing given adjacent pairs of test levels (e.g., Grade 3 students completed both Levels 1 and 2).

Roughly 108,000 students participated in the spring 2000 test standardization. The normative sample closely matched the 1999 U.S. Census population profile. Various normative scores are available, including grade equivalent, national percentile, and NCE scores.

COMMENTARY. All conceivable bases (e.g., accommodations involving nonstandard administrations) have been covered. Test booklets are professional in appearance. Manuals and reports are colorful and clear.

Online administration has considerable appeal. The administration screens pictured in documentation suggest very thoughtful design of this administration protocol. However, less information is available about the scores generated by the online administration.

SUMMARY. Group administered tests given to students representing diverse ability levels have inherent limitations in accuracy and efficiency. This is why tests such as the Graduate Record Exam (GRE; T6:1076) are now administered in a computerized adaptive test (CAT) format.

At some future date computerized adaptive testing will be plausible even in elementary school contexts. Until that time, the InView test warrants serious consideration for measuring a broad array of cognitive abilities across a wide range of grade levels. The opportunity to use InView with the conormed TerraNova measure also has appeal.

REVIEWER'S REFERENCES

Fan, X., & Thompson, B. (2001). Confidence intervals about score reliability coefficients, please: An EPM guidelines editorial. *Educational and Psychological Measurement, 61*, 517–531.

Thompson, B. (2000). Ten commandments of structural equation modeling. In L. Grimm & P. Yarnold (Eds.), *Reading and understanding more multivariate statistics* (pp. 261–284). Washington, DC: American Psychological Association.

[115]

Iowa Early Learning Inventory.

Purpose: Designed to "describe a student's acquisition of skills and behaviors related to the academic parts of the school curriculum."

Population: Grades K–1.

Publication Date: 2003.

Acronym: IELI.

Scores, 6: General Knowledge, Oral Communication, Written Language, Math Concepts, Work Habits, Attentive Behavior.

Administration: Individual or group.

Price Data: Available from publisher.

Time: (10) minutes.

Comments: Teacher-completed rating scale; computer scoring and group score summaries available through Riverside scoring service.

Authors: H. D. Hoover, S. B. Dunbar, D. A. Frisbie, and A. L. Qualls.

Publisher: Riverside Publishing.

Review of the Iowa Early Learning Inventory by LESLIE EASTMAN LUKIN, Director of Assessment and Evaluation Services, ESU 18/Lincoln Public Schools, Lincoln, NE:

DESCRIPTION. The Iowa Early Learning Inventory (IELI) is an observational instrument that is designed to measure six behavioral areas that are purportedly related to school learning and is intended to be administered in conjunction with a measure of achievement such as the Iowa Test of Basic Skills (ITBS; T6:1268). The primary purpose of the IELI is to provide information about student behaviors so that "information from it can be used to focus instruction and improve achievement" (teacher's directions and interpretive guide, p. 1). The six behavioral areas included in the IELI are: (a) General Knowledge, (b) Oral Communication, (c) Written Language, (d) Math Concepts, (e) Work Habits, and (f) Attentive Behavior. The instrument is to be used with students in kindergarten through early first grade. The instrument is to be completed by a student's classroom teacher and takes about 10 minutes to complete. There are 44 items distributed across the six behavioral areas. For each item, the teacher is asked to indicate the frequency with which the identified behavior occurs on a 3- or 4-point scale that ranges from *never* (none) to *often*. National norms are used to generate a developmental description of each behavioral area. The three developmental levels that are used for reporting are delayed, developing, or developed.

The authors of the Iowa Early Learning Inventory provide useful information concerning appropriate and inappropriate uses of the instrument. Appropriate uses include things such as describing the developmental level of a student with regard to behavioral dimensions, identifying students who may be at risk because of developmental delays, providing information that can be used as a part of instructional planning, and monitoring change in developmental levels over time.

The authors warn against inappropriate uses such as selecting students for enrollment in kindergarten programs, retaining students in kindergarten, evaluating the effectiveness of an educational program, or evaluating the instructional effectiveness of a teacher. The general warning that is provided concerning inappropriate uses is that no important educational decision should ever be based on information from a single assessment instrument.

The authors also provide several suggestions for improving the quality of the teacher ratings including things such as making sure that the person completing the inventory has had an opportunity to observe a wide range of behaviors of all children in a group prior to rating an individual child. The authors also provide cautions about the need for uniform interpretations of student behavior, careful consideration of when and how often to use the instrument, a careful consideration of the frequency needed to justify ratings, and whether to rely on multiple observations to rate a behavior or the most recent observation.

There are two options for scoring the IELI: processing through the Riverside Scoring Service or local hand scoring. If the inventories are scored by Riverside, there are three types of score reports available including a group diagnostic report, a profile narrative, and a group summary of student scores. A fairly detailed description of each type of report is provided including information about the primary purpose and intended users for each report. A section is also included that provides clear guidance and specific suggestions on how to use reports for instructional planning.

DEVELOPMENT. The section on development indicates that the behaviors targeted for inclusion in the inventory are those behaviors that support student learning and are therefore related to a child's success in school. The authors developed a number of criteria for including a behavior in the inventory: Things such as the behavior must be related to achievement, the behavior can be further developed as a result of experience, delayed development of the behavior is not considered to be a disability, and the behavior must be able to be observed in a classroom. In addition, the authors consulted state and large-city guides for the preschool and Kindergarten curriculum and published reports to identify potential behaviors for inclusion in the inventory. Once behaviors were identified, operational definitions were written for each behavioral area and these definitions were used to guide the development/selection of items. In order for a behavior to be included in the inventory the authors indicated that the behavior must be observable and must occur frequently enough in a classroom setting for a teacher to rate it.

In April 1999 the authors conducted item tryouts. Kindergarten and first grade teachers from various regions of the U.S. reviewed items and used them in their classes. No specific information about how many teachers participated in the item tryouts was provided. The teacher comments and ratings that resulted from the item tryouts were used to revise items and develop the final form. Early childhood specialists reviewed the final form for content relevance, appropriateness of items, and potential bias. This section of the interpretive guide could be strengthened by providing additional information about whom these content specialists were, how many content specialists participated in the review, and the nature of the specific guidance that was provided to the reviewers. The nature of the guidance provided is particularly important for the bias review. No empirical analysis of bias was conducted.

TECHNICAL.

Standardization (norming). The normative data were collected in the spring of 2000. The standardization sample included 2,108 Kindergarten students from 47 different states and included 217 different districts. The authors indicated that the standardization study was conducted concurrently with the national standardization of the Iowa Test of Basic Skills. No specific information was provided about the standardization sample beyond the number of students, states, districts, and classrooms included in the sample. There was no indication that a stratified sampling procedure was employed to ensure appropriate representation of variables such as gender, socioeconomic status, urbanicity, or ethnicity. The inclusion of additional information in this section would have allowed the reviewer to determine to what extent this sample matches information available from the U.S. Census and, therefore, how representative this sample is of a national sample.

Reliability. The interpretive guide provides estimates of internal consistency reliability coefficients (coefficient alpha) for each of the six behavior scales. All estimated reliability coefficients are well within an acceptable range (.8–.9).

Validity. The empirical evidence of validity that is reported in the interpretive guide includes correlations among the six IELI behavior scores and correlations between six IELI scores and scores from the subtests of the Iowa Test of Basic Skills (ITBS). The correlations are fairly high among the six IELI scores ranging in value from a low of .594 to a high of .865. The general pattern of correlations is what one would expect. The highest correlations are among the four cognitive skills (General Knowledge, Oral Communication, Written Language, and Math Concepts) or between the two behavior skills (Work Habits and Attentive Behavior). The lowest correlations are between scores on the cognitive skills and scores on the behavior skills. The correlations between the six IELI scores and ITBS subtest scores demonstrate low to moderate correlations ranging in value from .178 to .570. In general, the cognitive skills on the IELI were more highly correlated with the scores on the ITBS than the two behavioral skills.

Taken as a whole, the empirical evidence that is provided does document important information about how the IELI functions; however, the information does not yet provide compelling evidence that the test is valid for the intended use. Additional studies that provide evidence that the scores on the IELI are both predictive of individual student achievement and show evidence of changing over time (developmental), particularly in response to instructional interventions, would be helpful. This sort of evidence would further support the use of this instrument as part of the instructional planning process, one of the major intended uses.

COMMENTARY. There are a number of areas of concern. First, not much detail is provided concerning the national standardization sample. The sample appears to be of an adequate size; however, not much descriptive information about the sample is provided. Because of the lack of information it is impossible to tell just how representative this "national" sample is. Given that the standardization study for the IELI was conducted concurrently with the national standardization of the Iowa Test of Basic Skills it would be tempting to conclude that sufficient attention was paid to this issue, but the data provided in the interpretive guide do not warrant this conclusion. Second, insufficient information is provided concerning how the score ranges associated with each of the

developmental classifications (delayed, developing, and developed) were derived. Given the central role that these classifications play in the reporting and interpretation of individual student scores, more information about this decision should be provided. Finally, as mentioned above, additional empirical evidence that supports the use of this instrument for instructional planning purposes is needed.

SUMMARY. Overall, the IELI appears to be a viable measure of behaviors that are potentially related to academic success. The inventory appears to be relatively easy to complete and score. Although some empirical evidence exists that suggests that the IELI scores are related to student achievement (as measured by the ITBS) additional information is needed to support the use of this instrument as a part of the instructional planning process.

Review of the Iowa Early Learning Inventory by CAROL M. McGREGOR, Associate Professor of Education, Brenau University, Gainesville, GA:

DESCRIPTION. The Iowa Early Learning Inventory (IELI) is an observational assessment of young children's knowledge and behavior that seems to be linked to school success. The Teacher's Directions and Interpretive Guide (TDIG) states that an effort was made to create a test applicable to all students, including those with different linguistic backgrounds and those with special needs. The assessment tool is made up of six areas of early learning: General Knowledge—general information expected of children of "this age" (TDIG, p. 2); Oral Communication—general communication, ability to describe what is seen and heard, and ability to ask questions; Written Language—recognition of and ability to write letters or simple words; Math Concepts—understanding and use of beginning mathematical processes; Work Habits—persistence, resourcefulness, and independence in completing assigned tasks; and Attentive Behavior—sustaining attention on class activities.

Although the TDIG states that the IELI is to be used in primary grades, it then specifies prekindergarten through late first grade for those who began the year at a low developmental level. Norms are based on a subsample of kindergarten students from the spring 2000 standardization of the Iowa Tests of Basic Skills (ITBS).

Materials include a four-page inventory booklet and the TDIG. Time required for completing the assessment tool is 10 minutes per student. The IELI can be hand scored with results indicated as "Developed," "Developing," or "Delayed" for each scale. Alternatively, the Riverside Scoring Service will provide a Group Diagnostic Report, a Profile Narrative describing the developmental levels of each student, and a Group Summary of Student Scores. This last report provides the same information as the hand scoring process.

The TDIG defines appropriate purposes for using the IELI as: using behavioral dimensions to describe student learning behaviors; supplemental information to the ITBS; describing learning-related behaviors of children with special needs or who have a different language background; identifying students at risk academically; monitoring change in developmental levels; providing a baseline from which to work; helping plan instructional activities; and reporting to parents.

The TDIG warns against using this assessment as a single measure for any important decision including enrollment, retention, placement into special education, or program or staff effectiveness. The classroom teacher is the best person to administer the IELI and should rate behaviors based on multiple occasions that are relatively recent.

DEVELOPMENT. According to the TDIG, item selections for the IELI were gained from reviewing state and large-city guides for preschool and kindergarten curriculum, research reports on child behavior related to learning, and current instruments in use. From this the six areas of interest were developed. Items were selected to cover each domain based on three criteria: (a) item validity based on its content relevance, (b) a specific behavior a teacher can observe, and (c) a reoccurring behavior demonstrated in the classroom often enough for a teacher to rate.

In April 1999, kindergarten and first-grade teachers in various regions of the country were asked to review and use the assessment tool in their classrooms. Their comments were used to design the format and revise items for standardization. Along with this, early childhood educators from various backgrounds were asked to comment on content relevance, appropriateness of items, and indicators of bias. Their comments were also incorporated into the final instrument for standardization.

The TDIG is laid out specifically for giving teachers a step-by-step guide in how to use and administer the IELI. Rationale is provided for why the separate scoring profiles were developed and how to use them. Examples of each with specific directions are included. The purposes of the reports are to give the teacher methods to analyze each student's strengths and weaknesses in achievement-related activities (Class Diagnostic Report), a graph of the class as a whole (Class Summary of Student Scores), and the Profile Narrative meant for reporting to parents.

TECHNICAL. The standardization of the IELI was done in conjunction with the spring 2000 national standardization of the ITBS. Participating schools were public, parochial, and non-denominational private schools from small rural to large urban. The 2,108 students in the standardization were from 392 kindergarten classes in 47 states. Roughly, the findings indicated that 7% of students were in the "Delayed" category, 30% were in the "Developing" category, and 63% were in the "Developed" category for each of the six domains.

The only measure of reliability reported was internal-consistency reliability using coefficient alphas for each domain. These ranged from .80 to .93, which are adequate. Standard error of measurement was not reported and this is a relevant issue. In such an assessment tool, where teachers are doing subjective ratings, interrater reliability would be an important statistic and this was not computed.

A table of "Correlations Among IELI Scores for Kindergarten-Spring 2000" (TDIG, p. 27) appears to be a measure of construct validity. Because the same teachers rated students on all scales, the correlations in the .59 to .86 ranges are not surprising. Correlations among academic skills show a greater relationship than do correlations among skills and behaviors. Content validity is not mentioned in this portion of the manual. The authors have attempted to make this manual teacher-friendly and in doing so may have failed to include some of the data that would attest to its potential strengths or weaknesses. Number of students used to determine the analyses provided is not known and it can only be assumed that the entire standardization group was used.

The only scores used are "Score Ranges for Developmental Classifications" (TDIG, p. 33). Because the range is used and the classifications are not definitive, a mean and standard deviation are not used. These statistics for the six domains are available in the TDIG, but there are no explanations about how these were used in deriving the score ranges eventually used.

COMMENTARY. The IELI focuses on behaviors that support learning. The TDIG states how the results of the inventory are to be used but provides no basis for how these decisions were made. The instrument is highly subjective and no interrater reliabilities were computed to determine how this might affect results or uses of the inventory. One example of use is to measure "Change" but no method is given for determining the lack of or significance of the change. The test can be used with preschool to late Grade 1 children although the standardization group was kindergarteners in the spring. Therefore, what would a "Delayed" score mean for a spring preschooler or what would a "Developed" score mean for a late first grader? These score levels appear meaningless with some of the specified age groups. No information was provided to indicate the effects of linguistic differences or the presence of disabilities on the outcome of the inventory. With the technical assistance available, a great deal more could have been done to give users more definitive data that would make using this assessment tool more worthwhile.

SUMMARY. The purposes of the IELI are commendable and it focuses on behaviors needed to support learning rather than academic skills. The test is user friendly and takes little time to administer. Its weaknesses lie in technical reporting of issues in reliability, validity, effects of differences of certain populations, and standardization norming for all groups to which the inventory purports to be useful.

[116]

Iowa Tests of Educational Development, Forms A and B.

Purpose: Designed to "provide objective, norm-referenced information about high school students' development in the skills that are the long-term goals of secondary education."

Population: Grades 9–12.

Publication Dates: 1942–2003.

Acronym: ITED.

Administration: Group.

Levels, 3: 15, 16, 17/18.

Forms, 2: A, B (parallel forms).

Price Data: Available from publisher.

Authors: R. A. Forsyth, T. N. Ansley, L. S. Feldt, and S. D. Alnot.

Publisher: Riverside Publishing.

a) CORE BATTERY.

Scores, 7: Vocabulary, Reading Comprehension, Language: Revising Written Materials, Spelling, Mathematics: Concepts and Problem Solving, Computation, Total.

Time: (160) minutes.

b) COMPLETE BATTERY.

Scores, 10: Vocabulary, Reading Comprehension, Language: Revising Written Materials, Spelling, Mathematics: Concepts and Problem Solving, Computation, Analysis of Social Studies Materials, Analysis of Science Materials, Sources of Information, Total.

Time: (260) minutes.

Cross References: For reviews by William A. Mehrens and Michael J. Subkoviak of an earlier edition, see 13:160 (7 references); see also T4:1281 (4 references); for a review by S. E. Phillips of an earlier edition, see 10:156 (3 references); for reviews by Edward Kifer and James L. Wardrop of an earlier form, see 9:534 (5 references); see also T3:1193 (14 references) for reviews by C. Mauritz Lindvall and John E. Milholland of an earlier form, see 8:20 (15 references); see T2:20 (85 references); for reviews by Ellis Batton Page and Alexander G. Wesman of earlier forms, see 6:14 (23 references); for reviews by J. Murray Lee and Stephen Wiseman, see 5:17 (9 references); for a review by Eric Gardner, see 4:17 (3 references); for reviews by Henry Chauncey, Gustav J. Froelich, and Lavone A. Hanna, see 3:12.

Review of the Iowa Tests of Educational Development, Forms A and B by ALAN C. BUGBEE, JR., Assistant Dean of Assessment/Associate Professor, School of Education, North Carolina Agricultural and Technical State University, Greensboro, NC:

DESCRIPTION. The Iowa Tests of Educational Development (ITED) focuses on educational growth, regardless of curriculum or whether knowledge, etc. is acquired in or out of school. "[T]he primary reason for using the ITED batteries is to gather information that can be used to improve instruction" (guide to research and development [Guide], p. 2). The ITED is the most recent addition to a long line of tests designed to evaluate student achievement in high school. The test battery reviewed here consists of two different forms (A and B). The ITED covers nine areas: Vocabulary, Reading Comprehension, Language: Revising Written Materials, Spelling, Mathematics: Concepts and Problem Solving, Computation, Analysis of Social Studies Materials, Analysis of Science Materials, and Sources of Information. The test has two batteries: the Complete Battery

Tests and Core Battery Tests. The latter consists of Vocabulary, Reading Comprehension, Language: Revising Written Materials, Spelling, Mathematics: Concepts and Problem Solving, and Computation. Composite scores are provided for Reading Total (Vocabulary and Reading Comprehension), Mathematics Total (Computation and Mathematics: Concepts and Problem Solving), Core Total without Computation (the average of the Reading Total + Language + Mathematics: Concepts and Problem Solving), and Core Total with Computation, the previous scores with the Mathematics Total score replacing the Mathematics: Concepts and Problem Solving score, averaged together. There are also two Complete Composite scores, one with Computation and one without. The difference between them is the use of the Mathematics Total score in the former and the Mathematics: Concepts and Problem Solving score in the latter. Both are averages.

The ITED Complete Battery has 378 test questions and requires 260 minutes of testing time. The Core Battery has 240 questions and requires 160 minutes of testing time. There is no distinction in the number of questions or the amount of testing time between the different levels of the tests (15, 16, and 17/18) on both test Forms A and B. The questions are all 4- or 5-option multiple-choice. The tests are scored without correction for guessing.

DEVELOPMENT. As has been the case since its initial development in 1942 (Guide, p. 1; Mehrens, 1998), the ITED is part of the integrated Iowa Tests set that includes the Iowa Tests of Basic Skills (ITBS), the Iowa Writing Assessment for TAP/ITED (TAP = Tests of Achievement Proficiency), and the Constructed Response Supplement to The Iowa Tests. Although the Iowa Writing Assessment and the Constructed Response Supplement are not part of the ITED, their respective development, standardization, and score characteristics are reported in the ITED Guide (pp. 105–109). The ITED and the Cognitive Abilities Test (CogAT) were standardized on the same population at about the same time and under the same conditions.

The ITED, together with the ITBS, provides an integrated scale of Grades 4 through 12 as reported in the ITED manuals. (The Iowa Tests cover kindergarten through 12th grade. Whether kindergarten to Grade 3 is scaled on this continuum is unknown to this reviewer.) A scaled score of 200 represents the median score for student performance in the spring of the 4th grade. A scaled score of 280 represents the spring of the 12th grade. This standard scoring scale is based on a study conducted in 1992 that related the three different grade groups (primary—kindergarten through 3rd, middle—3rd through 9th, and high school—8th through 12th) to a common scale that allows comparison across these different grades.

The test battery went through rigorous development, following the path of its predecessors. The test questions had a national item tryout in 1998 and 1999, and normed in 2000. Both Forms A and B were assembled concurrently to the same specifications, using the item pool that had been in the national item tryout.

TECHNICAL. The ITED is supported by superior technical merits. Following the tradition of its predecessors, Forms A and B are presented as useful and dependable examinations. The guide for research and development provides comprehensive information about the test batteries and how they were developed. In addition, the interpretive guide for school administrators and the interpretive guide for teachers and counselors provide detailed information about what the tests report and mean, and how the score should and should not be used. These manuals are quite laudable.

Standardization. Form B is equated to Form A. The equating was done in the 2000 fall national standardization. In addition, in a study of about 2,300 students, the forms are equated to one another at each test level by having the students take both Forms A and B. The manual also provides a detailed discussion of the relationship between these forms and the previous forms of this test.

The reviews of prior test Forms K, L, and M (Mehrens, 1998; Subkoviak, 1998) indicate that there once were separate norms for special populations. This reviewer could not find this type of norm in the materials provided. [Editor's Note: The publisher advises that Catholic/Private and High SES norms are available and documented in the ITED Guide to Research and Development.] The manuals do provide very detailed information about the tests and their items, with particular attention to the subtests.

As befits a national examination developed by a university renowned for its measurement programs, the ITED uses a normative sample from schools in all 50 states and the District of Columbia, dealing with many types of schools— public, Catholic, and private (non-Catholic). Public school samples were stratified nationally by geographic region (four areas), district enrollment (nine sizes), and socioeconomic status (five levels). Catholic school samples were stratified by geographic region (four areas) and enrollment size of the diocese (five sizes). The Private (non-Catholic) school samples were stratified by geographic areas (four). Schools within these areas were randomly selected. Comprehensive details about the stratifying variables are provided in the Guide. This guide also provides a list of the schools used in the sample, broken down by state.

The ITED also had detailed investigation of the differences in performance by gender and race/ethnicity—White, Black/African American, Hispanic. The tests within the battery were also analyzed for readability in several different ways— Bormuth formula, Dale-Chall 1995 formula, and the 1958 Dale-Chall formula. The analyses showed that reading levels of the test questions were appropriate and consistent.

Reliability. The reliability estimates(KR-20) for the ITED, Form A, tests range from a low of .84 for Spelling in Level 15 (Grade 9) to a high of .93 for Revising Written Materials in Level 17/18. The total reliability estimates for Core Test Batteries (six tests) are all greater than .95. The KR-20 reliability estimates for the Complete Composite Test Batteries all equal or exceed .98.

The ITED also presents a large study of the stability of Form A scores between spring and fall administrations. In this study, the lowest reliability estimate for a test was in Sources of Information between Level 16 (Grade 10) and Level 17/18 (Grade 11), .64. The highest reliability estimate for a test was in Reading Vocabulary, .82. This was for both Level 15 (Grade 9) to Level 16 (Grade 10) and Level 17/18 (Grade 11) to Level 17/18 (Grade 12).

Another reliability study was the stability of parallel forms (A & B). Here, the lowest reliability estimate for a single test was .63. This occurred for both Mathematics: Concepts and Problem Solving and Sources of Information between Level 16 (Grade 10), Form A, and Level 17/18 (Grade 11), Form B. The highest single test reliability was .84 for Reading Vocabulary between Level 15 (Grade 9), Form A, and Level 16 (Grade 10), Form B.

Validity. As is expected for a test battery that is 60 years old, the materials present a great deal of evidence about the validity of the ITED in measuring educational achievement. To help the user better understand about the nature of the test battery and its uses, the Guide provides some very good explanations about validity and how the tests were developed.

Interestingly enough, there have been a number of studies on the predictive validity of the ITED. This has included studies in the prediction of high school grade point averages (gpa), ACT Composite scores, SAT-V, SAT-M, College first year gpa, and final college gpa. According to these studies, the ITED Composite scores or Core Total scores are particularly good predictor ($r = .85$ to .89) of ACT Composite scores. They are less so for SAT-V (.71 to .83) and SAT-M (.58 to .78). Prediction of first year college gpa shows a lower correlation ($r = .24$ to .50). Surprisingly, the only study cited for predicting final college gpa (Ansley & Forsyth, 1983) showed a correlation from .45 to .47. Further investigation of this would be quite interesting.

The ITED also reports results from a factor analysis of the structure of the tests in the complete battery. In this oblique, least-squares analysis, Vocabulary, Analysis of Social Studies Materials, Analysis of Science Materials, and Sources of Information load on one factor ("Verbal Reasoning or Comprehension"). It is interesting to note that only the Vocabulary test is part of the Core Battery Tests. Mathematics: Concepts and Problem Solving and Computation load on the second factor ("Mathematical Reasoning"). The third factor ("Aspects of Written Language") is composed of Revising Written Materials, Spelling, and, again, Vocabulary. It would have been interesting to know what higher order orthogonal analyses would have revealed about factor structure.

COMMENTARY. The Iowa Tests of Educational Development, Forms A and B, are very good instruments that can provide useful information to school districts, teachers, counselors, administrators, parents, and students about high school student's levels of achievement. Laudably, the ITED goes to great lengths to explain uses of its scores. The explanations are aimed towards specific groups—teachers, counselors, school administrators, students, and parents—in order to help assure that everyone understands the nature and purpose of these tests. This is a very detailed test set with very detailed information about its use(s), scoring, development, and interpretation. The booklet entitled "A message to parents" is a very good idea. It seems somewhat long, however.

The ITED has many excellent qualities. However, there are some points where either more or better work could have been done and presented by the test owners and the test developers. For example, there is no explanation of why some tests are part of the Core Test Battery and others are not. Although it is certainly interesting that these tests have been around for over 60 years, that alone does not justify their structure. This structure does not seem to fit with the reported factor structure mentioned previously.

Perhaps because it is so well established, the ITED may not be providing all of the available information about its development to the end-users. For example, nowhere in the extensive set of manuals could this reviewer find why the test for Grades 11 and 12 (called Level 17/18 by the ITED) is combined. That is, both grades take the same test, although they are—rightly—scaled differently. This unification seemed odd. An explanation would be welcome.

Other than the materials presented, it is not clear how the Analysis of Social Studies Materials and the Analysis of Science Materials are particularly different from one another. They appear to be applying the same analytical process to different materials. The fact that they loaded on the same factor as one another, along with Vocabulary and Sources of Information, also may indicate this. Further information about what they are measuring would be helpful.

Although these points do not suggest that the ITED has fundamental problems that disallow its use, they should be addressed by the test developers and owners in the future. Although longevity can help make a test more credible, it alone does not obviate the need for explanation of how or why the test battery or its components were developed. It is the obligation of the test owner to make all of this clear to a potential user (American Educational Research Association, American Psychological Association, & National Council on Measurement in Education, 1999, Standard 6.2).

SUMMARY. The Iowa Test of Educational Development, Forms A and B, is a comprehensive battery of nine tests that provide measures of student achievement levels in high school. They are based in sound psychometric studies, and with a few exceptions, provide useful and meaningful information for all of the parties involved in the high school enterprise—administrators, teachers, counselors, parents, and students. The ITED is the high school portion—complementing the kindergarten to eighth grade Iowa Test of Basic Skills—of The Iowa Tests. This makes the ITED especially useful if a school district is already using the ITBS. Even if this is not the case, the ITED is a very useful instrument to assist school districts in improving instruction, its basic intention.

REVIEWER'S REFERENCES

American Educational Research Association, American Psychological Association, & National Council on Measurement in Education. (1999). Standards for educational and psychological testing. Washington, DC: American Educational Research Association.

Ansley, T. N., & Forsyth, R. A. (1983). Relationship of elementary and secondary school achievement test scores to college performance. Educational and Psychological Measurement, 43, 1103–1112.

Mehrens, W. A. (1998). [Review of the Iowa Tests of Educational Development, Forms K, L, and M.] In J. C. Impara & B. S. Plake (Eds.), The thirteenth mental measurements yearbook (pp. 547–550). Lincoln, NE: The Buros Institute of Mental Measurements.

Subkoviak, M. J. (1998). [Review of the Iowa Tests of Educational Development, Forms K, L, and M.] In J. C. Impara & B. S. Plake (Eds.), The thirteenth mental measurements yearbook (pp. 550–552). Lincoln, NE: The Buros Institute of Mental Measurements.

Review of the Iowa Tests of Educational Development, Forms A and B by WILLIAM D. SCHAFER, Affiliated Professor (Emeritus) of Measurement, Statistics, and Evaluation, University of Maryland, College Park, MD:

DESCRIPTION.

History. The Iowa Tests of Educational Development (ITED) are designed to assess the progress of students in Grades 9–12 toward ultimate educational goals, such as the skills and processes needed by educated, adult citizens. They have been used since 1942 and have been reviewed in eight earlier editions of these *Yearbooks*. The Iowa tests, which include the Iowa Tests of Basic Skills (ITBS) for lower grades, are the foundation of one of a handful of testing programs that are extremely well known and highly respected by measurement professionals and by broad segments of the general public throughout the United States.

There have been several new forms and some changes in the constructs tested over the years. The current forms, A and B, were normed in 2000, which is subsequent to the last *Mental Measurements Yearbook* ITED review. Nevertheless, the changes in the forms do not fundamentally alter the program and the earlier reviews still apply. Only Form A was available for this review.

Form B is intended to be a parallel form with supporting information like that for Form A.

Purpose and nature. These tests are designed to assess a general construct of educational development of students, independent of specific courses they have taken. The focus is on skills needed in both work and postsecondary education. There are nine separate tests: Vocabulary, Reading Comprehension, Language (Revising Written Materials), Spelling, Mathematics (Concepts and Problem Solving), Computation, Analysis of Social Studies Materials, Analysis of Science Materials, and Sources of Information; a Core Battery excludes the last three. Scores are provided for each of these and for a core of Reading (composed of Vocabulary and Reading Comprehension), Mathematics (Concepts and Problem Solving, and Computation), a Core Total (Reading, Language, and Mathematics), and an overall Composite.

For each Level, the Core Battery consists of 240 selected-response items and takes 160 minutes of testing time; the additional three tests add 138 selected-response items and 100 minutes. Constructed-response supplements are available in Reading, Language, and Mathematics; they are not part of this review.

DEVELOPMENT.

Equating. Forms A and B were generated by a close-to-random process from a combined pool of items in order to make their domains equivalent. Data from the 2000 standardization's equivalent-groups design were used with smoothed equipercentile equating for these two Forms. Although the process is described, there is little material in the guide to research and development that can be used to evaluate the success of the equating of Forms A and B.

Norms. The standardization data were gathered in 2000. The spring standardization sample (N = 37,168) was generated from a sample of public school districts randomly selected within strata defined by combinations of four geographic regions, nine enrollment sizes, and five percent-below-poverty-level categories. Backup districts were selected in case of refusals. Private schools were stratified—randomly sampled separately for Catholic and non-Catholic populations. The spring sample (median administration of April 30) was administered Form A only; approximately 2% received one or more accommodations (for special education or English-language-learner status) as determined by local school policies in relation to general guidelines. The fall standardization sample (median administration of October 22) was a subset of the spring sample, augmented to increase accuracy for both equating and estimating item difficulty. The fall sample took Forms A and B on an alternate-seat basis within classrooms. All data were weighted within the stratification categories and smoothed to produce raw-to-scale-score and other derived-score estimates for the total population.

Average percent correct national standardization norms are available on an item-by-item basis and within subclassifications for the fall and the spring, with interpolated midyear percents, for 9th graders (on Level 15), 10th graders (on Level 16), 11th graders (on Level 17/18) and 12th graders (on Level 17/18). Also shown are the skills (content and process) tested with some items appearing more than once. Materials are available for teachers and counselors that describe these skills in detail. These may be used to interpret item-level reports.

Scales. Quarter-month (i.e., weekly) norms were generated from spring 2000 and fall 2000 standardization data. Interpretive information is given for both student scores and school average scores. There are six scores provided: raw scores, developmental standard scores, grade-equivalents (discouraged by the publisher), national percentile ranks, national stanines, and national normal curve equivalents. Local percentile ranks are also available for student scores. The developmental standard scores were designed to represent both a vertical scale and a scale that allows comparisons among the scores for different subtests. The developmental scales extend downward to the Iowa Tests of Basic Skills (ITBS).

As with any vertical scale, a scale score on one test may not represent the same achievement level as the same scale score on another test, primarily because of differences in content tested. Perhaps this issue is less important in tests that represent general achievement constructs such as these. However, it would be helpful for the test materials to include a discussion of the assumptions under which interpretations of growth are reasonable and how to evaluate the importance of these assumptions in representative situations.

TECHNICAL COMMENTARY.

Reliability evidence. KR20 estimates from the national standardization data are given for each subtest for the appropriate form for Grades 9,

10, 11, and 12, separately. These range from a low of .84 (Spelling, Grade 9) to a high of .93 (Revising Written Materials, Grade 12). Composites of subtests generally show higher KR20 estimates. Reliabilities of differences between subtests were largely above .60.

Standard errors of estimate are given overall and for score ranges. For some subtests, the overall standard errors are overestimates of the conditional standard errors at the subtest means and in other cases they are underestimates. Use of conditional standard errors in score interpretations seems more appropriate.

Validity evidence. An important issue needs to be addressed at the outset: Can scores from a test like the ITED, with an emphasis on broad skills, be used validly to evaluate student progress in their classes (and schools) and/or school effectiveness in educating students toward the content they are supposed to be studying (i.e., instructional standards of the school, the district, and/or the state). To the extent that content standards vary among entities (e.g., states), any test designed to have broad appeal will not have equivalent validity across contexts. Thus, in choosing a test, the comparative fit with existing instructional standards should be considered carefully, as should the possible need to augment the test (or perhaps even just part of it) with locally developed items, if the scores are to be used for either evaluation of students or of schools.

The test materials recommend that persons considering using the tests actually take them in order to satisfy themselves about whether the questions tap appropriate skills and abilities that fit with local content and instructional standards. This is a question of alignment. Several statewide studies have been conducted using standard methodologies that compare the domains assessed by the ITED with state content standards. Clearly these studies fill a need on the part of test users. It would be helpful for the ITED to present the results of these studies where they are available and to provide materials that facilitate alignment studies in situations where they do not exist.

The constructs assessed by the ITED are described in the guide to research and development. The process of item development, review, tryout, evaluation, revision, further tryout, further evaluation, and acceptance into the assessment or rejection is state-of-the-art, as is expected of such

a mature and successful program. Evidence showing that ITED scores are correlated with various external assessments such as high school grades and test scores, as well as college grades, is generally supportive of validity.

The 2000 standardization sample data were factor analyzed to study relationships among the nine tests. Three factors resulted: a verbal factor, a mathematics factor, and a written language factor. These generally support the subscore level reports generated in the testing program.

As in earlier standardizations, members of the 2000 standardization sample also took the Cognitive Abilities Test (CogAT), which yields Verbal, Quantitative, and Nonverbal scores along with a Composite. A total of 24,475 students were able to be matched for the analysis. The pattern of correlations was consistent with expectations.

Returning to the issue at the beginning of this section, it would be helpful for the authors of the ITED to generate consequential evidence of validity. Questions that could be addressed include whether the skills that are tapped by the assessments reflect the outcomes of instruction and, if so, whether the results lead to positive instructional change. It is recommended that students and educators focus on discrepancies between the ITED results and other data; that seems reasonable, but no evidence is presented to show that the comparisons result in useful insights. Suggestions to educators are given in the interpretive guide for teachers and counselors, but that they can result in improved ITED (and other tested) performance is not documented.

Utility. Students and parents receive a report that expresses their results in terms of national and local percentile ranks. The report also estimates predicted score ranges on the ACT, the SAT-V, and the SAT-Q. The report should be helpful, especially because it suggests students focus on their scores in relation to what they have learned about themselves in other contexts, such as classroom grades.

Educators receive reports that show performance for individuals and for groups. These include percent-correct reports at the test, subdomain, and item levels for any groupings the school or district requests.

SUMMARY. The ITED deserve their solid reputation. They are among the best general-purpose assessments of high school students' educational development available. They are part of a state-of-the-art assessment program, but improvements are always possible. The suggestions made in this review, offered in a constructive spirit, should not be interpreted as uniquely applicable to the ITED. Efforts in similar directions could improve virtually all assessment programs in this category.

[117]

IRAOS: Interview for the Retrospective Assessment of the Onset and Course of Schizophrenia and Other Psychoses.

Purpose: Designed to provide "a retrospective assessment of symptoms, disability and social development in schizophrenic and affective illness."
Population: Adults who have schizophrenia.
Publication Dates: 1992–2003.
Acronym: IRAOS.
Scores: Item scores only.
Subtests, 5: General Information, Socio-Demographic and Case History Information, Episodes and Intervals of Mental Disorder, Indicators of Psychiatric Illness, Evaluation of Success of Information.
Administration: Individual.
Price Data: Price data for manual (2003, 60 pages), score sheets, interview forms, and survey aids available from publisher.
Time: (90–120) minutes.
Authors: Heinz Häfner, Walter Löffler, Kurt Maurer, Anita Riecher-Rössler, and Astrid Stein.
Publisher: Hogrefe & Huber Publishers.

Review of the IRAOS: Interview for the Retrospective Assessment of the Onset and Course of Schizophrenia and Other Psychoses by ALLEN K. HESS, Distinguished Research Professor of Psychology, Auburn University at Montgomery, Montgomery, AL:

BACKGROUND. The IRAOS: Interview for the Retrospective Assessment of the Onset and Course of Schizophrenia and Other Psychoses was developed during the A (age), B (beginning), C (course) schizophrenia study (Hafner et al., 1998; Hafner, Riecher, Meissner, & Maurer, 1992; Hafner, Riecher-Rossler et al., 1992). It traced the course of the social history, symptoms, disability, and treatment from the first signs or indicators of the illness until the time of the interview. The A B C sample was composed of 232 first-episode schizophrenics. The IRAOS aims to provide a fine-grained data set of six key social roles, breaks in social development of the patients, and information about the current and prior episodes of the

illness. The authors describe the acceptance of the IRAOS and the interest in early onset of major psychiatric illness as impetuses to extend the IRAOS to articulate with the ICD—10 and to extend its scope to include affective psychoses. The most compelling finding cited in the A B C study was "the overwhelming part of social losses and disabilities happen long before the first treatment contact" (manual, p. 3). The symptoms section of the IRAOS reflects both ICD—10 criteria and several major psychopathology symptom scales (Present State Examination [PSE], Wing, Cooper, & Sartorius, 1974 and Scales for the Assessment of Negative Symptoms [SANS], Andreasen, 1983).

MATERIALS. The instrument consists of the interview booklet, the test manual, score sheets, forms, and survey aids (time schedule and calendar of episodes). IRAOS consists of five parts: I. General Information (gender, informant description, and information sources such as case notes); II. Socio-Demographic (education, vocation/occupation, living conditions, and biographical information including developmental delays and interruptions) and case history information; III. Episodes and Intervals of Mental Disorder (details about the course of the episode and the treatment); IV. Indicators of Psychiatric Illness (retrospective data on symptom course and diagnostic criteria; and V. Evaluation of Sources of Information (interviewer assesses the quality of the informants' data). Information is gathered from at least three sources: family or close friends, the patient, and a knowledgeable professional such as the patient's psychotherapist.

TECHNICAL.

Reliability: Interjudge. Interjudge reliability was determined by Kappas, which ranged from .62 (Education) to 1.0 (Vocational training and Partner and family). These are acceptable but also worrisome in how education can be assessed so variably. Pairwise Agreement Rates (PAR) ranged from .77 (Partner and family) to .97 (Vocational training), all acceptable.

Reliability: Test-retest. A disappointingly small subsample of 18 patients were interviewed between 7 and 15 months after the first interview. PARs were above .60 for three-quarters of the items. Unsatisfactory PARs below .40 occurred in 4.5% of the items. Kappas were poor, with more than 72% below .39. One wonders whether the symptom picture changed (as it should if treatment or even time elapsed affected changes in the patients), hence the test-retest intervals were too long. What is interpreted as error might be change in the patient or in the views of informants as they learn about the patient and become more accurate in their assessments.

Validity. Interviews as tests pose particular validation problems. On the one hand, what is assessed is self-evident. That is, a finding of social isolation means just that. IRAOS is content valid. On the other hand, an instrument and its manual should detail the validational evidence so we can determine the soundness of any inferences based upon the instrument. As to concurrent validity, the authors conflate its construction and reliability with validity: "We have already pointed out the validity of the content of the IRAOS is well-founded—mainly due to its construction on the basis of expert assessments and the orientation of the research criteria to those in the ICD-10- is well founded …. We were able to compare the results from three independent sources; the interview with the patient, the interview with a close person and an IRAOS, which was based on clinical case notes or information provided by the practitioner in charge" (manual, p. 10). In a sense, the argument is that if the ICD is valid, the IRAOS must be, too. This is a mirror of the relationship between the Structured Clinical Interview for the DSM (SCID) and the DSM. Still, any user of the IRAOS (and the SCIDs) would be comforted if appropriate data were presented in the manual (or even referenced) that showed the relationship in convergent and discriminant validity studies of the relationships between the IRAOS variables and various psychoses and their stages. Alas, this is lacking.

It would be similarly useful for us to know the relationships between the IRAOS and the SCIDs, and how each relates to independent measures. Research with the biodata (biographical) measure of Owens and Schoenfeldt (1979) would be one way to examine concurrent validity. It would be comforting for research on predictive validity to be forthcoming, too. None is presented.

Uses. In addition to the clinical and research uses possible for the IRAOS, it seems to have pedagogical potential. That is, the authors have trained a number of clinicians in the use of the IRAOS. Might they explore its use in training novice clinicians? The IRAOS might well serve as a framework in teaching structured interview skills. Again, research as to its effectiveness as an educational tool is desirable.

SUMMARY. The IRAOS is a diagnostic anamnestic-structured interview procedure constructed to help make informed ICD diagnoses, parallel to what the SCIDs are to the DSM. As such, the IRAOS authors need to establish more substantial reliability levels to assure users that findings are reliable. Moreover, studies are needed to establish concurrent and predictive validity, independent of the ICD and the IRAOS respondents. The IRAOS does provide a more systematic method for ICD assessments. Finally, studies validating its use as a pedagogical device to teach introductory psychiatric/psychological interviewing are needed.

REVIEWER'S REFERENCES

Andreasen, N. (1983). The Scale for the Assessment of Negative Symptoms (SANS). Iowa City: University of Iowa.

Hafner, H., Riecher, A., Meissner, S., & Maurer, K. (1992). *Interview zur retrospektiven Einschatzung des Erkrankungsbeginns (IRAOS)*, Selbstverlag.

Hafner, H., Riecher-Rossler, A., an der Heiden, W., Maurer, K., Meissner, S., & Loffler, W. (1992). *Interview for the retrospective assessment of the onset of schizophrenia (IRAOS)*. Translation: G. Patton, published by the first author.

Hafner, H., Maurer, K., an der Hieden, W., Munk-Jorgensen, P., Hambrecht, M., & Riecher-Rossler, A. (1998). The ABC-schizophrenia study: A preliminary overview of the results. *Social Psychiatry and Psychiatric Epidemiology, 33*, 380–386.

Owens, W. A., & Schoenfeldt, L. F. (1979). Toward a classification of persons. *Journal of Applied Psychology, 64*, 569–607.

Wing, J. K., Cooper, J. E. & Sartorius, N. (1974). *Measurement and classification of psychiatric symptom: An instruction manual for the PSE and CATEGO program*. London: Cambridge University Press.

Review of the IRAOS: Interview for the Retrospective Assessment of the Onset and Course of Schizophrenia and Other Psychoses by JANET V. SMITH, Assistant Professor, Department of Psychology and Counseling, Pittsburg State University, Pittsburg, KS:

DESCRIPTION. The IRAOS: Interview for the Retrospective Assessment of the Onset and Course of Schizophrenia and Other Psychoses involves a highly structured interview format for the assessment of early symptoms and development of schizophrenia and other psychoses. The IRAOS consists of an interview booklet with detailed questions to guide the interviewer in his or her collection of clinical data, including assessment of indicators and symptoms associated with the onset and course of psychotic disorders. These indicators and symptoms are charted in a longitudinal manner, allowing identification of onset of the illness as well as documenting their impact on various aspects of functioning. Although the instrument was designed for retrospective use, the authors point out that data can be collected in an ongoing manner to chart progress of symptoms and indicators on a monthly, or for some aspects, weekly basis. Data can be collected from a variety of sources, including client interview, informant interview (usually a close family member of the client), and review of professional information such as case notes and conversations with practitioners.

Part I, General Information, is a brief section that covers basic demographic data such as date of birth and gender, along with details about sources of information. Part II, Socio-Demographic and Case History Information, addresses such areas as education, employment, relationships, living situation, and family history. These areas are assessed in terms of well-defined time frames, so that changes over time can be evaluated in the context of the mental illness. Part III, Episodes and Intervals of Mental Disorder, charts the course of the disorder over time, including history of treatment. Part IV, Indicators of Psychiatric Illness, documents presence or absence of 128 specific signs and symptoms and their course over time. Finally, Part V, Evaluation of Sources of Information, is a brief section that provides the interviewer with a format to assess the quality of data collected.

Data collected during the interview, as well as from other sources, are coded in the interview booklet and then transferred to a coding sheet. In addition, data can be arranged in chronological order on a time schedule sheet to provide a clear time frame of important events. In addition, there is a calendar of episodes record sheet to assist in documenting course of symptoms and indicators.

DEVELOPMENT. Two main types of procedure were used to guide the development of the IRAOS. First, existing international instruments and other measures of psychopathology were used to generate initial items. According to the manual, a pool of 776 items was extracted from a total of 21 established psychopathology instruments. This initial pool was reduced to 240 variables by elimination of multiple occurrences of the same symptom. Second, these indicators were then evaluated by a group of 61 experienced psychiatrists to rate their suitability for determining the onset of schizophrenia. The instrument has been in use since 1987, initially published privately in 1992. According to the manual, the current publication represents an amendment of that earlier version, including expansion of symptoms and clearer guidelines for use.

TECHNICAL. The manual does directly address psychometric properties of the IRAOS, although scant information is presented in this section. Interrater reliability evidence is based on the original version of the scale, but is generally high. In a 1990 study, interrater reliability coefficients range from .62 to 1.00, with almost all variables having a rating above .80. Test-retest reliability was documented using a sample of 18 patients, with a time interval ranging between 7 and 15 months. These data are presented in summary form, showing pairwise agreement rates of .80 or above for only 27.3% of items and pairwise agreement rates below .60 for 25.7% of items. In terms of validity, the manual notes that content of the IRAOS aligns with ICD-10 diagnostic criteria for research as well as with DSM-III-R prodromal symptoms. In addition, the manual reports evidence of validity based on consistency of results concerning onset of illness from multiple sources. Data from a 1995 study involving 142 patients showed consistency between self-report, information from a close other person, and information from practitioners.

COMMENTARY. Overall, the IRAOS does appear to meet the authors' goal of increasing objectivity of retrospectively collected data. Once coded, the data can be directly entered into a database, such as Microsoft EXCEL or SPSS, which is an invaluable asset from a researcher's perspective. However, although clear information is provided on coding of responses, it appears that this system would be quite complex to learn initially, and the manual states that "a training course of several days arranged with the authors is recommended." In addition to demands on the examiner, the structured interview format would appear to place a high level of demand on the client. However, the manual reported a 96.7% compliance rate, based on a sample of 267 inpatients, close to being discharged. This would suggest that use of the IRAOS is feasible with patients, at least in those individuals whose psychotic symptoms have mainly subsided.

It would have been desirable to have more information included on psychometric aspects of the instrument. For example, interrater reliability data are impressive in that they show a high consistency between different raters. But it would have been preferable to include more information on number of participants and level of training, as well as have data on the current version of the instrument. It is quite possible that interrater reliability would be just as high with the current version, especially given that one of the changes has been to improve clarity of directions. But there are no data presented in the manual to support this assumption. Some of the test-retest data are rather low, but are based on a very small sample size. Given such a large range in the test-retest data, it would have been helpful to identify which aspects of the instrument have the highest and lowest test-retest reliability. The manual does provide an extensive list of recommended project publications and bibliography. It would have been useful to include more data from some of these sources to provide a more complete description of the psychometric properties of the instrument.

SUMMARY. The IRAOS provides a very thorough method for documenting early symptoms and course of schizophrenia and other psychoses. The instrument involves considerably more detail and structure than would be needed for a regular clinical assessment and is not intended as a diagnostic instrument. The authors specifically caution that, at this point, the IRAOS has no data to support prognostic use of the instrument. However, as a research tool, the IRAOS appears to be a valuable instrument. The main limitations may be the initial complexity of learning the coding system plus it would have been desirable to see more extensive psychometric data included in the manual. But once mastered, the instrument allows a comprehensive assessment of multiple aspects related to the development and course of schizophrenia and other psychotic disorders. It is especially appealing that the coding system allows for a diverse range of information to be quantified and entered into a database, considerably increasing ease of analysis.

[118]

Jesness Inventory—Revised.

Purpose: Designed to be used as a personality inventory for delinquent and conduct-disordered youths and adults.

Population: Ages 8 and over.

Publication Dates: 1962–2003.

Acronym: JI-R.

Scores, 24: Randomness Scale, Lie Scale, Asocial Index, Social Maladjustment, Value Orientation, Immaturity, Autism, Alienation, Manifest Aggression, Withdrawal-Depression, Social Anxiety, Repression, Denial, Conduct Disorder, Oppositional Defiant Disorder, Undersocialized/Active [Unsocialized/Aggressive], Undersocialized/Passive [Unsocialized/Passive], Conformist [Immature Conformist], Group Oriented [Cultural Conformist], Pragmatist [Manipulator], Autonomy-Oriented [Neurotic/Acting-Out], Introspective [Neurotic/Anxious], Inhibited [Situational], Adaptive [Cultural Identifier].

Administration: Group.

Price Data, 2005: $165 per complete kit including technical manual, 10 item booklets, 25 response forms, and scoring templates; $62 per technical manual; $20 per 10 item booklets; $46 per 25 response forms; $156 per 100 response forms; $66 for scoring templates; $4 per assessment for computer administration and scoring.

Time: (30–45) minutes.

Comments: Mail-in/fax-in scoring service available; web administration available.

Author: Carl F. Jesness.

Publisher: Multi-Health Systems, Inc.

Cross References: For reviews by Robert M. Guion and Susana Urbina of a previous edition, see 14:188; see also T5:1341 (3 references) and T3:1209 (9 references); for a review by Dorcas Susan Butt of an earlier edition, see 8:595 (14 references); see also T2:1249 (5 references); for a review by Sheldon A. Weintraub of the Youth Edition of the earlier edition, see 7:94 (10 references); see also P:133 (3 references).

Review of the Jesness Inventory—Revised by ELIZABETH KELLEY RHOADES, Associate Professor of Psychology, West Texas A&M University, Canyon, TX:

DESCRIPTION. The Jesness Inventory—Revised is a paper-and-pencil self-report personality inventory. The 160-item questionnaire provides subtype information for the classification and treatment of juvenile offenders and youth with conduct problems. The current restandardization includes norms for males and females aged 8 years and up.

The test taker reads the items in the item booklet and marks True or False on the response form. The examiner then uses a series of scoring templates to handscore the responses. There is also a computerized version of the test that may be used for administration and/or scoring. A mail-in/fax scoring service is also available.

Based on these responses, the test provides *T*-scores on 11 personality scales (Social Maladjustment, Value Orientation, Immaturity, Autism, Alienation, Manifest Aggression, Withdrawal-Depression, Social Anxiety, Repression, Denial, and Asocial Index), 9 subtype scales, and 2 DSM-IV scales (Conduct Disorder and Oppositional

Defiant Disorder). Subtypes include Undersocialized Active/Unsocialized Aggressive, Undersocialized Passive/Unsocialized Passive, Conformist/Immature Conformist, Group-Oriented/Cultural Conformist, Pragmatist/Manipulator, Autonomy-Oriented/Neurotic Acting-Out, Introspective/Neurotic Anxious, Inhibited/Situational Emotional Reaction, and Adaptive/Cultural Identifier.

The measure includes two validity scales. The Random Responding Scale consists of five sets of similar items. Individuals who give inconsistent responses to four or five of these item sets are judged to have an excessive rate of random responding and their overall data may be suspect. The Lie Scale consists of five items that indicate a tendency to respond in an unrealistically "good" way. If the participant responds in the unrealistic direction on four or five of these items, then they may be suspected of faking their responses in the positive direction and their remaining scores may be suspect.

DEVELOPMENT. The current measure is basically a restandardization of the original Jesness Inventory that was developed in the 1960s to classify juvenile delinquents to aid in their understanding and treatment. A total of 250 items were used in the original normative and validation studies with the 155 that best discriminated between the various groups being retained. The test was revised for use with older male adolescents in the 1960s, for use with adults and females in the 1970s, and based on the results of a longitudinal prediction study in the 1980s.

The Jesness Inventory—Revised is the result of a lengthy restandardization process. First, all inventory items were examined for readability and datedness resulting in minor changes in 10 items. The existing item scales were retained and the Conduct Disorder and Oppositional Defiant Disorder Scales were created resulting in the addition of 5 new items for a test total of 160 items.

This modified measure was administered to 3,421 nondelinquent individuals recruited through schools (elementary through university), local testing by the test publisher, and online data collection. The "controlled online data collection" was not described and the extent to which it was used and the nature of this testing is unclear. Although there is ample evidence of sufficient cell sizes, age by gender, there is no evidence that these individuals were representative of the population in terms of geographic location or socioeconomic status.

The measure was also administered to 959 delinquent individuals from various facilities, the large majority from the Jetson Correction Center for Youth in Louisiana. Again the sample sizes by age and gender appear adequate but the geographic representation of this sample appears very poor and there are no data on their socioeconomic status (SES). One of the most serious concerns about the norm groups is that the nondelinquent sample was largely (over 80%) white whereas the delinquent sample was largely (over 70%) nonwhite. Similarly, the adults in the nondelinquent sample had a much higher average level of education.

The Social Maladjustment Scale is defined as "the extent to which the individual shares attitudes and opinions expressed by persons who do not meet the demands of living in socially approved ways" (technical manual, p. 13). This scale was originally developed by comparing all responses to 250 test items between a group of youthful offenders (ages 8 to 14) and a group of nonoffending youth. The 71 items that differentiated between these two groups were then used in a study of older youths and the 63 items that continued to vary between the two groups were retained. A follow-up study of arrest records of youth who had taken the original Jesness Inventory 4 years previously (i.e., 4th grade) was used to further modify the scale in 1986, resulting in the addition of 12 items and removal of 10 items. The current restandardization resulted in a slight modification of three items, dropping 3 items, and the addition of 4 items.

The Values Orientation Scale is a measure of the individual's attitudes that are common to those of low SES. The scale on the original Jesness Inventory was developed by comparing item responses of youth based on their fathers' occupations and selecting the 39 items that differentiated between the groups.

The Immaturity Scale is based on the test taker's attitudes that are typical of younger rather than older individuals. Items selected for this scale on the restandardized test were the 29 items that differentiated between age groups in the nonoffending portion of the norm group.

The remaining personality scales (Autism, Alienation, Manifest Aggression, Withdrawal-Depression, Social Anxiety, Repression, and Denial) were based on a cluster analysis of the adjudicated males in the original norm sample aged 13 to 17.

The original Asocial Index was derived through discriminant function analysis to develop a scale using data from all the other scales that best differentiated between 963 juvenile offenders and 925 nonoffenders. A separate discriminant function analysis was run for the female sample. The Conduct Disorder and Oppositional Defiant Disorder Scales are new to the Jesness Inventory—Revised and consist of a tally of items that appear to meet the DSM-IV criteria for these diagnostic classifications.

TECHNICAL. Concerns about the norm sample were described in the previous section.

The developers of the Jesness Inventory—Revised assessed the reliability of the instrument in two ways. They measured internal consistency using Cronbach's alpha and odd-even correlation coefficients. Overall correlations were fairly consistent across the delinquent and nondelinquent samples and ranged from relatively high (.91 for Social Maladjustment in nondelinquents) to relatively low (.61 for Repression in nondelinquents).

Test-retest reliability was evaluated by retesting 131 delinquent individuals 8 to 12 months after their original evaluation. Correlations between their performance on the earlier and later testing varied considerably by personality scale with a high of .67 for Manifest Aggression and a low of .35 for Immaturity. Reliability of subtype classification was more variable.

The test developers provided several sources of data on the validity of the Jesness Inventory—Revised. Based on ANOVAs, several of the scales were found to discriminate between offenders and nonoffenders. The Asocial Index and the Social Maladjustment Scale were found to be the best at differentiating between the two groups. Validity of the subtype classifications is more difficult to determine with no real evidence of predictive validity of the subtypes.

COMMENTARY. The Jesness Inventory—Revised has a number of strengths including a long history of test development and research. The directions are clear and the materials are well-organized.

However, there are some areas of concern, one of the most serious of which is in the area of the standardization sample. The delinquent and nondelinquent norm groups are highly different in terms of education level and racial background. The delinquent group is not representative geographically and comes largely from a single facility. These weaknesses cast doubt as to the generalizability of the test results. Also, the reported fourth grade reading level of the test may be an underestimate (words like mischief, outwit, and self-conscious appear to be at a higher level) and a significant number of individuals may be unable to read the test items independently.

The various scales and subtypes are developed utilizing different techniques (discrimination between groups, cluster analysis, tallying of responses that appear similar to a list of DSM-IV criteria) and are thus highly variable in terms of their overall technical characteristics and validity. It would appear that the Social Maladjustment Scale and the Asocial Index may be the most robust in terms of differentiating between offenders and nonoffenders. The Immaturity Scale appears to lack reliability and the Conduct Disorder and Oppositional Defiant Disorder Scales have only limited evidence of validity.

SUMMARY. The Jesness Inventory—Revised is a restandardization of the original Jesness Inventory. Although there are serious concerns about the normative sample, it may be able to differentiate between delinquents and nondelinquents with some accuracy, based largely upon its measures of social maladjustment and asocial behavior. The other scales should be interpreted with some caution.

Review of the Jesness Inventory—Revised by GEORGETTE YETTER, Postgraduate Researcher, Gevirtz Graduate School of Education, Center for School-Based Youth Development, University of California—Santa Barbara, Santa Barbara, CA:

DESCRIPTION. The Jesness Inventory—Revised (JI-R) is a recent revision of an instrument designed to measure the attitudes and perceptions of juvenile delinquents and to aid clinicians in tailoring treatment plans and measuring response to intervention. Together with the Minnesota Multiphasic Personality Inventory (MMPI; T6:1623) and the California Psychological Inventory (CPI; 15:43), the Jesness has been one of the most used instruments with this population.

Like the previous versions of this inventory, the JI-R profiles individuals along 11 personality dimensions and classifies them along nine I-level developmental subtypes derived from integration-level theory, a stage theory of interpersonal maturity. Detailed information about the development of the personality scales is discussed in Mooney's (1984) extensive review. Further information about I-level theory is provided in the manual and in Jesness (1988).

DEVELOPMENT. The JI-R updates and expands on the previous edition. Its enhancements include adding clinical and "validity" scales, improving its sensitivity to maturity, updating the norms on a larger and more diverse sample, and offering more administration and scoring options.

The revised instrument introduces four new scales: two clinical scales to help determine the extent to which individuals meet the DSM-IV criteria for Conduct Disorder and Oppositional Defiant Disorder (American Psychiatric Association, 1994) and two "validity scales" that signal the presence of the favorable and random response sets.

The new clinical scales are intended to flag response patterns that identify individuals likely to meet the DSM-IV criteria for Conduct Disorder or Oppositional Defiant Disorder (American Psychiatric Association, 1994). Most of the 14 Conduct Disorder and 16 Oppositional Defiant Disorder items were contained in the previous edition of the inventory; five new items were added to increase content coverage. As a result, the JI-R is slightly longer than the prior edition (160 vs. 155 items). Other items that appeared on the previous version of the inventory are grouped into a Lie Scale and a Random Response Scale, two new "validity scales" that screen for invalid response patterns. The manual describes these scales as experimental.

Besides expanding the inventory to include DSM-IV oriented clinical scales and "validity scales," the JI-R features a substantially revised Immaturity scale. Sixteen items were removed and 29 items retained that were empirically shown to correlate with age for nondelinquents, and the manual reports a correlation of $r = .15$ with the previous version of the Immaturity scale. The internal consistency of this subscale is much improved, with alphas ranging from .77 to .83 for nondelinquents and from .73 to .87 for delinquents. Validity evidence shows that the revised scale discriminates among groups of individuals by age and that it shows lower levels of immaturity for older individuals.

Minor revisions also have been made to the other personality scales to enhance their internal consistency, with correlations of $r = .91$ to 1.00 between their previous and revised versions (median .98). In addition, the names of the I-level developmental subtypes have been updated with the intent of making them seem less pejorative. For example, the original categories of "Manipulator" and "Neurotic Anxious" are renamed "Pragmatist" and "Introspective," respectively.

The JI-R's normative data were updated between 2000 and 2002 on over 4,000 individuals. The new standardization sample includes respondents from age 8 to over 35 from across the U.S. and from Canada, a broader geographic distribution than the inventory's original sample. Another improvement over the previous norm sample is the inclusion of approximately equal numbers of females and males, especially in the older age ranges and among nondelinquents. However, the new norm group does not represent delinquents under age 12, and the delinquent and nondelinquent normative groups also have very different racial/ethnic characteristics, with the delinquent normative sample predominantly Black and the nondelinquents mostly White.

Because most of the personality subscales showed different age and gender distributions, the manual reports separate personality subscale norms by age group (8–11, 12–14, 15–17, 18–35, and over 35), and separate norms by gender. For the I-level subtype scales, age-specific norms also are provided, but separate norms are not reported according to gender. I-level classification rates are reported for delinquents and for nondelinquents, further broken down for delinquents by racial/ethnic group.

TECHNICAL. The reliability and validity data reported in the manual include both new findings that pertain to the current revision and results previously reported on the prior version of the inventory. The manual also includes an annotated bibliography of research conducted using the Jesness Inventory over the past 30 years.

JI-R scales with strong internal consistency include Social Maladjustment, Value Orientation, Manifest Aggression, Undersocialized Aggressive, Undersocialized Passive, and Inhibited. These scales showed alpha coefficients consistently above .8 for all groups. Scales with lower internal consistency (alphas generally at or below .7) include

Repression, Withdrawn-Depression, Introspective, and the Conduct Disorder and Oppositional Defiant scales. Not only do these new clinical subscales show generally weak internal consistency, but limited external validation procedures are reported. As the manual notes, these scales should be seen as screening devices rather than as definitive diagnostic measures. Test-retest reliability is reported only for the previous version of the inventory and not for this revision.

According to the manual, nearly all of the personality and I-level scales distinguish delinquent from nondelinquent groups. However, these analyses failed to consider race and ethnicity. In light of the considerable racial and ethnic differences between the delinquent and nondelinquent norm samples, it is conceivable that at least some of the measured differences are attributable to cultural/social differences.

The manual describes evidence of concurrent validity of the JI-R with the State-Trait Anger Expression Inventory using a small sample of university students. Clinically relevant scales of the State-Trait Anger Expression Inventory showed correlations with several JI-R personality scales and I-level subtype scores.

The JI-R offers several new administration and scoring options. Current options include paper-and-pencil administration, either hand-scored using templates or computer-scored using the revised JI-R Version 5 for Windows software; computerized administration and scoring; and web-based administration and scoring. All the scoring options produce standard scores (T-scores) and profile graphs for the personality scales and I-level developmental subscales. The computer and web-based scoring options also provide detailed interpretive reports.

This reviewer found the test very readable and the hand-scoring straightforward. A separate spiral-bound template book contains a set of 22 templates for hand-scoring. To tabulate raw scores, the scorer aligns the response sheet with each template. The I-level subtype classifications are found using the algorithm shown in the manual. For each subtype, detailed descriptions of typical personality characteristics, together with brief suggestions for treatment planning, are presented in the manual.

COMMENTARY. The Jesness Inventory is a well-researched instrument for assessing the attitudes of delinquent individuals. Although this revision makes several notable improvements, there are areas in which the inventory could be further improved. For example, some of the items lack face validity for the adult population. Although the internal stability of the personality scales is improved from previous editions, several scales show relatively low internal stability, most notably Repression, Withdrawn-Depressed, and the new clinical scales. Further validation is needed for the clinical scales. Also, the new "validity scales" are not as carefully constructed as might be desired, especially compared with Pinsoneault's (1998) elegantly designed scales for the previous edition of the Jesness. Further study is needed to better understand the predictive validity of scores from this instrument across ethnic groups, and additional validation is also needed for delinquent children under age 12.

Perhaps a more subtle limitation of this instrument pertains to the comprehensiveness of its underlying model of delinquency. It seems that the JI-R fails to measure at least one construct that is potentially important for understanding delinquency, namely, attitudes toward sexual behavior. It is likely that such attitudes are important predictors of delinquency and furthermore, it would be valuable to assess individuals' attitudes regarding sexual acting-out behavior. The user should be aware that additional measures may be needed to assess for these and other variables that are not assessed by the Jesness.

SUMMARY. Over the past 40 years a solid research base using the Jesness has accumulated (a PsycInfo search showed 27 studies between 1998 and 2003). The inventory is relatively easy to administer and score. The current revision is more sensitive to respondents' maturity than previous editions, and the new norms include a larger proportion of females. The JI-R expands on previous editions by introducing new scales for detecting certain response sets and scales that screen for the DSM-IV disorders most commonly diagnosed among delinquents (American Psychiatric Association, 1994).

REVIEWER'S REFERENCES

American Psychiatric Association. (1994). *Diagnostic and statistical manual of mental disorders* (4th ed.). Washington, DC: Author.

Jesness, C. F. (1988). The Jesness Inventory classification system. *Criminal Justice and Behavior, 15,* 78–91.

Mooney, K. C. (1984). [Review of the Jesness Inventory.] In D. J. Keyser & R. C. Sweetland (Eds.), *Test critiques* (vol. I, pp. 380–392). Kansas City: Test Corporation of America.

Pinsoneault, T. B. (1998). A variable response inconsistency scale and a true response inconsistency scale for the Jesness Inventory. *Psychological Assessment, 10,* 21–32.

[119]
Job Challenge Profile.

Purpose: "Designed to help managers better understand and see their job assignments as opportunities for learning and growth."

Population: Managers, leaders, and executives.

Publication Date: 1999.

Acronym: JCP.

Scores, 10: Unfamiliar Responsibilities, New Directions, Inherited Problems, Problems with Employees, High Stakes, Scope and Scale, External Pressure, Influence Without Authority, Work Across Cultures, Work Group Diversity.

Administration: Group.

Price Data, 2002: $27 per Facilitator's Guide (76 pages); $14 per Participant's Workbook/Survey (49 pages); quantity discounts available.

Time: 15(25) minutes.

Comments: Revision of the Developmental Challenge Profile (DCP; no longer available); self-scored; Facilitator's Guide includes details of workshop procedures, reproducible overheads, and handout masters; Participant's Workbook contains test items and action guide.

Authors: Cynthia D. McCauley (Facilitator's Guide, Participant Workbook/Survey), Patricia J. Ohlott (Facilitator's Guide, Survey), and Marian N. Ruderman (Facilitator's Guide, Survey).

Publisher: Center for Creative Leadership.

Cross References: For reviews by Jean Powell Kirnan and Kristen Wojcik and by Eugene P. Sheehan of The Developmental Challenge Profile, see 13:94 (2 references).

Review of the Job Challenge Profile by LAURA L. B. BARNES, Associate Professor of Educational Research and Evaluation, Oklahoma State University, Tulsa, OK:

DESCRIPTION. The Job Challenge Profile (JCP) is a 50-item rating scale designed to assess 10 developmental components of managerial jobs. Managers rate the degree to which their current jobs reflect these dimensions. Five items measure each dimension. The dimensions are organized into the following five clusters with the respective developmental components scales in parentheses: (a) experiencing a job transition (Unfamiliar Responsibilities); (b) creating change (New Directions, Inherited Problems, Problems with Employees); (c) managing at high levels of responsibility (High Stakes, Scope and Scale); (d) managing boundaries (External Pressure, Influence Without Authority); and (e) dealing with diversity (Work Across Cultures, Work Group Diversity). The authors designed the self-scored instrument to be administered as part of a training program, either in a workshop setting or in one-on-one training. Scores are obtained for each of the 10 dimensions and profile interpretations are facilitated by comparing respondents' scores with those of a normative sample of managers. The sample's score distribution for each dimension is trisected into low, moderate, and high scores. These score categories are referred to as "relative scores" (facilitator's guide, p. 25).

After managers complete the instrument, the workshop materials instruct them to identify the most relevant developmental job components based on any of the following criteria: (a) they rated the component as quite descriptive or extremely descriptive based on an actual score of 20 or higher; (b) they earned a high relative score on the component; or (c) they feel particularly challenged by this component. The choice of criteria for selecting the most relevant components is described as somewhat subjective and may vary depending on the participants' score patterns. For instance, managers who have high relative scores on most components might be encouraged to identify as most relevant those dimensions with the highest absolute scores. Others might be encouraged to focus on a component with which they know they are struggling, regardless of the absolute rating. Participants then complete a series of exercises for the three or four components they identified as most relevant.

DEVELOPMENT. The JCP is a revision of the Developmental Challenge Profile (DCP, 1993). The authors report the JCP had its origins in a series of research projects on managerial learning, growth, and change beginning in the early 1980s at the Center for Creative Leadership. These studies suggested that job assignments were key to the development of successful executives. Components of these assignments were initially identified through content analysis of interviews with managers and ultimately 155 items based on managers' verbatim responses were developed to assess these job components. The DCP was formed through item analysis procedures that reduced this item set to 113 items covering 15 job dimensions. Subsequent analyses suggested the elimination and restructuring of the job component dimensions. Items were written to tap two new components focused on managing diversity and additional item analyses were conducted. The result was the current 50-item version of the JCP—shorter, more focused, and more easily scored.

TECHNICAL.

Standardization. The JCP uses the term "relative scores" to refer to the scores obtained from a normative sample. In the training presentation examinees are told how to score their tests and they are provided instruction in using the norms charts. The patterns of the participants' job component scores (all high, all low, all moderate, or mixed) can be used to guide the training as described above. In general, we are provided very limited information about the norms. It is not at all clear that the normative sample is representative of managers in general—it was made up of workshop participants of unspecified age, ethnicity, and geography. Approximately 1,100 managers who completed the JCP between 1992 and 1996 as participants in a management development program comprise the sample. The only information provided is that the sample is about equally male and female, represents various companies, and is described as normally distributed by organizational level (i.e., a larger percentage from middle management with fewer from executive and supervisory levels). In a separate section the manual states that for the current version of the JCP the authors expanded the sample to include a "significant number" of African Americans (facilitator's guide, p. 5). However, the manual does not explicitly state that this refers to the normative sample because there are three different samples used in data analysis, nor is the actual number of African American individuals given. Formal norms are not presented, but rather the score range is simply trisected into low, moderate, and high scores. The basis for determining the cutpoints for the scales is not provided though they appear to be derived from the normative sample because the cutpoints are higher for scales with higher reported scale means.

Reliability. Internal consistency reliability coefficients computed on the normative sample were on the low end of acceptable ranging from .63 (Scope and Scale) to .80 (Inherited Problems) with a median reliability coefficient of .70. Four to 6-week test-retest coefficients computed on a smaller sample ($n = 50$) who took an earlier version of the test (without the two diversity scales) ranged

from .78 to .87 with a median of .835. These managers were primarily from one professional organization. The authors report that long-term stability was not examined because of the tendency for jobs to change over time.

Validity. Interscale correlations range from zero to .49 with a median of .24. The 10 scales are said to form five clusters as described above; however, factor analytic results to support this claim are absent from the report on psychometric properties in the facilitator's guide. Correlations of the JCP scales with various criterion measures are presented. These measures include managers' ratings of job challenge, how developmental the job is, a composite self-report rating of how much they have learned from their jobs, whether their current jobs represent first experiences in a variety of areas, and stressful emotions of challenge, threat, and harm. The correlations reflect a fairly complex pattern of relationships, with some scales correlating moderately with several of the criteria and other scales showing little association with any criteria. For instance, the Unfamiliar Responsibilities and Scope and Scale dimensions showed reasonable correlations (.21 to .36) with the composite learning index and managers' ratings of current jobs as challenging and developmental. The Influence without Authority scale, however, correlated less than .10 with all criterion measures except the stressful emotions of threat and harm ($r = .13$ and .11). Of the 110 criterion validity coefficients reported, over half were .10 or smaller (11 were negative) and only 4 were .30 or greater. Some of the results make intuitive sense—for example, scores from Work Across Cultures correlate more strongly with the job being a first international assignment than with any of the other "firsts." It is unfortunate that the authors chose to interpret negligible, yet statistically significant correlations as small as $r = .07$. The significance, of course, is due to the large sample size ($n = 1,143$). It is very difficult to make sense of the large number of coefficients that are presented, especially in light of their small magnitude and relatively low score reliability for some JCP scales and unknown reliability in the criterion measures. It would enhance the presentation of validity evidence if the authors would provide an interpretation based on a theoretically based examination of patterns of relationships; structural equation modeling would be very helpful here.

COMMENTARY. The instrument is grounded theoretically in research that examined the pivotal role that job assignment played in the development of top executives. A strength of the JCP lies in its use as a tool for self-improvement. It is well integrated into a management development program and appears to provide a potentially useful means of organizing work experiences for career development purposes. Managers' patterns of scores help them focus their training on those components that are most relevant to their jobs. Though normative comparison is not the only way managers identify the job components on which to focus training, it is the first step in the process. Test users should have confidence that the sample used to make these comparisons is representative in relevant ways. They should also have confidence that the basis for categorizing scores as low, moderate, or high was not arbitrarily established. The failure to adequately describe the normative sample and how the cut scores were developed are shortcomings.

The low internal consistency of several of the scores is also of some concern. Reviewers of the Developmental Challenge Profile (DCP), the previous version of the JCP, were concerned about the low internal consistency reliabilities of some of the scales. This characteristic of the test has improved a bit though half of the scale internal consistency reliabilities are still .70 or below. Reviewers of the DCP (Kirnan & Wojcik, 1998; Sheehan, 1998) also noted that more information regarding the standardization sample was needed; however, less information apparently is provided now than previously.

SUMMARY. The JCP is an integral part of a comprehensive set of materials for providing development training to managers. As noted by reviewers of the previous version, it is an interesting instrument and has an impressive developmental background. Validity evidence is not overwhelming but is probably adequate to support the instrument in its intended use. The manual should be supplemented with an expanded description of the standardization sample and a description of how cut scores were obtained. Because the instrument itself is not used for high stakes purposes, but rather as a means of guiding training, this may mitigate some of the psychometric limitations.

REVIEWER'S REFERENCES

Kirnan, J. P., & Wojcik, K. (1998). [Review of the Developmental Challenge Profile: Learning from Job Experiences.] In J. C. Impara & B. S. Plake (Eds.), The thirteenth mental measurements yearbook (pp. 350–353). Lincoln, NE: Buros Institute of Mental Measurements.
Sheehan, E. P. (1998). [Review of the Developmental Challenge Profile: Learning from Job Experiences.] In J. C. Impara & B. S. Plake (Eds.), The thirteenth mental measurements yearbook (pp. 353–354). Lincoln, NE: Buros Institute of Mental Measurements.

Review of the Job Challenge Profile by JEAN POWELL KIRNAN, Professor of Psychology, The College of New Jersey, Ewing, NJ:

The reviewer gratefully acknowledges the contributions of Melissa Siino to this review. Her diligence and perspectives were greatly appreciated.

DESCRIPTION. The purpose of the Job Challenge Profile (JCP) is to help managers develop an understanding of how challenging job assignments can be used as tools for their own growth and development. This instrument is an outgrowth of a larger project conducted by the Center for Creative Leadership (CCL), undertaken in the 1980s to uncover how leaders and top-level managers develop their skills. Although not specifically stated in the publisher's materials, it appears that an initial product of that study was the Developmental Challenge Profile (DCP), a precursor to the JCP, which was reviewed in the Thirteenth Mental Measurements Yearbook in 1998 (Kirnan & Wojcik, 1998).

The JCP measures 10 challenging work components that are presented in five clusters: (a) experiencing a job transition (Unfamiliar Responsibilities); (b) creating change (New Directions, Inherited Problems, Problems with Employees); (c) managing at high levels of responsibility (High Stakes, Scope and Scale); (d) managing boundaries (External Pressure, Influnce Without Authority); and (e) dealing with diversity (Work Across Cultures, Work Group Diversity). The 50 items used to measure these components (5 items per component) use a Likert scale ranging from 1, not at all applicable, to 5, extremely applicable. All of the test items are worded in the same direction with higher numbered responses indicating a greater challenge in the participant's current job. The self-scoring instructions are brief, straightforward, and uncomplicated. Overall, the items are clearly worded although a few are conditional, making responding difficult.

A trained facilitator or human resource specialist should administer the test. Administration can be either individual or group and includes eight steps that constitute a 2.5- to 3-hour training session. These consist of: (a) introduction and explanation of the JCP; (b) administration of the questionnaire; (c) brief lecture with overheads about learning from job assignments; (d) scoring, with an explanation of relative and component scores; (e) reflective exercises on the learning potential of the job of participants; (f) introduction of three learning strategies that allow for increasing the developmental power of the job; (g) summary worksheet focusing on the learning potential in the participants' job; and (h) explanation of the use of job components as tools for developmental processes.

One area of difficulty is the organization of the overheads in the facilitator's guide. The overheads are located in Appendix A of the facilitator's guide, but are listed out of order, making it difficult to locate the proper overhead.

This is a self-development tool with transparent items. Due to the obvious nature of the items and the fact that the instrument is self-scored, benefits can only be derived if participants are honest in their responses. Scoring is simple and brief, and interpreted by the participants. There is a sense in the interpretation that if you score high on several components, you have a very challenging job. Scoring high on a particular component will determine which specific area of your job is challenging, and from there a description and strategies are presented to help capitalize the learning potential.

Scores in each component range from 5 to 25 with a higher score in a job component indicating a greater challenge in that component. The scores are also interpreted relative to those experienced by other managers in the normative sample. From this normative group the following score interpretations were derived: High scores consist of 20–25, Medium scores range from 11–19, and Low scores include 5–10. Participants are encouraged to further explore a job component if their actual score is high, the relative score is high (compared to their other scores), or it is an area in which they feel challenged. It is suggested that they restrict themselves to three or four components to explore and develop strategies for learning and growth. A list of suggested tasks, responsibilities, and assignments are provided for each of the 10 job dimensions and range from minor changes (resolving a conflict between two parties) to major changes (loaning yourself out for 1-year to a non-profit organization). In addition to viewing and developing job assignments as learning strategies, participants are also encouraged to review learning

opportunities available through feedback, relationships, and training.

A concern is raised here in the selection of which components to pursue more intently and for which to develop learning strategies. The presence of a high raw score or a high relative score indicates that the job has a lot of challenge in this area, not that the individual is challenged. Perhaps more emphasis in selecting components on which to concentrate should lie in those that one feels challenged. For example, Work Group Diversity is listed as a challenge. With the increasing diversity of the workforce, this may not be considered a challenge for some individuals.

DEVELOPMENT. A series of in-depth interviews were conducted on four occasions with successful executives regarding key events that influenced the way they manage. The initial two studies utilized a combined sample of 191 mostly male executives. The third data collection expanded the research findings in a sample of 76 female executives. Finally, in the 1990s a sample with a significant number of African American managers was assessed. The common finding through all these interviews was that the majority of key events that shaped the respondents as managers were related to job assignments. Although other learning strategies (i.e., feedback, relationships, and training) are effective in job growth, aspects of one's work assignment accounted for the bulk (56%) of the cited growth factors.

Following a thorough content analysis of the interviews, 155 items were developed. Using responses from a variety of managers, statistical analyses were conducted to remove inadequate items and to develop item clusters. The resulting 15 dimensions were confirmed in another sample of managers. The initial 113-item instrument (believed to be the DCP, although not specifically stated as such in the support materials) was introduced. After a period of time, data collected on approximately 1,000 managers were used in qualitative and statistical analyses to further refine the instrument. The current version consists of 50 items, 5 for each of 10 dimensions. Following factor analysis, these 10 dimensions were grouped into the five clusters mentioned earlier.

TECHNICAL. Data from a large sample of 1,143 managers of approximately equal numbers of males and females from a variety of companies were used to calculate internal consistency measures. These reliability coefficients ranged from .63 to .80 for the 10 components. A smaller group of 50 managers from one company were used in a test-retest assessment of the temporal stability of the JCP over a 4- to 6-week interval. These coefficients ranged from .78 to .86 although "Work Across Cultures" and "Work Group Diversity" were not assessed in the test-retest. The reliability coefficients reported here are considered acceptable to good for these types of psychological constructs.

The normative data appear to be based on about 1,000 managers who completed the JCP between 1992 and 1996. These individuals were from a variety of companies and most were in middle management positions. No information is provided in the manual regarding the gender or ethnic composition of the norm group and should be supplied. It is not clear if this is the same large sample used in the internal consistency study cited above.

By the very nature of the JCP's purpose, it is difficult to gather validity evidence. Attempts were made to derive some measures of construct validity by correlating scores on the 10 components with responses to a variety of questions. The sample of 1,143 managers rated the amount of challenge on the job; seven of the components correlated significantly with those questions. Additionally, they were asked to indicate if their job had any of four "firsts" such as a first time in an international assignment. All but one of the components correlated significantly with at least one "first" question. When the sample of 1,143 managers and a sample of 264 managers (about two-thirds males and one-third female) responded to a question on the level of development in their current job, six of the components in the large sample and five of the components in the smaller sample correlated significantly with the question. Finally, the smaller sample rated the degree to which they felt one of three stressors. Seven of the components correlated with one stressor and three correlated with two. Thus, each of the dimensions had significant correlations with some of the questions. But some dimensions clearly seemed stronger than others as they correlated with many of the questions asked.

COMMENTARY AND SUMMARY. The JCP is a well-developed measure of the degree of challenge that is presented in a managerial or executive job position. The instrument provides a positive outlook on the perspective of job challenges as a way to develop new skills and other opportunities for growth. However, the JCP measures the job and not the incumbent. Whether the incumbent is challenged by the job tasks is not assessed. This would seem to be a minor drawback of the instrument; however, it should be noted that assessment of the incumbent is not cited in the purpose of the test provided by the publishers.

REVIEWER'S REFERENCE

Kirnan, J. P., & Wojcik, K. (1998). [Review of The Developmental Challenge Profile: Learning from Job Experiences.] In J. C. Impara & B. S. Plake (Eds.), *The thirteenth mental measurements yearbook* (pp. 350–353). Lincoln, NE: Buros Institute of Mental Measurements.

[120]

Job Search Attitude Inventory, Second Edition.

Purpose: Helps identify personal attitudes about looking for a job.

Population: Adult and teen job seekers and career planners.

Publication Date: 2002.

Acronym: JSAI.

Scores, 4: Luck vs. Planning, Uninvolved vs. Involved, Help from Others vs. Self-Help, Passive vs. Active.

Administration: Group or individual.

Price Data, 2003: $39.95 per 25 inventories including copy of administrator's guide (8 pages).

Time: (10–15) minutes.

Comments: Self-administered and self-scored; revised edition features simplified language and directions, plus added practical advice for becoming more self-directed in a job search.

Author: John J. Liptak.

Publisher: JIST Publishing, Inc.

Review of the Job Search Attitude Inventory, Second Edition by JOHN W. FLEENOR, Director of Knowledge Management, Center for Creative Leadership, Greensboro, NC:

DESCRIPTION. According to its publisher, the Job Search Attitude Inventory (JSAI) provides a brief assessment of the motivation level of individuals who are in the process of searching for a job. The purpose of the JSAI is to provide these individuals with a snapshot of their attitudes towards the job search process, and to make suggestions to job seekers on how they can be more motivated to find a job. The JSAI yields scores on four scales (a) Luck vs. Planning, (b) Uninvolved vs. Involved, (c) Help from Others vs. Self-Help, and (d) Passive vs. Active. Possible uses of the JSAI include outplacement counseling, employment counseling, job search assistance, career counseling, rehabilitation counseling, and correctional counseling.

The instrument is designed to make job seekers more aware of their attitudes toward the job search. The attitudes measured by the instrument were identified by a review of the literature, case studies, and interviews with unemployed adults. The publisher suggests that the instrument will be useful for (a) predicting who will be more likely to find a job, (b) determining who will better benefit from job search services, and (c) for use as a pre- and posttest to measure the effectiveness of job-search training programs. Because self-motivated individuals can benefit from relatively inexpensive services (e.g., job search assistance), the JSAI is touted as a cost-effective method of determining which services a job seeker should receive.

According to the publisher, the second edition of the JSAI has been improved in the following areas as compared to the first edition of the instrument: (a) simplified language and instructions, and a six-panel design, which makes it easier for users to read, complete, and score the instrument; (b) concrete suggestions for job seekers on how to be motivated to find work; (c) new research on learned helplessness; (d) better documentation of the estimates of reliability and validity; and, (e) additional research indicating that self-directed attitudes are likely to result in individuals finding jobs in less time.

ADMINISTRATION AND SCORING. The instrument can be administered individually or in groups. There is no time limit. Online administration is also available.

The respondents indicate their level of agreement on 32 items using a 4-point Likert scale ranging from *strongly agree* to *strongly disagree*. Test takers respond to each item directly in the test booklet. They then self-score their responses and copy these scores to a graphic profile, which presents the four dimensions measured by the JSAI. Step-by-step scoring instructions are included in the test booklet. Higher scores indicate the likelihood that individuals will find their own jobs. Guidelines for interpreting the scores are presented in the manual.

DEVELOPMENT. The Job Search Attitude Inventory is based on the premise that increasing individuals' self-esteem can enhance their self-directed motivation to search for a job (cf., Helwig, 1987). Research indicates that the most important factor in finding a job is the individual's attitudes towards unemployment and the job search process itself. Individuals who fail to display self-directed motivation in the job search often exhibit tendencies of learned helplessness. According to Helwig, personal motivation to find a job can be more important than job search skills themselves.

A rational-empirical method (Crites, 1978) was used in the development of the instrument. The author employed a review of the literature, case studies, and interviews with unemployed adults to develop the scales and the item content. The resulting pool of 50 items was reviewed by professional counselors, who assigned the items to one of the four scales. Intercorrelations among the four scales were calculated using the sample of 135 adults described above. These intercorrelations were in the acceptable range.

TECHNICAL.

Sample. The manual presents the means and standard deviations for a sample of 135 adults (70 males and 65 females). Descriptive statistics are also presented for 521 convicted offenders, 235 welfare-to-work clients, 325 college students, and 285 youths (ages 12 to 18).

Reliability. The author reports the usual estimates of reliability, including split-half, coefficient alpha, and test-retest reliabilities. These reliabilities were calculated using the scores of the sample of 135 adults described above. The reliability estimates were generally in the acceptable range; however, the split-half reliability of the Uninvolved vs. Involved scale was somewhat low (.53).

Validity. In general, validity evidence was based on a content validation strategy. No evidence of criterion-related validity is presented in the manual; therefore, the test results should be interpreted with caution.

COMMENTARY AND SUMMARY. The JSAI appears to have some utility as a measure of the attitudes of job seekers. The test is a short, self-scored instrument for which the interpretation is relatively straightforward. A strength of the instrument is that test-takers and counselors receive immediate feedback, which is presented graphically. The reported reliability estimates are acceptable, with the exception of the Uninvolved vs. Involved scale. However, no evidence of criterion-related validity is presented in the manual. It is not known, therefore, if the instrument can accurately predict how well an individual will do in the job search process. Because the instrument is not a normative measure, no norms are available for comparison purposes. Before the instrument can be recommended without reservation, some evidence of criterion-related validity is necessary. Additionally, all evidence of reliability and validity should be based on larger sample sizes.

REVIEWER'S REFERENCES

Crites, J. A. (1978). *Theory and research handbook for the Career Maturity Inventory* (2nd ed.). Monterey, CA: CTB/McGraw-Hill.
Helwig, A. A. (1987). Information required for job hunting: 1,121 counselors respond. *Journal of Employment Counseling, 24,* 184–190.

Review of the Job Search Attitude Inventory, Second Edition by THOMAS R. O'NEILL, Psychometrician, National Council of State Boards of Nursing, Chicago, IL:

DESCRIPTION. The Job Search Attitude Inventory, Second Edition (JSAI) is a pencil-and-paper questionnaire composed of 32 statements in which the respondent is asked to indicate the extent of their agreement to each statement using a 4-point Likert scale. The stated purpose of the instrument is "to make job seekers more aware of their self-directed attitudes about their search for employment" (cover of administrator's guide). It does this by reporting their attitudes on four scales: Luck vs. Planning (LP), Uninvolved vs. Involved (UI), Help from Others vs. Self-Help (HS), and Passive vs. Active (PA). Although the author identifies these attitudes as conceptually related to the overarching construct of self-directedness, the subscales are separately computed and never explicitly combined.

The questionnaire is a self-report measure that is designed to be self-administered and self-scored. It can also be administered online. The administrator's guide suggests that this instrument can be useful for out-placement counseling, job search assistance, career development workshops, correctional counseling, employment counseling, career counseling, rehabilitation counseling, and group assessment. The format of the survey makes using it intuitive and the instructions are quite easy to understand. The entire process of responding to the statements, scoring the responses, plotting the scale scores, and interpreting the results according to the directions is rather straightforward. Scoring is accomplished by summing the ratings of each of the eight statements within each of the four scales. Negatively worded statements are "reverse scored" to make higher ratings correspond to more self-directedness. One shortcoming of the administrator's guide is the lack of a specific description for whom this survey was appropriate. There was no description regarding how well this survey worked across gender, ethnicity, age groups, and type of work (blue-collar or white-collar).

DEVELOPMENT. The materials provided by the publisher included a cursory explanation of the questionnaire development process. The four scales (LP, UI, HS, and PA) were conceived first, mostly on the basis of a literature review, prior research, case studies, and interviews. Subsequently, statements were drafted to represent these scales and then the statements were refined and distilled down to a set of 32. A cursory examination of the statements should reassure the user that the content is related to the construct of self-directedness with regard to job searches. However, there were a few phrases such as "job search process" and "job search skills" that sounded more like counselors' jargon than the language of a typical respondent. Also, the interspersed negatively worded statements may cause some confusion for the respondents.

TECHNICAL. Although not explicitly stated, the measurement model used is true score theory, but without any discernable connection to a norm group or to specific criteria for interpreting results. Although there are detailed descriptions of what the score ranges (labeled: LOW, AVERAGE, and HIGH) mean, there is no description, empirical or theoretical, of how the thresholds between these categories were established. In fact, if the sample of 135 adults described in the administrator's guide is assumed to be a norming sample, it is clear from the Table of Means that the thresholds for the AVERAGE category should be different for each of the four scales, rather than the uniform thresholds that are found on the scoring chart.

It would have been helpful with regard to examining construct validity evidence if the author provided a table of the statements in difficulty (of endorsement) with the thresholds between categories (SD, D, A, SA) marked, similar to the techniques used by Linacre (1997) or Smith (1997). Articulating the construct probabilistically and displaying it visually would permit the construct to be more easily understood and the misfit of responses could be identified by visual inspection. Similarly, a differential item functioning study to demonstrate that the construct was stable across gender, ethnicity, and other relevant groups would have been useful.

Overall, reliability estimates are good for this sample. When using Cronbach's alpha as the indicator of internal consistency, all the scales indicated that the items did a reasonably good job of accounting for the variance among the respondents. Yet, it is curious that using the same sample, another indicator of internal consistency, the split-half reliability, was low for UI. The test-retest reliability across a 3-month interval ranged from .60 to .76, depending on the scale.

The author suggests that the low to moderate interscale correlation between scales (-.21 to .58) supports the notion that the scales are independent. The author erroneously refers to this as "concurrent validity" (administrator's guide, p. 6). Because the author's interpretation of the correlations is that the scales measure different constructs, it is more properly described as "divergent" or "convergent-divergent" validity. To demonstrate concurrent validity, the author must find other indicators of these attitudes and establish a respectable correlation between these indicators and this questionnaire.

COMMENTARY. With regard to what is being measured, it is unclear whether the author intends the user to think of self-directedness as a unitary construct. Although the author identifies LP, UI, HS, and PA as conceptually related to self-directedness, the subscales are separately computed and never explicitly combined. Yet, there are three elements found in the scoring section of the form that imply that these scales can be combined (averaged or added) in ways never stated by the author. These elements are: (a) each scale has the same raw score range (8–32), (b) the graphic representations of these scales are stacked on top of each other and then aligned, and (c) each scale has the same thresholds for LOW, AVERAGE, and HIGH.

To the author's credit, he does not attempt to assign percentile rankings to the different scale scores. I doubt anyone cares about the ranking within identified groups. What consumers will care about is what does this score imply about current and future performance. In this regard, the most useful piece of the interpretation has been left out. If a person has a particular score or set of scores, how many applications or resumés will they likely submit this week? What is their likelihood of getting an interview? What is their likelihood of becoming employed? A framework to answer these questions would make this questionnaire a powerful survey. This test seems to be a fairly new test. It is hoped that subsequent versions will retain its strengths and improve upon its weaknesses.

SUMMARY. The content seems relevant to the construct, the ease of use is quite good, and the price is reasonable. However, the psychometrics behind the instrument appear to be minimal and the suggested interpretation of scores seems tenuous. This instrument seems like a good tool for beginning a discussion regarding job search attitudes and strategies and, therefore, the author has successfully accomplished the stated purpose of the questionnaire. However, until it has a better psychometric foundation, it should not be used to measure these attitudes in high-stakes situations or when it is important that the measure possess interval scale qualities.

REVIEWER'S REFERENCES

Linacre, J. M. (1997). Instantaneous measurement and diagnosis. *Physical Medicine and Rehabilitation: State of the Art Reviews, 11*(2), 315–324.
Smith, R. M. (1997). The relationship between goals and functional status in the patient evaluation and conference system. *Physical Medicine and Rehabilitation: State of the Art Reviews, 11*(2), 333–343.

[121]

Kaplan Baycrest Neurocognitive Assessment.

Purpose: "Test of neurocognitive functioning."
Population: Ages 20–89.
Publication Date: 2000.
Acronym: KBNA.
Scores: 8 index scores: Attention/Concentration, Immediate Memory Recall, Delayed Memory Recall, Delayed Memory Recognition, Spatial Processing, Verbal Fluency, Reasoning/Conceptual Shifting, Total Index.
Administration: Individual.
Price Data, 2002: $239 per complete kit including manual (188 pages), stimulus book (94 pages), 8 response chips, cassette, 25 response booklets, 25 record forms, and response grid (packaged in a box); $70 per manual; $70 per stimulus book; $43 per 25 response booklets; $43 per 25 record forms; $11 per response grid.
Time: (60–90) minutes.
Comments: Test contains 25 subtests (Orientation, Sequences, Numbers, Word Lists 1, Complex Figure 1, Motor Programming, Auditory Signal Detection, Symbol Cancellation, Clocks, Word Lists 2, Complex Figure 2, Picture Naming, Sentence Reading—Arithmetic, Reading Single Words, Spatial Location, Verbal Fluency, Praxis, Picture Recognition, Expression of Emotion, Practical Problem Solving, Conceptual Shifting, Picture Description—Oral, Auditory Comprehension,

Repetition, Picture Description—Written); detailed analysis of neurocognitive functioning can be obtained through examination of 94 component Process Scores; Process Scores are categorized as below average, equivocal, or average.

Authors: Larry Leach, Edith Kaplan, Dmytro Rewilak, Brian Richards, and Guy-B. Proulx.

Publisher: PsychCorp, A brand of Harcourt Assessment, Inc.

Review of the Kaplan Baycrest Neurocognitive Assessment by RAYMOND S. DEAN, George and Frances Ball Distinguished Professor of Neuropsychology, Neuropsychology Laboratory, Ball State University, and JOHN J. BRINKMAN, JR., Associate Director, Neuropsychology Laboratory, Ball State University, Muncie, IN:

DESCRIPTION. The Kaplan-Baycrest Neurocognitive Assessment (KBNA) is a comprehensive battery of individually administered tests that provides normative and qualitative data assessing a broad range of neuropsychological abilities for adults aged 20–89 years. It is grounded in behavioral neurology and was developed to assist in the localization and etiology of neurological dysfunction. It includes 25 subtests, each of which was designed to measure a specific aspect of neurocognitive functioning. The information from these subtests then contributes to eight indexes of neurocognitive functioning: Attention/Concentration, Immediate Memory Recall, Delayed Memory Recall, Delayed Memory Recognition, Spatial Processing, Verbal Fluency, Reasoning/Conceptual Shifting, and a Total Index.

The KBNA is written in English and administration takes approximately 60 to 90 minutes to complete. Nonclinically trained personnel can administer and score the test protocol under supervision. However, only individuals with appropriate or professional training in assessment should provide an interpretation of the KBNA.

The KBNA is organized according to six areas of cognitive functioning or domains. The domains include Attention/Concentration, Declarative Memory, Visuioconstruction/Visuoperception, Praxis, Language, and Reasoning/Problem Solving. The cognitive domains are then represented by eight indexes (noted earlier). The test indexes are measured by 10 of the 25 subtests in the battery. The other 15 subtests provide qualitative information on neurocognitive functioning. Below is a short description of the 10

subtests organized according to their contribution to the KBNA's Indexes.

Attention/Concentration (AC) is the first index and is composed of the Sequences and Spatial Location subtests. Sequences requires the examinee to sequence both forward and in reverse the months of the year, identify letters of the alphabet that rhyme with the word "key," identify curved printed capital letters, and count backwards by fours. Spatial Location assesses the examinee's ability to correctly place dots on a response grid that exactly matches a stimulus design. The second index, Memory-Immediate Recall (MIR), is made up of Word-Lists 1-Recall and Complex Figure 1-Recall. Word-Lists 1-Recall requires the examinee to immediately recall a list of 12 words. Complex Figure 1 assesses the examinee's ability to copy and immediately recall an abstract, complex figure. The third index is Memory-Delayed Recall (MDR), which is composed of Word List 2-Recall and Complex Figure 2-Recall. Word List 2 includes a delayed free recall, a delayed cued recall, and a delayed recognition of words from Word List 1. Complex Figure 2 requires the examinee to draw, from memory, the figure from Complex Figure 1 and recognize the major parts of that design. Word List 2-Recognition and Complex Figure 2-Recognition also contribute to the fourth index, Memory-Delayed Recognition (MDRec). This subtest requires the examinee to recognize target words from Word List 1 and to identify and draw parts of the complex figure previously presented in Complex Figure 1.

The fifth index is Spatial Processing (SP) and is made up of Complex Figure 1-Copy and Clocks. The Spatial Processing index assesses only the copy portion of Complex-Figure 1. The Clocks subtest evaluates the examinee's ability to draw a complete clock, add the numbers and hands to set the time on a predrawn clock, tell time on clocks without numbers, tell time on clocks with numbers, and copy a clock. Verbal Fluency (VF) is the sixth index. The subtest Verbal Fluency Phonemic and Semantic Scores contributes to it. Verbal Fluency evaluates the examinee's ability to generate as many words as possible within 60 seconds from three categories: words that begin with the letter "C," names of animals, and first names. This subtest assesses phonemic fluency for words that begin with the letter "C" and semantic fluency for names of animals, and first names. The seventh index, Reasoning/Conceptual Shifting (RCS), is composed of Practical Problem Solving and Conceptual Shifting. Practical Problem Solving requires the examinee to respond to a series of practical problems and state possible solutions (e.g., what would you do if you smelled smoke in your house or apartment?). Conceptual Shifting assesses the examinee's ability to group three of four line drawings by two separate common attributes. The eighth and final index score is represented by totaling the seven indexes to obtain a Total Index (TI) score of overall neurocognitive functioning.

A short description of the additional 15 tests is provided below. Although these tests do not contribute to the indexes, they provide qualitative information that aids in evaluating neurocognitive functioning consistent with a behavioral approach to neurological assessment. Orientation is the first subtest. It consists of questions that assess the examinee's orientation to date, time, location, and personally relevant information (e.g., age, date of birth). Repetition evaluates the ability of the examinee to repeat a series of orally presented words and sentences. Auditory Comprehension requires the examinee to respond "yes" or "no" to a series of questions (e.g., is there a chair in this room?). The examinee's ability to discriminate the letter "A" in a series of orally presented letters is evaluated in the Auditory Signal Detection subtest. The Symbol Cancellation subtest requires the examinee to circle a designated target that is presented on a page with over 200 different geometric figures. Motor Programming evaluates the examinees' ability to open and close each hand simultaneously and oppositionally. Praxis requires the examinee to perform both transitive (i.e., tool-based movements) and intransitive (i.e., expressive/communicative) hand movements with both the dominant and nondominant hand, as well as perform buccofacial movements. The subtest, Expression of Emotion, asks the examinee to produce a series of facial expressions that correspond to common emotional states.

Picture Naming assesses the examinee's ability to identify pictures of common objects. Picture Description-Oral asks the examinee to describe orally the events depicted in a line-drawing. Picture Description-Written, requires the examinee to describe in writing the events in the same line-drawing depicted in Picture Description-Oral.

Reading Single Words requires the examinee to read both real and pseudowords. The subtest Sentence Reading-Arithmetic asks the examinee to read aloud two problems and work them out using paper and pencil and to complete a page of arithmetic problems. Numbers requires the examinee to recall a set of telephone numbers of 7 and 10 digits in length both orally and through a written response. Finally, Picture Recognition asks the examinee to identify the pictures presented earlier in Picture Naming.

Scoring is done by hand to obtain three scores: Process scores, Subtest Scaled scores, and Index scores. All raw scores are converted to Process scores, which are then converted to percentiles. Total raw scores for the eight test indexes discussed above are converted to Scaled scores and Index or T-scores. The total raw scores for the eight indexes are entered on the Subtest Score Conversion Chart to obtain Scaled scores. The Scaled scores for the eight indexes are then entered on the Index Score Conversion Chart to obtain an Index or T-score, a confidence interval, and a percentile rank. A graphic representation of the percentile rank for the eight indexes and a place for Behavioral Observations are also provided. No summary sheet or conversion chart is provided for the additional 15 subtests that are not part of the indexes.

DEVELOPMENT. The KBNA was developed to be a comprehensive test of neuropsychological functioning. Its development was driven, at least in part, by concerns regarding current clinical practices. Specifically, the concerns were the tendency of clinicians to rely on brief tests of cognitive functioning (e.g., Mini-Mental State Exam) and on nonstandardized mental-status exams developed by neurologists. Further, although other comprehensive exams existed, many lacked norms for 55 years of age and older and had long administration times. Because of these concerns, the authors set several goals for the development of the KBNA that included the following criteria: assessing several domains of cognitive functioning; developing individual subtests that contributed to a scale that would tap a principle cognitive domain; designing subtests that would be sensitive to a range of neuropsychological and neurological disorders thereby allowing for prediction of impairments; and an administration that would take no more than 2 hours.

TECHNICAL. The KBNA was normed using a standardized sample of 700 adult participants representative of the 1999 U.S. Bureau of the Census data for sex, age, race/ethnicity, educational level, and geographic region. The sample population consisted of both male (46%) and female (54%) participants. The sample population of 700 was divided into seven age groups with 100 participants per group. The groups included the following age ranges: 20–29, 30–39, 40–49, 50–59, 60–69, 70–79, and 80–89. The sample was also broken down by race/ethnicity including 531 White participants (77%), 80 African American participants (11%), 65 Hispanic participants (9%), and 24 other participants (3%). The sample was further separated by educational level to include ≤8 years (11%), 9–11 years (12%), 12 years (34%), 13–15 years (24%), and ≥16 years of education (19%). Finally, the population was divided by geographic region with 20% from the Northeast, 27% from the North Central, 33% from the South, and 20% from the West. The normative sample included only "normal" participants and excluded individuals with neurological deficits (e.g., color-blindness), neurological impairments (e.g., head injuries), cognitive impairments (e.g., memory difficulties), those being treated for alcohol or drug dependence, and those with medical or psychiatric conditions that could affect cognitive functioning (e.g., bipolar disorder).

Reliability was estimated using split-half reliability, standard error of measurement, test-retest reliability, and decision consistency. All reliability estimates were estimated for both the subtest scores that make up the index scores and the individual index scores themselves. Split-half reliability coefficients were calculated by correlating the scores of the two half-tests using the Spearman-Brown formula. Average reliability estimates for the subtest coefficients ranged from .64 for Verbal Fluency-Phonemic to .90 for Word Lists 2-Recall, with the average index scores ranging from the .70s to the .80s. The standard error of measurement was also calculated for the subtest and index scores. The standard error of measurement for the subtest scores ranged from 1.5 to 2.3, with index scores ranging from 1.4 to 2.3. Test-retest reliability was also estimated with a 2- to 8-week retest interval. The sample size ($n = 94$) was similar to the normative sample of participants for sex, level of education, and (less so) for race/ethnicity. Test-retest estimates for subtest scores ranged from $r = .42$ for Practical Problem Solving/Conceptual Shifting Combined to $r = .80$ for Sequences, with index scores ranging from $r = .42$ for Reasoning/Conceptual Shifting to $r = .81$ for Attention/Concentration. Further test-retest reliability estimates were assessed on all 25 subtests using decision consistency. Decision consistency estimates ranged from 100% for numerous subtests to 55% for Word Lists 2-Recognition False Positives-Related.

The validity of the KBNA was estimated using content, construct, and criterion validity. The authors suggest that the KBNA has content validity because the contents of the subtests are similar to tasks contained in the most frequently administered clinical tests including the Wechsler Adult Intelligence Scale—Third Edition (WAIS-III), the Wechsler Memory Scale—Third Edition (WMS-III), and the California Verbal Learning Test (CVLT).

Construct validity was estimated by evaluating intercorrelations between the KBNA subtest scores and the Index scores. Though the intercorrelations had a broad range from as low as .02 to as high as 1.0, the authors suggest that the overall pattern of correlations supports the theoretical foundation of the test.

Finally, criterion-related validity was estimated using convergent and divergent validity between the KBNA and other selected neuropsychological tests. Several studies were conducted to evaluate the relationship between the KBNA and the following measures: Wechsler Adult Intelligence Scale—Revised (WAIS-R); WMS-III; Dementia Rating Scale (DRS); CVLT; Rey-Osterrieth Complex Figure Test (Rey-O); Boston Naming Test (BNT); the Controlled Word Association Test of the Multilingual Aphasia Examination; and the Grooved Pegboard. The first study evaluated general intelligence and attention and found overall associations ranging from $r = .215$ for the WMS-III Mental Control to $r = .82$ for the DRS. The second study assessed memory and spatial processing and found overall relationships ranging from $r = .20$ for the Rey-O Complex Figure Immediate Recall to $r = .81$ for the Rey-O Complex Figure Direct Copy. The third study examined language for both the BNT and the Controlled Word Association Test of the Multilingual Aphasia Examination with overall correlation values of $r = .65$ and $r = .50$, respectively. The last study evaluated fine motor speed using the Grooved Pegboard and found overall correlations for both the dominant and nondominant hand of $r = -.65$ and $r = -.71$, respectively. The authors suggest that the results from these comparison studies should be considered preliminary due to the small sample size ($n = 111$) and the diversity of the clinical groups.

COMMENTARY. The KBNA is a well-designed test of neurocognitive functioning measuring a broad range of neuropsychological abilities. The KBNA uses a psychometric approach and a behavioral neurological approach to offer both a quantitative and a qualitative interpretation of neurocognitive abilities. The KBNA is easy to administer in less than 2 hours and scoring the indexes is facilitated with the subtest score conversion and index score conversion charts. Though the protocol is easy to use, for ease of interpretation, the test authors should have included a summary sheet for the 15 additional tests that are not part of the indexes.

The authors met most of their original design goals. The KBNA provides norms for adults over the age of 55 years, requires a relatively short administration time (i.e., less than 2 hours), assesses several cognitive domains, and has a number of subtests that contribute to a single domain. However, the authors did not achieve all of their goals. Although six cognitive domains were evaluated, the authors did not include an interpretation of each domain in their overall index score. For example, motor functioning was assessed by the Motor Programming, Praxis, and Expression of Emotion tests, but no overall motor index was provided. A measure of auditory processing could be conceived in the same way. The Auditory Signal Detection, Auditory Comprehension, and Repetition subtests were included, but no overall index for auditory processing was provided. The authors also suggested that the KBNA would be sensitive to a range of neuropsychological and neurological disorder, thereby allowing for the prediction of impairment, yet they offered no data to support such an assertion.

Though the KBNA is a well-designed test of neurocognitive functioning, the interpretation should proceed with caution for five reasons. First, the KBNA purports to measure six areas of cognitive functioning by the eight test indexes provided; however, one of the domains, Praxis, is not represented in any index. Second, the authors provide no rationale as to why or how test construction and domain-to-index transformations were developed. For example, there was no explanation provided as to why the 15 additional subtests were not represented in the test indexes. Third, the KBNA has only modest reliability and validity estimates, with validity estimates that have not been well established due to the diversity of the sample and the small sample size ($n = 111$). Although the authors suggested that the KBNA has content validity because the tasks are similar to tasks contained in frequently administered tests (e.g., WAIS-III, WMS-III, CVLT), no information was provided on the process involved or how the decision was made to draw such a conclusion. Fourth, even though sensory and motor functioning was assessed, none of the test indexes were specifically designed to measure and interpret these functions. Finally, no information was provided on how the qualitative subtests should be interpreted and the advantage of using this additional information.

The advantage of having only modest psychometric properties for this test is that the estimates apply to only 10 of the 25 subtests. The other subtests rely on more of a qualitative interpretation of functioning. Thus, this makes the KBNA a broad measure able to incorporate qualitative with quantitative data. However, the extensive presence of such qualitative data (15 of the 25 subtests) requires the clinician to have extensive training and/or experience with a range of neuropsychological disorders for an accurate interpretation of test results.

SUMMARY. The KBNA is a measure designed to assess neurocognitive functioning from both a quantitative and qualitative perspective. It was developed to be a comprehensive assessment battery providing reliable and normative data covering a range of neuropsychological abilities for adults aged 20–89 years. It is grounded in behavioral neurology and was developed to assist in the localization and etiology of neurological dysfunction. It includes 25 subtests, each of which was designed to measure a specific aspect of neurocognitive functioning. The KBNA is easy to administer in less than 2 hours and scoring the indexes is facilitated with the subtest score conversion and index score conversion charts. Because the psychometric properties have not been well established, the test's strengths lie in its ability to assess qualitative information. Both the qualitative and quantitative data along with the collection of medical history, psychosocial history, and observations will contribute to a sound comprehensive neuropsychological assessment.

Review of the Kaplan Baycrest Neurocognitive Assessment by HARRISON D. KANE, Assistant Professor, Western Carolina University, and SHAWN K. ACHESON, Assistant Professor, Western Carolina University, Cullowhee, NC:

DESCRIPTION. The Kaplan Baycrest Neurocognitive Assessment (KBNA) is an individually administered test of neurological functioning intended for adults aged 20 to 89 years. According to the authors, the KBNA was conceived as a viable alternative to longer and more cumbersome neuropsychological batteries. The primary application of the KBNA is to diagnose and rule out neuropsychological disorders. A secondary application is to help the clinician form positive and negative predictions of impairment that may link directly to intervention. The authors do not cite a specific theoretical basis for the development of the KBNA. Rather, selected subtests and procedures are intended to maximize clinical utility.

The KBNA consists of 25 subtests, most of them derived from extant neuropsychological tests (e.g., Bells Test, the Clock Test, and Rey Complex Figure Test) and published mental status exams. Each subtest is hypothesized to tap a specific process (e.g., expression of emotion, selective attention, verbal fluency, and motor coordination) contributing to six principal domains of neurocognitive functioning: attention/concentration, primary memory, declarative memory, visuoconstruction/visuoperception, praxis, language, and reasoning/problem solving. Subtests are administered in the order in which they appear on the record form. There is no abbreviated administration; thus, all subtests must be administered to arrive at an estimate of overall functioning. The authors report that the KBNA can be administered in a single session lasting 60–90 minutes, although this estimate seems a bit optimistic. Administration of some subtests requires a stopwatch and tape player. Test materials (i.e., a stimulus book, tape cassette, and response grid) are compact, easily handled, and unobtrusive during administration. According to the authors, trained technicians can administer the KBNA under supervision.

For most subtests, all items are administered. The KBNA is not a power test, and therefore basal and ceiling levels of performance are not established. The majority of the KBNA subtests call for objective scoring. For subtests demanding some degree of subjectivity (e.g., subtests requiring the examinee to reproduce drawings), a scoring guide is provided in the administration manual. Record forms are straightforward and bear strong resemblance to the familiar Wechsler scales (e.g., WAIS-III), also published by The Psychological Corporation.

The KBNA yields a variety of scores based on age-equivalent peer groups, including process scores, subtest scaled scores, and index scores. Process scores may be converted to percentile ranks and are solely designed to help the clinician distinguish between Average, Equivocal, and Below Average ranges of neurocognitive functioning. Subtest scores are scaled to a metric with a mean of 10 and standard deviation of 3, with a range of 1 to 19. The KBNA assumes an implicit three-stratum hierarchical factor structure. Subtests that are believed to share a common source of variance combine to yield seven index scores: Attention/Concentration, Memory-Immediate Recall, Memory-Delayed Recall, Memory-Delayed Recognition, Spatial Processing, Verbal Fluency, and Reasoning/Conceptual Shifting. These second-order index scores contribute to a Total Index that provides an overall estimate of neurocognitive ability. Scoring procedures maximize the amount of information yielded during test administration. That is, several subtests yield multiple raw scores that are intended to enhance diagnostic sensitivity and specificity. For example, semantic and phonemic cues recorded during the Picture Naming subtest are designed to assist in distinguishing between Alzheimer's dementia and visual agnosia. The interpretive guidelines offered for the subtests and index scores are adequate for the trained professional. However, beyond a few references and brief examples, interpretive guidelines for additional data obtained during administration (i.e., errors, cues, and omissions) are limited.

DEVELOPMENT. The standardization is adequately described in the administration manual. The KBNA standardization sample is stratified by age, sex, race, education, and geographic region to reflect the 1999 U.S. census. The standardization sample consists of 700 adults, 100 participants at each age group. Data were collected concurrently during the standardizations of the Wechsler Abbreviated Scale of Intelligence (Wechsler, 1999), the Delis-Kaplan Executive Function System (Delis, Kaplan, & Kramer, 2001), and the California Verbal Learning Test-Second Edition (Delis, Kramer, Kaplan, & Ober, 2001). Predictably, the standardization sample mirrors the representation of Whites, Hispanics, and African Americans in the general population. For the most part, the standardization procedures of the KBNA are a significant improvement over most neuropsychological tests, which are either outdated, ambiguous, or absent entirely.

TECHNICAL. Reliability estimates generally affirm the internal consistency of the various KBNA subtests, ranging from .64 (Verbal Fluency) to .90 (Word Lists). As expected, coefficient alphas for the index scores are higher than those reported for individual subtests, ranging from .77 (Reasoning/Conceptual Shifting) to .87 (Memory-Immediate Recall). Test-retest stability estimates are more problematic, however. To establish the stability of the KBNA, a subsample of 94 participants was retested at 2- to 8-week intervals. Reliability estimates indicate some instability among constructs measured by the subtests. Significant practice effects are noticeable for three of seven index scores. In addition, even when corrected for attenuation, test-retest stability coefficients for two of the remaining index scores are below .50. Given the nature of some subtests, the attenuated coefficients are likely attributable to truncated and irregular subtest distributions. However, the necessary information to affirm this supposition is not provided. The authors report decision consistency coefficients across the repeated test administrations (i.e., the consistency of assignment to the qualitative classifications of Below Average, Equivocal, and Average). These coefficients are considerably higher, on the order of .80 to .90 across subtests.

The content, presentation, and response format of the KBNA subtests are similar in nature to those contained in widely accepted clinical instruments such as the Wechsler Adult Intelligence Scale—Third Edition (WAIS-III; T6:2691) and the California Verbal Learning Test (CVLT; 13:42). However, evidence to support the construct validity is limited. Intercorrelations of the KBNA subtest scaled scores and index scores are

offered, but without the requisite factor analyses, these data are difficult to evaluate. As a means of determining the convergent and divergent validity, a number of comparison studies were conducted during the KBNA standardization. However, some of the referenced instruments do not have current norms (e.g., Rey-Osterrieth Complex Figure Test) or lack established validity (e.g., Grooved Pegboard Test). Moreover, the average sample size of these comparative studies ($N = 12$) precludes any meaningful evaluation of the data. As evidence of the clinical sensitivity of the KBNA, the authors cite a single study in which the KBNA was administered to normal and clinical samples. Unfortunately, unreported sample sizes and the heterogeneous composition of the clinical sample undermine the authors' conclusion that the KBNA is sensitive to a range of neurological impairments. There is no information available regarding the incremental validity of the KBNA over other common measures of neurocognitve functioning, such as the Halstead Russell Neuropsychological Evaluation System (HRNES, Russell & Starkey, 1993; T6:1115), Luria's Neuropsychological Investigation (Christensen, 1989), or the Woodcock-Johnson Tests of Cognitive Ability, Third Edition (WJIII, Woodcock, McGrew, & Mather, 2001; 15:281). Finally, exploratory and confirmatory evidence that would support the structural fidelity of the KBNA (i.e., seven index scores and a total index) is absent. Although the KBNA is conceptualized as primarily a clinical instrument, many researchers would argue strongly that construct validity is a prerequisite for clinical validity (Messick, 1995).

CONCLUSIONS. The KBNA holds several advantages over commonly used neuropsychological tests and mental status exams. Namely, the KBNA has norms for older age groups, imposes standardized procedures for administration and scoring, distinguishes between mild domain-specific impairment and normal functioning, permits ipsative analysis, and provides verbal and nonverbal formats for examinee response. Given the complexity of the KBNA (i.e., many tests offer multiple scores) and the importance of behavioral observation in neuropsychological assessment, only experienced and trained professionals should administer the test and interpret results.

The KBNA successfully updates several tests that are common to batteries designed to measure neurocognitive impairment. Unfortunately, comprehensive reliability and validity data are not readily available. The effectiveness of the KBNA to monitor interventions is questionable. Presently, there is little empirical evidence of incremental validity over that of other neurocognitive tests and batteries the KBNA was designed to supplant. With the limited information at hand, the KBNA is best used as an initial screening instrument. Certainly, publications will provide data beyond the information offered in the manual, and these references should expand its clinical utility considerably.

REVIEWERS' REFERENCES

Christensen, A. (1989). Luria's Neuropsychological Investigation. Copenhagen: Munksgaard.
Delis, D. C., Kaplan, E., & Kramer, J. (2001). Delis-Kaplan Executive Function System. San Antonio, TX: The Psychological Corporation.
Delis, D. C., Kramer, J., Kaplan, E., & Ober, B. A. (2001). California Verbal Learning Test—Second Edition. San Antonio, TX: The Psychological Corporation.
Messick, S. (1995). Validity of psychological assessment: Validation of inferences from persons' responses and performance as scientific inquiry into scoring meaning. American Psychologist, 9, 741–749.
Russell, E. W., & Starkey, R. I. (1993). Halstead Russell Neuropsychological Evaluation System (HRNES). Los Angeles: Western Psychological Services.
Wechsler, D. (1999). Wechsler Abbreviated Scale of Intelligence. San Antonio, TX: The Psychological Corporation.
Woodcock, R. W., McGrew, K. S., & Mather, N. (2001). Woodcock-Johnson Tests of Cognitive Ability, Third Edition (WJIII-COG). Itasca, IL: Riverside.

[122]
Katz Adjustment Scales—Relative Report Form.

Purpose: Designed to assess aspects of community adjustment of psychiatric patients "to identify whether follow-up rehabilitation services are required."
Population: Adults with psychiatric, medical, or neurological disorders.
Publication Dates: 1961–1999.
Acronym: KAS-R.
Administration: Individual.
Parts, 3: General Behavior, Socially Expected Activities, Use of Leisure Time.
Price Data, 2005: $104 per complete kit including manual (1998, 94 pages), response card, and 25 AutoScore™ answer forms; $55 per manual; $36.50 per 25 AutoScore™ answer forms; $19.50 per 10 Spanish language test forms; $15.50 per 5 response cards; $16.50 per mail-in answer booklet; $240 per 25-use PC disk; $15 per 50 PC answer booklets; volume discounts available.
Time: (35–45) minutes; (10–15) minutes for Short Form.
Comments: Informant (relative or close friend) completes behavior rating scale; computer scoring available; formerly a subscale of the Katz Adjustment Scale; Spanish language form available for research purposes; Short Form includes General Psychopathology, Stabil-

ity, Social Aggression Index, Emotionality Index, Disorientation, Withdrawal Index, and Psychopathology Index.
Authors: Martin M. Katz and W. Louise Warren.
Publisher: Western Psychological Services.
  a) GENERAL BEHAVIOR.
  Scores, 16: Inconsistent Responding, General Psychopathology, Stability, Social Aggression Index (Belligerence, Negativism, Verbal Expressiveness), Emotionality Index (Anxiety Index [Anxiousness, Nervousness], Depression Index [Depression, Helplessness]), Disorientation/Withdrawal Index (Confusion, Expressive Deficit, Withdrawal/Retardation), Severe Psychopathology Index (Bizarreness, Hyperactivity, Suspiciousness).
  b) SOCIALLY EXPECTED ACTIVITIES.
  Scores, 3: Level of Performance of Socially Expected Activities, Level of Expectations for Performance of Socially Expected Activities, Expectation/Performance Discrepancy.
  c) USE OF LEISURE TIME.
  Scores, 2: Level of Performance of Leisure Activities, Level of Satisfaction with Leisure Activities.
Cross References: For information on an earlier edition of the Katz Adjustment Scales, see T4:1340 (30 references), T3:1240 (18 references), 8:599 (3 references), T2: 1255 (12 references), and P:138 (10 references).

Review of the Katz Adjustment Scales—Relative Report Form by ROGER A. BOOTHROYD, Associate Professor, Department of Mental Health Law and Policy, Louis de la Parte Florida Mental Health Institute, University of South Florida, Tampa, FL:

DESCRIPTION. The Katz Adjustment Scales—Relative Report Form (KAS-RR) is a 178-item, key-informant self-report measure primarily used to assess the community adjustment of individuals following receipt of psychiatric care. Significant others, typically family members, rate patients' behavior during the previous several weeks in three broad domains: (a) general behavior (100 items), (b) social roles (32 items), and (c) use of leisure time (46 items). Although the original scales developed in the 1960s were available in two forms—Self-Report and Relative Report—the Relative Report form has proven more useful over time and is the focus of this revision and review.

The general behavior portion of the KAS-R (Part I) produces a total of 22 scores and indices. These scores include a General Psychopathology score, a Stability score, Social Aggression (including Belligerence, Negativism, and Verbal Expansiveness subscores), Emotionality (consisting of an Anxiety Index with Anxiousness and Nervousness subscores, and a Depression Index with Depression and Helplessness subscores), Disorientation/Withdrawal (with Confusion, Expressive Defect, and Withdrawal/Retardation subscores), and Severe Psychopathology (containing Bizarreness, Hyperactivity, and Suspiciousness subscores). In addition, a score for Inconsistent Responding is also generated to help the user assess the validity of respondents' ratings. Part II of the KAS-R assesses patients' socially expected activities and generates two scores: Performance of Socially Expected Activities and Expectations for Performance of Socially Expected Activities. Part III of the KAS-R examines patients' use of leisure activities and also produces two scores: Performance of Leisure Activities and Expectations for Performance of Leisure Activities.

The KAS-R has been used in various research studies as an outcome measure to assess changes in patients' behavior over time and is also used by clinicians to help inform treatment planning and identify service needs. The authors stress, however, that information from the KAS-R should be combined with other sources of information when making treatment decisions.

ADMINISTRATION. The manual provides detailed information regarding the administration and scoring of the KAS-R. A relative or someone who has been in close contact with the individual during the previous 2 or 3 weeks should complete the KAS-R. The KAS-R can be completed independently by the informant or as part of an interview in instances where the informant requires assistance with reading or responding to the items. The measure is written at a fifth grade reading level.

In Part I, the informant rates the individual on the frequency of occurrence of 100 psychiatric symptoms (e.g., "gets tired and blue," "acts helpless") during the past 2 to 3 weeks using a 4-point Likert-type scale ranging from 1 = *Almost never* to 4 = *Almost always*. In Part II, informants assess both the individual's current performance and expected performance on 16 social behaviors (e.g., "goes to church," "work") using a 3-point Likert-type scale ranging from 1 = *Is not doing* to 3 = *Does (or Expects patient to do) regularly*. A respondent uses "0" to denote behaviors that are not applicable to the individual. In Part III of the KAS-R, the

informants are asked to assess the frequency of individuals' current involvement in 23 leisure activities using a 3-point Likert-type scale ranging from 1 = *Frequently* to 3 = *Practically never*. Additionally, informants rate their satisfaction with the amount of time the individuals spend engaged in each activity using a 3-point Likert-type scale ranging from 1 = *Satisfied with what he/she is doing* to 3 = *Would like to see him/her do less*. Respondents again use "0" to denote activities that are not applicable to the individual. Administration time for the KAS-R can vary from 10 to 45 minutes depending on whether all three parts of the measure are being completed and whether Part I involves the long (100-item) or short (48-item) form. Recommended protocol administration procedures for the KAS-R are described in the manual (e.g., quite comfortable setting, instructing the informant to complete all of the items, thanking respondent).

SCORING. The KAS-R can be hand-scored or scored through several computerized scoring options (i.e., mail-in or PC-based) offered through Western Psychological Services Test Report Services. Hand-scoring the KAS-R is straightforward. For each of the three parts of the KAS-R, the informant completes the ratings using an AutoScore™ form, a detachable, carbon-backed form that automatically transfers the raters' responses to the scoring sheet on the inside of the answer form. When the completed answer form is opened, the scorer transfers (by hand) the respondent's circled rating on each item to a box representing the scale on which that item clusters. In the absence of missing responses, raw scores are simply the sum of the item responses within that symptom domain (which is a column on the scoring form). If responses are missing, the scorer is instructed to substitute the median score for that item from the standardization sample. These scores are printed directly on the scoring sheet making it easy for the scorer to obtain them. The authors state that if more than 20% of the items are missing from any portion of the measure, the user should document this because the interpretation of the scores will likely be impacted. Raw scores are then converted to *T* scores by plotting them on the profile sheet attached to the scoring sheet. Case examples and detailed instructions for scoring each part of the KAS-R are provided in the manual.

INTERPRETATION. Extensive information is provided in the manual regarding the interpretation of KAS-R scores. A detailed description of the meaning of each item cluster (i.e., index or subscale score) is provided along with the meaning of an elevated score on that cluster, defined as a T score of 60 or higher. In addition, four case studies are provided that include completed KAS-R profile sheets to assist users in determining how the scores can be used "in evaluating the need for mental health services and in developing plans for treatment" (manual, p. 28).

DEVELOPMENT. The KAS-R has an extensive developmental history dating back over 40 years to its predecessor, the KAS. Part I of the KAS-R (i.e., General Behavior) evolved from an original version consisting of 127 behaviorally oriented items describing symptoms and disturbed social behaviors. Common symptom domains (e.g., depression, anxiety) guided KAS-R item generation, and symptom descriptions were developed using everyday language (e.g., "afraid something terrible may happen"). McDowell and Newell (1996) noted that the measure was developed with the view that psychiatric treatment should enhance "the patient's adjustment to living in the community" (p. 146). Development of the short form (i.e., 48-item version) entailed a series of analyses to identify at least 2 items from each index area that were most closely associated with the General Psychopathology and Stability scores as well as each index score.

The 16 items within the Socially Expected Activities portion of the KAS-R (i.e., Part II) were developed to assess behavioral domains related to family and social responsibilities and activities, self-care, home adjustment, and community activities. The authors note that the 23 items in Part III of the KAS-R related to leisure time activities were based on items from the Activities and Attitudes Scales developed by Cavan, Burgess, Havighurst, and Goldhamer (1949).

The magnitude of the intercorrelations among the various scores on the 100-item version of the KAS-R range from .07 to .75 for individuals in nonclinical settings suggesting the relative independence among the scales. As would be expected, the Stability score is negatively correlated with each of the other symptomatology subscales. Similar relationships among the scales were found in a sample of newly admitted psychiatric inpatients on a reduced number of scales that were examined.

During scale development, the factor structure of the KAS-R was examined to identify the various symptom dimensions using data from both an adult non-clinical community-based sample and a sample of adult psychiatric inpatients. The factor solutions obtained from both samples were similar, supporting the stability of the KAS-R scale structure although a few differences were noted on several scales (e.g., withdrawal and helplessness) between the two samples, suggesting some differences in the performance of the measure between groups.

TECHNICAL.

Standardization. Standardization of the KAS-R was conducted using data collected on a relatively large-size community-based sample of 1,864 adults from three states. Participants were generally selected using geographic methods, and quota sampling was employed to ensure that the final sample was representative of the general population in these areas. Although not detailed in the manual, the norming samples seemingly were collected at different points in time and pooled using meta-analytic techniques. The sample is primarily composed of Caucasian respondents, although the Hawaii site did provide more cultural diversity. Only 5% of the standardization sample is Black/African American and apparently no Hispanic respondents were included.

Descriptive data on the KAS-R scores are presented by respondents' age, gender, race/ethnicity, and socioeconomic status. The effects of these respondent characteristics were examined in relation to KAS-R scale scores. Although slight differences were found between the ratings of men and women, the authors concluded that the "differences are small" and do not "suggest a need for separate norms" (manual, p. 45). Similarly, small but sometimes significant differences were found in KAS-R scores across various age, racial/ethnic, and socioeconomic status groups but again the authors concluded that these differences "are not of a magnitude that is likely to be of clinical importance" (manual, p. 45). Given this conclusion, a single set of norms is provided.

Reliability. Three forms of evidence associated with the reliability of scores from the KAS-R are reported in the test manual: internal consistency, interrater, and test-retest. Internal consistency reliability estimates are generally acceptable ranging from .61 to .87 (median = .73) on the 11 scales for which estimates are available on the clinical samples and from .62 to .98 (median = .74) across the full 23 scales administered to the standardization sample. Internal consistency estimates on the 48-item short form are, as would be expected, somewhat lower ranging from .68 to .86 (median = .78). The correlations between the short and long forms of the KAS-R are quite acceptable ranging from .87 to .98 (median = .94). A few studies are summarized in the manual in which the interrater and test-retest reliability estimates were examined. Although only moderate interrater agreement was found between mothers' and fathers' assessments of their adult children diagnosed with schizophrenia, the estimates are based on small samples. Two studies examining the test-retest reliability of the KAS-R are summarized. These studies also reported a moderate level of reliability but in one study ratings were obtained before and after treatment and thus may have lowered these stability estimates.

Validity. Evidence supporting the KAS-R's construct, predictive, and discriminant validity is provided. Evidence of the construct validity of the KAS-R is supported by the fact that the KAS-R correlates as well with other measures of psychopathology such as the Minnesota Multiphasic Personality Inventory (MMPI; Hathaway & McKinley, 1943), Brief Psychiatric Rating Scale (Overall & Gorham, 1962), and the Psychotic Reaction Profile (Lorr, 1961) as these measures correlate with each other. Other evidence of the measure's construct validity is supported by the high correlation (.87) between parents' KAS-R ratings and their ratings on the Interpersonal Checklist (Leary, 1956), another measure of personality traits. Parents' KAS-R ratings also correlate highly with clinician and staff ratings of adjustment, although the level of agreement has been found to differ according to the patient's clinical syndrome.

A number of studies are cited in the manual supporting the predictive validity of the KAS-R. For example, KAS-R scores obtained on individuals with psychiatric disorders at admission to day treatment programs were found to be significantly higher among those who had relapsed within a year after treatment compared to those who did not. Among patients with head injuries, higher KAS-R scores on the Nervousness and Helplessness subscales are associated with increased difficulties during recovery.

Evidence of the KAS-R's discriminant validity is amply reported. Studies have found the KAS-R can adequately discriminate among subclasses of individuals diagnosed with schizophrenia, individuals with varying psychiatric diagnoses, as well as among individuals with differing levels of head injuries. In one study, Zimmerman, Vestre, and Hunter (1975) reported the KAS-R could discriminate among individuals with various diagnoses as well as the MMPI. The KAS-R can also differentiate among individuals in nonclinical settings from those with head injuries or psychiatric disorders.

COMMENTARY. The KAS-R is clearly a well-established measure that has been used with regularity to assess the adjustment of individuals with psychiatric disorders. The significance and acceptance of the KAS-R is noted by the fact that Waskow and Parloff (1975) included this measure in their core battery of psychotherapy outcome measures recommended by the National Institute of Mental Health. The manual is well written and includes adequate information on the development, administration, scoring, interpretation, and psychometric properties of the measure. The KAS-R has well-documented and acceptable psychometric properties. However, many of these psychometric studies are dated and the KAS-R has not been validated against other newer measures of community adjustment such as the Multnomah Community Ability Scale (Barker, Barron, McFarland, & Bigelow, 1994). The standardization sample lacks Hispanic respondents and thus questions arise regarding the performance of this measure and the adequacy of its use within this subpopulation. Information on test-retest reliability should be evaluated with larger samples in nontreatment context. Additionally, further study of the KAS-R's interrater reliability would be helpful.

Although initially developed to assess adjustment and functioning among individuals with psychiatric disorders, the use of the KAS-R has been expanded for use with individuals with head injuries as well as various medical (e.g., heart surgery) and neurological (e.g., epilepsy) conditions. The KAS-R can be quickly scored by hand and scoring is easy and straightforward. Administration of the complete version, however, can be time-consuming for relatives, particularly in situations where multiple follow-up assessments are desired, making the short version more desirable.

SUMMARY. The KAS-R is a key-informant, self-report measure for assessing the community adjustment of individuals with psychiatric disability. The measure more recently has been used for assessing the adjustment among individuals with other medical conditions. The measure has been widely used for over 40 years for clinical as well as research purposes. The KAS-R has good psychometric properties and is a useful measure of community adjustment.

REVIEWER'S REFERENCES

Barker, S., Barron, N., McFarland, B., & Bigelow, D. (1994). *Multnomah Community Ability Scale*. Multnomah County, OR: Network Behavioral Health and Multnomah County.

Cavan, R. S., Burgess, E. W., Havighurst, R. J., & Goldhamer, H. (1949). *Personal adjustment in old age*. Chicago: Science Research Association.

Hathaway, S. R., & McKinley, J. C. (1943). *The Minnesota Multiphasic Personality Inventory*. Minneapolis: University of Minnesota Press.

Leary, T. (1956). *Interpersonal diagnosis of personality: A functional theory and methodology for personality evaluation*. New York: Ronald.

Lorr, M. (1961). *The Psychotic Reaction Profile manual*. Los Angeles: Western Psychological Services.

McDowell, I., & Newell, C. (1996). *Measuring health: A guide to rating scales and questionnaires*. New York: Oxford University Press.

Overall, J. E., & Gorham, D. R. (1962). The brief psychiatric rating scale. *Psychological Reports, 10*, 799–812.

Waskow, I. E., & Parloff, M. B. (1975). *Psychotherapy change measures*. Rockville, MD: National Institute of Mental Health.

Zimmerman, R. L., Vestre, N. D., & Hunter, S. H. (1975). Validity of family informants' ratings of psychiatric patients: General validity. *Psychological Reports, 38*, 555–564.

[123]
Kaufman Assessment Battery for Children, Second Edition.

Purpose: Designed to measure the "processing and cognitive abilities of children and adolescents."
Population: Ages 3–18.
Publication Dates: 1983-2004.
Acronym: KABC-II.
Scores, 7–23: Sequential (Number Recall, Word Order, Hand Movements, Total), Simultaneous (Block Counting, Conceptual Thinking, Face Recognition, Pattern Reasoning [Ages 5 and 6], Rover, Story Completion [Ages 5 and 6], Triangles, Gestalt Closure, Total), Planning [ages 7–18 only] (Pattern Reasoning, Story Completion, Total), Learning (Atlantis, Rebus, Atlantis Delayed, Rebus Delayed, Total), Knowledge (Expressive Vocabulary, Riddles, Verbal Knowledge, Total), Nonverbal Index, Mental Processing Index, Fluid-Crystallized Index.
Administration: Individual.
Price Data, 2004: $724.99 per complete kit, including 4 easels, manual (2004, 236 pages), all necessary stimulus and manipulative materials, 25 record forms, and soft-sided briefcase; $49.99 per manual; $49.99 per 25 record forms; $99.99 per computer ASSIST scoring software.
Time: [25–70] minutes.

Comments: Nonverbal scale available for hearing impaired, speech-and-language disordered, and non-English-speaking children (an adaptation that examiners can make when verbal concerns are present).
Authors: Alan S. Kaufman and Nadeen L. Kaufman.
Publisher: AGS Publishing.
Cross References: See T5:1379 (103 references) and T4:1343 (114 references); for reviews by Anne Anastasi, William E. Coffman, and Ellis Batten Page of an earlier edition, see 9:562 (3 references).

Review of the Kaufman Assessment Battery for Children, Second Edition by JEFFERY P. BRADEN, Professor of Psychology, North Carolina State University, Raleigh, NC, and SANDYE M. OUZTS, Graduate Student in Psychology, North Carolina State University, Raleigh, NC:

DESCRIPTION AND DEVELOPMENT. The Kaufman Assessment Battery for Children, Second Edition (KABC-II) is both similar to and different from the original K-ABC. The KABC-II retains Luria's processing model to guide development and interpretation, but adds the Cattell-Horn-Carroll (CHC) broad and narrow abilities model as well. The Simultaneous and Sequential scales appear on both the KABC and KABC-II, although a new scale (Planning) is added to the KABC-II. Also, some achievement tests migrate from the original KABC Achievement domain into the new Knowledge domain, which is included as a cognitive (not achievement) index. Some KABC subtests (e.g., Magic Windows) are deleted from the KABC-II, whereas others (e.g., Atlantis) were added. Original subtests retained on the KABC-II have new items to accommodate a wider age range (now to 18 years of age, rather than 12). In short, there is plenty that is familiar, but enough that is new to clearly demonstrate the KABC-II is more than just a superficial update of its predecessor.

The KABC-II is composed of 18 core and supplementary subtests. The number of core and supplementary subtests depends on the age of the child and the model the clinician chooses to use (either the Luria or CHC model). However, the same core subtests are administered for each scale whether the examiner uses the Luria or CHC model to interpret results. The KABC-II was conormed with the KTEA-II to provide conormed tests of intelligence and achievement.

The KABC-II yields four or five scales, depending on which interpretive model examiners use. The CHC model organizes subtests according to Short Term Memory (*Gsm*), Visual Processing (*Gv*), Long-Term Storage & Retrieval (*Glr*), Fluid Reasoning (*Gf*), and Crystallized Ability (*Gc*) scales, yielding a Fluid-Crystallized Index composite estimated from all five scales. The Luria model simply renames these scales Sequential Processing, Simultaneous Processing, Learning Ability, and Planning Ability, and yields a Mental Processing Index global scale based on four of the five scales (excluding the *Gc* scale). The number of core subtests using the CHC model ranges from 7 to 10, depending on the child's age, and the number of core subtests using the Luria model ranges from 5 to 8 (due to the elimination of the two subtests comprising the Knowledge scale). In addition, the Nonverbal scale yields the Nonverbal Index and is composed of four or five subtests, depending on the child's age, that include language-reduced instructions and nonverbal responses. All subtest scale scores are normed to a mean of 10 (*SD* = 3), whereas Index scores are normed to a mean of 100 (*SD* = 15).

TECHNICAL. The KABC-II was standardized on a large national sample of 3,025 children. The norm sample mirrors 2001 U.S. Census data with respect to gender, ethnicity, parental education level, geographic region of the U.S., and educational and psychological classifications (i.e., gifted and talented and specific learning disabled).

Reliability. Subtest reliability coefficients are mostly good (.80) to excellent (.90), although a few are fair (.70) to poor (below .70), particularly for younger children. The consistency of global and individual scales is good to excellent (.81 to .97), with coefficients for the Nonverbal Index being the lowest of the global scales. Subtest stability coefficients, based on 205 children subdivided into three age groups, are poor to excellent (.50 to .92). Global and individual scale stability coefficients are mostly fair to excellent (.72 to .95), with coefficients for the Nonverbal Index being the lowest of the global scores. Norms for the KABC-II yield MPI scores that are 6–7 points lower than those obtained with the original KABC, which is consistent with the increasing trend toward higher IQs in Western populations over time.

Validity. The test developers claim the KABC-II can be interpreted using either the Luria model or a CHC model. The KABC-II manual presents an extensive and well-organized discussion of these models, recommending that examiners use CHC theory to guide administration and interpretation unless the examinee is likely to have knowledge (crystallized ability) deficits due to nonstandard learning opportunities (e.g., language difference, lack of schooling). However, the manual also allows for examiner preference to shape the decision, stating that examiners "with a firm commitment to the Luria processing approach" (p. 5) may use it instead of the CHC model. The manual justifies why crystallized ability/knowledge is omitted from the Luria model, but it does not justify why the same subtests/scores can be interpreted in two different ways (e.g., why the same tests reflect simultaneous processing in one examinee, but would reflect visual processing in another—or even the same examinee if the examiner adopts a different model). Although the structural/interpretive model is not consistent across all ages, the changes are justified by developmental trends showing younger children have more global/less articulated cognitive structures than older children. The Nonverbal Scale/Index is justified by reduced verbal content; the manual does not link the scale to either (Luria or CHC) interpretive framework.

Unfortunately, the KABC-II does not explicitly use the current standards (AERA, APA, & NCME, 1999) to organize and present validity evidence. Nonetheless, it presents substantial evidence of validity in three of the five domains identified in the standards (i.e., content, relationships within the test, and relationships to other tests). The evidence provided with respect to content validity appears to be comprehensive and appropriate. The intratest relationships and structure (e.g., item characteristics, subtest consistencies, stabilities, correlations, and factor structure) all strongly support the expected outcomes for the test. The relationships presented in the manual include correlations and other statistics showing that the KABC-II relates to other tests of intelligence and achievement in ways one would expect, with a few exceptions (e.g., KABC-II *Gv* has a lower correlation with other *Gv* measures than measures of *Gf*). Additional information showing means and standard deviations for clinical groups suggests there is little evidence of test score patterns (i.e., profiles) to discriminate among individuals with different types of learning disabilities or ADHD, but means for other groups are congruent with expectations. The presentation of these technical characteristics is detailed, yet accessible, providing a clear and concise record for those who want to better understand test development procedures, decisions, and results.

Because the original and current versions of the test claim to yield smaller ethnic group differences, substantial detail is provided relating to item bias and mean group differences. The data suggest the goal of reducing ethnic group differences is not entirely achieved. The manual emphasizes between-group differences adjusted for parental education level, which are about half the magnitude of those found on other tests of intelligence. However, unadjusted group differences are only slightly smaller than unadjusted differences on other tests (e.g., the mean difference between blacks and whites in the larger/older age group is 10 points). Socio-cultural norms, included in the KABC, are absent from the KABC-II. Finally, it is worth noting that predictive bias data are not presented, which is odd in part because the data available for calculating these indexes are certainly available (e.g., prediction bias for KTEA-II scores).

COMMENTARY. The KABC-II retains many of the strengths of its predecessor (e.g., intriguing subtests, reduced emphasis on prior learning, Luria interpretive model), and overcomes some of the limitations of the original KABC (e.g., poor floors/ceilings, no norms beyond 12 years of age, nonrepresentative norm sample at some ages). The addition of new subtests appears to strengthen psychometric characteristics, and the assignment of subtests to scales adheres more closely to the available evidence than in the KABC. Finally, the KABC-II adopts clear and psychometrically defensible procedures for identifying intra-individual differences (i.e., identifying strengths/weaknesses), which other, newer tests (e.g., WISC-IV, SB-5) have adopted.

However, the KABC-II also retains two flaws that plagued the KABC. First, the KABC was widely criticized for claiming to reflect Luria's processing approach despite substantial evidence that it was little more than a poorly organized measure of more traditional intellectual abilities (see Kamphaus & Reynolds, 1987). The current effort to resolve this problem (i.e., providing two interpretive models) is unsatisfying, and smacks of trying to have (and market) it both ways. Surely the composite drawn from the simultaneous scale

does not mysteriously morph from reflecting visual processing to simultaneous processing just because the examinee might lack standard education or native English proficiency, or because the examiner is strongly committed to one paradigm over another. The Cognitive Assessment System (Naglieri & Das, 1997) provides a verbal/vocal (i.e., nonvisual) test of simultaneous processing, suggesting the KABC-II's characterization of the interchangeability of CHC and Luria frameworks is inappropriate. The KABC-II directions on choosing between models are illogical (e.g., it is more logical to use Gc measures with examinees from nonstandard backgrounds as a means to test for the effects of nonstandard experiences than to presume such individuals process information in a wholly different way), and the absence of direct evidence to support one model over another should leave examiners wondering what the KABC-II really tests.

The second and far more serious flaw inherent in the KABC-II is its complete lack of evidence supporting the utility of test data for driving educational or psychological interventions. Concerns over the value or utility of cognitive assessment results to enhance client outcomes have become increasingly prominent. The claim that "the definition of specific learning disability (SLD) undoubtedly will continue to stipulate that the child must have a disorder in one or more basic psychological processes" (manual, p. 58) is ironic, as recent changes in federal legislation have eliminated cognitive testing altogether as a requirement for SLD diagnosis—in part because of the failure to demonstrate the psychoeducational utility of cognitive tests.

The more elaborate claims of utility that accompanied the KABC have been replaced by more modest, and more easily accomplished, claims. For example, the claim that KABC-II "offers information that can facilitate clinical and educational diagnoses, educational planning, treatment planning, and placement decisions" (manual, p. 9) is both benign and vague (e.g., what information facilitates such activity, and how does it do so?). Psychological and educational utility for test results are implied but are not explicit; the conclusion that "the multiple constructs offered by the KABC-II are consistent with all of these contemporary practical and clinical perspectives" (manual, p. 53) promises much while claiming little.

SUMMARY. The KABC-II is a new and improved version of its predecessor, and provides a plausible option for measuring cognitive abilities (and, with the conormed KTEA-II, academic achievement) in children and young adults. The improvements over the KABC are ones of degree (e.g., better technical characteristics), but not of kind. Although the KABC-II offers some features bound to appeal to many examiners (e.g., interesting subtests, somewhat smaller score differences between ethnic groups), it overlooks questions about the value of psychological testing for guiding educational and psychological interventions. Examiners may want to consider using other measures of CHC abilities (e.g., the WJ-III) or Luria's cognitive processing model (e.g., the CAS) that more broadly represent their conceptual frameworks than the KABC-II. Although the KABC-II provides a reasonable, well-normed, clinically appealing, and technically sound approach to measuring cognitive abilities and generating diagnoses, its meaning is ambiguous, and its value for guiding interventions is unsupported.

REVIEWERS' REFERENCES

American Educational Research Association, American Psychological Association, & National Council for Measurement in Education. (1999). *Standards for educational and psychological testing.* Washington, DC: American Educational Research Association.

Kamphaus, R. W., & Reynolds, C. R. (1987). *Clinical and research applications of the K-ABC.* Circle Pines, MN: American Guidance Service.

Naglieri, J. A., & Das, J. P. (1997). Cognitive Assessment System. Itasca, IL: Riverside Publishing.

Review of the Kaufman Assessment Battery for Children, Second Edition by ROBERT M. THORNDIKE, Professor of Psychology, Western Washington University, Bellingham, WA:

DESCRIPTION. "The Kaufman Assessment Battery for Children, Second Edition (KABC-II) is an individually administered measure of the processing and cognitive abilities of children and adolescents aged three through eighteen" (manual, p. 1). Like its predecessor, the Kaufman Assessment Battery for Children (K-ABC), the primary theoretical focus of the KABC-II is derived from Luria's neuropsychological theory, specifically as a measure of simultaneous and sequential processing. Users familiar with the K-ABC will have little trouble seeing the family resemblance. The new test also retains the separation of subtests into a relatively short (8 or 10 subtests) core battery and supplementary subtests. About half of the subtests are new to this second edition.

Also new to the KABC-II is a link to the Cattell-Horn-Carroll (CHC) three-stratum theory of cognitive abilities. In fact, the test authors propose an equivalence of the four elements of the Luria model with four of the 9 (or 10) broad factors of the CHC model (Simultaneous Processing (Sim) = Visual Processing [Gv], Sequential Processing (Seq) = Short-Term Memory [Gsm], Learning Ability (Lrn) = Long-term Storage and Retrieval [Glr] and Planning Ability (Plan) = Fluid Reasoning [Gf]). Each of the paired constructs is measured by the same two core subtests. In addition, two core subtests and one supplemental subtest at each age level after age 3 measure Crystallized abilities (Gc) or Knowledge. These tests are used only if the examiner adopts the CHC model. A Nonverbal Index composed of four (age 3) or five (all other ages) subtests that require no reading or spoken instructions is also provided for use with nonnative English speakers and examinees with hearing impairments.

The theoretical structure of the KABC-II changes, depending on the examinee's age. At age 3 only a single score, called the Mental Processing Index (MPI) in the Luria model and the Fluid-Crystallized Index (FCI) in the CHC model, is computed. This is roughly equivalent to general cognitive ability. At ages 4–6 the Luria model produces Seq, Sim, and Lrn as well as MPI, whereas in the CHC model one obtains scores for Gsm, Gv, Glr, Gc, and FCI. By age 7 the full array of four processes or five abilities has been differentiated. These changes in complexity of intellectual structure are roughly consistent with milestones of intellectual development that have been identified by other theorists and investigators such as Piaget.

DEVELOPMENT. There are 18 subtests available on the KABC-II, but only 8 or 10 of them (depending on whether Gc is included) are used in the core battery. Not all subtests are appropriate for all ages, and tests that are in the core battery at some ages are supplementary at other ages. Supplementary tests are included for administration in case one of the core tests is spoiled or the examiner wants to probe a particular area further.

The manual for the KABC-II gives detailed descriptions of the processes followed in item and subtest selection, development, and refinement. Justification is offered for each subtest dropped from the original instrument as well as for inclusion of each new test. One major improvement is substituting a subtest called Verbal Knowledge for the original Faces and Places knowledge test. Instead of identifying individuals and scenes, which can become dated, the items require the child to select the picture from a set of six pictures, that best exemplifies a particular concept or piece of information read by the examiner.

The initial tryout battery included 11 subtests from the K-ABC and 10 new subtests. Subtests were subjected to expert review for fairness by sex, socioeconomic status, ethnicity, and disability. They were also scrutinized for suitability for use with special populations and for fit with current thinking in cognitive psychology. Using input from the tryout data and professional reviews, tests and items were modified or eliminated as needed, resulting in a 20-subtest battery used for standardization.

TECHNICAL. Standardization data were collected over a 16-month period beginning in September 2001. "A nationally representative sample of 3,025 examinees aged 3 through 18 was tested at 127 sites in 39 states and the District of Columbia" (manual, p. 75). The publisher seems to have made every reasonable effort to obtain a standardization sample that would reflect the performance of the American preschool and school-age population. Subtest score distributions for each age were smoothed and scaled to yield means of 10 and standard deviations of 3. These scaled scores were then combined and scaled to produce scale index scores and composite index scores with means of 100 and standard deviations of 15.

As is usual with standardization of tests like this, examiners were carefully trained and closely monitored, a practice that results in the highest quality of measurement that can be obtained with the instrument. Consequently, scores on the standardization sample are likely to show higher reliability and greater fidelity to the authors' theoretical model than can ordinarily be obtained in practice.

Subtest reliabilities are about what one would expect for a well-constructed test of this kind. Mean corrected split-half subtest reliabilities for ages 3–6 are all .75 or above with the exception of the two supplementary tests, Hand Movements and Gestalt Closure, and most are above .80. Average within-age standard errors of measurement are mostly in the .86 to 1.52 range. In the 7–18-year age range, the average subtest reliabilities are all above .74 and *SEM*s are generally 1.47 or below (mean 10, *SD* 3). With a few exceptions, scale scores have composite reliabilities between .85 and .95. The MPI and FCI composites have within-age reliabilities of .95 or higher with three exceptions at the lowest ages. The Nonverbal Index reliabilities are somewhat lower, averaging .90. Standard errors of measurement are generally below 5.50.

Test-retest reliability was assessed over a period of 2 to 8 weeks on children in three age ranges (*N* generally between 60–80 at each age level). Mean reliabilities for the four Luria/CHC scales ranged from .77 to .81. The Knowledge/*Gc* scale came in around .90. MPI and FCI scores yielded mean reliabilities of .87 to .92 with the Nonverbal Index giving values of .77–.88. Retesting showed score gains of as high as 14 index-scale points (about one standard deviation), but most gains were in the 2- to 10-point range, reasonable for such a short retest interval.

One of the main objectives of the KABC-II was to produce a test with minimal differences between demographic groups. Here the authors appear to have been quite successful. Means by gender generally differ by 3 points or less. Means sorted by parental education show the expected pattern of increase with increasing education. In the area of greatest concern, ethnicity, scale means for African American, American Indian, Asian American, Hispanic, and White examinees typically differed by less than 7 points (one-half standard deviation) on the scales, with Hispanics usually scoring lowest. Differences were slightly larger on the composite indexes.

Three sources of evidence are offered for the validity of the KABC-II as measuring what the authors claim it measures: restricted factor analysis, correlations with selected other tests, and clinical studies. I will consider these three lines of evidence separately.

I have certain reservations about taking reports of restricted factor analyses (RFA) at face value after finding that some authors (not these) omit some information crucial to evaluating their fit claims, so I ran my own replication analysis of the core battery and full test for ages 13–18 on the correlation matrix published in the manual using EQS. I am happy to report that I was able to replicate the authors' results within rounding error and conclude that the claims made in the manual for the factor structure of the KABC-II are probably correct. Using RFA it is possible to fit a model consistent with the authors' theory to the correlation matrix with very satisfactory results.

The validity evidence from correlations with other instruments yielded results that were generally what one would expect. Subscale and index-score correlations are presented with the K-ABC, with the index and IQ scores of the WISC-III, WISC-IV, and WPPSI-III, with the KAIT, and with the Cognitive clusters of the Woodcock-Johnson III. Correlations of KABC-II scales with the like-named clusters of the WJ III Cog battery reveal weak discriminant validity. That is, KABC-II scales correlate only slightly higher with WJ III Cog scales with the same name than with some dissimilar scales. In particular, MPI and FCI show almost identical correlations (.78) with WJ III General Cognitive Ability, suggesting that they are really measures of the same thing called by different names.

Most of the clinical studies reveal mean differences between the group with disabilities and the norm group, but the pattern of differences for the various scales is relatively flat, suggesting little diagnostic utility. The only groups where possibly useful patterns emerged were Autistic Disorder, ADHD, and emotional disturbance. To their credit, the authors warn about overinterpreting small scale discrepancies and provide tables of statistically significant differences and demographically unusual patterns. Clearly, we must gather much more experience with these scales before practitioners can use scale patterns with confidence for diagnosis and treatment.

COMMENTARY. The authors assert that "The examiner must select either the Luria or CHC model before testing the child or adolescent" (manual, p. 4). They also argue that processes and abilities are distinct, but do not explain how a single test can measure two distinct constructs. That is, there is an operational isomorphism between the Luria and CHC models (with the exception of *Gc*) that seems somewhat at variance with what the theories themselves say. It is also not at all clear from the test manual what kinds of differences are implied by score patterns using the two theories.

One piece of validity evidence that I expected to see was conspicuous by its absence. The test battery that is most explicitly designed to assess the Luria processing model is the Cognitive Assessment System (CAS) of Das and Naglieri (Naglieri & Das, 1997; T6:743). No mention is ever made of this instrument by the KABC-II authors. Given all the work that has been done to validate the CAS, it would seem that this is the most crucial instrument with which to validate the Luria model as assessed by the KABC-II.

Seven of the subtests involve timing, and on some tests a score bonus is given for rapid responding. This can place a burden on the examiner, particularly when, as is the case with Triangles, up to 2 bonus points can be awarded depending on the precise time taken. For Face Recognition and Atlantis, precise timing of exposure to the stimulus material is required. I expect that Atlantis will be a particularly difficult test to administer correctly because not only must the examiner keep accurate exposure time, she or he must also keep a running total of the child's score to use the stopping rules correctly. An additional small concern is that Rover may lack interest for teenagers.

SUMMARY. If you liked the K-ABC, you will probably like the KABC-II. The test materials are well made and should stand up to prolonged use. The response records have been structured to facilitate scoring and score interpretation, and the soft-sided carrying case is large enough that one does not have to worry about putting the materials into it in exactly the right way. It remains to be seen whether practitioners will find it a desirable substitute or alternative to the Wechsler scales and how it will fit into such schemes as Flanagan and Ortiz's Cross-Battery Assessment (Flanagan & Ortiz, 2001).

REVIEWER'S REFERENCES

Flanagan, D. P., & Ortiz, S. (2001). *Essentials of cross-battery assessment.* New York: Wiley.
Naglieri, J. A., & Das, J. P. (1997). Cognitive Assessment System. Itasca, IL: Riverside.

[124]

Kaufman Test of Educational Achievement—Second Edition, Comprehensive Form.

Purpose: Designed to measure "achievement in reading, mathematics, written language, and oral language."
Population: Ages 4.6–25.
Publication Dates: 1985–2004.
Acronym: KTEA-II.
Scores, 23: Reading (Letter and Word Recognition, Reading Comprehension, Composite), Mathematics (Math Concepts and Applications, Math Computation, Composite), Written Language (Written Expression, Spelling, Composite), Oral Language (Listening Comprehension, Oral Expression, Composite), Comprehensive Achievement Composite, Phonological Awareness, Nonsense Word Decoding, Sound-Symbol Composite, Decoding Composite, Word Recognition Fluency, Decoding Fluency, Reading Fluency Composite, Associational Fluency, Naming Facility, Oral Fluency Composite.

Administration: Individual.

Forms, 2: Parallel forms A and B.

Price Data, 2004: $549.99 per complete form A and B kit including Comprehensive Form A and Form B kits with 2 manuals (2004, 442 pages) and 2 norms books; $299.99 per comprehensive kit (Form A or B) including 2 easels, manual, norms book, 25 record forms, 25 student response booklets, 25 error analysis booklets, 2 each of 3 Written Expression booklets, all necessary stimulus materials, administration CD, puppet, and tote bag; $34.99 per manual; $34.99 per norms book; $59.99 per 25 record forms and 25 student response booklets; $24.99 per 25 error analysis booklets; $9.99 per 10 Written Expression booklets; $99.99 per Computer ASSIST computer scoring program.

Time: (30–85) minutes.

Comments: Computer and hand scoring available.

Authors: Alan S. Kaufman and Nadeen L. Kaufman.

Publisher: AGS Publishing.

Cross References: For reviews by John Poggio and William D. Schafer of an earlier edition, see 14:191; see also T5:1386 (26 references) and T4:1348 (5 references); for reviews by Elizabeth J. Doll and Jerome M. Sattler of an earlier edition, see 10:161.

Review of the Kaufman Test of Educational Achievement—Second Edition, Comprehensive Form by MIKE BONNER, Assistant Professor, Department of Psychology, University of Nebraska at Omaha, Omaha, NE:

DESCRIPTION. The Kaufman Test of Educational Achievement—Second Edition (KTEA-II) is a revision of the 1985 original KTEA (Kaufman & Kaufman, 1985) that had previously provided normative data updates (KTEA-NU; Kaufman & Kaufman, 1997). The Second Edition is available in three forms, the Comprehensive Form (with parallel Forms A and B) and the Brief Form. This review is limited to the Comprehensive Form. The KTEA-II provides scores for academic achievement in Reading, Mathematics, Written Language, and Oral Language composite areas, as well as several reading-related skill areas.

The Reading Composite is made up of subtests for Letter and Word Recognition and Reading Comprehension. Letter and Word Recognition contains tasks of letter identification, letter-sound understanding, and single word reading. Reading Comprehension retains the structure of the original version in that it is composed of picture-word matching, "commands" ("Do what this says."/Eat), and short passages followed by literal and inferential comprehension questions.

The reading-related subtests include composites for Sound-Symbol (Phonological Awareness and Nonsense Word Decoding subtests), Decoding (Nonsense Word Decoding subtest and the Letter and Word Recognition subtest from the Reading Composite), Oral Fluency (Associational Fluency and Naming Facility—rapid automatized naming), and Reading Fluency (Word Recognition Fluency and Decoding Fluency).

The Math Composite is composed of a Math Computation subtest sampling numeration, basic operations, fractions, decimals, algebra, roots and exponents, signed numbers, binomials, and factorial expansion. The Math Concepts and Application subtest measures the application of math concepts to problem-solving and reasoning tasks. The Written Language Composite assesses Spelling, in a very traditional way, and Written Expression in a very novel way (detailed later in this review). The Oral Language Composite includes single subtest measures for Listening Comprehension and Oral Expression.

The materials include easel books for presenting all 14 subtests, a primary pencil, record forms, a manual, and a separate norms book. A student response booklet is used for Math Computation, Spelling, and Written Expression for prekindergarten and kindergarten (Level 1). Written Expression Booklets for Grade 1 through age 25 (Levels 2–4) are also included. An administration CD for use in presenting Listening Comprehension passages provides administration and scoring demonstrations for Phonological Awareness, Letter and Word Recognition, and Nonsense Word Decoding subtests. Additional materials include cards with items for use with the Word Recognition Fluency, Decoding Fluency, and Naming Facility (RAN) subtests. There is also an Error Analysis Booklet with forms for use with the Math Computation, Letter and Word Recognition, Nonsense Word Decoding, and Spelling subtests. A chapter in the manual describes procedures for conducting error analysis. Finally, the kit includes "Pepper," a dog puppet to be used in administration of the Phonological Awareness subtest.

DEVELOPMENT. Content development followed a general strategy of developing a content blueprint for each achievement domain targeted in the KTEA-II. Conceptual definitions are described as being developed from a review of literature and written feedback from expert advisors in each content area. Item development then followed to operationalize the definitions. In addition to experimental analysis of novel item format design, expert advisors were again cited as contributing feedback on the utility of original KTEA items and suggestions for content and item format for new subtest areas. In each subtest content area this process occurred and is well described in the manual (in a chapter titled Content Development).

The authors state that the rationale for why the Reading Composite was limited to Word Recognition and Reading Comprehension subtests is to better discern measurement of reading outcome from measurement of discrete skills, and to provide balance between comprehension and decoding on the composite. This likely will prove to be a strength of the KTEA-II design as assessors will be able to target testing to obtain global reading outcome measures, measures of selected skill areas, or both. Another strength that remains from the original version is the measurement of reading comprehension. The revised KTEA-II subtest follows the general format of the original by presenting "commands" at early items and short passages with the requirement to respond to literal and inferential questions. Passage content varies from 50 to 225 words, with both fiction and nonfiction topics, and the range of questions asked was increased to 2–5 questions per passage.

The structure of the oral language subtests, Listening Comprehension and Oral Expression, was designed to parallel the Reading Comprehension (with Listening Comprehension) and Written Expression (with Oral Expression) measures to provide global indicators of general language comprehension and expression. The Listening Comprehension subtest was designed with the intent of approximating the "kind of listening comprehension that students must do in school—that is, comprehension of relatively formal speech" (manual, p. 67). Basically, students listen to passages presented on CD and answer questions. The Oral Expression subtest was designed to measure pragmatic language along with syntax and grammar. Stimulus items are presented through a contextual scenario designed to allow for a more "conversational" administration.

The Written Expression subtest is uniquely designed to provide context for the writing demands. Consulting with researchers in the area of written expression, the task is designed to encourage responses from reluctant writers, avoid a reading confound, and use illustrations throughout the stimulus. The result is three response booklets, which utilize an interactive "storybook" format, and limit the demand to produce sustained writing (i.e., essay) to the upper limit of the subtest.

The KTEA-II underwent a tryout process preceding the standardization process. This allowed for preliminary examination of reliability and content coverage, item analysis, and formative evaluation of administration procedures. This process included a review of the test by 34 "experts" who evaluated the representation of the achievement domains. The KTEA-II was normed and standardized according to the March 2001 Current Population Survey. The manual states that younger age ranges were targeted for larger sampling to better account for the developmental nature of academic skills acquisition. Essentially, this translated to a sample size of 220 for Kindergarten, 200 for Grades 1–8, 160 for ninth grade, and 140 for Grades 10–12. There were 2,400 participants in the total normative sample. Grade and age groups were matched to the U.S. population for gender (nearly a perfect 50–50 representation across grades), geographic region, education level of the examinee's mother/female guardian, ethnicity, and parental education within each ethnic group. Across these dimensions the standardization sample is impressively matched with few exceptions. The sample was further controlled for percentage of students receiving special education, having an ADHD diagnosis, or enrolled in gifted/talented programs. The sample for ages 18–25 was further controlled for educational status of the examinee. After the standardization process, item analysis procedures were repeated to make adjustments to the subtest content, scoring rules, and administration procedures (including start points, basal and discontinue rules, and item sequence).

TECHNICAL.

Reliability. Internal consistency coefficients by age and grade are generally impressive by traditional psychometric standards, and follow a typical pattern: The highest stability is associated with the Reading Composite, Math Composite, Spelling, and Nonsense Word Decoding subtests (generally .93–.97). As is typical with standardized achievement tests of this sort, the Written Expression, Listening Comprehension, and Oral Expression subtests are somewhat lower (ranging from

.78 to .85), yet customary for these type of tests. The internal consistency coefficients for the other reading-related subtests (Phonological Awareness, Associational Fluency, and Naming Facility) range from .73 to .89.

Alternate-form reliability was computed by administering the parallel forms (half the pool taking Form A first, the other half taking Form B first) after a 3–4-week interval (on average). The correlation coefficients show a similar pattern to the internal-consistency analysis, but are not as strong. One can conclude from the data presented ($N = 62$ for Grades K–1, $N = 83$ for Grades 2–6, and $N = 79$ for Grades 9–12) that forms are equivalent, with some variations of note, although interpretation of data is confounded with test-retest interval. Standard errors of measurement also follow the typical pattern described previously, with the more reliable subtests having *SEM*s between 3–5 standard score points, and between 6–8 points for subtests with lower reliability.

Interrater reliability coefficients are available for Written Expression, Oral Expression, Reading Comprehension, Listening Comprehension, and Associational Fluency, as all are subtests requiring examiner judgment in scoring. Fifty cases from each of two grade levels (2 or 3 and 8) were scored by three or four raters who had no involvement with the KTEA-II development process, but who met examiner qualification standards. The data presented show that scoring can be highly reliable, but this is best interpreted as preliminary, not conclusive, evidence.

Validity. Intercorrelations of subtests and composites are reported, as is an explanation of confirmatory factor analysis of the eight core subtests (Reading, Math, Written and Oral Language Composites). Correlations were obtained with other achievement measures (original KTEA, Wechsler Individual Achievement Test-II, Woodcock-Johnson 3 Tests of Achievement, Peabody Individual Achievement Test—Revised/Normative Update, and the Oral and Written Language Scales). Analysis of these coefficients perhaps sheds more light on the measurement of achievement constructs than on validity of the KTEA-II. For example, the Reading Composite shows highest correlations with the original KTEA and the PIAT-R/NU (early Grades 1–5), and lowest with the WJ-III at upper grades (6–10). The KTEA-II Reading Composite correlates .85 with the WIAT-II across all grades, despite the WIAT-II overem-

phasis on decoding skills, as KTEA-II authors might argue. With the WJ-III, the correlation is .82 for early grades, and .76 for upper grades. Despite significantly different designs in measurement of written language, the correlations with WIAT-II are .87 across the grades, and with the WJ-III are .92 (early grades) and .84 (later grades). Oral Language subtests are recent additions to achievement batteries such as the KTEA-II, motivated in part to help identify language learning disabilities. However, correlations between these subtests are very low, calling into question any measurement of oral expression and listening comprehension. As an illustration, the correlations between the Oral Expression subtests of the KTEA-II with the WIAT-II are .46 at upper grades and .41 with the OWLS for 53 students in Grades K–10.

Correlations with measures of cognitive ability were also reported, with the overall KTEA-II Comprehensive Achievement Composite correlating about .8 with general measures of cognitive ability. Mean score differences for disability groups are reported, which the authors suggest is evidence that the KTEA-II can distinguish between nonclinical and clinical (identified disabled) children.

COMMENTARY. The KTEA-II represents an extensive revision of the original test. Furthermore, it was developed from technically sound procedures over several years. This is a model for how to develop a test instrument. Standardization procedures were solid, and reliability evidence is impressive, albeit preliminary. Evidence of traditional validity is the weakest section of this manual. Although the authors rightfully detailed their content development process, they did not present enough discussion of important conceptual validity issues in the manual, especially as it relates to how and why they selected the statistical evidence they presented, and what it suggests for the validity of the test. The inclusion of the error analysis form with chapter explanation is a welcome addition. The manual claims that the parallel forms (A & B) make the KTEA-II suitable for progress monitoring, but no data are presented to back up this claim. Without data to the contrary, it cannot be assumed that item coverage combined with norm-reference standard scores are sensitive enough to detect change (in any of the specific domains or over any specific time frame).

Despite this, there are many things to like about the KTEA-II. The clean composite for reading is much appreciated. As early literacy skill measurement has gained favor, the temptation might be strong for test developers to include these skills in a composite measure of reading. In my opinion, the KTEA-II is appropriately organized into reading outcome and reading-related tasks. The tables in the manual detailing the scope and sequence of the skills measured by the two math subtests are an excellent source for understanding the sampling offered by these tests. The written language scales are well designed, and although significantly different in stimulus design from the WIAT-II, there is a strong and consistent correlation between the two measures. Thus, from an administration standpoint, the KTEA-II would be the preferred measure for written language because of its high face validity (for children) and ease of administration and scoring. Like all other tests that include measures of listening comprehension and oral expression, these subtests and the resulting composite need to be interpreted cautiously, if at all. There is little incremental validity to be gained, and much measurement error to be added by interpreting these types of measures along with direct and functional assessment approaches in these skill areas.

SUMMARY. The KTEA-II is a well-designed, conceptually clear, and highly reliable measure of general achievement domains. The material and the manual are comprehensive and well organized. The original KTEA was a solid, no-nonsense test when the assessment goal was to obtain nationally normed reference measures of achievement. The KTEA-II strives to update this solid history through sophisticated and admirable test development, and has largely succeeded. Nevertheless, the problems inherent with these kinds of general measures of achievement (e.g., instructional utility, curriculum-content overlap, sensitivity to change) are likely to persist, despite the increased psychometric sophistication, until further data are offered. For those times when the assessment questions are geared toward a general measure of achievement with a national norm reference, the KTEA-II should be a top consideration.

Review of the Kaufman Test of Educational Achievement—Second Edition, Comprehensive Form by C. DALE CARPENTER, Professor of Special Education and Associate Dean, College of Education and Allied Professions, Western Carolina University, Cullowhee, NC:

DESCRIPTION. The Kaufman Test of Educational Achievement—Second Edition (KTEA-II) is an individually administered achievement test for ages 4-6 through 25 composed of 14 separate subtests in Form A and Form B. Eight subtests, two in each area, form composites in Reading, Math, Written Language, and Oral Language. These same subtests combine to form the "comprehensive achievement composite." The other six subtests, not described here, contribute to four additional composites: Sound-Symbol, Decoding, Oral Fluency, and Reading Fluency.

Letter-Word Recognition and Reading Comprehension make up the Reading composite. Letter-Word Recognition requires students to identify letters and pronounce phonetically irregular words. Reading Comprehension requires students to read passages and orally answer questions about the passage.

Math Concepts and Applications and Math Computation comprise the Math composite. Students respond to oral questions with a visual stimulus in different mathematical areas ranging from number concepts to geometry and higher math concepts in Math Concepts and Applications. Math Computation requires students to write solutions to printed problems up to and including algebra.

The Written Language composite has two subtests: Written Expression and Spelling. New for this edition, Written Expression requires students to write responses to a combination of oral stimuli, pictures, and incomplete sentences in a student booklet. An essay is also required. Pre-kindergarten and kindergarten children trace and copy letters and write letters from dictation. The Spelling subtest requires students to write words from dictation.

The Oral Language composite includes Listening Comprehension and Oral Expression subtests. Both of these subtests are new to this edition and both are oral versions of other subtests. Listening Comprehension is similar to the Reading Comprehension subtest. However, passages are read to the student using a prerecorded CD and the student is required to answer verbal questions about the passage orally. Oral Expression is similar to the Written Expression subtest with the student responding orally in the context of a real-life scenario. Language tasks on this subtest are in the areas of pragmatics, syntax, semantics, and grammar.

The KTEA-II requires extensive preparation and training to administer, score, and interpret results similar to the preparation needed for other individually administered comprehensive tests of academic skills. Examiners are required to become familiar with and handle multiple materials including easel-type booklets, individual record forms, student response forms, separate stimulus cards, a puppet, and a CD player. Examiners must follow different basal and ceiling rules for each subtest and some subtest starting points are determined by scores on other subtests. Smooth, efficient, and accurate administration and scoring requires substantial examiner preparation and practice. Average administration time during standardization of the eight subtests described above and comprising the Comprehensive Achievement composite was 75 minutes for students in Grades 3 through 5 and 85 minutes for students in Grades 6 through 12.

Standard scores with confidence intervals and percentile ranks are available for subtests and composites based on age or grade norms. The record form and manual provide directions for using scores to make subtest comparisons, composite comparisons, and other analyses. The manual and record forms also provide directions for clinical error analysis.

DEVELOPMENT. The KTEA-II is a major revision of the original Kaufman Test of Educational Achievement. Five subtests were retained and revised and three new subtests were added, which in combination combine to form the Comprehensive Composite. Six more new subtests were added to provide the additional composites. Although major aspects of the original were retained, KTEA-II is a new test with significant changes, a new norm sample, and new qualitative and quantitative technical aspects.

Prospective users may find that although the manual provides 13 pages of information about content and item development of the subtests, the information may be inadequate to make an informed decision about the appropriateness of the test for a certain purpose, given that the test is composed of 14 separate subtests in complex areas such as reading spanning skills from prekindergarten through Grade 12. Nevertheless, the manual describes conceptualization of the skills measured and rationale for the format used. The developers utilized expert panels, referenced resources such as the standards of the National Council of Teachers of Mathematics, and other

well-known instruments to conceptualize and develop blueprints for the subtests.

TECHNICAL. Standardization of the KTEA-II between September 2001 and May 2003 involved a national sample of 3,000 in the age-norm sample and 2,400 students in kindergarten through Grade 12 in the grade sample. The KTEA-II—Comprehensive Form was co-normed with the Kaufman Assessment Battery for Children, Second Edition (KABC-II; 123) and a total of 2,520 students were administered one form of the KTEA-II and the KABC-II. The sample matches the national population for key demographic variables (e.g., sex, parental education, ethnicity, geographic region, educational placement, and educational status) and an adequate number of people were included in each age and grade level. The publisher includes information about students in the norm sample identified as receiving special services such as those with a learning disability, mental retardation, or gifted and talented. For those in the upper age ranges, information is provided about the number of years of schooling completed. Some prospective test users will note that no information is provided about the inclusion of students with Limited English Proficiency.

Reliability information is provided in the form of internal consistency, alternate-form reliability, and interrater reliability. Split-half reliability coefficients for the subtest and composites described above are typically .90 or above with the exception of the oral language areas. The mean reliability coefficient across grades for the Oral Expression subtest is .78 representing one of the lowest mean internal consistency estimates. The manual states that Oral Expression has a low ceiling and is designed more to identify problems than to assess sophisticated abilities of older students. Alternate-form reliability coefficients follow the same pattern and are sufficiently high. Because five of the subtests require judgment in scoring, interrater reliability was studied on 100 students for each subtest and the coefficients were above .90 on all but Oral Expression where coefficients were .82 for Grade 2 students, .88 for Grade 8 students, and Associational Fluency at Grade 2 of .82.

Validity information consists of intercorrelations of subtests and composites, factor analysis, correlation with other achievement tests and aptitude measures, and special population studies. The correlation of scores on the two subtests for each composite of reading, math, and written language are around .70, but the two composites for oral language correlate at lower levels, generally in the .40–.50 range. That may be expected given that the two subtests measure very different skills in Oral Expression and Listening Comprehension. The manual describes a factor analysis process to investigate relationships among subtests and to use the data to organize subtests into groups and the subsequent composites in the final product. Prospective users may be more interested in clearer evidence that shows how each subtest and composite yields usable information for users.

Scores on the KTEA-II were correlated with scores on several well-known achievement and aptitude tests. Forty or more individuals participated in each study of individually administered achievement tests and results generally indicate high correlations in the areas of reading, written expression, and math. Correlations for oral language are lower. Correlations with tests of cognitive abilities are also generally high overall.

The manual provides information on studies about the performance of eight different groups of students including those with learning disabilities, emotional/behavioral disorders, deaf or hard-of-hearing, and gifted. These data document mean scores for each of the groups discrepant from the norm sample showing lower mean scores where expected and higher mean scores for those in the gifted group. The number of students in each study ranged from 27 (mental retardation) to 134 (reading disability).

COMMENTARY. The KTEA-II—Comprehensive Form should be considered a new test because it represents significant revision of some older subtests, several new subtests, and a different approach to academic achievement and assessment than the original test. The addition of oral language in the form of Oral Expression and Listening Comprehension subtests provides test users with interesting data. However, the utility of the data is uncertain because of questionable reliability and validity data and the uncertainty of the need of educators and others for the data.

Materials are attractive and usable. The use of a CD to aid in the administration of some subtests and to provide pronunciation guides for others is helpful if used. Scoring is clearly described and assistance is provided in the manual for subtests that require judgment. The KTEA-II, like similar tests, assumes an experienced, trained examiner because of its individual format and comprehensive nature.

Two alternate forms of the test provide an opportunity to use the test to document progress and to confirm, or refute, results when the results of an administration of the test are suspect. Another attractive feature of the KTEA-II—Comprehensive Form is co-norming with the KABC-II. This allows examiners to compare cognitive ability and educational achievement for students with confidence that scores are being compared to the same norm group. Comparisons of cognitive ability with educational achievement are popular, although not universally accepted, for assistance in diagnoses of learning disabilities.

Technical characteristics are acceptable for most subtests and composites for an educational achievement test. However, when comparisons between abilities and composites or between subtests are made, the correlation between the scores must be carefully reviewed because many of the measures being compared are highly correlated with each other and require that difference scores must be very large to be meaningful. The manual provides adequate information but users must be diligent in their use of the data.

Co-norming of the KTEA-II with the KABC-II is a potential benefit for users when comparing results from both tests for the same individual, but only if the KABC-II is the test of cognitive ability of choice for the user. Otherwise, to realize the benefit provided by the same norm sample, the KABC-II must be administered. The time and cost of the additional administration of the KABC-II may not be worthwhile.

SUMMARY. The Kaufman Test of Educational Achievement—Second Edition, Comprehensive Form is new and improved over the original test. Prospective users have available in the KTEA-II an individually administered set of measures for reading, math, written language, and oral language with adequate technical characteristics and stated purposes. Furthermore, the KTEA-II offers equivalent alternate forms and the same norm group as the KABC-II. Competitive instruments like the Woodcock-Johnson Tests of Achievement (Woodcock, McGrew, Mather, & Schrank, 2001; 15:281), and the Wechsler Individual Achievement Test, Second Edition

(Wechsler, 2001) also offer desirable attributes. A decision to use the KTEA-II over a competing instrument with similar technical characteristics and comparable features may hinge on preference for the content and format of the KTEA-II. Each of the areas measured is complex and each of the areas has proponents for different theories and different ways to usefully measure achievement. For example, the Oral Expression subtest is unique and a prospective user must decide if its content and format are acceptable for the uses intended in addition to the technical characteristics associated with it.

REVIEWER'S REFERENCES

Wechsler, D. (2001). Wechsler Individual Achievement Test, Second Edition. San Antonio, TX: The Psychological Corporation.
Woodcock, R. W., McGrew, K. S., Mather, N., & Schrank, F. A. (2001). Woodcock-Johnson III. Itasca, IL: Riverside Publishing.

[125]

Keirsey Temperament Sorter II.

Purpose: Designed to be used "for assessing temperament, character, and personality."
Population: College and adult.
Publication Dates: 1978–2003.
Acronym: KTS-II.
Scores, 16: Artisan-Promoter (ESTP), Artisan-Crafter (ISTP), Artisan-Performer (ESFP), Artisan-Composer (ISFP), Guardian-Supervisor (ESTJ), Guardian-Inspector (ISTJ),Guardian-Provider (ESFJ), Guardian-Protector (ISFJ), Rational-Fieldmarshal (ENTJ), Rational-Architect (ENFP), Rational-Mastermind(INTJ), Rational-Inventor (INTP), Idealist-Champion (ENFP), Idealist-Header (INFP), Idealist-Counselor (INFJ), Idealist-Teacher (ENFJ).
Administration: Group.
Price Data, 2004: KTS-II may be taken free online; $14.95 per Classic Temperament Report; $19.95 per Career Temperament Report; $27.95 per Career Personality Package; price information available from publisher for Statistical Study (2003, 89 pages) and for Academic Platform or Corporate Platform delivery; $15.95 per "Please Understand Me II" (1998, 352 pages).
Foreign Language Editions: Available in American English, Spanish, French, German, Italian, Polish, Portuguese, and Japanese.
Time: (10–15) minutes.
Authors: David Keirsey (instrument and "Please Understand Me II") and Alpine Media Corporation (Statistical Study).
Publisher: AdvisorTeam, Inc.

Review of the Keirsey Temperament Sorter II by PETER ZACHAR, Associate Professor of Psychology, Auburn University Montgomery, Montgomery, AL:

The Kiersey Temperament Sorter II (KTS-II) is a personality test designed to measure fundamental personality predispositions that each individual inherits at birth. The predispositions measured by this test are based on the personality theory of the psychiatrist Carl Jung and Isabelle Briggs-Myers's attempt to measure Jung's types using a paper-and pencil questionnaire, called the Myers-Briggs Type Indicator (MBTI). The KTS-II is a refinement and reconceptualization of MBTI constructs for use in organizational consultation, personnel selection, educational settings, and couples work.

DESCRIPTION AND DEVELOPMENT. The KTS-II measures eight bipolar personality preferences. In order of importance to the theory, they are Sensing-Intuiting (S-N), Thinking-Feeling (T-F), Judging-Perceiving (J-P), and Extroversion-Introversion (E-I). Sensing refers to a preference for using information that is concrete and observable. Intuiting refers to a preference for information that is abstract and oriented toward possibilities. Thinking describes a tendency to evaluate information impersonally whereas feeling describes a tendency to evaluate information with respect to its personal implications. Judging involves being more comfortable with having things decided and closed. Perceiving involves being more comfortable with keeping options open. Extroversion refers to deriving one's energy from other people whereas introversion refers to deriving one's energy from periods of solitude.

The author of the KTS-II, David Keirsey, has organized these preferences into four temperaments. Keirsey sorts the preferences differently than Myers did, and believes that his alternative sorting is more informative. He initially separates people into two broad groups—either sensing or intuiting. Although Jung believed that extroversion-introversion was the primary trait dimension, what Jung meant by E and I is not measured by either the KTS-II or the MBTI. One could argue that the SN dimension as operationalized in these tests has some overlap with Jung's original notion of extroversion-introversion. In support of Keirsey's approach, factor analytic research suggests that the S-N dimension accounts for more "variance" among the items than any other dimension.

Another unique feature of Keirsey's approach is that he uses thinking versus feeling to make distinctions with the intuiting group, and uses judging versus perceiving to make distinctions within the sensing group. The resulting clusters are his four temperaments, for which he provides commonsense names: Artisan (SP), Guardian (SJ), Idealist (NF), and Rational (NT). Furthermore, each species of temperament is sorted into four different varieties. The varieties are also given commonsense names, for example, there are four varieties of Artisan: Crafter, Composer, Performer, and Promoter.

Artisans are impulsive, spontaneous, and creative. They are intellectually concrete, and utilitarian in achieving goals. Utilitarian in this sense means doing whatever they need in order to reach their objective. *Guardians* are obsessive, ordered, controlled, and traditional. They are also intellectually concrete, but prefer to work toward goals cooperatively. *Idealists* are romantics, concerned with the deeper meanings of events and achieving personal authenticity. They are intellectually abstract and prefer to work with others to achieve goals. *Rationals* are logical, skeptical, scientifically oriented, progressive kinds of people. They are intellectually abstract, individualistic, and practical with respect to achieving their goals.

TECHNICAL AND FURTHER COMMENTARY. The KTS-II is available in both paper-and-pencil and computer formats. The 70-item paper-and-pencil version can by found in Keirsey's 1998 book *Please Understand Me II*. The computer version is available on http://www.advisorteam.com. The web site is maintained by AdvisorTeam, a consulting firm that markets the KTS-II to corporations and schools. The web site also sells interpretive reports. Although a psychologist, Keirsey has not appeared to be interested in developing his test psychometrically, and his book does not contain the kinds of references to research studies that a scientist would like to see. Rather than science, Keirsey sells his experience and his ideas. He believes that he has conceptualized this model of personality assessment better than did Isabelle Myers.

Written for a general audience, the book is easy to read. It describes the underlying theory, the four temperaments, and makes applications to leadership, parenting, and mating. In some cases, Keirsey overgeneralizes, especially when he attempts to fit the history of temperament theory from Plato through Fromm into the Procrustean bed of his four categories. In his favor, Keirsey does not write down to his audience.

Although Keirsey has not attempted to assess the test scientifically, a professional consultation company that specializes in test development, Alpine Media Corporation, has begun this process and published a test manual (2003). Their analyses utilize data collected from the web-based version of the KTS. The manual indicates that they used some of the results of an item-response theory (IRT) analysis to modify the on-line version of the test. This means the paper-and-pencil version and the web version are not the same test, and the manual refers primarily to the web version. Interpretation is, however, left to Keirsey's book.

The manual is clearly written and uses modern rather than classical psychometric techniques to evaluate the test. There are probably too many direct quotes from the *Standards for Educational and Psychological Testing*. At one point the manual refers to Lee Cronbach as Lee J. Cornball and Samuel Messick as Samuel Homesick. I will assume this was an editorial blunder.

The statistical assessment of the test is based on a population of over 77,000 people. The manual reports both reliability and validity evidence. To the credit of the test, the reliability coefficients appear to be respectable. Unfortunately, the statistics are reported in unconventional ways, and in many cases the manual does not present enough data for a psychometrically inclined reader to evaluate the conclusions reached. For example, it reports the results of a principal components analysis that is supposed to support the distinction between SN, TF, JP, and EI, but without providing the actual items and their loadings on each component, the reader has to take the interpretations presented on faith.

With such a large number of protocols, it is surprising that more normative data are not presented. Although some analysis of gender differences is reported, no information about race differences or age differences is presented. Although the scores on the various dimensions are not the focus of interpretation, it would have been helpful to present means and standard deviations for the scales so that users would have some idea about what actually counts as a low, average, and high score.

An important problem with the manual and the psychometric assessment of the KTS is that the reliability and validity evidence was largely assessed with respect to the basic dimensions, SN, TF, JP, and EI, and not assessed with respect to

the four temperaments: Artisan, Guardian, Idealist, and Rational. This is puzzling because those
temperaments are the categories from which inferences about people are being made. There needs
to be a dual level strategy with tests of this kind.
First, the scales SN, TF, JP, and EI are being used
to predict a person's category membership, so they
need to be assessed using traditional methods.
Secondly, the categories themselves should be
evaluated.

The items on the basic trait dimensions SN,
TF, SP, and EI all appear to be measuring the
same construct. This is called internal consistency
reliability, and it is very desirable. For future
editions of the manual, a confirmatory factor analysis would provide better support for the test than
the analyses reported in the manual, and it should
be easy to do with such a large data set.

If a person scores very high on any pole of a
particular dimension, then the odds that she would
score high on that pole 30 days later are 90% or
better. This is called test-retest reliability. My
primary concern here is that the manual describes
traditional test-retest reliability as measured by a
Pearson correlation coefficient, but does not report those correlations. SN, TF, JP, and EI should
be evaluated in this manner. To its credit, the
manual also reports a percentage of agreement
measure to assess assignment to types. If someone
is typed as an extrovert on an initial testing, there
is a good chance that she will be typed as an
extrovert on a second testing, as long as she had a
relatively high score on that scale. The next logical
step would have been to evaluate the temporal
stability of the four temperaments—but that information was not presented.

The same considerations noted above apply
to the validity analysis. In the KTS-III, scores on
quantitative dimensions are being used to construct dichotomous categories where a person either is or is not a member of the category. Most
psychologists eschew this kind of typing because
so much information is lost. For example, extroversion is not an either-or construct, rather, there
are degrees of extroversion represented by scores
on a scale from low to high. Future editions
should provide a traditional analysis of the validity
of the underlying scales using correlational methods, and then proceed to evaluate the four temperaments. For example, the temperaments could
be used as categories in an analysis of variance

design where differences between them on variables of interest are investigated.

In the current manual, validity information
is sparse. Research using the KTS often focuses on
the scales of SN, EI, etc., rather than on the four
temperaments. The research reported suggests that
the KTS-II (paper-and-pencil version) might be
useful for the kind of personal exploration done in
career counseling, and maybe for understanding student learning styles. Broad use in these settings has
not yet been supported. Evidence for use in organizational settings is mixed, and no evidence for use in
couples work is reported. Contrary to the authors'
claim, the appeal of a test does NOT speak to its
validity. The manual also presents evidence that the
KTS-II is correlated with the MBTI. The amount of
research done with the MBTI dwarfs the work done
with the KTS-II, and it is conceivable that some of
that research could provide support for other uses
of the KTS-II.

SUMMARY AND CONCLUSIONS. The
Jungian typology as measured by the Myers-Briggs
Type Indicator and The Keirsey Temperament II
sorter is intuitively appealing. The underlying
theory has given rise to its own culture, and a
culture that is closer to popular psychology than it
is to scientific psychology. The culture is also more
familiar to counselors and laypersons than it is to
clinical psychologists. Psychologists, of course, do
not own personality or even personality assessment.
They should, however, have an important vote on
what counts as adequate and ethical assessment. To
put it in Keirsey's terminology, psychometricians are
supposed to be logical, skeptical rational types, and
their skills are well-suited for refining psychological
tests, and making sure that the interpretations made
from test scores are justified. This is even more
important with tests such at the KTS-II because
intuitive plausibility has a way of creating a confirmatory bias in favor of the test, whether or not it really
does what its authors claim. Tests have to be
subjected to critical scrutiny. The authors of the
test manual have begun some of this important
work, but there is much yet to be done.

[126]

Kent Visual Perceptual Test.

Purpose: Designed to "identify and characterize visual processing deficits in school or neuropsychological
settings."
Population: Ages 5–11, 18–22, 55–91.

Publication Dates: 1995–2000.

Acronym: KVPT.

Administration: Individual.

Price Data, 2005: $207 per complete kit including 10 copy tests, memory test stimuli, discrimination test stimuli, 10 scoring and error analysis booklets, and manual (2000, 128 pages).

Time: (25–30) minutes.

Author: Lawrence E. Melamed.

Publisher: Psychological Assessment Resources, Inc.

    a) KENT VISUAL PERCEPTION TEST—DISCRIMINATION.

    Purpose: Designed to assess visual discrimination skills.

    Acronym: KVPT-D.

    Scores, 2: Error Analysis, Total.

    b) KENT VISUAL PERCEPTION TEST—COPY.

    Purpose: Designed to assess visual reproduction skills.

    Acronym: KVPT-C.

    Scores, 4: KVPT-C1, KVPT-C2, KVPT-C3, Total.

    c) VISUAL PERCEPTION TESTS—IMMEDIATE MEMORY.

    Purpose: Designed to assess immediate memory.

    Acronym: KVPT-M.

    Scores, 2: Error Analysis, Total.

Cross References: For a review by Annie W. Ward, see 14:193.

Review of the Kent Visual Perceptual Test by RALPH G. LEVERETT, Professor, Department of Education, Union University, Jackson, TN:

DESCRIPTION. Three subtests comprise the Kent Visual Perception Test (KVPT). Among its claims is a reduction in the subjectivity required in scoring similar tests. The test is suitable for children from 5 to 11 years of age. The stimuli are based upon "the parameters of two-dimensional forms" (professional manual, p. 1). A multiple-choice format is utilized for much of the instrument. The KVPT-D subtest assesses Discrimination. Examinees compare alternatives to a standard form. A Memory subtest, the KVPT-M, follows a similar pattern; however, the standard is presented briefly, and the individual chooses among alternatives. One subtest, the KVPT-C, requires the individual to Copy a pattern. The first two subtests minimize subjectivity. Although the developer has reduced the subjectivity of scoring the latter subtest, it is not entirely objective. The examiner is still required to ascertain the accuracy of angles and orientation of patterns. The suggestion of the author of this test overall is that it requires less

examiner judgment than similar instruments. Test materials are to be positioned so that the examinee views the stimulus items consistently throughout the test's administration. As support for this orientation, there is some discussion of "developmental surface dyslexia" (professional manual, p. 2), and its relationship to visual discrimination tasks. The test may be given by persons without a psychology background who have received training from qualified personnel (persons with backgrounds in psychology). The interpretation of the test, however "should only be performed by individuals with the requisite professional training" (professional manual, p. 3). The professional manual includes several completed facsimile test forms for students of the targeted age levels. These are especially valuable because they include application of the error analysis procedure as well as a narrative of the errors (Integrated Analysis of Errors). Three advantages are cited for the KVPT. One is the analysis of error types. A second claim is the "dissociating" of levels of disorders. Finally, "judgment calls" are minimized due to the detailed criteria for the evaluation of copying tasks.

DEVELOPMENT. The construct of the KVPT varies from some other widely recognized tests of visual perception. In contrast to the Gestalt theory, which guided developers of "most current instruments," the KVPT is based upon a perceptual processing model. As a result, rather than referring to figure-ground tasks and familiar related terms, the taxonomy that defines the functions of this test includes classifications based upon Sensory Encoding, Perceptual Integration, Memorial Classification and Retrieval, and Cognitive Abstraction. Although the terminology related to the actual tasks (designs) is familiar (e.g., pattern discrimination and pattern recognition), a child's performance would be interpreted in terms related to perceptual processing. So, although the execution of the tasks on the KVPT (their visual form) would appear similar to those of related tests, the interpretations of the examiners would vary.

TECHNICAL. The discussion of normative procedures is brief. Although the primary focus of the test is children between the ages of 5 and 11 years, norms for adolescents and adults between 18 and 22 are available for the KVPT-D and KVPT-M subtests. The norms for the latter group were gathered from "ongoing research on adult visual-perceptual skills" (professional manual, p.

2). Separate norms are included for boys and girls. The author is candid in describing evidence for reliability. He describes the reliability of the KVPT-C (Copying) as "very reliable." Reliability of the remaining subtests is "more modest." Evidence for validity is based primarily upon the discussion of construct validity. The conclusions related to validity seem tenuous. The following statement is representative of this conclusion, "To compare performance on other 'perceptual processing' instruments is problematic given their less involved association with constructs from perceptual science" (professional manual, pp. 83–84). It appears, then, that this test represents a theoretical alternative to more common measures of visual perceptual skills; however, its perspective is so different as to make satisfying statements of validity difficult at this time. Of interest is the discussion of performance differences between individuals with right and left hemisphere lesions. Although these would seem foundational to overall research in visual perception, in this context, they seem only peripherally related to the children, who are the primary focus of the test. Additionally, these data are based upon a total of only 30 people, presumably adults.

COMMENTARY. At first glance, the KVPT appears to offer an intriguing alternative to traditional tests of visual perception. It is built upon a theoretical foundation that differs from similar tests. Although on the surface the test appears to have increased the examiner's confidence in scoring the responses, the test is so different in its perspective that it ultimately diminishes that sense of security. As a test that is essentially the lone example based upon a "processing model" in a field of more familiar alternatives, the KVPT seems to lack the technical integrity most examiners would require. Additionally, the format of the manual seems awkward and difficult to follow, with almost excessive detail that appears unrelated to the test's basic administration and interpretation. With this in mind, the examples of scored tests provided in the manual become essential. Overall, the feel is that of a very "clinical" test. If that perception is accurate, it would likely have less appeal to the examiner of young children.

SUMMARY. Although the KVPT is based upon a model that would seem to have direct application to the nature of visual perceptual problems, its own uniqueness and apparent lack of technical support make it a cautious choice for the examiner. The test appears to have promise, but its publication seems premature. Perhaps further research will substantiate the processing approach to assessing visual perceptual disorders and will result in a test that offers a viable alternative to traditional visual perception tests.

Review of the Kent Visual Perceptual Test by KATHARINE A. SNYDER, Assistant Professor of Psychology, Methodist College, Fayetteville, NC:

DESCRIPTION. The purpose of the Kent Visual Perceptual Test (KVPT) is to allow for the neuropsychological assessment of three major classes of visual-motor deficits using a common pool of stimuli. To accomplish this, the Kent Visual Perceptual Test (KVPT) is composed of three sections, a figure discrimination test (KVPT-D), a figure copy test (KVPT-C), and a figure memory test (KVPT-M). Order of presentation proceeds from the KVPT-D, to the KVPT-C, to the KVPT-M. Individuals using the battery should be highly qualified (e.g., school psychologists, clinical psychologists, neuropsychologists).

Administration of the KVPT-D begins with two practice items. Respondents are instructed to view a figure and then select that form from five alternatives. Error analysis on the KVPT-D leads to five aggregate scores, which are converted to standard scores and percentile ranks. These five scores are as follows: Total Score (all 26 items), Single Feature Errors (17 items), Multiple Feature Errors (9 items), Rotational Errors (possible on 22 items), and Nonrotational Errors (possible on 17 items). Individual feature errors factored into the five aggregate scores are also as follows: Errors of intersection (I), rotation (R), reflection (Rf), vertical element reflection (RfV), vertical element rotation (Vr), incorrect vertical elements (V), incorrect vertical lengths (Vl), incorrect horizontal elements (H), incorrect horizontal lengths (Hl), horizontal lines off center (Hc), incorrect spacing of elements (S), incorrect number of elements (En), incorrect size of elements (Es), and/or incorrect angle of intersection (A). Rotation Error Scores are the sum of R, Rf, RfV, and Vr error scores, whereas the Nonrotation Error scores are the sum of all other feature errors.

Administration of the KVPT-C begins with instruction to draw copies of items in the booklet. Respondents work through all 42 items, with 3 items per page, and no time restrictions. In addition to a total KVPT-C score, three subscores are obtained. The first subscore (KVPT-C1; Items 1–18) is based on figures with only one form feature, which differ only in the angle of rotation, whereas the second subscore (KVPT-C2; Items 19–30) is based on figures composed of two lines that differ in orientation, angle, point of intersection of constituent lines, relative lengths, and the extension of lines beyond the intersection. Finally, the third subscore (KVPT-C3), consists of all these errors as well as Gestalt feature errors like symmetry and closure. Scoring the KVPT-C is rather rigorous, requiring the precise use of a protractor, a compass, and a ruler. Line drawing features factored into the aggregate scores include the following: Is the drawing a line, is the angle of orientation and intersection correct, do the lines extend 2/16th beyond the intersection, is the relative length of lines correct, is the point of intersection correct, etc. Curved drawing features factored into the aggregate scores also include the following: Is the drawing a curve, are the curves continuous, is there a point of maximum curvature, is the angle of orientation correct, are the points of curvature within 2/16th of each other, etc.

DEVELOPMENT. Underlying development of the KVPT is the perceptual information processing model proposed by Zusne in 1970 (as cited in the professional manual). In sum, the theory proposes a taxonomy of perceptual information processing functions beginning with the senses (Level 1) and concluding with perceptual integration in the brain (Level 4). Although a linear, bottom-up, flow of information is implied, the researchers emphasize the critical role of top-down, bidirectional processes.

All items of the KVPT were selected from the same pool of figures, namely forms necessary for the perception of letters (Massaro & Sanocki, 1993, as cited in the professional manual). Zusne's model emphasizes transpositional (e.g., rotation, reflection), informational (number of sides), and configurational (organization) features of figures as related to the perception of letters. Hence, the ideal was to select forms that varied in transposition (e.g., rotation), information (e.g., number of lines), and configuration (e.g., relative length of the lines). The final selection of 42 forms was reportedly based on the developmental progression of abilities to copy figures varying on these three dimensions. For instance, from a sample of 700 children, an accuracy rate of 30% for 5-year-

olds, 45% for 6-year-olds, etc., was reported. Items for the KVPT-D and KVPT-M were randomly selected from 42 figures chosen for the KVPT-C.

TECHNICAL. KVPT norms were based on a sample of 741 children, 365 boys and 376 girls. Children were from lower middle to middle socio-economic backgrounds in northeastern Ohio. Less than 10% of the sample comprised minority children. A concern addressed throughout the manual is that the scores on the KVPT are in many instances not normally distributed. Standard scores are recommended for descriptive purposes only, yet in case exemplars they are used for clinical interpretation. Percentile ranks are also given.

Reliability of the KVPT is assessed through use of Cronbach's alpha, test-retest, and interrater methods. Although median Cronbach's coefficient alphas were high for the KVPT-C (.92), they were relatively low for the KVPT-D (.60) and KVPT-M (.51). For the test-retest assessment, 30 children (10-year-olds) from the original sample were given the KVPT again, approximately 14 days later. The test-retest coefficient for the KVPT-C was .83, whereas the KVPT-D and KVPT-M coefficients ranged between .40 and .50. An interrater reliability study was carried out with the KVPT-C. Two evaluators scored the inventories of 232 randomly selected children. Interrater reliability coefficients are .98 for the KVPT-C1, .97 for KVPT-C2, .97 for KVPT-C3, and .99 for the KVPT-C.

Construct, content, and criterion validity were evaluated in the KVPT through the use of factor analytic methods, intercorrelational studies, and predictive utility. Factor analysis revealed significant loadings on two factors. The first factor loaded heavily on the KVPT-D, moderately on the KVPT-C, and nearly zero on the KVPT-M, whereas the second factor exhibited the opposite pattern. It is suggested that these factor loadings represent Levels 2 and 3 of Zusne's theory. Performance on the KVPT-C is correlated with performance on the Beery Developmental Test of Visual Motor Integration (DTVMI). There are also numerous correlations between the KVPT subtests, the Metropolitan Achievement Test (MAT), and the Iowa Test of Basic Skills (ITBS). Finally, two studies were carried out to assess criterion-related validity. The KVPT-D and KVPT-C were found to predict academic performance (.50–.60 coefficients) for first through third graders by Melamed and Rugle, 1989, as cited in professional manual.

COMMENTARY. The major concern of this reviewer is the lack of findings of a normal distribution. Normal distributions were reported for the KVPT-C, KVPT-C1, KVPT-C2, KVPT-C3, four of seven age groups on the KVPT-M, and five of seven age groups for the KVPT-D for girls. Conversely, normal distributions were reported for four of the seven age groups for both the KVPT-D and KVPT-C for boys. Details on which age groups were normally distributed are not provided. Little detail is given as to the nature of other distributions, except general statements that skewness seems more apparent for older children and that there could be restriction of range in KVPT-C2/KVPT-C3 scores for younger ages as well as KVPT-D scores for older ages.

Providing more details about the data would be very useful. It is noteworthy that the KVPT evaluates numerous features, yet scores are limited to totals, rotation/nonrotation errors, and single/multiple feature set size errors. Distribution data on the feature errors subsumed by these categories would be very useful and may help in determining why all of the data were not normally distributed. It is also noteworthy that significant effects were found for both age and gender on the KVPT, with less errors occurring with advancing age and girls having significantly more rotation errors than boys. However, it would be useful to see the post hoc comparison tests for the significant age factor.

Another concern is that the purpose of the KVPT is to assess perceptual processes in children, yet pilot studies were done with other age groups. Normative data are given for the following age groups: 5 years, 6 years, 7 years, 8 years, 9 years, 10 years, 11 years, 18–22 years, and 55–91 years. Sample sizes for age groups beyond 11 years were far too small and far too compounded (e.g., 55–91 years of age) to come to any clear extension of the findings to respondents older than 11 years of age. However, forthcoming research appears to be promising, suggesting that stroke patients perform significantly more poorly on all KVPT subtests than both hospitalized and nonhospitalized controls (Strenger, 1998).

SUMMARY. The KVPT is a good measure of visual perceptual skills for children aged 5 to 11 years. Addressing the transpositional, informational, and configurational aspects of Zusne's model is a valuable way of adding to the literature on Gestalt principles.

REVIEWER'S REFERENCE

Strenger, V. E. (1998). Use of the Kent Visual Perceptual Test in neuropsychological assessment of the stroke patient [abstract]. *Dissertation Abstracts International, 60* (1-B), 0377.

[127]

Khan-Lewis Phonological Analysis—Second Edition.

Purpose: "Recommended for use in the diagnosis and description of articulation or phonological disorders."
Population: Ages 2-0 to 21-11.
Publication Dates: 1986–2002.
Acronym: KLPA-2.
Scores, 11: 5 Reduction Processes (Deletion of Final Consonants, Syllable Reduction, Stopping of Fricatives and Affricates, Cluster Simplification, Liquid Simplification), 3 Place and Manner Processes (Velar Fronting, Palatal Fronting, Deaffrication), 2 Voicing Processes (Initial Voicing, Final Devoicing), Total Score.
Administration: Individual.
Price Data, 2002: $114.95 per kit including manual (2002, 206 pages), 25 analysis forms, Sound Change booklet, and 25 Phonological Summary and Progress Report worksheets; $59.95 per manual; $21.95 per analysis forms.
Time: [10–30] minutes.
Comments: Revision of the Khan-Lewis Phonological Analysis (KLPA), old edition still available; supplements the Goldman-Fristoe Test of Articulation—Second Edition (GFTA-2; 15:109); scores based on responses to the Sounds-in-Words subtest of the GFTA-2; to complete the KLPA-2, examiner needs both complete KLPA-2 kit and complete GFTA-2 kit.
Authors: Linda M. L. Khan and Nancy P. Lewis.
Publisher: AGS Publishing.
Cross References: See T5:1394 (13 references) and T4:1356 (1 reference); for a review by Donald E. Mowrer of an earlier edition, see 10:164.

Review of the Khan-Lewis Phonological Analysis—Second Edition by CARLOS INCHAURRALDE, Professor of Linguistics and Psychologist, University of Zaragoza, Zaragoza, Spain:

DESCRIPTION. The Khan-Lewis Phonological Analysis—Second Edition (KLPA-2) is a test for analysis of overall phonological process usage that was designed as a companion tool to the Goldman-Fristoe Test of Articulation—Second Edition (GFTA-2; 15:109) and makes use of 53 target words also elicited by GFTA-2 Sounds-in-Words, in order to provide further diagnostic information. The test analyzes 10 phonological processes in the speech of participants aged 2 to 21 years. These processes are categorized into three areas: Reduction Processes (Deletion of Final Consonants, Syllable Reduction, Stopping of Fricatives and Affricates, Cluster Simplification, Liquid Simplification), Place and Manner Processes (Velar Fronting, Palatal Fronting, Deaffrication), and Voicing Processes (Initial Voicing, Final Devoicing). The materials provided include a manual, 25 Analysis Forms, a Sound Change Booklet, and a pad of 25 Phonological Summary and Progress Report worksheets. To complete the test, the examiner also needs a complete GFTA-2 kit, which is sold separately. The KLPA-2 should be used after administration of the GFTA-2 Sounds-in-Words, which normally takes from 5 to 15 minutes. The typical time required to complete the KLPA-2 is between 10 and 30 minutes.

This test is to be administered by speech-language pathologists with training in phonetics and in the nature of articulation and phonological disorders. It starts with the recording of identifying information for the individual examined and the calculation of his or her chronological age. The examiner then elicits the 53 GFTA-2 Sounds-in-Words stimulus words and transcribes phonetically the responses, marking sound changes in the Analysis Form. Raw scores are obtained by counting the number of checkmarks in each of the columns corresponding to the 10 phonological processes analyzed. The 10 subtotals are then summed, giving a Total Raw Score. Raw scores can later be converted to standard scores, percentile ranks, and test-age equivalents.

DEVELOPMENT. The KLPA-2 is the first revision of the original Khan-Lewis Phonological Analysis (KLPA), developed to identify the phonological processes present in several types of errors, including those related to phonemic context. The original idea was to develop a companion phonological process analysis for the GFTA, extending the assessment provided by that test. The GFTA provided an efficient method for recording phoneme production, but the KLPA is argued to be more responsive to the needs of clinicians because it provides a more detailed analysis of phonological processes involved in errors. In addition, the GFTA and the KLPA can be used together, in a single administration, with minimal additional scoring and analysis time.

The second edition of the GFTA was published in Spring 2000, and this called for a revision of the KLPA as well, with the goal of obtaining a more user-friendly product than in the first edition.

There were several changes: The number of phonological processes scored decreased from 15 to 10, the KLPA Analysis Form was improved with a realignment and new categorization of phonological processes, a Sound Change Booklet (which makes the Analysis Form easier to use) was created, and a Phonological Summary and Progress Report (as a separate form) was also introduced for the first time.

TECHNICAL. The standardization of this test is linked to the standardization of the GFTA-2. The same stimuli are used for both tests, and the collection of data for the development of national norms for the GFTA-2 Sounds-in-Words and for the revision of the Khan-Lewis Phonological Analysis took place at the same time. In the standardization administration procedures, participants were prompted to identify pictures and the examiner recorded the responses with misarticulations.

The general plan for standardization was very comprehensive. Two stratified random samples of 1,175 females and 1,175 males were used, and special care was taken in selecting samples that were representative in terms of race or ethnic group, geographical region, and socioeconomic status. The distribution in these parameters was selected to match the U.S. Census data from the *Current Population Survey, March 1998* (Bureau of the Census, 1998). The sample was subdivided into age groups (1-year intervals from 2 to 8:11 years, 2-year intervals from 9 to 14:11 years, and then a single interval from 15 to 21:11 years) to facilitate the analysis of the data. Geographical distribution of the sample was accomplished by means of a distinction between four regions (Northeast, North Central, South, and West). Socioeconomic status was assumed on the basis of the examinee's mother, father, or parent guardian's education. This is acknowledged to be questionable by the authors themselves when they say in the manual that "Recent research has shown correct consonant production not to be significantly related to mother's education level" (p. 55). However, they also assume that the parents' education is a variable that can be considered, on the grounds of an easier collection of information. Race or ethnic group was categorized according to the ethnic groups derived from U.S. Census classifications. All these groups had a distribution in the sample that matched the distribution in the U.S. population.

A coding system of the GFTA-2 data was then developed for misarticulated responses, so that the resulting data could be used in the Khan-Lewis Phonological Analysis system. This coding system was to be reflected later in a scoring system.

Internal reliability estimates were calculated using coefficient alpha (Crocker & Algina, 1986), which was very high in all age ranges (>.95 in most of the cases; the only value below .90 was .89, for male participants between 13 and 14 years of age). The median reliability coefficients were .96 for females and .95 for males. For these reliability measures, the KLPA-2 has a median Standard Error of Measurement of 3.0 standard score points for females and 3.4 points for males. This is equivalent to one-fifth standard deviation of the standard score.

Test-retest reliability, valuable for knowing about the temporal stability of the test, was evaluated using a smaller sample of 53 examinees, who underwent two separate tests (interval ranged from 1–34 days). The results were then marked by the same examiner in both tests. The majority (167 out of 250) of the phonological processes in each target had a 100% test-retest consistency rate. Nearly all the rest of the processes had a value higher than .90.

A sample of 34 examinees was used for the calculation of interrater reliability. The results were similar to those of test-retest reliability (177 out of 250 had a 100% value, and except for 3 examinees, the rest had an agreement index higher than .90).

Both content and construct validity evidence was reported for the KLPA-2. Content validity is demonstrated by having 23 of the 25 sounds recognized as Standard American English included in the GFTA-2 and they are, therefore, available for sampling and analysis in the KLPA-2. However, it should also be pointed out that phonological process usage is only addressed through the production of single words and there is no provision for that kind of analysis in connected speech. Construct validity evidence is also presented based on the fact that total raw scores change with age according to the developmental expectations (fewer errors in older individuals). This type of validity is also based on the relationship of this test with the GFTA-2. Both tests have a high correlation in total raw scores (so high, in fact, that it is argued that the KLPA-2 can be considered to be an extension of the GFTA-2).

COMMENTARY. This test has the advantage of not requiring much time for its administration, provided that the GFTA-2 is also used, because the target words are the same as those in the GFTA-2 Sounds-in-Words subtest. However, the fact that it is so heavily dependent on the GFTA-2 is also one of its weaknesses because both tests have to be used together. It is not possible to administer it without using the GFTA-2 Sounds-in-Words. At the same time, although the analysis forms and other accompanying materials have a very clear layout and administration is not complicated, there is always the need, as is customary with any test measuring phonological processes, for the examiner to have training in phonological discrimination. This requirement, however, is very clearly stated in the manual.

The rationale behind the test is not explained with much detail, although there is mention of the different approaches that have taken place (e.g., traditional, distinctive-feature, context-based). Also, there is an important reference to the evidence shown in the literature of the few differences in overall phonological profile in single word production and connected speech production, which justifies the usage of single words as targets for identification of phonological errors.

SUMMARY. This is a test that has undergone a comprehensive standardization process and has clear materials for its administration. Provided that the examiner has the suitable training, and assuming that the GFTA-2 is administered jointly with it, the KLPA-2 can be a useful tool for identifying the kind of phonological errors that children produce. If it is unclear from the start whether the child's production is good or not, the joint administration of the GFTA-2 and the KLPA-2 is recommended because the former identifies possible faulty production patterns and the latter helps identify in more detail the types of mistakes that are made.

REVIEWER'S REFERENCES

Crocker, L., & Algina, J. (1986). *Introduction to classical and modern test theory.* New York: CBS College Publishing.
Current Population Survey, March 1998. (1998). Washington, DC: Bureau of the Census.

Review of the Khan-Lewis Phonological Analysis—Second Edition by STEVEN LONG, Assistant Professor, Speech Pathology and Audiology, Marquette University, Milwaukee, WI:

DESCRIPTION. The Khan-Lewis Phonological Analysis—Second Edition (KLPA-2) is a "companion tool" used to produce a phonological process analysis of phonetic data taken from the

Goldman-Fristoe Test of Articulation—Second Edition (GFTA-2, Goldman & Fristoe, 2000; 15:109). Users of the KLPA-2 must therefore also possess the GFTA-2. The KLPA-2 is solely a supplementary analysis; it has no test stimuli of its own. It consists of an analysis form and a manual containing procedures for scoring and normative data for the KLPA-2 raw score. The norms are derived from the GFTA-2 standardization sample and thus are suitable for speakers of Standard American English in the age range 2–21 years.

Unlike an articulation test such as the GFTA-2, which does not score every phoneme contained in a target word, the KLPA-2 takes into account *all* sound changes that occur. This requires the examiner to record the entire response of the speaker, by writing out each word production phonetically or by marking up the phonetic transcription printed on the analysis form. Either way, the KLPA-2 requires training in broad phonetic transcription. Distortion errors are not analyzed as phonological processes and therefore are ignored in the calculation of the KLPA-2 raw score.

To generate the raw score, the examiner must review all target words and note on the analysis form those sound changes that represent "developmental phonological processes" (manual, p. 39). Those processes, 10 in number, are divided into three groups: reduction processes (Deletion of Final Consonants, Syllable Reduction, Stopping of Fricatives and Affricates, Cluster Simplification, and Liquid Simplification); place and manner processes (Velar Fronting, Palatal Fronting, and Deaffrication); and voicing processes (Initial Voicing and Final Devoicing). Only sound changes analyzed as one of these 10 processes are counted toward the raw score. Other sound changes involving consonants and all vowel changes are merely noted on the analysis form. To simplify the process of identifying both scored and unscored phonological processes, the KLPA-2 offers three procedures. First, the analysis form contains a grid that shows which of the 10 developmental processes are applicable for each target word and provides check boxes to record occurrences. Second, a Sound Change booklet included with the KLPA-2 shows a matrix for each target word that identifies the target consonants in that word, all possible sound changes that could occur to those consonants, and what the resulting phonological process would be in each instance. Third, the

manual contains the same matrix as the Sound Change booklet but displays the information sorted by target sound rather than by target word. All three procedures are designed to save time and improve scoring accuracy. They do not teach phonological concepts but rather assume that the examiner possesses this knowledge prior to using the KLPA-2.

The time needed to complete the KLPA-2 analysis form is estimated in the manual at 10–30 minutes, depending on the severity of the sample. This does not include the time needed to administer the GFTA-2 (about 15 minutes). It also does not include the time—another 5–10 minutes—that would be needed to complete an optional summary form used to construct a phonetic inventory by sound position and to calculate percentage frequencies for each of the 10 developmental processes.

DEVELOPMENT. The KLPA-2 is the first revision of the KLPA, originally published in 1986. The revision was necessitated by the 2000 publication of the GFTA-2, which, because of changes to the target words, rendered the original KLPA obsolete. The new version reduces the number of scored phonological processes from 15 to 10 on the grounds that the processes removed occurred infrequently and failed to show a developmental trend. All other changes in the KLPA-2 pertain to the analysis forms and materials designed to help complete those forms. What was a quite bulky single form in the original KLPA has been replaced by two considerably streamlined forms in the KLPA-2. The developmental phonological processes have been grouped into three categories and are arranged in an order that reflects their impact on speech intelligibility.

The overall rationale and design of the KLPA-2 are the same as its predecessor. The instrument is intended as a supplement to the GFTA-2, to provide a more thorough phonological description and aid in the planning of intervention, especially for children with more extensive error patterns that serve to compromise their intelligibility. In principle, the combination of the GFTA-2 and KLPA-2 provide an evaluation and assessment tool that can address the multiple needs of speech-language pathologists: a norm-referenced score that can qualify a child for clinical services; a criterion-referenced phonological assessment that can help determine intervention goals; and an instrument that can be administered repeatedly to measure the effects of that intervention.

TECHNICAL. The normative scores for the KLPA-2 were obtained by re-analyzing the data from the standardization sample of the GFTA-2. Hence comments made in the *Mental Measurements Yearbook* review of the GFTA-2 also apply to the KLPA-2 (Long, 2003). To summarize these comments, the sample was not evaluated for use of dialect nor are the norms tabulated by ethnicity or region. This makes it impossible to compare a dialect speaker to his or her linguistic peers.

All norm-referenced measures of developing phonological skill must adapt to the fact that, beyond the age of 4, the distribution of accuracy scores becomes highly skewed. By that age, most children produce speech that is highly accurate, with a few residual errors occurring on sounds such as strident /s/, liquids /r/ and /l/, and consonant clusters. In the case of the KLPA-2, the problem of skewing is even greater than with other articulation tests where the raw score is based on the number of speech errors. This is because the KLPA-2 raw score is based on the number of phonological processes, many of which are suppressed by the great majority of children at very young ages (Grunwell, 1987). As a result, the standard scores of the KLPA-2 must be used cautiously and always in comparison to the percentile rank scores. For example, the usual interpretation that a standard score of 70 (mean of 100, standard deviation of 15) places a child in the bottom 2%–3% of the standardization sample is not correct on the KLPA-2. This point is made clearly and emphatically in the test manual discussion but does not appear anywhere in the table of norms.

The KLPA-2 is fundamentally an analysis tool. However, the analyses produced by the KLPA-2 can only be as good as the accuracy of the phonetic transcriptions obtained from the GFTA-2. The KLPA-2 assumes that test users possess a level of transcription skill comparable to those clinicians who participated in the collection of standardization data. Unfortunately, there is no way to compare the two, such as a training tape to assess the user's skill. A similar problem exists for the scoring procedure of the KLPA-2. The test manual reports acceptable values for test-retest and interexaminer reliability, mostly at .90 or higher for an administration window from 0–34 days. Two cautions apply, however. First, the three—and only three—examiners who participated in the reliability studies are not identified and therefore cannot be evaluated for how well they represent the typical KLPA-2 user. It seems likely that many test users will be less proficient at transcription and phonological process identification than the individuals selected by the test developers. Second, the authors do not report the severity of the samples compared for reliability purposes. One hopes that they were samples with numerous errors, as this is the clinical population most targeted by the KLPA-2. The reliability of perceptual judgments is greatly inflated when the sample(s) to be judged contain mostly normal behaviors (Kearns & Simmons, 1988).

COMMENTARY. The KLPA-2 is designed to provide users with the clinical insight that can be gained only through phonological analysis of a speech sample but without the huge investment of time and effort that such analysis ordinarily requires. In most respects, the KLPA-2 achieves its goal, though anyone considering the instrument should carefully assess their own skill in phonetic transcription and knowledge of phonological process categories to ensure their skills are adequate to the task.

Like the GFTA-2 on which it is based, the KLPA-2 can be used as a norm-referenced test to help in qualifying children for clinical services. To use the KLPA-2, one must first administer the GFTA-2. In view of this, clinicians are likely to have two norm-referenced scores, one from the GFTA-2 and one from the KLPA-2. Surprisingly, the issue of how the *two* scores should be interpreted is not addressed in the test manual. The same standardization sample served as the source of the norms for both instruments, which suggests that they should yield the same clinical interpretation. However, there are differences in how the GFTA-2 and KLPA-2 are scored, the former using a simple error count, the latter a count of phonological process occurrence. A child with numerous distortion errors might achieve a GFTA-2 score that identifies him as speech impaired but those same errors would be ignored on the KLPA-2. This difference in outcome is understandable, as the KLPA-2 is targeted at the identification of phonological disorders whereas the GFTA-2 is sensitive to both phonetic and phonological problems. Some discussion of this point is warranted in the KLPA-2 manual.

Clinicians must take special care to apply the KLPA-2 norms appropriately. This new version allows examiners to express performance as a standard score or a test-age equivalent score, but both should be avoided in clinical use because of the test's nonnormal distribution of scores. Standard scores are provided for use in research, where their statistical properties are essential.

The strength of the KLPA-2 is in assessment, the identification of a child's strengths and weaknesses that can be used as the basis for intervention planning. If both analysis forms are completed, there is information available about a child's phonetic inventory, phonemic inventory, and phonological processes or patterns of sound change. Interpreted wisely, such information should enable clinicians to evaluate the nature of a child's disorder and to render appropriate recommendations for treatment. However, the wisdom needed for these judgments must lie within the clinician using the test. The KLPA-2 itself contains no procedure for rating the severity of a phonological disorder, for estimating its impact on speech intelligibility, or for generating treatment recommendations based on a particular model of remediation.

SUMMARY. The KLPA-2 can be used as a norm-referenced instrument to document the existence of an articulation impairment, though it is time-consuming if used only for this purpose. Its more time-efficient application is in the identification of phonological patterns that could be applied in treatment planning, especially with individuals who demonstrate severe articulation disorders. A comparable test that is based on a more specific remediation model is the Assessment of Phonological Processes—Revised (APP-R; T6:209). The other option to be considered is computer software designed to yield phonological analyses of input phonetic data.

REVIEWER'S REFERENCES

Goldman, R., & Fristoe, M. (2000). Goldman-Fristoe Test of Articulation—Second Edition. Circle Pines, MN: American Guidance Service, Inc.
Grunwell, P. (1987). *Clinical phonology* (2nd ed.). Baltimore, MD: Williams & Wilkins.
Kearns, K. P. & Simmons, N. N. (1988). Interobserver reliability and perceptual ratings: More than meets the ear. *Journal of Speech and Hearing Research, 31,* 131–136.
Long, S. H. (2003). [Review of the Goldman Fristoe Test of Articulation—Second Edition]. In B. S. Plake, J. C. Impara, & R. A. Spies (Eds.), *The fifteenth mental measurements yearbook* (pp. 410–413). Lincoln, NE: Buros Institute of Mental Measurements.

[128]

Khatena-Torrance Creative Perception Inventory.

Purpose: Developed as measures of creative personality.
Population: Age 10–adult.
Publication Dates: 1976–1998.

Acronym: KTCPI.
Administration: Group.
Price Data, 2001: $57.65 per starter set including instruction manual (1998, 96 pages), 35 SAM checklists, 35 WKOPAY? checklists, and 35 scoring worksheets; $32.75 per instruction manual; $38 per package of 35 SAM checklists, 35 WKOPAY? checklists, and 35 scoring worksheets; $18.90 per specimen set including instruction manual (abridged), 1 SAM checklist, and 1 WKOPAY? checklist.
Time: (10–20) minutes per checklist.
Comments: Includes 2 self-report checklists designed to identify candidates for creativity programs.
Publisher: Scholastic Testing Service, Inc.

a) WHAT KIND OF PERSON ARE YOU?
Purpose: Designed to "yield an index of the individual's disposition or motivation to function in creative ways."
Acronym: WKOPAY?
Scores: 5 factors: Acceptance of Authority, Self-Confidence, Inquisitiveness, Awareness of Others, Disciplined Imagination.
Author: E. Paul Torrance.

b) SOMETHING ABOUT MYSELF.
Purpose: Designed as an autobiographical "screening device for the identification of creative people."
Acronym: SAM.
Scores: 6 factors: Environmental Sensitivity, Initiative, Self-Strength, Intellectuality, Individuality, Artistry.
Author: Joe Khatena.
Cross References: See T5:1396 (5 references); for reviews by David L. Bolton and William Steve Lang of a previous edition, see 13:168 (2 references); for a review by Philip E. Vernon of an earlier edition, see 9:569 (3 references).

Review of the Khatena-Torrance Creative Perception Inventory by CAROLYN M. CALLAHAN, Professor of Educational Psychology, University of Virginia, Charlottesville, VA:

DESCRIPTION. The Khatena-Torrance Creative Perception Inventory (KTCPI) is composed of two self-report checklists, What Kind of Person Are You? (WKOPAY?) and Something About Myself (SAM). The tests are described in the manual as tests of creative self-perceptions, and the manual identifies purposes of the checklists to include: identification of school- or college-age creative individuals for purposes of research or placement in gifted programs. A second specified purpose is for use in business or industrial settings in the identification of individuals who can contribute creative ideas and to maximize creative functioning of an individual through use of the instruments for diagnostic assessment. The authors state that the two checklists are measures of "relatively different dimensions" of the creative personality, but advise that one can add and average the standard scores from the two checklists. Although group or individual administration is acceptable for those 10 years or older, the checklists are to be individually administered to children between the ages of 6 and 9.

The WKOPAY? presents a series of paired statements, and the examinee is directed to check the statement that best describes his or her characteristics. The SAM requires the examinee to consider a list of statements and check all statements descriptive of himself or herself. A scoring key for the WKOPAY? provides guidance in assigning one point to each "right" answer. An individual receives one point for each item checked on the SAM. Norms tables provide standard score equivalents for total summed scores (T-scores and stanine scores) for both total scores and subscales of the WKOPAY? (Acceptance of Authority, Self-Confidence, Inquisitiveness, Awareness of Others, Disciplined Imagination), and the SAM (Environmental Sensitivity, Initiative, Self-Strength, Intellectuality, Individuality, and Artistry). Norms are provided for "regular subjects" and for gifted students, but no description of the gifted population is provided.

DEVELOPMENT. Both instruments were developed based on the assumption that biographical instruments are useful in the identification of creative talent. The authors contend that "the individual has a psychological self comprised of subselves relative to creative and noncreative ways of behaving" (instruction manual, pp. 5–6) that are reflected in the WKOPAY?. The SAM was developed based on the rationale that "creative functioning is reflected in the personality characteristics of the individual, in the way he thinks or the kind of thinking strategies he employs, and in the products that emerge as a result of his creative strivings" (instruction manual, p. 6). Items for the WKOPAY? were derived from a survey of the literature by one of the authors. The 84 characteristics in this review were reduced to 66 characteristics assumed to differentiate between more and less creative persons. The results of a Q-sort using creative productivity as a criterion were used to create pairs of characteristics representing high

and low creativity (I give my whole attention to what I do/I am respectful, polite). The authors report that the items were selected for the SAM based on previous research findings and hypotheses relating to creativity, but no definition of creativity used in the selection of the research was included in the review. The initial 100 items were reduced to 74 by an unspecified process, and then the number was reduced to 50 by combining items that correlated more than .30 or "appeared" to provide the same information as other items. Items include both items that reflect judgments of self (I am imaginative) and those that are descriptive of past behaviors (I have created a new dance or song).

TECHNICAL.

Reliability. Interrater reliability of total scores on both instruments is very high (r = .97 to .99). Internal consistency of the WKOPAY? as measured by the split-half measure ranges from r = .75 to .98 on samples of college students. An estimate of split half reliability for the WKOPAY? on a sample of "regular students" in Grades 1–12 was .59 and for gifted students across Grades 1–12 was .66. Test-retest reliability reported on adult college age samples ranged from .71 to .97 for periods of 1 to 6 weeks.

Split-half estimates of reliability on the SAM ranged from .68 to .96 on adolescent and adult populations. The split-half estimate on a regular student population (Grades 1–12) was .80 and on a gifted population was .79. Test-retest reliability on college-age students was reported as ranging from .77 to .98 for a period of 1 day to 4 weeks. No stability data are provided for school age children on either measure, and no reliability data is provided for subscale scores.

Validity. Validity is based on explicit statements of the purposes of a test that provide a clear conceptual framework for the construct measured and evidence that the test fulfills those purposes. The manual for the WKOPAY? and the SAM provides considerable data on studies using the checklist, but the lack of a clear definition of the construct of creativity as measured by this instrument and apparent relationships between the evidence presented and the proposed uses of the test limit interpretation of validity of the instruments. There are considerable data from a variety of studies that correlate the checklists with other nonbiographical assessments of creativity with moderate correlations and a small but significant correlation with another self-perception instrument (.14–.18). The correlations between the two checklists on college age adult populations ranged from .36–.38. These data provide moderate evidence of concurrent validity. Evidence of construct validity is difficult to interpret because of the absence of a clear definition or theoretical framework for the creativity construct assessed. Groups identified as high creatives on two creative productivity measures (by the same authors) scored significantly higher on the SAM than those identified as low creative. In other studies there were mixed results when subscores on the Torrance Tests of Creative Thinking were used as criterion measures. Other data on the Runner Studies of Attitude Patterns and the Style of Learning and Thinking also produced mixed results without clear interpretation.

If one of the purposes of the instrument is for identification of students as gifted and talented, one would expect some predictive validity evidence. Aside from the presentation of one study with concurrent data comparing gifted students (not clearly defined as to what dimension of giftedness had been used in the identification of those students) and "regular students," no such data were presented. Further, no predictive validity data were provided on creative productivity of adults.

Nearly all reliability and validity data for the SAM and WKOPAY? were collected before 1980. *Normative data.* Norms are provided for total scores; however, the data all appear to have been collected in the 1970s with no updated norms collected or presented. Norms for Grades 1–12 are all presented in one table with no further breakdown by age or grade. Further, although norms are provided for subscores, no reliability data are available on subscores. Standard errors of measurement are not provided for the total scores or the subscales.

COMMENTARY. Reliance on self-report relating to the behaviors that require considerable self-knowledge and reflection is a very tenuous assessment strategy, and thus, requires considerable attention to the establishment of both reliability and validity of perceptions. Although some of the reliability data are adequate, absence of stability data on such an instrument is a serious shortcoming. Dated norms and dated reliability and validity evidence are also problematic. More important, the vague presentation of the constructs and consequent ambiguity regarding the nature of what is being measured by the Khatena-

Torrance Creative Perception Inventory or the two checklists presents the most serious shortcoming of the instrument.

SUMMARY. Use of the Khatena-Torrance Creative Perception Inventory should be limited to research purposes or to stimulate discussion of the traits underlying the construct of creativity. The dated norms and unclear evidence of validity would make it unsuitable as a diagnostic tool or measure to be used in the identification of gifted students.

Review of the Khatena-Torrance Creative Perception Inventory by GREGORY SCHRAW, Professor, Department of Educational Psychology, University of Nevada—Las Vegas, Las Vegas, NV:

DESCRIPTION AND DEVELOPMENT. The Khatena-Torrance Creative Perception Inventory (KTCPI) provides two separate measures of creative self-perception. The What Kind Of Person Are You? (WKOPAY?) scale, assesses the extent to which an individual reports creative and noncreative ways of behaving. The Something About Myself (SAM) scale assesses strategies and characteristics associated with creativity. The two measures are assumed to provide independent assessments of the creative personality.

Both tests have a number of factors that load on the test. The WKOPAY? test contains five factors, including Acceptance of Authority, Self-Confidence, Inquisitiveness, Awareness of Others, and Disciplined Imagination. The SAM contains six factors, including Environmental Sensitivity, Initiative, Self-Strength, Intellectuality, Individuality, and Artistry. Normative data in the manual reveal that most of these factors are not significantly correlated.

Both the WKOPAY? and SAM include 50 items, which consist of two options. For example, Item 37 on the KTCPI includes the following options: "I am sure of myself" and "I'm timid." The test taker selects one of these two options, which is compared to a scoring key in the manual.

The tests can be group administered to individuals over the age of 10, and administered individually to children between the ages of 6 and 9. Each test requires 10 to 20 minutes to complete, but has no time limit. Test scores range from 0 to 50. A scoring key is included in the manual indicating whether a response is scored as a 1 or 0. Scores of 1 correspond to responses more characteristic of high-creativity individuals.

TECHNICAL. The KTCPI is accompanied by a 96-page manual, complete with information about administration, scoring, reliability and validity, interpretation, development, and standardization of the instruments. The manual is clearly written and concise. There is extended discussion for both the WKOPAY? and SAM tests regarding criterion-related validity. However, most of these studies were conducted in the 1960s and 1970s. In addition, virtually all of the studies are correlational in nature, in which the KTCPI is correlated with other self-report instruments. There was no study that examined whether the KTCPI predicted observable creative performance in any domain. The manual indicates that the KTCPI is correlated moderately (e.g., .40 to .60) with other personality instruments, though there is no evidence that it is related to artistic performance or achievement.

The manual provides a concise but thorough discussion of reliability and validity. Internal consistency for the overall test typically exceeded .80, although reliability is not reported for the individual factors from the WKOPAY? It is likely that the individual factors have low reliability (i.e., < .60). Construct validity for the SAM was assessed in two ways. The first was to perform an exploratory factor analysis of the full scale. This yielded 16 factors that explained 53% of variation in the sample data. The second was to compare performance on the test with gifted and regular students. Gifted students consistently scored higher on the test, although the effect size usually appeared to be in the .20 to .40 standard deviation range. These results suggest that gifted students report different personality characteristics than regular students, although it is unclear whether these differences are attributable to creative personality characteristics. In contrast, correlations between the WKOPAY? and the Torrance Tests of Creative Thinking reveal relatively low correlations, typically .40 or below. These correlations suggest that self-reported creative characteristics are not strongly correlated with performance on a creative thinking test.

COMMENTARY. The strengths of the KTCPI include (a) easy administration and scoring, (b) a well-written manual, (c) high reliability, and (d) an adequate amount of construct validity data. Weaknesses include a lack of predictive validity with creative thinking or measures of cre-

ative performance. One major concern is that recent research suggests that personality characteristics are not predictive of creative thinking or performance (Csikszentmihalyi, 1996). Although the attempt to assess creative dispositions is laudable, the reliability and validity of scores from these instruments remains largely unproven.

SUMMARY. Overall, the KTCPI provides a quick measure of potential correlates of the creative personality. It provides specific information about two major subscales, the What Kind Of Person Are You? scale, which assesses the extent to which an individual reports creative and noncreative ways of behaving, and the Something About Myself scale, which assesses strategies and characteristics associated with creativity. These indices may provide useful information about personality characteristics relayed to creative thinking; thus, they may serve some usefulness in screening for gifted and talented programs.

REVIEWER'S REFERENCE

Csikszentmihalyi, M. (1996). *Creativity: Flow and the psychology of discovery and invention.* HarperCollins Publishers: New York.

[129]

Kindergarten Diagnostic Instrument— Second Edition.

Purpose: "Designed to assess developmental readiness skills in children."

Population: Children ages 4–6 years or older children with known or suspected developmental delays.

Publication Date: 2000.

Acronym: KDI-2.

Scores, 22: 13 subtest scores (Body Awareness, Concept Mastery, Form/Letter Identification, General Information, Gross Motor, Memory for Sentences, Number Skills, Phonemic Awareness, Verbal Associations, Visual Discrimination, Visual Memory, Visual-Motor Integration, Vocabulary), 6 subskills (Form Identification, Letter Identification, Verbal Associations—Similarities, Verbal Associations—Opposites, Visual Discrimination—Similarities, Visual Discrimination—Differences), Nonverbal Factor Score, Verbal Factor Score, Total Test Score.

Administration: Individual.

Price Data, 2004: $175 per complete test kit including administration manual (146 pages), 3 stimulus booklets, 13 1-inch wooden blocks, and 25 student response booklets in a carrying case; $495 per assessment bundle including complete test kit, 50 student response booklets, 50 My Kindergarten Fun Books-II (40 pages), and scoring program for Windows; $32 per 25 student response booklets; $50 per 25 My Kindergarten Fun Books-II; $275 per KDI-2 Scoring Program for Windows (one-time license fee, additional cost applies for sites screening more than 300 children annually); $30 per training video; quantity discounts available on all items.

Time: (35–45) minutes.

Comments: KDI-2 Scoring Program for Windows stores students' pre-kindergarten and kindergarten data, generates local schoolwide norms, assesses performance compared to local norms, generates individual reports, test-retest reports; contact publisher for KDI-2 Scoring Program system requirements.

Authors: Daniel C. Miller (KDI-2, Training Video, My Kindergarten Fun Book-II) and Michie A. Miller (Training Video, My Kindergarten Fun Book-II).

Publisher: KIDS, Inc.

Review of the Kindergarten Diagnostic Instrument—Second Edition by GLEN P. AYLWARD, Professor of Pediatrics and Psychiatry, Southern Illinois University School of Medicine, Springfield, IL:

DESCRIPTION AND DEVELOPMENT. The Kindergarten Diagnostic Instrument—Second Edition (KDI-II) is a screening instrument designed to assess developmental readiness skills in children 4 to 6 years of age. The original KDI was developed in the mid-1970s as part of a doctoral dissertation. Ten years later, a revised version was standardized on a sample of 1,391 children. The current KDI-Second Edition was restandardized in 1999, using 893 children. The test contains 13 subtests and reportedly requires 35–45 minutes to administer. Individual or group administration (using four or five screening stations for the latter) is possible. No special training is required, except that the examiner needs to have experience working with young children. A prescriptive, 41-page handbook, *My Kindergarten Fun Book,* was designed to complement the KDI-II. The authors indicate that the combination of the two components enables users to pinpoint areas of concern (via use of the KDI-II) and help remediate weaknesses in basic developmental skills (*Fun Book*). A computer-scoring program disk is included.

The authors indicate that the KDI-II was designed to measure processes underlying specific skills rather than the specific skills themselves. The KDI-II subtests are: (a) Body Awareness (a draw-a-person task), (b) Concept Mastery* (knowledge of basic concepts such as left, right, most, bottom), (c) Form/Letter Identification* (basic shapes, letter identification skills), (d) General Information* (knowledge of basic facts), (e) Gross Motor (jumping, catching, balance), (f) Memory for Sentences* (formerly called Auditory Memory; recall of strings of words), (g) Number Skills* (number recognition, counting, simple mental computations), (h) Phonemic Awareness* (rhyming), (i) Verbal Associations* (verbal opposites, similarities), (j) Visual Discrimination (discriminate shapes, match similar and different shapes), (k) Visual Memory (short term visual memory for pictures), (l) Vocabulary* (knowledge of word meanings), and (m) Visual-Motor Integration (copying shapes with a pencil). Eight subtests comprise a Verbal factor (indicated above with an asterisk), and five load on a Nonverbal factor. Stepwise multiple regression has produced an abbreviated or short form that contains five subtests, accounting for 86% of the variance: Body Awareness, Concept Mastery, Form/Letter Identification, General Information, and Gross Motor. The authors indicate that future research is necessary to determine the predictive utility of the short form in comparison to the entire KDI-II.

Raw scores (range 0–36, depending on subtest) are converted to *T*-scores, and there is a "*T*-score to Percentile Conversion Table." Raw scores are summed to produce the Verbal and Nonverbal Factor Scores (maximum raw scores of 117 and 83, respectively), which in turn are combined to generate a Total Test Score (maximum score = 200). These composites also have corresponding *T*-scores. Of note is the fact that norms are combined for children 4 to 6 years of age, and older children would most likely obtain higher scores. Because younger children would typically have lower *T*-scores, interpretation of findings is difficult. Standardization sample norms are used to determine "instructional" or "mastery" status based on raw scores on individual subtests (usually the maximum raw score is indicative of mastery). A *T*-score of <30 (2 *SD* below the mean) is considered "significantly below average," 30–39 "below average," 40–60 "average," 61–70 "above average," and >70 is considered "significantly above average." A test results summary score sheet is found in the manual; it is suggested by the authors that this be copied to use as an aid in interpreting a child's raw scores to parents or teachers. This form would be more useful if it were included in a separate packet in the test kit. However, once again, this form potentially may be misinterpreted, due to the age range problem indicated previously.

Subskill analyses for nine subtest components are included on the summary form, with a box that can be checked to indicate instructional or mastery level.

With respect to development, a pilot version of the KDI-II was given to 50 children and this resulted in a KDI-II standardization edition. This standardization edition differed from the original KDI in that items were added, combined, or deleted; graphics were redone; subtests were redesigned; and the phonemic awareness subtest was a totally new entry. The standardization sample consisted of 893 4- to 6-year-old children (no specifics on the age distribution are provided) drawn from nine sites in five states. Six sites were in the Midwest (mostly Ohio), two were South-Central, and one was located in the West. Of these children, 88% were White, 4.25% were Hispanic, 1.75% were Black, 1.75% American Indian, and 2.78% were "Other." Hence, minorities were not adequately represented, nor was there adequate geographic sampling. With respect to parental education, 12%–15% had less than a high school diploma, and approximately 40% had a greater than high school education; 12% of families had less than $15,000 annual income. This again raises questions regarding the demographic representativeness of the sample.

TECHNICAL. Much of the information regarding the psychometric qualities of the test that is included in the manual involves master's theses and doctoral dissertations on the original KDI. However, although the two-factor Verbal and Visual (Nonverbal) factor structure (accounting for 50%–53% of total variance); two test-retest reliability (interval = 3 weeks) studies ($r = .87$ & $r = .91$; range .16–.81, depending on subtest); and concurrent validity with the Woodcock-Johnson Tests of Cognitive Ability and Achievement ($r = .80$–.85), the DIAL-R ($r = .68$, range .46–.67 for domain scores), and the Gesell School Readiness Test ($r = .75$) are reported, these values might be markedly different with the KDI-II. Obviously, new studies are needed. Construct validity was measured by administering the KDI "along with the new KDI-II items" in 727/893 children, although the actual scoring method was not clear. Nonetheless, the authors report correlations ranging from $r = .58$–.98. With respect to internal consistency, Cronbach alphas ranged from .43 (Visual Discrimination) to .93 (Form/Letter To-

tal); most scores range from .60–.68. The Cronbach Alpha value for the Verbal factor was .93; for the Nonverbal Factor, .80; and for the Total Test Score, .93. Factor analysis of the KDI-II revealed a two-factor solution that accounted for 44.7% of the variance, supporting a verbal and nonverbal dichotomy. Gender differences were found, with girls obtaining a mean test score of 122.06, and boys, 116.59; females did better than males on both the nonverbal and verbal scores. With respect to age, 4-year-olds obtained a mean test score of 112.97; 5-year-olds, 118.83; and 6-year-olds, 123.31. This difference is statistically significant and underscores the need to have norms for each age group. Because the description of the standardization sample is vague, it is difficult to assess any gender x age interaction. Children with preschool experience also obtained higher mean scores than peers.

The 41-page, *My Kindergarten Fun Book* is reported to be a prescriptive handbook for children to share with parents and teachers. It consists of listings of 3–13 simple activities that are geared to address areas of weakness indicated by the KDI-II. It may be too simplistic to consider the booklet prescriptive or that the activities could adequately address these areas of deficit. Provision of general activity guidelines as well as specifics would be more helpful.

SUMMARY. There are problems in the representativeness of the subject sample with respect to ethnicity, geographic location, and other demographics. The combination of 4-, 5- and 6-year-old norms, particularly in light of age group differences, is a major shortcoming. Because of this issue, the usefulness of *T*-scores is compromised. Moreover, it is difficult to tease out specific aspects of the subject sample. Better description of the psychometric qualities of the KDI-II is also warranted. Although the overall approach is reasonable, further test development is needed. One cannot depend on theses or dissertations for such data. Finally, although this might be an issue of semantics, the title of the test includes the term "diagnostic," yet the test is a screening instrument. Use of both terms is incongruous, as in developmental testing, screening tests are indicative, *not* diagnostic.

Review of the Kindergarten Diagnostic Instrument—Second Edition by LISA F. SMITH, Associate Professor, Psychology Department, Kean University, Union, NJ:

DESCRIPTION. The Kindergarten Diagnostic Instrument—Second Edition (KDI-II) is intended to screen children ages 4–6 on developmental readiness skills. The administrative manual states, "A best practice for kindergarten screening is to identify a profile of strengths and weaknesses of each child and tailor an intervention program designed to meet the unique needs of that child" (p. 3), rather than keeping an at-risk child home for an additional year without early interventions. Special training for administrators is not required. Although ideally the KDI-II is given on an individual basis, it can be used to screen small groups of up to five children, possibly during a "kindergarten round-up." Instructions are given for group administration using a screening team approach. A shortened form of the KDI-II may be used by those districts not able to administer the full assessment; however, the shortened version must use the KDI-II scoring program to calculate the total test score. Subtests to be included on a shortened form are specified, although other combinations involving other subtests can be chosen.

The KDI-II response booklet has four sections. Section I contains identifying information. Section II is used to record observations for each subtest made by the administrator. Section III contains the directions, answer sheets, and scoring criteria for the subtests. Section IV is the summary score sheet. When opened, the front and back pages allow for straightforward data entry into the KDI-II scoring program.

In brief, the subtests are: Body Awareness, which requires the child to draw a person to assess visual-motor coordination and knowledge of body parts; Concept Mastery, which assesses basic concepts such as right and left; Form/Letter Identification, for shapes and letter identification; General Information, to determine knowledge of basic facts, such as "What does a fireman do?"; Gross Motor, related to physical coordination; Memory for Sentences, measuring oral recall; Number Skills; Verbal Associations, assessing verbal reasoning skills through use of verbal similarities and opposites; Visual Discrimination, in which a match to a stimulus measures discrimination of similarities and differences; Visual Memory, in which the child is shown a stimulus and then must choose it from a group of pictures to assess short-term memory; Visual Motor Integration, in which the child copies simple shapes to measure eye-hand coordination and fine motor skills; and Vocabulary, to measure knowledge of word meanings; and a new subtest, Phonemic Awareness, which uses rhyming words in sentences.

Directions for administration are clear. Some materials are not provided, including: large pencils, masking tape, a standard 12-inch playground rubber ball, and a stopwatch or watch with a second hand.

The items on the assessment, almost without exception, seem appropriate. Areas of concern include the final three items (out of eight items) on the Number Skills subtest that address the concepts of part/whole, addition, and subtraction. On the Verbal Associations subtest, the correct response to "What part of your body lets you move your leg?" is knee. A child could reasonably answer foot or hip but receive no credit for this item. On the Visual Discrimination subtest it is not clear whether unlimited time is allowed.

Scoring, with the exception of the Visual-Motor Integration subtest, is straightforward and is done as the KDI-II is administered. The Visual-Motor Integration subtest is scored after the administration and may take some time and practice, but detailed instructions and numerous examples are provided. The administrative manual also provides standardization sample norms in the form of *T*-scores and percentiles. *T*-score ranges are grouped into five classifications, from "Significantly Below Average" to "Significantly Above Average." As an alternative, the KDI-II scoring program (provided on disk) may be used to generate local norms and print reports. The authors recommend that districts build local data bases. However, they caution that false positives in this age group are possible and scores for those children should not be included in calculating local norms.

The *My Kindergarten Fun Book* (Second Edition) included with the KDI-II is engaging and informative. Along with information and advice for caretakers, it contains games and activities that parallel the screening tasks in the KDI-II. These may help prepare the child for kindergarten, and possibly help remediate basic skills and identify areas of concern.

DEVELOPMENT. The KDI-II is a revision of the KDI, based on feedback from KDI users and pilot tests with several samples. It takes less time to administer than the earlier version. Other changes include the addition of the Phonemic

Awareness subtest, improved scoring, and additions/deletions/modifications of items to permit administration down to age 4.

TECHNICAL. The standardization sample for the KDI-II was 893 children aged 4–6 from five locations in Ohio, and one location each in Indiana, Louisiana, Texas, and California. The majority of the sample was Caucasian (88%) with preschool experience (72%) and living with both biological parents (68%). Father's educational level, mother's educational level, prior preschool experience, child's ethnicity, and mean family income accounted for 20% of the variance of the total test score. The authors caution that school districts with different demographics should develop local norms.

For each subtest, the administration manual shows the distribution of standardization sample scores, means and standard deviations for each subtest item, Cronbach's alpha, correlations of each item to the subtest total score, and when applicable, the correlation of the KDI items to the KDI-II items. The authors state that the correlations of the item to subtest scores provide evidence of content validity and the correlation of the items on the two versions of the assessment provide evidence of construct validity; these are not technically accurate statements. For the most part, the distributions, means, and standard deviations look reasonable. There is something of a ceiling effect shown on the Gross Motor subtest. Cronbach's alpha reliabilities mostly range between .56 and .75, with a low of .43 on the Visual Discrimination subtest and a high of .93 on the Form/Letter Identification subtest. These are somewhat low; however, children this young are difficult to test in a reliable fashion.

A factor analysis yielded a two factor solution that accounted for 45% of the variance. Factor 1 is a verbal factor that accounts for 37% of the total test variance; Factor 2 is a nonverbal factor that accounts for 8% of the total test variance. The Form/Letter Identification subtest and the Number Skills subtest load on both factors. Cronbach's alpha was .93 for the total test score, .80 for the nonverbal factor, and .93 for the verbal factor.

Significant gender differences favoring females were found on the total test score, the verbal factor, the nonverbal factor, and five subtests (Body Awareness, Form/Letter Identification, Gross Motor, Visual Memory, and Visual-Motor Integration). The point differences were roughly 5 points on the total test score, 3 points on the

factors, and 1 point or less on the subtests. As such, the authors plan to reevaluate in a future study whether separate norms by gender are needed.

There were no significant age differences on the total test score. Significant differences between the 4-year-old group and the 6-year-old group on the nonverbal factor score, the Body Awareness subtest, and the Visual-Motor Integration are not surprising.

Prior preschool experience was associated with higher scores on total scores, both factor scores, and eight subtests (Form/Letter Identification, General Information, Gross Motor, Memory for Sentences, Phonemic Awareness, Visual Discrimination, Visual-Motor Integration, and Vocabulary).

From the KDI-II standardization sample, the primary caregiver for 753 children also completed the Kindergarten Inventory of Social-Emotional Tendencies (KIST; Miller & Miller, 1997). Seven percent of the KDI-II total test score is explained by three KIST domains: Sleeping and Eating Skills, Communication Skills, and Socialization Skills. This provides evidence of divergent validity; the authors indicate that additional studies with other kindergarten readiness tests are in progress.

The validity and reliability evidence presented is generally supportive. However, the data do not necessarily support the fundamental notion that the scales are the appropriate ones to have in a kindergarten diagnostic measure, or that the items measure what the scale names suggest they do. This is not to say that the scales are not the proper ones or that the items do not measure the skills, but the supporting evidence is not strong. For example, there are no studies involving kindergarten teachers rating the scales or studies providing predictive validity information for the measure.

COMMENTARY/SUMMARY. Overall, for children matching the standardization sample the KDI-II seems to be a useful instrument for kindergarten screening. Its strengths are that administration requires little training, it may be given individually or in small groups, and it takes just over half an hour to administer. In addition, the instructions are clear and the scoring is fairly straightforward. The test items seem engaging for its intended examinees. It is attractively packaged. It has an added benefit of scores being easily communicable to parents. The *My Kindergarten Fun Book* (Second Edition) provides an enjoyable guide for parents and children to work on skills.

All indications are that results of future studies will allow for additional generalizability.

REVIEWER'S REFERENCE

Miller, D. C., & Miller, M. A. (1997). Kindergarten Inventory of Social-Emotional Tendencies. Denton, TX: KIDS, Inc.

[130]

Kindergarten Inventory of Social-Emotional Tendencies.

Purpose: "Designed to screen for social skill deficits and signs of emotional immaturity in preschool and kindergarten aged children."

Population: Ages 4–6.

Publication Date: 1997.

Acronym: KIST.

Scores: 7 domains: Communication Skills, Daily Living Skills, Hyperactive/Inattentive Behaviors, Maladaptive Behaviors, Separation Anxiety Behaviors, Socialization or Peer Relation Skills, Sleeping & Eating Behaviors.

Administration: Individual.

Price Data: Available from publisher.

Time: (10) minutes.

Comments: Ratings by child's primary caregiver, or by a teacher who knows the child well.

Authors: Daniel C. Miller and Michie A. Miller.

Publisher: KIDS, Inc.

Review of the Kindergarten Inventory of Social-Emotional Tendencies by AMY M. REES, Assistant Professor of Counseling Psychology, Lewis & Clark College, Portland, OR:

DESCRIPTION. The Kindergarten Inventory of Social-Emotional Tendencies (KIST) is a behavior rating instrument designed to use as a screening, prescriptive, and research tool for assessing social skills and emotional maturity in preschool and kindergarten children aged 4–6. A primary caregiver or teacher who knows the child well completes 50 items based on observations over the past 3 months with behaviors rated as *Never, Rarely, Sometimes, Often,* or *Always*. All items start with "My Child …" and end in a string designed to vary positive (e.g., … can sit still) and negative (e.g., … is bossy with other children) responses. The items are grouped into a validity index and seven domains: Communication Skills, Daily Living Skills, Hyperactive/Inattentive Behaviors, Maladaptive Behaviors, Separation Anxiety Behaviors, Socialization or Peer Relationship Skills, and Sleeping & Eating Behaviors. The interpretation section of the manual includes brief basic recommendations for inter-ventions in each domain, and further references for educators and parents.

The KIST is a sealed, pencil-and-paper instrument with access to scoring on the inside of the protocol. Domain raw scores are calculated on the protocol. Tables in the manual are used to determine *T*-scores, confidence intervals, percentile ranks, and qualitative labels from one of four possible norm groups: 4-year-olds, 5-year-olds, 6-year-olds, and General. Qualitative labels range from "Significantly Above Average" to "Significantly Below Average" in increments corresponding to the *T*-score standard deviation. The Validity Index is a rating of consistency in item response on six item pairs. The authors encourage users to answer all items, but a system for prorating is available when there are missing items. The authors recommend that the instrument be used only qualitatively if prorating is used. A separate critical item form is included. This form includes all but one item and is grouped into the seven domains plus "Supplemental Items." This sheet is used to record items answered at the extremes of the scale (*Often, Always, Rarely, Never*).

DEVELOPMENT. Although described as a tool that can be used independently, the KIST was developed to complement an academically oriented kindergarten readiness instrument also developed by one of the authors. The suggested use of the KIST is primarily as a tool to identify young children at-risk of school difficulties due to social skills deficits and/or emotional immaturity. Neither descriptions nor operational definitions for social skills deficits and emotional immaturity are provided. The instrument is described as conceptually divided into two areas: adaptive behaviors and maladaptive behaviors. However, the items were psychometrically grouped into the domains based on results of factor analysis. Each domain contains a mixture of items that could be described as adaptive or maladaptive. In addition, definitions and titles for each of the domains varies depending on which portion of the manual one is reading. For example, "Socialization," "Social Skills or Peer Relations," and "Socialization or Peer Relationship Skills" are all used to describe the same domain.

Two research editions and a standardization version of the KIST preceded the current instrument. The initial item pool of 150 was developed "by the authors on a basis of face validity and constructs believed to be related to social and emotional skills needed for successful kinder-garten adjustment" (manual, p. 23). The manual provides only basic information about the samples and methods used in the development of the first two editions. Factor analytic methods were used to reduce the item pool on the second and third editions. The first edition contained 90 items and was administered to 571 parents of primarily Anglo-American, middle-class kindergarteners. The second edition contained 80 items and was administered to 392 parents described as ethni-cally diverse and varied in socioeconomic levels. The current instrument contains 50 items derived from the standardization version.

STANDARDIZATION. The third version, referred to as the standardization version, con-tained 60 items and was administered to 658 parents of kindergarten children. Detailed demo-graphic information is provided for the standard-ization sample. The sample is described as ap-proximating the 1995 U.S. Census data in ethnicity with 73.6% Anglo-American, 11.1% African American, 8.4% Hispanic-American, 2.6% Asian American, .7% Native-American, and 3.6% Other. The sample was gathered from three states and was therefore not geographically representative. Mean family income was greater than the U.S. average. Although children ranged in age from 4.6 to 6.5, the majority of the children (n = 487–504 depending on domain) were aged 5.0 to 5.11, with much smaller numbers represented in the younger (n = 66–69) and older (n = 24–26) age groups. Given that most children enter kindergarten at approxi-mately 5 years of age, the age distribution is to be expected. No explanation is offered for the differing sample sizes across the domains. The sample con-tained roughly equal numbers of males and females. Significant differences between sexes and between different ages were found on some domains.

Factor analysis of the 60 items was used to identify the domains and reduce the final number of items to 50. Reliability and validity data were gener-ated from this data set. A cutoff raw score on the Validity Index was set as criteria for an invalid protocol. Invalid protocols were removed from the analysis.

Reliability. Cronbach's coefficient alphas are reported for the domains. Reliabilities on most domains are adequate for a screening instrument, but too low to use for clinical decisions. In addi-tion, the authors recommend that the Separation

Anxiety and Sleeping & Eating Behaviors do-mains are best interpreted qualitatively due to low reliability scores (.50 and .64, respectively).

Validity. Support for construct validity is offered from analysis of the standardization ver-sion. Item-domain correlations were generally good. Interdomain correlations ranged from .16 to .60 and are described by the authors as "fairly independent from each other" (manual, p. 35). Fac-tor analysis indicated that a nine-factor solution accounted for 40.9% of the variance. Sleeping & Eating Behaviors separated into two factors, but were retained as one domain. Two items loaded on a separate factor but were added to the Maladaptive Behaviors domain arbitrarily. The authors suggest that confirmatory factor analytic studies are needed. The authors are in the process of conducting a study to demonstrate criterion-related validity.

To support the convergent and divergent validity of the KIST the authors conducted stepwise regression analysis to predict scores on the Kin-dergarten Diagnostic Instrument (KDI), a mea-sure of academic readiness administered to the standardization sample. Only 25% of the variance on KDI total test was explained by portions of the KIST. In addition, regression analysis of socioeco-nomic variables as predictors of the KIST domain scores indicate that only minimal variance is shared with these variables. Mean family income was a small but significant predictor on all domains. Group differences in sex and age are also reported.

COMMENTARY. The stated purpose of the KIST is as a screening and prescriptive tool to identify the level of social skills and emotional maturity for preschool- and kindergarten-aged children to identify appropriate interventions. The KIST presents a number of challenges in practical use. The manual provides limited guidance in the interpretation section, with some important rec-ommendations located only in the Technical Prop-erties chapter. A difficulty in using the instrument is choosing a norm group. Although there are norms for three age groups and general norms, the variability in sample sizes and domain scores by age and sex makes it difficult to choose a norm group. The general norm group provides the larg-est sample size, and presumably would compare the child to the "typical" kindergartener. However, the user should also be familiar with the age and sex differences in the standardization sample to aid in interpretation. Appropriate interpretations would need to take multiple factors into account. In addition, the instrument generally measures skills related to expectations in a typical educational environment in the United States that values independence and self-control. Caution should be exercised in applying some of the items to children from all cultures. For instance, sleeping alone, adjusting to caretakers outside of the family, and using a spoon and fork are valued abilities on the instrument.

An additional difficulty is in determining interventions. Although the placement of items in the domains was supported by factor analysis, each domain tends to represent a relatively large area. For instance, Communication contains both receptive and expressive communication skills items and Maladaptive Behaviors includes headaches, using a spoon and fork, talking back, and other items. The interventions section of the manual is very brief and acts mostly as a reference to additional resources. The section on inattention primarily lists resources for ADHD, which could be misleading because the instrument is not designed as a measurement of attention disorders. The instrument may be adequate as a screening tool, but weak as a prescriptive tool. Further assessment of a child's areas of difficulty would be necessary to design effective interventions.

SUMMARY. Reliability and validity of the Kindergarten Inventory of Social-Emotional Tendencies (KIST) are fairly well supported for the initial development. The authors generally acknowledged the psychometric difficulties with the KIST and acknowledged the need for additional validation studies. They also indicate that some portions of the KIST should only be interpreted qualitatively. The KIST appears to be adequate for its intended use as a screening instrument, but is not recommended for use to make clinical or educational decisions related to specific services or placement. The manual does not identify the level of training recommended for the user of the KIST, nor does it offer significant guidance on administration and interpretation for those not well trained in assessment. If kindergarten teachers without significant assessment training are administering the KIST, it should be under the supervision of a qualified professional (i.e., school psychologist, special education diagnostician). Scores on the KIST need to be interpreted in light of the aforementioned difficulties including low reliability of some domains, norm group variability, and weakness as a prescriptive tool. Culturally sensitive use is also necessary.

Review of the Kindergarten Inventory of Social-Emotional Tendencies by CYNTHIA A. ROHRBECK, Associate Professor of Psychology, The George Washington University, Washington, DC:

DESCRIPTION. The Kindergarten Inventory of Social-Emotional Tendencies (KIST) is designed to measure social skills deficits and emotional immaturity in preschoolers and kindergartners ages 4–6. It can be given with an academic readiness measure to more comprehensively assess overall "readiness" for kindergarten. The scale consists of 50 items that measure how often behaviors were observed in the last 3 months on a 5-point scale from 1 = *Never* to 5 = *Always*. Some items are phrased positively whereas others are worded negatively. Scale items cover seven domains including Communication skills (7 items), Daily Living Skills (6 items), Hyperactive/Inattentive Behaviors (9 items), Maladaptive Behaviors (9 items), Separation Anxiety Behaviors (4 items), Socialization or Peer Relationship Skills (5 items), and Sleeping & Eating Behaviors (6 items). A "Validity Index" built into the KIST helps to identify instances in which raters presumably have randomly completed the measure.

The KIST may be completed by either a caretaker or a teacher who knows the child well (for at least 3 months across several settings). It is estimated that a rater can complete the measure in 10 minutes. The answer sheets include a self-scoring template, although item scores still need to be transferred and added in each domain on a separate page. The Validity Index is easily computed; it is the sum of the discrepancies between pairs of similar items. T scores and percentile ranks are available for different norm groups including 4-year-olds, 5-year-olds, and 6-year-olds from a standardization sample.

The manual includes a helpful overview of skills in the seven KIST domains and remedial suggestions and references for deficits in those areas. It should be noted that the KIST is called the Kindergarten Inventory of Social/Emotional Adjustment in the manual's title. The manual requires additional editing; it includes many such spelling/typographical errors.

DEVELOPMENT. As described in its manual, KIST items were generated by its authors "on a basis of face validity and constructs believed to be related to social and emotional skills needed for successful kindergarten adjustment" (p. 23). The initial 150 items were reduced in subsequent versions to 90 and 80 items. After factor-analysis, 60 items were retained. It is unclear how those 60 items were reduced to the final 50 in the current KIST. In 1996, the KIST was standardized on 658 kindergarten children, ages 4 1/2 to 6 years in school districts in Ohio, Texas, and New Jersey. That sample resulted in norms for 4-, 5-, and 6-year-olds. The sample was similar to the 1995 U.S. Census data for ethnicity, and had a slightly higher mean family income than the national census.

TECHNICAL. Some item means in the standardization sample may indicate a ceiling effect, with mean values close to 5. Correlation coefficients suggest low to adequate internal consistency for the seven domains, ranging from .50 to .83. The internal consistency for the measure as a whole is .91; most likely the lower values for domains reflect the smaller number of items in the domains. No test-retest reliability data are provided for the KIST. Item-domain correlations are reported as evidence of content validity; however, those correlations are more indicative of internal consistency or reliability. There is no evidence of content validity, concurrent validity, or criterion validity presented in the 1997 manual. An overall MANOVA analysis showed age group differences across the three age groups on the seven domain scales, although there were not always significant differences between the 5- and 6-year-olds. The authors suggest that the 6-year-old group may over-represent children with developmental delays (some of those children may have started kindergarten later than usual due to such delays). An overall MANOVA also showed gender differences, in particular on the domain of Daily Living Skills.

COMMENTARY. Given substantial variability in the rate of normal child development among young children of similar ages, it is not clear how useful the norms for 4-, 5-, and 6-year-old kindergarten students will be. Because most states use 5 as the age for entering kindergarten, the 4-year-old norms may reflect "older fours" whereas the 6-year-old norms may include "younger sixes." If boys are overrepresented in the older group and underrepresented in the younger group, there may be confounds between age and gender on the norms provided. Perhaps norms based on only 5-

year-olds, or all 4-, 5-, and 6-year-olds, regardless of school status, would be more useful.

An important goal for "readiness" assessments is to demonstrate that they yield scores that are valid, and measure what they say they measure. In this respect, the KIST falls short. Preferably, items would have been developed after review by early childhood researchers, teachers, and parents. Discriminant validity, or evidence that the measure could distinguish between those children hypothesized to be less "ready" than others, would also provide support for use of scores from the KIST. Although the KIST provides some evidence of internal consistency, evidence of test-retest reliability is also critical.

Given these problems, the KIST may not be the best choice for social or emotional kindergarten readiness assessment at this time. It is hoped that its authors can provide evidence of validity of its scores in the future.

SUMMARY. The KIST was developed to assess social skills and maturity deficits in potential kindergartners, and to supplement more traditional kindergarten readiness measures. At this time, there is insufficient evidence of the validity of its scores to suggest its use as a screener.

[131]
Knox's Cube Test, Revised.

Purpose: A nonverbal mental test designed to measure attention span and memory of children and adults.
Population: Ages 3 and over.
Publication Dates: 1980–2002.
Acronym: KCT-R.
Scores: Total score only.
Administration: Individual.
Price Data, 2003: $105 per complete kit including manual, tapping cubes, and 15 test/record booklets; $25 per 15 report booklets.
Time: Administration time not reported.
Comments: Items unchanged from previous edition; Junior and Senior forms have been eliminated.
Author: Mark H. Stone.
Publisher: Stoelting Co.
Cross References: See T5:1407 (5 references) and T4:1367 (7 references); for reviews by Raymond S. Dean and Jerome M. Sattler of the previous edition, see 9:574 (2 references).

Review of the Knox's Cube Test, Revised by CAROLYN M. CALLAHAN, Professor of Educational Psychology, University of Virginia, Charlottesville, VA:

DESCRIPTION. The 2002 revision of the Knox's Cube Test, Revised (KCT-R) is the latest version of a test originally developed in 1915. Developed to evaluate mental impairment of immigrants, the stated purpose is now to measure attention span and short-term memory. Based on the assumption that when attention span and short-term memory are measured by number of words or digits recalled, performance is influenced by the verbal or numeric knowledge or skills of the examinee, the tasks in the KCT-R seek to eliminate the influence of meaningfulness of materials in order to assess a purer construct. The tasks that comprise the test require the examinee to use a 1-inch cube to duplicate the examiner's demonstration of increasingly complex and longer series of taps on four 1-inch cubes fastened to a wooden base in a line 2 inches apart. The exam begins with the simplest task and proceeds until there are five successive failures. Each successful reproduction of a series of taps is scored "1" and each failure is scored "0." Correct and incorrect responses are recorded on a report page and are then transferred to a record page according to a complex set of directions. The record page allows for translation of the examinee's performance into a "median ability level" score representing upper and lower boundaries of an age range of years ranging from 3 to 23. The record page also provides information on the median difficulty levels of each tapping series, the median difficulty levels of the reverses in direction required to complete a series, and median difficulty level of each distance traveled across blocks. The manual also provides limited direction for assessing attention deficits and for detecting when there has been an invalid performance on the test.

DEVELOPMENT. The KCT-R has evolved through various iterations of a fundamental task of repeating the examiner's example of tapping cubes in a particular sequence. The KCT-R was created by first examining item difficulty from items of the 1947 version of the test. Then items were added in the middle range of difficulty as well as items at easier and more difficult levels (to extend the range of assessment) and those items were integrated into the new form by calibrating all items using the Rasch scaling model (using a sample of 101 individuals). These new items were selected from other versions of the test or were newly created. The author used Rasch scaling based on data from prior versions of the test and the new items to create the norm tables provided in the manual. Extensive elaboration on the development of the former versions of the test is provided as justification for use of the newer version. Earlier Junior and Senior test forms apparently have been abandoned in this revision.

TECHNICAL.

Reliability. The reliability data presented are a translation of a Rasch test separation value of 38.22 into a corresponding test reliability of .99 and the Rasch person separation value of 2.54 into a corresponding reliability of .87. Stability was estimated as .96 for 260 people, ages 50–60. The length of time elapsed for the estimate is not provided in the manual. No other reliability data are provided.

Validity. The primary purpose of the KCT R is to measure short-term memory and attention. The manual for the KCT-R provides considerable evidence of the characteristics of earlier versions of the test instruments, but little in the way of validation of the current instrument except evidence from Rasch scaling that the items fit expected patterns of increasing difficulty. The authors do caution that the KCT-R is not a comprehensive assessment of learning or memory functioning. However, evidence of construct validity for even limited application is limited. Factor loadings of earlier versions of the KCT on factors identified as visual and auditory attention and nonverbal, visual-spatial abilities in one study (Bornstein, 1983) are offered as further evidence of the construct validity of the test.

In the manual's discussion of use of this instrument as an indicator of diffuse organic involvement, little evidence is offered except data that suggest that scores on earlier forms of the measure correlate higher with WAIS verbal IQ than WAIS performance IQ and that subtests on the WAIS not requiring memory had the highest correlation with the earlier forms of the KCT (Golden, 1979; Silberberg & Bourestem, 1968). The author concludes that there is also a motoric component of functioning measured, but does not indicate how this affects the assessment of memory and attention. Other data from earlier versions of the test were offered as supporting sensitivity to organic involvement.

The author notes that the test gives an indication of attention span by examining patterns of correct and incorrect responses. Irregular and regular pattern illustrations are provided to guide the examiner in interpretations of "attention disorders." No validity data are presented to support these interpretations.

Normative Data. Age norms are provided on the record form for total scores ranging from 3 to 23 years. Unlike usual age scores, only whole number age scores are reported. Data for the norming tables are apparently derived from administrations of the various versions of the test administered in 1915, 1947, and 1965 and a small sample of people assessed for calibrating the current form. The manual identifies the population as 3,173 persons spanning ages 3–84 from Midwestern states with an adequate mix of racial/ethnic groups. Only five percentile rank scores are available (2, 16, 50, 84, and 98) for comparison on the age norms. Standard errors of measurement are implied with the age bandwidths that are provided for the total scores on the record form; however, the process for establishing these bands is not provided. Standard errors of measurement, cumulative frequencies, and percentile ranks are provided in a separate table. These norm tables do not allow for the comparison of individuals over the age of 23 with comparable age groups.

Although the Rasch model provides the statistical means to combine these data, the lack of clear descriptions of the population, the apparent overweighting of impaired individuals in the sample, and the lack of appropriate norm tables by age seriously limits the usefulness of the norms.

COMMENTARY. The current version of the KCT-R has successfully increased the difficulty range of items presented to assess attention and memory; however, the test is still deficient on several dimensions. First, the developers have ignored current thinking regarding information processing in labeling the test a short-term memory test when it would be more appropriately considered a test of visual or visual-spatial memory.

Second, the scales and scores offered are not carefully defined. Little information is provided to the test user regarding appropriate use of vaguely defined scores such as the median difficulty levels of each tapping series, the median difficulty levels of the reverses in direction required to complete a series, and the median difficulty level of each distance traveled across blocks.

It is not a test of short-term memory. There is a lack of strong evidence for the validity of the current revision and a lack of carefully established normative groups and statistics. Limitation of the

norms to only whole year age scores and the limited range (3–23), as well as lack of a current national norming sample and norms by age group, further detract from the usefulness of the test.

SUMMARY. The author does caution that the KCT-R is not a comprehensive assessment of learning or memory. However, the KCT-R does not provide adequate psychometric supporting data for validity or norms. At this point, there is not sufficient information to warrant its use as a diagnostic tool, as a measure of attention disorders, or as measure to be used in the identification of organic involvement.

REVIEWER'S REFERENCES

Bornstein, R. A. (1983). Construct validity of the Knox Cube tests as a neuropsychological measure. *Journal of Clinical Neuropsychology, 5*(2), 105–114.
Golden, C. J. (1979). *Clinical interpretation of objective psychological tests.* New York: Grune and Stratton.
Silberberg, N. E., & Bourestem, N. C. (1968). The Knox cubes as a screening measure of intelligence for hemiparetic patients. *Journal of Clinical Psychology, 24,* 348–349.

Review of the Knox's Cube Test, Revised by ANITA M. HUBLEY, *Associate Professor of Measurement, Evaluation, and Research Methodology, University of British Columbia, Vancouver, British Columbia, Canada:*

DESCRIPTION. Knox's Cube Test, Revised (KCT-R) is described as a measure of attention span and short-term memory that can be used with both children and adults. This particular version of the Knox Cube Test (KCT), and its immediate predecessor (Stone & Wright, 1980), used a Rasch measurement model to calibrate items and order them by difficulty level. Materials consist of four 1-inch cubes attached, 2 inches apart, to a wood base, and a fifth unattached cube.

Administration of the KCT-R is straightforward. There are two practice items of two taps each, which are repeated until mastered. For each of the 26 test items, the examiner uses the fifth cube to tap out a series, ranging from two to eight taps, on the other cubes at the rate of one tap per second. The examinee then reproduces the tapped series. No administration time is reported, but it should not exceed 10–15 minutes.

Scoring of the KCT-R is also straightforward. Each item is scored either correct or incorrect. The total score is the number of correct items. A report page is used to record all correct and incorrect items, the total score, any "surprising responses" (i.e., items the examinee should not have gotten correct or incorrect according to the Rasch model), as well as the Mastery Units (MITs), median taps, reverses, and distances, and age norms (i.e., median ability level on the KCT-R for each age) that correspond to the total score. Surprising responses are used to determine if an examinee's performance is valid or not. Four examples demonstrate possible patterns of "surprising responses" (manual, p. 14). Although these examples are somewhat helpful, more guidance is needed to standardize examiners' decision making about the validity of performance. It is unclear why the age range for the norms is so limited and typographical errors in the manual make it unclear what the actual age range should be. It is also important to note that no guidance is provided to help the examiner properly interpret the MITs, median taps, reverses, and distances, or norms.

DEVELOPMENT. A nice summary of differences in materials and items among nine versions of the KCT is given, but surprisingly few details about the test development process are provided. Several studies appear to have been conducted using Rasch's (1960) measurement model with data from children and adults to calibrate items from different versions of the KCT as well as some new items. However, only two initial studies are described in any detail. No information is provided about the development of any of the new items. Nor is any rationale offered for the selection of the 26 items (from the item bank) that form the KCT-R. An additional problem is that at least five figures and tables referred to in the text are not provided.

Considerable evidence is presented to demonstrate that the KCT-R fits the Rasch measurement model. The variable of interest in the presented analyses (i.e., fit analysis, principal components analysis, item residual analysis, item-to-score correlations) is item difficulty. The results of these analyses generally support the calibrations of the KCT-R items in terms of item difficulty. Further analysis suggests item calibrations for males and females do not differ substantially, with the exception of Item 1. Unfortunately, none of the analyses, or the accompanying tables and figures, are presented in a manner that is easily understandable to the typical practitioner.

TECHNICAL. Normative data are based on 3,173 individuals (49.5% male) ages 3–84 years from four Midwestern U.S. states. The majority of this sample was White (66%), with 29% Black, 4% Hispanic, and 1% Asian. No information is provided about the sample distribution across the age span; nor is it clear when or how the normative data were obtained. The manual indicates that KCT-R age norms were based on the Pintner (1915), Arthur II (1947), and Babcock (1965) versions, studies by Gellerman (1952), Levinson (1960), and Sterne (1966), as well as data from Stone and Wright (1976, 1977, 1978 [cited but not referenced in manual]). However, it is difficult to reconcile the individual sample sizes and ages from these sources with the overall normative sample size and ages reported. In addition, although the normative sample ranged in age from 3 to 84, it is not clear whether the normative data are applicable to this entire age range. Age trends reported in the manual and the age norms provided on the report page suggest that dependable age norms are only available for children and adolescents. However, an age norm plot showing the 2nd, 16th, 50th, 84th, and 98th percentile ranks for individuals ages 3 to 63 is also presented in the manual. One table in the manual presents logit measures, normed scores ($M = 500$, s = 100), standard errors, and percentile ranks associated with total KCT-R scores, but it is unclear to what ages these norms can be appropriately applied.

Reliability was quantified using Rasch item and person separation indices. Unfortunately, the concept of a separation index is not well known to many test users and the description and tables provided in the manual do little to rectify this situation. The separation index values reported basically indicate that the item difficulties are more replicable than the responses of individuals on the KCT-R, but both suggest adequate reliability. A test-retest reliability estimate of .96 was obtained for 260 individuals ages 5–60. Unfortunately, the interpretation of this classical test theory estimate is hampered because no retest interval is reported.

Although considerable attention has been paid to providing evidence that the KCT-R fits the Rasch model, no validity evidence is presented to support that scores obtained on this test can be interpreted as indicators of attention span and short-term memory.

COMMENTARY. The KCT has a long history in cognitive testing that is nicely recorded in the manual. The strength of all versions of this test lies in the relative simplicity of its administration and scoring. Strengths of this most recent version are the attempt to order the items in a meaningful way and the equating of total scores, in terms of MITs, from the Pintner, Arthur II, Babcock, and the 1980 Junior and Senior KCT versions using a calibrated item bank.

Unfortunately, there are several critical weaknesses to the KCT-R. The most noticeable weakness is the sloppiness in the reporting of information throughout the manual and the accompanying "technical manual" (Stone & Yumoto, 2002), which makes it very difficult to have much faith in the quality of the test development and norms. Simply put, these materials are poorly organized and contain an appalling number of typographical errors. Critical information about norms, reliability, and validity are difficult to locate quickly. Numerous tables and graphs referred to in the text are not provided, whereas, in other cases, existing tables and graphs are poorly labeled, occasionally mislabeled, and poorly explained. A number of citations, including the central Stone and Wright (1976, 1977, 1978) studies, are missing from the references.

The key weakness, however, is the inadequate description of the KCT-R test development and norming process as detailed earlier, as well as the lack of strong validity evidence (e.g., convergent and discriminant evidence), as established in the *Standards for Educational and Psychological Testing* (AERA, APA, & NCME, 1999). The Rasch model, which underlies this version of the KCT, is unfamiliar to many test users and yet the description of this model and its related statistics in the manual is poor. Frequently mentioned terms, such as logits and MITs, are often left unexplained. Likewise, the assumptions of Rasch measurement that underlie the selection and ordering of the KCT-R items and, in turn, constrain interpretation (e.g., "invalid" performance) are not made clear to the test user. The lack of guidance provided to the test user in the proper interpretation of scores obtained on this test suggests that this version of the KCT was simply an exercise in applying the Rasch model.

SUMMARY. Stone and Yumoto (2002) indicate that the "purpose of the latest revision was to cross-validate test properties and provide new norms" (p. 4), but the authors are never explicit about what cross-validation took place or what new norms were provided. It is also unclear whether the revisions made justify the addition of the term "revised," as per the *Standards* (AERA, APA, &

NCME, 1999). A strength of this particular version of the KCT may be the use of the Rasch measurement model to calibrate items and order them by difficulty level. However, in choosing to use the KCT-R, test users need to understand the assumptions of the Rasch model and be willing to accept the constraints that it places on the validity and interpretation of an examinee's performance. For example, inconsistent performance that suggests attentional deficits is also likely to be declared invalid according to the Rasch model. Important weaknesses of the KCT-R include the inadequate description of test development and norming, lack of adequate validity evidence, lack of guidance in interpreting test information, and a poorly presented test manual. Caution must be exercised in using the KCT-R for clinical purposes. In choosing a spatial measure of attention span, test users may want to consider versions of the KCT by other authors as well as other available tapping measures (e.g., Wechsler Memory Scale-III [T6:2695] Spatial Span subtest, Wechsler, 1997; Stanford-Binet V [233] Block Span subtest, Roid, 2003).

REVIEWER'S REFERENCES

American Educational Research Association, American Psychological Association, & National Council on Measurement in Education. (1999). *Standards for educational and psychological testing.* Washington, DC: American Educational Research Association.

Arthur, G. (1947). *A point scale of performance tests, Revised form II.* New York: The Psychological Corporation.

Babcock, H. C. (1965). The Babcock Test of Mental Deficiency. Beverly Hills, CA: Western Psychological Services (with permission of Stoelting Co.).

Gellerman, S. W. (1952). Forms I and II of the Arthur performance scales with mental defectives. *Journal of Consulting Psychology, 16,* 127–131.

Levinson, B. M. (1960). A research note on the Knox Cubes as an intelligence test for aged males. *Journal of Gerontology, 15,* 85–86.

Pintner, R. (1915). The standardization of Knox's cube test. *Psychological Review, 22,* 377–401.

Rasch, G. (1960). *Studies in mathematical psychology I: Probabilistic models for some intelligence and attainment tests.* Oxford, England: Nielsen & Lydiche.

Roid, G. H. (2003). Stanford-Binet Intelligence Scales, Fifth Edition. Itasca, IL: Riverside Publishing.

Sterne, D. M. (1966). The Knox Cubes as a test of memory and intelligence with male adults. *Journal of Clinical Psychology, 22,* 191–193.

Stone, M. H., & Wright, B. (1980). Knox's Cube Test. Wood Dale, IL: Stoelting Co.

Stone, M. H., & Yumoto, F. (2002). *Psychometric properties of Knox's Cube Test—Revised (KCT-R).* Wood Dale, IL: Stoelting Co.

Wechsler D. (1997). *WMS-III: Administration and scoring manual.* San Antonio, TX: The Psychological Corporation.

[132]

Krug Asperger's Disorder Index.

Purpose: To identify individuals who have Asperger's Disorder, to target goals for intervention on the IEP, and for use in research.

Population: Ages 6-0 to 21-11.

Publication Date: 2003.

Acronym: KADI.

Scores: Total score only.

Administration: Individual.

Price Data, 2003: $76 per complete kit; $54 per examiner's manual (39 pages), $15 per 50 profile/examiner record forms (specify ages 6-11 or ages 12-22).
Time: Untimed.
Comments: Ratings by parents, close relatives, teachers, educational assistants, or counselors.
Authors: David A. Krug and Joel R. Arick.
Publisher: PRO-ED.

Review of the Krug Asperger's Disorder Index by LEAH M. NELLIS, School Psychologist, RISE Special Services, Indianapolis, IN:

DESCRIPTION. The Krug Asperger's Disorder Index (KADI) is designed as a "norm-referenced screening instrument that provides useful information for determining the diagnosis of Asperger's Disorder" (examiner's manual, p. 1) for use with individuals 6 through 21 years of age. The test authors support the use of the KADI for three purposes. The primary purpose is stated as the identification of individuals with Asperger's Disorder. Additional uses include targeting goals for intervention and research. The KADI consists of 32 items (behaviors) that the rater endorses if the statement accurately describes the person being rated. Items are reportedly written at a sixth grade level and are to be completed by parents, relatives, teachers, counselors, or educational assistants. Two forms, one for elementary and one for secondary, are included although only 5 items are different and these have only slight wording variations. Items are organized into two sections with the 11 items in the first section reportedly being behaviors that best differentiate between those with Asperger's Disorder and those without delay. Raters complete the first 11 items and if the score meets a specified criterion, the remaining items in Section 2 are completed. If the criterion is not met, completion of the KADI is discontinued and evidence of Asperger's Disorder is not supported. The total raw score is based on 30 items (2 items from Section 1 do not contribute because they did not differentiate between Asperger's and high functioning Autism). The total raw score is converted into a standard score and percentile rank.

DEVELOPMENT. The manual briefly covers the literature base regarding Autism Spectrum Disorders citing a small number of case histories, DSM-IV criteria, and supporting the separate diagnosis of Asperger's Disorder. Readers may benefit from a more complete description of the various pervasive developmental disorders and differences between the separate diagnoses. Given that differential diagnosis was the stated primary purpose for the KADI, the background and conceptual information is weak and limited. The process of item development and selection was described as occurring through three processes including review of existing screening checklists/questionnaires and resource materials, expert review, and pilot testing of an initial pool of 106 items. The scope of the existing rating scales was limited and the description of the pilot study was without essential details, such as who completed the pilot version, procedures, ages, and criteria for previous diagnoses. The selection and organization of the 32-item final version was discussed within the validity section of the manual and it is unclear if additional modification of test items occurred during the development process. The final 32 items were grouped into two sections based on the ability to differentiate between normal, Asperger's, and Autism. According to the manual, Section 1 consists of 11 items that were found to best differentiate between those with Asperger's Disorder and those with no identified delay. Section 2 consists of 21 items that best differentiated between those with Asperger's Disorder and high functioning Autism Disorder.

TECHNICAL. The manual describes three populations: those identified with Asperger's Disorder ($n = 130$), those diagnosed with high functioning Autistic Disorder ($n = 162$) and those with no identified developmental delay ($n = 194$) under the section of Normative Information. However, careful reading revealed that these three populations were utilized during reliability and validity studies but were not all included in the standardization sample. The standardization sample consisted only of 130 individuals identified as the Asperger's Disorder Sample. However, a demographic characteristic table notes that 11 of these 130 did not have a diagnosis but no further explanation was provided.

The identified samples were primarily male and between the ages of 6–11 years. The Asperger's and Autistic samples were recruited from 32 states and 10 countries whereas those with no delay were from Oregon and Washington. The samples were not described with regard to ethnicity or socioeconomic status.

The manual reports split-half reliability estimates for the Asperger's Disorder sample ($r =$

.89), test-retest coefficients for a sample of 25 individuals with Asperger's ($r = .98$) over a 2-week interval, and high interrater agreement. Validity evidence included chi-square analyses and item analysis that reportedly resulted in 32 items that significantly differentiated between individuals with a diagnosis of Asperger's Disorder, high functioning Autism Disorder, and no identified developmental delays. Test authors provided sensitivity and specificity indexes as well as positive predictive values that reportedly support the KADI's ability to identify those with a previous diagnosis of Asperger's Disorder.

COMMENTARY. The identification and differentiation of Asperger's Disorder is a complex issue and in need of high-quality instrumentation. Thus, the purpose of the KADI is important and timely for clinical practice. However, there are numerous levels of concern associated with the development of the KADI that result in caution regarding its use. Specifically, the authors refer to the tool as a screening instrument but support its use for diagnosis and differential diagnosis. This purpose is highly overstated and the presented data do not support such utility. The manual is lacking critical information about the procedures in development, description of the clinical samples, and background information. Specifically, no information is provided about the selection criteria for the individuals in the clinical samples. This is especially concerning given the variability in diagnostic decision making in the area of pervasive developmental disabilities. Further, the authors combine Asperger's and high functioning Autism samples for some analyses but state that the scale can be used to differentiate between groups. This conclusion does not appear justified by the presented data. In addition, standard scores should be used cautiously because they offer only a comparison to individuals with a previous diagnosis. Comparing the KADI to existing rating scales and interview formats and investigating the factor structure could have enhanced validity evidence.

SUMMARY. Although the KADI was developed to fill a needed and complex assessment role, many levels of concern are noted that limit its utility at the present time. Future research with the scale may provide additional data to support its clinical usage.

Review of the Krug Asperger's Disorder Index by STEPHEN E. TROTTER, Associate Professor, Department of Psychology, Tennessee State University, Nashville, TN:

DESCRIPTION. The Krug Asperger's Disorder Index (KADI) is a norm-referenced, 32-item test, administered as a paper-pencil rating scale. All items are of the weighted scores type. Recommendations are made for the examiner to follow the instructions described in the manual for completing, scoring, and interpreting the KADI. The rating scale is appropriate for individuals ranging in age from 6 years to 21 years 11 months. The test has both elementary and secondary school-age forms.

A variety of professionals who have the necessary training and background may administer the KADI. The examiner must have studied the KADI manual. He or she must (a) understand the diagnostic criteria for Asperger's Disorder as listed in the DSM-IV, (b) be conversant with the construction and statistical characteristics of the KADI, (c) be proficient in the administration of the KADI, and (d) have a working knowledge of the guidelines for interpreting the results of the KADI. The KADI yields three types of scores: raw scores, standard scores, and percentile ranks. The raw score is the sum of the weighted scores circled in Column B of the profile/examiner record form. The raw scores are used primarily for research purposes. Standard scores provide the clearest indication of an individual's possible diagnosis of Asperger's Disorder. Percentile ranks indicate the percentage of the distribution that is equal to or below a particular score.

The instrument is one page printed on both sides and can be completed quickly by an informant. The front side provides for identifying data, record of scores, and standard score analysis.

DEVELOPMENT. The KADI consists of 32 items derived from a study that listed 106 distinct behavior statements gleaned from careful consideration of several sources: the DSM-IV diagnostic criteria, the considerable literature describing Asperger's Disorder, input from knowledgeable professionals, and personal and professional experience with individuals with this disorder. The final 32 items were derived after considerable research on the survey results.

The final version of the KADI was standardized on 486 individuals. Of these individuals, 130 had a diagnosis of Asperger's Disorder, 162 had a diagnosis of Austic Disorder, and 194 were "normal." The KADI has three stated goals: identification, IEP goal development, and usage as a research tool.

TECHNICAL. The manual is brief. Information describing the norming process is provided. The manual makes reference to administration and scoring procedures, interpretation, normative data, and reliability and validity coefficients. The administration and scoring section is very brief and an inordinate amount of time is spent addressing deriving the chronological age computation. A completed profile sheet is provided that is more helpful than the text. The profile layout is easy to read and the usage of shading areas in the "likelihood for Asperger's Diagnosis" is very helpful. KADI informants must have at least a sixth grade reading level to successfully complete the checklist. Responses to the KADI yield three score types: raw, standard, and percentile ranks. This indicates that Type II errors may be a concern when using this instrument.

In terms of reliability, the KADI shows well-documented internal reliability of .89 and excellent test-retest reliability as demonstrated by an r value of .98 over a 2-week period.

Visual examination of the items suggests that the wording and behaviors addressed are not redundant. Therefore, the reliability coefficients suggests a high degree of stability across a number of dimensions.

Validity procedures are well documented in the manual. The KADI manual addresses and provides supporting data for content, criterion, and predictive validity. The test items are related to five of the six DSM-IV criteria for Asperger's. The 32 items in the final version of the KADI demonstrated significance in discriminating between individuals classified as high level functioning with Autism and Normal versus Asperger's Disorder.

SUMMARY. The KADI provides a quick and easily administered screening instrument for the diaagnosis of individuals with Asperger's Disorder. It is a brief, 32-item instrument that shows evidence of sound technical properties. The test appears to be well normed with an Asperger's sample size of 130, High Functioning Autistic sample of 162, and finally a "normal" population of 194. The strong reliability and validity coefficients suggest that the KADI is a welcome addition in the area of Asperger's diagnosis.

[133]

LARR Test of Emergent Literacy.

Purpose: Designed to provide "a simple measure of young children's level of literacy on entry to compulsory schooling."
Population: Students entering school.
Publication Date: 1993.
Acronym: LARRTEL.
Scores: Total score only.
Administration: Group.
Price Data: Available from publisher.
Time: (25) minutes.
Comments: Based on the Linguistic Awareness Reading Readiness (LARR) Test (T6:1434).
Author: National Foundation for Educational Research.
Publisher: NFER-Nelson Publishing Co., Ltd. [England].

Review of the LARR Test of Emergent Literacy by JILL ANN JENKINS, Consultant Child & School Psychologist, Barcelona, Spain:

DESCRIPTION. The LARR Test of Emergent Literacy (LARRTEL) is a 19-question paper-and-pencil task that is specifically meant to be used with children between the ages of 4.0 and 5.3 years, who are just entering the formal school system. It may also be used for younger children who are advanced in reading, or for older students who are delayed to identify a reading readiness age equivalent. The test aims to identify children who have entered school with knowledge about reading and writing and those who have not and to "identify those children who will need further experience of reading and writing activities in order to develop their knowledge and awareness of the concepts and conventions of print" (teacher's guide, p. 1). It also asserts to provide "detailed diagnostic information for individual children" (teacher's guide, p. 1), which can then be applied to teaching methods. In addition, the test can be used to obtain baseline information for class groups or for individual students.

It is recommended that students are tested approximately 7 weeks after entering school. Each child who is tested receives a small booklet with pictures and words, within which children are to circle their responses to questions asked by the administrator. Questions 1 through 5 test recognition of readable material in various forms, Questions 6 through 8 test recognition of when reading and writing are taking place, and Questions 9 through 19 test understanding of the basic technical terms associated with reading. The LARRTEL can be administered individually or in small group settings of no more than four children. The testing time is approximately 25 minutes. One raw score is found at the end of the testing, which is converted to a standardized score that correlates with one of five bands, from highest to lowest. The testing booklets are easy to handle and engaging to children.

The LARR Test of Emergent Literacy was developed in England and Wales and it is written in British English. One test item, "Circle each full stop" would be confusing to American children, who would be more familiar with the term "period."

DEVELOPMENT. The LARRTEL is the second version of the LARR, initially published in 1983. The authors of the LARRTEL state that the initial test was constructed as a part of a study of reading readiness and was "based firmly on original research" by Marie Clay, John Downing et al. They state that "research shows that linguistic awareness and related concepts are more closely related to progress in learning to read and write than such factors as visual and auditory perception of letter-naming knowledge" (teacher's guide, p. 1). The teacher's guide does not reference this background history and research. It would be helpful to have a true "technical guide" that gives great details to the history and development of the test, so that those, other than teachers (i.e., researchers, psychologists, and psychometricians) may have this information at their fingertips when evaluating a test.

The development of the original LARR Test originated from cross cultural testing of children and found that developing concepts on the functions of writing are dependent on home background and its emphasis (or lack thereof) of reading. The LARR was adapted by an inner city Local Education Authority (LEA) in England for use in its planned evaluation of children entering school, resulting in the LARRTEL. The changes, according to the teacher's manual, included "selecting, redrawing and anglicizing questions from the original Canadian test. The layout was also changed so that only one question was printed per page, as early trials showed this improved children's understanding of the tasks" (teacher's guide, p. 16).

TECHNICAL.

Standardization. Initial development and piloting of the LARR Test of Emergent Literacy were conducted by an inner city Local Education Authority (LEA). A 20-item version of the test was compiled and administered to $N = 277$ pupils. The test publisher then analyzed these responses and developed the marking scheme. One test item was eliminated because it was found to be "inadequate," resulting in the 19-item, current version of the LARRTEL.

The national sample, used for standardization of the LARR Test of Emergent Literacy, was based on a normative sample of $N = 2,831$ participants. This sample included two subgroups: "Nursery," or those who would be aged 4 in the current academic year ($n = 484$) and "Reception," or those who would be aged 5 in the current academic year ($n = 2,347$). Random samples of schools were drawn from England and Wales. The sample was stratified to ensure representative proportions of schools: in different regions, within metropolitan/nonmetropolitan LEAs, of different sizes, of maintained/independent status, and for the Reception sample, of different age ranges. There was a fairly even distribution of males and females among the two groups (Nursery: $n = 232$ males and $n = 252$ females; Reception: $n = 1,177$ males and $n = 1,169$ females).

Test results and feedback from the Nursery sample indicated that the testing was too rigorous for the LARRTEL, concluding that it was only appropriate for a small minority of very advanced Nursery aged children. Test norms for this sample were therefore not developed.

The description indicates the ages of children in Nursery and Reception by dividing each group into age bands of 4 months. In Nursery, $n = 138$ children were less than 3.6 years, $n = 146$ were between 3.6 and 3.9 years, and $n = 184$ were between 3.10 years and 4.1 years. In Reception, $n = 43$ children were between 3.10 years and 4.1 years, $n = 499$ were between 4.2 and 4.5 years, $n = 744$ were between 4.6 and 4.9 years, $n = 989$ were between 4.10 and 5.1 years, and $n = 16$ were more than 5.1 years.

Although we can hope that through the random sampling appropriate representation of children throughout England and Wales was completed, it would have been helpful for the authors to have presented information on demographics, ethnic backgrounds, bilingual speakers, and socioeconomic status of the children who were actually used for the normative sample.

Reliability. Authors stated that the reliability of the Reception group, which was used for the normative sampling, was .85 using the Cronbach's alpha index of internal consistency. Test-retest reliability was not reported.

Validity. The content validity was discussed by the authors, but was not statistically analyzed. Although the test does appear to test for the three areas that it sets a goal to evaluate (including recognition of readable material in various forms, recognition of when reading and writing are taking place, and understanding of the basic technical terms associated with reading), it is unclear why the test is heavily loaded on the final factor, with 10 of the 19 questions devoted to basic terms associated with reading. The authors do warn that the LARRTEL be used only as a *part* of initial assessment, in conjunction with other measures of importance such as matching and phonic skills.

Predictive validity was not assessed before publication of the teacher's guide. The publisher did provide this reviewer with a great amount of information gained after the test publication, which indicates very impressive predictive validity of the LARRTEL, especially when used in conjunction with teacher checklists.

Strand (1997) discusses a follow-up study, in which $n = 1,669$ of the original participants were used for the standardization of the LARRTEL. Results indicated that a combination of teacher-completed checklists and the LARRTEL were significantly correlated with Key Stage 1 (KS1) testing at age 7. Another study by Strand (1999c) indicated correlation coefficients of around .4 between $N = 1,223$ students tested with the LARRTEL at reception and their KS1 scores at approximately age 7. When combined with teacher checklists this correlation improved even further.

A very impressively large study of $n = 11,000$ children who were initially evaluated with the LARR between 1993 and 1997 were also evaluated at the end of KS1 (Strand, 1999a). Results indicated that there were positive predictive validities with later school attainment, most especially when combined with teacher-completed checklists. The author also found significant differences in baseline attainment (initial LARRTEL results) associated with pupil's age, sex, length of nursery education, economic disadvantage, ethnic group, and home language. Another study by Strand (1999b), analyzing the educational progress of $n = 5,000$ students who were first evaluated with the LARRTEL at reception, and then again at age

7 (end of KS1), indicated that initial baseline and further KS1 scores are affected by ethnic background, socioeconomic status, and gender.

Researchers Day and Day (1991) examined the concurrent validity of the original LARR, the Written Language Assessment Test, the Test of Early Reading Ability, and the Concepts About Print (CAP). They found that the intercorrelations of the total and subtest scores indicated generally low concurrent validity between these four tests of metalinguistic awareness. Concurrent validity evidence between the LARRTEL and other reading-readiness tests do not appear to have been undertaken.

COMMENTARY. The LARR Test of Emergent Literacy was based on initial research by Marie Clay et al., in the early 1980s. Contemporary research suggests that reading readiness is influenced by more factors than those tested by this examination, which include: recognition of readable material, recognition of when reading and writing are taking place, and understanding of the basic technical terms associated with reading. Other abilities, such as phonological skills (Blaiklock, 2004; Snowling; 1995), linguistic and conceptual organization (Jiménez & Artiles, 1990), alphabet knowledge (Johnston, Anderson, & Holligan, 1996), and left-right visual coding skills (Fisher, Bornstein, & Gross, 1985), have also been shown to have a predictive relationship with learning to read.

It is clear that the material provided by the test publishers (the teacher's guide) is meant specifically for teachers. It certainly reaches its goal of instructing them on how to use the test and gives enough background information on the test and its development for application to the classroom. It is not, however, a technical manual. This very successful test falls short in providing an international audience of researchers the background information that they would require on the rationale and theories that went into the development of the LARRTEL, including a full list of references. It also does not include any of the impressive studies on predictive validity of the LARRTEL, which were achieved after its publication.

It would also be helpful for the test publishers to provide potential users of the LARRTEL with the "teacher checklist" that they so often have used in conjunction with the LARRTEL. When used in combination, the validity of the test use did improve. To replicate the good predictive nature of the LARRTEL, the use of the same teacher checklist would be warranted.

SUMMARY. The LARRTEL could be categorized as a "reading readiness" test that was developed in England and Wales as a revision from the original Canadian test, the LARR. This test has been shown to have impressively high predictive value. When administered at age 4, studies have shown that there are high correlations with school attainment at age 7, most especially when used in combination with teacher checklists.

The test can be easily undervalued by the lack of information provided for the potential user. The publishers are highly cooperative at providing this information, but in the end, this test does not as of yet have a technical manual and those interested in understanding this test at a deeper level will need to "do their homework" by reading literature that has been published post hoc to test development. In addition, knowing the history of a test and its development is highly important and is not covered in any great detail in the current teacher's guide, nor are references given to support this background for the researchers or examiner who would like to further delve into the topic (despite their existence).

There are a lot of positives to the LARRTEL. It is an easy-to-use screening test that is engaging to children and takes relatively little time.

Although the test does provide a good baseline of a child's reading readiness, this reviewer would highly disagree with the publisher's claim that it can provide "detailed diagnostic information for individual children." This is a screening device only. Detailed information on any child must take place with individual testing that looks at a great many more skills than those indicated on the LARRTEL. Examinations better suited for individual diagnostics include the Woodcock Diagnostic Reading Battery (Woodcock, 1997) and the Wechsler Individual Achievement Test—II (The Psychological Corporation, 2001).

REVIEWER'S REFERENCES

Blaiklock, K. E. (2004). The importance of letter knowledge in the relationship between phonological awareness and reading. *Journal of Research in Reading, 27,* 36–57.

Day, K. C., & Day, H. D. (1991). The concurrent validity of four tests of metalinguistic awareness. *Reading Psychology, 12,* 1–11.

Fisher, C. B., Bornstein, M. H., & Gross, C. G. (1985). Left-right coding and skills related to beginning reading. *Journal of Developmental and Behavioral Pediatrics, 6*(5), 279–283.

Jiménez, J., & Artiles, C. (1990). Factores predictivos del éxito en el aprendizaje de la lectoescritura (Predictive factors of success in reading and writing acquisition). *Infancia y Aprendizaje, 49,* 21–36.

Johnston, R. S., Anderson, M., & Holligan, C. (1996). Knowledge of the alphabet and explicit awareness of phonemes in pre-readers: The nature of the relationship. *Reading & Writing, 8*(3), 217–234.

Psychological Corporation. (2001). The Wechsler Individual Achievement Test—Second Edition. San Antonio, TX: Psychological Corporation, Harcourt Assessment Company.

Snowling, M. J. (1995). Phonological processing and developmental dyslexia. *Journal of Research in Reading, 18*(2), 132–138.

Strand, S. (1997). Pupil progress during Key Stage 1: A value added analysis of school effects. *British Educational Research Journal, 23*(4), 471–487.

Strand, S. (1999a). Baseline assessment results at age 4: Associations with pupil background factors. *Journal of Research in Reading, 22*(1), 14–26.

Strand, S. (1999b). Ethnic group, sex and economic disadvantage: Associations with pupils' educational progress from baseline to the end of Key Stage 1. *British Educational Research Journal, 25*(2), 179–202.

Strand, S. (1999c). *LARRTEL and KS1 English Assessment outcomes.* (Online). Retrieved November 10, 2004, from http://www.nfer-nelson.co.uk/downloads/indicators/larrr/larrsummary.pdf

Woodcock, R. W. (1997). Woodcock Diagnostic Reading Battery. Itasca, IL: The Riverside Publishing Company.

[134]

Leadership Skills Inventory [Consulting Resource Group International, Inc.].

Purpose: To examine skills commonly used by effective leaders.

Population: Adults.

Publication Dates: 1992–1999.

Acronym: LSI.

Scores, 6: Self-Management Skills, Interpersonal Communication Skills, Counseling and Problem Management Skills, Consulting Skills for Developing Groups and Organizations, Versatility Skills, Total Score.

Administration: Group.

Editions, 2: Self, Other.

Price Data: Available from publisher.

Time: Administration time not reported.

Comments: Condensed and streamlined version of the self-assessment contained throughout the book, Transforming Leadership: Equipping Yourself and Coaching Others to Build the Leadership Organization (2nd ed.), which serves as manual; self-administered; self-scored.

Author: Terry D. Anderson.

Publisher: Consulting Resource Group International, Inc.

Cross References: For reviews by Mary Henning-Stout and George C. Thornton, III of an earlier edition, see 13:176.

Review of the Leadership Skills Inventory [Consulting Resource Group International, Inc.] by ALAN D. MOORE, Associate Professor of Educational Leadership, University of Wyoming, Laramie, WY:

DESCRIPTION. The Leadership Skills Inventory (LSI) is a 56-item self-assessment intended to help leaders evaluate their own skills related to a model of leadership termed "Transforming Leadership" advocated by the author, T. D. Anderson. It is a condensed version of the self-assessment contained throughout a book by the author (Anderson, 1998), which serves as the manual. It is intended for use as an assessment for personal development or as part of leadership training within an organization. A parallel version for others to rate the skills of a leader is available from the publisher. Both versions emphasize that the instrument is intended to focus on the "people" side of management, rather than technical management skill. This instrument should not be confused with an earlier instrument, the Leadership Skills Inventory (LSI; T4:1413; Karnes & Chauvin, 1985), designed to assess leadership skills of students in Grades 4–12.

The instrument comprises five "skill sets": Self-Management Skills, Interpersonal Communication Skills, Counseling and Problem Management Skills, Consulting Skills for Developing Groups and Organizations, and Versatility: Role, Style and Skill Shifting. Each section contains 12 skills to rate, except the last, which contains 8 skills. Each item is presented with a single word or phrase, followed by a more detailed explanation. For example in the first skill set, "Self-management," two items are "Grounding: control attention to focus in the present (not in the past or future)," and "Values Identification: identify, prioritize and live out a set of personal values."

A leader completing the assessment is asked to rate his or her skill level on a 10-point scale related to how well he or she can perform a given skill. A total for each skill set can be calculated, together with a grand total of all five sections. A score of 80% or higher for a section is interpreted to indicate "a high degree of confidence in your ability to perform the skills of a particular section. [A score less than 80%] indicates that you would likely benefit from some type of training in some of the specific skills of that section" (test booklet, p. 9).

DEVELOPMENT. The LSI is the second version of an earlier instrument published in 1992 and reviewed by Henning-Stout (1998) and Thornton (1998). No information about the development of the instrument is available in either the stand-alone version or the book, though it is claimed that the LSI "is based on research in applied behavioral science" (test booklet, p. 2). In an interview, Anderson reported that it grew out of his doctoral dissertation.

TECHNICAL. No information is provided concerning the standardization of the instrument. No rationale is offered for setting the threshold for a sufficiently high score on a skill to be at 80%. No normative data are reported. The instrument can be seen as standardized only in the sense that a printed version is available, so the items and response formats are identical across people and administrations.

No reliability information is provided with the inventory or in the associated book. Though test-retest estimation of reliability may not make sense for a self-description instrument, studies of internal consistency for subscales, together with factor analysis, would provide reliability estimates. Additionally, studies of interrater agreement among a leader's self-assessment and others' assessments of the leader would support interrater reliability.

The content validity evidence for the instrument is based on the degree to which items reflect a general model of "transforming leadership." According to the author, "[f]rom the … bodies of research and theoretical formulations have emerged 'chunks' of applicable knowledge or sets of easily learned and teachable qualities and skills" (Anderson, 1998, p. 53). A review of supporting literature cited by the instrument author revealed that most sources were theoretical rather than research-based. It is not clear how the particular items were chosen to represent the theory on which the inventory is based. As with most self-report instruments, responses to these items would appear to be especially susceptible to effects of social desirability, leniency, and situational factors. No evidence of construct validity or criterion-related validity is contained in the book, other than cursory references to a small percentage of leaders who score high on all skill sets. A search of literature indexed in ERIC found no studies where the validity of the LSI could be judged.

COMMENTARY. The value of this instrument appears to be in its use for helping readers of Anderson's book to understand elements of the leadership model advanced. It could also be useful as a focusing tool in a leadership-training environment. However, without more information about its development, and with no evidence of its reliability and validity, the user must be cautious in ascribing too much credence to results of the assessment. The recommendations of a reviewer of the previous version should still be followed: "Before this instrument can be recommended for use, the author must provide empirical data indicating that the supposed benefits will be attained, including accuracy of assessment and effects on development of leadership skills" (Thornton, 1998).

SUMMARY. The LSI is an informal self-administered, self-scored instrument for rating by a leader or by others of a leader's skills related to a model of "transformational leadership." The instrument is based on a premise that most managers lack important skills of leadership but that those skills can be identified and learned, with the result that both the leader and the organization benefit from this learning. Unfortunately, this instrument has limited evidence of its ability to measure proficiency in these skills or in assessing the development of these skills.

REVIEWER'S REFERENCES

Anderson, T. D. (1998). *Transforming leadership: Equipping yourself and coaching others to build the leadership organization* (2nd ed.). Boca Raton, FL: St. Lucie Press.

Henning-Stout, M. (1998). Test review of the Leadership Skills Inventory. From J. C. Impara & B. S. Plake (Eds.), *The thirteenth mental measurements yearbook* [Electronic version]. Retrieved August 2, 2004, from the Buros Institute's *Test Reviews Online* website: http://www.unl.edu/buros.

Karnes, F. A., & Chauvin, J. C. (1985). *Leadership Skills Inventory.* East Aurora, NY: DOK Publishers.

Thornton, G. C., III. (1998). Test review of the Leadership Skills Inventory. From J. C. Impara & B. S. Plake (Eds.), *The thirteenth mental measurements yearbook* [Electronic version]. Retrieved August 2, 2004, from the Buros Institute's *Test Reviews Online* website: http://www.unl.edu/buros.

Review of the Leadership Skills Inventory by NAMBURY S. RAJU, *Distinguished Professor, Institute of Psychology, Illinois Institute of Technology, Chicago, IL:*

DESCRIPTION. The Leadership Skills Inventory (LSI) consists of 56 Likert-type items, broken into five sections (Self-Management, Interpersonal Communication, Counseling and Problem Management, Consulting, and Versatility: Role, Style and Skill Shifting). Each item is scored on a 10-point (1–10) scale. The LSI can be used by a manager or leader (or anyone else) for assessing himself or herself or by others to provide feedback to the manager or leader. The LSI is designed to help managers/leaders develop their ability to handle the "people" side of management.

The first four sections of the LSI consist of 12 items each with a maximum possible score of 120. The last section consists of 8 items with a maximum possible score of 80. The LSI is designed for self-scoring and interpretation. It is stated in the LSI that a score of 96 (out of 120) in Sections 1–4 indicates that the manager has a high degree of confidence in his or her ability to perform the noted skills. A score of less than 96 would be an indication of a need for training in some skill areas. It is recommended that a manager compare his or her scores with scores given to him or her by others to better identify the strengths and the need for training.

DEVELOPMENT. The rationale underlying the development of the LSI and how to use the results from the LSI to transform leadership in organizations is detailed in a book by the LSI author: *Transforming Leadership* (2nd Edition). Chapters 2–8 in this book provide additional information about the 56 items (or skills) included in the LSI and describe an integrative model for developing self, others, and organizations.

TECHNICAL. No psychometric information was provided.

SUMMARY. The LSI offers interested individuals (managers/leaders) a mechanism for assessing their strengths and weaknesses of the skills essential for managing people. The book, *Transforming Leadership,* offers additional information about the LSI and describes methods that one could use to train for and maintain these essential skills. This reviewer is unable to assess the psychometric quality of the LSI (reliability, validity, score interpretation, and normative data) because the necessary psychometric data are not available to this reviewer.

[135]
Leadership Skills Profile.

Purpose: Designed to analyze "the strengths and weaknesses of managerial and executive candidates."

Population: Ages 18 and over.

Publication Date: 2003.

Acronym: LSP.

Scores: 42 Leadership Dimensions: Technical Orientation, Analytical Orientation, Decisiveness, Creativity, Thoroughness, Objectivity, Risk Taking, Open-Mindedness, First Impression, Interpersonal Relations, Sensitivity, Social Astuteness, Conflict Management, Communication, Formal Presentation, Persuasiveness, Negotiation, Listening, Achievement/Motivation, Self Discipline, Flexibility, Independence, Self Esteem, Emotional Control, Dependability, Ambition, General Leadership Effectiveness, Assuming Responsibility, Vision, Emphasizing Excellence, Organizational Spokesperson, Subordinate Involvement, Facilitating Teamwork, Inspirational Role Model, Short-Term Planning, Strategic Planning, Organizing the Work of Others, Delegation, Monitoring and Controlling, Motivating Others, Attracting Staff, Productivity.

Administration: Individual.

Price Data, 2003: $197 per administration; volume discounts available.

Time: [40] minutes.

Comments: Internet administration available; publisher scoring service provided via internet, fax, or mail.

Author: Douglas N. Jackson.
Publisher: Sigma Assessment Systems, Inc.

Review of the Leadership Skills Profile by PHILIP G. BENSON, Associate Professor of Management, New Mexico State University, Las Cruces, NM:

DESCRIPTION. The Leadership Skills Profile (LSP) is 352 items in length, and can be administered via the Internet, or completed manually on a provided answer sheet that can be returned to the publisher via mail or fax. All items utilize the very common Likert five-anchor answer options of *Strongly Disagree* through *Strongly Agree* (i.e., SA, A, N, D, SD). The LSP is untimed. Actual time to complete is likely to vary among test takers (although about 40 minutes is suggested as typical), and the manual suggests that any quiet environment is acceptable, including allowing the person to take the test home for completion.

Scores on the LSP are reported along 42 dimensions of expected job performance. These are further categorized into four major areas of leadership (cognitive managerial skills; interpersonal managerial skills; personal managerial qualities; and teamwork, supervision, planning and productivity). The report provided for each assessment gives scores on the 42 scales as percentile ranks, and also gives a bit more detail in reports by dimension that place the candidate in a general category (average, slightly above average, below average, etc.), and then lists the kinds of behaviors and tendencies the person is likely to display given the score on that dimension.

The test is intended for use in the workplace with executives and managers, and can be used for staffing decisions. The manual and other supporting materials also suggest the use of the test in succession planning. The test can also be used with these populations developmentally, as part of a coaching/mentoring program or other developmental activity.

DEVELOPMENT. The LSP is a relatively new test (copyright 2000, supporting material copyright up to 2003), but has a long history behind it. Developed by Dr. Douglas N. Jackson, and based heavily in his earlier work on the Personality Research Form (PRF), the Jackson Personality Inventory-Revised (JPI-R), and the Survey of Work Styles (SWS), the LSP can be thought of as having a near half-century of development work

behind it. The LSP drew from items and research from all of those earlier tests in its development.

The use of personality tests for employment decisions was highly criticized in the 1970s, but in recent decades a case has again been made for their application in these settings. The manual briefly reviews some of this recent research, although the earlier controversial nature of these tests is not really acknowledged. Potential users of the LSP should have at least a cursory understanding of the criticisms, even if later research can be cited to support this type of test.

Supporting materials for the LSP include a 33-page manual and an example of a "typical" sample report for a fictitious test taker. The manual in particular is relatively sophisticated in comparison to test manuals in general, and has both item analysis information and validation reports.

TECHNICAL. Reasonable technical information and analyses are provided in support of the LSP. However, the normative sample is not described as well as it could be. Although a sample of "well over a thousand" (manual, p. 19) respondents was used to select items for inclusion in the scales, little else is said. Reliability and validity data are also not as complete as would be desired—much is based on data for the SWS, and specific data on the LSP should be given. Validity data do include some correlations between LSP scales and 360 degree performance ratings, and reported correlations are solid, generally from the mid-.30s to high-.40s. However, significant details are lacking; for example, are all reported values for unique leaders, or do multiple raters evaluate the same leaders in at least some cases? It appears that the manager is the unit of analysis, and that multiple raters (coworkers) give information that is somehow combined into a total performance measure. I assume that each manager is only included once, but is rated by multiple raters in that process. In addition, details on the validation sample are notably lacking, including demographic data, basic job information, and other such details. Although it seems that there is empirical support for the LSP, greater detail in the manual would be helpful.

COMMENTARY. My greatest concern over the use of the LSP is that only a moderate level of sophistication is required to administer and use the test on a superficial level, but many of the applications are quite sophisticated, and the typical user is given little direction on how to use the LSP in practice. For example, the reports provided to users are very detailed, with lots of percentiles, graphs, and so forth, but it is not clear that the average user can relate all of this information to a specific job, and little is said about how to determine just which dimensions of the LSP are likely to be most important in a specific organization. In particular, just how complex patterns of scores relate to performance in jobs requires at least some knowledge of profile analysis, and the test's documentation is notably silent on such topics. The manual also talks about the potential use of the LSP in succession planning, but again, it is only a suggestion, and it is unlikely that all users will have a clear idea on how this should be done.

As mentioned above, there is still substantial controversy in the use of personality tests for employee selection. Although this is more commonly done now than it was 25 years ago, these issues need to be addressed in the supporting materials, especially the test manual.

SUMMARY. This test is likely one worthy of consideration in measuring the role of personality factors in job performance, especially at the managerial level. Although the LSP is itself a relatively new test, it is based on earlier, well-established tests, and thus has a substantial "history." The test is grounded in solid theoretical foundations, and has all appearances of being technically solid. However, because of the limited coverage of technical background issues in the manual, users should exercise moderate caution. With that caveat, the test is recommended.

Review of the Leadership Skills Profile by JOHN S. GEISLER, Professor of Counselor Education and Counseling Psychology, Western Michigan University, Kalamazoo, MI:

DESCRIPTION. The Leadership Skills Profile (LSP) is a 352-item instrument that utilizes selected items from previously published personality tests to predict scores on 42 job performance dimensions. All responses to item statements are on a 5-point Likert scale (*Strongly Disagree, Disagree, Neutral, Agree, Strongly Disagree*). The items are self-report in nature and are related to personal values, beliefs, attitudes, and interests related to the world of work. The responses to LSP items are then related to the 42 dimensions of leadership that are categorized into four groups: (a) Cogni-

tive Managerial Skills (Technical Orientation, Analytical Orientation, Decisiveness, Creativity, Thoroughness, Objectivity, Risk Taking); (b) Interpersonal Managerial Skills (Open-Mindedness, First Impression, Interpersonal Relations, Sensitivity, Social Astuteness, Conflict Management, Communication, Formal Presentation, Persuasiveness, Negotiation); (c) Personal Managerial Qualities (Listening, Achievement/Motivation, Self-Discipline, Flexibility, Independence, Self-Esteem, Emotional Control, Dependability, Ambition, General Leadership Effectiveness); and (d) Teamwork, Supervision, Planning and Productivity (Assuming Responsibility, Vision, Emphasizing Excellence, Organizational Spokesperson, Subordinate Involvement, Facilitating Teamwork, Inspirational Role Model, Short-Term Planning, Strategic Planning, Organizing the Work of Others, Delegation, Monitoring and Controlling, Motivating Others, Attracting Staff, Productivity).

In addition, the LPS Executive Summary section of the profile report also provides scores on three additional dimensions: Overall Expected Leadership Performance, Interpersonal Leadership Effectiveness, and Task Orientation. The latter two scores are also plotted on a grid. All scores are reported as percentile ranks. The responses to the LSP can be scored on-line, or sent to the publisher by FAX or regular mail. Scores are reported in a profile booklet (Leadership Skills Profile) that provides percentile ranks and bar graphs for each scale. A narrative interpretation is also provided for each scale that reports the relative ranking for each score (Very Low, Low, Below Average, Slightly Below Average, Average, Slightly Above Average, Above Average, High or Very High); the characteristics of each scale; and an analysis of the strengths and weaknesses of the candidates' predicted LSP scores.

DEVELOPMENT. The origins of the LSP lie in the author's (Douglas N. Jackson) previously published instruments (Jackson Personality Inventory-Revised [JPR-R], Personality Research Form [PRF], and the Survey of Work Styles [SWS]). Correlation coefficients between responses to these instruments and work performance ratings of 243 senior managers and executives were computed. Items for which responses met rigorous standards became part of the LSP. These item responses also ranked high on a differential reliability index, had minimum correlations with other scales, and had high rankings on an efficiency index.

The 243 persons in the normative group were enrolled in a program to develop and improve management and leadership skills. They were either sent to the program or volunteered to attend. They were all senior managers and executives holding titles such as president, vice-president, chief financial officer, general manager, etc. They performed job functions such as administration, accounting, research and development, finance, etc. They represented 62 different organizations. The work performance ratings were based on "360-degree feedback ratings from an average of more than 17 judges per participant" (manual, p. 3). The LSP scale scores do not come directly from the instrument itself, but are actually predictive scores based on 42 job performance dimensions.

TECHNICAL. Multiple correlation coefficients are reported between the LSP personality scale scores and job leadership performance (rated by coworkers). The coefficients ranged from .31 to .51 ($p<.05$). In addition, the leadership skill job measures were subjected to a factor analysis that produced six factors. These factors became the "criterion battery" that was used as the criteria for LSP scores prediction.

The reliability of the LSP is unknown. The author indicates that the three instruments that form the basis for the LSP have good reliability data. However, the only reliability data reports come from a study on the SWS (.71 to .90, total $N = 396$). Also, because the number of items from the SWS that are included in the LSP is unknown, these data are not meaningful.

The author also reports that two of the predecessor instruments (JPI-R and PRF) have demonstrated convergent and discriminate validity. Studies to support this contention are cited. However, because it is not known which or how many items from these instruments are included in the LSP, it cannot be assumed that studies conducted on them are relevant to the new instrument.

No information is provided on the reliability or validity of the 360-degree feedback instrument. No information is reported on the nature of this instrument, how it is scored, the types of scores derived, its origins, rationale, development, or theory.

COMMENTARY. The developers should be congratulated for the manner in which the LSP items were selected. The statistical procedures used in the selection of the items were rigorous, detailed, and complete. The procedures for selection were spelled out in detail, with formulas and explanations that were thorough and informative. The empirical nature of the item development is commendable. However, there are some drawbacks that need to be mentioned.

There is no information provided as to the nature, derivation, or rationale for the three Executive Summary Scores. This instrument may be utilized by human resource personnel for selection purposes, therefore, more information needs to be provided. Criteria for the scale scoring narrative statements (Very Low, Low, etc.) are missing (i.e., What percentile ranges = Very Low?) Also, percentile ranks may not be the best score reporting system for this type of assessment. Percentile ranks only report relative standing in a group. It would be much more helpful to have scores related to performance criteria.

Reliability and validity data are seriously lacking. Relying on reliability and validity data from predecessor instruments is not appropriate in an attempt to establish the worthiness of a "new" instrument. Also, no information is available about which items from the predecessor instruments are included in the LSP. The author of the manual also states "37 personality scales [are] contained in the LSP question booklet" (manual, p. 17). No support for such a statement is provided. The 42 LSP scores are predicted work/job leadership performance scores. Convergent and discriminate validity data are incomplete and the normative group is quite small and highly selective. The author reports that a factor analysis was conducted and that six factors emerged. However, the nature, description, and analysis of the factors were not provided.

SUMMARY. The developers have a good start on an interesting approach to work leadership assessment. Using personality test scores to predict how well persons would rate on leadership qualities as they relate to the world of work is innovative and has potential. The empirical research conducted to date on the LSP is most worthy and commendable. However, much more research must be reported before the instrument can be accepted for general use. The LSP must be considered as an experimental instrument at this time. Caution must be used when using the results. Reliability; validity; types of scores; normative group; factor analysis reporting; the origin, nature, and description of the work/job leadership instrument; and origin, description, and rationale for the Executive Summary scores are all factors that need improvement.

[136]
Learning Accomplishment Profile Diagnostic Edition.

Purpose: "Designed to provide the teacher of the young child with a simple criterion-referenced tool for systematic assessment of the child's existing skills."
Publication Dates: 1992–1997.
Administration: Individual or group.
Parts, 4: LAP-D Normed Assessment, LAP-D Screen, LAP (Revised Edition), Early LAP.
Comments: May be administered in station or individual format.
Publisher: Kaplan Early Learning Company.

a) LEARNING ACCOMPLISHMENT PROFILE DIAGNOSTIC EDITION NORMED ASSESSMENT.
Purpose: "Facilitates standardized, norm referenced assessment ... of developmental skills."
Population: Ages 30–60 months.
Publication Date: 1992.
Acronym: LAP-D.
Scores, 8: 4 development areas: Fine Motor (Writing, Manipulation), Language (Comprehension, Naming), Gross Motor (Body Movement, Object Movement), Cognitive (Counting, Matching).
Price Data, 2001: $624.95 per Normed Assessment including examiner's manual (62 pages), technical report, scoring booklets, and training manual (55 pages); $25.95 per 20 scoring protocols; $19.95 per technical report; $9.95 per examiner's manual; $12.95 per 10 Partial Person pads; $9.95 per 10 Plain Paper pads or 10 Diamond Design Cutting pads; $199.95 per single-user software (diskette or CD-ROM); $899.95 per 5-user site license (diskette); $1,799.95 per 10-user site license (diskette).
Time: (45–90) minutes.
Comments: "Designed to assist in making relevant educational decisions with regard to young children and to enable the teacher to develop developmentally appropriate instructional objectives and strategies"; hand or computer scoring available; LAP-D Windows software Version 3.5 system requirements: Windows 3.1, 3.51, or 98, 80486 or higher microprocessor, VGA or higher resolution screen supported by Windows, 8MB or more RAM, Windows-compatible printer.
Authors: Aubrey D. Nehring, Ema F. Nehring, John R. Bruni, Jr., and Patricia L. Randolph.

b) LEARNING ACCOMPLISHMENT PROFILE DIAGNOSTIC EDITION NORMED SCREEN.
Purpose: "Quick initial developmental instruments designed as entry level to the diagnostic process."
Population: Ages 3–5 years.
Publication Date: 1997.
Acronym: LAP-D Screen.
Scores, 6: 4 developmental areas: Fine Motor (Writing, Manipulation), Language (Comprehension, Naming), Gross Motor, Cognitive.
Price Data: $124.95 per Screen kit (specify age 3, age 4, or Kindergarten) including examiner's manual, 25 scoring booklets, 3 Kindergarten Progress Charts, and screening items (specify English or Spanish); $349.95 per ages 3/4/5 Screen package (specify English or Spanish); $9.95 per 30 scoring profiles (specify age 3, age 4, or Kindergarten, specify English or Spanish); $52.95 per Screen manuals for ages 3, 4, and 5 (specify English or Spanish).
Time: (12–15) minutes, untimed.
Comments: Designed to be completed by the child's classroom teacher; items selected from LAP-D Standardized Assessment.
Author: Kaplan Press.

c) LEARNING ACCOMPLISHMENT PROFILE—REVISED EDITION.
Purpose: "A systematic, ongoing, criterion-referenced assessment of a child's existing skills in fine and gross motor, cognitive/language, personal/social, and self-help skills."
Population: Ages 3–6 years.
Publication Date: 1995.
Acronym: LAP-R.
Ratings, 7: Gross Motor, Fine Motor, Pre-Writing, Cognitive, Language, Self-Help, Personal/Social.
Price Data: $274.95 per kit including manipulatives, supplies, toys for use during assessment, 380 Learning Activities for Young Children cards, 20 scoring booklets, instruction manual (132 pages), and IEP forms; $89.95 per 10 manuals (specify English or Spanish); $6.50 per Social or Self-Help Observation Checklist.
Time: Administration time not reported.
Authors: Anne R. Sanford and Janet G. Zelman.

d) EARLY LEARNING ACCOMPLISHMENT PROFILE.
Purpose: "An ongoing, criterion-referenced assessment system covering gross motor, fine motor, cognitive, language, self-help, and social/emotional domains."
Population: Birth to 36 months.
Publication Date: 1995.
Acronym: E-LAP.

Ratings, 6: Gross Motor, Fine Motor, Cognitive, Language, Self-Help, Social/Emotional.

Price Data: $334.95 per Early Learning kit including manipulatives, toys, supplies, 20 scoring booklets, Early Learning Activity Cards, and instruction manual (111 pages); $89.95 per 10 manuals (specify English or Spanish); $22.95 per 20 scoring booklets (specify English or Spanish); $9.95 per manual.

Time: Administration time not reported.

Authors: M. Elayne Glover, Jodi L. Preminger, and Anne R. Sanford.

Review of the Learning Accomplishment Profile Diagnostic Edition by LORAINE J. SPENCINER, Professor of Special Education, University of Maine at Farmington, Farmington, ME:

DESCRIPTION. The Learning Accomplishment Profile Diagnostic Standardized Assessment (LAP-D) (1992) is a norm-referenced instrument for assessing children between the ages of 30 and 72 months of age. The instrument covers three developmental domains: Cognitive, Language and Motor, with the latter subdivided into Gross and Fine Motor skills. Each domain includes two subscales: (a) Fine Motor: Writing and Manipulation; (b) Cognitive: Matching and Counting; (C) Language: Naming and Comprehension; (d) Gross Motor: Body Movement and Object Movement.

Additional items that come with the LAP-D Standardized Assessment include: a kit containing materials to use during the assessment, manuals that provide instructions and scoring criteria for each of the subscales, an examiner's manual (1992), a training manual (n.d.), and a technical report (1992). The training manual includes specific instructions, examples of administration, and practice exercises for learning how to use the instrument. Assessment information is recorded in a scoring booklet. There is also a booklet, a *Guide for Developing an Individual Education Program*, which contains a list of annual goals and objectives with space for individual objectives to be checked, depending on the child's needs.

The purpose of the LAP-D Standardized Assessment is "to assist in making relevant educational decisions with regard to young children and to enable the teacher to develop instructional objectives and strategies that are developmentally appropriate" (examiner's manual, p. 1). Administration time ranges from 45–90 minutes depending on the age of the child. Examiners can report results using percentile ranks, age equivalent scores, and normal curve equivalents (NCE). According to the technical report, the LAP-D Standardized Assessment may be used by teachers, psychometrists, psychologists, or others who have been trained in its administration. This instrument does not require a specific educational level, licensure, or certification.

In addition to the LAP-D Standardized Assessment, other assessment materials that may be purchased in this series include screening instruments and criterion-referenced instruments. The LAP-D Screens (1981, 1994), normed screening instruments for children ages 3–5 years, were developed by using items from the LAP-D Standardized Assessment. These screening instruments are not normed per se; but rather the norms of the LAP-D Screens are based on the full LAP-D Standardized Assessment.

The criterion-referenced assessments provide comprehensive assessments for preschoolers as well as infants and toddlers. The Learning Accomplishment Profile-Revised Edition (LAP; 1981, 1995), for children ages 3 to 6 years, assesses a child's skills and knowledge in all five developmental domains including: Cognitive, Communication, Motor (Gross, Fine, and Pre-Writing), Adaptive (Self-Help), and Personal/Social. The Early Learning Accomplishment Profiles (Early-LAP; 1988, 1995) for very young children, birth to 36 months, also assesses the five developmental domains. Each of these assessments includes a profile sheet that can be used to record initial results as well as follow-up assessment results. By examining the profile sheet, a teacher or parent can readily see the child's areas of strengths and needs as well as areas where the child is demonstrating scatter skills.

DEVELOPMENT. The LAP-D Standardized Assessment was originally developed in 1977 by the Chapel Hill Training-Outreach Projects. Between 1990 and 1992, the publisher (Kaplan Press) and personnel from the Chapel Hill Training-Outreach Project revised the LAP-D, reducing the number of items, updating materials, norming the instrument, and conducting a small study (30 children) concerning concurrent validity.

TECHNICAL. During the 1990–92 standardization process, normative data were collected from a sample of 792 children within seven 6-

month age groupings, between 30 and 72 months of age. The sample was chosen based on the 1990 U.S. Census and stratified by sex and race. The data were collected in 10 locations throughout the U.S.; unfortunately, none of the LAP-D Standardized Assessment manuals identify the locations or their geographic regions.

Reliability and validity information and studies reported in the technical report include internal consistency, content validity, concurrent validity, and construct validity. Concurrent validity shows a moderate correlation between the LAP-D Standardized Assessment and the Battelle Developmental Inventory (BDI), a norm-referenced assessment, and the Developmental Indicators for the Assessment of Learning—Revised (DIAL-R), a screening instrument.

COMMENTARY. During screening and assessment of young children, examiners gather information about a child's development in one or more of the developmental domains including Cognitive, Communication, Motor, Adaptive, and Social/Emotional. The LAP Screens and the LAP-D Standardized Assessment address only three areas. Thus, neither the LAP Screens nor the LAP-D Standardized Assessment provide a comprehensive measure for either screening or assessment of a young child's development.

That said, the LAP-D Standardized Assessment includes a variety of test items in three development domains, including Cognitive, Communication, and Motor Skills (Gross and Fine). The depth of this information would be valuable for educators and other team members to use in developing outcomes or goals for the individualized program, planning, and monitoring instruction for children with needs in one or more of these three areas. The *Guide for Developing an Individual Education Program with the LAP-D* could be a helpful reference for teachers as part of this process; however, it should be used with caution. Because the individual objectives are linked directly to test items, there is major concern that the teacher would "teach to the test." Furthermore, because many of the objectives are based on specific test items, they are narrow in focus and do not address more functional skills.

In addition to these limitations, the LAP-D manuals illustrate a lack of consistency that may result in misuse of this instrument. The examiner's manual and the training manual are not consistent in stated purposes for which the LAP-D Standardized Assessment may be used. The examiner's manual states that "the LAP-D is designed to assist in making relevant educational decisions with regard to young children and to enable the teacher to develop instructional objectives and strategies that are developmental appropriate" (p. 1). A broader purpose is stated in the training manual: "*To identify/place special needs students, *To assist in program planning, *To design an individualized program, *To design intervention strategies, *To validate early intervention programs, *To evaluate a program's effectiveness (i.e. Head Start, Title I), and *To fulfill Head Start OSPRI guidelines and requirements" (p. 4). The lack of consistency in stated purpose is troublesome and leads one to question for which purpose(s) was this assessment designed?

The LAP-D Standardized Assessment further lacks consistency in the discussion and recording of derived scores. The technical report states that examiners can report results using percentile ranks, age equivalents scores, and normal curve equivalents (NCE); yet, the training manual also includes a table to convert percentile ranks to t scores or z scores. The child's scoring booklet includes a place to record and plot z scores but no place to record and plot t scores. The scoring booklet does not include a place to record NCEs. These inconsistencies may be careless errors on the part of the publisher but examiners should demand a higher standard of quality control from developers and publishers of assessment instruments. Well-developed materials are consistent across manuals and protocols.

The LAP-D Standardized Assessment lacks technical adequacy, based on standards for educational testing described in *Standards for Educational and Psychological Testing* (American Educational Research Association, American Psychological Association, & National Council on Measurement in Education, 1999). The norms are over 10 years old and the norming sample is small (792 children). The instrument should be restandardized using an adequate norming sample. Additional studies are needed concerning the reliability and validity of this instrument.

In contrast to the LAP-D Standardized Assessment and the LAP Screens, the criterion-referenced assessments, the LAP and the Early LAP, cover all five developmental domains. Each of the domains is well-represented in number of test items. Depending on the child's age, one of these two instruments could provide a wealth of information concerning the child's current level of functioning at the beginning of the year. Later, teachers and other professionals could use the instrument periodically to monitor the child's progress.

SUMMARY. This review examined the LAP-D Standardized Assessment and other assessment instruments associated with the LAP series including the LAP Screens and the LAP criterion-referenced assessments. The LAP-D Standardized Assessment (1992) is a normed-referenced instrument for assessing children between the ages of 30 and 72 months of age. This standardized assessment focuses on the Cognitive, Communication, and Motor domains of development. According to the training manual, the instrument can be used as part of a multidisciplinary assessment to determine eligibility or in planning and monitoring a child's progress. The instrument needs to be restandardized and renormed. Additional information regarding technical adequacy should be included with the restandardization. The LAP-D Screens for children 3, 4, and 5 years of age should not be used because the instrument was not normed, per se; rather, the norms for these screens were based on the LAP-D Standardized Assessment. The LAP and Early LAP criterion-referenced instruments provide a comprehensive snapshot of a young child's development. Both instruments include a wide variety of items across all five developmental domains. The profile summary sheet available in both the LAP and Early LAP is a useful way to display assessment information and record individual child progress.

REVIEWER'S REFERENCE

American Educational Research Association, American Psychological Association, & National Council on Measurement in Education. (1999). *Standards for educational and psychological testing*. Washington, DC: American Educational Research Association.

[137]

Listening Comprehension Test Series.

Purpose: Designed to "assess the communication skills that enable a child to listen, understand and respond appropriately to information."
Population: Ages 4–14.
Publication Date: 1999.
Scores: Total score only.
Administration: Individual or group.
Levels, 5: A, B, C, D, E.

Price Data: Price data for starter set including teacher's guide group record sheet, 20 pupil booklets, At-a-Glance Guide, and audiocassette available from publisher.
Time: Untimed.
Comments: Linked to the National Curriculum for England and Wales, the Scottish 5–14 Guidelines, and the Northern Ireland Curriculum.
Authors: Neil Hagues, Rifat Siddiqui, and Paul Merwood.
Publisher: NFER-Nelson Publishing Co., Ltd. [England].

Review of the Listening Comprehension Test Series by MICHAEL D. BECK, President, BETA, Inc., Pleasantville, NY:

DESCRIPTION. The Listening Comprehension Test Series is composed of five test levels, A through E, designed to assess the current level of listening comprehension of children from ages 4 through 14. Each of the five levels is intended for a pair of age levels, with the five levels being statistically interconnected to enable cross-level score interpretation. The content at each test level is three or four listening selections, each followed by several multiple-choice and/or true-false items. Total test length ranges from 24 items at Level A to 38 at Level E to 45 at Level C. Listening selections are presented via an audio tape provided for each level. The other materials comprising the attractively packaged series at each test level are student test booklets containing the test questions and a score-summary page; a teacher's guide describing the series, providing development and technical information, and administration and scoring instructions; and an At-a-Glance Guide that summarizes the series and repeats the administration procedures. Test administration and scoring directions are clear; interpretive information is sound though sketchy. The test is untimed, but can generally be administered in 45–60 minutes.

Test administration proceeds by playing the audio tape for a selection, followed by the teacher's reading the test items aloud to test-takers, repeating the audio, then rereading the items. The first iteration of passages and questions, during which time students simply listen but do not attempt to respond, is designed to "focus" students on the task. When the selections and items are then immediately repeated, students respond to the questions. According to the publisher, repetition permits test-takers to become aware of what to listen for and minimizes any potential issues of inaudibility or distraction during test administration.

DEVELOPMENT. The content of the listening selections for each level is designed to offer a wide range in level of formality and style. Passages at the various test levels include short- and medium-length expository, opinion, and narrative texts; multiple-speaker interactions; poems; scenarios; first- and third-person accounts; and assorted "classroom-type" events. The selections at each level, although limited to three or four situations, reflect a broad range of practical situations, primarily but not exclusively school-based, in which children would be expected to evidence the ability to listen carefully. According to the teacher's guide, the selections "reflect something of the range of listening contexts in which pupils' skills may be assessed" (p. 7).

Selections are professionally read and tapes are of high audio quality. It is important to stress that the test was developed in the United Kingdom. As such both accents and, not infrequently, word choice will pose somewhat of a problem for United States students. This concern also applies to the wording of many of the subsequent test items.

Each listening selection is followed by from 5 to 12 questions based upon the passage. The majority of questions are four-option multiple-choice items, although several at each test level are true-false (or, at the highest two levels, true-false-can't tell) items. At two levels of the tests, several of the latter items are scored in pairs, with correct answers to both questions required in order to receive a raw score of credit. Other than this curiosity (unexplained in the teacher's guide), test scoring is easy and straightforward. At all levels, students respond by circling the correct answer choice, perhaps a common response procedure in the U.K., though unusual after primary school in the U.S. Most test-item options are presented in graphic form; most words that are presented are also represented with a drawing. Because teachers dictate all test items and answer choices, no student reading is required to respond to the questions. This pertains even to the true-false questions for which a check mark is presented as the symbol for True and an X represents False. To this reviewer, this symbolic representation of primary-level words seems unnecessary. Artwork is generally of acceptable clarity though some is confusing, and many drawings have an unclear link to the

verbal options (e.g., artwork of a pencil representing the answer option "a drawing" or a drawing of a tent to represent "a camper"). The artwork is of uneven quality, disappointing for the product of a major test-publishing house.

Test items are generally a mix of literal, simple inferential, and synthesis items dependent on the students' understanding of key elements of the texts, with a preponderance of the former items. Wording of most items is straightforward and clear, although the test's U.K. development would pose a nontrivial problem for U.S. students for several questions at each level. For several selections, at least one per test level, too many questions focus on the same elements of the story (e.g., at Level D, all six of the multiple-choice questions for one selection focus on "who" took a certain action, all such items using the same answer choices). Aside from issues regarding the sampling of key and representative content, such items and redundant answer choices create cueing issues for test-takers.

TECHNICAL. The Listening Comprehension Test Series was normed throughout the U.K. in 1999 using sizable and apparently representative samples of students. Norming involved students only of the middle age group for each level, with adjacent age norms developed via extrapolation. Resulting normative scores include month-by-month "standardized scores" (scaled scores with a mean of 100 and standard deviation of 15 at each age level) and percentile rank conversions for each age group. Standardized scores are interpreted via a 90% confidence band. Girls slightly outperform boys across all levels (by about 1 raw score point); other subgroup data are not provided. Given the location of the norming, potential U.S. users would likely find the normative metrics of unknown and questionable value. The series also provides "Progress Scores" for gauging student growth across successive levels of the tests.

Test difficulty by level is somewhat of an issue normatively. These problems are primarily a result of the apparently overly broad age span of each test level and/or the minimum amount of "growth" over age in the assessed construct. Examples of the normative issues include the following: Level A, designed for ages 4 through 6-3, is inappropriate for typical children below age 5. The median raw score for age 4-3, for example, is 6 out of 24—far too challenging a task for 4-year-olds. Norms for levels beyond A have little "top"; above-average students even at the youngest of the ages for which each level is designed answer correctly the overwhelming majority of items. Level C (for ages 8-0 through 10-3) is very easy overall, with the median raw score at age 8-0 being 24 of 34. After Level B, the test norms show almost no "growth" across the various levels' age span. For example, median raw-score change across the 2+ years for Levels C and D is only about 3 raw score points on a 34-point scale. These data make it curious, perhaps even unfortunate, that the publisher decided to extrapolate normative data on a month-by-month basis. The extreme of this lack of student growth is seen in Level 5 (ages 12-0 through 14-9) for which the raw score-to-standardized score conversions are *identical* for every month. Given the apparent lack of growth over age in the construct being assessed (or, a more bothersome hypothesis, inadequate vertical equating across adjacent test levels), the publisher's decision to provide monthly normative conversions after age 6 or 7 was regrettable.

Test reliability is acceptable for such a short test. Kuder-Richardson 20 reliability estimates are generally about .80; 1-week test-retest correlations are in the mid-.70s, with retest means approximately 2 to 6 raw-score points higher, likely reflecting a combination of memory for the selections and "format effect."

Little discussion of test validity is provided in the teacher's guide. Reference to the importance of listening skills in national curriculum guides in U.K countries is made, but no data or discussion of the mapping of these curricula onto the Listening Comprehension Test content are provided.

SUMMARY. For potential U.K. users, the Listening Comprehension Test, assuming content validity can be documented locally, appears to be a product worthy of consideration. Listening is a construct infrequently assessed in districtwide situations despite its importance in elementary instruction and prominence in published curriculum guides. However, because essentially the entire interpretive framework of the tests is normative, the tests could not be recommended for a U.S. population. Issues of wording, terminology, and accent in the selections and wording of the questions would pose problems for U.S. students, especially youngsters.

Listening Practices Feedback Report—360 Degrees.

Purpose: Designed "to provide self-knowledge about a person's listening behaviors at work."
Population: Adults.
Publication Dates: 1987–1999.
Acronym: LPFR-360°.
Scores, 7: Attention, Empathy, Respect, Response, Memory, Open Mind, Overall Listening Practices.
Administration: Individual or group.
Forms, 2: Self, Observer.
Price Data: Not available.
Time: Untimed.
Comments: Compares participant's and associates' reports of extent of use of 28 "good listening practices"; may be used as part of a listening training program for workers in business, industry, and government; system requirements: Windows 3.1/95/98.
Authors: Richard C. Brandt (LPFR), Janice D. Brandt (LPFR, "Psychometric Properties of the LPFR"), Victoria Emmert ("Psychometric Properties of the LPFR"), and Philip Emmert ("Psychometric Properties of the LPFR").
Publisher: Brandt Management Group.
[Editor's Note: The publisher advised in April 2004 that this test is now out of print.]

Review of the Listening Practices Feedback Report—360 Degrees by BRUCE THOMPSON, Professor and Distinguished Research Scholar, Texas A&M University, College Station, TX:

DESCRIPTION. The Listening Practices Questionnaire (LPQ) is a 28-item paper-and-pencil questionnaire completed both by each target listener using the Self form, and by six associates using the Observer form. The items on the forms differ only in the stem as regards the use of "I, the listener _____" or "The listener _____." The instrument is targeted at measuring perceived listening behaviors of workers in the business setting.

The LPQ items are represented as measuring six aspects of listening: (a) Attention, (b) Empathy, (c) Respect, (d) Response, (e) Memory, and (f) Open Mindedness. Related materials include an administrator's guide, a participant's guide, and a technical manual. Software is available that allows entry of data and then generates score reports for both individuals and the work group as a whole. The score report presents mean scores for both self- and observer ratings, and differences between these two sets of ratings on the 28 items (no total score differences). Also included is a facilitator's guide to assist in the use of LPQ data to improve listening in a given setting.

DEVELOPMENT. The LPQ was developed in the early 1980s. Workers at 22 companies provided developmental data. The set of 278 usable responses included criteria that participants felt differentiated good and poor listeners. The final set of items emerged from these data and a review of related literature.

The basis for organizing the 28 items into the six areas is difficult to discern. Apparently scale scores on the six areas are not generated, yet cutoffs for "high" performance in these six areas are noted on the score report. No factor analysis confirming these dimensions is reported. The relationship of some items to listening (e.g., ability to keep confidences, or following up with prompt action) is not fully clear.

TECHNICAL. Regarding what is described as "content/face" validity, the technical manual notes that the LPQ has been administered to over 1,500 business people, and that "no one has ever reported that the results were not a true description of their listening behaviors" (p. 4).

The LPQ invokes a 10-point Likert scale response format. It is not clear that the word anchors assigned to these numbers are psychologically equidistant. Thus, it may be inappropriate to assume the interval scaling required for computing means in score reports or in research uses of the scores.

Reliability was evaluated by computing coefficient alpha. These coefficients are evaluated in the technical manual by testing the null hypothesis that alpha equals zero. As noted elsewhere, this practice is questionable, because a small and completely unacceptable alpha may still be deemed statistically significant if sample size is reasonably large (Fan & Thompson, 2001).

For the Self form, alphas for the six scales are no higher than .66 and two are less than .45. One of the scales on the observer protocol had an alpha of .63. The utility of scores at even the scale level thus seems questionable. The manual refers to these results as if they were solely a function of the test, rather than of a variety of study features, including the sample itself (Thompson, 2003).

Validity evidence includes validity coefficients of LPQ scores with scores on the Listening Preference Profile. The largest of these values was $r^2 = .22$. LPQ scores were also compared with preference scores on the Myers-Briggs Type Indicator (MBTI). This was a bit unusual, because the manual notes that the LPQ "is not a personality profile" (p. 11), yet the MBTI is exactly that.

COMMENTARY. The value of LPQ scores from a measurement perspective is quite limited. The data yielded by the protocol may not be intervally scaled, or reasonably reliable, or valid except for cursory use in facilitating open-ended group discussions or self-reflection.

SUMMARY. Most psychological measures are useful principally as a vehicle for self-exploration or reflection with others. The LPQ has value from this perspective, even if the evidence regarding the psychometric properties of LPQ scores is quite limited. Where the use of scores is high stakes, or involves research, other measures that have been studied more thoroughly might be preferred.

REVIEWER'S REFERENCES

Fan, X., & Thompson, B. (2001). Confidence intervals about score reliability coefficients, please: An *EPM* guidelines editorial. *Educational and Psychological Measurement, 61,* 517–531.

Thompson, B. (Ed.). (2003). *Score reliability: Contemporary thinking on reliability issues.* Newbury Park, CA: Sage.

Review of the Listening Practices Feedback Report—360 Degrees by CLAUDIA R. WRIGHT, Professor, Educational Psychology, California State University, Long Beach, CA:

DESCRIPTION. The Listening Practices Feedback Report (LPFR-360°) was designed to measure individual- and other-based perceptions of listening skills and practices in the workplace for individualized feedback and group discussion. The typical test setting described is corporate or business, although anyone interested in how others perceive his or her listening skills may find the information derived from the report valuable for enhancing interpersonal communication.

The LPFR-360° is a 28-item-statement questionnaire with two forms representing the perceptions of (a) one's own listening skills ("Self" form) and (b) those listening skills held by others about a particular individual ("Associate Observer" form). A 10-point Likert-type response format is employed for both forms with anchors ranging from *almost never* (1) to *almost always* (10). The items are organized for presentation of feedback into 6 categories: (a) Attention (5 items), emphasizing focused conversations with others; (b) Empathy (5 items), understanding another's perspective; (c) Respect (4 items), sincerely considering another's viewpoint; (d) Response (5 items), preparing for and clarifying ideas; (e) Memory (4 items), maintaining consistency between agreements and outcomes; and (f) Open Mind (5 items), freedom from bias or emotions by emphasizing content and logic.

The LPFR-360° is marketed by the Brandt Management Group in conjunction with a 3-hour structured workshop that can be singularly focused on listening practices or integrated with other training topics. Four manuals are provided: (a) Facilitator's Guide, (b) Administrator's Guide, (c) Participant's Guide, and (d) Psychometric Properties of the Listening Practices Feedback Report. The Facilitator's Guide offers detailed directions for conducting workshops that include information about listening practices and the role of individual and group feedback for enhancing communication in the workplace. The Administrator's Guide provides helpful suggestions and detailed, step-by-step instructions for scheduling seminars, administering the LPFR-360°, collecting and compiling data, and explaining findings to participants. Computer software is included for scoring the questionnaires and generating summary reports. In the Participant's Guide, a conceptual description is presented for each item contained in each of the six LPFR-360° categories. Information about the questionnaire's development, reliability and validity information, and selected findings from research studies that have employed the LPFR-360° are discussed in the Psychometric Properties of the Listening Practices Feedback Report.

DEVELOPMENT. During the initial developmental phase of the instrument, 860 individuals from 22 companies were asked to identify colleagues they considered "good," "moderate," or "poor" listeners and to report the criteria ("five qualities or habits") they used to make such judgments; 278 surveys were returned (constituting a 32% response rate) yielding 2,780 criterion statements and 1,500 names of individuals classified as "good," "moderate," or "poor" listeners. From the list of criteria generated for the three listener classifications and based upon a literature review, 28-item-statements were constructed.

From the sample of 1,500 names provided, those classified as "good listeners" by at least three colleagues were assigned to the "good listener" group (n = 43); the same criterion was applied for "bad listeners" (n = 66). Questionnaire packets were sent to both groups inviting participation;

each packet of materials included one "Self" and six "Associate" forms for distribution to colleagues known to the respondent. Thirty respondents from the "good listener" group and 35 from the "bad listener" group returned completed packets representing a 69% and 53% response rate, respectively. A discriminant analysis based upon data compiled from the "Associate" questionnaires yielded 100% accurate classifications for both groups. All 28 item-statements were retained.

TECHNICAL.

Administration and scoring. The authors recommend that the test administrator be someone from within the organization who maintains confidentialities, handles data entry tasks, and enjoys some level of authority to contact employees who have not submitted their questionnaires. The LPFR-360° Questionnaire Scoring Software program computes an individualized report that includes a total score and a subscore for each of the six listening categories, a corresponding set of averaged "Associate" scores for each individual, and a set of group scores for the same measures when grouped data are requested. Detailed guidelines are provided for describing feedback individually and in groups. The authors cite appropriate cautions in interpreting self-report data and offer helpful suggestions for addressing culturally sensitive practices, specifically with respect to eye contact.

Reliability evidence of LPFR-360° scores. Based on a sample of 192 respondents (both individuals and associates) from several settings (bank, hospital, general management, instructional design, and nonprofit), internal-consistency (Cronbach alpha) estimates of reliability were calculated for the six categories of the LPFR-360° ("Self") and ranged from .44 to .66 (mdn = .56). Scores for the Total LPFR-360° ("Self") yielded an alpha of .84. In addition, Cronbach alphas for "Associate" scores compiled for three categories (Appropriateness, Business/Professional Listening, and Supportiveness) were .90, .84, and .63, respectively. (Note: the "Supportiveness" variable was not defined.) "Associate" total scores on the LPFR-360° produced an alpha of .94. No internal-consistency estimates were provided for the six subscores of responses derived from the "Associate Observer" form that correspond to those in the "Self" form and that appear in the feedback reports.

In general, internal-consistency estimates for "Associate" scores were higher than those obtained for "Self" scores due, in part, to the larger number of participants generating an averaged score for the associate analyses. The estimate for the "Supportiveness" dimension may have been lowered, however, if it represented a collection of items that involved more than one factor. Although the obtained Cronbach alphas for total scores fall in the acceptable range, the modest internal-consistency estimates obtained for the subscore categories indicate that caution is warranted when using these subscores as separate variables.

Validity evidence of LPFR-360° scores. The technical manual includes some support for the content, construct, and criterion-related validity of LPFR-360° scores. The evidence for content validity is detailed in the procedures employed during the developmental phase of the instrument (see the section on Development of the LPFR-360° in this review). The creation of subscore categories was based upon expert opinion.

Construct validity was examined by Emmert, Emmert, and Brandt (1994), who correlated LPFR-360° scores with scores on the Listening Preference Profile (LPP; Barker, Watson, & Weaver, 1992), a self-report measure designed to assess listener preferences for attending to messages that are action-, people-, content-, or time-press-oriented. No information was provided about the sample size or sample characteristics in this study. Further, no information was provided with respect to the reliability and validity evidence of LPP scores. Emmert et al. (1994) are cited as reporting statistically significant, moderate negative correlations between the LPFR-360° "Attention" scores and scores on the LPP subscales "Action" (r = -.47) and "Time Press" (r = -.43) suggesting that those respondents who expressed preferences for "listening to take action" and those "pressed for time" expressed difficulty paying attention to a listener, bringing proper closure to a topic, and being preoccupied with other concerns. Low moderate positive correlations were observed between scores on the LPFR-360° "Response" and LPP "People" scales (r = .30) and between scores on the LPFR-360° "Respect" and LPP "Content" scales (r = .31). The authors interpreted these findings to support the view that respondents who perceived themselves as seeking to maximize understanding (paraphrasing, seeking clarification), listened to connect with people; and those who tended to come to conversations prepared and tracked ideas with appropriate notes were more likely to listen to obtain information. In addition, those scores on the LPFR-360° "Associate" form that were designated as the "Supportiveness dimension" yielded a low moderate correlation with the LPP "action-oriented" scores (r = .30). In other words, associates tended to view those individuals who "listen to take action" to be more supportive listeners.

Criterion-related validity was provided by examining correlations among LPFR-360° total scores and subscores obtained from 110 respondents and their scores on the Myers-Briggs Type Indicator (MBTI; see 14:251). In a study conducted by Emmert, Emmert, and Brandt (1993), it was predicted that individuals classified as Extravert (E), Intuitive (N), Feeling (F), and Perceptive (P) on the MBTI would be rated as "better listeners." No other foundation was provided for these hypotheses. Approximately 110 participants completed both the LPFR-360° and the MBTI. No statistically significant outcomes were found supporting the hypotheses. With respect to the LPFR-360° subscores, two statistically significant outcomes were reported: (a) compared with those classified as Extraverts (E) on the MBTI, Introverts (I) rated themselves higher on "Listening Receptivity" (I = 14.8/E = 13.5; t(108) = -2.47, p < .05); and (b) "Associates" rated those classified as E higher than those classified as I on the "Supportiveness" dimension (E = 12.6/I = 12.0; t(108) = 2.91, p < .01).

Gender comparisons yielded statistically significant outcomes for females perceiving themselves as "better" listeners than men on the total LPFR-360° score and two subscores ("Attention" and "Response"). In addition, "Associates" rated females higher than males on two subscores ("Professionalism" and "Supportiveness"). All p < .05.

SUMMARY. Overall, it appears that the LPFR-360° has demonstrated some success as a vehicle for stimulating examination and discussion of listening practices in the workplace. In addition, the LPFR-360° shows promise for research purposes. In particular, the method appears sound for the initial development and content validation of the 28 item-statements.

The technical manual for the LPFR-360° would benefit from more detail and from a revision of outdated text. For example, the following information would be helpful to test users: (a) a description of the procedures used to select companies and to sample within a company-if the companies were "self-selected," these data should be identified; (b) sample sizes; (c) gender, ethnic, and job title breakdowns; (d) a description of the number and types of industries represented; (e) a description of the corporate climates/settings; and (f) because the labels for subscores have changed over time, a text revision to resolve inconsistencies in term usage. Additional useful psychometric information would include (a) stability estimates of scores that are not confounded by workshop participation; (b) internal-consistency estimates of reliability, particularly for the six categories of scores generated for the "Associate Observer" form; (c) a multitrait-multimethod analysis; and (d) a factor analytic approach to examine the factor structure of the LPFR-360° scores and to build subscales.

REVIEWER'S REFERENCES

Barker, L. L., Watson, K. W., & Weaver, J. B. (1992). *Development and validation of the Listening Preference Profile.* Paper presented at the International Listening Association Convention, Seattle, WA.
Emmert, V. J., Emmert, P., & Brandt, J. D. (1993). *An analysis of the Myers-Briggs Type Indicator differences on the Listening Practices Feedback Report.* Paper presented at the International Listening Association Convention, Memphis, TN.
Emmert, V. J., Emmert, P., & Brandt, J. D. (1994). *An analysis of pre- and post-listening training scores on the Listening Practices Feedback Report.* Paper presented at the International Listening Association Convention, Boston, MA.

[139]
Martin and Pratt Nonword Reading Test.

Purpose: Designed to "investigate the [phonological] recoding skills of students."
Population: Ages 6–16.
Publication Date: 2001.
Scores: Total score only.
Administration: Individual.
Forms, 2: A, B.
Price Data, 2002: A$120 per starter set including record booklet, stimulus book, and manual (60 pages); A$16.50 per 10 record booklets (A or B); A$35 per stimulus book; A$60 per manual.
Time: (5–10) minutes.
Authors: Frances Martin and Chris Pratt.
Publisher: Australian Council for Educational Research Ltd. [Australia].

Review of Martin and Pratt Nonword Reading Test by KRIS L. BAACK, Assistant Professor of Speech Pathology, University of Nebraska—Lincoln, Lincoln, NE:

DESCRIPTION. Designed to "investigate the [phonological] recoding skills of students" (manual, p. 12), the Martin and Pratt Nonword Reading Test is suitable for individual administration to students aged 6 to 16 years. The purpose of this instrument is to determine a students' ability to recode nonwords phonologically. The Martin and Pratt Nonword Reading Test contains a manual, test book, and 54 items on both Form A and Form B.

The test is to be administered by teachers, guidance counselors, speech-language pathologists, or other qualified educational professionals. In addition, administration of this instrument requires familiarity with phonetics and the ability to listen and understand the utterance phonetically. Both Form A and Form B contain seven practice phonemes prior to starting the test. The test follows the practice items with 54 test items listed in order of difficulty. Testing should be discontinued when the student has failed on 8 consecutive items. However, the authors suggest the student be allowed to finish all items on that page. Any item correctly stated after the eight consecutive errors is not included in the raw score.

Scoring for the Martin and Pratt Nonword Reading Test is in determining responses as phonetically correct or incorrect. The authors provide a pronunciation guide and recommend the administrator practice listening and transcribing the sounds phonetically until competent. However, administrators unable to transcribe may still obtain a raw score as long as they can determine acceptable pronunciations of the items. When testing is completed, the administrator will total the number of correct responses by summing any scores of 1 scored before the discontinued level was reached. This number is recorded as the raw score. Other scores that can be obtained from the test include: interval scores, standard scores, percentile ranks, and age-equivalent scores.

DEVELOPMENT. According to the authors, the development of this instrument is to monitor recoding skills and to determine reading difficulties associated with poor phonological recoding skills. To insure reading in alphabetic languages, skilled word recognition relies on the acquisition and application of phonological skill and knowledge (Adams, 1990; Byrne, 1998; Garton & Pratt, 1998). In the early stages of reading, students must become aware of the alphabetic principle (letters on a page are the sounds of the language), if they are to learn to read successfully. This letter-sound mastery, referred to as phonological recoding, allows students to become efficient readers. Martin and Pratt acknowledge that some argue students do not need to acquire good phonological recoding skills and can rely on context to identify words they cannot read. The authors deem this as not an effective strategy for reading generally and for learning new words specifically. They state the extent that context predicts what an unknown word is may vary from less than 10% to a maximum of 30% (Finn, 1978; Garton & Pratt, 1998; Gough, 1983).

Item selection began with constructing 763 nonwords. Two- and three-letter nonwords were constructed by combining consonants and vowels from the lists to include all legal vowel and consonant combinations. More difficult items that included all possible vowel and digraph pronunciations and consonant clusters were constructed for the upper primary and secondary classes and to ensure that a representative sample of nonwords was included. Items were compiled from the Lindamood Syllable Construction Chart (Lindamood & Lindamood, 1992) and charts from Smelt (1976). Possible vowel settings and consonant clusters were randomly combined to form 182 of the 763 nonword items. If an item had more than one possible pronunciation, it was removed from the list; 567 two- to eight-letter nonwords remained.

Continued testing of the 567 nonword items narrowed the list to 441 items, to 350 items, to 54 items for Form A and 54 different items for Form B. At the 567 level, items were categorized as easy (items said correctly by 60% of the student sample and the correlation of the item with grade was at least .3 and at least .3 with the total items correctly pronounced), medium (items said correctly by 30–60% of the student sample and the correlation of the item with grade was at least .5 and at least .6 with all correct items), or hard (items said correctly by less than 30% of students, with the correlation of these items with grade and all other items at least .3). The 441 items were evaluated by a speech pathologist and items with more than four legal pronunciations or without legitimate phonological strings were removed. Any items that were foreign words with a common English usage or were abbreviations of common words were eliminated. To narrow the items from 441 to 350, 150 students ages 5–11 read all items with results correlated to the Coloured Standard and Progressive Matrices and Neale Analysis of Reading Ability—Revised. Equivalence of item difficulty and content was maintained by assigning an equal number of items from each reading age to each form. Items on both forms gradually increase in their difficulty from digraphs to single-syllable nonwords to multiple-syllable words.

TECHNICAL. The standardization sample for the Martin and Pratt Nonword Reading Test was made up of participating students from schools in southern Tasmania. They were randomly selected from class lists to obtain an equal number of male and female students from each year (Grades Prep–10) and represented ages 6–16 years. A total of 863 students were tested on both Forms A and B.

Although the ages and grade levels are appropriate for standardization, there is a challenge with the lack of diversity in the population. According to the authors, southern Tasmania has limited social diversity and there is no mention of cultural or ethnic diversity.

When examining the mean and standard deviation, student performance on both Forms A and B shows a gradual improvement with age that indicates a developmental improvement in phonological recoding ability.

Reliability was examined three ways: test-retest (mean administration interval of 3 months), alternative-form, and internal consistency. There is a high test-retest reliability coefficient for both Form A and Form B and they are highly reliable alternative forms providing a consistent measure of the ability to recode phonetically. Finally, the Kuder-Richardson procedure, showed a high reliability of both Form A and B for each age category, suggesting both forms are internally consistent.

To examine validity, the authors gathered a massive amount of data from other diagnostic instruments (27 tests or subtests). Results indicate the correlations between the Martin and Pratt and other measures of verbal ability and comprehension are stronger for those tests involving reading than for tests that emphasize listening and speaking.

COMMENTARY. There are many strengths to the Martin and Pratt Nonword Reading Test: ease of administration and scoring, test items are accurately identified as those needed for reading, timeliness, alternative forms, validity, and reliability. Challenges with this instrument appear generally and specifically. Generally, there is the issue of the professional's personal opinion on the use of a nonword-testing instrument. For many educators and speech-language pathologists the issue of context is paramount when testing or teaching reading. Thus, these individuals would have a philosophical difference with an instrument for which test items are nonwords. A specific challenge is the lack of social or cultural diversity in the standardization sample. The validity evidence for the instrument and other nonword reading tests is very high, which would help counter the social and cultural challenge.

SUMMARY. If the professional is of the mind-set that nonword reading tests are preferred over word reading tests, this instrument would be one to use. Martin and Pratt have provided solid background and rationale for using their instrument. In addition, they were thorough in their development of items and standardization procedures. The Martin and Pratt Nonword Reading Test is an easy-to-administer instrument that measures a student's phonological recoding skills.

REVIEWER'S REFERENCES

Adams, M. J. (1990). *Beginning to read: Thinking and learning about print.* Cambridge, MA: MIT Press.
Byrne, B. (1998). *The foundation of literacy: The child's acquisition of the alphabetic principle.* Hove, UK: Psychology Press.
Finn, P. J. (1978). Word frequency, information theory, and cloze performance: A transfer feature theory of processing in reading. *Reading Research Quarterly, 78,* 508–537.
Garton, A. F., & Pratt, C. (1998) *Learning to be literate: the development of spoken and written language* (2nd ed.). Oxford, UK: Blackwell Publishers.
Gough, P. B. (1983). Context, form and interaction. In K. Rayner (Ed.), *Eye movements in reading: Perceptual and language processes.* San Diego, CA: Academic Press.
Lindamood, C. H., & Lindamood, P. C. (1992). *Auditory discrimination in depth.* Austin, TX: PRO-ED.
Smelt, E. D. (1976). *Speak, spell and read English.* Melbourne, Australia: Longman.

Review of the Martin and Pratt Nonword Reading Test by ANNABEL J. COHEN, Professor, Department of Psychology, University of Prince Edward Island, Charlottetown, Prince Edward Island, Canada:

DESCRIPTION. The Martin and Pratt Nonword Reading Test measures English phonological recoding skills of children of ages 6 to 16 years. Norms for each 6 months of age, based on a Tasmanian (Australian) sample, aim to identify poor performers who may require remedial work or special attention. Early identification of phonological problems is important in order that appropriate phonological skills can be acquired from the outset.

The test entails asking the child to read a given nonword out loud. In the Martin and Pratt test, all nonwords are supposedly equally unfamiliar to those who take the test because none of the nonwords has ever been seen before.

The manual suggests three applications of the Martin and Pratt Nonword Reading Test. The first and most obvious is the monitoring of phonological recoding ability in school and detecting difficulties from as early as 6 years of age. Secondly, the types of errors that are made can indicate specific problems and suggest the direction for follow-up diagnostic tests and remediation. Finally, the test may be helpful in research on reading.

Administration and scoring. The manual recommends that the administrator of the test be a teacher, guidance officer, speech pathologist, or other relevant professional. The test entails 7 single-letter practice items followed by 54 test items listed in order of increasing difficulty. The test scoring ends when eight consecutive errors are made. Familiarity of the administrator of the test with the speech sound correspondence to the letters is obviously essential.

The two forms of the test, A and B, are essentially equivalent so that retesting, should it be of interest, would employ the form not yet used. Testing is carried out in a quiet room. The test administrator presents each page of one form of the test to the child. The test book is made of a heavy cardboard, 45 pages in length, the first half for Form A, and the last half for Form B. The coil binding makes it easy to show one page at a time to the student. There are six nonwords per page, with the exception of the initial page of seven practice letters.

The most informative scoring by the test administrator entails use of the 44-item phonetic alphabet. However, if the administrator is not fluent with this alphabet, noting the confusions made by the student in terms of English letters will be still helpful. Even a score of right or wrong is useful, though not as useful as the two other levels of scoring, which provide more detailed information about particular problems. In the event of a poor score, it is advised for the test to be readministered by a test administrator familiar with the phonetic code and using the alternate form not yet seen by the student. Accents of students or speech impediments can be accommodated so that scores are not lowered.

Conversion and interpretation of scores. A variety of scores are provided by the Martin and Pratt Nonword Reading Test. The test manual emphasizes that the norms reported in the manual were established in the state of Tasmania. Raw scores are converted to standard scores (mean = 100, *SD* = 15), percentile ranks, and age-equivalent ranks for A and B Forms of the test from age 6 years 0 months to 8 years 11 months at intervals of 6 months, and then for ages 10 to 16 at yearly intervals.

DEVELOPMENT. Items were compiled from the Lindamood Syllable Construction Chart and charts presented "in Smelt (1976) of all possible English vowels, digraphs and consonant clusters" (manual, p. 39). A pool of 763 nonword items was created. Retaining items with only one pronunciation left a pool of 567 nonwords. Approximately 200 students representing the ages of just under 6 years to just under 12.5 years each read one quarter of this set in order to assign a difficulty level to each nonword with respect to age, grade, and gender of the speaker. Items were classified as easy, middle, or difficult based on percent of students at each grade level answering correctly.

There were 441 words left after excluding items that were not in one of these categories. Of these any that had more than four legal pronunciations according to inspection by a speech pathologist, any that appeared as a word in an Oxford Dictionary or an Australian dictionary (Macquarie), or any that were abbreviations were excluded. The remaining pool of 350 nonwords was read by 150 Tasmanian (city of Hobart) primary school and high school students of 5 to 11 years of age.

Items were excluded if they were correlated at less than .3 with all correctly pronounced items or with reading age. Of the remaining items, retention depended on correct performance by between 40–60% of the students at one reading age or at two consecutive reading ages, assuring the inclusion of items of medium difficulty for each age. It is not clear from the manual exactly how the final set of 108 items was chosen although it is pointed out that items of similar content were distributed equally across the two forms of the test.

TECHNICAL. Standardization involved 863 students attending schools in southern Tasmania and controlled for age, grade, gender, community size, and economic status of school location. Age ranged from 6 to 16 years. Students were randomly selected from class lists from Grades Prep–10 and were tested on both Forms A and B. The selection of schools was in accordance with a stratified sampling design to match the 1991 Census distribution of the socioeconomic characteristics of a southern Tasmanian government school population in the three school districts of Southern Tasmania. In the standardization sample, 29 students had parents with a first language other than English.

A validity sample of approximately 200 children representing the ages of 6 years 0 months to 15 years 11 months was administered tests in four 1-hour sessions to obtain correlations between both raw and standardized measures of phonological recoding, phonological awareness, reading rate, word reading, reading and listening comprehension, verbal ability, IQ, and several other abilities tapping such well known resources as the Woodcock Reading Mastery Tests—Revised (WRMT-R), Peabody Picture Vocabulary Test—Revised, Oral and Written Language Scales (OWLS), Woodcock-Johnson Psycho-Educational Battery—Revised: Cognitive Ability Tests, Kaufman Test of Educational Achievement, Neale Analysis of Reading Ability—Revised, Raven's Standard Progressive Matrices, and the Wechsler Intelligence Scale for Children (WISC-III). The authors note that correlations were stronger for tests that involve reading than those that involve speaking.

Three measures of reliability are provided. Test-retest reliability was carried out on approximately half the validity sample and produced reliability estimates of .96 for Form A and .95 for Form B. Alternative forms reliability based on the entire standardization sample of 863 gave raw score reliability of .96 and standard scores of .92. Internal consistency obtained through split-half reliability was also greater than .90 for both Form A and B within each age, and over all ages. Reliability is, therefore, impressive although the alternative forms reliability for standard scores might be higher.

COMMENTARY. The Tasmanian/Australian context of the test raises several issues. The test originates in the Australian state of Tasmania and has been normed for Tasmania. Because of their isolation, islands might be less than ideal for creating norms for the larger mainland. One can only assume that the use of Tasmania for data collection was based on practicality and expedience, along with the assumption that the construct under investigation was highly robust and would change little from one locale to another given the uniformity of the Australian educational system.

The manual does make a point of noting early on that the difficulty levels were based on Australian children and that the choice of nonwords reflects letter combination to which Australian children would be normally exposed.

Reference to the problem of accents of the students gives the example of a New Zealand accent, which is common in Australia but uncommon in America. In this particular example, pronunciation of pin as pen would be acceptable if the student were from New Zealand, but not if he or she were from Australia. Differences between American and Australian accents could require a revision to the phonetic coding of the form for broad use in America.

One of the assumptions about the use of nonwords is that they are equally unfamiliar to all. It is noted that the authors resist making the suggestion that semantic processing is avoided. No doubt semantic associations are brought to mind by these nonwords, some more than others.

It would have been useful if the length of time required to learn the phonetic recoding system were given during the discussion of the test administration. This information appears in the section on technical information. One hour of instruction and 3–4 hours of practice were required for those who administered the test to the standardization group.

Although the alternate forms reliability correlation is extremely high, different norm tables are required for each form. Differences are small and do not suffer the problems of lack of form equivalence such as those that characterized the ACER Applied Reading Test (Daniel, 1995). Considerable detail is provided about the validity sample.

SUMMARY. The Martin and Pratt Nonword Reading Test can be quickly and easily administered to assess the phonological recoding skills of children 6 to 16 years of age. Tables of norms, based on an Australian sample, facilitate interpretation. The test appears to be directed to the Australian audience, and several relatively minor aspects make it less suitable for use in other English-speaking countries, at least on a grand scale. The authors argue persuasively that every school child is owed such a test in order to be assured that phonological skills are acquired early on and are developing normally. Alternative forms enable testing for reliability. Empirically based validity and reliability measures are impressive. Sensitivity to age is greatest for younger ages, where it is most needed. The test is useful as a screen for reading difficulties, for monitoring improvement, and for research.

REVIEWER'S REFERENCE

Daniel, M. H. (1995). [Review of ACER Applied Reading Test]. In J. C. Conoley & J. C. Impara (Eds.), *The twelfth mental measurements yearbook* (pp. 9–12). Lincoln, NE: The Buros Institute of Mental Measurements.

[140]

Maslach Burnout Inventory, Third Edition.

Purpose: Constructed to measure three aspects of burnout.

Population: Members of the helping professions including educators and human service professionals.

Publication Dates: 1981–1996.

Scores, 3: Emotional Exhaustion, Depersonalization, Personal Accomplishment.

Administration: Group.

Price Data, 2001: $65 per review kit including Human Services Survey booklet, Educators Survey booklet, General Survey booklet, set of scoring keys, and manual (1996, 56 pages); $28 per 25 nonreusable survey booklets (specify Human Services, Educators, or General); $17.50 per 25 Human Services Survey or Educators Survey demographic data sheets; $14 per 25 scoring keys; $42 per manual.

Authors: Wilmar B. Schaufeli, Michael P. Leiter, Christina Maslach, and Susan E. Jackson.

Publisher: CPP, Inc.

a) HUMAN SERVICES SURVEY.

Acronym: MBI-HSS.

Population: Staff members in the Human Services profession.

Time: (10–15) minutes.

b) EDUCATORS SURVEY.

Acronym: MBI-ES.

Population: Educators.

Time: (5–10) minutes.

c) GENERAL SURVEY.

Acronym: MBI-GS.

Population: Other workers in the service professions.

Time: (10-15) minutes.

Cross References: See T5:1590 (69 references) and T4:1552 (30 references); for reviews by David S. Hargrove and Jonathan Sandoval of an earlier edition, see 10:189 (34 references).

Review of the Maslach Burnout Inventory, Third Edition by ROBERT FITZPATRICK, Consulting Psychologist, Cranberry Township, PA:

DESCRIPTION. The Maslach Burnout Inventory (MBI) is the overall name for three versions of a questionnaire intended to measure burnout. The original 22-item Human Services Survey (HSS) is designed for human services staff members required to work directly with clients, who are referred to as *recipients*. The Educators Survey (ES) is the same as the HSS except that the word *students* is used rather than *recipients*. For these two versions, the authors define burnout as "a syndrome of emotional exhaustion, depersonalization, and reduced personal accomplishment that can occur among individuals who work with people in some capacity" (manual, p. 4). The third, most recently developed version is the 16-item General Survey (GS), for which burnout is defined as "a state of exhaustion in which one is cynical about the value of one's occupation and doubtful of one's ability to perform" (manual, p. 20).

The respondent is to rate each item on a 7-point scale ranging from *Never* to *Every day*, to describe the frequency with which the respondent experiences the feeling described in the item. Each version produces three scores, which are collectively thought to indicate the extent of burnout. For the HSS and ES, the scores are the summed ratings for three aspects: Emotional Exhaustion (nine items reflecting fatigue or stress), Depersonalization (five items referring to feelings of callousness or indifference in regard to recipients or students), and Personal Accomplishment (eight items about feelings of enthusiasm and effectiveness in working with the people). The GS version also has three scores, but these are somewhat different from those of the other versions: Exhaustion (five items identical or highly similar to five of the HSS/ES items), Cynicism (five items indicating detachment from or cynicism about one's work), and Personal Efficacy (six items describing feelings of accomplishment in or worth of one's job). The scoring key does not indicate how the GS should be scored, but the manual suggests computing the mean rating for each of the three sets of items. Each version may be administered by untrained staff or self-administered by the respondent. There is no provision for missing responses, so administrators are urged to be sure that all items are completed.

The authors recommend no way of combining the three scores into an overall index of burnout. The manual suggests that modern multidimensional statistical methods make it readily possible to work with three scores rather than one. The manual also suggests that scores not be used for individual diagnosis or assessment but rather to provide feedback to the individual and to identify group or organizational trends in the three scored aspects.

DEVELOPMENT. Exploratory research on the popularly understood concept of burnout produced a preliminary form of the HSS with 47 items, derived from the general experience of the researchers. The items were studied in further research using factor analytic techniques and reduced in both number and style of response. Three factors were shown to be predominant and to be measured to the researchers' satisfaction. The final version of the HSS was chosen solely on the basis of factor analytic results. Later research has shown that two items are loaded on two of the three primary factors; the manual recommends the continued use of these items except in conducting analyses that are "sensitive to mild departures from the predicted factor structure" (p. 11).

The ES version was developed simply by substituting *students* for *recipients*. Statistical checks have been consistent in suggesting that the ES version functions in basically the same way as the HSS.

Research on the GS version started with a 28-item form, with items similar to those in the HSS/GS in the Exhaustion factor, but somewhat modified for Professional Efficacy and substantially so for Cynicism. After several studies, the final form with 16 items was decided upon.

TECHNICAL. Norm information in the manual is derived from a number of studies of each version. The total sample for the combined HSS/ES norms is 11,067 workers in various occupations. For the GS, the sample is 5,259 in several occupations from 3 countries. Separate HSS/ES norms are provided for various demographic groups. However, there apparently has been no effort to develop a normative sample that is representative of any broad group of respondents. Normative information is presented in two ways: by reporting means and standard deviations of scores obtained for each norm group, or by showing score ranges that divide a study sample into upper, middle, and lower thirds. It appears that the standard deviations are measures of variation for individuals; users should be aware that the standard deviation for a group will be smaller. More systematic norms are needed, preferably in the form of percentile ranks.

Though the questionnaires are short, reliability seems adequate. Internal consistency is fairly high within scales. Test-retest reliability is only moderate, but that seems appropriate for scales that might be used to measure change over time.

The items appear to measure attitudes that might plausibly be associated with a concept called burnout. However, it should be remembered that, in spite of extensive research efforts, the burnout concept is not one that has been conclusively defined and distinguished from other states such as depression, stress reactions, or boredom. One problem is that burnout presumably would happen after a good start on the job—something cannot burn out if there was no fire. But most of the items in all the MBI versions refer to current state only, rather than to a deteriorated or burned-out status.

Some evidence for the validity of the MBI scales resides in the results of numerous factor analytic studies confirming the three-factor structure of the attitude complex viewed as burnout. Note, however, that the factors are not quite the same in the GS version as in the HSS/ES. The manual reports that groups who do not work directly with clients do not achieve that same factor structure; that is the main rationale for the development of the GS version. There have apparently been no studies comparing HSS/ES with GS.

The MBI, especially the HSS/ES, has been studied in conjunction with a number of other constructs such as depression and stress. In general, correlations have been moderate and the usual interpretation has been that the MBI measures a related but separately identifiable entity (or trilogy).

The manual also claims validity evidence in that a number of small studies have found correlations between the MBI scores and reports of behavior or attitude by coworkers, spouses, and the respondents themselves.

The manual does not discuss in any detail the potential benefits and problems involved when the MBI is administered. Is it possible, for example, that some people's feelings of frustration with their jobs might be increased by the experience of completing one of the MBI questionnaires?

COMMENTARY. The authors of the MBI are deeply involved in research on burnout. Much of the manual is devoted to discussion of this research and suggestions for further research. Thus, the mundane matters of scoring and norms are somewhat neglected. The authors and others have pointed out that interventions shown to prevent or mitigate burnout are conspicuously lacking—not an encouraging sign to potential users who may wish to use the MBI as part of a program to promote good work motivation.

Just what is burnout? To say that it consists of three aspects is not entirely clarifying, especially because the aspects are said to differ depending on the type of work in which the respondent is engaged. As measured by the MBI, burnout is

thought to be substantial when two scale scores are high and the third is low, but what if one indicates burnout and the others do not? Some researchers have used a total score as an index of overall burnout but the manual labels one such study "unorthodox" (p. 16) and implies that use of a single score is to distance oneself from the main body of burnout research.

SUMMARY. As the manual points out, the MBI is "recognized as the leading measure of burnout" (p. 1). Although burnout is a controversial concept, an extensive body of research and application has involved the MBI or something similar. If one is to study or apply the idea of burnout, it may be advantageous to tie in with that research through use of the MBI. The psychometric characteristics of the MBI appear to be at least adequate and the scores have good intuitive appeal. Evidence for validity is not strong, but on the other hand there is little basis for saying the MBI is *not* meaningful and useful. It is hoped that better evidence about the concept of burnout and the technicalities of its measurement will be forthcoming.

Review of the Maslach Burnout Inventory, Third Edition by CLAUDIA R. WRIGHT, Professor, Educational Psychology, California State University, Long Beach, CA:

DESCRIPTION. The Maslach Burnout Inventory (MBI), Third Edition, was constructed as a self-report instrument to assess perceived levels of three factorially derived affective dimensions of the construct "burnout"—a complex phenomenon involving a sense of exhaustion, detachment, and lack of effectiveness with respect to one's job and/or one's interactions with other people on the job. The MBI includes three formats: (a) the 22-item Human Services Survey (MBI-HSS), designed for personnel working in the health, mental health, law, and protection-related professions; (b) the 22-item Educator's Survey (MBI-ES) that employs the same content as that for the MBI-HSS with the exception that items have been modified by replacing all reference to "recipients" with the term "students"; and (c) a newly created form called the MBI-General Survey (MBI-GS) made up of 16 items that make no reference to "recipients" in any form and which was constructed for individuals who work in other service-related professions and for whom intense person contact is considered to be less prevalent than for those in human services or educational settings. For both the MBI-HSS and MBI-ES, factor analytic studies support the following three scales: (a) Emotional Exhaustion (nine items) provides a measure of fatigue that comes from managing stressors stemming from problem solving encountered when working with people in crisis or with a continuous stream of individuals seeking assistance or guidance; (b) Depersonalization (five items) assesses the extent of accommodation one makes to minimize the effects of highly charged situations by distancing oneself from others; and (c) Personal Accomplishment (eight items) reflects one's sense of progress, the attainment of one's goals, and other successes. The three scales for the MBI-GS parallel those just described and are labeled (a) Exhaustion (five items), which includes selected items from the original MBI-HSS Personal Exhaustion scale and deals with the perception of fatigue or emotional drain without reference to people as the source; (b) Cynicism (five items) refers to one's awareness of a developing indifference towards work; and (c) Professional Efficacy (six items) emphasizes one's expectations for success in the workplace. All three forms of the MBI use a 7-point Likert-type response scale with "frequency" anchors ranging from *never* (coded 0) to *every day* (coded 6).

DEVELOPMENT. The development of the MBI over the course of nearly three decades has followed traditional procedures for item construction and validation of scores employing relatively large samples of respondents from the United States, Canada, and other countries. The first two editions of the MBI catapulted the MBI-HSS and the MBI-ES to the forefront of research on burnout in the U.S. Two primary changes prompted the introduction of a third edition: (a) the development of the MBI-GS and (b) the removal of the "intensity" response scale from all forms of the MBI.

Typically, studies have supported the hypothesis that Personal Accomplishment scores are inversely correlated with Emotional Exhaustion and Depersonalization scores (i.e., the greater the perceptions that one's physical, mental, and emotional reserves have been depleted, the greater tendency to distance one's self from others and to cast one's personal accomplishments in a negative light). However, when the MBI-HSS and MBI-ES forms (with or without revised wording) were administered to samples of workers outside hu-

man services and education, a factor analysis of responses to Emotional Exhaustion and Depersonalization items revealed a single factor. Revisiting this problem and based on interviews with respondents, the authors distinguished between a perceived "crisis in one's relationship with work," and "one's relationship with people at work," leading to the construction of the 16-item MBI-GS with a focus on "one's relationship with work" generating scores for three scales (Exhaustion, Cynicism, and Professional Efficacy).

The decision to remove the 7-point Likert-type scale that employed anchors along an "intensity" dimension for each of the three scales (Emotional Exhaustion, Depersonalization, and Personal Accomplishment) was based on the observation of moderately high correlations between frequency and intensity scores and concerns that the intensity scores, because of similarity in response format to other attitudinal measures, would produce spurious correlations with like variables and contribute little to the validation of scores. Retained for all three versions of the MBI is the 7-point Likert-type scale with "frequency" anchors.

TECHNICAL. The demographic data for the normative samples employed for the MBI-HSS and MBI-ES were collected nearly 10 years ago and were based on responses from 11,067 examinees that included 4,163 teachers (Grades K–12), 635 postsecondary teachers, 1,538 social service workers, 1,104 medical workers including physicians and nurses; 730 mental health workers (including psychologists, psychotherapists, counselors, mental hospital staff, and psychiatrists); and 2,897 others (including legal aid employees, attorneys, police, probation officers, ministers, librarians, and administrators). Males represented about 40% of the sample; and Caucasians represented slightly more than 82%.

Acceptable levels of internal-consistency reliability estimates (Cronbach's alpha) and stability estimates are reported for the three MBI-HS scores from a large sample of workers in the human-services professions. Cronbach's alphas were .90, .79, and .71 for Emotional Exhaustion, Depersonalization, and Personal Accomplishment, respectively. Several studies were cited in which test-retest coefficients for the three scale scores were reported for various samples; for example, over a few weeks (.82, .60; and .80, respectively); 3 months (.75, .64, and .62, respectively); and up to 1 year (.60, .54, and .57, respectively).

Derived from the original database described in the demographics discussion, a useful table is displayed in the manual that organizes subsamples by occupation and cutoff scores for one of three levels of "burnout" (low, average, and high). Although sample data may vary, this classification guide for scores can assist in interpreting outcomes for individuals or groups; but authors appropriately caution against the use of such data in statistical analyses and emphasize the use of scale scores instead.

In the technical manual, a summary is presented of various studies designed to examine the validity of MBI-HSS test scores. A drawback is that all of the research cited was conducted no later than the early 1990s. Moderate to low correlation coefficients have been reported among MBI scale scores provided by the previously described demographic sample for Emotional Exhaustion with Depersonalization, .52, and with Personal Accomplishment, -.22. The correlation between Depersonalization and Personal Accomplishment scores was -.26.

An appendix is provided that lists convergent validity coefficients from five studies that sampled respondents from a variety of occupational settings and that examined relationships between performance on the MBI-HSS subscales and (a) peer ratings of respondents (e.g., observations of emotional and physical well-being); (b) characteristics of the job (e.g., more or less contact with people, feedback levels); (c) personal assessments of the job (e.g., level of satisfaction, perceived meaningfulness of one's work); and (d) other variables (e.g., substance abuse, changes in interpersonal relationships). Sample sizes ranged from 40 to 180. In general, the coefficients were low to moderate and absolute values ranged from .15 to .56 (*mdn* = .26). Although nearly all were statistically significant at the .05 level or lower, out of 44 coefficients listed, only 8 (20%) attained a value of .40 or larger and 9 (20.5%) ranged from .31 to .38. The strongest coefficients were observed for a small sample of mental health workers (*n* = 40) between peer observations of respondent "fatigue" and respondents' scores on the Emotional Exhaustion scale (*r* = .42); and on the Depersonalization scale, peer reports of respondent appearing "emotionally drained by the job" (*r* = .56) and "physically fatigued" (*r* = .55) (manual, p. 45). In a study that included nurses, social workers, and mental health workers (*N* = 180), Depersonalization scores were negatively correlated with perceived co-worker satisfaction (*r* = -.41) and growth satisfaction (*r* = -.47); whereas Personal Accomplishment scores were positively correlated with these two variables (*r* = .40 and .41, respectively).

In addition, discriminant validity investigations of MBI-HSS scores were designed to clarify the relationships between scores on the MBI scales and on measures involving such constructs as job satisfaction, social desirability, depression, and occupational stress for which concerns had been raised about possible confounding with the construct "burnout." In general, the authors provided credible evidence that "burnout," as measured by scores on the MBI, is relatively independent of the examined constructs.

Demographic information reported for the MBI-GS was based on responses collected in the mid-1990s from 1,717 workers in the Netherlands (about 56% were civil servants and 44% were classified as "rural workers"); 289 examinees in Finland, holding computer jobs; and 3,253 employees in Canada. About 51% of the Canadian sample was made up of individuals commonly associated with "human services" including nurses (38%) and psychiatric workers (13%). The remaining 49% of respondents worked in jobs classified as clerical (19%), technology (16%), management (10%), or military (4%).

For the newly constructed MBI-GS, internal-consistency estimates of reliability (Cronbach's alpha) based on data obtained from 3,727 respondents in the North American sample, 941 in Holland, and 290 in Finland, similar patterns across groups were observed for Exhaustion (.89, .87, and .87, respectively); Cynicism (.80, .73, and .84, respectively), and Professional Efficacy (.76, .77, and .84, respectively). An examination of intercorrelations among the MBI-GS scale scores obtained from nine subsamples that comprised three international samples (Dutch, Finnish, and Canadian) revealed patterns of correlations similar to those observed among the three scales for the MBI-HSS and the MBI-ES. Scores on the Exhaustion and Cynicism scales were positively correlated (.44 to .61, *mdn* = .48; compare with .52 on the MBI-HSS) and scores on the Professional Efficacy scale correlated negatively with both the

Exhaustion (-.04 to -.34, mdn = -.23; compare with -.22 on the MBI-HSS) and Cynicism scales (-.38 to -.57, *mdn* = .44; compare with -.26 on the MBI-HSS). No other validity-related information was reported in the technical manual for the MBI-GS.

COMMENTARY. The publication date for the third edition of the MBI technical manual is 1996, at least 8 years ago. Although the application of various and appropriate statistical procedures reported in the manual provide comparable psychometric properties that attest to the reliability and validity of MBI-HSS and MBI-ES scores, reliance on reports by numerous investigators over nearly 3 decades raise concerns about the currency of these data. Further, an open question remains about the generalizability of findings to individuals from cultures other than Euro-American and European as the bulk of the data employed to established norms was obtained from Caucasian respondents constituting approximately 82% of the sample.

The foregoing notwithstanding, the addition of the MBI-GS appears promising. The idea of creating items with face validity for a broader segment of workers in various professions expands the utility of the instrument for both research and applied purposes. However, the lack of research reported in the manual that supports the validity of MBI-GS scale scores is an oversight that should be remedied with a revised publication.

With greater access to educational and employment opportunities in all professions, it would be helpful to have data that confirm the relevance of norms as well as the reliability and validity of subscale scores for each of the three MBI forms for traditionally underrepresented groups in the U.S. including African Americans, Latino-Americans, the various subgroups of Asian-Americans, and Native Americans. As the MBI is a widely used instrument cited in research and published in a variety of outlets, it is incumbent upon the authors to summarize and incorporate this information for test users.

SUMMARY. Over the years, evidence supporting the validity of MBI scores has stimulated interest in the problem of "burnout" among workers and the use of this measure with individuals in a variety of professions. The administration of the MBI-HSS and the MBI-ES for research and applied purposes has a history of nearly 3 decades, a confirmation of the utility of the instrument. In general, the reliability and validity evidence reported for the MBI-HSS and the MBI-ES remains sound but incomplete—although the authors include provocative suggestions for future research agendas. Of particular interest is the welcomed addition of the MBI-GS for assessing perceptions of "burnout" for workers in jobs outside of the helping professions and education.

[141]

Math-Level Indicator.

Purpose: Designed to survey the basic mathematical skills of students.
Population: Grades 4–12.
Publication Date: 2003.
Acronym: MLI.
Scores: Total score only.
Administration: Group.
Price Data: Available from publisher.
Time: (30) minutes.
Author: Kathleen T. Williams.
Publisher: AGS Publishing.

Review of the Math-Level Indicator by ZANDRA S. GRATZ, Professor of Psychology, Kean University, Union, NJ:

DESCRIPTION. The Math-Level Indicator (MLI) is a 60-item math assessment designed to measure basic math skills of youngsters in Grades 4 through 12. The manual suggests that the MLI may be used with youngsters suspected of below level math skills, students whose math skill level is unknown, and those being considered for pre-algebra or algebra classes. Items use a multiple-choice format and include both numeric and word problems. The first 20 items are considered relatively easy whereas the last 40 are more difficult. In an effort to motivate test takers to try all items, the final 40 items are not arranged in order of difficulty. This distinction is explained to test takers in the administration directions. Two forms of the MLI are available.

Although the MLI manual describes three administration methods, their primary difference is the extent to which the test taker may write in the test booklet. For those choosing to use an answer sheet and scrap paper, the test booklets are reusable. Scoring stencils are available for use with the answer sheet. Although there is no time limit for the MLI, average administration time is 25 minutes with a range of 16 to 45 minutes to complete. Each form of the MLI begins with two sample items.

The manual suggests that the items may be grouped to form one of seven clusters: Addition and Subtraction of Whole Numbers, Multiplication and Division of Whole Numbers, Operations with Fractions, Operations with Decimals, Algebra, Word Problems, and Concepts and Communication. The number of items per cluster ranges from 5 to 13. Worksheets are provided to support computation of cluster scores. The manual presents tables to enable raw score to percentile rank and raw score to w-ability (equal interval) score conversions.

DEVELOPMENT. The MLI items are a subset of the items generated as part of the development of the Group Mathematics Assessment and Diagnostic Evaluation (G•MADE). The original G•MADE item pool was developed subsequent to a study of state standards, curricula, research on best practices, and *Principles and Standards for School Mathematics of the National Council of Teachers of Mathematics* (NCTM, 2000). In 2002, items were field tested in order to examine item difficulty as well as to perform Rasch model goodness-of-fit tests of each item to "identify any items that were not consistent with others in a particular subtest" (manual, p. 30). Items were also examined by consultants and by Rasch model estimates to identify items that appeared unfair or biased. Items considered not to fit the model or to appear biased were eliminated. Of the remaining items, Rasch item difficulty estimates and item content considerations were used to develop two equivalent MLI forms.

TECHNICAL. Technical data for the MLI were generated from the Fall 2002 G•MADE standardization sample of over 14,000 youngsters in kindergarten through Grade 12. Percentiles by grade level were based on G•MADE ability scores, which were then used to generate MLI item and total scores and percentile ranks. Rasch ability estimates of items were used to generate all reliability estimates. These included alternate form reliability estimates that ranged from .84 to .90 with a median reliability estimate of .89. Coefficient alpha estimates of reliability ranged from .82 to .88 with a median estimate of .87. Split half reliability estimates ranged from .83 to .90 with a median estimate of .88. Content validity is offered by examination of the list of skills measured by each item and cluster. Evidence of construct validity is offered via the development process of the

MLI. In particular, in connection to the development of G•MADE, a test structure was generated based on review of curriculums, texts, and national standards. In particular, the MLI reports to measure all five of the content standards and three of five process standards of the National Council of Teachers of Mathematics (NCTM, 2000).

COMMENTARY. The MLI relies on G•MADE data to support its technical efficacy and interpretation guidelines. No actual administration of the MLI is reported in the manual, rather inferences and conclusions about the efficacy of the MLI are based on scores imputed from Rasch ability estimates and other extrapolations of G•MADE development data. Efforts to confirm the psychometric properties of the MLI, based on an actual administration of the MLI, are needed.

In particular, data from an actual administration of the MLI would provide information about the stability of test scores. No test-retest estimates of reliability are reported in the manual. This is of particular concern in that among the recommended uses of the MLI are: for "research that requires a test-retest structure[,] program evaluation[,] the tracking or monitoring of growth" (manual, p. 3). These uses require evidence that the MLI is dependable over time; alternate form estimates based on the one-time-administered G•MADE standardization sample are not sufficient.

The manual suggests that in addition to an overall score, seven cluster scores may be computed and used. The Rasch model, used to generate many of the psychometric indices reported in the manual, assumes one variable is being measured (Andrich, 1988). This brings into question the viability of either the use of the Rasch model or the seven distinct clusters the MLI reports to measure. Beyond this, despite recommendations to interpret and compute cluster scores, no information as to the reliability of cluster scores is reported in the manual.

The MLI manual calls to the attention of the reader the impact of the attenuated range of imputed MLI scores on percentile ranks for youngsters in Grades 9 through 12. This suggests that one measure may not be suitable for such a large grade span (4 through 12). Further calling into question the use of one measure across so many grade levels is that five of the nine levels of G•MADE cover the grade levels recommended for the MLI.

The name of the measure, Math-Level Indicator, suggests that the MLI may be used to help identify the particular math level of a youngster. Similarly, the manual suggests that the MLI is recommended for "any group whose math skill level is unknown" and results may be used to "select the appropriate level of follow-up testing" (manual, p. 3). Despite these suggestions, no data are offered to indicate a link between MLI test scores and either G•MADE test level or instructional level. Local studies are needed if the MLI is to be used to assign youngsters to a particular math instructional level. This points to the more broad concern that no evidence of either predictive or diagnostic validity is reported in the manual.

SUMMARY. The MLI is an easy to use math assessment with what might be considered only preliminary psychometric data for review. More studies as to its psychometric properties are needed prior to confidently using the MLI.

REVIEWER'S REFERENCES

Andrich, D. (1988). *Rasch models for measurement*. New York: Sage University Paper.

National Council of Teachers of Mathematics. (2000). *Principles and standards for school mathematics*. Reston, VA: National Council of Teachers of Mathematics.

Review of the Math-Level Indicator by DIXIE McGINTY, Associate Professor of Educational Research, Western Carolina University, Cullowhee, NC:

DESCRIPTION. The Math-Level Indicator (MLI) is a brief, individual- or group-administered, norm-referenced test of basic mathematics skills, appropriate for students in Grades 4–12. The test is intended not as a comprehensive assessment, but rather as a screening instrument for a variety of purposes. For example, the developers suggest that the MLI may be used to identify individuals performing below grade level in math; to assess the skills level of students new to a school or school district; to select students for an algebra or pre-algebra curriculum; or as a prereferral for a special education evaluation. Two parallel forms ("Red" and "Blue") are available; each consists of 60 multiple-choice items. Skill clusters addressed include Addition and Subtraction of Whole Numbers, Multiplication and Division of Whole Numbers, Operations with Fractions, Operations with Decimals, Algebra, Word Problems, and Concepts & Communication. Scores include (in addition to total raw scores) skills cluster summary scores, percentile ranks by grade, and w-ability scores (a scaled score useful for determining growth;

see Woodcock & Dahl, 1971). Tables in the user's manual allow for easy conversion of raw scores to these derived scores.

The MLI is an untimed test. According to the developers, it can usually be completed in 30 minutes or less. It can be easily administered by individuals without special qualifications. Examinees may mark their answer choices directly in the test booklets, or they may use optional answer sheets. Thorough, clear administration instructions are provided in the user's manual, along with guidelines for using the MLI with individuals with literacy difficulties, reading difficulties, or physical handicaps.

Tests may be scored by hand using an answer key (for responses in the test booklet) or a handscoring template (for answer sheets), or by using electronic scanning equipment. Software for scanning and scoring the tests is available from the publisher but must be ordered separately.

DEVELOPMENT. The user's manual provides evidence that the MLI was developed in accordance with sound principles and procedures widely accepted by the measurement community. The items on the MLI were drawn from the item pool for a more comprehensive mathematics assessment, the Group Mathematics Assessment and Diagnostic Evaluation (G-MADE), by the same developer (Williams, 2004). According to the MLI manual, the blueprint for the G-MADE was based primarily on the *Principles and Standards for School Mathematics* of the National Council of Teachers of Mathematics (NCTM, 2000), as well as a year-long study of several state standards and curriculum guides, widely used mathematics textbooks, and a review of current research on the teaching and learning of mathematics. The manual does not, however, specify which states' standards were examined, nor which textbooks were reviewed.

Excellent detail is provided in the user's manual about tryout of the G-MADE items, which was conducted from January to March 2002 using a sample of over 10,000 students in kindergarten through Grade 12 at 51 sites nationwide. Items were calibrated using the one-parameter logistic item response theory (IRT) model (the "Rasch" model). The manual's description of this analysis is sufficient for readers trained in psychometrics, but will mystify the average user; a paragraph introducing item response theory in layperson's terms would have been a welcome addition to this otherwise extremely user-friendly and informative manual.

The developers of the MLI have taken more than adequate steps to identify and eliminate biased items and otherwise offensive content. Statistical analyses of potential bias were conducted using the variables of gender and ethnicity. This was done by obtaining a separate set of Rasch item difficulty estimates for each examinee subgroup of interest, then comparing these difficulty parameters across subgroups. Items showing any statistically significant differences in difficulty were eliminated from the pool. This is a widely accepted method of identifying potentially biased items, and, in fact, one of the more conservative of such methods; thus the MLI is unlikely to contain items favoring one subgroup or another. In addition, the developers convened a panel of consultants—whose names are given in the appendix to the manual—to review all test materials and identify any potentially offensive or biased content.

TECHNICAL. Percentile scores given in the user's manual for the MLI are based on the administration of G-MADE items to a standardization sample of over 14,000 students between September 2002 and January 2003 at 72 sites nationwide. Sufficient detail about the standardization sample and administration conditions is provided to allow the user to determine the appropriateness of using the derived scores in his or her own situation. The user should be aware that, in the standardization process, not every item was administered to every examinee, due to the fact that some skill clusters or items are not appropriate at certain grade levels. The raw scores on which the percentile ranks are based were thus derived in part theoretically using the Rasch model, rather than from the actual performance of examinees.

Internal consistency reliability is reported for both the Red and Blue forms, for each grade level from 4 through 12. Alpha reliabilities range from .82 to .88, with a median of .87 for both forms. Split-half reliabilities, using the Spearman-Brown adjustment for length, range from .83 to .90, with a median of .88 for both forms. These values indicate adequate reliability for this type of test, given its intended purpose. Note that all reliability estimates for the MLI, like the derived scores, were generated partly from "imputed" rather than empirical item scores.

Users who desire to use both forms of the MLI can be reasonably confident about the equivalence of the two forms. Alternate-forms reliability coefficients range from .84 to .90, depending on the grade level; these values indicate that it is reasonable to treat the Red and Blue forms as parallel testing forms. The developers have also carefully matched the two forms with regard to content; this is evident by visually inspecting the test booklets, but is also documented in an appendix to the manual, which lists item objectives for each form.

The validity of a test, by definition, is its appropriateness for the specific purposes for which it will be employed. The developers of the MLI have provided evidence that the items on the test address basic math skills that are included in some state curricula, some textbooks, and the NCTM Standards; however, potential users should carefully consider whether the content on the test is a good match to *their* own curriculum or to *their* specific testing purpose. To the developers' credit, the user's manual includes detailed summaries of the skills clusters and objectives represented on the test. Neither concurrent nor predictive validity evidence is provided for the MLI. This does not mean that the test should not be used for its intended purposes; however, information about the relationship between MLI outcomes and scores on other basic math skills assessments—particularly more comprehensive ones—would aid users in deciding whether the MLI is as effective for their purposes as a longer, less economical test.

COMMENTARY. The MLI is, in general, a soundly constructed instrument that is adequate for its intended purposes. The developers have provided an excellent user's manual that discusses appropriate uses of the test and interpretations of scores; a number of interpretational caveats are included, which the user should heed. This test should not be used for high-stakes purposes, nor as a comprehensive assessment.

The user should also be warned that the MLI's relationship to the NCTM Standards may be overstated in the test's promotional materials and the user's manual. The manual states that the NCTM standards were the "cornerstone" for the test blueprint (p. 25). Although it is true that each item can be justified based on the Standards, the test as a whole does not reflect many of the conceptual emphases of that document. As the MLI developers point out, 44 out of 60 items on each form are based on the Number and Operations standard. Many important areas of the Standards are not addressed. For example, virtually no questions are based on a visual stimulus such as a graph, chart, or diagram; the test is, in fact, remarkably—though not totally—devoid of graphics. Items are mostly of the "basic skills" type—serviceable, but unsophisticated, addressing primarily the lower levels of Bloom's taxonomy of educational objectives. Educators who are enthusiastic about assessing the NCTM Standards may thus be disappointed to find that the MLI addresses the Standards only in a limited way.

SUMMARY. The MLI is a suitable instrument for screening of basic mathematics skills, if the user determines that its content is appropriate for the specific purpose at hand. It is likely to be useful for quickly and economically identifying students who need further diagnostic testing with a more comprehensive assessment. Test materials are attractive and user-friendly, and the test can be administered and scored with ease. The test was developed in accordance with sound principles, and its technical properties are acceptable. The MLI is not a test of higher order thinking skills in mathematics, but will be useful to those seeking to identify deficits in mathematical functioning on a basic-skills level.

REVIEWER'S REFERENCES

National Council of Teachers of Mathematics. (2000). *Principles and standards for school mathematics.* Reston, VA: National Council of Teachers of Mathematics.

Williams, K. T. (2004). Group Mathematics Assessment and Diagnostic Evaluation. Circle Pines, MN: AGS Publishing.

Woodcock, R. W., & Dahl, M. N. (1971). *A common scale for the measurement of person ability and test item difficulty* (AGS Paper No. 10). Circle Pines, MN: American Guidance Service, Inc.

[142]

Mathematics 5–14.

Purpose: Designed to provide "information on pupils' skills and understanding in maths."
Population: Ages 5–14.
Publication Dates: 1994–2001.
Scores: Total score only.
Administration: Group.
Levels, 10: 5, 6, 7, 8, 9, 10, 11, 12, 13, 14.
Price Data: Available from publisher.
Time: (30–70) minutes.
Comments: Separate Teacher's Guide for each level; related to the National Curriculum for England and Wales, the Northern Ireland Curriculum, and the Scottish 5–14 Guidelines.
Publisher: NFER-Nelson Publishing Co., Ltd. [England].

a) MATHEMATICS 5.
Population: Age 5.
Publication Date: 2001.
Time: (30–50) minutes.
Authors: Neil Hagues, Tandi Clausen-May, Hanna Vappula, Joanne Morris, National Foundation for Educational Research, with Peter Patilla.
b) MATHEMATICS 6.
Population: Ages 6–7.
Publication Date: 1999.
Time: (30–50) minutes.
Authors: Neil Hagues, Louise Caspall, Helen Claydon, National Foundation for Educational Research, with Peter Patilla.
c) MATHEMATICS 7.
Population: Ages 7–8.
Publication Date: 1994.
Time: (30–50) minutes.
Authors: Neil Hagues, Denise Courtenay, National Foundation for Educational Research, with Peter Padilla.
d) MATHEMATICS 8.
Population: Ages 8–9.
Publication Date: 1994.
Time: (30–50) minutes.
Authors: Same as Mathematics 7.
e) MATHEMATICS 9.
Population: Ages 9–10.
Publication Date: 1994.
Time: (60) minutes.
Authors: Same as Mathematics 7 and 8.
f) MATHEMATICS 10.
Population: Ages 10–11.
Publication Date: 1994.
Parts, 2: A (items completed with calculator), B (noncalculator items).
Time: (65) minutes.
Comments: Parts given in separate testing sessions.
Authors: Same as Mathematics 7, 8, and 9.
g) MATHEMATICS 11.
Population: Ages 11–12.
Publication Date: 1994.
Parts, 2: A (items completed with calculator), B (non-calculator items).
Time: (70) minutes.
Comments: Parts given in separate testing sessions.
Authors: Same as Mathematics 7, 8, 9, and 10.
h) MATHEMATICS 12.
Population: Age 12.
Publication Date: 1998.
Parts, 2: A (items completed with calculator), B (noncalculator items).
Time: (65) minutes.
Comments: Parts may be taken successively or in separate testing sessions.

Authors: Keith Mason, Neil Hagues, National Foundation for Educational Research, with Peter Patilla.
i) MATHEMATICS 13.
Population: Age 13.
Publication Date: 1998.
Parts, 2: A (items completed with calculator), B (noncalculator items).
Time: (65) minutes.
Comments: Parts may be taken successively or in separate testing sessions.
Authors: Same as Mathematics 12.
j) MATHEMATICS 14.
Population: Age 14.
Publication Date: 1998.
Parts, 2: A (items completed with calculator), B (noncalculator items).
Time: (65) minutes.
Comments: Parts may be taken successively or in separate testing sessions.
Authors: Same as Mathematics 12 and 13.

Review of the Mathematics 5–14 by MARK J. GIERL, Associate Professor of Educational Psychology, University of Alberta, Edmonton, Alberta, Canada, and XUAN TAN, Research Associate, Department of Educational Psychology, University of Alberta, Edmonton, Alberta, Canada:

DESCRIPTION. Mathematics 5–14 is a series of 10 tests designed for group administration to school children in the final term of the academic year when they reach the ages 5 to 14, respectively. The Mathematics 5–14 series serves as a revised extension to the Mathematics 7 (1987) and 8-12 (1984) series (for reviews of Mathematics 7, see Camilla Persson Benbow, 1992 and Kevin Menefee, 1992). The tests in the Mathematics 5–14 series are intended to assess the mathematical knowledge and skills of students who are educated in England, Wales, Northern Ireland, and Scotland, given the items on the tests are aligned closely to mathematics curriculum in these countries. The tests are also designed to yield diagnostic information. Mathematics 5 covers the topics of number, shape, space, measures, and some classification aspects of information handling. Mathematics 6 to 11 cover all the topics in Mathematics 5 as well as all aspects of information handling. Mathematics 12 to 14 cover even more topics by adding algebra, handling data, and probability to the content areas that exist on the previous tests. In addition to content area classifications, items are also categorized into process

areas designed to reflect different levels of thinking and problem solving. For Mathematics 5, the four process categories include understanding number, non-numerical processes, computation and knowledge, and mathematical application. Mathematics 6 to 11 add one new process category to the existing four, mathematical interpretation. Mathematics 12 to 14 contain five different process categories: computation and knowledge, application of skills, application of concepts, interpretation and evaluation, and application of patterns and relationships. Content specifications and process category definitions are provided in the teacher's guide. These specifications and definitions provide a clear description of the processes required to solve the test items in each content area. Each test in the Mathematics 5–14 series includes a teacher's guide, an at-a-glance guide (which serves as a concise summary of the test, including administration and marking procedures), a curriculum links sheet, a group record sheet, and pupil booklets.

Each test is administered by a teacher to a group of students. The teacher's guide for Mathematics 5 sets a group size limit to five students, but there is no suggested group size limit for the other tests. Test instructions are read aloud to students writing the Mathematics 5 to 8 tests. This approach is designed to try to ensure that reading ability does not interfere with the test performance of younger students. Students are instructed to work through the items by themselves for the Mathematics 9–14 tests. Test lengths vary from 24 to 50 items. The tests include both multiple-choice and constructed-response formats. Mathematics 10 to 14 are divided into two testing sessions, one with calculators and one without calculators. Administration time varies from 30 to 70 minutes, depending on the test.

The teacher scores each student's response and assigns a mark on each pupil booklet. A raw score is calculated using number-right scoring and then recorded on the front of the booklet. The teacher also has the option of recording item responses on the group record sheet for further analysis. The raw scores are converted to age-equivalent standard scores ($M = 100$, $SD = 15$) that take into account students' age differences at the time of testing. Students with extreme scores that fall below the standard score of 70 and above the standard score of 140 are not assigned scores (the test developers claim that extreme scores are unreliable because few students in the standardization sample received these scores). Unfortunately, this scoring convention can be problematic because performance levels cannot be differentiated for all age groups. For example, students who receive a raw score between 0 and 8, at the age of 5 years and 4 months in Mathematics 5, will be assigned the same standardized score of 70. In addition to standardized scores, percentile ranks and confidence bands, which are derived from the standardized scores, can also be reported.

A large section in the teacher's guide is devoted to score interpretation. Score interpretation is divided into three sections. First, the developers explain, in detail, how the standardized scores, percentile ranks, and confidence bands are derived from the normal distribution. These explanations may help teachers, who have little knowledge about statistical scoring procedures, better understand the meaning of the test scores. Second, the developers describe the use of progress scores, which can be used to help monitor students' progress from age 5 to 14. Students' raw scores in the individual tests can be converted onto a single score scale across the 10 tests in the series so student performance can be compared across adjacent years. The test developers also provide a table with average gain scores for pairs of adjacent tests to allow teachers to analyze their students' progress in mathematics. Third, the developers describe how diagnostic information can be garnered from the tests in the Mathematics 5–14 series to promote instructional improvements. The proportion correct for each item from the standardization sample is presented in the group record sheet. This information allows teachers to compare the group performance for their students against the standardization sample. Because items are categorized into process categories, the item analysis can help teachers identify specific areas of strength and weakness.

DEVELOPMENT. The content areas measured on the tests in the Mathematics 5–14 series are anchored to the national curriculum in England, Wales, Northern Ireland, and Scotland. Items for the tests in Mathematics 7 to 12 were based on the previous versions of the tests (all items from the previous forms were evaluated and, if necessary, replaced with new items for the current series). Items for Mathematics 5, 6, 13, and 14, were developed, presumably for the first time, for inclusion in this series. Field testing of the items was conducted for each test, from November 1993 to February 2001. The item pools ranged in sizes from 40 to 100 items. These items were administered to samples ranging from 290 to 400 students. The field test data were then used for item analyses which, in turn, guided item selection. The number of items on the final form of each test ranges from 24 to 50 items. There is no description of the sample composition for the field tests; therefore, it is not possible to evaluate the representativeness of the field test samples. Further, the test developers claim the items on the final forms represent appropriate content coverage and contain adequate statistical characteristics, but there is no empirical evidence in the teacher's guide to support this statement.

TECHNICAL.

Standardization. Each test in the Mathematics 5–14 series was standardized separately between 1993 and 2001. The standardization samples were stratified on a number of variables designed to represent the testing population in the United Kingdom, including country (i.e., England, Wales, Scotland, and Northern Ireland), school type, school performance in Key Stage 1 mathematics, and capital/noncapital area. The sample sizes ranged from 2,110 to 2,850 students. Clearly, care was taken to obtain representative samples on several key stratification variables. Yet, some obvious and potentially important stratification variables were also overlooked, including gender, ethnicity, and socioeconomic status.

Reliability. Internal consistency, score precision, and score stability are reported in the teacher's guide for Mathematics 5–14. Kuder-Richardson 20 (KR 20) reliability, which is a measure of internal consistency, was obtained from the standardization samples. The results ranged from .81 to .94. The standard error of measurement, which indicates score precision, ranged from 3.6 to 6.6 standard score units. Test-retest reliability, which serves as a measure of score stability, was obtained from a subsample of the standardization sample who were tested, again, after 1 week. The correlations between the standardized scores across the two test administrations ranged from .78 to .94. However, it should be noted that the characteristics of the samples used for the test-retest reliability estimates were not described in the teacher's guide. This omission makes it difficult to judge the representativeness of the test-retest samples relative to the standardization samples when attempting to evaluate the accuracy of the reliability estimates. The testing interval of 1 week could also pose a threat to the accuracy of the information on score stability because this interval is relatively short.

Validity. The validity section in the teacher's guide for the Mathematics 5–14 series is outdated. More than a decade ago, Sam Messick (1989) devoted an extensive chapter in the third edition of the influential handbook, *Educational Measurement,* to a unified approach to test validation. The influence of Messick's view is apparent in the latest edition of the *Standards for Educational and Psychological Testing* (AERA, APA, & NCME, 1999) where different sources of validity evidence are presented and discussed. The developers of the Mathematics 5-14 series do not present a unified treatment of test validity. Instead, they limit their discussion to the content, concurrent, and predictive validity of tests. Content validity, they argue, is established by fiat because the tests contain items that measure content in national curriculum. However, no evidence is presented to demonstrate the adequacy or accuracy of the item-by-curriculum fit. No evidence is available to support the concurrent validity of the tests. Instead, teachers are encouraged to provide the test developer with information about relationships between the tests in the Mathematics 5–14 series with other math tests. Finally, the developers claim the tests in the Mathematics 5–14 series are highly correlated with the Key Stage mathematics tests (although no correlations are presented in the teacher's guide) and, thus, the tests possess predictive validity. Taken together, the validity evidence designed to support the use of these tests is very limited.

COMMENTARY AND SUMMARY. The Mathematics 5–14 series has some noteworthy strengths: It has clear content specifications based on a national mathematics curriculum; it is easy to administer; and it contains a resourceful guide on scoring tests and interpreting test scores. The suggested diagnostic analysis is also attractive because it could be useful to teachers. A small improvement could be made by adding an introduction to the whole series. This introduction could provide a succinct overview of the entire series thereby eliminating the need to read 10 different

teacher's guides. The Mathematics 5–14 series also has some important weaknesses, particularly from a psychometric view. For example, the developers provide little information on the test development process; the standardization sample excludes potentially important stratification variables such as gender, ethnicity, and socioeconomic status; and the samples for the test-retest reliability analyses are poorly described. But, above all, the tests in the Mathematics 5–14 series lack evidence to support the validity of intended score inferences. And because of this fundamental weakness, it is difficult to evaluate the usefulness of the scores produced from these tests.

REVIEWERS' REFERENCES

Benbow, C. P. (1992). [Review of the Mathematics 7.] In J. J. Kramer & J. C. Conoley (Eds.), *The eleventh mental measurements yearbook* (pp. 513–514). Lincoln, NE: Buros Institute of Mental Measurements.
Menefee, K. (1992). [Review of the Mathematics 7.] In J. J. Kramer & J. C. Conoley (Eds.), *The eleventh mental measurements yearbook* (pp. 514–515). Lincoln, NE: Buros Institute of Mental Measurements.
Messick, S. (1989). Validity. In R. L. Linn (Ed.), *Educational measurement* (3rd ed., pp. 13–103). Washington, DC: American Council on Education.
American Educational Research Association, American Psychological Association, & National Council on Measurement in Education. (1999). *Standards for educational and psychological testing.* Washington, DC: American Educational Research.

Review of the Mathematics 5–14 by ARTURO OLIVAREZ, JR., Associate Professor of Educational Psychology, Texas Tech University, Lubbock, TX:

DESCRIPTION. The Mathematics 5–14 test series is a comprehensive set of 10 examinations covering a wide array of multinational curriculum standards from England, Wales, Scotland, and Northern Ireland. The primary purpose of the series is to assess processes in mathematical applications, mathematical interpretation, non-numerical processes, computation and knowledge, application of skills and concepts, interpretation and evaluation, and application of patterns and relationships, and understanding numbers. The series is intended for school-aged pupils ranging from 5 to 14 years of age. Each color-coded evaluation pack includes the exam booklet, teacher's guide (manual), group record sheet, at-a-glance guide, curriculum links sheet, and a response sheet. The teacher's guide provides the general description of the test with a clear and concise set of directions for administration, scoring, interpreting, and reporting of test results, plus technical information regarding the psychometric evidence obtained from the standardization sample on the final test forms. The at-a-glance guide provides a brief overview of the test background, administration, marking, and actual test questions. With younger pupils, the test can be given individually or with small groups no larger than five students. For most tests in the series, group administration is preferred. The teacher reads each question and assists those who may have limited English proficiency. The tests can be used at any time during the academic year, but are best suited for end of academic year administration. None of the tests in the series have time limits. The administration time ranges from 30 to 70 minutes.

For each test level, each item is dichotomously scored and correct responses are summed to produce a total score. The total raw score is then transformed to a scale score by the use of conversion tables for each age level. Typically the teacher can administer, score, and interpret any of the tests because the raw score is easily converted into a scale score. The scale score is standardized by using a mean of 100 and standard deviation of 15, irrespective of the level of difficulty of the test. These standardized scores can be converted to percentile ranks for each test level and 90% confidence bands may be constructed around each standardized score. Additionally, teachers may use these scores to predict results that pupils may obtain at the National Curriculum levels. The teacher can provide feedback to pupils and their parents about students' current level of performance against the national norms, and the teacher can set targets for individual pupils or classes. These types of information are known as concurrent and value-added indicators (www.nfer-nelson.co.uk). Progress scores from one year to the next are also possible as long as the pupils take adjacent tests. For all the tests in the series, the developers have provided a section on Implications for Teaching. This section focuses on the importance of error analysis to determine areas of student difficulty on any of the process areas in mathematics learning. The curriculum link sheets provide a detailed description of the items in each test and their correspondence to the various national standards.

DEVELOPMENT. The developers of the original series were a team of researchers from the National Foundation for Educational Research in England. The first series of mathematics tests was started in 1984, and this updated version was revised from 1994 to 1999. The main goal in selecting items for each of the 10 tests was to capture two important aspects of teaching mathematics—process and content. The content was drawn from the various mathematics curricula of England, Wales, Scotland, and Northern Ireland and the National Numeracy Strategy for England.

The developers' goal was to enable teachers to assess the performance of their pupils against a national standardization sample. For all levels in the series, item pools were created to generate tryout items, and multiple forms for the tests were subjected to preliminary pilot testing. The final forms for each of the series tests reflected appropriate content coverage (links to the National Curriculum) and statistically appropriate levels of item difficulty and group discrimination were observed, also. In order to motivate the student to complete the exam, the developers strategically spread "easy" items throughout the exam. The developers emphasized the importance of treating the individual test's content as a whole measure by assessing the overall mathematics attainment at a particular point in a pupil's school career. The process is replicated for the development of each of the 10 tests in the series.

TECHNICAL. The standardization process for each test in the series included samples that were proportionally stratified by region and country; primary school type; and metropolitan and nonmetropolitan Local Education Agencies within England, Wales, Scotland, and Northern Ireland. The sample sizes for the standardization samples ranged from a low of 2,100 pupils (Math 7) to a high of 2,850 pupils (Math 9) with a comparable representation of boys and girls in all of the standardization samples. The average number of schools participating in the 10 standardization samples was approximately 139 schools. The developers provided brief statistical results on the entire sample and by gender. Boys and girls tended to perform very similarly on each of the individual tests.

The developers provided two types of reliability measures for each of the tests. First, Kuder-Richardson 20 was used to estimate the internal consistency of test scores. The internal consistency indexes for all the tests in the series ranged from a low .81 (Math 5) to a high of .94 (Math 11, 12, 3, and 14). Second, the Pearson product-moment correlation coefficient was used to determine the 1-week test-retest stability of test scores. The stability indexes for the tests in the series ranged from a low .78 (Math 6) to a high of .94 (Math 10). These stability indexes were obtained from samples that were tested 1 week apart and the sample sizes ranged from a low of 168 pupils (Math 8) to a high of 368 (Math 12) pupils.

The developers of the series focused only on evidence of content-related validity procedures for all the tests. In order to provide evidence of content validity, the developers relied heavily on the detailed curricular links of mathematical process and content established within the various national mathematics curricula. The developers mentioned concurrent and predictive types of validity evidence for the test scores; however, to date, no descriptions of research results were provided in the manual for any of the 10 tests in the series. However, research on predictive validity is available on the publisher's website (www.nfer-nelson.co.uk).

Each of the test scores in the series has been linearly equated or linked to provide a continuous scale. This linking allows for valid comparisons to be made of a pupil's scores on two adjacent tests in the series, thus permitting teachers, pupils, and parents to determine whether progress has been made from one grade level to the next. The test manual instructs test-users that equating formulae for monitoring year-to-year progress can be done only with adjacent tests.

COMMENTARY. One of the most significant hurdles a test developer faces is developing a reliable and valid measure. To this end, the developers of the series set out to meet the challenge by creating a relevant and relatively useful measure of mathematics achievement for school-age pupils. The series provides a wide array of tests that cover more than 40 different mathematical components within six or seven different mathematical processes as dictated by several National Curricula. Once the developers were able to construct the first test specimen, then the blueprint for the rest of the tests was just a matter of adhering to the original test specifications. There are several aspects that make the series a useful tool for assessing pupil's mathematical attainment. First, the tests are easy to administer and interpret for both individual and group purposes. The tests provide a quick overview of what a student is capable of doing in key mathematical concepts, and identify some of the individual students' areas of difficulty. Second, the tests allow school teachers to determine each individual student's relative standing within the class or against the national standardization norm. Third, the administration procedures for each of the 10 tests are very clear,

consistent, flexible, and simple to follow, even for a nonspecialist. Finally, the students' test booklet content is well organized and inspection of the individual test items for all the tests in the series show their close adherence to the targeted content and process mathematics areas.

Some cautionary notes, however, should be made. First, administration of all the tests in the series allows for a 20-minute break per test session or for two separate sessions of the exam. Given that students' test booklets are handed to all students and all test items are within reach of the student, it is of particular concern that students may potentially have access to those items not yet attempted and get a glimpse into what content areas are next. This may compromise the accuracy and validity of the interpretation of the pupil's test score. More specific instructions are needed here for what exactly needs to occur while the students are on their break or waiting to conclude the second part of the test. Second, gains were observed when the subsample of pupils was selected for retesting in every test in the series. This indicates that there were some carry-over effects observed and the lag period of 1 week was not long enough to prevent this occurrence. Third, upon examination of the curriculum link sheet for each test, an uneven representation of some content areas was observed. There is overemphasis in numerical computation in all levels of the series. Developers can easily balance this by noting that there are other key content areas in which a pupil must be proficient. Fourth, upon examination of the distribution item difficulty levels for all the tests, it was found that for the first four tests there is an overrepresentation of "easy" items whereas for the last six tests there is an overrepresentation of "moderate to very difficult" items. Use of one-parameter model IRT item analyses procedures can assist in making the tests more balanced and fair for the older students. Finally, after more than 10 years of use, the developers could have very easily done analyses of the predictive validity of the tests, but no such research was reported in the manual.

SUMMARY. In attempting to evaluate the entire Mathematics 5–14 test series, it seems appropriate to point out that the present form of the series is a marked improvement over the previous version of the same due to the diligence its developers placed on updating and establishing clear links to current National curricula. Each test in the series is user-friendly and simple to administer by nonspecialist personnel in the schools. The length of each test increases appropriately as the pupils develop age-wise and mathematically. This is one of the unifying themes for each of the 10 mathematics tests in the series. To the developers' credit, the series appears to have served its constituency of test-users and test-takers well for over 10 years in schools in the United Kingdom. These types of tests tend not to last very long in other parts of the world due to the changing pedagogical and political contexts within which they are used. Overall, the series can be strengthened, first, by providing technological updates such as computerized adaptive testing, scoring, and interpretation and, secondly, by providing additional psychometric information as it relates to evidence of concurrent and predictive validity of all its tests or even better, the establishment of clear evidence of the tests' construct-related validity. I commend the developers of the series for their efforts in creating an assessment tool that has many positive attributes which makes it unique in the field. I recommend this series for its diagnostic power and also because of its power to assess students' overall level of mathematics attainment based on crucial mathematics standards. It is hoped that the developers will incorporate all the suggested changes in this review and those changes currently being considered by the National Foundation for Educational Research (www.nfer.ac.uk/aboutus/amd31.asp).

Review of Mathematics 5–14 by JOHN J. VENN, Professor, College of Education and Human Services, University of North Florida, Jacksonville, FL:
DESCRIPTION. Mathematics 5–14 is a series of 10 norm-referenced, group-administered, screening tests for measuring the performance of students near the end of the academic year. The content reflects the mathematical skills taught in schools in the United Kingdom, and the tests provide a way to continuously assess the achievement of students from ages 5 to 14. Generally, the tests evaluate five process categories: (a) understanding numbers, (b) non-numerical processes, (c) computation and knowledge, (d) mathematical interpretation, and (e) mathematical application. The specific items on each test vary by age level. For example, the proportion of mathematical application items increases on the tests for older students reflecting the mathematics curriculum in

the higher grades. The number of items on each test also increases with age. For instance, the age 5 test contains 24 items, whereas the age 11–14 tests contain 50 items. The test items reflect the National Curriculum guidelines in the United Kingdom and correlate with the content of mathematics textbooks used in schools throughout the United Kingdom.

The purpose of the Mathematics 5–14 series is to provide profiles of student's strengths and needs; to provide a system for monitoring the progress of individual students, classes, and schools each year; and to assist schools and teachers in establishing instructional goals. The content was derived from the mathematics curricula and standards used in England, Wales, Scotland, and Northern Ireland. Because of this, the test is best when used with students in the United Kingdom.

The Mathematics 5–14 materials include a teacher's guide, student booklets and response sheets, a group record sheet, an "at-a-glance" guide, and a curriculum-links sheet. In addition, the publisher provides follow-up resources including math worksheets for student support and practice. For example, Maths Workout Copymasters are available for Levels 6–11 of the test series, and each level offers over 100 activity sheets that address specific math weakness identified by the tests.

The test manuals, referred to as teacher's guides, contain valuable information regarding administering, scoring, interpreting, and reporting test results. The manuals are attractively arranged, and the material is clearly presented with excellent instructions and useful supporting information. The scoring and interpretation discussions are clearly written for users with little or no knowledge of measurement and statistics terminology. For example, the meaning and use of psychometric terms, such as standardized scores, percentile ranks, and confidence bands, are described in detail. The manuals also provide helpful information for interpreting and using test score results.

The tests were designed to be given to students in groups, and they take about an hour to administer. Instead of writing answers on bubble-in scoring sheets, the students write their answers directly in the scoring booklet. The teacher then scores the tests and fills in the results on the front page of each booklet. With younger students the tests usually take slightly less than an hour to give. With older students the tests may take slightly longer than an hour. The administration procedures call for giving the test in two sessions with a break of at least 20 minutes. For students age 10–14 the tests are divided into a calculator section and noncalculator section with a break after the calculator section. The tests produce standard scores, percentile ranks, and scaled scores. The standard scores have a mean of 100 and a standard deviation of 15. The scaled scores are used to monitor a student's progress from one year to the next.

DEVELOPMENT. The Mathematics 5–14 tests are a revision and update of the original series of tests published in the 1980s. As part of the revision process the authors reviewed the original tests to identify questions that were no longer appropriate, and they identified curriculum content not covered on the original tests. The revised tests were then developed using questions from the original tests, newly developed questions, and questions from an unpublished test series. The new tests were revalidated in a pilot study. The final questions selected for the normative studies were the statistically discriminating questions that reflected appropriate content coverage and range of difficulty. Easier questions were distributed throughout the test to motivate students to attempt the entire test.

TECHNICAL. Norms for the Mathematics 5–14 tests were derived from a proportionately stratified sample using variables for region and country, school type, and metropolitan and nonmetropolitan area. The norm sample groups ranged in size from 2,110 students for the age 7 test to 2,850 for the age 9 test. The average sample group size for all 10 tests was 2,621 students. These sample sizes were more than adequate, and the norms appear to be excellent.

Test reliability was estimated using measures of internal consistency and test-retest reliability. Internal consistency was calculated using the Kuder-Richardson 20 (K-R 20) formula. The K-R 20 reliability coefficients ranged from .81 for the age 5 test to .94 for the age 11–14 tests. The authors appropriately suggest that the relatively low coefficient of .81 for the age 5 test is adequate for a screening test containing 24 questions, 9 of which are in a multiple-choice format. The coefficients of .94 for the tests for older age students are suitably high. Retest reliability was measured at an interval of approximately 1 week using small subsamples from the larger normative sample groups. The retest subsample sizes ranged from 168 for the age 8 test to 368 for the age 12 test. The test-retest correlation coefficients between the standard scores on the two test administrations ranged from .78 for the age 6 test to .94 for the age 10 test. These results indicate adequate test-retest reliability. Overall, the reliability evidence presented in the manual is very good.

In contrast to the excellent norms and the very good reliability, the developers fail to provide sufficient evidence to support the overall validity of the Mathematics 5–14. The basis for examining validity rests almost entirely on its content, and although the manual does describe the analysis of various curricula and guidelines in developing the test items no other information about content validity was reported. The authors explain that content validity was established by including the variety of mathematical processes included in the England and Wales National Curriculum, the Scottish 5–14 Guidelines, the Northern Ireland Curriculum, the National Numeracy Strategy Framework, and, for some tests, the Early Learning Goals. This content validity information is useful, but the developers provide little data or information about other forms of test validity such as concurrent, predictive, and construct validity. This lack of additional validity evidence must be considered a serious shortcoming of the tests. [Editor's Note: The publisher advises that validity information is now available on their website: http://www.nfer-nelson.co.uk/indicators/mathematics.asp]

COMMENTARY. The Mathematics 5–14 tests are significantly revised and improved compared with the earlier editions. Although Mathematics 5–14 results provide a useful overall view of a student's achievement from year to year, users should not rely on the results to diagnose specific mathematics deficits in individual students. Likewise, the results are helpful for reviewing the general progress of groups of students, but users should be wary of using the results to examine student performance in the five process categories as suggested in the manual. This practice is ill-advised because group screening instruments like the Mathematics 5–14 tests do not contain enough items to accurately measure subscale performance. Further, the test developers provided no supportive basis for grouping items into different categories. As a result, users should disregard the process categories and avoid any type of subscale analysis.

SUMMARY. The Mathematics 5–14 tests were designed to assess student's mathematics achievement at the end of each school year in the United Kingdom. The tests contain items that reflect the content on the most widely used mathematics textbooks and curriculum guidelines developed by education agencies in the United Kingdom. Because the tests are brief screening instruments, the results are best when used to provide an overall assessment of the mathematics achievement of individuals and groups of students. Care should be taken to avoid using the results for making placement decisions with individual students. Fortunately, this limitation is carefully explained in the test manuals. Users who follow the developer's guidelines will most likely find the Mathematics 5–14 tests to be a valuable tool for measuring the yearly progress of students in mathematics skill development.

[Editor's Note: The publisher advises that a revised set of these tests has been published, now entitled Progress in Maths 4–14. These materials were not available to these reviewers and will be reviewed in a future *Mental Measurements Yearbook*.]

[143]

Mayer-Salovey-Caruso Emotional Intelligence Test.

Purpose: Designed to assess emotional intelligence, measuring a person's capacity for reasoning with emotional information.
Population: Age 17 and older.
Publication Date: 2002.
Acronym: MSCEIT.
Scores, 4: Managing Emotions, Understanding Emotions, Using Emotions, Perceiving Emotions.
Administration: Individual or group.
Price Data, 2002: $50 per user kit including user's manual (100 pages), 1 profile summary report, and 1 item booklet; $40 per user's manual; $30 per mail-in/fax-in report.
Time: (25–35) minutes.
Comments: Self-completed.
Authors: John D. Mayer, Peter Salovey, and David R. Caruso.
Publisher: Multi-Health Systems, Inc.

Review of the Mayer-Salovey-Caruso Emotional Intelligence Test by S. ALVIN LEUNG, Professor, Department of Educational Psychology, The Chinese University of Hong Kong, Hong Kong, China:
DESCRIPTION. The Mayer-Salovey-Caruso Emotional Intelligence Test (MSCEIT) is a measure based on an ability model of emotional intelligence. According to the user's manual, the MSCEIT was constructed to measure objectively "how well people perform tasks and solve emotional problems" (p. 1).

The MSCEIT could be administered through a test booklet and an answer sheet. The answer sheet must be sent to the test publisher for scoring. The MSCEIT could also be taken via the Internet. In either case, a narrative report with test scores and interpretive comments is generated and sent to the test administrator for interpretation. According to the user manual, the MSCEIT is designed for individuals 17 years of age and older, and test items are written at an eighth grade (North America) reading level. Even though there is no time limit for completing the test, most test takers could complete the test in about 30 to 45 minutes.

The MSCEIT is designed to be used in a variety of settings, including corporate, educational, clinical, correlational, and research settings. Mental health practitioners without formal psychological training who are interested in administering this test are strongly encouraged to enroll in certification programs offered by the test publisher before using the test.

The MSCEIT is anchored on a Four-Branch Model, in which emotional intelligence is conceptualized as having an experiential and a strategic domain or area. Experiential Emotional Intelligence (EEIQ) is further divided into two branches named Perceiving Emotions and Facilitating Thoughts. Similarly Strategic Emotional Intelligence (SEIQ) is further divided into two branches called Understanding Emotions and Managing Emotions.

Each of the four branches of emotional intelligence is assessed by two tasks in the MSCEIT. Perceiving Emotions are assessed by two sets of items (Face Task and Picture Task) in which emotions have to be identified from facial expressions and pictures of ambiguous stimuli (e.g., landscape, patterns). Facilitating Thoughts are assessed by a Sensation Task and a Facilitation Task. In the Sensation Task, a test taker is asked to compare emotions with sensations expressed through modalities such as light, temperature, and color. In the Facilitation Task, a test taker has to identify emotions that would facilitate a range of cognitive and interpersonal tasks. Similarly, two tasks are used to assess Understanding Emotions. In the Blends Tasks, a test taker has to identify different emotions that might co-exist in one situation. In the Changes Tasks, a test taker has to identify "chains" of related emotions differing in intensities, as well as situations/experiences that might cause transitions of emotions through these chains. Meanwhile, Managing Emotions is assessed by two tasks (Emotion Management Task and Emotional Relations Task) related to emotion management strategies and coping strategies in interpersonal situations in which emotions are involved.

The above conceptual framework serves as a guide to the arrangement of scales and subscales in the MSCEIT. The eight tasks formed the eight subscales of the MSCEIT. Based on scores from these subscales, four branch scores, two area scores, and a total emotional intelligence (EIQ) score are generated. In addition to the above, there are three supplemental scales related to response style. The scatter score indicates the variation of scores across the eight task scores. The positive-negative bias score indicates the degree that a test taker responds to items with pictoral stimuli with positive or negative emotions. The number of omitted items is also presented as a score. If more than 10% of items are missed, the validity of test scores would become questionable.

Test items could be scored using the "general consensus" or "expert consensus" scoring method. In the general method, the responses of the test taker are compared to those in the normative sample (n = 5,000), and the score assigned to each possible response for an item is the proportion of individuals in the normative sample who had selected that as a correct response. Similarly, in the expert scoring method, the responses of a test taker are compared to those of 21 international experts on emotions. The correlation between the two methods of scoring was high. The range of correlation coefficients between scores derived from the two methods for the overall, area, branch, and task scales ranged from .93 to .99. The authors suggested that the general consensus method is "suitable for most applications" (user's manual, p. 12).

Similar to methods used in cognitive intelligence tests, all MSCEIT scores are converted to standard scores with a mean of 100 and a standard deviation of 15. Guidelines for interpretation of different ranges of test scores are given in the user's manual.

DEVELOPMENT. The MSCEIT was initially called the Multifactor Emotional Intelligence Scale (MEIS) developed by the same authors. The MEIS had 402 items, with 12 emotional intelligence subscales. Based on statistical findings generated from the initial normative sample, the MEIS was revised to become the MSCEIT (RV 1.1), with the total of items reduced to 292, forming 12 subscales. In an effort to further reduce the number of items and to strengthen the reliability of items and subscales, the current version (Version 2.0) of MSCEIT was formed in which there are 141 items forming eight subscales.

The evolvement of the MEIS to the MSCEIT seemed to reflect a parallel but systematic process of conceptual clarification and scale development. The structure of the MSCEIT is guided by how emotional intelligence is conceptualized by the authors, as a set of abilities that are used to understand and manage emotions to enhance intelligence, rather than as a mixture of personality attributes or socioemotional qualities. The user's manual did not provide detailed information on how test items were developed, except that they were written by the authors. If emotional intelligence was operationalized as sets of skills, the content of test items should be sampled more broadly from diverse sources to ensure they represented a spectrum of situations typical to test takers in which these skills are called for.

TECHNICAL. The normative sample (n = 5,000) of the MSCEIT was an aggregation of several subsamples taking paper-and-pencil or computerized versions of the MSCEIT (Versions 1 or 2). The user's manual reported that the demographic characteristics of the normative sample did not adequately reflect those in the United States, and a procedure to weight cases in the normative sample "to mimic" the U.S. Census Bureau demographic characteristics was conducted. However, it was not clear how the weighting procedure was carried out, and whether cases were deleted from the normative sample in the process to achieve the stated purpose.

There were gender, age, and ethnic differences in the MSCEIT scores. Women scored higher than men in all the scales. Older individuals also scored higher than younger individuals. In relation to ethnic differences, Whites scored higher than Blacks and Asians in 14 of 15 scales. Possible reasons behind these differences were not discussed in the user's manual.

The test-retest reliability estimate for the MSCEIT total score was .82 (*N* = 62), but the test-retest time period as well as test-retest reliabilities for the subscales were not reported. Split-half reliability estimates for the total, area, and branch scores ranged between .79 and .93 for general scoring, and between .76 and .91 for expert scoring. Internal consistency reliabilities for the eight task scores ranged between .64 and .88 (mean = .71) for general scoring, and ranged between .56 and .87 (mean = .68) for expert scoring. Although reliabilities for the total, area, and branch scores were adequate, reliabilities of some task scores were lower than expected.

Findings from a number of studies related to the validity of the MSCEIT were summarized in the user's manual. Most of these studies were conducted using earlier versions of the test (MEIS and MSCEIT, v.1). There was evidence to show that the MSCEIT scales were not related to scales with little conceptual relationship to emotional intelligence (e.g., SAT scores, scores on depression and suicidal ideation). The correlation between MSCEIT scores and tests of intelligence was low to moderate (e.g., correlation with the Vocabulary scale of the WAIS-III was .15). The correlation between MSCEIT scores and scores from a number of personality instruments were mostly in the low to moderate range. For example, in a study (*N* = 97) on the correlation between the MSCEIT and the NEO-PI, the correlation was .13 with Neuroticism, .04 with Extraversion, .33 with Openness, and .25 with Conscientiousness. With the exception of the correlation with Extraversion, all the correlations were in the expected direction. In general, the findings were supportive of the convergent and discriminant validity of the MSCEIT.

Findings from several "field studies" were also reported. High EIQ individuals were found to be more effective in their performance in management than those with low EIQ across a number of organizational settings (e.g., hospital, business). Individuals with higher EIQ scores were more likely to choose occupations in the "Social" area, but less likely to choose occupations in the "Enterprising" area. They were also more secured in their attachment style, and less likely to engage in problematic behavior such as drug use and violence. The authors suggested correlation between EIQ scores and these "life criteria" supported the relevance as well as validity of the MSCEIT.

Based on normative data, confirmatory factor analyses were conducted to examine the structural validity of the MSCEIT. Overall, the findings were supportive of the Four-Branch model that was the conceptual framework behind the MSCEIT.

COMMENTARY. Overall, the MSCEIT is a well-developed instrument that is based on a clear theoretical structure. Through the Four-Branch Model, emotional intelligence was assessed via multiple tasks and channels. Evidence accumulated so far on the reliability and validity were mostly favorable.

There are five areas in which further research is needed. First, given the very high correlation between the general method and expert method of scoring (>.90), it is not clear if there are clear distinctions between the two methods of scoring. If both methods were to be employed, further research should examine how the two methods could generate different information for test takers. Second, the meanings and validity of the supplemental scales are not clear, and further research efforts are needed to enrich the meanings of these scales as well as their validity. Third, based on normative data, Asians and Blacks are more likely to be assessed as having lower EIQ than Whites. Further research and conceptual clarification should be done to examine the social and cultural reasons behind these ethnic differences, to reduce bias that might arise from such observed differences. Last and foremost, the MSCEIT is claimed to be a test of emotional intelligence that is based on a skill model. Existing evidence on the validity of the instruments has shown that test scores were related to a range of related personality characteristics (e.g., emotional sensitivity) and relational qualities (e.g., attachment). There was, however, little evidence to show that the test scores actually reflect skills that could be used to facilitate cognitive intelligence in real life situations.

SUMMARY. The MSCEIT is a well-constructed measure of emotional intelligence. Given that emotional intelligence is still a somewhat fuzzy concept that is often too broad and vague to operationalize, the MSCEIT offers helping professionals an assessment tool in which emotional intelligence is more narrowly defined as a set of skills. The preliminary evidence related to the reliability and validity of the instrument is promising. Further research to examine the external validity of the instrument, especially on the assertion that it is a measure of skills related to emotions, should be conducted.

Review of the Mayer-Salovey-Caruso Emotional Intelligence Test by CATHERINE COOK-COTTONE, Assistant Professor, and SCOTT T. MEIER, Professor, Department of Counseling, School, and Educational Psychology, The University at Buffalo, Buffalo, NY:

DESCRIPTION. The Mayer-Salovey-Caruso Emotional Intelligence Test (MSCEIT) is an ability-based scale designed to assess emotional intelligence, the ability to reason using feelings and to use feelings to enhance thought. Intended for those 17 years of age or older, the MSCEIT measures how well individuals perform emotion-related tasks and solve emotional problems. The MSCEIT yields a Total score indicating level of emotional intelligence, four Branch scores (Perceiving Emotions, Facilitating Thought, Understanding Emotions, and Managing Emotions), and two Area scores (Experiential Emotional Intelligence, consisting of Perceiving Emotions and Facilitating Thought scores, and Strategic Emotional Intelligence, consisting of Understanding Emotions and Managing Emotions scores).

Following the Four-Branch Model of emotional intelligence (Mayer & Salovey, 1997), the measure assesses four postulated areas of emotional intelligence, that is, the abilities to (a) accurately perceive emotions; (b) use emotions to facilitate thinking, problem solving, and creativity; (c) understand emotions; and (d) manage emotions for personal growth. Specifically, perceiving emotions is the ability to recognize emotions in a variety of stimuli (e.g., self, others, art, stories, and music). Facilitating thought is the ability to generate, use, and feel emotions as needed to communicate or employ feelings in cognitive processes. Understanding emotions involves the ability to understand emotional information, to understand how emotions combine and progress through relational transitions, and to appreciate emotional meanings. Finally, managing emotions is the ability to be open to and modulate feelings in oneself and others so as to promote personal understanding and growth.

The MSCEIT is recommended for use by qualified psychologists or other professionals familiar with psychometrics, testing, normal human behavior, and psychopathology. It can be adminis-

tered individually or to groups using the booklet and mail-in/fax-in response sheet or by using the online MSCEIT. In all cases, scores and reports are produced by the publisher and returned to the administrator. The test is untimed, and respondents typically take 30-45 minutes to complete the 141 items.

Each domain is measured with two tasks, which are composed of individual items or item parcels (e.g., a group of items that ask about the same facial expression; Mayer, Salovey, Caruso, & Sitarenios, 2003). Item stimuli include pictures of human faces, landscapes, and abstract images as well as written problems and scenarios with related questions. Respondents are required to choose a response from five possible answers (indicated as choices 1–5). The five choices represent varied answer formats throughout the test, including Likert-type scales using written responses (e.g., *not useful* to *useful*), Likert-type scales using drawings of faces (e.g., a neutral face to a very happy face), and multiple choice.

DEVELOPMENT. The concept of emotional intelligence is relatively new and has come to represent somewhat divergent popular and scientific constructs. The scientific concept of emotional intelligence originally evolved from research integrating cognition and affect, theories of multiple or multifaceted intelligences, progress in the development of artificial intelligence, and brain research. In 1990, Salovey and Mayer published a literature review explicating the first theory of emotional intelligence as a distinct ability; the same year, Mayer, DiPaolo, and Salovey (1990) published a study using the first ability scale designed to measure emotional intelligence.

Mayer, Salovey, and Caruso maintain that the MSCEIT is distinctly different from tests measuring the popular notion of emotional intelligence or psychological well-being introduced by Goleman (1995). Mayer and colleagues' theory of emotional intelligence is based on the ideas that (a) intelligence involves, above all else, the capacity to carry out abstract reasoning; (b) emotions are signals that convey regular, discernable meaning about relationships; and (c) at least some basic emotions are universal.

Initial work with an earlier version of the instrument indicated a unified and independent construct of emotional intelligence with three separable subfactors corresponding well to the theoretical branches: perceiving emotions, understanding emotions, and managing emotions (Mayer, Caruso, & Salovey, 1999). However, limited evidence was found supporting the facilitating thought branch of emotional intelligence (Mayer et al., 1999). Also problematic was the scale's length (at 402 items) making it impractical for many applications, as well as low correlations between expert and consensus scoring of items. Thus, the MSCEIT Research Version 1.1 (RV 1.1) and the MSCEIT Version 2.0 were developed to improve the scale's psychometric properties and practical utility. Confirmatory factor analysis (CFA) of normative data was utilized to analyze the 122 MCEIT items and provide support for the validity of the test structure. To control for the natural item grouping and variations in item format (e.g., image versus sentence format) a methods factor was built into the CFA. Multiple criteria were used to assess goodness-of-fit of the MSCEIT V2.0's eight subscales, four Branches, and two Area scores. Findings indicate acceptable goodness-of-fit indices for the model as a whole and use of the Total Score.

TECHNICAL.

Standardization. Normative data for the MSCEIT V2.0 are based on a compilation of data from three samples totaling 5,000 respondents. The normative sample is 52% females (N = 2,599), 37.3% male (N = 1,866), and 10.7% unreported and ranged in age from 17–79 with a majority of the sample under age 30 (i.e., 72%). However, the authors report in the user's manual that each age group (i.e., 17–19, 20–29, 30–39, 40–49, 50+, and unreported) was adequately sampled (Ns ranging from 187–1,851). Matches of the demographic characteristics of the normative group to the U.S. population are adequate as the normative group included four ethnic classifications (White, Asian, Black, and Hispanic) with significant variation in representation (n = 2,041, n = 920, n = 189, n = 171, respectively). As several data collection sites used university settings, the sample overrepresents individuals with some college experience (n = 2,902, 58% of sample). Finally, individual score analysis does not include age-based comparisons to the normative sample as is typically done with more traditional tests of general intelligence. As with general intelligence, there may be increases in emotional ability that coincide with an individual's development (Mayer et al., 1999). Significant but small age, gender, and ethnic effects were observed

in the normative sample, and the test authors include scoring options to adjust scores for any or all of these effects at the test user's discretion.

Reliability. Test developers assessed internal consistency using data from the standardization sample. Full scale internal consistency is good with a split-half reliability value of .93 and with adequate to good internal consistency reported at the Area score level (Strategic EI = .88 and Experiential EI = .90). In general, Branch score internal consistencies were adequate (.79–.91). Adequate test-retest reliability (at 2 weeks) was reported for the full scale (r = .86) but the representativeness and size of the test-retest sample were inadequate (n = 62).

Validity. For the MSCEIT, there is evidence of content validity, structural validity, and predictive validity. For content validity, the authors reported that items were rationally and systematically chosen to represent abilities explicated in the Four-Branch Model of emotional intelligence. In the test manual, the test developers report factor analytic results consistent with the proposed structure of the measure. Discriminant validity is suggested by studies finding Total EQ to show small to moderate correlations with other measures of intelligence, social desirability, mood, and perceived emotional IQ. Convergent correlations between EQ scores and indicators of job performance (r = .28), customer service ratings (r = .46), ranking of team leaders' effectiveness (r = .51), and peer-related violence (r = .45) suggest that EQ scores are related to occupational interests and performance, the quality of interpersonal relationships, and interpersonal violence.

Some published evidence provides support for the MSCEIT's predictive utility. For example, a qualitative study of very high and very low EQ scoring individuals indicated differences in leadership styles between the two groups with high EQ individuals demonstrating a more collaborative approach (Vitello-Cicciu, 2001). EI appears to show small correlations with overall academic performance, though it may not have incremental predictive utility beyond that already accounted for by general intelligence (e.g., Brackett & Mayer, 2003).

COMMENTARY. Evidence about the MSCEIT's construct validity is supportive but preliminary. Initial studies suggest that the potential importance of EQ-related constructs may have less to do with academic performance than with behavior in interpersonal situations, particularly in occupational settings where it is important to regulate affect during work with others in emotionally intense situations. Additional theory-driven research should provide a more solid grounding for emotional intelligence as a construct and more meaningful interpretation of MSCEIT scores. Does emotional intelligence, for example, actually have no correlation with neuroticism as Salovey, Mayer, Caruso, and Lopes (2004) found? Emotional intelligence should also be related to constructs such as emotional labor, affective events theory, and emotions in facial expressions (Ashkanasy, Hartell, & Daus, 2002; Ekman, 2003).

Additional empirical evidence of test-rest reliability is needed. This is especially true in light of the authors' assertion that emotional intelligence is a stable ability rather than a skill. And likely due to the recent publication of the MCSEIT, much of the data presented in the manual (particularly for predictive validity) is in the form of manuscripts in preparation, unpublished dissertations and theses, and manuscripts under review.

SUMMARY. The test developers have produced a measure of emotional intelligence that offers promise for both theoretical and applied work. The MSCEIT is noteworthy for its theoretical basis and use of performance tasks. Additional reliability estimates and study of related constructs and predictive criteria should deepen the theory on emotional intelligence and strengthen evidence regarding the MSCEIT's validity.

REVIEWERS' REFERENCES

Ashkanasy, N. M., Hartell, C. E. J., & Daus, C. S. (2002). Diversity and emotion: The new frontiers in organizational behavior research. *Journal of Management, 28,* 307–338.

Brackett, M. A., & Mayer, J. D. (2003). Convergent, discriminant, and incremental validity of competing measures of emotional intelligence. *Personality and Social Psychology Bulletin, 29,* 1147–1158.

Ekman, P. (2003). *Emotions revealed: Recognizing faces and feelings to improve communication and emotional life.* New York: Times Books/Henry Holt and Co.

Goleman, D. (1995). *Emotional intelligence.* New York: Bantam.

Mayer, J. D., Caruso, D. R., & Salovey, P. (1999). Emotional intelligence meets traditional standards for an intelligence. *Intelligence, 27,* 267–298.

Mayer, J. D., DiPaolo, M. T., & Salovey, P. (1990). Perceiving affective content in ambiguous visual stimuli: A component of emotional intelligence. *Journal of Personality Assessment, 54,* 772–781.

Mayer, J. D., & Salovey, P. (1997). What is emotional intelligence? In P. Salovey & D. Sluyter (Eds.), *Emotional development and emotional intelligence: Educational implications* (pp. 3–31). New York: Basic Books.

Mayer, J. D., Salovey, P., Caruso, D. R., & Sitarenios, G. (2003). Measuring emotional intelligence with the MSCEIT V2.0. *Emotion, 3,* 97–105.

Salovey, P., & Mayer, J. D. (1990). Emotional intelligence. *Imagination, Cognition, and Personality, 9,* 185–211.

Salovey, P., Mayer, J. D., Caruso, D. R., & Lopes, P. N. (2004). Measuring emotional intelligence as a set of abilities with the MSCEIT. In S. J. Lopez & C. R. Snyder (Eds.), *Positive psychology assessment.* Washington, DC: American Psychological Association.

Vitello-Cicciu, J. M. (2001). *Leadership practices and emotional intelligence of nurse leaders.* Unpublished doctoral dissertation, The Fielding Institute, Santa Barbara, CA.

[144]

Memory Test for Older Adults.

Purpose: Designed as a brief instrument to assess verbal and visuospatial learning and memory in older adults.

Population: Ages 55–84.

Publication Date: 2002.

Acronyms: MTOA, MTOA:S, MTOA:L.

Scores, 8: Free Recall Word List Total Score, Free Recall Word List Retention, Free Recall + Cued Recall Word List Total Score, Free Recall + Cued Recall Word List Retention Score, Recognition Score, Geometric Figure Total Score, Geometric Figure Retention Score, Geometric Figure Copy Score.

Administration: Individual.

Forms, 2: Long, Short.

Price Data, 2005: $168 per complete kit including long form (MTOA:L) and short form (MTOA:S) geometric cards, 25 short form record forms, 25 long form record forms, and technical manual; $45 per 25 record forms (specify long form or short form); $51 per technical manual; $75 per MTOA:Long kit including MTOA:L geometric card, 25 MTOA:L record forms, and technical manual; $75 per MTOA:Short kit including MTOA:S geometric card, 25 MTOA:S record forms, and technical manual.

Time: Administration time not reported.

Authors: Anita M. Hubley and Tom M. Tombaugh.

Publisher: Multi-Health Systems, Inc.

Review of the Memory Test for Older Adults by STEPHEN J. FREEMAN, *Professor and Chair, Department of Counseling, Texas A&M University-Commerce, Commerce, TX:*

DESCRIPTION AND DEVELOPMENT. The Memory Test for Older Adults (MTOA) is a brief test for assessing verbal and visuospatial learning and memory performance in older adults age 55–84 years. The test has two versions, MTOA:L (long form) was designed to be used with persons "who are suspected of having some type of learning or memory deficit that has not yet been diagnosed" (technical manual, p. 1). MTOA:S (short) was designed for use with individuals who are already diagnosed or whose cognitive impairment is obvious. The authors' rationale for developing the test was that many of the memory tests used with older adults were originally developed for use with a younger age group and have high performance ceilings that make it difficult to identify older adults with impaired performance. The MTOA was developed to better assess the needs of older adults.

The kit contains a manual and two color-coded record forms (L = green and S = blue).

Both the MTOA:S and L use the same paradigms to assess learning and memory, a verbal task (i.e., word list) and a visuospatial task (i.e., a geometric figure). Word lists were patterned after those used in the Learning and Memory Battery (LAMB; Schmidt & Tombaugh, 1995; Tombaugh & Schmidt, 1992). Geometric figures were developed to be less difficult and frustrating for older adults than other complex figures such as the Rey-Osterrieth.

MTOA:S contains a 10-item word list with three learning trials and a 9-component simple geometric figure. MTOA:L contains a 15-item word list with five learning trials and a 13-component complex geometric figure. Eight scores are obtained for both versions: Free Recall Word List Total Score, Free Recall Word List Retention, Free Recall + Cued Recall Word List Total Score, Free Recall + Cued Recall Word List Retention Score, Recognition Score, Geometric Figure Total Score, Geometric Figure Retention Score, and Geometric Figure Copy Score. Raw scores are converted to cumulative percentiles and compared to normative data. Normative data for both versions are provided for three age groups: 55–64 years, 65–74 years, and 75–84 years.

Administration time for the test was not reported in the manual; however, it is estimated that a skilled examiner can administer the short form in approximately 30–45 minutes and the long form in approximately 45–60 minutes. These estimates were obtained with testing average participants. Testing procedures are easy to follow; however, the authors state that administration and interpretation on the MTOA require an examiner trained in the principles and limitations of psychological assessment and cognitive psychology and neuropsychology with an emphasis on learning and memory. The manual includes case studies and scoring keys for the geometric figure (both versions).

TECHNICAL. The norming sample consisted of males and females age 55–84 years. The MTOA:L normative sample consisted of 187 individuals. The MTOA:S sample consisted of 213 individuals. The sample was divided into three age groups 55–64, 65–74, and 75–84 years for both MTOA versions. Each age group consisted of at least 50 participants. It appears that a smaller interval (e.g., 5 years) and a larger sample would be more consistent with the goal of sensitivity to older adults. Individuals with a history of cognitive risk factors or unusually low performance in the study that might be related to a history of head injury or organic disease were excluded from the study.

The manual reported three estimates of reliability for both versions of the MTOA: internal consistency, standard error of measurement, and interscorer reliability. Internal consistency was estimated for each age group using Cronbach's coefficient alpha. MTOA:L alpha coefficients ranged from .68 to .87 on total acquisition and .24 to .81 on retention. MTOA:S alpha coefficients ranged from .35 to .76 on total acquisition and .30 to .72 on retention. Because these reliability coefficients vary greatly, serious caution is advised when using scores from groups with lower reliability values as stand-alone criteria. Standard error of measurement was reported for both versions of the MTOA by group; however, because SEMs are derived from the reliability coefficients, caution should also be applied when interpreting these data. Estimates of interscorer reliability were included owing to the fact that scoring of the geometric figures involves a degree of subjectivity. Two measures of interscorer reliability were reported: interscorer consistency and interscorer agreement. Estimates of interscorer consistency for the MTOA:L ranged from .84 to .97 and for interscorer agreement ranged from .81 to .97. Estimates of interscorer consistency for the MTOA:S ranged from .75 to .99 and for interscorer agreement from .70 to .99.

Evidence supporting the MTOA is a limited ongoing process. Although loquacious support for statistical validity was provided, efforts to support concurrent validity by examining a dementia sample and a depression sample were limited by sample sizes (n = 8, 12, 18, 19, 33), which negated this attempted endorsement.

Studies are needed to examine cultural test bias with the MTOA scores by ethnic group and by gender. No instrument can be recommended for use with ethnic minorities without such supporting studies.

SUMMARY AND CONCLUSIONS. There have been relatively few studies of the psychometric properties of the MTOA. The sample size of the validity studies reported severely limit the overall support and generalizability of these findings. However, the MTOA does warrant further research in order to continue its development and to document its validity as a clinical diagnostic tool. The potential usefulness of the MTOA will be contingent on the outcome of this research. Until such supportive research is forthcoming, clinical use of the MTOA is not recommended.

REVIEWER'S REFERENCES

Schmidt, J. P., & Tombaugh, T. N. (1995). *LAMB: Learning and Memory Battery manual.* Toronto: Multi-Health Systems, Inc.

Tombaugh, T. N., & Schmidt, J. P. (1992). The Learning and Memory Battery (LAMB): Development and standardization. *Psychological Assessment, 4,* 193–206.

Review of the Memory Test for Older Adults by W. JOEL SCHNEIDER, Assistant Professor of Psychology, and MARK E. SWERDLIK, Professor of Psychology, Illinois State University, Normal, IL:

DESCRIPTION. The Memory Test for Older Adults (MTOA) consists of two separate but similar tests designed for use with adult populations aged 55 and older. The MTOA:L is a longer and more difficult test designed to be used to identify memory deficits in older adults. The MTOA:S is a shorter and easier version of the test designed to be used in cases in which the impairments are obvious. The MTOA:S can be used to track severe impairments over time. Both versions of the test contain one verbal task and one visuospatial task.

The MTOA measures verbal learning with a word list learning task (similar to the Rey Auditory Verbal Learning Test and the WMS-III Word Lists subtests). In the MTOA:L, the examinee is given five trials in which to learn a 15-word list. During the learning trials, the examinee is given a cue immediately after all failed items (e.g., "Which word was a type of animal?"). Ten minutes after the five learning trials, the examinee is given three retention trials: a free recall trial, a cued recall trial, and an optional recognition trial. The MTOA:S word list task is similar to the longer version, except that it uses a 10-item word list and has only three learning trials.

The MTOA measures visuospatial learning with a complex figure drawing task similar to the Rey-Osterrieth Complex Figure Test. The MTOA is different from the Rey-Osterrieth in that it has three learning trials (30 seconds each for the MTOA:L and 15 seconds for the MTOA:S). Ten minutes after the last learning trial, a retention trial is administered. Finally, the examiner can also give a copy trial after the retention trial. The MTOA:L and MTOA:S complex figures differ from each other in their complexity and number of parts (13 and 9, respectively).

TECHNICAL. The normative sample of the MTOA:L consists of 187 men and women aged 55 to 85 years. The normative sample was recruited through volunteer hospital groups, community organizations, seniors' buildings, volunteer booths at shopping centers, and personal contacts. The manual does not state how many participants were found with each recruiting method. Participants were excluded from the normative sample if they were classified as cognitively impaired on the Mini-Mental State Examination or moderately depressed on the Geriatric Depression Scale. The manual does not describe any attempt to ensure that the normative sample was representative of the U.S. population. Although data on education, age, and gender are reported, no information on race or socioeconomic status of the normative sample is available. The normative sample for the MTOA:S is similar to that of the MTOA:L except that it consists of 213 men and women aged 55 to 84 years.

The reliability of the Total Acquisition scores of the MTOA:L, as measured by Cronbach's coefficient alpha, ranged from .68 to .87. The reliability of the MTOA:L Retention scores was lower, ranging from .24 to .81. The reliability of the MTOA:S was generally much lower than that of the MTOA:L, ranging from .30 to .76. The authors attribute the low reliability scores to a relative lack of variability in performance in the normative samples, particularly with the MTOA:S. In contrast, the interscorer reliability was quite high (greater than .96 except for the Complex Figure Copy interscorer reliability of .84).

Confirmatory factor analyses suggest that a two-factor structure fits best. The verbal and visuospatial factors were moderately correlated at .59.

Further analyses found that, as expected, performance improved over trials, decreased with increasing age, and improved with increased retrieval support (i.e., was better with a recognition format than with a free recall format).

To bolster the validity of the MTOA:L, a dementia sample (*n* = 33) and a depression sample (*n* = 19) were given the test and were compared with matched control samples of the same size, respectively. The dementia sample performed much worse than the control sample on all measures except for the complex figure copy task. The depression sample performed better than the dementia sample but not as well as the control sample. The depression sample made better use of the cued recall format than the dementia sample and was characterized by a faster learning rate. No concurrent validity studies were reported in which the MTOA was given along with more established memory tests.

COMMENTARY. The MTOA manual is well written and clear. The test materials are simple and well-designed. The test is easy to learn, administer, and score. Furthermore, the MTOA is laudable for adding a number of innovative features to well-established test formats. It is clear that the test was designed to meet special needs of questions working with older adults. With its especially low floor, the MTOA can be used to measure cognitive declines even in cognitively impaired individuals.

Because the cued recall format is interwoven with the free recall format, frustration is minimized in low performing adults. Utilizing both formats at the same time also allows the astute clinician to disentangle the effects of poor encoding and poor retrieval.

Another helpful feature of the MTOA is that the performance of the individual on each trial can be plotted on a graph and can be compared with general population norms. Thus, the clinician can note unusual patterns of performance that might have diagnostic significance.

Unfortunately, despite all of these strengths, problems related to the size and representativeness of the normative sample make it very difficult to recommend this test. Within each of the three age groups of the normative samples for the MTOA:L and for the MTOA:S there are 57 to 74 individuals. Normative samples this small are probably sufficient to create norms capable of differentiating between the healthy and the grossly impaired. Normative samples of this size are insufficient for differentiating between the healthy and the mildly to moderately impaired. To illustrate, the 10th percentile is defined by six or seven people, 5th percentile is defined by only three or four people, and the bottom percentile is not defined at all. MTOA scores are given in cumulative percentiles rather than the more common standard scores (e.g., *T*-scores, index scores, or scaled scores). Standard scores were not used, probably because of the skewed nature (i.e., the low ceiling) of the norms. Unfortunately, the use of cumulative per-

centiles may give the illusion that the scores are more precise (i.e., reliable) than they are.

More troubling than the small size of the standardization sample is the manual's failure to demonstrate that the standardization sample is representative of older adults. The manual does not mention the geographical region(s) from which the sample was recruited. There is no account in the manual of any attempt to ensure that the normative sample was similar to the U.S. population in terms of education, income, and ethnic composition. Without these assurances, it is impossible for the clinician to have confidence in the meaning of the scores.

After the problems of the standardization sample have been addressed, an important subsequent step in the validation research of the MTOA would be to conduct some studies in which older adults are given both the MTOA and more established memory tests such as the Wechsler Memory Scale—Third Edition (WMS-III; T6:2695), Rey Auditory Verbal Learning Test (RVLT; T6:2114), California Verbal Learning Test, Second Edition (CVLT-II; 41), and Rey-Osterrieth (15:37). Given the similarity of formats, it is likely that the MTOA measures abilities similar to those measured by more popular tests. However, it is important to show that the MTOA yields at least some information that would result in either more accurate diagnostic decisions or similar diagnostic decisions in less time than is possible with these more established memory tests.

SUMMARY. The Memory Test for Older Adults (MTOA) is a brief measure of verbal and nonverbal memory. The test has a longer version and a shorter (and easier) version. Both tests are considerably easier than the typical memory test designed for adults of all ages. The MTOA's very low floor allows clinicians to measure the memory of adults with more severe cognitive impairments. Despite a number of innovative features in the MTOA, problems with the normative sample make it difficult to recommend this test other than as a gross screener.

[145]

Mental Mathematics 6-14.

Purpose: "A series of nine standardized tests (designed) to assess children's mental agility skills in maths year-on-year."
Population: Ages 6–14.

Publication Date: 1999.
Scores: Total score only.
Administration: Individual or group.
Levels, 9: 6, 7, 8, 9, 10, 11, 12, 13, 14.
Manual: No manual; each level includes a teacher's guide (33–35 pages).
Price Data: Price data for starter set including teacher's guide, 20 pupil booklets, At a Glance Guide, 2 group record sheets, and audiocassette (specify level) available from publisher.
Time: Administration time not reported.
Comments: Test administered via audiocassette.
Authors: Tandi Clausen-May, Helen Claydon, and Graham Ruddock, National Foundation for Educational Research.
Publisher: NFER-Nelson Publishing Co., Ltd. [England].

Review of the Mental Mathematics 6–14 by JERRY JOHNSON, Professor of Mathematics, Western Washington University, Bellingham, WA:

DESCRIPTION. Mental Mathematics 6-14 is a series of nine standardized tests designed to accompany the Mathematics 6–14 test series. In terms of educational use, the test series serves as an assessment tool for students of ages 6–14, making it compatible with Levels 1–7 of the national mathematics curricula in England, Wales, and Northern Ireland and Levels A-F in Scotland. The mathematical areas addressed include Number, Algebra, Measures, Shape and Space, Data Handling, and Probability.

The two series of tests differ in that the focus of Mental Mathematics 6–14 is specifically on those mathematical understandings and skills that can be assessed in a mental test context. It is important to note that this focus is consistent with the National Numeracy Strategy I that was introduced as an important part of the U.K. national curriculum in 1999. As part of this Strategy, teachers teach a daily mathematics lesson that uses a three-part structure, starting with oral work and mental calculation, followed by a main part of the lesson that introduces new topics or consolidates previous learning, and concluding with a closure that reviews and integrates what has been learned.

Using a prerecorded audio tape and individual test booklets, all nine tests can be administered either individually or to a group. Though the expected time length for test administration at all nine levels is only 20 minutes, it is possible to administer the test in parts (A, B, and C). To accommodate the needs of special education students, the teacher's guide suggests specific adaptations that can be made in the tests' administration, and thereby overcome the limitations of a paced audio tape.

The designers of the test series claim that the individual assessments have multiple uses. As a summative diagnostic tool, a single test can be used to assess a student's strengths and weaknesses in mental mathematics. As a formative diagnostic tool, parts of a single test can be used to assess specific skills and concepts in mental mathematics, such as the use of mental number strategies and visual images. For each of the nine tests, the teacher's guide includes the section "Issues for Teaching and Learning," which provides detailed examples of how a test can be used to develop a student's "mental agility" with numbers.

The teacher's guide includes administration instructions, a transcript of the recording on the cassette tape, directions and exemplars for scoring, and the interpretation of test results. By design, the nine tests in series form a "school" unit in that the testing approach (cassette recording), test booklets, and teacher's guide are all uniform, thereby making it easier to both implement and use the test series across multiple classroom levels.

DEVELOPMENT. Minimal information is provided regarding the development of the Mental Mathematics 6–14, which raises multiple concerns about the test series that are amplified by the technical information made available. At best, the questions, scoring process, and standardization effort are all products of the staff at the National Foundation for Education Research.

The development of the questions apparently was guided by the stated intent to both "address areas of the curriculum that can be assessed through a mental test" (Teacher's Guide 14, p. 6), and be consistent with current practices and goals in the U.K. National Curriculum in mathematics. However, though specific content areas are mentioned (e.g., Number, Algebra, Measures, Shape and Space, Data Handling, and Probability), no information was provided as to criteria for item selection or the matching of questions to a content matrix.

Specific teaching or learning strategies are provided, designed to complement the diagnostic aspects of the tests relative to mental mathematics agility. However, no information is provided as to how these strategies were generated, let alone their "roots" in either expert teacher advisory groups or in the considerable research literature that is available.

TECHNICAL. The standardization of Mental Mathematics 6-14 was done in January and February of 1999, with sample sizes for the specific tests varying from $n = 1,114$ (Mental Mathematics 6) to $n = 1,578$ (Mental Mathematics 10). The stratified sample was defined by criteria such as sex, geography (England, Scotland, Wales, Northern Ireland), prior mathematics results (Key Stage One to Three in England), school type, and setting (metropolitan vs. nonmetropolitan).

The sample for each of the nine tests included children of age ranges that bracketed the intended age range (e.g., for Mental Mathematics 14, the age range was 13 years to 15 years). However, the test designers note that the number of students at the extremes of each standardized score range is so small that the extrapolated standard scores and confidence bands should be used with caution.

The Kuder-Richardson 20 formula was used to estimate the reliability of each test, obtaining values that ranged over the nine tests from .83 ($SEM = 6.2$) to .89 ($SEM = 5.1$). In the table used to generate standardized scores, a 90%-confidence band was used.

A special feature of the Mental Mathematics 6–14 series was the "linking" of scores on the tests to form a continuous scale, thereby allowing the comparison of student scores on adjacent tests administered in subsequent years. During the standardization process, subsamples of students took two adjacent test versions (in both orders) and then their scores were linked using linear equating. To their credit, the test designers mention the underlying assumption that the test levels were "parallel in function," but made no apparent effort to validate the veracity of this assumption. Also, no measures of test-retest stability are reported.

The concept of test validity is mentioned, but not attended to on any level. That is, the issue of content validity is dismissed as being evident on the basis of the test script. No measures of concurrent validity or predictive validity are provided, but an appeal is made for users of the test to share scores with the test designers.

COMMENTARY. On a surface review, the Mental Mathematics 6–14 series has merit as it includes test questions similar to those used by researchers to measure skills and understandings associated with mental mathematics. Consistent emphases are given to the use of visual images of number, visual images of geometrical relationships, estimation techniques, and alternative computation algorithms. These aspects are all positive, especially because this test series proposes to be consistent with emphases of the U.K. National Curriculum and is designed to complement the Mathematics 6–14 series.

The concerns raised in this review outweigh the positives, however. Given the nature of the tests and their purported value, it is important that attention be given to the issue of validity. That is, users of these tests can calculate standard scores, but cannot be sure what a score means. The situation is compounded negatively because the test purports to produce diagnostic information related to mental mathematics abilities of students.

A final review concern is the casual use of statistics in the standardization process, especially in the use of linear equating to produce "progress scores." Attention must be given to the unwarranted assumption that the adjacent tests were "parallel in function."

Tests in the area of mental mathematics are needed, especially for diagnostic purposes. Though perhaps a step forward in several ways, this test unfortunately falls short of what is needed due to a lack of validity evidence.

SUMMARY. The Mental Mathematics 6–14 test series was designed to measure the mental mathematics agility of students (ages 6–14) in a manner that the Mathematics 6–14 test series cannot. In turn, the importance of Mental Mathematics 6–14 lies in its "assumed" compatibility with the U.K.'s National Numeracy Strategy, in the areas of Number, Algebra, Measures, Shape and Space, Data Handling, and Probability.

The basic standardization of the Mental Mathematics 6–14 series on the surface level is satisfactory and comprehensive. However, those educators intending to use the test series must carefully consider the concerns regarding test validity, which should limit its eventual use and interpretations.

[146]
Metropolitan Achievement Tests, Eighth Edition.

Purpose: Designed to provide assessment of students' achievement in reading, mathematics, language arts, science, and social studies at appropriate levels.

Publication Dates: 1931–2001.
Acronym: METROPOLITAN8.
Administration: Group.
Forms, 2: Complete Battery, Short Form.
Price Data, 2002: $31.50 per multiple-choice Complete Battery examination kit (for preview only) including Complete Battery test booklet, directions for administering, practice test with directions (Preprimer through Intermediate 4 only), separate answer document (Elementary 1 through Secondary 3 only), and open-ended assessment preview brochure (specify level); $16 per multiple-choice Complete Battery 25 practice tests (specify Level Preprimer through Intermediate 2/3/4); $7 per directions for administering practice tests; $122.50 per 25 machine-scorable multiple-choice Complete Battery test booklets (specify preprimer–Elementary 1); $93 per 25 reusable multiple-choice Complete Battery test booklets (specify Elementary 1–Secondary 3); $76 per 100 Complete Battery machine-scorable answer documents (specify Elementary 1–Secondary 3); $11.50 per directions for administering (specify level); $7 per 25 test booklet place markers; $31.50 per multiple-choice Complete Battery response key-list of correct responses (specify level); $16 per 25 multiple-choice Short Form practice tests (specify Primary 1–Intermediate 2/3/4); $7 per directions for administering Short Form practice tests; $104 per 25 multiple-choice Short Form machine-scorable test booklets (specify Primary 1–Elementary 1); $83 per 25 multiple-choice Short Form reusable test booklets (specify Elementary 2–Secondary 3); $11.50 per directions for administering (specify Primary 1–Secondary); $69 per 100 multiple-choice Short Form machine-scorable answer documents (specify Elementary 1–Secondary 3); $31.50 per multiple-choice Short Form response key-list of correct responses (specify level); $14 per 25 Parent Guide to METROPOLITAN8 (specify English or Spanish); $66 per norms book (specify Fall or Spring); $60 per technical manual; $40 per Compendium of Instructional Objectives (also available in CD-ROM version); $25 per Guide for Classroom Planning (specify Primary 1/2, Elementary 1/2, Intermediate 1/2/3/4, or Secondary 1/2/3); $21 per Understanding Test Results (specify Primary 1/2–Secondary 1/2/3); price information for scoring and reporting services available from publisher.
Author: Harcourt Educational Measurement.
Publisher: Harcourt Assessment, Inc.
  a) PREPRIMER.
  Population: Grades K.0–K.5.
  Scores, 4: Sounds and Print, Mathematics, Language, Complete Battery.
  Time: (90–100) minutes.
  b) PRIMER.
  Population: Grades K.5–1.5.
  Scores, 4: Same as for Preprimer.

Time: (90–100) minutes.
  c) PRIMARY 1.
  Population: Grades 1.5–2.5.
  Scores, 12: Sounds and Print, Reading Vocabulary, Reading Comprehension, Total Reading, Mathematics Concepts and Problem Solving, Mathematics Computation, Total Mathematics, Language, Spelling, Science, Social Studies, Complete Battery.
  Time: (265–292) minutes.
  d) PRIMARY 2.
  Population: Grades 2.5–3.5.
  Scores, 12: Same as for Primary 1.
  Time: (270–296) minutes.
  e) ELEMENTARY 1.
  Population: Grades 3.5–4.5.
  Scores, 12: Same as for Primary 1.
  Time: (275–328) minutes.
  f) ELEMENTARY 2.
  Population: Grades 4.5–5.5.
  Scores, 11: Same as for Primary 1 minus Sounds and Print.
  Time: (255–298) minutes.
  g) INTERMEDIATE 1.
  Population: Grades 5.5–6.5.
  Scores, 11: Same as Elementary 2.
  Time: (275–316) minutes.
  h) INTERMEDIATE 2.
  Population: Grades 6.5–7.5.
  Scores, 11: Same as for Elementary 2.
  Time: (275–316) minutes.
  i) INTERMEDIATE 3.
  Population: Grades 7.5–8.5.
  Scores, 11: Same as for Elementary 2.
  Time: (275–316) minutes.
  j) INTERMEDIATE 4.
  Population: Grades 8.5–9.5.
  Scores, 11: Same as for Elementary 2.
  Time: (275–316) minutes.
  k) SECONDARY 1.
  Population: Grade 9.
  Scores, 9: Reading Vocabulary, Reading Comprehension, Sounds and Print/Total Reading, Mathematics, Language, Spelling, Science, Social Studies, Complete Battery.
  Time: (240–288) minutes.
  l) SECONDARY 2.
  Population: Grade 10.
  Scores, 9: Same as for Secondary 1.
  Time: (240–288) minutes.
  m) SECONDARY 3.
  Population: Grades 11–12.
  Scores, 9: Same as for Secondary 1.
  Time: (240–288) minutes.
Cross References: See T5:1657 (25 references); for reviews by Carmen J. Finley and Ronald K.

Hambleton, see 12:232 (37 references); see also T4:1618 (31 references); for reviews by Anthony J. Nitko and Bruce G. Rogers of an earlier edition, see 10:200 (44 references); for reviews by Edward H. Haertel and Robert L. Linn, see 9:699 (30 references); see also T3:1473 (89 references); for reviews by Norman E. Gronlund and Richard M. Wolf and an excerpted review by Joseph A. Wingard and Peter M. Bentler of an earlier edition, see 8:22 (41 references); see also T2:22 (20 references) and 7:14 (25 references); for reviews by Henry S. Dyer and Warren G. Findley of an earlier edition, see 6:16 (16 references); for a review by Warren G. Findley, see 4:18 (10 references); see also 3:13 (7 references); for reviews by E. V. Pullias and Hugh B. Wood, see 2:1189 (3 references); for reviews by Jack W. Dunlap, Charles W. Odell, and Richard Ledgerwood, see 1:874. For reviews of subtests, see 8:283 (1 review), 8:732 (2 reviews), 6:627 (2 reviews), 6:797 (1 review), 6:877 (2 reviews), 6:970 (2 reviews), 4:416 (1 review), 4:543 (2 reviews), 2:1458.1 (2 reviews), 2:1551 (1 review), 1:892 (2 reviews), and 1:1105 (2 reviews).

Review of the Metropolitan Achievement Tests, Eighth Edition by MICHAEL R. HARWELL, Department of Educational Psychology, University of Minnesota—Twin Cities, Minneapolis, MN:

INTRODUCTION. Some tests are so poorly conceptualized, and their psychometric properties so flimsy, that if they were reincarnated as cars they would have an exterior made of rice paper, be powered by a lawnmower engine, and run on plastic wheels. Others like the Metropolitan Achievement Tests, Eighth Edition (METROPOLITAN8) are made of sterner stuff and only require regular maintenance to continue to perform at a high level. The METROPOLITAN8 is a revision of a popular test designed to assess achievement in reading, language arts, mathematics, science, and social studies for Grades K-12. The rationale for revising this popular test is to (a) update test content coverage so that it is aligned with current curriculum trends; (b) provide new normative data for more valid student and school comparisons; (c) broaden and improve information for interpreting test results; and (d) improve formatting and artwork of the test. Descriptions of the METROPOLITAN8 are available at http://www.hemweb.com/trophy/achvtest/mat8info.htm.

DESCRIPTION. The Metropolitan Test was first published in the 1930s and has been revised frequently, the last time in 1993. The popularity of this test has been matched by generally positive reviews in the *Mental Measurements Yearbook* (e.g., Hambleton, 1995; Nitko, 1989). The METROPOLITAN8 is a paper-and-pencil test battery that uses the idea of test levels rather than grade to guide administration and interpretation. For example, there are two tests available for kindergartners, one for midway through the school year referred to as test level PP, and a second appropriate for the end of the year and referred to as test level PR. Similarly, test level P1 refers to Grades 1.5–2.5, test level P2 to Grades 2.5–3.5, and so on for a total of 13 test levels. Most subtests (e.g., Reading Vocabulary, Reading Comprehension, Open-Ended Reading, Mathematics Concepts and Problem Solving) are available for all test levels except PP and PR. Similarly, short forms are available for reading, mathematics, and language for all test levels except PP and PR. The addition of open-ended items, available for reading, mathematics, and writing, responds to earlier concerns about the absence of performance assessments in the MAT7 (Hambleton, 1995). The multiple-choice and open-ended items are constructed so that they can be used jointly or independently.

DEVELOPMENT OF THE METROPOLITAN8. The test specification, item development, and item tryout process continues to be a strength of this test. The process began by examining recent editions of major textbook series in each subject area, current state and district curricula and educational objectives, and educational trends and directions identified by national professional organizations (e.g., National Council of Teachers of Mathematics). The technical manual states that the MAT7, the predecessor of METROPOLITAN8, was also reviewed. Items were developed that reflected the various content areas at each test level and were reviewed by external curriculum specialists. Next, a committee of professional educators examined the items for evidence of bias, and those items identified as possibly showing bias were revised or eliminated. The number or percentage of items revised or deleted is not given. Nor is there any information about the guidelines or instructions provided to committee members, which is unfortunate because these details are important and should be public.

Items subsequently found to show evidence of differential performance using the Mantel-Haenszel statistical procedure were likewise modified or removed, but no information about the number or percentage of these items is given. Moreover, specific information that users (and test reviewers) need to evaluate the application of the Mantel-Haenszel procedure to the METROPOLITAN8 is not provided. The absence of this important information is particularly puzzling given Hambleton's (1995) comment that the Mantel-Haenszel technique cannot detect nonuniform bias. A detailed description of the efforts to detect and correct for bias, including nonuniform bias, is needed.

On the heels of the above efforts came the statement in the technical manual that "items that did not meet the specified statistical criteria might nevertheless be selected for inclusion if they were the only or the best available items measuring critical content. In the case of bias, every effort was made to counterbalance any items that appeared to favor one group over another with other items that appeared to favor the second group over the first" (technical manual, p. 12). After the work of the committee of professional educators, the results of the Mantel-Haenszel statistical procedure, and the description of absence of bias as a criterion for selecting items, it comes as a surprise that biased items still appear on the test. No information is provided about the number or percentage of such items, examples of the balancing of biased items, or the distribution of biased items across content areas.

The criteria used to select items were (a) appropriate content, (b) appropriate difficulty, (c) good discrimination between high and low scorers, (d) appropriate clarity and interest, (e) absence of bias, and (f) good spread of students choosing each distractor. Multiple-choice items were also balanced with respect to the cognitive level (research skills, thinking skills) they assess. Research skills include the ability to locate and use information from a variety of sources, and thinking skills include the ability to analyze and synthesize information, to evaluate information to determine cause and effect, and to interpolate and/or extrapolate beyond available information to draw conclusions, make predictions, and hypothesize. Items are arranged such that, where possible, difficult items are surrounded by easier items with the goals of reducing the frustrations students may encounter when items are arranged from easiest to most difficult, and increasing student motivation to complete the test.

The number of multiple-choice items across the subtests range from 20 to 50, along with suggested times that students should be given to complete that subtest. For example, the technical manual suggests that students in test level I1, covering Grades 5.5–6.5, be given 50 minutes to respond to 48 multiple-choice items in Mathematics Concepts and Problem Solving. This pattern, in which the number of items is close to the time (in minutes) suggested for testing, occurs for all test levels. The technical manual provides evidence that the recommended times should be sufficient for most students to complete the subtests, and states that students should be given extra time if needed. Students also have 50 minutes to respond to 9 open-ended items in each content area of Reading, Mathematics, and Writing. No information about scoring rubrics for the open-ended items is given.

For the first time, scores are used to place students into performance standards categories (Advanced, Proficient, Basic, Below Basic). The process used to arrive at the performance standards began with the development of categories based on the recommendations of 24 groups of 10–15 teachers possessing particular content expertise. Interestingly, this process was done online and included a general orientation, training session, chat session, and interaction via email. The publisher apparently takes it on faith that similar performance standards would be generated had this process been done face-to-face.

SAMPLING. Four national research programs were associated with METROPOLITAN8 and provided normative data for (a) Fall Standardization, (b) Equating of Levels, (c) Spring Standardization, and (d) Equating to MAT7 Setting Performance Standards. One sample consisting of approximately 80,000 students from 151 school districts was tested in the Fall of 1999, and another, smaller, sample was tested in the Spring of 2000. Both were apparently obtained using a stratified cluster sampling scheme that identified school districts throughout the U.S. for possible participation. Socioeconomic status, urbanicity, and ethnicity served as stratification variables and classrooms as clusters. Samples were chosen to be proportionally representative of the U.S. school population (e.g., low, median, and high socioeconomic status groups). Students in the standardization samples also took the Otis-Lennon School Ability Test, Seventh Edition.

There is no mention of the number of school districts invited to participate that were already using the MAT, the number of districts that declined to participate, or whether those districts that declined differed in important ways from those that agreed to participate. The discrepancy between the initial sample of school districts agreeing to participate and the characteristics of the U.S. school population was apparently large enough to lead the publisher to employ a weighting process in which some student records were randomly duplicated or deleted. The intent was to increase the similarity of the characteristics of the sample to those of the national school population. No information about the numbers of student records duplicated or removed is provided. This information would be helpful because it appears that the duplicated records were used in establishing the statistical and psychometric properties of the tests.

After the weighting process there was generally good agreement between the characteristics of the standardization samples and the U.S. school population with one exception: Rural classrooms are overrepresented in the Spring 2000 sample (51.3% compared to 29.6% nationally) and urban classrooms are underrepresented (10.1% compared to 31.9% nationally). No explanation of these substantial discrepancies is provided, leaving users wondering about how representative the Spring 2000 sample is of rural and urban classrooms. Additional details of the sampling and weighting process are needed.

TEST ADMINISTRATION. Users should find the METROPOLITAN8 straightforward to administer. The directions provide an introduction to the test, a description of what the subtests are measuring, suggested testing times, and answers to questions that anyone administering the test might ask (e.g., why should directions be read rather than simply telling the students what to do?). Although detailed, the directions still offer teachers the flexibility to accommodate particular needs of their class (e.g., giving students additional time to read a sample story before beginning work on the Reading Comprehension subtest).

SCORING. Multiple-choice items are scored as correct-incorrect and vary in number across test levels and content areas. Each open-ended item is scored 0–3. The technical manual contains a very readable description of the scores reported for the METROPOLITAN8 (e.g., scaled, grade equivalent), and how the Rasch item response theory model was used in the Equating of Levels research

program to rescale scores so that they are expressed in a common metric. The manual also cites the one-to-one link between ability estimates and raw scores as an important justification for using the Rasch model rather than other models. As noted in Hambleton's (1995) review of the MAT7, the Rasch model requirement that items show equal discrimination with no guessing requires special attention in the technical manual. This is because the effect of items showing unequal discrimination and guessing is likely to be poor model-data fit, which can affect ability estimation and test equating.

Hambleton (1995) noted that the MAT7 failed to provide information about the fit of the Rasch model to test items, an omission that continues with the METROPOLITAN8. Because it is unlikely that all of the (hundreds) of METROPOLITAN8 items showed adequate model-data fit, there is a need to describe how these cases were handled. Hambleton (1995) also highlighted the need for information about certain aspects of each item's performance, such as item biserial correlations. This information is missing from the METROPOLITAN8 technical manual.

NORMS. Norm information for scaled scores is presented in the technical manual for each grade and content area for selected percentiles (90, 75, 50, 25, 10). This gives users a general idea of the relative standing of students with particular scores, but makes connecting specific scores to particular percentiles difficult. No normative information is provided for the open-ended items.

RELIABILITY. KR-20 reliabilities for subtests are reported in 27 tables in the technical manual and are generally quite high, with many exceeding .90 based on sample sizes ranging from approximately 900 to several thousand. Two exceptions are the Science and Social Studies subtests for the early grades, which tended to have lower KR-20 values. This pattern was also evident in the MAT7 but no explanation is offered. Standard errors of measurement are also reported for the subtests.

VALIDITY. Validity evidence focuses on content, criterion, and construct validity for the multiple-choice items. Unfortunately, only a few paragraphs in the technical manual are devoted to describing this evidence. Within this space the publisher gives priority to content validity, which is defined as the extent to which test content represents an appropriate sample of the skills, knowledge, and understanding that are the goals of instruction. The manual wisely notes that evidence of content validity is specific to each school district and is obtained by mapping the METROPOLI-TAN8 content and a district's curricula. Missing from the materials reviewed was a detailed description of test content and instructional objectives that could assist school districts in this mapping process.

Evidence of criterion validity is in the form of item p-values for each grade for each content area. The argument is that students will find material covered earlier in an instructional sequence more difficult, reflected in lower p-values, and somewhat easier as they progress and reflected in higher p-values. This is assumed to provide evidence that what the subtests measure is affected by instruction (as it should be). Evidence of an increase in p-values as grade increases is also used as evidence of criterion validity, along with changes in means and standard deviations over time for scaled scores. Other evidence of criterion validity is reported as correlations between MAT7 and MET-ROPOLITAN8, which typically exceed .65 and suggests validity evidence for the MAT7 can be added to that for the METROPOLITAN8. The technical manual also reports the median biserial correlation for each subtest at each test level as evidence of the ability of subtests to distinguish between high and low scoring students and, hence, as validity evidence. These values are generally above .55 but the absence of biserial correlations for each item is an important omission.

Correlations among the METROPOLI-TAN8 subtests and the METROPOLITAN8 and the Otis-Lennon School Ability Test, Seventh Edition are offered as evidence of construct validity. As Hambleton (1995) noted, these correlations reflect the relationship between various school subjects and the relationships between tests measuring school ability and school achievement. Most correlations among METROPOLITAN8 subtests fall between .60 and .85, although the Spring standardization sample sometimes produced much smaller correlations at lower grades. Most correlations among the METROPOLITAN8 subtests and the Otis-Lennon School Ability Test fall between .60 and .80. Correlations between a given test level and the next lower test level are also used as evidence of construct validity, and are described as reflecting the extent to which levels are consistent in measuring the same aspects of achievement.

Although the case for construct validity is strong, it could be strengthened even further by reporting correlations between METROPOLITAN8 scores and student grades (Hambleton, 1995).

Correlations between subtest scores based on multiple-choice items and open-ended assessments are reported for each content area. On the assumption that the validity evidence for the multiple-choice items is compelling, these values, which typically exceed .50, provide validity evidence for the open-ended subtests. No evidence of the validity of placing students in a performance standards category (Advanced, Proficient, Basic, Below Basic) is provided.

SUMMARY. The METROPOLITAN8 continues the psychometrically impressive tradition of its predecessors. Test specifications, item development and tryouts, item analyses, and reliability and validity evidence suggest a high quality test that will continue to serve the educational community well. The one notable deficiency is the publisher's failure to provide additional technical information, the availability of which would probably only further enhance the appeal of this test. This is a problem with historical roots, as attested to by the similar requests for information in a number of previous reviews. Indeed, users who read reviews of previous versions of the MAT and the request for technical information in the current review may quickly recall Yogi Berra's comment that "It's déjà vu all over again."

REVIEWER'S REFERENCES

Hambleton, R. K. (1995). [Review of the Metropolitan Achievement Test, Seventh Edition]. In J. C. Conoley & J. C. Impara (Eds.), *The twelfth mental measurements yearbook* (pp. 606–610). Lincoln, NE: Buros Institute of Mental Measurements.

Nitko, A. J. (1989). [Review of the Metropolitan Achievement Test, Sixth Edition]. In J. C. Conoley & J. J. Kramer (Eds.), *The tenth mental measurements yearbook* (pp. 510–515). Lincoln, NE: Buros Institute of Mental Measurements.

Review of the Metropolitan Achievement Tests, Eighth Edition by LESLIE EASTMAN LUKIN, Director of Assessment and Evaluation Services, ESU 18/Lincoln Public Schools, Lincoln, NE:

DESCRIPTION. The Eighth Edition of the Metropolitan Achievement Tests (METROPOLITAN 8) is the most recent in a long line of norm-referenced K–12 achievement tests designed to measure, according to the authors, content reflecting "current curricula nationwide" (technical manual, p. 7). The METROPOLITAN8 consists of 13 levels of tests that are designed to be administered from Kindergarten (Preprimer) to junior or senior year in high school (Secondary 3). There appears to be only one form (V) for this most recent version, with the availability of both Complete Battery and Short Form test booklets. The Complete Battery includes tests of Reading, Math, Language, Science, and Social Studies. Science and Social Studies are introduced beginning at Grade 2. The Short Form is designed to measure only "core" areas. "Core" areas are defined by the authors as including Reading Comprehension, Math Concepts and Problem Solving, and Language. In addition, open-ended versions are available for Reading and Math. The METROPOLITAN8 also includes a separate test of Writing. An entire range of support materials designed to be used by parents, teachers, and school administrators were also developed by the authors. The support materials include practice tests, directions for administration, parent guides, a complete compendium of the instructional objectives measured, and numerous guides for instructional planning. Finally, a wide array of scoring services are available, including the option of local scoring.

Specific revisions associated with Eighth Edition. According to the authors, the most recent revision was undertaken in order to: (a) align the content of the test with the most recent curricula, (b) expand the scope of the test to include items designed to measure both basic and higher order thinking skills, and (c) update the norms. There are a number of notable changes in the Eighth Edition. One major change was going from 14 levels to 13 levels by eliminating Secondary 4, the level that was designed to be administered during the senior year of high school. The administration manual for the Eighth Edition suggests that Secondary 3 is appropriate for both juniors and seniors in high school. A second change was the addition of two new tests, Sounds and Print (K—Grade 3) and a separate test of Spelling (Grade 1 and up). The "Sounds and Print" test was designed to measure phonemic awareness and word recognition and was no doubt added in response to the resurgence of instruction in phonics at the primary grades. A third change was the implementation of timing guidelines in lieu of specific timing requirements.

Another notable change is associated with the test of Reading Comprehension. This change involves the application of the Lexile framework. The Lexile system has two major components. One part of the Lexile system is an analysis of text samples that yields a Lexile score that ranges in value from 0 to 2,000. The text analysis portion of the Lexile system relies on sentence length and word frequency (a proxy for word familiarity). This approach is very similar to other readability formulas that have historically been used to "level" text samples, such as the Dale-Chall, Fry, and the Spache formulae. Presumably, the text analysis portion of this system was used to identify appropriateness of "level" for each of the text samples that were included in the test materials. In addition, the Lexile system includes a bank of titles of reading materials that have been assigned a Lexile score. In theory, this allows a student's level of reading achievement to be matched to appropriate titles. According to the authors, the intent of using the Lexile system with the METROPOLITAN8 was to provide instructional recommendations for individual students.

Other changes in the METROPOLITAN8 include: (a) the availability of an open-ended version of math and reading tests, (b) the inclusion of picture prompts on the writing assessment to eliminate the reading demands placed upon the test taker, (c) the deletion of separate norms for calculator use on the math test, and (d) the updating of the layout of the test booklets. The new layout is designed to look more like instructional materials, but at the same time, to facilitate the test taker's ability to negotiate through the materials. This is achieved, in part, by using boxes to set off individual items.

DEVELOPMENT. Summary information about test development can be found in both the Fall and Spring Norms Book and the technical manual for the METROPOLITAN8. Based on the information provided by the authors, it appears that an appropriate set of review procedures was employed with the METROPOLITAN8. This included: (a) reviewing recent editions of major textbooks and state and district curricula to define the educational objectives that would be measured, (b) monitoring recent trends and directions identified by national organizations, and (c) reviewing the content, structure, and format of the MAT7 to determine what was worth retaining. Based on the results of this review process, a table of specifications was developed. The table of specifications included information about the organization of tests, specific content to be measured, and the number of items to include. In turn, the development of the final form was based on the table of specifications. A number of other variables were also considered when choosing items for inclusion in the final form, such as item statistics from item try-outs, target *p*-value means and distributions for sets of items, and approval by a bias review committee. In addition, appropriate statistical analyses, Mantel-Haenszel procedures, were conducted as a further check for potential bias. These results were also considered during the selection of items for the final form. Unfortunately, the technical manual provides little information about the use of the Mantel-Haenszel or the results generated; therefore, it is difficult to draw any real conclusions about the appropriate employment of this analysis to detect bias.

TECHNICAL.

Standardization (norming). Based upon the information provided in the norms books and the technical manual, we know that normative data were collected in both the fall (September 15—October 15, 1999) and the spring (April 1—30, 2000). The fall standardization study included approximately 80,000 students from 151 different districts. No specific numbers were provided for the spring standardization study. A stratified cluster sampling procedure was employed, with classroom as the clustering factor. The stratification variables were socioeconomic status, urbanicity, and ethnicity. The demographic variables for the target school population were defined using data from the 1990 and 1995 Census of Population and Housing and the 1997–98 National Center for Educational Statistics. The percentage of student representation for each stratification variable in the fall and spring standardization samples are reported in both the Fall and Spring Multi-Level and Norms Books and the technical manual. An inspection of these percentages suggests that standardization samples, overall, appear to be representative of the target population. However, there are some minor problems with the spring sample (e.g., there appears to be a slight overrepresentation of rural students and an underrepresentation of Asian American students). In addition, for both the fall and spring samples, data about the participation of students with disabilities suggest that approximately 5% of the students included were identified as having some type of disability. Given the recent levels of occurrence of these disabilities in school age populations, 5% may indicate an underrepresentation. It is also interesting that the authors chose to include data about students who are English language learners under the heading of "disabilities."

Horizontal and Vertical Equating. According to the technical manual, approximately 15,000 students were included in a vertical equating study. Adjacent levels were administered to this sample with one level being on-grade and one level being one grade lower. Approximately half of the students took the Reading and Language tests and the other half took Math, Science, and Social Studies. A counterbalanced order of presentation was employed. According to the authors, the Rasch model (an IRT method) was used for equating. Although IRT can be used for equating purposes, few details are provided about the use of the Rasch model for horizontal equating; therefore, it is difficult to make a judgment about the appropriateness of this analysis. At the very least, information about the fit of the model would have been important to include given the potential impact of model fit on the results generated. One assumption of the Rasch model is that items vary only in terms of difficulty. Insufficient data were provided about item discrimination (median biserial correlations) to draw any conclusions about the homogeneity of item discrimination values. In addition, no information was provided about either the design or the method for the horizontal equating of the METROPOLITAN8 to the MAT7.

Reliability. The technical manual provides estimates of internal consistency reliability coefficients (KR_{20} and KR_{21}) by subtest and by level for both the fall and spring standardization samples. Estimates of the Standard Error of Measurement are also provided. The majority of the estimated reliability coefficients are well within an acceptable range (.8—.9). The lower estimates are generally associated with the lower grade levels (kindergarten through Grade 2) or the Short Form battery. Unfortunately, no information is provided about the reliability of the content cluster scores that are available in a number of reporting options. Content cluster scores represent the major instructional objectives that are included in each subtest and are often based on a small number of items (less than 10). Given the small number of items that contribute to the content cluster scores, the reliability is likely to be quite a bit lower than the subtest scores. If test users are going to be given these scores for use, it is essential that estimates of reliability be provided.

It is very odd that the authors chose to report both KR_{20} and KR_{21}, when KR_{20} is clearly the preferred formula. The advantage of KR_{21} lies in the ease of calculation given that it requires summary statistics rather than information about individual items (p and q values). The disadvantage of KR21 is that it will tend to underestimate reliability, particularly when the items are of varying levels of difficulty (p-values). Based on the p-values provided in the technical manual, we can conclude that the KR_{21} values represent underestimates of reliability. Given that the authors estimated reliability using the KR_{20} formula, there is no value added by calculating KR_{21}.

Although there is no mention of any other data in the section entitled reliability in the technical manual, there are tables in appendix D with test/retest reliability estimates. No information is available about the design that was used to collect these data. In particular, it would be important to have information about the interval of time that elapsed between the first and second administration of the test. The title of the appendix suggests that the sample was the same sample that was used for horizontal equating (equating of forms). Despite the lack of information about the collection of these data, the estimated reliability coefficients appear to be within an acceptable range. The majority range in value from .7 to .9, with the lower values associated with Social Studies, Science, or supplemental scores (research or thinking skills).

Validity. Empirical evidence of validity is reported in the technical manual, including student completion rates, item p-values, median point biserial correlations, summary data about scaled scores, intercorrelations amongst the subtests of the METROPOLITAN8 and correlations between the METROPOLITAN8 and other measures, such as the MAT7 and the Otis-Lennon School Ability Test. The data provided are what one would expect: (a) high completion rates, (b) typical range of p-values for a norm-referenced test, (c) reasonably high median biserial correlations, (d) expected progression of scaled scores, and (e) moderate to strong correlations with other measures.

Taken as a whole, the empirical evidence documents important information about how the METROPOLITAN8 functions; however, the information does not provide compelling evidence that the tests are valid for the intended uses. The authors suggest that the primary consideration with regard to validity should be the match of the METROPOLITAN8 with local curriculum. They

go on to suggest that this judgment can be made by scrutinizing the information available in the *Compendium of Instructional Objectives.*

Although content-related evidence of validity is extremely important for a measure of achievement, additional research that is based on the intended uses of METROPOLITAN8 scores would be very helpful. It is important to note that the types of evidence provided in the documentation for the METROPOLITAN8 are fairly typical for a K–12 norm-referenced achievement test and is not out of line when compared to other major competitors. The point is that the status quo probably is not sufficient given the widespread use of these tests to support data-based decision making.

COMMENTARY. There are a number of areas of concern. Several of these concerns can be summarized under the heading, *insufficient information provided in the technical manual.* Generally, the problem is a lack of description of samples, designs, and statistical methods employed, particularly in the areas of empirical analysis of bias, equating, reliability, and validity. In a number of cases, there simply is not enough information provided for the reader to draw conclusions about the appropriateness of the statistical analyses.

Another area of concern centers on the use of the Lexile system in the area of Reading Comprehension. As mentioned earlier, the Lexile system employs a readability formula to identify the level of text difficulty. The International Reading Association warns that use of readability formulas as the sole method for establishing text difficulty is potentially problematic because there are a number of important text characteristics that are not considered in the calculations. These characteristics include things such as information/idea density and conceptual complexity. Research has shown that quantitative (formula) and qualitative analyses of text complexity can yield very different conclusions about the level of text (Lukin, Brunsman, & Friesen, 2001). This can be particularly problematic when lists of "leveled" texts are recommended based on students' scores on a measure of reading comprehension, as is the case with the METROPOLITAN8. The consumer of these instructional recommendations needs to be very cautious in using this information.

With regard to timing, although it appears that a shift from specific timing requirements to time guidelines is a positive step because it firmly establishes the METROPOLITAN8 as a "power" test and not a "timed" test, there may be some problems in the implementation of these guidelines. With regard to standardized tests, teachers have little practice in making a professional judgment about when it is no longer productive to allow a student to continue working on an exam. The problem arises because some students appear to be incapable of making the decision that they are done taking the exam. Unless an adult intervenes, they will continue to sit in front of the exam for an indefinite amount of time. Teachers will need reassurance that it is their responsibility to intervene in these cases and terminate the test administration. Without this reassurance, teachers may allow students to sit in front of the exam for hours, because the test is not "timed." Although this is not likely to be a problem for the majority of students, the negative impact on the handful of students who may be affected should not be underestimated.

SUMMARY. Although there are some problems associated with a lack of documentation in the technical manual, overall the METROPOLITAN8 appears to a viable norm-referenced measure of K–12 academic achievement. The content coverage is carefully researched to ensure an acceptable representation of current curricula nationwide. In addition, the technical characteristics that are adequately documented in the accompanying manuals (test development, standardization, and reliability) appear to be of high quality. The major problems with the METROPOLITAN8 are the omissions of information about certain aspects of the test analyses, such as empirical analysis of bias and equating. There is no reason to conclude that there are problems in these areas, but there is also not enough specific information to conclude that these areas are without problems.

REVIEWER'S REFERENCES

Lukin, L. E., Brunsman, B. A., & Friesen, P. A. (2001, April). *A new approach to rating text difficulty: Trait-based qualitative rubrics.* Paper presented at the annual meeting of the American Educational Research Association, Seattle, WA.

[147]

METROPOLITAN8 Writing Test.

Purpose: Designed to provide a "norm-referenced measure of student achievement in written expression."
Population: Grades 1–12.
Publication Dates: 1931–2001.
Acronym: METROPOLITAN8 Writing.
Scores: Analytical Scoring option yields Content Development, Organizational Strategies, Word Choice, Sentence Formation, Usage, and Writing Mechanics scores; Holistic Scoring option yields total score only.
Administration: Group.
Levels, 11: Primary 1 and 2; Elementary 1 and 2; Intermediate 1, 2, 3, and 4; Secondary 1, 2, and 3.
Forms, 22: 2 forms for each level.
Price Data: Available from publisher.
Time: Untimed (40–50 minutes).
Comments: Scoring and reporting services available from publisher; may be used alone, or in combination with the Metropolitan Achievement Tests (146) Language Test.
Author: Harcourt Educational Measurement.
Publisher: Harcourt Assessment, Inc.

Review of the METROPOLITAN8 Writing Test by STEPHEN L. BENTON, Professor of Educational Psychology, Kansas State University, Manhattan, KS:

DESCRIPTION. The METROPOLITAN8 (METROPOLITAN8) Writing Test is a direct assessment of writing for students in Grades 1 through 12. Like its predecessor, the METROPOLITAN8 Writing Test prompts students with interesting and grade-appropriate pictures to facilitate free-response writing. Each test booklet contains an ambiguous sketch of children or adolescents engaged in some activity (e.g., canoeing, running a race, opening an overstuffed school locker). Students are directed to "Write about the picture. Tell what happened earlier, what is happening now, and what might happen next."

The publisher reports that the METROPOLITAN8 version has been enhanced in two ways over the Metropolitan Achievement Test, Seventh Edition (MAT7) version. First, two writing prompts are now available at each of 11 grade levels (Grades 11 and 12 are combined). Second, testing conditions are designed to facilitate writing processes (i.e., prewriting, composing, editing). To facilitate prewriting, a blank page precedes the writing prompt. Students are told to spend 5 to 10 minutes organizing their thoughts by writing down notes or outlines. Then students compose for approximately 35 minutes on three lined pages. Following this, the administrator or student reads nine questions intended to facilitate the editing process. Students then have 10 minutes to revise their written response.

Teachers are qualified to administer the METROPOLITAN8 Writing Test and may choose between local scoring and scoring done by the Harcourt Assessment Scoring Center. In either case, holistic and/or analytic scoring is available. Holistic scores range from 1 ("On topic, but sparse") to 6 ("Writing is complete and unified"). When scoring is done by the Harcourt Scoring Center, two independent raters assess each writing sample, and the final holistic score is the sum of the two ratings (i.e., scores range from 2 to 12). Analytic scores are assigned to two clusters: Organized Content and Correct Expression. Organized Content is composed of three features: Content Development, which concerns how well students present ideas and elaborate on them; Organizational Strategies, which concern how well students organize their thoughts; and Word Choice, which concerns appropriateness and precision of words chosen. Correct Expression is broken down into Sentence Formation (i.e., sentence structure, length, variety), Usage (e.g., subject-verb agreement, correct tense), and Writing Mechanics (i.e., punctuation, capitalization, spelling). Within each analytic feature, raters assign a score from 1 to 4, with high scores indicating greater writing proficiency. At the Harcourt Scoring Center, each writing sample receives a single reading and is assigned a score for each analytic feature.

The Harcourt Assessment Scoring Center provides each teacher with summary information about each student's writing achievement. An Individual Student Report can be formatted to indicate holistic and/or analytic raw scores, along with national and local standard scores for the holistic rating. In addition, teachers receive a Master List of Test Results for all students tested.

DEVELOPMENT. The METROPOLITAN8 is the latest edition of a test that has been under development since the 1930s. Changes in school curricula and the need to update norms and manuals led the publisher to produce the new version. Development began with analysis of recent editions of major subject-area textbooks, state and district standards, and current educational trends. In addition, the MAT7 was reviewed to ascertain which items to retain or discard, and any changes needed in content, objectives, test arrangements, item formats, and testing times. This review led to new test specifications subsequently critiqued by editorial staff and measurement professionals. An advisory panel, representative of educators from diverse cultures, also examined the test for instances of bias. In addition, Mantel-Haenszel procedures were employed to examine differential item functioning between majority and minority student groups after matching the groups on test scores.

The publisher furnishes a technical manual and norms book that provide adequate information about test development, sampling procedures, and standard scores. However, no information is provided specifically about how the Writing Test was developed. The Writing Test Manual for Interpreting provides neither information about how the writing prompts were created nor about how discriminations were made in question wording at each grade level. The manual does provide helpful descriptions of scoring principles and procedures, diverse examples of students' writing samples, suggestions for improving students' writing, and references to relevant research. No guidance is given, however, regarding the expected level of scorer agreement if scoring is done locally.

TECHNICAL. The description of the norming sample and process is adequate. Fall and spring standardizations were conducted on large samples from fall 1999 to fall 2001. Student records were randomly duplicated or deleted within a sampling cell to approximate proportional representation of the total U.S. school enrollment with respect to geographic region, socioeconomic status, and ethnicity. Students with disabilities and English Language Learners were also included in the standardization.

Information about the intended domain (i.e., writing genre) and test specifications is lacking. The writing prompts were apparently designed to emit narrative prose from students because they ask students to write about a chronology of events related to a picture. Such prompts were most likely preferred over expository prompts to prevent the influence of students' prior knowledge. However, students who have more knowledge and interest about a topic (i.e., canoeing, running a race) might write lengthier and qualitatively better narratives than do those with less knowledge and interest (Benton, Corkill, Sharp, Downey, & Khramtsova, 1995).

Descriptions of the meaning and limitations of raw and derived scores are helpful. The technical manual also provides adequate descriptions of the norming samples, sampling procedures, weightings of the samples, dates of testing, and descriptive statistics. Percentile ranks, stanines, and scaled scores corresponding to Grades 1 through 12 holistic raw scores are provided.

The manual contains no information about interrater agreement on holistic scores. More troubling is the fact that analytic scores are assigned by only one reader. Both interrater consistency in scoring and within-examinee consistency over repeated measurements should have been demonstrated, but they were not. Neither alternate-form nor test-retest reliability information is presented. Teachers should, therefore, interpret individual holistic and analytic scores with much caution.

Validity evidence is almost nonexistent. Information should have been reported about how holistic and analytic scoring procedures and anchors were developed. There is no evidence that the test actually assesses the writing processes of prewriting, composing, and editing. Holistic and analytic scores are apparently based on what is composed on the three lined pages, not on what students write on the blank page preceding the writing prompt. Furthermore, there is no way of knowing what students actually do during the 10-minute editing phase. The structure of the two analytic scoring clusters-Organized Content and Correct Expression-is assumed; however, factor analytic procedures should have been applied to confirm that the six analytic features do in fact load differentially on the two clusters. At the very least, intercorrelations among the six features should have been reported. No information is provided on convergent, discriminant, or test-criterion evidence.

COMMENTARY. The METROPOLITAN8 Writing Test provides teachers with inadequate information about students' writing achievement for several reasons. First, it samples only narrative writing about chronological events. Expository writing is completely neglected. Second, the reliability and validity of the holistic and analytic scores are unsubstantiated. Given the restricted range on analytic features (1 to 4), and the fact that they are scored by only one rater, one can probably assume a standard error of measurement large enough to render the scores virtually meaningless. Although the holistic ratings receive two ratings, one must still assume sizeable error in a reported score. No evidence exists that (a) the six analytic features load differentially on separate constructs, and (b) holistic and analytic scores represent different aspects of writing. In addition, scores on the Writing Test have not been correlated with any criterion measure. If students achieve at a level different than what the teacher might have expected, a follow-up interview should be conducted with them to determine how much knowledge they have about the topic (e.g., canoeing). Theoretically, topic knowledge could be related to the holistic score and analytic scores pertaining to Organized Content (Benton et al., 1995).

SUMMARY. The METROPOLITAN8 Writing Test offers teachers a standardized assessment of students' free-response narrative writing. Students can complete the assessment in approximately 55 minutes. The time allotted for students is adequate for them to plan and organize their thoughts prior to writing and to revise subsequent to the composing process. Teachers can choose between local scoring and scoring done by the Harcourt Assessment Scoring Center. Both holistic and analytic scores are available. Standard scores are reported for holistic raw scores in Grades 1 through 12, in both fall and spring semesters. However, because the validity and reliability of the holistic and analytic scores are not fully documented, teachers and students might be better served with curriculum-based assessments.

REVIEWER'S REFERENCE

Benton, S. L., Corkill, A. J., Sharp, J. M., Downey, R. G., & Khramtsova, I. (1995). Knowledge, interest, and narrative writing. *Journal of Educational Psychology*, *87*, 66–79.

Review of the METROPOLITAN8 Writing Test by NATALIE RATHVON, Director of Accountability and Assessment, Center City Consortium Schools, Washington, DC:

DESCRIPTION. The METROPOLITAN8 Writing Test is a norm-referenced, group-administered test designed to assess achievement in written expression for students in Grades 1 through 12. A component of the Metropolitan Achievement Test, Eighth Edition (METROPOLITAN8), it may be used alone or administered in combination with the METROPOLITAN8 Multiple Assessment. The METROPOLITAN8 Writing Test consists of 11 levels, with 1 level per grade for Grades 1 and 10 and a combined level for Grades 11 and 12. Although the test materials indicate that the assessment has two forms, only Form V was available for review. Intended to reflect the shift toward a process approach to writing, the test requires students to respond to a prompt (pictorial and written). Prompts are designed to elicit narrative-descriptive writing, although other modes, such as persuasive and expository, are also scorable. Student booklets are organized according to a three-step writing process, with an unscored page for prewriting, three ruled pages for story writing, and an editing checklist on the inside back cover. No information is provided regarding optimal or maximum group size; presumably the test could also be administered individually.

Although the METROPOLITAN8 Writing Test is untimed, it is intended for administration during a 50-minute class period. Guidelines provide 10 minutes for planning, 25 minutes for writing, and 10 minutes for editing at the Primary levels and 30 to 35 minutes for planning and writing and 10 minutes for editing at the Elementary through Secondary levels. At the Primary levels, the teacher leads students through the three writing stages, whereas at the upper levels, the teacher encourages students to spend 5 to 10 minutes planning and prompts them to begin editing after 35 minutes have elapsed. No rationale or empirical evidence is offered in support of the length or format of the three stages. No guidelines are provided to help teachers determine what kinds of accommodations, if any, should be afforded to English-language learners or students with disabilities or when students are no longer being productive and testing should be terminated.

Administration. In addition to a set of highlighted directions, which are intended to be read verbatim, the Directions for Administering manuals include an identical set of "special considerations" that consist of supplementary instructions on legibility, quantity versus quality, and other writing aspects. With no indication as to how or when teachers are to deliver these instructions, the test is vulnerable to interexaminer variance (Rathvon, 2004). Although the picture prompts are attractive and developmentally appropriate, the written directions differ across levels only for the initial sentence describing the picture and may seem simplistic to high school students. Moreover, the nine-item editing checklist, also identical across levels except for type size, is likely to be too advanced for primary grade students, notwithstanding the fact that the teacher reads it aloud at those levels. Contrary to the publisher's assertion that an entire blank page is provided for prewriting, the white box designed for that purpose occupies a little more than half of the page in the Primary level booklets and less than half a page at the other

levels, which may be insufficient for older, more proficient writers.

Scores. Two types of scores are available: holistic and analytic. Scored on a 6-point scale, the holistic score is intended to represent an overall impression of the student's written response, encompassing characteristics such as organization, development, and fluency. When the METROPOLITAN8 Writing Test is scored at the publisher's scoring center, each test receives two readings by two independent raters, and the final holistic score is the sum of the two ratings (raw score range = 2 to 12 points). Norm-referenced scores (scaled scores, percentile ranks, normal curve equivalents, and stanines) are available only for the holistic score. Also available is an analytical scoring option, which yields six criterion-referenced scores (Content Development, Organizational Strategies, Word Choice, Sentence Formation, Usage, and Writing Mechanics), each scored on a 4-point scale.

The Writing Manual for Interpreting provides rubrics for holistic and analytic scoring, but score point descriptions for both approaches are common to all levels, rather than linked to level-specific or grade-specific standards. Because of the developmental nature of writing skills, separate rubrics should be developed for each level of the test. Both holistic and analytic scoring services are available from the publisher (analytic scoring incurs an additional cost). No information is provided regarding the process for resolving interrater discrepancies. Moreover, the manual provides no information on training for analytic scorers, other than the fact that each test receives only a single reading when analytic scoring is done at the publisher's scoring center. The METROPOLITAN8 Writing Test can also be scored locally, using norms tables in the Writing Manual for Interpreting and a training packet, which was not included in the sample materials.

Interpretation. Interpretation of analytic scoring results is based on two feature clusters: Organized Content (Content Development, Organizational Strategies, and Word Choice) and Correct Expression (Sentence Formation, Usage, and Writing Mechanics). According to the authors, the clusters provide diagnostic information about students' strengths and weaknesses relative to content development and writing conventions, respectively.

The Writing Manual for Interpreting includes samples of three reports: an Individual Student Report designed for teachers; an Individual Narrative Report, written in the form of a letter and designed for parents; and a Master List of Test Results. Providing test information in tabular or graphical as well as narrative form would improve the readability of the Individual Narrative Report.

The manual includes a section with suggestions for improving writing instruction. The strategies, which relate to writing across the curriculum and teaching writing as a process, are useful, but the only instructional resources cited are more than a decade and a half old. Moreover, no individual or case examples based on METROPOLITAN8 Writing results are included to provide a context for the recommendations.

DEVELOPMENT. According to the Writing Manual for Interpreting, the latest version of the METROPOLITAN8 Writing Test, like its predecessor, is designed to reflect the shift from instruction focusing primarily on writing mechanics and conventions to instruction focusing on the writing process. Changes to this edition include implementation of time guidelines rather than specific time limits, separate time allocations for each of the three writing stages, and provision of two prompts or forms for each of the 11 levels. Inspection of the reference list suggests that the current edition, despite a publication date of 2001, does not incorporate the most recent research in writing assessment, instruction, and intervention. Of the 15 entries, 14 date from the 1980s.

TECHNICAL. No technical information specific to the METROPOLITAN8 Writing Test in either narrative or tabular form could be located in any of the test materials received, other than norms tables in the Writing Manual for Interpreting. The METROPOLITAN8 technical manual presents information about development, standardization, reliability, and validity for the multiple-choice assessment battery but only a single sentence referring to the development of constructed-response reading, mathematics, and writing assessments. Although presumably the METROPOLITAN8 Writing Test was included in the Metropolitan Achievement Test, Eighth Edition development and validation process, it is not included in the METROPOLITAN8 Scope and Sequence table. Similarly, although tables in the METROPOLITAN8 technical manual present mean raw scores for the open-ended Reading and Mathematics assessments and correlations between those assessments and related METROPOLITAN8 multiple-choice tests, there are no entries for the METROPOLITAN8 Writing Test.

Norms. For users selecting the local scoring option, the Writing Manual for Interpreting provides norms tables for converting raw holistic scores to scaled scores, percentile ranks, and stanines, with spring norms for Grade 1 and fall and spring norms for Grades 2 through 12. Normal curve equivalents should also be provided for progress monitoring and accountability purposes. Considering that the test has such a limited raw score range, it is not surprising to find floor effects at numerous grade levels. For example, for spring of Grade 1, the lowest possible raw score (2) yields a percentile rank of 21, indicating that the test is unable to differentiate among students with low average, low, and very low writing skills at that administration window. Item gradient violations are also frequent, especially near the medians of the score distributions, indicating that the test is not sensitive to individual differences across the entire range of skill development. For example, for fall of Grade 8, a raw score of 7 yields a percentile score of 44, whereas a raw score of 8 yields a PR of 71.

Reliability. No reliability evidence is presented. Especially of concern is the lack of information on interrater consistency, which is critical not only to the reliability but also the validity of score interpretations from performance assessments (e.g., Clauser, 2000; Engelhard, 2002; Harwell, 1999). In addition to reliability evidence based on classical test theory approaches, evidence derived from generalizability studies, which permit the simultaneous estimation of multiple potential sources of score variability, is also essential in assisting users in evaluating the utility of performance-based assessments such as METROPOLITAN8 Writing for accountability purposes (Miller & Linn, 2000; Swartz et al., 1999). The Writing Manual for Interpreting describes training for holistic scorers, but it is not clear if this description, which is written in general terms, refers to the publisher's training procedures for METROPOLITAN8 Writing Test raters. Information about the type and comprehensiveness of the training procedures is also needed because different training and scoring models can produce differences in obtained scores (Moon & Hughes, 2002).

Validity. Content validity evidence is sparse. The authors present a brief review of the direct approach to writing assessment in support of their contention that METROPOLITAN8 Writing requires higher order thinking skills and is more closely aligned with typical classroom instruction than traditional indirect assessment measures, but they include no citations from the research literature or empirical evidence to document those claims. The picture prompts depict individuals from a variety of racial/ethnic groups and portray both children and adults in nonstereotyped activities and attire, but it is not clear whether the advisory panel identified in the METROPOLITAN8 technical manual reviewed the picture prompts or any other METROPOLITAN8 Writing materials to determine if the pictorial or written content might be offensive. Nor is it clear if the differential item functioning procedures used to evaluate potential bias on the METROPOLITAN8 were applied to METROPOLITAN8 Writing. No criterion-related or construct validity evidence is presented, such as information concerning the test's relationship to other validated writing measures, teacher ratings, or school grades; utility in predicting future writing achievement; or ability to distinguish between poor or proficient writers.

COMMENTARY. Although the METROPOLITAN8 Writing Test is attractive, can be easily administered, and employs a format that is consistent with current trends in writing assessment, face validity is no substitute for evidence documenting the meaningfulness of the inferences that can be made from the results. Without information on psychometric characteristics critical to performance-based writing assessments, such as the adequacy of content coverage; development, validation, and equating of the prompts; reliability and validity of the scoring approaches; and score consistency and stability, it is impossible to evaluate its technical soundness. With today's emphasis on data-based educational decision making, it is especially unfortunate that the authors present no evidence to support their contention that the results can be used to help establish instructional priorities for individuals or groups of students. Evidence should also be provided in support of the three-stage test organization, including how the Editing Checklist was developed and its effect on writing productions of students at different grade levels during field testing. In addition, in view of the gender, racial, and native-language differences that have been identified on constructed-response writing assessments (e.g., Abedi, 2002; Gabrielson, Gordon, & Engelhard, 1995; Ryan & DeMark, 2002), information on subgroup performance should be provided.

SUMMARY. Although efforts have been directed toward making this edition of the Metropolitan Writing Assessment reflect the process approach to writing instruction, the dearth of information about its psychometric properties makes it impossible for potential users to be confident that it measures writing achievement in a consistent or meaningful way. In view of the floor and item gradient violations noted above, it should not be used as a decision-making tool at the individual student level. Its efficacy in evaluating the quality of writing programs is also unknown because of the lack of evidence regarding the relevance and representativeness of test content, score consistency, and stability, and its relationship to other measures of writing achievement. Because this lack of comprehensive technical information is the norm rather than the exception among the relatively few commercially available large-scale direct writing assessments, it is not surprising that so many states are developing their own instruments.

REVIEWER'S REFERENCES

Abedi, J. (2002). Standardized achievement tests and English language learners: Psychometrics issues. *Educational Assessment, 8*, 231–257.

Clauser, B. E. (2000). Recurrent issues and recent advances in scoring performance assessments. *Applied Psychological Measurement, 24*, 310–324.

Engelhard, G. (2002). Monitoring raters in performance assessments. In G. Tindal & T. M. Haladyna (Eds.), *Large-scale assessment programs for all students: Validity, technical adequacy, and implementation* (pp. 261–287). Mahwah, NJ: Erlbaum.

Gabrielson, S., Gordon, B., & Engelhard, G. (1995). The effects of task choice on the quality of writing obtained in a statewide assessment. *Applied Measurement in Education, 8*, 273–290.

Harwell, M. (1999). Evaluating the validity of educational rating data. *Educational and Psychological Measurement, 59*, 25–37.

Miller, M. D., & Linn, R. L. (2000). Validation of performance-based assessments. *Applied Psychological Measurement, 24*, 367–378.

Moon, T. R., & Hughes, K. R. (2002, Summer). Training and scoring issues involved in large-scale writing assessments. *Educational Measurement: Issues and Practice, 21*(2), 15–19.

Rathvon, N. (2004). *Early reading assessment: A practitioner's handbook.* New York: Guilford Press.

Ryan, J. M., & DeMark, S. (2002). Variation in achievement scores related to gender, item format, and content area tested. In G. Tindal & T. M. Haladyna (Eds.), *Large-scale assessment programs for all students: Validity, technical adequacy, and implementation* (pp. 67–88). Mahwah, NJ: Erlbaum.

Swartz, C. W., Hooper, S. R., Montgomery, J. W., Wakely, M. B., de Kruif, R. E. L., Reed, M. et al. (1999). Using generalizability theory to estimate the reliability of writing scores derived from holistic and analytic scoring methods. *Educational and Psychological Measurement, 59*, 492–506.

[148]

Michigan English Language Institute College English Test—Listening.

Purpose: "Designed to provide information about the English language competence of adult non-native speakers of English who have high-intermediate to advanced level English skills."

Population: Adult nonnative speakers of English.
Publication Date: 2003.
Acronym: MELICET-L.
Scores: Total score only.
Administration: Group.
Forms, 2: A1, B1.
Restricted Distribution: Distribution restricted to authorized educational institutions and researchers.
Price Data: Available from publisher.
Time: 30(45) minutes.
Comments: Tests available to colleges for local administration.
Authors: Jeff S. Johnson, Barbara Dobson, and Amy D. Yamashiro.
Publisher: English Language Institute, The University of Michigan.

Review of the Michigan English Language Institute College English Test—Listening by MARSHA BENSOUSSAN, Chair, Department of Foreign Language, University of Haifa, Haifa, Israel:

DESCRIPTION. The Michigan English Language Institute College English Test—Listening (MELICET-L) is designed to provide information about the English language listening competence of adult nonnative speakers of English with high-intermediate to advanced level English skills. It is also designed to assess their ability to pursue academic study in an English-language college or university.

MELICET-L is a 50-item, 45-minute, paper-and-pencil test. Each item has three multiple-choice options, printed in a test booklet. The test has three parts: (a) short question and short statement items, (b) emphasis items, and (c) a two-person conversation and a short lecture.

The MELICET-L provides educational institutions approved by the English Language Institute, University of Michigan (ELI-UM) and researchers with information about the English language competencies of their own students, employees, or research participants. Nonstandard administrations (with modifications in timing, setting, mode, or presentation) for examinees with disabilities (vision or hearing limitations, physical handicaps, dyslexia, etc.) are also available from ELI-UM.

Test takers receive a test booklet with an answer sheet and hear recorded prompts only once. Procedural instructions, including an example of each type of item, are printed on the first page of the test booklet and recorded on a cassette tape or compact disk for examinees to listen to before they begin the test. In Part 3, examinees are instructed to take notes and are given visual aids (e.g., graph, map, chart). Test-taking conditions are standardized in terms of examination procedures, room and seating arrangements, listening conditions, examiner/examinee ratio, and security measures. Total raw scores are converted to scaled scores, ranging between 30 and 100, to enable comparison between Forms A1 and B1 and interpretation.

DEVELOPMENT. MELICET-L, produced by ELI-UM in 2003, was originally designed as part (Part 2) of a secure test battery, the Michigan English Language Assessment Battery (MELAB; T6:1584). Forms A1 and B1 are slightly modified retired forms of the MELAB Listening section tests.

The development of MELICET-L reflects an attempt to achieve optimal construct validity in terms of language authenticity and discourse structure (Buck, 2001). Standard American English is used, with alternating male and female voices in conversations and in the multiple-choice questions. Natural language is used, reflecting elisions, reductions, false starts, and phonological patterns characteristic of spoken English, at a normal delivery rate (about 150 wpm).

The textual context of the questions ranges from minimal in Parts 1 and 2 (short question and short statement items, and emphasis items) to maximal in Part 3 (a two-person conversation and a short lecture). Emphasis items are meant to test examinees' comprehension of meaning conveyed by suprasegmentals or prosodic aspects of a speaker's utterance.

The examinee assumes the role of participant or eavesdropper. Although no particular content knowledge is required, the listener is expected to be familiar with conversational routines. The listener is required to work out a speaker's intended meaning to predict how the speaker would continue.

TECHNICAL. The percentile ranking for various scaled MELICET-L scores is based on a sample of 259 examinees who took the MELICET-L in late 2002 and early 2003. Examinees were volunteers from English as a Second Language (ESL) programs at universities in Texas, Alabama, Illinois, and Wisconsin, and several English as a Foreign Language (EFL) institutions in Colombia. Drawn from geographically diversified ESL and EFL programs, the sample is representative of the university population of potential examinees. However, a slight bias towards higher grades may stem from their voluntary status, which may have lowered the usual state of anxiety accompanying typical high stakes testing.

Central tendency statistics and dispersion statistics provide one source of evidence for score consistency. Forms A1 and B1 have similar means = 75.90 (Form A1), 75.78 (Form B1); medians = 76 (Form A1 and Form B1); SD = 7.31 (Form A1), 7.15 (Form B1).

Two estimates of reliability are given. Alternative forms reliability, estimated when groups of ESL and EFL learners took both MELICET-L forms on same day, yielded the following Pearson product-moment correlation, based on the A1/B1 scaled score: r(A1/B1) = .73. Internal consistency reliability coefficients were estimated using Cronbach's alpha on data from participants for both the MELICET-L form equating study and the MELICET-L/LCT equating study. Cronbach's alpha reliability coefficient estimate = .851, SEM = 3.19 (Form A1), Cronbach's alpha reliability coefficient estimate = .873, SEM = 3.08 (Form B1).

In addition, a conversion study between the MELICET-L and the Listening Comprehension Test (LCT) based on the examinations of 417 ESL/EFL learners enrolled at institutions of higher learning in Wisconsin and Colombia, yielded a scaled score Pearson correlation of r = .80.

Reliability levels can vary, depending on the homogeneity of the tasks and the ability range of the test-takers (Buck, 2001, p. 208). Thus, the present moderate levels of reliability may reflect the variety of tasks in the three parts of the test (minimal to maximal context) and the wide ability range of the examinees.

The MELICET-L is an instrument to measure English language competence for academic study. Although it is a predictor of student success, no evidence appears demonstrating the correlation between MELICET-L scores and subsequent achievement in further studies. However, as the test was produced recently (2003), it is still early for these results.

The user's manual instructs users to interpret scores cautiously. The manual reminds the user that validation is a continuing process, and that test users have the responsibility of collecting evidence about the appropriateness of interpretations of MELICET-L scores for their own examinees and purposes.

Test Forms A1 and B1 contain short and long conversations about daily life, academic activities, and lectures on college grades and tourism. The content constitutes a representative sample of behavior domain that the test aims to measure. The MELICET-L is intended to measure the ability to comprehend spoken English, including the ability to understand the meaning of short utterances, brief conversational exchanges, and extended, semiplanned discourse as spoken by university-educated, native speakers of standard American English in an academic or professional setting.

The MELICET-L reflects current theoretical models of listening comprehension proficiency (see, e.g., Buck, 2001). It is based on the assumption that listening comprehension ability involves many component abilities:

> vocabulary knowledge; predictive abilities; background knowledge; awareness of stress and intonation; comprehension of characteristics of spoken discourse such as unfinished sentences, contractions, ellipses, etc.; ability to recognize relationship between ideas in extended discourse; knowledge of grammar in a communicative context; pragmatic knowledge; and inferencing ability. (user's manual, p. 12)

It is only indirectly possible to show that a test is indeed examining some theoretical attribute. The user's manual shows that the test measures a single construct, which is demonstrated with strong intersubsection correlations between the subsections of MELICET-L, and also by factor analysis.

Correlations are moderate, in the .31 to .60 range, with average value of .47. Moderate or strong subsection correlations provide evidence that each is measuring a similar trait. The weakest correlations are between Part 2 items (emphasis items) and other item types, indicating that this item type is somewhat unique.

Evidence of a common trait for each MELICET-L subsection (item type) is shown on the factor analysis of Form A1 and Form B1. The single factor solution explains over 60% of total variance for each test form (eigenvalues = 2.42), with high subsection score loadings on the factor, ranging from .48 to .81. Again, the weakest factor loadings were for the emphasis item type.

COMMENTARY. MELICET-L is a carefully planned and well made test. It is user-friendly: The recordings are clear, the topics are interesting, and the test booklet is well organized. There is a clear effort to maintain construct validity. The test goes beyond grammar into sociolinguistic knowledge and academic discourse.

MELICET-L has two weaknesses: test security and lack of evidence for predictive validity. The ELI-UM website warns that the test is considered nonsecure because it is sold to many institutions, and a student may have seen a particular form of the test at another institution. Therefore, the developers recommend it for internal use only, not as an admissions test. Moreover, no evidence is given that grades on the test reflect subsequent student achievement at the university.

Another issue is the extent to which listening competence can be assumed to reflect general language competence. The test user may need to consider range of language competencies when making decisions.

SUMMARY. This is a well-designed and professionally crafted test. The texts are reasonably authentic samples of academic English. The test is efficient in its brevity, with each of the three parts evaluating another aspect of the listening process. Alternative high-quality tests of American academic listening comprehension exist but are longer and/or more expensive.

REVIEWER'S REFERENCE

Buck, G. (2001). *Assessing listening*. Cambridge, MA: Cambridge University Press.

Review of the Michigan English Language Institute College English Test—Listening by CATHERINE P. COOK-COTTONE, *Assistant Professor of School Psychology, State University of New York at Buffalo, and* JENNIFER PICCOLO, *Doctoral Student of School Psychology, State University of New York at Buffalo, Buffalo, NY:*

DESCRIPTION. The Michigan English Language Institute College English Test—Listening (MELICET-L) was designed to assist in the assessment process of proficiency in English as a second language for academic study. The target population of the test includes adult nonnative speakers of English who possess high-intermediate to advanced level English skills. The MELICET-L is recommended for use "by teachers, administrators, and researchers who need to assess students, candidates for professional development programs, or research participants" (user's manual, p. 1). The user's manual provides examples of appropriate uses, including administra-

tion as an exit exam for students in an intensive English program, or as a reassessment of the English language skills of college or university students. Of importance, it is intended for internal purposes only and should not be used for initial university admissions.

Two alternate forms (A1 and B1) of the MELICET-L are available. The test consists of 50 multiple-choice items, divided into three parts, and takes approximately 45 minutes to complete. The test may be administered individually or to a group. Instructions and test items are verbally presented using an audio recording (cassette tape or CD), and examinees choose answers from a multiple-choice test booklet and record their responses on a separate answer sheet. Parts 1 and 2 include short question and statement items and items assessing interpretation of prosody variation, respectively. Part 3 assesses comprehension skills needed for success in a classroom. Specifically, this section consists of a two-person conversation accompanied by a map or diagram and a short lecture accompanied by a chart or graph. Instructions and examples of some item types are included in the test booklet and on the test recording for examinees to listen to before beginning. The MELICET-L is scored using a punched scoring stencil.

Raw scores are converted to scaled (or equated) scores using the Equivalency Table provided in the user's manual. MELICET-L scaled scores reflect levels of proficiency established by earlier versions of the Michigan English Language Assessment Battery (MELAB; T6:1584) and have been refined using equipercentile equating and other techniques based on Item Response Theory (J. Johnson, personal communication, January 31, 2005). Alternate forms of the test are not equivalent in difficulty at all score levels. This should be considered when making comparisons between Forms A1 and B1. Scaled scores can be converted to percentile rankings based on the test's normative group of 259 examinees from ESL programs at universities in Texas, Alabama, Illinois, and Wisconsin, and several EFL institutions in Colombia who took the MELICET-L in late 2002 and early 2003. The manual provides general cut scores for graduate schools, undergraduate programs, and community colleges, and directs users to the MELICET-GCVR user's manual and the MELAB technical manual for "more information about approximate cut scores required for various test applications" (user's manual, p. 2). The authors of the manual caution against rigid adherence to a specified cut score but assert that MELICET-L scores can complement decision-making processes.

DEVELOPMENT. The MELICET-L consists of slightly modified retired forms of the Listening component of the MELAB. Of note, the MELICET-L differs from the MELAB in several key ways. The MELAB is a secure test battery consisting of three sections: (a) a 30-minute written composition on an assigned topic; (b) a test of listening comprehension; and (c) a grammar, cloze, vocabulary, and reading (GCVR) section. The MELICET-L is considered nonsecure and is solely a test of listening comprehension. In addition, the MELAB is administered solely by the University of Michigan English Language Institute and its authorized examiners, whereas the MELICET-L is available to be administered by educational institutions and researchers for use within their institutions. Further, MELAB scores are used to provide educational and professional institutions with official evidence of English proficiency that can be used to meet admissions requirements whereas MELICET-L scores are used to "provide educational institutions and researchers with information about the English" proficiencies "of their own students, employees, or research participants" (user's manual, p. 3).

The test utilizes several different types of listening items based on varying degrees of context and does not require particular content knowledge. Items based on minimal context assess knowledge of conversational routines and the ability to comprehend the unexpected. Authors report a multi-step item selection process that began with the development of the MELAB. First, items were written according to established content and format specifications. Specifically, items were designed to reflect theoretical models of listening comprehension, which suggested the inclusion of listening items based on both minimal and extended context (Johnson, 2003). Items that appeared to be working well after preliminary pretesting were then presented to approximately 5,000 examinees in a University of Michigan English Language Institute annual overseas proficiency certificate test. An item analysis of 600 of these tests was performed and the best functioning items (i.e., item-test correlations of .30 or higher and

proportion correct in the range of .30 to .85) were compiled to form an item bank over several years and used to create two MELAB test forms.

TECHNICAL.

Standardization. The MELICET-L was normed in late 2002 and early 2003 using a sample of 259 participants, taking both forms of the test, from ESL programs at universities in Texas, Alabama, Illinois, and Wisconsin, and several EFL institutions in Colombia. No further demographic information (e.g., age, gender, race, ethnicity, and native language) is provided in the user's manual to validate the adequacy of the test's normative sample.

Reliability. Using data provided by the participants in both the form equating study and a MELICET-L and Listening Comprehension Test (LCT; Upshur, Koba, Spaan, & Strowe, 1986) equating study, adequate internal consistency was reported (Cronbach's alpha: Form A1 = .85, Form B1 = .87). Acceptable standard errors of measurement of 3.19 and 3.08 were reported for Forms A1 and B1, respectively. Possibly reflecting the test form equivalency issues, a Pearson product-moment correlation of .73 was reported for alternative forms based on the normative sample. Information regarding test-retest reliability is not provided.

Validity. The user's manual discusses both the content and construct validities of the MELICET-L. The MELICET-L and LCT conversion study reported a scaled score Pearson correlation of .80 between the two tests. Further, the manual states that the content of the MELICET-L reflects current theoretical models of listening comprehension proficiency, which assumes that listening comprehension involves many elements including "vocabulary knowledge, predictive abilities, background knowledge, awareness of stress and intonation, comprehension of characteristics of spoken discourse, ability to recognize the relationship between ideas in extended discourse, knowledge of grammar in a communicative context, pragmatic knowledge, and inferencing ability" (user's manual, p. 12).

Authors assert that the test measures a single construct (i.e., English language proficiency for academic study) and provides evidence of construct validity in the form of intersubsection correlations as well as factor analysis. Intersubsection (item type) correlations are moderate, ranging from .31 to .60, with an average of .47. The weakest correlations are between the prosody emphasis items (Part 2) and other item types (Form A1: .46 with Part 1 short questions and statements, .39 with lecture items, .34 with conversation items; Form B1: .41 with Part 1, .37 with lecture items, .31 with conversation items), suggesting that this type of item is unique. A factor analysis of the test (Form A1, N = 525; Form B1, N = 512) indicated that a single factor solution explained approximately 60% of the total variance for each test form (eigenvalues = 2.42). Item-type score loadings on the factor were moderate to high, ranging from .48 to .81. Short statement and question items had the strongest factor loadings (Form A1 = .81, Form B1 = .78) and emphasis items had the weakest factor loadings (Form A1 = .54, Form B1 = .48).

COMMENTARY. The MELICET-L appears to possess moderate to strong content and construct validity evidence. The item content seems to reflect the domain of English language proficiency most relevant in an academic setting. However, no independent studies to evaluate the MELICET-L have been published to date. Additional research is needed. It is recommended that users establish local norms when using the MELICET-L as part of their language assessment process. As emphasized in the manual, scores are an estimate of an individual's English language proficiency and should be used as only one part of any decision-making process.

SUMMARY. The MELICET-L is based on a well-established test of English language proficiency (MELAB). Additional research on this particular portion of that test could provide users with a more thorough understanding of the characteristics of the MELICET-L. Because of its practical content, the MELICET-L seems to be a useful tool for institutions seeking a valid measure of nonnative English speakers' language proficiency and progress.

REVIEWERS' REFERENCES

Johnson, J. (2003). *Michigan English Language Assessment Battery (MELAB) technical manual.* Ann Arbor, MI: Testing and Certification Division, English Language Institute.

Upshur, J., Koba, H., Spaan, M., & Strowe, L. (1986). Listening Comprehension Test (LCT). Ann Arbor, MI: Testing and Certification Division, English Language Institute.

Review of the Michigan English Language Institute College English Test—Listening by ALAN GARFINKEL, Professor of Spanish and Education, Purdue University, West Lafayette, IN:

DESCRIPTION. The Listening section of the Michigan English Language Institute College English Test (MELICET-L) is a 50-item test administered with a recorded cassette and an answer sheet. There are three sections. In the first section, one listens to a question or a statement and is asked to select which of three choices is either an answer to one of the questions or about the same as one of the statements. In the second section one must select a fragment that is likely to follow the one that is recorded or select the best of three responses to recorded questions. The third section allows note taking on the answer sheet and allows the test taker to listen to a lecture and, later, a conversation after which he or she is asked select a proper summary or response. The MELICET-L is to be used by authorized educational institutions and researchers who want a test that can be locally administered and scored. According to the MELICET-L users manual, possible applications include "an exit test for students in an intensive English program" (p. 1). Even though the test is not standardized in its present form, it is likely to discriminate more accurately along with being more valid and reliable than one written by an instructor because its items are slightly modified versions of items retired from the Michigan English Language Assessment Battery (MELAB; 14:233) also published by the Michigan English Language Institute.

DEVELOPMENT. As noted above, the user's manual indicates that the items in the MELICET-L are slightly modified versions of items of a more comprehensive battery of tests that includes more than listening. Materials furnished by the developer include the two forms of the MELICET-L, the user's manual, and cassette recordings of the prompts for the test. The manual indicates that the recordings were made at a "normal" pace of about 150 words per minute. The subsections in each form provide for testing skills such as comprehending the meaning of short utterances, brief conversational exchanges, and more extensive segments spoken by university-educated native speakers of standard American English.

TECHNICAL. The MELICET-L is not offered as a standardized test. However, the manual does provide an extensive discussion of both reliability and validity of scores from the test. Because the forms are different from one another, the only way to compare performance on one form with that on another is to use the scaling device provided in the manual. The test preparers note that using raw scores to make a comparison would not properly account for differences in the forms. They also point out that the range of equated or scaled scores is from 30 to 100. These scores reflect neither the number of correct answers nor the percentage of correct answers. The manual does provide percentile ranks for scores from each form and cautions (p. 7) that "rigid adherence to a specified cut score for any purpose is strongly discouraged." The percentile ranks are for volunteers from English as a Second Language (ESL) programs at several major American universities and from English as a Foreign Language (EFL) institutions in Colombia who took both forms of the MELICET-L in late 2002.

Internal consistency reliability estimates for both forms are reported at high levels (.85 and .87, with standard error of measurement values between 3.08 and 3.19). Test validity is examined with the proviso that validity changes depending on how the test is used. The content validity is clearly demonstrated. The observable skills that are included in the test are explained in detail.

COMMENTARY. The test publishers have adhered to the standards established by the American Educational Research Association and two other professional groups in writing the test manual. The test items realistically reflect standard spoken English.

SUMMARY. The MELICET-L is offered as a classroom test that can be used for local administration. As such, there is less need for information on providing norms for the test than there would be in the case of items standardized in their present form. The fact that the items are very similar to those retired from the more comprehensive and standardized MELAB test makes a strong case for concluding that scores from the MELICET-L test would be both valid and reliable for the kinds of purposes for which it is offered.

[149]

Minnesota Handwriting Assessment.

Purpose: "Used to assess manuscript and D'Nealian handwriting of students."
Population: Grades 1–2.
Publication Date: 1999.
Acronym: MHA.
Scores, 6: Rate, Legibility, Form, Alignment, Size, Spacing.
Administration: Group or individual.

Price Data, 2002: $56 per kit including 25 manuscript sheets, 25 D'Nealian sheets, and manual (99 pages).
Time: (2.5–10) minutes.
Author: Judith Reisman.
Publisher: Harcourt Assessment, Inc.

Review of the Minnesota Handwriting Assessment by KATHY J. BOHAN, Assistant Professor of Educational Psychology, Northern Arizona University, Flagstaff, AZ:

DESCRIPTION. The Minnesota Handwriting Assessment (MHA) is designed to be an objective measure of young students' manuscript handwriting. It can be used with students from mid first grade through second grade. Two versions assess either manuscript (e.g., Palmer, Zaner-Bloser) or D'Nealian handwriting. Students copy words from a stimulus sheet onto lines provided below the text examples. The eight words chosen for the assessment come from a commonly used sentence for handwriting assessment, "the quick brown fox jumped over the lazy dogs." This sentence includes every letter in the English alphabet at least once. The MHA stimulus mixes the word order to reduce memory effect for better readers when copying the various letters during the timed portion of the test.

The administration can be completed as a group assessment in a classroom or individually. Students are timed for 2.5 minutes to obtain a Rate score. Then students are encouraged to continue to copy the complete stimulus. A total of 34 letters are copied for later grading of quality categories: Legibility, Form, Alignment, Size, and Spacing.

The assessment can be administered by professionals who train to become proficient in the scoring system. The test was developed by an occupational therapist, but might also be used by physical therapists, special and regular education teachers, psychologists, and researchers. The manual provides specific scoring guidelines along with a self-guided tutorial to practice scoring. A clear 6-inch ruler is required to measure responses to determine any quality category errors. General and specific guidelines along with examples of scored responses are provided. Correct scores in each category are added and entered on the Record Form under the appropriate grade level (i.e., first or second grade) and assessment period (i.e., January, April, October). Cut scores are assigned for classifying whether students' errors are typical of same grade peers or atypical. The top 75% of the standardization sample was identified to be at the "Performing Like Peers" range. Students whose scores fell within the bottom 5% to 25% range were classified as "Well Below Peers." According to the author, students attaining scores in this range should be monitored to determine if they need more direct instruction or practice to develop skills. The bottom 5% of students in the normative sample were identified as students "Performing Well Below their Peers" (manual, p. 43). The author indicates that these students should be considered for further evaluation.

DEVELOPMENT. A pilot version of the MHA was developed by Reisman in 1991. This version was untimed and provided information about handwriting legibility, form, alignment, and size. Scoring procedures were developed through a review of the literature, as well as consultation with occupational therapists and primary teachers. The final version added a timed component as a measure of rate of copying letters. Guidelines for scoring spacing within words were also added. The final scoring directions were established through majority opinion of a convenience sample of 12 primary teachers.

TECHNICAL. The final standardization study included approximately 2,000 students from 11 states. Normative sample data provided in the manual include sample sizes and means for ages at the various marking periods for first and second grade. Percentages of the normative sample by gender, hand preference, handwriting style (i.e., manuscript, D'Nealian), and ethnicity are also given. Percentages generally match general population demographics with the exception of ethnicity. The sample is 80–85% Caucasian; however, this underrepresentation of ethnic diversity is identified as a limitation by the test author.

The manual reports interrater reliability studies from the pilot and final development phases. Although good to excellent interrater coefficients are reported (ranging from .77 to .98), the studies compared ratings by the primary author of the test with only one to six novice raters. Although the scoring guidelines are presented clearly and a self-tutorial provides practice opportunity, more evidence of interrater reliability with scoring would add to the confidence that scores provide meaningful data for interpretation. Additionally, the author reports two studies addressing test-retest stability. Both

studies found only moderate consistency for the Legibility and Rate categories, whereas relatively good stability was found with the Form, Spacing, Size, and Alignment categories. Thus, caution should be used with interpretation of some categories.

Content validity evidence emphasizes the selection of the stimulus sentence as representative of all letters in the alphabet with words that are generally within the reading level of most first and second graders. The near-point copying task uses lined paper similar to what is most commonly provided in classroom instruction. Scoring based on rate and measurement criteria attempts to objectively measure handwriting skills.

A special group study reported correlations between the MHA and the Test of Visual Motor Skills (TVMS). The TVMS was selected because "many occupational therapists have assumed that the ability to copy letters and the ability to copy forms are related" (manual, p. 91). This comparison is presented as an assumption rather than citation of empirical data. The study's sample size of 239 students included 21 special education students and 10 students receiving occupational therapy. Results found moderate to high correlations for first graders, special education, and occupational therapy students, whereas low correlations were obtained with second graders' scores. The author hypothesized that the relationship between copying letters and handwriting decreases as visual motor maturity increases. To the author's credit, a recommendation is made for further research with larger groups of participants.

COMMENTARY. The manual is well written with concise directions for administration. Common administration and scoring questions are anticipated and addressed using specific examples and illustrations. Once an examiner has mastered the scoring guidelines, a Quick Reference scoring chart makes future scoring more efficient. Although the author states that the MHA is a handwriting assessment tool, it would seem to be more appropriate to consider it to be a screener. Cutoff scores along with other information about the student can assist with referral decisions for further evaluation. The lack of interrater reliability evidence beyond the small studies with the test developers as well as moderate test-retest reliability evidence limits the confidence of some scores. Additionally, further research to substantiate the validity of scores from the measure is also needed.

SUMMARY. The test author's purpose in developing the MHA was to provide a norm-referenced, standardized assessment for identifying handwriting ability in young students. As such, the MHA clearly provides a more objective means of identifying young children who might benefit from monitoring and intervention than the current practice of subjective impressions made by teachers and therapists.

Review of the Minnesota Handwriting Assessment by ANDREW A. COX, Professor, Department of Counseling and Psychology, Troy State University, Phenix City, AL:

DESCRIPTION. The Minnesota Handwriting Assessment (MHA) is designed to evaluate manuscript handwriting for first and second grade students. The assessment uses an eight-word mixed order stimulus sentence "the quick brown fox jumped over the lazy dogs." Using a regular pencil, test takers copy these words from a printed stimulus sheet onto a lined answer sheet. Stimulus sheets for both manuscript and D'Nealian style handwriting are available with the test taker using the particular stimulus document for the handwriting style utilized within the classroom or instructional setting.

The instrument can be administered by educators, psychologists, occupational and physical therapists, and other practitioners interested in children's handwriting. The manual indicates that the instrument should be interpreted by evaluators with an understanding of handwriting processes and the underlying perceptual and motor skills associated with this process.

Scores are provided for handwriting rate, legibility, form, alignment, size, and spacing. Scoring is completed by consulting the detailed scoring instructions provided within the manual. The manual includes a self-guided tutorial with scoring examples for each score area to assist examiners in mastering scoring rules. A quick reference scoring guide is provided to facilitate scoring for accomplished evaluators. Other than in handwriting rate, each letter within the stimulus sentence is scored for errors to evaluate legibility, form, alignment, size, and spacing.

The record form contains raw score intervals for first and second grade students with qualitative interpretations indicating whether the test taker is performing consistent with, somewhat below, or well below grade peers. The interpretative levels correspond to students within the bottom 5%, 5 to 25%, and those within the top 75% of the normative sample. The record form also allows the test administrator to evaluate student progress over multiple administrations of the MHA. Tables are provided within the manual for the standardization sample's means and standard deviations for both first and second grade students. Suggestions for remediation of handwriting deficits are also included within the instrument's manual.

DEVELOPMENT. The Minnesota Handwriting Assessment was initially developed by occupational therapists with a Minnesota school district. A pilot version of the instrument was administered to 225 first and second grade students. The manual does not describe the nature of this pilot sample or the manner in which it was obtained.

The later development of a research version of the MHA included an additional timed test and a word/letter spacing scoring category. This edition included data for 90 California and Maine second graders collected by occupational therapists. Characteristics or the manner in which these children were sampled are also not described.

The stimulus sentence used to administer the MHA was selected on the basis of young children's learning and developmental characteristics. All alphabet letters are used at least one time within the stimulus sentence. Words are short in length with most first and second grade students having familiarity with these words within their learning settings.

TECHNICAL.

Standardization. The current edition of the Minnesota Handwriting Assessment was standardized on more than 2,000 students residing in California, Colorado, Illinois, Kentucky, Maine, Massachusetts, Minnesota, New Jersey, South Carolina, Washington, and Wisconsin. The manual does not describe the standardization sample's selection other than data being provided by teachers and occupational therapists. It is also not known if the standardization sample was designed to represent various United States population demographic characteristics. Tables describing the standardization sample's age, gender, ethnicity, hand preference, and instructional handwriting style are provided within the manual. The test developer notes but does not describe efforts made to obtain a sample of students from both urban and rural school districts across several states. The test developer also notes that the standardization sample does not represent ethnic diversity as reflected within the general population. Review of tabled data suggests that the number of ethnically diverse students within the standardization sample is small, being approximately 7% or less of the total sample.

Validity. Validation for scores from the instrument is supported through content validity and a specialized validation study using the Test of Visual-Motor Skills. The rationale for the stimulus sentence used to administer the test; the use of near-point, lined paper, alternate lines, and triangles on the stimulus answer document; and the instrument's scoring categories are presented as evidence of content validation. This appears to be limited as content validation does not appear to be based upon formal validation studies.

One validation study using the Test of Visual-Motor Skills with a sample of 239 regular education, special education, and special education coupled with occupational therapy first and second graders is reported. Grade, gender, ethnicity, hand preference, instructional handwriting style, and educational placement data are described in tabular form for this sample. Correlation coefficients for this sample are provided as evidence supporting a relationship between visual-motor maturity, handwriting, and letter copying.

Reliability. Interrater, intrarater, and test-retest reliability estimates are presented as evidence for reliability. Interrater reliability analyses were conducted during development of the pilot and research version of the MHA. Reliability coefficients for inexperienced scorers ranged from .77 to .88. Inexperienced as compared to experienced scorer coefficients ranged from .87 to .98 depending upon the scoring category. Intrarater reliability is reported to examine individual rater variability. A small group of experienced and inexperienced scorers was used to determine this characteristic. Excellent intrarater reliability is suggested with coefficients ranging from .96 to 1.0.

Two test-retest reliability studies are reported. One study used a sample of 99 second grade students from three different school districts in three states within the Northeastern and Midwestern regions of the United States. A second study included 56 first and second grade at-risk, economically deprived students. Both of these studies suggest moderate to high instrument reliability with reliability estimates varying according to the evaluation categories.

COMMENTARY. The Minnesota Handwriting Assessment appears to have value as a measure of handwriting. The test developer has attempted to standardize and develop technical characteristics consistent with the *Standards for Educational and Psychological Testing* (American Educational Research Association, American Psychological Association, & National Council on Measurement in Education, 1999). The manual is well organized, readable, and interpretable. Scoring and administration guidelines are detailed and easy to follow. Efforts have been made to standardize scoring guidelines and insure consistency as some scorer judgment and interpretation is inherent in the handwriting scoring process.

The MHA would be useful for a variety of users with interest in children's handwriting performance. These users would include regular and special education teaching personnel, occupational and physical therapists, and those interested in educational diagnosis and remediation, particularly for children with educational limitations or deficiencies in need of remediation.

The user of this measurement would be required to be knowledgeable of handwriting instruction and assessment particularly manuscript (Palmer or Zaner-Bloser) and D'Nealian methods. The manual provides almost no information describing these instructional methods. A manual section providing an overview of such instruction would be highly recommended.

Information regarding placement of students in descriptive categories as noted on the instrument's record form appears to be diffuse. Descriptive information details performance of children in the range of less than 5 to 25% and those within the top 75% category. Clarification of this interpretative process is needed for potential test users.

Relative to technical characteristics, enhancement of the instrument's standardization sample is needed. Though the current standardization sample is impressive relative to number of children and geographical locale, there is a need to make the standardization sample more reflective of United States population demographics.

There also needs to be more work substantiating the instrument's psychometric properties. Concurrent validation studies with instruments such as those described in McLoughlin and Lewis (1994) could be undertaken by the test developer. Additional reliability studies would also be recommended.

SUMMARY. The Minnesota Handwriting Assessment is an instrument not commonly found within the repertoire of assessment measures for utilization by educational, psychological, developmental, and other practitioners assessing children's development. As noted by Ediger (2002), handwriting is often a neglected area of instruction and attention within the educational curriculum of today. This instrument could be readily integrated within the instructional setting with the caution that the MHA content be consistent with classroom instructional methods. The MHA is also only appropriate for learners using English as their primary language. It may not be appropriate for the increasingly diverse language background found in today's educational environment.

In practice, this measure should be utilized in conjunction with classroom samples of young people's handwriting work. Informal assessment and analysis techniques such as those described by McLoughlin and Lewis (1994) and Overton (1996) can be used to supplement MHA assessment to provide a broader and more valid assessment of children's handwriting. The supplemental use of such assessments would be important considering the instrument's limited validity data. Item analysis techniques could be used with the MHA making it useful in evaluating the nature of the learner's errors and promoting remediation.

The MHA appears to be a good beginning in the assessment of manuscript handwriting for young children. With additional standardization and validation data, the measure should become an excellent measure for those practitioners interested in assessing children's handwriting, assisting in the development of remediation intervention, and research into the nature of children's development.

REVIEWER'S REFERENCES

American Educational Research Association, American Psychological Association, & National Council on Measurement in Education. (1999). *Standards for educational and psychological testing.* Washington, DC: American Educational Research Association.

Ediger, M. (2002). Assessing handwriting achievement. *Reading Improvement, 35,* 103–110.

McLoughlin, J. A., & Lewis, R. B. (1994). *Assessing special students* (4th ed.). New York: Maxwell Macmillan International.

Overton, T. (1996). *Assessment in special education: An applied approach* (2nd ed.). Upper Saddle River, NJ: Merrill.

[150]
Mirror Edition of the Personal Values Inventory.

Purpose: Designed to describe how a person uses his/her personal strengths in relationships.
Population: Adolescents and adults reading at sixth grade level or above.
Publication Dates: 1973–1997.
Scores, 20: 7 Motivational Values.

Administration: Individual or group.
Price Data, 2001: $4.50 per test booklet; $30 per manual (1996, 146 pages).
Time: (20–40) minutes.
Comments: Manual is entitled Relationship Awareness Theory Manual of Administration and Interpretation (9th Ed.).
Author: Elias H. Porter.
Publisher: Personal Strengths Publishing.

Review of the Mirror Edition of the Personal Values Inventory by RIC BROWN, Vice President for Academic Affairs, California State University—Sacramento, Sacramento, CA:

DESCRIPTION. The Mirror Edition of the Personal Values Inventory (PVI) is a measure designed for helping individuals understand their personal strengths through self-reflection and feedback from others. This instrument is a companion to the original PVI (T6:1876; a self-assessment tool). The "mirror" refers to use by others to reflect on the individual to be rated. Thus, the Mirror Edition of the PVI is a measure of values, relationships, motivation, and understanding. Author Elias Porter (who notes working closely with Carl Rogers) attempted to create an instrument to assist individuals to have positive interpersonal relationships. The manual devotes approximately 30 pages to the underpinnings of relationship awareness theory.

As outlined, the author suggests that the Mirror Edition, along with other instruments in the relationship awareness theory arsenal (the Strength Deployment Inventory [SDI], the Job Interaction Inventory, and the original PVI), can be utilized for leadership training, supervisory skills, team building, conflict management, assertiveness training, time management, career development, sales training, customer relations, personal counseling, marital relations, and emergency response team training.

DEVELOPMENT. The manual of administration and interpretation discusses very broadly the scales mentioned above in a manner suggesting that they all reflect the same dimensions, but from different perspectives. Thus, development of the dimensions does not seem distinguishable from one scale to the other.

To develop the dimensions, items were written (and color-coded) along concepts of Altruistic-Nurturing (blue—behaving in ways that are more likely to be trusting, optimistic, helpful, etc.); Assertive-Directing (red—behaving in ways that reflect self-confidence, ambition, risk taking, etc.); Analytic-Autonomizing (green—behaving in ways exhibiting caution, order, and conserving of resources, etc.).

On the Mirror Edition, those rating others are asked to assign points (totaling no more than 10) across three categorizing responses to prompts under two general scenarios: When things are going well, and then another set of prompts, when there is conflict and opposition. For each scenario there are 10 prompts. After all 20 questions are answered, 6 scores emerge: 2 red scores (1 for when things are going well and 1 for when there is conflict or opposition) and so on.

An example of an item when things are going well includes: He/she feels best when … the main choices have been made by others and he/she knows how to be of help (Altruistic-Nurturing); others count on him/her to make the main choices and tell them what to do (Assertive-Directing); he/she has had time to study a choice and decide what is best for him/her (Analytic-Autonomizing).

An example of an item when faced with conflict and opposition includes: When someone strongly disagrees with him/her, he/she usually … gives in and does it their way (Altruistic-Nurturing); challenges them right away and argues as hard as he/she can (Assertive-Directing); stays cool and backs off until he/she is sure of where he/she stands (Analytic-Autonomizing).

TECHNICAL. Although very vague and sketchy, there is a chapter devoted to reliability and validity evidence for the dimensions in general. Again, it appears that the same dimensions are components of all the scales developed to measure relationship awareness theory. Thus, it is not made clear from which scale the data are presented. With that caveat, 6 days to 2 weeks, test-retest coefficients in the .7 range are shown for the three major dimensions. Longer test-retest issues are discussed, with no data presented.

Validity is generally discussed for the SDI and PVI, suggesting, for example, that among nurses (noting, except those in administration), most scored highest on the Altruistic-Nurturing behavior. Again no data are presented. Cross-cultural verification is suggested with no supporting evidence.

COMMENTARY. For the feedback receiver (the focus of the relationship awareness), the Strength Deployment Inventory or the Personal Values Inventory are completed. For the rater, the manual suggests that they also complete the SDI or PVI and become familiar with relationship awareness theory. They then complete the Mirror Edition of the PVI on the ratee. The provider of the feedback, not necessarily the rater, plots all 12 scores (6 from the ratee's PVI and 6 from the Mirror Edition) about the ratee on a multicolored triangle for interpretation. Those charts are discussed with the ratee in a one-on-one setting or a group setting for multiple ratees. Several chapters of the manual are devoted to scoring and interpretation.

SUMMARY. At a very broad level, the concepts of relationships awareness theory are interesting and presented clearly at a theoretical level. However, quantitatively measuring the constructs leaves much to be desired from a psychometric perspective. Administration seems to be labor intensive and the plotting of scores on a color-coded triangle is tedious.

The manual itself (really a short text on the theory) does not offer much assistance to a potential user. Although there are several chapters devoted to scoring, charting scores on the color-coded triangle, and interpretation, they are not easy to follow. Unfortunately, as interesting as the theory may be, the Mirror Edition of the PVI does not seem to offer much in the way of a usable instrument.

[151]

Morrisby Profile.

Purpose: "Designed to give a complete statement, in objective terms, about the basic mental structure of a person."

Population: Age 14–adults.

Publication Dates: 1955–1992.

Acronym: MP.

Scores: 12 tests: Compound Series, General Abilities-Verbal, General Abilities-Numerical, General Abilities-Perceptual, Shapes, Mechanical Ability, Speed Tests 1–4 (Modal Profile), Speed Tests 5–6 (Dexterity).

Administration: Group.

Price Data: Available from publisher.

Time: 180(210) minutes.

Comments: Previously called the Differential Test Battery.

Author: The Morrisby Organisation.

Publisher: The Morrisby Organisation [England].

Cross References: For information on the Differential Test Battery, see T3:733 (2 references), T2:1070 (6 references); for reviews by E. A. Peel, Donald E. Super, and Philip E. Vernon, see 5:606.

Review of the Morrisby Profile by PATRICIA A. BACHELOR, Professor of Psychology, California State University—Long Beach, Long Beach, CA:

DESCRIPTION. The Morrisby Profile (MP) is designed to appraise an individual's mental and personality profile. The MP consists of 12 subtests designed to assess five areas—Abstract Reasoning, Information Processing Abilities, Practical Abilities, Manual Dexterity, and Personality. Abstract Reasoning, measured by the Compound Series Test (CST), is a speeded, pattern completion task without verbal or numerical acquired knowledge required to successfully perform the tasks. The CST items increase in difficulty through the use of more complex combinations of sizes, colors, and shapes. Three information processing areas are assessed by General Abilities Tests (Gat) designed to capture Verbal (Gat-V), Numerical (Gat-N), and Perceptual or Diagrammatic (Gat-P) content. Each Gat consists of two subsets—Sequences and Analogies. Practical abilities involve routine, everyday activities. A person's score will result in placement along a bipolar continuum of preference toward dealing with discrete or whole systems. Practical abilities encompass spatial and mechanical abilities. Spatial abilities are measured by the Shapes test. The Mechanical Abilities Test (MAT) is a multiple-choice test composed of diagrams that represent practical problems involving mechanical content.

The remaining two general areas—Personality Characteristics and Manual Dexterity—are assessed by six speeded tests (ST-1 to ST-6) developed specifically to capture these characteristics. The six tests are administered last and completed within 35 minutes or less. The four personality characteristics tests (ST-1 to ST-4) are scored and then interpreted in comparison of the strength of relation to the subject's other personality traits. The traits assessed include ST-1 (Awareness), ST-2 (Perseveration), ST-3 (Inner Confidence), and ST-4 (Outer Confidence). The four personality scores are interpreted with respect to three dimensions. The first dimension categorizes a test taker as Flexible, Inflexible, or Tenacious. The second dimension evaluates the individual as Personally Confident, Outwardly Confident, or Matched in Confidence. The third dimension classifies the test taker as Non-Confident, Confident, or Even. Manual Dexterity tests assess manual

speed (ST-5) and manual skill (ST-6). These test scores generate a person's profiles as fast/slow, skillful or not, and dominant characteristic.

DEVELOPMENT. The current MP (1992) is the result of a series of revisions to the Morrisby Differential Test Battery (DTB). Fundamentally, the update's focus was to change the presentation and content of the test to improve the measurement of personal characteristics and mental abilities and to eliminate or revise items that are irrelevant or culturally biased. Correlations (ranging from .62 to .93) between MP subtests and the DTB reveal substantial consistency across tests, hence, the revisions successfully captured the originally theorized attributes.

The revisions to the DTB to create the MP were driven by a series of item analyses and Rasch analyses. The first set in a series of analyses guided several test modifications and was piloted on 678 students in high school and college. The results of that study led to revisions piloted on a stratified sample of 3,016 students from over 40 schools in the United Kingdom with approximately equal numbers of males and females, more than 200 ESL students, and 9% ethnic minorities. The scores from this sample were used to estimate internal consistency and test-retest reliability coefficients as well as suggest further revisions. These analyses facilitated further changes to the test, which was administered to 1,000 graduates, technicians, and managers.

The aforementioned series of revisions were empirically based. A summary of the revisions follows. Items on any subtest that discriminated on the basis of language or ethnicity were eliminated. Items on the CST were reordered by difficulty level. The General Abilities subtests were designed to capture potential, not acquired, vocabulary or arithmetic skills; hence, test items that involved increasingly difficult word comparisons or items that required addition or multiplication tasks under speeded conditions were eliminated in favor of items that correctly categorized individuals with the ability to manipulate verbal and numerical content. Items were reordered on the Shapes Test based on Rasch analyses. MAT items were rewritten to simplify the language, to eliminate the need of formal mechanical training, and to balance test figures by gender. A section comparing pairs of shapes was added to the ST-1. The ST-4's time limit was doubled to 2 minutes and required examinees to label their diagrams within this time limit. ST—5 and ST—6 items were presented in a slightly simplified style.

TECHNICAL.

Standardization. Extensive revisions to create the MP from its prior form, the DTB, were detailed in the manual. Several standardization samples were used in the revision process, yet, full disclosure of the demographic characteristics about the samples was lacking. The information provided has been presented in the relevant section of this review. Unfortunately, the demographic information provided was not sufficient to enable a researcher to make meaningful comparisons or to evaluate the MP's use with other groups.

Reliability. Cronbach's alpha was used to estimate the internal consistency reliability of the MP subtests. A total of 341 high school students—169 female and 172 male—in the 11th and 12th grades comprised the standardization sample. The reported values of alpha for the subtests ranged between .79 and .96 with a median of .88 for the 12 subtests. These values are, without question, compelling evidence for the claim of internal consistency reliability.

Intercorrelations between the 12 subtests and the MP battery—the sum of scores on all subtests—were the evidence presented in support of test-retest reliability. The subtest correlations ranged from .72 to 92 (with a median of .82). The intercorrelation of MP battery was .95. Unfortunately, the length of time between the test administrations was not provided. The knowledge of the time between testing sessions is imperative; hence, despite substantial correlations offered to demonstrate stability via test-retest; reliability evidence is inadequate.

Validity. A currently accepted technique to examine concurrent criterion-related validity is to correlate the scores on the test undergoing a validation assessment with current scores on a widely established instrument measuring the same attribute, skill, or ability. Raven's Progressive Matrices, Bennett's Mechanical Comprehension Test, the Alice Heim Tests 5 and 6 (which assess verbal, numerical, and diagrammatic content), Witkin's Embedded Figures test, and the Verbal subtest of the Differential Assignment Theory (DAT) were identified as tests that measured the same traits as the MP; hence, these tests and/or subtests are appropriate criteria for the validation of the MP subtests. A total of 103 individuals were adminis-

tered Raven's Progressive Matrices (RPM), which is a measure of visual, spatial, and diagrammatic abilities. Students' scores on the RPM correlated significantly with the CST ($r = .56$), Gat-V ($r = .47$), Gat-N ($r = .57$), Gat-P ($r = .65$), Shapes ($r = .60$), MAT ($r = .53$), and ST-1 ($r = .35$). Significant correlations existed between Alice Heim Tests 5 and 6 and the Gat-V ($r = .58$ and .54, respectively); the Gat-N ($r = .59$ and .49, respectively); and the Gat-P ($r = .49$ and .50, respectively). Clearly, these correlations are convincing evidence of concurrent criterion-related validity of the MP subtests. Due to space limitations, further validation studies, factor analyses, and differential validity assessments are not presented here; interested readers are directed to the manual.

COMMENTARY. The manual of the Morrisby Profile includes a thorough presentation of the theoretical issues surrounding the measurement of mental abilities. This discussion served as a foundation to the empirical development of the DTB and the MP. Extensive descriptive information about each subtest's purpose, development, scoring rubrics, and interpretation were documented as was the extensive revision process.

Evidence of internal consistency reliability was demonstrated with values of Cronbach's alphas ranging from the .80s to .90s; yet an acceptable description of the sample was lacking. Substantial intercorrelations between subtest scores and MP battery scores were used as evidence of test-retest reliability; unfortunately, the time between test administrations was omitted. This omission prevents any positive or substantial conclusion about the evidence submitted for test-retest reliability. The assessment of concurrent criterion-related validity conformed with current standards of test construction. Correlations between criterion measures and MP subtests attained statistical significance. This would be compelling support if norm groups were adequately described. It is imperative that future publications detail time frames and demographics of samples comprising each psychometric investigation.

SUMMARY. The Morrisby Profile (MP) consists of 12 subtests designed to generate a profile of five general areas of intellectual and personality attributes. The MP is an extensive revision of the Differential Test Battery (DTB) originally created by Morrisby to reflect his perception of the conceptual underpinnings of differential theories of human intellectual abilities and their assessment. The procedures used to support the psychometric qualities of the MP were appropriate but ample demographic information of the samples used in the various standardization samples was lacking; hence, meaningful comparisons cannot be made. Internal consistency reliability was demonstrated by alpha values in the range of the .80s and .90s. Despite substantial correlations between subtests and the total score on the MP, no reasonable conclusions about test-retest reliability can be made without information regarding the time frame between test administrations. Criterion-related validity was demonstrated by significant correlations between MP subtests and several well-accepted standardized tests measuring the criteria of interest.

[152]
Motor-Free Visual Perception Test, Third Edition.

Purpose: Designed to assess an individual's "visual perceptual ability without any motor involvement needed to make a response."
Population: Ages 4–94.
Publication Dates: 1972-2003.
Acronym: MVPT-3.
Score: Total score only.
Administration: Individual.
Price Data, 2004: $120 per test kit including manual (2003, 95 pages), test plates, and 25 recording forms in portfolio; $30 per manual; $65 per set of test plates; $25 per 25 recording forms.
Time: (20-30) minutes.
Comments: Revision includes updated norms.
Authors: Ronald P. Colarusso and Donald D. Hammill.
Publisher: Academic Therapy Publications.
Cross References: For reviews by Nancy B. Bologna and Theresa Volpe-Johnstone of an earlier edition, see 14:241; see also T5:1725 (8 references) and T4:1677 (6 references); for a review by Carl L. Rosen of an earlier edition and an excerpted review by Alan Krichev, see 8:883 (9 references).

Review of the Motor-Free Visual Perception Test, Third Edition by GARY L. CANIVEZ, Professor of Psychology, Eastern Illinois University, Charleston, IL:

DESCRIPTION. The Motor-Free Visual Perception Test, Third Edition (MVPT-3) is an extension and new standardization of the MVPT-R. To increase the utility of the MVPT with adults, it was necessary to add items of increasing difficulty to better assess visual perception in adulthood. It was also necessary to expand norms to the adult population and to obtain a nationally representative standardization sample, characteristics lacking in earlier editions. An additional "Response Time Index" was developed for the MVPT-3 so that speed of visual perceptual skills may also be assessed.

The MVPT-3 purports to measure visual perception skills as defined by Chalfant and Scheffelin (1969): spatial relationships, visual discrimination, figure-ground, visual closure, and visual memory. The authors of the MVPT-3 acknowledge the interaction of visual perception and cognition in the responses to item content of the MVPT-3, suggesting that "perception, as used in the real world, most often involves a combination of perceptual skills, so the overlapping of constructs in MVPT-3 tasks is to be expected" (manual, p. 14).

DEVELOPMENT. The MVPT-3 was expanded to better assess visual perception among adults. An additional 31 items were created and following item analysis, 29 items were selected (4 sample items, 25 test items), added to the original 40 MVPT-R items, and included in the standardized version. The MVPT-3 uses black-and-white line drawings in stimuli and response choices where the individual selects from among four choices the answer matching the stimulus. As such, no physical manipulation is required in making responses rendering the MVPT-3 "motor free."

TECHNICAL. The standardization version of the MVPT-3 was administered to 2,005 individuals, 1,856 of whom comprised the normative sample. The remaining individuals were part of validity samples. Standardization data were collected in 118 cities from 34 states from across the continental United States and Alaska by 166 examiners who were mostly occupational therapists. Examiners were asked to randomly select students from regular classrooms or non-head-injured adults from hospitals or institutions where the examiner worked. No details were provided on how random selection was done. Various disability groups were also sampled and data used for validity studies. Overall, stratification variables of geographic region, race/ethnicity, gender, residence (urban/rural), and disability fairly closely matched the U.S. population based on the 2000 Census; however, stratification by age, race/ethnicity, and geographic region resulted in some significant over- and underrepresentation of some groups, which was reportedly statistically corrected using weighting procedures. For example, there were no Asian American or Black/African American individuals in the age range of 55–69 and there was only one Asian American individual and there were no Black/African American individuals between 70–84+. Details on weighting procedures were not provided.

Raw scores on the MVPT-3 are transformed to standard scores ($M = 100$, $SD = 15$) and percentile ranks. Standard score confidence intervals (85% and 90%) based on the standard errors of measurement within age groups are also provided. Although the MVPT-3 includes items from five different areas, only an overall total score is computed as with earlier editions. Although age equivalent scores are provided, problems with this metric (Sattler, 2001), including correct interpretation of age equivalent scores, suggest that it, like grade equivalent scores from other tests, should not be used.

Reliability of MVPT-3 scores was assessed with internal consistency and test-retest stability estimates. Internal consistency (r_{alpha}) estimates for the standardization sample ranged from .69 to .87 (*Mdn* r_{alpha} = .80) for ages 4–10 and ranged from .86 to .90 (*Mdn* r_{alpha} = .89) for ages 11–84+. Based on these internal consistency estimates, the MVPT-3 should only be used for group decision making or screening for 4–10-year-olds (Salvia & Ysseldyke, 1991). The short-term ($M = 34$ days) test-retest stability estimate for an unacceptably small sample ($n = 28$) of 4–10-year-olds was .82 (uncorrected) and showed a moderate gain of 8.44 points (Glass's delta = .56) suggesting practice effects. The short-term ($M = 34$ days) test-retest stability estimate for the 11–84+-year-old group ($n = 75$) was .72 (uncorrected) and showed smaller practice effects with a gain of 3.87 points (Glass's delta = .26). Practice effects were similar to those found with nonverbal/perceptual ability measures on tests such as the WISC-III and WISC-IV (Wechsler, 1991, 2003). The test-retest interval range was not indicated in the manual for either sample so differences between the younger and older age groups in practice effect may be the result of differences in the retest intervals between the two groups. Demographic data on these two samples are collapsed in the MVPT-3 manual and illustrate that mostly college-educated Whites comprised the sample but this obviously pertains to the older group. Response Time Index scores were

also examined for reliability for 87 individuals in a test-retest stability study. The retest interval was between 5 and 125 days ($M = 35.0$, $SD = 38.9$) and the stability coefficient equaled .91. Additional investigation and replication of the reliability of MVPT-3 scores is necessary.

Validity of MVPT-3 scores was reported in content, criterion-related, and construct validity domains. Content validity was reported via item discrimination and item bias studies as well as content "developed to represent the areas of visual perception that have been identified by previous research and that occupational therapists and other users of the test have found to be the most discriminating" (manual, p. 56). There was no mention of content analysis by experts in measurement or in visual perception skills or what criteria were used to determine how "discriminating" the areas were. Criterion-related validity investigations with other tests of visual perception are presented in the MVPT-3 manual but these studies pertain to the first edition of the MVPT and not the MVPT-3. Apparently, there are no current criterion-related studies supporting the MVPT-3. Construct validity of MVPT-3 scores was provided by examining scores across chronological age and illustrated the theoretical developmental change in visual perception skills from early childhood through old age. As such, the MVPT-3 showed increases in scores from age 4 through age 39 and then slow, steady decline into late adulthood. This also parallels the development of fluid, visual, and perceptual reasoning abilities in the cognitive domain (Kaufman & Lichtenberger, 2002). Construct validity was also examined with comparisons to cognitive ability and academic achievement where it was hypothesized that low correlations would be obtained. Given the authors' hypothesis that correlations between the MVPT-3 and tests of cognitive ability and achievement would be low, this would be indicative of divergent or discriminant validity. Of the three small sample studies reported in the manual, only one was for the MVPT-3 and compared scores with the Wechsler Intelligence Scale for Children—Third Edition (Wechsler, 1991). The sample size was unacceptably small for calculation of correlation coefficients, but correlations were calculated and ranged from .22 to .37. These were not statistically significant. The final method of construct validity was the distinct group difference method by comparing various exceptional (disabled) groups' performance on the MVPT-3. Three different samples were obtained and included 38 "Developmentally Delayed," 48 "Head Injured," and 51 "Learning Disabled" students. How individuals were classified into these groups is not clear but investigation of demographic data provided in the MVPT-3 manual suggests some irregularities. For example, among the sample of "Learning Disabled" the age range was 5–62, and 29 individuals (56.9%) reportedly were in the 4+ Years College group. Thus, this sample of "Learning Disabled" individuals may well differ from those typically encountered by assessment professionals in schools. A similar phenomenon was observed with the sample of "Developmentally Disabled" where the age range was 4-52, and 22 (57.9%) were reportedly in the 4+ Years College group. All three "exceptional" groups demonstrated MVPT-3 scores that were statistically significantly lower than the population mean. Only the "Developmentally Delayed" group performed more than 2 SD below the mean. Other exceptional distinct groups comparisons reported in the MVPT-3 manual pertained to earlier editions of the MVPT and not the current version. Other than a comparison of U.S. and Canadian examinees, no other "validity" studies have been reported for the Response Time Index. "Validity" of MVPT-3 Response Time Index scores was assessed by comparing the U.S. sample to a Canadian sample and found no significant differences between the two groups. No other method of validity was presented so the meaning and interpretability of this index is unclear. Based on the validity studies reported in the MVPT-3 manual, it is obvious that additional investigation is necessary before judgment on the adequacy of the MVPT-3 or its interpretation can be rendered.

COMMENTARY. The MVPT-3 remains easy to administer and score. The instructions seem clear and test items are clearly presented for the examinee. Reliability estimates suggest the MVPT-3 is adequate for individual decision making for those 11 and older but inadequate for individual decision making below age 11. Interpretation of the MVPT-3 is limited due to the limitations in validity studies presented. What is most disappointing is the general lack of empirical studies supporting the MVPT-3 score reliability and validity. Many of the studies reported in the MVPT-3 manual pertain to earlier editions of the MVPT and these studies are fairly limited in scope. Although distinct group differences are presented as evidence of construct validity, this is a necessary but not sufficient condition for determining the diagnostic utility of a test. Studies examining other types of construct validity such as discriminative validity (diagnostic efficiency/utility), incremental validity, and factorial validity would be more useful determinants of construct validity than the distinct group differences presented in the manual.

Norm tables were divided into 3-month intervals for ages 4–10, 6-month intervals for ages 11–15, 1-year intervals for ages 16–19, 5-year intervals for ages 20–49, and 2-year intervals for ages 50–93. Examination of sample sizes within age groupings of the standardization sample suggests that although the proportions of individuals at younger ages (4–10) may be adequate for estimating the population, there appear to be too few individuals to adequately divide the 50–93 age group into 2-year intervals. Specific details as to the exact number of individuals within each 2-year interval is not provided but simple calculation suggests an average of less than 9 individuals per age group; which seems insufficient for providing a norm-based score.

The MVPT-3, like earlier editions, was constructed to measure visual perceptual abilities; however, item types like visual short-term memory and spatial orientation seem to require "cognitive" skills in addition to "perceptual" skills. This confound is acknowledged by the authors in that "real world" tasks require both perception and cognition, so the overlap in constructs (tasks) in the MVPT-3 is expected. However, if one is constructing a test to measure "perceptual" skills then tasks should minimize the influence of "cognitive" skills. It appears that the perception and cognition in visual short-term memory and spatial orientation tasks may be too confounded to be good measures of "perceptual" skills, the goal of this measure. In fact, tasks of short-term (working) memory and spatial orientation are typically included in measures of cognitive ability (Horn & Noll, 1997; Kaufman & Lichtenberger, 2002; Sattler, 2001). Clarification of just what these tasks measure (perceptual vs. cognitive) should be the topic of validity research.

SUMMARY. The MVPT-3 is an easy-to-administer test of visual perception and cognitive skills with a fairly nationally representative standardization sample. Limited reliability and validity data are presented and further research is necessary, particularly in validity of MVPT-3 scores. Construct validity studies with larger samples and utilizing methods such as discriminative validity, incremental validity, and factorial validity would be much more helpful than the distinct group differences in judging the utility of this test.

REVIEWER'S REFERENCES

Chalfant, J. C., & Scheffelin, M. A. (1969). *Central processing dysfunctions in children: A review of the research* (Contract PH-43-67-61). Bethesda, MD: Department of Health, Education, and Welfare.
Horn, J. L., & Noll, J. (1997). Human cognitive capabilities: Gf-Gc theory. In D. P. Flanagan, J. L., Genshaft, & P. L. Harrison (Eds.), *Contemporary intellectual assessment: Theories, tests, and issues* (pp. 53–91). New York: Guilford.
Kaufman, A. S., & Lichtenberger, E. O. (2002). *Assessing adolescent and adult intelligence* (2nd ed.). Boston, MA: Allyn and Bacon.
Salvia, J., & Ysseldyke, J. W. (1991). *Assessment* (5th ed.). Boston, MA: Houghton Mifflin.
Sattler, J. M. (2001). *Assessment of children: Cognitive applications* (4th ed.). La Mesa, CA: Jerome M. Sattler, Publisher.
Wechsler, D. (1991). Wechsler Intelligence Scale for Children—Third Edition. San Antonio, TX: The Psychological Corporation.
Wechsler, D. (2003). *WISC-IV technical and interpretive manual.* San Antonio, TX: The Psychological Corporation.

Review of the Motor-Free Visual Perception Test, Third Edition by JOHN D. KING, Professor Emeritus, University of Texas at Austin, Licensed Psychologist, National Health Service Provider, Licensed Specialist in School Psychology, Austin, TX:

DESCRIPTION. The Motor-Free Visual Perception Test, Third Edition (MVPT-3) is a 65-item test that is designed to assess overall visual perceptual ability without requiring the use of motor responses. According to the manual, the MVPT-3 is an alternative to commonly used measures of visual perception that require examinees to draw or copy figures. Such instruments assess motor problems or visual-motor integration rather than visual perception. The MVPT-3 was designed for use with individuals ranging in age from 4 to 95 years of age and above. The test is untimed and individually administered, and all items are multiple choice. Visual perceptual tasks included in the MVPT-3 are spatial relations, visual discrimination, figure-ground, visual closure, and visual memory. The test provides a single score representing general visual perceptual abilities. Test authors strongly caution that the MVPT-3 is intended only for use as a general screening of visual perceptual skills and that it is not designed to produce subtest scores or to reveal specific strengths or weaknesses on any of the visual perception tasks.

Clinicians such as school psychologists, occupational therapists, teachers, or other professionals can administer the MVPT-3. The manual indicates the test can also be administered by nonclinical staff if they are trained and supervised by "a professional familiar with the principles of educational and psychological assessment and interpretation" (p. 21). Administration takes approximately 20 to 30 minutes. Directions are presented in the manual. They are clear and easy to follow. Examinees are presented with a series of test plates and asked to choose the correct answers from four alternatives for each item. A spiral-bound easel is used to present the test plates. For children under 11 years of age, Items 1 through 40 are administered. Items 14 through 65 are administered to children over 11 years and adults. The examinee may indicate the answer by saying the letter corresponding to the answer choice or by pointing to the choice.

According to the manual, scoring takes approximately 10 minutes. A single raw score is calculated and used to obtain derived scores. Three main types of derived scores are available including standard scores, percentile ranks, and age equivalents. Procedures for obtaining derived scores are clearly described in the manual and examples are provided. Norm tables and information on interpretation of scores are included in the manual as well.

DEVELOPMENT. This test is the third version of the MVPT, which was originally developed in 1972. Earlier editions were normed only on children. Unlike previous versions, norms for the MVPT-3 were based on a nationally representative sample of the population and were expanded to include individuals from 4 to 95 years of age and up. All 40 items of the MVPT-R were retained in this edition, and 31 new items were added. New items were designed to be more difficult in order to allow for assessment of older children, adolescents, and adults.

The manual (Colarusso & Hammill, 2003) includes a thorough description of procedures used to evaluate new items for the development of the MVPT-3; however, there is no information about the development of original test items. For this edition, new test plates were developed and then administered to 136 young adults to determine how difficult items were and to get feedback from examinees. Based on findings from that preliminary tryout, new items were created that were similar to preliminary items with an item difficulty in the .20 to .80 range. A normative study using the 40 original items and the 31 new items was then conducted. Item analysis was used in order to determine which new items would be retained. Test authors also conducted item bias studies in order to determine whether or not the MVPT-3 is fair to use with all segments of the general population. Results indicated no significant differences between groups based on demographic characteristics.

TECHNICAL. Procedures for collection of standardization data and characteristics of the standardization sample are thoroughly described in the manual. A total of 1,856 participants were selected for inclusion in the norm group in order to meet a variety of demographic criteria. Testing was conducted in 118 cities in 34 states across the United States. Testing took place in public, private, and parochial schools and in private practice settings. A detailed description of sample characteristics is included in the manual, and test authors provide evidence that the overall sample compares to the characteristics of the U.S. population based on information from the 2000 U.S. Census.

Evidence to support the reliability of scores from the MVPT-3 is provided. In order to estimate internal consistency, Cronbach's alpha was computed for each of the age groups in the standardization sample. For children 4 through 10 years of age, estimates ranged from .69 to .87. For participants who were 11 years of age or older, estimates ranged from .86 to .90. For ages 5 through 10, reliability coefficients approach or exceeded .80, and for ages 11 and up, coefficients were at or near .90. Based on that information, test authors concluded that the MVPT-3 "can be used with confidence for ages 5 and above" (manual, p. 52) but that it "is best used as a screening instrument" (manual, p. 52) for children who are 4 years of age. To provide evidence of test-retest reliability, 103 participants from the standardization sample were retested by the same examiner with an average time of 34 days between tests. For children ages 4 to 10 years, the corrected test-retest correlation was .87, and for individuals 11 years of age and up, a corrected test-retest correlation of .92 was found. Based on those findings, it can be concluded that the test scores are adequately stable over time.

Evidence to support the validity of the MVPT-3 was presented as well. The authors suggest that evidence of content validity can be found in the methods used to develop the test. For example, a test format was selected that does not require the use of motor skills, and the content was developed based on previous research and information from experts in the area of visual perception. In addition, test items "were required to meet rigorous criteria of item discrimination and item bias studies" (manual, p. 56). Criterion-related validity is evidenced by findings of moderate to high correlations of the MPVT with other tests that purport to measure the same abilities; however, the original version the test, not the MVPT-3, was used for those studies. Evidence of construct validity is provided, but most of the studies reported used previous versions of the test. In reported studies, low correlations were found between the MVPT and measures of cognitive ability and academic achievement. Studies also found that, as expected, individuals with head injuries or academic difficulties performed poorly compared to the normal population. Other validity studies suggest that the MVPT can be used with individuals who have motor difficulties, stroke patients, patients with ALS, and those with schizophrenia. Although evidence that lends support to the validity of scores from this test is presented, many of the findings reported were based on older versions of the test. Correlations between the older versions of the MVPT and the MVPT-3 were not reported, and one would expect that due to the addition of new items, the MVPT-3 is much different than its earlier versions. As a result, it is unclear how the validity findings reported in the manual pertain to the MVPT-3. The authors acknowledge that evidence is limited and encourage further study.

COMMENTARY. The MVPT-3 is an improvement over earlier versions due to its expanded age range and the use of a nationally representative norm sample. There is evidence that it measures the construct of visual perception, as it was developed based on previous research and expert opinion in the area. It also appears that the test can be used reliably for individuals 5 years of age and up with a wide variety of demographic characteristics. The MVPT-3 has been used in a variety of settings to assess a number of problems, and because of its design, it may be particularly useful for individuals with motor impairments. A limitation of the test is that its focus is very limited. It is designed only to screen for potential visual perception problems and gives no information about the particular deficit or the source of the problem. An additional concern is the fact that most validity studies are based on older versions of the test, and it is unclear how the older versions relate to the MVPT-3.

SUMMARY. The MVPT-3 is quick and easy to administer and score, and the directions are clearly explained in the manual. The usefulness of the test was improved by the changes made to this version. Although its focus is very limited, it appears to be a useful tool for the assessment of visual perception.

[153]

Multiphasic Sex Inventory II.

Purpose: "To assess a wide range of psychosexual characteristics of the sexual offender."
Population: Adult males, ages 18–84.
Publication Dates: 1984–2003.
Acronym: MSI II.
Scores: 42 scales and indices: Suicide, Sexual Ethics, Sex Knowledge and Beliefs, Repeated Items, Infrequency, Social Sexual Desirability, Sexual Obsessions, Dissimulation, Lie, Molester Comparison, Rapist Comparison, Child Molest, Rape, Exhibitionism, Voyeurism, Sex Harassment, Net Sex, Obscene Call, Pornography, Transvestism, Fetishism & NOS Paraphilias, Bondage Discipline, Sexual Sadism, Masochism, Physiologic Dysfunction, Desire, Premature Ejaculation, Body Image, Social Sexual Inadequacies, Emotional Neediness, Cognitive Distortion and Immaturity, Antisocial Behavior, Conduct Disorder, Sociopathy, Domestic Violence, Substance Abuse, Denial, Justification, Scheming, Superoplimism, Gender Identity, Treatment Attitudes.
Administration: Group.
Price Data: Available from publisher.
Foreign Language Edition: Spanish language version available.
Time: (45–120) minutes.
Comments: May be administered via audio cassette or paper-pencil; computer scoring done by publisher.
Authors: H. R. Nichols and Ilene Molinder.
Publisher: Nichols & Molinder Assessments.
Cross References: See T5:1744 (8 references) and T4:1689 (2 references).

Review of the Multiphasic Sex Inventory II by PAUL A. ARBISI, Staff Clinical Psychologist, Minneapolis VA Medical Center, and Associate Professor, Department of Psychiatry, University of Minnesota, Minneapolis, MN:

DESCRIPTION. The Multiphasic Sex Inventory II (MSI II) is a 560-item self-report questionnaire that was designed to identify a wide range of psychosexual characteristics in a sexual offender population. All items are keyed true or false. The authors claim that the 40 resultant scales and indices are "theory driven" and provide a means to assist the clinician in evaluating and treating sexual offenders. Candidate items designed to assess test-taking behavior and a wide range of attitudes, behaviors, drug and alcohol problems, and attitudes toward sex were identified, and through a series of poorly described and idiosyncratic steps, some items were modified and others deleted. From this pool of items, indices and scales were derived using several different procedures including rational, empirical, "summated," and "compound scaling," as well as a factor analytic strategy. This process resulted in the derivation of 13 indices through rational item selection (Sex Knowledge/Beliefs, Obscene Call, Pornography, Fetishism, Bondage/Discipline, Sado-Masochism, Physiological Dysfunction, Impotence, Premature Ejaculation, Gender Identity, Body Image, Substance Abuse, and Treatment Attitude. Two scales, Molester Comparison and Rapist Comparison, were constructed through a criterion-oriented procedure by contrasting item responses between a "normal" control group and either a child molester or a rapist group. Seventeen scales (Social Sexual Desirability, Sex Obsessions, Lie, Child Molest, Rape, Exhibitionism, Voyeurism, Sexual Inadequacies, Hypercritical Sexuality, Sexual Repression, Emotional Neediness, Cognitive Distortion/Immaturity, Conduct Disorder, Sociopathy, Scheming, Superoptimism, Manipulation Awareness) were developed through a summated scaling method in which items were selected based on the average correlation among items, although not all scales achieved the specified level across all developmental samples. The Domestic Violence and Dissimulation scales were formed using a combination of rational, content, and summation approaches. The Denial and Justification scales were formed using "coaxial items" where a "bivariate scaling method" (handbook, p. 31) was developed by the authors to better assess the excuses and justifications used by the sex offender. The items comprising these scales are purported to be composed of two axes of information, a general component and a specific indication (e.g., "My sex offense happened because I was sexually molested as a child"). Finally, two sections containing information related to referral issues and social history are also included in the profile.

The MSI II is predicated on the willingness of sexual offenders to admit to their offences and is primarily composed of various indices and "scales" made up of items associated with the admission of sexual deviance, sexual dysfunction, and disorder of conduct. The MSI II is to be used with individuals who have either been charged with or convicted of criminal sexual misconduct. The test is administered to the offender and the completed answer sheet sent to the authors to be computer scored and profiled. A professional-to-professional consultation report is developed and "a customized report and four page MSI II profile form" (handbook, p. 65) is returned to the clinician. The manual does not contain an example of the customized report or an example of an interpreted profile. A Spanish-language version of the MSI II is also available.

DEVELOPMENT. The authors solicited clinicians throughout the United States who worked with sexual offender populations to administer a group of tests (MMPI, Shipley Institute of Living IQ Screening Test, Draw-A-Person-In-The-Rain-Test, Semantic Differential, Symptoms Checklist, and the MSI II research form) to sexual offenders. The clinicians then sent in the raw data and for a fee received a report from the authors. The research form of the MSI II consisted of the 300 original MSI items plus 408 items rationally derived by the authors. A "normal" nonsex-offending group was also identified. A number of comparison groups were used in the development of scales and indices for a "semi-final" MSI II including 100 "normal" males, two groups of 100 child molesters, 100 rapists, 100 exposers, 100 individuals who were found guilty but denied their crimes, and 75 individuals at the end of treatment after committing a sexual offense. In the normal sample, there were no Asian Americans, 10 African Americans, 1 Hispanic American and 1 Native American. Cross validation of the semifinal MSI II took place through two additional cross-validation studies that were mentioned in the manual, but not described.

From a group of 9,000 test protocols gathered from 45 sites located in 12 states and Canada, the authors identified a group of 1,951 valid protocols through a process of stratified random sampling.

Offender groups of interest (e.g., rapists, child molesters, exposers) were then selected from the broader pool. Also, two groups of 100 normal males were selected mostly from the West Coast. Neither of these groups of normals conformed to the 1990 U.S. Census with regard to educational level. The latter set of samples served as the source of "validation studies" where criterion offender groups were compared across the different MSI II scales and indices to each other and to the normal groups.

As mentioned above, scales and indices were developed through a rather idiosyncratic and unsystematic process that alternatively used empirical keying by contrasting offender groups with the "normal" nonoffending males, rational item selection, reliance upon the psychometric coherence of items, and a combination of strategies. For the majority of the scales, the criterion for retention of scales or indices was the authors' conviction that the indices or scales were theoretically relevant to sexual offender populations (content-rationale strategy).

TECHNICAL. Reliability estimates for the MSI II scales were not reported for the "normal groups." Further, the MSI II scale and indices intercorrelations and the correlations between the MSI II scales and the collateral measures were not reported for the normal group. In the offender groups, the alphas range from nonexistent (Pornography, .05) to moderate (Obscene Calls, .80) to high (Girl Molester sample: Child Molest, .94). Test-retest reliabilities across an interval of "approximately 15 days average time between testing periods" (handbook, p. 46) for 50 child molesters ranged from .96 for Rape to .66 for Body Image. Education and IQ were related to the MSI II Lie scale, Molester Comparison, and Rape Comparison scales as well as Antisocial Behavior, Domestic Violence, and Substance Abuse scales, and indices in the offender sample. Despite the claims in the manual (see p. 49) that none of the demographic variables affect the MSI II scales in any appreciable way because none of the correlations exceed .29, the magnitude of the relationship between demographic variables and MSI II scales is hardly negligible.

Each scale appears to have been standardized on a separate sex offender population. These standardized samples varied from 1,200 child molesters to 40 voyeurs. Some scales use T scores as measurement units, others use a z score. A number of the scales have too few items that have low endorsement rates to develop into a scale, but were still felt to be useful. Consequently, a multiple-item rule was invoked where a minimum of three items must be endorsed on the index for the index to be "functional." Finally, eight scales have "unique" measurement units. This use of "unique" measurement units is counterintuitive and defeats the purpose of using a unit of measurement in the first place.

COMMENTARY. The MSI II is a self-published instrument that represents a major change from the original 300-item MSI. There is little information contained in the manual that describes what changes were made between the instruments (other than the addition of 260 items) and which of the 300 items contained on the original MSI were retained in the MSI II intact. This is an extremely significant omission because the authors assert (without support) that the MSI II has been admitted as evidence to provide supplemental information to the courts. Given that a literature review did not turn up any citations referencing the MSI II, it is hard to imagine that the MSI II would be admissible under Daubert without relying upon the original 300-item MSI, which has appeared in peer-reviewed publications. Therefore, without knowing which items and to what degree each scale or index was changed from the MSI to the MSI II, an examiner will be hard pressed to support his or her opinions regarding an offender if the MSI II served, in part, as the basis for those opinions.

The MSI II is purported to be theory driven yet limited evidence is provided of the construct validity of the instrument. The manual makes claims for the utility of the MSI II in capturing these constructs, yet provides limited evidence that the instrument is accomplishing any such thing. The authors claim a theoretical framework for sexual deviance and attempted to construct scales to capture this framework. Within this framework, the authors attempted to capture theoretical constructs associated with sexual motivation, sexual socialization, and deviant arousal, as well as actual behaviors subsumed under the rubric of "stimulus field" such as universal sex offender behaviors and individual behaviors. The authors also hypothesized three levels (stages?) in the behavioral chain or sequence resulting in any sexual offence: deviant arousal, pre-assault behavior, and sexual as-

sault/ aggravated assault. Given the supposed theory driven underpinnings of the MSI II, these levels and constructs should emerge through factor analysis of the instrument. Support for the proposed underlying theoretical structure was not found. An exploratory item level factor analysis was performed, but without an adequate number of subjects. At the scale level, a 10-factor solution was derived, which does not appear to conform well to the authors' proposed theoretical structure of sexual deviance. Despite the text, no evidence is contained in the manual or in the literature that the MSI II provides information that is not readily available in the arrest and trial record of individuals charged and/or convicted of criminal sexual conduct.

SUMMARY. The MSI II is an instrument that appears held together by baling wire and string. The manual is marred by poor writing and organization and the development and validation of the instrument is hard to understand. An example of the impact of the poor organization was that after reading the section entitled "Initial Test Construction and Cross Validation Studies" on page 33 and thinking that I had a handle on the tangled skeins of logic used in the development of the various scales and indices, I was surprised to learn on page 93 that Principal Components Factor Analysis (PCA) was also used to develop another set of indices (Social Sexual Inadequacies, 14 items; Emotional Neediness, 21 items; and Cognitive Distortion and Immaturity, 16 items). The authors state on page 67 that "the Multiphasic Sex Inventory II (MSI II) is essentially a personality inventory." Without tying any of the MSI II scales or indices to personality dimensions represented in either normal or abnormal populations and without presenting validity data related to real world criteria, the authors should ·not make this claim. Consequently, the use of this instrument for any reason other than research is questionable and reliance upon the instrument to make clinical judgment is risky.

Review of the Multiphasic Sex Inventory II by ALBERT BUGAJ, Professor, Department of Psychology, University of Wisconsin—Marinette, Marinette, WI:

DESCRIPTION. The Multiphasic Sex Inventory II (MSI II) is designed to assess the "psychosexual characteristics" (handbook, p. 1) of the sexual offender. The inventory, consisting of

40 scales and indices and a compact social history, is based on an extensive "cognitive-emotional-behavioral" (handbook, p. 4) model of sexual deviance developed by the test authors. The details of the theory are presented in the test manual. Detailed guidelines for the administration of the test, how to interpret its results, and its proper use in forensic evaluation and assessing the progress of treatment are also provided.

The MSI II is a paper-and-pencil test consisting of 560 true-false items. The test-taker indicates whether each item is, or is not, self-applicable. Additional information is collected on the time of the alleged sexual offense, type of offense, whether the test-taker has admitted to the behavior, and information concerning the nature of the alleged victim and the circumstances of the alleged offense. Demographic information concerning the offender and a brief health and life history are also obtained.

The test instructions are clear and straightforward. However, the test administrator must send the completed answer sheet to the test publisher for machine scoring. The publisher then prepares and returns a customized report and a four-page MSI II profile to the referring clinician.

A Spanish-language version of the MSI II has been developed. For individuals who have difficulty reading, audiocassette editions of the test have been developed in both Spanish and English.

DEVELOPMENT. In developing the MSI II, a preliminary version of the test, combining the 300 items of the first edition of the test with 408 new items, was first constructed. This was administered to specific groups of sex offenders, offenders who had undergone treatment, and normal males. Most groups contained 100 individuals, although one consisted of 75. The groups were matched as closely as possible to the 1980 U.S. Census demographics by age, education, occupation, marital status, and ethnicity. Based on an examination of internal consistency (Cronbach's alpha), several scales and items were eliminated, and new scales developed. The result was the 560-item MSI II.

In the second stage 9,000 test protocols were gathered from 45 sites in 12 states and the province of Quebec. Elimination of protocols for reasons such as a high number of omitted responses resulted in a database consisting of 6,975 protocols. From this set, 1,951 protocols were randomly

selected and divided into 22 groups, which again included specific types of offenders, offenders who had undergone treatment, and normal males. Most groups consisted of 100 individuals, although three were smaller (ns = 55, 40, and 21). Data provided by these groups were used in determining the norms of the MSI II, and evidence for validity and reliability.

Methods used to develop the norms of the MSI II were dependent on the psychometric properties of the data and scales. Normally distributed data were converted to t-scores, whereas data with skewed distributions were converted to z-scores. Some scales consist of very few items. In this case cutoffs are used; endorsing three items is said by the test authors to make that scale "functional" for the test-taker. Finally, a number of scales have "unique measurement" units that are spelled out fully in the manual. Depending on the nature of each scale, particular groups were used in developing the norms. For example, the "domestic violence" scale was normed using data obtained from sex offenders who admitted to having committed physical abuse on a spouse, mate, or girlfriend.

In the development of the Spanish language version of the test, a bilingual therapist first translated the MSI II into Spanish, which was then critiqued by two additional bilingual therapists. During field-testing, Spanish-speaking test-takers were also asked to list any items they found difficult. Additionally, the Spanish-language version was back-translated into English by another bilingual clinician, and again checked for accuracy.

TECHNICAL.

Validity. The MSI II has strong evidence for content validity. Many items were constructed utilizing textbooks regarding human sexuality, and on the basis of relevant Axis I and II disorders found in the DSM-III-R (American Psychiatric Association, 1987). Discriminant validity was examined by determining the correlations between the scales on the MSI II, IQ, and the demographic variables of age, education, occupation, ethnicity, and marital status. The sample tested consisted of 1,551 census-matched, pretreatment sex offenders. No demographic variable exhibited a correlation higher than .29 with any MSI II scale, with most correlations falling between .00 and .20. Four MSI II scales were related with intelligence (correlations ranging between .31 and .44), and these relationships are fully discussed in the manual.

The constructs measured by the MSI II are thus for the most part independent of variables with which they should be independent.

In the same study, convergent validity was demonstrated by finding 11 scales on the MSI II were correlated with 7 scales on the Minnesota Multiphasic Personality Inventory (MMPI). Several scales within the MSI II were also intercorrelated. These relationships are logically explained by the test's authors and in most cases are highly important and expected. For example, a scale on the MSI II designed to measure dissimulation is related to the MMPI Lie scale ($r = .53$). Data from this study were also subjected to two principal components factor analyses, first with varimax rotation, then with oblique rotation. Results of both analyses were similar, and the test authors provide adequate theoretical explanations of the results.

Two examinations of criterion-related validity were performed. In the first, 12 samples of child molesters, matched by age, education, occupation, and marital status were tested ($n = 1,090$). With the exception of a few scales (discussed in the manual), the results indicated no differences between groups based on ethnicity, region in the United States, sex of victim, or whether the molesters acted within or outside the family. In the second study 8 known groups were compared, including non-sex-offending normal males, child molesters, end-of-treatment child molesters, rapists, and exposers. Except for the group of child molesters ($n = 1,090$) each group consisted of 100 individuals. Analysis of variance followed by Scheffé's test of multiple comparisons indicated the test distinguished between normal males and sex offenders. Specific groups of sex offenders were distinguished by their scores on theoretically logical scales. Pretreatment, incarcerated, and end-of-treatment sex offenders also received differential scores.

Reliability. Internal consistency of the MSI II was estimated using the national sample of 1,551 participants. Cronbach's alpha ranged from .31 to .94. Twenty-four of the scales achieved acceptable levels of internal consistency. Of the remaining scales the authors state that aside from two scales, low alphas were expected because they measure heterogeneous characteristics with a small number of items. Cronbach's alphas for specific groups in the study are also reported for each scale. Most of these are acceptably high (.70 or higher).

However, a few are close to zero, although the authors reasonably indicate that this is due to low sample sizes, or the inappropriate nature of specific scales for specific groups.

Test-retest reliability figures are reported for only one group tested over a short period of time. A group of 50 child molesters was tested at an average of a 15-day interval. Exact times between tests ranged from 5 to 30 days. Except for one scale resulting in a test-retest correlation of .66, all correlations were above .76.

COMMENTARY. The use of the MSI II can be highly recommended, although cautionary notes must be made. Although it has undergone rigorous tests of validity, the Spanish-language version was apparently not subjected to statistical analyses. The exact nature of the validity of that version of the test cannot therefore be ascertained, so it should only be used with great care. The same holds true for the audiocassette versions of the test.

On the other hand, the English-language version of the test is commendable. The development of the test itself, as described in the manual, is an excellent example of construct validation. The test is based on an elaborate theory, and the studies of its validity were based on hypotheses drawn from that theory. The MSI II has strong evidence for convergent validity; the interrelationships between its scales, and with other tests measuring theoretically related constructs, are all acceptably high. Tests of known groups also led to expected results.

The internal consistency estimates of the test's scales are satisfactory. The MSI II also has strong short-term test-retest reliability. One disappointment is the lack of long-term reliability estimates. This is an area that should be pursued in future research. Such testing is needed before an unconditional recommendation can be forthcoming.

SUMMARY. Although the Spanish-language and audiocassette versions of the MSI II should be used with caution, the English-language version of the test is highly creditable. The development of the test is an excellent example of construct validity. The evidence for criterion-related validity of the test is exceptionally strong and it has strong short-term test-retest reliability. However, an unconditional recommendation cannot be made until further data are produced regarding the long-term reliability of the test.

REVIEWER'S REFERENCE

American Psychiatric Association. (1987). *Diagnostic and statistical manual of mental disorders—revised* (3rd ed.). Washington, DC: Author.

[154]

Multiple Affect Adjective Check List—Revised.

Purpose: "To measure both state and affect traits."
Population: Ages 20–79.
Publication Dates: 1960–1999.
Acronym: MAACL-R.
Scores, 7: Anxiety, Depression, Hostility, Positive Affect, Sensation Seeking, Dysphoria, Positive Affect and Sensation Seeking.
Administration: Group.
Price Data, 2005: $11 per 25 hand-scoring or machine-scoring lists (specify State or Trait) [$41.75 per 100, $166.50 per 500]; $16.50 per scoring key; $28.75 per manual (1999, 71 pages); $26.75 per bibliography (1991, 1,000 references); $31 per specimen set including manual and 1 copy of all forms.
Time: 5(10) minutes.
Comments: Previous edition still available.
Authors: Marvin Zuckerman and Bernard Lubin.
Publisher: EdITS/Educational and Industrial Testing Service.
Cross References: See T5:1745 (89 references) and T4:1690 (96 references); for a review by John A. Zarske of an earlier edition, see 10:205 (84 references); see also 9:734 (47 references), T3:1547 (108 references), 8:628 (102 references), and T2:1293 (56 references); for reviews by E. Lowell Kelly and Edwin I. Megargee of an earlier edition, see 7:112 (60 references); see also P:176 (28 references).

Review of the Multiple Affect Adjective Checklist—Revised by GERALD E. DeMAURO, Managing Education Assessment Scientist, American Institutes for Research, Washington, DC:

DESCRIPTION. The Multiple Affect Adjective Checklist—Revised (MAACL-R) 1999 Edition provides 132 adjectives that test users can check or not to describe their affect. The stated purpose of the assessment is to provide a measure of both affect States and affect Traits. A wide variety of applications of the instruments are described below.

Users are instructed to either check those adjectives that describe how they "generally" feel (Trait Form) or that describe how they feel "now-today" (State Form). These two forms take about 3 minutes each to complete. The State Form norms appear to be applicable over a small range of reference time periods. *T* score and percentile conversion tables are provided for both forms, based on normative information (see below). The authors report development of a short form (66 adjectives) and ongoing development of translated forms.

Use of the Trait Form norms is best-supported for noninstitutionalized adults. The State Form is intended more for within subject analyses over time, and therefore would seem to have broad application.

The authors state that factor analytic studies (described below) have identified three levels of affect measured by the MAACL-R: (a) factored domains that include anxiety, depression, hostility, positive affect, and sensation seeking; (b) higher order affects composed of summing scaled scores for anxiety, depression, and hostility to yield dysphoria and summing positive affect and sensation seeking to yield well-being; and (c) 12 components or facets identified by principal component analysis (not cited in the psychometric research).

DEVELOPMENT. The original Multiple Affect Adjective Check List (MAACL) was published in 1965. To improve the discriminant validity of the scales, the authors revised the structure of the original three basic scales (Anxiety, Depression, and Hostility), added new scales, controlled for the tendency to check adjectives regardless of content (response acquiescence), and separated indices of positive and negative affect so that one is not merely the absence of the other.

Two classes for a total of 536 college undergraduates were administered the State Form twice, separated by 5 days. One class was administered the form in a stressful environment (course examination). Principal-axis factor analyses with varimax rotations for each class and each administration (four analyses) produced five factor solutions accounting for 47–51% of the common variances: Positive Affect (PA, 17–20%), Anxiety (A, 5–11%), Depression (D, 5–11%), Hostility (H, 7–11%), and Sensation Seeking (SS, 4–8%). Items were retained that had loadings of .30 or higher on three of the four factor analyses (a few exceptions were noted on the SS scale) and that loaded more heavily on one scale than on the others.

Factor analytic studies also defined the scales for the Trait Form. Results from a nationally stratified sample of 780 females and 763 males identified all factors retained by the State Form except SS. An analysis of responses of 746 adolescents decomposed the Checklist to broad positive and negative factors, hostility, sensation seeking, and "shyness." The authors decided to retain the factors identified for adults in the college undergraduate study of the State Form to maintain comparability of the two forms. Dysphoria (Dys, A + D + H) and positive affect (PASS, PA + SS) are derived by adding raw scores of the component scales shown.

TECHNICAL.

Standardization. Norms are available for both forms based on opportunistic samples and on a national representative adult sample (Trait Form). The manual describes the sample as being 1,543 adults representing the United States in sex, race, region, education, and income. Sampling was based on a Gallup organization survey of noninstitutionalized adults of 18 years or older in the United States, prestratified on community type and adjusted with reference to U.S. Census data. Other demographic characteristics that were measured within the sample included: occupational levels, marital status, religion, regions of the United States, and size of municipality. The target and obtained distributions are not reported in the manual. The norms are conditioned both on the total numbers of adjectives checked and sex.

For the general adult population, females checked higher numbers of adjectives for all of the Trait scales but SS. It raises the interesting criterion-referenced question of whether the scales have the same interpretation for each group. If so, separate norming for males and females might mask differences of diagnostic importance. Appendix A of the manual provides means and standard deviations for the general and specialized populations on the State and Trait forms. Frequency distributions by sex of the number of adjectives checked could help interpret the magnitude of differences related to these two variables. Data presented for the general sample show standardized sex differences of: Anxiety = -.32, Depression = -.21, Hostility = -.08, Positive Affect = -.13, Sensation Seeking = .14 (the only scale in which male scores are higher), Dysphoria = -.22, and Positive Affect plus Sensation Seeking = -.07.

To control for response acquiescence, the general norming sample was divided into the six groups defined by sex and the total number of adjectives checked. Raw scores within scale were converted to *T* scores specific to the six groups and correlated with the total numbers of adjectives checked. The correlations were lower than raw score correlations suggesting control of the threat of response acquiescence to discriminant validity. Perhaps this decrement can be attributed to the restriction of range that ensues from conditioning the *T* scores on numbers of adjectives checked. The question arises again of whether there is interactivity with numbers of adjectives checked that is obscured by separating the norms. A description of how the total number of checks was derived that define the three groups would help score interpretation.

Examination of the norms tables shows that the relatively low means and standard deviations reported for the A, D, H, and composite Dys scales result in very large *T* scores for smaller numbers of adjectives checked, especially for those groups that checked fewer adjectives overall. The authors warn that large *T* score results should be validated by evaluation of subject faking (see below).

Reliability. Internal consistency and test-retest reliability coefficients are reported for each MAACL-R form. On the State Form, internal consistency measures for seven nonreferred and two referred groups ranged from .62 to .95. The groups varied in size from 237 to 1,392 for the nonreferred groups and from 105 to 126 for the referred groups. On the Trait Form the range was .69 to .95 for four nonreferred groups (sizes ranged from 858 to 1,543) and three referred groups (sizes ranged from 48 to 109). In general, the State Form test-retest reliability estimates were low, as expected, ranging over studies from -.08 (college students) for Hostility over a 5-day interval to .53 for Dysphoria over a 1-day interval (female normal adults). For the Trait Form, the test-retest reliabilities from .10 for Hostility over a 2-week interval (college students) to .92 for Sensation Seeking over a 6-week interval. The manual presents ranges of *T* scores that suggest the need for intervention. Decision reliability estimates for these scores would address the stability of these interpretations.

Validity. The preponderance of validity data address the discriminant and convergent properties of the scales. Data also suggest that the trait constructs transcend immediate settings and conditions whereas the state constructs are responsive to the immediate influences on affect.

The State Form scales evidence convergent and discriminant properties for a variety of samples over a range of instruments including those that measure similar constructs (cf. the State-Trait Personality Inventory, Spielberger, 1980), those that measure extensions of the construct (cf. Profile of Mood States, McNair, Lorr, & Droppelman, 1971; the Toronto Alexithymia Scale, Taylor, Ryan, & Bagby, 1985; and the Affect Intensity Measure, Larsen, Billings, & Cutler, 1996), and Likert-like 1–5 self-ratings of adolescents and community college students. The State Form scales also are sensitive to a large variety of status changes, induced anxiety, psychiatric status (Lubin, Van Whitlock, Thieszen, & Leak, 1997), and predictive of dropout status in Air Force basic training (Lubin, Fiedler, & Van Whitlock, 1999).

The Trait Form scales were found to agree only moderately with all of the corresponding State Form scales except for PA and PASS scales, which yielded high correlations among college students. Good convergent and discriminant properties are reported with Likert-like self-ratings among referred samples (Zuckerman & Lubin, 1985), peer ratings of male veterans, counselor Likert-like ratings (moderate relationships), and instruments that measure related constructs among adolescents (cf. the Piers-Harris Children's Self-Concept Scale, Piers, 1984). Equivocal results are reported for correlations with corresponding scales of the Profile of Mood States (McNair, Lorr, & Droppelman, 1971). Good convergent and discriminant properties are reported with a variety of instruments that are theoretically related to the Trait Form constructs, and with self-reported social activities. The Minnesota Multiphasic Personality Inventory scales (Hathaway & McKinley, 1983) converge with the Trait Form better than with the corresponding scales of the State Form among three referred groups, and provide discriminant validity evidence for the PA, SS, and PASS scales. Scale differences were reported among depressed, diagnosed schizophrenic, other patients, and normals, and also between normals and a group including diagnosed anxiety disorders. Self-ratings of health were also related to the appropriate Trait Form scales.

The MAACL-R offers a Random Response scale designed from most and least frequently checked positive and negative items, as well as Fake Good and Fake Bad subscales. These have suggested cut scores. The authors recommend validating results by checking that the number of items checked is in an acceptable range and applying the Random Response, Fake Good, and Fake Bad scales.

COMMENTARY. The MAACL-R has been studied in many settings with many populations. The evidence suggests that it is a simple instrument to administer and that it measures constructs of theoretical import with adequate reliability even for the scales with few adjectives. It is important that instruments of this type are used in conjunction with observations and careful evaluation by practitioners. On the other hand, the MAACL-R provides an additional and readily acquired source of useful information.

One of the weaknesses of the reported information is a lack of clarity about how scoring ranges were identified as criterion values for judgments. It is not clear why certain T scores are associated with certain conclusions, and the test could benefit by some attention to the incidence of clinical Anxiety or Depression, for example and its incidence in the samples on which the T scores are based. Related to this is the specification of different norms by gender and numbers of items checked. More information about how criterion numbers of items checked was identified and why it is important to consider female results and male results differently would aid the score interpretation.

Finally, the research indicates that the State Form instructions could be altered to provide different time span references. It would be interesting to define a time range on the State Form that is long enough to approximate trait evaluations, that is, to identify a reference of time where measurement moves from focus on states to focus on traits, both for clinical and general populations, or to identify the endurance of state affects and their contribution to traits.

SUMMARY. The MAACL-R offers an impressive background in development and data in support of score interpretation. With the cautions mentioned above, it appears to be a useful tool for providing information about affective states and traits.

REVIEWER'S REFERENCES
Hathaway, S. R., & McKinley, J. C. (1983). *The Minnesota Multiphasic Personality Inventory manual.* New York: Psychological Corporation.
Larsen, R. J., Billings, D. W., & Cutler, S. E. (1996). Affect intensity and individual differences in information style. *Journal of Personality, 64,* 185–207.
Lubin, B., Fiedler, E. R., & Van Whitlock, R. (1999). Predicting discharge from Air Force basic training by pattern of affect. *Journal of Clinical Psychology, 55,* 71–78.
Lubin, B., Van Whitlock, R., Thieszen, K., & Leak, J. (1997). *Mood as an index of psychiatric inpatient progress in managed care settings.* Manuscript submitted for publication.

McNair, D. M., Lorr, M., & Droppelman, L. F. (1971). *Profile of Mood States: Manual.* San Diego, CA: Educational and Industrial Testing Service.

Piers, E. V. (1984). *Revised manual for the Piers-Harris Children's Self-Concept Scale.* Los Angeles, CA: Western Psychological Services.

Spielberger, C. D. (1980). *Preliminary manual for the State-Trait Personality Inventory (STPI).* Unpublished manuscript.

Taylor, G. J., Ryan, D., & Bagby, M. (1985). Toward the development of a new self-report alexithymia scale. *Psychotherapy and Psychosomatics, 44,* 91–99.

Zuckerman, M., & Lubin, B. (1985). *Multiple Affect Adjective Check List-Revised: Manual.* San Diego, CA: Educational and Industrial Testing Service.

Review of the Multiple Affect Adjective Check List—Revised by PAUL RETZLAFF, Professor of Psychology, University of Northern Colorado, Greeley, CO:

DESCRIPTION. The Multiple Affect Adjective Check List—Revised (MAACL-R) has "been around forever." It is a classic. The test form is a single sheet with 132 adjectives. Participants are to check the box in front of the adjectives that describe their feelings. There are two forms. One is a state form requesting endorsement as the participant feels "today," and the other a trait form associated with how they feel "generally." Only the instructions change, not the adjectives.

Five unique scales are scored: Anxiety, Depression, Hostility, Positive Affect, and Sensation Seeking. These are then combined into two "higher order affects." The first is Dysphoria, which is the sum of the first three (Anxiety, Depression, and Hostility). The second is Well-being which is the sum of the final two (Positive Affect and Sensation Seeking). The manual mentions 12 "components or facets" in the first paragraph but these are never mentioned again, nor are there scoring keys or templates.

The MAACL can be scored either by computer or by hand. By hand, there are five fairly crude scoring overlays for the five scales. There are also *T*-score profile sheets but, inexplicably, these only include the first 3 scale scores.

There is a newer manual published in 1999 that is far superior to either the 1965 manual or the 1985 manual. The only exception is that the newest manual fails to include the items keyed to each of the five scales.

DEVELOPMENT. Reviewing the three manuals, it is apparent that the test was primarily developed prior to 1965. The original version included the first three scales, Anxiety, Depression, and Hostility. In 1985, the other two scales (Positive Affect and Sensation Seeking) were added. There appears also to have been item-keying changes between 1965 and 1985. Particularly, it appears that most of the "false keyed" (no

check mark) items were eliminated. With the 1999 manual, the only substantive change seems to be the dropping of the remaining four "false keyed" items from the Sensation Seeking scale.

As it stands, Anxiety has 10 items, Depression 12, Hostility 15, Positive Affect 21, and Sensation Seeking 8. All items require positive endorsement of the keyed adjective. The manual fails to list the items or the number of items per scale. Only reviewing the overlays allows for such information. Interestingly, it becomes apparent that only 66 of the 132 items are actually used in scales.

The origin of the items is varied. The very first "version" of the test was simply to assess anxiety. As such, the initial item set was probably written with this domain in mind. In 1965, items were added to assess the depression and hostility dimensions. Here, again, items were undoubtedly written expressly for those scales. Moving from the 1965 version to the 1985 version, the Positive Affect and Sensation Seeking scales were added without writing any unique items for them.

The test was developed exclusively through factor analysis. All scales were created, defined, and keyed through the analysis of factors and factor loadings. This also explains the authors' ability to change item keying across the versions.

TECHNICAL. The psychometric information of the test is very well documented. There are literally hundreds of studies on the test.

Cronbach alpha internal consistency reliability estimates for the state form across nine samples are all high and almost invariably above .70. The softest scale is the Sensation Seeking scale and this is probably due to the reduction in the number of items to eight in this revision of the test. The trait form has reliability estimates in the .80s and .90s.

Given the development of the test, it is interesting to note that the first three scales actually suffer from a lack of specificity. Anxiety, Depression, and Hostility all intercorrelate in the .50s and .60s. These numbers approach and, in some cases, exceed the validity coefficients for the scales. There were no intercorrelations of trait form in the manual.

There are quite a few tables in the manual demonstrating construct validity against other tests of affect such as the Profile of Mood States (POMS; T6:1995) and the Positive Affect and Negative Affect Schedule (PANAS; Watson, Clark, & Tellegen, 1988). The results are quite mixed with same/similar domain correlations ranging from the .20s to the .60s. Also, there often is a lack of differential validity across the scales.

COMMENTARY. There are many attractive things about the MAACL-R. It is a "classic." It is quick and not expensive. It is intuitive and transparent to users. It is easy to score. It allows for easy pre- and posttesting.

Its "classic" status, however, is also its problem. Each version of the test adds a little bit to the test but never questions the underlying fundamentals. For example, if only 66 items are scored, why not print a 66-item form? And having a 66-item form, why not use a carbonless scoring template?

It would be nice if the authors and publisher would come out with a totally new version. That version should include only scored items, include at least 15 items per scale, drive the specificities of the scales up, and provide user-friendly scoring and profiling. Such a version would be even more reliable but more importantly, it would be more valid and differentially valid.

SUMMARY. The Multiple Affect Adjective Check List—Revised (MAACL-R) is a classic. It is quick and easy. It provides some useful information. It does, however, need a true revision. There are several competitors. They, however, usually suffer from the same problems of age, too few items, and idiosyncratic development. The world needs a new adjective test of moods. If tests like the MAACL-R do not dramatically change, some publisher will come up with a new, modern approach and we will lose the MAACL-R to history.

REVIEWER'S REFERENCE

Watson, D., Clark, L. A., & Tellegen, A. (1988). Development and validation of brief measures of positive and negative affect: The PANAS Scales. *Journal of Personality and Social Psychology, 54,* 1063–1070.

[155]
Multiple Assessment Series for the Primary Grades.

Purpose: Designed to "provide criterion-referenced measures of student performance."
Population: Grades 1–3.
Publication Dates: 1998–1999.
Scores, 18: Reading (Constructing Meaning—Fiction, Extending Meaning—Fiction, Constructing Meaning—Nonfiction, Extending Meaning—Nonfiction, Total), Mathematics (Patterns/Algebra, Problem Solving, Number Relations, Geometry, Measurement, Estimation, Data Analysis, Total), Writing (Content, Organization, Language, Conventions, Total).
Subtests: Subtests available as separates.

Administration: Individual or group.
Levels, 3: Grades 1, 2, 3.
Price Data, 2003: $35 per 25 test booklets (specify content area and grade level); $8.25 per teacher directions for administration (specify content area and grade level); $8.75 per scoring guide (for Grades 1–3, specify content area); $3.92 per student, per content area; basic service scoring includes Individual Performance Profile, Class Roster Report, Class Performance Profile, Building Performance Profile, and District Performance Profile.
Time: (60–150) minutes.
Author: Riverside Publishing.
Publisher: Riverside Publishing.

Review of the Multiple Assessment Series for the Primary Grades by KAREN MACKLER, School Psychologist, Lawrence Public Schools, Lawrence, NY:

DESCRIPTION. The Multiple Assessment Series for the Primary Grades provides criterion-referenced assessment in the areas of Reading, Writing, and Mathematics. Riverside Publishing developed this series to provide diagnostic information about performance in content-area skills and information for Title 1 reporting. The test is in a pencil-and-paper format and can be administered individually or in groups. The test is appropriate for students in Grades 1, 2, and 3 and may be used as a formal measure of year-end achievement or as an informal measure of students' strengths and weaknesses.

Materials include an individual testing booklet in each of the content areas for each grade level. For each content area test, there is a corresponding Teacher Directions for Administration Guide, containing test preparation information as well as scripted text to read to the students during administration. There is a separate scoring guide for each content area, which spans the three grades tested. Scoring options include sending the tests out to Riverside for scoring, or local scoring based upon examples provided in the scoring guides.

The Reading component assesses the ability to construct and then extend meaning in a text. Students in Grade 1 listen to reading passages and then answer related questions, whereas students in Grades 2 and 3 are required to read the passages on their own. Each reading assessment is composed of four or five reading selections including fiction, nonfiction, and poetry, from previously published works. Many of the selections are accompanied by pictures or graphic organizers. Questions are multiple choice, short answer, or extended response. Short answer and extended response questions are scored using either 2-point (short answer) or 4-point rubrics. Questions cover information regarding literal and abstract comprehension, vocabulary, prediction, and recall. The time required to complete the test should be about an hour, but the authors state that the students may have up to 2.5 hours.

The Writing component assesses writing proficiency. The measure encourages students to utilize strategies in classroom writing process, including prewriting/planning, writing, and revising. Objectives of this measure are content, organization of thought, expressive language skills, and mechanics. Students write two pieces on this test, a longer piece such as a report or narrative, and a shorter piece such as a letter or invitation. The scoring rubric is constructed on a 4-point numerical scale, for each of the two pieces. The first grade Writing component is given over two sessions, on consecutive days, for a maximum of 3 hours, whereas the Grade 2 and Grade 3 components are administered in one session for a total of 2.5 hours. All directions are read aloud to all students.

The Mathematics component measures knowledge of mathematics content, analysis of mathematical information, problem solving, and communication skills in the area of mathematics. There is an expectation that as a student progresses from Grade 1 to Grade 3, there is an increase in conceptual understanding and application and problem solving. Seven areas are assessed: patterns/algebra, problem solving, number relations, geometry, measurement, estimation, and data analysis. Questions are multiple choice, short answer, and extended response. Extended response answers are scored on a 4-point rubric. Total time allotted for this component is 2.5 hours. All directions are read aloud to all students.

DEVELOPMENT. The authors developed a test blueprint from their surveys of state learning standards across the nation, standards documents representing professional educational organizations, and current textbooks. These standards were deemed meaningful and developmentally appropriate. Test questions were generated by test development specialists in each of the three content areas.

A large pool of questions was written so that some could be discarded after the research phase. Riverside staff, including content area test development specialists, measurement experts, and a focus group of educators reviewed each question for adherence to learning standards, grade-level appropriateness, bias/sensitivity, clarity, and relevancy. Questions that passed through this procedure were presented in research booklets to students to gather item difficulty and bias information.

TECHNICAL. A research study was conducted in Ohio in the spring of 1995. Approximately 29,400 students representing 26 school districts were evaluated. These districts represented different socioeconomic levels and geographic areas. Nothing is known about the types of learners represented, such as students with special needs or second language learners, making it difficult to ascertain if the sample is representative of the nation. This study also did not include Grade 1 Writing, which was included in a second study conducted in spring 1997 on 3,000 students. Test questions were analyzed for the final form of the test. Attention was given to characteristics such as item difficulty, item discrimination, and overall test reliability. The technical manual is not written very concisely, and data regarding the final sample of students used to provide stable statistics are unclear.

Descriptive summary statistics were obtained, although the final Grade 1 Writing assessment was not available at the time the data were collected. Reliability estimates ranged from .66 for the Grade 3 Writing component to .87 for Grade 2 and Grade 3 Reading.

Cut scores were obtained from the spring 1997 data set, culled from frequency distributions for the total raw score and strand scores of each of the content areas in each grade level. High, middle, and low groups were created for each grade. The low group attained 50% or lower correct on the test, the middle group attained 51–89% correct and the high group attained a score of 90% or higher. Cut scores were aligned to these cutoffs to adjust for test difficulty.

Content validity for this test appears high in that the assessments contain a wide range of reading, writing, and mathematical questions. These tests look similar to others of this nature. No studies aimed at assessing concurrent or predictive validity were mentioned in the technical manual.

COMMENTARY. The Multiple Assessment Series for the Primary Grades provides a well-intended opportunity for students to practice test-taking skills in preparation for state-mandated high-stakes testing. It is unclear why the publishers separated reading and writing into two distinct competency areas, as most students are currently taught that language arts is an integrated set of skills involving both reading and writing. The length of these tests for young children is problematic, especially for first graders. Research limited to a specific region, with no mention of diversity among testing groups, is troublesome as well. Poor data collection in regard to the writing component of this series in Grade 1 makes its use meaningless, especially when the same information can be gathered on a local level within a specific school building or district.

SUMMARY. The Riverside Publishing Company has developed a set of questions produced in booklet form, which they state can be used as a means of assessing content area competencies or individual strengths or weaknesses in the areas of Reading, Writing, and Mathematics. They assert that the test could be administered in either a group or individual format, although at 2.5 hours per administration, it would make little sense for individual testing. Although instructions for local scoring are given, it seems subjective at best, making their offer for scoring more attractive. Although this assessment might be very useful to the students of Ohio, it is recommended that most other consumers use caution in using this measure for the purpose of test preparation for high-stakes mandated testing or for Title 1 reporting.

Review of the Multiple Assessment Series for the Primary Grades by TIMOTHY SHANAHAN, Professor of Urban Education, University of Illinois at Chicago, Chicago, IL:

DESCRIPTION. The Multiple Assessment Series for the Primary Grades is a group-administered, criterion-referenced assessment of Reading Comprehension, Writing, and Mathematics for Grades 1–3. The assessments provide multiple-choice, short answer, and extended-response items that are designed to evaluate higher order thinking skills for use in instructional planning and Title 1 reporting. The Reading tests have 4–5 passages along with 23–31 questions. Most of the questions (18–22) are multiple-choice items, but there are some short answer items (4–7), and 1 or 2 extended response questions at each level as well. The passages include poems, short stories, and brief science articles. These passages are illustrated and are similar to materials in many textbooks.

The Math test includes 30–35 items, again, with most of these being multiple-choice (23–26 items), but with some short answer items (6–7), and 1–2 extended items. These items focus on a wide range of grade-appropriate skills including telling time, counting, measuring, geometric shapes, understanding the value of coins, estimation, translating story problems into algebraic equations, and recognizing number patterns. The Writing assessment requires students to compose two pieces at each grade level: one longer piece such as a personal narrative or informational report, and a shorter one such as a letter or invitation. The Writing assessments provide students with a literary example, a prewriting assignment, and then the two writing tasks.

DEVELOPMENT. Test developers reviewed state learning standards, standards put forth by professional groups, and popular textbook series to identify grade-level appropriate skills. Content area specialists wrote items and designed scoring rubrics based upon these standards. Items were then reviewed for content, grade level appropriateness, and sensitivity and bias. The Math and Reading items were administered to 29,400 students in 26 school districts in Ohio who were selected to represent a range of socioeconomic levels. The Writing assessment was tried out on a separate sample of 3,000 students from Ohio. Test scorers were trained to use the scoring rubrics and 80% agreement between the scorers' results and a head scorer was accomplished. The data from these administrations were used to select the final items for inclusion and items that had p-values in the range of .35 to .90 were selected. Cut scores were then established for each measure—including the various subtest scores—by selecting a criterion that identified students who scored 90% or higher, 51–89%, and 50% and lower.

TECHNICAL. The test was standardized on a group of 58,500 students from urban and rural populations in Ohio during the spring of 1997. This sample obviously does not reflect the regions of the nation, and the technical manual provides no statistical breakdown concerning other demographic characteristics such as race, ethnicity, or gender. The manual does provide assurances that the sample was diverse with regard to SES and region (rural/urban), but no normative descriptions of these characteristics are provided.

Reliability coefficients and standard errors of measurement are provided for total scores only, except at Grade 1 where no reliability data were available for Writing. No reliability data are provided for the cut score results or for any of the 14 subtest and total scores. The technical manual fails to define which form of reliabilities are being reported, but there is only a single form of each test and no repeated administration was described, so these coefficients are either interrater reliabilities (which seems likely for Writing), or alpha coefficients (which seems likely for Math and Reading given the predominance of multiple-choice items). In any event, reliabilities for Reading range from .78 (at Grade 1) to .87, for Mathematics from .80–.84, and the Writing measures are .66–.73. Given that the purpose of this test is to make individual instructional decisions, these reliabilities are a bit on the low side, especially considering that the subtest scores and cutscore decisions are going to be less reliable than these. Of course, if these are interrater reliabilities, as seems likely with Writing, these reliabilities would be very low—certainly lower than useful for making instructional decisions.

Content validity is the only aspect of validity addressed in the Multiple Assessment Series for the Primary Grades. These tests include items that reflect a wide range of instructional objectives. However, test development began approximately a decade ago, and most states have revised their instructional standards during that period, particularly in reading. The federal government now requires an emphasis on five essential elements of reading (phonemic awareness, phonics, oral reading fluency, vocabulary, comprehension) in the primary grades within federally supported programs such as Reading First or Title 1 (NICHD, 2000). The Multiple Assessment Series reflects only current primary grade reading content in one of these five areas—Reading Comprehension. There are no statistical analyses of the validity of these measures such as correlations with other tests. However, this is meant to be a criterion-referenced measure capable of identifying specific weaknesses or strengths in students' performance. Given that, it is not a correlation with other assessments that is most needed to validate this measure, but evidence that the classifications of children lead to improved instruction. No such data are provided here.

COMMENTARY. The Multiple Assessment Series for the Primary Grades is at best an adequate measure of reading comprehension, writ-

ing, and mathematics for some testing situations. Although the test manual claims this measure can be used for Title I evaluations, new regulations would not permit the use of this kind of a test for that purpose. The Reading test, because it fails to address so many key elements of the reading curriculum at these grade levels, would have to be set aside. Normally, a test like this could be used as a partial assessment in federal programs (this could be used to assess reading comprehension, for instance, and the school would be required to have measures of the other curricular elements), but the lack of any statistical validation evidence would militate against its use even in that context. The same would be true of the Math and Writing assessments (and the latter bears the additional burden of not being especially reliable either). It is surprising, given the extensive try-out and standardization administrations, that no demographic breakdown of the samples is provided. Therefore, it is impossible to determine the appropriateness of these measures for use with particular students.

These assessments have some valuable features that would make them useful for classroom assessment purposes, however. The Reading test passages, for example, are comparable to those in many instructional programs in terms of types and length of the material, and test questions focus on a diverse set of widely accepted reading skills including main idea, sequence, vocabulary, and inference. Few literal recall items are included at any grade level, with most items requiring some interpretation, although a few questions are passage independent (children could answer them correctly without reading the passages). The Math items are equally well drawn, and are representative of the skills taught at these grade levels and asked in a manner that will require that students truly think mathematically. The use of both multiple-choice and open-ended questions in the Reading and Math assessments is a great feature, as it requires some children to do more than guess. The questions are asked in a manner consistent with how a teacher might try to get at these concepts in the classroom. The same could be said of the Writing assessment that takes students through a prewriting exercise to prepare for the writing tasks—very much what one would expect to see in a primary grade writing lesson. As useful as these measures are for instructional planning assessment, the length of administration time and the single forms of the tests will circumscribe their usefulness for this purpose. Furthermore, the open-ended questions, while providing a more direct representation of classroom thinking, require complex scoring rubrics; teachers will have to spend extended time evaluating student responses or the tests will have to be sent for scoring.

SUMMARY. This test is likely to have a narrow range of use. Although the developers have made an ambitious effort to represent the school curriculum in three key areas (reading, mathematics, and writing), there have been important changes to curriculum standards and federal testing regulations since test development began. The test items are generally of high quality, and the administration and scoring manuals are thoughtful, easy to follow, and sound. However, insufficient information about the standardization sample, lack of reliability and validity evidence, neglect of key portions of the reading curriculum, and the provision of scores in categories that will often fail to match well with particular programs, will severely limit the value of this instrument.

REVIEWER'S REFERENCE

National Institute of Child Health and Human Development (NICHD). (2000). *Report of the National Reading Panel. Teaching children to read: An evidence-based assessment of the scientific research literature on reading and its implications for reading instruction. Reports of the subgroups* (NIH Publication No. 00-4754). Washington, DC: U.S. Government Printing Office. [Also available on-line: http://www.nichd.nih.gov/publications/nrp/report.htm]

[156]

Multiscale Dissociation Inventory.

Purpose: To assess the clinical severity of dissociative disturbance.
Population: Adults with a history of psychological trauma.
Publication Dates: 1998–2002.
Acronym: MDI.
Scores, 6: Disengagement, Depersonalization, Derealization, Emotional Constriction, Memory Disturbance, Identity Dissociation.
Administration: Individual or group.
Price Data, 2004: $112 per introductory kit including professional manual (2002, 40 pages), 25 test booklets, and 25 profile forms.
Time: (5–10) minutes.
Comments: Self-report; requires 6th grade reading level.
Author: John Briere.
Publisher: Psychological Assessment Resources, Inc.

Review of the Multiscale Dissociation Inventory by FREDERICK T. L. LEONG, Professor of Psychology, University of Tennessee, Knoxville, TN:

DESCRIPTION. Dissociation has been of interest to clinicians for a long time and many different instruments have been developed to measure this phenomenon. The Multiscale Dissociation Inventory (MDI) is a recently developed measure within this collection that can be administered individually or in groups requiring approximately 5–10 minutes. It is an objective, standardized, 30-item measure of six types of dissociative responses: Disengagement, Depersonalization, Derealization, Emotional Constriction, Memory Disturbance, and Identity Dissociation. As pointed out in the professional manual by Briere, author of the MDI, dissociation has been tied closely to the trauma literature resulting in over 1,600 references within the Published International Literature On Traumatic Stress (PILOTS) bibliographical database maintained by the U.S. Department of Veterans Affairs (1991). According to Briere (1996, as quoted in professional manual), the defining feature of dissociation is "the notion of an alteration or reduction in conscious awareness that arises, in part, from a separation in the normally existing connections between thoughts, feelings, memories, and behavior" (professional manual, p. 2).

DEVELOPMENT. Development of the MDI followed the best practices within the field. It began with the generation of an initial pool of potential items. Using a rational approach as opposed to an empirical approach, 90 statements that tap each of six types of dissociative symptomatology were identified for Disengagement, Depersonalization, Derealization, Emotional Constriction, Memory Disturbance, and Identity Dissociation. Based on consultations with experienced clinicians, 30 items were eliminated for each of the following reasons: redundancy with other items, inadequate indicators of the intended construct, or were in some other way problematic. The remaining 60 items were then administered to the participants from a general population sample. Responses were then submitted to item analyses that resulted in an additional 30 items being discarded. The remaining 30 items became the final version of the MDI.

Based on a stratified, random, national sampling frame, the author identified an initial sample consisting of 620 participants from the general population. From this group, 444 individuals who had at least one traumatic experience were selected as the standardization sample. The racial/ethnic composition of this sample was as follows: 80% Caucasian, 6% African American, 3% Hispanic, 3% Asian, 2% Native American, 1% Other, with 4% of Unspecified race/ethnicity. A discriminant function analysis of participant sex and MDI scores was conducted and the results indicated no significant differences across gender on this measure. This in turn was followed by a series of one-way ANOVAs that also indicated no race/ethnicity difference for any of the six MDI scales. Having established the representativeness of the standardization sample, the author went on to develop normative data based on this sample using T-score transformations.

TECHNICAL. Using samples from a university ($N = 573$), a community ($N = 70$) and a clinical setting ($N = 93$), the author provided evidence of good reliability and validity for the MDI. In terms of internal consistency, the mean alpha coefficients ranged from .77 to .92 across the various samples. The alphas ranged from .74 to .91 for the standardization sample and were in the same range for the combined clinical-community sample. However, for the university sample, two subscales had relatively low alphas (i.e., Memory Disturbance [.65] and Identity Dissociation [.68]).

Validity was examined in terms of factorial analysis and the correspondence of the factor structure to the six theoretical dimensions underlying the MDI. Based on a principal components analysis, followed by varimax rotation of all factors with eigenvalues of 1.0 or greater, the author found partial evidence for the validity of the MDI with the general population sample where seven factors were identified. Of these seven factors, the first three represented scales from the MDI (i.e., Disengagement, Depersonalization, Emotional Constriction), whereas the remaining factors split among the remaining scales (i.e., Memory Disturbance and Identity Dissociation). With the assumption that the dimensions of MDI may not be well represented within a general nonclinical population, the author conducted a second factor analysis using the clinical sample and found a closer approximation to the subscales with four factors accounting for almost 77% of the variance (compared to 65% for the general population).

Related to construct validity, the author provided additional validity evidence in the form of significant MDI correlations with theoretically meaningful variables such as history of trauma and

diagnosis of Post-Traumatic Stress Disorder (PTSD) and Dissociative Identity Disorder (DID). Finally, the author also provided some evidence of convergent and discriminant validity in relating the MDI to other dissociation measures (convergent) and nondissociative components of a trauma measure, the Trauma Symptom Inventory (discriminant).

COMMENTARY. Overall, this is a well-developed and psychometrically strong instrument that adds to the measurement of dissociation above and beyond the existing measures. The MDI stands on a firm theoretical foundation in correcting the mistakes of previous instruments. For example, many clinicians and the existing instruments operate with the erroneous assumption that dissociation is a single unitary psychological phenomenon when considerable evidence supports a multidimensional structure to this clinical syndrome. Briere points to the example "that psychogenic amnesia differs in important respects from depersonalization, which, in turn, is quite different from a fugue state, all of which seemingly have little in common with the hallmark symptoms of Dissociative Identity Disorder" (professional manual, p. 2).

Despite strong evidence that dissociation may be a multidimensional phenomenon, The Dissociative Experiences Scale (DES; Bernstein & Putnam, 1986), which is the most popular existing measure, does not distinguish between different types of dissociative experiences and therefore lacks clinical specificity. Although the DES does have good reliability (internal consistency and test-retest) and evidence of discriminant validity, it lacks standardized norms in addition to being unidimensional. The MDI has been carefully developed in response to these weaknesses within the DES, namely to provide a multidimensional measure of dissociation with good reliability, validity, and normative data. The last point is particularly important for a clinical measure in providing a basis for cutoff scores and the determination of "caseness."

SUMMARY. In conclusion, the MDI is a well-developed and psychometrically sound multidimensional measure of dissociation. It corrects some of the weaknesses in previous measures of dissociation and was developed using some of the best practices in test construction. Nevertheless, there are two major elements missing in terms of the validity of the MDI. In arguing strongly that the MDI improves upon previous measures such as the Dissociative Experiences Scale (DES; T6:828), it is incumbent upon the author to provide data to demonstrate the incremental validity of the MDI above and beyond other measures of dissociation such as the DES. Identifying and correcting for weaknesses in previous instruments is only the first step. The second step is to demonstrate empirically that the new and improved measure is indeed superior in some respects to previous measures. Relatedly, additional studies will be needed to demonstrate that the subscales of the MDI will also be useful in either incremental validity or differential validity. Internal validity (factorial and structural analysis) will have to be coupled with external or criterion-related validity for the subscales.

REVIEWER'S REFERENCES

Bernstein, E. M., & Putnam, F. W. (1986). Development, reliability, and validity of a dissociation scale. *Journal of Nervous and Mental Diseases, 174*, 727–734.
U.S. Department of Veterans Affairs, National Center for Post-Traumatic Stress Disorder. (1991). *Published International Literature on Traumatic Stress [PILOTS], 1991* [Bibliographical database]. Available from National Center for Post Traumatic Stress Disorder Web site and retrieved March 2002, http://www.ncptsd.org

Review of the Multiscale Dissociation Inventory by PAUL RETZLAFF, Professor of Psychology, University of Northern Colorado, Greeley, CO:

DESCRIPTION. The Multiscale Dissociation Inventory (MDI) is a 30-item, six-scale test of various dissociation elements. The six scales include Disengagement, Depersonalization, Derealization, Emotional Constriction, Memory Disturbance, and Identity Dissociation. There is no "Total" score. The items take the form of verbal phrases such as "Absent-mindedness or forgetfulness" and are endorsed on a 1 to 5 Likert scale. Scoring is accomplished through a carbonless form and typical profile sheet. The manual emphasizes the use of the MDI in cases of psychological trauma.

DEVELOPMENT. There is a brief description of the development of the MDI in the manual. The two paragraphs talk about the test as a whole and not at a scale level. The author states that 90 items were initially written to map the six areas. It is inferred that the author alone wrote the initial items. The manual then indicates that 30 of these items were eliminated by expert judges as redundant, poor indicators of the dimension, or psychometrically suspect. The remaining 60 items (presumably 10 per scale) were then cut down through item-total correlations. The type of subjects or number of subjects in this step is not specified. The author apparently kept the 5 best items per scale.

TECHNICAL. The psychometric information for the test was gathered using three subject samples: 573 Canadian college students, 93 general clinical patients, and 70 community members. Norms are available for several samples in the manual. The student and community sample have very low means near the minimum possible scores. With six items and 5-point scales, scores can vary from 5 to 30. Most means are around 5.5. The Cronbach alpha reliability estimates are all quite high with only a few in the student sample falling below .70. Indeed, they are remarkably high given the lack of variance in the samples.

The specificity of the scales is seen in the table of intercorrelations. The scales correlate against one another quite highly. Indeed, 9 of the 15 correlations are above .50 and the median is .53. This suggests a lack of scale specificity.

Validity evidence is provided in two ways. The traditional construct validity is developed through the correlation of these scales against other scales of dissociation. Here the MDI has a median convergent validity of .68. Divergent validity is only a bit lower and has a median of .46.

The second form of validity was examined with individuals with some degree of dissociation or PTSD. When all is said and done there appear to have been only 13 participants with clinician-judged dissociative disorder. Although the ANOVAs are all significant, this is a limited test of validity. The PTSD work included both "interpersonal trauma" and "PTSD" identification. It is not clear in the manual what cutscores were used to identify those with "interpersonal trauma." Effect sizes are quite small. For those with outright PTSD ($N = 25$) the effect sizes are similarly small but with significant ANOVAs.

COMMENTARY. There are two major problems with this test. First, there are only 5 items per scale. With a total of only 30 items, it is difficult to develop six good scales. This is an important area and it deserves a test that takes more than 5–10 minutes to take. I do not see any advantage in a test so brief.

The second problem is that the test was built largely without benefit of participants with dissociative disorder. If an author sets out to build a test of anxiety, one would seek out several hundred anxious patients. The MDI supports its validity on a mere 13 dissociative patients. It is acknowledged that it is difficult to find dissociative patients but this is a requirement for good test construction. Many more PTSD patients are identified but all this does is to provide evidence that this test is a valid PTSD test. Most of the validity data are provided by the general clinical patients. My concern here is that many diagnostic groups would score at the 10 and 15 raw score level given the item content. For example, most drug and alcohol patients would rate many of these items at a 3 or greater. Items such as "Absent-mindedness or forgetfulness," "Knowing that you are upset, but not being able to feel it," "Feeling like you were in a dream," "Spacing out," and "Not being able to feel emotions" are all nonspecific and many patient groups including, for example, drug and alcohol patients would endorse these.

SUMMARY. The Multiscale Dissociation Inventory (MDI) is intended as a multiple-scale test of dissociation. It is too brief. It has good reliability eidence but has not yet demonstrated validity against the intended diagnostic group.

[157]

Musical Aptitude Profile [1995 Revision].

Purpose: Designed to evaluate music aptitude.
Population: Grades 5–12.
Publication Dates: 1965–1995.
Scores, 11: Tonal Imagery (Melody, Harmony, Total), Rhythm Imagery (Tempo, Meter, Total), Musical Sensitivity (Phrasing, Balance, Style, Total), Total.
Administration: Group.
Price Data, 2001: $140 per complete kit; $25 per 100 answer sheets; $30 per 100 profile cards; $2 per class record sheet; $25 per sensitivity compact disc; $25 per tonal and rhythm compact disc; $20 per scoring masks (with school purchase order only; $20 per manual (1995, 162 pages).
Time: (110) minutes.
Comments: Test must be scored manually.
Author: Edwin E. Gordon.
Publisher: GIA Publications, Inc.
Cross References: See T5:1752 (1 reference); for reviews by Annabel J. Cohen and James W. Sherbon of an earlier edition, see 12:251; see also T4:1697 (2 references); T3:1552 (4 references); 8:98 (25 references), and T2:209 (11 references); for reviews by Robert W. Lundin and John McLeish, see 7:249 (33 references).

Review of the Musical Aptitude Profile [1995 Revision] by CHRISTOPHER M. JOHNSON, Professor of Music Education and Music Therapy, University of Kansas, Lawrence, KS:

DESCRIPTION. The Musical Aptitude Profile (MAP) is one of the most recognized tests of all of music testing. It has been administered, used as a model, and reported on more than any other test in the industry. It is purported to measure seven different dimensions of musical aptitude. The stated purposes of these measures are to: (a) identify musically talented students who can profit most from and contribute most to school music activities; (b) adapt music methods and materials to the individual needs and abilities of students by compensating for their specific musical weaknesses and by enhancing their specific musical strengths; (c) aid in the formulation of educational plans in music; (d) compare the collective musical aptitudes of groups of students; and (e) apprise parents of the musical aptitudes of their children.

The test is designed for students from the 4th through the 12th grades. No prior formal music training is required as a prerequisite for taking the test. A normal general exposure to the sound of music and a "seriousness of purpose" are the only listed requirements.

The dimensions being measured are claimed to be stable, and therefore it is recommended that the test be completed on 3 different days. The manual claims that these 3 days can be spread out over weeks or even months, and as formal music education has no impact on the test results, no level of time passage between sections should affect the outcomes.

The three main sections of the test are Tonal Imagery, Rhythmic Imagery, and Musical Sensitivity. The first two sections have two components, and the third area has three subsections. Each main section takes 50 minutes to complete, though the actively engaged listening portions require roughly 15 minutes for each subsection. It is asserted by the author that there is an unequivocally correct or best answer to the items of the tests of the first two divisions. Consequently, the author finds it convenient to refer to these tests as nonpreference tests. The tests in the third division, on the other hand, are intended as measures of musical expression and creativity. These tests are referred to as preference tests because the correct answers have been determined by conformance with the consensus of student and professional responses to the items. Two separate tests or subtests are provided for each of the nonpreference divisions. They are Melody and

Harmony for the Tonal Imagery division, and Tempo and Meter for the Rhythm Imagery division. The preference test division, Musical Sensitivity, involves three separate tests or subtests titled Phrasing, Balance, and Style. The author claims that in addition to providing for diagnostic appraisal of specific aspects of tonal and rhythmic aptitudes, the test battery also provides an appraisal of appreciation for musical expression and musical creativity.

The complete battery of seven tests, including practice exercises and directions, is recorded on compact disks. The test items consist of original short selections composed for violin and cello and performed by professional artists playing real acoustic (not electronic) instruments. The recording quality is high and the timbres are pleasant.

DEVELOPMENT. The original Musical Aptitude Profile was published in 1965. Over the next 30 years it has gone through several versions, and the test reviewed here is the fourth revision, which carries a 1995 publication date.

The first edition of the MAP consisted of five subtests: Melodic Variations, Harmonic Variations, Rhythmic Variations, Melodic and Rhythmic Balance, and Phrasing. This original battery of test questions was given to 1,200 students residing in the Racine, Wisconsin public schools. Test items that did not meet with minimum criteria were then discarded in order to create the first revision.

This first revision was then examined with an administration of the test to 1,200 students in Centerville, Iowa. Again, some test items were discarded following this examination. Item order effects were also examined, and found to be of little consequence.

The second revision showed a greater degree of change. Items were added to the two preference tests (Melodic and Rhythmic Balance and Phrasing) bringing the item count to 40 in each part. Also, a new section titled Interpretation was added. This revision was administered to 1,000 students in Shenandoah, Iowa. The results of this testing showed that the Harmonic Variations and Melodic Variations met the criteria. The best of 30 of the 40 items of the preference tests were retained. The Rhythmic Variations portion of the test retained only the best 20 items. It was stated that the Interpretation section of the testing did meet with as much success as the other two main tested sections.

The third revision of the test maintained the same sections of the test, but modified the number of items in an effort to make it shorter to administer.

TECHNICAL. The fourth revision of the Musical Aptitude Profile features a completely new test of Rhythmic Variations that has been simplified from the previous editions as they were deemed too difficult. Furthermore, the instructions for each subtest have been simplified and streamlined. This revision was administered to more than 1,000 students in Grades 4 though 12 in Sandusky, Ohio. The manual reports that the reliability coefficients were satisfactory, but does not provide any numbers for the reader. The manual features separate norms for each grade from 4 through 12. Special norms for students participating in school music organizations are also provided for three levels: elementary school (Grades 4, 5, and 6); junior high school (Grades 7, 8, and 9); and senior high school (Grades 10, 11, and 12).

Reliability coefficients of scores from the tests are as high as those generally reported for academic and diagnostic achievement tests. Reliability coefficients differ from grade to grade and from test to test, but are generally in the .70s and .80s for individual subtests, in the .80s and .90s for main division composites, and in the .90s for the total battery. Means, standard deviations, and standard errors of measurement for each test for each grade, and the intercorrelation among the tests, are also reported.

A discussion of the absence of any absolute index of the validity of any test is presented in the manual. It is stated that the user must feel confident that the factors measured here do measure aptitude, though many might think there are more aspects to aptitude than just those measured in this test. Nevertheless, there are correlations given between test results and teachers' ratings, and also correlations with a somewhat more objective Performance Criteria, albeit they are substantively lower. There is also a reference to some longitudinal data, though those are not based on the current version, and in fact, are actually from the original 1965 battery. The most striking issue might be the extremely low correlations between the teachers' estimations of the students' aptitudes and their scores on the MAP.

COMMENTARY. As mentioned above, this is perhaps the most famous instrument currently available to investigate musical aptitude. This test has also spawned eight other aptitude and related tests. Furthermore, countless other tests have adopted the concepts and rubrics as the guiding model. There is probably no other musical aptitude test that has more data to support its use than the MAP. Most of these data are readily accessible through the manual as well as the other four booklets included with the test package.

The value of the MAP is that it is a very reliable source of information and has been well researched. I would have no problem recommending to a researcher or public school system that this could be a valuable tool.

The administration of this test, although a bit taxing on younger students, is straightforward and can easily be done in a group setting. Also, instructions are very clear, so mistakes in administration are unlikely. Scoring, though by hand, is not a difficult task, and there is more than enough support to help with appropriate interpretation of scores.

There are three nagging issues that should be noted. First, Professor Gordon is the author of this test and of almost all of its research reports. When he was not the principal investigator using this instrument, one of his doctoral students almost always was. It calls into question (though ever so slightly) the objectivity of the studies. It would be helpful if an objective third party were to take an interest in verifying some of the claims made in the included materials. This concern is also reflected in that the test and the included monographs are all published by GIA Publishing, which is also wholly controlled, if not owned, by Professor Gordon.

A second concern is regarding the validity of interpretations based on scores from the test itself. Though validity measures are presented in the included monographs and the manual, many of those data are on early versions of the test, and frankly, are not that strong. Many musicians, scholars, and researchers have questioned what the MAP is really testing. To his credit, the author does acknowledge that the person administering this test has the discretion of determining what they thought was being measured, and then to apply meaning to that carefully before major decisions based on these test results are made.

The final concern of this reviewer relates to the fifth purpose of the test: To apprise parents of the musical aptitudes of their children. One might

be seriously concerned regarding the psychological benefits and problems arising from providing students with their profiles. It seems that the possibility for mishandling this is enormous, and many students, after being informed of their "aptitude" might become discouraged about music education and choose to abandon these activities entirely. In fact, how could this be handled properly? Research has shown that this information in the hands of a competent instructor can help in the teaching/learning task, but I cannot support the idea that the student ever needs this information.

SUMMARY. The Musical Aptitude Profile is the most complete and researched test in the area of aptitude for music. The manual is outstanding, as are the other included materials. The test administration is clear and precise. The only drawbacks stem from issues related to the meaning and use of the obtained results.

Review of the Musical Aptitude Profile [1995 Revision] by JAMES W. SHERBON, Professor Emeritus of Music, School of Music, University of North Carolina at Greensboro, Greensboro, NC:

DESCRIPTION. The Musical Aptitude Profile (MAP) was published in 1965 and revised in 1988–the current revision was published in 1995. Edwin Gordon created the MAP to serve as an objective instrument for the evaluation of music aptitudes of students and it appropriately reflects the author's long-standing dedication toward music education and students' musical needs. The MAP was created in the context of defining and unlocking the mysteries of music aptitude by the pioneering of an instrument specifically composed for the purposes of evaluating students' music aptitudes and enhancing instruction. The test is principally structured on theories of audiation, although this term does not appear in the 1965 manual. Within the educational and research literature and in contemporary and prevalent psychometric practice, however, "audiation" has assumed a prominent and meaningful position. Gordon defines audiation as the foundation of music aptitude, specifically: "the ability to hear and to comprehend music for which the sound is not physically present, … is no longer physically present, … or may never have been physically present (manual, p. 8). Herein lies the core of the MAP: The assessment of tonal audiation, rhythm audiation, and expressive/aesthetic audiation.

The test battery consists of three major tests that may be administered on separate days. The tests and approximate working times are: Tonal Imagery (29 minutes), Rhythm Imagery (36 minutes), and Musical Sensitivity (45 minutes). Within this global structure are seven subtests consisting of Melody and Harmony within Tonal Imagery; Tempo and Meter within Rhythm Imagery; and Phrasing, Balance, and Style within Musical Sensitivity. The complete battery requires administration time of approximately 1 hour and 50 minutes, but the structure of the battery's tests and subtests allows administration in three 50-minute class periods.

An important strength of the MAP is its setting in a musical context, manifest by original item stimuli composed by Gordon and performed by professional artists on violin and violoncello. Withstanding almost 40 years of research, evaluation, revision, and application, the test content is unaltered in the 1995 revision. In keeping with Gordon's penchant for continued development and improved quality, however, the principal element changed in the 1995 revision is that of remastered recordings, from cassette tape in the 1988 revision to digital format in the 1995 revision in which test stimuli are now presented by means of two compact disks.

DEVELOPMENT. Before publication of the MAP in 1965, the test construction comprised a process involving broad and inclusive research, development, and study by the author. The development of the tests also received support and study from other researchers focused on the measurement of music aptitude. Throughout the construction and evolution of the original test battery, Gordon enlisted many resources and field-based testing environments couched in practical and real-life venues. These structured procedures provided solid anchors of empirical substance, ensuring the development of a test of music aptitude that not only is constructed on substantial test theory, but also a test that manifests practical foundations of item determination, difficulty, and global representativeness of music aptitude—all backed by the administration and study of obtained data from students in schools throughout the nation.

The processes of test standardization continued in the same scientific manner as employed during the initial construction. Students within 20 schools throughout the nation were selected on the basis of region, demographic factors, and so-cioeconomic considerations to ensure representativeness. The cumulative developmental detail and compositional thoroughness implemented by Gordon during the development stages obviously documented stability and research-tested accuracy that have ensured the maintenance of identical core content throughout the life of the MAP. Consequently, all supportive, explanatory, statistical data, and elements of standardization remain unchanged also in the 1995 revision. Gordon justifies the retention of the original standardization by stating that "stabilized music aptitude is known not to vary except, perhaps, in relation to an overall increase in music achievement in a society at large" (manual, p. 66). He continues this justification by citing support for the stability of student music achievement over a period of 20 years (Gordon, 1994).

TECHNICAL. The 1995 revision of the MAP is mainly cosmetic, with the exception of the previously mentioned remastering of the test stimuli from cassette tape to two compact disks. The answer sheet, class record and profile chart, and cumulative record folder show slight functional enhancements, but essentially remain unchanged. Hand scoring employs the 1988 version of the tag board scoring masks. The machine-scoring service offered previously is no longer available.

The 1995 test manual is improved in readability, clarity of the printed page, and overall layout; however, a word-by-word comparison with the 1988 revision primarily reveals only stylistic enhancements and clarification of terminology. The tables in the 1995 revision, although remaining somewhat physically compacted, present substantial improvements in format and clarity. A table is provided for converting raw scores to standard scores with comprehensive tables of percentile norms for the standard scores ranging from Grades 4 through 12. Norms are also provided for student members of performance ensembles. The test administrator who wants to obtain maximum results from the MAP will find the manual's content to be logical, thorough, utilitarian, theoretical, and concomitantly void of verbal subjectivity—the subject areas enforced by objective research and concrete data. The manual contains information of value for both the professional and novice.

Worthy of reinforcement from the 1988 revision is the presence of extensive and conclusive research on the MAP dealing primarily with longitudinal predictive and diagnostic validity.

Gordon's (1967) classic longitudinal study, *A Three-Year Longitudinal Predictive Validity Study of the Musical Aptitude Profile*, is appropriately reported as well as later longitudinal studies: *Fourth-Year and Fifth-Year Final Results of a Longitudinal Study of the Musical Achievement of Culturally Disadvantaged Students* (Gordon, 1975) and *Final Results of a Two-Year Longitudinal Predictive Validity Study of the Instrument Timbre Preference Test and the Musical Aptitude Profile* (Gordon, 1986). Also worthy of note is the addition of 70 entries to the 1995 bibliography. Significance herein points to strong evidence of the MAP's validity as well as its prominence among scholars and educators. The presence of extended published research on validity as well as empirical focus on its position and applicability in music education is impressive.

COMMENTARY. The Musical Aptitude Profile has served educators, psychologists, and researchers as the principal instrument within the field of standardized music aptitude tests for almost four decades. Although Gordon continues unparalleled productivity in the testing and evaluation of music aptitude, the MAP has pioneered an era of attention toward music aptitude, manifesting itself as an embryonic icon while simultaneously distinguishing itself as a fully developed and mature classical fixture in music aptitude evaluation. The test obviously will continue to serve as a catalyst for future research and facility while focusing on the evaluation of students' music aptitudes and associated fulfillment of instruction and individual musical human needs.

A candid contrast, however, is the fact that we live in an age of computerization and technical facilitation. Optical scanned answer sheets, online testing, and test responses transmitted from students to staging servers resulting in descriptive statistics arriving instantaneously in teachers' hands cause some disquietude regarding practical, facilitative, and outdated features present in the MAP, remaining unchanged in the 1995 revision. For example, Gordon's Advanced Measures of Music Audiation (AMMA, 1989; T6:95), a music aptitude test requiring an administration time of 20 minutes, may be more realistic than the MAP with its admission time of approximately 1 hour and 50 minutes. The AMMA, therefore, might be more expeditiously used with older students followed by the MAP to gain more diagnostic information for special music students.

Perhaps Gordon's more recent creativity such as the Primary Measures of Music Audiation (1979; T6:1976), Intermediate Measures of Music Audiation (1982; T6:1236), or Advanced Measures of Music Audiation (1989; T6:95) may someday dislodge the contemporary father of music aptitude tests, the Musical Aptitude Profile. The current status and value of the latter, however, are presently manifest in the third revision (1995) while awaiting the arrival of future revisions that are compatible with and expedited by the 21st Century of Internet and Web-based interactions between students and teachers.

SUMMARY. Considering purpose, content, and product, the Musical Aptitude Profile remains the ultimate test of music aptitude currently in print. The MAP retains its stature as the best test of its kind available to the music performance and music education profession today. Gordon obviously has not discarded the MAP in lieu of his more recent work and research; however, a 1995 revision that does not reflect the age of technology and computer processing raises many questions about the viability of tests that are not current with technology, record forms that require hand-written information, and answer sheets that can only be scored by use of a paper template.

In view of the extensive amount of study, research, and testing that underlies the MAP, one cannot fail to recognize the contributions this test of music aptitude has made to the evaluation of students' music aptitude and educational enhancement of students' musical needs. Gordon has indeed made a monumental contribution to the vast area of music aptitude testing and how the musical aptitudes of students may be recognized. The definition, enhancement of identity, and evaluation of music aptitude are credited to Edwin Gordon in many exemplary ways, and the Musical Aptitude Profileis but one of the contributions this researcher, author, and teacher has made to the evaluation of music aptitude. Practitioners, consumers, and music educators will be well-served to study the origins, foundations, theories, research applications, and results that emerge from the MAP. Regardless of future generations and technological enhancements of the MAP, those involved in the musical education of our current generations of the youth of America should be cognizant of the origins and theories underlying Gordon's Musical Aptitude Profile so that the future of music education can better meet the musical and educational challenges of the music aptitude of our students and the innate requirements of human needs in music.

REVIEWER'S REFERENCES

Gordon, E. E. (1967). *A three-year longitudinal predictive validity study of the Musical Aptitude Profile.* Iowa City: The University of Iowa Press.

Gordon, E. E. (1975). Fourth-year and fifth-year final results of a longitudinal study of the musical achievement of culturally-disadvantaged students. *Experimental Research in the Psychology of Music, 10,* 24-52.

Gordon, E. E. (1979). Primary Measures of Music Audiation. Chicago: GIA Publications.

Gordon, E. E. (1982). Intermediate Measures of Music Audiation. Chicago: GIA Publications.

Gordon, E. E. (1986). Final results of a two-year longitudinal predictive validity study of the Instrument Timbre Preference Test and the Musical Aptitude Profile. *Bulletin of the Council for Research in Music Education, 89,* 8-17.

Gordon, E. E. (1989). Advanced Measures of Music Audiation. Chicago: GIA Publications.

Gordon, E. E. (1994). *A comparison of scores on the 1971 and 1993 editions of the Iowa Tests of Music Literacy: Implications for music education and selecting an appropriate string instrument for study using the Instrument Timbre Preference Test.* West Berne, NY: Gordon Institute for Music Learning.

[158]
My Worst Experience Scale.

Purpose: Designed to "assess youngsters' reports of their most stressful experiences and their thoughts, behaviors, and feelings associated with those experiences."

Population: Ages 9–18.

Publication Date: 2002.

Acronym: MWES.

Scores, 12: DSM IV PTSD Criterion subscales (Impact of the Event, Re-experience of the Trauma, Avoidance and Numbing, Increased Arousal), Symptoms Subscales (Depression, Hopelessness, Somatic Symptoms, Oppositional Conduct, Hypervigilance, Dissociation and Dreams, General Maladjustment), Total.

Administration: Group or individual.

Price Data, 2005: $115 per test kit including 25 AutoScore™ answer forms, manual (78 pages), and 100 school alienation and trauma survey forms; $45 per manual; $49.95 per 25 AutoScore™ answer forms; $24.50 per 100 school alienation and trauma survey forms; $250 per 25-use disk; $15 per PC answer booklet; $12.50 per mail-in answer booklet; volume discounts available.

Time: (20–30) minutes.

Comments: Self-report questionnaire; computer administration and scoring available.

Authors: Irwin A. Hyman, and Pamela A. Snook (scale and manual), J. M. Berna, M. A. Kohr, J. DuCette, and G. Britton (scale).

Publisher: Western Psychological Services.

Review of the My Worst Experience Scale by FREDERIC J. MEDWAY, Professor of Psychology, University of South Carolina, Columbia, SC:

DESCRIPTION. The My Worst Experience Scale (MWES) is a self-report measure of children's thoughts, behaviors, and emotions in reaction to one stressful event. The test was designed to assess Posttraumatic Stress Disorder (PTSD) in children according to DSM-IV criteria and to measure symptoms common to children and adolescents (ages 9–18) who experience extreme stress or trauma. A test manual describes the development of the measure, administration and scoring, interpretation, standardization, and test characteristics.

The MWES consists of two major parts. In Part I, the respondent is asked to check their "worst experience" from 21 choices that include various presumed traumatic events and disasters (e.g., death of a parent, loss of a pet, family fighting, and school problem) and to indicate various information about the event (e.g., the child's age at time of event and whether the child still is bothered by the event). In Part II, children read 105 behavioral statements and are asked how many times they experienced this particular feeling or reaction after the traumatic event occurred and whether the reaction lasted more than 1 month. The test uses an automatic scoring form to transfer respondents' answers to appropriate test factors and a computer test-scoring and interpretation diskette is included. The latter generates a score report and can also be used for computer administration of the test.

The MWES produces two major types of scores. First, it yields an index of Inconsistent Responding (INC) that serves as a measure of accurate, reliable reporting. Second, the MWES produces, using T scores, a total score and subscale scores. The total score is an overall distress composite that can be used to differentiate clinical and nonclinical groups. Of the subscale scores, one subset is used to assess PTSD based on four DSM-IV criteria: Impact of the Event, Re-experience of the Trauma, Avoidance and Numbing, and Increased Arousal. For each criterion, from 4 to 24 items are used in scoring. Another group of the subscale scores measures seven categories of assorted stress-related symptoms: Depression, Hopelessness, Somatic Symptoms, Oppositional Conduct, Hypervigilance, Dissociation and Dreams, and General Maladjustment. These scales are for differential diagnosis and to suggest areas for further psychological examination.

DEVELOPMENT. Whereas most of the current children's measures of PTSD were developed to assess the impact of community (e.g., crime victimization) and environmental (e.g., disasters) stressors, the MWES grew initially out of the first author's longstanding interest in the impact of corporal punishment on children, school paddling, and his observations that paddling and spanking may result in PTSD symptoms in children that do not meet standard adult diagnostic criteria. This observation led to several case studies and empirical investigations that showed the range and nature of children's responses to "extreme" stress and showed that some of these stressors would not be considered necessarily traumatic for adults. The original version of the MWES was specific to the school setting but the current version is now expanded well beyond the school context. And a separate measure, the Student Alienation and Trauma Survey, also included in the MWES test manual, specifically assesses school traumas. The final selection of MWES items was based on case studies of victimized children, the research literature, and on analysis by professionals in the child trauma field. Items were designed to be developmentally appropriate, and were written at a third to sixth grade level. The PTSD scales were based on items with pertinent content; the seven Symptom subscales were derived based on content and factor analysis.

TECHNICAL. The standardization sample was 1,255 children ranging in age from 9 to 18. However, there were only 48 students in the 9–10-year age group. The sample is not entirely representative of the U.S. population. The sample is underrepresentative of African American and particularly Hispanic minority groups, and does not include any Native Americans. Further, low SES groups are underrepresented and children from the Northeastern region of the U.S. are overrepresented. Nevertheless, effect size differences are negligible for gender, ethnicity, and age. Measures of internal consistency yielded quite high correlation coefficients for the Total score (.97) and respectable coefficients for the Symptom subscales (.69–.94). Similarly, measures of test-retest reliability yielded high correlation coefficients for the Total score (.88–.95) and excellent coefficients for the Symptom subscales (median correlation of .77). However, the test-retest administration period did not exceed 6 weeks. Construct, concurrent, and discriminant validity indices are reported.

Factor analysis generally supports the subscale structure of the test, although some items load on other than the intended factors and the Dissociation and Somatic subscale items do not produce identifiable factors. The test manual reports that trauma symptoms correlate negatively with positive indices such as overall self-concept on the Piers-Harris Scale and moderately positively with indices of anger and aggression (e.g., the Children's Inventory of Anger). The MWES was found to differentiate children diagnosed with PTSD from a nonclinical group based on the four PTSD criteria and stress symptoms reported. The MWES also has been shown to discriminate children suffering divorce trauma, hurricane trauma, sexual abuse, and conduct disorder.

COMMENTARY. Great care and considerable insight into the parameters of PTSD in children appears to have gone into the design and validation of the MWES. Test design is based on contemporary views of PTSD in children and scientific studies that provide a strong rationale for test design. The test is easy to administer, can be computer administered, and can be used in individual or group (for screening purposes) administration. The INC index is useful to eliminate test protocols that may not reflect children's true feelings or may be contaminated in some way. The manual is clear, logically organized, and presents four clinical case studies to aid in interpretation. However, given that the scale initially developed out of the study of school-based traumas, one concern is whether the "worst experiences" elicited by this measure are indeed traumatic or exceptionally stressful for children at all. Specifically, whereas the majority of the standardization sample were upset by and continue to be bothered by the named experience, for many, the experiences named are arguably normative and developmental challenges (e.g., 24% death of someone other than parent; 6% loss of a pet; 8% problems with friends at school). In one of the case studies dealing with loss of a pet it is clear that another significant stressor, physical abuse, contributed highly to the particulars of the case. Further, stresses such as car and other accidents, parent incarceration, or parent military service are not included in the named list even though these are fairly common and upsetting to children. Clinicians may have to determine how much the symptoms reported such as depression reflect the impact of the particular trauma or more generalized tendencies, and may have to determine if these emotions are transitory or stable. Thus, careful clinical interviewing and administration of other personality and behavior rating scales would appear to be essential to confirm any diagnoses.

From a technical standpoint, the MWES has ample clearly written items to sample the domains of interest, and the authors report very good initial reliability and validity statistics. The authors acknowledge the limitations and representativeness of the standardization sample. Given that younger children often have difficulty describing trauma, it is unfortunate that more children at or below age 10 were not included in the standardization sample, or that the scale was not designed to be appropriate for children a few years younger than age 9. Further, considering that community and school trauma is often high in minority groups (particularly Native Americans and those living in poverty), a decided weakness of this measure is its failure to sample these groups and also to include handicapped children in the standardization sample.

As originally developed the MWES filled a needed void for a comprehensive measure of PTSD in children that was aligned with DSM-IV criteria. Whereas this scale is supported by well-designed reliability and validity studies, there is no information regarding potential false positives identified by this test and no information regarding the sensitivity of the measure to clinical intervention aimed at addressing children's trauma. The validation studies do not include any research showing how this test compares with others with a similar stated purpose. Additionally, in recent years, there have been a growing number of child PTSD scales (e.g., Child PTSD Symptom Scale [Foa, Johnson, Feeny, & Treadwell, 2001], Childhood PTSD Interview [Fletcher, 1996], Children's PTSD Inventory [Saigh, Yasik, Oberfield et al., 2000]) and considerable future research is needed to compare the MWES with these other measures so that examiners fully understand the strengths and weaknesses of each one.

SUMMARY. The MWES is a well-constructed instrument with good reliability and adequate validity evidence. Although it may overlap with other measures of PTSD in children and may lean toward identification of less than extreme stressors, its use in school and community settings is well demonstrated. Additional normative data on younger age groups and minorities are needed,

as well as future data on the stability of the constructs measured, their susceptibility to intervention, and the scale's advantages compared to other instruments with similar objectives.

REVIEWER'S REFERENCES

Fletcher, K. (1996). Psychometric review of the Childhood PTSD Interview. In B. H. Stamm (Ed.), *Measurement of stress, trauma, and adaptation* (pp. 87-89). Lutherville, MD: Sidran Press.
Foa, E. B., Johnson, K. M., Feeny, N. C., & Treadwell, K. R. H. (2001). The Child PTSD Symptom Scale: A preliminary examination of its psychometric properties. *Journal of Clinical Child Psychology, 30,* 376-384.
Saigh, P. A., Yasik, A. E., Oberfield, R. A. et al. (2000). The Children's PTSD Inventory: Development and reliability. *Journal of Traumatic Stress, 13,* 369-380.

Review of the My Worst Experience Scale by HEIDI K. MOORE, *Research Scientist, Healthcare Technology Systems, Inc., Madison, WI:*

DESCRIPTION. The My Worst Experience Scale (MWES) is a 111-item instrument developed to measure children's self-reports of their thoughts, behaviors, and feelings associated with their most stressful experiences. Children ages 9-18 can complete the MWES via either paper-and-pencil (AutoScore(tm)) or computer forms. The test kit also includes the Student Alienation and Trauma Survey (SATS) that is designed to measure traumatic events that occur in a school setting. Given the lack of information in the manual about the development and technical properties of the SATS, it will not be reviewed here, and users should administer the SATS only for research purposes.

The MWES contains two parts. Part I is intended to gather details about the respondent's most stressful event. From a list of 21 events, children check the event they experienced as their "worst." The list was generated based on the first author's experiences with children who experienced a traumatic event. Next, children complete six questions about when the event happened and its emotional burden. Part II contains 105 items about children's behavioral and emotional reactions to the event (e.g., "I had nightmares"). Response to items is via a 6-point Likert scale ranging from 0 (*Did not happen*) to 5 (*All the time*). The instructions seem poorly worded as they ask the respondent to "circle the number under the answer that tells how many times you felt or acted that way" and may result in children circling, for example, the number 3 for a response that happened three times when 3 actually means *More than a few times*. Additionally, although the manual states that most children can complete the instrument in 20–30 minutes, children with emerging reading skills or those who have experienced severe trauma may require more time and possibly breaks. The authors report readability statistics suggesting the items were written at a second- or third-grade reading level. However, the two reported readability studies were conducted with eighth-grade students and students ages 13–18. These samples seem weighted toward the higher end of the stated age range of 9–18. Readability studies with children between the ages of 9–10 would be more informative. The manual recommends that an adult read items to "younger children" but does not give suggestions for determining reading levels and does not acknowledge the potential for bias if the items are read aloud.

The MWES yields two groups of subscale scores and a total score. The first group of subscales is designed to correspond to Criteria A, B, C, and D of the Posttraumatic Stress Disorder (PTSD) diagnosis according to the *Diagnostic and Statistical Manual of Mental Disorders, Fourth Edition* (DSM-IV; American Psychiatric Association, 1994). The authors appropriately state that the MWES is not designed to diagnose PTSD and recommend gathering additional information before making a diagnosis. The second group of subscales, the Symptom subscales, measures a broader group of symptoms associated with PTSD and are based on the authors' 15-year research working with children diagnosed with PTSD. The subscale scores and the total score are reported as *T*-scores (Mean = 50, *SD* = 10) and are interpreted similarly to scores on the Minnesota Multiphasic Personality Inventory-2 (Butcher, Dahlstrom, Graham, Tellegen, & Kaemmer, 1990). The MWES also includes an Inconsistent Responding index that contains 16 pairs of similar items (e.g., "I lost my appetite" and "I stopped eating"). Inconsistent responses to 7 or more of the 16 pairs suggests the respondent may not have considered his or her answers carefully, and the administrator should initiate a discussion with the child and exercise caution when interpreting the scores.

The manual states that the MWES can be administered individually or in a group. The authors appropriately mention that children may experience emotional distress when completing the MWES and also discuss the potential for some children who have experienced severe trauma to avoid distressing items and deny symptoms. Given the content of the instrument and the potential for young survivors of traumatic events

to re-experience the trauma for several years after the event, the MWES may be best administered individually. In addition, a trained administrator should be prepared to assist with emotional responses, including re-experiencing, and to discuss incomplete or inconsistent responses with the child.

DEVELOPMENT. The MWES was developed partially in response to the first author's experience with a child who responded with PTSD-like symptoms to a traumatic experience at school. In addition, the manual cites research suggesting that children and adolescents respond to stressors and exhibit PTSD differently than adults. The items were initially developed based on clinical experiences with first-grade children who experienced a traumatic incident at their school. These items were combined with a second set of items based on the DSM-III-R PTSD criteria (American Psychiatric Association, 1987). A third set of items was developed based on ongoing research with child and adolescent survivors of traumatic stressors. Although not stated in the manual, it is assumed that these three item sets were combined to form Part II of the MWES. A panel of local and national experts in childhood trauma reviewed the item bank and provided evidence for content and face validity. The results of these reviews and any changes to the items are not presented in the manual. To support the seven Symptoms subscales, the manual presents interscale correlations and results from a factor analysis fully presented in an unpublished doctoral dissertation. Given that readers of the manual cannot easily access an unpublished doctoral dissertation, it would have been helpful to include more detailed information about the reliability and underlying factor structure of the MWES in the manual.

TECHNICAL. The standardization sample included 1,255 children between the ages of 9 and 18. Most participants completed the MWES in a public school setting, apparently administered in a group. The sample contained more females (53%) than males (47%). In addition, ethnic and racial minorities were quite underrepresented. Less than 1% of the sample identified themselves as Hispanic, compared to 15% in the U.S. population. Geographically, the Northeast was overrepresented whereas the West was underrepresented. Although the manual does not present tests of statistical significance for scores observed in the standardization sample, females score higher than males, and older children reported more symptoms than younger children. The manual presents the mean scores for the small racial and ethnic minority samples but does not compare these values to those obtained for the Caucasian sample. In addition, although the manual states "For ethnic background, all effect sizes were small" (p. 39), no effect sizes are reported.

As evidence for reliability, the authors present internal consistency estimates using Cronbach's alpha from the standardization sample. For the full sample, the reliability estimate for the total score was .97, and values for the PTSD subscales ranged from .69 to .92, and the Symptom subscales values ranged from .76 to .94. Interage coefficients for the subscales are generally good, with a low of .59 for the General Maladjustment Symptom subscale among 11–12-year-olds.

Correlations between scores on the MWES and scores on similar measures, such as the Piers-Harris Self-Concept Scale (Piers, 1996) and the Children's Inventory of Anger (Nelson & Finch, 2000) are presented as evidence for concurrent validity. Most correlations are in expected directions, although weak. As evidence for "discriminant validity" (manual, p. 47), that appears more similar to criterion validity, the authors present results from four studies comparing children who experience different traumas, such as divorce and surviving a hurricane, to children without such experiences. In all studies, children who experienced trauma scored higher than children who did not. However, the authors fail to present results from the tests of statistical significance, other than p values. As most of these studies are also based on unpublished doctoral dissertations, providing this information for the reader would have been appreciated. The test manual should be revised to include more detail for unpublished studies that have not been peer-reviewed and that interested readers cannot obtain.

SUMMARY. The MWES is grounded in a wealth of clinical experience and may provide a resource to researchers interested in trauma among children and adolescents. Although recommended by the test authors, group administration of such an instrument does not seem wise. With additional research, the instrument could also serve as a useful tool in identifying young people who may need further evaluation for PTSD. This research should include more representative samples and provide further evidence for reliability and valid-ity. In its current form, the MWES should be used for research purposes only. Future research will assist in directing other applications.

REVIEWER'S REFERENCES

American Psychiatric Association. (1987). *Diagnostic and statistical manual of mental disorders* (3rd ed., revised). Washington, DC: Author.
American Psychiatric Association. (1994). *Diagnostic and statistical manual of mental disorders* (4th ed.). Washington, DC: Author.
Butcher, J. N., Dahlstrom, W. G., Graham, J., Tellegen, A., & Kaemmer, B. (1990). The Minnesota Multiphasic Personality Inventory-2. Minneapolis, MN: University of Minnesota Press.
Nelson, W. M., III, & Finch, A. J., Jr. (2000). Children's Inventory of Anger (ChIA): Manual. Los Angeles, CA: Western Psychological Services.
Piers, E. V. (1996). *Piers-Harris Children's Self-Concept Scale: Manual.* Los Angeles, CA: Western Psychological Services.

[159]

Naglieri Nonverbal Ability Test—Individual Administration.

Purpose: Designed to provide a brief nonverbal measure of general ability.

Population: Ages 5-0 to 17-11.

Publication Date: 2003.

Acronym: NNAT-I.

Scores: Total score only.

Administration: Individual.

Price Data, 2004: $233 per complete kit including manual (139 pages), stimulus book, 25 parent reports, and 25 each of record forms A and B; $110 per stimulus book; $55 per manual; $55 per 25 record forms (specify Form A or B); $55 per 25 parent reports.

Time: (25–30) minutes.

Comments: This test and the Naglieri Nonverbal Ability Test (Multilevel Form) (T6:1680) are the second editions of the still in-print Matrix Analogies Test (Expanded Form and Short Form) (T6:1531).

Author: Jack A. Naglieri.

Publisher: PsychCorp, A brand of Harcourt Assessment, Inc.

Cross References: See T5:1607 (15 references) and T4:1566 (8 references); for a review by Robert F. McMorris, David L. Rule, and Wendy J. Steinberg of the Matrix Analogies Test, see 10:191 (1 reference).

Review of the Naglieri Nonverbal Ability Test—Individual Administration by CONNIE T. ENGLAND, Department Chair, Grad Counseling & Guidance, Lincoln Memorial University, Knoxville, TN:

DESCRIPTION. The Naglieri Nonverbal Ability Test—Individual Administration (NNAT-I) is a brief nonverbal measure of general ability in children and adolescents aged 5 to 17 years. The NNAT—Individual (NNAT-I) is a companion to the NNAT—Multilevel Form and is the revision of the Matrix Analogies Test—Expanded Form (MAT—Expanded Form).

The NNAT-I is designed for use with a large population of examinees including those individuals who may have language delays due to hearing impairments or other communication difficulties or who come from different cultural or linguistic backgrounds. The NNAT—I requires minimal examinee motor capabilities, and is therefore appropriate for those individuals with motor impairments.

The NNAT-I consists of the manual with administration, scoring, and technical data; stimulus booklet with Forms A and B; record forms for Forms A and B; and a parent report form. The NNAT-I yields four types of scores: raw score (i.e., total points awarded an examinee), standard score (mean = 100 and a standard deviation of 15), percentile rank, and age equivalent score.

Assessment professionals and trained technicians under the supervision of a qualified assessment professional may administer and score the NNAT-I. Test result interpretation, however, requires appropriate graduate level training. The NNAT-I takes an average of 25 to 30 minutes to administer and should be completed in one sitting. Examiners may repeat instructions, clarify examinees' responses, and prompt examinees to answer.

The record form has typical demographic information and a place to calculate the examinee's chronological age. Start points are based on examinee age. A basal level is obtained with four consecutive correct responses and the discontinue criterion is met at four consecutive incorrect responses. The response form has a space for the examinee's response, a space with the correct response listed, and a space for the item score, entered as either a "1" for correct or a "0" for incorrect.

There are two sample items for each of the two forms with directions in English provided on the record form. Test administration directions for these items are also provided in Spanish and French and are found in Appendix C of the manual. Feedback on the examinee's response is allowed only for the sample items.

Raw scores are calculated by adding correct responses, including points awarded for unadministered items before the basal level. Raw scores are converted to standard scores and percentile ranks with confidence intervals provided at the 90th and 95th percentile. Only the total raw score is used to obtain the age equivalent. The parent report form is intended to be used as an aid to test result interpretation and discussion. It includes a bell curve figure upon which the examinee's results can be depicted. Definitions of standard score and percentile rank are also included on the parent report.

DEVELOPMENT. The NNAT-I is composed of figural matrix items. Items are solved through pattern identification and selection of the answer that best completes the pattern. The manual lists several rules used in the development of the items. Pattern Completion, considered to be the easiest among the test items, is intended for elementary school-aged examinees. These items require the examinee to look at the design in a large rectangle with a missing portion and select the answer that completes the pattern. The second rule is Reasoning by Analogy. These items require the examinee to discover the logical relationship between several geometric figures. Determining the correct answer requires examinees to recognize how the shapes change as they move across the rows or down the columns. For these figural items examinees must attend to multiple dimensions simultaneously. Serial Reasoning is the third rule used in item development. These items are constructed of a series of shapes that change both across the rows and down the columns throughout the design. To determine the correct answer the examinee must recognize the shift in the sequence of shapes. Items become more difficult by using different characteristics of the shapes (e.g., size, color, rotation). Spatial Visualization is the fourth rule—requiring the examinee to determine how designs would appear if combined.

A total of 64 additional items were added to the NNAT—Multilevel. Based on a minipilot study of approximately 500 examinees, 22 items were added to allow for accurate measurement of examinees with the lowest ability and 42 were added to measure examinees with the highest abilities.

TECHNICAL. A total of 1,585 examinees were included in the standardization sample. U.S. Bureau of Census data (2000) provided the basis for stratification and included the following variables: Age, gender, race/ethnicity, geographic region, and parent education level. All examinees were enrolled in public or private school. Approximately 6% of the standardization sample consisted of examinees who were classified as having mental retardation or who were receiving gifted/talented services. Examinees diagnosed with Attention Deficit Hyperactivity Disorder were also included in the sample. Separate clinical validity studies were conducted for examinees classified as gifted or talented; having mental retardation; having a learning disability; language or hearing impairment; or who spoke English as a second language.

Test-retest reliability estimates are based on a subset of 200 examinees who were given Form A of the NNAT-I. Stability coefficients for the various age groups fell within the moderate range with $r = .73$. Equality measures between Form A and Form B suggest test items are parallel for the alternate forms yielding an overall correlation of .89 for the various age groups.

Content and construct validity evidence is based on correlations between the NNAT-I and the MAT-EF, which yield a corrected correlation coefficient of .74. Racial/ethnic comparisons suggest similar mean standard scores for African American/White and Hispanic/White groups.

Concurrent and predictive criterion-related evidence of validity is also presented. When compared to the Raven's Standard Progressive Matrices (RSPM) and the Test of Nonverbal Intelligence—Third Edition (TONI-3) the NNAT-I shows corrected correlation coefficients of .78 and .63, respectively. When compared to the Wechsler Intelligence Scale for Children—Fourth Edition (WISC-IV) the NNAT-I was most closely related to the Matrix Reasoning subtest, with a corrected correlation coefficient of .62. Predictive validity data, based on comparisons with the Wechsler Individual Achievement Test—Second Edition (WIAT-II), revealed a corrected coefficient of .55.

COMMENTARY. As a brief nonverbal measure of overall ability, the NNAT-I appears to be a good choice. The test developer reports sufficient data to support the efficacy of using this instrument with a variety of children with varying English language proficiency. One caveat noted is the comparison study conducted with hearing-impaired students. In this comparison study, students with hearing impairments scored higher than the matched control group. The developer suggests further investigation of these unexpected findings. One explanation for these unexpected findings may be that the unidimensional design of the instrument (i.e., figural matrices) makes the NNAT-I both a nonverbal measure of ability, and a measure of nonverbal ability.

SUMMARY. The NNAT-I adds to the growing number of nonverbal measures of ability. As a brief, psychometrically sound instrument it appears to be an excellent choice. However, if a global measure of intellectual ability is needed, possibly an instrument with a multidimensional item base would be a better option.

Review of the Naglieri Nonverbal Ability Test—Individual Administration by BRIAN F. FRENCH, Assistant Professor of Educational Psychology, Purdue University, West Lafayette, IN:

DESCRIPTION. The Naglieri Nonverbal Ability Test—Individual Administration (NNAT-I) is an individually administered nonverbal instrument that is claimed to measure general ability through the use of nonverbal content and stimuli, independent of verbal, math, and reading skills, with little requirement of the use of motor skills. The examinee's task is to view a stimulus, identify the pattern, and select an answer from the given choices that completes the pattern. Ability is estimated based on the total number of correct responses. The instrument is composed of figural matrix items that contain common shapes and designs and include: Pattern Completion, Reasoning by Analogy, Serial Reasoning, and Spatial Visualization. Items on each form ($N = 72$ per form) are arranged in order of difficulty from easy to hard.

This brief (i.e., 25–30 minutes) instrument is appropriate for a wide range of examinees ages 5 through 17, who may come from economically, linguistically, or culturally diverse backgrounds, as well as examinees with motor or communication problems. The NNAT-I also may be useful for (a) identification of gifted examinees, (b) evaluation of the hearing impaired, (c) identification of mental retardation, and (d) predicting achievement (manual, p. 1). The test should be administered, scored, and interpreted by a trained professional who knows the standards specified in the *Standards for Educational and Psychological Testing* (AERA, APA, & NCME, 1999) and has graduate training in individual administration of educational and psychological testing. Trained personnel may administer and score the NNAT-I under the supervision of a qualified professional who will interpret the scores.

The NNAT-I test kit includes a manual, a stimulus book, record forms for Forms A and B, and parent report sheets. The record form provides space for examinee demographic and score information. The parent report provides score in-

formation (numerical and graphical) to aid interpretation, a brief description of the NNAT-I, and
two sample items. The manual provides detailed
instructions including examples for administration, scoring, interpretation, and completion of
the parent report, as well as sample items and
instructions used at the start of administration in
English, Spanish, and French. Tables containing
standard scores, confidence intervals, percentile
ranks, and age equivalent scores are provided.

DEVELOPMENT. The predecessor of the
NNAT-I is the Matrix Analogies Test—Expanded
Form (MAT-EF; Naglieri, 1985), which has had
substantial use for academic and research purposes. The NNAT—Multilevel Form (Naglieri,
1997) provided the foundation for the NNAT-I.
The NNAT-I was designed to provide current
norms, better psychometric qualities, and practical
utility in comparison to its predecessor. The design of the items and the structure of the test
follow four rules, and resulted in the four item
types. These rules include being able to recognize
(a) the missing component of a pattern, (b) logical
relationship between geometric shapes, (c) shifts
in the sequence of shapes, and (d) how designs
would appear if combined. Item development involved administration of the NNAT-Multilevel
items to examinees ($N = 500$) from three age
ranges (i.e., 5–6, 10–11, and 16–17 years) and of
diverse geographic, socioeconomic, and ethnic
backgrounds. Additional items were then created
to assess the lowest and highest levels of ability
($n_{items} = 22$, $n_{items} = 42$, respectively), which were
tested at each of the two ability levels. A detailed
description of the theoretical basis and item generation procedures were not given. The manual
states that an item analysis including examination
of differential item functioning (DIF) with item
response theory (IRT) methods was conducted.
However, details (e.g., results of the analyses, IRT
model employed, groups compared, sample size)
were not provided. Thus, it is not possible to
evaluate the extent of item invariance across the
groups.

TECHNICAL. Standardization data ($N = 1,585$) were collected in 2002 and employed a
stratified random sampling procedure. The sample
was composed of 52% and 48% females and males,
respectively, with an average of 132 examinees at
each age level. The demographic characteristics
(e.g., geographic region, race/ethnicity) matched

the 2000 U.S. Bureau of the Census data very well
(e.g., all categories within 2%). The sample also
consisted of examinees classified as having mental
retardation (approximately 3%) or enrolled in gifted
education programs (approximately 3%). Examinees classified as having learning, speech, hearing,
motor, or language difficulties were included in
validity studies. Standard scores were determined
for each age group by converting raw scores to
standard scores (i.e., $M = 100$, $SD = 15$) through
normalization and smoothing the distributions to
"eliminate minor irregularities" (manual, p. 35).
Appropriateness of the normalization procedure
and a detailed description of the equating procedure of Forms A and B were not provided.

Reliability of the NNAT-I scores was estimated using internal consistency reliability (coefficient alpha) and test-retest methods. Coefficient
alphas were provided for each age group and
ranged from .88 to .95 with an average of .91 for
Form A. Alphas for Form B based on a smaller
sample ($n = 394$) were .94, .93 for ages 5-8, and
.94 for ages 9-17. As the test is recommended for
use with many diverse groups, reliability coefficients reported by various subgroups would be
appropriate (AERA, APA, & NCME, 1999).
The standard error of the estimate for the NNAT-
I scale scores was reported for each age group with
a range of 3.19 to 4.57 ($M_{FormA} = 4.09$, $M_{FormB} = 3.57$). Confidence intervals based on estimated
true scores were provided for the standard scores.
Intervals for Form B were computed using the
alpha estimates from Form A. Test-retest reliability was reported for Form A based on examinees
($n = 200$) across age groups with a range of 14-49
days between tests. Values ranged from .71 to .78
($M = .73$). Parallel forms reliability for Form A
and Form B was examined ($n = 394$) with an
average of 24 days between tests. The average
value was .89, with values of .87 and .79 for the 5–
8- and 9–17-year-olds, respectively.

Several types of validity evidence were reported. Content validity evidence was provided by
the author, who created and reviewed all items,
and made a professional judgment about the validity of the item content. Other experts were involved in this process but their qualifications were
not provided. The correlation between the MAT-
EF and the NNAT-I ($r = .66$, $N = 90$) was
reported but does not provide validity evidence as
the "NNAT-I is a revised version of the MAT-

EF" (manual, p. 44) and some items appear in both tests. Samples of Hispanic and African American examinees were compared to matched White examinees on mean performance and revealed moderate to low differences (Cohen's d = .22 and .68, respectively), with White examinees scoring slightly higher. Based on this evidence, the author claims "this nonverbal test has utility for fair assessment of these diverse populations" (manual, p. 46). Mean differences or a lack of differences does not provide sufficient evidence that an instrument is fair or unbiased. Additionally, it is not clear why other subgroups were not examined. Investigations of differential item functioning or factor structure invariance would provide the appropriate evidence to support these claims.

Criterion-related validity evidence consisted of correlations between the NNAT-I scores and scores from several tests, including abstract reasoning tests (Raven's Standard Progressive Matrices; RSPM; Raven, Raven, & Court, 1998; and Test of Nonverbal Intelligence—Third Edition; TONI-3; Brown, Sherbenou, & Johnsen, 1997), an ability test (Wechsler Intelligence Scale for Children—Fourth Edition; WISC-IV; 2003), and an achievement test (Wechsler Individual Achievement Test—Second Edition; WIAT-II; The Psychological Corporation, 2002). Correlations between the RSPM and the NNAT-I and the TONI-3 and the NNAT-I were .71 and .56, respectively. Correlations of the NNAT-I with the 15 WISC-IV subtests ranged from .07 (Cancellation) to .65 (Matrix Reasoning). Additionally, correlations between the WIAT-II subscales and the NNAT-I ranged from .32 (Reading Composite) to .56 (Mathematics Composite). These correlations were low to moderate.

Other validity evidence consisted of the examination of mean differences between seven matched control groups and seven subgroups including individuals (a) in gifted programs, (b) classified with mental retardation, (c) classified with hearing impairments, (d) who do not speak English as their primary language, (e) classified with learning disabilities, (f) classified with language impairments, and (g) who were given instructions in Spanish. Examinees in gifted programs scored significantly higher whereas examinees classified as having mental retardation scored significantly lower than their respective control groups. No other significant differences

were found. However, there was a moderate difference (Cohen's d = .47), although not significant, between examinees classified as having hearing impairments and a control group. The hearing-impaired sample's higher scores were "unexpected and require further investigation" (manual, p. 52). No validity evidence was provided for the (a) prediction of school grades or classroom achievement, (b) functioning of items across groups, or (c) test structure.

COMMENTARY. The NNAT-I appears to be a useful and quick nonverbal measure of general ability. Evidence supports the use of the test as a component of the assessment process for identification of children who may be classified as gifted or having mental difficulties. However, a few main concerns should be mentioned. First, the NNAT-I does not provide information about verbal ability. This is of concern if scores are used to make judgments about or to predict student's academic achievement. [Editor's Note: The publisher emphasizes that the NNAT is NOT an achievement test.] Second, additional validity evidence is necessary. In particular, studies are recommended to examine (a) predictive validity for classroom achievement, (b) the test structure, and (c) item and structure invariance, especially as the test is claimed to be appropriate for several diverse populations. Third, even with adequate reliability and validity evidence, recommending scores for diagnostic purposes is difficult as the author states "a fundamental assumption underlying the use of the NNAT-I is that the examiner determines whether or not the test is an appropriate instrument for answering diagnostic question(s)" (manual, p. 43).

SUMMARY. The NNAT-I manual provides clear instructions for administration, scoring, and interpretation. The NNAT-I appears to be an acceptable instrument to obtain a quick estimate of general ability through nonverbal methods. The NNAT-I does have adequate psychometric properties for this purpose. However, further evaluation of these properties is warranted. The NNAT-I has the potential to become a very useful tool with certain populations of children with the support of additional validity evidence. Persons who need to use an individually administered, multidimensional nonverbal intelligence test may consider the Universal Nonverbal Intelligence Test (T6:2636; Bracken & McCallum, 1998).

REVIEWER'S REFERENCES

American Educational Research Association, American Psychological Association, & National Council on Measurement in Education. (1999). *Standards for educational and psychological testing.* Washington, DC: American Educational Research Association.

Bracken, B. A., & McCallum, R. S. (1998). Universal Nonverbal Intelligence Test. Itasca, IL: Riverside Publishing.

Brown, L., Sherbenou, R. J., & Johnsen, S. K. (1997). Test of Nonverbal Intelligence—Third Edition. Austin, TX: PRO-Ed.

Naglieri, J. A. (1985). Matrix Analogies Test—Expanded Form. San Antonio, TX: Psychological Corporation.

Naglieri, J. A. (1997). Naglieri Nonverbal Ability Test—Multilevel Form. San Antonio, TX: Psychological Corporation.

The Psychological Corporation. (2002). Wechsler Individual Achievement Test—Second Edition. San Antonio, TX: The Author.

Raven, J., Raven, J. C., & Court, J. H. (1998). *Manual for Raven's Standard Progressive Matrices and Vocabulary Scales.* Oxford, United Kingdom: Oxford Psychologists Press.

Wechsler, D. (2003). Wechsler Intelligence Scale for Children—Fourth Edition. San Antonio, TX: The Psychological Corporation.

[160]

National Survey of Student Engagement.

Purpose: Designed to provide colleges and universities information about the student experience and institutional performance to use to improve undergraduate education, inform accountability and accreditation efforts, and facilitate national and sector benchmarking efforts.

Population: Undergraduate students at 4-year colleges and universities.

Publication Dates: 2000–2002.

Acronym: NSSE.

Scores, 7: Level of Academic Challenge, Active and Collaborative Learning, Student Interactions with Faculty Members, Enriching Educational Experiences, Supportive Campus Environment, Background Information, Consortium Questions.

Administration: Group.

Price Data, 2002: $275 institutional participation fee and $2,700 to $6,000 student sampling fee (includes customized institutional report with means and frequency distribution by item, along with sector and national comparisons, response rates and sampling error, student response data on a CD-ROM, national report and institutional benchmarks of effective educational practice, and a sample presentation); $6 each for paper oversampling; $2 each for web-only mode oversampling for first 1,000 students and $1.50 each for additional students over 1,000; $1.50 for locally administered oversampling; additional fees for participating in consortium or special analyses; $30 per Technical and Norms Report (2001, 290 pages); $300 special peer comparison reports that compares institution against select group of 8–10 other participating institutions.

Time: (10–15) minutes.

Authors: George D. Kuh (test and technical report); J. C. Hayek, R. M. Carini, J. A. Oimet, R. M. Gonyea, and J. Kennedy (technical report).

Publisher: Indiana University Center for Postsecondary Research and Planning, Bloomington.

Review of the National Survey of Student Engagement by WILLIAM I. SAUSER, JR., Associate Dean and Professor, Business and Engineering Outreach, Auburn University, Auburn, AL:

DESCRIPTION. Are you searching for a professionally developed, independently administered measure of a college or university's undergraduate student learning environment, a measure that could replace or supplement popular guidebook or magazine rankings of colleges and universities? Do you agree that a high-quality learning environment for undergraduate students is one that (a) challenges students academically, (b) fosters active and collaborative learning, (c) encourages student interactions with faculty, (d) provides enriching educational experiences, and (e) maintains a supportive campus environment? Would you like to have access to a carefully constructed survey instrument that provides comparative and normative information for hundreds of colleges using data collected from hundreds of thousands of representative freshmen and seniors? If so, then you should give high consideration to the National Survey of Student Engagement (NSSE).

The NSSE makes use of a survey instrument known as the "College Student Report." The instrument consists of 95 (on the 2003 version) short, behaviorally based items for college students to rate on scales ranging from 2 to 7 points using a simple "mark the box" format. The items themselves are clearly worded and unambiguous; they are designed to measure the five aspects of a high-quality learning environment listed above, plus gather three overall estimates of satisfaction as well as demographic information used to build detailed normative tables. The instrument is available in paper and Web versions and takes about 15 minutes to complete. Its purpose, as stated in the *2002 Annual Report,* is to "provide data to colleges and universities to use for improving undergraduate education, inform state accountability and accreditation efforts, and facilitate national and sector benchmarking efforts" (p. 5). This reviewer believes this versatile instrument is singularly well developed to meet this purpose and several more, including those mentioned elsewhere (p. 7) in the *2002 Annual Report:* assessment and improvement, curricular reform, benchmarking, alumni outreach, accountability, advising, grant writing, institutional research, institutional advancement, accreditation, self-studies, retention, and state system performance reviews.

Beginning with the year 2000, when the NSSE moved from pilot-testing and development into full operation, 4-year colleges and universities have been invited to participate in an annual survey, using the "College Student Report," of representative samples of freshman and senior students. As of the *2002 Annual Report*, "more than 285,000 students at 618 different four-year colleges and universities" had participated, with "more than 400 schools...registered for the spring 2003 program" (p. 5). Once an institution has accepted the invitation to participate, the following action steps are taken: (a) The institution chooses mode of survey administration, either standard or Web only; (b) the institution provides information and materials to NSSE, including an institutional data file of all freshman and senior students from which NSSE selects a random sampling; (c) NSSE contacts students and collects surveys; (d) NSSE conducts follow-up with students, including survey tracking and contacts with nonrespondents (technical and norms report, pp. 42–43).

Once the national survey is complete, NSSE reports data using several formats. First, an annual report is issued summarizing findings from across the nation. The 2001 and 2002 reports supplied to this reviewer are well written in language understandable to general readers and higher education professionals alike. They provide benchmark data on five factors related to student learning (Level of Academic Challenge, Active and Collaborative Learning, Student-Faculty Interaction, Enriching Educational Experiences, Supportive Campus Environment); highlight key themes as well as both encouraging and disappointing findings from the composite data; and include anecdotes, case examples, and other information designed to encourage "best practices" in higher education. Each participating institution also receives a detailed individual report including analyses of each question on the survey plus comparative information using national and selected comparison group norms. The individual report is detailed enough that strengths and weaknesses can be pinpointed and action steps can be formulated to improve the learning environment. Other reporting formats include PowerPoint slides and informational brochures. The technical and norms report includes voluminous breakdowns of the data from almost

every perspective imaginable, plus normative data for freshmen and seniors on each item by gender, enrollment status, race, age, and major.

What kinds of questions are found on the survey? Here are a few representative ones: How often during the current school year have you made a class presentation? How often have you come to class without completing readings or assignments? How many reports of 20 pages or more have you written? Have you participated in community service or volunteer work? How many hours per week do you spend relaxing or socializing? To what extent does your institution emphasize using computers in academic work? If you could start over again, would you go to the *same institution* you are now attending?

DEVELOPMENT. Funded by charitable foundations and guided by "blue ribbon" technical and advisory panels, the developers of the NSSE have provided a textbook example of excellent practice in survey construction. The project began with a review of 25 years worth of literature on educational practices demonstrably effective in helping students learn (*2002 Annual Report*, p. 2). Experts whose works were reviewed include Alstete, Astin, Banta, Bloom, Chickering, Ewell, Goodsell, Johnson, Kuh, McKeachie, Pace, Pascarella, Sorcinelli, Terenzini, and The Wingspread Group, just to name a few (technical and norms report, pp. 282–283). The five benchmark categories were identified, and items exemplifying each benchmark were either written or "derived from other long-running, well-regarded college student research programs" (technical and norms report, p. 8). Because the NSSE relies on self-reports, the "College Student Report" was intentionally designed to meet five general conditions for validity spelled out in detail in the technical and norms report (pp. 8–9). Extensive pilot testing was then undertaken, followed by item analyses, reliability studies, and validity studies. Extensive norms tables were constructed following the inaugural (2000) national survey administration, and have been updated following each subsequent national survey.

TECHNICAL. The 288-page technical and norms report provides a wealth of information about the psychometric characteristics of the NSSE. The 20 "college activities" items found on the first page of the survey were subjected to a series of principal components factor analyses (oblique rotation) that produced a four-factor solution consisting of (a) student-faculty and student-student active learning; (b) engaging and educationally meaningful conversations; (c) cooperative communications among students, especially through technology; and (d) academic challenge. Similar factor analyses were employed to investigate the construct validity of the other portions of the survey, with similarly useful solutions.

Standardized item alpha reliability scores were .82 for the 20 college activities items, .88 for the 14 educational and personal growth items, and .83 for the 10 items measuring "opinions about your school" (pp. 16–17). Three different methods were employed to investigate reliability/stability. Correlations of concordance of institutional benchmark scores from 2000 and 2001 ranged from .83 to .92 for freshmen and .76 to .89 for seniors. Matched sample t-tests (from the 2000 and 2001 administrations) resulted in all coefficients being statistically significant, ranging from .60 to .96. A test-retest reliability study yielded a coefficient of .83 (N = 569) across all items (administration interval not reported). All in all, evidence indicates that the NSSE is a psychometrically sound instrument for the uses for which it was designed, measures what it is intended to measure, and yields interpretable benchmark scores for comparison across institutions.

COMMENTARY. This reviewer's highly positive impression of the NSSE can be gleaned from the glowing comments presented above. The developers of this instrument are to be applauded for constructing a survey that yields theoretically meaningful information in a highly pragmatic manner, for thoroughly documenting the development and psychometric qualities of the instrument, for packaging it in an attractive and useful manner, and for providing national and institutional-specific reports that can truly lead to positive change. Equally impressive are the many anecdotes, comments, and brief case studies found in the annual reports. These provide qualitative substance to the quantitative data presented in the reports.

SUMMARY. The developers of the NSSE set out to create an instrument that "documents dimensions of quality in undergraduate education and provides information and assistance to institutions and other organizations to improve student learning" (*2002 Annual Report,* p. 1). This reviewer believes they have succeeded admirably and commends this painstaking and important work.

Leaders of institutions of higher education who are serious about measuring and improving the learning climate for their undergraduate students are well advised to participate annually in the NSSE program. The cost to participate may be daunting to some institutions, but the wealth of information obtained-tailored to meet the needs of each participating institution-more than justifies the investment. The NSSE appears destined to become an indispensable survey for evaluating higher education across this nation.

Review of the National Survey of Student Engagement by EUGENE P. SHEEHAN, Dean, College of Education, University of Northern Colorado, Greeley, CO:

DESCRIPTION. The increased focus by institutes of higher education on accountability and assessment has resulted in the development of many measures of student performance, learning, and student satisfaction with their university experience. Universities employ grades, course-embedded assessments, licensure and professional examination results, student satisfaction questionnaires, and other indicators of transition point achievement both to assess student progress and to demonstrate institutional quality. Accreditation bodies such as The Higher Learning Commission and The National Council for Accreditation of Teacher Education place much emphasis on the collection and use of such data for program assessment and improvement.

The National Survey of Student Engagement (NSSE) is an instrument that provides very useful data to universities that can assist in program assessment, accreditation, and improvement. The survey is designed to provide universities with information about how often students engage in various activities including in-class (e.g., made a class presentation), course-related activities (e.g., number of drafts of papers students develop), and interactions with faculty (via e-mail and in advising sessions) and peers. Estimates of time spent on education and noneducation activities are also provided. Respondents indicate how much emphasis their coursework places on memorizing, analyzing, synthesizing, making judgments, and applying theories and also how much reading and writing they have done in their courses. The survey also requests students to reflect on how their educational experience has contributed to both their knowledge and personal development. The last three evaluative questions on the instrument ask students to provide summative ratings regarding academic advising and their entire educational experience at the institution and also to indicate the probability of attending their current institution again (if they could start over). A key feature of the NSSE is that the questions asked represent behaviors shown by the research to be related to positive learning and personal development outcomes.

The NSSE is administered to first-year and senior college students across the U.S. Thus, it permits institutions to make internal comparisons between new and more experienced students, assessments about the effectiveness of program changes over time, and comparisons with national norms. For those concerned with voluntary participation by students in studies of institutional quality, administration time is approximately 15 minutes.

There is an institutional participation fee of $275 and a student sampling fee that ranges from $2,250 to $5,000. These costs cover an institutional report that contains much useful information including descriptive statistics by item and national and sector comparisons. Further, the report indicates whether an institution's students differ significantly in their responses from students in aggregate groups. For an additional fee, institutions can obtain a report that compares the institution against a select group of other participating institutions.

DEVELOPMENT. The NSSE was initially funded by a grant from the Pew Charitable Trusts to Professor Kuh at Indiana University. The concept underlying this instrument is that the questions asked represent areas of the university experience (pertaining to, for example, academics, in-class activities, and advisement) that are central to student success. The word "engagement" in the survey title is a very accurate descriptor of the type of questions asked of students. The majority of the questions do measure the level of student engagement or involvement. The authors provide many references to research studies that support the assertion that level of engagement is directly related to quality of student learning and their total educational experience. Indeed, the research reviewed is extensive.

A technical report provides information regarding instrument development. Several drafts of the instrument were reviewed prior to pilot testing in 1999. The success of the pilot persuaded The Pew Charitable Trust to launch a national admin-istration. Focus groups and psychometric analyses informed revisions to the 2001 version.

TECHNICAL. The psychometric evidence provided in support of this instrument is impressive, both in terms of quantity and quality. Much effort has been devoted to a sophisticated analysis of the instrument, including an analysis of nonrespondents. The psychometric data are based on studies of large groups of respondents.

The technical and norms report provides descriptive statistics broken down by academic major, age, enrollment status, gender, and race for both first-year students and seniors. The report also contains information regarding response rates by several demographic variables. Clearly, the sample upon which the NSSE is normed matches the population for which the instrument is designed.

Reliability data show the NSSE to provide scores that are consistent. For example, the Cronbach's alpha coefficient for those items measuring college activities was a respectable .82. Other subscales have alpha coefficients of above .75. Interitem correlations are in the expected directions and are at appropriate levels. Estimates of stability over time are, for the most part, high. Similarly, overall test-retest for the NSSE was .83 (interval not provided).

Discussion of validity analyses are equally thorough. The technical and norms report contains a description of how items were selected to accurately assess the appropriate construct. Arguments regarding plausible and expected relationships between scales or between subgroups are also made. For example, patterns of responses between first-year students and seniors suggest the items have validity. The report also describes steps taken to assess the accuracy of the self-report data provided. Overall, the psychometric evidence presented indicates the NSSE can accomplish its purpose—to assess student engagement along several dimensions.

COMMENTARY. The NSSE provides universities with valuable information concerning student engagement. The instrument is based on the robust theoretical assumption that student engagement is predictive of student success and student satisfaction with the university experience.

The impact of an instrument such as the NSSE can be gauged by the number of uses of the instrument and ease with which the data can be used. The materials provided in support of the instrument are excellent. They provide thoughtful examples and suggestions of how the data from the survey might be used. Indeed, this is one of the main strengths of the instrument. The data generated by the NSSE can be used for several purposes at different institutional levels. The data certainly will aid assessment, accountability, and accreditation efforts at the college and university level. Individual programs and departments will also find the data useful as they reflect on the responses of students to questions about writing in courses or about the availability and friendliness of faculty advisors. Individual faculty members will, in turn, be able to adjust their teaching and advising behaviors. The NSSE can be used to close the feedback loop in assessment: Recommendations for program improvement and enhancement should be obvious from the data provided.

SUMMARY. University administrators seeking ways to collect meaningful information regarding student learning and student satisfaction will find the NSSE to be just the instrument they are looking for. The NSSE is based on a well-researched link between student engagement and student success. The instrument is psychometrically sound—the survey developers have devoted much effort to ensure the standardization, reliability, and validity of the instrument all meet high standards. Best of all, the NSSE can be used for many functions by many groups across a university campus.

[161]
Neale Analysis of Reading Ability: Second Revised British Edition.

Purpose: Designed to measure reading accuracy, comprehension and rate and to provide diagnostic information about children's reading difficulties.
Population: Ages 6-0 to 12-11.
Publication Dates: 1958–1997.
Acronym: NARA II.
Scores, 3: Comprehension, Accuracy, Rate; plus 4 supplementary diagnostic scores (Discrimination of Initial and Final Sounds, Names and Sounds of the Alphabet, Graded Spelling, Auditory Discrimination and Blending).
Administration: Individual.
Forms, 3: 1, 2, Diagnostic Tutor Form (not norm referenced).
Price Data: Available from publisher.
Time: (20) minutes.
Comments: Revision includes new norms and larger standardization sample.
Authors: Marie D. Neale (test and manual); Second Revised British Edition and standardization by Chris Whetton, Louise Caspall, and Kay McCulloch.

Publisher: NFER-Nelson Publishing Co., Ltd. [England].
Cross References: See T5:1765 (36 references) and T4:1714 (7 references); for reviews by Cleborne D. Maddux and G. Michael Poteat of an earlier edition, see 11:257 (41 references); see also T3:1567 (13 references) and T2:1683 (7 references); for reviews by M. Alan Brimer and Magdalen D. Vernon, and an excerpted review, see 6:843.

Review of the Neale Analysis Of Reading Ability: Second Revised British Edition by MARIE MILLER-WHITEHEAD, School of Education, University of North Alabama, Florence, AL:

DESCRIPTION. The Neale Analysis of Reading Ability: Second Revised British Edition (NARA II) is a standardized, norm-referenced, individual measure of reading comprehension, oral reading fluency, and accuracy for use with children from the ages of 6 to 12. However, the assessment has been used with older students and adults for diagnostic purposes. The assessment yields scores for Rate, Accuracy, and Comprehension of oral reading skills for six levels of graded reading passages. A full-page illustration accompanies each reading passage. The test consists of two forms (6 reading passages each) and 7 supplementary diagnostic reading passages, for a total of 19 reading passages. With the exception of the Level 1 passage, which has four comprehension questions, all other Levels have eight questions. Although most of the comprehension questions are factual, several require that the student make an inference or prediction. Students do not see or hear the questions prior to reading the passage. Supplementary diagnostic tests measure discrimination of initial, medial, and final sounds; names and sounds of the alphabet; graded spelling; and auditory discrimination and blending.

The author estimates that a standardized assessment using the NARA II should take about 20 minutes. Reading topics are of general interest, and although the assessment is specifically designated as the British Edition, there are few examples of vocabulary or spelling that would differentiate reading passages from their American counterparts. These variants include the use of hyphenation of words such as no-one and tea-time. Materials consist of a spiral-bound reader, a manual for schools, and individual records forms for each of the two test forms and the diagnostic tutor. There is a separate manual for psychological services, which the publisher indicates provides more detailed information than previous editions. However, the manual for schools includes conversion tables so that scores can be reported with 68% confidence bands for Reading Age. The manual also provides information about the NARA II norm populations, and test reliability and validity evidence for this latest edition. A demonstration cassette accompanies the materials.

The manual for schools provides detailed directions for administration of the test and includes a list of essential equipment the examiner will need, as well as explicit instructions for timing and computing the reading rate. Directions for establishing a basal level are provided, with directions to give students full credit for all levels below the established basal level. Each level consists of progressively longer reading passages. In this edition the Level 1 reading selection contains 26 words and the Level 6 selection has either 139 or 141, depending upon whether it is Form 1 or 2. The Diagnostic Tutor has an additional set of nine reading passages (two passages for Level 1–3), also of increasing length and difficulty, and an Extension Passage. A Level 1 passage had a reading grade level of 1.5 according to the Flesch-Kincaid readability index and a Level 6 passage had a reading grade level of 12.6, more because of difficulty of vocabulary than because of complex syntactical structures. The Diagnostic Tutor includes passages for Levels 1 through 6 and an Extension Passage that had a reading grade level of 16 on the Flesch-Kincaid index.

A limitation of this test is that several of the Supplementary Diagnostic Tests contain relatively few items; for example, there are just eight pairs each for discrimination of beginning, medial, and ending phonemes. The Supplementary Diagnostic Tests are not standardized and, according to the publisher, should not take the place of hearing and vision tests administered by professionals in these areas. However, because the manual for schools includes multiple ways that scores can be reported to parents, test results may assist parents in obtaining specialized help for their children who differ markedly from the norm on the standardized tests. Score discrepancy tables for comparison of NARA II scores and scores on the British Ability Scales, Second Edition (BAS II) provide some guidance for those who do not have a copy of the Manual for Psychological Services. For example, a child younger than 8 years of age who received a standard score on the BAS II of between 100–104 and a NARA II score of ≤ 88 would have a significantly low NARA II, because the expected range of corresponding NARA II scores is between 92–110. On the other hand, NARA II scores ≥ 112 would be significantly higher than expected, given a BAS II of 100–104 for the same child.

DEVELOPMENT. According to the publisher, since its inception in 1958, the NARA II has become one of the most widely used reading tests in the United Kingdom, Australia, and New Zealand. The test has undergone several revisions since 1958, with the 1996 revision prompted by the introduction of a national curriculum in the U.K. and the publisher's subsequent need to restandardize and renorm the assessment. Because some of the norm population also took the Phonological Assessment Battery and the British Ability Scales, Second Edition, correlations between these scores and the NARA II are available. Also, the publisher included more schools and students in the present standardization than in previous versions of the assessment.

TECHNICAL. The NARA II was standardized on a representative stratified random sample of nearly 3,500 children representing 610 schools over a period of 7 years, twice as many as the previous edition. Parallel form reliability estimates were highest for Accuracy, ranging from .84 for age 10–11:11 to .92 for age 6–7:11, followed by Comprehension, ranging from .65 for age 12-12:11 to .87 for age 6-7:11. Lowest parallel form reliability estimates were for Rate, ranging from .50 for ages 12–12:11 to .83 for ages 10–11:11. The manual also reports parallel form reliability values for two presentation orders; there was no evidence of a presentation order effect on the reliability coefficients. Internal consistency as measured by Cronbach's alpha was higher for Comprehension, ranging from .93 to .95 for the 44 questions, than for Accuracy, ranging from .81 to .88 for six reading passages. The manual for schools also provides mean raw score and standard deviations for each age group, each reading passage, and each form of the test, with numbers of participating students. Scores are disaggregated by gender only for each age group for Form 1 and Form 2. Correlations with other assessments and evidence of predictive validity are provided in the NARA II Manual for Psychological Services.

COMMENTARY. I liked the publisher's use of color-coding the forms of the test; this is particularly helpful if the alternate forms will be used as a pretest and posttest. The results of the Auditory Discrimination and Blending test may certainly be indicative of a child's ability to identify English phonemes. Published studies that examine correlations between reading rate and comprehension (O'Connor & Hermelin, 1994) and reading training and comprehension (McGee & Johnson, 2003; Reason & Morfidi, 2001; Sen & Blatchford, 2001) have found various subscales of the NARA series helpful as a dependent variable, often in conjunction with another literacy or ability assessment.

A difference between the NARA II and some other tests of reading comprehension is that students do not see or hear the comprehension questions prior to reading the comprehension passages. Some students may be more concerned about rate and fluency than about comprehension, although they are instructed that they will be asked about what they have read. Therefore, comparison of student comprehension scores on the NARA II and on an assessment that presents questions prior to reading might provide helpful information about student retention of reading material.

SUMMARY. This assessment is nicely packaged, and the score reports are relatively simple to complete and compute. I would recommend this test only for the users for which it was developed. A similar assessment, designed for use with a wider range of age groups, is the Gray Oral Reading Tests—Fourth Edition (GORT—IV; 15:111). Those who do use the NARA II should review the demonstration cassette carefully, as it may answer the kinds of questions that usually arise during an actual test administration.

REVIEWER'S REFERENCES

McGee, A., & Johnson, H. (2003). The effect of inference training on skilled and less skilled comprehenders. *Educational Psychology, 23*, 49–59.
O'Connor, N., & Hermelin, B. (1994). Two autistic savant readers. *Journal of Autism and Developmental Disorders, 24*, 501–515.
Reason, R., & Morfidi, E. (2001). Literacy difficulties and single-case experimental design. *Educational Psychology in Practice, 17*, 227–244.
Sen, R., & Blatchford, P. (2001). Reading in a second language: Factors associated with progress in young children. *Educational Psychology, 21*, 189–202.

Review of the Neale Analysis of Reading Ability: Second Revised British Edition BY ELIZABETH KELLEY RHOADES, Associate Professor of Psychology, West Texas A & M University, Canyon, TX:

DESCRIPTION. The Neale Analysis of Reading Ability: Second Revised British Edition is an individually administered test of children's oral reading abilities in three areas—accuracy of decoding skills, comprehension, and the speed or rate of reading. The test is designed to provide both normative data on the individual child's reading achievement and diagnostic information to assist in designing interventions for the struggling reader, ages 6 to 12.

The test includes two alternate forms, Form 1 (gold) and Form 2 (green). Each form consists of two sample passages and a series of six graded passages that the child reads aloud while receiving prompting and correction by the examiner. The child's reading is timed and all errors are noted and analyzed by category. The child is then asked a series of questions following each passage. These raw scores for each section are totaled and the examiner uses a chart to determine standard scores in the areas of Accuracy, Comprehension, and Rate. Percentile ranks, confidence bands, stanines, and reading age equivalents may also be obtained. Each form also includes a set of Supplementary Diagnostic Tests that provide nonstandardized measures of the child's skills in the areas of auditory discrimination of beginning and ending sounds, alphabet naming and letter/sound associations, spelling, and auditory discrimination and blending.

In addition to Forms 1 and 2, which provide normative data, the Diagnostic Tutor Form (blue) contains further reading passages at levels similar to those found in Forms 1 and 2. The examiner is encouraged to use these passages for further analysis of the child's reading behaviors and errors. This nonstandardized form has no norms.

DEVELOPMENT. The Neale Analysis of Reading Ability: Second Revised British Edition is a revision of the Neale Analysis of Reading Ability, first published in 1958. The test has undergone several revisions including the development of versions appropriate for use in Australia, England, and Wales. The current instrument is a revision designed to address changes in instructional methods and reading standards in England and Wales (owing to the introduction of the National Curriculum) and to provide current norms.

TECHNICAL. The test standardization occurred during the summer of 1996 during the final school term. The norm group included approximately 3,500 children for Forms A and B, with about 2,000 girls and 1,500 boys from schools across Scotland, Northern Ireland, England, and

Wales. The norm group was found to be relatively close to national data in terms of metropolitan versus nonmetropolitan schools, type of schools, and area of the country. The match was somewhat less satisfactory in terms of the percentage of free school meals and National Curriculum Assessment results, requiring weighting of the sample.

One area of concern in the test administration is the lack of a clearly specified ceiling. Although the examiner must stop testing when the child makes 16 or 20 errors on a passage (the number specified by the passage's difficulty level), he or she may stop earlier when the child has made as few as 8 errors and the child has "had difficulty" with the practice passage or the evaluator believes that the child "would be unable to master the next level of difficulty" (manual for schools, p. 11).

Test reliability was measured through the use of alternate forms testing for 364 children in the normative sample. Correlations between alternate forms of the test on the Accuracy measure ranged from .92 to .84 across the various age groups, with an average of .89. Comprehension scores across Forms 1 and 2 correlated from .65 to .87, with an average of .82. Rate scores correlated from .50 to .83 across the forms, with an average of .66.

Reliability was further measured through an examination of internal consistency. Cronbach's coefficient alpha for the Accuracy items ranged from .81 to .88 and from .93 to .95 for the Comprehension items. No test/retest data were provided (using the same test form).

The test appears to have content validity for the content area—oral reading skills. There is no evidence that it has any validity as a measure of a child's silent reading performance. Thus, it may be useful primarily at the beginning levels of reading instruction and achievement. No evidence on the measure's correlations with other reading tests is provided in the Manual for Schools although they are described in the NARA Manual for Psychological Services. There was no evidence presented of the test's correlations with other, nontest measures of reading such as grades or teacher ratings, nor any evidence of the measure's ability to predict later reading performance in the classroom.

COMMENTARY. The Neale Analysis of Reading Ability: Second Revised British Edition has many positive attributes. The test includes a demonstration cassette, an audiotape that provides examples of test administration and teacher prompts and corrections. This is a nice tool for the novice examiner or the psychologist with less experience in providing cues during a child's oral reading. The directions are clear and easy. The administration of the Phonological Assessment Battery and portions of the British Ability Scales—Second Edition to a subset of the children in the norm group provides some useful data for comparisons. The practice passages provide assurance that the test participant can understand the appropriate response set required before test items begin to count towards the actual score. Analysis of the child's oral reading errors and examination of the categories into which these errors fall should provide useful diagnostic information for individualized reading instruction.

However, much useful information on the test's standardization and psychometric characteristics is generally not provided to the individual test user/purchaser. These data are presented in the NARA Manual for Psychological Services that must be obtained separately. The alternate forms reliability on the Rate measure is relatively low and therefore results should be interpreted with caution. It may be useful only as a diagnostic measure. It appears that the test may be most useful at the early stages of reading development because it does not measure silent reading performance that is a key ability in the skilled reader.

Although the test materials are well designed and easy to use, they are not particularly attractive. The pictures in the reader are in black and white and there is little to grab a child's interest.

SUMMARY. The Neale Analysis of Reading Ability: Second Revised British Edition is a brief (about 20 minutes) individually administered measure of children's oral reading skills, specifically accuracy, comprehension, and the speed of reading. It may provide some useful data about a beginning reader's word attack and comprehension skills when reading aloud. It may be less useful for the more advanced or skillful reader.

[162]

Neurobehavioral Functioning Inventory.

Purpose: "Designed to measure the frequency of neurobehavioral problems associated with traumatic brain injury and other neurological disorders."

Population: Patients ages 17 and older.

Publication Date: 1999.

Acronym: NFI.

Scores, 6: Depression, Somatic, Memory/Attention, Communication, Aggression, Motor.
Administration: Individual or group.
Price Data, 2002: $137 per complete kit including manual (120 pages), 25 Family record forms, and 25 Patient record forms; $79 per manual; $39 per 25 record forms (Family or Patient).
Time: (30) minutes.
Comments: Self-scoring self-report forms.
Authors: Jeffrey S. Kreutzer, Ronald T. Seel, and Jennifer H. Marwitz.
Publisher: PsychCorp, A brand of Harcourt Assessment, Inc.

Review of the Neurobehavioral Functioning Inventory by RAYMOND S. DEAN, George and Frances Ball Distinguished Professor of Neuropsychology, Neuropsychology Laboratory, Ball State University, and JOHN J. BRINKMAN, JR., Associate Director, Neuropsychology Laboratory, Ball State University, Muncie, IN:

DESCRIPTION. The Neurobehavioral Functioning Inventory (NFI) is a 76-item self-administered test designed to describe neurobehavioral functioning in patients 16 years and older. It was developed to complement psychological and neuropsychological measures by providing relevant information on the presence and frequency of behaviors characteristic of individuals with head injuries and neurological disabilities that impact daily living (e.g., depression, aggression, attention).

The NFI is written in English and self-administered in approximately 20 to 40 minutes. The 76 items contribute to the six scales. These scales include Depression, Somatic, Memory/Attention, Communication, Aggression, and Motor. Items reflective of each scale are scattered throughout the instrument to avoid a response bias. The NFI also includes 6 Critical Items independent of the six scales. The 6 Critical Items include: Blackout Spells, Seizures, Threatens to Hurt Self, Cannot Be Left at Home Alone, Misses or Cannot Attend Work/School, and Double or Blurred Vision. These items call attention to the severity of symptoms and need for immediate intervention.

As noted above, six neurobehavioral scales are identified in the NFI. The content of each scale is based on characteristic symptoms/behaviors of the respective scale. For example, the Depression scale includes helplessness, low self-esteem, anhedonia, social isolation and discomfort, frustration, rumination, and fearfulness. The Somatic scale includes headaches, appetite and digestive difficulties, inner ear problems, and sleep disturbance. The Memory/Attention scale contains symptoms of forgetfulness, poor concentration, distractibility, confusion, and disorientation. Difficulties in speech initiation and execution and problems with spelling, reading, and writing constitute the Communication scale. The Aggression scale reflects behavioral tendencies toward argumentativeness, verbal and physical abusiveness, and destructiveness. Physical slowness and weakness, incoordination, and balance disturbances are Motor scale symptoms. Identification of specific symptoms and behaviors are meant to provide information on neurobehavioral functioning, guide report writing, and aid in the conceptualization of diagnostic and treatment implications.

Two parallel forms of the NFGI are offered, one to be completed by the patient and the other by a family member or a knowledgeable informant. The Patient Form and the Family Form are to be filled out separately with collaborative efforts discouraged. Responses to items are meant to reflect the patient's "current level of functioning." The items on each form are endorsed and their frequency noted on a 5-point Likert-type scale with responses ranging from *never* to *always*. Normative tables for both forms are provided based on the patient's age and the amount of time he or she remained unconscious at the time of injury. Beyond normative comparisons, the NFI can be analyzed and interpreted through qualitative item analysis and thematic considerations.

Nonclinical personnel may administer and score the test protocol. However, only licensed professionals should interpret the NFI. Further, the results should be interpreted within the context of a comprehensive examination including a review of records, patient history, emotional status examination, and measures of cognitive and sensorimotor functioning.

Scoring and interpretation for both forms, patient and informant, are completed in the same fashion. Scoring is done by hand and facilitated by the *Ready to Score Answer* document. Scores provided include a total raw score, percentile rank, and *T*-score. Endorsement of Critical Items is also recorded on a record form for qualitative interpretation. Total raw scores are computed by summing the Likert values for items on each individual scale. Raw scores for each scale are then converted to *T*-scores and percentile ranks. The total raw score, percentile rank, and *T*-score are recorded on the profile page along with a graphic representation of the *T*-score profile. Guidelines are provided for addressing missing data, scoring protocols, and interpreting valid profiles.

Scores may be interpreted in three ways: through qualitative analysis, scale scores related to neurobehavioral themes, and normative comparison. The first type of interpretation, qualitative analysis, involves the interpretation of individual items to identify extreme response sets, endorsement of critical items, and a comparison of the patient's and informant's item responses. Extreme responses (i.e., *Never* or *Always*) for almost all items should be interpreted with caution. Extreme response sets may reflect a patient's or informant's attempt to present the patient in a positive or negative manner. When critical items are endorsed, a follow-up interview with the patient is recommended to address the presence and severity of these symptoms and to determine the need for immediate attention or intervention. An interpretation of the comparison of the patient's and informant's individual item responses may also be done to identify differences in their perceptions of problems.

The second type of interpretation involves the analysis of scale scores for the identified scales: Depression, Somatic, Memory/Attention, Communication, Aggression, and Motor. Scale score analysis includes identifying areas of least and greatest concern, correspondence between the perceptions of impairment and medical data, agreement between patient's and informant's perceptions of impairment, and changes over time. Areas of least and greatest concern allow for the identification of the frequency of problem behaviors and those areas that require attention. An analysis of the correspondence between the perceptions of impairment and available medical data provide information on expected results, as the scores should be consistent. Lower scores may reflect impaired awareness, denial, or attempts to present the patient in a positive manner. Higher scores may reflect an attempt to exaggerate symptoms, extreme psychological distress, or a "cry for help" (Kreutzer, Seel, & Marwitz, 1999). An analysis of the agreement between the patient's and informant's scores provides information about their perceptions of adjustment among the six scales. High agreement represents similar points of view, whereas low agreement may repre-

sent limited awareness, denial, or an attempt to obtain secondary gain.

Finally, the patient's profile can be compared to a normative sample of patients for frequency of patient difficulties. The normative sample is composed of patients of similar age and severity of impairment. The patient's scale score can be compared to matched peers and divided into five categories based on this comparison. The categories include: Very High (>1.5 *SD* above the mean); High (>2/3 *SD* above the mean); Average (2/3 *SD* above or below the mean); Low (>2/3 *SD* below the mean); and Very Low (>1.5 *SD* below the mean).

DEVELOPMENT. The NFI represents the third phase of development for the original inventory, the Brain Injury Problem Checklist (BIPC). The original version was developed in the 1980s and consisted of 105 items. This inventory was organized into five categories based on face validity. The original categories included Somatic, Cognitive, Behavior, Communication, and Social problems. The original items were developed by a review of the literature on outcomes after neurological injury, a review of the content of existing neurobehavioral assessment protocols, and by interviewing patients and family members regarding the patient's symptoms. In the original version, items were endorsed using a Likert-type scale responding to one of four answers: *Never, Sometimes, Often,* or *Always.*

The second phase of test development included using principal components and confirmatory factor analytic methodology to create the NFI. The second version consisted of only 70 items from the original 105-item BIPC. The reduction in test items was due to a two-step decision rule for inclusion of test items. First, inclusion was based on having factors with loadings of .40 or higher. Second, to maintain independence between scales, items had to have a loading of .09 or higher than the loadings on all other scales for inclusion. The 70 items broke down into six categories that included Depression, Somatic Difficulties, Memory/Attention Difficulties, Communication Deficits, Aggressive Behaviors, and Motor Impairment. This second version also provided reliability and validity estimates. Research supported internal consistency within the scales and criterion-related validity. The authors also suggested that the scales were correlated logically with other measures of neurobehavioral functioning (Kreutzer, Marwitz, Seel, & Serio, 1996; Kreutzer et al., 1999).

The third phase of development represented the final version of the NFI. This version is the same as the second version with the addition of the six Critical Items and the expansion of the Likert-type scale to include the choice, "Rarely." The six Critical Items were included so that the severity of symptoms and need for immediate intervention was called to attention. The choice "Rarely" was added between "Never" and "Sometimes" to reduce the asymmetrical distribution of item responses thereby reducing the positive skew originally found in the distribution.

TECHNICAL. The NFI was normed on a sample of 520 patients and 520 informants referred for services at an outpatient Level I trauma center. No regional information was provided about where data collection occurred. The sample ranged in age from 4–81 years at time of injury with a mean age of 31.3 years (SD = 12.7). The sample contained both males (66%) and females (34%) and was broken down by ethnic background: 77% were Caucasian, 21% were African American, and 2% were from other ethnic backgrounds. No information was provided on the level of education for the sample. Medical data were collected on the sample population with 80% of the patients in the sample having been involved in vehicular accidents. Length of time in a coma was recorded for the sample population with a mean of 14.6 days (SD = 33.1) and a median of .25 days. Evaluations were performed, on average, 2.9 years post-injury with a median of 1.3 years.

Reliability was estimated using interrater reliability and internal consistency. No estimate of test-retest reliability was conducted due to the variability of neurobehavioral symptoms changing over short periods of time (e.g., from day to day). Interrater reliability was evaluated by comparing the agreement of ratings for the patient and the ratings of the patient by the informant. Interrater reliability was estimated with five studies using a sample of 301 pairs of patients and informants. The first study looked at the percent of agreement between the patient and the informant for the 70 items. The percentage of agreement ranged from 48% to 84% with no more than 35% of the patients rating their problems as occurring more frequently than the informants' ratings. The authors concluded that the patient and the informant rated problems with equal frequency.

The second study looked at the frequency of difference between the patients' and the informants' responses for each of the 70 items. Pairs of responses were evaluated by subtracting the Likert-type patients' rating from the informants' Likert-type rating. No difference in scores indicated that the informant and the patient rated the problem occurring at the same frequency. Analysis revealed that paired responses with identical scores (i.e., a zero difference score) ranged from 55% to 69%. Ninety-two percent of the paired responses had either exact agreement or a difference of 1 point. The authors again concluded that the patients and the informants rated problems with equal frequency.

The third study analyzed the differences between the patients' rating and the informants' rating by matched pair t tests for each of the 70 items. The analysis revealed no statistical difference between the ratings for 57 of the 70 items with 13 showing statistical differences. The differences were attributed to patients rating items as occurring more frequently than the informants' ratings, with Communication and Memory/Attention having the largest differences.

The fourth study analyzed the differences between the patients' and the informants' mean NFI scale score. For this analysis, six-matched pair t tests were conducted and no statistical differences were found for five of the six mean scale scores. The sixth scale score, Communication, showed a significant difference with the informants' scores being significantly less than the patients' scores.

The last study analyzed the difference of the patients' scores and the informants' scores by injury severity. Injury severity was based on the number of days a patient was unconscious. The groups were as follows: Mild = 20 minutes or less (n = 161); Moderate = greater than 20 minutes and less than 24 hours (n = 21); Severe = greater than or equal to 24 hours and less than 7 days (n = 20); Very Severe = 7 days or greater (n = 47). One-way analyses of variance were conducted on the mean difference scores for each of the six scales. The independent variable was injury severity. Significant differences were observed for three of the scales: Memory/Attention, Communication, and Motor. Internal consistency reliability estimates were also computed using coefficient alpha. The internal consistency reliability estimates obtained within each scale ranged from r = .86 to r = .95

with an estimate for all items exceeding $r = .97$. Although these correlations seem high, the test authors expected such results due to the majority of patients in the sample having experienced diffuse impairment (i.e., closed head injury).

Validity of scores from the NFI was estimated examining the criterion-related validity between the NFI and selected neuropsychological tests and the NFI and selected clinical scales of the Minnesota Multiphasic Personality Inventory—2 (MMPI-2). Bivariate correlations were conducted between the NFI and the following neuropsychological tests: the Rey Auditory Verbal Learning Test, Wechsler Memory Scale—Third Edition, Gray Oral Reading Test, Controlled Oral Word Association Test, Symbol Digit Modalities Test, and the Grooved Pegboard. For statistical analysis, each measure was assigned to one of three groups to include (a) attention, memory, learning; (b) visuoperception and motor functioning; and (c) language and communication functioning. Correlations of the NFI and neuropsychological assessment instruments were conducted using the scores from the NFI Family Record Form. The first study evaluated Group 1 (attention, memory, and learning) and found that the Communication scale of the NFI correlated significantly ($p<.001$) with five measures including: the Rey Auditory Verbal Learning ($r = -.18$), MCV Paragraph Immediate Recall ($r = -.24$), MCV Paragraph Delayed Recall ($r = -.21$), Wechsler Memory Immediate Recall ($r = -.34$), and Wechsler Memory Delayed Recall ($r = -.32$). The second study evaluated Group 2 (visual and motor functioning) and also found that the Communication scale correlated significantly ($p<.001$) with two scores from the Symbolic Digit Modalities-Oral test ($r = -.31$) and the Grooved Pegboard test ($r = .20$). Further, significant scores were found between the NFI Memory/Attention scale score and the Symbol Digit Modalities Test-Oral test ($r = -.18$). The third study evaluated Group 3 (language and communication functioning) and again found that the Communication scale score correlated significantly ($p<.001$) with scores from the Gray Oral Reading Test-Comprehension ($r = -.20$), Controlled Oral Word Association test ($r = -.21$), and the Gray Oral Reading Test—Accuracy ($r = -.26$).

The criterion-related validity studies on the NFI and the MMPI-2 included only five of the clinical scales in the MMPI-2 because of their sensitivity to brain injury populations. These included Hypochondriasis (Scale 1), Depression (Scale 2), Hysteria (Scale 3), Psychasthenia (Scale 7), and Schizophrenia (Scale 8). The correlations for the MMPI-2 scales and the NFI scales were as follows: Scale 1 was most related to scores on the Somatic ($r = .65$) and Motor ($r = .53$) NFI scales; Scale 2 was related to all six NFI scale scores ($r = .18$ to .34); Scale 3 was related to Somatic Complaints ($r = .50$) and Motor Difficulties ($r = .42$); Scale 7 was related to Depression ($r = .43$) and Somatic Complaints ($r = .40$); and Scale 8 was related to Depression ($r = .40$) and Memory/Attention ($r = .36$).

COMMENTARY. There are many advantages to using the NFI as a measure of neurobehavioral functioning. First, the NFI is an easy-to-administer inventory as it is self-administered. Second, the test can be given in a relatively short period of time, taking approximately only 20 to 40 minutes to complete. Third, it is relatively easy to score as it uses the *Ready Score Answer Document* requiring a transfer of only a few numbers to the scoring and profile pages. Fourth, it provides a comprehensive interpretation with three distinct ways to interpret the scores. Fifth, it provides useful scales with behavioral and symptom identification that guide intervention and treatment planning and contain critical items necessary in evaluating the patient's current level of functioning and possible need for immediate intervention. Finally, having both a Patient Form and a Family Form allows for the collection of the patient's symptoms even if the patient is unable to provide accurate information due to impaired self-awareness or denial. In addition, having parallel forms may discourage patients or family members looking to obtain secondary gain.

Despite all of the advantages of the NFI, there are three shortcomings. First, the NFI does not provide any suggestions for intervention and treatment planning for the scales discussed. Second, the authors should have employed other measures of reliability such as test-retest reliability. The authors make a point to explain why they did not use test-retest reliability as neurobehavioral symptoms are variable and change over short periods of time. Yet, research does not agree with such variability after a period of 2+ years. It would have been advantageous to employ a sample of patients with symptoms that would have remained relatively stable over time (e.g., patients with post-stroke depression). Third, of the six scales, only the Communication scale provided criterion-related validity with other neuropsychological tests. This calls into questions the appropriateness of the other scales as measures of neurobehavioral functioning, suggesting that additional studies need to be conducted with more appropriate neuropsychological tests. Moreover, the higher validity estimates found with the MMPI-2 may differentiate the NFI as a measure of emotional functioning rather than a test of neurobehavioral functioning.

Further, the use of the NFI as a measure of neurobehavioral functioning appears to be a well-designed measure of associated symptoms for patients who have endured brain injury. However, the NFI should be interpreted with caution for two important reasons. First, the generalizability of the NFI may be questionable as the standardization sample consisted of a majority of patients who had a brain injury due to a vehicular accident. Thus, further investigation is needed to assess the generalizability of the NFI to a wider array of neuropsychological disorders. Second, only a modest amount of data was collected on older adults over the age of 45 and little information was provided on diseases associated with aging populations. Therefore, an interpretation of diseases associated with aging (e.g., dementia) may be inadequate. Alternatively, if the NFI can be demonstrated to be a generalized measure of brain damage, then it may prove to be an established measure of neurobehavioral functioning and could provide an array of clinical uses across a range of disorders.

SUMMARY. The NFI is a measure used to assess "neurobehavioral" functioning, which includes behaviors that are characteristic following neurological impairment. The NFI is composed of six scales (Depression, Somatic, Memory/Attention, Communication, Aggression, and Motor) and has a set of "critical items." The NFI includes two parallel forms, one to be completed by the patient and the other by a family member or a knowledgeable informant. The NFI may be used as an adjunct to a comprehensive neuropsychological examination or as a screening tool to identify if additional assessment is required. Further, the NFI may be used as an overall quality of life measure and for treatment recommendations. The NFI is easy to administer and score, and provides three distinct ways to interpret scores. Though it provides useful scales with behavioral and symptom identification that guides intervention and treatment planning, no suggestions for intervention and treatment planning for the scales were discussed. It has modest reliability and validity estimates that need to be further investigated. Though the generalizability of the measure to all neuropsychological disorders, including those associated with an aging population, may be questionable, further studies could prove to establish this measure as a standard in the assessment of brain injury.

REVIEWERS' REFERENCES
Kreutzer, J. S., Marwitz, J. H., Seel, R., & Serio, C. D. (1996). Validation of a neurobehavioral functioning inventory for adults with traumatic brain injury. *Archives of Physical Medicine and Rehabilitation, 77*(2), 116-124.
Kreutzer, J. S., Seel, R. T., & Marwitz, J. H. (1999). Neurobehavioral Functioning Inventory. San Antonio: The Psychological Corporation.

Review of the Neurobehavioral Functioning Inventory by THOMAS McKNIGHT, Psychologist, Private Practice, Spokane, WA:

DESCRIPTION. The Neurobehavioral Functioning Inventory (NFI) is a self-report instrument, designed to "complement psychological and neuropsychological tests" (manual, p. 4) by providing information about patient symptoms, problems with daily living, and functional limitations, noted by the patient, family members, and other close acquaintances. It describes a "wide spectrum" (manual, p. 5) of post-injury behaviors and symptoms related to neurological damage that are encountered daily by patients and family members or caretakers. The NFI was developed with factor analytic techniques to "empirically reveal unidimensional scales" (manual, p. 5) associated with neurological impairment. The NFI addresses the limitations of earlier neurobehavioral assessment tools, involving issues related to interrater reliability, construct validity, and criterion-related validity.

According to the manual, the NFI can be used to measure the frequency of specific problems reported by patients and others; describe performance in broader functional categories; identify discrepancies of the patient's functioning, perceived by various responders; compare reported daily living problems with performance on rather traditional neuropsychological measures; and provide useful information about the patient's overall quality of life. The authors note interpretation of the NFI is "best accomplished by a licensed mental health professional" (manual, p. 7) and interpreted in conjunction with other information about the patient. The instrument consists of a Patient Form and a Family Form, each with the same 76 symptoms, rated: "never, rarely, sometimes, often, always" (manual, p. 6). It is designed to be used with patients, age 16 or older, who have known or suspected brain injury. Responses are purely subjective and respondents are not given any guidelines for the meaning of the choices on the rating scale.

DEVELOPMENT. The Brain Injury Problem Checklist, with 105 items, was the forerunner of the NFI, which includes 70 of the original items, grouped into six categories: Depression, Somatic Difficulties, Memory/Attention Difficulties, Communication Deficits, Aggressive Behaviors, and Motor Impairment, with Cronbach's alpha ranging from .86 to .95. Later, six "critical" items, from the earlier instrument, were added to the NFI questionnaire, to "provide information that reveals areas where further investigation of the patient's situation may be warranted" (manual, p. 10). It seems none of the critical items factors loaded on any of the NFI scales. With additional study, the authors concluded that a 70-item, six-factor model most "closely met the goodness-of-fit criteria" (manual, p. 19) and was superior to other options. Confirmatory factor analysis found all items loaded on the predicted factor with t values of p <.05; chi-square to degrees of freedom ratio less than 2.0; and CFI of .89, close to "the minimum criterion of .90 for goodness of fit" (manual, p. 20).

Normative information was based on responses by 520 patients and 520 informants. Demographic and medical information for the patients is reported in the manual and data collection procedures are generally clear. Although the authors note the NFI is not intended to be a diagnostic tool, standardized scores for patient ratings and family ratings, were established for various ages and length of unconsciousness. One-way ANOVA found no main effect related to ethnic background of patients but there was a main effect for sex on Somatic Complaints and Motor Impairment; a main effect for severity of injury on Somatic Complaints, Memory/Attention Difficulties, Communication Deficits, and Motor Impairment; and a main effect for age on Somatic Complaints, Memory/Attention Difficulties, and Motor Impairment.

TECHNICAL. Interrater reliability was based on ratings by 301 patients and others with significant knowledge of the patients' functioning.

Matched pair t tests examined the differences in ratings on the 70 item scores on the six scales. Statistical analysis found agreement of ratings varied from 48% to 84% and no more than 35% of patients indicated various problems occurred more often than the frequency reported by family members. Even on the 13 items where there was statistical difference, none was reported more frequently by family members than by patients. High levels of internal consistency are reported, with Cronbach's alpha values ranging from .86 to .95. The authors note that test-retest reliability has not been empirically evaluated. Correlation studies between the NFI and various measures of neuropsychological functioning and the MMPI are reported in the manual and are generally impressive.

Information about gender, ethnicity, and age are reported in the manual but there is no real information about educational level at the time of injury or the patient's geography. The total number of cases used in the study is small and does not reflect population data from the U.S. Bureau of Census.

COMMENTARY. Directions for administering and scoring the Neurobehavioral Functioning Inventory are generally clear. There is no information about test-retest reliability, reportedly because the instrument was designed to measure characteristics that "endure over a relatively short period of time" and scores reflect these changes (manual, p. 37). However, research in this area is warranted. The information on interrater reliability will likely be confusing to a significant number of "licensed mental health" professionals who use this instrument. Reliability studies of ratings by different family members are needed. The instrument is based on a limited number of cases. There is no information about overreporting or the relationship between changes on the NFI and changes on various measures of neuropsychological functioning. Factor analysis and goodness of fit statistics are impressive.

SUMMARY. The Neurobehavioral Functioning Inventory is expected to find immediate use in assessing patient response to rehabilitative programs or evaluating perceived changes in behavioral functioning that might require a different level of care. However, additional standardization research is needed and there is a need for more information about secondary gain, outcome ratings for patients with various levels of education at the time of injury, and interrater reliability. The authors' notation that the "NFI will prove to be most valuable when results are considered along with standardized testing, interviews, and a thorough review of records" (manual, p. 65) must be remembered.

[163]
Neuropsychological Assessment Battery.
Purpose: "Developed for the assessment of a wide array of cognitive skills and functions in adults with known or suspected disorders of the central nervous system."
Population: Ages 18–97.
Publication Dates: 2001–2003.
Acronym: NAB.
Administration: Individual.
Forms, 2: Form 1, Form 2 (equivalent forms).
Price Data: Available from publisher.
Time: Administration time not reported.
Comments: Software portfolio available for use on Windows 95/NT with Internet Explorer 4.0 or higher or Windows 98/ME/2000/XP and CD ROM drive; modules may be administered individually.
Authors: Robert A. Stern and Travis White.
Publisher: Psychological Assessment Resources, Inc.
  a) SCREENING MODULE.
  Scores, 6: Attention, Language, Memory, Spatial, Executive Function, Total.
  Comments: May be used to determine whether more in-depth, follow-up examinations are necessary.
  b) ATTENTION MODULE.
  Scores, 12: Digits (2), Dots, Numbers & Letters (7), Driving Scenes, Total.
  c) LANGUAGE MODULE.
  Scores, 6: Oral Production, Auditory Comprehension, Naming, Writing, Bill Payment, Total.
  d) MEMORY MODULE.
  Scores, 5: List Learning, Shape Learning, Story Learning, Daily Living Memory, Total.
  e) SPATIAL MODULE.
  Scores, 5: Visual Discrimination, Design Construction, Figure Drawing, Map Reading, Total.
  f) EXECUTIVE FUNCTIONS.
  Scores, 5: Mazes, Judgment, Categories, Word Generation, Total.

Review of the Neuropsychological Assessment Battery by TIMOTHY J. MAKATURA, Adjunct Professor of Psychology, Capella University, Minneapolis, MN:
DESCRIPTION AND DEVELOPMENT. The Neuropsychological Assessment Battery (NAB) is a recently developed, modular instrument that is intended for the assessment of cogni-

tive functions in adults aged 18 to 97. This battery was designed with the dual purpose of providing a screening and/or comprehensive assessment of critical neuropsychological domains including Attention, Memory, Language, Spatial, and Executive Functioning. The authors report that the NAB was developed to meet the continuing need in the neuropsychological community for a brief, integrated test battery while maintaining acceptable psychometric characteristics, extensive normative and validation data, and a level of comprehension that was sufficient to answer varied referral questions as well as facilitate systematic research.

Many of the decisions regarding format and content of the NAB were based on the results of a rather extensive 1997 survey of neuropsychological assessment practices (Stern & White, 2000). In this survey, each respondent in a group of 888 predominantly doctoral-level, neuropsychology practitioners rated the importance of 79 specific neuropsychological functions derived from the literature. Each function that was sufficiently rated by greater than 33% of the sample was included in the NAB. Functions receiving ratings below this threshold were included in multifactorial tests. The test also incorporates suggestions from the NAB Advisory Council that consists of six distinguished neuropsychologists and a language/aphasia consultant. Two specific functions, Writing Ability and Oral Production, were included on the sole recommendation of the language/aphasia consultant.

The NAB consists of 30 individual subtests divided into five modules or domains as well as a Screening Module that consists of selected items from the five domains. The Attention Module consists of 6 subtests involving the answering of orientation questions, recitation of digits forward and backward, visual identification of subtle changes in visual stimuli, letter cancellation task, and identifying differences between two landscapes. The Language Module consists of 6 subtests involving Oral Production, Auditory Comprehension (varied formats), Naming, Reading Comprehension, Writing, and a simulated Bill Payment task. The Memory Module consists of 10 subtests involving word List Learning with delayed recall and recognition trials, Shape Learning with delayed recognition trials in two formats, Story Learning with delayed recall trials, medication instructions with delayed recall and recognition trials, and demographic information with a delayed recall and recognition trials. The Spatial Module consists of 4 subtests involving Visual Discrimination, Design Construction, Figure Copy and immediate recall, and Evaluation of a Map. The Executive Function Module consists of 4 subtests involving Mazes, Judgment in varied situations, Categories, and Word Generation. The Screening Module consists of 12 subtests including 2 subtests derived from the Attention Module, 2 subtests derived from the Language Module, 2 subtests derived from the Spatial Module, 4 subtests derived from the Memory Module, and 2 subtests derived from the Executive Functions Module.

For the Screening and Main Modules, raw scores from each of the subtests are converted to z scores, T scores, and/or percentile ranks based on a normative sample consisting of either a demographically corrected sample or a U.S. Census matched sample. Standard scores for selected subtests are summed to create a composite score that is converted to a standard score and percentile rank with either a 90% or 95% confidence interval. Composite scores from the Screening Module are used to determine if assessment with the respective Main Module is necessary. The accuracy of this classification ranges from .67 to .95 with greater accuracy noted for the impaired scores than above average scores. The NAB kit includes software that automates many of the steps involved in obtaining these normative scores.

The NAB provides two sets of norms that may be used for interpretation. The Demographically Corrected Norms are based on a sample of 1,448 individuals categorized by age, gender, and educational level. The U.S. Census Matched Norms are based on a sample of 950 individuals proportionally matched to the current population in terms of education, gender, ethnicity, and geographic region by age group. Standard exclusionary criteria for these samples are noted including significant primary sensory loss, color blindness, current psychotropic medication use, suspected cognitive impairment, psychiatric history, or significant substance use.

TECHNICAL. Measures of internal consistency resulted in quite diverse average alpha coefficients that ranged from .20 to .87. Standard errors of measurement (*SEM*) for the Screening Domains ranged from 4.5 to 10.06. *SEM*s for index scores ranged from 3.97 to 6.87. Test-retest reliability estimates for subtest and module index

scores on Forms I and II of the test are based on a sample of 95 participants with a test-retest interval of approximately 6 months. The reliability coefficients for the primary scores were quite diverse, however. Reliability coefficients for the module indexes ranged from .52 to .87. Equivalent forms reliability is evaluated according to generalizability theory and based on a sample of 100 individuals after an average 25-day (*SD* = 6.3 days) interval. Approximately 50% of subtest scores in the Language and Memory modules did not meet the stated criteria for very good reliability; however, median coefficient for each of the modules did meet the criteria for very good reliability. Interrater reliability estimates were calculated for the Writing, Story Learning, Figure Drawing, Judgment, and Categories subtests based on 60 randomly selected protocols and ranged from .83 to 1.00.

The evidence for content validity of the NAB scores comes from the extensive survey of neuropsychological assessment practices carried out by Stern and White (2000) as well as guidance provided by the NAB Advisory Board and other consultants. In addition, a number of subtests are similar in style and format to tests that are frequently used in neuropsychological assessment.

The evidence for construct validity is based on convergent lines of reasoning involving intercorrelations, factor analysis, and comparison studies. The intercorrelations between and among screening, subtest, and index scores are provided for the Demographically Corrected Standardization Sample. Relatively independent factors are indicated with higher correlations noted between Screening Domain scores and their respective Main Module Index scores, and among the subtests that comprise individual modules. Factor analytic procedures for subtest scores from the Screening and Main Modules resulted in plausible factorial representation that closely corresponds to the NAB modular structure. However, certain subtests had significant loading on more than one factor.

In addition, correlations based on the performance of 50 individuals were identified between the NAB Modules/Screening Domains and external measures of general cognitive function, attention, language, memory, spatial processing and executive functioning. Screening scores tended to correlate in a similar fashion as the respective index scores. Specifically, the Total NAB Index correlates with the Modified Mini-Mental State

Exam, the Mini-Mental State Exam, and the Repeatable Battery for the Assessment of Neuropsychological Status (RBANS) total score in the .40 to .65 range. Correlations between the Total Index and the Reynolds Intellectual Screening Test also fall within this range but are based on the total sample of 1,448 individuals. Correlations between the NAB Attention index score and certain scores from the Wechsler Memory Scale-III (WMS-III), Trail Making Test (TMT), RBANS, and Ruff 2 & 7 Selective Attention Test range from .27 to .65. Correlations between the NAB Language index score and certain scores from the Boston Naming Test, Token Test, Verbal Fluency Test (FAS), and RBANS range from .09 to .41. Correlations between the Memory index score and certain scores from the WMS-III, California Verbal Learning Test—II, and RBANS range from .11 to .53. Correlations between the Spatial index score and certain scores from the WMS-III, Wechsler Adult Intelligence Test-III (WAIS-III), Boston Qualitative Scoring System for the Rey-Osterrieth Complex Figure, RBANS, and Judgment of Line Orientation range from .02 to .43. Correlations between the Executive Function index and certain scores from the Wisconsin Card Sorting Test, WAIS-III subtest, and Porteus Maze Test ranged from -.27 to .41. The authors additionally provide extensive correlations between these external measures and all subtests of the NAB. The authors further provide specific information regarding performance on the NAB by persons with specific disabilities including dementia, aphasia, traumatic brain injury, HIV/AIDS, multiple sclerosis, rehabilitation inpatients, and adults with ADHD. Additional information is also presented from a simulated malingering study.

SUMMARY. The NAB is a recently developed neuropsychological instrument that has met the rather lofty objectives of the authors for a brief, comprehensive, and integrated test battery with extensive normative and validation data. This instrument provides an innovative design that allows for the screening of a particular domain to determine if a more comprehensive assessment is warranted, avoids floor/ceiling effects, provides data regarding malingering, and incorporates items that are ecologically valid. It also includes parallel forms and coverage of critical functional domains. The NAB does have some minor weaknesses including a lack of standard scores for certain subtests and a

conversion process that raises questions about the relative contribution of individual subtest scores. However, these issues as well as limited evidence for validity should be amended as investigators conduct further research using the NAB.

REVIEWER'S REFERENCE

Stern, R. A., & White, T. (2000). Survey of neuropsychological assessment practices [Abstract]. *Journal of the International Neuropsychological Society, 6*, 137.

Review of the Neuropsychological Assessment Battery by WILFRED G. VAN GORP, Professor of Clinical Psychology and Director, Neuropsychology, Columbia University College of Physicians & Surgeons, Department of Psychiatry, New York, NY, and JASON HASSENSTAB, Doctoral Candidate in Clinical Psychology, Fordham University, Department of Psychology, New York, NY:

DESCRIPTION. The Neuropsychological Assessment Battery (NAB) consists of two equivalent forms, Form 1 and Form 2, which were developed "for the assessment of a wide array of cognitive skills and functions in adults aged 18 years to 97 years, with known or suspected disorders of the central nervous system" (manual, p. 1). It is aimed at individuals 18–97 with corresponding norms. The test consists of multiple modules assessing specific cognitive domains with each module containing a screening component and a more comprehensive assessment component. Modules include Attention, Language, Memory, Spatial, and Executive. The screening component, which is optional, can be used to determine whether more in-depth follow-up examination of the domain is needed. Individual modules can be administered individually without requiring that other modules also be administered.

The Neuropsychological Assessment Battery (NAB) contains a comprehensive battery of 36 neuropsychological tests, organized into six modules: Screening, Attention, Language, Memory, Spatial, and Executive Functions. Two equivalent forms are provided (Form 1 and Form 2). Normative data were gathered on a large sample of healthy individuals across four geographic regions. The NAB provides both demographically corrected norms (n = 1,448) and census-matched norms drawn from the same sample (n = 950). The modules can be administered and scored as part of a complete battery or as individual stand-alone tests. Alternatively, scores from administration of the Screening module can be used to identify areas of functioning that require further investigation using the appropriate domain-specific module. Standard scores, percentile ranks, and interpretive categories are provided for Attention, Language, Memory, Spatial, and Executive Functions modules, as well as for an overall NAB Index score. Within the modules, individual tests provide one or more primary test scores, and in some cases, secondary scores and/or qualitative information.

The NAB can be administered by a trained technician; however, its interpretation is limited to a trained professional referred to in the manual as a "professional clinician" (manual, pp. 21–22). Administration of all six modules, including the Screening module, typically takes less than 4 hours. Scoring can be accomplished both by hand and by assistance from the optional scoring software for PC, which greatly reduces scoring time.

DEVELOPMENT. The NAB was devised, according to the authors, to meet the need for an integrated and comprehensive battery of neuropsychological measures, which would provide theoretically and ecologically valid and reliable test data in a relatively brief assessment period using a common normative sample. To this end, the test authors designed and distributed a detailed survey of neuropsychological assessment practices to a cadre of practicing neuropsychologists. The data from approximately 1,000 returned surveys were compiled from which a model was constructed and employed throughout the initial design of the battery.

An advisory council consisting of internationally recognized experts in the field of clinical neuropsychology was involved throughout the process of developing the NAB. These advisors provided preliminary guidance regarding the spectrum of neuropsychological functions that the NAB should assess. Also, the advisory council rated the initial pool of test items, questions, and stimuli on potential biases, test satisfaction, and difficulty. These ratings were used to narrow the pool of possible items and to divide the items into alternate forms.

In an effort to ensure that a wide range of difficulty levels was represented, pilot testing, including difficulty analysis, was conducted on a heterogeneous sample of healthy individuals as well as on individuals with known neurological conditions. Results from pilot testing were used to further refine the item pool and revise administration, recording, and scoring procedures.

The resultant battery, the NAB, was designed to assess multiple domains of cognitive functioning in adults aged 18 to 97 with known or suspected disorders of the central nervous system.

TECHNICAL. From a psychometric perspective, the reliability coefficients for scores from the NAB were quite variable, but were generally adequate. Internal consistency estimates (Cronbach's alpha) for the various subtests range from .24 to .86. The authors were careful to point out mitigating factors such as construct heterogeneity, range of expected scores, and variability of scores when interpreting the reliability coefficients. Test-retest reliability was documented for both Form 1 and Form 2 on roughly equivalent samples at a test-retest interval of more than 6 months. Test-retest reliability values for the various subtests ranged from .11 to .71. Again, the authors were careful to point out mitigating factors. In this case, they explain the low stability coefficients in terms of the variability of scores. Equivalent forms reliability measures for Form 1 and Form 2 yielded mean generalizability (G) scores for the modules ranging from .62 to .83, and each module primary score exceeded a G score of .60. Subsequent confirmatory factor analytic studies reported in the manual have demonstrated adequate fit for a five-factor model corresponding to the five domain-specific modules. However, a six-factor model, including a factor for speed of processing, appears to provide a significantly better fit. The authors further provide useful data on the validity of scores from the battery by comparing performance on the Screening module for seven different clinical populations. In addition, there are comparison data for each domain-specific module for four different clinical populations including TBI, HIV/AIDS, MS, and Adult ADHD. An aphasia comparison group is provided for the Language module as well as the Memory module.

COMMENTARY. The NAB represents a significant step forward in the evolution of neuropsychological tests in that it provides an ecologically valid assessment of multiple cognitive domains using a common normative sample representative of the United States population. Demographically corrected norms are available for all subtests, another attribute of the test. Another distinct advantage of the NAB is that it provides a validated screening approach so that an entire test battery need not be administered unless there is evidence of impairment in a given domain. Other advantages include an alternate form so that test-retest may be accomplished while minimizing practice effects, and the manual provides data on true positives, false positives, etc., for various clinical conditions, addressing issues that can potentially arise in the forensic arena regarding admissibility of scientific data in the courtroom.

The test is not without its drawbacks, however. Research to date is limited to that conducted by the authors and reported in the manual (though this will no doubt soon change). The test will often need to be supplemented by other tests, such as an IQ test and/or a personality test, hence increasing administration time for a "comprehensive assessment." The test is expensive, relative to other neuropsychological tests. Though the test has ecological face validity, it has yet to be determined how well it assesses ability to accomplish everyday tasks and demands.

SUMMARY. The NAB represents a screening and comprehensive follow-up assessment of neuropsychological function for adults using two equivalent forms. It has solid psychometric properties, and its common normative database across tests, tied to the U.S. Census, represents a major step forward compared to prior neuropsychological measures. The test is encouraging in both its psychometric and clinical properties, and seems to provide varying profiles in different clinical samples. Expense and time for administration, often supplemented by IQ or personality tests, are drawbacks, though they seem outweighed by the advantages noted above.

[164]

New Standards Reference Examinations: English Language Arts.

Purpose: Designed to assess student performance "in the areas of reading and writing."
Population: Elementary, middle, and high school students.
Publication Dates: 1996–2003.
Acronym: NSRE: English Language Arts.
Scores, 4: Reading: Basic Understanding, Reading: Analysis and Interpretation, Writing: Effectiveness, Writing: Conventions.
Administration: Group.
Levels, 3: Elementary, Middle, High School.
Forms, 2: E, F.
Price Data: Available from publisher.
Time: Three 55-minute sessions.
Comments: Scoring service provided by publisher.
Author: National Center on Education and the Economy; Learning Research and Development Center, University of Pittsburgh.
Publisher: Harcourt Assessment, Inc.

Review of the New Standards Reference Examination: English Language Arts by DOROTHY M. SINGLETON, Associate Professor of Education, Winston-Salem State University, Winston-Salem, NC:

DESCRIPTION. There are E and F forms for the New Standards Reference Examinations: English Language Arts (elementary, middle, and high school). The purpose of the tests is to assess student performance in the areas of reading and writing.

The Reading component of the test covers Basic Understanding and Analysis and Interpretation. The Writing component covers Rhetorical Effectiveness and Conventions.

The tests require students to do an independent writing task that asks them to use details to respond to a constructed-response prompt; an integrated reading and writing task that asks them to read passages, answer short constructed-response questions, and produce a piece of text-based writing to demonstrate comprehension of the passage; and to do a multiple-choice examination that asks students to read a number of passages and respond to questions that deal with either reading comprehension, inference and analysis, or editing rules and guidelines (teacher's guide, pp. 7–8).

Each exam is divided into three parts. The recommended administration is three sittings of 55–65 minutes each, designated for 3 consecutive school days. This schedule allows for 55 minutes of actual testing and 5 minutes for administrative tasks. Allow 10 extra minutes, if needed.

Form F (elementary level) of the test consists of Part 1: Independent Writing; Part 2 consists of Reading and Writing; and Part 3 consists of Reading Comprehension and Editing. This test has 43 multiple-choice items.

Form E (elementary level) of the test consists of Part 1: Independent Writing; Part 2 consists of Reading and Writing; and Part 3 consists of Reading Comprehension and Editing. This test has 43 multiple-choice items.

Form F (middle grades) of the test consists of Part 1: Independent Writing; Part 2 consists of Reading and Writing; and Part 3 consists of Reading Comprehension and Editing. This test has 43 multiple-choice items.

Form E (middle grades) of the test consists of Part 1: Independent Writing; Part 2 consists of Reading and Writing; and Part 3 consists of Reading Comprehension and Editing. This test has 43 multiple-choice items.

Form F (high school) of the test consists of Part 1: Independent Writing; Part 2 consists of Reading and Writing; and Part 3 consists of Reading Comprehension and Editing. This test has 51 multiple-choice items.

Form E (high school) of the test consists of Part 1: Independent Writing; Part 2 consists of Reading and Writing; and Part 3 consists of Reading Comprehension and Editing. This test has 53 multiple-choice items.

The tests are student-friendly. The writing prompts and reading passages are appropriate for all levels. The topics cover current issues and the vocabulary is consistent with each grade level. The test booklets have excellent reading and writing topics.

Teachers will administer the tests to their students. All teachers must follow the guidelines written in the teacher's guide. There are guidelines and accommodations for both typical and atypical students. The accommodations for atypical students (students with special needs) should be adhered to before and during the administration of the tests. Harcourt Assessment, Inc. will score the test items.

Before the administration of the original tests, the New Standards Released Tasks manual has been suggested for teachers to use in preparation for the test. It is an excellent tool for teachers to use with their students and for teachers to use among themselves. The manual provides a way for teachers to assess their students according to national standards; for looking at criteria based on national standards; the use of rubrics and commentaries to describe students' work; and to supply models of students' work with different score points. Teachers can follow the manual for elementary, middle, and high school students.

The New Standards Released Tasks manual also provides students with activities that will enhance their reading and writing skills, as practice, before the tests. Teachers will be able to score the students' tests by using the rubric provided for them. Scoring guides or rubrics are provided so that teachers would have a clear understanding of how the work of students is scored.

Harcourt Educational Measurement offers practice tests. Scoring guides and rubrics are provided so that teachers and school administrators can see how the work their students do on the Reference Examination is scored.

DEVELOPMENT. The last copyright of the English Language Arts Reference Examination materials provided to this reviewer was in 2001; the publisher advises that Form F was published in 2003. The English Language Arts Reference Examination Released Tasks were last copyrighted in 1995. The test was designed to assess student performance in the areas of reading and writing. There are two forms of this test (E & F). There are three parts to the English Language Arts tests. They are listed as Part I: Independent Writing, Part 2: Reading and Writing, and Part 3: Reading Comprehension and Editing.

These tests are standards based, which means that the tests measure how well students master the specific skills identified for each grade level based on Performance Standards. The tests were developed for Grades 4, 8, and 10.

The National Assessment of Educational Progress (NAEP), commonly known as the Nation's Report Card, has collected national representative data since 1969 about what American children know and can do in a variety of key subject areas. Those subject areas include Reading, Writing, Mathematics and Science for children in Grades 4, 8, and 12 (website at: http://nces.ed.gov/nationsreportcard).

TECHNICAL. The test items are based on national standards students should know in the areas of Reading and Writing. As reported in the Released Tasks manual, these tests are:

Designed to measure student performance in relation to a standard or set of standards. The New Standards Reference Exam ties to the New Standards Performance Standards for reading, writing, and conventions. It does not attempt to measure the range of what is required to meet these three standards because the amount of work required to meet any one of them is substantial; the writing standard alone calls for proficiency in six different genres. What the Reference exam does is to provide a snapshot of the kinds of work students can do in an on-demand situation. Essentially, it is designed to work in conjunction with a portfolio to provide additional information about student performance. (Released Tasks, 1995; p. 1)

The tests provide both qualitative and quantitative data for an accurate assessment of students' performance at the 4th, 8th, and 10th grade levels. Based on the number of items on all three parts of the tests, the test items have been proven to be both reliable and valid.

Background information is also collected on each student. Examples of information collected from the student questionnaire consist of (a) How often do you speak in front of the class? (b) How often do you work on English assignments in small groups? (c) How many books do you read each year? and (d) What is the highest educational level reached by your most educated parent?

The publisher does not report any significant statistics about the English Language Arts Reference Exam (elementary, middle, high school). The publisher has suggested rubrics and score guides to assess students' performance. In the English Language Arts Reference Examination Released Tasks, the Writing rubrics range from 5–0 score points (*exceeds the standards—unscorable*). Criteria for scoring are based on (a) organization and coherence, (b) controlling conventions, and (c) elaboration of ideas. The Conventions rubric for all types of writing has score points of 5, 4, 2, and 1. Score 3 is not applicable. The categories for the Conventions rubric range from *exceed the standard* to *limited responses.*

The same scoring guide is used for the Reading component of the exam (5–0). Criteria for scoring are based on (a) textual understanding and (b) evidence of interpretation.

COMMENTARY. Overall, the English Language Arts Reference Exam is an excellent assessment for students in Grades 4, 8, and 10. It is designed to do what it is purported to do. The assessment covers three parts to measure student performance in relation to a standard or set of standards. Of course, the Reference Exam is very similar to the National Assessment of Educational Progress (NAEP) report. There are Demonstration Booklets that cover similar material. The website for this report is http://nces.ed.gov/nationsreportcard/pdf/demo_booklet/2005demobkG4.pdf.

Some concerns about this assessment are as follows: (a) the Reference exam is compatible with many of the end-of-grade tests in many of the states; (b) the end-of-grade tests are designed to infuse national standards; (c) the latest copyright of the tests in the Released Tasks manual is 1995 for Grades 4, 8, and 10; and (d) lack of technology (website links) for additional practice for preparation of tests.

SUMMARY. The English Language Arts Reference Examinations reinforce the idea that reading and writing are highly integrated activities

in any given curricula. Reading and writing skills can be infused in any lesson designed by the teacher and presented to the students.

> The assessment does not include all the different types of reading and writing that appear in the standards, but it does emphasize skills that are fundamental to many types of reading and writing: for example, the careful selection of details and the ability to relate specific details to an overall theme or idea. (teacher's guide, p. 8)

Performance assessments can only infer what students know by what they write in response to a question. Therefore, students should attempt to answer every question. There is no penalty for wrong answers—only credit for correct ones. There are special accommodations for students with special needs.

This is a paper/pencil test. The Reference Examination was designed, field tested, and benchmarked and will be scored assuming that students were tested during a 3-day period.

[165]
New Standards Reference Examinations: Mathematics.

Purpose: Designed to assess student performance in mathematics.
Population: Elementary, middle, and high school students.
Publication Dates: 1996–2003.
Acronym: NSRE: Mathematics.
Scores, 3: Skills, Concepts, Problem Solving.
Administration: Group.
Levels, 3: Elementary, Middle, High School.
Forms, 2: C, D.
Price Data: Available from publisher.
Foreign Language Edition: Spanish edition available.
Time: Three (55–65) minute sessions.
Comments: Scoring service provided by publisher.
Author: National Center on Education and the Economy; Learning Research and Development Center, University of Pittsburgh.
Publisher: Harcourt Assessment, Inc.

Review of the New Standards Reference Examinations: Mathematics by MARÍA DEL R. MEDINA-DÍAZ, Professor, Department of Graduate Studies, Program of Educational Research & Evaluation, School of Education, University of Puerto Rico-Río Piedras, San Juan, PR:

DESCRIPTION. New Standards Reference Examination: Mathematics (NSRE-M) is a group standard-based performance assessment tool designed to determine how well fourth, eighth and tenth grade students have learned the mathematics skills, concepts, and tasks described on the New Standards Performance Standards (NSPS, developed by the National Center on Education and the Economy [NCEE] and the University of Pittsburgh in 1997). These standards as well as other practice materials, such as the Mathematics Reference Examination Release tasks, are available from the publisher and NCEE. Classroom test packages include: 25 student assessment booklets, 1 teacher's guide; 25 formula sheets (for middle and high school); and 25 rulers (if provided with the examination). Spanish and English students' assessment booklets are available. Forms D and E (the latest NSRE edition), in both languages, were reviewed. The publisher provided the technical data report of NSRE for Mathematics and English Language Arts of Forms E and F.

Primarily, the NSRE-M items and tasks include mathematical skills (SK), conceptual understanding (CP), and problem solving (PS). Each school level (elementary, middle, and high school) test consists of three parts to be answered in 55 minutes each. The first part includes 20 multiple-choice (MC) items to be answered in 20 minutes. The second and the third parts of Form E, for example, include a combination of 15, 18, or 20 short, medium, and long constructed-response tasks (for high school, elementary school, and middle school, respectively). These tasks are the same for English and Spanish test forms and many of them resemble real-life situations. MC items are different in the Spanish and English versions of the test Forms D and E. Apart from the time suggested for working on the tasks, there is no additional discussion about the differences among the items and tasks. According to the teacher's guide, the short tasks normally require just an answer and no explanation is expected whereas the other tasks require the test taker to show their response method or explanation.

Teachers should administer the test on 3 consecutive school days. The recommended time for each sitting is 60 minutes: a 5-minute administrative period at the beginning of the testing session for general directions and to fill-in student's information, and a full 55-minute period for working on the test. The teacher's guide includes clear directions for the test administration, security, sittings, and room conditions. Teachers may choose to read aloud the directions for each part or let the students read to themselves and when they have finished reading, "briefly paraphrase the directions, drawing attention to the two different kinds of tasks" (teacher's guide, p. 36). It also lists specific testing accommodations that are permitted for students with special needs. Teachers should mark in the section "For teachers only use" on the back cover of the student booklet what accommodations, if any, were applied to his or her work on the test.

Each student must work individually on the test, keep her or his pace in the time required to complete each part, and write the answer in the test booklet, using No. 2 pencils only. The student can use a calculator, the mathematics textbook, a ruler (with metric and standard units), and any other materials she or he uses in class. She or he must write, show, or explain all of his or her work in the booklet, in order to get credit for the response. Guessing is permitted and there is no penalty for wrong answers.

Student's name and school information in the test booklet can be supplied by pre-identification labels or by the student on the first day of testing. Also, the student should provide demographic information (such as gender, age, and ethnic group) on the booklet back cover during second day of testing as well as answer a brief questionnaire on the inside back cover, during last day of testing. For elementary students, the teacher will complete the ethnic identification box. The category of "multi-ethnic/biracial" included in this box is misleading because it does not indicate what are the sources of multiplicity or duality (i.e., To what combination of races or ethnic groups it refers?). For all school levels, the teacher should provide student's information about his or her participation in special school programs, fluency in English, and parents' involvement in school activities.

DEVELOPMENT. According to the authors, the NSRE-M is an approach to assess student achievement in comparison to the eight NSPS: Arithmetic and Number Concepts, Geometry and Measurement Concepts, Function and Algebra Concepts, Statistics and Probability Concepts, Problem Solving, Mathematical Reasoning, Mathematical Communication, and Putting Mathematics to Work. The materials supplied by the publisher provide minimal information regarding test development and how it matches the NSPS. The technical data report includes a one-page description of each cluster and of the possible reasons for low scores. No further explanation is included about the instructional validity of the scores and inferences.

The technical data report indicates that a student's scores are reported as profiles in three clusters of performance standards in mathematics (SK, CP, and PS) and his or her performance on a particular cluster is described in five levels: (a) achieved the standard with honors, (b) achieved the standard, (c) nearly achieved the standard, (d) below the standard, and (e) little evidence of achievement. No details are included about how the publisher scores the student's responses, how the student's profile is derived from the responses to different test items and tasks, and how the raw or scaled scores are translated to these levels of achievement. Also, it is not clear which rubrics or criteria are used for scoring the student's responses and how the student's raw score is obtained. The released tasks booklet includes several examples of scoring rubrics for different tasks. However, there is no indication if the same rubrics are applied in the NSRE-M.

The technical data report lists a multifaceted strategy for creating cutoff scores for each cluster and school levels on Form E. This procedure used various sources of data such as judges' recommendations of cut scores (no data about the number of judges and qualifications are included), and comparison with Form D cut scores and equating raw score distributions. Results of the final set of cut scores by cluster, performance, and school levels are shown for Forms E and F (English and Spanish versions). Statistics of the accuracy and consistency for the cut scores based on combined performance levels (meet the standards or not) are included. Results show accurate and consistent decisions across school levels and mathematics clusters and total (ranging from .81 to .94, and .74 to .92, respectively). False positive and negative classifications ranged from .03 to .09, and .03 to .11, respectively. Accordingly, the mathematics total (MT) score provides the most accurate and consistent classification of student's performance. Item statistics (such as item difficulty, item discrimination, differential item functioning, and item information function) are not reported.

The revised Spanish versions of Forms E and D are adequately translated from English but no information is provided about the translation or adaptation procedures. No rationale was presented for the differences in the MC items in both languages. If the Spanish version of the test will be administered to different Hispanic/Latino groups in the United States, specifically Puerto Ricans, some words should be changed (e.g., "maceta," "plátano," "rebanadas," "naranjas," "listón," "pay," "pastel," "bote," "duraznos," nickels, dimes), and additional research about construct and content equivalence is required. Also, two translations should be revised because of their different meanings in mathematics: A line segment is not a "recta" (or straight line), and a task is not the same as "problema" (problem). Gender stereotypes can be identified in items or task situations such as: Men are always driving; usually, women are either shopping or posing as teachers.

TECHNICAL. Form E of the NSRE-M was administered in spring 2001 to a large sample of students in each school level (19,967 fourth, 18,763 eighth, and 16,419 tenth graders). Number and percentage of students at the five performance levels in the three mathematics clusters are reported. There is no additional description regarding the sample selection, representativeness and characteristics.

Descriptive data of test Forms E and F show scores mean, standard deviation, reliability, and *SEM*. In Form E, the internal consistency reliability estimates (using Cronbach alpha coefficient) for MT scores are higher than the rest of the clusters. They ranged from .91 (44 items in elementary school) to .94 (42 items in high school). The reliability of the clusters ranged from .68 (Skills, 9 items in middle school) to .91 (Concepts, 27 items in high school). Using 2002 Form E administration, the lowest *SEM* values for the MT score are in elementary and high school levels and in the SK cluster for all groups. Considering that tests include constructed-tasks, scorer consistency or generalizability coefficients are missing.

Correlations and confirmatory factor analysis are used as sources for sustaining the construct validity of the NSRE-M results. High intercorrelations are reported among the mathematics clusters and the total score for each test level (ranged from .82 to .97). Form E intercorrelations among clusters are lower (ranged from .59 to .88). Results of confirmatory factor analysis indicate a satisfactory fit between the test internal structure and the three-factor model proposed for each school level (either for Form E or F). Also, the unidimensionality assumption was met.

However, evidence based on the test content is not covered in detail. Also, criterion-related validity evidence was not presented in the technical data report. At least there are no specifications to illustrate the matching between each of the three performance standards clusters, the mathematics content, and the test items and tasks. The released tasks are helpful because they include examples about the links between the tasks and the performance standards. Also, an examination of students' response processes should be an important source for assessing mathematical communication, reasoning, and problem solving.

COMMENTARY. The NSRE-M materials describe partially its conceptual and technical features. The framework and rationale for developing the NSRE-M was not fully delineated for sustaining the purpose of assessing student performance against the NSPS. Although items and tasks apparently relate to the mathematical content taught in the three school levels as well as the eight standards, there is not enough conceptual and empirical evidence to support the test's adequacy and scores' interpretations. In consequence, the categorization of student's performance in five levels can be misleading.

SUMMARY. Overall, the NSRE-M includes a challenging set of mathematics performance tasks accompanied by good black-and-white illustrations. It has a convenient format for writing the responses in the same booklet. Student's instructions and test items and tasks, both in Spanish or English, are clear. The released tasks booklet provides useful examples for teaching purposes. High internal consistency of overall students' responses is reported. However, given the concerns expressed about its development, scoring, and validity, the test developers should present additional evidence regarding the fulfillment of the test purpose and uses.

Review of the New Standards Reference Examinations: Mathematics by CAROL S. PARKE, Assistant Professor, School of Education, Duquesne University, Pittsburgh, PA:

DESCRIPTION. The New Standards Reference Examinations (NSRE) for Mathematics measure students' math achievement according to a set of standards, the New Standards Performance Standards, that describe important math skills and concepts that students should know and be able to do. Although the Standards themselves were not reviewed, based on descriptions in the materials provided to the reviewer, it appeared that the Standards are reflective of the National Council of Teachers of Mathematics (NCTM) Principles and Standards for School Mathematics (2000).

The NSRE is not considered a norm-referenced exam because student performance is not based on comparison to norm samples. Rather, student test performance is compared to math standards. As stated in the technical data report, tests are designed "so that preparation for the exam (1) pays off (hard work is rewarded with good performance) and (2) is time well spent learning the curriculum" (p. 9). Several aspects of the NSRE support this statement. Each test booklet consists of a combination of multiple-choice items and constructed-response tasks that assess worthwhile math concepts and require students to solve complex math problems, demonstrate solution strategies, and/or explain their reasoning. Practice test documentation provides examples of performance tasks and rubrics for use in the classroom. An effort is made during test administration to simulate the classroom environment as closely as possible. All students are given rulers and calculators, and middle and high school students are given formula sheets. It is strongly stated in the teacher's guide that "students MUST be allowed to use the customary resources and materials used in the classroom while taking this examination" (p. 28). This includes their math textbook and other resources such as protractors.

The NSRE for Math is available in three test levels: elementary, middle, and high. Although test booklets are labeled as such, a few statements in the manuals refer to Grades 4, 8, and 10. The target population was not explicitly described, and so it was unclear as to whether the tests are only appropriate for use in fourth, eighth, and tenth grades or if a broader interpretation of the three levels is acceptable. The test is administered in three parts over a period of 3 consecutive days. The first includes 20 multiple-choice items and a set of constructed-response tasks that focus on skills and concepts, and the remaining two parts contain only constructed-response tasks that focus on concepts and problem solving. A Spanish version is also available. The teacher's guide provides clear and detailed instructions about test security, accommodations, and test administration. The recommended length of time for each day is 60 minutes, but time may be extended if students are still working productively.

In addition to the Total Math score, three cluster scores in Skills, Concepts, and Problem Solving are produced. Using the Rasch model of Item Response Theory, scaled scores are provided on a range from 100 to 200. Total Math raw scores and corresponding scaled scores are listed for each form and level. Scoring procedures for constructed-response tasks were not described. It was unclear if tasks classified as "short," "medium," and "long" were evaluated using the same scale. Rubrics for released tasks showed a scale of 0 to 4, but a scale of 0 to 3 was mentioned briefly in the manual. Five achievement levels further describe student performance on each cluster. The two highest levels represent performance that "Meets the Standards." Students at these levels are consistently performing at the level of the standard or higher than the standard. The remaining three levels (Nearly Achieved the Standard, Below the Standard, and Little Evidence of Achievement) are classified as "Do Not Meet the Standards."

DEVELOPMENT. Items are categorized into three clusters. As described in the manual, the Skills cluster contains items measuring basic skills in number and operations, geometry and measurement, functions and algebra, and statistics and probability. Items in the Concepts cluster emphasize math ideas and conceptual understanding. The Problem Solving cluster consists only of constructed-response items, which reflect the application of math knowledge to solve complex, realistic problems. Items are said to be linked to the *New Standards Performance Standards*, but steps in the item development process are not provided. There is no information on test specifications, initial creation of items, pilot or field testing, examination of potential item bias, selection of final items, or development of procedures to score the open-ended responses. Thus, a test user would find it difficult to evaluate the appropriateness of the items for measuring the intended constructs. Further, development of the Spanish versions was not described.

Because Form E did not have items in common with the four previous NSRE forms, new cut scores had to be created to define the performance levels. The strategy was multifaceted and included judgments from panelists within a standard setting procedure, information from cut scores on an earlier form, item calibration results, and matching a previous form's distribution to Form E's distribution. The equating and scaling methods using the Rasch Model are described. A fixed item-parameter method was used to equate Form F to Form E, and cut scores for performance levels on Form F were generated during the process. Although cut scores are displayed in the manual by cluster, score ranges for each cluster were not provided nor can they be accurately obtained from the information given. This makes the performance level information somewhat difficult for the test user to interpret.

TECHNICAL. Based on 2002 and 2003 administrations of Forms E and F, percentages of students at each performance level are shown by test level and cluster. Total sample size ranged from 16,419 to 20,284. For Skills, more than half the students at each level are classified as Meets the Standards, and only small percentages of students performed at the two lowest standards. In general, results appeared to be more favorable at the elementary level than at the middle or high school level. Demographic characteristics of this sample were not provided.

As a measure of internal consistency, coefficient alphas are provided for cluster and total scores. All alphas for total scores are excellent (>.90). Alphas for clusters were somewhat lower, ranging from a low of .68 for Form E, Middle Grades, Skills to a high of .91 for Form E, High School, Concepts. Of the 18 alphas, 8 were in the .70 range and 8 were in the .80 range. There was a tendency for estimates to be higher for Concepts compared to Skills or Problem Solving.

The accuracy of decisions based on performance levels (i.e., classification of a student into Meets the Standard versus Does Not Meet the Standard) was shown to be high. The proportion of accurate classifications was ≥.90 for Math Total and >.80 for each cluster. Similar to the reliability results above, Skills tended to have lower accuracies and Concepts had higher accuracies. Proportions in the "false positives" and "false negatives" misclassifications were similar. Values for the consistency of decisions were slightly lower than those for accuracy. The lowest three proportions were in the Skills cluster (.74, .80, and .77 for elementary, middle, and high, respectively).

Goodness-of-fit statistics showed that the proposed structure for the NSRE (a global factor including the three clusters as group factors) appeared to be confirmed. For each form and level, the GFI was ≥.90 and the RMSEA was <.05. The Tucker Lewis reliability index was only slightly lower than .90 for one case (Form E, Middle, .87). An intercorrelation matrix of cluster and total scores was used to show evidence of concurrent validity. Because cluster scores are components of the total score, it was not surprising that correlations between the total and each cluster were high (from .82 to .98). If cluster scores are thought to measure distinct mathematics constructs, the intercorrelations should be somewhat low; but on Form F, seven of the nine correlations were ≥.80. On Form E, correlations were a bit lower, ranging from .59 to .88, with six correlations <.80. In general, correlations at the elementary level were lower than at the middle and high levels, and the two lowest correlations occurred between skills and problem solving (.59, Form E and .69, Form F).

Several important aspects of validity and reliability were not addressed. For instance, information was not available regarding the content validity of items, interrater reliability for constructed response tasks, examination of potential gender or ethnicity bias, and comparisons of NSRE scores to external measures of math constructs.

COMMENTARY. A major strength of the NSRE is that it measures important, worthwhile mathematics that students in elementary, middle, and high school grades should be expected to know, and it does so by simulating a classroom atmosphere as closely as possible. There are no strict time limits and students are allowed to use customary materials in their classroom. The assessment and its accompanying materials provide teachers with models of good performance tasks. A packet of released tasks gives an analysis of the mathematics involved in each released task and links it to the Standards. Possible student responses and a detailed rubric for each task describes various solution methods and explains common flaws and errors. Responses for which more instruction is needed are distinguished from responses for which only revisions are necessary. Extensions are also described for further exploration of the particular math concept.

Along with test score results, the NSRE score reports give "feedback on what can be done to improve student performance on the assessment" (technical data report, p. 9). Suggestions are made when the performance level shows that further instruction on the math assessed by the task is needed. Although the suggestions are broad and not intended to be prescriptive, they describe possible causes for low scores, such as lack of practice with core basic skills, more time needed for direct instruction and practice, lack of in-depth coverage of concept, lack of frequent opportunities for explaining concepts, and lack of experience in applying math to solve complex problems.

However, as mentioned throughout the review, there are major omissions with regard to the assessment's technical quality. Item development and evidence for content validity were not presented. The process of translating the English versions into the Spanish versions was not mentioned, thus the equivalency of items could not be evaluated. Due to the lack of information on scoring the constructed-response tasks (including the background of the raters, the training and rating procedures, and interrater reliability and validity) it was difficult to determine the validity of these scores. Characteristics of the calibration samples were not provided, and there were no descriptions of studies to examine potential item bias or differential item functioning. Finally, concurrent validity evidence comparing NSRE performance to external measures of math performance was lacking.

SUMMARY. Schools will find that the NSRE for Mathematics has several desirable characteristics. It offers them a way to assess students' achievement levels in relation to a set of standards describing important math competencies. The assessment maintains a nice balance with regard to measuring core basic skills, conceptual understanding, and complex problem solving. A combination of multiple-choice items and short, medium, and long constructed-response tasks allows students to demonstrate their knowledge in a variety of ways. Accompanying materials, such as the released task packets, are valuable to teachers in that they promote the development and use of performance tasks in classroom instruction. Although most of the information supplied in the technical data report appears to be solid, the missing technical evidence is necessary in order for test users to evaluate the quality of items and to determine the validity of test use in assessing a variety of student populations. As indicated in the *Standards for Educational and Psychological Testing* (AERA, APA, & NCME, 1999), these important aspects of validity and reliability must be addressed.

REVIEWER'S REFERENCES

American Educational Research Association, American Psychological Association, & National Council on Measurement in Education. (1999). *Standards for educational and psychological testing.* Washington, DC: American Educational Research Association.

National Council of Teachers of Mathematics. (2000). *Principles and standards for school mathematics.* Reston, VA: NCTM.

[166]

The New York Longitudinal Scales Adult Temperament Questionnaire.

Purpose: Measures temperament in adulthood.
Population: Adults.
Publication Dates: 1995–2003.
Acronym: NYLS ATQ.
Scores, 9: Activity, Rhythmicity, Adaptability, Threshold, Approach, Distractibility, Intensity, Persistence, Mood.
Administration: Group.
Price Data, 2003: $69.95 per complete kit including test manual (2003, 28 pages), user's guide, and 25 questionnaires including scoring and profile slides; $49.95 per 25 questionnaire refills including scoring and profile sheets; $34.95 per 25 questionnaire refills only; quantity discounts available.
Time: (10–15) minutes.
Comments: Scoring and report software available for online administration.
Authors: Stella Chess and Alexander Thomas.
Publisher: Behavioral Developmental Initiatives.

Review of The New York Longitudinal Scales Adult Temperament Questionnaire by JAMES A. ATHANASOU, Faculty of Education, University of Technology, Sydney, Australia:.

DESCRIPTION. The purpose of The New York Longitudinal Scales Adult Temperament Questionnaire (ATQ) is to provide users with a brief assessment of nine temperaments derived from the New York Longitudinal Scales (NYLS) of temperament. The nine temperaments assessed are considered to be distinct from dimensions of personality and are: Activity Level, Regularity, Adaptability, Approach, Intensity, Mood, Persistence, Distractibility, and Threshold. The intended use of the test is for a group or individual assessment in clinical, personnel, or educational settings as well as for research purposes in health settings.

The test comprises 54 items and nine self-ratings. The test content is based on self-report using a 7-point Likert scale from *hardly ever* to *almost always*. The meaning of terms such as *rarely, once in a while, sometimes, often,* or *very often* is left to the respondent. Items are straightforward and almost all refer to personal preferences or actions. A sample preference item is "I prefer a hobby which has a lot of…." Some refer to hypothetical situations, such as, "If someone messes up my room or apartment I get very angry…." A third form of item refers to the reactions of others, "People think I am a cynic because…."

It is administered in a paper-and-pencil format or in a computer-administered version. It is straightforward to administer and the instructions are largely self-explanatory for both administrators and users. Scoring is also straightforward but requires attention to detail so that clerical or computational errors do not occur. The scoring procedure involves transferring responses to a scoring sheet and tallying the number of responses for each of the nine temperaments. Results are transferred to a scoring profile on which self-ratings of personality are also indicated.

DEVELOPMENT. The development of the ATQ was described briefly but clearly. It derived from a 140-item version developed originally in 1982 for the New York Longitudinal Studies of adult temperament. It was developed from a larger pool of 345 items and the final 54-item version was based on the responses of 135 participants in the longitudinal study.

The underlying assumption or model that guided the assessment was observations of infant temperament and the categorization of nine temperaments. These were later assessed by questionnaire and a briefer version of the ATQ was developed using the same framework. The central thesis of the ATQ is that "temperament continues to exist as a measurable component of behaviour that influences how we interact with the environment" (test manual, p. 4). The item development was entirely from the pre-existing version and involved the construction of nine separate scales with reasonable internal consistency based on responses from a college sample. The final selection of items was designed to produce nine temperament scales containing six items with maximal internal consistency (.69 to .83).

TECHNICAL. The norm sample comprised 135 NYLS participants aged 20–30 years and is not defined in terms of gender or demographic details. The NYLS sample is unlikely to match a general population and the value of the published norms cannot be determined readily for different gender or ethnic culture groups.

The major evidence for score consistency is the test-reliability study conducted across 1 month on 25 college students and the internal consistency indices that are reported. The test-retest reliabilities varied from .66 to .90 and are acceptable for a survey or research questionnaire but some caution may be required for individual clinical or counselling use of the results. The sample used for these estimates would not normally represent an adequate basis for generalization to other future studies using the ATQ. Consistent with current notions about reliability for research studies it is recommended that separate test-reliability coefficients should be determined in each future instance where the ATQ will be used.

The interpretation of the results appears to be adequate for group purposes that do not involve high-stakes assessments but validity data for individual use are not substantiated in the manual. The studies designed to gather evidence of the valid use of the ATQ are few in number. They rely partly on the earlier longitudinal investigations. For instance, reference is made to concurrent validity studies conducted on an earlier form of the ATQ. The external criterion was interview ratings. No data are provided on the differential validity across gender, racial, ethnic, and culture groups. It is definitely the case that additional evidence on the applicability of the ATQ is required before a recommendation for everyday use in applied settings is recommended.

COMMENTARY. The overall strength of the test is that it was derived from clinical observations made on temperament differences. The adequacy of the theoretical model is not addressed in the manual or user's guide and the reader is referred to sources cited in the references; however, the most recent of these is 1997.

SUMMARY. The ATQ represents a typical paper-and-pencil questionnaire of personality and temperament that reflects a survey of human characteristics. The development of the ATQ is not psychometrically sophisticated. Current research supports five major personality factors, which are not congruent with the nine temperaments listed in the ATQ. Potential users might better be served and referred to the Eysenck Personality Questionnaire that provides an assessment of fundamental personality temperaments, the NEO five-factor

questionnaires (T6:2110), or the Cattell Sixteen Personality Factor Questionnaire (16PF; T6:2292), or even the Minnesota Multiphasic Personality Inventory (MMPI; T6:1623) for more useful and externally validated assessments supported by up-to-date research and better normative samples.

Review of The New York Longitudinal Scales Adult Temperament Questionnaire by STEPHEN N. AXFORD, Assistant Director of Special Services and Licensed Psychologist, Falcon School District 49, Colorado Springs, CO:

DESCRIPTION AND DEVELOPMENT. The New York Longitudinal Scales Adult Temperament Questionnaire (ATQ) is an assessment instrument intended to be used by clinicians and researchers in the measurement of primary reaction patterns or temperament traits. It is based on the pioneering work of Thomas, Chess, Birch, Hertzig, and Korn (1963). The ATQ was preceded by a 140-item self-report instrument (NYLS Young Adult) used in a published research study (Thomas, Mittelman, Chess, Korn, & Cohen, 1982), standardized on college-aged individuals. This was followed up with longitudinal studies, leading the researchers to conclude that temperament traits significantly contribute to behavioral and psychological adjustment (Chess & Thomas, 1984, 1989), particularly within the context of person-environment interaction.

The impetus for developing the ATQ was to provide a brief standardized measure of temperament, accomplished in the development of a 54-item, 7-point Likert-type scale, self-report measure. The ATQ measures nine temperament traits: Activity, Regularity, Adaptability, Threshold, Approach, Distractibility, Intensity, Persistence, and Mood. The self-report protocol provides simple, clear instructions. The questionnaire items are also unambiguous and well constructed. Nine additional items are included at the end of the 54-item questionnaire, one for each of the nine temperament traits, allowing the respondent to provide their general or overall impression for each trait. For the evaluator, an easy-to-use scoring sheet and profile sheet are provided, with brief but clear instructions on each. Also available is software for administration, scoring, and interpretive report writing. Based on examination of the testing materials, this reviewer believes the ATQ has good face validity.

In constructing the ATQ, an item analysis was conducted on the original 140-item questionnaire data utilizing 135 participants in their 20s and 30s. The purpose of the reanalysis was to identify 6 items for each temperament trait, creating a brief measure still having satisfactory reliability. The NYLS Young Adult questionnaire yielded internal consistency reliability coefficients in the .80s and, according to the authors, acceptable test-retest reliability (one-month interval). The analysis revealed the requisite number of 6 items for each temperament trait, yielding a 54-item instrument, the ATQ, with reliability coefficients all at the .70 level or higher.

As an indicator of self-awareness, the nine General Impressions items were added to the ATQ, using a 6-point rather than 7-point scale. The general impression items, however, are not factored into the nine temperament indices derived from the item analysis. The authors seem to suggest that research (Carey & McDevitt, 1995) based on infants and children examining the relationship between ratings and perception has clinical relevance for adults with respect to helping them gain insight into their own temperament profiles. This view has pragmatic appeal. However, empirical research should be conducted examining efficacy of treatment based upon this notion of gaining self-awareness of temperament characteristics. With regard to this point, worth noting is that the authors emphasize the ATQ as a research tool. Temperament self-awareness as a treatment dimension would be a promising area for further research.

Clear guidelines are provided for administering and scoring the ATQ. Clear descriptions are provided for each of the nine temperament categories. A user's guide is also provided, which gives an overview of ATQ software available for administration, scoring, interpretation, and data reporting. Thus, the ATQ can be administered and scored through the traditional paper-and-pencil format or by computer yielding an interpretive report. The ATQ software allows the examiner to generate raw scores, z scores, a bar graph, written interpretation of the temperament profile, and validity checks requiring login of a password. The specific validity checks include: social desirability response set with established cut points for z scores; and ratings/perception discrepancy comparing norms for the ATQ standardization sample

and self-perceptions corresponding to the General Impressions ratings.

TECHNICAL. Normative data are provided for both the 54-item brief version (N = 135) and the 140-item original version (N = 70) of the NYLS. Different standardization samples were used for the two NYLS versions. The standardization samples are relatively small, raising issues of demographic representation and generalization. Further standardization efforts, utilizing larger and broader demographic standardization samples would, of course, be recommended for future editions. Noteworthy, however, is the discussion provided by the authors (p. 17) regarding interpretive limitations of the ATQ considering its limited standardization sample (i.e., middle-class European-American). The authors note the following additional limitations: reading and educational level, lack of exposure to an urban American environment on which the items are based, the vagaries of self-report, and age factors given the ATQ were standardized on young adults. Regarding the data interpretation problems with self-report, the authors recognize various sources of response bias. With the computerized version of the ATQ, validity scales address this concern, a psychometric issue often overlooked by test developers.

Internal consistency (N = 135) and test-retest reliability (N = 25) analyses for the ATQ consistently yielded satisfactory coefficients. Item analysis data employing the NYLS sample yielded alpha reliability coefficients ranging from .69 to .83, with a median of .76, indicating internal consistency similar to the 140-item version of the NYLS (.72–.87, median = .82). The test-retest analysis, employing Winona State University college students reevaluated with the ATQ after 1 month, yielded coefficients of .89 for the total scale, with a range of .64 to .90 across categories.

Assumptions about concurrent validity for the ATQ are based upon research (Thomas et al., 1982) involving the original 140-item version of the NYLS, correlating interview ratings with the questionnaire data. Given the ATQ was developed from the original or Young Adult version, this research has relevance for the ATQ. However, additional research should be conducted specifically addressing the concurrent validity of the ATQ.

The authors note additional research should also be conducted addressing construct validity, specifically as to how temperament relates to perhaps better known and validated personality traits.

Nevertheless, the authors report findings from a principal components analysis of the ATQ standardization data, employing a varimax rotation, and using the nine temperament dimensions as variables. Analysis of the factor structure supported the nine-category interpretation of temperament.

The authors note, related to predictive validity, based on research involving the earlier or 140-item version of the NYLS, moderate correlation has been observed within the early adult period for longitudinal stability of temperament scores. However, as the authors also note, longitudinal stability of the ATQ requires additional research. Other psychometric and theoretical issues requiring further study, according to the authors, include: correspondence between ATQ data and current/future behavior; relationships between temperament and clinical diagnosis and development of psychopathology; genetic versus environmental predisposition within adulthood; and the course of adult temperament development after age 40.

COMMENTARY AND SUMMARY. As the authors concede, the major limitation of the ATQ is its limited standardization sample, in terms of number of subjects and demographic representation. Nevertheless, the quality of what has been done to this point in developing the ATQ is quite good. The ATQ is probably most appropriately used at this time as a research tool because of the standardization limitations. It should not be used as a high stakes measure, although it holds great promise as a useful clinical tool as future research in the validation of the ATQ and the temperament construct is conducted. This reviewer hopes the ATQ will spark interest in the further investigation of clinical applications focusing on the nine temperament categories.

REVIEWER'S REFERENCES

Carey, W. B., & McDevitt, S. C. (1995). *Coping with children's temperament: A guide for professionals.* New York: Basic Books.

Chess, S., & Thomas, A. (1984). *Origins and evolution of behavior disorders from infancy to early adult life.* New York: Brunner-Mazel.

Chess, S., & Thomas, A. (1989). The practical applications of temperament to psychiatry. In W. Carey & S. McDevitt (Eds.), *Clinical and educational applications of temperament research* (pp. 23–35. Amsterdam: Swets & Zeitlinger.

Thomas, A., Chess, S., Birch, H. G., Hertzig, M., & Korn, S. (1963). *Behavioral individuality in early childhood.* New York: NYU Press.

Thomas, A., Mittelman, M., Chess, S., Korn, S., & Cohen, J. (1982). A temperament questionnaire for early adult life. *Educational & Psychological Measurement, 42,* 593-600.

[167]
Non-Verbal Reasoning.

Purpose: Designed to assess "a pupil's ability to recognise similarities, analogies and patterns in unfamiliar designs."

Population: Ages 7.3–15.3.
Publication Date: 1993.
Scores: Total score only.
Administration: Group.
Levels, 3: Age 8 and 9; Age 10 and 11; Ages 12–14.
Price Data: Available from publisher.
Time: (40–45) minutes.
Authors: Pauline Smith and Neil Hagues.
Publisher: NFER-Nelson Publishing Co., Ltd. [England].

Review of Non-Verbal Reasoning by SALLY KUHLENSCHMIDT, Professor of Psychology, Western Kentucky University, Bowling Green, KY:

DESCRIPTION. The Non-Verbal Reasoning test is a measure designed to be used by teachers to assess a pupil's "ability to recognize similarities, analogies and patterns in unfamiliar designs" (teacher's guide, p. 1) and how easily children acquire new concepts and new material. The standardization sample (consisting of school children in England and Wales) included students aged 7-9 to 14-9. The test is broken into three measures, one for 8–9-year-olds (42 items), one for 10–11-year-olds (54 items), and one for 12–14-year-olds (52 items). The authors suggest that it is appropriate for pupils with language disabilities or for whom English is one of several languages. The test is designed for group administration and takes about 40 to 45 minutes (15 for instruction and a practice test and a 25- to 30-minute time limit). A test kit for each age group includes 20 test booklets and a teacher's guide, as well as an "At a Glance Guide" for administration. A technical supplement is available. Instructions are very clear and the test is easy to administer. Scoring instructions and a key are included. The highest score that can be earned is 140 and the lowest is 70 for some ages.

DEVELOPMENT. Items consist of the presentation of a geometric design and four, five, or six options. Four types of nonverbal items are included, those that require finding another element of a set (classification) and those requiring either a matrix, analogy, or series. Questions that failed to discriminate high from low scorers, were too difficult, or were gender biased were eliminated. Tests for ethnic bias were not done because of the unreliability of the categorization and the small numbers of some ethnic populations.

The tests were developed from various unpublished and published measures created in the late 1980s and early 1990s, including some items from the Non-Verbal Test BD and DH. No information regarding the theoretical basis of the test items was provided, making it impossible to judge the appropriateness of the items. The technical supplement reports they conducted what seems to be from 1 to 2 trials of each of the three measures during development. The nature of the trials appears to have been to evaluate items for discrimination and gender bias.

TECHNICAL. The standardization sample is reported to be a nationally representative group of students aged 7-9 to 14-9 from England and Wales. The technical manual does not provide census data so one cannot judge how closely their sample matches national data. Stratification variables were three regions of England and Wales, metropolitan or not, and four types of schools. It is not clear if gender was a stratification variable. Norms are simply for age, not by gender or ethnic groups.

The authors provide two measures of reliability of the test. The internal consistency estimates (KR20) for the three measures are .94 (8–9-year-old), .93 (10–11-year-old), and .92 (12–14-year-old). Twelve-month stability correlations for the 8–9-year test are .69, .80 for the 10–11, and .80 for the 12–14. They report that the raw scores rose from 6 to 8 points over that period whereas standardized scores varied from 4 to 5 points.

Concurrent validity was assessed by comparing the unpublished test with the current version. Correlations range from .74 to .81. However, because some of the items on the current version are derived from the unpublished version, it is unclear what these correlations mean for validity. They do provide point biserial correlations for items with the total score. The correlations range from .19 to .66 but no summary data are provided.

COMMENTARY. The materials for teachers provided with this test are attractive and user-friendly and yet retain sophistication about psychometric matters. It is a well-constructed test with clear instructions, scoring, and reasonable interpretation. The claims for the test seem in line with the evidence for the test quality. As is common, extreme scores present a challenge, particularly the weak floor for each of the age groups. It would be desirable to provide data for standardization samples for other parts of the world. The lack of data on ethnic group differences is also a weakness. Given how long the test has been available,

it is disappointing that more validity information is not available. The test is promising, but more research on its relationship to other measures of nonverbal reasoning as well as the relationship to verbal measures is necessary for effective interpretation and application.

SUMMARY. The Non-Verbal Reasoning test has a separate measure for each of three age groups: 8–9-year-olds (42 items), 10–11 (54 items), and 12–14 (52 items). It takes about 40 minutes to administer to a group and has clear administration and scoring instructions. The test has potential for broader use than its current grounding in England and Wales. It would be worthwhile for researchers to build on the foundation by adding more standardization samples and validity data, such as correlations with other measures (e.g., the Matrix Analogies Test, an individually administered nonverbal measure, Naglieri, 1985; T6:1531). The theoretical basis of the test should be presented more explicitly.

REVIEWER'S REFERENCE

Naglieri, J. (1985). Matrix Analogies Test—Expanded Form. San Antonio, TX: Harcourt Assessment, Inc.

Review of Non-Verbal Reasoning by JULIA Y. PORTER, Assistant Professor of Counseling, Mississippi State University, Meridian, MS:

DESCRIPTION. The Non-Verbal Reasoning (NVR) test series assesses students' reasoning abilities using classification questions, series questions, and matrix questions. Test takers are asked to identify similarities, analogies, and patterns in shapes and designs. Test developers' purposes include: identifying individual's current level of reasoning functioning, predicting an individual's ability to acquire new concepts and master new material, providing a tool to inform teaching strategies, and documentation of teaching effectiveness.

The NVR test series is based on age and is divided into three categories: (a) NVR 8 and 9 (4 examples, 6 practice test items, 42 test items); (b) NVR 10 and 11 (4 examples, 6 practice test items, 54 test items); and (c) NVR 12 to 14 (3 examples, 4 practice test items, 52 test items). Recording the test taker's age and the testing date accurately are essential for accurate test results.

Each test in the series is designed to be administered in a group setting using a pencil-and-paper format. The NVR 8 and 9 presents four choices per test item, the NVR 10 and 11 presents five choices per test item, and the NVR 12 to 14 presents six choices per test item. Approximate testing time is 40–45 minutes. Each test in the series estimates 15 minutes for instructions, examples, and practice tests. Administration of the NVR is timed (25 minutes for the NVR 8 and 9 and the NVR 10 and 11; 30 minutes for the NVR 12 to 14).

Raw scores on the NVR range from 0 to 42 for the NVR 8 and 9, 0 to 54 for the NVR 10 and 11, and 0 to 52 for the NVR 12 to 14. A standardization table is provided for converting the raw scores to standardized scores. Percentile Rank and 90% Confidence Bands are also provided in table format.

DEVELOPMENT. According to the NVR teacher's guide, test items were carefully selected from "a much larger number of items" (p. 4). Items were eliminated based on unsuitable level of difficulty, gender bias, or low discriminate value between high and low scorers. Statistical data were not provided about item selection. Although the developers discuss the value of reasoning in general terms, specific references to the theoretical base and statistical data used in the development of the test series would be useful to test administrators when comparing the NVR with other instruments for test selection (Whiston, 2000).

Test developers presented test items as shapes and designs to help eliminate bias. This format was chosen instead of words and sentences to help eliminate scoring differences that might be the result of a deficiency in language skills rather than a deficiency in reasoning skills. Pictorial material was not used in the test items because some pictorial material requires culturally specific knowledge. Although test developers indicate mathematical knowledge and spatial visualization levels for items are low, specific level information would help administrators use the test series more effectively.

TECHNICAL. First published in 1993, the NVR 8 and 9 were developed during the late 1980s. Test items were selected based on the developers' literature review of relevant research. After several administrations of the pilot test, 42 items were chosen based on statistical discrimination. Test items are arranged in order of difficulty. The NVR 8 and 9 was standardized in 1992 in Wales and England using 204 schools. Over 6,000 students were tested with approximately half being girls and half being boys. The same norming procedures were followed for the NVR 10 and 11 and the NVR 12 to 14. Additional data are needed about the characteristics of the norm groups to determine how generalizable the results are for groups other than the norm sample.

Detailed instructions are provided for calculating the examinee's age and for calculating raw scores. One point is awarded for each correct answer. Incorrect answers are not penalized. Detailed instructions are also given for converting raw scores to standardized scores, for determining percentile ranks, and for determining 90% confidence bands. Results are reported on the front cover of the student test booklet. Standardized scores are on a scale from 70 to 140 with a standard deviation of 15.

The Kuder-Richardson 20 (K-R 20) was used to measure internal consistency of the test. The reliability for NVR 8–9 is .935 with a standard deviation of 14.8 and a standard error of measurement of 3.8. According to NVR developers, reliability is established through prescribed administration instructions and the objective marking key. The standardization process compares students of the same chronological age to eliminate differences in scores that are the result of differences in age.

Concurrent validity for NVR 8–9 was documented by administering the Non-Verbal Reasoning Test BD and the NVR 8 and 9 within a few days to 331 students. The test scores showed a .76 correlation between raw scores and .74 correlation between standardized scores. The teacher's guide states that scores from the NVR correlate favorably with scores from other nonverbal reasoning tests, but examples are not cited to support this statement.

COMMENTARY. Developers have made efforts to ensure test reliability and validity through test item selection and standardization of testing and scoring procedures. A 90% confidence band is provided in the interpretation of test results to more accurately identify the range within which the test results will fall if there were no errors.

In addition to standardized testing procedures, the NVR teacher's guide offers suggestions to facilitate the process of administering and scoring tests. The teacher's guide also includes explanations of the basic statistical terms used to describe NVR results.

Test developers note several limitations of the NVR: (a) Even though reasoning is a part of intelligence, the NVR should not be called an "Intelligence Test" or used to report "Intelligence";

(b) very low test scores need to be interpreted with caution (suggestions for analyzing the testing process to determine the validity of the low score are included in the teacher's guide); (c) to eliminate the possibility of learning effects from testing, the NVR should not be administered again to the same individuals in less than a year.

SUMMARY. The Non-Verbal Reasoning test series was designed to measure reasoning ability in children and adolescents. The NVR is appropriate for use with individuals who have language deficiencies. The teacher's guide provided with the test materials is written to accommodate new test administrators as well as those who are experienced. Administration instructions and scoring instructions are standardized. The teacher guide is easy to follow and a one-page administration summary is provided for each test in the series. The NVR series should be used and interpreted with caution because limited data are available about the statistical methods used in developing the NVR and about the norm groups used for standardization of the NVR (American Educational Research Association, American Psychological Association, & National Council on Measurement in Education, 1999). The NVR can provide a useful analysis of reasoning ability as part of an assessment program to compare with other assessment instrument results.

REVIEWER'S REFERENCES

American Educational Research Association, American Psychological Association, & National Council on Measurement in Education. (1999). *Standards for educational and psychological testing.* Washington, DC: American Educational Research Association.

Whiston, S. C. (2000). *Principles and applications of assessment in counseling.* Belmont, CA: Wadsworth/Thomson Learning.

[168]
Numeracy Impact Tests.

Purpose: "Designed to assess the impact of intervention strategies which are intended to raise the level of achievement of pupils who are working on the borderline between levels 3 and 4 in mathematics."
Population: Ages 10–11.
Publication Date: 2000.
Scores: Total score only.
Administration: Group.
Forms: 2 tests: A, B.
Price Data, 2003: £18.90 per 10 test booklets; £16.80 per evaluation pack.
Time: (30) minutes.
Authors: Tandi Clausen-May, Helen Claydon, and Graham Ruddock.
Publisher: NFER-Nelson Publishing Co., Ltd. [England].

Review of the Numeracy Impact Tests by DIXIE McGINTY, Associate Professor of Educational Research, Western Carolina University, Cullowhee, NC:

DESCRIPTION. The Numeracy Impact Tests are a pair of short, group-administered tests designed to address the National Curriculum for mathematics in the United Kingdom. Specifically, the tests are appropriate for students who are working at or toward Level 4 of the curriculum in England, Wales, and Northern Ireland (Level D in Scotland). According to the developers, the two tests (Test A and Test B) are intended to be used as a pretest and posttest to assess the impact of instructional intervention strategies. The teacher's guide includes suggested intervention strategies for each item on Test A, which is the recommended pretest.

Content areas addressed on the tests include Number, Algebra, Measures, Shape and Space, and Data Handling. Each test consists of five questions that are read aloud to the students, followed by a section of written questions, for which 30 minutes are allowed. Items are open-ended in format, with the exception of a few multiple-choice items; examinees write their answers in the test booklet. Calculators are not permitted.

The tests can be easily administered and scored by teachers without special training. The teacher's guide contains adequate administration instructions and a script for the oral items. A detailed scoring scheme is provided, with examples of acceptable and unacceptable answers. A group record sheet is provided to aid the teacher in computing total scores and item p-values; p-values for the standardization sample are conveniently given on this sheet for comparison purposes. Each test yields a total raw score of up to 30 points; no subscale or individual objective scores are generated due to the small number of items.

DEVELOPMENT. The Numeracy Impact Tests were first published in 2000. Materials provided to the user contain no information about any aspect of the development of the tests (e.g., item development, item selection, item tryout). Limited information is provided about the standardization process; this will be described in the next section.

TECHNICAL. According to the teacher's guide, the tests were standardized in October 1999 using a sample of approximately 2000 "rising 10- and 11-year-old pupils" (p. 25). The purposes of the standardization were (a) to obtain a set of scaled scores that would allow comparisons between performance on the Numeracy Impact Tests and the National Curriculum tests and (b) to place performance on the two Numeracy Impact Tests on the same scale. The teacher's guide provides tables for converting raw scores to scaled scores and for predicting the likely achievement level on National Curriculum tests.

The sample is reported to have been proportionately stratified by region (northern, middle, and southern regions of England, Scotland, Wales, and Northern Ireland), school type, and "1998 KS2 math results in England" (p. 25). These variables are not explained further, and no additional description of the standardization process is provided. Raw score means and standard deviations are given for the total sample, and also by gender, for each of the two tests, but there is no evidence that scores have been disaggregated based on any other variable. The teacher's guide provides neither norm tables nor any type of standard scores.

Reliability evidence provided for the Numeracy Impact Tests is inadequate for its intended purpose. If the tests are to be used as pre- and postmeasures to assess students' progress, evidence of the equivalence of the two test forms is essential, yet the developers make no mention of alternate-forms reliability. The fact that the two tests have been "equated" is not sufficient to ensure their comparability with regard to content. Indeed, examination of the items on the two test forms reveals some striking disparities in content. For example, Test B requires the use of an angle measurer, and 4 of the possible 30 points hinge on the student's understanding of angles; Test A contains no items addressing angles. In addition, some of the questions on Test A, for which a suggested intervention is given, address skills that are not addressed at all on Test B.

Internal consistency reliability estimates using the Kuder-Richardson 20 (KR-20) formula are provided (.91 and .90 for Tests A and B, respectively). Though these values would normally be considered to indicate high reliability, they are likely to be inflated in this case due to a substantial amount of dependency among individual items on the tests. Many questions on the tests consist of two or more individual items that are related, but scored separately. In a few of these instances, a correct answer to one item depends upon a correct answer to the previous one. For example, the first of a pair of two related items is the following: "A carton holds 6 eggs. Yasmin has 50 eggs. How many cartons can she fill?" The second item asks, "How many eggs will be left over?" The two items are scored separately, for 1 point each, yet an examinee who misses the first item will also miss the second item, barring a correct guess. The tests also include at least two items in which 1 point is awarded for what essentially amounts to partial credit, whereas 2 points are awarded for a fully correct answer. A close examination of the items revealed four pairs of clearly dependent items (representing a total of 8 score points) on Test A and three pairs (6 points) on Test B. In estimating internal consistency, it would thus have been more appropriate to treat these pairs of items as single, nondichotomously scored items and use a different reliability measure (e.g., coefficient alpha).

Validity evidence presented in the teacher's guide is also inadequate. The authors claim that the tests have content validity, which "may be established by examining the content of the Numeracy Impact Tests in the test scripts themselves" (p. 26). It is further claimed that "the tests assess a variety of aspects of mathematics that are included in the curricula for England, Wales, Scotland and Northern Ireland" (p. 26). Yet, no evidence is provided of the match between test items and the curriculum, nor are the development and selection of items described at any point in the materials provided. Concurrent validity coefficients (.87 and .84 for Tests A and B, respectively) indicate a moderately strong relationship between the Numeracy Impact Tests and the QCA Year 5 optional test in mathematics; detail about the process of collecting this information is scant. Predictive validity evidence is not provided; instead, the teacher's guide states that "predictive evidence will, by definition, become available only after a period of time" (p. 26).

COMMENTARY. The Numeracy Impact Tests have several appealing features. They consist of unambiguous, well-constructed items that are free from obvious flaws. Educators familiar with the National Curriculum in the U.K. may find these tests to have high face validity. Further, the tests will appeal to many users because they are quick and easy to administer and score.

The weaknesses of these tests lie in their lack of documented technical quality. In assessing the seriousness of these weaknesses, it is important to consider the intended purpose(s) of the tests. Because the tests are not intended to serve a norm-referenced purpose, the lack of standard scores and norm tables is not a serious flaw. However, potential users of these tests to measure student progress—the stated purpose of the tests—should be aware of two very serious issues. First, it is questionable whether these tests can be reliably used as pretest/posttest measures, especially given the small samples of items on each test, and the lack of evidence that the two test forms are parallel. Second, the tests purport to assess students' achievement with regard to the National Curriculum, but the developers have provided no information linking items to any specific objectives in the curriculum. Potential users would be well advised to contact the publisher and request, for each of the two tests, a specific breakdown of the curricular areas covered, and the number of items addressing each.

SUMMARY. The Numeracy Impact Tests may be useful to teachers in the U.K. who desire a set of practice items for the National Curriculum mathematics tests at this level, and who prefer not to construct the items themselves. The tests may also be used to predict, with a moderate degree of accuracy, whether a student's performance on National Curriculum tests is likely to reach Level 4. Use of these instruments as pretest and posttest to measure the effects of intervention strategies may lead to erroneous conclusions. Potential users are urged to request more detailed technical information from the publisher.

Review of the Numeracy Impact Tests by GEORGETTE YETTER, Postgraduate Researcher, Gevirtz Graduate School of Education, Center for School-Based Youth Development, University of California—Santa Barbara, Santa Barbara, CA:

DESCRIPTION. Numeracy Impact is a standardized, norm-referenced assessment system and teaching aid designed to help British school teachers measure students' response to instruction in Level 4 of the National Mathematics Curriculum in England, Wales, and Northern Ireland (Level D in Scotland). It consists of two tests that address the topics of number, algebra, measures, shape, and space, and data handling and is targeted to students ages 8–14.

Materials include pretest booklets (Test A), an At-A-Glance Guide outlining the purpose and procedures involved in administering and scoring the test, posttest booklets (Test B), and Group Record Sheets to help teachers keep track of their students' scores. The materials also include a teacher's guide that includes detailed instructions, tables for converting raw scores to scaled scores and predicting students' performance on the National Mathematics Exam, and suggestions for interpreting and using the test results to enhance instruction.

Test A contains 13 items and is intended to identify advanced Level 3 students' strengths and areas of need and to provide a baseline measure of students' math skills in the Level 4 curriculum prior to instruction. The teacher's guide offers suggestions for teaching students how to solve each question on Test A. These suggestions incorporate multiple teaching modalities and emphasize ways to help students avoid common errors. They seem especially likely to be helpful to novice teachers. Posttest scores allow teachers to measure students' math skills following instruction and to estimate students' likely performance on Level 4 of the National Mathematics Examination. Test B contains 14 items. It is intended to identify students for whom more extensive instruction is warranted prior to sitting for the National Exam and to help teachers individualize instruction by pinpointing students' most prominent areas of need.

The teacher's guide states that teachers can use pretest-posttest changes to track progress for both individual students and for groups, and also evaluate the effectiveness of instruction over time periods as short as 2 weeks. Examination of group-level performance is facilitated by use of the group record sheets, which allow for calculation of percent correct for an entire class, and facilitate comparison with the standardization sample.

DEVELOPMENT. The Numeracy Impact tests are relatively new. They were normed in 1999 using a geographically diverse sample of approximately 2,000 10- and 11-year-old students from 90 schools, stratified by geographical region, school type, and, for English students, their Level 2 mathematics test results.

Both tests start with a section of five oral questions to be read aloud by the teacher. Students are allowed 10 seconds to respond to each oral question. This section is followed by 8–9 written questions for which students are allowed a total of 30 minutes to complete. Both tests are teacher-scored. The teacher's guide contains detailed descriptions of correct and incorrect responses to facilitate standardized scoring. The guide also contains tables to allow teachers to convert raw scores to scaled scores and to predict students' likely achievement on the National Examination. Another table allows teachers to compare their students' progress from Test A to Test B compared with the normative sample.

TECHNICAL. The teacher's guide reports high internal consistency for both of the Numeracy Impact tests, with Kuder-Richardson 20 reliability coefficients of .91 for Test A and .90 for Test B.

The concurrent validity of Tests A and B was checked by calculating their correlations with the performance of 800 students on the Qualifications and Curriculum Authority (QCA) Year 5 Test in Mathematics. That test covers material from Levels 3, 4, and 5 of the National Curriculum and follows the same format as the National Mathematics Examination. For that sample of students, the correlation with performance on the QCA Test was .87 for Test A and .84 for Test B. These correlations show good concurrent validity. However, the predictive validity of these tests has not yet been examined vis-à-vis student performance on the National Mathematics Examination.

COMMENTARY. The Numeracy Impact tests are easy-to-administer, relatively easy-to-score, brief tests that can be administered to either individuals or groups. These tests can be used to evaluate student performance, to diagnose strengths and weaknesses, and to establish teaching goals and objectives. However, they do not come close to covering comprehensively the extensive content of Level 4 of the National Mathematics Curriculum. The teacher's guide provides no rationale for deciding which portions of the curriculum are included.

Also, although the teacher's guide advocates the use of Numeracy Impact Tests A and B as pre- and posttests, it does not provide a strong basis for confidence that these tests can be used reliably to measure student response to instruction. For one, the strength of the relationship between student performance on Test A and Test B is not reported. Another reason to question their use as pre- and posttests is that they are not parallel forms. Not only does the teacher's guide describe Test B as easier, but the tests have slightly different content emphases. Test A includes relatively more calculation problems, whereas Test B includes more

geometry questions. In view of these differences, it is especially unfortunate that the authors did not report the correlation between Tests A and B to support their use as pre- and posttests.

SUMMARY. The Numeracy Impact Tests A and B seem useful for measuring the performance of British Level 4 mathematics students, especially in light of the recent emphasis on accountability in education. These tests were recently standardized and normed on a geographically diverse sample. They have high internal consistency and good evidence of concurrent validity with the QCA Year 5 Test in Mathematics. However, teachers should be aware that these tests do not comprehensively sample student performance across the Level 4 National Mathematics Curriculum. Also, although there is a great deal of overlap in their content coverage, the two Numeracy Impact tests emphasize slightly different skill areas, leaving open to question the extent to which they can reliably be used as pre- and posttests to measure student learning.

[169]

Nurse Entrance Test.

Purpose: "Designed … as a diagnostic instrument to assist nursing programs evaluate the academic and social skills of new applicants to their programs."

Population: Adult applicants to nursing schools.

Publication Dates: 1998–2001.

Acronym: NET.

Scores, 28: 7 Essential Math Skills scores (Whole Numbers, Number System Conversions, Algebra Equations, Percentage Operations, Decimal Operations, Fraction Operations, Essential Math Skills), 3 Reading Comprehension scores (Reading Rate, Reading Rate Placement, Reading Comprehension), 3 Critical Thinking Appraisal scores (Main Idea of Passage, Inferential Reading, Predicting of Outcomes), Testtaking Skills score, 2 Social Interaction Profile scores (Passive, Aggressive), 5 Stress Level Profile scores (Family, Social, Money/Time, Academic, Work Place), 6 Learning Styles (Auditory Learner, Solitary Learner, Visual Learner, Social Learner, Oral Dependent Learner, Writing Dependent Learner), Composite Percentage.

Administration: Group.

Price Data, 2002: $17 per test by computer; $10.50 per test; $8 per answer sheet; $27.50 per Study Guide.

Time: (150) minutes.

Comments: Generates a Diagnostic Report including NET Group Report, individual Student Reports; Group Report provides group-level mean percentages and normative comparisons for the 28 scores; optional Study Guide offers testtaking strategy tips and practice tests.

Author: Michael D. Frost.
Publisher: Educational Resources, Inc.

Review of the Nurse Entrance Test by MARK A. ALBANESE, Professor of Population Health Sciences, University of Wisconsin, Madison, WI:

DESCRIPTION. The Nurse Entrance Test (NET) is designed, primarily, as a diagnostic instrument to assist nursing programs in evaluating the academic and social skills of new applicants to their programs. For each examinee, over 30 diagnostic scores are generated that programs can use to more objectively screen applicants for admission as well as provide an academic/social profile of a class already admitted. The NET consists of an eclectic combination of seven subtest areas: Essential Math Skills (60 items, 60 minutes), Social Decisions (30 items, 10 minutes), Stressful Situations (50 items, 12 minutes), Learning Styles (45 items, 20 minutes), Reading Comprehension (33 questions, 30 minutes), Reading Rate (1 minute), and Testtaking Skills (30 questions, 20 minutes). The Essential Math Skills and Reading Comprehension tests are the only scored sections. They are combined into a composite score as well as reported separately. Further, these two scores have been equated to the corresponding subtests on the ACT exam. The correlation of these scores and their ACT equivalents has been in excess of .80. The remaining sections are primarily diagnostic. The Social Decisions subtest has two sections. The first section has respondents answer either Agree or Disagree to a series of 18 statements that characterize themselves in social situations. The second section has respondents indicate, for 12 items, which of two activities or occupations they "like better." The Stressful Situations subtest has respondents answer either Agree or Disagree to 50 statements that can intuitively be seen to either contribute to increase or lower one's stress level, depending on how one would answer the question (money problems, performance tendencies in school, fear of losing a job, etc.). The Learning Styles subtest has respondents answer Agree or Disagree to 45 statements reflecting preferences for learning in various situations. The Testtaking Skills subtest consists of 30 multiple-choice questions that assess a variety of information pertaining to taking tests, including tendencies for instructors to use various flawed item writing practices, interpreting what is meant by words

commonly used in essays, etc. In total, the exam takes 153 minutes of direct testing time to complete.

DEVELOPMENT. The NET was developed by the Examination Committee of Educational Resources (ECER), a geographically balanced standing committee composed of faculty who are actively involved in both teaching and academic counseling in health occupations programs. Specific questions were written by a larger pool of faculty based on their educational and professional credentials. Although it is never specifically stated that a test blueprint or other systematic approach was employed in item creation, the specificity of the feedback provided in the diagnostic reports suggests that one was employed in the test design. The final pool of items was reviewed and evaluated by the ECER in what the authors term as screening. The items that survived this process were then administered to a norming group of 1,385 entering nursing students in a geographically representative sample between January-December 1989. Item analysis and intense review of items was used to reduce any item ambiguity.

TECHNICAL.

Scoring. The NET reports scores in various ways. Generally, scores are reported in terms of percentage of items answered correctly and in terms of percentile rank from the norming population. In the cases of Essential Math Skills and Reading Comprehension, a descriptive score is provided placing the student's score as a function of their relative progress in the educational system (Pre Junior High, Junior High, High School, Post High School). Reading Rate is reported in words per minute as well as the relative percentile rank of that reading rate. For the Testtaking Skills, Stress Level Profile, Social Interaction Profile, and Learning Style, additional descriptors are used to characterize the examinee's performance.

Standardization. The NET was standardized by equating its individual Composite Percentile (and the individual Math and Reading Comprehension scores) with the ACT Composite scores (and its individual Math and Reading Comprehension scores) for the norming sample.

Reliability. Split-half (odd versus even) correlations served as the reliability estimate from the norming sample. The two splits ultimately became separate alternate forms of the examination. Reliability estimates for the subscores range from a low of .81 for the Math subtest to .98 for Reading Comprehension. The Math subtest is the only one to report reliability estimates below .90. The manual provides some confusing information about the subtest reliability because the values reported in text differ from those reported in a tabular format.

Validity. The Technical and Development Report addresses content, criterion-related, and diagnostic validity. Content validity is argued for because the NET was based upon a needs assessment of a representative sample of health occupation program directors from across the United States.

Criterion-related validity evidence of the NET is based upon the relationship of the NET Composite score to the Composite score on the ACT, which ranged between .79–.83. The sample used to obtain these values is not specified. Here again, discrepancies exist between the information reported in text compared to that tabulated. In a case study, NET scores accounted for 33% of the variance in first year grades in nursing school, further supporting the criterion-related validity of the NET.

To support the diagnostic validity of the NET, mean scores on each subtest of 365 graduating nurses were compared to the norm means via *t*-tests. Although no data are provided on these comparisons, the text reports "for each subtest the performance of the graduating students was significantly higher than the average of the norms established for entering students" (p. 6). One case study reported that using the NET has "facilitated the early identification of the at-risk student, and retention strategies have been implemented" (p. 21).

COMMENTARY. The NET is an eclectic combination of subtests that have strong intuitive appeal as diagnostic instruments to identify students who are in need of either academic or personal support systems. It depends heavily on what appears to be almost a redundancy with the ACT Math and Reading scores for its validity. Using this relationship as a bedrock, detailed feedback is provided on student performance on these tests as well as on a broad mix of academic and personal diagnostic scores. Case studies suggest that schools have found the instrument to provide useful information for identifying students needing remediation.

The main problems with the NET pertain to its weak developmental foundation, both conceptually and empirically. The construct validity of many of the subtests is not demonstrated and there is little literature cited to support their existence. Learning style has been a notoriously difficult concept to operationalize and the approach used in the NET is susceptible to the same self-report bias that has kept such instruments limited to low stakes purposes. Excepting the Math and Reading subscales, the same can be said for the subscales reported on the NET. They are dependent upon respondents making open and honest answers in order to make constructive use of the information. Any attempt to use the NET for selection or screening purposes has the potential to distort the results such that they are likely to be meaningless. The only exceptions to this are the Math and Reading subtests, and they owe their validity to the close relationship they have with the ACT. Because the ACT has demonstrated high reliability and validity, it would be a much better instrument to base any high stakes decisions upon than would be the NET. The weaknesses in the empirical data used to support the reliability and validity of scores from the NET are magnified by errors in reporting such data in the technical report.

Although the data to support the reliability and validity of uses of scores of the NET are limited, it does report an appealing assortment of diagnostic scores for an institution concerned with helping their students succeed in a demanding educational program. The case studies reported indicate that the NET has proven useful in some situations in helping identify at-risk students for early intervention. If an institution is having problems with students experiencing severe problems at points that are too late for intervention, the NET may be of benefit. Its value, however, will need to be established on a case-by-case basis.

SUMMARY. The NET is designed, primarily, as a diagnostic instrument to assist nursing programs in evaluating the academic and social skills of new applicants to their programs. Over 30 diagnostic scores are generated for each examinee, and programs can use these scores to "more objectively screen applicants for admission" as well as provide an academic/social profile of a class already admitted. It consists of an eclectic combination of seven subtest areas: Essential Math Skills (60 items, 60 minutes), Social Decisions (30 items, 10 minutes), Stressful Situations (50 items, 12 minutes), Learning Styles (45 items, 20 minutes), Reading Comprehension (33 questions, 30 minutes), Reading Rate (1 minute), and Testtaking Skills (30 questions, 20 minutes). The Essential Math Skills and Reading Comprehension tests are the only scored sections. They are combined into a composite score as well as reported separately. Further, these two scores have been equated to the corresponding subtests on the ACT exam. The correlation of these scores and their ACT equivalents has been in excess of .80. The remaining sections are primarily diagnostic. In total, the exam takes 153 minutes of direct testing time to complete.

The NET has the potential to be useful for identification of at-risk students for early intervention. Its use as a screening instrument is discouraged. The evidence supporting its use for this purpose is extremely weak and would be vulnerable to any challenge. Institutions wishing to use it as a screening tool need to establish their own evidence for its validity for this purpose. The alternate form reliability of the NET appears to have been established reasonably well, but other forms of reliability and especially validity estimates are currently inadequate.

Review of the Nurse Entrance Test by PATRICIA A. BACHELOR, Professor of Psychology, California State University—Long Beach, Long Beach, CA:

DESCRIPTION. The Nurse Entrance Test (NET) was designed for use by nursing programs in the evaluation of applicants to their programs. The NET is designed to assess applicants on seven academic and social/personal factors (Essential Math Skills, Reading Comprehension, Critical Thinking Appraisal, Social Decisions, Stressful Situations, Learning Styles, and Testtaking Skills) in an effort to select applicants who have the highest probability of success in a nursing program. The three academic factors—Essential Math Skills, Reading Comprehension, and Critical Thinking Appraisal—comprise seven, three, and three subtests, respectively. The seven Math subtests are: Whole Numbers, Number System Conversions, Algebra Equations, Percentage Operations, Decimal Operations, Fraction Operations, and Essential Math Skills. The three Reading Comprehension subtests are: Reading Rate, Reading Rate Placement, and Reading Comprehension. The three Critical Thinking Appraisal subtests are: Main Idea of Passage, Inferential Reading, and Predicting of Outcomes. There is

one Testtaking subtest. The two Social Interaction Profile scores are derived from the Passive/ Aggressive subtests. There are five Stress Level Profile subtests (Family, Social, Money/Time, Academic, and Work Place). The six Learning Styles assessed are: Auditory Learner, Solitary Learner, Visual Learner, Social Learner, Oral Dependent Learner, and Writing Dependent Learner. There is also an Overall Composite Percentage. Hence, the NET yields a total of 31 scores, which can be used for diagnostic and academic counseling purposes. The NET also provides a Diagnostic Report, which includes Group-level mean percentages and normative comparisons for each of the 31 scores, individual student reports, and an optional study guide with testtaking strategy information along with practice tests. The NET is administered in groups with a time limit of about 150 minutes.

DEVELOPMENT. Educational Resources, Inc. (ERI) was responsible for the development of the NET. In that effort, ERI formed an Examination Committee composed of faculty actively involved in the teaching and academic counseling of students in health occupations programs. Members of the committee were sought to represent professional preparation and experience from the West, South, Midwest, and Northeast regions of the country. Item writers were health occupation faculty and counselors with the education and/or professional credentials to be considered proficient and current in the content areas or student behaviors for which a subtest was being developed. Upon completion of the item writing, the examination committee reviewed and evaluated the items and sample answers for alignment with the content or student behavior to be assessed in the subtest. After this first round of test item screening, the items were then administered, as a trial test, to a sample of nursing students during the first 2 months of their first semester. In an attempt to have a representative sample of nursing students, students from the four aforementioned regions of the country were tested. The examination committee used statistical analyses of the responses on the trial test to edit/revise/add/delete items, as needed, so that there was adherence to the guidelines established by the committee with respect to the content areas and social/personal behaviors to be assessed in each subtest. Test questions were expected to distinguish between students with or without adequate skill level in the areas of essential math skills, critical thinking, and reading comprehension; to identify students who were and were not experiencing stress; and to correctly identify students' learning styles.

TECHNICAL.

Standardization. Representative client schools were selected to reflect the four previously identified general regions of the country, level of education, and type of location (suburb, city, or rural). A purposive sample of nursing schools in inner-city core areas was included in the sample. The sample consisted of 85 nursing schools. Unfortunately, this is the extent of information about the selected schools. Normative comparisons are, thereby, difficult. Tests administered at each school were arranged in different orders so that each examination would be administered to a sample of students (of at least 200) in each school. No further information was provided about students' demographics, or the process by which students were recruited. The lack of descriptive data about the students' demographics seriously limits the normative comparisons and assessment of the appropriate use of the NET. It is hoped that these data will be forthcoming.

Reliability. The reliability of scores from the NET was assessed using the split-half reliability procedure. The split-half method, with an adjustment using the Spearman-Brown equation, is considered within the rubric of estimating internal consistency reliability. However, the Spearman-Brown equation adjustment was not made in the case of the NET subtests. Rather, NET subtests administered to students, when scored, were converted into two halves (odd-numbered items were scored as Form A and even-numbered items were scored as Form B). Then, students' scores on Form A were correlated with their scores on Form B. These correlations on NET subtests were .81 for Essential Math Skills, .98 for Reading Comprehension, .97 for Stress Decisions, .92 for Social, and .91 for Learning Styles. Based on these correlations, the content in each half of the aforementioned NET subtests is internally consistent. However, to correctly complete the assessment of split-half internal consistency reliability of the subtests, the Spearman-Brown Equation should be used to compute the estimated reliability of all items on the subtest. The correct calculations of estimates of split-half internal consistency reliability are in the ranges of .90s for subtests mentioned above.

Validity. The items and objectives of the NET were developed after a survey of the literature. Guidelines by state licensing boards were also utilized to assure that the test assessed the curricula of schools of nursing. A test blueprint was thereby developed upon careful review of the current texts, recent literature, standards established by state nursing boards, and current educational practices of the experts who teach and counsel students in health occupation areas. Item writers who possessed the appropriate credentials and expertise wrote subtest items that were reviewed by the examination committee for conformity to the subtest objectives. Evidence of content validity of the NET was the agreement between the specified item content and test expert's rating of the items as evaluating the specified content area.

Criterion-related validity of the NET was demonstrated by the correlation between students' NET Composite Percentage Score and their ACT Composite Score. The correlations ranged between .79 and .83; hence, the NET has a very strong relationship to the ACT. If the ACT is considered a meaningful test of successful performance after high school, then the Composite Percentage Score on the NET possesses substantial criterion-related validity.

COMMENTARY. The test manual for the NET provided a thorough yet concise presentation of the development and psychometric features of the NET. Efforts were made to seek a purposive sample to demonstrate the psychometric merits of the NET. The development of the NET was extensively researched to reflect current health occupation content. Items were written to capture current and relevant content, then judged and evaluated, and carefully revised. The elaborate, ongoing plan for test revision is noteworthy. Five research studies were included in the manual. One such study investigated the existence of a cultural bias in items of the NET but found none. A considerable amount of consistency and dependability has been demonstrated on the subtests discussed in the NET's manual. Content validity is demonstrated by the construction and revision of the NET. The high positive correlation between the Composite NET and ACT supports the claim of criterion-related validity.

SUMMARY. The NET is designed to evaluate the academic skills and social/personal traits of applicants to nursing programs. Initial test development and ongoing revisions were appropriate and resulted in a thorough and theoretically based representation of targeted content areas. The description and the demographics of the standardization sample were lacking as were the details of selection of the sample; hence, meaningful comparisons are limited. Applicants' 31 subtest scores on the NET are translated into group and individual normative scores to assist normative comparisons. Internal consistency reliability, when corrected with the Spearman-Brown equation, should fall within the .90s for most subtests. Content and criterion-related validity of the NET have been adequately demonstrated for the purposes stated. In conclusion, the psychometric properties of the NET were well within acceptable ranges; hence, the NET is a suitable and thoughtful option for selection and counseling applicants to nursing programs.

[170]

Object-Oriented Programmer Analyst Staff Selector.

Purpose: To measure knowledge of object-oriented terminology and C++.
Population: Candidates for the position of object-oriented programmer analyst.
Publication Date: 1994.
Acronym: OOPS.
Scores: Total Score, Narrative Evaluation, Ranking, Recommendation.
Administration: Group.
Price Data, 2001: $350 per candidate; quantity discounts available.
Time: (120) minutes.
Comments: Scored by publisher.
Author: Bruce A. Winrow.
Publisher: Walden Personnel Performance, Inc. [Canada].

Review of the Object-Oriented Programmer Analyst Staff Selector by DENNIS DOVERSPIKE, Professor of Psychology, University of Akron, Akron, OH:

DESCRIPTION. The Object-Oriented Programmer Analyst Staff Selector (OOPS) was developed to be used by organizations in the selection of object-oriented programmers, a specialized type of computer programmer. This test is probably best described as a test of technical knowledge, although it also attempts to tap logic and programming skill. There are six sections or types

of problems: Object-Oriented Knowledge, C++ Knowledge, Reasoning, Procedure Creation, Specifications, and Symbolic Programming.

The test is administered via paper and pencil. The first section or problem uses a matching format. The second section is multiple choice. The third, fifth, and sixth sections are fill-in-the-blank. The fourth section asks the respondent to correctly order steps in a sequence. Technical knowledge is required to respond to the problems and each problem could be considered to be a low-fidelity simulation of a real-world programming problem.

The test can be administered by clerical staff to either a group or an individual. The instructions are fairly simple to follow.

A scoring service is provided by the publisher. Tests can be submitted for scoring using regular mail, courier, or fax. Additional scoring options are also offered. The scoring service includes an individualized candidate report, which can be provided by mail, courier, fax, or email. The candidate report provides an overall score, a normative rating, and scores on each of the problem areas. In addition to the overall rating, a recommendation regarding the potential for success is provided.

DEVELOPMENT. The problem with evaluating the OOPS test is that the content validation study supplied was not clearly labeled as to whether it was used in the development of the test or whether it is intended as an example of the type of validation report that would be provided to a client. The OOPS appears to have been developed based upon a content validation strategy. That is, a job analysis was conducted to identify the tasks performed by a programmer analyst. Then, the essential knowledge, skills, and abilities corresponding to each task were identified. Based on the knowledge, skills, and abilities, the relevant problems were identified. Again, this appears to be the procedure, but it is unclear from the manual.

Thus, the test appears to have been developed based upon a content validity strategy where critical knowledge elements were identified. However, the exact nature of this study was unclear. The materials provided by the developer provide minimal information on the actual initial test development.

TECHNICAL. No real technical information was provided in the materials supplied by the developer. There appears to be some type of normative or standardization sample, because the candidate reports provide a type of normative or standardized score. However, the exact nature of this standardization sample was not discernable from the materials provided. Therefore, no judgment can be made concerning its appropriateness for various gender or ethnic groups.

Based on the nature of the test, it is likely that internal consistency reliability is high. However, no information on reliability was identified in the test manuals.

It appears that the intent is to provide a validation study for each client. This validation study would be based upon a transfer study, which is described as a content validation study in the provided manual. The transfer study demonstrates that there is sufficient overlap between the tasks and knowledge, skills, and abilities for the company's jobs and the original validation sample. It is not clear whether the test can be administered without a local validation study.

COMMENTARY. The OOPS appears to represent a reasonable attempt to measure the knowledge, skills, and abilities required for an entry level programmer analyst position. However, more information is needed on the technical aspects of the test including its standardization, reliability, and validity.

Several questions can be asked regarding the construction of the items for the test. As mentioned above, the first section is matching. One wonders whether a multiple-choice format might have been more effective.

In addition, the second section is multiple choice. However, the multiple-choice questions violate many of the basic rules of multiple-choice item construction. Alternatives include "all of the above," "none of the above," and "both a and c" types. The problem with these types of alternatives is that it makes the existence of a single defensible best answer or correct answer questionable.

SUMMARY. The OOPS does provide a standardized approach to measuring the knowledge, skills, and abilities required for an entry level programmer analyst position. However, better documentation is needed with regard to technical issues. The test items could also use rewriting following the rules for multiple-choice item construction. The question a company, the most likely user, would have to ask is whether it is better to use a test such as the OOPS or whether it would be better to invest in developing a locally validated and constructed test tailored to the organization's jobs.

Review of the Object-Oriented Programmer Analyst Staff Selector by MATTHEW E. LAMBERT, Assistant Clinical Professor of Neuropsychiatry, Texas Tech University Health Sciences Center, Lubbock, TX:

DESCRIPTION. The Object-Oriented Programmer Analyst Staff Selector Test (OOPS) was designed to evaluate candidates for the employment position of Object-Oriented Programmer Analyst using the C++ programming language. It is to be used as part of their overall evaluation prior to employment. The OOPS consists of six problems designed to assess basic technical knowledge, logic, and analytical skills. Aspects of job criteria include: Object-Oriented Knowledge, C++ Knowledge, Reasoning, Procedure Creation, Specifications, and Symbolic Programming. It is administered in a paper-and-pencil format either individually or in a group setting. A 2-hour time period is provided to complete the instrument.

Once completed, the OOPS must be submitted to the test publisher for scoring and interpretation. Submission options include regular mail, courier service, fax service, or a "Super-Fast" service that provides reports within 24 hours. The interpretive report offers an overall score that is based on the number of points obtained in each problem. A rating is then provided indicating whether the candidate's performance reflects the potential to have a successful career as an object-oriented programmer analyst. Unfortunately, the exact range of the ratings is not provided in any of the OOPS's supporting materials. The report also provides a problem-by-problem analysis of the candidate's performance followed by a recommendation based on the rating that predicts the potential for a successful career. Finally, the interpretive report provides a graph of the candidate's individual problem performance on a 1 to 9 scale with 1 being "Below Average" and 9 being "Above Average."

The supporting documentation for the OOPS includes a bound report of the content validation study used in development of the OOPS and a four-page test manual. The test manual provides a general description of the instrument, a sample interpretive report, administration instructions, and scoring service instructions.

DEVELOPMENT. Information regarding the development is included in a content validation report conducted in response to a "request of the Employment Manager of XYZ Systems, Inc. to establish content validity" of the OOPS for their use in selecting programmer analysts. XYZ Systems, Inc. is described as a holding company based in New York that provides telecommunications, data, and information services through its subsidiaries. According to the content validation study report the OOPS was developed, through a job analysis, by identifying 14 key tasks to be completed by a Programmer Analyst in performing the responsibilities associated with the programmer analyst job. The 14 tasks, however, vary in their importance to performing the job. To accomplish those tasks, 64 traits deemed as essential were identified and organized to be assessed by one or more sections of the test. Additionally, 10 secondary traits were identified as "nice but not necessary" (content validation study, p. 12) for the Programmer Analyst job. The documentation provided indicates that an unweighted overlap of the essential skills tested versus essential skills identified was 56.3%, and a weighted (minus those skills deemed company specific) overlap of 71.87%.

Although these statistics are adequate, there is no information to indicate how the items were constructed, or whether they were chosen from a larger group of items. There is also no information related to the individuals who actually wrote the items. As well, there is no discussion of how the job analysis upon which the essential skills were determined was conducted. All in all, there is little basis for understanding how the OOPS was constructed other than to say it was designed to assess essential skills thought important to the performance of the job of programmer analyst.

TECHNICAL. Unfortunately, there is a complete absence of any other psychometric information related to the statistical properties of the OOPS. No reliability information of any type is reported. There is also no information reported regarding internal consistency of the items nor their discriminatory ability. Unfortunately, the reliability of the instrument will ultimately impact its validity.

Although content validity is essential to meeting EEOC guidelines as providing a basis for using the instrument in an employment setting, it does not in and of itself make the instrument a valid tool. Again, no information is provided that relates to the instrument's predictive validity, which would seem related to the specific purpose for which the instrument is to be used. No studies appear to have been conducted to determine if the instrument is effective in predicting candidates' success in the position of a programmer analyst. One can only assume that if those studies were conducted they are viewed as proprietary and therefore not published in a test manual format. If those studies were not conducted then there is a deficit in the basis for using the OOPS.

COMMENTARY. The OOPS was developed to assist in the selection of candidates for the position of Programmer Analyst in a C++ programming environment. Although the instrument appears to take a standard approach to that endeavor, there is little information with which to judge the instrument's utility and efficacy. A single content validation study is presented as the sole basis for the instrument's use. No predictive validity information was made available, which seems somewhat curious as the purpose of the instrument is to predict success. More troubling, however, is the lack of information regarding the individual item development and basic measures of reliability and internal consistency. It can only be assumed that this information is viewed as proprietary or was not obtained at all. In either case, without presentation of this information to potential consumers it cannot be said that this instrument should be widely used in employment screening. Although it may meet the letter of EEOC guidelines, as presented it certainly does not meet the spirit. It is this spirit that may pose problems for consumers if challenges to its use in employment screening are actually made.

[171]

Occupational Aptitude Survey and Interest Schedule—Third Edition.

Purpose: To assist in career development.
Population: Grades 8–12 and adults.
Publication Dates: 1983–2002.
Administration: Group or individual.
Time: (30–45) minutes per survey.
Comments: Machine scoring is available.
Author: Randall M. Parker.
Publisher: PRO-ED.

a) APTITUDE SURVEY.
Acronym: OASIS-3:AS.
Scores, 6: General Ability, Verbal Aptitude, Numerical Aptitude, Spatial Aptitude, Perceptual Aptitude, Manual Dexterity.
Price Data, 2004: $164 per complete kit including 10 student test booklets, 50 handscorable

answer sheets, 50 profile sheets, and examiner's manual (2002, 45 pages); $40 per 10 student test booklets; $40 per 50 handscorable answer sheets; $28 per 50 profile sheets; $56 per examiner's manual.

b) INTEREST SCHEDULE.

Acronym: OASIS-3:IS.

Scores, 12: Artistic, Scientific, Nature, Protective, Mechanical, Industrial, Business Detail, Selling, Accommodating, Humanitarian, Leading-Influencing, Physical Performing.

Price Data: $174 per complete kit including 25 student test booklets, 50 handscorable answer sheets, 50 profile sheets, 50 scoring forms, and examiner's manual (2002, 53 pages); $40 per 25 student test booklets; $28 per 50 handscorable answer sheets; $28 per 50 profile sheets; $27 per scoring forms; $56 per examiner's manual.

Cross References: For reviews by Laura L. B. Barnes and Thomas E. Dinero of an earlier version of the Aptitude Survey, see 12:263 (2 references); see also T4:1862 (2 references). For reviews by Robert J. Miller and Donald G. Zytowski of an earlier version of the Interest Schedule, see 12:264; see also T4:1863 (2 references); for reviews by Christopher Borman and Ruth G. Thomas of an earlier edition, see 20:244 (1 reference).

Review of the Occupational Aptitude Survey and Interest Schedule—Third Edition by MICHAEL B. BUNCH, Vice President, Measurement Incorporated, Durham, NC:

DESCRIPTION.

General. The Occupational Aptitude Survey and Interest Schedule—Third Edition (OASIS-3) consists of the OASIS-3:AS (Aptitude Survey) and the OASIS-3:IS (Interest Schedule). Together, these instruments may be used to determine the occupational aptitudes and interests of students in Grades 8 through postsecondary education. The program consists of the two student test booklets, two administration manuals, answer sheets, scoring forms, student profile sheets, and an interpretation workbook. The instruments may be scored by hand or by a computerized scoring service.

The Aptitude Survey. The Aptitude Survey (AS) consists of five subtests: Vocabulary (40 items), Computation (30 items), Spatial Relations (20 items), Word Comparison (100 items), and Making Marks (160 items). Student responses to these items yield scores on the following factors: General Ability (G; derived by summing Vocabulary and Computation); Verbal Aptitude (V; equal

to the Vocabulary score); Numerical Aptitude (N; equal to the Computation score); Spatial Aptitude (S; equal to the Spatial Relations Score); Perceptual Aptitude (P; equal to the Word Comparison score); and Manual Dexterity (M; equal to the Making Marks score).

The 40 Vocabulary items require examinees to find synonyms or antonyms in lists of four words (e.g., Dry, Hot, Dusty, Cold, with the correct pairing being Hot/Cold). The Computation subtest consists of 30 multiple-choice mathematics problems of one step, typically requiring only one of the four basic functions, square root, or algebra with one unknown. The Spatial Relations subtest requires examinees to match 20 flat depictions of three-dimensional shapes with their 3-D forms. For each of these three subtests, items are ordered by difficulty. The Word Comparison subtest is a clerical accuracy test that requires examinees to compare 100 pairs of entries in 5 minutes to determine which are exact matches and which are not. The Making Marks subtest requires examinees to make 160 asterisk-like marks (*) inside 160 small square boxes in 1 minute. Tests may be scored by hand or sent to the publisher for computerized scoring.

The Interest Schedule. The Interest Schedule (IS) consists of 120 job titles and 120 job activities that test takers mark on a 3-point scale: Like (L), Neutral (N), and Dislike (D). Each of the 12 scales listed above is represented by 10 job titles and 10 activities. Scoring consists of adding the Likes (2 points) and Neutrals (1 point) for each job or activity associated with a particular scale. The items are arranged in the test booklet and answer sheet in a way that makes this process quite simple.

Students and adults are guided through a series of steps to help narrow their vocational choices. The author employed a 12-scale model within which test takers make these decisions: (1) Artistic (ART); (2) Scientific (SCI); (3) Nature (NAT); (4) Protective (PRO); (5) Mechanical (MEC); (6) Industrial (IND); (7) Business Detail (BUS); (8) Selling (SEL); (9) Accommodating (ACC); (10) Humanitarian (HUM); (11) Leading-Influencing (LEA); and (12) Physical Performing (PHY).

Scores on these 12 factors are interpreted against norms based on the responses of 1,505 students in Grades 8–12 and a sample of 500 postsecondary students in 1997–2001. There is no attempt to compare the scores of students to those of job incumbents. Scales yielding high stanine scores are considered worthy of further exploration, and the materials in the kit provide extensive aids to further exploration, including average starting salaries, job growth projections through 2008, and a host of Web sites for additional information.

DEVELOPMENT.

The Aptitude Survey. The AS is based on the General Aptitude Test Battery (GATB; U.S. Department of Labor, 1970). The five factors represent a streamlining of the 9-factor GATB, based on research that showed a stable five-factor solution to the correlation matrix of the 12 GATB subtests. The developers then adapted or developed new items to measure these five factors. The new items were patterned after GATB items.

All items were administered to 1,505 students in Grades 8–12 and 500 adults in postsecondary settings. The author used both quota and purposive sampling (i.e., they kept a running tally of the demographic characteristics of subjects as they added to the sample). In terms of geography, ethnicity, and gender, the demographics of the norming sample are quite close to 1996 U.S. Census data.

The Interest Schedule. The IS is based on earlier work by the U.S. Employment Service (USES). The 12 interest factors extracted by Cottle (1950), based on 307 activity items, are identical to those listed above. The 120 job activities in the IS were selected to represent activities in the *Guide for Occupational Exploration* (Farr, Ludden, & Shatkin, 2001; U.S. Department of Labor, 1979), whereas the 120 job titles were selected to be representative of the 12 interest factors and 66 subareas listed in that same work. These 120 job titles and 120 activities were translated into 240 items by the addition of the 3-point rating scale to each. The 240 items were administered to the same 1,505 students in Grades 8–12 and 500 adults in postsecondary settings who also responded to the AS.

TECHNICAL.

The Aptitude Survey. The five-factor solution to the GATB item correlation matrix was applied to the development of the OASIS:AS. A sixth factor (General Ability) was derived by summing Verbal and Numerical Aptitude scores. The item correlation matrix for the AS yielded two factors, with eigenvalues of 2.16 and .99, that accounted for 63.2 percent of common variance.

Three scores (Vocabulary, Computation, and Spatial Relations) loaded significantly on the first factor, whereas two (Word Comparison and Making Marks) loaded on the second. Factor loadings showed clear distinctions between the two overall factors, which might well be called General Ability and Perceptual-Motor Skill.

Item difficulties (percent correct) ranged from 8% to 94% for Vocabulary, 7% to 93% correct for Computation, and 15% to 95% correct for Spatial Relations. Subtest or factor score reliability coefficients are not reported. Instead, the examiner's manual reports item/total correlation coefficients, which range from the .20s to the .60s, with most in the .30s and .40s.

Results of several studies comparing AS scores to scores on other measures are reported in the examiner's manual. In general, the correlations support the claim that the AS measures the variables it purports to measure. As the AS is based on the GATB, the most compelling evidence of construct validity is found in the table of correlations between AS scores and comparable GATB scores. The correlations range from .74 (Manual Dexterity) to .87 (Perceptual Aptitude). It is noteworthy that the remaining correlations are all significantly lower than the target correlations, providing very satisfactory evidence of convergent/divergent validity.

The Interest Schedule. Reliability coefficients reported for each IS scale are generally quite high. Coefficients by group are also reported and are also typically high, although some are in the .75 range. The publishers report reliability of difference scores and offer both standard errors of measurement (*SEM*) and standard errors of difference (*SED*), a necessity for an instrument of this sort. Correlations with other interest measures are also reported, and the correlations generally support the notion that the IS measures the 12 interest scales it purports to measure.

COMMENTARY. The OASIS demonstrates many fine qualities. The most striking quality emerges from even a casual reading of the two examiner's manuals. Beyond the clear directions and detailed technical information is a consistent body of text that projects the authority of experienced vocational counselors. Even the introductory comments reveal a wealth of experience and understanding of students and vocational counseling. There are no attempts to overinterpret; in fact, there are several cautions to the contrary. To their credit, the publishers offer interest test norms by sex only when there are significant differences between male and female responses. Indeed, they have made every effort (with success) to eliminate or minimize gender bias.

The publishers have attempted to provide up-to-date job market projections and other crucial nontest information. The Web sites listed in the manuals provide additional information that should be even more current. The various information sources are very neatly tied together.

Any flaws in the tests should be considered minor, perhaps even picky. The sample sizes seem rather small, but reasonably representative. The two-factor solution includes one factor with an eigenvalue of only .99. Such factors always present difficult decisions. The first factor accounts for 43% of the variance and is reasonably reliable. The second factor adds 20% to variance explained but has no reliability. Does one opt for reliable factors or more explained variance? Some of the validity studies also seemed to be of marginal value, particularly those attempting to predict postsecondary major or learning style. In fact, the OASIS/GATB intercorrelation matrix should be sufficient to convince anyone that the OASIS is a viable tool for vocational guidance. This should be considered a very minor criticism. The materials are of uniformly high quality.

SUMMARY. The test booklets, scoring sheets, manuals, and interpretive guides are well produced and easy to use. The experience of the publishers and authors is quite evident throughout. Every page of the instructions and interpretive materials conveys authority and experience. Anyone looking for an exceptional tool to help junior high, high school, or postsecondary students explore vocational options would do well to pay very close attention to the OASIS.

REVIEWER'S REFERENCES

Cottle, W. (1950). A factorial study of the Multiphasic, Strong, Kuder, and Bell inventories using a population of adult males. *Psychometrika, 15,* 25–47.
Farr, J. M., Ludden, L., & Shatkin, L. (2001). *Guide for occupational exploration* (3rd ed.) Indianapolis, IN: JIST Works.
Norusis, M. (1998). *SPSS 8.0: A guide to data analysis.* Englewood Cliffs, NJ: Prentice Hall.
U.S. Department of Labor. (1970). *Manual for the USES General Aptitude Test Battery.* Washington, DC: U.S. Government Printing Office.

Review of the Occupational Aptitude Survey and Interest Schedule—Third Edition by WILLIAM B. MICHAEL, Professor Emeritus, University of Southern California, Los Angeles, CA:

The Occupational Aptitude Survey (OASIS-3:AS) and Interest Schedule (OASIS-3:IS) were constructed to facilitate career development by examining (a) achievement-related dimensions measured by performance on the OASIS-3:AS and (b) vocational interest and preference factors related to various occupations assessed by the OASIS-3:IS. The instruments were originally devised for students enrolled in Grades 8–12 and now have been revised to include adult norms that can serve postsecondary students through graduate school. Presented separately in the two major sections that follow, the reader will find a review for the two batteries of the OASIS with closing remarks in a final summary section that addresses both instruments.

DESCRIPTION. This form of the Occupational Aptitude Survey and Interest Schedule: Aptitude Survey (OASIS-3:AS) was designed to identify those aptitude/achievement factors hypothesized to be important in learning activities that might tend to support success in a variety of vocations. The essential rationale was that those students who demonstrate a relatively high level of performance on selected academic skills and perceptual tasks would be expected to hold an affinity for selected jobs that require similar abilities. A practical aspect of the scale is its use as a comparatively quick assessment of aptitudes that can provide a foundation from which to examine career options for students in Grades 8–12 and for individuals with postsecondary levels of education.

The OASIS-3:AS is a six-scale, 35-minute timed test. The subtests accompanied by a statement of the number of items and the time required for completion of each section are as follows: (a) Vocabulary (40 items; 9 minutes) gives the examinee four words from which he or she identifies either a pair of synonyms or a pair of antonyms; (b) Computation (30 items; 12 minutes) requires completion of arithmetic calculations; (c) Spatial Relations (20 items; 8 minutes) presents items that rely on the tasks of visualization and prediction of sequences in the construction of an object such as a cube or cylinder; (d) Word Comparison (100 items; 5 minutes) lists pairs of names, letters, or numbers and asks the examinee to determine whether these pairs contain the same or different elements—an activity known to measurement specialists as a perceptual speed factor; and (e) Making Marks (two 30-second sections) is a fine-motor coordination-type test in which the examinee makes as many pencil marks as possible of a specified form in a designated space. The scores from the Vocabulary and Computation subtests are combined to form a sixth subtest score called General Ability.

DEVELOPMENT. The development of OASIS-3:AS has been influenced by the research and constructs developed for such well-known instruments as the General Aptitude Test Battery (GATB; T4:2868), the Armed Services Vocational Aptitude Battery (ASVAB; T4:196), and the Differential Aptitude Test (DAT; 12:118). It is noteworthy that the OASIS-3:AS subtests were constructed through factor analytic studies of the GATB in which consideration was given to the reduction of the nine GATB factors to a smaller subset.

Accompanying the detailed examiner's manual are student test booklets, answer sheets, and student profile forms. Test administrators are instructed to follow the guidelines set out in the manual and common testing procedures are described for conducting a testing session, organizing materials, setting up the testing environment to maximize performance and minimize cheating, and adhering to established time limits for each subtest. It is recommended for every 30 examinees that a trained proctor be provided. Both hand-scored or machine-scored answer sheets are available. The test examiner directs examinees through each phase of the five OASIS-3:AS subtests by reading a detailed script that provides a sample item, the correct response option, and instructions for marking the answer sheet. Explicit directions are furnished for scoring the two types of answer sheets and a student profile can be generated that lists raw scores and corresponding percentile ranks and stanines for each of the six subtests presented in a typical chart format. The examiner's manual provides clearly written guidelines for interpreting OASIS-3:AS subtest scores and student profiles as well as for presenting this information to the examinee. Sample scenarios are offered for additional instruction.

TECHNICAL. The standardization of OASIS-3:AS scores for generating norms was based on two samples: (a) 1,505 public school students in Grades 8–12 described in the second edition of the OASIS published in 1991 and (b) 500 individuals enrolled in postsecondary educational settings and cited in the third edition in 2002. Efforts to gain representative samples employed quota (for selecting geographical regions) and purposive

sampling procedures. Regions included the South, which made up about 36% of the normative sample, with the Midwest, West, and Northeast contributing 24%, 21%, and 19%, respectively. Student characteristics collected for Grades 8–12 included gender, race (White, Black, or Other), residence (urban/suburban or rural), and grade level. For the adult sample, region, age, gender, and ethnicity (African American, European American, Hispanic, or Other) were tracked.

Two separate tables have been provided for conversion of raw scores to standard scores and percentile ranks; one for Grades 8–12 because no statistically significant differences were found among grade levels or between genders on the various subtests; and one for postsecondary students. The author suggested that test users develop local norms for OASIS-3:AS scores.

Appropriate estimates of reliability for the six subscale scores were applied to a sample of 357 student responses from each of the five grade levels (sample sizes ranged from 44 to 119). Internal-consistency estimates using Cronbach's alpha yielded the following range of coefficients for Vocabulary (.87 to .92, *mdn* = .88); Computation (.82 to .88, *mdn* = .84); and for the related composite subtest, General Ability (.89 to .90, *mdn* = .90). Split-half reliability estimates for scores on the Spatial Relations subtest ranged from .70 to .92 (*mdn* = .78). Estimates derived from separately timed, parallel forms were obtained for Word Comparison (.85 to .94, *mdn* = .90) and Making Marks (.86 to .93, *mdn* = .89). In a separate analysis, reliability estimates were provided for males and females, which approximated the median estimates reported for subtest scores obtained for students in Grades 8–12. Stability estimates were obtained from a small sample of 54 secondary school students over a 2-week period. Coefficients ranged from .76 (Spatial Relations) to .94 (Making Marks) (*mdn* = .86). The author appropriately cautioned the test administrator not to use these scores as predictors of job performance but rather emphasized their use for vocational self-exploration.

For the total sample of 500 postsecondary adults, alpha coefficients were computed for Verbal (.90), Numerical (.83), the General Aptitude composite (.91), and Spatial (.70). Parallel-forms estimates were obtained for Perceptual (.89) and Manual Dexterity (.91). In addition, coefficients were generated for gender and ethnicity categories for each of the OASIS-3:AS subtests revealing similar patterns to those obtained for the total sample.

It is worth mentioning that the technical manual includes corresponding standard errors of measurement that may contribute to an increased understanding of subtest scores by the test user. A level of confidence, expressed as a range within which a particular subtest score is expected to fall, is generated for each score and displayed in the student profile.

Evidence of construct validity was provided by an examination of the intercorrelation matrix obtained from a sample of 1,363 respondents that revealed low to moderate correlations among the five subtest scores suggesting relative independence among the variables. Coefficients ranged from .07 to .51 (mdn = .28) with the strongest coefficients found between Computation and Vocabulary (r = .51) and Word Comparison (r = .40). The intercorrelation matrix was factor analyzed and produced two factors (factor loadings are presented in parentheses). The first factor included Vocabulary (.68), Computation (.67), and Spatial Relations (.40) and was labeled a "general ability factor" (manual, p. 23). However, as the Spatial Relations loading was low (.40), it was excluded from the General Ability composite score. The second factor was described as a perceptual-motor factor made up of Word Comparison (.53) and Making Marks (.56).

Concurrent validity evidence was reported in studies designed to investigate convergent and discriminant validation of the subtest scores. Correlation coefficients were examined between each of the six OASIS-3:AS subtest scores and subtest scores on (a) the Iowa Tests of Educational Development (ITED; 13:160), (b) the SRA Achievement Series (SRA; Naslund, Thorpe, & Lefever, 1973), and (c) the GATB (T4:2868). Based on a sample of 145 Arizona students in Grades 9–12, moderately high correlations were observed between the OASIS-3:AS Vocabulary and the ITED Reading, Grammar, and Math subtest scores (.68, .61, and .62, respectively), and between the OASIS-3:AS Computation and the ITED Math subtest scores (.64). In a second study of 175 Texas students enrolled in Grades 10–12, correlations among OASIS-3:AS and SRA subtest scores yielded moderately high coefficients between Vocabulary and the SRA Composite (.77), Reading (.74), Language (.72), Composite (.77), Math

(.65), Social Studies (.65), Science (.69), and Sources (.72). The OASIS-3:AS Computation (.31 to .44, mdn = .34) and Spatial Relations subtest scores produced moderately low coefficients with all SRA subtest scores (.30 to .49, mdn = .39). And, finally, for a small sample of 72 respondents, high correlations were observed between each of the six OASIS-3:AS subtest scores with each of the corresponding GATB subtests scores (.74 to .87, mdn = .82).

COMMENTARY. Extensive, thoughtful psychometric work with the OASIS-3:AS has been accomplished; no additional statistical procedures are suggested. However, it is recommended that additional efforts be undertaken to expand the norms to include broader sampling of underrepresented groups, particularly African American, Latino, Native American, and Asian subgroups.

The conceptual framework supporting the OASIS-3:AS is steeped in the rich tradition of aptitude testing and its subtests have been skillfully derived both conceptually and psychometrically from well-known instruments in the field. The five major constructs and one composite represent a distillation of commonly described aptitudes, the sense of which can be communicated readily to individuals with no testing expertise.

Testing time for the administration of the OASIS-3:AS has the advantage of being less than one third that required for the DAT (12:118) and other aptitude measures. However, career planning should not rely solely on the outcomes of one's performance on the OASIS-3:AS.

DESCRIPTION. The Occupational Aptitude Survey and Interest Schedule: Interest Schedule (OASIS-3:IS) organizes interest and preference factors judged to be important in various occupations. The rationale was that those individuals who respond in a manner consistent with such factors would be expected to enjoy success in and satisfaction with identified vocations at a higher level than would those students who express relatively low levels of preference or interest. A key feature of the scale is its intended use as a tool for vocational interests clarification and career exploration for those examinees in the eighth grade through postsecondary education levels.

The OASIS-3:IS is a 240-item, 12-scale instrument to which the examinee expresses his or her level of interest in various jobs and activities by providing 1 of 3 possible responses ("like," "neutral," or "dislike"), carrying score values of 3, 2, or 1, respectively. Each of the following 12 scales is made up of 20 items, 10 of which are occupation titles and 10 of which pertain to related activities: (a) Artistic (ART) deals with a variety of common methods of expression typically associated with the fine and performing arts and includes writing; (b) Scientific (SCI) emphasizes applied and research-related activities in mathematics and the sciences; (c) Nature (NAT) relates to work, management, or service in outdoor settings; (d) Protective (PRO) refers to interests compatible with law enforcement, fire fighting, or related jobs; (e) Mechanical (MEC) pertains to the application of mechanical principles and related technical-scientific endeavors; (f) Industrial (IND) focuses on supervisory and repetitive tasks such as those that occur in factory settings; (g) Business Detail (BUS) includes items associated with office work; (h) Selling (SEL) takes into account interest in product information and persuasion; (i) Accommodating (ACC) covers hospitality-related services; (j) Humanitarian (HUM) corresponds with the helping professions; (k) Leading-Influencing (LEA) stresses jobs that require leadership skills; and (l) Physical Performing (PHY) includes careers that involve demonstrations before various audiences as in professional sports. Along with the examiner's manual, the publisher provides answer sheets, profile sheets, and scoring forms.

DEVELOPMENT. The development of the OASIS-3:IS grew out of interest research influenced by Cottle (1950) and conducted through the U.S. Employment Service (USES). An initial 307 items were generated dealing with activities thought to be involved with most types of work. The items were administered to a sample of 1,115 high school seniors, college students, and workers affiliated with the USES. A principal components analysis yielded 11 interpretable factors for the total sample, factors that were invariant for the male and female subsamples. Next, 66 job groups were identified and classified into 1 of the 11 dimensions; those occupations that did not fit were assigned to a 12th factor. The 12 USES factors correspond to the names given to the 12 scales of the 240-item OASIS-3:IS and used in the development of the *Guide for Occupational Exploration* (GOE; Farr, Ludden, & Shatkin, 2001) and the *Enhanced Guide for Occupational Exploration* (Mayall & Maze, 1995); both texts are

considered helpful resources for interpreting OASIS-3:IS scores.

Careful attention has been paid to controlling for gender bias in the construction of OASIS-3:IS items and scales, with particular emphasis placed on gender-neutral wording to meet the *National Institute of Education (NIE) Guidelines for Assessment of Sex Bias and Sex Fairness in Career Interest Inventories* (NIE, 1974) and to insure gender-balance for the item pool and scales so that the same test form can be administered to both males and females.

Test administrators receive guidelines for administering, scoring, interpreting, and presenting findings to examinees with adequate cautionary notes included for the interpretation of scores, particularly for those scores that are based on same-sex norms. In addition, descriptive scenarios and a helpful guide to resources are provided to aid interpretation. The examiner's manual for the OASIS-3:IS includes information of similar detail as that described for the OASIS-3:AS.

TECHNICAL. The reader is referred to the technical section of the OASIS-3:AS in this review for a description of the two samples (1,505 students in Grades 8–12; and 500 postsecondary students) that also were employed for providing normative data for OASIS-3:IS scores. Four norm tables used to convert raw scores to standard scores (stanines) and percentile ranks are included in the manual; three tables were generated for Grades 8–12 and one for postsecondary students. Statistically significant differences were identified for secondary school males and females on 5 IS scales including MEC, BUS, ACC, HUM, and PHY requiring separate tables. No statistically significant gender differences were found for these students on the remaining 7 scales and no gender differences were noted for scores on the 12 OASIS-3:IS scales for the postsecondary sample.

Both internal-consistency estimates of reliability (Cronbach's alpha) and stability estimates were provided for scores obtained from the two samples (secondary school and post-secondary students) for each of the 12 OASIS-3:IS scales. Alpha coefficients displayed by gender for a sample of 177 respondents in Grades 8–12 revealed similar patterns for males and females, with a range from .87 to .95 (*mdn* = .89) for males; and .85 to .92 (*mdn* = .89) for females. For a sample of 260 secondary school students, an examination of coefficients for the 12 scales grouped by Grades 8, 10, and 12, produced ranges of .86 to .93 (*mdn* = .90), .86 to .94 (*mdn* = .90), and .78 to .94 (*mdn* = .88), respectively. Two-week test-retest reliability estimates for each of the 12 OASIS-3:IS scale scores obtained from a sample of 54 secondary school students ranged from .66 to .91 (*mdn* = .82). With respect to the total sample of 500 postsecondary students, alpha coefficients for the 12 OASIS-3:IS scale scores produced a range of .84 to .96 (*mdn* = .92). When the scores were grouped by gender, the range for males was .86 to .95 (*mdn* = .92) and for females, .83 to .96 (*mdn* = .92). Similar patterns were observed for four ethnic classifications (European American, African American, and Hispanic American, and Other). Two-week test-retest coefficients yielded a range of .82 to .91 (*mdn* = .87). Standard errors of measurement for stanine scores and corresponding levels of confidence are listed for each of the 12 scores presented in the respondent's profile providing an aid to the interpretation of scores.

Principal components analyses provided factorial validity evidence for the 12 hypothesized interest factors for data examined by gender as well as for the total sample. However, for the postsecondary adult sample, 11 of 12 factors were identifiable with Mechanical and Industrial items loading on the same factor.

Construct validity evidence was built upon 15 hypotheses generated by Gottfredson and Holland (1996) on the correspondence between OASIS-3:IS areas (the same as for the GOE) and Holland's Self-Directed Search (SDS; 10:330) classifications. In general, using the criterion of $r \geq$ .45, correlations obtained from one small study of 90 college students confirmed 10 of the following 15 hypotheses (correlation coefficients are presented in parentheses): Holland's "Realistic" classification would align with NAT (.62), PRO (.50), MEC (.64), IND (.60), and ACC (n.s.); "Investigative" with SCI (.54); "Artistic" with ART (.77); "Social" with ACC (n.s.), HUM (.76), LEA (n.s.), and PHY (n.s.); "Enterprising" with SEL (.67), ACC (n.s.), and LEA (.51); and "Conventional" with BUS (.67). These findings suggest congruence between the two measures and tend to support the constructs underlying the OASIS-3:IS scores.

In a study of 147 community college students, relationships were examined among several variables including learning style (classified as Accommodators, Convergers, Divergers, or Assimilators on Kolb's [1976] The Learning Styles Inventory), vocational interest (OASIS:IS scales), aptitude (OASIS:AS subtests), and selection of an academic major. The findings from a stepwise discriminant analysis indicated that the best discriminators among the four learning styles were, in order, academic major, ACC and SCI scores on the OASIS-3:IS, and Numerical Aptitude (NUM) scores on the OASIS-3:AS. Basically, "divergers," who are defined as people-oriented and creative, tended to have higher scores on ACC (meeting needs of others), to be undecided with respect to college major, and scored lower on NUM; "convergers," who prefer working with things, scored higher on SCI and lower on ACC; and "assimilators," described as inductive thinkers, scored highest on NUM and decisiveness regarding a college major. And, finally, no distinctive pattern among the variables was observed for those classified as "accommodators."

In another study, performance on the OASIS-3:IS and the OASIS-3:AS was examined for a sample of 135 community college students who identified a major as (a) undecided; (b) mechanical engineering; (c) business; (d) humanitarian, including nursing physical therapy, or psychology; and (e) professional, including law, nutrition, or education. Mechanical engineering students scored higher on MEC, SCI, PHY, and General Ability, compared to other major classifications; business majors had higher scores on BUS; and humanitarian majors, on HUM. In a follow-up study with 126 community college students and seven majors, art majors scored highest on ART, science majors on SCI, mechanical majors on MEC, business majors on BUS, and humanitarian majors on HUM.

COMMENTARY. The OASIS-3:IS is linked conceptually to research conducted by the U.S. Employment Service and to the *Guide for Occupational Exploration* (Farr et al., 2001). Test administration is an advantage with respect to ease, clarity of directions, and time required. Conscientious efforts have been made to prepare an empirically and psychometrically sound foundation although studies cited have relied on small samples raising legitimate concerns about the representativeness of the scores. Applicable to the OASIS-3:IS is the recommendation made for the OASIS-3:AS to expand the norms to include broader sampling of underrepresented groups, particularly

African American, Latino, Native American, and Asian subgroups.

SUMMARY. The Occupational Aptitude Survey and Interest Schedule: Aptitude Survey (OASIS-3:AS) and Interest Schedule (OASIS-3:IS) can serve as useful instruments for identifying common aptitudes and vocational interests to help focus career exploration for secondary school students and young adults particularly when used together and with the guidance of a trained career counselor.

In the examiner's manual for the OASIS-3:AS, an appendix is offered that groups occupations by the minimum level of aptitude performance as measured by the 6 OASIS-3:AS subtests thought to be required to successfully execute the jobs listed. Also, in the examiner's manual for the OASIS-3:IS, an appendix is offered that groups occupations by occupational interests organized by the 12 OASIS-3:IS scales. In addition, cross-referenced for each job listed are the corresponding occupation codes from the U.S. Department of Labor (1991) publication, *Dictionary of Occupational Titles* and the *Guide for Occupational Exploration* (Farr et al., 2001).

REVIEWER'S REFERENCES

Cottle, W. (1950). A factorial study of the Multiphasic, Strong, Kuder, and Bell inventories using a population of adult males. *Psychometrika, 15,* 25–47.

Farr, J. M., Ludden, L., & Shatkin, L. (2001). *Guide for occupational exploration* (3rd ed.). Indianapolis, IN: JIST Works.

Gottfredson, G., & Holland, J. (1996). *Dictionary of Holland occupational codes* (3rd ed.). Odessa, FL: Psychological Assessment Resources.

Kolb, D. (1976). *The Learning Styles Inventory: Technical manual.* Boston, MA: McBer.

Mayall, D., & Maze, M. (Eds.). (1995). *The enhanced guide for occupational exploration* (2nd ed). Indianapolis, IN: JIST Works.

Naslund, R. A., Thorpe, L. P., & Lefever, D. W. (1973). *SRA Achievement Series* (and SRA Assessment Survey). Chicago, IL: Science Research Associates, Inc.

National Institute of Education. (1974). *Guidelines for assessment of sex bias and sex fairness in career interest inventories.* Washington, DC: Department of Health, Education, and Welfare.

U.S. Department of Labor. (1991). *Dictionary of occupational titles* (4th ed.). Washington, DC: U.S. Government Printing Office.

[172]

O*NET Career Interests Inventory: Based on the "O*NET Interest Profiler" Developed by the U.S. Department of Labor.

Purpose: To allow users to rank six career interest areas and relate them to specific careers.
Population: Youth and adults.
Publication Date: 2002.
Scores: 6 interest categories: Realistic, Investigative, Artistic, Social, Enterprising, Conventional.
Administration: Group or individual.
Price Data, 2003: $29.95 per 25 inventories including copy of administrator's guide (8 pages).
Time: (20–60) minutes.

Comments: Twelve-panel foldout; a compact, shorter, and less expensive version of the Department of Labor's "O*NET Interest Profiler"; based on the "O*NET Interest Profiler" developed by the U.S. Department of Labor.
Author: JIST Publishing, Inc.
Publisher: JIST Publishing, Inc.

Review of the O*NET Career Interest Inventory: Based on the "O*NET Interest Profiler" Developed by the U.S. Department of Labor by MARK POPE, Associate Professor, Division of Counseling and Family Therapy, University of Missouri—St. Louis, St. Louis, MO:

DESCRIPTION. The O*NET Career Interests Inventory (OCII) is a reformatted commercial version of the Department of Labor's (DOL) O*NET Interest Profiler (OIP), Version 3.0 (174). The OCII was developed to "help people identify their work interests or values and then use this information to explore career, learning, and lifestyle alternatives" (administrator's guide, p. 1). Items from the United States Employment Service (USES) Interest Inventory, USES Interest Checklist, and Job Search Inventory (Mueller, 1998; Zedeck, 1998) were used in the initial development of items.

The OCII is a 12-page consumable, combined administration/items/responses/profile/interpretive form that can be self-scored, self-administered, and self-interpreted. It utilizes a four-step process rather than simply a conventional inventory format. In this way it is similar to the Self-Directed Search (Holland, 2003; T6:2238) or other self-scored career interest inventories.

The first step consists of the presentation of 180 items that use a response format of Like, Unsure, and Dislike. Items consist of selected work activities such as "market a new line of clothing" (reported in the administrator's guide, p. 1).

In Step 2, the test-takers' Like responses are counted in the six Interest Areas (RIASEC areas: Realistic, Investigative, Artistic, Social, Enterprising, and Conventional) with 30 items used to develop a score in each Interest Area.

In Step 3, using an ipsative methodology, Interest Areas are then rank ordered for use in this interpretative step. Information is also provided for each of the six Interest Areas, specifically a brief definition followed by the job titles from O*NET that are related to each Area and categorized by "job zones," (i.e., DOL categories based on ordered levels of training, education, and experience, where "1" corresponds to "little or no preparation needed" to "5" described as "extensive preparation needed").

Finally, Step 4 describes a process that allows test takers to research career options that interest them most and develop appropriate information for successful career decisions. Two behaviorally anchored forms are included here. The first is a "job information worksheet" that identifies the type of occupational data that would be useful for the test taker in their job choice and the second is a "develop an action plan" worksheet that requests the test taker to identify actions to be accomplished in 30 days, 3 months, 6–12 months, 1–2 years, and 5 years.

There were four primary goals in the development of the original OIP: (a) develop an instrument that has strong technical characteristics that would provide clients with accurate and useful information; (b) develop an unbiased instrument that would serve the needs of clients from a variety of ethnic, cultural, and socioeconomic backgrounds; (c) develop an instrument that included items representing the entire world of work; to insure that it would provide useful information to individuals with different work-related goals and interests; and (d) develop an instrument that could be used as a self-assessment tool that individuals could self-administer, self-score, and self-interpret to empower clients to take control of their career exploration efforts.

The OCII is printed on 25.5 by 22 inches (width/length) heavy multicolored paper that has been folded into an 8.5 by 11 inches booklet of 12 same-sized panels, 6 panels on a side. The OCII uses a color-coordinated scheme in the presentation of the survey items that is then used in the scoring process as well as in an interpretative section to highlight descriptive information regarding the six Interest Areas.

The inventory is designed for group administration. It is designed to be easily self-scored and the administrator's guide states that it "can be self-scored and self-interpreted even by persons with no technical training of any kind" (p. 4). The lower age limit is 14 years and the reading level is eighth grade. The time required for administration of the OCII is 20 to 60 minutes.

DEVELOPMENT. How this inventory (OCII) or the inventory on which it is based (OIP) were developed was not addressed any-where in the administrator's guide other than to say that the U.S. Department of Labor did it. There is, in the OIP user's guide, an exhaustive explanation of the development of the OIP. That explanation leaves a knowledgeable reader feeling quite secure about the initial rationally derived item and scale development as well as the research used to validate the completed item selection and scale development. Also, because the OCII uses the same 180 items selected for the OIP in the same item order and same page design, there should be no substantial differences from the reliability and validity data for the OCII.

In the OIP user's guide, the DOL addressed the issues of bias in the instrument in a straight-forward way and provide evidence of reducing bias at each step in the development of the instrument. One of the primary goals in the development of the OIP was to "develop an unbiased instrument that would serve the needs of clients from a variety of ethnic, cultural, and socioeconomic backgrounds" (user's guide, p. 31). The DOL developers made a substantive effort to meet this goal by first training item writers and item reviewers to write items that would "reduce spurious gender and race/ethnic endorsement rate differences" (p. 34). In the first pilot study, items with large gender differences or large race/ethnic differences were removed. Next, the remaining items underwent a seven-step screening process that included the elimination of items that would be offensive to particular segments of the user population. A panel representing diverse ethnic and racial groups reviewed each item for possible bias against or offensiveness to racial, ethnic, or gender groups. Next, the pool of remaining items was piloted using a large representative sample that included approximately equal numbers of males and females, a high degree of ethnic diversity, a broad distribution of age groups, and represented a variety of education and employment situations. There were also other procedures that were employed to reduce bias.

TECHNICAL. An important issue for any consumer of these materials is the stability of vocational interests over time because, if interests change substantially, it would limit the application of the scores received on any career interest measure. In the administrator's guide, the publisher addresses research supporting the reliability and validity of the OCII. In a section titled "Validity of the Instruments," a summary of these data is presented. Internal consistency data are reported for the Interest Area scales ranging from .93 to .96, but such data are not reported by individual scale. Test-retest reliability values are reported to range from .81 to .92 for a "short time." No specific time frames were reported in the administrator's guide, but Rounds, Walker et al. (1999) reported that there was approximately 1 month between administrations. The publisher also reported that the "correlation to the Holland scales suggests a problematic Enterprising scale, since it correlates too closely to the Artistic scale, likely due to the instrument's inclusion of many low-level jobs that were not in the original Holland model" (p. 3). Each of these statements is accurate and mirrors similar detailed statements along with specific data in the DOL's OIP User's Guide from a study by Rounds, Smith, Hubert, Lewis, and Rivkind (1999).

COMMENTARY. The main question for any user of the OCII should be: What are the differences between the OCII and the OIP? Why should I purchase the OCII instead of the OIP? According to the publisher of the OCII, there are three reasons: (a) lower price, (b) simpler to administer and use, and (c) easier purchasing and better customer service because they are not a government agency.

Regarding cost, this is not as significant as the publisher would have users believe. The cost for purchase of the OCII is US$1.20 per booklet and the cost for the purchase of the OIP is US$5.92 for each user (the instrument is US$1.72 and the interpretive score report is US$4.20). The one large caveat is that the OIP is available for free if you download it from the DOL O*NET website (http://www.onetcenter.org). The DOL also provides two different versions on their website: one for those who want to produce single copies or small volume duplication (PDF files) where print quality is not an important issue and another for those who wish to print larger quantities for either private or public uses as these downloadable files (ZIP files) are suitable for generating print film and for reproduction using professional printing equipment. The following materials are available for download at no cost: the O*NET Interest Profiler instrument, the Score Report, the User's Guide, the O*NET Occupations Master List, and the O*NET Occupations Combined List: Interests and Work Values. If the indirect costs of downloading and color duplication are calculated, users might find they are better off financially to bite the bullet and order the OCII.

Regarding the simplicity of administration and use, there are substantial format differences between the OCII and the OIP. The OCII has been reformatted to fit into one booklet that is only 12 pages in length whereas the OIP is more than 60 pages in length. A substantial amount of information has been deleted to shrink 60 pages into 12 pages, but the substance remains intact. The OCII is described in the administrator's guide as a shortened version of the OPI. That is accurate, but the survey section has not been abbreviated—there are still 180 items. It is only the instructions and other descriptive materials that have been substantially edited to produce this version so that it would fit on these 12 pages. Although the OCII retains the psychometric properties of the survey sections, the original OIP instructions and other descriptive materials provided substantially more information and made the process more understandable and usable. Regarding ease of purchasing and better customer service, it is difficult for this reviewer to adequately assess these claims with limited experience.

The reformatting used in the OCII is succinct and attractive. The actual inventory section (Step 1) and the scoring section (Step 2) are exactly the same as used in the OIP. The interpretive sections (Steps 3 and 4) are practical and useful.

The "Administrator's Guide," as it is presented here, contains more than information for the "administration" of the OCII. It is a mini "user's guide" that includes a summary of the reliability and validity information as well as substantial interpretive resources. These interpretive resources include a section titled "Administration Tips for JIST's Inventories." This section is very useful as it provides realistic and creative suggestions on using the OCII in a group, using the inventory in a short session, and using the inventory to help structure one or more career exploration sessions. The last use section was obviously written by someone who actually does career counseling and uses such instruments regularly and effectively. It was also noted that the personal pronoun "I" appears in this section twice even though no specific author is given credit anywhere in the guide.

The OCII is a 12-page consumable, combined administration/items/responses/profile/interpretive form that contains very detailed and user-friendly instructions that enable the test taker to easily complete the administration and scoring process almost unaided by a counselor/test administrator. In this self-scorable format (as with any self-scorable format with large numbers of items) there is substantial room for error. The OIP user's guide, however, directly addressed this issue and stated that "an examination of client's ability to self-score the instrument revealed a low percentage of scoring errors and, more importantly, a minimal presence of individuals identifying the wrong top interest due to scoring errors" (p. 42). The user's guide did not, however, provide any specific data on error rates associated with the instrument; these data were found in Rounds, Walker et al. (1999).

Nowhere in the administrator's guide or the OIP user's guide was there an explanation of how the jobs were categorized into RIASEC classes. Only in Rounds, Smith et al. (1999) was this addressed and, although this study was available on the O*NET website, it should also be addressed in the user's guide as part of the development of the OIP.

SUMMARY. The OCII has substantial reasons to recommend its use with junior high and high school students and with adults. It is low cost. It is up-to-date. It has substantial research providing good evidence of validity and reliability. The administrator's guide is not a technical manual, nor does it purport to be, and user's of the OCII are referred to the OIP user's guide for technical information. It would be helpful, however, to have a comprehensive and substantial technical manual instead of the variety of studies available on the O*NET website. It is difficult to find all of the development research when it is spread all over the website in separate PDF files. The data are there and are substantive, but the delivery is not user-friendly.

REVIEWER'S REFERENCES

Holland, J. (1995). Self-Directed Search. Odessa, FL: Psychological Assessment Resources.
Mueller, R. O. (1998). [Review of the Job Search Inventory.] In J. C. Impara & B. S. Plake (Eds.), The thirteenth mental measurements yearbook [Electronic version]. Retrieved January 18, 2004, from the Buros Institute's Test Reviews Online website: http://www.unl.edu/buros
National Center for O*NET Development. (2000). O*NET Interest Profiler user's guide. Raleigh, NC: Author.
Rounds, J., Smith, T., Hubert, L., Lewis, P., & Rivkind, D. (1999). Development of occupational interest profiles for O*NET. Raleigh, NC: National Center for O*NET Development.
Rounds, J., Walker, C. M., Day, S. X., Hubert, L., Lewis, P., & Rivkind, D. (1999). O*NET Interest Profiler: Reliability, validity, and self-scoring. Raleigh, NC: National Center for O*NET Development.
Zedeck, S. (1998). [Review of the Job Search Inventory.] In J. C. Impara & B. S. Plake (Eds.), The thirteenth mental measurements yearbook [Electronic version]. Retrieved January 18, 2004, from the Buros Institute's Test Reviews Online website: http://www.unl.edu/buros

*Review of the O*NET Career Interests Inventory: Based on the "O*NET Interest Profiler" Developed by the U.S. Department of Labor by ELEANOR E. SANFORD, Vice-President of Research and Development, MetaMetrics, Inc., Durham, NC:*

DESCRIPTION. The O*NET Career Interests Inventory developed by JIST Works is based on the O*NET Interest Profiler (IP), Version 3.0 (see 174), developed by the U.S. Department of Labor (2000). The O*NET Career Interests Inventory is a tool to help users explore careers and learning options based on their interests. The O*NET Career Interests Inventory was developed to be a low-cost, simple to administer and score version of the Department of Labor's inventory. It employs the same 180 test items, uses the same response layout, and employs the same scoring protocol as the IP. As a result, JIST Works states that "we did not change the important content that underlies the validity of the instrument" (administrator's guide, p. 3).

The O*NET Career Interests Inventory was designed for career exploration, career planning, and vocational counseling. It has not been validated for use in making employment or hiring decisions or for screening applicants for jobs or training programs. Six occupational interest scores are derived—Realistic, Investigative, Artistic, Social, Enterprising, and Conventional—based upon the work of John Holland. Holland hypothesized that individuals could be classified into six personality types and that there are six corresponding work environments. He concluded that individuals seek out work environments that match their personality types. When the personality type of the individual matches the work environment, the individual will be satisfied and productive.

ADMINISTRATION. The O*NET Career Interests Inventory can be self-administered and can be completed in 20 to 60 minutes (additional time may be needed for score interpretation and career investigation). It can be administered individually, in a group setting, or in some combination. The assessment is administered by paper and pencil using one six-panel foldout. The examinee is asked to respond to 180 work activities "that represent a wide variety of occupations as well as a broad range of training levels" (Lewis & Rivkin, 1999, p. 1). The examinee is asked to respond to each work activity in terms of whether he or she would like the activity, whether he or she would dislike the activity, or unsure whether he or she would like the activity.

The O*NET Career Interests Inventory was designed to be self-scored. The examinee tallies the number of "Likes" that he or she indicated for each of the six interest areas. The results are then transferred to the "Work Interests to Careers Chart." This chart is organized using Holland's six occupational interest scales and then, within each scale, by training level (job zone). The training levels range from "little or no preparation needed" to "extensive preparation needed." Job titles are presented for each of the five job zones in each occupational interest area. The examinee selects job titles within his or her top three occupational interest areas for further investigation.

DEVELOPMENT. The O*NET Interest Profiler (IP) was developed through a seven-phase process (Lewis & Rivkin, 1999). Initially, the items on three existing Department of Labor interest instruments were examined. Based upon this review, the design of the IP was delineated. The items from the three instruments served as the initial item pool for the IP. The 453 items were reviewed, revised, and/or replaced and then administered during the initial pilot study. In addition, 288 new items were created to fill in gaps identified during the review process. After the field study, 532 items were retained.

The next phase of the process was to structure the items based on a work content area taxonomy (Holland's R-I-A-S-E-C model) and a training level taxonomy. Each item currently in the pool was reviewed and categorized within each of the two taxonomies. Where necessary, additional items were developed. A pilot study was conducted of the 804 items in the pool. Based upon the results of the pilot study, 28 items were deleted. Items with extreme means, large gender differences, or large race/ethnicity differences were deleted. The main source of item deletion was the comparison of endorsement rates for items with similar content.

The fifth phase of the item development process involved extensive item reviews. The retranslation review examined whether the item represented the intended RIASEC construct. The sensitivity review examined whether the item exhibited possible bias against or offensiveness against racial, ethnic, or gender groups. The comprehensibility review examined the reading demand of the item to ensure that junior high school students could comprehend it (the lowest level of intended users). The familiarity review examined how familiar the work activities were to all levels of intended users. The training requirement review was conducted to ensure that items represented the broad range of training requirements specified by the taxonomy. The duplication review was conducted to identify items with very similar content. The copyright review was conducted to identify those items that were very similar to items on other specified interest inventories. A total of 226 items were deleted from the item pool. A large-scale field study was conducted with 1,123 examinees. Based on item statistics criteria, 39 of the 500 items were deleted from the item pool. Using the remaining items, 180 were selected that (a) demonstrated strong conformity to Holland's hexagonal model, (b) maximized coverage of the two taxonomies, and (c) minimized gender and race/ethnicity differences.

TECHNICAL.

Reliability. The internal consistency estimates (coefficient alpha) across the six occupational interest scales on the O*NET Interest Profiler range from .93 to .96. Test-retest reliability was examined using the results from 132 examinees administered the O*NET Interest Profiler twice over a 1-month period. The correlation coefficients between the two administrations ranged from .81 to .92 across the six occupational interest scales.

Validity. The construct validity of the O*NET Interest Profiler was examined by having a group of 1,061 examinees take the O*NET Interest Profiler and the Interest-Finder developed by the Defense Manpower Data Center. The correlations between scales measuring the same construct on the two assessments ranged from .73 to .84. Correlations between scales on the O*NET Interest Profiler ranged from .10 to .50. The principal components analysis indicated that the two instruments had similar factor loadings, with the first factor for the O*NET Interest Profiler accounting for 44% of the variance and the next two factors accounting for 16% and 13%, respectively. The factor analytic results for the O*NET Interest Profiler are consistent with other research conducted with assessments of Holland's hexagonal model of occupational interests.

Inconsistent results were obtained for the Enterprising scale between the two assessments. It was hypothesized that the O*NET Interest Profiler contains a more diverse range of training requirements for this scale than is found on other assessments. Based on an examination of the correlations between the items on the Enterprising scales and the level of training required, it was shown that training level accounted for 61% of the variation in strength of association between the O*NET Interest Profiler Enterprising items and the Interest-Finder Enterprising scale.

SUMMARY. The O*NET Career Interests Inventory is an easy-to use and interpret assessment of occupational interests. The assessment is faithful to the design and development of the Department of Labor's O*NET Interest Profiler in that the same 180 activity statements are used, the same scoring scheme is used, and the same list of O*NET occupations is used for interpretation and investigation.

Because of its similarity to the O*NET Interest Profiler, the O*NET Career Interests Inventory has adequate validity and reliability for the intended uses. In contrast to other career interest assessments, the items on the O*NET Interest Profiler are work activities. This leads to a more balanced assessment in terms of training levels and a more relevant assessment for examinees with less formal preparation, especially students in junior-high and high school.

REVIEWER'S REFERENCES

Lewis, P., & Rivkin, D. (1999). *Development of the O*NET™ Interest Profiler.* Raleigh, NC: National Center for O*NET Development, Employment Security Commission.

Rounds, J., Walker, C. M., Day, S. X., Hubert, L., Lewis, P., & Rivkin, D. (1999). *O*NET™ Interest Profiler: Reliability, validity, and self-scoring.* Raleigh, NC: National Center for O*NET Development, Employment Security Commission.

U.S. Department of Labor, Employment and Training Administration. (2000). *Interest Profiler: User's guide.* Washington, DC: Author.

[173]

O*NET Career Values Inventory: Based on the "O*NET Work Importance Locator" developed by the U.S. Department of Labor.

Purpose: To allow users to rank six work values and relate them to specific careers.

Population: Youth and adults.

Publication Date: 2002.

Scores: Achievement, Independence, Recognition, Relationships, Support, Working Conditions.

Administration: Group or individual.

Price Data, 2003: $29.95 per 25 inventories including administrator's guide (8 pages).

Time: (20–60) minutes.

Comments: Twelve-panel foldout; a compact, shorter, and less expensive version of the Department of Labor's "O*NET Work Importance Locator"; based on the "O*NET Work Importance Locator" developed by the U.S. Department of Labor.

Author: JIST Publishing, Inc.

Publisher: JIST Publishing, Inc.

*Review of the O*NET Career Values Inventory: Based on the "O*NET Work Importance Locator" developed by the U.S. Department of Labor by KATHY GREEN, Professor of Quantitative Research Methods, University of Denver, Denver, CO:*

DESCRIPTION. The O*NET Career Values Inventory (CVI) is a paper-and-pencil card sort task, the purpose of which is to help people identify and order their most important work values. The goal is to help identify occupations that the test user may find satisfying. The O*NET Work Importance Locator, the assessment upon which the CVI is based, is intended for use in career counseling and career planning. Twenty statements printed on cards are sorted into five importance levels yielding six values scores: Achievement, Independence, Recognition, Relationships, Support, and Working Conditions. Scoring is ipsative. The CVI can be self-administered, self-scored, and self-interpreted. The six values are described and a list of jobs requiring minimal to extensive preparation that are likely to include each work value is provided. The CVI is appropriate for students 14 years of age and older and adults with an eighth grade + reading level who are making career or career change decisions and who are seeking to explore career choices. The CVI is based on the O*NET Work Importance Locator (WIL) developed by the U.S. Department of Labor. Reference to sources of additional information and to the Department of Labor website is provided. As the CVI is a version of the WIL, the extensive information provided on the Department of Labor website applies to the CVI.

Because the CVI is self-administered, it can be used individually as well as in group sessions. Administration time is listed as 20–60 minutes. To take the CVI, the user separates the 20 cards provided on a sheet of heavy, perforated paper, sorts the card statements by importance, places the cards on a fold-out sheet, computes scores for each of six values, copies scores to the reverse side of the fold-out sheet, and reads the information provided matched to the highest values. Scoring requires transcribing single-digit numbers, adding, and multiplying. The card sort task is similar to a Q-sort.

DEVELOPMENT. The CVI is a repackaging of the WIL, which was released in 2001 in booklet format and is available from the U.S. Government Printing Office. The CVI uses the same statements, card sort and scoring, and occupation lists but uses a fold-out paper format. Although no information on initial test development is provided in the CVI or the administrator's guide, both sets of materials explicitly direct the administrator or user to the O*NET website, which archives test development information on the WIL.

The WIL was developed from the Minnesota Importance Questionnaire (MIQ; Rounds, Henly, Dawis, Lofquist, & Weiss, 1981), which was a product of work begun in 1957 on the Work Adjustment Project at the University of Minnesota. The MIQ was itself based on earlier questionnaires. The Theory of Work Adjustment (Dawis & Lofquist, 1984) stresses the fit of an individual's needs and abilities with the ability requirements and reward systems of the employer. Individuals' preferences for certain kinds of job rewards or satisfiers were identified based on this theory. The MIQ is a publisher-scored assessment with complex scoring, and so not amenable to self-administration. WIL items were adapted from the original 21 statements on the MIQ. To create the WIL, 1 MIQ item was dropped and 11 items were reworded, 6 with minor changes and 5 with moderate to substantial changes. Values were relabeled and the scoring system was changed.

Three development studies were then conducted. The prepilot and pilot studies yielded information used to improve WIL items and administration procedures. The main study yielded psychometric data and information about gender, race, ethnic, and educational level differences in value importance.

TECHNICAL. No information is provided on psychometric quality of the CVI in the administrator's guide. The administrator is referred to the U.S. Department of Labor user's guides for the WIL, from which the following information was obtained (McCloy et al., 1999).

Test-retest reliability coefficients for items ranged from .26 to .62 (median = .42) over a 4–8-week time period. The WIL developers attempted a correction for ipsative scoring yielding reliability coefficients that were slightly higher (.33 to .61 with a median of .52). Consistency in selection of the most important values from the WIL paper-and-pencil version to a computerized version was 62% for the top value and 80% for the top two values with assessment about 6 weeks apart. The correlation between values profiles over time was $r = .62$. Internal consistency reliabilities were quite low (median alpha = .20), argued to be a result of ipsative scoring. The median alternate forms correlation between the WIL paper-and-pencil and the computerized version was .77 with a correction used for ipsatization. Sample size for the main study was 1,199 usable cases. Research participants were in junior college classes, clients of employment centers, employed, unemployed, high school students, members of a community group, or in the military. The sample was roughly balanced by gender, and had adequate numbers of participants from three ethnic/racial groups (African American, White, Hispanic). Although reliability at the statement or item level is questionable, consistency of top value choices was acceptable.

Validity was assessed by correlation with the MIQ. Item level correlations ranged from .27 to .63, with value-level correlations of .30 to .49. All items with correlations less than .40 had changes in item wording from the MIQ to the WIL. Decision consistency for the two measures was 57% for the top value and 79% for the top two values. The correlation for the values profile was .57. Sample sizes ranged from 134 to 670. Research participants were unemployment insurance clients, displaced workers, vocational/technical students, and community college students.

Some statistically significant differences in value importance were found by gender, race, and ethnicity but effects were small. More substantial differences were found by level of education.

Validity studies of the WIL are limited to correlation with the parent measure, the MIQ. Additional validity studies are needed that support the use of the WIL and CVI in job placement, choice of educational field of study, relationship with level of job satisfaction, and job tenure. Differences, if any, in these validity coefficients based on gender, educational level, race, or ethnicity are also of interest. Such studies would extend the potential use of the WIL/CVI beyond a career exploration tool. Supporting use of the WIL/CVI for career exploration are reported favorable participant reactions to the measure. More systematic summary self-reports of WIL/CVI users about whether it was helpful in career exploration would also support use for its stated purpose.

No normative studies were reported with the WIL/CVI.

COMMENTARY. The value of the WIL/CVI is limited by problems with reliability, possibly due to ipsative scoring, but the consistency of the most important value choice is moderate to high. Validity evidence is limited to correlations with one measure and anecdotal reports of favorable participant reactions to the measure. Low to moderate correlations with the MIQ were explained by changes in item wording. However, these low to moderate correlations with the MIQ make generalization of extensive work with the MIQ to support of the WIL/CVI questionable.

The inventory provides a fast, simple, interesting means of identifying important work values and seems to do so with some consistency. The strong theoretical basis for the MIQ (and so the WIL and CVI) suggests these work values contribute to job satisfaction if they are characteristic of the chosen position. The WIL/CVI has strong face validity for its stated purpose of career exploration. Evidence of reliability and validity for other uses, such as prediction of job satisfaction or job tenure, is lacking.

SUMMARY. The CVI developers have produced an attractively formatted, color-coded version of the WIL that is as easy to use and less expensive. The CVI is based on strong theory. Although reliability and validity information is minimal, being based on only one study, and available information leads to questions about the quality of the inventory for prediction of career choice or satisfaction, the CVI seems suited to its stated primary purpose, which is to provide information for career exploration. The inventory and the administrator's guide provide no information about psychometric quality, but clearly direct the reader to the website archiving that information. The website also links to extensive career information. The WIL is quite new; the CVI is newer; both lack any but the most minimal study.

REVIEWER'S REFERENCES

Dawis, R. V., & Lofquist, L. J. (1984). *A psychological theory of work adjustment.* Minneapolis, MN: University of Minnesota Press.
McCloy, R., Waugh, G., Medsker, G., Wall, J., Rivkin, D., & Lewis, P. (1999). *Development of the O*NET Work Importance Locator.* Raleigh, NC: National Center for O*NET Development.
Rounds, J. B., Henly, G. A., Dawis, R. V., Lofquist, L. H., & Weiss, D. J. (1981). *Manual for the Minnesota Importance Questionnaire: A measure of needs and values.* Minneapolis, MN: University of Minnesota, Department of Psychology.

*Review of the O*NET Career Values Inventory: Based on the "O*NET Work Importance Loca-tor" developed by the U.S. Department of Labor by RICHARD E. HARDING, Director of Research, Kenexa Technology, Lincoln, NE:*

DESCRIPTION AND DEVELOPMENT. The O*NET Career Values Inventory as published by JIST Publishing Company is a repackaging of the O*NET Career Values Inventory developed by the U.S. Department of Labor and released in the second half of 2001. In the brief administrator's guide, the publisher indicates the cost of their version is approximately one-fifth of what the government would charge. The publisher also indicates that they feel that their version is simpler to administer and easier to use. The purpose of this review is not to evaluate the research done by the Department of Labor in developing the O*NET Career Values Inventory, but rather to examine the effort by JIST Publishing in the repackaging of that tool.

The purpose of the O*NET Career Values Inventory is to help people identify what work values are important to them in the job or in a workplace. Indications suggest the results should be used for "career exploration, career planning, and vocational counseling purposes only, and no other use is authorized or valid" (Cover of Inventory). The authors further caution that the Inventory results should not be used for pre-employment hiring decisions or screening of applicants.

The tool can be administered individually or in a group format. The booklet provided makes it very easy for an individual to complete the assessment, score it, and interpret the results. The respondents are given scores in six major values: Achievement, Independence, Recognition, Relationships, Support, and Working Conditions. It is indicated in the manual that the higher the score, the higher the level of importance for the individual and presumably the jobs listed with that particular work value would have a higher appeal to the individual. There are approximately 1,000 jobs listed across those six work values. Furthermore, the jobs are split into job zones by the Department of Labor. Job Zone 1, for example, requires little or no preparation whereas Job Zone 5 lists jobs in which extensive skills, knowledge, experience, and preparation may be required. An example of Achievement in Job Zone 1 is general farm workers whereas Achievement under Job Zone 5 indicates teachers, engineers, physicians, dentists, zoologists, etc.

The actual tool uses a five by four grid where columns are ordered from most important to least important in work value. Respondents are asked to sort, using a "q sort" technique, 20 statements that are prefaced by "on my ideal job it is important that." Examples of the statements are "I make use of my abilities," "my coworkers would be easy to get along with," "I could plan my work with little supervision," etc.

Each of the 20 statements has a letter associated with it ranging from A to T. The respondent then sorts each of those statements into the importance level that they would give it in the work environment on their ideal job. After sorting, the respondent should have four statements that are the most important, four that are next most important, continuing on to the four that are the least important to their work values. Based upon card placement, there is a very easy to follow scoring section where a weighting is provided for each of the 20 cards. Each card is associated with one of the work values. The cards are then placed into their work value scoring formula and a score is derived for each of the six work values. Each of the values is scaled from a minimum score of 6 to a maximum of 30. The higher the score, presumably, the more important the work value is to the respondent.

Respondents then transfer their top three scoring work values to a form that has a definition of each work value as well as the occupations listed in each of the five zones. As indicated earlier there are about 1,000 occupations listed across the six zones. The lists are very extensive. Presumably, the Department of Labor in developing this concept has evidence as to why various jobs were placed in each of these six work values. One is left wondering why certain jobs were listed under Achievement and not under, for example, Recognition. It is interesting to note that chemical engineers and chemical teachers were listed under Achievement in extensive preparation needed. However, chemical engineers were also cross listed under Recognition, extensive preparation needed, but chemical teachers were not. There are other similar examples that leave one still wondering why occupations were placed into the various zones.

After listing the top three work values and then scanning the other work values for possible interesting jobs, the next step involves a researching of the top career options. There are many useful points in this page in the documentation

that include other things to consider such as interests, abilities, education, earnings, level of responsibility, lifestyle choices, etc. Also provided is a job information work sheet that the respondent can fill out with as many jobs in which they have interest. This seems to be a very useful page for the respondent in that it asks the respondent many questions about the job such as job descriptions, key skills and abilities, working conditions, training/education, other qualifications needed, earnings, negatives about the job, positives about the job, barriers faced, and how they can begin preparing for the job. This leads to the respondent actively researching their top job choices in order to answer all of the questions.

Finally, there is a very basic action plan form that is segmented in time increments of 30 days, 3 months, 6 to 12 months, 1 to 2 years, and 5 years. The respondent is asked to figure out what they can do to move towards their objective for their top career or job interest in those time parameters.

TECHNICAL. There is a section in the eight-page administrator's guide that mentions reliability and validity. The authors of the administrator's guide indicate that the user can obtain more detailed information on validity and reliability of the tool by going to the O*NET center website. They further indicate that the Department of Labor provides downloadable files regarding the development, reliability, validity, and other psychometric properties of the value of the O*NET Career Values Inventory. The authors do not provide any summary of the development, reliability, or validity of the process in the administrator's guide. A summary of at least a half page or a full page outlining the various psychometric properties of this particular tool would have been useful. The downloading of the appropriate technical report takes some time and determination to find the right report and then to download it. Most people using the tool will probably not download the reports and will rely only on the administrator's guide in its very brief assertions regarding the reliability and validity of the Inventory.

COMMENTARY. The guide does indicate that the intended audience is people 14 years of age or older and the tool can be used with many different types of individuals ranging from junior high students to unemployed adults or workers in transition. The guide also indicates that a reading level of eighth grade or higher is necessary for complete understanding of the tool and its concepts. It is also delineated that the time required to complete will be anywhere from 20 to 60 minutes. The administrator's guide also gives tips on using the tool in a group and in structuring career exploration sessions. The administrator's guide, although very brief, is relatively useful.

SUMMARY. This paper repackaging of the Department of Labor tool is relatively easy to use, follow, and score. The interpretation and follow-up materials are clear, concise, and easy to understand. There are appropriate cautions as to the limitations of the tool, particularly for what it can and cannot be used. However, these cautions are in very small print and one needs to read carefully to find them. The authors rely on the development and psychometric properties of the Department of Labor research and have made no attempt to further the knowledge in this other than offering researchers the chance to have free access to the tool to use in their own research and, ultimately, the publishing of those research results. Finally, this version of the O*NET Career Values Inventory has much to recommend for its use in career exploration.

[174]
O*NET Interest Profiler.

Purpose: "Provides ... self-knowledge about [one's] ... vocational personality type ... [and] fosters career awareness."

Population: Age 14 and older.

Publication Dates: 1985-2000.

Acronym: IP.

Scores, 11: Interest Areas (Realistic, Investigative, Artistic, Social, Enterprising, Conventional), Job Zones (Little or No Preparation Needed, Some Preparation Needed, Medium Preparation Needed, Considerable Preparation Needed, Extensive Preparation Needed).

Administration: Group.

Price Data: Available from publisher.

Time: (20-60) minutes.

Comments: Replaces the Job Search Inventory (T5:1351); self-administered and self-scored; pencil-and-paper format; Computerized Interest Profile is administered and scored on computer; part of the O*NET Career Exploration Tools; intended for career exploration, planning, and counseling purposes only; results should not be used for employment or hiring decisions.

Author: U.S. Department of Labor, Employment and Training Administration.

Publisher: U.S. Department of Labor, Employment and Training Administration.

Cross References: For reviews by Ralph O. Mueller and Sheldon Zedeck of the Job Search Inventory, see 13:163.

*Review of the O*NET Interest Profiler by MICHAEL B. BROWN, Associate Professor of Psychology, East Carolina University, Greenville, NC:*

DESCRIPTION. The O*NET Interest Profiler is a self-assessment vocational interest instrument used for career exploration. There is a paper-and-pencil version along with a similar computerized version available. The O*NET Interest Profiler is one part of a series of career exploration tools developed by the U.S. Department of Labor. Other tools in this series include a Work Importance Profiler that identifies work satisfactions and an Ability Profiler that identifies activities that the client does well. Included with the instrument is a detailed user's guide, an instructive score report that guides the user in the scoring and interpretation process, and two Occupations Lists. The O*NET OnLine system is an automated jobs database that replaces the previously published *Dictionary of Occupational Titles* (U.S. Department of Labor, 1991a).

The instrument is designed for use with persons who are 14 years of age or older and requires an eighth grade reading level to adequately understand the materials. The Interest Profiler is self-administered and self-scored, and requires 20 to 60 minutes to complete. The instrument is compatible with Holland's Theory of Vocational Personality and provides scores that use the familiar RIASEC typology. Once scored, the user develops a primary and secondary interest score based on the RIASEC categories. The O*NET Occupations Master List shows occupations based on their primary interest code and is divided into "Job Zones" based on level of educational preparation required for the occupation. Further information about jobs is also available at the O*NET OnLine website.

The user's guide provides a very well-written procedure for guiding users in self-administration of the instrument. The guide includes a notation of possible challenges for clients at different steps in the process along with suggestions on how the challenges might be overcome (for example, clients may have difficulty understanding the differences between Job Zones). The instrument can also be used in a group administration format, where the use of the Interest Profiler by several clients is guided by a professional leader. The user's guide also outlines a variety of interpretation activities that can be incorporated into a group vocational exploration program or class.

DEVELOPMENT. The O*NET Interest Profiler was developed to be well-constructed, fair, and useful for persons from a variety of ethnic, cultural, and socioeconomic backgrounds. The instrument was conceived to be self-administering and self-scoring and representative of the entire range of available jobs. An initial item pool of 569 items was developed that included 281 items from existing Department of Labor interest instruments (such as the USES Interest Inventory and the USES Interest Checklist) and 288 new items to supplement the existing items. A pilot test for acceptability to a wide audience reduced the item pool to 532. The Holland RIASEC constructs provided the taxonomy for developing job groups and the existing Specific Vocational Preparation Scale (U.S. Department of Labor, 1991b) formed the basis for identifying training levels within the job groups. Trained judges placed each of the items into respective RIASEC content areas; a total of 272 new items were developed to provide approximately 100 items per scale. A pilot test of the resulting 804 items reduced those of duplicate content; a pool of 776 items remained.

The item pool underwent a comprehensive screening process that included the use of trained judges along with panels of persons representing diverse ethnic and gender groups. This step was aimed at assessing the proper assignment of items to content areas, sensitivity to the needs of diverse individuals, and ensuring that the items were sufficiently familiar to diverse individuals. Reading comprehension was also evaluated and set at the eighth grade level. Only 500 of the items remained after this step in the development process. These items were then tested on 1,123 participants who also completed a demographic questionnaire, feedback forms, and the Interest-Finder (Defense Manpower Data Center, 1995), an established interest inventory. The scales were analyzed to identify a 180-item questionnaire that would conform to the RIASEC model, have maximum representation of occupations, and minimize differential endorsement based on race, ethnicity, and gender. Final consideration was given to the presentation of the instrument, obtaining client feedback about the layout, the directions, and the scoring procedures.

TECHNICAL. The majority of the data on reliability and validity were gathered using a group of 1,061 individuals from four states of the United States. The participants were from a variety of settings, including employment service offices, junior colleges, trade schools, and other agencies. The group was administered the Interest Profiler and the Interest-Finder in a counterbalanced fashion. Test-retest studies were administered to 132 junior/vocational college students and college students with 1-month retest period. Participants found the instrument easy to use and score and there was a low percentage of scoring errors.

The internal consistency coefficients ranged from .93 to .96 for the scales, which is indicative of strong internal consistency reliability. The test-retest reliabilities were reported to range from .81 to .92, which provides evidence of satisfactory reliability of scores over a short period of time. Convergent validity was examined by comparing the factor structures of the Interest Profiler and the Interest-Finder. Both instruments had similar factor structures and the equivalent scales from both instruments were highly correlated. Two problems were noted with the Interest Profiler. The Enterprising scale correlates too highly with the Artistic scale and not highly enough with the Social scale. The range of lower-level activities on the Enterprising scale are apparently not consistently viewed by users as Enterprising activities. Also, the correlation between the Realistic and Conventional interest scales is too low, which the user's guide identifies as a problem common to other Holland-type measures.

COMMENTARY. The O*NET Interest Profiler is a well-constructed instrument that has many strengths. The instrument has sound technical characteristics. Its compatibility with the Holland RIASEC model means that the instrument can be easily included in the practice of career counselors who are familiar with the theory. The instrument appears easy to use and self-score, which enhances a client's sense of responsibility for career exploration and decision-making. It is also appropriate for use in a group format for a career exploration class or for group career counseling. The administration and scoring time is very reasonable, and the Profiler can be used alone, with the other components of the O*NET system, or with other proprietary instruments. The range of occupations is quite broad and would appeal to users with a wide variety of occupational interests and training levels. The user's guide is very well-done and provides the professional user with a solid technical background and guidelines for use. That the Master Occupations List is based on single Holland codes rather than the combination codes is a criticism; the Combined Interest and Work Values list does, however, include a two-code breakdown. The O*NET OnLine system is a nice supplement that provides a wealth of additional information on occupations. Unfortunately, the O*NET OnLine taxonomy does not translate directly from the RIASEC framework. Clients wishing to consult this useful resource will have to search by job families or by entering an SOC code provided in the occupations lists.

SUMMARY. The O*NET Interest Profiler is an attractive, well-constructed instrument that should find widespread use in career exploration and counseling services. It can be used as both an individual counseling tool and for group instruction and exploration. It is versatile and can be used alone, with other O*NET tools, or with other instruments that the counselor may already use. The supplemental materials are well-done and the online component offers considerable additional information for counselors and clients and offers the advantage of more frequent updates than with print-only materials.

REVIEWER'S REFERENCES.
Defense Manpower Data Center. (1995). *ASVAB 18/19 counselor manual.* Monterey, CA: Author.
U.S. Department of Labor. (1991a). *Dictionary of occupational titles.* Rev. 4th ed.) Washington, DC: U.S. Government Printing Office.
U.S. Department of Labor. (1991b). *The revised handbook for analyzing jobs.* Washington, DC: U.S. Government Printing Office.

*Review of the O*NET Interest Profiler by* WILLIAM B. MICHAEL, *Professor Emeritus, University of Southern California, Los Angeles, CA:*

DESCRIPTION. Developed for use as a tool to provide information for career exploration and vocational counseling, the 180-item O*NET Interest Profiler (IP) yields scores in each of six 30-item subscales that serve to operationalize the six constructs or factors compatible with Holland's theory of six vocational personality types: Realistic, Investigative, Artistic, Social, Enterprising, and Conventional.

The Realistic subscale includes items representing an interest in hands-on practically oriented work activities involving machines, tools, wood, and outside activity distinct from participating in persuasive assignments or manifesting

social interests. Reflecting work activities dealing with ideas and intellectual pursuits, the Investigative subscale items minimize any form of physical activity or persuasive or competitive behaviors. The items of the Artistic subscale are conceived with preferences for work activities associated with the arts broadly considered in a context offering considerable autonomy and opportunities for self-expression. The Social subscale items portray an interest in behaviors that are directed toward helping others and in interacting with people, as in teaching, nursing, or some other service-oriented occupation. The Enterprising subscale comprises items that emphasize persuasive and leader behaviors that pertain to initiating and completing challenging projects, especially in a business venture requiring one to make decisions, lead others, and take risks. In the Conventional subscale, the items reflect working activities that are directed toward following routines and carrying out procedures with clear-cut lines of authority having been specified.

All items allow the test taker one of three response alternatives of Like (L), Unsure (?), or Dislike (DL). In the scoring of items, each one marked L receives 1 point with the other two responses being given no points. Thus, the scores on any one of the six subscales will vary between zero and 30 points for any examinee. Subsequently, a profile of scores on the six subscales can be formed to identify clusters in working activities differing in level of interest. The higher score on a given subscale constitutes what is called the primary interest area, and the second highest score in a subscale indicates a secondary interest area. In the event of a tie in scores on two subscales or the presence of a difference of six or fewer points, a third subscale with the next highest scores can be chosen. Each of the selected interest areas creates a job zone for which clusters of numerous occupations requiring differing levels of education, training, and experience are listed on the pages of a separate comprehensive manual or booklet entitled O*NET Occupational Combined List: Interest and Work Values. This manual furnishes a list of an almost countless number of occupational alternatives for the client and vocational counselor to explore and to evaluate.

DEVELOPMENT. The development of the IP was dependent to a considerable degree on prior research and publications of the United States Department of Labor. In its Interest Profiler,

User's Guide is an overview of the primary goals for the latest developmental efforts to complete a revision of the IP in terms of eight phases that are paraphrased as follows: (a) an examination of currently available instruments; (b) a review, revision, and administration of existing items from the Department of Labor; (c) preparation of an item taxonomy based on a review of numerous sources; (d) placement of retained items in appropriate categories of the taxonomy accompanied by the creation of new items subject to field testing; (e) comprehensive screening of new items according to stringent criteria; (f) item tryout accompanied by item analysis and development of preliminary subscales subject to content review comprising use of appropriate taxonomy categories, application of psychometric procedures, and minimization of possible gender and racial/ethnic bias; (g) creation of a suitable format design for ease of administration and scoring; and (h) evaluation of the reliability of scores and of self-scoring skills required. The final result was a six-factor scale reflecting a dedicated effort to achieve a workable and improved instrument.

TECHNICAL. Although extensive psychometric procedures were employed in the development of the IP, the user's guide sets forth only a limited data base in tables placed near the end of the guide. For a total sample of 1,123 participants, means, standard deviations, internal-consistency estimate of reliability (alpha coefficients), and intercorrelations of scores for the six subscales are reported. Means and standard deviations of scores for subgroups differentiated by gender and ethnic membership (White Non-Hispanic, African American, and Hispanic) are presented. Intercorrelation of scores on the six subscales varied between .38 and .66 with a median value of .52. Reliability coefficients fell between .95 and .97. Normative data have to be internal from the mean and standard deviation of scores reported for each of the subscales. Mean scores placed between 10.3 (Realistic) and 16.2 (Social) with 30-point maximum possible score. No additional psychometric data were reported.

COMMENTARY. It is evident that comprehensive and exhaustive efforts were made to develop an occupational inventory based on an appealing theory of vocational personality type proposed by Holland (1965). Missing, however, have been extensive and readily interpretable normative data. There is an absence of follow-up information linking job success of employee in a given family of interrelated jobs hypothesized to be assorted with scores on a given subscale previously taken by the employees. The relatively high intercorrelations of scores among the six subscales would suggest that a comparatively small number of higher order interest areas might possibly furnish a somewhat simplified basis for matching clients (test takers) with a greater variety of jobs. Nevertheless, with its current six subscales, the IP along with the use of job zones and listing of occupations corresponding to these zones is a useful tool for vocational exploration and counseling.

SUMMARY. The IP with its updated manual and related publications offers a workable and appealing basis for assisting both the vocational counselor and client and providing a viable means for exploring and identifying possible occupations in which the client has expectations of being successful and satisfied. Intended to operationalize the six constructs of Holland's (1965) job interest theory of six vocational personality types, the six 30-item subscales of the IP bear the same names and work activities as those hypothesized in the theory: Realistic, Investigative, Artistic, Social, Enterprising, and Conventional. The test-taking client uses his or her two or three highest subscale scores to identify corresponding job zones for which a manual, O*Net Occupational Master List, provides a large number of occupations hypothesized to be relevant to that job zone. Subsequently, the vocational counselor and client can explore and evaluate the several available alternatives. Although great care was exercised in the exhaustive efforts to develop the IP, a great need exists for follow-up validation studies and for the creation of extensive and easy-to-read normative data. Nevertheless, the IP is a useful and competitive instrument for vocational exploration and counseling.

REVIEWER'S REFERENCE

Holland, J. (1965). *Making vocational choices: A theory of vocational personalities and work environments* (2nd ed.). Englewood Cliffs, NJ: Prentice Hall.

[175]

O*NET Work Importance Locator.

Purpose: "Helps users identify what is important to them in a job."
Population: Ages 16 and older.
Publication Date: 2000.
Acronym: WIL.
Scores, 6: Achievement, Independence, Recognition, Relationships, Support, Working Conditions.

Administration: Group.
Price Data: Available from publisher.
Time: (15–45) minutes.
Comments: Available in paper-and-pencil format only; related Work Importance Profiler is administered and scored on computer; part of O*NET Career Exploration Tools; intended for career exploration, planning, and counseling purposes only; results should not be used for employment or hiring decisions.
Author: U.S. Department of Labor, Employment and Training Administration.
Publisher: U.S. Department of Labor, Employment and Training Administration.

*Review of the O*NET Work Importance Locator by KARL N. KELLEY, Professor of Psychology, North Central College, Naperville, IL:*

DESCRIPTION. The U.S. Department of Labor developed the O*NET Work Importance Locator (Version 3) to assess an individual's core work values. The goals of this test include increasing an individual's sense of self-knowledge, specifically in terms of career awareness and to connect this information to occupations listed on O*NET online. Utilizing a Q-sort method, participants arrange 20 work value cards on a sorting sheet with five categories ranging from *most important* to *least important*. The information on these work value cards includes statements such as "on my ideal job it is important that I could do things for other people" and "on my ideal job it is important that I could do something different every day." Participants sort these cards imagining their ideal job. It is recommended that participants use the Card Sorting Sheet in order to ensure that the cards are evenly distributed among the categories (four cards per category). Following Dawis & Lofquist's (1984) Theory of Work Adjustment, six work values scales are computed. These scales are Achievement, Independence, Recognition, Relationships, Support, and Working Conditions. Each of these scales represents a cluster of work needs. For example, the value of Independence includes needs for creativity, responsibility, and autonomy.

The target audience for this self-administered test is anyone 16 years of age or older (and with an eighth grade reading level) interested in exploring career options. The test takes between 15–45 minutes to complete, including scoring. The procedure involves minimal adding (at most five values ranging from 1 to 5) and simple multi-plication. The test is designed to be administered to individuals or groups in a single session.

Interpretation of this test focuses on the two highest scale scores. Although most clients will be able to use the Work Importance Locator Score Report to understand their scores, it is recommended that a trained staff member be present to address any questions or concerns that the client may have.

DEVELOPMENT. The primary goal for the developers of this test was to create a simple and useful self-scoring instrument assessing key work values. The Work Importance Locator is based on the Minnesota Importance Questionnaire (MIQ; Rounds, Henly, Dawis, Lofquist, & Weiss, 1981), which is an established measure of work values. The problem with the MIQ is that the scoring protocol is complex and does not lend itself to easy self-scoring. The items on the Work Importance Locator were patterned after the 21 items of the MIQ. Developers reworded the items to better fit a sorting task. Although using the same basic items, these two tests label the dimensions differently.

In the initial version of the WIL, participants sorted the 21 cards into seven categories (3 cards per category). The scoring protocol for this version was deemed overly complex, requiring a participant to use a weighted score table to transform scores before adding and multiplying. Using a logical deductive procedure (as opposed to an empirical one) the developers dropped 1 item (need for social status) thus reducing the total items to 20. These 20 items neatly fit into a five category scoring procedure. Two small pilot studies ($n = 21$ and $n = 48$) were conducted to make sure participants understood the instructions and could compute their scores accurately. After some minor modifications in the instrument, most participants reported understanding the instructions and scoring the test was easy to do (although almost 19% made computational errors in computing their scores).

The third version of this test consists of the 20 value cards (labeled A through T for easy reference), the card-sorting sheet with instructions and five importance columns with four card rectangles under each column for card placement, and instructions/scoring booklet.

TECHNICAL. Psychometric information provided in the Work Importance Locator is sparse. However, some preliminary evidence is provided on reliability and validity.

If this test is to be useful in making predictions about the future, the measured construct must be reasonably stable. A 2-month test-retest reliability study that used a sample of 230 community college students reported correlations ranging from .35 (for Achievement) to .58 (for Support). Specific test-retest reliability indices for the other four dimensions were not reported. Although scores on the specific dimensions varied over this time period, the top work value (highest score) remained the same for 62% of the participants. These data suggest that, at least when measured in this manner, scores on this test tend to fluctuate over time, indicating a concern about using this instrument to make solid predictions about work values.

An internal reliability study was conducted using 1,199 employment service clients and junior college students. In general, the internal consistency of the scales was also generally low. Although information for specific scales was not provided, the developers reported a median coefficient alpha of .20; when corrected for ipsatization, this value increased to .38. These patterns raise concerns about the internal consistency of this instrument.

Scores on this test were compared to an online version (the WIP) available online at www.onetcenter.org/WIP.html. For this study, a sample of 230 vocational/technical and community college students took both of these tests. The median correlation between the work value scores was .77 suggesting that these two versions of the test are generally yielding similar test scores.

Construct validity for this test was assessed by comparing scores on the MIQ (the Minnesota Importance Questionnaire) with those on the Work Importance Locator. A large sample (n = 550) of unemployment insurance clients, displaced workers, vocational students, and community college students yielded correlations ranging from .30 to .49. No specific correlations between scales were reported. Although there was little agreement on the scale scores, the top scores were the same in about 57% of the cases.

COMMENTARY. There is minimal psychometric support for this test. Both reliability and validity indices indicate concerns with using this test. These results suggest that scores on this test should be interpreted with extreme caution. The only interpretable pattern supported was the use of the top score. As assessed by this test, an individual's

top core work value does seem to remain somewhat stable over time.

Because the test is a self-report instrument, it is difficult to tell if participants are reporting what they value or what they think the test administrator wants to hear. Participants may also have difficulty responding to the forced-choice format where many of the descriptors may be equally appealing (or equally unappealing). In these cases, it is not surprising to see low internal reliability coefficients.

SUMMARY. The goal of this test is a first step in beginning a career exploration process. At best, this test will give someone a place to start exploring career options. Although there are many potential problems with using this test, if it is used according to the intent and guidelines provided with this test, it can be of some benefit to many clients. This test could be used in academic settings in high schools and college classes to get students to start thinking about careers and career options. Even when used in these settings, participants should be strongly cautioned about using the entire profile as only the highest work value is stable over time. It is clear that this test should not be used as a selection tool or even as a primary instrument in career development. When used according to the recommendations in the user's guide, this test has limited, but reasonable, value in beginning the process of career exploration.

REVIEWER'S REFERENCES

Dawis, R. V., & Lofquist, L. H. (1984). *A psychological theory of work adjustment*. Minneapolis: University of Minnesota Press.
Rounds, J. B., Henly, G. A., Dawis, R. V., Lofquist, L. H., & Weiss, D. J. (1981). *Manual for the Minnesota Importance Questionnaire: A measure of needs and values*. Minneapolis: University of Minnesota, Department of Psychology.

*Review of the O*NET Work Importance Locator by WILLIAM B. MICHAEL, Professor Emeritus, University of Southern California, Los Angeles, CA:*

DESCRIPTION. The O*NET Work Importance Locator (WIL) is a self-guided, 20-item-statement survey, limited for use to career exploration and vocational counseling for adults 16 years of age or older. The WIL is based on the premise that those individuals who work in jobs for which there is correspondence between their personal characteristics and work demands will experience greater satisfaction, better job performance, and resolve to stay longer on the job. The WIL was designed to assess the perceived importance of the following six work-related values, which are considered to be linked with the requirements of various occupations: (a) Achievement (2 items)—an interest in applying one's skills and observing the results of one's own efforts; (b) Independence (3 items)—a preference for calling upon one's own initiative in the workplace; (c) Recognition (3 items)—a penchant for prestige, leadership, and opportunities for advancement; (d) Relationships (3 items)—a priority for service to others; (e) Support (3 items)—a leaning toward jobs where management is viewed as competent and fair-minded with respect to workers; and (f) Work Conditions (6 items)—a focus on job security, compensation, and one's particular work style. Respondents calculate a score for each of the six work-value areas to identify the two highest ranking work-related values for guiding their career exploration activities.

A detailed step-by-step instruction booklet guides the examinee through the testing procedure, which requires the careful consideration of 20 Work Value cards, each displaying a statement associated with work within the context of an "ideal job." Then, the respondent sorts the 20 statements using an 11-inch x 17-inch Work Value Card Sorting Sheet that displays a 4-by-5 grid of empty boxes. A 5-point Likert-type "importance scale" creates the columns with a range from 5 (*most important*) to 1 (*least important*). Four cards are assigned to each of the five importance ratings. The WIL Score Report guides the examinee through the calculation of the weighted work-value scores generated from the assessment and their interpretation. The test developers indicate that the testing procedure takes about 15–45 minutes. It appears that the sorting task may take from 15 to 30 minutes, maybe longer, depending upon the care with which the examinee approaches the activity; the calculations may take 5 to 15 minutes; and, depending upon one's thoroughness, from several minutes to over an hour for consideration of how the assessed work-related values and level of preparation align with selected occupations. Also, respondents are referred to the *Work Importance Locator O*NET Occupations Master List*, another career exploration tool that lists more job titles and descriptions not provided in the WIL Score Report.

DEVELOPMENT. The 20-item WIL represents a modification of the 21-item Minnesota Importance Questionnaire (MIQ; 11:243), which is based on Dawis and Lofquist's (1984) Theory of Work Adjustment that includes several key constructs thought to facilitate vocational adaptation including personal characteristics of the worker (e.g., abilities, preferences for work conditions, and working style) and characteristics of the job requirements. A key idea is that the more coherence between a worker's characteristics and the job demands, the greater likelihood he or she would be satisfied and productive in a chosen vocation. Recognizing a need for individuals to have direct access to career planning tools that could be easily interpreted without assistance, the authors of the WIL considered the MIQ as inappropriate for self-assessment because of its complex scoring requirements. Thus, the developers of the WIL worked in collaboration with the authors of the MIQ to construct an efficient self-assessment instrument that would retain features similar to those of the MIQ to support validity concerns.

An examination of the statements employed by the two instruments reveals that the 20 item-statements for the WIL correspond to those for the MIQ with minor to moderate wording changes and appear to retain the general meaning. In addition, efforts have been made to use labels for work-value categories that are relatively jargon free to enhance the clarity of the concepts for the untrained user. Appropriate, standard procedures were employed for piloting the newly constructed instrument including administration of the instrument with small samples to evaluate patterns of errors that involved sorting, scoring calculations, ranking work values, or interpreting instructions.

The WIL can be administered either individually or in a group and either with or without assistance. Detailed instructions are provided for administration of the WIL by either a test administrator or by the examinee.

TECHNICAL. The reliability of the six WIL work-value scores have been examined in a variety of contexts but only summary data have been provided in the technical manual. Two-month stability estimates were reported for scores obtained from a sample of 230 students enrolled in either vocational programs or in community colleges. The assumption that work values would be stable over time for this young-adult sample was only moderately supported with stability coefficients for work-value scores ranging from a low of .35 for Achievement to a high of .58 for Support. The percent of agreement between a respondent's highest ranked work-value over the 2-month period was reported to be 62%. The authors correctly point out that although the performance on the WIL may be useful for identifying one's top-ranked work value, the six scores taken together cannot be meaningfully interpreted.

For the same sample of 230 students, an analysis of reliability estimates for the six work-value scores derived from parallel forms of the WIL (the noncomputerized version and the computerized version called the O*NET Work Importance Profile) produced moderate to high correlations that ranged from .70 to .80 (mdn = .77). For a sample of 1,199 adults drawn from 23 sites representing community college students and employment service clients, the authors report low to moderate internal-consistency reliability coefficients for the six work-value scores. Specifically, the average coefficient was .20. However, when scores were corrected for ipsatization, in an effort to reduce the effects of data that are rank ordered, the average coefficient was reported to have increased by .38. In addition to the ipsative nature of the rank-order format, the small number of items included for each work-value score likely contributed to the low reliability estimates.

The validity evidence for the six WIL work-value scores is limited to a single study in which the relationships were examined between scores obtained on the WIL and scores on the MIQ, the instrument from which the WIL was derived. The sample was made up of 550 respondents that included unemployment insurance clients, displaced workers, and students enrolled either in a community college or in vocational-oriented programs. Correlations between the corresponding work-value scores on the WIL and MIQ ranged from .30 to .49 (the six coefficients were not reported, so a median coefficient is not available). The relatively low reliability estimates previously reported for the WIL scores may explain this outcome. Moreover, the authors suggest that those WIL scores, which produced correlations of .40 or lower with corresponding MIQ scores, may be related to a possible problem with wording changes. In another approach, the authors examined the consistency between the highest work-values scores obtained on the two measures and found the highest value was the same for each pair for about 57% of the cases and for 79% of the cases if one matched the top WIL work value against the top two work values obtained on the MIQ.

COMMENTARY. The O*NET Work Importance Locator (WIL) is a self-study guide that can be viewed as a useful instrument for career planning activities with several cautionary notes. Although the WIL has been built upon sound theoretical principles and its items parallel those from a measure that has been shown to be psychometrically sound, the reliability estimates of test scores are low to moderate depending upon the method employed and the validity evidence provided is marginal. The authors indicate that forthcoming research will be designed to examine the content validity of item statements and the criterion-related validity of scores. In addition, investigators might find it fruitful to consider gender and/or cultural differences that might affect the interpretation of scores and support the development of norms. The authors admonish test administrators to guard against the use of work-value scores on the WIL (and its companion tools) for making employment-related decisions. Further, as with any self-study measure, the examinee should exercise caution in relying upon his or her own interpretation of outcomes. In particular, an examinee should not rely on the WIL as the only source of information when engaged in career planning but make sure he or she has obtained the guidance of a career counselor who includes input obtained from the respondent's performance on abilities and interests assessments, information about personal experience, education, and specialized training. Thus, the utility of the WIL can best be realized by employing it in conjunction with information obtained from other O*NET career planning tools and with feedback from a skilled career counselor.

SUMMARY. Published by the U.S. Department of Labor, Employment, and Training Administration (DOL/ETA), the O*NET Career Exploration Tools have been designed for the purpose of providing career-related exploration, planning, and counseling guidance for adults. The tools include the O*NET Work Importance Locator, which is the focus of this review, as well as the O*NET Interest Profiler (see 174) and the O*NET Ability Profiler for which detailed reviews have been provided elsewhere. It is the expressed intent of the test developers that the three tools would be used together as "part of a whole-person approach to the assessment process" (Work Importance Locator User's Guide, p. i) to aid the examinee in clarifying his or her work-related interests and abilities and identifying which occupations may be more satisfying. To further enhance accessibility, computerized versions of the tools are available from DOL/ETA: (a) the O*NET Work Importance Profiler parallels the O*NET Work Importance Locator, and (b) the O*NET Computerized Interest Profiler corresponds to the O*NET Interest Profiler.

REVIEWER'S REFERENCE

Dawis, R. V., & Lofquist, L. H. (1984). *A psychological theory of work adjustment*. Minneapolis: University of Minnesota Press.

[176]

OQ-45.2 (Outcome Questionnaire).

Purpose: Designed to measure "patient progress in therapy."

Population: Adult therapy patients.

Publication Dates: 1996–2004.

Scores, 4: Symptom Distress, Interpersonal Relations, Social Role, Total.

Administration: Individual.

Price Data, 2004: Price data for manual (2004, 54 pages), questionnaire, and scoring services available from publisher.

Foreign Language Editions: Spanish, German, French, Dutch, Swedish, Norwegian, Hebrew, and Japanese editions available.

Time: (5–15) minutes.

Comments: Designed for repeated administration over the course of therapy; computer scoring available; may be administered orally.

Authors: Michael J. Lambert, Jared S. Morton, Derick Hatfield, Cory Harmon, Stacy Hamilton, Rory C. Reid, Kenichi Shumokawa, Cody Christopherson, and Gary Burlingame.

Publisher: OQ Measures LLC.

Review of the OQ-45.2 (Outcome Questionnaire) by WILLIAM E. HANSON, Assistant Professor, Department of Educational Psychology, University of Nebraska—Lincoln, Lincoln, NE; and BRAD M. MERKER, Clinical Neuropsychology Pre-Doctoral Intern, University of Miami Medical School, Miami, FL:

DESCRIPTION. The OQ-45.2 (OQ©) is a norm-referenced, 45-item self-report instrument. According to the manual, it is "a brief screening and outcome assessment scale that attempts to measure the subjective experience of a person, as well as the way they function in the world" (p. 2). Specifically, it attempts to measure how a person is feeling (e.g., depressed, anxious), getting along with others (e.g., friends, family), and functioning in important life tasks (e.g., school, work). It consists of a total score and three subscale scores and may be used with a wide range of adult clients, ages 17–80. Target populations include University Counseling Center (UCC) clients, Employee Assistance Program (EAP) clients, inpatients, and outpatients, among others. The OQ© may be used for a number of different purposes, including to screen clients, assist in making initial treatment decisions and recommendations, monitor overall client progress, and identify clients who are "on track" treatment-wise, as well as those who may be at imminent risk of "treatment failure" (manual, p. 24). It may be administered by hand or, under special circumstances, orally. Total administration time typically ranges from 3 to 15 minutes, with most clients completing it in 5 minutes. It uses a 0 (*never*) to 4 (*almost always*) 5-point Likert scale and may be scored by hand, using simple, template-free procedures, or by computer, fax to file, web, or direct scanning procedures. It is important to note that 9 of the 45 items are reverse scored. The authors recommend using computer-based scoring procedures, primarily "to take advantage of quality assurance tools" that are available to prospective users (e.g., clinical support/feedback tools; manual, p. 3). Recommendations for handling "missing data" are included on page 3 of the manual, though it is unclear how many items may be omitted/substituted before the reliability and validity of the scores are called into question.

DEVELOPMENT. The OQ-45.2 is the latest version of the original OQ©, which was first published in 1994. According to the manual, the items are "essentially the same as those found on the original form, with a few cosmetic alterations" (p. 43). The authors used a combination of rational and empirical methods to develop/select the 45 items (e.g., reviews of relevant literature, fit with DSM criteria, interitem correlations). Generally speaking, items were developed with the following considerations in mind: (a) they should address a commonly occurring disorder, problem, or complaint; (b) they should tap symptoms that occur across a wide range of clients; and (c) they should measure "quality of life" types of issues. Also, "the number of items was limited so that administration of the OQ© assists, rather than hinders, customary clinical practice" (manual, p. 1). That said, no other details related to the development and selection of items were reported in the manual (e.g., specific results of item analyses, factor loadings, or pilot testing), making it difficult to readily evaluate the appropriateness of the criteria and decision rules used to choose the items/create the subscales.

Nevertheless, as noted earlier, the OQ© consists of a total score and three subscales: Symptom Distress (SD), Interpersonal Relations (IR), and Social Role (SR). The total score has, as the name of the test implies, 45 items and may be considered an overall "index of mental health" (manual, p. 10). Scores on this scale may range from 0–180. The SD subscale has 25 items and is a measure of "subjective (symptom) distress," particularly as it relates to mood, anxiety, and adjustment disorders, stress-related illnesses, and substance abuse (manual, p. 1). The IR subscale has 11 items and is a measure of "satisfaction with, as well as problems in, interpersonal relations" (manual, p. 2). The SR subscale has 9 items and is a measure of "dissatisfaction, conflict, distress, and inadequacy in tasks related to … employment, family roles, and leisure life" (manual, p. 2). Scores on the SD, IR, and SR subscales may range from 0–100, 0–44, and 0–36, respectively.

Additional versions of the OQ© are available currently (e.g., OQ©-10.1, LSQ©-30). These abbreviated versions are, however, available for research purposes only. Also, to date, the OQ© has been translated into at least eight different languages, including Dutch, German, and Spanish—the three foreign-language versions that have received at least some empirical attention. The conceptual equivalence of the items and scores has, it seems, yet to be firmly established cross-culturally.

TECHNICAL INFORMATION. Normative information is available for six samples: college undergraduates (n = 538), community volunteers (n = 815), UCC clients (n = 486), EAP clients (n = 441), Community Mental Health Center (CMHC) clients/outpatients (n = 342), and inpatients (n = 207). Specific details related to pertinent sample characteristics/demographics are not reported completely in the manual. For example, details related to *gender* are reported for four of the six samples and to *age* and *ethnicity* for one sample. Details related to *education* and *SES* are not reported at all. Consequently, it is not possible to determine the representativeness of the normative samples (relative to either U.S. Census data or the intended populations). Scores derived from the

OQ© should therefore be interpreted cautiously and, to the extent possible, in the context of available research. Preliminary research has shown, for example, that clients 20 years of age and younger, as well as those who are Asian American/Pacific Islander, may score significantly differently than their older, European American counterparts. Prospective users are strongly encouraged to familiarize themselves with studies cited in the manual, as well as those published elsewhere in the literature. They are also encouraged to, in their use and interpretation of OQ© scores, attend closely to important moderator variables, such as a client's level of psychocultural adjustment (e.g., biculturation, ethnic identity, and worldview), which, to the authors' credit, are alluded to on page 6 of the manual.

RELIABILITY AND VALIDITY. Reliability estimates of OQ© scores are provided in the manual. These estimates are based primarily on two samples. The first is a sample of 157 undergraduate students (54 men, 103 women, >90% European American) from a large western university and the second is a subset of 298 EAP clients of unreported gender and ethnicity. Estimates of internal consistency ranged, in these samples, from "fair" ([.70] SR subscale score) to "excellent" ([.93] total score; Cicchetti, 1994). Test-retest reliability estimates ranged, over a 3-week timeframe, from .78 (SD subscale score) to .84 (total score). Ten-week stability coefficients ranged, in an altogether different sample of 56 undergraduate students, from .82 (Week 1) to .66 (Week 10). Standard error of measurement (*SEM*), a common method of estimating the reliability of a given respondent's test score, is reported to be .93. The reliability estimates cited here, it should be noted, easily meet traditional professional standards of acceptability.

Preliminary evidence of construct validity (i.e., convergent validity), criterion-related validity (i.e., concurrent validity), and test score sensitivity and specificity are also provided in the manual. Evidence of convergent validity, which the authors refer to as "concurrent" validity (manual, p. 8), is based on correlations between OQ© scores and scores on 10 other tests that measure similar constructs (e.g., BDI, STAI, SCL-90-R). Reported correlation coefficients are satisfactorily high (in the .44–.92 range) and are, at least for the total score, generally in the expected direction. Specific evidence of discriminant validity is lacking. Also lacking is discussion/elaboration of results of initial factor analysis (e.g., item-factor loadings). Thus, the amount of variance accounted for by one-, two-, and three-factor solutions is unknown. Of note, OQ© total and subscale scores appear to be highly correlated (in the .83–.93 range), leading the authors to conclude that "they effectively represent a single factor" (manual, p. 38). This conclusion raises serious doubts about the theoretical (and empirical) basis of the test's original three-factor organizational/conceptual scheme.

Evidence of concurrent validity is based on correlations between OQ© scores and therapist-rated Global Assessment of Functioning scores and computer-administered SCID interviews. These correlations are .78 and .87, respectively. Specific evidence of predictive validity is lacking.

Test score sensitivity, the extent to which a score accurately detects the presence of a condition/phenomenon (e.g., subjective distress), is reported to be .84. Test score specificity, the extent to which a score accurately detects the absence of a condition/phenomenon, is reported to be .83. Empirically derived cut scores of 63 were used to calculate these estimates. According to the manual, "when a patient's score falls at or below 63, it is more likely that they are part of the community sample than the patient sample" (p. 20).

In addition to the aforementioned validity data, data related to item sensitivity (including item-level effect sizes), subscale cut scores, and reliable change indices (RCIs; cf. Jacobson & Truax, 1991) are also provided in the manual. Although more research is clearly needed (especially with respect to differential score validity across various age groups, U.S. ethnic groups, and groups of international respondents), the authors are to be commended for their concerted efforts to rigorously and systematically study/document the reliability and validity of OQ© scores.

COMMENTARY. The OQ© has a number of strengths and weaknesses. Its most obvious strengths include: its brevity and ease of administration, scoring, and interpretation; that it may be used for multiple clinical and research purposes, including the identification of potential "treatment failures" (manual, p. 24); that it is cost effective, that the majority of its items and scores have been shown to be highly sensitive to change; that it utilizes empirically derived cut scores and

RCIs; and that its total score has been shown to be a *reliable* and *valid* "index of mental health" (manual, p. 10). In contrast, its most obvious weaknesses include: incomplete scale development and norming information (though this relates more to the manual than the test); the "unidimensional" nature of the total and subscale scores (manual, p. 38); the fact that it does not measure any symptoms of psychosis; and, like other self-report tests, its susceptibility to undetected "faking."

Strengths and weaknesses notwithstanding, five important questions remain unanswered: (a) What reading level is required to complete the OQ©? (b) How many items may be omitted without negatively affecting/jeopardizing the reliability and validity of its scores? (c) What criteria and decision rules were used to select items/create the subscales (e.g., item-factor loadings, scree plots, interpretability)? (d) How much variance is accounted for by the original 3-factor solution? (e) What percent of the normative samples are men, women, African American, Latino/a, and so on? How old are they? What are their educational levels? Social status? Answers to these questions, and possibly others, would be helpful in evaluating the true merits of the OQ©. They should, we believe, be included in future editions of the manual.

SUMMARY. The OQ© is an innovative, practical, and highly promising screening/outcome assessment instrument. It may be used with a wide range of adult clients, for a variety of clinically meaningful and relevant purposes. Its ability to identify potential "treatment failures" is one of its most distinguishing and compelling features. Generally speaking, it is recommended that, at this point in time, only the *total score* be used, especially for clinical purposes. And, until more substantive information is known, it is also recommended that it be used cautiously with clients who are ethnically diverse (e.g., Asian American/Pacific Islander, American Indian) and/or from other countries.

Given the OQ©'s multiple uses, psychometric soundness, and overall treatment utility, it will likely become, in the very near future, a popular test of choice for clinicians and researchers alike.

REVIEWERS' REFERENCES

Cicchetti, D. V. (1994). Guidelines, criteria, and rules of thumb for evaluating normed and standardized assessment instruments in psychology. *Psychological Assessment, 6*, 284–290.

Jacobson, N. S., & Truax, P. (1991). Clinical significance: A statistical approach to defining meaningful change in psychotherapy research. *Journal of Consulting and Clinical Psychology, 59*, 12–19.

Review of the OQ-45.2 (Outcome Questionnaire) by STEVEN I. PFEIFFER, Professor, Psychological Services in Education, Florida State University, Tallahassee, FL:

DESCRIPTION. The OQ-45.2 (Outcome Questionnaire) is a 45-item self-report instrument designed to measure patient progress in psychotherapy. The OQ-45.2 asks patients to rate their feelings on a 5-point Likert scale ranging from *never* (0) to *always* (4). The instrument is designed to measure three aspects of a patient's life: Symptom Distress, Interpersonal Relations, and Social Role performance.

The OQ-45.2 is self-administered and requires no instructions from a therapist or technician for the patient to complete. The manual recommends that the test administrator encourage the patient to complete the scale in an honest and conscientious manner; however, there is no truthfulness or lie scale. The test takes approximately 5 to 10 minutes to complete, and under special circumstances can be administered orally.

The Symptom Distress (SD) scale consists of 25 items, the Interpersonal Relations (IR) scale consists of 11 items, and the Social Role (SR) scale consists of 9 items. Scoring is a straightforward totaling of item values ranging from 0–4. The manual recommends using a computer-scanned scoring method or software program to avoid errors due to the 9 items that are scored in reverse. The OQ-45.2 yields a Total Score (TOT), which is the sum of the patient's self-ratings across all 45 items, and three scale scores (SD, IR, and SR). The higher the patient's total and/or scale scores, the more disturbed or dysfunctional the patient's subjective discomfort, interpersonal relations, and/or social role performance.

The manual provides cutoff scores for the total and three scale scores based on the midpoint between the nonpatient standardization sample and standardization data combining a number of clinical samples. The manual also provides the user with a reliable change index (RCI) for the total and scale scores, based on the work of Jacobson and Truax (1991). The RCI allows the clinician to determine whether the patient has evidenced reliable change (i.e., improvement or deterioration) during the course of treatment from one session to the next (or however frequently the OQ-45.2 is administered).

In addition to measuring patient progress in therapy, the OQ-45.2 is designed as a baseline screening tool to be used in treatment planning and as a clinical instrument to assist in treatment outcomes assessment. The OQ-45.2 is *not* designed to be used for making a psychiatric diagnosis.

DEVELOPMENT. The OQ-45.2 is based on the psychotherapy outcome and dose-response-to-treatment work of Michael Lambert and his associates at Brigham Young University, dating back more than 20 years (Lambert, 1983). Items were selected that are typically present in a wide variety of clinical disorders, at a high frequency of occurrence.

Lambert and associates constructed three scales, guided by a view that the OQ-45.2 should measure, to be clinically useful, the degree of symptom distress, the quality of interpersonal relations, and social role performance related to work, family, and leisure time. The manual reports that the SD scale was derived from a 1988 National Institute of Mental Health study and a review of the 1992 Human Affairs International data on the most frequently diagnosed *DSM-III-R* diagnostic codes. Not surprisingly, a majority of the 25 items on the SD scale represent signs or symptoms of anxiety and depression. The 11 items on the IR scale were derived from the marital and family therapy literature, and the 9 items on the SR scale were based on the quality of life literature.

Neither the manual nor a chapter on the Outcome Questionnaire by Lambert and Finch (1999) provide information on item construction or final selection. It does not appear that test development included a pilot or item tryout prior to standardization. There is no indication that the authors employed a review panel of experts or preliminary statistical analyses to review, revise, or discard any of the original items.

TECHNICAL. The manual reports that normative data were drawn from several samples collected across a variety of geographic regions. There are, in fact, two normative samples, a clinical and nonclinical norm group. The clinical samples consist of clients who were seen in a university counseling center (n = 486), employee assistance program (n = 441), outpatient clinics (n = 342), and inpatient settings (n = 207). The nonclinical normative samples consist of undergraduate students (n = 538) and a community-based sample (n = 815). Sample sizes for both the clinical and nonclinical norm groups are quite adequate.

It is not clear whether the nonclinical and clinical normative samples are representative of the populations they intend to denote. The selection of the samples does not appear to have been guided as much by ensuring two representative norm groups by important standardization sample characteristics as by convenience. The manual does not provide demographic information on important sample characteristics such as the mean age, education and income level, and geographic region of the two normative samples—information that would bolster the confidence that the nonclinical normative sample is representative of the population at large (e.g., similar to U.S. Bureau of Census data) and that the clinical normative sample is representative of individuals seeking psychotherapy.

The manual provides empirical data that the OQ-45.2 total score does not differ across age (17–80) or gender. However, it is unclear whether these analyses are based on unique samples or a subset of the normative sample. The manual cites a study by Gregersen, Nebeker, Seely, and Lambert (2005) that ethnic differences were found in OQ-45.2 total score and response patterns.

Support for the internal consistency and test-retest reliability of the OQ-45.2, as reported in the manual, was obtained using an undergraduate sample of 157 students and 298 patients. Coefficient alpha was high for the Total and SD scales for both the nonclinical and clinical samples (ranging from .91–.93). Coefficient alpha scores were adequate for the other two scales for both the nonclinical and clinical samples (ranging from .70–.74). Test-retest reliability for the same nonclinical sample ranged from .78–.84; the manual does not report the time interval between test administrations. The manual reports a second test-retest reliability study with a nonclinical sample (undergraduate students), with stability scores ranging from .66–.86 over a 10-week period.

A concurrent validity study using a nonclinical sample (undergraduates) compared the OQ-45.2 with 11 different instruments (e.g. Beck Depression Inventory, Taylor Manifest Anxiety Scale, Symptom Checklist SCL-90-R, SF-36 Medical Outcomes Questionnaire). Correlation coefficients were all significant at the .01 level, ranging from .43–.88 for the three scale scores and .54–.88 for the Total score. Sample sizes for these samples were not reported in the manual.

A second validation study used a clinical sample and compared the OQ-45.2 with the SCL-90-R, Inventory of Interpersonal Problems, and Social Adjustment Rating Scale—Self-Report Form. All validity coefficient values were significant at the .05 level. The OQ-45.2 Total Score and SD scale correlated highly with the General Severity Index of the SCL-90-R (ranging from .78–.92). Validation of the IR and SR scales was not as strong. The manual states, "this finding suggests that all three scales measure similar constructs despite attempts to distinguish functioning in different areas ... The status of the three subscales is less certain" (p. 10). An ambitious factor analytic study did not find strong support for a three-factor solution. There was equal support for a one-factor solution and a two-factor solution (SR and IR scales collapsed into a life functioning scale).

Construct validation of the OQ-45.2 was measured employing a test of sensitivity to change. The rationale was that detectable improvement should occur by the eighth therapy session (Lambert & Ogles, 2004), and therefore the OQ-45.2 should discern significant improvement in scores after seven therapy sessions. Forty patients were followed over at least seven therapy sessions, yielding a significant t test between pretest and posttest scores. The most significant change occurred with the Total score (17.47-point average improvement). The three scale scores did not generate nearly as large a change (9.55-point average for SD; 3.85-point average for SR; 2.68-point average for IR). Unfortunately, the manual does not report the overall standard deviation statistic for the nonclinical and clinical standardization samples. This compromises the ability to test sensitivity to change using the standard deviation and standard error of measurement for the standardization sample.

The manual includes a handful of additional validation studies conducted by Lambert and his associates indicating that the OQ-45.2 is sensitive to identifying change in patient status as a result of therapy. The studies concur that the total score is the most effective index in discerning sensitivity to patient change. The authors report a study on the ability of the OQ-45.2 to classify individuals correctly as either members of a nonclinical or patient group. Test sensitivity ("true positives") was .84 and specificity ("true negatives") was .83 for the sample. Information on the sample, including sample size, was not reported.

COMMENTARY. Dating back to 1996, at least 12 studies have been published in peer review journals on the OQ-45.2, the great majority with

Michael Lambert as a coauthor. This reviewer located an additional 19 unpublished studies, dissertation research, that have investigated the OQ-45.2 instrument. These numbers suggest that the OQ-45.2 is generating considerable interest. Managed care is increasingly interested in the effectiveness and efficiency of the provision of behavioral health care services (Pfeiffer & Shott, 1996), making the OQ-45.2 an attractive and timely outcome tool.

The OQ-45.2 is an instrument that is inexpensive and easy to administer and score. There is theoretical logic and clinical support for conceptualizing and measuring change in patient status in terms of three domains: symptom or subjective distress, quality of interpersonal relations, and adequacy of social role performance. An inspection of the 45 items reveals that they all enjoy face validity; no item stands out as irrelevant, inappropriate or quirky. They are the kinds of items that a therapist would want to monitor in evaluating the progress that their patient is making in therapy.

The authors are to be commended for designing a test consistent with their substantial work in the psychotherapy outcome research. The incorporation of a Reliable Change Index (RCI) to measure improvement, recovery, and deterioration is particularly noteworthy. The authors recommend that interpretation includes analysis of 4 "critical items" that screen for potential suicide, substance abuse, and violence—a useful enhancement of the instrument.

The OQ-45.2 is not without its weaknesses. The manual does not articulate in any clear fashion how or why the standardization samples were recruited. It is unclear whether either the nonclinical normative sample or the patient normative sample is representative of the larger populations that they are intended to represent. The manual does not synthesize the many sample data sets into two visually clear, coherent normative sample tables—a nonclinical norms table and a clinical norms table—that the user could turn to when comparing scores obtained with their patients.

The reliability and validity of the Total score is adequate for clinical practice; however, the use of the scale scores, based on less strong reliability or validity data, is questionable. At this time, it would be advisable for therapists to rely on the Total score and place less weight or value on the individual scale scores in monitoring patient progress. Although the extant OQ-45.2 research does not necessarily yet "disprove" the ability to reliably measure interpersonal relations, social role performance, and symptom distress, there is presently not enough support for viewing these three scales as unique or independent.

Lambert and Finch (1999) report that persons who have a sixth-grade reading level and who are age 18 or older can complete the scale. The authors were remiss in not reporting an analysis of the readability of the scale, easily enough calculated using methodology first described by Kincaid and McDaniel (1974).

SUMMARY. The OQ-45.2 is an important new tool that is designed to measure patient progress in therapy. It fills a critical need in the behavioral health care field at a time when managed care is requiring providers to document both the effectiveness and efficiency (cost-savings) of the interventions that they provide. The scale is easy to use, score, and interpret, and the items are consistent with what most patients would expect to be asked as part of their treatment. A growing body of research conducted by Michael Lambert, first author, and his colleagues suggests that the OQ-45.2 is effective in monitoring treatment progress, identifying potential treatment failures and treatment-resistant patients, and even serving as an early warning system signaling which patients might require treatment adjustments to change their outcome trajectory. It is not clear if the OQ-45.2 is a better choice than the SCL-90-R or the mental health scale of the SF-36 Medical Outcomes Questionnaire. Provision of an easy-to-understand Reliable Change Index makes the OQ-45.2 an attractive choice.

REVIEWER'S REFERENCES

Gregersen, A. T., Nebeker, R. S., Seely, K. I., & Lambert, M. J. (2005). Social validation of the Outcome Questionnaire: An assessment of Asian and Pacific Islander college students. *Journal of Multicultural Counseling and Development, 33.*

Jacobson, N. S., & Truax, P. (1991). Clinical significance: A statistical approach to defining meaningful change in psychotherapy research. *Journal of Consulting and Clinical Psychology, 59,* 12–19.

Kincaid, J. P., & McDaniel, W. C. (1974). *An inexpensive automated way of calculating Flesch Reading Ease scores* (Patent Disclosure Document N. 031350). Washington, DC: U.S. Patent Office.

Lambert, M. J. (1983). Introduction to assessment of psychotherapy outcome: Historical perspective and current issues. In M. J. Lambert, E. R. Christensen, & S. S. DeJulio (Eds.), *The assessment of psychotherapy outcome* (pp. 3–32). New York: Wiley.

Lambert, M. J., & Finch, A. E. (1999). The outcome questionnaire. In M. E. Maruish (Ed.), *The use of psychological testing for treatment planning and outcome assessment* (pp. 831–869). Mahwah, NJ: Lawrence Erlbaum Associates.

Lambert, M. J., & Ogles, B. M. (2004). The efficacy and effectiveness of psychotherapy. In M. J. Lambert (Ed.), *Bergin and Garfield's handbook of psychotherapy and behavior change* (5th ed., pp. 805–821). New York: Wiley.

Pfeiffer, S. I., & Shott, S. (1996). Treatment outcomes assessment: Conceptual, practical and ethical considerations. In C. E. Stout (Ed.), *The complete guide to managed behavioral healthcare* (pp. 1–11). New York: Wiley.

[177]
Ordinate Spoken English Test.

Purpose: Measures speaking and listening skills over the telephone and measures facility in spoken English, which includes the ease and immediacy in understanding and producing basic conversational English.

Population: Ages 17–79.

Publication Dates: 2000–2004.

Acronym: SET-10.

Scores, 5: Overall Score, Sentence Mastery, Vocabulary, Fluency, Pronunciation.

Administration: Individual.

Forms, 2: 5 minutes, 10 minutes.

Price Data, 2003: $24 per 5-minute test; $40 per 10-minute test.

Time: (5–15) minutes.

Comments: Test administered via telephone; previously titled PhonePass Spoken English Test.

Author: Ordinate Corporation.

Publisher: Ordinate Corporation.

Review of the Ordinate Spoken English Test by DENNIS DOVERSPIKE, Professor of Psychology, University of Akron, Akron, OH:

DESCRIPTION. The Ordinate Spoken English Test (SET-10) was developed to be used by organizations, and any interested parties, in assessing the English-language vocabulary, speaking, and listening skills of nonnative speakers over 15 years of age. This test is probably best described as a sample or simulation of speaking and listening ability. There are five tasks or types of problems: (a) Read simple sentences, (b) repeat back sentences heard over the phone, (c) give short answers to questions, (d) build sentences out of words, and (e) answer three open-ended questions.

The test is administered by phone, although there are paper test forms and instructions. The paper forms include the test identification number and the sentences that are read during the phone-based administration.

The test can be taken 24 hours a day. There are two versions of the test. One version takes 5 minutes to complete and the other version takes 10 minutes. This review is based on the 10-minute version.

No special software or training is required. Scoring is performed by machine (i.e., by voice recognition software based upon a number of criteria). The scoring is completed by the publisher. Scores can be provided by regular mail, email, or the web.

An overall score is reported. In addition, scores are provided on sentence mastery, vocabulary, fluency, and pronunciation. Scores are reported on a 20-80 scale. The score report form is very well laid out. It is easy to read and provides a lot of information on the meaning of the total score and the scale scores. Information is provided for translating the overall score into a score on the Educational Testing Service Test of Spoken English scale.

A validation manual is available for the SET-10 version of the Ordinate Spoken English Test. This validation manual is very well done, very professional, and provides information on test development, reliability, and validity.

DEVELOPMENT. The SET-10 is a measure of the construct of facility in spoken English. It assesses the ability to understand spoken English and to respond within normal conversation. It is based on a model of conversational speech that involves tracking what is said, extracting meaning, and producing a response. Through a series of prompts or questions, it tests this ability to listen and then speak in normal conversational English. As such, it can be seen as tapping the construct of engaging in conversational speech. It does this in what amounts to real time. Thus, it measures a person's ability to encode spoken language and formulate a response in a simulated real time environment.

The SET-10 was based on cognitive and communication literature and appears to rely primarily on a construct-content validity approach to development. The content of the SET-10 was designed so as to reflect this emphasis and concentrates on simple to understand phrases, although the phrases are described as reflecting a range of skill levels and skill profiles. The vocabulary is based upon words most frequently used in telephone conversations and has been tested to ensure its applicability across diverse populations of native and nonnative speakers. The content was balanced in order to apply to speakers of English other than those from the United States. The content was also balanced for geography and gender.

TECHNICAL. The validation manual for the SET-10 contains a great deal of technical detail on the development of the test, the content of the test, reliability, and validity. This includes detailed information on comparisons between machine and human scoring.

Prototype versions of the SET-10 have been administered to over 4,000 native and nonnative speakers. The native norming group was diverse in terms of age, sex, and race. The nonnative norming group was representative in terms of native languages and gender. Over 40 languages were represented in the norming group.

As would be expected, the test effectively discriminates between native and nonnative speakers. The correlation between the current version of the SET-10 and the previous version was close to 1, $r = .98$. The correlations between different scale scores were relatively high, although this may reflect the unidimensionality of the underlying construct or overlap in the underlying tasks. The reported reliability estimates were relatively high, whether machine or human scored, although it is not clear what type of reliability was being reported. It appeared to be some type of rerate reliability. The reported reliability estimates were mostly above .90. Correlations between machine and human scoring also tended to be above .90.

Correlations were also presented between the SET-10 and various tests such as the TOEFL. Generally, the correlations are high, .70 or above, providing evidence for the concurrent validity of the test.

The SET-10 can be used for employment purposes. However, no validation studies were reported in the manual dealing with the prediction of job performance.

COMMENTARY. The SET-10 appears to represent a practical, reliable, and valid measure of proficiency in spoken, conversational English for nonnative speakers. The test was developed based upon a model of conversational English. The reliability and validity data are strong, suggesting that this is a technically sound instrument. Overall, this is an excellent example of both how to develop a test and how to present data on the development of a test.

A great deal of care and professional effort were put into the development of this test. Although I find it to be remarkable from a technological standpoint, it is also strong from a psychometric perspective. The technical manual provides extensive documentation on the test. It would be nice to see data on the prediction of job performance.

SUMMARY. The SET-10 appears to represent a practical, reliable, and valid measure of proficiency in spoken, conversational English for nonnative speakers. The reliability and validity data suggest that this is a technically sound instru-

ment. The manual indicates that the test was carefully and professionally developed. Great attention was paid to the development of norms and the validation of machine scoring. In future versions, I would like to see data on the test as a predictor of job performance.

Review of the Ordinate Spoken English Test by ALAN GARFINKEL, Professor of Spanish and Education, Purdue University, West Lafayette, IN:

DESCRIPTION. The Ordinate Spoken English Test (SET-10) is an automated test that is administered over the telephone. It contains five separate parts that ask the examinee to read printed sentences aloud, repeat items verbatim, give opposites, answer simple questions, and to answer questions on such things as preferences with a 20-second response. The examinee is given a test number that appears on the test instruction form and is identified by pressing numbers on the phone's keypad. The last section is recorded but not scored by machine, thus making it possible to post scores on a secure website within minutes. Test purchasers have the option of using another secure website to gain access to scores and the open-ended answers to give some consideration to answers to the open-ended responses. There is a test of half the duration available under the same conditions for a lower fee.

DEVELOPMENT. The SET-10 was copyrighted in 2000 and 2002 by the Ordinate Corporation of Menlo Park, CA. CTB/McGraw-Hill is a distributor for both versions. Materials furnished by the publisher include a four-page test manual (*Validation Summary for PhonePass SET-10*) and a supplementary sheet of correlations. A description of the test's development that is included in the manual reports that "Lexical and stylistic patterns of actual conversation have been used in developing all item material" (p. 1). Also reported is the fact that conversations from 540 North Americans were used to design test items. The "opposite" and short answer questions were pretested on diverse samples of native and nonnative speakers. Items retained in the test were answered correctly by at least 90% of native speakers of English.

TECHNICAL. The SET-10 reflects strong face and content validity. A team of scorers led by master scorers graded thousands of exams by hand in order to estimate the reliability of the machine-scoring system used on the telephone. Other more empirical measures to demonstrate that the test actually does test what it is supposed to test are absent. The test manual does not comply with the *Standards for Educational and Psychological Testing* (AERA, APA, & NCME, 1999).

COMMENTARY. The test's publisher included a working test number that the reviewer, a native speaker of English, was invited to take. This experience was not positive. This leads one to wonder about using this intimidating test alone for making so important a decision as whether or not to employ a given job candidate. In the corporate world, employers would not be likely to pay for a second chance to take the test. It seems that this might be a test used for very high stakes. The publishers assure that the test and its manual meet standards expressed by the United States Equal Opportunity Commission's *Uniform Guidelines for Employee Selection Procedures.* Considering the context of the test's use, some will allege that no other standards need be observed.

SUMMARY. It is unrealistic to think that this test will not be widely used simply because it does not supply some statistics on validity. It is a high stakes test and the publisher might be well advised to consult the AERA, APA, and NCME Standards when preparing future versions of the test manual.

REVIEWER'S REFERENCE

American Educational Research Association, American Psychological Association, & National Council on Measurement in Education. (1999). *Standards for educational and psychological testing.* Washington, DC: American Educational Research Association.

[178]

Organizational and Team Culture Indicator.

Purpose: Designed to "assess an organization or team's unconscious archetypal stories and to discover how these are related to its values and strengths."
Population: Adults.
Publication Dates: 2003–2004.
Acronym: OTCI.
Scores: 12 Archetypes: Creator, Everyperson, Hero, Caregiver, Innocent, Magician, Jester, Lover, Sage, Ruler, Explorer, Revolutionary.
Administration: Individual or group.
Restricted Distribution: Distribution of Professional Report is restricted to persons who have completed the publisher's or author's training course.
Price Data, 2004: $45 per manual (204, 151 pages); $18 per Basic Report (print version) including 1 instrument, 1 self-scorable report form, and 1 Understanding Archetypes in Your Organization (2003, 110 pages); $15 per Basic Report (online version).

Time: Administration time not reported.
Comments: Results are available in either Basic or more comprehensive Professional Report Format; Basic Report is available for online or self-scored administration and Professional Report Format is available only through qualified professionals.
Authors: Carol S. Pearson and Allen L. Hammer.
Publisher: Center for Applications of Psychological Type.

Review of the Organizational and Team Culture Indicator by STEPHEN B. JOHNSON, Managing Partner, RPM Data, Greensboro, NC:

DESCRIPTION. The Organizational and Team Culture Indicator (OTCI) is designed to assess an individual's perceptions of an organization or team with regard to 12 "unconscious archetypes" (such as the Magician or Ruler), based on the theories of Jung. The OTCI helps identify the dominant archetype(s), with the "goal of identifying the attitudes, behaviors, unwritten rules and taboos" (manual, p. 1) of the group.

The OTCI is an untimed assessment that can be administered to groups or individuals over the Internet or in a pencil-paper format. The OTCI consists of 96 five-point Likert type questions anchored by *Almost Never* to *Almost Always.* The respondent is asked to rate their team or organization and not themselves. Each administration takes an average of 40 minutes and can be administered under conditions set by the test administrator.

There are two available item sets that provide different reports. The OTCI Basic is used by individuals to rate their organization or team; it can be self-administered and self-scored. This version provides a Basic Report that can be used as part of a team-building exercise, or as part of individual counseling. The OTCI Professional is administered to all team or organization members and allows for an aggregated assessment. It is available only through qualified trainers.

The Professional Report has nine parts: (a) Identification and review of the dominant archetypes; (b) Assessment of team or organizational values; (c) Assessment of team or organizational strengths/competencies; (d) Review of the alignment between values and strengths; (e) Review of archetypes with low scores indicating blind spots or weaknesses; (f) Orientation or style under which the group operates (Stability/Structure, People/Belonging, Results/Mastery, Learning/Freedom, based on Maslow's [1954] hierarchy of needs); (g) Assessment of the four major organizational subsystems (Material, Human Community, Production, Learning); (h) A summary of the relationship between dominant archetype(s), organizational orientation, and organizational subsystems; and (i) Review of the Public or Brand Identity associated with the dominant archetype.

DEVELOPMENT. The OTCI was developed from the author's work on organizational dynamics. The stated aim of the instrument is to allow identification of the dominant archetypes of the team/organization. By identifying unconscious archetypal stories, teams and organizations can learn what motivates their leaders and employees, what values are deeply held by their corporate cultures, and what brand identities will help them connect more readily with customers.

The OTCI material is professionally presented with regular attempts to make it understandable to a wide audience. Clear definitions are provided about the archetypes with examples of how the archetypes may play out in organizational behaviors.

Initially, 188 items were developed to assess values, strengths, and challenges for each of the 12 archetypes. After administration to 800 individuals across three organizations, an assessment of coefficient alpha and item-total correlations eliminated 44 items, leaving 4 items to assess each of the values, strengths, and challenges for each of the 12 archetypes. Further data were collected from administration in 10 organizations to assess the reliability of these remaining items. The 48 items assessing challenges for the 12 archetypes were subsequently dropped as they showed inconsistent patterns of relationships with values and strengths across different types of organizations. Alternative anchors for the scales were tested using *Strongly Agree* to *Strongly Disagree*, with data indicating that the coefficient alpha was lower for six of the archetype scales. Eleven items were also reworded in response to feedback from non-U.S.-English-speaking users, with coefficient alphas showing an improvement for five of the six scales affected.

TECHNICAL. Scores for the OTCI (values, strengths, total archetype, and orientation) are reported as standard scores with a mean of 50 and a standard deviation of 10. The range of possible scores is not clear. Scores for individuals are combined to yield team/organizational scores using a multistep standardization and averaging process.

The authors use Cohen's (1988) work on effect size to judge the relative strength of the different archetypes and determine which are "significantly higher" than the other archetypes. The authors state that a difference of 2 points (.2 standard deviation units) represents a "minimum separation required to conclude that the difference between the two archetypes is meaningful" (manual, p. 71).

Internal consistency reliability estimates for the individual archetype scales are presented through analysis of data from eight organizations representing a variety of organizational types. The Cronbach alpha values range from .34 to .93 with the majority in the range of .80 to .90. Some of the organizations had a very low number of respondents (as few as 12). The different Ns for each organization could explain the wide range of reliabilities across organizations and archetypes. Differences in consistency may also reflect the level of English comprehension and understanding of organizational jargon required by respondents (e.g., "Encourages self-organizing teams"). There are no data on the correlations between the different scales, nor is there any confirmatory factor analysis of the instrument.

Evidence for test-retest reliability has been collected from three organizations. Reliability was checked through assessing the ranking of the archetype scores using Spearman's rho. This resulted in correlations of .78, .83, and .95. The Ns for the test-retest were small (16, 12, and 13), with the testing occasions separated by 30 days.

The validity evidence presented for the OTCI is limited, failing to meet traditional or modern concepts of validity (e.g., Messick, 1995). There are no validity data that explore the OTCI's relationship with measures of organizational functioning or performance that may be affected by alignment with organizational archetypes (e.g., employee morale). Instead, the manual presents as validity data a series of ANOVA tests using total archetype, values, strengths, and orientation scores as dependent variables with the independent variables of years of service, organizational position, level in the organizations, ethnicity, and gender. There was no consistent pattern for which organization or dependent variable was significantly different for the independent variables. However, not all organizations provided information and some Ns were very small. For example, only one organization had data on ethnicity. It is not clear to this reviewer how these results contribute to a validity argument.

The authors also present data showing that rankings of archetypes differed across organizational type, though seven of eight organizations ranked the Hero archetype in the top three. Again, it is not clear how this relates to the OTCI's validity argument. It also suggests to this reviewer that there may be some bias in responding to archetypes based on their social desirability. For example, the Hero archetype is a competitive concept, an arguably socially desirable trait in the U.S.

COMMENTARY. Different theories of organizational development have at their core a focus on helping organizations change. Most change processes begin by assessing the current situation and identifying areas that will meet organizational objectives. Recent models of organizational development emphasize the importance of members candidly discussing their views and experience of an organization. The OTCI is firmly rooted in this model, through its focus on team members using the tool to discuss the team and organizational values, strengths, and orientations. The OTCI materials repeatedly stress that the instrument is a tool to promote discussion and provides plenty of supplementary materials to support this intent.

The statistical evidence for the OTCI is of mixed quality. For the most part, the authors use accepted approaches to show reliability. However, the use of effect size to infer meaningful distinctions between archetypes and other scores is problematic in two ways. First, Cohen himself was hesitant in giving absolute meanings to effect sizes, as he (and others) believe that effect sizes must be interpreted in context. Second, the effect size statistic reflects the impact of a treatment on independent groups, not a difference in magnitude between constructs as measured in a single group. The authors seem to have confused standardized scores with effect sizes

The evidence for validity is weaker than the reliability evidence, most particularly because the authors do not attempt to connect the OTCI to other measures of organizational functioning or performance. The statistical analysis provided in support of validity is idiosyncratic and not aligned with any traditional or modern theory.

A review of the items and the data indicates that the language may need more research for readability and comprehension. The concepts expressed in some of the items may not be suited to groups where English comprehension is limited, or for individuals with limited exposure to organizational language. For example, there were differences in ratings for some archetypes based on organizational position and years of service, and this reviewer's assessment of the readability of two items (Recognizes the restorative value of recreation; Values consensual decision making) indicated that they are at the 12th grade level (Flesch-Kincaid Grade Level) and had a low Flesch Reading Ease (16; where most documents aim for a score of 60 to 70). A more detailed research program on the impact of ethnicity and age/experience on comprehension is needed.

SUMMARY. The authors are to be admired for having a deep theory and for development of an instrument that matches their theoretical perspective. There is evidence of strong work in getting the reliability indices right. However, the authors appear to be struggling to provide validity evidence, especially to connect to other aspects of organizational behavior. If the OTCI theory holds, then organizations with a consistent message, and understanding of the message, should show aspects of improved functioning (e.g., reduced turnover, high morale). These aspects would serve as a good model to assess important aspects of validity.

The OTCI requires investment in interpretation. This is not a tool for teams or organizations wanting a quick assessment of values and strengths. The highly interpretive nature of the archetypes, and the theoretical tradition of these concepts, requires a long-term relationship with an organizational development consultant

REVIEWER'S REFERENCES

Cohen, J. (1988). *Statistical power analysis for the behavioral sciences* (2nd ed.). Hillsdale, NJ: Lawrence Erlbaum Associates.
Maslow, A. H. (1954). *Motivation and personality.* New York: Harper & Brothers.
Messick, S. (1995). Validity of psychological assessment: Validation of inferences from persons' responses and performance as scientific inquiry into scoring meaning. *American Psychologist, 9,* 741–749.

[179]

Parent Success Indicator.

Purpose: Designed to identify "favorable qualities of parents and aspects of their behavior where education seems warranted."

Population: Parents of children ages 10 to 14.

Publication Date: 1998.

Acronym: PSI.

Scores, 6: Communication, Use of Time, Teaching, Frustration, Satisfaction, Information Needs.

Administration: Group or individual.

Forms, 2: Parent, Child.

Price Data, 2003: $74 per starter set including manual (58 pages), 20 parent inventory booklets, 20 child inventory booklets, and 20 profiles; $16 per manual; $63 per additional forms package including 20 parent inventory booklets, 20 child inventory booklets, and 20 profiles; $20 per sample set.

Foreign Language Editions: Spanish, Japanese, and Mandarin editions available (manual available in English only).

Time: (15–20) minutes.

Comments: Parents report self-impressions; children report observations of the parent.

Authors: Robert D. Strom and Shirley K. Strom.

Publisher: Scholastic Testing Service, Inc.

Review of the Parent Success Indicator by C. RUTH SOLOMON SCHERZER, Associate Professor, Département de psychologie, Université de Montréal, Montreal, Quebec, Canada:

DESCRIPTION. The purpose of the Parent Success Indicator (PSI) is to evaluate parenting skills in order to identify areas of parenting that may be problematic for parents' interactions with their 10- to 14-year-old children. According to the authors, the information obtained by the PSI may be used in several ways: designing curriculum for parent education groups, as a pre- and postmeasure of the effects of a parent education program, as a survey instrument of parental self-perceptions and of how adolescent sons and daughters view their parents.

The PSI is composed of three booklets. Two of the booklets contain identification forms and include questions, the responses to which can be used to compare respondents from different demographic groups or on other variables such as time spent with a child and performance at school. Each booklet contains 60 closed statements and a 61st statement that solicits individual comments.

One booklet is to be filled in by parents, the other by the children. The statements (items) in each booklet are the same except for changes in grammar at the beginning and end of each statement. Parent booklet statements begin with "I" and child booklet statements begin with "my parents." Thus, parents rate themselves and children rate parents on the same items. Examples of statements are "I am good at listening to my child." ("My parent is good at listening to me.") "I am frustrated by the way my child follows rules." ("My parent is frustrated by the way I follow rules.")

Each of the 60 statements is followed by a choice of four answers, *Always, Often, Seldom,* or *Never,* one of which the participant circles.

The third booklet, the Parent Success Indicator Profile provides parents with feedback from their self-evaluations. It is designed in the same format as the other two booklets. It can also be used before and after an educational program in order to evaluate the effects of the program.

The 60 individual statements compose six 10-item subscales on which the parents' strengths or weaknesses are evaluated. The subscales are Communication (skills of advising and learning from children); Use of Time (making decisions as to how time is used); Teaching (the scope of child guidance that is expected of parents); Frustration (child attitudes and behaviors that bother parents); Satisfaction (aspects of being a parent which bring satisfaction); and Information Needs (things parents need to know about a child). The authors provide a rationale for each subscale which is based on currently accepted principles in the childrearing literature.

Parents are invited to complete the PSI in person or by mail. Children may complete the PSI in person or at school with directions provided by a teacher. Children are asked to complete one form for each parent with whom they live. When filled in at school, teachers are requested to read the items aloud if a child has poor reading skills. The teachers are also asked to verify the responses of each child to be sure that all the items are completed. Children generally take 15 to 20 minutes to complete the PSI.

The same scoring key is used for both the parent and child versions of the PSI. Responses seen as indicating parent strength are attributed a score of 4 and scores of 3, 2, and 1 are attributed for decreasing levels of parental strength. After the values have been assigned to each response, mean scores are derived for each subscale. The Parent Success Indicator Profile is then prepared and may be presented to the parents with items scored as 4 identified as Highly Favorable, 3 as Slightly Favorable, 2 as Slightly Unfavorable, and 1 as Highly Unfavorable.

In addition to their own profile, parents may compare their performance with the group responses of their child's peers and overall group scores of other mothers and fathers. For feedback purposes, item mean scores of 2.5 to 3.0 are interpreted as slightly favorable and scores of 3.0 to 4 as highly favorable. All item mean scores of 2.0 to 2.5 are interpreted as slightly unfavorable and scores of 1 to 2 as highly unfavorable. For subscales the interpretation values are the same.

DEVELOPMENT OF THE INSTRUMENT. As stated in the manual, the PSI was generated from the findings of an open-ended survey administered to parents, teachers, and children. The survey was conducted in a mostly upper-middle-class suburb of Phoenix, Arizona. The randomly selected sample involved 1,286 parents, 907 children, and 700 teachers at the elementary and high school levels. It was composed of questions such as "What things does your child do that you consider frustrating?" Corresponding items appeared on the child and teacher forms. Concerns implicating parent competence were identified and ranked in order of importance for each grade level. A 96% rate of interrater agreement was obtained for the coding of 33,000 responses.

Topics with the highest priority for families with children ages 10–14 were then used to formulate a Likert-type instrument called the Parental Strengths and Needs Inventory (PSNI). Validity tests of the PSNI led to the creation of new subscales and the revision, deletion, and replacement of various items on the other subscales. The revised instrument is the Parent Success Indicator.

TECHNICAL.

Reliability. Internal consistency analysis of the 60 items of the PSI and each of the expected six subscales showed high overall Cronbach's alphas for the scores of African American, Caucasian, and Mexican American parent and child subject groups ($N = 1,634$ child and parent participants). Reliability checks showed the estimates of internal consistency for parent and child populations from economically and culturally diverse groups ($N = 900$) to be uniformly high.

Validity. To assess construct validity the PSI item responses were subjected to a principal component extraction solution followed by a varimax rotation. The factor analysis supported the six proposed PSI subscales.

Comparison studies. The authors summarize the results of a number of research studies that used the PSI. The studies involved African American mothers and children, mothers and fathers of gifted children, immigrant parents and grandparents, mothers and fathers of mentally challenged children, Chinese mothers and fathers of one child and deaf parents and their hearing children. The authors conclude that the PSI is a very useful instrument for obtaining important information about parenting skills in all of these studies, but do not provide details about the role, use, and results of the PSI therein. [Editor's Note: The publisher has provided copies of some recently published articles that provide many more details. However, these were provided in response to this review and were not made available to the reviewer prior to April 2004 when the review was completed.]

COMMENTARY. The Parent Success Indicator is grounded in generally approved criteria for improving relations between parents and their 10- to 14-year-old children. The individual items and resulting scales address parents' current problems and needs. It is an easy instrument to use; the wording is clear and simple and should be easily understood by most parents and children to whom it is addressed. It appears to have two main values. The first would be to use the parent version to quick start discussions in parent education groups. Similarly, it could be used as a starting point for discussion in family or mother-child therapy. The second value would be to gather parent self-perceptions and child opinions for various surveys of parents and children in order to use them for other purposes. The instrument seems to be limited, however, by the same problem as are self-report instruments in general, that is, a lack of participant insight or a tendency to inflate their abilities and behaviors. In the case of the PSI, this limit appears to be illustrated in the tables that show the mean scores for the individual items obtained by 857 mothers. Only 13 of 60 means are under the 2.5 cutoff score that would result in an unfavorable interpretation and no means lie between the scores of 1 and 2. Most of the mean scores are over 3 (highly favorable). Taking the standard deviations into account does not modify this impression. The tendency of parents to underestimate their needs for help undermines the value of the PSI. A further contributor to the high mean scores may be the organization of the scales. The items composing each scale are all grouped together rather than being dispersed at random throughout the booklet(s) (and then regrouped for scoring purposes). This type of organization of items usually leads to circling or checking off the same scoring choice, in part because it is quick and easy, and in part because of a desire for consistency in responding. This last comment would also hold for the child version booklet.

For research purposes, obtaining children's perceptions of their parents is helpful. For parent education purposes, however, the manual is not clear about how it is helpful to parents to provide them with the mean scores of their children's peers and not with the evaluations made by their own children.

The manual also does not make clear how issues of confidentiality and privacy are addressed when teachers are involved. Teachers are sometimes asked to read the items to the children who may not be able to read well and have them circle their answers in their presence, and teachers are asked to make certain that all the items have been completed by all the children who complete the PSI at school.

The PSI appears to have good construct validity evidence but no external validity evidence is provided. Similarly, the internal reliability is high but no test-retest reliability estimates are provided.

The authors report that the PSI has been used with various demographic groups, and with fathers, and they have children use it to evaluate their stepfathers. However, no normative data are provided about any of these groups. The manual provides information only about African American, Caucasian, and Mexican American mothers and children. [Editor's Note: The publisher has advised that some recently published articles do provide some of this information.]

CONCLUSION. The PSI has some merit but needs further work in order to be a more valuable instrument.

Review of the Parent Success Indicator by SUZANNE YOUNG, *Associate Professor of Educational Research, University of Wyoming, Laramie, WY:*

DESCRIPTION. The Parent Success Indicator, published in 1998, is designed to examine parents' strengths and weaknesses. The inventory is appropriate for parents of 10- to 14-year-old children and for children of that same age group. It has two very similar forms: one for parents to self-evaluate their skills and the second for children to evaluate a parent's skills. The inventory can be used in a number of ways such as allowing parents to evaluate and reflect on their own performance, designing an educational program for a

group of parents with similar characteristics, and understanding how children view their parents.

Both forms of the inventory have 60 items that form six subscales related to parenting: Communication, Use of Time, Teaching, Frustration, Satisfaction, and Information Needs. The respondent is also asked to complete an identification page, although, depending on the purpose of the data collection, that information may not be necessary. The directions are easy to understand and there is no time limit for either form.

In the manual, the authors include a sample letter to be sent to parents inviting them to complete the inventory, a sample form requesting permission from parents for their children to participate, a sample consent form for children to sign, and directions for teachers to read to students before they begin the inventory. The authors suggest that the parent form be administered by mail and that the child form be administered to groups of students in a classroom setting. The forms have also been translated into Spanish, Mandarin, and Japanese.

Scoring is done by the test administrator and the manual explains how to score each item as well as each subscale. The authors explain that parents can be told only their own scores. In other words, parents will not be given their own child's scores. However, overall group scores, both parent and child, can be given to parents so they can compare their performance to the group. Results, whether individual or grouped, are communicated to parents by a Parent Profile form. The form is completed by the test administrator and indicates behaviors that are seen as highly favorable, slightly favorable, slightly unfavorable, and highly unfavorable. Also, if the parents are involved in an educational intervention, the inventories can be used as pretest and posttest measures. The Profile Form is used to show both sets of scores and how they differ.

DEVELOPMENT. Using a grounded theory approach, the authors began the development of the inventory by soliciting information from 2,893 parents, children, and teachers. They responded to open-ended questions about parental behavior; raters analyzed and coded the responses. Also, the authors examined the literature on parent success in order to support their analysis. Based on the coding, the authors created a two-generational measure titled the Parental Strength and Needs

Inventory. The reliability of the two forms (parent and child) was assessed using a sample of 900 economically and culturally diverse parents and children. Internal consistency was found to be between .88 and .96 for the entire inventory; subscale reliabilities ranged from .67 to .93. Preliminary validity was examined using a factor analysis and was based on 612 low to middle income racially mixed parents and children. Based on this analysis, items on the scale were rearranged, revised, or deleted; the revised scale is called the Parent Success Indicator.

TECHNICAL. Validity and reliability estimates were found for the revised instrument. Data were collected from 1,634 African American, Caucasian, and Mexican American mothers and children. The mothers' and children's characteristics are described in detail in the manual, as well as means and standard deviations of subscales and frequencies of item responses.

Total scale reliability estimates were high, ranging from .92 to .95 for the parents and children in the three populations. The six subscale reliability estimates were also high, ranging from .77 to .86 for Communication, .75 to .84 for Time, .83 to .88 for Teaching, .81 to .90 for Frustration, .82 to .88 for Satisfaction, and .91 to .95 for Information.

Construct validity for the two forms of the inventory was assessed using factor analysis. Initially, the authors used a principal component extraction method without constraining the number of factors; they found 10 factors with eigenvalues greater than one. Factors 7 through 10, those with the smallest communalities, had 3, 1, 2, and 0 items, respectively, with factor loadings of .40 or greater. The authors retained 6 factors because (a) the scale was hypothesized to contain six subsets of 10 items each and (b) the 6-factor solution was the best fit with the most simple structure. Four of the 6 factors are very clearly defined, with all 10 items loading clearly on a single factor. The other two factors, Factor 4 (Communication) and Factor 5 (Satisfaction), had 9 and 8 items, respectively, that loaded significantly. Overall, the factor analysis supported the presence of six hypothesized subscales.

COMMENTARY. The careful development of the two forms of the Parent Success Indicator is impressive. The authors used large and diverse samples of parents, children, and teachers to develop the initial scale. Along with a careful review

of the literature regarding the basic aspects of parenting, their grounded theory approach to analysis provided strong evidence of content validity. The authors examined the initial scale for its consistency and its demonstration of six subscales. Based on that analysis, the scale was revised and analyzed again. The reliability of the revised scale is high for all responding groups (African American, Caucasian, and Mexican American) of parents and children (10 to 14 years old) and it conformed very cleanly to the hypothesized six-factor structure.

The authors intend for this inventory to be used for parents (defined as fathers, mothers, custodial parents, and stepparents) to be able to gain insights about their strengths and their needs. As the inventory was developed, the authors made use of parent samples that were culturally, racially, and economically diverse. In the sample used for the reliability and validity analysis of the final instrument, the authors report parent information for mothers only. If the comparison populations are mothers, it seems this instrument should be used only with a female parent. Further studies should focus on male parents.

SUMMARY. The authors of the Parent Success Indicator have developed an instrument that appears to be sound in its technical aspects. Reliability estimates for various ethnic groups are high; evidence of content validity and construct validity is very strong. The two forms of the inventory, one for a parent and the second for a child to complete, are well designed. However, this reviewer recommends that the authors continue developing this instrument for use with male parents. Also, potential users of the present inventory should consider administering it to female parents only.

[180]

Pearson-Marr Archetype Indicator.

Purpose: "Designed to be a comprehensive measure of a system of twelve archetypes" and to identify "the heroic archetypal theme(s) most active in a person's current life."

Population: Adolescent—adult.

Publication Dates: 1989–2003.

Acronym: PMAI.

Scores: 12 archetypes: Innocent, Orphan, Warrior, Caregiver, Seeker, Lover, Destroyer, Creator, Ruler, Magician, Saga, Jester.

Administration: Group.

Price Data, 2003: $12 per introductory manual (2003, 61 pages), questionnaire, and individualized scoring sheet; $12 per online administration; price information for manual (2003, 116 pages) available from publisher.
Time: Administration time not reported.
Comments: Self-administered and self-scored; can also be administered and scored online.
Authors: Carol S. Pearson and Hugh K. Marr.
Publisher: Center for Applications of Psychological Type, Inc.

Review of the Pearson-Marr Archetype Indicator by CARL ISENHART, Coordinator, Addictive Disorders Section, VA Medical Center, Minneapolis, MN:

The Pearson-Marr Archetype Indicator (PMAI) is a 72-item self-report questionnaire that assesses the extent an individual agrees with statements that describe 1 of 12 different archetypes. The authors define archetypes as "broad emotional, cognitive, and behavioral styles. Each style has its own theme, goals, adequacies, and potential difficulties" (manual, p. 1). The test was developed from the authors' previous publications (Pearson, 1989; Pearson, 1991; Pearson & Marr, 2002) and clinical experience with archetypes and Jungian psychology. The authors devote a chapter to discussing the concept of archetypes, where they describe each archetype: Innocent, Orphan, Warrior, Caregiver, Seeker, Lover, Destroyer, Creator, Ruler, Magician, Sage, and Jester. The authors stress that the PMAI is not a test of psychopathology and does not "categorize" a person; rather the instrument is a "well-person instrument, designed to help individuals capitalize on their strengths and recognize and predict areas of difficulty" (manual, p. 2).

The test has been studied on people ranging in age from "late adolescence" to "late sixties"; a minimum of a third-grade reading level is required. The test comes in two formats: paper-and-pencil (the format reviewed at this time) and online. The paper-and-pencil format comes with a test booklet, scoring worksheet, and an interpretation guide. For the online version, immediate results are available from computer scoring, and an electronic version of the interpretation guide is available. The examinee indicates the extent of agreement with the statement describing the features of an archetype by using a scale of 1 (*strongly disagree*) to 5 (*strongly agree*). The test is self-scored by the examinee by summing the individual scores to produce a score for each archetype. These scores can then be transferred to a "wheel" that displays the 12 archetypes, and the examinee can compare his or her scores on each archetype. In addition, each archetype can be combined into one of three groups titled "ego," "soul," and "self."

The interpretation guide provides a step-by-step process of understanding the results, provides descriptions of the archetypes, and offers suggestions on how to use the results. The manual provides information on how to interpret individual "high," "midrange," and "low" scores; combinations of high scores; and "conflictual" and "complementary" archetypal pairs. The manual also provides information regarding the ethical use of the results: protecting the client's confidentiality and maintaining a high level of sensitivity to the client's reactions to the results. Finally, to further aid the interpretation of the results, the manual contains a chapter of case histories that demonstrates the use of the test results.

The authors state in the manual that, because the archetypes that are most influential in a person's life change over time, the PMAI can be administered from every 6 months to 1 year to "chart the course of his or her journey" (manual, p. 23). The authors indicate that the instrument can be used by "psychotherapists, counselors, coaches, and spiritual directors" (manual, p. 15). Overall, they state that the test can be used to help individuals increase self-awareness, motivation, and enthusiasm; improve working relationships; reduce stress; and provide clients with more options for thinking and behaving. They provide information about using the test in psychotherapy (to promote recovery and in family therapy), for personal growth, in educational settings (by teachers and professors), for leadership development, and for team building and developing organizations. There is also a brief discussion of using the instrument with other assessment instruments (e.g., the Myers-Briggs Type Indicator) and of using the PMAI in research.

DEVELOPMENT. The PMAI is based on Jungian psychology and the authors' previous work in archetypes. The original form was developed to accompany Pearson's (1989) book and consisted of a 36-item test that was titled the "Personal Myth Index." This instrument assessed 6 archetypes; however, with the eventual addition of 6 additional archetypes, a new test was needed. Consequently, summaries of the 12 archetypes were developed, statements were elaborated that reflected each archetype, and the items were reviewed by judges who matched the statements to what they thought was the most appropriate archetype. (These judges had little familiarity with Pearson's theory or with Jung's concepts). Some items were retained for each archetype, but it was necessary to remove several items (because they were matched with an archetype other than what they were originally intended) and write several new items. These items were again reviewed and critiqued, which resulted in a 103-item scale. The scale was then piloted on 64 volunteers; reliability estimates were calculated, item analyses performed, and discrimination indices were generated. These analyses resulted in the 72-item, 6 items per archetype, scale. Two additional studies were completed to assess the technical aspects of the PMAI, one consisting of 309 individuals and the other consisting of 738 individuals.

TECHNICAL.

Standardization. The initial group of 64 individuals had a mean age of 39, and they were mostly Caucasian females with a graduate level of education. The authors noted for the group that "the distribution included some racial, gender, and educational diversity" (manual, p. 59). The 309-participant sample were 70% female and 76% White/not Hispanic; the participants were recruited from an undergraduate psychology "pool," community college students, graduate students and professors from a social science "external degree program," and administrative and professional staff from urban community mental health centers and from a VA medical center. There were no demographic data provided on the 738-participant sample.

Reliability. Test-retest reliability was calculated with the 64-participant sample, and the mean correlation was .76; however, the interval between test and retest was not stated. The item analysis of this sample was also studied; however, no specific data were provided in the manual other than to state that "The elimination of inconsistent items resulted in sufficiently high alpha for all archetypes" (manual, p. 59). Test-retest reliability was assessed, using a 2-week time period, using the 309-participant sample. The correlations ranged from .59 to .84, with an average of .72. The internal consistency (alpha) results ranged from .21 to .69, with an average of .55. The internal

consistency results for the 738-participant sample ranged from .58 to .77.

Validity. The authors attempted to assess the instrument's validity by comparing the scores with tests that measure similar concepts and by completing factor analytic studies. The authors acknowledged that one problem with assessing this kind of instrument is that there are few other validated instruments that assess archetypes; therefore, the authors attempted to "indirectly" demonstrate concurrent validity by comparing the PMAI with instruments that assess similar concepts. For example, one instrument was the Marlowe-Crowne Social Desirability Scale. It was assumed that there would be some high and low correlations between the Marlowe-Crowne and the scores for the 12 archetypes. They reported two correlations that seemed to "confirm[ing] the hypothesis" (manual, p. 63). However, the correlations, though significant, were low (-.13 and -.11) and represent less than 2% shared variance.

Construct validity was assessed by examining age and gender differences in scores and career satisfaction. The theory is that men and women progress through different archetypes at different ages. The authors completed a MANOVA and found that, for some scales, men and women experience different archetypes at different ages. However, regarding the relationship between career satisfaction and archetypes, most of the hypotheses were not supported. Finally, a factor analysis was completed using the 309-participant sample. One concern is the number of participants per test item; typically a minimum of 5 participants per item is required for a factor analysis. Therefore, a minimum of 360 participants should be used for a 72-item scale. An initial scree plot identified 18 factors; however, this was considered to be too many. Therefore, 11-, 12-, and 13-factor solutions were considered. Unfortunately, this is a very liberal way to identify the number of factors to retain and likely overestimated the actual number of dimensions for the scale. The factor analysis of the 738-participant sample found that "twelve factors emerged" (manual, p. 71). However, there was no discussion regarding the decision to retain that number of factors, and it is likely that number of factors is again an overestimate of actual dimensions.

COMMENTARY. The theoretical background of the PMAI is based on Jungian theory, and the authors have a lot of experience studying and publishing in this area. The test materials are easy to use and understand, the test is straightforward to administer and score, and the materials include a guide to understanding archetypes. Technically, the test has been standardized on groups of individuals with somewhat limited demographic features, there are some reliability data that support the consistency of the instrument, but the validity data are lacking. Part of the problem with studying the validity of this type of instrument is that there are few criteria against which this test could be compared.

SUMMARY. The PMAI appears to be part of a process that could be used in helping people develop more self-awareness and understanding. However, the professional using the instrument needs to be mindful of how the demographic background of the client differs, if at all, from the standardization sample, and the instrument is clearly not a tool to assess psychopathology. Also, the concept of archetype is quite abstract, and not only will the clinician need to be very familiar with the concepts, but also able to help the client "translate" the results into action.

REVIEWER'S REFERENCES

Pearson, C. S. (1989). *The hero within: Six archetypes we live by.* New York: Harper & Row.
Pearson, C. S. (1991). *Awakening the hero within: Twelve archetypes that help us find ourselves and transform our world.* San Francisco: HarperCollins.
Pearson, C. S., & Marr, H. K. (2002). *Introduction to archetypes: The guide to interpreting results from the Pearson-Marr Archetype Indicator instrument.* Gainesville, FL: Center for the Application of Psychological Type, Inc.

Review of the Pearson-Marr Archetype Indicator by WILLIAM E. MARTIN, JR., Professor of Educational Psychology, Northern Arizona University, Flagstaff, AZ:

DESCRIPTION. The Pearson-Marr Archetype Indicator (PMAI) is described by the author as a "well-person" instrument designed to help individuals capitalize on their strengths while recognizing and predicting areas of difficulty. The PMAI consists of 72 items using a Likert response format (*Strongly Disagree, Disagree, Neutral, Agree, Strongly Agree*). The PMAI is designed to measure 12 archetypes. The archetypes are defined by the author as broad emotional, cognitive, and behavioral styles, each having a theme, goals, adequacies, and potential difficulties. The 12 archetypes are named Innocent, Orphan, Seeker, Warrior, Caregiver, Destroyer, Creator, Lover, Sage, Magician, Ruler, and Jester. According to the authors, the PMAI has been researched with individuals from late adolescence to individuals in their late sixties. The reading level of the test is third grade but the concepts may be too complex for younger persons to fully understand. The authors indicate that the PMAI has uses in psychotherapy, personal growth, education, leadership development and team building, and organizational development.

The questions and response categories of the PMAI are clearly presented on the inner two pages of a self-scorable four-page folder. The responses to the questions are placed in 12 columns. The respondent totals the numbers in each column and each total represents the score for a particular archetype. These 12 total archetype scores are then transferred to the PMAI Scoring Worksheet. A graphical wheel of archetypes is presented for the respondent to shade in the appropriate area in the wheel that corresponds with the number value from the 12 total scores. There are standardized instructions for administering the PMAI in the manual. In addition to the manual, there is a Guide to Interpreting Results from the PMAI. The PMAI also can be taken online.

DEVELOPMENT. The PMAI is grounded in the theoretical framework of Carl Jung's archetypal psychology. The original form of the PMAI was a self-help test called The Personal Myth Index (Form A) that was included in a 1989 book by Carol Pearson to assist readers to determine which of the six heroic archetypes were most active in their lives and, then, use the self-assessment information to apply the contents of the book. The instrument was totally revised when six additional archetypes were added as described in a subsequent book by Carol Pearson in 1991. The item development process began with written summaries of the 12 archetypes that were used by judges to categorize questions. Items from original forms of the questionnaire and items solicited from people familiar with the theory were categorized using the written summaries and evaluated on several other criteria. A total pool of 144 items (12 items per archetype) was generated. These items were presented to three judges who sorted the questions by the written archetype summaries and other items were added resulting in 103 items used for a pilot study. Item analysis using the alpha if item deleted and a discrimination index for each item was used on the pilot study responses resulting in a total of 72 items (6 items per archetype).

TECHNICAL. A larger scale sample of 309 persons was collected following the pilot study to focus on validity and reliability evidence. The sample was composed primarily of college students and professionals. Seventy percent were females and 76% were White, not Hispanic. The average alpha coefficient for the PMAI archetype scales was .55. The average test-retest (2-week time interval) correlation was .72. The PMAI scales Innocent and Jester were correlated with the Marlowe-Crowne measure of social desirability to indicate concurrent validity. The Marlowe-Crowne measure negatively correlated to Jester and positively correlated to Innocent as expected by the authors, although neither showed a strong relationship. Other results of concurrent validity studies entailed correlating the PMAI with the Questionnaire of Meaning resulting in several low correlations.

Studies of construct validity reported in the manual compared the archetype scales with predictions that can be made of "differential paths through the archetypes" (manual, p. 64) by age and gender, career satisfaction and archetypal influences, and factor analyses. Males and females differed on PMAI scores when age was accounted for. Although there was an overall effect, there was limited support for specific career hypotheses comparing PMAI archetypes and Holland's hexagonal model of vocational personality. The results of two factor analyses resulted in 7 and 12 factor solutions. Although there was some consistency in factors across the two samples, there also were clear differences.

Standardization sample scoring norms are not used with the PMAI. The authors explain this by asserting, "A comparison to any norm group does not make much sense for this kind of assessment because whether a person scores higher on a given archetype than most people is not as useful as knowing which archetype is the highest for the person taking the instrument" (manual, p. 27). Instead, interpretation points for facilitators are identified that include the identification of: (a) high, midrange, and low scores; (b) complementary pairs (high/high, high/low); (c) archetypes in the orientation quadrants (stability, people, results, learning); and (d) archetype levels (ego, soul, self). Five case histories are presented in the manual using the PMAI. Finally, more information about the 12 archetypes and working with archetypes is presented in the Guide to Interpreting Results from the PMAI.

COMMENTARY. The steps of administration and scoring the PMAI are clear and straightforward to employ. The manual and the Guide for Interpretation are well written and provide additional information needed to more fully understand the uses and interpretation techniques when working with individuals who have taken the PMAI. Studies have been conducted to document the reliability and validity of scores from the PMAI; however, more studies are needed using samples reflecting more diversity in gender, age, career orientation, and ethnocultural background.

Concern exists with the underlying theoretical construct of the PMAI, which is problematic and unstable. The foundation of the PMAI is built on a combination of Carol Pearson's (PMAI author) and Carl Jung's theories. Indeed, information from the manual states, "her definitions make Jung's archetypal theory accessible to instrumentation, hence the creation of the PMAI instrument" (manual, p. 2). In relation to Jung's theory, Ryckman (2004) stated "Many of its concepts are also highly ambiguous. For example, archetypes are metaphysical concepts that have multiple meanings and few clear referents in external reality" (p. 104). Problems with precision, testability, and parsimony of Jung's theoretical model are amplified when adding the ideas of another individual without a defensible rationale articulated to support the union. Moreover, the two factor analyses conducted resulted in factor structures that differed from the 12 archetypes weakening the stability of the construct. The reported measures of internal consistency are not consistently strong.

There is a lack of evidence to support how the cutoff scores were selected for interpreting high, midrange, and low scores. Moreover, there is limited information as to how the complementary archetypal pairs, archetypes in the orientation quadrants, and archetype levels were derived. Furthermore, evidence is needed to justify the origins and validation of the recommended interpretation guidelines.

SUMMARY. The PMAI is user friendly and has useful supporting materials. Efforts have been made by the authors to demonstrate the reliability and validity of scores from the instrument. There are weaknesses in the content and construct validity of the PMAI. There is no evidence to validate the cutoff scores and interpretation procedures recommended for use with the PMAI. I recommend caution in using the PMAI, especially in psychotherapy and counseling. Alternative tests to consider are the Revised NEO-PI-R (T6:2110), the Sixteen Personality Factor Questionnaire (16PF; T6:2292), and the California Psychological Inventory (CPI; 15:43).

REVIEWER'S REFERENCE

Ryckman, R. M. (2004). *Theories of personality* (8ᵗʰ ed.). Belmont, CA: Wadsworth/Thomson Learning.

[181]
Personal Characteristics Inventory™.

Purpose: Designed to "help organizations hire more effectively" and provide feedback to employees regarding "strengths and areas where improvement is necessary"; used in the hiring process and for developmental purposes.

Publication Dates: 1995–2002.

Acronym: PCI.

Scores, 26: Agreeableness (Cooperation, Consideration, Total), Extraversion (Sociability, Need for Recognition, Leadership Orientation, Total), Conscientiousness (Dependability, Achievement Striving, Efficiency, Total), Stability (Even Temperament, Self-Confidence, Total), Openness (Abstract Thinking, Creative Thinking, Total), Occupational Score (Manager, Sales, Clerical, Production, Driver), Teamwork, Integrity, Learning Orientation, Commitment to Work.

Administration: Group or individual.

Price Data, 2005: $27.50 per inventory; $137.50 per 5 inventories; $550 per 25 inventories; $1,925 per 100 inventories (volume discounts available).

Foreign Language Editions: French and Spanish editions available.

Time: [25–30] minutes.

Comments: On-line administration available with Microsoft Internet Explorer Version 5.5 or higher or Netscape Navigator Version 6.0 or higher.

Authors: Michael K. Mount, Murray R. Barrick, and Wonderlic Consulting.

Publisher: Wonderlic, Inc.

Review of the Personal Characteristics Inventory by SUSAN M. BROOKHART, Coordinator of Assessment & Evaluation, School of Education, Duquesne University, Pittsburgh, PA:

DESCRIPTION. The Personal Characteristics Inventory is designed for employers making decisions about job applicants and also for developmental purposes with current employees. It is based on a five-factor model of personality (called the "Big Five"). Scale scores on these five factors, with subscale scores indicated in parentheses, are as follows: Agreeableness (Cooperation, Consid-

eration); Extraversion (Sociability, Need for Recognition, Leadership Orientation); Conscientiousness (Dependability, Achievement Striving, Efficiency); Stability (Even-Temperament, Self-Confidence); and Openness (Abstract Thinking, Creative Thinking). Five Occupation scores, representing different linear combinations of the previous scores, are available: Manager, Sales, Production Worker, Driver, and Clerical Employee. Four Success scales are reported, apparently based on the same items: Teamwork, Integrity, Commitment to Work, and Learning Orientation. There are also three types of Accuracy Indices: Self-Presentation, Response Pattern (reported separately for Agree, Neutral, and Disagree patterns), and Infrequency.

The constructs underlying the five primary factors are defined briefly in the manual and supported with references to the personnel psychology literature, where the constructs are defined more theoretically and empirically for readers who wish to pursue this information. Score interpretation information for the five primary factors, the 12 subscales, the occupation scores, and the success scores are described in detail in Appendix A of the manual, in language aimed at employers. Descriptions are provided for high, average, and low scorers on each of these scales.

Test takers respond to a 150-item, multiple-choice instrument. Each item is a brief statement (e.g., "My feelings can be easily hurt") followed by three choices: Agree, Neither agree nor disagree, and Disagree. The test is not timed; the manual reports that most test takers use between 25 and 30 minutes to respond. The paper-and-pencil version of the test is clear and visually well designed, as is the answer sheet. On-line administration is available with Microsoft Internet Explorer version 5.5 or higher or Netscape Navigator version 6.0 or higher. This reviewer did not have access to the on-line version.

DEVELOPMENT. The authors date the origin of the PCI to a meta-analysis they did (Barrick & Mount, 1991) at the start of a research agenda beginning in 1990, where they investigated the relationships between personality traits and work performance outcomes. The development of the items on the instrument itself is not documented in the manual.

TECHNICAL.

Standardization. The norms that are reported in the manual come from a variety of different studies with different samples. Separate norms on the five primary scales are provided for two samples of managers, two samples of sales representatives, two samples of production workers, a sample of registered nurses, and one of truck drivers. Combined sample size for all of these occupations was 1,125. Norms tables are also provided for "all occupational groups," including both applicants and incumbents, with incumbent scores adjusted to those of applicants. Total sample size for "all occupational groups" is listed as 1,891. No specific norms for job applicants, the primary intended population, are given.

Similarly, separate norms on the five primary scales are provided for MBA students, undergraduate business students, and Air Force cadets. Combined sample size for all student samples was 2,334. Norms for the five primary scales are also given for a "Total Sample" of 4,556. Because this total is not the sum of the occupational groups plus the student groups, the exact composition of the sample is not clear, but it is certainly reflective of a large number of college students. Dates of data collection were not given, although given the history of the project these data had to be from some time during the 1990s.

A section on Fairness in the manual presents score differences for gender, "Race Groups" (Caucasian, African American, Hispanic, and Asian American), and age (over/under 40). Differences across gender and race are pronounced "minimal," as are differences for age. This reviewer does not agree with that conclusion. On three of the five primary scales, for instance, the difference between men and women is greater than .2 standard deviations. Cohen (1988, p. 25) defined this as a "small" effect size. With the reported difference of z = -.23, for example, on the Extraversion scale, identified in the manual as particularly important for managerial and sales occupations, the average woman would be expected to score at the 41st percentile of the men's distribution of Extraversion. There are differences of this magnitude or greater for Hispanic and Asian American samples and for the Over 40 samples. With z = -.31, the average test taker over 40 would be expected to score at the 38th percentile of the under 40 distribution on Conscientiousness, identified by the manual as important for all five of the occupations studied.

Reliability. Reliability values for the five primary scales and their 12 subscales are adequate and are reported. Internal consistency for the five primary scales ranged from .82 to .87, and .70 to .80 for the subscales. Test retest reliability in three samples with fairly long intervals (4, 6, and 9 months, respectively) ranged from .61 to .91 for these scales and subscales, quite high for intervals of that duration. No reliability data were presented for the Success scales; because these were rearrangements of items on the primary scales, the values of interest to this reviewer would be internal consistency.

Validity. The manual recommends that employers do a job analysis, benchmark analysis (test their current employees), and/or local validation study (for example, a job analysis plus a predictive validity study) before using the PCI for a local purpose. This is sound advice.

The manual also reports many different sources of evidence for the validity of score interpretations. Criterion-related validity evidence in the form of correlations with supervisors' ratings or other productivity measures from what appear to be 15 different samples (although the reader needs to make some inferences about which correlations are based on the same samples) are given. The results of meta-analytic studies about the predictive validity of the five primary personality dimensions are cited and reported. Convergent and discriminant validity evidence from correlations of other "Big Five" instruments with the primary scales are reported. Factor analytic results are offered to show that the appropriate subscales load on their intended factors, although the method appears to have been exploratory rather than confirmatory, a fact inferred from a table title that indicated a varimax rotation was used. Validation evidence for the Occupation scales is given by reporting predictive validity (true-score correlation, corrected for unreliability) for the linear combinations (regression weights) that were used to compute occupation scores from primary scale scores; these ranged from .31 to .51. Validation evidence for the Success scales is presented, citing empirical evidence in all cases. Studies of stability in prediction after controlling for response distortion, and studies of the validity of using the PCI in combination with measures of general mental ability, are also presented.

This reviewer agreed with the manual's interpretation of the validity evidence it presented, as being comprehensive, with coefficients of expected size and import, with two exceptions. The first is the interpretation of the "fairness" information discussed in the Standardization section above.

The second is a concern that, at first glance, the main criterion related validity coefficients do not seem large enough. Even the correlations that have been corrected for unreliability range from -.45 to .57, with a median of .12.

There are at least two reasons for the low validity coefficients. The first is a "theory-meets-practice" issue. Theoretically, not all of the personality traits are expected to be good predictors for any given occupation. So, for example, success as a manager is expected to be best predicted by Extraversion and Conscientiousness, whereas success as a production worker is expected to be best predicted by Conscientiousness and Stability. Thus there are a lot of expected low correlations on the other, less relevant personality scores. Practically, it would be very important that the users of this test either read the manual carefully or use their consultants' services carefully. Simply looking for "high" scorers, something many employers might be expected to do, would not be a valid thing to do. Yet the personality traits all sound good. What employer would not want an "Agreeable" employee, for instance? This practical approach to scores, however, is not valid score interpretation, according to the evidence.

Counting only the coefficients on personality dimensions reported as expected to be relevant to occupational success for the respective occupations, the true-score coefficients range from -.29 to .57, with a median of .28—not high for coefficients corrected for unreliability. This is apparently not a new problem. In the original meta-analysis, the authors wrote about this phenomenon. About the low validity coefficients, they wrote:

> Before discussing the substantive findings, a comment is in order regarding the relatively small observed and true score correlations obtained in this study. We would like to re-emphasize that our purpose was not to determine the overall validity of personality; in fact, we question whether such an analysis is meaningful. Rather, the purpose was to increase our understanding of the way the Big Five personality dimensions relate to selected occupational groups and criterion types. (Barrick & Mount, 1991, p. 17)

It does appear that this problem is handled with the linear combinations constructed for the Occupation scores. The various true-score corre-

tions reported from the prediction studies ranged from .31 to .51, with a median of .40.

COMMENTARY. This instrument is strong where many are weak; namely, it comes with a solid academic and theoretical background for the constructs it purports to measure. Inquiry into the utility of these constructs for predicting job success has been the academic work of both authors and several of their students for over a decade. Conversely, its documentation is weak in more pedestrian areas (e.g., a description of item development is lacking). However, because this work has been presented in so many academic venues, item development may well be represented in some of the conference papers listed in the Reference section. If so, this reviewer recommends having those conference papers available as technical reports.

This reviewer was surprised, given the obvious academic understanding of the authors, at the lack of norms developed specifically for the intended population of applicants for positions in management, sales, production, driving, and clerical jobs. This reviewer was also surprised at the interpretation of gender, ethnic, and age differences as minimal.

SUMMARY. The personality characteristics behind this inventory are well researched and well documented in the academic literature. The authors have devised a simple, clear measure of these characteristics that may be helpful in some personnel work. Presently available evidence suggests more development work would be necessary, particularly in creating norms for job applicants and in further investigation of the effects of gender, ethnicity, and age, before this reviewer could recommend its use.

REVIEWER'S REFERENCES

Barrick, M. R., & Mount, M. K. (1991). The Big Five personality dimensions and job performance: A meta-analysis. *Personnel Psychology, 44,* 1–26.
Cohen, J. (1988). *Statistical power analysis for the behavioral sciences.* Hillsdale, NJ: Lawrence Erlbaum.

Review of the Personal Characteristics Inventory by MARK L. POPE, Associate Professor, Division of Counseling and Family Therapy, University of Missouri—St. Louis, St. Louis, MO:

DESCRIPTION AND DEVELOPMENT. The Personal Characteristics Inventory (PCI) was developed in the early 1990s by Murray R. Barrick and Michael K. Mount, University of Iowa faculty, a result of their work investigating the validity of personality traits for predicting job performance, looking to see if there were meaningful relationships between personality traits and performance outcomes at work.

The PCI is a 150-item personality inventory that has as its stated objective to measure the five-factor model of personality (FFM). The FFM was originally derived in the 1960s and 1970s by two independent research teams—Paul Costa/Robert McCrae (National Institutes of Health) (Costa & McCrae, 1976) and Warren Norman (University of Michigan)/Lewis Goldberg (University of Oregon) (Goldberg, 1990; Norman, 1963; Norman & Goldberg, 1966)—who took slightly different routes to arrive at the same results: Most human personality traits can be boiled down to five broad dimensions of personality, regardless of language or culture. These five dimensions were derived by asking hundreds of questions to thousands of people and then analyzing the data with a statistical procedure known as factor analysis. Five dimensions emerged from their analyses of these data. The FFM is now the most widely accepted and used model of personality and is composed of five personality dimensions (OCEAN): openness to experience, conscientiousness, extraversion, agreeableness, and neuroticism.

The PCI factors that are measured are labeled somewhat differently from the traditional FFM dimensions and include Openness (20 items), Conscientiousness (30 items), Extraversion (30 items), Agreeableness (20 items), and Stability (20 items) (called "neuroticism" in the FFM). It also measures 12 different subfacets of this model (Cooperation, Consideration, Sociability, Need for Recognition, Leadership Orientation, Dependability, Achievement Striving, Efficiency, Even-Temperament, Self-Confidence, Abstract Thinking, and Creative Thinking), five Occupational scores (Manager, Sales, Production Worker, Driver, and Clerical Employee), and four Success scales (Teamwork, Integrity, Commitment to Work, and Learning Orientation). As with most personality inventories, the administration of the PCI is not timed, but the inventory is usually completed within 25–30 minutes.

The PCI can be administered through either a paper-and-pencil or an online version. Results from either version are available in minutes and are emailed or faxed to the test administrator.

The PCI question booklet consists of four 11 x 17-inch pages, saddle-stitched and using heavy-weight white paper. The booklet was prepared using a multicolor printing process. The items are clearly printed and arranged ergonomically for ease of reading and understanding. The 11 x 17-inch answer sheet, folded in half, is printed on only one side for ease of machine scoring. The arrangement of item responses on the answer sheet is in six consistently spaced 25-item columns where respondents answer "A" for agree, "D" for disagree, and "N" for neither agree nor disagree.

The result of the scoring process is a 12- to 15-page narrative/interpretive report that includes: (a) a cover page; (b) a 1-page summary report (profile report) that graphically presents the scores on each subscale along with "accuracy indices" to check for a variety of potential problems in the responses of the test-taker; (c) 1–2 page interpretive reports on each of the five factors and their related subscales; (d) a short interpretive paragraph on each of the four Success subscales (Teamwork, Integrity, Commitment to Work, and Learning Orientation); and (e) a 1-page interpretive report on the general occupation that the test-taker chose for comparison (Manager, Sales, Production Worker, Driver, and Clerical Employee).

TECHNICAL. The 110-page technical manual is divided into five sections: (a) an overview (22 pages); (b) technical overview (5 pages); (c) legal issues and fairness in testing (6 pages); (d) references (6 pages); and (e) appendices (68 pages) on score interpretation (26 pages), normative data (8 pages), and history and validation evidence including a more detailed technical section (33 pages). Reading level is reported as third-fourth grade on certain scales and eighth-ninth grade on others.

The "technical overview" is intended for a novice test user, and consists of five pages in a narrative format that attempts to educate the reader about the general psychometric issues involved in developing an inventory of this type as well as to evaluate the specific data available on this particular instrument. The authors' presentation of the general psychometric issues was especially very well done. It was clear and easy to understand even if one is not that knowledgeable of such issues. On the other hand, the summary sentences regarding the evaluation of the actual data were too brief.

Data are provided for the stability of scores over time—the test-retest reliability. Data for three small samples (N = 43, 63, and 88) over 6 months, 9 months, and 4 months, respectively, had stability coefficients that ranged from .66 to .91 for the five primary scales and from .61 to .87 for the subscales. The authors state that this is "quite high"; however, the coefficients for the Agreeableness scale were .66, .74, and .77, respectively. If this scale is actually measuring a trait, it should not degrade so quickly. This may be an effect of the wording of the items. Several items on the PCI seemed to be susceptible to the "it depends" approach to item interpretation more so than on other similar personality inventories. This alone might account for much of the variance in the stability coefficients.

Data assessing the construct validity of the PCI are also provided to allow comparisons with similar scales on similar instruments, such as the NEO-PI. In such situations, we expect to see high correlations (.80 or higher), but not perfect ($r = 1.00$); otherwise, the two scales would be measuring exactly the same construct. If the validity coefficients are too low, however, authors of one inventory then would argue that their measure is a more pure measure of the construct in question. The key is to select comparison measures that have strong and proven evidence of construct validity as the PCI authors have done and hope for high correlations between the two scales. Unfortunately, the relationships between the PCI primary scales and similar scales are in the moderate or moderate-to-high range (.39 to .71, with a median of .64), none are above .80.

The bottom line for any personnel selection instrument is its predictive ability or criterion-related predictive validity—how well a trait predicts some relevant external criteria (future behavior, such as job performance). This is critical for this type of instrument. Data are provided for 15 different occupational samples (some samples were compared on two or three different criteria). The criteria included supervisor ratings of performance (in most cases), but other quite concrete external criteria were also used in some cases such as sales volume, account maintenance, new accounts, and others. The authors used tests of statistical significance to make their argument for criterion-related validity. Some of the correlation coefficients reported as statistically significant are relatively small (e.g., -.13 for 147 long-haul drivers, Agreeableness and voluntary turnover). I would suggest that actual probabilities be reported in future revisions of the technical manual.

Finally, the samples and sample sizes are rather narrow and small at this time. In future revisions of the manual, I would expect broader and larger samples to be reported.

COMMENTARY. An important issue for employers who might want to use this inventory as a personnel selection tool is the quality of the job description/job analysis they are using as a benchmark. The PCI does not provide a "matching" section in the interpretive report where the qualities of the test-taker are compared to a successful employee for a specific job. It is left to the employer to develop occupational descriptions for successful workers and then try to intuit if the test-taker/job-seeker matches with their profile of a successful plumber, for example. The PCI does provide information for the five generic occupations through its occupational scores (Manager, Sales, Production Worker, Driver, and Clerical Employee); however, this is not a substitute for specific comparisons for successful workers.

The authors of the PCI attempt to address these issues in a section on "meta-analytic findings," where they report that two factors (Conscientiousness and Stability) have been found to be general predictors of job performance and that the other three factors are specific predictors of job performance for specific occupations or with some criterion types. This is useful information, but it still does not relieve the test authors of responsibility for providing more data.

The authors are to be applauded for their comprehensive approach to educating the users of their instrument about the legal and ethical issues in personnel selection testing. The sections that are included in the manual are well written and user-friendly. Also, the customer service people at Wonderlic, Inc. were knowledgeable, friendly, efficient, and fast.

SUMMARY. The PCI is a good first step in the development of a personnel selection instrument. Developing a good personnel selection instrument is a huge undertaking that requires, at the least, long-term commitment to an instrument. There are some important reliability and validity issues the authors must address in their revisions. It is always important to note that instruments such as the PCI should only be used as part of a comprehensive personnel selection process.

REVIEWER'S REFERENCES

Costa, P. T., & McCrae, R. R. (1976). Age differences in personality structure: A cluster analytic approach. *Journal of Gerontology, 31,* 564–570.

Goldberg, L. R. (1990). An alternative "Description of Personality": The Big-Five factor structure. *Journal of Personality and Social Psychology, 59,* 1216–1229.

Norman, W. T. (1963). Toward an adequate taxonomy of personality attributes: Replicated factor structure in peer nomination personality rating. *Journal of Abnormal and Social Psychology, 66,* 574–583.

Norman, W. T., & Goldberg, L. R. (1966). Raters, ratees, and randomness in personality structure. *Journal of Personality & Social Psychology. 4,* 681–691.

[182]

Personal Experience Screening Questionnaire for Adults.

Purpose: Designed to "screen for the abuse of alcohol and other drugs by adults."

Population: Ages 19 and over.

Publication Date: 2003.

Acronym: PESQ-A.

Scores, 2: Problem Severity, Defensiveness.

Administration: Individual or group.

Price Data, 2005: $82.50 per kit including Autoscore™ test forms and manual; $37.50 per 25 Autoscore™ test forms; $48 per manual; volume discount available.

Time: (10) minutes.

Comments: Self-report behavior inventory.

Author: Ken C. Winters.

Publisher: Western Psychological Services.

Review of the Personal Experience Screening Questionnaire for Adults by JODY L. KULSTAD, Assistant Professor of Professional Psychology and Family Therapy, Seton Hall University, South Orange, NJ:

DESCRIPTION. The Personal Experience Screening Questionnaire for Adults (PESQ-A) is a 46-item brief screening tool used to identify individuals needing referral for a more complete substance abuse evaluation. It is not intended as a diagnostic tool, and should only be used in clinical settings to provide initial screening information. The PESQ-A is particularly useful in settings where routine screening is undertaken, but complete evaluation is typically precluded (e.g., medical offices, hospital ERs, EAPs).

The PESQ-A is appropriate for adults over age 19. Administration and scoring are clear and easily completed, which allows for use by paraprofessionals though the author cautions that use should be under the supervision of a trained health professional and only undertaken by those who have an adequate understanding of test administration and scoring procedures, as outlined in the manual. Interpretation, though, is limited to trained and experienced substance abuse service providers, mental health professionals, or social science researchers.

The PESQ-A can be administered to an individual or group. With a fourth grade reading level and short, grammatically simple items, the PESQ-A should be able to be completed in less than 10 minutes, though there is no time limit. For those with reading difficulties, the instrument can be read by the examiner or via an audiotape. Substance affected individuals should not be given the assessment. Respondents need only the autoscore paper form and ballpoint pen/pencil. Respondents first complete the demographic portion, ensuring sex is marked due to sex-specific cutoffs, and then the remainder of the instrument. A check is made to ensure that the form is completed correctly.

SUBSCALE INFORMATION, SCORING, AND INTERPRETATION. PESQ-A items are organized into three sections: The Problem Severity section comprises 25 items relating to activities associated with substance involvement over the past year. Responses are rated on a 4-point scale including *never, once or twice, sometimes,* and *often.* The Defensiveness and Psychosocial Indicators section comprises 10 items addressing psychosocial adjustment and 5 items (items on both indicators are dichotomous yes/no) measuring whether the respondent is answering in a defensive manner (e.g., faking good). Section III, Recent Drug Use, asks frequency questions related to drug and alcohol use in the past 12 months (ranging from *none* to *40+ times*).

"Formal scores" are obtained in six steps, with instructions available on the inside of the autoscore form. Scoring yields a red or green flag for Problem Severity and Defensiveness (Response Distortion). For Problem Severity, gender specific cutoff points are used and are available in the autoscore form. Not intended to yield summary scores, the Psychosocial Indicators and Recent Drug Use sections yield "supplemental scores" also shown on the scoring page of the autoscore form. These sections are reviewed and which items are endorsed is noted.

In the manual, two case studies are available that show scoring and interpretation. Interpretation follows a three step process: ascertaining protocol validity, determining whether a substance abuse problem exists and needs further assessment, and reviewing psychosocial and recent drug use information. Forms that have a red-flagged DEF Total score (indicative of positive distortion or "faking good") have questionable validity and interpretation should be done with this in mind. Though there are no criteria set for a negatively distorted profile, several tips for assessing this are provided by the author. As with profile validity, Problem Severity is interpreted by evaluating whether the section has a red or green flag. A red flag suggests a problem likely needing further evaluation. The author does note that further clinical evidence gleaned from the supplemental areas can further support referral. Though not included in the formal scoring, the supplemental areas can provide important interpretive information. Item endorsement in Section II, Psychosocial Indicators, is reflective of problems that may or may not be substance use related such as psychological and/or emotional distress, family/interpersonal problems, abuse, unsafe sex practices, and heavy smoking. Items from Section III, Recent Drug Use, can provide information on substance use severity, and can signal a need for referral even when the Problem Severity section has a green flag.

DEVELOPMENT. The three sections were developed using different procedures. Problem Severity items were taken directly from the PEI-A's Personal Involvement with Drugs scale (the manual does provide an overview of this but see Winters, 1996, for complete scale development information), which in turn was based on the adolescent PEI's (1989) Personal Involvement with Chemicals Scale. Information was not included about how any of these items were modified for the PESQ-A. The Defensiveness Scale was developed using items taken from the Marlowe-Crowne Social Desirability Scale (Crowne & Marlowe, 1960). No information is provided on the criteria used for selecting items from this scale. The Psychosocial Indicators items were "rationally selected based on the high priority typically assigned to their content in clinical settings" (manual, p. 14). No other information is provided about item selection. The Recent Drug use section was developed based on checklist items from several nationally conducted substance use surveys and includes a listing of the major substances of abuse.

PSYCHOMETRIC INFORMATION.

Standardization sample. The sample used to provide standardization information was taken from the original standardization sample of the PEI-A and not based on evaluations after the scale was constructed. As such, it appears that only the Problem Severity section was evaluated. Included in the sample were inpatient (n = 394) and outpatient (n = 501) substance abuse clients, criminal offenders (n = 410), and nonclinical participants (n = 690). Males outnumbered females except for the nonclinical sample, and Euro-Americans were more prevalent in drug clinic and nonclinical samples, whereas ethnic minority participants made up the majority of the criminal offender sample (68.1%). The manual describes data collection procedures for the three groups. Red flag cutoffs were developed using discriminant function analysis for two-thirds of the drug clinic and nonclinical samples, the remaining one-third of each group was set aside for the cross-validation sample.

Reliability. Internal consistency and temporal stability reliability estimates were computed on the sample. The internal consistency (coefficient alpha) estimates for the Problem Severity scores ranged from .87 to .95 for the three samples. Test-retest reliability for the Problem Severity scores were based on the initial administration and at 1-week and 1-month intervals. Test-retest reliability coefficients (Pearson r correlations) ranged from .76 at 1 week, to .62 at 1 month. The author notes that though the coefficients in the 1-month interval is lower, the scores remained consistent within individuals, suggesting both stability and change.

Validity. The PESQ-A evidences good content, construct, and criterion validity. Good internal consistency estimates discussed earlier provide partial evidence for content validity. The author notes that methods for scale development and item selection for the Problem Severity scale are also suggestive of content validity. Construct validity is shown through good correlations (ranging from .62 to .66.) with the Alcohol Dependence Scale and items from the Recent Drug Use section of the PESQ-A. Further evidence was provided by comparing those in the drug clinic sample with and without a drug treatment history; those with a history of drug treatment had statistically higher Problem Severity scores than those with no history. Finally, 101 of the drug clinic clients' significant others completed the Significant Other Questionnaire. Results suggested that clients' and significant others' observations are quite consistent and that the responses are not unduly affected by the self-report format. Using staff ratings for the drug clinic clients, criterion validity was shown by reviewing referral patterns and through intake diagnosis. Those with higher scores on Problem Severity were more likely to be referred to more intensive treatment and those with substance dependence also scored higher than those who did not receive a dependence diagnosis; the scores for those with a dependence diagnosis also exceeded the red flag cutoff. Additionally, comparisons between the two drug clinic samples and the nonclinical sample yielded significantly higher scores for those in the inpatient sample and significantly lower scores for those in the nonclinical sample; scores for outpatient clients were in between the two samples. In a separate study, 251 individuals receiving drug abuse evaluation completed the PESQ-A. Their scores were compared to the referral recommendation for further assessment by an assessor who was blind to their PESQ-A results. In 94% of the cases, those whose PESQ-A results were above the red flag cutoff for Problem Severity were also referred for further evaluation, whereas 92% were correctly classified as not needing a referral, for an overall classification rate of 93% accuracy.

Additional information. According to the author, the PESQ-A can serve as a valuable tool for use in community surveys when prevalence of substance abuse information is sought and in research settings to provide individual information necessary for group assignment in treatment studies as well as a pre-post measure of treatment effectiveness.

COMMENTARY. The scale was derived from a strong, and often recommended measure, the PEI-A, which could be a logical next step should a client need further evaluation. Overall, administration, scoring, and interpretation are easily completed, and could be undertaken by a paraprofessional with some training. Though the author notes that interpretation should only be done by a trained mental health, substance abuse, or social science researcher, it would seem that a paraprofessional could be trained to provide referrals, but perhaps not any extensive verbal interpretation based on score patterns.

Information on the scale development was somewhat incomplete, and largely based on the PEI-A. More information on how the items were selected for the Defensiveness and Psychosocial Indicators scales would be useful. Also, though the author notes that service providers were involved in each stage of scale development, it really only appears that this was the case for the Problem

Severity scale. This does not limit scale validity, but does suggest more specific information is necessary on just how they were involved in the total scale development as their involvement adds to perceptions of the instrument's credibility.

The PESQ-A has good psychometrics for the Problem Severity scale, but no attention was paid to the other sections of the measures. The major problem in this area is that the standardization sample was derived from those who responded to the PEI-A, and then the items pertaining to the PESQ-A were selected out for review. As a result, only those items on the PESQ-A that were on the PEI-A could be evaluated for psychometric quality. Additional review is necessary to further support the psychometric quality of the instrument. Finally, though noted as an epidemiological survey tool or a research tool, these uses were not discussed in the manual so use in this manner should be undertaken with caution.

SUMMARY. Health, interpersonal, psychological, and emotional problems often stem from substance abuse, but too often go unnoticed. Use of a screening tool such as the PESQ-A is a valuable adjunct to standard psychosocial history taking. In conclusion, though the manual could benefit from further information, the instrument itself appears solid and valuable as a screening tool for substance abuse problems.

REVIEWER'S REFERENCES

Crowne, D. P., & Marlowe, D. (1960). A new scale of social desirability independent of psychopathology. *Journal of Consulting Psychology, 24,* 249–254.

Winters, K. C. (1996). *Personal Experience Inventory for Adults (PEI-A): manual.* Los Angeles, CA: Western Psychological Services.

Winters, K. C., & Henley, G. A. (1989). Personal Experience Inventory. Los Angeles, CA: Western Psychological Services.

Review of the Personal Experience Screening Questionnaire for Adults by WILLIAM E. MARTIN, JR., Professor of Educational Psychology, Northern Arizona University, Flagstaff, AZ:

DESCRIPTION. The Personal Experience Screening Questionnaire for Adults (PESQ-A) is a brief, self-report measure designed to screen for the abuse of alcohol and other drugs by adults 19 years of age or older. The PESQ-A is composed of 46 items with three parts. The first part (Problem Severity) has 25 items that address drug use behaviors, experiences, and attitudes requesting respondents to use a 4-point response scale (*never, once or twice, sometimes, often*). Fifteen items (yes or no response options) make up the second part (Defensiveness and Psychosocial Indicators) and focus on detecting psychosocial problems and the tendency to fake good. Part III (Recent Drug Use) of the PESQ-A consists of six questions, with varying response options that measure the use of alcohol or drugs over the preceding year.

The test author suggests that the PESQ-A can be used by a wide range of health professionals who have appropriate training in test construction and the principles of testing. Moreover, users should be knowledgeable of the contents of the test manual, standards for educational and psychological testing, and background in substance abuse, mental health, or social science research. The PESQ-A has a fourth grade reading level and takes most persons 10 minutes or less to complete. Test takers use a ballpoint pen or hard pencil to respond to questions. The response marks are automatically transferred onto a scoring sheet inside the questionnaire form. After tearing along the perforation of the form and discarding the carbon, there are six scoring steps identified within the inside of the form to follow. The scoring yields a Defensiveness total score (five items) and when the score falls within a certain range (5–8) the term Green Flag is circled and Red Flag is circled if the total score falls within a range of 9–10. A Red Flag indicates that the validity of the protocol is questionable; however, it is not clear how the cutoff scores were derived. Additionally, a Problem Severity total score is calculated from 25 items and a Green Flag or Red Flag is circled based upon a score range and whether the respondent is male or female. A Red Flag designation identifies an individual who probably has a drug problem and suggests referral for further assessment. The Red Flag cutoff scores were identified using a discriminant function analysis. Responses to the six items of the Psychosocial Indicators and Recent Drug Use section do not culminate in a total score. Instead, the responses generate supplemental information that can be used for such purposes as identifying problems unrelated to drug abuse and the need for follow-up interviewing and an assessment referral. Two case studies are presented, one showing how the PESQ-A can be used to illustrate the stages of drug abuse and the second case study illustrates its use with understanding the interplay between complex drug abuse and chronic stress.

DEVELOPMENT. The 25 items of the Problem Severity scale of the PESQ-A were taken from the Personal Involvement With Drugs scale

of the Personal Experience Inventory for Adults (PEI-A). The PEI-A was developed by examining the content of the Personal Involvement With Chemicals (PICS) scale of the PEI adolescent substance abuse inventory. Researchers and drug treatment service providers reviewed and rated each PICS item. Additional items related to tolerance and withdrawal were added to the favorably reviewed items of the PICS to form the PEI-A Personal Involvement With Drugs scale and the Problem Severity scale of the PESQ-A.

The Defensiveness (Response Distortion) scale of the PESQ-A consists of 5 items taken from the Marlowe-Crowne Social Desirability Scale to measure "faking good." The 10 yes/no items that make up the Psychosocial Indicators section were "rationally selected based on the high priority typically assigned to their content in clinical settings" (manual, p. 14). The last section (Recent Drug Use) of the PESQ-A has 10 items that were adapted from instruments used in a national study of high school students and young adults.

TECHNICAL. A normative sample of 1,995 individuals for the PEI-A also are used for the PESQ-A. The individuals represented drug clinic clients, criminal offenders, and nonclinical participants. Oversampling was used to increase participants who were inpatients of drug clinics, ethnic minority nonclinical participants, and nonclinical participants who were under age 40. Two additional normative samples were collected for the PESQ-A. The first sample was composed of drug clinic and criminal offender groups from five U.S. states and Canada. The number of participants in this sample was not provided. The second sample consisted of 690 nonclinical participants from Minnesota.

Internal consistency measures were reported for the Problem Severity scale of the PESQ-A. The alpha coefficients ranged from .87 to .95 across gender, race/ethnicity, and clinical/nonclinical category. Test-retest reliability intraclass correlations were reported for the drug clinic sample at 1 week (.70) and 1 month (.54). The test-retest reliability correlations could have been affected by the participants receiving treatment after the first test.

The high, consistent internal consistency measures are identified as evidence for content validity. Another indication of internal consistency was attributed to the use of items from the often used Marlowe-Crowne Social Desirability Scale. Correlations between the PESQ-A Problem Severity Scale and the Alcohol Dependence Scale (.63), the Recent Drug Use (.66), and the Significant Other Questionnaire (.62) were identified as evidence for construct validity. Moreover, the results of a study were reported that showed that high scores on the PESQ-A Problem Severity scale significantly identified clients with prior history of drug treatment compared to those clients with no prior treatment. The results of six studies were used to demonstrate criterion validity of the PESQ-A Problem Severity scores. The studies show accurate classifications of referral recommendations, clinical group status, and alcohol, marijuana, and cocaine intake diagnoses using the PESQ-A Problem Severity scale. Finally, a supplemental study demonstrated that the Red Flag cutoff resulted in correct assignment of 94% of those referred for further evaluation.

COMMENTARY. The PESQ-A meets the overall purpose of the instrument to be a brief, self-report measure to screen for the abuse of alcohol and other drugs. The automatic scoring form provides ease of administration, scoring, and interpretation. The Red Flag cutoff score system is unique and efficient for screening of problem severity. Although there is evidence for arriving at the cutoff score ranges of the Problem Severity Scale, more clearly integrating how the use of means-standard deviations relates to the discriminant function analysis information would be beneficial. More evidence is needed about how the Red Flag cutoff scores were developed for the Defensiveness scale. The development of items for all of the scales needs to be more clearly articulated. How the items for the most important scale (Problem Severity) were developed is clouded by their origin from two other instruments. Also, there needs to be a description of the expert panel of researchers and drug treatment services providers and how they were used to review and rate items. Moreover, the strategies used to select 5 items from the Marlowe-Crowne Social Desirability Scale and 10 items for the Psychosocial Indicators section need to be provided. Finally, an expanded description of the two additional normative samples collected for the PESQ-A is warranted.

SUMMARY. The PESQ-A has an appealing system for obtaining, scoring, and interpreting respondent information. The results appear to have value for screening adults for alcohol and drug abuse with the primary purpose of making a decision about referring individuals for further assessment. However, some degree of caution is recommended until there is more evidence of content and construct validity of scores from the instrument.

[183]
Personality Inventory for Children, Second Edition.

Purpose: "Assesses both broad and narrow dimensions of behavioral, emotional, cognitive, and interpersonal adjustment."

Population: Ages 5–19 years (Kindergarten–Grade 12).

Publication Dates: 1977–2001.

Acronym: PIC-2.

Administration: Group.

Forms, 2: Standard Form, Behavioral Summary.

Price Data, 2002: $175 per kit including 2 reusable administration booklets, 50 answer sheets, 1 set of scoring templates, 25 Behavioral Summary AutoScore forms, 50 Standard Form profile sheets, manual (2001, 212 pages), 25 Behavioral Summary profile sheets, and 50 Critical Items summary sheets; $50 per manual; $25 per reusable administration booklet, quantity discount available; $19.50 per 5 Spanish translation administration booklets, quantity discount available; $19.50 per 100 answer sheets; $32.50 per set of scoring templates.

Foreign Language Editions: Spanish editions available for both forms.

Comments: Complete revision and restandardization of Personality Inventory for Children, Revised (PIC-R); old edition no longer available; coordinates with Personality Inventory for Youth (PIY, T6:1884) and Student Behavior Survey (SBS, 15:250).

Authors: David Lachar and Christian P. Gruber.

Publisher: Western Psychological Services.

a) STANDARD FORM.

Scores, 33: 9 Adjustment Scales and 21 Adjustment Subscales: Cognitive Impairment (Inadequate Abilities, Poor Achievement, Developmental Delay), Impulsivity and Distractibility (Disruptive Behavior, Fearlessness), Delinquency (Antisocial Behavior, Dyscontrol, Noncompliance), Family Dysfunction (Conflict Among Members, Parent Maladjustment), Reality Distortion (Developmental Deviation, Hallucinations and Delusions), Somatic Concern (Psychosomatic Preoccupation, Muscular Tension and Anxiety), Psychological Discomfort (Fear and Worry, Depression, Sleep Disturbance/Preoccupation with Death), Social Withdrawal (Social Introversion, Isolation), Social Skill Deficits (Limited Peer Status, Conflict With Peers), 3 Response Validity Scales (Defensiveness, Dissimulation, Inconsistency).

Price Data: $19.50 per 100 Standard Form profiles or 100 Critical Items summary sheets.
Time: (40) minutes.
Comments: Hand-scored; computer scoring option will be available 2003 and will include mail, fax, or computer disks; system requirements DOS 3.0 or above, 512K memory, 286 processor, 1 MB free disk space, 3.5-inch high-density floppy drive.
b) BEHAVIORAL SUMMARY.
Scores, 12: 8 Short Adjustment Scales (Impulsivity and Distractibility—Short, Delinquency—Short, Family Dysfunction—Short, Reality Distortion—Short, Somatic Concern—Short, Psychological Discomfort—Short, Social Withdrawal—Short, Social Skill Deficits—Short), 3 Composite Scales (Externalization—Composite, Internalization—Composite, Adjustment—Composite), Total Score.
Price Data: $29.95 per 25 Behavioral Summary AutoScore answer forms, quantity discount available; $19.50 per 100 Behavioral Summary profiles.
Time: (15) minutes.
Comments: "A quick screening version of the Standard Form; focuses on current behavior that can support the development of a treatment plan; can be administered using standard PIC-2 test materials"; hand-score only.
Cross References: See T5:1962 (23 references) and T4:1998 (21 references); for a review by Howard M. Knoff of an earlier edition, see 10:281 (20 references); for reviews by Cecil R. Reynolds and June M. Tuma of an earlier edition, see 9:949 (5 references); see also T3:1796 (5 references).

Review of the Personality Inventory for Children, Second Edition by RADHIKA KRISHNAMURTHY, Associate Professor of Psychology and Director of Clinical Training, Florida Institute of Technology, Melbourne, FL:

DESCRIPTION. The Personality Inventory for Children, Second Edition (PIC-2) is a 275-item inventory of child and adolescent personality and functioning, intended to assess multiple areas of psychological and interpersonal adjustment in 5- through 19-year-olds. As young children are often unable to provide accurate self-assessments, and parent report is a useful source of information for minors of all ages, the inventory is completed by a parent or caretaker who is knowledgeable of the child's functioning. Item responses are provided in a True/False format to identify the presence or absence of problem characteristics.

Similar to its predecessors, the original PIC (Wirt, Lachar, Klinedinst, & Seat, 1977) and the PIC-R (Lachar, 1982; Wirt, Lachar, Klinedinst, & Seat, 1984), the PIC-2 is most suited for evaluating referred children and adolescents in clinical and educational settings. This second edition shares its central purpose, item-response format, basic administration and scoring procedures, and validity scales with its antecedent forms. On the other hand, substantial revisions have been made in the structure of the inventory including the number and content of items and scale names and organization. For example, the current version is reduced in length to approximately half of the previous 600-item versions with corresponding reduction in test-completion time. The General Screening scale and the 12 clinical and 17 supplemental scales of the PIC/PIC-R have been replaced by 9 adjustment scales and their 21 subscales. The PIC-2 also provides a 96-item short form known as the Behavioral Summary that can be employed for screening and retesting purposes. The 4 broad-band factor scales of the PIC/PIC-R are reduced and modified into the 3 Composite Scales of the Behavioral Summary. The reading proficiency requirement of the inventory has been reduced from the sixth-to-seventh grade level to a fourth grade level.

PIC-2 administration procedures are straightforward with paper-and-pencil and computer administration options. Materials for the paper-and-pencil form consist of an administration booklet and answer sheet, both containing clear instructions. Responding is made easy by asking the respondent to mark an "X" in either the "T" or "F" box for each item. Computer administration guidelines are provided separately instead of being integrated into the manual. The test manual reports familiarity with the test as the only qualification for being a test administrator, but specifies that interpretation is to be done by appropriately trained professionals.

Hand scoring of the Standard Form, Behavioral Summary, and Critical Items is done by the use of a series of templates placed directly over the response sheet to obtain a tally of raw scores. The method is simpler than might be inferred by reading the guidelines in the manual. Raw scores for scales of the Standard and Behavioral Summary forms are transferred to their appropriate profile sheets to locate the corresponding *T* scores. The Composite scores and Total Score of the Behavioral Summary are derived through some additional calculations, simplified by use of the AutoScoreTM Form.

The computer-scoring program is available in a somewhat-dated floppy disk form.

DEVELOPMENT. PIC-2 development began with the construction of a 390-item research version that contained the first 280 items of the PIC-R in a largely unmodified form and 110 new items. The methodology used in the earlier versions, involving a combination of rational and empirical approaches, was employed to revise and/or develop items and scales. For example, the older items were rationally examined and revised to eliminate double-negative wording, achieve equitable reference to both parents, and improve item clarity, and new items were rationally developed to address specific issues such as eating disorders and substance abuse. Items were placed into relabeled scales in a manner intended to parallel their membership in corresponding PIC-R scales. The use of expert judgment in such decisions appears to have been successful. Factor analysis was subsequently employed to identify subscales for the nine adjustment scales. Other statistical evaluations involved examining item-to-scale correlations, intercorrelations between PIC-R and PIC-2 scales, and between PIC-2 Standard Form scales and Behavioral Summary scales as part of the process to examine the valid use of test scores. PIC-2 scales are largely nonoverlapping in item content with the exception of 16 items that have been permitted to appear on two or three scales, reflecting an acceptable compromise in item-to-scale placement decisions.

TECHNICAL. The central limitations of the PIC and PIC-R with reference to composition of the standardization sample and norms have been addressed in the PIC-2. In contrast to the previous geographically restricted sampling, the PIC-2 standardization sample (N = 2,306; 1,208 girls and 1,098 boys) was derived by use of national sampling methods and includes children and adolescents from urban and rural areas across the four major regions of the U.S. The sample reflects a broad range of socioeconomic levels and includes ethnic minorities in proportion to 1998 Census data. Most of the 14 age groups represented contain more than 150 children, with the exception of ages 5 (n = 96), 15 (n = 126), and, notably, ages 18+ (n = 67). The clinical referred sample (N = 1,551) obtained from referrals from school, clinic, and juvenile justice settings is sufficiently large and diverse in pertinent demographic

variables. Once again, however, adolescents ages 18+ are underrepresented (n = 13). Norms are provided separately for boys and girls but not by age groups, based on analyses of moderator effects.

The PIC-2 manual does not delineate the method used for deriving T-score equivalents of raw scores, nor provides the normative mean and standard deviation for the scales in T-score values. Rather, a table of raw score means and standard deviations is provided that has limited meaning. On the other hand, the manual describes the procedure used to evaluate T-scores across four T-score ranges to determine optimal cutting scores for scale interpretation, yielding two cutting score levels of ≥ 60 and ≥ 70 T. The norms shown on the test profile range from a T-score of 40 through 90, reflecting greater emphasis on high-range scores, and Appendix A of the manual provides the complete T-score conversion table.

Reliability and validity assessments of the PIC-2, as described in the manual, suggest that this inventory has good psychometric foundations. Internal consistency reliability estimates for the adjustment scales indicate strong alpha coefficients for both the standardization sample (.75 to .91) and the referred sample (.81 to .95). As expected, alpha coefficients are lower for the subscales but they are quite acceptable with median coefficients of .73 and .80 for the standardization and referred samples, respectively. The Behavioral Summary short scales, Composite scores, and Total score also yielded acceptable-to-strong alphas. Overall, internal consistency coefficients are stronger than those found for the PIC-R with Standard Error of Measurement values falling largely in the acceptable range of 3 to 6 points. One-week test-retest reliability estimates obtained from a nonclinical sample of 110 students and clinical referred sample of 38 students are also strong across all scales and subscales with median coefficients of .77 or higher. However, small effect size differences in scores were noted in the direction of lower scores at retest for the clinical sample, leading the authors to extend an appropriate caution about response bias. As was done for the PIC-R, the PIC-2 authors also furnish information about interrater (mother-father) agreement, evaluated in subsets of the standardization sample (n = 60) and referred sample (n = 65), and report overall strong agreement rates with median coefficients of .68 or higher. These figures reflect notable improvement over those obtained for the PIC-R. However, the authors do not appear to have implemented a statistical correction for chance agreement and these values may therefore be somewhat inflated. It is further noted that fathers of referred children tend to report slightly fewer problems than mothers, suggesting the need for further evaluation of the *accuracy* of father and mother reports on the PIC-2.

The test authors have put considerable effort into establishing and evaluating the validity of PIC-2 scores for identifying child/adolescent problem areas. These include the previously mentioned item-to-scale correlations that furnish evidence of appropriate item membership on scales, and correlations between PIC-R and PIC-2 scale scores that provide evidence of continuity between the two versions of the inventory. Additionally, factor analytic results identify five factors—externalizing symptoms, internalizing symptoms, cognitive deficits, interpersonal adjustment, and family dysfunction—based on the Standard Form Adjustment subscales, and a two-factor (externalizing and internalizing problems) structure based on the Behavioral Summary Adjustment scales that support the construct validity of the test. Evidence of criterion-related validity is convincing, based on the reported convergence of PIC-2 scores with clinician, teacher, and student self-ratings. Of particular usefulness are the data concerning differential correlate patterns across 11 diagnostic groups. These data could be bolstered with evaluations of sensitivity, specificity, and overall classification accuracy of the scales. Overall, the PIC-2 appears to hold a good degree of validity for the purpose of evaluating emotional, behavioral, cognitive, and social maladjustment in children and adolescents.

COMMENTARY. The PIC-2 rests on strong foundations provided by a well-devised original test and its subsequent reorganization that provided direction for the current revision, and by a meaningful set of research studies and scholarly writings about its applications in clinical child assessment. The second edition appears to have succeeded in reversing the flaws in the earlier versions particularly in terms of achieving a representative standardization sample. The provision of contemporary norms and the continuity of this second edition with the earlier forms of the inventory enables continued use of the test in the present and future, and the test's applicability is broadened by the availability of a Spanish edition. The psychometric properties of the test have been strengthened in the current revision, but more evidence of discriminant validity is warranted. The suitability of the test for assessing adolescents age 18+ requires further evaluation, given their relatively low representation in the standardization sample. Further evaluation may also be needed to determine if age-specific norms are needed, given the evidence of small age effects for some PIC-2 scales.

The PIC-2 makes minimal demands on reading capacity and test-taking time, making it a convenient measure to administer to parents in evaluative settings. The structure of the PIC-2 Standard Form, consisting of validity scales, adjustment scales, and subscales, permits a systematic assessment of child and adolescent disorder. The revised adjustment scales appear to align better with the types of presenting problems seen in typical clinic and school referral settings than the earlier versions. A particular strength of the Standard Form, shared with its predecessors, is the provision of validity scales that offer a means of gauging the accuracy of the profiles; this is certainly important in light of likely motivational sets operating among parents of troubled children. In contrast, the Behavioral Summary results are markedly limited by the absence of validity scales.

PIC-2 scoring can be done in a relatively effortless manner. PIC-2 interpretation is facilitated by the authors' provision of sets of descriptions corresponding to two cutting score levels in the test manual, and by multiple case examples involving markedly different profiles to guide the test interpreter. The accuracy of adjustment scale interpretation is also facilitated by the new set of subscales. The test manual is generally thorough and clear except for containing insufficient information about the development of derived scores and test norms.

A key asset of the PIC was the empirically derived typology of PIC profiles furnished by Gdowski, Lachar, and Kline (1985) to elaborate the interpretation of individual PIC scales. The PIC-2 would benefit from a similar effort and by other methods of configural analysis.

SUMMARY. At the time of its development, the original PIC was unique as a parent-reported measure of emotional and behavioral disorder in children as young as age 3. Despite the subsequent development of rival measures, the PIC-2 holds the distinction of being a multidimensional measure of child and adolescent adjustment with a strong actuarial base and a substantial literature that supports and refines test interpretation. Overall, the PIC-2 represents a good revision that should prove useful in the assessment of child and adolescent maladjustment. The future of the test rests both on its experienced utility and on the development of a new research base to support and extend its applications.

REVIEWER'S REFERENCES

Gdowski, C. L., Lachar, D., & Kline, R. B. (1985). A PIC profile typology of children and adolescents: I. An empirically-derived alternative to traditional diagnosis. *Journal of Abnormal Psychology, 94,* 346–361.

Lachar, D. (1982). *Personality Inventory for Children (PIC): Revised format manual supplement.* Los Angeles: Western Psychological Services.

Wirt, R. D., Lachar, D., Klinedinst, J. K., & Seat, P. D. (1977). *Multidimensional description of child personality: A manual for the Personality Inventory for Children.* Los Angeles: Western Psychological Services.

Wirt, R. D., Lachar, D., Klinedinst, J. K., & Seat, P. D. (1984). *Multidimensional description of child personality: A manual for the Personality Inventory for Children* (1984 revision by David Lachar). Los Angeles: Western Psychological Services.

Review of the Personality Inventory for Children, Second Edition by SUSANA URBINA, Professor of Psychology, University of North Florida, Jacksonville, FL:

DESCRIPTION. The Personality Inventory for Children, Second Edition (PIC-2) is an objective instrument aimed at evaluating the adjustment of children and adolescents, aged 5 to 19, with regard to behavioral, emotional, cognitive, and interpersonal functioning. It has been designed to help in diagnosis, treatment planning, and outcome assessment for its target population. Like its predecessors, the PIC and the PIC-R, this questionnaire is meant to be completed by the parents or parent surrogates of the child in question. The Standard Form of the PIC-2 consists of 275 true-false items that take about 40 minutes to complete. It yields scores on (a) three response validity scales: Inconsistency (INC), Dissimulation (FB), and Defensiveness (DEF); (b) nine adjustment scales: Cognitive Impairment (COG), Impulsivity and Distractibility (ADH), Delinquency (DLQ), Family Dysfunction (FAM), Reality Distortion (RLT), Somatic Concern (SOM), Psychological Discomfort (DIS), Social Withdrawal (WDL), and Social Skill Deficits (SSK); and (c) 21 adjustment subscales. Each of the adjustment scales has two or three subscales made up of relatively homogeneous subsets of items within their respective scales. For example, the 47-item DLQ scale comprises an Antisocial Behavior subscale (13 items), a Dyscontrol subscale (17 items), and a Noncompliance subscale (17 items).

Overlap of items across the adjustment scales and subscales has been kept to a minimum.

The PIC-2 provides a Behavioral Summary version made up of the first 96 items of the Standard Form. The briefer version can be administered with the same booklet and answer sheet as the Standard Form or with a separate AutoScore Form and can be completed in less than 15 minutes. It includes eight short adjustment scales, three composite scales, and a total score. Although both the Standard Form and the Behavioral Summary can be hand scored, scoring and interpretation software for both are also available from the publisher. All of the PIC-2 scale and subscale raw scores are converted to *T*-scores prior to interpretation. A Critical Items Summary and scoring template are also available for the Standard Form.

DEVELOPMENT. The PIC-2 is a revised and newly standardized version of the Personality Inventory for Children (PIC), an instrument conceived in the 1950s, and originally published in 1977, with the express aim of providing a multidimensional and objective tool for the assessment of personality in children that would serve roughly the same purposes as the Minnesota Multiphasic Personality Inventory (MMPI) did for adults and older adolescents. Like the MMPI, the PIC stemmed from Minnesota and was normed there; it was also atheoretical in nature and cumbersome to complete, both because of its length-600 items-and because of its frequently awkward or obscure wording. Although the PIC was improved through the format changes instituted in the 1980s, in the PIC-R and in the revised 1990 edition, the PIC-2 is by far the most thorough revision this instrument has undergone.

One of the primary goals in developing the PIC-2 was to increase its similarity to the Personality Inventory for Youth (PIY), a self-report measure for children and adolescents aged 9 to 18 that can be used in tandem with the PIC-2 in individual assessment. Thus, the PIC-2 and the PIY now have the same validity and adjustment scales and extensive item overlap, with six out of the nine adjustment scales sharing 82% or more of the items.

Development and standardization of the PIC-2 took place over the period of 1995 to 2000. In addition to a slight reduction in the total number of items, the PIC-2 adjustment scales are now more saturated with manifest item content and the validity scales are either new or substantially revised. Other improvements of item content include the elimination of double negatives, expansion of items to cover areas of contemporary concern such as substance abuse and eating disorders, and a decrease in the reading skills needed to respond to the inventory down to the fourth grade level. Furthermore, the items now refer to "the child's parent(s)" instead of the "father," so the wording of items no longer assumes that the child's mother will be the respondent. As a consequence, either parent can serve equally well as the informant.

TECHNICAL. Two distinct sets of data were collected in developing and standardizing the PIC-2. The first of these involved a referred sample of 1,551 cases from clinical and special education facilities in 17 states, primarily in the South and Midwest, ranging in age from less than 5 to over 18 years. Consistent with referral patterns, boys in this sample significantly outnumbered girls (68% versus 32%). Approximately 30% of the referred sample came from ethnic minority groups. The second data collection effort consisted of a standardization sample of parents of 2,306 students, aged 5 to 18+ years, in kindergarten through 12th grade regular education classes from 23 schools in 12 states from all regions of the United States. Overall, this sample was fairly representative of American school children in terms of gender, age levels, geographic region, parents' educational level, and socioeconomic status, as well as ethnic background. Approximately 67% of the children were from households where both biological parents were present and the rest were from single-parent homes, homes with stepparents or other relatives, and foster homes. The majority of the respondents in the standardization sample (82%) were mothers, 15% were fathers, and 3% were other caregivers, mostly female.

As expected, the standardization and referred samples differed significantly on all PIC-2 scales. Effect sizes for these differences, measured by Cohen's *d*, ranged from medium to large, with the exception of the Social Introversion adjustment subscale, which had a small *d* of only .16. Statistically significant differences were also obtained with regard to gender and age. The impact of gender differences on PIC-2 score interpretation is acknowledged through the provision of gender-specific norms in separate profile forms. However, because the practical impact of age differences was considered to be too small for most scales, no age-specific norms are provided.

Reliability. Internal consistency estimates of score reliability were obtained for both the standardization and referred samples. For the adjustment scale scores, Cronbach's alpha coefficients ranged from .75 to .91 for the standardization sample and from .81 to .95 for the referred sample, with most alpha values in the .80s. As expected, internal consistency alpha coefficients for the adjustment subscales and for the short adjustment scales of the Behavioral Summary were somewhat lower than for the full adjustment scales and ranged from .49 to .92, with median values in the .70s and .80s, depending on the sample. Alpha coefficients for the response validity scores across both samples ranged from .52, for Inconsistency, to .91, with a median value of .82. The total and composite scores of the Behavioral Summary form produced alpha values ranging from .78 to .95.

Test-retest reliability coefficients were gathered from a nonclinical sample of 110 students who were a subset of the standardization sample and from 38 clinically referred students who were attending an outpatient psychiatric facility. Both groups were retested after a 1-week interval. For the nonclinical sample the test-retest correlations for the adjustment scales ranged from .66 to .90 (median = .82) and for the subscales from .63 to .87 (median = .77). The retest coefficients for the clinical sample were somewhat higher. In addition, the mean differences between the test and the retest scores of several individual scales were significant among the clinical sample, in the direction of fewer reported symptoms upon retesting.

Interrater agreement between mothers' and fathers' responses was assessed for a nonclinical subset of 60 students from the standardization sample and for 65 clinically referred cases. These coefficients were higher for the nonclinical subset than for the clinical sample. Median coefficients for the nonclinical group were .80 for both the adjustment scales and subscales; the corresponding median coefficients for the clinical group were .73 and .71, respectively. Furthermore, whereas in the nonclinical group there were no reliable differences between the responses of mothers and fathers, in the clinical group there was a small but significant trend for fathers to report fewer problems than mothers on several of the scales.

Altogether, with few exceptions, the various reliability estimates for the PIC-2 scores appear to be quite acceptable for an instrument of this type.

Variations in the magnitude of the coefficients are in most cases consonant with the content and length of the different scales and with the make-up of the samples used in obtaining the estimates.

Validity. The development of the PIC-2 proceeded through a series of steps based on logical and empirical grounds. Item placement in the adjustment scales was initially determined on the basis of logic and item-scale correlations; this process resulted in an overlap of only 6% across the total item set. Subscale structure was determined on the basis of factor analysis of each of the full adjustment scales, resulting in nonoverlapping homogeneous subscales.

In the PIC-2 manual, considerations regarding validity begin with the data on internal consistency of the scales, previously discussed, followed by correlations between the Standard Form (SF) and the Behavioral Summary (BS) and between the PIC-R and the PIC-2 obtained from the referred sample of 1,551 parents who completed a research version of the PIC-2, which included all the PIC-R items. These data show good correspondence among the various forms and correlation patterns that underscore the emphasis on content that characterizes the PIC-2.

Factor analysis of SF scores from the referred sample resulted in five factor dimensions. The first one, Externalizing Symptoms, had the largest weights on the ADH and DLQ subscales; the second factor, Internalizing Symptoms, was defined primarily by five of the seven RLT, SOM, and DIS subscales. These patterns were replicated with the BS short adjustment scales and provide the basis for the Externalization and Internalization composites of the BS. Two of the three COG subscales and one of the RLT subscales comprise the third factor dimension, which is seen as representing the presence of cognitive deficits. The fourth dimension is defined as a measure on interpersonal adjustment and consists of the WDL and SSK subscales; this factor corresponds to the Social Adjustment composite index of the BS. The final dimension represents family dysfunction and includes both of the FAM subscales.

Two types of criterion-related validation data are presented in the manual. One of these consists of concurrent correlations between PIC-2 measures and independent ratings completed by (a) clinicians on a symptom checklist, (b) teachers on the Student Behavior Survey (SBS), and (c) students themselves on the PIY. The resulting patterns of intercorrelations appear to be reasonably consistent with the constructs the PIC-2 aims to assess. However, the variety of informants, contexts, and instruments represented in this set of data makes it difficult to interpret and, thus, not very informative.

The second set of criterion-related data presented consists of differences in PIC-2 scores among 11 groups created based on diagnostic characteristics. These groups comprised 754 children from the referred sample. MANOVA and ANOVA results as well as effect sizes for group differences were analyzed. Mean scores for each of the 11 groups on all PIC-2 scales and subscales are presented as are the effect sizes for differences between children in each group compared to children in all other groups, many of which are significant. By and large, these data are consonant with the adjustment dimensions assessed by the PIC-2.

Three chapters of the PIC-2 manual are devoted to issues related to interpretation. One of these provides guidelines for the Standard Form, with special focus on the nine adjustment scales; clinicians are likely to find the information in this chapter, which includes special attention to the response validity scales, quite useful. A second chapter is devoted to interpretation of the Behavioral Summary version, which unfortunately lacks response validity scales. An additional chapter provides guidance for users on applications of the PIC-2 and its related family of instruments, namely, the PIY and SBS, as well as profile correlates and case studies.

COMMENTARY AND SUMMARY. Undoubtedly, the PIC-2 is a carefully developed instrument and constitutes a significant improvement over its predecessor, the PIC-R, in terms of its length, structure, content, and normative base. Its manual has been fully revised as well and is rich in material that may provide the basis for clinical inferences regarding problems of adjustment in children and adolescents, especially when used in tandem with the PIY and SBS.

Although the Standard Form takes longer to complete than the Behavioral Summary, it provides a sufficient amount of additional data-especially through its response validity and cognitive impairment scales-to make the time investment worthwhile. However, additional investigation of the diagnostic efficacy of the PIC-2, preferably from sources independent of its developers, would be highly desirable.

When the original PIC was conceived and developed there were no other instruments of its kind. At present there are a number of choices in the field, including several instruments—such as the Achenbach System of Empirically Based Assessment (see 3) and the Behavior Assessment System for Children (T6:280)—that provide a fully coordinated approach to the evaluation of adjustment problems in this population through multiple informants. Each one of these contemporary instruments has some strengths and weaknesses, ably summarized by Kamphaus and Frick (2002). Potential users are thus in a position to choose among them based on their preferences (e.g., ratings versus true-false formats) and on the requirements of their specific settings after careful comparison of the features provided by each.

REVIEWER'S REFERENCE

Kamphaus, R. W., & Frick, P. J. (2002). *Clinical assessment of child and adolescent personality and behavior* (2nd ed.). Boston: Allyn and Bacon.

[184]

Personality Self-Portrait [Revised].

Purpose: Designed to illustrate "the wide range of normal personality styles that combine to create each individual's unique personality profile and demonstrates how each personality style influences relationships, work and home life."

Population: Ages 18 and over.

Publication Dates: 1995–1996.

Acronym: PSP.

Scores, 14: Vigilant, Solitary, Idiosyncratic, Adventurous, Mercurial, Dramatic, Self-Confident, Sensitive, Devoted, Conscientious, Leisurely, Aggressive, Self-Sacrificing, Serious.

Administration: Individual.

Price Data, 2005: $137 per complete kit including the New Personality Self-Portrait book (1995, 463 pages), 5 reusable item booklets, and 20 Quikscore forms/interpretation guides; $32 per 5 Quikscore forms/interpretation guides; $42 per 5 reusable item booklets; $24 per 20 Quikscore forms; $87 per 20 interpretive guides, $5 per web-based profile report (minimum purchase of 20).

Time: [30] minutes.

Comments: Self-report questionnaire; online administration available.

Authors: John M. Oldham and Lois B. Morris.

Publisher: Multi-Health Systems, Inc.

Review of the Personality Self-Portrait [Revised] by GREGORY J. BOYLE, Professor of Psychology, Bond University, Gold Coast, Queensland, Australia:

DESCRIPTION. The Personality Self-Portrait [Revised] is a 107-item self-report questionnaire purported to measure 14 distinct personality styles. Although not intended as a clinical diagnostic tool, the instrument nonetheless is intended to provide quantitative measures of the normal nonpathological versions of personality disorders listed in the DSM-IV (American Psychiatric Association, 1994). These 14 personality styles have been labelled respectively: Vigilant, Solitary, Idiosyncratic, Adventurous, Mercurial, Dramatic, Self-Confident, Sensitive, Devoted, Conscientious, Leisurely, Aggressive, Self-Sacrificing, and Serious. The personality styles are combined to identify functioning within six broad domains labelled: Self, Relationships, Work, Emotions, Self-Control, and Real-World perceptions. An individual's particular profile (portrait) across the various personality styles is useful, for example, in providing insight into his or her own personality makeup, and/or in charting the outcomes of psychological therapy or counselling.

The Personality Self-Portrait [Revised] is intended for use by laypersons, who are encouraged to self-administer and self-score their own personality portraits. The accompanying book *The New Personality Self-Portrait: Why You Think, Work, Love, and Act the Way You Do* (Oldham & Morris, 1995) provides detailed case histories that highlight for each personality style, common traits and behaviors, tips for living and working, and exercises to strengthen one's character weaknesses. The book also provides an indication of possible personality disorders as defined in the DSM-IV.

The Personality Self-Portrait [Revised] is also accompanied by an interpretation guide (Oldham & Morris, 1996) that includes plausible if somewhat subjective insights into basic differences in personality styles. Scoring of the Personality Self-Portrait self-test is relatively straightforward, and requires only that the raw scores for each item within each of the 14 scales be added and the total scores be entered into the relevant column of the Personality Self-Portrait graph included on the inside cover of the interpretation guide (no standardized scores are required to be computed). Each of the scores in the Personality Self-Portrait graph is then joined by a single interconnecting line, thereby revealing an individual's idiosyncratic personality profile/portrait.

TECHNICAL. Neither *The Personality Self-Portrait Interpretation Guide* nor the accompanying book *The New Personality Self-Portrait* includes any data on the psychometric properties of the instrument pertaining to its reliability and validity. At the very least, data on the test-retest reliability (both dependability and longer term stability), item homogeneity (cf. Boyle, 1991), concurrent and discriminant validity, and construct validity including factor analytic structure of the instrument are needed. Failure to report these essential psychometric data is a serious omission.

In view of the high face validity and transparency of the items included in the Personality Self-Portrait self-test, the validity of an individual's responses to the items depends entirely upon the person's honesty and self-insight in answering the questions. Clearly though, as with the vast majority of self-report personality instruments, use of self-report methodology is a substantial weakness, not only because of response sets and motivational distortion, but also because individuals may not be fully aware of, and may lack insight into, their own personality. This problem of item transparency associated with self-report and observer rating instruments has been discussed elsewhere (Boyle, 1985, 1987). In view of this difficulty, it is especially surprising that there are no validity scales to correct for faking good, faking bad, or other types of motivational distortion. Such correction scales have for decades been incorporated explicitly into the design of many standardized personality instruments such as the Minnesota Multiphasic Personality Inventory (MMPI; Hathaway & McKinley, 1943), the Sixteen Personality Factor Questionnaire (16PF; Cattell, Eber, & Tatsuoka, 1970), the Eysenck Personality Questionnaire (EPQ; eysenck & Eysenck, 1975), or the Comrey Personality Scales (CPS; Comrey, 1970).

COMMENTARY. It is important to note that the DSM-IV classification of personality disorders itself has come under increasing scrutiny in recent years, and the adequacy of the DSM-IV classifications has been seriously challenged (e.g., Beutler & Malik, 2002) thereby raising concerns about the actual selection of personality traits/styles included in the Personality Self-Portrait itself.

To their credit, Oldham and Morris (1995, 1996) have produced a creative and novel approach to the self-assessment of normal personality styles linked to DSM-IV personality constructs

that can be administered, scored, and interpreted relatively easily. Also on the positive side, the instrument includes relevant self-test items, employs a straightforward trichotomous response scale, and avoids colloquial or slang expressions. The Personality Self-Portrait [Revised] appears to make a useful contribution to the self-measurement of personality styles. It has the added benefit of providing relevant information to individuals that may enable them to take actions to counteract weaknesses and liabilities in their own personality makeup.

SUMMARY. Extensive research needs to be undertaken into the psychometric properties of the Personality Self-Portrait [Revised] and data need to be included in the accompanying manuals regarding the important psychometric issues of reliability and validity, as well as factor analytic evidence (cf. Boyle, Stankov, & Cattell, 1995; Gorsuch, 1983) because the structural dimensionality of the instrument remains uncertain.

REVIEWER'S REFERENCES
American Psychiatric Association. (1994). *Diagnostic and statistical manual of mental disorders* (4th ed.). Washington, DC: Author.
Beutler, L. E., & Malik, M. L. (Eds.). (2002). *Rethinking the DSM: A psychological perspective.* Washington, DC: American Psychological Association.
Boyle, G. J. (1985). Self-report measures of depression: Some psychometric considerations. *British Journal of Clinical Psychology, 24,* 45–59.
Boyle, G. J. (1987). Review of the (1985) "Standards for educational and psychological testing: AERA, APA and NCME." *Australian Journal of Psychology, 39,* 235–237.
Boyle, G. J. (1991). Does item homogeneity indicate internal consistency or item redundancy in psychometric scales? *Personality and Individual Differences, 12,* 291–294.
Boyle, G. J., Stankov, L., & Cattell, R. B. (1995). Measurement and statistical models in the study of personality and intelligence. In D. H. Saklofske & M. Zeidner (Eds.), *International handbook of personality and intelligence* (pp. 417–446). New York: Plenum.
Cattell, R. B., Eber, H. W., & Tatsuoka, M. M. (1970). *Handbook for the Sixteen Personality Factor Questionnaire.* Champaign, IL: Institute for Personality and Ability Testing.
Comrey, A. L. (1970). *Manual for the Comrey Personality Scales.* San Diego, CA: Educational and Industrial Testing Service.
Eysenck, H. J., & Eysenck, M. W. (1975). *Manual of the Eysenck Personality Questionnaire.* San Diego, CA: Educational and Industrial Testing Service.
Gorsuch, R. L. (1983). *Factor analysis* (rev. 2nd ed.). Hillsdale, NJ: Erlbaum.
Hathaway, S. R., & McKinley, J. C. (1943). The Minnesota Multiphasic Personality Inventory. Minneapolis, MN: University of Minnesota Press.
Oldham, J. M., & Morris, L. B. (1995). *The New Personality Self-Portrait.* New York: Bantam Books.
Oldham, J. M., & Morris, L. B. (1996). *The Personality Self-Portrait: Interpretation guide.* North Tonawanda, NY: Multi-Health Systems Inc.

Review of the Personality Self-Portrait [Revised] by SANDRA D. HAYNES, Interim Dean, School of Professional Studies, Metropolitan State College of Denver, Denver, CO:

DESCRIPTION. The Personality Self-Portrait was designed for a lay audience as "a system for defining [a person's] personality style" (interpretation guide, p. 1). Based on the idea that personality disorders represent one extreme of a continuum ranging from normal to pathological, the Personality Self-Portrait was designed to measure the normal end of this spectrum of these personality traits. The first edition of the assessment was modeled after the Axis II Personality Disorders identified in the *Diagnostic and Statistical Manual, Third Edition, Revised* (DSM-III-R). When the DSM was again revised in 1994 (DSM-IV), the authors found it necessary to revise the Personality Self-Portrait. Rather than selecting only traits from those disorders found in the DSM-IV, however, traits from personality disorders as well as the appendices of both the DSM-III-R and the DSM-IV were also included. The decision to include all identified personality disorders and potential personality disorders was based on clinician reports that these patterns are the primary focus of treatment in many patients, although no reference was provided on the origins of these data. The authors further believe that these patterns more accurately represent a broad range of normal as well as abnormal human behavior. Thus, the range of personality traits of this assessment tool includes the following personality disorders: Paranoid, Schizoid, Schizotypal, Antisocial, Borderline, Histrionic, Narcissistic, Avoidant, Dependent, Obsessive-Compulsive, Passive-Aggressive, Sadistic, Self-Defeating, and Depressive. Because the assessment is designed to measure the normal end of the personality spectrum, the authors have derived the following names for the traits measured: Vigilant, Solitary, Idiosyncratic, Adventurous, Mercurial, Dramatic, Self-Confident, Sensitive, Devoted, Conscientious, Leisurely, Aggressive, Self-Sacrificing, and Serious. The degree to which people exhibit traits in each of the identified personality areas is representative of their personality style.

In the text, the authors differentiate between personality traits and personality disorders. They also differentiate between personality disorders and Axis I disorders. Careful and frequent cautions are provided that the new Personality Self-Portrait is not designed to diagnose personality or other disorders. They, likewise, offer the recommendation for obtaining a professional opinion if the individual taking the test believes they may have a serious disorder.

The questionnaire itself is composed of 107 statements. The examinee is asked to rate each question "Y" if the statement is completely true most of the time, "M" if the statement is sometimes or somewhat true, or "N" if the statement is completely false. The new Personality Self-Portrait takes approximately one-half to one hour to complete. The authors urge accuracy and honesty when responding to each statement and to make certain the examinee takes the time necessary to ensure such.

Once completed, scores are transferred to the score sheet. Each question is listed down the left side of the score sheet and is followed by 14 columns representing the 14 personality characteristics. One or two of these columns in each row contains the letters Y, M, and N in subcolumns (a, b, c). Answers are recorded in the column or columns with these letters by circling the appropriate letter. The first two subcolumns are then summed. The first subcolumn (a) is multiplied by 2 before adding the total to the second subcolumn (b). The scores in the third subcolumn (c) are not used in the score. Scores are then transferred to a graph with the personality traits identified along the bottom and columns of numbers above them ranging from 0–14, 16, or 18 depending on the trait.

One more calculation can be made. Using The Personality Self-Portrait Interpretation Guide, a separate publication, a domain table can be completed. Domains are defined as the "six key areas of life": Self, Relationships, Work, Emotions, Self-Control, and Real World (interpretive guide, p. 9). The Self domain includes sense of self, self-esteem, and self-image. The Relationships domain is a measure of how important people are in the examinee's life. The Work domain is a measure of how the individual completes tasks, takes and/or gives orders, makes decisions, plans, handles external and internal demands, takes or gives criticism, obeys rules, takes and delegates responsibility, and cooperates with other people. Usual moods and emotional states are considered in the Emotions domain and the Self-Control domain is an indicator of the impulsiveness of the person. Finally, Real World measures the extent to which the individual is rooted in conventional shared realities or believes in realities beyond the apparently tangible. Each personality style primarily influences one or more domains.

Interpreting the test is vaguely described. Essentially, the examinee is asked to look first at those characteristics that have the highest score. These are the strongest or dominant personality styles. Low scores are assessed as weaker influences on personality style but not unimportant in determining one's overall personality. Examinees are asked to consider how all the styles blend together to create the overall personality assessment. When high and low personality style scores are identified, interpretations can be found in the later chapters of the book or in the interpretive guide. The interpretive chapters in the book begin with a description of normal style for each category and then the personality disorder on which the style is based is explained. although meant to help define normal from abnormal, including the disorder description can be misleading and appears contradictory to the stated purpose of the book to not diagnose personality disorders.

Comparisons can be made between people in relationships to help them to understand how they are alike and how they are different. The interpretive chapters also include a section on dealing with other people who exhibit the personality characteristics described. However, although these comparisons have purpose, the authors are again contradictory about making other comparisons. They caution people not to share their answers to specific questions but to freely share overall results. A more responsible approach would be to encourage sharing to the extent one is comfortable.

DEVELOPMENT. Very little information is given on the development of this assessment tool. Dr. Oldham speaks of his role in the development of DSM-IV and the Personality Disorder Examination (PDE). It is assumed that this work helped in the creation of the Personality Self-Portrait but no direct links are given. Research on test development is alluded to in the acknowledgments and preface but never described in any part of the text. The chapter notes and bibliography include excellent sources of information regarding personality and personality disorders but, again, no description of development exists in the book.

TECHNICAL ASPECTS. As with development, no technical information is given by the authors. No information is given even on the basic technical aspects of validity and reliability.

SUMMARY. The *New Personality Self-Portrait: Why You Think, Work, Love, and Act the Way You Do* (title of accompanying text), was clearly developed for a lay audience. As such it is easy to administer and score and the books are straightforward and easy to read. What is missing is the technical information that would allow for evaluation of the efficacy of the measure. The authors claim that much research has been conducted on the test. It is hoped that the researchers had more information on which to base their conclusions.

[185]
Personalized Achievement Summary System.

Purpose: Designed to provide information useful for monitoring academic progress, selecting curriculum and evaluating and planning instructional programming in home school settings.
Population: Grades 3–8.
Publication Dates: 1981–1993.
Acronym: PASS.
Scores, 20: Reading (Word Meaning, Literal Comprehension, Interpretive Comprehension, Evaluative Comprehension, Total); Mathematics (Numeration and Number Systems, Fractions, Decimals/Percent/and Currency, Geometry and Measurement, Graphs/Charts/and Statistics, Word Problems and Problem Solving, Computation, Total); Language Usage (Grammar, Capitalization, Punctuation, Composition, Study Skills, Spelling, Total).
Administration: Individual.
Price Data: Available from publisher.
Time: (210–330) minutes.
Comments: Items taken from the Portland Achievement Level Tests (PALT).
Authors: Hewitt Research Foundation.
Publisher: Hewitt Homeschooling Resources.

Review of the Personalized Achievement Summary System by DOUGLAS F. KAUFFMAN, Assistant Professor of Education, Eastern Connecticut State University, Willimantic, CT:

DESCRIPTION. The Personalized Achievement Summary System (PASS) is described by the authors as an achievement-level test designed to "provide longitudinal standardized test information for the students served by Hewitt instructional programs" (technical manual, p. 1). The authors argue that the rationale for developing an *achievement* level (rather than grade level) test system was to assign a test to students on which they can succeed. Further, the achievement level test should: (a) ensure students were able to respond correctly on 60–90% of the items, increasing the likelihood that they will find the items challenging, but not frustrating; and (b) make the test shorter than the typical grade-level test.

The PASS is administered individually to Grade 3–8 students in three separate parts, including Reading, Mathematics, and Language Usage. The mathematics portion is further divided into lower grades (third through fall fifth grade) and upper grades (spring fifth grade through eighth grade).

Each section of the test is divided into 8 to 10 separate, but overlapping achievement levels. Students are tested at one of these levels based on either previous achievement or on a brief placement test. The test authors argue that the use of latent-trait scaling allows them to standardize and thus compare the various levels of achievement with each other. Additionally, they argue that this approach allows for more efficient assessment. Unfortunately, the technical manual is unclear as to how this is specifically accomplished.

DEVELOPMENT. The Personalized Achievement Summary System (PASS) was developed from items from the Portland Achievement Level Test (PALT). Nearly all the information provided by the authors in the technical manual describes the assessment and the development of the PALT rather than the PASS. Consequently, it is difficult to describe the development of the PASS itself other than to say the items were taken from the existing pool of PALT items.

The authors describe using Rasch units to report the average scores and ranges for each of the levels on the four tests. It was difficult to understand how exactly this was accomplished as the authors never really clearly described the process used when administering or scoring the PASS. The authors do provide a list of objectives for each section of the test. It is difficult to determine, however, whether the items were developed (selected) because they match the objectives or if the objectives were written after the items were chosen.

TECHNICAL. In this section, I will first describe the reported validity evidence followed by reliability and standardization.

Validity. It is a bit difficult to interpret validity information on the PASS because the authors report using the PALT test bank in order to construct the PASS test. Consequently, much information in the technical manual was about the PALT rather than the PASS. The authors do report that the PASS was constructed to "provide a balance of curriculum content across the spectrum of achievement in each basic skill area" (technical manual, p. 2). Unfortunately, there seems to be no substantive information provided in the manual as to how this was accomplished for the PASS. Specifically, the only information provided regarding how to decide at what level to test

students is "based on previous achievement" (technical manual, p. 2) or a brief placement test. At best, it appears from the manual that the authors are trying to argue that there is some convergent validity evidence because the PASS items were taken from the PALT test bank. Without proper evidence, however, this seems to be a relatively weak description of validity evidence for the PASS.

Reliability. The authors provide reliability estimates in the form of internal consistency scores (KR20) for each level on the three PASS tests. In all cases the reported reliability estimates appear to be well within the acceptable range. On the Reading test, for example, KR20s range from .78–.93. Likewise, on the Language Usage tests, KR20s range from .82–.94. Finally, KR20s on the Lower and Upper Math tests range from .83–.91 and .88–.95, respectively. Interestingly, although the manual states the reliability estimates are acceptable, the authors describe them as underestimates due to the fewer extreme scores at each level of the tests.

Other technical issues. One potential problem with the PASS relates to bias and appropriateness of items. According to the copyright information at the bottom of page 1 of each test booklet, this test was developed approximately 20 years ago. As a result, the test's layout, terminology, and item content are, in some cases, potentially out of date. For example, one item in the Reading section relates to the topic of "nuclear proliferation," which was arguably a much more relevant topic in 1985 than it is today. Likewise, the wording on the instructions is potentially biased and/or misleading. For example, the sample item on the Reading test asks "What is a food" and then gives four choices (book, shoe, rice, or ball). Problems related to clarity and/or ethnic/cultural bias seem to be prevalent throughout the test.

COMMENTARY. My review of the technical manual and the test booklets themselves suggests the development, validity, scoring, and usability of the PASS are questionable at best. Although the use of Rasch modeling in and of itself is certainly appropriate under certain conditions, the materials provided in the technical manual make it unclear as to whether the authors of the PASS have used the described methods appropriately. It is unclear, for example, how decisions are made regarding at what level students are placed. For example, if educators know that a student is at Level 6, then why test him or her to begin with? Based on all the available information, I cannot recommend this test be used and my recommendation is to approach it with caution.

SUMMARY. In sum, the Personalized Achievement Summary System (PASS) was designed to "provide longitudinal standardized test information for the students served by Hewitt instructional programs" (technical manual, p. 1). My review of the technical manual suggests that the items were designed for another purpose (test) and consequently the majority of validity information is for another test altogether. Finally, specific information regarding how to decide at what level to test students is unavailable. Consequently, I cannot recommend this test for use.

Review of the Personalized Achievement Summary System by MICHAEL S. TREVISAN, Associate Professor, Department of Educational Leadership and Counseling Psychology, Washington State University, Pullman, WA:

DESCRIPTION. The Personalized Achievement Summary System (PASS) is a collection of achievement tests in reading, language arts, and mathematics. For each subject, the tests assess a basic skills curriculum for Grades 3—8. Each subject maintains broad curriculum goals. The purpose of the tests is to provide standardized, longitudinal achievement information for home-schooled students. PASS was first administered in 1988 and is published by the Hewitt Research Foundation.

PASS consists of four test booklets in reading, language arts, lower grades mathematics, and upper grades mathematics, respectively. These booklets contain sets of tests (referred to as levels) of increasing difficulty that are linked by a common scaling technique. The reading booklet for example, contains eight test levels that span the curriculum and associated scale.

For each subject, scores are provided in terms of Rasch Unit scores or RITs. RIT scores are scaled to have equal intervals. Each scale point represents an equal amount of achievement, and has the same interpretive meaning, regardless of the test level. Thus, RIT scores can be compared between students taking lower level tests with those from upper level tests. RIT scores can also be compared from year to year for a particular student. Parents can track their child's progress through the curriculum by observing the incremental gain in RIT scores across levels.

Placement tests are available in each subject to match the achievement level of the student with the appropriate test level. Students first take the locator test. Depending on the number of items correct, students then take the designated test level. Conversion tables and instructions are provided with the placement tests. Placement tests contain 11—12 items.

All tests were designed for administration in one 45-minute class period. The number of items per test ranges from 44 to 61, with a lower number of items on the reading tests, as these tests generally take more time than the others. Subject test specifications illustrate the goals assessed, and the number of items that assess each goal, by test level. All tests are multiple-choice in format. Reading and language test items are composed with four options per item. Options are labeled 1 through 4, respectively. Mathematics items have five options with labels a through e, respectively. No rationale is provided for the difference. Detailed, clear instructions for test administration are provided. Scoring services and reports are available from the publisher. In addition to RIT scores, score reports provide descriptive, evaluative feedback for each goal assessed.

DEVELOPMENT. According to the technical manual, items constituting the PASS tests were obtained from item banks developed and calibrated during the 1970s in the Portland Public Schools. The item banks contain over 11,000 items across a variety of subjects and levels. Each item was field tested with 300 to 5,000 students. The items are keyed to instructional goals for each subject. Microsystems for Education and Business, Inc. provided the items and technical expertise for the original PASS development. The Northwest Evaluation Association in Portland, Oregon now maintains the item banks (P. Hendrickson, personal communication, November, 14, 2003).

Each level test was constructed to overlap with adjacent levels. The rationale is to give students more options. In addition, each level test is scaled to encompass approximately 20 RIT scale points of the curriculum scale. With this strategy, each level test represents approximately the same amount of achievement, and together, span the curriculum scale.

Although few specifics are provided in the technical manual about item development, the authors do mention that item development was accomplished with committees of teachers and curriculum specialists. Items were screened for gender and ethnic bias. The items are linked to achievement goals established through the tri-county region of Portland, Oregon, during the 1970s.

TECHNICAL. The psychometric procedure used to scale items places the item difficulty on the same scale as student achievement. Thus, items are measured in RITs. Item calibration data are provided in the technical manual. This includes item difficulty estimates, as well as point biserial correlations. Acceptable internal consistency reliability data are also presented. The authors argue that validity is established through links to achievement goals (i.e., content validity).

Linking studies were done between the PASS test and the Metropolitan Achievement Test (MAT), making it possible to convert from RIT to percentile rank scores for Grades 3—8. The linking sample was composed of students who were administered the PASS in the fall of 1988. These students were also administered the MAT. Conversion tables are located in the technical manual.

Comparisons between students taking the PASS test and students taking the Portland Achievement Levels Test in fall 1988 and spring 1989 are provided. Comparisons are also provided between students taking the PASS and students in the 1993 Oregon Statewide Assessment. The Oregon Statewide Assessment tests Grade 3, 5, and 8 students in basic skills. Descriptions of the PASS sample for this comparison were not provided.

COMMENTARY. The levels test technology that constitutes the PASS has had a long and for the most part, distinguished history in the Pacific Northwest. Although the history is not well documented, levels test methodology continues to be well regarded in some circles, thriving in many school districts in this region, and was recently adopted for the statewide achievement testing program in Idaho.

The notion of calibrated items linked to achievement goals is compelling, if not for its precision then certainly the efficiency, cost effectiveness, and soundness with which customized tests can be developed, stored, and maintained. Thus, the levels test methodology used by PASS will likely continue for the foreseeable future.

There are some limitations to PASS as well as the methodology that potential users should be aware. First, the documentation associated with the PASS is incomplete. A call to the publisher indicated that no documentation other than the review materials exists. Although a technical report comes with the review materials, there is little in the way of documentation that could meet the information needs of parents, presumably the primary users of the PASS.

Examination of the materials shows poor print copy, as several letters are missing from words in the technical manual. In addition, the technical information is poorly organized and formatted. Statistical information about the items is presented without explanation. There are grammar and syntax errors in the text. In short, the review materials, which include the PASS booklets, appear as if they have been produced expeditiously and then neglected. Potential users will be challenged to make sense of the documentation and, therefore, the PASS.

Second, the items and achievement goals are nearly 30 years old. The linking to the Metropolitan Achievement Test is outdated as revisions to this achievement test have occurred since the original linking study. At minimum, work is needed to determine if the quality of the items have changed over time. Linking to a current achievement test is also needed.

Third, the PASS assesses basic skill outcomes only. As this test is multiple-choice in format, assessment of any other outcome is difficult or impossible. Current state and national achievement standards include outcomes that require the use of constructed response and, in some cases, performance assessments. The PASS is clearly limited in this regard.

Fourth, achievement comparisons of users of PASS materials, who are presumably home-schooled students, to students in the Portland Public Schools and Oregon students statewide, consistently show PASS users outperforming these comparison students. Results also show greater gains for PASS users. The results should not be a surprise as home-schooled students are a unique group, and somewhat homogeneous, compared to the diversity of students public schools must educate. No explanation about this phenomenon is provided in the review materials. Without explanation, the results could imply better outcomes for students, simply by using PASS. A balanced appraisal and interpretation of these achievement comparisons is needed to properly convey to potential users, particularly parents, accurate information about the PASS.

SUMMARY. PASS provides home-schooled students with basic skills achievement information to help track progress through a standard reading, language, and mathematics curriculum. PASS tests received sound, rigorous psychometric development but in many respects are outdated. Updating the tests, therefore, is strongly recommended. Revising the review materials for clarity is needed.

[186]

Personalysis®.

Purpose: Constructed "to inventory personality characteristics of individuals at five different levels" yielding information on "how to maximize personal, interpersonal, and group effectiveness in the work place."

Population: Leaders, employees, families, individuals.

Publication Dates: 1975–2001.

Scores, 32: Preferred Style—Rational Self (Authoritative, Democratic, Structured, Self Directed), Communication Expectations—Socialized Self (Direction, Involvement, Methodology, Input), Motivational Needs—Instinctive Self (Authority, Influence, Control, Understanding), Defensive Self (Coerce, Provoke, Resist, Reject), Irrational Self (Hostile, Rebellious, Stubborn, Withdrawn); Act, Adapt, Analyze, and Assess scores for Preferred Style—Rational Self, Back-Up Style—Socialized Self, and Functional Stress—Instinctive.

Administration: Individual or group.

Price Data: Available from publisher.

Time: Untimed.

Comments: Self-administered.

Author: James R. Noland.

Publisher: Personalysis Corporation.

Cross References: For reviews by George Engelhard, Jr. and L. Alan Witt of an earlier edition, see 12:291.

Review of the Personalysis® by JACK GEBART-EAGLEMONT, President, International Institute for Personality Assessment and Therapy, Watsonia, Victoria, Australia:

DESCRIPTION. The Personalysis is a self-description questionnaire, which consists of a set of 94 forced-choice binary questions developed by James R. Noland, initially to assess "sales profiles" (1979). According to the booklet, the questionnaire takes about 20 minutes to complete. It is scored ipsatively, but the scoring system was not sufficiently described by the materials submitted for this review. The completed questionnaires must be sent to Personalysis Corporation for scoring.

The computer-generated report presents scores on the six Basic Traits expressed in terms of a typological description: Extroverts, Humanistic, Introverts, Pragmatists, Individualists, and Conformists at the three Ego Levels. The results also include the scores on the 12 "primary" scales: Insistence, Activeness, Assertiveness, Sociability, Supportiveness, Adaptability, Conceptuality, Empathy, Imaginativeness, Precision, Control-Minded, and Predictability. Some interpretations of the profiles are also supplied. The interpretations are expressed in a jargon specific to Personalysis, which is incompatible with any current psychological system (e.g., Red = Rational, Yellow = Instinctive). Even more confusing is the fact that in different materials submitted for this review the names of the scales and dimensions are often different: For example, the Rational Self is sometimes described as Preferred Style, and sometimes as Adult. Even the meaning of the same score changes rapidly depending on the context: The extroverted sensing type from the manual changes into "Authoritative" (within the Instinctive Self) in the client's report, on the next page of the same report dealing with the Socialized Self, the same dimension is called "Direct," the next page again, discussing the Rational Self, it changes back to "Authoritative." The terminology of Personalysis appears generally chaotic and unstable.

DEVELOPMENT. The theoretical origins of the Personalysis are somewhat unconventional. The underlying theory represents an attempt to combine some Jungian concepts with the basic Freudian ideas as well as with Eric Berne's "Ego States" structure of human behavior. The Jungian typology, based on Extroversion versus Introversion, co-classified with Sensing, Intuition, Thinking, and Feeling, originally results in the eight basic types. These were "distilled" by Noland "into a theoretical and semantic base through deductive reasoning, winding up with" only four types (manual, p. 2). These types are described as Action Oriented, Socially Oriented, Communication Oriented, and Analysis Oriented. To make things more kaleidoscopic, Noland "color-coded them after Lusher, assigning the colors of Red, Yellow, Blue, and Green, respectively" (manual, p. 2). This four-dimensional classification is then expressed in three Ego States variably described as Child (Instinctive), Parent (Socialized), and Adult (Rational). The configuration of the four dimensions within each Ego State is then expressed in terms of the six Basic Traits. The "secondary" traits are apparently calculated from configurations of the four dimensions across the various Ego States.

TECHNICAL. The materials submitted for this review do not demonstrate sufficient evidence of reliability, which indicates that much work is needed to develop Personalysis into a psychometric instrument. Interestingly, there is some weak indication of validity of two "primary" scales (BS "Blue Parent" and YS "Yellow Parent") in one study, but the entry methods of different tests used in multiple regressions appear questionable and are not well explained or properly presented (Hamilton, 1988). In the other study, described in the Personalysis manual, in which the Personalysis dimensions were correlated with Personality Research Form E, there were only two correlation coefficients above .4. These were "Yellow Rational" with Affiliation, .49; and "Yellow Rational" with Play, .43. This may indicate that some scores on Personalysis are simply related to social desirability dimensions. The data concerning validity are scanty and come from small and specific samples; the questionnaire had not been subjected to rigorous studies attempting to examine its reliability and validity with large and representative samples.

COMMENTARY. The ipsative system of scoring makes it impossible to compare individuals in relative terms, which to some extent defies the central purpose of psychological measurement in selection or diagnostic processes. In other words, everybody is good on at least one scale (because the total of all four scales within each Ego State is always 12.0), and therefore any meaningful comparison of composite merits between individuals is virtually impossible; rather, the scales merely reflect configurations of dimensions within individuals. The declared number of derived scores seems rather implausible concerning the small number of items. These characteristics make this instrument rather difficult to assess from the perspective of the standard psychometric point of view. Some hope can be associated with the 12 secondary "traits." They are derived from scores across two Ego States (e.g., Sociability equals "Yellow" in Rational + Socialized states); however, we face a logical contradiction because the "primary" traits may be present in different states at different levels by definition. The system of "secondary" traits appears to have a weak rationale.

Perhaps a proper factor analysis of all items can reveal some real primary traits, which in turn could be factor analyzed again in order to calculate psychometrically valid secondary dimensions. But such steps would first require a translation of ipsative scoring into an additive system before subjecting the raw scores to any factor-analytic operations. A psychometrically oriented scoring system for ipsative items is mathematically possible (if preceded by proper standardization and normalization), but the materials submitted for this review do not indicate that such an effort has been attempted. The operation would also require sufficiently large standardization and normalization samples.

The items of the questionnaire demonstrate an obviously high level of face validity. This fact may make an instrument easy to fake. The lack of any control scales increases enormously this inherent vulnerability. On the other hand, the existence of three levels of interpretation (Rational/Preferred style, Socialized/Communication expectations, and Instinctive/Motivational needs) seems to approach this problem to at least some extent: Preferred style means simply that people present themselves in a way in which they want to be perceived; Communication expectations means self-presentation, which is socially expected according to the respondent's perception; and Motivational needs mean what the respondent really needs in work-related situations. The differences among the expression of traits at different levels probably could be used as measures of social desirability. One can pose a hypothesis that Personalysis is in fact a device measuring social desirability. Significant discrepancies among the three levels subsequently can be treated as an expression of the strength of this trait.

The author of this review agrees with one of the previous reviewers (Witt, 1995) that Personalysis may probably demonstrate "a capability of capturing hidden motivation." But these possibilities are not in any way reflected in summaries or presentations of the results.

SUMMARY. The theoretical origins of the questionnaire demonstrate a creative approach, which indicates that there may be inherent potential in Noland's product. The attempts to directly utilize psychoanalytic theories in organizational psychology measurements were so far limited. For example, the idea of the presentation of personality in three Ego States is very interesting, albeit very difficult to further develop psychometrically. Consequently, the Personalysis is difficult to assess following the standard psychometric approach. The modern approach to personality measurement assumes the existence of some factor-based traits, which are expected to demonstrate internal consistency, as reflected by the high levels of correlation between items measuring each trait. The idea of the same trait expressed at different levels within each Ego State is therefore generally difficult to test and at least disputable from the point of view of the factor-analytic approach. Subsequently, the questionnaire fails to demonstrate reliability and sufficient validity in the traditional sense, and therefore cannot be compared with the existing psychological instruments. Moreover, the materials provided for a review did not include any normalization data, which rules out, in an obvious way, the use of this questionnaire in any attempts to justifiably compare individuals for selection or assessment purposes. At this stage of its development, Personalysis fails to demonstrate sound psychometric qualities, although the items may have some diagnostic potential, which may be indicated by a high level of face validity and transparency. The instrument feasibly may be used as a measure of social desirability (selective preference in self-presentation and adjustment of self-presentation according to the perceived social expectations). The high level of face validity and the obvious "transparency" of the items would greatly facilitate such a development. But such objectives were not declared in the materials submitted for this review.

The questionnaire needs to be subjected to rigorous psychometric studies to examine the reliability and validity of the declared traits. The scales measuring social desirability should be included and psychometrically validated against the existing SD scales. The weakness of the Personalysis may actually be turned into its strength. The attempts to assess faking using specialized tests in other fields of psychological measurement, such as the area of cognitive functioning, have been proven highly successful (for example Validity Indicator Profile) and reviewed (Gebart-Eaglemont, 2001; Ivens, 2001). A well-structured and methodologically sound test specifically assessing social desirability in the area of personality measurement is indeed needed. The items and the three-level structure of Personalysis are eminently suitable for this purpose.

Overall, the use of Personalysis in its present form for any selection, evaluation, or assessment purposes in the workplace is not advisable. At the present stage of its development, the instrument cannot be considered a fully developed psychological measurement because solid research-based indications of its reliability were not demonstrated. There are some weak indices of validity (especially regarding social desirability), but the samples were small and not representative of the population of workers. The perpetually changing language of the system, sometimes lacking precision and clarity, and at the same time serving lots of colorful displays, may confuse and baffle the clients. In the opinion of the author of this review, any occupational decisions based on the Personalysis scores concerning individuals in the workplace would be very difficult to justify from the point of view of professional psychology. The author of this review recognizes the theoretical merits and the developmental potential of the Personalysis, and would like to encourage the further psychometric development of the instrument.

REVIEWER'S REFERENCES

Gebart-Eaglemont, J. E. (2001). [Review of the Validity Indicator Profile]. In J. C. Impara & B. S. Plake (Eds.), *The fourteenth mental measurement yearbook* (pp. 1302–1304). Lincoln, NE: Buros Institute of Mental Measurements.

Hamilton, E. E. (1988). The facilitation of organizational change: An empirical study of factors predicting change agents' effectiveness. *The Journal of Applied Behavioral Science, 24,* 37–59.

Ivens, S. H. (2001). [Review of the Validity Indicator Profile]. In J. C. Impara & B. S. Plake (Eds.), *The fourteenth mental measurement yearbook* (pp. 1305–1306). Lincoln, NE: Buros Institute of Mental Measurements.

Witt, L. A. (1995) [Review of the PERSONALYSIS]. In J. C. Conoley & J. C. Impara (Eds.), *The twelfth mental measurements yearbook* (pp. 769–770). Lincoln, NE: Buros Institute of Mental Measurements.

Review of the Personalysis® by S. ALVIN LEUNG, Professor, Department of Educational Psychology, The Chinese University of Hong Kong, Hong Kong, China:

DESCRIPTION. Personalysis is an inventory designed to help individuals understand their personality characteristics, and to identify how these characteristics might enhance or interfere with effective performance in organizations. The test publisher did not clearly specify the age and types of individuals who would benefit from taking this test, but it is clear from the test content and description that the Personalysis targets individuals who work in business and organizational settings. There is no information on who could administer the test or the training requirement for test administration and interpretation. It seems that Personalysis could be administered only through trained personnel from the test publisher.

The Personalysis test booklet consists of 94 forced-choice items divided into three sections, which "generally takes about twenty minutes for a subject to fill out" (technical manual, p. 3). Personalysis could also be taken on-line via the website of the test publisher. For each item, a test taker has to choose between two descriptions related to work nature, work preference, or personality style. The first section is about "which do you like better, to work" (10 items). The second section is divided into three subsections (each subsection has 26 items), with the following instructions, "which type of work do you feel you should do," "in describing yourself, which words better fit your personality," and "most people feel under pressure when things go wrong, under intense stress, you tend to become," respectively. The third section (16 items) consists of another set of personality descriptions and a test taker is instructed to choose "which best describes you."

Completed test booklets must be sent to the test publisher to be scored. A test report is generated with test scores and narrative descriptions of a test taker's personality characteristics, and how they are expressed in organizational settings. The test report is to be interpreted by a trained facilitator through individual or workshop formats. A self-paced computerized "report guide" could also be used to assist test takers to explore and understand their test reports.

Personalysis measures personality styles in two major dimensions. The first dimension is Ego States. There are three Ego States, which are Rational, Socialized, or Instinctive. The second dimension is Primary Trait. There are four Primary Traits related to how energy and information are used. The four Primary Traits are named in terms of color. Red denotes highly focused energy but little use of conception. Blue denotes low physical energy, high mental energy, and high focus on information. Yellow denotes expanded energy and information, but used in unfocused manner. Green denotes contracted energy and information, in which both are conserved and stored. The three Ego States and four Primary Traits combination resulted in the 12 scales of the Personalysis.

Test scores for each of the 12 scales range from 0 (lowest intensity) to 6.0 (highest intensity). Each increment of test scores is set at .5, but the rationale for this arrangement is not given. The aggregate total of four trait scores for each Ego State is always 12.0, indicating that the distribution of higher intensity in one trait category would result in lower intensity in another trait category.

Within each Ego State, two traits (or colors) with the highest intensities are combined to form the so-called "color cluster." A color cluster is identified by summing the two highest color scores in an Ego State. The two scores have to be higher than 2.0, and the aggregate total has to be at least 6.5. The four colors resulted in six possible combinations, which are Red/Blue, Green/Yellow, Yellow/Blue, Red/Green, Yellow/Red, and Green/Blue. The six color clusters formed six basic personality traits, which are given the labels Individualism, Conformity, Divergence, Convergence, Extraversion, and Introversion. The interpretation of the color cluster is one of the major highlights of the interpretation.

The procedure and key to scoring are not given in the technical manual. It is not clear which items are used in computing different test scores. The technical manual indicates that Personalysis "is scored ipsatively and is related to norms developed by Personalysis Corporation as it works with its client companies" (technical manual, p. 3). However, it is not clear how individual ipsative scores are compared to the norms, and whether raw scores are transformed to standard scores. The size and characteristics of normative populations are not given.

DEVELOPMENT. According to the technical manual, Personalysis is theoretically anchored in conceptual constructs of Sigmund Freud, Carl Jung, and Eric Bernes. More specifically, the test was based on "Freud's multilayered understanding of consciousness" (technical manual, p. 1). The test was also strongly influenced by Jung's conception of psychological functions in relation to thinking/feeling, extroversion/introversion, and Bernes' view of personality structure. The three components of personality structure suggested by Bernes, which were Child, Parent, and Adult, were relabeled as Instinctive, Socialized, and Rational, respectively. The four color-coded Primary traits were influenced to some extent by Jung's conception of psychological functions.

There is no information on how items were developed, and how these items were written to reflect the theoretical constructs upon which the test was anchored. Also, there is no information on whether a scientific process was involved in selecting test items from an item pool.

TECHNICAL. Whereas the technical manual mentioned that normative reference is involved in generating scores, no information is given on the characteristics of norms. It is important for any credible psychological test to disclose to test users information regarding characteristics of the normative populations such that implications and limitations of test scores in the interpretation process could be delineated.

The technical manual reported a study on test-retest reliability of the instrument. Two versions of the tests (Form A and Form B) were given participants in a customer-service training program at two time points separated by 3 months. For Form A, in all of the three Ego States, the percentage of cases in which one of the top two colors identified in the pretest emerged also as one of the top two colors in the posttest ranged from 99 to 100. The percentage of cases in which the same two top colors emerged in both the pretest and posttest ranged from 56.1 to 63.3. Similarly, for Form B, the percentage of getting one of the top two pretest colors in the posttest ranged from 96.8 to 98.0, and the percentage of getting the same top two colors ranged from 54.1 to 72.4. Given the emphasis on the "color clusters," the above information suggested that between 30% to 40% of test takers were classified into a different color cluster in the posttest, which did not suggest a high degree of reliability.

There is no test-retest information on test scores. The technical manual stated that information about stability of test scores is less significant as long as there is reliability on the classification of types. There is no information on the internal consistency reliability of different scales.

Several studies examining the validity of scores from the Personalysis are reported in the technical manual. One was a study by Hamilton (1988) in which certain traits (blue socialized and yellow socialized) as measured by Personalysis were found to relate to organizational effectiveness among Navy OD consultants (N = 105). In another unpublished study, Johnson (1984) found that, among students in organizational effectiveness classes offered through the U.S. Navy (N = 144), a number of Personalysis personality dimensions (e.g., yellow socialized and blue socialized) were predictive of organizational effectiveness

measured by performance checklist scores and peer ratings. In a third study, members of a religious congregation were administered Personalysis, and were asked to indicate whether they "agreed" or "disagreed" with the test scores and descriptions. The percentage of participants who chose "agreed" ranged from 96 to 100. It was claimed that such evidence supported the validity of the instrument.

COMMENTARY. Personalysis is an instrument that is developed specifically for individuals in organizational settings. The colorful profiles and individualized reports are designed and structured to convey a professional image. However, in a number of ways, there is not yet sufficient evidence to support the reliability and validity of this "product." First, there is no clear evidence that test items were generated in a systematic manner. Similarly, there is no evidence that different personality scales were formed based on empirical findings (e.g., internal consistency reliability measures, factor-analytic and structural analysis). Second, test reports provide test takers with very specific comments about who they are, their strengths and areas needing improvement, and how they could move toward a level of peak performance. With evidence generated from only a few research studies conducted in the 1980s summarized above, the empirical foundation of these specific comments is quite weak. Third, there is no built-in safeguard against response sets that might influence the validity of a profile. The technical manual reported a small-scale study (N = 24) in which findings "strongly suggest that an individual is unlikely to consciously skew the Personalysis profile that meets the expectations of a prospective employer" (p. 49). Nevertheless, the empirical basis of such conclusion was not clearly explained. Fourth, without sufficient information about the normative population, it is hard to judge if the meanings and interpretation of test scores are valid.

Meanwhile, the technical manual was not comprehensive and informative. Considerable information key to understanding the quality of the instrument—including information about test item development, characteristics of norms, and how different scales were scored—was not given. The sections on reliability and validity were not written in a clear and concise manner. A good proportion of materials presented in these sections were actually taken word-by-word from Hamilton (1988) and Johnson (1984) without sufficient extrapolation on the meaning and implication of findings.

Theoretically, Personalysis conveniently blended concepts from Jung and Bernes. It is, however, not clear how Jung's personality functions influenced how traits and color clusters were defined. The theoretical framework is complex, with terms such as primary traits, personality traits, colors, color clusters, and ego states being used in different places. It is not clear why "colors," instead of descriptors that might convey meanings, are used to denote the personality traits.

SUMMARY. Personalysis is an instrument designed to help individuals in organizational settings to learn about their personality styles, and how these styles might impact their approach to managerial and interpersonal tasks. The test report provides test takers with extensive narrative feedback and suggestions. However, from a scientific perspective, Personalysis is not developed through a vigorous and systematic research process. At this point, there is not sufficient empirical evidence to support the reliability and validity of Personalysis. Test takers should use it cautiously and with reservations.

REVIEWER'S REFERENCES

Hamilton, E. E. (1988). The facilitation of organizational change: An empirical study of factors predicting change agents' effectiveness. *The Journal of Applied Behavioral Science, 24,* 37–59.

Johnson, C. A. (1984). *Personality characteristics of highly successful organizational effectiveness students.* Unpublished internal document, Personalysis Corporation.

[187]

Phonics-Based Reading Test.

Purpose: "Designed to assess reading skills" and "To measure an individual's ability to apply phonics concepts when reading single words and connected text."
Population: Ages 6-0 to 12-11.
Publication Date: 2002.
Acronym: PRT.
Scores, 4: Decoding, Fluency, Comprehension, Total Reading Standard Score.
Administration: Individual.
Price Data, 2002: $82 per test kit including manual (109 pages), stimulus book, and 25 student test booklets; $25 per stimulus book; $27 per 25 student test booklets; $30 per manual.
Time: (20–30) minutes.
Comments: Norm- and criterion-referenced.
Author: Rick Brownell.
Publisher: Academic Therapy Publications.

Review of the Phonics-Based Reading Test by *KAREN MACKLER, School Psychologist, Lawrence Public Schools, Lawrence, NY:*

DESCRIPTION. The Phonics-Based Reading Test (PRT) is an individually administered reading test that takes approximately 15 to 20 minutes to administer and 10 minutes to score, once familiar with all the scoring grids. The test administration can be broken down into more than one session for younger students or for students with special needs. The age range assessed on this measure goes from 6 years through 12 years of age. The test can be administered by nonclinical staff with appropriate supervision and training.

The purpose of the PRT is to ascertain knowledge of a student's phonics skills and how the skills affect fluency and comprehension. This test provides both criterion-referenced scores, which are helpful in instructional planning, and normed scores, which are needed to determine if additional intervention is warranted.

The test is composed of two subtests. The Decoding subtest presents the student with a list of nonsense words. Words are grouped into 14 phonics clusters, consisting of five pseudowords following a specific pattern, such as short vowels, or multiple syllables. This format allows for information regarding mastery of a specific phonics concept. A composite score for the Decoding subtest may be obtained as well.

The Fluency and Comprehension subtest requires the student to read passages out loud and then answer five comprehension questions based on the passage read. The student is not permitted to refer back to the selection to answer the questions. Responses are either scored as correct or incorrect. The subtest is composed of eight passages that were specifically constructed for the development of this test. Each passage corresponds to a level of skill typically taught in a given grade, ranging from letter names and sounds in kindergarten to multisyllabic words typically taught in Grades 3 and 4. Each reading selection contains many words common to that level and includes words from the earlier, easier levels. The passages also contain sight words. Students are expected to read the paragraphs orally, so the examiner can track miscues and record the time taken to read through the paragraph. This process yields a rate and accuracy score for each selection. A composite of these scores results in a Fluency index score. A

Comprehension score may be computed based on the accuracy of responses to five open-ended questions following each passage. Performance on this section may indicate at what point a student begins to falter on more complex material, leading to dysfluency and subsequently poorer comprehension of text.

A Total Reading Score may be obtained by adding the Decoding Score to the Fluency and Comprehension scores, giving an overall picture of reading performance. Given a student's chronological age, raw scores can be converted to standard scores, percentile ranks, and age/grade equivalent scores. The manual also presents data for other derived scores such as NCEs, scaled scores, *T*-scores, and stanines.

DEVELOPMENT. Word lists and words included for reading selections were chosen based on a scope and sequence developed from supplemental phonics programs, basal reading programs, and professional resources. From the scope and sequence, decoding skills were grouped into eight levels that follow a hierarchical sequence of increasingly complex phonics skills. Both nonsense word lists and reading passages were constructed based on this hierarchy. Sentence length and complexity were also controlled throughout the passages. Comprehension questions are mostly literal in nature, and aim to find out if the student derived meaning from the text. Several revisions of the test were piloted over a 2-year period. The final form of the test was administered to 1,282 students from January 2001 through January 2002. The final standardization sample was based on 820 students taken from this pool of subjects.

TECHNICAL. The correlation of task difficulty to task order for the standardization sample on each of the three subtests was at least .99, indicating a strong relationship between task order and task difficulty. The Comprehension subtest scores at the upper ages indicated some evidence of ceiling effects, which might be expected given the literal content of the questions.

The final standardization sample was similar to the demographics of the United States. Students were chosen from 63 cities in 30 states. The remainder of the sample was used for validation studies. Students attended public, private, and parochial schools. The sample appears to be adequately diverse, and contains students with special needs. There were some categories of over- or underrepresentation, such as an overrepresentation of white students with highly educated parents.

Internal consistency reliability estimates were obtained using Cronbach's coefficient alpha. On the Decoding subtest, coefficients were consistently high for all age groups with the median reliability coefficient at .97. For the Fluency scores, coefficients ranged from .95 at the older ages up to .98 at age 10. Coefficients for the Comprehension scores were within the low .90s for the younger ages and lower at the 11- and 12-year-old ranges (.75 and .86). Total reading coefficients were very strong, ranging from .95 to .98, indicating a high level of homogeneity. Test-retest reliability was assessed on a sample of 37 students tested on average 20 days between administrations. Correlations ranged from .87 to .95, indicating that the test is stable over time. Standard score gains of 2 to almost 5 points were evidenced, which would be typical given the short time span between the two administrations, indicating a certain amount of practice effects.

Content validity appears high. Decoding, Fluency, and Comprehension are all major components so the reading process and tasks were aligned to a developmental scope and sequence.

Concurrent validity was assessed by correlating the PRT with other widely used reading tests. The Decoding subtest correlations ranged from .52 to .70 with a median of .66. Fluency correlations ranged from .60 to .87 with a median of .79 and Comprehension from .32 to .71 with a median of .58. Total reading scores correlated with the other tests from .61 to .83 with a median of .77. These correlations indicate that this test is measuring skills similar to those of the other tests, although it appears that tasks are not standard across measures.

Construct validity analysis reveals that PRT skills increase with chronological age. Subtest intercorrelations are high, ranging from .60 to .80, indicating that general reading skills account for the common variance between subtests. Performance on the PRT for individuals with lower intelligence levels was poorer than for those individuals with higher IQs. Correlations between the PRT and the Wechsler Intelligence Scale for Children (WISC-III) were low to moderate, with higher correlations found for the Verbal Scale scores. The PRT shows differences between students representing exceptional group membership, such as mental retardation, learning disability, and language delay.

COMMENTARY. The PRT is an easily administered measure to use when screening a student for possible intervention in the area of decoding. The Decoding subtest begins at the letter level and builds up in a hierarchical manner, giving the evaluator an opportunity to assess the point at which a breakdown in skills occurs. However, because there is no opportunity for the young or struggling student to feel success at reading a known sight word or two, it may set up a situation where the student stops trying. Use of the Fluency/Comprehension subtest might be problematic for struggling readers, as even the first passage has six sentences, containing words that may not be known at this level, such as "rug" and "got." There are no picture cues to assist a reader who is unsure about the content. For more accomplished readers, the comprehension subtest might be difficult because the passage is taken away, causing a student to rely on memory to answer the questions. Children with learning problems often have concomitant memory issues, and this task makes it difficult to differentiate between the two. Having the student read aloud is beneficial, as the evaluator can analyze miscues as part of the assessment, leading to better instructional planning. Although the scoring profile is full of important information, it appears difficult for an inexperienced evaluator to complete, which may lead to mistakes.

SUMMARY. The Phonics-Based Reading Test may have a place in a screening battery. It is a quickly administered measure, with many benefits, such as words presented in a hierarchical fashion, leading to take-off points for instruction. This would be helpful in assisting a teacher in planning phonics-based lessons. The test may not be sensitive enough for the young or struggling reader, as there are few opportunities for demonstrating predecoding skills, such as matching picture to word, or using sight words as a confidence builder. The fluency piece is a helpful addition, as fluency is most certainly an important indicator of reading success. The comprehension piece appears limited, due to the limited scope of questions, and the difficulty in differentiating between comprehension and auditory memory. Practitioners might want to use this measure as part of a screening process when considering further evaluation or assessment.

Review of the Phonics-Based Reading Test by ANNITA MARIE WARD, *Associate Professor of Education and TESL, Salem International University, Salem, WV:*

DESCRIPTION. The Phonics-Based Reading Test (PRT) is an individually administered reading test for which the purpose is to test reading skills of children within the age range of 6 years, 0 months, through 12 years, 11 months.

There are two parts to the test: Part 1, Decoding Task, consists of a list of 70 nonsense words that test examinees read, using their knowledge of phonics to figure out how to pronounce each word. Words are grouped together to test a specific phonics skill or generalization, starting with Names of Letters (five stimulus letters offered) and moving through more complex skills to end with difficult words containing such syllables as *tion* and *ture*. Part 2, Comprehension and Fluency Task, consists of eight reading passages about which test-takers are asked comprehension questions. Each of these passages focuses on a specific set of phonics skills and as the test-taker progresses through the passages, each passage is supposed to present more of a challenge to decoding skills than did previous ones. Task 1 yields a Decoding score and Task 2 yields a Comprehension score and a Fluency score. These scores totalled yield a Total Reading score.

The test can be administered by classroom teachers and others who are not specifically training in educational testing, but administrators must follow procedures outlined in the test manual and should have several trial administrations before giving the test to an actual examinee. Administration time for the test is about 15 to 20 minutes with about 10 additional minutes required to score the test.

In administering the Decoding task (Part 1), the examiner must do critical range testing in order to determine where students should begin reading from the list of 70 words. In fact, everyone begins reading with Word 11 (within the Short Vowels section) but examinees who miss any of the 5 words that illustrate the short vowel generalization must go back to the beginning of the 70-word list and read the five items in the Letter Names section and the five items in the Letter Sounds section. Once the examinee has read the 5 nonsense words that illustrate the short vowel generalization or the five items for testing letter sounds, then the examinee moves on to Word 14, which is in the groups of words that illustrate long vowel generalizations. Other vowel skills and generalizations illustrated by the nonsense words are consonant blends, consonant digraphs, controlled-r, variant vowel pairs, diphthongs, silent letters, spelling patterns, inflectional endings, multiple syllables, and difficult words.

Examinees go through the list of 70 words, pronouncing the five items that illustrate each of the phonics skills. Although examinees pronounce nonsense words from a stimulus list, examiners mark items missed in a test booklet. Examinees may stop reading when they have mispronounced at least 4 nonsense words in two consecutive lists.

When test-takers have completed Part 1, Decoding Task, they move on to the second task. On this particular task children under age 8 begin the test by reading aloud the first passage from the stimulus booklet whereas examinees over age 8 begin reading the third passage. When the examinee begins reading, the test administrator sets a timer and while the examinee is reading, the administrator marks in the test booklet words the student has incorrectly decoded. After readers finish reading each passage, they are asked five very literal comprehension questions. The examiner asks these questions orally and students are not allowed to look back in the story to find answers.

In scoring results, administrators enter information on three charts in the test booklet, the Phonics Performance Evaluation Chart, the Reading Skills Performance Summary, and Words Correct Per Minute Calculations. From Information entered, test administrators use a chart found on the bottom of page 5 of the test booklet to determine if the student's score in each area puts the student's performance at the frustration, instructional, or mastery level. Using tables found in the testing manual, administrators can convert raw scores entered on the Reading Skills Performance Summary chart to age equivalent and grade equivalent scores. Total Reading Scores can be converted to percentile ranks.

DEVELOPMENT. The PRT was developed over a 2-year period during which several versions of it were developed and piloted. A final version of the test was given to 1,282 participants between January 2001 and January 2002.

In developing the test, Academic Therapy Publications examined various phonics programs, reading programs, and professional references to determine the scope and sequence for the introduction and instruction of phonics skills. Eight levels of phonics skills were identified; Levels 1 through 5 were skills taught in Grade 1; Levels 6 through 8 were skills taught in Grades 2 and 3.

Task 1, Decoding Task, was developed as a single word task to test students' ability to use phonics generalization to pronounce new words. For Task 2, Comprehension and Fluency Task, eight passages, one for each level of the phonics skills levels, were created. Each passage contains at least 10 words that illustrated the phonics generalization being tested at that particular level. In each passage all other words, besides those 10 illustrating the generalization being tested, illustrate phonics generalizations tested in previous passages or are sight words taken from a list of basic sight words.

TECHNICAL. In standardizing the test, test administrators at 78 sites in 30 states across the United States gave the PRT to 1,282 children from January 2001 to January 2002. From this group of test-takers, 820 were randomly chosen for inclusion in norm groups. The remaining examinees' scores were included in various validity samples.

Test developers calculated raw scores and from these developed standard scores, percentile ranks, and age and grade equivalencies. T-scores, scaled scores, and stanines were derived from standard scores, which were themselves derived using Angoff's method, which was offered in 1971.

In order to assess internal consistency, Cronbach's coefficient alpha was calculated for each subtest at each age level. All coefficients were .90 or above except for the Comprehension coefficients for 11- and 12-year-olds. Test-retest reliability was assessed by having the same examiner give the test twice to 37 examinees. Duration between first and second test administrations averaged 20 days. Corrected test-retest correlations ranged from .87 to .95. Standard score gains obtained between the first and second test administrations ranged from 2.10 to 4.65. According to the Phonics-Based Reading Test manual, such gains can be attributed to practice effect.

Developers of the PRT believe the content validity of the test was documented by their review of supplemental phonics programs, basal reading texts, and professional sources in order to establish the scope and sequence for teaching and development of phonics skills. The final series of tasks on the test are the result of 2 years of pilot studies on a test developed based on these initial reviews of scope and sequence of phonics skills.

Criterion-related validity was examined through concurrent validity testing relating test scores on the PRT to examinees' scores on other tests, such as the Stanford Achievement Test, Ninth Edition (SAT-9), the Wechsler Individual Achievement Test (WIAT), and the GATES. Correlations between PRT Total Reading scores and composite scores on such tests ranged from .61 for WIAT to .83 on CTBS/TerraNova Reading Comprehension. Criterion-related validity was also assessed by correlating teachers' assessment of students' reading ability to each score obtained on the PRT. These correlations ranged from .57 on the Comprehension score to .71 for the Total Reading and Fluency score.

Internal correlations were examined to judge construct validity. These ranged from a correlation of .60 between the Comprehension score and Decoding score to a correlation of .94 between the Total Reading Score and Fluency.

COMMENTARY. According to the Phonics-Based Reading Test manual, the PRT was developed "to assess reading skills in students aged 6 to 12" (p. 5). However, page 50 of the same manual explains that the PRT "was developed to evaluate a student's reading level relative to his or her ability to use phonics decoding skills."

In fact, the purpose stated on page 5 of the manual is a comprehensive view of the process of reading and that stated on page 50 is a reductive view of reading. The PRT does reduce reading to what is mainly a decoding activity, and, therefore, the true purpose of the test is stated on page 50 of the manual. The testing manual (p. 10) admits that there are many aspects of reading, such as knowledge, vocabulary, reasoning, and metacognitive strategies, which the PRT does not assess.

What is more, one has to wonder how much of what is assessed by the PRT is actually related to real reading tasks, and, thus, how useful a score from the PRT would be for predicting reading success. Although the test developers claim that correlations of .61 to .83 between scores on the PRT and other reading tests indicate "moderate to high" relationships, it seems more accurate to say such correlations are low to moderate. No task on the PRT corresponds to a real reading task that students might find in their classroom or in the everyday world. Whether one sees reading as "getting" meaning or as "constructing" meaning, the reading process always involves meaning. A word list, such as the one offered in Task 1 of the PRT, which has no real words on it, is not really a reading task as one cannot derive meaning from a list of nonsense words. Very short passages that include no more than 75 words and that have been written to test knowledge of phonics generalizations, rather than to convey meaning, are not terribly useful in assessing reading problems that may result from limited background knowledge or from problems associated with information processing. What is more, by orally asking the examinees reading comprehension questions, the examiner has the possibility of mistaking problems with auditory processing or other listening comprehension problems as reading comprehension problems. As test administrators are cautioned not to allow students to look back in the text to find answers to comprehension questions, the comprehension task is a memory and listening task, not a reading task.

Finally, the best that can be said about the grade equivalent and age equivalent scores for the PRT is that they represent grade equivalent and age equivalent scores for phonics skills, not reading skills. It is important to remember that phonics is a useful tool for some people as they learn to read. However, phonics skills and reading skills are not equivalent. It is obvious that some people could have phonics skills equivalent for their age group, but still be poor readers. It is also possible that some people who rely on visual cues and background knowledge when reading, rather than on auditory cues, might be better readers than a score on this test would indicate.

The only real uses for the PRT would be, first of all, to identify phonics skills that a particular examinee may not have developed. (This identification is almost always done by early childhood teachers and early elementary teachers without the need of standardized tests.) Second, the test might be administered before and after students participate in a phonics development program in order to assess prior knowledge and developed knowledge.

Aside from judgment about phonics, it would be very dangerous to make any other judgments about reading skills based on results from the PRT.

SUMMARY. Developers of the PRT have provided an inexpensive, easy-to-administer test that is accompanied by a very well-written, easy-to-follow testing manual. They have also provided extensive tables, charts, and statistics to indicate various aspects of the validity and reliability of the test.

However, the underlying ideas for this test make it somewhat limited as either a diagnostic tool for many struggling readers or as a tool for evaluating learners' reading performance or for assessing reading programs' effectiveness. This is because it is wrong to equate reading skills to phonics skills as reading *always* involves meaning. What is more, the Fluency score on this test is tied to the underlying idea of testing phonics skills. Automatic recognition of words is essential to fluency and that involves not only knowledge of phonics generalizations, but also a well-developed sight vocabulary as well as application of linguistic knowledge and of background knowledge.

[188]

Piers-Harris Children's Self-Concept Scale, Second Edition (The Way I Feel About Myself).

Purpose: Designed to aid in the "assessment of self-concept in children and adolescents."
Population: Ages 7–18.
Publication Dates: 1969–2002.
Acronym: Piers-Harris 2.
Scores, 7: Behavioral Adjustment, Intellectual and School Status, Physical Appearance and Attributes, Freedom From Anxiety, Popularity, Happiness and Satisfaction, Total.
Administration: Group or individual.
Price Data, 2004: $105 per complete kit including 20 AutoScore™ answer forms, manual (2002, 135 pages), 2-Use Disk (PC with Windows) and 2 PC answer sheets; $38.50 per 20 AutoScore™ answer forms; $55 per manual; $15.95 per 20 Spanish answer forms; $17.50 per mail-in answer sheet; $260 per 25-Use Disk (PC with Windows); $15 per 100 PC answer sheets; $10 per fax scoring.
Foreign Language Edition: Spanish answer forms available.
Time: (10–15) minutes.
Authors: Ellen V. Piers (test and manual), David S. Herzberg (test and manual), and Dale B. Harris (test).
Publisher: Western Psychological Services.
Cross References: See T5:1991 (108 references) and T4:2030 (123 references); for reviews by Jayne H. Epstein and Patrick J. Jeske of an earlier edition, see 9:960 (38 references); see also T3:1831 (107 references), 8:646 (95 references); and T2:1326 (10 references); for a review by Peter M. Bentler of an earlier edition, see 7:124 (8 references).

Review of the Piers-Harris Children's Self-Concept Scale, Second Edition (The Way I Feel About Myself) by MARY LOU KELLEY, Professor of Psychology, Louisiana State University, Baton Rouge, LA:

DESCRIPTION. The Piers-Harris Children's Self-Concept Scale, Second Edition (Piers-Harris 2) is a 60-item questionnaire, subtitled The Way I Feel About Myself. The Piers-Harris 2 is a self-report measure for children and adolescents age 7–18. Respondents indicate whether each item is true or not true of them. The items are very easy to read and interpret. English and Spanish versions are available. The Piers-Harris 2 is a revision of the previous, identically titled questionnaire and contains the same Self-Concept and Validity scales. Specifically, the scales consist of a total (TOT) score and six domain and two validity scales. The domain scales assess self-concept across a variety of areas including perceptions about school and intellectual functioning, appearance, and social acceptance. The self-concept scales are scored so that higher scores indicate more positive self-evaluation. The validity scales assess response bias, inconsistent responding, and exaggerated responding.

Several methods of scoring are available in this revised edition. These include the AutoScore™, which is scored manually with the use of carbons, mail/fax-in forms, and a PC program that generates a report based on online or offline administration. Raw scores are converted to standard scores (normalized *T*-scores, percentile ranks). Scoring using the AutoScore™ is very straightforward and easily accomplished by someone with minimal training. The authors warn, however, that interpretation and use of the scores should only be conducted by someone trained in psychological assessment. Norms are based on the total standardization sample and are not broken down according to respondent age, gender, or ethnicity. The authors state that ethnicity did not appear to be a moderating variable in any of their analyses.

The technical manual is well written and clearly describes the measure and its development, scoring procedures, and psychometric studies. Instructions for calculating scores for the validity scales and high/low domain scores were quite clear and examples were provided. The authors presented several case examples illustrating how the scores were useful for screening and as a part of a psychological evaluation. The authors describe precisely how the current instrument differs from the previous version, which is important for those who use the instrument in research contexts. The various chapters are short yet adequately detailed.

The technical manual describes various approaches to reducing respondent bias and provides suggested oral instructions as well as cautions against use of the word "test" when describing the scale to children.

DEVELOPMENT. The Piers-Harris 2 is a revision of a measure originally developed in the early 1960s and revised in 1984. The current version is an improvement over earlier versions in three important ways. First, the items were updated and trimmed from 80 on the earlier version to 60. An item was eliminated if it contributed only to the total and not to domain score, contained outdated or gender-specific content, or required additional information to answer. Thus, the current version is more contemporary, less ambiguous, and less time-consuming to complete. Second and perhaps of most importance, the scale has been standardized on a national sample in contrast to the use of a homogeneous, rural sample collected in the 1960s. The current sample consists of 1,387 students aged 7 to 18 recruited from school systems across the nation. The use of a heterogeneous sample addresses one of the most significant limitations cited in a previous *MMY* review (Epstein, 1985). The third change in the Piers-Harris 2 cited by the authors is the availability of computer scoring.

TECHNICAL. Descriptions of the restandardization were clear and adequately detailed. The authors assessed whether age, gender, socioeconomic status, and ethnicity produced different norms. The results indicated that significant differences in scores were not obtained for any of these variables in almost all cases, although the authors indicated that further research on potential moderating effects of demographics should be pursued.

With regard to reliability, internal consistency estimates for the total and domain scores were adequate with almost all Cronbach alphas being above .70. Test-retest reliability studies were not conducted with the new standardization data but studies using the earlier scale were acceptable.

The validity of scores from the Piers-Harris 2 was evaluated in a number of ways. The authors examined content validity using a judge's ratings

as to whether the deleted items continue to be represented by the remaining items of each domain. The rating process was not described and thus, exactly what was judged is uncertain. Construct validity was assessed via factor analysis and generally supported the rationally generated domains. However, findings across studies are somewhat inconsistent according to the authors.

The convergent validity of the Piers-Harris was assessed by evaluating self-concept scores with various other psychological measures. Generally, studies show that positive self-concept is inversely related to measures of psychological problems. Overall, studies suggest that the Piers-Harris has support for the validity of the instrument although the majority of studies were conducted with the original version of the scale. The authors aptly note that additional studies on the reliability and validity of the Piers-Harris 2 are needed.

COMMENTARY. The Piers-Harris is one of the best if not *the* best questionnaire of its type, given the long history of research findings supporting the reliability and validity of the scale. It is very easy for children to use and probably is best used as a screening instrument as illustrated in the case examples described in the technical manual.

SUMMARY. The Piers-Harris 2 is a revision of a previous scale that is well known and well researched. The revised scale is an improvement over the previous scale in several ways. The scale was renormed using a relatively large, demographically and geographically diverse sample. The scale was shortened, eliminating ambiguous, outdated, and psychometrically limited items. Finally, the scale can be computer scored. However, the scale retained many of the positive features of the original scale. The items are straightforward and require a yes or no endorsement. The questionnaire is easy to score and the manual is clear and straightforward. Numerous psychometric studies support the reliability and validity of the earlier version but additional studies are needed using the revised scale.

REVIEWER'S REFERENCE

Epstein, J. H. (1985). [Review of the Piers-Harris Children's Self-Concept Scale (The Way I Feel About Myself).] In J. V. Mitchell, Jr. (Ed.), *The ninth mental measurements yearbook*, (pp. 1167–1169). Lincoln, NE: Buros Institute of Mental Measurements.

Review of the Piers-Harris Children's Self-Concept Scale, Second Edition (The Way I Feel About Myself) by DONALD P. OSWALD, Associate Professor of Psychiatry and Psychology, Virginia Commonwealth University, Richmond, VA:

DESCRIPTION. The Piers-Harris Children's Self-Concept Scale, Second Edition (The Way I Feel About Myself) (Piers-Harris 2) is a 60-item self-report scale designed for the assessment of self-concept in children and adolescents. The scale is designed for children ages 7 to 18 who are able to read and comprehend at a second grade level. The scale can be completed by most respondents in 10-15 minutes. The instrument may be administered in an individual or group format and can be administered and scored by teachers or paraprofessionals; however, interpretation of results should be provided by "a professional with appropriate training in psychological assessment" (manual, p. 4).

The Piers-Harris 2 is a revision of The Piers-Harris Children's Self-Concept Scale, a self-concept scale originally constructed in the 1960s. The instrument has been shortened from the original 80 items to reduce administration time and to eliminate items that included outdated language or were of less value psychometrically. In most respects, however, the Piers-Harris 2 preserves the character and content of the original version. Like the original, the instrument yields a total score and six domain scale scores, originally constructed on the basis of a factor analytic study (Piers, 1963). The items included in the domain scales are virtually identical; two domain scales lost two items from the original instrument and one domain scale lost one item. One original domain scale, "Anxiety" has been renamed "Freedom from Anxiety" to more accurately reflect the direction of scores, and the scale originally called "Behavior" has been given the more descriptive name: "Behavioral Adjustment." The remaining domain scale names are unchanged (i.e., Intellectual and School Status, Physical Appearance and Attributes, Popularity, and Happiness and Satisfaction). The second edition of the instrument adds two validity scales (Inconsistent Responding and Response Bias) that are designed to detect random responding and excessive yea-saying or nay-saying.

The instrument may be administered using several alternative formats depending on the preferred scoring method. Scoring alternatives include an AutoScore Form that can be scored manually by the examiner, mail-in response forms that are computer scored by the publisher, and a personal computer program that generates a report based on responses keyed in by the respondent or by the examiner from a paper record form.

The Piers-Harris 2 includes a disk with a computerized scoring program that allows the user to complete and score two administrations of the instrument. The program requires activation via phone or the internet. The program is easily installed and produces a score report, including a table and graph of total and domain scores, and a narrative describing the scores.

The Total score and all domain scale scores are calculated as T-scores (mean = 50; SD = 10) and the "normal" range is considered to be between 40 and 60. The profile sheet for the AutoScore form also provides percentile equivalents for all T-Scores.

The manual provides a thorough discussion of the interpretation of validity and self-concept scores as well as a summary of some of the relevant literature on the psychometrics of the original Piers-Harris. An appendix provides an extensive bibliography of studies that involved the original instrument.

TECHNICAL. The Piers-Harris 2 is essentially a restandardization of the instrument based on a national sample of 1,387 students recruited from school districts across the U.S. The sample was intended to match U.S. Census data but Hispanic/Latino students are substantially underrepresented as are students from the West region of the country. The sample is relatively evenly distributed across the age span of 7–18 years.

Some new psychometric studies accompany this revision. Internal consistency data for the total scale and the domain scales are provided at each age level; alpha coefficients range from .60 to .93. Interscale correlations among the domain scales are modest, ranging from .30 to .69; some of the higher correlations between domains may be attributed in part to shared items. As indications of convergent validity, the authors investigated relationships between Piers-Harris 2 scores and scores on measures of anger, aggressive attitudes, symptoms of Post-Traumatic-Stress Disorder, and thoughts and attitudes related to obesity. However, no new test-retest reliability studies or concurrent validity studies involving other self-concept instruments are presented in the manual.

The manual includes a thoughtful discussion of potential moderator variables that might affect scores on a test independently of the target construct, including age, sex, ethnicity, SES, geographic region, and intelligence/academic achievement. For each of these potential moderator variables (except intelligence/academic achievement, for which no data were available) the authors provide evidence of minimal moderating effects. As a consequence, all children's scores are derived from the same conversion table, regardless of age, sex, or ethnicity.

COMMENTARY. One criterion for judging a revision of an existing instrument is the extent to which the revision addresses the weaknesses that have been identified in the literature. Criticism of the original Piers-Harris over the years has included considerable emphasis on the limited nature of the standardization sample. This weakness has been substantially addressed in the Piers-Harris 2. The present standardization sample is drawn from a far more representative pool, although the underrepresentation of Hispanic/Latino students is unfortunate in view of the recent growth of the Latino population in the U.S. and the anticipated continued expansion of this minority group.

The original Piers-Harris was often criticized for the fact that the domain scales are not unique (i.e., there are many items that appear in more than one domain scale). The authors indicate that removing the overlapping items substantially lowered internal consistency of the domain scales and, as a result, they chose to retain them. The original instrument has also been criticized for inadequate test-retest reliability (Keith & Bracken, 1996); the failure to undertake new studies of test-retest reliability constitutes a weakness of the current revision.

Another recurring criticism of the original Piers-Harris has been that the instrument is fundamentally unidimensional. The current domain scales were derived from a factor analysis of the original Piers-Harris items; however, these domain scales have not been consistently replicated in succeeding factor analytic studies. Indeed, the literature is inconsistent regarding the factor structure of the scale to the point that the validity of the domain scales is called into question. The authors of the Piers-Harris 2 undertook a new factor analysis of the present scale and reported finding six factors that support the six domain scales. However, the correspondence between factors and domains is far from perfect and, for two of the domain scales (Physical Appearance and Attributes; and Happiness and Satisfaction), fewer than half of the items load on a single factor.

SUMMARY. The Piers-Harris 2 represents an incremental improvement on the original instrument by virtue of a more representative standardization sample and reduced administration time. However, the authors of the Piers-Harris 2 appear to have placed a high value on preserving continuity with the original instrument (e.g., keeping the domain scales virtually intact) and such continuity comes at a substantial price. The theoretical and empirical basis of the instrument has been subjected to considerable criticism over the past three decades and these critiques are not effectively addressed in the Piers-Harris 2. Much scholarly work has been done in the area of children's self-concept and there is now considerably more competition in the field of self-concept assessment. Given the alternatives available, the instrument may well be supplanted by another tool with a stronger theoretical and empirical basis.

REVIEWER'S REFERENCES

Keith, L. K., & Bracken, B. A. (1996). Self-concept instrumentation: A historical and evaluative review. In B. A. Bracken (Ed.), *Handbook of self-concept* (pp. 91-170). New York: John Wiley & Sons, Inc.
Piers, E. V. (1963). [Factor analysis for the Piers-Harris Children's Self-Concept Scale]. Unpublished raw data.

[189]
Polish Proficiency Test.

Purpose: "Designed to evaluate the level of proficiency in Polish attained by American and other English-speaking learners of Polish."
Population: Postsecondary to adult.
Publication Date: 1992.
Acronym: PPT.
Scores, 3: Listening Comprehension, Reading Comprehension, Structure.
Administration: Group.
Price Data, 2002: $25 per test; quantity discounts available.
Time: (150) minutes.
Comments: Machine-scorable.
Author: Center for Applied Linguistics.
Publisher: Center for Applied Linguistics.

Review of the Polish Proficiency Test by JACK GEBART-EAGLEMONT, President, International Institute for Personality Assessment and Therapy, Watsonia, Victoria, Australia:

DESCRIPTION. The Polish Proficiency Test (PPT) is a measure of general language proficiency in listening and reading in Polish attained by American and other English-speaking learners of this language. The authors indicate that the major focus of the test is "on assessing the examinee's ability to function in situations typical of real-life language use" (test interpretation manual, p. 1). The test covers proficiency levels from Novice High to Superior, following the national proficiency guidelines defined by the American Council on the Teaching of Foreign Languages. The above defined levels correspond to skills levels present at the end of the first year of study at the college level. The uses of the PPT include: testing for admission to a Polish study program, placement within a Polish study program, exemption from a Polish language requirement, application for a scholarship or an appointment, language competency testing, certification of Polish language proficiency for occupational purposes, and evaluation of Polish instructional programs.

The test consists of 135 items (4-option multiple choice). The response sheet is provided separately from the test booklet. The author of this review, as a native Polish speaker, would like to comment that some of the items are outdated and may therefore appear strange, considering rapid changes of the Polish society during the last two decades. The PPT contains three sections: Listening Comprehension (50 items), Reading Comprehension (50 items), and Structure (35 items). The Listening Comprehension's materials include a tape recording composed of text read by a single individual, samples of conversations between two speakers, and passages representing typical samples of news broadcasts, advertisements, and public announcements. The response sheet is machine-scorable. Testing time is defined as 2 hours: Listening Comprehension 40 minutes, Reading Comprehension 50 minutes, and Structure 30 minutes.

DEVELOPMENT. The Polish Proficiency Test was developed in a project funded through a grant from the U.S. Department of Education in 1992. The project was coordinated by the Division of Foreign Language Education and Testing of the Center for Applied Linguistics in Washington, DC. The development program utilized the collaboration of language scholars and teachers in the United States and Canada.

TECHNICAL. The normative data were initially based on a sample of 70 North American students studying Polish at the college level in a given year. The final norms were developed on the basis of responses of 129 examinees who participated in the field testing of the PPT. The quartile distribution is presented for each year (first, second, and third) and for each section of the test separately. Mean scores for each scale are also presented for each year of study.

Internal consistency reliability of the PPT was estimated using the Rasch equivalent of the KR-20 formula. The resulting reliability coefficients were high: Listening = .92, Reading = .90, and Structure = .88. The standard error estimates for each section were also very satisfactory (Listening = 6, Reading = 7, and Structure = 7).

Content validity was assessed by language experts following the requirements specified by the American Council on the Teaching of Foreign Languages, who confirmed that the PPT items have been drawn from real-life use of Polish language. Concurrent validity was assessed using the correlation coefficients between the PPT and the ratings on proficiency at the Foreign Service Institute (FSI) and at the Defense Language Institute. The scores obtained on the proficiency scale of the Interagency Language Roundtable (ILR) were used for this purpose. The correlations were as follows: PPT Listening and ILR Speaking, .78; PPT Reading and ILR Reading, .75; PPT Listening and ILR Listening, .58; PPT Reading and ILR Reading, .77. Concurrent validity of the Structure section was not sufficiently investigated, and the sample size was quite small (10). Construct validity was examined using the calculated percentages of misfitting items for each scale. The percentages were 6% for the Listening scale, 4% for the Reading Scale, and 14% for the Structure scale. The intercorrelations between the scales were high to very high (Listening and Reading, .84; Listening and Structure, .82; Reading and Structure, .92), which indicates a considerable conceptual homogeneity of the instrument and supports overall construct validity of the entire test.

COMMENTARY. The test materials submitted for this review are clear and easy to understand. The instructions are easy to follow. It would be advisable to update and amend some items from time to time, reflecting the changing social conditions and realities of the language and culture over time. The statistics concerning normative data are satisfactorily presented. The existing measures of reliability indicate a high degree of internal consistency. Test-retest reliability indices were not presented, but it is not absolutely necessary because the practice effect would somehow contaminate the indices and would be difficult to correct for, considering the skill-type nature of the items involved. The indices of Content Validity, Concurrent Validity, and Construct Validity are satisfactory to excellent.

SUMMARY. The PPT should be considered a psychometrically sound test as it meets the psychometric requirements for an instrument used for the defined purposes, such as educational assessment, selection, and skill evaluation. The authors should be encouraged to update the items systematically. The systematic continuation and expansion of the statistical investigation of the test is also advisable, considering the fact that the initial sample sizes were quite small. Because the Structure section demonstrates a slightly lower internal consistency coefficient, a higher percentage of misfitting items, and at the same time contains significantly fewer items, it would be advisable to expand this section, probably to 50 items, which could be then comparable with the size of other sections and may improve its reliability coefficient. More sophisticated assessment methods of reliability could also be applied, in order to assess the precise contribution of each item to the overall reliability of the scale. Such a step would also greatly facilitate the potential improvement and correction of the misfitting items. Some additional testing of validity of this section is also needed. The overall standard of presentation of test materials submitted for this review was very high.

[190]
Postpartum Depression Screening Scale.
Purpose: Designed to assess the presence, severity, and type of postpartum depression symptoms.
Population: New mothers ages 14–49.
Publication Date: 2002.
Acronym: PDSS.
Scores, 10: Inconsistent Responding Index, Sleeping/Eating Disturbances, Anxiety/Insecurity, Emotional Lability, Mental Confusion, Loss of Self, Guilt/Shame, Suicidal Thoughts, Short Total Score, Total Score.
Administration: Group.
Price Data, 2005: $72.50 per kit including manual (59 pages) and 25 AutoScore™ test forms; $32.50 per 25 AutoScore™ test forms; $45 per manual; $17.50 per 10 test forms in Spanish.
Time: (5–10) minutes; (1–2) minutes for short form.
Comments: May be orally administered; allows for detection of women in need of psychiatric evaluation; short form consists of just 7 items and yields a short total score.

Authors: Cheryl Tatano Beck and Robert K. Gable.
Publisher: Western Psychological Services.

Review of the Postpartum Depression Screening Scale by PAUL A. ARBISI, Staff Clinical Psychologist, Minneapolis VA Medical Center, and Associate Professor, Department of Psychiatry, University of Minnesota, Minneapolis, MN:

DESCRIPTION. The Postpartum Depression Screening Scale (PDSS) is a 35-item instrument designed to identify women who are at risk for developing postpartum depression (PPD). Embedded in the full version of the PDSS is a PDSS short form consisting of the first 7 items on the PDSS questionnaire. The short form identifies women who are in need of referral for psychiatric evaluations, but does not provide information regarding content areas. The PDSS has recently been made available in a Spanish-language version for use with Hispanic groups in the United States (Beck & Gable, 2003). The PDSS is a self-report, paper-and-pencil instrument that contains a single validity scale to assess inconsistent or random responding composed of 10 item pairs that if endorsed in opposite directions represent an inconsistent response set and seven symptom content scales: Sleeping/Eating Disturbances (5 items); Anxiety/Insecurity (5 items); Emotional Liability (5 items); Mental Confusion (5 items); Loss of Self (5 items); Guilt/Shame (5 items); and Suicidal Thoughts (5 items). The items are scored on a 5-point Likert scale anchored between *Strongly Disagree* and *Strongly Agree.*

Administration for the short form takes between 1 and 2 minutes and for the full form 5 to 10 minutes. The respondent's answers are transferred by carbon paper to the corresponding values on the scoring worksheet. Using the worksheet, the examiner calculates the validity scores and raw scores for the total and symptom content scores and transfers the scores to the summary sheet. The summary sheet provides interpretive guidelines for the total score and for the symptom content scores. The interpretive guidelines are based on analyses of a developmental sample ($n = 525$) consisting of 463 new mothers recruited primarily from the Northeast and Midwest of the United States, and 62 women recruited through a postpartum support group, and a diagnostic sample ($n = 150$) that was recruited through childbirth classes and newspaper advertisements.

DEVELOPMENT. The PDSS was designed to be "a brief, easily administered, self-report inventory to assess the presence, severity, and type of postpartum depression" (manual, p. 1). Although instruments specifically designed for the assessment of general depression and PDD such as the Beck Depression Inventory II (BDI-II; T6:273) and the Edinburgh Postnatal Depression Scale (EPDS) are widely used and well-validated, the authors contend that the item content of the PDSS reflects the phenomenology of new motherhood and postpartum depression more specifically than the other instruments. The PDSS was developed through the first author's qualitative research on the subjective experience of postpartum depression. A thematic content analysis of extensive clinical interviews with women suffering from PPD resulted in the identification of seven dimensions that reflect the symptomatology of PPD. Items were then written that mirrored the actual content of the clinical interviews within these seven dimensions. A panel of five experts in PPD then examined the candidate items. Of those experts, four had experienced PPD themselves. Items were also reviewed by a focus group consisting of 15 graduate students in nursing whose specialties were either obstetrics or psychiatry. Based on the responses of the experts and the focus group, some items were removed and replaced with more effectively worded items, new items were added, and editorial changes were made on the remaining items. This process resulted in a 56-item pilot version of the PDSS.

The psychometric properties of the items were examined in two separate samples. The first sample, designated the developmental sample, was described above and consisted of 525 women. A second sample, designated the diagnostic sample, consisted of 150 women recruited through prenatal childbirth classes and newspaper advertisement. These women were administered a number of self-report instruments (PDSS, EPDS, BDI-II) and the Structured Clinical Interview for DSM-IV Axis I Disorders (SCID). All of the coefficient alphas for the content scales from the 56-item version were above .75 and a decision was made to delete items from each scale to achieve a briefer version of the instrument. Thus, 3 items were deleted from each content scale to reach the final version of the PDSS based on the content of the item and the impact of removal of the item on the item total correlations for each content scale.

TECHNICAL. The PDSS total score and content scales display good to excellent internal consistencies across both samples (total score alpha for the developmental sample was .97 and for the diagnostic sample .96; range for content scales was .80 to .94). The content scales are all relatively highly intercorrelated with the exception of suicidal thoughts. This is reflected in the exploratory factor analysis that yielded seven factors with a large first factor representing a component of general emotional distress that correlated with items from the Mental Confusion and Loss of Self and, to a lesser extent, the Emotional Liability content scales. Confirmatory factor analysis was supportive of the seven-factor model and reflects the seven content scales.

The cutoff for the PDSS total score was established by examining the area under the Receiver Operating Characteristic Curves for screening the women in the diagnostic sample for major postpartum depression. The cutoffs for the symptom content scores were established in a somewhat more arbitrary manner by designating it as a standard deviation above the mean raw score for each content scale in the diagnostic sample with the exception of the Suicidal Thoughts scale where any score above the minimum possible score (5) was considered significant. There were no predictive validity studies reported in the manual to support the selection of these decision rules. The concurrent validity evidence of the PDSS appears to be quite good and comparable to the EPDS in detecting major postpartum depression in the diagnostic sample. Further, in a recent independent study conducted in Australia, the PDSS and the EPDS both identified the same women who were experiencing depression at an 8-week postpartum health visit (Hanna, Jarman, & Savage, 2004).

COMMENTARY. The PDSS represents an admirable integration of contemporary psychometric techniques and procedures in the development of a relatively short self-report instrument that can be used for screening women for postpartum depression. The manual is exceptionally well-written and provides information related to the development of the instrument as well as the psychometric properties and performance of the PDSS. For example, the authors provide information regarding the incremental validity of the PDSS (relative improvement in prediction of structured interview defined depression diagnosis) above other more established instruments. Further, the manual provides antecedent probabilities for prediction of DSM-IV Major Depressive Disorder at various cut scores. Of particular utility to the clinician is presentation of Positive Predictive Power and Negative Predictive Power rather than simply Sensitivity and Specificity at each cutoff score. This allows the clinician to determine the trade-off between errors of omission (failing to detect a depressed mother) or errors of commission (labeling a mother as depressed who is not in fact depressed) at various cutoff scores. The reported parameters are fairly impressive given the base rate in the sample of between 12% for MDD (Major Depressive Disorder) and 31% for both MDD and Depression NOS (Not Otherwise Specified). The manual provides detailed instructions for interpretation of the PDSS and presents case examples that are well described and useful in illustrating the interpretive process. A question that is not addressed in the manual is to what extent the PDSS is a selective measure of postpartum depression as claimed by the authors and not another measure of general distress or demoralization? In other words, how good is the discriminant validity of the PDSS? Can the PDSS distinguish between postpartum depression and other forms of affective disturbance such as a generalized anxiety disorder or panic disorder better than the BDI-II or the EPDS or would the PDSS simply identify women in the general population who have not recently given birth but who are generally upset?

SUMMARY. The PDSS is a 35-item tool to be used for screening women at least 2 weeks after giving birth for major postpartum depression. Interpretation of the PDSS is straightforward and facilitated by the scoring sheet. The manual is well written and easily followed. It contains sufficient psychometric information and validity data to allow the reader to evaluate the utility of the instrument and provides a refreshingly sophisticated presentation of the incremental validity of the PDSS and classification accuracy of the instrument. Further, the authors do not make unsubstantiated claims and caution against reliance on the shorter, less reliable content scales or single items in decision making or interpretation. The PDSS demonstrates a strong relationship between other measures of general depression and postpartum depression both in the validation study presented in the manual and also in a recent study

conducted independent of the scale's authors. The discriminant validity of the PDSS has not been established. However, if the sole clinical purpose of the PDSS is to identify women who are in need of further psychiatric/psychological evaluation and services, then the PDSS is certainly a reasonable choice based on the available data.

REVIEWER'S REFERENCES

Beck, C. T., & Gable, R. K. (2003). Postpartum depression screening scale: Spanish version. *Nursing Research, 52*(5), 296–306.

Hanna, B., Jarman, H., & Savage, S. (2004). The clinical application of three screening tools for recognizing postpartum depression. *International Journal of Nursing Practice, 10*(2), 72–79.

Review of the Postpartum Depression Screening Scale by DELORES D. WALCOTT, Associate Professor, Counseling and Testing Center, Western Michigan University, Kalamazoo, MI:

DESCRIPTION. The Postpartum Depression Screening Scale (PDSS) is a 35-item self-report inventory that can be administered either by paper and pencil or orally. The PDSS was designed to assess the presence, severity, and type of postpartum depression symptoms. The scale is also used to determine if the respondent needs to be referred for additional diagnostic evaluation and provides a description of the individuals' symptoms, which helps to facilitate the development of a treatment plan. The 5-point Likert-type response scale items consist of statements about how a mother feels after the birth of her child. The PDSS was developed for new mothers ages 14–49 who can read and comprehend at the third grade level or higher. If the respondent's reading is not adequate for the task, the test administrator can choose to read the test items out loud. The PDSS can be completed in 5 to 10 minutes. The short form, which takes 1 to 2 minutes to complete, consists of 7 items and yields a short total score. However, as indicated in the manual, the short form does not screen for individual symptoms. The PDSS provides content scales for seven symptom areas: Sleeping/Eating Disturbance, Anxiety/Insecurity, Emotional Lability, Mental Confusion, Loss of Self, Guilt/Shame, and Suicidal Thoughts. The screening scale also includes an Inconsistent Responding (INC) index to screen for response validity. The PDSS yields a separate score for each of the seven scales, and the manual provides guidelines for interpreting elevated scales. The PDSS can be used in both clinical and research settings. The PDSS manual suggests that health care professionals such as those in obstetrics, pediatrics, and psychiatry can use the PDSS to screen the mother for postpartum depression.

According to a separate insert provided by the authors, the PDSS should be administered to the new mother no earlier than 2 weeks postpartum. In addition, the PDSS is not appropriate for use during pregnancy. It was designed specifically to assess depression in the context of new motherhood. The administration and interpretation of the PDSS requires the utilization of the AutoScore Form. The respondent is asked to complete the demographics on the front side and then read the directions for the PDSS on the back of the form. The PDSS Summary Sheet is detached from the AutoScore Form before administration. The testing environment should be quiet, free from distractions, and allow for privacy.

DEVELOPMENT. The PDSS was developed specifically by the authors to address a major public health problem that affects mothers in the United States. Beck and Gable report that 10% to 15% of new mothers (up to 400,000) experience reported symptoms of PDSS. However, despite the high incidence of postpartum depression researchers found that as many as 50% of all cases go undetected. Postpartum depression is treatable, but only when women are identified, creating the need for an assessment instrument. Extensive research, conducted by the first author and others, has shown that living with and being socialized by a depressed mother may harm a child's development. Furthermore, children of depressed mothers appear to have more behavior problems and poorer cognitive functioning, creating a need for intervention.

The PDSS is based on a series of research studies that included the first author's subjective assessment of postpartum depression in women. These studies were based on clinical interviews with women who were suffering from postpartum depression. In generating items for the PDSS, the phenomenological flavor of these women's experiences was captured. A thematic content analysis of the clinical interview was carried out and led to the identification of seven dimensions of symptomatology. The seven symptom dimensions served as the organizing principles for the creation of pilot items. Five experts who were experienced with this mood disorder and 15 graduate students in nursing (obstetrics or psychiatry) who comprised a focus group were provided with the conceptual basis for the PDSS and an operational definition.

This group was asked to rate how well each item fit the symptom dimension to which it had been assigned. It should be noted that background information, on the experts and the graduate students regarding their ethnic, cultural and socioeconomic status, was not provided. The mean rating of fit ranged from 4.00 to 5.00 for the experts and from 3.73 to 5.00 for the student focus group. This process resulted in the creation of a 56-item pilot version. The pilot version was then employed in two studies to standardize the measure and establish the psychometric properties.

TECHNICAL. The development sample for the PDSS consists of 525 women; 463 were new mothers recruited from seven data collection sites located in Connecticut, Massachusetts, Rhode Island, New Jersey, Ohio, and Indiana. These data collection sites included several obstetrics offices, a large public hospital, and an organization providing in-home clinical services to women in a low socioeconomic status. An additional group of 62 women was recruited through Postpartum Support International (PSI), an organization that disseminates information. The mean age of the sample was 27.6. The predominant race/ethnic groups were White (79%), Black (11%), Hispanic (7%), and Asian American (less than 1%). The development sample was slightly skewed toward more highly educated individuals. Thirty-seven percent had high school education or less and the remaining 63% had some college. Nineteen percent reported a history of depression prior to their most recent depression. Participants were 8 weeks postpartum when they completed the PDSS.

The diagnostic sample was used to provide reliability and validity evidence of the PDSS and determine the cutoff scores for use in screening postpartum depression. The diagnostic sample was recruited from a childbirth class in the northeast region and through newspaper advertisements. Details regarding population who received advertisements were not provided in the manual. The participants met the following inclusion criteria: 18 years of age or older; able to speak and read English; between 2–12 weeks postpartum; had delivered a live, healthy infant; and had no history of diagnosable depression during pregnancy. Each mother completed three self-reported depression inventories in random order: the PDSS, the Edinburgh Postnatal Depression Scale (EPDS), and the Beck Depression Inventory-II (BDI-II).

Each mother was also interviewed using the Structured Clinical Interview for DSM-IV Axis I Disorder. Reportedly, the interviewers were blind to scores on depression questionnaires.

This group consisted of 150 women, 122 recruited through prenatal classes and 28 recruited through the newspaper advertisements. The mean age was 31.2 years. The women were predominantly White (87%) and married (89%). The sample was skewed towards highly educated women, with 80% having a college degree or higher and 27% having a master's degree. Seventeen percent of the participants reported a previous history of depression. At the time of the study these women were 5.5 weeks postpartum.

Reliability estimates were obtained by Cronbach's alpha and item analysis. Reportedly, reliabilities on each subscale were calculated for the 35-item development sample of the PDSS using the development sample data. Excellent internal consistency values for the final version are presented with an alpha coefficient of .97 for the Total score and coefficients ranging from .83 to .94 for the seven symptom content scales. The diagnostic sample alpha PDSS Total Score yielded an alpha coefficient of .96 with the content scale alphas ranging from .80–.91. Reportedly, a measure of an emotional construct should have a minimum coefficient alpha of .70. As noted the PDSS exceeds the acceptable range. Furthermore, the individual items in the final item set have moderate to high correlation with their respective content scales.

The content validity of the PDSS was demonstrated by means of two expert rater studies; where experts, in the area of postpartum depression, rated the extent to which the PDSS pilot items correctly described the symptoms content of this disorder. Criterion validity was used in relation to a structured diagnostic interview and two self-reported depression inventories. Construct validity of the PDSS was examined to look at the interrelatedness among the scales. The interscale correlation coefficients for both reference samples (diagnostic and development) correlate from moderate to high with each other.

Confirmatory factor analysis of the PDSS of the development sample yields a standardized weight that was sufficiently high with minimum t values of 14.79, which indicates that all the items fit the hypothesized model with a Tucker-Lewis

index of .87. Post hoc exploratory factor analysis examines how each PDSS item loads on all extracted factors, yielding seven factors with eigenvalues greater than 1. The exploratory factor analysis confirms the interrelatedness of certain content scales. Convergent validity was calculated using the PDSS Total score; and total scores from the EPDS, BDI-II, and depression diagnostic status, as derived from the SCID interview. The authors' findings showed that the PDSS is highly associated not only for other established self-report depression inventories, but also with depression status as ascertained by different methods (i.e., interviews). Concurrent validity studies showed that the PDSS can predict the assignment of women to depressed or nondepressed groups.

COMMENTARY. It is a known fact that manuals can never give all the information that might be desirable. However, the PDSS technical manual is impressive, organized, and detailed. The authors emphasized the importance of introducing the PDSS to the new mother in a clinically sensitive manner. This is particularly important given the symptomology of women with postpartum depression. Therefore, the authors warn that the interpretation of PDSS should be carried out with caution; as factors such as cognitive dysfunction, attentional lapse, and social stigma are usually associated with postpartum depression. They also indicated that administration or supervision by an experienced professional with psychometric knowledge is imperative when using the PDSS, as numerous factors may compromise the accuracy of the respondent's rating. The PDSS scale is easily administered, which makes it an attractive choice. The PDSS AutoScore form is used to administer and interpret this test. This form contains scoring aids that were designed to make scoring rapid, while eliminating the potential for key errors. Responses are transferred through to the underlying pages where the administrator can follow steps for scoring. However, if the client fails to press hard and/or erases a response after being told not to do so, the scoring will become smudged and difficult to read. Likewise, it is important that the scorer proceed with caution when transferring raw scores from the worksheet to the summary sheet because an error could result in the interpretation.

Evidence of validity and reliability studies were included in the manual, along with other relevant research data on target domain (postpartum depression). As reported in the manual the diagnostic sample differed from the development sample on several demographic variables. Women in the diagnostic sample were significantly older, have fewer biological children, and were closer to childbirth. In terms of education, more participants in the diagnostic group had achieved at least a college degree and there were also significantly more married women in this group. The two groups did not differ significantly in racial composition or in their self-report of previous depression. However, there was no mention of differential validity studies of test scores across racial, ethnic, and cultural groups, as these variables might have a significant impact on generalizability to other populations.

SUMMARY. Although the PDSS is available as a clinical tool and as a screening instrument, several cautions must be emphasized. It is a known fact that self-reporting is vulnerable to underreporting, distortions due to response style bias, inaccurate reporting, defensiveness, and denial. This is true with most self-reporting measures, but particularly true given the mental state of women suffering from postpartum depression. Therefore, test users should proceed with caution when interpreting tests results. Although self-reports have clear limitations, they have some validity related to standardization, economics, and limited training required for administration and administration time. When used with other assessments, the PDSS can be a valuable tool for diagnosing and treating women with postpartum depression.

[191]
Posture and Fine Motor Assessment of Infants.

Purpose: Designed to identify motor delays in infants and to monitor progress in the first year of life.
Population: Ages 2–12 months.
Publication Date: 2000.
Acronym: PFMAI.
Scores, 2: Posture, Fine Motor.
Levels, 2: PFMAI-I (2–6 months), PFMAI-II (6–12 months).
Administration: Individual.
Price Data, 2001: $55 per manual (99 pages).
Time: (25–30) minutes.
Authors: Jane Case-Smith and Rosemarie Bigsby.
Publisher: Harcourt Assessment, Inc.

Review of the Posture and Fine Motor Assessment of Infants by LINDA K. BUNKER, Professor, B. ANN BOYCE, Associate Professor, and GREGORY HANSON, Ph.D. Candidate, Department of Human Services, University of Virginia, Charlottesville, VA:

DESCRIPTION. The Posture and Fine Motor Assessment for Infants (PFMAI) can provide diagnostic information for the identification of infants with motor delays and should be used in conjunction with other types of diagnostic tools (i.e., norm-referenced tests and interviews). The PFMAI was designed for use by physical and occupational therapists as well as other health professionals (trained psychologists) with knowledge of infant motor patterns (see chapter 1 of the PFMAI user's guide). This criterion-referenced assessment tool utilizes qualitative measures to note deficiencies in early motor development of infants. The PFMAI is divided into two age levels: the PFMAI-I for infants from 2 to 6 months, who require assistance to sit and the PFMAI-II for infants from 6 to 12 months, who can sit either independently or with minimum assistance. Both levels of this instrument are further subdivided into postural control and fine motor facility. The Posture Control Scale assesses the child's ability to balance, dynamically shift weight, rotate, and maintain upright posture. The Fine Motor Scale evaluates the infant's reaching and grasping patterns while rating arm, hand, and finger movements.

Testing should take place in a naturalistic setting with postural control evaluated with the infant moving freely and fine motor facility gauged through the child's play with selected toys. During testing, parents are encouraged to stay near the infant and the therapist functions as an observer who can introduce toys or moves to help the infant exhibit his or her highest level of motor performance. The main body of the test is composed of a rating scale where the health professional scores the infant on a 4-point scale with 4 denoting the highest level of performance to 1 signifying the lowest level for items in the Posture and Fine Motor sections of the test. In addition to the rating scale, this instrument also collects information via open-ended questions from the parents and health professional. The professional's open-ended comments require him or her to provide information on the interpretation of the test scores as well as goals and objectives for the child. Information gleaned from the application of this qualitative diagnostic tool can form the foundation for early intervention strategies. Further, the authors state that the sensitivity of the PFMAI to detect small changes in motor performance could be useful in charting an infant's progress. However, no research evidence was cited to support the notion of the PFMAI's sensitivity to change.

DEVELOPMENT.

Theoretical overview. The Dynamical Systems Theory (DST; see chapter 2 of the user's guide) forms the conceptual basis of the PFMAI and is contrasted in the user's guide with the less useful Neuromaturation Theory. The DST proposes that the "organization of movement" (p. 7) facilitates the infant's development of movement patterns. Based on the task and environmental demands, the infant must organize his or her movement patterns to produce movement and thereby establish motor schema. This organization of movement patterns is the result of the "heterarchy" (user's guide, p. 7) of several brain structures (e.g., cortical, central brain, cerebellum, and brain stem) that work together to produce movement. In addition to the structures in the brain, sensory systems (visual, tactile, proprioceptive, auditory, and vestibular) via afferent signals adapt the movement pattern. Thus, movement behaviors seem to be generated in the central brain but adapted through the input of the sensory systems. The PFMAI attempts to capture the infant's self-organizing motor behavior through testing in a naturalistic environment that is familiar to the child while at the same time presenting a series of novel stimuli that elicit the child's true level of motor performance.

Development of the PFMAI. The PFMAI-I was originally developed in 1988. Research that compared the PFMAI with other measurement tools of motor function (e.g., Peabody Developmental Motor Scale, Bayley Scales of Infant Development) was undertaken (see Case-Smith, 1989; Case-Smith, 1992) and the resulting correlations were within an acceptable range from a low of .67 to a high of .85. Further, research that examined the age (in months) and the current version of the PFMAI yielded correlation scores between .48 and .74; this range represents a low to a moderate positive correlation. Last, the research of Case-Smith and Bigsby (1997) revealed that an infant's grasping pattern varies by age and object.

TECHNICAL.

Administration. The PFMAI identifies motor delays in infants from 2 to 12 months of maturity and shows the progression in motor development related to the child's posture and fine motor performance. The authors also suggest that the PFMAI can be used with older infants with identified motor delays but state that the standard testing protocol and cutoff scores should not be used with this population. Unfortunately, they do not offer suggestions related to an appropriate testing process or cutoff score. Occupational and physical therapists as well as trained psychologists can administer this test. The authors recommend that the health care professional practice using the test on one or two infants and achieve 85% agreement with another professional. Other ways to determine appropriate interrater agreement are also suggested but are not clearly explicated.

The observation portion of the test should take approximately 25 to 30 minutes to complete with either the PFMAI-I or PFMAI-II. Testing should take place in an environment familiar to the infant where the room is warm, because the infant is dressed only in a diaper. A family member or caregiver is encouraged to stay for testing and can assist in handling and offering toys for the fine motor portion of the test. A list of toys is provided in the user's manual and can be provided by either the health professional or the caregiver. Prior to formal assessment (observation of Posture and Fine Motor skills), the caregiver is interviewed regarding her or his impressions and concerns regarding the infant. Questions are provided in the reproducible documents of the PFMAI-I and PFMAI-II.

Suggestions for the observation include determining the infant's sensory preferences (e.g., tactile sensitivity, visual or auditory input) and then interpretation of the test based on this information. When administering the PFMAI-I, it is best to begin the test with the Posture items (because they involve little handling of the infant who is observed in prone and supine positions) and then give the Fine Motor assessment. The reverse order of the tests is recommended for the PFMAI-II. The scoring directions for the PFMAI were subject to interpretation by the evaluator with regard to the "consistency" issue related to the child's movement patterns. Also it would help if the authors designated the numbers on the scale

(1 to 4) as #1 as low and #4 as high, even though this information was specified in the actual PFMAI scoring guide found in Appendix A. Specific directions for each test (PMFAI-I & II) with subsections (Posture and Fine Motor Scale) are delineated in the user's guide. Directions for this section were helpful with strategies and contingencies for test administration given as well as time recommendations for those who need extra time to correctly assess their highest level of performance.

Scoring and interpretation. Raw scores for each item in the PFMAI-I or PFMAI-II are summed for each of the Posture and Fine Motor scales and then comparisons are made to the mean criterion reference scores for "mean/average" or "at-risk" or "delayed" categories listed by age (in months) found in Appendix B of the users guide. These scores are judged in accordance with how the existing environmental constraints (e.g., noise level, infant activity level) may have impacted the infant's performance. The authors suggest that motor performance may be depressed in the area of posture if the child is tired or anxious or fine motor performance may be negated by a hungry or frightened infant. A strong recommendation was made to interpret scores as they relate to patterns that emerge in subareas (e.g., prone posture in the PFMAI-I) as opposed to the summed score for the entire Posture section of the PFMAI. Retesting was recommended 3 months after the collection of baseline information. In addition, the authors warned against direct comparisons of the PFMAI-I and PFMAI-II because the scales are different and are administered in a different order. Differences in symmetries between right and left sides should also be noted as a part of the evaluation.

PFMAI scoring guide. The scoring guide presented a description for each scoring level on a 1- (low) to 4- (high) point scale with some levels accompanied by pictures to help with the evaluation process. This portion of the testing guide lacked clarity, especially with such statements as "the child should demonstrate some consistency with that response" (p. 51). It is unclear how a practitioner should interpret that statement.

Scoring table. The PFMAI-I and PFMAI-II recording forms are straightforward and easily understood. They would be even better if they included the evaluation criteria. With many tests, such as the Peabody Developmental Motor Scales (15:184), the grading form also provides descrip-

tions of the scoring criteria. This is very convenient and eliminates the need to continually refer to the test manual.

Confidence intervals. The confidence intervals should have been more fully discussed in terms of how this information could help the evaluator interpret the test scores. The occupational therapist who examined this instrument noted that the manual is lacking with regard to a clear explanation as to how the evaluating therapist should use intervals. What if, for example, a 6-month-old infant receives a Fine Motor score of 62? The at-risk score is 61. Does this mean that because of the confidence interval that this child should also be considered at-risk? More guidance is needed in this section to clarify the use of confidence intervals. [Editor's Note: The publisher advises that Appendix C of the manual does provide information on how to calculate the lower and upper ends of the confidence interval.]

SUMMARY COMMENTS. The biggest drawback to this evaluation tool is that the authors recommend that it needs to be completed in addition to other assessment tools. Although this reflects an understanding that no one assessment tool could or should provide all the information needed, the problem becomes one of time. Many of the items on the PFMAI are very similar to those included in the Peabody and other developmental tools. Thus, practicing therapists may find it difficult to justify using the PFMAI if they already have much of the information via another assessment tool.

Additionally, the PFMAI is purported to be based upon dynamical systems theory but maintains a structure that is based upon developmental progressions (e.g., developing grip patterns). Therefore, it is unclear if the PFMAI will lead therapists to a treatment approach that is different from that which would be utilized having administered a more classical developmental motor scale in combination with good clinical observation skills.

REVIEWERS' REFERENCES

Case-Smith, J. (1989). Reliability and validity of the Posture and Fine Motor Assessment of Infants. *Occupational Therapy Journal of Research, 9,* 259–272.

Case-Smith, J. (1992). A validity study of Posture and Fine Motor Assessment of Infants. *American Journal of Occupational Therapy, 46,* 597–605.

Case-Smith, J., & Bigsby, R. (1997). *A study of the reliability and validity of the Posture and Fine Motor Assessment of Infants, Part I and Part II.* Report submitted to the American Occupational Therapy Foundation.

Review of the Posture and Fine Motor Assessment of Infants by JOHN J. VENN, Professor, College of Education and Human Services, University of North Florida, Jacksonville, FL:

DESCRIPTION. The Posture and Fine Motor Assessment of Infants (PFMAI) is a developmental scale for infants from 2 to 12 months of age who exhibit motor delays. The instrument is useful for obtaining diagnostic information, developing intervention goals, and measuring progress. The PFMAI includes a Posture scale and a Fine Motor scale, and it is divided into two age levels. The PFMAI-I is for infants from 2 to 6 months who need external support to sit. It contains 18 Posture items and 21 Fine Motor items. The PFMAI-II is for infants from 6 to 12 months who sit independently or need minimal external support. It includes 13 Posture items and 17 Fine Motor items. It takes 25 to 30 minutes to administer the instrument. The instrument was especially designed to measure the movement patterns of infants with central nervous system impairment, and it can be given to older infants who are performing below 12 months in motor development. The authors created the assessment for occupational and physical therapists and other professionals with knowledge of infant movement patterns. Because the PFMAI is an informal, criterion-referenced tool, the developers recommend using it together with norm-referenced tools when making placement and classification decisions.

The instructor's manual includes guidelines to acquaint new evaluators with the PFMAI administration and scoring procedures. The guidelines include a list of needed equipment and toys, directions for the caregiver interview, observation guidelines, and scoring requirements.

Administration begins with an informal caregiver interview and general observation of the infant. The administration sequence is responsive to the needs of infants who may be hypersensitive to touch and resistive to excessive handling and repositioning. Rather than giving each item in sequence, evaluation information is gathered during facilitated play activities. The Posture scales assess postural control, proximal stability, and proximal mobility in both supine and upright positions. The Fine Motor scales evaluate reaching, grasping, releasing, moving fingers and thumbs, and manipulation during interaction with three different toys.

With the PFMAI-I, administration begins with the posture items. The evaluator scores these items by nonobtrusively observing the infant in prone and supine positions. This part of the evaluation involves almost no handling. Administration then moves to the Fine Motor items in which the infant plays with selected toys while positioned in an infant seat. During this part of the assessment, the evaluator interacts with the infant by presenting toys and observing how the infant interacts with, reaches for, and manipulates the objects.

PFMAI-II administration begins with the Fine Motor scale by positioning the infant in a stable sitting position in a high chair with a tray. The evaluator observes the infant's grasping and movement strategies with toys placed on the tray. The infant is given time to interact with three toys: a movable parts toy, one-inch cubes, and pellet-sized objects such as dry cereal. The PFMAI-II posture scale evaluates stability and mobility while the infant is sitting, engaged in quadruped movement, and standing with support. For example, to observe stability and mobility in quadruped movement, the evaluator presents toys just out of reach and encourages the infant to move forward on hands and knees to play with the toys. Likewise, to evaluate standing stability and mobility, the evaluator stands the infant in front of a chair with toys on the seat. The infant holds on to the chair seat for stability while reaching for and interacting with the toys.

The individual PFMAI items are scored with a 1, 2, 3, or 4 based on the infant's best response. A score of 4 indicates the highest performance level. For each item, the manual includes descriptive scoring criteria for every level from 1 to 4. Although evaluators may score some items by parent report if necessary, the best evaluation is obtained by scoring all items from direct observation. The manual provides photographs of infants illustrating the assessment procedure for each group of items. After scoring the individual items, the evaluator calculates summary scores for the posture and fine motor subtests. These summary scores can be compared to mean, at-risk, and delayed criterion-referenced scores listed by age in months. This enables evaluators to estimate an infant's age level of performance for each subtest. The manual includes five comprehensive case studies demonstrating how to analyze movement and identify problems, interpret scores, relate findings to functional performance, and develop intervention strategies. These are very helpful in understanding how to best use the instrument.

DEVELOPMENT. The PFMAI was originally developed in 1988, and it has undergone significant revision and improvement since then. The authors created the first version of the scales by revising and structuring informal clinical protocols used for observation of infants with motor delays. The authors designed the PFMAI to assess the motor movements that provide the foundation for skillful motor function during infancy and later development. A dynamic systems model served as the theoretical basis for developing the instrument. This model stresses the importance of measuring how well infants with motor delays (a) make transitions to higher level skills, (b) dynamically connect perception with movement, (c) acquire meaningful motor patterns through play, and (d) learn new functional movements through phases of disorganization and variation. Other developmental principles incorporated into the instrument include the importance of natural observations and interviews with primary caregivers.

TECHNICAL. The reliability research conducted with the PFMAI included two interobserver studies using the original PFMAI-I. In these studies, one evaluator administered the items; this evaluator, along with another trained evaluator, independently scored the items. Interobserver correlations were .97 in both studies. A study with the current version of the PFMAI-I with 13 infants and two raters produced correlations of .97 for the Posture scale and .99 for the Fine Motor scale. A similar study of the PFMAI-II with 18 infants and two raters yielded correlations of .98 for the posture scale and .96 for the fine motor scale. These investigations provide evidence to support the interobserver reliability of the instrument. Unfortunately, descriptions of the participants and examiners were not provided, and it is unclear how much experience evaluators had with the instrument. Although the overall results are impressive, more studies with varying types of infants and evaluators need to be completed to thoroughly examine interobserver reliability.

Test-retest reliability research included a 1989 study using the initial version of the PFMAI-I that produced moderate to high coefficients and a 1992 study with a pilot version of the current instrument. The time intervals between administrations were not reported. The 1992 study included 8 infants and yielded a coefficient of .90 for the Posture scale and .49 for the Fine Motor scale.

A study with the PFMAI-II using 18 infants and two raters resulted in coefficients of .94 for the Posture scale and .77 for the Fine Motor scale. Unfortunately, the investigations with the earlier version of the scales provide limited evidence of the reliability of the current instrument. Further, although the findings support the consistency of the Posture scale scores, they call into question the reliability of the Fine Motor scales. As a result, further investigations with larger sample sizes are necessary to examine the test-retest reliability of the PFMAI, especially the motor scales.

Internal consistency was estimated using the final version of the instrument in an investigation with 59 infants. The Cronbach alphas in this study were .97 for the PFMAI-I Posture scale and .99 for the PFMAI-I Fine Motor scale. A sample of 126 infants was used to gauge the internal consistency of the PFMAI-II. The resulting Cronbach alphas were .95 for the Posture scale and .96 for the Fine Motor scale.

Several studies provide the basis for evaluating the validity of the PFMAI. Again, some of these investigations relied on an earlier version of the instrument. In 1989, Case-Smith examined the relationship between the scores of 32 infants on the PFMAI-I and the Peabody Developmental Motor Scales (PDMS). The correlation between the PFMAI-I Posture scale and the PDMS Gross Motor scale was .83, and the correlation between the Fine Motor scales was .67. In 1992, Case-Smith examined the correlation between the PFMAI-I and two instruments: the PDMS and the Bayley Scales of Infant Development (BSID). The correlation between the PDMS Gross Motor scale and the Posture scale was .83, and the correlation between the Fine Motor scales of the two instruments was .67. Scores from 25 infants were used to calculate these correlations. The correlation of scores between the BSID Psychomotor scale and Posture scale was .75. The correlation between the BSID Mental scale and the Fine Motor scale was .85. These comparisons were based on scores from 23 infants. Although these concurrent reliability studies support the effectiveness of scores derived from the PFMAI-I, the use of an earlier version of the instrument limits the extent to which the results apply to the current version.

Further evidence of the validity of the PFMAI was provided in a study of the relationship between age and PFMAI scores. Using a sample of 59 infants, Pearson correlation coefficients were .74 between age and the PFMAI-I Posture scale and .64 between age and the Fine Motor scale. Correlation coefficients of .48 were found between age and the PFMAI-II Posture scale and .56 between age and the Fine Motor scale. These coefficients were derived from a sample of 126 infants.

Criterion-referenced age scores were developed from a sample of 185 full-term infants from eight childcare centers in central Ohio. The sample included 59 infants assessed with the PFMAI-I and 126 infants assessed with the PFMAI-II. The sample was about equally divided by gender. The sample included infants from diverse ethnic backgrounds. This sample was used to develop scoring tables by age in months with scores divided into the categories of average, at risk, and motor delay. Thus, evaluators may obtain scores for the Posture and the Fine Motor scales that estimate an infant's developmental performance level in months. Because these scores are derived from a small and limited sample, evaluators should use them cautiously.

COMMENTARY. The PFMAI is one of several evaluation tools emphasizing dynamic assessment of infant movement organization and functional performance. Similar instruments include the Toddler and Infant Motor Evaluation (Miller & Roid, 1994) and the Alberta Infant Motor Scale (Piper & Darrah, 1994). In contrast, traditional evaluation approaches gather more static assessment information about infant progress in acquiring specific motor milestones and reflexes. The PFMAI dynamic movement approach relies heavily on observation in natural settings to assess how well infants interact with functional items, such as toys, and maintain postural stability across environments and situations. Even though therapists often use this approach in clinical observations, the PFMAI provides standardized administration and scoring procedures that produce objective assessment information about how infants organize and reorganize movements in response to the task and the environment. Thus, scales like the PFMAI yield structured diagnostic data that are especially sensitive to changes in infant movement. This helps evaluate qualitative differences in motor development through analysis of motor components. The PFMAI is especially useful for identifying the unique movements of infants with severe deficits who have extensive motor delays.

SUMMARY. The PFMAI is a helpful tool for obtaining detailed diagnostic information, and professionals may use this information to identify the performance of infants with motor delays, to formulate intervention goals, and to measure progress over time. The PFMAI emphasizes precise, structured measurement of infant postural and fine motor movements in naturalistic, functional, play-like settings. The administration and scoring directions are well presented and clear. Thus, the PFMAI is useful to therapists and other professionals with specific knowledge of infants who have problems with reciprocal movements, postural stability, and coordinated fine motor movement patterns. Drawbacks include technical deficits, such as research using older versions of the instrument, and the need for additional studies with larger sample sizes to more clearly examine reliability and validity. When used cautiously by trained professionals who recognize the strengths and limitations of criterion-referenced assessment, the PFMAI is a valuable assessment instrument. The PFMAI is best when used to develop intervention plans for remediating specific deficits. It is also ideal for measuring individual progress. When making identification decisions, the PFMAI should be used together with other measures including a norm-referenced test. Overall, the PFMAI provides relevant, appropriate, and detailed diagnostic information for planning interventions and gauging the development of infants with motor delays.

REVIEWER'S REFERENCES
Case-Smith, J. (1989). Reliability and validity of the Posture and Fine Motor Assessment of Infants. *Occupational Therapy Journal of Research, 9,* 259–272.
Case-Smith, J. (1992). A validity study of the Posture and Fine Motor Assessment of Infants. *American Journal of Occupational Therapy, 46,* 597–605.
Miller, L. J., & Roid, G. H. (1994). The T.I.M.E.: Toddler and Infant Motor Evaluation: A standardized assessment. Tucson, AZ: Therapy Skill Builders.
Piper, M. C., & Darrah, J. (1994). Alberta Infant Motor Scale. Orlando, FL: W. B. Saunders Co.

[192]

Power and Performance Measures.

Purpose: Battery of nine aptitude and ability tests designed to measure both potential and achievement in a wide range of occupational settings.
Population: Ages 16 and over.
Publication Dates: 1990–1996.
Acronym: PPM.
Scores: Verbal Reasoning, Verbal Comprehension, Perceptual Reasoning, Spatial Ability, Numerical Reasoning, Numerical Computation, Mechanical Understanding, Clerical Speed and Accuracy, Applied Logic.
Administration: Group or individual.

Price Data, 2001: £55 per technical handbook (1996, 54 pages); £6.50 per question booklet; £2.75 per answer sheet; £133 per specimen set.
Time: (3–12) minutes.
Author: James S. Barrett.
Publisher: The Test Agency Ltd. [England].

Review of the Power and Performance Measures by KURT F. GEISINGER, Vice President of Academic Affairs, Professor of Psychology, The University of St. Thomas, Houston, TX:

DESCRIPTION AND DEVELOPMENT. The Power and Performance Measures (PPM) instrument is a battery of nine aptitude and ability tests developed in Great Britain for occupational/personnel testing purposes. As such, it is intended to be appropriate for adults of normal working age. Each of the nine cognitive tests can be administered singly or in combination with some or all of the other tests. The manual reports that the instrument should be used in "making improvements in selection, development and career counselling" (technical handbook, p. 6) and suggests that most users will administer only a small number of the tests of the battery.

The goal of this battery is to provide relatively short measures of specific abilities and skills so that relative strengths and weaknesses can be assessed or diagnosed. The ability measures are components of intelligence. This approach is in opposition to that of making an assessment of general mental ability or general intelligence. When using results from the entire battery, however, a measure of Full Scale Intelligence can be calculated.

The terms, Power and Performance, as used in the title of the battery, are defined in the manual and differ somewhat from the ways these terms have historically been used in personnel testing. Performance is considered to be reasoning ability. Performance measures, on the other hand, involve past experience on the part of the test taker. The author of the manual states that Performance "relates more strongly, though not inevitably, to the presence of experience" (technical handbook, p. 7). A concern this reviewer has with this dichotomy is that it implies that the Power (or reasoning) tests do not involve experience and are, hence, genetically based. Obviously, both Power and Performance measures assess developed abilities and involve experiences in their enhancement.

The measure divides the separate tests into a model much like that of Wechsler or Thurstone,

that is, into what might be called verbal and performance intelligence, and which this author calls "Power IQ" and "Performance IQ." Subtests composing the Power IQ are Abstract Reasoning (the test for which is entitled Applied Power), Verbal Reasoning, Numerical Reasoning, and Perceptual Reasoning. Those making up the Performance IQ include Verbal Comprehension, Numerical Computation, Spatial Ability, Mechanical Understanding, and Clerical Speed. Taken together, of course, these are the nine tests making up the PPM battery. The battery is also conceptualized in a matrix format with the two matrix dimensions being Stimulus and Process. There are three levels of the Stimulus factor: Visual (Perceptual Reasoning, Applied Power Test, and Spatial Ability), Verbal (Processing Speed, Verbal Reasoning, Numerical Reasoning, Verbal Comprehension, and Numerical Computation), and Motor (Mechanical Understanding). There are four levels of the Process factor: Speed (Processing Speed), Reasoning (Perceptual Reasoning, Applied Power Test, Verbal Reasoning, Numerical Reasoning, and Mechanical Understanding), Design (Spatial Ability), and Memory (Verbal Comprehension, Numerical Computation). Of this 4x3 matrix, 6 of the 12 cells are filled; the author portends that these are the ones most relevant for personnel selection. The manual provides fine definitions of what each test is intended to measure, the number of items on that test, and the length of time for the test. The entire battery would entail 108 minutes of testing time, but there would certainly need to be time between individual tests. The testing times range from 6 minutes for Processing Speed to 16 minutes for Applied Power.

The test is administered in group settings and can be machine scored, although most test administrators would do so by hand. Test booklets may be re-used, although answers sheets can be used only once.

A critical aspect of the PPM battery is that it can be administered quickly. That is, relative to other employment batteries, the PPM attempts to minimize test length while keeping reliability in the acceptable range. (Test length is one of the primary determinants of test reliability.) As noted previously, the test author suggests that only 3–4 tests will normally need to be administered for most positions. He provided some four sample batteries. For Technical/Systems (IT) positions, for example, the Applied Power, Numerical Reasoning, and Perceptual Reasoning tests would be employed. For Sales and Marketing, the Verbal Reasoning, Verbal Comprehension, and Numerical Reasoning tests are suggested.

The manual provides generally excellent instructions to the test administrator. More specific information would be useful, however. For example, the statement, "The first [task] is to provide an atmosphere which is conducive to every individual giving of their best with as much calmness and control as is feasible" (technical handbook, p. 14) could use a number of more precise behavioral suggestions. Specific wording for the test administration is provided, especially in regard to oral instructions. It is not clear why the answer sheet requires the provision of age and sex, as these variables are not involved in the computation of scores and may provide extraneous information in an employment setting.

Gridding answers (that is, filling in the bubbles) to some questions is rather complex. For the Applied Power Test, the test taker must fill four bubbles for each answer, a difficult enterprise. Furthermore, the test instructions include the following statement. "There is no point in simply guessing since wrong answers count against you" (technical handbook, p. 15). There is no penalty for guessing for the Applied Power Test, however. Moreover, the remaining tests have different numbers of options, sometimes varying even within a test. This scoring is confusing and would place test-wise examinees at something of a disadvantage if they attempt to guess selectively to maximize their scores. Furthermore, the manual informs those computing final scores (rights minus a proportion of wrongs) that they must round the wrongs to whole numbers. This system is confusing and unnecessarily difficult. Moreover, the norms in the manual provide a number of different scales, including z-scores, T-scores, and IQs. This reviewer was rather surprised to see the use of the IQ scale for a variety of measures other than intelligence per se. The manual reports that this scale is especially useful because it is so well known. Because so many nonprofessionals misinterpret IQs, however, would be a reason why one would not wish to use this scale. On the other hand, the manual does suggest that an IQ "can only really be measured accurately by taking the scores from all of the tests in the battery and looking at the results as a whole" (technical handbook, p. 20). This caution appears correct, but too little a warning.

TECHNICAL. In terms of reliability information, the author provides coefficient alpha results for the nine tests. No description of the size or nature of the population upon which these estimates of reliability tests were based is provided, however. Furthermore, it is generally inappropriate to use such measures for highly speeded tests and several of these tests are speeded, most notably, the Processing Speed measure. The reliability indices provided are likely to be overestimated. The range of indices provided range from .74 for Perceptual Reasoning to .89 for Processing Speed. Test-retest information would be useful. No information on the speededness of the measures is provided. Standard errors of measurement are provided for each of the scales in raw score units. This information is less helpful than might be hoped, as standard errors in terms of the preferred scaled scores are not supplied. Reliability coefficients for the entire battery or for the various suggested test groupings are not provided, a significant detriment.

Intercorrelations of the nine measures are also provided based upon data from 337 professional managers and these are on the order of what should be expected. The range of the intercorrelations is from .14 to .59 and the median, as computed by this reviewer, .36–.37.

Some concurrent validation information is provided in terms of correlational results with established tests. Correlations among appropriately matched tests from the Employee Aptitude Survey range in the .60s and .70s. With some of the Saville and Holdsworth's (SHL) tests, the correlations are rather lower, ranging from .30 to .60. These data are too preliminary and the manner in which they are provided in the manual, with little descriptive information and without peer review, fails to meet accepted professional standards. That no predictive validity information is provided for a measure that is to be used in personnel selection is not acceptable.

Some preliminary norms data are provided. These data are very poorly described. A few studies are summarized in one table in an appendix but it is not clear how they were used in the determination of norms. Presumably, some of these data were used for the norms. Perhaps even more concerning, however, is the fact that the populations or samples upon which the norms tables are based are largely undefined. The norms tables themselves are broken down first by four recommended battery groupings (administrative/clerical, engineering/technical, graduates/managers/professionals, and technological/systems). The author neither presents the numbers of individuals upon which these composites are based nor provides a description of the samples. The author provides percentile ranks for varying groups. One norm table, entitled "British Working Population," again has neither a sample size nor a sample description imparted. Percentiles and T-scores are then provided for a variety of groupings (e.g., senior managers, professional managers). The sample sizes for these norms range from 132 to 337, with only one table including more than 200 individuals. Such numbers are too small for a measure administered in group settings. A final table provides a system for converting test scores to IQ-equivalents based on the British general population (undefined sample, but with 1,600 test takers).

No data on minority or subgroup performance are provided. Given that measures such as these often lead to adverse impact against certain groups that have been historically underrepresented in the working population, this omission is a considerable problem for this cognitive measure. Some of the studies described in a table in an appendix provide correlations with age, however, and many of these are significant negative correlations, which would appear somewhat problematic. They range as high as -.37, indicating that the test may be more speeded than may be desirable. (Another explanation is that the older groups have considerably less education.)

SUMMARY. In conclusion, this battery is a relatively recently published measure. At present it appears to lack the necessary validity data to permit its use in high stakes situations, such as employment settings. Its administration has some problems, primarily related to speededness and the correction for guessing. It may prove useful in time and its use in research studies is recommended.

[193]
Practical Adolescent Dual Diagnostic Interview.

Purpose: "To elicit information relevant to the identification and diagnosis of mental health and substance use disorders in adolescents."

Population: Ages 12–18.
Publication Date: 2000.
Acronym: PADDI.
Scores, 17: Major Depressive Episode, Manic Episode, Mixed Episode, Psychotic Symptoms, Panic Attacks, Anxiety and Phobias, Posttraumatic Stress Disorder, Obsessions/Compulsions, Conduct Disorder, Oppositional Defiant Disorder, Personality Disorders, Paranoid Personality Traits, Dependent Personality Traits, Sexual Orientation, Substance Abuse Disorders, Dangerousness to Self or Others, Child Abuse—Victimization.
Administration: Individual.
Price Data: Available from publisher.
Time: (20–40) minutes.
Comments: A structured diagnostic interview compatible with the DSM-IV diagnostic criteria; can be administered by paraprofessionals as a screening device.
Authors: Todd W. Estroff and Norman G. Hoffmann.
Publisher: Change Companies.

Review of the Practical Adolescent Dual Diagnostic Interview by C. G. BELLAH, Director of Special Services, Parker College, Dallas, TX:

DESCRIPTION. The Practical Adolescent Dual Diagnostic Interview (PADDI) is a 164-item structured interview designed to facilitate diagnosis of mental disorders for an adolescent population in accordance with criteria outlined in the *Diagnostic and Statistical Manual of Mental Disorders, Version IV* (DSM-IV; American Psychiatric Association, 1994). The PADDI is appropriate for use by both professionals and paraprofessionals in a variety of applied settings, such as: community mental health centers, juvenile detention centers, adolescent addictions treatment centers, and private clinics. However, the authors caution that, although professionals may find the PADDI effective in gathering information for use in deriving diagnoses, its utility for the paraprofessional is necessarily limited to gathering information that may facilitate consultations and expedite referrals.

Administration of the PADDI may be completed in 1 clinical hour and is eased by a stipulation that all items must be read to each respondent exactly as they are written in the test manual. This caveat is meant to ensure standardization of test administration and to promote efficiency and accuracy in recording interview data. Scoring of the PADDI protocol is relatively simple and straightforward. The test administrator is directed to the one-page "PADDI Scoring Summary" that is attached to the answer sheet. Test administrators are instructed to sum the raw scores of items that are relevant to each of 32 nonoverlapping "problem categories." Summative scores are then compared to normal ranges of score values that are anchored with interpretive statements that facilitate differential diagnosis.

Overall, 129 of the 164 items are dichotomously scored, with "0" indicating "No" and "1" indicating "Yes" to assessment questions and ostensibly either the presence or absence of a given sign or symptom. Seven of the additional 35 dichotomous items are demographic questions, and 7 others are endorsed by the interviewer and represent observational data, including 5 Likert-Type ratings and 2 qualitative listings with more than one possible rating. The remaining 21 items have qualitative or graduated multiple-choice formats wherein the respondent selects the statement that best answers the question. In sum, 130 of the 164 items are scored for diagnostic purposes, including 101 items that represent "mental health conditions" and 29 items that represent "substance use."

DEVELOPMENT. The authors report that the PADDI is based on the DSM-IV and provides the clinician with a standard set of questions that cover specific diagnostic criteria. Unfortunately, the test manual provides no detailed information regarding item pool generation or pilot testing procedures. Beyond rationale, no empirical support is presented that provides either confirming or disconfirming evidence of several operating assumptions of the PADDI, namely the number and content of specified "problem categories," as well as the condition of nonoverlapping items between categories.

Specifically, it is reported in the manual that data analyses suggest the items within each diagnostic category are highly related and identify distinct clusters of syndromes as defined by the DSM-IV. However, the manual proffers no discussion of the method or type of analyses that were conducted for this purpose, nor is there any presentation of any numerical results of these analyses. Therefore, the empirical question of whether each item is truly a manifest indicator of a single distinct category is ultimately inconclusive at the current time.

Moreover, the manual does not provide the reader with any empirical evidence of orthogonality in their specification of "distinct" clusters of syndromes, nor is any empirical evidence presented that indicates this particular sample of items adequately represents the domain of discourse in adolescent psychopathology. Consequently, the lack of empirical support for the proposed structural model necessarily calls into question the veracity of the specified scoring procedures and leaves the reader with many unanswered questions regarding the design and development of the PADDI.

TECHNICAL. A "Normal Range" of summative scores is employed for each of the specified problem categories on the PADDI scoring summary. However, no information is provided to the reader regarding the derivation of these ranges of scores, nor is there any presentation of parameter estimates, sampling procedures, standard scores, percentile ranks, or any descriptive statistics that identify demographic characteristics of the standardization sample. It is reported in the manual that the data were drawn from a population of predominantly white adolescents being evaluated in substance abuse treatment centers. However, the test manual does not present any normative data (e.g., averages, standard deviations) or any discussion of the racial composition of the standardization sample. Thus, generalizability of the authors' findings to a known population of respondents is compromised, which necessarily limits the scope of its utility in specialized areas of interest.

RELIABILITY. Although 130 of the 164 items of the PADDI are scored for diagnostic purposes, the manual includes estimates of internal consistency for only 88 items that comprise 10 "diagnostic groupings." It is noteworthy that these 10 "diagnostic groupings" represent a subset of the 32 specified "problem categories," which leaves roughly one-third of the diagnostic portion of the assessment unaccounted for (32.31%). Nevertheless, reliability estimates for the 10 diagnostic groupings ($N = 144$) range from .922 (Major Depressive Episode) to .671 (Conduct Disorder). Only 3 of the 10 diagnostic groupings are listed with reliability estimates of .90 or greater, which is the recommended benchmark for diagnostic tools (Nunnally & Bernstein, 1994, p. 265).

The manual also presents test-retest reliability estimates for 14 areas of "problem indication" based on a sample of 23 teens in residential addiction treatment programs. The listed test-retest reliability coefficients range from .92 (Manic Episode) to .61 (PTSD), and the authors caution that the time between administrations of the PADDI varied considerably (2 to 4 weeks) among the 23 participants. It is also noteworthy that the aforementioned areas of "problem indication" do not correspond to the ten "diagnostic groupings" that were used in estimation of internal consistency, which were themselves discordant with the 32 specified "problem categories" that comprise the PADDI scoring summary. Overall, in review of the psychometric properties of the PADDI, it remains unclear how the authors intend for the user to score and interpret the assessment data, and sufficient evidence does not exist to warrant use of the PADDI as a reliable diagnostic tool.

VALIDITY. With respect to validity of the PADDI, the authors of the manual introduce the subject by stating, "Content validity refers to whether the instrument includes the content intended. This is also known as face validity" (p. 54). Given that most scholars consider content validity and face validity to be separate and complimentary aspects of psychological assessment (Cronbach, 1990, p. 703), it remains unclear how the authors envisioned the validation of the PADDI. Although the authors note their use of the DSM-IV criteria as evidence of content/face validity, the test manual also indicates that PADDI items account for all the diagnostic criteria of some clinical syndromes (e.g., depression, substance use) but not others (e.g., generalized anxiety, panic). Thus, the content/face validity of the PADDI is not uniform across the spectrum of its design, which consequently leads one to conclude that the PADDI may only be appropriate for use in conjunction with supplemental assessments of the clinical syndromes that are underrepresented by PADDI items.

In addition to content/face validity of the PADDI, the manual presents results of analyses that provide some evidence of modest construct validity, although there is no discussion of criterion validity or differential item functioning in any of the accompanying test materials. Overall, the interpretive statements that are germane to the scored items and their relative problem categories appear to be in the preliminary stages of test validation and warrant further study.

COMMENTARY. The PADDI has a number of uses for the clinician that merit mention. As a structured interview, it may be said that the PADDI provides a mechanism for consistent data gathering that ideally extenuates many of the factors that impinge upon interrater reliability in applied settings. Moreover, the PADDI's versatility makes it useful in a variety of applications, such as treatment planning, consulting, and making professional referrals. Also, given the PADDI's interview format, a respondent's reading level is not a factor in gathering information.

SUMMARY. Although the strength of the rationale for the PADDI is evident, there appears to be a paucity of empiricism in support of that rationale. Several assumptions in design of the PADDI have apparently remained untested, particularly the number and content of identified "problem categories" and the specification of nonoverlapping items. It is recommended that the authors of the PADDI consider providing descriptive norms (e.g., averages, standard deviations), correlations, demographics, and standard scores of samples from applicable populations, as well as item analyses, a clarification of scoring procedures, and validation studies of interpretive statements used in the interpretation of PADDI scores.

REVIEWER'S REFERENCES

American Psychiatric Association. (1994). *Diagnostic and statistical manual of mental disorders* (4th ed.). Washington, DC: Author.
Cronbach, L. J. (1990). *Essentials of psychological testing* (5th ed.). New York: Harper Collins.
Nunnally, J. C., & Bernstein, I. H. (1994). *Psychometric theory* (3rd ed.). New York: McGraw-Hill.

Review of the Practical Adolescent Dual Diagnostic Interview by MICHAEL G. KAVAN, Associate Dean for Student Affairs and Associate Professor of Family Medicine, Creighton University School of Medicine, Omaha, NE:

DESCRIPTION. The Practical Adolescent Dual Diagnostic Interview (PADDI) is a structured interview designed to identify the "prevalent conditions" (Hoffmann, n.d.) found in adolescents ages 12 to 18 years in both treatment and juvenile justice populations. Although not specifically stated in the manual, it is assumed from its title that the "prevalent conditions" refer to mental health and substance abuse problems seen in this age group. According to Hoffmann, the content of the PADDI is based on the *Diagnostic and Statistical Manual of Mental Disorders, Fourth Edition* (DSM-IV; American Psychiatric Association, 1994). The PADDI covers 10 Axis I mental health diagnostic areas as well as substance abuse and dependence, dangerousness to self or others, child abuse victimization, and sexual orientation. It also includes a set of four questions that act as an "Intellectual Functioning Screen" along with several observational items.

According to the manual, the PADDI is designed to be used in a variety of settings that include community mental health centers, adolescent addiction treatment facilities, juvenile justice detention centers, and private clinics. Both paraprofessionals and professionals may use this instrument in order to collect information necessary for a diagnostic workup. It may also be used to seek consultations or to make referrals. The PADDI consists of 164 items that are either asked of the patient or observed during the interview. The first set of questions covers general demographic issues. These are followed by a set of questions that act as a mental status screen. The remaining items cover various mental health and substance use disorders and include seven questions in which the interviewer is given the opportunity to rate the interviewee on several behaviors observed during the interview. The authors recommend that the clinical items be read as written without probing. Most questions may be answered with a simple "yes/no" or a close-ended response. Typical administration time is estimated to be between 20 and 40 minutes although it is certainly conceivable that much more time would be necessary for examinees providing more thorough responses.

Scoring is accomplished by transferring individual question responses to the scoring summary sheet, which is on the back of the front page of the instrument. The scoring summary sheet provides a "normal range" and "indications" section for each problem category area. For example, any positive response on items in the "Dangerousness to Self or Others" problem category warrants the following indication: "Any positive response indicates need for immediate psychiatric consultation." In another example, a positive score in all four areas in the problem category entitled "Posttraumatic Stress" results in the following indication: "PTSD is indicated."

The authors note that the PADDI scoring sheet may be used to determine DSM-IV diagnoses, signs of dangerousness, history of abuse, evidence of co-occurring disorders, and the severity of problems. They continue by reporting that it may also be used to guide further assessment, generate a narrative report, assist in the production of a diagnostic report, guide treatment planning, or make a referral. In addition, results may be used to educate and motivate patients and/or their parents, communicate among professionals, and assist with quality assurance.

DEVELOPMENT. The items within the PADDI are based on several DSM-IV disorders. Materials furnished by the publisher (i.e., a test manual and a "Research Update" handout) provide no additional information regarding test development.

TECHNICAL. The authors report that the PADDI items are drawn from the diagnostic criteria of the DSM-IV. Internal consistency (Cronbach alpha) was determined in a sample of 144 cases (the authors state that "these data are drawn from a variety of programs, but most of the cases are Caucasians"). No other information on these cases is provided in the manual. Internal consistency ranges from .671 (Conduct Disorder) to .922 (Major Depressive Episode). Test-retest reliability data are available on 8 females and 15 males between the ages of 14 and 17 years who are in residential addiction programs; all but one being Caucasian. No information is provided on the interviewers other than most had received no training in the use of the PADDI. The percent agreement (i.e., agreement on whether a condition is present) ranges from a low of 74% (PTSD) to a high of 100% (Conduct Disorder and Severe Substance Dependence) for the various problem areas. Cohen's kappa, which corrects for chance levels of agreement, ranged from .40 for the Mixed States (i.e., depression and mania) problem category to 1.0 for both the Conduct Disorder and Severe Substance Dependence problem categories. Although there is some disagreement regarding the interpretation of kappa, Spitzer, Fleiss, and Endicott (1978) suggest that values greater than .75 demonstrate good reliability, values between .50 and .75 suggest fair reliability, and values below .50 connote poor reliability. Using these criteria, six of the PADDI's problem areas (i.e., Key Depressive Symptoms, Thoughts of Harming Others, Panic Attacks, Conduct Disorder, Oppositional Defiant Disorder, Severe Substance Dependence) would be considered to have good reliability, four (i.e., Major Depressive Episode, Manic Episode, Psychotic Symptoms, Obsessive/Compulsive Indications) have fair reliability, and four (i.e., Mixed States, Thoughts of Self-Harm, Anxiety/Phobia Symptoms, PTSD) have poor reliability. It should be noted these data were collected on a small number of patients and that the time between administrations varied greatly from case to case. In fact, they ranged from 1 day to over a month with the median time between the two interviews being 2 weeks. No other reliability data are provided within the manual.

In terms of validity, the authors note that the PADDI items are derived from the DSM-IV and therefore the instrument has content validity. Although the PADDI provides screening questions for various DSM-IV diagnoses, it is not comprehensive in its coverage in each area. However, in fairness to the authors, they do note that those disorders that are more prevalent and more likely to adversely affect persons with substance use disorders are covered more thoroughly by the PADDI; yet, they fail to elaborate on or provide support for this.

Construct validity is demonstrated by the PADDI having content validity with respect to the diagnostic criteria represented by the questions, through its profile of symptoms, and through its internal consistency reliability. No information is provided for concurrent or predictive validity and no documentation is provided to support the use of the PADDI in managing youth, enhancing motivation, and assisting with treatment planning and placement.

No normative data are provided within the manual. In fact, the authors report, "although the statistical properties of a test are important for interpretation of findings, they are secondary to the consistent coverage of problem behaviors" (manual, p. 2). They continue by stating that statistics may be developed by individual users or through services available through the publisher.

COMMENTARY. The purpose of the PADDI is to provide paraprofessionals and professionals with a structured diagnostic interview that can identify mental health and substance abuse problems in adolescents. As long as the interviewer adheres to the script, it is an easy to use questionnaire that provides data on a variety of problems. Internal consistency and test-retest reliability are fairly good, although the latter were obtained on a rather small sample. As such, there is a need for further reliability studies.

The validity of scores from the PADDI is suspect. Although the authors provide limited support for content and construct validity, the question that must be addressed with any structured interview is: Does the PADDI do what it purports to do (i.e., assess mental health problems and assist with treatment planning and placement)? Whereas the PADDI items address several DSM-IV disorders, it is most likely a stretch to say, as the publisher's website reports, that the PADDI is a "comprehensive diagnostic assessment" that "rapidly collects detailed information." Those using the PADDI may benefit from rapid assessment, but may have to look to supplemental assessment information to obtain a comprehensive clinical assessment because detailed diagnostic information is not available for each diagnostic category. In addition, the PADDI fails to address whether symptoms produce significant impairment in important life functioning and it fails to include any exclusion criteria, both of which are important when using the DSM-IV for diagnostic purposes.

The authors also miss out on the opportunity to demonstrate concurrent validity by comparing it to more well-established structured interviews or predictive validity by assessing its ability to affect a variety of treatment-related issues. The authors should consider validating the PADDI by using what Spitzer (1983) refers to as the LEAD standard (i.e., Longitudinal observation by Experts using All available Data).

Finally, a lack of normative data is troublesome. Although the authors are correct in their directive to users to develop local norms, the lack of any such data makes interpretation of the PADDI difficult.

SUMMARY. As with any other diagnostic interview, the PADDI has its strengths and weaknesses. Strengths include its easy administration by paraprofessionals with little or no training, its coverage, limited as it is, of DSM-IV disorders, and its decent reliability. Weaknesses include scant validity data, no normative data, and no documented support for its advertised use in treatment planning. Although the PADDI looks promising, users are cautioned to use it as a research instrument or with supplemental data when forming diagnoses or planning treatment. In order to be truly helpful to both paraprofessionals and professionals, additional studies must be conducted before the PADDI can be used confidently for its stated purposes. Interested readers are urged to read Summerfeldt and Antony (2002) for a comprehensive review of other diagnostic interviews.

REVIEWER'S REFERENCES

American Psychiatric Association. (1994). *Diagnostic and statistical manual of mental disorders* (4th ed.) Washington, DC: Author.

Hoffmann, N. G. (n.d.) *PADDI findings for adolescents in treatment.* Retrieved January 20, 2004, from http://www.evinceassessment.com/paddi_251findings.pdf

Spitzer, R. L. (1983). Psychiatric diagnosis: Are clinicians still necessary? *Comprehensive Psychiatry, 24,* 399–411.

Spitzer, R. L., Fleiss, J. L., & Endicott, J. (1978). Problems of classification: Reliability and validity. In M. A. Lipton, A. DiMarco, & K. Killam (Eds.), *Psychopharmacology: A generation of progress* (pp. 857–869). New York: Raven.

Summerfeldt, L. J., & Antony, M. M. (2002). Structured and semistructured diagnostic interviews. In M. M. Antony & D. H. Barlow (Eds.), *Handbook of assessment and treatment planning for psychological disorders* (pp. 3–37). New York: Guilford.

[194]

Preschool and Kindergarten Behavior Scales, Second Edition.

Purpose: "Designed for use in evaluating social skills and problem behaviors of preschool and kindergarten-age children."

Population: Ages 3–6.

Publication Dates: 1994–2002.

Acronym: PKBS-2.

Scores, 12: Social Skills (Social Cooperation, Social Interaction, Social Independence, Total), Problem Behavior (Externalizing Problems, Internalizing Problems, Total), Supplemental Problem Behavior Subscales (Self-Control/Explosive, Attention Problems/Overactive, Antisocial/Aggressive, Social Withdrawal, Anxiety/Somatic Problems).

Administration: Group.

Price Data, 2002: $107 per complete kit including examiner's manual (2002, 103 pages) and 50 profile/record forms (specify English or Spanish); $69 per examiner's manual; $40 per 50 record forms (specify English or Spanish).

Foreign Language Edition: Spanish version available.

Time: (8–12) minutes.

Comments: Ratings by home-based raters or school-based raters; Supplemental Problem Behavior Subscales can be used to identify more specific symptoms of emotional and behavioral problems.

Author: Kenneth W. Merrell.

Publisher: PRO-ED.

Cross References: See T5:2036 (1 reference); for reviews by David MacPhee and T. Steuart Watson of an earlier edition, see 13:237.

Review of the Preschool and Kindergarten Behavior Scales, Second Edition by DOREEN WARD FAIRBANK, Associate Professor of Psychology, Meredith College, Raleigh, NC:

DESCRIPTION. The Preschool and Kindergarten Behavior Scales, Second Edition (PKBS-2), originally published in 1994, is a behavior rating scale used to evaluate social skills and problem behaviors in preschool children, ages 3 through 6 years. The PKBS-2 has 76 items divided between two scales: Social Skills (34 items) and Problem Behavior (42 items). Both scales include subscales that are helpful in identifying cluster areas of social skills and behavior problems. The three subscales for the Social Skills Scale include Social Cooperation (12 items), Social Interaction (11 items), and Social Independence (11 items). The Problem Behavior Scale includes two subscales and includes Externalizing Problems (27 items) and Internalizing Problems (15 items). There are also five specific supplemental subscales that can also be formed from the items on the Problem Behavior Scales. The first three are from the Externalizing Problem subscale and the last two are derived from the Internalizing Problem subscale. These can be used to identify more specific symptoms of emotional and behavioral problems in preschool children. These areas include Self-Centered/Explosive (11 items), Attention Problems/Overactive (8 items), Antisocial/Aggressive (8 items), Social Withdrawal (7 items), and Anxiety/Somatic Problems (8 items).

The PKBS-2 Summary/Response Form may be completed by school-based raters (anyone working with the child) or by home-based raters (any guardian of the child) and separate normative data and score conversion tables exist for each type of rater. Each item is rated on a 4-point scale (0 = *never*, 1 = *rarely*, 2 = *sometimes*, and 3 = *often*). The PKBS-2 Summary/Response Form usually takes between 8 to 12 minutes for the specific rater to complete. The form includes the following four sections: Child Information, Rater Information, the Instructions and Scales, and Additional Information. After completion of this form, a qualified user completes scoring and interpretation. The examiner's manual states that scoring is straightforward and no special expertise is required after the manual has been read carefully. However, individuals who interpret the results should have a basic understanding of the principles of education and psychological testing. Most trained professionals, such as psychologists, social workers, counselors, speech-language pathologists, educational diagnosticians, and teachers who receive appropriate training in educational and psychological measurement may interpret the results. Scoring is completed by calculating the raw scores for each of the subscales and then converting them to standard scores, percentile ranks, and risk levels. The subscale standard scores for the Social Skills Scale and Problem Behavior Scale are summed to create the composite scores, which are then converted to composite standard scores. The composite scores are then converted to percentile ranks and risk levels for the Social Skills Scale and Problem Behavior Scale. The manual also describes the scoring process if the supplemental problem behavior subscales are to be used. Once the scoring process has been completed, the manual discusses several methods of developing and implementing Functional Behavior Assessments and linking assessment to intervention planning and monitoring.

DEVELOPMENT. According to the examiner's manual, the PKBS-2 was developed to serve five purposes. The first purpose was as a screening tool to identify preschool- and kindergarten-age children who exhibit at-risk behavior that would benefit from early intervention. The second area was to be used as a multimethod, multisource, multisetting assessment to help identify, classify, and determine service eligibility for young children with significant social and behavioral problems (Merrell, 1999). The third purpose was to assess deficiencies in social skills and behavioral problems in order to develop appropriate interventions. The next purpose was as a measurement tool for monitoring behavior change during an intervention. The final purpose was the use of this instrument as a research tool to study behavioral, social, and emotional characteristics and patterns of young children.

The Social Skills Scales include items that describe positive social skills that are typical of well-adjusted children of similar ages, whereas the Problem Behavior Scale includes items that describe problem behaviors commonly seen with children of this age and to represent the domains of internalizing and externalizing problems.

The second edition retained the same test items and rating format, but increased the norming sample to enhance the racial/ethnic diversity and to conform to the demographic data of the 2000 U.S. Census. The reporting procedure has been simplified and now includes risk levels as a clinical guide to assist in interpreting the scores. The second edition includes a Spanish-language rating form.

TECHNICAL. The PKBS-2 was standardized with a nationwide sample of 3,313 children ages 3–6. The 458 cases of the 3,313 collected between 1996 and 2000 were used to increase the original normative sample and to field test the Spanish-Language Summary/Response Form. This added sample is more representative of the current ethnic makeup of the U.S. population based on the 2000 Census. Ethnicity, socioeconomic status, and special education classification of the norming sample are very similar to those characteristics of the U.S. population based on the 2000 Census.

Internal consistency reliability, as determined by Cronbach's coefficient alpha and the Spearman-Brown split-half reliability formula, was calculated using data from the PKBS-2 normative sample and from the samples used to develop the Home Rater norms and School Rater norms. Both measures demonstrated high coefficients of internal reliability across samples. The coefficients ranged from .81 to .97 in all areas of age, scale total, and subtests. The examiner's manual also demonstrates strong test-retest and English-Spanish Alternate Form reliability coefficients.

The manual provides substantial evidence for content validity. Convergent and discriminant construct validity was demonstrated through seven sets of comparison between the PKBS-2 and other child behavior rating scales. Validity was demonstrated for both scales. The examiner's manual reports on a variety of research studies that have been conducted with the PKBS-2 to demonstrate that it is a valid measure for clinical use as well as research applications.

SUMMARY. The PKBS-2 is designed to be used as a screening tool for early detection of developing social-emotional problems, as part of a multimethod assessment battery for classifications and eligibility purposes, to develop intervention programs and gauge subsequent behavioral change, and as an early childhood research tool. The PKBS-2 examiner's manual contains extensive descriptions and data from research that has been conducted with the instrument since its inception and demonstrates a test based on sound practice and research.

REVIEWER'S REFERENCE

Merrell, K. W. (1999). *Behavioral, social, and emotional assessment of children and adolescents.* Mahwah, NJ: Erlbaum.

Review of the Preschool and Kindergarten Behavior Scales, Second Edition by RONALD A. MADLE, School Psychologist, Shikellamy School District, Sunbury, PA, and Adjunct Associate Professor of School Psychology, The Pennsylvania State University, University Park, PA:

DESCRIPTION. The Preschool and Kindergarten Behavior Scales, Second Edition (PKBS-2) is designed to measure social skills and problem behaviors in children from ages 3 to 6. Although there are multiple stated uses of the PKBS-2, the author clearly favors using it to develop intervention goals and plan strategies.

The PKBS-2 kit includes an examiner's manual and 25 record forms. The record forms include identifying information, directions, a scoring summary, and space for additional comments. The 76 items, which the manual states can be completed in about 8 to 12 minutes, cover two pages.

The PKBS-2 now consists of five subscales organized under two major scales. Thirty-four items are used to assess Social Cooperation, Social Interaction, and Social Independence under the major area of Social Skills. Raters use a 4-point scale to indicate whether each behavior occurs *Never, Rarely, Sometimes,* or *Often* based on their knowledge of the child over the past 3 months. The ratings then are converted to standard scores (mean = 100; standard deviation = 15) and percentile ranks, as well as descriptive risk levels. The same scores are obtained for the 42 items that assess the well-established categories of Externalizing Problems and Internalizing Problems under a major scale called Problem Behaviors. The five subscales used on the original instrument—Self-Centered/Explosive, Attention Problems/Overactive, Antisocial/Aggressive, Social Withdrawal, and Anxiety/Somatic Complaints—are now considered supplemental scales. They can be derived using a separate scoring sheet from the manual.

The manual includes clear administration and scoring directions, as well as the needed qualifications for both raters and users of the scale. An additional chapter on interpretation, based on a three-level strategy involving standard scores, risk levels, and qualitative inspection of individual items, uses an integrated case study to illustrate the interpretive process. Introductory materials in the manual include a useful discussion of early childhood behavioral development, as well as issues in using behavior rating scales, in particular the need to employ them as only one component of a multimethod, multisource, and multisetting evaluation.

DEVELOPMENT. The stated goals for the second edition included improving the norming sample, providing separate norms for home and school raters, developing a Spanish language form, adding derived scores for scales and composites, simplifying risk level descriptors, and summarizing available research on the scale.

Even though the factor structure of the scale has been updated, all items and wording from the original PKBS (Merrell, 1994) have been retained. These had been developed using a rational-theoretical approach, with content validation based on examination by 16 early childhood professionals (e.g., preschool teachers, daycare operators). Any items rated as less than "fair" were dropped for the development version of the scale, with several more being eliminated after factor analytic studies were completed.

TECHNICAL.

Standardization. The normative data for the original PKBS were obtained from 2,855 preschool- and kindergarten-aged children during 1992 to 1994 with roughly equivalent numbers of males and females. Rather than true renorming, the PKBS-2 retains these data and adds an additional 458 cases collected between 1996 and 2000. This was done to increase the sample size and improve the ethnic composition of the norms. Recruitment for data collection both times was done through schools, preschools, and pediatric medical clinics.

The final norm tables are presented with separate tables for home and school raters, but are collapsed across gender and age. Attempts were made to approximate the 2000 U.S. Census on several key variables. Racial and ethnic distribution has improved greatly from the original scale, with no major deviations. Census approximation is also adequate for gender and special education status. Socioeconomic status shows some small deviations, most notably an overrepresentation of professional and managerial parents and underrepresentation of technical, sales, and administrative support workers. However, geographic region shows large mismatches with the Census. Seventy-seven percent of the sample came from the West, whereas the remaining 6%, 8%, and 9% came from the Midwest, Northeast, and South, respectively. The manual reports this has no practical impact based on a post hoc study. Unfortunately, the data are not presented to allow users to decide. The largest difference, which is reported in the text, shows nearly a one-third standard deviation difference between groups.

A second potential problem area with the norms is the use of a single age group for obtaining derived scores. Although minimized in the manual, there were distinct trends toward decreased problem behaviors and increased social skills with age. Three-year-olds in particular are relatively underrepresented ($N = 311$), yet show considerably different mean scores on the scales. Because of this a child retaining the same relative position with respect to other children can have an 8 to 10 standard score point change in a favorable direction between ages 3 and 4.

Reliability. Both Cronbach's coefficient alpha and Spearman-Brown split-half reliability for the total sample across PKBS-2 primary subscales and age groups generally meet or exceed the recommended .90 criterion, although Social Independence estimates are in the upper .80s. Internal consistency estimates for the total scores ranged from .94 to .97. As typically seen, reliabilities for home raters are somewhat lower than for school raters. Unfortunately, although standard error of measurement values are provided in the manual to allow for construction of confidence intervals, there is no place on the form to note this important piece of information. Test-retest reliabilities were .58 to .87 at 3 weeks and .66 to .78 at 3 months. The supplemental problem behavior scales had better test-retest reliabilities but showed lower internal consistency estimates than the primary scales.

Interrater agreement for teachers and teacher aides was found to be moderate for both Social Skills (.36 to .61) and Problem Behavior (.42 to .63). The usual lower level of cross informant agreement between home and preschool raters (.20 to .57 for Social Skills, .13 to .42 for Problem Behavior) is also present.

Validity. Content validity was established principally through item-total correlations, which were all quite satisfactory. Both exploratory and confirmatory factor analyses were used and supported the factor structure of the PKBS-2. Results of the factor analyses and intercorrelations are presented in the manual as evidence of factorial validity of the scale.

Considerable information is reported about the convergent and divergent validity of the PKBS-2 through correlational studies with seven other widely used social skills and problem behavior rating scales. Some scales used were the Social Skills Rating System (Gresham & Elliott, 1990), Achenbach Teacher's Report Form (Achenbach, 1991), and the Adjustment Scales for Children and Adolescents (McDermott, Marston, & Stott, 1993). Moderate to strong correlations were found with scales measuring related social skills constructs across studies. Similarly, the problem behavior sections of comparison scales showed the expected positive correlations with the corresponding PKBS-2 problem behavior scales. Inverse relationships were found between measures of social skills and problem behaviors across all measures, as were nonsignificant correlations with tangentially related constructs.

Several studies are reported that examined differences between typically developing children and those with some type of at-risk or clinical status. These showed significant differences for children who were being screened for or were identified with developmental delays, had ADHD, or were nominated by teachers as having internalized or externalized problems.

COMMENTARY AND SUMMARY. The primary weakness of the PKBS-2 is its normative information. The norms appear to be based on an accumulation of cases rather than a planned representative sample. Assurances that this has not compromised the norms are not always accompanied by the data needed for the user to verify this. In addition, some important uses might be limited by the structure of the PKBS-2 normative tables. Rather than providing for accurate monitoring of changes during the early preschool period, which should be a strength of this scale, changes could be difficult to interpret because of the failure to separate norm tables by age. Although changes across 4- to 6-year-old children appear to be relatively small on the average, raw score changes from ages 3 to 4 are substantial. For example, the mean externalizing problems raw score for boys changes from 34.22 at age 3 to 25.72 at age 4. This results in derived score changes from the 72nd to the 54th percentiles. Similar changes appear to be present throughout the distribution, causing apparent positive changes in children who have maintained the same relative position. This same phenomenon also could have an impact on identification rates because an excessive number of 3-year-olds, in particular, would be noted as having extreme problems. As a result, the PKBS-2 is not recommended for use with 3-year-olds except as an inventory of behaviors.

Other than these problems, the PKBS-2 appears to be a scale that effectively samples many important social skills and problem behaviors in young children. The scale is brief, easy to use, and measures important constructs throughout the entire preschool period. Technical information shows a high degree of reliability and validity, as well as a consistent factor structure. The PKBS-2 should serve users well as part of a multifactored assessment, especially when information for program planning and development, the use clearly favored by the author, is needed. The availability of a Spanish language form is also a positive aspect of the scale.

REVIEWER'S REFERENCES
Achenbach, T. M. (1991). Teachers Report Form for Ages 5-18. Burlington, VT: University of Vermont Department of Psychiatry.
Gresham, F. M., & Elliott, S. N. (1990). Social Skills Rating System. Circle Pines, MN: American Guidance Service.
McDermott, P. A., Marston, N. C., & Stott, D. H. (1993). Adjustment Scales for Children and Adolescents. Philadelphia, PA: Edumetric and Clinical Science.
Merrell, K. W. (1994). Preschool and Kindergarten Behavior Scales. Austin, TX: Pro-ED.

[195]

Preschool and Primary Inventory of Phonological Awareness.

Purpose: "Designed to identify children who have poor phonological awareness" and are at risk for literacy problems.
Population: Ages 3 to 6-11.
Publication Date: 2000.
Acronym: PIPA.
Scores: 6 subtests: Syllable Segmentation, Rhyme Awareness, Alliteration Awareness, Phoneme Isolation, Phoneme Segmentation, Letter Knowledge.
Administration: Individual.
Price Data, 2005: $158.42 per complete kit including record forms, stimulus booklet, and manual (54 pages).
Time: (25–30) minutes; (5) minutes per subtest.
Comments: A version with U.S. norms, the Pre-Reading Inventory of Phonological Awareness (2003), is available from Harcourt Assessment (USA) and will be reviewed in the next Mental Measurements Yearbook.
Authors: Barbara Dodd, Sharon Crosbie, Beth McIntosh, Tania Teitzel, and Anne Ozanne.
Publisher: Harcourt Assessment [England].

Review of the Preschool and Primary Inventory of Phonological Awareness by CARLOS INCHAURRALDE, Professor of Linguistics and Psychologist, University of Zaragoza, Zaragoza, Spain:

DESCRIPTION. The Preschool and Primary Inventory of Phonological Awareness (PIPA) is a test designed to identify children (of ages 3 to 7) with poor phonological awareness. It consists of six subtests (Rhyme Awareness, Syllable Segmentation, Alliteration Awareness, Phoneme Isolation, Phoneme Segmentation, Letter Knowledge), which take 4–5 minutes each to administer. The total time for completion of the whole test is 25–30 minutes. The materials provided consist of a manual (with information about theoretical background, test design and development, administration procedures, scoring and interpreting the test, and normative data), a stimulus booklet, and record forms.

This test is to be administered by speech and language therapists, teachers, or professionals assessing a child's literacy skills, and the examiners are explicitly required to have experience in standardized test administration, scoring, interpretation, and children's assessment. The test should be administered individually in a quiet, well lit room. Rapport should be established with the child and appropriate feedback provided to his or her answers during testing. The examiner uses picture stimuli in the stimulus booklet and standardized instructions to elicit answers from the child. Scores are recorded reflecting the performance of the child on the subtest being administered. Each item of the six subtests has three possible score values: 1 for each correct response, 0 for an incorrect response, and NR for no response. The raw scores are converted into a normalized standard score using different tables for U.K. children (Appendix A of manual) or Australian children (Appendix B of manual). Percentile scores may be calculated by looking at another table of the manual (Appendix D).

DEVELOPMENT. This test was developed based on the assumption that the measurement of phonological awareness can predict early reading and spelling skills more accurately than any other single variable. Thus, early identification of problems in that area could allow appropriate intervention to prevent reading and spelling failure. Phonological awareness can be identified with three main components: syllable, onset-rime, and phoneme awareness (Hoien, Lundberg, Stanovich, & Bjaalid, 1995). Five subtests were designed corresponding to these components: Syllable Segmentation (addressing syllable awareness), Rhyme Awareness (addressing onset-rhyme awareness), Phoneme Isolation, Phoneme Segmentation (addressing phoneme awareness), and Alliteration Awareness. A sixth subtest, Letter Knowledge, was added for assessment of grapheme-phoneme knowledge.

The first five PIPA subtests were standardized initially in Brisbane, Australia during 1995 and 1996. The standardization study was conducted by two pediatric speech and language therapists, with 583 children between the ages of 3 years and 6:11 years. In 1999 the Letter Knowledge subtest was included and another standardization study was conducted, this time in the United Kingdom, with 595 children. This testing was conducted by trained undergraduate and postgraduate students of the University of Newcastle.

TECHNICAL. The manual devotes chapter 4 to technical information. Concerning standardization, it details the Australian normative sample by age, by gender, and by socioeconomic status. The United Kingdom normative sample is also grouped according to age, gender, and socioeconomic status, but separation by geographical area is included, too. There are no further details about the standardization procedure.

Reliability is claimed to have been evaluated by means of three methods: calculation of internal consistency reliability coefficients, a test-retest procedure, and interrater scores. Internal consistency coefficients were obtained for the U.K. sample using coefficient alpha, with acceptable values for the six subtests (all of them above .7). The test-retest procedure was used on a sample of 42 children from ages 3 to 7 years, using a test interval of 2 weeks. The mean age was 5 years and the same examiner administered the test and the retest. The resulting correlation coefficients exceeded .7, except in the Phoneme Segmentation subtest (.3), which suggests that the stability of scores on this subtest is lacking. Finally, a small group of 6 children were videotaped and scored a second time by another speech and language pathologist. There were no significant differences between the scorers, but the sample chosen was very small for reaching a significant conclusion about interscorer reliability.

Concerning validity, the technical section of the manual claims content, concurrent, criterion-related, and construct validity for this test. Content validity (that is, whether the subtests are real measures of phonological awareness) is assumed on the grounds of what is documented in the literature addressing phonological awareness. However, there is no concrete reference to research that

provides evidence to support content validity. Concurrent validity (that is, the correlation with other tests that are valid measures of the same facts) was obtained by comparing scores of the Phonological Abilities Test (PAT) (Muter, Hulme, & Snowling, 1997) concerning Rhyme Detection and Letter Knowledge. They were significantly correlated (>.6 in all cases). However, there are no concurrent validity values for the other four subtests. Criterion-related validity (the value of the test as a predictor of performance on a criterion measure) was evaluated by comparing performance on the PIPA and the Test of Early Reading Ability (TERA; Reid, Hresko, & Hammill, 1989) because it is assumed that phonological awareness is a predictor of reading ability. Thirty children ages 4 to 6:4 years were included in the sample. Significant correlations were found between scores on the five subtests measuring phonological awareness and the TERA. Finally, construct validity (whether the subtests evaluate the ability they are supposed to evaluate, phonological awareness) was evaluated by examining the intercorrelations among subtests, with the result that all correlations were significant. The highest correlations were between Letter Knowledge and Alliteration Awareness (.73), and Letter Knowledge and Phoneme Isolation (.79). The weakest correlation was between Syllable and Phoneme Segmentation (.33).

COMMENTARY. This test deserves praise for the clarity of the materials provided. The record forms provide instructions for the completion of the different subtests in a very clear, straightforward manner, and the stimulus booklet also provides good stimuli, with big and colorful pictures that should be motivating for children. The manual is also clear and not too technical. However, this clarity and conciseness can also be a weakness because the manual lacks detailed information about the standardization procedure, and the rationale behind the test is not sufficiently supported with references to studies about the relationship between phonological awareness and early reading and spelling skills. The only reference mentioned is Bryant, MacLean, Bradley, and Crossland (1990).

SUMMARY. This is a test that should not be difficult to administer provided that the examiner has some experience in phonetic assessment. The evaluation of Syllable Segmentation, Rhyme Awareness, Alliteration Awareness, Phoneme Isolation, Phoneme Segmentation, and Letter Knowledge is carried out in a clear way, and the calculation of standard scores and percentiles is also easy, even for the noninitiated, as the manual gives very clear instructions concerning these matters. The test shows that scores tend to be reliable. There is also evidence that scores may be integrated as intended (validity). The record forms provide a good, systematic way of recording the assessment of phonological awareness. In short, this is a test that can be used with few problems.

REVIEWER'S REFERENCES

Bryant, P. E., MacLean, M., Bradley, L., & Crossland, J. (1990). Rhyme and alliteration, phoneme detection and learning to read. *Developmental Psychology, 26,* 429–438.

Hoien, T., Lundberg, I., Stanovich, K., & Bjaalid, I. (1995). Components of phonological awareness. *Reading and Writing, 7,* 171–188.

Muter, V., Hulme, C., & Snowling, M. (1997). Phonological Abilities Test. London: The Psychological Corporation.

Reid, D. K., Hresko, W., & Hammill, D. (1989). Test of Early Reading Ability. Austin, TX: PRO-ED.

Review of the Preschool and Primary Inventory of Phonological Awareness by GENE SCHWARTING, Associate Professor, Education Department, Fontbonne University, St. Louis, MO:

DESCRIPTION. The stated purpose of the Preschool and Primary Inventory of Phonological Awareness (PIPA) is to identify those children age 3 to 7 years with impaired understanding of the sound structure of the English language, as well as the decreased ability to manipulate units of sound. The authors note the importance of such abilities in the development of reading and written communication skills, and that identification of those with impairments should be done early so that intervention can be provided. The PIPA consists of an administration/technical manual, an easel-style stimulus booklet with color artwork, and record forms. The instrument assesses children in the following areas: Rhyme Awareness, Syllable Segmentation, Alliteration Awareness, Phoneme Isolation, Phoneme Segmentation, and Letter Knowledge. Each of these subtests has separate norms, and consists of 2 or more practice items followed by 12 test items (except Letter Knowledge, which has 32 items). Subtests may be administered out of order, except that those with similar formats should not be used sequentially. All begin with the first item so there are no basal rules, and only three of the subtests have ceilings. The PIPA may be used by speech and language therapists, teachers, and "professionals" who are experienced in the use of standardized tests. Administration time is estimated at 25-30 minutes.

Each subtest has a mean of 10 and a standard deviation of 3, with conversion of these standard scores to percentile ranks, as well as 68% and 95% confidence intervals, being provided.

DEVELOPMENT. The PIPA is based on the concept that the three principal components of phonological development are syllable, onset-rime, and phoneme awareness. However, information is not provided as to how the relationship of subtest content to the three components was determined, the development of the test format or items, or any field testing that was conducted.

TECHNICAL. Standardization of the PIPA occurred twice, resulting in two norm groups. The first took place in 1995–1996 in Brisbane, Australia with 583 children—approximately 70 at each 6-month age interval between 3 and 7 years. There is fairly even representation of genders and socioeconomic status, but other information on the sample is not provided. The second standardization occurred in the United Kingdom in the Summer of 1999 with 595 children, and included the Letter Knowledge subtest, which was not part of the instrument in Australia. There was an overrepresentation of 4.5- to 5-year-old children, and an underrepresentation of children less than 4.5 years of age within this group. In addition, the majority of this sample came from the low socioeconomic group although representation by geographic location was uneven.

Reported reliability information for the United Kingdom sample indicates that internal consistency ranges from .70 for Phoneme Segmentation to .98 for Letter Knowledge; and test-retest with a 2-week interval varies from .33 to .98 for the same subtests. A validity study with an unidentified sample, comparing the PIPA and the Phonological Abilities Test, found relationships of .63 for the Rhyme Detection and .92 for the Letter Knowledge subsets common to both instruments. A criterion-related validity study in Australia involving 30 children, comparing the PIPA subtests and the Test of Early Reading Ability, found correlations ranging from .39 to .50. And, review of the PIPA subtest intercorrelations notes variation from .33 to .79.

COMMENTARY. In recent years, the emphasis on early assessment and identification of future learning problems, as well as the importance of phonological development to the acquisition of reading and written communication ability, have increased. Therefore, instruments such as the PIPA seem particularly relevant because other instruments in the field are designed for older children. The PIPA attempted to develop an objective assessment—however, concerns exist about the ability of examiners to accurately and objectively assess young children's verbal responses, particularly for those children with dialects, disfluencies, or articulation impairment. The two sets of norms are useful for residents of Australia and the United Kingdom, but would be confusing to residents of other countries, especially in that there are significant differences in the raw to standard score conversions. In addition, some picture stimuli demonstrate cultural bias and the issue of accent or dialect is not addressed.

SUMMARY. On first appearance, the PIPA appears to fill a need. Administration directions are simple and straightforward and the instrument is user-friendly. However, the absence of information about development, the two sets of discrepant (and somewhat dated) norms, limited information about reliability and validity, and the lack of U.S. or Canadian norms raise significant questions as to its use outside of Australia and the U.K.

[196]
The Pre-School Screening Test.

Purpose: To screen children for special educational needs.
Population: 3 years 6 months to 4 years 5 months.
Publication Date: 2001.
Acronym: PREST.
Scores, 14: PREST 1 (Rapid Naming, Bead Threading & Paper Cutting, Digits & Letters, Repetition, Shape Copying, Corsi Frog, At-Risk Total), PREST 2 (Balance, Phonological Discrimination, Digit Span, Rhyme, Sound Order, Teddy and Form Matching, At-Risk Total).
Administration: Individual.
Price Data, 2001: $120.28 per complete kit including score sheets, card sets, beads, sound order audiotape, training videotape, and manual (98 pages).
Time: (10–30) minutes.
Authors: Angela Fawcett, Rod Nicholson, and Ray Lee.
Publisher: Harcourt Assessment [England].

Review of The Pre-School Screening Test by SHERRY K. BAIN, Associate Professor, Department of Educational Psychology & Counseling, and YOUNG JU LEE, Doctoral Student in School Psychology, University of Tennessee, Knoxville, TN:

DESCRIPTION. Developed and normed in England, the general purpose of The Pre-School Screening Test (PREST) is to provide an initial decision-making step in identifying children who may be at risk for Special Education Needs and need further assessment. Other recommended uses include serving as a "basis for important records of the child's development," and for profiling strengths and weaknesses to guide the development of "in-school support" (manual, p. 2). Age levels appropriate for use of this test are 3 years, 6 months to 4 years, 5 months.

The PREST can be administered as a short form, called PREST1, or as a full test. The short form should take between 10 and 15 minutes to administer, and can be used to identify children who are potentially at risk and should be administered the second part, PREST2, taking another 10 to 15 minutes to obtain the composite score. Information offered in the manual of the Pre-School Screening Test on how these recommendations are derived is brief; more details would be helpful.

The PREST was easy to administer within the time frames suggested. Children appear to enjoy taking the test, which switches quickly to interesting stimuli and new skills. The manual does not state the level of qualifications for the test administrator, but directions are generally clear and concise, suggesting that anyone with testing experience and practice could administer the PREST. A welcome addition to administration aids would be the inclusion of written stimulus words to accompany the Rhyming Sheet (Section B). The stimulus card for this test supplies drawings that easily could be misnamed by the examiner to ruin the rhyming arrangement (e.g., calling the "pig" a "hog").

The 12 individual tests making up the PREST yield percentile rank scores, each of which can be categorized at five interpretive levels from double minus (--) representing highly at risk, to double plus (++) representing above average. The rationale for the criterion scores that divide these categories is not offered. Divisions do not follow standard deviations in the population (e.g., double minus represents 1st to 10th percentiles, minus represents 11th to 25th percentiles).

Test results also provide a composite score, called the At-Risk Quotient (ARQ), based on a weighted score procedure. Individual test scores categorized as double minus (highly at risk) are assigned weighted scores of 2; test scores categorized as minus (at risk) are assigned weighted scores of 1; test scores at higher percentile categories are assigned 0. The ARQ is calculated by averaging the weighted scores. An ARQ of .9 or higher is considered an indicator of the child being generally at risk. Among the participants in the standardization sample, 13% acquired ARQ scores of .9 or more; 3.8% acquired scores of 1.25 or more; and 1%, scores of 1.5 or more.

The authors recommend that the test may be re-administered to a child after 6 months, to document growth in skills following intervention. A description of an intervention program based upon identification of deficits based upon PREST results is offered in the manual. The intervention program was still in progress at the printing time of the manual, and explicit data concerning the PREST's sensitivity in documenting growth due to intervention were not offered.

DEVELOPMENT. The authors' rationale for developing the PREST is the current shift away from play activities toward formal instruction at preschool levels, mandated by the (British) National Curriculum for primary school children. The PREST is apparently a downward extension of The Dyslexia Early Screening Test (Nicholson & Fawcett, 1996) designed for use with children 4.6–6.5 years of age.

The authors state they selected items for the PREST to conform to each of three primary hypotheses involving dyslexia: (a) a phonological deficit hypothesis, (b) a neurologically based hypothesis, and (c) a hypothesis involving difficulties in automatization of skills. A breakdown of the relationship of the 12 tests to respective hypotheses is given in the manual.

Information on the standardization sample is somewhat sketchy in the manual. The sample consisted of over 500 children from "selected nursery schools in various areas of England" (p. 60). An effort was made to stratify the sample across ages. Cities and counties that were sampled appear to be from the northern portions of England exclusively. Samples from urban areas such as London, or from southern, eastern, southwestern regions, or the Midlands are absent. Information about the ethnic or racial makeup of the sample, socioeconomic status, and the fit of the sample to current census data is also absent. One might question the appropriate use of this screener in areas of England not represented in the standardization sample, as well as in regions of the United Kingdom such as Scotland, Wales, or Northern Ireland. Additionally, without more information about demographic characteristics of the standardization sample, use of the screener with students from ethnic or racial minority groups is questionable. Local or regional normative information is recommended before using this screener outside of the northern region of England.

TECHNICAL. The manual offers information on test-retest reliability, based on approximately a 1-week interval, with 12 children from 4 years to 4 years 5 months of age participating. Excluding Sound Order, which yielded a reliability coefficient of .57, the range across the remaining 11 tests was .71 (Rapid Naming) to .93 (Digit & Letter Names). Across the 12 tests, reliability averaged .82, which seems a respectable average coefficient for a screener, considering the rather small sample size.

Intercorrelations of the 12 tests, based upon results from 470 participants, are provided in tabular format in the manual. These results are not addressed qualitatively by the authors and could benefit from interpretive explanations. For example, Rapid Naming correlates negatively with all other tests. Without an explanation by the authors, a newcomer to the test would have to check scoring procedures in another section of the manual to confirm the reason for the negative relationship.

In terms of validity, information offered in the manual tends to be sparse or contradictory. The authors offer a broad statement: "It is clear from the case studies we have run ... that both PREST1 and PREST2 identify children known to be at risk" (manual, p. 63). However, only one case study is presented in the manual.

In lieu of further validity evidence, the authors pose three questions, providing answers that they feel are appropriate to address the validity issue. The first question concerns the relationship of the PREST to three hypothesized views on dyslexia (discussed above under Development). A discussion of the relationship between individual tests and the relevant hypotheses follows this question. Disabilities besides dyslexia that might become evident when screening young children are briefly addressed (e.g., disabilities involving low intelligence, other learning disabilities) but clearly, the authors are primarily interested in identifying early problems that relate to dyslexia.

The second and third questions asked by the authors concern the relationship of the PREST to other screening tests for early childhood, and the relationship of the PREST to assessment methods used with older children. While specific assessment instruments are identified in the answer to each question, statistical data comparing the PREST to tests in either of these two categories are not offered. In an earlier statement, the authors had suggested that evidence of concurrent validity was not possible because of the absence of comparable tests, and construct validity would involve an "exhaustive series of tests" (manual, p. 63) to determine the presence or absence of learning disabilities. The contradiction between this statement and the eventual naming of related tests is difficult to resolve. Empirical evidence of validity is badly needed, and should be obtained.

The issue of test bias is not addressed in the manual. Without more information about demographic characteristics of children in the standardization sample, or information about minority groups who might be administered this screener, the question of bias is indeed difficult to address. Research addressing bias issues, including gender bias, ethnic/racial bias, socioeconomic bias, and regional bias, should be an integral part of test development.

COMMENTARY AND SUMMARY. The PREST represents a modest effort in test development for an age group that could benefit from easy and effective screeners. However, without a broader standardization sample; adequate information on demographic characteristics; evidence of concurrent, construct, and predictive validity; and examination of test bias, potential users should be cautious, opting for alternative screening instruments that have been reasonably validated. With appropriate evidence of validity, the PREST might represent a viable choice for use with children from the northern region of England, as this is where the standardization sample is located. Interested researchers are encouraged to investigate issues of validity and bias for this instrument.

REVIEWERS' REFERENCE

Nicholson, R. I., & Fawcett, A. J. (1996). Dyslexia Early Screening Test. London, England: The Psychological Corporation.

Review of The Pre-School Screening Test by GENE SCHWARTING, Associate Professor, Education Department, Fontbonne University, St. Louis, MO:

DESCRIPTION. The Pre-School Screening Test (PREST) was developed to screen children ages 3 1/2 to 4 1/2 years of age for special education needs, to record a child's development, to profile strengths and weaknesses, and to guide development of in-school support for such children. The instrument consists of two parts: PREST 1 with six subtests (Rapid Naming, Bead Threading and Paper Cutting, Digits and Letters, Repetition, Shape Copying, and Corsi Frog [visual memory]) is estimated to take 10 to 15 minutes for a routine screening. Those children found to be "at risk" on the PREST 1 are to be tested with the PREST 2, consisting of six additional subtests (Balance, Phonological Discrimination, Digit Span, Rhyming, Sound Order, and Teddy and Form Matching), which requires an additional 10–15 minutes.

The PREST was designed for use by school professionals, nursery school teachers, and nurses. The test kit includes, in addition to the manual, a number of large cards with drawings, manipulatives (large enough that a preschooler's swallowing them is not a major concern), scoring keys, a cassette audio tape, and a training video. Additional items that the administrator provides include a cassette tape player, a container for the provided beads, children's scissors, a stopwatch, paper and pencils, and duplicated copies of one of the provided cards.

The subtests include provision for teaching/demonstrating the items and have neither basals nor ceilings. Raw scores are translated using the norms tables (3-month intervals) into percentile score bands. These bands include a large average group with a converted score of "0" including the 25th to 75th percentiles. Two smaller bands exist above the average, with converted scores of "+" and "++", as well as two below the average, with converted scores of "-" and "- -". In addition, total scores may be obtained by adding the subtest results and an "At Risk Quotient" through dividing this total score by the number of subtests. A quotient of .5 or more on the PREST 1 should result in administering the PREST 2, whereas an overall quotient of .9 or greater is regarded as strong evidence of being at risk.

DEVELOPMENT. The goals indicated by the test authors for the PREST were that it be quick, simple, and enjoyable for preschool-age children; a reliable predictor of primary school failure; provide a profile of strengths and weaknesses; and meet the requirements of baseline assessment for school entrance. The authors have extensive experience in dyslexia research, incorporating in the development of the PREST aspects of a previously developed instrument, the Dyslexia Early Screening Test (DEST; Nicholson & Fawcett, 1996; 15:88) as well as items from the Middleton in Teesdale Screening Test (MIST; Lee, 1994). The resulting subtests, which are based upon commonly used measures in early childhood, were field-tested and modified several times prior to final selection of items followed by norming.

TECHNICAL. Norming was done completely in England by a number of trained nursery school teachers on whole classes of preschool-age children in unspecified locations. The group consists of "around" 100 children each at ages 3 1/2, 3 3/4, 4, and 4 1/4 with no data presented about gender, race/ethnicity, or socioeconomic status. The presence of a norms table for ages 4-3 to 4-5 in the absence of children of this age group in the norming is not explained. Scores for each age group were then ranked and utilized to develop percentile ranks that were converted into the bands previously described.

Reliability data are provided only from a very small ($n = 12$) study using a test-retest format "around a week apart" (manual, p. 62) of children from 4 years to 4 years and 5 months of age. The coefficients from this study are mostly in the .8–.9 range, with the lowest being .57 (Sound Order) and the highest .93 (Digit and Letter Names).

Validity data are not presented, with the authors indicating in the manual that it was not possible to obtain such information. Intercorrelations of the subtests are provided, with most coefficients falling in the -.3 to +.3 range.

COMMENTARY. As indicated, this instrument was developed and normed in England, raising questions regarding the usefulness of the norms tables in other countries. Many of the subtests and items are commonly used in assessing children of this age range, and the materials mainly seem appropriate although there are some directions for the examiner and test materials that are distinctly British. The absence of validity information, extremely limited reliability data, and incomplete normative information are cause for significant concern. In addition, some of the tasks appear difficult developmentally for the ages for which they are intended, whereas others appear to have little discriminative value (spatial memory and discrimination subtests have the same score conversions for every age group).

SUMMARY. Because the subtests and items themselves seem appropriate, use of the instrument to develop local norms for screening could be defended. However, the use of other instruments with better norms, and with reliability and validity evidence such as is provided for the Developmental Indicators for the Assessment of Learning, Third Edition (DIAL-III; Mardell-Czudnowski & Goldenberg, 1998; T6:790) would be strongly encouraged.

REVIEWER'S REFERENCES
Lee, R. (1994). The Middleton in Teesdale Screening Test. Middleton in Teesdale, England: Bramblewood Education.
Mardell-Czudnowski, C., & Goldenberg, D. (1998). Developmental Indicators for the Assessment of Learning, Third Edition. Circle Pines, MN: American Guidance Services, Inc.
Nicholson, R. I., & Fawcett, A. J. (1996). Dyslexia Early Screening Test. London, England: The Psychological Corporation.

[197]

Preschool Language Assessment Instrument—Second Edition.

Purpose: Designed to test "children's discourse abilities" in "aspects of early educational exchanges."

Population: Ages 3-0 to 5-11.

Publication Dates: 1978–2003.

Acronym: PLAI-2.

Administration: Individual.

Forms, 2: Age 3 years, Ages 4–5 years.

Price Data, 2003: $197 per complete kit including examiner's manual (2003, 71 pages), picture book, 25 profile/examiner record booklets—3-year-olds, and 25 profile/examiner record booklets—4/5-year-olds; $52 per examiner's manual; $77 per picture book; $40 per 25 profile/examiner's record booklets for 3-year-olds; $40 per 25 profile/examiner's record booklets for 4/5-year-olds.

Time: (30) minutes.

Comments: Includes nonstandardized procedures for analyzing adequacy of response and interfering behaviors.

Authors: Marion Blank, Susan A. Rose, and Laura J. Berlin.

Publisher: PRO-ED.

a) AGES 3 YEARS.

Scores, 6: Discourse Ability (Matching, Selective Analysis, Reordering and Reasoning, Receptive, Expressive, Total).

b) AGES 4–5 YEARS.

Scores, 7: Discourse Ability (Matching, Selective Analysis, Reordering, Reasoning, Receptive, Expressive, Total).

Cross References: See T5:2044 (6 references) and T4:2083 (2 references); for reviews by William O. Haynes and Kenneth G. Shipley of a previous edition, see 9:979.

Review of the Preschool Language Assessment Instrument–Second Edition by KORESSA KUTSICK MALCOLM, School Psychologist, Augusta County Public Schools, Fishersville, VA and Adjunct Faculty Member, Mary Baldwin College, Staunton, VA:

DESCRIPTION. The Preschool Language Assessment Instrument–Second Edition (PLAI-2) is the revision of the Preschool Language Assessment Instrument, an experimental test of a young child's discourse functioning that was published in 1978. The PLAI-2 attempted to modernize the presented stimuli of its predecessor and to provide a normative base for the test. The test's developers also wanted to preserve what they believed was the PLAI's unique approach to assessing language functioning in young children.

The PLAI-2 is built around four constructs of language abstraction (Matching Perception, Selective Analysis Perception, Reordering Perception, and Reasoning Perception); two modes of responding (Receptive and Expressive); and two aspects of pragmatic behavior (adequacy of response and interfering behaviors a child might exhibit while responding to an item). The authors maintained that in a typical social encounter, such as in a preschool classroom, children are expected to respond to many rapid shifts in linguistic demands. For example, they might be asked to identify an object, answer a question about the possible outcomes of a story, make comparisons between objects, describe an object or place, and follow a series of directions all within a very short time frame. The PLAI-2 attempts to reflect these demands as items are presented in a steady flow of different language tasks. Children respond to verbal and pictorial stimuli in order to demonstrate their understanding of various language constructs. Examiners record verbatim responses, mark the response as being right or wrong, and then complete ratings regarding the adequacy of the responses. Any interfering behaviors, which might have been a factor in the response, are also noted.

The administrative and scoring format of the PLAI-2 is rather straightforward. The test stimuli are presented in an easel format. The visual stimuli are bright, attractive and appropriate for the targeted population. Two different record books are offered for the 3-year-olds and for the 4- to 5-year-olds. These different record books reflect the developmental expectations for the type of responses that should be given by younger and older children. Because items are not arranged in any sort of hierarchical sequence, fatigue factors from successive failures are not an issue for this test. Standard scores, percentile ranks, and age equivalencies can be computed for the overall Discourse Ability Scale as well as for the Matching, Selective Analysis, Reordering, and Reasoning subtests. The test's observation section is scored following a nonstandardized system.

The PLAI-2 was designed for children ages 3 years to 5 years, 11 months of age. The authors of this test stated that the PLAI-2 is appropriate for children "who can understand the directions, who are able to formulate the necessary responses, and who can speak English" (examiner's manual, p. 9). Because the test items are presented in English, this latter prerequisite is easy to understand. The other requirements, that the child can understand the directions and can form necessary responses, would seem to negate the utility of the test for children who have possible language delays.

Reviews of the original PLAI maintained that a major strength of the test was that it offered a different approach to the assessment of a young child's language competencies. This difference involved the test's format of item presentation that deviated from standard groupings of items by task demands or developmental levels. This continues to be a unique feature for a test that yields more than one overall standard score.

DEVELOPMENT. The PLAI-2 manual contains little specific information regarding the development process of this test. As mentioned above, the PLAI-2 is a revision of the PLAI. The PLAI had no normative information and little statistical data to its credit and was deemed to be a research tool. No information was provided as to how items were developed or selected for either version of the test. The authors contend that examiner feedback, previous test reviews, and personal observations were factors that contributed to the revision of the PLAI-2. No specifics regarding these factors were discussed, however.

TECHNICAL. Statistical information presented in the PLAI-2 manual seemed to mark more of a good starting point in the test's developmental history than its end product. The standardization sample, although noted to be representative of the general U.S. population demographics for geographics, gender, race, ethnicity, socioeconomic factors, disability status, and subject age, was rather small for a national study (*n* = 463). The selection process for this sample was also of concern. Examiners in 16 states were asked to test 10–30 children who matched the demographic makeup of their communities. It seemed this selection process might not have yielded a true representative sample for the norming group.

Reliability information provided for the PLAI-2 was based on measures of internal consistency, examination of the standard error of measurement for the subtest and total test scores, and one test-retest study. Results of these analyses indicated that the Overall Discourse Ability Scale was the most reliable of the possible scores with correlation coefficients ranging from .92 to .95 across three age levels for the test. Moderate to high coefficients ranging from .70 to .85 were obtained for the internal consistency scores of the subtests at the same age levels. Noting Salvia and Ysseldyke's (2001) recommendation that educational decisions should be made from scores with reliability levels of .90 or higher, the authors note that only the Discourse Ability score should be utilized for placement decisions. In the one test-retest study offered (no time interval specified), resulting correlation coefficients ranged from .73 to .93 for the various groupings by sex and ethnicity categories. The lowest of these coefficients were obtained on the Reordering and Reasoning subtests, raising some questions as to the stability of the scores of these two subtests over time.

Validity information provided for the PLAI-2 was based on a review of the test's content, criterion-related studies, and review of the test's factor structures. For verification of content validity, the authors focused on a discussion of how the PLAI-2 was similar to the PLAI test item content. Because little or no information was presented on the appropriateness of the PLAI item content, this did not seem to be a strong argument for the revised test. A stronger presentation for the test's content validity might have included a discussion of relevant language development research that drove the item development process. The manual did review some information regarding item analysis techniques utilized to examine item responses generated by the standardization sample. This discussion, however, did not describe how the analysis related to the selection or removal of items for the final version of the test. Although the factor analytic study presented in the manual

did lend support for the factor structures of the test, additional studies in this area would make a stronger case for this aspect of the PLAI-2.

The authors of the PLAI-2 contend that the available validity information demonstrated that the test was nonbiased with regard to gender and race variables. Although test results were similar between males and females, it was noted that African American children and Hispanic American children consistently scored lower than European American children on all dimensions of the PLAI-2 with the exception of the Matching subtest. With this pattern in scores, examiners should use caution when using the PLAI-2 with minority group children.

COMMENTARY. Several areas of weakness were noted for the PLAI-2. There needs to be a comprehensive review of preschool language literature provided to build a rationale for the test's purpose, structure, and development process. In administration of the test, the flow of items, attempting to capture more natural language demands, might prove difficult for young children. In real language encounters, a child would have many cues (such as facial expressions, voice tones, environmental stimuli) to help them deal with rapid shifts in language demands. In the testing environment, without context cues, children never seem to get into a mode of responding. With their limited testing experiences, preschool children should be given more items of a kind presented together to help them understand the demands of the task. It was also noted that the length of some of the examiner directions presented seemed to be too long for young children. Even in real life encounters, teachers and parents tend to ask questions and share information with language levels more consistent with the developmental level of children than the test presented.

With regard to the statistical properties of the PLAI-2, additional reliability and validity studies are needed before examiners could feel comfortable using this test in clinical settings. More studies need to examine the use of the PLAI-2 with minority groups. It might be helpful to add additional subgroups broken by factors such as ethnicity and socioeconomic levels when examining the validity of the test's scores. It will also be important to compare the PLAI-2 to other tests of language development to determine if the test really does assess language functioning and if it does so in a unique manner that would be useful to professionals studying a young child's language patterns. In addition, studies comparing the PLAI-2 with measures of general development and/or intellectual functioning could help discern the role of these variables in the PLAI-2 scores.

SUMMARY. The PLAI-2 appears to be an instrument still in its early stages of development as a test of language functioning in preschool children. The test warrants further investigation into its value to the assessment world. Examiners who choose to use this test in clinical settings should only use it as a supplemental measure. Examiners searching for tests of preschool language functioning might consider the Preschool Language Scale–Fourth Edition (Zimmerman, Steiner, & Pond, 2002; see 198).

REVIEWER'S REFERENCES
Salvia, J., & Ysseldyke, J. E. (2001). *Assessment* (8th ed.). Boston: Houghton Mifflin.

Zimmerman, I. L., Steiner, V. G., & Pond, R. E. (2002). Preschool Language Scale: Fourth Edition. San Antonia, TX: The Psychological Corporation.

Review of the Preschool Language Assessment Instrument—Second Edition by REBECCA McCAULEY, Professor, Communication Sciences, University of Vermont, Burlington, VT:

DESCRIPTION. This instrument consists of a standardized, norm-referenced measure of children's discourse skills as well as two "nonstandardized" procedures designed to guide examiner's observations of children's pragmatic skills in discourse. The instrument differs from many existing measures of young children's language skills in its focus on children's use of language during teacher-child communication. It is intended for use with children who are 3 years to 5 years, 11 months of age, with slightly differing subtest structures for the 3-year-olds versus 4- to 5-year-olds. The authors advocate the instrument's use for six purposes: the identification of children who are functioning below their peers, the description of a child's strengths and weaknesses in dealing with abstract language, the documentation of progress, the determination of differences in expressive versus receptive language, the examination of receptive skills in children who are not using expressive language, and the measurement of discourse skills for research.

Administration of the test is estimated to require about 30 minutes, but the authors recommend the use of short breaks, completion of testing at a second session, or even re-administration of the test at a later time as needed to ensure the perceived validity of the child's test results. Children are to be administered all items unless they do not use expressive language, in which case expressive items are omitted. Specific training recommendations are given to prepare an examiner to use the instrument. Scores available for interpretation include standard scores ($M = 10$, $SD = 3$), percentile ranks, and age-equivalent scores for six subtests (four related to level of language abstraction: Matching, Selective Analysis, Reordering, and Reasoning; as well as two related to mode of response: Receptive and Expressive) and an overall Discourse Ability score. In addition, general guidelines are provided to aid users in the interpretation of a nonstandardized assessment of pragmatic language function.

DEVELOPMENT. This instrument is a revision of a 1978 experimental test that was not normed. Like the earlier version, the Preschool Language Assessment Instrument—Second Edition (PLAI-2) is designed to examine children's attainment of language performance at four levels of abstraction: (a) matching perception, (b) analyzing perception, (c) reordering perception, and (d) reasoning about perception. Also retained from the earlier version of the instrument is the interspersing of items at each of these levels throughout testing as a means of capturing the variety of demands present in normal discourse.

Other constructs embodied in the PLAI-2 include the long-established distinction between receptive and expressive language and a novel examination of two aspects of pragmatic language function: adequacy of response and the presence of interfering behaviors. Although the Expressive-Receptive distinction is represented in subtest scores, the Pragmatic function is examined in an accompanying informal assessment. In the informal pragmatic assessment, the adequacy of children's pragmatic responses is described for expressive items only, with items rated as fully adequate, acceptable, ambiguous, or inadequate. Within the description of pragmatic skills, interfering behaviors are characterized as underresponsive (nonresponsive, delayed, low volume) or overresponsive (extra actions, excessive verbalization, loud volume).

Major elements of the revision included enhancements in item selection designed to improve the aility to measure receptive discourse skills and allow for interpretation of the newly added Pragmatic assessment described above. Methods used in the process of item selection included traditional indices of item performance such as item discrimination and item difficulty, as well as more recently developed methods. Specifically, differential item functioning (DIF) analysis techniques were used to identify items that function differently for different groups across all ability levels, thus serving as a means for detecting item bias. This method verified a lack of item bias when used to compare the performance of items in three groups: male versus female, African American versus non-African American, and Hispanic American versus non-Hispanic American.

TECHNICAL.

Standardization. The normative data were collected in Spring 1999 and Fall 2000 from 463 children in 16 states who were identified by individuals who had participated in previous test development projects of the publisher. Demographic characteristics of the sample, consisting of geographic region, gender, race, ethnicity, family income, parental educational attainment, and disability, appeared to match well those of the U.S. population for 1999. No description of methods used to identify the language status (bilingual vs. monolingual English speakers) of the Hispanic American participants was provided.

Reliability. Internal consistency using Cronbach's coefficient alpha method was used to examine the homogeneity of items within subtest and the overall Discourse Ability scores for the normative data, calculated for each of the three age groups, as well as for gender, racial, ethnic, and language-disordered subgroups. These measures were also used in the calculation of standard errors of measurement for age groups within subtest and overall scores. Across all of these calculations, coefficient alpha ranged from .67 to .95. As acknowledged by the authors, a generally held standard for coefficient alpha is .80. This level was achieved most consistently for the subtest scores related to Expressive and Receptive language and for the overall Discourse Ability score (the latter often achieved coefficient alpha values of .90 and above). However, whether examined within ages or within the subgroups based on gender, race, etc., the coefficient alpha values for subtest scores associated with levels of language abstraction often failed to meet this standard, with most falling in the .70s.

Test-retest reliability was examined for 60 children in each of the three age groups. Although sampling of gender and ethnic/racial groups approximated that of the overall normative sample, the children came from just three Northeastern states and the time between test administrations was not specified. In addition, children with disabilities were not studied. Test-retest reliability measures consisted of subtest and Discourse Ability score correlations between Time 1 and Time 2, corrected for restricted range as needed. If one uses the criterion of .80 as indicative of adequate reliability, the Discourse Ability score, Expressive Language subtest, Receptive Language subtest, and three of the subtest scores related to level of language abstraction achieved or exceeded this level.

Validity. The content validity evidence for this measure consisted of a detailed description of the test's structure with rationales and the item analyses described in the previous section of this review entitled "DEVELOPMENT."

Evidence that scores from the PLAI-2 could predict performance on a relevant criterion consisted of a correlational study involving 38 children who were given both the target instrument and the Test of Early Language Development—Third Edition (TELD-3; Hresko, Reid & Hammill, 1999). The children in the sample were from three Northeastern states and were about equally divided by age and gender. Ethnicity and racial differences were also reasonably represented in the sample. Correlations between standard scores were given for the PLAI-2 subtest and overall score with the Expressive Language subtests, Receptive Language subtests, and overall score for the TELD-3. Correlation coefficients ranged in size from a low of .40 for the Expressive Language subtests of the two measures to a high of .91 for the overall Discourse Ability score with that same Expressive Language TELD-3 subtest. The size of these correlations was deemed sufficient by the authors, but in the absence of a discussion of the relative purposes of the two measures, this interpretation is less than completely persuasive to this reviewer.

Evidence showing that the construct for which the test was developed was sufficiently measured using the PLAI-2 was provided using five commonly used strategies. First, because of the developmental nature of language development, it was predicted that age and performance on the PLAI-2 would be positively correlated.

This prediction was borne out in a correlation of standard scores with age for each of the PLAI-2 subtests. Second, the authors compared seven groups of children to examine the degree to which the PLAI-2 differentiated groups in a manner predicted by the authors. Although not tested statistically, what appeared to be substantially lower scores (approaching one standard deviation below the mean) were obtained by a small group ($n = 32$) of children with speech-language disorders, but not by children with articulation problems ($n = 50$), findings in keeping with expectations of performance if the PLAI-2 is a valid measure of language function. Comparison of ethnic and racial subgroups (European American, African American, and Hispanic American) suggested similar scores across groups, except that the Hispanic children received the next to lowest scores of any group. This finding caused the authors to caution users of the test to determine the language proficiency of children's parents prior to use of the instrument, presumably as a means of obtaining indirect information about the child's language status. A third method of construct validation used by the authors was a confirmatory factor analysis. In that analysis, the standard scores of the older two groups (4- and 5-year-olds) were examined to determine the extent to which a single underlying factor, labeled Overall Discourse Ability, explained the variance observed in the four subtest scores related to level of language abstraction. This model represented a good fit to the data, as determined using three different methods. The fifth construct validation method used by the authors was the computation of a correlation coefficient between the Receptive and Expressive subtest scores. The finding of a correlation coefficient of .70 suggests a high degree of relationship between the two measures, as expected. Finally, the authors pointed to the size of item discrimination indices calculated during the test's development as a fifth indicator that the test was constructed in such a way as to maximize the likelihood that it would successfully target the intended construct.

COMMENTARY. This instrument appears to be unique in its efforts to examine children's abilities to deal with different levels of language abstraction, a construct that is thought to be particularly important to understanding a child's discourse abilities in a child-teacher interaction. Its inclusion of informal methods for the description of pragmatic functions is also a special feature. A further strength is that the test's authors have included several steps to avoid bias related to gender, race, ethnicity, and disability. Of particular note in this regard is their normative sampling methods and their adoption of the DIF method for examining item bias as part of the development process. Although they appear to have been successful in avoiding bias at the level of individual items, they may not have succeeded in avoiding overall bias affecting children who are Hispanic Americans. Because mean differences in performance appeared to disfavor this group, additional statistical testing and data are needed. Also helpful, but absent, in sorting out this potential problem would have been information about the way in which children were screened for language dominance prior to inclusion in that group.

As a more general caveat, it should be noted that adequate reliability was most consistently obtained for the overall Discourse Ability score and for the subscores related to Expressive and Receptive Language, but not for the four subscores related to differing levels of language abstraction. Methods used in validating the measure were conventional and provided a general pattern of results supporting the utility of this measure for use in examining overall discourse skills, as well as those skills broken down by expressive versus receptive modes of responding. Support for the central construct of examining levels of language abstraction was considerably less convincing, with the strongest evidence being the rationale given for content within each subtest and the tendency for each of these levels to correlate positively with age.

SUMMARY. This revision represents a substantial improvement over the 1978 experimental measure that it replaces. Particular strengths include the representativeness of the normative sample, a substantial expansion of information regarding the test's technical properties, and the provision of information related to the authors' examination of potential bias affecting important subgroups of children. Given these data, however, the use of this instrument should be approached cautiously for children who are Hispanic American. In addition, the reliability and validity data fail to provide sufficient evidence documenting the merit of the more creative aspect of subtest structure—namely, the subtests organized by level of language abstraction. Given this latter limitation, it is not clear that this measure represents an advance over the numerous competitors available to assess expressive and receptive language in 3- to 5-year-olds. One example of such a measure is Carrow-Woolfolk's Oral and Written Language Scales (1995; Graham, 2001).

REVIEWER'S REFERENCES

Carrow-Woolfolk, E. (1995). Oral and Written Language Scales: Listening Comprehension and Oral Expression. Circle Pines, MN: American Guidance.

Graham, S. (2001). [Review of Oral and Written Language Scales: Listening Comprehension and Oral Expression.] In B. S. Plake & J. C. Impara (Eds.), *The fourteenth mental measurements yearbook* (pp. 860-862). Lincoln, NE: Buros Institute of Mental Measurements.

Hresko, W. P., Reid, D. K., & Hammill, D. D. (1999). Test of Early Language Development—Third Edition. Austin, TX: PRO-Ed.

[198]

Preschool Language Scale, Fourth Edition.

Purpose: Designed to "identify children who have a language disorder or delay."

Population: Ages birth to 6-11.

Publication Dates: 1969–2002.

Acronym: PLS-4.

Scores, 4: Auditory Comprehension, Expressive Communication, Total Language, Articulation.

Administration: Individual.

Price Data, 2003: $235 per English basic kit with manipulatives including examiner's manual (2002, 287 pages), picture manual, 15 record forms, and 23 manipulatives; $185 per English basic kit without manipulatives including examiner's manual, picture manual, and 15 record forms; $60 per examiner's manual; $109 per picture manual; $37 per 15 English record forms; $59 per set of manipulatives.

Foreign Language Edition: Spanish edition available.

Time: (20–45) minutes.

Comments: Fourth edition adds supplemental subtests and norms based on 2000 U.S. Census figures.

Authors: Irla Lee Zimmerman, Violette G. Steiner, and Roberta Evatt Pond.

Publisher: Harcourt Assessment, Inc.

a) ARTICULATION SCREENER.

Purpose: Designed to evaluate articulation in single words.

Population: Ages 2-6 to 6-11.

Scores: Total score only.

Time: (2) minutes.

Comments: "Criterion-referenced" optional subtest.

b) LANGUAGE SAMPLE CHECKLIST.

Purpose: Designed to evaluate spontaneous speech.

Population: Ages 1 to 6-11.

Scores: No scores.

Time: (15–60) minutes.

Comments: Supplemental checklist allows validation of information obtained from the Expressive Communication subscale.

c) CAREGIVER QUESTIONNAIRE.

Purpose: Designed to "enable parents/caregivers to provide information about the child's communication behaviors" at home or preschool.

Population: Ages birth to 2-11.

Scores: Not scored.

Time: (15–20) minutes.

Comments: Supplemental questionnaire; may be administered as an interview.

Cross References: See T5:2045 (6 references); for reviews by J. Jeffrey Grill and Janet A. Norris of a previous edition, see 13:241 (26 references); see also T4:2084 (24 references); for an excerpted review by Barton B. Proger of a previous editions, see 8:929 (3 references); see also T2:2024 (1 reference); for a review by Joel Stark and an excerpted review by C. H. Ammons, see 7:965.

Review of the Preschool Language Scale, Fourth Edition by TERRI FLOWERDAY, Assistant Professor of Educational Psychology, University of New Mexico, Albuquerque, NM:

DESCRIPTION. The Preschool Language Scale, Fourth Edition (PLS-4) is a norm-referenced instrument designed for use with children age birth through 6 years, 11 months. The PLS-4 is an individually administered test used to identify children with language disorder or delay. The PLS-4 consists of two core subscales, the Auditory Comprehension subscale (AC) and Expressive Communication subscale (EC). Three supplemental assessment instruments are also available: Language Sample Checklist, Articulation Screener, and Caregiver Questionnaire.

The AC subscale is used to assess the child's ability to understand spoken language. It includes items designed at three developmental levels: infants and toddlers, preschool, and 5–6-year-olds. Infant/toddler items focus on precursors for language, such as ability to pay attention and object play. Preschool items emphasize comprehension of basic vocabulary, concepts, and grammatical markers. The items designed for ages 5–6 assess ability to understand complex sentences, make comparisons, and inferences.

The EC subscale is used to assess the child's ability to communicate with others. Infant/toddler tasks focus on vocal development and social communication. Preschool items ask children to name and describe common objects, express quantity, and to use prepositions, grammatical markers, and appropriate sentence structure. Children ages 5–6 are assessed on preliteracy skills such as phonological awareness, ability to sequence a short story, and use of language to define words.

The core subscales (AC and EC) should be administered and scored by qualified users who might include speech-language pathologists, early childhood specialists, psychologists, educational diagnosticians, and others with training in assessment. Administration time is estimated at 20–45 minutes. The PLS-4 yields three norm-referenced scores: AC score, EC score, and Total Language (TL) score (a composite of AC and EC). Standard scores, percentile ranks, and age equivalents are available for age birth to 11 months (3-month intervals) and 1 year through 6 years, 11 months (6-month intervals).

The three supplemental assessments are designed to provide additional information and to assist in evaluation. The Language Sample Checklist can be used with children capable of producing connected utterances. This instrument gives an overview of the content and structure of the child's spoken language by calculating mean length of utterance (MLU) and summary profile. The Articulation Screener, designed for children age 2 years, 6 months through 6 years, 11 months, yields age-appropriate cut scores that help a clinician determine if further articulation testing is advisable. Criterion scores are reported for children ages 2 years, 6 months through 6 years, 11 months. The Caregiver Questionnaire provides specific open-ended questions to be answered by the child's caregiver and is designed for use with children age birth to 3 years. This instrument provides supplemental information about the child's behaviors at home and gives the caregiver an opportunity to share perspective and provide input.

The PLS-4 comprises the following components: examiner's manual (required), picture manual (required), record form (required), and manipulatives (optional). The examiner's manual contains information about administration, scoring, and interpretation of the tests. In addition, information about test development and psychometric evaluation of the instruments is provided. The picture manual is a spiral-bound, cardboard flip chart with an easel back. It provides color picture stimuli necessary for administration of test items. The record form (20 pages) provides the user with abbreviated directions for administration, recording, and scoring of test items. It includes information about Articulation Screener and Language Sample Checklist. Manipulatives are required for test administration primarily with children age birth through four years and can be purchased from the test maker or acquired separately. The user must have a medium-sized ball, 5 blocks, 2 small bowls, box with lid, bubbles, 2 small toy cars, a cloth, crackers, 3 small cups, 3 keys on a key ring, paper, small sealable sandwich bag, 3 plastic spoons, rattle, squeaky toy, teddy bear, several age appropriate books/toys, a watch with a second hand, and a windup toy.

DEVELOPMENT. The PLS-4 is the latest version (copyright 2002) of a test that has been under development since 1969. The differences between the PLS-3 (1992) and the PLS-4 (2002) are as follows: new standardization data collected in 2001 and U.S. Census data from 2000 replaced old data from 1991 and 1980, respectively; increased emphasis on early childhood assessment, especially infant/toddler age level; improvement in the test's psychometric properties; provision for collecting additional information, particularly with regard to criterion-referenced assessments and caregiver input.

Item/task development and selection procedures were described in detail. The authors conducted an extensive literature review to update information on best practices and research findings. Clinicians were surveyed for feedback about issues of concern with the PLS-3. Some initial changes were made based on this input. New task development and subitem writing was done by a pool of speech-language pathologists with extensive experience using the PLS-3 to assess children. Items tested in the Tryout phase totaled 229 tasks and more than 700 subitems. These items were reviewed and modified by a panel of experts to insure appropriateness for children of diverse backgrounds. The Bias Review Panel members (14) are listed with contact information. After modification by the Bias Review panel, a pilot test was conducted with 15 children. Based on these data, additional adjustments were made and the Tryout Phase of data collection was conducted. In this phase, 661 children were tested at 227 sites in 46 states. In addition to this sample, 53 children with diagnosed language disorders were tested. Results of the Tryout Study were reviewed by a second

Tryout Bias Review Panel consisting of an additional 6 speech pathologists/psychologists in 4 states and Puerto Rico. Final revisions were made based on feedback from this panel.

TECHNICAL. Standardization procedures using 2001 data are discussed at length. Noting a population shift occurring between 1980 and 2000, the authors recognized the need to update. For example, 1980 Census data indicated that 31% of the U.S. population was of nonmajority background. In 2000, this figure had increased to 37%. The standardization sample of the PLS-4 reflects this shift, including 38% ethnic minority participants. The standardization sample consisted of 2,400 "children who could speak and understand English" (examiner's manual, p. 175). Data were collected at 357 sites in 48 states. Males and females were represented equally, as were age levels. A representative, stratified sample, based on 2000 Census data included proportionate numbers of ethnic minority participants, participants at various SES levels, and participants from diverse geographic areas. A criticism of the PLS-3 suggested insufficient numbers of children diagnosed with language disabilities or delay in the standardization sample. In the PLS-4 the authors included 13.2% participants with "identified conditions/ diagnoses" (examiner's manual, p. 179).

A concern with the PLS-4 standardization sample is the lack of bilingual speakers (or the lack of reporting such). The authors indicate that 3.4% of the sample reported speaking Spanish and 3.4% reported speaking Chinese. The development of language and/or language disorders in bilingual children is not directly addressed in the examiner's manual. Specific instructions are not included with regard to scoring and code shifting in the English version. The PLS-4 could do more to advise examiners about the unique characteristics of children who are English language learners (Kester & Pena, 2002) and who now constitute a large percentage of the U.S. population.

Several types of reliability evidence were described and tested. Evidence of test-retest reliability supported consistency of scores. The test was administered on two separate occasions (administration interval = 2 to 14 days, with a mean of 5.9 days) to a subsample of 218 children randomly selected from the standardization sample. Analyses indicated subscale stability coefficients of between .82 and .95. Cronbach's alpha ranged

from .81 to .97 for the total language scale. A third measure used to document reliability was the standard error of measurement (*SEM*). A smaller *SEM* and confidence interval are evidence of more reliable scores. Reliability coefficients are presented for each subscale measure at 16 different age levels. They range from .66 to .97 with means of .86 on AC, .91 on EC, and .93 for TL.

The authors state, "most of the PLS-4 tasks are objectively scored; however, some Expressive Communication tasks are subject to the scorer's interpretation" (examiner's manual, p. 189). Although scoring rules are discussed in chapter 6 of the examiner's manual, the person doing the testing must make decisions about how to score any given response. The authors suggest that study data provided evidence of interrater reliability at .99%. Evidence of interrater reliability would be more convincing if at least two examiners tested a number of children (each examiner testing each child) under similar conditions. The scores assigned each child by each of the two raters could then be compared for degree of similarity. This was not done. Instead, the authors offer as evidence, the data provided by 15 elementary school teachers who "scored" 100 protocols selected from the standardization protocols. "Each PLS-4 Standardization protocol was scored by two different scorers, under the supervision of the test developers" (examiner's manual, p. 190). Only scores on the open-ended tasks were used in the evaluation of interrater reliability, and we are not told how many tasks nor which tasks are considered open-ended. The protocols selected from the standardization sample had, in essence, already been scored. The teachers participating in the interrater reliability study did not do the original testing. The influence of any differences in examiners' test administration would not be represented in these comparisons. The reliability of scoring is a concern. As mentioned by the authors, the time taken to administer the tests can vary by as much as 100%. One test administered and scored in 20 minutes could have a different result from a second test administered and scored in 40 minutes, and personal inquiry has suggested that many scorers take as long as 60 minutes on a given test. Because the user is given directions for administering the test only in written form in the manual, inconsistencies in administration are possible. A training video would be helpful providing review of genuine testing situations with discussion of the scoring rationale. In addition, a training session could be included to encourage a higher degree of user consistency.

Evidence of validity has been provided based on extensive expert checks throughout instrument development. Evidence of validity based on response process would be indicated by responses that are not attributable to processes other than the targeted process. The English version has been closely scrutinized by experts in the field and seems solid. There are some concerns with the Spanish version of the test that will be discussed in the commentary. Internal structure has been discussed and is largely acceptable. Convergent evidence is presented that suggests the PLS-4 elicits similar responses, scoring, and interpretation as the Denver II, an instrument designed to assess language development levels in children. In addition, with a sample of 104 children, scores on the PLS-3 and PLS-4 were correlated at .65 (AC) and .79 (EC).

COMMENTARY. The PLS-4 English version appears to be a reasonably sound instrument for the assessment of language development and/ or language disorders. The manipulatives can be distracting for some children and the test makers might consider placing all tasks that use manipulatives together in the sequence. This would eliminate the need to periodically "take toys out" and "put toys away" when administering the test. Testers need to be well trained to insure consistent, standardized administration of the instruments. A video and/or standardized training session would be beneficial. Special instructions for proper administration and scoring of this instrument with English-language learners should be developed.

The PLS-4 Spanish version raises concerns. The PLS-4 (English) included in its standardization sample an appropriate representation of children speaking several English dialects, and consideration was taken in the suggested scoring for speakers of each dialect. The PLS-4 (Spanish) indicates that 81% of the standardization sample came from homes where Mexican Spanish was spoken. This could introduce bias into the scoring, particularly with regard to Spanish speakers whose Spanish language origin is other than Mexico.

SUMMARY. The PLS-4 is a norm-referenced instrument used for assessment of language development and language disorders in preschool children. Both the English version and Spanish

version have undergone rigorous psychometric evaluation throughout development and the examiner's manuals provide evidence for adequate levels of reliability and validity, although interrater reliability could be reassessed. A training video or training session might improve the consistency of instruction and scoring during administration. Special care is recommended when using the PLS-4 (English) for assessing children who are English-language learners. The PLS-4 Spanish version would benefit from some modifications in language usage (examiner's manual instructions), and revisions to the picture manual. Overall, the PLS-4 should be considered a useful instrument for assessing language development and disorders in preschool children. For purposes of diagnosis, the PLS-4 should be used in conjunction with other assessments, never alone.

REVIEWER'S REFERENCE

Kester, E. S., & Pena, E. D. (2002). Language ability assessment of Spanish-English bilinguals: Future directions. *Practical Assessment, Research & Evaluation, 8*(4). Retrieved January, 16, 2004 from http://PAREonline.net/getvn.asp?v=8&n=4.

Review of the Preschool Language Scale, Fourth Edition by HOI K. SUEN, Professor of Educational Psychology, Pennsylvania State University, University Park, PA:

DESCRIPTION. The Preschool Language Scale, Fourth Edition (PLS-4) is an individually administered test designed to identify young children from birth to 6 years 11 months old who have a language disorder or delay. It consists of two subscales for the assessments of Auditory Comprehension and Expressive Comprehension, respectively. It also provides three supplemental measures, which include an Articulation Screener, a Language Sample Checklist and a Caregiver Questionnaire. The materials provided for the administration of the test include an examiner's manual that spells out the administration, scoring, and interpretation procedures; a record form that provides all the items of the test; a picture manual that contains color pictorial stimuli needed for many of the test items; and a box of manipulatives (e.g., ball, bowls, rattles, windup toy, cloth) needed for interactions with the child during test administration. There are a grand total of 68 task items. However, almost all of these items/tasks are better described as testlets than items as each of them contains anywhere between 2 to 8 related subitems/ tasks. Dependent on the age of the individual child, the administration time is reported to be between 20 and 45 minutes.

DEVELOPMENT. The steps followed in the development of the PLS-4 were careful and comprehensive. First, a review of the literature was conducted to identify appropriate developmental milestones and current trends in developmental theories. Next, a survey of clinicians who had used the previous version of the scale, PLS-3, was conducted in 1999 to obtain feedback and suggestions for modifications. Based on these, some PLS-3 tasks were modified accordingly. Additionally, a list of new tasks needed was established. A set of criteria for task design was also established for each age group. Based on these, a number of item writers/task designers, including a pool of speech-language pathologists, were used to create new tasks. These new tasks along with the necessary accompanying pictorial stimuli and manipulatives were submitted to a diverse panel of experts for a sensitivity review to identify potentially biased items. After removal or modification of potentially biased items, the resulting items were tested through a two-stage process—a pilot study and a tryout study—to help identify the final set of items. The pilot study involved only a very small sample of 9 males and 6 females in San Antonio, Texas. The purpose of that was to further identify potentially problematic items. Subsequently, items were further modified before the tryout study. The tryout data were collected from 661 children from 46 states in the continental United States. Classical item analyses were conducted on these data. Additionally, a second sensitivity review was done by a different diverse panel of experts to further identify potentially biased items among the items used in the tryout. Based on results of the item analyses, on results from the second sensitivity review, and on feedback from examiners, a final set of items was identified.

TECHNICAL. Responses to the final set of items were collected from a large standardization sample consisting of 2,400 children throughout the 48 lower states of the United States in 2001. The sample was stratified on the basis of parental education, geographic region, and race. Data show that this sample is representative of the U.S. population as described in the 2000 Census on these three variables. Scoring rules were established and refined after a careful compilation of alternative responses. Additionally, a panel of dialect reviewers was used to further refine the scoring rules to be consistent with known dialect rules and usage.

Normative subscale scores and total scores were derived based on the standardization sample. Normalized standard scores with a mean of 100 and standard deviation of 15 are used. Additionally, age-equivalent scores are provided.

Several approaches to classical reliability were used to estimate reliability and standard error of measurement. A test-retest method (administration interval = 2 to 14 days, with a mean of 5.9 days) was used on a random subsample of 218 children from the standardization sample. The resulting reliability estimates for various age groups range between .82 and .97. The Cronbach's alpha approach was also used on the response data for a subsample of 1,534 children. The results are mostly above .82, and some are as high as .97. This is with the exception of the reliabilities for the sample of 9- to 11-month-olds, for whom the Cronbach's alphas range between .67 to .81. Finally interrater reliabilities were estimated using 15 raters and the percent-agreement indices and correlations were found to be .99.

Evidence of validity was gathered in a very comprehensive manner consistent with the latest professional standards, set forth by the Joint Committee for Testing Standards (AERA, APA, & NCME, 1999). The 1999 Standards suggested that validation is a process of evidence accumulation to support interpretation and use. Evidence may come from many different sources and may be in different forms. However, the Joint Committee specifically identified five possible sources of validity evidence: evidence based on content, on response processes, on internal structure, on relationships with other variables, and on consequences. The developers of the PLS-4 gathered evidence from all five sources. Particularly impressive is the evidence based on test content. This was gathered through a literature review, user survey, a delineation of test scope (specifications), and the mapping of tasks on the areas in the scope to ensure correspondence between tasks and specifications, content and sensitivity reviews, and a comprehensive set of task analyses. The care and comprehensiveness of the process of gathering content evidence from multiple sources is rare in commercially published tests. Evidence based on internal structure was based on the correlation between the two subscales and Cronbach's alpha coefficients. Although the evidence is strong that the two subscales correlate with one another, the case for the distinctiveness of the two subscales is not compelling.

Evidence based on relations with other variables was gathered from a number of angles, including relationship with the Denver II and with PLS-3 and through estimation of sensitivity and specificity indices for the identification of known groups, including children with language disorder, those with a developmental language delay, those diagnosed with autism, and those with hearing impairment. Results from all these analyses are supportive of the validity claim. No information regarding long-term predictive utility is available.

Evidence based on response processes and that based on consequences are two sources of validity evidence typically not considered prior to the 1999 Standards. As such, PLS-4 represents one of the pioneers in the practice of gathering evidence from these two sources. Response process evidence was gathered from a detailed task analysis, from examiner feedback in the tryout process, from results of the pilot test with the 15 children, from an examination of item difficulty in the tryout sample, and from interviews of 4–6-year-old children in the sample to determine why they selected or gave a certain response. Information gathered from these sources was used to modify and refine the tasks to ensure that appropriate responses would be elicited. Concerns of consequential evidence of validity were addressed in the test manual for PLS-4. No direct evidence was provided. The test developer only pointed out that "to date, there is no evidence to suggest that the PLS-4 has any negative consequences for children when it is used as intended" (examiner's manual, p. 218). Indeed, evidence based on consequences is not easily gathered by developers, but is generally considered a shared responsibility of the test user. The developers of the PLS-4 provided careful and detailed recommendations regarding the intended uses of the test and suggested steps to minimize potentially negative impact of testing children who differ from the mainstream population.

COMMENTARY. The development process, the standardization process, the estimation of score reliabilities, and the gathering evidence of validity for the PLS-4 are all very impressive, careful, and comprehensive. The steps followed in the validation process also used a state-of-the-art, most sophisticated conceptual framework. This is consistent with the usual high standard of quality of other tests published by The Psychological Corporation (Harcourt Assessment, Inc.). There is little doubt that the PLS-4 produces very reliable scores. Evidence of validity is also reasonably cogent.

However, no test is perfect and there are areas that can use some fine-tuned improvements. These areas of imperfections are not expected to lead to any problems in the use of the PLS-4 in general, but may be problematic in some situations. Improvements in these areas will likely make an already good test even better. One such area is the standard error of measurement. The standard errors of measurement are relatively large for many age groups. For example, a 95% confidence interval can be as large as plus or minus 18 points for certain subscales for certain age groups. This is substantial in light of the fact that the standard deviation of the scores is only 15 points wide. For example, for those subscales and age groups with such large standard errors, the 95% confidence interval could suggest a child's range of possible scores being between the 12th and the 88th percentile—a range too large to be meaningful or useful. Such large standard error of measurement limits the utility of the test, particularly for classification decisions. The test developer is apparently aware of this limitation in that they have provided the range of scores for a 90% confidence interval and that for a 95% confidence interval for all scores in the norm tables. Users need to be aware of these often-large ranges and use caution when making important classification decisions.

Another area that is less than optimal is the insurance against potential ethnic/cultural biases. The test developer did perform two separate sensitivity reviews as well as dialect reviews to minimize the potential for cultural bias. However, it is generally known that sensitivity reviews are inadequate in the identification of potentially biased items. More formal differential item functioning (DIF) analyses are usually needed to isolate these items.

In terms of reliability, classical methods were used. The testing design, however, involves a trained rater observing a child's response to specific tasks and assigning scores according to the scoring rubric. The design is in fact a complex two-faceted design with nested raters. For such a complex design, classical methods are inadequate, particularly with regard to the nesting of raters. The reliability estimates would have been more definitive had a Generalizability approach been used.

Validity evidence based on the internal structure of the test was claimed by looking at the correlation between the two subscales. This piece of evidence would have been more conclusive had factor analyses been performed. These were not done, possibly due to sample size limitations for age subgroups and substantial missing data in the use of basal and ceiling rules. Perhaps future research may focus on conducting such factor analytic studies.

Because the test is designed to identify children with language disorders or delays, perhaps the most critical piece of validity evidence is clinical utility. In this area, the developer has looked into measures of sensitivity and specificity. However, from a clinical utility perspective, it is more important to determine and report the degrees of positive predictive power and negative predictive power. Also, longitudinal predictive accuracy data are not available. Finally, although the composite and subscale scores are highly reliable, information regarding classification reliability/consistency is missing.

SUMMARY. The strongest area of the PLS-4 is in the cogency of the validity evidence to support interpretation. Particularly compelling and thorough is the evidence based on test content. Evidence to support the recommended use of identifying children with language disorder or delays, however, is not as compelling. Overall, the PLS-4 is a well-designed and carefully developed instrument, meeting a standard of quality substantially above that of most other commercial tests. A user can be quite confident of the accuracy of scores and appropriateness of using PLS-4 scores as indicators of language skills of preschool children. There is some, but not strongly compelling, evidence that it is useful in the identification of children with language disorder or delay.

REVIEWER'S REFERENCE

American Educational Research Association, American Psychological Association, & National Council on Measurement in Education. (1999). *Standards for educational and psychological testing*. Washington, DC: American Educational Research Association.

[199]

Process Assessment of the Learner: Test Battery for Reading and Writing.

Purpose: "Designed for assessing the development of reading and writing processes in children in kindergarten through grade 6."
Population: Grades K–6.
Publication Date: 2001.

Acronym: PAL.
Administration: Individual.
Levels, 3: Kindergarten, Grades 1–3, Grades 4–6.
Price Data, 2002: $260 per complete kit in a box including examiner's manual (180 pages), 2 stimulus booklets, 25 record forms, 25 response forms, stylus-wood, word card, audiotape, and shield; $285 per complete kit in a bag including examiner's manual, 2 stimulus booklets, 25 record forms, 25 response forms, stylus-wood, word card, audiotape, and shield; $150 per PAL Scoring Assistant for Windows (CD ROM or 3.5-inch diskette); $64 per manual; $48 per 25 record forms or response forms; $80 per stimulus book (specify Book 1 or Book 2); $11 per word card and audiotape; PAL Test Battery Training Video available (contact publisher for price information); quantity discounts available.
Time: (30–60) minutes if all subtests for a specific grade are administered; (1–6) minutes per subtest.
Comments: Subtests may be administered separately; PAL Scoring Assistant for Windows available.
Author: Virginia Wise Berninger.
Publisher: PsychCorp, A brand of Harcourt Assessment, Inc.
　a) KINDERGARTEN.
　Scores, 10: Alphabet Writing, Receptive Coding—Tasks A and B, Rapid Automatized Naming—Letters, Rapid Automatized Naming—Digits, Rhyming—Tasks A and B, Syllables, Phonemes—Tasks A and B, Story Retell, Finger Sense, Copying—Task A.
　b) GRADES 1–3.
　Scores, 14: Alphabet Writing; Receptive Coding—Tasks A, B, and C; Rapid Automatized Naming—Letters; Rapid Automatized Naming—Words; Rapid Automatized Naming—Digits; Rapid Automatized Naming—Words and Digits; Syllables; Phonemes—Tasks A, B, and C; Rimes—Task A; Word Choice; Pseudoword Decoding; Finger Sense; Sentence Sense; Copying—Tasks A and B.
　c) GRADES 4–6.
　Scores, 17: Alphabet Writing; Receptive Coding—Tasks C, D, and E; Expressive Coding—Tasks A, B, and C; Rapid Automatized Naming—Letters; Rapid Automatized Naming—Words; Rapid Automatized Naming—Digits; Rapid Automatized Naming—Words and Digits; Note-Taking—Task A; Syllables; Phonemes—Task D; Rimes—Task B; Word Choice; Pseudoword Decoding; Finger Sense; Sentence Sense; Copying—Tasks A and B; Note-Taking—Task B.

Review of the Process Assessment of the Learner: Test Battery for Reading and Writing by KAREN E. JENNINGS, LaMora Psychological Associates, Nashua, NH:

DEVELOPMENT. Four goals guided the development process of the Process Assessment of the Learner: Test Battery for Reading and Writing (PAL-RW). The first goal was the creation of a process test wherein a student's strengths and weaknesses can be measured and described. The second goal was the creation of an instrument to supplement other cognitive and achievement measures (e.g., the Weschler intelligence and achievement scales). The PAL-RW was developed to provide a three-tiered assessment/intervention process for all school-aged children in kindergarten to sixth grade. This measure was developed to facilitate the creation of assessment driven interventions.

The author developed this battery on the basis of a model of neurodevelopmental mastery of reading and writing skills. She described a very coherent and cogent summary of the literature on the nature and the acquisition of reading and writing skills (phonological analyses of aural and oral material, and orthographic analyses of single letters and complex combinations of letters). Her summary included discussions on the developmental course of expressive and receptive aspects of language. She also discussed the developmental course of automatized and non-automatized skills. Subtests of the battery were designed to assess aspects of these skill components.

The author conducted two tryout studies to assess the following types of information: interitem correlations, percent correct statistics, internal consistency estimates, item difficulty estimates, item bias, item-total correlations, and the progression of mean scores across grades. The best items from these analyses were retained and utilized in the standardization process. The author also devised impressive quality control procedures to ensure that examiners were adequately trained in individual assessment practice and in the administration of the PAL-RW. Additional bias minimizing safeguards included the application of a double-blind procedure for raters of the standardization protocols.

TECHNICAL.

Standardization. The standardization sample for the PAL-RW was composed of 868 (469 male and 399 female) students aged 5 through 13. These students attended Grades K–6 in public and private schools in the Northeastern U.S., Southern U.S, Western U.S, and North Central U.S. The sample was representative of the population of students estimated by the 1998 U.S

Census. Students were selected via a stratified sampling procedure. The 1998 U.S Census Bureau stratification variables (grade, race/ethnicity, geographic region, and parent education) were incorporated into this study. The author did not discuss whether she instituted the principle of randomness in the selection of participants. [Editor's Note: The publisher advises that "The Psychological Corporation, Harcourt Assessment, employs a stratified random sampling model in selection of participants."]

Reliability. Three types of evidence for the reliability of this battery were discussed: internal consistency, test-retest, and interscorer agreement. Estimates of internal consistency of subtests were variable. Intersubtest coefficients ranged from .52–.98. Test-retest estimates (14–49-day interval) ranged from moderate high to very high correlations (61–.92). Interscorer agreement estimates were surprisingly variable. The Alphabet Writing subtest interscorer correlations ranged from .64–.85). On the other hand, the Copying subtest coefficients were quite variable and ranged from .26–.79. Unfortunately, other than the author's useful discussion about the potential implications of restriction in range on interscorer correlations, the absence of a detailed discussion on the meaningfulness of these data for the user and its impact upon the quality of the findings of this battery was problematic.

Validity. The author presented three sources of evidence for the validity of this battery: content, construct, and criterion evidence. Content-based evidence was provided by experts in the field and the interitem analyses conducted during development and standardization. Three types of evidence for construct validity were presented: subtest intercorrelations by grade, cross-sectional data on developmental differences in performance, and convergent evidence. The subtest intercorrelations were variable (ranging from negative [-.60] to positive correlations [.99]) across grade levels. Motor skills subtests demonstrated a positive correlation with other motor skills; random automatized letter and word naming subtests demonstrated a strong positive correlation (.71). The mean scores on subtests within grade levels were posited as evidence of a developmental progression in mastery of specific skills. The author did not present any evidence for the statistical or practical significance of the differences amongst these mean scores. A discussion of these data would have been useful in order to more fully evaluate this information.

Convergence and divergence with other measures of academic achievement in reading and writing (Wechsler Individual Achievement Test—Second Edition [WIAT-II]; Peabody Picture Vocabulary Test—Third Edition [PPVT-III[; Visual-Motor Integration Test [VMI], and Clinical Evaluation of Language Fundamentals—Third Edition [CELF-III]) was presented as evidence for the validity of this battery. The correlations between selected PAL-RW and WIAT-II subtests were variable. The PAL-RW Story Retell subtest yielded minimal correlation with the WIAT-II Word Reading subtest (.07). Receptive language skills were important to the Story Retell subtest performance; whereas, phonemic analysis was critical to the participants' performance on the Word Reading subtest. On the other hand, the PAL-RW Word Choice and WIAT-II Reading Comprehension subtests demonstrated a strong correlation (.89). These data illustrate the convergence of the PAL-RW subtests with complementary skill modalities and dissociation of dissimilar modalities sampled by the WIAT-II.

The nature of the relationship between the PAL-RW and the PPVT-III is a complex one (expressing both inverse and positive correlations). The correlation coefficients demonstrated a negligible relationship between the PAL-RW Expressive Coding subtest and the total score of the PPVT-IV (.12). On the other hand, Word Choice and the PPVT-III total score demonstrated a moderately high correlation (.64). RAN Letters and PPVT-III total score coefficients demonstrated a moderately strong inverse relationship (-.65).

Correlations between selected subtests of the PAL-RW and VMI total score were variable. The selected PAL-RW subtests measure a variety motor speed, sensory perception/integration, and fine motor skills. The VMI measures fine motor skill, developmental acquisition of visuospatial analysis, and visuomotor organization and construction. Motor speed subtests in the PAL-RW and VMI demonstrated a moderately high correlation. Tactile perception and analysis (Fingertip Writing) and the VMI were found to demonstrate a minimal correlation (.12). Aspects of both intersecting and distinct neurocognitive skills were assessed by these measures.

Correlations between selected subtests of the PAL-RW and CELF-III demonstrated complex relationships. The selected subtests of the PAL-RW measured a variety of skills essential to expressive language, receptive language, and phonemic analysis. The CELF subtests measure skills salient to the oral expression of language. Similar skill domains demonstrated stronger positive correlations than distinct skill domains. Word Choice (PAL-RW) and Sentence Structure (CELF-III) manifested a moderately high positive relationship (.68). The PAL-RW Phonemes subtest demonstrated a negligible relationship to the CELF-III concept and directions subtest (-.10) These findings supply evidence of convergence and divergence of the PAL-RW from other measures of interrelated constructs.

Criterion-based evidence of validity was examined in the presentation of an analysis of the current research and literature of functional reading and functional writing systems. The author cogently presented the intersection of her theorizing about the nature of these language systems and cited research that supported elements of these systems. She discussed the theoretical importance of aspects of these language systems (i.e., orthographic, phonemic, word-specific recognition, word finding, and rapid automatized aspects), in an erudite and fascinating manner. The author provided an interesting treatise of relevant literature. Unfortunately, this discussion did not inform the reader as to the applicability of this information to the question of the evidence for validity of this battery.

COMMENTARY. The strengths of the PAL-RW lie in its daunting effort of operationalizing theoretically salient aspects of academic skills. The battery enables the examiner to investigate the child's level of mastery of components of skills and interactions among components of skills. This battery investigates not only the product of a child's academic skills but also provides for the "process assessment" in articulating the specific components implicated in the child's performance. The author's goal of creating a process assessment is eminently important and laudable. The battery is also a nice integration of academic and neurocognitive assessment devices. This battery has the potential to be very useful in both clinical and research applications.

The weaknesses of the battery lie in some of its psychometric properties. Although the quality assurance components of the development of this battery were quite detailed and strong, interscorer reliability data were surprisingly variable. The sample selection method requires more discussion and analysis by the author. The apparent absence of random selection of participants may introduce bias and limit the utility of the battery. [Editor's Note: Publisher points out that stratified random sampling approach was used.] The author's assistance in explaining the presence of safeguards for minimizing the potential effects would have been a welcome addition to the manual (Heinsman & Shadish, 1996).

Validity data illuminated complex relationships among battery subtests and related measures of academic achievement. Evidence for content and construct validity was presented. Construct-based evidence for validity is in process. The author has elucidated a fascinating theoretical foundation and justification of a need for this battery. Additional research, and quantification of construct related evidence, is requisite.

SUMMARY. The PAL-RW is a very useful instrument in the evaluation of possible learning problems of school-age children. This instrument assesses several theoretically based dimensions of academic skills necessary for academic success. It provides the examiner an analysis of how a child approaches reading and writing such that problems can be conceptualized as a process rather than a product. This perspective easily lends itself toward the coordinated assessment and intervention of academic problems. Additional elaboration in the PAL-RW manual about potential sampling problems, inconsistent interrater reliability coefficients, and evidence of validity would be most useful to the test user.

REVIEWER'S REFERENCE

Heinsman, D. T., & Shadish, W. R. (1996). Assignment methods in experimentation: When do nonrandomized experiments approximate answers from randomized experiments? *Psychological Methods, 1*(2), 154–169.

[200]

Programmer Analyst Aptitude Test [One-Hour Version].

Purpose: To evaluate the candidate's aptitude and potential for programming and analyzing business problems.

Population: Entry-level and experienced applicants for programmer analyst positions.

Publication Date: 1997.

Acronym: PROGANI.

Scores: Total Score, Narrative Evaluation, Ranking, Recommendation.

Administration: Group.

Price Data, 2001: $235 per person; quantity discounts available.

Foreign Language Edition: Available in French.

Time: (60) minutes.

Comments: Available in booklet and Internet versions; scored by publisher; must be proctored.

Author: Bruce A. Winrow.

Publisher: Walden Personnel Performance, Inc. [Canada].

Review of the Programmer Analyst Aptitude Test [One-Hour Version] by SUZANNE YOUNG, Associate Professor of Educational Research, University of Wyoming, Laramie, WY:

DESCRIPTION. The purpose of the Programmer Analyst Aptitude Test is to predict programmer analyst abilities in a business environment. The test is appropriate for those who are entry level or those with experience in computer science. It does not assume any knowledge of programming but rather evaluates the person's ability to perform the kinds of skills needed on the job.

The test includes four lengthy problems that require skills in thinking logically, solving problems that might occur in a business setting, and using symbolic logic to make sense of problems. This is a 1-hour test and directions for the test taker are included in the booklet. The directions are easy to understand and include a suggested time estimate for each problem. The test is to be taken in a quiet place with no distractions or opportunity for interactions with others. All work is to be done in the test booklet and recorded on the answer sheet provided on the last page of the booklet. The instructions require a test administrator to fill out a brief section and send the answer sheet (by mail or fax) to the testing company for scoring.

Total scores on the four problems range from 0 to 100. An interpretation is provided for the total test score, indicating the test taker's likelihood for success as a program analyst. However, there is no explanation for how the interpretations (and their cutoff scores) were determined. Also, the authors do not explain how the total test score is determined or how much of the total is generated by each of the four problems.

DEVELOPMENT. Materials provided by the authors include a test manual and a content validation study. The study describes a job analysis that was based on information given in a job description for a programmer analyst. The study took place in 1997; however, the job description that formed the basis of the analysis was written in 1989.

Fourteen essential functions of a programmer analyst emerged from the job analysis. Fifty-six traits of a programmer analyst were identified that related to the 14 functions of the job. Of these 56 traits, 37 were assessed at least once on the test, for a 66.1% overlap. A weighted overlap was also calculated for these skills, based upon each function's importance; the overlap was found to be 73%.

Twenty-two secondary traits were also identified in the job analysis; of these, the test assessed five traits in at least one test item. The overlap of secondary traits with the test was 23%. These secondary traits were described as nonessential ("nice but not necessary") for a programmer analyst.

The content validation study also included two articles (dated in the 1970s) supporting the notion of content validity as sufficient in establishing test validity. The *Standards for Educational and Psychological Testing* (AERA, APA, & NCME, 1999) support the use of job analysis as the primary basis of validity when tests are used for employment decisions. A third article, dated 1982, was also included and it provides support for the idea of validity generalization. According to the *Standards for Educational and Psychological Testing* (AERA, APA, & NCME, 1999), validity generalization is based on test-criterion relationships. The authors have not provided predictive or concurrent validity evidence; it is unclear if that is their intent.

TECHNICAL. The correspondence between test items and the essential and desired traits of a programmer analyst is very well documented. The 1997 job analysis shows that 66% of the test items are also identified as essential traits for a programmer analyst; 23% of test items are identified as nonessential, desirable traits. Statistics reported in the test manual include a table showing descriptive statistics for a sample of 1,541 test takers. Other than these statistics that illustrate the frequency of test scores and a comparison of apparently male and female scores (identified by M and F), there is no further description of the sample.

Evidence of content validity (overlap between the test and the traits determined by the job analysis) was provided. The job analysis was thoroughly and carefully described. Criterion validity evidence was not given or discussed; test items were not correlated with other measures. No test reliability evidence is provided.

COMMENTARY. The match between job skills and test items constitutes the primary evidence of the test's validity for assessing the aptitude for a programmer analyst. The content validity study is well done and convincing. However, a reanalysis of the essential and secondary (nonessential) functions of a programmer analyst's job seems important; it is highly likely that a programmer analyst's job functions will have changed significantly since 1989. Also, because the test is meant to predict the degree of success that a candidate would have as a programmer analyst, evidence of criterion validity would add to the credibility of the test. The original version of the test was developed and published in the 1990s; the developers have had ample time to examine the relationship between test scores and actual job performance for those working in the field. In addition, reliability is not addressed at all. The statistics illustrating the test performance for a sample are provided but it is not clear if this is meant to be a norm sample; if so, a description of the sample's demographics as well as when the data were collected would assist prospective test users in determining the appropriateness of the test.

SUMMARY. In previous *Mental Measurements Yearbook* reviews of the Programmer Analyst Aptitude Test (Basic Version) (Bassai, 1992; Darr, 1992), reviewers recommended that the test developers add more information to support the technical aspects of the test, including details about the sample used for norming. A content validation study was conducted following that review and the results of the study (a job analysis) were added to the test materials. The test was revised, although it is unclear what revisions were made and why. The authors of the test have not provided evidence of reliability. In addition, they have not described the sample that was used to report test norms, if indeed the scores they report are test norms. This reviewer recommends that potential users consider administering this test along with a test such as the Campbell Interest and Skill Inventory or the Strong Interest Inventory.

REVIEWER'S REFERENCES

American Educational Research Association, American Psychological Association, & National Council on Measurement in Education. (1999). *Standards for educational and psychological testing.* Washington, DC: American Educational Research Association.

Bassai, F. (1992). [Review of the Programmer Analyst Aptitude Test (Basic Version).] In J. J. Kramer & J. C. Conoley (Eds.), *The eleventh mental measurements yearbook* (pp. 708–709). Lincoln, NE: Buros Institute of Mental Measurements.

Darr, R. F., Jr. (1992). [Review of the Programmer Analyst Aptitude Test (Basic Version).] In J. J. Kramer & J. C. Conoley (Eds.), *The eleventh mental measurements yearbook* (pp. 709–710). Lincoln, NE: Buros Institute of Mental Measurements.

[201]

Progress in English 5–14.

Purpose: Designed as "a comprehensive standardized English test series that assesses reading and writing skills."
Publication Dates: 1994–2001.
Acronym: PiE 5–14.
Administration: Group.
Price Data: Available from publisher.
Comments: Assessments linked to curriculum guidelines for England and Wales, Scotland and Northern Ireland.
Publisher: NFER-Nelson Publishing Co., Ltd. [England].

a) PROGRESS IN ENGLISH 5.
Population: Ages 4.0–6.03.
Scores, 3: Initial Literacy, Understanding of Whole Text, Total.
Time: (40) minutes.
Authors: Lynn Howard, Anne Kispal, and Neil Hagues, National Foundation for Educational Research.

b) PROGRESS IN ENGLISH 6.
Population: Ages 5.0-7.05.
Scores, 5: Early Reading, Early Reading-Spelling, Understanding of Whole Text, Understanding Language in Context.
Time: (40-45) minutes.
Authors: Anne Kispal, and Neil Hagues, National Foundation for Educational Research.

c) PROGRESS IN ENGLISH 7.
Population: Ages 6.0–8.05.
Scores, 5: Understanding of Whole Text, Understanding Language in Context, Grammar, Spelling, Total.
Time: (60) minutes.
Authors: Anne Kispal, and Neil Hagues, National Foundation for Educational Research.

d) PROGRESS IN ENGLISH 8.
Population: Ages 7.0–9.5.
Scores, 5: Spelling, Grammar, Understanding of Whole Text, Understanding Language in Context, Total.
Time: (60) minutes.
Authors: Anne Kispal, Neil Hagues, and Graham Ruddock, National Foundation for Educational Research.

e) PROGRESS IN ENGLISH 9.
Population: Ages 8.0–10.05.
Scores, 6: Same as *d* above.
Time: (60) minutes.
Authors: Anne Kispal, Neil Hagues, and Graham Ruddock, National Foundation for Educational Research.

f) PROGRESS IN ENGLISH 10.
Population: Ages 9.0–11.05.

Scores, 6: Spelling, Grammar, Understanding of Whole Text, Vocabulary(Frequency and Spelling), Style, Total.
Time: (60) minutes.
Authors: Anne Kispal, Neil Hagues, and Graham Ruddock, National Foundation for Educational Research.

g) PROGRESS IN ENGLISH 11.
Population: Ages 10.0–12.05.
Scores, 6: Same as *f* above.
Time: (60) minutes.
Authors: Anne Kispal, Neil Hagues, and Graham Ruddock, National Foundation for Educational Research.

h) PROGRESS IN ENGLISH 12.
Population: Ages 11.0–13.05.
Scores, 6: Same as *f* above.
Time: (60) minutes.
Authors: Anne Kispal, Neil Hagues, and Graham Ruddock, National Foundation for Educational Research.

i) PROGRESS IN ENGLISH 13.
Population: Ages 12.0–14.05.
Scores, 6: Same as *f* above.
Time: (60) minutes.
Authors: Anne Kispal, Neil Hagues, and Graham Ruddock, National Foundation for Educational Research.

j) PROGRESS IN ENGLISH 14.
Population: Ages 13.0–15.05.
Scores, 6: Same as *f* above.
Time: (60) minutes.
Authors: Anne Kispal, and Neil Hagues, National Foundation for Educational Research.

Review of the Progress in English 5-14 by ANDREW A. COX, Professor, Department of Counseling and Psychology, Troy State University, Phenix City, AL:

DESCRIPTION. The Progress in English 5–14 is a nontimed assessment of proficiency in the use of English language concepts. It can be used with learners age 4 through 15-5 years. There are 10 tests each for a specific age group. The measure assesses knowledge of spelling, grammatical, language stylistic, and reading comprehension competencies. Questions are of varying difficulty in order to differentiate levels of student attainment. For test Levels 7 and above, test exercises are divided into editing and reading exercises. Editing exercises involve correcting spelling, grammar, and stylistic errors in a text format. Reading tasks require tests takers to read passages and insert missing words, phrases, or clauses. Reading items measure knowledge of contextual language and whole text comprehension. Test Level 5, appropriate for ages 4 to 6, does not use editing skills but assesses whole text understanding, graphical knowledge, and grapheme/phoneme correspondence. Test Levels 9 and above contain a section that involves defining common idioms or terms in open-ended question format. All tests other than Level 5, assess writing skills through short editing exercises. An assessment checklist assessing the qualitative aspects of writing rather than derived scores is provided for this test section. All items and administration procedures appear to be appropriate for the intended test taker's developmental level.

Several purposes for the test are advanced. Evaluation of student language performance as compared to age peers is an assessment goal. The test also promotes monitoring progress over the course of several academic years. The measure also includes a criterion-referenced purpose measuring student performance as compared to United Kingdom national curricular attainment criteria.

There are 10 test kits corresponding to each test level. Each kit provides a teacher's guide, test booklets, a group record sheet for facilitating scoring and derived score conversion, curricular links sheet relating test exercises to the various United Kingdom educational curricular, and an At a Glance Guide summarizing test administration rules. A technical supplement (Kispal, Hagues, & Ruddock, 1995) for Progress in English Test—Levels 8 through 13, and the publisher's website (http://www.nfer-nelson.co.uk/indicators/indicators.asp) provides additional updates on research available for this instrument.

The teacher's guide contains detailed test administration instructions, and scoring guidelines needed to obtain raw and derived scores. The test can be administered by classroom personnel and others familiar with standardized test administration basics. All tests can be administered in both individual and group/whole class administration formats with the Level 5 test designed for small group administration. Each test requires approximately 1 hour for completion with Level 5 and 6 requiring about 40 to 45 minutes.

Progress in English 5–14 yields raw scores with tables within the teacher's guide allowing raw score conversion to age-related standard scores, percentile ranks, and standard score 90% confidence bands. Standard scores have a mean of 100,

standard deviation of 15, and range from 70 to 140. The manual details procedures for denoting scores that are higher or lower than this score interval.

A table is also provided for converting raw scores to scale scores. According to the teacher's guide, this allows comparison of student performance and progress across all 10 tests using a single scale. The test developer cautions, however, against comparing progress greater than one test level below or above the level completed by the test taker. The scale score's statistical qualities relative to mean and standard deviation are not provided within the test's descriptive materials.

DEVELOPMENT. Test items consist of reading exercises selected from various children's literature texts. Items for younger children were selected from children's fiction whereas those for older children were selected from autobiographical and adult literature. Culture and gender issues were considered in item selection. Both small and large scale item field testing was conducted using teachers and students in local British schools. It is noted that selected students included British as well as other ethnic background children. Selected test exercises are described as being relevant to both native English and bilingual students. Field testing descriptive information is not described within available materials.

TECHNICAL.

Standardization. Each test within the Progress in English 5–14 series was standardized using a stratified sample on over 2,000 United Kingdom students drawn from the North, Midlands, South of England, Scotland, Wales, and Northern Ireland. Students were randomly selected from a national register of maintained and independent schools. Various school types depending upon the age level for the test and schools located within metropolitan and nonmetropolitan areas were involved in sample selection.

Standardization was completed for most tests in 1994. However, test Levels 6, 7, and 14 were standardized in 1999 and Level 5 in 2001. Standardization differences are noted for test Levels 5 and 14 relative to metropolitan/nonmetropolitan sampling. The number of schools and gender characteristics of the sample are described. Data descriptions for any ethnic or cultural groups sampled are not indicated.

Reliability. All Progress in English 5–14 tests present internal consistency and test-retest reliability estimates. Kuder-Richardson 20 formula reliability coefficients range from .92 to .95. Test-retest coefficients range from .88 to .95 with a 1-week retest interval. Linear equating procedures were used to assess the reliability of progress scores and the use of a continuous scale score. A subsampling of approximately 500 students within the standardization sample for each test level completed two adjacent test levels to provide data for this equating process. From this procedure and using a linear equating formula, the publisher determined that student progress scores could be reliably interpreted for adjacent school levels.

Validity. Content validity evidence is reported for all Progress in English 5–14 series tests. Test content was compared to the England and Wales National Curriculum, Scottish Guidelines, and Northern Ireland Curriculum. Depending upon the test age level, curriculum reading, writing, spelling, and listening target goals and National Literary Strategy concepts were used. Concurrent validity evidence is reported for test Levels 7 and 14 compared to Key Stage 1 and 3 National Curriculum English Tests. Data for these comparisons are not reported. Concurrent validation evidence is not described for other series tests.

Predictive validity is mentioned but not described within the teacher's guide. Series tests are indicated to be "highly correlated with end of Key Stage English Tests" (Level 5 teacher's guide, p. 23) but no information regarding this correlation is reported. Series Test 11 does not include the above noted predictive validity statement. This test indicates that "predictive validity will, by definition, only become available after a period of time" (Level 11 teacher's guide, p. 27). Validation evidence relative to various gender, racial, ethnic, or cultural groups is not provided within descriptive information for this test series.

The test publisher maintains a website with additional research-based information for this measure. Review of this website indicates additional correlations for selected tests within the Progress in English 5-14 series and Key Stage testing and student progress for 31031 students using 2000 and 2001 data (NFER-Nelson, 2001a, 2001b).

COMMENTARY. The Progress in English 5-14 appears to have value as a relatively brief small to large group measure of English language proficiency. Items appear to be appropriate for various age levels with whom the test may be used.

The instrument possesses good standardization with samples selected from various regions of the United Kingdom. Content validation appears adequate with items sampled from this nation's national educational curriculum. Educational practitioners can administer, score, and interpret the instrument with ease. Hand scoring promotes utilization of results by stakeholders with minimal test administration/scoring turn-around.

The test would be appropriate only for students and educators within the United Kingdom as the instrument is based solely upon a standardization sample and curricular aspects unique to this nation. Weaknesses are noted in descriptive data regarding the standardization sample. No data are reported relative to standardization sample characteristics or usage of the measure with cultural or ethnic minorities within the United Kingdom. The test is indicated to be of limited value to students with reading or other language difficulties or limited English language fluency as the standardization is based upon students able to read test material.

Validation is based predominantly upon content validation. Though concurrent and predictive validation is reported, these data are nonspecific or nonexistent in available descriptive information. No validation data relative to different ethnic or cultural groups within the United Kingdom are described. Accordingly, additional validation work to address these deficiencies would be required for this instrument.

It is suggested that descriptive data regarding the standardization sample, various validation data, and subsequent information such as that described within the publisher's website be included in a technical supplement or published periodically within teacher's guide revisions. This would make this information more accessible and useable by test users.

SUMMARY. The Progress in English 5–14 test series would appear to be useful for educators and other educational practitioners within the United Kingdom. Individuals administering and interpreting these tests should be knowledgeable of United Kingdom instructional and curricular concepts and competencies. Sampling, content validation, and reliability are instrument strengths. It would be of limited utility with students lacking English language fluency or those with special educational needs. The test appears to meet both norm-referenced and criterion-referenced assessment goals. With additional validation and descriptive information, this measure should serve a useful role in language arts assessment and instruction in the United Kingdom.

REVIEWER'S REFERENCES

Kispal, A., Hagues, N., & Ruddock, G. (1995). *Progress in English 8–13 Technical Supplement.* Windsor, Berkshire, UK: NFER-Nelson.
NFER-Nelson (2001a). *Progress in English 5–7 and KS1 progress tables: Autumn, 2001.* Retrieved on October 11, 2004 from: http://www.nfer-nelson.co.uk/indicators/indicators.asp.
NFER-Nelson(2001b). *Progress in English 7–11 and KS2 progress tables: Autumn, 2001.* Retrieved on October 11, 2004 from: http://nfer-nelson.co.uk/indicators/indicators.asp.

Review of the Progress in English 5–14 by NATALIE RATHVON, Project Director, Early Reading Initiative, Center City Consortium Schools, Washington, DC:

DESCRIPTION. Progress in English 5–14 (PiE 5–14) is a group-administered, norm-referenced achievement series assessing reading, writing, spelling, and listening skills for students between the ages of 4 and 15 years. Published by the nferNelson in England, the series consists of 10 tests linked to the national curriculum guidelines in England, Wales, Scotland, and Northern Ireland, so that it is a form of curriculum-based assessment. Purposes of the PiE noted by the authors include formative and summative assessment, progress monitoring, and evaluating student performance in terms of attainment criteria (i.e., National Curriculum levels in reading and writing).

At each level (except Levels 5 and 6), the test consists of reading and editing tasks, termed "exercises," that are linked to extracts from authentic texts. Texts for reading exercises are derived from contemporary children's fiction at the lower levels and autobiographical and adult literature at the upper levels. Editing exercises are based on texts originally written by students and contain some of the actual errors made by the student authors. All of the items require production-type responses. For the reading exercises, students first listen to or read a selection and then write words or phrases in blanks that have been inserted in a summary of the passage, in a type of modified cloze procedure. At the lower levels, students select from among several words printed on the page. Skills assessed at the lower levels include phonological awareness and early literacy skills, such as letter-name and letter-sound knowledge. Reading exercises at the upper levels, which include one open-ended task, are designed to assess both contextual comprehension and vocabulary

knowledge. Editing exercises, which begin at Level 7, require students to correct spelling, word division, and grammatical and stylistic errors in contextual material. The PiE is untimed, with time guidelines ranging from 40 to 45 minutes at Levels 5 and 6 to 50 to 60 minutes for Levels 7 through 14.

Administration. According to the authors, the tests are most appropriate for administration in the second half of the school year but can be administered at any time during the year. Because all normative data were collected in the spring, however, results from other administration windows should be interpreted cautiously. Directions in the teacher's guide are summarized in a laminated "At-a-Glance Guide" so that the teacher does not have to refer to the guide during administration. PiE 5 (ages 4 to 6) is intended for small-group administration, with a recommended group size of five or six students. Test materials are very attractive, formatted for readability, and color-coded by level. The engaging texts on which the reading and editing exercises are based were carefully selected to reflect cultural diversity and balanced gender representation and should retain students' interest.

Scoring. Scoring is dichotomous for all items. Teacher's guides list only a few of the most frequently occurring acceptable answers, as well as common unacceptable responses, and in some cases, the criteria are unclear, at least to this reviewer. For example, for Item 50 on PiE 14 Exercise 4, which refers to solving a mathematics problem, *finding (out)* and *working out* are listed as acceptable synonyms for *discovering,* but *figuring out* is listed as unacceptable (PiE 14 teacher's guide, p. 12). Raw total scores can be converted to standard scores (mean = 100, *SD* = 15), percentile ranks, and "progress scores" (scaled scores). Norms are in 1-month increments across all levels. Scaled scores (range of -19 to 76), derived from linear equating procedures, span all levels, making it possible to track changes in performance over time. According to the authors, when the original PiE 8–13 was extended downward, scaled scores at the low end of the raw score range for PiE 5, 6, and 7 were left negative so that scores for the other levels did not have to be rescaled. Only raw scores are available for the exercises.

Interpretation. A section in the teacher's guides entitled "Interpreting and Reporting Test

Results" provides readable explanations of the derived scores and methods for calculating confidence bands, as well as a description of the process of deriving the scaled scores that is unusually detailed for a publication designed for teachers. Although the authors offer cautions about administering the test to students with very limited English skills, a paragraph entitled "Interpreting Unexpectedly Low Scores" makes no mention of the potential impact of English language proficiency on standardized test performance (see Abedi, 2002). Moreover, no suggestions are provided about communicating test results to students or parents.

Group record sheets included in the test kits list the percentage correct for each item so that teachers can compare individual and classroom item performance with norm group percentage correct. Teacher's guides include a suggestion for a follow-up free writing exercise linked to test content but provide no individual or group case examples illustrating the scoring and interpretive process or guidelines for using results to target instruction.

DEVELOPMENT. PiE Levels 8 through 13 were first published in 1994. Since then, there have been two extensions—the first in 1999 (Levels 6, 7, and 14) and the second in 2001 (Level 5).

TECHNICAL ADEQUACY. Information about test development and psychometric characteristics is scattered across the 10 teacher's guides, a 1995 technical supplement for Levels 8 through 13 obtained from the publisher, and three documents, dated 2001, available on the publisher's web site. According to the authors, test materials were piloted with thousands of students across the United Kingdom, and tasks and items that were disliked, too easy, too difficult, or otherwise inappropriate were eliminated, but specific details about the task and item development process are not provided.

Standardization. For Levels 8 through 13, standardization data were collected in the spring of 1994 from a sample randomly selected from the national register of maintained and independent schools and stratified by region and three additional variables for England and Wales (metropolitan vs. nonmetropolitan, size-of-year group, and school type). Because data tables do not include United Kingdom population statistics for comparative purposes, however, it is impossible to evaluate sample representativeness. No information about the norm group in terms of other

important demographic variables, such as race/ethnicity, English language proficiency, family socioeconomic or educational status, and disability status, is presented. Norm group sizes are adequate, ranging from 2,030 to 2,737 examinees per level. Subgroup age sizes vary markedly but are also within the acceptable range (i.e., at least 100 examinees per interval). Several subgroup differences were observed for PiE 8 through 13, with significantly higher standard scores for girls, Scotland, small-year groups in secondary schools, and grammar and independent schools. The additional levels were standardized in the spring of 1999 and 2001 on random samples of schools stratified by region, school type, and metropolitan versus nonmetropolitan status. Norm group and subgroup sample sizes are adequate, but no details about subgroups are given.

Reliability. KR-20 reliability coefficients for total test are in the .90s for all levels, indicating that the test is generally reliable enough for individual decision making in terms of this criterion. These coefficients are based on the entire normative group at each level, however; reliability estimates for subgroups based on any of the stratification variables or on demographic variables such as gender and ethnicity are not presented. Moreover, reliability coefficients are not provided for the exercise scores, which represent the major instructional objectives and are intended to be used for diagnostic and instructional purposes. Test-retest reliabilities (approximately 1-week interval) are in the .80s for Levels 5, 9, and 14 and in the .90s for the other levels. No evidence of interscorer reliability is presented in any of the test materials—a very serious omission. Given the degree of subjective judgment involved in the scoring, the sketchy nature of the scoring guidelines, and the all-or-nothing nature of the decision criteria, PiE is highly vulnerable to interscorer inconsistency, compromising both the reliability and validity of the results.

Validity. Content validity evidence is limited. Teacher's guides include brief descriptions of the test development process and the content of the exercises. According to the authors, the PiE was designed to assess the "secretarial" aspects of writing, such as spelling, punctuation, and grammatical errors rather than creative aspects such as content and style in order to keep testing time to a reasonable length. Because fewer items can be included in constructed- versus selected-response measures, given the same testing times, a theoretical rationale and empirical evidence should be presented to demonstrate that content coverage is representative and adequate for the intended purposes.

Item difficulty values reported in the technical supplement and on the group record sheets are generally in the acceptable range. Item discrimination values, reported only for Levels 8 through 13, are also in the acceptable range. According to the authors, items displaying potential cultural or gender bias were omitted during field testing, but no details regarding either judgmental or statistical reviews to detect possible bias are given.

Test-curriculum alignment is documented in a curriculum links sheet in each test kit, which displays the relationship between the exercises and the National Curricula for England and Wales, Scottish 5-14 Guidelines, Programmes of Study and Attainment Targets of Northern Ireland, and National Literacy Strategy, but there is no indication as to how the process of aligning test content to the curricula was conducted. Similarly, no theoretical rationale or empirical documentation is offered to support the selection of test format or item types, some of which are quite unusual (e.g., fill-in-the-blank items for which the first letter, word, or words of the response have been supplied).

Concurrent and predictive validity evidence is presented in three documents available on the publisher's web site comparing PiE scores with National Curriculum English and Key Stage levels. Although the documents and web site indicate that these "performance indicators" are revised each year, the documents are undated, and the web links are dated 2001. Tables display estimates of students' current National Curriculum Level in English based on PiE raw score intervals, but there is limited information as to the size and characteristics of the samples from which they were derived. Predictive validity evidence consists of correlations between PiE standard scores and Key Stage National Curriculum English Tests taken in the same year for samples ranging from 1,500 to 25,000 students. (In the United Kingdom, students are tested at the end of each Key Stage, that is, at ages 7, 11, 14, and 16). PiE scores are moderate to strong predictors of Key Stage Reading, Writing, and Spelling test levels, although only a single summary coefficient for the three Key Stage tests is provided for PiE Levels 7 through 14. Estimates of Key Stage test levels

based on PiE scores are also provided in the form of expectancy tables and charts that display the percentage of students at each of 12 PiE standard score intervals achieving each Key Stage test level.

Evidence of construct validity is sparse. Mean raw scores for total test increase across levels, with the largest increases at the lower levels, as expected. No rationale is offered to indicate how the exercises at each level contribute to an overall construct of reading and writing proficiency. Moreover, because the authors fail to report correlations among the exercise scores and the results of factor analytic studies, there is no way to determine the degree of independence of the subscores. Given the lack of information about the reliability and independence of the exercise scores, which are based on as few as three items, interpretation should be based on total score.

COMMENTARY. PiE is an interesting and attractive literacy battery that incorporates several trends in large-scale assessment, including the use of performance-based measures, content based on authentic materials, and alignment with national curriculum standards. The texts on which the exercises are based include some of the most engaging materials that this reviewer has ever encountered on a standardized test. There is also some evidence that PiE scores are effective predictors of important student outcomes, such as national curriculum and Key Stage test levels. Unfortunately, PiE also illustrates many of the concerns that have been expressed regarding the reliability and validity of performance-based assessments (e.g., Clauser, 2000; Miller & Linn, 2000). Documentation of the adequacy and representativeness of content coverage is limited, scoring is time-consuming and vulnerable to error, estimates of internal consistency and stability estimates are available only for the total score, and evidence of interrater reliability is conspicuous by its absence. Studies comparing PiE results with results obtained on other selected- or constructed-response instruments designed to assess the domains of reading and writing are also lacking. Moreover, no evidence is presented regarding the reliability and validity of the exercise scores. In the absence of this information, their use for general instructional planning, much less evaluating individual student achievement, cannot be recommended.

SUMMARY. PiE represents a commendable effort to develop an authentic, large-scale literacy assessment aligned with national curriculum standards. Although predictive evidence is encouraging, a comprehensive evaluation of the PiE's technical adequacy is limited by insufficient evidence relative to task and item development, subscore independence and reliability, interscorer consistency, and criterion-related validity, including evidence that PiE results can be used to make instructional decisions. Its usability is also limited by the lack of an alternate form for more frequent progress monitoring and, for non-British test consumers, alignment with a British curricular framework. Differences between British and American spelling (e.g., favourite, colour) as well as the use of British terms and idioms in the texts and directions (e.g., cheeky, tick [check] the box) may also serve as sources of construct-irrelevant variance (Messick, 1989) for non-British examinees. Practitioners searching for a group-administered multilevel literacy battery have two viable alternatives, both of which provide more adequate technical documentation as well as software scoring and reporting programs—the selected-response Group Reading Assessment and Diagnostic Evaluation (GRADE; Williams, 2002; 15:113) and the Basic Early Assessment of Reading (BEAR; Riverside, 2002; 23), which includes both selected- and constructed-response items.

REVIEWER'S REFERENCES

Abedi, J. (2002). Standardized achievement tests and English language learners: Psychometrics issues. *Educational Assessment, 8*, 231–257.

Clauser, B. E. (2000). Recurrent issues and recent advances in scoring performance assessments. *Applied Psychological Measurement, 24*, 310–324.

Messick, S. (1989). Meaning and values in test validation: The science and ethics of assessment. *Educational Researcher, 18*, 5–11.

Miller, M. D., & Linn, R. L. (2000). Validation of performance-based assessments. *Applied Psychological Measurement, 24*, 367–378.

Riverside Publishing. (2002). Basic Early Assessment of Reading. Itasca, IL: Author.

Williams, K. T. (2002). Group Reading Assessment and Diagnostic Evaluation. Circle Pines, MN: American Guidance Service.

[202]
Project Leader Skills Evaluation.

Purpose: To assess essential skills needed for the position of Project Leader.

Population: Candidates for Project Leader position.

Publication Date: 1993.

Scores: Total Score, Narrative Evaluation, Ranking, Recommendation.

Administration: Group.

Price Data, 2001: $235 per candidate; quantity discounts available.

Foreign Language Edition: Available in French.

Time: [60] minutes.

Comments: Scored by publisher; available in booklet and Internet versions; must be proctored.

Author: Bruce A. Winrow.

Publisher: Walden Personnel Performance, Inc. [Canada].

Review of the Project Leader Skills Evaluation by LAURA L. B. BARNES, Associate Professor of Educational Research and Evaluation, Oklahoma State University, Tulsa, OK:

DESCRIPTION. The Project Leader Skills Evaluation (PLSE) was developed to "evaluate the suitability of candidates for the position of Project Leader, by measuring essential skills including business judgment, supervisory practices, problem solving and knowledge of project organization, control, scheduling, and planning concepts" (test manual, p. 1). The instrument is said to be appropriate for the following positions: project leaders, project managers, business analysts, and systems analysts. The test manual recommends that applicants have at least 2 years of experience.

The PLSE consists of five sections (called problems in the test): Knowledge of general project leadership practices; problem solving in a business situation; general business judgment; application of acceptable supervisory practices; and project plan analysis. The items associated with the problems are selection-type-multiple-choice and ranking—except for the section requiring the analysis of a project plan that uses fill-in-the-blank items. The problems are generally measured with 5 or 6 items each. The time requirements for the sections (8 to 30 minutes) reflect varying reading loads—two sections have dense reading passages.

Examinees record their answers on an answer sheet supplied with the test. Directions call for the answer sheet to be faxed, mailed, or air couriered to the publisher for scoring. Optionally, for immediate scoring, at additional cost, the consumer may phone the scoring service, read the answers over the phone or fax the answer sheet, and within 2 hours receive a "GO/NO GO" result (test manual, p. 4). A bar graph in the test manual from a sample report depicts a score range of 1–9 for each problem with descriptive anchors of *below average, average,* and *above average* performance. The actual score ranges for the problems vary so this range appears to correspond roughly to a percentage correct range of 10%–90% with actual endpoints of 0 and 100%. An interpretive narrative adds the terms "high average" and "superior" to describe performance of a sample examinee on each of the problems. The total score is the sum of the problem scores and forms the basis for an overall rating and recommendation regarding the candidate's suitability for a career as a project leader. Examinees scoring above 75% are given a rating of "above average" with a strong recommendation that the individual has the "potential for a successful career as a Project Leader" (test manual, p. 4). Those scoring between 60% and 74% are rated "average" and recommended for Project Leader if further training is provided. For those scoring between 48% and 59% ("satisfactory" rating) the Project Leader recommendation goes only to those who are highly motivated with an intensive and well-supervised training course. Those scoring below 48% ("below average") are not recommended for Project Leader. No information is provided regarding how these cut scores were established.

DEVELOPMENT. No information regarding the development of this instrument was provided for review.

TECHNICAL.

Reliability. No information was made available regarding score reliability for this instrument. The word reliability did not appear in any of the materials provided for review.

Validity. An analysis of the test content was provided as evidence for validity. In 2000, a job analysis for the position of project leader was conducted for a corporation of 38,000 employees in 126 manufacturing facilities in 27 U.S. states, Canada, Mexico, and 10 European countries. Company employees identified eight major job functions. The functions were weighted in order of importance; essential and secondary traits, skills, or knowledge for the tasks were identified; and the corresponding items from the PLSE were identified. The ratio of number of essential traits tested to number of essential traits identified for the job was about 69%. When weighted by the importance of the tasks, the ratio is reported to be 83.2%. No empirical validation procedures were reported. The manual reports that the publisher can perform a validation of the test at a moderate cost.

Standard setting. The test manual provides no information regarding how the cutscores were established. Evidence of a procedure for establishing a linkage between ranges of test score performance and the likelihood of successful job performance is completely absent in the documentation provided for review.

COMMENTARY AND SUMMARY. The PLSE may be an adequate test for its stated purpose. The content validation study that was reported suggests the test content may overlap reasonably well with an intended job domain. However, in the absence of information regarding the basis for the instrument's development or the reliability of test scores, or evidence that the recommended cutscores were not arbitrarily established, I would not recommend the use of this test.

Review of the Project Leader Skills Evaluation by ALAN D. MOORE, Associate Professor of Educational Leadership, University of Wyoming, Laramie, WY:

DESCRIPTION. The Project Leader Skills Evaluation is intended for use as a pre-employment test to help companies assess the skills of prospective employees. The stated purpose of the instrument is to "evaluate the suitability of candidates for the position of Project Leader, by measuring essential skills including business judgment, supervisory practices, problem solving and knowledge of project organization, control, scheduling and planning concepts." (test manual, p. 1).

The test manual says the test is appropriate for project leaders, project managers, business analysts, and systems analysts. It also says the test should be used to aid in the selection of Project Leader applicants with at least 2 years of experience. It is unclear what kind of experience is recommended.

The test is administered under clerical supervision in the employer's office or over the internet. It takes approximately 70 minutes to complete. For the print version, an answer sheet is submitted to the testing firm and a score report is returned to the employer within 2–5 days or sooner, for a higher fee. For the online version, the score report is immediately e-mailed to the employer.

The instrument consists of 25 items embedded in five problems. Problems areas are (a) generally accepted project leadership practices, (b) analysis of a business situation and development of a structured problem-solving approach, (c) common working situations that determine the test-takers' general business judgment, (d) candidate's supervisory abilities, and (e) analysis of a project plan to determine such issues as estimated time of completion, slack, and manpower requirements.

Sixteen items are multiple-choice, 6 are short fill-in constructed response, and 3 are ranking tasks. Score points are 16 for Problem 1, 15 for Problem 2, 12 for Problem 3, 15 for Problem 4, and 17 for Problem 5, for a total of 75 score points. Scores of *Above Average* (75–100%) are interpreted to mean that the individual is strongly recommended as having the potential for a successful career as a Project Leader. For an *Average* score (60–74%) the individual is recommended for the position, provided further training is supplied. With a score of *Satisfactory* (48–59%) the individual is recommended only if highly motivated and if an intensive, well-supervised training course is available. *Below Average* (0–47%), the individual is not recommended for the position of Project Leader.

DEVELOPMENT. There is no information in the test manual about the process of test development, item development pilot testing, or revision.

TECHNICAL. There is no information available about how the cut points between different score bands were determined. The rating category labels imply that they are based on some sort of normative study. Scores are interpreted as above average, average, satisfactory, or below average, but there is no information reported to support these normative interpretations. No information is provided about how groups of examinees have performed on the test, so it is impossible to judge the level of performance relative to a norm group. Consequently, it is also impossible to judge how free the test is of gender, ethnic, or cultural bias. In addition, there are no available estimates of the reliability of test scores.

A content validation study was conducted by the test publisher in which all the major tasks required for the Project Leader position were identified based on data supplied by a group of employees of Sample Test Corporation. Each task was ranked in order of importance to the overall functions required for the job. Next, the essential traits, skills, or knowledge required to perform these tasks were identified to determine whether or not those essential traits were evaluated by a relevant test question or by some other means. A total of 35 traits were identified as essential to accomplishing the first eight tasks contained in the job description. Of these 35 traits, 69% were judged to be reflected in one or more of the problems in the test. When the essential traits were weighted by importance, 83% of the traits were reflected in at least one test item.

For any kind of personnel selection test, it is essential to establish criterion-related validity. Test scores should correlate positively with indicators of job performance, such as measures of work proficiency, supervisory ratings of job performance, length of service, regularity of attendance, and properly measured success in job-relevant training. For the Project Leader Skills Evaluation, no studies of criterion-related validity are available, so the extent to which scores on the test predict these indicators of job performance is unknown.

COMMENTARY. This test contains items related to knowledge about project leadership practices, problem solving ability, general business judgment, generally accepted supervisory practices, and interpretation of a PERT (Program Evaluation and Review Technique) diagram. The one existing validity study supports the content validity of the test for knowledge and skills necessary for the Project Leader for Sample Test Corporation. To the extent that this set of knowledge and skills is the same for project leaders in other settings, the content validity of the test may be high. However, without criterion-related validity information, it is impossible to determine how useful the test is in employment screening. Because this test is intended as only one part of an evaluation procedure, there should be available job performance data for a wide range of test scores on the Project Leader Skills Evaluation, on which criterion-related validity studies could be based. The test manual is woefully inadequate, containing only a description of the test and its purpose, instructions for administration, a score report example, and fee schedule for scoring. It presents no information to help the user assess the technical properties of the test.

SUMMARY. The Project Leader Skills Evaluation is a pre-employment test intended to help employers evaluate the knowledge and skills needed to be a successful Project Leader. The test is administered by the employer, takes up to 70 minutes to complete, and is scored by the testing firm. Scores are reported in percent of items correct and in four categories of above average, average, satisfactory, or below average. Although there has been one study supporting the content validity of the instrument, there is little other information available about its development or the validity and reliability of test scores. The user should be cautious in the interpretation of scores of individual examinees, unless local studies of the content validity of items, together with studies of how well scores predict job success, are conducted.

[203]

The Psychiatric Diagnostic Screening Questionnaire.

Purpose: "Designed to screen for the DSM-IV (Diagnostic and Statistical Manual of Mental Disorders, Fourth Edition) Axis I disorders most commonly encountered in medical and outpatient mental health settings."

Population: Adult psychiatric patients.

Publication Date: 2002.

Acronym: PDSQ.

Scores, 14: Major Depressive Disorder, Posttraumatic Stress Disorder, Bulimia/Binge-Eating Disorder, Obsessive-Compulsive Disorder, Panic Disorder, Psychosis, Agoraphobia, Social Phobia, Alcohol Abuse/Dependence, Drug Abuse/Dependence, Generalized Anxiety Disorder, Somatization Disorder, Hypochondriasis, Total.

Administration: Individual.

Price Data, 2005: $104 per test kit including manual, 25 test booklets, 25 summary sheets, and CD containing 13 follow-up interview guides (one for each disorder); $45 per manual; $39.50 per 25 test booklets; $26.50 per 100 summary sheets; volume discounts available.

Time: (15–20) minutes.

Comments: Self-report questionnaire.

Author: Mark Zimmerman.

Publisher: Western Psychological Services.

Review of The Psychiatric Diagnostic Screening Questionnaire by MICHAEL G. KAVAN, Associate Dean for Student Affairs and Associate Professor of Family Medicine, Creighton University School of Medicine, Omaha, NE:

DESCRIPTION. The Psychiatric Diagnostic Screening Questionnaire (PDSQ) is a self-report instrument designed to screen for *Diagnostic and Statistical Manual of Mental Disorders, Fourth Edition* (DSM-IV; American Psychiatric Association, 1994) Axis I disorders that are most commonly seen in medical and outpatient mental health settings. It is designed to be completed by individuals 18 years of age and older prior to their initial diagnostic interview. The PDSQ covers 13 Axis I areas including Major Depressive Disorder, Posttraumatic Stress Disorder, Bulimia/Binge-Eating Disorder, Obsessive-Compulsive Disorder, Panic Disorder, Psychosis, Agoraphobia, So-

cial Phobia, Alcohol Abuse/Dependence, Drug Abuse/Dependence, Generalized Anxiety Disorder, Somatization Disorder, and Hypochondriasis. It also provides a PDSQ Total score, which acts as a global measure of psychopathology.

According to the manual, the PDSQ is designed to be used in "any clinical or research setting where screening for psychiatric disorders is of interest" (manual, p. 2). It may be administered and scored by any appropriately trained and supervised technician; however, clinical interpretation should only be undertaken by a professional with appropriate psychometric and clinical training.

The PDSQ consists of 125 items in which respondents are requested to answer yes or no to each test booklet question according to "how you have been acting, feeling, or thinking" during the past 2 weeks or 6 months, depending on the symptom cluster. Typical administration time is between 15 and 20 minutes. Scoring is completed by hand and entails counting the number of yes responses on each PDSQ subscale and entering that number in the space provided on the accompanying summary sheet. Subscale scores are then compared to cutoff scores to determine whether follow-up interviewing is indicated. In addition, the scorer is to circle critical items to which the respondent answered "yes." All subscale scores are then summed in order to obtain a PDSQ Total raw score. Finally, the PDSQ Total raw score is transferred to a PDSQ Score Conversion table that converts the total score into a *T*-score. On the back side of the summary sheet is a table that includes diagnosis percentages of persons who endorsed each item and either qualified or failed to qualify for a subscale diagnosis. An accompanying CD provides follow-up interview guides for all 13 disorders. These may be printed and then used to gather additional diagnostic information regarding these syndromes.

As noted previously, scores from the PDSQ are then used to facilitate the initial diagnostic evaluation. The author notes that "results should be verified whenever possible against all available information, including the results of patient interviews, clinical history, professional consultations, service agency records, and the results of additional psychological tests" (manual, p. 11).

DEVELOPMENT. The PDSQ was developed to be a relatively brief, self-administered questionnaire for the assessment of various DSM-

IV Axis I disorders in psychiatric patients. Development of the measure began over 10 years ago with an instrument entitled the SCREENER, which was originally designed to screen for psychiatric disorders in primary care settings and later in outpatient mental health settings. Following subscale revisions, the SCREENER became a 102-item version of the PDSQ. Through additional modifications the PDSQ took its present form as a scale of 125 items.

TECHNICAL. The author stresses the importance of patients being able to understand any self-administered instrument. As such, readability studies of the initial version of the PDSQ were conducted and ranged from a 5.8 grade level (Flesch-Kincaid method) to a 9.2 grade level (Bermuth formula). Additional understandability studies using psychiatric outpatients demonstrated that PDSQ items were "written at a level that most individuals ... would understand" (manual, p. 27). The author acknowledges that one-third of the sample patients were college graduates and only 5% of the sample patients had less than a high school diploma.

Initial and replication studies were conducted to estimate internal consistency and test-retest reliability on 112- and 139-item versions of the PDSQ. Samples were large, but dominated by white, married or single, and educated females. Internal consistency values (Cronbach alpha) for the initial study on 732 psychiatric outpatients ranged from .73 (Somatization Disorder) to .95 (Drug Abuse/Dependence), whereas a replication study involving 994 psychiatric outpatients found internal consistency estimates to range from .66 (Psychosis and Somatization Disorder) to .94 (Posttraumatic Stress Disorder). Test-retest reliability coefficients on a subsample of these patients ranged from .66 (Bulimia/Binge-Eating Disorder) to .98 (Drug Abuse/Dependence) for the initial study (mean interval of 4.8 days) and from .61 (Mania/Hypomania) to .93 (Drug Abuse/Dependence) in the replication study (mean interval of 1.6 days).

The author reports that 27 of the 112 items did not achieve a minimum endorsement base rate of 5% during the initial study and were not used to determine test-retest reliability. Eighty-three of the 85 remaining items had a Cohen's kappa coefficient, which corrects for chance levels of agreement, between .67 and .92. In the replication study, only two items were excluded in the test-retest reliability study. Cohen's kappa for the remaining items ranged from .50 to .83. Although there is some disagreement regarding the interpretation of kappa, Spitzer, Fleiss, and Endicott (1978) suggest that values greater than .75 demonstrate good reliability, values between .50 and .75 suggest fair reliability, and values below .50 connote poor reliability. In the initial study, 7 subscales (Major Depressive Disorder, Dysthymic Disorder, Bulimia/Binge-Eating Disorder, Mania/Hypomania, Agoraphobia, Generalized Anxiety Disorder, and Hypochondriasis) would be considered to have fair reliability and 7 (PTSD, Obsessive-Compulsive Disorder, Panic Disorder, Psychosis, Social Phobia, Alcohol Abuse/Dependence, and Somatization Disorder) would be considered to have good reliability (1 subscale did not meet the base rate standard). In the replication study, 14 subscales would be considered to have fair reliability and 1 (Drug Abuse/Dependence) would be considered to have good reliability.

To document discriminant and convergent validity, corrected item/subscale total correlation coefficients were calculated between each item and subscale. The mean of the correlations between each subscale item and that subscale's total score were compared to the mean of correlations between each subscale item and the other 14 subscale scores. The author points out that in 90.2% of the calculations the item/*parent*-subscale correlation was higher than each of the item/*other*-subscale correlations. A similar pattern emerged from the replication study with 97.1% of items having a higher correlation with their parent subscale. Data are not provided on correlations between each subscale mean and other *individual* subscales within the PDSQ.

The PDSQ subscales were also compared to "other measures of the same construct versus measures of different constructs" (manual, pp. 31–32). In all instances, the PDSQ subscale scores were significantly correlated with measures of similar syndromes. In addition, correlations were higher between scales assessing the same symptom domain than scales assessing other symptom domains. Interpretation is somewhat clouded by the manual's lack of clarity regarding the nature of these measures.

Finally, criterion validity was documented by comparing the scores of respondents with and without a particular DSM-IV diagnosis. In both the initial and replication studies, the average PDSQ score was significantly higher for those with versus those without the disorder (the only exception was Mania-Hypomania, which was subsequently dropped from the PDSQ).

Cutoff scores are provided based on a study of 630 psychiatric outpatients who were interviewed with the Structured Clinical Interview for DSM-IV Axis I Disorders (SCID; First, Spitzer, Gibbon, & Williams, 1997). Based on results from this study and the fact that the PDSQ is intended to be used as an aid for conducting an initial diagnostic evaluation, the author has recommended a cutoff score resulting in diagnostic sensitivity of 90%. These cutoff scores are provided on the PDSQ Summary Sheet. In addition, a table within the manual includes cutoff scores, sensitivity, negative and positive predictive values, and separate columns estimating the rates of occurrence among psychiatric patients and the general population—the latter being based on information obtained from the DSM-IV.

Limited data are provided within the manual on the PDSQ Total Score. The author states that it is the only norm-referenced score in the instrument. The Total Score is expressed as a standard *T*-score and is a means for "comparing the patient's level of symptom endorsement with that of the average patient seen for intake in a clinical psychiatric outpatient setting" (manual, p. 11). Apparently, it provides a "rough measure of the overall level of psychopathology and consequent dysfunction that a patient reports" (manual, p. 11). However, the author states that it is only loosely related to the distress a patient may be experiencing and it should not be used as an index of severity.

COMMENTARY. The purpose of the PDSQ is to screen for DSM-IV Axis I disorders that are most commonly seen in outpatient mental health settings. With any measure such as this, the real question is: Is it accurate and does it improve efficiency? In regard to accuracy, the PDSQ has respectable internal consistency and test-retest reliability. In addition, convergent and discriminate validity studies demonstrate that PDSQ items are correlated more strongly with their parent subscale than with other subscales within the PDSQ. Also, the PDSQ items were more strongly correlated with other measures of the same construct versus measures of different constructs; although the manual is somewhat unclear as to the nature of these "measures." Finally, it appears as though the PDSQ has decent sensitivity and specificity and

does well at identifying both principal and comorbid disorders. A problem, however, is that the PDSQ has no validity indices, thereby allowing patients to misrepresent themselves on the instrument. Any interpretation should, therefore, be done cautiously and with corroborating information.

In regard to the question of efficiency, the author admits that this, as well as the issue of accuracy, remain empirical questions. Despite the lack of supportive data within the manual, the PDSQ does appear to readily guide the interview toward symptom areas requiring more detailed assessment. In and of itself, this should streamline the diagnostic interview.

Potential PDSQ users are cautioned about several other areas. The first relates to the samples used in studying the PDSQ. Although numbers are typically adequate, the generalizability of findings are somewhat limited by rather homogeneous (i.e., mostly white, female, married/single, and well-educated patients) samples used within the various studies. Finally, users of the PDSQ are reminded of the fairly high reading level necessary for self-administration and the lack of validity indices within the instrument.

SUMMARY. The author should be commended for developing a self-report screening measure that is relatively easy to administer and score and has acceptable evidence of reliability and validity. As noted by the authors, the PDSQ "is not a substitute for a diagnostic interview .... There are no special questions on the PDSQ that allow it to detect psychopathology that otherwise would go undetected during a clinical evaluation" (Zimmerman, 2003, p. 284). Nonetheless, the PDSQ will likely guide clinicians toward those areas of clinical concern that need additional assessment. In doing this, the PDSQ should serve its intended purpose of increased clinical diagnostic accuracy and efficiency. Additional studies will need to be completed to determine the overall impact of the PDSQ on these issues and whether it leads to improved treatment outcome.

REVIEWER'S REFERENCES

American Psychiatric Association. (1994). *Diagnostic and statistical manual of mental disorders* (4th ed.). Washington, DC: Author.
First, M. B., Spitzer, R. L., Gibbon, M., & Williams, J. B. W. (1997). *Structured clinical interview for DSM-IV Axis I Disorders (SCID)*. Washington, DC: American Psychiatric Association.
Spitzer, R. L., Fleiss, J. L., & Endicott, J. (1978). Problems of classification: Reliability and validity. In M. A. Lipton, A. DiMarco, & K. Killam (Eds.), *Psychopharmacology: A generation of progress* (pp. 857–869). New York: Raven.
Zimmerman, M. (2003). What should the standard of care for psychiatric diagnostic evaluations be? *Journal of Nervous and Mental Disease, 191,* 281–286.

Review of The Psychiatric Diagnostic Screening Questionnaire by SEAN P. REILLEY, Assistant Professor of Psychology, Morehead State University, Morehead, KY:

DESCRIPTION. The Psychiatric Diagnostic Screening Questionnaire (PDSQ) consists of 125 items (111 numbered items, 2 with multiple parts) that tap symptoms of several DSM-IV Axis I disorders commonly seen in outpatient settings. The PDSQ can be completed on-site in as little as 20 minutes or at home in advance of an appointment. Respondents use one of three time frames (past 2 weeks, past 6 months, lifetime recollection) to specify the presence ("Yes") or absence ("No") of symptoms. Responses can be rapidly handsummed into raw subscale scores and converted to *t*-scores by clinicians and appropriately trained staff. The inventory yields a total score and 13 subscale scores, denoted in brackets, which tap *mood* [Major Depressive Disorder], *anxiety* [Posttraumatic Stress Disorder, Obsessive Compulsive Disorder, Panic Disorder, Agoraphobia, Social Phobia, Generalized Anxiety Disorder], *eating* [Bulimia/Binge-Eating Disorder], *somatoform* [Somatization Disorder, Hypochondriasis], *substance abuse/dependence problems* [Alcohol Abuse/Dependence, Drug Abuse/Dependence], and *psychotic* [Psychosis] symptoms. Summary sheets assist with identification of 45 possible critical items and comparison of subscale scores with recommended clinical cutting scores. A compact disc containing follow-up interview guides with prompts related to DSM-IV criteria is available from the test publisher for each subscale.

DEVELOPMENT. The PDSQ is an atheoretical inventory. Items were written to reflect symptom criteria for DSM-IV Axis I disorders most common in epidemiological surveys and in published research articles. Most items adequately represent the DSM-IV nosology except those comprising the Alcohol and Substance Abuse/Dependence and the Psychosis subscales. The former reflect abuse/dependence symptoms broader than those required by the DSM-IV, whereas the latter assess critical symptoms of several nonspecific psychotic disorders. During the item revision process, 89% of items successfully passed four criteria established by the developer. The addition of new and revised items was not successful in meeting five additional subscale retention criteria for: Anorexia Nervosa, Body Dysmorphic Disorder, Mania/Hypomania, Dysthymic Disorder, Generalized Anxiety Disorder, Psychosis, Somatization, and Hypochondriasis subscales. The latter four subscales were retained, however, partially based on adequate diagnostic performance with outpatient clinical groups, but could benefit from further modification. The 13 subscales comprising the current version of the PDSQ contain uneven item distributions ranging from 5 to 22 items. This, in addition to a lack of items to assess response bias, raises concern. Namely, endorsement of a single transparent item for some subscales is sufficient to exceed the clinical screening criterion, which could potentially lower their positive predictive power. The developers do offer practical suggestions for detecting response bias using the PDSQ Total score. However, this indicant is norm referenced and not criterion referenced like subscale scores. Thus, prior to acceptance, bias detection procedures using the PDSQ Total score need empirical validation with clinical groups.

TECHNICAL. Multiple, adult, medical, and psychiatric outpatient samples, of at least four hundred individuals (over 3,000 combined) per sample, were used to standardize the PDSQ. Although certainly commendable, these data are predominantly from Caucasian (range 85 to 94%) high school graduates (89 to 94%) living in Providence, RI. The impact of gender on PDSQ norms is not reported, despite women outnumbering men by a 2:1 ratio in all standardization samples. Because several DSM-IV syndromes tapped by the inventory show marked gender differences (e.g., Major Depressive Disorder), gender impact studies are needed. Perhaps more salient is the need for a broader and more representative normative sample to improve the generalizability of the PDSQ for diverse populations including rural, multi-ethnic, and geriatric adults, as well as those with lower education and/or socioeconomic status.

Readability analyses using the Flesch-Kincaid and Bermuth methods indicate PDSQ items range from fifth to ninth grade reading levels. Studies employing simpler forced-choice procedures (Understand/Don't Understand) suggest greater than 95% of adults with a high school degree or equivalency understood all PDSQ items. Despite these initial data, no minimum level of reading skill is recommended in the manual.

Reliability estimates are reported for previous PDSQ versions that include items and subscales not found on the present version. Extrapolating from these data, the Cronbach alpha coefficients of subscales common to the current PDSQ are adequate (.66) to excellent (.94). To date, internal consistency estimates have been used to estimate the latent variables comprising the PDSQ. No attempts are reported to validate its primary factor structure. This could be accomplished using advanced modeling procedures such as confirmatory factor analysis or structural equation modeling. Test-retest estimates for approximately a week are borderline adequate (kappa = .56) to excellent (kappa = .98) at the item level, and slightly higher at the subscale level (rs ranging .72 to .93). Studies involving longer test-retest durations are needed to bolster initial data, given the longer temporal requirements of several DSM-IV syndromes (e.g., Major Depression; 2 weeks, PTSD; 4 weeks) tapped by the PDSQ.

Data concerning convergent and discriminant validity of the PDSQ are based on initial outpatient (n = 732) and replication samples (n = 994) using multiple methods. Across studies, the mean corrected item-parent PDSQ subscale correlations (rs ranging .42 to .85) are significantly higher than 90% of those afforded by item-other PDSQ subscale relations (rs ranging .15 to .35). Subscale-specific correlations with externally recognized instruments are modest (r = .25) to very good (r = .77), and higher than those afforded by nonspecific PDSQ subscales (rs ranging .15 to .35). Thus, initial internal and external comparisons of PDSQ subscales suggest appropriate convergence and discriminant validity. Adequate criterion validity is initially examined by showing significantly higher diagnosis-specific PDSQ subscale scores (e.g., Major Depressive Disorder) among outpatient groups with the corresponding DSM-IV disorder than for those without the disorder. Absent from the manual, however, are comparisons of non-diagnosis-specific PDSQ scores between outpatient groups. Inclusion of these data could further bolster the criterion validity evidence of the PDSQ.

The initial sensitivity, specificity, and positive and negative predictive power of PDSQ cutting scores for primary DSM-IV diagnoses are based on a single sample of psychiatric outpatients (n = 630). Subscale sensitivity is generally adequate (75%) to very good (100%) in this sample with less variability noted for rates of specificity (range 83 to 100%). The developer recommends a sensitivity level of 90% for establishing cutting scores for clinical practice. However, four subscales, Obsessive Compulsive Disorder (89%), Psychosis (75%), and both Alcohol (85%) and Drug (85%) Abuse/Dependence, fail to reach this sensitivity level. Using the most liberal cutoff scores, positive predictive values range considerably (18 to 100%), whereas negative predictive values are high and fairly consistent (97 to 100%). Seven subscales yield positive predictive values below 60%, which, in part, may be due to low base rates of disorders tapped by Bulimia/Binge Eating Disorder, Somatization Disorder, Hypochondriasis, and Psychosis subscales. However, as noted, Drug Abuse/Dependence and Psychosis subscales provide less than an adequate mapping of the DSM-IV nosology, which may negatively impact their predictive ability. Finally, the differential validity evidence of all PSDQ cutting scores needs to be clarified for gender and diversity considerations.

COMMENTARY. The PDSQ appears to be a potentially valuable screening instrument for common DSM-IV Axis I disorders in outpatient settings. Several issues need to be addressed in order to firmly anchor the psychometrics and generalizability of the PDSQ. First, a more representative standardization sample needs to be collected using the current version of the PDSQ. In that sample, gender and diversity contributions to PDSQ scores need clarifying and a minimum reading level should be established. Second, response bias needs to be addressed either by inclusion of new items or additional studies designed to empirically validate bias detection techniques using the PDSQ Total Score. Third, factor analysis or structural equation modeling is needed to adequately assess the overall PDSQ factor structure and to address less than adequate homogeneity in several subscales. Fourth, longer test-retest studies are needed to bridge the existing stability of several subscales with specific temporal requirements of several selected DSM-IV disorders. Finally, the positive predictive power of Psychosis, Bulimia/Binge Eating Disorder, Generalized Anxiety Disorder, Somatization Disorder, Hypochondriasis, and Alcohol and Drug Abuse/Dependence subscales needs to be improved.

SUMMARY. The developer, to his credit, has produced a potentially valuable screening instrument, and one of the first that directly incorporates the DSM-IV nosology for common Axis I disorders. Significant care was taken in initial studies to evaluate PDSQ items and subscales using multiple reliability and validity indices. In order for this instrument to become a gold standard, a more representative standardization sample is needed. Careful, continued validation work will also be required to solidify the PDSQ factor structure, to enhance the homogeneity and test-retest reliability of specific subscales, and to improve their positive predictive power. As a whole, this inventory is recommended for screening purposes with an eye to its current limitations.

[204]
Psychological Processing Checklist.

Purpose: Designed to "measure psychological processing difficulty."
Population: Kindergarten–Grade 5.
Publication Date: 2003.
Acronym: PPC.
Scores, 7: Auditory Processing, Visual Processing, Visual Motor Processing, Social Perception, Organization, Attention, Total.
Administration: Individual.
Price Data, 2005: $69 per complete kit including technical manual (96 pages), and 25 QuikScore™ forms; $50 per technical manual; $36 per 25 QuikScore™ forms; $122 per 100 QuikScore™ forms.
Time: (15) minutes, plus 10–15 minutes for scoring.
Comments: Teacher-completed rating scale.
Authors: Mark E. Swerdlik, Peggy Swerdlik, and Jeffrey H. Kahn.
Publisher: Multi-Health Systems, Inc.

Review of the Psychological Processing Checklist by BRUCE A. BRACKEN, Professor, School of Education, The College of William & Mary, Williamsburg, VA:

DESCRIPTION. The Psychological Processing Checklist (PPC) is an innovative instrument that may contribute to the diagnosis of learning disabilities (LD) by providing a third-party behavioral anchor that can be combined with traditional LD diagnostic tools (e.g., intelligence tests, achievement tests). As such, the PPC might add an additional component toward the "triangulation" of diagnostic information from multiple sources and multiple instruments.

The scale includes an 82-page manual and a package of Quikscore Forms. Each Quikscore Form separates along perforated lines to create a series of documents, including a 35-item behavioral checklist, scoring grid, male and female profiles, and a sheet used to calculate and display scale score differences to aid interpretation.

Using a frequency-of-occurrence item format (i.e., Never, Seldom, Sometimes, Often), teachers rate students' educational behaviors consistent with deficits in six processing areas (i.e., Auditory Processing, Visual Processing, Visual-Motor Processing, Social Perception, Organization, Attention). Operational definitions are provided for each of these processing deficits.

Teachers can easily rate students in kindergarten through Grade 5 in approximately 5 to 10 minutes with the PPC; however, scoring and interpreting the PPC requires another 10 to 15 minutes. As a result, the PPC may serve as a convenient, low-cost (i.e., time and money) screener for teacher-raters, although it will not be as convenient or inexpensive for professionals who score and interpret these ratings.

DEVELOPMENT. Development of the PPC began as a result of a local school system's need to better identify the processing deficits of children assessed for learning disabilities. The original instrument included 85 items distributed across nine processing areas, using two forms—one form was intended for kindergarten through fifth grade students and the second form was for Grades 6 through 12. After piloting the PPC and subsequent assessment of its technical characteristics and structure, the instrument was reduced to a single 35-item kindergarten through fifth grade form.

The manual is well written and provides considerable detail about the development, description, uses, and applications of the PPC, as well as a description of assessor qualifications. The record form includes a carbon-free "tear-apart" document with several imbedded sheets that facilitate responding, scoring, and interpretation. Rater's responses recorded on the front page of the record form are carried through to the inside pages where item scores can easily be transposed to their respective processing areas, summed to form part-scores and a total scale score (i.e., percentile ranks and T scores), profiled, and interpreted.

PPC items are fairly evenly divided across the six processing areas, with five to seven items assigned to each area. In most instances, PPC items present behaviors that are clearly processing in nature, but on several items the behaviors could be related to either physical or processing deficits. For example, a teacher might endorse the item "Has difficulty forming letters when printing or writing" due to a child's motoric (physical) difficulties or the child's perceptual-motor (processing) difficulties. Similarly, children may have difficulty "seeing similarities in pictures" as a result of problematic visual acuity (physical) or visual processing. In this sense, the PPC items do not clearly discern the important differences between educational behavioral deficits that result from physical or processing underpinnings.

The PPC manual provides clear directions for administering, scoring, and interpreting the instrument. These related chapters also include a separate example for scoring the PPC and several case studies that together depict items with their respective ratings, transposed raw scores, standard score determinations and graphing, scale difference score calculations, and scale interpretation.

Scale difference scores can be calculated for each possible pair of processing deficit areas and the total score, resulting in 21 possible paired scale contrasts. There is no indication in the manual that protection against alpha slippage was built into the application of the Standard Error of the Difference when calculating significant scale differences. In any child's profile, one or more significant scale differences would likely result from chance variation at either the .05 or .01 alpha levels.

Scale interpretation is based on a straightforward, but tedious 10-step process. This section of the manual provides descriptions (i.e., percentile ranks, T score, classifications) and comparisons of standard scores across the total scale and processing deficit areas, as well as comparisons of rated students' raw scores with a known sample of special education students. Also, the manual provides a useful but brief collection of instruments that might be combined with the PPC to create a "multi-source/multi-method" assessment of processing difficulties. The list does not include several current and important comprehensive, multidimensional behavior rating scales, perceptual or processing measures, or nonverbal intelligence tests that may be especially useful in the diagnosis of both language-related and nonverbal learning disabilities.

TECHNICAL. The PPC examiner's manual provides appropriate information on the normative and special education samples, as well as the psychometric properties of the PCC. This information is clearly presented and mostly reflects well on the instrument. However, this section lacks some strength, specificity, or clarity that would make the instrument more interpretable and useful.

The PPC was normed using 944 students in kindergarten through fifth grade from 10 rural or suburban school districts throughout Illinois. This sample size is adequate, with more than 140 students at every grade level, except kindergarten. Gender representation in the normative sample is fairly even across all age levels. Across the total sample the authors have provided a fairly representative distribution of African American (10%), Caucasian (74%), and Hispanic (13%) students. Ethnicity is presented for the total sample, but not as a function of gender or grade level; socioeconomic status is not reported.

An anomaly of the PPC is that it produces considerable raw score variability across the age range, but the variability does not appear related to developmental phenomena (e.g., predictable age progression or decline). For example, the mean PPC total raw score across the grade levels ranges from a low of 15.12 (Grade 5) to a high of 33.39 (Grade 4), with fourth grade students performing less well on average than kindergarten students (mean = 30.39) and much worse than second grade students (mean = 19.65). Second and fifth grade students are more comparable than second grade students and either first (mean = 25.65) or third grade students (mean = 28.06). The authors concluded, "This finding is likely due to nonrandom sampling and corresponding confounding effects of school districts" (technical manual, p. 51). This finding is exacerbated by the fact that the instrument was normed in a single midwestern state, which seriously limits the generalizability of the norms across grades or states.

The PPC evidences strong internal consistency for both the overall normative sample and the special education sample, with coefficients alpha ranging from .86 to .93 (total scale = .98) for the normative sample; .78 to .91 (total score = .95) for the special education sample. PPC interrater reliability also appears to be quite strong based on small sample analyses.

Evidence for validity is mixed and is not as strong as it might have been if better criterion measures had been selected for convergent and discriminant contrasts. Because the PCC is not an intelligence test, it was unfortunate that intelligence tests were the primary measures employed for convergent and discriminant validity. Where coefficients are not as strong as or in the direction that one might anticipate, the reader should question whether the fault lies with the predictor (i.e., PPC) or the criterion (i.e., intelligence test). For example, the PPC Auditory Processing scale correlated -.50 with the WJ-R Visual Matching subtest (discriminant validity) as compared to -.36 and -.13 with Memory for Sentences and Incomplete Words, respectively (convergent validity). Similarly, the PPC Visual Processing scale correlated only slightly higher with Visual Matching (-.38; convergent validity) than with Memory for Sentences (-.31; discriminant validity). When contrasted with the CAS, the PPC Attention scale correlated -.29 with the CAS Attention scale, but -.51 with CAS Planning. The PPC Organization scale correlated moderately and appropriately ($r = -.48$) with CAS Planning.

The hypothesized structure of six processing deficit scales is generally supported through confirmatory factor analyses. Although RMSEA, SRMR, and CFI criteria were not optimal, item factor loadings were high and appropriately placed on corresponding factors.

SUMMARY. The PPC is a brief, third-party rating system intended for the identification of processing deficits in six educationally related areas (i.e., Auditory Processing, Visual Processing, Visual Motor Processing, Social Perception, Organization, and Attention). The instrument permits raw score comparisons between the rated child and a small special education sample, as well as norm-referenced interpretation based on a sample of nearly 1,000 Illinois children in kindergarten through Grade 5. The PPC has strong internal consistency and interrater reliability for the total sample, but validity evidence is somewhat less supportive. The strengths of the instrument include its contribution to the triangulation of data in a multisource, multimethod assessment of learning disabilities and its brevity, ease of administration, strong reliability, and useful targeted behaviors. Its weaknesses include items that can be interpreted from either a processing or purely physical deficit manner, a normative sample limited to a single state, unexplained and

nondevelopmentally consistent variation in scores across grade levels, and limited validity evidence.

Review of the Psychological Processing Checklist by KEITH F. WIDAMAN, Professor of Psychology, University of California, Davis, CA:

DESCRIPTION. The Psychological Processing Checklist (PPC) is a short, paper-and-pencil test designed as a screening device to assess dimensions relevant to the diagnosis of learning disabilities. The federal special education law, titled the Individuals with Disabilities Education Act (IDEA), and guidelines from professional organizations specify that learning disabilities are based on deficits in basic psychological processes that influence learning, and these deficits in processing are thought to be due to central nervous system dysfunction. States were directed to develop laws that operationalize the IDEA requirements related to specific learning disabilities, and the PPC was developed as a standardized measure of several of the processing dimensions identified by the Illinois State Board of Education (ISBE). The ISBE list of processing dimensions includes nine dimensions, and the PPC assesses six of these dimensions.

The PPC comprises 35 items, each of which is answered on a 0–3 scale, with options varying from 0 = "Never, does not engage in the behavior," to 3 = "Often, exhibits behavior one to several times per day." The PPC can be completed by teachers, but teachers should know a child for a reasonable period of time (e.g., at least 6 weeks) before completing the PPC to ensure a valid description of the child's behavior. PPC ratings can be completed in 15 minutes or less, and scoring requires an additional 10 minutes. Raw scores on each of the six dimensions and the total score can be converted into scaled or standardized scores on a T-score metric ($M = 50$, $SD = 10$) or can be converted into percentile ranks (median = 50, range = 1 to 99+).

DEVELOPMENT. The initial version of the PPC consisted of 85 items designed to assess all nine dimensions of processing identified by ISBE, and two forms—one for kindergarten through Grade 5 and a second form for Grades 6 through 12—were initially developed. During pretesting, it became clear that three of the nine dimensions of processing were difficult to assess reliably using a rating scale format. Moreover, the authors found it difficult to arrive at consensus on behaviors by older students that are relevant to particular dimensions of processing. Therefore, the focus of the PPC was restricted to the six dimensions of processing that could be validly assessed using this teacher-report format and to the earlier grades of kindergarten through 5, as this is the time when most learning disabilities are initially diagnosed and greater consensus on relevant behaviors was attained.

The six dimensions assessed by the PPC are Auditory Processing (7 items), Visual Processing (7 items), Visual-Motor Processing (6 items), Social Perception (5 items), Organization (5 items), and Attention (5 items). During the initial rounds of pilot scale development, the PPC was subjected to several sets of item analyses to select the best items for inclusion in the scale.

TECHNICAL. Norms were based on samples of students from 10 school districts in Illinois, consisting of 944 students in general education classrooms and 99 students with learning disabilities in special education, distributed approximately equally across the six grade levels from kindergarten to Grade 5. Data from students in general education classrooms were used to establish the conversions from raw scores to T-scores and percentile ranks. Approximately half of these students were males and half were females, and about one-fourth of the students in general education classrooms were members of ethnic minority groups. Data from the students with learning disabilities were used to establish quartiles to aid the interpretation of PPC scale scores. Over two-thirds of students with learning disabilities were male and about one-third were members of ethnic minority groups, consistent with trends often observed for this population. The presence of consistent sex differences in levels of processing deficits led the authors to develop separate conversion tables for males and females; ethnic differences were found, but the relatively small samples of minority students makes interpretation difficult.

Two kinds of reliability coefficients were reported for PPC scores. Internal consistency reliability estimates across the 944 general education students ranged between .86 and .93 (median of .91) for the six PPC scales; the comparable value for the total score was .98. Reliability estimates for the 99 students with learning disabilities were lower, ranging between .78 and .95, as might be expected. Interrater reliability estimates were some-

what lower, with values ranging between .75 and .92; because these were based on rather small samples, the estimates are preliminary and should be verified on larger samples. The initial results suggest that the PPC has adequate levels of internal consistency reliability, but further evaluations of reliability (e.g., test-retest) should be performed.

Several forms of validity information were also reported. Content validity was assessed in the usual fashion, using expert judgments by teachers and school psychologists having experience with students with learning disabilities. Known-groups validity was documented by showing that the students in general education classrooms differed significantly on all dimensions when compared with students with learning disabilities in special education. The authors also conducted a confirmatory factor analysis to verify whether the items developed to assess each dimension did so satisfactorily. A six-factor model fit the data far better than did a single factor model, and the median factor loading of .81 for items was rather high. However, two of the factors—Organization and Attention—were perfectly correlated, implying that the solution was, in effect, a five-factor solution, and the correlations among these five factors tended to be rather high, ranging between .54 and .97. Thus, the discriminant validity for several of the dimensions is questionable, a finding noted by the authors of the PPC.

Correlations of PPC scores with scores on ability batteries were reported. Five scores from the PPC—Auditory Processing, Visual Processing, Organization, Attention, and Total PPC scores—tended to correlate about equally with the same tests from the Woodcock-Johnson Test of Cognitive Ability Revised (Woodcock & Johnson, 1989), tests identified as Memory for Sentences, Visual Matching, Analysis-Synthesis, and Broad Cognitive Ability, correlations that ranged between -.31 and -.49. The preceding five scores from the PPC also correlated in similar ways with the Simultaneous, Successive, and Planning subtest scores and full scale scores from the Cognitive Assessment System (Naglieri & Das, 1997), correlations ranging between -.36 and -.51. The remaining two scores from the PPC—Visual-Motor Processing and Social Perception—correlated at lower, nonsignificant levels with the ability dimensions.

Correlations of PPC scores with scores from educational achievement test batteries were somewhat stronger. Each of the seven scores from the PPC had at least one significant correlation with the Reading, Language, or Mathematics subtests from the Iowa Tests of Basic Skills (Hoover, Dunbar, & Frisbie, 2001), and these correlations ranged between -.31 and -.57. Finally, most scores from the PPC tended to correlate with the Verbal scale, but not with the Quantitative or Nonverbal scales, from the Cognitive Abilities Test (Thorndike & Hagen, 1993).

COMMENTARY. The PPC is a simple-to-use screening device that can be used to provide an initial assessment of processing deficits that are related to learning disabilities. The initial standardization of the PPC has produced scores that meet standard levels of reliability for individual decisions. However, at least four concerns should be raised about the PPC, its standardization, and the quality of its scores. First, the standardization sample was not large and was not assuredly representative of any particular population. This may account for the somewhat haphazard trends in the means for raw scores across grade levels. If larger and more representative norming samples were used, the resulting age trends would likely be more regular and the associated conversions to T-scores and percentile ranks could be used with greater confidence.

Second, the psychometric properties of PPC scores are encouraging, but deserve replication and extension across larger samples. Additional forms of reliability, such as test-retest reliability, should be examined, and all forms of reliability should be replicated across samples to ensure their stability.

Third, the structure of the instrument should be verified in additional samples. At present, it appears that the instrument can support only five, rather than six, separable dimensions of processing, and these five dimensions are fairly highly correlated. The high correlations among these dimensions could be related to construct-relevant sources of variance, such as high comorbidity for processing problems in elementary school populations, or to construct-irrelevant sources, such as bias in teacher ratings. Further research should attempt to resolve these issues.

Fourth, because the PPC was developed as a screening instrument, item gradients do not allow precise placement of persons along dimensions. That is, for three of the PPC scales, raw scores vary only from 0–15, so discrimination among individuals is not optimal at all points along a dimension. This is not crucial for a screening instrument, which provides only a first indicator of problems in an area to be verified with further testing. If the nature of the PPC as a screening device is emphasized, the gaps in raw score to T-score conversions should pose no problem.

SUMMARY. The developers of the PPC have produced a multidimensional screening device for processing deficits related to learning disabilities that can be administered and scored in an efficient manner. Scores derived from the PPC have strong levels of reliability, although assessments of reliability should be supplemented. Furthermore, the discriminant validity of PPC scales has not been firmly documented, although whether this reflects on the particular instrument or on levels of comorbidity that may exist in the population is not clear. For its intended purpose as a screening device to identify possible bases for learning disabilities, the PPC appears to offer a usable, quite useful option. Future versions of the PPC will likely only improve on this promising first edition.

REVIEWER'S REFERENCES

Hoover, H. D., Dunbar, S. B., & Frisbie, D. A. (2001). Iowa Tests of Basic Skills. Itasca, IL: Riverside Publishing Company.
Naglieri, J. A., & Das, J. P. (1997). Cognitive Assessment System (CAS). Itasca, IL: Riverside Publishing Company.
Thorndike, R. L., & Hagen, E. P. (1993). Cognitive Abilities Test. Itasca, IL: Riverside Publishing Company.
Woodcock, R. W., & Johnson, M. B. (1989). Woodcock-Johnson Psycho-Educational Battery—Revised. Allen, TX: DLM Teaching Resources.

[205]

Quest, Second Edition.

Purpose: Designed to identify students who "have difficulties in aspects of language and mathematics through group screening tests," then "assess pupils' learning difficulties in these areas of the curriculum through individual diagnostic tests."

Population: Ages 6 to 8.

Publication Dates: 1983–1995.

Administration: Individual and group.

Price Data: Available from publisher.

Comments: Assessment program is linked to the national curricula of England and Wales, Northern Ireland, and Scotland.

Authors: Alistair Robertson, Ann Robertson, Joanna Fisher, Anne Henderson, and Mike Gibson.

Publisher: NFER-Nelson Publishing Co., Ltd. [England].

a) THE READING SCREENING TEST.

Scores: Total score only.

Administration: Group.

Parts, 2: PMs 1A and 1B.

Time: (30) minutes.

b) THE NUMBER SCREENING TEST.
Scores: Total score only.
Administration: Group.
Parts, 3: PMs 2, 3, and 4.
Time: (35) minutes.
c) DIAGNOSTIC READING TEST.
Scores, 13: Pre-Reading (Auditory Discrimination, Auditory Sequential Memory, Visual Discrimination, Visual Sequencing, Visuo-Motor Skills,) Word Attack Skills (Sight Vocabulary, Letter Recognition, Simple Blends, Beginnings and Endings, Digraphs, Silent "E" Rule and Silent Letters, Word-building and Multisyllabic Words, Reading Comprehension).
Administration: Individual.
Time: (30) minutes.
d) DIAGNOSTIC NUMBER TEST.
Scores, 12: Pre-Number (Visual Perception, Visuo-Motor Coordination, Auditory Memory), Number Concepts (Ordering, Addition, Subtraction), Number Skills (Ordering: Oral, Ordering: Written, Computation: Oral, Computation: Written), Money/Time (Money Within 10p, Time: O'clock and Half Past).
Cross References: See T5:2134 (1 response); for reviews by G. Gage Kingsbury and Christine Novak of an earlier edition, see 12:317.

Review of the Quest, Second Edition by GABRIELE VAN LINGEN, Visiting Associate Professor in School Psychology, University of the Virgin Islands, U.S. Virgin Islands:

DESCRIPTION. Quest, Second Edition (Quest) is described as a set of resources for teachers for identifying, assessing, and providing learning supports for pupils 6 to 8 years old who have difficulties in reading and mathematics. Quest stands for Quick, Useful, Easy to use, Structured, and Teacher produced and tested. This second edition of Quest consists of the original Screening Tests in Reading and Number (1983), updated and refined Diagnostic Tests in Reading and Number, and revised Workbooks: Reading Quest 1 to 10, Looking Quest 1 and 2, Writing Quest 1 and 2, and Number Quest 1 to 5. Screening and diagnostic activities each take approximately 35 minutes for each subject area.

The Quest kit contains materials appropriate to these items, including photocopy masters for the screening and diagnostic tests, pupil profiles, and workbook activity sheets along with the teacher's manual and procedural guidelines. The three major parts (Screening Tests, Diagnostic Tests, and Workbooks) can be used flexibly. Overall, Quest is intended to identify students who are having difficulties in reading and mathematics at the beginning of their third year of schooling, to develop a diagnostic Pupil Profile, and to provide individualized workbooks tailored to the pupil's needs based on the National Curriculum in England and Wales. It can also be used to monitor pupil progress and establish a baseline of skills for school transfers.

The group-administered Reading and Number Screening Tests are unchanged from the first edition of Quest. The Reading Screening Test assesses basic word identification and reading comprehension, whereas the Number Screening Test assesses basic number concepts (e.g., cardinality, ordinality, addition, subtraction). The individually administered Diagnostic Reading and Number Tests have been revised from the 1983 version. The Diagnostic Reading Test retains original items on auditory and visual perception, but has added new and more carefully graded items in phonics, writing patterns and free writing, word-building, and reading comprehension. The Diagnostic Number Test has deleted items on the concept of belonging and difference, while retaining items on auditory and visual skills, number labeling, ordering, addition, and subtraction. New test items related to time and money and additional oral items on addition and subtraction have been included. The workbooks have also been revised.

The teacher's manual provides directions for administration and scoring criteria. For both the Reading and Number Screening Tests a range of scores is provided that identify pupils with significant difficulties (lowest 5%), some difficulties (the lowest 6% to 20%), and those without notable difficulties. Pupils within the first two categories should be given the Diagnostic Tests.

The Reading Diagnostic Tests include Test 1: Auditory Discrimination of initial, medial, and final sounds of one-syllable words; Test 2: Auditory Sequential Memory of digits, tapping rhythms, and word sequences; Test 3: Visual Discrimination of letter sequences and words; Test 4: Visual Sequencing of pictures telling a story; Test 5: Visuo-Motor Skills based on pencil control (Mazes), continuation of writing patterns, copying letters and sentences, and writing from memory; Test 6: Sight Vocabulary; Test 7: Letter Recognition (sounds), followed by three tests of word reading; Test 8: Simple Blends; Test 9: Beginnings and endings; Test 10 Digraphs, silent "e" rule and silent letters; Test 11: Word-Building and Multisyllabic Words; and Test 12: Reading Comprehension using pictures and a cloze format. Items range from 2 to 25 per test section, and most items receive a correct score of 1. The four parts of Test 5: Visuo-Motor Skills, are based on qualitative comments, with an overall rating based on a 5-point scale of "satisfactory/fairly satisfactory/fair/fairly poor/poor."

The Quest Diagnostic Number Tests also consists of 12 tests. Test 1: Visual Perception has four parts involving copying patterns/numbers of blocks, matching shapes, and finding shapes to complete a puzzle. Test 2: Visuo-Motor Coordination consists of copying figures, writing, and copying numbers. Test 3: Auditory Sequential Memory involves repeating a series of random digits. Test 4: Ordering by Quantity entails identifying the most and the least of a number of items, and sequencing cards by quantity of pictured items. Test 5: Addition uses blocks for basic numeration and addition items. Test 6: Subtraction presents problems similarly. Test 7: Ordering—Oral asks the pupil to count in various ways to 10 and to identify numbers "before" and "after" within that series. Test 8: Ordering—Written requires the pupil to write numbers up to 100 to dictation and to order numbers from smallest to largest. Test 9: Computation—Oral presents simple addition and subtraction problems orally, whereas Test 10: Computation—Written presents written addition and subtraction problems up to 20. Test 11: Money requires the pupil to identify and complete problems using British coins. Test 12: Time—O'Clock and Half Past expects the pupil to show and tell time.

The results of the Diagnostic Tests are recorded on well-designed test sheets and transferred to a Pupil Profile that provides both numeric and graphic displays of the results. A section for comments, references to pages of the teacher's manual for relevant interventions, and linkages to associated Quest workbooks are provided. The teacher's manual also presents a section of "Links between Quest Workbooks and Diagnostic Test Items," and a brief case study for a pupil with a reading problem and one with a math problem.

DEVELOPMENT. The test developers describe the Quest as criterion-referenced rather than norm-referenced. It was the result of a research project undertaken by a college of education and a child guidance center. The screening

tests were piloted first, with the tests then "developed over a five- to seven-year period" (teacher's manual, p. 4). No information is presented on item selection, item tryout, item analysis efforts, or the rationale for the construction and formats of the screening and diagnostic tests.

TECHNICAL. The interpretation of the Quest screening and diagnostic tests is based on results obtained from annual administrations in over 30 schools in partly rural and partly "urban new town" regions, resulting in a research sample of 2,046 pupils. These pupils were tested at the end of their second year and the beginning of their third year of schooling. There is no additional information about the characteristics of the sample.

To facilitate the identification of students who need extra support, a skewed distribution was produced that "separated out" the lower scores. Initially working with a 5% cutoff on the Screening Tests for identifying students that would receive diagnostic testing and support, the second edition extended this to the 6% to 20% range. Tables are provided for base rates (frequency and cumulative percentages) for Reading and Number Screening Test scores of pupils within a given age range. Additional tables and figures, displaying the ranges for the classification of scores into "significant" and "some" difficulties are presented. There are no outcome studies related to the effectiveness of the supports or interventions provided to identified pupils.

The teacher's manual provides very limited information on reliability and validity. A test-retest reliability study was carried out on a sample of 40 students with a time interval of 1 month. It was reported that the correlations for reading and number were significant at the 1% level. For evidence of validity, the developers reported that a test of internal validity was conducted in addition to using other group tests (Young's). "These checks provided evidence of validity at a level of chance which was less than one per cent" (teacher's manual, p. 97). These studies apply to the Screening Tests only. Another study, with similar results, is reported for the Quest Diagnostic Reading Test in relation to the Burt and/or Holborn reading tests. There is no list of references.

COMMENTARY AND SUMMARY. The Quest presents criterion-referenced screening and diagnostic tests for primary-school-aged children, end of second grade, beginning third grade, in the areas of reading and mathematics as articulated by the British national curriculum. The test kit contains record and pupil profile forms that are well designed and easy to use. The teacher's manual provides clear guidelines for administration and scoring rules, as well as interventions for pupils who need support. Associated workbooks present drill and practice worksheets for subskills of reading and mathematics. They do not consist of high interest materials.

The tests and their items appear to have content validity, based on the types of items selected; however, the number of items per test section is limited to the point that reliability of measurement is compromised. Moreover, some Diagnostic Reading Test items do not appear to reflect the aspect of reading intended to be measured based on the title of the test. Technical information provided for the Quest is extremely limited, including information on test development, standardization, reliability, and validity. This would advise against the use of the Quest in favor of better developed instruments. For the assessment of preliteracy and basic skills of pupils in the United States, curriculum-based measurement (CBM) techniques, such as those developed by Shapiro (2004) and Dynamic Indicators of Basic Early Literacy Skills (DIBELS) would provide preferred alternatives for non-U.K. groups, especially as Quest is based on the British curriculum.

REVIEWER'S REFERENCES

DIBELS—Official site at the University of Oregon. Retrieved March 1, 2005 from: http://dibels.uoregon.edu/index.php
Shapiro, E. S. (2004). *Academic skills problems: Direct assessment and intervention* (3rd ed.). New York: The Guilford Press.

[206]

Racial Attitude Survey.

Purpose: Measures attitudes toward an examiner-selected group of people using a generic semantic differential method.
Population: Adults.
Publication Dates: 1989–1996.
Scores, 9: Physical, Ego Strength (Dominance, Control, Anxiety, Ethics, General Social, On-the-Job), Social Distance, Casual Contact.
Administration: Individual or group.
Manual: No manual.
Price Data: Available from publisher.
Time: Administration time not reported.
Comments: Previously entitled Racial Attitude Test; technical information provided is from thesis by Cynthia Lewis.
Author: Thomas J. Rundquist.
Publisher: Nova Media, Inc.

Review of the Racial Attitude Survey by DEBORAH L. BANDALOS, *Professor of Educational Psychology, University of Georgia, Athens, GA:*

DESCRIPTION. The Racial Attitude Survey (RAS) is a self-report instrument composed of 75 items. For the first set of 62 items, respondents are presented with adjectives such as "clean," "independent," and "radical" and are directed to indicate the degree to which they believe a given racial group possesses the quality represented by each adjective. The response format for these ratings is a 5-point scale ranging from *strongly disagree* to *strongly agree,* making this part of the scale a sort of Likert/semantic differential hybrid.

It should be noted at the beginning of this review that there is no manual for this questionnaire. The only information on the instrument available consisted of an unpublished Master's thesis in which the instrument was used. What little information I have on the technical qualities of the instrument was gleaned from this manuscript.

The 62 adjectives in the first part of the instrument are arranged under two main headings labeled "Physical," comprising 14 adjectives, and "Ego Strength," with the remaining 48. "Ego Strength" is divided into six sections: "Dominance," "Control," "Anxiety," "Ethics," "General Social," and "On-the-Job." Control has eight adjectives associated with it, Anxiety and General Social each have six adjectives, and Ethics contains four adjectives. I have deliberately avoided use of the terms "scale" or "subscale" to describe these groupings because there is no theoretical or empirical evidence presented to demonstrate that the adjectives included under a heading measure distinguishable or even logically consistent constructs.

The remaining 13 items are grouped under two headings: "Social Distance" and "Casual Contact." Under Social Distance, eight referents such as "boss," "neighbor," and "marriage partner" are presented with the stem "You would be accepting as." I found the wording of this section somewhat confusing. For example, the literal reading of an item would be "You would be accepting as neighbor." Because this is an awkward construction, it may be that the author intended the instruction to read "You would be accepting of as" rather than "You would be accepting as." Although this is speculation on my part, it seems likely that some respondents may interpret the set of items in this way, which could lead to very different answers.

The five items grouped under the heading Casual Contact include situations such as "in the same bus" or "in the same bar," with instructions that simply state "You would be accepting" using the same 5-point scale as the items under Social Distance. As with the previous set of items, no evidence relative to the factor structure or theoretical basis of these groupings is presented.

DEVELOPMENT. No information is presented regarding how the instrument was developed, or whether the numbers of items under each heading are based on their relative importance, the availability of salient adjectives, or some other criterion. Similarly, the reason for selection of the categories of Physical, Ego Strength, Social Distance, and Casual Contact is not given.

TECHNICAL. No information on standardization is provided. With regard to reliability, the Master's thesis described earlier reports the following values for Cronbach alpha: Physical traits, .85; Ego Strength, .92; Social Distance, .94; and Casual Contact, .99, based on a large national sample of 747. However, although respondents in this study were instructed to base responses on their perceptions of one of four different racial groups, only one set of reliability coefficients is presented. Possibly these values are based on responses averaged across all racial groups, but this is problematic because attitudes may well vary across the four groups. It is, therefore, difficult to know how to interpret these values. In particular, the value of .99 for the five Casual Contact items is somewhat questionable given that these five items represent fairly different situations: "in the same bus," "in the same theater," "in the same bar," "in the same restaurant," and "in the same college." Moreover, the situations are such that not all respondents would necessarily have experienced all of them. For example, not everyone frequents bars or goes to college.

Because the purpose of this test was not provided in the materials given, it was not possible to evaluate any validity evidence that might have been provided by the scale developer. It is, therefore, perhaps serendipitous that none was. Information on the ability of some of the RAS scores to differentiate those giving positive and negative ratings of advertisements featuring models from different racial groups is provided in the Master's thesis described earlier. However, given the proscribed nature of this task, the generalizability of these findings as well as the degree to which they relate to the validity of the instrument is limited. Clearly much more work in this area is needed for this scale to be considered seriously.

SUMMARY. The Racial Attitude Survey is a poorly constructed and awkwardly worded instrument with little to no evidence of acceptable psychometric properties. The author of this instrument is apparently either unaware of professional standards in testing or has chosen to disregard them. I would recommend that those interested in measuring such attitudes look elsewhere.

[207]
Reading Style Inventory 2000.

Purpose: Designed to identify "the way each student learns best then (match) those strengths to the most effective reading methods, materials and strategies."

Population: Grade 1 to adults.

Publication Dates: 1980–2000.

Acronym: RSI.

Scores: 52 elements: Global Tendencies, Analytical Tendencies, Perceptual Strengths (Auditory Strengths, Visual Strengths, Tactile Strengths, Kinesthetic Strengths), Reading Methods (Carbo Recorded-Book Method, Fernald Method, Individualized Method, Modeling Methods, Language-Experience Method, Orton-Gillingham Method, Phonics Method, Whole-Word Method, Recorded Books, Computers), Preferred Reading Environment (Quiet—No Talking, Quiet—No Music, Dim Light, Warm Temperatures, Informal Design, Highly Organized), Emotional Profile (Peer Motivated, Adult Motivated, Self-Motivated, Persistent, Responsible), These Students Prefer (Choices, Direction, Work Checked), Sociological Preferences (Read to a Teacher, Read with Peers, Read Alone, Read with Peers/Teacher, Read with One Peer), Physical Preferences (Intake While Reading, Read in the Morning, Read in Early Afternoon, Read in Late Afternoon, Read in Evening, Mobility), Reading Materials (Audio-Visuals, Basal Reader Phonics, Basal Reader Whole-Word, Computers, Fernald Materials, Reading Activities, Orton-Gillingham Materials, Reading Kits, Recorded-Books, Tradebooks, Newspapers, etc.; Workbooks and Worksheets).

Administration: Group.

Forms, 3: Primary, Intermediate, Adult.

Price Data, 2003: Price per administration varies by volume.

Time: Administration time not reported.

Comments: Available online only.

Author: National Reading Styles Institute.

Publisher: National Reading Styles Institute.

Cross References: See T5:218 (2 references); for reviews by Jeri Benson and Alice J. Corkill of a previous edition, see 11:328 (1 reference).

Review of the Reading Style Inventory 2000 by ALICE CORKILL, Associate Professor, Department of Counseling and Educational Psychology, University of Nevada, Las Vegas, Las Vegas, NV:
DESCRIPTION AND DEVELOPMENT. The Reading Style Inventory 2000 (RSI Online) is designed to help practitioners identify a person's "reading style." It is based on the Dunn and Dunn model of learning styles. Each individual who completes the RSI Online receives a personal reading style profile that claims to pinpoint the individual's Global/Analytic Tendencies, Perceptual Strengths, best Reading Environment, Emotional Profile, and Sociological Profile. In addition, the profile includes suggestions for the most effective reading methods and materials to use with each individual.

The RSI Online is available in three different versions. The Primary version is appropriate for individuals in Grades 1 and 2. The Intermediate version is appropriate for individuals in Grades 3 through 8. The Adult version is appropriate for individuals from Grade 9 through adult. Based on information from the RSI Online website, it appears the Primary version can only be administered via the internet. The Intermediate and Adult versions may be administered via the internet or by means of a paper-and-pencil version that may be accessed from the website and printed locally. The Primary version recommends the use of auxiliary audio provided by the website. Use of the audio is extremely important as the Primary version includes several listening tasks in which information is presented auditorally and the examinee must listen and respond to a subsequent question. The Intermediate and Adult versions do not have this requirement.

Each version of the inventory has approximately 68 items. Roughly half of the items require the respondent to read and make a selection among three alternatives. For the other half, respondents make a dichotomous selection. For a three-response item, for example, the respondent would read and select from the following three alternatives (taken from the Adult version): "A) I like my reading assignment checked as soon as I finish it. B) I like my reading assignment checked about one day after I finish it. C) It's not important to me to have my reading assignment checked often."

For a dichotomous response item, for example, the respondent would read the following two alternatives (taken from the Intermediate version): "A) I like to make and build things. B) I don't like to make and build things." If the respondent is completing the inventory on the internet, the respondent reads the alternatives and then selects a response by locating and clicking the computer mouse over the response that most closely fits their attitude or belief. The same is true for individuals who complete the Primary version.

The three versions of the inventory (Primary, Intermediate, Adult) include similar, and sometimes identical, items with one exception. The Intermediate and Adult versions ask respondents to self-report on their memory abilities. Respondents who complete the Primary version are given simple memory tasks to complete as a part of the inventory. For example, on the Intermediate or Adult version of the inventory, respondents would see the following item: "A) It's hard for me to remember the directions that someone tells me. B) It's easy for me to remember the directions that someone tells me." The respondent then selects the option that he or she believes best describes himself or herself. On the Primary version, the respondents are given a listening task instead. The respondent is told to listen carefully to a set of directions. The directions are then spoken and the respondent is asked a question directly related to the directions they just heard. The Primary version has approximately 10–15 items that require respondents either to demonstrate their memory skills or to examine a display of information presented on the computer screen and make comparisons to several confusably similar displays.

The inventory is scored automatically by the website and three separate individual profiles are provided: (a) a complete RSI profile, (b) a condensed RSI profile, and (c) a report for parents. Each profile provides similar information presented in a different format.

The complete profile provides the greatest amount of information. It includes a series of diagnoses as well as recommendations relative to the best strategies for teaching reading to the respondent for each diagnosis provided. The diagnoses fall into six or seven categories (six categories for the Primary inventory; seven categories for the Intermediate and Adult inventory): (a) Global/Analytic Tendencies (not reported on the Primary profile)—information relative to use of humor, stories, or games in learning to read (global tendencies) and use of routines, rules, directions, and details in learning to read (analytic tendencies); (b) Perceptual Strengths—information relative to auditory, visual, tactile, and kinesthetic strengths; (c) Preferred Reading Environment—information relative to what the respondent prefers with respect to noise, lighting, temperature, and setting; (d) This Student Is—information relative to whether the respondent is motivated by others or by himself or herself as well as information about their persistence and level of motivation; (e) This Student Prefers—information relative to whether the respondent would appreciate choices with respect to reading material, direction from the teacher, and how often his or her work is reviewed and by whom; (f) Sociological Preferences—information relative to whether the respondent prefers to read alone, read to, or read with others; and (g) Physical Preferences—information relative to when the respondent prefers to read (morning, early noon, late noon, in the evening), whether the respondent prefers to read for long or short periods of time, as well as whether the respondent would appreciate having a snack available.

The complete RSI profile also includes recommendations for the best reading method for the individual who completed the inventory. This reviewer had the opportunity to create two profiles by completing the inventory online (an Adult and a Primary profile) and to peruse an adult profile available on the RSI Online web pages. On the Adult profiles, "highly recommended," "recommended," and "not recommended" reading methods were provided. On the Primary profile, "highly recommended," "recommended," "acceptable," and "not recommended" reading methods were provided. In each instance, despite several diagnoses that were diametrically opposed, the Carbo Recorded-Book method was listed first in the "highly recommended" method category. The complete profile also includes a brief section that makes suggestions for how reading instruction might be modified for the individual who completed the inventory and a section that makes recommendations as to appropriate reading materials. Again, on the three profiles available to this reviewer, despite the diagnostic differences on the profiles, the Carbo Method materials were first on the list of recommended reading materials.

The report for parents is written in letter format, which explains to parents that their child completed the inventory and provides a profile for parents that includes the same six or seven diagnostic categories included on the complete profile. Parents are not given information about reading method recommendations, special modifications for the student, or reading material recommendations.

TECHNICAL. The reliability of the RSI Online has, apparently, not been assessed. The reliability information provided on the RSI Online web pages appears to be based on previous (paper-and-pencil) versions of the inventory. Reliability estimates for the Primary version of the inventory are based on two samples (one with 105 New York City first and second grade students; the other with 158 first and second grade students from Kansas, Missouri, New York, and Washington). Reliability coefficients ranging from .67 to .89 are reported. Reliability estimates for the Intermediate version of the inventory are based on one study with 210 students (from Kansas, Michigan, New York, Oklahoma, and Washington) with coefficients ranging from .63 to .87. Reliability estimates for the Adult version of the inventory are based on one study with 220 individuals (ages ranging from 16 to 22 from the states of New York, Oklahoma, and Washington) with coefficients ranging from .65 to .90. In each instance, reliability coefficients are based on test-retest, with a 3-week retest interval.

Separate reliability coefficients are reported for several RSI subscales on the Intermediate and Adult versions of the inventory. The subscales reported do not align with either the diagnostic categories included on the profiles or with the elements of reading style that are described on the RSI Online web pages. The RSI Online web pages report five elements of reading style: (a) environmental stimuli, (b) emotional stimuli, (c) sociological stimuli, (d) physical stimuli, and (e) psychological stimuli. Each element is briefly defined on the web pages. The RSI subscales listed in the reliability reports available on the RSI Online web pages include sound, light, intake, design, auditory perception, visual perception, tactile perception, and kinesthetic perception (it is unclear whether this is an exhaustive list of subscales). This curious mismatch between profile diagnostics, elements of reading style, and RSI subscales calls into question the underlying theory of the inventory as well as its psychometric properties.

The validity of the RSI Online has also apparently not been assessed. Information provided on the RSI Online web pages appears to be based on previous versions of the inventory. Evaluation of the content (face) validity of the inventory was examined by a call to interested parties via an article in *Educational Leadership* in 1981 and another article in the *Learning Styles Network Newsletter* also in 1981. Eighty-seven educators responded and the majority of them (93%) indicated that the items on the inventory appeared to be items that would assess elements of reading style.

Attempts to examine concurrent validity have resulted in a mishmash of claims based on everything ranging from comparing parental observations with inventory results to comparing teacher observations with inventory results to comparisons between the RSI and Dunn and Dunn's Learning Style Inventory. Concurrent validity of the RSI has yet to be firmly examined. Claims of predictive validity are equally, if not more, insubstantial.

The RSI web pages provide a detailed account of how construct validity has been documented, but provide no specific, technical information that corroborates these claims. In addition, virtually all of the research cited to support the validity of the RSI was published in the 1970s and 1980s (77% of the citations on the RSI web pages are from research, dissertations, or master's theses published or completed between 1970 and 1983 with only three publications—less than 6%—from the 1990s). Clearly no new validity studies have been conducted since the publication of the original version of the RSI.

SUMMARY. The Reading Style Inventory 2000 (RSI Online) makes extravagant claims without having the technical or psychometric evidence to support them. At best, the RSI Online may give practitioners a suggestion or two as to individual learner's preferences with respect to reading environments (e.g., prefer bright versus dim lighting). At its worst, the RSI Online may simply be a vehicle for promoting the Carbo reading materials and methods.

Review of the Reading Style Inventory 2000 by THOMAS EMERSON HANCOCK, Associate Professor of Educational Psychology, George Fox University, Newberg, OR, and KATHLEEN ALLEN, Assistant Professor of Reading Education, St. Martin's College, Lacey, WA:

DESCRIPTION. The Reading Style Inventory 2000, or RSI, is an on-line self-report designed to measure a person's unique style of reading. It also attempts to recommend reading methods and materials that match each person's unique style. The RSI is available in both English and Spanish, in three forms: primary (Grades 1—2), intermediate (Grades 3–8), and adult (Grades 9–adult). The adult and intermediate versions each have 68 questions and the primary has 52 questions.

The inventory can be accessed at www.rsi-on-line.com. The home page includes links to the RSI login menu, a description of the instrument, sample reporting profiles, reference to related research, and user support information. In the user support section, there are provisions for "assigners," such as a school administrator or principal. The assigners can distribute RSIs after on-line purchase. Users can then administer the RSI to students or themselves. Various recommendations are provided to the administrator for increasing the likelihood of meaningful student responding, such as providing 2 to 4 weeks of experiences related to those addressed in the instrument's questions.

To complete the RSI, some computer knowledge is assumed. However, no list of required computer skills is included in the directions. A user completes the RSI items one screen per question. In the Grade 1–2 version, text is presented along with a recorded voice. Each of the RSI items provides two or three response selections for self-judged preferences about stimuli, reading, and learning styles. For example the respondent is to choose between the two statements, "I like to read at night" and "I do not like to read at night," or between three alternatives such as, "I almost always use my hands a lot when I talk," "I sometimes use my hands when I talk," and "I almost never use my hands when I talk." There is no discernible way for the test taker to change a response once selected. However, the test administrator can change responses when the testing session is over, but only before the profile has been generated.

Immediately after test administration, various group summary profiles and individual profiles can be viewed and printed out. The individual profiles for the intermediate and adult versions consist of seven categories containing 32 strategy statements for teaching reading. Two categories appear to be mostly focused on learning styles— global/analytic tendencies and perceptual strengths, and five on preferences related to reading-environment for reading, motivation to read, self-direction to read, who to read with, and physical preferences such as preferred time to read. The individual profiles for the primary version consist of 30 elements in six categories, without the global/analytic category of the other versions. The profile report for all three versions also includes recommendations for reading method (e.g., the Carbo Recorded Book method) and materials (e.g., "trade books, magazines, short stories, articles"). The methodology for translating a respondent's choices on the 52- or 68-item RSI into profile statements is not described at the site nor is the manner in which instructional recommendations are determined. It appears that response selections for 26 items of the inventory are each reworded to provide 26 recommendations of strategies for teaching reading. For example, one of the RSI item selections is "When I read, I like to sit on something soft, like pillows, a soft chair or a rug." In the preferred reading environment section, the associated strategy recommendation for teaching reading is "Provide soft chairs, couches, rugs, pillows."

With minor wording variation, all three versions of the RSI use the same question content and the same recommended strategies, except that the primary version does not include the 16 items that presumably measure global/analytic techniques. There are no directions in Spanish for the Spanish versions.

In our testing of the instrument, we found that the intermediate and adult RSIs were fairly easy to administer. However, the graphics for the primary version seemed confusing to some students because they consisted of line drawings where the delineation between the choices was not always evident. Most primary students do not have the subtlety of reasoning for such fine distinctions. Photographs of the real rooms with a clear choice would seem to be much more effective for learners who are at the concrete level developmentally.

The test authors are to be commended for having an oral direction component for the primary test. However, the slow, sing-song voice, the multiple-step directions, and the "cute" storyline with "Tic, Tac, and Toe" should be left out. If there were one-step questions stated in a normal tone of voice, more valid data would be likely.

DEVELOPMENT. The foundation for the RSI is the proposal that all people have different learning strengths and that reading instruction should match strengths. The RSI grew out of the Learning Styles model of Dunn and Dunn that identifies five types of stimuli to consider when diagnosing learning styles:environmental (sound, light, temperature, design); emotional (motivation, persistence, responsibility, structure); sociological (peers, self, pairs, team, adults, varied); physical (perceptual, intake, time, mobility); and psychological (analytic/global, cerebral dominance, impulsive/reflective).

However, there is no clear explanation for how the actual RSI items were developed. It is simply stated that "the items on the RSI were developed as the result of careful comparisons between a youngster's actual behavior as observed randomly by at least two trained individuals, and the student's self-reported behavior." That was followed by an invitation to readers of *Educational Leadership* and the *Learning Styles Network Newsletter* to evaluate the clarity, appropriateness, and representativeness of the RSI items. Eighty-seven educators responded and 93% stated "that the RSI accurately measured the elements of reading style."

TECHNICAL. There has been no standardization reported for the RSI.

The primary version (1 and 2) of the RSI was tested for reliability with two studies. In the first, 105 first and second graders produced reliability coefficients from .67 to .89, with the highest (.77 to .89) obtained for the perceptual subscales. The second study, with 158 first and second graders, yielded test-retest reliability coefficients for subscales that ranged from .69 to .87 with the highest reliability coefficients (.78 to .87) obtained for the perceptual subscales. Test-retest reliability for the intermediate inventory was examined with 210 children in Grades 3, 5, and 6. The reliability coefficients for the RSI subscales ranged from .63 to .87 and averaged .76. The reliability of the adult inventory was tested with 220 individuals drawn from groups ranging in age from 16 to 22 years. A 3-week retest interval yielded reliability coefficients ranging from .58 to .90, with most RSI subscales clustering around the mid 70s. These results indicate that there is fair to good test-retest reliability evidence for the RSI and particularly for the perceptual subscales. However, these studies were not conducted in the online format of the current RSI.

The "Validity" section at the RSI site reports evidence according to traditional categories. The content validity evidence is scant, as reported above in the Development section. The concurrent validity evidence seems impressive: Learning styles experts concur with the results of the RSI, practitioners testify to the accuracy of the RSI diagnoses, RSI results are correlated with the Learning Styles Inventory results, and RSI printouts are matched to teacher observations. However, the weight of these studies should be balanced by noting that the confirmatory evidence may be from those who are already predisposed toward such measures. It is not clear whether those experts and teachers are unbiased. Similarly, correlations between the RSI and the Learning Styles Inventory are not sound validity evidence because the two contain similar items drawn from the same conceptual base. In the construct validity section, the bulk of the evidence focuses on differences across gender, ages, and ability levels. Though these differences would generally be desirable validity evidence, in this case it is not clear why variance in reading styles between these groups provides validity evidence for the RSI. On the contrary, the popular appeal of the RSI is that everyone has a different learning style and that effective instruction needs to be matched to style.

The volume of predictive validity evidence is likewise impressive. However, we are cautioned that simply providing numbers and stating that research supports a measure is not adequate. The methodologies must be studied. However, it was difficult to access the three pivotal research studies cited for demonstrating reading gains associated with the RSI. We contacted the RSI authors for help in finding those papers. They graciously provided abstracts for those and dozens of other studies. With two exceptions, the research updates they provided did not include detailed methodologies, so it was impossible to verify validity claims. However, in reading only the abstracts several confounding factors could be identified. For example, there was a recurring intact groups problem. That is, treatment varied with classroom or school, so that any effect reported may have been due to the difference in groups and not the RSI treatment. Also, significant effects were reported when the experimenter (sympathetic to the RSI) taught both the control and treatment groups.

We were hard-pressed to find convincing evidence that those studies reporting positive effects were clearly due to the RSI results and not, for instance, to the diligent application of novel instructional methods. For example, in the first of the two complete research studies provided by the authors, the methods were detailed on applying various Carbo promoted instructional materials but sketchy on other methods. Compounded with other serious methodological concerns, it is plausible that the effect reported was not due to the use of the RSI instrument.

The other detailed research study that was provided along with all the abstracts does report somewhat sound methods and the results are positive, though not strong. However, the showcase research paper should be much more convincing, in view of the great volume of other research cited. We cannot ignore this one study nor the many other studies cited, but it is difficult to recommend the RSI as providing valid data, in view of the paucity of convincing methodological evidence from other studies.

COMMENTARY AND SUMMARY. Several strengths of the RSI are evident: (a) easy accessibility online, (b) recognition that children do have varied environmental and physical preferences (this information may be used for classroom environment design, lesson planning, and homework guidelines), (c) attempts to provide differential instruction based on individual differences, and (d) efficiency of feedback to parents and educators in the profile reports.

Several weaknesses could be easily addressed to improve the RSI 2000. Given the research on effectiveness of providing feedback to students, a student-friendly version of the profile report would be an easy but welcome addition. The adult version could be rewritten with language that does not assume the user is a student. The needs of teachers could be more solidly addressed if all of the method and materials recommendations were not only categorized but also matched to actual products that the teacher could efficiently find and use. The test authors should describe in detail how their items were developed and precisely how reading style diagnoses and strategy recommendations are determined. Research should be more completely discussed and links should be provided to the complete papers that are used for supporting evidence. The Spanish population's needs could be better addressed if the Spanish versions of the RSI were accompanied with Spanish instructions, support material, and validity evidence. The functionality of the website could be improved by making all the hotlinks properly operational, finishing subpages that are "under construction," providing a way back to the home page from every other page, upgrading the design quality of some of the subpages, explaining security precautions that have been taken, providing email contact information, and using tooltips instead of occupying screen real estate to explain the main menus.

Several other weaknesses are more problematic. First, the language used throughout the RSI site implies that students' rating of their preferences is the same as actually measuring their behaviors. At best we are measuring perceptions, which perceptions may be inaccurate and sometimes are only guesses by the respondent. Second, a student's preference for some reading modality is not necessarily the most effective modality for reading and learning. Third, although there is a differentiation in the test for primary, intermediate, and adult readers, the reading methods, strategies, and materials suggestions are generally the same for each. For example, it is hard to find sound justification for every user receiving recommendations that Carbo materials are the preferred match to profiles. The idea of providing differential instruction that matches individual differences is quite appealing. However, there is the need for empirical support for those strategies, materials, and methods that are recommended. In all seven of the RSIs that we had completed, varied reading styles profiles were always paired with the Carbo materials as the strongly recommended instructional tools. Another serious problem is that many of the other methods included in the recommendations are from special education practice in the 1970s and 1980s, whereas instructional reading methods that have evolved in the last 10 years are not included. It appears that the orientation of the RSI is overly rooted in the behavioristic paradigm that was more dominant when it was created. More value should accrue if measures of individual differences in reading style were more explicitly rooted in the current cognitive research.

Finally, in responsibly commenting on the validity of the RSI, the meta-analysis of 39 studies by Kavale and Forness (1987) must be mentioned. In their article, "Substance over Style," modality preference groups could not be clearly differentiated. Furthermore, the average effect size of learning styles interventions was . 04, or nearly zero. They conclude that, although intuitively appealing, the modality model should be dismissed.

Thus, the reported validity evidence of the RSI would need to be particularly strong for it to be seriously considered as a valuable instrument. However, as has been discussed above, the evidence is not strong and is mixed at best. Thus, we cannot confidently recommend the Reading Styles Inventory 2000 as likely to yield valid data.

REVIEWERS' REFERENCE
Kavale, K. A., & Forness, S. R. (1987). Substance over style: Assessing the efficacy of modality testing and teaching. *Exceptional Children, 53*(3), 228–239.

[208]

Receptive-Expressive Emergent Language Test, Third Edition.

Purpose: Designed to identify babies or young children with delayed language acquisition, to determine discrepancy between receptive and expressive processes of emergent language and to document intervention effects.

Population: Ages 0–36 months.

Publication Dates: 1971–2003.

Acronym: REEL-3.

Scores, 3: Receptive Language Ability, Expressive Language Ability, Language Ability.

Administration: Individual.

Price Data, 2003: $88 per complete kit including examiner's manual (2003, 98 pages) and 25 profile/examiner record booklets; $55 per examiner's manual; $39 per 25 profile/examiner record booklets.

Time: (20–30) minutes.

Comments: Informants knowledgeable about child's language behavior are interviewed; first edition titled The Bzoch-League Receptive Expressive Emergent Language Scale: For the Measurement of Language Skills in Infancy.

Authors: Kenneth R. Bzoch, Richard League, and Virginia L. Brown.

Publisher: PRO-ED.

Cross References: See T5:2189 (7 references); for reviews by Lyle F. Bachman and Lynn S. Bliss of a previous edition, see 12:323 (2 references); see also T4:2238 (3 references) and T3:338 (5 references); for excerpted reviews by Alex Bannatyne, Dale L. Johnson, and Barton B. Proger of the first edition, see 8:956 (5 references); see also T2:2067 (2 references).

Review of the Receptive-Expressive Emergent Language Test, Third Edition by DAVID P. HURFORD, Director of the Center for the Assessment and Remediation of Reading Difficulties and Professor of Psychology and Counseling, Pittsburg State University, Pittsburg, KS:

DESCRIPTION. The Receptive-Expressive Emergent Language Test, Third Edition (REEL-

3) is a test designed to assess the receptive and expressive emerging language abilities of children from birth to 36 months of age. Although the REEL-3 has no time limits, administration typically is completed within approximately 20 to 30 minutes. The REEL-3 assesses two components of emergent language: receptive and expressive language. The REEL-3 also includes a vocabulary inventory and supplementary questions, the purpose of which is to further probe the informant's understanding of the infant's or young child's emergent language abilities.

Although certainly not an unusual or unreasonable procedure for assessing infants' and young children's language ability, the REEL-3 utilizes structured questions presented to parents, guardians, or caregivers who are very familiar with the child's language behaviors (i.e., informants). It is practical to ask informants about the acquisition of language behaviors given the time and highly specialized knowledge that would be required to assess directly the actual language acquisition behaviors of children. The REEL-3 has 66 questions to be answered by the informant regarding expressive language and 66 questions to be answered by the informant regarding receptive language. Although there is a total of 132 questions on the REEL-3, an informant would not respond to all of these questions. Entry into the test is determined by the child's age with informants of older children starting at later questions and informants of younger children most likely ending at earlier items.

The authors believe that the REEL-3 has four intended uses: (a) to identify infants or young children who are delayed in their language acquisition, (b) to determine if there are significant discrepancies between receptive and expressive language, (c) to document the progress of interventions designed to improve the emergent language abilities of children, and (d) to measure expressive and receptive language abilities in research studies. The REEL-3 has only one form, hence no alternative form. As a result, the use of the REEL-3 for research purposes is limited to studies that do not assess language processing more than once. Research designs typically require that alternative forms of a test be used at different times of testing to reduce the likelihood of time of measurement or practice effects.

The record booklet has sections for identifying information (e.g., child's name; gender; informant's name; preschool, daycare, or school; school district; language spoken in the home or daycare; examiner's name and title), age (date of testing, date of birth, chronological age, prematurity adjusted age), and recording the scores (e.g., raw scores, age equivalents, ability scores [standard scores], percentile ranks, *SEM*, confidence intervals, score range, and descriptive ratings). The subtests along with their brief instructions are contained within the record booklet.

The manual is complete and easy to comprehend. The novice user of the REEL-3 will not find it difficult to comprehend the administration or scoring procedures. The manual provides very useful information regarding adaptive assessment (nonstandardized administration geared to further probe to clarify the informants' responses), how to share the results of the REEL-3 with parents and other potential nonprofessionals, how to develop local norms if local norms are desired or needed, and how to develop intervention goals that utilize parents and caregivers. This section of the manual is quite thorough and valuable.

DEVELOPMENT. The REEL-3 was standardized with a norming group of 1,112 infants and young children from 32 states with 91% of the sample having no disability, 2% having language disabilities, and 7% having "other" disabilities. The normative sample was very similar to the demographic characteristics of the population of the United States. The REEL-3 provides standard (ability) scores, percentiles, and age equivalents for the receptive and expressive language subtests. A language ability (composite standard) score is also provided. Although age equivalents have been extensively criticized, they are provided as a normative score. However, if test authors would stop providing these psychometrically deficient values, agencies might become less dependent upon them and, thus, authors of future tests would be less obliged to provide them.

TECHNICAL. Reliability was assessed with internal consistency, test-retest reliability, and interrater reliability coefficients. Internal consistency was assessed by computing coefficient alphas for the Receptive and Expressive Language subtests and the Language Ability Composite score for each of the 23 age levels (birth to 36 months). Coefficient alphas ranged from .71 (for 3-month-olds on the Expressive Language subtest) to .98 (for 36-month-olds on the Expressive Language subtest and the Language Ability Composite score) with a mean of .92, .93, and .93 for the Receptive and Expressive Language subtests, and the Language Ability Composite score, respectively. Coefficient alphas were also calculated for males, females, European Americans, African Americans, Hispanic Americans, Asian Americans, and children with speech or language impairments, by subtest and composite score. These values were quite similar to those reported above with a range of .95 to .98 with an average .963. These values indicate that the REEL-3 provides a reliable measure of emergent language ability in infants and young children from birth to 36 months regardless of gender, minority group status, or speech or language impairment.

Test-retest reliability was evaluated by assessing 44 infants and toddlers aged 0 to 36 months of age residing in Austin, Texas. Of the 44 infants and toddlers, 20 were male and 24 were female, 58% were European American, 36% Hispanic American, 2% African American, 2% Asian American, and 2% Native American. The time between the two administrations of the REEL-3 was 2 weeks. The correlation coefficients for the Time 1 and Time 2 administrations of the Receptive and Expressive Language subtests and the Language Ability Composite were .89, .78, and .80, respectively. These values represent adequate test-retest reliability values.

Interrater reliability was assessed utilizing Cohen's kappa (a measure of interrater reliability that is used when the items are categorical, such as the items on the REEL-3). Two raters each independently scored the mothers' responses to the REEL-3 from the test-retest study described above. The kappa values ranged between .69 and 1.00 (mean of .99), and .79 and 1.00 (mean of .99) for the Receptive and Expressive Language subtests. The mean kappa score for the Language Ability Composite was .99 (ranges were not reported in the manual).

Validity was assessed with content validity (including item rationale, conventional item analysis, and differential item functioning analysis), criterion-related validity, and construct validity. With regard to content validity, the Receptive and Expressive Language subtests that comprise the REEL-3 were developed as a function of several avenues. First, the items on the original REEL were created from refinements of clinical observations of infants' and young children's utterances. The items on the REEL-3 were reformatted to

more adequately reflect contemporary theories of language development and acquisition. Supplementary items were created by examining 10 well-known sources that assessed language development (e.g., Bayley Scales of Infant Development—Second Edition) and using items that could be found on at least three of these sources. The Expressive and Receptive Language subtests, therefore, seem to quite adequately assess language ability.

The manual also provides reasonable arguments for utilizing caregivers as informants for the purpose of collecting information concerning language acquisition and development rather than trained observations of the infant's or young child's actual behavior. Young children, particularly infants, are not capable of participating in the assessment process. As a result, the options simply are to have trained observers spend considerable amounts of time observing the language ability of the young children or to query informants who are very knowledgeable of the young child's language development. Others have determined that parents or caregivers are valid sources of information for assessing language development. In terms of practical considerations for assessment, the argument for informants is compelling. Using information from informants as a first step in assessing the emergent language abilities of young children also allows the clinician to make appropriate decisions concerning the most promising avenues to pursue if evaluating the young child's emergent language abilities directly is necessary.

The items on the REEL-3 were calibrated using Item Response Theory parameters of item discrimination and difficulty. Item discrimination analysis assesses the ability of an item to differentiate between respondents. The analysis utilizes the Pearson product-moment correlation to measure the relationship between each item and the remaining items on the REEL-3. Item discrimination scores should be approximately .35 or better. The median item discrimination scores ranged between .33 and .69 (mean of .528) for the Receptive Language subtest and between .29 and .72 (mean of .532) for the Expressive Language subtest.

The item difficulty for a test, the percentage of respondents who pass an item, should be between 15% and 85% for individual items and approximately 50% for the total test. Median item difficulty scores for the Receptive Language subtest ranged between .21 and .96 with a mean of .616, and between .35 and .97 with a mean of .668 for the Expressive Language subtest. The item discrimination and item difficulty scores fall within values that support the validity of the REEL-3.

To examine the possibility of item bias in the REEL-3, items were examined for potential gender and ethnic bias. Items were also examined to determine the possibility that any of them might potentially be offensive to an informant. The items that were deemed appropriate for the REEL-3 were then subjected to Differential Item Functioning (DIF) analysis. DIF analysis highlights items in which the various groups examined perform differently. The particular type of DIF analysis that was utilized examined two logistic regression solutions. The first examined subtest scores to predict item performance. The second solution used subtest scores and group membership to predict item performance. If the second solution provided a better solution than the first, it would have indicated that group membership was important in predicting item performance, thus suggesting that the items were biased toward particular groups. Three hundred ninety-six DIF comparisons were carried out (one for each item for both subtests for each of the three groups mentioned above being examined). Of the 396 comparisons, 13 were determined to be significantly different (2/66 for males/females on the Receptive Language subtest, 4/66 for males/females on the Expressive Language subtest, 3/66 for African Americans/Non-African Americans on the Receptive Language subtest, 1/66 for African Americans/Non-African Americans on the Expressive Language subtest, and 3/66 for Hispanic Americans/Non-Hispanic Americans on the Expressive Language subtest. Although the authors indicate that the 13 significant comparisons had negligible effect sizes, they did not report the effect sizes. Even so, the analyses indicate that the REEL-3 does not appear to be biased.

Criterion-related validity was examined with two studies. The first examined the relationship between the REEL-3 and the Developmental Assessment of Young Children (DAYC). Fifty-eight children (31 males and 27 females) between birth and 29 months (87% European American, 5% African American, 5% Asian American, and 3% Native American) participated. The correlation coefficients between the standard score on the DAYC Communication subtest and the standard

scores from the Receptive and Expressive subtests, and the Language Ability Composite score were .55, .62, and .57, respectively.

The second study examined the relationship between the REEL-3 and the Early Language Milestone Scale (Second Edition; ELM-2). Thirty-six children (17 males and 19 females) between 2 and 35 months of age (54% European American, 40% Hispanic American, 3% African American, and 3% other) participated. The ELMS-2 provides Auditory Receptive, Auditory Expressive, and General Language standard scores. These scores were correlated with the analogous standard scores from the REEL-3. The correlation coefficients for the Expressive and Receptive subtests were .71 and .53, respectively, and .62 for the General Language and Composite standard scores. The above two studies indicate that the REEL-3 has sufficient criterion validity.

Finally, construct validity was assessed utilizing age differentiation and group differentiation. Age differentiation is another means to examine the validity of a test. Emergent Language abilities should improve with age. Data provided in the manual indicate that the means for the various subtests increase with age, thus supporting validity. Group differentiation, like age differentiation, can be used to support validity. If a test of emergent language can differentiate between groups of young children who are known to have poor or delayed emergent language development, such as individuals with speech and hearing disabilities, validity would be further supported. This group should perform significantly worse than individuals who are not speech and hearing delayed. Data reported in the manual indicated that individuals who were speech and language delayed had low average standard scores for Receptive Language (.93) and significantly below average standard scores for Expressive Language (.84) and the Language Ability Composite (.86). Individuals who are speech and hearing delayed would be expected to be near average on Receptive Language, but significantly lower on Expressive Language and the Composite score. Very little information was provided in the manual regarding the disability status group other than 2% of the normative sample was language impaired.

Measures of language ability have been found to be moderately related to intelligence. The authors of the REEL-3 examined the relationship between the REEL-3 and the Cognitive Abilities Scale—Second Edition (CAS-2) in 27 young children between 6 and 18 months of age. The resulting correlation coefficients between the Receptive Language, Expressive Language, and Language Ability Composite for the CAS-2 were .59, .38, and .48, respectively. These values are consistent with other studies that examined the relationship between intelligence and emergent language.

In summary, the case for validity is strong. Age differentiation data indicated that performance on the REEL-3 increased with age, which supports validity given that emergent language abilities are purported to develop with age. The case for group differentiation also supported validity in that speech and hearing delayed children performed significantly worse than nondelayed children. There was a moderate relationship between the REEL-3 and the CAS-2, which would be anticipated if the REEL-3 was a valid measure of emergent language abilities.

SUMMARY. The REEL-3 is a test that assesses the emergent language abilities of individuals aged 0 to 36 months of age. Employing informants, the REEL-3 has sound psychometric properties for its intended uses: identifying infants or young children who are delayed in their language acquisition, determining if there are significant discrepancies between receptive and expressive language, documenting the progress of interventions designed to improve the emergent language abilities of children, and measuring expressive and receptive language abilities in research studies.

Review of the Receptive-Expressive Emergent Language Test, Third Edition by GABRIELLE STUTMAN, Private Practice, Westchester and Manhattan, NY:

DESCRIPTION. The Receptive-Expressive Emergent Language Test, Third Edition (REEL-3) is the second revision of the original 132-item checklist first published in *Assessing Language Skill in Infancy* (Bzoch & League, 1971). It uses parents/caregivers as informants to identify babies or young children (from birth to 3 years) with delayed language acquisition, to determine if there is a discrepancy between receptive and expressive linguistic development, and to document intervention effects. It assesses children's receptive and expressive spoken English language competence in the areas of semantics, syntax, and phonology. A

supplementary assessment of lexical development, designed as a screening device, is also provided.

The manual gives guidelines for interviews, interventions, and assessments of the parent/caregiver's ability to participate in planned interventions, along with a brief summary of its foundation in contemporary linguistic theory, a glossary of terms, and resources for further assessment. Improvements over the previous editions include a reduction of professional language, updated information on reliability, validity, and updated norms.

PURPOSE AND USE. The REEL-3 was developed to identify infants and young children (birth to 3 years) in need of early intervention, document their level of expressive and receptive language development, structure intervention, monitor progress, and measure language development for research studies. It consists of a Receptive Language Ability subtest, an Expressive Language Ability subtest, and a Composite Ability score to measure emergent language. A supplemental Vocabulary inventory provides specific words that are characteristic of the child's developing language. The REEL-3 appears appropriate for its intended population, practioners, and uses.

ADMINISTRATION AND SCORING. The REEL-3 can be administered to parent/caregivers by anyone with testing expeience in the fields of education, language, or psychology. The administration and scoring chapter provides full instructions. The administrator asks a series of "yes" and "no" questions that reflect increasing levels of expressive and receptive language development. Testing begins with the item that corresponds to the child's age (to establish a basal score) and continues until a ceiling is reached; the child earns 1 point for each "yes" response. Open-ended questions are provided to check questionable responses and to gain a more detailed picture of the quality of linguistic functioning. "Yes" responses are summed to derive Expressive, Receptive, and Composite Language raw scores. No time limits are imposed on the test; administration time varies between 20 and 30 minutes. Norms (ability scores) have a mean of 100 and a standard deviation of 15, and can be converted into percentile ranks and age equivalents. The subtest's standard scores may be compared to assess the relative strengths and weaknesses of the two linguistic functions.

The Vocabulary inventories, used for screening, are divided into 2 forms: Form A from 12 through 24 months, and Form B from 25 through 36 months. The raw score is converted to a stanine.

TECHNICAL. Sample selection procedures, demographic characteristics, reliability, and validity measures are fully documented. Clear definitions and explanations of each type of reliability, validity, source of error variance, and the procedures used to gather the evidence are given.

Reliability was measured by errors of content sampling (Cronbach's coefficient alpha), time sampling (2-week time lapse), and interrater reliability (using Cohen's kappa). All coefficient alpha values ranged from .80 to .98 except for the newborns (.79, Receptive Language) and 3-month-olds (Receptive = .77, Expressive = .71, and Composite = .74). The test was also shown to be unbiased for the population subgroups: males, females, European Americans, African Americans, Hispanic Americans, and Asian Americans, and for language impaired infants and toddlers. The test-retest reliability coefficients evidence a consistently high degree of reliability across all three types of test error. Interrater reliability was estimated at .99. However, the manual lacks a table of coefficients to partial out practice effects when retesting to assess intervention effectiveness.

Three types of validity evidence were investigated: Content validity (analyzed in terms of item selections, the choice of caregivers as informants, and conventional item and differential item functioning analysis procedures to determine item discrimination, item difficulty, and to ensure against fostering stereotypes), criterion validity (assessed by correlating REEL-3 scores with the Developmental Assessment of Young Children Communication subtest and the Early Language Milestone Scale—Second Edition), and construct validity (the identification of test traits, and the extent to which they reflect the theory on which they are based). The median coefficient between the Receptive Language Ability score and the criterion tests was moderate (.55). However, the Expressive Language Ability score (.62) and Composite score (.60) correlations are high. When test results from a delayed language group were compared with the population, the composite for the delayed subgroup was Low Average. The assumption that receptive and expressive speech should correlate with each other, with the Composite score, and with intelligence is validated (significant at $p < .01$). There is also a moderate

relationship between the REEL-3 and the General Cognitive Quotient (GCQ) of the Cognitive Abilities Scale—Second Edition (.49).

NORMATIVE INFORMATION. The normative sample, comprising 1,112 infants in 32 states, was tested from 2001 to the spring of 2002. The sample was weighted with regard to geographic region, gender, ethnicity, race, family income, educational level of parents, and disability condition as estimated by the *Statistical Abstract of the United States* (U.S. Bureau of the Census, 2000) for the population of children under 5 years old. However, whenever possible, local norms should be developed and used.

Norms are presented in tables for the two subtests of language abilities and for the Composite; these have a mean of 100 and a standard deviation of 15. The tables of normative values are listed by monthly intervals from birth to 12 months, by 2-month intervals from 13 through 24 months, and by 3-month intervals from 25 through 36 months. Percentile ranks are also provided.

SUMMARY. The REEL-3, a cost-effective evaluative and diagnostic tool for measuring early receptive and expressive language deelopment, and targeting goals for remediation, serves its stated purpose well. The manual provides a brief summary of the developmental data and theory upon which it is based, a glossary of terms, a guide for assessing potential caregiver effectiveness, and resources for further assessment. High interrater reliability provides justification for using caregivers as informants. The REEL-3 is relatively free of bias, has acceptable reliability, and has generally good evidence of validity.

REVIEWER'S REFERENCES

Bzoch, K. R., & League, R. (1971). *Assessing language skill in infancy.* Austin, TX: PRO-ED.
U.S. Bureau of the Census. (2000). *Statistical abstract of the United States.* Washington, DC: Author.

[209]

Receptive One-Word Picture Vocabulary Test—Spanish-Bilingual Edition.

Purpose: Designed to provide "an assessment of an individual's combined Spanish and English hearing vocabulary."

Population: Ages 4.0–12.11.

Publication Date: 2001.

Acronym: ROWPVT-SBE.

Scores: Total score only.

Administration: Individual.

Price Data, 2003: $140 per test kit including manual (92 pages), test plates, and 25 Spanish-Bilingual record forms in portfolio; $38 per manual; $27 per 25 Spanish-Bilingual record forms; $75 per book of test plates.

Time: (15–20) minutes.

Comments: Co-normed with the Expressive One-Word Picture Vocabulary Test—Spanish-Bilingual Edition (88) to allow for comparisons of an individual's expressive and receptive vocabulary.

Author: Rick Brownell.

Publisher: Academic Therapy Publications.

Review of the Receptive One-Word Picture Vocabulary Test—Spanish-Bilingual Edition by S. KATHLEEN KRACH, School Psychologist, Henry County Schools, McDonough, GA:

DESCRIPTION. The Receptive One-Word Picture Vocabulary Test—Spanish-Bilingual Edition (ROWPVT-SBE) is described as a measure of "bilingual hearing vocabulary" (manual, p. 10). Specifically, it measures a child's combined receptive language vocabulary by providing credit for answers given in either English or in Spanish. Therefore, either the person administering the test or the translator working with the examiner should be fluent in both English and Spanish.

The ROWPVT-SBE is administered individually to children of various levels of English and Spanish combined proficiency between the ages of 4 and 12. Items are presented from a two-sided, spiral-bound easel, with four color pictures on each page denoting possible vocabulary answers. A word is read aloud in the child's dominant language, determined by a brief questionnaire at the beginning of the test. The respondent selects an answer from one of the four pictures. If the answer is incorrect, the child is given a second opportunity to answer the item in the nondominant language. If the answer is correct in either language, the child receives full credit for that item.

This measure provides a standard score, a confidence interval for the standard score, a percentile rank, and an age equivalent. In addition, it provides a comparison of the statistical significance of score differences between the ROWPVT-SBE and the Expressive One-Word Picture Vocabulary Test—Spanish-Bilingual Edition (EOWPVT-SBE), which was conormed with ROWPVT-SBE. The purposes of the ROWPVT-SBE listed by the publisher in the manual include "assessing the extent of hearing vocabulary; assess-

ing cognitive ability; diagnosing reading difficulties; comparing bilingual language acquisition to monolingual language proficiency; diagnosing expressive aphasia; screening preschool and kindergarten children; assessing vocabulary with a nonverbal response requirement; monitoring growth; and evaluating program effectiveness" (manual, pp. 12-13). The developers specify that the ROWPVT-SBE should neither be used as a measure of Spanish and/or English proficiency, nor as a single measure in making a diagnosis of any type.

DEVELOPMENT. The ROWPVT-SBE is an updated version of the original Spanish translation of the Receptive One-Word Picture Vocabulary Test (ROWPVT), developed in 1985. That translation provided only translated items with no consideration for item selection, and did not provide bilingual norms. To correct these weaknesses, the current ROWPVT-SBE was designed as a separate test from the 2000 revised version.

The authors of the ROWPVT-SBE decided to create a bilingual test instead of two separate tests, one each in Spanish and English, because of concerns that two monolingual assessments done in each language might provide an underestimate of overall language skills. Given this, all items were selected for administration in both English and Spanish instead of one or the other.

Of the 170 items available on the English-only version of the ROWPVT, only 150 are used in the ROWPVT-SBE. The other 20 of the original items from the English-only version are skipped because content screening and item analysis determined them to be problematic in the assessment of bilingual students. Specifically, a group specializing in the production of Spanish educational materials eliminated the first 9 items after a general review of the test items. The other 11 items were eliminated based on statistical analyses run on both Classical Test Theory (item difficulty, item discrimination, and item reliability index) and Item Response Theory (item calibrations and goodness-of-fit data). With these 11 items removed, the overall correlation of item difficulty to item order for the entire test was .97.

TECHNICAL. The normative sample for the ROWPVT-SBE included 1,050 bilingual children from 17 states. Although the sample is described as a close approximation of demographics in the United States, the test developers report an overrepresentation of children who speak a Mexican dialect and children who live in the western United States.

Reliability studies were performed using measures of internal consistency and temporal stability. Internal consistency was assessed using Cronbach's coefficient alpha and split-half reliability coefficients. All of the coefficients listed (coefficient alpha, corrected split-half, and uncorrected split-half) across all age groups fell at or above .95. Temporal stability was measured by retesting 32 children from the standardization sample 20 days after the first testing. Test-retest corrected correlation was a .92; uncorrected, the correlation was .80. Given the results of both types of reliability assessed by the developers, it appears that the ROWPVT-SBE is sufficiently reliable.

The developers address content, criterion-related, and construct validity in the manual. Content validity was addressed during the development stage by minimizing the impact of other skills on the scores and by selecting individual items considered to be nonbiased. Criterion-related validity was measured using concurrent validity correlations between the ROWPVT-SBE and the Vocabulary test on the English-only, SAT9 (correlation = .38) and the EOWPVT-SBE (correlation = .24).

Construct validity was discussed for appropriate use across chronological age, cognitive ability, academic achievement, receptive and expressive vocabulary, and exceptional group differences. When chronological age was correlated with raw score data (correlation = .70), data showed that, in general, the raw score increased along with age. Cognitive ability was supported by data generated from comparing 13 children considered mentally retarded to the normative group. These children performed at a statistically significantly lower level. A correlation study of the ROWPVT-SBE and the English-only SAT9 Reading (.46 correlation) and Language (.61 correlation) assessed the validity of the ROWPVT-SBE as an estimate of achievement.

Receptive and expressive vocabulary differences were assessed by correlating the EOWPVT-SBE and the ROWPVT-SBE (correlation = .43). The correlation was considerably lower than that calculated across the English-only versions of the EOWPVT and the ROWPVT. The test developers ascribed this difference to language proficiency issues in the bilingual examinee and/or the test materials. Finally, exceptional group differences were examined for children with nonacademic-impacting and academic-impacting disabilities. All of the means across four academic-impacting dis-

abilities were found to be significantly different from the normative mean, and the nonacademic group mean was not found to be significantly different.

Given the data presented by the test developers, it would seem that content validity was considered in the development of the ROWPVT-SBE. Criterion-related validity and several areas of construct validity data from the manual showed that the measures used for comparison frequently were not sufficient to make a determination of validity. Specifically, the English-only version of the SAT9 (language and reading) probably measures a different construct due to the monolingual nature of the SAT9 and the bilingual nature of the ROWPVT-SBE. Construct validity assessments do indicate that the ROWPVT-SBE is related to chronological age, cognitive ability, and exceptional group differences.

COMMENTARY. The ROWPVT-SBE is a very good measure of bilingual receptive vocabulary. Two strengths of this test are that each item allows for a bilingual response, and that norms were provided for bilingual children living in the United States.

However, one of the greatest problems with this test is related to those strengths. There are so few measures of bilingual receptive language on the market (in fact, a comprehensive search found no other truly bilingual school-age measures) that the user may wish to generalize the data beyond what it really measures. The developers request that users consider this test only as one measure in diagnosing a disorder.

Therefore, practitioners may have to go beyond normative-based measures and administer criterion-based measures or informal measures in addition to the ROWPVT-SBE to support diagnoses in any of these areas. For the inexperienced, this may require additional training. This problem of overgeneralizing test results is compounded by the developers' statements that the ROWPVT-SBE can be used as more than a test of receptive vocabulary. Although some of the data presented in the manual support that this test can be used as a broad screener for other assessment areas, the validity data do not support using it as a primary measure to test anything but hearing vocabulary.

Practical bonuses to this measure include its light physical weight, as well as its ease of learning, use, and scoring. However, it is sometimes unclear which stimulus word to present, and the measure is further hampered by its dependence on a short questionnaire to determine the child's dominant language, and by allowing the examinee two chances to answer the same question. In addition, the basal and ceiling rules are different for the ROWPVT-SBE and the EOWPVT-SBE, so examiners who use both should be careful when choosing which items to administer.

SUMMARY. The ROWPVT-SBE is a fine measure of receptive vocabulary. The developers put much effort into assuring it is a psychometrically sound test for its intended purpose (hearing vocabulary). However, some usages described by the developers appear to overreach the validity data indicated in the manual. This is particularly problematic as practitioners have few norm-referenced measures available to measure other areas (other than vocabulary) of bilingual receptive language skills. So long as the ROWPVT-SBE is used only for its appropriate purpose, it should be considered a valuable addition to any practitioner's toolkit.

Review of the Receptive One-Word Picture Vocabulary Test—Spanish-Bilingual Edition by MARÍA DEL R. MEDINA-DÍAZ, Professor, Department of Graduate Studies, Program of Educational Research & Evaluation, School of Education, University of Puerto Rico-Río Piedras, San Juan, PR:

DESCRIPTION. The Receptive One-Word Picture Vocabulary Test—Spanish-Bilingual Edition (ROWPVT-SBE) is a standardized, norm-referenced, individual, multiple-choice test. It is designed for bilingual examinees from 4 years-0 months to 12 years-11 months old, who speak Spanish and English with varying levels of proficiency. "The primary objective is to assess general vocabulary competence—independent of the particular language" (manual, p. 8). The test case contents a manual, a set of 170 color test cards in a spiral booklet with fold-out easel, and 25 record forms.

Professionals in education- and psychology-related fields who administer and score the ROWPVT-SBE should be fluent in Spanish and English, or have assistance of someone fluent in the language not spoken by the principal examiner; have training in assessment; and perform several test trials. Formal training may be required for interpreting test results. To administer the test, the examiner should determine the child's dominant language either by asking teachers, parents,

or the child. Ten questions, in both languages, are provided for the child's interview. The examiner classifies the examinee in one of four categories of language proficiency based on the degree in which she or he speaks Spanish and English at home or school. The instructions for the examinee are provided in that language, but during the administration it can be switched to present the stimulus words.

The examinee is required to listen to a stimulus word that is read by the examiner in the examinee's dominant language; the examiner shows a card with four pictures, and the examinee must point out the picture that matches the "meaning of the word." Only 150 out of 170 cards are used in the test administration; and from these only the cards within the examinee's range of ability are used. If the examinee answers incorrectly in his or her dominant language, the stimulus word is read in the nondominant language. Thus, the examinee has two chances to respond. If she or he does not know the answer, the examinee is encouraged to take his or her best guess. A point is scored for each correct answer. The examinee's raw score corresponds to the number of correct responses, "up to the last item in the ceiling level" (manual, p. 26).

Depending on the examinee's chronological age, there are different test cards for starting the test administration. Because the test items are arranged by level of difficulty, only a series of items are administered according to the examinee's ability. In order to determine the basal level of eight correct responses, the examiner starts the administration with a test card suggested by age group; but the examiner can change it. Determining the basal level may be difficult when the administration of the items has to be done back and forth (as shown in the manual's example). Directions are provided when the basal or ceiling levels cannot be established. The scoring system is also another challenge for the examiner. It could be useful to provide another example with double basal and ceiling levels, and of the scoring procedures.

Total time administration is 15 to 20 minutes in one session. The test manual suggests that adaptations can be made for different examinees such as young children or examinees with reluctance, negative behavior, or who are motor handicapped. In such cases, more than one administration session may be needed. Instructions are present for testing environment and preparation. However, there is no information available about the possible effects of these modifications in the validity and reliability of test results.

The instructions regarding what the examinee must do on the test are not as clear in Spanish as they are in English. Also, the Spanish version uses the pronouns "tu" and "usted" interchangeably and for some children this may be awkward. For example, when we talk with Puerto Rican children we use "tu" instead of "usted." In contrast, for a Mexican-American child, it is more common to use "usted" in a conversation. Some substitutions for Spanish words are included but not for English. Other substitutions of Spanish words may be necessary because their usage varies among Hispanic/Latino groups.

DEVELOPMENT. This test is an adaptation of the 2000 edition of the Receptive One-Word Picture Vocabulary Test (ROWPVT) for assessing English hearing vocabulary. According to the author, items were translated to Spanish by a firm specialized in developing Spanish educational materials and a group of Spanish-bilingual educators reviewed test items for cultural bias. The selection of stimulus words was based on children's familiarity or exposure at home or school, regardless of gender and cultural backgrounds. Details of the procedure used in the translation and cultural adaptation of the test are not included. Hispanic/Latino groups from the Caribbean and from Central and South America do not frequently use some of the stimulus words in Spanish. Various words require checking spelling and the accuracy of the translation. Also, some pictures may cause confusion because it may be difficult for a child (or even for an adult) to identify what is the possible association between them and the stimulus word. No additional information is provided about the item representation of the content, difficulties, and differential functioning by age levels and Hispanic/Latino groups.

TECHNICAL. ROWPVT-SBE and the Expressive One-Word Picture Vocabulary Test (EOWPVT-SBE) were conormed. The sample answered first the EOWPVT-SBE and then the ROWPVT-SBE. The correlation between the scores in the two tests was .43. Difference scores are included in the test manual. No estimation of the reliability of the difference scores is reported. Test norms (i.e., standardized scores, percentile ranks, and age equivalents) were derived from a standardized administration (in January to December 2000) to 1,050 children in 17 states across the United States. The sample size by age group ranged from 71 to 143 (4- and 12-year old children composed the smallest sample). Sample characteristics and test norms are presented in the test manual.

The standardized sample was not randomly selected across the United States. Test sites and examiners were chosen from the test publisher's client files. Mexican-American children (84.5%) and children who are living in the west region (65.8%) were overrepresented in the sample. There are also representation disparities with the Hispanic/Latino population regarding gender, country regions, and place of residence.

Mean and standard deviation of the distribution of ROWPVT-SBE's scores are not included; however, median raw scores and standard deviations are presented. Classical test theory item statistics are reported at each age level for the standardized sample. There are no data about the performance of the Hispanic/Latino groups on the test items. Although the manual indicates that Item Response analysis Theory (IRT) was performed, no results are included. Because the adaptive features of the test are intended to match the difficulty of the items to the ability level of the examinees, basic IRT data analysis could help to support the use of test results and inferences (e.g., item difficulty, examinee's ability estimate, item difficulties by age levels, ability estimates at each age level, test characteristics curves, and test information function at each age level). Descriptive and correlation statistics are not sufficient for determining accurately the examinee's ability in an adaptive or tailored test (Lord, 1980; Hambleton & Swaminathan, 1985). Moreover, the rationale for choosing eight and six items, respectively, to establish the basal and ceiling levels as well as the following sequence of items is not fully explained in the manual.

Very high internal consistency values at each age level (from .96 to .98) were found using Cronbach's alpha and split-half coefficients in the standardized sample. Also, test-retest reliabilities are reported with a small sample of 32 examinees and 20 days apart for administration. Acceptable *SEM* values by age groups for raw scores ranged from 3.33 (12 years old) to 2.70 (4 years old); and for standard scores, *SEM* values ranging from 2.12 (8 to 11 years old) to 3.00 (4 years old) are reported.

Various sources of evidence addressed validity concerns. Based on the assumption that the ROWPVT-SBE, the EOWPVT-SBE, and the Stanford Achievement Test-9th Edition (SAT-9) measure similar vocabulary skills, concurrent validity evidence showed low-moderate correlations between their scores. Construct validity was addressed determining the relationship between the ROWPVT-SBE scores with chronological age (.70 with the all standardized sample); SAT-9 reading and language scores (.44 and .61 with samples of 42 and 40 examinees, respectively); and scores of 13 low-cognitive ability examinees. No information concerning the predictive use of ROWPVT-SBE results and its consequences as well as differential validity across different Hispanic/Latino groups is presented.

COMMENTARY. The responsibility of developing a test is intrinsically tied to the validity of its inferences. Children with different levels of language proficiency (in Spanish or English) come from families with diverse socioeconomic, ethnic, and educational backgrounds. This requires more appropriate evidence for using ROWPVT-SBE with bilingual Hispanic/Latino groups across the United States. The evidence provides partial support for "evaluating the hearing vocabulary of Spanish-bilingual individuals" (manual, p. 66). In the test materials, there is no sufficient theoretical and empirical evidence for sustaining the inferences regarding all the purposes and uses claimed.

SUMMARY. The most salient feature of the ROWPVT-SBE is the examinee's opportunity to respond to either the Spanish or the English stimulus word, based on his or her proficient language. This is recorded in the scoring sheet as well as his or her picture selection. Because the test does not require an oral response, it can be administered to pre-school children, shy children, or to those who are unable to provide a verbal response. The color test cards are generally adequate and the instructions easy to follow. The test norms are recent and relevant but the representativeness is questionable.

Despite the above limitations, ROWPVT-SBE is a reliable tool that can be used, with caution, to identify examinee's hearing vocabulary, either in Spanish or English. More studies are necessary to address its accuracy and appropriateness for measuring the same construct in different groups of examinees.

REVIEWER'S REFERENCES

Hambleton, R. K., & Swaminathan, H. (1985). *Item response theory: Principles and applications.* Boston: Kluwer-Nijhoff Publishing.
Lord. F. M. (1980). *Applications of item response theory to practical testing problems.* Hillsdale, NJ: Erlbaum.

[210]

Rehabilitation Survey of Problems and Coping.

Purpose: Intended for use as a symptom rating and disability management tool.
Population: Age 14 and over.
Publication Date: 2002.
Acronym: R-SOPAC.
Scores, 12: Overall Total, Problem Total, Coping Total, Emotional Overall, Emotional Problem, Emotional Coping, Physical Overall, Physical Problem, Physical Coping, Cognitive Overall, Cognitive Problem, Cognitive Coping.
Administration: Group.
Parts, 2: Survey of Problems, Survey of Coping.
Price Data, 2005: $81 per complete kit including technical manual (124 pages) and 25 QuikScore™ forms; $63 per technical manual; $38 per 25 QuikScore™ forms; $125 per 100 QuikScore™ forms.
Time: (10–15) minutes.
Comments: One of several measures comprising a broad battery of rehabilitation-oriented instruments together entitled the Rehabilitation Assessment Series (RAS).
Authors: J. Douglas Salmon and Marek Celinski.
Publisher: Multi-Health Systems, Inc.

Review of the Rehabilitation Survey of Problems and Coping by THEODORE L. HAYES, Research Director, the Gallup Organization, Washington, DC:

DESCRIPTION. The technical manual for the Rehabilitation Survey of Problems and Coping (R-SOPAC) states that "The R-SOPAC instructs the client to rate his/her level of symptom coping in reference to his/her perceived ability to live a normal life in spite of existing problems. Such an instruction is intended to broadly stimulate the client's own understanding of what resources he or she has been using to help function on the level approximating normalcy, be it in a conscious or a habitual way" (p. 19). The R-SOPAC is composed of 25 self-report items, each of which describes a clinical symptom and asks the respondent to indicate first how problematic the symptom is, and then how well the respondent believes he or she is coping with each symptom. Additional (but unused) overall impairment and overall coping responses are also requested, as is whether the symptom existed previous to any recent trauma.

Respondents should be at least 14 years old with an English reading level proficiency of at least a fourth grader. The expected completion time for this paper/pencil survey is 15 minutes. Scoring is to be completed onsite by a test administrator via simple scoring guidelines. Output includes total scores based on item endorsements regarding symptomatic emotional problems, cognition problems, and physical problems; coping scores for these dimensions are also reported; and finally, an overall coping and overall problem score are derived based on total scores within each germane set of dimensions. The rehabilitation specialist may administer the assessments every few weeks to chart progress in terms of impairment and coping.

DEVELOPMENT. A significant strength of the R-SOPAC is its content and construct coverage. The R-SOPAC is one of a suite of assessments by the same publisher and/or authors. These assessments purport to evaluate different levels or facets of a broader impairment-treatment-coping model that is in turn based on a wide-ranging review of rehabilitation theory and findings. Practitioners who subscribe to a different model may regardless find that the R-SOPAC has sufficient coverage for the assessment of client symptomology and coping strength. A noteworthy feature of the R-SOPAC is the authors' treatment of potential client malingering/dissimulation. Finally, because this is the first edition of the R-SOPAC, it is likely that further refinements and linkages to other measures may be unveiled in future editions.

TECHNICAL. The validity of scores from the R-SOPAC arises primarily through the authors' clinical experience and their review of the theoretical and practice-based issues in trauma and rehabilitation. The R-SOPAC focuses upon symptom-oriented self-report and not rehabilitation process/progress self-report, and so even if one might subscribe to a different rehabilitation model, the content and construct validity of the instrument for describing impairment and coping seem strong.

The criterion-oriented validity evidence of the R-SOPAC might charitably be described as premature. There are two prominent deficiencies in the validation information reported in the manual. First, the authors rely primarily upon two

clinical validation referent groups: one of between 54 to 194 motor vehicle accident victims, and one of between 222 to 296 workers' compensation claimants. The size of these groups varies significantly and inexplicably from table to table beyond what one could attribute to partially missing data. Results for ancillary groups appear in some tables (e.g., some with psychological adjustment disorders, some without) without explanation of whether these are independent of the two main validation groups. Most annoyingly, the authors regularly introduce validation evidence from studies performed with initial or parallel instruments that predated the R-SOPAC, or sometimes with the instrument scored using a previous algorithm.

The second deficiency arises from the psychometrics reported in the manual. The best evidence for the validity of the R-SOPAC would be indication of change after rehabilitation intervention, or correlation to independent/non-self-report indicators. On the first marker, the authors make the argument that, perversely, some patients may not report improvements in coping (i.e., they malinger) in order to keep their insurance benefits; thus, the authors recuse themselves from presenting evidence of improvement as criteria for the R-SOPAC. Though this is a sympathetic argument on the surface, it is nihilistic: If the instrument cannot be relied upon to forecast improvement, then it is essentially a paperwork exercise. The authors advise that the R-SOPAC be administered every few weeks to indicate change. The manual does not indicate how much change should be expected; in fact, the only test-retest reliability is presented for 13 individuals over 2-6 days, and unsurprisingly the stability of the instrument is quite high.

The R-SOPAC also is lacking from the perspective of discriminant validation and multimode validation. The internal reliability estimates of the measure vary by scale between .77 to .92, with the overall score internal reliability at .87. Thus, there is essentially one dimension in the instrument. This dimension does not differentiate the referent groups in the manual; in part this is because the few groups are so small, and in part it is because the authors—who refer to discriminant validity at one point as "face validity"—present data from an earlier version of the R-SOPAC and claim differentiation based on scale score differences under 1 scale point; eventually, one cannot rule out the possibility that the R-SOPAC simply does not reliably differentiate clinical groups. This is most problematic when the authors present their rationale for clinical cutoffs (it also does not help that they present this rationale with a previous version of the instrument).

The authors present multitrait validation data to little obvious effect. The two main external measures are their clients' scores on the Beck Depression Inventory (Beck, 1987) and the Millon Clinical Multiaxial Inventory (1997). In short, individuals with high R-SOPAC scores for symptom intensity are anxious and depressed, and do not cope well. The authors' claims about the superiority of one correlation of an R-SOPAC scale to an MCMI Axis score relative to another correlation of scales and axes ignore the fact that these are not independent correlations, that is, the same person made responses to all measures. Also, it bears noting that none of these multi*trait* correlations are multi*method* correlations—there is no independent index of coping or symptom intensity. Thus, although the R-SOPAC is convergent with other trait-oriented measures, results do not support the strong interpretation that the R-SOPAC dimensions are highly differentiated, and one cannot rule out the possibility that the correlations of the R-SOPAC to external scales are due simply to shared method variance.

On a final technical note, the manual itself is poorly edited. It was noted earlier that tables refer to different versions or scoring algorithms of the R-SOPAC. In addition, in several instances, the authors describe results in the text that are not found in the tables. This is not a matter of interpretational differences; literally, the data are not presented. One cannot help having the sense that the authors were not well-served by their editor.

COMMENTARY. The rationale underlying the R-SOPAC is more convincing than that for other measures, such as the Health Status Questionnaire 2.0 (Hayes, 2003). That measure had little obvious diagnostic value, and its publisher suggested that the same or better information "should be drawn" through other means. The R-SOPAC may be a better choice because its conceptual underpinning is stronger. However, as the R-SOPAC assesses only perceived health status, and because there are no external criterion-oriented validity data for the R-SOPAC, it too should be considered as only one among many options for rehabilitation specialists.

SUMMARY. The R-SOPAC provides measurements of perceived impairment and coping status. These measurements have strong conceptual validity and internal reliability. It may be better used as an indicator of the patient's overall emotional well-being at the time of the appointment rather than an indicator of rehabilitation process. The instrument may be useful to professionals who wish to employ a standardized intake interview, or possibly to corporate health survey sponsors who wish to create localized databases of patient perceptions. Further claims as to its diagnostic or predictive value are currently unwarranted, though future research may substantiate them.

REVIEWER'S REFERENCES
Beck, A. (1987). *Beck Depression Inventory manual.* San Antonio, TX: The Psychological Corporation.
Hayes, T. L. (2003). [Review of the Health Status Questionnaire 2.0.] In B. S. Plake, J. C. Impara, & R. A. Spies (Eds.), *The fifteenth mental measurements yearbook* (pp. 442-444). Lincoln, NE: Buros Institute of Mental Measurements.
Millon, T. (1997). *Millon Clinical Multiaxial Inventory–III manual* (2nd ed.). Minneapolis, MN: National Computer Systems.

Review of the Rehabilitation Survey of Problems and Coping by NAMBURY S. RAJU, Distinguished Professor, Institute of Psychology, Illinois Institute of Technology, Chicago, IL:

DESCRIPTION. The Rehabilitation Survey of Problems and Coping (R-SOPAC) consists of 25 items or problem areas, each with a 7-point scale. The R-SOPAC is designed to serve as a disability management tool for rehabilitation professionals. The primary objectives of the R-SOPAC are "(1) to facilitate differential diagnosis, (2) to facilitate the determination of reasonable and necessary treatment needs …, (3) to monitor treatment progress and, (4) to determine the clients' risk for psychological impairments and barriers to rehabilitation" (technical manual, p. 5). The R-SOPAC is part of a battery of rehabilitation-oriented instruments, called the Rehabilitation Assessment Series (RAS).

In Part 1 of the survey (Survey of Problems), the participant is asked to indicate the degree to which the condition specified in each item has been a problem over the past few weeks, ranging from 0 (Not a Problem) to 6 (Extreme Problem). Examples of items included in the survey are Sleep, Sexual Activity, and Muscle Tension. In Part 2 of the survey (Survey of Coping), the participant is asked to indicate how well he or she has been able to cope with the problem on a 7-point scale ranging from 0 (*Cannot Cope At All*) to 6 (*Can Cope Very Well*). In this part of the survey, there is a provision for an NA (Not Applicable) response. The survey is consumable and designed for hand scoring. It yields three different global scores: Overall Total, Problem Total, and Coping Total. The Overall Total is simply the sum of Problem Total and Coping Total scores. In addition, there are three subscales (Emotional Subscale, Physical Subscale, and Cognitive Subscale), each with three separate scores (Overall, Problem, and Coping). In all, a total of 12 different scores are obtained for each participant.

DEVELOPMENT. The inclusion of specific items/symptoms in the R-SOPAC was based on a careful review of the published literature. The relevance of symptoms to the domain-specific scores (Physical, Emotional, and Cognitive) is also noted. Although the review of the published literature appears to be quite thorough, how the final set of 25 symptoms was selected and the role of the subject matter experts (SEMs) in that selection was not always clear. If SEMs were used, information is needed about the degree of consensus and the associated interrater reliability. Such information would be helpful to rehabilitation practitioners and professionals.

In addition to the emphasis on system-coping and coping process, the selection of items for the survey also emphasized the symptoms that are known to develop as a result of psychotraumatic events, such as head injury and whiplash.

TECHNICAL. The technical manual describes procedures for hand-scoring the R-SOPAC and presents the psychometric information on the reliability and validity of the R-SOPAC. These aspects of the R-SOPAC are reviewed and evaluated in this section.

Hand-scoring. Procedures for hand-scoring the R-SOPAC are easy to follow and well documented. The authors also provide guidelines for handling omits and blanks, which are probably unavoidable.

Interpretation of R-SOPAC scores. The technical manual also provides information on the interpretation and use of the R-SOPAC scores. As the authors note, the R-SOPAC can be used for assessment and treatment planning as well as for determining ongoing treatment needs. Five different case studies are presented and discussed, highlighting the scoring, use, and interpretation of the R-SOPAC scores. Some of the clinical situations considered in the five case studies include severe bodily injuries with leg amputation, mild head injury, and serious concussive head injury. The manual offers rehabilitation practitioners good guidance on how to use and interpret scores from the R-SOPAC. The clinical situations considered in these case studies are a real strength of this guidance.

Intercorrelations of subscales. Intercorrelations among the nine subscales and the overall totals are reported for two samples. Subscales (Cognitive, Physical, and Emotional) within the Intensity (Problems) category have significant positive correlations with each other; the same is also true of the subscales within the Coping category. The intercorrelations of subscales across categories (Intensity vs. Coping), however, are negative and substantial. This trend is also true for the overall scales. Within the Overall category, Coping and Intensity have a high negative correlation (-.87), meaning that the higher the intensity of the problem, the less the ability to cope with the problem. The Overall Total, which is simply the sum of scores on the overall Coping and Intensity scales, has a very high correlation of .97 with the Intensity scale. Given the definition of the Overall Total and the high negative correlation between the Coping and Intensity scores, this result (very high positive correlation between the Overall and Intensity Totals) appears to reflect a high degree of ipsativity between the Coping and Intensity scales. An explanation of this not so obvious result is desirable and should prove useful to practitioners.

Underlying structure of R-SOPAC. Results from the principal components analysis with varimax rotation appear to confirm the (original and revised) underlying structure (Cognitive, Physical, and Emotional) proposed by the authors. These findings are informative and should prove useful to rehabilitation professionals.

Reliability. Internal consistency estimates of reliability for the nine subscales and the overall totals are high, mostly in the .90s, for individual subscales, except for the Physical subscale. The reliability estimates for the totals are reported simply as the average of the reliabilities of the components that make up a given total. A more appropriate estimate of total reliability could have been obtained with the stratified alpha formula (Feldt & Brennan, 1989).

There are no data on the means and standard deviations of the subscales and totals, nor are there data on the standard errors of measurement

(*SEM*s). The data on *SEM*s could be especially helpful to practitioners in evaluating the changes over time. Given the nature of the instrument, it is probably extremely difficult to develop parallel forms of the R-SOPAC and assess its parallel-form reliability. The test-retest reliabilities (time interval of 2–6 days) are based on a sample of 13 individuals, which may severely restrict the generalizability of these data.

Validity. There are substantial empirical data concerning the validity of scores from the R-SOPAC. Given "the constraints imposed by the institutional policies and practices that play a significant role in determining recovery stances and outcomes of clients" (technical manual, p. 73), the authors emphasized the pathology-related predictive validity rather than the outcome-related predictive validity. Under the circumstances, this appears to be a sound strategy for assessing the validity of the R-SOPAC.

Information about symptom patterns across different client groups is presented. Item, subscale, and total means are presented for five different groups. The data on means are useful and informative, but they may be difficult to interpret without additional statistical analyses. For example, some type of a profile analysis would help identify where the real (statistically significant) differences are across the five client groups. The same is also true of the means reported for the psychological versus no psychological diagnosis groups. It is strongly recommended that the authors report the specific sample sizes and standard deviations for the items and subscales in order to facilitate a better and more reliable interpretation of the reported data.

Correlations between the R-SOPAC scales and the MCMI Axis I scales are shown. Correlations are also reported between the R-SOPAC scales and the Beck Depression Inventory. These data are offered as evidence of the construct, convergent, and divergent validity of the R-SOPAC scales. Information is presented concerning the discriminant validity of the Cognitive, Physical, and Emotional subscales in separating those with mild and severe impairment from those with no diagnosis. Again, information about the standard deviations and post-hoc analyses would have been very helpful. The data presented offer empirical support for the discriminant, convergent, and divergent validity of the R-SOPAC scales.

The technical manual also presents information about the Intensity and Coping abilities across several ethnic samples (English, French, Italian, Portuguese, Spanish, Greek, Hindi, Asian, and European). Also given are the means and standard deviations on the Intensity, Coping, and Overall Totals for three different samples: employed, unemployed, and clinical. The mean differences are in the expected direction, providing validity evidence for the R-SOPAC scales. Overall, the validity information presented in this chapter is substantial and significant, although there is a need for additional statistical analyses of the same data to offer a more integrated and understandable picture of the validity of the R-SOPAC scales.

SUMMARY. The R-SOPAC, designed to serve as a disability management tool for rehabilitation professionals, appears to enjoy strong psychometric credentials for its development, score interpretation, and technical properties. These credentials can be made even stronger by performing additional statistical analyses of the current validity data (and thus leading to a better explanation of the validity information), offering more reliable test-retest data, and reporting standard errors of measurement and explaining their usefulness in interpreting scores from the R-SOPAC.

REVIEWER'S REFERENCE

Feldt, L. S., & Brennan, R. L. (1989). In R. L. Linn (Ed.), Educational measurement (3rd ed., pp. 105–146). New York: American Council on Education/ Macmillan.

[211]

Reynolds Adolescent Depression Scale—2nd Edition.

Purpose: Designed "to assess the severity of depressive symptomatology in adolescents in school and clinical settings."

Population: Ages 11–20.

Publication Dates: 1986–2002.

Acronym: RADS-2.

Scores, 5: Dysphoric Mood, Anhedonia/Negative Affect, Negative Self-Evaluation, Somatic Complaints, Depression Total.

Administration: Individual or group.

Price Data, 2004: $127 per introductory kit including professional manual (2002, 172 pages), 25 hand-scorable test booklets, and 25 summary/profile forms; $62 per professional manual; $47 per 25 hand-scorable test booklets; $27 per 25 summary/profile forms.

Time: (5–10) minutes.

Comments: Self-report measure; hand scored; may be administered aloud; test booklet is titled "About Myself."

Author: William M. Reynolds.
Publisher: Psychological Assessment Resources, Inc.
Cross References: See T5:2230 (21 references) and T4:2274 (11 references); for reviews by Barbara J. Kaplan and Deborah King Kundert of an earlier edition, see 11:333 (6 references).

Review of the Reynolds Adolescent Depression Scale—2nd Edition by KIMBERLY A. BLAIR, Assistant Professor of School Psychology, Duquesne University, Pittsburgh, PA:

DESCRIPTION. The Reynolds Adolescent Depression Scale—2nd Edition (RADS-2) does not provide a formal diagnosis of depression, but rather is an empirically derived screening measure of the severity of depressive symptomology. As a screening measure, the RADS-2 is helpful in assessment of general depressive symptomology and in the identification of adolescents who may be at risk for serious, diagnostic forms of depression. This self-report measure is appropriate for use with adolescents 11 through 20 years of age, requiring a third-grade reading level. Alternatively, it may be administered aloud to adolescents with reading problems or developmental delays.

The RADS-2 consists of 30 items, evaluating a wide range of symptoms including those assessing emotional, cognitive, affective, and somatic complaints of depression. It can be administered individually or in group testing situations and typically can be completed in approximately 5 minutes. Responses are scored on a 4-point Likert-type scale in which adolescents are asked to endorse if they feel specific symptoms *Almost never, Hardly ever, Sometimes,* or *Most of the time.* The test booklet can be hand-scored with a built-in scoring key and a Summary/Profile Form provides a score summary table for converting raw scores to T scores and percentile ranks. A Depression Total score is provided, as well as scores for four subscales representing dimensions of depressive symptomology in adolescents including: Dysphoric Mood, Anhedonia/Negative Affect, Negative Self-Evaluation, and Somatic Complaints. Adolescents who exceed the "cutoff score" of $61T$ on the Depression Total score are thought to be in need of further evaluation.

DEVELOPMENT. The RADS-2 is an updated version of the original Reynolds Adolescent Depression Scale. The original scale was developed to provide mental health professionals with a brief self-report measure of adolescent depression, with items written specifically for adolescents.

The original RADS items were based on symptomology for major depression and dysthymic disorder outlined by the DSM-III (American Psychiatric Association, 1980) and Research Diagnostic Criteria. No changes to the RADS content have been made for the RADS-2, yet the content remains consistent with a wide range of sources of depressive symptomology including the DSM-IV (American Psychiatric Association, 1994) and ICD-10 (World Health Organization, 1992).

Several updates have been made to the original RADS version. Four factorially derived subscales have been included that assist in the analysis of depressive symptomology in adolescents (Dysphoric Mood, Anhedonia/Negative Affect, Negative Self-Evaluation, and Somatic Complaints). Additionally, the RADS-2 extends the age range to include adolescents between 11 and 12 years of age and between ages 19 and 20. The RADS-2 was also restandardized with a large (N = 3,300) sample corresponding to the 2000 U.S. Census with regards to ethnicity. Other updates include: the addition of T-scores for ease of interpretation, new carbonless test booklets, Summary/Profile Forms for plotting scores, and an updated manual with extensive psychometric information and expanded guide for interpretation.

TECHNICAL. Extensive evidence documenting the reliability and validity are presented in the RADS-2 professional manual, including studies conducted with the original RADS. Over 20 years of research documents the clinical and psychometric quality of the RADS/RADS-2. Given the abundance of information on the psychometric qualities of this measure, a summary will necessarily focus primarily on the new data provided for the RADS-2.

The development and restandardization of the RADS-2 involved an ethnically and socioeconomically heterogeneous group of 9,052 adolescents (3,772 males, 4,864 females) in school settings from seven states and one Canadian province. A school-based restandardization sample of 3,300 adolescents was drawn from this group to reflect ethnicity proportions based on 2000 U.S. Census data and was heterogeneous with regards to SES. Reliability and validity data for the RADS-2 were obtained utilizing both the school-restandardization sample and clinical samples.

Standardization. The RADS-2 includes norms for the entire restandardization sample for the total sample (n = 3,300), as well as for gender: 1,650 males and 1,650 females; for age: 11 to 13 years (n = 1,100), 14 to 16 (n = 1,100), and 17 to 20 years (n = 1,100); and for gender by age. Percentile ranks and T scores are provided for the Depression Total scale and subscales.

Reliability. The RADS-2 professional manual provides considerable evidence to document the RADS-2 as having strong reliability evidence. Internal consistency was computed for the RADS-2 across gender and age/norm group stratification. Cronbach's alpha coefficients are relatively consistent across all strata, ranging between a low of .78 (Somatic Complaints subscale) and a high of .94 (Depression Total scale). The RADS-2 establishes high internal consistency reliability for the Depression Total scale for the total school sample (.93), school-based restandardization sample (.92), and a subsample of 101 adolescents with DSM-III-R/DSM-IV diagnoses pulled from the clinical sample described above (.94). For the RADS-2 subscales, moderately high internal consistency reliability is reported for the total school sample (range = .80 to .87), school-based restandardization sample (range = .79 to .89), and clinical subsample (range = .81 to .87).

The RADS-2 reports good test-retest reliability estimates for a scale measuring depression, where some fluctuations over time are expected. Over approximately a 2-week period, test-retest reliability estimates were found to be high for the Depression Total scale (.85) and moderately high for the subscales for the total school sample (range = .77 to .84), as well as for the school-based restandardization sample (Depression total = .86; subscale range = .77 to .85) and a subsample of 70 diagnosed adolescents from the clinical sample (Depression total = .89; subscale range = .81 to .87). Low mean T-score differences for each sample were also reported, providing further evidence of this scale's high test-retest reliability.

Validity. Numerous studies conducted by the authors and multiple independent investigators provide impressive empirical support for the validity of scores from the RADS-2. Extensive studies of content, criterion-related construct, convergent and discriminant, and clinical and contrasted groups validity of the RADS/RADS-2 are provided in the RADS-2 professional manual. The authors also provide persuasive evidence supporting the clinical validity of using the 61 T cutoff

score on the Depression Total score as compared to the usual T score of 65 selected for other multidimensional assessment tools, citing the higher base rate of depression among adolescents.

The professional manual presents convincing evidence supporting the validity of including four subscales in the measure's second edition. The inclusion of four factorially derived subscales in the RADS-2 is a result of several exploratory factor analyses of the original RADS measure, conducted by the author as well as other researchers. Each study resulted in either a four or five factor solution, along remarkably similar dimensions of depressive symptomology. These studies provided a solid empirical basis for the inclusion of factorially derived subscales in the RADS-2 to assist users in the analysis of depressive symptomology in adolescents.

The factor analysis of the RADS-2 using the total school sample resulted in the four clinically significant factors with high internal consistency reliability. Each factor consists of seven or eight items with only four items yielding factor loadings below .400 (range = .292 to .325 for the four lowest items; range = .406 to .869 for majority of items). In almost all cases, items clearly loaded on one of the four factors: Dysphoric Mood (range = .292 to .776); Anhedonia/Negative Affect (range = .535 to .869); Negative Self-Evaluation (range = .298 to .600); and Somatic Complaints (range = .325 to .593).

COMMENTARY AND SUMMARY. The RADS-2 is a exceptional brief measure of the severity of depressive symptomology for adolescents age 11 through 20. As a screening measure of depression in adolescents, it is useful in identifying those who may be in need of more comprehensive psychological evaluation. The RADS-2 can also make a valuable component of a comprehensive assessment battery, helpful in evaluating the severity of adolescent depressive symptomology as well as for monitoring the effectiveness of therapeutic interventions over time.

The RADS-2 represents a significantly improved version of an already extremely well-developed assessment tool for depression. It is apparent that considerable effort was made in developing an extremely well-written and well-constructed instrument, which is useful in school, clinical, and research settings. The most striking addition to the previous edition is the empirical evidence supporting the psychometric qualities of the RADS-2. The abundance of research presented supporting the reliability and validity of the measure is impressive. When a brief self-report measure of adolescent depressive symptomology is needed, the excellent psychometric properties of the RADS-2 make it an excellent choice. However, as with any assessment instrument, clinicians are advised to utilize multiple sources of data to complete a thorough and comprehensive assessment.

REVIEWER'S REFERENCES

American Psychiatric Association. (1980). *Diagnostic and statistical manual of mental disorders* (3ʳᵈ ed.). Washington, DC: Author.
American Psychiatric Association. (1994). *Diagnostic and statistical manual of mental disorders* (4ᵗʰ ed.). Washington, DC: Author.
World Health Organization. (1992). *International classification of diseases and related health problems* (10ᵗʰ ed.). Geneva, Switzerland: Author.

Review of the Reynolds Adolescent Depression Scale-2ⁿᵈ Edition by JANET F. CARLSON, Professor and Department Head, Department of General Academics, Texas A&M University at Galveston, Galveston, TX:

DESCRIPTION. The Reynolds Adolescent Depression Scale-2ⁿᵈ Edition (RADS-2) is a revision of the first edition, published in 1986. The RADS-2 provides a direct assessment of the severity of depressive symptomatology for individuals between the ages of 11 and 20. It is an extremely brief, paper-and-pencil, self-report measure that may be administered aloud, either in groups or individually.

The RADS-2 uses frequency of occurrence, as reported by respondents, to determine the severity of depressive symptoms. Respondents are asked to indicate the extent to which each of the 30 statements presented on a single page of the test booklet represents how they feel. Responses are hand-scored, using the carbonless response form. Scoring is quick and easy. Results are used to derive scores for four subscales that correspond to dimensions of depression, as well as a total scale score, which ranges from 30 to 120. Higher scores indicate greater severity of depressive symptomatology. All responses contribute to one of the four subscales and to the total scale.

Appropriately, the test author points out that the RADS-2 is not a diagnostic instrument, as it screens solely for depression. Although the use of this instrument cannot replace a more comprehensive evaluation, knowledge of an adolescent's symptoms of depression may be helpful in guiding diagnostic efforts.

DEVELOPMENT. Item content of the RADS-2 is identical to the original RADS. With the second edition, a number of modifications were implemented concerning scoring and interpretation, as well as ease of administration and scoring. Factor analytic techniques were applied to establish four subscales, corresponding to recognized dimensions of depression: Dysphoric Mood, Anhedonia/Negative Affect, Negative Self-Evaluation, and Somatic Complaints. In addition to percentile ranks, RADS-2 raw scores may be converted to T scores for each of the subscales and the Depression Total score.

Various amenities add to the ease of administration and scoring. The carbonless record form also provides the template for hand scoring responses, with the numerical score for each item being circled by the test taker, as he or she responds to test items. The addition of a Summary/Profile form allows for graphic presentation of results. Case illustrations provide guidance for clinical application and interpretation.

TECHNICAL. The RADS-2 extended the age range of the first edition by 1 year, to include adolescents as young as 11, and used a standardization sample with demographic features that, according to the test author, align with the 2000 U.S. Census Bureau data. The test manual describes the demographic characteristics of the various samples used to develop and restandardize the instrument, and to document evidence for reliability and validity. A total of 9,052 adolescents comprised the total sample. Participants were drawn from varied socioeconomic backgrounds and school settings in eight states and one Canadian province. The total sample composition favored females (55%) over males (45%); 23% of the sample reported they were not Caucasian. The proportion of non-Caucasian individuals in the RADS-2 total school sample is a very close match to the Census Bureau data. Comparable demographic characteristics of the school-based restandardization ($n = 3,300$) and clinical ($n = 297$) samples are provided in the test manual, which does not provide actual Census Bureau data for direct comparison of demographic features. Norms were developed using the total school-based restandardization sample of 3,300 adolescents. The test author recommends the use of this sample as the primary comparison group when converting raw scores to T-scores and percentile ranks for the four subscales and the Depression Total score. The test manual also provides normative data by gender and age group.

The RADS-2 demonstrates sound test-retest reliability. Reliability estimates were obtained from subsamples of the school (*n* = 1,765), school-based restandardization (*n* = 676), and clinical (*n* = 70) samples, with a retesting interval of about 2 weeks. Coefficients for Depression Total scores were .85, .86, and .89, respectively. Coefficients for the subscales ranged from .77 to .84, from .77 to .85, and from .81 to .87, respectively .

Good internal consistency reliability estimates are reported in the test manual. Coefficients were in the .80s for the four subscales and .93 for the Depression Total score for the total sample (*n* = 9,052). The test manual also reports median item-with-total scale correlations from .55 to .67 (.53 for Depression Total) and mean interitem correlations from .37 to .47 (.30 for Depression Total). Internal consistency reliability coefficients are reported by gender as well, with values that are quite similar to those reported for the total sample.

The test manual presents substantial evidence for the validity of using test results from the RADS-2 as an indicator of depressive symptomatology among adolescents. Results from extensive validation studies conducted by the test author and other investigators are reported in support of content, criterion-related, construct, and clinical validity. RADS-2 items were designed to address the main features of depression, as articulated in standard diagnostic frameworks. Test items are easily mapped onto specific symptoms of depression listed in the *Diagnostic and Statistical Manual of Mental Disorders—Fourth Edition* (American Psychiatric Association, 1994). Item-total scale correlations for the restandardization sample ranged from .27 to .67 with a median value of .53.

Two studies pertaining to criterion-related validity are presented in the test manual. In the first study, the correlation coefficient between the RADS-2 and the Hamilton Depression Rating Scale interview was .82 for the Depression Total score. Coefficients ranged from .54 to .72 for the four RADS-2 subscales. In the second study, the coefficient was .76 for the total score, and ranged from .47 to .70 for the subscales. Criterion-related validity also was examined from the standpoint of other self-report measures of depression, using a clinical sample of 62 inpatient and outpatient

adolescents with a range of psychiatric diagnoses. Among other calculations, coefficients were determined for the RADS-2 Depression Total score and three other scales—the MMPI Depression scale and the Major Depression and Dysthymic Disorder scales of the Adolescent Psychopathology Scale (APS). The resulting values of .78, .76, and .74, respectively, offer solid support for the criterion-related validity of the RADS-2.

Evidence of construct validity derives in part from evidence that supports convergent and discriminant validity. Convergent validity was evaluated using measures of self-esteem, anxiety, suicidal behaviors, and other constructs viewed as theoretically or phenomenologically akin to depression. Extensive and highly significant correlations are reported in the test manual between the RADS-2 scales and the Suicidal Behaviors Interview, Suicidal Ideation Questionnaire, Revised Children's Manifest Anxiety Scale, Rosenberg Self-Esteem Scale, Academic Self-Concept Scale—High School Version, Hamilton Anxiety Scale, and the Beck Hopelessness Scale. A study using a clinical sample of 167 adolescent patients who completed both the RADS-2 and the APS revealed a similar pattern of convergence, with highly significant correlations in the moderate to moderately high ranges for select scale scores. Discriminant validity was examined in a series of studies, with sample sizes ranging from 665 to 1,134, in which RADS-2 scales were compared to academic achievement and/or the Marlowe-Crowne Social Desirability Scale—Short Form. Although some of the resulting coefficients were statistically significant, they were uniformly low, ranging from -.25 to .11. The RADS-2 Depression Total score was compared to IQ values for 66 adolescents from the clinical sample. The resulting correlation coefficient of .12 was not significant. Additional evidence of discriminant validity is provided in the test manual.

The test author investigated the clinical efficacy of the RADS-2 cutoff score, by matching 107 adolescents with a primary diagnosis of Major Depression with adolescents in the restandardization sample. Participants were matched on age and gender. Various cutoff scores were considered, as far as their ability to differentiate school-based adolescents from those carrying a diagnosis of Major Depression. Ultimately, the selected cutoff score of 61 *T* produced a hit rate of about 88%, a specificity level of about 84%, and a sensitivity level of 92%. Approximately 16% of the restandardization group and 92% of the clinical group scored at or above 61T, a pattern that offers clear support for the clinical efficacy of the RADS-2 cutoff score.

COMMENTARY. The RADS-2 provides a convenient first look at depressive symptomatology among adolescents. It is easy to understand, administer, and score. It may appear to prospective users to be easily interpreted as well. However, test users are advised to heed the numerous caveats offered by the test author concerning interpretive issues. The test author is extremely careful not to overstate what the RADS-2 offers; test users should be equally circumspect in recognizing that the use of this instrument provides a means to begin to understand the severity of depressive symptoms in adolescents.

The RADS-2 can provide a solid indication of who among its respondents may need more comprehensive evaluation, so its use as a screening measure is likely to be considerable. The symptom clusters that comprise its subscales are recognized as the mainstays of depression in the most widely used diagnostic and classification systems. It is theoretically and psychometrically sound when used for its intended purposes.

SUMMARY. The RADS-2 uses a pencil-and-paper, self-report format to screen and evaluate the severity of depressive symptomatology in adolescents. Its subscale scores were derived via factor analyses and align well with current perspectives on the major domains that comprise depression. It is reasonably priced, exceptionally brief, and easy to administer and score, using individual or group administration procedures. Documentation provided in the RADS-2 manual is thorough and compelling in its coverage. On balance, the RADS-2 would be a good choice for test users who wish to screen adolescents, singly or as a group, for the presence and severity of depressive symptoms.

REVIEWER'S REFERENCE

American Psychiatric Association. (1994). *Diagnostic and statistical manual of mental disorders* (4th ed.). Washington, DC: Author.

[212]

Reynolds Bully-Victimization Scales for Schools.

Purpose: Designed to evaluate "school-related violence and its impact on students."
Publication Date: 2003.
Acronym: RBVSS.
Administration: Individual or group.

Levels, 3: Bully-Victimization Scale, Bully-Victimization Distress Scale, School Violence Anxiety Scale.
Price Data, 2003: $160 per complete kit including manual (181 pages), 30 Bully-Victimization Scale forms, 30 School Violence Anxiety Scale forms, 30 Bully-Victimization Distress forms, Bully-Victimization Scale scoring key—English/Spanish, and Bully-Victimization Distress Scale scoring key—English/Spanish; $65 per manual; $30 per 30 Bully-Victimization Scale (specify English or Spanish); $30 per 30 School Violence Anxiety Scale (specify English or Spanish); $30 per 30 Bully-Victimization Distress Scale (specify English or Spanish); $10 per Bully-Victimization Scale scoring key—English/Spanish; $10 per Bully-Victimization Distress Scale scoring key—English/Spanish.
Foreign Edition: Spanish edition available.
Time: (5–10) minutes per scale.
Comments: Scales may be used individually or as a battery; automated group testing available.
Author: William Reynolds.
Publisher: PsychCorp, A brand of Harcourt Assessment, Inc.

a) BULLY-VICTIMIZATION SCALE.
Purpose: "Designed to measure bullying behavior and victimization among peers in or near school settings."
Population: Grades 3–12.
Acronym: BVS.
Scores, 2: Bullying, Victimization.

b) BULLY-VICTIMIZATION DISTRESS SCALE.
Purpose: Designed to "evaluate the dimensions of students' psychological distress specific to being bullied."
Population: Grades 3–12.
Acronym: BVDS.
Scores, 3: Total Distress (Externalizing, Internalizing, Total).

c) SCHOOL VIOLENCE ANXIETY SCALE
Purpose: Designed to "measure student anxiety about schools as unsafe or threatening environments."
Population: Grades 5–12.
Acronym: SVAS.
Scores: Total score only.

Review of the Reynolds Bully-Victimization Scales for Schools by CHRISTOPHER A. SINK, Professor and Chair, School Counseling and Psychology, Seattle Pacific University, Seattle, WA, and CHER I. EDWARDS, Assistant Professor, School Counseling and Psychology, Seattle Pacific University, Seattle, WA:

DESCRIPTION. The Reynolds Bully-Victimization Scales for Schools (RBVSS) manual provides considerable information on three self-report norm-referenced measures designed to estimate in children and youth (Grades 3–12, ages 7–20) various dimensions of school-related bullying, victimization, and the accompanying psychological distress. The 46-item Bully Victimization Scale (BVS) appraises bullying behavior and victimization among peers in or around schools. Although no total score is computed, subtest scores for the Bullying Scale (23 items) and Victimization Scale (23 items) are reported. The 35-item Bully-Victimization Distress Scale (BVDS) is composed of an Externalizing Distress Scale (14 items) and the Internalizing Distress Scale (21 items). A BVDS total scale score is calculated. The 29-item School Violence Anxiety Scale (SVAS) examines student anxiety about schools as unsafe or threatening places across three domains of symptom expression (cognitive, physiological, and behavioral). It may also be used as an evaluation tool for school- or community-based violence reduction/prevention programs or as a school-based needs assessment. Spanish-language versions of the scales are available as well.

Individual scales within the RBVSS battery can be administered in several convenient formats (e.g., individually, small groups, or school- or grade-wide as a screening device) by an assessment-trained professional. According to the author, the BVS and BVDS require about 10 minutes or less for younger children to complete and 5 to 10 minutes for older students. The entire battery can be administered in 15 to 20 minutes. The testing procedures are coherently described. The hand scoring procedures for each measure are relatively simple to follow and require only minutes to complete. Raw scores are readily converted into T scores and percentile ranks. Standard scores are then plotted across seven RBVSS dimensions on a profile chart, providing a clear and readily interpretable graphic representation of the child's performances.

Using the total standardization sample norms, T scores can be categorized into one of four descriptive levels (normal, clinically significant, moderately severe, or severe. What these levels actually denote in concrete terms is described sufficiently in the manual. Respondent scores can also be designated as indicating a functional problem in the area assessed by the scale. Because these cutoff scores vary from scale to scale, score patterns must be carefully considered before accurately interpreting them. How these

functional problems reveal themselves in school settings are underdocumented.

DEVELOPMENT. The scale development and standardization process are logically and satisfactorily described in the test manual. In 1996, the BVS was first created, and subsequently, the SVAS was developed as a complementary measure. In an effort to evaluate various psychosocial responses to bully victimization, the BVDS was then designed.

Although further theoretical development and empirical research on bullying and victimization need to be conducted (e.g., Ireland, 2003; Smith, 2004), each scale's theoretical underpinnings and relevant supportive research were sufficiently reviewed in the manual. Key concepts and constructs were defined and elaborated upon. In addition, each scale was cogently overviewed about its fundamental nature/attributes, purpose, and applications.

Each measure appeared to go through several stages of revision and refinement. The sample sizes for final phase of scale development were acceptable ($N = 2,405$ for the BVS and the BVDS, and $N = 1,850$ for the SVAS) and generally representative of the target population. Regrettably, specifics on various item analyses conducted on the scales during the test development period were sparse. The author appears to have reduced the language requirements needed to complete the scales, while making sure their content was reflective of the underlying constructs. To secondary-age students the items may read as somewhat simplistic.

TECHNICAL. The standardization process appears to have been conducted in a rigorous manner. The standardization sample was sufficiently large ($N = 2,000$), representing students in Grades 3–12 from 37 schools across 11 diverse states. The norm group approximated the demographic characteristics of the general population as reported in the 2000 U.S. Census. About 200 respondents for each grade level were assessed on the RBVSS measures. The Spanish-language versions of the scales were administered to a sample of 104 Spanish-speaking Hispanic American students drawn mainly from the western region of the U.S. As such, any definitive scale score interpretations derived from this norm group are probably suspect.

Reliability evidence for the RBVSS is reviewed in the manual as internal consistency coefficients (Cronbach alphas) and stability estimates (Pearson rs). The magnitude of the alphas reported for each of the three scales was strong (e.g.,

English-language versions using the total standardization sample: BVS [Bullying and Victimization], r = .93; BVDS total score, r = .96; SVAS total score, r = .95). Alphas of approximately .90 or higher were also found across gender and grade level subsamples. Test-retest stability coefficients were estimated from a smaller student group (N = 207, Grades 3–12) following a hiatus of approximately 1 to 2 weeks after the initial testing. These correlations were in the moderately high to high range (e.g., .80 [BVS Victimization subscale] to .87 [SVAS total score]).

The manual reports in some detail three separate validity studies conducted on the RBVSS. First, content validity of the RBVSS was demonstrated through a series of item analyses. Whether or not the items themselves were scrutinized by outside experts in the school violence field was not discussed. The author provided solid evidence for the convergent, discriminant, and criterion validity of the BVS and BVDS. For the SVAS, however, these psychometric properties were less well supported. Factorial validity evidence for the RBVSS was sufficient. In short, the empirical documentation marshaled in support of the instruments' construct validity was more than passable for self-report screening inventories.

COMMENTARY. The value of the RBVSS battery to accurately estimate respondents' perceptions of the level of bullying and victimization in their schools, as well as what impact these problems have had on their psychosocial functioning, are well documented in the manual. The English-language versions of the BVS and BVDS appear to be valid screening measures for use in school settings. Because the evidence supporting the validity of the SVSS is limited and its standardization sample fails to include younger children in Grades 3 and 4, interpreting derived scores from this scale requires some caution. Before endorsing the Spanish-language RBVSS as a reliable and valid screening tool, additional research needs to be garnered with much larger samples to confirm the soundness of its psychometric properties.

It is also worth noting that this test battery can be employed as a screening device in clinical and mental health settings, as well as in juvenile detention and incarceration milieus. Because the developmental activities (pilot studies) were completed in schools, much of the evidentiary research is school-based, and the norms were drawn from a large student base, data collected from respondents in nonschool environments may be less reliable and valid as the ratings provided by students. Thus, care must be exercised when using nonstudent ratings as professionals plan therapeutic interventions and measure their effectiveness. The case study provided in the manual is a very helpful guide for practitioners to follow in their work with children and youth, either in schools or clinical venues.

In terms of scoring and participant response consistency, potential users should be aware that for the BVS a "0" rating on a 4-point scale is assigned "never" as its descriptor, whereas for the BVDS, a "0" is designated as "never or almost never." For each of the items on the SVSS, a "0" response is anchored by the "almost never" label. Because many students are likely to be administered the entire battery in one sitting, some uncertainty may arise about what a "0" means as they move from items on one scale to the next. This area of potential confusion should be pointed out to students prior to testing.

Finally, the test manual explores several applications for the RBVSS in which teachers and administrators are considered the primary educators attending to issues of bullying and its effects. Given that school counselors and school psychologists also work closely with students at risk and individuals with bullying problems as well as their victims, these other professionals should be identified as potential users of the battery. In short, the scales's applications and explanations should be extended to all relevant professionals.

SUMMARY. The three scales that comprise the RBVSS (English-language versions) are user friendly, highly reliable, and efficient instruments to appraise student perceptions of bullying, victimization, and school violence. They can be readily administered and scored by a variety of trained educators. Score interpretation should be left to assessment competent professionals (e.g., special educators, school counselors, and school psychologists). School-based validity evidence for the BVS and BVDS falls well within the accepted professional testing standards for attitudinal-like screening surveys. Although the SVAS requires further validation research, its scores can be applied cautiously to evaluate the efficacy of bullying intervention/prevention programs. The SVAS could be also deployed as an inexact school-wide needs assessment tool. Mental health professionals outside school settings must take into account the test battery's school-based focus and norms as they appropriately interpret and apply respondents' scores. At present, the Spanish-language versions of the scales should be used only for research purposes.

REVIEWERS' REFERENCES

Ireland, J. L. (2003). Attachment, emotional loneliness, and bullying behaviour: A study of adult and young offenders. *Aggressive Behavior, 30,* 298–312.

Smith, P. K. (2004). Bullying: Recent developments. *Child & Adolescent Mental Health, 9,* 98–103.

Review of the Reynolds Bully Victimization Scales for Schools by SUSAN M. SWEARER, Associate Professor of School Psychology, University of Nebraska—Lincoln, and KELLY BREY LOVE, Doctoral Student, University of Nebraska—Lincoln, Lincoln, NE:

DESCRIPTION. The Reynolds Bully Victimization Scales for Schools (RBVSS) consists of three self-report scales designed to evaluate "school-related violence and its impact on students" (manual, p. 8). The battery comprises three individual scales: The Bully Victimization Scale (BVS), the Bully-Victimization Distress Scale (BVDS), and School Violence Anxiety Scale (SVAS). The BVS is a 46-item scale designed to measure bullying behavior and victimization among students in Grades 3 through 12 in and out of school settings. The BVDS is a 35-item scale designed to evaluate students' psychological distress as a result of being bullied. The BVDS is also administered to students in Grades 3 through 12. The SVAS is a 29-item scale designed to measure students' anxiety toward school as unsafe or threatening for Grades 5 through 12. The total test battery for Grades 3 and 4 consists of 81 items (BVS+BVDS) and the total battery for Grades 5–12 consists of 110 items (BVS+BVDS+SVAS). The RBVSS can be individually administered, administered in small groups, or administered in large groups as a screening process to identify students' involvement in bullying and/or victimization. All scales are hand scored, using scoring templates.

The RBVSS are totaled individually, deriving a separate score for each scale. Each scale utilizes a Likert type scale, ranging from 0–3. The scale for the BVS is 0 = *Never;* 1 = *Once or twice;* 2 = *Three or four times;* and 3 = *Five or more times.* On the BVDS, the scale is 0 = *Never or almost never;* 1 = *Sometimes;* 2 = *A lot of the time;* and 3 = *Almost all of the time.* The scale for the SVAS is almost identical to that on the BVDS, except 0 = *Almost never.* Administration and scoring of the RBVSS are relatively simple. According to the manual, completion of each scale

takes approximately 5–10 minutes, and approximately 2–3 minutes to score. Administrators of the RBVSS should have background in testing and measurement, as well as a familiarity with child and adolescent self-report measures.

Several scores can be derived from the RBVSS: a Bullying raw score; a Victimization raw score (BVS); an Internalizing Distress, Externalizing Distress, and Total raw scale score (BVDS); and a School Violence Anxiety raw score (SVAS). The raw scores are converted to standard scores in the form of T scores. The BVS Bullying score contains 14 items focusing on physical bullying behavior, 6 items on verbal behavior, and 3 that can be defined as either physical or verbal behaviors. The Victim score of the BVS contains 14 items focusing on physical victimization, 4 items focusing on verbal victimization, and 5 items that can be defined as either physical or verbal victimization.

DEVELOPMENT. The initial version of the BVS was developed in 1997. The scale consisted of 48 items, and was pilot-tested with 417 children in fourth through seventh grades in 1998. Item analysis reduced the scale to 44 items, and was administered to 355 students in Grades 7 to 12. This 44-item scale was revised again to lower the reading level and to add questions regarding harassment and social exclusion. This final scale consisted of 47 items, and was administered to a national sample of 2,405 students in Grades 3–12. The reading level is calculated at 2.1, at a reading ease of 96.5%.

Development of the BVDS initially consisted of 36 items, to reflect various symptoms of internalizing and externalizing distress. After administration to a national sample of 2,405 children, one item was removed from the scale. This resulting 35-item scale has a reading level of 3.4 and a reading ease of 94%.

Development of the SVAS initially consisted of 32 items, designed to evaluate students' responses to and perception of school violence and safety in the school environment. This initial sample was pilot-tested with 355 students in Grades 7 through 12. From these results, 3 additional items were added to the scale. This final 32-item scale was administered to a national sample of 1,850 students from Grades 5–12. Results from this administration resulted in removal of 3 items with low item with total scale correlations, resulting in a final 29-item scale. The SVAS has a reading level of 4.6, and a reading ease of 85%.

TECHNICAL.

Standardization. The RBVSS was normed on 2,000 students in Grades 3–12 in 2002. The manual advises against using group-specific norms when evaluating individual students; instead the consumer is advised to use the total standardization sample. The sample was stratified by gender, grade, ethnicity, geographic region of the country, and parent education level. Thirty-seven schools from 11 states participated in the standardization of the RBVSS. Two hundred students from each grade were sampled. The Spanish version of the RBVSS was standardized on 104 Spanish-speaking students in Grades 3–12, with a relatively equal number of male and female participants. Another sample was analyzed using Hispanic students who completed the English version of the RBVSS. This sample matched the gender, grade, and geographic region of the Spanish sample, and was used to examine the equivalence of scores on the two language versions. The norm scores are converted from raw scores to percentile ranks and standard scores. Standard scores are computed with a mean of 50 and standard deviation of 10 points.

Validity. The manual reports potential use of the RBVSS as an individual assessment tool, a school-wide screening device to identify students at-risk for bullying and victimization, a school-wide needs assessment, a program evaluation tool, and a research measure. The developer of the scale reports high item-with-total scale correlations as evidence of content validity.

Criterion-related validity is demonstrated by teacher ratings on the Teacher Bully-Victimization Rating Scale (TBVRS; Reynolds, 2002) of bullying and victimization with the BVS Bullying and Victimization scales. Moderate correlations of .43 and .46 were demonstrated between the TBVRS and the BVS Bullying and Victimization scales. The manual indicates a correlation of .70 between the Beck Youth Inventories of Emotional and Social Impairment (BYI; Beck, Beck, & Jolly, 2001) and the SVAS, illustrating criterion and convergent validity. Additionally, the BVS Bullying scale correlated .40 with the number of times student was sent to the office in the past 6 months.

Convergent validity is reported in the manual between the BVS and BYI Disruptive Behavior Scale $r = .54$, and the BYI Anger scale $r = .38$. The BVS Victimization Scale correlated with BYI scales of Anxiety $r = .58$ and Depression $r = .50$, and $r =$ .32 with BYI Disruptive Behavior, providing evidence of convergent and discriminant validity. The manual also reports a correlation coefficient of .61 between Victimization scale and BYI Anger scale. The BVS Bullying scale has an $r = .48$ correlation with the RAASI (Reynolds Adolescent Adjustment Screening Inventory) Antisocial Behavior subscale, and $r = .60$ with the RAASI Anger Control subscale.

Discriminant validity is demonstrated between the SVAS and the BYI Disruptive Behavior scale with a low correlation of .23. The correlation between the BVS Bullying scale and RAASI Emotional Disturbance scale is .08, also demonstrating discriminant validity. Factorial validity is also described at length in the manual.

Reliability. Reliability estimates are provided in the manual. Test-retest reliability was analyzed using scores from 207 students in Grades 3 through 12. The analysis was conducted 1–2 weeks after initial testing. The test-retest reliability coefficients for all six scales (using total retest sample) were .80 to .87, with a median of .84.

Internal consistency reliability was reported for the BVS Bullying and BVS Victimization scale, using the general standardization sample and various subgroups across gender and grade. The internal consistency reliability for the total standardization sample for the two scales was reported as an alpha coefficient of .93. Internal consistency reliability for the BVDS was calculated as .95 for the Internalizing Distress subscale, .92 for the Externalizing Distress subscale, and .96 for the total score. Internal consistency reliability for the standardization sample was .95. Item-with-total scale correlations were calculated on all three scales (English version) and ranged from .43 to .77, with 90% of items demonstrating item-with-total correlations of .50 or higher.

Internal consistency reliability was also calculated for the Spanish versions of the RBVSS, and are reported as follows: BVS Bullying Scale = .92, BVS Victimization Scale = .90, BVDS Internalizing Distress Scale = .95, BVDS Externalizing Distress Scale = .95. Reliability coefficients for the BVS Bullying Scale were .89 and .91 for the BVS Victimization Scale. Standard error of measurement was calculated for the English and Spanish versions of the RVBSS, with *SEM* values ranging from 2.00 to 3.61.

COMMENTARY. Although the three scales can be used to comprehensively assess students' experiences and responses to bullying and victimization, the RVBSS manual is not very user friendly. At several points throughout the manual, a topic is initially addressed and then the reader is directed to another chapter to obtain further results. Construct validity was calculated using three scales, two of which were written by the same author as the RVBSS. Perhaps the veracity of the construct validity would have been more defensible if other widely used behavior and/or bullying scales had been used. Teacher ratings of bullying and victimization behaviors and number of office referrals were used as evidence of criterion validity. Teachers were instructed to think of the bullying instances in the previous 6 months, whereas the scales prompt students to think of "how often this has happened to you in the past month." This timing discrepancy between the student and teacher versions is problematic. The RVBSS is also more sensitive to physical forms of bullying, and includes few questions regarding the relational aspects of bullying (i.e., exclusion, rumors, name-calling, cyber bullying, etc.) This is a major omission of the RBVSS, given that research clearly demonstrates that girls engage in social aggression as a primary mode of bullying (Underwood, 2003). This omission likely contributes to an under identification of females as bullies or victims when using the RBVSS. The scale developer advocates for use of the overall norm sample to evaluate individual students. This overall sample is not divided by gender or grade, thus the wide age range of students (Grades 3 through 12) would likely produce a high number of false positives, as well as potential under- or overreporting at the low and high ends of the grades (i.e., the cutoff for clinical significance is the same for students in 3rd grade as it is for those in 12th grade). The ease of scoring the RBVSS would be greatly increased if there were a computerized scoring program for the scales.

SUMMARY. The Reynolds Bully Victimization Scales contain three separate self-report scales: the Bully Victimization Scale (BVS), the Bully-Victim Distress Scale (BVDS), and the School Violence Anxiety Scale (SVAS). The BVS is designed to measure bullying behavior and victimization among peers in or near school settings. The BVDS is designed to evaluate students' psychological distress as a result of being bullied. The SVAS is designed to measure student anxiety about schools as unsafe or threatening environ-

ments. Administration, scoring, and interpretation may be completed in a relatively short amount of time. The large nationally stratified norm sample used for the RVBSS is one of the strengths of the scales. Test-retest reliability evidence is also strong. The RVBSS appears to possess strong construct validity. Of greatest concern is the overrepresentation of items measuring physical forms of bullying and victimization and the limited number of items assessing relational aspects of bullying. This omission likely underidentifies girls' involvement in bullying and victimization. However, despite this limitation, the RBVSS seems to be an effective self-report tool for school personnel who are interested in assessing the scope of bullying and victimization and/or responses to bullying prevention and intervention programming in their schools.

REVIEWERS' REFERENCES

Beck, J. S., Beck, A. T., & Jolly, J. B. (2001). Beck Youth Inventories. San Antonio, TX: The Psychological Corporation.
Reynolds, W. M. (2002) Teacher Bully-Victimization Rating Scale. Unpublished measure.
Underwood, M. K. (2003). *Social aggression among girls*. New York: Guilford Press.

[213]

Reynolds Intellectual Assessment Scales and the Reynolds Intellectual Screening Test.

Purpose: Designed to assess verbal and nonverbal intelligence and memory.

Population: Ages 3–94.

Publication Dates: 1998–2003.

Administration: Individual.

Price Data, 2003: $349 per RIAS/RIST combination kit including 3-volume set of stimulus books, 25 RIAS record forms and 25 RIST record forms, and professional manual (2003, 267 pages); $80 per professional manual.

Authors: Cecil R. Reynolds and Randy W. Kamphaus.

Publisher: Psychological Assessment Resources, Inc.

   a) REYNOLDS INTELLECTUAL SCREENING TEST.

   Purpose: Designed to identify quickly those who need a more comprehensive intellectual assessment.

   Acronym: RIST.

   Scores, 3: Guess What, Odd-Item Out, Total RIST Index.

   Time: (10–15) minutes.

   Comments: Brief screening test comprising two RIAS subtests.

   b) REYNOLDS INTELLECTUAL ASSESSMENT SCALES.

   Purpose: Designed to measure intellectual level.

Acronym: RIAS.

Scores, 10: Verbal Intelligence Index (Guess What, Verbal Reasoning), Nonverbal Intelligence Index (Odd-Item Out, What's Missing), Composite Intelligence Index, Composite Memory Index (Verbal Memory, Nonverbal Memory).

Time: (30–35) minutes.

Review of the Reynolds Intellectual Assessment Scales and the Reynolds Intellectual Screening Test by BRUCE A. BRACKEN, *Professor, School of Education, The College of William & Mary, Williamsburg, VA:*

DESCRIPTION. The Reynolds Intellectual Assessment Scales (RIAS) is an intelligence test designed for use with individuals between the ages of 3 and 94 years. The test is packaged in a convenient canvas carrying case, with three small easels, an examiner's manual, and a set of record forms. The easels and manuals are bound well, are very sturdy, and are very easily manipulated (e.g., the spiral bindings do not catch). The RIAS has no extraneous testing materials (e.g., blocks, puzzles) for examinees to manipulate; the test is easel-administered, allowing pointing and verbal responses. The RIAS artwork is quite variable in quality and ranges from primitive black-and-white and four-color clipart to some artist-produced four-color pictures. Record forms are spacious and laid out well, with Start Rules, Reverse Rules, End Rules, and Scoring Rules clearly presented to facilitate administration of each subtest.

With six subtests in the total battery, the RIAS produces subtest scores based on a *T*-score metric and four scale indices based on an IQ metric (i.e., Verbal Index, Nonverbal Index, Composite Memory Index, and the total test score—Composite Intelligence Index). There is little innovation in the RIAS cognitive tasks and subtests. The first verbal subtest, Guess What, requires the examinee to deduce an object or concept based on presented clues. This subtest is very similar to the Kaufman Assessment Battery for Children (K-ABC; T6:1316) subtest, Riddles. Verbal Reasoning presents a verbal analogy with one or two words that will complete the proposition. This subtest is similar to the Opposite Analogies subtest on the McCarthy Scales of Children's Abilities (T6:1536). To assess nonverbal reasoning, the RIAS includes Odd-Item Out, with very similar task demands to those of the Columbia Mental Maturity Scale (T6:613), which presents a set of

objects with one among the set that does not belong perceptually or conceptually. The RIAS What's Missing subtest is essentially the same measure as the Wechsler Picture Completion subtest, with nearly identical response prompts. The RIAS memory subtests include Verbal Memory, which is very similar to sentence/story memory subtests found across the ages on the Stanford-Binet (233) and the McCarthy Scales (T6:1536), as well as other measures. The Nonverbal Memory subtest is very similar to the Object Memory subtest from the Universal Nonverbal Intelligence Test (T6:2636). As such, the RIAS contributes little new to the process of assessing intelligence, but it does employ well-tested and proven measures of intelligence.

Although the Verbal Index is clearly verbal in nature with verbal directions and verbal content, the Nonverbal Index is a bit of a misnomer. The two "nonverbal" subtests on the RIAS are presented with verbal directions, and What's Missing essentially requires a verbal response. This index would have been better represented with a more accurate descriptor.

The Reynolds Intellectual Screening Test (RIST) is composed of two of the six standard battery subtests (i.e., Guess What and Odd-Item Out). Using the same standardization sample as the RIAS, the RIST has very similar psychometric characteristics as the complete instrument, including strong reliability.

DEVELOPMENT. The RIAS professional manual cites eight primary goals that guided the development of the instrument. The RIAS was developed with the goals of providing a sound measure of general intelligence that accurately predicts academic achievement across a broad age range, while eliminating or reducing examinee reading and motor coordination requirements and reducing bias in testing by using a simple, brief, and easy administration format. The manual provides a fairly detailed set of additional development goals that address perceived shortcomings of other approaches or niches the authors believe need to be filled by measures of intelligence. A lengthy rationale for not endorsing subtest profile analysis is presented, which is both instructive and supportive of the test authors' interpretation approach.

With six subtests and a 30- to 35-minute administration, the RIAS provides a nice option as compared to the majority of extant language-loaded intelligence tests that seem to have grown longer every year. The RIAS administration and scoring guidelines are carefully explicated, including identifying and dealing with potential sources of examiner, examinee, and test error. Subtest administration guidelines provide clear directions, excellent examples, and appropriate prompts.

Overall, the section of the manual that addresses RIAS development, administration, and scoring provides a nice tutorial for graduate students who are acquiring assessment skills and for practitioners who may have forgotten important issues.

TECHNICAL. The RIAS was normed on 2,438 individuals residing in 41 states. By single age levels, the sample varies from a low of one hundred 6- and 10-year-olds to 170 children who were 4-year-olds. At the adolescent and adult age levels, samples tend to be larger than 100, but also include a broader range of ages. Considering the combined age levels, the sample ranges from 121 in the 15–16-year age range to 333 individuals in the 35–54 age level. As such, the RIAS includes sample sizes that are sufficient for developing norms. In many instances, the RIAS sample is at variance with population estimates provided by the U.S. Census Bureau by fairly large amounts. For example, considering ethnicity as a variable, the RIAS overrepresents Whites by as much as 8 to 10% in some age ranges and underrepresents African Americans, Hispanics, and others by as much as 4 to 5%. Similarly, discrepancies are found in gender and education levels. As a result of the less than ideal variable match of the sample to the U.S. demographics, the RIAS data were weighted accordingly during norms development.

The RIAS professional manual provides considerable and strong support for the reliability of scores from the instrument (i.e., internal consistency, stability), with internal consistency coefficients mostly in the .90s for the subtests and composites across gender, ethnicity, and age groupings. Obtained and corrected stability coefficients are reported. The obtained stability coefficients are generally in the .70s to .80s for the subtests and indices across the age levels; the corrected coefficients are higher, but inappropriately inflated due to the use of a formula to correct for attenuated reliability rather than restriction in range.

In terms of validity, the RIAS manual presents factor analyses and content and construct validation efforts, including concurrent validity and clinical/psychiatric group studies. Although the authors' goal was primarily to provide a strong measure of psychometric "*g*," many of the subtest *g*-loadings are in the fair to poor range (i.e., *g* loadings ≤.70), with only the two verbal subtests, Guess What and Verbal Reasoning, consistently providing strong measures of general intelligence (i.e., >.70). The two "nonverbal" and memory subtests typically produced *g*-loadings in the .40s to .60s across the age levels.

Although the primary loadings of the verbal and nonverbal subtests on their respective factors were quite strong, they frequently produced secondary loadings on the opposite factor at or above .35 and sometimes as high as .50. The RIAS factor analyses provide preliminary, but only moderate support for the theoretical foundation of the instrument. To the authors' credit, they provided several factor analyses on subsamples, including age, gender, and ethnicity.

Concurrent validation evidence of the RIAS was demonstrated in comparisons with the WISC-III and WAIS-III, as well as the Wechsler Individual Achievement Test. Consistent with the results of the factor analyses, the concurrent validity studies also provided modest results. Although the RIAS produced mean scores comparable to those of the WISC-III and WAIS-III, the convergent and discriminant validity coefficients were sometimes counterintuitive. For example, although the RIAS Verbal Scale correlated higher (*r* = .86) with the WISC-III VIQ than it did with the PIQ (*r* = .44), the RIAS Nonverbal Scale also correlated higher with the VIQ (*r* = .60) than the PIQ (*r* = .33, n.s.). This finding shows that the RIAS Nonverbal Scale is not only not nonverbal, it is very much a verbal scale. It also should be noted that the concurrent validity coefficients are all inflated due to significant and uncorrected expansion in range (i.e., with standard deviations as high as 21 points). The total test scores of the RIAS and the WAIS-III correlated at a strong level (*r* = .75); however, this coefficient resulted in large part from a RIAS total score standard deviation of 17.84 and a WAIS-III total score standard deviation of 20.48. When corrected for expansion in range in both the predictor and the criterion variables, this coefficient would drop to a much more modest level.

COMMENTARY AND SUMMARY. The RIAS is a brief, easily administered intelligence test with two verbal, two nonverbal, and two memory subtests. The RIST is a two-subtest screener composed of one verbal and one nonverbal subtest from the standard battery. Both instruments are designed and normed for use with a broad age range (i.e., ages 3 to 94 years). RIAS subtests and cognitive tasks are very similar in design, administration, scoring, and even the use of specific prompts as subtests found on several existing batteries.

The strengths of the RIAS include its high quality covers, bindings, and packaging; a well-written professional manual; well-organized and easily used record forms; and strong evidence of reliability (i.e., internal consistency and stability) for the total sample and several demographic subsamples (e.g., age, gender, ethnicity). The RIAS limitations are associated more with validity evidence. Factor analysis of the RIAS yielded promising, yet less pure than desirable evidence of the instrument's structure. Although subtests generally loaded predominately on their identified factor, many subtests had large (i.e., ≥.35) secondary loadings on the opposite factor. Although the RIAS was intended as a sound measure of psychometric g, the majority of the subtests have loadings on the g factor that would be considered fair or poor measures of the construct. Concurrent validity studies with the WISC-III and WAIS-III yield comparable mean scores and overall strong positive correlations; however, RIAS "nonverbal" measures correlated as high or higher with the Wechsler VIQs as with the PIQs—possibly due to the administration requirements of the nonverbal measures that present verbal directions and allow/encourage verbal responses. The strong RIAS-Wechsler validity correlations are inflated due to uncorrected expanded range, which when corrected will result in coefficients in a more modest range.

Review of the Reynolds Intellectual Assessment Scales and the Reynolds Intellectual Screening Test by GREGORY SCHRAW, *Professor, Department of Educational Psychology, University of Nevada—Las Vegas, Las Vegas, NV:*

DESCRIPTION. The Reynolds Intellectual Assessment Scale (RIAS) provides a measure of intelligence based on the Horn and Cattell (1966) model of intelligence. The RIAS consists of two composite scales. The Composite Intelligence Index (CIX) contains four tests, divided into the Verbal Intelligence Index (VIX), which includes the Guess What (62 items) and Verbal Reasoning tests (48 items); and the Nonverbal Index, which includes the Odd-Item Out (51 items) and What's Missing tests (40 items). The Composite Memory Index (CMX) includes the Verbal Memory (88 items) and Nonverbal Memory (46 items) tests. The RIAS may be used for a variety of purposes, including diagnosis of learning disabilities, mental retardation, and memory impairment.

The complete RIAS takes roughly 30 to 35 minutes to administer for an experienced tester. The instrument is appropriate for ages 3 to 94. Each of the individual tests contains items that are ordered from least to most difficult. Children of age 3 begin with the first item, whereas older children and adults begin with later items. The manual specifies at which item to begin depending on the age of the test taker. Starting, reverse, and ending rules are described clearly in the manual. The general ending rule is two or three consecutive incorrect responses.

The RIAS is accompanied by a 258-page manual, complete with information about administration, scoring, reliability and validity, interpretation, development, and standardization of the instruments. The manual is clearly written and concise. The manual does an excellent job of providing a rationale for the RIAS, how the test might be used in diagnostic settings, and tips for administering the test.

The RIAS can be interpreted at several levels. The easiest is to use the overall Composite Intelligence Index (CIX). However, comparing performance (or percentile ranks) on the Verbal Intelligence Index (VIX) and Nonverbal Intelligence Index (NIX) may help examiners distinguish between these two types of intelligence. In addition, comparing the CIX to the Composite Memory Index (CMX) may help identify test takers with memory impairments.

The RIAS includes clear and concise record forms that enable the test giver to record raw scores, convert these scores using tables in the manual to age-adjusted T scores, and to graph the RIAS subtest profiles.

TECHNICAL. This is the first version of the RIAS. The RIAS was standardized on a sample of 2,438 individuals. Samples matched key demographic variables of the United States population. Approximately equal numbers of males and females were used across three ethnic categories.

The manual presents scores from the standardization sample broken down by gender, age, ethnicity, and educational attainment.

The manual provides a concise but thorough discussion of reliability and validity evidence. Reliability for each subtest is excellent across all age groups for all subtests, ranging from .84 for 3-year-old children to .96 for adults. Reliability is equally good when broken down by gender, age, and ethnicity. Corrected test-retest reliability coefficients range from .69 to .91 for subtests, and .78 to .99 for composite scores.

Construct validity was assessed in two ways. The first was to perform a number of confirmatory factor analyses of the full scale. These analyses generally yielded a one-factor solution consistent with Cattell and Horn's (1966) model of intelligence. The second way construct validity was assessed was to correlate the scales with another test of intelligence such as the Weschler Intelligence Scale for Children (WISC-III) and Weschler Adult Intelligence Scale (WAIS-III). Correlations ranged from .61 to .79 using the VIX, NIX, and CMX composite scores from the RIAS, and three composite scores from the WAIS-III. However, it should be noted that these comparisons were made on samples of 54 and 31 test takers, respectively. Further construct validation work is necessary to document the construct, criterion-related, and predictive validity of the RIAS.

COMMENTARY. The strengths of the RIAS include (a) easy administration and scoring, (b) a well-written manual, and (c) high reliability. Weaknesses include (a) the small norming sample for validity, (b) lack of predictive validity data, and (c) a moderate correlation with the WISC-III and WAIS-III. Although the manual provides a clear rationale for the test, it is not clear at this point whether the RIAS is a better instrument than other measures of intelligence. More validation research is needed before this issue is resolved.

SUMMARY. Overall, the RIAS provides a quick and efficient measure of overall intellectual functioning. It provides specific information about three major subscales, including the verbal ability, nonverbal ability, and memory indices. The RIAS appears to be most useful when used to diagnose major intellectual and memory impairments .

REVIEWER'S REFERENCE

Horn, J. L., & Cattell, R. B. (1966). Refinement and test of the theory of fluid and crystallized general intelligences. *Journal of Educational Psychology, 57*, 253-270.

[214]

Ruff Neurobehavioral Inventory.

Purpose: Designed to measure cognitive, emotional, physical, and psychosocial problems both before and after a specified event—usually an injury or neuropsychiatric illness.
Population: Ages 18–75.
Publication Date: 2003.
Acronym: RNBI.
Scores, 26: Inconsistency, Infrequency, Negative Impression, Positive Impression, Cognitive Composite, Emotional Composite, Physical Composite, Quality of Life Composite, Attention & Concentration, Executive Functions, Learning & Memory, Speech & Language, Anger & Aggression, Anxiety, Depression, Paranoia & Suspicion, Posttraumatic Stress Disorder, Substance Abuse, Neurological Status, Pain, Somatic Complaints, Abuse, Activities of Daily Living, Psychosocial Integration & Recreation, Vocation & Finance, Spirituality.
Administration: Individual or group.
Price Data, 2005: $149 per introductory kit including 25 reusable item booklets, 25 answer booklets, 25 profile booklets, and professional manual (123 pages); $39 per 25 reusable item booklets; $51 per 25 answer booklets; $26 per 25 profile booklets; $45 per professional manual.
Time: [30–45] minutes.
Authors: Ronald M. Ruff and Kristin M. Hibbard.
Publisher: Psychological Assessment Resources, Inc.

Review of the Ruff Neurobehavioral Inventory by ANDREW S. DAVIS, Assistant Professor of Psychology, Ball State University, and W. HOLMES FINCH, Assistant Professor of Educational Psychology, Ball State University, Muncie, IN:

DESCRIPTION. The Ruff Neurobehavioral Inventory (RNBI) is a self-report questionnaire that is structured to assess cognitive, emotional, physical, and psychosocial intrapersonal and interpersonal problems from a neurobehavioral perspective. Designed for use with adults age 18 to 75, this instrument is constructed to assess individuals before and after an injury or neuropsychiatric illness. Information on this self-report instrument is collected via the patient completing a Likert-type scale that has four options, ranging from False to Very True. The patient is required to read and respond to 243 questions, with the first 124 questions referring to current functioning and the remaining 119 referring to premorbid functioning. Respondents darken the corresponding oval on a response sheet separate from the test booklet. The test booklet and answer sheet are the only items with which the patient interacts for the RNBI. A profile-scoring sheet is provided for examiners to calculate the results of the measure.

Because subjective questionnaires depend upon the honesty and concentration of the patient, the test authors have provided four validity scales to assess accuracy and truthfulness. The Inconsistency scale is based on 12 pairs of questions that essentially ask the same question. Patients providing inconsistent answers to each pair may be responding to the questions in a random fashion. The Infrequency scale comprises 12 items, which were rarely endorsed at the extreme end of the Likert scale by respondents in the standardization sample. The Negative Impression scale is designed to identify individuals who are trying to "fake bad" by endorsing the 12 items that would indicate they are suffering from very serious problems. The Positive Impression scale, also consisting of 12 items, are constructed to recognize individuals who are endorsing multiple items in order to "fake good" or cast themselves in a positive light.

The RNBI is designed to measure four broad neurobehavioral domains. The Composite scales are crafted from a series of Basic scales, and premorbid and postmorbid scores are generated. The Cognitive domain assesses the individual's neuropsychological functioning with questions from four subdomains: Attention and Concentration, Executive Functions, Learning and Memory, and Speech and Language. The Emotional domain examines the patient's self-perception of their emotional state by looking at six subdomains: Anger and Aggression, Anxiety, Depression, Paranoia and Suspicion, Posttraumatic Stress Disorder, and Substance Abuse. The Physical domain is assessed through three subdomains that examine physical functioning: Neuropsychological Status, Pain, and Somatic Complaints. The patient's perception of their quality of life is assessed through four subdomains: Abuse, Activities of Daily Living, Psychosocial Integration and Recreation, and Vocation and Finance. An additional scale of Spirituality is included, which is the only scale that is assessed postmorbidly only. Scoring and administering the RNBI is very simple and convenient. The respondent's answers pass through the top page onto another page, which allows the examiner to sum the raw scores, and the manual contains easy-to-read charts for the conversion of raw scores into *T*-scores.

DEVELOPMENT. The RNBI was developed due to the authors' need to construct a comprehensive, quantitative, and psychometrically sound questionnaire that could supplement a clinical interview for patients who had suffered a neurotraumatic event. Moreover, the authors note that many traditional questionnaires, such as the Minnesota Multiphasic Personality Inventory–Second Edition (MMPI-II; Butcher, Dahlstrom, Graham, & Tellegen, 1989) were not designed for individuals with neurotraumatic injuries, and they tend to provide only emotional information regarding the patient. The RNBI was designed to address these issues by providing additional information on cognitive functioning, physical functioning, and quality of life issues for patients who had suffered a traumatic event. The authors constructed an initial item pool that contained 1,272 items that were chosen after an extensive literature review and were designed to operationalize the constructs of the RNBI. After reviewing the items for appropriateness, length, reading level, and slang, the item pool was reduced to just over 1,000 items. The item pool was further reduced to 502 items after analysis for content and bias, and then increased to 570 items after the inclusion of the validity scales and a scale for executive functioning. A 4-point Likert scale was used to administer the items to 80 patients in a rehabilitation setting who were being treated for conditions like traumatic brain injury, strokes, spinal cord injuries, and chronic pain. The items were also administered to 230 individuals with no history of neuropsychiatric illness. The 570 items were also administered to three additional groups; the number of participants was not included in the manual to investigate the validity items. The final 243 items were chosen after analysis for theoretical relevance and psychometric properties.

TECHNICAL. The normative data for the RNBI were collected on an adequately sized sample of 1,024 adults who were contacted by e-mail after expressing an interest in completing surveys to an Internet research company. Each individual completed an online version of the RNBI. Strangely, a negative history of neurotraumatic injury, mental disorders, or physical problems did not seem to be a prerequisite for participation in the standardization sample, as indicated by the manual. A possible concern is that the normative sample completed the RNBI via the Internet, without a face-to-face meeting. Hence, it is difficult to ascertain the integrity of responses from the normative sample regarding demographic characteristics such as age, gender, and prior history of injury. Additionally, because the RNBI is administered with paper and pencil, the normative sample was not collected with the same standardized instructions patients receive with the RNBI.

Information is provided in the manual regarding the standardization sample in terms of gender, age, ethnicity, education, and marital status, and the test manual provides information about these effects. The normative age ranges available in the manual are 18–25, 26–35, 36–45, 46–55, 56–65, and 65–75. This sample has a disproportionately large representation of Caucasian individuals (81.4%) and a small number of Asians. A multivariate analysis of variance (MANOVA) was used to assess the possibility of differences between minority and nonminority participants on the RNBI subscales. Results of this analysis indicate racial differences on the premorbid scale scores Activities of Daily Living, Anger and Aggression, Paranoia and Suspicion, and Posttraumatic Stress Disorder. Racial differences on the postmorbid scale scores include Pain, Somatic Complaints, Spirituality, and Paranoia and Suspicion. The test authors suggest that race-based norms are unnecessary given the relatively small number of scales exhibiting racial differences and the small size of the differences in terms of mean differences. In addition to the normative sample, a clinical sample is provided that included 195 patients with pain disorders, cerebral vascular accidents, traumatic brain injuries, and spinal cord injuries. Demographic information is included in the manual. The clinical group took the paper-and-pencil version of the RNBI, and the results were used to examine the psychometric properties of the RNBI.

The test manual provides extensive reliability information about the RNBI in the form of detailed text and tables. A test-retest study was conducted with 75 college students during intervals ranging from 2 to 4 weeks. The majority of the scales achieved moderate to high correlation coefficients, though the average test-retest correlation for the four validity scales was somewhat low (.67). The Composite scales demonstrated moderate to high temporal stability, with the Emotional scale obtaining a coefficient of .96 and the Physical scale obtaining a coefficient of .65.

Internal consistency, in the form of Cronbach's alpha, was calculated for the standardization sample. The internal consistency of the Basic scales was generally acceptable, with five falling below .70. The manual breaks down the coefficient correlations for both the premorbid and postmorbid scales. The test authors indicate that some scales are below .70 because the RNBI was designed to assess a wide range of domains, which caused a limited number of test items to be available for each scale, as the authors also wanted to make the RNBI time-efficient. The internal reliability estimates for the Composite scales for the standardization sample were generally good ranging from .67 to .85. Reliability information is also provided for the clinical sample and is in general equivalent to the standardization sample, which the test authors note could indicate the robustness of the Internet data collection for the standardization sample.

Akin to the reliability information, the test authors do a commendable job reporting the validity information about the RNBI. Concurrent validity studies were conducted with the Millon Clinical Multiaxial Inventory-III (MCMI-III; Millon, 1997), the Quality of Life Enjoyment and Satisfaction Questionnaire (Q-LES-Q; Endicott, Nee, Harrison, & Blumenthal, 1993), and the Mayo-Portland Adaptability Inventory (MPAI; Malec, Smigielski, DePompolo, & Thompson, 1993). Correlation coefficients were obtained between the MCMI-II and the RNBI from a sample of 83 college students. The authors report statistically significant correlations between MCMI-III validity scales and corresponding components of the RNBI. At the same time, the largest of these validity coefficients is .48, which falls into Cohen's moderate effect size classification for correlations. In terms of the premorbid and postmorbid RNBI scales, moderate correlations were found with the MCMI-III scores, with the largest being .65. The authors note that the pattern of correlations supports the concurrent validity of the RNBI. At the same time, they found a number of statistically significant correlations between RNBI and MCMI-III scales that did not appear to be conceptually related.

The authors report that the correlation coefficients between the RNBI and the Q-LES-Q demonstrated concurrent validity for some of the subscales. The values range from less than .20 to .56, with the highest values occurring between the Cognitive domain measures of the RNBI with the

Work and School Work scales of the Q-LES-Q. The authors also indicate that there are no corresponding measures on the Q-LES-Q for their Abuse scale, though they did find moderately large negative correlations between Abuse and several of the Q-LES-Q scales. As with the correlations between the RNBI and the MCMI-III subscales, the vast majority of the correlations with the Q-LES-Q fall into the small to moderate range based on Cohen's recommendations.

The final concurrent validity study was conducted using 40 members of the original clinical sample who completed the MPAI. The authors state that the MPAI is comparable to the RNBI Postmorbid scales. And indeed, the correlations between the MPAI scale scores and the Postmorbid subscales of the RNBI are generally strong, with just under half of the correlations being classified as large. The correlations between the MPAI and RNBI Premorbid scale scores are much lower, as the authors predicted they would be. Furthermore, these correlation values appear to support the pattern of relationships expected by the authors, with the MPAI Physical/Cognitive scale strongly correlated with the RNBI Cognitive domain subscales. However, the authors note that the Cognitive domain scores were also correlated fairly strongly with the Pain/Emotion and Social Participation scores from the MPAI. The authors find these results, along with the other two concurrent validity studies described above, to support the concurrent validity of the RNBI.

Exploratory factor analyses of each of the Premorbid and Postmorbid scales were used to assess the construct validity of the RNBI using the standardization sample of 1,024. The authors found that for both the Premorbid and Postmorbid scales, a three-factor solution was optimal, with 60% and 70%, respectively, of the variance explained. They concluded that the results generally support the presence of three constructs represented by the items, including an emotional/quality of life factor, a cognitive factor, and a physical dysfunction factor in both scales.

The final type of validity to be assessed by the authors of the RNBI was done by contrasting scores from selected clinical samples with a sample of 50 individuals taken from the standardization sample. The clinical samples included 50 individuals suffering from chronic pain, 42 stroke victims, 51 people having suffered a traumatic brain injury, and 37 patients with spinal cord injury. MANOVA was used to compare the means on the RNBI scales for each of these clinical groups with the sample of 50 nonclinical individuals. Reported results indicate that the clinical samples did indeed differ from the nonclinical sample in ways that supported contrasting groups' validity. In general, there were very few significant differences between the nonclinical sample and the Premorbid scores for the four clinical groups, whereas a number of differences did exist when comparing Postmorbid scale scores for the groups.

COMMENTARY. The RNBI appears to be a very promising, useful self-report instrument that should assist psychologists and neuropsychologists during the initial stages of assessment for individuals who have suffered a neurotraumatic injury. A wide array of information can be collected about many interpersonal and intrapersonal domains, and to further complement the Basic and Composite scales, information can be viewed both premorbid and postmorbid of the injury. The RNBI is easy to administer and score, and the examiner does not need to be present when the test is completed. The authors have provided four separate validity scales that should help neuropsychologists identify malingering, misrepresentation, consistency, and honesty. A well thought out series of Composite and Basic scales assess an individual's cognitive, emotional, and physical state, as well as their perception of quality of life.

The normative sample size is adequate, with over 1,000 participants, broken down into six normative age ranges. The information in the manual regarding the demographics of the normative sample is excellent, with gender, ethnicity, age, education, and marital status provided in an easy-to-read table. The reliability coefficients of the RNBI appears to be lower than would be hoped for in a diagnostic instrument, yet the RNBI was not necessarily designed as a diagnostic instrument. It seems that the primary utility of the RNBI would be to provide additional and quantitative information during the intake, or information-collecting phase, of an assessment. Indeed, the test authors state, "Although the RNBI does not replace the clinical interview, it should be used to generate inferences and hypotheses about the individual" (manual, p. 9). In light of the somewhat low reliability for some scales, the RNBI may have included too many scales, or too few items per scale, especially because each scale can be viewed premorbidly and postmorbidly. The reliability of the measure could have been improved by reducing the number of scales while maintaining the same number of test items, or by adding additional test items. However, the addition of items to increase reliability presumes that they are parallel to the current set. If not, the reliability of the instrument could actually be decreased. In general, the reliability of any self-report measure is destined to be lowered by the nature of the scale.

The validity evidence for the instrument appears to be satisfactory, with particularly strong evidence of the RNBI's ability to distinguish between clinical and nonclinical groups. The MANOVA models used to assess this aspect of validity were appropriate; however, no attempt appears to have been made to correct for an inflated Type I error rate, which probably should have been done given the number of such analyses that were conducted using the same nonclinical group. The criterion-related coefficients were generally in the moderate range, though they did not uniformly provide consistent evidence of the scales' validity, with some values being negligible. In addition, some scales of the RNBI were not only correlated with the corresponding scales on the other instruments examined, but also with scales that are conceptually not related. This situation indicates that there is not always a clear delineation of the constructs being measured by the RNBI. Construct validity as assessed by the factor analysis supported the presence of three latent traits in both the Premorbid and Postmorbid scales, roughly corresponding to domains of emotional/quality of life, and cognitive and physical dysfunction. The factor analysis appears to have been done well, and conclusions drawn from it seem reasonable.

At this time there is no observer rating scale with which to compare patients' answers, although the test authors report that future research studies will develop an observer rating scale. This would be a useful addition to the instrument allowing a patient's answers to be validated beyond the four validity scales. Of some minor concern is the manner in which the normative sample was collected compared to the administration of the RNBI (i.e., Internet compared with paper and pencil). The test authors have done an admirable job in listing validity and reliability studies in the manual, yet like any new instrument, the RNBI will benefit

from independent validation studies on different clinical populations.

SUMMARY. The test authors have produced a very useful self-report measure that provides a broadband view of an individual's interpersonal and intrapersonal functioning from a premorbid and postmorbid approach. This easy-to-score and administer test will provide clinicians with a much-needed addition to standard intake and history-taking forms. The comprehensive and extensive reliability and validity information contained in the manual should render practitioners comfortable with employing this measure. Although some questions remain about the low reliability of some of the scales, the validity evidence of the instrument seems to be solid, particularly in terms of the underlying constructs being measured and the differentiation of disparate groups. In summary, if clinicians do not extrapolate the results beyond what the test authors intended, this measure should be a welcome addition to any clinician's or researcher's battery of tests.

REVIEWER'S REFERENCES
Butcher, J. N., Dahlstrom, W. G., Graham, J. R., & Tellegen, A. (1989). *Manual for the restandardization of the Minnesota Multiphasic Personality Inventory: MMPI-2.* Minneapolis: University of Minnesota.
Endicott, J., Nee, J., Harrison, W., & Blumenthal, R. (1993). Quality of Life Enjoyment and Satisfaction Questionnaire: A new measure. *Psychopharmacology Bulletin, 29,* 321–326.
Malec, J. F., Smigielski, J. S., DePompolo, R. W., & Thompson, J. M. (1993). Outcome evaluation and prediction in a comprehensive-integrated post-acute outpatient brain injury rehabilitation programme. *Brain Injury, 7,* 15–29.
Millon, T. (1997). *The Millon inventories, clinical and personality assessment.* New York: Guilford Press.

Review of the Ruff Neurobehavioral Inventory by WILFRED G. VAN GORP, Professor of Clinical Psychology and Director, Neuropsychology, Columbia University College of Physicians & Surgeons, Department of Psychiatry, New York, NY, and JASON HASSENSTAB, Doctoral Candidate in Clinical Psychology, Fordham University, Department of Psychology, New York, NY:

DESCRIPTION. The Ruff Neurobehavioral Inventory (RNBI) is a 243-item self-report questionnaire intended to measure cognitive, emotional, and physical complaints as well as quality of life issues in individuals whose lives have changed as a result of a major illness or injury. A unique feature of the RNBI is that it allows clinicians to assess an individual's impression of his or her functioning both before and after a catastrophic event in one inclusive measure. It was designed for individuals 18–75 years with corresponding norms. The test consists of a Premorbid section and a Postmorbid (current functioning) section. There are four validity scales and 17 basic scales in the Premorbid section, whereas in the Postmorbid section, there are four validity scales and 18 basic scales. Within each of the two sections, the basic scales are organized into four domains represented by four composite scores. The four domains include a Cognitive Domain, an Emotional Domain, a Physical Domain, and a Quality of Life Domain. Results from both Premorbid and Postmorbid sections are reported as linear T-scores, which are then manually plotted together on a profile sheet for visual comparison and difference analyses.

DEVELOPMENT. The RNBI was devised, according to the authors, to meet the need for an integrated and comprehensive assessment of the presenting complaints of patients with neurological or physical injuries. In addition, the authors perceived a need for an instrument to assess these complaints that utilizes a research-driven conceptual framework and a common normative sample. To this end, a conceptual model was constructed that organizes functioning along two domains: intrapersonal and interpersonal. The intrapersonal component of the RNBI evaluates neurobehavioral functions including cognition, emotion, and physical functioning. The interpersonal component evaluates spirituality, financial and vocational stability, and social and recreational functioning. The 17 basic scales of the RNBI were derived from this conceptual model and a large pool of 1,272 items was developed. Approximately 270 items were dropped following an initial round of item rating by a panel that included the authors. An independent bias review panel was then assembled to ensure that items that were biased or unfair to minority groups would be eliminated. The bias panel did not recommend the removal of any of the actual test items. Following the bias panel review, a panel of highly qualified experts in rehabilitation and neuropsychology sorted the items within each scale. The use of an 85% agreement cutoff resulted in a reduction of 500 items. In response to recommendations from the expert sorting panel, an Executive Functioning Domain was added to the Cognitive Domain. The four validity scales were tested on "coached" response style groups and only items with optimal psychometric properties were kept. The final pool of items was selected by the authors and a psychologist from Psychological Assessment Resources, Inc.

The final 243-item version was designed to assess the "current status of individuals whose lives have been altered by a catastrophic event such as a major illness or injury" (professional manual, p. 1).

TECHNICAL. The RNBI is divided into two sections, Premorbid functioning and Postmorbid functioning. Both sections include four validity scales. Response accuracy is measured with the Infrequency and Inconsistency scales, which were developed to identify arbitrary or careless responding. Response honesty is measured using the Negative Impression and Positive Impression scales, which were designed to detect unrealistically positive or negative attributes and symptoms. The 17 basic scales load onto four composite scales representative of four domains: Cognitive, Emotional, Physical, and Quality of Life. The basic scales within each domain contain six questions in the Premorbid section and six questions in the Postmorbid section. The Cognitive domain includes basic scales for Attention & Concentration, Executive Functioning, Learning & Memory, and Speech & Language. The Emotional domain includes basic scales for Anger & Aggression, Anxiety, Depression, Paranoia & Suspicion, Posttraumatic Stress Disorder, and Substance Abuse. The Physical domain includes basic scales for Neurological Status, Pain, and Somatic Complaints. The Quality of Life domain includes basic scales for Abuse, Activities of Daily Living, Psychosocial Integration & Recreation, and Vocation & Finance. Also included in the Quality of Life domain is the Spirituality scale, which is measured only in the Postmorbid section and is not included in the composite score for this domain. Normative data were gathered online via a private Internet research company using a computerized version of the RNBI. The standardization sample consisted of 1,024 community-dwelling individuals. Additionally, a clinical sample was collected, which was composed of 195 individuals with diagnoses of pain disorders, cerebral vascular accident, traumatic brain injury, or spinal cord injury. The RNBI provides age-matched norms for ages 18–45 and ages 46–75. T scores from both Premorbid and Postmorbid sections are plotted together on a profile sheet for visual comparison and difference analyses. T score and difference scores are provided for each of the 17 basic scales as well as for the four composite scales. Critical items are displayed separately in the response booklet for convenience.

The RNBI can be administered and scored by a trained technician but its interpretation is limited to a "qualified professional" (professional manual, p. 6). Administration typically takes less than 45 minutes and scoring can be accomplished in 15 minutes. Scoring software is currently not available for the RNBI.

In terms of psychometrics, the reliability estimates from the RNBI were quite variable, but were generally adequate. In the standardization sample, internal consistency estimates (Cronbach's alpha) for the various Premorbid basic scales ranged from .43 to .88, whereas the Postmorbid estimates ranged from .68 to .90. In the clinical sample, Premorbid basic scale internal consistency estimates ranged from .58 to .90, whereas the Postmorbid estimates ranged from .57 to .90. The authors emphasize that the low number of test items in each scale may have resulted in artificially low internal consistency estimates, pointing to the necessity of a trade-off between reliability and overall test length. Test-retest reliability was calculated on a relatively small sample of college students (n = 94) at a test-retest interval of 2 to 4 weeks. Test-retest reliability estimates for the various basic scales in the Premorbid section ranged from .47 to .99. In the Postmorbid section, test-retest reliability estimates ranged from .37 to .88. Again, the authors were careful to point out mitigating factors. In this case, they attribute the lower stability coefficients to sample characteristics. Factor analytic studies were conducted separately for the Premorbid and Postmorbid basic scales. A three-factor solution accounting for approximately 60% of the variance best fit the Premorbid basic scales. For the Postmorbid basic scales, a three-factor solution, which accounted for approximately 70% of the variance, provided the best fit. The authors further provide useful data on the validity of scores from contrasting groups validity studies, including samples from groups with chronic pain, stroke, traumatic brain injury, and spinal cord injury.

COMMENTARY. The RNBI addresses an important need in neuropsychological assessment—surveying premorbid and postmorbid report of the patient/evaluee as it relates to neurocognitive functioning. However, there are some cautions that must be considered with this test. First, it is well known that persons with neurocognitive impairment are often inaccurate observers (and hence reporters) of their abilities or condition. Thus, though the scores obtained may be reliable data, it will likely need corroboration by external sources of information. This will be an important caveat

for clinicians to consider when interpreting these scores—they will likely need external validation, not because the patient may be "malingering" or feigning, but simply because some people, particularly if depressed, will over- or underreport their abilities in many domains.

The norms of the test are stratified by only two age groups: 18–45 and 46–75, although Appendix D has "descriptive statistics" divided into 10-year age groups, but has no T-score conversion, rendering them unhelpful. In the future, it would be good for the normative data to represent smaller age groupings.

An interesting point was raised in the description of the norming procedure. The administration directions read as follows for the Premorbid functioning section: "please rate how much each statement applied to you at an earlier time (or times) in your life." Note that it is not specified that the respondent should focus on a time before their illness or injury. The authors note that in the norming process with a clinical sample, if the respondent asked, "does this mean before my (accident, stroke, etc.)?" the examiner would affirm this. If the respondent did not ask, it was just assumed that they would take the directions to mean prior to their respective incident. So, the question here is one of a sampling irregularity, which could affect the normative sample.

A computer-based scoring program would be very helpful to the clinician. Scoring is laborious and time-consuming. There is a good potential for scoring error as well without a computer-based program, as there is a lot of summing across rows and columns required, all of which is likely to introduce error.

Some materials are clumsy, with carbon-copy bubble sheets, poor perforations, etc. The professional manual is difficult to navigate. Future editions might consider more sturdy materials.

Finally, there was limited sampling of minority populations. This should be addressed in future editions.

SUMMARY. The RNBI represents a useful development in clinical neuropsychology—the assessment of the patient's perspective of his or her functioning both pre- and postmorbidly. Psychometrically sound assessments of these abilities are much needed in neuropsychology. That said, evaluees often unintentionally distort their report of their functioning, by factors related to depression, anosagnosia, etc. Future editions of the test might focus on refining the norms into smaller age groupings, development of a computerized scoring for the test, and more sturdy and user-friendly test materials. The test at this time warrants cautious acceptance.

[215]

Rust Advanced Numerical Reasoning Appraisal.

Purpose: Measures the ability to recognize, understand, and apply mathematical and statistical reasoning abilities.
Population: Adults.
Publication Dates: 2001–2002.
Acronym: RANRA.
Scores: Total score only.
Administration: Group or individual.
Price Data, 2002: $251.20 per complete kit.
Time: (40) minutes.
Author: John Rust.
Publisher: Harcourt Assessment [England].

Review of the Rust Advanced Numerical Reasoning Appraisal by CEDERICK O. LINDSKOG, Professor, Pittsburg State University, Pittsburg, KS:

DESCRIPTION. The Rust Advanced Numerical Reasoning Appraisal (RANRA) is an instrument devised and standardized in the United Kingdom (U.K.) for use with adults in the workplace. According to the author, it is intended to measure higher level numerical reasoning using deduction, interpretation, and evaluation. It is intended for use with working age adults, and "assesses the ability to recognize, understand, and apply mathematical and statistical reasoning" (manual, p. 1.1). It is intended to measure "higher level numerical skills involving deduction, interpretation, and evaluation" (manual, p. 1.1). The RANRA has available both paper-pencil and computerized scoring versions.

The materials furnished are for the paper-pencil type administration, and include test items in British measures (e.g., currency measures were cited in pounds and pence), limiting use outside the U.K. The RANRA is intended to be a power test; however, the author suggests 30 minutes is adequate if a time limit is desired.

The author indicates the RANRA for use as either norm or criterion referenced, and provides suggestions for establishing local norms. The RANRA consists of two 16-item sections for a total of 32 multiple-choice items. The two sections are Comparison of Quantities (comparing different distances, fractions, and the like) and Sufficiency of Information (determine if there is enough information to confirm statement accuracy). Each test item is in the form of an item composed of two statements. The examinee must indicate if the statements are equal, or A is less than, equal to, or greater than B, or the information is insufficient for the Quantities section, and similar decisions are to be made for two statements in each item of the Sufficiency of Information section.

DEVELOPMENT. The instrument was published in 2001, and conormed with the Watson-Glaser Critical Thinking Appraisal (WGCTA-UK; T6:2687), which is not reviewed here. The author indicates the RANRA is a measure of numerical critical reasoning intended to complement the verbal critical reasoning measured by the WGCTA.

TECHNICAL. The test scores are expressed as either a RANRA Score or a RANRA Score Corrected for Guessing, which is most useful if the test was timed or the examiner knows there was a significant amount of guessing. In either scoring, the test gives a raw score and a T-score. Tables are provided to transform the scores to percentile rankss, stanines, z-scores, or sten scores.

The standardization sample consisted of 1,546 individuals from diverse occupations in the U.K., with approximately a 2:1 male to female ratio. The population had an age range of 17 to 72, with a mean of 29.97 years, and a standard deviation of 8.13. Education levels are described, and the ethnicity of the standardization population was "with certain caveats" (which were not explained), representative of the population for which this test is intended. No charts to compare this population to national census figures were provided.

Percentile scores were matched "to a transformation that would ensure that the resultant distribution closely matched the equation of the normal curve" (manual, p. 7.14). The technical approach for this transformation is briefly explained in the manual.

The test reliability is addressed by internal consistency and split-half calculations for both subtests and total score. Cronbach alphas range from .62 to .78. There is no significant difference between the reliability coefficients for the RANRA scores and corrected for guessing scores, indicating that the RANRA scores are adequate for use unless the examiner feels there is guessing due to time limits. Odd-even split-half reliabilities ranged from .60 to .78. The *SEM* for both composite *T*-scores was 4.7 to 4.9, based on the split-half reliability estimate.

The author provided construct validity data by comparing the RANRA to the Watson-Glaser Critical Thinking Appraisal subtests, which yielded correlations ranging from .29 to .44 for the two scales and .36 to .48 for the total RANRA score. These data were derived from the conorming of the RANRA and the WGCTA. Also provided is factor analytic support for most items loading into one of the two subtests (Comparison of Quantities and Sufficiency of Information), and also the total score, supporting separate function of each section and total scores.

COMMENTARY. This instrument may be of use to business managers in the U.K. wishing to assess numerical reasoning skills in employees. The RANRA is limited by several factors. Because it has language and norming specific to the U.K., its use is limited to the U.K., and although the author provided a cursory description of the standardization sample, one cannot tell if the sample is reflective of a national or subpopulation of the U.K. without researching an appropriate census document.

The reliability statistics are acceptable, but the evidence for validity is insufficient to accept the author's conclusion that because there is a stronger relationship between the two sections of the RANRA than between the RANRA and the WGCTA, the RANRA measures a "distinctly different aspect of critical thinking." In fact, the only apparent validity evidence besides factor analysis appears to be a product of the conorming instrument. The RANRA needs further documentation of reliability and validity before any application beyond experimental applications or studies limited to using local norms.

SUMMARY. The RANRA is an assessment of adult numerical reasoning recommended for use with the WGCTA, a measure of critical thinking. It has two 16-item sections of multiple-choice questions. It was normed in the U.K. on a population of over 1,500, which may or may not be representative of the larger group of U.K. adults in the workplace. The reliability measures referenced seemed adequate, but in the opinion of the reviewer, the RANRA is particularly lacking concurrent validity evidence, and as such, can only be used in the U.K. with caution in interpretation.

Review of the Rust Advanced Numerical Reasoning Appraisal by ELEANOR E. SANFORD, Vice-President of Research and Development, MetaMetrics, Inc., Durham, NC:

DESCRIPTION. The Rust Advanced Numerical Reasoning Appraisal (RANRA) was designed to assess an individual's ability to recognize, understand, and apply mathematical statistical reasoning. The assessment emphasizes analytical skills-deduction, interpretation, and evaluation-rather than straightforward computation skills. The RANRA consists of two subtests: Comparison of Quantities and Sufficiency of Information. These subtests are based on a theoretical "model that identifies mathematical abilities that have a clear relevance for managers and other decision makers in organisations" (manual, p. 1.1). Results from the two subtests are combined into one overall score that can be used as is or corrected for guessing. The total score is reported as a standard score with a mean of 50 and a standard deviation of 10. Percentile ranks can also be used to report the results to individual respondents.

Administration. The RANRA is a group-administered assessment. It can be administered by paper-and-pencil or through the Estrado software program developed by The Psychological Corporation. The RANRA is a power test so specific time limits are not part of the administration procedures. The manual states that the typical respondent can complete the assessment in approximately 30 minutes. The manual shows great concern with the assessment being administered according to the standardized test administration conditions to minimize any consequences on the reliability and validity of the results.

On the Comparison of Quantities subtest, the respondent is presented with two statements for which he or she must state which quantity is larger, if the quantities are equal, or if no comparison can be made. On the Sufficiency of Information subtest, the respondent is first presented with a scenario. The respondent is then asked to identify which of the two statements alone is sufficient to solve the problem, if both statements are necessary, or if neither statement is sufficient to solve the problem.

The RANRA can be scored by hand using acetate scoring keys (templates) or with the Estrado software program. The Estrado program also allows the user to integrate the results of the RANRA assessment with the results of the Watson-Glaser

Critical Thinking Appraisal (WGCTA^UK) if administered.

DEVELOPMENT. The RANRA was initially developed in 2000 and is based upon and extends the foundation built for the assessment of thinking skills by the WGCTA^UK. During the conceptual analysis of the role of critical thinking in mathematics, two subconstructs were identified: comparison of quantities and sufficiency of information. Eighty items were constructed and administered to a small sample of students and staff. The items were analyzed for difficulty, quality of the distracters, and relationship to the overall construct of mathematical statistical reasoning. Based upon the results, 32 items were selected (16 for each subtest) for use on the operational form of the assessment.

The RANRA was normed in the United Kingdom with 1,546 respondents who were also part of the restandardization of the WGCTA for use in the United Kingdom. The sample included a broad range of job applicants and incumbents at all levels of education and across 50 different occupations.

TECHNICAL. Because the RANRA is used for employee selection, the technical manual presents a complete chapter on issues related to fairness in selection testing. The author describes how mathematical reasoning may be different for various subgroups within each of the respondent classifications: gender; English language proficiency; age; training, learning, and education; and multicultural contexts. Some evidence from the standardization study is presented that shows there may be group differences between males and females on the RANRA (males, mean = 50.5; females, mean = 48.8; $p < .002$) and between various age groupings (less than 21 years, mean = 48; 21 to 29 years, mean = 51; 30 to 34 years, mean = 50; 35 years and older, mean = 48; $p < .01$).

Reliability. The manual for the RANRA presents split-half reliability coefficients and coefficient alpha coefficients for each subtest and the assessment as a whole. The coefficients for the subtests range from .60 to .71, with coefficients of .78 for the assessment as a whole. Given that individual decisions are to be made using the results from the RANRA, the level of reliability is low.

Validity. The manual describes four types of validity for the RANRA: face, content, criterion-related, and construct. The manual states that the

RANRA "has high face validity," but says only that respondents "easily understand its relevance to both scientific and technical performance and to the skills required by those who deal with figures or project planning" (p. 8.7). The manual does not describe any specific studies conducted with respondents or human resource personnel who would be using the assessment. The content validation of the RANRA is left to the user to determine the match between the content of the test and the specific jobs with which the test is being used. Evidence of the criterion-related validity of the RANRA is presented from the standardization sample in terms of the relationship between RANRA scores and gender (males scored higher than females, $p = .001$) and educational level ($F = 21.81$, $p < .001$). Evidence of the construct validity of the test is presented in the form of a factor analysis showing the test is composed of one overall factor of mathematical reasoning and two subfactors corresponding to the two subtests. In addition, from the standardization sample, the two subtests correlate .53, which is lower than the reliability of either subtest.

SUMMARY. The RANRA assesses two skills that can reasonably be considered important in the selection of managers and those employees who deal with project management and numbers. Little evidence is provided at this time showing the development and validation of the assessment. The technical manual is very thorough in describing how studies should be conducted and how the assessment can be used in a fair and unbiased manner for employee selection.

[216]
Sales Skills Test.

Purpose: Designed "to evaluate the knowledge, skills, and abilities for a sales position."
Population: Adult sales position applicants.
Publication Dates: 2001–2002.
Scores, 6: Sales Principles, Sales Terms, Vocabulary, Sales Comprehension, Sales Situations, Math/Logic & Attention to Detail.
Administration: Individual.
Price Data: Available from publisher.
Time: (65) minutes.
Comments: Scoring available by mail, courier service, fax service, telephone, or "super-fast" fax service.
Author: Bruce Winrow.
Publisher: Walden Personnel Testing and Consulting, Inc. [Canada].

Review of the Sales Skills Test by JoELLEN V. CARLSON, Carlson Consulting, Indian Rocks Beach, FL:

DESCRIPTION. The Sales Skills Test is intended for companies to use in the selection of candidates for sales positions. The publisher claims that the instrument is appropriate for four positions: Sales Clerk, Sales Representative, Store Manager, and District Sales Manager.

The test consists of six timed "problems." Each "problem" is a collection of items testing knowledge or choosing the best course of action, for which the candidate writes responses; there appear to be no items directly measuring sales *skills*. With the exception of a very few items for which the candidate supplies a one-word or one-number response, the item types are multiple-choice, matching, true-false, and sequencing. Some items are not well constructed. The candidate is given the booklet containing all "problems" and instructed to work through at a recommended pace; the time recommended for each "problem" ranges from 5 to 18 minutes.

Before beginning the test, the candidate must sign a disclaimer/release form and consent to the "procedure whereby the organization administering this test will receive the evaluation report derived therefrom" (test booklet, p. 2) but not to the use of the results. It appears that the candidate for a position at a company using the test must grant the *publisher* permission to provide a copy of the evaluation report to other clients of the publisher to whom the candidate may apply for a position in the future; none of the materials describes how this would work.

Along with the test booklet, a test manual and a document entitled, "Content Validation Study" are provided. The test manual provides brief administration directions, recommended testing times, and two sample questions without answers. Nearly two pages are devoted to a sample score report and the options for receiving score reports (e.g., mail, courier, fax, collect call).

The test manual includes an evaluation table (Evaluation Guide) listing score bands (range of percents), a rating (hiring recommendation), and a prediction (which the publisher calls a "recommendation") associated with each (e.g., "Candidate will likely be a below average performer in a sales position.").

Though responses all can be scored objectively, no scoring key is provided. The user must return each test booklet to the publisher for scoring.

DEVELOPMENT. The publisher provides absolutely *no information* on the development of the instrument, either in the print materials provided for this review or on the publisher's website.

TECHNICAL. The publisher provides no acceptable data on psychometric characteristics of the instrument—from the most basic reliability estimates for these "sections" to evidence of content, concurrent, or predictive validity. There is no discussion of how the content basis for the sections or their content was identified. There is no discussion of how the score bands and their accompanying evaluations and "recommendations" were derived.

Accompanying the test and the test manual is a document entitled, "Content Validation Study." This document appears to be a hypothetical case or, at best, a study for a single, disguised company exemplifying what a company would receive if it purchased the "validation study" at a "moderate cost," as advertised in the test manual. Its statements are broad and sketchy at best and are not specific about the personnel or procedures of the "study." Further, the conclusions represent overgeneralizations, such as "the test represents a content valid evaluation device for that position."

Apparently, this "validation" service includes cross-referencing the description of each position for which a company wishes to use this instrument with what the publisher calls the "prime traits evaluated in" the test. The results then indicate the percentage of "essential skills" for a position covered by the test. There are charts indicating a correspondence between items and such skills, but there is no information about how this chart was derived or who contributed to it.

COMMENTARY. Though the publisher indicates that the purpose of this instrument is "to evaluate the knowledge, skills, and abilities for a sales position" (test manual, p. 1), there is no evidence of its acceptability or utility for this purpose. It remains the responsibility of the publisher to provide or point to basic evidence of the utility and defensibility of the instrument and the interpretations to be made of the scores derived from it. This is true regardless of the publisher's desire to sell the service of conducting a study of validity specific to a company that is considering use of the instrument.

SUMMARY. This reviewer cannot recommend the use of this test for any purpose without some evidence of the background of its development and its psychometric properties. Further, if the "Content Validation Study" sample submitted for review is indicative of the procedures that would be followed in conducting such a study for a specific company and the validity claims that would be made, it is questionable how much such a service would contribute to the defensibility of this instrument and its use in making employment decisions.

Review of the Sales Skills Test by PAUL M. MUCHINSKY, Joseph M. Bryan Distinguished Professor of Business, University of North Carolina at Greensboro, Greensboro, NC:

DESCRIPTION. The Sales Skills Test (SST) is designed to evaluate the potential of candidates for sales jobs. It is stated as being appropriate for making personnel selection decisions for specific job titles including sales clerk, sales representative, store manager, and district sales manager. The SST is administered in paper-and-pencil format and has a 65-minute time limit. Six scales are measured by the test: "knowledge of general sales principles, knowledge of sales terms, relevant vocabulary skills, understanding of issues that can affect the sales process, ability to deal with several sales situations, and basic mathematical and calculation skills, as well as logic and attention to detail" (test manual, p. 1). There are various formats to the questions: multiple choice, matching, true/false, fill in the blank, and ranking.

The results of the SST can be returned to the administering organization in four possible time frames: 2–5 days, 24 hours, 8 hours, and 2 hours, depending on cost. The test is available only in the English language.

DEVELOPMENT. The SST was first developed in 2001, and apparently has not been revised. Materials furnished by the publisher are the SST, test manual for the SST, and content validation study of the SST. There is no reference to any theory or other body of work that guided the development of the SST, or how this test compares to similar tests designed with a comparable purpose.

TECHNICAL. A very large amount of technical information regarding the SST is nonexistent. First, no information is provided as to how the correct answers to the questions in three of the six scales (i.e., understanding of issues that can affect the sales process, knowledge of general sales principles, and ability to deal with several sales

situations) were determined. Second, no information is provided as to how the interpretation of the total test score was determined. Four possible interpretations of the total test score are provided by the developer: strongly recommended for hire (85%–100%); recommended (70%–84%); recommended limited use (60%–69%); and not recommended (59% or less). The basis for these cut scores and ranges is unspecified. Third, separate scores are provided for the six scales assessed by the SST, but no information is provided to legitimate compensatory scoring into a total score. Fourth, no narrative information of any nature is provided (either in terms of total score, scale scores, by job, by race or gender of the applicant, etc.). Fifth, no reliability data of any nature are provided. Sixth, no information is presented on the statistical relationships among the six scales. Seventh, no information is provided on the correlation between scores on the SST and any other type of assessment of any kind. Eighth, no information is presented on adverse impact (or the lack thereof). Ninth, no criterion-related validity data of any kind are provided on the SST.

The only basis of validational evidence is a detailed account of how the SST was developed from a content validity perspective. The developer conducted a job analysis of sales jobs; identified the knowledge, skills, and abilities (KSAs) associated with performance in these jobs; and then designed the test to assess these KSAs. Based upon a weighted overlap analysis of the content of the job and the content of the test, the developer concluded that 81% of the content of a sales job is measured by the content of the SST.

COMMENTARY. In my opinion offering content validational evidence to support the use of the SST is an embodiment of the distinction between "doing things right" and "doing the right thing." Without any doubt, the method of content validation described by the developer is a textbook example of how it should be done. The developer is clearly skilled in conducting content validation studies. Indeed, the individual who developed the SST is described as someone who has "conducted several 'content validation' studies for large corporations to ensure EEOC compliance" (Content Validation Study, p. 37). However, sole reliance on content validity is totally inappropriate to justify use of the SST for making personnel selection decisions in sales. Success in sales is best understood at the construct level and is based heavily on dispositional factors such as ambition, tolerance for rejection, interpersonal relations, and social perceptiveness (not just job knowledge). The SST ignores such factors in favor of assessing dimensions of general mental ability (vocabulary and arithmetic) and knowledge of sales-related terminology (e.g., "cold calling"). At its core the SST combines a measure of *g*, sales terminology, and situational job knowledge (with unsubstantiated correct answers). In a classic article Guion (1977) documented the problem with using content validity in lieu of criterion-related validity to substantiate a test's capacity to predict job performance. Knowing the difference between a rebate and a sales quota, for example, is not necessarily predictive of success in sales. Given the complete absence of any criterion-related validity of any kind to support the use of the SST, there is no basis to assume scores on this test are predictive of performance in sales. As such, the justification for using this test is as stated, to help ensure EEOC compliance. The fact there is no evidence the SST actually predicts sales performance is more than trifling.

SUMMARY. There is no empirical evidence whatsoever to justify use of the SST to select applicants who will become successful sales personnel. However, the test may have possible value as a developmental aid for people new to sales. Although the generic vocabulary and arithmetic scales serve no such purpose, the other scales present relevant sales terminology, and pose practical situations a retail sales person might confront with customers. These questions have high face validity and might invite a lively discussion among sales trainees as to the range of possible responses to such situations. It is evident the developer of the SST has considerable knowledge of sales contexts. Such knowledge can be used to help develop sales skills in others. However, mere possession of knowledge and the effective application of that knowledge in sales are not equivalent. Therein lies the problem in using the SST to make personnel selection decisions. Published research indicates it is difficult to accurately predict success in sales. Tests have been developed to do so, with the vast majority providing little or no compelling evidence for their predictive accuracy. The SST is one of them.

REVIEWER'S REFERENCE

Guion, R. M. (1977). Content validity: The source of my discontent. *Applied Psychological Measurement, 1*, 1–10.

[217]

SCAN-C: Test for Auditory Processing Disorders in Children—Revised.

Purpose: Designed to identify children who have auditory processing disorders.
Population: Ages 5-0 to 11-11.
Publication Dates: 1986–1999.
Acronym: SCAN-C.
Scores, 5: Filtered Words, Auditory Figure-Ground, Competing Words, Competing Sentences, Composite.
Administration: Individual.
Price Data, 2002: $149 per kit including 25 record forms, compact disc in a vinyl album, and examiner's manual (2000, 129 pages); $34 per 25 record forms; $58 per examiner's manual.
Time: (30) minutes.
Comments: Formerly called SCAN: A Screening Test for Auditory Processing Disorders.
Author: Robert W. Keith.
Publisher: PsychCorp, A brand of Harcourt Assessment, Inc.
Cross References: See T5:2300 (1 reference); for a review by Sami Gulgoz of an earlier edition, see 11:341 (2 references).

Review of the SCAN-C: Test for Auditory Processing Disorders in Children—Revised by ANNABEL J. COHEN, Professor, Department of Psychology, University of Prince Edward Island, Charlottetown, Prince Edward Island, Canada:

DESCRIPTION. The SCAN-C: Test for Auditory Processing Disorders in Children—Revised presents a battery of four auditory tests by compact disk and headphones to a child whose imitative responses are recorded by the test administrator on a supplied response sheet. Raw scores on the subtests can be transformed to standard scores for comparison with norms for the U.S. population for each of the ages of 5 through to 11 years (ages 10 and 11 years combined). A composite score is also generated with an associated standard score. Because some of the tests are dichotic, raw measures of ear asymmetry are obtained, and these can be transformed into a standard score for which norms are provided. Standard scores below the normal range are suggestive of an auditory processing disorder. The SCAN-C is generally used in conjunction with other tests rather than for definitive diagnosis on its own. Additional behavioral and electrophysiological tests can be administered for further clarification.

The test manual recommends administration by a professional experienced with auditory testing. However, given the detailed instructions in the manual and the ease of use of the test materials on the CD, nonclinical staff could potentially administer, score, and interpret the test assuming they had the skills to communicate with children and particularly with children having communication or behavioral problems, learning disorders, or low IQ. Once the test is administered, it is a simple matter to total the scores.

DEVELOPMENT. The SCAN-C Revised is the latest version for children of the more general SCAN test that has been under development since 1986. The present version is an advance over the former in several respects. The test including instructions is presented via a compact disc (CD) player. A CD does not degrade with use as does an audiotape, and quality is typically higher for digital than analogue playback machines, other than the most professional. It is claimed that instructions are more appropriate to children than the previous version, and the Competing Words subtest is reduced in length. The previous SCAN had only three subtests. The SCAN-C Revised adds a test of Competing Sentences.

Subtests 1 to 4 represent increasing complexity of the auditory material presented, moving from identification of single filtered words that one might encounter on a small audio-electronic device like a portable telephone, to auditory figure-ground in which words are heard against background speaker babble, to dichotically presented words, and then dichotically presented sentences. These are situations similar to those that children might face in everyday life.

For the Filtered Words test, the child is asked to repeat a word of one syllable presented binaurally and lacking low frequency acoustic information below 1000 Hz. For the Auditory Figure-Ground test, the child must repeat a word of one syllable presented binaurally against a background of babbling. For the Competing Words test, the child is asked to repeat a pair of words presented dichotically, that is, simultaneously, a different word in each ear. First the child is asked to focus attention on the right ear and to repeat the word that arrives there first, followed by the word presented to the left ear. On a subsequent list of words, the child is asked to repeat the word first that arrives in the left ear. For the Competing Sentences test, simultaneous sentences replace the single words. The child is asked again to focus on

one sentence at a time, but to repeat the sentence arriving at the attended ear, ignoring completely the sentence in the other ear.

Materials furnished in the SCAN-C kit include the compact disc, record forms, and the examiner's manual. The manual is generally straightforward. Certainly the guidelines for administering and scoring the tests are clear. As well, it is noted that below average performance on this test, as with any behavioral test, can arise from factors unrelated to the auditory system (e.g., poor concentration, anxiety disorders, and memory disorders). The manual provides guidelines for distinguishing between central auditory processing disorder (CAPD) and Attention Deficit Hyperactivity Disorder (ADHD).

TECHNICAL.

Item construction. Words and sentences are the same as those in the adolescent/adult version of the test, SCAN-A (T6:2190); however, all of the words and sentences originate in other standardized sources in the literature (full references are given in the manual). One sentence was adjusted as a result of feedback from an expert reviewer. The materials were recorded professionally with high quality equipment. Before making the final CD recording, two expert reviewers provided feedback on all aspects of the test, and several changes, such as clarification of instructions and number of practice items, were made as a result.

Standardization. Standardization on 650 children between the ages of 5 years 0 months and 11 years 11 months took place over a period of 10 months. The sample was stratified by age, gender, race/ethnicity, region, and parent education level in accordance with demographic percentages based on the 1997 U.S. Census for the age range examined. Only those children were included who could take the test in English, could speak without articulation errors, and had normal audiometric results for the tones 500, 1000, 2000, and 4000 Hz.

Normative data are reported at 1-year intervals for ages 5 through 9 years, with one combined group for the ages of 10 and 11 years. Raw scores on each of the subtests for the standardized sample systematically increase for each age. These data are consistent with the maturing of the auditory system, but they are also consistent with generally improving test-taking skills.

Standard scores for each of the six child age groups were derived from the distribution of scores from the four subtests. These were normalized by converting the percentile rank associated with each raw score to a normalized z score. These z scores were then converted to subtest standard scores with a mean of 10 and a standard deviation of 3, resulting in a range of standard scores from 1 to 19. Composite standard scores were also developed using a distribution of the scores created by summing the four subtest standard scores leading ultimately to standard scores with a mean of 100 and standard deviation of 15.

Reliability estimates included test-retest and internal consistency, the latter using coefficient alpha. In both cases the results for the composite score provided acceptable levels of reliability ($>.80$) whereas the subtests generally did not. This was true for the test-retest reliability on all but one subtest; however, for the Competing Words subtest, for all ages the reliability coefficients for internal consistency were $>.85$ with the exception of the 10–11-year-olds. Also regarding internal consistency, Filtered Words produced one reliability coefficient $>.80$, and two were produced by Competing Sentences. In general, performance on the subtests is not highly reliable, although performance on the composite is.

Criterion validity was measured by comparing scores of 80 children on the original SCAN with their scores on SCAN-C. For some unspecified reason, the administration of the original SCAN tests used well-worn audiocassettes, up to 12 years of usage, which, as the manual claims, may have deteriorated over time and added to the noise. Unfortunately, means are not provided, only the correlations between the three SCAN scores and composite with the four SCAN-C scores and composite. All correlations are below .80 and run as low as .19 for SCAN Filtered Words with SCAN-C Competing Sentences. More encouraging is the correlation of the two Composite scores, which is .79.

To examine discriminant validity, SCAN-C was administered to 144 children, covering the standardization age range, who were suspected of a central auditory processing disorder (CAPD). Each possible CAPD child was matched for age, gender, and race/ethnicity with a member of the standardization sample. IQ was not measured. For the CAPD group, mean performance was significantly lower for all subtest scores and the composite score. The manual states "You could then conclude that this test is a good measure of audi-

tory processing skills" (p. 82). However, other factors have not been ruled out such as other types of disorders that may have characterized the so-called CAPD group, IQ differences, and test-taking skills.

In support of the provision of content validity, a rationale is provided for the inclusion of the four subtests based on what other researchers have said about the value of similar tests to measuring CAPD. Support here is weakest for the Competing Sentences test, which is arguably not a precognitive test in view of the benefits of grammatical analysis, analysis of word and sentence meaning, exploitation of contextual meaning, and memory strategies.

Five case studies are provided that use several other tests of CAPD among other verbal and behavioral tests. These profiles will be of interest to users of the test. The provision of the multiple tests provides an example of what might be expected for future sources of evidence of the validity of the SCAN-C. As it is, the subtest reliability and the construct validity are not the strongest aspects of the SCAN-C, and of greater value is the ability to obtain quickly some results on auditory processing that can be compared with national norms for particular chronological ages.

COMMENTARY. As with any test construct, defining the construct of auditory processing disorders is a challenging problem. Auditory processing includes all of hearing really, but the SCAN-C test is designed to establish evidence for hearing problems that are not associated with basic hearing sensitivity: when sound gets in but meaning does not. On the surface, SCAN-C, as an imitative test, has nothing to do with meaning. Meaning is never tested, at least not directly. In theory, a child who did not understand English but had reasonable command of English phonology could do well on the test. All that is required is to repeat the sounds that were heard. However, understanding English is, in fact, a likely implicit requirement of doing well on the test. Being able to repeat the words most likely means that the words were understood. Yet the SCAN-C aims to assess the "primary reception" (or perception) stage of precognitive auditory processing. However, the tests are not precognitive if the child cannot help but benefit from linguistic encoding. Until such a time as the construct of auditory processing disorder is clearly delineated, tests of the disorder will always face a problem of construct validity. Nevertheless, by providing norms, such tests as SCAN-

C do a great service by giving guidelines as to normal development of the particular auditory processing skills that are examined.

The manual is confusing on several points, fortunately none of which interferes with the execution or scoring of the tests. The first concerns the relation between SCAN and SCAN-C Revised. It is clear that SCAN came first but it is unclear whether the SCAN-C Revised came directly from SCAN or whether there was an intermediary SCAN-C. Reference is obliquely made to SCAN-A. A paragraph on the relation between SCAN-C and SCAN-A would have been welcome. Clarification of what "Revised" refers to is also needed.

A further confusion surrounds the inconsistent use of terminology to describe the construct of interest. Presumably this is auditory processing disorders, but we cannot be sure because considerable reference is made to central auditory processing disorders (CAPD).

A distinction is made between precognitive and cognitive processing. Keith argues that his tests are of the precognitive processes; confusion enters again with the rationale for the competing sentences test, which allows a comparison of "findings obtained with both simple and more complex linguistic levels of auditory stimuli" (manual, p. 4). Surely processing of linguistic complexity entails cognitive processes. The manual refers to "central nervous system disease" (p. 68) that may be related to a "reduced ability to respond to auditory information from both ears." It is unclear what "central nervous system disease" means here, because surely central auditory processes are part of the central nervous system, or are they meant to be exempt from this particular ailment?

Another confusion arises from the use of the terms "development of the auditory system, and auditory maturation" in a list of abilities reflected by the Competing Words and Competing Sentences subtests. Yet another unclear distinction is that between an auditory system that is "disordered" versus one that is "damaged" (manual, p. 62).

CONCLUSION. Quite independent of any issues regarding the construct of central auditory processing, one great value of SCAN-C is in Keith's (the author) words that "SCAN-C results can help you to identify how a particular child's pattern of auditory skills compares to a national sample of children" (manual, p. 54). The tasks of the four subtests resemble real-life situations of extracting speech information in noise. Identification of abnormal performance is a first step to diagnosis, management, and remediation. A second important benefit is that the tests can be administered to children, even to some children as young as 3 years of age. Thus, if a problem is suspected early on, information beyond simple observation is available. Especially because of early brain plasticity, catching problems early may have great lifelong benefit. Twenty-five minutes with SCAN-C is time well spent for both the child and the test administrator. Simplification and clarification of the theoretical part of the manual is recommended for a next revision and reports of tests of convergent and discriminant validity are needed.

Review of the SCAN-C: Test for Auditory Processing Disorders in Children—Revised by JACLYN B. SPITZER, Professor, Clinical Professor of Clinical Audiology and Speech Pathology in Otolaryngology/Head and Neck Surgery, Columbia University College of Physicians and Surgeons, New York, NY and ABBEY L. BERG, Assistant Professor, Department of Communication Studies, Pace University, New York, NY and Assistant Professor of Clinical Audiology and Speech Pathology in Otolaryngology/ Head and Neck Surgery, Columbia University College of Physicians and Surgeons, New York, NY:

DESCRIPTION. The purpose of this test is to identify children between the ages of 5.0 years and 11.11 years suspected of having a perceptive-type auditory processing dysfunction. The four subtests of the SCAN-C—Revised include Filtered Words, Auditory Figure-Ground, Competing Words, and Competing Sentences. The addition of the Competing Sentences subtest is new to this edition. The tasks require the ability to repeat words and sentences. The test can be administered in approximately 25 minutes and scored in 10 minutes. Raw and composite standard scores, percentile ranks, and cumulative prevalence of ear advantage (Competing Words only) are easily computed. The SCAN-C was designed to address and correct problems found in the previous edition. Specifically, instructions given to children are simplified for ease of understanding, a CD is used to eliminate inherent noise present in audiocassettes, and the normed sample better represents the population in terms of geographic region, gender, and race/ethnicity. The test is intended to be used by speech-language pathologists, audiologists, neuropsychologists, and other qualified specialists familiar with concepts of test administration and interpretation.

DEVELOPMENT. The SCAN-C was developed to describe multiple perceptive auditory processing abilities. The Filtered Words and Auditory Figure-Ground subtests examine the child's ability to perceive speech in a distorted condition or in the presence of background noise. The Competing Words and Competing Sentences subtests are dichotic listening tasks that examine the child's ability to understand competing speech signals assessing ear advantage, auditory maturation, and hemispheric dominance for language. Both degraded speech and dichotic measurements are accepted assessments for identification of dysfunction in the auditory nervous system.

TECHNICAL. Data were collected and participants were recruited according to geographic regions, gender, race/ethnicity, and parent education level reflective of the U.S. 1997 Census of Population Update. The 114 examiners who participated in the standardization and validation studies included speech-language pathologists, audiologists, and audiology graduate students. Examiners were given detailed instructions and procedures for the administration and scoring of tests. Trained personnel at The Psychological Corporation reviewed for accuracy practice cases administered by examinees.

RELIABILITY. Thorough standardization data are included in the manual. Cronbach's alpha was used to estimate internal consistency coefficients: Reliability coefficients ranged between .56 (for Auditory Figure-Ground) and .89 (for Competing Words) for the subtests and between .86 and .92 for the composite standard scores. These reliability coefficients indicate that the SCAN-C should be administered in its entirety, rather than to rely on any one individual subtest. Subtest test-retest reliability (time interval: 2 days–6 weeks; mean 6.5 days) ranged from .65–.82 for 5- to 7-year-olds and .67–.78 for 8–11-year-olds, acceptable for clinical repeated measures. Standard error of means ranged from .99 (for Competing Words) to 1.99 (for Auditory Figure-Ground); these values are clinically acceptable.

VALIDITY. Content and construct validity procedures are well described, referenced, and documented. Both the SCAN-C and SCAN were administered to 80 children. Data collected included age, gender, and race/ethnicity diversity. A correlation of .79 was found between the SCAN-C composite standard score and SCAN composite standard score, which is clinically acceptable. Construct validity was evaluated by discriminant analysis on 144 children with documented auditory processing dysfunction to a matched group (age, gender, race/ethnicity) of children not diagnosed with an auditory processing dysfunction and not receiving special education services. Mean scores were lower for children diagnosed with auditory processing dysfunction compared to the control group of children, suggesting that the SCAN-C is a valid measure of perceptive auditory processing skills.

COMMENTARY. The test manual is exceptionally clear, well-organized, and well-written. Instructions for test administration are user friendly. It is important to note that proper instrumentation and calibration are essential to accurate test administration. An audiologist would use a two-channel audiometer with CD player. Other professionals would be able to use the test with a CD player with stereo earphones. Control of ambient noise is essential.

SUMMARY. The SCAN-C meets the requirements purported—speed and ease of presentation, high internal consistency, and test-retest reliability. The discriminant analysis and use in clinical settings indicates that it has high hit, low miss, and low false alarm rates. The SCAN-C is a test that would add useful information about the perceptive auditory processing abilities in children between the ages of 5.0 to 11.11 years when used in conjunction with other neurologic, behavioral auditory processing, and electrophysiologic measures.

[218]

School Social Behavior Scales, Second Edition.

Purpose: Designed to "evaluate social competence and antisocial behavior of children and youth."
Population: Grades K–12.
Publication Dates: 1993–2002.
Acronym: SBSS-2.
Scores, 8: Social Competence Scale (Peer Relations, Self-Management/Compliance, Academic Behavior, Social Competence Total), Antisocial Behavior Scale (Hostile/Irritable, Antisocial/Aggressive, Defiant/Disruptive, Antisocial Behavior Total).
Administration: Individual.
Price Data, 2002: $34 per 25 rating forms; $47 per user's guide (2002, 114 pages).

Time: (8–10) minutes.
Comments: Companion to Home and Community Social Behavior Scales (107); rated by teachers or other school personnel.
Author: Kenneth W. Merrell.
Publisher: Assessment-Intervention Resources.
Cross References: For reviews by Stephen R. Hooper and Lesley A. Welsh of a previous edition, see 13:277 (2 references); see also T4:2369 (1 reference).

Review of the School Social Behavior Scales, Second Edition by ROSEMARY FLANAGAN, Assistant Professor/Director, Masters Program in School Psychology, Adelphi University, Garden City, NY:

DESCRIPTION. The School Social Behavior Scales, Second Edition (SSBS-2) is a 64-item, norm-referenced, standardized instrument developed to be used by school personnel to rate the social competence and antisocial behavior of youth aged 5–18. A companion instrument, the Home and Community Social Behavior Scales (107; HCSBS; Lund & Merrell, 2001), is used to evaluate home behavior; together these scales comprise the Social Behavior Scales, a cross-informant rating system. Particular uses include functional behavior assessment and the linking of assessment to intervention.

The SSBS-2 is composed of two scales: Social Competence and Antisocial Behavior. The Social Competence Scale is composed of 32 items rated on a 5-point scale; higher scores indicate greater social competence. There are three subscales: Peer Relations, Self-Management/Compliance, and Academic Behavior. The Antisocial Behavior Scale is a 32-item scale, divided into three subscales: Hostile/Irritable, Antisocial/Aggressive, and Defiant/Disruptive. Similarly, the items are rated on a 5-point scale, with higher scores indicating greater tendency to antisocial behaviors. The items in the scales are believed to rate peer-related and adult-related social adjustment.

Administration and scoring are straightforward. The rater can complete the scales in 8–10 minutes. The overall scales are each printed on separate inside pages of the four-page record form. The directions on the record form are clear and the scoring summary should be self-explanatory to individuals familiar with similar behavior rating scales; details for completing the form are clearly explained in the manual. Noteworthy is that all items must be completed to produce a valid record; procedures for dealing with missing data are explained in the manual.

Interpretation procedures are outlined in the manual, and are conceptually similar to those commonly used in the field. Interpretation is made by first examining T-scores and percentiles, followed by the social functioning levels that the scores correspond to, followed by item analysis.

DEVELOPMENT. The SSBS-2 is an updated version of the SSBS (Merrell, 1993). Additional cases were added to the norming sample for the SSBS to create the current sample (2,280 youth). This was done to make the norms for the SSBS-2 more comparable to the U.S. population and to those for the HCSBS, by having the ratings made by school personnel and parents for a common group of youth. A few items were rewritten for the second edition, to better coincide with the concurrently developed HCSBS. The connection between the norming samples, as well as this rationale, is not well explained, although it is clearly desirable to have common norming samples. The new normative sample is more diverse so as to reflect the Year 2000 U.S. Census data, and is oversampled in regard to special education students. Among the norming variables are race/ethnicity, socioeconomic status, gender, dwelling area, school setting, and grade level.

The number of youth at each grade level from K–12 is uneven. There is minimal variation in raw scores over the age span of the instrument. The author indicates there is no compelling reason to have separate norms for males and females, and reports the data at each age level for both genders to make the point. There is admission, however, that the genders score somewhat differently on the two major scales, possibly due to societal expectations. For this reason, one set of norms for both genders is used to limit errors. The normative sample was split, however, into two groups for the development of separate norms for Grades K–6 and 7–12. T-scores and percentile ranks are available for the total scores on Social Competence and Antisocial Behavior, as well as each respective subscale. For Social Competence and its subscales, scores at the 5th percentile or lower are considered *high risk*; scores at the 80th percentile and above are considered *high functioning*. For Antisocial Behavior and its subscales, scores below the 80th percentile are considered *average*, scores between the 18th and 94th percentiles are considered *at risk*, and scores at or above the 95th percentile are *high risk*. Although cutting scores are not parallel, the divisions seem appropriate to limit the possibility of false positives as well as false negatives.

TECHNICAL. Reliability is reported in terms of internal consistency, test-retest, and interrater reliabilities. Internal consistency is strong and is reported as coefficient alpha (.94–.98) as well as split-half (.91–.97) reliabilities for the entire sample of 2,280 youth. Test-retest reliability estimates at a 1-week interval ranged from .86–.94 for the subscales; at a 3-week interval, this decreased (.68–.82). The data are difficult to interpret because different subsamples were used. Interpreter reliability is high, ranging from .55–.82 for the subscales, with stronger agreement for subscales measuring aspects of social competence rather than antisocial behavior. Although informative, the ratings reflect differing relationships and circumstances. Nevertheless, the SSBS-2 demonstrates acceptable reliability on the basis of several types of evidence.

Several types of validity evidence are presented: evidence based on test content, internal structure, the relationship to other measures (i.e., construct validity), and group separation. Content validity was demonstrated on the basis of item-whole correlations, ranging from .60–.87 for the subscales and from .78–.90 for the total scores, which exceed the criteria of .25–.30 suggested by Salvia and Ysseldyke (2000). Construct validity was examined by exploratory and confirmatory factor analysis. Noteworthy is that some subscale names were changed from the first edition to better represent the content and to be consistent with the HCSBS. For a subset of normative data, three-factor solutions for both Social Competence and Antisocial Behavior were found. Data from a second sample were analyzed and the result was replicated. Confirmatory factor analysis was conducted for a number of models; the best fit was observed for a three-factor solution for each scale. Intercorrelation among scales indicates that interpretation according to two main scales is appropriate.

Data reported in the manual show the relationships between the SSBS-2 and several measures that assess similar constructs. Correlations between the SSBS-2 subscales and the Conners' Teacher Rating Scale (CTRS-39; Conners, 1990) and the Child Behavior Checklist (CBCL; Achenbach, 1991), among others, are in the expected directions. Considerable data are reported for several samples at different age levels, demonstrating evidence of convergent and discriminant

validity. Other evidence includes correlations with behavioral observations and sociometric data, and group separation data based on educational status (gifted, special education). The treatment utility of the instrument is promising, as it was used to successfully evaluate an anger management program as well as a prevention program.

COMMENTARY. There is no mention in the manual of the possibility of cohort effects negatively impacting the normative sample. Although the manual initially describes the instrument as theory-based, it is later stated in the manual that the SSBS-2 is literature-driven, which is more accurate. Technical properties of the scale are adequate, and the author attends to detail sufficiently so others may evaluate the statistical treatment of the data. Of concern is that the names of the scales appear on the fourth page of the record form, as part of the scoring summary. Respondents might be less than forthright, as clearly desirable and undesirable behaviors are rated.

SUMMARY. The SSBS-2 is similar to the first edition. The main purposes for the development of a new edition were to revise the scale to have a greater similarity to a companion rating form (HCSBS) for home behavior and to have some comparability in the norming samples. Psychometric properties are adequate. Although use of the instrument seems appropriate for research purposes and to evaluate the effectiveness of interventions, its use for diagnostic purposes seems premature. The main advantage over an omnibus measure of social and behavioral functioning is that the measure is briefer.

REVIEWER'S REFERENCES
Achenbach, T. M. (1991). *Child Behavior Checklist for ages 5-18.* Burlington, VT: Center for Children, Youth and Families, University of Vermont Department of Psychiatry.
Conners, C. K. (1990). *Manual for the Conners' Rating Scales.* North Tonawanda, NY: Multi-Health Systems.
Lund, J., & Merrell, K. W. (2001). Social and antisocial behavior of children with learning and behavior disorders: Construct validity of the Home and Community Social Behavior Rating Scales. *Journal of Psychoeducational Assessment, 19,* 112–122.
Merrell, K. W. (1993). *School Social Behavior Scales.* Eugene, OR: Assessment Intervention Resources.
Salvia, J. & Ysseldyke, J. E. (2001). *Assessment* (8th ed.). Boston: Houghton-Mifflin.

Review of the School Social Behavior Scales, Second Edition by MICHAEL J. FURLONG, Professor of Counseling/Clinical/School Psychology, and ALICIA SOLIZ, Doctoral Student, Counseling/Clinical/School Psychology, University of California—Santa Barbara, Santa Barbara, CA:

DESCRIPTION. The School Social Behavior Scale, Second Edition (SSBS-2) is a teacher-completed rating scale to assess the social competence and antisocial behavior of children and youth ages 5–18. It represents a minor modification of the original SSBS. These changes were undertaken with the development of a new companion instrument, Home and Community Social Behavior Scales (HCSBS; see 107), which provides assessment across school, home, and community settings. The SSBS-2 is used to (a) identify children and youth who are behaviorally at-risk; (b) identify, classify, and determine service eligibility for children and youth with significant social skills deficits and antisocial behavior problems; (c) assess social skill deficiencies and antisocial behavior problems to develop appropriate interventions; (d) monitor child and adolescent behavior change during the course of an intervention, as well as evaluate the effectiveness of the intervention; and (e) research the social-behavioral characteristics and patterns of children and youth.

Users of the SSBS-2 may find it confusing that the manual has a tendency to refer to early SSBS studies and related information by using the new SSBS-2 label. The reader must carefully examine the manual to distinguish updated information from old information that is mislabeled as involving the SSBS-2 version.

DEVELOPMENT. An understanding of the context and sequence of revision of the original SSBS should be kept in mind when examining the manual. The SSBS was originally published in 1993 by PRO-ED. In 1998, the author began the development of the companion HCSBS and simultaneously sought to enhance the SSBS. Based on previous research and experience, the author made minor modifications—a few minor item wording changes were made and one item was dropped. This resulted in a 64-item scale with 32 items each in the Social Competence and Antisocial Behavior domains.

Once these minor changes were made, the author tackled a more pressing matter—the original norm sample had inadequate representation of the students across sociocultural groups. With the intention of selecting student to match population patterns, 158 cases from the original norm sample were dropped and 580 cases were added producing an SSBS-2 norm sample of 2,280 students. This sample was more representative of the U.S.A. student population, but oversampled students in special education programs (22.3% vs. 12.8% in U.S.A.; in fact, 272 of the 580 new cases were

from special education classes). A notable oversight is that the author does not point out that the SSBS-2 also oversampled males (1,203 males to 1,077 females); however, there are 180 fourth-grade females compared to 100 fourth-grade males. This is important because the manual presents analyses showing that females obtained significantly higher scores on the Social Competence domain total score and that males obtained higher scores on the Antisocial Behavior domain total score. No rationale is provided for this oversampling of males, and despite these significant gender differences, separate norm tables are not provided for males and females (on this matter also see a review of the SSBS by Kreisler, Mangione, & Landau, 1997). Curiously, norm tables are provided for Grades K–6 and 7–12 even when the analysis indicates that there were no significant age-related differences. The author suggests that the rationale for not providing separate gender norms is that it may overidentify females and underidentify males as having social adjustment problems. Such an approach is at odds with all other similar social skill and antisocial behavior rating scales.

TECHNICAL CONSIDERATIONS. The SSBS-2 builds on a solid research record supporting its psychometric properties and, in many regards, it provides a model of the breadth of information that should be included in any test manual. However, the SSBS-2 manual mixes information about the original SSBS and the SSBS-2 in such a manner that it is at times difficult to assess what is new information about this instrument.

Reliability. The internal consistency indices of the SSBS-2 are updated; however, all other reliability information is taken from studies using the SSBS, even if mislabeled in the manual. For the Social Competence and Antisocial Behavior domain scales, the alpha and split-half reliability coefficients were substantial, ranging from .96 to .98 across the three samples (for both Grades K–6 and 7–12). Several SSBS studies reported in the manual evaluated the test-retest reliability over 1-week (students in Grades 1–5, range: .86–.94) and 3-week intervals (middle school students, range: .60–.83). Interrater reliability information was obtained using ratings obtained from special education resource room teachers and paraprofessional classroom aides of 40 elementary-age students (Grades 2–6) with learning disabilities. The coefficients across raters ranged from .72 to .86 on the Social Competence scales, and from .53 to .71 on the Antisocial Behavior scale scores. These reliability coefficients are favorable, although the 3-week stability coefficients seem low given the types of behaviors being assessed.

Validity. Previous SSBS validity studies are presented in some detail and they demonstrate the substantial effort made by the author to gather evidence about validity. For the updated SSBS-2 version most of the new validity information involves content and construct validity analyses.

To assess the content validity of the SSBS-2, correlations between individual items and their respective domain total scores (Social Competence or Antisocial Behavior) and subscale scores were determined. The item-total correlations for the Social Competence Scale ranged from .62 to .86, and the item-subscale correlations ranged from .78 to .90. The item-total correlations for the Antisocial Behavior scale ranged from .60 to .87, and the item-subscale correlations ranged from .78 to .90. These construct validity coefficients are impressive. It would also help if the author would provide information about the item-to-other-subscale correlations. There is some evidence that the subscales tap into highly correlated behavioral domains and additional information showing how specific items correlated with out-of-subscale total scores would aid interpretation. For example, some of the Antisocial Behavior domain items appear to be mirror opposites of Social Competence domain items (e.g., Social Competence Item 31, "Shows self-control," and Antisocial Behavior Item 30, "Acts impulsively without thinking"). In addition, at least at the face validity level, it is unclear why some Social Management/Compliance items (e.g., Item 12, "Is accepting of other students" and Item 1, "Cooperates with other students") do not load on the first subscale (Peer Relations). More detailed information about out-of-subscale item characteristics would aid interpretation and research.

Separate exploratory factor analyses of the original SSBS Social Competence and Antisocial Behavior domains produced factor solutions with three subscales within each domain. The first Social Competence factor (Interpersonal Skills and renamed Peer Relations in the SSBS-2) accounted for 59.1% of the variance, the second factor (Self-Management and renamed Self-Management/Compliance) accounted for 6.7% of the variance, and the third factor (Academic Skills and renamed

Academic Behavior) accounted for 5.9% of the variance. The first Antisocial Behavior domain factor (Hostile/Irritable) accounted for 61.4% of the variance, the second factor (Antisocial/ Aggressive) accounted for 4.7% of the variance, and the third factor (Disruptive/Demanding and renamed Defiant/Disruptive in the SSBS-2) accounted for 3.6% of the variance. These exploratory factor analysis results show that the first factor in each domain, by far, accounts for the bulk of the interitem variation. Given that the author suggests that the total scores themselves provide the most salient information to be taken from the SSBS, and given the substantial intersubscale correlations, it would be of interest to further explore the viability of a brief unidimensional domain instrument (with no subscales) that could be used for research and program evaluation purposes.

The SSBS-2 manual adds important new validity information by presenting construct validity analyses using exploratory and confirmatory factor analyses (CFA), which are based on previous analyses of the SSBS and a CFA with a preliminary subset of the SSBS-2 norm sample. The presentation of these analyses is incomplete in an otherwise very detailed manual presentation. The item-subscale, item-total domain scale, and factor loadings for all six subscales are presented, but cross-factor loadings are not. This is important because the author acknowledges that there were some double-loaded items, yet these were retained in the instrument and are not specifically identified. Furthermore, the exploratory factor analyses used orthogonal rotation, even though subsequent information shows that the intersubscale correlations were all substantial (r = .76–.86). Such a condition would typically argue for an oblique rotation factor solution. Furthermore, why the CFA analyses did not include the final norm sample of 2,280 is not explained. The information presented indicates that several alternative models were tested; however, these models are not shown and it is unclear if a model was tested that controlled for the substantial intersubscale correlations. Such information is needed in future research.

COMMENTARY. The SSBS-2 provides conormed information about positive and challenging student behaviors, which is unique for a school-based scale. However, as the author acknowledges, any instrument is constantly in a state of development and the SSBS-2 can be enhanced by further research.

In the tradition of rating scale development, the SSBS-2 has strong internal reliability characteristics. However, as is the custom among developers of rating scale instruments, the data are gathered for a sample of students, some of whom are rated by the same teacher. Thus, although the total number of individual student ratings is substantial, the manual provides no information regarding the number of teachers who actually provided these ratings, although in a previously published SSBS study, it was mentioned that 688 teachers provided ratings of three students (first, middle, or last three on their class list; Merrell, 1993). To the extent that data were gathered by having the same teacher rate multiple students in her or his class, then the manual should include information about who the raters were, how they were selected, and which students in the class were rated. Such information is needed to better understand any potential source bias in the ratings obtained.

A second major aspect of future research should focus on completing confirmatory factor analyses with independent, diverse samples of students. Such analyses should provide detailed information about the type of factor analysis completed and comparative indices for all models tested. Without such analysis, users of the SSBS-2 may want to heed the author's own suggestion to interpret only the two total domain scores and not the six subscale scores.

SUMMARY. Given the increasing demands being placed on schools to assess the social, emotional, and character development of students, the SSBS-2 is one of the better empirically validated instruments available. Along with the Social Skills Rating System (T6:2321) it is an instrument of choice to use when school-based behavior is the focus of interest (Demaray, Ruffalo, & Carlson, 1995). The SSBS-2 author recognizes the need for additional research to be conducted and has created a web site to provide updated information to support research and school-based program evaluation projects.

REVIEWERS' REFERENCES

Demaray, M. K., Ruffalo, S. L., & Carlson, J. (1995). Social skills assessment: A comparative evaluation of six published rating scales. *School Psychology Review, 24,* 648–671.

Kreisler, T. A., Mangione, C., & Landau, S. (1997). Review of the School Social Behavior Scales. *Journal of Psychoeducational Assessment, 15,* 182–190.

Merrell, K. W. (1993). Using behavior rating scales to assess social skills and antisocial behavior in school settings: Development of the School Social Skills Behavior Scales. *School Psychology Review, 22,* 115–133.

[219]
Science Assessment Series 1 and 2.

Purpose: Designed to assist teachers in "checking children's understanding of the science taught" during primary and secondary education.
Publication Date: 2001.
Administration: Group.
Levels, 2: Series 1, Series 2.
Price Data: Available from publisher.
Comments: Designed to correspond to the national curricula of England and Wales, Northern Ireland, and Scotland.
Authors: Terry Russell and Linda McGuigan.
Publisher: NFER-Nelson Publishing Co., Ltd. [England].
a) SCIENCE ASSESSMENT SERIES 1.
Population: Ages 5–9.
Scores: 5 subtest units: Humans and Other Animals, Planets, Materials, Light and Sound, Electricity and Forces.
Time: (45) minutes per unit.
b) SCIENCE ASSESSMENT SERIES 2.
Population: Ages 8–13.
Scores: 8 subtest units: Humans and Other Animals, Planets, Living Things in the Environment, Materials, Changing Materials, Electricity, Light and Sound, Forces and the Earth and Beyond.
Time: (45) minutes per unit.

Review of the Science Assessment Series 1 and 2 by BRUCE G. ROGERS, Professor Emeritus of Education, University of Northern Iowa, Cedar Falls, IA:

DESCRIPTION. The Science Assessment Series 1 and 2, (abbreviated in the teacher's guide, and in this review, as the Series) was developed in England for the express purpose of "checking children's understanding of science" (teacher's guide, p. 5), according to the authors of the Series. (Quotes in this review are from the Teacher's Guide, Series 1, hereafter referred to as the "manual," and identified by page number.) The terminology is thus reflective of Great Britain (including Wales, Northern Ireland, and Scotland). In U.S. terminology, the Series are appropriate for Grades K through 8 and are designed to be given "at any point" within that grade span. Because good teachers and science educators continually emphasize the need for understanding basic scientific concepts, there is a need for appropriate instruments to focus on those cognitive skills. The two authors of the Series emphasize the value of giving feedback to both teachers and pupils to help improve teacher pedagogy and pupil learning of generalizable constructs.

Scientific constructs have been studied by science educators to determine which ones are most appropriate at what grade in the school curriculum. Because England has a National Curriculum, the Series reflects those concepts. Although there is no official national curriculum in the U.S., science educators will see that the units of the Series are basically compatible with the science curriculum of any good school, and any good science textbook sequence.

DESCRIPTION. Series 1, which has a suggested age range of 5 through 9 years, is composed of five units, entitled: Humans and Other Animals, Plants, Materials, Light and Sound, and Electricity and Forces. Series 2 covers these same units, plus three more: Forces and the Earth, Living Things, and Changing Materials. The objective type items are multiple-choice and matching, using both words and pictures. By asking the student to draw lines to connect pictures, many variations of these forms are created. The nonobjective-type items require a response ranging from a single word to a complete sentence. Each unit is scored with a maximum of 30 points, but there are between 11 and 19 items, with some items receiving up to 3 points. Teachers are expected to administer each unit following the teaching of the corresponding material. Each unit was designed to include questions covering science processes, knowledge and comprehension, and conceptual probes. There are no time limits, although the authors estimate a 45-minute average time.

DEVELOPMENT. Unfortunately, the teacher's guide (manual) provides no information about the actual development of the Series, other than to say that the "tests were developed in response to a specific need identified by teachers. They asked for a means of checking children's understanding of the science taught at any point during primary and early secondary education" (p. 5). Because no further information is given, it is probably safe to assume that the Series were designed, and the items were written, by the two authors alone. Although there are many drawings and photographs, one must assume that the authors worked alone, because no credit is given to others. The authors state that the "Series are designed to span key stages 1 and 2 of the National Curriculum for England and Wales" (p. 5) but no further information is given. It would be useful if extended explanations could be made available in future editions.

TECHNICAL.
Standardization. The authors arranged for Series 1 to be administered to a group of about 1,800 pupils during a 3-year period. Series 2 was given to about 2,000 pupils. For each of the units, the mean, standard deviation, and coefficient alpha were reported. For each unit, the mean for boys and girls was reported. This constituted the entire report of the data, without any reports for age or grade level.

Reliability. The Cronbach alpha values ranged from .72 to .89. The standard error of measurement was reported to be "consistently around 2.0" (p. 71). Because there appears to be only one form of the test, alternate form reliability was not possible to obtain. It should be noted that the Cronbach alpha procedure was used because many of the items were constructed for the awarding of up to 2 or 3 points. Because the items that were nonobjective required a judgment to assign points, it would be useful to have an estimate of interrater reliability. Unfortunately, there is no mention of this in the manual. Potential users of the Series could have more confidence in the reliability estimates if the authors had reported who did the scoring of the tests, classroom teachers or others, and had arranged for some estimate of expected interrater reliability of the scoring.

Because the reliability data were not reported by grade or age, the reported reliability values may be artificially inflated. No mention was made of conformity to any technical standards, and thus the reported reliability values cannot be compared with the values from other standardized tests for which reports follow technical standards.

Validity. Unfortunately, no evidence of any type was given in the manual for validity. This reviewer suggests that the publisher assemble a panel of educators to analyze the items and make judgments about content validity. Data could be gathered from both teachers and students relating to the "face validity" of the Series. Correlation with other measures of science achievement would also be appropriate to give evidence of concurrent and predictive validity.

Norms. The previously mentioned data of means and standard deviations are the sole data reported for norms. No information was given concerning how the sample was selected, other than it was claimed to be "representative" and "stratified by size of school and overall science achievement" (p. 67). Thus, it is not possible to evaluate the data collection procedures. Furthermore, because the data were not reported by age or grade, no age or grade norms could be reported. Instead, a statistic called Levels was created, with values of 1, 2, and 3, corresponding to low, medium, and high. According to the authors, for each group taking a unit test, a "teacher-assessed level" was obtained (p. 16).

COMMENTARY. How convenient will teachers find these series to administer, score, and interpret in actual classroom use? How convenient will students find the test as they interact with it? The manual states that the Series do not require any additional staff in the class to administer the test, but it is clear that the teacher will be very busy accommodating the needs of the children. No mention is made in the manual of how teachers or children reacted to the administration, which is a deinite limitation.

The manual provides detailed scoring instructions for every item. For those items requiring a free response (constructed response), several acceptable answers are given, along with several nonacceptable answers. Although this is very helpful, it will require considerable time for the teacher to score all of the items. Pupils may find open-response items to be very broad. In reading the items, this reviewer imagines that many students may react to an item by "trying to guess" what the authors had in mind for an answer. A common rule for item writing is to set a clear task for the pupil. This reviewer feels that some of the items may be perceived by children as not setting a clear task. Some of the questions are so broad that the authors listed seven or more acceptable responses in addition to the nonacceptable responses. This reviewer perceived that many of these items could be cast as multiple-choice items with good foils created from the nonacceptable responses.

Among the positive aspects of this series are the objective type items. There is a creative use of drawings and photographs. Pupils are asked to select the best picture or draw lines connecting appropriate pictures. Some of these require the student to demonstrate both knowledge and understanding, which is the main purpose of the Series. There has been an obvious attempt by the authors to achieve a gender representation in the photos and a balance in taking the lead part. There is also an attempt to show a variety of races represented.

There is an emphasis on intuitive ideas about science, such as pushing toy cars to show force and graphs to show the relationships of applying heat and resulting temperature. Two batteries are connected in series to show an increase in the brightness of a light bulb. Balls are rolled down an inclined plane to show the effect of slope. There is an emphasis on making a "fair test," a term used for an experiment to control for extraneous factors. The authors have demonstrated creativity in preparing many of the test items. In the nonobjective items, there is an emphasis on writing skills, but the request for an entire sentence may, in some cases, result in less emphasis on scientific principles. The test was not designed to measure writing skills, but that appears to be a major factor in some of the items.

SUMMARY. The Science Assessment Series is a test that was designed to measure understanding of scientific principles. It reflects an emphasis on reasoning about basic principles. Children and teachers will find many of the items to be interesting and thought-provoking. Test constructors can gain insight into novel ways of constructing items. The booklets are attractive and the printing is very legible. However, the Series appears to this reviewer to be still in the first draft stage. As the test publisher continues the development process, several steps might be considered. A panel of science educators could look at the content validity of the test plan and items. Pilot tests could be run to generate item analysis data for item improvement. Feedback could be obtained from teachers and children to address "face validity." In standardizing the test, grade level should be collected in order to generate percentile scores within grades, and reliabilities within grades, in accordance with established guidelines for standardized tests. The authors are advised to use published technical standards to allow this instrument to evolve into one that teachers will find convenient to administer, score, and interpret. While waiting for that to occur, this reviewer urges caution in adopting the Series.

Review of the Science Assessment Series 1 and 2 by WILLIAM D. SCHAFER, Affiliated Professor (Emeritus) of Measurement, Statistics, and Evaluation, University of Maryland, College Park, MD:
DESCRIPTION.
Purpose and Nature. Initially developed in 2001, these tests were designed to assist teachers

in determining the level of science achievement of their students. Series 1 is intended for early primary students (ages 5 through 9) and Series 2 for later primary students (ages 8 through 13). They are intended to be given in either group or individual format and may optionally be supported by manipulatives, although they are not necessary.

There are five tests in Series 1: Humans and Other Animals, Plants, Materials, Light and Sound, Electricity and Forces. Series 2 contains eight tests: Humans and Other Animals, Plants, Living Things in Their Environment, Materials, Changing Materials, Electricity, Light and Sound, Forces in the Earth and Beyond. Each test is tied to units in the National Curricula of England, Northern Ireland, Scotland, and Wales; each Series has available a sheet that shows which items are tied to which curriculum strands (threads or elements linked across grades) for each of these four divisions of the United Kingdom.

Each test consists of several selected-response or short constructed-response items. Sometimes more than one response is to be selected by the student. Scoring is accomplished using a guide that gives sample responses that receive and do not receive credit. Sometimes a response pattern among the items is necessary to receive credit. Possible scores range from zero to 30 on each test.

Within each test, items were selected in an attempt to balance equally three levels of demand (low, or Level 1; medium or Level 2,; high or Level 3) within each of three item types (process on science inquiry, knowledge and understanding, conceptual). The levels have meaning in relation to the National Curriculum in England and Wales.

DEVELOPMENT.

Equating. Series 1 and 2 are intended for separate age ranges with some overlap. There was no stated attempt to vertically equate the Series such that scores from one Series could be compared with the other. However, users will find that scores in Series 1 are related to achievement ranges 1 through 3 and in Series 2 they are related to achievement ranges 2 through 5. A link between the two Series at Levels 2 and 3 is implied but neither made explicit nor evaluated.

Norms. Separate norming studies were conducted for each of the Series. The samples were stratified by school size and overall science achievement and otherwise are described as representative, but how they were selected, recruited, and tested is not described. Norms are provided separately for each test, but each student took only one of the tests in the standardization. The sample sizes for the various tests ranged from 211 to 411. These seem too small for anything but preliminary norms. For each test, students were further separated into years (1, 2, and 3 for Series 1 and 3, 4, and 6 for Series 2), but the meaning of a year is not documented. Raw score means and standard deviations are reported for each test overall and within years for boys and girls separately and combined. As expected, the means increase with increasing years with the exception of a decrease in Year 3 after Year 2 for the Series 1 test on Electricity and Forces. These means are based on sample sizes of only 205 for Year 2 and 81 for Year 3, which at the same time (a) suggests an explanation for the out-of-order results (instability in the means) and (b) underscores the point that the sample sizes used for the norms are low.

Scales. Each test is scored by summing item scores. The resulting raw scores can be converted to level scores on a scale from 1 to 5. This was done using teacher judgments of which level in the norming sample their students were in (except for Year 6 students in England, where a national science test replaced teacher judgment). On a graph with raw score on the abscissa and level on the ordinate, the regression of level on raw score was estimated and the most satisfying polynomial (linear, quadratic, or cubic) was selected. Raw score cutoffs for levels are where the polynomial crosses the horizontal lines halfway between the levels (e.g., at the raw score corresponding to 2.5 for Level 3). Scalings into levels denoted by letters are provided for Scotland.

Scaling was done using only raw item sums and classical psychometric theory. Most modern tests are now developed using item response theory, which may have proven more helpful for the developers of these tests.

TECHNICAL COMMENTARY.

Reliability evidence. Alpha coefficients are given for each subtest. These range from .72 to .85 for Series 1 and from .82 to .89 for Series 2. Using the standard deviations given, unconditional standard errors range from 1.69 to 2.15 and the manual suggests simply using 2 as the standard error for all the tests. Because these are low-stakes tests that are recommended as supplemental information that teachers may use for student (and curriculum) evaluation, these standard errors seem reasonable to use, as does the approximation of 2. However, if more importance is attached to the results, then it would be helpful to have conditional standard errors along with other information that would result from a more ambitious norming study.

The process that was used in scoring the norming assessments was not described. It is possible that the same person scored all of the items on each test. Because the scoring of the constructed-response items may sometimes be ambiguous, it is possible that the alpha coefficients overestimate the reliabilities of the tests in practice.

Some of the items appear to be dependent (e.g., a scored result and then a scored explanation of how the result was determined). There was no evaluation of the effects of these dependencies on reliability.

Validity evidence. Content evidence of validity is presented by tying items to curriculum strands and levels. However, the matching is not very precise within broad categories of science. For example, items in the Series 1 Humans and Other Animals test are matched to only two content areas in England's curriculum: Scientific Enquiry and Life Processes and Living Things. One would need to look at the actual items to determine alignment of any of these tests with any other curriculum not detailed, and perhaps for alignment even with England's curriculum.

Item development and evaluation are not described. Data for Year 2 and Years 4 and 6 trials samples are given but what those students took and how their results were used is not presented. There may have been no evaluation of differential item functioning.

Gender means and standard deviations are provided for each test, overall, and within years. Four of the 52 comparisons were statistically significant, but the small sample sizes may have provided insufficient power for the other comparisons. Effect sizes would have helped the reader evaluate the degree to which the differences are important.

Utility. The tests are easy to administer and score and appear engaging for students. They appear suited only for low-stakes uses, however.

SUMMARY. These tests may provide interesting information that teachers could use in planning instruction and administrators might find valuable in evaluating curriculum for possible enhancements. However, the norms for each test are based on too few students and useful interpretations seem supportable only at the item level.

[220]

Sensory Profile.

Purpose: "To measure a child's sensory processing abilities."

Publication Dates: 1999–2002.

Administration: Individual or group.

Levels, 2: Infant/Toddler Sensory Profile—Clinical Edition, Sensory Profile.

Price Data, 2002: $150 per software kit including user's manual (1999, 146 pages), e-record forms, and 1-year subscription; $105 per software stand-alone including 1-year subscription for e-record forms; $65 per manual; $45 per e-record forms including subscription renewal for 1-year.

Foreign Language Edition: Available in Spanish.

Comments: Profiles completed by child's caregiver; can be administered and scored electronically using personal computer or PDA (Windows and Palm OS), contact publisher for details.

Publisher: PsychCorp, A brand of Harcourt Assessment, Inc.

a) INFANT/TODDLER SENSORY PROFILE—CLINICAL EDITION.

Population: Birth to 36 months.

Publication Date: 2002.

Scores, 6: General Processing, Auditory Processing, Visual Processing, Tactile Processing, Vestibular Processing, Oral Sensory Processing.

Price Data: $119 per Infant/Toddler Sensory Profile complete kit including user's manual (2002, 21 pages), 25 English caregiver questionnaires, and 25 summary score sheets; $75 per user's manual; $31.50 per 25 caregiver questionnaires (English or Spanish); $16.50 per 25 summary score sheets.

Time: 15(25) minutes.

Comments: Ages birth to 6 months: 5 scores (General Processing, Auditory Processing, Visual Processing, Tactile Processing, Vestibular Processing).

Author: Winnie Dunn.

b) SENSORY PROFILE.

Population: Ages 3–10.

Forms, 2: Sensory Profile, Short Sensory Profile.

Scores, 23: 6 Sensory Processing categories (Auditory Processing, Visual Processing, Vestibular Processing, Touch Processing, Multisensory Processing, Oral Sensory Processing); 5 Modulation categories (Sensory Processing Related to Endurance/Tone, Modulation Related to Body Position and Movement, Modulation of Movement Affecting Activity Level, Modulation of Sensory Input Affecting Emotional Responses, Modulation of Visual Input Affecting Emotional Responses and Activity Level); 3 Behavioral and Emotional Responses categories (Emotional/Social Responses, Behavioral Outcomes of Sensory Processing, Items Indicating Thresholds for Response); 9 Factor Scores (Sensory Seeking, Emotionally Reactive, Low Endurance/Tone, Oral Sensitivity, Inattention/Distractibility, Poor Registration, Sensory Sensitivity, Sedentary, Fine Motor/Perceptual).

Price Data: $119 per Sensory Profile complete kit including user's manual, and 25 each of each of caregiver questionnaires, short sensory profiles, and summary score sheets; $65 per user's manual; $32 per 25 caregiver questionnaires (English or Spanish); $15 per 25 short sensory profiles (English or Spanish); $19 per 25 summary score sheets (English or Spanish).

Time: (15–30) minutes.

Comments: 125-question profile.

Author: Winnie Dunn.

c) SHORT SENSORY PROFILE.

Purpose: "To help service providers in screening settings quickly identify children with sensory processing difficulties."

Population: Ages 5–10.

Acronym: SSP.

Scores, 8: Tactile Sensitivity, Taste/Smell Sensitivity, Movement Sensitivity, Underresponsive/Seeks Sensation, Auditory Filtering, Low Energy/Weak, Visual/Auditory Sensitivity, Total.

Time: (10) minutes.

Authors: Daniel N. McIntosh, Lucy Jane Miller, Vivian Shyu, and Winnie Dunn.

Review of the Sensory Profile by DOREEN W. FAIRBANK, Associate Professor of Psychology, Meredith College, Raleigh, NC:

DESCRIPTION. The Sensory Profile is a judgment—based caregiver questionnaire that measures a child's sensory processing abilities and helps determine their effect on daily functioning. The Sensory Profile has three separate editions that can be used to evaluate children: The Sensory Profile, the Short Sensory Profile (SSP) and the Infant/Toddler Sensory Profile, Clinical Edition. The Sensory Profile, the main edition, is for children 5-10 years old but can be adapted for those 3 and 4 years old. This consists of 125 items divided into three main sections: Sensory Processing, Modulation, and Behavioral and Emotional Responses. Sensory Processing measures general responses to the basic sensory system and is divided into six sensory processing systems: Auditory, Visual, Vestibular, Touch, Multisensory, and Oral Sensory Processing. Modulation reflects the regulation of neural messages through facilitation

or inhibition of various types of responses and is divided into five areas of sensory modulation: Sensory Processing Related to Endurance/Tone, Modulation Related to Body Position and Movement, Modulation of Movement Affecting Activity Level, Modulation of Sensory Input Affecting Emotional Responses, and Modulation of Visual Input Affecting Emotional Responses and Activity Level. Behavioral and Emotional Responses reflects the behavioral outcomes of sensory processing and is divided into Emotional/Social Responses, Behavioral Outcomes of Sensory Processing, and Items Indicating Thresholds for Response. Items on the Caregiver Questionnaire also form nine meaningful factors: Sensory Seeking, Emotionally Reactive, Low Endurance/Tone, Oral Sensory Sensitivity, Inattention/Distractibility, Poor Registration, Sensory Sensitivity, Sedentary, and Fine Motor/Perceptual. These factors characterize children by their responsiveness to sensory input.

A caregiver completes the Caregiver Questionnaire and each item is rated on a 5-point scale (1 = *always*, 2 = *frequently*, 3 = *occasionally*, 4 = *seldom* and 5 = *never*). The Sensory Profile usually takes 30 minutes for the specific rater to complete. After completion of this form, a qualified user completes scoring and interpretation, which can take about 20–30 minutes. Scoring is straightforward and no special expertise is required as the manual provides a framework for interpreting the caregiver's responses. However, individuals who interpret the results should have a basic understanding of the principles of sensory processing and its impact on performance. The Summary score sheet includes demographic information, the Factor Grid, the Factor Summary and the Section Summary. The Factor Grid summarizes the scores from each of the nine factors (e.g., Sensory Seeking, Emotionally Reactive) and then these scores are transferred to the Factor Summary. The scores are then determined to be in one of three classification systems: typical performance, probable difference, and definite difference. This system helps the examiner to determine areas of concern. If there are areas of concern, the manual gives detailed information on interpreting threshold patterns (high or low) for evaluating the child's pattern of performance. The Section Summary provides a visual summary of the child's sensory processing, modulation, and behavior/emotional response abilities and also uses the same three classification systems.

The user's manual also gives suggestions to begin intervention in each area of concern.

The Short Sensory Profile (SSP), primarily a screening and research tool, contains 38 items from the Sensory Profile and is used to specifically target sensory modulation. The sections of the SSP include Tactile Sensitivity, Taste/Smell Sensitivity, Movement Sensitivity, Underresponsive/Seeks Sensation, Auditory Filtering, Low Energy/Weak, and Visual/Auditory Sensitivity. The SSP is completed using the same rating scale and takes about 10 minutes to complete. Scoring for the SSP is a similar format to the Sensory Profile but only using the summary section for the seven areas. The total score is the most important score and gives the examiner a quick indication of a child's sensory processing ability. If a child receives a score in the Definite Difference range, it is suggested that the complete Sensory Profile be administered.

The Infant/Toddler Sensory Profile was developed to evaluate infants and toddlers between birth and 36 months of age. The Infant Toddler Sensory Profile—Clinical Edition—Caregiver's Questionnaire (58 items) takes about 15 minutes to complete and about 10 minutes for the professional to score. It contains six areas: General Processing, Auditory Processing, Visual Processing, Tactile Processing, Vestibular Processing and Oral Sensory Processing. The score sheet is grouped into four age divisions and gives typical performance and performance at-risk for each division.

DEVELOPMENT. The Sensory Profile was originally developed to test sensory integration theory and to determine how sensory processing affected the daily routines and expectations in a classroom. This indicated that intervention could positively affect the children's sensory processing. The Sensory Profile was developed from 1993–1999 and underwent extensive pilot testing until the present 125 items were selected. A principal-components factor analysis helped to determine the item categories. The SSP was developed primarily as a screening instrument and as part of a research protocol. After several pilot studies, the Sensory Profile items were reduced to 38 items that were indicative of sensory modulation process rather than direct sensory events. The Infant/Toddler Sensory Profile, Clinical Edition was developed to evaluate the sensory processing issues with infants and toddlers between birth and 36 months of age. This was developed to be included

as part of a comprehensive assessment of performance. The test is also available in Spanish.

TECHNICAL. The Sensory Profile was researched and standardized with a nationwide sample of over 1,200 children with and without disabilities between the ages of 3 and 14. Separate validity studies took place with children with ADHD, PDD, Fragile X Disorder, or a sensory modulation disorder. Ethnicity, socioeconomic status, region, and special education classification of the norming sample are discussed in the user's manual. The manual for the SSP and the Infant/Toddler Sensory Profile, Clinical Edition also discussed their separate standardized procedures.

Internal consistency reliability, as determined by Cronbach's coefficient alpha, was calculated using data from the normative sample. The coefficients of internal reliability ranged from .47 to .91 in the various sections. The SSP had coefficient alpha from .70 to .90.

The manual provides substantial evidence for content validity. Convergent and discriminant construct validity was demonstrated through comparison between the Sensory Profile and the School Function Assessment.

The Infant/Toddler Sensory Profile, Clinical Edition was researched and developed on a national sample of 401 infants and toddlers without disabilities between the ages of birth to 36 months. The user's manual does not report reliability and validity data at this time. Research regarding standardization is currently being conducted with a large national sample according to the manual.

COMMENTARY. The Sensory Profile, SSP, and The Infant/Toddler Sensory Profile, Clinical Edition appear to be very useful evaluation instruments to assess the sensory processing abilities in children. The user's manual is well written and contains adequate information regarding administrating, scoring, and interpreting the results. Some information regarding intervention in the various areas of concern is given. However, a background in the area of sensory processing appears to be needed in order to interpret the results and develop an appropriate intervention program. The additional information regarding the clinical group studies, specifically with autism and ADHD, appears to be very useful to anyone wanting to assess sensory processing with these disability areas.

SUMMARY. The Sensory Profile was designed to be used as an evaluation instrument to obtain information regarding a child's sensory processing abilities that support and/or interfere with a child's functional performance. The combination of the three instruments allows for screening or a full evaluation on infants/children from birth to 10 years old. The test was developed on sensory integration theory and research and should benefit anyone interested in obtaining sensory processing information regarding a child.

Review of the Sensory Profile by JOHN J. VACCA, Assistant Professor of Individual and Family Studies, Developmental School Psychologist, University of Delaware, Middletown, DE:

DESCRIPTION. The Sensory Profile has three forms: Infant/Toddler Sensory Profile-Clinical Edition, Sensory Profile, and Short Sensory Profile. The conceptual model for all three forms is based on the constructs of Neurological Threshold and Behavioral Response/Self-Regulation. Central to Neurological Threshold is the determination of how much sensory input is needed to develop a balance or homeostasis whereby the right amount of excitatory and inhibitory neurons are activated to allow the individual to function optimally within their environment.

Each version of the Sensory Profile comes with an examiner's manual, scoring protocols, and summary sheets. The response patterns identified through completion of the caregiver questionnaire are compared against a normative sample of children without disabilities.

The Infant/Toddler Sensory Profile-Clinical Edition was originally designed for professionals to use while the normative version of the Infant-Toddler Sensory Profile was being completed. The additional items on the Clinical Edition are common among very young children with identified disorders in self-regulation. Total completion time is approximately 15 minutes, and total scoring time is approximately 10 minutes. In terms of user qualifications, the author specifies that many professionals from different disciplines can administer it, yet those professionals whose training is not in neurodevelopment are urged to seek consultation from someone whose training is in this area for interpretation.

The Sensory Profile, a 125-item questionnaire, is designed for use with children ages 3 years to 10 years, although the author states that it is most appropriate for children ages 5 to 10 years. The intended purpose is the same as that specified

for the infant and toddler version. With the Sensory Profile, the 125 items are grouped into three main sections: Sensory Processing, Modulation, and Behavioral and Emotional Responses.

The Short Form Sensory Profile was designed to examine sensory modulation only. The author recommends the 38-item tool be used for screening and/or research purposes.

DEVELOPMENT. The Sensory Profile was originally designed as a result of research that focused on the need to identify sensory integrative functions and related difficulties in young children so that consultative interventions could be delivered within the daily routine of the classroom to support learning. Initially, 99 items were developed and pilot tested, after which 26 additional items were added to make the existing instrument.

The author provides a description of the children who were included in the sample. A total of 1,037 children without disabilities between the ages of 3 and 10 years were included (524 girls, 510 boys), and they were provided by the examiners participating in the research. Children were excluded from the sample if they were receiving special education and were on regular dosages of prescription medication. In terms of demographics, there was an even distribution of children across ages and geographic regions. There was more unevenness of representation with respect to race/ethnicity and with household income. In the sample, 91.4% of the children were White compared to 1.5% of the children who were African American. This constitutes a major flaw, especially with providing data on generalizability of sensory integrative functioning for individuals from varying ethnic backgrounds. Review of related literature does not provide sufficient detail on the implications of genetics with sensory functioning.

Research studies were also conducted on a smaller scale with children with specific disabilities to examine validity of score use. The sample included children with attention deficit/hyperactivity disorder (n = 61, ages 3–15), autism/pervasive developmental disorder (n = 32, ages 3–13), Fragile X Syndrome (n = 24, ages 3–17), and sensory modulation disorder (n = 21, ages 4–9).

Measures of validity were determined in a manner similar to that done with the child version. Adequate support was determined for use of the tool with very young children with suspected sensory integrative dysfunction.

TECHNICAL. The authors identify that descriptive statistics, multivariate analysis of variance, and principal component factor analysis were used in the formulation of the scoring structure for all versions of the instrument. Examination of reliability indicates values for internal consistency to range from .47 to .91 (Cronbach's alpha). The authors provide a table that specifies these values for each factor identified in the development of the instrument (i.e., Sensory Processing, Modulation, Behavioral and Emotional Response, and general factors). The one subfactor found to have the lowest value (.47) was Items Indicating Thresholds for Response. Although all of the other subfactor items are well above this (.58 to .91), there is an overarching concern that the ability to determine the point at which a child encounters difficulty due to the lack of homeostasis in their central nervous system (i.e., threshold for responding) is not strong. This contradicts a major premise of the tool itself. Furthermore, there is a need to not only identify setting events that influence children's learning but to identify the point at which a child may not be able to remain autonomous in their learning abilities. It is the determination of such a threshold that holds considerable value for the professional working with the child so that they can adequately plan for children in anticipation of stressful events that will impede learning.

Reliability involved calculations of internal consistency and test-retest reliability. Similar values were received for the infant and toddler version compared to that reported for the child version.

Other values of reliability are not reported. The author comments on the difficulty of estimating test-retest reliability given that the sensory abilities of individuals changes over time. Although this is an important point, documentation of these changes should be investigated in order to monitor the stability of sensory functioning over time and to identify strategies that can be implemented to support such stability and to support the ability of the central nervous system to create new integrative skills to adapt to the changing environment.

Another aspect of reliability not reported and that represents a major flaw considering the judgment-based nature of this tool is interrater reliability. Although many professionals were involved in the development of the tool, there is no mention of comparing observations among these professionals with the children who were involved in the study. Considering the emphasis on team collaboration and functioning in service delivery systems for very young children, there is a need to use tools that are complementary of each other in order to provide a forum for consensus among the professionals on the team. The author is encouraged to pursue aggressive research that examines reliability between multiple observers to strengthen the consistency of information one receives over time and to help with the evaluation of predictive validity.

In terms of validity, the authors examined both content and construct validity. Content validity was adequately supported by the methods of a literature review, expert review, and category analysis. Construct validity was determined by examining values of convergent validity resulting from comparison of the Sensory Profile and the School Function Assessment. Minimal information is provided indicating these values, and the justification for using the School Function Assessment is not substantiated. Extreme caution should be used whenever comparing two or more assessment tools because the theoretical model from which each is based can be different, thereby affecting how the tool is organized, scored, and interpreted. To better evaluate concurrent validity it would have been better to include the review of tools similar to the Sensory Profile that look at similar areas. Having said this, the author acknowledges that low correlation values were received following comparison of the two instruments, and that the Sensory Profile is a tool that assesses more "global sensory processing" versus specific sensory skills tapped within specific tasks that are assessed by the School Functioning Assessment.

Values for discriminant validity are well documented in the groups of children with disabilities that were included in the normative sample. The author is encouraged to pursue ongoing analyses with other children, however, to provide support for how the Profile is consistent with behaviors seen in children with identified sensory integrative functions.

COMMENTARY. Researchers and professionals in the early childhood community are continuing to document the increasing numbers of children entering early care and education programs with suspected or known sensory integrative dysfunction. The author of the Infant/Toddler Sensory Profile and Sensory Profile is to be commended for providing the pediatric community with a useful tool to accompany the other tools they routinely use to provide a comprehensive picture of the child's strengths, needs, learning styles, and sensory integrative skills.

SUMMARY. The three versions of the Sensory Profile represent an innovative approach in gathering information about a child's ability to take in and manage sensory information and carry out daily activities within the natural environment. This information has implications for all aspects of learning and development. It also provides a foundation for appropriate interventions and activities to be developed in order to support children's learning and skill acquisition. Ongoing research should continue with this and other similar tools, however, to provide information about generalizability across individuals and to document how the sensory abilities of individuals change across the lifespan.

[221]

Sigma Survey for Police Officers.

Purpose: "Designed to identify job applicants possessing the cognitive skills necessary to use sound practical judgement in police situations, and to write meaningful and credible police incident reports."
Population: Ages 18 and over.
Publication Dates: 2001–2002.
Acronym: SSPO.
Scores, 6: Incident Report Writing (Spelling, Grammar, Vocabulary, Total), Police Problem Solving, Total.
Administration: Individual or group.
Price Data, 2003: $25 per report (1–99); volume discounts available.
Time: (35) minutes.
Comments: Computer, internet, and fax-in scoring service available through publisher; available in Canadian format and American format; publisher recommends use of the SSPO in conjunction with the Employee Screening Questionnaire (see 86).
Author: Douglas N. Jackson.
Publisher: Sigma Assessment Systems, Inc.

Review of the Sigma Survey for Police Officers by THOMAS M. DUNN, Assistant Professor of Psychology, University of Northern Colorado, Greeley, CO:

DESCRIPTION. The Sigma Survey for Police Officers (SSPO) is a brief screening instrument designed for selecting job candidates to be police officers. Specifically, the test purports to identify individuals who have the cognitive ability to make good decisions when performing law

enforcement duties and who also have the ability to write competent police reports. It is also likely that this test reasonably could be used to assess persons applying for similar occupations, such as a security officer or customs agent. The instrument takes 35 minutes to complete and can be administered individually or in a group setting. The test comprises two parts, an Incident Report Writing Aptitude portion and a Police Problem Solving part. Both parts are administered by pencil-and-paper and are forced-choice tests, with the candidate selecting true/false, or choosing the best response among four possibilities. Incident Report Writing is composed of Spelling (finding misspelled words), Vocabulary (identifying meaning of words), and Sentences (correcting grammar errors). In Police Problem Solving, the candidate is asked to respond to a number of situations that are "relevant to the work of a police officer" (p. 5), including: reading a map, matching an offense with a particular charge, putting vignettes into chronological order, and responding to scenarios of crimes being committed.

It appears that no special training is required to administer the instrument. The manual provides step-by-step directions to be followed by a police supervisor who proctors the test. The response sheet is then faxed to a toll-free number for scoring; the scored profile sheet is to be faxed back in about 15 minutes. The profile sheet has two pages. One side is a "detection summary," designed to compare the original response sheet to verify accurate transmission of the marked items. The second side of the profile sheet includes two fields. The first is a "notes" field that can include remarks about whether there were duplicate responses, errors in scoring, or about unreadable responses. The "results" field reports six scores: Spelling, Vocabulary, and Language Usage scores from the Incident Report Writing Aptitude; Total Writing Aptitude (the mean of the three previous scores); Police Problem Solving; and an Overall Score (the mean of Total Writing and Problem Solving). These percent scores are also plotted on a bar graph ranging from "low" to "high." The person responsible for making hiring decisions then has data about Report Writing aptitude and Police Problem Solving to assist in selecting candidates to be police officers.

DEVELOPMENT. The SSPO is in its first edition (copyright, 2001). Although the manual does state that the SSPO is based on the Sigma Survey for Security Officers (223), there is a meager amount of information about test development. The author also specifies that items "in each section were developed by using carefully defined, theoretically based concepts of what each section should measure" (technical manual, p. 2), but these definitions, theories, and concepts are not in the manual.

TECHNICAL. The normative sample for this instrument is quite large, with scores taken from 4,465 individuals. It should be noted that these scores are described as "provisional norms" (technical manual, p. 5), because the norms are from job candidates applying to be security officers for a "large, international security company" (technical manual, p. 5). There is no information about the proportions of age, gender, ethnicity, or education level in this provisional normative group. Nor is it clear from what country the candidates from this "international" company were. The only data about the provisional normative group are descriptive statistics regarding their performance on the two parts of the instrument. However, these scores do not precisely match with the scales on the test (e.g., no vocabulary score). The manual does acknowledge that it is desirable to replace the provisional normative group and states "We are currently in the process of obtaining norms for police officers" (p. 5).

Reliability data are reported from both the provisional normative group and also from a 2000 study (Jackson, Harris, Ashton, McCarthy, & Tremblay, 2000) with 187 police officers with at least 6 months of experience. Internal consistency is impressive, with Cronbach's alpha scores on the Incident Report Writing Aptitude (including Spelling and Sentences) and Police Problem Solving scale, and a Total Scale score, ranging from .90 to .96 in the Jackson et al. (2000) police officer study. The coefficients reported from the provisional normative group were a little lower, ranging from .77 to .89; however, the author explains this disparity by the lower standard deviation values associated with the larger sample of job applicants in the provisional normative group.

Validity data are scarce. There is no comparison of this instrument with others purported to measure police officer ability; however, there are few such tests on the market. It should also be noted that there is controversy in the field about instruments that cogently measure police officer candidates (Sanders, 2003). Instead, there are va-

lidity coefficients reported between Incident Report Writing Attitude, Spelling, Sentences, Police Problem Solving, and Total scores and a criterion work-sample incident report rated by two judges who rated reports written by the Jackson et al. (2000) police officer study. These validity coefficients ranged from a very acceptable .43 to .57. A secondary analysis was also done by ranking SSPO total test battery scores and plotting them across four quartiles. The manual reports that 100% of the 187 respondents in the Jackson et al. (2000) study who scored in the top quartile produced incident reports judged to be satisfactory, whereas only 17% of the bottom quartile were able to achieve similar scores, showing good separation.

COMMENTARY. The author of the SSPO was a highly regarded psychologist who is widely noted for personality inventories. This instrument is relatively inexpensive, very easy to administer in a group setting, and dispenses with the uncertainty of results that come from scoring the instrument by hand. A scored profile is faxed back from the publisher after receiving the answer sheet (also by fax). Although percent scores are present (presumably percent correct), there are no instructions for interpreting the scored profile (such as cut scores). Although the scores do range from "low" to "high" there is no corresponding interpretation regarding how low is still an acceptable score.

It is unfortunate that the SSPO relies on a "provisional" normative group and has not yet been normed on police officer candidates, nor police officers. The manual reports a 187-participant research study (Jackson et al., 2000) of police officers and 4,500 security officer candidates instead. It is unclear if candidates to work in private security are an acceptable analog to police officers or police officer candidates. Obviously, the instrument will be far more credible and valid with police officer norms. The publisher acknowledges this in the manual.

Finally, there are items in the Police Problem Solving section that were spelled with the British convention (e.g., "neighbourhood," p. 24) and some problems used metric measurement, such as liters and meters. This gives the test a European or Canadian flavor at times. It is possible that the "international security" firm mentioned earlier is European or Canadian. [Editor's Note: The SSPO is available in to formats: a Canadian and an American. Items on the Canadian format contain British spelling conventions and use the metric system. Items on the American format contain American spelling conventions and use the imperial measurement system.]

SUMMARY. The SSPO has several strengths. Its author is a well-known and highly respected psychologist in the area of test construction. It can be administered by anyone who can read directions and supervise test takers. It is brief (35 minutes) and can be administered to a large group. Possible errors in scoring are reduced by faxing the completed test to the publisher for scoring. It is cost effective. Naturally, there are some limitations to this instrument. It contains a "provisional normative group," with data based on police officers forthcoming. The validity data are promising, but are incomplete and do not come from the normative group. Finally, the scored profile is relatively unsophisticated with few instructions about how to interpret high or low scores. The SSPO fills a niche because it has a large (but provisional) normative group, can be administered in 35 minutes by a police supervisor, and is cost efficient. As the publisher suggests, it is likely best used with another employment screening instrument that is not specific to law enforcement. For those who are concerned about the provisional normative group, there are few alternatives; however, the Police Selection Test (T6:1921) offers a normative group of over 2,000 police officer candidates and has similar scales.

REVIEWER'S REFERENCES

Jackson, D. N, Harris, W. G., Ashton, M. C., McCarthy, J. M., & Tremblay, P. F. (2000). How useful are work samples in validation studies? *International Journal of Selection and Assessment, 8*, 29–33.
Sanders, B. A. (2003). Maybe there is no such thing as a "good cop." Organizational challenges in selecting quality officers. *Policing: An International Journal of Police Strategies and Management, 26*, 313–328.

Review of the Sigma Survey for Police Officers by CHOCKALINGAM VISWESVARAN, Associate Professor of Psychology, Florida International University, Miami, FL:

DESCRIPTION. The Sigma Survey for Police Officers (SSPO) is designed to assess the report writing skills and problem-solving skills of police officer applicants. It is a standardized test that can be administered in group formats. There are two parts and it takes 35 minutes to administer both parts. The first part focuses on incident report writing aptitude, an aptitude that is assessed in three sections: Spelling, Vocabulary, Sentences. The Spelling section lists 28 words and the examinee has to indicate whether each one is correctly or incorrectly spelled. The Vocabulary

section has eight words, each embedded in a sentence and four words are listed after each sentence. The examinee should identify which of the four words best reflects the meaning of the word embedded in the sentence. The Sentences section has eight sets of four sentences each and the examinee has to identify which of the four sentences in each set is grammatically correct.

The second part of the SSPO is a test of Problem Solving Skills. There are eight situations described followed by questions that assess the quality of judgments made by the examinee. For example, a map could be provided with the current location of a police squad car and the report of a disturbance in another location. The examinee has to indicate which route is best to take. Detailed instructions are given to the test administrator and the procedures to follow are clearly outlined. The examinees read the questions in the test booklet and bubble in their responses on a separate sheet that gets faxed to the test publisher. Scores are faxed back within 15 minutes and instructions are given for troubleshooting if problems arise in this automated process. The report generates scores for Spelling, Vocabulary, and language usage (Grammar) subtests as well as scores for Incident Report Writing Aptitude and Problem Solving Skills. A total score is also provided.

DEVELOPMENT. The items were rationally developed based on a careful delineation of the content domain. The objective was to choose culture-fair items but no empirical data have been provided in the technical manual about score differences (or lack of score differences) across ethnic groups. No item analyses data (difficulty levels, discrimination indices, item-total correlation, average inter-item correlations, differential item functioning, etc.), either for the final set of items or for the initial pool of items, are provided in the technical manual. The materials provided for this review included a 21-page technical manual, a copy of the test booklet, an answering sheet, and a 1-page promotional flier.

TECHNICAL. Empirical data based on two samples are provided in the technical manual. The first sample consists of responses from 262 police officers (incumbents) of whom 187 provided complete data. Each of the officers had at least 6 months of job experience and none had been selected using the SSPO. A work sample criterion of incident report writing was collected from the participants. Two judges who were not acquainted with the police officers and who did not see the test scores evaluated these reports. The criterion ratings were obtained on a 7-point scale and it is stated in the technical manual that the judges "demonstrated excellent agreement on what were good and poor incident reports" (p. 16). The internal consistency reliability estimates of Incident Report Writing scores, Spelling section scores, Sentences section scores, Problem Solving scores, and Total scores were .93, .95, .93, .90 and .96, respectively. No reliability estimates are provided for the third section of the first part (Vocabulary). The observed validities are reported for the Spelling section scores, Sentences section scores, Problem Solving scores, and Total scores (.43, .47, .53, and .57, respectively).

The second sample is presented as the tentative normative sample and includes responses from 4,665 job applicants in a large international security company. The internal consistency reliability estimates of Incident Report Writing scores, Spelling section scores, Sentences section scores, Problem Solving scores, and Total scores were .86, .82, .70, .77 and .89, respectively. Again, no reliability estimates are provided for the third section of the first part (Vocabulary). The test publisher notes that lowered reliabilities in the second sample are due to a restriction in the variability of scores, a statement that raises some concerns about the motivational framework of the first sample of police incumbents. No validity data are available on this second sample.

COMMENTARY. Accurate report writing and good judgment are essential skills for a police officer. The SSPO has items with excellent face and content validity to assess these skills. Although the test publisher makes the narrow claim that this test measures report writing skills and problem-solving skills, I suspect it is a good measure of general mental ability. I would like to see more data on the construct validity of this measure that include correlations with other standard tests of mental ability. If my assumptions are true, I would expect to see group differences in these scores that could result in adverse impact for minorities. Again, future data collection should check for these potential problems.

The test publisher should also include more information on item selection, item analyses, and refinements in the technical manual. Specifically, information should be provided on the item diffi-

culties, discriminability, etc. An assessment of (potential) differential item functioning should also be presented. Information on reliability should be expanded. In addition to internal consistency estimates, some information on temporal stability should be provided.

Validity data should be augmented. Diverse samples with different criteria should be obtained. The criterion description given for the one validity study in the technical manual is inadequate. For example (see Technical section of this review), if two judges rated the reports on a 7-point scale, what does it mean to say that there was excellent agreement on deciding good and poor reports? What was the excellent agreement?

SUMMARY. Although I have pointed out what additional information needs to be gathered and included in the technical manual, I believe this test has made a good beginning. The items are face valid and the test publisher had made an earnest effort to collect supporting data. With the collection of the data recommended in the Commentary section of this review, I believe this will be an excellent test. Given the need to assess report writing and problem-solving skills in police applicants, this test will be of value in police selection.

[222]

Sigma Survey for Sales Professionals.

Purpose: Designed to analyze "the strengths and weaknesses of sales and sales manager job candidates on 28 dimensions of expected job performance."

Population: Ages 18 and over.

Publication Dates: 2002–2003.

Acronym: 3SP.

Scores, 28: Technical Orientation, Creativity, Thoroughness, Risk Taking, Open Mindedness, First Impression, Interpersonal Relations, Sensitivity, Social Astuteness, Communication, Formal Presentation, Persuasiveness, Negotiation, Listening Skill, Achievement and Motivation, Self-Discipline, Flexibility, Independence, Self Esteem, Emotional Control, Dependability, Ambition, Organizational Spokesperson, Assuming Responsibility, Vision, Short-Term Planning, Strategic Planning, Productivity.

Administration: Group.

Price Data, 2003: $47 per administration; volume discounts available.

Time: (40) minutes.

Comments: Publisher scoring service available via internet, fax, or mail.

Author: Douglas N. Jackson.

Publisher: Sigma Assessment Systems, Inc.

Review of the Sigma Survey for Sales Professionals by MARTHA E. HENNEN, Manager, Employment Programs, United States Postal Service, Washington, DC:

DESCRIPTION. The Sigma Survey for Sales Professionals (3SP) is a 352-item inventory that may be administered either over the internet or via paper-and-pencil administration with fax-back scoring services. Items are rated on a 5-point Likert rating scale ranging from *Strongly Disagree* to *Strongly Agree*. The 3SP is intended for use in selection and placement of job applicants for professional and management level sales personnel, succession planning, as well as coaching and development. It provides summary results against 28 personality scales for sales professionals and sales managers. These scales include: Technical Orientation, Creativity, Thoroughness, Risk Taking, Open-Mindedness, First Impression, Interpersonal Relations, Sensitivity, Social Astuteness, Communication, Formal Presentation, Persuasiveness, Negotiation, Listening Skill, Achievement & Motivation, Self-Discipline, Flexibility, Independence, Self-Esteem, Emotional Control, Dependability, Ambition, Organizational Spokesperson, Assuming Responsibility, Vision, Short-Term Planning, Strategic Planning, and Productivity. The first half of this list of dimensions is broadly categorized as Cognitive and Interpersonal Sales Skills, and the second half is broadly categorized as Personal Sales Qualities.

The 3SP is computer scored and interpretation reports are provided by Sigma Assessment Systems. Nontechnical staff can administer the instrument. Reports are available immediately via Sigma Assessment System's website at http://www.sigmatesting.com. A fax-returned report could also be generated at additional cost.

Sigma Assessment Systems provides an interpretive report for each examinee. The report contains three sections. The first section provides overall summary scores calculated as an overall sales performance percentile rank, as compared to the norm group. Both an Interpersonal Sales Skills and a Task Orientation broad dimension score are also calculated. It is not clear from the technical documentation how the 28 individual dimensions roll up or relate to the Interpersonal Sales Skills or Task Orientation summaries. The detailed results section of the report provides percentile rank profiles for each of the 28 performance dimensions. The final section provides specific definitions for each of the

28 dimensions as well as examples of behavior representative of those scoring in the same range.

Although the 3SP was designed to be used by a nontechnical audience, users are cautioned that proper interpretation of individual results requires both an understanding of the job requirements and to "try to focus on the overall pattern of interpretations, rather than on single interpretations" (Abbreviated Sample Report, p. 1). No guidance is provided on how the user should go about this interpretation. Nor is the user guided in how to evaluate the relative importance of different dimensions to a particular position or job.

DEVELOPMENT. The 3SP was developed by combining items from three other personality inventories offered by Sigma Assessment Systems and authored by Douglas Jackson: the Personality Research Form (PRF), the Jackson Personality Inventory-Revised (JPI-R), and the Survey of Work Styles. The section of the technical documentation describing this development procedure provides a great deal of information about the decision rules that were used in refining the item pool for this new measure. The technical manual describes the steps undertaken to develop and refine the initial scales providing the basis for the 3SP.

According to the manual, the research procedures included first a careful theoretical study of each construct; second, development of a large pool of items bearing conceptual relation to the underlying constructs. Internal editorial review was followed by pilot administration to a large pool of respondents. Finally, a series of decision rules were applied to the psychometric results for each item to identify the final item set for the new measure. The description of these procedures demonstrates the care with which Jackson and his colleagues have designed their personality measures. The technical documentation does not provide detail on the research participants or even on the number of potential items included in the pilot administration, which is unfortunate, as this research provides the clearest support for the quality of measurement provided by the 3SP. It is also not explicitly stated, but the manual implies that no new item development was undertaken in creating the new 3SP. The items comprising each of these other measures were apparently reviewed against the constructs underlying sales performance and evaluated for inclusion in the 3SP.

The technical manual does provide a detailed description of the various statistical decision rules applied to the pilot test data in defining the final scale content. Items were retained for further consideration only if the relationship of an item to the theoretically hypothesized scale was higher than its relation to any other scale, including the Desirability scale, and if the item failed to show any extreme endorsement proportions (i.e., less than 20% or greater than 80% endorsement for any one response alternative). Items were ranked on a Differential Reliability Index (DRI) summarizing the relationship between each item and its intended scale versus a Desirability scale, and the desired number of items for each scale was selected from those with the highest rankings. Note that no minimally acceptable level of this statistic was established to protect against different scales being more or less saturated with socially desirable responding. Such statistical decision rules help to ensure that the final item sets demonstrate high internal consistency and discriminant measurement properties.

Using an algorithm developed by the author in concert with J. A. Neill and described in Neill and Jackson (1976), a summary statistic was computed for ranking each item as to its relative same scale versus other scale variance. Ranking items on this Item Efficiency Index (IEI) empirically controls the degree to which items and scales are interrelated in the final scale. Finally, the items were reviewed for editorial considerations such as representativeness of content, lack of item ambiguity, and editorial style. All of these development steps support this set of items as providing a personality questionnaire that includes scales with optimal reliability, minimal content redundancy, and including content relevant, readable items that are relatively free from irrelevant variance.

TECHNICAL.

Standardization. The norms established for the 3SP are based upon the responses of "243 participants drawn from a variety of organizations. Although some of the participants were from sales backgrounds, a variety of other business functions were contained in the sample" (technical manual, p. 8). The norm group represents a relatively diverse population who volunteered to participate in this research effort in hopes of developing and improving business skills. The technical manual also reports that Sigma Assessment Systems would be willing to work with a large organization to define local norms.

Reliability. No reliability information for the newly developed 3SP scale is provided. According to the manual, "The PRF, JPI-R, and SWS have displayed substantial evidence of internal consistency and test-retest reliability" (technical manual, p. 27). Although it is undoubtedly true that these other measures demonstrate strong reliability, it is not clear that the scales comprising the 3SP are either exact duplicates of these other measures or that the reliability would be exactly the same.

Validity. The technical manual reports results of research undertaken to compare scores on the 3SP with 360° feedback ratings on 25 sales performance dimensions recorded by co-workers of the 243 participants in the norming research. Multiple correlations between those dimensions and the 3SP personality dimension scores are reported, and adjusted multiple Rs for each dimension range from .25 to .47. The data from this research were also analyzed using canonical correlation to predict factor analyzed components of the 360° ratings of sales performance. Five canonical variates emerge as significant from this analysis, ranging in value from .38 to .65. The authors draw the conclusion that "It is clear that the personality scales contained in the 3SP have important implications for sales performance" (technical manual, p. 29).

COMMENTARY. The justification for using the 3SP as a separate measure, particularly for selection or placement decision making, does not seem strong. It is clear that the items comprising this measure are drawn from well-respected instruments of personality with long research support. It is not clear that a more specific inventory is needed for the intended purpose. The norming study included a relatively small sample. Normative data based upon voluntary participation motivated by personal development may be very different than the data that might emerge from a sample participating in hopes of selection or promotion.

It would be beneficial for Sigma Assessment Systems to clarify the research studies that support use of the 3SP. It is not clear from reading the technical documentation what or how constructs in the underlying personality inventories were modified to match the dimensions intended for the 3SP. The description of the only research that appears to have been conducted specifically evaluating the 3SP, the 243 volunteers who simultaneously participated in a 360° assessment, is similarly poorly described.

Without good information to compare the 3SP with its constituent measures, it is particularly concerning that the reliability coefficients are not reported specific to the 3SP. The user is referred back to the three underlying measures. *The Standards for Educational and Psychological Testing* (AERA, APA, & NCME, 1999) require the user to evaluate the reliability of the scale as it would be used for decision making.

SUMMARY. Given the care with which Sigma Assessment Systems has targeted the items for inclusion in the 3SP and given the quality of the measures underlying it, the psychometrics of this new scale are likely to prove strong in the long run. However, it appears that Sigma has published this instrument without providing statistics on the scale reliability to support using this instrument for its stated purpose. Stronger research support for the normative conclusions to be drawn and the scale's validity evidence would also enhance the case for using this instrument. Given the degree to which the user must determine what aspects of sales performance are important for the job of interest, it is not clear that the Jackson Personality Inventory—Revised (T6:1278) or the Personality Research Form (T6:1885) are not better choices for hiring or placing sales professionals. With additional research data, the 3SP may show stronger relationships with later sales performance, but the data are not yet convincing on that question.

REVIEWER'S REFERENCES

American Educational Research Association, American Psychological Association, & National Council on Measurement in Education. (1999). *Standards for educational and psychological testing.* Washington, DC: American Educational Research Association.
Neill, J. A., & Jackson, D. N. (1976). Minimum redundancy item analysis. *Educational and Psychological Measurement, 36,* 123–134.

Review of the Sigma Survey for Sales Professionals by STEPHEN B. JOHNSON, Managing Partner, RPM Data, Greensboro, NC:

DESCRIPTION. The Sigma Survey for Sales Professionals (3SP) is an untimed 352-item test, administered either in paper-pencil format or on the Internet. All items are 5-point Likert type anchored by *Strongly Disagree* and *Strongly Agree*, with a *Neutral* midpoint. There are no qualifications required for the test users and the test can be administered under conditions set by the test user. The test takes an average of 40 minutes to complete.

The 3SP is designed to provide information on the strengths and weaknesses of sales professionals and sales managers on 28 sales performance dimensions. The 3SP is designed to aid in selection, placement, professional development, or coaching. The dimensions include 14 Cognitive and Interpersonal Sales Skills (Technical Orienta-

tion, Creativity, Thoroughness, Risk Taking, Open-Mindness, First Impression, Interpersonal Relations, Sensitivity, Social Astuteness, Communication, Formal Presentation, Persuasiveness, Negotiation, and Listening), and 14 Personal Sales Qualities (Achievement and Motivation, Self-Discipline, Flexibility, Independence, Self-Esteem, Emotional Control, Dependability, Ambition, Assuming Responsibility, Vision, Organizational Spokesperson, Short Term Planning, Strategic Planning, and Productivity).

A report generated by the publishers is available online, by fax, or mail. The report provides the test taker's percentile ranks on the 28 sales performance dimensions compared to an "executive comparison group" and narratives of typical behaviors for individuals with those scores. The data are presented in three sections. The first is an executive summary that includes the test taker's percentile rank for a scale labeled Overall Expected Sales Performance, and two additional concepts: Interpersonal Sales Skills and Task Orientation. There is no further information on these dimensions. The second section provides the test taker's percentile ranks on the 14 Cognitive and Interpersonal Sales Skills, and the 14 Personal Sales Quality factors. The third section provides a narrative description of the test taker's strengths and weaknesses for the 28 sales performance factors. The third section also describes for each of the 28 sales performance dimensions whether the test taker's responses put them above, below, or at the average, and then provides a series of bulleted statements about the test taker's personal qualities. There appears to be a series of fine graduations in the ratings including below average, slightly below average, average, slightly above average, above average, high, and very high. There is no further information on these ratings.

The 3SP is intended for a variety of applications with the test user making decisions on which of the 28 dimensions are important for the position being assessed. The test user is encouraged to use other sources of information, such as cognitive ability assessments and interviews, to make decisions about placement and recruitment. The test developers do not recommend the test as a tool for "dehiring."

DEVELOPMENT. The 3SP is constructed on the foundations of the author's previous personality measures, the Jackson Personality Inventory—Revised (JPI-R), the Personality Research

Form (PRF), and the Survey of Work Styles (SWS). Jackson's model of personality does not map to the "Big Five" (Extraversion, Emotional Stability, Agreeableness, Conscientiousness, and Openness to Experience: Vinchur, Schippmann, Switzer, & Roth, 1998) but rather is based on 25 personality factors. In the interest of flexibility, Jackson endeavored to develop measures that are independent, span a wide range of behaviors, and are specific enough to be readily understandable by the lay reader.

Jackson extended his earlier work in personality by analyzing "relevant reference works, theory, and research" to develop a series of 28 theoretical constructs regarding sales performance. From a large pool of items developed for the author's previous personality work, relevant items were selected for each sales performance construct. After an initial review of p-values, items were then tested for their ability to reliably measure the sales performance construct while minimizing the correlation between the different sales performance measures. The items were then judged for their content representativeness, ambiguity, cogency, simplicity, and compactness of style. The judgement process is not specified. As per the author's intent to allow flexibility in use, the definitions of the resulting scales are broad, though some behavioral examples for each scale can be obtained from sample reports. It is not clear how the items load, or whether items can load on more than one scale.

TECHNICAL. The standardization sample included 243 people. The sample included individuals with a variety of functions (e.g., administration, sales, marketing, accounting and finance, R&D, HR) and industries (e.g., defense, pharmaceuticals, IT, health care). Information on the normative sample, especially a breakdown of the sample by business function, industry, age, sex, and years of experiences, is not available.

There is no information on the test-retest reliability of scores from the instrument, and the reliabilities of the 3SP items are not reported. The reader is referred to "substantial evidence" of the internal consistency and test-retest reliability of the author's other measures (i.e., SWS, JPI-R, and PRF).

The reader is also referred to evidence obtained for the SWS, JPI-R and PRF for convergent and discriminative validity information. Predictive validity evidence for the 3SP is based on 360-degree feedback on 243 test takers' job performance by multiple raters. A table provides the correlations between the 360-degree feedback and the 3SP sales performance dimensions, which range from .32 to .55. There is no information on the types of questions raters were asked, nor how many raters provided information. The authors do not provide other types of validity evidence. The authors state that other types of performance measures, such as sales figures, can be contaminated by factors such as the size of the geographic area covered by the sales person, or the specific type of product (communication with publisher).

There is no information on how the scales for Overall Sales Performance and Interpersonal Sales Skills and Task Orientation are constructed, that is, how the 28 sales performance measures are combined to create these overall measures.

The technical manual notes that a principal component factor analysis of the 28 sales performance constructs, using data for 243 test takers, extracted six factors. Using canonical correlation analysis the author identified five "combinations of personality factors that predict sales leadership behaviors" (technical manual, p. 29). This information appears to support a "Big Five" model of personality, a point of potential confusion.

COMMENTARY. The potential impact of a successful salesperson is significant, especially for small and medium sized businesses. A sales person can intimately affect an organization, both financially and through the relationships they build or fail to build. They operate, often unacknowledged, as their organization's public face. As a consequence, organizations are very concerned with identifying sales persons who not only have the potential to make sales but also will reinforce their organization's image.

For most organizations the 3SP would be inappropriate due to its lack of an interpretative framework (e.g., how well does this sales person compare to other sales people?). For such organizations there exist tools that are built on proven sales models (e.g., Resource Technologies' Impact Three Sales Building System [www.resource-technologies.com] based on the IMPACT sales model), which provide a comprehensive report that answers questions directly related to sales performance: can they sell, how do they sell, will they sell, and why do they sell?

In studies where an organization has the resources for developing its own interpretive framework, the 3SP may offer an assessment around which an organization could develop an internal selection and development program. Such an organization must be able to build a comprehensive database of 3SP profiles for different positions and develop a research program to relate these profiles to actual job performance.

The documentation of the 3SP is very weak, and the author relies on the user's familiarity with related personality assessments. This seriously undermines the credibility of the instrument as a tool to identify and develop sales staff. This credibility gap is widened by the lack of information on the normative sample and the inclusion of individuals who do not have a sales function. The largest credibility gap is the lack of evidence relating the dimensions to sales revenue. A rule of thumb in the business world is that less than 10% of your sales people generate 90% of your revenue. As a consequence, the lack of research on the 3SP's relationship with sales revenue would be of little comfort for a business owner or an HR Director charged with identifying sales performers. There is research documenting the relationship between personality traits and sales performance (e.g., Vinchur et al., 1998), so the absence of such data is very troubling. It is necessary for Sigma Assessment Systems to aggressively address this credibility gap because it fails to meet its goal to "identify the underlying factors for effective sales performance of job candidates" (technical manual, p. 17).

SUMMARY. The 3SP suffers a credibility gap. Improved documentation, appropriate normative group(s), evidence of links to sales performance (including sales volume and relationship capabilities), and more detailed descriptions of behaviors would substantially address this problem. The lack of an interpretive framework makes the 3SP inappropriate for organizations that do not have the time, expertise, or resources to create one.

REVIEWER'S REFERENCE

Vinchur, A. J., Schippmann, J. S., Switzer, F. S., & Roth, P. L. (1998). A meta-analytic review of predictors of job performance for salespeople. *Journal of Applied Psychology, 83*, 586–597.

[223]

Sigma Survey for Security Officers.

Purpose: Designed as a "test for screening job applicants for the position of security officer."
Population: Ages 18 and over.
Publication Dates: 1996–2003.
Acronym: SSSO.
Scores, 5: Security Officer Problem Solving, Incident Report Writing Aptitude (Spelling, Correct Sentences, Total), Overall Score.

Administration: Individual or group.
Parts, 2: Situations, Language Use.
Price Data, 2003: $17 per administration (1–99); volume discounts available.
Time: (35) minutes.
Comments: Computer, internet, and fax scoring services available through publisher; recommended by publisher for use in conjunction with the Employee Screening Questionnaire (86).
Authors: Douglas N. Jackson, Julie M. McCarthy, and Michael C. Ashton.
Publisher: Sigma Assessment Systems, Inc.

Review of the Sigma Survey for Security Officers by JAMES T. AUSTIN, Research Specialist 2, and ERICH C. FEIN, Senior Program Associate, Center on Education and Training for Employment, College of Education, The Ohio State University, Columbus, OH:

DESCRIPTION. The Sigma Survey for Security Officers (SSSO) provides scores proposed for evaluation of candidates for job positions in the occupation, thus the stakes of testing may be high. The security officer occupation is expected to grow, at least through 2012, according to the Occupational Outlook Handbook entry (retrieved January 9, 2005 at www.bls.gov/oco/ocos159.htm#outlook). A slice of the criterion domain for this occupation, namely security problem solving and preparation of incident reports, was selected as the focus of measurement. The 35-minute test yields multiple scores from two sections. A Security Problem Solving score is based on responses to five testlets (scenarios) each with four associated multiple-choice items. This format seems to represent situational judgment. An Incident Report Writing Aptitude score is based on Spelling and Correct Sentences scores. The Spelling test presents 28 words relevant to the security officer occupation—around 50% are misspelled. The response required is indication of the words that are spelled incorrectly. The Correct Sentence test presents eight sets of four sentences of which one sentence is grammatically correct. The response required is selection of the correct sentence.

DEVELOPMENT. This test may have been constructed within a conceptual framework, but it was not clear in the manual beyond the assertions of the developers. Provision of a framework, perhaps in graphic format, would satisfy a key criterion from the *Standards For Educational and Psychological Testing* (AERA, APA, & NCME, 1999).

The stated purpose of the test in the manual and the one-page brochure is to provide a comprehensive assessment yielding scores that can be used in personnel selection. The content of the test specification apparently was drawn from interviews with security industry personnel and corporate clients that elicited abilities and behaviors. There are, however, no details of the test planning process. This lack of documentation runs against the SIOP Principles for the Validation and Use of Personnel Selection Procedures (2003). The test specification and any item specifications were not discussed in the manual except in general terms.

TECHNICAL. Two types of materials were provided for review. One was a manual of 11 pages developed by Jackson, McCarthy, and Ashton (2003). The other was a folder containing a shrink-wrapped rapid-fax answer form and test booklet, a sample score report intended for the test user, and a 1-page brochure of the SSSO containing descriptions and pricing. We address each in turn.

Manual. The brief manual in three parts seems to combine elements of a technical manual and an administrator's manual. The first part addresses administration and scoring of the Sigma Survey for Security Officers in four subsections: nature and purpose, format, administration, and issues in the construction of the SSSO. The initial section on nature and purpose deals with broad overview, including the definition, content development, administration time, and recent research support. The section on format describes the two parts and their subsections. The section on administration takes a proctor through the process by providing specific steps as well as material to be read aloud to test-takers. The subsection ends with short paragraphs on scoring (only by computer, not by hand) and the normative sample. The section on issues in construction asserts that careful theoretical conceptions were used to develop items in each section, but there are no test specifications or content inputs to document this claim. The developers discuss ease of administration as a positive feature of the SSSO, then discuss objective scoring, and broad applicability across groups. This section seems misplaced on pages 4–5 and might be better placed at the beginning of the manual.

The second part of the manual presents an "empirical evaluation" of the test. First, the authors discuss the background of the study that evaluated the SSSO and its details. An initial sample of 262 was reduced to an achieved sample of 187. Individuals completed the SSSO and also wrote incident reports, which were evaluated by two independent, blind raters. The results of the study are presented as alpha estimates for the SSSO sections (Situations .90, Language Usage .93, Spelling .95), as corrected reliability of work sample judgments (interrater for both incidents and the total, plus split half for the total), and as validity in the form of correlations of predictor scores with the work sample criterion. An overview of the empirical evaluation is provided, and it seems to have been competently done. References and appendices comprise the last page of the manual (four references appear, although published articles on situational judgment tests that are accumulating were not cited).

Additional materials. The rapid fax answer form is specific to Sigma Assessment Systems, Inc. The front of this form, which is not faxed back, presents instructions to job candidates on the left and to administrators on the right. The back of this form, which is faxed back for scoring promised within 30 minutes, provides at the top a place for examiners to enter the fax-back number to receive the report (the test user), followed by space to print the name of the job candidate, followed by scannable areas to enter responses to the two parts of the test. Second, the sample report is a single page with the test name at the top of the page. The name and serial number from the answer form make up the second layer of detail, followed by an explanation of the score. Immediately following is a statement that the score report should not be shared with the job candidate. A notes section indicates if there were unreadable or duplicate responses. The results form the bottom layer of the page and show five scores (more clearly than described in the manual). Percentage scores are four: Security Officer Problem Solving, Incident Report Writing Aptitude consisting of Spelling and Correct Sentences, and Total Writing Aptitude. The fifth, Overall Score, is shown as a percentile rank. Percentage and percentile rank results are displayed graphically.

Third, the descriptive and advertising material is a single sheet that presents sections on application (purpose is selection), overview, description, development, reliability and validity, administration, and a section titled "We recommend," which advocates using SSSO with the

Employee Screening Questionnaire for work-related personality measurement (dependable and counterproductive scores implied). One additional section, as well as the left border, provides contact information for Sigma Assessment Systems, Inc. The pricing, with volume discounts, is listed at the bottom right of the sheet.

COMMENTARY. Validity is a unified argument constructed to explain how scores can be interpreted and used. Content, criterion, and construct claims were made by the developers, and should be supported. Ideally a series of studies would be done to relate scores on the SSSO to different criteria, or to other tests claiming to measure the same or similar constructs. There is no evidence that this was done, and no discussion in the manual that would indicate that it is contemplated. One of the key choices made by the test developers is the range of the job domain sampled, here situation analysis/judgment and incident report writing. Even there, the components of spelling and correct sentences rather than the actual writing of incident reports are assessed.

Security officers comprise an important and growing occupation. Test developers have considerable liberty in selecting narrower constructs for measurement. But what is unclear is how the scores provided by the SSSO fit into the general occupational criterion domain. There have been cases, perhaps few in number, in which the misapplication of a "use of force continuum" by a security officer leads to civil lawsuits and monetary losses. There are a number of deficiencies in the materials provided for review that make it difficult to recommend the SSSO without reservation. Information on content validation and item tryouts is not provided in the manual, nor is it mentioned. It is unclear whether there are multiple forms, which might enhance retesting if that is indicated. A normative sample of 4,040 job candidates is mentioned briefly in the manual, but further details and breakdowns are not provided. Reliability is mentioned in the brochure differently than in the manual (.94 figure cited in brochure). There is no evidence about possible differential item functioning in the normative data. A single study was presented in support of the SSSO, and it seemed to be competently done and supportive, finding a validity coefficient of .65 between SSSO scores and a criterion of incident report quality as assessed by two independent raters.

SUMMARY. Based on the limited evidence available and the gaps in evidence, it is not possible to recommend widespread use of this tool until additional details are provided. At a minimum the additions include normative data and subgroup analyses to investigate differential item functioning, whereas over time we would anticipate additional studies supporting the criterion and construct validity of the SSSO measure. An example of the former might be studies using training reactions and knowledge acquisition as outcomes; an instance of the latter might be studies that investigate convergent and discriminant validity of the SSSO with other measuring tools used in the criminal justice and security domain.

REVIEWERS' REFERENCES

American Educational Research Association, American Psychological Association, & National Council on Measurement in Education. (1999). *Standards for educational and psychological testing.* Washington, DC: American Educational Research Association.
Society for Industrial and Organizational Psychology. (2003). *Principles for the validation and use of personnel selection procedures* (4th ed.). Bowling Green, OH: Author. Retrieved January 10, 2005, from www.siop.org/principles

Review of the Sigma Survey for Security Officers by DAVID J. PITTENGER, Associate Provost: Academic Administration, The University of Tennessee at Chattanooga, Chattanooga, TN:

DESCRIPTION. The publisher of the Sigma Survey for Security Officers (SSSO) presents the instrument as an employee selection tool designed specifically to help identify potentially successful security officers. More specifically, the publisher describes the SSSO as an instrument that will evaluate applicants' cognitive skills, judgment, and ability to prepare credible incident reports.

The instrument consists of a single-use test booklet and a single-page answer sheet. The SSSO contains three broad categories of questions—spelling, grammar, and problem solving. The spelling section consists of 28 words, 17 of which are misspelled, and requires the applicant to indicate whether the spelling of each word is correct or incorrect. For the grammar section, which contains eight items, the applicant identifies which of four sentences is free of grammatical errors. The remainder of the test consists of 20 multiple-choice questions that follow brief scenarios related to the work of a security officer. Applicants receive 35 minutes to complete the whole test; there are no time limits for the subcomponents of the SSSO.

When completed, the user faxes the answer sheet to the publisher for scoring. In return, the user receives a summary profile of the applicant's performance on the test. The summary presents the percentage correct for each category of questions and an overall percentile ranking of the applicant's score. The test does not offer a manual scoring option. Therefore, it appears that one must purchase individual booklets for each applicant taking the test.

DEVELOPMENT. Readers of the SSSO's manual will be greatly disappointed by the limited and often vague presentation of the steps used to create the instrument. According to the manual, the test reflects the needs of a large corporation that wished to hire security officers who could write incident reports that were relatively free of spelling and grammatical errors, and that accurately reported the critical events of the incident. There is no information describing the development of the items used in the SSSO and only limited information regarding its reliability and validity.

What one does learn reading the manual is that the SSSO's developers asked a group of security officers, with at least 6 months of experience, to "prepare incident reports to occur presented in the form of sets of drawing" (quoted verbatim from p. 7 of manual). Apparently, the security officers wrote two incident reports that were then evaluated on their quality by two judges, using a 7-point rating scale. The interrater reliability between the raters was high as was the correlation of the ranking of the two incidents. The researchers then examined the relation between test scores on the SSSO and the judges' scores of the incident reports as a measure of convergent validity.

TECHNICAL. The section of the manual reviewing the reliability and validation of scores from the SSSO is as thin on detail as the section describing the evolution of the instrument. In essence, one finds the correlation between test scores and judges' scores of incident reports for the 187 officers who completed the task. Interestingly, 262 officers began the task. The authors of the manual make no mention of the missing 75 participants, their characteristics, or how their departure may have affected the results. The manual reports moderate correlations between the tests scores and the quality of the incidents.

Searching through the manual, one finds a two-sentence description of the normative data used to generate the summary statistics for the SSSO's evaluation of the applicant. These sentences reveal only that the sample consists of 4,040 applicants for security officer jobs from various parts of the United States. The manual provides no additional normative data regarding this population.

COMMENTARY. The utility of this instrument is difficult to describe and defend. If the sole purpose of the instrument is to identify security officers who can write complete sentences and accurately describe a critical event, then one wonders whether a general measure of writing skills let alone the simple evaluation of a writing sample would not be more cost effective and equally informative. The manual offers little useful information to judge the adequacy of the test or the inferences made from scores produced by the test. At most, the data indicate a hint of convergent validity, but little else.

The manual supplies no information that would allow one to describe the basic psychometric properties of the instrument. There is no information regarding the characteristics of the population against which applicants are compared. Notably absent are the conventional statistical summaries of the total score and the subtests. Equally conspicuous in their absence are additional data reflecting the psychometric properties of the test. Given the single focus on convergent validity, one would expect data related to discriminant validity for the sake of comparison and context.

Those who wish to say only that they use systematic testing procedures to evaluate their applicants will be able to fulfill this claim using the SSSO. Those who wish to say that they use cost-effective and amply validated selection instruments with no evidence of adverse impact will need to pass over the SSSO as a selection tool.

SUMMARY. The SSSO is an instrument consisting of 56 items that purportedly index the applicant's ability to use good judgment and to recognize misspelled words and grammatically in correct sentences. There is no attempt to measure other traits one might expect in a security officer such as dependability or honesty. Although the test may well measure the basic traits it was intended to measure, there is little evidence to support its use. Those wishing to hire employees who have mastered basic writing skills would do well to pass over the SSSO and continue their search.

[224]

Signposts Early Assessment System.

Purpose: Designed to provide an overall measure of literacy development focusing on prereading and reading skills.

Population: Grades K–3.5.
Publication Dates: 2000–2001.
Scores: Total score only.
Subtests: 4 components: Early Literacy Battery, Pre-DRP Tests, Performance Tasks, Informal Assessments.
Administration: Group.
Levels, 5: SA-1 (Grades K–K.5), SA-2 (Grades K.5–1.4), SA-3 (Grades 1.0–1.9), SA-4 (Grades 1.7–2.7), SA-5 (Grades 2.5–3.5).
Price Data, 2003: $50 per examination set including 1 test booklet of each level, administration procedures, handbook (2001, 68 pages), and norms book (2001, 31 pages); $99 per classroom set including 25 test booklets (specify level) including administration procedures, a class record, handbook, and norms book; $72 per 25 test booklets (specify level) including administration procedures and a class record sheet; $10 per scoring key (specify level); $24 per handbook; $20 per norms book.
Time: (110–165) minutes.
Comments: Scoring keys must be purchased separately.
Author: Touchstone Applied Science Associates, Inc.
Publisher: Touchstone Applied Science Associates, Inc.

Review of the Signposts Early Assessment System by THOMAS P. HOGAN, Professor of Psychology, University of Scranton, Scranton, PA:
DESCRIPTION. The Early Literacy Assessment System (ELAS) has four components: the Early Literacy Battery (ELB), the Pre-DRP Tests, the Performance Tasks, and the Informal Assessments. In combination, they are designed to provide a comprehensive picture of a child's literacy development in the grade range kindergarten through Grade 3. ELAS defines literacy as including speaking, listening, reading, and writing.

The ELB has five battery levels, each successively more difficult with some overlapping of items. The levels are labeled as forms (Forms SA-1 to SA-5), not to be confused with equivalent forms of approximately equal difficulty. The test booklets range in size from 24–32 pages, with numbers of items ranging from 68–88. All items in the ELB are multiple-choice, with three options predominating for the lowest levels and moving to four or five options for more advanced levels. All printing is black-on-white, thus appearing a bit drab in comparison with the usual multicolored materials typical in the lower grades. Content ranges from letter identification and sound-letter matching up to the reading of con-nected discourse. Each ELB test form has a separate book of Test Administration Procedures, containing a brief description of the complete ELAS, general directions for administering, and the specific directions for administering the items at that level.

The Pre-DRP Tests occur at three levels, with recommended grade ranges of K.5–1.4, 1.0–1.9, and 1.7–2.7. Numbers of items range from 28–32. All items are multiple-choice. A single Test Administration Procedure manual covers all three levels. The tests are untimed; the handbook indicates that the tests are usually completed in 45 minutes. Items range from reading single words, to sentences, to paragraphs, the latter using the modified cloze format of the DRP tests. Both ELB and Pre-DRP tests are hand-scored.

Performance Tasks occur in five levels, spanning the grade range K.0–3.5. Types of tasks vary by level, with some overlap of tasks between levels. There are six types of tasks, not all appearing at all levels. The types include: listening (to a story) and drawing a picture (about the story), listening and retelling, listening and writing a summary, reading and completing a story, reading and writing a summary, and writing from dictation.

Each teacher's manual for the Performance Tasks begins with a succinct, useful summary of the entire ELAS and the particular function of the performance component. At the heart of the teacher's manuals are the directions for administering the tasks and the scoring rubrics. Most frequently, the scoring rubrics are 5-point scales, with 0 being *no response or indecipherable*. The other points have simple descriptors such as "5 *Full Understanding*" and "2 *Some Understanding*."

The Informal Assessments occur at three levels: kindergarten, Grade 1, and Grades 2/3 (i.e., Grades 2 and 3 combined). At each level, the assessments are miscellaneous collections of relatively simple, usually brief tasks to be administered individually. The teacher makes copies of the forms to be used. Separate teacher's manuals for each level present the tasks and the administration procedures. Examples of tasks are: making a list of books read during the month, simple writing tasks, and giving the sound associated with a letter.

The handbook states that "The Student Profile is the element of the system that permits the integration of information from each of the other elements of the system as well as that from other sources" (p. 7). Unfortunately, as of November, 2003, this apparently crucial document has not been published. Therefore, it is not clear how the publisher intends to coordinate the various components of the ELAS and exactly what is to be reported.

DEVELOPMENT. For the conceptual framework for ELAS, the handbook refers to standard documents in the early literacy field, such as those from the International Reading Association and the National Reading Panel. The sources cited are appropriate to the task of defining the intended content. Beyond that, the handbook provides minimal information about the procedures used to develop the various components of the ELAS. The final forms of the ELB and Pre-DRP tests came from two forms used in standardization. However, the handbook does not indicate how final items were selected from these preliminary forms. No information is given about the selection of materials for the Performance Tasks and Informal Assessments, other than reference to such guiding documents as mentioned above. The handbook makes little of the point, but it seems clear that the Pre-DRP test is intended as a downward extension of the well-established Degrees of Reading Power (see 69) test. In turn, the ELB is a downward extension of the Pre-DRP tests.

TECHNICAL INFORMATION. Technical information for the ELB and Pre-DRP are given in the handbook and in the norms booklet. There is no technical information of any sort (e.g., norms or reliability data) for either the Performance Tasks or Informal Assessments. Hence, the following remarks are confined to the ELB and Pre-DRP components.

The Signposts norms booklet describes the norm groups for ELB and Pre-DRP in terms of geographic region, school district size, socioeconomic status, and ethnicity. Numbers of students involved in the twice per year norming ranged from 689–1,982 per period. Considering all of the data, it appears that the norm groups will yield a slightly "hard" norm. Minority students and low SES groups were somewhat underrepresented in the norm groups. It is surprising that the publisher did not use a weighting procedure, now a fairly common practice, to bring the norm group into better alignment with national data on crucial variables. The norms booklet indicates that actually two forms at each level were administered in the standardization. From these came what the handbook (p. 35) refers to as the "shelf forms." It is not clear how the norms for these shelf forms arose.

The Pre-DRP scores and a Pre-DRP subtest embedded in Level 5 of ELB permit conversion of scores into DRP units. The norms booklet and the handbook seem to assume that the potential user is already familiar with the concept of DRP units; the documents provide little description of this type of unit and its use for selecting reading materials. For persons already familiar with the DRP tests, the conversion tables will be useful. Persons not familiar with the DRP tests would need to develop such familiarity for meaningful use of these conversions.

For reliability, the handbook reports internal consistency (alpha) coefficients for each level of the ELB and Pre-DRP tests. For ELB, values range from .92–.97, with a median of .94. For Pre-DRP, values range from .82–.94, with a median of .93. There is one odd form with a value of .82. All of the reliability data are for the two separate forms involved in the standardization. Data are not provided for the "shelf forms," the forms actually available for use. The handbook provides standard errors of measurement, but only in original raw score units. *SEM*s should be provided in converted score units.

The handbook makes no reference to reliability of subscores on the ELB or Pre-DRP tests. One would infer from this absence that the publisher does not intend interpretation below the level of total scores. However, a brochure made available with specimen materials points to subscore areas on the Class Record Sheet and calls for "Identify[ing] your students' strengths and weaknesses on critical literacy tasks" (p. 6). This is a major mismatch between the technical materials and advertising materials. If subscores are a basis for interpretation, then reliability information must be provided for them.

The discussion of validity concentrates primarily on content validity, especially through reference to the source documents for defining literacy, as identified above. The discussion is straightforward. The handbook also provides the correlation matrix for individual tasks within the ELB and for selected tasks in ELB and Pre-DRP tests. Finally, the handbook presents results of several studies relating scores on the Pre-DRP tests to other criteria such as reading rate in a 1-minute period and scores on another reading test. The data seem generally supportive, but samples for these latter studies are not described sufficiently to permit firm conclusions.

COMMENTARY. The ELAS test booklets have a clean, simple layout, with clear drawings and appropriate type size. The test items should function well for most children in the target age groups. The directions for administering are also clearly presented and easy to follow.

It would have been better to label the ELB forms as levels rather than forms. The term "forms" can easily be confused with equivalent forms. It would also have been preferable to use a different title for the ELB component. The title "Early Literacy Battery" is easily confused with the title of the complete package, "Early Literacy Assessment System."

The ELB and Pre-DRP tests provide fairly standard coverage of prereading and early reading skills, beginning with simple matters such as letter identification and proceeding to reading connected discourse. Reliability estimates of total scores on the tests are good.

Directions for the Performance Tasks and Informal Assessments are clearly presented. Scoring rubrics for the Performance Tasks are quite general. One would anticipate substantial interteacher variation and perhaps intrateacher variation in the application of the rubrics. The manuals contain no exemplars or benchmark responses for the scoring rubrics.

The Performance Tasks and Informal Assessments represent the best and the worst of purely criterion-referenced assessment. On the positive side, the activities appear meaningful and appropriate. The representation of various facets of literacy, beyond what is covered in ELB and Pre-DRP tests, is wholesome. On the negative side, completion of the tasks will be time-consuming and burdensome. Further, it is not at all clear how much useful, reliable information a teacher will obtain from these tasks beyond what is available through textbook-based and other ordinary classroom activities. There is no information about how reliably teachers actually use any of the scoring rubrics on the tasks.

The ELAS aims to cover literacy, defined to include reading, listening, speaking, and writing. It is apparent that the components of the system with any semblance of technical information are limited almost entirely to the reading domain. The other three domains are covered almost exclusively with the Performance Tasks and Informal Assessments, for which there is no technical information.

SUMMARY. The ELAS is a work in progress. Parts of the system appeared in 2001, other parts in 2003. A key reporting mechanism, the Student Profile, is not yet available. The ELB and Pre-DRP Test components, the parts of the system with technical information, merit some further development, especially in terms of norms. For schools heavily dependent on accurate national norms for the reading component of literacy, alternative instruments such as the Metropolitan Readiness Tests (MRT; T6:1581) or the Stanford Early School Achievement Test (SESAT; T6:2361) may be preferable. For schools already using the Degrees of Reading Power (DRP; 69) tests in upper grades, these two components may provide a useful downward extension that ties into the DRP reporting framework. The Performance Tasks and Informal Assessments may be useful adjuncts to ordinary classroom materials, but they do not move much beyond such materials.

Review of the Signposts Early Assessment System by JUDITH A. MONSAAS, Executive Director of P-16 Assessment and Evaluation, University System of Georgia, Atlanta, GA:

DESCRIPTION. The Signposts Early Assessment System is designed to assess the literacy development of children in kindergarten through the middle of Grade 3. The purpose of the assessments is to monitor the literacy development of children in the primary grades. There are four components to the assessment system. The Early Literacy Assessment System measures the prereading and reading skills to obtain an overall assessment of a child's literacy development. There are five levels of this battery and five categories of tasks (Sounds, Letters, and Words; Vocabulary; Reading; Listening; and Language). The Pre-DRP provides holistic measures of "the ability of emerging and beginning readers" (Handbook, p. 23). There are three Pre-DRP test levels and alternate forms at each of the levels. One of the alternate forms of the Pre-DRP is embedded in three of the Early Literacy forms, so if one administers the Early Literacy Assessment System, one would not administer the Pre-DRP at the same time. The two additional components of the assessment system, Performance Tasks and Informal Assessments, are more specifically targeted at literacy skills and designed to be used to assess student progress in the classroom.

Test administration booklets are provided for each form of the Early Literacy Assessment System and the Pre-DRP tests. Procedures for standardization of the administration are clearly spelled out. The tests do not have to be administered by someone with a testing background, but the manual recommends that the test administrator be someone with whom the students are familiar. The tests are group administered, but the recommended size of the group depends on the age of the students. Teacher's manuals are provided for each form of the Performance Tasks and Informal Assessments. These clearly describe how to administer the assessments. Follow-up instructional activities are also provided with the Performance Tasks and Informal Assessments.

A student profile integrates information from the various assessments and can be used to track student development over time. A class record sheet is also provided for the Early Literacy Assessment System. All materials needed to administer the assessments are provided.

Both Early Literacy Assessment System and Pre-DRP raw scores can be converted into scale scores. These scale scores are vertically equated so progress can be determined across test levels. Scale scores can be converted to percentile ranks and stanines. For Grades 2 and 3 students, percentile ranks on the Pre-DRP tests or the Pre-DRP subscale can be converted to DRP (Degrees of Reading Power) scores. These DRP scores can be used to match students' reading level to appropriate reading materials. Brief descriptions of the use of DRP scores to select appropriate materials are explained in the resource materials, but in order to use the DRP scores to plan literacy/reading instruction, further resources would need to be consulted by the teacher. The Early Literacy and Pre-DRP assessments can be reported as norm-referenced or standards-based test scores. In order to provide standards-based test scores, it is necessary to map the tasks of the assessments to the state or local standards. Then information from the class record sheet can be used to describe student performance on the standards.

Standards-based scores are available on the Performance Tasks and the Informal Assessments. The test user can reference the scores to national standards (e.g., NAEYC) or to state or local standards if they map those standards against the tasks. The scoring guides/rubrics for the performance tasks are fairly clear, but would be enhanced with examples of student responses that are appropriate for each response level.

DEVELOPMENT. The procedures used for the development of the Early Literacy Assessment System and the Pre-DRP Tests are clearly described in the handbook. Several sets of national standards were released during the development of these assessments and they were used to gain validity evidence for the assessments. Test specifications were created; items were developed and field tested. Bias and content reviews were conducted. A norming study was conducted and final forms developed.

The Performance Tasks and Informal Assessments were developed using national literacy and reading standards. No evidence of field testing of these assessments was provided.

TECHNICAL.

Standardization. The Early Literacy Assessment System and Pre-DRP tests were normed on a national sample during Fall and Spring of 1999. Approximately 9,900 students in Kindergarten through the first half of third grade participated in the norming study. The tables provided in the manual show that the norming sample approximated the nation in terms of geographic regions, school district size, socioeconomic status, and ethnicity. Demographic breakdowns were not reported for gender. Tabulations across demographic groups (e.g., geographic region by ethnicity) were also not reported.

Reliability. Internal consistency reliability coefficients were provided for each form of the Early Literacy Assessment System. The reliability coefficients were all in the mid .90s, indicating strong reliability for each of the forms. Reliability coefficients for the Pre-DRP were all in the .90s except for the Kindergarten level, which was .89 and .82 for the two K forms of this test. The standardization sample was used for calculating reliability coeefficients so all Ns were adequate. No reliability data were provided for the Performance Tasks and Informal Assessments. The authors recommend selecting items to match standards, making it unlikely that the entire set of tasks would be administered in a standard testing situation. Evidence of scorer reliability on the Performance Tasks would have been helpful.

Validity. Content validity evidence for the Early Literacy Assessment System is based on the process used in the development of the assessments, a thorough review of the research on early literacy, and the use of the current standards for early literacy development. Additionally, items were reviewed by a panel of experts. Tables showing growth from kindergarten into Grade 3 are provided as evidence that the assessment reflects growth over time. Tables showing the internal correlations of tasks are used to demonstrate construct validity evidence. The tasks are all positively correlated and the patterns of lower and higher correlations suggest that the skills assessed are logically interrelated. The last set of evidence to support the construct validity of the Early Literacy Assessment System includes the conceptual and empirical links of the Pre-DRP subtest and the Degrees of Reading Power (DRP) tests. The case for consequential validity is somewhat ambiguous. According to the handbook, "Consequential validity concerns the consequences of using test scores to make decisions. This aspect of validity is one that should be taken very seriously in the case of all measures of achievement, but especially in those that are designed for young children. One must be mindful that a number of competencies contribute to emergent literacy and that variability in the speed and pattern of development is more the rule than the exception" (p. 39). This is a useful reminder, but one expects more information in a section concerning consequential validity.

The validity evidence supporting the Pre-DRP is provided by a description of the developmental nature of the items included on the test. The evidence of construct validity is largely based on the relationship of the Pre-DRP with the DRP. Item Response Theory is used to demonstrate that the Pre-DRP and DRP ability estimates form an underlying construct that is being measured by both assessments. The correlations between the Pre-DRP and other elements of the Early Literacy Assessment System reflect stronger relationships with the Pre-DRP and comprehension tasks and lower correlations with foundational tasks that need to be mastered before students begin reading.

Validity evidence was not provided to support the Performance Assessment Tasks and the Informal Assessments. These two assessments serve as "assessment banks" for teachers to use in the classroom. The alignment of the Performance Tasks with national standards and the integration of literacy strands within the tasks support the content validity of these tasks. The Informal Assessments are based on national standards and recommendations made by national organizations.

A sequence chart shows what tasks match which area of literacy development. Although a section entitled "validity" may be appropriate for these assessments, the supporting documentation shows that both sets of assessments reflect appropriate content for classroom use.

COMMENTARY AND SUMMARY. This system of assessment tools appears to be a useful contribution to the assessment of early literacy. The standardized assessments (Early Literacy Assessment System and Pre-DRP) assess the development of early literacy in students in kindergarten through the middle of Grade 3. They are supplemented by sets of classroom tasks that teachers can use to monitor student growth throughout the school year. The administration and interpretation materials are user-friendly and a classroom teacher or aide would have little trouble administering any of the assessments. Interpreting the tests should be left to the classroom teacher.

The technical information is fairly strong and appears to be well grounded in early literacy theory and research and supported by national standards. The assessments appear to be a downward extension of the DRP assessments and those assessments are used to provide validity support. Reviewer recommendations include adding more detailed descriptions of the norming sample and exemplars for the rubrics with the Performance Tasks and/or scorer reliability evidence. In all, this battery is a strong addition to the repertoire of assessment tools for early literacy.

[225]
Single Word Spelling Test.

Purpose: "Designed to assess the attainment in spelling."
Population: Ages 5-9 to 14-9.
Publication Date: 2000.
Acronym: SWST.
Scores, 2: Total Score, Progress Score.
Administration: Group.
Levels, 9: A for Age 6, B for Age 7, C for Age 8, D for Age 9, E for Age 10, F for Age 11, G for Age 12, H for Age 13, I for Age 14.
Price Data, 2004: £36.75 per complete package including manual, photocopiable answer sheets, and group record sheets.
Time: (30) minutes per test.
Authors: Lesley Sacre and Jackie Masterson.
Publisher: NFER-Nelson Publishing Co., Ltd. [England].

Review of the Single Word Spelling Test by JENNIFER N. MAHDAVI, Assistant Professor of Special Education, California State University, Los Angeles, CA:

DESCRIPTION. The Single Word Spelling Test (SWST) is a norm-referenced, group-administered paper-and-pencil assessment of English spelling ability. The SWST can be used to collect information for progress monitoring, compare student achievement to that of expected spelling ability, and analyze spelling errors to inform instruction. There are nine separate tests of 30–50 words each that are designed to assess mastery of spelling skills expected of students of ages 6 through 14 who attend school in the United Kingdom.

The directions state that the person administering the test should first read the target word aloud, then read the provided sentence using the target word in context and finally repeat the target word. Students are to write the word on a response sheet and may ask to have the words repeated. All items are to be administered and the test takes about 30 minutes.

Raw scores can be converted to standardized scores, percentile ranks, spelling age, and progress scores. Spelling age is an age-equivalent score based on the mean raw score on a test level of students of a particular age. Progress scores purport to show growth in spelling after a year of schooling. A progress score can be determined if the student has taken two consecutive test levels (e.g., A then B), approximately 12 months apart. However, when test developers initially calculated the progress scores, they used students who took two levels of the test at the same time, rather than taking a higher level test a year later. The manual therefore urges caution in interpreting progress scores.

DEVELOPMENT. Although no specific theory is cited regarding the development of the test, the authors discuss the importance of improving children's writing ability by making correct spelling an automatic function. Automaticity in spelling is expected to free a student to focus on content, organization, advanced vocabulary use, and the like.

The authors used national curricula from England, Scotland, Wales, and Northern Ireland to determine spelling patterns that should be mastered by a particular grade or age. Comparisons between National Curriculum writing levels and raw scores on the SWST are offered. The words presented for each level appear to reflect expecta-tions for the corresponding age/grade accurately. A fairly extensive portion of the test manual is devoted to classifying the words used in the SWST by spelling patterns as well as delineating types of phonological and visual errors so that teachers can analyze the spelling errors made by their students. This work is continued with a section about instructional strategies to help students improve their spelling.

No pilot testing information is offered in the test manual. There is no description of how words were selected for each test, who participated in selecting them, or whether the test items were designed to demonstrate variability among students taking the test. The raw scores appear to translate to standardized scores mathematically, not by test item construction and selection.

TECHNICAL.

Standardization. The norm sample came from randomly selected schools from the national register of schools, but locations and numbers of participating schools are not included in the manual. Between 35 and 50 school sites were used to norm each level of the test, but the total number of schools participating across the levels is not provided. The manual says that the sample was stratified by school attainment data (such as national test scores) and school type (such as maintained, infant, or junior); however, no description of the results of stratification is presented. Furthermore, there is no attempt to stratify the sample according to socioeconomic status, setting (such as urban or rural), region, or any other school-based characteristics.

Information about student participants in the norming sample is limited to age and gender. A total of 7,952 students took part in the norming process—3,901 boys and 4,051 girls. Between 819 and 983 students took each level of the test. Raw and standardized score comparisons are made by gender for each level of the test, but statistical discussions of the significance of the differences in mean score by gender are not offered. No data are presented about ethnicity, socioeconomic status, primary language, or whether any of the students had identified disabilities.

Reliability. Kuder-Richardson 20 (K-R 20) measures of internal consistency ranged between .94 and .97, with Levels D and E for the middle grades attaining the greatest K-R 20 scores. In addition, test-retest reliability measures were conducted with 507 students from England and Wales on Levels A, E, and I. The subsamples were not further described. Taking the same test a second time, approximately 1 week later, yielded strong reliability estimates: A = .96, E = .95, and I = .87. Additional information about the reliability of the SWST should be provided.

Validity. To support their claims of good content validity, the authors direct the reader to the National Curriculum guides of England, Scotland, Wales, and Northern Ireland, as well as the National Literacy Strategy. No effort is made in the manual to draw parallels between these documents and the SWST. As such, content validity should not be considered documented.

To examine concurrent validity, the authors correlate the SWST standardized scores to the National Curriculum Teacher Assessment (TA) in the areas of reading and writing. Between 567 and 806 students from England were included at each level of the SWST to yield moderate correlations between the tests ranging between .51 and .79, with the lowest correlations appearing at the highest grade levels. In addition, 150 students who took Level 5 of the SWST were compared to the British Spelling Test Series; the correlation between raw scores on the two tests was .94.

Discussions of concurrent validity with other tests in England are not convincing. In addition, concurrent validity with tests given in Scotland, Northern Ireland, or Wales is not addressed.

COMMENTARY. As a norm-referenced, standardized measure, the SWST has little to recommend it. Technical adequacy measures are poorly described throughout the manual and only cursory attention is paid to issues of reliability, validity, and standardization. Despite having a large number of students in the norm group, only gender and age are mentioned as variables of interest. No attempt is made to justify omitting other factors.

No theory or research is cited to support the test design or item selection. Administration instructions leave room for teachers to interpret them in ways that may interfere with test reliability. The authors recommend testing students of like ability together, in groups ranging from two to an entire class, faster or slower, all according to student needs. In terms of students with special needs, the authors recommend administering to students with achievement scores of 18 months or

more below or above their grade level the "spelling test closest to their estimated spelling ability" (p. 3).

However, as a curriculum-based measure, the SWST has value for classroom teachers in the United Kingdom. The manual is very friendly to a person without a background in test construction or test theory, explaining the derived scores and their uses clearly. The SWST can provide a good baseline measure of spelling ability and may be used as a formative evaluation of progress over time, especially given the relatively short amount of time that is necessary to administer it to a group of students. In addition, the authors of the test provide a method for analyzing spelling errors as well as some basic instructional ideas that might help the teacher gear classroom instruction toward the needs of individual students.

SUMMARY. The Single Word Spelling Test should be used as a norm-referenced measure of spelling ability with caution. The presentation of technical adequacy information leaves the reader with more questions than confidence about the standardization, reliability, and validity of the test. Although the SWST is a weak norm-referenced measure, it does have strengths as a curriculum-based assessment. For educators looking for an organized system for progress monitoring and error analysis, the SWST might be quite useful.

Review of the Single Word Spelling Test by JOHN W. YOUNG, Associate Professor of Educational Statistics and Measurement, Rutgers University, New Brunswick, NJ:

DESCRIPTION. The Single Word Spelling Test (SWST) is a series of nine tests designed to assess the spelling attainment of pupils ages 5 to 14, with one test for each year. Each word is administered orally in a sentence that puts the word in context. The tests are intended for group administration, and the tests take approximately 30 minutes each to administer. The tests were developed, normed, and intended for use with students in the United Kingdom. The SWST can be used to identify gaps in a student's knowledge of spelling and for tracking a pupil's progress over time. The test administrator reads aloud each word, followed by a sentence using the word, then says the word again, while students write their responses on the answer sheet provided. With the exception of the first three tests, which have 30, 35, or 45 words, all of the spelling tests contain 50 words. There are some words in common among the nine tests.

DEVELOPMENT. Spelling is considered to be an important skill because it raises both writing standards and an individual's self-esteem. The content domain for the words used in the SWST is based on the national writing curricula of England, Northern Ireland, Scotland, and Wales. In addition, words proposed by the National Literacy Strategy of the United Kingdom (a framework for teaching literacy in primary schools), have been included in the SWST. The SWST series was normed in June of 2000 using a nationally representative sample of schools. Each of the tests was administered to a sample of over 800 students, with a total standardization sample of 7,952. SWST results are reported in terms of raw scores, standardized scores, percentile ranks, progress scores, and spelling age.

TECHNICAL. Evidence in two areas, content and criterion-related, was provided to support the validity of scores from the SWST. With regard to content validity, the developers indicate that the SWST assesses spelling skills referred to in the national writing curricula of the four countries of the United Kingdom as well as the National Literacy Strategy. Evidence on the criterion-related validity of the SWST is provided in terms of its concurrent validity with National Curriculum test results (TA levels). All English schools that participated in the SWST standardization were asked to provide their students' National Curriculum results in reading and writing. For each of the nine SWST tests, based on samples of 567 to 806 pupils, correlations of SWST raw scores and TA reading ranged from .51 to .79, with an unweighted average of .64. Correlations of SWST raw scores and TA writing ranged from .53 to .79, with an unweighted average of .67. The test's developers did not provide any evidence with regard to the predictive validity or construct validity of the SWST.

The reliability of the SWST was estimated using two methods: test-retest and internal consistency. Test-retest reliability was computed for three of the SWST tests, using samples ranging from 155 to 182 students. The correlation between standardized scores from two administrations, held 1 week apart, ranged from .87 to .96, with an unweighted average of .93. The internal consistency of the SWST tests was computed

using the Kuder-Richardson 20 (K-R 20) formula. The internal consistency of all nine tests is high, with K-R 20 values ranging from .94 to .97. The standard error of measurement (*SEM*) is approximately 3 points, ranging from 2.57 to 3.47, for the standardized scores from each of the nine tests.

COMMENTARY. The SWST tests appear to hold potential as a diagnostic tool for use with students in the United Kingdom or as an assessment tool for research. The use of the national writing curricula and the National Literacy Strategy, as a basis for choosing words for inclusion on the SWST, has yielded a representative sampling of the content domain of words commonly used in the primary grades. However, the evidentiary basis to support the SWST is, at present, limited. For example, the authors acknowledge that no predictive validity studies have been conducted to date because the SWST tests are so new. In addition, there is no information provided in the test manual regarding the construct validity of scores from the SWST. An explanation for the theoretical basis behind the SWST tests is necessary to judge whether the tests are, in fact, scientifically sound. The SWST tests, in their present form, appear to be potentially useful assessment tools. However, because they are so new, and because there have been few validity studies conducted to date, users are urged to proceed cautiously in making decisions based on results from these tests.

SUMMARY. The SWST series is designed to assess the spelling attainment of pupils ages 5 to 14, and is intended primarily for use with students in the United Kingdom. The words on the SWST are drawn from the national writing curricula of the United Kingdom countries and the National Literacy Strategy. The limited validity evidence for the SWST tests indicates that the tests appear promising for use as diagnostic tools, but because they are so new, cannot be strongly recommended, at this time, until additional supporting validity evidence becomes available.

[226]

Social-Emotional Dimension Scale—Second Edition.

Purpose: "Designed to provide school personnel ... with a means for rating student behavior problems that may interfere with academic functioning."

Population: Ages 6.0–18.11.

Publication Dates: 1986–2004.

Acronym: SEDS-2.
Administration: Individual.
Price Data: Available from publisher.
Comments: Norm-referenced behavior rating scale.
Authors: Jerry B. Hutton and Timothy G. Roberts.
Publisher: PRO-ED.
  a) SCREENER FORM.
  Scores: Total score only.
  Time: (5–8) minutes.
  b) COMPREHENSIVE FORM.
  Scores, 8: Externalizing Behavior (Interpersonal Relationships, Conduct Problems, Total), Internalizing Behavior (Inappropriate Behavior, Depression, Anxiety/Inattention, Total), Overall Social-Emotional Disturbance.
  Time: (15–20) minutes.
  c) FUNCTIONAL ASSESSMENT INTERVIEW.
  Scores: Not scored.
  Time: (30) minutes.
Cross References: For a review by Jean Powell Kirnan of the earlier edition, see 11:368.

Review of the Social-Emotional Dimension Scale—Second Edition by MARK D. SHRIVER, Associate Professor, Pediatric Psychology, Munroe-Meyer Institute for Genetics and Rehabilitation, University of Nebraska Medical Center, Omaha, NE:

DESCRIPTION. The Social-Emotional Dimension Scale—Second Edition (SEDS-2) is purported to assist with identifying students at risk for behavior problems that interfere with academic performance. The SEDS-2 consists of three parts: a 15-item behavior rating form to be used as a screening measure (Screener Form), a 74-item behavior rating form to be used as a comprehensive assessment of a student's social-emotional functioning (Comprehensive Form), and a Functional Assessment Interview. It is intended to be used with students between 6-0 and 18-11 years. The rating forms are completed by teachers familiar with the student in question. Items are in a likert format with ratings from 1 (*never*) to 5 (*always*). The Screener Form provides a total score. Subscales (i.e., Dimensions) on the Comprehensive Form include Interpersonal Relationships, Conduct Problems, Inappropriate Behavior, Depression, and Anxiety/Inattention. Composite scores on the Comprehensive Form include Externalizing Behavior, Internalizing Behavior, and Overall Social-Emotional Disturbance. The Functional Assessment Interview consists of six questions. Raw scores, *T* scores, and percentile ranks are computed for the Screener Form and Compre-

hensive Form. The authors emphasize, however, that *T* scores were computed based on a linear transformation of the raw scores representing a skewed normative distribution and therefore *T* scores cannot be used for comparisons between subscales, with other tests, or for clinical interpretation. It is recommended that interpretations of a student be based solely on percentile rank scores. Percentile rank score ranges are given qualitative descriptors of "Not At Risk," "At-Risk," "High Risk," and "Very High Risk." The Screener Form is intended to be completed by more than one teacher. If 50% or more of the teachers rate a student "At Risk," then it is suggested that the Comprehensive Form be administered.

DEVELOPMENT. Bower's definition of emotional disturbance served as a model for item and scale development (Bower, 1969). In addition, items were developed based on reviews of the literature, review of IDEA (1990, 1997) definitions of emotional disturbance, review of definitions of emotional disturbance from the National Mental Health and Special Education Coalition (Forness & Knitzer, 1992), and review of existing behavior rating scales. It is unclear who, besides the authors, did the reviews and how decisions were made to include specific items. Eighty-eight additional items were created in addition to the original 32 items on the first edition of the SEDS. An undefined group of teachers sorted this item pool into six previously created categories. Empirical or theoretical/logical information about how these categories were developed is not provided. These categories appear to be the precursors to the subscales currently used on the Comprehensive Form. After further undefined review, 98 items were kept. Items were placed in a rating scale format and given to 486 students with learning disabilities, mental retardation, and emotional/behavior disorders and 741 students without identified disabilities. Items that did not differentiate between the disabled and nondisabled groups were removed. Finally, factor analyses were conducted to determine the final subscale structure and the final 74 items were retained. Discriminability Indexes were calculated for items across gender and total sample and indicated good item discrimination. It is unclear how the items for the Screener Form were identified. Information is not provided for the empirical or theoretical/logical basis for development of the Screener Form. It is also unclear how the questions for the Functional Assessment Interview were developed.

TECHNICAL.

Standardization. The normative sample consisted of 1,700 students ages 6 to 18. The demographic characteristics of the normative samples are largely comparable to the 2001 U.S. Census data; however, the Western geographic area of the U.S. appears underrepresented. In addition, African American and Hispanic American students are underrepresented. Differential item functioning (dif) analyses were conducted and indicated that items performed equally across race and ethnicity.

Significant differences were identified in mean raw scores between males and females and separate tables for normative comparisons were developed based on gender. The authors recommend using the gender-specific normative tables rather than the table for the total sample. Somewhat surprisingly, differences were not noted in mean raw scores across the age ranges. Therefore, separate standard score tables were not created for age groups.

Reliability. Several different sources of reliability evidence are provided in the manual. Coefficient alphas are .88 for the Screener Form for both male and female samples. This is acceptable for a screening measure. The coefficient alphas are all in the high .80s and .90s for the Comprehensive Form subscales and in the .90s for the composite scores. The standard error of measurement (*SEM*) values follow a similar pattern. The Overall Social-Emotional Disturbance score is very good with *SEM*s of 2 and 1, respectively, for female and male samples. The *SEM*s are a 4 for the Screener Form across both genders and this may be too large. A 95% confidence interval would be computed to be +/- 7.84. For a female attaining a mean *T* score of 50 that *SEM* computes to a percentile rank range between 22 to 80 and for a male between 21 to 77. Interpretation of this range of scores is problematic as a student with this range of scores may or may not be at risk.

Test-retest reliability coefficients computed on administration of the SEDS-2 over 2 weeks with a sample of 32 students with learning disabilities or emotional disturbance indicated high reliability for both the Screener and Comprehensive Form. Similar administration with 133 students in general education indicated less stability over 2 weeks with coefficients in the .80s except for the total score of the Comprehensive Form, which was .90. Interrater

reliability for the Screener Form was good at .91 and for the overall score for the Comprehensive Form at .95. The other subscales had good interrater correlations in the high .80s to .92.

Validity. Content validity evidence is provided in the description of item and test development and through analyses of item discrimination and differential item functioning. This evidence is most clearly presented for the Comprehensive Form. Except for item discriminability analysis, evidence is not provided for the content validity of the Screener Form. Criterion-related evidence is provided through correlative studies of the SEDS-2 Screener and Comprehensive Forms with the earlier edition of the SEDS, the Walker-McConnell Scale of Social Competence and School Adjustment (Walker & McConnell, 1995), and the Child Behavior Checklist—Teacher Report Form (Achenbach, 1991). The sample size for the comparison with the Walker-McConnell Scale and SEDS was 31 and for the CBCL-TRF it was 59 with good representation of ethnic/racial groups and children in special education. The correlations with the measures are in the expected direction and largely moderate to very good. The SEDS-2 actually has higher correlations with the CBCL-TRF than with the SEDS. The SEDS-2 appears to be measuring some of the same constructs as the CBCL-TRF.

Sensitivity, specificity, and positive predictive values were computed for the ability of the Screener Form to predict the Overall Social-Emotional Disturbance score on the Comprehensive Form. The values were good with Sensitivity Index at .80, Specificity Index at .99, and Positive Predictive Value at .95. In a study that examined the ability of the Overall Social-Emotional Disturbance score to predict a student's need for a behavior management plan the values were lower. The sample included 84 students in kindergarten through Grade 12. Minorities were underrepresented in the study. The Sensitivity Index was very good at 1.00, but the Specificity Index was low (.56), reflective of a high rate of false positives. The authors caution that the SEDS-2 is to be used as part of a comprehensive assessment and that this may assist in reducing number of false positives.

In an effort to provide evidence regarding subgroup performance, a table of *T* score means is provided for selected subgroups from the normative sample including gender, race/ethnicity, and special education label. However, interpretation of the means is complicated by the fact that the individual subgroups probably have different score distributions and given the linear transformation used with the T scores, comparisons of T scores across subgroups is not possible and interpretations regarding comparability of performance are unclear.

Other than the correlations with the CBCL-TRF, there is no information provided regarding the construct validity of the subscales in the Comprehensive Form. In other words, it is not clear that the Depression subscale measures depression or that Anxiety/Inattention measures anxiety or inattention and so forth.

COMMENTARY. General and specific intervention suggestions are provided in the manual. The suggestions are largely a laundry list of interventions one might attempt for someone with characteristics of depression, anxiety, conduct problems, or inattention. The interventions are prescriptive and not based on a functional assessment, although a functional assessment is recommended in the manual. Two case studies are presented that highlight how the SEDS-2 may contribute to decision making for a student with a possible social-emotional disorder. Neither case study demonstrates how the SEDS-2 data lead to development of a specific intervention plan to improve a child's social-emotional functioning. The first was a student who did not demonstrate social-emotional difficulties. She was referred due to academic difficulties. Treatment consisted of providing the student with more appropriate instructional activities matching her skill level and as needed consultation with a special education teacher. The second case study was for a 10-year-old male receiving special education services as a child with learning disability and a diagnosis of Attention Deficit Hyperactivity Disorder. He was rated to be at risk across all subscales of the SEDS-2 except Conduct Problems and Depression. Treatment recommendations included placement in a self-contained classroom, social skills training, and referral to a pediatric neurologist. These case studies do not provide useful evidence regarding the treatment utility of the SEDS-2 or of the incremental validity of the SEDS-2. In addition, there is no other evidence provided in the manual regarding the treatment validity or incremental validity of this measure.

With the exception of the *SEM* values for the Screener Form, the reliability evidence for the SEDS-2 is good and one may have some confidence that data obtained are stable across 2 weeks and across raters. Likewise, the content validity evidence is good and there is preliminary evidence that the SEDS-2 measures similar constructs as the Walker-McConnell scale and CBCL-TRF. The potential user should feel most confident using the Overall Social-Emotional Disturbance percentile rank score. Evidence for the construct validity for the Screener Form and individual subscales is lacking. In addition, empirical evidence is not presented for the cutoff scores regarding who is "At-Risk" and who is "Not At Risk." Empirical evidence is not provided for the decision rule to administer the Comprehensive Form if 50% or more teachers rate a student "At-Risk" on the Screener Form. Finally, evidence is not provided regarding the reliability, validity, treatment utility, or incremental validity of the Functional Assessment Interview and use of that form is not recommended.

SUMMARY. The SEDS-2 appears to be a definite improvement over the earlier edition and the authors have clearly attempted to respond to earlier reviews of the SEDS. Initial reliability and validity evidence is supportive of this measure. Concerns persist, however, regarding the contribution of data from this measure for purposes of decision making regarding eligibility, diagnosis, treatment development, and progress monitoring. At this time, use of other more established behavior rating measures, such as the Child Behavior Checklist (Achenbach, 1991) and the Behavior Assessment System for Children (Reynolds & Kamphaus, 1998) is recommended.

REVIEWER'S REFERENCES

Achenbach, T. M. (1991). *Child Behavior Checklist—Teacher Report Form.* Burlington: University of Vermont, Department of Psychiatry.

Bower, E. (1969). *Early identification of emotionally handicapped children in the school* (2nd ed.). Springfield, IL: Thomas.

Forness, S. R., & Knitzer, J. (1992). A new proposed definition and terminology to replace "serious emotional disturbance" in the Individuals with Disabilities Education Act. *School Psychology Review, 21,* 12–20.

Reynolds, C. R., & Kamphaus, R. W. (1998). Behavior Assessment System for Children. Circle Pines, MN: American Guidance Services.

Walker, H. M., & McConnell, S. R. (1995). Walker-McConnell Scale of Social Competence and School Adjustment. Austin, TX: PRO-ED.

[227]

Social Problem-Solving Inventory—Revised.

Purpose: Designed to measure people's "ability to resolve problems of everyday living."

Population: Ages 13 and over.

Publication Dates: 1990–2002.

Acronym: SPSI-R.

Administration: Individual.

Price Data, 2003: $86 per complete kit including technical manual (2002, 114 pages), 25 long forms, and 25 short forms; $61 per Long Version kit including technical manual and 25 long QuikScore™ forms; $59 per Short Version kit including technical manual and 25 short QuikScore™ forms; $37 per technical manual; $30 per 25 long QuikScore™ forms; $107 per 100 long QuikScore™ forms; $28 per 25 short QuikScore™ forms; $103 per 100 short QuikScore™ forms; $40 per specimen set including technical manual, 3 long forms, and 3 short forms.

Foreign Editions: Also available in Spanish.

Authors: Thomas J. D'Zurilla, Arthur M. Nezu, and Albert Maydeu-Olivares.

Publisher: Multi-Health Systems, Inc.

a) LONG VERSION.

Acronym: SPSI-R: L.

Scores, 9: Positive Problem Orientation, Negative Problem Orientation, Rational Problem Solving (Problem Definition and Formulation, Generation of Alternative Solutions, Decision Making, Solution Implementation and Verification), Impulsivity/Carelessness Style, Avoidance Style.

Time: (15–20) minutes.

b) SHORT VERSION.

Acronym: SPSI-R: S.

Scores, 4: Positive Problem Orientation, Negative Problem Orientation, Impulsivity/Carelessness Style, Avoidance Style.

Time: (10) minutes.

Review of the Social Problem-Solving Inventory—Revised by PAM LINDSEY, Associate Professor, Curriculum and Instruction, Tarleton State University, Stephenville, TX:

DESCRIPTION. The Social Problem-Solving Inventory—Revised (SPSI-R) is described as a self-report instrument that assesses individuals' ability to resolve problems in their everyday lives. The instrument offers an English and Spanish version and a long and short form. The long form has 52 items and the short form has 25 items. The protocol uses a Likert-type scale format asking respondents to rate their responses on a scale from 0 (*Not at all true of me*) to 4 (*Extremely true of me*). The response items are based on the authors' model of social problem solving. The revised instrument's 52 items were developed through factor analyses of the original SPSI's (D'Zurilla & Nezu, 1982, 1999) 70 items.

The SPSI-R purports to measure two constructive and three dysfunctional dimensions of problem solving in respondents ages 13 and older. The constructive dimensions are defined as posi-tive problem orientation and rational problem solving. The dysfunctional dimensions are negative problem orientation, impulsivity/careless style, and avoidance style. Each dimension has a raw score that is converted to a standard score and an overall problem-solving score is also computed. The instrument has a mean score of 100 and a standard deviation of 15, which makes it easy to compare with other standardized assessment instruments typically used for assessing adaptive behavior skills.

Respondents read and circle the number (0–4) that is most like their typical behavior. The scores for each item are summed and converted into standard scores. The protocol and scoring matrices are bound together on NCR paper.

A full description of the skills measured in each dimension is provided along with several case studies that guide assessment professionals in interpreting the scores. The manual suggests that data from the SPSI-R are useful to clinicians, educators, parents, and others interested in the "relationship between social problem solving abilities and adjustment or effective functioning" (technical manual, p. xi) in the everyday world.

User qualifications are described in the manual as those persons with an understanding of the basic principles and limitations of psychological testing. The authors contend that the instrument is easily administered and scored by "untrained individuals." They stipulate, however, that interpretation and recommendations should be made by a "mature professional who realizes the limitations of such screening and testing procedures" (technical manual, p. 2).

DEVELOPMENT. The SPSI-R is the most current version (copyright 2002) of an instrument that has been under development since 1982. The definitions for each dimension of problem solving are brief, but clear.

The original version of the scale had 70 items that used a 7-point Likert scale format and used the same theoretical basis of social problem solving as the revised instrument. The 52 items for the long version and 25 items for the short version of the revised instrument were generated through an item analysis of the original SPSI's 70 items and a pool of 300 test items. The authors report a series of exploratory and confirmatory factor analyses led to the formulation of the revised item sets.

TECHNICAL. The revised scale used a population of 2,312 in the normative sample and included what the authors describe as "normal" and "distressed" individuals (p. 53). The sample included a range of ages from adolescents to elderly adults as well as a range of the types of "distressed" individuals. The normative sample is described in detail. The instrument was also normed on a group of Spanish-speaking individuals ranging in age from 17–53 for the Spanish version of the interview. The manual discusses the age, gender, and ethnic effects associated with the instrument based on the authors' research.

Reliability evidence for the SPSI-R was generated using internal consistency and test-retest data. Internal consistency data were collected on the four normative samples, namely, adolescents, young adults, middle adults, and elderly adults and for all five scales of social problem-solving ability. The alpha coefficients ranged from .60–.95 with most falling in the .80+ range. The high coefficients may be explained by the repetition of the same items stated in a different way, which is an inherent characteristic of self-report formats.

Test-retest reliability was reported in the technical manual for a small number of young adults over a 3-week period ($N = 138$) and an additional sample of nursing students over a 6-week period ($N = 221$). The samples were mixed in gender and ethnicity. The estimates were reported as adequate to high: .68 to .91. These estimates suggest that the SPSI-R has relatively stable test-retest reliability. Test-retest reliability data were also analyzed to determine practice effects. The authors reported that this effect was minimal.

Validity analysis consisted of structural, concurrent, and predictive validity. Concurrent validity data were reported comparing the Problem Solving Inventory (Heppner, 1988; Heppner & Peterson, 1982) and the SPSI-R. Correlations ranged between .33 and .75, with most falling in the .40–.60s. The authors stated that these ranges are moderate to high, therefore suggesting that the SPSI-R has met adequate standards of concurrent validity with an instrument purported to measure social problem-solving skills.

Predictive validity was calculated through correlations between the SPSI-R scales and several measures of psychological distress in samples of college students. Correlations ranged from .00–.68 with most falling in the .25–.40 range. When compared to the Reynolds Adolescent Depression Scale (Reynolds, 1986), the SPSI-R appeared to be associated with predicting depression in high school students.

Overall, the technical data reported in the manual appear to support with some degree of confidence the reliability and validity of the instrument to assess an individual's ability to solve problems and make effective decisions in the course of his or her everyday life, which is the authors' construct for the assessment.

COMMENTARY. As with all self-reports, the inherent problem is response bias, which the authors define and describe. The technical manual is very careful to describe the types of response bias that may occur and how that bias would adversely impact the reliability and validity of the obtained scores. In addition, the authors are clear in describing the SPSI-R as a psychometric screening instrument that has an intrinsic degree of measurement error. Therefore, it is suggested that the results should be interpreted with caution and in conjunction with other client data. The inclusion of these cautions is a plus for this instrument's usefulness.

The instrument is easy to give and score and the case study examples are very helpful in interpreting specific profiles. Sample scoring guides are provided for the long and short forms and norm tables are provided for each age group and problem-solving dimension.

The title of the test is a bit misleading as is the description in the authors' preface. At first glance, it appears that the SPSI-R measures adaptive behavior when, in fact, what it really measures is an individual's approach to and basic style for making important decisions. The test protocol explains, in small print, exactly what skills the test purports to measure; however, it seems a misnomer to call it a social problem-solving test rather than a test of individual decision-making abilities.

SUMMARY. Used as a screening device for the specific purpose of adding to a body of information about an individual's ability to deal with stressful events in his or her life, the SPSI-R has merit. It should be used as is typical of a screening device to estimate or approximate an individual's functioning, but as the authors caution, should not be used as the sole decision-making data. Users need to keep in mind the inherent bias of a self-report instrument.

REVIEWER'S REFERENCES

D'Zurilla, T. J., & Nezu, A. M. (1982). Social problem-solving in adults. In P. C. Kendall (Ed.), *Advances in cognitive-behavioral research and therapy* (vol. 1). New York: Academic Press.

D'Zurilla, T. J., & Nezu, A. M. (1999). *Problem-solving therapy: A social competence approach to clinical intervention* (2nd ed.). New York: Springer.

Heppner, P. P., (1988). The Problem Solving Inventory. Palo Alto, CA: Consulting Psychologists Press.

Heppner, P. P., & Petersen, C. H., (1982). The development and implications of a personal problem-solving inventory. *Journal of Counseling Psychology, 29,* 166-175.

Reynolds, W. M. (1986). *Assessment of depression in adolescents: Manual for the Reynolds Adolescent Depression Scale.* Odessa, FL: Psychological Assessment Resources.

Review of the Social Problem-Solving Inventory—Revised by GRETCHEN OWENS, Professor of Child Study, St. Joseph's College, Patchogue, NY:

DESCRIPTION. The Social Problem-Solving Inventory—Revised is a theory-based self-report measure designed to assess adolescents' and adults' self-appraisal of their skill at solving problems that they experience in everyday living. The 52-item Long Form (SPSI-R:L) and the 25-item Short Form (SPSI-R:S) both require examinees to circle the number (0 through 4) that best describes how they might "think, feel, and act when faced with problems in everyday living" that bother them a lot. Sample problems are mentioned (e.g., their health or appearance; their relationships with other people; money problems; or problems with things they own, such as a car or house). Though individual administration in the presence of an administrator is recommended, directions are provided for group administration, for reading the instructions and items aloud, for at-home administration, and for administration using an interpreter, if any of these should be necessary. There is also a Spanish version, but this was standardized in Spain, so the norms may not be accurate for Spanish speakers from countries other than Spain.

Scoring is done by lifting the response page to reveal a grid used to calculate raw scores for each of the scales and subscales. There are five scales: two adaptive problem-solving dimensions (Positive Problem Orientation and Rational Problem Solving) and three dysfunctional dimensions (Negative Problem Orientation, Impulsivity/Carelessness Style, and Avoidance Style). The four subscales appear only on the longer, 52-item form, for which Rational Problem Solving is broken down into four steps that the authors consider necessary for effectively solving problems: Problem Definition and Formulation, Generation of Alternative Solutions, Decision Making, and Solution Implementation and Verification. Step-by-step directions are provided that walk the scorer through the arithmetic procedures needed to normalize the raw scores and to reverse-score the maladaptive scales so a total raw score can be calculated. A profile sheet shows the standard scores (mean of 100, standard deviation of 15) for each of the five scales and four subscales, as well as the total SPSI-R. Throughout the test, high scores are desirable for positive dimensions (e.g., Positive Problem Orientation), whereas for the negative dimensions (such as Avoidance Style) low scores indicate better problem-solving skills. Though the SPSI-R can be administered and scored by untrained individuals such as research assistants, the manual recommends that interpretation of scores should be done only by professionals with postgraduate training in assessment.

The authors suggest that the SPSI-R can be used in a variety of settings. In clinical, medical, and educational settings, the intent is to assess problem-solving skills and identify specific areas of strength and/or weakness, with the implied goal being to then increase individuals' adaptive functioning and minimize their maladaptive approaches to solving personal problems. The authors also recommend its use in corporate, government, and military settings without specifying particular applications, though the reader must surmise that the purpose of these nonclinical uses would be to rank individuals in terms of their level of problem-solving ability in order to make staffing decisions. In either case, the authors caution that scores from the SPSI-R must be supplemented by observations, interviews, and other psychometric measures to give a comprehensive view of the individual's problem-solving ability.

DEVELOPMENT. The original SPSI (1990) was developed based on D'Zurilla's earlier research with Goldfried (1971) and his collaborations with Nezu during the 1980s. In the 1971 theoretical model, the distinction was made between social problem *skills* (now referred to as "styles") and *attitudes* (currently described as "orientation"). The 1990 SPSI therefore included a Problem Orientation Scale (broken into cognitive, emotional, and behavioral subscales to match the theoretical model) and a Problem-Solving Skills Scale broken into subscales reflecting the four steps of problem solving. An informal content validity study using 10 clinical psychology graduate students indicated that all 138 items that had passed a redundancy screening addressed the relevant subscales to which they had been assigned. A sample of 260 undergraduates then took the 138-item version, and the test authors selected the

10 items from each subscale that correlated best with their own subscale and scale scores, yet least with scores on divergent scales and subscales. The resulting 70-item measure was subjected to psychometric analyses, which demonstrated mostly acceptable levels of validity and reliability.

For the current revision, the authors gave the original version to two new samples of college students (N = 924 total) and then conducted factor analyses. This led to a five-factor solution and allowed the authors to reduce the number of items from 70 to 52. The four skills subscales were retained, but the orientation scale has been broken into a Negative (dysfunctional) Problem-Solving Orientation and a Positive (facilitative) one, and the three style scales were added. Further, to provide an instrument that could be administered in an even shorter period of time, the authors devised a 25-item version (the SPSI-R:S), for which the authors selected five items within each factor that they believe represent the definition of that dimension best.

TECHNICAL. Normative data were obtained from multiple independent samples, some contributed by the authors, others by independent researchers. The total sample consisted of 708 "normal" adolescents (56% females); 1,020 young adults (college students at a "major northeastern university," 52.5% females, who were tested in group testing sessions as a course requirement); 100 middle-aged adult community residents who responded to requests made by civic, social, and religious organizations (70% females, 98% White); and 100 elderly community residents (70% females, 93% White). Each group was from a single geographic area, with no specification in the manual of where, and no information was given regarding the racial/ethnic breakdown of the college sample; the user must locate published studies reporting the data if he or she wishes to obtain further sample information. In addition, five psychiatric (distressed) samples were tested. They included 100 adult psychiatric inpatients (70% females), 63 adolescent psychiatric patients (62% females), 117 medical patients with cancer (72% females, 72% White), 43 clinically depressed adult outpatients (75% White, no information on sex provided), and 61 suicidal inpatient adults (61% females). A Spanish sample of 777 undergraduates at the University of Barcelona (84% females) provided additional data for the SPSI-R:S QuikScore form.

Analyses showed significant age, gender, and ethnic differences. The norms take only the first of these into account, providing separate norms for adolescents (ages 13–17), young adults (ages 17–39), middle-aged adults (ages 40–55), and elderly adults (60–80 years). No individuals aged 56–59 were tested, so normative data are not available for this age group. In regard to gender, in three independent samples (college students, inpatient psychiatric adults, and suicidal inpatient adults), women scored consistently higher than men on the Negative Problem Orientation scale, and other significant differences—almost all in favor of men—appeared in at least one of the three samples. Regarding ethnicity, one study has shown Asian-American college students scoring higher on Negative Problem Orientation and on the Impulsivity/Carelessness Style, but other ethnic differences have not yet been investigated.

Reliability and validity data are based upon re-analyses of data obtained for the original SPSI (1990). The authors rescored protocols from some of the earlier samples using only the items that made it into the new SPSI-R, then redid their factor and correlational analyses. Reliability was tested in the four normative (nondistressed) samples only. Nine of 36 internal consistency estimates (coefficient alpha) exceeded .90; an additional 15 were in the .80s, with the remaining 12 ranging from .60–.79. In a second sample of 582 college students, coefficients ranged from .80–.95 for the five scales. Test-retest reliability estimates (3-week period) for a subsample of 138 of the young adult group ranged from .72–.88, and for an additional sample of 221 nursing students (6-week period) they ranged from .68–.91, suggesting relative stability for Negative Problem Orientation and the total SPSI score, but less for subscales. The standard error of measurement for the standard scores of the five SPSI-R scales, subscales, and overall score ranged from 3.00 (for the total score for middle-aged adults) to 9.49 (Positive Problem Orientation for adolescents). More than half were over 6.

In the validity section, the authors note that they verified the structural validity of the instrument via factor analyses, using results from two independent samples of college students who took the original SPSI (the analyses that led to the current revision). To demonstrate concurrent validity, they rescored the original SPSI measures, then calculated correlations between the resulting

SPSI-R scores and scores on another, more extensively researched, self-report measure, the Problem Solving Inventory (Heppner, 1988). Coefficients were all significant and in the moderate to moderately high range (.33–.75).

The manual then provides a lengthy literature review as an argument for predictive validity. This section has interesting clinical implications because the authors and other researchers have found significant associations between SPSI-R scores and various measures of psychological stress and symptomatology in secondary-level and college students, middle-aged and elderly adults, general admissions and suicidal psychiatric inpatients, adult caregivers of Alzheimer's patients, and cancer patients. Evidence is also presented that SPSI-R scores are significantly related to positive well-being (self-esteem, life satisfaction, social adjustment, and social skills) in secondary and college students, to health-related behaviors and to aggression in college students, to sexual aggression in a sample of incarcerated male sex offenders, and to externalizing behavior in adolescents. However, with a paucity of prospective studies, it is difficult to see how the bulk of this research demonstrates predictive validity because the SPSI/SPSI-R and the psychological measures were mostly administered at the same time. To be accurate, the term predictive validity should be reserved for studies that demonstrate "how accurately a person's current performance estimates that person's performance on the criterion measure *at a later time*" (Salvia & Ysseldyke, 2003, p. 152, italics added).

The convergent and discriminant validity data are definitely a move in the right direction, with the authors demonstrating overlap (but not redundancy) with locus of control, optimism and pessimism, and positive and negative trait affectivity. In another analysis, they determined that only the Impulsiveness/Carelessness scale was related to academic aptitude as measured by SAT scores, so the SPSI does not appear to be measuring simply cognitive skill. Finally, they describe a study by the second author that showed SPSI-R scores improving in response to training in problem-solving skills for highly distressed adult cancer patients.

To obtain the norms and gain information about the psychometric properties of the short form of the SPSI-R, the authors reanalyzed the data from the SPSI-R:L using only the items included in the SPSI-R:S, rather than re-administering the short form to another large sample. Not surprisingly, analyses show strong similarities between the reliability and validity data for the long and short forms. However, future studies will be needed to confirm that individuals respond similarly to the same items when asked 52 questions as when they respond to only 25.

COMMENTARY. As with any self-report measure, the danger exists of a bias toward socially desirable responses and even of blatant misrepresentation if the SPSI-R is being used to help others make decisions about whether the person will be hired or promoted. This and other self-report measures of problem-solving ability have been studied principally in college students who complete them anonymously as part of the course requirements for introductory psychology courses, or among college-age or older individuals who have sought psychological counseling. These groups usually have little reason to misrepresent themselves in order to appear in a more socially desirable light, and in fact, the SPSI has been shown in several peer-reviewed studies to correlate significantly with various markers of psychological adjustment and mental health, both concurrently and some months into the future. On the other hand, users should be extremely cautious about using it in corporate, government, or military settings, where individuals can potentially derive benefits from responding in a socially desirable way, as most motivated individuals will have little difficulty determining which response will be scored as "better."

More importantly, users must remain cognizant that the SPSI-R is not an objective measure of problem-solving skill, but rather a measure of how individuals view themselves as problem solvers. The authors frequently lose this distinction. For example, they assert on page 4 of the manual that "The SPSI-R offers a strong measure of general problem-solving ability and skills" and describe their measure in published studies as a "measure of problem-solving ability" (e.g., D'Zurilla & Sheedy, 1991). Despite multiple studies that have used the SPSI, and well over 100 that have utilized Heppner's (1988) Problem Solving Inventory, little information is available in the literature about whether self-appraisal of problem-solving skills reflects actual problem-solving skill or some other underlying construct (such as self-confidence or possibly a propensity toward positive or negative affect). Indeed, Burns and D'Zurilla

(1999) found correlations of only .13–.19 between adolescents' scores on the SPSI-R and ratings by their peers of their interpersonal competence, associations that may be statistically significant in large enough samples, but are nonetheless relatively meaningless. Other research has shown little congruence between client self-ratings and ratings by counselors (Lambert & Hill, 1994, cited by Heppner, Cooper, Mulholland, & Wei, 2001). Especially if the SPSI-R is to be used in applied settings other than counseling, it is important to establish that individuals' scores on the SPSI-R do in fact reflect real-life problem-solving skills.

Other difficulties relate to the questionnaire itself rather than theoretical issues. Despite the instruction to mark how you "usually" think, feel, and act, examinees may be thinking of a particular situation as they fill out the form, which is likely to affect their responses. Second, there is considerable range restriction built into the SPSI-R. As individuals age and their comparison group becomes generally more skilled at problem solving, it becomes very difficult to score outside the average range unless the individual endorses only the most extreme statements for nearly every item (marking *not at all true of me* or *extremely true of me*, rather than *slightly true of me* or *very true of me*), a response mode that seems in itself to contradict the instruction to mark how you "usually" think, feel, and act. Adults who are skilled at problem solving will probably have learned through their experiences that sensitivity to situational differences and flexibility in problem-solving responses lead to more successful outcomes, because the same solution, such as problem-focused action, will not work for every situation (Cornelius & Caspi, 1987). Dealing with a serious illness does not require the same set of problem-solving skills as being worried about a grown son or daughter's choice of partner. Having learned this, older respondents are likely to become less willing to endorse all-or-nothing statements.

One other practical difficulty with the SPSI-R is that interpretation can become confusing because high scores on some scales are considered adaptive, whereas for other scales high scores indicate deficiencies. Because the dysfunctional scales are ultimately reverse-scored to obtain a total score, it would seem fairly straightforward to do the reverse scoring of these *before* arriving at standard scores so that high standard scores would consistently indicate more positive self-appraisals on all scales and subscales.

One final quibble is that calling the measure the Social Problem-Solving Inventory implies that it applies to social situations only, so most potential users are likely to think that the instrument measures interpersonal skills. Though the manual and the directions to the examinee make fairly clear that the measure takes a broader approach to problem-solving skills by including nonsocial problems such as money difficulties, users who are looking for a measure of their clients' or students' interpersonal skills should be cautious about SPSI results, and the authors may wish to consider a name change in subsequent revisions (perhaps the *Personal* Problem Solving Inventory).

SUMMARY. The SPSI-R appears to be a rather interesting research measure that wants to be a traditional standardized test. The scorable forms are in fact an improvement over hand scoring a questionnaire, but there are a number of psychometric problems (in particular, an incompletely described and disproportionately female norm group, normative data that came from the original SPSI and are therefore at least 15 years old, and some omissions and confusing data encountered in the validity section of the manual) that do not meet accepted testing standards. Nevertheless, the SPSI-R appears appropriate at this time for research, and it also may be useful in clinical settings because it correlates significantly with a number of markers of psychological functioning and can serve as a useful outcome measure to supplement other indicators of therapeutic change. However, applied use in nonclinical settings is especially problematic because we do not yet know whether individuals' performance on the SPSI or other self-report measures reflects their behavior in actual situations, and individuals can easily select their answers to achieve a desired outcome.

Nevertheless, a person's appraisal of his or her problem solving seems to be an important dimension of actual problem solving. Further research using the SPSI-R may lead to advances in both theoretical and applied domains, and researchers interested in a self-report approach to assessment of problem solving will find a review of studies employing the SPSI in the validity section of the manual. The most directly competitive measure is the Problem Solving Inventory (Heppner, 1988), which has been used more extensively and has somewhat better psychometric properties.

REVIEWER'S REFERENCES

Burns, L. R., & D'Zurilla, T. J. (1999). Individual differences in perceived information processing styles in stress and coping situations: Development and validation of the Perceived Modes of Processing Inventory. *Cognitive Therapy and Research, 23,* 345–371.

Cornelius, S. W., & Caspi, A. (1987). Everyday problem solving in adulthood and old age. *Psychology and Aging, 2,* 144–153.

D'Zurilla, T. J., & Goldfried, M. R. (1971). Problem-solving and behavior modification. *Journal of Abnormal Psychology, 78,* 104–126.

D'Zurilla, T. J., & Sheedy, C. F. (1991). The relation between social problem-solving ability and subsequent level of psychological stress in college students. *Journal of Personality and Social Psychology, 61,* 841–846.

Heppner, P. (1988). *The Problem Solving Inventory.* Palo Alto, CA: Consulting Psychologists Press.

Heppner, P. P., Cooper, C., Mulholland, A., & Wei, M. (2001). A brief, multidimensional, problem-solving psychotherapy outcome measure. *Journal of Counseling Psychology, 48,* 330–343.

Salvia, J., & Ysseldyke, J. E. (2003). *Assessment in special and inclusive education* (9ᵗʰ ed.). Boston: Houghton Mifflin.

[228]

Social Skills Training: Enhancing Social Competence with Children and Adolescents.

Purpose: Designed to measure social skills problems and help design appropriate intervention programs to develop social competence.

Population: Ages 5–18.

Publication Date: 1995.

Administration: Individual.

Price Data, 2004: Price data for user's guide (267 pages) photocopiable resource book, 8 photo cards, and research and technical supplement (37 pages) available from publisher.

Time: Administration time not reported.

Comments: Assessments are incorporated in Social Skills Training: Enhancing Social Competence with Children and Adolescents program.

Author: Susan H. Spence.

Publisher: NFER-Nelson Publishing Co., Ltd. [England].

a) SOCIAL COMPETENCE WITH PEERS QUESTIONNAIRE.

Forms, 3: Parent, Teacher, Pupil.

Scores, 3: Total score for each form.

b) SOCIAL WORRIES QUESTIONNAIRE.

Forms, 3: Parent, Teacher, Pupil.

Scores, 3: Total score for each form.

c) SOCIAL SITUATION CHECKLIST.

Scores, 1: Total score only.

d) SOCIAL SKILLS QUESTIONNAIRE.

Forms, 3: Parent, Teacher, Pupil.

Scores, 3: Total score for each form.

e) ASSESSMENT OF PERCEPTION OF EMOTION FROM FACIAL EXPRESSION.

Scores, 1: Total score only.

f) ASSESSMENT OF PERCEPTION OF EMOTION FROM POSTURE CUES.

Scores, 1: Total score only.

Review of Social Skills Training: Enhancing Social Competence with Children and Adolescents by

KATHLEEN M. JOHNSON, Psychologist, Lincoln Public Schools, Lincoln, NE:

DESCRIPTION. Social Skills Training: Enhancing Social Competence with Children and Adolescents is intended by the author, Susan Spence, to be a comprehensive and integrated model of assessment and intervention for interpersonal functioning. A user's guide (with an overview of the materials and session-by-session intervention guide), a photocopiable resource book and a research and technical supplement are provided. According to the author, the materials are designed for use by school professionals and therapists who have a "good understanding of the nature of social competence, the causes of relationship difficulties, the assessment of interpersonal problems and the effectiveness of intervention methods" (user's guide, p. 2). The Social Skills Training (SST) is a product from Australia and contains some vocabulary that may cause slight confusion to parents, teachers, and students outside that country.

The SST materials are designed for use with children and adolescents, ages 8 to 18. The 252-page user's guide provides an overview of the social competence concept, defined as "the consequences or outcomes of a person's interaction with other people" (p. 7). The author reviews relevant issues such as skill versus performance deficits and overt versus cognitive social skills. The materials include multiple questionnaires to aid in assessment of general social competence (personal and situational), peer acceptance (sociometric forms), responses to specific situations, basic social skills, social worries, and perceptions of emotions. To allow comparisons, parent, teacher and student forms are provided for most of the assessment questionnaires. Spence also presents rubrics for rating specific social skills of students and a trainer evaluation form in the user's guide. In addition to the use of the questionnaires, the author recommends the use of interviews and direct observations to supplement the overall assessment process in order to plan social skill interventions. Detailed outlines for the interviews are provided by Spence. The author recommends using a process of screening for overall interpersonal difficulties by using general social competence ratings and sociometrics. More detailed follow-up involves the use of her more in-depth and detailed social skill assessments. Spence developed several questionnaires (as described in the research and technical supplement) as a basis for targeting specific social/interpersonal skills that warrant intervention.

Most of the content in the user's guide focuses on strategies for improving social competence and skills. The author outlines various intervention methods for enhancing overall social competence by improving overt/behavioral social skills (e.g., direct instruction, modeling, role-play/practice with feedback and reinforcement, use of homework tasks), social perception skills (e.g., learning about feelings, understanding and using social cues), relaxation skills, and social problem solving. Spence also addresses general intervention issues such as maximizing the generalization and maintenance of acquired skills, determining the size and make-up of social skill groups, and the value of parent and teacher involvement. The instructions for administering the questionnaires are printed on each form. The assessment questionnaires are reproducible, easy to read, and simple to score. Total scores for the questionnaires are sums of the numerical ratings that can be compared to the mean and standard deviation values from the norm group. Included in the SST materials are teacher and peer sociometric nomination forms and two previously developed assessments: the Social Situation Checklist for screening purposes and the Basic Social Skills Assessment Chart (includes rubric) for observations (Spence, 1980). Spence also provides eight laminated cards (each containing six photographs) for use in assessing a student's perceptions of emotions from the facial expressions and postural cues in the pictures. The author states that these materials are not presented as psychometric tests, and no normative data are provided.

DEVELOPMENT. Spence developed and organized the SST materials on the basis of a review of pertinent literature, her own previous publications, and clinical practice. The questionnaires were developed to allow users to screen and assess for social skill deficits and design relevant interventions. The social skill training plans are organized to incorporate components of all typical social skill interventions, again based on the author's review of relevant research and her professional experiences.

Item selection for the questionnaires started with a large pool on items reportedly generated from relevant research and professional opinions. Spence conceptualized the items as reflecting three groups: (a) general social competence, (b) specific social skills, and (c) social anxiety. The items were selected by being consistently categorized into one of the three types by two independent judges. The final version of the Social Competence with Peers Questionnaires (SCPQ) are brief scales designed to focus on the consequences of a student's social interactions with peers. The 9-item teacher questionnaire emphasizes school-based outcomes (e.g., peers like to sit next to him/her in class), whereas the 9-item parent questionnaire emphasizes home-based social competence (e.g., gets invited to parties). The 10-item student questionnaire includes both home and school outcomes of social interactions. For the Social Competence Questionnaires no description is provided for the final item selection process (except for the focus on peer social interactions). Item responses consist of a 3-point scale (0 = *Not true*, 1 = *Sometimes true*, 2 = *Mostly true*).

For the Social Skills Questionnaires (SSQ), the author reported that the final 30 items were selected from 77 initial items. Items were selected through a process of pilot work and field testing. The author reported that these specific behavioral items were retained "if the phrasing of the item was positive" and "if the item-total correlation exceeded .20 for all three versions" (supplement, p. 2) of the SSQ. The items are similar across versions (raters), for example: shares things with other kids his/her age (parent), shares things with peers (teacher), and I share things with other kids (pupil). The items of the Social Worries Questionnaires (SWQ) were reportedly selected on the basis of being about situations that are commonly feared and involve some form of evaluation by others. The situations and number of items vary across versions for parents, teachers, and students based on situational differences. No mention is made by the author about the methods of item selection for the SWQ.

TECHNICAL. The SST standardization sample consisted of 376 children and adolescents, ages 8 to 17, attending Catholic Schools in Sydney, Australia. Only 313 teacher questionnaires and 187 parent questionnaires were returned. The author described the sample make-up as typical of Australian society ethnically and mostly lower to middle income. The questionnaires were administered to students on a class basis and all items were read aloud to the students. The three questionnaires were presented in counterbalanced order across student classes. Responses for all final versions used the 3-point Likert-type scale (0 = *Not true*, 1 = *Sometimes true*, 2 = *Mostly true*). The alpha coefficients for the questionnaire total scores are as follows: SCPQ-Teacher .95; SCPQ-Parent .81; SCPQ-Pupil .75; SSQ-Teacher .96; SSQ-Parent .92; SSQ-Pupil .85; SWQ-Teacher .96; SWQ-Parent .94; and SWQ-Pupil .84. Fairly similar split-half reliability values are also reported in the supplement. Data analyses indicated that overall mean scores adequately represent the data for the three parent and pupil questionnaires. In contrast, mean scores for each gender and each of three age groups (8–11 years, 12–14 years, 15–17 years) better reflect the teacher questionnaire data. The author states that the same factor structure (three highly correlated factors) was found for all the questionnaires although the specific factor analysis results were not reported in the technical supplement. Construct validity is reported as evidenced by the "association between pupil, parent and teacher responses to the questionnaires and children's sociometric status in the peer group" (supplement, p. 12).

COMMENTARY. The Social Skills Training user's guide is primarily a descriptive process of methods for gathering data relevant to planning and implementing social/interpersonal interventions. Most of the information in the guide focuses on various aspects of intervention. Details about the assessment questionnaires are contained in a few pages of the technical supplement. Reliability and validity data for the assessments are limited and additional investigation would be useful in this area. Redundancy of information occurs between the user's guide and the supplement, and it might have been more effectively organized and integrated. The author has developed and provided many assessment devices but outlined no clear model or method for aligning the assessment results with the interventions or with best practice (Gresham, 2002). Likewise, little attention is given to the use of the questionnaires or other assessment data to evaluate intervention effectiveness. A very comprehensive set of assessments and interventions is outlined, but to use all the materials would be extremely time-consuming for students and practitioners. The author appropriately notes that the materials can and should be individualized to address the needs of students and situations and recognizes the struggles associated with generalizing interpersonal skills to natural environments. The reproducible resource book is a

nice feature that provides a cost-effective method of individualizing the use of the materials. The "home tasks" designed by the author are ways to involve parents in the social skill learning process, provide opportunities for practicing and generalizing skills, and provide measures of treatment integrity and possibly skill progress.

SUMMARY. The Social Skills Training: Enhancing Social Competence with Children and Adolescents is primarily an intervention guide that also contains some data gathering materials. Educators who work with small groups of students with behavioral/social challenges, counselors, and psychologists may find the materials useful. The author has developed several questionnaires and organized other assessments for use in screening for and specifying interpersonal difficulties. The user's guide provides a thorough and detailed description of various social/interpersonal difficulties, assessments and interventions that are consistent with other literature (Elliott, Sheridan, & Gresham, 1989; Jenson, Rhode, & Reavis, 1994; Sheridan, 1995). The SST materials address important issues such as the need for using a multimethod (data from more than one rater, environment, and skill area) and integrated approach to assessing and treating social/interpersonal difficulties.

REVIEWER'S REFERENCES

Elliott, S. N., Sheridan, S. M., & Gresham, F. M. (1989). Assessing and treating social skills deficits: A case study for the scientist-practitioner. *Journal of School Psychology, 27*, 197–222.

Gresham, F. M. (2002). Teaching social skills to high-risk children and youth: Preventive and remedial strategies. In M. R. Shinn, H. M. Walker, & G. Stoner (Eds.), *Interventions for academic and behavior problems II* (pp. 403–432). Bethesda, MD: National Association for School Psychologists.

Jenson, W. R., Rhode, G., & Reavis, H. K. (1994). *The tough kid tool box.* Longmont, CO: Sopris West.

Sheridan, S. M. (1995). *The tough kid social skills book.* Longmont, CO: Sopris West.

Spence, S. H. (1980). *Social skills training with children and adolescents: A counsellor's manual.* Windsor: NFER Publishing Co.

Review of Social Skills Training: Enhancing Social Competence with Children and Adolescents by CAROLINE MANUELE-ADKINS, *Vice-President, Institute for Life Coping Skills Inc., Stamford, CT:*

DESCRIPTION AND DEVELOPMENT. Social Skills Training is designed to be used as a comprehensive assessment and intervention system by teachers and counselors. It can be used to assess the difficulties of children (ages 8–18) in social interactions and to identify the skills they lack that contribute to their social competence problems. It also provides a social skills group training curriculum. The assessment part of the system consists of a variety of questionnaires covering six areas—social competence, social skills, social worries, unhelpful attitudes, beliefs and thoughts, problem-solving skills, and physiology—all with attention to parent, teacher, child, and peer perceptions of functioning in these areas. Guidelines for clinical interview protocols are also included if more in-depth or specific information is needed.

The Social Skills Training curriculum includes outlines for 16 different sessions with detailed descriptions of methods and techniques such as role-playing, problem-solving, self-instruction methods, friendship skills, basic conversation and listening skills, relaxation skills, conflict situations, and social perception. It also includes handouts, task sheets, exercises, and photo-cards. To understand the system the user needs to consult three manuals: (a) the Social Skills user's guide, (b) the photocopiable resource book, and (c) the research and technical supplement manual.

The questionnaires are basically self-report, parent-report, and teacher-report, paper-and-pencil-measures with varying item numbers ranging from 9 items on one to 60 items on another. In most instances, items are rated on Likert scales as being (0) *Not true,* (1) *Sometimes true,* and (2) *Mostly true.* Item scores are simply added up and the technical supplement manual says that "higher scores indicate greater social skills and social competence and greater levels of social worries" (research and technical supplement, p. 11). Mean scores for different age groups and for teachers and parent groups are provided with the normative data for the questionnaires.

The user's guide and the research and technical supplement provide extensive descriptions of social skills and competence theory and reviews of other social skills assessment measures. It is presumably from this knowledge base that items were derived for the questionnaires, interview protocols, and training curriculum. A direct link is not made, however, between item development and specific theoretical constructs. According to the manual, a general pool of items was developed and then selected by "two independent judges" (p. 1) for inclusion in the questionnaires and for subsequent pilot-testing. Attention was paid by the judges to items that differed for parents, teachers, and older and younger children and that focused on positive behaviors that could be trained.

TECHNICAL. Norms were developed by administering the questionnaires to samples of

376 children (age range 8–17), 313 teachers, and 187 parents, all from four Catholic schools in Sydney, Australia. Ethnicity and social-economic status were not measured in the sample but are described as diverse, being of overseas European origin, and in lower to middle income brackets. Gender scores are present for teacher and parent ratings but surprisingly not for pupil self-ratings.

In the analysis of normative data, some attention is paid to scoring differences between older and younger students, boys and girls (as rated by teachers), popular and unpopular children, but the interpretation of what a specific score means is elusive, other than that it is a higher or lower score. Normative scores should have been related to how they really vary for students who have different levels of social competence, who are more socially anxious or socially avoidant, or who lack specific skills. Practitioners then would have more confidence in interpreting what a given score means for an individual student or for groups of students. It is also unclear from the standardization sample whether or not the measure really distinguishes between child and adolescent behavior.

The technical manual presents reliability and validity data for each of the questionnaires. In general, internal reliability estimates are robust, with split-half reliabilities ranging from .77 to .94 and coefficient alphas ranging from .75 to .96. Test-retest reliability information is not provided. Medium range item-total correlations figures, varying from .20 to .77, are also provided as measures of internal consistency suggesting that the scales are measuring somewhat homogenous factors.

Content and face validity are basically good, in that items appear to be related to social functioning and behavior and derived from the author's extensive review of the literature in the areas of social skills, social phobia, and social functioning. Other evidence for score validity is presented in the form of factor analytic studies that for the most part indicate that the questionnaires are measuring a single homogenous factor. How different these factors are we do not know. One of the main methods for establishing construct validity was by examining the relationship between the independent ratings of parents, teachers, children, and peers. The manual concludes that these intercorrelations are good, but closer examination reveals that in some cases, the correlation between parent and teacher ratings is .40, between teacher and student ratings

.17, and between parent and child .25. More agreement and less variation between the various perspectives would have been expected.

Validity information is somewhat difficult to extract in an organized way from the technical manual text. Organizing the text with reliability and validity subheadings would be helpful. Presenting data in several correlation matrix tables would also be more concise and efficient than requiring the reader to search through diverse parts of the text. Of most importance is the fact that no attempt has been made to explore how scores achieved on these questionnaires are related to any external criteria, such as scores achieved on other established tests of social skills or tests of related constructs such as quality of interpersonal relationships or ratings of in-situ social behaviors.

COMMENTARY. An integral part of Social Skills Training is the actual training curriculum that is provided. Many practitioners will be much more interested in the curriculum lessons, training techniques, and tools the program provides than in the assessment part of the system. It will appeal to those who are looking for something to actually use in their classroom or group counseling sessions. The session-by-session guide is based on relevant theory and research and involves the training of basic skills and the application of these skills to social problem-solving and behavior in social settings. The curriculum appears to be well designed but a major issue is the fact that no outcome data are provided to indicate that the intervention is really effective in helping students acquire the social skills they need. And like many programs of this type, there is no information about the transferability of these trained skills to real-life social situations. More attention also needs to be paid to how the group functions with this intervention. How the trainer develops, maintains, and uses the group to provide the context for learning complex social behaviors needs to be described in more detail for the average users of such an intervention.

Social Skills Training is presented as a system, but the assessment and training parts appear to be quite separate, with weak relationships between the two (e.g., concepts and scores on the questionnaires are not necessarily related to the skills covered in the training program core). Future development needs to be directed at making it a better system, in which assessment, diagnosis, and intervention would become more congruent. Most practitioners will find the assessment part of the system too complex to use with its multiple questionnaires and subquestionnaires. This part of the system seems to have been developed for research purposes, and it is most likely that it will be of greatest appeal to people who are doing social skills research.

SUMMARY. Overall this system reflects good professional underpinnings. Its development is based on theory and research. Each of the three user manuals provides a great deal of information about social skills assessment and functioning. It suffers from some technical issues that include the need for more construct validity studies so that users can have more confidence in knowing that it is measuring what it purports to measure. Standardization samples need to be more varied, with populations that include adolescents, special education students, and students with disabilities, so one can understand what variations in scores really mean. More attention to gender and socioeconomic issues would be essential.

Outcome studies for the Social Skills curriculum also need to be done, because we have no way of knowing how effective the program really is, or how different groups react to it. Because this system was developed in Sydney, Australia, questions of cultural relevance and applicability have to be raised if it is used outside Australia. The user can have confidence in the system's content and face validity, but future research could include studies that examine its applicability in other English-speaking countries (e.g., in the United States with our diverse cultural and socioeconomic groups).

[229]

Socio-Sexual Knowledge and Attitudes Assessment Tool—Revised.

Purpose: Designed to assess sexual knowledge and attitudes of individuals with developmental disabilities.
Population: Developmentally disabled adults (ages 16–71), can be used with other adults.
Publication Dates: 1976–2003.
Acronym: SSKAAT-R.
Scores, 8: Anatomy, Women's Bodies and Women's Knowledge of Men, Men's Bodies and Men's Knowledge of Women, Intimacy, Pregnancy/Childbirth and Child Rearing, Birth Control and STDs, Sexual Boundaries, Total.
Administration: Individual.

Price Data, 2003: $275 per complete kit including easel, stimulus cards, 20 record forms, and manual (2003, 47 pages); $50 per 20 record forms.
Time: Untimed.
Author: Dorothy Griffiths and Yona Lunsky.
Publisher: Stoelting Co.
Cross References: For a review by Edward S. Herold of an earlier edition, see 9:1152; see T3:2237 (1 reference).

Review of the Socio-Sexual Knowledge and Attitudes Assessment Tool—Revised by MARY M. CLARE, Professor, Graduate School of Education and Counseling, Lewis & Clark College, Portland, OR:

DESCRIPTION. The Socio-Sexual Knowledge and Attitudes Assessment Tool—Revised (SSKAAT-R) has been specifically designed for use with adolescents and adults who have developmental disabilities and are interested in sexual relationships. The SSKAAT-R is not a diagnostic test, but rather evaluates knowledge and attitudes referred to by the authors as "information persons with developmental disabilities have about their bodies, socio-sexual intimacy, relationships and issues of abuse" (manual, p. 1). As such, this assessment is for use in cases of "a specific purpose that will benefit the individual" (manual, p. 11).

This instrument was revised from the original Socio-Sexual Knowledge and Attitude Test (SSKAT; Wish, McCombs, & Edmonson, 1979) to reflect changes over the past two decades in the interests and concerns of people with developmental disabilities. A primary objective of the authors was to shift the instrument from being used as a diagnostic tool to being used as an assessment capable of describing knowledge and attitudes and thereby supporting responsive service delivery to developmentally disabled clients. The authors also express interest in providing a measurement capable of meeting the necessity for evaluating the effectiveness of sexuality education for clients with developmental disabilities. Revisions and extensions of narrative and visual representations of physical, ethnic, and sexual-orientation diversity are also part of the SSKAAT-R.

The SSKAAT-R is composed of seven subscales: Anatomy (12 items), Women's Bodies (for women only, 31 items), Men's Bodies (for men only, 22 items), Intimacy (35 items), Pregnancy, Childbirth, and Child Rearing (32 items), Birth Control and STDs (35 items), and Healthy Socio-Sexual Boundaries (27 items). In both the easel used to administer the SSKAAT-R and the scoring protocol, blue ink indicates select items that compose a screening option.

The authors suggest the SSKAAT-R be administered in a place familiar and comfortable to the client but also public and preferably with a second clinician or observer present to prevent later misunderstanding about the conversation and activity of the assessment. The authors also suggest matching gender of assessor and client, particularly in cases of known sexual victimization.

Scoring of responses occurs both during and after administration of the SSKAAT-R. Knowledge items are scored 0, 1, or 2 to indicate the level of a client's expressed knowledge. Responses to the attitude items interspersed through the seven subscales are recorded, but not scored. Once administration is completed, scores may be summarized and compared with knowledge levels obtained for the norm sample representing the level of developmental disability best describing the client. Normative data are available for subscale and full-scale scores when either the entire assessment or the screening portion of the assessment has been completed.

DEVELOPMENT. The authors of the SSKAAT-R provide little overt explanation of the theoretical underpinning of the instrument. They emphasize the importance of using the SSKAAT-R as a descriptive and not a diagnostic tool. Consistent with this emphasis, the authors' description of the shifts in the interests and concerns of adolescents and adults with developmental disabilities anchors the assessment tool in the practical experiences of this population. For example, the manual holds scattered discussion of the need for sexuality education and accountability on the part of agencies providing that education. The authors also mention the empowering educative potential of the assessment experience itself, in particular with people who have histories of being shamed about speaking candidly about sexuality. The authors' inclusion of items depicting same- and other-gender dating, sexual interaction, and marriage indicates interest in normalizing sexuality across and within genders. Consistent with these content decisions, the descriptive nature of this assessment characterized by the initial instruction to clients that there is no right or wrong answer implies a constructivist philosophical basis and practically allows for a client's free expression of knowledge and opinions.

The SSKAAT-R is the result of thoughtful development strategy. To begin, the authors systematically surveyed 80 parents, educators, and clinicians about what they observe as the primary challenges to the socio-sexual relating of the people who have developmental disabilities. The data from these surveys indicated shifts in caretakers' perceptions (e.g., in 1999, masturbation, knowledge of body parts, and intercourse were the top three concerns; in 1979, birth control, intercourse, and the transmission of venereal disease were the top three concerns). Although these data served as a primary basis for the revision, the authors do not provide description of the surveyed group of 80 people; thus, representation by role, ethnicity, geographic location, etc. is unclear.

The authors convened a small focus group (*n* = 14) of people with developmental disabilities. Their responses to questions about sexuality indicated overlap with caretakers' responses around considerations of knowledge of body parts, intercourse, and inappropriate physical touch. However, focus group members were more interested in childbirth and sexual contact than were caretakers.

Additional approaches to instrument development included the authors' careful survey of SSKAT users regarding what of the original to keep and what to revise. Throughout the revision process, the authors repeatedly evaluated the new version alongside the SSKAT. The authors also reviewed the content of three sexuality education programs, basing the seven sub-scales of the instrument on that review. Finally, the authors enlisted field researchers in "over 20 sites" (manual, p. 31) across North America to conduct field tests and gather normative data for the revision.

Some of the items in the instrument are visually explicit. Given the general sexual squeamishness of North American culture, both professionals and clients may respond negatively to this content. The authors make no excuses for the content, but clearly indicate ways users may elect to omit sections of the assessment.

Early in the manual the authors suggest there are *core* items assessing general information, and *optional* items assessing more advanced or explicit knowledge ("questions of a sensitive nature," p. 4) in the assessment, but nowhere in the easel used for administration or in later sections of the manual is there indication of which questions fit which category. Related to this consideration is the absence of suggestion for how to make scoring accommodate such omissions. In the easel, warnings and opportunities for the client to decline viewing explicit images are inconsistent—given directly before two separate sketches of a naked man and a naked woman, then given several items (as many as 10) prior to explicit sketches of sexual activity.

However, in contrast to these oversights and consistent with their implied philosophical basis in respect and advocacy for people with developmental disabilities, the authors offer solid advice on confidentiality, client consent, individual disability conditions as they affect a client's ability to respond, and the importance of a familiar yet public location for administration of the SSKAAT-R. The guidance in these sections of the manual includes attention to a client's potential discomfort or need to process thoughts and feelings that might follow exposure to assessment content. We who serve people without developmental disabilities have much to learn from these respectful and thorough procedures.

TECHNICAL CONSIDERATIONS. Norms for the SSKAAT-R are based on a sample of 276 adolescents and adults ages 16–71 (mean age, 37; 60% men, 40% women, 46% Canadian, 54% U.S. citizens, 98% English-speaking, 87% White). The psychometric investigations accomplished with this sample indicate strong reliability (internal consistency, Cronbach's alphas between .81 and .92; test-retest [3–8-week intervals], $r = .96$; interrater, r between .89 and .96) and validity (convergent with SSKAT total score, $r = .84$; convergent with SexKen-ID total score, $r = .96$; significant differences between scores of college students and the norm sample; and significant differences prior to and following sex education, $n = 16$).

Based on reported psychometrics, the SSKAAT-R is a technically sound assessment instrument. One primary weakness of this assessment resides in its inadequately representative normative sample. A second weakness is perhaps unavoidable. The SSKAAT-R cannot predict behavior, it can only measure knowledge or attitudes. The authors illustrate this weakness with description of the uncertain link between actual condom use and either understanding of the purpose of condoms or demonstrated skill with putting a condom on an anatomical model.

COMMENTARY. As I spent time with this instrument, two questions came to mind. First, does the SSKAAT-R assess what the authors want to assess? The authors offer no clarifying definition of the term *socio-sexual relationships*, leaving the reader to interject her or his own meaning. Parallel to this question, and perhaps more illustrative of its point, is consideration of what this assessment teaches. Assessments carry culture. Of necessity, they are both products and purveyors of the worldviews of their authors. Wittingly or not, the particular combination of questions composing the SSKAAT-R teach (among many other things) that sexuality is associated cautiously with positive feelings like romance, and less subtly with violence (e.g., the prompt, "Show me the pictures of things that are bad for a woman to do when she's pregnant," referring to photos including one of a pregnant woman being beaten by a man—this photo a correct selection for the item). Perhaps administering sections of the assessment separately and offering linked opportunities for the client to process her or his responses would be helpful for making the distinction between sexuality as an expression of affection and physical violations that involve sex organs but are distinctly harmful.

A second question arose as I read. Are there equity issues at play here? The authors' commitment to addressing such questions with the SSKAAT-R is clear throughout its documents, and questions of equity have a way of pushing us further and further into clarity. It is not surprising that more questions emerge with every revision.

The representation of the norm sample relative to the general population seems limited. The authors do not give clear information on socioeconomic status, geographic location, and sexual orientation of the sample and, as indicated above, the ethnic representation of the norm group is quite limited.

SUMMARY. The SSKAAT-R is a reliable and potentially valid assessment of the knowledge and attitudes of adolescents and adults with developmental disabilities. The norm sample for this revision is inadequately representative of the diversity within this population and limits the validity of the scale. Sexuality has profound, if often socially stigmatized, meaning to all people, its meaning varying according to a person's socialized experience. As a clinical tool, the SSKAAT-R

seems valuable so long as users recognize the necessary cultural loading of the items presented and use the instrument as the authors intend—as a tool and not as an unquestioned representation of the truth.

REVIEWER'S REFERENCE
Wish, J. R., McCombs, K. F., & Edmondson, B. (1979). The Socio-Sexual Knowledge and Attitude Test. Wood Dale, IL: Stoelting.

[230]
Spanish Reading Inventory.

Purpose: To help teachers and other professionals determine a student's reading proficiency in Spanish.
Population: Grades 1–4+.
Publication Date: 1997.
Scores, 7: Independent, Instructional, Frustration, Word Recognition in Isolation, Word Recognition in Context, Comprehension-Oral, Comprehension-Silent.
Administration: Individual.
Forms, 2: A, B.
Price Data, 2003: $52.95 per complete kit (specify Form A or Form B); $32.95 per performance booklets (specify Form A or Form B).
Time: Administration time not reported.
Author: Jerry L. Johns.
Publisher: Kendall/Hunt Publishing Company.

Review of the Spanish Reading Inventory by SALVADOR HECTOR OCHOA, Associate Professor, Department of Educational Psychology, Texas A&M University, College Station, TX:

DESCRIPTION. The purpose of the Spanish Reading Inventory is to ascertain a student's grade level reading ability in Spanish. There are two forms of this inventory. Form A is designed to assess oral reading; Form B is used to assess silent reading. This test can be administered to Spanish-speaking pupils who are at the preprimer to fourth grade level. Each form has two parts. The first part of the test, "Word Recognition in Isolation," contains word lists at four levels: preprimer, primer, first grade, and second grade. Each of these lists contains 20 words. The second section of this inventory, "Word Recognition in Context," contains one graded reading passage at each of the following six levels: preprimer, primer, and first to fourth grade.

Each student is given both parts of the inventory. With respect to the first section, each student is directed to read the 20 words on a list at a respective level. The child is then given a second opportunity to read any word that he or she initially missed. If the student is able to read at least 14 of the 20 words on the graded word list, he or she is given another more advanced level word list to read. If the student reads 13 or less words correctly on a given level, he or she is deemed to be at the Frustration level for that particular level. Students who read 14 to 18 out of 20 words correctly for a given grade level are classified as being at the Instructional level for that given level of word difficulty. Students who read at least 19 out of the 20 possible words correctly for a given grade level are classified as being at the Independent level for that given level of word difficulty.

Based on their performance on the first section of the test, a starting graded reading passage level is selected for the second part of the inventory. The examiner should select the reading passage that is "two levels below the highest independent level achieved on the graded word lists" (administration manual, p. 6). Each reading passage in this section of the inventory will yield two scores. The first score is the Word Recognition in Context score that is used to ascertain a student's reading level. The second score is the Comprehension score that is also used to ascertain a student's reading level. The test manual provides sufficient information on how to administer this portion of the inventory and obtain the Word Recognition in Context and Comprehension score.

As a student reads each graded passage, the examiner marks the reading errors made by the student in a performance booklet. An examiner can count the "total miscues" and/or "significant miscues" made by the student (administration manual, p. 17) in order to arrive at a Word Recognition in Context score. The following errors should be noted and counted by the examiner as total miscues: substitutions, omissions, and insertions. According to the test manual, examiners are given discretion whether to count self-corrections made by the student while reading as errors. "Significant miscues alter the meaning of the passage" (professional manual, p. 19). The test performance booklet provides a scoring guide to ascertain the particular reading level (Independent, Independent/Instructional, Instructional, Instructional/Frustration, and Frustration) for both total miscues and significant miscues for each graded reading passage level.

In order to obtain a comprehension score, the examiner poses comprehension questions to the student. There are 5 comprehension questions for the preprimer graded reading passage. There are 10 comprehension questions for the other five graded reading passages (primer, first to fourth grade). These questions are in the test performance booklet. The test performance booklet also provides a scoring guide to ascertain the particular reading level (Independent, Independent/Instructional, Instructional, Instructional/Frustration, and Frustration) based on the number of comprehension questions missed by the student for each graded reading passage level.

The test manual provides examiners with alternative methods to evaluate comprehension. These procedures include story retelling and a combination of story retelling and comprehension questions. The test manual does not provide sufficient information on how to use and score these alternative procedures.

DEVELOPMENT. This inventory was developed by translating and adapting the Basic Reading Inventory into Spanish. The Basic Reading Inventory was also developed by Dr. Jerry Johns. In order to develop the first portion of the inventory, graded word lists, the test developer reported that he used both published and unpublished sources to obtain appropriate words in Spanish. The test developer, however, did not appear to review some of the commercially available basal reading series available in Spanish when developing the graded word lists. Given that these commercial basal reading series are developed by consultants with experience and expertise in Spanish reading instruction, this would have provided much content validity evidence for the graded word lists.

The second portion of the inventory, reading passages, was also developed by translating and adapting the English reading passages of the Basic Reading Inventory. The test author reported that individuals from six Latin American countries and five states provided feedback on "passage content, specific word choices, and the comprehension questions" (administration manual, p. 34). The test author, however, fails to provide information concerning the number of reviewers used in this process and their qualifications to provide such feedback.

The test author also reported that three different readability formulas were utilized to ascertain that reading passages assigned to a particular graded category (preprimer, primer, first grade, second grade, third grade, and fourth grade) were appropriate. These readability formulas included: (a) Spaulding's readability formula for Spanish, (b)

Fry Readability Adapted for Spanish Evaluation (FRASE) developed by Vari-Cartier, and (c) the Gilliam, Peña, and Mountain formula. The test author, however, acknowledged that one of these three reading formulas was not designed to be used with elementary reading texts: "The FRASE readability formula was developed to evaluate the readability of Spanish textbooks used at the secondary level" (administration manual, p. 35).

Thus, only information from the other two readability formulas will be reviewed in this critique. Johns states: "The revised difficulty scores from the Spaulding formula increase from the first passage in each form" (administration manual, p. 35). This statement is incorrect based on the information found on Table 4.1 of the test manual. The data on Table 4.1 report that the revised difficulty score for the Form A primer level is 55, which is higher than the revised difficulty score for the Form A first grade level of 48. Both the primer and first grade reading passages were categorized as "very easy." Moreover, the revised difficulty scores for Form B are the same at the primer and first grade level. Both levels on this form had a score of 55 and both were categorized as "very easy." The Gilliam, Peña, and Mountain formula "confirm[ed] a gradual increase in difficulty for the passages within each form" (administration manual, p. 35). It is important to note, however, that the primer reading passage and the first grade level reading passage of Form A were both classified as being at the first grade level. Thus, the difficulty levels obtained by the two aforementioned readability formulas for the primer and first grade levels reading passages for Form A do not provide support that these two reading passages differ in their level of difficulty.

The test developer also provides information about the final field testing procedures that were undertaken. A total of 240 elementary-school-age students took part in the final field testing for Form A. The composition of this group by grade level was: 44 first graders, 119 second graders, 54 third graders, and 23 fourth graders. Moreover, these students were from California, Florida, Illinois, and Texas. No other information about these students was provided in the test manual. No indication was provided as to why the numbers of children participating by grade level varied from 23 to 119. There are insufficient numbers of children at certain grade levels. Moreover, the

number of first graders participating in this field testing is unclear because Table 4.2 appears to report contradictory data. Data on this table indicate that 44 first graders (20 males and 24 females) participated in the field testing procedures. However, in the word list column of this table, the data indicate that 45 first graders were administered the first preprimer word list.

Similarly, a small sample of elementary-school-age students ($n = 104$) were used in the final field testing for Form B. The composition of this group by grade level was: 29 first graders, 42 second graders, 23 third graders, and 10 fourth graders. These students appear to be from the same four aforementioned states. No other information about these students was provided in the test manual. There are insufficient numbers of children at all grade levels.

The test author also provided information regarding whether Forms A and B were comparable. Twelve second graders and 14 third graders were used to compare the results of the graded word lists section of Forms A and B. The test author reports that 42 comparisons were undertaken for the 12 second graders. "Of these comparisons, 31 (74%) indicated the same level … . A similar comparison with a group of … third graders … revealed 78% agreement when 85 comparisons were made" (administration manual, p. 36). The author also reports that the comparability of the graded reading passages of Form A with Form B was conducted with the same number of second graders. Johns reported: "Of 21 passages compared, the same level was achieved in 13 (62%) of the instances" (administration manual, p. 36). There were an insufficient number of students used to examine the comparability of the graded word lists and graded reading passages of Form A with Form B. Additional research with more students needs to be conducted to further ascertain if Form A and B are comparable.

TECHNICAL. The test manual fails to provide any information about reliability. The test manual does provide information about content validity stating that the test developer reviewed relevant sources and sought feedback by outside sources from foreign Latin American countries as well as from within the United States. As previously mentioned, the test author did not appear to review some of the commercially available basal reading series available in Spanish when developing the graded word lists. Moreover, the test developer did not provide information concerning the number of reviewers used in this process and their qualifications to provide such feedback. Given these two limitations, further evidence for the content validity appears warranted. The test manual does not provide any information regarding concurrent validity regarding the reading levels obtained by this measure with other formal and/or informal reading achievement tests or classroom performance. Moreover, the construct validity of the graded reading passages was examined by utilizing three readability formulas. As previously mentioned, there appears to be some question regarding whether the difficulty levels for the primer and first grade reading passages of Form A differ.

COMMENTARY. Although the Spanish Reading Inventory evidences some strengths, it has some significant weaknesses. With respect to positive features, the test author did use professional literature to establish appropriate criteria as to what constitutes independent, instructional, and frustration levels of reading. Moreover, the author did employ readability formulas in order to document if the graded reading passages increased in difficulty by grade level. The results of the formulas appear to indicate that most passages have been assigned to the appropriate grade level.

There are some weaknesses that need to be considered by individuals using this inventory. First, the test-retest reliability evidence for this inventory is lacking. Second, further evidence is needed to examine content validity. Third, concurrent validity has not been evaluated. Fourth, the educational context/history of students who participated in the field testing procedures was not discussed in the manual. Thus, it is unknown if this factor was considered. The manual does not provide any information concerning how this factor was considered and/or incorporated when the test was developed. The educational context/history of Spanish-speaking elementary-school-aged students can vary considerably. For example, were these Spanish-speaking elementary-school-aged pupils educated in bilingual education programs? If so, for how long and in what type of bilingual education program? These three factors can greatly impact the reading performance of English language learners.

SUMMARY. The psychometric data supporting this informal Spanish Reading Inventory are lacking. Additional research needs to be con-

ducted to examine its reliability. Moreover, research examining the concurrent validity of this measure needs to be conducted. The test author failed to provide important contextual information regarding the small number of students included in the final field testing procedures. The comparability of Forms A and B needs to be established with a larger group of elementary-school-aged students. Individuals who use this measure should recognize the limitations of test results in light of the concerns included in this test review.

[231]

Spatial Reasoning.

Purpose: Designed to assess "a pupil's ability to manipulate shapes and patterns."
Population: Ages 5.4–15.5.
Publication Date: 2002.
Scores: Total score only.
Administration: Group.
Levels, 4: Age 6 and 7; Age 8 and 9; Age 10 and 11; Ages 12–14.
Price Data: Available from publisher.
Time: 20(35–40) minutes for Age 6 and 7; 27(40–45) minutes for Age 8 and 9; 28(45) minutes for Age 10 and 11; 33(45–50) minutes for Ages 12–14.
Comments: Designed to complement the publisher's Verbal (258) and Non-Verbal Reasoning (167) series of tests.
Authors: Pauline Smith and Thomas R. Lord.
Publisher: NFER-Nelson Publishing Co., Ltd. [England].

Review of Spatial Reasoning by KATHY BOHAN, Assistant Professor of Educational Psychology, Northern Arizona University, Flagstaff, AZ:

DESCRIPTION. The NFER-Nelson's Spatial Reasoning tests are part of a series of tests designed as a complement to the British Ability Scales: Second Edition (BAS II). The tests in the nferNelson series were developed to assess the three general thinking abilities that emerged as constructs in the BAS II, namely verbal reasoning, nonverbal reasoning, and spatial processes. In addition to the Spatial Reasoning tests, the NFER-Nelson Verbal and Non-Verbal Reasoning series are also available (see 258 and 167). The manuals are labeled as "Teacher's Guide," suggesting that the intended consumers of the test are classroom teachers. Yet, examiner qualifications are not clearly stated in the materials. The authors indicate that exposure and practice may improve scores; thus, it might be inferred that the tests can provide teachers with a greater understanding of pupil differences leading to differential instruction methodologies. However, the authors also state that pupils demonstrate varied aptitudes with spatial tasks, and that this information may also assist in guiding instruction.

The Spatial Reasoning test series purports to measure abilities on tasks that include shape and space, including combining, rotating, and imagining views of shapes from different perspectives. The various timed subtests are designed to be administered in group settings. Various age-level materials are administered to children age 6–7, 8–9, 10–11, and 12–14 years. Additionally, scores can be extrapolated for children as young as 5 years 4 months, and as old as 15 years 5 months. Administration time, depending upon the age level, requires between 35 and 50 minutes. Depending upon the age group, subtests include Windows, Hidden Shapes, Stacks, Jigsaws, Sections, Wallpaper, and Right Angles.

For administration, test instructions are read to pupils as they are asked to mark their responses in their individual booklets. The booklets include written directions so the pupil can follow along as the examiner reads them. Practice items are provided with each subtest. Although the booklet is generally attractively designed, each page includes several items. This may present additional challenges to pupils with distractibility, concentration, figure/ground problems, or other perceptual difficulties independent of spatial reasoning. Each subtest is timed and pupils who finish early are instructed to check their work. After administration, correct answers are tallied and errors are ignored to obtain a total raw score. This score is then converted into a standard score and percentile rank.

Interpretive guidelines indicate consideration of the relationship of the pupil's score with other test scores and background information. The authors note that even though very low spatial reasoning scores do not in themselves suggest evidence of dyslexia, research suggests that "on average, spatial ability tends to be relatively high compared with verbal ability in the more severe levels of dyslexia" (teacher's guide, p. 6). Although this may be consistent with the research literature related to dyslexia, it would behoove the authors to provide additional references to studies that support or contradict this finding. Additionally, the authors link assessment to "follow-up activities" and cite four references. However, only very general implications are discussed in the manual.

DEVELOPMENT. The manual and materials provided included very limited information regarding the development and standardization of the tests; however, the manual noted that additional information can be obtained through the test publisher. Item development was apparently based on a survey of the research literature and trials with samples of children of various ages. The time limits were reportedly established according to speed of working, attention span, and test length. However, the manual does not provide specifics as to how items were selected or how procedures were determined.

TECHNICAL. The Spatial Reasoning tests were standardized from a sample of children who attended several maintained and independent schools in the United Kingdom in 2002. The manual reports that the sample was proportionally stratified by region (e.g., North, Midlands and South of England, Wales and Scotland) and by size of school. However, all pupils within a year group were administered the test. Thus, total numbers of pupils included in the samples varied from year to year. For example, the lowest number of pupils were in the Year 1 sample ($N = 493$), whereas the largest sample included Year 4 pupils ($N = 872$). Additionally, it is unclear as to the heterogeneity of the normative sample—such as whether it included pupils with learning disabilities, mental retardation, or other disabilities—is unclear. Standard scores are calculated in increments of 2 months, yet data are not provided specifying the number of pupils in the standardized sample reflected at each age group.

The various manuals report generally high internal consistency (.87–.92) using the Kuder-Richardson 20 formula. However, additional measures of reliability such as test-retest reliability or split-half techniques were not reported. The Spatial Reasoning tests are described as both power and speed tests; however, due to the limited description of test reliability methods, it is unclear as to whether the reported coefficients take into account any individual differences with speed versus accuracy.

The test developers contend that the validity of the various measures is evident through the research and comparisons with other spatial reasoning tests. The developers state that the test "can be trusted as a modern and reliable test for which the item types and the questions themselves have been carefully selected" (teacher's guide, p. 5). It would have been advantageous to include evidence supporting this promise. Because the tests were developed to complement the BAS II, it would seem appropriate that reporting correlations between these tests would lend credence to this statement.

COMMENTARY. The NFER-Nelson Spatial Reasoning tests, along with the Verbal and Nonverbal Reasoning tests in this series, are group-administered tests of children's cognitive processing. As such, classroom teachers interested in gaining greater understanding of individual differences in thinking abilities may find value in administration, scoring, and interpretation of these findings. The administration instructions are clearly presented and scoring is easy. However, the time involved with administration and scoring for a classroom of pupils should be carefully weighed to determine whether results can translate into meaningful implications for instruction. Teachers should also be cautioned to consider that the standardization sample appears to be a largely homogeneous, as well as small group of pupils attending schools in the U.K. These demographics may not provide an appropriate comparison to other classroom settings in different cultures. Because the test's directions are orally presented, a verbal component to the test is introduced that may impact some pupil's understanding of the nature of the various tasks. Thus, the tests likely are not "pure" measures of spatial ability. Finally, a single total score is attained on the test. This score provides an overall ranking for comparison with other pupils in the normative sample. Yet, it does not provide the examiner with information about differences in performance with various subtests or in regard to accuracy versus speed. As with other tests, some level of item analysis along with consideration of other contributing factors may be required with interpretation of pupils attaining particularly low scores. These points, along with sparse details of evidence of reliability and validity, suggest that the measure should be used with caution.

SUMMARY. The NFER-Nelson Spatial Reasoning series offers educators a group-administered measure of these abilities. As such, the tests may be useful for educational psychologists wanting confirmatory evidence as an adjunct to other cognitive assessments. However, this use of the tests was not articulated in the manuals. Rather, the intended consumer appears to be teachers desiring information regarding the thinking processes of students in their classrooms. Although this information may prove useful for some teachers in some settings, the value of these data should be considered in conjunction with the costs (e.g., time, effort) required to fully implement this assessment procedure. In the environments that such information would seem to be most useful, the test developers fail to provide specific demographic information so that teachers have knowledge of whether their pupils can be adequately compared.

Review of Spatial Reasoning by BETH DOLL, Professor of Educational Psychology, University of Nebraska—Lincoln, Lincoln, NE:

DESCRIPTION. NFER-Nelson's Spatial Reasoning test is a measure of children's ability to solve cognitive tasks involving shape and space, such as imagining how shapes would look from different perspectives, or rotating and combining shapes. Spatial Reasoning is an important cognitive domain in the United Kingdom, because it is one of three major thinking skills assessed by the British Ability Scales: Second Edition (BAS II; Elliott, Smith, & McCulloch, 1996; 37), a prominent individual intelligence scale developed in that country. Whereas the BAS II must be individually administered and interpreted by a trained psychological examiner, the Spatial Reasoning test is intended for administration by classroom teachers using a convenient, group format. The purpose is to allow teachers to identify the underlying cognitive abilities of their students, so that they can capitalize on spatial strengths throughout the curriculum. The remaining two BAS II skills are Verbal Reasoning and Non-Verbal Reasoning, and NFER-Nelson also offers teacher-friendly, group measures of these two skills (see 258 and 167).

TEST DESCRIPTION. There are four parallel forms of the Spatial Reasoning test for students from 6 to 14 years of age (6–7, 8–9, 10–11, and 12–14). All tasks are timed, and the test varies in length from 20 minutes for the age 6–7 form to 33 minutes for the age 12–14 form. The tasks that comprise the Spatial Reasoning test are inventive and interesting. Spatial reasoning is assessed by (a) showing drawings of a design from outside a shop window, and asking students to imagine what it would look like from inside the shop; (b) asking students to find the hidden shapes in complex designs; (c) showing drawings of stacked shapes, and asking students to identify the shape that is at the very bottom of the stack; (d) asking students to imagine what a shape would look like if sliced through its midsection; (e) showing students a collection of shapes and asking them to imagine these assembled like a puzzle; (f) asking students to imagine the pattern printed on a cutout from a larger "wallpaper" design; and (g) asking students to identify the line that would form a right angle when moved next to another line. Because these spatial tasks vary in difficulty, different combinations of tasks are included at different age levels.

Items on the test are objectively scored. Raw scores on the test are converted to standard scores with a mean of 100 and a standard deviation of 15. An additional table is provided to convert the standard scores to percentile ranks, and the front of each pupil booklet directs the teachers to construct 90% confidence intervals around each score.

Each form of the Spatial Reasoning test is accompanied by a 30-page teacher's guide and a 4-page "At a Glance" guide. Over half of the teacher's guide is dedicated to specific directions for administering, marking, and scoring the test, using verbatim scripts for test instructions. Then the guide carefully explains the test's standard scores, percentile scores, and confidence intervals in language appropriate for teachers with minimal training in assessment principles. From the simplicity of the explanation, it is apparent that the Spatial Reasoning test is designed for independent use by teachers. Each guide concludes with a very brief 3-page description of the test's standardization, and information about reliability and validity.

DEVELOPMENT. Only very general information is provided about the development of the Spatial Reasoning test. The authors note that test construction began with a large item pool, and that items were subsequently discarded if they were too easy or too difficult for the intended age group, or if they did not discriminate well between high and low scorers on the test.

TECHNICAL PROPERTIES. The Spatial Reasoning test was standardized on 6,593 students, with roughly equivalent numbers of participants drawn from the five geographic regions of the United Kingdom. The sample was 51% male and 49% female. Within each of the four forms, separate norms are provided for every 2 to 3 months of age. Although the standardization samples were of adequate size, the manual omits critical information about participants' ethnicity and socioeconomic status, reporting only their gender and a general comment that their geographic distribution was representative.

The standardization data were used to examine the internal consistency of scores from the test at each age level, using the Kuder-Richardson 20 formula. Results show consistently strong reliability, ranging from a low of .868 in the fifth year to a high of .921 in the ninth year. Despite this evidence of strong internal consistency reliability, there is no evidence of score stability over time.

Unfortunately, no similar evidence is provided for construct or predictive validity. The authors argue that there were no equivalent measures of spatial reasoning with which to compare the test, and that the test was released before predictive validity evidence could be accrued. At other points in the manual, the authors argue that the validity of test scores depends on the careful construction of spatial reasoning tasks. Only a single, unpublished concurrent validity study is described with 113 ninth year students and yielding a very modest correlation of .491 between the Spatial Reasoning Test and the Test of General Abilities Spatial (ACER, 2004).

The lack of validity information is particularly concerning because the authors recommend that results of the Spatial Reasoning test be used to individualize educational instruction to students' specific needs. Even though the tasks look like measures of spatial abilities, there is no empirical evidence that performance on these items has any relevance to school success. The test also purports to assess the abilities measured by the British Ability Scales: Second Edition, but there is no empirical examination of the relation between performance on this group-administered test and the individually administered BAS II.

COMMENTARY AND SUMMARY. The NFER-Nelson Spatial Reasoning test provides an intriguing set of spatial tasks, but its standard scores are derived from a large but incompletely described sample of elementary and secondary students in the United Kingdom. Although there is good evidence of internal consistency reliability, there is no evidence that the test relates in any meaningful way to the educational success of students, or to the Spatial Reasoning tasks of the British Ability Scales. The manual does not reference any additional publications on the test's development, tasks, or standardization, and no related references were identified in a search of the Psychlit database of peer-reviewed literature or a broad-based internet search. Consequently, although it is very difficult to judge the quality of research from which the Spatial Reasoning test was derived, it is clear that this work has not been held up to the scrutiny of peer review.

It is especially concerning that the Spatial Reasoning test is being marketed to teachers who would be interpreting these results without the benefit of consultation from an educational psychologist with expertise in individual cognitive abilities. Instead, until additional empirical investigations are conducted of its technical properties, the Spatial Reasoning test should only be used as a very preliminary research measure and should not be used in actual practice.

REVIEWER'S REFERENCES

Australian Council for Educational Research. (2004). Test of General Abilities. Camberwell, VIC: Author.
Elliott, C. D., Smith, P., & McCulloch, K. (1996). British Ability Scales: Second Edition. London: NFER-Nelson.

[232]
Stanford Achievement Test, Tenth Edition.

Purpose: Measures student achievement in reading, language, spelling, study skills, listening, mathematics, science and social science.
Population: Grades K.0–12.9.
Publication Dates: 1923–2003.
Acronym: Stanford 10.
Administration: Group.
Forms, 4: A, B, D, E.
Levels, 13: Stanford Early School Achievement Test 1, Stanford Early School Achievement Test 2, Primary 1, Primary 2, Primary 3, Intermediate 1, Intermediate 2, Intermediate 3, Advanced 1, Advanced 2, Stanford Test of Academic Skills 1, Stanford Test of Academic Skills 2, Stanford Test of Academic Skills 3.
Price Data: Available from publisher.
Comments: A variety of assessment options are available including full-length and abbreviated multiple-choice batteries; large-print and Braille editions are available.
Author: Harcourt Assessment, Inc.
Publisher: Harcourt Assessment, Inc.
 a) STANFORD EARLY SCHOOL ACHIEVEMENT TEST 1.
 Population: Grades K.0–K.5.
 Acronym: SESAT 1.

Forms, 2: Basic Battery, Complete Battery.
Scores, 6: Reading (Sounds and Letters, Word Reading, Total), Mathematics, Listening to Words and Stories, Environment.
Time: (105) minutes for Basic Battery; (135) minutes for Complete Battery.
b) STANFORD EARLY SCHOOL ACHIEVEMENT TEST 2.
Population: Grades K.5–1.5.
Acronym: SESAT 2.
Forms, 2: Basic Battery, Complete Battery.
Scores, 7: Reading (Sounds and Letters, Word Reading, Sentence Reading, Total), Mathematics, Listening to Words and Stories, Environment.
Time: (140) minutes for Basic Battery; (170) minutes for Complete Battery.
c) PRIMARY 1.
Population: Grades 1.5–2.5.
Forms, 4: Basic Battery, Complete Battery, Abbreviated Battery, Language.
Scores, 11-12: Reading (Word Study Skills, Word Reading, Sentence Reading, Reading Comprehension, Total), Mathematics (Mathematics Problem Solving, Mathematics Procedures, Total), Language, Spelling, Listening (not available in Abbreviated Battery), Environment.
Time: (295) minutes for Basic Battery; (325) minutes for Complete Battery; (212) minutes for Abbreviated Battery.
d) PRIMARY 2.
Population: Grades 2.5–3.5.
Forms, 4: Same as *c* above.
Scores, 10-11: Reading (Word Study Skills, Reading Vocabulary, Reading Comprehension, Total), Mathematics (Mathematics Problem Solving, Mathematics Procedures, Total), Language, Spelling, Listening (not available in Abbreviated Battery), Environment.
Time: (265) minutes for Basic Battery; (295) minutes for Complete Battery; (189) minutes for Abbreviated Battery.
e) PRIMARY 3.
Population: Grades 3.5–4.5.
Forms, 4: Same as *c* above.
Scores, 11-12: Reading (Word Study Skills, Reading Vocabulary, Reading Comprehension, Total), Mathematics (Mathematics Problem Solving, Mathematics Procedures, Total), Language, Spelling, Listening (not available in Abbreviated Battery), Science, Social Science.
Time: (280) minutes for Basic Battery; (330) minutes for Complete Battery; (203) minutes for Abbreviated Battery.
f) INTERMEDIATE 1.
Population: Grades 4.5–5.5.
Forms, 4: Same as *c* above.

Scores, 11-12: Same as *c* above.
Time: (280) minutes for Basic Battery; (330) minutes for Complete Battery; (201) minutes for Abbreviated Battery.

g) INTERMEDIATE 2.
Population: Grades 5.5–6.5.
Forms, 4: Same as *c* above.
Scores, 10-11: Reading (Reading Vocabulary, Reading Comprehension, Total), Mathematics (Mathematics Problem Solving, Mathematics Procedures, Total), Language, Spelling, Listening (not available in Abbreviated Battery), Science, Social Science.
Time: (260) minutes for Basic Battery; (310) minutes for Complete Battery; (187) minutes for Abbreviated Battery.

h) INTERMEDIATE 3.
Population: Grades 6.5–7.5.
Forms, 4: Same as *c* above.
Scores, 10-11: Same as *g* above.
Time: (260) minutes for Basic Battery; (310) minutes for Complete Battery; (187) minutes for Abbreviated Battery.

i) ADVANCED 1.
Population: Grades 7.5–8.5.
Forms, 4: Same as *c* above.
Scores, 10-11: Same as *g* above.
Time: (260) minutes for Basic Battery; (310) minutes for Complete Battery; (186) minutes for Abbreviated Battery.

j) ADVANCED 2.
Population: Grades 8.5–9.9.
Forms, 4: Same as *c* above.
Scores, 10-11: Same as *g* above.
Time: (260) minutes for Basic Battery; (310) minutes for Complete Battery; (185) minutes for Abbreviated Battery.

k) STANFORD TEST OF ACADEMIC SKILLS 1.
Population: Grades 9.0–9.9.
Acronym: TASK 1.
Forms, 4: Same as *c* above.
Scores, 8: Reading (Reading Vocabulary, Reading Comprehension, Total), Mathematics, Language, Spelling, Science, Social Science.
Time: (180) minutes for Basic Battery; (230) minutes for Complete Battery; (160) minutes for Abbreviated Battery.

l) STANFORD TEST OF ACADEMIC SKILLS 2.
Population: Grades 10.0–10.9.
Acronym: TASK 2.
Forms, 4: Same as *c* above.
Scores, 8: Same as *k* above.
Time: Same as *k* above.

m) STANFORD TEST OF ACADEMIC SKILLS 3.
Population: Grades 11.0–12.9.
Acronym: TASK 3.

Forms, 4: Same as *c* above.
Scores, 8: Same as *k* above.
Time: Same as *k* above.

Cross References: See T5:2484 (15 references); for reviews by Ronald A. Berk and Thomas M. Haladyna of an earlier edition, see 13:292 (80 references); for reviews of the Stanford Achievement Test-Abbreviated-8th Edition by Stephen N. Elliott and James A. Wollack and by Kevin L. Moreland, see 12:371; for information on an earlier edition of the Stanford Achievement Test, see T4:2551 (44 references); for reviews by Frederick G. Brown and Howard Stoker, see 11:377 (78 references); for reviews by Mark L. Davison and by Michael J. Subkoviak and Frank H. Farley of the 1982 Edition, see 9:1172 (19 references); see also T3:2286 (80 references); for reviews by Robert L. Ebel and A. Harry Passow and an excerpted review by Irvin J. Lehmann of the 1973 edition, see 8:29 (51 references); see also T2:36 (87 references); for an excerpted review by Peter F. Merenda of the 1964 edition, see 7:25 (44 references); for a review by Miriam M. Bryan and an excerpted review by Robert E. Stake (with J. Thomas Hastings), see 6:26 (13 references); for a review by N. L. Gage of an earlier edition, see 5:25 (19 references); for reviews by Paul R. Hanna (with Claude E. Norcross) and by Virgil E. Herrick, see 4:25 (20 references); for reviews by Walter W. Cook and Ralph C. Preston, see 3:18 (33 references). For reviews of subtests, see 9:1173 (1 review), 9:1174 (1 review), 9:1175 (1 review), 8:291 (2 reviews), 8:745 (2 reviews), 7:209 (2 reviews), 7:537 (1 review), 7:708 (1 review), 7:802 (1 review), 7:895 (1 review), 6:637 (1 review), 5:656 (2 reviews), 5:698 (2 reviews), 5:799 (1 review), 4:419 (1 review), 4:555 (1 review), 4:593 (2 reviews), 3:503 (1 review), and 3:595 (1 review); for a review of the Stanford Test of Academic Skills [1982 Edition] by John C. Ory, see 9:1182; see also T3:2298 (3 references); for reviews by Clinton I. Chase and Robert L. Thorndike of an earlier edition, see 8:31.

Review of the Stanford Achievement Test, Tenth Edition by RUSSELL N. CARNEY, Professor of Psychology, Southwest Missouri State University, Springfield, MO:

DESCRIPTION. The Stanford Achievement Test, Tenth Edition (Stanford 10) is the latest in a long line of distinguished achievement test batteries dating back to 1923. The Stanford 10 replaces the Ninth Edition, which was published in 1996. Designed to measure students' achievement in Reading, Mathematics, Spelling, Language, Science, Social Science, and Listening, this new edition is said to continue "the tradition of testing excellence" (technical data report, p. 5) established by prior Stanford Achievement Test batteries. The Stanford 10 can be administered as either the Full-Length Battery or the Abbreviated Battery. Braille and large print editions are available. The Stanford 10 is untimed. The directions indicate that students be allowed to continue working on a test as long as they are working productively. Suggested times are for planning only.

The Stanford 10 consists of 13 test levels that cover kindergarten through Grade 12. Specifically, the first two levels are the Stanford Early School Achievement Test (SESAT: K–first half of Grade 1), the next eight levels are the Stanford Achievement Test (second half of Grade 1–Grade 9), and the last three levels comprise the Stanford Test of Academic Skills (TASK: Grades 9–12). Except for the two levels of the SESAT, all the tests have equivalent forms. The test offers a variety of formats. These include multiple-choice, open-ended items for which partial credit can be received, writing prompts "that elicit performance in one of four modes" (Directions for Administering, p. 5), or any combination of these.

Several reasons for the development of the Tenth Edition are presented. These include changes in school curricula, national assessment trends, and the need to update norms and test materials. Regarding the latter, the new test is purported to be the *only* achievement test battery providing realistic, full-color illustrations. These illustrations resemble students' everyday instructional materials, and their provision is thought to improve student motivation. Another unique feature of the battery is that the reading selections are written specifically for the Stanford 10 by children's authors. Other improvements include improved navigation through the multiple-choice test and answer sheets, and color-enhanced, simplified reports.

DEVELOPMENT. The content of the test was based on a careful review of national and state instructional standards, content-specific curricula, and standards outlined by various professional organizations, such as the Standards for the English Language Arts, Principles and Standards for School Mathematics, National Science Education Standards, Benchmarks for Science Literacy, and Expectations for Excellence: Curriculum Standards for Social Studies. The academic standards for the various states and National Assessment of Educational Progress (NAEP) test framework were also considered.

Test blueprints were devised, calling for new test items for all levels of the battery. The blue-prints were reviewed by test professionals and content experts and were revised as needed. Blueprints were followed by the development of test item specifications for the multiple-choice items. A number of the items were written to get at higher order problem-solving processes. Test items were written by trained professionals, the majority being practicing teachers. Internal screening of the items included content experts, measurement experts, and editorial specialists.

Analysis of item tryouts provided useful statistical information, such as item difficulty, item discrimination, as well as the mean square fits for the items. Mantel-Haenszel bias analyses were conducted.

Beyond use of the Mantel-Haenszel differential item functioning (DIF) analyses, procedures were in place throughout the development of the test to reduce bias. Citing the *Standards for Educational and Psychological Testing* (AERA, APA, & NCME, 1999), the authors define bias as "construct-irrelevant components that result in systematically lower or higher scores for identifiable groups of examinees" (AERA et al., 1999, p. 76). With this in mind, they made a concerted effort to minimize bias in areas such as gender, ethnic, cultural, disability, SES, or stereotyping. In particular, a diverse, 20-member "Bias Review Advisory Panel" screened the items.

Over 170,000 students participated in their national item tryout program. Also, more than 10,000 teachers completed questionnaires as to the "match" of the test to their curriculum, layout, color illustrations, clarity of directions, and so forth.

The final forms of the test were developed based on the extensive data gathered during the tryout program—with a key criterion being the fit of the item's content with the test blueprint. Test items were said to be "balanced" in regard to whether they assessed "Basic Understanding" or higher order "Thinking Skills."

STANDARDIZATION. Norms for the Stanford 10 reflect the K–12 population (2002). Both spring and fall norms are provided. The spring standardization involved 250,000 students, and the fall standardization involved 110,000. School districts were chosen based on a stratified cluster sampling design that included variables such as geographic region, SES, urbanicity, and ethnicity. Stratification variables reflected the 2000 Census of Population and Housing and the 2000–2001 National Center for Education Statistics.

Special education students who would routinely be tested were included in the standardization samples. The norms are presented in the Spring Multilevel Norms book and the Fall Multilevel Norms book.

An "Equating of Levels Program" led to the creation of a continuous (vertical) score scale, allowing for comparisons across levels. Developers also equated the Stanford 10 with the Stanford 9. A group of students (approximately 1,000 per grade test level) were administered both the Stanford 9 and Stanford 10. Performance standards had been derived via a group of teachers who made judgments about the various items of the Stanford 9. Then equating was used to translate these standards for the Stanford 10.

SCORING. The Stanford 10 reports several types of scores: raw scores, scaled scores, individual percentile ranks, stanines, grade equivalents, Normal Curve Equivalents (NCEs), Achievement/Ability Comparisons (AACs), group percentile ranks and stanines, content cluster and process cluster performance categories, and performance standards. According to the technical data report, scaled scores "express student performance across all test levels of any given subtest on a single scale." However, "they are not comparable from one content area to another or across subtests within a content domain total" (p. 34). The technical report does an excellent job of describing the various scores. For example, they caution the test user as to the ease with which Grade Equivalent scores can be misinterpreted, and provide an example of such misinterpretation. The Achievement/Ability Comparisons allow for comparisons between the Stanford 10 and the Otis-Lennon School Ability Test, Eighth Edition (OLSAT 8).

TECHNICAL. According to the *Standards for Educational and Psychological Testing* (AERA et al., 1999), reliability "refers to the consistency of such measurements when the testing procedure is repeated on a population of individuals or groups" (p. 25). In this regard, the technical report states that the battery exhibits a "high degree" of internal consistency reliability. Indeed, a review of the multitude of tables of KR20 coefficients for the full-length test (Forms A and B) shows the majority of them to be in the mid-.80s to .90s—certainly satisfactory for the purposes of this test. As would be expected, the coefficients for the abbreviated test tend to be a bit lower, with the majority falling in the .80s. Corresponding standard errors

of measurement (*SEMs*) are provided in the various reliability coefficient tables as well.

Alternate-form reliability measures the equivalency of the different forms of the test. Here, for Forms A and B, correlations across the various tables ranged from .53 to .93, but were usually in the .80s for the various tests composing Forms A and B. Composite scores, such as "Total Reading" and "Total Mathematics" were generally close to .90. These alternate-form comments do not apply to the SESAT tests because equivalent forms were not developed for the two levels of the SESAT. No test-retest reliability was reported.

The technical report cites the *Standards for Educatonal and Psychological Testing* (AERA et al., 1999) in defining validity as: "the degree to which evidence and theory support the interpretations of test scores entailed in the use of tests" (p. 9), and interprets validity as an integrated concept. In that regard, and as indicated earlier, the Stanford 10 has good internal-consistency reliability. Next, content validity has been built into the test through their well-defined test blueprint and their careful development process. Test reliability and content validity are probably the two most important requirements for validity in an achievement test. That said, and echoing a prior reviewer (Berk, 1998), it is up to the user to determine that the content of the test matches the curricula and goals of the particular school.

Further, an appendix in the technical data report provides numerous correlations between the various subtests and totals of the Stanford 10 levels with the subtests of the Stanford 9. These correlations (which run in the .70s–.80s) provide evidence of convergent validity. Also, correlations between the Stanford 10 and the OLSAT 8 provide additional evidence of construct validation. The authors of the technical data report argue that, because the abbreviated version represents a subset of the items on the full-length version, the validity evidence applies "equally" to the abbreviated version.

COMMENTARY. The materials comprising this K–12 test battery are numerous. Hence, this review is based primarily on a reading of the technical data report (2004) and a review of selected test materials at different levels.

The test appears to have been carefully developed according to high measurement standards. Given this, the battery should provide students, parents, and schools with useful information as to what students know in the areas of reading, mathematics, spelling, language, science, social science, and listening. The flexibility of this instrument is a plus, with both full and abbreviated versions, and other options are available in terms of the test format. Test reliability and evidence for validity appear to be satisfactory, and care has been taken to minimize any test bias.

An interesting feature of the Stanford 10 is the arrangement of items within subtests. Rather than the typical "easy to hard" arrangement, the Stanford 10 mixes easy and difficult items. The rationale is that in the traditional arrangement, students tend to get frustrated as they get into consistently harder items and "give up." With the mixed arrangement, students are thought to be better motivated to keep working throughout the entire test.

The fact that the test is untimed should help to reduce test anxiety. Along these lines, the practice test provided for each test level, to be administered within a week of the actual administration, is a fine way of familiarizing students with the directions and format of the test, and in preparing the test administrator (e.g., the teacher) for the actual administration. The directions for administration are clearly written, as are the score reports.

Another aspect that may reduce student anxiety is the presence of attractive color illustrations. As the developers suggest, the test materials more closely resemble the picture-laden textbooks students are accustomed to studying. Thus, the test materials seem more "friendly" and authentic than more traditional test formats, and this may not only reduce anxiety but also help to maintain students' interest and motivation. Another function of the pictures is that they allow the test maker to add cultural diversity (e.g., via skin color) to the various items.

Items were "boxed" throughout the test—usually to good effect. However, in a spelling test, six sentences containing spelling items are presented per page, each outlined in long, brown, rectangular boxes. The effect makes the page overly busy, so much so that it was hard to focus on the sentences in the boxes. Less intrusive boxes (or no boxes) might have been less problematic.

SUMMARY. In short, the Stanford 10 maintains the high standards of the prior editions of this well-respected test. It provides a reliable and user-friendly assessment of students' achievement in seven academic areas across Grades K–12. School

systems, and their students, should be well served by this thoroughly updated test battery. At the same time, it should be noted that content validity is based on the "fit" of the test to what is taught in particular classrooms. Educators considering this test should judge for themselves how closely it matches their goals and curricula to ensure test validity for their purposes.

REVIEWER'S REFERENCES

American Educational Research Association, American Psychological Association, & National Council on Measurement and Education. (1999). *Standards for educational and psychological testing.* Washington, DC: American Educational Research Association.
Berk, R. A. (1998). [Review of the Stanford Achievement Test, Ninth Edition.] In J. C. Impara & B. S. Plake, (Eds.), *The thirteenth mental measurements yearbook* (pp. 925–928). Lincoln, NE: Buros Institute of Mental Measurements.

Review of the Stanford Achievement Test, Tenth Edition by DAVID T. MORSE, Professor, Counseling, Educational Psychology and Special Education, Mississippi State University, Mississippi State, MS:

DESCRIPTION. The Stanford Achievement Test, Tenth Edition (Stanford 10) comprises a series of 13 battery levels, covering Grades K–12. The Stanford Early School Achievement Test (SESAT) has two levels, intended for Grades K–1.5, the Stanford Achievement Test (SAT) has eight levels (Primary 1, 2, and 3; Intermediate 1, 2, and 3; and Advanced 1 and 2) covering Grades 1.5 through end of junior high, and the Stanford Test of Academic Skills (TASK) has three levels, covering Grades 9–12. The tests are intended as measures of school achievement that might be used in two ways. First, it can be used as a norm-referenced measure by school or district personnel to make judgments about attainment relative to a national norm group, as required by the No Child Left Behind legislation, or longitudinal progress via the vertically equated scaled scores. Second, it can be used as a source of feedback about sets of general skill areas (clusters) or more specific skills (standards) that might be useful in making some decisions about adequacy of instruction. All of the levels of the Stanford 10 have subtests in the disciplines of Reading, Mathematics, and Language. Specific subtests vary by level. As an example, for Primary 3 and higher, separate Science and Social Science subtests are included, but these are merged in a subtest called Environment in lower levels.

Administration of the Stanford 10 requires no special training, and tests may be scored locally or sent to the publisher for off-site scoring and reporting. Directions for administration are straightforward and should present no special difficulty for school staff or faculty. Use of calculators is permitted, but not required, for the Mathematics Problem Solving/Mathematics subtest, but may not be used on the Mathematics Procedures subtest. The technical data report indicates that there was not a distinguishable normative difference between those using and those not using a calculator for the Problem Solving/Mathematics subtests. Subtests are not timed and are intended to be power tests. Administration directions suggest that students be permitted to continue as long as they are working productively; however, a suggested time allocation is given for each subtest. According to the technical data report, most accommodations for testing conditions are considered not to endanger the utility of the normative data. One notable exception is that of Braille editions of the test, which are available, as are large print versions. Screening tests and separate norms are available for hearing-impaired examinees. Practice tests are available. To administer the full battery at any level requires considerable testing time, from 2 hours, 15 minutes for SESAT and from 1 to 5 hours, 30 minutes for Primary 3 or Intermediate 1. The core test items are multiple-choice, though the promotional literature mentions the availability of open-ended items and writing prompts.

Normative scores are available as percentile ranks, scaled scores, stanines, normal curve equivalents, or grade equivalents. Though there are many noteworthy deficiencies of grade-equivalent scores, some of which are noted by the technical data report, they are still available. Qualitative classifications of performance levels (e.g., "Below basic," "Basic," "Proficient," and "Advanced") are also available, and were derived from teams of teachers making Angoff-type judgments of Stanford 9 items (e.g., "What percent of 'minimally proficient' students would be able to answer this question correctly?"). Group percentile ranks and stanines are said to be available for class, building or district level, though these do not appear in either the Fall Multilevel Norms Book or the Spring Multilevel Norms Book.

DEVELOPMENT. The Stanford 10 is the newest version (2003 copyright) of an achievement series that first appeared in 1923. Revisions have been published in 1929, 1940, 1953, 1964, 1973, 1982, 1989, and 1996. Normative data were collected in April and September—October of 2002 for spring and fall norms, respectively. In the technical data report, the publisher lists many

textbook series and state and national standards guidelines and compendiums that were consulted during the development of this edition. The Stanford series has long been used as a norm-referenced, group-based test of academic achievement; the Stanford 10 continues that tradition. There were also preliminary, national item tryouts conducted over a 3-year period (1998–2000) prior to the final standardization in 2002. Before statistical analysis, item sensitivity reviews were conducted by trained panel members, looking for instances of concerns about the items based on gender, race/ethnicity, religion, geographic region, socioeconomic status, English proficiency, and disability.

Each item is keyed four ways: by a content cluster (typically two–four per subtest), a process cluster, a cognitive level (basic understanding or thinking skills), and an instructional standard (often taken from national discipline-based organizations). At elementary and middle/junior high levels, the tests typically assess concepts or skills taught in the second half of the school year and possibly the first half of the next school year. The TASK series, aimed at high school grades, are better characterized as basic skills tests. For these reasons, spring testing is recommended for summative decisions made from Stanford levels below TASK 1 or for measures of change from year to year, whereas the technical data report suggests that TASK levels are acceptable for use either in fall or spring testing.

Starting with the Primary 1 level, there are two variants of the test, one having a Language subtest that emphasizes mechanics and expression (Forms A/B), the other focusing on "actual writing processes" such as prewriting, composing, and editing subskills (Forms D/E). Form Pairs A & B and D & E are available as alternate forms. Individual subtests may be used, as may an abbreviated or full battery for a given level.

Materials available from the publisher include norms manuals, a technical manual, a compendium of instructional standards (that lists the specific skills measured by each subtest), parent guides, test administration manuals, and a wide array of score reports, both print and electronic forms. Individual reports, group reports, summaries with or without narratives, and detailed reading first reports are available for those using the full battery.

TECHNICAL. Overall, the standardization sample is typically within a few percentage points of mirroring the 2000 U.S. figures for geographic region, socioeconomic status, urbanicity, and ethnicity. Additionally, special norming samples were collected to allow for (a) comparison of separate answer sheets versus marking answers in test booklets for the Primary 3 version (separate norms are furnished); and (b) for Braille editions of the Stanford 10, for which separate norms are available.

The technical data report offers a traditional presentation of information (item p-values, median biserial and point-biserial coefficients by subtest, subtest intercorrelations, internal consistency reliability estimates, classical theory standard error of measurement (raw score units), and conditional errors of measurement (given as nomographs for the scaled scores). Though the one-parameter logistic item response ("Rasch") model was used for creating the scaled scores, conditional errors, and for vertical equating, little information is given as to some of the key decision points (e.g., which measure of fit was used, and what sort of threshold for a mean square fit index was used to cull items). Additional checks for differential item functioning, using the Mantel-Haenszel statistic were conducted for male-female, White-African American, White-Hispanic, and Regular education-Special populations comparisons.

Alternate forms reliability values for the Stanford 10 are virtually the same as the relationships between adjacent forms of the Stanford 10 (e.g., Primary 3 to Intermediate 1) that formed the basis for vertical equating or for the relationships of Stanford 9 to Stanford 10 subtests undertaken for equating (e.g., for those who wish to make longitudinal comparisons). One might have expected the alternate forms reliability values to have been typically higher. Data on the equivalence of alternate forms are given, and, for the most part, such pairs have means, standard deviations, median item-total correlations, and internal consistency reliability estimates that are, with few exceptions, close in value.

The reliability estimates from full-length subtests tend to be good enough for making judgments about individual examinees, according to guidelines such as those given by Cronbach (1990). However, there are some noteworthy exceptions to this, including: some abbreviated-length subtests, some of the constituent subtests of a discipline area (e.g., language prewriting), and some of the full-length subtests (e.g., Environment). Estimates

of reliability appear high enough in all cases to make judgments about groups of examinees.

A "Thinking Skills" score, both for abbreviated and full battery, is furnished, starting with the Primary 3 level. This raw score is computed by summing the number of correct answers across all items in all subtests that are classified by cognitive level as "thinking skill." Further, norms tables are given for this score. There is no reliability, error of measurement, or other technical information beyond mean item p-value for this score. This lack of reporting is not in accord with the *Standards for Educational and Psychological Testing* (AERA, APA, & NCME, 1999).

The conversion of the performance category thresholds (e.g., "Basic," "Proficient") from the Stanford 9, from which they were initially generated, to Stanford 10 was via the score equating process of Stanford 9 to Stanford 10, which required a special norming sample. Because many of the older to newer subtest score correlations are reported as being less than .80 according to the technical data report, it is not clear how accurately the cut points have survived the equating process. The classification accuracy/consistency tables are not satisfactorily explained and do not appear to have been developed from examinees who took alternate forms of subtests, which would have been the best evidence for the stability of classification of examinees into these performance categories.

Authors of the technical data report show evidence of having consulted the 1999 *Standards* (AERA, APA, & NCME, 1999), but evidence of relationships to external variables (whether convergent or discriminant) involves only Stanford 9, OLSAT 8 (Otis-Lennon School Ability Test, Version 8), and intercorrelations among subtests on Stanford 10; these data, though presented, are not interpreted. The magnitude of correlations of Stanford 10 subtest scores with OLSAT 8 scores—values in the .40s to the .60s are abundant—would not warrant the use of OLSAT 8 scores to predict Stanford 10 scores or vice versa.

COMMENTARY. The Stanford 10 offers a linked set of school achievement measures for which relatively recent national normative data are available. As such, it would appear to be a viable option for schools needing national "benchmarks" for gauging the attainment of their students. The tests cover the traditional discipline areas, do not require special training for administration or interpretation, and do have both fall and spring norms available. Within subtests, the layout of items on the page is easy to follow, and color is used generously to make the pages and items more visually appealing.

The option of versions (Forms D/E) having Language subtests that emphasize elements of the writing process might be of interest to some educators. Though these subtests do include questions about topic selection, organizing and finding information, the "actual writing processes" are mostly manifested as micro-editing type tasks, using multiple-choice format. No direct writing samples are included in versions of the core tests. Any potential user of the Stanford 10, or any other academic achievement series, should carefully review the skills measured, as well as how they are measured, to determine the degree of fit to the local curriculum.

The vertical equating allows for the scaled scores to be used as a way of tracking performance across grades. Users of the series need to understand that median year-to-year increases in scaled scores diminish in size with increasing grade level and can, with some subtests of the TASK, show little or no increase or even a decrease.

Though scores may be disaggregated to the cluster or standard level, only the cluster level tends to have potentially sufficient items within subtests to warrant interpreting scores for individuals. There are typically too few items at the standard level to recommend making decisions about specific examinees. For class, school, or district-wide summaries, these disaggregated scores might be of interest. No reliability, error of measurement, or, beyond the general discussion of content coverage and generation, validity information is presented for cluster-level or standard-level percent correct summaries. The ersatz Thinking Skills score is also made available without reliability information, though normative scores are given.

SUMMARY. The Stanford 10 can serve as a vehicle for comparing local students' academic attainment to that of a national norms group in traditional subject areas. The subtests are easy to administer, can be scored locally or sent to the publisher, may be used for small or large groups of examinees (with appropriate proctoring assistance), include practice items, and practice tests may be purchased. The utility of any achievement series, though, rests in large part on the extent to which

the skills assessed reflect outcomes important to the user of the test scores.

Anyone looking for a nationally normed measure that features "authentic" assessment of student attainment or accomplishment beyond the multiple-choice framework of the core test will be disappointed with the Stanford 10. However, for those who judge the Stanford 10 to tap important skills in an appropriate manner, the developers have succeeded in updating an achievement battery that can help educators satisfy some of the seemingly endless assessment demands emerging at both the state and national levels.

REVIEWER'S REFERENCES

American Educational Research Association, American Psychological Association, & National Council on Measurement in Education. (1999). *Standards for educational and psychological testing*. Washington, DC: American Educational Research Association.
Cronbach, L. J. (1990). *Essentials of psychological testing* (5th ed.). New York: Harper Collins Publishing.

[233]

Stanford-Binet Intelligence Scales, Fifth Edition.

Purpose: Designed to assess "intelligence and cognitive abilities."

Population: Ages 2-0 to 89-9.

Publication Dates: 1916–2003.

Acronym: SB5.

Scores, 13: Nonverbal Fluid Reasoning, Verbal Fluid Reasoning, Nonverbal Knowledge, Verbal Knowledge, Nonverbal Quantitative Reasoning, Verbal Quantitative Reasoning, Nonverbal Visual-Spatial Processing, Verbal Visual-Spatial Processing, Nonverbal Working Memory, Verbal Working Memory, Nonverbal IQ, Verbal IQ, Full Scale IQ.

Subtests and Partial Batteries: Abbreviated Battery (Nonverbal Fluid Reasoning and Verbal Knowledge).

Administration: Individual.

Price Data: Available from publisher.

Time: (45–75) minutes; (15–20) minutes for Abbreviated Battery.

Author: Gale H. Roid.

Publisher: Riverside Publishing.

Cross References: For information on an earlier edition, see T5:2485 (245 references) and T4:2553 (120 references); for reviews by Anne Anastasi and Lee J. Cronbach, see 10:342 (89 references); see also 9:1176 (41 references), T3:2289 (203 references), 8:229 (176 references), and T2:525 (428 references); for a review by David Freides, see 7:425 (258 references); for a review by Elizabeth D. Fraser and excerpted reviews by Benjamin Balinski, L. B. Birch, James Maxwell, Marie D. Neale, and Julian C. Stanley, see 6:536 (110 references); for reviews by Mary R. Haworth and Norman

D. Sundberg of the second revision, see 5:413 (121 references); for a review by Boyd R. McCandless, see 4:358 (142 references); see also 3:292 (217 references); for excerpted reviews by Cyril Burt, Grace H. Kent, and M. Krugman, see 2:1420 (132 references); for reviews by Francis W. Maxfield, J. W. M. Rothney, and F. L. Wells, see 1:1062.

Review of the Stanford-Binet Intelligence Scales, Fifth Edition by JUDY A. JOHNSON, Assistant Professor of Psychology in the School Psychology Program at the University of Houston-Victoria, Victoria, Texas, and RIK CARL D'AMATO, Assistant Dean and Director of the Center for Collaborate Research in Education, College of Education and Behavioral Sciences, M. Lucile Harrison Professor of Excellence, School of Professional Psychology, University of Northern Colorado, Greeley, CO:

DESCRIPTION. The Stanford-Binet Intelligence Scales, Fifth Edition (SB5) is the latest version of one of our fundamental assessment instruments for which the original version was created almost 100 years ago. The SB5, which took 7 years to complete, is the long-awaited update of the Fourth Edition, which was published in 1986. The SB5, like its predecessors, is a comprehensive, norm-referenced individually administered test of intelligence and cognitive abilities. The SB5 can be used with examinees who range from 2 years old to over 85 years old. This expansive age range has always been one of the most remarkable features of this instrument. Typical uses of the SB5 include diagnosing exceptionalities and developmental disabilities in adults, adolescents, and children.

The scales yield a Full Scale IQ, two domain scores (Nonverbal IQ and Verbal IQ), and five factor Indexes (Fluid Reasoning, Knowledge, Quantitative Reasoning, Visual-Spatial Processing, and Working Memory). Unlike previous editions, the means of the IQ and factor index scores are 100 with a standard deviation of 15. The Full Scale IQ is based on the administration of 10 subtests and is the global measure of cognitive ability. Each of the five factors are considered using both verbal and nonverbal measures. The SB5 has 10 subtests including 2 special routing subtests (Nonverbal-Fluid Reasoning: Object Series/Matrices and Verbal-Knowledge: Vocabulary), which are administered at the beginning of the SB5. These routing subtests determine the developmental starting point for the remaining subtests.

Depending on the examinee's performance on the routing subtests, the examiner is directed to begin at Level 1, 2, 3, 4, or 5. This unique way of addressing development is a longstanding tradition with the Binet scales.

The SB5 subtest names and the activities that make up the subtests for a specific level are listed below. The SB5 Nonverbal subtests include Nonverbal Knowledge (Picture Absurdities [Levels 4–6] and Procedural Knowledge [Levels 2–3]); Nonverbal Quantitative Reasoning [Levels 2–6]; Nonverbal Visual-Spatial Processing (Form Board [Levels 1–2] and Form Patterns [Levels 3–6]); and Nonverbal Working Memory (Block Span [Levels 2–6] and Delayed Response [Level 1]). The Verbal subtests include Verbal Fluid Reasoning (Early Reasoning [Levels 2–3], Verbal Absurdities [Level 4], and Verbal Analogies [Levels 5–6]); Verbal Quantitative Reasoning [Levels 2–6]; Verbal Visual-Spatial Processing (Position and Direction [Levels 2–6]); and Verbal Working Memory (Memory for Sentences [Levels 2–3] and Last Word [Levels 4–6]). These subtests yield a scaled score with a mean of 10 and with a standard deviation of 3. The SB5 also yields an Abbreviated Battery IQ that is based on the two routing subtests and can be used to supplement another battery of tests that has been administered or when a brief measure of intelligence is sufficient.

The administration time of the SB5 varies from 15 to 75 minutes, depending on which scales are given. Most of the SB5 items are not timed and time bonuses are not admissible. The estimated time to acquire a Full Scale IQ is 45 to 75 minutes, whereas the Abbreviated Battery IQ takes 15 to 20 minutes to administer to a client. Further, the examiner can choose to administer only the Verbal IQ (based on the five Verbal subtests) or the Nonverbal IQ (based on the five Nonverbal subtests); each of these takes about 30 minutes to complete. The technical manual states the Nonverbal IQ can be used for assessing those with hearing impairments, autism, communication disorders, limited English-language backgrounds, and other areas where verbal ability is limited. This is a unique and helpful feature of the instrument.

For ease of administration, the SB5 is organized into three item books printed on an easel format that includes all administration directions. The easel format allows examinees to easily view test materials, but also allows the examiner to easily record and score responses behind the easel. The first item book includes the two routing subtests, whereas the second item book contains Levels 1–6 of the Nonverbal subtests. The third Item book contains Levels 2–6 of the Verbal subtests.

A variety of scores are derived from the raw test data. In addition to standard scores for each composite score, subtest scaled scores, percentile ranks, confidence intervals, age equivalents, and Change-Sensitive Scores may be computed. Change-Sensitive Scores (CSS), based on item response theory, provide a means to identify a client's change in scores over a period of time. The SB5 may be hand scored, but scoring can be made easier by using the SB5 Scoring Pro. The SB5 Scoring Pro is a Windows-based program that allows the examiner to enter background information, age, and raw scores. The resulting report includes an extended score report and a brief, narrative summary report that, if desired, can be exported to a word processing file for editing.

DEVELOPMENT. Several significant changes were made from the SB4 to the SB5. First, the SB5 was renormed on a large, representative sample that ranged from preschool age to mature adults. The SB5 made a significant change to the structure of the test by adding another factor, Working Memory. Working Memory was added because it has been shown to be related to both reading and math achievement, and, in fact, is a deficient area in many of those children and adults with learning problems. It is also a novel area that is not covered on many traditional tests of intelligence. Another important change included enhanced coverage of nonverbal intelligence. The Nonverbal IQ, unlike other cognitive measures, is composed of nonverbal items that cover the five factors of Fluid Reasoning, Knowledge, Quantitative Reasoning, Visual-Spatial Processing, and Working Memory. Because the U.S. population is becoming more and more diverse, increasing the nonverbal coverage (where items require no or a minimal verbal response) was an important change.

Other changes in the new edition have included updated items that extend the scales upward and downward as well as allowing assessment of individuals who display very high or very low levels of functioning. Materials have also been "revamped" to be more appealing to both examinees and examiners. The SB5 includes "child friendly" toys and manipulatives that are appealing to younger clients. Examiners will also welcome the easel-style item books and computerized scoring program, which can make the assessment process more user friendly. Further, the examiner-friendly record form includes directional arrows when sums are to be transferred to another area on the record form, bold print to identify correct answers for the examiner, as well as lightly printed areas, which show the total points possible on a specific subtest.

The SB5 includes comprehensive technical (Roid, 2003c) and examiner's manuals. The technical manual guides the examiner through the test development process, which is consistent with the *Standards for Educational and Psychological Testing* (American Educational Research Association, American Psychological Association, & National Council on Measurement in Education, 1999). In addition, the technical manual highlights the history of the measure, theoretical foundations, evidence of reliability and validity, and provides detailed descriptions of professional and ethical use of the SB5. Further, the examiner's manual succeeds in familiarizing the examiner with test user qualifications, assessment of special populations with the SB5, as well as key administration, scoring, and interpretive guidelines. A more detailed SB5 interpretive manual is available, but it is disappointing that it must be purchased separately. [Editor's Note: The publisher advises that beginning in 2006 the manual may be purchased as part of the kit.]

TECHNICAL. The SB5 is based on the Cattell-Horn-Carroll (CHC) theory of cognitive functioning that has been investigated empirically over several decades (D'Amato, Fletcher-Janzen, & Reynolds, in press). Several other recent intelligence tests have also been based on elements of CHC theory, and studies on earlier versions of the Binet scales revealed distinguishable CHC factors. The SB5 is composed of 5 factors (out of 10) of the CHC model including (CHC factors in parentheses): Fluid Reasoning (Fluid Intelligence or Gf), Knowledge (Crystallized Knowledge or Gc), Quantitative Reasoning (Quantitative Knowledge or Gq), Visual-Spatial Processing (Visual Processing or Gv), and Working Memory (Short-Term Memory or Gsm).

The selection of only five of the CHC factors for the SB5 was based on research of the relations of the factors to achievement, giftedness, and reasoning ability, as well as earlier versions of the Binet scales. Three of the CHC factors on the SB5 (Gf, Gc, and Gq) have the highest *g* loadings in the model and are seen as key factors in general reasoning ability. Further, the factors most predictive of school achievement (Gc, Gsm, Gq) are also included on the SB5. Finally, Roid has stated in the technical manual that these five factors have been identified in earlier editions of the Binet scales. Overall, these reasons, as well as practical considerations (ease of test administration, total testing time, factors measured by other tests, etc.), led to the selection of five factors after eight CHC factors were extensively researched for the SB5. The other two factors, Reading and Writing (Grw) and Decision Speed/Reaction Time (Gt) were not chosen for the SB5 because they are usually included in other batteries.

The norming of the SB5 is one of the most impressive aspects of the instrument. A sample of 4,800 participants, ranging from age 2 to over 85 were closely matched to variables in 2001 U.S. Census Bureau documents. The stratification variables included sex, age, race/ethnicity, socioeconomic level, and geographic region. The sample included 1,400 young children (ages 2–5), 1,000 children (ages 6–10), 1,322 adolescents/young adults (11–20), and 1,078 adults (21–80+). The geographic regions in the Census (Midwest, South, Northeast, and West) were used in stratifying the sample for the SB5. Socioeconomic status was indicated by educational attainment (years of education completed) in the normative sample. Five percent of the school-aged normative sample included students in special education programs who were included in regular classrooms for more than 50% of the day. However, no significant changes in SB5 administration were made for participants included in the normative sample and those with significant medical conditions, limited English skills, severe communication or sensory deficits, and severe emotional or behavior disorders were excluded. Overall, the technical manual describes a norm group that is representative of those in the United States.

Reliability for the SB5 was estimated using several methods including the split-half method, test-retest reliability, and interscorer agreement. The coefficients for subtests were calculated by the split-half method. The scores were then corrected by using the Spearman-Brown formula. Average reliability coefficients for the Nonverbal subtests ranged from .85 to .89, whereas those for the

Verbal subtests ranged from .84 to .89. Reliability for the IQ and Factor Index scores were computed using "the formula for a reliability of a sum of multiple tests" (technical manual, p. 63). Average reliability coefficients for the Full Scale IQ (.98), Nonverbal IQ (.95), Verbal IQ (.96), and the Abbreviated Battery IQ (.91) were extremely high. When reliability coefficients were computed for the Factor Index scores, the average values included the following: Fluid Reasoning (.90), Knowledge (.92), Quantitative Reasoning (.92), Visual-Spatial Processing (.92), and Working Memory (.91).

Four studies of test-retest stability were included in the technical manual. In the first study, 96 young children 2 to 5 years old were administered the SB5 on two different occasions. The Pearson correlations were corrected for sample variability. Test-retest correlations ranged from .92 to .95 for the IQ scores (Full Scale IQ, Nonverbal IQ, and Verbal IQ), .82 to .92 for the Factor Index scores, and .76 to .91 for the subtest scores. A similar study with participants ranging in age from 6 to 20 years (*n* = 87) found test-retest correlations ranged from .90 to .93 for the IQ scores (Full Scale IQ, Nonverbal IQ, and Verbal IQ), .85 to .92 for the Factor Index scores, and .76 to .91 for the subtest scores. Further, test-retest reliability was studied with adults ranging in age from 21 to 59 years. Test-retest correlations ranged from .89 to .95 for the IQ scores (Full Scale IQ, Nonverbal IQ, and Verbal IQ), .79 to .94 for the Factor Index scores, and .66 to .93 for the subtest scores. Finally, a study was conducted to measure test-retest reliability in a sample of mature adults over 60 years old (*n* = 92). For this sample, test-retest correlations ranged from .93 to .95 for the IQ scores (Full Scale IQ, Nonverbal IQ, and Verbal IQ), .83 to .95 for the Factor Index scores, and .77 to .91 for the subtest scores. The test-retest interval in the above four studies ranged from 1 day to 39 days. In light of the above studies, test-retest reliability of the SB5 seems adequate. It would also be interesting to see test-retest reliability studies with a longer interval between tests. In most of the studies included in the manual, the test-retest interval was about a month.

Another critical aspect of reliability is interscorer agreement—the correlation of item scores for the same client when rated by two different examiners. The technical manual reports, on all polychotomous items, correlations that ranged from .74–.97 (median of .90) in the investigations into interscorer agreement on the SB5. These findings show adequate interscorer agreement on the SB5.

Preliminary evidence of content-related, criterion-related, concurrent, and construct-related validity is presented in the SB5 technical manual. Of course, validity of the SB5 will also be gathered after publication as it is used in the field and in research studies. The test development of the SB5, which was a 7-year process, underwent extensive expert review of items and subtests, numerous pilot studies, and reviews of the tryout edition. Additionally, the SB5 was found to be highly correlated with major cognitive tests such as the Wechsler scales and previous editions of the Stanford-Binet. Studies were conducted with special populations (such as those classified as gifted or with mental retardation) and expected results were found using the SB5. Further, confirmatory factor analyses of the SB5 subtests provided evidence for a five-factor solution. Throughout the test development process, the items of the SB5 were reviewed for fairness in regard to gender, race/ethnicity, culture, and religious background. Studies of item and test bias were conducted and problematic items were deleted from each successive version. Overall, the SB5 appears to have adequate validity for clients of a great variety of backgrounds.

COMMENTS AND SUMMARY. The SB5 is the long-awaited revision of the Stanford-Binet 4 and the publication of the SB5 was worth the wait. The test development process followed the *Standards for Educational and Psychological Testing* (AERA, APA, & NCME, 1999) and resulted in a well-designed, technically sound instrument that follows in the footsteps of earlier editions of the Binet scales but also integrated new research on intelligence into the measure. Especially impressive is the structure of the new test that now includes working memory, a neuropsychological area that will be especially useful in assessing those with learning problems. Additionally, the expanded emphasis on nonverbal intelligence will be useful in the assessment of a variety of clients in our changing world. The scoring software will also reduce clerical errors and save examiners a great deal of time.

Of course, improvements could be made on the SB5. The interpretive manual is not included with the test materials and the interpretative data in the SB5 technical manual and

examiner's manual are limited. Further, it would be helpful to see appropriate evidence-based intervention recommendations generated from SB5 data included with the test materials. For the SB5 to have the most utility in educational settings, there needs to be additional research on how the results of the SB5 can be linked to successful interventions. However, the strengths of the SB5 clearly outweigh its weaknesses. The SB5 is an outstanding measure with few significant weaknesses. For those who require an individually administered, norm-referenced intelligence test, the SB5 is clearly an exceptional instrument. The SB5 may again take its place as one of the seminal and primary measures of intelligence in our field. Many of the unique features of the SB5 make it the ideal choice when selecting an instrument from the long list of currently available intelligence tests.

REVIEWERS' REFERENCES

American Educational Research Association, American Psychological Association, & National Council on Measurement in Education. (1999). *Standards for educational and psychological testing*. Washington, DC: American Educational Research Association.
D'Amato, R. C., Fletcher-Janzen, E., & Reynolds, C. R. (Eds.). (in press). *The handbook of school neuropsychology*. Hoboken, NJ: John Wiley and Sons.

Review of the Stanford-Binet Intelligence Scales, Fifth Edition by JOSEPH C. KUSH, Associate Professor, Duquesne University, Pittsburgh, PA:

DESCRIPTION. The Stanford-Binet Intelligence Scales, Fifth Edition (SB5) is an individually administered intelligence test designed for examinees between the ages of 2 and 85+ years. The test consists of five verbal and five nonverbal subtests. Verbal subtests can require individuals to read, speak, and comprehend age-appropriate English. Nonverbal subtests expect minimal receptive language and additionally require fine-motor coordination to manipulate toys and puzzle pieces, and to be able to point to correct answers. The SB5 utilizes very few time limits, and bonuses for speeded performance are not given. Unlike previous versions, however, the SB5 now utilizes a metric common to all other major tests of intelligence: a mean of 100 and a standard deviation of 15.

Administration and scoring. The test begins by presenting participants with two routing tests that are used to determine the proper starting level for the remainder of the subtests. The first routing subtest, Vocabulary, has been used in all previous editions of the SB scale. Beginning with the Fifth Edition, the nonverbal subtest Object Series/Matrices has been added as a second routing subtest. The Full Scale IQ Battery normally takes between

45 and 75 minutes to administer, the Verbal and Nonverbal IQ scales each take approximately 30 minutes to administer, and the Abbreviated Battery takes between 15 and 20 minutes to administer.

Consistent with guidelines established by the American Psychological Association (APA, 2000), the SB5 examiner's manual describes user qualifications as assuming that all test users "have the college and/or graduate-level training in general measurement and statistical concepts essential for understanding test scores" (p. 8). Additionally, "All test users should have a thorough understanding of the standardized administration procedures for the SB5 and the scoring procedures for calculating accurate raw scores, subtest scaled scores, and all other scores on the SB5 Record Form." Finally, "Supervised administration should include a sufficient number of practice cases to establish reliable, standardized testing skills. Typically, supervised testing is completed as part of training workshops or graduate-level testing courses" (examiner's manual, p. 8).

In considering changes from earlier editions of the instrument, the SB5 examiner's manual indicates that beyond "a general modernization of artwork and item content", the SB5 has: (a) added a fifth factor to the scale (Visual-Spatial Processing); (b) increased the number of toys and colored manipulatives, primarily used by young children; (c) increased the nonverbal content of the instrument; (d) added new items that measure very low and very high functioning; (e) redesigned the record form and item books for easier administration and interpretation; and (f) expanded the norms to include the measurement of elderly examinees' abilities. Additionally, the two routing tests can be combined to calculate an abbreviated IQ (ABIQ), and the SB5 is linked to the Woodcock-Johnson III Tests of Achievement, an addition designed to enhance the identification of students with learning disabilities. The number of subtests contained on the SB5 has also been reduced from 15 (SB4) to 10. This reduction now guarantees that individuals of all ages will complete identical subtests reflecting an important improvement over the SB4; critics of the SB4 were troubled by the fact that depending on their ages and performance on the routing test, two different individuals might produce a Full Scale IQ that was derived from a different combination of the 15 subtests.

DEVELOPMENT. The author of the SB5 indicated that the development of the instrument was heavily influenced by the theoretical work of Carroll (1993). The SB5 was constructed on a five-factor hierarchical model of human intelligence. The hierarchy flows from overall, Full Scale IQ or *g*, to a second level consisting of two domains (Verbal and Nonverbal) and five factors (Fluid Reasoning [FR], Knowledge [KN], Quantitative Reasoning [QR], Visual-Spatial Processing [VS], Working Memory [WM]) to a third level consisting of 10 subtests, then a fourth level consisting of five to six testlets per subtest, and finally to the individual item level. Although the Cattell-Horn-Carroll (CHC) theory identifies 8 to 10 factors believed to comprise human intelligence, the author of the SB5 selected the five factors that required no specialized timing or test apparatus and that were thought to be most heavily related to school achievement. Additionally, it appears that the content of the memory factor now places greater emphasis on working memory than on the often-criticized emphasis on short-term memory found on the SB4. One theoretical inconsistency of the SB5, however, relates to the decision to include the verbal and nonverbal domains. As presented on page 25 of the examiner's manual "subtests are combined into either one of the two domains or one of the five factor indexes. At the most general level, either the two domains or the five factor indexes combine to form the Full Scale IQ (FSIQ)." It is not clear why an instrument so heavily influenced by CHC theory would include verbal and nonverbal domains as neither is contained as a CHC Stratum I (Narrow) or Stratum II (Broad) ability. Certainly a test that includes a verbal/nonverbal dichotomy offers clinical advantages for certain types of referral questions (e.g., motor-impairment, limited English proficiency); however, the decision to retain this terminology is theoretically inconsistent. As a result, it is not clear when users of the SB5 should attempt to make test interpretations based on the two verbal/nonverbal domains or instead on the five factor scores.

TECHNICAL.

Standardization and norms. Careful attention was given to the standardization of the SB5 and the norms will generalize to most segments of the United States population. The sample was matched to percentages of the stratification variables in the most recent United States Census

(2001). The norming sample consisted of a total of 4,800 individuals who were stratified into 30 age groups, by gender, and by race/ethnicity (White or Anglo American, Black or African American, Hispanic [Latino or Spanish], American Indian and Alaskan Native, Asian, and Native Hawaiian or Other Pacific Islander). Additionally, the category of Other included 2.7% of the standardization sample, consistent with the percentage included in the U.S. Census and typically described as individuals of mixed origins.

Two final SB5 stratification variables included geographic region (Northeast, Midwest, South, and West) and socioeconomic level, defined as educational attainment. For adults, educational attainment was defined as the number of years of completed education; for children under age 18, educational attainment was defined as the number of years of education completed by parents or guardians. Although not included as stratification variables, community size, type of school attended, and special education or clinical treatment were recorded and included in the SB5 technical manual. Additionally, 11% of the SB5 normative sample attended parochial or private schools and 6.8% received special services. Approximately 2% of the sample were identified as intellectually gifted students. Finally, the technical manual reports a series of studies in which 1,365 students receiving special education or clinical service were oversampled. Although the number of students included in each of these separate studies was relatively small, their resulting score profiles were typical for their special education classification (e.g., learning disabled, attention deficit disorder) providing a promising base for future research that examines the characteristics of exceptional populations. This future research will also extend the important, but preliminary, findings presented in the technical manual that were conducted on test items for possible gender, ethnic, religious, and socioeconomic test bias.

Like the SB4, when over- or underrepresentation of individuals occurred in particular normative categories, the imbalance was adjusted through a weighting procedure. Although this is a common practice for many current psychological tests, the practice can magnify sampling error. This approach introduces error that consists of systematic bias, in addition to naturally occurring random error; thus, the sample is less representative of the true target population. In this approach one individual's profile is given more weight to represent a larger proportion of minority profiles in the sample.

Reliability. The SB5 technical manual provides considerable evidence in support of the reliability of scores from the instrument. Internal consistency reliability coefficients ranged from .95 to .98 for IQ scores and from .90 to .92 for each of the five Factor Index scores. Spearman-Brown corrected, split-half reliabilities are also reported for each of the subtests, IQ, and Factor Index scores by age. Again, all reliability coefficients were quite high and appropriate for an instrument of this magnitude. As would be expected due to increased length, Full Scale IQ reliability exceeded Factor Index reliability, which in turn exceeded individual subtest reliability. Subtest reliabilities were also strong with an average of .84 to .89 reported for the 10 individual subtests.

Standard errors of measurement are also reported for IQs and Factor Indexes across age levels. The overall *SEM*s of the SB5 across age levels are a respectable 2.30 for Full Scale IQ, 3.26 for Nonverbal IQ, and 3.05 for Verbal IQ. The technical manual also does a nice job of describing the concept of *SEM* as well as appropriate suggestions for interpretation, including the use of confidence intervals.

Additionally, the technical manual reports that Rasch modeling techniques, a one-parameter logistic item response theory (IRT) model, were used to estimate item difficulty, examinee ability (based on the Rasch W metric), and test precision (information and standard errors at each ability level). Using the Rasch model, items from previous editions, all previous SB4 items, and newly created SB5 items were formed to create a calibrated item bank. Items were in turn formed into the five cognitive index scales. Roid reports in the 2003 interpretive manual (p. 20) that "Each scale showed excellent fit to the one-parameter Rasch model." However, the specific criteria for fit are not reported. Although the Rasch model certainly is theoretically preferred in its model simplicity and its resultant unit weighted items, the criterion that all items must be equally discriminating is quite stringent for ability tests. In reporting the test information curves of related change-sensitive scores (CSS), Roid writes "the SB5 CSS provide high levels of precision (high information) throughout the average age-equivalent range of the test

(CSS values of 430 to 520, ...). Also the shapes of the curves show the greatest precision in the advanced levels of performance ..., an excellent attribute for a test such as the SB5 that is widely used in gifted screening" (technical manual, p. 68). An examination of the CSS curves presented in the technical manual supports this conclusion but also reveals that corresponding *SEM*s are not equivalent across ability levels (CSS). The presentation of unequal precision across ability reflects a distinct advantage of IRT over classical standard errors of measurement. Although it appears that the SB5 does produce tighter *SEM*s and, thus, more precise ability estimates for gifted examinees, less precision is offered for examinees at the lower end of the ability continuum: children and adolescents with cognitive impairments. Such a finding is not atypical in ability measurement. However, given that the IRT findings indicate unequal *SEM*s across ability levels, future research might report actual SB5 *SEM*s across ability levels (rather than by age alone, see Figure 3.2 in technical manual), so that psychologists and educators who work with exceptional populations will have more accurate information for making diagnostic and placement decisions.

Differential Item Functioning (DIF) was detected using the Mantel-Haenszel approach. This approach is appropriate only if the Rasch model fits the data, further justifying the need for more specific reporting of fit statistics. That is, if items do not fit the Rasch model, it does not make sense to compare poorly estimated item difficulties, even using observed score data. Furthermore, more detail is needed regarding the DIF analysis, including whether purification was used, as per Holland and Thayer (1988), the criterion for DIF determination, and the sample sizes for each analysis.

Test-retest reliability is also reported in a series of studies across four age groups (*N*s = 96, 87, 81, and 92). The amount of time between test sessions ranged from 1 to 39 days with a median of 5, 8, 7, and 7 days, respectively. Reported test-retest coefficients (as well as coefficients corrected for range restriction) were good, with corrected test-retest coefficients ranging from .66 (Nonverbal Working Memory at ages 21 to 59) to .93 (Verbal Knowledge at ages 21 to 59). The test-retest studies reported for the SB5 are much improved over the SB4. Unfortunately, however, one critique of SB4 test-retest studies at the younger

ages of the instrument (Cronbach, 1989) continued to be ignored, "Far too little was invested in retest studies .... Retests with a change of examiners should be made on 100 cases at each early age and at spaced later ages" (p. 774). Although this is a stringent requirement for any test publisher, it is hoped that future independent research studies will address this issue. For the most part, SB5 coefficients reflect credible stability for the SB5 for intervals of time between testing sessions of up to approximately 1 month; future research should examine SB5 consistency across longer intervals of time and across ethnic groups and clinical populations, with a particular focus on the stability of the instrument for young children.

Finally, the SB5 technical manual indicates that numerous interrater reliability studies were performed during the initial tryout and standardization phases of the instrument. Items that demonstrated poor interrater agreement at that time were eliminated from the final published edition of the scale. The only study included in the technical manual, following the final publication, reported that a single pair of examiners each rescored selected subtests of 120 protocols. Specifically, each of two new examiners rescored polychotomous (scored 0, 1, or 2) items and compared their scoring with the results of the original standardization examiner. Interscorer agreement ranged from .95 to .98 across the Vocabulary routing test; Picture Absurdities correlations ranged from .90 to .97; Verbal Absurdities yielded correlations of .82 to .89; and Form Patterns test-retest correlations ranged from .87 to .94. Although these results reflect a promising beginning for the instrument, additional research should examine inter-rater agreement across all subtests.

Validity. In an initial attempt to examine the criterion validity of the SB5, the technical manual describes a study in which 104 individuals received the SB5 and the SB4 in counterbalanced order. The correlation between Full Scale scores was .90, representing good criterion-related evidence of validity. Consistent with the Flynn Effect (Flynn, 1985, 1987), the SB5 Mean Full Scale Score was lower than the SB4 Mean Composite Score (SB5 = 107.9, SB4 = 111.4). Similar results were found in a second study that compared the Full Scale Scores of the SB5 and the SB L-M (*r* = .85). Additional evidence of criterion-related validity was found in studies that compared the SB5 with the Wechsler Preschool and Primary Scale of Intelligence—Revised (WPPSI-R) (r = .83); the Wechsler Intelligence Scale for Children—Third Edition (WISC-III) (r = .84); the Wechsler Adult Intelligence Scale—Third Edition (WAIS-III) (r = .82); and the Woodcock-Johnson III Tests of Cognitive Abilities (r = .78).

Next, the SB5 technical manual presents a series of studies that compare the instrument with tests of academic achievement. Two studies are presented that compare the SB5 with the Woodcock-Johnson III Tests of Achievement and the Wechsler Individual Achievement Test-II. The resulting pattern of correlations is quite varied with coefficients ranging from .33 to .84. Depending upon the pragmatic orientation of the user, these correlations will either support or not support the utilization of the instrument. If, for example, the SB5 (and most other commercially available IQ tests) is perceived as a predictor of school success, then the SB5-Achievement correlations will be seen quite favorably. The SB5 is clearly highly correlated with tests of academic achievement and users of the SB5 will be able to make accurate predictions about the academic performance of students who complete the test. In contrast, users of the SB5 who are instead looking for a measure of "pure" intelligence will interpret many of the correlations with achievement as "too high" (e.g., SB5—WJ III Reading Comprehension, r = .84; SB5—WJ III Math Reasoning, r = .80; SB5—WIAT-II Math, r = .79) and will argue that the SB5 is too heavily achievement-loaded. With correlations in the .80 range, approximately two-thirds of the information contained on the SB5 and tests of academic achievement reflects shared variance or overlapping content, a figure that may be too high for instruments thought to be measuring related yet discrete constructs.

Finally, a series of studies is described in support of the construct validity of the SB5. Although the SB4 was based on a four-factor model, the SB5 was constructed on a five-factor hierarchical model. All SB5 subtests, across all ages, demonstrated average principal component loadings of greater than .70 on the g, or general factor, indicating that each subtest was a good measure of g. The proportion of SB5 variance accounted for by the g factor ranged from 56% to 61%, depending on the factoring method. These percentages are slightly higher than found on the SB4 but are comparable for other current IQ tests.

Confirmatory (CFA) analyses were also performed in an attempt to provide further support for the construct validity of the SB5. The technical manual indicates that a CFA, conducted on five age groups from the SB5 normative sample, examined one- through five-factor models and indicated that the five-factor model yielded the best fit when compared to other models in the analysis. In examining these results it is important to note that in order for the CFA analysis to be performed, the test author were forced to split each subtest in half so that 20 variables could be analyzed. Without this adaptation, the test author did not have an identified model. Additionally, the CFA fit statistics presented in the technical manual are not as good as would be desired according to some measurement standards (Hu & Bentler, 1998, 1999). Finally, it is unclear why a hierarchical model was explicitly hypothesized yet a hierarchical model CFA was not performed.

To their credit, the developers of the SB5 attempted to provide an empirically supported method for interpretive analyses. The presentation of the two-stage clustering technique contained in the interpretive manual provides users with 10 core profiles identified in the SB5 standardization sample. These patterns of subtest profiles allow users a normative comparison from which interpretive hypotheses can be generated, in contrast to a purely speculative "armchair" approach that looks at an individual's pattern of subtest strengths and weaknesses in isolation. Additional information about the cluster analysis, however, would assist users in the development of more accurate interpretations. Specifically, additional justification could be provided as to why a two-stage rather than a three-stage analysis was performed (McDermott, 1998). Additionally, it is not clear (a) why an average linkage method was utilized instead of Ward's technique; (b) why only one stopping rule (profiles identifying less than 5% of the population were dropped) rather than multiple stopping rules was employed; (c) how many cases were relocated in the second stage of the analysis; and (d) what standard deviation values correspond to the 10 identified core profiles. Future research should address these questions as well as examine the stability and utility of these profiles in both regular and exceptional populations.

SUMMARY. The publication of the newest revision of this well-established test of intelligence continues an almost 100-year-old tradition of evolution and refinement. Despite some technical and statistical limitations (e.g., lower stability for young children and individuals with low cognitive abilities, problematically high correlations with achievement, uncertain factor structure) the SB5 offers important improvements over the previous version of the scale and remains one of the premier instruments for the assessment of cognitive abilities of children, adolescents, and adults.

REVIEWER'S REFERENCES

American Psychological Association. (2000). *Report of the task force on test user qualifications.* Washington, DC: Author.

Carroll, J. B. (1993). *Human cognitive abilities: A survey of factor analytic studies.* New York: Cambridge University Press.

Cronbach, L. J. (1989). [Review of the Stanford-Binet Intelligence Scale, Fourth Edition.] In J. C Conoley & J. J. Kramer (Eds.), *The tenth mental measurements yearbook* (pp. 773–775). Lincoln, NE: Buros Institute of Mental Measurements.

Flynn, J. R. (1985). Wechsler intelligence tests: Do we really have a criterion of mental retardation? *American Journal of Mental Deficiency, 90,* 236–244.

Flynn, J. R. (1987). Massive gains in 14 nations: What IQ tests really measure. *Psychological Bulletin, 101,* 171–191.

Holland, P. W., & Thayer, D. T. (1988). Differential item performance and the Mantel-Haenszel procedure. In H. Wainer & H. I. Braun (Eds.), *Test validity* (pp. 129–145). Hillsdale, NJ: Erlbaum.

Hu, L.-T., & Bentler, P. M. (1998). Fit indices in covariance structure modeling: Sensitivity to underparameterized model misspecification. *Psychological Methods, 3,* 424–453.

Hu, L., & Bentler, P. M. (1999). Cutoff criteria for fit indexes in covariance structure analysis: Conventional criteria versus new alternatives. *Structural Equation Modeling, 6,* 1–55.

McDermott, P. A. (1998). MEG: Megacluster analytic strategy for multistage hierarchical grouping with relocations and replications. *Educational and Psychological Measurement, 58,* 677–687.

U. S. Census Bureau. (2001). *Census 2000 Summary File 1 United States.* Washington, DC: Author.

[234]

STAR Math®, Version 2.0.

Purpose: Designed as a computer-adaptive math placement test with database.

Population: Grades 1–12.

Publication Dates: 1998–2002.

Scores: Total score only.

Administration: Individual.

Price Data, 2003: $499 per single-computer license kit (40 students) including installation guide (2002, 32 pages), quick reference card, and software manual (2002, 62 pages); $1,499 per school license kit (up to 200 students) including installation guide, quick reference card, and software manual.

Time: (15) minutes.

Comments: Available for Macintosh computers and computers running Windows.

Author: Renaissance Learning, Inc.

Publisher: Renaissance Learning, Inc.

Cross References: For reviews by Joseph C. Ciechalski and Cindy M. Walker of an earlier version, see 15:241.

Review of STAR Math, Version 2.0 by MARY L. GARNER, Associate Professor of Mathematics, Kennesaw State University, Kennesaw, GA:

DESCRIPTION. STAR Math, Version 2.0, is a computerized adaptive achievement test in mathematics for students in Grades 1 through 12. Each test consists of a different set of 24 multiple-choice items, 8 from numeration concepts (e.g., place value, fractions, decimals, powers, roots), 8 from computation processes, and 8 from six possible strands depending on the student's grade level-word problems, estimation, data analysis and statistics, geometry, measurement, and algebra. Items are selected from a bank of 1,974 items. The student is initially given an item that is easy for his or her grade level; the algorithm for choosing that item varies according to the student's grade level. Items are then chosen that the student could answer correctly 75% of the time. There is a 3-minute time limit on any single item, and the test requires less than 15 minutes to complete

The test can be used to determine a student's mathematics achievement level relative to national norms, and it can be used to track growth in achievement across school years. Scaled scores, percentile ranks, grade equivalent scores, and normal curve equivalent scores are provided. A variety of useful reports can be generated describing the performance of individual students or groups of students. Most notable is a diagnostic report in which scores for a specific testing session and a specific student are clearly reported and explained, and diagnostic information is provided. In addition, a growth report for individual students or groups of students can be generated.

The 60-page software manual, 32-page installation manual, and 130-page technical manual are all very well-written, clear, and easy to follow. The software includes a management program for teachers to set up access for students and a separate student program. Students must successfully answer two out of three practice questions before taking the actual test. The software keeps track of what items are administered to a student so that a student cannot be given the same item within a 6-month period. It is recommended that students be tested no more than three times a year. Students are not allowed to use calculators.

DEVELOPMENT. STAR Math, Version 2.0, was developed by Renaissance Learning, Inc., and published in 2002. Version 1.0 was originally published in 1998. Notable differences between the two versions include a larger item bank (1,974 vs. 1,434), a greater number of objectives covered (214 vs. 176), and an algorithm that selects items that the students could answer correctly 75% of the time rather than 50% of the time.

The items were designed to parallel curriculum objectives most commonly found in curriculum guides, textbooks, recommendations of the National Council of Teachers of Mathematics, and objectives of the tests designed for the National Assessment of Educational Progress (NAEP) and the Third International Mathematics and Science Study (TIMSS). The technical manual includes a list of all objectives and a table indicating exactly how many items are selected from each content strand according to the student's grade level. Distractors for items were chosen to be representative of most common errors. In addition, rules for item writing included instructions for keeping the reading level as low as possible and avoiding cultural loading, gender bias, and ethnic stereotyping.

In 2001, 2,471 items that included items from Version 1.0 and new items were pilot-tested on a national sample of 44,939 children from Grades 1 through 12. The sample was stratified according to geographic region, school size, and socioeconomic status; it included 261 schools from 45 states. There were seven levels of fixed test forms with fixed sets of items used for horizontal and vertical anchoring. Each form included 36 to 46 items and required 30 to 40 minutes to complete. Both traditional analyses and analysis with the Rasch measurement model were used to determine the appropriateness of the items. Of the 2,471 items, approximately 2,000 were determined to be acceptable.

TECHNICAL. The test was normed in 2002 on a U.S. random sample stratified according to geographic region, per-grade district enrollment, and socioeconomic status. The final sample included 29,185 students from 312 schools and 48 states. All schools that participated in the study are listed in the technical manual, along with characteristics of the schools. Each student took a computer-adaptive version of the test, not a fixed form as in the pilot-testing conducted in 2001. All schools began testing in February and were finished testing in mid-April. Subsets of the sample were used for reliability and validity studies described below.

Evidence for the reliability of the test took three forms. "Generic" reliability coefficients ranged from .79 to .88. Split-half reliability coefficients were calculated for all students used for norming, and these ranged from .78 to .88. Alternate form reliability coefficients were calculated for 7,517 of the students used for norming, and these values ranged from .72 to .80. Standard errors of measurement for scaled scores (1 to 1,400) ranged from 37 to 42.

Content validity of the test was supported by procedures used for test design and pilot-testing of items. Construct validity was supported with two kinds of evidence: correlation with other standardized tests and correlation with teacher ratings. During the norming process, scores on approximately 30 achievement tests were correlated with STAR Math scores for more than 17,000 students. The correlations for each test ranged from .58 to .70, providing strong evidence for the validity of the test. Complete tables of correlations are provided in the technical manual. In addition, teacher ratings were collected on 17,326 students, using teacher-rating forms developed by Renaissance Learning, Inc. Correlations between scaled scores on STAR Math and teacher ratings for each grade level ranged from .38 to .58, with an overall correlation of .85.

COMMENTARY. The strength of STAR Math is in its technical development and validation, its ease of use, and the information that it provides. The pilot-testing and norming procedures appear to be well-conceived and executed, and the evidence for the reliability and validity of the test is impressive. The technical manual for the test is clear and well-written. A final chapter with answers to frequently asked questions is most informative. The software is easy to use. The test provides a quick, easy way for the classroom teacher and school principal to track students' growth in mathematics as compared to the national population.

On the other hand, the test does not allow use of calculators, as do many standardized tests, particularly at the higher grade levels. Because two-thirds of the test includes items from numeration and computation strands, and the time limit is 3 minutes per item, the emphasis is on basic skills, quick answers, not higher order thinking or open-ended problem solving. Advanced high school students would not be very well-served by the test. The test should therefore not be used exclusively to judge mathematical prowess.

SUMMARY. This is a technically sound, very convenient way to assess students in Grades 1 through 12 on basic mathematical skills, compare their performance with the national population, and track their growth in these basic skills. It should not be used exclusively, however, to assess a student's mathematical achievement.

Review of the STAR Math, Version 2.0 by G. MICHAEL POTEAT, Director of Institutional Effectiveness, East Carolina University, Greenville, NC:
DESCRIPTION AND DEVELOPMENT. The STAR Math 2.0 is described by the publisher as a computer-adaptive, norm-referenced, mathematics test and database. The authors assert that with the STAR Math 2.0, one can assess the math performance of students in Grades 1-12 in only about 15 minutes. The STAR Math is contained on a single CD ROM and once installed the test requires no examiner intervention except for entering student data and providing administrative oversight. The STAR Math 2.0 provides scaled scores (SS) that range from 1 to 1400, a grade equivalent (GE) with a range of 0.0 to 12.9, a percentile rank (PR) of 1 to 99, and a normal curve equivalent (NCE) with a mean of 50 and standard deviation of 21.06 (in the normative sample).

The technical information for the STAR Math 2.0 is contained in a PDF file under a folder labeled "extras" on the CD ROM. The first edition of the STAR Math was reviewed by Ciechalski (2003) and Walker (2003) and I strongly recommend that potential purchasers look at those reviews and especially at Walker's comments. Improvements to the STAR Math 2.0 are listed in the technical manual (pages 4-5) and include:

1. The item bank was increased from 1,434 to 1,974 items.

2. The number of objectives covered by the item bank was increased from 176 to 214.

3. The number of items administered that measure a single objective has been limited.

4. Content balancing specifications were implemented.

5. The distribution of items from the STAR Math 2.0 strands has been changed with one-third of the items in each test coming from each of the three broad areas.

6. The difficulty of the level of test has been lowered.

7. New norms have been developed.

8. The diagnostic report has undergone major changes.

The STAR Math 2.0 has eight strands (or content areas): Numeration Concepts, Computation Processes, Estimation, Geometry, Measurement, Data Analysis and Statistics, Word Problems, and Algebra. Numeration Concepts and Computational Process constitute two-thirds of the items presented and the other one-third come from the other five strands that are labeled Other Applications. So five of the eight strands constitute one-third of the test and Numeration Concepts and Computational Processes make up the other two-thirds.

TECHNICAL. The norms for the STAR Math 2.0 were based on a sample of 29,185 students from 312 schools. The characteristics of the normative sample are reasonably close to the national population. Estimates of split-half reliability range from .78 to .88 by grade. The alternate-forms reliability estimates ranged from .72 to .80 by grade. Aggregate (across grade level) reliabilities for both split-half and alternative forms are reported to exceed .90. The validity evidence for the STAR Math 2.0 is based on a number of correlations between the STAR Math 2.0 and other tests of math achievement. The correlations ranged from .58 to .70 with a median of .64. Also, for 17,326 students in the normative sample, teachers completed a math skills rating scale. These ratings were compared to the scaled score from the STAR Math 2.0. The overall correlation was .85. Overall, the STAR Math 2.0 has good normative data, acceptable reliability, and moderate evidence of validity.

COMMENTARY. Even if the STAR Math 2.0 had excellent psychometric characteristics, it would be a difficult instrument to recommend. First, the computer interface for managing the STAR Math 2.0 is somewhat awkward and there does not appear to be any method that allows the teacher or administrator to easily import a classroom roster. Instructions are given for importing ASCII files but not for spreadsheets or other common computer data sets. Consequently, the instructor or test administrator has to enter data on students manually using an interface reminiscent of an old DOS-based program given a graphical face-lift.

Worse, although the STAR Math 2.0 is easy to administer to anyone who can sit in front of a computer terminal and punch the A, B, C, and D keys, it does not provide more than a superficial evaluation of student skills. In an attempt to evaluate the STAR Math 2.0, I completed the STAR Math 2.0 after logging on as a fictional student of different ages and grade levels and varying my performance to see how well the STAR Math 2.0 adapted to performance and to examine the usefulness of the information produced. The STAR Math 2.0 does adapt the level of difficulty to the student's performance and most students would probably take less than 15 minutes to complete the assessment.

Unfortunately, the information provided by the STAR Math 2.0 is of only limited value. For a student in the second grade who performed poorly, the computer-generated report provided a GE of .8, a PR of 1, and SS of 287. The report recommended that the student: (a) Learn to rapidly recognize the numeral and number words for 1-10; (b) Practice counting groups of objects to 10; and (c) Learn the addition and subtraction facts for sums to 10. The hypothetical student was also described as performing near the bottom of the range for the STAR Math 2.0.

For a fifth grade student who performed well, the computer-generated report provided an SS of 906, GE of 12.9+, and a PR of 99. The report stated that the hypothetical student had likely mastered all of the concepts and skills in K–8 basic math and suggested that algebra be introduced. It is interesting to note that the STAR Math 2.0 did not test the student on beginning algebra concepts (presumably because the hypothetical student was only in the fifth grade).

Finally, for a hypothetical 11th grade student who was very advanced, the computer-generated report provided an SS of 1093, a GE of 12.9+, and a PR of 98. Given the difference in the ages and grade levels of the hypothetical students, the SS and PR seem reasonable but the identical grade equivalents of 12.9+ are difficult to interpret. None of the items on the Key Math required any math skills that would challenge the typical high school student who had completed Algebra 1. The most difficult problems involved solving the Pythagorean Theorem, finding the roots of a second-degree polynomial, and graphing the area of an ellipse.

SUMMARY. STAR Math 2.0 is not recommended. The publisher provides considerable technical details and the standard score and other normative information are probably relatively accurate. However, the instrument provides limited diagnostic information, which is not the STAR Math's claimed purpose, even though it produces a "diagnostic" report. It is easy to administer and students should be able to complete the computer protocol with minimal instruction. Evidently, the STAR Math 2.0 is part of a larger package that includes instructional materials. Perhaps the combination of the test and instructional materials would be helpful for a school system with personnel with very limited backgrounds in math education. It could provide a rough index of math performance for students in Grades 1 through early high school. To assess the performance of college-bound high school students there are better instruments available free on the internet (e.g., tcc.math.berkeley.edu/).

Because assessment and curriculum are aligned in many states, use of curriculum-based assessments to identify students' deficits in mathematics is recommended, not a general norm-referenced test. As Walker (2003) summarized, "Overall, this test is not very well aligned with current research in mathematics or NCTM (National Council of Teachers of Mathematics) standards" (p. 868). There is a vast amount of material on evaluating mathematics performance and effective teaching available for little or no cost. A good place to begin is at the University of Tennessee Math Archives (archives.math.utk.edu/).

REVIEWER'S REFERENCES

Ciechalski, J. C. (2003). [Review of the STAR Math.] In B. S. Plake, J. C. Impara, & R. A. Spies (Eds.), *The fifteenth mental measurements yearbook* (pp. 864-866). Lincoln, NE: Buros Institute of Mental Measurements.
Walker, C. M. (2003). [Review of the STAR Math.] In B. S. Plake, J. C. Impara, & R. A. Spies (Eds.), *The fifteenth mental measurements yearbook* (pp. 866-868). Lincoln, NE: Buros Institute of Mental Measurements.

[235]

Stirling Eating Disorder Scales.

Purpose: Developed as a comprehensive measure of anorexia and bulimia.

Population: Adolescents and adults.

Publication Dates: 1995–1996.

Acronym: SEDS.

Scores: 8 scales: Anorexic Dietary Cognitions, Anorexic Dietary Behavior, Bulimic Dietary Cognitions, Bulimic Dietary Behavior, Perceived External Control, Low Assertiveness, Low Self-Esteem, Self-Directed Hostility.

Administration: Individual.

Price Data, 2002: $94.46 per complete kit including scales, profile forms, and manual (1995, 33 pages).

Time: (30) minutes.
Authors: Gwenllian-Jane Williams and Kevin G. Power.
Publisher: Harcourt Assessment [England].

Review of the Stirling Eating Disorder Scales by JEFFREY A. ATLAS, Clinical Psychologist, St. Christopher-Ottilie Services for Children and Families, Queens, NY:

DESCRIPTION. The Stirling Eating Disorder Scales (SEDS), although developed as a comprehensive measure of anorexia and bulimia, should not be confused with a diagnostic instrument or test. The authors specify that "the SEDS questionnaire cannot replace a clinical diagnostic interview" (manual, p. 28). Instead, the purpose of the SEDS is to screen suspected patients, by comparing summary scores to those obtained in a standardization group of anorexic and bulimic patients in Scotland. Due to the restricted geographic range of subjects (although there is no reason to believe they differ substantially from groups in other industrialized regions), and the small number of subjects in the criterial groups, the SEDS is best seen as a (promising) work-in-progress.

The 80-item, two-page questionnaire is carbonized, to leave an examiner score key and summary columns underneath. A separate "Test Profile" sheet duplicates the summary columns, with indications of tentative cutoff scores suggesting clinical significance. The items presume a 9-year-old's reading level. The examinee is required to endorse "True" or "False" for each item, which makes for ease of administration and scoring but yields some likely contaminating factors in assessment. Faced with a nonnuanced, forced response (all True/False) format, some examinees might abandon a reflective response set and haphazardly answer such items as "I have a positive attitude about myself" or "I feel my family have [sic] control over me." Other items presume the cognitions and behaviors being screened (e.g., "When I binge I feel disgusted with myself"). Finally, in view of the common proclivities toward hiding problem eating behaviors, one wonders how accurate this scale may be on a case-by-case basis. Given the transparency of many of the items, a general practitioner or mental health worker might disperse with the 30-minute assessment and directly ask about, and probe conditions surrounding, binging and/or purging. The scale itself contains no alerts for participants "faking bad" or "faking good."

DEVELOPMENT. The authors submit as an enticing postulate, that is not elaborated, that more systematized study into eating disorders has suggested cognitive/emotional characteristics underlying an "eating disorder personality." Ultimately presented are four component scales of anorexic and bulimic cognitions and behaviors, together with four scales related to disordered self-validation that do seem to relate to depressive personality disorder.

The pool of items for each intended scale was presented to a panel of clinical experts to assess the weighting of each item and its unambiguity. From this set 10 items, with severity weighting ranging from 1 to 7, items were selected for each scale, based upon a second expert panel's agreement of over 60% on proper item conceptualization relative to the eight scales.

STANDARDIZATION. The standardization sample consisted of recruited participants falling into three groups: anorexia nervosa ($n = 40$) or bulimia nervosa ($n = 38$) hospital patients diagnosed in accordance with the DSM-III R, and normal control ($n = 76$) individuals who were Stirling University staff and students or the general public.

Comparison of the three groups on demographic characteristics of age, height, weight, marital status, and socioeconomic status did not reveal any significant differences, except for the expectant lower weight of the anorexic individuals. The mean age of mid-20s and typical marital status of "single" is broadly consistent with the presence of eating disorders in industrialized populations. Responses were not affected by gender of the respondents.

RELIABILITY. Internal reliability estimates were calculated to examine the homogeneity of the eight scales: Anorexic Dietary Cognitions, Anorexic Dietary Behavior, Bulimic Dietary Cognitions, Bulimic Dietary Behavior, Perceived External Control, Low Assertiveness, Low Self-Esteem, and Self-Directed Hostility. Cronbach alpha coefficients and split-half correlations within the three groups were all significant at the .001 level. Test-retest correlation across scales after 3 weeks was also reported to yield rs significant at the .001 level. Overall, the data presented are suggestive of adequate score consistency.

VALIDITY. Construct validity was assessed by comparing the anorexic, bulimic, and control groups across all eight scales utilizing one-way

ANOVA, followed by Scheffe contrasts. The three groups differed significantly at the .01 level in the four cognitive-behavioral eating disorder categories in the expected directions. This finding suggests the scale's discriminative potential in differentiating anorexic and bulimic individuals, and these from normal controls in the realm of eating disorders. The associated scales of Perceived External Control, Low Assertiveness, Low Self-Esteem, and Self-Directed Hostility differentiated the normal group from each eating-disordered group, but did not distinguish anorexics from bulimics. One might view such data as suggestive in a view of eating disorders as related to, or superimposed upon, depressive personality.

Concurrent validity was assessed via a correlation matrix of each SEDS scale with measures of anorexia, bulimia, assertiveness, self-esteem, and shame and guilt. The higher order and highly significant correlations of each scale with its associated measure supported validity of the separate scales as aspects of eating disorder.

Some associated research reported in the manual bears upon issues of construct validity. The completed SEDS of 36 anorexic and 36 bulimic patients in treatment tended to show the expected changes in each scale at 3 and 6 months, demonstrating the use of the scale in treatment monitoring. Another study featured comparisons between recruited groups of eating disorder, depressed, panic disorder patients, and normal controls on the SEDS and on measures of anxiety and of depression, the latter represented by the Beck (1967) Depression Inventory. The four scales of eating pathology discriminated all groups, as did the four cognitive/emotional scales for eating disorder, anxiety disorder patients, and normal controls. On these latter scales the eating disorder and depressed group were not significantly different, except in Self-Directed Hostility, a scale on which the eating disorder patients scored higher. The authors argue, correctly, I believe, for the clinical importance of including in the SEDS core characteristics shared by both eating disorder and depressed patients. If one returns to the conception of eating disorders as often related to or built upon types of personality disorder, especially depressive, inclusion of such cognitive/emotional components would be important aspects to consider in assessment and treatment.

COMMENTARY. The authors of the SEDS offer it as a screening device for potential patients, and provide preliminary cutoff scores for the eight scales. The cutoffs seem weakened by a number of factors. There is no preliminary cutoff for the aggregate SED score, even though this score is cited in the manual in one of the comparisons of treatment effect. The SEDS Profile Form has little utility, as the cutoffs are not proportionately scalar (i.e., they do not use a metric such as T-scores to allow for cross-scale comparison). The cutoffs also appear quite low. For example, one of two SEDS items the present reviewer endorsed, "I cut my food into very small pieces in order to eat more slowly" merited a scale score of 4.3. If I had also endorsed "I keep to a very strict diet regime" (as referring to vegetarianism) and earned an additional 5.2, my score on Anorexic Dietary Behavior would have reached the eating disorder range, as it surpasses the cutoff of 9 for this scale. The low floor of at least this cutoff does not inspire confidence in the prevention of false-positives.

SUMMARY. The Stirling Disorder Scales is a brief, self-administered and hand-scorable measure of eating-related cognitions and behaviors as well as a set of indices of self-concept that can aid in screening for eating disorders. In its present preliminary format, there are too few standardization data and there are inconsistencies in psychometrics that make the instrument problematic for diagnostic purposes. It could play a useful role in monitoring relative change during treatment and in further research in the field of eating disorders.

REVIEWER'S REFERENCE
Beck, A. T. (1967). *Depression.* New York: Harper & Row.

Review of the Stirling Eating Disorder Scales by RONALD A. BERK, Professor of Biostatistics and Measurement, School of Nursing, The Johns Hopkins University, Baltimore, MD:

DESCRIPTION. The Stirling Eating Disorder Scales (SEDS) consist of eight scales, 10 items each, which are administered as a paper-and-pencil self-report questionnaire to patients with eating disorders. All 80 statements are answered as "True" (applies to you usually or all the time) or "False" (rarely or never applies to you). Scores are produced for the eight scales: Low Assertiveness, Low Self-Esteem, Self-Directed Hostility, Perceived External Control, Anorexic Dietary Cognitions, Anorexic Dietary Behavior, Bulimic Dietary Cognitions, and Bulimic Dietary Behavior.

The SEDS is designed to be administered and used by clinicians and medical personnel to screen, profile, and monitor movements in severity during treatment of eating disorder patients. Clinical researchers can also use SEDS as a multiscale assessment tool for studies of eating disorders. According to the manual of the SEDS, the total questionnaire takes only 15 minutes to complete for all except the most severely disordered patients. The answer forms are self-scorable, but should always be conducted by the clinician or researcher. The scores are hand calculated using a matrix of item weights for the eight scales previously determined by a panel of clinical experts. The final scores can then be referenced to established cutoff scores for anorexic and bulimic patients. Patients scoring at or above any of the cutoffs are assumed to be in the range of eating disorder severity. Although such performance does not indicate a firm diagnosis, it can screen suspected patients. The SEDS is not intended to replace a clinical diagnostic interview.

DEVELOPMENT. The SEDS was developed more than a decade ago (copyright, 1992) and subsequently published in 1995 by The Psychological Corporation in Great Britain. The sparsity and quality of eating disorder instruments available at that time stimulated the development of the SEDS. Although theoretical, empirical, and anecdotal evidence is mentioned, no references are cited or a concrete framework presented to substantiate the eating disorder psychopathology used to build the SEDS. The manual states only that the "review of the literature and discussion with clinicians" (p. 16) led to the criteria for structuring the instrument: (a) independent scaling of four core personality characteristics (assertiveness, self-esteem, perceived control, and self-directed hostility), (b) coverage of dietary behaviors, (c) coverage of dietary cognitions that require different therapeutic approaches, and (d) comprehensive assessment of eating disorder symptoms for both anorexia and bulimia.

A modified Thurstone method of scaling was chosen to construct the SEDS. Three steps were described. First, a large pool of items was created. Each item was then rated by a panel of clinical experts on a scale of 1–7 for severity and ambiguity. These ratings produced a severity weight and degree of ambiguity for each item. Ten items were selected for each scale to ensure a variance of weights and low ambiguity. Second, "concept validity" was measured by having another panel of experts sort the 80 items into the appropriate SED scales. Only those items with a 60% or higher

panel match were retained; the remainder were dropped and replaced. Finally, a "true-false" response format was chosen for ease of completion by the respondents.

The foregoing procedures constituted the only information provided in the manual. No details were given on (a) the size of the initial item pool, (b) the number and qualifications of the clinical experts used for both panels, (c) the 7-point rating scale (with or without anchors) for severity and ambiguity, (d) descriptive statistics on the item ratings, (e) the number of items that met the 60% criterion and the process for replacing and retesting new items, and (f) the meaning of the frequency response scale compressed into a true-false format. Despite this frequency scale, seven items also contained frequency terms, such as "often," "all of the time," "never," and "rarely." It is not clear how patients would answer those items. The only item analyses conducted were calculation of the Spache-Dale readability formula and positive and negative statement intercorrelations within each scale. The correlations ranged from .64 to .87, from which the authors concluded there was no response bias. No item-subscale, item-total scale, or interitem correlations were computed.

TECHNICAL. Standardization of the SEDS was based on a norm sample of 154 persons—78 patients (anorexia nervosa, $n = 40$, and bulimia nervosa, $n = 38$) recruited from hospitals throughout Scotland who were diagnosed with eating disorders according to DSM-III-R criteria by psychiatrists and psychologists, and 76 normal people who were staff and students from Stirling University and members of the general public with no history of eating disorders. No systematic sampling design, inclusion and exclusion selection criteria, population sizes, and participation and nonparticipation rates were presented. The demographic profile of the three groups included only age, height, weight, marital status, and socioeconomic class. There was no evidence that other variables such as gender, ethnicity, or education were taken into account. The norms for the three very small samples were expressed as means and standard deviations. No standard scores were given.

Reliability was estimated for all eight scales using coefficient alpha, split-half correlations, and test-retest (3-week interval). Alphas ranged from .83 to .92, split-halves ranged from .73 to .99, and retest coefficients ranged from .85 to .97. The scale with the lowest coefficients was Perceived External Control. There was no explanation of this finding or of any of the other coefficients. No standard errors were computed. Unfortunately, the manual does not report whether the reliability estimates were based on the total norm sample or any of the subsamples, although it does say that the correlations within the three groups "remained high and significant" (pp. 15, 19). The magnitude of the coefficients is adequate for all scales except Perceived External Control, Low Assertiveness, and Self-Directed Hostility, which are borderline and warrant caution when interpreting patient profiles.

Procedures related to content validity were described previously. There were no detailed content specifications or behaviors from which the items on the scales were generated. Only core personality characteristics and areas of behavior and symptoms were identified from the literature. There was also no indication of how the pool of items was written. The "concept validity" analysis was the closest approximation to content validity. However, the representativeness of each scale sample of items in relation to the domain of items that could have been written for each scale topic was not addressed.

One primary use of the SEDS scores is to screen patients suspected of having anorexic and bulimic eating disorders. Evidence of discriminant validity was inadequate. The major analysis pertinent to this use was a one-way analysis of variance among the three groups identified previously. Statistically significant differences were found between both eating disorders groups and the normal group on all eight scales and between the anorexic and bulimic groups on the four disorder-specific scales in the expected direction. No effect sizes were computed to assess the clinical significance of those differences, although most appeared to be quite large. In addition to these analyses, cutscores were established for the eight SEDS for anorexic and bulimic groups to facilitate ease of screening. Unfortunately, no method was described for how these cutoffs were set, nor were any classification accuracy estimates reported, particularly false positives and false negatives. Such evidence is essential to evaluate the clinical utility of the SEDS.

Concurrent validity evidence was obtained by correlating the eight SEDS with several comparison measures. Validity coefficients ranged from .83 to .90 for seven of the scales; the Perceived External Control scale correlated .37 to .76 with related health locus of control scales. No scale correlated more highly with any other comparison measure than with its direct comparison, although none of these correlations were reported. There was no interpretation of any of these coefficients.

Other validity evidence was presented related to treatment sensitivity. Because the SEDS is also intended to monitor changes in patients' profiles as the patients progress through treatment, a 6-month study was conducted with 36 anorexic and 36 bulimic patients to assess changes in their attitudes and behaviors. Repeated measures analysis of variance results indicated differences over the first 3-month period for all scales, but only differences for five of the scales over the second 3-month period. The authors concluded that the scores on the SEDS can be used to monitor patient changes.

Gender bias was examined by computing t tests between the males and females in the normal group for the eight scales. No significant differences were found. Other validity studies were mentioned, but no citations or specific evidence were provided. Conspicuously omitted was any construct validity evidence in the form of a factor analysis of the 80 items or intercorrelations among the eight scales to furnish an empirical confirmation for the a priori judgmental eight-scale structure.

COMMENTARY. The SEDS and the research upon which it is based are dated. The SEDS was designed to fill the need for a clinically useful instrument to measure eating disorders. However, from the beginning of the effort, the mission was doomed without any explicit definition of the construct derived from a theoretical and empirical research foundation. Starting with a list of eight topics, the authors developed a pool of items. No procedures were described to specify how the items were written. The underlying frequency scale, compressed into a true-false format, confounded the scale structure and interpretation of ratings. Why not simply use four to six frequency anchors as the response options? Details about the expert panel and its reviews were not presented. The evidence of content validity that was given was inadequate.

All of the technical reliability and validity studies that followed were based on unrepresentative field-test size "norm" samples of less than 50 patients per eating disorder group. Reliability coefficients for these samples were not reported. Discriminant validity evidence related to the screening purpose of the scale scores failed to address the classification accuracy of patients based on the recommended cutoff scores. Concurrent validity coefficients of the SEDS with comparison measures were relatively high for seven of the eight scales. The treatment sensitivity study provided preliminary evidence for very small samples.

SUMMARY. The authors of the SEDS manual state, "Any new instrument must be methodologically and statistically adequate if clinicians are to have confidence in the profiles produced" (p. 7). As this review has repeatedly indicated, the SEDS falls far short of this psychometric goal. Despite the numerous studies that were conducted, the faulty foundation of a deficient construct definition and content specifications, several flawed items with ambiguous and inappropriate response anchors, unsystematically selected and inadequate norm samples, and incomplete psychometric evidence to support the intended uses of the scores render the SEDS as unworthy of recommendation as a tool to screen patients for eating disorders. A structured clinical diagnostic interview may furnish more reliable and accurate information to screen anorexic and bulimic patients than the SEDS.

[236]
Structured Photographic Articulation Test II Featuring Dudsberry.

Purpose: Designed to assess children's articulation and phonological skills.
Population: Ages 3-0 through 9-11 years.
Publication Dates: 1989–2001.
Acronym: SPAT-D II.
Scores: Total score only.
Administration: Individual.
Price Data: Available from publisher.
Time: Administration time not reported.
Comments: Forty photographs are used to assess 59 singleton consonants and 10 consonant blends; revision of the Structured Photographic Articulation Test Featuring Dudsberry (SPAT-D).
Authors: Janet I. Dawson and Patricia J. Tattersall.
Publisher: Janelle Publications, Inc.
Cross References: For reviews by Clinton W. Bennett and Susan Felsenfeld of the earlier edition, see 12:376.

Review of the Structured Photographic Articulation Test II Featuring Dudsberry by MILDRED MURRAY-WARD, Professor, Department of Advanced Studies, California Lutheran University, Thousand Oaks, CA:

DESCRIPTION. The Structured Photographic Articulation Test II Featuring Dudsberry (SPAT-D II) is a revision of the version published in 1989. The purpose of the test is to identify and analyze articulation errors and identify patterns of articulation to aid in determining therapy types and focus for children ages 3-0 through 9-11 years.

The SPAT-D II continues to use the format from the SPAT-D involving photographs of Dudsberry, a young golden retriever who engages in a number of activities designed to stimulate children to emit the targeted phonemes. The photographs are in a spiral-bound booklet. The manual is generally easy to read and the assessment process is straightforward. The child's responses are recorded on a color-coded form with areas specifically designated for different types of analyses. In addition to the directions involving emitted responses, other directions are provided to the examiner on production of modeled responses from the children.

DEVELOPMENT. The new version is a complete restandardization and contains 40 updated photographs, reduced from the 48 used in the previous version. Using the first 30 photographs, the instrument explores a child's articulation of 59 consonants in initial, medial, and final positions. The final 10 photographs are used to examine performance on 10 initial consonant blends. In addition, nine phonological processes most commonly used by phonetically disordered young children are assessed. The processes are described and there are some directions to assist in the assessment of these processes.

A total of 40 photographs were chosen from 391 original ones using a process of examination of the photographs and their ability to elicit the correct target responses. The photographs were updated and revised to avoid bias and present more current representation of sounds. Speech-language personnel were involved in the modification of the photos and eliciting statements.

The test was normed on 2,270 children from ages 3-0 to 9-11, an increase from the 710 children used in the SPAT-D (Bennett, 1995; Felsenfeld, 1995). The sample represented 23 states and the four major U.S. geographic regions. However, the sample did not represent the U.S. Census, with only African American children represented in the appropriate proportion. Hispanics and other ethnic groups were underrepresented, whites were overrepresented, and less than 1% of the children were nonnative English speakers.

TECHNICAL. The SPAT-D II is scored by determining the number of correct items and comparing it to the mean score for the child's age. Consideration of dialectic influences are suggested in the scoring process and examples of dialectic variations are included in the examiner's manual. The raw scores are converted to standard scores with a mean of 100 and standard deviation of 15. The standard scores are then used for normative comparisons of children by gender and age groupings.

Norms are separately reported for males and females up through age 6 because gender-based differences were noted through that age. Norms combining both genders are reported for ages 7 through 9-11. The authors note that by the age of 9 years, few children make more than one error, resulting in a negatively skewed distribution of scores.

A variety of scores are available. The Percentage of Consonants Correct (PCC) and the Percentage of Consonants Correct—Revised (PCC-R) may be calculated, but their descriptions and usability are not thoroughly discussed. In addition, percentile ranks, confidence intervals, and scaled scores are provided. However, the user is informed that use of normed scores must be done with caution because of the negatively skewed distribution of errors.

Reliability was assessed on 219 children; however, the process of selection of this sample is not discussed in the manual. Reliability studies include test-retest (with a 2-week interval), internal consistency, and interjudge estimates. The estimates of test-retest reliability had a median of .98. The interjudge reliability coefficient was .98. The estimate of internal consistency reliability based on all of the children in the norming sample (n = 2,270) was .88.

Validity of the SPAT-D II was explored through content, construct, and concurrent validity studies. The content validity of the test was well supported with reference to literature establishing common sounds and error patterns.

Construct validity was explored through the construct of speech as developmental, with fewer errors appearing in normal children as they approach 9 years of age. The authors examined the error rates in their norming sample and found just such a pattern. Interestingly, the authors did not

complete a validity study involving analysis of children with and without speech disorders, as they had done with the SPAT-D (Bennett, 1995; Felsenfeld, 1995). Lack of this information leaves in question the appropriateness of using the SPAT-D II for determining type or focus of therapy.

Concurrent validity was explored through test score correlations of the scores of 43 children with normal speech with their scores on the Goldman Fristoe Test of Articulation—Second Edition. The resulting correlation on 68 common items was .97.

COMMENTARY. The SPAT-D II is a good quality instrument that may be used to describe a child's current level of articulation of common English sounds. The sounds are well documented through the literature. However, it should be noted that although the discovery of patterns is well supported in the manual, the claim for aid in determining therapy types and foci are not explored or substantiated by validity studies.

The norming procedures are sound, but the results are problematic in that the sample of children did not represent the U.S. Census and the number of nonnative English speakers was quite small. Thus, the usability of the instrument in communities of large numbers of English-language learners may be limited.

The content, construct, and concurrent validity studies do lend support to the descriptive value of the instrument. However, the absence of a study exploring the scores of children with normal and nonnormal speech articulation keeps use of the instruments somewhat limited.

Use is particularly problematic because although the authors state that the test can be used to determine the type or focus of therapy, no numerical guidelines or cut scores are provided for determining these aspects of therapy. The authors also note that speech errors have nonnormal distributions at most ages, and are quite skewed at older ages. The authors further state that although normative data have been provided to identify deficits for referral, subjective information from the assessment is best. Unfortunately, only limited guidance for this process is provided in the manual.

Reliability studies do show that the instrument is stable and internally consistent. In addition, interjudge reliability estimates show that the observations made on children's responses are consistent.

SUMMARY. The SPAT-D II is an easy-to-administer and interesting assessment of articulation patterns of young children. The test employs a well-documented set of consonant and vowel sounds and processes used in pronunciation of those sounds. The test should provide a clear description of the child's articulation and processes. However, the test's technical qualities do not support its use for determining the type or focus of therapy. Furthermore, because of the limitations in the norming sample, individuals should be cautious in use of this instrument with ethnic minority and nonnative English-speaking children.

REVIEWER'S REFERENCES

Bennett, C. W. (1995). [Review of the Structured Photographic Articulation Test Featuring Dudsberry]. In J. C. Conoley, & J. C. Impara (Eds.), *The twelfth mental measurements yearbook* (pp. 1005–1006). Lincoln, NE: Buros Institute of Mental Measurements.

Felsenfeld, S. (1995). [Review of the Structured Photographic Articulation Test Featuring Dudsberry]. In J. C. Conoley, & J. C. Impara (Eds.), *The twelfth mental measurements yearbook* (pp. 1006–1007). Lincoln, NE: Buros Institute of Mental Measurements.

Review of the Structured Photographic Articulation Test II Featuring Dudsberry by ROGER L. TOWNE, Associate Professor and Head, Department of Communication Disorders, Northern Michigan University, Marquette, MI:

DESCRIPTION. The Structured Photographic Articulation Test II Featuring Dudsberry (SPAT-D II) is a revision of the original SPAT-D, which was first published in 1989. The authors noted that this revision was undertaken due to feedback from users of the original SPAT-D and a need to make the test suitable for children with greater severity of articulation disorder and diversity. Therefore, the revised edition of the test contains similar but updated stimulus pictures and new normative data reflecting the most recent U.S. Census data.

The SPAT-D II is designed to test the articulation of children ages 3-0 through 9-11 years utilizing 40 full-color photographs of Dudsberry, a golden retriever dog, engaged in various activities and playing with various objects. As with other articulation tests, each photograph contains content designed to elicit a specific targeted word containing selected phonemes in the initial, medial, or final syllable position. There are also specific eliciting statements that the examiner can use if a spontaneous response is not given. In all, 59 single consonants and 10 consonant blends are assessed. In addition, there are 8 other photographs ("Dudsberry's 1st Birthday") selected to elicit phoneme production in connected speech. The 4 x 6-inch photographs are neatly contained in a bound album. Instructions for administering

and scoring the SPAT-D II and the normative data are found in the test manual, which also contains appended information relative to dialectical variations, phonological process identification, and vowel production assessment.

The test kit comes with a packet of 30 color-coded response forms for recording the child's verbal responses and documenting test performance. Performance data recorded on the response form consist of the child's transcribed verbal responses and any articulation errors made on targeted sounds. Noted articulation errors are then transferred to two other sections of the form; one for consonant error classification relative to manner of phoneme production, and the other for consonant cluster error analysis. Raw scores, or the total number of correct responses made by the child, are also recorded and a percent of correct consonant production calculated. The raw scores can also be converted to standard scores, confidence intervals, and percentile rank for gender and age, as well as raw score age equivalencies. Finally, if "Dudsberry's 1st Birthday" was used to test for phoneme production in connected speech, the back of the response form has a place for recording a child's verbal responses and analyzing their error pattern.

Test administration is straightforward. Each of the photographs is presented to the child along with the appropriate eliciting statement, which the child completes using the target word. The child's verbal response (target word) is then recorded on the response form and any errors on the selected phoneme(s) noted. Additional prompting is used when a spontaneous response is not initially given. There are no basal or ceiling criteria; therefore, all 40 photographs are presented. If testing of consonants in connected speech is to be done, the photographs for "Dudsberry's 1st Birthday" are then presented and, depending on their reading skills, the child is asked to either read or repeat a sentence describing the picture.

DEVELOPMENT. Selection of the photographs to be used as stimuli and their eliciting statements was based on two trial test presentations made to children. The first trial consisted of 391 photographs and statements presented to 47 children from which 96 were selected for the second test presentation. The second test presentation was made to 38 children from which 48 stimuli having a 90% or better probability of eliciting the targeted word were then selected for potential use in the SPAT-D II. These 48 stimuli were then field tested by speech-language pathologists; their feedback resulted in the selection of the final 40 pictures used in the revised test.

Test stimuli are organized so that 54 singleton consonants are elicited by the first 30 photographs and consonant blends (plus 5 additional singleton consonants) are elicited by the next 10 photographs. In addition, the stimuli also allow for the assessment of nine phonological processes commonly used by preschool and school-aged children. Most often a single stimulus word allows for the assessment of more than one sound or process, keeping the number of photographs and stimulus words manageable. Most of the singleton consonants are tested in the syllable initial (prevocalic), syllable medial (intervocalic), and syllable final (postvocalic) positions. However, six singleton consonants are tested only in their most commonly occurring syllable positions. All consonant clusters are only tested in the syllable initial position.

TECHNICAL. The SPAT-D II was standardized on 2,270 children between the ages of 3-0 and 9-11 living in 23 different states throughout the country. Speech-language pathologists were recruited and asked to test children in day care centers and schools meeting specific demographic requirements relative to age, region, ethnicity, and gender. Test performances of these children were then used to determine standard scores, percentile ranks, and age equivalency ranges for the test. Test-retest reliability was determined by retesting 219 children across the age range with genders being approximately equal and representing a variety of ethnic groups. Test-retest correlation coefficients (approximate 2-week interval) ranged between .85 and 1.00 (median = .98) across the 7-year age groups. Interjudge reliability using 43 children and two testers had a correlation of .98, whereas internal consistency ranged between .77 and .95 (median = .88, mean = .87). Data are also presented to support the premise that the SPAT-D II demonstrates adequate content and construct validity. Concurrent validity was demonstrated by comparing the performance of 43 children on the SPAT-D II with their performance on the Goldman-Fristoe 2 Test of Articulation (Goldman & Fristoe, 2000). Correlation of performance between the two tests was found to be .97 whereas the average percentage for agreement for the presence and/or absence of errors was 98.2%. Based on the data presented by the test's authors, the SPAT-D II appears to demonstrate both excellent reliability and validity measures.

COMMENTARY. In general the design of the SPAT-D II is little different than most available standardized articulation tests. Pictures are utilized to elicit a specific verbal response (word) from a child from which targeted speech sounds are judged relative to their accuracy of production or type of articulation error committed. The test also conveniently provides a means by which articulation in contextual speech (reading) can also be assessed in older children. Perhaps the test's greatest strength and uniqueness is in the utilization of very cute photographs of a golden retriever dog as the stimulus items. For younger children especially, these photographs should be highly entertaining and verbally stimulating. I would suspect that many children spontaneously provide more than just a single word response to the items thus providing additional contextual speech samples for analysis.

The SPAT-D II also suffers an inherent weakness that is common among most other articulation tests as well. That is, judgments regarding a child's overall articulation behavior must be made using data from a relatively small sampling of the child's speech collected within a fairly narrow context. This would be especially true of reticent children who restrict their verbal responses to only one or two words. It is, therefore, incumbent upon the tester to use additional data collected in a variety of environments, activities, and contexts before reaching conclusions regarding a child's articulation behavior. No single test, including the SPAT-D II, can provide all the data necessary for accurate and reliable conclusions to be reached.

SUMMARY. There are several standardized articulation tests available for the evaluation of articulation performance in children. They vary primarily by the type of visual stimulus items used, the words the stimuli are designed to elicit, and the specific sounds in the words targeted for analysis. All provide a relatively small sample of speech from which overall articulation behavior is assessed. Clinicians should have several of these tests at their disposal so they can select the one that appears most likely to elicit the most natural and spontaneous speech sample possible. The SPAT-D II would seem to be a test that would particularly meet these needs for younger children, and, therefore, would be desirable to have available for use.

REVIEWER'S REFERENCE

Goldman, R., & Fristoe, M. (2000). Goldman-Fristoe 2 Test of Articulation. Circle Pines, MN: American Guidance Service.

[237]

Suffolk Reading Scale 2.

Purpose: Designed to assess "reading ability."
Population: Ages 6.0 to 14.11.
Publication Dates: 1986–2002.
Acronym: SRS2.
Scores: Total score only.
Administration: Individual or group.
Levels, 3: 1 (Ages 6.0 to 8.11), 2 (Ages 8.0 to 11.11), 3 (Ages 10.0 to 14.11).
Forms, 2: A, B.
Price Data: Available from publisher.
Time: (50) minutes.
Author: Fred Hagley.
Publisher: NFER-Nelson Publishing Co., Ltd. [England].
Cross References: See T5:2556 (3 references); for reviews by Robert B. Cooter, Jr. and Richard Lehrer of an earlier edition, see 11:392.

Review of the Suffolk Reading Scale 2 by JEN-NIFER N. MAHDAVI, Assistant Professor of Special Education, California State University, Los Angeles, CA:

DESCRIPTION. The Suffolk Reading Scale 2 (SRS2) is a norm-referenced, standardized, group-administered assessment of reading ability, revised from the Suffolk Reading Scale (1987). The test is designed for students in the United Kingdom, ages 6-0 through 14-11. It is broken into three levels by age (1, 2, 3) with each level of the test having two forms (A and B).

Test items are in the cloze format, with students selecting the best of five word choices to fill in the blank in a sentence. For Levels 1 and 2, students fill in the bubble corresponding to the correct answer in the test booklet; for Level 3, answers are marked on a separate answer sheet. Tests take approximately 30 minutes to administer, with 20 minutes of preparation time. Administration directions recommend that alternate forms are given to students sitting next to one another to reduce the probability of cheating. Guidelines, rather than a script, are provided for teachers to use when giving instructions to the students. As teachers interpret administration directions differently, the test results should not be considered to be a consequence of standardized procedures. Students are to complete all the items they can within

a 30-minute time limit. The SRS2 can be either handscored or sent to the publisher for machine scoring.

Raw scores, the total items correct, can be converted into standard scores, percentile ranks, and age equivalent scores. Tables are also provided to compare a class or school's group mean to the national one to determine whether there is a significant difference in scores.

DEVELOPMENT. The SRS, reviewed in *The Eleventh Mental Measurements Yearbook* (11:392), was the foundation for the SRS2. No research about reading development is cited in the manual of the new edition, nor do the authors offer any theoretical underpinnings for this test. They state that the National Curricula of England, Scotland, Wales, and Northern Ireland informed the choice of test items, which are meant to reflect real-life reading tasks. The SRS2 is also designed to be easy to administer and score and to provide a method for monitoring progress over time.

The revision was based on item analyses of the results of the SRS administered in 2000 by the Newcastle Education Authority to over 21,000 students, as well as critical feedback from the Suffolk County Literacy Manager. Developers decided to change some items to address outdated vocabulary and to strengthen the link between the SRS and the National Curriculum. Items biased by gender or ethnicity were also identified and eliminated or changed. No examples of items that were changed are included in the manual. A total of 262 items were tested (160 of these from the first edition of the test) on 900 children at three grade levels and analyzed using Rasch and classical item analysis. Results of these analyses are not presented in the test manual, but the authors write that 212 items were retained, put in order by difficulty and by their ability to discriminate among students, and then divided into three levels of two forms each. Of the 212 items, 70 are unchanged from the SRS and 77 are new.

The format of the test, cloze sentence reading items with multiple-choice answers, provides a rough estimate of children's reading ability in the extent to which they can decode text and recognize appropriate vocabulary to complete sentences when presented with a time limit. The SRS2 does not provide insight into a student's ability to comprehend what he has read or what strategies he might use when reading.

TECHNICAL.

Standardization. The manual states that a nationally representative sample of 23,508 students was drawn by region from England, Scotland, Wales, and Northern Ireland, stratified for type of school and for scoring level on the National Curriculum Assessment. Specific information about how many students represented each region, or even how large each region was, is not included. Stratification information is not included, nor are numbers of participating schools included.

Although the total number of students in the norm group is large, no information is given about their gender, ethnicity, socioeconomic status, primary language, or any other demographic characteristic. The standardization procedures are vague and the norm group poorly described.

Reliability. Internal consistency reliability, in the form of Cronbach's alpha, is given by level, year group, and form and is strong (.91–.96). In addition, 250 students at each level took both Forms A and B, within an unspecified time period, to yield parallel form reliability between .85 and .93. No other measures of test reliability are offered.

Validity. Concurrent validity statistics are presented comparing the SRS2 to the National Curriculum Teacher Assessments in the United Kingdom. These correlations range from a low of .55 between the Scottish 5-14 level test and the SRS2's Level 1 Form B to a high of .77 between the same Scottish test and Level 3 Form B of the SRS2. These correlations are moderate, at best.

In addition to concurrent validity statistics reported above, the SRS2 manual includes a table that enables test administrators to convert raw SRS scores to SRS2 raw scores and then convert to standard scores.

No attempt was made to compare the content of the SRS2 with any other standardized or curriculum-based measure of reading ability. Content validity is not specifically addressed in the test manual.

Considering the number of students included in the norm sample, there is a disappointing lack of effort in examining measures of the technical adequacy of the SRS2. The discussion of the technical aspects of the test is unconvincing.

COMMENTARY. The Suffolk Reading Scale 2 purports to be a measure of reading ability. However, the format of the test is very limited and does not allow students to truly demonstrate how well they can read. In addition, the group adminis-tration of this multiple-choice test does not allow teachers to conduct error analysis that would help make decisions about the students' reading strengths and needs and necessary instruction. That the test is quick and easy to administer and score is not a very powerful recommendation in the face of the limited information that the test yields.

The discussion of how the update of the original SRS was made is vague. Only one person is named as contributing feedback about the earlier test. Statistics arising from Rasch and item analysis are not presented in the manual. Moreover, beyond the mention of the National Curriculum, which is made with no evidence to show how it was used in the development of the SRS2, no theory or research is cited to support the choices made in revising or designing this test.

The utter lack of technical adequacy demonstrated in the SRS2 manual is also an area of concern. Researchers should not use the SRS2 as a measure to compare students' reading ability or as an outcome measure for an intervention study.

SUMMARY. The SRS2 has few strengths, beyond ease of administration. It can offer only a very rough estimate of reading ability and has no demonstrated instructional relevance. Its technical adequacy is poorly presented. This test likely would not be useful as a scientific measure of reading ability nor as a teaching tool. Researchers should consider selecting a better described and more technically adequate test. Classroom teachers should use an instructionally relevant curriculum-based or criterion-referenced assessment to make decisions about how to teach reading.

Review of the Suffolk Reading Scale 2 by HOWARD MARGOLIS, *Professor, Department of Educational and Community Programs, Queens College of CUNY, Flushing, NY:*

DESCRIPTION. The Suffolk Reading Scale 2 (SRS2) is a group-administered test that uses a "multiple-choice sentence completion format" (teacher's guide, p. 5) or maze procedure to measure students' reading ability. The SRS2 has three levels: Level 1 is for students age 6:00 to 8:11, Level 2 for 8:00 to 11:11, and Level 3 for 10:00 to 14:11. All levels have parallel forms.

The SRS2 was designed for teachers to administer to their classes. As such, the SRS2 is supposed to be quick and simple to administer. This goal has been achieved. All items follow the same format, making administration simple; the testing period, including time for teachers to explain the directions and time for students to practice items, is 50 minutes; students have 30 minutes to complete the test. Scoring is straightforward and should not take much time; optical scanning and computerized scoring are available.

When administering the SRS2, teachers are supposed to follow a specific set of guidelines. The "exact wording" used with the students, however, is "left to the teacher" (teacher's guide, p. 11). As discussed later, under Commentary, this is problematic.

The SRS2 manual is easy to understand. To its credit, it cautions teachers to use confidence bands, explains the use and limitations of age equivalents, discusses how to use the SRS2 to monitor progress, and discusses what to do when obtaining unexpected results.

DEVELOPMENT. The SRS2 is a revision of the 1987 Suffolk Reading Scale. Although the multiple-choice sentence-completion format remained the same, some original items were eliminated, some revised, and new ones added. Items were carefully assessed to determine difficulty. Consequently, the manual asserts that the tests devised from these items represent the full range of reading ability that each level of the SRS2 was designed to assess. The SRS2's development procedures appear to support this assertion.

TECHNICAL. The SRS2 manual states that the test was standardized on a nationally representative sample of 23,508 students from England, Northern Ireland, Scotland, and Wales. Unfortunately, how students were chosen is unclear. Moreover, the manual fails to report critical demographic information, such as ethnicity and socioeconomic status.

The SRS2's internal consistency reliability is good. For Levels 1, 2, and 3, Cronbach's alpha ranged from .93 (Level 3) to .96 (Level 1). Parallel form reliability is also good, but suggests that for individual students the forms are not interchangeable, that one-third of students may obtain scores that differ by 6 or more standard score points. For parallel forms, the standard score correlation for Level 1 was .91, for Level 2 it was .89, and for Level 3, it was .87.

COMMENTARY. Reviews of the original Suffolk Reading Scale (Cooter, 1992; Lehrer, 1992) had criticized it for ignoring recent advances in the understanding of reading, ignoring reading theory, offering little guidance for classroom instruction, and failing to demonstrate validity. The reviews stated that the test was not a comprehensive test of reading skill and that it should not be used for more than school or district reporting. Unfortunately, the same criticisms hold for the SRS2, making it important that prospective SRS2 users understand that only tentative, narrow conclusions about students' reading abilities can be drawn from the SRS2, that SRS2 scores should not be a major factor in selecting reading materials, and that SRS2 scores are inadequate for instructional planning. Prospective users should also know that allowing teachers to independently phrase administrative directions might affect student performance, that some students may have difficulty with the SRS2's page layout and computer scoring sheet, and that the SRS2 is inappropriate for use in American schools.

Tentative conclusions. The SRS2 uses a modified cloze or maze procedure. The degree to which this procedure fully measures reading comprehension is suspect, as are the cognitive processes activated by the procedure and the underlying abilities influencing it (Layton, Robinson, & Lawson, 1998; Parker, Hasbrouck, & Tindal, 1992). For teachers planning instruction, the degree that SRS2 performance generalizes to other reading tasks is uncertain. Consequently, conclusions reached on the basis of a student's SRS2 performance must be tentative. Conclusions must also be tentative because the SRS2 is a group test; as such, extraneous factors, factors that may go unnoticed in group situations, and factors that are more obvious when tests are individually administered (fatigue, poor motivation, high anxiety, low self-efficacy, poor self-regulatory abilities, temporary emotional strain, difficulty using computer scoring sheets) can adversely affect a student's score. Thus, the SRS2's authors should be commended for recommending that "in most circumstances it will be advisable to take further action with low-scoring pupils, [this may involve] further testing and observation" (teacher's guide, p. 29).

Reading materials. The SRS2 manual states that the test "may be used to … assist in gauging what each pupil is able to read and thereby help the teacher to choose suitable reading materials" (teacher's guide, p. 3). This, to a very limited extent, may be true. However, several factors militate against making the SRS2 a major part of such decision making, especially in American schools. First, because the test was standardized in Great Britain and Northern Ireland, the norms are inappropriate for American schools. Second, the reading passages are exceedingly short—the longest item is about two dozen words, and most have far fewer words. As such, they do not reflect the length and complexity of typical school reading assignments, especially beyond the second grade; they do not assess the ability of students to comprehend and synthesize information from more than one sentence, a critical component of cloze processing. Third, SRS2 scores neglect students' motivation, background, and self-regulatory abilities. Fourth, and perhaps most important, the manual fails to present validity data demonstrating that the SRS2 helps teachers to accurately place students, especially struggling readers, in reading materials.

Instructional planning. Because the SRS2 measures one rather than several clearly delineated aspects of reading, and because it is group administered, it has no diagnostic value other than identifying students who may be foundering or excelling in reading. This limits its use to that of a screening test or a test for making gross group comparisons. The test manual implies that the developers recognized this limitation: "It was decided not to attempt to produce sub-scores of supposed diagnostic significance. It was felt that a more detailed analysis of reading difficulties should be done on an individual basis" (teacher's guide, p. 5).

Unique wording. Although the SRS2 manual provides logically derived test administration guidelines, the SRS2 asks teachers to explain these guidelines in their own words. This can be beneficial as it allows teachers to match their instructions to the specifics of the situation, including students' particular needs and characteristics. However, the extent to which teachers' words differ is the extent to which standardization, and thus the applicability of the SRS2's norms, may be vitiated. Because research had not adequately addressed this problem, the authors needed to—but did not—present data showing how differences in teachers' wording affected student performance.

Page layout and computer scoring sheet. Some students with learning disabilities may have difficulty with the test, even if they know the correct answers, because each page contains too many items, too close together. Others, taking the Level 3 SRS2, may get confused by the crowded computer answer sheet. Similarly, students with motor coordination problems may have difficulty with the SRS2's response requirements. For such students, these problems reduce the accuracy and thus the validity of SRS2 scores.

SUMMARY. The SRS2 is an easy-to-administer series of tests that attempts to measure overall reading ability. The degree to which it succeeds is highly suspect. Although it may prove to be an adequate screening device in Great Britain and Northern Ireland, its use for matching students to reading materials and for planning instruction is unsupported. Finally, because the SRS2 was standardized in another country, using it and its norms in American schools is unjustified.

REVIEWER'S REFERENCES

Cooter, R. B., Jr. (1992). [Review of the Suffolk Reading Scale.] In J. J. Kramer & J. C. Conoley (Eds.), *The eleventh mental measurements yearbook* (pp. 892-893). Lincoln, NE: Buros Institute of Mental Measurements.
Layton, A., Robinson, J., & Lawson, M. (1998). The relationship between syntactic awareness and reading performance. *Journal of Research in Reading*, 21, 5-23.
Lehrer, R. (1992). [Review of the Suffolk Reading Scale.] In J. J. Kramer & J. C. Conoley (Eds.), *The eleventh mental measurements yearbook* (pp. 893-894). Lincoln, NE: Buros Institute of Mental Measurements.
Parker, R., Hasbrouck, J. E., & Tindal, G. (1992). The maze as a classroom-based reading measure: Construction methods, reliability, and validity. *The Journal of Special Education*, 26, 195-218.

[238]

Supports Intensity Scale.

Purpose: Designed to help service providers "understand the support needs of people with intellectual disabilities (i.e., mental retardation) and closely related developmental disabilities."

Population: Individuals ages 16–72 with intellectual or closely related developmental disabilities.

Publication Date: 2004.

Acronym: SIS.

Scores, 9: Home Living, Community Living, Lifelong Learning, Employment, Health and Safety, Social, Support Needs Index, Exceptional Medical Needs, Exceptional Behavioral Needs.

Administration: Individual.

Price Data, 2004: $125 per complete set including user's manual (128 pages) and 25 interview forms; $95 per user's manual; $38.75 per 25 interview forms.

Time: Administration time not reported.

Comments: Semistructured, multiple informant interview format.

Authors: James R. Thompson, Brian R. Bryant, Edward M. Campbell, Ellis M. Craig, Carolyn M. Hughes, David A. Rotholz, Robert L. Schalock, Wayne P. Silverman, Marc J. Tassé, and Michael L. Wehmeyer.

Publisher: AAMR American Association on Mental Retardation.

Review of the Supports Intensity Scale by SANDRA A. LOEW, Associate Professor of Counse-

lor Education, University of North Alabama, Florence, AL:

DESCRIPTION. The Supports Intensity Scale (SIS) is a planning tool to assist agencies and/or organizations in developing Individualized Service Plans (ISP) for people with mental retardation or developmental delays. There are three sections of the SIS that are filled out during interviews with one to three people who provide support or know the individual receiving services. It is recommended that the interviewer have extensive experience or a bachelor's degree in a human services field.

The first section consists of 49 life activities that are grouped into subscales: Home Living Activities, Community Living Activities, Lifelong Learning Activities, Employment Activities, Health and Safety Activities, and Social Activities. Each activity is assessed based on the frequency of support, the daily support time, and the type of support required for the individual to complete that activity. The scale ranges from zero to either 1, 2, 3 or 4. A person who needs support every time he does an activity, but that support takes only 5 minutes and\or consists of monitoring, would have a high "frequency" number (4), but a low "daily support time" number (1) and a low "type of support" number (1) for that activity. The standard scores for each activity provide a pattern and each score is converted to a standard score that is graphed on the SIS Profile Form.

The second section is the Supplemental Protection and Advocacy Scale, which consists of eight questions. The four highest scoring activities are listed on the Profile Form. This is scored the same as the first section with the same ranges for frequency, daily support time, and type of support.

The third section deals with Exceptional Medical and Behavioral Support Needs. There are two subscales: Medical Supports Needed and Behavioral Supports Needed. The possible scores in these areas are: zero (no support needed), 1 (some support needed), and 2 (extensive support needed). The completed form provides a planning tool that shows the supports a person needs to function in one's community.

DEVELOPMENT. The SIS is the result of a 5-year endeavor that relied on the expertise of numerous contributors. The developers provided a manual that has a comprehensive literature review concerning the societal changes that have occurred

that impact the services that are available to, and are required for, persons with intellectual disabilities. This instrument is not a diagnostic tool and does not take the place of intelligence tests and behavioral rating scales; instead it is to be used after an initial diagnosis is made. The developers clearly state that the SIS is a planning tool to be used in developing Individualized Service Plans. The manual has a comprehensive section on the development of the instrument, which includes references.

TECHNICAL. This instrument was normed on a convenience sample of 1,306 adults who were diagnosed with an intellectual disability and were from 33 states and 2 Canadian provinces.

Each subscale of the SIS has a normalized standard score with a mean of 10 and standard deviation of 3, like many popular intelligence tests and behavior rating scales. In this case, higher scores mean more needs for supports. Percentile ranks are also available but the developers caution interviewers in using them.

Internal consistency reliability was computed using Cronbach's alpha method with coefficients ranging from .86 to .98. The high reliability coefficients might be related to the fact that some of the activities in the different subscales may be very similar. Test-retest reliability coefficients (approximately 3-weeks period) ranged from .74 to .94, which is within an acceptable range. The retests were given by the same interviewer who had given the first test. The interrater reliability coefficients ranged from .55 to .90, which is disturbing. Given that a case manager in an entry level position would probably be the interviewer using this instrument and then when it is time for follow-up or review of Individualized Service Plans, there would probably be a new case manager in that same entry level job, interrater reliability would be very important.

To document content validity the developers did an extensive literature review to identify support needs of persons with intellectual disabilities and found 130 potential indicators. They asked professionals in the field of developmental disabilities to use a Q-sort methodology to put each indicator into 1 of 12 areas. They retained 8 of those areas and proceeded with a pilot of the instrument. They conducted four field tests to refine the instrument, that became the SIS. To quantitatively assess the content validity, the developers ran an item analysis that supported the items in the subscales.

There do not seem to be other standardized instruments that could be used to address criterion-related validity. Unfortunately, the developers devised a Likert-type scale for interviewers to assess the support needs of clients that the interviewer filled out prior to using the SIS. Not surprisingly, the criterion-related validity was acceptable when the SIS was compared to this other scale.

The SIS subscales were correlated with intelligence scores for some of the norming sample and were found to have sufficient coefficients to support construct validity. As expected, there was an inverse relationship between intelligence level and need for supports.

COMMENTARY. The developers recognized a need and created an instrument that is a useful tool in developing Individualized Service Plans. Its strengths are that it is grounded in research and based on current best practices. The manual is well-written and carefully explains the theoretical background of the instrument. There are three case studies with completed SIS forms in the manual to help the interviewer understand the scoring system, and there are example questions for an interviewer to ask. The scoring is simple with easy-to-use conversion tables. The graph that gives a picture of support needs is also a helpful tool.

The first section that deals with supports needed and the intensity of those supports seems to provide the most useful information. The third section that looks at medical or behavioral supports is an important area that impacts the level of supports needed and is crucial in developing an appropriate ISP. The second section explores Protection and Advocacy areas but it is unclear how this information is to be used. This might be useful information but an overworked case manager may not see the point of asking for it if there is no apparent relevance to it.

The developers of the SIS encourage users to aggregate data to use in program planning, resource allocation, funding analyses, and program evaluation. Although this is not the primary purpose of the SIS, it may be used to assist decision makers in those areas.

Although the psychometric properties of the instrument are adequate for the most part, the most troubling aspect is low interrater reliability. The reality for many agencies is a large turnover in staff, which means that a consumer might be served by the same agency for years but be interviewed by a number of different case managers during those years. The discrepancies that might result from low interrater reliability should be of concern for anyone using this instrument.

SUMMARY. The SIS is a valuable tool to assist agencies in the development of Individualized Service Plans. It does not take the place of diagnostic tests but is used after a diagnosis is made to determine the supports needed and the intensity of those supports for a person to be a functioning member of the community. The SIS is well-researched and easy to use and score with a comprehensive manual that is easy to read and use. Because it is such a useful and well-constructed instrument, it is essential for any agency that chooses to use the SIS to conduct regular training in the use and scoring of the instrument so that interrater reliability within the agency is in acceptable ranges. The developers encourage users to share the results of using the SIS with different samples so that information can be included in subsequent manuals. It is clear that they recognize that although they have made an excellent start, there is still room for improvement.

Review of the Supports Intensity Scale by *DAVID J. PITTENGER, Associate Provost: Academic Administration, The University of Tennessee at Chattanooga, Chattanooga, TN:*

DESCRIPTION. The Supports Intensity Scale (SIS) is a semistructured interview that allows professionals serving persons with developmental disabilities to determine the level and the intensity of support required for various activities of daily living. The interview also identifies the necessity of medical services required of persons in this population. Using a single-use booklet, a trained interviewer asks questions of one or more people who know the client's abilities. For most items, the respondent estimates the frequency and intensity of the types of support required for various life activities.

The scope of activities included in the review is broad, and ranges from ability to perform a host of activities of daily living to the ability to advocate and protect one's self-interests. The first section of the SIS consists of six subscales. The Home Living activities subscale assesses basic activities of daily living including hygiene and other self-care activities. The Community Living subscale assesses the individual's ability to use public transportation, community services, and perform basic shopping tasks. The questions in the Lifelong Learning subscale indicate the quality of interactions with others, participation in various training activities, and ability to learn appropriate health and self-management strategies. The Employment section includes questions related to ability to learn tasks, level of interaction with coworkers, and general efficiency while working. The purpose of the Health and Safety section is to assess the level at which the person can attend to his or her health needs including taking prescribed medication and seeking health services as needed. Finally, the Social subsection assesses the extent to which the individual is able to socialize beyond the context of home and work. A second section assesses the extent to which the person can assert his or her rights, avoid exploitation, and make appropriate decisions. The third section reviews the level of medical intervention required of the person and the extent to which he or she may suffer medical or behavioral maladies characteristic of persons with a developmental disability.

The instrument consists of an eight-page booklet that lists the specific categories to be assessed and associated rating scales. The booklet includes clear instructions for determining the subscale scores and converting these into a percentile score. Once completed, the booklet could easily be stored in the client's permanent file for future reference. Although the instrument is not a diagnostic tool, one can use the SIS to determine the level of various services required of a client and to track the client's progress.

DEVELOPMENT. The authors of the SIS began development of the instrument by preparing a host of questions they believed to be representative of critical information that service providers require. The authors then requested professionals working in the field to participate in a Q-sort task to identify and modify critical questions that became a part of the SIS. The authors then asked 68 professionals working in the field to administer the SIS to clients under their care. This step yielded a sample of 1,306 evaluations from 33 states about persons who lived in various settings.

TECHNICAL. The manual provides ample information on the ideal procedures for administering the SIS, its scoring, limitations, and psychometric properties. The reported assessment of internal consistency indicates that the coefficient alphas are extremely high for each of the SIS's support needs subscales: Home Living, Community Living, Lifelong Learning, Employment, Health and Safety, and Social. The authors report no statistical analysis justifying the creation of the separate subscales. Indeed, the intercorrelations among the subscales are moderate to high, suggesting a common factor among the subscales. Nevertheless, the questions within each subscale appear to provide relevant information regarding a specific domain of the client's ability and need for supervision and assistance.

The test-retest (with a 3-week administration interval) and interrater reliability indices indicate a high level of test-retest reliability, but only moderate levels of interrater reliability. The latter observation is not surprising given the nature of the instrument and the methods for collecting the information. The interrater reliabilities vary considerably among the subscales. For example, the Home and Living, and Health and Safety subscales evidence relatively robust interrater reliabilities. By contrast, the Lifelong Learning and Employment subscales evidence notably lower levels of interrater reliability.

The information regarding the validity of the SIS includes several perspectives. The manual provides a lengthy description of the Q-sort techniques used to select and modify the items included in the instrument. The theme of this section is that the authors of the SIS exercised extreme care in selecting items that appeared relevant to decision making among professionals working with the persons with developmental disabilities. The manual also reviews empirical information demonstrating statistically significant negative correlations between the subscale score and measures of intelligence.

COMMENTARY. Semistructured interviews are becoming a popular means of providing objective information regarding client needs in a number of health care and social service domains. Use of such instruments is clearly an improvement over anecdotal and ad hoc assessment of a client's needs and level of functioning. To the extent that a service agency focuses on the well-being of persons with developmental disabilities, the SIS appears to offer an efficient and useful means of objectively assessing the important life and social skills of persons with developmental disabilities.

SUMMARY. The SIS is a carefully designed semistructured interview instrument that allows persons with limited training and supervision to assess quickly the level of functioning and needs of a person with developmental disabilities. The construction of the instrument reveals careful attention to detail and the assurance that it produces useful information. Moreover, the instrument is sufficiently flexible to ensure its use in a number of settings.

[239]

Survey of Teenage Readiness and Neurodevelopmental Status.

Purpose: "Provides an overview of an adolescent's own perceptions of his or her functioning and performance strategies across a variety of neurocognitive and psychosocial domains."

Population: Ages 13–19.

Publication Date: 2001.

Acronym: STRANDS.

Scores, 13: Attention, Memory, Sequencing, Language, Visual Processing, Motor Functions, Organization and Strategies, Higher-Order Cognition, School Skills, School Life, Social Life, School and Work Preferences, Reasons.

Administration: Individual.

Price Data, 2002: $81.15 per complete set including manual for administration, scoring and interpretation (114 pages), 12 student questionnaires (15 pages), 12 student interview booklets (30 pages), and 12 profile sheets; $21.85 per specimen set including manual for administration, scoring, and interpretation, 1 student questionnaire, and 1 student interview booklet; $19.75 per manual; $68.65 per 12 pair of student questionnaires and student interview booklets; $5.75 per 12 profile sheets (quantity discounts available).

Time: (40) minutes for Student Interview; (20) minutes for Student Questionnaire.

Comments: Examines the relationship between metacognitive knowledge and actual strategic behavior; consists of 2 parts: structured clinical student interview (closed- and open-ended questions), student-completed questionnaire.

Authors: Melvin D. Levine and Stephen R. Hooper.

Publisher: Educators Publishing Service, Inc.

Review of the Survey of Teenage Readiness and Neurodevelopmental Status by SCOTT T. MEIER, Professor, Department of Counseling, School, and Educational Psychology, The University at Buffalo, Buffalo, NY:

DESCRIPTION. The Survey of Teenage Readiness and Neurodevelopmental Status (STRANDS) consists of a structured interview and a self-administered, self-report measure designed to assess adolescents' metacognitive and psychosocial abilities. Completing both requires about 1 hour and a third-grade reading level. The structured Student Interview assesses eight conceptual domains: Attention, Memory, Sequencing, Language, Visual Processing, Motor Functions, Organization and Strategies, and Higher-Order Cognition. In addition to questions answered in a Likert scale, the interview includes open-ended questions designed to tap into the "student's knowledge, insight, and strategy deployment" (manual, p. 2), which the examiner can record along with clinical impressions and observations. Similarly, the self-report Student Questionnaire assesses 5 domains: School Skills, School Life, Social Life, School and Work Preferences, and Reasons (for school performance).

The usefulness of the STRANDS rests on an assumption that Hooper and Levine (the authors) term the *insightful adolescent*. They maintain that research on study skills and reading strategies, among others, provide support for the idea that adolescents can provide reliable reports. They also cite literature indicating that self-report measures "have proven to be quite useful in attempting to understand specific neurocognitive functions and dysfunctions, in guiding additional testing efforts, and in developing treatment hypotheses" (manual, p. 1).

DEVELOPMENT. The test developers report that the STRANDS is based on the theoretical work of Flavell (1985, 1999) and others, who distinguish between two types of metacognition: *knowledge*, a person's insights into her or his cognitive processes, and *regulation*, a person's flexibility and fluency in problem solving. The STRANDS taps the former because "individuals of all ages can describe their knowledge of their cognitive processes better than they can describe how they regulate these processes" (manual, p. 3). Flavell distinguished between knowledge of self, knowledge of task, and knowledge of self relative to task, and the developers of the STRANDS employed these categories and their clinical experiences in developing test items for both interview and self-report measures.

Five experts in adolescent development and learning then reviewed items and provided feedback about their conceptual relevance. A small pilot study with 54 high school students provided data for initial reliability and validity estimates of items that were then rewritten or deleted.

TECHNICAL. The standardization sample consisted of adolescents ages 13 to 19, with the test developers seeking 100 participants per age band. Most participants were from the North Carolina area, although the authors attempted to match the 1995 U.S. Census for race and SES for each age band. Full-time special education students were excluded. The final sample included 388 males and 398 females; 644 of those participants were Caucasians and 106 were African Americans. The authors noted that only 17% of the standardization sample were persons of color compared to 33% in the Census.

The authors reported reliability and validity estimates for a variety of subsamples in the standardization pool. Low coefficient alphas were found for the Sequencing Scale (.42 for one sample of males, .47 for females), Visual Processing Scale (.51 males, .53 females), Motor Functions Scale (.36 males, .57 females), School Life Scale (.58 males), and Social Life Scale (.48, males). The authors note in the manual that only 68% of the computed reliability coefficients were above .70, although the lowest estimates were primarily found for the scales with the fewest items. Test-retest reliability estimates were computed with only 20 students from the standardization sample—too few to offer dependable information about temporal stability.

Similar difficulties are apparent during validity evaluations where low correlations were found between STRANDS scales and a variety of scales such as the Wechsler Intelligence scales and the Stroop Color and Word Test.

COMMENTARY. The STRANDS is a test in search of a purpose. The test developers suggest the STRANDS be employed to identify areas of functioning that require additional testing or intervention; the measures' strength lies in the broad range of domains sampled. From a research perspective, adolescents' perception of their cognitive and social functioning is an area of considerable interest and practical importance, and here the STRANDS represents a tool of potential usefulness.

Considerable doubt remains, however, about what the STRANDS measures. Should the STRANDS scales evidence high or low correlations with performance measures of intellectual and cognitive functioning? Interview and self-report remain questionable approaches to ascertaining cognitive functioning, particularly if one's purposes center on performance rather than per-ception. STRANDS scales do not provide information about whether a particular adolescent being tested has sufficient self-awareness to provide useful reports. Indeed, the authors note that "it will be up to the astute interviewer to determine the ultimate validity of the responses provided by the student" (manual, p. 6).

SUMMARY. In its present stage of development, the STRANDS should be considered an experimental measure primarily of interest to individuals interested in investigating adolescents' reports about intellectual, academic, and social functioning. As the test authors note, interpretation of STRANDS results "should be made by individuals with a knowledge base in metacognitive theory, information processing, and general cognition" (manual, p. 6). Professionals interested in assessing adolescents' cognitive and social functioning would be better served through traditional intelligence tests or a measure such as the Social Skills Rating Scales (Gresham & Elliott, 1990; T6:2321).

REVIEWER'S REFERENCES

Flavell, J. H. (1985). *Cognitive development* (2nd ed.). Englewood Cliffs, NJ: Prentice Hall.
Flavell, J. H. (1999). Cognitive development: Children's knowledge about the mind. *Annual Review of Psychology, 50*, 21–45.
Gresham, F. M., & Elliott, S. N. (1990). *Social Skills Rating System manual.* Circle Pines, MN: American Guidance Service.

[240]

Swallowing Ability and Function Evaluation.

Purpose: "Designed for evaluating and treating dysphagia."
Population: Ages 30 and over.
Publication Date: 2003.
Acronym: SAFE.
Scores, 3: Physical Examination, Oral Phase, Pharyngeal Phase.
Administration: Individual.
Price Data, 2002: $114 per complete kit including examiner's manual (37 pages), Treatment and Resource Manual (235 pages), and 50 profile/examiner record forms; $49 per examiner's manual; $41 per Treatment Manual; $27 per 50 profile/examiner record forms.
Time: (20–25) minutes.
Authors: Peggy Kipping and Deborah Ross-Swain.
Publisher: PRO-ED.

Review of the Swallowing Ability and Function Evaluation by CAROLYN MITCHELL PERSON, Nationally Certified and Licensed Speech Pathologist, Associate Professor, Special Education Department, and Director, Research Roundtable (Title III) and Southern University Online at Southern University and A&M College, Baton Rouge, LA:

DESCRIPTION. The Swallowing Ability and Function Evaluation (SAFE) is a screening test designed for evaluating and treating oropharyngeal dysphagia (swallowing disorders that affect the oral phase or early pharyngeal phase of the swallow) in adolescents and adults. Additionally, it is designed to "provide clinicians with a standardized, efficient, systematic, and comprehensive format for the clinical evaluation of swallowing" (examiner's manual, p. 3). As it is designed to be one part of a comprehensive evaluation, the purpose is not "to provide a definitive diagnosis or label of dysphagia" (examiner's manual, p. 3).

The three components of the SAFE are the examiner's manual, profile/examiner record form, and the treatment and resource manual. The profile/examiner record form is used to record severity ratings and diagnostic observations derived from a three-stage evaluation during which a physical examination of the oropharyngeal mechanism is conducted as well as a functional analysis of swallowing and an evaluation of general information related to swallowing ability. The materials included in the treatment and resource manual assist the clinician in implementing the treatment plan that is established following the administration of the SAFE if treatment is indicated.

DEVELOPMENT. The SAFE was administered to 159 individuals living in California and Texas. The sample consisted of 47 males and 53 females between the ages of 32 and 99 years. Even though the authors state that the SAFE is for use with adolescents and adults (examiner's manual, p. 3), there are no adolescents represented in the sample as evidenced by the age range of the participants. The individuals included in the sample had been previously diagnosed with some degree of dysphagia associated with cardiovascular, pulmonary, gastrointestinal, musculoskeletal, neurologic, or other medical disorders. The demographics do not include race or ethnicity. The severity of the dysphagia for each participant was not mentioned.

The SAFE was administered by "therapists who participated in gathering the standardization data" (examiner's manual, p. 25). No other specific information was provided about the therapists or whether training was provided by the authors of the SAFE for the administration, rating, scoring, and interpretation of the physical examination of the oropharyngeal mechanism, the functional analysis of swallowing, or of the diagnostic observations that comprise the subscales of the SAFE.

TECHNICAL. The quality of a test can be judged by three major standards: (a) reliability, (b) validity, and (c) fairness. The authors state that "the study of a test's reliability centers on estimating the amount of error associated with its scores" and that "content sampling reflects the degree of homogeneity among items within a test or subscale" (examiner's manual, p. 24). Therefore, the reliability status of the SAFE subscales was investigated relative to content sampling error. The internal consistency reliability was calculated with scores from the SAFE subscales items using Cronbach's coefficient alpha. The coefficient alpha for the Oral Mechanism, Oral Phase, and Pharyngeal Phase subscales was found to be high (.97, .82, and .73, respectively).

The authors state that because stanine scores are "particularly useful to determine which adults require additional assessment and treatment" (examiner's manual, p. 23), such scores were computed on the entire sample of 159 individuals. Percentile ranks for use in scoring the SAFE were calculated directly from the stanines. The standard error of measurement, theoretically describing a range of scores around each individual's true score, was calculated for the stanines obtained on the Oral Mechanism, Oral Phase, and Pharyngeal Phase subscales and reported as .35, .85, and 1.04, respectively.

Validity is the extent to which judgments based on a test or subtest are accurate and appropriate for the intended purpose. The intended purpose of the SAFE is twofold. One purpose is for the evaluation of dysphagia using the results of the Oral Mechanism, Oral Phase, and Pharyngeal Phase subscales with general information and observations. The second purpose is for the design, plan, and implementation of treatment if indicated by the stanines and severity ratings resulting from subscale scores. The SAFE subscales correspond to stages of its administration. In Stage 1 the physical examination of the oropharyngeal mechanism is conducted and corresponds to the Oral Mechanism subscale whereas in Stage 2 the functional analysis of swallowing is conducted and corresponds to the Oral Phase (Swallowing Evaluation) subscale and the Pharyngeal Phase (Swallowing Evaluation) subscale. In Stage 3 observations of cognitive and behavioral factors known to influence swallowing ability and participation are recorded. Evidence for the validity of scores from the SAFE is provided from information about two types of validity: content-description validity (content validity) and construct-identification validity (construct validity) (examiner's manual, p. 25).

In an effort to address content-description validity, a detailed qualitative rationale providing evidence-based support for the abilities chosen to be measured in the three stages of the SAFE administration is provided. The authors also describe quantitative evidence for content-description validity by reporting the discrimination power of each subscale. The discrimination power of each subscale was derived by calculating individual item discrimination indexes that represent a relationship between a particular item and the other items on the test. This information is not displayed in any tables, graphs, or charts. The authors discuss sources who suggest that accepting discrimination indexes of .35 or higher is appropriate and report the discrimination power of each subscale as .71, .68, and .45 (Oral Mechanism, Oral Phase, and Pharyngeal Phase, respectively). There is no information provided to help the reader make the transition from discrimination indexes for individual items to discrimination indexes for subscales.

The investigation of construct-identification validity was based on three constructs relating to (a) the SAFE differentiated between people with dysphagia and those without, (b) the SAFE subscales correlated with each other, and (c) the items of each subscale correlated with the total score of that subscale. Group differentiation was studied by evaluating the individuals with dysphagia from the normative sample and 20 individuals between the ages of 30 and 72 without dysphagia. Raw scores were transformed to stanines. The mean stanines are reported as being supportive of construct-identification validity and differentiation between people with dysphagia and those without. SAFE's subscales should be significantly intercorrelated. The correlation coefficients were calculated and are reported to "represent a high to very high degree of relationship" (examiner's manual, p. 27); therefore, the SAFE subscales appear to correlate with each other. The authors refer to the discriminating powers of individual subscale items (reported as discrimination power for each subscale) as evidence that a strong correlation exists between the items of each subscale and the total score of that subscale.

The SAFE is to be administered "by experienced clinicians who have the necessary proficiencies, knowledge, and skills as identified by the American Speech-Language-Hearing Association's Task Force on Dysphagia" (examiner's manual, p. 5). A patient with a cognitive or communicative loss should be given a thorough language assessment prior to the administration of the SAFE. Before beginning the assessment, the examiner should make sure that the patient is seated with hips flexed at a 90 degree angle. The examiner should also administer the evaluation in its entirety, and complete the scoring following the assessment.

Scoring the SAFE requires the examiner to rate various swallowing behaviors during the physical examination of the oropharyngeal mechanism (Stage 1: Subscale 1), the oral phase swallowing evaluation (Stage 2: Subscale 2), and the pharyngeal phase swallowing evaluation (Stage 2: Subscale 3) by indicating whether the swallowing behavior is severely impaired (score 0), moderately impaired (score 1), mildly impaired (score 2), or is within functional limits (score 3). Operational definitions of severity scores for the subscales and an explanation of the marks used to record diagnostic observations are provided. Using the severity scores to rate the swallowing behaviors requires the use of clinical judgment regarding the effectiveness and efficiency of those behaviors. When the examiner believes that a patient exhibits a mild to moderate level of impairment during any stage of the evaluation, the authors recommend that the impairment should be scored as moderate. Diagnostic observations for oropharyngeal structure and sensation, various liquid and solid viscosities and food textures, as well as general information related to swallowing ability should be recorded in Stage 3.

Several scores are provided, including raw scores, stanines, percentile ranks, and severity rankings. Raw scores are the total points accumulated by a patient on a subtest. Raw scores can be converted to stanines and percentile ranks using the table provided in the examiner's manual. Severity levels indicate the degree of the problem for the swallowing function measured by each subscale.

A treatment plan suited to the patient's particular situation results from an analysis of the results of the SAFE along with a careful review of the patient's medical chart and history. According to the authors, "treatment plans established for the management of dysphagia should also include patient or caregiver education about the nature of the disorder and necessary precautions" (examiner's manual, p. 21). The accompanying SAFE treatment and resource manual provides material designed to help the therapist develop a coordinated, multidisciplinary dysphagia program or to enhance a current dysphagia program. Using the manual will allow swallowing therapists to focus on patient care and staff training rather than use valuable personal and professional time searching for and developing resources for their dysphagia programs.

Test developers must give careful attention to questions about ethnic, racial, gender, and regional bias. There is no discussion about whether or not the authors took steps during test development, validation, and norming to minimize the influence of ethnolinguistic factors on individual scores. Neither race nor ethnicity is included in the sample demographics. The authors state that "the SAFE can be administered to non-English speaking patients without confounding the assessment results" (examiner's manual, p. 7); however, no supporting evidence is provided.

COMMENTARY. After reviewing the SAFE, the reviewer has several concerns. First, the standardization sample is not described in detail. As the sample was composed of patients with some degree of dysphagia and other medical conditions (examiner's manual, p. 23), the diagnosis of these patients could be reported and the severity of their medical conditions stated.

Second, there is no mention of how the therapists who participated in gathering the standardization data were trained to administer the SAFE to ensure standardized procedures. One factor that might influence the administration of the SAFE is the experience of the therapists. This is an important consideration because the authors state that "scoring the responses to the SAFE items calls for the use of clinical judgment as to the effectiveness and efficacy of the patient's swallowing behaviors" (examiner's manual, p. 7). Even though therapists may have the necessary proficiencies, knowledge, and skills as identified by the American Speech-Language-Hearing Association's Task Force on Dysphagia as required by the authors of the SAFE, clinical judgment is developed from experience over time in providing evidence-based dysphagia evaluation and treatment as well as continuing education.

Third, minimal reliability and validity information is provided. Additionally, the use of stanines as indicators of which adults require additional assessment and treatment needs to be explained with more detail and supporting evidence.

SUMMARY. Evaluation and treatment of dysphagia is a growing area of concern for many health care professionals. If a patient has apparent oropharyngeal dysphagia, "best practices" call for therapists to determine the main swallow dysfunction, including: (a) an inability or delay in initiating the pharyngeal swallow, (b) aspiration, (c) nasopharyngeal regurgitation, or (d) residue within the pharynx after swallowing. The subscales of the SAFE, representative of dysphagia best practices, are designed to determine the main swallow dysfunction as one part of a comprehensive assessment battery. Some weaknesses exist in terms of the standardization sample; reporting of training of therapists to ensure standardized procedures in administering, scoring, and interpreting results; reporting of reliability and validity data; and in the provision of evidence to support the use of stanines as indicators of which adults require additional assessment and treatment. The potential of the SAFE appears to lie in its use to meet its authors' goal to provide consistency of evaluation and to improve quality of care.

[241]

Taylor-Johnson Temperament Analysis® [2002 Edition].

Purpose: Designed to "measure a number of ... personality variables or attitudes and behavioral tendencies which influence personal, social, marital, parental, family, scholastic, and vocational adjustment."

Population: Ages 11 and up.

Publication Dates: 1941–2002.

Acronym: T-JTA®.

Scores, 11: Nervous vs. Composed, Depressive vs. Light-Hearted, Active-Social vs. Quiet, Expressive-Responsive vs. Inhibited, Sympathetic vs. Indifferent, Subjective vs. Objective, Dominant vs. Submissive, Hostile vs. Tolerant, Self-Disciplined vs. Impulsive, Attitude, Total.

Administration: Individual or group.

Forms, 4: Regular Edition (criss-cross and self-report forms); Form "S" for Adolescents (criss-cross and self-report).

Price Data, 2005: $259 per complete kit (for handscoring and computer software scoring); $249 per complete kit (for scoring using computer software); $129 per computer scoring package (for use with mail-in scoring service); $129 per test manual; $47.50 per handbook.

Foreign Language Edition: Available in Spanish, German, French, Portuguese, Japanese, Chinese, Korean, and Danish; norms for Spanish and German editions only.

Time: Untimed.

Comments: Can be used as a self-report questionnaire or as a tool for obtaining perceptions of another person (criss-cross form); Form S can be used with adolescents or with adults with poor reading skills; 2002 Edition based upon new 2002 norms.

Authors: Original edition by Roswell H. Johnson, revision by Robert M. Taylor, Lucile P. Morrison (manual), W. Lee Morrison (statistical consultant), and Richard C. Romoser (statistical consultant).

Publisher: Psychological Publications, Inc.

Cross References: For reviews by Michael J. Sporakowski and Stephen E. Trotter of the 1996 Edition, see 14:381; for reviews by Jeffrey A. Jenkins and Barbara J. Kaplan of an earlier edition, see 13:315; see also T4:2690 (3 references); for reviews by Cathy W. Hall and Paul McReynolds, see 10:357; see also T3:2396 (1 reference) and T2:840 (3 references); for a review by Robert F. Stahmann, see 8:692 (18 references); for a review by Donald L. Mosher of an earlier edition, see 7:572 (1 reference); see also P:264 (3 references) and 6:130 (10 references); for a review by Albert Ellis of the original edition, see 4:62 (6 references); for a review by H. Meltzer of the original edition, see 3:57.

Review of the Taylor-Johnson Temperament Analysis® [2002 Edition] by STEPHEN N. AXFORD, Assistant Director of Special Services and Licensed Psychologist, Falcon School District 49, Colorado Springs, CO:

DESCRIPTION AND DEVELOPMENT. The Taylor-Johnson Temperament Analysis® (T-JTA) is a 180-item, dichotomously rated (yes/no, and undecided), self-report questionnaire designed as a tool for family and career counseling, normed on adolescents and adults. It is the latest version of the Johnson Temperament Analysis (JTA) developed by Roswell H. Johnson in 1941 and published in 1966. The current version is substantially modified from the original and offers not only handscoring but also personal computer scoring and computerized scoring via mail through Psychological Publications. Brief and more comprehensive Interpretive Reports are available providing normative data and analysis.

Similar to The New York Longitudinal Scales Adult Temperament Questionnaire (see 166), the T-JTA is designed to measure nine temperament dimensions considered to be common personality traits or behavioral tendencies impacting interpersonal, scholastic, and career adjustment. It is intended to be used by "counselors" to measure client self-and interpersonal perception, with particular application to "early identification of emotionally troubled individuals" (manual, p. 1) as a preventative measure in avoiding the development of "acute" disturbance and interpersonal conflict. The test developers caution that although the T-JTA provides indicators of psychopathology, it "is designed for use in the more ordinary counseling situation, such as individual, pre-marital, marital, and family counseling, and in student and vocational counseling and guidance" (manual, p. 1). As noted by the authors, T-JTA symptomatic indicators of psychopathology may require further clinical evaluation, as with psychiatric referral. Thus, it is clear that the T-JTA is intended for counseling as opposed to clinical use (i.e., DSM-IV diagnosis), focusing on enhancing normal development and resolving life's usual challenges as opposed to identifying and treating serious psychopathology.

The nine temperament scales representing the T-JTA include: Nervous/Composed, Depressive/Light-Hearted, Active-Social/Quiet, Expressive-Responsive/Inhibited, Sympathetic/Indifferent, Subjective/Objective, Dominant/Submissive, Hostile/Tolerant, and Self-Disciplined/Impulsive. Three versions of the T-JTA questionnaire measuring the nine temperament traits are available: Regular Edition, Regular Non-Criss-Cross Edition, and Secondary (Form-S) Edition. Items for each T-JTA booklet edition are essentially the same, differing only with respect to whether or not a blank space is provided for name insertion, allowing the respondent to apply the question to himself/herself or someone else (fiancée, family member, etc.) in "Criss-Cross" fashion. The "Criss-Cross" feature provides a measure of interpersonal perception, considered to be useful in premarital, marital, and family counseling. In general, the test booklets provide clear directions with well-constructed items. Although easy-to-use handscoring answering sheets are provided with client-friendly profile sheets for graphing results (sten profile), computer answer sheets are available if the Psychological Publications scoring service is elected.

The T-JTA manual is a comprehensive and thoughtfully constructed publication. It provides detailed information on test development, descriptions of materials, scoring and interpretation, appropriate application, and validation. The manual should serve as an excellent resource to the counselor employing the T-JTA.

TECHNICAL. Two-week interval (N = 81) and 1- to 3-week interval (N = 50) reliability estimates for the nine T-JTA temperament scales were calculated based on two separate studies. Correlation coefficients ranged from .71 to .87 (2-week interval) and from .62 to .88 (1- to 3-week interval, reliability of sten scores). Internal consistency was estimated by split-half (N = 1,138) and analysis of variance (N = 200) techniques. Regarding split-half reliability, Spearman-Brown corrected correlations ranged from .71 to .86. Gutman's estimated minimums ranged from .71 to .86. Split-half reliability coefficients by gender ranged from .71 to .90 for males (N = 477) and from .65 to .87 for females (N = 661). ANOVA coefficients (N = 200) ranged from .76 to .90. ANOVA coefficients by gender ranged from .79 to .91 for men (N = 100) and from .71 to .89 for women (N = 100). Construct validity was assessed by examining patterns of correlation between the T-JTA and the 16PF (N = 129) and the MMPI (N = 200). In general, the T-JTA was observed to concur as predicted with the 16PF and MMPI. Intercorrelations of the T-JTA scales (N = 922) yielded further evidence of construct validity, with predicted patterns observed.

To its merit, the T-JTA provides a validity scale, the T-JTA Attitude Scale, addressing response bias, specifically tendencies (conscious or unconscious) to self-deprecate or to conceal weaknesses. The K Scale from the MMPI was selected as the criterion. (A high K score indicates response bias resulting in false "good" scores or perceived positive attributes; a low K score indicates excessive false "bad" scores exaggerating perceived defects.) The T-JTA and MMPI were administered to 657 people (289 men, 368 women; 15–81 years of age). Observed K Scores were correlated with the 180 T-JTA questions, yielding 18 T-JTA items with strong predictability of response bias. Internal consistency of the T-JTA Attitude scale was then assessed through an ANOVA study involving 1,215 people (585 men, 630 females), yielding a coefficient of .83. For these same individuals, the Attitude scale scores correlated .72 with K scores (the MMPI was also administered).

The T-JTA would benefit from additional validation. However, the available data support its technical adequacy, particularly within the parameters of its intended use as a counseling and guidance tool as opposed to a high stakes clinical measure.

COMMENTARY. With respect to application, an underlying assumption of the T-JTA, as well as with much of counseling theory, is that self-awareness will lead to enhanced development. Of course, this is an empirical question requiring ongoing investigation. In other words, do the counselor's interventions (i.e., guidance) based on T-JTA data really result in better interpersonal relations, more functional families, and more satisfying work situations for clients? The T-JTA appears to be technically sound. However, the fundamental question of its utility will require further research.

SUMMARY. The test developers, to their credit, have produced a measurement of the nine temperament traits that is user friendly not only to the client but also the counselor. The surveys and scoring materials are professional in appearance and easy to use. Computerized scoring options are an added technological plus for the T-JTA. The manual is very well organized, offering ample information about the instrument's history and development, and reviewing available validation studies. The manual also sufficiently addresses limitations for interpretation and use of the T-JTA. All in all, although further validation is recommended, the T-JTA offers a useful tool to counselors in their advisement of clients related to gaining insight into client temperaments as this may relate to interpersonal functioning in family and work systems.

REVIEWER'S REFERENCES

Chess, S., & Thomas, A. (1995–98). *The New York Longitudinal Scales Adult Temperament Questionnaire.* Scottsdale, AZ: Behavioral-Developmental Initiatives.
Dahlstrom, W. G., & Walsh, G. S. (1960). *An MMPI handbook: A guide to use in clinical practice and research.* Minneapolis: The University of Minnesota.

Review of the Taylor-Johnson Temperament Analysis® [2002 Edition] by GREGORY J. BOYLE, Professor of Psychology, Bond University, Gold Coast, Queensland, Australia:

DESCRIPTION AND DEVELOPMENT. The Taylor-Johnson Temperament Analysis® (T-JTA) is a 180-item questionnaire that has a long history with several revisions going back as early as 1941. The most recent revision was undertaken in 2002. The T-JTA is purported to measure a variety of temperament and behavioral variables relating to personal, interpersonal, and scholastic/career factors and outcomes that are useful, for example, in counseling and educational arenas. Although not intended as a clinical diagnostic tool, the T-JTA instrument nonetheless provides quantitative measures of nine bipolar temperament traits labelled respectively: Nervous vs. Composed, Depressive vs. Light-Hearted, Active-Social vs. Quiet, Expressive-Responsive vs. Inhibited, Sympathetic vs. Indifferent, Subjective vs. Objective, Dominant vs. Submissive, Hostile vs. Tolerant, and Self-Disciplined vs. Impulsive.

Supplemental scales are labelled: Overall Adjustment, Emotional Stability, Self-Esteem, Outgoing/Gregarious, Interpersonal Effectiveness, Alienating, Industrious/Persevering, Persuasive/Influential, and Consistency. T-JTA Trait patterns include Anxiety, Withdrawal, Hostile-Dominant, Dependent-Hostile, Emotionally Blocked—Inhibited, Emotionally Repressed, and Socially Effective Pattern. In addition there is an Attitude Scale, purported to measure test-taking bias derived from the K-scale of the MMPI, that is intended to measure defensiveness against psychological weakness on the one hand, versus self-deprecation at the other extreme of the bipolar continuum. Data included in the test manual indicate that the T-JTA Attitude Scale is very highly correlated with the K Scale, although doubts have been cast on the adequacy of the K Scale itself (cf. Helmes & Reddon, 1993).

The T-JTA with its unique "criss-cross" method of scoring, and its use of profiling of the temperament variables, is rather innovative in its approach to psychological assessment and counseling. For example, the test manual provides sample premarital and marital criss-cross profiles that illustrate the utility of this feature of the T-JTA in providing counseling advice to couples.

TECHNICAL. The test manual includes a chapter on the psychometric properties of the T-JTA. For example, in regard to reliability, 2-week test-retest stability coefficients are reported as ranging from .71 to .87 for the nine trait scales. Likewise, 1- to 3-week stability coefficients for the raw scores range from .74 to .90, and for the corresponding sten scores from .62 to .88. Immediate test-retest (dependability) coefficients are not reported, and likewise, longer term stability coefficients over 6 to 12 months are not reported,

so the actual reliability of the T-JTA over longer time intervals remains somewhat uncertain.

Split-half coefficients (ranging from .71 to .90 for males; from .65 to .87 for females; and from .71 to .86 for the combined groups) are reported as though they reflect internal reliability ("internal consistency") of the separate scales. However, no information is provided on the homogeneity of the items, so it is not clear whether the T-JTA scales have redundant items (due to item overlap) and are therefore somewhat narrow measures of the particular constructs (cf. Boyle, 1991).

The test manual provides concurrent and discriminant validity data on the T-JTA as follows: Correlations between the nine T-JTA scales and the 16PF scales range from -.48 to .70 showing that the T-JTA scales correspond as expected with the 16PF scales. The manual also reports the results of a second-order "Little Jiffy" factor analysis (principal components plus varimax rotation) of the scale intercorrelations of the T-JTA and 16PF. It is difficult to draw definitive conclusions from these results, because the sample size was only 129 undergraduates, and because the "Little Jiffy" method has been shown to be unreliable and provides only crude approximations to simple structure solutions (cf. Boyle, Stankov, & Cattell, 1995; Gorsuch, 1983). Intercorrelations between the T-JTA and the MMPI range from -.56 to .66 showing that the T-JTA scales correspond as expected with the MMPI scales. Likewise, the results of a crude second-order "Little Jiffy" factor analysis of the combined T-JTA/MMPI scale intercorrelations ($N = 200$) are reported. Using the standardization sample of 922 members of the general adult population, intercorrelations of the T-JTA scales range from -.50 to .73 showing that there is considerable overlap between the T-JTA scales in the variance measured.

COMMENTARY. The use of self-report methodology in the Secondary Edition question booklet (and ratings of others in the Regular Edition question booklet and also in the Regular Edition Non-Criss-Cross question booklet is a substantial weakness, not only because of response sets and motivational distortion, but also because individuals may not be fully aware of, and/or lack insight into, their own temperament. This limitation of item transparency of self-report and observer rating instruments has been discussed elsewhere (Boyle, 1985, 1987). In view of this problem, it is especially surprising that there are no validity scales, other than the basic T-JTA Attitude Scale, to correct specifically for faking good, faking bad, and/or other types of motivational and response distortion.

SUMMARY. To their credit, Taylor and Morrison (the authors of the 2002 T-JTA manual) have produced a creative and novel approach to the assessment of temperament variables that can be administered, scored, and interpreted in a relatively cost-effective manner. Also on the positive side, the T-JTA includes relevant items, employs a straightforward trichotomous response scale, and avoids colloquial or slang expressions. The T-JTA has been used extensively in a wide range of studies, and there are numerous published reports suggesting its popularity. The T-JTA appears to make a useful contribution to the measurement of individual differences in temperament. Although the test manual is relatively informative, much further detail is needed to be included particularly regarding psychometric issues such as factor analytic evidence because the structural dimensionality of the T-JTA remains uncertain. Clearly, further research is needed to refine the factor structure and psychometric properties of the T-JTA instrument.

REVIEWER'S REFERENCES

Boyle, G. J. (1985). Self-report measures of depression: Some psychometric considerations. *British Journal of Clinical Psychology, 24*, 45–59.

Boyle, G. J. (1987). Review of the (1985) "Standards for educational and psychological testing: AREA, APA and NCME." *Australian Journal of Psychology, 39*, 235–237.

Boyle, G. J. (1991). Does item homogeneity indicate internal consistency or item redundancy in psychometric scales? *Personality and Individual Differences, 12*, 291—294.

Boyle, G. J., Stankov, L., & Cattell, R. B. (1995). Measurement and statistical models in the study of personality and intelligence. In D. H. Saklofske & M. Zeidner (Eds.), *International handbook of personality and intelligence* (pp. 417–446). New York: Plenum.

Gorsuch, R. L. (1983). *Factor analysis* (rev. 2nd ed.). Hillsdale, NJ: Erlbaum.

Helmes, E., & Reddon, J. R. (1993). A perspective on developments in assessing psychopathology: A critical review of the MMPI and MMPI-2. *Psychological Bulletin, 113*, 453—471.

[242]

Teele Inventory for Multiple Intelligences.

Purpose: "Designed to examine the dominant intelligences of students in kindergarten through the twelfth grade."

Population: Grades K–12.

Publication Dates: 1992–1997.

Acronym: TIMI.

Scores, 7: Linguistic, Logical-Mathematical, Musical, Spatial, Bodily-Kinesthetic, Intrapersonal, Interpersonal.

Administration: Individual or group.

Price Data, 2004: $250 per complete kit including 35 pictorial inventories, teacher's manual (1997, 3 pages), 35 answer sheets, and 1 scoring transparency; $25 per single complete set; $10 per 35 scoring sheets plus transparency; $325 per test kit plus set of 25 rigid polished vinyl overhead transparencies for presentations.

Time: (30–45) minutes.

Author: Sue Teele.

Publisher: Sue Teele & Associates.

Review of the Teele Inventory for Multiple Intelligences by ALLEN K. HESS, Distinguished Research Professor of Psychology, Auburn University at Montgomery, Montgomery, AL:

DESCRIPTION. Teele constructed the Teele Inventory for Multiple Intelligences (TIMI) to help the teacher "reach all students and honor their diversity" (teacher's manual, p. 1). The TIMI is to accomplish this by "identifying their [the teacher's] student's dominant intelligences" and providing "methodologies that reach all seven intelligences" (teacher's manual, p. 1). The student (Teele claims the test's range is from preschool to college) can then have learning programs tailored for their peak intelligences (each student possessing all seven intelligences to varying degrees).

Gardner's view of multiple intelligences represents a departure from the usual g versus s (general vs. specific) theories. He addressed the "learning" style by which we garner and retrieve information about the world. In fact, for Gardner, all people have different worlds (some are linguistic, others are bodily kinesthetic, and still others are interpersonal) by which we learn. Teele constructed the TIMI to help the teacher "reach all students and honor their diversity." TIMI is to accomplish this by "identifying their student's dominant intelligences" and provide "Methodologies that reach all seven intelligences" (teacher's manual, p. 1). The student (Teele claims the test's range is from preschool to college) can then have learning programs tailored for their peak intelligences (each student possessing all seven intelligences to varying degrees).

TIMI MATERIALS. The three-page teacher's manual contains directions for administering and scoring the TIMI, as well as a brief interpretive guide of two-thirds of a page. The test booklet contains 14 pages; each containing two items. An item pairs two black-and-white drawings, each showing one or more pandas performing an activity representing one of Gardner's learning styles. For example, Item 2A shows a panda playing a guitar (Musical style) and 2B portrays two pandas kicking a soccer ball to each other (Bodily-Kinesthetic style). The student chooses which he or she prefers. Thus all seven styles are shown eight times, paired with each of the other styles, in 28 items composed of pairs of pictures. The administration and scoring are straightforward. This reviewer was provided with a letter from Dr. Teele to the Buros Institute with an accompanying study concerning the TIMI (Teele, 2004).

Standard 6.1, and the next four (6.2–6.5) as well, require test documentation, usually in the form of test manuals, technical manuals, user's guides, and supplemental materials (American Education Research Association, American Psychological Association, & National Council on Measurement in Education, 1999). Unless the unpublished study sent in a letter to the Buros Institute constitutes the latter and is sent to all test consumers, then there is simply nothing to evaluate. Without a test or technical manual, there is nothing to evaluate. Given that the test has been used for over a decade in "more than 28 countries plus throughout the United States on more than 4,000 students" (Dr. Sue Teele, January 19, 2004) the lack of a technical manual is astonishing. However, let us examine psychometric properties that were detailed in the letter's appended 1995 © unpublished report.

DEVELOPMENT. No evidence is presented that a drawing in fact taps the learning style that it is supposed to depict.

TECHNICAL.

Reliability. All parametric statistics will be compromised by the ipsative nature of the test, as described above. That is, because the scales balance each other—a student selecting Musical must necessarily reject the paired style—there is a built-in statistical dependency that would inflate parametric correlations. No mention is made on the type of correlation nor how it was computed (one must assume the score of the seven scales was used, but use of the rank would obviate the ipsative problem with correlations). The reported correlations range from 1 day to 4 weeks; one would like to see how trait-like these aptitudes, or preferences for aptitudes, are if curriculum planning depends on TIMI results, and see 3-, 6- and 12-month data. The correlations for 1 day are in the .80s but fall to about .50 in three of the seven scales at the 4-week test-retest interval. One would like to see more robust reliability data when children's learning fates are at stake.

Validity. The only reports concerning validity are two brief case studies selected from 4,000

cases. In short, there is no validity evidence presented. Teele used the Metropolitan Achievement Test in describing the two cases so she presumably had the MAT results available for statistical comparisons. Yet she reports no concurrent validity. And there is no report of any results concerning the outcomes of any students for whom the TIMI was used over the past decade. Simply put, there are no validity data.

The ipsative nature of the measure tells about the relative strengths of a preference of a style from the person's repertoire but does not tell anything about the person's strength of preference relative to anyone else's style. Also, this means two people scoring seven on the Intrapersonal style might have quite different actual strength of preferences; one person's seven may not be another's but merely indicates that Intrapersonal is strongest for both people.

Finally, there are no prescriptive curricula to which the author ties the TIMI. To be useful, the TIMI or measures of curricular aptitude or preference should lead to learning prescriptions. None are offered.

COMMENTARY. The test assesses the learner's preference, *not* the learner's aptitude. Because of the way the test is set up, it is easy for the consumer to overlook this critical point. And the difference cannot be overemphasized. One might assume that a student prefers what he or she is good at performing but preference is simply *not* performance. The test user might incorporate the student's preference into curriculum planning but needs to include a measure of learning style itself as the foundation for such planning.

CONCLUSION. The seemingly appealing TIMI suffers grave psychometric (modest reliabilities and no validity studies), formal (no test manual; no peer-reviewed publications regarding reliability or validity studies; no independent researchers' publications), and conceptual problems (assesses preference and not aptitude, as the manual claims: "This inventory will assist teachers in identifying the student's dominant intelligences," teacher's manual, p. 1). It simply fails to meet minimum psychometric, formal, or conceptual standards to warrant its use.

REVIEWER'S REFERENCES

American Educational Research Association, American Psychological Association, & National Council for Measurement in Education. (1999). *Standards for educational and psychological testing.* Washington, DC: AERA.
Teele, S. (2004). [Letter to Buros Institute accompanied by unpublished study.] Redlands, CA: Author.

Review of the Teele Inventory for Multiple Intelligences by SALLY KUHLENSCHMIDT, Professor of Psychology, Western Kentucky University, Bowling Green, KY:

DESCRIPTION. The Teele Inventory for Multiple Intelligences (TIMI) is a 28-item measure derived from Gardner's Theory of Multiple Intelligences. It takes from 30–45 minutes to complete. The stated purpose of the test is to identify the "strengths or dominant intelligences each participant possesses" (teacher's manual, p. 1). The manual does not directly indicate the appropriate age range for the scale although there is a clear implication that the test is addressing public school teachers. In materials not included with the test materials (Teele, 1995), the author indicates that it was developed for kindergarten through 12th grade but has been used in higher education institutions. After instructions are read, the examinee makes a forced choice between two pictures of panda bears engaged in various activities. In 12 items English words or numbers are included in the images that may impact cultural generality. Scoring is accomplished by marking each choice according to which of the seven "intelligences" it indicates. The four "intelligences" with the highest scores are considered to be the dominant intelligences or strengths. There are no directions concerning tie scores or what constitutes a significant difference between two scores. Interpretation suggestions consist of a definition of each of the seven "intelligences." The test can be administered to an individual (recommended for K–1) or a group and comes in a "classroom" packet of 35 stimulus booklets and 35 answer sheets along with a scoring template. Brief instructions for administration to "a handicapped individual" are included.

DEVELOPMENT. Minimal information is provided about the development of the TIMI other than a statement that it is based on Howard Gardner's Theory of Multiple Intelligences. In supplemental information provided by the author (Teele, 1995) she reports that the images were field tested at one elementary school. She says an item-by-item analysis was done but does not explain of what that analysis consisted. She says pictures were modified on the basis of this analysis.

Examination of the answer sheet reveals that items are not counterbalanced across first and second places on the test, nor across halves of the test, nor in matches. That is, Intelligence 1 is matched one time to each of the other intelligences plus an additional time to Intelligence 7 and 6. Clearly there is room for order effects on this scale. Teele provided no evidence of having evaluated the role of order in answer selection nor has she controlled for the possibility.

In addition, a number of the images display multiple panda bears in hierarchical relationships and it is unclear how this would influence a person's decision about why a bear is "like me." A bear telling a story could presumably be chosen for the Linguistic, the Intrapersonal, or the Interpersonal elements.

The scale has an underlying assumption that selecting an item as "like me" means that the respondent therefore possesses or is inclined toward that intelligence. However, the flaws of self-response are well known and require greater levels of reliability and validity evidence than have been provided.

Apart from these construction difficulties, the images, although presumably appropriate for grade school children, seem likely to be considered childish by middle school, high school, and college students and users may well have substantial cooperation problems in having older persons complete the inventory.

TECHNICAL. The manual provides no standardization information. Scores are not transformed but are simply point sums. Therefore, we do not know what a typical score is nor what score would indicate a strength or weakness relative to other children. Nor is there any discussion of gender or ethnic/culture effects.

The teacher's manual provides no information on reliability or validity. Teele (1995), in an unpublished manuscript, attempts to provide reliability and validity data but it is woefully inadequate. The author misapplies or misreports psychometric terms. For example, she says she has "proven" reliability, a misinterpretation of the basic logical positivism assumptions of science.

Teele (1995) attempts to present data on test-retest reliability (currently more commonly called stability) collected from a sample of roughly 50 students. The reported correlations for a 2-week interval for the seven intelligences fall in a range from .45 to .88, with three scales below .65. For a 4-week interval (N approximately 600) the Rs range from .48 to .66. These are not satisfactory levels of reliability, particularly given that stability usually errs toward a higher correlation. She apparently did several studies using teachers to complete the scale, a population outside of the targeted group. For example, in one study 69 teachers took the scale with a 2-month interval separating administrations. Correlations ranged from .54 to .74.

Her attempt to demonstrate validity consists of showing how the scores on standardized tests of two individuals are consistent with the scores on the TIMI. She makes reference to a comparison between an all Anglo Kentucky school first grade and a high minority California first grade. But she does not thoroughly explain the method, the rationale for the comparison, nor the statistical analysis, if any. She only lists that the same three "intelligences" were dominant in both situations. She claims she addressed content validity during development but did not explain her procedure or controls for bias.

COMMENTARY. The strengths of the TIMI include a simple manual and clear illustrations. Scoring is straightforward and the connection to the Theory of Multiple Intelligences is likely to be popular. What the TIMI lacks, however, is a research foundation that would allow one to be confident it was measuring something and that the something being measured was worthwhile. It is unclear to me how the information provided by this scale would be used to improve services, particularly because the scientific evidence for the Theory of Multiple Intelligences is poor, at best. Assuming that the Theory does have support, then the author needs to demonstrate, by correlations with relevant measures, that her subscales reflect these intelligences and no others. That is, there should be no or minimal correlations among the various "types" of intelligences. The score interpretation section presents a series of hypotheses about how students who fall in the various categories of intelligence react to certain stimuli or approach learning activities. These hypotheses need to be examined before they are presented as certain paths to instructional nirvana. The scale is also missing a discussion of how it performs with various genders and ethnic/racial groups.

SUMMARY. The Teele Inventory for Multiple Intelligences is likely to appeal to the public school teacher seeking insight into student learning behavior. The materials are attractive and easy for young children. However, the psychometric information is risky. Using it to make curricular or child placement decisions in the absence of basic test development or psychometric information is risky. Simply asking a child his or her preferences or directly observing child learning habits is preferable as there are fewer inferences.

REVIEWER'S REFERENCE

Teele, S. (1995). *Statistical analysis of the Teele Inventory of Multiple Intelligences.* Unpublished manuscript.

[243]

Telephone Interview for Cognitive Status.

Purpose: Designed to serve as a "brief test of global cognitive functioning" for administration over the telephone.

Population: Ages 60–98.

Publication Dates: 1987–2003.

Acronym: TICS.

Scores: Total score only.

Administration: Individual.

Price Data, 2005: $68 per introductory kit including manual (2003, 31 pages) and 50 record forms; $21 per manual; $52 per 50 record forms.

Time: (10) minutes.

Authors: Jason Brandt and Marshal F. Folstein.

Publisher: Psychological Assessment Resources, Inc.

Review of the Telephone Interview For Cognitive Status by RONALD J. GANELLEN, Associate Professor, Department of Psychiatry and Behavioral Sciences, Northwestern Medical School, Chicago, IL:

DESCRIPTION. Brandt and Folstein, two respected researchers whose names are associated with several widely used assessment instruments (e.g., the Hopkins Verbal Learning Test [Brandt, 1991] and the Mini-Mental Status Examination [Folstein, Folstein, & McHugh], respectively) developed the Telephone Interview for Cognitive Status (TICS) to be used as a brief screening of cognitive functioning for adults ages 60 through 98. The TICS is intended to be used in situations in which face-to-face cognitive screening is impossible or impractical, such as when an individual is unable to travel; for large-scale population screening and epidemiologic surveys; or for direct evaluation of persons who are visually impaired, whose reading or writing skills are limited, or who are illiterate. The authors acknowledge the TICS should be considered a brief screening measure of cognitive impairment, which cannot be used to diagnose specific neurological or psychiatric disorders.

The TICS was designed to be administered over the phone. The 11 items on the TICS assess orientation, the ability to count backwards from 20 to 1, immediate recall of a list of 10 words, serial sevens, the ability to name an object after hearing a description of it, repetition of a phrase and a short sentence, praxis, and simple reasoning skills. Responses are recorded on the TICS record form which provides clear scoring criteria. Item scores are summed to obtain a total score. The TICS record form indicates whether the total score should be considered to fall in the range indicating no cognitive impairment, questionable performance, mild impairment, or moderate to severe impairment.

DEVELOPMENT. Items on the TICS are familiar as they are adaptations or variations of questions and probes used frequently to assess mental abilities in clinical practice. As the TICS is intended to be a brief screening instrument, the developers attempted to assess basic domains of cognitive functioning with as few items as possible, mostly 1 item per ability. The authors do not provide any further conceptual or empirical rationale for selection of the 11 items that comprise the TICS. Because each domain of cognitive functioning is assessed by 1 or 2 items, one should not expect any of these dimensions of cognitive functioning to be evaluated thoroughly, particularly because the range of difficulty is quite limited. Furthermore, one can have little confidence that the TICS is able to reliably identify any pattern of strengths or weaknesses.

Brandt and Folstein acknowledge that as the TICS is intended to be administered over the phone, several mental abilities involving visual abilities are not assessed. These include memory for nonverbal material, perception of spatial relationships, visual-motor coordination, constructional apraxia, nonverbal reasoning, and motor speed and dexterity. Although the TICS assesses immediate recall of a list of 10 words, it does not assess delayed recall or recognition recall of this material.

Potential users of the TICS must recognize that (a) the TICS assesses only a limited set of cognitive abilities and (b) those cognitive abilities that are screened are assessed in a very cursory manner. This indicates that the TICS is likely to identify only a subset of individuals with cognitive impairment and is likely to be sensitive to those individuals with gross, significant deficits while being relatively insensitive to mild, subtle deficits.

TECHNICAL. The TICS was normed on data obtained from a sample of 6,338 women, ages 60 to 89. All participants were nurses. Some of these women completed a 2-year nursing program, others completed 3- or 4-year programs, and others obtained master's or doctorate degrees in nursing.

The composition of the sample is noteworthy in several respects. First, all participants were female. The authors suggest that the norms based on this large sample of women can be applied to men. The manual cites a study by Mangione et al. (1993), which showed that men obtained significantly higher scores on the TICS than women, but suggested that these findings may have been due to the effects of age and education. Further research is needed to substantiate the position that existing norms for the TICS can be applied to both men and women.

Second, all participants in the normative sample were high school graduates who went on to obtain additional education. Brandt and Folstein conducted a multiple regression analysis and found that within the normative sample, education was not related to the TICS total score. However, other studies cited in the manual suggest that education is significantly related to performance on the TICS, particularly for individuals with less than a high school education. This raises concerns that although the TICS is described as being useful for individuals who are illiterate or who have limited academic skills, individuals with less than 12 years of education may be misclassified by the TICS. The authors should consider adjusting TICS scores, taking into account level of education, in the future.

As expected, the test-retest reliability estimate of the TICS over a short period of time, 4–6 weeks, is high. Studies reported in the manual show the TICS Total score discriminates between nonpatient samples and samples of patients with Alzheimer's dementia or stroke. Other indications of construct validity include reports of significant correlations between the TICS Total score and scores on the Mini-Mental Status Examination. Alternatively, one might consider that high correlations between the TICS and MMSE reflect substantial overlap of items and shared method variance rather than providing evidence of construct validity.

The authors present two methods to use to evaluate the significance of TICS Total scores. In the first method, the TICS Total score is converted to a T-score based on three age-groups (e.g., 60–69, 70–79, and 80–89). The manual notes that because these T-scores were developed using a sample of women who completed at least the 12th grade, it is not advisable to convert the Total score to *T*-scores for individuals who did not graduate from high school.

The second method converts TICS Total scores into MMSE equivalent scores based on data from a sample of 100 outpatients with dementia and 440 elderly community residents with low cognitive performance. The manual notes that this method of determining equivalent MMSE and TICS scores is based on samples of individuals aged 65–98 "with less than 12 years of education" (p. 11). Thus, it appears that the second method should be used only for individuals with less than a high school education. It would have been preferable if the authors had developed one method of interpreting scores to be used with all individuals correcting for level of education rather than different methods depending on the individual's level of education.

COMMENTARY AND SUMMARY. The TICS was developed to be used as a brief screening instrument administered over the phone to detect cognitive impairment when it is impractical to administer more comprehensive instruments face-to-face. The TICS appears to have some value for this limited purpose. Potential users of this screening tool should be aware that the TICS does not provide any information at all about a number of domains of cognitive functioning, particularly nonverbal, visual-spatial, and motor abilities, and that the dimensions it does address are assessed using a small number of items with a very restricted range of difficulty. Given the way the TICS was developed, one may expect it will accurately identify individuals who require a more in-depth evaluation because they exhibit obvious deficits in cognitive functioning, but should anticipate that the TICS is likely to be relatively insensitive to mild, subtle impairment. At this point in time, there is no evidence that the TICS is useful in differential diagnosis or in identifying patterns of cognitive strengths and weaknesses.

As described above, the TICS normative sample was composed entirely of women who graduated high school and then became nurses. The application of the TICS to men and to individuals with less than a 12th grade education is questionable.

REVIEWER'S REFERENCES

Brandt, J. (1991). The Hopkins Verbal Learning Test: Development of a new memory test with six equivalent forms. *The Clinical Neuropsychologist, 5*, 125–142.
Folstein, M. F., Folstein, S. E., & McHugh, P. R. (1975). "Mini-Mental State": A practical method for grading the cognitive state of patients for the clinician. *Journal of Psychiatric Research, 12*, 189–198.

Mangione, C. M., Seddon, J. M., Cook, E. F., Krug, J. H., Jr., Sahagian, C. R., Campion, E. W., et al. (1993). Correlates of cognitive function scores in elderly outpatients. *Journal of the American Geriatrics Society, 41*, 491–497.

Review of the Telephone Interview for Cognitive Status by ROBERT M. THORNDIKE, Professor of Psychology, Western Washington University, Bellingham, WA:

DESCRIPTION. The Telephone Interview for Cognitive Status (TICS) is a very short screening test for dementia or very low cognitive functioning intended for use with English-speaking clients over 60 years of age. There are 11 questions with point values ranging from 2 to 10 points (depending on the number of responses required) that can be administered over the telephone and scored by an examiner who has a modest level of training. The single total score can range from zero to 41. Interpretation guidelines suggest that a score of 20 or below indicates modest to severe impairment, 21–25 mild impairment, 26–32 ambiguous as to whether impairment is present, 33 and above nonimpaired. The authors provide tables for converting raw scores to *T*-scores, based on the score distribution of the norm group, and to the scale of the Mini-Mental State Examination (MMSE).

The test protocol anticipates that there will be another person, called the proctor, present in the room while the test is being administered. This person is expected to answer the telephone, confirm that the person who will be responding is the named client, and ensure that a testing environment free of distractions is maintained during the interview. Because none of the items require that the examinee view any stimulus material, the TICS is also offered as an instrument that can be used with clients with visual impairments.

DEVELOPMENT. The TICS was developed in the late 1980s "to survey the basic cognitive functions that are affected by dementia and delirium: orientation, attention, language, praxis, calculation, and memory" (professional manual, p. 13) and apparently has not been revised, although it is unlikely that any of the items would become dated. The 2003 copyright date refers to the publication of the test manual and the record forms. Norms data were collected at an unspecified time (but apparently prior to 1988) on a group of 6,338 retired nurses ranging from 60 to 89 years of age, all of whom had at least a high school education plus nurses' training. An equating study with the MMSE was conducted with a group of 440 individuals in a study of Memory and Medical Care,

57% of whom were African American. Clearly, both the norm group and the equating sample were samples of convenience and no attempt was made to represent any defined population. Given the highly specialized purpose of the test, it is not clear that this lack of representativeness presents a problem.

TECHNICAL. The professional manual provided with the TICS (21 pages plus references) reports only the one normative study of retired nurses. Separate T-score conversions are given for people in their 60s, 70s, and 80s because age was found to affect scores, but education was not found to significantly affect scores. The lack of a relationship with education may have been due to restriction of range. Also, the fact that the norm sample was 100% female may limit generalizability of the interpretive categories. These issues are not addressed in the manual.

Reliability of the TICS appears to be adequate for the rough screening for which the test is offered. A Brown-Spearman-corrected split-half reliability based on the combined norm sample and Memory sample is reported to be .75, yielding a standard error of measurement in the T-score metric of 5.0. Two test-retest coefficients, .97 for 34 Alzheimer's disease (AD) patients over 6 weeks and .90 for 36 stroke patients over 4 weeks, show scores to have moderate stability.

A subgroup of the norming sample was used to assess validity for detecting Alzheimer's disease. Mean scores for 100 AD patients was 13.2, whereas the mean score for 33 spouses of the patients was 35.8. Correlation with the MMSE in the AD group was .94. In a sample of 36 stroke patients the TICS correlated .86 with the MMSE and the clinical group scored significantly lower that an age- and education-matched subsample of the norm group. Comparisons of mean scores for various clinical groups with different diagnoses are also offered as evidence of validity. A correlation of -.40 between the TICS and a measure of functional impairment in a sample of 440 provides further evidence of the validity of the TICS as a measure of cognitive impairment.

COMMENTARY. The TICS strikes me as an adequate instrument for coarse screening for cognitive impairment, but it is not clear what the likely applications would be. With a standard error of measurement of 5 T-score points, it lacks sufficient precision for diagnosis and would pick up only relatively gross changes in cognitive status.

There is a certain convenience to being able to administer an evaluation over the telephone, but I wonder how often this would be done in practice. All of the applications that the authors cite seem to be for research purposes.

The TICS has been translated into other languages such as Spanish and Italian. The authors rightly warn that these versions should not be assumed to be equivalent to the English (actually, American) version. For example, knowing the current president and vice president of the United States might be much more difficult in Europe.

The authors mention in several places that the test does not suffer from a ceiling effect, and this may be true for a population in which there is concern about decline. However, in a general population of elderly the only item that looks like it might differentiate at all in the upper half of the distribution is the requirement to recall 10 unrelated words. That is, if you restrict use of the test to people with impairments, there may be no ceiling effect, but this seems to presuppose selection of a lower functioning group.

SUMMARY. The TICS appears to be an adequate instrument for the purpose for which it is offered, as a coarse screen for suspected mental impairment in the elderly. Whether there would be many practitioners who would use it as a telephone interview may be questionable.

[244]

Temperament and Atypical Behavior Scale.

Purpose: Designed to measure temperament and dysfunctional behavior.

Population: 11–71 months.

Publication Date: 1999.

Acronym: TABS.

Scores, 5: Detached, Hyper-Sensitive/Active, Undereactive, Dysregulated, Temperament and Regulatory Index.

Administration: Individual.

Price Data, 2003: $85 per complete set including manual (122 pages), screener with 50 forms, and 30 assessment tools; $25 per 50 screener forms; $30 per 30 assessment tool forms; $40 per manual.

Time: (5) minutes for screener; (15) minutes for assessment tool.

Comments: Ratings by parents, surrogates, or other professionals.

Authors: John T. Neisworth, Stephen J. Bagnato, John Salvia, and Frances M. Hunt.

Publisher: Brookes Publishing Co., Inc.

Review of the Temperament and Atypical Behavior Scale by HAROLD R. KELLER, Professor and Chair, Department of Psychological and Social Foundations, University of South Florida, Tampa, FL:

DESCRIPTION. The Temperament and Atypical Behavior Scale (TABS) consists of a 15-item Screener and a 55-item Assessment Tool, designed to provide early childhood indices of developmental dysfunction. Specifically, the TABS is intended to identify children who are developing atypically or are at-risk for atypical development. Authors suggest the measure can be used for screening, determining eligibility for special programs, planning educational and intervention programs, monitoring program effectiveness, and conducting research. The norm-referenced measure is individually administered with caregivers of (or professionals who have interacted with) infants and young children 11–71 months of age. Respondents are to mark a "Yes" box if the listed problematic behavior or characteristic is currently a problem, and "No" if it is not a problem. For each item checked "yes," respondents are to mark "Need Help" whenever they have a special concern or want assistance for that problem. Norms are provided for a Temperament & Regulatory Index (TRI) standard score (mean 100, *SD* 15), and four factor *T*-scores (Detached, Hyper-Sensitive/Active, Underreactive, Dysregulated, with mean 50, *SD* 10) and percentile ranks. Examples of items from each factor include: "seems to look through or past people," "flaps hands over and over" (Detached); "upset by every little thing," "has wild temper tantrums" (Hyper-Sensitive/Active); "doesn't pay attention to sights and sounds," "shows no surprise to new events" (Underreactive); "can't comfort self when upset," "often cries too long" (Dysregulated).

DEVELOPMENT. Items were developed through research with earlier versions that drew items from literature reviews, clinical judgments, and retrospective ratings of parents of children with and without disabilities. An original 154-item pool was subjected to field tests with 949 children. Composite scores were created for sets of items believed to represent totals and four factors underlying the TABS. A series of point-biserial correlation coefficients were calculated between each of the 154 items and the composite scores, yielding 65 items with a point-biserial coefficient equal to or greater than .375 with at least one of the composites. Those items were retained for subsequent factor analyses.

A principal components factor analysis with varimax rotation of the 65 items resulted in a four-factor solution, and dropping 3 items with insufficient loading on any factor. The remaining 62 items were examined as a function of age, sex, and severity of disability of the 833 children in the norm sample. Most items showed random fluctuation for age and sex, with substantial increases across disability risk levels. Seven items not showing that pattern were dropped, leaving the final item pool of 55 items. Factor analyses were again conducted, yielding a four-factor solution. TABS Screener items were selected on the basis of three criteria: high correlation with the TRI, correlation with the Screener raw score, and large differences between children with and without disabilities.

TECHNICAL. A normative sample of 621 children without disabilities between 11 and 71 months of age was selected from agencies across the United States and Canada, to provide estimates of prevalence of the behaviors. A sample of 212 children with disabilities from the same agencies provided validation data for the TABS. The behaviors sampled by the TABS are associated with syndromes or neurologically based disorders believed to be aberrant across social class, geographic area, and cultural group, so representativeness of the sample was less of a concern. About half (52%) of the sample without disabilities were 2 years old or younger. Child's sex was omitted in about 60% of the cases. When known, sex of the children was distributed evenly (53% boys, 47% girls). There were no sex differences, and analyses of age revealed no systematic and orderly differences among ages. Therefore, no separate sex or age norms were created. The sample of children with disabilities had a 2 to 1 ratio of boys to girls, with child's sex unavailable in 15% of the cases. About 55% of the sample were 3 years old or younger. A wide range of severe disabilities was included in the sample, with children with mild speech, language, or articulation problems excluded from the sample with disabilities. No systematic age differences occurred for any of the TABS scores. The total TRI and each subtest (factor score) means for the children with disabilities were all significantly higher than the means for children without disabilities.

Internal consistency estimates, via split-half methods, yielded coefficients ranging from .81 to .95 with the disabled sample, .66 to .84 for the nondisabled sample, and .79 to .95 for the pooled sample. The highest coefficients were for the TRI score, with the factors having the fewest items yielding the lowest coefficients. The lower reliabilities for the nondisabled sample are due to the minimal variability among that sample. The TRI, Detached, and Hyper-Sensitive/Active coefficients are of sufficient magnitude for individual decision making, whereas those for Underreactive and Dysregulated are too low and useful only for screening and research purposes. Stability coefficients (over a 2–3-week interval) were of similar magnitude. Internal consistency for the Screener was .83, adequate for screening purposes.

Standard error of measurement data are provided, which are comparable to similar measures. The authors also provide significance data on subtest differences. They provide appropriate cautions against their use, and emphasize significant subtest differences do not mean that the differences are rare or meaningful differences. Because only two of the factor scores are of sufficient reliability for individual decision making, one questions the advisability of providing the data and enabling misuse of the data.

Content validity for the items and factors is theoretically meaningful. Scores were consistent with expectations (i.e., highly skewed with most being either 0 or 1 problematic behaviors, no relationship with age, no relationship with sex for children without disabilities, males more problematic than females among children with disabilities, and generalization of aberrant behaviors across contexts both within and across raters), adding to construct validity. The TABS factor structure overlaps with the Diagnostic Classification 0-3 (Zero to Three: National Center for Infants, Toddlers, and Families, 1994). There are no other measures designed to address these behaviors with this age group, so concurrent validity with other independent measures is not available. Score distributions for the samples of children with and without disabilities enabled authors to establish categories for the TRI and Screener (not at-risk, at-risk, and temperament and regulatory disorders/potentially having disorders). The Screener resulted in 83.1% accurate classification on the TRI, with 2.4% false negatives and 14.5% false positives.

COMMENTARY. The TABS represents a well-developed measure for an area and age group

(i.e., extremes of temperament and self-regulation in infants and young children) with a dearth of research and available measures. The authors provided an excellent set of guidelines for intervention within an ecological approach, one that is respectful of the role of parents and caregivers. They also provide a set of research-based specific interventions linked to behaviors on the TABS. There is a need for treatment-linked validity research, conducted within the context of varying ecological supports for the interventions (Barnett, Lentz, & Macmann, 2000). The severity of the behaviors sampled is such that demographic variables in the normative samples are less pertinent than for other measures. At the same time, it would be helpful to have a more comprehensive description of the characteristics of the samples of children with and without disabilities.

SUMMARY. The TABS appears to be a psychometrically sound measure of aberrant behaviors in infants and young children. The overall TRI score, and the Detached and Hyper-Sensitive/Active factor scores have sufficient support for individual decision making, whereas the Screener and other TABS factor scores appear adequate for screening and research purposes. The guidelines for intervention and suggested research-based specific interventions linked to problem behaviors are well worth the read, and subsequent treatment-linked validity research will likely enhance the value of this measure.

REVIEWER'S REFERENCES

Barnett, D. W., Lentz, F. E., & Macmann, G. (2000). Psychometric qualities of professional practice. In E. S. Shapiro & T. R. Kratochwill (Eds.), *Behavioral assessment in schools: Theory, research, and clinical foundations* (2nd ed., pp. 355-386). New York: Guilford Press.
Zero to Three: National Center for Infants, Toddlers, and Families. (1994). *Diagnostic classification: 0-3.* Washington, DC: Author.

Review of the Temperament and Atypical Behavior Scale by LORAINE J. SPENCINER, Professor of Special Education, University of Maine at Farmington, Farmington, ME:

DESCRIPTION. The Temperament and Atypical Behavior Scale (TABS) is a norm-referenced, individually administered checklist for assessing atypical behavior of young children between the ages of 11 and 71 months of age. The TABS consists of three components: the TABS Screener, the TABS Assessment Tool, and the TABS Manual. Both the Screener and the Assessment Tool may be completed by the parent (or by a professional who is familiar with the child's daily behavior).

The TABS Screener is a 15-item checklist that describes behaviors most commonly associated with temperament and self-regulatory problems in young children. The procedure for using the Screener begins with the examiner discussing the checklist with the parent or professional. The TABS Manual suggests that the examiner explain that although many screens identify what the child can do, this checklist is designed to identify areas of difficulty. Each test item describes a specific type of problem behavior that might be observed in young children. The examiner encourages the parent to consider the degree that the child's behavior presents a problem currently, particularly regarding intensity or duration. The parent then indicates the problem behavior(s) by checking each item as yes/no. The Screener takes about 5 minutes to complete. The examiner totals the screening items to obtain a raw score and refers children with low raw scores for additional assessment with the TABS Assessment Tool.

The TABS Assessment Tool consists of 55 specific behaviors, divided into four subtest areas: Detached, Hyper-Sensitive/Active, Underreactive, and Dysregulated. According to the manual, the instrument may be used alone or as part of a comprehensive assessment battery. The examiner uses a similar procedure described above to introduce the checklist to the parent and, like the Screener, each item is scored yes/no. When items are scored yes, the parent may further indicate if the parent would like help with the problem behavior. The manual also includes suggestions for specific interventions for targeted behaviors, which could be useful at a later date as team members design the child's Individualized Family Service Plan (IFSP) or Individualized Education Program (IEP). The Assessment Tool usually takes less than 15 minutes to complete.

The TABS Assessment Tool yields percentile ranks and standard scores (mean = 100; standard deviation = 15) for each of the four subtests as well as a total score, or Temperament & Regulatory Index (TRI). The authors recommend that the examiner use only the TRI score in reporting and interpreting the assessment results because "the TRI is sufficiently reliable and stable to be used in making a variety of important decisions" (manual, p. 23). Whereas, "we caution clinicians that subtest scores (as well as differences between subtests) are less reliable than the full TRI" (manual, p. 24).

DEVELOPMENT. The authors of the TABS spent over 10 years of research focusing on typical and atypical developmental patterns of early self-regulatory behaviors and behavioral styles or temperament in young children. The manual provides an in-depth discussion of these constructs and interesting summaries of the early research of well-known works such as those by Thomas and Chess, Kopp, and DeGangi. The manual also includes a brief discussion of the classic diagnostic framework, *The Diagnostic Classification: 0-3*, published in 1994 by the national organization Zero to Three.

TECHNICAL. The normative sample consisted of 621 children between the ages of 11 and 71 months of age, with a greater number of children 2 years old or younger (52% of the sample). Information concerning gender of the children was omitted in about 60% of the sample; the remaining 40% was distributed about evenly between boys and girls. Additional information about the sample was not collected because the authors believe that the atypical behaviors being assessed by the TABS are atypical in any social class, geographic area, and cultural group (manual, p. 40). That said, the manual does include the names of the agencies and sites in 33 states and 3 Canadian provinces that participated in the sampling procedure.

According to the manual, internal consistency was measured by correlating equivalent halves of each of the subtests and the total test. Total test reliability ranged from .84 (for children not at risk) to .95 for children with disabilities and the pooled samples. Scores for the Detached and Hyper-Sensitive/Active subtests were higher (.91 and .90, respectively, for the pooled sample) than reliabilities for the Underreactive and Dysregulated subtests (.86 and .79, respectively, for the pooled sample).

The manual reports a small study (157 children) that examined the stability of TABS scores over time (2–3 weeks between test/retest) for children not at risk, for children with disabilities, and for the pooled sample. For all groups, the coefficients fr TRI and the Hyper-Sensitive/Active subtest exceeded .90. Other subtest scores ranged from .73–.80 (children not at risk); .78–.91 (children with disabilities); and .81–.92 (pooled sample). The authors state, "We do not recommend using TABS subtest profiles for more precise diagnoses, because only some of the subtests have sufficient reliability for this purpose" (manual, p. 55).

A validity study of the TABS Screener to identify only those children in need of further assessment was conducted using a sample of 833 children. The Screener correctly identified 83% of the children. Of the children incorrectly identified, 2.4% of the children who actually needed further assessment were not identified (false negatives) and 14.5% of the children were identified as needing further assessment, actually did not need it (false positives) (manual, p. 61).

COMMENTARY. Based on a conceptual framework appropriate for understanding behavior in young children, The Temperament and Atypical Behavior Scale (TABS) provides both a Screener and a more extensive Assessment Tool for identifying difficulties in dysfunctional behavior. The inclusion of case studies, a detailed discussion of test score interpretation, and the constructs that the test intends to measure provide evidence of the validity of the TABS. According to the *Standards for Educational and Psychological Testing* (American Educational Research Association, American Psychological Association, & National Council on Measurement in Education, 1999), "The process of validation involves accumulating evidence to provide a sound scientific basis for the proposed score interpretations. It is the interpretations of test scores required by proposed uses that are evaluated, not the test itself" (p. 9).

Both instruments are designed to be completed by parents and support a family-centered philosophy, one of the cornerstones in delivering services to young children with special needs. The TABS may be completed by the parent alone or together with the examiner who may read the test item, explain, or translate the item. This flexibility in administration would prove helpful to professionals in many ways (e.g., when working with families who are newcomers to this country or when a parent has difficulty articulating concerns about the child's behavior).

Because the TABS is designed for children of 11–71 months, many individual test items that would not be considered a problem for younger children could be considered a problem for older children. Thus, the examiner must have a solid knowledge of typical child development when working with a parent to complete the items and when interpreting the results. Both the Screener and Assessment Tool are easy to learn how to use for most individuals with at least a bachelor's degree and training in early intervention/early childhood special education and assessment. How-

ever, examiners and clinicians need to be carefully trained in interpreting the results of the TABS, as in any norm-referenced instrument used in identifying children with disabilities. Unfortunately, the manual does not state the qualifications for examiners using and interpreting the TABS. This information should be included in all standardized instruments to ensure that qualified professionals are making appropriate decisions regarding assessment information.

SUMMARY. The Temperament and Atypical Behavior Scale (TABS) is a norm-referenced, individually administered checklist for assessing atypical behavior of young children between the ages of 11 and 71 months of age. The TABS consists of three components: the TABS Screener, the TABS Assessment Tool, and the TABS manual. Both the Screener and the Assessment Tool may be completed by the parent (or by a professional who is familiar with the child's daily behavior). The manual is well-written and provides adequate information about the test development as well as evidence that the TABS is technically sound. The design of the TABS makes the instrument easy to use. The involvement of the parent in completing the instrument represents best practice in the fields of early intervention and early childhood special education. This instrument should be a valuable tool when assessing concerns regarding a young child's temperament or atypical behavior.

REVIEWER'S REFERENCE

American Educational Research Association, American Psychological Association, & National Council on Measurement in Education. (1999). *Standards for educational and psychological testing.* Washington, DC: American Educational Research Association.

[245]

TerraNova, The Second Edition.

Purpose: "A comprehensive, modular series offering multiple measures of both English- and Spanish-language student achievement."

Population: Grades K-12.

Publication Dates: 1997-2002.

Administration: Group.

Levels, 12: 10 (Kindergarten), 11 (Grade 1), 12 (Grade 2), 13 (Grade 3), 14 (Grade 4), 15 (Grade 5), 16 (Grade 6), 17 (Grade 7), 18 (Grade 8), 19 (Grade 9), 20 (Grade 10), 21/22 (Grades 11, 12).

Forms, 2: C, D (2 forms of the Plus Tests also available).

Price Data, 2002: $47.70 per Teacher's Guide to TerraNova, The Second Edition (2000, 320 pages), quantity discount available; $47.70 per Technical Bulletin (2002, 310 pages), CD-ROM version only; $31.80

per Pre-Publication Technical Bulletin (82 pages), CD-ROM version only; $5.85 per Assessment Accommodations Supplement (17 pages); $2.10 per class record sheet for hand scoring; $42.40 per norms book including student diagnostic profile, CD-ROM with all norms tables (Fall, Winter, or Spring, specify season).

Foreign Language and Special Editions: Available in English and Spanish editions (Supera); Braille and large print editions available.

Time: Administration time varies by test and level.

Comments: Also called California Achievement Test, Sixth Edition (CAT6); total remake of the TerraNova (T5:2654) including all new items and thematic content, new norms; TerraNova, The Second Edition, Forms C and D are designed as parallel test forms to the Comprehensive Tests of Basic Skills (CTBS; 1997) Forms A and B; Basic Battery, Basic Multiple Assessments measure only Reading, Language, Mathematics; Survey, Complete Battery, Multiple Assessments measure Reading, Language, Mathematics, Science, Social Studies; Plus Tests measure additional skills (Word Analysis, Vocabulary, Language Mechanics, Spelling, Mathematics Computation); tests may be administered alone or in any combination; 2 formats: paper and pencil, CD-ROM; both Windows and Macintosh versions available; system requirements for Windows: 486 processor or faster, Windows 95 or later, 20 MB hard disk; system requirements for Macintosh: Power Macintosh, Apple OS 7.5.3 or later, 60 MB hard disk; also requires 6 MB RAM, CD-ROM drive, Adobe Acrobat Reader 4.0 or later; full-service scoring available through publisher; reports and data available on CD-ROM; electronic report delivery available; information regarding numerous customized and packaged scoring and reporting services available from publisher; optional locator tests available to assist teachers in identifying appropriate testing level for individual students; optional practice activities available to help familiarize students with test-taking mechanics, item formats, test design elements; website (www.ctb.com) provides sample test questions and answers, information about instructional strategies, report interpretation for teachers, parents, administrators, students.

Author: CTB/McGraw-Hill.

Publisher: CTB/McGraw-Hill.

a) CAT SURVEY AND SURVEY WITH PLUS.

Purpose: Designed to "yield norm-referenced and some curriculum-referenced information in a minimum of testing time."

Price Data: $107.05 per 25 consumable Survey test books (Levels 12–13, specify level) including manipulatives, and Test Directions for Teachers; $42.95 per 25 consumable Plus test books for use with Survey (Levels 12–13, specify level) including manipulatives, and Test Directions for Teachers; $93.30 per 25 reusable Survey test books (Levels

14–21/22, specify level); $36.05 per 25 reusable Plus test books for use with Survey (Levels 14–21/22, specify level); $44.50 per 50 Survey CompuScan answer sheets (Levels 14–21/22) including Plus answer grid; $1,125 per 1,250 continuous form (Trans-Optic) answer sheets for precoding (Levels 14–21/22) including Plus answer grid; $635 per 2,500 student information sheets; $59.35 per 2 Survey or Survey with Plus acetate scoring stencils (Levels 14–21/22); $7.40 per 30 Survey ancillary pieces additional manipulatives (Levels 12–13); $11.65 per 50 Survey ancillary pieces additional manipulatives (Levels 14–22); $17.50 per Test Directions for Teachers (Levels 12–22, specify level); Basic Service scoring: $3.51 per Basic Survey book (Levels 12–13); $2.05 per Survey answer sheet (Levels 14–21/22); $3.89 per Survey with Plus book (Levels 12–13); $2.43 per Survey with Plus answer sheet; $59.95 per Survey accommodation kit (Levels 12–22, specify level).

Comments: Provides norm-referenced scores; all items use selected-response format.

Time: Varies by level; Reading and Language Arts: 60–80(70–90) minutes; Mathematics: 35–40(45–50) minutes; Science, Social Studies: 20–25(30–35) minutes each; 135–170(155–190) minutes total; 215–235(260–280) minutes total with Plus tests.

1) *Levels 12–13.*

Population: Grades 2–3.

Scores: 5 Survey scores (Reading, Language, Mathematics, Science, Social Studies); 5 Plus scores (Vocabulary, Language Mechanics, Spelling, Mathematics Computation, Word Analysis).

2) *Levels 14–21/22.*

Population: Grades 4–12.

Scores: 5 Survey scores (Reading, Language, Mathematics, Science, Social Studies); 4 Plus scores (Vocabulary, Language Mechanics, Spelling, Mathematics Computation).

b) CAT COMPLETE BATTERY AND COMPLETE BATTERY PLUS.

Purpose: "Generates norm-referenced achievement scores and a full complement of objective-mastery scores."

Price Data: $138.85 per 25 consumable Complete Battery test books (Levels 10–13, specify level); $143.10 per 25 consumable Complete Battery Plus test books (Levels 11–13, specify level); $103.90 per 25 reusable Complete Battery test books (Levels 14–21/22, specify level); $112.35 per 25 reusable Complete Battery Plus test books (Levels 14–21/22, specify level); $44.50 per 50 complete Battery CompuScan answer sheets (Levels 14–21/22) including Plus grid; $1,125 per 1,250 continuous form (Trans-Optic) answer sheets for precoding (Levels 14–21/22) including Plus answer grid; $635 per 2,500 student information sheets; $59.35 per 3 Complete Battery Plus acetate scoring stencils (Levels 14–21/22); $7.40 per 30 Battery ancillary pieces additional manipulatives (Levels 12–13); $11.65 per 50 Battery ancillary pieces additional manipulatives (Levels 14–21/22); $17.50 per additional Test Directions for Teachers (Levels 10–21/22, specify level); Basic Service scoring: $3.51 per Complete Battery book (Level 10–13); $2.05 per Complete Battery answer sheet (Levels 14–21/22); $3.89 per Complete Battery Plus book (Levels 11–13); $2.43 per Complete Battery Plus answer sheet; $59.95 per Complete Battery accommodation kit (Levels 10–22, specify level).

Comments: Combines Survey items with additional selected-response items; yields detailed diagnostic information; provides norm-referenced scores.

Time: Varies by level; Reading and Language Arts: 55–100(65–110) minutes; Mathematics: 40–70(50–80) minutes; Science, Social Studies: 20–40(30–50) minutes each; 95–250(115–270) minutes total; 95–315(140–360) minutes total with Plus tests.

   1) *Level 10.*

   Population: Kindergarten.

   Scores: 3 Complete Battery scores (Reading, Language, Mathematics); 2 Plus scores (Language Mechanics, Spelling).

   2) *Level 11.*

   Population: Grade 1.

   Scores: 5 Complete Battery scores (Reading, Language, Mathematics, Science, Social Studies); 2 Plus scores (Language Mechanics, Spelling).

   3) *Levels 12 and 13.*

   Population: Grades 2–3.

   Scores: 5 Complete Battery scores (Reading, Language, Mathematics, Science, Social Studies); 5 Plus scores (Language Mechanics, Spelling, Vocabulary, Mathematics Computation, Word Analysis).

   4) *Levels 14–21/22.*

   Population: Grades 4–12.

   Scores: 5 Complete Battery scores (Reading, Language, Mathematics, Science, Social Studies); 4 Plus scores (Language Mechanics, Spelling, Vocabulary, Mathematics Computation).

c) CAT BASIC BATTERY AND BASIC BATTERY PLUS.

Purpose: Designed to "provide the same information as the Complete Battery, targeting the basic areas of reading, language arts, and mathematics."

Price Data: $131.45 per 25 consumable Basic Battery test books (Levels 11–13, specify level) including manipulatives, and Test Directions for Teachers; $42.95 per 25 consumable Plus test books for use with Basic Battery (Levels 11–13, specify level) including manipulatives, and Test Directions for Teachers; $102.80 per 25 reusable Basic Battery test books (Levels 14–21/22, specify level); $36.05 per 25 reusable Plus test books for use with Basic Battery (Levels 14–21/22, specify level); $44.50 per 50 Basic Battery CompuScan answer sheets (Levels 14–21/22) including Plus answer grid; $1,125 per 1,250 continuous form (Trans-Optic) answer sheets for precoding (Levels 14–21/22) including Plus answer grid; $635 per 2,500 student information sheets; $59.35 per 3 Basic Battery or Basic Battery with Plus acetate scoring stencils (Levels 14–21/22); $7.40 per 30 ancillary pieces additional manipulatives (Levels 12–13); $11.65 per 50 ancillary pieces additional manipulatives (Levels 14–21/22); $17.50 per additional Test Directions for Teachers (Levels 10–21/22, specify level); Basic Service scoring: $3.51 per Basic Battery book (Levels 10–13); $2.05 per Basic Battery answer sheet (Levels 14–21/22); $3.89 per Basic Battery Plus book (Levels 11–13); $2.43 per Basic Battery Plus answer sheet.

Comments: Reading/Language Arts and Mathematics tests same as for Complete Battery.

Time: Varies by level; 55–100(65–110) minutes for Reading and Language Arts, 40–70(50–80) minutes for Mathematics, 95–170(140–215) minutes total; 170(215) minutes total with Plus tests.

   1) *Levels 10 and 11.*

   Population: Kindergarten–Grade 1.

   Scores: 3 Basic Battery scores (Reading, Language, Mathematics); 2 Plus scores (Language Mechanics, Spelling).

   2) *Levels 12 and 13.*

   Population: Grades 2–3.

   Scores: 3 Basic Battery scores (Reading, Language, Mathematics); 5 Plus scores (Language Mechanics, Spelling, Vocabulary, Mathematics Computation, Word Analysis).

   3) *Levels 14–21/22.*

   Population: Grades 4–12.

   Scores: 3 Basic Battery scores (Reading, Language, Mathematics); 4 Plus scores (Language Mechanics, Spelling, Vocabulary, Mathematics Computation).

d) CAT MULTIPLE ASSESSMENTS AND MULTIPLE ASSESSMENTS WITH PLUS.

Purpose: Designed "to provide data on students' problem solving and reading skills."

Price Data: $143.10 per 25 consumable scannable CAT Multiple Assessments test books (Levels 11–21/22, specify level); $42.95 per 25 consumable Plus test books for use with Multiple Assessments (Levels 11–13, specify level); $36.05 per 25 reusable Plus test books for use with Multiple Assessments (Levels 14–21/22, specify level); all test book sets include manipulatives and Test Directions for Teachers; $15.90 per scoring guide for CTBS Multiple Assessments (Levels 11–21/22, specify level); $95.40 per Multiple Assessments scoring guide (CD-ROM, Levels 11–21/22); $19.10 per 30 Multiple Assessments ancillary pieces additional manipulatives (Levels 11–21/22); $17.50 per additional Test Directions for Teachers (Levels 11–21/22, specify level); Basic Service scoring: $11.88 per Multiple Assessment (all levels); $12.26 per Multiple Assessment with Plus (all levels); $59.95 per Multiple Assessments accommodation kit (Levels 11–22, specify level).

Comments: Combines selected-response items from Survey with constructed-response items allowing students to produce their own short and extended responses; constructed-response items scanned electronically, hand scored by publisher; produces norm-referenced and curriculum-referenced scores.

Time: Reading and Language Arts: 100–120(110–130) minutes; Mathematics: 50–90(60–100) minutes; Science: 45–60(55–70) minutes; Social Studies: 45–65(55–75) minutes; 240–335(280–375) minutes total; 290–400(355–465) minutes total with Plus tests.

  1) *Level 11.*
  Population: Grade 1.
  Scores: 5 Multiple Assessments scores (Reading, Language, Mathematics, Science, Social Studies); 3 Plus scores (Vocabulary, Mathematics Computation, Word Analysis).
  2) *Levels 12 and 13.*
  Population: Grades 2–3.
  Scores: 5 Multiple Assessments scores (Reading, Language, Mathematics, Science, Social Studies); 5 Plus scores (Vocabulary, Mathematics Computation, Language Mechanics, Spelling, Word Analysis).
  3) *Levels 14–21/22.*
  Population: Grades 4–12.
  Scores: 5 Multiple Assessments scores (Reading, Language, Mathematics, Science, Social Studies); 4 Plus scores (Vocabulary, Mathematics Computation, Language Mechanics, Spelling).

e) CAT BASIC MULTIPLE ASSESSMENTS AND BASIC MULTIPLE ASSESSMENTS PLUS.
Price Data: Available from publisher.
Time: Varies by level; 150–210(195–255) minutes total; 200–275(245–320) minutes total with Plus tests.

Comments: Includes both selected-response and constructed-response items; selected-response items scored electronically; constructed-response items hand scored by publisher; Reading/Language Arts and Mathematics tests same as for Complete Multiple Assessments.

  1) *Level 11.*
  Population: Grade 1.
  Scores: 3 Basic Multiple Assessment scores (Reading, Language Arts, Mathematics); 3 Plus scores (Vocabulary, Mathematics Computation, Word Analysis).
  2) *Levels 12–21/22.*
  Population: Grades 2–12.
  Scores: 3 Basic Multiple Assessment scores (Reading, Language Arts, Mathematics); 5 Plus scores (Vocabulary, Mathematics Computation, Language Mechanics, Spelling, Word Analysis).

f) TERRANOVA ALGEBRA TEST.
Purpose: "Measures how students use algebraic processes to manipulate expressions and model mathematical situations."
Population: Students in grades 7–12 who have completed Algebra I.
Scores: Available from publisher.
Price Data: $75.25 per 25 test books; $57.25 per 50 answer sheets; $11.65 per additional Test Directions for Teachers; $1,430 per 2,500 continuous form answer sheets; $25 per Technical Resource manual; $28 per Algebra specimen set including test book, answer sheet, and test directions); Basic Service scoring: $1.84 per Algebra answer sheet; $1.35 per Algebra individual report; $0.81 per Algebra summary report; $3.60 per Algebra Plan 1 including Basic Service scoring, Algebra individual report, and Algebra summary report.
Comments: Results are reported separately from those of TerraNova, The Second Edition.
Time: 45(50) minutes.

g) SUPERA.
Purpose: "The Spanish-language version of the assessment series, offering multiple measures of student achievement."
Population: Grades 1–10.
Levels, 9: 11, 12, 13, 14, 15, 16, 17, 18, 19/20.
Scores: 3 Supera scores (Reading, Language Arts, Mathematics); 5 Plus scores (Word Analysis, Vocabulary, Language Mechanics, Spelling, Mathematics Computation).
Price Data: $36.70 per Teacher's Guide; $17.30 per Norms Book (specify Fall or Spring); $43.45 per Test Coordinator's Handbook; $20 per Supera Technical Report disk; $10.80 per Handbook of Instructional Objectives (specify Survey, Multiple Assessments, or Plus Edition).

Comments: Uses Spanish "common to all dialects"; designed as a parallel test form of English TerraNova tests; separate norms "allow comparison with either Spanish- or English-speaking peers"; Custom Assessments (Evaluaciones Desarolladas a su Preferencia) also available.

1) *SUPERA Survey (Evaluaciones Esenciales) and Survey Plus.*

Price Data: $152.25 per 30 consumable test books (Levels 11–13, specify level); $119.90 per 30 reusable test books (Levels 14–19/20, specify level); $45.35 per 50 CompuScan answer sheets (Levels 14–20); $34.05 per 25 SCOREZE answer sheets (Levels 14–20); $2,268 per 2,500 continuous form answer sheets (Levels 14–20); $39.95 per scoring stencil (Levels 14–20, specify level); $41.05 per 30 Supera Plus consumable test books (Levels 11–13, specify level); $41.05 per 30 Supera Plus reusable test books (Levels 14–20, specify level); $45.35 per 50 CompuScan Plus answer sheets (Levels 14–20); $1,145 per 1,250 continuous form Plus answer sheets (Levels 14–20); $34.05 per 25 Supera Plus SCOREZE answer sheets (Levels 14–20, specify level).

Time: Reading/Language Arts test: 110–160(155–205) minutes; Mathematics test: 70–100(115–145) minutes; Supera Plus tests: 25–30 minutes for Word Analysis, 20–40 minutes for Vocabulary tests, 25–35 minutes for Language Mechanics tests, 20–25 minutes for Spelling tests, 25–30 minutes for Mathematics Computation tests.

2) *SUPERA Multiple Assessments (Evaluaciones Multiples) and Multiple Assessments Plus.*

Price Data: $126.35 per 30 consumable scannable test books (specify level); $16.20 per scoring guide (specify level).

h) PERFORMANCE ASSESSMENTS.

Purpose: "Available for educators who wish to use extended open-ended assignments."

Population: Grades 3–12.

Levels, 6: 13/14, 14/15, 16/17, 17/18, 19/20, 21/22.

Scores, 10: 6 Communication Arts strands (Establish Understanding, Explore Meaning, Extend Meaning and Examine Strategies, Evaluate Critically, Write Effectively, Write Fluently); 4 Mathematics Competencies (Problem Solving, Communication, Reasoning, Data and Information Processing).

Comments: Open-ended response items require students to "move through a series of activities culminating in a final product or summative activity."

Price Data: $88 per 30 consumable test books including test directions (Communication Arts or Mathematics, specify level); $6.35 per scoring guide (Communication Arts or Mathematics, specify level); $10.60 per additional copy of test directions (Communication Arts or Mathematics, specify level); $36.55 per 30 test materials and accessories for practice activities (Communication Arts or Mathematics, specify level); $79.50 per Communication Arts video cassette (specify level).

Cross References: For reviews by Judith A. Monsaas and Anthony J. Nitko of an earlier edition, see 14:383; for information on the Comprehensive Tests of Basic Skills, see T5:665 (95 references); see also T4:623 (23 references); for reviews by Kenneth D. Hopkins and M. David Miller of the CTBS, see 11:81 (70 references); for reviews by Robert L. Linn and Lorrie A. Shepard of an earlier form, see 9:258 (29 references); see also T3: 551 (59 references); for reviews by Warren G. Findley and Anthony J. Nitko of an earlier edition, see 8:12 (13 references); see also T2:11 (1 reference); for reviews by J. Stanley Ahmann and Frederick G. Brown and excerpted reviews by Brooke B. Collison and Peter A. Taylor (rejoinder by Verna White) of Forms Q and R, see 7:9. For reviews of subtests of earlier editions, see 8:721 (1 review), 8:825 (1 review), 7:685 (1 review), 7:514 (2 reviews), and 7:778 (1 review).

Review of the TerraNova, The Second Edition by GREGORY J. CIZEK, Professor of Educational Measurement and Evaluation, University of North Carolina—Chapel Hill, Chapel Hill, NC:

DESCRIPTION. The second edition of the TerraNova achievement test (TN2) is an updated version of its popular predecessor the TerraNova, first published in 1997. The purpose of the test is to provide users with norm-referenced and criterion-referenced information on concepts, processes, and skills taught throughout the nation. The following subsections of this review describe the test materials and relevant supporting documentation.

Test materials. To begin, referring to the TN2 generically is somewhat imprecise. TerraNova is actually the name given to a family of products published by CTB/McGraw-Hill. TerraNova, The Second Edition can refer to any of a number of recent incarnations of its California Achievement Tests (CAT) series. The family of TN2/CAT-6 products includes several different versions or "modules," and the array can be somewhat confusing.

Basically, the versions vary in terms of subjects tested, overall length, testing time required, and item/task formats used. The configuration for a complete version of TN2 provides measurement of student achievement in Reading and Language

Arts, Mathematics, Science, and Social Studies. What are referred to as optional "Plus" modules add Word Analysis, Spelling, Vocabulary, Language Mechanics, and Mathematics Computation to the normal configuration. Trimmed versions of the complete configuration include only Reading, Language Arts, and Mathematics. Brief descriptions of the most common TN2 combinations follow.

The Complete Battery version of TN2 comprises only multiple-choice format items for the five areas tested. It is the only version that includes a test appropriate for kindergarten-aged students. The length of the Complete Battery ranges, depending on grade level, from 70 to 217 items, with shorter length associated with lower grade levels. The amount of time for testing ranges from 1 hour and 35 minutes to 4 hours and 10 minutes, again depending on grade level, and with an additional time allotment required for administration activities. The "Plus" configuration of the Complete Battery brings the range of test length to 192–297 items and testing time to 3:30–5:15 hours for Grades 1 and 12, respectively. (A "Plus" version is not available for kindergarten.)

A Survey version of the TN2 is available for Grades 2 through 12. This version, too, comprises only multiple-choice format items for the five areas tested and is shorter than the Complete Battery, though still measuring the same subject areas. The length of the Survey version ranges from 111 to 145 items depending on the grade level; actual testing time ranges from 2:15 to 2:50 hours, again depending on grade level, with total testing time somewhat longer when administration activities are included. Adding the "Plus" configuration of the Survey version brings the range of test length to 211–222 items and testing time to 3:35–3:55 hours for Grades 2 and 12, respectively.

The Basic Battery version of the TN2 is a scaled-down version of the Complete Battery. It consists only of the Reading/Language Arts and Mathematics portions of the longer test. (The Science and Social Studies portions are omitted.) Test length for the Basic Battery ranges from 70–137 items (K–12) and testing time ranges from 1:35–2:50 hours. The "Plus" version of the Basic Battery comprises from 152 to 237 items (Grades 1–12) with testing time ranging from 2:50–3:55 hours.

Perhaps the version of TerraNova that most commonly comes to mind is the version that includes a mix of selected-response and con-structed-response items, known as TerraNova Multiple Assessments. It was this version that broke new ground in standardized norm-referenced achievement testing when it was introduced. The Second Edition continues to provide the same features that resulted in wide acceptance among many educators seeking an alternative to traditional, multiple-choice-only assessments. Full versions of the TN2 Multiple Assessments have been developed for Grades 1 through 12. The full versions measure achievement in Reading, Language Arts, Mathematics, Science, and Social Studies, with total test lengths ranging from 144 to 182 items (testing time = 4:00 to 5:35 hours, with administration activities adding additional time). As with other versions of the TN2, "Plus" configurations of the full versions are available; these add between 60 to 80 items and 50 to 65 minutes of testing time. Because a primary distinguishing characteristic of TN2 Multiple Assessments is the inclusion of constructed-response items, the relative proportion of such item types is relevant. In the form appropriate for second graders, constructed-response items comprise approximately 48% of the raw score points possible; the percentage at 12th grade is similar (50%).

Basic Multiple Assessments versions have also been developed. These combine focused assessment of Reading, Language Arts, and Mathematics only, using a mix of selected- and constructed-response formats. The length of the Basic Multiple Assessments versions range from 87–112 items for Grades 1–12 with time required for testing ranging from 2:30 to 3:30 hours, the "Plus" option boosts the range of test length to 147–184 items and testing time to 3:20–4:35 hours.

A Spanish-language version of the TerraNova, called Supera, is available. In each configuration, this assessment is limited to measurement of Reading, Language Arts, and Mathematics. Supera is available in Survey (Evaluaciones Essenciales) or Multiple Assessments (Evaluaciones Multiples) versions with or without the same supplemental "Plus" tests as the English-language versions. Braille and large-print English-language versions are also available. The balance of this review pertains to the English-language, standard version of the TN2 for which the preponderance of technical data were collected and reported in various documentation.

As with most standardized achievement tests, the TN2 allows users to obtain a variety of indicators of individual student and group-level performance. These include traditional norm-referenced scores such as national or custom percentile ranks, grade equivalent scores, and normal curve equivalents. The TN2 also reports a developmental scale score, which ranges from approximately 100 to 900 and can be used to track student progress across the grade levels. Test results are also summarized in ways that are as user-friendly as possible. For example, on each score report, norm-referenced indices are supplemented by graphic displays and narrative interpretations that tell the same story as the statistical summary.

Like other commercial norm-referenced measures, the TN2 has also attempted to broaden the information gleaned from student test performance beyond indices of relative rank. Three such standards-references scores warrant specific mention.

First, an "Objective Performance Index" (OPI) provides an objectives-referenced score on small groupings of items reflecting narrower areas of knowledge or skill. For example, in Reading, OPI scores are given for the areas of Basic Understanding, Analyzing Text, Evaluating/Extending Meaning, and Identifying Reading Strategies. A student's OPI score can range from 0–100 and is an estimate of the number of items in the subdomain that a student would be expected to answer correctly if he or she had attempted 100 such items.

A second innovation is the incorporation of a Lexile score (Wright & Stenner, 1999) into what is called the "Reading Links Report." This report essentially gives a different developmental scale score unique to reading—a Lexile score. Based on the student's Lexile score, the report provides a list of readily accessible reading materials at an instructional level corresponding to his or her measured reading ability. Thus, the score provides teachers and parents with at least one piece of individualized, instructionally useful information.

Finally, the TN2 incorporates performance levels consisting of five categories bearing the labels: Step One, Progressing, Nearing Proficiency, Proficient, and Advanced. (At Grades 1 and 2, the label "Starting Out" is used instead of Step One.) These categories indicate hierarchical levels of performance similar to the familiar Basic, Proficient, and Advanced used on the National Assessment of Educational Progress (NAEP). The Bookmark procedure (Mitzel, Lewis, Patz, & Green, 2001) was used to establish performance levels on the TN2.

DOCUMENTATION. One of the strengths of the TN2 documentation is the abundant information on test preparation and test administration practices that should be implemented and monitored to promote validity of test score interpretations. In particular, the documentation for the TN2 provides a fairly good treatment of appropriate test accommodations and proper interpretation of scores obtained under nonstandard conditions. An *accommodation* is defined in the teacher's guide as "changes in the setting in which a test is administered, the timing of the test, the scheduling of a test, the ways in which the test is presented, and the ways in which the student responds to the test ... that do not alter in any significant way what the test measures or the comparability of scores" (2001, p. 276). A specific example of how to interpret a mathematics test score obtained under conditions such as "teacher reads the test directions, stimulus material, and questions" [to the examinee] (p. 272) is provided, along with test administration guidelines for "ensuring valid and equitable test results" (p. 3).

Other documentation is equally helpful, including an *Assessment Accommodations Supplement* (CTB/McGraw-Hill, 2000a) and a separate document titled *Guidelines for Using the Results of Standardized Tests Administered Under Nonstandard Conditions* (CTB/McGraw-Hill, 2000b). The latter provides a compilation of information on accommodations in a single, brief (10 pages) booklet format that is probably more user-friendly and more likely to be reviewed by those actually administering and interpreting scores from the TN2 (as opposed to the teacher's guide). One weakness of the booklet—which is probably more a reflection of the state of knowledge about accommodations—is that there are still far too many instances of advice that scores obtained under nonstandard conditions should be interpreted "with caution" or "in light of the accommodation." Such vagaries cannot be operationalized in any specific way, and such advice is not likely to be very helpful in a practical sense: It would seem that *any* score, no matter how obtained, should be interpreted with caution and in light of relevant departures from standard administration conditions.

Overall, it appears that the publisher gave serious attention to developing the supporting documentation in a variety of materials and formats to promote appropriate test use and interpretation. On the other hand, it is probably impossible for any publisher to satisfy all potential audiences for a product it develops. Some aspects of the TN2 and supporting materials that make the product more useful for some audiences may make it less appealing to others. For example, in the case of some of the materials targeted toward teachers and other school personnel, users are prompted to click on a link on the publisher's web site in order to "download the complete technical quality document" for the TN2. Unfortunately, that document contains virtually no technical information. Another resource developed to be as user-friendly as possible—a compact disc titled "Introducing TerraNova, The Second Edition"—provides somewhat more information on the development and quality of the test, though it is still rather skimpy in terms of actual detail on technical characteristics. Both of these products would be better classified as marketing tools than technical documentation.

On the other hand, abundant technical information can be located in two other sources: (a) a CD titled *CAT Technical Bulletin 1* and (b) a paper called *TerraNova, The Second Edition Teacher's Guide*. Though the information provided in these materials is laudable, some reorganization might be considered. First, the teacher's guide appears to be the primary source of content validity evidence. It is unclear whether many teachers would actually be interested in reviewing the list of state curricula, textbooks, standards, and so on consulted in the development of the TN2, but it is certain that this kind of information should be a part of the validity documentation provided in the technical bulletin. Also, if the technical bulletin is not routinely provided in paper form, it should be.

DEVELOPMENT. Two important aspects of test development distinguish the TN2 from the first edition of TerraNova. First, the second edition does not simply represent a cosmetic change or minor modification of the first edition. The new version was built using all new items and tasks, all of which were subjected to a degree of scrutiny prior to inclusion that would be expected of a high-quality standardized achievement battery. For example, items and tasks were developed to meet content specifications; examined by content, editorial, and sensitivity reviewers; field-tested to gauge difficulty level and to ensure construct-relevant discrimination; and so forth. Linkages were established to previous versions of the Comprehensive Tests of Basic Skills (CTBS), the California Achievement Tests (CAT), and to the previous version of TerraNova, permitting comparisons of student performance on these tests to performance on the TN2.

Although the items are new, the second edition retains the distinctive characteristic that accounted in large part for the success of the first. Namely, the test booklets, items, and constructed-response tasks have been formatted to—as much as possible—resemble the kinds of instructional classroom materials that students would be exposed to at the grade level the test targets. The publisher refers to many usability studies that were intended to make the assessment process less novel, and less discomforting—especially for younger students—and to foster optimal motivation and engagement in the testing process. At extra cost, users of the TN2 may also purchase "Practice Activities Booklets," which give students additional exposure to the test format.

Regardless of whether these changes to the look and feel of the TN2 actually improve the accuracy of the measurement process, the improved face validity likely increases the appeal of the tests to both educators and students. On the other hand, as a reviewer of the previous edition of the TerraNova observed, it is still "doubt[ful] that students will forget that they are taking a test" (Monsaas, 2001, p. 1224).

A second substantial aspect of the new edition is the updated norms. The publisher is to be commended for undertaking the large investment necessary to ensure recency and representativeness for norm-based score interpretations. Norms data for the TN2 were gathered during the 1999–2000 school year. The norming sample comprised approximately 280,000 students; 429 schools were included in the fall sample, 202 in the winter, and 689 in the spring. The sampling strategy was a stratified approach using individual schools as the sampling unit. Stratification was based on type of school (three levels: public, private, parochial), region of the U.S. (four levels), community type (seven levels), and socioeconomic status (two levels). Sampling was also done to ensure that special needs students and students requiring testing accommodations were included. A list of schools and school districts that participated in the norming study is provided. A table provided in the technical bulletin demonstrates that the sampling strategy for obtaining the norm group resulted in a very close representation of important demographic characteristics of U.S. school children.

The TN2 was normed concurrently with a new version of the publisher's ability measure called InView (114). This cognitive ability test serves the same purpose as its predecessor, the Test of Cognitive Skills, which is to obtain a traditional, norm-referenced index of ability, and to permit achievement/ability comparisons to identify over- and underachievement.

TECHNICAL. Technical information on reliability indicates that users of the TN2 can have confidence in scores yielded by the measure. For constructed-response item formats, interrater agreement indices (intraclass correlations) are almost all in the high .90s and weighted kappa coefficients (agreement corrected for chance agreement) are uniformly high. Overall, the technical bulletin reports that exact agreement between raters on individual items "was obtained on approximately 80 to 100 percent of the check-set papers across all grade levels and content areas" (CTB/McGraw-Hill, 2002, p. 87), indicating a strong tendency for raters to agree on scores assigned to student responses.

Alpha coefficients and/or KR-20 estimates calculated to express internal consistency reliability are reported for every level of the TN2, for Reading, Language Arts, Mathematics, and Total Score, and for both fall and spring administrations. Standard errors of measurement for raw scores are reported; the technical bulletin indicates that *SEMs* for scaled scores will be provided in a future revision of the bulletin. Alphas for total test, fall and spring administrations, respectively, range from .95 and .95 on the Level 12 form (Grade 2) to .96 and .96 on the Level 21/22 form (Grade 12). All internal consistency estimates for subareas (i.e., Reading, Language Arts, Mathematics) are in the mid- to low .90s. It is especially noteworthy that these values span the range of grades for which the TN2 is intended, putting to rest concerns about the reliability of test scores for young children.

Although the reliability information provided supports confidence in total and subscores, three seemingly important pieces of evidence are not reported. I suspect that many of those who might review the technical foundation of the TN2 would gladly trade some of the 70 pages of individual item difficulty statistics for a paragraph or two on test score equivalence and stability.

First, two forms of the TN2 (Forms C and D) are available. According to the technical bulletin, the forms "were designed and are considered to be parallel test forms that can be used interchangeably with the TerraNova Forms A and B" (p. 1). Unfortunately, information on both aspects of comparability is missing.

Information on comparability of Forms C and D can be inferred from the fact that a computer-facilitated test construction procedure was used, promoting content and statistical equivalence between the two forms. However, the bulletin indicates that actual evidence on the extent to which Forms C/D can be used interchangeably with Forms A/B will be presented in a future publication. Oddly, even information bearing on the parallel forms reliability of the TN2 (i.e., Forms C and D) is not presented in the technical bulletin, and no advice on when such information might be forthcoming is given. Finally, information on the stability of scores is lacking. Some indication of the extent to which scores (and Performance Categories) might differ from one administration to another (i.e., test-retest reliability) would be useful.

A moderate degree of validity evidence supports the TN2. First, the technical bulletin reports that studies of speededness find less than 5% of students fail to complete the entire test in the time provided. Further, extensive editorial review, sensitivity review, item-to-model fit, and differential item functioning (DIF, for African American and Hispanic subsamples) analyses suggest great attention to minimizing the influence of construct-irrelevant variables on students' performance.

For these procedures, however, some improvements might be warranted. For example, the system for considering DIF is novel; it consists of the creation of four (for gender) and five (for ethnicity) categories that indicate differential functioning. However, the classifications are not ordinal reflections of the degree of DIF, but nominal categorizations in which, for example, Category 1 represents no DIF favoring African American or Hispanic students, Category 2 represents DIF favoring African Americans but not Hispanics, Category 4 represents DIF in favor of one ethnic group and against the other, and so on. The technical bulletin identifies the number of items flagged for DIF or poor fit and indicates that these were "avoided as much as possible" (p. 50) in test construction.

As regards the most important validity evidence for an achievement test—that is, the extent to which the content of the test is drawn from relevant sources—the evidence is abundant. Though one might have expected to find this information in the technical bulletin, it is actually found in the teacher's guide. It consists of extensive documentation of the specific content and skills assessed by each item or task on the test, as well as the specific materials (curriculum guides, state curriculum frameworks, textbook series, professional standards, and other resources) that served as the sources for the test content.

Construct validity evidence is comparatively skimpy. The only correlations reported involve the TN2 and the companion ability measure, InView. Further, in several places, it is claimed that the TN2 is aligned with specific standards, such as the National Council of Teachers of Mathematics *Principles and Standards for School Mathematics.* One shortcoming—though this seems common in the context of similar alignment statements by other test producers—is that such alignment is usually claimed but not documented.

Some construct-related validity evidence was anticipated in the previous version of the TerraNova. A *Mental Measurements Yearbook* review of that version by Monsaas noted that "criterion-related validity studies were being planned at the time the various manuals were published. The publishers plan to correlate the TerraNova with the National Assessment of Educational Progress (NAEP), the Third International Mathematics and Science Study (TIMSS), and the SAT and ACT .... These data are necessary to determine whether scores on this new test are related to other independent measures of achievement" (2001, p. 1225). However, as yet, that information has not been included in the most recent technical documentation. Supporting detail on the actual degree of alignment with any particular criterion, along with simple correlations between scores on the TN2 and related measures is still desirable.

SUMMARY AND COMMENT. The first edition of the TerraNova broke new ground in large-scale measurement of school achievement. With the TN2, it is evident that much attention has been paid to retaining and enhancing the characteristics that distinguish it from an earlier generation of standardized, norm-referenced tests. The test continues to be marked by materials that students are likely to find to be highly similar to the kinds of materials they regularly encounter in the classroom. Score reports, interpretive materials, guidelines for test administration, and other documentation appear to have been designed with parents, educators, and other users in mind.

The latest version of the TerraNova incorporates two major technical improvements. First, the test was built using all new items and includes constructed-response tasks. Second, norms for the TN2 are recent and highly representative of American students, ensuring users of accurate, meaningful derived scores. These scores are supplemented by helpful objective- and standards-based information, such as the Objectives Performance Index, Achievement Levels, and Lexile scores for reading.

Procedures for building the TN2 ensured that scores yielded by the new test can be compared to scores from the original version. The variety of TN2 combinations (e.g., Basic, Complete, Survey, Plus, and so on) means that all users should be able to find a combination that meets their needs for test information, subject areas tested, time available for testing, and format preferences.

Room for further improvement exists. Noteworthy by its absence is information that might be considered routine for tests like the TN2—namely, equivalent forms reliability estimates, test-retest information, and correlations between the TN2 and other achievement measures. And, concrete evidence of alignment, when claimed, should be provided. Overall, however, the reliability and validity information provided for the TN2 suggests that scores on the test can be interpreted with confidence to reflect student achievement of currently accepted knowledge and skills that are broadly endorsed as important and relevant in the grades and subjects tested.

REVIEWER'S REFERENCES

CTB/McGraw-Hill. (2000a). *Assessment accommodations supplement.* Monterey, CA: Author.
CTB/McGraw-Hill. (2000b). *Guidelines for using the results of standardized tests administered under nonstandard conditions.* Monterey, CA: Author.
CTB/McGraw-Hill. (2001). *Teacher's guide to TerraNova, The Second Edition.* Monterey, CA: Author.
CTB/McGraw-Hill. (2002). *TerraNova, The Second Edition: Technical bulletin 1.* Monterey, CA: Author.
Mitzel, H. C., Lewis, D. M., Patz, R. J., & Green, D. R. (2001). The Bookmark procedure: Psychological perspectives. In G. J. Cizek (Ed.), *Setting performance standards: Concepts, methods, and perspectives* (pp. 249–282). Mahwah, NJ: Erlbaum.
Monsaas, J. A. (2001). [Review of the TerraNova.] In B. S. Plake & J. C. Impara (Eds.), *The fourteenth mental measurements yearbook* (pp. 1223–1226). Lincoln, NE: Buros Institute of Mental Measurements.
Wright, B. D., & Stenner, A. J. (1999). Using Lexiles. *Popular Measurement, 2*(1), 41–42.

Review of the TerraNova, The Second Edition by ROBERT L. JOHNSON, Associate Professor, Educational Psychology, University of South Caro-

lina, Columbia, SC, and *DAWN MAZZIE, Teacher, Richland One Public Schools, Columbia, SC:*

DESCRIPTION. The TerraNova, The Second Edition measures students' achievement in Grades K–12 with tests of Reading and Language Arts, Mathematics, Science, and Social Studies. Three versions of the test are available: Survey, Complete Battery, and Multiple Assessments. Each version also has additional tests, referred to as Plus tests, that support the measurements of the main content areas. The Plus tests use selected-response items to measure skills in Word Analysis, Vocabulary, Language Mechanics, Spelling, and Mathematics Computation.

The Survey and the Complete Battery consist solely of selected-response items. The Survey edition is the shortest version of the TerraNova with the number of items ranging from 111–142 across grade levels. The developers suggested that this test be used when time is a major concern. The Complete Battery combines the Survey items with additional selected-response items. The number of items ranges from 70–217 across grade levels. Finally, the Multiple Assessments version combines selected-response items with constructed-response items that allow students to produce their own responses. The number of items for the Multiple Assessments ranges from 144–183 across grade levels. Each Plus test contains 20 additional items. The TerraNova, The Second Edition also offers practice activities for certain tests and levels to familiarize students with the test-taking mechanics, item formats, and page design elements.

A teacher's guide provides a good description of the specific tests and a table of specifications in order for teachers to be familiar with test content. The guide also provides information on different score reports. The Home Report shows a student's percentile rank for the subjects tested, indicates the national average with a color band at the 50th percentile, and gives an overall description of the skills assessed on the subtests. The Individual Profile Report indicates the specific objectives and the student's level of mastery. The guide also provides an explanation of the performance level scores (e.g., Nearing Proficiency, Proficient, and Advanced) that TerraNova provides for standards-referenced interpretation. Other reports provided are Group Lists, Group Performance Report, and an Algebra Summary Report.

In addition, the guide provides suggestions on communicating the results to all interested parties.

DEVELOPMENT. The developers of TerraNova, The Second Edition described it as an alternate form of the TerraNova and indicated that the content rationale and specifications for the TerraNova apply to the TerraNova, The Second Edition. The test developers claimed that TerraNova, The Second Edition measures the same constructs in the same manner as the TerraNova and the information about students' knowledge, skills, and abilities would be the same for both.

Test development for the TerraNova, The Second Edition is well described and documents the thoroughness of the process. In planning the content of the TerraNova, the test developers met with educators from all areas of the United States; they reviewed the content standards and curriculum frameworks of educational bodies to determine common educational goals; and they examined current textbook series, instructional programs, and national standards publications.

Developers of the TerraNova, The Second Edition wrote assessment specifications to guide the development of items and stimulus materials. A staff of item-writers, which included experienced teachers, developed a pool of items for tryout material. Items were reviewed for content and editorial accuracy and graphic and textual clarity.

Test developers also attended to possibility of bias associated with ethnicity, race, gender, region, and age. The writing and review of materials were guided by the policies and guidelines outlined in *Reflecting Diversity: Multicultural Guidelines for Educational Publishing Professionals* (Macmillan/McGraw-Hill, 1993) and *Guidelines for Bias-Free Publishing* (McGraw-Hill, 1983). In addition, educators of various ethnic groups reviewed materials for bias in language, subject matter, and representation of people. In the final versions of the tests, it is evident that the developers were aware of diversity issues and made specific attempts to include a wide range of ethnic groups, some representations of the physically challenged, and a variety of authors, perspectives, and geographic locations.

Test development occurred in two phases: tryout and standardization. In the tryout phase, testing included more than twice as many items as were needed for the final form. The items were field tested nationally. Items were administered across several grades for which they were thought appropriate (e.g., fifth grade items tested in Grades 4–6). Tryout booklets were created and anchor items from the TerraNova accompanied the new items for linking purposes. In the tryout phase, items were administered to more than 100,000 students. Teachers who participated in the tryout phase were asked to comment on accuracy, validity, and grade appropriateness of the items. In other reviews, teachers, parents, and others evaluated items in all of the content areas.

Statistical information about items from the tryout sample was used by the content developers to select items for the final forms. In the selection, developers reviewed the proportion of students answering the item correctly, the point-biserial correlation between the item and the number-correct score on the rest of the test, and the mean number-correct score of students selecting the correct answer. For each constructed-response item, the statistics included the proportion of students at each performance level and the mean raw score. The developers also used item-response theory (IRT) analyses to estimate the national difficulty of items, fit ratings, and differential item functioning (DIF). DIF was assessed for African Americans, Hispanics, males, and females. Items that displayed DIF were examined to determine if construct irrelevant variance contributed to disparate difficulty by ethnicity or gender.

The primary criterion for item selection for TerraNova, The Second Edition was to meet the content specifications of the TerraNova. Next, developers selected items most statistically similar to TerraNova items. In addition, the developers minimized the number of items displaying DIF. Item selection was also guided by similarity of the distracter performance, item fit, and discrimination with TerraNova items. Developers also selected items that minimized measurement error throughout the range of student performance.

TECHNICAL.

Norming. The national standardization (i.e., norming) occurred in the fall of 1999 and spring of 2000. Fall norming included Grades 1–12 and spring norming included Grades K–12. Standardization also occurred in the winter of 2000 for Grades K and 1.

A total of 1,320 schools from 778 districts participated in the standardization of the TerraNova, The Second Edition. More than 264,000 students participated in Grades K–12:

114,312 in the fall, 12,859 in the winter, and 149,798 in the spring. Selection of schools for the norming sample was based on the stratification variables of geographic region (eastern, southern, midcontinent, western), community type (large central city, midsize central city, urban fringe of large central city, urban fringe of midsize central city, large town, small town, rural), socioeconomic status (high and low based on number of students eligible for Title 1 funding), and special needs.

In the development of the norms, the developers indicated that they weighted students' scores on the TerraNova to represent national proportions.

Schools participating in standardization were asked to test all students normally tested, including those with accommodations. This decision by the developers is congruent with the current emphasis of the inclusion of all students in a testing program. The examiners were asked to record the areas of special needs, as well as any testing modifications specified in the student's individual education plan (IEP). Special needs categories included learning disabled, physically disabled, emotional disabled, and mentally disabled.

The TerraNova, The Second Edition was co-standardized with two tests of cognitive skills: the Primary Test of Cognitive Skills (PTCS) (Kindergarten and Grade 1) and InView (Grades 2–12). Both were included in the standardization of spring of 2000. When TerraNova is administered with these tests of cognitive skills, InView and PTCS produce anticipated achievement scores that are a function of the student's grade and age, as well as his or her scores on the cognitive skills test. The developers stated that "The difference between a student's obtained and anticipated scores is an estimate of the student's achievement above or below the average of students with similar attributes and it can help screen students for a potential-actual discrepancy requiring further diagnostic testing" (technical manual, p. 53).

In order for TerraNova, The Second Edition to be on the TerraNova scale, student scores on TerraNova, The Second Edition were equated with their scores on Form A of the TerraNova. Approximately 1,000 students in Grades 1–12 were administered subtests from TerraNova, The Second Edition, Forms C and D, and TerraNova Form A. Students in the first grade were administered the Complete Battery Plus edition and students in Grades 2–12 completed the Survey with Plus edition. Different students completed different sets of subtests. The data from TerraNova, The Second Edition and TerraNova Form A anchor subtests were used for item calibration and equating to the TerraNova scale.

The TerraNova, The Second Edition: Technical Bulletin 1 provides tables of scale score information: mean, standard deviation, and median. The developers stated that the scale means for the fall standardization reflected steady growth in average performance across grades. They noted a similar pattern in the spring data. In some cases, scale means reflected a decline when going from the spring of one grade to the fall of the next grade. The developers indicated that these declines were not unusual and linked them to summer slumps in student performance.

Scoring of the TerraNova can use either raw scores or IRT-based item-pattern scores. The developers recommended the use of item-pattern scoring because it results in more accurate scores for students. The test developers indicated that a subsequent publication will include the standard error of measurement curves that reflect the reliability of scores based on IRT.

Standard-setting. Student performance can be compared normatively, as described above, or in a standards-based manner. Standards-referenced scores are based on performance levels that describe the knowledge, skills, and abilities of students within each performance level. CTBS used the Bookmark Standard Setting Procedure™ to establish cut scores to classify student performance in one of five levels: Step 1, Progressing, Nearing Proficiency, Proficient, and Advanced. Cut scores were established for Reading, Language, Mathematics, Science, and Social Studies. To set the cut scores for the performance levels, the TerraNova developers used teachers and curriculum specialists.

Reliability. For the tests with multiple-choice items only, KR20 was reported as a measure of internal consistency. Reliability estimates for the Survey with Plus test ranged from the high .80s to mid .90s for the Reading Composite, Language Composite, Mathematics Composite, and the Total test. The developers appropriately recommended caution in the use of scores based on the individual tests associated with the Survey with Plus edition due to low KR20 values; some of the individual tests, such as Vocabulary and Language

Mechanics, have KR20 reliability estimates only in the high .70s and low .80s.

For the Complete Battery Plus test, internal consistency ranged from the high .80s to high .90s for the Reading Composite, Language Composite, Mathematics Composite, and the Total test. Given the Complete Battery has more items for the individual tests of Reading, Language, Mathematics, Science, and Social Studies, for these tests the reliability is typically in the upper .80s to lower .90s. The Plus tests maintain the same number of items and the reliability estimates range from the high .70s to the low .80s.

For the Multiple Assessments with Plus, the alpha coefficient was used as a measure of internal consistency. Alpha coefficients ranged from the high .80s to high .90s for the Reading Composite, Language Composite, Mathematics Composite, and the Total test. For the tests of Reading, Language, Mathematics, Science, and Social Studies, the Multiple Assessment with Plus typically has fewer items than the Complete Battery Plus. The reliability estimates for these tests range from the high .80s to the low .90s. The reliability estimates for the Plus tests remain the same: high .70s to low .80s.

For the Multiple Assessments, the consistency of scoring of the constructed-response items by readers was assessed through the use of interrater agreement indices, expressed as an intraclass correlation and a weighted Kappa coefficient. The agreement levels typically were in the .90s. However, for some items, interrater agreement was in the .60s and .70s based on Kappa. The authors stated that "Kappa values between .40 and .74 represent good agreement beyond chance" (technical manual, pp. 84–85); however, they offered no basis for the statement. Given that students' scores are based on all the items within a test, and not any one constructed-response item, an occasional low interrater agreement estimate is not especially troublesome if the test-level score is in the high .80s and above.

Validity. In their discussion of validity, the developers of TerraNova cited the *Standards for Educational and Psychological Testing* statement that "Validity refers to the degree to which evidence and theory support the interpretations of test scores entailed by proposed uses of tests" (American Educational Research Association [AERA], American Psychological Association [APA], & National Council on Measurement in Education

[NCME], 1999, p. 9). Admirably, the developers of TerraNova then explicate its proposed uses. They wrote that the purpose of TerraNova is to "provide achievement scores that are valid for most types of educational decision making" (technical bulletin, p. 253). They also identified the use of scores to track progress over years and grades, to make decisions in a criterion-referenced manner about individual student's strength and weaknesses, to plan additional instruction, and to report student's progress to parents.

They presented content validity evidence in terms of the correspondence between the test and instructional content. In support of this correspondence, the developers of TerraNova described their comprehensive curriculum review (see the description in the Development section above). They noted the correspondence between test and instructional content was strengthened by thematically integrating the content and developing graphics to be congruent with the materials that students encounter in their daily lives. In addition, teacher and student questionnaires collected information on test clarity and appropriateness of the material for the grade level.

Construct validity. The test developers collected construct validity evidence by examining the patterns of correlations between the TerraNova tests to determine if the test demonstrates convergent and discriminant validity. Such evidence requires that "tests designed to measure similar skills should correlate more highly than tests designed to measure distinctly different skills" (technical bulletin, p. 254). The developers presented tables of intercorrelations of TerraNova tests for Grades 2–12 and indicated that the correlations provided convergent and discriminant validity evidence. To support this claim, the developers noted that Reading correlated more highly with Language scores than Reading with Mathematics or Language with Mathematics. Evidence of convergent and discriminant validity also appears to hold when contrasting the tests associated with language arts (i.e., Language Arts and Language Mechanics) with those of mathematics.

The developers also correlated TerraNova scores with InView, a test of academic abilities. InView has five subscales: Verbal Reasoning—Words, Verbal Reasoning—Context, Sequences, Analogies, and Quantitative Reasoning. According to the test developers, the two Verbal Reason-

ing subscales gauge students' ability to solve verbal problems and were expected to correlate more highly with Reading, Vocabulary, Language Arts, and Language Mechanics than with either Mathematics or Mathematics Computation. In contrast, the InView tests of Sequences, Analogies, and Quantitative Reasoning were expected to correlate more highly with the Mathematics or Mathematics Computation tests than the Reading and Language Arts tests of the TerraNova. A review of the correlations provided in the Technical Bulletin 1 shows a pattern of slightly higher correlations between the Reading tests of TerraNova and the verbal skills of InView as compared to the correlations between the Reading tests and the quantitative subtests of Sequences, Analogies, and Quantitative. However, the correlations between the TerraNova Mathematics tests and the InView Quantitative tests were of nearly the same magnitude as those between TerraNova Mathematics tests and the Verbal Reasoning tests in InView.

The technical manual also contains a series of construct validity statements that describe the skills, concepts, and processes measured in each area. These statements allow the consumer to determine the congruency of test content with their conceptualization of the subject area. For example, for Reading and Language Arts, the developers wrote that two main goals in the development of TerraNova were "1) to integrate assessment of the major communication skills—reading comprehension, language expression, vocabulary, and reference skills—and 2) to present the materials in a context that provides meaning and purpose" (technical bulletin, p. 267).

Differential item functioning. A differential item functioning analysis was conducted on the items used in the standardization. Separate DIF analyses were conducted for the categories of gender and ethnicity. The DIF analyses for ethnicity included students who were African American, Hispanic, and Other. Asian students were not included in the DIF analyses due to small numbers. Across grade levels and subject areas, out of over 3,500 items, of the items flagged for DIF, 11 items functioned in favor of African American students and 44 against these students. Thirteen items functioned in favor of Hispanic students and 45 against these students. Only 2 items functioned in favor of students classified as Other and 2 against these students. In terms of gender, 3 items functioned in favor of males and 21 against males; whereas, 8 functioned in favor of and 14 against females.

COMMENTARY. The developers of the TerraNova have described test development procedures that lend credibility to the assessment. They conducted an extensive curriculum review, guided the item development with assessment specifications, employed a staff of item writers that included teachers, and submitted items for review to editors and a committee of educators for bias. The developers then completed a national tryout of items and used the statistical information to select items that functioned appropriately and displayed characteristics similar to items on the TerraNova.

For the final forms, the developers of the TerraNova, The Second Edition presented evidence about validity and estimates of reliability. In the presentation of validity evidence, the test developers first specified the purpose and uses of the test and then presented evidence to support the use of the test scores for making inferences about student achievement. Content validity evidence derived from the curriculum review that was completed in the development stage. In their review of construct validity, the developers of TerraNova examined convergent and discriminant evidence. The low correlations between the Reading and Language tests with Mathematics tests provided discriminant validity evidence for Mathematics. The constructs of reading and language were less distinct because correlations of Reading tests with Language Arts tests were of similar magnitude as the correlations between Reading with Vocabulary and Language with Language Mechanics. However, current views in the English language arts consider reading and language arts as overlapping constructs and, in this view, the high correlations between the tests of Reading and Language would be expected.

Reliability levels appear reasonable for students' scores when based on the Total test. Individual test scores require caution in the interpretation because in some instances they are only in the upper .70s and .80s. Interrater agreement indices were generally in the .90s for constructed-response items; however, some items were associated with estimates as low as the .60s and .70s. If scores for individual items are only reported as part of a Total score, then these low reliability estimates should not prove problematic.

Standardization for the TerraNova included over 264,000 students from a total of 1,320 schools in 778 districts. To make the norming sample as representative of the nation as possible, test developers selected schools based on the stratification variables of geographic, community type, socioeconomic status, and special needs. In the development of the norms, the developers indicated that students' scores on the TerraNova were weighted to reflect national percentages.

DIF was reviewed for the results from the standardization. Few items display DIF; however, a small percentage do and districts and states should review the implications prior to adopting this or any other instrument.

SUMMARY. The TerraNova measures student achievement in Reading, the Language Arts, Mathematics, Science and Social Studies. It appears to be a well-developed instrument. Reliability and validity evidence support its use as one measure of student achievement. Potential consumers will want to compare the representativeness of the TerraNova standardization sample with the representativeness of the standardization samples of other achievement tests. In addition, districts and states will want to compare the prevalence of items with DIF in TerraNova with the number of items with DIF in other tests of achievement.

REVIEWERS' REFERENCES

American Educational Research Association, American Psychological Association, & National Council on Measurement in Education. (1999). *Standards for educational and psychological testing.* Washington, DC: American Educational Research Association.
Macmillan-McGraw Hill. (1993). *Reflecting diversity: Multicultural guidelines for educational publishing professionals.* Monterey, CA: Author.
McGraw-Hill Book Company. (1983). *Guidelines for bias-free publishing.* New York: McGraw-Hill.

[246]

Test of Early Mathematics Ability, Third Edition.

Purpose: Designed as a test of early mathematical ability.
Population: Ages 3-0 to 8-11.
Publication Dates: 1983–2003.
Acronym: TEMA-3.
Score: Math Ability Score.
Administration: Individual.
Forms, 2: A, B.
Price Data, 2003: $256 per complete kit including examiner's manual (2003, 71 pages), picture book Form A, picture book Form B, 25 examiner record booklets Form A, 25 examiner record booklets Form B, 25 worksheets Form A, 25 worksheets Form B, assessment probes, 5"x8" cards, 20 blocks, 20 tokens, and mesh bag; $51 per picture book A or B; $25 per 25 Form A or Form B examiner record booklets; $19 per 25 Form

A or Form B worksheets; $35 per Assessment Probes manual (2003, 82 pages); $48 per examiner's manual; $19 per objects kit.

Time: Untimed.

Authors: Herbert P. Ginsburg and Arthur J. Baroody.

Publisher: PRO-ED.

Cross References: See T5:2681 (2 references); for a review by Jerry Johnson and Joyce R. McLarty of an earlier edition, see 11:428 (1 reference); for a review by David P. Lindeman, see 9:1252.

Review of the Test of Early Mathematics Ability, Third Edition by KEVIN D. CREHAN, Professor of Educational Psychology, University of Nevada—Las Vegas, Las Vegas, NV:

DESCRIPTION. The Test of Early Mathematics Ability (TEMA) was originally developed as a means for identification of learning difficulties or the likelihood of developing learning difficulties for children in kindergarten through third grade. The test also was intended to provide useful information on the strengths and weaknesses of children without learning difficulties. The test is now in its third edition and has been expanded to include tasks for children as young as 3 years. The TEMA-3 consists of 72 items designed to measure both school and nonschool learning of mathematics skills and concepts. The testing materials consist of an examiner's manual, test booklet, recording booklet, manipulatives, suggested assessment probes, and recommended instructional activities. In addition to the initial uses of the TEMA, the authors suggest that the TEMA-3 provides guidance for individualized instructional activities and is a means for documentation of children's progress. They also suggest that the TEMA-3 has uses as a research measure.

The test is individually administered with a starting point determined by the child's age. Testing is continued until the child passes five consecutive items (basal) and misses five consecutive items (ceiling). Average testing time is estimated to be between 45 and 60 minutes. Items that are not administered below the basal level are scored correct and items that are not administered above the ceiling are scored incorrect. Tables are provided for conversion of raw scores to math ability scores and age and grade equivalents. A table for conversion of math ability scores to percentile ranks is also included.

DEVELOPMENT. Item and test development was based on a body of research conducted by the authors and others that showed that mathematical skills develop from a foundation of informal mathematical thinking that emerges before the child begins formal schooling. Items range from showing one finger and recognition of more or less dots to formal multiplication facts and mental arithmetic.

The TEMA-3 materials provide more than a test of mathematics. The accompanying *Assessment Probes and Instructional Activities* presents an item-by-item set of useful guides to the understanding of each task and the child's responses. The author describes the task, comprehension of the task, underlying thought processes, probes to stimulate response, and suggested instructional activities.

TECHNICAL. The authors report that the norm sample for the TEMA-3 was 1,228 children (637 Form A and 591 Form B) tested in 2000 and 2001 in 15 states. However, they list 16 states by name and the list excludes South Dakota, which is named as a standardization site. It appears that the norm data were collected primarily at each of four testing sites in New York, South Dakota, Texas, and Oregon. Additional data came from the participation of volunteers solicited from the publisher's customer database. The breakdown among the data sources is not given. Observations were weighted to the U.S. Census population at age levels (3 through 8) by geographic region, gender, and ethnicity.

The authors report using a counterbalanced random groups design to collect data for equating the two forms of the test. However, they state that "examinees at each testing site were grouped according to age … Child 1 was tested with Form A, Child 2 was tested with Form B, and so on. These procedures were followed to ensure that approximately the same numbers of examinees were tested with both forms" (examiner's manual, p. 25). This is a bit confusing because, if a counterbalanced design had been used, then each child would have been tested with both forms.

In one paragraph, the authors describe how math ability scores were derived for the raw score norm data. They report using polynomial regression to develop normalized standard math ability scores (mean 100, standard deviation 15) at each 3-month age interval, which "were smoothed somewhat to allow for a consistent progression across age levels" (examiner's manual, p. 25).

Coefficient alpha reliability estimates and standard errors are reported at each age level for each form. The median reliability estimate is .95 and the median standard error is three. Alternate forms reliability is estimated at .97 based on a sample of 46 children and corrected for restriction of range. This same sample was retested after 2 weeks on alternate forms. The correlation, corrected for restriction of range, was .93. Test-retest correlations (corrected for restriction of range, 2-week interval) were .82 for 49 children on Form A and .93 for 21 children on Form B. A summary table of all reliability estimates is provided but unfortunately, the table's columns are not aligned correctly.

The validity chapter presents a lengthy and detailed description of the test's content related to age that tracks the development of mathematical knowledge from nonverbal recognition of number concepts through application of formal and informal procedures to solve mathematical questions. The developmental progress is supported by citation to theory, research, and national standards.

Results of item analyses for the norm sample are reported by age level and test form. The item-total correlations are quite high with a range of .45 to .68 and a median of about .55. The reported age by grade median item difficulties seem to suggest some anomalies. The year-to-year median item difficulties range from .03 for the Form B 3-year-old sample to .87 for the Form B 8-year-old sample. The year-to-year changes in median difficulty for Form A range from .14 to .28. Changes in year-to-year difficulty for Form B range from .06 to .29. Differences in median difficulty between forms within age groups range from .01 for age 3 to .20 for age 8. The results for median difficulties seem to conflict with the raw score means reported later. Raw score means show a generally smooth increase in means over ages and little difference in means between forms within ages. It would seem that form by age median item difficulties would agree more closely with form by age mean raw scores. The authors do not comment on this apparent irregularity.

The authors describe a recommended sensitivity review to assure that test content is free of offensive content, stereotypes, ethnocentrism, and gender bias. Additionally, they conducted differential item functioning (DIF) analyses that resulted in no items being eliminated for reason of DIF.

Evidence of correlation with other measures of mathematics is reported for seven mathematics subtests selected from the KeyMath-R/NU, Wood-cock-Johnson III-ACH, Diagnostic Achievement Battery-3, and Young Children's Achievement Test. It is not clear whether the correlations are to be interpreted as concurrent or predictive evidence because no indication of time intervals is given. Sample sizes for the seven correlations ranged from 43 to 62 and the correlations had a median of .65. The reported correlations were corrected for attenuation and restriction of range so should be treated as theoretical estimates.

Additional evidence, labeled construct-identification validity, is presented which shows average mean raw scores increasing with age, high correlations of score with age, and a difference between mean scores for low mathematics achievement groups and "normal" children.

COMMENTARY. Reviews of earlier versions of the TEMA (9:1252; 11:428) were generally complimentary of the test as a useful measure of children's mathematical knowledge and thinking and the reviewers of the TEMA-2 were impressed with the addition of the *Assessment Probes and Instructional Activities*. However, these earlier reviewers were critical of some of the supporting technical data. The present review follows along these same lines. The TEMA-3 provides the user with a broad range measure of children's mathematics attainment. Additionally, the supporting materials include the profile/examiner record booklet and the *Assessment Probes and Instructional Activities*. A completed profile/examiner record booklet gives a ready reference to the child's performance with brief clear item descriptions. A review of this document is likely to fulfill three of the stated purposes of the TEMA-3; to identify children with learning difficulties, to provide useful information of the child's strengths and weaknesses, and to document a child's progress in learning arithmetic. As mentioned earlier, the *Assessment Probes and Instructional Activities* presents an item-by-item account describing each task, comprehension of the task, underlying thought processes, probes to stimulate response, and suggested instructional activities. Although not actually part of the test, this supplement should provide the skilled tutor with useful diagnostics and prescriptive actions. Additionally, it fulfills a fourth stated purpose of the test. The fifth stated purpose of the test is for use in research. The case for this use is not made and the test is likely to be of too broad a range for most research applications.

Although not diminishing the usefulness of the test, the supporting technical documentation remains in need of improvement and/or more detailed explanation in some areas. A few concerns are noted. Directions for scoring the test indicate that all items below the basal level are scored correct and all items above the ceiling are scored incorrect. The implied rationale for this scoring protocol is that items are ordered by difficulty. However, ordering items by empirical difficulty level is no assurance that a child would miss items above his or her ceiling or correctly respond to items below his or her basal level. Assuming this scoring procedure was used with the norm sample, a number of concerns follows. First, item difficulties for the lower numbered items would tend to be inflated and item difficulties for the higher numbered items would be depressed. This problem would extend to the further concern of magnified item-total correlations. This in turn extends to inflated coefficient alpha estimates and correlations between the TEMA-3 and other measures. Because most of the reliability and validity evidence is based on correlations, the concern is broad based.

One average length paragraph is not sufficient to describe the method of derivation for the seminal math ability score. This procedure needs greater explication, documentation, and justification. In future revision, the authors may even want to consider a different approach using applications of item response theory. Also, it is not clear what the reporting of grade and age equivalents adds to the interpretive information for the test.

The manual provides information in the form of score discrepancies for statistically significant and clinically useful interpretations. The methods used to arrive at these estimates are questionable, especially the formula used to estimate a correlation between two measures from the two reliability estimates of the measure involved. If appropriate methods are available to estimate a clinically useful discrepancy, the discrepancy should be reported as a range based on the standard error of the estimate.

Even though the authors clearly say that "validity is a relative rather than an absolute concept" (examiner's manual, p. 33), they state that the TEMA-3 is a "valid" measure on three occasions in the manual (pp. 4, 5, & 42).

SUMMARY. THE TEMA-3 was designed to improve on its predecessor in a number of ways.

Additional items were added for younger children and some items were revised to provide more specific assessment. Descriptive item names were added to the profile/examiner record booklet to facilitate communication of results and IEP writing. The addition of an alternate form enhances the TEMA-3 use as a pre- and posttest assessment. These improvements and the supplemental *Assessment Probes and Instructional Activities* make the TEMA-3 an attractive choice for the skilled professional. Although there are a number of weaknesses in the technical documentation and some quality indices are likely to be overestimates, more appropriate methods would likely yield quite acceptable estimates. If the purposes of the TEMA-3 mesh with your needs, the instrument deserves attention.

Review of the Test of Early Mathematics Ability, Third Edition by JUDITH A. MONSAAS, Executive Director of P-16 Assessment and Evaluation, University System of Georgia, Atlanta, GA:

DESCRIPTION. The Test of Early Mathematics Ability, Third Edition, (TEMA-3) is designed to assess the informal and formal mathematics ability of children from ages 3-0 to 8-11. The purposes of the test are to identify young children who have learning difficulties and who are likely to develop problems in mathematics and to provide information about mathematical strengths and weaknesses of children, with or without learning difficulties. It also provides suggested instructional practices for students who miss specific items. The test measures mathematics learned in everyday situations (informal) and in more formal situations such as school (formal) as well as concepts and skills. The test has two forms and is individually administered.

The materials provided are attractively packaged and include: an examiner's manual with administration and technical information; a picture book with administration and scoring information for each item and pictures for use with some items; an administration booklet (called "Assessment Probes and Instructional Activities") with additional probes for each question, explanations of why students may answer incorrectly, and strategies for teaching the skill; a profile/examiner record booklet for recording student information, item performance, interpretation, and comment; manipulatives that are to be used with certain questions; and a pad of student worksheets for use with select items. The examiner's manual explains how TEMA-3 is an improvement over TEMA and TEMA-2. The authors have responded to feedback on earlier editions and improved both the content, the ease of use, and technical characteristics of the test. The TEMA-3 has added an alternate form that is useful for researchers and for teachers wishing to monitor student progress over time. Examiner qualifications and administration procedures, scoring, etc., are all clearly spelled out so, after practice, any qualified person, such as a classroom teacher, should be able to administer the test.

The 72 items are arranged in ascending difficulty. Administration begins at an entry point based on the child's age and continues until 5 consecutive items are answered incorrectly, the ceiling. The basal is the highest 5 items answered correctly. All items below the basal are considered correct. Scoring instructions are clearly described. Standard scores (mean = 100, standard deviation = 15), percentile ranks, and age and grade equivalents are provided. A section addressing discrepancy analysis for Forms A and B and between TEMA-3 and other tests provides guidance for using the test in research and in clinical practice. A table showing the difference scores required for statistical significance and clinical significance is provided. The section on cautions in interpreting test scores and accounting for situation and child error should be read by any test user.

DEVELOPMENT. The TEMA was developed in 1983 to fill the gap in the assessment of the mathematical knowledge of young children. It has a sound theoretical and research base. The developers of the TEMA-2 and TEMA-3 have responded to critiques and each subsequent test has been an improvement over its predecessors. There appears to have been more substantive change in TEMA-3, with several items added based on recent research on children's acquisition of number and on the "big ideas" that underlie mathematical understanding. Traditional discrimination and difficulty analyses were used for item selection. Data were not provided showing the number of new items pilot tested and the number with acceptable psychometric characteristics. Median item discrimination and difficulty indices are provided for each grade level. Even though these indices are quite high, the item-test correlations are probably inflated because of the method of scoring all items below the basal as correct and

those above the ceiling as incorrect. Item response theory (IRT) procedures might provide better evidence of item quality.

TECHNICAL.

Standardization. The TEMA-3 was normed on a sample of 1,228 children who took one of the two forms of the test. The standardization sites reflected the four major demographic regions as designated by the U.S. Bureau of the Census. The sample approximated the school-age population in terms of geographic area, gender, race, and ethnicity. In terms of socioeconomic status, income levels were higher than the general population and for parents' educational attainment, "less than bachelor's degree" (examiner's manual, p. 22) was combined into one category that included the majority of the sample and the school-age population (approximately 74%) so it is impossible to determine if the sample accurately reflected the lower end of the educational spectrum. Norms were calculated using weighted samples.

Counterbalanced random samples were used to collect normative data for the alternate forms of the TEMA-3. The forms were equated using linear equating procedures allowing for differences between forms to vary along the scale. Formulas recommended by Kolen and Brennan (1995) were used to make adjustments in scale scores.

Reliability. Coefficient alpha, test-retest, and alternate form reliability with immediate and delayed administration reliability analyses were performed. All the coefficients reported were over .90 except for test-retest reliability for Form A, which was .82. It is unclear why grade level and demographic breakdowns were reported for coefficient alpha only. These data would be useful for the test-retest and alternate forms reliability, which tended to be slightly lower than the coefficient alphas.

Validity. The authors rely on Anastasi and Urbina (1997) to structure their validity claims. The authors provide a detailed, well-articulated rationale for the "content-description validity" (examiner's manual, p. 33) of the test. The research base for the structure of the test and the item development/selection is particularly strong. Conventional item analyses and differential item functioning analyses were performed to further support the content validity and provide evidence that the items are relatively bias free.

"Criterion-prediction validity" (examiner's manual, p. 40) evidence is supported by the correlation of the TEMA-3 with other tests that measure early mathematics ability. These correlations range from moderate to very high, which supports the claim that the TEMA-3 is measuring concepts similar to those assessed by other related tests. The authors use fairly traditional methods for assessing the construct-related validity of the test. Age differentiation means and standard score means for various demographic groups are in the predictable direction. Item validity evidence in support of the test is also used to support the construct validity of the test.

According to the *Standards for Educational and Psychological Testing*, "Validity refers to the degree to which evidence and theory support the interpretations of test scores entailed by the proposed uses of the tests" (AERA, APA, & NCME, p. 9). The authors provide a sound basis for the content of the test but they do not take the next step and tie the validity evidence to the purported uses of the test. Of the two purported uses of the test, (a) to identify children who have or are likely to develop learning difficulties and (b) to provide useful information about the mathematics strengths and weaknesses of children, the validity evidence provides stronger support for the second use than the first. More direct evidence should be provided that the test is useful for identifying young children with learning difficulties.

COMMENTARY AND SUMMARY. With each new successive edition of the TEMA, the test is improved. The theory and research base supporting the test is strong.

The test is user friendly. All materials are included in the packet with clear directions for use. Administration and scoring instructions are clearly spelled out. The development of alternate forms is useful for assessing change after interventions with children. The technical characteristics continue to improve as the authors expand the norming samples and include additional reliability and validity studies.

Nonetheless there is still room for improvement. Validity evidence linked to the recommended test uses would strengthen the test and bring the validity studies more in line with the current standards. More specific demographic breakdowns of the norming samples (e.g., educational attainment of parents) and the reliability estimates (e.g., test-retest) would strengthen those sections as well.

Overall, this is a strong tool in the repertoire of tests of the mathematical knowledge of young

children. As with previous editions, it is anticipated that the next version will provide stronger technical evidence supporting the test as has been the case with each successive version.

REVIEWER'S REFERENCES
American Educational Research Association, American Psychological Association, & National Council on Measurement in Education. (1999). *Standards for educational and psychological testing*. Washington, DC: American Educational Research Association.
Anastasi, A., & Urbina, S. (1997). *Psychological testing* (7th ed.). Upper Saddle River, NJ: Prentice Hall.
Kolen, M. J., & Brennan, R. L. (1995). *Test equating methods and practices.* New York: Springer.

[247]

Test of Narrative Language.

Purpose: Designed to measure "children's ability to understand and tell stories."
Population: Ages 5-0 to 11-11.
Publication Date: 2004.
Acronym: TNL.
Scores, 3: 2 subtests: Narrative Comprehension, Oral Narration, plus Narrative Language Ability Index.
Administration: Individual.
Price Data, 2004: $148 per complete kit including examiner's manual (119 pages), picture book, and 25 examiner record booklets; $55 per examiner's manual; $57 per picture book; 440 per 25 examiner record booklets.
Time: (15–20) minutes.
Authors: Ronald B. Gillam and Nils A. Pearson.
Publisher: PRO-ED.

Review of the Test of Narrative Language by ABIGAIL BAXTER, *Associate Professor, Department of Special Education, University of South Alabama, Mobile, AL:*

DESCRIPTION. The Test of Narrative Language (TNL) is designed for use with children between the ages of 5 years 0 months and 11 years 11 months. The authors claim it is a "norm-referenced, efficient, and accurate way of assessing children's ability to listen to and tell narratives (i.e., stories)" (examiner's manual, p. 1) that can be used to identify language impairments, compare narrative comprehension and production discrepancies, document changes resulting from intervention, and in research studies.

The TNL is individually administered and requires the audio taping of every task for scoring purposes. It consists of six tasks on narrative comprehension or oral narration subtests that are assessed by three different narrative formats. Scripted examiner instructions and prompts are provided. Administration time is approximately 15–25 minutes.

The Narrative Comprehension tasks are scored during administration and validated by the audiotape. Acceptable and unacceptable answers for each task are in the test manual. For the Oral Narration tasks, the scorer must listen to the audiotape of each task at least three times and follow a scoring guide that assesses both the macrostructure and microstructure of responses. Scoring, by an experienced examiner, may take 20 minutes.

The TNL yields many scores. Raw scores for each task are combined into Narrative Comprehension and Oral Narration subtest raw scores. Subtest age equivalents, percentile ranks, and standard scores are available. The Narrative Language Ability Index (NLAI) is a standard score (mean = 100, standard deviation = 15) based upon the sum of the two subtest standard scores.

DEVELOPMENT. The TNL manual presents little information on the development of specific items. Research concerning the dimensions of narrative discourse, components of narratives, and factors affecting narration abilities are discussed and support the importance of assessing overall narrative language abilities and its components. Information supporting the three formats used on the TNL is presented. Item discrimination and item difficulty analyses led to 26 items being removed from the TNL.

The administration instructions in the manual are easy to follow; however, the scripted directions are difficult to discern because the font is similar to the other text. One item on the TNL appears problematic. On the McDonald's story, question 6 asks, "Where did they eat?" In the story the family is not described as eating. It ends with the family having ordered their food and the mother discovering she has left her purse at home. A response indicating that the story did not tell if the family ate at McDonald's or not is coded as incorrect. Better wording of the question may be to ask where the family went to eat.

TECHNICAL.
Standardization. The standardization sample was 1,059 children, between the ages of 5 and 11 years, who lived in 20 states. Compared to the U.S. population the two groups are similar in terms of geographic area, gender, and race. The age groups (by year) are not equally represented in the norm group. Upper income groups ($35,000/ year and above) are slightly overrepresented in the norm group, which is problematic because of the language abilities of children from more advantaged backgrounds (Hart & Risley, 1992). Children with

disabilities are included but many appear to have disabilities that would specifically impact narrative language. The manual states that children with hearing impairments and unintelligible speech should not be tested with the TNL; however, the norm group had such children. Data indicate no significant gender performance differences although there is some evidence of racial differences.

Reliability. Internal consistency, interscorer, and test-retest reliability estimates are presented. Most coefficient alphas for the subtests and all items for the entire norm group, genders, and racial groups exceed the minimum criteria of .80. Interscorer reliability was assessed for a subsample of the norm group using point-to-point and Cohen's kappa procedures. Raters scoring protocols using directions in the manual were reliable with scorers trained by the test developers. Scorings from audiotapes were reliable with scorings from written transcripts. Test-retest reliability (2-week window) analyses involved a convenience sample of 27 children from Austin, TX between 5 and 10 years of age who were predominantly European American and had a disability (a group that may be less likely to show changes in these skills). Only the uncorrected Narrative Comprehension subtest score meets the .90 criteria for use of tests to make individual educational decisions about children (Salvia & Ysseldyke, 2004). Test-retest reliabilities were not separately calculated for different ages. Thus, the test-retest data are based on a small nonrepresentative group and are not strong enough for clinical decision making.

Validity. The manual presents evidence of content, criterion-prediction, construct, and factor analytic validity. Content validity was documented through a review of the literature concerning format and narrative skills. Item discrimination, bias, and difficulty analyses were conducted. Criterion-prediction validity included comparing the TNL and Spoken Language Quotient of the Test of Language Development—Primary: Third Edition (TOLD-P: 3) for 47 language-impaired children between the ages of 5 and 10 years. Their scores were similar; however, the TOLD–P: 3 is normed only for children between the ages of 4-0 and 8-11. TNL scores and language samples collected from TNL audio recordings for a sample of 105 children with and without disabilities were similar but it is very possible that the TNL language samples may not be as rich as samples taken in different situations. Evidence of construct validity was demonstrated by increased performance on the TNL with age, differentiation between children with and without language disabilities, and the ability of the TNL to accurately identify children with and without language disabilities. The authors also claim that comparisons of scores for European Americans, African Americans, and Hispanic Americans on the subtests and NLAI support the TNL's construct validity. However, inspection of the means suggests that the subtests and composite may not measure the same thing in the three groups. The subtest standard scores vary between 9 and 10 for the two latter groups whereas that of the European Americans is 10. On the NLAI, the groups' average standard scores are 102, 95, and 94, suggesting that the scores for African American and Hispanic American children are 1/3 of a standard deviation away from the mean and 7 and 8 points, respectively, below the European American children. This suggests that these skills are influenced by culture (e.g., Berman, 2001), and the TNL is assessing the differences. Exploratory factor analysis identified the two subtest factors. Confirmatory factor analysis confirmed the development of the NLAI from the tasks.

COMMENTARY. There are several concerns about the quality of the TNL as a measurement tool. A larger norm group with all ages more equally represented in the sample would improve the strength of the TNL. The relatively fewer number of 5-year-olds in the norm group has important implications for the psychometric qualities of the test and for clinical uses.

Inclusion of some of children with disabilities related to oral language skills in the norm sample is also problematic. It is possible that these children lowered the raw scores of the group analyses in which they were included. A supplementary norm group of children with disabilities might have solved this problem.

The test-retest reliability estimates are of concern. The use of a small convenience sample "primarily composed of children who had been identified as language disordered and who were receiving language intervention services" (examiner's manual, p. 44) that did not represent all ages suggests that the reliabilities may not be accurate estimates for the entire population. Test-retest reliability and how it was determined is crucial because of the proposed use of this test for the identification of language problems. Small numbers of participants in some of the other reliability and validity studies are problematic.

There are also questions about the utility of the TNL in real-world applications. The manual states on page 8 that one of the TNL's uses is to "identify children who have language impairments"; on the next page it suggests its use in evaluating the language disorders in children while it notes that "not all children who score below average on the TNL have language disorders" (examiner's manual, p. 9). Thus, using the TNL as a tool to determine eligibility for special education and related services is not supported. Rather, the TNL may be helpful to teachers and therapists trying to understand the nature of a child's language impairment or learning disability.

SUMMARY. The TNL is a norm-referenced test that assesses the narrative comprehension and oral narration skills of children between the ages of 5 and 12. The authors have developed the test on a sound theoretical basis and have attempted to assess more than one dimension of narrative development. The test is easy to administer, engaging for children, and easy to score. However, many limitations in terms of test development and psychometric characteristics exist. The TNL may be best suited to help teachers and/or clinicians understand one aspect of children's language development and look for progress in this specific skill.

REVIEWER'S REFERENCES

Berman, R. A. (2001). Setting the narrative scene: How children begin to tell a story. In K. E. Nelson & A. Aksu-Koc (Eds.), *Children's language: Developing narrative and discourse competence* (vol. 10, pp. 1–30). Mahwah, NJ: Lawrence Erlbaum.

Hart, B., & Risley, T. (1992). American parenting of language-learning children: Persisting difference in family-child interactions observed in natural home environments. *Developmental Psychology, 28,* 1096–1105.

Salvia, J., & Ysseldyke, J. E. (2004). *Assessment in special and inclusive education* (9th ed.). Boston: Houghton Mifflin.

Review of the Test of Narrative Language by GABRIELE VAN LINGEN, Visiting Associate Professor in School Psychology, University of the Virgin Islands, U.S. Virgin Islands:

DESCRIPTION. The Test of Narrative Language (TNL) is a norm-referenced assessment instrument designed to measure children's comprehension and production of the connected speech used in telling stories. The authors, Ronald B. Gillam & Nils A. Pearson, state that it has four major uses: "(a) to identify children who have language impairments, (b) to determine whether there is a discrepancy between narrative comprehension and oral narrative production, (c) to document progress in narrative language as a result of language intervention, and (d) to measure narrative language in research studies" (examiner's manual, pp. 8–9). It is composed of six tasks related to story telling. It is designed to assess the language of children between the ages of 5-0 and 11-11. Although not specifically stated in the manual, the administration is conducted on an individual basis, using a tape recorder, examiner record booklet, and picture book. The examiner's manual states that administration time can vary between 15 and 25 minutes, with an additional time of 20 minutes needed for scoring by an experienced examiner.

The six tasks are divided into two sections or subtests labeled "Narrative Comprehension" and "Oral Narration." The authors describe Narrative Comprehension as the ability to recall and understand information, as well as make inferences about stories produced by others. Oral Narration measures "the ability to weave words and sentences into stories that contain characters who engage in goal-directed actions that are related to complicating events, consequences, and resolutions" (examiner's manual, p. 32). It provides measures of the child's use of well-formed simple and complex sentences, proper nouns, action verbs, temporal adverbs, and causal adverbs.

Each of the three tasks in the two subtests follows a similar format: The first type of format involves story narration by the examiner with no picture cues, followed by questions for Narrative Comprehension or a story retell for Oral Narration. For the second type, the examiner again reads a story while the child is provided with sequenced pictures in the picture book with similar response demands. The third task involves the presentation of a single picture in the picture book. For the Narrative Comprehension task, the examiner reads a related story and asks structured literal and inferential questions of the child. For the Oral Narration task the child is asked to freely generate a story, which is analyzed on a macrostructure (setting information, episode structure, holistic judgment) and microstructure level (vocabulary, sentence structure and grammaticality, cohesive ties). Examiners record responses in the examiner record booklet and also tape record the child's responses. Scoring instructions are provided on the record booklet and expanded in the examiner's manual. Scores can range from 0 to 2,

based on either quantitative or specifically described qualitative criteria. Both the record booklet and the manual provide sample responses for ease of scoring. Examiners are instructed to play back the audiotape to review their scoring of the comprehension questions and to score the story retelling and generation tasks. They are cautioned to listen to each story at least three times while making scoring judgments.

The results are transferred to the face sheet of the examiner record booklet, which also allows for noting identifying information about the examinee, the examiner, and incidental observations related to the examinee's speech production, fluency, and voice. Raw scores are recorded and summed for the two subtests, Narrative Comprehension and Oral Narration. For each subtest, age equivalents, percentile ranks, and standard scores are provided. Age equivalents were based on the average scores of all examinees at 2-month intervals from ages 5-0 through 8-11 and at 1-year intervals from ages 9-0 through 11-11. Standard scores are based on a normalized distribution of raw scores, using continuous norming procedure. Subtest standard scores have a mean of 10 and a standard deviation of 3. A classification system of seven categories with associated percentages based on the normal curve ranges from "Very Poor" to "Very Superior" in order to assist in the interpretation of subtest standard scores. A Narrative Language Ability Index (NLAI) was derived from the summation of the two subtest standard scores, using Guilford and Fruchter's (1978) procedure for pooling variances. The NLAI has a mean of 100 and a standard deviation of 15. A classification system similar to that provided for the subtest standard scores provides guidelines for interpreting the NLAI. These results can be used as a measure of a child's overall narrative language ability. It is seen as one part of a comprehensive evaluation of a student's language comprehension and production abilities. Although the results of the TNL can contribute to the selection of a student's long-term communication goals, they should not form the basis for planning daily instructional interventions. The authors caution that "the measures on the TNL assess too few of the critical aspects of narration to warrant using the subtest items for instructional planning" (examiner's manual, p. 35).

The qualifications for examiners of the TNL are successful completion of a basic course in assessment or psychometrics. Desirable qualifications include supervised practice in test administration, scoring, and reporting. Students and assistants are expected to be supervised by certified or licensed professionals.

DEVELOPMENT. The examiner's manual of the TNL provides a clear rationale for the development and relevant definitions of the constructs of the instrument. Moreover, it presents a synopsis of narrative language development for children between the ages of 5 and 12, as well as an overview of the research related to the narrative abilities of children with language disorders. However, the relationship between the definitions and constructs presented and the actual scores resulting from the TNL are not always clear and deserve greater elucidation.

TECHNICAL. The TNL was normed on a sample of 1,059 children in 20 states during 2001-2002 stratified by geographic area, gender, race, ethnicity (Hispanic/non-Hispanic), family income, exceptionality status, and age. Based on the tables provided, the norming sample seems quite representative of school-age and total population data of the 2001 U.S. Census. Exceptions include an overrepresentation of children in families with incomes over $35,000 and a much lower number of 5-year-olds in the sample when compared to the other age groups. The authors also present the demographic characteristics by age and region and by age and income, thereby allowing the examiners to determine the appropriateness of the sample for their more specific purposes.

The selection of formats—no picture, sequenced pictures, single picture—has been modified based on documented previous research on the assessment of narrative language. A similar process was used to identify appropriate measures. For Narrative Comprehension, literal and inferential questions were included, and for Oral Narration measures that included both a micro- and a macrostructure of analysis was used. The measures are listed and defined by examples in table format. The authors report that item analyses were conducted in order to determine each item's discriminating power, level of difficulty, and differential item functioning (DIF) at several stages of test development. The basis for the item analysis is not clearly stated. Moreover, the tables provided only report the median discriminating powers and difficulty level for the two subtests by age, based on the entire normative sample. The median discriminating power for Narrative Comprehension ranges from .23–.37, with only one median at age 6 surpassing .35; for Oral Narrative the corresponding range is .25–.33. Median difficulty level for Narrative Comprehension appears to be high (range .55–.87), with four ages having medians .80 or above. For Oral Narration the median difficulty levels range from .22–.63. A logistic regression procedure developed by Swaminathan and Rogers (1990) was used to detect DIF. Although five items were found to exhibit DIF according to the authors' criteria, they were retained in the TNL because of their "good discrimination and difficulty characteristics" (examiner's manual, p. 56) and because they represented less than 1% of the test items.

Evidence to support the validity of the TNL is reported by studies related to criterion-prediction validity, construct-identification validity, and factor analysis. For criterion-prediction validity, Gillam and Pearson report a study on the relationship between the TNL and the Spoken Language Quotient (SLQ) from the Test of Language Development—Primary: Third Edition (TOLD-P:3) using a subsample of 47 children classified as language impaired. The moderate to very large relationships are presented for the SLQ and TNL Narrative Comprehension, Oral Narration and NLA scores, based on the use of uncorrected and corrected coefficients, respectively. The large to very large correlations were most frequently obtained between the TNL Oral Narration score and the SLQ. A second study that correlated the stories of 105 children for Oral Narration subtest with an analysis of the same stories using the Systematic Analysis of Language Transcripts (SALT; Miller & Chapman, 1998) resulted in moderate to large correlations based on Hopkins' (2002) criteria.

Three types of studies were reported to substantiate Construct-Identification Validity: Age differentiation, group differentiation, and the identification of children with language problems. Support for age differentiation was provided for the Narrative Comprehension and Oral Narration subtests. A comparison of selected subgroups with the total sample on all three measures of the TNL showed the greatest difference for children with language disorders. In addition, a series of positive predictive outcome analyses for identifying children with language disorders was conducted using the NLAI scores of 76 children who were independently classified as language impaired compared to a matched group of 76 normally developing children. It was found that the indices of sensitivity, specificity, and positive prediction for the NLAI all exceeded .85 providing evidence for the test's validity for identifying children with language disorders.

Principal components factor analyses were also performed in order to provide evidence for the TNL's Construct-Identification Validity. The first analysis resulted in one factor, which the authors labeled as "general narrative ability." When a two-factor solution was specified using the Promax rotation method, three of the Narrative Comprehension tasks loaded on one factor, two of the Oral Narration tasks on another, and a third Oral Narration task loaded nearly evenly on both factors. Although confirmatory factor analysis appears to provide evidence for the authors' conclusion that these studies "support the construct validity of the TNL" (examiner's manual, p. 67), the data also point to the need for additional research that clarifies the relationship between Narrative Comprehension and Oral Narration.

COMMENTARY. The TNL is a promising instrument as a measure of children's spoken discourse and story telling. Comprehending and producing narratives require the integration of all other aspects of language development—phonology, morphology, syntax, semantics, and pragmatics. The TNL represents an important beginning in measuring this important aspect of language and therefore determining its relationship to other language measures pertaining to the elementary-school-aged child, both oral and written. The authors have provided information related to the standardization and technical qualities of the instrument that would recommend its thoughtful implementation. Questions remain related to each of these issues. The manual gives little information as to whether a pilot and try-out phase were part of test development. There is a lack of clarity regarding the items that were actually used for item analyses. Reliability and validity concerns persist, especially those involving the differentiation of the construct of narrative language into Narrative Comprehension and Oral Narration, despite their intuitively acceptable presentation. The fact that the authors caution against the use of these subtest scores for planning interventions recapitulates this need. Moreover, additional in-

formation as to how to best use the results for assisting individual children who are identified by the TNL as having a language problem is needed.

The materials of the TNL are quite helpful for assessment purposes, with a well-designed examiner record booklet, that provides instructions for administration and initial but detailed scoring rules. Administration and scoring rules are additionally explained in the examiner's manual, which also presents helpful information related to the construct and prior measures of narrative language as well as technical procedures. The inclusion of an example of a scored TNL and the scoring practice examples are especially helpful for scoring children's narratives. The pictures in the picture book are clearly related to their purpose. However, the box that contains these materials tends to collapse easily.

SUMMARY. The authors of the TNL have developed an intriguing instrument for measuring children's narrative language that can be administered efficiently and with some practice, scored effectively. The materials are useful and suited to their purpose. Test development included standardization on a representative norming sample, and relevant scores are provided (standard scores, percentile ranks, age equivalents). Standard scores use the same means and standard deviations as most psychological and educational tests. Considerable evidence for reliability and validity are presented in the manual, but these areas need additional studies, which the authors acknowledge. The main weakness with the instrument lies in the questionable differentiation of two narrative language abilities as represented by the subtests Narrative Comprehension and Oral Narration. Another major weakness is that the TNL does not stand alone as an assessment tool, although it does provide an assessment of overall narrative language ability. Considering that the alternative to the TNL is the analysis of language samples that consist of major commitments of time and effort, the TNL is overall a welcome addition to the assessment of narrative language.

REVIEWER'S REFERENCES

Guilford, J. P., & Fruchter, B. (1978). *Fundamental statistics in psychology and education.* New York: McGraw-Hill.

Hopkins, W. G. (2002, June 23). A scale of magnitude for the effect statistics. In *A new view of statistics.* Retrieved March 1, 2005, from http://sportsci.org/resources/stats/effectmag.html

Miller, J. F., & Chapman, R. S. (1998). *Systematic analysis of language transcripts.* Madison, WI: Language Analysis Laboratory, Waisman Research Center.

Swaminathan, H., & Rogers, H. J. (1990). Detecting differential item functioning using logistic regressions procedures. *Journal of Educational Measurement, 26,* 55–66.

[248]

Test of Phonological Awareness in Spanish.

Purpose: To assess phonological awareness in children whose first language is Spanish.
Population: Ages 4-0 to 10-11.
Publication Date: 2004.
Acronym: TPAS.
Scores, 5: Phonological Awareness Ability, Initial Sounds, Final Sounds, Rhyming Words, Deletion.
Administration: Individual.
Price Data: Available from publisher.
Time: (10–15) minutes.
Authors: Cynthia A. Riccio, Brian Imhoff, Jan E. Hasbrouck, and G. Nicole Davis.
Publisher: PRO-ED.

Review of the Test of Phonological Awareness in Spanish by CARLOS INCHAURRALDE, Professor of Linguistics and Psychologist, University of Zaragoza, Zaragoza, Spain:

DESCRIPTION. The Test of Phonological Awareness in Spanish (TPAS) is a norm-referenced measure of phonological skills for use only with Spanish-speaking children of ages 4 years 0 months to 10 years 11 months. It is provided in a kit consisting of a 70-page examiner's manual and a 5-page examiner record booklet. This booklet has the following sections to be filled in: (Child's) Identifying Information, Record of Scores, Interpretation and Notes, and Record of Performance (with a battery of four subtests of between 20 and 30 items each: Initial Sounds, Final Sounds, Rhyming Words, Deletion). The test is to be administered only to children who speak Spanish as their first (or only) language and there is a very explicit warning on page 5 of the examiner's manual not to use it with children who are not Spanish-dominant speakers except under some research conditions. The examiners should be fluent speakers of Spanish with some formal training in assessment. The entire test is given in Spanish, which means that if no trained assessment personnel can be found with fluency in this language, it is possible to employ Spanish-speaking personnel without extensive testing experience if they receive basic training about administration of the TPAS and they are supervised by someone with the appropriate training and expertise. The interpretation of the results, however, should never be left to untrained personnel.

The scoring procedure is simple and straightforward. After doing four practice items, the child starts answering the questions of the actual test items. In subtests 1 to 3 (Initial Sounds, Final Sounds, Rhyming Words) the items enquire whether concrete sounds in two different words are comparable (similar or rhyming). In subtest 4 (Deletion) the child is asked to delete a sound from a word in each item. Responses are scored either correct (1) or incorrect (0) and the raw score of each of the four subtests is the sum of the items answered correctly. In the deletion test there is also a ceiling (three consecutive incorrect answers indicate the examiner should terminate the test). With the raw score of the four subtests and the information about the children collected in Section 1 of the examiner record booklet it is also possible to calculate percentile ranks, scaled scores for the subsets, an ability score for the composite, and age and grade equivalents.

DEVELOPMENT. The TPAS was developed in order to fill a gap in the field of phonological awareness testing. Although there were many tests available for phonological awareness in the English language, there are very few available for Spanish, lacking in any case comparable measuring criteria. Other tests for Spanish, which are related to and for which development is connected with the development of the TPAS, are the Test of Early Language Development (Hresko, Reid, Hammill, Ramos, & Ramos, 2004) and the Spanish Photo Articulation Test (Ramos, Ramos, & Hresko, 2004). In the examiner's manual provided with the TPAS there is extensive information concerning the norming process used in its development, but there is not a clear explanation of why there was a choice of four subtests. Some theoretical background can be found in the manual, but without a clear reference of why these four types of subtests are the most important or comprehensive enough. The reader is referred ultimately to Torgesen and Mathes (2000) as a more comprehensive source of information for phonological awareness and phonological processing research and findings.

TECHNICAL. Chapter 4 of the examiner's manual describes the norming process of the TPAS. The normative sample chosen comprises 1,033 students from Mexico, Spain, and the United States. The sample from Mexico and the United States is very comprehensive, with participants from 7 and 11 states, respectively. However, the sample from Spain is very small and not at all representative of European Spanish. The data were collected in Sta. Cruz de Tenerife, Islas Canarias, a Spanish region with a pronunciation standard that more resembles that of many types of American Spanish (very noticeable in features like the pronunciation of the sounds /s/ and /x/, for instance) rather than the most characteristic varieties of peninsular Spanish. In any case, this fact should not be important for the norming process if we assume that the test is to be used mostly with North American speakers of Spanish. The sampling process in Mexico was systematic and there was correction for gender and socioeconomic status by using parental income. In the United States, data were gathered from professionals who submitted information about students in their areas, and from bilingual educators, speech-language pathologists, and other professionals who agreed to use custom-made materials to test students whose demographic characteristics matched those of their community.

With this sample, norms for the four different subtests were created. These norms are presented in the examiner's manual in terms of scaled scores having a mean of 10 and a standard deviation of 3. This type of distribution is widely used in intelligence tests and other tests of phonological awareness, which facilitates reading and interpretation of results on comparable grounds.

Reliability of scores from this test has been analyzed empirically for three types of error: Content sampling error (internal consistency), time sampling error (stability of results through time), and scorer differences (examiner variability). Internal consistency has been computed with the help of Cronbach's coefficient alphas calculated at seven age intervals in the whole normative sample. The averaged coefficients for the subtests yield results of .92, .92, .93, and .96. The average coefficient for the composite yields a value of .97. In all cases, the resulting figures show good reliability. The second type of reliability (time sampling error) was measured with a test-retest correlation method using two different groups of 30 and 40 students (with the same number of males and females in both cases). The test was administered twice to each group with an intervening time of 2 weeks, and the correlations between the scores obtained were around .80 and above in most cases. This is an acceptable result for a test-retest measure. Finally, interscorer differences were measured using a small sample of examiners who were asked to score 50 completed TPAS protocols. The

results of the scorings were correlated and the resulting coefficients meet or exceed .97 in all instances. This is also a good indicator of high reliability, although in this case a better explanation of the number of examiners chosen would have helped in the evaluation of the result.

Concerning validity, the authors have analyzed three main types: content-description validity, criterion-prediction validity, and construct-identification validity. There is a good explanation of validity issues for this test in Chapter 6 of the examiner's manual. In the content validation process, careful determination of item content has been important through different steps: detailed review of phonological awareness within existing materials and published tests, examination of the TPAS content by relevant professionals, and conformity to the *Standards for Educational and Psychological Testing* (AERA, APA, & NCME, 1999). The list of published awareness tests used by the authors is mostly for English, due to the lack of materials for Spanish. The authors acknowledge this problem, but this fact does not help much in finding a suitable comparison in the search for validity evidence.

Apart from qualitative evidence of content validity, the authors also provide quantitative evidence concerning item discrimination and item difficulty. The index chosen with this goal in mind has been the item-total-score Pearson correlation index. Discrimination indexes higher than .35 (exceptionally .20) were chosen in most cases. The arrangement of items was in an easy-to-difficult order, with items distributed between 15% and 85% being generally considered acceptable. Tables are provided with median item difficulty and discrimination values that in most cases are higher than .50. Additionally, the authors use statistical techniques to detect item bias (or differential item functioning), more concretely Nagelkerke's R^2. Biased elements according to this analysis correspond only to less than 2% of the test items, which suggests acceptable levels regarding gender and Spanish dialect. In this respect, it is necessary to repeat here the comment made above about the Spanish variety chosen for the norming process.

Criterion-prediction validity was measured by correlating scores obtained in the TPAS with scores from the experimental edition of the Comprehensive Test of Phonological Processing (CTOPP; Wagner, Torgesen, & Rashotte, 1999). This is a measure of concurrent validity (as opposed to predictive validity, cf. Anastasi & Urbina, 1997, p. 118) by comparison with a test developed for measuring phonological awareness of standard American English. The test's developers again refer to the lack of comparable tests for Spanish. In any case, the phonological processes measured by the TPAS seem to be very similar to those measured by the CTOPP.

Construct-identification validity is demonstrated by the results obtained in a three-step procedure in which first several relevant constructs were identified, then hypotheses based on these constructs were generated, and finally the hypotheses were verified by logical or empirical methods. The eight basic constructs identified connected performance in the TPAS with chronological age differences, demographic variables, correlation across the different subtests, oral language proficiency, intelligence tests, and reading fluency in Spanish and English. They also assumed relationships between the different subtests. Because this kind of validity also relates to the degree to which the underlying features of a test can be identified and the extent to which they reflect the theoretical model used, confirmatory factor analyses were also used. More concretely, two indexes of goodness-of-fit were calculated: Bentler's (1990) comparative fit index (CFI) and Bentler and Bonnett's (1980) normed fit index (NFI). Both indexes for the TPAS had values of .91, which confirms good construct validity. It seems to be the case that the TPAS is a valid indication of general awareness ability, according to the data provided by the authors.

COMMENTARY. This test fills an important gap in the field of phonological awareness testing because it is aimed at speakers of Spanish, whereas most similar available tests only test phonological awareness in English. This is the reason why, at the same time, this test cannot be compared properly with other existing materials, and its developers have had to rely on the previous experience of tests for English in the whole development and norming process. The test is also mostly based on varieties of Spanish spoken in the United States and Mexico, which makes it valid only for speakers of those varieties. However, the test can be administered very easily, it is well documented, and shows evidence of good reliability and validity values. These facts support its suitability for measurement of phonological awareness in Spanish in contexts in which this kind of assessment is needed.

SUMMARY. The TPAS is a test for assessing phonological awareness in Spanish of Spanish-speaking children aged 4 to 10 in educational settings. It can be easily administered and scored and it is a very convenient tool for assessment of phonological awareness problems linked to other educational problems. The test is to be used only with speakers of North American varieties of Spanish, because these are the varieties that were used in the norming process. This seems suitable with most Spanish speakers in the United States, where this test appears to be a very useful tool with high levels of reliability and validity and no competitors in sight.

REVIEWER'S REFERENCES

American Educational Research Association, American Psychological Association, & National Council on Measurement in Education. (1999). *Standards for educational and psychological testing.* Washington, DC: American Educational Research Association.
Anastasi, A., & Urbina, S. (1997). *Psychological testing* (7th ed.). New York: MacMillan.
Bentler, P. M. (1990). Comparative fit indexes in structural models. *Psychological Bulletin, 107,* 238–246.
Bentler, P. M., & Bonnett, D. G. (1980). Significance tests and goodness of fit in the analysis of covariance structures. *Psychological Bulletin, 107,* 238–246.
Hresko, W. P., Reid, D. K., Hammill, D. D., Ramos, M., & Ramos, J. (2003). *Test of Early Language Development—Third Edition, Spanish Version.* Austin, TX: PRO-ED.
Ramos, M., Ramos, J., & Hresko, W. P. (2004). *Spanish Photo Articulation Test.* Austin, TX: PRO-ED.
Torgesen, J. G., & Mathes, P. G. (2000). *A basic guide to understanding, assessing, and teaching phonological awareness.* Austin, TX: PRO-ED.
Wagner, R. K., Torgesen, J. K., & Rashotte, C. A. (1999). *Comprehensive Test of Phonological Processing.* Austin, TX: PRO-ED.

Review of the Test of Phonological Awareness in Spanish by VINCENT J. SAMAR, Associate Professor, Department of Research, National Technical Institute for the Deaf, Rochester Institute of Technology, Rochester, NY:

DESCRIPTION. The Test of Phonologial Awareness in Spanish (TPAS) is a norm-referenced paper-and-pencil instrument for evaluating phonological awareness skills in Spanish speaking children between 4 and 10 years of age. The kit contains the instrument's comprehensive and highly accessible examiner's manual and the examiner record booklet for administering the instrument to individual children and recording their responses. The TPAS contains four subtests, rationally chosen based on the extensive scientific literature on phonological awareness. The four subtests assess distinct aspects of phonological awareness that constitute necessary precursor skills for reading acquisition. The TPAS subtests are Initial Sounds, Final Sounds, Rhyming Words, and Deletion. These tests measure the child's ability to isolate and compare the initial and final sounds of words, to identify rhyming words, and to segment and blend phonemes within words, respectively. Scaled scores, percentile ranks, age equivalents, and grade equivalents are provided for each of the subtests. An overall standardized phonological awareness ability score (PAAS) is reported, and a table is presented for converting an obtained PAAS to a z-score, *T*-score, or stanine score.

Uses of the TPAS. The three major uses of the TPAS, as presented in the manual, are: "(a) to identify those Spanish-speaking children who may be significantly below their peers in phonological awareness ability, (b) to monitor remediation and intervention progress, and (c) to provide a tool for research in the development of phonological awareness and early reading" (examiner's manual, p. 3). The TPAS manual provides a cogent description and rationale for each of these uses. The comprehensive attention that the authors have given to constructing and validating scores from the TPAS, and to providing the user with an excellent manual to guide administration and interpretation of results, enhances the probability that the TPAS will enable these educational and research applications.

DEVELOPMENT. The TPAS was developed in response to the growing national concern about high illiteracy, poor grade retention, and high dropout rates among Hispanic youth. As the test's authors note, it is predicted that one in four children in U.S. schools will be Hispanic by 2020. Many of these children will have Spanish as their first language and will have limited English proficiency when they enter school. We know from linguistic and psychophysical studies that Spanish and English differ significantly in their phonological properties, such as the saliency of syllable structure, the distribution of stress patterns, and the psychoacoustic location of distinctive feature boundaries for categorical phoneme perception. In order to accurately assess the phonological awareness of many Hispanic children, it is therefore optimal and probably necessary to use an assessment instrument tailored to the phonological properties of their native language. Because phonological awareness is a trainable critical prerequisite for reading acquisition, such an instrument would be a boon to researchers and educators committed to improving literacy instruction and minimizing dropout rates for Hispanic children in the U.S. The TPAS is a phonological assessment instrument developed to fill this need.

TECHNICAL.

Normative sample. The TPAS was normed on a sample of 1,033 students residing in three countries: Mexico, Spain, and the U.S., including Puerto Rico. Sampling in Mexico and in the U.S. was systematic over several states, and provided a representative normative sampling of these countries. The Spanish sample was localized to a specific city. Care was taken to mathematically weight the sample in order to make it representative of U.S. student population proportions according to gender, geographical region, and Spanish dialect spoken.

Reliability. Each of the TPAS subtests has been shown to be highly reliable on three key indices of reliability. The adequacy of content sampling for the four subtests at each chronological age between 4 and 10 years was assessed using internal consistency reliability. Coefficient alphas ranged from .87 to .97 for the individual subtests. The coefficient alphas for the overall PAAS ranged from .95 to .98 among the chronological age groups.

To check for bias in the reliability of the TPAS within selected subgroups in the TPAS sample, coefficient alphas were computed for males and females, separately; speakers with Mexican dialects in the U.S. and in Mexico, separately; and speakers with dialects from Puerto Rico, Spain, Central and South America, and Cuba, separately. The coefficient alphas among all subgroups and subtests, collapsed across chronological age, ranged from .90 to .98. Coefficient alphas over the subgroups for the PAAS ranged from .96 to .98. These data suggest equivalent high reliability across gender and dialect subgroups.

Time sampling reliability was assessed using the test-retest technique. With a 2-week test-retest interval, the reliability coefficients ranged from .79 to .98, indicating generally good testing reliability over time.

Interscorer reliability, based on parallel scoring of 50 TPAS protocols by two fluent Spanish-speaking graduate students ranged from .97 to .98 across the four subtests, and was .97 for the overall PAAS.

Validity. The authors have expended every effort to construct an inventory of items that samples a representative range of phonological awareness behaviors of relevance to bilingual assessment. Item choice was negotiated through expert review by professionals in bilingual speech pathology and language assessment. Particular attention was paid to the special linguistic properties of Spanish that distinguish it from English, and must therefore be taken into account in assessing phonological awareness in Spanish speakers. These properties include a greater sensitivity to syllables than to single phonemes in Spanish, language differences in the salience and distribution of stress patterns, and language and dialectal differences in rhyme patterns. Final item choice was validated by conventional item analysis of each item's discriminating power as well as differential item functioning analysis to detect item bias with respect to gender and dialect subgroup.

Good construct validity was documented by careful correlational studies and confirmatory factor analyses of the ability of TPAS performance to differentiate among ages and dialect groups, to express factorial distinctiveness among subtests, to relate to spoken language proficiency, to relate to an intelligence measure, and to relate to Spanish and English reading fluency. The overall outcome of this thorough validation procedure is that the TPAS has been demonstrated to be a solidly valid measure of phonological awareness for a broad and representative sample of Hispanic children, and to be a measure of choice for individuals for whom other phonological awareness tests might be biased.

Test bias. The authors have been exceptionally vigilant in designing and in empirically confirming an unbiased measure of phonological awareness for Hispanic children of different genders and different dialect subgroups. Much to their credit the authors have gone further and included a compellingly written chapter in their manual that explicitly discusses the nature of test bias and how to control it when assessing children using the TPAS as well as other tests. Responsible management of test bias in bilingual and bicultural assessment is absolutely essential to the educational and developmental welfare of children in our multicultural nation.

TPAS examiner record booklet and examiner's manual. The TPAS examiner's record booklet is an easy-to-use response form for testing individual children. Conveniently, instructions to be read to the child are printed at the top of the booklet pages in Spanish along with the English translation in parentheses.

The TPAS manual is a model of concise and accessible writing. It is comprehensive in presenting the motivation for the TPAS, its test development history, and the extensive statistical evidence of reliability and validity. The manual also presents normative conversion tables in an easy-to-use conventional format. In addition, the manual is carefully designed to provide the reader with a comprehensible background discussion of the nature of test development in general and of the scope of important defining concepts underlying reliability and validity determination. The manual has an appealing tutorial flavor and provides an excellent introduction or review of basic test development concepts for educational assessment providers and other professional test consumers.

COMMENTARY. Generally, the extensive literature on phonological awareness training and reading acquisition has supported the importance of developing and validating effective methods of literacy instruction that maximize phonological awareness training during preschool and kindergarten. However, very few existing studies have examined the specific language-related factors that must be considered when designing effective literacy instruction for normal and reading-disabled *biliterate* populations such as Hispanic children in the U.S. The TPAS overcomes one barrier to this important and necessary line of research, namely the lack of reliable and valid phonological awareness assessment instruments for Hispanic children. The TPAS is therefore a timely, necessary, and welcome addition to reading achievement and reading disability assessment batteries for use in the nation's schools. It is equally significant for reading researchers concerned with ultimately improving bilingual education and with ameliorating the many socially costly and personally disabling consequences of reading failure within a substantial proportion of the nation's large Hispanic community.

SUMMARY. The TPAS is a valuable and excellently developed instrument. It is well poised to support the needs of Hispanic children for reading-related assessment and of the educational research community as they pursue increasingly important issues surrounding reading achievement and bilingual education.

[249]

Test of Phonological Awareness—Second Edition: PLUS.

Purpose: Designed to measure "young children's ability to isolate individual phonemes in spoken words and their knowledge of relationships between letters and phonemes in English."

Population: Ages 5–8.

Publication Dates: 1994–2004.

Acronym: TOPA-2+.
Scores: 2 subtests: Phonological Awareness, Letter Sounds.
Administration: Individual or group.
Levels, 2: Kindergarten, Early Elementary.
Price Data, 2004: $203 per complete kit including examiner's manual (2004, 78 pages), 50 Kindergarten summary forms, 50 Early Elementary summary forms, 25 student booklets for Kindergarten, and 25 student booklets for Early Elementary; $71 per examiner's manual; $28 per 50 Kindergarten summary forms; $28 per 50 Early Elementary summary forms; $45 per 25 Kindergarten student booklets; $45 per 25 Early Elementary student booklets.
Time: (30–45) minutes for Kindergarten version; (15–30) minutes for Early Elementary version.
Authors: Joseph K. Torgesen and Brian R. Bryant.
Publisher: PRO-ED.
Cross References: For reviews by Steven H. Long and by Rebecca McCauley of a previous edition, see 13:333 (3 references).

Review of the Test of Phonological Awareness—Second Edition: PLUS by RAY FENTON, President, FentonResearch, Tucson, AZ:

DESCRIPTION. The Test of Phonological Awareness—Second Edition: Plus (TOPA-2+) is a standardized norm referenced measure of the ability of young children to recognize phonemes in spoken words and the relationship between letters and phonemes in English. The test may be administered to individuals or groups of students ages 5 through 8. The Kindergarten version may be administered anytime during kindergarten but it is best given during the second half of the year. The Early Elementary version may be administered at any time during first or second grade.

The TOPA-2+ is a revision and expansion of the popular Test of Phonological Awareness introduced in 1994. New subtests of Letter Sound recognition are added. The Kindergarten TOPA-2+ includes a Letter Sounds subtest where children mark which letter from a set of four corresponds to a specific phoneme (15 items). Test takers also respond to 10 items where students match an initial phoneme in one word with one of three words starting with a similar sound, and 10 items where a word starting with a dissimilar sound must be selected from a group of four where three agree. The Early Elementary version is similar in format to the Kindergarten version but the same sound and different sound items call for identification of the last rather than the first sound

in words. The new letter sound items of the advanced version have students spell 18 simple pseudowords that are presented as the names of "funny animals" along with a rhyming English word. The pseudowords are one or two syllables in length and vary from two to five phonemes.

The TOPA-2+ examiner's manual provides a clear introduction to the test with detailed information on test administration and scoring. The Kindergarten version may be administered in 30 to 45 minutes whereas the Grade 1 or 2 version may be given in from 15 to 30 minutes. Tests are hand scored by counting correct responses and then looking up age-based standard or percentile score information from tables. A record sheet/reporting form is available for recording item performance, scoring the test, and for reporting scores to parents or "other responsible persons eligible to receive information" (examiner's manual, p. 20). Scores commonly reported are raw scores, percentile rank scores, and one standard score. Space is available on the score report for comments on the testing situation and on the performance of the student. The examiner's manual includes a discussion of the meaning and interpretation of the various types of available scores.

DEVELOPMENT. The TOPA-2+ is a direct outgrowth of the TOPA, which was first published in 1994 as a group-administered indicator of phonological awareness that was easily administered and would be useful to teachers and researchers. The items included in the original test were broadly sampled from phonemes that could be articulated by children and had been found to be pronounced accurately by almost all children. The two 20-item TOPA tests proved popular and became widely used to indicate phonological awareness in young children, to provide early identification of students at risk for reading difficulties, and for research into phonemic awareness.

The TOPA-2+ builds on the TOPA. The old TOPA subtests have some revised items and new pictures. The new subtests are designed to increase overall reliability of the test and the utility of the test for early screening for reading difficulties. At kindergarten, the added subtest assesses knowledge of letters and the sounds that they usually represent in English. Second and third grade students are presented with rhyming pseudowords that students must write out to demonstrate their knowledge of English phonemes.

These additions are consistent with commonly used teacher-developed informal assessments and directly relate to skills that have been associated strongly with early spelling and reading ability.

TECHNICAL. The TOPA-2+ examiner's manual provides a detailed discussion of the methods used to generate and evaluate normative information, explore the internal validity and reliability of test scores, and argue for the validity of intended uses of the test.

Norming was done with a selected sample of 1,035 students for the Kindergarten version and 1,050 students for the Early Elementary version. The demographic characteristics of the normative sample were matched with the school-age population reported by the U.S. Bureau of the Census in 2001. Norming studies took place between the spring of 2000 and the summer of 2003. No special effort is reported to explore the performance of students with disabilities, students with limited English proficiency, or students with diverse home linguistic experience as part of the norming process.

Initial studies of the internal consistency and test-retest reliability of the TOPA-2+ are reported. Coefficient alpha values range from .80 to .90 for Phonological Awareness and Letter Sound subtests for students of different ages and analysis groups. Standard errors of measurement are close to one third of a standard deviation for the various age-based scores. The evidence presented is convincing that the TOPA-2+ has reasonable internal consistency and test-retest reliability for a group-administered standardized test for young children. The TOPA-2+ has demonstrated improved reliability over the original TOPA.

Evidence is presented to support the validity of scores from the test including a detailed description of test format and content, rationales for the specific content of each subtest with an emphasis on the newly added Letter Sounds subtests, and brief discussions of related research. Post hoc item analysis and differential item functioning studies are presented to support overall validity and the consistency of the measure for various racial and gender groups.

Limited studies of the correspondence of TOPA 2+ scores to other indicators are presented as evidence of criterion or predictive validity. First, a concurrent administration of TOPA 2+ and elements of the Dynamic Indicators of Basic Early Literacy Skills (DIBELS): Initial Sound Fluency,

Phonological Awareness, and Phoneme Segmentation subtest to 128 kindergarten and 148 Florida first grade students and 22 Oregon kindergarten students is reported. Combined data show median correlation coefficients of .51 and .43 for Phonological Awareness and .40 and .54 for Letter Sounds with DIBELS subtests. Another study had teachers rate students on scales based on the Learning Disabilities Diagnostic Inventory and correlated the results with TOPA-2+ subscales. Overall, the associations found from the reported studies are moderate and do suggest an association.

COMMENTARY. The TOPA-2+ is a revised and extended version of the TOPA that should prove popular with teachers and those interested in early grade screenings of students. It is one of the few quick and easy-to-administer standardized norm-referenced indicators of early language skills that has a record of successful use and good evidence of test reliability and validity. The new subtests of the TOPA-2+ make it a better potential predictor of student success in the acquisition of reading skills. Additional research in this area would be helpful.

Although the TOPA-2+ is easy to administer, care must be taken in the administration to ensure the validity of scores. Differences in the pronunciation of phonemes may affect results. Test results may also be affected by differences in dialect between the examiner and the tested children. As with any group test with young children, the administrator must be well prepared for the test administration and observant to ensure that students are engaged in the testing process, giving their own answers, and making meaningful responses to test items.

The TOPA-2+ may be used with confidence as a measure of phonological awareness and letter sound knowledge with regular education program students. Care should be taken in the administration of the test to students with disabilities, particularly a hearing disability, and students who are English Language Learners or from environments where nonstandard English is spoken. More work needs to be done to examine the validity of the TOPA-2+ with nonstandard English speakers (see e.g., Geisinger & Carlson, 1992) and the link between Phonological Awareness and Letter Sound knowledge scores and learning to read prior to reliance on the TOPA-2+ as a general indicator of future student success in reading or language arts. Individual scores should be considered in conjunction with other evidence of student performance prior to assignment of a student for remedial instruction.

The TOPA-2+ examiner's manual is well written and should be read carefully by any educator or researcher planning to use the instrument. The manual provides useful guidance related to test administration and interpretation that is important to understanding the strengths and the limitations of the instrument. The section on sharing test results is of particular importance because the reporting forms do not include an indicator of measurement error, which is of particular importance when scores are used to diagnose performance or provide guidance to parents or make decisions about students or programs (see *Standards for Educational and Psychological Testing*, AERA, APA, & NCME, 1999).

SUMMARY. The TOPA-2+ is a well-made standardized norm-referenced test of phonological awareness and letter-sound knowledge that is consistent with early grades English language learning. It is a useful tool for educators seeking information on the early linguistic performance of students. The test is attractive, easy to administer, and readily available to use as part of early grades screening programs.

REVIEWER'S REFERENCES

American Educational Research Association, American Psychological Association, & National Council on Measurement in Education. (1999). *Standards for educational and psychological testing*. Washington, DC: American Educational Research Association.
Geisinger, K. F., & Carlson, J. F. (1992). Assessing language-minority students. *Practical Assessment, Research and Evaluation, 3*(2).

[250]

Test of Phonological Awareness Skills.

Purpose: Designed to "measure varied aspects of phonological awareness."
Population: Ages 5-0 to 10-11.
Publication Date: 2003.
Acronym: TOPAS.
Scores, 5: Rhyming, Incomplete Words, Sound Sequencing, Phoneme Deletion, Phonological Awareness.
Administration: Individual.
Price Data: Available from publisher.
Time: (20–30) minutes.
Authors: Phyllis L. Newcomer and Edna Barenbaum.
Publisher: PRO-ED.

Review of the Test of Phonological Awareness Skills by CATHERINE P. COOK-COTTONE, Assistant Professor of School Psychology, State University of New York at Buffalo, and JENNIFER

PICCOLO, Doctoral Student of School Psychology, State University of New York at Buffalo, Buffalo, NY:

DESCRIPTION. The Test of Phonological Awareness Skills (TOPAS) is an individually administered test designed to measure specific types of phonological awareness skills of children 5 years 0 months to 10 years 11 months. Based on a model of conceptualizing and assessing phonological awareness delineated by Torgesen and Mathes (2000), the TOPAS subtests (i.e., Rhyming, Incomplete Words, Sound Sequencing, and Phoneme Deletion) yield an overall phonological awareness composite, or the TOPAS Ability Score. The subtests are administered in sequence with an increasing level of task complexity. Specifically, Rhyming (Subtest 1) measures sound comparison skills. Incomplete Words (Subtest 2) assesses phoneme blending skills. Sound Sequencing (Subtest 3) and Phoneme Deletion (Subtest 4) measure phoneme segmentation skills. Of note, for 5-year-olds only the Rhyming and Incomplete Words subtests make up the composite. For other ages, all four subsets are used. Subtests have no time restrictions and total time required for test administration is reported to vary from 20 to 30 minutes.

For the 31-item Rhyming subtest, the child is asked to complete a sentence by supplying a word that rhymes with a word that has been emphasized by the examiner. For example "I hurt my *knee* falling out of a _____" (examiner's manual, p. 6). To administer the 29-item Incomplete Words subtest, the examiner articulates parts of words and asks the child to supply the missing sounds and pronounce the word. To illustrate, the examiner would say "ba_ana," which would correctly be pronounced by the child as "banana" (examiner's manual, p. 6). The 27-item Sound Sequencing subtest requires the child to listen to a nonword sound sequence and arrange colored blocks (each assigned to a particular sound) according to that sequence. To correctly respond to an item (e.g., /b/ /a/ /b/), a child must sequence, in left-to-right order, the appropriate colored blocks (e.g., blue, red, blue). The 22-item Phoneme Deletion subtest requires the child to repeat the stimulus word and then to say the word again without specified sounds. For example, the examiner might ask the child to say "top" and then ask the child to say the word again without the /t/ sound.

Protocols are provided for recording of the child's identifying information, test scores and conversions, summary of testing conditions, and interpretation and recommendation notes. Administration instructions are explicitly provided and correct responses indicated. Each subtest is administered beginning with the first item and testing is discontinued when a child misses five consecutive items. Correct responses are scored with a 1 and incorrect with a 0. Raw scores are calculated by adding up the number of correct responses and are converted to standard scores (called scaled scores) based on a normal distribution with a mean of 10 and a standard deviation of 3. The TOPAS Ability Scores for the composite are obtained by summing the scaled scores of appropriate subtests, based on age, and converting this value to a standard score by using the conversion table provided in the manual. Ability Scores are based on a mean of 100 and a standard deviation of 15. Tables are also provided for age and grade equivalents as well as percentile ranks. Additionally, descriptive ratings are provided for Ability Score and Scaled Score ranges (i.e., Very Superior, Superior, Above Average, Average, Below Average, Poor, and Very Poor).

Authors report that children who demonstrate adequate ability on the TOPAS (i.e., with an Ability Score > 90) reliably have awareness of and access to the phonological structure of oral language. Subtest analysis is recommended for children whose Ability Scores fall below 90. Subtest findings should be interpreted only in terms of specific item content and skills measured. Instructions for determination of statistically significant differences and guidelines for clinical utility of difference score findings are provided. The manual includes instructions for addressing situational and child error as well as cautions for interpretation of test results.

Created for clinical, diagnostic, and research use, it is recommended that the TOPAS be administered by individuals with a basic understanding of testing statistics, test administration, scoring, and interpretation, as well as specific knowledge about the evaluation of phonological awareness skills. Specific applications include: identification of children who are significantly below peers in phonological awareness ability, determination of relative strengths and weakness of phonological awareness abilities, documentation of progress in intervention programs, and for measurements of phonological awareness in research studies.

DEVELOPMENT. The development of the TOPAS follows increasing interest in the role phonological awareness processes play in learning. Particularly, accumulating empirical evidence implicates phonological awareness as a longitudinal predictor of early reading development (e.g., Parrila, Kirby, & McQuarrie, 2004). Phonological awareness is defined as an oral language skill, which although important to the development of emergent literacy and reading, is distinct from constructs that pertain to the relationships between sounds and letters in written language (e.g., the alphabetic principal, graphophonics, and phonics). In accordance with the Torgesen and Mathes (2000) model, the TOPAS measures phonological awareness via the assessment of three major types of skills: (a) sound comparison, (b) phoneme blending, and (c) phoneme segmentation. Specifically, sound comparison is defined as the ability to recognize the relationships between sounds in spoken words. Phoneme blending is the child's ability to blend the sounds that make up common multisyllabic nouns. Finally, phoneme segmentation is defined as the ability to manipulate the sound segments of words. Although the authors acknowledge the lack of an empirically supported model of a developmental progression of phonological skills, existing literature suggests that, in regard to skill complexity, sound comparison can be considered easy, phoneme blending as moderate, and phoneme segmentation as difficult. Each TOPAS subtest was selected to assess one of the three major skill areas: Rhyming (sound comparison), Incomplete Words (phoneme blending), Sound Sequencing (phoneme segmentation), and Phoneme Deletion (phoneme segmentation).

TECHNICAL.

Standardization. The TOPAS was normed on 926 children (ages 5-0 to 10-11) from 14 states representing the four general regions of the continental United States through a data collection project running from 1997 to 2001. Comparative tables provided in the examiner's manual demonstrate that sample characteristics (i.e., geographical, gender, race, ethnicity, family income, educational level of parents, and disabling conditions) are adequately representative of the 2001 U.S. Census data. Representativeness of normative data was also demonstrated through stratification of demographic information by age. Subtest scaled scores were developed using a continuous norming procedure in which a polynomial regression fits the progression of means, standard deviations, skewness, and kurtosis across age groups. Fitted values were estimated across 6-month intervals and the shape of the distribution of scores was determined. The 6-month intervals appear appropriate given item gradients. Next, percentiles were derived and consequently converted to standard scores for each age interval. Subtest floors are best for children ages 9-0 to 10-11. Caution should be used when interpreting low scores for younger children. Subtest item gradients are adequate with all violations occurring generally beyond two standard deviations from the mean. The TOPAS Ability Score was calculated using a procedure that involves pooling the scaled scores of the subtests. The composite test floors and item gradients are adequate. Subtest and composite percentile ranks were obtained directly from normal-curve tables. Age and grade equivalents were created using interpolation, extrapolation, and smoothing procedures and authors warn that these scores should be interpreted with caution.

Reliability. Test reliability was evidenced by measures of internal consistency, standard error of measurement, test-retest method, and test scorer reliability. Coefficient alphas suggest high reliability at the subtest ($.87 \leq \alpha \leq .97$) and composite ($.91 \leq \alpha \leq .97$) levels and are provided for each age group, as well as by gender and selected ethnic groups (i.e., European American, African American, and Hispanic American). Psychometrically sound standard errors of measurement are also provided for six age intervals at the subtest ($SEM = 1$) and composite (SEM ranging from 4 to 5) levels. Though good (Ability Score = .90), the 3-week-interval, test-retest data are limited to a study of 30 children in kindergarten through the second grade. Subtest and composite interscorer reliability was excellent ($r = .98$–.99). Of note, evaluator administration of items, rather than a recorded stimulus, may be a potential source of error.

Validity. Evidence is provided for content, criterion, and construct validity. Content validity is evidenced via a detailed rationale for both items and testing format. Further, item discrimination indexes are good for each of the six age intervals ($.40 \leq r \leq .74$). Item difficulties are generally acceptable. According to differential item functional analyses, the TOPAS was found to be nonbiased in regard to gender, race, and ethnicity. Evidence for criterion-prediction validity was based on a sample of 101 children and yielded moderate

to high correlations with the Comprehensive Test of Phonological Processing (CTOPP; Wagner, Torgesen, & Rashotte, 1999), the Lindamood Auditory Conceptualization Test—Third Edition (LAC-3; Lindamood & Lindamood, 2004), and the Diagnostic Achievement Battery—Third Edition (DAB-3; Newcomer, 2001). Finally, several forms of construct identification are presented including confirmatory factor analysis and unpublished data correlating TOPAS scores with various spoken language, reading, writing, and intelligence measures. Further published empirical evidence is needed.

COMMENTARY. The TOPAS is a solid contribution to the field of assessment of phonological awareness skills. Authors addressed many psychometric challenges and created a measure useful for both clinical and research purposes. Strengths include a strong theoretical and empirical foundation for both item content and format. Standardization is representative. Reliability and validity evidence is generally good. There is a need for published research.

SUMMARY. The TOPAS appears to be an adequate measure of phonological awareness strongly anchored in the Torgesen and Mathes (2000) model. Strengths include sound construct validity evidence, a well-designed protocol and manual making for ease of administration and scoring, and adequate psychometric properties given the challenges inherent in assessing emerging phonological awareness. Although caution is noted for interpretation of very low scores for younger children, the TOPAS is a good measure and demonstrates utility in regard to clinical, intervention, and research applications.

REVIEWERS' REFERENCES
Lindamood, P. C., & Lindamood, P. (2004). *Lindamood Auditory Conceptualization Test (LAC-3)*. Austin, TX: PRO-ED.
Newcomer, P. L. (2001). *Diagnostic Achievement Battery—Third Edition (DAB-3)*. Austin, TX: PRO-ED.
Parrila, R., Kirby, J. R., & McQuarrie, L. (2004). Articulation rate, naming speed, verbal short-term memory, and phonological awareness: Longitudinal predictors of early reading development? *Scientific Studies of Reading, 8*, 3–26.
Torgesen, J. K., & Mathes, P. G. (2000). *A basic guide to understanding, assessing, and teaching phonological awareness skills*. Austin, TX: PRO-ED.
Wagner, R. K., Torgesen, J. K., & Rashotte, C. A. (1999). *Comprehensive Test of Phonological Processing*. Austin, TX: PRO-ED.

[251]
Test of Silent Word Reading Fluency.

Purpose: Measures the ability to recognize printed words accurately and efficiently.
Population: Ages 6-6 to 17-11.
Publication Date: 2004.
Acronym: TOSWRF.

Scores: Total score only.
Administration: Group.
Forms, 2: A, B.
Price Data: Available from publisher.
Time: 3 minutes per form.
Authors: Nancy Mather, Donald D. Hammill, Elizabeth A. Allen, and Rhia Roberts.
Publisher: PRO-ED.

Review of the Test of Silent Word Reading Fluency by MICHAEL D. BECK, President, BETA, Inc., Pleasantville, NY:

DESCRIPTION. The Test of Silent Word Reading Fluency (TOSWRF) assesses "the ability to recognize printed words accurately and efficiently" (examiner's manual, p. 1). Group administered in 3 minutes, the TOSWRF is published in two forms, with a single test form usable throughout an age range of 6-6 to 17-11 years, essentially the entire Grades 1 through 12 span. A norm-referenced instrument, the TOSWRF provides a full range of normative score metrics. It can be administered by anyone with basic training in standardized test administration, although test scoring requires some incremental training and practice. The publisher claims the instrument assesses "reading fluency," defined as a combination of word identification and speed. As discussed below, the TOSWRF is more accurately described by its title—word reading fluency—not reading fluency in general. The publisher lists three primary uses: identification of poor readers as a screening instrument, monitoring reading development or growth, and research in the area of reading or, more broadly, literacy.

DEVELOPMENT. The format of the TOSWRF is clever and rather unique. The test itself is contained on a single sheet of paper, to which students of all ages respond. Test content is simply strings of letters that form words of varying length. The letters are presented without spaces between words; the test-taker's task is to read the lines of letter sequences as quickly as possible and to segment the letter strings into words. The entire test is a set of 32 lines each of approximately 4 inches of these running letter strings. Normative data indicate sufficient floor and ceiling for the intended age range. A sample for the test is presented as:

ofgoliketwobig/
onheupyesget/

Test-takers respond to this sample simply by drawing a line between consecutive words as follows:

of/go/like/two/big/
on/he/up/yes/get/

Scoring, well explained in the manual, essentially involves crediting students for all words correctly segmented. "Imbedded" words are of steadily increasing difficulty and length as test takers proceed through the page. Initial words are primary-level and short; the end of the page contains words that are generally infrequently used and lengthy.

The examiner's manual explains the TOSWRF development history, including its content/format grounding in previous research and instruments. The test's gradient of word difficulty is described, although empirical evidence of the "leveling" is absent. Although the test appears interesting and manageable for test-takers, one caution about the likely impact of the unique item-response format is evident in test-retest data presented. Across grades, a large sample of test-takers showed an average score gain over a 2-week period of nearly 1/3 of a *S.D.* This unexplained gain appears to reflect a rather troubling "format effect."

The examiner's manual is well-written and generally on an appropriate level for the intended user. Test directions, scoring, and conversion procedures are well explained and thorough. Very limited interpretive information is included. The provision of a set of 10 "practice tests" to train prospective test scorers is a very positive feature.

TECHNICAL. On the whole, the evidence presented is consistent with capable test-construction techniques and technically sound underpinnings. The test suffers technically from problems encountered by any first-edition test—limited data to support validity-related qualities. However, although the data presented are somewhat sketchy and derived from limited sources, this is a minor objection.

Reliability evidence, calculated predominately on the normative sample, is sound. Typical alternate-form reliability coefficients by age are in the mid-.80s, solid for a test of such short duration. Because the TOSWRF can be administered so quickly, users desiring higher reliability could administer both forms of the test in less than 10 minutes, with significant increment in score reliability. Tabled alternate-form standard scores (mean of 100, *S.D.* of 15) do not support the claim of form equivalence—the near-identical data are an artifact of the scaling process—but the two forms are roughly comparable statistically. To the publisher's credit, they provide other reliability estimates—immediate and delayed test-retest and interscorer data.

It would have been informative to include data on the validity of the scoring procedure. Students receive full credit for all responses preceding the last two consecutive lines that were fully correct. This process essentially assumes a Likert-type graded difficulty of the words, at least on a line-by-line basis. Although there is no reason to refute this assumption based on the surface features of the words, the soundness of the process should be empirically demonstrated because it is the foundation of each examinee's score.

Although the reliability estimates are acceptably high for individual-student use as a screening instrument, a pervasive problem with the manual prevails. That is the tendency for the authors to "promote" or "hype" the data. Data presented support the TOSWRF's use for the purposes intended; the extended claims are not supported. It is regrettable that the authors and/or publisher chose to use the test manual as a promotion vehicle.

Validity is discussed according to the three major categories proposed by Anastasi and Urbina (1997). The content-description section primarily discusses the evolution of the TOSWRF item type and its grounding in a cell of Guilford's Structure of Intellect model. The criterion-prediction validity section provides correlations with several assessments of various elements of reading. Samples upon which these data were collected were heavily learning-disabled, limiting generalizations. The manual adopts an unusual and overly "kind" interpretive scale for the correlations, all of which are already corrected for attenuation. According to this curious scale, uncorrected correlations as low as .3 are labeled "moderate," and values as low as .5 are termed "large." Even using these (to this reviewer) generous descriptors, presented correlations are unimpressive. For example, TOSWRF corrected correlations with Woodcock-Johnson Passage Comprehension, derived by collapsing students across a several-year age span, average in the mid-.40s for Form A, disappointingly low for a test purportedly assessing "reading fluency."

This section also provides supposed evidence for the claim that the TOSWRF assesses reading comprehension or, more broadly, general reading ability. Data fail to provide this evidence. In fact, a sound measure of mathematics applications, hardly a measure of reading ability, would correlate as highly with the various comprehension measures as does the TOSWRF. Again the authors/publishers overreach and claim more for the TOSWRF than the data support.

Construct-identification data are limited, not surprising for a young instrument. Most data moderately support the construct of word-identification fluency, although some curiosities obtain. For example, a rather sizable sample of preidentified "gifted and talented" students had mean TOSWRF scores less than a standard deviation above average; large samples of minority students averaged near the 45th percentile nationally—encouraging, but far from the gap typically seen on literacy measures; Form A of the test correlates (uncorrected) less than .5 with the Broad Reading section of the Woodcock-Johnson Psycho-Educational Battery; and even the disattenuated correlation with the WISC-III Verbal scale is below .4 for Form A.

A general problem crossing many of the data sets is the unfortunate combining of scores across a 12-year age span. This process artificially inflates correlations, obscuring the more relevant grade-by-grade relationships. Although such combining increases sample sizes and stabilizes data, to subsequently statistically further "correct" resulting correlations for attenuation strikes this reviewer as indefensible.

Finally, a few comments should be made concerning the norms. The sample, spanning ages 6 through 17, totaled nearly 3,600 students. Although neither indefensible nor impressive, it is important to recognize that this averages approximately 300 students per grade level. Even though all normative conversions were smoothed analytically using accepted procedures, the fact remains that sample sizes are small.

Representativeness of a norming sample is, of course, far more important than size. The TOSWRF sample, admirably described in the manual, was moderately representative of the nation's school population. Of particular concern, nearly 20% of the sample was "exceptional," a figure markedly exceeding national percents. Regional and gender representations in the sample are good; average socioeconomic status (using parental education as a proxy) was acceptable, but disappointingly variable by age of student. On the whole, the TOSWRF norms appear to be sound for the intended screening and "identification" purposes.

COMMENTARY. Of significant concern is the curious labeling of the TOSWRF as a measure of "reading fluency." The content validity section of the manual clearly, and more accurately, describes the test as a measure of the speed of word recognition. Indeed, in a footnote, the authors "define reading fluency as speed of word recognition" (p. 1). However, both in this footnote and at several later locations in the manual, the authors define "reading fluency as speed of word recognition" (p. 15). This is an unfortunate extension of the construct actually assessed to a broader, albeit a generally more important, one. "Reading fluency" as used by most literacy professionals certainly includes speed of word recognition. Yet it almost invariably also includes one or more additional elements including, particularly, some indication of comprehension or meaning. It is unfortunate that the authors extrapolated beyond the actual skill assessed and claimed, absent compelling data, assessment of a much broader skill. Similarly regrettable is the labeling of the age-based normative data as "reading age." Despite obvious commercial reasons for such labeling, the TOSWRF data do not support this reach. TOSWRF assesses an important reading skill and does so efficiently and reliably. It is not a measure of "reading fluency" as this term is generally accepted in the profession.

SUMMARY. The TOSWRF has much to recommend it. It is a very efficient instrument with significant promise for screening students for reading difficulties. It is easily administered and scored, and has two parallel forms and a full range of normative data for interpretive purposes. For someone charged with screening large numbers of students, this reviewer considers TOSWRF worthy of consideration.

Perhaps the major objection to the TOSWRF is, in this reviewer's opinion, that the data provided furnish modest support for the instrument's use, but not the definitive support claimed. Further, but along the same line of criticism, the TOSWRF provides an adequate measure of exactly what its label indicates: silent word reading fluency. The TOSWRF provides a sound, quick assessment of a child's word identification ability, likely a good indicator of reading skills or problems.

REVIEWER'S REFERENCE

Anastasi, A., & Urbina, S. (1997). *Psychological testing* (7th ed.). Upper Saddle River, NJ: Prentice-Hall, Inc.

Review of the Test of Silent Word Reading Fluency by JOHN W. YOUNG, Associate Professor of Educational Statistics and Measurement, Rutgers University, New Brunswick, NJ:

DESCRIPTION. The Test of Silent Word Reading Fluency (TOSWRF) is designed to measure the skills of word identification and word comprehension, using printed rows of words. It is intended for use with individuals between the ages of 6 years 6 months and 17 years 11 months, and can be administered in 10 minutes or less. Students are given 3 minutes to draw lines between the boundaries of as many words as possible (no spaces appear between the words). Each of the two equivalent forms (A and B) contains 32 rows of words, ordered by reading difficulty. Speed of word recognition is important because slow processing is thought to be the most substantial impairment in poor readers (Stein, 2001). The test manual claims that TOSWRF scores are valid estimates of general reading ability and can be used to identify poor readers.

DEVELOPMENT. Developers of the TOSWRF were influenced by Wordchains (Miller-Guron, 1999), a test that consists of 400 nouns, verbs, and adjectives in chains of three to four words. In designing the TOSWRF, the developers selected words from a graded word frequency list—EDL Core Vocabularies in Reading, Mathematics, Science, and Social Studies (Taylor, et al., 1989)—so that words could be ordered by difficulty level. The TOSWRF was normed on a sample of 3,592 persons in 32 states tested in 2001 and 2002. Examiners from around the country who agreed to participate were asked to test two classes of students in their area whose demographic makeup matched that of their community. The sample used for norming cannot be considered truly representative of the national population because: (a) It is somewhat less diverse with regard to race and ethnicity, (b) the parents of students in the norming sample have significantly lower educational attainment, and (c) a number of states, primarily in the upper Midwest and the Rocky Mountain region, did not have any students included. In addition, the effects on the norming statistics, due to self-selection among the examiners who agreed to participate, are unknown.

TOSWRF results are reported in terms of standard scores, percentile ranks, and age and grade equivalents.

TECHNICAL. Evidence in three areas—content, criterion-related, and construct—was provided to support the validity for use of scores from the TOSWRF. With regard to content validity, the developers point to the success of the Wordchains measure as a method of identifying poor readers. The TOSWRF is similar to Wordchains in format, but the words used in the TOSWRF span a larger range of difficulty levels. In addition, earlier research by Meeker, Meeker, and Roid (1985) and Guilford (1959) provided the theoretical foundation for the TOSWRF. The criterion-related validity evidence included studies based on four samples of students who were administered the TOSWRF and one or more additional measures of reading ability. Correlations of the TOSWRF with measures of speeded word identification (such as the Test of Word Reading Efficiency) ranged from .36 to .82 with most values in the range of .60 to .75. Correlations with measures of nonspeeded word identification (such as the Woodcock Reading Mastery Test—Revised) were somewhat lower, ranging from .47 to .53. Correlations of the TOSWRF with the Passage Comprehension subscore from the Woodcock-Johnson Psycho-Educational Battery—Revised were .33 and .39, and from .59 to .74 with Reading Comprehension from the Stanford Achievement Test. Correlations corrected for restriction of range were also reported, but it is questionable as to whether these values would be considered more accurate in representing the relationship of TOSWRF scores to other measures. Construct validity of the TOSWRF was demonstrated through differentiation based on chronological age, and between groups previously identified as having either good or poor reading skills. For the standardization sample, correlations of scores from the two TOSWRF forms with age were .77 and .76. Students identified as belonging to a group with a disability or disorder and those identified in one of the criterion-related studies as being poor readers obtained below average TOSWRF scores. In addition, TOSWRF scores were shown to be moderately correlated with several subscores from the Woodcock-Johnson Psycho-Educational Battery—Revised, and to have low to moderate correlations with the main subscales of the Wechsler Intelligence Scale for Children—Third Edition.

The reliability of TOSWRF scores, based on alternate forms and test-retest, was computed, as well as interrater reliability for scoring. Alternate forms reliability, based on immediate administration of the two forms, was calculated using the entire norming sample. The alternate forms reliability coefficients for each of 13 subgroups ranged from .73 to .87, with most of the coefficients at or above .85. The reliability of the alternate forms, administered 2 weeks apart, averaged .64 for five samples of students. Test-retest reliability coefficients, with an intervening period of 2 weeks and based on the same five samples of students used in the delayed alternate forms administrations, averaged .69 (.68 for Form A and .70 for Form B). Scoring reliability was assessed using a sample of 486 protocols, each scored independently by two raters. Scoring reliability was extremely high with correlations between the two sets of scores at .99 (overall, and for each of the two forms).

COMMENTARY. In the TOSWRF test manual, the authors acknowledge that study of the test's validity has only begun, and that their work in this area is preliminary. The authors' honesty regarding the degree of evidence on the test's validity is commendable. However, in order to improve the instrument, additional theoretical development is also needed. At present, the theoretical basis for the content and construct validity of the TOSWRF is weak. The use of a 1989 word frequency list in determining the words for use in the TOSWRF appears to be both outdated and limited in scope. In terms of construct validity, a more explicit theoretical model for the TOSWRF as a measure of reading ability is necessary. At present, the evidence on the construct validity of this instrument is negligible, as the results do not rule out the possibility that the TOSWRF may be measuring general academic aptitude or achievement. Although the TOSWRF is a timed instrument, it should still be possible to compute the internal consistency reliability based on the number of words correctly identified for each line. An estimate of internal consistency can be useful in determining whether the words chosen are from a single content domain or whether the words may be drawn from different domains.

SUMMARY. The initial development of the TOSWRF seems promising, but further theoretical development and empirical analyses are needed before the instrument can become highly recommended. In addition, the current norming sample seems marginally adequate and should be supplemented with additional examinees so as to be more truly representative of students nationally. Ease and speed of administration and scoring are some of the positive features of the TOSWRF. Nevertheless, until further refinements and additional validation studies have been carried out, it is premature to recommend the TOSWRF as a measure of reading ability or as a method of identifying weak readers over other already established methods.

REVIEWER'S REFERENCES

Guilford, J. P. (1959). Three faces of intellect. *American Psychologist, 14*, 469-470.

Meeker, M., Meeker, R., & Roid, G. H. (1985). Structure of Intellect Learning Abilities Test—1985 Edition. Los Angeles: Western Psychological Services.

Miller-Guron, L. (1999). *Wordchains: A reading test for all ages, teacher's guide.* Windsor, Berkshire, England: NFER-NELSON.

Stein, J. (2001). The neurobiology of reading difficulties. In M. Wolf (Ed.), *Dyslexia, efficiency, and the brain* (pp. 3-21). Timonium, MD: York Press.

Taylor, S. E., Frackenpohl, H., White, C. E., Nieroroda, B. W., Browning, C. L., & Birsner, E. P. (1989). *EDL core vocabularies in reading, mathematics, science, and social studies.* Orlando, FL: Steck-Vaughn.

[252]

The Toglia Category Assessment.

Purpose: Designed "to examine the ability of adults with brain injury or psychiatric illness to establish categories and switch conceptual set."

Population: Adults 18 and over who have neurological impairment.

Publication Date: 1994.

Acronym: TCA.

Scores: Total score only.

Administration: Individual.

Price Data: Price data for "Dynamic Assessment of Categorization TCA: The Toglia Category Assessment (1994, 43 pages), score sheets, and manipulatives available from publisher.

Time: (10–20) minutes.

Authors: Joan Toglia assisted by Naomi Josman.

Publisher: Maddak Inc.

Review of The Toglia Category Assessment by THOMAS McKNIGHT, Psychologist, Private Practice, Spokane, WA:

DESCRIPTION. According to its authors, The Toglia Category Assessment (TCA) is designed to examine the ability of adult patients, who have brain injury or psychiatric disorders, to "establish categories and switch conceptual set" (manual, p. 2) by sorting plastic eating utensils according to size, color, and type. There is a notation in the manual that the TCA "is not diagnostic and is not intended to replace other

standardized measures of categorization and deductive reasoning" but was "designed to supplement conventional measures of categorization and reasoning and provide information relevant to rehabilitation planning." Additionally, there is specific notation in the manual (p. 2) that the instrument was "not designed to be used in isolation of other tests."

The TCA reportedly uses a "dynamic interactional" approach to assessment, estimating the "degree" that the patient's "performance can be modified or changed" with feedback. The examiner is instructed to provide cues or alter the procedures for test administration in response to the patient's difficulty with each task. The authors note that focus is on the conditions that elicit the patient's best performance, thereby addressing "weakened skills" that are lying "just beneath the surface but have the potential for function" (manual, p. 4). The material used for the assessment includes two sizes (large and small) of green, red, and yellow plastic spoons, forks, and knives. The patient is required to "sort these utensils into groups, so that the items in one group are different from those of the other group in at least one way" (manual, p. 11). When the initial sorting is finished, the patient is required to "sort these items another way" and "once more in a different way" (manual, p. 11) for the third sort. A number of verbal cues are offered, as necessary, for each sorting task and scores are based on the amount of "general cueing," "general feedback," or "specific feedback" the patient needs.

After the three tasks are finished, the patient earns a cue level score (0–33) and an awareness score. But the authors specifically note the awareness score method was "primarily developed for the purposes of research" (manual, p. 14) and must be "tested for reliability and validity" (manual, p. 14).

DEVELOPMENT. The Toglia Category Assessment was developed by occupational therapists to be used by "cognitive rehabilitation professionals" including speech and language pathologists, psychologists, and occupational therapists, with "experience in working with cognitively impaired adults" (manual, p. 2).

TECHNICAL ASPECTS. According to the manual, the instrument can be administered in 10–20 minutes, is easily transported, and can be used at the bedside of patients. The authors note that preliminary reliability and validity studies have been conducted, apparently using 35 "brain injured" patients and 35 "schizophrenic subjects," but interrater reliability of .87, according to the manual, was based on 5 subjects (3 schizophrenic patients and 2 brain-injured patients). There is no information about test-retest reliability. Rasch analysis found item separation reliability ranged from .83 to .94 and person separation reliability ranged from .58 to .78, for the two groups of patients. Of interest is the authors' notation that most neuropsychological tests are unable to differentiate between chronic schizophrenic and brain-injured subjects while stating that the TCA was not designed for this purpose. The authors reported that concurrent validity, with the Riska Object Classification Test, ranged from .43 to .51. Even though these coefficients were statistically significant, they reflect modest correlation with an instrument of dubious distinction. Thus, technical quality is questionable, given the paucity of data reported in the manual.

COMMENTARY. Directions for administering and scoring the Toglia Category Assessment are generally clear. Information about interrater reliability is severely limited and no information about test-retest reliability is reported in the manual. Concurrent validity is demonstrated with the Riska Object Classification Test but coefficients are modest and the authors note the "TCA should be examined in relationship to other categorization tasks such as the Wisconsin Card Sorting Test (manual, p. 37). Future studies should also include the Halstead Category Test and it is unclear why these studies were not pursued before the Toglia was offered to the public. Although the authors note the TCA was designed to supplement conventional measures of categorization and reasoning and provide information relevant to rehabilitation planning, the manual provides limited technical information to justify its use in either arena.

SUMMARY. The Toglia Category Assessment might be attractive to occupational therapists but neurophysiologists are expected to find no use for the instrument. Reliability and validity studies, reported in the manual, are seriously limited and there is nothing about the TCA to suggest it will supplement conventional measures of categorization and reasoning. More research, including normative data and better reliability and validity studies, will be necessary before this instrument can be considered for use in any clinical or applied setting.

Review of The Toglia Category Assessment by SCOTT A. NAPOLITANO, Assistant Professor, Lincoln Pediatric Group, and COURTNEY MILLER, Lecturer, Educational Psychology, University of Nebraska—Lincoln, Lincoln, NE:

DESCRIPTION. The Toglia Category Assessment (TCA) examines the "ability of adults with brain injury or psychiatric illness to establish categories and switch conceptual set" (manual, p. 2). The TCA, consisting of 18 large and small colored plastic utensils, can be administered relatively easily within 10 to 20 minutes. The test kit includes a test manual, score sheets, and the set of utensils. The TCA is intended to be used with "adults 18 years of age and older who have neurological impairments such as cerebral vascular accident, brain tumor, head injury, cerebral hemorrhage" (manual, p. 10). This test has also been used with persons diagnosed with schizophrenia. To ensure reliable administration, those assessed should be able to follow two-step directions; discriminate between size, color, and form; and have the ability to attend to a task for at least 15 minutes.

Results are reported in terms of a Total Cue Score based on the examinee's ability to sort the utensils in three different categorical ways (i.e., color, type, size). The score sheet also provides the examiner with five levels of general to specific cueing guidelines, with possible prompts to assist the examinee if he or she is unable to complete the task. In addition, the TCA assigns an Awareness Score based on questions answered by the examinee prior to and after administration, specifically assessing the examinee's perception of his or her thinking ability and perceived difficulty of the task. The TCA has also been administered as a preliminary tool to assess deductive reasoning but currently does not have evidence for reliability and validity.

DEVELOPMENT. In the manual, the authors provide a synopsis of general concepts relative to static versus dynamic assessments as well as a brief overview of six standardized categorization tests. Vygotsky's principle of zone of proximal development is discussed as it relates to dynamic interact ional assessment and provides the theoretical background for the TCA. In addition to this principle, relevant research is presented with regard to awareness of cognitive deficits and categorization. Additional discussion in terms of deficits of categorization, categorization with brain injury and psychiatric populations, characteristics of sorting task, and factors underlying categorization tasks is provided.

Although relevant literature is cited and provides a basis for the TCA, there is limited information detailed in the manual regarding specific test development. Normative data are not available for the TCA. Preliminary analysis of this instrument was based on a sample of 70 people, which included 35 brain-injured and 35 schizophrenic individuals. It is unclear how this sample was selected or under what conditions the TCA was administered. Demographic variables of ages, gender, and education are provided but no information is given for the ethnic composition of the sample.

TECHNICAL. In reporting estimates for reliability, Rasch analysis was used. The Rasch method is described as examining the person and item separation reliability and bases reliability on the ratio of true variance to observed variance in a person's scores. Person separation reliabilities for total sample, brain-injury sample, and psychiatric sample were .69, .58, and .78, respectively. For item separation, total sample reliability was .94, brain injury .91, and psychiatric .83. An item analysis using the Rasch method revealed that classification of size was the hardest and classification according to color the easiest. A T-test was conducted between means ($t = 1.23$), indicating no significant difference between brain injury and schizophrenic adults sampled.

The TCA was compared to the Riska Object Classification Test (ROC; Josman, 1993, as cited in TCA manual), which was also administered to the sample of 70 individuals in an effort to examine validity. The authors report that a moderate positive correlation was found between the two tests for both populations; however, only the p-value of <.001 is provided to support this correlation. Several differences were noted in terms of significant correlations on the TCA and ROC subtests for the populations; the authors suggest that some aspects of these tests may be assessing different abilities, although no speculation of these abilities is given. Overall, the technical quality of the TCA remains questionable, given the limited sample size of each population used in the analyses and lack of normative data.

COMMENTARY. The authors commendably include in the manual a list of limitations of the TCA as well as directions for future research. Limitations cited include the requirement of language skills, excluding persons with moderate or severe aphasia; the TCA also cannot be used to measure change across time. Directions for research as noted by the authors encompass a more rigorous research approach to examining subsets within the brain injury and schizophrenic populations, examining populations with equivalent education levels (in the current sample, there was a correlation of .59 [p<.00] between level of education and TCA), as well as possible inclusion of an adolescent population. Additional areas to research include gathering normative data, possibly revising the cue level to increase test difficulty, and further comparing the TCA to other categorization tasks. The reliability of the awareness questions also needs to be addressed, with responses from different populations compared.

Given the infancy of the TCA in terms of development and research, users should view this instrument as more of an informal, observational tool to be integrated with other forms of assessment. Although the TCA provides a Total Cue Score, this score is more or less meaningless without a normative sample. The authors also provide a table in the manual on the relationship of estimation (i.e., how difficult the examinee perceives the task) to the TCA score; however, no explanation is given in terms of how these expectancies were arrived at or through what manner it was determined that if an examinee has an Awareness score of 1 or easy, his or her expected TCA score would be in the range of 30–33. Although this comparison certainly has utility value, it should be viewed more as observational than confirmatory in nature. The authors point out the intention to link the information obtained through the TCA to treatment and provide the user guides to analyzing responses to cues as well as two case examples. Again, the information obtained from the TCA may be very useful in helping to determine further assessments as well as guide planning but must not be used as the sole determinant for treatment.

SUMMARY. The TCA may be a useful tool for gathering observational information with brain injury and schizophrenic populations. More research is certainly needed to improve the utility of this instrument and lend further credibility to its treatment implications. Users may wish to couple the TCA with a standardized categorization test such as the Wisconsin Card Sorting Test (WCST; Heaton, Chelune, Talley, Kay, & Curtis, 1993) until further empirical support for the TCA is established.

REVIEWERS' REFERENCE

Heaton, R. K., Chelune, G., Talley, J. L., Kay, C. C., & Curtis, G. (1993). Wisconsin Card Sorting Test, Revised Expanded. Lutz, FL: Psychological Assessment Resources, Inc.

[253]
Transition Behavior Scale–Second Edition.

Purpose: "Developed to be an educational-relevant measure of predicted success in employment and independent living based upon school personnel's observation of a student's behavior or skills."
Population: Ages 12–18.
Publication Dates: 1989–2000.
Acronym: TBS-2.
Scores, 3: Work-Related, Interpersonal Relations, Social/Community Expectations.
Administration: Group or individual.
Price Data, 2005: $125 per complete kit including 50 school version rating forms, 50 self-report rating forms, school version technical manual (2000, 41 pages), self-report technical manual (2000, 36 pages), and IEP and intervention manual (2000, 188 pages); $35 per 50 school version rating forms; $35 per 50 self-report rating forms; $15 per school version technical manual; $15 per self-report technical manual; $25 per IEP and intervention manual.
Time: (15–20) minutes.
Authors: Stephen B. McCarney and Paul D. Anderson.
Publisher: Hawthorne Educational Services, Inc.
Cross References: For reviews by Martha Blackwell and David O. Herman of the original edition, see 12:404.

Review of the Transition Behavior Scale–Second Edition by SUSAN K. GREEN, Associate Professor of Education, Winthrop University, Rock Hill, SC:

DESCRIPTION. The Transition Behavior Scale–Second Edition is a 62-item scale designed for rating 12–18-year-olds' behaviors associated with making a successful transition into adult roles after high school. The Second Edition, which uses the same items as the First Edition, has both a restandardized School Version for school personnel and a new Self-Report Version for students. Both take 15–20 minutes to complete. As in the First Edition, both scales are divided into three subscales, Work Related, Interpersonal Relations, and Social/Community Expectations. Items range from very specific ("have necessary materials for specified activities") to very broad ("demonstrate stability (e.g., maintain consistent patterns of acceptable behavior, emotions, etc.)"), and all are written to describe the appropriate rather than the inappropriate behavior. Students use a 5-point scale for rating themselves from 0 (*do not demonstrate the behavior or skill*) to 4 (*demonstrate the behavior or skill at all times consistently*). The School Version rating scale has been expanded from 3 points in the First Edition to a 6-point scale that parallels the 5-point student version, with one additional choice, "is not developmentally appropriate for the student's age group." The Self-Report Version is a commendable addition to the instrument because transition plans are likely to be more successful if students have some voice in the process. A valuable resource accompanying the test is the Transition Behavior Scale IEP and Intervention Manual. This volume contains sample objectives and intervention strategies for each of the 62 items. The intervention suggestions are practical and plentiful and may stimulate additional strategies for a team working on a student's transition.

DEVELOPMENT. The items were developed for the first edition based on predictors of employment and social success recommended by employers and school personnel. No new items have been added for the second edition.

TECHNICAL.
Standardization. Randomly selected school systems from the major geographic regions of the U.S. were solicited to participate in standardization procedures. For the Self-Report Version, 21 schools participated, which included 2,605 students from 17 states. Demographic characteristics of the sample approximately represented the U.S. population on several important dimensions including gender, geographic area, and father's occupation and residence (urban/suburban vs. rural). Some minorities and certain mothers' professions appear to be somewhat underrepresented.

For the School Version, 30 schools participated, which included 2,624 students from 20 states. This sample also approximately represented the U.S. population in terms of ethnicity, gender, and geographic area, with urban/suburban students somewhat underrepresented. Both samples were randomly selected from the participating schools and therefore represented typical students rather than special education or other clinical populations.

Scoring for both the School Version and the Self-Report Version appears to be clearer than in the first edition. Standard scores, percentile ranks, and standard error of measurement are easily found in tables clearly marked by age and gender. The manual also recommends prioritizing individual items from low to high scores to determine priority weaknesses to be addressed in the transition program using the Transition Behavior Scale IEP and Intervention Manual.

Reliability. For the Self-Report Version, test-retest reliability was performed on scores of self-ratings 30 days apart for 93 standardization sample subjects. Correlations ranged from .67. to .79. Coefficient alpha was used to examine internal consistency resulting in scores for the three subscales and the total scale at or above .90. Alpha coefficients were also computed separately for five ethnic subgroups producing similar high levels of internal consistency. Test authors used these data as evidence of low levels of bias for these subgroups; however, additional evidence would be required to make this claim.

The School Version had test-retest reliability evidence presented in the second edition manual from the first edition (N = 203) showing correlations between .87–.92, as well as a smaller sample (N = 21) using the second edition with correlations ranging from .85 to .92. For both of these samples, ratings were completed 30 days apart. Data on interrater reliability from the first edition were also included showing high levels of agreement between raters (.87–.92). Coefficient alpha was used to examine internal consistency of the second edition resulting in scores for the three subscales and the total scale at or above .90. These strong coefficients not only indicate high internal consistency, they also suggest that items for the three subscales are categorized on the basis of face validity rather than technical evidence.

Validity. For the Self-Report Version and the School Version, content validity evidence is based on the original development of the first edition of the scale, which had input from 42 educators and employers. For the Self-Report Version, criterion-related validity evidence comes from comparisons of self-ratings by over 180 students on this scale and either the Youth Self-Report (YSR; Achenbach, 1991) or the Behavior Assessment System for Children: Adolescent Self-Report of Personality (BASC:ASRP; Reynolds & Kamphaus, 1992). Correlations with both measures of similar constructs ranged from .29 to .65 and fall within an acceptable range. For the Self-Report Version, construct validity was investi-

gated primarily through factor analysis. A principal components analysis revealed a dominant first factor explaining 38% of the variance, with other factors accounting for no more than 2.7% of the variance. When three factors were used based on the three subscales, 46 of 62 items loaded on at least two factors with loadings above .30. Additional evidence of high correlations (r = .84 or higher) among the subscales and between the subscales and the total scale (r = .94 or higher) suggests that the evidence for treating subscales as separate domains is limited.

For the School Version, criterion-related validity evidence was examined by comparing teacher ratings on the Transition Behavior Scale—Second Edition with ratings on the Adaptive Behavior Evaluation Scale—Revised (ABES-R; McCarney, 1995) (N = 2,624), the Adaptive Behavior Inventory (ABI; Leigh, 1986) (N = 40), and the AAMR Adaptive Behavior Scale—School Second Edition (AAMR ABS-S:2; Lambert, Nihira, & Leland, 1993) (N = 40). On subscales where both instruments measure the same construct, correlations ranged between .45 and .83 and fall within the acceptable range. Construct validity for the second edition was investigated primarily through factor analysis for the School Version. A principal components analysis revealed a dominant first factor explaining 60.6% of the variance with other factors accounting for no more than 3.2% of the variance. When three factors were used based on the three subscales, 58 of 62 items loaded on at least two factors with loadings above .30. The pattern of evidence presented suggests that treating subscales as separate domains may not be warranted for the School Version.

COMMENTARY. The scale appears to be most useful for pinpointing particular types of behaviors needing remediation in anticipation of transition rather than for comparing a given student's summary scores to national norms. Indeed, the manual states, "Individual item ratings are one of the most valuable sources of specific information that may be gained from the TBS-2" (School Version manual, p. 24; Self-Report Version manual, p. 23). Individual items may prove more practically significant than scale scores particularly because the principal components factor analysis showed a very dominant first factor explaining 38% of the scale's variance for the Self-Report Version and 60.6% of the variance for the

School Version, with no other factors explaining more than 3% of the variance in either version. Use of individual items can be reinforced by the use of the accompanying IEP and Intervention Manual for specific practical interventions.

SUMMARY. The Transition Behavior Scale–Second Edition consists of carefully developed and useful items related to preparing students for the transition from school to the world of adulthood. Improvements from the First Edition include clearer scoring procedures and the addition of a Self-Report Version for students. Norms for both the Self-Report Version and the School Version approximately represent the U.S. population with a few exceptions that should be noted when generalizing results. Because of the technical evidence suggesting that use of the subscales may not be technically justifiable, the most useful aspect of this instrument may be analysis of individual items in the service of developing appropriate transition plans for students.

REVIEWER'S REFERENCES

Achenbach, T. (1991) *Manual for the Youth Self-Report and 1991 Profile.* Burlington, VT: University of Vermont Department of Psychiatry.
Lambert, N., Nihira, K., & Leland, H. (1993). *AAMR Adaptive Behavior Scale–School Second Edition examiner's manual.* Austin, TX: PRO-ED.
Leigh, J. E. (1986). *Adaptive Behavior Inventory examiner's manual.* Austin, TX: PRO-ED.
Reynolds, C. R., & Kamphaus, R. W. (1992). *Behavior Assessment System for Children manual.* Circle Pines, MN: American Guidance Service.

Review of the Transition Behavior Scale— Second Edition, by MICHAEL S. TREVISAN, Associate Professor, Department of Educational Leadership and Counseling Psychology, Washington State University, Pullman, WA:

DESCRIPTION. The Transition Behavior Scale—Second Edition (TBS-2) is a 62-item behavioral assessment used to ascertain readiness for transition from school to work life or from home life to independent living. The authors offer the TBS-2 for students 12–18 years of age.

The TBS-2 is composed of three subscales and can be administered in 15–20 minutes. The subscales are: (a) Work Related, (b) Interpersonal Relations, and (c) Social/Community Expectations. A self-report and school version of the TBS-2 are available. Separate norms tables accompany each version.

The authors recommend the assessment for individualized transition planning. Of particular importance is the use of the TBS-2 in developing Individualized Educational Plans (IEP) for special education students. A manual accompanies the assessment, specifying goals, objectives, and tran-

sition activities. The goals, objectives, and activities are keyed to specific items on the TBS-2 and provide the basis to develop a transition support program for students.

DEVELOPMENT. The same 62 items developed for the first edition are used in both versions of the TBS-2. The development of a self-report version is a new feature in the TBS-2. As rationale for this version, the authors cite literature that advocates self-evaluation as an essential component of successful transition planning. Brief scoring instructions are provided in the manuals for both self-report and school versions of the TBS-2.

New norms are provided for both versions. Though the documentation reports that teachers provided the ratings for both versions, an inquiry to the publisher regarding this issue clarified that students, in fact, provided the ratings for the self-report norms, as one would logically expect. The publisher mentioned that appropriate corrections would be made in future publications (A. Laird, personal communication, September 30, 2003).

One other change from the first edition is the number of choice points in the rating scale (referred to as "quantifiers" in the documentation). In the first edition, a 3-point rating scale was applied to all items. In the TBS-2, the self-report version uses a 5-point rating scale, whereas the school version employs a 6-point scale. No rationale was provided for the increase in choice points from the first to the second edition, or the difference between the self-report and school versions.

TECHNICAL. The standardization sample for both versions was drawn in relation to the 1998 United States Census. Sample characteristics include the variables gender, ethnicity, residence, geographic location, and mother's and father's occupation. When comparing the percent of the TBS-2 norm samples for a particular variable with the corresponding variable in the census sample, most appear comparable, with the exception of ethnicity. In this case Whites are overrepresented whereas African Americans, Hispanic origin, and Asian or Pacific Islander are all underrepresented. Caution is recommended when using norms tables with any individual not well represented within the norm sample characteristics.

Conversion from raw scores to percentile ranks, subscale standard scores, and quotient scores is accomplished through use of the norms tables. The subscale standard score has a mean score of 10 with a standard deviation of 3. The authors offer the quotient score as an overall measure of a student's ability to make successful transition as compared to the norm group. The quotient score has a mean of 100 and a standard deviation of 15. Scores under one standard deviation below the mean signify transition difficulty in work or independent living. For students with these scores the authors recommend developing a transition support system, using in part the goals, objectives, and transition activities provided in the accompanying manual.

Factor analyses were used in an attempt to provide an evidentiary basis for retaining three subscales. However, for each version, one dominant factor emerged from the factor analyses. Further complicating the results were a large number of overlapping items across subscales after rotation, and only small amounts of variability accounted for by the other factors. Thus, many of the items do not differentiate behavior among the subscales, and the two subsequent factors retained account for little of the information in the original data. The authors acknowledged the factor analytic findings, yet went ahead and retained three factors anyway, with the justification being: "due to theoretical scale construction and comparative purposes" (McCarney & Anderson, 2000; p. 10). In short, the empirical results do not justify three factors and thus, their rationale and solution is unsatisfying. This issue was also a criticism in reviews of the first edition (Blackwell, 1995; Herman, 1995) and it appears the authors have not adequately addressed the problem.

In addition to the factor analyses, a variety of reliability indices were computed. Traditional item analyses were conducted. The authors state that content validity was built into the item development process by initially referring to the literature to guide item development and then obtaining feedback from a variety of education and allied health professionals in order to obtain refined, finished items. Correlations with similar measures were also computed, showing low to moderate correlations across subscales.

COMMENTARY. There are three issues surrounding the TBS-2 that make recommendation of this instrument problematic. First, the construct validity evidence is weak, and poorly integrated. This starts with the untenable argument for retaining three subscales, as previously mentioned. In addition, a form of criterion-related validity was offered but no justification for correlating scores on specific, related measures was provided. The validity documentation reads like a checklist of tasks that were accomplished, rather than well-thought, integrated construct validity evidence. The TBS-2 is in need of a validity argument and framework that will guide the production of validity data and, therefore, properly build the foundation for appropriate use.

Two, the authors make a solid case for self-evaluation, and thus, the rationale for the self-report version. Besides the brief scoring instructions, however, no training procedures or scoring guidelines are offered that could assist students in obtaining consistent, accurate self-evaluations. Nor are there any recommendations for integrating the self-report ratings with those from the school version.

Three, the documentation is confusing in parts, also a criticism in reviews of the first edition (Blackwell, 1995; Herman, 1995). In addition to the confusion over the norms, the section on item development reads as if it was part of the construction of the TBS-2. However, cross checking references and dates, as well as confirmation from the publisher, indicates that the items are part of the development of the first edition. At minimum, these confusions undermine confidence in the instrument.

To the authors' credit, they have identified an important component of personal development and constructed an instrument that could be used by a variety of school and health professionals. The service to special education through the IEP process with the TBS-2 has the potential to have wide impact. With the addition of the self-report version, the authors have developed instruments that meet many of the expectations of the Individuals with Disabilities Education Act Amendments of 1997 (IDEA 97). And these are not ad hoc instruments. The authors thoughtfully identified a literature base to inform at least the beginning stages of the development of the TBS-2.

SUMMARY. The TBS-2 has potential to become a useful tool for educators and health specialists serving teenagers as they transition from youth to independence and adulthood. A good deal of work, however, is needed to ensure the construct validity underlying the use of the instrument. Clarity in the technical documentation is also essential. Guidelines to assist students in rating themselves with the self-report version would be helpful. At this time, caution is recommended for use of the TBS-2. The authors are urged to address the criticisms in this review and when relevant, criticisms in reviews of the first edition.

REVIEWER'S REFERENCES

Blackwell, M. (1995). [Review of the Transition Behavior Scale.] In J. C. Conoley & J. C. Impara (Eds.), *The twelfth mental measurements yearbook* (pp. 1073-1074). Lincoln, NE: Buros Institute of Mental Measurements.

Herman, D. O. (1995). [Review of the Transition Behavior Scale.] In J. C. Conoley & J. C. Impara (Eds.), *The twelfth mental measurements yearbook* (pp. 1074-1076). Lincoln, NE: Buros Institute of Mental Measurements.

Individuals with Disabilities Education Act, PL 101-476, 104 STAT, 1103-1151.

McCarney, S. B., & Anderson, P. D. (2000). *Technical manual, self-report version, Transition Behavior Scale* (2nd ed). Columbia, MO: Hawthorne Services, Inc.

[254]
Trauma and Attachment Belief Scale.

Purpose: Measures beliefs related to five need areas that are sensitive to the effects of traumatic experiences.
Population: Ages 9–18, 17–78.
Publication Date: 2003.
Acronym: TABS.
Scores, 11: Self-Safety, Other-Safety, Self-Trust, Other-Trust, Self-Esteem, Other-Esteem, Self-Intimacy, Other-Intimacy, Self-Control, Other-Control, Total.
Administration: Group.
Forms, 2: Profile Sheet, Profile Sheet for Youth.
Price Data, 2003: $79.50 per kit including 25 AutoScore™ test/profile forms, and manual (52 pages); $36.50 per 25 AutoScore™ test/profile forms; $48 per manual.
Time: (10–20) minutes.
Comments: Previously known as Traumatic Stress Institute (TSI) Belief Scale.
Author: Laurie Anne Pearlman.
Publisher: Western Psychological Services.

Review of the Trauma and Attachment Belief Scale by EUGENE V. AIDMAN, Senior Lecturer, University of Adelaide, Adelaide, Australia:

DESCRIPTION. The Trauma and Attachment Belief Scale (TABS) is an 84-item self-report, paper-and-pencil questionnaire designed to assess cognitive schemas sensitive to the effects of traumatic experiences. The instrument is based on the constructivist self-development theory (CSDT; McCann & Pearlman, 1990). Its subscales correspond to the psychological needs—Safety, Trust, Esteem, Intimacy, and Control—hypothesised by the CSDT model as the most vulnerable to disruption by traumatic life experiences.

According to the test developer, the TABS is intended for assessment of trauma survivors in a range of clinical and counselling settings, including domestic partner abuse, childhood sexual abuse, and other forms of intrafamilial victimization. Administration is not timed, taking between 10 and 20 minutes to complete. Manual scoring is assisted with an AutoScore Form, which is claimed to be able to reduce both time and scoring errors.

DEVELOPMENT. The instrument's development followed the CSDT model. Items were generated from statements by trauma survivors, which were reviewed and refined for content validity by a panel of clinical psychologists. However, no details of this evaluation procedure are presented (e.g., the size and composition of the expert team remains unknown). The resulting scales utilize a 6-point Likert scale format and include Safety, Trust/Dependency, Self-Esteem, Other-Esteem, Self-Intimacy, Other-Intimacy, High-Power, and Low-Power. The instrument has evolved from the initial 1988 version called McPearl Belief Scale through the 1991 Traumatic Stress Institute Belief Scale, the 1994 Revision L, and the current TABS. The test manual presents a comprehensive study of equivalence between Revision L and the current TABS.

TECHNICAL. TABS reliability was evaluated simultaneously with its parallel form evaluation study (Revision L versus the current TABS). Internal consistency estimates reported in the manual were obtained on a sample of 260 college students and ranged from .67 for Self-Intimacy subscale to .87 for Other-Intimacy and .96 for the total TABS score. Median retest reliability (administration interval = 1–2 weeks) of TABS subscales on the same sample was .72 and .75 for the total TABS score, with subscale estimates ranging from .60 for Other-Intimacy to .79 for Other-Trust.

Validity. Transparency of TABS items and test takers' general acceptance of their TABS scores as accurate are presented as evidence of face validity in the test manual. No other empirical evidence is reported to support the instrument's content validity.

Intercorrelations between the 10 TABS subscales range from .20 to .88, which indicates a considerable variance overlap between most of the 10 TABS scales. Factor analyses reported in the manual reveal latent variable structures that (a) are partially consistent with the TABS' intended subscale structure and (b) indicate the presence of a second-order (global) factor set comprising three factors: Self, Other, and Safety.

Correlations between TABS and Trauma Symptom Inventory scores on a sample of 207 outpatients with chronic disturbances ranged from .23 to .67, mostly in the directions supporting convergent validity of TABS subscales. The test manual does not discuss issues of discriminant validity—an important omission, especially given the subscale overlap mentioned above.

Criterion validity is represented by predictable differences in TABS scores between known groups (e.g., psychiatric patients who report a history of child sexual abuse versus those who do not) and by the effects of vicarious victimization (e.g., elevated TABS scores among counsellors who had a higher caseload of trauma survivors). This type of evidence appears to be more relevant to construct validity considerations. At the same time, neither concurrent nor predictive validity are discussed in the test manual.

Standardization. The standardization sample (N = 1,743) is a combination of several research samples. Although age, gender, and ethnic background data presented in the test manual leave an impression of convenience sampling, the manual makes no assertion about how representative the TABS normative sample is of the general population. All TABS scales are scored in T-scores (mean of 50 and standard deviation of 10).

CONCLUSION. Overall, the TABS appears a solid instrument, with a reasonable conceptual foundation and considerable empirical justification. However, evidence of its validity and standardization, as currently documented, is incomplete. Caution is recommended in using it as a standard clinical instrument, until more validation data become available for peer scrutiny, such as evidence of criterion validity (especially, predictive) and normative data (i.e., purpose-developed standardization sample).

REVIEWER'S REFERENCE

McCann, I. L., & Pearlman, L. A. (1990). *Psychological trauma and the adult survivor: Theory, therapy and transformation.* New York: Brunner/Mazel.

Review of the Trauma and Attachment Belief Scale by ADRIENNE GARRO, Assistant Professor of Psychology, Kean University, Union, NJ:

DESCRIPTION. The Trauma and Attachment Belief Scale (TABS) is an 84-item self-report, paper-and-pencil instrument developed to assess beliefs that are affected by traumatic experiences. The TABS was designed for clinical use with survivors of traumatic life experiences, though the test manual notes that it can be applied in any therapeutic situation where relationship issues are

a concern. The estimated time of administration is 10–20 minutes for most respondents. All of the TABS items are answered on a Likert scale from 1–6 (1 = *Disagree strongly,* 6 = *Agree strongly*) using an AutoScore packet that allows the item response values to be transferred to a worksheet inside the packet. According to the manual, the TABS can be administered by a trained technician, though it recommends that reporting and interpretation of test scores should only be done by those with training and experience in the use of clinical psychological instruments.

The beliefs measured by the TABS, described as cognitive schemata by the author, are related to five areas—Safety, Trust, Esteem, Intimacy, and Control. For each of these five areas, there are beliefs about self and beliefs about other people. Thus, the completed TABS yields 10 subscale scores as well as a total score. Raw scores are converted into normalized T-scores and percentile ranks. According to the test manual, the TABS scores indicate the degree of "disruption" affecting the respondent's interpersonal relationships. A "disruption" is defined as a restriction of beliefs that negatively influences the ability to relate to others in a healthy manner. Higher scores indicate greater disruption for each of the 10 subscales and the total scale. Also, the manual provides descriptive interpretations based upon the T-scores that range from Extremely low (very little disruption) to Extremely high (substantial disruption).

Unfortunately, the origins and basis for these descriptive terms are not given. According to the manual, therapists can use the TABS score profile, in combination with other assessment measures, to make clinical diagnoses, identify themes in clients' relationships, and formulate effective treatment approaches.

DEVELOPMENT. The TABS is the latest version of an instrument that was originally developed in 1988. The first version, known as the McPearl Belief Scale consisted of nine subscales with 76 total items and was designed for clinical use with trauma survivors. Item development for this scale was based upon statements from clients who had experienced trauma and subsequent review by experts in the field of trauma. Between 1988 and 1991, research studies, reliability checks, and item modifications were conducted with the scale; the specifics of these are not described in the manual. In 1991, the instrument was renamed as the Trauma Stress Institute Belief Scale. After further study and review, it was restructured into self-oriented and other-oriented scales, resulting in the 1994 version (Revision L) consisting of 80 items. The current edition of the TABS is very similar to the 1994 version with the exception that items were simplified to make them easier to read. All versions of the instrument were designed using constructivist self-development theory (CSDT). This theory is briefly described in the manual as a blending of psychodynamic and cognitive behavioral theories to explain how trauma influences individuals. However, the manual provides little empirical support for this theory.

To the developer's credit, all of the 10 TABS subscales are clearly and concisely defined in the test manual. Although these definitions are helpful, there is some overlap and considerable intercorrelations among the subscales. Based upon the CSDT model, these intercorrelations are described as expected. However, the overall factor structure for the TABS is confusing, and the constructs underlying the subscales require better theoretical and empirical support.

TECHNICAL. The norming process for the TABS is partially explained. Dates for the norms are not clearly specified. The standardization sample consisted of 1,743 adults ages 17–78 who participated in research projects asking about the effects of trauma. The sample is described as "non-clinical," but additional information would be helpful to clarify the use of this descriptor. The sample was disproportionately female (73%), and younger participants ages 17–29 were overrepresented (68%). To the developer's credit, gender-specific, age-specific, and race/ethnicity-specific norms are given in the manual, Also, effect size calculations were done to consider the clinical meaning of score differences between genders, age groups, and racial/ethnic groups. However, because the numbers of males and older individuals were relatively low, these norms still need to be applied and interpreted with caution. In addition, the race/ethnicity norms should be interpreted carefully because a relatively large proportion of the sample (38%) did not report this characteristic. Subgroup norms, based upon a number of research studies, are provided for adults with histories of child abuse, outpatients with and without trauma history, and prisoners. The use of these norms also warrants caution due to the small size and limited description of some subgroups.

[Editor's Note: A new Youth Profile Form is now available for ages 9–18. It is based on a sample of N = 1,242. This Form was not yet available at the time this review was written.]

The items for the TABS are clear, easy to read, and are linked to the content of the associated scales. About 80% of the items are worded in a socially undesirable manner such that agreeing with the item suggests the presence of a problem. Although this may be a deterrent to truthful responding in some cases, the scale does not use labels or focus on overt pathology symptoms. The TABS does not have specific scales or items to detect response sets, but the manual does provide general guidelines to identify these sets.

There is some evidence of internal consistency reliability and test-retest reliability for the current version of the TABS, but additional studies are warranted. The manual reports one study involving 260 college students, which yielded a Cronbach's alpha value of .96 for the Total Scale and values ranging from .67 for the Self-Intimacy subscale to .87 for the Other-Intimacy subscale. This same study indicated moderate test-retest correlations using an interval of 1–2 weeks. These ranged from .60 for the Other-Intimacy subscale to .79 for the Other-Trust subscale and a value of .75 for the Total Scale.

Evidence to support the validity of the TABS is mixed. As noted previously, the factor structure is somewhat confusing. The manual suggests that a 10-factor model is most applicable, but the factor analysis results do not support this. Interestingly, a three-factor model by Varra (2001) is also explained. There are no specific data given in support of this model, but it is described as a potentially viable framework for understanding the TABS results. Other research indicates that TABS scores do correlate significantly with scores from the Trauma Symptom Inventory, thus providing some support for the construct validity of the instrument. Criterion validity information for the TABS is presented from several studies, many of these involving contrasted groups. For example, Pearlman and Mac Ian (1995) found that therapists with personal histories of trauma had higher TABS scores than those who did not have such personal histories. For other contrasted groups research, the validity evidence is weakened by small sample sizes or unclear rationale for the group comparisons. Other research by Dutton,

Burghardt, Perrin, Chrestman, and Halle (1994) indicated that TABS scores were correlated with posttraumatic stress symptom scores in a sample of battered women. Overall, there is some preliminary information supporting the criterion validity of the TABS, but additional data are needed.

COMMENTARY. The value of the Trauma and Attachment Belief Scale rests upon the user's need for a formal, specific measurement tool. The content of the TABS is clearly relevant to therapeutic work with individuals who have experienced trauma and/or are struggling with relationship issues. As a clinical instrument that is part of a comprehensive assessment, it is useful in gathering basic qualitative information about belief systems that strongly influence interpersonal relationships. Because these beliefs are shaped by many factors, not just traumatic experiences, the TABS should not be used as a means for identifying trauma victims or diagnosing trauma syndromes. The manual emphasizes the need for clinicians to not overrely on TABS scores and to employ multiple methods of assessment in making diagnostic and treatment decisions. This point cannot be overstressed.

As a formal norm-referenced instrument, the TABS is compromised in a number of areas. As previously noted, there is little empirical support for CSDT, the model from which the TABS originated, and the underlying constructs require clarification and better differentiation. Secondly, although there is some preliminary evidence for the TAB's reliability and validity, additional studies are clearly warranted. In addition, the norms for the scale have restricted utility and must be applied with caution due to lack of information about race/ethnicity, the underrepresentation of males and people over age 29, and the small size for some subgroups. Finally, the descriptors accompanying different *T*-score ranges are vague. Due to these factors, a TABS score profile should only be viewed as a very general indicator of an individual's disrupted beliefs.

SUMMARY. The TABS is a unique instrument in that it focuses on beliefs affected by trauma and not on the traumatic experience itself or its associated psychological symptoms. The developer, to her credit, has developed a scale that is easy to administer, pertinent in many therapeutic environments, and relatively nonthreatening to respondents. The TABS is thorough in covering beliefs both about self and others across a number of key areas that have an impact on relationships. This is definitely a positive aspect of the instrument that will be valued by clinicians. In addition, it is clear that the development of the instrument has been guided by direct information from the field of trauma (victim statements) and an integrated theoretical framework. From a psychometric standpoint, however, the TABS is missing some key elements including sufficient reliability and validity evidence and representative norms. It is appropriate for use in a therapeutic context when normative information is not needed.

REVIEWER'S REFERENCES

Dutton, M. A., Burghardt, K. J., Perrin, S. G., Chrestman, K. R., & Halle, P. M. (1994). Battered women's cognitive schemata. *Journal of Traumatic Stress, 7,* 237–255.

Pearlman, L. A. & Mac Ian, P. S. (1995). Vicarious traumatization: An empirical study of the effects of trauma work on trauma therapists. *Professional Psychology: Research and Practice, 26,* 558–565.

Varra, E. M. (2001, December). The need for trauma assessment beyond the DSM-IV. In L. A. Pearlman (Chair), *Objective theory-based assessment from adaptation perspective: The TSI belief scale.* Paper presented at the 17th annual meeting of the International Society for Traumatic Stress Studies, New Orleans, LA.

[255]

Utah Test of Language Development, Fourth Edition.

Purpose: Designed to "identify children who are significantly below their peers in language proficiency."
Population: Ages 3-0 to 9-11.
Publication Dates: 1958–2003.
Acronym: UTLD-4.
Scores, 8: Picture Identification, Word Functions, Morphological Structures, Sentence Repetition, Word Segmentation, Total Language Composite, Content Composite, Form Composite.
Administration: Individual.
Price Data: Available from publisher.
Time: (15–30) minutes.
Comments: Earliest edition of this test was called the Utah Verbal Language Development.
Author: Merlin J. Mecham.
Publisher: PRO-ED.
Cross References: See T5:2801 (3 references) and T4:2872 (1 reference); for a review by Lynn S. Bliss of the third edition, see 11:454 (2 references); for reviews by Joan I. Lynch and Michelle Quinn of an earlier edition, see 9:1306 (3 references); see also T3:2541 (5 references) and T2:2097 (4 references); for reviews by Katharine G. Butler and William H. Perkins of an earlier edition, see 7:973.

Review of the Utah Test of Language Development, Fourth Edition by DAVID P. HURFORD, Director of the Center for the Assessment and Remediation of Reading Difficulties and Professor of

Psychology and Counseling, Pittsburg State University, Pittsburg, KS:

DESCRIPTION. The Utah Test of Language Development, Fourth Edition (UTLD-4) is a test designed to assess the language abilities of children between the ages of 3-0 and 9-11. The UTLD-4 has no time limits; however, administration typically is completed within approximately 15 to 30 minutes.

The UTLD-4 has four intended uses: (a) to identify children who need special assistance due to language delay or disorder, (b) to determine a child's strengths and weaknesses in the process of diagnosing language disorders, (c) to guide remediation strategies based on the diagnosis process, and (d) for use in research projects addressing language.

The UTLD-4 is composed of five subtests: Picture Identification, Word Functions, Morphological Structures, Sentence Repetition, and Word Segmentation. These reflect the theorized language components of content and form and the theorized linguistic areas of semantics, grammar, and phonology.

The record booklet has sections for identifying information (e.g., child's name, school, grade, gender; examiner's name and title, and reason for referral), age (date of testing, date of birth, chronological age), and recording the scores (e.g., raw scores, percentiles, age equivalents, standard scores, and descriptive ratings). The subtests along with their brief instructions are contained within the record booklet. In addition, the manual is complete and easy to comprehend. The novice user of the UTLD-4 will not find it difficult to comprehend the administration or scoring procedures.

The picture book for the Picture Identification subtest contains black and white drawings. The materials for this subtest are not stimulating or exciting, but are adequate.

DEVELOPMENT. The various subtests that comprise the UTLD-4 were developed as a function of current theory in linguistic and language development. The subtests reflect the theorized linguistic areas of semantics (Picture Identification and Word Functions), grammar (Morphological Structures and Sentence Repetition), and phonology (Word Segmentation). The subtests also reflect children's language abilities in terms of content (Picture Identification and Word Functions) and form (Morphological Structures, Sentence Repetition, and Word Segmentation). Once

the test items were created, based on contemporary theory, the items were field tested to determine their appropriateness for the various ages. In addition, only items that represented acceptable levels of item difficulty and discrimination were retained.

TECHNICAL. The UTLD-4 was standardized with a norming group of 841 children from 14 states in which 93% of the sample had no disability, 5% had speech and language disabilities, and 2% had "other" disabilities. The normative sample was weighted, which resulted in a sample that was very similar to the demographic characteristics of the population of the United States. The UTLD-4 provides standard scores, percentile ranks, and age equivalent scores for each subtest, and composite standard scores for Content, Form, and Total Language. Although age equivalents have been extensively criticized, they are provided as a normative score. However, if test authors would stop providing these psychometrically deficient values, agencies might become less dependent upon them and, thus, authors of future tests would be less obliged to provide them.

Reliability was assessed with internal consistency and test-retest reliability. The authors do not provide evidence of interrater reliability. Internal consistency was assessed by computing coefficient alphas for the five subtests and three composite scores for the age levels 3, 4, 5, 6, 7, 8, and 9 years. Coefficient alphas ranged from .75 (for the Sentence Repetition subtest for the 9-year-olds) to .93 (for the Word Segmentation subtest for the 6-year-olds) with a mean of .90, .93, and .95 for the Content, Form, and Total Language composite scores, respectively. Coefficient alpha coefficients were also calculated for males, females, European Americans, African Americans, Hispanic Americans, Asian Americans, children with articulation disorders, and children with low language achievement, by subtest and composite score. These values were quite similar to those reported above with a range of .87 to .98 with an average of .94. These values indicate that the UTLD-4 is a reliable measure of language ability in children between the ages of 3-0 and 9-11 regardless of gender, minority group status, or speech or language disability.

Test-retest reliability was evaluated by assessing 45 children between the ages of 3 and 9 years of age residing in Austin, Texas. Although the author indicated that the children were in regular education classes, no information regarding gender or race was given. The time between the two administrations of the UTLD-4 was approximately 2 weeks. The correlation coefficients for the Time 1 and Time 2 administrations of the Picture Identification, Word Function, Morphological Structures, Sentence Repetition, and Word Segmentation subtests were .78, .88, .85, .86, and .93, respectively; and the coefficients for the Content, Form, and Total Language composites were .85, .91, and .92, respectively. These values represent adequate test-retest reliability values.

The author argued that because interrater reliability coefficients for earlier versions of the UTLD-4 rarely were lower than .98, they would not be included in the manual. This is an unfortunate omission. Interrater reliability provides further evidence of reliability if interrater reliability is properly assessed. Information regarding interrater reliability is generally very useful in providing a case for the reliability of a test.

Validity was assessed with content validity (including item rationale, conventional item analysis, and differential item functioning analysis), criterion-related validity, and construct validity.

The item difficulty for this type of test, the percentage of respondents who pass an item, should be between .15 and .85 for individual items and approximately .50 for the total test. Median item difficulty scores ranged between .11 (Word Segmentation for the 5-year-olds) and .87 (Sentence Repetition for the 9-year-olds) with a mean of .49.

Item discrimination analysis assesses the ability of an item to differentiate between respondents. The analysis utilizes the Pearson Product-Moment correlation to measure the relationship between performance on each item and performance on the remaining items on the UTLD-4. Item discrimination scores should be approximately .35 or better. The median item discrimination scores ranged from .33 (Picture Identification for the 8-year-olds) to .64 (Sentence Repetition for the 3-year-olds) with a mean of .46. The item discrimination and item difficulty scores fall within values that support the validity of the UTLD-4.

To examine the possibility of item bias in the UTLD-4, items were examined for potential gender and ethnic bias. The items that were deemed appropriate for the UTLD-4 were then subjected to Differential Item Functioning (DIF) analysis. DIF analysis highlights items on which the various groups performed differently. The particular type of DIF analysis that was utilized examined two logistic regression solutions. The first examined subtest scores to predict item performance. The second solution used subtest scores and group membership to predict item performance. If the second solution provides a better solution than the first, it would indicate that group membership was important in predicting item performance, thus suggesting that the items were biased toward particular groups. The groups that were examined included males versus females, African Americans versus non-African Americans, and Hispanic Americans versus non-Hispanic Americans. Three-hundred and sixty-six DIF comparisons were carried out (one for each item for each of the three group comparisons). Of the 366 comparisons, only 10 were determined to be significant. Although the author indicated that the 10 significant comparisons had negligible effect sizes, they did not report the effect sizes. Even so, the analyses indicate that the UTLD-4 does not appear to be biased.

Another source of validity evidence to indicate that the test measures what it is intended to measure is how well scores on the test relate to scores on other tests that measure the same construct. Criterion-related (concurrent) validity is examined by analyzing the relationship between scores on a particular test with scores on other tests that purport to measure the same construct, in this case, language ability. The scores on the UTLD-4 were correlated with scores from the Test of Language Development-Primary (3rd Edition, TOLD-P:3) and the Kindergarten Language Screening Test (2nd Edition, KLST-2). There were 58 children between the ages of 4 years and 9 years (32 males and 26 females; 37 European Americans, 4 African Americans, 10 Hispanic Americans, and 7 Asian Americans) who participated in the study examining the relationship between the UTLD-4 and the TOLD-P:3. The coefficients ranged between .30 and .84 with a mean of .59. There were 31 children between the ages of 3 years and 6 years (14 males and 17 females; 15 European Americans, 3 African Americans, 12 Hispanic Americans, and 1 Asian American) who participated in the study examining the relationship between the UTLD-4 and the KLST-2. The coefficients ranged between .38 and .88 with a mean of .74. The coefficients support criterion-related validity.

Construct validity was assessed utilizing age and group differentiation. Age differentiation is another means to examine the validity of scores from a test. When assessing young children, linguistic abilities should improve with age. Data provided in the manual indicated that the means for the various subtests increased with age, thus supporting validity. Group differentiation, like age differentiation, can be used to support validity. A test of language development should be able to differentiate between groups of young children who are known to have low language achievement and those who do not have low language achievement. Data that were reported in the manual indicated that individuals who had low language achievement had low average to below average subtest scores and below average composite standard scores for Content, Form, and Total Language (i.e., 88, 86, and 85, respectively). The individuals who had articulation disorders had subtest scores that ranged from 8 (low average) to 10 (average). Composite scores for this group were also within the low average to average range (i.e., 96, 92, and 93 for Content, Form, and Total Language, respectively). It was crucially important that the UTLD-4 be able to differentiate between language disordered and nondisordered children. However, the etiology for articulation disorder is multifaceted and may have less to do with language development than motoric discrepancies. Thus, one would anticipate that the group with articulation disorder would have scores on a language development test near normal values.

Finally, confirmatory factor analysis was used to assess the appropriateness of the composite scores to reflect the model on which they were based. The first model examined supported a two-factor solution based on a goodness-of-fit criterion (i.e., how closely the data would fit a solution that included the composite scores of Content and Form). The second model examined the adequacy of a one-factor solution (Total Language) also based on goodness-of-fit criterion. The results indicated that both models were supported by the data and that the subtests were correctly assigned to the composite scores. The results also support the Total Language Composite as an appropriate measure of general linguistic ability.

In conclusion, the case for validity is strong. Age differentiation data indicated that performance on the UTLD-4 increased with age, which supports validity given that emergent language abilities are purported to develop with age. The case for group differentiation also supported valid-

ity in that children with low language achievement performed less well than children with appropriate language achievement. The results of the confirmatory factor analysis also supported the validity of the UTLD-4.

SUMMARY. The UTLD-4 is a test that assesses the language abilities of individuals aged 3-0 to 9-11. It was developed to identify children who need special assistance due to language delay or disorder, to determine a child's strengths and weaknesses in the process of diagnosing language disorders, to guide remediation strategies based on the diagnosis process, and for use in research projects addressing language. The UTLD-4 has only one form. Therefore, with no alternative form, it is limited to research studies that do not assess language processing more than one time of measurement. Research designs typically require that alternative forms of a test be used at different times of testing to reduce the likelihood of time of measurement or practice effects. The most recent edition of the UTLD-4 provides a technically sound measure of language development in children aged 3-0 to 9-11.

Review of the Utah Test of Language Development, Fourth Edition by JUDITH R. JOHNSTON, Professor, School of Audiology and Speech Sciences, The University of British Columbia, Vancouver, British Columbia, Canada:

DESCRIPTION. The Utah Test of Language Development, Fourth Edition (UTLD-4) is the latest revision of a test first published in 1967. The preface to the examiner's manual provides a brief history of the test, and identifies areas of change. In particular, the fourth edition has a new subtest structure, new normative data, and a wider range of statistical tests of bias, construct validity and reliability.

The UTLD-4 now focuses exclusively on expressive language and is "designed to identify children who are significantly below their peers in language proficiency" (examiner's manual, p. 2). The test is organized into five sections: Picture Identification (child names pictures, mostly of objects; examiner asks for a second word for each); Word Function (child explains "what you do with" various objects); Sentence Repetition (child repeats sentences of increasing grammatical complexity); Grammatical Morphological Structures (child completes sentences with inflected words, or makes up sentences containing inflected words);

and Word Segmentation (child repeats words, omitting designated portions). The first two subtests assess vocabulary knowledge and are considered tests of language Content. The remaining three subtests assess grammar and phonological awareness and are considered tests of language Form.

Performance on the UTLD-4 yields five subtest scores and three composite scores: Content, Form, and Total. Norms are provided for children aged 3:00–9:11, at 3-month intervals, and all scores are presented as percentile ranks, standard scores, and age equivalents. Task instructions and scoring criteria are straightforward.

The examiner's manual is comprehensive, clearly written, and includes a general discussion of the use and limitations of standardized tests, providing reasons to question their suitability for diagnosis or for setting educational goals. The record booklets are well designed, and contain all the information needed to administer the tasks. The set of line drawings used for Picture Identification are the only materials required, and are unimaginative but adequate.

DEVELOPMENT. Test items for the UTLD were selected to "best achieve the objective or purpose of the particular subtest," "provide a broad coverage," "keeping the number of items down," and to represent a "wide range of … difficulty" (examiner's manual, p. 32). The only development details that are provided concern the last two criteria. Items for all subtests were selected from larger pools, in field testing, primarily on the basis of difficulty and discrimination power.

TECHNICAL.

Standardization. The normative sample consists of 841 children in 14 states, generally 125 from each year between the ages of 3:0 and 9:11. Data were collected in two phases. First, personnel with experience and training in test standardization administered the UTLD-4 to 440 children in five cities selected to represent the four major regions of the U.S. Then volunteer professionals from around the country, contacted via the publisher's mailing list, contributed data on an additional 400 children. The characteristics of the resulting sample closely mirror those of the school-aged population described in the 1999 report of U.S. Census data in regard to geographic area, gender, race, ethnicity, family income, residence (urban, rural) parental education, and disability status (none, speech-language disorder, other handicap). Weighted scores were used in the final

construction of norms to bring the sample values even closer to those in the population. Distribution of the sample by geographic region may be less satisfactory than claimed, however, because the cities designated as test sites may not be typical of their regions: Austin, Texas (South); Grandview, Missouri (Midwest); Salt Lake City, Utah, and San Dimas, California (West); Kennet Square, Pennsylvania (Northeast).

Reliability. The examiner's manual includes data on item homogeneity within subtest (Cronbach's alpha) for groups defined by age and by other demographic characteristics. Values fall within acceptable ranges. The stability of standard scores over a 2-week period was also measured for a sample of 45 children spanning the test's age range. Correlation coefficients for both the subtest and composite scores fell between .85 and .93, except for Picture Identification at .78.

Validity: Content-description. The five subtests of the UTLD-4 cover their intended domains with varying degrees of success. Discrimination indices and other psychometric features of test items are generally in the acceptable range. However, some items appear to be difficult or discriminating for the wrong reasons, particularly in the three tests of Form. In the Sentence Repetition subtest, at least 5 of the 23 sentences are highly improbable ("a girl that is little likes cake") if not ungrammatical ("I see a blue and a red book"). Success in reproducing these forms may be compromised if their meanings are unclear. In the Morphological Structures subtest, higher level items require children to create sentences that include a specific inflected word (e.g., "taken"). The author makes the arguable claim that children must understand the inflection before they can create a suitable sentence. Even if this were true, the task clearly requires much more than knowledge of grammatical morphology. The fact that this subtest correlates most strongly with a vocabulary subtest is not surprising. Finally, in the Word Segmentation subtest, higher level items seem to test literacy as well as metaphonology. Children are instructed to repeat a word, omitting a particular syllable or sound. It is not clear whether the examiner is to pronounce letter names or sounds for the elements to be omitted (i.e., "es—tee" or /st/). The ambiguity is moot, however, because both are problematic. Using letter names presumes literacy, which is clearly beyond the intended scope of the test. Using sounds, on the other hand, is likely to be confusing due to co-articulation effects. The sound of "r" in isolation is quite different from the sound of "r" in the words *try* or *true*. It is not clear how one could reasonably tell a 6-year-old to say the word "true" but omit the "r." In sum, many items in the Form subtests do not seem well designed from a linguistic point of view although they meet quantitative criteria. This is likely to lead to interpretive errors if the subtest labels are taken at face value.

Unlike prior editions, the UTLD-4 does not include tests of language comprehension. The author's rationale for this change is that "if children produce language structures correctly, they should be able to comprehend them" (examiner's manual, p. 4). This argument ignores the fact that many school-age children have difficulty processing the language they hear and do not "comprehend" in real-time even though they have knowledge of the forms. Despite the arguable premise, there are a number of comprehension tests available and this lacuna is not fatal. A more significant gap in the scope of the UTLD-4 is the lack of any subtest devoted to discourse. Although the author aims to cover those aspects of expressive language that can be readily assessed formally, there is no subtest in the realm of pragmatics. Language use in conversation is admittedly difficult to test, but language use in narrative *is* amenable to testing and a brief story-telling activity would have been useful and important, particularly for the 7–9-year-old groups.

Other validity analyses. Differential item functioning analysis was used to determine whether there were gender, race, or ethnicity biases in performance on test items. The analysis is poorly described, but seems to indicate the absence of bias. Predictive validity was assessed via concurrent scores from 30–60 children on the UTLD-4 and two other language tests, the Test of Language Development: Primary, Third Edition (TOLD-P:3), and the Kindergarten Language Screening Test—Second Edition (KLST-2). Correlations between scores on the TOLD subtests and the UTLD-4 subtests fell in the .4 to .7 range and were generally significant. The UTLD-4 vocabulary tests, however, correlated most strongly with TOLD measures of grammar, suggesting that the UTLD-4 tests of Content actually tap into more general language competencies. Correlations between pertinent composite scores on the

two tests were stronger than the subtest values, falling between .54 and .84. The KLST-2 yields only a total score. Correlations between this test and UTLD-4 composite scores were strong, falling in the range from .8–.87.

Additional analyses of construct validity demonstrated that subtest scores increase with age, are reasonably intercorrelated, and can differentiate between persons with and without developmental disabilities. This latter conclusion was, however, based on data from an unsystematic collection of only 20 disabled children. Results from a factor analysis are presented to assess the degree to which the UTLD instantiates its theoretical model (i.e., the division of language competencies into Form and Content). The author concludes that the model is supported, but the findings again indicate considerable overlap between the two domains. This overlap, along with the item design problems described earlier, muddies test interpretation and challenges the value of the new subtest structure.

COMMENTARY AND SUMMARY. The UTLD-4 aims for a unique—and potentially useful—niche in the universe of language assessment, attempting to measure two different aspects of expressive language in a brief, easy to administer, test. Except for concerns about the geographical distribution of the normative sample, the psychometric properties of this edition are reasonably strong. The manual is clear and comprehensive, and the author offers sound advice on the use of test scores. Ultimately, however, the UTLD falls short of its aims due to the poor design of items on the Form subtests, overlap in the competencies tapped by the Form and Content tasks, and failure to test discourse abilities. These shortcomings make test interpretation difficult and greatly mitigate the value of the test.

[256]

Valpar Test of Essential Skills.

Purpose: Designed to "help examinees demonstrate in a relatively short period of time important basic English and math skills required of workers in most of the occupations or training programs in the United States and Canada."

Population: Ages 15 and over.

Publication Dates: 1998–1999.

Acronym: VTES.

Administration: Individual or group.

Price Data, 2000: $30 per manual (1998, 80 pages), $75 per 25 answer sheets; $50 per 10 math test booklets (specify Form A or Form B); $50 per 10 English booklets (specify Form A or Form B); $50 per Evaluation Kit including 1 manual, 10 answer sheets, 2 math test booklets, 2 English test booklets, and scoring software.

Comments: Time limited; criterion-referenced; computer scoring only; requires IBM PC or compatible, 486 or higher.

Authors: Bryan B. Christopherson and Alex Swartz.

Publisher: Valpar International Corporation.

a) VTES ENGLISH.

Scores, 6: Vocabulary/Grade Equivalent, Spelling/Grade Equivalent, Usage/Grade Equivalent, Reading/Grade Equivalent, Total/Grade Equivalent, Total/General Educational Development-L (GED-L).

Forms, 2: Alternate Forms: Form A and Form B.

Time: (60) minutes.

b) VTES MATH.

Scores, 6: Computation/Grade Equivalent, Usage/Grade Equivalent, Total/Grade Equivalent, Computation/General Educational Development-M (GED-M), Usage/General Educational Development-M (GED-M), Total/General Educational Development-M (GED-M).

Forms, 2: Alternate Forms: Form A and Form B.

Time: (45) minutes.

Review of the Valpar Test of Essential Skills by ARTHUR S. ELLEN, Senior Psychometrician, National League of Nursing, New York, NY:

DESCRIPTION. The Valpar Test of Essential Skills (VTES) includes two parallel tests— Forms A and B. Each form consists of criterion-referenced vocational tests in English and math for people 15 years of age or older. The academic content of the tests spans material covered in Grades 6 to 10 in English and Grades 4 to 10 in math. The English test covers Vocabulary, Spelling, English Language Usage, and Reading Comprehension. The math test has two subtests: Computation and Math Usage (short word problems). The VTES bases its vocational content upon the General Educational Development (GED) scale from the *Revised Handbook for Analyzing Jobs* (U.S. Department of Labor, 1991). It covers the Language scale (GED-L) from Levels 2 to 4 and the Math scale (GED-M) from Levels 1 to 4.

The examiner's manual provides explicit directions, making the administration of each 1-hour test straightforward. Examinees answer on optical scan sheets, which may be scanned into the accompanying software. Alternatively, users can manually transfer

responses into the easy-to-use database for storage and report generation. The database facilitates correct entry with functions for field checking and double entry. Only the software generates reports; there is no hand scoring. The report contains: examinee identifying information, scores reported by grade and GED levels, a breakdown by subtests, and an explanation of test scores and the test's rationale. Optical scan sheets can also be returned to the publisher for scoring and reporting.

DEVELOPMENT. The VTES test plan generally involved selecting several items at specified grade levels for each subtest, and coordinating the subtests' content with the GED scale. Then grade and GED levels determine scoring and reporting, which was done differently for the English and math tests. Furthermore, the authors developed a scale that denotes below test-level performance with a minus sign (e.g., -6) and above- or between-grade level performance with a plus sign (e.g., 6+). The definition for this between-level scoring is no more detailed than "plus signs indicate a high level of performance at grade level" (manual, p. 20).

Six subtests form the English test and all questions have five options. There are three vocabulary subtests: synonyms (10 items), completion of a simple sentence with a synonym (10 items), and antonyms (5 items). The 5-item Spelling test has the test-taker choose the one correctly spelled word. The 10-item English Language Usage subtest requires the choice of one sentence with an error. These sentences contain errors in subject-verb agreement, verb tense, capitalization, pronoun agreement, sentence construction, and use of double negatives. For the 10-item Reading Comprehension subtest, the examinee selects the main idea from 10 different passages.

The grade levels for the Vocabulary and Spelling subtest items were determined by sampling from a graded word list. The authors did not determine the grade level for the items of the English Language Usage subtest. Grade levels for the Reading Comprehension passages were determined with readability software, only after calibrating the program with texts from known grade levels. It was not reported which readability formula or approach was chosen. Two items from each of the six grade levels were included on the Comprehension subtest. Although a similarly even distribution of items for the Vocabulary and Spelling subtests appears reasonable, this was not indicated.

Each subtest's raw score is converted to a grade-level score; two conversion tables are provided for this, one for the 10-item subtests and another for the 5-item subtests. These tables were apparently constructed by having the center of the grade level match the average grade level for each subtest, but this is not spelled out. The total grade-level score is derived from the average of each of the six grade-level scores. It is not explained why the 5-item subtests are given the same weight as the 10-item subtests. Although tables are exhibited for the grade level to GED-L conversions, it is not reported how these tables were developed or if they were taken from another source.

The math test consists of a 20-item Computation subtest and a 21-item Math Usage subtest; each question has four options. The manual provides tables identifying the grade and GED level for each question along with a description of item content. For the Computation subtest, 4 items are placed at each grade level from 4th to 8th grade, and the test's content comes from GED-M Levels 1 and 2. For the Math Usage subtest, the number of items at each grade level varies slightly from 6th grade to 10th grade, and GED-M ranges from Level 2 to 4. More than half the math items come from GED-M Level 2. Additionally, the assignment of items to grade levels occasionally appears questionable, especially when an item like "John had 7 marbles and found 5 more. How many does he have now?" is assigned to Grade Level 4.

A table precisely indicates the number correct required to obtain grade and GED-M level scores. For example, to obtain a grade level of 6, an examinee must correctly answer all sixth grade items or miss only 1 and correctly answer 3 of 4 items at the prior grade. Subtest scores are reported as the number correct at each grade and GED-M level.

TECHNICAL. In developing two parallel test forms, Valpar field tested approximately 600 people with 380 items divided between four English and four math tests. To place all items on the same difficulty scale, they linked exams by test section adjusting the item difficulties based upon the values of 20 total common items (a procedure superficially similar to test banking using common item equating). Because this linking ostensibly used raw item difficulties with fewer than 20 items for each test section, this may well have resulted in an arbitrary common scale. Test content, question format, and item difficulties were used to create two similar test forms. Items were statistically examined for sex and ethnic bias by using a chi-square procedure that first controlled for examinee ability level. The high ratio of statistical tests to subjects and the high reported p values would have resulted in inconsistently overidentifying biased items.

The test's reliability—internal consistency, alternate form reliability, and decision consistency—was examined based upon 50 people who had taken alternate test forms. Total raw score Cronbach's alphas (KR-20) were .95 for both English forms and .88 and .82 for Math Forms A and B, respectively. Subtest alphas ranged from .56 to .83. Correlations between alternate form total grade levels and GED levels ranged from .68 to .78. Decision consistency was reported as percentage agreement between Forms A and B for grade and GED levels. A typical pattern of score consistency emerged with higher proportions of agreement at the ends of the scale, where there are fewer and more extreme scores, than at the center, where there are typically more cases. However, percentage agreement inflates estimates of reliability compared to a chance corrected agreement index such as coefficient kappa.

The manual reports two concurrent validity studies. The first, with the 50 people who had taken the alternate test forms, examined the relationships between self-reported grade completion and test-score levels. Correlations for total score levels ranged from .26 to .51, with higher relationships found for the math tests. The second study correlated proxy English and math test scores formed by using only items that survived the field testing with various achievement tests similar to the VTES. Although these correlations generally indicated evidence of concurrent validity, some of the sample sizes were too small for reasonable inference and the proxy scores were at best an indirect measure of actual VTES scores.

COMMENT. Criterion-referenced testing requires not only a clear description of the domain to be measured but also explicit performance standards (Popham, 1978). Although there were clearly visible rules for score conversions involving the math test, the GED-L and grade conversions for the English tests were obscure. This was particularly so for the English test's raw score to grade-level conversions, grade-level to GED-L conversions, the assignment of grade level to the English usage test, and the differential weighting of 5- and 10-item subtests. Whereas the authors do not claim that the VTES is a comprehensive assessment of the GED domains, there is an unexplained emphasis at the lower end of the GED-M scale. For both tests, tables of blueprints, including item counts, organized by grade level and GED content areas would have been helpful.

When a test report fails to exhibit a thorough attention to detail and does not display effective information for test users, surety in a test declines. The VTES report erroneously prints places for between level score information for the English subtests when no such scores exist. Although the math subtest report provides readily comprehensible counts of items correct at each grade and GED-M level, the English subtest scores are reported as counts correct without such clear and helpful reference points. Finally, the table reporting counts of occupations based upon the cross-classification of GED-L and GED-M levels would increase its informative value if a few examples of selected occupations were printed.

SUMMARY. The VTES depends upon content validity for test scoring and meaning, yet insufficient detail about English test scoring makes test interpretation difficult. Furthermore, technical shortcomings in test construction, limited math coverage, and inadequately established concurrent validity are all current test limitations. These problems may lead to errors in vocational placement and incorrect suggestions for educationally relevant job choices. Hence, use of the VTES is currently not recommended.

REVIEWER'S REFERENCES

Popham, J. W. (1978). *Criterion-referenced measurement.* Englewood Cliffs, NJ: Prentice-Hall.

U.S. Department of Labor, Employment and Training Administration. (1991). *The revised handbook for analyzing jobs.* Washington, DC: U.S. Government Printing Office.

Review of the Valpar Test of Essential Skills by SHAWN POWELL, *Associate Professor, and* MICHELLE A. BUTLER, *Associate Professor, Department of Behavioral Sciences and Leadership, United States Air Force Academy, USAF Academy, CO:*

DESCRIPTION. The Valpar Test of Essential Skills (VTES) in English and Math is designed to assess "important basic English and math skills required of workers in most occupations or training programs" (user's manual, p. 1). The VTES is a criterion-referenced, timed test of English and mathematics skills. It has two forms,

A and B. It is intended to be administered to individuals 15 years of age and older. To complete the VTES, individuals solve English and mathematics problems and then record their answers on an answer sheet. The time requirement is approximately 2 hours, 1 hour for the English test and 1 hour for the mathematics test. The VTES reportedly can be used in work training programs, adult vocational educational programs, and for employee selection.

The VTES is a criterion-referenced test linked to the Department of Labor's (DOL) General Levels of Educational Development (GED) and job standards from the Dictionary of Occupational Titles (U.S. Department of Labor, 1991). Through this comparison, VTES results are intended to represent an individual's capability to successfully perform various occupations. The VTES assesses the following areas: Vocabulary, Spelling, Grammar/Usage, Reading Comprehension, Mathematics Computation, and Mathematics Usage. Scores in the form of GED levels and scholastic grade levels are provided for each area the VTES evaluates. Additionally, a total English score and a total Mathematics score are given. Both VTES versions use multiple-choice formats with test items arranged from easy to more difficult.

The English tests consist of 50 items designed to measure language skills commonly taught in Grades 6 to 10. The Vocabulary test includes 10 synonym knowledge items, 10 items that require a synonym to be chosen to complete a short sentence, and 5 items measuring antonym knowledge. The Spelling section consists of 5 items. The Grammar/Usage section consists of 10 items and the Reading Comprehension section has 10 items.

The Mathematics test has 41 items. These items include 20 Mathematics Computation items and 21 Mathematics Usage items. The Mathematics Computation section is intended to evaluate arithmetic skills routinely taught in Grades 4 to 8. The Mathematics Usage section is designed to assess arithmetic skills taught in Grades 4 to 10+.

Administering the VTES does not require specific training and it can be given by anyone who can serve as a test proctor. The VTES must be computer scored. A software program produces a computer-generated report containing scores an individual achieves and occupational information related to the Department of Labor's GED levels in English and mathematics. Interpretation of the VTES report requires specific training in testing, knowledge of the VTES, GED levels, scholastic grade levels, and the *Dictionary of Occupational Titles* (U.S. DOL, 1991). With accurate interpretation by a trained professional VTES results can be used to assist in making occupational decisions such as job placements and training program selections.

DEVELOPMENT. The VTES was developed to assess basic English and mathematics skills to assist various organizations in making occupational decisions. It was designed to measure academic skills required for the majority of occupations contained in the *Dictionary of Occupational Titles* (U.S. DOL, 1991). The VTES was intentionally constructed to measure occupational skills related to GED Mathematics Levels 1 to 4 and GED Language Levels 2 to 4. In developing the VTES, efforts were taken to have the content of the tests represent typical school curriculum. To accomplish this goal, VTES items were developed based on samples of English and mathematics educational materials from eight states (i.e., Alabama, Arizona, California, Florida, Kansas, New York, North Carolina, and Texas).

In choosing words for the VTES vocabulary tests, a thorough procedure was followed to ensure selected words adequately reflect the grade level content they were developed to measure. This procedure involved making alphabetical grade level lists of "several thousand potentially suitable words" (user's manual, p. 24) from *The Living Word Vocabulary* (Dale & O'Rourke, 1976). Potential subject words paired with their synonyms or antonyms and distractors were randomly selected from these grade level lists. Spelling test items were selected from the same word lists used for the vocabulary tests. The VTES grammar or language usage items were selected to measure the ability to discern various types of errors in capitalization or sentence construction. To measure reading comprehension, 10 short passages were chosen using two items per grade level from Grades 6 to 10.

The VTES Mathematics test items were specifically selected to measure arithmetic skills directly related to the DOL's GED levels. The mathematics computation items are intended to correspond to skills taught in Grades 4 to 8 and GED Levels 1 to 2+. These items range from adding whole numbers without carryover to dividing fractions. The mathematics usage items were developed to represent skills ranging from single step whole number addition to simple trigonom-etry ordinarily taught in Grades 4 to 10+ and GED Levels 2 to 4+.

TECHNICAL. The VTES manual indicates two different samples were used for its reliability and validity studies. One sample had 50 participants and the other had 228 participants. The larger sample's African American/Black representation was 31%, compared to 12.3% African American/Black representation in the U.S. population (U.S. Census Bureau, 2000). The smaller sample's Hispanic representation was 32%, compared to 12.5% Hispanic representation reported in the 2000 Census. The larger sample was drawn from six states (i.e., Florida, Indiana, Missouri, Oklahoma, South Dakota, and Texas).

For internal consistency estimation, K-R 20 was used. The coefficients for the English sections range from .56 to .71. Internal consistency estimates for Form A and B's total English score is .95. The mathematics sections' internal consistency estimates range from .61 to .83 and the total Mathematics scores' internal consistency estimates are .88 for Form A and .82 for Form B. Alternate forms reliability correlations range from .40 to .78. Reported means for Forms A and B are similar with small standard deviations suggesting both forms produce similar results. As the VTES is criterion-referenced, evidence of its reliability is also presented in the form of P and agreement indexes. The VTES P indexes range from .76 to 1.00. The VTES agreement indexes show a high level of concurrence.

Evidence of content and construct validity for the VTES is provided. For content validity correlations between reported years of education and obtained VTES scores range from .07 to .64. For construct validity, comparisons of the VTES to other educational tests are provided; however, it should be noted these comparisons reflect data collected over the course of a year. Criterion validity is not discussed.

COMMENTARY. As a criterion-referenced measure of work-related skills, the VTES appears to have incremental validity when used by organizations to assist them in making occupational decisions. Although a proctor is required, administration of the VTES is easily accomplished as the manual contains good instructions. The VTES can be administered in individual or group formats. Its two alternate forms could be used for pre- and posttraining outcome assessments.

The VTES content areas are reportedly linked to occupational requirements across a variety of jobs. Although the VTES is purportedly linked to DOL occupational standards, its psychometric properties are problematic. The first concern is the absence of a large normative group representative of the U.S. population. For reliability and validity purposes two samples are reported; however, due to their small sizes both samples are inadequate. Additionally, neither sample reflects the current U.S. population's racial/ethnic demographics. The second concern is the lack of criterion validity data comparing VTES results to actual job performance. The method in which construct validity data were obtained is also troubling. The comparisons of the VTES to other educational achievement tests are based on test results accumulated over a year. This is problematic as the VTES measures basic academic skills and a person's level of achievement would be expected to change over the course of a year, especially for individuals involved in training programs.

The content of the VTES English tests is limited as it only reflects curriculum materials from eight states, thus the English skills being tested are especially problematic. The Mathematics portion of the VTES is more robust in this regard as schools across the U.S. tend to follow a more similar curriculum for mathematics instruction compared to language arts. The mathematics tests appear to have a good representation of various problems to assess a person's skill level.

The software program required to score the VTES is easy to install and has a straightforward technical manual. Technical support from Valpar is readily available and very responsive. The test report is comparable to other computer-generated reports.

SUMMARY. The VTES offers a relatively quick assessment of an individual's basic English and mathematics skills. Its intended use in making occupational decisions is readily apparent as the skills it measures are linked to the DOL's job standards. Organizations could use VTES results to assist in determining job placements and training selections. It is easy to administer, score, and interpret. It can be given in either individual or group settings. Its psychometric properties deserve additional research, most notably an adequate normative group and evidence of criterion validity. Nonetheless, as a criterion-referenced test linked to the DOL occupational standards, the VTES offers a solid addition to the assessment of job-related academic skills.

REVIEWERS' REFERENCES

Dale, E., & O'Rourke, J. (1976). *The living word vocabulary.* Chicago: World Book-Childcraft International. Inc.

U.S. Department of Labor, Employment, and Training Administration. (1991). *Dictionary of occupational titles* (4th rev. ed.). Washington DC: U.S. Government Printing Office.

U.S. Census Bureau. (2000). *Census 2000.* Retrieved November 20, 2003, from http://factfinder.census.gov/servlet/QTTable?ds_name=DEC_2000_SF1_U&geo_id=01000US&qr_name=DEC_2000_SF1_U_DP1

[257]
Verbal Motor Production Assessment for Children.

Purpose: "Designed to aid in the systematic assessment of the neuromotor integrity of the motor speech system in children ... [with] speech production disorders."

Population: Speech-disordered children ages 3–12.
Publication Date: 1999.
Acronym: VMPAC.
Scores, 8: Global Motor Control, Focal Oromotor Control, Sequencing, Connected Speech and Language Control, Speech Characteristics, Auditory, Visual, Tactile.
Administration: Individual.
Price Data, 2005: $115 per complete kit including examiner's manual (206 pages), 11 stimulus cards, 15 record forms, and training videotape (45 minutes); $80 per examiner's manual; $32 per 15 record forms; $32 per stimulus cards; $43 per training videotape.
Time: (30) minutes.
Authors: Deborah Hayden and Paula Square.
Publisher: PsychCorp, A brand of Harcourt Assessment, Inc.

Review of the Verbal Motor Production Assessment for Children by KATHARINE SNYDER, Assistant Professor of Psychology, Methodist College, Fayetteville, NC:

DESCRIPTION. The purpose of the Verbal Motor Production Assessment for Children (VMPAC) is to assess motor speech functions in children, ages 3 through 12, to identify speech disorders, recommend treatment modality (auditory, visual, tactile), and document progress over time. To accomplish this, the VMPAC consists of three primary areas (Global Motor Control, Focal Oromotor Control, Sequencing) and two supplemental areas. Area 1, Global Motor Control (20 items), assesses Tone (head, neck, and trunk stability during rest, ambulation, and phonation), Respiration (thoracic and diaphragmatic activity during phonation), Reflexes (e.g., rooting, Babkin's, mouth opening, biting), and Vegetative Functions (e.g., chewing or swallowing).

Area 2, Focal Oromotor Control, consists of 17 nonspeech single or double oromotor items (e.g., mandible, labial-facial, or lingual movements) and 29 speech oromotor movements (e.g., single, double, or triple phoneme movements, word sequences, and sentences). Administration of Area 2 proceeds along three sensory modality cues, depending upon the needs of the child. The auditory modality is utilized first and a command is given (e.g., "show me how you smile and kiss"). If accurate production is not achieved after one attempt, the visual modality is added. For instance, an examiner would say, "look at me and do what I do," then model a smile and a kiss. If there still is not accurate production of the item, the tactile modality is added, with the examinee saying "now I am going to help you smile and kiss," then guiding the movements by touching the appropriate facial muscles.

Area 3, Sequencing (23 items), consists of double or triple oromotor phoneme sequences and oromotor speech within word sequences or sentences. For example, the examiner states, "Now we're going to put some sounds together," then says "/a-u/." Children are given a Motor Control (MC) score as to their ability to speak smoothly, precisely, and symmetrically without jaw sliding. An MC score of 2 means that both movements were precise in both parameters, whereas an MC score of 1 signifies that one or both movements were not accurate on one or both phonemes. An MC score of zero occurs when one or both phoneme movements are severely inaccurate, a phoneme is substituted, or both phonemes are not stated. Next, the examiner says the "/a-u/" sequence four times, each time pointing to the picture of a block on a stimulus card. The ability of the child to say the sequence back four times is used to obtain the Sequencing score (SC). An SC of 2 indicates that all four repetitions were accurate, whereas an SC of 1 signifies that there were either three correct repetitions or there were more than the original four. A zero SC means that the child repeated the sequence either less than two or more than six times. On the word sequence and sentences items (61-66) of Area 3, children are shown picture cards and then asked to repeat words or sentences. The child is to repeat the words correctly for the MC score and the word sequence or sentence correctly for the SC score.

Connected Speech and Language Control (Area 4) and Speech Characteristics (Area 5) comprise the supplemental section. For Area 4, children are to put four stimulus cards in an order that makes up a story. The MC score is assessed by evaluating production of the four sentences that correspond to each card. Within Area 5, children are asked to either count to 10 or recite the alphabet. Finally, for Area 5, the evaluator scores pitch, resonance, voice quality, intensity, prosody, and rate based on clinical judgment.

Test items are arranged in increasing difficulty. This has clinical utility. A child exhibiting smooth and precise movements for single items, but not double or triple items, may have a sequencing problem. Similarly, a child may have difficulty sequencing items on the test, yet have little difficulty on tasks that are previously learned (e.g., counting to 10 or saying the alphabet). This also suggests a sequencing problem.

For each of the five areas, total raw scores are obtained and then converted into percent scores. The examinees' percent scores are placed on Standardized Sample graphs for their age groups. Standardized Sample graphs include plots of the 95th percentile, mean, and fifth percentile scores for each normative sample (age 3, age 4, age 5, age 6, and ages 7–12). Whether or not scores are within acceptable limits or are impaired is based upon clinical judgment as to the placement of the plot of scores for the child being tested relative to the normative sample plots.

DEVELOPMENT COMMENTARY. The hierarchical model (the five areas) is supported by prior research and proceeds from basic neurophysiological capabilities to higher level sequencing skills. This progression is designed to identify the point at which the articulatory/phonological problems begin and to assess the level of support most helpful to the child (auditory, visual, tactile). Originally, the VMPAC was created to distinguish children with articulatory/phonology problems with or without motor speech deficits. The VMPAC was also designed to distinguish phonological problems from dysarthrias or apraxias as well as level of therapeutic support necessary (auditory, visual, tactile).

Allegedly, the VMPAC can be useful to any child with one or more of the following afflictions:

Articulation disorder, phonological disorder, developmental dysarthria, developmental apraxia of speech, developmental verbal apraxia, developmental delay with concurrent speech production disorder, neurodevelopmental disorder with concurrent speech production disorder, pervasive developmental disorder with concurrent speech production disorder, autism with concurrent speech production disorder, specific language impairment of expression, receptive/expressive language delay or disorder, acquired brain injury with concurrent speech production disorder, acquired aphasia with concurrent speech production disorder, oral/facial genetic disorders with concurrent speech production disorder, congenital oral/facial structural disorders with concurrent speech production disorder, delayed speech development. (examiner's manual, p. 2)

Standardization research was conducted during the 1997–1998 academic year on a stratified sample (1995 U.S. Census) of 1,434 children ranging in age from 3 to 12 years. A total of 180 licensed and/or certified speech-language pathologists from across the country served as examiners. Stratification was based on age, gender, race/ethnicity, primary caregiver education, and geographic region. Children in the standardization sample were able to attend to and complete the test. Researchers state the following: "All items were statistically analyzed and evaluated for difficulty, reliability, differential item functioning (bias), and discrimination within and across each age group. Final item selection was based on these analyses" (examiner's manual, p. 24). Further details of these analyses are not provided.

TECHNICAL COMMENTARY. Reliability of the VMPAC was assessed through test-retest and interrater studies. From the original standardization sample, 115 children were retested with the VMPAC. Test-retest coefficients (7–14-day interval) were as follows: Global Motor Control (.60), Focal Oromotor Control (.90), Sequencing (.88), Connected Speech and Language (.62), and Speech Characteristics (.56). The lower correlations, those less than .70, are reported to be due to the smaller number of items in these areas. From the original standardization sample, 119 children were also given the test with an observer present to establish interrater reliability, which resulted in correlations ranging from .93 to .99.

Content and discriminant validity were addressed in the manual. Content validity of the VMPAC is argued from previous research and clinical practice. However, studies correlating the VMPAC areas with other assessments in the field would be very useful. Discriminant validity of the VMPAC is argued by assessing intercorrelation of the five areas as well as cross-sectional age comparisons. In support of the discriminant validity, there are low correlations between the Global Motor Control Scores and Sequencing scores (-.03 to .29). Data such as these reportedly support prior research on the distinction between behaviors mediated by the cortico-bulbar pathway and primary motor cortex (e.g., Global Motor Control) as compared to more anterior frontal function (e.g., volitional control of sequencing). From observation of the cross-sectional comparisons, researchers report an increase in mean percent scores with advancing age. Observational data such as this are reported to support prior research of increasing cortical specialization and overall speech production capabilities with age.

Clinical utility was assessed through the study of four clinical groups. Generally, in the four clinical group studies, the worse the impairment, the poorer the scores on the VMPAC. Best to worst performance is as follows: Group 1 (148 children with therapy responsive articulation/phonological pathology), Group 3 (65 children with therapy resistant articulation/phonological pathology), Group 4 (130 children with oromotor functional problems), and Group 2 (51 children with generalized motor pathology).

SUMMARY. The VMPAC is a reasonable measure of Global Motor Control, Focal Motor Control, and Sequencing for children 3 to 12 years of age. What is especially useful from the VMPAC is the determination as to whether adding the tactile component to therapy will be beneficial.

[258]
Verbal Reasoning Tests.

Purpose: Designed to "assess a pupil's verbal skills."
Publication Date: 1993.
Scores, 5: Vocabulary, Relationships, Sentences, Reasoning, Symbol Manipulation.
Administration: Group.
Levels, 3: 8 and 9, 10 and 11, 12 and 13.
Price Data: Available from publisher.
Authors: Neil Hagues and Denise Courtenay.
Publisher: NFER-Nelson Publishing Co., Ltd. [England].
   a) VERBAL REASONING 8 and 9.
   Population: Ages 7.3–10.3.
   Time: (40) minutes.

b) VERBAL REASONING 10 and 11.
Population: Ages 9.3–12.3.
Time: (45) minutes.
c) VERBAL REASONING 12 and 13.
Population: Ages 11.3–14.3.
Time: (50) minutes.

*Review of the Verbal Reasoning Tests by HOI
K. SUEN, Professor of Educational Psychology, Pennsylvania State University, University Park, PA:*

DESCRIPTION. The Verbal Reasoning
Tests are designed to be measures of intelligence
that can be administered in group settings. They
are composed of three sets of tests designed for 8–
9, 10–11, and 12–13 years of age, respectively.
These tests can be administered individually or in
groups. The test for the 8–9-year-olds consists of
65 items. The time needed for administration is
estimated to be 40 minutes. This test is to be
preceded by a 34-item familiarization test. The
10–11-year-old version consists of 75 items estimated to take 45 minutes, with a 36-item familiarization test. Finally, the test for 12–13-year-
olds consists of 85 items and takes 50 minutes to
administer, in addition to a 36-item familiarization test. Each of these paper-and-pencil tests
features a variety of item types including completion of small crossword puzzles, multiple-choice items,
matching items, word-finds, and fill-in-the-blanks.
Questions are designed to measure five areas of
verbal reasoning: Vocabulary, Relationships between
words, Sentence structure, Reasoning, and Symbol
Manipulation. Those designed to measure Vocabulary include items that require the test-taker to find
hidden words within an unrelated sentence; to find a
missing letter that will simultaneously form the end
of one given word and the beginning of another
given word; to form new words by combining words;
and to form new words by adding and subtracting
letters. Items designed to measure relationships are
matching items that identify antonyms, homonyms,
and synonyms. Sentence items include tasks requiring the rearrangement of words within sentences and the determination of missing letters
from key words within a sentence to make the
sentence meaningful. Reasoning items are primarily symbol decoding items and deductive reasoning items based on given verbal information. Finally, Symbol Manipulation items are primarily
pattern-recognition items. A student's raw score is
determined by the total number of items responded
to correctly across all these areas.

Each of the familiarization tests contains an
example plus two or three questions for each item
type. The purpose of these tests is to help students to
understand and get used to these item types. These
familiarization tests may be given earlier in the same
day or on the day before the main test. Teachers may
go over the familiarization tests after students have
attempted them to ensure that the students fully
understand how each question works.

Although not explicitly stated in the test
manual, the Verbal Reasoning Tests are intended
to be used as intelligence tests. According to the
National Foundation of Educational Research of
England (NFER, 2004), which is the sponsor of
these tests, the testing of verbal reasoning is designed to assess what Cattell (1963) coined as
crystallized general intelligence. The authors suggested that results from the Verbal Reasoning
Tests could be used to guide curriculum planning
for schools and to help placement decisions for
individual students in secondary schools.

DEVELOPMENT. According to the authors,
the National Foundation of Educational Research
(NFER), a nongovernmental national organization of local education authorities, teachers' associations, and other teaching and learning organizations in England and Wales, maintains a large
verbal reasoning item bank. The authors examined
the range of item types in this item bank and chose
16 types as potential item types to be used in the
Verbal Reasoning Tests. A total of 103, 121, and
133 new items were then constructed, respectively,
for the three age groups. The exact proportions of
various item types were not reported. Test specifications either were not used or are not reported
in the test manuals. In a technical supplement
(Hagues, Smith, & Courtenay, 1993), the rationale for the choice was stated as being based on an
earlier publication by Whetton (1985) and another by Smith (1986). These new items were
pilot tested in 1991 on 320, 250, and 320 pupils,
respectively, for the three age groups. No description of the sampling method used to select the
pilot samples of pupils is provided in the manual
or in the technical supplement. Based on classical
item difficulty and discrimination statistics estimated from the pilot study, 65, 75, and 85 final
best items were selected, respectively, for the three
ages. The pilot data were also used to conduct
differential item functioning (DIF) analyses to
attempt to identify items that were potentially

biased in favor of one of the sexes. The items identified as DIF were discarded. According to the technical supplement, five different DIF analytic techniques that were common in the early 1990s were used. Unfortunately, due to various practical concerns, DIF analyses across ethnicities were not conducted.

TECHNICAL. In 1992, data were collected from large stratified samples of school children for the purpose of standardizations and the estimation of score reliabilities. Specifically, for each of the three age groups, between 4,600 and 5,400 pupils from 174–194 schools in Wales and in the North, Midlands, and South regions of England were tested. Scores were normed based on these samples and were scaled on a standard score metric with a mean of 100 and a standard deviation of 15. From the technical supplement, these appear to be normalized standard scores. The norm tables provided are broken down to the level of month-in-age such that one can convert from the raw score to the standard score for the exact month within a certain age. No information is provided as to exactly how these detailed levels of standard scores were derived. It is possible that some form of interpolation operation was used. The technical supplement reported the use of a nonlinear transformation process to adjust for ceiling effects and provided no detail of the process. The norm tables also extrapolated scores beyond the range of age for the sample by 6 months on both ends of each of the age ranges.

Score reliabilities were estimated via the KR-20 and the test-retest approach. The authors reported KR-20 estimates to be around .96 for all age groups. Test-retest reliability estimates (administration interval = 1 year) were also very high—around .88 for 10/11 and 12/13 age groups and .81 for the 8/9 age group.

It appears that evidences of validity were gathered following a somewhat outdated model of validity commonly used prior to the 1980s. Under this model, there are three to four types of validity, including content validity, concurrent validity, predictive validity, and construct validity. The authors suggested that they had evidence of content and concurrent validity. However, upon closer examination, content validity proved to be only a claim by the authors without impartial third party judgment. Specifically, content validity was claimed on the basis that an examination of the item types in the Verbal Reasoning Tests by the authors themselves shows that the inferential and deductive skills are reflected in the individual questions of the tests. Concurrent validity was claimed on the basis that scores on the Verbal Reasoning Tests were found to correlate at levels of between .78 and .89 with the corresponding older version of the same tests. The authors also discussed predictive validity but only offered hints of potential evidence by pointing out that scores on other verbal reasoning tests in general had been found to correlate well with subsequent academic performance. Overall, evidence of validity is rather weak to nonexistent.

COMMENTARY. Many of the important areas of concern often not addressed in a large portion of published tests have been addressed in the development of the Verbal Reasoning Tests. Many of the technical aspects, including the use of large stratified samples, DIF analyses, reliability, and standardization methods, are generally sophisticated for the time period when it was published. These have led to very reliable scores. However, the Achilles heel is in the most important area of concern (i.e., the area of validity). Evidence of validity is lacking.

Although not explicitly stated in the test manual, the construct of interest for the Verbal Reasoning Tests is general intelligence. It appears that, for these tests, verbal reasoning or general intelligence is defined as consisting of vocabulary, ability to determine relationships between words, understanding sentence structures, reasoning ability, and symbol manipulation ability. To measure these subconstructs, the authors selected from the item bank of NFER 16 item types and created the items for the tests accordingly. It is not clear as to how the exact number of each item type, and thus the implicit weight given to that item type, was determined. Consequently, there is no explicit formal basis to claim that the composite scores for these tests constitute the optimal or even a valid indicator of verbal reasoning.

The above problem of uncertain construct representation could have been somewhat ameliorated had there been a review of items for their representation and relevance by an independent panel of recognized specialists in theories of intelligence in a formal content validation exercise. Unfortunately, this review was only done by the authors themselves informally. Finally, the question of appropriateness of the composition of items for the tests could also have been answered to some degree had there been factor analyses conducted to show that these items indeed reflect those five intended areas faithfully. Given the large samples available, this could have been accomplished easily, but was unfortunately not done or not reported.

The claim of concurrent validity is based on an approach that is a departure from the generally accepted method of gathering concurrent evidence. Specifically, scores on the Verbal Reasoning Tests were correlated with scores on a previous version of the same test. One of the existing methods to distinguish classical reliability from concurrent/convergent validity, which were two approaches used for the attempt to validate the Verbal Reasoning Tests, is that reliability is the correlation between two maximally similar measures of the same construct whereas convergent/concurrent validity is the correlation between two maximally dissimilar measures of the same construct (Campbell & Fiske, 1959). According to this definition, the approach used for concurrent validity for the Verbal Reasoning Tests resembles reliability more so than validity. It is, in fact, reliability estimated via the equivalent forms method. Therefore, given the inadequate content validity methodology and the lack of concurrent, predictive, or construct validity, not to mention other sources of validity evidence recommended by more recent standards, one can only conclude that there is little evidence of validity.

The norm tables are rather detailed and standard scores are listed by month in age. The scores for each month interval may be based on empirical data or mathematical interpolation. From the tables, they appear to be interpolations. The exact mathematical form for interpolation was not reported but appears to be linear. Implicit in the chosen mathematical form is an assumption regarding the nature of child development. For example, a linear interpolation would assume that a child's maturation is linear, which would be inconsistent with known child development models. The tables also provided extrapolated scores beyond the age range of children actually tested in the standardization samples. Again, these extrapolations are based on untested mathematical assumptions and are potentially risky and harmful. Finally, the provision of detailed month-in-age norms in the particular structure of the norm tables makes it potentially tempting for users to convert from raw scores to age-equivalent scores, which are scores that are known to be highly susceptible to misinterpretation. Given the problems of interpolation/extrapolation and age-equivalent scores, it might have been more appropriate simply to provide major age norms without the month-in-age level of detail.

DIF analyses were reported in the technical supplement. Comparisons between males and females were done and items found to be potentially biased against one or the other sex were discarded. DIF analyses across ethnicities were not done due to various practical concerns. This is unfortunate. If these tests are to be used beyond England and Wales, analyses of potential cultural bias are needed. A superficial examination of the contents of items in these tests suggests that many of these items would have high potentials of cultural bias against children in other English-speaking countries, including the U.S. For example, the correct response to one of the items for 10–11-year-olds requires the child to be familiar with the English practice of staying at a farmhouse on holidays. (Not to mention that the meaning of "holidays" are different in different cultures. In the U.S., for instance, the concept conveyed by "holidays" in this test is referred to as "vacations.") An item for 8–9-year-olds requires the child to know the meaning of "£11.5," "a £5 note," and "a 50p piece." One analogy item requires a child to associate lemon with the color yellow, which is a classic DIF problem found in the SAT when researchers realized that lemons in Central and South America were green. These and other items suggest a need to conduct thorough DIF analyses with appropriate subsequent modifications before these tests are appropriate for use in the U.S., Canada, Australia, New Zealand, India, or other English-speaking countries.

SUMMARY. Classical score reliabilities for the Verbal Reasoning Tests are uniformly high regardless of the exact estimation procedure used. Therefore, we can conclude that the Verbal Reasoning Tests produce highly stable scores with little measurement error. Given the careful stratified sampling method used, the norms are likely to be relatively accurate for children in England and Wales. The proper interpretation and use of these scores and norms for decisions, however, are much more uncertain, due to a lack of validity evidence. Given the norming sample as well as the lack of information regarding potential item or test bias in favor of or against children with cultural backgrounds different from those of England and Wales, the appropriateness of these tests for children in English-speaking nations outside of England and Wales is suspect.

REVIEWER'S REFERENCES

Campbell, D. T., & Fiske, D. W. (1959). Convergent and discriminant validation by the multitrait-multimethod matrix. *Psychological Bulletin, 56,* 81–105.

Cattell, R. B. (1963). Theory of fluid and crystallized intelligence: a critical experiment. *Journal of Educational Psychology, 54,* 1–22.

Hagues, N., Smith, P., & Courtenay, D. (1993). *Verbal and Non-verbal Reasoning: Technical supplement.* Windsor, UK: NFER-Nelson.

NFER. (2004). [Website for National Foundation of Educational Research of England.] Retrieved October 18, 2004, from http://www.nfer.ac.uk/aboutus/amd35.asp

Smith, P. (1986). Application of the information processing approach to the design of a non-verbal reasoning test. *British Journal of Educational Psychology, 56,* 119–137.

Whetton, C. (1985). Verbal reasoning tests. In T. Husen & N. Postlethwaite (Eds), *The international encyclopedia of education.* Oxford: Pergamon.

Review of the Verbal Reasoning Tests by ROSEMARY E. SUTTON, *Professor, Department of Curriculum and Foundations, Cleveland State University, Cleveland, OH, and* JEREMY GENOVESE, *Assistant Professor, Department of Curriculum and Foundations, Cleveland State University, Cleveland, OH:*

DESCRIPTION. These three instruments measure verbal reasoning and replace earlier versions of the tests (called Verbal Reasoning Tests BC, D, EF). There are five types of questions in the three NFER-Nelson tests: Vocabulary, Relationships (analogies), Sentences (meaning in context), Reasoning (logical argument), and Symbol Manipulation. Verbal reasoning assessments encompass the deductive and inferential skills involving the production and use of language, can be thought of as ability measures, and have historically been used in Great Britain.

The NFER-Nelson Verbal Reasoning Tests are attractively printed. The tests can be administered and scored by teachers or other school personnel. A familiarization test is included because students may not be familiar with verbal reasoning problems. Instructions for administering the assessment are included in both the test manual and on a convenient "At a Glance Guide." The manual provides an answer key, a table to convert raw scores into standardized scores and percentile ranks, and a table of the 90% confidence bands around the standardized score ranges. Machine scoring is not available.

DEVELOPMENT. The NFER-Nelson Verbal Reasoning Tests were developed out of item trials conducted in November of 1991. Statistically discriminating items were selected for the appropriate range of difficulty and some individual items were dropped because of gender bias.

TECHNICAL. The manual gives little information about the theoretical constructs that these instruments purport to measure and no reference is made to the peer-reviewed literature. Readers are referred to a special technical supplement for additional information on validity. The new tests show reasonable concurrent validity with previous versions and the technical supplement provides regression formulae for the comparison of old and new scores. Unfortunately, data on predictive validity were not available when the supplement was published but are promised in future editions. Standardization was conducted in June of 1992 and included more than 170 schools in both metropolitan and nonmetropolitan areas of Great Britain (Wales, North, Midlands, and South of England). Verbal Reasoning 8 and 9 was standardized on 2,229 Year 3 and 2,951 Year 4 students and the internal consistency reliability estimates (Kuder-Richardson 20 formula) were .96 for each age sample. Verbal Reasoning 10 and 11 was standardized on 2,806 Year 5 and 2,644 Year 6 students and the internal consistency reliability estimates (Kuder-Richardson 20 formula) were .96 for each age sample. Verbal Reasoning 12 and 13 was standardized on 2,471 Year 7 and 2,161 Year 8 students and the internal consistency reliability estimates (Kuder-Richardson 20 formula) were .95 for the Year 7 sample and .96 for the Year 8 sample.

Concurrent validity coefficients with older versions of the tests ranged from .78 to .87 for standardized scores. No other validity evidence was provided for this review.

COMMENTARY. The NFER-Nelson Verbal Reasoning Tests were standardized on large samples and have high reliability estimates. However, Primrose, Fuller, and Littledyke (2000) reported large changes in individual scores over time.

Group administered tests are often used to predict academic achievement so the lack of information about predictive validity is a significant weakness. The NFER-Nelson tests reflect a traditional approach to ability testing that differs from the current U.S.A. emphasis on the use of cognitive measures for individual diagnostic purposes in education.

SUMMARY. The instructions are clear, the instrument can be easily administered and scored by school personnel, and the reliability estimates are high. The lack of current information about predictive validity is a serious weakness. These instruments may be a sensible choice for the assessment of verbal reasoning in children ages 8 to 13 for those who wish to assess verbal reasoning from a traditional approach.

REVIEWERS' REFERENCE

Primrose, A. F., Fuller, M., & Littledyke, M. (2000). Verbal reasoning test scores and their stability over time. *Educational Research, 42,* 167-174.

[259]

ViewPoint.

Purpose: An assessment of work attitudes designed for use in employee selection.

Population: Applicants for nonexempt or entry-level positions in industries.

Publication Dates: 1998–2003.

Scores: 10 scales: WorkView Total, ServiceView Total, Conscientiousness, Trustworthiness, Managing Work Pressure, Getting Along with Others, Drug/Alcohol Avoidance, Safety Orientation, Carelessness, Faking.

Administration: Group or individual.

Price Data, 2005: Available from publisher for test materials including technical manual (1999, 62 pages), Technical Report Addendum: A meta-analysis of the Validity of ViewPoint (2001, 13 pages), and examiner's manual (1998, 43 pages).

Comments: Published in five different forms, each one covering a different combination of work and service attitudes; computerized versions are available.

Authors: W. M. Gibson, M. L. Holcom, S. W. Stang, and W. W. Ruch.

Publisher: Psychological Services, Inc.

a) WORKVIEW 6.
Acronym: W6.
Time: (15–20) minutes.
b) WORKVIEW 4.
Acronym: W4.
Time: (10–15) minutes.
c) SERVICEVIEW.
Acronym: SV.
Time: (10–15) minutes.
d) WORKVIEW 6 + SERVICE.
Acronym: W6SV.
Time: (20–30) minutes.
e) WORKVIEW 4 + SERVICE.
Acronym: W4SV.
Time: (20–25) minutes.

Review of ViewPoint by ROBERT FITZPATRICK, Consulting Psychologist, Cranberry Township, PA:

DESCRIPTION. ViewPoint (VP) is a self-descriptive survey of work attitudes designed to evaluate suitability of applicants for nonexempt

jobs. The survey is offered in three major versions: WorkView6 (W6) includes scales measuring the six "dimensions" of Conscientiousness, Trustworthiness, Managing Work Pressures, Getting Along with Others, Drug/Alcohol Avoidance, and Safety Orientation. In addition, there are supplementary measures of Carelessness (in responding consistently to the survey) and Faking. WorkView4 (W4) covers the same aspects except Drug/Alcohol Avoidance and Safety Orientation. ServiceView (SV), which deals separately with attitudes about providing service to others, may also be scored in combination with W6 or W4 to form W6SV or W4SV. VP uses four types of items:

> (1) *Attitudes/Opinions* toward disapproved or illegal behavior or activities; (2) *Admissions* of disapproved or illegal behavior or activities; (3) *Self-descriptions* of one's attitudes, behaviors, or thoughts; and (4) *Hypothetical situations* for assessing one's judgment or likelihood of action in realistic work situations. All items use a multiple-choice response scale, with the majority of response scales reflecting agreement, likelihood, or frequency. (technical manual, p. 3)

The scales are short, averaging 16 items each. There is no time limit; it is expected that almost all respondents will complete the longest combination (W6SV) in no more that 30 minutes. No special training is required to administer the VP.

The VP is scored by the publisher. The client may send completed answer sheets by mail or fax and receive in return a score report for each candidate showing composite scores, a score for each of the dimensions, and levels of carelessness and faking. The score report also shows the percentile rank (and a confidence interval) for each composite score and dimension in comparison to a specified norm group. An optional feature provides examples of statements endorsed by the respondent that are considered to be of critical importance. An internet-based computer version is also available, with equivalent scoring arrangements.

DEVELOPMENT. The initial item production was based on an extensive literature review and a series of job analyses. A guide for item production was produced and several hundred items were developed. These were narrowed to the final set of items after extensive review and tryout. Some pains were taken to insure the appropriateness, clarity, and plausibility of items while minimizing intrusiveness and ethnic or gender bias. "Language suggestive of a clinical disorder, impairment or psychological diagnosis was avoided" (technical manual, p. 22).

TECHNICAL. Normative information is available in a separate supplementary norms report for a number of occupations and industries. A default set of percentile norms is based on a mix of respondents chosen to be representative of a general United States working population; sample sizes range from 1,100 (for W6SV) to 3,850 (for W4).

Internal consistency reliabilities, in the form of alpha coefficients and standard errors of measurement, were estimated from a study of 1,024 job applicants. Alpha coefficients ranged from .90 to .95 for the five major packages and from .68 to .77 for the six dimensions. The Faking scale reliability was .70 and the Carelessness value was .50. This study also showed substantial intercorrelations among the elements of VP, the highest of these being .69 between SV and Getting Along with Others. A single factor appears to dominate the variance in the VP scales.

The careful planning and implementation of item content constitute a strong basis for a claim of content validity for VP. The correlations of VP elements with cognitive tests are low positive, consistent with expectations. The technical manual does not report correlations with other types of tests. Six criterion-related validity studies are reported and meta-analyzed in a 2003 addendum to the technical manual. The meta-analysis suggests an overall validity between .32 (W6) and .40 (W4) against a criterion of job performance; and a range of .16 (SV) to .23 (W6) for training success.

The technical manual presents evidence that differences in average scores between gender, age, ethnic, and racial groups are lower with VP than they would likely be with cognitive tests. Given the low correlation between VP and cognitive tests, it appears that a combination of VP with one or more cognitive tests should yield a satisfactory overall validity along with less advantage to white males than normally obtains with cognitive tests alone.

COMMENTARY. The VP documentation is generally sound and comprehensive, and is frequently updated to include new research. In addition, the publisher offers support in response to queries by users. It appears that VP has good evidence for validity and other psychometric characteristics (though some evidence of test-retest reliability would be welcome).

VP is relatively simple to administer and scoring can be carried out accurately if accurate information is supplied to the publisher. However, those who use fax-back scoring should take very seriously the publisher's advice to check answer sheets carefully and remove improper marks before faxing them to be scored. Major errors can occur, and there is some evidence to indicate that errors are more likely in this type of scoring arrangement than in other methods.

W6 includes two more dimensions than W4, but the validity evidence is comparable for W6, W4, and SV, suggesting that all are effective in predicting job performance. It is suggested in the technical manual that "employers may wish to use the longer survey configurations to ensure representation of content areas that are important for certain positions" (p. 18).

SUMMARY. ViewPoint was carefully developed and designed to be convenient for users. Norms are extensive, reliability evidence appears to be adequate, and the publisher provides evidence of validity for a wide variety of applications. A number of self-description inventories purport to measure such constructs as temperament, integrity, honesty, reliability, and workplace citizenship; ViewPoint appears to be one of the better ones, worthy of serious consideration by an employer seeking to hire superior employees.

[260]
Vigil Continuous Performance Test.

Purpose: Designed to "measure a person's ability to concentrate on a simple or relatively complex task over time."

Population: Ages 6 to 90.

Publication Dates: 1996–1998.

Scores, 4: Errors of Omission, Errors of Comission, Hit Rate, Reaction Time.

Administration: Individual.

Price Data, 2003: $545 per complete kit including Windows Version Binder and three 3.5-inch disks.

Time: [8] minutes.

Comments: Test is computer administered and scored; requires IBM compatible 386 or 486, 20 MB hard drive, 3.5-inch disk drive, Windows 3.1, mouse, Color VGA or Super VGA monitor, and Sound System compatible with Sound Blaster Pro Deluxe Soundboard.

Author: The Psychological Corporation.

Publisher: PsychCorp, A brand of Harcourt Assessment, Inc.

Review of the Vigil Continuous Performance Test by JOSEPH C. KUSH, Associate Professor, Duquesne University, Pittsburgh, PA:

DESCRIPTION AND DEVELOPMENT. The Vigil Continuous Performance Test is a computer-administered test of attention intended by the authors to create tests that assess "concentration and vigilance (sustained attention) as well as tests that require higher levels of cognition in addition to concentration and vigilance" (user's guide, p. 1). Vigil is a proprietary version of the Continuous Performance Test (CPT), a test initially developed by Rosvold (1956). The test requires an IBM-compatible computer, a display monitor, and a standard keyboard. Test takers are presented a series of alphanumeric symbols or graphics in a visual or auditory format. Users can modify the timing, complexity, order, and clarity of the target stimuli. Test takers are required to press a key on the keyboard, as quickly as possible, each time the target stimuli is presented. The number of trials and test length are determined on an individual basis by the test user. The users guide indicates that the test is appropriate for people between the ages of 6 and 90.

Vigil requires an IBM-compatible computer with a 386 processor or higher and at least 4 MB of RAM, a color or mono VGA or Super VGA monitor, a high density, 3.5-inch (1.44 MB) floppy diskette drive, approximately 10 MB of free hard drive space, a mouse, Microsoft Windows 3.1 or higher, or MS-DOS version 5.0 or higher. Vigil is MCI and Soundblaster compatible. With a sound card installed, the test is capable of providing instructions orally through digitized speech (a procedure recommended by the authors). Vigil comes with three floppy disks and a 61-page manual.

Although a variety of user alternatives are available, Vigil comes with two standard batteries of normal vigilance: K and AK. Under both conditions the letter K serves as the target stimulus. During the K condition users press a key (normally the space bar) each time the letter K is presented. Under the AK format they press the space bar *only when* the target letter K is immediately preceded by the letter A. Under this condition, the authors describe the letter A as a "priming stimulus" (user's guide, p. 25). Under both conditions, stimuli are presented to the user for a default time of 85 msec. The user's guide inconsistently reports (p. 26) the interval between stimuli

as 850 msec. but later as 900 msec. Again, although many modifications can be made, norms for the instrument were developed after presenting test takers with white colored stimuli on a black background, using Stick font. A total testing situation normally consists of four trial blocks, with 36 targets per block and 120 stimuli per block.

The Vigil produces several test variables thought to relate to vigilance performance. Hit Rate, the overall accuracy of target discrimination, is computed by dividing the total number of targets correctly discriminated by the total number of targets presented. False Alarm reflects the incorrect anticipation of a target when no target was presented. This value is computed by dividing the total number of Errors of Commission by the total number of targets presented. An Error of Commission is the total number of incorrect target anticipations. In contrast, Errors of Omission are represented by the frequency of missed targets. Vigil also calculates Reaction Time as "the average time from the onset of each stimuli to the initiation of each response" (user's guide, p. 3). Additionally, Perseverations are calculated by totaling the number of responses (greater than one) made during the interstimulus intervals. Finally, two nonparametric measures of signal detection, A' and H', can also be calculated.

TECHNICAL. The standardization of the Vigil, as presented within the user's guide, is poorly described and technically inadequate. The Vigil was standardized on 324 participants between the ages of 6 and 90. The Vigil user's guide does indicate "The sociometric status and educational levels of the population were mixed, from lower to higher SES levels. Similarly, education levels varied widely" (user's guide, p. 27); however, more detailed information describing this consideration is not provided. Additional demographic variables such as gender, ethnic status, level of education, intellectual level, or geographic region were not considered, and as a result, it is not clear that the norms for this instrument are representative of the United States population.

Very minimal reliability estimates for the K and AK measures are presented. Partial (age held constant), alpha, and split-half reliability coefficients are reported; however, they are derived from an unspecified number of participants. In general, the reported reliability coefficients are adequate (.80 to .90 range); however, several coefficients are exceptionally low (e.g., K Partial False Alarm =

.64; AK Partial Hit Rate = .37; AK Alpha Hit Rate = .38) and explanations for these spurious values are not presented. Additionally, test-retest reliability was calculated for 69 participants, in each of seven age groups, within a 3-month interval. The majority of the resulting coefficients were somewhat low, typically falling in the mid-.70 range. Unfortunately, separate test-retest reliabilities are not reported for each of the age groups, a particularly troubling omission given the highly developmental nature of vigilance. Without developmentally disaggregated test-retest information (as well as corresponding standard errors of measurement), potential users of the Vigil are unable to determine whether changes across time reflect normal developmental growth or, in contrast, the possibility of abnormal developmental etiology. In the absence of reported standard errors of measurement it is also impossible to determine the extent variables such as fatigue, anxiety, and guessing will influence Vigil scores. Similarly, the influence of practice effects is never addressed.

The description of psychometric validity contained in the user's guide is also wanting. Regrettably, the most detailed section merely describes the face validity of the instrument. In an attempt to provide evidence of criterion validity, Table 5 in the user's guide provides "Intercorrelations of Vigil and other attention related tests" (p. 34). However, this information is problematic for several reasons: (a) the names of these related tests are not provided, only acronyms (e.g., SST, SSO, UAT); (b) the number of subjects from which the resulting correlations were derived is not provided; and (c) many of these correlation coefficients are actually quite low (many correlations in the .20 to .30 range). The user's guide continues by mentioning that in an additional study, the Vigil was correlated with the Mesulam Figure Cancellation Tasks and a second measure described only as the FAS. Without reporting any descriptive statistics reflecting the characteristics of the sample, or the results, the user's guide concludes "The results of these tests were significant and consistent with the hypothesis that these tests assess common processes" (p. 35). Despite the absence of solid, empirical evidence for even minimal criterion or construct-related validity, the user's guide inappropriately concludes, "Vigil appears to be significantly correlated with tests that are face valid instruments assessing attention processes" (p. 35).

The test manual concludes with examples of several case studies and some very basic normative information. Case study information is presented describing several individuals with pathological problems (e.g., a child with ADHD; an adult with severe closed head injury) and presents sample Vigil scores and interpretations. Six tables of normative information are also presented including the variables errors of omission, errors of commission, hit rates, reaction time, and A' and H' scores. Each table provides raw scores for participants disaggregated by gender and seven levels of age. In all instances, information contained within these tables is presented in raw score format and no percentile ranks, stanines, T-scores, or other types of standard scores are provided. A careful examination of these tables indicates that the distribution of data is extremely skewed and, as a result, psychometrically problematic. For example, on errors of omission, 15–19-year-old males produced a mean score of 3.58 and a standard deviation of 7.96. In any situation where a measured variable produces a standard deviation greater than its mean, the psychometric properties that characterize the variable are extremely compromised. Equally troubling are trends such as those presented in errors of commission and reaction time tables where mean values decrease developmentally until ages 50–64, at which point they begin to rise. It is not clear whether these trends reflect some underlying developmental trajectory or if it is merely due to sampling error.

COMMENTARY. The absence of any standard scores makes intersubtest comparisons and interpretations difficult. For example, 6–8-year-old male participants produced an average error of commission score of 44, an average hit rate of .68, and an average reaction time of 492.82. Without a common metric, users of the Vigil are limited to subscale interpretations that merely say that the test taker produced a score that was above or below the average of the normative comparison group. The question of "how much" above or below average would require the user to calculate standard scores by hand; the Vigil fails to provide even minimal assistance in this regard.

SUMMARY. Taken collectively, current standardization and psychometric shortcomings make the utilization of the Vigil, as a diagnostic instrument, problematic. The normative comparison group is quite small and does not appear to be representative of many important demographic characteristics. Perhaps users of the scale, as a research instrument, will be able to provide a better normative comparison base for both normal and clinical samples and will engage in a more rigorous validation process. Future research conducted with this instrument would also do well to focus on the diagnostic accuracy of the instrument including the rate of identified false positives and false negatives.

REVIEWER'S REFERENCE

Rosvold, H. E., Mirsky, A., Sarason, L., Bransome, E. D., & Beck, L. H. (1956). A Continuous Performance Test of brain damage. *Journal of Consulting and Clinical Psychology, 20,* 343–350.

[261]
Visual Association Test.

Purpose: "Designed to detect anterograde amnesia and certain brain disorders it is connected with."
Population: Ages 16–94.
Publication Date: 2003.
Acronym: VAT.
Scores, 7: Trial 1 & 2, Trial 3, Delayed Reproduction, Form A (Trial 2), Form A (2 Trials), Form B (2 Trials), A (2 Trials)-B (2 Trials).
Administration: Individual.
Forms, 3: Form A, Form B, Long Form.
Price Data: Available from publisher.
Foreign Language Editions: Dutch and German editions available.
Time: Administration time not reported.
Comments: Based on the Visual Association Method; manual includes section for each language.
Authors: J. Lindeboom and B. Schmand.
Publisher: PITS: Psychologische Instrumenten Tests en Services [The Netherlands].

Review of the Visual Association Test by STEPHEN J. FREEMAN, Professor and Chair, Department of Counseling, Texas A&M University-Commerce, Commerce, TX:

DESCRIPTION. The Visual Association Test (VAT) is designed to detect anterograde amnesia and certain brain disorders connected with it. The author's rationale for the test's development was that anterograde amnesia is marked by deficient performance on tests of learning and memory, the possible exception being tests involving visual recognition. Memory-impaired patients benefit as much from visual associations as nonimpaired individuals, except that the effect is negligible in cases of anterograde amnesia. There are three forms of the test: Form A, Form B, and a Long Form. Form A is identified for use with individuals age 65 years and above. Form B may be used as a parallel form of Form A. The Long Form is identified for use with individuals age 62 years and younger. The authors intended the instrument to be useful across a wide range of individuals between the ages of 16 to 84 years of age (excluding ages 63 and 64).

For Forms A and B, the assessment consists of three steps. Step 1: Presentation of cue cards; Step 2: Presentation of association cards; and Step 3: Reproduction. For the Long Form, the administration consists of Step 1: Presentation of the association cards; Step 2: Reproduction; and Step 3: Second trial. A total of seven scores may be obtained: Long Form (Trial 1 & 2, Trial 3, Delayed Reproduction), Form A (2 Trials), Form A (Trial 1 only), Form B (2 Trials), Form A (2 Trials) minus Form B (2 Trials). Scoring of the VAT is uncomplicated, 1 point is given for each correct response. Individual test record sheets are also straightforward.

No administration time is reported in the manual; however, experience suggests a trained examiner can administer the VAT in approximately 20–30 minutes (50–60 minutes with delay). Information required to administer and score the VAT is abundant. Cutoff scores based on percentile scores are used to interpret the VAT. Testing procedures are relatively easy to follow.

TECHNICAL. Psychometric data presented in the manual were disappointing. Information describing the norming process was incomplete. In the data reported there was limited information on how the information was collected, no demographic information (i.e., gender, socioeconomic level, educational level, ethnicity, and geographic region) was presented, and the reader was referred to the referenced studies to retrieve what data were reported. Information reported came from published and unpublished studies by different researchers dating from 1991 to 2003. Participants in the research studies ranged in age from 16–84; however, no other information was provided (i.e., age groupings or intervals, gender information, or number of participants in each group). Given the numerous problems noted, the exactitude of the information presented must be called into question.

The evidence supporting the reliability of the VAT is somewhat terse and presented with limited data in the manual. Little to no information was provided as to age, gender, ethnicity, or other relevant characteristics. Reliability estimates were reported for internal consistency, test stability, and equivalent forms.

Internal consistency reliability coefficients were reported to range from .82–.84. Because no other meaningful information was provided, the coefficients, though acceptable, must be viewed skeptically. Coefficients estimating test stability (interval = 1 year) ranged from .74 for one trial to .81 for two trials. Alternate forms reliability coefficients were provided and ranged from .74–.84; however, the manual noted that scores on Form B were on average lower than on Form A, the difference increasing with additional trials. This raised questions as to the true equivalance of the two forms for which the manual offered no explanation.

Evidence supporting the validity of the VAT is as sparse as all the psychometric data reported. The manual purports to examine construct (discriminative validity), concurrent, and criterion-related validity. The studies cited appear to support the ability of the VAT to discriminate (construct validity) between patients with and without anterograde amnesia. Criterion-related validity also appeared to be supported by a study on the relationship between medial temporal lobe atrophy and performance on the VAT. As expected, patients with clear medial temporal lobe atrophy confirmed by MRI scored low on the VAT whereas high scores were obtained by patients with no atrophy. Concurrent validity was moderately supported by correlations of the VAT (Form A) scores with scores from the cognitive section (orientation and memory) of the Cambridge Examination for Mental Disorders of the Elderly. Although cited research studies appear to provide support for the validity of the VAT to detect anterograde amnesia and certain disorders connected with it, sufficient information is not provided in the test manual to support its claim of validity.

COMMENTARY. The value of the Visual Association Test to detect anterograde amnesia is questionable at best. This is primarily due to the absence of information on the norm sample and limited information regarding the reliability and validity of the instrument. Psychometric data reported came from research studies that span 12 years without adequate support indicating that the same instrument without revisions was used in all of the studies.

SUMMARY. The VAT appears to suffer from a serious lack of clear technical strength that calls into question its ability to accomplish its mission. Given the problems with the standardization sample and the woeful lack of technical information demonstrating acceptable levels of reliability and validity, no support for the use of the VAT can be made.

[262]
Wechsler Intelligence Scale for Children—Fourth Edition.

Purpose: Designed to assess "the cognitive ability of children."
Population: Ages 6-0 to 16-11.
Publication Dates: 1971–2003.
Acronym: WISC-IV.
Scores, 15 to 20: Verbal Comprehension (Similarities, Vocabulary, Comprehension, Information, Word Reasoning, Total), Perceptual Reasoning (Block Design, Picture Concepts, Matrix Reasoning, Picture Completion, Total), Working Memory (Digit Span, Letter-Number Sequencing, Arithmetic, Total), Processing Speed (Coding, Symbol Search, Cancellation, Total), Total.
Administration: Individual.
Price Data, 2003: $725 per Basic Kit including administration manual (2003, 282 pages), technical manual (2003, 183 pages), stimulus book #1, stimulus book #2, 25 record forms, 25 response booklet #1, 25 response booklet #2, blocks, symbol search scoring template, coding scoring template, and cancellation scoring templates; $775 per Basic Kit in hard or soft case; $840 per Basic Kit with Scoring Assistant; $890 per Basic Kit with Scoring Assistant in hard or soft case; $1,075 per Basic Kit with Writer in soft case; $85 per 25 record forms; $53 per 25 response booklet #1, $50 per 25 response booklet #2; $320 per 100 record forms; $199 per 100 response booklet #1; $188 per 100 response booklet #2; $165 per scoring assistant; $350 per writer.
Time: Core subtests (65–80) minutes; Supplemental: (10–15) minutes.
Author: David Wechsler.
Publisher: PsychCorp, A brand of Harcourt Assessment, Inc.
Cross References: See T5:2862 (740 references); for reviews by Jeffrey P. Braden and Jonathan Sandoval of an earlier edition, see 12:412 (409 references); see also T4:2939 (911 references); for reviews by Morton Bortner, Douglas K. Detterman, and by Joseph C. Witt and Frank Gresham of an earlier edition, see 9:1351 (299 references); see also T3:2602 (645 references); for reviews by David Freides and Randolph H. Whitworth, and excerpted reviews by Carol Kehr Tittle and Joseph Petrosko, see 8:232 (548 references); see also T2:533 (230 references); for reviews by David Freides and R. T.

Osborne of the original edition, see 7:431 (518 references); for a review by Alvin G. Burnstein, see 6:540 (155 references); for reviews by Elizabeth D. Fraser, Gerald R. Patterson, and Albert I. Rabin, see 5:416 (111 references); for reviews by James M. Anderson, Harold A. Delp, and Boyd R. McCandless, and an excerpted review by Laurance F. Shaffer, see 4:363 (22 references).

Review of the Wechsler Intelligence Scale for Children—Fourth Edition by SUSAN J. MALLER, Associate Professor, Purdue University, West Lafayette, IN:
DESCRIPTION. The Wechsler Intelligence Scale for Children—Fourth Edition (WISC-IV) is the newest revision of Wechsler's intelligence tests for children and adolescents. The WISC-IV is an individually administered intelligence test designed for examinees aged 6 years 0 months to 16 years 11 months. The WISC-IV has updated theoretical foundations with more emphasis on fluid reasoning (as per Carroll, 1997; Cattell & Horn, 1978), working memory, and processing speed. Traditional Verbal and Performance IQs are not calculated, although the test yields Full Scale IQ (FSIQ) and four Index scores: Verbal Comprehension Index (VCI), Perceptual Reasoning Index (PRI), Working Memory Index (WMI), and Processing Speed Index (PSI). The WISC-IV contains 15 subtests in total (10 core, 5 supplemental), 10 from the Wechsler Intelligence Scale for Children—Third Edition (WISC-III) with modifications or new items. Object Assembly, Picture Arrangement, and Mazes are not included, partly to decrease performance time emphasis. VCI subtests are (in the remainder of this review, supplemental subtests will be followed by asterisks): Similarities, Vocabulary, Comprehension, Information*, and Word Reasoning*. The PCI includes: Block Design, Picture Concepts, Matrix Reasoning, and Picture Completion*. The WMI includes: Digit Span, Letter-Number Sequencing, and Arithmetic*. The PSI includes: Coding, Symbol Search, and Cancellation*. Up to one supplemental subtest may be substituted for a core subtest in composites, yet potential effects on WISC-IV psychometric properties are not stated.

The WISC-IV includes seven Process scores, based on variations (e.g., untimed, last item completed) of Block Design, Digit Span, and Cancellation*, and cannot be used in composites. As per Kaplan (1988), Process scores are intended to assist in "neuropsychological evaluations, qualita-tive interpretation of test performance, analysis of errors, and testing of the limits" (as quoted in administration and scoring manual, p. 5).

ADMINISTRATION. The WISC-IV core battery administration requires approximately 65–80 minutes, with an additional 10–15 minutes for supplemental subtests. The WISC-IV generally has very understandable administration and scoring instructions, clear artwork, and easy-to-use manuals. Letter-Number Sequencing scoring is ambiguous. Examiners should be familiar with the *Standards for Educational and Psychological Testing* (AERA, APA, & NCME, 1999), have completed graduate training in assessment or be supervised by such a person, and have specialized training when testing persons from unique linguistic, cultural, or clinical backgrounds.

TECHNICAL.
Standardization sample. The standardization sample included 2,200 examinees (Arithmetic* included 1,100 examinees), representative of the March 2000 U.S. Bureau of the Census data in terms of age, gender, race ethnicity, parent education level, and four geographical regions. Large areas within regions exclude examinees, without clarification (e.g., eight sites included from Idaho, yet only one from Nevada).

Reliability. Evidence for internal consistency reliability for all subtests, Process scores, and Composite scales (Indexes and FSIQ) was obtained on the standardization sample using the split-half method with Spearman-Brown correction, without specification regarding how halves were divided. For speeded subtests, test-retest reliability coefficients appropriately were reported. Average coefficients across age groups ranged from .79 to .90 for core subtests and .79 to .88 for supplemental subtests. Except for Processing Speed coefficients, all Index coefficients were at or above .90 at all ages. FSIQ reliability was impressive, with coefficients $\geq$ .96 for every age.

The administration manual reports confidence intervals around estimated true scores, thus allowing for regression effects. Traditional standard errors of measurement are preferred, because norms, percentile ranks, and descriptive classifications based on observed scores as unbiased estimates of true scores (Feldt & Brennan, 1989; Sabers, Feldt, & Reschly, 1988) are available in the technical manual.

Test-retest reliability coefficients present evidence of score stability based on a sample of

243 examinees (*n* = 18 to 27 in each age group). Time intervals ranged from 13 days to 2 months, with an average interval of approximately 1 month. Information is needed per age group regarding sample sizes, demographic characteristics, and retest time intervals. Subtest coefficients (corrected for restriction of range) generally were in the .70s or .80s, whereas, Index coefficients ranged from .84 for WMI (ages 8 to 9) to .95 VCI (ages 14 to 16). The FSIQ reliability coefficient was at or above .91 for each age group.

Validity evidence. Content validity was based on extensive literature reviews, and input from panels, consultants, and various psychologists. During the national tryout phase (*n* = 1,270 with an oversample of 252 African American and 186 Hispanic children), items were reviewed by "content and bias experts" (administration manual, p. 11). Information provided regarding the statistical detection of item bias (also known as differential item functioning or DIF) is as follows:

> Results from traditional Mantel-Haenszel bias analysis (Holland & Thayer, 1988) and item response theory (IRT) bias analyses (Hambleton, 1993) provided additional data on potentially problematic items. (technical and interpretive manual, p. 11)

Detail is needed regarding DIF detection analyses including: comparison groups (ethnic, gender, special populations) and sample sizes; IRT models and fit statistics; estimation procedures; criteria for flagging or removing items; effect of DIF on ceiling rules; whether DIF was uniform (difficulty differences only) or nonuniform (discrimination differences); and at least some summary of the results. The literature (Maller, 2001) on gender DIF in the WISC-III standardization sample and other special populations was not addressed, yet the majority of items from the retained WISC-III subtests appear in the WISC-IV.

The WISC-IV internal structure was investigated via exploratory (EFA) and confirmatory factor (CFA) analyses. EFA and CFAs were conducted on core subtest scores for the entire standardization sample and both core and supplemental subtest scores of 1,525 children from the standardization sample, across age and within four age groups. The EFA was completed first, regardless of the a priori theoretical model presented in the technical manual. Conducted on the same data, subsequent CFA fit statistics were data-driven on EFA results. Nonetheless, principal axis EFA with oblique rotation results indicate most loadings as salient (≥ .3; Comrey & Lee, 1992), loading on expected factors. Loadings vary considerably, suggesting substantial differences in relationships to respective factors, yet subtests are equally weighted when computing composite scores.

CFAs tested competing one, two, three, four, and five factor models. The four factor model, corresponding to WISC-IV Index scores, was concluded as the best fitting model with impressive fit statistics. More detail is needed regarding the analysis (e.g., input matrix, estimation, model parameters). Of concern, the models compared were not nested. Because the one factor model does not reside within the two factor model, they should not be compared using a difference chi-square test. Notably, the two negative chi-square difference tests would not occur with nested model comparisons unless there were unreported estimation problems or differential missing data. Also, and noted elsewhere (Flanagan & Kaufman, 2004; Keith, Fine, Traub, Reynolds, & Kranzler, 2004), a hierarchical model with FSIQ at the apex, and the four Index scores is the only model of interest. This is the theoretical model advocated by the publisher and the model on which scores are based. Had this model been tested and found not to fit the data, exploratory analysis or restructuring of the test would be appropriate. Finally, evidence of factorial invariance is not reported for gender, ethnic, or other special groups.

Rather than presenting traditional concurrent and predictive validity evidence, the technical manual refers to Campbell and Fiske's (1959) terminology of convergent and discriminant (sometimes switching to "divergent") validity. Loose use of this terminology apparently avoided the dilemma of what to call a correlation that could be considered a reliability, concurrent validity, or predictive validity coefficient, depending on when tests were administered. Correlations (corrected for variability) between the WISC-IV and several tests are presented, such as the WISC-III, Wechsler Individual Achievement Test-Second Edition (WIAT-II), and Children's Memory Scale (CMS). Samples sizes ranged from *n* = 145 to *n* = 550. Demographic characteristics vary considerably. Based on 244 examinees with somewhat different demographic characteristics than the WISC-IV standardization sample, the WISC-IV and WISC-III were correlated .89 (average FSIQ decrease of 2.5 points). Correlations between WISC-IV FSIQ or Index scores and WIAT-II subtests were moderate to high, although Cancellation* was a poor predictor of all achievement subtest scores (all $r \leq .18$). Correlations between the WMI and CMS subtests were low to moderate, with the exception of .74 for the CMS Attention/Concentration subtest. The WMI still appears to be mostly a measure of distractibility.

Data for 16 "special groups" were collected. Results reported include means, standard deviations, and t-tests comparing matched controls. Some of these groups (e.g., Autistic Disorder) have large standard deviations, and practitioners might question why such children vary markedly. Some samples are small for reliability studies and of questionable representativeness, ranging from $n = 12$ (Autistic Disorder) to $n = 89$ (ADHD). The administration manual includes a lengthy section regarding WISC-IV appropriateness for deaf children. Although a consultant and "experienced specialists" provided judgments regarding subtest appropriateness, deaf children were excluded from validity studies. Thus, judgments were not based on empirical research, as per recommendations of the *Standards for Educational and Psychological Testing* (AERA et al., 1999). The manual's recommendation for further research cannot be understated, given countless deaf examinees regularly are evaluated with tests that lack necessary psychometric evidence.

Both WISC-IV manuals promote the use of profile analysis for interpreting an examinee's strengths and weaknesses, providing tables for conducting numerous significance tests even at the .15 alpha level (between Index scores, subtest and mean scores, individual subtests, etc.). Practitioners should be wary that this method increases the likelihood of findings due to random chance and potential overinterpretation. Profile analysis has been criticized, because profiles generally lack evidence of reliability and predictive validity, and generally do not differ from those in the population (Konold, Glutting, McDermott, Kush, & Watkins, 1999; McDermott, Fantuzzo, Glutting, Watkins, & Baggaley, 1992). Lacking are prevalence rates of expected profiles in the standardization sample and rigorous methods for normative comparisons (as per Konold et al., 1999; McDermott, 1998).

SUMMARY AND CONCLUSIONS. The WISC-IV is likely to hold its place in history as a dominant force among individually administered intelligence tests. The name alone is likely to keep the test a major player, even though David Wechsler is no longer alive to approve of revisions. The publisher has managed to assemble a set of materials that are familiar enough to practitioners and incorporate newer theoretical perspectives. The new version has minimized the emphasis on timed tasks, reducing potential speed confounding effects. The standardization sample is representative of the U.S. Census, and the test appears to be highly reliable, especially in terms of the composite scores.

As the test retains its place in history, it also retains its flaws. As measurement methods become more sophisticated, it would be refreshing to see them incorporated in clinical measurement. The newest version still fails to report sufficient evidence concerning item and test bias studies. The factor analytic methods were poorly executed and do not provide fit statistics for a model including FSIQ. The use of profile analysis is advocated without normative profile comparisons, despite published criticisms. Sample sizes for many special group studies were small and of questionable representativeness, and lengthy recommendations were made for the administration to deaf examinees in the absence of empirical validity evidence.

The WISC-IV looks good, is consistent, and pretty much still feels like a Wechsler. We all count on the Wechsler, even if we have to ignore the fact that it could have been so much better if the publisher would have used state-of-the art psychometric methods; however, the truth is those methods are expensive and the test probably would have been much more pricey. Hence, the Wechsler keeps on selling and continues to be used to test our children.

REVIEWER'S REFERENCES

American Educational Research Association, American Psychological Association, & National Council on Measurement in Education. (1999). *Standards for educational and psychological testing*. Washington, DC: Author.

Campbell, D. T., & Fiske, D. W. (1959). Convergent and discriminant validation by the multitrait-multimethod matrix. *Psychological Bulletin, 56*, 81–105.

Carroll, J. B. (1997). The three-stratum theory of cognitive abilities. In D. P. Flanagan, J. L. Genshaft, & P. L. Harrison (Eds.), *Contemporary intellectual assessment: Theories, tests, and issues* (pp. 122–130). New York: Guilford Press.

Cattell, R. B., & Horn, J. L. (1978). A check on the theory of fluid and crystallized intelligence with description of new subtest designs. *Journal of Educational Measurement, 15*, 139–164.

Comrey, A. L., & Lee, H. B. (1992). *A first course in factor analysis* (2nd ed.). Hillsdale, NJ: Erlbaum.

Feldt, L., & Brennan, R. L. (1989). Reliability. In R. L. Linn (Ed.), *Educational measurement* (3rd ed., pp. 105–146). Washington, DC: American Council on Education.

Flanagan, D. P., & Kaufman, A. S. (2004). *Essentials of WISC-IV assessment*. Hoboken, NJ: Wiley.

Hambleton, R. K. (1993). Principles and selected applications of item response theory. In R. L. Linn (Ed.), *Educational measurement* (3rd ed., pp. 147–220). Phoenix, AZ: Oryx Press.

Holland, P. W., & Thayer, D. T. (1988). Differential item performance and the Mantel-Haenszel procedure. In H. Wainer & H. I. Braun (Eds.), *Test validity* (pp. 129–145). Hillsdale, NJ: Erlbaum.

Kaplan, E. (1988). A process approach to neuropsychological assessment. In T. J. Boll & B. K. Bryant (Eds.), *Clinical neuropsychology and brain function: Research, measurement, and practice* (pp. 129–167). Washington, DC: American Psychological Association.

Keith, R. Z., Fine, J. G., Traub, G. E., Reynolds, M. R., & Kranzler, J. H. (2004). *Hierarchical, multi-sample confirmatory factor analysis of the Wechsler Intelligence Scale for Children—Fourth Edition: What does it measure?* Manuscript submitted for publication.

Konold, T. R., Glutting, J. J., McDermott, P. A., Kush, J. C., & Watkins, M. M. (1999). Structure and diagnostic benefits of a normative subtest taxonomy developed from the WISC-III standardization sample. *Journal of School Psychology, 37*, 29–48.

Maller, S. J. (2001). Differential item functioning in the WISC-III: Item parameters for boys and girls in the national standardization sample. *Educational and Psychological Measurement, 61*, 793–817.

McDermott, P. A. (1998). MEG: Megacluster analytic strategy for multistage hierarchical grouping with relocations and replications. *Educational and Psychological Measurement, 58*, 677–686.

McDermott, P. A., Fantuzzo, J. W., Glutting, J. J., Watkins, M. W., & Baggaley, A. R. (1992). Illusions of meaning in the ipsative assessment of children's ability. *Journal of Special Education, 25*, 504–526.

Sabers, D. L., Feldt, L. S., & Reschly, D. J. (1988). Appropriate and inappropriate use of estimated true scores for normative comparisons. *Journal of Special Education, 22*, 358–366.

Review of the Wechsler Intelligence Scale for Children—Fourth Edition by BRUCE THOMPSON, Professor and Distinguished Research Fellow, Texas A&M University, College Station, TX, and Adjunct Professor of Family and Community Medicine, Baylor College of Medicine (Houston), Houston, TX:

DESCRIPTION. The Wechsler Intelligence Scale for Children—Fourth Edition (WISC-IV) is a comprehensive, individually administered measure for assessing the intelligence of children ages 6 years 0 months through 16 years 11 months. The WISC-IV yields a score measuring full scale IQ (FSIQ), and four index scores: Verbal Comprehension (VCI), Perceptual Rreasoning (PRI), Working Memory (WMI), and Processing Speed (PSI). The WISC-IV includes 10 core subtests and 5 supplemental tests. Supplemental tests are administered to obtain additional clinical information or, in some cases (e.g., a core subtest is invalidated, a child has fine motor difficulties), as substitutes for core subtests. Scores are intended for use in formulating intervention and placement decisions in clinical and educational settings.

Item administration for a scale is discontinued when a specified number of item scores of 0 occur. These discontinue rules were specified by determining at what point fewer than 2% of children in normative samples gave no additional correct responses after a given sequence of errors. Thus, test administration times vary from child to child. According to the technical manual, completion times for 90% of children identified as gifted, normative, or mentally retarded were 104, 94, and 73 minutes, respectively. Items on six subtests are

strictly timed and on selected subtests bonus points are awarded to recognize correct responses involving rapid processing speed.

The administration, scoring, and interpretation of the WISC-IV requires graduate-level training and experience in conducting psychological assessments. Administrator experience in testing children of diverse ages and cultural and linguistic backgrounds may also be necessary. Scoring in some cases requires the exercise of general scoring principles guided by selected scoring examples provided in the administration and scoring manual.

DEVELOPMENT. The Wechsler Intelligence scales have been published in four editions over the last 60 years. The previous edition was published in 1991. The WISC-IV administration and scoring manual notes that the present edition "is not simply a normative update" (p. iv). Indeed, this 2003 revision can only be characterized as major.

Three subtests from the WISC-III were dropped, and 5 new subtests were developed for the WISC-IV. For the 10 subtests retained, administration procedures were changed for 9 of 10 subtests, recording/scoring was changed for all 10 subtests, and new items were created for 9 of 10 retained subtests. The number of new items per subtest is considerable (e.g., for verbal Similarities subtest, 12 items are old, 11 are new; for verbal Comprehension, 10 items are old, 11 are new). According to the administration and scoring manual, this redesign presumes that "When it comes to learning, clinical research has shown that processing speed, working memory, and fluid reasoning are among the most important cognitive abilities to have emerged in the literature" (p. iii).

During revision, in addition to the normative sample, data were also collected from 16 special groups (e.g., gifted, ADHD, autistic). Both easier and harder items were added to item pools to insure adequate coverage at both test floors and ceilings. Items were subjected to various DIF procedures prior to being considered for use on the final measure.

TECHNICAL. Test revision was guided by data collected in various pilot studies, a national tryout study ($n = 1,270$), and a standardization study. The standardization study involved 2,200 children divided into 11 age groups, 200 per group, but the Arithmetic subtest was normed on a sample of 1,100 children. The standardization sample matched 2000 U.S. Census data reasonably well as regards child age and sex, parent education level, and geographic region.

The technical manual espouses contemporary views of reliability, insofar as reliability seems to be recognized as a property of scores, and not of tests (Thompson, 2003). It is especially noteworthy that the technical manual acknowledges "that there are serious limitations in the use of null hypothesis testing" (p. 33). Even more exemplary (Thompson, 2002), the technical manual eschews the rigid use of Cohen's effect size benchmarks, noting that these "were meant to be general guidelines, and, depending on the situation, the importance associated with a particular effect size might be very different from those suggested by these guidelines" (p. 33).

Both internal consistency and test-retest reliability coefficients were computed. The reliability coefficients for the subtests, index, and full scale scores are all quite high across ages and special groups. For example, the FSIQ scores had internal consistency coefficients of either .96 or .97 across the age groups.

Myriad correlation coefficients are presented as evidence for score validity. In addition to correlations of WISC-IV subtests with each other, also reported are correlations of WISC-IV scores with WISC-III, WPPSI-III, WAIS-III, WASI, WIAT-II, CMS, GRS, BarOn EQ, and ABAS-II scores.

Both exploratory and confirmatory factor analyses of subtest scores are reported in the technical manual. In both cases factors were correlated, in some cases quite considerably (e.g., r^2 = 53%). In such cases, in both EFA and CFA (a) both factor pattern and factor structure coefficients should be reported and interpreted, and (b) higher order factors are implied and should be extracted (Thompson, 2004). Neither precept was followed in the technical manual, although these analyses were otherwise quite thoughtful and supportive of views that scores are reasonably valid.

COMMENTARY. The WISC-IV appears to have been developed in an extremely thoughtful manner, and also represents an improvement over the WISC-III. For example, most reliability coefficients for WISC-IV scores on the 10 retained subtests improved substantially (e.g., Arithmetic, from .78 to .88), and scores on the five new WISC-IV subtests tended to have reliability coefficients (.79 to .90) higher than those for WISC-III subtest scores.

Obviously, considerable resources have been invested in developing the present Wechsler revi-

sion. The marriage of resources and reflection inexorably yields impressive progeny.

SUMMARY. According to the WISC-IV technical manual, revision was undertaken with the objectives of updating the measure's focus given contemporary theory, enhancing clinical utility, increasing developmental appropriateness, improving score psychometrics, and increasing test user-friendliness. These objectives appear to have been achieved.

Of course, test psychometrics are essential. But the ultimate proof of the pudding lies in the utility of such measures to help us understand and impact the learning of children. As the administration and scoring manual notes, "after all, what is intelligence if not, at the least, the ability to learn?" (p. iii).

REVIEWER'S REFERENCES

Thompson, B. (2002). What future quantitative social science research could look like: Confidence intervals for effect sizes. *Educational Researcher, 31*(3), 24—31.

Thompson, B. (Ed.). (2003). *Score reliability: Contemporary thinking on reliability issues.* Newbury Park, CA: Sage.

Thompson, B. (2004). *Exploratory and confirmatory factor analysis: Understanding concepts and applications.* Washington, DC: American Psychological Association.

[263]

Wechsler Memory Scale—Third Edition Abbreviated.

Purpose: Designed to survey auditory and visual immediate and delayed memory.

Population: Ages 16–89.

Publication Dates: 1997–2002.

Acronym: WMS-III Abbreviated.

Scores, 12: Total Memory Composite, Delayed Memory Composite, Immediate Memory Composite, Logical Memory I, Family Pictures I, Logical Memory II, Family Pictures II, Logical Memory I—Family Pictures I, Logical Memory II—Family Pictures II, Immediate Memory Composite—Delayed Memory Composite, Predicted WMS-III General Memory Index Score, FSIQ—Predicted Total Memory Composite Score.

Administration: Individual.

Price Data, 2003: $150 per complete kit including manual (2002, 207 pages), stimulus book, and 25 record forms; $55 per manual; $35 per 25 record forms; $72 per stimulus book.

Time: 15–20 (40–55) minutes.

Comments: Abbreviated adaptation of the Wechsler Memory Scale—Third Edition (T6:2695).

Author: David Wechsler.

Publisher: PsychCorp, A brand of Harcourt Assessment, Inc.

Review of the Wechsler Memory Scale—Third Edition Abbreviated by RONALD K. HAMBLETON, Distinguished University Profes-

sor, School of Education, University of Massachusetts at Amherst, Amherst, MA:

DESCRIPTION. The Wechsler Memory Scale—Third Edition Abbreviated (WMS-III Abbreviated) was designed to provide users with an instrument that could quickly measure auditory and visual memory abilities. It is a subset of the Wechsler Memory Scale—Third Edition (WMS-III) and includes four of the subtests measuring auditory and visual immediate and delayed memory, specifically, Logical Memory I, Family Pictures I, Logical Memory II, and Family Pictures II. From these four subtests three composite scores are formed: Immediate Memory Composite, Delayed Memory Composite, and Total Memory Composite. The instrument has been normed on 1,250 examinees ranging in age from 16 to 89. According to the publisher, the goal of the instrument is to provide clinicians with an estimate of an examinee's general memory functioning, when the results from a full assessment of memory is not necessary or not possible. So, for example, the instrument might be useful when a clinician is simply screening for memory problems in a standard evaluation.

The administration of the four subtests is convenient, clear, and straightforward: First, the administrator administers the Logical Memory I subtest. The administrator reads a story, and the examinee repeats what he or she can remember. A second story is read, and again, the examinee repeats what he or she can remember. For Family Picture I, the administrator shows the examinee a family with several members, and then four different scenes. The examinee is asked to repeat the events in the four scenes. After a delay of 25 to 35 minutes, the examinee is administered Logical Memory II and asked to recall as much of the stories from Logical Memory I as he or she can. Finally, Family Pictures II is administered, and the examinee is asked this time to recall as much as possible about the family scenes presented in Family Pictures I. Detailed scoring guides are available. Basically, examinees receive points for the information they can recall from the stories and family scenes.

According to the technical manual, a decision about whether to administer the long or short version of the WMS-III depends on the clinical questions being asked, the level of detail of information that is needed, and the amount of time available to assess memory functioning. In the context of a standard review requiring an assess-

ment of memory functioning, the short form would appear to suffice. Specifically, it is stated in the manual that the short version could be used to assess diagnosis and identification of memory impairment, early identification of dementias and degenerative conditions, quantification of memory impairment, serial assessment of memory to document change in cognitive status, comparison of auditory versus visual memory impairments, and identification of relative strengths and weaknesses for treatment or educational planning.

DEVELOPMENT. Research on memory has had a long history in psychology, and that theory, briefly presented, appears in the technical manual. The Wechsler Memory Scale has received wide use by researchers and clinicians over the years. Now in its third edition, the Wechsler Memory Scales—Third Edition Abbreviated is based on four of the subtests. According to the technical manual, the criteria for the selection of only four subtests included the following: good psychometric qualities, relatively easy to administer and score, high correlations with other memory measures, evidence of sensitivity to memory impairment in clinical studies, assessment of immediate and delayed recall, and the use of both visual and verbal modalities of presentation. As the selection does not attempt in any way to draw a representative sample of subtests from the full version, it cannot be considered to be a form of the WMS-III, and this point ia emphasized in the technical manual.

The WMS-III went through five developmental steps: Existing items in the WMS-II were reviewed and new items and subtests were developed; pilot testing was carried out; a national tryout took place with emphasis on item analysis, item bias, functioning of the subtests, and factor analysis to study test structure; a national standardization study to compile norms data, more item bias data, validity data, and evidence to assist in the selection of final subtests; and additional studies to compile a wide array of reliability and validity information. It is from the final version of the WMS-III that the WMS-III Abbreviated was constructed.

TECHNICAL. Reliability estimates (based on the corrected split-half reliability method) are reported for each of the four subtests and three composite scales in 13 age groups. For the subtests, average reliability estimates (across the age groups) ranged from .79 to .88, and for the longer composite scales, average reliability estimates (across the age groups) ranged from .87 to .92. Test-retest reliability coefficients with much smaller samples showed a general drop in value (e.g., the subtest reliabilities ranged from .61 to .80, and the composite scale reliabilities ranged from .71 to .81) with an administration interval ranging from 2 to 12 weeks. These results clearly support the view that when using the scores in diagnoses, focus should be on the composite scores. One interesting finding was the small but practically significant practice effect, and so clinicians need to be alert to the small expected gain simply due to the experience of examinees taking the instrument a second time. Interrater reliabilities of scoring seemed to be high—for all of the subtests, interrater reliabilities were in excess of .90.

The amount of validity data reported in the technical manual is substantial. Evidence to support the selection of the four subtests is provided—they were strong in technical quality and among the best subtests to measure the underlying factors found in the WMS-III. Evidence was provided to show high correlations among the three composite scores on the WMS-III Abbreviated with the WMS-III Index scores. These results definitely lend credibility to the WMS-III Abbreviated scores. Extensive convergent validity evidence, concurrent validity evidence, and criterion group evidence shows that the findings from scores on the WMS-III Abbreviated were very consistent with expectations, and thus support the validity of the WMS-III Abbreviated scale scores for the various intended uses.

Norms for the WMS-III Abbreviated are very ambitious and could serve a model for compiling norms data on all tests. Using information from the 1995 U.S. Census, stratified samples were drawn for persons ranging from 16 to 89 years. Variables that were part of the sample stratification included sex, race/ethnicity, educational level, and geographic region. Substantial details about the sampling and some of the minor quirks are provided in the technical manual. For example, because women outnumber men in the older age groups, a larger proportion of women were drawn for the norm group.

One of the few concerns I had was the validity of the norms for the four subtests when the normative information was compiled within the full battery administration. I worried that with the short version of the instrument, an examinee might be more attentive and score higher than

they would on the full version. As a result, percentile scores for all examinees taking the Abbreviated Form would be inflated, misleading, and could lead to underdiagnosis of memory problems. My hypothesis seems to be a good one, but the fact is that the author's research suggests that examinee performance on the Abbreviated and Full versions of the memory tests was more or less the same. Two small studies were carried out with samples matched to the WMS-III and these samples were administered the WMS-III Abbreviated. The differences in mean test performance between the special samples and the norm group samples were small, though I would have preferred to see these important studies carried out with larger and very carefully matched samples.

COMMENTARY. The Wechsler Memory Scales have a long history of use in psychology and education and the technical manual reflects it. The technical documentation is superb. I did notice that a common error is still being made when it comes to interpreting confidence bands. I believe that a probability statement about the location of true score for an examinee cannot be made. What can be said about a 95% confidence band set up around an observed score, is that across all examinees, about 95% of the time, these confidence bands set up around test scores will contain the true score.

I also noticed that both 90% and 95% confidence bands appear in the technical manual. I appreciate the focus on confidence bands. All too often in educational and psychological testing, test authors and publishers are in violation of the 1999 AERA, APA, and NCME *Test Standards* on this point. But 90% and 95% confidence bands are so very close that I fail to see the merit of presenting both. If I were to present two sets of confidence bands, I might choose 68% and 95%, or 68% and 90% but not 90% and 95%.

SUMMARY. A highly reliable and valid instrument to measure auditory and visual memory abilities in 15 to 20 minutes of examinee time will be of great interest and value to researchers and clinicians. Even if readers have little need for an instrument to measure memory in their own research program and/or clinical practice, they should read the technical manual. It is a superb example of how technical manuals should be written: comprehensive, technically sound, and highly readable.

REVIEWER'S REFERENCE

American Educational Research Association, American Psychological Association, & National Council on Measurement in Education. (1999). *Standards for educational and psychological testing.* Washington, DC: American Educational Research Association.

Review of the Wechsler Memory Scale—Third Edition Abbreviated by JOYCE MEIKAMP, Professor of Special Education, Marshall University, South Charleston, WV, and CAROLYN H. SUPPA, Associate Professor of Counseling, Marshall University, South Charleston, WV:

DESCRIPTION. The Wechsler Memory Scale—Third Edition Abbreviated (WMS-III Abbreviated) is a measurement of auditory and visual immediate and delayed memory abilities tapping constructs associated with declarative episodic memory processes. It is intended for use with English-speaking individuals aged 16–89 and is derived from its predecessor, the Wechsler Memory Scale—Third Edition (WMS-III), a widely used and well researched comprehensive individual assessment of a wide range of memory functioning. Although the WMS-III Abbreviated is a short form of the WMS-III, it is not a parallel form in that a comparability study was performed with the sample for the WMS-III Abbreviated meeting the same inclusion/exclusion criteria as the WMS-III sample. The WMS-III Abbreviated was designed to provide a fast, reliable alternative to the WMS-III as a method of identifying general memory dysfunction when extended memory testing is not feasible or indicated. The WMS-III technical manual warns that for more specific inferences, the WMS-III battery should be used.

The WMS-III Abbreviated contains four subtests (Logical Memory I, Family Pictures I, Logical Memory II, and Family Pictures II) that form three composites (Immediate Memory Composite, Delayed Memory Composite, and Total Memory Composite). These are called composites in order to avoid confusion with the indexes of the WMS-III. The subtests of the WMS-III-Abbreviated were selected from the WMS-III based on relative ease of administration and scoring, favorable psychometric properties, high correlation with other memory measures, and ability to exhibit sensitivity to memory impairment. To support the selection of the included subtests, subtest correlations and results of factor analytic research were reviewed.

When used in the context of other evaluative information, the WMS-III Abbreviated can assist the clinician in understanding the degree to which the examinee's memory impairments contribute to current functional impairments, diagnosing and identifying memory impairments, identifying onset of dementias and degenerative conditions, documenting change in cognitive status, comparing auditory and visual memory impairments, and identifying relative strengths and weaknesses for treatment and educational planning. Clinical studies were conducted with disorders including Alzheimer's Disease, Huntington's Disease, Parkinson's Disease, Traumatic Brain Injury, Multiple Sclerosis, Temporal Lobe Epilepsy, Chronic Alcohol Abuse, Korsakoff's Syndrome, Schizophrenia, AD/HD and Learning Disabilities. Results indicated the WMS-III Abbreviated is sensitive to these disorders associated with amnesia and dementia.

Like the WMS-III, the WMS-III Abbreviated is conormed with the Wechsler Adult Intelligence Scale-Third Edition (WAIS-III; T6:2691). These studies suggest a moderate relationship between intelligence and memory performance on the two tests although further analyses would be helpful for clinical interpretation of joint scores. Correlations with other memory measures are provided in well-detailed tables.

The overview of the WMS-III Abbreviated in the technical manual initially states the instrument can be administered in 15-20 minutes. However, this is misleading in terms of the overall amount of time necessary to complete the administration because a 25–35-minute interval is required between the completion of Logical Memory I and the beginning of Logical Memory II. The manual states the subtests are to be administered in the following order: Logical Memory I, Family Pictures I, delay of 25–35 minutes, Logical Memory II, and Family Pictures II. Thus, although the actual testing time is only 15–20 minutes, the total administration time is closer to 1 hour. This additional time should be reflected in the overview as well. The manual gives suggestions from research for appropriate use of this required interval stating most cognitive tests other than those with a similar story-memory component could be administered at this time.

The WMS-III Abbreviated materials are easily used and explicit. Administration of the WMS-III Abbreviated requires skills similar to the WMS-III. The examiner must take care to use standard statements found in the manual and be proficient at recording responses not recalled verbatim. Although scoring criteria are tabled in the manual, the examiner must be competent in using judgment with both queries and variations within context.

DEVELOPMENT. The WMS-II Abbreviated standardization is based on a national sample from 1995 U.S. Census data representative of adults aged 16–89 stratified along age, sex, race/ethnicity, educational level, and geographic region. All potential participants were screened medically and psychiatrically by self-report. Well-organized tables detail the representativeness of the sample. Scoring studies involving both expert content reviews and empirical analyses were conducted on the scoring criteria for Logical Memory and Family Pictures. Overall, adequate quality assurance procedures were employed throughout development.

A pilot study comprised 92 individuals from the San Antonio area ranging in age from 17–87 years was conducted to ensure reducing the number of subtests from those found in the WMS-III did not affect the subtest norms. Two comparison samples extracted from the WMS-III standardization data were matched based on demographic characteristics and age. These results yielded no significant differences between scores obtained by the pilot sample and the control groups on any of the WMS-III Abbreviated composites and provide initial, although limited, evidence for the equivalence of the forms. A national tryout study concerning item bias and difficulty, subtest functioning, and factor structure was conducted concurrently with the investigation of the clinical groups.

Norms were developed by converting each age band's raw scores from most subtests to percentile ranks and then to a scaled score having a mean of 10 and a standard deviation of 3. After developing a frequency distribution, scaled scores for each subtest were calculated and smoothing of minor fluctuations and irregularities was performed. For each composite, actual age-corrected scaled subtest scores were summed to derive the composite score. Because analysis of variance and Bartlett's test data did not support a significant variance based on age, age groups were combined to construct the tables of composite score equivalents of sums of scaled scores. Then the smoothed and normalized distribution of the sums of scaled scores was converted to a scale with a mean of 100 and a standard deviation of 15 for each composite.

TECHNICAL. Reliability information for scores from the WMS-III Abbreviated was examined by dividing each subtest form into two half-tests and the variances of the half-tests were compared to ensure equivalence. The reliability coefficient of each subtest was the result of the correlation between the total scores of the two half-tests corrected by the Spearman-Brown formula for the full subtest. The average reliability coefficients across age groups for the subtest scores range from .79 to .88. The average reliability coefficients for the composite scores are even higher ranging from .87 to .92. Tables for standard errors of measurement and confidence intervals are provided.

Test-retest stability as assessed in a separate study indicated for all WMS-III Abbreviated measures that there is a significant practice effect from Time 1 to Time 2 (mean of 35.6 days between administrations). The manual warns this practice effect should be considered when serial assessments are conducted and provides suggestions for addressing this. Interscorer agreement was evaluated in another separate study that yielded coefficients on all subtests of .90 or greater suggesting the subtests can be scored reliably even though they require scoring judgment.

Validity evidence for the WMS-III Abbreviated is drawn from research conducted for standardization of the WMS-III and the WAIS-III as well as from data collected specifically for the WMS-III Abbreviated. Ample information regarding the application of this instrument in relation to its predecessor and to specific clinical populations and in association with other measures of memory and cognitive functioning is provided in the manual.

COMMENTARY. Because the WMS-III Abbreviated is a shorter, although not parallel, version of the WMS-III, it inherently holds some of the advantages and disadvantages of the WMS-III. The WMS-III is well-researched and is generally considered to be an excellent instrument for measuring a wide range of memory functioning. However, research has shown the WMS-III can take up to 100 minutes to administer. The WMS-III Abbreviated provides a shorter, reliable alternative when screening, rather than comprehensive testing, is a choice. However, the manual does not clearly state in the overview that the WMS-III Abbreviated requires a 25–35-minute interval between two of the subtests in addition to the 15–20 minutes of actual testing time, thereby lengthening the total time of administration. Other information provided in the manual is presented in a detailed manner.

The WMS-III Abbreviated is a well-organized and developed instrument with sound psychometric properties. Administration skills are easily transferable from the WMS-III but do require skill in clinical judgment. As with the WMS-III, instructions for Logical Memory could be improved by including guidelines for reading speed, intonations, pauses, or inflections, thereby reducing the potential for error particularly based on regional or cultural differences in speech patterns and rate of speech. The fold-out summary chart on the record form assists with scoring. Although additional research was conducted to support the abbreviated version, concerns similar to those voiced about the WMS-III such as a need for cross-cultural validation as well as studies of item bias across race, ethnicity, and gender still exist. Support has been provided for use of the WMS-III Abbreviated with various clinical populations where amnesia and dementia often exist. It should be expected that a serial administration would yield a similar or higher score on the second assessment due to the practice effects identified in test-retest reliability studies. Further information on using the WMS-III Abbreviated in combination with the WAIS-III would be helpful.

SUMMARY. The WMS-III Abbreviated offers a shorter, reliable option to the widely used WMS-III when the clinical question requires less information regarding memory function and/or there is less time for administration. Also, it can be used as a screener for neurological testing. Validity studies support the use of the abbreviated version for identifying general memory dysfunction in a variety of clinical settings and populations with both adolescents and adults. Due to the significant practice effect found when the same individual is tested twice over time, results of serial assessment should be scrutinized. Additional guidelines for administering the Logical Memory subtests and further information on cross-cultural validity, item bias, and patterns of performance across race, ethnicity, and gender as well as suggestions for use of the WMS-III Abbreviated in combination with the WAIS-III would be helpful.

[264]
Wechsler Objective Language Dimensions.

Purpose: Designed to assess language skills.
Population: Ages 6 to 16-11.
Publication Date: 1996.
Acronym: WOLD.

Scores, 4: Listening Comprehension, Oral Expression, Written Expression, Total Composite Score.
Administration: Individual.
Price Data, 2003: £134.50 per complete kit including manual (209 pages), stimulus booklet, and 50 record forms; £6 per 50 record forms.
Time: (20–40) minutes.
Author: John Rust.
Publisher: Harcourt Assessment [England].

Review of the Wechsler Objective Language Dimensions by JUDITH R. JOHNSTON, Professor, School of Audiology and Speech Sciences, The University of British Columbia, Vancouver, British Columbia, Canada:

DESCRIPTION. The Wechsler Objective Language Dimensions (WOLD) is the U.K. version of three language subtests from the Wechsler Individual Achievement Tests (WIAT): Listening Comprehension, Written Expression and Oral Expression. "The primary object ... was to achieve a valid normative frame of reference for the assessment of language in the UK in the 6–16 age range"(manual, p. 99). To this end, the various tasks from the WIAT were Anglicized and standardized on children in U.K. schools. This review will consider only those aspects of the WOLD that are unique to the U.K. version.

DEVELOPMENT AND TECHNICAL.

Anglicization. The test developers planned for a U.K. edition of the WIAT from the outset and designed tasks and items with both the U.K. and the U.S. in mind, thereby minimizing the changes that would later be needed to achieve anglicization. The eventual changes mostly concern lexical preferences (i.e., "animal shelter" in the U.S. version was anglicized to "stray dogs home").

Standardization. The standardization plan was designed "to clarify the relationship between achievement levels in the UK and the US and to generate sufficient additional data to support the preparation of a set of UK transformation tables for WOLD" (manual, p. 99). A random sample of 418 children was selected for inclusion, stratified on age, gender, SES, race/ethnicity, and geographic region. Distribution of these variables in the sample closely matched values taken from the 1989 U.K. census.

The WOLD manual provides the norms that resulted from the U.K. standardization effort. Normative data are presented as standard scores, percentile ranks, and age equivalents. There is also information about the size of the observed discrepancies between the three WOLD subtests. However, the algorithm by which any of these data were derived from the U.S. data is not presented, nor is there any discussion of the magnitude or direction of difference between the two samples/populations. The manual also provides the WOLD subtest and composite scores that would be predicted from the Wechsler Intelligence Scale for Children, Third Edition (WISC-III) FSIQ along with information about the size of discrepancies between the two measures. These aptitude-achievement relationships are, however, based entirely on the performance of children in the U.S. because children in the U.K. normative sample did not complete the WISC-III.

Two further facts about the composition of the standardization sample raise additional concerns about the interpretation of the WOLD. First, the Wechsler Individual Achievement Test (WIAT) sample and the WOLD sample most probably differ in regard to their inclusion of children with severe language learning difficulties. This can be inferred from the fact that in the U.K. such children are schooled in special schools that were excluded from the sample whereas in the U.S. they are generally schooled in regular schools and were, therefore, not excluded. Secondly, both the WIAT and the WOLD fail to deal with important differences among bilingual children. The manual states that for both samples, children were tested if they could speak and understand English. This criteria would appear to be underspecified because there are many possible degrees of proficiency in a second language. As applied by parents, teachers, and even test administrators, this criterion could easily lead to the inclusion of bilingual children who differ widely in their ability to use English. Because 7–10% of each sample came from immigrant communities known to be language-preserving, and another 2–3% from communities likely to be language preserving, this is not a trivial consideration. This lack of attention to the realities and academic implications of bilingualism is particularly disappointing in a test of language achievement.

Reliability and validity. The validity and reliability data refer only to studies conducted in the U.S. Both the tables and the text are somewhat misleading because they refer repeatedly to the WOLD, but are actually studies of the WIAT.

Although the authors of the manual express their confidence that the U.S. standardization project results confirm that the WOLD achieves high levels of reliability, they provide no analyses to support this judgement. In the absence of any data regarding the differences, or similarities, between the raw scores earned by children in the U.K. and the U.S. it remains possible that the U.K. scores are less reliable, less predicted by the WISC-III, etc. The fact that the wording and content of items in the two versions of the WOLD differed only slightly in no way reduces this possibility, particularly for a test battery that focuses on achievement rather than aptitude and could well reflect differences in school practice.

SUMMARY. Professionals concerned with educational assessment in the U.K. will appreciate the publication of the WOLD with its "transformed" norms and anglicized tasks. There are, however, potential problems in interpretation because (a) the manual does not distinguish clearly between analyses that do and do not reflect the performance of U.K. children, (b) the U.K. and U.S. samples differ in their inclusion of children with severe language disorders, and (c) both samples are likely to include bilingual children who have not yet reached full English proficiency.

Review of the Wechsler Objective Language Dimensions by DOLORES KLUPPEL VETTER, Professor Emerita, University of Wisconsin—Madison, Madison, WI:

DESCRIPTION. The Wechsler Objective Language Dimensions (WOLD) was designed to provide information about children's oral comprehension of language, as well as oral and written expression of language for the age range of 6 to 16 years in the U.K. It is made up of three subtests, Listening Comprehension, Oral Expression, and Written Expression; they may be administered individually, but the use of all three subtests allows for the most complete picture of the individual's strengths and weaknesses. Two subtests, Listening Comprehension and Oral Expression, may be combined into a composite Language score that reflects overall oral abilities. Standard scores, percentile ranks, age equivalent scores, and stanines are provided. The WOLD has two basic purposes: (a) to ascertain a child's oral and written language abilities in order to determine what forms of assistance, if any, may be required for him or her to take full advantage of the educational experience in the U.K.; and (b) to provide oral and written language subtests that could be considered extensions of the Wechsler Intelligence Scale for Children—Third Edition (WISC-III) so that discrepancies between ability and achievement might be determined and a diagnosis of specific learning disabilities applied when warranted.

Listening Comprehension has a total of 36 items; the first 9 require the child to point to one of four foils as a response to an orally presented word. The remaining items, also ordered in difficulty, require oral responses that reflect passage comprehension. To be successful the child may, among other things, be required to recognize details, sequence events in time, or draw inferences, while holding the examiner's stimulus statement in memory. Oral Expression is composed of 16 items. The first 10 require the child to produce the correct target word in response to the word's oral definition and picture. The remaining items require the child to produce statements that reflect the functional aspects of language: informing, instruction, and explaining. The final subtest, Written Expression, requires that the child write for 15 minutes on a topic to a standardized prompt. Perhaps because of the debate over the relative merits of analytic and holistic scoring of written language, either or both methods of scoring the written response may be used.

The WOLD must be administered by a trained examiner, most often an Educational or Clinical Psychologist; access to others is determined on a case-by-case basis. Even so, the administration and scoring must be learned through study and practice. Scoring of the initial items for Listening Comprehension and Oral Expression is "correct-incorrect"; for later items, the examiner must make judgments or determine if criteria have been met to award points. The manual provides extensive documentation and examples for assigning credit for a response. Because the criteria differ by item, the examiner must be fully acquainted with the scoring procedure. The subtest Written Expression is more complex to score. The first decision is whether to use the analytic or the holistic procedure. If comparisons between oral and written expressive language are of interest, the evaluator must score Written Expression analytically because these were the scores chosen for transformation to standard scores. For analytic

scoring, six components (e.g., organization, vocabulary, capitalization) are each assigned a score ranging from 1 to 4. Holistic scoring allows the examiner to provide a global assessment of the written passage; criteria are provided for the assignment of scores from 1 to 6. A process of self-training is specified, and the manual suggests that the examiner practice scoring transcripts with another individual competent in English, if necessary.

DEVELOPMENT. The Wechsler Objective Language Dimensions (WOLD) came out of a Wechsler scales development program (U.S. and U.K.) involving the third revision of the Wechsler Intelligence Scale for Children (WISC-III) and the Wechsler Individual Achievement Test (WIAT) and published in 1996. The original instrument, the WIAT, was standardized in the United States. Basically, an initial pool of items was developed; the items were field tested, reviewed for curriculum content, and analyzed statistically; items were revised or eliminated; and a final version of the instrument was constructed. The initial standardization project was conducted in the U.S. with over 4,000 children chosen for the stratification variables of age, grade, gender, race/ethnicity, geographic region, and parent education based on the 1988 U.S. Census.

In the U.K. the WIAT subtests were organized into three instruments: the Wechsler Objective Reading Dimensions (WORD; 266), the Wechsler Objective Numerical Dimensions (WOND; 265), and the Wechsler Objective Language Dimensions (WOLD). Further discussion will be restricted to the WOLD. Given linguistic and cultural differences between the U.S. and the U.K., some items were anglicized (e.g., *pounds* for *dollars*, *soccer* for *football*, changes in spelling and some prepositions). Then an additional validation project was undertaken in the U.K. with 400 children chosen for the stratification variables of age, gender, race/ethnicity, geographic region, and socioeconomic status based on the 1989 Census and 1985/86 Labor Force Surveys. Examiners were trained to administer and score the WOLD and were informed of differences with the WISC-III[UK]. Final scores were determined by an independent assessor in the event of a discrepancy.

TECHNICAL. Information concerning the development of the items, the U.S. standardization project, the anglicization of the items, and the U.K. validation study is presented extensively in the manual. Each study used national census information to determine the variables to be used for stratification. Although age and gender were comparable variables in the two studies, there were differences in the composition of the race/ethnicity populations (Black, Hispanic, White, and Other in the U.S., and Indian, Pakistani or Bangladeshi, West Indian or African, White, and Other in the U.K.) and in defining socioeconomic levels (parent education level in the U.S. and head-of-household employment in the U.K.). These differences obviously reflect the manner in which census information has been codified given the make-up of each nation. The data presented indicate that the samples chosen closely matched their respective stratification goals, although the sample sizes differed dramatically (i.e., 4,252 individuals in the U.S. and only 400 subjects in the U.K.).

Split-half reliability correlation coefficients are presented by age and by subtest, for the Language composite score, and then averaged across ages (using Fisher's Z transformation). They range from .76 to .92 for the individual subtests; the averaged correlation coefficients are .83, .91, .81, and .90 for Listening Comprehension, Oral Expression, Written Expression, and the Language Composite score, respectively. Standard errors of measurement and confidence intervals are also provided for individual ages and for the average. These values appear to be derived from the U.K. validation study.

Test-retest reliability information presented in the manual is from the U.S. standardization study conducted at five different age bands (Grades 1, 3, 5, 8, 10) on a total of 367 children. The interval between tests was 12 to 52 days, with a median of 17 days. Correlation coefficients, corrected for the variability in the scores at the time of the first test, ranged from .56 to .88; in general, the older the children, the poorer the correlations. Interscorer agreement was also determined in two studies with data taken from the U.S. project. One study used 50 protocols with four scorers independently evaluating each protocol. The average correlation among pairs of scores was .98. The second study was of Oral and Written Expression and used an intraclass correlation. The correlation for Oral Expression was .93; for Prompt 1 of Written Expression, it was .89 and .79 for Prompt 2.

Evidence for content validity was based upon expert judgments and item analysis. All aspects of the items were evaluated at each stage of the development of the instrument. Item content was compared to curriculum objectives and to textbooks by expert reviewers. Item analyses were also used to provide evidence of the degree to which each item was empirically consistent with the other items in the subtest.

The construct-related evidence and criterion-related evidence presented in the manual are apparently based upon the U.S. standardization data. Construct-related evidence includes intercorrelations among subtest scores at each age, correlations with measures of ability (i.e., FSIQ from the WISC-III), and group differences in performance among various clinical groups. Criterion-related evidence is derived from studies of comparisons when children were given other achievement tests (i.e., Woodcock-Johnson Psycho-Educational Battery—Revised, Tests of Achievement, and the Peabody Picture Vocabulary Test—Revised) or were rated by teachers. All validity evidence appears to support the assertion that the WOLD subtests are measures of the underlying abilities that they purport to measure.

COMMENTARY. The WOLD, designed to be used in the U.K., is made up of three subtests taken from the WIAT, with items anglicized as needed. Much of the reliability and evidence of validity for the WOLD is based on the original standardization of the WIAT and other research conducted in the U.S. In and of itself, that is not a negative. If the examiner is willing to accept that there are basically no differences between the two versions of the oral and written language subtests (WOLD and WIAT), except that one is used in the U.S. and the other in the U.K., then there is acceptable reliability and validity information presented in the manual. The major criticism of the manual is that it does not provide sufficient stipulations or reminders to the reader of which standardization sample is the referent for a particular discussion of reliability or validity. It may be necessary for the examiner to review the manual multiple times in order to be sure of the test or standardization sample being referenced.

A second concern is that the U.K. validation of the WOLD was completed and the manual published in 1996. Since that time, the Woodcock-Johnson III, Tests of Achievement has been published (Woodcock, McGrew, Mather, & Schrank, 2001; 15:281). It had been noted in the

WOLD manual that the earlier version of the Woodcock-Johnson was not well known in the U.K., and that was part of the justification for the validation of the WOLD, WORD, and WOND in the U.K. Now, however, this updated version of a comprehensive achievement test has been standardized in the U.S. If, or when, this instrument is validated in the U.K., it may provide for a more comprehensive assessment of learning abilities/disabilities as well as permit a discrepancy analysis between achievement and ability.

SUMMARY. The WOLD appears to be an appropriate instrument to use to assess the oral language comprehension and production and the written language expression of children 6 to 16 years old in the U.K. Part of its value lies in its linkages with other Wechsler scales (i.e., WISC-III) co-normed in the U.K. and the U.S. It permits the determination of ability-achievement discrepancies that may relate to specific learning disabilities. Even though a newer revision of the Woodcock-Johnson has been recently published in the U.S. (i.e., the Woodcock-Johnson III, Tests of Achievement, 2001) the WOLD may continue to be the most appropriate option for assessing oral and written language in the U.K. until a validation study of it is accomplished.

REVIEWER'S REFERENCE

Woodcock, R. W., McGrew, K.S., Mather, N., & Schrank, F. A. (2001). *Woodcock-Johnson III, Tests of Achievement, Standard and Extended Battery*. Itasca, IL: Riverside Publishing.

[265]
Wechsler Objective Numerical Dimensions.

Purpose: Intended to assess a child's progress in acquiring fundamental numeracy skills.
Population: Ages 6 to 16-11.
Publication Date: 1996.
Acronym: WOND.
Scores, 3: Composite Score, Mathematics Reasoning, Numerical Operations.
Administration: Individual.
Price Data, 2003: £134.50 per complete kit including manual (134 pages), stimulus booklet, and 50 record forms; £46 per 50 record forms.
Time: (20) minutes.
Author: John Rust.
Publisher: Harcourt Assessment [England].

Review of the Wechsler Objective Numerical Dimensions by MARY L. GARNER, Associate Professor of Mathematics, Kennesaw State University, Kennesaw, GA:

DESCRIPTION. The Wechsler Objective Numerical Dimensions (WOND) consists of two tests, Mathematical Reasoning and Numerical Operations, designed to identify and quantify difficulties in achievement of basic mathematical skills in children 6 to 16 years of age. Scores on each test are produced as well as a composite score. In addition, the two tests may be used to compare the child's level of achievement in mathematics with ability in mathematics as measured by the Wechsler Intelligence Scale for Children—Third Edition (WISC-III). The tests are individually administered and require 15 to 20 minutes to complete.

The first test, Mathematical Reasoning, consists of 50 items that are administered both visually and verbally. Students deliver most answers verbally and are allowed to use pencil and paper. The items are divided into four sets of increasing difficulty. The examiner is instructed to begin with the set of items that correspond to the age of the student. If the student incorrectly answers any item in the first set administered and the student did not start with the first set of items, the examiner is instructed to administer preceding sets in reverse order until the student correctly answers five consecutive items. If the student correctly answers all items in the first set administered, the examiner continues with subsequent sets of items until the student incorrectly answers four consecutive items. The items are tied to topics in the mathematics curriculum and include simple word problems and problems that involve place value, counting, comparing and ordering numbers, interpreting graphs, simple geometry, and measurement. There is no indication in the manual as to whether students may use a calculator.

The second test, Numerical Operations, consists of 40 items. The items appear in a booklet and are organized into 10 sets. Except for the first set of items, which requires students to write numbers said by the examiner in the spaces provided in the booklet, the student is instructed to work on a set of 4 items by himself or herself over a period of 5 to 7 minutes. The problems are not read aloud. The examiner begins with the set of items appropriate for the student's age. The "reverse" and "discontinue" rules for this test are similar to those for the Mathematical Reasoning test. The items in this test are strictly computational—addition, subtraction, multiplication, division of whole numbers, fractions, and decimals.

Calculator use would seem inappropriate for this test. Students are not required to explain or justify their procedures.

A clear and well-written manual is provided, along with easy-to-use scoring booklets, response booklets for the Numerical Operations test, and a stimulus booklet that contains the visual presentation of the items in the Mathematical Reasoning test. Raw scores can be converted to standard scores with a mean of 100 and standard deviation of 15; also available are percentile ranks, stanines, and age equivalents for both the individual tests and the composite score. Simple instructions for a discrepancy analysis are provided, allowing the examiner to compare WOND scores to WISC-III scores.

DEVELOPMENT. The WOND was developed by The Psychological Corporation in both the United States (U.S.) and the United Kingdom (U.K.) as part of a larger program for the development of a variety of Wechsler scales. Development and testing of the U.K. version was directed by Dr. John Rust at Goldsmiths' College, University of London.

The items were designed to parallel curriculum objectives most commonly found in curriculum guides, textbooks, and recommendations of national organizations such as the National Council of Teachers of Mathematics. The skill addressed by each item in the tests is identified in the scoring booklet. The items were pilot tested in 1989 on a sample of 2,238 children in the U.S., consisting of 48% female, 52% male, and 28% minority. Approximately 300 children in each of seven grade levels were chosen; those grade levels were kindergarten, 1, 2, 4, 6, 8, and 10. Most items were administered to the children in groups, but beginning items of both subtests were administered individually.

The data from the pilot study were used to conduct both conventional item analysis and item analysis based on Rasch measurement theory. The level of difficulty of the items was established using Rasch difficulty indices. Two methods were used to analyze bias of items. The number of items discarded after the pilot study was not reported.

TECHNICAL. In the U.S., in 1989, the test was standardized using a stratified random sample of 4,252 children from 13 age groups ranging from 5 though 19 years of age and representing all Grades K through 12. The number of children within each age group and grade ranged from about 200 to almost 400. The children were se-

lected from both public and private schools in four geographical regions according to the 1988 U.S. Census data. Approximately 39% of the children were from the South, 25% from North Central, 20% from the West, and 16% from the North East. Approximately 49% were male and 51% were female. Approximately 15% were classified as Black, 11% Hispanic, and 4% other. All students in the sample had to be able to speak and understand English.

A sample of 1,284 children was selected from the original U.S. sample used for standardization, and these children were administered Wechsler intelligence scales so that performance on the ability scales might be linked to WOND scores. The demographic profile of these students approximately matched the larger sample.

In the U.K., in 1994 and 1995, the standardization performed in the U.S. was validated on a stratified random sample of 400 students from 11 age groups ranging from 6 to 16 years, with 26 to 40 students from each age. Approximately 52% were male and 48% were female. The sample was stratified according to geographic region, race/ethnicity, and socioeconomic status in a manner consistent with U.K. Census data. Thirteen of the 50 items in the Mathematical Reasoning test had to be altered to reflect the culture of the U.K. Some differences in order of difficulty of the items were found during standardization and items were reordered based on the patterns observed on testing children in the U.K. A linking sample was not used. Although the sample is well described, no analysis is provided of the results of the standardization.

Split-half reliability coefficients for each subtest at each age group in the U.S. sample ranged from .82 to .92, whereas the reliability coefficients for the composite score ranged from .90 to .95. Standard errors of measurement averaged 4.3 for the standard composite score, 5.18 for the standard score on the Mathematics Reasoning test, and 6.03 for the standard score on the Numerical Operations test. In a separate study involving 367 children from Grades 1, 3, 5, 8, and 10, the test-retest reliabilities were .86 for Numerical Operations, .89 for Mathematics Reasoning, and .91 for the composite score. No evidence for interrater reliability is presented.

Extensive evidence for the validity of the WOND scores was provided by expert judgments, item analysis, and correlations with achievement tests and with ability tests. Correlations between WOND composite scores and WISC-III scores for each age group in the U.S. sample ranged from .51 to .79. Correlations between scores on the two subtests for each age group ranged from .66 to .78. Correlations between the WOND composite score and other mathematics achievements tests were approximately .8 or higher. The pattern of results obtained by testing special groups of children, such as those who are gifted, have severe learning difficulties, have emotional disorders, have attention-deficit disorder, or are hearing impaired, also support the validity of the WOND scores.

Two ways of comparing WOND scores with WISC scores are described. Tables are provided for interpreting the significance of differences between WOND and WISC scores and between WOND scores predicted from WISC scores and actual WOND scores. Evidence is presented for the validity of the interpretation of the score differences in the U.S. standardization sample but not the U.K. sample.

COMMENTARY. The strength of the WOND is in its technical development and validation. As with other well-respected Wechsler scales, the standardization procedure appears to be well conceived and executed, and the evidence for the reliability and validity of the test is extensive. The manual for the test is clear and well written. The materials provided are well organized and easy to use. More evidence for the reliability and validity of the tests within the U.K. sample could be provided.

The weaknesses of the WOND are in the range of skills tested and in its emphasis on answers rather than process. As stated in the manual, the test emphasizes very basic mathematical skills and would not be appropriate for students taking a strong high school curriculum including algebra, trigonometry, or precalculus. Furthermore, there are only a few items in each skill area and students might easily get none or all items correct, thus providing little useful information. Although specific weaknesses in the student's repertoire of mathematical skills can be identified, the test does emphasize correct answers rather than the processes used to obtain the answers. The authors point out in the manual that the correct answer may be obtained for the wrong reason, and that the recent emphasis in mathematics education is on justifying procedures, estimating answers, and using manipulatives and technology to represent

mathematical operations and explore mathematical conjectures. WOND subtests do not reflect this emphasis.

SUMMARY. In general, the two WOND subtests provide a technically sound instrument for identifying and quantifying weaknesses in very basic mathematical reasoning and computation skills. It also offers a means of identifying and quantifying discrepancies between ability and achievement through its links with the WISC-III.

Review of the Wechsler Objective Numerical Dimensions by JERRY JOHNSON, Professor of Mathematics, Western Washington University, Bellingham, WA:

DESCRIPTION. The Wechsler Objective Numerical Dimensions (WOND) uses two distinct subtests to assess numeracy skills of children of ages 6 to 16 in the United Kingdom. Mathematical Reasoning, the first WOND subtest, involves 50 items that assess a child's ability to reason mathematically in contexts that involve geometry, measurement, money, and time. Numerical Operations, the second WOND subtest, involves 40 items that assess a child's ability to write dictated numerals, solve computational problems involving the four standard operations, and solve simple algebraic equations. Though both subtests can be used independently and have their own score conversion table, they are designed to be used together where a composite score is computed and reflects an overall performance level of numeracy.

The Mathematical Reasoning test is administered orally using the WOND stimulus booklet, whereas the Numerical Operations test is administered using a special response booklet. The estimated time for administration of both subtests is 20 minutes, dependant on the child's ability to respond correctly to suggested entry points keyed to the child's age. For example, the Mathematical Reasoning Test suggests starting points of Item 1 (for up to 8 years), Item 10 (for 9–12 years), and Item 20 (for 13 years and above). A special Reverse Rule and Discontinue Rule guides the subtests' administration in those instances when a child does not score with five correct responses from the suggested entry point.

The WOND is one component of the full Wechsler assessment program, which includes the Wechsler Intelligence Scale for Children (WISC-III), the Wechsler Objective Reading Dimensions

(WORD), and the Wechsler Objective Language Dimensions (WOLD). Through the use of an overlapping sample, the scores on these tests are linked and "ability-achievement discrepancies" can be determined.

DEVELOPMENT. While the Wechsler Intelligence Scale was being revised into the WISC-III, the Wechsler Individual Achievement Test (WIAT) was developed in the United States to measure specific learning disabilities. Involving a battery of eight subtests, the WIAT included two subtests for the areas of mathematics calculation and mathematics reasoning. To enable usage with children in the U.K., the WOND is the result of both the Anglicization of the content of mathematics subtests in the WIAT and the necessary standardization using a sample of U.K. children to ensure a valid normative frame of reference. The WOND manual provides an interesting overview of the changes needed to produce an Anglicized version of the Mathematical Reasoning subtest (as no changes were necessary in the Numerical Operations subtest), including the use of character names, the substitution of familiar monetary and measurement units, and some adjustments in the order of item difficulty.

The development of the WIAT and WOND was guided by the intent to produce tests that were not only consistent with current practices and goals in mathematics education but also could serve as an extension of the WISC-III profile. For the Mathematical Reasoning subtest, specific development steps included item specifications that ensured increasing levels of difficulty, a balance of traditional items and innovative items that reflect the daily use of mathematics, and compatibility with national curriculum standards in the U.S. and U.K. The Numerical Operations subtest resulted from item specifications that measured the child's ability to write numerals, compute with fractions and decimals, and solve simple algebraic equations. Subsequently, the WIAT and WOND were field tested and subjected to careful item analysis using U.S. and U.K. samples, respectively, prior to the full standardization.

TECHNICAL. The field-testing of the WIAT involved a total pilot sample of 2,238 U.S. children who reflected diverse geographical regions, socioeconomic levels, and ethnicity. To provide a normative linking, a subset of this sample (1,284 U.S. children) was administered the WISC-III. Results from this field-testing and an item analysis process determined the Start Points, Reverse Rule, Discontinue Rule, and standard score conversions for each subtest. The sum of a child's raw scores on each subtest are added and converted to produce a standard score for the cumulative test package. The subtest and cumulative standard scores reflect the use of a statistical procedure (i.e., linear transformations) to "smooth" the scores within and across grade levels. In turn, the WOND, as an Anglicized version of the WIAT, was standardized and validated using a stratified sample of 418 children reflective of 12 geographic regions across the U.K. This standardization effort capitalized on the more comprehensive U.S. standardization process, while also providing enough baseline information to "clarify the relationship between achievement levels in the UK and the US" (manual, p. 34).

The reliability evidence for the WOND is described using multiple statistical techniques. First, to document internal consistency, reliability coefficients for both the subtests and the composite test (ranging from .82 to .95 across the grade ranges) were determined using the split-half method, and corrected for the full-length test using the Spearman-Brown formula. It is important to note that the split-half method was specifically chosen for reasons of consistency, as this method was also used to describe the reliability of the other WISC-III subtests. The reliability coefficients and population standard deviations were used to compute the standard error of measurements, which can in turn be used to construct confidence intervals centered on a child's obtained score.

Test-retest stability over time was examined in an assessment of 367 U.S. children tested twice, with an intervening time interval of 12 to 52 days. The resultant test-retest reliability coefficients, averaged across the full age range, were .89 for Mathematics Reasoning, .86 for Numerical Operations, and .91 for the combined WOND assessment. To help the test administrator, the WOND manual gives some attention to interpretation of observed differences between standard scores on the two subtests, which may be either meaningful or statistical fluctuations.

The content validity of the WOND was initially examined using expert judgments (e.g., by mathematics curriculum specialists) during the development, pilot, and standardization phases.

This was followed by an item analysis to ensure that each test item was empirically consistent with the other items. Any item with a correlation value of .20 or less was either revised or replaced. The construct validity of the WOND was documented in four ways: (a) using intercorrelations of the two subtests at each age level; (b) correlations between the WOND and the WISC-III (ranging from .35 to .75); (c) analysis of expected differences of raw scores across different age and clinical groups (e.g., gifted children, underachievers, hyperactive children, children with severe learning disabilities); and (d) correlations between the WOND standard scores and scores on three U.S. achievement tests-the Stanford Achievement Test ($r = .69$), the Iowa Test of Basic Skills ($r = .67$), and the California Achievement Test ($r = .78$).

Criterion-related validity evidence for the Mathematical Reasoning and Numerical Operations subtests of the WOND was derived from using correlations with other accepted tests, such as the Basic Achievement Skills Individual Screener (.82, .79), the Kaufman Test of Educational Achievement (.87, .81), the Wide-Range Achievement Test (.77 for second subtest only), the Woodcock-Johnson Psycho-Educational Battery (.67, .68), and the Differential Ability Scales (.75, .70). As an additional check on criterion-related validity, composite WOND scores were correlated with teacher-assigned grades in mathematics, with a value of $r = .43$. This low value was explained as being due to the lack of reliability in teacher ratings.

COMMENTARY. The value of the WOND is directly connected to the value of the WIAT, in that it is basically a U.K.-version of the WIAT. Because the WIAT is well-accepted and respected as an assessment device within the U.S., it is an easy step to claim that the WOND will be accepted and respected within the U.K. The Anglicization effort and standardization process are both sufficient enough to merit this acceptance and respect.

As a reviewer, my biggest concerns lie in some of the claims made regarding the mathematical content of the two subtests. That is, what is being assessed may be reliable and valid, but is that what should be assessed in the area of mathematics? For example, many mathematics educators would argue that the WOND's view of "math-ematical reasoning" falls short of the mathematics being emphasized in classrooms today. For example, identification of a cylinder from line drawings of other 3-D shapes (Item 22) is a rather low-level skill and is not considered to be reasoning in a geometrical context. Also, as the NAEP results have clearly shown, computation of areas of rectangles with given side-lengths is a rote skill using a formula; it is not reasoning in a measurement situation and certainly does not equate to demonstrating an understanding of area as a concept. As a final example, mathematical reasoning in a statistical context involves much more than the reading of data from a table and the calculation of a mean.

In a similar fashion, the Number Operations subtest does not fit well with the modern interpretation of numeracy. For example, the focus is on the four standard operations, with no attention to concepts such as reasonableness of results, estimation, number size, and the use of alternate algorithms. In defense of the WOND, its manual specifically states that its focus is on obtained answers and not the algorithms used, but this seems to miss the essence of what numeracy entails.

SUMMARY. The WOND as a U.K. standardization of the WIAT is worthy and well-done. It provides useful information across a wide age range, while meeting all of the normal criteria for reliability and validity. An earnest attempt has been made to ensure its value as a measure of mathematical reasoning and numerical operation abilities. But this success has led to suggested limitations as to its use and interpretations.

These suggested weaknesses in the WOND are perhaps reflective of its developmental process. First, the WOND and its predecessor, the WIAT, were first developed and then standardized using mathematics education curricula, national standards, and expert input relevant to a specific time period. In the subsequent 10-plus years, great changes have occurred in mathematics education, making the mathematics implications of both the WOND and WIAT less relevant. That is, they may be reliable and valid in measuring what it is claimed they measure, but their value has been lowered because they no longer are consistent with the mathematics concepts and skills being emphasized in today's classrooms.

Wechsler Objective Reading Dimensions.

Purpose: Designed to assess literacy skills.
Population: Ages 6 to 16-11.
Publication Dates: 1990–1993.
Acronym: WORD.
Scores, 4: Basic Reading, Spelling, Reading Comprehension, Total Composite Score.
Administration: Individual.
Price Data, 2003: £134.50 per complete kit including manual (1993, 157 pages), stimulus booklet, and 50 record forms; £46 per 50 record forms.
Time: (20) minutes.
Authors: John Rust, Susan Golombok, and Geoff Trickey.
Publisher: Harcourt Assessment [England].

Review of the Wechsler Objective Reading Dimensions by THOMAS EMERSON HANCOCK, Associate Professor of Educational Psychology, George Fox University, Newberg, OR:

DESCRIPTION. The Wechsler Objective Reading Dimensions (WORD) was designed as an individually administered assessment of the literacy skills of students ages 6 to 16. Its purpose is to address the needs of local administrators, teachers, and parents who have become concerned about a pupil's educational progress. WORD consists of three subtests: Reading Comprehension, Spelling, and Basic Reading, with separate norms for each. These scores, and a composite score, may be used as part of the decision-making process involved in determining certain literacy-related needs of students. When used concurrently with the Wechsler Intelligence Scale for Children— Third Edition (WISC-III), WORD can provide basic information about ability-achievement discrepancies and thus help in decisions regarding eligibility for special educational programs.

The tests can typically be administered in about 20 minutes. The manual for WORD provides administration, recording, and scoring information. It would be helpful if directions or examples facilitated the students' understanding that correct answers should be more literal and less personally elaborated. Scoring for the Basic Reading (word identification) and Spelling subtests is a dichotomous rating of correct or incorrect. Scores for the Reading Comprehension are based on administrator judgment of the match between student responses and common correct and incorrect responses. Tables are pro-vided for transforming raw scores according to the appropriate norming group.

DEVELOPMENT. The developing of subtest and item specifications, field testing, and item analysis were facilitated by specialists in cognitive assessment, in speech and language assessment, and in reading assessment. Thoroughness is evident in the creation of all three subtests. The words for the Basic Reading subtest were selected from graded lists and included various word types and vowel-consonant combinations. Words for the Spelling subtest were selected based on occurrence in children's writing, from lists of common words, and to sample both regular and irregular spellings. In addition, words were ordered by difficulty and grouped by age level and are presented in the context of a sentence. The Reading Comprehension subtest items involves recognizing stated details, sequencing, recognizing cause-effect, inferencing, comparing, and for younger children using picture clues. However, there is no table of specifications that would enable users to efficiently link particular items with various reading skills. Passages were constructed with thorough consideration of various readability scales and graded word lists. Except for item bias analysis, there is no consideration of the match between the content or tone of the passages themselves with the varied schemas of students of diverse age, gender, or cultural subgroups.

The field testing for WORD was extensive in both the U.K. and the U.S., with impressive sampling procedures in each case. In addition, the item analysis, which was based on conventional and item-response theory, seems to have been thorough. The order of items in the final instrument was determined by using Rasch analysis. The items were analyzed for bias by experienced reviewers; the particular methods of analysis were not explained or referenced.

One of the stated goals for WORD was creating a standardized "test relevant to current educational thinking" (manual, p. 32). A related goal was addressing the literacy concerns of teachers and parents about their students reading words in isolation and being good spellers. The manual mentions "recent debate" regarding these goals. There are no citations and no discussion of how reading words in isolation is a crucial part of facilitating students' literacy development. It was stated the Spelling subtest might be used to access the "strategies and errors evident in children's reading" (manual, p. 32). There is no explicit citation and no discussion of such strategy analysis.

An underlying reason for the creation of WORD was the facilitation of simple "profile analysis" by means of the link to the WISC-III results. This provides for efficiency in making discrepancy-achievement decisions, and in particular for the dichotomous decision whether a student qualifies for special education or not. The manual goes on to state that a related reason for the development of WORD and its link to the WISC-III was to "be used flexibly to address a range of assessment questions" and to offer "a number of permutations and differing depths of assessment" (manual, p. 32). Some discussion about that flexibility and depth of assessment could be helpful to students and to those who make important educational decisions for them.

TECHNICAL. The standardization and reliability evidence for WORD as well as the criterion-related validity evidence are impressive indeed. The norm samples are a good match for intended users. The various reliability calculations indicate good consistency. And the criterion related evidence for each subscale is good. For those who want to look at details, the WORD manual is recommended.

Regarding other validity evidence, a few comments are in order here. It was reported that the WORD subtests and items were matched to the curricula used in the schools and to other achievement tests, as well as to emerging curricular trends, and to the opinions of recognized educational experts. It is hard to independently verify such content validation because the particular curricular trends were not discussed in detail nor were the experts identified. No evidence has been provided that the Spelling and Basic Reading scores do anything more educationally than simply adding more data to the ability-achievement discrepancy. And it is regrettable that although volumes of data are reported in the manual, there is limited evidence showing that WORD can indeed identify those who had already been marked as learning disabled. Yet this seems to be one of the major purposes of the test.

And finally, there is no discussion at all of consequential validity. For example, what is the test's impact on the teachers, administrators, and community? How do the results address the parents' and teachers' concerns related to literacy and are they satisfied? Are the students less at-risk due to the test? In the acknowledgements section of the manual it is recognized that the students tested were "long-suffering" and that their performance is "enshrined with the transformation tables" (p. 4). Indeed, the psychometric properties of the WORD are excellent. That excellence would be more fitting if there were more responsibility taken for the consequences to the children and in the broader educational environment.

COMMENTARY AND SUMMARY. The WORD is an excellent tool for making norm-referenced judgments about students' learning of spelling, word identification, and reading comprehension skills. It is also an efficient tool for identifying students whose achievement does not match their ability. Popular or legislative demands for spelling, decoding, and reading comprehension assessment and for efficiently determining achievement-ability discrepancies can easily be addressed with this instrument.

When WORD was created, assessment professionals were primarily concerned about psychometrically sound instruments. By today, we are progressing toward more detailed test results that will most directly relate to what each child specifically needs for becoming literate. Meeting parents' interests in their desires to see certain kinds of literacy progress is important to consider, especially as we realize the impact of legislation. And making tests match curricula that are in place is understandable and even needed. However, when the consequences are that teachers tend to lose the art in their instruction and minimize the creation of meaningful experiences with text, and instead become locked into the achievement of high scores (e.g., with spelling and decoding), then our well-intentioned efforts are not efficiently focused on their becoming better readers, which eventually should be the purpose of assessment efforts such as with WORD. It is hoped that the next version of WORD will yield results with more specific feedback and guidance for helping students in their development of the broad array of comprehension strategies that are tested by WORD.

In addition, that WORD has been normed with the WISC-III is a laudable effort. However, in implementation, teachers and parents deserve more than an efficient way to identify who will receive special help. It would be most desirable if The Psychological Corporation could focus on helping teachers use the rich storehouse of data from the pairing of the WISC-III and WORD to yield instruction that is targeted to more detailed cognitive profiles of each student. Such reporting is now occurring with the Woodcock-Johnson III (Woodcock, McGrew, & Mather, 2002). The potential is indeed great! Research (Evans, Floyd & McGrew, 2002) demonstrates that aspects of cognitive functioning such as are measured by the WISC-III, do correlate with reading achievement. It is likely that reading achievement will improve more dramatically when instruction is targeted appropriately, both to comprehension strategies and also to the specific aspects of the cognitive profile underlying ability-achievement discrepancies. It seems likely that the skilled professionals at The Psychological Corporation will be addressing these concerns with the next iteration of WORD.

Along this line, it is hoped that there will be a more transparent and specific linkage with each of the precise and relevant objectives for the test with the tables of specification. If these tables were clearly related to the specific theoretical base for the instrument, including citations, then we might more efficiently connect the instrument to the current thinking in the literature and more intelligently and profitably use the instrument.

REVIEWER'S REFERENCES

Evans, J. J., Floyd, R. G., & McGrew, K. S. (2002). The relations between measures of Cattell Horn-Carroll (CHC) cognitive abilities and reading achievement during childhood and adolescence. *School Psychology Review, 31,* 246–262.
Woodcock, R. W., McGrew, K. S., & Mather, N. (2001). Woodcock-Johnson Psycho-Educational Battery, Third Edition. Itasca, IL: Riverside Publishing.

Review of the Wechsler Objective Reading Dimensions by ALFRED P. LONGO, Instructor in Education, Social Science Department, Ocean County College, Toms River, NJ:

DESCRIPTION. The Wechsler Objective Reading Dimensions (WORD) provides reliable assessment in the key area of language attainment for children aged 6 to 16. There are three separate components, each of which is designed to make a distinctive contribution to the overall assessment. The WORD has a direct and consistent linkage with other Wechsler scales, namely the Wechsler Intelligence Scale for Children, Third Edition (WISC-III; Wechsler, 1991), U.K.; the Wechsler Preschool and Primary Scale of Intelligence—Revised (WPPSI-R); and the Wechsler Adult Intelligence Scale—Revised (WAIS-R). The linked data derived from the above should provide a rather complete picture for diagnosing and assess-ing learning difficulties and in calculating ability versus achievement discrepancies.

The three WORD subtests are Basic Reading, Spelling, and Reading Comprehension. Taken as a whole, the subtests measure a child's attainment of fundamental literacy skills, a composite literacy score, which is a combined score for the three subtests. If needed, scores from subtests may be reviewed separately for more specific analysis. Subtests have their own score conversion tables.

The Basic Reading subtest contains a series of pictures and words in print. In order to assess decoding and reading ability, the participant either points to the "correct" word in initial test items or orally responds to the words on subsequent items.

The Spelling subtest consists of dictated sounds and words that allow measurement of spelling ability. The participant responds in writing.

The Reading Comprehension subtest relies upon oral questioning and response to printed passages. Some of these passages are accompanied by pictures. All are one or more sentences in length. Questioning endeavors to assess the ability to recognize stated (specific) detail and/or make inferences based upon passage content.

Raw scores, standard scores, percentile ranks, stanines, and age-equivalent data are all available by subtest.

DEVELOPMENT. Development of the WORD focused on the attainment of three distinct goals: the creation of a test that would reflect current thinking in literacy and deals with word meaning in isolation and in context; the creation of a reading test that linked data with WISC-III (U.K.); and development of an instrument that is adaptable to a broad spectrum of literacy concerns across a number of age levels.

For each subtest, selections of words were predicated on previous scholarship at the highest level. The research used for development of test items includes work done by noted practitioners including Dale and Chall (1948), and Kincaid and Fishburne (1977).

Field testing occurred in 1989 with an initial United States sampling over 300 children aged 5 through 16. Total sampling was based on the responses of over 2,200 children fairly well distributed over gender, ethnic, and minority identities.

Conventional and item-response theory were utilized in the review of specific items. It also appears that a dedicated and productive review of item bias was conducted. The authors state that "flawed, potentially biased and psychometrically inferior items were deleted or, ... rewritten" (manual, p. 40). It appears that this review resulted in the reduction of most, if not all, items that could be considered troublesome in this regard.

A full United States standardization was also well conducted as it considered census data, private and public schooling, and an exceptional student population in its sampling techniques. Diligence is evident in assembling a sample that is truly representative. While much of this work was conducted in the U.S., a U.K. "project" was completed that was utilized as a foundation for WORD (U.K.). Grammatical and spelling differences in the languages of the two countries were addressed in the WORD and some items (printed words, passages, and illustrations) that may have caused confusion were rewritten or eliminated. For example, in one illustration a cricket bat was used in place of a baseball bat.

TECHNICAL. The technical data underpinning the WORD are impressive. They reflect vigorous attempts to address issues of accuracy and the resultant interpretations of scores. Data presented in table form in the test manual are clear and complete. Internal consistency, interscorer reliability, and test/retest stability estimates show more than acceptable levels of accuracy and attention to precise detail.

Content validity is strong. Correlations with other Wechsler achievement scales range from .30 to .70. Tests correlated with the WORD include The Basic Achievement Skills Individual Screener (1988), the Kaufman Test of Educational Achievement (Kaufman & Kaufman, 1985), the Wide Range Achievement Test—Revised (Wilkinson, 1993), and the Differential Ability Scales (Elliott, 1990; U.S. version of the British Ability Scales; Elliott, Murray, & Pearson, 1983).

In the discussion of literacy and overall intelligence a review of special populations, including the gifted, those with severe learning difficulties and/or hearing impairment, and hyperactive children, was conducted. Means and standard deviations are presented in the testing manual.

With reference to reliability, reliability coefficients at age Levels 6 through 16 average (across age groups) .95 for Basic Reading, .92 for Spelling, and .91 for Reading Comprehension. Test-retest stability coefficients are also significant as

they average .94 for Basic Reading and Spelling (administration interval = 12 to 52 days with a median interval of 17 days). The Reading Comprehension coefficients are .85. Though less precise, scores on reading comprehension subtests sometimes fall victim to nuances in inferential comprehension, issues of cultural differences, and interscorer discrepancies, despite the authors' attempts to remove bias. The .85, however, remains positively significant.

Finally, a review of interscorer reliability for the "objective" subtests of Spelling and Basic Reading are obviously free from variance. When analysis of scores from different raters for the Reading Comprehension subtest were presented, the correlation between score pairs was a robust .98. In the procedure used to obtain this, 50 completed papers, randomly selected, were independently scored by four readers. Statistical data presented support the construct validity, consistency, and reliability of the scores from the WORD.

COMMENTARY. The WORD is an instrument that reflects recent literacy theory, fosters linkage with more comprehensive tests of intelligence, and provides data extremely useful in determining decoding and encoding ability of children across a range of 10 years of development. The testing package includes a manual that is comprehensive as it outlines the context of the assessment including limitations, the use of scores, and specific testing considerations. The quality evidenced in the manual is also witnessed in the testing materials. For example, the WORD record form includes a section for reporting behavioral observations and creating an ability-achievement discrepancy analysis using data from the Wechsler FSIQs. Testing time ranges from 14 to 20 minutes depending on age.

It should be noted that results of WORD testing are not complete in and of themselves (i.e., they must be interpreted in the light of a participant's total history and results from more comprehensive instruments). Although they do give a precise analysis of literacy development, it may be possible for the interpretative usefulness of the instrument to be skewed by results from other present and to-be-developed intelligence tests. Although the authors correlate the instrument to other broad-based measures of intelligence, with what appears to be a dependence on other Wechsler scales, they cannot possibly account for linkages for all such measures. This is not to be considered a flaw in this particular assessment but is a condition that nonetheless exists, and should be considered in revisions of this instrument and by practitioners in their use of the results derived from the WORD.

Data for special populations need to be reviewed. This reviewer concurs with the authors' acknowledgement that the sample of students in these special populations was both small and not randomly stratified and, therefore, needs to be reviewed in the future.

SUMMARY. The Wechsler Objective Reading Dimensions (WORD) is a well-developed measure of several critical aspects of reading. The authors are to be commended for their thoroughness in developing, refining, and assembling the instrument. The test is easy to administer and interpret. Meaningful analysis of a student's encoding and decoding proficiencies can be gained in a short amount of time.

REVIEWER'S REFERENCES

Dale, E., & Chall, J. S. (1948). A formula for predicting readability. *Educational Research Bulletin, 27,* 11–20, 37–54.
Elliott, C. D. (1990). *Differential Ability Scales: Administration and scoring manual.* San Antonio, TX: The Psychological Corporation.
Elliott, C. D., Murray, D. J., & Pearson, L. S. (1983). The British Ability Scales. Windsor, Berks: NFER-Nelson.
Kaufman, A. S., & Kaufman, N. L. (1985). The Kaufman Test of Educational Achievement. Circle Pines, MN: AGS Publishing.
Kincaid, J. P., & Fishburne, R. P. (1977). Readability formulas for military training materials. *Human Factors Society Bulletin, 20*(7), 10–12.
The Psychological Corporation. (1988). Basic Achievement Skills Individual Screener. San Antonio, TX: The author.
Wechsler, D. (1991). Wechsler Intelligence Scale for Children-Third Edition. San Antonio, TX: The Psychological Corporation.
Wilkinson, G. S. (1993). The Wide Range Achievement Test–Third Edition. Wilmington, DE: Wide Range.

[267]

Wechsler Preschool and Primary Scale of Intelligence—Third Edition.

Purpose: Developed "for assessing the intelligence of children."

Publication Dates: 1949–2002.

Acronym: WPPSI-III.

Administration: Individual.

Price Data, 2002: $685 per complete box kit including all necessary stimulus and manipulative materials, examiner manual (2002, 267 pages), technical manual (2002, 228 pages), 25 record forms for ages 2-6 to 7-3, 25 record forms for ages 2-6 to 3-11, and 25 response booklets; $735 per complete kit including materials listed above (specify attaché or soft-sided case); $115 per complete manual including both examiner and technical manuals; $85 per examiner manual; $45 per technical manual; $80 per stimulus booklet (specify 1 or 2); $50 per 25 response booklets; $190 per

100 response booklets; $81 per 25 record forms; $307 per 100 record forms.

Author: David Wechsler.

Publisher: PsychCorp, A brand of Harcourt Assessment, Inc.

  a) 2:6–3:11 AGE BAND.

  Population: Ages 2-6 to 3-11.

  Scores, 7 to 9: Verbal (Receptive Vocabulary, Information, Picture Naming [supplemental], Total), Performance (Block Design, Object Assembly, Total), Global Language Composite [supplemental], Total.

  Time: (30–45) minutes.

  b) 4:0–7:3 AGE BAND.

  Population: Ages 4-0 to 7-3.

  Scores, 10 to 19: Verbal (Information, Vocabulary, Word Reasoning, Comprehension [supplemental], Similarities [supplemental], Receptive Vocabulary [optional], Picture Naming [optional], Total), Performance (Block Design, Matrix Reasoning, Picture Concepts, Picture Completion [supplemental], Object Assembly [supplemental], Total), Global Language Composite [optional], Total.

Cross References: See T5:2864 (146 references) and T4:2941 (38 references); for reviews by Bruce A. Bracken and Jeffery P. Braden of an earlier edition, see 11:466 (118 references); for a review by B. J. Freeman, see 9:1356 (33 references); see also T3:2608 (280 references), 8:234 (84 references), and T2:538 (30 references); for reviews by Dorothy H. Eichorn and A. B. Silverstein, and excerpted reviews by C. H. Ammons and by O. A. Oldridge and E. E. Allison, see 7:434 (56 reference).

Review of the Wechsler Preschool and Primary Scale of Intelligence—Third Edition by RONALD A. MADLE, School Psychologist, Shikellamy School District, Sunbury, PA, and Adjunct Associate Professor of School Psychology, The Pennsylvania State University, University Park, PA:

DESCRIPTION. The Wechsler Preschool and Primary Scale of Intelligence-Third Edition (WPPSI-III) is designed to measure intelligence in children between the ages of 2 years 6 months and 7 years 3 months. The test kit comes with two manuals, two stimulus books, manipulatives, a scoring template, and an initial supply of test booklets.

The WPPSI-III is a considerably different test than its predecessor, mostly due to changes in the subtests used. In particular, there is a reduced reliance on visual-spatial tasks with an increase in tasks that measure fluid reasoning. As with earlier versions, the child's general intellectual functioning is represented using a Full Scale IQ (FSIQ) with a mean of 100 and standard deviation of 15. The same metric is employed for all composites, and the subtests retain the familiar Wechsler mean of 10 and standard deviation of 3. The FSIQ continues to be derived from a combination of verbal items and items that involve reduced verbal content. These items form the two secondary composites, the Verbal IQ (VIQ) and the Performance IQ (PIQ), respectively. In a change from earlier versions, however, the WPPSI-III now includes additional tasks that can be used to obtain a General Language Composite (GLC) and, at older ages, a Processing Speed Quotient (PSQ).

The WPPSI-III now is a two-level test that uses different subtests for two age ranges. It also has research-based starting and stopping points. These both have shortened the administration time considerably. At ages 2-6 through 3-11 the FSIQ, VIQ, and PIQ can be obtained in 30 to 45 minutes using four core subtests. Testing for ages 4-0 to 7-3 involves seven core subtests and takes about 40 to 60 minutes. In addition to the core subtests, which are used to obtain the FSIQ, VIQ, and PIQ, the WPPSI-III now contains supplemental and optional subtests. Supplemental subtests are administered to obtain the PSQ or, for younger children, the GLC. Supplemental subtests can be used diagnostically, substituted for spoiled core subtests, or used as alternatives when core subtests may be adversely affected by a child's associated disabilities, such as poor motor skills. A maximum of only one substitution on the Verbal scale and one on the Performance scale is allowable. In addition, for older children two optional subtests are used to get the GLC. These cannot be substituted for any other subtests.

All administration instructions and scoring criteria are contained in the self-standing administration and scoring manual, which is well designed with clear instructions for administering and scoring the test. All materials are durable, colorful, and should be useful in holding a child's attention.

The various derived scores—standard scores, percentile ranks, confidence intervals, and age equivalents—are presented in the technical and interpretive manual, as are the recommended descriptive classifications. Age equivalents are provided with the now obligatory stipulation that their use is not recommended. This manual also presents a top-down interpretive procedure that emphasizes the FSIQ followed by description and interpretation, when appropriate, of the differences between the remaining composites. Procedures are then presented for analysis of variation both between and within subtests to further clarify a child's strengths and weaknesses when appropriate. There are a number of interpretive tables that show when such variation is common and when it should be interpreted as other than normal variation. Additionally, information is provided on using the GLC to determine the possible impact of language on a child's obtained intelligence scores. Finally, procedures and tables for completing ability-achievement discrepancy analysis with the Wechsler Individual Achievement Test—Second Edition (WIAT-II; The Psychological Corporation, 2001) are presented, using both simple difference and predicted achievement methods.

DEVELOPMENT. The manual presents a number of development goals for the WPPSI-III. A primary one was to bring it into greater alignment with contemporary research and theory on cognitive abilities, particularly providing for the assessment of more specific cognitive abilities. The two major changes in this area were to add a PSQ for older preschoolers and to provide better assessment of fluid reasoning, which has been conspicuously limited in the Wechsler scales until recently. This latter change was accomplished by adding the Picture Concepts, Matrix Reasoning, and Word Reasoning subtests to the scale. Second, a number of changes were planned to make it more clinically useful, such as lowering the age range, linking it to the WIAT-II, improving psychometric properties, updating norms, extending ceilings and floors, examining item bias, and providing enhanced information on reliability, validity, and differences between common diagnostic groups.

Another area addressed was updating the test to make it more interesting and user friendly. These changes included reorganizing the manual and record form; simplifying administration procedures; reducing testing time; and providing updated, enlarged, and colorized stimulus materials.

Finally, particular attention was paid to prior criticisms of the Wechsler Preschool and Primary Scale of Intelligence—Revised (WPPSI-R; Wechsler, 1989) while developing this edition. Instructions for the child were simplified and numerous teaching items, queries, and prompts were added. In fact, with few exceptions, prompts to ensure the child's understanding and task orientation are almost unlimited. Additionally, changes were made to accommodate the greater limitations of young children's vocabulary and motor skills. More emphasis was placed on meaning rather than verbatim content of verbal responses and less emphasis was placed on well-developed expressive language, motor precision, and response speed.

TECHNICAL.

Standardization. The WPPSI-III standardization sample of 1,700 children is divided into nine age groups. There are 200 children included at each 6-month interval between ages 2-6 and 5-11, with 200 children in the group of 6-year-olds. For ages 7-0 to 7-3 there are a total of 100 children. For each age group the children are equally split between boys and girls.

The normative sample was planned to be comparable to the 2000 U.S. Census across a number of key variables, including age, sex, race/ethnicity, parental education, and geographic region. Examination of the sample demographics shows that it is well stratified on race/ethnicity and parental education level. Geographic region, on the other hand, shows a small but noticeable oversampling of the south region and undersampling of the west and northeast regions.

Reliability. As with earlier versions, the WPPSI-III's split-half reliability estimates are acceptable at the subtest level across ages (.83 to .95), with only a few subtests being less than .80 at specific ages. The average Full Scale internal consistency coefficient of .96 is excellent, with all age groups having an internal consistency of .95 or higher.

The three remaining composites show internal consistency coefficients between .89 and .95 across ages, with only Processing Speed being less than .90. Interscorer agreement is high. Even the three more subjectively scored subtests are .97 or higher at the total score level. Test-retest stability ranged from .86 to .92 over an average interval of 26 days. The FSIQ increased by an average of 5.2 points over that time interval.

Validity. WPPSI-III validity information is quite extensive for a new test. In fact, the manual provides 59 pages of validity studies. The initial line of evidence examined is the WPPSI-III's internal structure. As expected, scales tended to correlate more highly with other subtests in the

same composite than with those from other composites, with a few exceptions. However, Picture Completion and Picture Concepts did load across Verbal and Performance tasks. Based on earlier Wechsler scales the developers anticipated that the Verbal-Performance dichotomy would be found for both age groups, whereas Processing Speed would emerge as a third factor for the older age group. Exploratory factor analysis of the core subtests showed strong support for this theoretical structure at all ages until age 6, where Picture Concepts switched loading from the Performance to the Verbal scale. When all subtests were included, more cross loadings were noted at the 4-year-old level, where some Performance subtests cross loaded on Processing Speed. These were interpreted as changes in the cognitive demands of the tasks at these levels. Subsequent confirmatory factor analysis showed good model fit for the a priori structures proposed at both age groups.

Validity evidence is also presented involving the relationship with other measures. For all studies the instruments were administered in a counterbalanced order with an average of 2 to 4 weeks separation. When the Wechsler Preschool and Primary Scale of Intelligence—Revised (WPPSI-R) and WPPSI-III were administered to 176 children the results supported the view that the scales measure similar constructs. Corrected correlations were .86, .70, and .85 for Verbal, Performance, and FSIQs respectively. The lower correlation for the Performance scale was thought to be from the WPPSI-III's increased emphasis on fluid ability over greater preponderance of visual-spatial tasks on the WPPSI-R.

Because the WPPSI-III overlaps with the Wechsler Intelligence Scale for Children—Third Edition (WISC-III; Wechsler, 1991) at older ages and the Bayley Scales of Infant Development—Second Edition (BSID-II; Bayley, 1993) at younger ones, studies also were done with these two scales. For the WISC-III with 96 primary-age children, the FSIQ was 4.9 points higher than the WPPSI-III FSIQ, with a correlation of .89. This again supported the measurement of similar constructs. At the lower end of the age range a correlation of .80 was found between the FSIQ and the BSID-II Mental Scale for 84 children 2 and 3 years of age. Not surprisingly, the BSID-II Motor Scale showed a lower correlation (.47).

Yet another frequently used preschool scale, the Differential Ability Scales (Elliot, 1990), showed an overall correlation of .87 at the Full Scale level when given to 164 children. The strongest correlations were between composites measuring similar constructs.

Another 40 children were administered the Children's Memory scale (CMS; Cohen, 1997), which showed low to moderate correlations with the WPPSI-III scores. The most notable correlation (.79) was between FSIQ and the CMS's Attention-Concentration Index.

When the WIAT-II was administered to 208 children to develop tables for determining significant differences and base rates, the expected moderate correlations were obtained. For example, the FSIQ correlated .66, .77, .62, and .67 with Reading, Mathematics, Written Language, and Oral Language, respectively.

Finally, a number of special group studies were conducted to provide additional support for the WPPSI-III's validity. Several of these comparisons were with groups that allow for clear-cut predictions because intelligence is a major element in their definition. For example, intellectually gifted children had an average FSIQ of 126.2, mildly mentally retarded children scored 62.1, and moderately retarded children averaged 53.1. Children with identified developmental delays (FSIQ = 81.8) and developmental risk factors (85.7) showed the expected mild delays in WPPSI-III scores. Other groups showed differences in scale patterns as would be predicted by the nature of their conditions. Autistic children evidenced significantly lower VIQs (70.6) than PIQs (88.2), as did children with limited English proficiency (80.2 versus 95.0). Additional supporting studies involved children with language impairments, motor impairments, and attention-deficit/hyperactivity disorder.

COMMENTARY AND SUMMARY. The WPPSI-R was one of the more psychometrically sound intelligence tests available for young children. This tradition has been continued and even improved upon in the WPPSI-III. The test continues to have excellent norms, reliability estimates, and validity evidence. The test norms provide ample ceilings and floors at all ages. The ceilings for all composites across ages are 150 or slightly higher. Floors for the FSIQs are at least an FSIQ of 41. These clearly meet the 3–4 standard deviations recommended by Bracken and Walker

(1997). The remaining composites also have floors and ceilings of at least three standard deviations. Equally important, however, are the item gradients that provide for smooth changes in standard scores that occur throughout the scale. Consistent with Bracken and Walker's (1997) recommendation there are from 3.0 to 5.4 raw score points per standard deviation at each age group.

The earlier versions of the WPPSI-III, with the exception of a few subtests, were primarily downward extensions of the WISC. This created some problematic aspects because preschool children are not merely smaller school-aged children. Reviews of an earlier version noted a number of problems (e.g., long administration time, complex instructions) that compromised its practicality with young children. These have been addressed systematically and effectively in the WPPSI-III's development. The WPPSI-III has commendably improved on virtually every weakness previously noted with the WPPSI-R.

There are two relatively small concerns with the WPPSI-III. One of these is the inclusion of a processing speed subtest in the estimate of intelligence for older children. There is still a lack of consensus that processing speed, although an important ability construct, should be considered an aspect of intelligence. In fact, its inclusion in some cases may artificially lower the intellectual estimate. The second minor criticism is the use of copy-protected gray paper for test booklets. Some individuals—examiners as well as children—may find that the lack of contrast creates problems when using a pencil to work on the page.

REVIEWER'S REFERENCES

Bayley, N. (1993). Bayley Scales of Infant Development—Second Edition. San Antonio, TX: The Psychological Corporation.

Bracken, B. A., & Walker, K. C. (1997). The utility of intelligence tests with preschool children. In D. P. Flanagan, J. L. Genshaft, & P. L. Harrison (Eds.), *Contemporary intellectual assessment: Theories, tests, and issues* (pp. 484–502). New York: Guilford.

Cohen, M. (1997). Children's Memory Scale. San Antonio, TX: The Psychological Corporation.

Elliot, C. D. (1990). Differential Ability Scales. San Antonio, TX: The Psychological Corporation.

The Psychological Corporation. (2001). Wechsler Individual Achievement Test—Second Edition. San Antonio, TX: The Psychological Corporation.

Wechsler, D. (1989). Wechsler Preschool and Primary Scale of Intelligence—Revised. San Antonio, TX: The Psychological Corporation.

Wechsler, D. (1991). Wechsler Intelligence Scale for Children—Third Edition. San Antonio, TX: The Psychological Corporation.

Review of the Wechsler Preschool and Primary Scale of Intelligence—Third Edition by MERILEE McCURDY, Assistant Professor of Educational Psychology, and LYNAE A. JOHNSEN, Graduate Student, University of Nebraska-Lincoln, Lincoln, NE:

DESCRIPTION. The Wechsler Preschool and Primary Scale of Intelligence—Third Edition (WPPSI-III) is an individually administered instrument for measuring the general intellectual functioning of children aged 2 years 6 months through 7 years 3 months (2:6–7:3). The WPPSI-III consists of composite scores that reflect intellectual functioning in specified cognitive domains (e.g., Verbal Intelligence Quotient and Performance Intelligence Quotient), as well as a composite score that represents a child's overall intellectual ability (i.e., Full Scale Intelligence Quotient). In addition, this revision has included composite scores for a Processing Speed Quotient and a General Language Composite. Of the 14 subtests included in the WPPSI-III, 7 are new subtests and the remaining 7 subtests have new items. This is a distinct revision from the WPPSI-III's predecessor, the Wechsler Preschool and Primary Scale of Intelligence—Revised (WPPSI-R; Wechsler, 1989), which was composed of 12 subtests divided into six Performance and six Verbal scales.

The manual indicates that administration of the core subtests requires approximately 30 to 50 minutes depending on the child's age. Administration of additional subtests will require increased administration time. When all subtests are administered, 95% of the standardization sample, ages 2:6 to 3:11, completed the assessment in 57 minutes. In the 4:0 to 7:30 age group, 95% of the standardization sample completed all subtests in 106 minutes.

Scoring of the WPPSI-III is generally an objective task, requiring minimal interpretation of scoring criteria for many of the subtests; however, increased professional judgment is necessary for the Vocabulary, Comprehension, and Similarities subtests where scoring requires awarding points based on the content of the child's response. Multipoint (2, 1, or 0) items are assigned a score based on the match in quality of the child's expression to sample responses. Borderline responses that require additional information from the examinee in order to make scoring decisions may present the most difficulty for the examiner. Thus, further query may be necessary for sound judgment in scoring.

The record form is provided to aid in the administration and scoring of the test. The form prompts the use of standardized procedural guidelines, such as starting points, discontinue rules, and time limits. The Summary Page of the record form facilitates the recording of raw scores and scaled scores for subtests, sums of scaled scores, and composite scores. In addition, profiles of subtest and composite scores can be plotted for a visual display of the child's performance. Also provided for use at the examiner's discretion are: (a) the Discrepancy Analysis Page of the record form, which provides space for making comparisons between composite and subtest scores, and strengths and weaknesses, and (b) the observation page for recording important information about the child's behavior during the test session.

DEVELOPMENT. The purpose of the revision of the WPPSI-R was to reflect recent advances in research as well as to take into account practical considerations and aesthetically appealing materials.

Specific to the WPPSI-III were five primary revision goals set forth during the test development process to address the shortcomings of previous test editions. The revision goals included the following: (a) update theoretical foundations, (b) increase developmental appropriateness, (c) enhance clinical utility, (d) improve psychometric properties, and (e) increase user-friendliness. These goals were developed based in part on an extensive review of literature from such areas as intelligence theory, cognitive development, intellectual assessment, and cognitive neuroscience.

As a means of updating the theoretical foundation, additional composite scores were incorporated into the test structure. More specifically, factor-based composite scores were included to simplify interpretation of findings and lend meaningful descriptions of cognitive ability. In addition, enhancing the measure of fluid reasoning and incorporating measures of processing speed were considerations undertaken to update theoretical foundations of the WPPSI-III.

Given the complex changes in cognitive development during early childhood, accounting for the developmental appropriateness of the test for children from ages 2:6 to 7:3 was a major goal in the revision of the WPPSI-R. The WPPSI-III age range was divided into two age bands: 2 years 6 months to 3 years 11 months and 4 years to 7 years 3 months based on practical need and empirical research related to early childhood development. The content among the two batteries reflects age-appropriate developmental differences in areas such as language development and reasoning processes. Moreover, the revised WPPSI-III provides the examiner with simplified instructions, more teaching items, and queries or prompts. In addition, the scoring criteria have been revised to account for the limited vocabulary of young children, and the emphasis of speed on a child's performance has been reduced.

Furthermore, the clinical utility of the WPPSI-III was enhanced through the delineation of several objectives in test development. In order to achieve this goal, special group studies were conducted during the scale's standardization in an effort to provide clinical validity evidence. In addition, the WPPSI-III was statistically linked to popular measures of achievement to provide the user with a comprehensive picture of the child's cognitive ability and the age range has been extended to reach younger ages as early in development as 2 years 6 months.

TECHNICAL.

Standardization. The normative sample for the WPPSI-III consisted of 1,700 children representative of selected demographic variables within the U.S. population of children aged 2:6–7:3. Stratification was based on the analysis of data gathered in 2000 by the U.S. Bureau of the Census along the variables of age, sex, race, parent education level, and geographic region. There were nine age groups that composed the standardization sample for the WPPSI-III, including 100 participants in the oldest age group and 200 children in each of the eight younger age groups. An equal number of male and female children comprised each age group. Similarly, the standardization sample consisted of an equal distribution of race/ethnicity groups among each age group of the U.S. population. Sampling of parent education level was stratified into levels according to years of schooling. Geographic regions included the Northeast, South, Midwest, and West. Efforts were made to sample a proportionate number of children from each area relative to the population within each geographic region.

Reliability. The split-half method was used to calculate internal consistency so the WPPSI-III reliability could be compared directly to WPPSI-R reliability. Internal consistency reliability coefficients ranged from .89 to .96 for the WPPSI-III composite scales in the 2:6-3:11 age group, whereas the 4:0-7:3 age group reliability coefficients ranged from .86 to .97. The overall reliability coefficients for the subtests ranged from .83 to .95, exhibiting

a dramatic improvement from the WPPSI-R to the WPPSI-III. The standard error of measurement (*SEM*) ranged from .60 to 1.50 for the subscales and 2.60 to 3.35 for the Full Scale across the age groups.

Test-retest reliability was assessed on 157 children from each of the nine age groups over a 14- to 50-day period to examine the stability of the test scores. By using Pearson's product-moment correlation coefficient, the stability coefficients fell in a range from .74 to .92 for subtests in the 2:6 to 3:11 age band and .69 to .93 for subtests in the 4:0 to 5:5 age band. Test-retest corrected reliability estimates for WPPSI-III composite scores ranged from .84 to .92 for the 2:6 to 3:11 age group and .87 to .93 for the 4:0 to 5:5 age group.

Interrater reliability for the WPPSI-III was based on ratings by two independent scorers responsible for double-scoring all protocols. The correlations ranged from .98 to .99 given that the majority of subtests are relatively simple and straightforward in their scoring criteria. However, Vocabulary, Similarities, and Comprehension subtests, which require more professional judgment in scoring, were evaluated under special studies to calculate interrater reliability. Reliability estimates at the item level were .92 for Vocabulary, .90 for Similarities, and .95 for Comprehension. Interrater reliability coefficients for the total subtest scores were .97 for Vocabulary, .99 for Similarities, and .97 for Comprehension.

In summary, the average reliability coefficients of the WPPSI-III subtests range from .83 to .95 for the overall standardization sample, which demonstrates good or excellent stability over time for all age bands. Furthermore, the reliability estimates indicate that subtests requiring more judgment can be scored reliably by independent raters.

Validity. Intercorrelation studies were conducted to provide information on the correlational patterns of relationships between subtests as a method of analyzing construct validity, convergent validity, and discriminant validity. It was found that all intersubtest correlations were significant, which supported the author's a priori hypothesis that all subtests were a measure of *g* or general intelligence. In addition, the data were supportive of the convergent and discriminant validity of the WPPSI-III.

The WPPSI-III is proposed to measure Verbal Comprehension and Perceptual Organization for ages 2:6 to 3:11 and to measure Verbal Comprehension, Perceptual Organization, and

Processing Speed for ages 4:0 to 7:3. Based on factor analysis, this pattern is very clear for the younger ages. However, when examining the older age bands, the pattern is less clear. For example, when looking at the factor loadings for the core and supplemental subtests at different age bands, the subtests of Matrix Reasoning and Picture Concepts do not load heavily on the Performance factor for the 4:0 to 4:11 age band. Although the authors explain many of these discrepancies, questions do exist about the three-factor theory at some age levels.

Validity was also examined by correlational studies, which examined the relationship of the WPPSI-III with other standardized test measures. The WPPSI-III was correlated with the WPPSI-R, WISC-III, BSID-II (Bayley Scales of Infant Development-II), DAS (Differential Ability Scales), WIAT-II (Wechsler Individual Achievement Test-II) and CMS (Children's Memory Scale). Correlations of composite scores ranged from .70 to .86 with the WPPSI-R (n = 176), from .69 to .89 for the WISC-III (n = 96), from .32 to .80 for the BSID-II (n = 84), from .38 to .87 (n = 164) for the DAS, and .31 to 78 on the WIAT-II (n = 208). The moderate correlational results of the composite scores across tests support evidence of the validity of the WPPSI-III and replicate data found in earlier research.

Finally, validity was examined by administering the WPPSI-III to several specific groups of children, such as children identified as gifted, children with mild or moderate mental retardation, developmental delays, developmental risk factors, autism, expressive and receptive language disorders, limited English proficiency, and ADHD. In general, for each group, the mean scores of all composites followed the pattern predicted of each group.

COMMENTARY. Materials and content that were in need of further refinement on the WPPSI-R were improved for a more complete and precise measure of intelligence. In addition, the developers of the WPPSI-III made a concerted effort to incorporate developmental research into the revision process, as evidenced by the addition of stratified age groups that serve to guide the structure and interpretation of test items and responses. Further, the test materials have been improved to increase their appeal to young children. The manipulables are colorful and the stimulus booklets include large pictures that can be easily viewed by children. In addition, the puzzle pieces required of the Object Assembly subtest should be easily handled by children.

Based on the information in the technical and interpretive manual, the psychometric components of the WPPSI-III are sound. Reliability evidence is moderate to strong for the subtests and composite scores. There is some question regarding the organization of the three factors for some age groups; however, many of these inconsistencies are rationally explained. As a caution, the WPPSI-III manual examines the scores of several specific groups of children to examine the "clinical utility" of the measure. It should be stated, and the authors do state, that a single instrument should not be used to make clinical decisions and that diagnostic decisions reliant on WPPSI-III assessment results are not appropriate.

SUMMARY. Overall, the revision to the WPPSI-R has been positive. The authors stated their main revision goals to be (a) update theoretical foundations, (b) increase developmental appropriateness, (c) enhance clinical utility, (d) improve psychometric properties, and (e) increase user-friendliness. In all aspects, improvements have been made.

REVIEWERS' REFERENCE

Wechsler, D. (1989). *Wechsler Preschool and Primary Scale of Intelligence—Revised manual.* San Antonio, TX: The Psychological Corporation.

[268]
Wechsler Test of Adult Reading.

Purpose: Developed as an assessment tool for estimating premorbid (pre-injury) intellectual functioning.
Population: Ages 16–89.
Publication Date: 2001.
Acronym: WTAR.
Scores: Total score only.
Administration: Individual.
Price Data, 2003: $99 per complete kit including manual (291 pages), 25 record forms, word card, and pronunciation audiotape; $69 per manual; $36 per 25 record forms.
Time: [5–10] minutes.
Comments: Co-normed with the Wechsler Adult Intelligence Scale—Third Edition (T6:2691) and the Wechsler Memory Scale—Third Edition (T6:2695).
Author: The Psychological Corporation.
Publisher: PsychCorp, A brand of Harcourt Assessment, Inc.

Review of the Wechsler Test of Adult Reading by NORA M. THOMPSON, Private Practice, Mountlake Terrace, WA:

DESCRIPTION. The Wechsler Test of Adult Reading (WTAR) is an assessment tool for estimating premorbid cognitive functioning in adults ages 16 to 89 years. The test can be used to generate predicted scores for the Wechsler Adult Intelligence Scale-III (WAIS-III) IQ and Index Scores as well as three of the Wechsler Memory Scale-III (WMS-III) Index Scores. The WTAR consists of a manual, record forms, word card, and pronunciation audiotape. The test can be administered by a trained and supervised technician or research assistant, although interpretation requires graduate or professional level training in assessment. While looking at the word card, the patient is asked to pronounce each word aloud until 12 consecutive errors are reached. The examiner is encouraged to review the pronunciation audiotape prior to assessment to familiarize themselves with the common and acceptable alternative pronunciations of the WTAR words. The WTAR is then hand-scored and the raw score converted to a standard score based on age with separate normative data for U.S. and U.K. samples. The predicted score is obtained from normative tables stratified by age, education level, gender, and race/ethnicity. The actual and predicted WTAR scores are compared for indication of significant difference. The user may choose whether to derive estimates of premorbid intellectual functioning from demographic markers alone, the WTAR score alone, or a combination of demographic markers and the WTAR score. The latter is recommended for most purposes, although it is generally available only for adults ages 17 and above. Using separate normative data for U.S. and U.K. samples, comparisons can be made between actual and predicted IQ and memory scores from the Wechsler tests third editions. The statistical significance of the actual predicted differences and their cumulative representation in the normative samples also can be determined in order to consider the probability of a clinically significant difference.

DEVELOPMENT. The WTAR was developed based on the methodology first used in the National Adult Reading Test (NART; Nelson, 1982) and its American counterpart (NAART; Blair & Spreen, 1989). The WTAR uses a reading recognition paradigm requiring pronunciation of words with irregular phoneme-grapheme correspondence. This approach emphasizes previously acquired reading abilities and minimizes require-ments for current phonetic decoding. Reading recognition has been shown to be relatively stable with aging and even in individuals with brain injury/disease, unless cognitive impairment is severe. The WTAR was conormed with the WAIS-III and WMS-III and thorough information is provided about the characteristics of the normative sample. There is scant information on the development of the word list and no specific studies are listed in spite of the manual claiming "multiple revisions based on clinical application, research studies, and professional reviews" (p. 23). The description of the statistical techniques used to generate the predicted scores and compare actual to predicted scores will likely satisfy most clinical users, as well as frustrate those who follow the large literature on the finer statistical aspects of estimating premorbid intelligence.

TECHNICAL.

Standardization. The normative sample is a strength of the WTAR and the manual presents information on the U.S. and U.K. sample characteristics. For the U.S. sample of 1,134 individuals, stratification was based matched to the 1999 U.S. Census reflecting age (13 age groups), sex, race/ethnicity, years of education, and geographic region. The U.K. sample of 331 participants was divided into four age bands (16–24, 25–44, 45–64, and 65–80 years) and stratified by age, sex, and into six educational levels. In the U.S. sample there are few Hispanic females ages 70 to 79. In general, middle-aged and old Hispanic adults were almost exclusively from the southern U.S.

Reliability. The manual presents data showing high internal consistency for the WTAR across age groups for both the U.S. and U.K. standardization samples. Test-retest reliability was investigated in a separate study of 319 U.S. participants tested an average of 35 days apart (2 to 12 weeks). Stability correlations (test-retest correlation coefficients corrected for sample variability) ranged from .92 to .94. There was no study of test-retest reliability available with a U.K. sample.

Validity. The manual addresses the content, construct, and concurrent predictive validity of the WTAR. The test correlates highly with the American NART (.90) and moderately high with other reading recognition tests (.73 to .78). The manual does not describe why the WTAR group mean score was 11 standard score points lower than the American NART. Correlations between the

WTAR and WAIS-III verbal intelligence are moderately high (.66 to .80) and in a moderate range with nonverbal intelligence (.45 to .66). Correlations between the WTAR and WMS-III scores were somewhat lower (.47 to .51) and particularly low in the 16- to 17-year age group (.32 to .37). A section on studies involving clinical groups is presented. Those groups included four types of dementia, as well as traumatic brain injury, chronic alcohol abuse, schizophrenia, depression, attention deficit disorder, learning disability reading, and learning disability math. Sample sizes, ages, and gender varied considerably and in directions predictable due to the etiologic characteristics of the clinical groups studied (e.g., dementia groups higher mean age than traumatic brain injury). The findings revealed WTAR scores in the average range in most groups with the exception of the more advanced dementia and learning disability reading groups. Finally, the manual reports several discriminant analysis studies exploring the utility of using actual and predicted WAIS-III and WMS-III scores to differentiate among specific clinical groups. Although the purpose of the test is to estimate premorbid intelligence, there were no studies of predictive validity presented in the manual based on records of prior cognitive ability (e.g., academic or military records).

COMMENTARY. The WTAR provides a welcome addition to the range of methods currently available for the estimation of premorbid intelligence and expands the practice to the prediction of additional cognitive and memory functions. The strengths of the WTAR are its large and nationally stratified sample, including separate normative data for U.S. and U.K. populations, as well as its reliance on the previously well-supported finding that reading recognition is less vulnerable to decline with brain injury/disease than many other cognitive abilities. Furthermore, the WTAR test development included concurrent intelligence and memory measurement with tests frequently used in clinical practice, strengthening its reliability and concurrent validity. The manual presents the user with clear instructions on the administration and scoring of the WTAR, along with limitations of its use for individuals ages 16–19 and in the extreme ranges of the IQ distribution. By combining reading recognition and demographic markers, the WTAR allows for improved prediction of premorbid intelligence within clinical groups. Limitations include predictions for ages 16 to 19, older Hispanic females, Hispanics residing outside of the U.S. southern region, and racial/ethnic minorities residing in the U.K.

SUMMARY. The clinical practice of generating estimations of premorbid cognitive functioning in adults with brain injury/disease is complex and should be undertaken only by those with professional and graduate level training in psychological and neuropsychological assessment principles and practice. The utility of using a reading recognition paradigm enhanced by the inclusion of demographic variables to estimate premorbid IQ has a long and well-supported tradition in the field of neuropsychology. The interested reader is referred to *Neuropsychological Assessment* (4th Edition) for an in-depth discussion of methodological issues involved in prediction of premorbid intelligence (Lezak, 2004). The WTAR compares favorably to currently available methods for estimating premorbid intelligence.

REVIEWER'S REFERENCES

Blair, J. R., & Spreen, O. (1989). Predicting premorbid IQ: A revision of the National Adult Reading Test. *The Clinical Neuropsychologist, 3,* 129–136.
Lezak, M. D. (2004). *Neuropsychological assessment* (4th ed.). Oxford: Oxford University Press.
Nelson, H. E. (1982). *National Adult Reading Test (NART): Test manual.* Windsor: NFER-Nelson.

Review of the Wechsler Test of Adult Reading by SANDRA WARD, Professor of Education, The College of William & Mary, Williamsburg, VA:

DESCRIPTION. The Wechsler Test of Adult Reading (WTAR) is a 50-item test designed to assess reading recognition for individuals aged 16–89 years. The authors cite research to indicate that reading recognition is relatively stable in the presence of cognitive declines associated with normal aging and brain insult. The intended use of the WTAR is to estimate premorbid intellectual and memory functioning of adults in this age range. The author emphasizes that the WTAR is not an appropriate instrument for the assessment and diagnosis of reading disabilities.

The WTAR is a standardized instrument in which the examinee is asked to pronounce a list of words that do not follow regular English grapheme-to-phoneme translation. The directions for administration and scoring are straightforward. The WTAR can be administered by individuals who have training and experience with the administration of "Level C" instruments, in addition to familiarity with the Wechsler Adult Intelligence Scale—Third Edition (WAIS-III; T6:2691) and the Wechsler Memory Scale—Third Edition (WMS-III; T6:2695). Although a trained technician can administer and score the WTAR under supervision, it is recommended that only those individuals with appropriate graduate and professional training interpret the results. It is essential that the examiner be familiar with the pronunciation of the item words. An audiotape of the item words is provided to assist the examiner with these pronunciations. It is recommended that the examiner listen to the word tape prior to administering the WTAR. The author cautions the examiner to be aware of alternate pronunciations for several words that are awarded credit. Although these alternate pronunciations are printed on the record form, they are not included on the word tape.

The raw score for the WTAR is converted into a standard score with a mean of 100 and a standard deviation of 15. A demographics-predicted WTAR score based on the examinee's age, race/ethnicity, and education level can be obtained by using tables in the manual. It is then possible to calculate the difference between actual WTAR and demographics-predicted WTAR scores. The results of this discrepancy test can be used as a guide to the validity of the actual WTAR score. Cumulative percentages of the differences also are provided. An analysis of the test-retest WTAR score differences can be completed. These differences can be used to assess changes in an examinee's cognitive functioning over time. Finally, the examiner can use WTAR scores for predicting WAIS-III and WMS-III scores in order to compare actual and predicted WAIS-III and WMS-III scores. Statistically significant differences and cumulative percentages are provided in the manual. All of these analyses can be completed on the record form, which is designed to facilitate this process.

DEVELOPMENT. The WTAR was developed and conormed with the WISC-III and WMS-III in the United States and the United Kingdom. The author states that the development of the WTAR is directly related to the National Adult Reading Test (NART), the American Version of the National Adult Reading Test (AMNART), and the North American Adult Reading Test (NAART). These tests are based on a reading recognition paradigm and share some item content. The authors cite several studies that support reading recognition as relatively stable in the presence of cognitive decline. Item selection

for the WTAR was based on an extensive review of words with irregular grapheme-to-phoneme translation. Pilot studies were conducted to determine the difficulty of potential items and the perception of bias. After a national standardization, items were re-evaluated for their adequacy of psychometric properties. Although the authors describe the procedures for test development in general terms, no specific information is provided about the expert review, pilot studies, or data analysis. This makes it difficult to evaluate the appropriateness of item selection.

TECHNICAL. The WTAR was standardized on a U.S. sample and a U.K. sample. Information describing the norming process is sufficient. All potential participants were medically and psychiatrically screened with a self-report questionnaire. Those individuals who met any of the exclusionary criteria were disqualified from the study. A complete list of these exclusionary criteria is provided in the manual. In the U.S. the WTAR was standardized on a nationally representative stratified sample of 1,134 adolescents and adults from 16-89 years of age. The sample was stratified on age, gender, race/ethnicity, years of education, and geographic region. The sample closely matched the U.S. Census data from 1999 on all demographic variables. The U.K. standardization sample included 331 participants who represented a subset of the WAIS-III U.K. standardization sample and who completed the WTAR. Although demographic data for this sample are provided, there is no indication of the degree to which these data represent the U.K. population.

The internal consistency and test-retest reliability coefficients in the manual are sufficient for the intended purpose of the WTAR in the U.S. Internal consistency coefficients ranged from .90–.97 across age levels for the U.S. sample. In the U.K. sample, internal consistency coefficients were slightly lower ranging from .87–.95. The standard errors of measurement were relatively small for both samples. Test-retest reliability for the WTAR in the U.S. sample was based on 319 individuals across four age groups with a mean test interval of 35 days. The correlations ranged from .90–.94, which supports the temporal stability of the WTAR. No test-retest data are presented for the U.K. sample.

Support for the instrument's content validity is inferred from steps taken in test development described in an earlier section. The test's content validity would be strengthened if the author reported the specific details of the expert review, pilot studies, and bias analyses. Without these data, the test user must rely on the authors' interpretations. Concurrent validity of the WTAR for use in the U.S. is demonstrated through comparisons with other measures of reading recognition, measures of intelligence, and measures of memory. The WTAR demonstrated high positive correlations (.73–.90) with measures of reading recognition. High positive correlations were found between the WTAR and measures of verbal intelligence (.66–.80). Moderate correlations (.45–.66) were evident between the WTAR and measures of visual perceptual abilities, working memory, and memory. These high correlations between the WTAR and measures of intelligence support the WTAR's use in predicting intellectual performance. The WTAR can be considered a moderate predictor of premorbid memory functioning. Although the authors correctly interpret correlations as "low," "moderate," and "high," there is no indication of the statistical significance of these correlations. The test user is left to assume that all correlations are significant.

The results of special groups studies in the U.S. indicated that there were no significant differences in performance on the WTAR between clinical groups and matched control groups for neurological disorders, traumatic brain injury, and neuropsychiatric disorders. These results support the WTAR's resistance to effects of neurological dysfunction with the exception of a group with moderate Alzheimer's dementia who performed lower on the WTAR. Additionally, the variability in the performance of individuals with developmental disorders suggests that the WTAR is not useful in predicting intellectual functioning of individuals with reading or math disorders. Due to the small sample sizes, these special group studies should be replicated. No data for special groups in the U.K. were reported.

Strong evidence is provided for the predictive validity of the WTAR. The WTAR was administered concurrently with the WAIS-III and WMS-III during standardization. Regression equations for predicting current intellectual and memory functioning from WTAR scores were developed. The data indicate that the WTAR is significantly related to the WAIS-III and WMS-III for the U.S. sample. The largest amount of predicted variance occurred for the Verbal IQ, Full Scale IQ, and Verbal Comprehension Index of the WAIS-III. The WTAR is not as strong a predictor of memory. Similar results were found for the U.K. sample. The inclusion of demographic variables improves prediction; however, the actual improvement in predicted variance is relatively small.

COMMENTARY. The WTAR is an instrument designed to estimate premorbid intellectual and memory functioning for individuals aged 16–89 years. Although the development of the WTAR is related to other established tests of reading recognition, specific information on item selection is lacking. The psychometric properties of the WTAR are strong for the U.S. sample; however, data are insufficient in some instances for the U.K. sample. The WTAR is well standardized, but the degree to which the U.K. standardization sample matches the population characteristics is unknown. Reliability coefficients support the intended use of the WTAR for the U.S. and U.K. samples. Test-retest reliability was not established for the U.K. sample. Information on content validity is vague. Evidence for concurrent and predictive validity of the WTAR is strong for both the U.S. and U.K. samples. The conorming of the WTAR with the WAIS-III and WMS-III enhances the linkage between the measures. The common sample allows for the creation of regression estimates and prediction error estimates, which increases the confidence in predictions produced by the WTAR. The authors provide an accurate and thorough summary of issues regarding WTAR use.

SUMMARY. The WTAR is a test of reading recognition that can be used to estimate premorbid intellectual and memory functioning in adults between 16–89 years of age. Administration and scoring of the WTAR is straightforward, and clear instructions are provided for the interpretation of scores. The WTAR was conormed with the WAIS-III and WMS-III. The WTAR yielded significant regression equations for all WAIS-III and WMS-III measures. The psychometric properties of the WTAR support its utility in predicting premorbid intellectual and memory functioning. The authors correctly assert that the WTAR should not be used as a direct measure of intelligence or to diagnose reading disabilities.

[269]

Weidner-Fensch Speech Screening Test.

Purpose: Designed "to be used in screening out children with speech difficulties from those who have normally developed speech."

Population: Grades 1–3.

Publication Date: No date.

Scores: Item scores only.

Administration: Individual.

Forms, 2: A, B.

Price Data, 2001: $4 per specimen set.

Time: (5–10) minutes.

Authors: William E. Weidner and Edwin A. Fensch.

Publisher: Psychometric Affiliates.

Review of the Weidner-Fensch Speech Screening Test by KRIS L. BAACK, Assistant Professor of Speech Pathology, University of Nebraska—Lincoln, Lincoln, NE:

DESCRIPTION. The Weidner-Fensch Speech Screening Test is designed as an instrument that distinguishes students with speech difficulties from those who have normally developed speech. This screening test is designed for students in Grades 1–3 and takes 5–10 minutes to administer, and is published in two forms (Test A and Test B). Each form consists of 33 pictures that contain 11 consonant sounds in the initial, medial, and final positions of words. The consonants are: s, z, th, l, r, j, k, sh, t, f and g.

The test is administered by presenting the object pictures one at a time and asking "What is this?" The examiner records any distortions or omissions with an "x" and phonetically transcribes the substitution in the respective columns. Weidner and Fensch state, "the purpose of this test is not primarily to 'derive a score' but to help a child. Since the latter is the primary purpose, the therapist making best use of the test may not even desire to compute a total score, but will simply detect the sounds on which the child needs training and proceed with that training" (manual, p. 2). Thus, scoring is based on whether a sound is articulated correctly or incorrectly and a norm table is given indicating the number of children who did articulate the word correctly.

DEVELOPMENT. According to the authors, "A good speech screening device should be so constructed that it does not of itself stimulate artificial, exceptional, or self-conscious speech mechanisms" (manual, p. 1). As a result the authors have adopted the "picture-naming" device to ascertain the child's ability to articulate the words correctly. Sounds selected were based on the authors' belief they are the "most often defective in children who have articulatory problems" (manual, p. 1).

All of the pictures used in the instrument, with the exception of nine, were given to 474 children in Grades 1–3, and elicited the word intended. Nine pictures were found to produce several responses causing the authors to make modifications of those pictures until "all object items now have high specific word recall recognition value" (manual, p. 1). All pictures are black drawings on white paper with three pictures per line and nine pictures per page. Each picture is numbered from 1–33. Drawings are unrefined; many are dated and appear disproportionate on the pages. There is also a question of appropriateness for some of the items (e.g., cigarette).

Score sheets include the number of the picture, the question being asked to stimulate the response, the word being elicited, the sound being tested and columns for distortions, substitutions, and omissions. Again, like the layout of the pictures, the score sheets are crowded and difficult to use.

TECHNICAL. For standardization there are two very general lists. One is entitled "Data Per Word On Correct Pronunciation" and lists each word with the number of children who stated the word correctly with $N = 321$. The other is percentile rank of children pronouncing various numbers of names correctly. The authors mention the test was administered to a sample of 1,150 children (496 first grade, 357 second grade, and 297 third grade) to further solidify their belief that all items have high specific word recall recognition value. Reliability and validity evidence is questionably nonexistent.

The population used to select the pictures is defined only by grade. There is no reference to gender or ethnic/cultural groups.

COMMENTARY. A speech screening instrument should be quick and easy to administer with results indicating the need for further assessment and/or treatment or that the student is functioning within a normal range for their age. There are no data or standardization for ages, and what is provided for grade levels is inadequate.

Information provided in the manual is incomplete and vague. The Weidner-Fensch is not based on theoretical constructs nor do the authors provide any rationale based on noted research. In addition, the authors do not provide normative data for any of their decisions. Finally, everything about the instrument is dated; the instrument appears to be from the 1950s in its selection of words, pictures, and layout. Most professionals would be unlikely to use this instrument.

SUMMARY. The Weidner-Fensch Speech Screening Test is based on no research or theories, has an incomplete manual, and unacceptable standardization. The instrument's pictures and score sheet are outdated. Most professionals would be more successful in screening students in Grades 1–3 informally rather than using this instrument.

[270]
Wellness Evaluation of Lifestyle [2004 Update].

Purpose: Designed to measure "the characteristics of healthy persons."
Population: Ages 18 and over.
Publication Dates: 1994–2004.
Acronym: WEL.
Scores, 21: Spirituality, Self-Direction, Sense of Worth, Sense of Control, Realistic Beliefs, Emotional Awareness and Coping, Intellectual Stimulation, Problem Solving and Creativity, Sense of Humor, Nutrition, Exercise, Self-Care, Stress Management, Gender Identity, Culture Identity, Work, Leisure, Friendship, Love, Total Wellness, Perceived Wellness.
Administration: Group or individual.
Price Data, 2003: 2003 price data: $30 per sampler set including one of each test component, question/answer sheet, and manual (2004, 39 pages); $120 per duplication set; $120 per PDF permission set; $10 per web-based administration.
Time: (15–20) minutes.
Authors: Jane E. Myers, Thomas J. Sweeney, and J. Melvin Witmer.
Publisher: Mind Garden, Inc.
Cross References: For reviews by Andrew A. Cox and Ashraf Kagee of a previous edition, see 15:277.

Review of the Wellness Evaluation of Lifestyle [2004 Update] by RICHARD F. FARMER, Senior Lecturer in Psychology, University of Canterbury, Christchurch, New Zealand:

DESCRIPTION. The Wellness Evaluation of Lifestyle [2004 Update] (WEL) is a self-report measure purported to assess "the characteristics of healthy persons" (manual, p. 4). The WEL is the most recent version of an instrument originally published over 10 years ago (Myers, Sweeney, & Witmer, 1993). Designed for persons 18 years and older, the WEL results in 20 different scores for

17 subscales, two composite scales ("Self-Direction" and "Total Wellness"), and a Perceived Wellness scale.

In the instructions for the WEL-S (the most recent version of the WEL), the respondent is asked to consider for each item "how you most often see yourself, feel, or behave" (manual, p. 24). Questionnaire items are written as self-statements, to which the respondent is asked to indicate agreement along a 5-point scale, from *Strongly Agree* to *Strongly Disagree* with *Undecided or Neutral* as the midpoint. It is difficult to discern from the manual and the sample test provided exactly how many items belong to the WEL-S. The instructions on the sample test in the manual's appendix suggest that there are 134 items to complete; however, the sample test form only contains 131 items (8 of which are demographic questions). Furthermore, the manual suggests that the WEL-S contains 105 items plus 3 Perceived Wellness items, with an additional 17 items identified as nonscored "distracter" items in the scoring key. When considered together, the numbers do not add up ([123 non-demographic items minus 3 Perceived Wellness items] minus 17 distracter items does not equal 105). The situation becomes even more confused when one compares data in Table 2 of the manual, which includes the numbers of items in each scale and subscale, with the numbers of items identified in the scoring key for each scale and subscale. There are several discrepancies in the numbers of items identified in these two sources, and the manual provides no description about how to reconcile these disparities. Consequently, uncertainty remains regarding the number of items that define the WEL-S scales and subscales.

The WEL can be administered in individual or group format, and can also be administered through an internet-based website. The WEL takes approximately 15–20 minutes to complete.

DEVELOPMENT. The WEL is based on the authors' lifespan model of wellness and illness prevention that is, in turn, primarily influenced by Adlerian theory. The authors (Myers, Sweeney, & Witmer, 2000) conceptualize wellness as "a way of life oriented toward optimal health and well-being in which the body, mind, and spirit are integrated by the individual to live more fully within the human and natural community" (p. 252). A pictorial representation of their wellness model (termed the "Wheel of Wellness") is presented (manual, p.

3), within which 18 characteristics or life tasks are depicted "that enable healthy persons to interact effectively with environment and ecological life forces" (manual, p. 1). The WEL was designed to measure each component of wellness depicted in the Wheel model.

During the course of scale development, 500 items were initially developed, and "after many initial trials and debate among the authors, the final pool was formed" (manual, p. 9). Absent from the manual are descriptions of processes involved in the determination of item retention and rejection. Initial trials were reported to consist of 10 years of psychometric evaluation studies, as well as feedback from persons who completed the WEL (e.g., workshop and conference attendees, university students). Over the course of scale refinement, four different versions of the measure were developed (WEL-O, WEL-R, WEL-G, and WEL-S). The WEL-S was subsequently developed based "on item analyses for the first three versions of the WEL and a series of factor analyses" (manual, p. 9). The item and factor analytic methods employed were not specified by the authors.

The manual provides scoring guidelines that are relatively straightforward and easy to follow. In an appendix of the manual (Part X), the authors present guidelines on how to use the WEL in counseling. No corresponding data are provided to support the therapeutic value of the guidelines suggested.

TECHNICAL. In the scoring of the WEL, raw scores for each scale are summed, and then divided by the total number of items within the subscale. The resultant percentage values are claimed to "represent a percent of total wellness" (manual, p. 16). This, however, is a dubious characterization of the meaning of resultant test scores given that the scaling method used is not a true ratio scale. This interpretive problem is only further compounded when one considers that most subscales (12 of 17, or 71%) contain only six or fewer items, thus severely constraining the content validity of the construct domains assessed by each subscale.

On page 1 of the manual, it is suggested that the interpretation of test scores can be done at the level of individual subscale scores, the total wellness score, or by an examination of patterns of scores. However, the authors provide few guidelines for scale interpretation, and no information concerning the interpretation of patterns of subscale scores.

The authors do suggest, however, that "a score of 100% would be interpreted as a high level of wellness" and that "scores not be interpreted in relation to norms, based on recent studies suggesting that high level wellness is not 'the norm' in the United States" (manual, p. 16). They further suggest that "scores of 80 or better are interpreted as being moderately well" and scores "below 80 reflect areas of importance for enhancing one's wellness" (manual, p. 16). How the authors arrived at these recommendations is not made explicit. The manual presents means and standard deviations of the WEL-S for a sample of 1,082 individuals (66% female, 55% university students, 78.7% White, 66.8% from a midsize town, large town/city, or metropolitan area), subdivided by sex and ethnic status.

As noted above, four different versions of the measure were developed. As noted by the authors, the internal consistencies of subscales in earlier versions of the WEL were often unacceptable. For example, only 3 of 16 scales of the WEL-O and WEL-R had alphas $\geq$.80. No internal consistency estimates were provided for the items used in the determination of the two composite scales for the WEL-O and WEL-R. Similarly, only 5 of 17 subscales of the WEL-G had alphas $\geq$.80, with no alpha coefficients provided for the composite scales. For the WEL-S, only 7 of 17 subscales are reported to have alphas $\geq$.80. The Self-Direction and Total Wellness composite scores have alphas of .80 and .84, respectively, and the three-item Perceived Wellness scale is reported to have an alpha of .70. Test-retest data are not presented for the WEL-R, WEL-G, and WEL-S.

The only validity data presented on the WEL are based on 229 graduate counseling students "who took the WEL and other instruments over a four-year period as part of courses in lifespan development and wellness" (manual, p. 12). It is not clear from the test manual which version of the WEL was employed in these studies. The validity data presented include correlations that a subset of WEL scales had with a self-report measure that also purportedly assesses components of wellness (i.e., the TestWell Scales). The authors reported that the WEL Total Wellness composite score correlated .77 with the TestWell composite score. Correlations among subscales identified as conceptually similar between the two measures tended to be more moderate (median r = .50). Also presented are correlations between certain WEL subscales and self-report devices that assess coping resources, psychosocial development, self-actualizing characteristics, locus of control, and death concerns. The theoretical rationale for using such measures to evaluate the construct validity of specific WEL subscales is either not provided or not often immediately apparent. For example, it is unclear why scores on measures of fear and anxiety associated with death, when correlated with the WEL Realistic Beliefs subscale (which is purported to assess "ability to process information accurately, to perceive reality accurately, not as one might want or desire it to be," manual, p. 5), would constitute a test of the WEL's validity.

In the test manual, the authors also cite as support of the validity of the WEL research by Hermon and Hazler (1999), who purportedly found a positive correlation between WEL subscales (unclear as to version) and happiness. However, wellness and happiness would seem to be different constructs, so the degree to which this finding supports the validity of the WEL is unclear. Similarly, the authors also cite an unpublished study from their lab (Dew, Myers, & Wightman, 2003) where a negative correlation was found between homophobia and wellness. Again, it is unclear how such data support the validity of the WEL.

In sum, several factors make it difficult to evaluate whether these data are supportive of the WEL-S's validity: (a) the theoretical bases underlying these validity analyses are unclear; (b) the construct validity data presented are selective, whereby correlations for only a subset of WEL subscales with one or more external measures are presented; (c) the correlations selected for presentation are often moderate at best; and (d) it is unclear as to which version of the WEL was used in these validity studies.

COMMENTARY. There are several unresolved difficulties associated with the WEL. As noted above, conclusions concerning the meaning of test scores appear to be unfounded and inconsistent with the design of the measure. The items themselves are often vague in content or assume a uniform set of personal values across persons. For example, the item "I am satisfied with my leisure activities" appears primarily to relate one's satisfaction with what one does during leisure time. However, the evaluation of satisfaction in this domain is something quite different than the engagement in behaviors that are health promoting (e.g., one can conceivably be satisfied by spending time after work drinking beer and consuming salty, high cholesterol snacks while watching sports on TV). Similarly, the item "I am satisfied with my spiritual well being" assumes that respondents embrace and share common knowledge about what constitutes "spiritual well being", which the authors define as including a "belief in a higher power" (manual, p. 4). In another example, the item "I eat a nutritionally balanced diet" assumes that the respondent knows what constitutes a nutritionally balanced diet. Such items have a presumptive or culturally biased quality. For other WEL items, the Likert response option format does not appear to be appropriate or optimal (e.g., "I do not use tobacco"). Many items appear to be susceptible to influence by response sets (e.g., "My perception of events is usually different from that of others"), and all but seven of the scored items are keyed in the same direction.

When one compares the descriptions of each of the scales in the manual against the items that define the scales, discrepancies are apparent. For example, the Nutrition subscale is suggested to assess "eating a nutritionally balanced diet, three meals a day including breakfast, consuming fats, cholesterol, sweets, and salt sparingly; maintaining a normal weight...and avoiding overeating" (manual, p. 5). However, there are no items within the scale that directly assess weight, overeating, or consumption of foods high in cholesterol, fat, sugars, or salt.

Essential psychometric data are lacking (e.g., test-retest reliability of the most recent form of the WEL, compelling validity data on a representative sample that link test scores to objective indices of wellness), and the data that do exist, namely alpha reliabilities for subscales and scales, often fall short of what is acceptable for research or clinical practice (Nunnally & Bernstein, 1994, p. 265).

Some of the claims made by the authors about the WEL appear to be clearly overstated given the existent data (e.g., what the subscales assess, what the total wellness score means, that the WEL "can be used as an adjunct to counseling to help people develop and maintain healthy lifestyles that promote well being over the lifespan, quality of life, and longevity," manual, p. 1). Finally, the manual could be written with greater care and clarity, as exemplified by inconsistent descriptions of the item contents of scales and subscales scales noted above.

SUMMARY. In its present form, the WEL suffers from a variety of problems that, in the aggregate, suggest extreme caution in the use of the measure. These include: (a) insufficient and/or inadequate psychometric data; (b) vague or biased item content, and/or nonoptimal response options given item content; (c) incongruities between what subscales are purported to assess and what they actually assess; (d) problems associated with the description of what scale scores mean; and (e) an absence of compelling interpretative guidelines supported by data. Consequently, the use of this measure in applied contexts is premature.

REVIEWER'S REFERENCES

Dew, B. J., Myers, J. E., & Wightman, L. (2004). *Wellness in adult gay males: Examining the impact of internalized homophobia, self-disclosure, and self-disclosure to parents.* Unpublished manuscript.
Hermon, D. A., & Hazler, R. I. (1999). Adherence to a wellness model and perceptions of psychological well-being. *Journal of Counseling & Development, 77,* 339–343.
Myers, J. E., Sweeney, T. J., & Witmer, J. M. (1993). *The wellness evaluation of lifestyle.* Palo Alto, CA: Mind Garden, Inc.
Myers, J. E., Sweeney, T. J., & Witmer, J. M. (2000). The wheel of wellness counseling for wellness: A holistic model for treatment planning. *Journal of Counseling & Development, 78,* 251–266.
Nunnally, J., & Bernstein, I. H. (1994). *Psychometric theory* (3rd ed.). New York: McGraw-Hill.

Review of the Wellness Evaluation of Lifestyle [2004 Update] by TRENTON R. FERRO, Professor of Adult and Community Education, Indiana University of Pennsylvania, Indiana, PA:

DESCRIPTION. The Wellness Evaluation of Lifestyle (WEL) is based on a "holistic model for wellness and prevention across the life span" (manual, p. 1) developed by Thomas Sweeney, Melvin Witmer, and Jane Myers (Myers, Sweeney, & Witmer, 2000; Sweeney & Witmer, 1991; Witmer & Sweeney, 1992). This theoretical model is illustrated by the Wheel of Wellness. Drawing upon Adler's personal psychology, "the Wheel includes five major life tasks which empirical data support as important characteristics of healthy persons and as central to healthy functioning" (manual, p. 2): work and leisure, friendship, love, and self-direction (labeled "self-regulation" on the Wheel). Self-direction, "viewed as functioning much like the spokes in a wheel to give strength to the wheel as a whole" (manual, p. 2), in turn, has 12 components. The authors define wellness as "a way of life oriented toward optimal health and well-being in which the body, mind, and spirit are integrated by the individual to live more fully within the human and natural community" (Myers et al., 2000, p. 252).

The purpose of the WEL is to help participants or clients "make healthy life choices" and "plan [their lives] more fully" (manual, p. 24). The WEL, which is self-administering and can be taken in either individual or group settings, can be completed in 15 to 20 minutes. The current Form S (as included in the manual) is composed of a total of 123 items, including 17 distractor items. Each item, a self-statement beginning with "I," is answered using a 5-item Likert scale: *Strongly Agree, Agree, Undecided or Neutral, Disagree,* or *Strongly Disagree.* The instrument concludes with eight demographic questions; however, the key does not provide any information on how to make use of responses provided for these items.

The scoring key breaks the 123 self-statements down into 17 discreet scales for the components of wellness (one each for Spirituality, Friendship, and Love; two for Work and Leisure; and 12 for Self-Direction or Self-Regulation), two composite scales (one for Total Self-Direction or Self-Regulation and one, combining all the previous scales, for Total Wellness), and a brief Perceived Wellness scale. The raw scores for each of these scales are converted into a percentage score. These scores, in turn, according to the authors, "are plotted graphically in a profile showing the relationship of all 19 scores" (manual, p. 16); unfortunately, a copy of that profile was not available for this review.

DEVELOPMENT AND TECHNICAL. The current form (WEL-S) is the fourth in the developmental sequence of the WEL. The reliability of each form has been tested by a fairly large convenience sample drawn from a rather broad range of settings (e.g., undergraduate and graduate students, Elderhostel participants, mental health clinic outpatients, professional counselors, and mid-level managers). The dates of each set of administrations are not provided. The alpha coefficients for the WEL-S (N = 1,082), with two exceptions, range from .70 to .89; the two exceptions are the Nutrition (.66) and Leisure (.61) scales. The latter scale was added to the third form of the instrument; hence, it has not gone through as many iterations as the other scales. The alpha coefficients for the composite scales, Self-Direction and Total Wellness, are .80 and .84, respectively.

Two approaches have been taken to test the validity of the various scales. In one the WEL (the authors do not indicate which form) was administered in concert with a 1983 version of TestWell, the exact nature of which is unclear from the current manual. Because the *Thirteenth Mental Measurements Yearbook* lists three forms of TestWell that were published in 1992 and 1993, it would appear that an earlier form of the WEL, as well, was used to test its validity. Further, the names of WEL scales provided in the table comparing the WEL and the TestWell scales do not match, in every case, the names of the scales in the WEL-S. Nevertheless, the correlations between 11 of the WEL scales and 13 of the TestWell scales range from .38 to .74 ($p < .01$), whereas the correlations for the Stress Management and Total Wellness scales are .31 and .77 ($p < .05$), respectively. In addition, correlations have been computed between 16 of the WEL scales and individual and/or total scales of five other instruments, with 23 correlations ranging between .34 and .72 ($p < .01$; one correlation is -.50) and another 8 ranging between .28 and .44 ($p < .05$); three comparisons did not show significant correlations.

COMMENTARY AND SUMMARY. Generally, the manual is well-designed and easy to use. In addition to providing a copy of the instrument and scoring key, the manual provides descriptions of the theoretical model and how the instrument was developed, definitions of the scales, tables containing the reliability and validity data and the norms established for the WEL, and suggestions for the use of the WEL in counseling. However, a copy of The WEL Workbook (Myers et al., 2003), which is recommended for client use, was not available for this review. There are some concerns. Although the manual carries two copyright dates, 2001 and 2004, it contains no mention of an earlier version, nor does it clarify what changes or additions may have been made to either the instrument or the manual between these two dates. As is also evident from the discussion of reliability and validity, it is not clear to which version of the WEL the data apply. In addition, the term "self-direction" is used rather consistently in the text of the manual; however, the term "self-regulation" is used in the figure of the Wheel of Wellness and the scoring key. Either greater consistency in the use of the terms or an explanation for the variation would be desirable. The section of the manual (pp. 22–23) containing the references has a number of inaccuracies and incomplete entries. A search of the literature provides a rather robust list of research articles and dissertations

that make use of the WEL. However, almost all of the authors have connections with the developers of the WEL. Further, the reviewer was unable to find any independent attempts to test the reliability and validity of the instrument.

REVIEWER'S REFERENCES

Myers, J. E., Sweeney, T. J., & Witmer, J. M. (2000). The Wheel of Wellness counseling for wellness: A holistic model for treatment planning. *Journal of Counseling and Development, 78*, 251–266. Retrieved March 12, 2005, from http://www.counseling.org/publications/jcd/jcd_summer00.pdf

Sweeney, T. J., & Witmer, J. M. (1991). Beyond social interest: Striving toward optimal health and wellness. *Individual Psychology, 47*, 527–540.

Witmer, J. M., & Sweeney, T. J. (1992). A holistic model for wellness and prevention over the lifespan. *Journal of Counseling and Development, 71*, 140–148.

[271]
Wide Range Achievement Test—Expanded Early Reading Assessment.

Purpose: Designed to measure "pre-reading and beginning reading skills."
Population: Ages 4.6–7.11.
Publication Date: 2003.
Acronym: ERA.
Scores, 7: Pre-Reading Skills (Letter/Word Discrimination, Letter-Sound Discrimination, Total), Reading Skills (Word Reading, Sentence Reading, Total), Total.
Administration: Individual.
Price Data, 2003: $195 per complete kit including manual (112 pages), flipbook, and 25 record forms; $55 per manual; $120 per flipbook; $45 per 25 record forms.
Time: (35) minutes.
Author: Gary J. Robertson.
Publisher: Psychological Assessment Resources, Inc.

Review of the Wide Range Achievement Test— Expanded Early Reading Assessment by LESLIE EASTMAN LUKIN, Director of Assessment and Evaluation Services, ESU 18/Lincoln Public Schools, Lincoln, NE:

DESCRIPTION. The Wide Range Achievement Test—Expanded Early Reading Assessment (ERA) is an individually administered norm-referenced achievement test designed to assess prereading and beginning reading skills in children 5 through 7 years of age. The ERA is intended to be used by educators and psychologists and takes about 40 minutes to administer. The ERA is broken down into two subtests: Pre-Reading Skills and Reading Skills. The Pre-Reading Skills subtest includes items designed to measure letter/word discrimination and letter-sound discrimination. The Reading Skills subtest includes items designed to measure word reading and sentence reading. There are 40 items on each subtest.

The ERA testing materials include a flipbook that contains all 80 items and directions for administering and scoring each item; record forms for recording student responses, scores, and results; and a technical manual.

The Early Reading Assessment is a companion test to the Wide Range Achievement Test (WRAT) and was concurrently normed with this test. The ERA supplements the information available in the WRAT by assessing prereading skills not measured by the WRAT such as letter/word and letter-sound discriminations.

The technical manual (WRAT—Expanded, ERA Manual) provides a number of pieces of useful information including the intended uses of this assessment, how to administer and score the assessment, and how to interpret and use test results. Although the section on intended uses was helpful, a brief discussion of inappropriate uses would strengthen the information that was provided. The authors suggest that the primary purpose of the ERA is to diagnose early reading difficulties; therefore, a key use of this information is placing students in appropriate instructional environments.

The section on test administration clearly outlined the necessary examiner qualifications and included the successful completion of graduate coursework in tests and measurements. The authors suggested that individuals without this education could be trained to administer the ERA, but that the interpretation is best left to those who have the requisite background knowledge. Clear directions are provided for administering the test, recording and scoring student responses, and translating raw scores into a variety of derived scores such as standard scores, percentile ranks, normal curve equivalent scores, stanines, and grade equivalent scores. An explanation of each type of derived score is provided including important information concerning how to interpret each type of score and common misconceptions to avoid. This section of the manual also provides a number of illustrative examples that further clarify the interpretation process.

DEVELOPMENT. The structure of the ERA is based upon an understanding of the development of early literacy as outlined in the professional literature. Careful consideration was given to the inclusion of measures of phonemic awareness in addition to comprehension skills and early reading comprehension (sentence reading). The letter-sound discrimination subtest that was designed to measure phonemic awareness was carefully constructed to include all three common types of sounds, beginning and ending consonants, and vowels. Detailed content specifications were developed and used to construct items for each of the four subtests of the ERA.

Item tryouts were conducted in the spring of 1997. During the item tryouts both statistical and qualitative information was obtained. A sample of approximately 200 kindergarten and first grade students from a single urban district in Florida participated in the item tryouts. Information about gender and ethnicity for this sample is provided in the manual. The sample appears to be representative of the U.S. population, at least with regard to these two variables. Item analyses were conducted using both classical and IRT methods. Under the classical approach, p-values, discrimination indices, and point-biserial correlations were calculated for each item. A one-parameter logistic (Rasch) model was also used to calibrate items.

The authors indicated that experts were asked to review the items that were being considered for inclusion in the final form. The experts were specifically asked to review items for content, clarity of the item, correctness of the answer key, and fairness (absence of bias). The information in the manual did not indicate how many experts were involved in the review process or who these experts were. Also, no specific information about the guidance that was provided to the reviewers was included in this section. An empirical analysis of bias was conducted using DIF analyses.

Both the feedback from the expert reviews and item statistics were used to select items for inclusion in the final form. In addition, the items on each subtest were ordered in terms of difficulty as estimated using the item calibrations calculated using the Rasch model.

TECHNICAL.

Standardization (norming). The normative data for the ERA were collected in conjunction with the standardization of the WRAT in 1998. Six hundred students were selected for inclusion in the normative sample for the ERA from the sample of school districts that were participating in the standardization of the WRAT. The 600 students were evenly divided into four age groups (4 years, 0 months to 4 years, 11 months; 5 years, 0 months to 5 years, 11 months; 6 years, 0 months to 6 years, 11 months; and 7 years, 0 months to 7 years, 11 months) with 150 students in each age group. A stratified sampling procedure was employed that focused on age, gender, race/ethnicity, parent education, and geographic region. The sample was drawn to match the U.S. population data from the Current Population Survey (March 2001) conducted by the Bureau of Labor Statistics. The data provided by the authors suggested that the ERA sample was representative of the national population.

Both age and grade norms are available for the ERA. A variety of derived scores are available including age- or grade-based scaled scores for subtests, composite scores, percentile ranks, stanines, normal curve equivalent scores, and grade equivalent scores. Information was provided about how each of the derived scores were generated.

Reliability. The technical manual provides estimates of internal consistency reliability coefficients (KR20) by subtest and by age and grade for the standardization sample. The majority of the estimated reliability coefficients are well within an acceptable range (.8—.9). The lower estimates are generally associated with the letter/word discrimination subtest and are lowest for the oldest students. This is most likely due to a lack of variability in the scores of the older students.

Test-retest reliability was estimated by administering the ERA to a group of 21 students with a 2- to 5-week lapse between administrations. The students participating in this study were diverse with respect to gender, age, and ethnicity. Again, the majority of the test-retest reliability estimates are within an acceptable range (.8—.9) and once again the lowest estimates were associated with the letter/word discrimination subtest for the same reasons mentioned above.

Estimates of the Standard Error of Measurement are also provided as well as a summary of how and why to construct confidence intervals to support score interpretation. In summary, the majority of the estimated reliability coefficients are well within an acceptable range (.8—.9) and sufficient description was provided of the sample used to estimate these coefficients.

Validity. In the section on validity, the authors stress the importance of viewing the validation process as an ongoing endeavor where both the test developer and user share the responsibility of accumulating the required evidence. The authors fulfill their obligation by reporting several different types of empirical evidence to support the use of ERA scores. The first section discusses evidence that the authors refer to as internal in nature. This section includes a discussion of the careful development process designed to ensure that the test measures what it purports to measure. In addition, intercorrelations among the ERA subtests are also reported. The intercorrelations are moderate to high indicating a strong relationship among the various subtests of the ERA. The authors also refer to the empirical analysis of bias that was conducted as part of the test development process as another source of evidence in support of the internal validity of the ERA scores.

Under the heading, "external evidence of validity," correlations between the ERA and the WRAT are presented. The correlations were based on a 124-child sample of 5-, 6-, and 7-year-olds who took both the ERA and the WRAT at about the same time. In addition, correlations between the ERA and individually administered intelligence measures such as the Wide Range Intelligence Test (WRIT), the Wechsler Intelligence Scale for Children—Third Edition (WISC-III), and the Kaufman Brief Intelligence Test (K-BIT) were also reported. The correlations between the ERA and the WRAT were generally moderate (.4–.5 range), whereas the correlations between the ERA and the various individual measures of intelligence were quite variable. For example, the correlation between the ERA and the WRIT were considerably lower (.12–.43 range) than the correlations between the ERA and the other individual measures of intelligence (.5–.7 range). As one would expect, the highest correlations occurred between the ERA and the verbal measures.

Taken as a whole, the empirical data presented in the technical manual provide good support for the conclusion that the ERA does indeed measure important prereading and beginning reading skills that are related to later measures of reading as well as other aspects of verbal performance. In the words of the authors, the data should be viewed as a good "beginning" and as such suggest that additional research will be necessary to support specific uses of this instrument.

COMMENTARY. Taken as a whole, the technical manual for the ERA is well written and provides good documentation of the technical quality of this instrument. As noted above, there are a few sections where additional information would help the reader draw conclusions about the rigor of the test development process (e.g., discussion of external reviewers and directions for reviews), but as a whole the information is fairly complete and easy to access.

SUMMARY. Overall the ERA appears to have utility as a measure of prereading and beginning reading skills. For an individually administered achievement measure, the ERA appears to be relatively easy to administer and score. Preliminary evidence suggests that scores on the ERA are correlated to measures of reading comprehension (WRAT), suggesting that the ERA may indeed measure skills that are predictive of later success in reading. The scores should be a useful source of information for educators who are responsible for planning and implementing appropriate instructional experiences for young students in the area of beginning literacy.

Review of the Wide Range Achievement Test— Expanded Early Reading Assessment by PATRICK P. McCABE, Associate Professor, Graduate Literacy Program, St. John's University, Queens, NY:

DESCRIPTION. The purpose of this test is to assess the early literacy development of children aged 4-6 to 7-11 years. There are four individually administered subtests; two assess Pre-Reading Skills (Letter/Word Discrimination and Letter/Sound Discrimination), and two assess Beginning Reading Skills (Word Reading and Sentence Reading). The manual states, "Within each of the subtests, the items are arranged in approximate order of difficulty, with the easier items occurring first, followed by harder items at the end of the subtest" (p. 8). Scaled scores, standard scores, and percentile ranks are provided, as well as a composite score profile with space for examiner comments.

DEVELOPMENT.

Letter/Word Discrimination subtest. This subtest has two parts. Part A tests Letter Knowledge, and Part B tests Word Discrimination. In Part A, the examiner points to and asks the child to name each of seven letters printed on one page. In Part B, the child identifies either target letters in words or entire target words from a choice of four words. The author took these words from the Educational Development Laboratories core vocabulary list, and used the Harris-Jacobson basic reading vocabulary list.

Unfortunately, there are problems with this subtest. According to the manual, the Letter Knowledge subtest contains one upper case letter and six lower case letters. However, on the actual test, there are two upper case letters and five lower case letters. In addition, in the Word Discrimination subtest, the directions for Item 15 do not specify that the letters must be in the same order as those in the target box, and the sample for that item appears nine items earlier. In fact, for Item 15, three choices contain the "same letters as those inside the box," albeit in a different order.

Letter-Sound Discrimination subtest. This subtest consists of Part A (Beginning Sounds/Vowels) and Part B (Ending Sounds). In Part A, there are 14 items for beginning sounds, and 3 items for vowels. Unfortunately, mislabeling of tasks is a problem in this subtest. For example, in Sample 2B and the items that follow (1–14), labeled "Beginning Sounds/Vowels," the child is not asked to identify any vowels, and in Sample 2C and the items that follow (15–17), labeled "Beginning Sounds/Vowels," the child is not asked to identify any beginning sounds. In fact, for these items, the examiner asks the child to identify the middle sound, a vowel. The eight items in Part B accurately assess final sounds.

Word Reading subtest. This subtest has two parts. In Part A, Word Knowledge, the child silently reads the word in the target box and locates the matching picture. In Part B, Sight Word Recognition, the examiner reads the target word and the child locates that word from among four word choices. This test is not timed; therefore, it is unclear why this is considered a "sight word" test. According to literacy experts, "sight words" are those that can be decoded immediately, without focusing on and sounding out individual letters or syllables. Also, some foils might need to be mediated (sounded out), an unnecessary and additional task that might frustrate some children. A more efficient sight word test would have been to put one word on a page and ask the child to read it. The problem here is the misuse of the term "sight words."

Sentence Reading subtest. The examiner asks the child to silently read 15 sentences, 10 declarative and 5 interrogative, and after each to identify the picture from among four choices that either represents the declarative sentence or answers the question sentence.

However, there were inconsistencies between the manual and this subtest also. According to the manual, the test contains 107 words, ranging from primer to Grade 3 (with one word unclassified). Table 4.4 (manual, p. 38) presents the grade level breakdown, and the 107 words in this table suggests each word appears once. However, there were actually 120 words with 14 used repeatedly. These repetitions ranged from 1 for nine of the words to 13 for one of the words (counting "girls" as separate from "girl's"). When I subtracted the total repetitions from 120, the result was 77, the number of different words that appeared in the sentences, not 107. Finally, the manual indicated that the longest sentence had 10 words; however, Sentence 14 contained 19 words.

TECHNICAL.

Standardization. According to the manual, 600 students participated in the standardization procedure with 150 in each of the following age categories: 4-0 to 4-11; 5-0 to 5-11; 6.0-6.11; and 7-0 to 7-11. Tables illustrating the variables (age, ethnicity, parental education level, and geographic area as they related to the US population) were included, and the author stated, "These data show that generally the students conformed rather closely to the national Census targets for the four levels of educational attainment used" (manual, p. 41/44). This statement is arguable.

The author acknowledged anomalies in the standardization sample. He stated, "Except for age 5, parental educational attainment and the over-representation from the South, the ERA sample of students tested showed close agreement with the national U.S. Census data and constitute a representative sample of students at these ages and grades" (manual, p. 44). However, the percentage of 5-year-olds' parents who had a college education was 33.6% in the sample compared to 19.6% in the U.S. population, and only 6.8% of the sample 5-year-olds' parents had less than a high school education compared to 16.5% of the U.S. population at large. Thus, the sample 5-year olds' parents were better educated than parents of 5-year-olds in the U.S. population. A recent analysis of reading ability (National Center for Educational Statistics, 2000) noted a positive relationship between level of parental education and literacy development; therefore, the reading performance of the 5-year-olds in the sample may have been higher than what could be expected from the U.S. population of 5-year-olds due to parental education, a critical variable. In addition, 63.5% of the total participants were from the South compared to 34.5% of the U.S. total. Another anomaly, although somewhat less pronounced, was that 68% of 4-year-olds in the sample were White compared to 56.8% of the U.S. population. Further, 10% of 4-year-olds were Hispanic in the sample compared to 20.6% of the U.S. population.

These issues raise questions about the appropriateness of this test, especially for 5-year-olds, and for Hispanic 4-year-old children.

Reliability. The author examined reliability by retesting 21 students over 13–36 days, and stated that the reliability data were reasonably consistent over a period of "about three weeks" (manual, p. 50). However, 36 calendar days is a little over 5 weeks and about 25 school days, excluding holidays; this is inconsistent with "three weeks." It is also of interest to note that 47.6% of the students (10) in the reliability sample were Hispanic compared to 14% Hispanics for the larger standardization sample (see test manual, Table 4.9, p. 42), another anomaly. Finally, 21 students is an inadequate sample size, especially given the limitations noted above.

Validity. The author conducted a Differential Item Functioning (DIF) analysis and stated, "DIF analyses per se do not automatically provide an indication of item bias. Such a determination can only be made by combining logical analysis with the DIF results to arrive at a judgmental decision about the presence or absence of bias in test items" (manual, p. 56). The ambiguity of the pictures (answer choices) for some of the items (17 in Test 2, Part A; 7 in Test 3, Part A; and 7 in Test 4), may have biased the results, which might not be apparent in a DIF.

COMMENTARY. Unfortunately, the discrepancies and other problems enumerated above severely limit the value of this test. The lack of congruence between the description of subtests in the manual and the actual test erodes confidence a user can have in the tables and other information presented in the manual.

These issues are particularly problematic, especially in the context of the "No Child Left Behind" legislation and its focus on early reading assessment and instruction. Psychologists and others using this test may inaccurately assess children's reading difficulty. If the information in the test manual is suspect, interpretation based on the scores from this test may misguide a practitioner as he or she plans literacy instruction and designs a literacy environment for the young child.

Also, interpretations of test results and instructional suggestions for four sample students appear in the manual. Of the three sample students for whom reading instruction was suggested, explicit phonics instruction was emphasized. Although children who read early are better able to name letters and identify phonemes than children who do not read early, teaching children to read by making sounds and letters the focus of the reading program, as this manual seems to suggest, is myopic and can be counterproductive. Children need numerous opportunities to read connected discourse in a curriculum that also incorporates writing, listening, and speaking with authentic, meaningful tasks and appropriate children's literature.

SUMMARY. As the author has indicated on page 31 of the test manual, "A student's performance always reflects much more than just a set of numbers, or scores. It is the blending of student background information with test score detail that results in a course of action most helpful and beneficial for the individual student." Anyone using this test should keep that in mind. Unfortunately, the inconsistencies noted above make it unadvisable to use this test in any but a most informal and cautious manner. I suggest, instead, the practitioner consult with a literacy professional in his or her school, or draw upon his or her literacy knowledge, to create an informal test of early literacy as well as an instructional plan based on the young child's environmental print.

REVIEWER'S REFERENCE

National Center for Educational Statistics. (2000). *NAEP 1999: Trends in academic progress: Three decades of student performance.* (NCES 2000-469). Washington, DC: U.S. Department of Education, Office of Educational Research and Improvement.

[272]

Wide Range Achievement Test—Expanded Edition.

Purpose: An achievement test battery "designed to assess the core curricular domains of reading, mathematics, and oral and written language."
Publication Dates: 2001–2002.
Acronym: WRAT-Expanded.
Comments: Designed to complement the WRAT-3.
Author: Gary J. Robertson.

Publisher: Psychological Assessment Resources, Inc.
a) WRAT-EXPANDED GROUP ASSESSMENT (FORM G).
Population: Grades 2–12.
Scores, 5: Reading (Basic Reading, Reading Comprehension), Mathematics, Nonverbal Reasoning.
Administration: Group.
Levels, 5: G-1 (Grade 2), G-2 (Grades 3–4), G-3 (Grades 5–6), G-4 (Grades 7–9), G-5 (Grades 10–12).
Price Data, 2003: $195 per WRAT—Expanded Group Assessment (Form G) comprehensive package including 10 booklets and scoring forms for each level, manuals for each level (2001, 71–75 pages each), and technical supplement (2001, 80 pages); $95 per 25 booklets, 25 scoring forms, and manual (specify level); $45 per technical supplement.
Time: (125–135) minutes.
b) WRAT-EXPANDED INDIVIDUAL ASSESSMENT (FORM I).
Population: Ages 5–24.
Scores, 5: Reading, Mathemaics, Listening Comprehension, Oral Expression, Written Language.
Administration: Individual.
Price Data: $195 per WRAT—Expanded Individual Assessment (Form I) reading/mathematics module package including reading and math flipbook, reading and mathematics manual (2002, 185 pages), 25 response forms, and technical supplement; $55 per manual; $120 per flipbook; $45 per 25 response forms; $45 per technical manual.
Time: [30] minutes.

Review of the Wide Range Achievement Test—Expanded Edition by GEORGE ENGELHARD, JR., Professor of Educational Measurement and Policy, Emory University, Atlanta, GA:

DESCRIPTION. The Wide Range Achievement Test—Expanded Edition (WRAT-Expanded) is an achievement test battery designed to assess the core curricular domains of Reading, Mathematics, Oral and Written Language, and Nonverbal Reasoning. The WRAT-Expanded consists of two forms: (a) Form G that is a group assessment designed to measure Reading (Basic Reading, Reading Comprehension), Mathematics, and Nonverbal Reasoning for students in Grades 2–12, and (b) Form I that is an individual assessment designed to measure Reading, Mathematics, Listening Comprehension, Oral Expression, and Written Language for examinees from ages 5–24. The WRAT-Expanded is organized in terms of five levels: Level 1 (Grade 2, 120 items), Level 2 (Grades 3–4, 121 items), Level 3 (Grades 5–6, 120 items), Level 4 (Grades 7–9, 119 items), and Level 5 (Grades 10–12, 120 items). The individualized component of the WRAT-Expanded (Form I) consists of 70 items in Reading and 75 items in Mathematics.

The WRAT-Expanded was designed to provide users with a group-administered achievement test closely linked to an individually administered test with similar content and interpretative systems. This integrated system is intended to provide an initial screen based on a group assessment (Form G) with an in-depth individual assessment (Form I) available for targeted students. According to the author, the WRAT-Expanded (Form G, group assessment) has six intended uses: preliminary screen to identify students for individual assessments, placement of new or transfer students, identification of special students, development of individual instructional goals and plans, periodic assessment of special groups of students, and research uses. Intended uses of Form I are to complement the WRAT3 assessment, follow-up assessment of students identified by results of Form G for preliminary screening, flexible assessment of students across a wide range of achievement, placement of students, assessment of ability-achievement discrepancies, and research uses.

DEVELOPMENT. The WRAT-Expanded consists of Reading, Mathematics, and Nonverbal Reasoning Tests. The content selected for the Reading Test is based on the assumption that the ability to read and understand printed material is necessary for success in school. Specifications for the Reading Test were developed by the author of the Stanford Diagnostic Reading Test (Dr. Bjorn Karlsen). Synthetic reading passages are used rather than authentic text. The Mathematics Test is designed to measure the ability to understand concepts and apply them to the solution of various types of mathematical problems. According to the author, the emphasis of the Mathematics Test is consistent with current National Council of Teachers of Mathematics standards. The Nonverbal Reasoning Test provides a brief measure of abstract reasoning ability that was designed to be independent of reading ability. The Nonverbal Reasoning Test consists of nonverbal classification items that are used in other ability tests, such as the Otis-Lennon School Ability Test and the Cognitive Abilities Test.

TECHNICAL. The author of the WRAT-Expanded provides a variety of manuals describing the psychometric characteristics of the instrument. General information about the instrument is provided in several administration manuals organized by levels (1 to 5), whereas more detailed psychometric information is provided in a separate technical supplement.

The group and individual forms of the WRAT-Expanded were normed concurrently in Grades 2–12 with common groups of students completing both Form G and Form I. The norms for Form G are based on 8,136 students from a variety of settings. The authors have been very careful to construct a normative sample that is demographically representative of the school-age population in the United States based on Census data. Out-of-level norms are also available. As expected, the normative data for the individually administered test (Form I) is based on fewer students ($N = 635$). Given the challenges of collecting this normative information for an individually administered test, the authors have done a good job. Detailed information provided in the technical supplement allows potential users to see the close match of the normative sample to the school-age population. Because the WRAT-Expanded covers a wide age range, the potential user needs to be reminded and cautioned about how few examinees actually were assessed within each grade or age group. A detailed description of the norms is provided in the technical supplement to the WRAT-Expanded and the manual for the individual assessment, but not in the administration manuals for the group assessments (Form G). Because users may not have access to the technical supplement, and because the description of the norms is essential for proper interpretation of the standardized scores, future versions of the group administration manuals should include a description of the norms. The author reports the following scores based on the normative sample: grade- and age-based standard scores, percentile ranks, stanines, Normal Curve Equivalents, grade equivalents, and Ability Scale Scores.

In the technical supplement, evidence regarding the precision of Form G is based on internal consistency reliability (KR-20) and test-retest reliability. Across grades, the KR-20 coefficients for the standardization sample (range across grades in parentheses) are as follows: Reading (.86–.91), Mathematics (.80–.88), and Nonverbal Reasoning (.80–.89). The test-retest reliability coefficients for the standardization sample (range across levels in parentheses) are as follows: Reading (.75–.90), Mathematics (.76–.90), and Nonverbal Reasoning (.75–.79). The WRAT-Expanded exhibits reliability coefficients that are comparable to those obtained with similar instruments. The author also provides standard errors of measurement with a clear description for potential users on how to interpret *SEM*s. Information regarding the precision of content skill areas is not provided. No scorer reliability information is provided for the individually administered test (Form I).

Validity information for Form G is presented in terms of internal evidence (content, intercorrelations between tests within the WRAT-Expanded, speed of responding, and differential item functioning), and external evidence (correlations between Form G and a variety of group and individually administered achievement and ability tests). Evidence regarding clinical validity is reported in terms of mean differences between two groups of students (learning disabled and gifted) as identified by their teachers and matched comparison groups of students. Validity evidence is comparable to what is found with other instruments similar to the WRAT-Expanded. The author is very clear that the validity evidence represents "only a start of the validation process for the WRAT-Expanded" (technical supplement, p. 52).

COMMENTARY. The WRAT-Expanded suffers from many of the problems encountered with wide-range achievement tests designed to measure educational performance over large age and grade ranges. There are very few items within each content area, testing time is quite short, and relatively few students are included in the norms for each grade and age group. Of course, some of these weaknesses can also be viewed as strengths by potential users who seek a quick and preliminary assessment of their students. Given the intended purposes of the instrument, the WRAT-Expanded has some nice features that potential users may find useful. In particular, the simultaneous norming of Forms G and I make comparisons between achievement and ability levels more meaningful.

One of the intended uses of the WRAT-Expanded is the identification of relative strengths and weaknesses of students in reading, mathematics, and nonverbal reasoning. The author provides very detailed and careful interpretations of these comparisons. However, the use of formal statistical tests to compare within student performance seems a bit of a stretch. It is not clear that the statistical tests recommended by the author are really appropriate. The scores are not really on the same scale, although the use of linking groups across Forms G and I provides some comparability. Perhaps the most straightforward interpretation is to view the comparisons in terms of normative data and the distribution of score differences obtained within the normative sample.

Rasch measurement theory was used to calibrate the WRAT-Expanded. Unfortunately, the author does not provide the psychometric information necessary to evaluate model-data fit. Traditional psychometric criteria are provided but the additional information available based on the use of Rasch measurement is not reported. The author should include information regarding item fit, reliability of person separation and other Rasch-based psychometric criteria. The WRAT-Expanded does not take full advantage of Rasch measurement and its useful features, such as variable maps and person fit displays, that can enhance the usefulness and interpretability of the scores. These additional features should be considered for inclusion in future editions of the instrument.

SUMMARY. The WRAT-Expanded is a new test designed to assess Reading, Mathematics, and Nonverbal Reasoning over a wide grade and age range using a linked group and individually administered assessments. Potential users should carefully consider the alignment between the content of the WRAT-Expanded, and the school curriculum when using the test as an achievement test. No validity evidence is currently available to support the accuracy of decisions based on the use of the WRAT-Expanded as a screen to identify students for individual assessments or the identification of students with special needs. As with other instruments that include individual assessments, the utility of the WRAT-Expanded depends fundamentally on the proper interpretation and use of the test by clinicians. Because the WRAT-Expanded is a new instrument, the final evaluation of its usefulness cannot be determined without additional research and use of the test.

Review of the Wide Range Achievement Test—Expanded Edition by BO ZHANG, Assistant Professor of Educational Psychology, and CINDY M. WALKER, Associate Professor of Educational Psychology, University of Wisconsin—Milwaukee, Milwaukee, WI:

DESCRIPTION. The Wide Range Achievement Test—Expanded Edition is designed to be used in conjunction with the Wide Range Achievement Test 3 (WRAT3; T6:2713) as an achievement test battery. The author states that this test can be used for identifying students with learning disabilities. The expanded version has two forms: a group form and an individual form. The group form has three subtests: Reading, Mathematics and Nonverbal Reasoning. The individual form has five subtests: Reading, Mathematics, Listening Comprehension, Oral Expression and Written Language (Individual Assessment manual for Reading and Mathematics, p. 2). However, at present, only the Reading and Mathematics subtests seem to be available as information on only these subtests was provided. Target users are ages 7–18 for the group form and ages 5–24 for the individual form. No explanation is provided about the discrepancy in content coverage and age difference between those two forms. Although the author did not specify situations in which one would choose to administer the group form rather than the individual form, or vice versus, it was recommended that the group form serve as a screening tool and the individual form as a more in-depth assessment of learning difficulty. This is because the individual form classifies students into finer categories. One might also decide to use this test if there was concern about only one single student.

The modifications made to the WRAT-Expanded resulted in a tool that appears to be much better at identifying possible learning deficiencies than the WRAT3. Although the WRAT3 is designed for ages between 5 and 74, the expanded version is targeted more to elementary and secondary school students. In addition, the administration format of the WRAT-Expanded is more flexible than that of the WRAT3. As the Reading and Mathematics tests of the group and individual forms were normed simultaneously, one major advantage of the WRAT-Expanded over the WRAT3 is that group test results are directly comparable to the individually administered test results. In other words, if some students were administered the group test while other students were given the individual test, normative scores have the same meaning. However, users should be cautious in linking the group and individual classifications because the group form classifies students into five different achievement levels whereas the individual form classifies students into eight achievement levels for Reading and nine achievement levels for Mathematics. The other advantage of the expanded version is that the aptitude-achievement discrepancy can be investigated as the WRIT (Wide Range Intelligence Test; 15:279) test scores were also obtained from the norming group.

TECHNICAL.

Standardization. The process of obtaining the norming group is described in detail in the technical supplement. Composition of the norming group was similar to that of the general population at each grade and age level. One drawback in the sampling process that was used to obtain the norming group is that private schools were excluded from the procedure. Only students from parochial schools were sampled for nonpublic schools. Thus, caution should be exercised when using this test in a nonparochial private school setting.

Age- and grade-based norms, in the form of standard scores, percentile ranks, stanines, and normal curve equivalents, are provided for both forms (i.e., group and individual) of the WRAT-Expanded. A detailed description of how the norms were developed is available in the manual. The relationship between these norms was presented in graphs, which are easy to read.

Reliability. For all three subtests of the group form, the internal consistency reliability coefficients (KR-20) is approximately .85 for each age and grade group, showing quite a consistent measure of the underlying skills by items. The internal consistency reliability coefficients for the individual form are a little higher than those of the group form, mostly above .90 for all subtests at each grade. But the statement "these reliability coefficients indicate that the WRAT-Expanded tests are measuring their designated constructs with sufficient consistency, or homogeneity, to yield dependable results" (technical supplement, p. 29) cannot be supported by those relatively high reliability coefficients. Whether the test is measuring those skills is a construct validity issue, as opposed to a reliability issue.

Test-retest reliability was obtained using a 1-month interval between test administrations. For both the group and individual forms, the test-retest coefficients were approximately .80 for the three subtests, also showing adequate stability of the measures. One shortcoming for the test-retest reliability study is the relatively small and nonrepresentative sample used. All students came from one parochial school. Sample size at five grade levels ranged from 19 to 124. For example, at Level 5, only 19 students were used to obtain the test-retest reliability estimate for the Reading subtest for the group form. No test-retest reliability coefficients were reported for the Mathematics and Nonverbal Reasoning subtests for that level. For the individual form, only 97 students from ages 5–17 were included in the test-retest reliability study.

Standard error of measurement (*SEM*) is provided for both grade and age level groups. The *SEM* is smaller for the individual form than for the group form, likely due to the higher reliability of the individual form. Confidence bands of test scores are reported in tables for convenient use. But whereas the 85% and 90% confidence bands were provided for scores of the group form, the 90% and 95% bands were offered for the individual form, causing an unnecessary discrepancy in test score interpretation.

Validity. The WRAT-Expanded test seems to show a high level of content validity. An informative description of the test development process is provided for both the group and individual forms in the technical manuals. Content experts were consulted to assist in developing the curricular domain for the Mathematics and Reading subtests. The reading skills assessed (literal comprehension, inferential comprehension, and word meaning in context) are important components of general reading ability. They certainly represent the domain of reading better than letter and word recognition used in the WRAT3. The author of the test also controlled the readability and the difficulty level of vocabulary, which should improve the content validity of the test. Facial bias was screened by content experts for possible racial and religious offenses as well as gender stereotypes. A problem one might have with the content validity of the Reading test is the lack of authenticity of the reading tasks. As all reading passages were written specifically for this test, they do not necessarily represent material that would be read in the "real" world.

The mathematics test was developed based on the *Principles and Standards for School Mathematics* (2000) from the National Council of Teachers of Mathematics. A detailed description of the content domains and subdomains are listed in the technical manual, which should facilitate the understanding of the skills measured for users of the WRAT-Expanded. As opposed to the WRAT3, the number of problems assessing computational skills was minimized on this test. Instead, understanding of mathematical concepts and problem-solving skills were emphasized. Effective measures were taken in the test development process to avoid the possible confounding effect of assessing reading ability on the Mathematics test, such as controlling of vocabulary level. All of these changes help to increase the content validity of the Mathematics test.

No underlying theoretical framework was given for the development of the Nonverbal Reasoning subtest. Instead, the types of items in the test were described. As no convergent construct validity evidence was provided for this subtest either, users must rely on their own wisdom to decide how well this test actually measures general cognitive ability independent of reading. The statement that this subtest can be used for students with limited English proficiency, such as ESL (English as Second Language) students, requires empirical support, which is not provided. ESL students come from different cultures. The nonverbal patterns and relationships assessed by this subscale might entail different meaning to them than for what the items were originally designed. A considerable amount of evidence was presented to demonstrate the construct validity of this instrument. Test results from the WRAT-Expanded were correlated with other achievement batteries, aptitude tests and intelligence tests. Some of the correlation coefficients provided are more relevant than others. As most validity coefficients are in the medium range and the strength of correlation varies across grades, it is not an easy task for users to conclude whether the subtests in which they are interested have enough validity evidence for their purpose. It would be helpful to users if the vast amount of information was condensed so that only meaningful and relevant information is provided.

Convergent validity evidence for the Reading and Mathematics subtests on the WRAT-Expanded seems sufficient. The high correlation between individual and group test results shows that student's reading and mathematic abilities are being measured in a consistent manner by the two forms. The correlation with similar measures, such as the CTBS and ITBS, was approximately .70 for most grades. One exception to this was for Grade 2 in which the correlation with the ITBS Reading test was only .25. The convergent evidence of the Nonverbal Reasoning Test with other similar measures was not reported, which is a drawback. Furthermore, the divergent evidence of the Nonverbal Reasoning subtest from the Reading subtest was not very clear. Although most correlations between the Nonverbal Reasoning test and the Reading test were low, others were in the moderate range. Test results from the WRAT-Expanded were also correlated with the WRAT3 to study its construct validity. As expected, the correlation was not very high as the two tests are actually quite different. The correlation between those two tests was approximately .6 for the group form and .5 for the individual form for Reading and Mathematics subtests.

To provide more construct validity evidence for the WRAT-Expanded, a factor analysis could be conducted to see whether items from the three subtests actually represent distinct factors. With regard to the convergent and divergent evidence, such evidence should be more focused on validity coefficients with other similar measures. For example, it is hard to interpret the reported correlation between the WRAT-Expanded Reading subtest and the CTBS Word Analysis subtest. What would be more relevant is the correlation between the Reading subtest on the WRAT-Expanded and the Total Reading score from the CTBS as more similar skills are being measured by these two scores.

COMMENTARY. The aptitude-achievement discrepancies can be investigated due to the standardization of the WRAT-Expanded and the Wide Range Intelligence Test (WRIT) on an overlapping sample of students. Convenient tables are provided to aid in the interpretation of score discrepancies obtained from the two tests. However, the composition of the sample of students who were given both tests differs from grade to grade and is sometimes quite inadequate. For example, for age 6, only 2 students were administered both the achievement and aptitude tests.

Another technical problem is with the item response models used for reading items in item tryout and differential item functioning analysis. As multiple items are asked from reading one paragraph, there is a testlet effect. That testlet effect was not accounted for in the item response models used.

SUMMARY. The WRAT-Expanded is a useful instrument in assessing the achievement of elementary and secondary school students and helping to identify students who may have a learning disability. The major strength lies in the flexibility of administration and the direct comparability of individual and group test forms. The expanded version successfully addressed several problems raised in the previous reviews of the WRAT3 test. The target users are more focused, making it possible to have more meaningful content domains than those used in the WRAT3. An adequate amount of information was provided on test development, standardization process, and technical features. The norms are clearly defined and should be easy to use. The internal consistency and test-retest reliability estimates of the Reading and Mathematics tests are high. However, the construct validity evidence of the test needs to be strengthened. Evidence should be collected on whether or not the three subtests actually measure what they were designed for and provide consistent information on the possibility of learning disabilities as other measures. The validity of the Nonverbal Reasoning subtest also needs to be further justified.

[273]

Wide Range Assessment of Memory and Learning, Second Edition.

Purpose: Designed for use in "clinical assessments of memory including evaluation of immediate and/or delay recall as well as differentiating between verbal, visual or more global memory deficits."

Population: Ages 5–90.

Publication Dates: 1990–2003.

Acronym: WRAML2.

Scores, 25: Verbal Memory (Story Memory, Verbal Learning, Total), Visual Memory (Design Memory, Picture Memory, Total), Attention/Concentration (Finger Windows, Number Letter, Total), General Memory; Optional scores: Working Memory (Verbal Working Memory, Symbolic Working Memory, Total), Verbal Recognition (Story Recognition, Verbal Learning Recognition, Total), Visual Recognition (Design Recognition, Picture Memory Recognition, Total), General Recognition, Sound Symbol, Sentence Memory, Story Memory Recall, Verbal Learning Recall, Sound Symbol Recall.

Administration: Individual.

Price Data, 2004: $475 per complete kit including administration and technical manual (2003, 245 pages), 25 examiner forms, 25 Picture Memory response forms, 2 Picture Memory Recognition forms, 2 china markers, 25 Design Memory response forms, 25 Design Memory Recognition forms, 4 Picture Memory plates, 5 Design Memory cards, 1 Finger Windows board, 2 Symbolic Working Memory boards, and soft canvas briefcase; $80 per administration and technical manual; $60 per 25 examiner forms; $40 per 25 Picture Memory response forms; $30 per 25 Design Memory response forms; $30 per 25 Design Memory Recognition forms; $55 per soft case with removable strap; $195 per scoring software.

Time: [60] minutes.

Authors: David Sheslow and Wayne Adams.

Publisher: Psychological Assessment Resources, Inc.

Cross References: See T5:2880 (7 references); for reviews by Richard M. Clark and Frederic J. Medway of a previous edition, see 11:470.

Review of the Wide Range Assessment of Memory and Learning, Second Edition by THOMAS M. DUNN, Assistant Professor of Psychology, University of Northern Colorado, Greeley, CO:

DESCRIPTION. The Wide Range Assessment of Memory and Learning, Second Edition (WRAML2) is the update to the 1990 instrument designed to assess memory in children. The original WRAML was one the first well-normed instruments that provided a comprehensive assessment of memory available to clinicians working with a child population. This most recent edition extends its effectiveness beyond children, with norms up to age 90. This instrument contains six core subtests: Story Memory, Verbal Learning, Design Memory, Picture Memory, Finger Windows, and Number/Letter. From these six subtests, three index scores can be derived: Verbal Memory, Visual Memory, and Attention-Concentration. Additional optional subtests include Sentence Memory, Sound Symbol, Verbal Working Memory, and Symbolic Memory. There is also the option to administer three delayed recall subtests and four recognition memory subtests. From the core subtests, a General Memory standard score can be computed, with seven other memory index scores also given depending on what optional subtests were administered. A "memory screening" option is also available, where the first four subtests are administered, taking about 20 minutes, and the result is strongly correlated ($r = .91$)

with the General Memory score. Some subtests are administered or omitted from the test depending on the age of the participant.

This instrument is administered individually with an examiner presenting items and recording responses. The examiner only needs experience giving other standardized psychometric tests, but interpretation of results is limited to those with graduate level training in cognitive assessment. Raw scores are converted into subtest scaled scores. These are then converted into index scores. Scores can be plotted across subtests and index scores in a profile grid for interpretation. A computerized scoring program is also available.

DEVELOPMENT. As mentioned above, this instrument is in its second edition (copyright, 2003), and has been in development since 1990. Although the original WRAML had norms only up to age 17, the WRAML2 has norms from age 5 to 90. Additionally, there are now two subtests to tap working memory (Verbal Working Memory and Symbolic Working Memory) and four recognition memory tasks (Story Memory, Verbal Learning, Design Memory, and Picture Memory). Items have been refreshed on other existing subtests, such as updated pictures on Picture Memory and revised stories in Story Memory. Revision of the instrument began with focus groups in 1998 to obtain first-hand information about improving the test. There was an item "tryout" followed by a standardization program.

The WRAML2 comes with a durable carrying case, a variety of subtest stimulus materials, test response booklets, and a comprehensive manual. The manual is well organized with a cogent explanation of construction of test scales, item selection, and the normative process. The scales are well conceptualized and thoughtfully cover a variety of memory processes. The authors convey a very reasonable rationale for their approach to their assessment of memory and learning, despite the conceptualization of such cognitive processes being very complex. Their discussion of memory is rich in its consideration of the literature, citing many classic studies. They also cite over 50 studies where the WRAML was used to assess memory.

TECHNICAL. The WRAML2 had a rigorous standardization process, testing 1,200 children and adults aged 5 to 90. Efforts were made to make the normative sample mirror the 2001 U.S.

Census, with testing conducted in more than a dozen states representing different geographical regions. Slight variations in the normative sample from census data were corrected with a statistical weighting procedure. The result is an instrument with a well-represented normative sample, albeit smaller than other instruments that have norms for young children as well as the elderly.

Reliability data from the WRAML2 indicate excellent person separation reliabilities from Rasch statistics ranging from .85 to .94 on the core subtests. Internal consistency is also shown to be very good, with Cronbach's alpha coefficients ranging from .82 to .96 on the core index scores, and from .71 to .95 across the six core subtests.

External validity was examined by comparing scores on the instrument with several other memory and learning measures, including the Wechsler Memory Scale—III (WMS-III) and the California Verbal Learning Test—II (CVLT-II). Correlations between the WRAML2 subtests and those of the WMS-III are adequate. Most notable is the .60 correlation between the WRAML2 General Memory index score and the WMS-III General Memory index score. Similar findings are noted on the CVLT-II. The WRAML2 is also noted to have moderate correlations with general intelligence measures, such as the Wechsler Adult Intelligence Scale—III and the Wechsler Intelligence Scale for Children—III.

COMMENTARY. The introduction of the WRAML in 1990 was important. Previously, it was difficult to assess children's memory with a well-normed test. This second edition of the WRAML is noteworthy, as the norms have been extended to include adults. This makes the WRAML2 a valuable tool for the assessment of memory in children, as it allows the clinician to use the same instrument as the child gets older. With good norms, solid technical qualities, and the ability to test a variety of memory processes, the WRAML2 is also an appropriate instrument to assess memory in adults up to age 90. As noted earlier, the normative group of 1,200 is somewhat smaller than some other instruments that have norms for young children to aged adults. For example, the Wide Range Achievement Test 3, with norms from age 5 to 74, has a normative group of 4,000.

Although the WRAML2 is of high quality, there are some minor things about the instrument that are slight drawbacks. First, it is a demanding

test to give and the examiner must keep track of many stimulus materials. If optional subtests are given, extra booklets are added to the primary scoring booklet. This can leave the examiner juggling quite a bit of material during the testing session. Because the test instructions are not listed on the scoring booklet, the manual adds one more item to manage during testing. There is also no place in the scoring booklet to note elapsed time from presentation of test materials and delayed recall. In interpreting results, it would be advantageous to be able to see if the interval of time between immediate and delayed recall was unusual.

Finally, it is interesting that the memory screening option on the WRAML2 correlates so highly with the General Memory index score ($r = .91$). One on hand, it is efficient to be able to administer four of the core subtests instead of a full battery and have a high correlation with the General Memory index. However, one might also note that with such a high correlation, there is considerable overlap of scales between the core subtests and those given for the screening.

SUMMARY. The WRAML2 is a robust, well-normed, psychometrically sound instrument for use of assessing memory. It is exceptional in that it has norms for young children as well as a geriatric population. The WRAML2 is a flexible instrument, in that it can be used as a reliable screening of memory. With additional subtests, however, it can provide a comprehensive measure of learning and memory with assessments of working memory, delayed recall, and recognition memory. For the clinician who wishes to assess children as they get older with the same instrument, the WRAML2 is extremely valuable.

Review of the Wide Range Assessment of Memory and Learning, Second Edition by SANDRA D. HAYNES, Interim Dean, School of Professional Studies, Metropolitan State College of Denver, Denver, CO:

DESCRIPTION AND DEVELOPMENT. As with the first edition, the second edition of the Wide Range Assessment of Memory and Learning (WRAML2) was designed to evaluate memory and learning. Knowledge about the structure and function of memory, both healthy and pathological, has greatly expanded in the 14 years since the development of the original WRAML. Hence the authors made a decision to revise the test to include new material to more accurately assess memory and learning as it is now understood. The new version was based on information from cognitive sciences, neuropsychology, and developmental research and includes elements of all of the following memory and learning concepts: Primacy and recency effects, immediate and delayed recall, recall of rote versus meaningful material, visual and verbal memory, semantic versus acoustic memory errors, working memory, sustained attention, short-term memory, recognition versus retrieval systems, incremental trial learning, learning curve, and memory decay.

Clearly, not all of these concepts are unique to the WRAML2. The second edition builds on the original WRAML to allow for broader, more in-depth analysis of memory and learning. The age range appropriate for measurement using the WRAML2 has also been significantly extended from 5–17 years for the WRAML to 5–90 years for the WRAML2. It is important to note that not all subtests are appropriate for all age levels. Sound Symbol and Sound Symbol Delay Recall were designed for individuals 8 years of age and younger. Verbal Working Memory and Symbolic Working Memory are only used for individuals 9 years of age and older.

Having six core subtests represents a change from the WRAML, which had nine subtests. The WRAML2 six core subtests are: Story Memory, Verbal Learning, Design Memory, Picture Memory, Finger Windows, and Number/Letter subtests. Each of these subtests supplies scores that make up one of three indexes: Verbal Memory index (Story Memory and Verbal Learning subtests), Visual Memory index (Design Memory and Picture Memory subtests), and Attention Concentration index (Finger Windows and Number/Letter subtests). These three indexes, in turn, contribute to the General Memory index and represent the three factor structures of the WRAML: Verbal, Visual, and Attention/Concentration. Although the WRAML also measured three factors, they were slightly different. The Learning factor in the WRAML was replaced by the Attention/Concentration factor in the WRAML2. This change made the WRAML2 a much more robust measure of memory and learning as attention and concentration are more relevant to the constructs being assessed.

In addition to the core, the WRAML2 has 11 optional subtests. The optional subtests provide the examiner the flexibility to explore areas of concern in greater depth. The optional subtests are divided into four categories: Working Memory, Delay Recall, Recognition, and Additional subtests. Working Memory consists of 2 subtests, Verbal Working Memory and Symbolic Working Memory. WRAML had no subtests in this category. Delay Recall consists of 3 additional subtests, Story Memory Delay Recall, Verbal Learning Delay Recall, and Sound Symbol Delay Recall. Although identified as Delayed Recall, the Recognition subtests are delayed memory tasks as well. The addition of these subtests to the Delayed Recall measure brings a total of seven measures of this concept. Again, this is a difference between the original version of the WRAML, which had four tasks of delayed recall. The Recognition subtests comprise Story Memory Recognition, Design Memory Recognition, Picture Memory Recognition, and Verbal Learning Recognition and represent a net increase of 3 subtests of recognition compared to the WRAML. The so-called "Additional Subtests" are Sound Symbol and Sentence Memory.

In addition to the changes noted above, common subtests of the WRAML and the WRAML2 have been updated for the second edition. Picture Memory has been updated with contemporary, full-color scenes. Story Memory has been updated, and lengthened to accommodate adults. Design Memory has an additional design bringing the total to five rather than four. Sentence Memory was updated using more contemporary language and changed from a core to an optional subtest. One subtest, Visual Learning, was eliminated.

With all the measures listed above, it is surprising that administration takes approximately 45 minutes for all subtests. Thus, a remarkable amount of information can be collected in a relatively short period of time.

TECHNICAL COMMENTARY. When scoring the WRAML2, raw scores are first converted into scaled scores ($m = 10$, $sd = 3$) for each subtest using norm tables divided into appropriate age groups. Standard scores ($m = 100$, $sd = 15$) or indexes are calculated by summing the scaled scores. Confidence intervals were carefully calculated and are provided in the manual for the index scores at the 68% and 90% confidence levels. Indexes represent the four overall categories of assessment of the WRAML2: Verbal Memory, Visual Memory, Attention and Concentration, and General Memory. The authors are careful to urge caution in interpretation of overall measures of memory without attention to the subtest scores and the presence of outliers that may skew the results. Age equivalent scores are available for young children and adolescents and percentile ranks and stanines are available for all age groups. Such a wide range of scores, both in type and in number of subtests and overall indexes, provides the examiner multiple means to unravel the data and make meaningful interpretations and comparisons.

The process of norming the WRAML2 was extensive. Test items were first subjected to "item tryout" with a relatively small number of individuals (140) from across the United States and an age range of 5–95. Based on the results of an item analysis of these data, a standardization edition of the WRAML2 was developed. This edition was administered to 1,200 individuals from all regions of the United States that included 22 states. The sample was highly representative of the U.S. population with regard to gender, ethnicity, and education. The age range used for standardization was slightly different from the "item tryout" sample with the high age being 90 years of age rather than 95. Additional item calibration was conducted after this administration and careful attention was given to the development of scaled and index scores as well as percentile ranks and age equivalents.

Scores from the WRAML2 are highly reliable. Measurements of internal consistency, using Cronbach's coefficient alpha, range from .82–.96 on core subtests. The range was greater for the optional subtests (.63–.96) but these coefficients still represent a quite respectable level of reliability. Test-retest reliability indicated a substantial learning effect from one test time to another (median administration lag of 49 days) with an overall gain of approximately +1 scaled score on subtests. Lower reliability correlations were thus found with correlations between .53 to .85 for core subtests and indexes and .47 to .80 for optional subtests. Interrater reliability was quite high (.98) even on subtests where some level of subjectivity is required for scoring.

Meticulous attention was paid to documenting the validity of the WRAML2. Internal validity was assessed via investigation of item content, subtest intercorrelations, exploratory factor analyses, confirmatory factor analysis, and differential item functioning. Separation reliabilities were found to be .98–1.00 when analyzing item content. Intercorrelations of the WRAML2 indexes and

subtests were likewise high. Results from factor analysis studies support the internal validity of the WRAML2.

External validity was assessed via correlations with other psychometric tests of memory and clinical studies. Moderate convergent and discriminant validities were noted when comparisons were made between the subtests of the WRAML2 and like subtests on the Wechsler Memory Scale—III (WMS-III), Children's Memory Scale (CMS), Test of Memory and Learning (TOMAL), and the California Verbal Learning Test (CVLT). Moderate correlations were also found with cognitive measures (i.e., Wechsler Adult Intelligence Scale [WAIS-III] and the Wechsler Intelligence Scale for Children—Third Edition [WISC-II]) and with achievement tests (i.e., Wide Range Achievement Test 3 [WRAT3], and the Woodcock-Johnson—Third Edition [WJ-III] Tests of Achievement).

Supporting documentation of external validity was provided by calculating effect size for each of the WRAML2 subtests and indexes for five clinical control groups: Alcohol Abuse, Alzheimer's Disease, Parkinson's Disease, Traumatic Brain Injury, and Learning Disabilities.

SUMMARY. The WRAML2 appears to be a carefully constructed and analyzed psychometric instrument. The manual is easy to follow, well-written, and thorough providing all necessary descriptions and caveats as deemed necessary by the American Educational Research Association, American Psychological Association, and the National Council on Measurement in Education in the 1999 edition of *Standards for Educational and Psychological Testing*. Significant improvements have been made over the original edition of the WRAML. The WRAML2 appears straightforward, requiring little training prior to use, and allows for a broad array of memory assessment in a short administration period.

REVIEWER'S REFERENCE

American Educational Research Association, American Psychological Association, & National Council on Measurement in Education. (1999). *Standards for educational and psychological testing*. Washington, DC: American Educational Research Association.

[274]

Wide Range Interest and Occupation Test, Second Edition.

Purpose: Designed to provide participants "with a better understanding of themselves, the types of occupations they prefer, their pattern of likes and dislikes among work-related activities, and the intensity and consistency of their response pattern."

Population: Ages 9–80.

Publication Dates: 1970–2003.

Acronym: WRIOT2.

Scores, 39: Occupational Cluster (Art, Music, Drama, Sales, Management, Clerical–Office, Personal Service, Food Service, Cleaning Service, Protective Service, Social Service, Science, Health Care, Build and Repair, Factory and Assembly Line, Heavy Equipment and/or Machine Operation, Plants and Animals); Interest Cluster (Spoken Words, Numbers, People, Things, Perceived Ability, Income, Leadership, Strenuous, Outdoors, Risk, Creative, Routine, Likes, Dislikes, Occupational Clarity, Inconsistency) Holland Type Cluster (Realistic, Investigative, Artistic, Social, Enterprising, Conventional).

Administration: Individual.

Price Data, 2004: $275 per complete kit including administration manual (2003, 174 pages), administration and scoring software (requires Windows 98 or above and 32 MB RAM), data disk, picture book and 25 response forms.

Time: (30) minutes.

Comments: A nonverbal measure of occupational interest; previous edition called the Wide Range Interest-Opinion Test.

Authors: Joseph J. Glutting and Gary S. Wilkinson.

Publisher: Psychological Assessment Resources, Inc.

Cross References: See T4:2959 (1 reference); for reviews by Louis M. Hsu and Caroline A. Manuele of a previous edition, see 9:1366; for a review by Donald G. Zytowski, see 8:1029.

Review of the Wide Range Interest and Occupation Test, Second Edition by ALBERT M. BUGAJ, Professor, Department of Psychology, University of Wisconsin—Marinette, Marinette, WI:

DESCRIPTION. The Wide Range Interest and Occupation Test, Second Edition (WRIOT2), designed for individuals ages 9 to 80, is a nonverbal test intended to assist people in choosing careers. It can be administered via computer or by paper-and-pencil. The WRIOT2 asks individuals "to indicate whether they like, dislike, or are undecided about work situations illustrated in 238 pictures" (manual, p. 1). The manual says the test is suitable for individuals who are English dominant and have college educations, who have limited English proficiency or little formal education, people with learning disabilities and/or reading problems, and individuals with mental retardation.

The WRIOT2 contains 39 scales organized into three clusters. The Occupational Cluster shows the extent to which test-takers like 17 career areas. The Interest Cluster consists of 16 scales evaluating needs, motives, and values influencing occupational choice. The final cluster is based on Holland's (1966, 1997) theory of occupational choice, identifying a person as a Realistic, Investigative, Artistic, Social, Enterprising, or Conventional type.

Scores on the WRIOT2 are expressed as percentile ranks and reported in comparison to general norms, with no breakdown according to gender or group. The computer-generated report provides a brief description of each scale, and extended, paragraph-length descriptions of the three highest scores on the Occupational cluster. Extended descriptions for additional scales in the Occupational Cluster, the Interest and Holland-Type Clusters, and career facts concerning the career areas assessed can also be printed. This information is also available in the test manual.

The manual itself is well written and informative. The computer program loads without difficulty and is easy to navigate. The instructions to the test-taker are straightforward. Both the computerized or paper-and-pencil formats of the test are easy to administer.

DEVELOPMENT. A preliminary set of 300 pictures was developed by revising items from the previous edition of the test. A panel of judges then placed each picture into what they felt were the appropriate occupational categories. The exact nature and backgrounds of the judges is not specified. The 17 occupational categories were devised to match 12 occupational areas specified by the Division of Testing of the U.S. Employment Service (U.S. Department of Labor, 1965) and other publications including the *Complete Guide for Occupational Exploration* (JIST, 1993). Items were retained only if interrater agreement yielded Kappa coefficients of reliability of .80 or higher. Additionally, items were retained only if their item-total point-biserial correlations were .30 or higher, first during pretesting of the items, and again following standardization. A similar three-step process was used to determine the content validity of the Interest and Holland-type clusters, resulting in the final 238 items. Pictures in the Holland-type scales were also statistically compared to similar listings in the *Dictionary of Holland Occupational Codes* (Gottfredson & Holland, 1996), resulting in a high rate of agreement as to the appropriate category of each item (K = .88).

The pictures were further rated by a panel of judges to determine how clearly they represented a single occupation and lacked ambiguity. The manual states that approximately 92% of the pictures in the WRIOT2 were rated as clear. Neither the nature of the scale used in the ratings, nor the number of judges, who are referred to as "experts and users," is provided. Although the ratings of the stimulus pictures for clarity are an improvement over the earlier edition, and the occupations illustrated might appear unambiguous to "experts and users," it cannot be ascertained if they are unambiguous to the range of individuals who are potential test-takers.

TECHNICAL.

Standardization. A stratified sample consisting of 1,286 participants was used in developing norms for the WRIOT2. The sample was constructed to be a close match to the U.S. population on the variables of age, gender, race/ethnicity, education, and geographic distribution as reported by the U.S. Bureau of the Census (2001). Minor weightings were applied to various groups in the sample to bring it into alignment with Census figures. No norms were developed for the specialized groups for whom the test is said to be suitable, such as individuals with mental retardation.

Reliability. Internal consistency of the WRIOT2 was determined by calculating Cronbach's alpha for each scale for six different age groups (total $n = 1,286$), the youngest ranging from 9 to 14, the oldest being 50 and above. With the exception of a scale designed to measure an inconsistent response pattern, Cronbach's alpha was above .82 for all scales. On the Inconsistency scale, the average alpha across age groups was .68. Because of the low reliability of the Inconsistency scale the manual states it should not be interpreted unless a test-taker receives an extreme score (percentile score of 97 or higher).

Test-retest reliability was determined for two age groups: adolescents ($n = 67$) and adults ($n = 49$). A median of 23 days elapsed between each administration. Test-retest reliability was lowest for the Inconsistency scale (.68 for adolescents; .44 for adults). Outside the Inconsistency scale, test-retest reliabilities generally ranged from .61 to .91, and tended to be somewhat higher for adults, especially on the interest and Holland-type scales.

These measures were not obtained on specific groups, such as individuals with limited English proficiency.

Validity. Convergent validity was determined by intercorrelating each scale on the WRIOT2. Most intercorrelations (ranging between .50 and .87) proved to be logically consistent. However, the same pictures are used for all three "clusters" on the test. As a result, some scales undoubtedly share many of the same items. This could result in inflated correlations between scales.

Several methods were used to determine the criterion and construct validity of the WRIOT2. First, using a contrasted-groups approach, 503 individuals from the standardization sample were placed into a Holland-type classification on the basis of their occupations. Analysis of variance indicated participants received significantly higher scores for their own type in comparison to highly incongruent types.

In another study, the WRIOT2 and the Strong Interest Inventory (SII) was administered to 72 adults. The criterion validity of the Holland-type scales was strongest, with each scale on the WRIOT2 correlating significantly only with its SII counterpart (rs ranging from .56 to .68). Correlations for occupational scales ranged from .40 to .73. Many of these were logical. In a final study the occupational scales of the WRIOT2 were also subjected to a discriminant function analysis. This resulted in five functions that were logically related to Holland types, although item overlap may have again affected the results.

COMMENTARY. The WRIOT2 can be recommended with some reservations for use with the general population. However, its use with specific populations, such as those with learning disabilities or limited reading ability must be called into question. The test's norms are highly appropriate for the general population, a group for whom rigorous methods were used in development. For more specific groups, no norms were developed, nor were validity and reliability data collected. Further, it cannot be ascertained if specific groups such as individuals with mental retardation would perceive the stimulus materials as unambiguous.

Of the three "clusters" on the WRIOT2, the Holland-type Cluster seems to be the most robust. Scores on this cluster correlate with their counterpart on the SII. Individuals already established in specific occupational areas also received appropriate scores on this cluster. The Occupational Cluster appears somewhat weaker. Although many of the scales correlate with their SII counterparts, no data using a known-groups procedure are provided for this cluster, data that could document strong criterion validity as found for the Holland-type Cluster. Measures of convergent and divergent validity analyzing the relationships between the scales on the WRIOT2 may also have been affected by item overlap.

The WRIOT2 does appear to have strong internal consistency, as measured by Cronbach's alpha. Short-term test-retest reliability is high, but no long-term reliability figures are presented. Additional testing of specific scales is also needed. For example, one scale (the "Likes scale") is designed to measure social desirability by counting the number of times a test-taker selects "like" as an option. However, social desirability bias could best be assessed by instructing a group of research participants to attempt to "fake good" on the test, using their response pattern as a criterion, or by examining the relationship of this scale to other tests measuring social desirability.

SUMMARY. The WRIOT2 can be recommended for use with the general population with reservations. It has strong short-term reliability. The procedures followed in developing the test's norms also make them representative of the general population, but may not be representative of populations such as non-English speakers, or special populations such as the learning disabled. For the general population, the Strong Interest Inventory (15:248) is a preferable test having undergone more extensive validity testing, and having reliability estimates determined over somewhat longer intervals (up to 6 months). Despite a lack of research on non-English-speaking populations, or on exceptional individuals, the WRIOT2 should also prove a useful research tool for studying the career interests of such individuals. However, it cannot be recommended as a counseling tool for those groups.

REVIEWER'S REFERENCES

Gottfredson, G. D., & Holland, J. L. (1996). *Dictionary of Holland Occupational Codes—Third edition.* Odessa, FL: Psychological Assessment Resources.
Holland, J. L. (1966). *The psychology of vocational choice.* Waltham, MA: Blaisdell.
Holland, J. L. (1997). *Making vocational choices: A theory of vocational personalities and work environments.* (3rd ed.). Odessa, FL: Psychological Assessment Resources.
JIST. (1993). *Complete guide for occupational exploration.* Indianapolis, IN: JIST Works.
U.S. Department of Labor. (1965). *Dictionary of occupational titles.* (3rd ed.; Vol. II: Occupational Classification). Washington, DC: U. S. Government Printing Service.

Review of the Wide Range Interest and Occupation Test, Second Edition by CAROLINE MANUELE-ADKINS, Vice-President, Institute for Life Coping Skills, Inc., Stamford, CT:

DESCRIPTION. The Wide Range Interest and Occupation Test, Second Edition (WRIOT2) represents a major revision of the 1972 and 1979 versions of the WRIOT (Jastak & Jastak, 1979). It remains a pictorial occupation-related interest inventory that can be used with children and adults who have limited reading or English-proficiency issues. The WRIOT2 uses a transitional format, as the user can choose between a paper-and-pencil or a computer version for administration.

All 238 items in the inventory are colorful pictures that depict people engaged in activities that represent a variety of occupations. Respondents are asked to indicate whether they Like, Dislike, or are Undecided about their preferences for each activity. The pictures in this version have been completely redone. They are not sex-stereotyped and issues of diversity have now been addressed. Ambiguity in the drawings was a problem and remains a problem. This reviewer had trouble with 23 of the items. As with previous versions, people from other countries or people with limited occupational and educational experiences may have trouble interpreting the nature of the pictured activities. Although the authors do not address this problem, they have added verbal descriptions of each picture in the manual with the recommendation that they be used for "the visually-impaired or for individuals with mental retardation" (manual, p. 155). It may be necessary to include these verbal descriptions for other populations as well.

The test, which can be administered individually or in groups and by picture book or computer, is easy to use. Clients with learning or literacy problems may require individual assistance to complete the test. The authors have improved on the prior scoring methods that were tedious and time-consuming by adopting computer scoring. Scoring for both formats is done on the computer, which means that the user must be computer literate. It also means that if the picture book and response form format is used, data must be hand entered into the computer to obtain individual scores and profile sheets.

The WRIOT2 includes 39 scales, which are organized in three clusters. The Occupational Cluster assesses the extent to which respondents like 17 types of careers. Changes in these scales include name changes to reflect current terminology, movement of the Outdoor scale to another cluster, deletion of the Literature scale, and collapse of the Social Service and Social Science scale into one. The second cluster is called an Interest Cluster. It has 16 scales that "evaluate the needs, motives, and values that influence a participant's occupational choice" (manual, p. 1). The Interest Cluster was formerly known as the Attitude Scale in earlier versions. Items in this cluster provide information about preferences for Functional Duties (people, data, things, activities), Chosen Skill Level, Social Rewards (e.g., Income), Conditions of Work, and Response Patterns. Cluster 3, Holland Types, is new to the WRIOT2. Items in the Occupational and Interest Cluster were coded and organized according to Holland types and like many other occupational interest inventories, the WRIOT2 now yields scores for Holland's six modal personality and occupational types—Realistic, Investigative, Social, Enterprising, Conventional, and Artistic.

Earlier versions of the WRIOT used standard T scores in their scoring procedures. The WRIOT2 uses normative percentile scores presented in profile format with percentile ranges and descriptive labels (e.g., 11 to 25, Below Average). Scores are norm referenced, which means that an individual's score is compared to scores obtained by large representative sample groups of "people in general." Interpreting scores requires training in assessment but the manual does include a long chapter on test interpretation. The chapter provides descriptions of each scale with corresponding items, information about gender differences, and questions to use when discussing scores to stimulate further career exploration.

DEVELOPMENT. Items (pictures) in the WRIOT2 scales were developed to represent a universe of occupational areas as defined in U.S. Department of Labor publications and other interest inventories. According to the manual, selection of items was based on input from "a panel of experts and users" (manual, p. 139) with interrater correlations of .80 or above needed to retain items in the final scales. Face validity of the items is good but absent from the development information is any reference to a theoretical context for criteria used to include items in the measure (e.g., theories of interests and how they relate to specific occupations). The Interest Cluster of scales claims

to evaluate needs, motives, and values but it is important to note that these characteristics are not directly assessed but surmised from respondents' expressed likes and dislikes for specific job activities. As in the Occupational Cluster, theoretical constructs are missing from this mix of scales. Why any of the scale groupings are included in this cluster is not known. They appear to combine a mix of unrelated, randomly selected concepts that may or may not relate to anything significant. This suggests that one cannot have too much confidence about what scores in this cluster really mean. More confidence can be placed on scores obtained on the Holland scale cluster that includes items and scales that are more congruent and matched to Holland types.

TECHNICAL. The standardization and normative samples for the WRIOT2 included a total of 1,286 males and females, divided into six age groups with ages ranging from 9 to 80 years. Efforts were made to make each sample group representative of the general population with race and ethnicity percentages reflective of U.S. Census proportions. Mean scale scores for the WRIOT2 sample scores are no longer provided and not needed for the machine-generated percentile scores but it would be interesting to know how sample scores vary by age group. Also of interest would be more normative data for sample groups who represent groups the WRIOT2 was designed to serve, including ESL populations, special education students, and people with certain disabilities. Information about score variance in groups with different socioeconomic and education levels would also be welcome. A major change in this version of the WRIOT2 is its change from gender-separate norms to the use of one set of norms for both genders. The authors cite progress made in occupational freedom for both genders as legal, social, and practical barriers have been removed.

The WRIOT2 includes expanded reliability analyses that include evidence of both internal reliability of test scores across scale items and test-retest reliability for consistency of test scores over time. Average alpha coefficients for the Occupation Scales Cluster range from .82 for Drama to .95 for Build and Repair. Interest Cluster coefficients range from .90 to .98. All coefficients for this cluster are high with one exception on the Inconsistency scale, which is .68. Test-retest reliability included studying two age groups, children and adolescents ranging in age from 9–18 years and adults ranging in age from 19–50 years. These groups were tested twice with median 23-day intervals between testing times. For both groups, test reliability averages on all scales ranged from .52 to .90 with reliabilities for the younger age group somewhat lower as would be expected. The generally high reliabilities here indicate good score reliability and stability over time.

The authors of the WRIOT2 have made some attempt to address the absence of validity data that was a serious shortcoming in the 1979 version. They describe content validity analyses with interrater agreement, interscale correlation analyses, scale-by-scale correlations to examine congruence and divergence, and studies that examine relationships to Holland codes and the Strong Interest Inventory Scale. The data from all these analyses support the measure's internal validity. Technically, these studies appear to be well constructed. Still missing is some sense of what is really being measured when the WRIOT2 is used. Given the absence of a strong theoretical context in the design of the measure and the lack of more external validity studies (e.g., how do scores on the WRIOT2 relate to actual occupational choice) questions still need to be raised about the validity of the measure.

COMMENTARY. In general, the WRIOT2 represents a significant advance over the 1979 version. Its authors have done some solid development work to address recommendations made by prior reviewers. The new computer version replaces the time-consuming hand-scoring version with a version that is easy to administer and score. The pictures are colorful and interesting though sometimes ambiguous. The new percentile scoring system is easier to use and interpret and the standardization sample with subsequent norms representative of the general population is an improvement. The manual has been improved with efforts made to provide more in-depth information about the measure's development. Most users will find the total assessment kit attractive and easy to understand and use.

Concerns about the WRIOT2 center mostly around the lack of theory and well-defined constructs underlying the measure. Item definition and selection is not tied to criteria other than saying they relate to U.S. Employment Service

occupational areas and constructs such as interests, values, and abilities are mixed up and poorly defined. Still needed are studies that demonstrate how scores on the WRIOT2 relate to choice of occupations, patterns of interests, level of education, and career decision making. Studies like these would convey more information about what the WRIOT2 is really measuring. Also needed is more information about how the populations the measure was designed for really perform on the measure. There is no evidence in the manual that populations with literacy or language issues have been studied. It would also be important to know more about score variations by age, gender, and socioeconomic status.

The user should also be aware of the fact that the measure itself seems slightly skewed toward including more items that relate to Realistic and Conventional occupations. It may be that these are easier to depict in drawings. This fact will affect how users should interpret the results and how they may need to further address "field and level" issues. More attention also needs to be paid in the manual to test interpretation issues.

SUMMARY. As with prior versions, WRIOT2 has no substantial competition when it comes to fulfilling a need for a pictorial interest inventory. There are many populations that need it and the user is well advised to try it out. Test developers also need to provide much mre information about these very populations so users can have more confidence that it really works for the populations for which it is intended.

REVIEWER'S REFERENCE

Jastak, J. F., & Jastak, S. (1979). Wide Range Interest-Opinion Test. Wilmington, DE: Wide Range, Inc.

[275]

Woodcock-Johnson® III Diagnostic Supplement to the Tests of Cognitive Abilities.

Purpose: Designed to expand "the diagnostic capabilities of the [Woodcock-Johnson III Tests of Cognitive Abilities] for educational, clinical, or research purposes."

Population: Ages 2–90+.

Publication Dates: 1977–2003.

Acronym: WJ III® Diagnostic Supplement to the Tests of Cognitive Abilities.

Scores, 11: Memory for Names, Visual Closure, Sound Patterns—Voice, Number Series, Number Matrices, Cross Out, Memory for Sentences, Block Rotation, Sound Patterns—Music, Memory for Names—Delayed, Bilingual Verbal Comprehension—English/Spanish.

Administration: Individual.

Price Data: Available from publisher.

Time: (5–10) minutes per subtest.

Comments: Tests from the Diagnostic Supplement can be combined with other tests from the Woodcock-Johnson III (15:281) Tests of Cognitive Abilities Standard and Extended Batteries and the WJ III Tests of Achievement to provide 14 additional interpretive clusters.

Authors: Richard W. Woodcock, Kevin S. McGrew, Nancy Mather, and Fredrick A. Schrank.

Publisher: Riverside Publishing.

Review of the Woodcock-Johnson® III Diagnostic Supplement to the Tests of Cognitive Abilities by TIMOTHY SARES, Director of Testing and Psychometrics, American Registry of Diagnostic Medical Sonography (ARDMS), Rockville, MD:

DESCRIPTION. The Woodcock-Johnson III (WJ III®) Diagnostic Supplement to the Tests of Cognitive Abilities consists of 11 testing measures intended to augment the WJ III Tests of Cognitive Abilities (WJ III COG). The supplemental tests are numbered 21–31 to coincide with tests numbered 1–20 on the WJ III COG. The Supplement is intended to provide further diagnostic capability for the standard and extended batteries of the WJ III COG and is especially useful as a complement in the assessment of bilingual persons and young children. The fundamental criteria for developing cognitive abilities in the Supplement are derived from the Cattell-Horn-Carroll (CHC) theory of cognitive abilities and are described in the WJ III COG examiner's manual (Mather & Woodcock, 2001) The broad CHC abilities covered on one or more of the supplemental tests are Long-Term Retrieval (Glr), Auditory Processing (Ga), Fluid Reasoning (Gf), Processing Speed (Gs), Short-Term Memory (Gsm), Visual-Spatial Thinking Comprehension (Gv), and Comprehension-Knowledge (Gc).

Several cognitive ability and broad CHC clusters can be evaluated in combination with the WJ III COG Standard and Extended Batteries. For example, Supplementary Test 21: Memory for Names, Test 22: Visual Closure, and Test 27: Memory for Sentences can be combined with the WJ III COG Standard Battery Test 1: Verbal Comprehension, Test 6: Visual Matching, and Test 8: Incomplete Words to derive a General

Intellectual Ability-Early Development (GIA-EDev) scale to assess young children or other individuals functioning at the preschool level. Two additional cognitive ability clusters identified are General Intellectual Ability-Bilingual (GIA-Bil) and Broad Cognitive Ability-Low Verbal (BCA-LV). The GIA-Bil is intended for English-dominant bilingual individuals. The BCA-LV is intended as a broad measure of cognitive ability requiring relatively minimal verbal expression or exchange.

The administration times may vary for the WJ III Diagnostic Supplement Tests as they adapt to the individual test-taker's progress. The manual states that supplemental GIA-EDev tests for preschool-age children generally require about 5–10 minutes per test to administer. Some tests in the supplemental battery may be suitable for assessing individuals in situations where attention span or response style is a concern.

The tests can be administered to individuals varying in ages from 2 to 90-plus years and is suitable for preschool, K–12, college and university undergraduate and graduate student educational levels, and also for adults over 14 years old not attending school. The following tests: Test 23: Sound Patterns—Voice, Test 27: Memory of Sentences, and Test 29: Sound Patterns—Music, require audio recording and audio equipment for administration. Test 26: Cross Out requires a stop watch, digital watch, analog watch, or clock with a second hand. Test 31: Bilingual Verbal Comprehension-English/Spanish is intended for administration by an examiner fluent in Spanish.

DEVELOPMENT. Items were written and reviewed by experienced teachers and psychologists serving as subject matter experts. Their overriding objective was to measure the narrowly defined applicable CHC ability construct. Support for structural validity is reported through intercorrelations of test scores for the Diagnostic Supplement Tests. Norms for the WJ III Diagnostic Supplement batteries are developed on test data from a national sample of over 8,000 individuals ranging in age from 2 years to over 90 years. The WJ III Diagnostic Supplement manual directs questions regarding the norming sample to the WJ III technical manual (McGrew & Woodcock, 2001). The norming sample was also administered the WJ III COG and the WJ III Tests of Achievement (WJ III ACH) and selected to resemble the demographic and community characteristics of the general U.S. population relative to geographic region, community size, gender, race, Hispanic origin, and type of school or college.

The test manual refers very briefly to the item selection criteria that follow stringent statistical fitting criteria of the Rasch model but provides very little useful basic information about the process, which leaves the reader questioning its sufficiency. As fit analysis criteria could signify item bias as well as extraneous content, no information is provided on what factor analysis, if any, was conducted to coincide with the fit analysis.

Test score intercorrelations and associated sample sizes are presented for the following age group ranges: 2–3, 4–5, 6–8, 9–13, 14–19, 20–39, and 40 and over. A rationale for selecting correlations for these age ranges is not provided in the testing manual. The correlations are based on sample sizes ranging from 42 (2–3 years) children to 1,984 (9–13 years). The intercorrelation of Block Rotation and Visual Closure in the smallest sample ($n = 42$, 2–3-year-olds) is fairly low ($r = .17$) and is even lower ($r = .10$) for the largest sample ($n = 1,984$) of 9–13-year-olds.

Approximate Age Equivalent (AE) scores and Grade Equivalents (GE) scores are shown in the Diagnostic Supplement on total number correct for all tests except Test 30: Memory for Names-Delayed. AE and GE scores for Test 30 can only be derived from the software-scoring program. AE and GE score estimates for the other batteries are shown alongside the score sheets for each test.

TECHNICAL. Overall internal construct validity is weakest for the four lower age groups (2–13 years) and strongest for the higher age groups (14 and older). For instance, low correlations are recorded between Delayed Memory for Names and Visual Closure ($r = .24$) at ages 40+, ($r = .06$) at ages 9–13, and Block Rotation ($r = .06$) at ages 6–8. The intercorrelations for Visual Closure produced somewhat inconsistent results across age groups. For age groups above 9 years old, the intercorrelation coefficients on visual closure are lowest for the 9–13-year age group. However, the intercorrelations for Visual Closure on the three youngest age groups reveal stronger relationships (than those shown for the 9–13-year-old age group) for all measures except Memory for Sentences (6–8 years) and Delayed Memory for Names (4–5 years). The cross-correlations between scores of the 2–3-year-old group on the five supplemental

tests reported are for Memory for Sentences and Visual Closure ($r = .52$), which are much higher than those reported in the 9–13-year-old group ($r = .12$).

The reliability estimates are derived from Rasch (Wright & Stone, 1979) standard error of measurement person measures, and split-half computational methods corrected for test length using the Spearman-Brown correction formula. The median reliability values are reported for each diagnostic test across all age level samples. A Rasch method is implemented for computing the reliability estimates for Test 26: Cross Out, Test 27: Memory for Sentences, and Test 28: Block Rotation, as split-half computational procedures are inappropriate for these tests. The reliability estimates for these tests are computed from unique estimates of the standard errors of measurement (*SEM*) for each person's raw score using the Rasch method as described in the WJ-R technical manual (McGrew, Werder, & Woodcock, 1991, p. 95).

The fact that median reliability coefficients are consistently high comes as no great surprise as the process of inputting all incorrect scores for measures above the ceiling or correct ones below the basal eliminates potential error variance for those responses. Reliability statistics are reported for as few as 17 individuals at age 4 for the number series construct ($r_{11} = .89$). The median reliability coefficient for Test 25: Number Matrices is .91 but is lowest for 5-year-olds ($r_{11} = .63$, $n = 173$). The reliability estimate for Test 26: Cross Out (median $r_{11} = .76$) is lowest for 5-year-olds and 18-year-olds ($r_{11} = .63$).

For ages 2 through 10, the standard score deviations are highest for the Number Series construct. For ages 11 and above, score standard deviations are about equally high for both the Number Matrices and Number Series constructs. The technical supplement of the testing manual reports two standard errors of measurement, one for the W-scale centered around 500 and a second for the standard score (SS) scale centered on 100 with standard deviation (*SD*) of 15.

Generally speaking, the confidence intervals are widest for Test 22: Visual Closure, Test 24: Number Series, Test 25: Number Matrices, and Test 26: Cross Out. The relatively wide confidence intervals for these measures increase as observed scores move out further from the scale centers for these measures. This occurs because Rasch standard errors of measurement are generally smaller near the scale centers. Although the median *SEM* and *SD* values are not presented with the median reliability coefficients, their values appear fairly large in regard to the score distributions. Overall, the *SEM* values differ greatly by test and by age group. For example, the *SEM* values range from 5.94 to 12.29 for Visual Closure and 3.53 to 12.77 for Number Series.

SUMMARY. The WJ III Diagnostic Supplement provides additional measures of CHC cognitive abilities intended for those seeking greater diagnostic assessment of an individual's cognitive skills. The tests are normed across a wide range of ages and educational levels. Test developers have given consideration for measurement biases on women, individuals with disabilities, and cultural and linguistic minorities. The tests appear as supplements to the WJ III COG and can be administered in as little as 3 minutes for Test 26: Cross Out, and range in length from 24 items on Test 28: Block Rotation, to 72 items on Test 21: Memory for Names, which can be cut short at one of two cutoff points.

The test battery provides additional diagnostic instruments intended to supplement the original WJ III COG test battery and provides support for their construct validity. The diagnostic supplemental tests also provide another mechanism for examining both narrow and broad CHC cognitive abilities that are applicable to a wide range of ages and educational backgrounds.

REVIEWER'S REFERENCES

Wright, B. D., & Stone, M. H. (1979). *Best test design.* Chicago: MESA Press.
Mather, N., & Woodcock, R. W. (2001). *Examiner's manual: Woodcock-Johnson III Tests of Cognitive Abilities.* Itasca, IL: Riverside Publishing.
McGrew, K. S., Werder, J. K., & Woodcock, R. W. (1991). *WJ-R technical manual.* Itasca, IL: Riverside Publishing.
McGrew, K. S., & Woodcock, R. W. (2001). *Technical manual: Woodcock-Johnson III.* Itasca, IL: Riverside Publishing.

Review of the Woodcock-Johnson® III Diagnostic Supplement to the Tests of Cognitive Abilities by DONALD L. THOMPSON, Professor of Counseling and Psychology (Adjunct), Troy University–Montgomery, Montgomery, AL:

DESCRIPTION. This review will provide an overview of the Diagnostic Supplement (DS) and examine its utility and empirical merits in terms of the test administration and interpretation process, and evidence for the test validity and reliability. The manual and various promotional materials for the Diagnostic Supplement (DS) indicate that it is intended to extend the diagnostic capabilities of the Woodcock-Johnson III Tests of Cognitive

Abilities. The DS includes 11 new tests, several new clusters, and new interpretive procedures that are intended to improve and enhance the diagnostic usefulness of the cognitive battery. By using the additional tests and clusters, the DS can provide a more complete evaluation of an individual's relative cognitive strengths and weaknesses. The DS is intended for use in educational, clinical, and research settings. It can be used with individuals who are age 2–90+. The Diagnostic Supplement is particularly useful for the assessment of bilingual individuals and young children. It is also recommended for use in any situation when a language-reduced cognitive ability score is required. In most cases, the DS will be used as a supplement to the Tests of Cognitive Abilities rather than a stand-alone test.

The complete WJ III contains two separate and distinct, conormed batteries: the WJ III® Tests of Achievement and the WJ III Tests of Cognitive Abilities. Although this review focuses only on the DS, it is important to know the characteristics of the complete WJ III battery to get a full understanding of the DS. Because this is beyond the scope of this review, the reader is referred to the most recent *Mental Measurements Yearbook* reviews of the Woodcock-Johnson III battery available in the *15th MMY* (Cizek, 2003; Sandoval, 2003).

The descriptive materials available on the website for the WJ III Tests of Cognitive Abilities indicates that the test "is based on the Cattell-Horn-Carroll (CHC) theory of cognitive abilities, which combines Cattell and Horn's Gf-Gc theory and Carroll's three-stratum theory" (Riverside Publishing, 2004). The Diagnostic Supplement includes 11 new tests that increase the breadth and depth of coverage for several broad and narrow abilities as defined by CHC theory. The subtests include: Memory for Names, Visual Closure, Sound Patterns-Voice, Number Series, Number Matrices, Cross Out, Memory for Sentences, Block Rotation, Sound Patterns-Music, Memory for Names-Delayed, and Bilingual Verbal Comprehension—English/Spanish.

The subtests of the DS can be combined with various subtests of the Standard Battery and/or Extended Battery of the WJ III Tests of Cognitive Abilities for selective testing to examine specific factors in three broad areas including intellectual ability (e.g., General Intellectual Ability-Bilingual), broad CHC clusters, and narrow CHC clusters. The manual identifies three intellectual ability clusters, two broad CHC clusters, and seven narrow CHC clusters. Logically, it would appear that test users might selectively combine various subtests to address specific questions for a particular client.

The administration of the 11 subtests is generally easy and straightforward. All subtests are presented using an easel from which both the examiner and examinee work. The examiner easel sheets provide the administration and scoring instructions for each subtest item. Three subtests are administered using a prerecorded tape provided with the test package. The test materials are of the highest professional quality, and the administration instructions and scoring procedures are described in excellent detail.

Scoring of the 11 subtests is done by hand during the test administration. Many subtests require that a ceiling level be established for the examinee, and several subtests require the establishment of a basal level. Although the subtests are scored by hand, the interpretation requires the use of the Compuscore® and Profiles software program that is included. This process is required because there are complicated scoring factors that, according to the manual, cannot be built into the printed score tables. The test interpretation is based principally on the relative clusters of tests because (as the online promotional material states), "cluster interpretation results in higher validity because scores are based on a broad, multifaceted picture of each ability instead of on a single, narrow ability" (Riverside Publishing, 2004).

DEVELOPMENT. As was noted earlier, the DS is an extension of the WJ III Tests of Cognitive Abilities, and as such was developed using the Cattell-Horn-Carroll (CHC) theory that was used in developing the other two components of the WJ III battery. The subtests were developed to provide measures that address the cognitive abilities conceptualized by that theory. The manual that accompanies the DS does not provide much detail regarding the test development process or how items were selected; however, it appears that the test development occurred concurrently with the work done in preparing the latest version of the WJ III Tests of Cognitive Abilities published in 2001. Other reviewers have described the development process in very positive terms, emphasizing that the effort used sound psychometric practices in the process (Cizek, 2003; Sandoval, 2003).

TECHNICAL. The standardization section of the manual provides information describing how the norm sample matches the intended user population. The DS was developed and normed using the same normative data that were used for the latest edition of the Woodcock-Johnson III (2001), and includes 8,818 individuals from more than 100 geographically diverse communities in the U.S. that theoretically represent the U.S. population from ages 2–90+. The norm sample includes college and university undergraduate and graduate students and a number of adults (nonstudents). The two MMY reviews cited earlier are generally very positive with regard to the norming and standardization of the WJ III, and this reviewer concurs that the development effort appears to represent good psychometric practices in test development.

The overall reliability and validity data provide empirical support for the DS when it is used in appropriate situations. Reliability data were generated using two primary means. Split-half reliabilities were calculated by age for eight of the subscales, whereas the reliability estimates for three subscales were calculated (also by age) using the Rasch analysis procedures. Split-half reliability coefficients for the eight subscales were in the acceptable range of .80 or above (five were <.90), and the Rasch procedures suggested acceptable reliability of the three scales examined in this manner. However, it was noted that some reliability coefficients for younger test subjects (ages 2 to 5) were lower. The reliability of 15 defined clusters was also examined, and all of the coefficients were above .80 (many were above .90).

Test validity was examined using a variety of methods including content, concurrent, and construct methods. Data reported in the test manual describe factor analyses that support the theoretical (CHC) factor structure indicating that hypotheses based on the theory were supported by the test results. Although it focuses on the Tests of Cognitive Abilities and does not specifically address the DS, one recent external study by Lohman (2003) provides additional empirical support for both the concurrent and construct validity of the WJ III Tests of Cognitive Abilities and the CHC theoretical model. Concurrent validity evidence is presented in the manual indicating the correlations between the DS subscales and clusters scores and other established measures of cognitive ability (e.g., WPPSI-R, WISC III, and WAIS III). The overall reliability and validity data provide empirical support for this instrument when it is used in appropriate situations.

COMMENTARY. Although the Woodcock-Johnson Tests of Achievement has long been a favorite of educators and clinicians, the Tests of Cognitive Abilities has never achieved the popularity of the Wechsler and Stanford-Binet for assessing general intellectual ability/IQ. However, with the addition of the Diagnostic Supplement to the Tests of Cognitive Abilities, this may change. Clearly the utility of the DS and its empirical qualities make it a test that should be considered by those who work with special populations/situations including bilingual assessment, early childhood assessment, or other purposes when a language-reduced cognitive ability score is needed. The administration and scoring procedures are easy to learn and simple to use. Because all parts of the WJ III are based on the same theoretical foundation, it potentially provides for more accurate and valid comparisons between different parts of the WJ III battery, and between and among the Cattell-Horn-Carroll (CHC) abilities than is possible if separately normed instruments are used for assessing ability and achievement (manual, p. 4). As with the other parts of the WJ III battery, the DS user may choose to administer only specific subtests in order to address particular questions about the test taker. Because of the flexible structure of the DS, test users have the option of choosing specific subtests to meet the needs of the client being assessed. Although some parts of the DS must be scored on-the-fly as the test is administered in order to establish basal and/or ceiling levels, the overall test interpretation must be done using the Compuscore and Profiles computer program. The scoring software works well and calculates scores using several variables, including time limits, test sections, age-equivalents, grade equivalents, and delay times.

There are some minor factors that detract from the overall excellence of the DS. Although the norm sample includes a significant number of college students and nonstudent adults, the nature of the stratification/sampling for these groups leaves questions as to whether they are truly representative of all college students/adults in the U.S. population. The manual that accompanies the DS provides little in the way of details regarding the test development process or how items were selected, but related information is included in the technical manual (McGrew & Woodcock, 2001) for the Woodcock-Johnson III. Although the DS can be purchased separately from other parts of the WJ III battery, and it is possible to use certain DS subtests for specific limited purposes independent of other parts of the battery, generally the DS should not be viewed as a stand-alone test. It is intended to be used as the title indicates, as a supplement to the Tests of Cognitive Abilities. A computer-based report program for the WJ III battery (Report Writer for the WJ III) is also available for purchase separately. This program generates reports that are comprehensive and will be useful in many counseling and placement situations; unfortunately, the results obtained from the DS are not supported by the program.

SUMMARY. The 2001 standardization of the Woodcock-Johnson III battery and the development of the Diagnostic Supplement have resulted in a well-developed and empirically sound instrument. It is easy to use and score and it has solid psychometric properties. One of the DS subtests can be used to test bilingual individuals. Although this represents a major strength of the test, it also requires bilingual proficiency on the part of the examiner (or an ancillary examiner). The manual is well written and comprehensive and fairly detailed regarding the standardization process as well as the test administration and scoring procedures. The software for computer-based scoring is a major plus. The software works well and makes for convenience and readily available results. Overall, this reviewer finds the DS used in conjunction with the Tests of Cognitive Abilities to be a particularly good choice for assessing clients who are younger, bilingual, or have some language-related deficiencies.

REVIEWER'S REFERENCES

Riverside Publishing. (2004). *The Woodcock-Johnson III product details*. Itasca, IL: Author. Available online at: http://www.riverpub.com/products/clinical/wj3/product.html
Cizek, G. J. (2003). [Review of the Woodcock-Johnson III.]. In B. S. Plake & J. C. Impara (Eds.), *The fifteenth mental measurements yearbook* (pp. 1020–1024). Lincoln, NE: Buros Institute of Mental Measurements.
Lohman, D. F. (2003). *The Woodcock-Johnson and the Cognitive Abilities Test (Form 6): A concurrent validity study*. The University of Iowa. Available online at http://faculty.education.uiowa.edu/pdf/cogat/WJIII_final_2col%202r.pdf
McGrew, K. S., & Woodcock, R. W. (2001). *Technical manual. Woodcock-Johnson III*. Itasca, IL: Riverside Publishing.
Sandoval, J. (2003). [Review of the Woodcock-Johnson III.]. In B. S. Plake & J. C. Impara (Eds.), *The fifteenth mental measurements yearbook* (pp. 1024–1027). Lincoln, NE: Buros Institute of Mental Measurements.

[276]

Word Identification and Spelling Test.

Purpose: Designed to "assess a student's fundamental literacy skills."

Population: Ages 7.0–18.11.

Publication Date: 2004.

Acronym: WIST.
Scores, 4: Word Identification, Spelling, Sound-Symbol Knowledge, Fundamental Literacy Ability Index.
Administration: Individual.
Levels, 2: Elementary, Secondary.
Price Data, 2004: $220 per complete kit including examiner's manual (142 pages), 25 Elementary examiner record booklets, 25 Secondary examiner record booklets, 50 Spelling response forms, word card-Regular Words, word card-Irregular Words, word card-Letter/Pseudo Words, Elementary Spelling card, Secondary Spelling card, and Irregular Spelling card; $50 per examiner's manual; $40 per 25 examiner's record booklets (specify Elementary or Secondary); $15 per 50 Spelling response forms; $15 per word card (specify Regular, Irregular or Letter/Pseudo Words); $15 per Spelling card (specify Elementary or Secondary).
Time: (40) minutes.
Authors: Barbara A. Wilson and Rebecca H. Felton.
Publisher: PRO-ED.

Review of the Word Identification and Spelling Test by W. JOEL SCHNEIDER, Assistant Professor of Psychology, and KATHRYN E. HOFF, Assistant Professor of Psychology, Illinois State University, Normal, IL:

DESCRIPTION. The Word Identification and Spelling Test (WIST) is designed to measure fundamental literacy skills in children and adolescents aged 7 to 18. The WIST consists of six item sets or tasks. Information from these item sets is used to generate norm-referenced scores and additional diagnostic information through informal methods. The WIST is designed to identify poor readers, poor spellers, and students requiring more intensive instruction, and to monitor annual progress in reading and spelling development.

The Word Identification subtest consists of the Read Regular Words item set (which consists of familiar and unfamiliar words that can be decoded with word attack skills) and the Read Irregular Words item set (which consists of high-frequency words with one or more orthographic irregularities). Likewise, the Spelling subtest consists of two item sets: Spell Regular Words and Spell Irregular Words. The Sound-Symbol Knowledge subtest consists of the Pseudo Words and Letters Sounds item sets. Both item sets measure the ability to identify a grapheme and recall its corresponding sound. The Fundamental Literacy Ability Index is a composite standard score consisting of the Word Identification and Spelling subtests.

Informal assessment procedures allow examiners to determine whether examinees are performing below, at, or above grade level on each of the six item sets. The WIST provides a procedure to conduct a sound-symbol analysis. On tasks that involve pronouncing regular words (i.e., Read Regular Words, Spell Regular Words, and Pseudo Words), all errors are classified and tallied. Error types include sound substitutions, additions, omissions, transpositions, and self-corrections. The WIST has an informal procedure to analyze spelling errors. Spelling error types include missing sounds, letter-sound confusion, using the wrong letters to generate the right sounds, unconventional spelling, schwa difficulties, and suffix errors. On the WIST examiner record booklet there is a checklist for problematic behaviors related to reading and spelling: poor attention, nervousness, immature vocabulary, dialectic differences, poor pronunciation, letter reversals, poor handwriting, word retrieval problems, rapid but wrong responses, and slow and accurate responses.

TECHNICAL. The normative sample of the WIST consists of 1,520 children and adolescents aged 7 to 18 years. The normative sample was recruited from 16 states representing all four major geographical regions of the United States. The normative sample was selected to match as closely as possible the characteristics of the 2000 U.S. Census according to geographic area, gender, ethnicity, parental educational attainment, exceptionality status, and age.

The three subtests and the composite have standard scores with a mean of 100 and a standard deviation of 15. Standard scores were developed with Roid's continuous norming procedure. Age-based and grade-based norms are available.

The reliability (i.e., internal consistency) estimates for the WIST subtests, as measured by Cronbach's coefficient alpha, ranged from .85 to .98 across all age levels. The average reliability of the Fundamental Literacy Composite was .97. Subsequent analyses suggested that the WIST is equally reliable for males and females, different ethnicities, and for people with learning disabilities. A subsample of 54 students was given the WIST twice over a 2-week period. Test-retest reliability coefficients of the WIST subtests ranged from .93 to .99. Forty WIST protocols were scored independently by two PRO-ED staff members to assess interscorer reliability. Interscorer reliability of the WIST subtests ranged from .95 to .98.

Confirmatory factor analyses of the six item sets suggest that a three-factor structure (isomorphic to the three subtests) fits best. The Word Identification factor is highly correlated with both the Spelling (.72 to .89) and Sound-Symbol Knowledge (.63 to .72) factors but the correlation between Spelling and Sound-Symbol Knowledge is more moderate (.30 to .34).

Criterion-related validity was investigated with five different samples of students. It was found that the WIST Word Identification subtest was highly correlated (.78 to .89) with untimed measures of Word Identification such as the WIAT-II Word Reading subtest and the Woodcock Reading Mastery Tests—Revised Word Identification subtest but moderately correlated with timed subtests such as the Test of Word Reading Efficiency and the Test of Silent Word Reading Fluency (.47 to .55). The WIST Spelling subtest was highly correlated (.80 to .87) with the WIAT-II Spelling subtest and the Test of Written Spelling—Fourth Edition.

COMMENTARY. The WIST manual is well written and clear. Its theoretical underpinnings appear to be reasonably sound and in agreement with most other tests measuring the same constructs. The normative sample is large and representative of United States children and adolescents. Reliability and validity data for the WIST are encouraging. One important omission in the validity data presented is that the relations between WIST scores and measures of reading comprehension have not been quantified, although it is likely that WIST subtests are just as correlated with reading comprehension tests as other word identification and spelling tests.

Although the WIST's norm-referenced subtests yield information that is highly similar to other commercially available tests, it is the informal features of the WIST that set it apart. The ability to identify specific types of spelling and decoding errors is especially valuable to clinicians needing to make specific recommendations for remediation service providers. Although the informal assessment procedures appear to be logically sound, their treatment utility has yet to be demonstrated empirically.

Although including a checklist with which to note behaviors that may have interfered with test performance (e.g., inattention, nervousness, dialectic differences) is a nice touch, few guidelines are presented to help clinicians decide how the presence of such factors should influence interpretation. Obviously clinicians should use their best judgment in such matters but it would be nice to have some validity data on the behavior checklist procedure.

Although the WIST provides three subtest scores, the manual does not provide much guidance on the meaning of various configurations of scores. For example, are the treatment implications different for a child with low Word Identification and Spelling scores but an average Sound-Symbol Knowledge score compared to the treatment implications for a child with low scores in all three subtests? Do the authors reject such procedures as unreliable forms of profile analysis? It would strengthen the case for using the WIST if longitudinal data were available to show the likely reading ability growth rates for children with different patterns of WIST scores.

SUMMARY. The WIST is a well-constructed and well-normed measure of fundamental literacy skills such as word identification, word decoding, and spelling. Although the norm-referenced subtest scores yield information almost identical to that which can be found using more established tests such as the Woodcock-Johnson III (WJIII; 15:281), Wechsler Individual Achievement Test—Second Edition (WIAT-II; 15:275), and the Kaufman Test of Educational Achievement — Second Edition (KTEA-II; 124), the more informal and qualitative analyses that can be conducted using the WIST make possible a more comprehensive analysis of reading difficulties than can be conducted using only the major batteries mentioned above. Unfortunately, the features with sound empirical backing in the WIST are not unique and the features that are unique to the WIST have little empirical backing. Thus, until more validity data supporting the use of the informal features of the test are available, the WIST will remain a merely promising instrument.

Review of the Word Identification and Spelling Test by JOHN T. WILLSE, Assistant Professor of Educational Research Methodology, University of North Carolina at Greensboro, Greensboro, NC:

DESCRIPTION. The Word Identification and Spelling Test (WIST) is designed for use with students with problems in reading, spelling, or both. It is not a generalized reading test; instead, it is focused on aspects of word-level reading and spelling. During the course of a 30–40-minute individualized assessment (modifications for partial group administrations are possible) six sets of items are administered to the examinee. Three subtest scores are produced at the conclusion of the assessment: (a) Word Identification, (b) Spelling, and (c) Sound-Symbol Knowledge. The Word Identification subscore and Spelling subscore are summed together to create the Fundamental Literacy Ability Index. The Sound-Symbol Knowledge subtest is considered an optional supplemental score. Two versions of the item sets are available, making the WIST appropriate for use with elementary (Grades 2–5) or secondary (Grades 6–12) students. Raw scores on the Fundamental Literacy Ability Index and the three subtests can be converted into percentile ranks, standard scores, descriptive ratings (e.g., "Above Average"), age equivalents, and grade equivalents.

For the Word Identification tasks, students read the list of words while the administrator marks the words as correctly or incorrectly pronounced in an examiner record booklet. For the Spelling task, which may be administered to groups, the examiner reads from the list of words while the student attempts to spell them. The Sound-Symbol Knowledge subtest requires examinees to read lists of pseudo words (i.e., nonsense words only readable by their phonetic structure) and lists of letter sounds and common letter groupings while the administrator scores the responses as correct or incorrect. Proper use of the WIST requires examiners with experience in the administration of standardized assessments.

Additional nonstandardized options for scoring examinees are available. Described as "informal analyses" in the examiner's manual, these nonstandardized procedures, which do not have associated norms, are intended to aid in the identification of categories of examinee mistakes. The test authors suggest that formative interventions to student learning can be planned from this information.

DEVELOPMENT. The WIST examiner's manual clearly describes the connection of difficulty with reading and spelling common words and letter combinations, the skills addressed by the WIST, to broader problems of basic reading literacy. The primary use of the WIST is the identification of students with these word level reading and spelling problems. The diagnostic information provided by the informal assessment can be used to plan appropriate instruction for students who have not mastered basic reading and spelling skills despite having received instruction.

The rationale for the structure of the test is most apparent in sections of the manual dealing with the informal assessment. Descriptions of common problems observed in assessment results are paired with general instructional guidelines. In a section on content validity, the authors provide explanations for the importance of each item set and explicitly link item sets to Orton-Gillingham-based programs.

Sophisticated item analyses, discussed in the section on validity, were part of the WIST's development. These analyses provide evidence of the utility and appropriateness of the norm-referenced scores. Additional analyses demonstrate that efforts have been made to control ethnic or gender related bias. None of the formal analyses, however, address the informally scored section of the WIST.

TECHNICAL. Descriptions of the normative process are clear. Efforts were made by the test's designers to create normative samples representative of the ethnic and geographic composition of the U.S. In mirroring the U.S. population, some subgroup samples (Asian American and American Indian) are quite small. Reasonable procedures were followed in creating norms from this sample.

A major concern regarding the testing materials is that they offer no summary of the psychometric properties of the informal diagnostic aspect of the WIST. Labeling one aspect of the test as "informal" does not free the test maker of responsibility for demonstrating its utility or appropriateness. Once test makers provide a scoring protocol and suggest uses for the resultant information, it is incumbent upon them to make a reasonable effort to provide evidence for the reliability of results and the validity of the intended interpretations (*Standards for Educational and Psychological Testing*, AERA, APA, & NCME, 1999).

Useful information is made available about the reliability and validity of the norm-referenced scores on the WIST. The internal consistency, test-retest, and interrater reliability estimates reported in the manual are all quite good. These high reliability coefficients even apply to the subscales, with only two reported coefficients falling below .95. The interrater reliability, however, is based on too small a sample (20 elementary and 20 secondary students). Additionally, the interrater reliability analysis was conducted on two raters employed by the publisher. Interrater reliability could be lower among the general pool of WIST users. This possibility seems especially plausible on the more subjective parts (e.g., when students must correctly pronounce words) of the WIST.

Validity evidence for the norm-referenced aspect of the WIST is well documented. Ample descriptions are provided for justifying the content aspect of validity. Criterion-related aspects of validity are demonstrated through appropriate correlational studies with other commercial reading/spelling tests. Additional evidence demonstrating a relationship between the WIST and related academic outcomes would be a useful addition to the validity evidence.

Construct validity is approached in two ways. First, WIST scores are shown to conform to theory by revealing relationships that are expected based on past research (e.g., scores increase with age). Second, results from confirmatory factor analyses indicate that factor structures correspond more closely with the organizing theories under which the WIST was designed than they do to factor structures based on competing theories. This factor analytic approach to establishing construct validity is a strong methodology.

COMMENTARY. The most clearly supported use of the WIST is in the application of the norm-referenced assessment for the identification of students with word-level reading and spelling problems. The development of the assessment and its connection to theory is clearly articulated. Procedures for administering and scoring the WIST are clear. Anyone familiar with the administration of standardized assessments to school-aged children should be able to appropriately use the WIST.

Some of the reliability information provided could be improved with larger sample sizes and by including general users of the WIST as raters (as mentioned previously). The most obvious shortcoming is the absence of any formal investigation of the technical properties of the informal assessment procedures.

SUMMARY. The WIST should provide users with a reliable way to identify students with word-level reading and spelling problems. The evidence supporting the validity of the norm-referenced aspect of this assessment is adequate. Unfortunately, many of the test's suggested uses follow from the "informal assessment" scoring procedures that are not supported by any direct

reliability or validity evidence. Potential users should be aware of this lack of supporting evidence in any applications of the informal assessment.

REVIEWER'S REFERENCE

American Educational Research Association, American Psychological Association, & National Council on Measurement in Education. (1999). *Standards for educational and psychological testing.* Washington, DC: American Educational Research Association.

[277]

Word Meaning Through Listening.

Purpose: Designed "to infer levels of semantic competence through response to receptive language."
Population: Ages 7–16.
Publication Date: 2002.
Scores: Total score only.
Administration: Group.
Forms, 2: A, B.
Price Data, 2002: £7.75 per complete kit including administrative and technical manual (18 pages) with computer disk scoring key and 25 Form A test booklets; £2.30 per manual and 3.5-inch disk scoring key; £5.25 per 25 test booklets (Form A or B).
Time: (20–25) minutes.
Author: Alan Brimer.
Publisher: Educational Evaluations [England].

Review of Word Meaning Through Listening by JAMES D. BROWN, Professor of Second Language Studies, University of Hawaii at Manoa, Honolulu, HI:

DESCRIPTION. The Word Meaning Through Listening (WMTL) test is a paper-and-pencil test designed for group administration to children in school years 3 to 11. The WMTL is available in two forms of 60 items each and is meant to be a direct measure of "the understanding of spoken English words through the recognition of pictures that represent their meaning" (p. 12), from which, it is argued, users can infer the students' "intelligent verbal interaction."

The test is designed for administration, scoring, and interpretation by nontechnical staff. During the test administration, the examiner reads a word while the students look at two pictures. The students then mark on each picture: drawing a tick mark if the picture represents the word that was read, a cross if the picture does not represent the word, or a line through the number of the item if the student does not know. One, none, or both of the pictures may represent the word that was read. WMTL includes two four-page test booklets (which are used up in the testing process as answer sheets), an administrative and technical manual, and a floppy disk used in scoring.

The test booklets (Forms A and B) start with questions about the students' biodata information. Then, the first page provides pictures used as examples in the directions. Each of the other three pages contains 20 pairs of pictures for a total of 60 paired-picture items. The pairs are clearly numbered, organized, and spaced so that it is easy for students to understand how to proceed. The pictures are fairly small (about 1 inch square) consisting of reasonably clear line drawings. Children in Grades 3 to 11 should be able to understand the pictures.

The administrative and technical manual is made up of three sections: Test Administration, Technical Data, and Scoring the Test. The Test Administration part provides proctor instructions, complete lists of the words used on Forms A and B, as well as tables for converting raw scores to standardized scores, and standardized scores to percentile ranks for various grade levels for Forms A and B separately. The Technical Data section explains the construct being tested, the structure of the test, the test history of the test construction, the derivation of the standardized scores, the validity evidence of the test and reliability information. The Scoring the Test section briefly explains how to use the floppy disk for scoring the test.

DEVELOPMENT. The WMTL was developed to provide a group-administered version of the Listening for Meaning Test (apparently developed in 1980, but not referenced). The LFMT was based on "approximately 1000 words" (p. 14) randomly selected from the *Shorter Oxford English Dictionary* (3rd ed., 1975). These words were screened by "four competent English speakers" and 327 were removed because they are not "in current use in English" (administrative and technical manual, p. 14). "Eventually, 576 words were successfully represented by drawings" (p. 14) and turned into trial items. The items were provisionally allocated to one of four difficulty levels defined as age group bands: below 7, 7–11, 12–17, and above average adult. Each item was piloted on 100 persons in the level to which it belonged as well as the adjacent levels. Thus the lowest and highest level items were piloted on 200 persons, and the two middle levels were piloted on 300 persons. Point-biserial correlation coefficients were used to eliminate items "which deviated in slope from the modal value" (p. 15). Then Rasch analysis was used to scale the items. The LFMT was

standardized, and then published in 1980. Person ability and item easiness estimates were derived, and a fit statistic (chi-square) was used to eliminate misfitting items (mostly very difficult or easy items). Nothing is said about eliminating misfitting persons. Later, in order to provide two forms of the test, the WMTL was compiled using the already existing items and item analysis statistics.

TECHNICAL. Standardization of the WMTL was based on over 1,000 applicants to "a new City Technology College" (administrative and technical manual, p. 15). No other information is provided about this norm sample; nor are norms provided for different gender or ethnic/cultural groups.

Because the WMTL employs a ceiling score and a correction for guessing, the author could not apply the traditional Kuder-Richardson formulas. He therefore used another approach vaguely defined as "calculated directly from item correlations with total score" (administrative and technical manual, p. 17). The result was .96 for both forms. The standard error of measurement was reported to be "three points of standardized score" (p. 17).

The validity of the WMTL is first defended in terms of the fit of the test content and the test tasks to the construct as described in the manual. Then the author presents concurrent validity correlations for the WMTL with the EPVT and SAST (which are not referenced), which were .51 to .71, respectively, based on relatively small samples of 169 and 171. A predictive validity argument was also offered in the form of correlations between the WMTL scores of 160 students and their SAT achievement test scores 4 years later. The correlations between the WMTL and English, Maths, Science, and Total scores on the SAT (again, this test is not referenced) were .61, .54, .32, and .59, respectively. The author claims that "The results are highly supportive of the predictive validity of the WMTL, given the four year time lapse" (administrative and technical manual, p. 17). I find neither the concurrent validity nor the predictive validity arguments particularly compelling. Worse yet, no mention is made of the relationship between test scores and any particular interpretation or use.

COMMENTARY. A number of potential problems exist in the design of the WMTL. First the words must be read aloud by the examiner (no cassette tape is provided). There is no explanation of how fast to read the words or how much time to allow between words. Second, some pictures on the test may not be clear to some nationalities or ethnic groups. As the author puts it, "Images are less easily controlled since the conventions of representation of meanings are culturally diverse" (administrative and technical manual, p. 12). Third, though designed for Grades 3–11, the author suggests that the WMTL could also be administered to students below Year 3. No explanation is given as to why a test normed for Grades 3–11 would be appropriate for younger students. The fourth and biggest problem with the WMTL involves the rather complex scoring procedures. Unfortunately, no means are provided for scoring the WMTL by hand without the computer program (written in Basic). Each student's responses to each picture on each item must be entered separately by hand for a total of 120 data points per student. Only then will the program print a raw score to the screen. Even with the raw score in hand, interpreting the test results requires first converting the raw scores to age-equivalent, IQ-like, standardized scores (using six pages of conversion tables) based on the form involved and each student's age in years (and months, if known). Those standardized scores must then be converted to percentile ranks using yet another table. My guess is that few practitioners would have the time or patience to deal with such complex scoring procedures.

For potential test uers outside the U.K., it should be noted that the words for this test were selected from a 1975 British dictionary, which suggests that they are representative of British dialects rather than the English used in other countries. In addition, though it is not clearly explained, the four English native speakers who judged whether the words were currently used in English were probably British as well. In addition, some of the words tested on the WMTL seemed odd to me as a speaker of North American English. For example, "Indian corn" (Form A, #44) is not the term I would use for maize, nor is "Red Indian" (Form B, #47) the phrase I would use to refer to Native Americans.

SUMMARY. The WMTL claims to use "the understanding of spoken English words to infer the level of intelligent verbal functioning of which a student is capable" (p. 2). The WMTL is *verbal* only in the sense that it is a passive-knowledge-of-vocabulary test. The students are not asked to use the vocabulary for anything, so it is difficult to see

how this is a test of *functioning*, verbal or otherwise. The word *intelligent* seems to be thrown gratuitously into the title.

Even if the construct were clearly defined, the computer program used to score the WMTL is very cumbersome. It could easily be modified to ask for the student's age and then automatically calculate and report the age-equivalent standardized scores and percentile ranks. In fact, many of the problems with the WMTL could be solved by computerizing it, so that students would (a) all hear the same speaker, speaking at the same speed, with pauses of the same length between words; (b) all see larger pictures on the screen; (c) all be able to answer directly on the keyboard (and to the computer's hard drive); and (d) all receive standardized and/or age equivalent percentile scores immediately upon completing the test. However, such a strategy would not solve the problems with construct definition and validation, both of which need considerable work.

Review of the Word Meaning Through Listening by CARLOS INCHAURRALDE, Professor of Linguistics and Psychologist, University of Zaragoza, Zaragoza, Spain:

DESCRIPTION. The Word Meaning Through Listening (WMTL) is a 60-item test that considers the understanding of spoken English words in order to infer the level of intelligent verbal functioning of students. It is to be administered to groups of students in Grades 3 to 11 (ages 7 to 16). There are two forms, A and B, for which usage is similar. Before taking the actual test, both forms have four examples and four practice exercises. All items have two pictures, which should be marked with a tick or with a cross according to whether they correspond to the same meaning or not of a word that is read aloud by the examiner. Raw scores are obtained by means of a computer program that is provided with the manual and the forms in a 3.5-inch floppy disk for PC-compatible computers. The examiner has to enter two digits for each item, corresponding to whether there was a tick (marked with 1) or a cross (marked with 0) for the two pictures in the item. Once all of the 60 items have been marked, the raw score is printed on the screen. The information can then be copied onto the front page of the test. It is possible to score several tests one after the other.

In order to represent the performance of students in comparison to a group, the raw scores are transformed to the normal curve with a common mean and standard deviation. These standardized scores can be used to obtain to percentile ranks, which can be used for comparison of a child's performance with those of children within a similar age range.

DEVELOPMENT. The WMTL test derives from the Listening for Meaning Test (LFMT), which was first published in 1980. This test was in turn a successor to the English Picture Vocabulary Tests (EPVT). The main difference between the WMTL and the LFMT is that the former is intended for administration within groups. According to the publisher, "the psychological model adopted is that of a multi-dimensional universe of publicly communicable meanings which is referenced by lexis. A person's holding of the universe is regarded as dynamic and as increasing with age" (administrative and technical manual, p. 12). The theoretical construct behind the test is explained in this paragraph and the following, but there are no references to research supporting this approach.

There is information about the development of the test in the manual. Trial tests for the WMTL were produced using a sample of words (a total of 480 trial items was needed) taken from the *Shorter Oxford English Dictionary, 3rd Edition*. A sampling fraction of 1:163 yielded approximately 1,000 words, which were chosen by stratifying the dictionary by page. Pages were then drawn at random; one word was chosen at random on each drawn page. The selected words were then surveyed by four English speakers who decided about the elimination of those that did not meet the requirement that they were in use in English speech. This led to the elimination of 327 words. A further step was to determine whether the remaining words could be represented by drawings. Eventually, 576 words were well represented by drawings.

TECHNICAL. There is very little information in the WMTL manual about standardization. Standardization began on the LFMT and it was only after a decade had passed that work on the WMTL started. Standardized scores were obtained by testing over 1,000 individuals, all of them applicants for admission to a new City Technology College (CTC), for whom scores on a nationally standardized test, whose name is not mentioned in the manual, were known. Calibration of the WMTL scores was carried out by means of an equipercentile method. The results were

norms for children aged 10 to 11. A similar procedure with smaller samples was used for extending norms to other groups. In any case, the manual warns that "norms for groups other than those aged 10:0 to 12:11 must be regarded as provisional" (administrative and technical manual, p. 16); therefore, more standardization studies are needed.

Concerning reliability, the WMTL uses a ceiling score and a correction for chance scoring, which invalidates the use of the Kuder-Richardson formulae for its estimation, because the variance of the test has more than two components. Therefore, the method used to measure reliability was direct calculation from item correlations with total test score. Both forms (A and B) of the test obtained reliability estimates of .96. It would have been interesting to determine correlation of scores obtained by the same individuals on the two forms of the test. However, this has not been done so far.

There are four ways in which the validity of the WMTL has been considered by the authors: the fitness of its content to the test construct, the fitness of the test task to the test construct, the relation of the test scores to those on other cognate tests, and the prognostic value of the test scores for future achievement. The authors argue that the first two criteria have been accounted for in the process of test construction because fitness of content is ensured by the choice of English words, and fitness of the test task is guaranteed by a careful screening of words not relevant to modern level speech and the grouping of the rest into difficulty levels. The adequate relationship of scores to those of other comparable tests was achieved during calibration because the EPVT and a sentence reading test were administered to students aged 11 to 12 who had already taken one form of the WMTL 2 years before. The correlation of WMTL scores with those of the EPVT was .71 for Form A and .69 for Form B, and the correlation with those of the SAST was .56 for Form A and .51 for Form B. These correlation coefficients are not high, but the time lapse of 2 years between tests may have had an influence on this. As for the predictive validity of the WMTL, the correlation of WMTL scores with SAT test results of achievement at Keystage 3 after a time lapse of 4 years shows values of .61 (English), .54 (Maths) and .32 (Science), with a combined total correlation of .59. This can be considered to be supportive of the prognostic value of the WMTL, especially for English and Mathematics.

COMMENTARY. In general terms, this test lacks some fine-tuning in the standardization process, which has not been completely finished except for the 10-years-old to 12-years-old range. More complete measures of reliability would also have been greatly appreciated by the potential user of this text. The theoretical construct on which the test is based also needs more extensive theoretical support. However, its administration and scoring system seem very simple and straightforward (provided one has a computer at hand and can use the scoring disk). The underlying notion that the understanding of spoken English words can be used for inferring the level of intelligent verbal functioning is intuitively sound and its validity is corroborated by the correlation values obtained with Scholastic Aptitude Test (SAT) test results. Although this test shows some weaknesses, it also has some virtues that should be taken into account, making it a useful tool in many situations.

SUMMARY. The WMTL can be a useful tool for assessing intelligent verbal functioning of students aged 7 to 16 when there is a need to carry out this assessment within groups. It can be easily administered and scored and it is therefore an interesting test for those educators or psychologists with that kind of need. However, whenever a more complex evaluation is required, other tests with a stronger verbal aptitude component should be used because there are still some gaps concerning evidence of reliability and the process of establishing norms according to age.

[278]
Wordchains: A Word Reading Test for All Ages.

Purpose: Designed to "screen for specific learning difficulties" and to help teachers "identify individual pupils with poor reading skills."
Population: Ages 7 and over.
Publication Date: 1999.
Scores, 2: Letterchains, Wordchains.
Administration: Individual or group.
Price Data: Available from publisher.
Time: (15) minutes.
Author: Louise Miller Guron.
Publisher: NFER-Nelson Publishing Co., Ltd. [England].

Review of Wordchains: A Word Reading Test for All Ages by COLIN COOPER, Senior Lecturer, School of Psychology, The Queen's University, Belfast, United Kingdom:

DESCRIPTION. Wordchains is a test designed as a quick, simple method of screening children or adults aged over 7 years for difficulty in reading words. Unusually, it can be administered in a group setting. The basic premise is straightforward. Participants are given a booklet containing 120 strings or three of four semantically unconnected words, without spaces (e.g., "brickcarfloor"). They are asked to draw two or three vertical lines in each string, to indicate the breaks between words. It is a highly speeded test, with a 3-minute time limit: no one can complete all items in the allocated time. The test is scored by counting the number of groups of words where the breaks are all correctly identified.

Performance on the test may be influenced by psychomotor speed or co-ordination rather than word recognition. Hence the test is preceded by the Letterchains test, which measures speed unconfounded by semantic processing. Participants identify the boundaries between strings containing three or four sequences of letters (e.g., ddddkkkrrrr) and have 90 seconds to complete 90 items. If a participant's Wordchains score falls below the "normal" range for their age (and fully 23% of those tested will do so) then their Letterchains score is also consulted. If the Letterchains score is within the "average" range then it is concluded that the individual may have a specific word processing difficulty, and further follow-up is recommended.

DEVELOPMENT. Wordchains is based on a Swedish test (Jacobson, 1996). The test has clearly been carefully constructed. The letter sequences have been chosen to remove ambiguities at the boundaries (e.g., "tinone" where the word "no" appears at the boundary). High frequency bigrams are also avoided at the boundaries (e.g., "pothappy") as have short utility words, such as "an" or "the," which may be overlooked.

Deviation norms (mean 100, *sd* 15) are presented for both Wordchains and Letterchains. These are apparently based on U.K. samples and show 3-month age bands. A table for converting scores into "word recognition age" (akin to mental age) is also provided. However, the composition and size of the normative samples is not specified, which is a major failing. Nor is the method of construction clear (e.g., whether smoothing or interpolation was used to estimate the scores for some age bands).

TECHNICAL. As the test is highly speeded with a single score being obtained from items of trivial difficulty, internal consistency measures of reliability should not be computed. One-week test-retest reliability for the Wordchains test was .85 in a sample of 181 children who were 11 years old. Similar figures are quoted for 12-month test-retest reliability for the Swedish version of the test, which was administered to pupils aged 7–12. The test-retest reliability of Letterchains is lower (.57 to .81), perhaps because it is so short. The correlation between Letterchains and Wordchains is .51 for the 11-year-olds (it varies from .39 to .51 in samples aged between 7 and 16 years); therefore, for the 11-year-olds the correlation between Letterchains and Wordchains is .72 when corrected for unreliability. The authors scrutinize the uncorrected correlation, and conclude that there is rather little overlap between Letterchains and Wordchains but this reflects the low reliability of the Letterchains task. There may be an appreciable psychomotor/perceptual speed component to Wordchains, and this issue could usefully be explored further.

Wordchains does, however, show an impressive degree of validity. The manual reports large and significant correlations with several other tests of reading ability and standard assessments of English performance taken between the ages of 5 and 16. The highest correlation is with the assessment of reading made at age 5 ($r = .73$), perhaps reflecting the vocabulary demands of the test. However, Wordchains also shows a correlation of .5 with performance on the GCSE (school-leaving) qualifications in English Language and English Literature in a large sample of pupils aged 16. This is most impressive for such a simple test. Letterchains also shows some significant correlations with performance in the preteenage children, although these are substantially smaller than for Wordchains. Correlations between Wordchains and teachers' ratings of reading skill were high—in the order of .8 for children in the 7–11-year age group. Children diagnosed with dyslexia scored a standard deviation lower than controls on Wordchains but not on Letterchains.

The manual reports little research into bias and fairness, other than noting a modest sex-difference favoring girls and poorer performance by students for whom English is not their first language. However, there seems to have been no attempt to explore whether the gender difference reflects bias or a genuine group difference, although the necessary data to check the equality of regression lines are clearly available.

COMMENTARY. The system of relating Wordchains scores to Letterchains scores is clearly flawed. The problem arises because it involves classifying the score on each test as either "normal" or "below normal." Consider the case where a child has a Wordchains score at the 22nd percentile (putting them in the below normal group) but a Letterchains score in the 24th percentile (just in the normal group). Because the former score is just below normal and the latter barely normal, it would be concluded that the child may show problems with word recognition, even though the two percentile scores are very similar. Yet a child whose Wordchains score was at the 24th percentile and whose Letterchains score was at the 99th percentile would not be diagnosed as having problems with word recognition, even though the difference is huge. It would be far better to develop a table showing the joint distribution of scores on Wordchains and Letterchains in order to show how frequently each particular difference occurs.

A second issue concerns vocabulary. If a child has not previously encountered a word shown as part of a word chain, they will probably find it harder to identify its boundaries. The manual suggests that "the words are likely to be familiar as spoken words to the beginning reader" (teacher's guide, p. 33) but no data are presented to support this assertion. It would be helpful if more information was provided on the familiarity of the words used, to ensure that the test is not assessing vocabulary in the very youngest age groups.

SUMMARY. Wordchains is a very short, highly effective group test for screening children for poor word-reading skills. Given its high predictive validity and its wide age range, it should be widely used. The method for determining whether a child's score indicates a problem with word recognition needs to be improved, and more information needs to be given about the nature and composition of the normative samples.

REVIEWER'S REFERENCE

Jacobson, C. (1996). *Manual: Ordkedjor.* Stockholm: Psykologiförlaget.

Review of the Wordchains: A Word Reading Test for All Ages by STEVEN R. SHAW, School Psychologist, The School District of Greenville County, Greenville, SC:

DESCRIPTION. The Wordchains test is an innovative method of screening for problems with word recognition. There are 120 three- or four-word chains. An example of a chain is: lampchairphone. The task is for the examinee to place strikes between the words with a pencil or pen (i.e., lamp/chair/phone). The time limit is 3 minutes. There is a preliminary task of letter chains. An example of a letter chain is rrrrrrdddddddkkkkk. The task is to make a strike between letter groups. There are 90 letter chains and a 90-second time limit. The purpose of this preliminary task is to practice visual motor skills, to raise confidence and motivation, to identify students who may not have understood directions or have a slow working speed, and to screen for visual motor deficits.

Wordchains is a test designed for students older than 7 years of age. There are four reported purposes for using Wordchains: (a) As a cost effective screening instrument to be used with groups of any size. (b) As a test of individual reading development. The manual reports that the same test could be used for students over time to track reading development. However, the data appear to show significant practice effects (i.e., an increase from 41.9 to 52.3 word chains correct over a 1-week period). Unfortunately, multiple parallel forms are not available. (c) As a method of evaluating remedial programs. The purpose would require a pre- and posttest. Without multiple forms the possibility of practice effects is present again. (d) As an indicator of whole class performance.

The sole materials are 12 page disposable test booklets for each student, teacher's guide, and the Easy Reference Marking Guide. Scores are presented as standard scores with a mean of 100 and a standard deviation of 15. Stanines, percentile ranks, and Word Recognition Age (i.e., age equivalent) are also provided.

DEVELOPMENT. The Wordchains test was developed in Sweden in 1987 as part of a large-scale research project on reading skill development. The Wordchains test was then used in some clinical settings in Sweden. The Wordchains test has been translated into Norwegian and into English in 1996. The reviewed version of Wordchains was published in England. However, there are no words that would be unfamiliar to readers in the U.S. (e.g., pram), nor are there words with different spellings in England versus the U.S. (e.g., behaviour). Although all standardization and norming data presented were based on an English

sample, there was a brief report in the manual about data on Wordchains in the U.S. Based on 135 students in the U.S., the author states tentatively that the U.S. scores follow a similar range of means and standard deviation to those in England and Sweden.

TECHNICAL.

Standardization. Data from a sample of 1,264 students were collected in October 1988. Different schools were used for each year group. Note that a year group is analogous to a grade (i.e., Year 3 in England is much like third grade in the U.S.). One class of approximately 25 students was selected from each school. For Year 7, Year 9, Year 10, and Year 11 samples were selected from eight different schools from different regions on England and Wales. For Year 3 and Year 12, 10 schools were sampled. Twelve schools were sampled for Year 5. There was an effort to match these samples with national census data in terms of urban/nonurban and socioeconomic status with mixed success. Normative data are sparse and not necessarily representative of the English population. Certainly, there are problems attempting to generalize these norms to a U.S. population.

Reliability. Reliability data are extremely limited. The only data presented were on a sample of 181 students from Year 7. These data were 1-week test-retest data. Correlation from Time 1 to Time 2 on letter chains was .59. Correlation from Time 1 to Time 2 on word chains was .85. As mentioned earlier, there was a significant increase in mean scores from Time 1 to Time 2 indicating a practice effect and "increased confidence in the task" (manual, p. 49). There is a paragraph reporting the 12-month test-retest reliability on Swedish Wordchains from Grades 1 to 6 ranges from .80 to .90.

Validity. There were several correlations of letter chains and word chains results with measures commonly used in England and Wales, but not in the U.S. Key Stage Tests 1 (Year 3 and 5), 2 (Year 7), and 3 (Year 9) were administered. The Key Stage tests consist of reading passages where students answer factual questions about the passages in writing. Teacher Assessment in Reading and Writing was used for Year 5 and Year 9. Teacher Assessments involve children reading passages aloud to teachers. The teachers then quiz students on what they read. GCSE (General Certificate of Secondary Education) assessment of English literature and English language was used for Year 12. The correlations between Wordchains results and all reading tests were significant and positive at the p <.001 level. Correlations ranged from .23 for Key Stage 3 to .73 for Key Stage 1. The correlations between these tests and letter chains were not as high. There was even a significant negative correlation between Teacher Assessment of Writing in Year 9 and letter chains. The validity data of Wordchains may be promising for future research, but are not compelling for a published assessment. Moreover, the majority of potential U.S. users will not have knowledge of the criteria used in the series of validity studies.

COMMENTARY. Wordchains is an innovative screening instrument for word recognition. It was developed in Sweden and adapted in England for an English-speaking population. In England, Wordchains is barely adequate as a 10-minute screening instrument for large groups of children. There remain questions on the quality of the normative group, reliability data, and validity data. Children scoring poorly on Wordchains would then require additional detailed assessment to determine the existence, nature, and severity of a reading problem. How much Wordchains adds to simple teacher judgment concerning a child's reading problems is not known. Wordchains is not recommended in the U.S., except as a research instrument. The standardization is not likely to be representative, the reliability data are too limited, and validity data are not based on criteria relevant to most U.S. schools. Moreover, as many school districts are developing local norms for curriculum-based measurement in oral reading it is unclear how much Wordchains would add. However, curriculum-based measurement in oral reading requires brief, but individual, administration with different reading probes for each grade level. Using Wordchains, an entire school could be assessed with one version of Wordchains in a total of less than 10 minutes. Research on the relationship between oral reading fluency as measured by curriculum-based assessment and Wordchains may be useful. In addition, multiple parallel forms of Wordchains would be ideal for assessing students at several points in time while minimizing practice effects.

SUMMARY. Wordchains is an innovative and potentially efficient method of screening large numbers of children for single word reading difficulties. There are significant technical issues such as quality of standardization sample, reported reliability data, and validity data. Wordchains was developed for a European audience. New normative data and updated technical information could make Wordchains an important screening instrument for schools in the U.S.

[279]
Work Personality Index.

Purpose: "Designed to identify personality traits that directly relate to work performance."
Population: High school to adult.
Publication Date: 2001.
Acronym: WPI.
Scores, 17: Teamwork, Concern for Others, Outgoing, Democratic, Attention to Detail, Rule-Following, Dependability, Ambition, Energy, Persistence, Leadership, Innovation, Analytic Thinking, Self-Control, Stress Tolerance, Initiative, Flexibility, and 5 factors: Achievement, Conscientiousness, Social Orientation, Practical Intelligence, Adjustment.
Administration: Group or individual.
Price Data: Available from publisher.
Foreign Language Editions: Available in English and French.
Time: (20–40) minutes.
Comments: May be administered via paper and pencil or on the Internet.
Authors: Donald Macnab and Shawn Bakker.
Publisher: Psychometrics Canada Ltd. [Canada].

Review of the Work Personality Index by JANET F. CARLSON, *Professor and Department Head, Department of General Academics, Texas A&M University at Galveston, Galveston, TX:*

DESCRIPTION. The Work Personality Index (WPI) provides a direct assessment of personality traits that relate to work performance for the normal adult population. It is a relatively brief, paper-and-pencil, self-report measure that may be completed individually or in groups by test takers with at least an eighth-grade reading level. The test authors recommend the measure for use with respondents who are at least 17 years old. Respondents are asked to indicate the extent to which they agree with the 153 statements presented in a four-page item booklet. Answer sheets may be mailed or faxed to the test publisher for scoring and interpretive reports. Hand scoring is not possible. On-line completion of the WPI also is available. Test users may request reports be returned by electronic or surface mail. The manual indicates that the test publisher provides two reports, although the website specified three reports: WPI Personal Effectiveness Report, WPI Select

Report, and the WPI Career Transition Report. At least for this reviewer, the three reports were returned promptly.

The WPI assesses 17 traits in five broad dimensions of personality, in the context of the workplace. The 17 Primary Scales provide information about an individual's personality style in the workplace that the test authors suggest may be used for personnel selection, team building, or career development. Interpretation is largely a function of automated scoring, the details of which are not provided in the test manual or accompanying materials.

DEVELOPMENT. The WPI was developed using specific criteria to ensure its ready application to the target population. The test developers wanted a measure that would assess work-related personality traits and would not require training in psychology or personality to administer and interpret. Developers of the WPI used the occupational classification system of the U.S. Department of Labor and reviewed the literature and existing personality measures to identify 17 personality traits that were "commonly found to relate to work performance" (user's manual, p. 19). The means by which such determinations were made is not specified in the test manual. Initially, 10 items were written to assess each of the 17 identified traits, using a few simple guidelines. An item tryout eliminated 17 of the original 170 items, based on alpha reliabilities.

TECHNICAL. American norms were developed using 6,000 individuals between the ages of 15 and 60. Males and females were equally represented in the norming group, 26% of whom were non-White. The test manual also reports educational level, employment status, and occupational areas of the norming sample. Results are reported as sten scores. Both high and low scores are considered meaningful. Scores are interpreted for all 17 scales.

Internal reliability estimates for the 17 scales range from .70 to .89 for the total sample ($n = 6,000$), with most coefficients above .80 and a median value of about .83. No other forms of reliability are addressed in the test manual.

The test manual presents data to support the validity of using WPI results in a wide variety of situations. Group differences were examined by age, gender, ethnicity, education, and occupation. Mean raw scores for the 17 scales are presented in a series of tables, corresponding to each of these factors. Statistical analyses of group differences are

occasionally mentioned but not completely or consistently reported. Instead, simplified, generalized conclusions about the pattern of mean raw scores are offered. Of note, statistically significant differences emerged among the five ethnic groups examined, for 8 of the 17 scales.

Evidence of construct validity derives in part from evidence that supports convergent and discriminant validity. Convergent validity of the WPI was evaluated using 1,463 individuals, most likely from the norming sample, who also provided a self-report of their Myers-Briggs Type Indicator preferences. Although the procedures employed in this empirical investigation are somewhat vague, the test authors present and interpret the findings as indicative of construct validation.

COMMENTARY. The WPI test manual contains only superficial descriptions of technical features, making the review process difficult for this reviewer or prospective users. It is impossible to ascertain the extent to which the norming process was appropriate and to understand how various demographic features are used in interpreting scores. Although the WPI answer sheet asks for one's sex and age, for example, nothing in the test manual specifies how or if these factors are taken into account during the interpretive process. The test manual states that a "number of minor gender effects were discovered," noting that "most of the differences are quite small in magnitude, [but] some are significant" (user's manual, p. 29). Nevertheless, these differences appear to be dismissed, with the rationalization that "the differences between the other [remaining] WPI scales were minimal" (user's manual, p. 29), so test interpretation would not be affected. Thus, it appears that a single set of norms is used to evaluate responses.

The test manual is not written at a sufficiently high level of sophistication to satisfy individuals with measurement expertise. It oversimplifies many technical constructs, such as reliability, to such an extent as to promote a false impression. For instance, the test manual suggests that internal consistency reliability is sufficient to establish the dependability of test results. Indeed, this is the only form of reliability for which supportive evidence is presented. With a brief, self-report measure such as the WPI, establishing consistency over time via test-retest reliability would and should be easily accomplished.

On balance, the evidence presented in support of validity is incomplete. Conclusions offered by the test authors are often unwarranted or overly simplified. This situation is complicated by numerous editorial oversights (e.g., what is stated on one page does not match what is presented elsewhere) such that one wonders how carefully validity evidence itself was gathered and analyzed. A particularly concerning instance of oversimplification involves the use of the WPI with different ethnic groups. As noted earlier, 8 of the 17 traits revealed mean raw score differences for various ethnic groups. However, the test authors dismiss these differences by saying (but not demonstrating empirically), "differences ... are virtually eliminated when converted to standard scores," and concluding that the "WPI can be used with different ethnic groups with little threat of adverse impact" (user's manual, p. 31).

The WPI itself is easily understood by test takers and is presented in a format that facilitates proper completion. Its items are rather transparent. It is easily administered and quickly generates a large volume of paper in its reports. The graphic displays of results provided in the WPI reports are colorful and easy to read. They give the appearance of containing a lot of information, although there is considerable redundancy from one report to the next. The main differences among the reports involve the target audiences and associated changes to report formats.

As far as the interpretive statements contained in WPI reports, Barnum effects loom large. Many interpretive statements are quite generic and would be widely accepted by most people as descriptive of their traits. Most people would agree that they "enjoy solving problems and like finding solutions that are both original and practical." Thus, it is not surprising that a large proportion of the 4,732 people who provided feedback about the WPI's descriptive accuracy believed it was "quite accurate" or "very accurate" (user's manual, p. 41).

SUMMARY. The WPI uses a pencil-and-paper, self-report format to evaluate 17 personality traits that bear on the work environment. It is brief and easily administered using individual or group administration procedures. Documentation provided in the WPI manual is lacking in many ways, but especially insofar as information needed to assess the technical adequacy of the measure.

Review of the Work Personality Index by JO-SEPH G. LAW, JR., Professor of Behavioral Studies, University of South Alabama, Mobile, AL:

DESCRIPTION. The Work Personality Index (WPI) is a 153-item inventory that may be administered in 20 to 40 minutes on the internet or by paper and pencil. It may be given individually or in group settings and has English and French versions. According to the 46-page manual, the WPI measures 17 personality traits that are related to work and have their origin in research conducted by the U.S. Department of Labor in the construction of the Occupational Information Network. There are five broad, global scales labeled as Achievement Orientation, Social Orientation, Practical Intelligence, Conscientiousness, and Adjustment. Individual traits are: Teamwork, Concern for Others, Outgoing, Democratic, Attention to Details, Rule-Following, Dependability, Ambition, Energy, Persistence, Leadership, Innovation, Analytical Thinking, Self-Control, Stress Tolerance, Initiative, and Flexibility. The test publisher maintains an easy-to-navigate web site from which one can download sample reports. Computer scoring of the 1-page answer sheet results in several possible report formats. The Select Report format is an 8-page report designed for the examiner. Results for the 17 traits are presented on a 10-point scale (stens) with a narrative discussion of the respondent's scores. The Personal Effectiveness Report is an 11-page report designed for the respondent. Each section gives a graphical depiction of the broad scales (e.g., Social Orientation) followed by a narrative explanation of that individual's traits and suggestions for improving personal effectiveness. The Job Match Profile is 6 pages long and enables employers to compare client traits to those trait requirements specified by the organization for each job. The web site contains a sample for a call center coordinator. There is a 21-page Career Transition Report that is designed to help workers in the midst of career change. The report helps the respondent identify those activities he or she is good at and likes to do as well as helping to develop career goals. There are exercises in the report that the respondent can use to improve career information, engage in self-exploration, learn to put into their own words career strengths identified by the WPI, and several pages for the individual to write about a career plan.

DEVELOPMENT. The authors indicate that items were designed to be easy to understand, measure a single construct, relate to work behavior, and be written in the first person. Their goal was to design an instrument that did not require a specialist in psychology or personality theory to interpret and was useful in personnel selection, team building, and personal development. Items were normed on 3,000 male and 3,000 female North Americans (American and Canadian) from 15 to 60 years of age. The manual contains a sample breakdown that is reported in six age bands. The largest age band is the 31- to 40-year group with 29.6% of the sample and the lowest is the 51- to 60-year age group with 7.1%. In terms of education, 31.6% had a bachelors degree, 15% a masters, and 3.8% a professional degree or doctorate. Only 17% of the sample had no college education. In terms of ethnic background, 74% were White/Caucasian, 7.9% African American/Canadian, 7.8% Latin, 3.7% Native American/Canadian, 2.7% Asian American/Canadian, and 3.9% Other. A breakdown by occupation found 56.6% employed, with the remainder being students (17.1%), homemakers (1.7%), those seeking employment (12.3%), self-employed (5.3%), or none given (6.5%). The most common occupational area was in management (24.7%) and the lowest was in journalism with 1.9%. Only .5% were employed in machine trades, .8% in construction, and .6% in agriculture. More common were those working in management, education, clerical/sales, law, science, medicine, social science, and human services.

TECHNICAL. The 46-page manual contains 7 pages on interpretation that are very easy to read and understand. There are 8 pages on the development of the inventory and 16 pages on technical properties. There are 23 figures and tables illustrating the characteristics of the norm group and other statistics. One table that depicts the age breakdown of the sample is a bit confusing because the number of years in the bands is not consistent. For example, 10 years are covered by the age groups of 31–40, 41–50 and 51–60. The 15–20 group has only 6 years and the 21–25 and 26–30 groups have only 5 years each. There are descriptive tables that indicate the means, standard deviations, and other statistics by trait. Internal consistency coefficients range from a low of .70 on the Democratic trait to a high of .89 on the Innovation trait. Validity is discussed in terms of its usefulness with different groups based on gender, ethnicity, education, and occupational background. The manual reports some statistical differences between various ethnic groups on some of the traits, but these were reported as minimal when transformed into standard scores. Implications are discussed in the manual. Construct validity evidence centers on a study of 1,463 individuals who were given the WPI and the Myers-Briggs Type Indicator. There is a brief mention of a factor analysis that identified five factors that the manual noted are similar to those of the Big Five personality traits (Barrick & Mount, 1991). There is a one-paragraph discussion of a feedback study of 4,732 people in which a large percentage gave high ratings to the accuracy of the WPI feedback. However, the usual cautions apply about interpreting such consumer satisfaction as evidence of validity.

COMMENTARY. The WPI has quite a few strengths. It contains traits based on the O*NET model, thus facilitating discussion among professionals and clients in terms of information readily available on the internet. The format of the answer sheet and the feedback reports are attractive and easy to read. The reports are well designed and written, with feedback that is easy for the respondent to apply to his or her work situation, and exercises that should assist in self-understanding and career planning. Additionally, there is a large normative population with fairly broad applicability to North American populations. The WPI is probably more applicable to individuals with some amount of college education who have backgrounds in sales, management, social services, and other white collar jobs than to those in skilled trades and the manual arts. There appears to be adequate internal consistency, but little evidence in the manual of test-retest reliability. More research needs to be conducted to support the validity and factor structure of this inventory.

SUMMARY. The Work Personality Index is designed to be a comprehensive career assessment tool for individual self-exploration of work-related personality traits and personnel selection and guidance. The inventory is easy to read, scoring is by computer, and the respondent is given well-organized written feedback in reports that are tailored to the demands of the situation (i.e., self-exploration, career planning, job selection). Construct validity data are supported by a study with one other inventory; however, there are no studies or test-retest reliability or predictive validity reported in the manual. The WPI is a new instrument that shows promise and should be a fruitful subject for quite a few research projects.

REVIEWER'S REFERENCE

Barrick, M. R., & Mount, M. K. (1991). The big five personality dimensions and job performance: A meta-analysis. *Personnel Psychology, 44,* 1–26.

[280]
Working Memory Test Battery for Children.

Purpose: To evaluate working memory in children and young adolescents.
Population: Ages 5–15.
Publication Date: 2001.
Acronym: WMTB-C.
Scores: 9 subtests: Digit Recall, Word List Matching, Word List Recall, Block Recall, Nonword List Recall, Listening Recall, Counting Recall, Mazes Memory, Backward Digit Recall.
Administration: Individual.
Price Data, 2005: £265 per complete battery including forms, stimulus books, and manual (183 pages).
Time: (60) minutes.
Authors: Susan Pickering and Sue Gathercole.
Publisher: Harcourt Assessment [England].

Review of the Working Memory Test Battery for Children by RAYNE A. SPERLING, Assistant Professor of Educational Psychology, and DANIEL L. McCOLLUM, ABD Educational Psychology, The Pennsylvania State University, University Park, PA:

DESCRIPTION. The Working Memory Test Battery for Children (WMTB-C) assessment is designed to measure working memory in children ages 5 to 15. Substantive research supports that processing constraints in working memory may result in various learning disabilities. Scores from the test battery can assist in identifying areas where individual children may have such processing constraints. The WMTB-C is a more comprehensive assessment than many commonly administered working memory assessments in that it better represents current research-based theories of working memory. The WMTB-C also employs more tasks than other measures of working memory. The assessment battery takes approximately 60 minutes to administer individually.

The WMTB-C assesses three components of working memory across nine subtests. The Listening Recall, Counting Recall, and Backward Digit Recall subtests assess the Central Executive. The Digit Recall, Word List Matching, Word List Recall, and Nonword List Recall subtests assess the Phonological Loop, and the Block Recall and Mazes Memory subtests assess the Visuo-Spatial Sketchpad.

Two types of raw scores are provided for each of the nine subtests assessed by the WMTB-C. These scores are a trials correct score, which provides the total number of correct trials achieved and is used to compute a standardized score, and a span score that indicates the highest level of difficulty achieved by the child on a given subtest. Percentile ranks are provided for each subtest by age. For most learners, subtest standard scores and component scores are then plotted to assist in further interpretation.

The assessment kit comes in a carry case that contains the test manual that includes information regarding the theoretical rationale for the assessment, the development and standardization of the assessment, strategies for insuring a productive testing environment, and the administration and scoring guide. The kit also includes the administration tools of Stimulus Book 1 that contains the mazes memory and backward digit recall stimuli, and Stimulus Books 2 and 3 that contain the counting recall cards. Word List Matching cards, Backwards Digit Recall cards, a Block Recall board, Maze response booklets, and record forms are also included.

DEVELOPMENT. Consistent with established research-based theoretical models (e.g., Baddeley, 1986, 1992), nine subtests of the WMTB-C assess three components of working memory: the Central Executive, the Phonological Loop, and the Visuo-Spatial Sketchpad. Tasks from many of these subtests are similar to those found in existing instruments. Most existing instruments, however, generally assess isolated components of working memory among other memory with limited tasks (e.g., The Children's Memory Scale, Cohen, 1997; Wechsler Intelligence Scales for Children, Wechsler, 1991).

The test manual presents limited information regarding item development and pilot testing. Items were developed for 12 subtests of the WMTB-C in the original, prototype, battery. Through analyses of a limited pilot administration with young participants, the instrument was modified and the original 12 subtests were reduced to the current 9. Other modifications were made based upon the pilot administration and experimental research with developed subtests. Among these modifications, the number of trials per subtest was increased, one-item blocks were included, the difficulty of the test was expanded for older participants, the number of practice trials was increased, and several modifications to subtests that address the Visuo-Spatial Sketchpad were made. Although ongoing research addresses and modifies our understanding of working memory, the final subtests of the WMTB-C represent a comprehensive, sophisticated coverage of working memory components.

TECHNICAL. The test manual provides psychometric information regarding the assessment. Approximately 750 students aged 4 to 15 years were included in the sample to standardize the WMTB-C. Special needs learners, as found in the classrooms from which the sample was drawn, were included in the sample. The manual reports that both rural and urban children were included in the sample. However, no additional demographic information is provided. The norming sample is limited in that no demographic information of the sample population is provided and that some age groups are not represented in the norming sample.

Test-retest reliability (2-week administration interval) was reported for a limited subset of the children in the norming sample. Across subtests, these reliability coefficients are generally lower than would be expected, with the majority under $r = .70$. Two administrators tested the children but the only inter-tester reliability information provided is for the Nonword List Recall subtest. Intertester reliabilities for this subtest both across administrators and live versus audio recording were adequate ($r > .85$).

Further, the reliability estimates did not cover the same age range as the standardization sample. The age range in the reliability sample covered 5 years, 4 months to only 11 years, 6 months. Therefore, the test-retest reliability (stability) of the test scores is unknown for the remaining ages, up to 15 years, for which the test is suggested. In addition, the authors noted that evidence of the stability of the construct in this particular age range is conflicting in past research. In as much, the stability of the test scores, or the stability of the constructs measured in this age range, is a critical piece of missing information. The assessibility of the construct toward early adulthood seems unclear. This appears to be a limitation of the assessment that may be consistent with theoretical limitations regarding the development of working memory.

Validity evidence was gathered by examining the factor structure of the WMTB-C and through assessing the relationship between the prototype version of the WMTB-C and several standardized measures of student performance. The correlation matrix for the WMTB-C indicates significant relations (range from $r = .41$ to $r = .72$) among subtests. The factor structure of the prototype version of the assessment supported the Central Executive and Phonological Loop subtests. Correlations among the Visuo-Spatial Sketchpad subtests on the WMTB-C were moderate. Confirmatory factor analyses (EQS) solutions for the WMTB-C across age levels indicate support for independence among the constructs. Taken together the WMTB-C appears to measure independent but related constructs as would be theoretically expected.

The manual reports on previous studies that employed the prototype version of the WMTB-C and other standard achievement measures. The phonological loop and the central executive measures were administered concurrently and again after a 1-year interval with a limited sample of 6- and 7-year-old children. Overall moderate correlations between the two factors and vocabulary, literacy, and mathematics were reported. In additional reviewed studies, the WMTB-C prototype version was related to school performance across subject areas. The manual also reports on two previous small investigations of special needs learners that indicated when compared to their general education peers, special education students performed lower on the working memory assessments.

The manual provides clear instruction for administration, scoring, and interpretation of the WMTB-C. These instructions should support the reliability and validity of scores obtained from the measure. Some limitations of the validity evaluation are that the external validity was assessed based upon the prototype, and not final, version of the instrument; that the youngest children were not included in the analyses because they did not complete all subtests; that an additional measure was included to assess the Visuo-Spatial Sketchpad; and the Word List Matching subtest was not included in the validity analyses.

COMMENTARY. One of the primary strengths of the WMTB-C when compared to many existing measures is the breadth of the assessment. The subtest items are often similar to items found in research studies and existing measures. Where item formats are unique, as with the Mazes Memory task, the rationale for the items is theoretically driven. Although ongoing research continues to modify our interpretation of working memory, the theoretical framework for the assessment is well established and the assessment is well grounded. The ability of the WMTB-C to assess children's working memory may facilitate appropriate diagnosis and placement of special needs learners. The breadth of assessment of the WMTB-C is also an asset for experimental research. Other strengths of the assessment are that the test manual provides clear direction for administration and scoring, and that the tasks are varied and not highly aversive to the child. There are also one-item trials and there is allowance for breaks in the administration to accommodate the learners being tested.

Drawbacks of the battery include little provided demographic information of previous examinees and a lack of normed information for particular age groups (11.9–12.9 and 13.11–14.8 years of age). Further, given that several subtests were too difficult for the youngest learners tested, some caution should be used in interpreting findings from learners under age 6.

SUMMARY. The WMTB-C provides a comprehensive means to assess individual components of working memory. The assessment appears to be appropriate for administration to most children. When used in conjunction with other informal and formal assessments, the WMTB-C may provide information to assist in the identification of learners' processing constraints and may be used to assist in identifying working memory limitations in special needs learners.

REVIEWERS' REFERENCES

Baddeley, A. D. (1986). *Working memory.* Oxford: Oxford University Press.
Baddeley, A. D. (1992). Is working memory working? *Quarterly Journal of Experimental Psychology, 44A*(1), 1–31.
Cohen, M. J. (1997). Children's Memory Scale. San Antonio, TX: The Psychological Corporation.
Wechsler, D. (1991). Wechsler Intelligence Scale for Children—Third Edition. San Antonio, TX: The Psychological Corporation.

[281]
World of Work Inventory.

Purpose: "Designed to assist clients in thinking about themselves in relation to their total environment" in relation to their personal career development.
Population: Ages 13–65+.
Publication Dates: 1970–2004.
Acronym: WOWI.
Scores, 35: Career Interest Activities (17 scores: Public Service, The Sciences, Engineering & Related, Business Relations, Managerial, The Arts, Clerical, Sales, Service, Primary Outdoor, Processing, Machine Work, Bench Work, Structural Work, Mechanical & Electrical Work, Graphic Arts, Mining); Job Satisfaction Indicators (12 scores: Versatile, Adaptable to Repetitive Work, Adaptable to Performing Under Specific Instructions, Dominant, Gregarious, Isolative, Influencing, Self-Controlled, Valuative, Objective, Subjective, Rigorous): Aptitude/Achievement (6 scores: Verbal, Numerical, Abstractions, Spatial-Form, Mechanical/Electrical, Clerical).
Administration: Individual or group.
Price Data, 2004: Online administration: $13 per single profile report with summary; $19.50 per profile report with interpretative report; and $189 online site license fee; Paper-and-pencil administration: $7 per test booklet and $19.95 per interpretation manual (2001, 70 pages).
Time: (60) minutes for online version; (90) minutes for paper-and-pencil short form.
Authors: Robert E. Ripley, Gregory P. M. Neidert, and Nancy L. Ortman.
Publisher: World of Work, Inc.

Review of the World of Work Inventory by JEFFREY A. JENKINS, Assistant Professor, Roger Williams University, Bristol, RI:

DESCRIPTION. The World of Work Inventory (WOWI) measures an individual's "work abilities, preferences, and styles" (interpretation manual, p. 1). Rather than focusing on interests alone, the WOWI seeks also to measure aptitudes and temperaments of individuals and match them to occupational characteristics. Thus, the WOWI provides scores in each of three domains: Career Interest Activities, which seek to measure respondents' preferences for various job tasks; Job Satisfaction Indicators, which focus on temperament for job aspects; and Vocational Training Potentials, which assess respondents' skill level or aptitude for training. Taken together, these three components of the WOWI provide a career counseling tool intended to be used as a "multiple purpose instrument" (manual, p. 2).

The Career Interest Activities (CIAs) consist of 136 items on which respondents rate the extent to which they like, dislike, or are neutral regarding a specific activity. For example, activities include "Planning river dams to control floods," "Determining how much a loan company should lend an applicant," and "Working alone at an outpost in the woods." The CIA activities are intended to reflect activities involved in performing 17 basic occupations found in the U.S. Department of Labor's *Dictionary of Occupational Titles:* Public Service, The Services, Engineering Related, Business Relations, Managerial, The Arts,

Clerical, Sales, Service, Primary Outdoor, Processing, Machine Work, Bench Work, Structural Work, Mechanical and Electrical Work, Graphic Arts, and Mining. The WOWI provides a scale score on each of these occupational titles.

Vocational Training Potentials (VTPs) attempt to measure six areas of aptitude or achievement: Verbal (28 items), Numerical (14 items), Abstractions (14 items), Spatial-Form (14 items), Mechanical-Electrical (14 items), and Clerical (14 items). A VTP scale score is reported in each of these areas. The VTPs consist of 98 items in multiple-choice (A, B, C, D) format.

Based on the *Dictionary of Occupational Titles*, the Job Satisfaction Indicators (JSIs) are reported as 12 temperament factors that relate to job satisfaction: Versatile, Adaptable to Repetitive Work, Adaptable to Performing under Specific Instructions, Dominant, Gregarious, Isolative, Influencing, Self-Controlled, Valuative, Objective, Subjective, and Rigorous. This scale consists of 96 items for which respondents rate whether they like, dislike, or are neutral about job-related tasks such as "Working against deadlines and meeting quotas" and "Doing work involving fine accuracy."

In addition to the CIAs, VTPs, and JSIs, respondents choose 2 of 12 Occupational Areas that they "have thought about or would like to do," as well as 2 of 12 "Best Liked Subjects" (manual, p. 14). These "Self-selected Choices" are intended to be compared to the CIAs to determine the respondent's level of "career directedness" (manual, p. 14).

The WOWI may be administered using an assessment booklet and scoring sheet or it may be administered online. Both the assessment booklet and scoring sheet are clearly organized and presented for straightforward administration. The publisher does not provide for hand scoring and, whether administered in person or online, the publisher scores the instrument and provides profile and interpretive reports. With some understanding of the makeup of the WOWI, these reports are clearly presented and explained in the interpretation manual.

DEVELOPMENT AND TECHNICAL. The publisher offers norms for each of the three areas measured that are reported to be based on a nationwide sample of 169,436 respondents. Although mean scores are reported by gender, education, and age, no information is provided regarding other characteristics of the norm group (such as occupation), how the norm data were collected, how the sample was selected, or the geographic distribution of the sample. This is surprising given the reported size of the norm group. Without this information, however, the WOWI cannot be used normatively. This is a serious shortcoming for using the instrument in the career counseling context.

In addition, the publisher provides little information about the technical characteristics of the WOWI, making evaluation of the instrument from a psychometric standpoint difficult. Apart from a discussion of the general theoretical basis for the three areas it purports to measure, the publisher does not discuss the procedures used for developing items or which items measure the scale to which they relate. [Editors' Note: This information was not included in the interpretation manual or other materials initially provided to the reviewers. However, extensive reliability and validity information is now available on their website (www.wowi.com).] Although the interpretation manual states that research on the instrument has established that it is "a valid and reliable career/vocational assessment" (p. 4), no information about or references to this research are given. Average validity coefficients "from numerous studies" are also given, ranging from .55 to .92 (including a coefficient for "conclusion" validity, which has no precedent in the measurement literature), yet neither a reference nor a summary of these studies is provided. Furthermore, it is not clear to what these coefficients refer, as the WOWI does not provide a total score, but rather 35 separate scale scores. Similarly, test-retest reliability coefficients are reported ranging from .51 to .92, with the only explanation that they were estimated "over several studies." [Editors' Note: See website for additional explanation.] These reliability estimates are reported separately for CIAs, JSIs, and VTPs, but if the reported values are averages (which is not stated in the manual), they do not reflect any of the scale scores in each of the three assessment areas and are therefore uninterpretable. To the extent that research has been done on the psychometric characteristics of the WOWI, it should be reported in detail or, at a minimum, made available to the test user by reference. Until this problem has been remedied, the WOWI cannot be recommended for use with individuals, including career counseling.

COMMENTARY AND SUMMARY. As a vocational and career exploration measure, the WOWI does approach career assessment in a useful manner by considering aptitudes, interests, and preferences of respondents as they relate to job requirements. The primary shortcoming of the WOWI is that its psychometric characteristics, including item development procedures, reliability, and validity, are not reported by the publisher in sufficient detail to justify confidence in its use. Therefore, it cannot be recommended for either clinical or educational purposes. It may be useful as a research instrument if levels of reliability and validity can be established by the researcher within the sample or population under study.

The WOWI does have a few strengths, however. First is the attempt of the authors to broaden the effectiveness of career assessment by attempting to create more than an interest inventory. Second is the ease of administration both online and using the assessment booklet. Third is the understandable profile and interpretive report that the company produces after scoring. Unfortunately, these strengths do not offset the serious and fundamental problem of recommending use of the instrument for individual decision making while failing to discuss procedures for developing the norms, and failing to justify the reliability and validity of uses of the instrument. These shortcomings do not satisfy the standards set out for such instruments in the *Standards for Educational and Psychological Testing* (AERA, APA, & NCME, 1999). Of particular importance is the need for evidence of concurrent and predictive validity comparing the WOWI to well-established measures such as the Strong Interest Inventory (15:248) or the Jackson Vocational Interest Survey (15:129), as well as the correlation between scores on the WOWI and measures of job success and satisfaction in various occupations. Until such information is provided, users should be very cautious about drawing any inferences about individual aptitudes, interests, or temperaments from scores on the WOWI scales. [Editors' Note: This information was not provided to the reviewers but has since been published and made available free of charge on the publisher's website. They now provide 11 tables comparing the WOWI to other instruments, including the Strong Campbell.]

REVIEWER'S REFERENCE

American Educational Research Association, American Psychological Association, & National Council on Measurement in Education. (1999). *Standards for educational and psychological testing.* Washington, DC: American Educational Research Association.

Review of the World of Work Inventory by EUGENE P. SHEEHAN, *Dean, College of Education, University of Northern Colorado, Greeley, CO:*

DESCRIPTION. The World of Work Inventory (WOWI) is a learning and development tool aimed at assisting counselors, teachers, and human resource professionals who work with clients (students or employees) to identify the client's vocational interests and strengths and weaknesses. Clients receive information on their career interests, job-related temperament factors, aptitude for learning, and academic achievement.

The WOWI measures several work-related topics. Respondents are first asked to select 2 general occupational areas, from a list of 12, in which they would like to work. They also provide information on their 2 best-liked academic subjects, again from a list of 12. Most of the inventory, however, focuses on three main areas: Career Interest Activities (CIAs), Vocational Training Potentials (VTPs), and Job Satisfaction Indicators (JSIs). The CIAs section asks respondents to indicate whether or not they would like to perform a job-related activity (e.g., binding covers to books; convincing people of your ideas) for at least 6 months or more. Respondents indicate their preference on a "like," "neutral," and "dislike" scale. There are 136 CIAs items. The CIAs section provides information on the respondent's interests in the 17 Basic Occupational Areas, as identified by the U.S. Department of Labor. According to the interpretation manual the "CIAs measure what job duties people like (and dislike), and how much they like (or dislike) engaging in them" (p. 44).

The VTPs section is a combination of achievement and aptitude test. This section is composed of several subsections: Verbal, Numerical, Mechanical/Electrical, Spatial-Form, Clerical, and Abstractions. There are 14 items in each section except for Verbal Reasoning, which has 28, for a total of 98 items.

JSIs items cover temperament factors related to work and motivation. In this section, respondents indicate whether or not they would like to perform a job-related activity (e.g., keeping things orderly and systematic; facing physical dangers) for at least 6 months or more. Respondents indicate their preference on a "like," "neutral," and "dislike" scale. There are 96 items in this section, all of which focus on job temperament factors. Responses to these items provide a profile of a respondent's disposition to 12 job temperament factors: Versatile, Adaptable to Repetitive Work, Adaptable to Performing Under Specific Instructions, Dominant, Gregarious, Isolative, Influencing, Self-Controlled, Valuative, Objective, Subjective, and Rigorous.

The WOWI has a very professional appearance. It is easily administered. Instructions are clear and straightforward. Respondents indicate their answers on a separate sheet. There is an on-line version of the inventory that provides instantaneous results. The profile developed and the interpretative report, based on an individual's responses, should provoke an exploration of individual's occupational preferences and choices. There is a very thorough website associated with the instrument. This website supports written materials and contains several sections including: sample reports, applications, and history and development.

DEVELOPMENT. An underlying tenet of the WOWI is that effective career counseling uses multiple sources of data. The instrument places a heavy emphasis on job relevance of items. The WOWI uses data concerning work-related tasks (CIAs), temperaments (JSIs), and abilities and aptitudes (VTPs) to provide a more global analysis of the client. The career counselor is to triangulate the data from these three sources, looking for patterns in the client profile that suggest a particular career or training path. Additionally, the data can be used to identify conflicts (e.g., between a client's ability and career interest).

Information on the development of the WOWI can be accessed on the inventory website. The developers followed a series of logical steps to ensure items on the scales are relevant to job activities. Items were reworded for clarity and job relevance. The website states that several judges, selected for their occupational experience and expertise, had to agree on the use of an item before it was placed in any scale. These scales were then subjected to standard analyses to norm the instrument and to determine reliability and validity.

TECHNICAL. Information describing the psychometrics behind the WOWI is available on the website. A table of norms indicates that the WOWI is normed on an impressive 169,436 individuals. However, beyond gender, education, and age no other demographic data are available on the popula-

tion on which the inventory is normed. The table of norms provides means and standard deviation for the VTPs, broken down by gender, education, and age.

The manual uses terms such as "reliable predictor" and "homogeneous and mutually exclusive" scales. Information provided supports these assertions. Data on reliability and validity are quite comprehensive. Reliability data are positive. For example, coefficient alphas for each scale are all higher than .81. They vary from .81 for the Valuative JSI, to .94 for the Verbal VTP. Indeed, 28 of the 35 scales have alpha coefficients of .85 or higher. Test-retest reliabilities are also quite high. Data are provided for 1-week, 6-week, and 2-year reliabilities. As would be expected, there is a decline as the time period increases. The 1-week test-retest reliabilities are .92 for the CIAs, .89 for the JSIs, and .70 for the VTPs.

Validity data are also positive. Face validity is obvious. Interitem correlations are generally in expected directions and at expected levels of significance. Some data are provided that indicate that certain groups that should differ in their scores do indeed differ. Tables demonstrating the correspondence between the WOWI and other career exploration instruments show anticipated relationships.

COMMENTARY. The WOWI has many strengths. From a face validity perspective the instrument clearly measures vocational interests, temperaments, aptitudes, and achievement. The questions are inherently interesting to a respondent, who should be motivated to provide accurate responses. Certainly, the results and the profile could be used to provoke a thoughtful analysis of an individual's occupational choices. The ability to use temperament, job activity, and skill and aptitude data to triangulate about a client's occupational interests and desires is also a strength. The interpretation manual provides the administrator with good advice on how best to use the instrument in career advising sessions. Further, the profile and interpretative report that the instrument produces can be used to provoke discussions about a client's potential career path.

The psychometric data provided support the view that the WOWI can accomplish its goal of assisting individuals with career exploration. Reliability and validity information are strong.

SUMMARY. The WOWI is designed to assess work-related interests, temperaments, abilities, and aptitudes. It consists of 330 items that measure preference for job-related activities, occupation potential, and indicators of job satisfaction. The emphasis on job relevance gives the items and scales strong face validity. The questionnaire can be easily and efficiently administered and scored, including an on-line version. There is an extensive website that provides supporting data on the interpretation and uses of the instrument. Psychometric evidence to support its use in career exploration is extensive. The section of the interpretation manual that describes the job preferences, temperaments, and abilities and aptitudes combined with the client profile and interpretative report could be used to provoke useful discussion with clients about their career path.

[282]
Youth Level of Service/Case Management Inventory.

Purpose: Designed for use in "assessing risk, need, and responsibility factors" in young offenders.
Population: Juvenile offenders, ages 12–17.
Publication Date: 2002.
Acronym: YLS/CMI.
Scores: 9 Risk Ratings: Offenses and Dispositions, Family Factors, Education and Employment, Peer Relations, Substance Abuse, Leisure/Recreation, Personality/Behavior, Attitudes/Orientation, Total.
Administration: Individual.
Parts, 7: Assessment of Risks and Needs, Summary of Risk/Need Factors, Assessment of Other Needs/Special Considerations, Your Assessment of the Client's General Risk/Need Level, Contact Level, Case Management Plan, Case Management Review.
Price Data, 2003: $145 per complete kit including user's manual (56 pages), 25 interview guides, 25 QuikScore™ forms, and 25 case management forms; $45 per user's manual; $60 per 25 interview guides; $225 per 100 interview guides; $35 per 25 QuikSore™ forms; $130 per 100 QuikScore™ forms; $20 per 25 case management forms; $75 per 100 case management forms; $55 per specimen set including user's manual, 3 interview guides, 3 QuikScore™ forms, and 3 case management forms.
Time: [30–40] minutes.
Comments: Risk assessment checklist completed on the bases of semistructured interview and record review; derived from the Level of Service Inventory—Revised.
Authors: Robert D. Hoge and D. A. Andrews.
Publisher: Multi-Health Systems, Inc.

Review of the Youth Level of Service/Case Management Inventory by PAM LINDSEY, Associate Professor, Curriculum and Instruction, Tarleton State University, Stephenville, TX:

DESCRIPTION AND DEVELOPMENT. The Youth Level of Service/Case Management Inventory (YLS/CMI) is the youth version of the Level of Service Inventory—Revised (LSI-R; Andrews & Bonta, 1995; T6:1421). It is based on the General Personality and Social Psychological Model of Criminal Conduct developed by the authors in the 1990s. The YLS/CMI is semistructured interview consisting of seven parts. The interview uses data from several informant sources including the youth, his or her parents, and professionals involved with the youth such as teachers, clinicians, or police. Data from the interviews may be used to evaluate the juvenile offender in terms of risk and need factors and to formulate a case management plan.

The technical manual describes Part 1: Assessment of Risks and Needs section as a 42-item semistructured interview of risk factors predictive of criminal activity and "criminogenic" need factors, those targeted for intervention, in young people (p. 2). The authors cite an extensive literature base as the theoretical background for the survey items. Survey items are administered to the target youth, his or her parents, and/or completed by professionals involved in the youth's case management. The interviewer uses the responses given and his or her professional judgment to make evaluations about the youth's risk and need factors for intervention.

The remaining five parts are interpretations that are made by analysis of the interviewee's responses on Part 1. These analyses include a summary of risk/need factors, assessment of other needs such as disabilities or environmental circumstances, general risk/need level, contact level, case management plan, and case management review. Each section is described in terms of how the information from the interview is used to complete the analysis and what types of decisions or judgments are appropriate.

Interviewer qualifications are not specified except "under ideal conditions" (p. 5), which the authors consider to be the client's probation officer or other professional. The authors contend that the assessment can still be used even when professionals do not have all the sources of information available, if the interviewee reports "the best information available" (p. 5) and the deficiency in information sources is noted and considered when interpreting the results.

The manual provides three sample case studies to guide the interviewer in making his or her evaluations of the interview data. Protocols are on NCR paper, which helps when data are to be shared among professionals and/or parents.

TECHNICAL. Construct and predictive validity were calculated between the YLS/CMI and the adolescent version of the Psychopathy Checklist. Calculations supported both construct and predictive validity between the two instruments.

Interrater agreement studies analyzing 33 cases with trained interviewers yielded a kappa coefficient of .69 and intraclass correlation coefficient of .75, both of which are in the acceptable range. In addition, the authors report that because the YLS/CMI was derived from the Level of Service Inventory—Revised (LSI-R; Andrews & Bonta, 1995), a highly used instrument for assessing adult offenders, it may be assumed that the youth version has considerable reliability and validity.

A study conducted in 2003 supported the use of the instrument as a reliable source of data for developing profiles of adjudicated youth. Results suggested that the YLS/CMI was particularly valid for predicting recidivism for at-risk youth (Flores, Travis, & Latessa, 2003).

The YLS/CMI's construct and criterion-related validity for the total risk/need score and the eight subscores was evaluated on a sample of 263 adjudicated offenders in northwestern Ontario, Canada and 62 youths with no criminal background. Both scores were reported as "significantly" (user's manual, p. 31) discriminating between the two groups. In addition, the authors reported predicted recidivism of the total offender sample. The user's manual reports a linear discrimination function value based on the eight subscores of 75.38% correct classification of prediction. A second study of predictive validity is reported with a linear discriminative function value of 91.28% correct classification using the same sample in a 2 year follow-up.

A third study is cited for construct and predictive validity of the risk/needs scores. The 2000 study was conducted with 150 male offenders between the ages of 12 and 15 who were referred to an inpatient assessment unit. Construct validity was supported by "significant correlations" (Lindsey's 2000 study as cited in the user's manual) between the scores of the YLS/CMI, the adolescent version of the Psychopathy Checklist (Hare, Forth, & Kosson, 1994 as cited in the user's manual), and the Behaviour Problem subscore

from the Brief Psychiatric Rating Scale for Children (Overall & Gorham, 1988, as cited in the user's manual).

Considering that the usefulness of the data collected on the instrument is highly dependent on professional judgment, the reliability and validity data seem adequate. In addition, the YLS/CMI is the youth version of the "highly successful" (p. ix) Level of Service Inventory—Revised (LSI-R; Andrews & Bonta, 1995), which, according to the publishers, is the highly reliable measure used to determine treatment targets for adult offenders. Therefore, the format and items appear to have a sound research base. One of the authors of the YLS/CMI, Andrews, co-authored the LSI-R, which seems to add face and content validity to the youth version.

COMMENTARY. The authors of the YLS/CMI report it to be a semistructured interview; however, the protocol looks more like a checklist that one person could complete without asking any questions. The protocol reports the instrument to be a "quantitative screening," however, it is unclear what is meant by that definition. Additionally, to complete the items with any reasonable assumption of reliability and validity, the interviewee would have to have considerable knowledge about the adjudicated youth. For example, Section 1 asks about the number of prior convictions, probations, and current convictions of the client. In another section, items refer to the client's behavior in school. The protocol appears to require several informants if the information is to be considered a reliable and valid data source.

The obvious difficulty with this, and any other semistructured interview used to make judgments or diagnosis about people's lives, treatment, or program options, is the bias of the person providing the answers to the interview questions and/or the interview skills of the person asking the questions (Sattler, 2001). Sattler (1992) suggested that interviewer bias is a critical factor in evaluating the validity and reliability of all interview data. Interviewer bias is defined as the intentional or unintentional expression of facts or suggestions by the interviewer that may cause the interviewee to distort his or her responses. Sattler (1992, 2000) suggested that training in interview skills such as establishing rapport, using summary statements, asking questions in several different ways, and/or re-asking questions when reliability is in question help to eliminate such bias. The authors of the

YLS/CMI suggest in the technical manual that under "ideal conditions" (p. 5) the youth's probation officer or other professional familiar with the juvenile should complete the protocol. However, they also contend that the interview information will still be useful if it is completed with the "best information available" (p. 5). No mention of specific training or qualifications for persons conducting the interviews is stipulated in the manual. The lack of specific training or suggested interviewer qualifications seems to compromise the reliability and validity of information collected by the instrument and makes it highly susceptible to interviewer bias. For example, one might suspect that the client's probation officer has had negative experiences with him or her or may have a bias about past clients with similar characteristics; therefore, the officer's responses might be distorted by his or her prior experiences.

A second concern is bias associated with the interviewee (Sattler, 1992). According to Bellack & Hersen's 1980 study (as cited in Sattler, 1992), the validity of interview information is dependent on the accuracy of the interviewee's information and the accuracy of his or her responses is dependent on such cognitive functions as selective memory, personal bias, personal interpretation of events, and/or personal experiences. Items on the YLS/CMI that ask interviewees to evaluate the quality of parenting provided to the target youth or whether or not he or she has inflated self-esteem are likely to have a great deal of interviewee bias based on his or her judgment of what makes a good parent or how the term "inflated self-esteem" is interpreted. The author's contention is that "professionals are capable of making these judgments" (user's manual, p. 5); however, it seems obvious that personal opinions, experiences, and bias could distort the interviewee's answers on such subjective areas of evaluation.

In an attempt to address the reliability and validity concerns inherent in the structured interview format, the authors stated that the YLS/CMI should be used to assist the professional in case planning, assessment of risk, and needs levels of clients. They further stipulate that the final decisions about the client should be in the hands of the individual/s responsible for his or her welfare, "as reflected in the Professional Override Principle" (user's manual, p. 5). The principle is included in Section IV of the instrument, which provides the interviewer with an opportunity to

"estimate" the risk level of the client based on all the information to which he or she has access.

SUMMARY. The authors have the expertise and experience to develop an instrument that assists professionals who work with juvenile offenders. They used the format of an instrument previously used with adult criminals and developed items appropriate to assess the needs of adjudicated youth. If the inherent validity and reliability problems associated with checklists and semistructured interviews are taken into account, the YLS/CMI seems to have merit as a screening tool. The LSI-R and YLS/CMI appear to be the most used of the instruments designated to assess criminal offenders. All other scales use a similar semistructured interview format. Therefore, professionals who work with youth offenders may find it a helpful tool to assist them in planning programs and/or interventions and making predictions about the likelihood that the youth will commit future criminal acts.

REVIEWER'S REFERENCES

Andrews, D. A., & Bonta, J. (1995). The Level of Supervision Inventory—Revised. Toronto, Ontario: Multi-Health Systems.

Bellack, A. S., & Hersen, M. (1980). *Introduction to clinical psychology*. New York: Oxford University Press.

Flores, A. W., Travis, F. T., III, & Latessa, E. J. (2003). *Case classification for juvenile corrections: An assessment of the Youth Level of Service/Case Management Inventory (YLS/CMI)* (Final Report, May, 2003). Abstract retrieved March 3, 2003, from www.uc.edu/criminaljustice/Project%20Reports/NIJYLSI.pdf

Hare, R., Forth, A., & Kosson, D. (1994). The Psychopathy Checklist: Youth Version (Research Version). Toronto, Ontario: Multi-Health Systems.

Lindsey, A. J. (2000). *Psychopathy: Risk/need factors, and psychiatric symptoms in high risk youth: Relationships between variables and their link to recidivism.* Unpublished doctoral dissertation, Simon Fraser University, British Columbia, Canada.

Overall, J. E., & Gorham, D. R. (1988). The Brief Psychiatric Rating Scale (BPRS): Recent development in assessment and scaling. *Psycho-Pharmacological Bulletin, 24,* 97–99.

Sattler, J. (1992). *Assessment of children: Revised and updated third edition.* San Diego: Sattler.

Sattler, J. (2001). *Assessment of children: Cognitive applications* (4th ed.). San Diego: Sattler.

Review of the Youth Level of Service/Case Management Inventory by STEPHEN E. TROTTER, Associate Professor, Department of Psychology, Tennessee State University, Nashville, TN:

DESCRIPTION. The Youth Level of Service/Case Management Inventory (YLS/CMI) is a norm-referenced, seven-part instrument. The YLS/CMI consists of an interview guide booklet and a seven-part instrument.

Part I of the YLS/CMI provides a survey of all the risk and needs factors that might be exhibited by the youth. The items in Part I are those identified in the literature as most predictive of criminal activity in young people. This section provides an assessment of the risk of continued criminal activity.

Part II of YLS/CMI then provides an overall risk/need score with a summary of the individual risk/need levels that were obtained in Part I.

Part III of the YLS/CMI provides a section where the assessor can record information about a range of variables.

Part IV of the YLS/CMI provides the assessor with a professional override. This feature allows the assessor to consider all the information about the client, then provide his or her estimate of the risk level involved.

On Part V of the YLS/CMI the assessor can record the level of contact that is appropriate for the case.

Part VI of the YLS/CMI focuses on setting specific goals for the youth and also addresses means for achieving these goals.

Part VII, the Case Management Review, is designed for use in reviewing case progress.

Recommendations are made for the examiner to follow the instructions described in the manual for completing, scoring, and interpreting the YLS/CMI. The instrument makes use of archival data, and self-report and collateral information. These data are used not only to predict recidivism but also to address responsivity factors that impact on case plan goals.

A variety of professionals who have the necessary training and background may administer the YLS/CMI. The examiner must have studied the YLS/CMI manual. He or she must (a) be conversant with the construction and statistical characteristics of the YLS/CMI, (b) be proficient in the administration of the YLS/CMI, and (c) have a working knowledge of the guidelines for interpreting the results of the YLS/CMI.

DEVELOPMENT. This YLS/CMI is based on the General Personality and Social Psychological Model of Criminal Conduct. The YLS/CMI was developed from the original Level of Supervision Inventory (Andrews, 1982), which was initially created to assist in decisions about parole release and parole supervision for adult offenders by assessing the level of risk for reoffending. After several revisions the current version is the Level of Service Inventory—Revised (LSI-R; T6:1421).

An earlier version of the LSI was adapted for use with children and adolescents; this was termed the Youth Level of Service Inventory (YLSI). This instrument was composed of 112 risk/need items divided into 10 subsections.

The YLS/CMI incorporates 42 of the 112 risk/need items from the YLSI. These items were selected due to previous research that indicated them to be the most strongly associated with youthful criminal activity. Other items incorporated into the YLS/CMI include responsivity items, a professional override feature, and a direct linkage with levels of supervision and case planning.

A fundamental assumption underlying the design of the instrument is that intelligent decisions about a youthful offender must be based on a valid and relevant assessment of the risk and need characteristics of the youth.

TECHNICAL. Information describing the norming process is comprehensive. The normative data were collected from January 1995 to January 1996. The data are based on a sample of 263 adjudicated youthful offenders. Respondent age ranged from 12–17 years. All the youths in the sample were serving either probation or custody sentences, and the sample consisted of 173 males and 90 females. The YLS/CMI forms were completed by the probation officers responsible for the youths at intake. The instrument may be best classified as a general risk or recidivism measure.

VALIDITY. Data bearing on the construct and predictive validity of YLS/CMI risk/need scores is provided by Lindsey (2000). Validity was supported by correlations between YLS/CMI scores and the adolescent version of the Psychopathy Checklist. Validity was also supported by significant correlations between the YLS/CMI scores and the Behaviour Problem subscore from the Brief Psychiatric Rating Scale for Children.

Predictive validity evidence was reported through the use of a linear discriminant function value based on the eight YLS/CMI subscores. This function yielded a 91.28% correct classification rate for reoffending data collected in the 2-year follow-up study. This demonstrated level of predictive validity suggests that the instrument is a valuable resource in determining the level of aftercare and supervision needed.

RELIABILITY. Satisfactory levels of reliability were reported for the total risk/need score: Kappa coefficient = .69; and intraclass correlation coefficient = .75. The values for the Kappa coefficient were reported to range from .38 to .90. The intraclass correlation coefficients were reported to range from .50 to .92.

SUMMARY. The strengths of the instrument center around the well-organized data collection format and subsequent case management tracking system. The manual is adequate for the stated purposes and the protocol is well laid out and articulated with the treatment or case notes section. The instrument appears to be useful in determining risk assessment with young offenders. The high level of recidivism among youthful offenders is an area of concern that might be addressed by a comprehensive interview and risk asseement protocol such as the YLS. The limited research available suggests the instrument is well positioned to add valuable information in determining level of care and supervision needed in treatment.

REVIEWER'S REFERENCES

Andrews, D. A. (1982). *The Level of Supervision Inventory (LSI): The first follow-up*. Toronto, Ontario: Ontario Ministry of Correctional Services of Ontario.
Lindsey, A. J. (2000). *Psychopathy, risk/need factors, and psychiatric symptoms in high-risk youth: Relationships between variables and their link to recidivism*. Unpublished doctoral dissertation, Simon Fraser University, British Columbia, Canada.

[283]
Youth Outcome Questionnaire (Y-OQ-2.01).

Purpose: Designed as a "measure of treatment progress for children and adolescents receiving psychological or psychiatric treatment."
Population: Ages 4–17.
Publication Date: 1996.
Acronym: Y-OQ-2.0.
Scores, 7: Intrapersonal Distress, Somatic, Interpersonal Relations, Critical Items, Social Problems, Behavioral Dysfunction, Total.
Administration: Individual.
Price Data: Price data for manual (1996, 27 pages) and questionnaires available from publisher.
Time: (7–20) minutes.
Comments: Behavior rating scale completed by parent or "significant adult figure."
Authors: Matthew J. Hoag, Carolen A. Hope, R. Scott Nebeker, Kimberly Konkel, Pamela McCollam, Gary Peterson, Mark Latkowski, Richard Ferre, and Curtis Reisinger (manual).
Publisher: OQ Measures LLC.

Review of the Youth Outcome Questionnaire by SUSAN K. GREEN, Associate Professor of Education, Winthrop University, Rock Hill, SC:

DESCRIPTION. The Youth Outcome Questionnaire (Y-OQ) is a 64-item measure designed for parents to report observed behavioral symptoms of children (ages 4–17) receiving psychological or psychiatric treatment. It was constructed to be sensitive to change over time and

takes 5–7 minutes to complete. The scale is divided into six subscales: Intrapersonal Distress (18 items address anxiety, depression, fearfulness, hopelessness, and self-harm), Somatic (8 items address headaches, dizziness, stomach aches, nausea, bowel difficulty, joint problems), Interpersonal Relations (10 items address attitudes toward others, communication and interaction with friends, cooperativeness, aggressiveness, arguing, defiance), Social Problems (8 items address truancy, sexual problems, running away from home, destruction of property, and substance abuse), Behavioral Dysfunction (11 items address ability to organize tasks, complete assignments, concentrate, handle frustration, inattention, hyperactivity, and impulsivity), and Critical Items (9 items address features associated with the need for inpatient treatment such as presence of paranoid ideation, obsessive-compulsive behaviors, hallucinations, delusions, suicidal feelings, mania, eating disorders). The respondent checks a box from 0 ("never or almost never") to 4 ("almost always or always"). Subscale scores are calculated by adding these ratings. Three subscales (ID, IR, and BD) have two positively worded items, and the SP subscale has one. These seven items are reverse scored from +2 to -2. Subtotals are summed for a total scale score.

DEVELOPMENT. A review of the general psychotherapy treatment literature for children and adolescents was conducted to specify empirically supported behavioral content domains sensitive to change (i.e., effect size of at least .5 after intervention). In addition, focus groups of medical providers (N = 10 groups) and former clients and parents (N = unspecified) drawn from a large western healthcare corporation were conducted to identify characteristic changes resulting from treatment of children. Finally, an unspecified number of hospital records were examined to determine behavior change goals typically addressed in treatment. The convergence of content from these three sources was used to develop 15–20 items for each subscale that were then reduced for duplicate content or diagnostic symptoms unlikely to be amenable to change. No more detailed information on appropriateness of domains or items is provided in the manual, except that focus groups from providers of inpatient care were instrumental in providing content for the Critical Items subscale. Subsequent exploratory factor analysis reported in Burlingame, Wells, Lambert, and Cox (2004) revealed two underlying factors for the total scale. This information suggests that individual subscale results should be interpreted with caution because of lack of evidence for six factors.

TECHNICAL.

Standardization. Normative data to establish cut scores and a reliable change index were collected from the U.S. Rocky Mountain region, primarily Utah and Idaho. A "normal" community sample (*N* = 650) was generated by randomly telephoning households in a community of 250,000. If the household had children between ages 4–17 who were not receiving mental health treatment and a respondent consented, they were sent a copy of the instrument to complete on one child. Approximately half of those who agreed to participate returned usable questionnaires. The normative information based on these respondents should be used with extreme caution given that demographic characteristics of the sample were not carefully described in the manual. For example, age range *N*s were listed (i.e., 6–8, *N* = 170; 9–11, *N* = 155; 12–14, *N* = 123; 15–17, *N* = 111) but 124 members of the sample were not classified by age. Gender totals were also listed (m = 361, f = 320) with 2 missing. No information on SES or race/ethnicity is reported. In addition, the 50% attrition rate was unlikely to be random. The sample cannot be assumed to accurately represent the U.S. population.

An inpatient sample (*N* = 174, m = 108, f = 65, 1 missing?) and an outpatient sample (*N* = 342, m = 208, f = 132, 2 missing?) were generated by the intake offices in Utah and Idaho of a large multistate western health care corporation from initial screenings of all children and adolescents who received treatment in a 9-month period. Age ranges, SES, and race/ethnicity on these two samples were not reported in the manual.

These three samples (community, inpatient, outpatient) were shown to be statistically significantly different from one another on total scores (community mean = 23.2, outpatient mean = 78.6, inpatient mean = 100) and on all but one subscale. Using these means, a cutoff score of 46 was calculated for evaluating treatment outcome based on work of Jacobson and Truax (1991). If patients' scores fall below this number, it is assumed that they are demonstrating behaviors no more severe than the normal community group. In addition, a reliable change index (RCI) of 13 points was also calculated based on these three sample means

rather than on actual changes in scores across time. The authors stipulate that for an individual's score to be reliably or clinically significantly changed over time, it must be 13 points higher than the initial score and must cross the cutoff score.

Reliability. Internal consistency reliability estimates using Cronbach's alpha based on several samples are quite high (.94), suggesting a strong single factor underlying the six subscales (Burlingame et al., 2004). Estimates for subscale reliability range from .51 to .90. In research subsequent to publishing the manual, test-retest reliability at 2 weeks and 4 weeks for a normal sample produced an average coefficient of .83 (Burlingame et al., 2004). No measures of interrater reliability were described.

Validity. Criterion-related validity evidence was collected by comparing total scores and parallel subscales from the Child Behavior Checklist (CBCL; Achenbach, 1991) and the Conners' Parent Rating Scale (Conners, 1990) with typical (*N* = 423) and outpatient (*N* = 61) samples (CBCL comparison only) for the manual and subsequent studies. Correlations with measures of similar constructs (e.g., CBCL anxious/depressed and Y-OQ intrapersonal distress) ranged from .48 to .78 and fall within an acceptable range. In addition, the total CBCL and Y-OQ scales correlated .78.

Additional validity evidence on the sensitivity (proportion of members of clinical groups correctly identified) and specificity (proportion of members of the normal group correctly identified) of the Y-OQ has been investigated for the manual and in subsequent studies (Burlingame et al., 2004). The most recent studies indicate that the Y-OQ will correctly identify clinical group members 82% of the time and normal group members 89% of the time with the cutoff score of 46. These figures compare favorably with sensitivity and specificity indices for the CBCL. Evidence of discriminant validity has been shown by the Y-OQ's ability to reliably distinguish between groups of normal, outpatient, and inpatient samples, with scores significantly rising with restrictiveness of setting.

Recent recommendations (Burlingame et al., 2004) suggest that the Y-OQ be administered on a weekly or biweekly schedule to detect change over time as a result of clinical intervention. When scales are used repeatedly, a retest artifact may occur because raters respond with carelessness or social desirability motives when asked to complete the same questionnaire many times. Research conducted by

Durham et al. (2002) explored this problem with a normal sample using the Y-OQ and found that the magnitude of the retest artifact increased as administration schedule increased (range was weekly to pre-post only over 9 weeks). That is, scores demonstrated less pathology the more frequently the Y-OQ was administered. The authors found no evidence for social desirability and mechanical responding influencing total scores, however.

COMMENTARY. At this time, the Y-OQ appears to be most useful as a screening tool. Because of the vague nature of the information on instrument development, the small number of items on several subscales, the lack of interrater reliability data, and the restricted norm group, it should not be used for diagnostic purposes, nor should data from subscales be used in isolation. This caveat is mentioned in recent writings (Burlingame et al., 2004) but not in the manual. Credible evidence for reliability and validity of the measure has been collected to validate use as a screening measure.

The authors also developed the measure with items that are intended to be sensitive to behavioral change with the goal of using the measure to detect impact of treatment over brief time periods. Although they developed a cutoff score and reliable change index to use for the purpose of detecting significant change over time, no evidence for the validity of this use is presented in the manual. There is evidence that total scores differ significantly between normal, outpatient, and inpatient populations, however. More recently, Burlingame et al. (2004) cite published studies indicating that the Y-OQ has been used to demonstrate the effectiveness of the instrument in assessing the usefulness of clinical programs, and Burlingame et al. (2001) reported that the changes in scores of a sample of children receiving treatment were significantly greater than the changes in scores of a sample of children not receiving treatment (17.7 points vs. 4.3 points) over an 8-week period. These findings are promising, but suggest continued caution in using the instrument as often as weekly or for purposes such as discontinuing or modifying treatment over short time periods.

SUMMARY. The Youth Outcome Questionnaire is a 64-item parent-report instrument containing six subscales that address behaviors purportedly sensitive to psychological or psychiatric treatment. Sufficient evidence of reliability and validity based on data from the Rocky Mountain region of the U.S. indicate its appropriate use as a screening measure. Promising research also suggests that this measure is sensitive to the impact of treatment over time periods of a few weeks.

REVIEWER'S REFERENCES

Achenbach, T. (1991) *Manual for the Child Behavior Checklist and 1991 Profile.* Burlington, VT: University of Vermont Department of Psychiatry.
Burlingame, G., Mosier, J., Wells, M., Atkin, Q., Lambert, M., Whooley, M., & Latkowski, M. (2001). Tracking the influence of mental health treatment: The development of the Youth Outcome Questionnaire. *Clinical Psychology and Psychotherapy, 8,* 361–379.
Burlingame, G., Wells, M., Lambert, M., & Cox, J. (2004). Youth Outcome Questionnaire. In M. E. Maruish (Ed.), *The use of psychological testing for treatment planning and outcome assessment* (3rd ed.). Mahwah, NJ: Lawrence Erlbaum Associates.
Conners, C. (1990). *Conners' Rating Scales manual.* North Tonawanda, NY: Multi-Health Systems.
Durham, C., McGrath, L., Burlingame, G., Schaalje, G., Lambert, M., & Davies, D., (2002). *Journal of Psychoeducational Assessment, 20,* 240–257.
Jacobson, N., & Truax, P. (1991). Clinical significance: A statistical approach to defining meaningful change in psychotherapy research. *Journal of Consulting and Clinical Psychology, 59,* 12–19.

Review of the Youth Outcome Questionnaire by JOHN HATTIE, *Professor of Education, University of Auckland, Auckland, New Zealand:*

DESCRIPTION. The Youth Outcome Questionnaire (Y-OQ) is a parent-report measure of treatment progress for children and adolescents (ages 4–17) receiving psychological or psychiatric treatment. It consists of 64 Likert-type items made up into six scales, and takes about 5–7 minutes to complete. The six subscales are Intrapersonal Distress (e.g., appears sad or unhappy), Somatic Distress (complains of dizziness or headaches), Interpersonal Relations (enjoys relationships with family and friends), Critical Items (thinks about suicide), Social Problems (deliberately breaks rules, laws, or expectations), and Behavioral Dysfunction (is fidgety, restless, or hyperactive).

DEVELOPMENT. One of the attractions of the Y-OQ is the care in its development. A comprehensive literature review and synthesis of meta-analyses identified content domains in which treated children were at least .5 *sd* different from untreated children. A series of focus groups of clients and of inpatient and outpatient provider groups identified a number of critical items that must be ameliorated or stabilized prior to discharge from inpatient treatment. Finally, the authors examined hospital records to assess the characteristic behavior change goals that were being addressed in treatment planning. From these three sources, the items and final six domains were developed.

TECHNICAL. The normative data, although constrained to one area of the U.S. (the Rocky Mountain area) seem reasonable. A group of 683 children and adolescents 4–17 year old who were not receiving mental health treatment were the controls, and a group of 174 inpatient and 342 outpatient children and adolescents were included in the normative groups. The means of the two latter groups are about 2 *sd* different from the community group. A cut score of about 1 *sd* above the community mean is recommended for evaluating treatment outcome. There are also cut scores for the individual scales, but for four of the six scales the differences between the means of the outpatient and community/control groups exceed or are very close to their cut score, which should be a reason for caution in using these cut scores.

The estimates of internal consistency reliability are all very high. The major issue is whether each scale adds sufficient unique variance to be worthwhile. The authors claim that the high reliability estimate suggests a strong single factor, but this is fallacious as reliability is no indicator of dimensionality. There is no factor analysis in the manual, but the correlations are provided in an article by the authors (Burlingame et al., 2001). A maximum-likelihood solution indicated that 70% of the variance can be explained by the first factor, which is indeed substantial. If two factors are requested, then Somatic, Intrapersonal Distress, and Critical Items load together, and perhaps raises the question as to whether these three could be combined into a Physical Incidents (recall Somatic measures headaches, bowel difficulties, pain; Intrapersonal Distress measures anxiety, self-harm; and Critical Items measures mania, eating disorders, paranoia). The other three scales are more related to Social or Mental Incidents. An equally important question is to ask whether a shorter version of the scale leading to only one total score is more appropriate, as there seems little information in each of the subscores. Whether one or two total scores are optimum needs to be addressed by further work, but certainly there seems little defense for all six subscores.

There are no reliable age group or gender differences on the total score. There are somewhat high correlations between "like" scales in Y-OQ and the Child Behavior Checklist (CBC; Achenbach, 1991; like scales average .51 vs. unlike scales .18) and for the Conners' Parent Rating Sale (Conners, 1990; like scales .55 vs. unlike scales .18). I would agree with the authors that this is "very promising" as this implies more work is needed: there are some concerns about the low .40 between the CBC somatic and the Y-OQ somatic, and .46 between the Conners Antisocial and Y-OQ social problems, and .54 between CBC attention and Y-OQ Behavioral dysfunction.

COMMENTARY AND SUMMARY. An impressive feature of the manual and related articles is the evidence about the sensitivity of the Y-OQ to psychopathology and to treatment. This surely is the major purpose of this instrument and its success at monitoring change makes this instrument worth considering, and certainly worthy of more investment in improving.

Such improvements could relate to demonstrating the worth of all 64 items, and the six subscales given the high dominance of one factor, more defense of the cut score beyond a statistical derivation (e.g., by demonstrating more evidence of the minimum number of real false positives and negatives relative to treatment providers' estimates), and more evidence of the differential information provided by the Y-OQ compared to other available scales. The Y-OQ is an easy-to-use instrument for parents, the items are well constructed, the sensitivity analysis impressive, and the use of the total score defensible, and thus it is a worthwhile instrument to use for documenting and tracking treatment outcomes.

REVIEWER'S REFERENCES

Achenach, T. M. (1991). *Manual for the Child Behavior Checklist and 1991 Profile*. Burlington, VT: University of Vermont, Department of Psychiatry.

Burlingame, G. B., Mosier, J. I., Wells, M., Atkin, O., Lambert, M., Whoolery, M., & Latkowski, M. (2001). Tracking the influence of mental health treatment: The development of the Youth Outcome Questionnaire. *Clinical Psychology and Psychotherapy, 8*, 361–375.

Conners, C. K. (1990). *Conners' Rating Scales manual*. North Tonawanda, NY: Multi-Health Systems.

APPENDIX

TESTS LACKING SUFFICIENT TECHNICAL DOCUMENTATION FOR REVIEW

Effective with The Fourteenth Mental Measurements Yearbook *(2001), an additional criterion was added for tests reviewed in* The Mental Measurements Yearbook. *Only those tests for which at least minimal technical or test development information is provided are now reviewed. This list includes the names of new and revised tests received since publication of the* Fifteenth Mental Measurements Yearbook *that are lacking this documentation. The publishers have been advised that these tests do not meet our review criteria.*

[284]
Analytical Reasoning Skills Battery.
Publisher: Walden Personnel Performance, Inc. [Canada].

[285]
The Career Exploration Inventory: A Guide for Exploring Work, Leisure, and Learning, Second Edition.
Publisher: JIST Publishing, Inc.

[286]
The Carolina Curriculum.
Publisher: Brookes Publishing Co., Inc.

[287]
Carolina Developmental Profile.
Publisher: Kaplan Early Learning Company.

[288]
Comprehensive Assessment of Mathematics Strategies II.
Publisher: Curriculum Associates, Inc.

[289]
Comprehensive Assessment of Reading Strategies II.
Publisher: Curriculum Associates, Inc.

[290]
Controller Staff Selector.
Publisher: Walden Personnel Performance, Inc. [Canada].

[291]
Criterion Test of Basic Skills [2002 Edition].
Publisher: Academic Therapy Publications.

[292]
Denver Prescreening Developmental Questionnaire II.
Publisher: Denver Developmental Materials, Inc.

[293]
Diagnostic Interview for Children and Adolescents–IV.
Publisher: Multi-Health Systems, Inc.

[294]
EYES [Early Years Easy Screen], Short Form.
Publisher: NFER-Nelson Publishing Company Ltd. [England].

[295]
Feedback Portrait of Overdone Strengths.
Publisher: Personal Strengths Publishing.

[296]
Guide to Early Movement Skills: A Portage-Based Programme.
Publisher: NFER-Nelson Publishing Co., Ltd. [England].

[297]
Hilson Adolescent Profile—Version S.
Publisher: Hilson Research, Inc.

[298]
Hilson Career Satisfaction Index.
Publisher: Hilson Research, Inc.

[299]
IDEA Feedback for Administrators.
Publisher: The IDEA Center.

[300]
IDEA Feedback for Deans.
Publisher: The IDEA Center.

[301]
Individual Employment Plan with 84-Item Employability Assessment.
Publisher: JIST Publishing, Inc.

[302]
Interest-A-Lyzer Family of Instruments.
Publisher: Creative Learning Press, Inc.

[303]
Inwald Survey 5.
Publisher: Hilson Research, Inc.

[304]
IPMA Correctional Officer Test.
Publisher: International Personnel Management Association.

[305]
IS Manager/Consultant Skills Evaluation.
Publisher: Walden Personnel Performance, Inc. [Canada].

[306]
Leadex: Leadership Assessment System.
Publisher: Karl Albrecht International.

[307]
Leisure to Occupations Connection Search.
Publisher: JIST Publishing, Inc.

[308]
The Middle Infant Screening Test.
Publisher: NFER-Nelson Publishing Company Ltd. [England].

[309]
Mindex: Your Thinking Style Profile.
Publisher: Karl Albrecht International.

[310]
Network Technician Staff Selector.
Publisher: Walden Personnel Performance, Inc. [Canada].

[311]
The Optimizer II™.
Publisher: Consulting Resource Group International, Inc.

[312]
Projective Storytelling Cards.
Publisher: Northwest Psychological Publishers, Inc.

[313]
Retail Store Manager Staff Selector.
Publisher: Walden Personnel Performance, Inc. [Canada].

[314]
Schedules for Clinical Assessment in Neuropsychiatry, Version 2.0.
Publisher: American Psychiatric Publishing, Inc.

[315]
Understanding Ambiguity: An Assessment of Pragmatic Meaning Comprehension.
Publisher: NFER-Nelsen Publishing Company Ltd. [England].

[316]
Vocational Decision-Making Interview, Revised Edition.
Publisher: JIST Publishing, Inc.

[317]
W-APT Programming Aptitude Test.
Publisher: Rose Wolfe Family Partnership LLP [Canada].

[318]
Warehouse/Plant Worker Staff Selector.
Publisher: Walden Personnel Performance, Inc. [Canada].

TESTS TO BE REVIEWED FOR THE SEVENTEENTH MENTAL MEASUREMENTS YEARBOOK

By the time each new Mental Measurements Yearbook *reaches publication, the staff at the Buros Institute have already collected many new and revised tests destined to be reviewed in the next* Mental Measurements Yearbook. *Following is a list of tests that meet the review criteria and that will be reviewed, along with additional tests published and received in the next year, in* The Seventeenth Mental Measurements Yearbook.

Abbreviated Torrance Test for Adults
Academic Intervention Monitoring System
Achievement Motivation Inventory
Anger Disorders Scale
Applicant Risk Profiler
The Assessment of Personal Goals
The Autobiographical Memory Interview
The Awareness of Social Inference Test

The Balloons Test
Basic Achievement Skills Inventory
Bateria III Woodcock-Munoz
Battelle Developmental Inventory, 2nd Edition
Battery for Health Improvement 2
Behavior Assessment System for Children, Second
    Edition
Behavioral Observation of Students in Schools
Behavioural Assessment of the Dysexecutive Syndrome
    in Children
Behavioural Inattention Test
Benton Laboratory of Neuropsychology: Selected Tests
Brief Battery for Health Improvement 2
Burns/Roe Informal Reading Inventory: Preprimer to
    Twelfth Grade, Sixth Edition

The Cambridge Prospective Memory Test
Career Directions Inventory [Second Edition]
Checking Individual Progress in Phonics
Child and Adolescent Risk Evaluation
Children's Depression Inventory [Revised]
Children's PTSD Inventory: A Structured Interview
    for Diagnosing Posttraumatic Stress Disorder
Children's Speech Intelligibility Measure
Clerical Skills Test
Clinical Assessment of Depression
Clinical Evaluation of Language Fundamentals Pre-
    school—Second Edition
Comprehensive Testing Program, 4th Edition
Computerized Articulation and Phonology Evaluation
    System
Cortical Vision Screening Test

Dean-Woodcock Neuropsychological Battery
Detroit Tests of Learning Aptitude—Primary: Third
    Edition
Doors and People
Dutch Eating Behaviour Questionnaire

Early Reading SUCCESS Indicator
Eating Disorder Inventory—3
Emotional Competence Inventory
Emotional Literacy—Assessment and Intervention
English Placement Test, Revised
ERB Writing Assessment [Revised]

Facial Expressions of Emotion: Stimuli and Tests
Feedback Edition of the Strength Development Inventory
Feedback Portrait of Personal Strengths

Graded Nonword Reading Test
Group Environment Scale, Third Edition
Group Mathematics Assessment and Diagnostic Evalu-
    ation
Gudjonsson Suggestibility Scales

The Hayling and Brixton Tests
Hodson Assessment of Phonological Patterns—Third
    Edition

Index of Teaching Stress
Iowa Tests of Basic Skills®, Forms A and B
IPT Early Literacy Test
IVA+Plus [Integrated Visual and Auditory Continuous
    Performance Test]

Kaufman Brief Intelligence Test, Second Edition

Leadership Spectrum Profile
Learning Styles Inventory, Version III
Level of Service Inventory—Revised [2003 Norms Up-
    date]
Level of Service/Case Management Inventory: An Of-
    fender Assessment System

Life Attitudes Schedule: A Risk Assessment for Suicidal and Life-Threatening Behaviors

Lindamood Auditory Conceptualization Test—Third Edition

Location Learning Test

Management and Organizational Skills Test—Revised Edition

Mechanical Understanding Test, Revised Edition

The Middlesex Elderly Assessment of Mental State

Millon Pre-Adolescent Clinical Inventory

Multidimensional Perfectionism Scale

Multifactor Leadership Questionnaire, Third Edition with Actual/Ought Feedback Report

Naturalistic Action Test

Nelson-Denny CD-ROM Reading Test

Nonverbal Personality Questionnaire and Five-Factor Nonverbal Personality Questionnaire

Orleans-Hanna Algebra Prognosis Test, Third Edition

Paced Auditory Serial Attention Test

Personnel Assessment Form

Pervasive Developmental Disorders Screening Test, Second Edition

Planning, Organizing, & Scheduling Test, Revised Edition

Pre-Reading Inventory of Phonological Awareness

Putney Auditory Comprehension Screening Test

Pyramids and Palm Trees Test

Quick Informal Assessment, Second Edition

Rapid Automatized Naming and Rapid Alternating Stimulus Tests

Reading Fluency Indicator

Risk-Sophistication-Treatment Inventory

Rivermead Assessment of Somatosensory Performance

The Rivermead Behavioural Memory Test—Extended Version

Sales Potential Inventory

Service Ability Inventory

Severe Impairment Battery

The Speed and Capacity of Language-Processing Test

Stanford-Binet Intelligence Scales for Early Childhood

Survey Ballot for Industry

Test of Everyday Attention

Test of Everyday Attention for Children

Test of Supervisory Skills, Revised Edition

Trauma Symptom Checklist for Young Children

Verb and Sentence Test

The Visual Object and Space Perception Battery

Visual Patterns Test

Wechsler Intelligence Scale for Children—Fourth Edition Integrated

The Wessex Head Injury Matrix

The Wilson Syntax Screening Test

Woodcock-Johnson III Diagnostic Reading Battery

Woodcock-Munoz Language Survey—Revised

Work Orientation and Values Survey

Workplace Skills Survey

NEW TESTS REQUESTED BUT NOT RECEIVED

The staff of the Buros Institute endeavor to acquire copies of every new or revised commercially available test. Descriptions of all tests are included in Tests in Print *and reviews for all tests that meet our review criteria are included in* The Mental Measurements Yearbook. *A comprehensive search of multiple sources of test information is ongoing, and test materials are regularly requested from publishers. Many publishers routinely provide review copies of all new test publications. However, some publishers refuse to provide materials and others advertise tests long before the tests are actually published. Following is a list of test titles that have been requested but not yet provided.*

The ABC Inventory-Extended

The Abel Assessment for Interest in Paraphilias

The Abel Assessment for Sexual Interest

Abilities Forecaster

Ability Test

Academic Profile

Accuracy Level Test

AccuRater

AccuVision

ACE Online Toolkit

Achiever

ACS California Chemistry Diagnostic Test

ACS Chemistry in the Community (Chem Com) Curriculum, High School Chemistry
ACS Examination in Instrumental Methods
ACT Assessment
The ACT Evaluation/Survey Service [Revised]
Actions, Styles, Symbols in Kinetic Family Drawings
Adaptability Test [Revised]
Adaptive Resilience Factor Inventory
Adjective Rating Scale
Admitted Student Questionnaire and Admitted Student Questionnaire Plus
The Adolescent Multiphasic Personality Inventory
Adolescent Self-Report and Projective Inventory
Adult Child Distortion Scale
Adult Health Nursing
Adult Measure of Essential Skills
Adult Memory and Information Processing Battery
Adult Placement Inventory
Adult Self-Perception Profile
Advanced Management Tests
Advanced Placement Examination in Comparative Government and Politics
Advanced Placement Examination in Computer Science
Advanced Placement Examination in Economics
Advanced Placement Examination in Environmental Science
Advanced Placement Examination in Government and Politics
Advanced Placement Examination in International English Language
Advanced Placement Examination in Macroeconomics
Advanced Placement Examination in Psychology
Advanced Placement Examination in Statistics
Advanced Placement Examination in United States Government and Politics
Advanced Placement Program: Psychology
The Advanced Problem Solving Tests
Air Conditioning Specialist
Algebra
Algebra Readiness Assessment
Alleman Leadership Development Questionnaire
Alleman Mentoring Activities Questionnaire
Alleman Relationship Value Questionnaire
Allied Health Aptitude Test
American Health and Life Styles
The American Tobacco Survey
Anatomy and Physiology
Angie/Andy Cartoon Trauma Scales
Aphasia Screening Test
Apperceptive Personality Test
Applicant Productivity Profile
Applied Natural Sciences
Applied Technology Series
APTICOM
Aptitude Assessment
Aptitude Test Battery for Pupils in Standards 6 and 7
The Arabic Speaking Test

The Area Coordinator Achievement Test
Areas of Change Questionnaire
Arithmetic Index [Revised]
Arithmetic Test, Form A
Arizona Basic Assessment and Curriculum Utilization System for Young Handicapped Children
Armed Services Vocational Aptitude Battery
Armstrong Naming Test
Assertiveness Profile
Assessing Semantic Skills Through Everyday Themes
Assessment of Collaborative Tendencies
Assessment of Competencies and Traits
Assessment of Organizational Readiness for Mentoring
Assessment of Sound Awareness and Production
Assessment of Stuttering Behaviors
The Assessment, Evaluation, and Programming System for Infants and Children
Associational Fluency
Attention Battery for Children
Attention Index Survey
Attitude Survey
Auditory Perception Test for the Hearing Impaired
Auditory-Visual Single-Word Picture Vocabulary Test—Adolescent
Authentic Assessment for the Intermediate Level in French
Authentic Assessment for the Intermediate Level in Spanish
Authentic Writing Screener
Auto Technician

Baccalaureate Achievement
Basic Academic Evaluation
Basic Banking Skills Battery
Basic Inventory of Natural Language
Basic Nursing Care I and II
The BASICS Behavioral Adjustment Scale
Basics in Nursing I, II, III
Battelle Developmental Inventory-Spanish
Beery-Buktenica Developmental Test of Visual-Motor Integration, 5th Ed.
Behavior Forecaster
Behavior Style Analysis
Behavioral Intervention Plan
Benchmarking Organizational Emotional Intelligence
Bilingual Classroom Communication Profile
Bilingual Health and Developmental History Questionnaire
Bilingual Language Proficiency Questionnaire
Bilingual Verbal Ability Tests-Normative Update
Bilingual Vocabulary Assessment Measure
BldgTest
Bloomer Learning Test-Neurologically Enhanced
Boston Diagnostic Aphasia Examination, 3rd Edition
BRIGANCE Inventory of Early Development-II
Building Maintenance Test
Business English Assessment
Business Personality Indicator

College Board SAT II: Biology E/M Subject Test
College Board SAT II: Biology Subject Test
College Board SAT II: Chemistry Subject Test
College Board SAT II: English Language Proficiency Test
College Board SAT II: French Subject Test
College Board SAT II: French with Listening Subject Test
College Board SAT II: German Subject Test
College Board SAT II: German with Listening Subject Test
College Board SAT II: Korean with Listening Subject Test
College Board SAT II: Latin Subject Test
College Board SAT II: Literature Subject Test
College Board SAT II: Mathematics Level IC and SAT II: Mathematics Level IIC
College Board SAT II: Modern Hebrew Subject Test
College Board SAT II: Physics Subject Test
College Board SAT II: Spanish Subject Test
College Board SAT II: Spanish with Listening Subject Test
College Board SAT II: Subject Test in Chinese with Listening
College Board SAT II: Subject Test in Italian
College Board SAT II: Subject Test in Japanese with Listening
College Board SAT II: World History Subject Test
College Board SAT II: Writing Subject Test
College Board SAT Program
College Portfolio Builder
College Student Expectations Questionnaire, Second Edition
Collegiate Assessment of Academic Proficiency [Revised]
Colorado Malingering Tests
Colorado Neuropsychology Tests
Combustion Control Technician
The Communication Behaviors Inventory II
Communication Competency Assessment Instrument
Communication Effectiveness Profile
Communication Effectiveness Scale
Communication Independence Profile for Adults
Communication Style Inventory
Community Health Nursing
Community Opinion Inventory [Revised]
COMPASS Managerial Practices Profile
Competence Assessment to Stand Trial for Defendants with Mental Retardation
Competency-Based Position Analysis
Comprehensive Nursing Achievement Test for Practical Nursing Students
Comprehensive Nursing Achievement-PN
Comprehensive Nursing Achievement-RN
Comprehensive Occupational Exams
Comprehensive Test of Adaptive Behavior-Revised
Computer Optimized Multimedia Intelligence Test
Computer Programmer Ability Battery

Computer Programmer Aptitude Battery
Comrey Personality Scales—Short Form
The Concise Learning Styles Assessment
Concussion Resolution Index
Conflict Style Instrument
Copeland Symptom Checklist for Attention Deficit Disorders
COPS Interest Inventory (1995 Revision)
Corporate Communication Assessment
Counterproductive Behavior Index
Creativity Questionnaire
Creativity/Innovation Effectiveness Profile
Cree Questionnaire [Revised]
Crichton Vocabulary Scale, 1988 Revision
Criterion Validated Written Test for Emergency Medical Practitioner
Criterion Validated Written Test for Fire Medic
Criterion Validated Written Tests for Firefighter [Revised]
Criterion-Referenced Articulation Profile
Critical Thinking in Clinical Nursing Practice-PN
Critical Thinking in Clinical Nursing Practice-RN
Critical Thinking Test
CRT Skills Test
Cultural Diversity and Awareness Profile
Culture for Diversity Inventory
Customer Satisfaction Practices Tool
Customer Satisfaction Survey
Customer Service Commitment Profile
Customer Service Listening Skills Exercise
Customer Service Profile
Customer Service Simulator
Customer Service Skills Assessment
Customer Service Skills Inventory
Customer Service Survey

Data Entry and Data Checking Tests
Data Entry Test
Dealing With Conflict Instrument
DecideX
Defendant Questionnaire
Denison Leadership Development Survey
Denison Organizational Culture Survey
DEST: Dental Ethical Sensitivity Test
Detention Promotions Test—Complete Service [Revised]
Developmental Eye Movement Test
Developmental Inventory of Learned Skills
Developmental Reading Assessment
The Devine Inventory [Revised]
Diagnostic Assessments of Reading, Second Edition
The Diagnostic Inventory of Personality and Symptoms
Diagnostic Prescriptive Assessment
Diagnostic Readiness Test-PN
Diagnostic Readiness Test-RN
Diagnostic Test for High School Math
Diagnostic Test for Pre-Algebra Math

Griffiths Mental Development Scales [Revised]
Group Literacy Assessment
Group Mathematics Test, Third Edition
Group Perceptions Inventory
Group-Level Team Assessment

Hare Psychopathy Checklist-Self-Report
Harmonic Improvisational Readiness Record and Rhythm Improvisation Readiness Record
Health and Illness: Adult Care
Healthcare Employee Productivity Report
The HELP Test-Elementary
High School and College Drop-Out Student Prediction Test
The Highly Effective Meeting Profile
Hill Interaction Matrix [Revised]
Hilson Adolescent Profile-Version D
Hilson Career Stress Inventory
Hilson Caregiver's Questionnaire
Hilson Cognitive Abilities Test
Hilson Job Analysis Questionnaire
Hilson Law Enforcement History Questionnaire
Hilson Life Adjustment Profile
Hilson Life Stress Questionnaire
Hilson Management Inventory
Hilson Management Survey
Hilson Parent/Guardian Inventory
HIlson Personal History Questionnaire
Hilson Relationship Inventory for Public Safety Personnel
Hilson Safety/Security Risk Inventory
HIlson Spouse/Mate Inventory
The Hindi Proficiency Test
Hiskey-Nebraska Test of Learning Aptitude
Hodder Group Reading Tests 1-3
HomeEducation Developmental Screen
Honesty Survey
Honesty Test
Human Job Analysis
Hydraulics

I-7 Impulsiveness Questionnaire
Impact of Event Scale
Independent Living Skills-Assessments for Life Skills
Indiana Student Scale: A Measure of Self-Esteem
Individual Directions Inventory
Individual Reading Analysis
Individualized Mathematics Program
Infant/Preschool Play Assessment Scale
Influencing Skills Index
The Influencing Skills Inventory
Influencing Skills Profile
Influencing Strategies and Styles Profile
The Influencing Style Clock
Initial Assessment: An Assessment for Reading, Writing and Maths [New Version]
Instruments for Assessing Understanding & Appreciation of Miranda Rights

Insurance Selection Inventory
Integrity Survey
Intercultural Communication Inventory
Interest Check List
Interest Inventory
Internal Customer Service Survey
InterSurvS
Intuitive Mechanics (Weights & Pulleys) [Revised]
Inventory of Gambling Situations
Inventory of Leadership Styles
Inventory of Marital Conflict (IMC)
Inventory of Parent-Adolescent Conflict
Inventory of Parent-Child Conflict
Inventory of Premarital Conflict (IPMC)
Inventory of Program Stages of Development
Inventory of Religious Activities and Interests
Invest in Your Values
Inwald Personality Inventory-Clinical
Inwald Personality Inventory—Short Version
Inwald Survey 2
Inwald Survey 2-Adolescent Version
Inwald Survey 3
Inwald Survey 4
Inwald Survey 6
Inwald Survey 8
Iowa Algebra Aptitude Test, Fifth Edition
The Iowa Developing Autonomy Inventory
Iowa Writing Assessment
IPI Performance Appraisal Questionnaires
Ironworker

The Janus Competency Identification & Assessment System
The Japanese Speaking Test
Job Effectiveness Prediction System
Job Skills Training Needs Assessment
Job Values Inventory
Job-O Enhanced
Jonico Questionnaire
Judgment of Line Orientation
The Julia Farr Services Post-Traumatic Amnesia Scale
Jung Type Indicator
Junior Scholastic Aptitude Test Battery (Standard 5)

The Kaufman Speech Praxis Test for Children
Kendrick Assessment of Cognitive Ageing
The Kendrick Assessment Scales of Cognitive Ageing
Kent Inventory of Developmental Skills (1996 Standardization)
Kindergarten Readiness Checklists for Parents
Kuder Career Search
Kuder Skills Assessment
Kuhlmann-Anderson Tests [1997 norms/standards]

Laboratory Technician (Mfg.)
Langdon Adult Intelligence Test
Language Processing Test-Revised

Negotiation Style Instrument
Networking & Relationship Building Profile
Neuropsychological Aging Inventory
The New Jersey Test of Children's Reasoning
The New Jersey Test of Reasoning [Adult Version]
New Reading Analysis
NOCTI Experienced Worker Assessments
NOCTI Industrial Assessments
NOCTI Job Ready Assessments
The Nonspeech Test
Nonverbal Form [Revised]
Nonverbal Reasoning [Revised]
Normal Nutrition
Normative Adaptive Behavior Checklist-Revised
Norris-Ryan Argument Analysis Test
NTE Specialty Area Tests: School Social Worker
Numeracy Progress Tests
Numerical Computation Test
Nurse Aide (Assistant) Program
Nursing Care During Childbearing and Nursing Care
  of the Child
Nursing Care in Mental Health and Mental Illness
Nursing Care of Adults with Pathophysiological Dis-
  turbances—Part I and II
Nursing Care of Adults, Parts I, II, and III
Nursing Care of Children
Nursing the Childbearing Family

Objective Risk Taking Test
Observation Ability Test for the Police Service
Occupational Clues
Occupational Interest Profile
Occupational Motivation Questionnaire
Occupational Personality Profile
Occupational Preference Inventory
Occupational Skills Inventory
Office Proficiency Assessment & Certification
Office Skills Assessment Battery
Office Skills Profile
Office Skills Tests [Revised]
Ohio Vocational Competency Assessment
O'Neill Talent Inventory
Online Sales Effectiveness Profile
The Opportunities-Obstacles Profile
OPQ32
OQ-10.2 (mini-OQ)
Oral Communication Battery
Organisational Transitions
Organizational Assessment Survey
Organizational Climate Survey
Organizational Focus Questionnaire
Organizational Survey System
OSHA Violations Safety Test

P.A.S.S. III Survey
Pacesetter
Pair Behavioral Style Instrument

Parent Opinion Inventory, Revised Edition [1995 Edition]
Parenting Stress Inventory
Partner Power Profile
Partnering Development Assessment
Passport
Pathognomonic Scale
Pathways to Independence, Second Edition
PCA Checklist for Computer Access
Pediatric Symptoms Checklist
Perceived Competence Scale for Children
Perceptual Archetypal Orientation Inventory
Performance Coaching
Performance Management Assessment System
Performance On-Line
Performance Skills Quality Teams Assessment
Performer
Personal Audit [Revised]
Personal Competency Framework
Personal Directions
Personal Dynamics Profile
Personal Effectiveness Profile
Personal Interest and Values Survey
Personal Learning Profile
Personal Productivity Assessment
Personal Profile Analysis
Personal Stress & Well-being Assessment
Personal Styles Inventory [PSI-120] [1999 Revision]
Personal Success Profile
The Personality Preference Profile
Personality Questionnaire
Personnel Security Standards Psychological Questionnaire
Personnel Selection Inventory [Revised]
The PETAL Speech Assessment
Pharmacology in Clinical Nursing
The Phonological and Reading Profile-Intermediate
Phonological Awareness & Reading Profile
The Phonological Awareness Profile
The Phonological Awareness Test
Phonological Screening Assessment
Physical Assessment
Pictorial Inventory of Careers
Pictorial Reasoning Test [Revised]
Picture Interest Exploration Survey
Pikunas Adult Stress Inventory
PIP Developmental Charts, Second Edition
PipeTest
PLAN [Revised]
Plotkin Index
Plumber-Pipefitter Test
PM Benchmark Kit
PN Fundamentals
PN Pharmacology
Police Administrator (Assistant Chief) 566
Police Administrator (Captain) 565
Police Administrator (Chief) 568
Police Administrator (Lieutenant) 564
Police Corporal/Sergeant Examination 562 and 563

School and College Ability Tests, Third Edition
School Child Stress Scale
School Diversity Inventory
School Improvement Follow-Up Survey
School Leaders Licensure Assessment
School Readiness Tests for Blind Children
School-to-Work Career Survey
Science Research Temperament Scale
Scoreboard
Secondary Reading Assessment Inventory
Secord Contextual Articulation Tests
The Security and Acuity of Psychiatric Illness Scales
Security Aptitude Fitness Evaluation-Resistance
Self-Directed Learning Readiness Scale [Revised]
Self-Directed Team Assessment
The Self-Perception Profile for Adults
Self-Perception Profile for Children
Self-Perception Profile for Learning Disabled Students
Seligman Attributional Style Questionnaire
Senior South African Individual Scale—Revised
Sensorimotor Performance Analysis
SEPO (Serial Position) Test for the Detection of Guilty/
    Special Knowledge
Serial Digit Learning
Service Skills Indicator
SF-12: Physical and Mental Health Summary Scales
SF-36: Physical and Mental Health Summary Scales
The Shapes Analysis Test
The Shorr Couples Imagery Test
The Shorr Parent/Child Imagery Test
Short Tests of Clerical Ability [Revised]
Side Effects Profile for Exceptional Children
SigmaRadius 360° Feedback
Situational Leadership II Leadership Skills Assessment
Situational Leadership [Revised]
16+ PersonalStyle Profile
Six Factor Automated Vocational Assessment System
Skil Scale Inventory
SkillCheck Professional Plus
Skillscape
Slosson Auditory Perceptual Skill Screener
Slosson-Diagnostic Math Screener
Slosson Intelligence Test-Primary
Slosson Intelligence Test-Revised (SIT-R3)
Slosson Oral Reading Test-Revised 3
Slosson Phonics and Structural Analysis Test
Slosson Visual-Motor Performance Test
Slosson Visual Perceptual Skill Screener
Slosson Written Expression Test
Social Competency Rating Form
The Social Support Scale for Children
Socially Appropriate and Inappropriate Development
SON—R2 1/2-7 and SON-R 5 1/2-17
Space Thinking (Flags) [Revised]
Spanish Articulation Measures
Spanish Language Assessment Procedures [Revised 1995
    Edition]

The Spanish Speaking Test
The Spanish Structured Photographic Expressive Lan-
    guage Test—II
Spanish Test for Assessing Morphologic Production
Special Abilities Scales
Specialty Practice Tests: End-of-Course Exams
Spectrum CPI 260 Instrument
SPELL: Spelling Performance Evaluation for Lan-
    guage and Literacy
Sr. Maint. Tech. Pipefitter
Staff Burnout Scale for Police and Security Personnel
The Staffordshire Mathematics Test
Stages of Concern Questionnaire
Stanford Spanish Language Proficiency Test
Station Employee Applicant Inventory
Station Manager Applicant Inventory
Step One Survey
Stephen's Oral Language Screening Test
Stones: Concepts About Print Test
Story Recall Test
Strategic Leadership Type Indicator [including 360-
    Degree Feedback Profile]
Strong Interest and Skills Confidence Inventory
Stroop Color and Word Test [Revised]
Structured Interview for Disorders of Extreme Stress &
    Traumatic Antecedents Questionnaire-Self Report
Student Aspiration Inventory
Student Instructional Report II
Student Opinion Inventory, Revised Edition [1995 Edi-
    tion]
Subordinate Behavior Rating
Super's Work Values Inventory-Revised
SuperSelect
Supervise Ability Scale
Supervisor's Role Rating
Supervisory Aptitude Test
Supervisory Proficiency Tests
Supervisory Simulator
Supervisory Skills Test
The Supplementary Shorr Imagery Test
Survey of Interpersonal Values [Revised]
Survey of Personal Values [Revised]
The Survey of Quality Values in Practice
System for Testing and Evaluation of Potential
System of Interactive Guidance Information, Plus
Systematic Assessment of Voice

Tangent Screen
TapDance
Teacher Opinion Inventory, Revised Edition [1995
    Edition]
Team Assessment System
Team Climate Inventory
Team Culture Analysis
Team Effectiveness Inventory
Team Empowerment Practices Test
Team Leader Competencies

Team Leader Skills Assessment
Team Management Index
Team Management Profile
Team Member Behavior Analysis
Team Performance Index
Team Performance Profile
Team Performance Questionnaire
Team Skills
Team Skills Indicator
Team Success Profile
Teambuilding Effectiveness
Team-Building Effectiveness Profile
Team-Review Survey
Technology and Internet Assessment
Telemarketing Applicant Inventory
Temperament Comparator
Temperament Comparator [Revised]
Temporal Orientation
Test Alert (Test Preparation)
Test Observation Form
Test of Academic Achievement Skills-Revised
Test of Adult Literacy Skills
Test of Auditory Processes
Test of Auditory Reasoning and Processing Skills
Test of Auditory-Perceptual Skills, Revised
Test of Auditory-Perceptual Skills, Upper Level
The Test of Everyday Reasoning
Test of General Intellectual Skills
Test of Grammatical and Syntactical Skills
Test of Handwriting Skills
Test of Inductive Reasoning Principles
Test of Mechanical Concepts [Revised]
Test of Oral Reading and Comprehension Skills
Test of Pictures/Forms/Letters/Numbers Spatial Orientation and Sequencing Skills
Test of Problem Solving-Adolescent
Test of Problem Solving-Revised-Elementary
Test of Relational Concepts [Norms for Deaf Children]
Test of Semantic Skills-Intermediate
Test of Semantic Skills-Primary
Test of Silent Reading Skills
Test of Visual-Motor Skills (Upper Level) Adolescents and Adults
Test of Visual-Motor Skills, Revised
Test of Visual-Perceptual Skills (Non-Motor) Upper Level: Revised
Test of Visual-Perceptual Skills (Non-Motor): Revised
Test of Visual-Perceptual Skills, Upper Level
Tests of Adult Basic Education, Forms 9 & 10
Tests of General Educational Development [The GED Tests]
The Texas Oral Proficiency Test
Theological School Inventory
Thinking Creatively with Sounds and Words
360 Degree Assessment and Development
360° Feedback Assessment

Thurstone Temperament Schedule [Revised]
Thurstone Test of Mental Alertness [Revised]
Time Management Effectiveness Profile
Time Management Inventory
Titmus Stereo Fly Test
Tobacco Use Survey
Tool Knowledge & Use
Torrance Tests of Creative Thinking [with 1998 norms]
Total Quality Management Survey
TotalView
TotalView Assessment System
Training Needs Assessment for Modern Leadership Skills
Training Needs Assessment Test
Training Proficiency Scale
Truck Driver Inventory
Trustworthiness Attitude Survey
The Two Cultures Test
Types of Work Index
Types of Work Profile

Undergraduate Assessment Program: Business Test
Understanding Communication [Revised]
Urban District Assessment Consortium's Alternative Accountability Assessments

Values and Motives Questionnaire
Visual Form Discrimination
Verbal Form [Revised]
The Vocabulary Gradient Test
Vocational Interest, Experience and Skill Assessment (VIESA), 2nd Canadian Edition

Warehouse & Shipping Reading
Welder, Repair & Maint.
What About You?
Window on Work Values Profile
Winterhaven Visual Copy Forms and Visual Retention Test
Wonderlic Employee Opinion Survey
Word Processing Aptitude Battery
The WORD Test-Adolescent
The WORD Test-R (Elementary)
The Word Test-R and The Word Test-Adolescent
Words List
Work Mate
Work Preference Questionnaire
Work-Readiness Cognitive Screen
Work Skills Series Manual Dexterity
Work Team Simulator
Working Together: An Assessment of Collaboration
Workplace Ergonomics Profile
Workplace Skills Survey
Workplace Skills Survey-Form E
Wright & Ayre Stuttering Self-Rating Profile

Y-OQ-SR 2.0

DISTINGUISHED REVIEWERS

Based on the recommendation of our National Advisory Committee, the Buros Institute of Mental Measurements is now making special recognition of the long-term contributions made by the individuals listed below to the success of the Mental Measurements Yearbook series. To receive the "Distinguished Reviewer" designation, an individual must have contributed to six or more editions of this series beginning with The Ninth Mental Measurements Yearbook. *By virtue of their long-term service, these individuals exemplify an outstanding dedication in their professional lives to the principles of improving the science and practice of testing.*

Phillip A. Ackerman
Mark A. Albanese
Jeffrey A. Atlas
Stephen N. Axford
Patricia A. Bachelor
Ronald A. Berk
Brian F. Bolton
Gregory J. Boyle
Michael B. Bunch
Linda K. Bunker
JoEllen V. Carlson
C. Dale Carpenter
Joseph C. Ciechalski
Gregory J. Cizek
Kevin D. Crehan
Gerald E. DeMauro
Beth Doll
George Engelhard, Jr.
Deborah B. Erickson
Robert Fitzpatrick
John W. Fleenor
J. Jeffrey Grill
Richard E. Harding
Patti L. Harrison
Michael R. Harwell
Allen K. Hess
Jeffrey A. Jenkins
Samuel Juni
Randy W. Kamphaus
Michael G. Kavan
Timothy Z. Keith
Mary Lou Kelley
Jean Powell Kirnan
Howard M. Knoff
Joseph G. Law, Jr.
Frederick T. L. Leong

S. Alvin Leung
Rick Lindskog
Cleborne D. Maddux
Rebecca J. McCauley
William B. Michael
Kevin L. Moreland
Anthony J. Nitko
Janet A. Norris
Judy Oehler-Stinnett
D. Joe Olmi
Steven I. Pfeiffer
G. Michael Poteat
Nambury S. Raju
Paul Retzlaff
Bruce G. Rogers
Michael J. Roszkowski
Darrell L. Sabers
Jonathon Sandoval
Eleanor E. Sanford
William I. Sauser, Jr.
Diane J. Sawyer
Gene Schwarting
Jeffrey K. Smith
Jayne E. Stake
Stephanie Stein
Terry A. Stinnett
Richard B. Stuart
Hoi K. Suen
Mark E. Swerdlik
Michael S. Trevisan
Wilfred G. Van Gorp
T. Steuart Watson
William K. Wilkinson
Claudia R. Wright
James E. Ysseldyke
Sheldon Zedeck

CONTRIBUTING TEST REVIEWERS

SHAWN K. ACHESON, Associate Professor of Neuropsychology, Western Carolina University, Cullowhee, NC

PHILLIP L. ACKERMAN, Professor of Psychology, Georgia Institute of Technology, Atlanta, GA

EUGENE V. AIDMAN, Senior Lecturer, University of Adelaide, Adelaide, Australia

MARK A. ALBANESE, Professor of Population Health Sciences, University of Wisconsin, Madison, WI

KATHLEEN ALLEN, Assistant Professor of Reading Education, St. Martin's College, Lacey, WA

JOHN O. ANDERSON, Professor and Chair, Department of Educational Psychology, University of Victoria, Victoria, British Columbia, Canada

PAUL A. ARBISI, Staff Clinical Psychologist, Minneapolis VA Medical Center, and Associate Professor, Department of Psychiatry, University of Minnesota, Minneapolis, MN

MICHELLE ATHANASIOU, Associate Professor of School Psychology, University of Northern Colorado, Greeley, CO

JAMES A. ATHANASOU, Faculty of Education, University of Technology, Sydney, Australia

JEFFREY A. ATLAS, Clinical Psychologist, St. Christopher-Ottilie Services for Children and Families, Queens, NY

JAMES T. AUSTIN, Research Specialist 2, Center on Education and Training for Employment, College of Education, The Ohio State University, Columbus, OH

STEPHEN N. AXFORD, Assistant Director of Special Services and Licensed Psychologist, Falcon School District 49, Colorado Springs, CO

GLEN P. AYLWARD, Professor of Pediatrics and Psychiatry, Southern Illinois University School of Medicine, Springfield, IL

KRIS L. BAACK, Assistant Professor of Speech Pathology, University of Nebraska—Lincoln, Lincoln, NE

PATRICIA A. BACHELOR, Professor of Psychology, California State University—Long Beach, Long Beach, CA

SHERRY K. BAIN, Associate Professor, Department of Educational Psychology & Counseling, University of Tennessee, Knoxville, TN

JOAN C. BALLARD, Clinical Neuropsychologist, Associate Professor of Psychology, State University of New York College at Geneseo, Geneseo, NY

DEBORAH L. BANDALOS, Professor of Educational Psychology, University of Georgia, Athens, GA

LAURA L. B. BARNES, Associate Professor of Educational Research and Evaluation, Oklahoma State University, Tulsa, OK

ABIGAIL BAXTER, Associate Professor, Department of Special Education, University of South Alabama, Mobile, AL

MICHAEL D. BECK, President, BETA, Inc., Pleasantville, NY

C. G. BELLAH, Director of Services, Parker College, Dallas, TX

PHILIP G. BENSON, Associate Professor of Management, New Mexico State University, Las Cruces, NM

MARSHA BENSOUSSAN, Chair, Department of Foreign Languages, University of Haifa, Haifa, Israel

SHERYL BENTON, Assistant Director of Counseling Services, Kansas State University, Manhattan, KS

STEPHEN L. BENTON, Professor of Educational Psychology, Kansas State University, Manhattan, KS

ABBEY L. BERG, Assistant Professor, Department of Communication Studies, Pace University, New York, NY and Assistant Professor of Clinical Audiology and Speech Pathology in Otolaryngology/Head and Neck Surgery, Columbia University College of Physicians and Surgeons, New York, NY

JENNIFER M. BERGERON, Graduate Student, University of Florida, Gainesville, FL

RONALD A. BERK, Professor of Biostatistics and Measurement, School of Nursing, The Johns Hopkins University, Baltimore, MD

FRANK M. BERNT, Associate Professor, Health Services Department, Saint Joseph's University, Philadelphia, PA

KIMBERLY A. BLAIR, Assistant Professor of School Psychology, Duquesne University, Pittsburgh, PA

CYNTHIA R. BOCHNA, Doctoral Candidate in Educational Psychology, The Pennsylvania State University, University Park, PA

KATHY J. BOHAN, Assistant Professor of Educational Psychology, Northern Arizona University, Flagstaff, AZ

MIKE BONNER, Assistant Professor, Department of Psychology, University of Nebraska at Omaha, Omaha, NE

SARAH BONNER, Doctoral Student, University of Arizona, Tucson, AZ

ROGER A. BOOTHROYD, Associate Professor, Department of Mental Health Law and Policy, Louis de la Parte Florida Mental Health Institute, University of South Florida, Tampa, FL

B. ANN BOYCE, Associate Professor, Curry School of Education, University of Virginia, Charlottesville, VA

GREGORY J. BOYLE, Professor of Psychology, Bond University, Gold Coast, Queensland, Australia

BRUCE A. BRACKEN, Professor, School of Education, The College of William & Mary, Williamsburg, VA

JEFFERY P. BRADEN, Professor of Psychology, North Carolina State University, Raleigh, NC

JOHN J. BRINKMAN, JR., Associate Director, Neuropsychology Laboratory, Ball State University, Muncie, IN

SUSAN M. BROOKHART, Coordinator of Assessment & Evaluation, School of Education, Duquesne University, Pittsburgh, PA

JAMES D. BROWN, Professor of Second Language Studies, University of Hawaii at Manoa, Honolulu, HI

MICHAEL B. BROWN, Associate Professor of Psychology, East Carolina University, Greenville, NC

RIC BROWN, Vice President for Academic Affairs, California State University—Sacramento, Sacramento, CA

BETHANY A. BRUNSMAN, Assessment Specialist, Lincoln Public Schools, Lincoln, NE

ALBERT M. BUGAJ, Professor, Department of Psychology, University of Wisconsin—Marinette, Marinette, WI

ALAN C. BUGBEE, JR., Assistant Dean of Assessment/Associate Professor, School of Education, North Carolina Agricultural and Technical State University, Greensboro, NC

MICHAEL B. BUNCH, Vice President, Measurement Incorporated, Durham, NC

LINDA K. BUNKER, Professor, Department of Human Services, University of Virginia, Charlottesville, VA

MATTHEW K. BURNS, Associate Professor of Educational Psychology, University of Minnesota, Minneapolis, MN

MICHELLE A. BUTLER, Associate Professor, Department of Behavioral Sciences and Leadership, United States Air Force Academy, USAF Academy, CO

CAROLYN M. CALLAHAN, Professor of Educational Psychology, University of Virginia, Charlottesville, VA

WAYNE J. CAMARA, Vice President of Research and Psychometrics, The College Board, New York, NY

MICHAEL H. CAMPBELL, Director of Residential Life and Food Service, New College of Florida, Sarasota, FL

GARY L. CANIVEZ, Professor of Psychology, Eastern Illinois University, Charleston, IL

KAREN T. CAREY, Professor of Psychology, California State University—Fresno, Fresno, CA

JANET F. CARLSON, Professor and Department Head, Department of General Academics, Texas A&M University at Galveston, Galveston, TX

JoELLEN V. CARLSON, Carlson Consulting, Indian Rocks Beach, FL

RUSSELL N. CARNEY, Professor of Psychology, Southwest Missouri State University, Springfield, MO

C. DALE CARPENTER, Professor of Special Education and Associate Dean, College of Education and Allied Professions, Western Carolina University, Cullowhee, NC

LINDA CASTILLO, Assistant Professor of Educational Psychology, Texas A&M University, College Station, TX

TONY CELLUCCI, Professor and Director of the Psychology Training Clinic, Idaho State University, Pocatello, ID

MARY "RINA" M. CHITTOORAN, Associate Professor of Educational Studies, Saint Louis University, St. Louis, MO

JOSEPH C. CIECHALSKI, Professor, East Carolina University, Greenville, NC

GREGORY J. CIZEK, Professor of Educational Measurement and Evaluation, University of North Carolina—Chapel Hill, Chapel Hill, NC

MARY M. CLARE, Professor, Graduate School of Education and Counseling, Lewis & Clark College, Portland, OR

ANNABEL J. COHEN, Professor, Department of Psychology, University of Prince Edward Island, Charlottetown, Prince Edward Island, Canada

D. ASHLEY COHEN, Forensic Neuropsychologist, CogniMetrix, San Jose, CA

THEODORE COLADARCI, Professor of Educational Psychology, University of Maine, Orono, ME

COLLIE W. CONOLEY, Professor of Educational Psychology, Texas A&M University, College Station, TX

CATHERINE P. COOK-COTTONE, Assistant Professor of School Psychology, State University of New York at Buffalo, Buffalo, NY

COLIN COOPER, Senior Lecturer, School of Psychology, The Queen's University, Belfast, United Kingdom

ALICE J. CORKILL, Associate Professor, Department of Counseling and Educational Psychology, University of Nevada—Las Vegas, Las Vegas, NV

ANDREW A. COX, Professor, Department of Counseling and Psychology, Troy State University, Phenix City, AL

KEVIN D. CREHAN, Professor of Educational Psychology, University of Nevada—Las Vegas, Las Vegas, NV

RIK CARL D'AMATO, Assistant Dean and Director of the Center for Collaborative Research in Education, College of Education and Behavioral Sciences, M. Lucile Harrison Professor of Excellence, School of Professional Psychology, University of Northern Colorado, Greeley, CO

ANDREW S. DAVIS, Assistant Professor of Psychology, Ball State University, Muncie, IN

RAYMOND S. DEAN, George and Frances Ball Distinguished Professor of Neuropsychology, Neuropsychology Laboratory, Ball State University, Muncie, IN

GEORGE J. DEMAKIS, Associate Professor, University of North Carolina at Charlotte, Charlotte, NC

GERALD E. DeMAURO, Managing Education Assessment Scientist, American Institutes for Research, Washington, DC

GYPSY M. DENZINE, Associate Professor of Educational Psychology, Northern Arizona University, Flagstaff, AZ

PHIL DIAZ, Assistant Professor of Psychology, Central Washington University, Ellensburg, WA

STEPHEN DILCHERT, Doctoral Student, Department of Psychology, University of Minnesota, Minneapolis, MN

JAMES C. DiPERNA, Assistant Professor, School Psychology Program, Pennsylvania State University, University Park, PA

R. ANTHONY DOGGETT, Assistant Professor of Educational Psychology, Mississippi State University, Starkville, MS

BETH J. DOLL, Professor of Educational Psychology, University of Nebraska—Lincoln, Lincoln, NE

DENNIS DOVERSPIKE, Professor of Psychology, University of Akron, Akron, OH

THOMAS M. DUNN, Assistant Professor of Psychology, University of Northern Colorado, Greeley, CO

KELLY EDER, Doctoral Student, Counseling Psychology, Indiana University, Bloomington, IN

CHER I. EDWARDS, Assistant Professor, School Counseling and Psychology, Seattle Pacific University, Seattle, WA

RICK EIGENBROOD, Associate Professor, Education and Director of Doctoral Studies, Seattle Pacific University, Seattle, WA

ARTHUR S. ELLEN, Senior Psychometrician, National League of Nursing, New York, NY

GEORGE ENGELHARD, JR., Professor of Educational Measurement and Policy, Emory University, Atlanta, GA

CONNIE T. ENGLAND, Department Chair, Grad Counseling & Guidance, Lincoln Memorial University, Knoxville, TN

DOREEN W. FAIRBANK, Associate Professor of Psychology, Meredith College, Raleigh, NC

RICHARD F. FARMER, Senior Lecturer in Psychology, University of Canterbury, Christchurch, New Zealand

ERICH C. FEIN, Senior Program Associate, Center on Education and Training for Employment, College of Education, The Ohio State University, Columbus, OH

RAY FENTON, President, FentonResearch, Tucson, AZ

TRENTON R. FERRO, Professor of Adult and Community Education, Indiana University of Pennsylvania, Indiana, PA

W. HOLMES FINCH, Assistant Professor of Educational Psychology, Ball State University, Muncie, IN

CORINE FITZPATRICK, Director of the Master's Program in Counseling, Manhattan College, Riverdale, NY

ROBERT FITZPATRICK, Consulting Psychologist, Cranberry Township, PA

ROSEMARY FLANAGAN, Assistant Professor/Director, Masters Program in School Psychology, Adelphi University, Garden City, NY

JOHN W. FLEENOR, Director of Knowledge Management, Center for Creative Leadership, Greensboro, NC

TERRI FLOWERDAY, Assistant Professor of Educational Psychology, University of New Mexico, Albuquerque, NM

STEPHEN J. FREEMAN, Professor and Chair, Department of Counseling, Texas A&M University—Commerce, Commerce, TX

BRIAN F. FRENCH, Assistant Professor of Educational Psychology, Purdue University, West Lafayette, IN

MICHAEL J. FURLONG, Professor of Counseling/Clinical/School Psychology, University of California—Santa Barbara, Santa Barbara, CA

RONALD J. GANELLEN, Associate Professor, Department of Psychiatry and Behavioral Sciences, Northwestern Medical School, Chicago, IL

ALAN GARFINKEL, Professor of Spanish and Education, Purdue University, West Lafayette, IN

MARY L. GARNER, Associate Professor of Mathematics, Kennesaw State University, Kennesaw, GA

ADRIENNE GARRO, Assistant Professor of Psychology, Kean University, Union, NJ

JACK E. GEBART-EAGLEMONT, President, International Institute for Personality Assessment and Therapy, Watsonia, Victoria, Australia

KURT F. GEISINGER, Vice President of Academic Affairs, Professor of Psychology, The University of St. Thomas, Houston, TX

JOHN S. GEISLER, Professor of Counselor Education and Counseling Psychology, Western Michigan University, Kalamazoo, MI

JEREMY GENOVESE, Assistant Professor, Department of Curriculum and Foundations, Cleveland State University, Cleveland, OH

MARK J. GIERL, Associate Professor of Educational Psychology, University of Alberta, Edmonton, Alberta, Canada

THERESA GRAHAM, Adjunct Faculty, Educational Psychology, University of Nebraska—Lincoln, Lincoln, NE

ZANDRA S. GRATZ, Professor of Psychology, Kean University, Union, NJ

KATHY E. GREEN, Professor of Quantitative Research Methods, University of Denver, Denver, CO

SUSAN K. GREEN, Associate Professor of Education, Winthrop University, Rock Hill, SC

PATRICK GREHAN, Assistant Professor, Derner Institute for Advanced Psychological Studies, Adelphi University, Garden City, NY

MANUELLA H. HABICHT, Director of Psychology, Queensland Health, Toowoomba Health Service District, Senior Lecturer, University of Queensland, Medical School, Rural Clinical Division, Honorary Senior Lecturer, University of Southern Queensland, Department of Psychology, Queensland, Australia

ATIQA HACHIMI, Lecturer & Coordinator of Arabic, University of Hawaii at Manoa, Honolulu, HI

RONALD K. HAMBLETON, Distinguished University Professor, School of Education, University of Massachusetts at Amherst, Amherst, MA

THOMAS EMERSON HANCOCK, Associate Professor of Educational Psychology, George Fox University, Newberg, OR

KARL R. HANES, Director, Cognitive-Behavioural Treatment Centre, Victoria, Australia, and Editor, Vangard Publishing, Victoria, Australia

GREGORY HANSON, Ph.D. Candidate, Department of Human Services, University of Virginia, Charlottesville, VA

WILLIAM E. HANSON, Assistant Professor, Department of Educational Psychology, University of Nebraska—Lincoln, Lincoln, NE

RICHARD E. HARDING, Director of Research, Kenexa Technology, Lincoln, NE

MICHAEL R. HARWELL, Professor, Department of Educational Psychology, University of Minnesota—Twin Cities, Minneapolis, MN

JASON HASSENSTAB, Doctoral Candidate in Clinical Psychology, Fordham University, Department of Psychology, New York, NY

JOHN HATTIE, Professor of Education, University of Auckland, Auckland, NZ

JAMES HAWKINS, Doctoral Student in School Psychology, University of Tennessee, Knoxville, TN

THEODORE L. HAYES, Research Director, the Gallup Organization, Washington, DC

SANDRA D. HAYNES, Interim Dean, School of Professional Studies, Metropolitan State College of Denver, Denver, CO

MARTHA E. HENNEN, Manager, Employment Programs, United States Postal Service, Washington DC

JAMES J. HENNESSY, Professor (Educational Psychology), Graduate School of Education, Fordham University, New York, NY

ALLEN K. HESS, Distinguished Research Professor of Psychology, Auburn University at Montgomery, Montgomery, AL

ROBERT W. HILTONSMITH, Professor of Psychology, Radford University, Radford, VA

JAMES M. HODGSON, Professor, Tennessee Center for the Study and Treatment of Dyslexia, Middle Tennessee State University, Murfreesboro, TN

KATHRYN E. HOFF, Assistant Professor of Psychology, Illinois State University, Normal, IL

THOMAS P. HOGAN, Professor of Psychology, University of Scranton, Scranton, PA

ANITA M. HUBLEY, Associate Professor of Measurement, Evaluation, and Research Methodology, University of British Columbia, Vancouver, British Columbia, Canada

DAVID P. HURFORD, Director of the Center for the Assessment and Remediation of Reading Difficulties and Professor of Psychology and Counseling, Pittsburg State University, Pittsburg, KS

CARLOS INCHAURRALDE, Professor of Linguistics and Psychologist, University of Zaragoza, Zaragoza, Spain

CARL ISENHART, Coordinator, Addictive Disorders Section, VA Medical Center, Minneapolis, MN

JEFFREY A. JENKINS, Assistant Professor, Roger Williams University, Bristol, RI

JILL ANN JENKINS, Consultant Child & School Psychologist, Barcelona, Spain

KAREN E. JENNINGS, LaMora Psychological Associates, Nashua, NH

CHRISTOPHER M. JOHNSON, Professor of Music Education and Music Therapy, University of Kansas, Lawrence, KS

JERRY JOHNSON, Professor of Mathematics, Western Washington University, Bellingham, WA

JUDY A. JOHNSON, Assistant Professor of Psychology in the School Psychology Program at the University of Houston—Victoria, Victoria, Texas

KATHLEEN M. JOHNSON, Psychologist, Lincoln Public Schools, Lincoln, NE

ROBERT L. JOHNSON, Associate Professor, Educational Psychology, University of South Carolina, Columbia, SC

STEPHEN B. JOHNSON, Managing Partner, RPM Data, Greensboro, NC

LYNAE A. JOHNSEN, Graduate Student, University of Nebraska—Lincoln, Lincoln, NE

JUDITH R. JOHNSTON, Professor, School of Audiology and Speech Sciences, The University of British Columbia, Vancouver, British Columbia, Canada

ASHRAF KAGEE, Professor of Psychology, University of Stellenbosch, Maitland, South Africa

HARRISON D. KANE, Assistant Professor, Western Carolina University, Cullowhee, NC

DOUGLAS F. KAUFFMAN, Assistant Professor of Education, Eastern Connecticut State University, Willimantic, CT

MICHAEL G. KAVAN, Associate Dean for Student Affairs and Associate Professor of Family Medicine, Creighton University School of Medicine, Omaha, NE

TIMOTHY Z. KEITH, Professor of Educational Psychology, The University of Texas—Austin, Austin, TX

HAROLD R. KELLER, Professor and Chair, Department of Psychological and Social Foundations, University of South Florida, Tampa, FL

KARL N. KELLEY, Professor of Psychology, North Central College, Naperville, IL

MARY LOU KELLEY, Professor of Psychology, Louisiana State University, Baton Rouge, LA

KEVIN R. KELLY, Head, Department of Educational Studies, Purdue University, West Lafayette, IN

JOHN D. KING, Professor Emeritus, University of Texas at Austin, Licensed Psychologist, National Health Service Provider, Licensed Specialist in School Psychology, Austin, TX

JEAN POWELL KIRNAN, Professor of Psychology, The College of New Jersey, Ewing, NJ

S. KATHLEEN KRACH, School Psychologist, Henry County Schools, McDonough, GA

RADHIKA KRISHNAMURTHY, Associate Professor of Psychology and Director of Clinical Training, Florida Institute of Technology, Melbourne, FL

SALLY KUHLENSCHMIDT, Professor of Psychology, Western Kentucky University, Bowling Green, KY

JODY L. KULSTAD, Assistant Professor of Professional Psychology and Family Therapy, Seton Hall University, South Orange, NJ

ANTONY JOHN KUNNAN, Professor, TESOL Program, Charter College of Education, California State University—Los Angeles, Los Angeles, CA

JOSEPH C. KUSH, Associate Professor, Duquesne University, Pittsburgh, PA

MATTHEW E. LAMBERT, Assistant Clinical Professor of Neuropsychiatry, Texas Tech University Health Sciences Center, Lubbock, TX

SUZANNE LANE, Professor of Educational Measurement and Statistics, University of Pittsburgh, Pittsburgh, PA

AIMÉE LANGLOIS, Professor, Department of Child Development, Humboldt State University, Arcata, CA

KELLY LAUGLE, Graduate Student in Psychology, North Carolina State University, Raleigh, NC

JOSEPH G. LAW, JR., Professor of Behavioral Studies, University of South Alabama, Mobile, AL

ROBERT A. LEARK, Associate Professor, Forensic Psychology Program, Alliant International University, Alhambra, CA

YOUNG JU LEE, Doctoral Student in School Psychology, University of Tennessee, Knoxville, TN

FREDERICK T. L. LEONG, Professor of Psychology, University of Tennessee, Knoxville, TN

S. ALVIN LEUNG, Professor, Department of Educational Psychology, The Chinese University of Hong Kong, Hong Kong, China

RALPH G. LEVERETT, Professor, Department of Education, Union University, Jackson, TN

PAM LINDSEY, Associate Professor, Curriculum and Instruction, Tarleton State University, Stephenville, TX

CEDERICK O. LINDSKOG, Professor, Pittsburg State University, Pittsburg, KS

SANDRA A. LOEW, Associate Professor of Counselor Education, University of North Alabama, Florence, AL

STEVEN LONG, Assistant Professor, Speech Pathology and Audiology, Marquette University, Milwaukee, WI

ALFRED P. LONGO, Instructor in Education, Social Science Department, Ocean County College, Toms River, NJ

KELLY BREY LOVE, Doctoral Student, University of Nebraska–Lincoln, Lincoln, NE

LESLIE EASTMAN LUKIN, Director of Assessment and Evaluation Services, ESU 18/Lincoln Public Schools, Lincoln, NE

KAREN MACKLER, School Psychologist, Lawrence Public Schools, Lawrence, KS

CLEBORNE D. MADDUX, Foundation Professor of Counseling and Educational Psychology, University of Nevada—Reno, Reno, NV

RONALD A. MADLE, School Psychologist, Shikellamy School District, Sunbury, PA, and Adjunct Associate Professor of School Psychology, The Pennsylvania State University, University Park, PA

JENNIFER N. MAHDAVI, Assistant Professor of Special Education, California State University, Los Angeles, CA

TIMOTHY J. MAKATURA, Adjunct Professor of Psychology, Capella University, Minneapolis, MN

KORESSA KUTSICK MALCOLM, School Psychologist, Augusta County Public Schools, Fishersville, VA, and Adjunct Faculty Member, Mary Baldwin College, Staunton, VA

SUSAN J. MALLER, Associate Professor, Purdue University, West Lafayette, IN

CAROLINE MANUELE-ADKINS, Vice-President, Institute for Life Coping Skills Inc., Stamford, CT

HOWARD MARGOLIS, Professor, Department of Educational and Community Programs, Queens College of CUNY, Flushing, NY

WILLIAM E. MARTIN, JR., Professor of Educational Psychology, Northern Arizona University, Flagstaff, AZ

MANUEL MARTINEZ-PONS, Professor of Education, Brooklyn College of the City University of New York, Belle Harbor, NY

DAWN MAZZIE, Teacher, Richland One Public Schools, Columbia, SC

PATRICK P. McCABE, Associate Professor, Graduate Literacy Program, St. John's University, Queens, NY

REBECCA McCAULEY, Professor, Communication Sciences, University of Vermont, Burlington, VT

DANIEL L. McCOLLUM, ABD Educational Psychology, The Pennsylvania State University, University Park, PA

MERILEE McCURDY, Assistant Professor of Educational Psychology, University of Nebraska—Lincoln, Lincoln, NE

DIXIE McGINTY, Associate Professor of Educational Research, Western Carolina University, Cullowhee, NC

CAROL M. McGREGOR, Associate Professor of Education, Brenau University, Gainesville, GA

THOMAS McKNIGHT, Psychologist, Private Practice, Spokane, WA

MARIA DEL R. MEDINA-DIAZ, Professor, Department of Graduate Studies, Program of Educational Research & Evaluation, School of Education, University of Puerto Rico—Rio Piedras, San Juan, PR

FREDERIC J. MEDWAY, Professor of Psychology, University of South Carolina, Columbia, SC

SCOTT T. MEIER, Professor, Department of Counseling, School, and Educational Psychology, The University at Buffalo, Buffalo, NY

JOYCE MEIKAMP, Professor of Special Education, Marshall University, South Charleston, WV

BRAD M. MERKER, Clinical Neuropsychology Pre-Doctoral Intern, University of Miami Medical School, Miami, FL

WILLIAM B. MICHAEL, Professor Emeritus, University of Southern California, Los Angeles, CA

COURTNEY MILLER, Lecturer, Educational Psychology, University of Nebraska—Lincoln, Lincoln, NE

DANIEL C. MILLER, Professor of Psychology, Texas Woman's University, Denton, TX

J. MONROE MILLER, Graduate Student, Educational Psychology, University of Florida, Gainesville, FL

M. DAVID MILLER, Professor of Educational Psychology, University of Florida, Gainesville, FL

MARIE MILLER-WHITEHEAD, Department of Education, University of North Alabama, Florence, AL

JUDITH A. MONSAAS, Executive Director of P-16 Assessment and Evaluation, University System of Georgia, Atlanta, GA

ALAN D. MOORE, Associate Professor of Educational Leadership, University of Wyoming, Laramie, WY

HEIDI K. MOORE, Research Scientist, Healthcare Technology Systems, Inc., Madison, WI

DAVID T. MORSE, Professor, Counseling, Educational Psychology and Special Education, Mississippi State University, Mississippi State, MS

PAUL M. MUCHINSKY, Joseph M. Bryan Distinguished Professor of Business, University of North Carolina at Greensboro, Greensboro, NC

MILDRED MURRAY-WARD, Professor, Department of Advanced Studies, California Lutheran University, Thousand Oaks, CA

SCOTT A. NAPOLITANO, Assistant Professor, Lincoln Pediatric Group, Lincoln, NE

LEAH M. NELLIS, School Psychologist, RISE Special Services, Indianapolis, IN

THOMAS R. O'NEILL, Psychometrician, National Council of State Boards of Nursing, Chicago, IL

SALVADOR HECTOR OCHOA, Associate Professor, Department of Educational Psychology, Texas A&M University, College Station, TX

JUDY OEHLER-STINNETT, Associate Professor, School of Applied Health and Educational Psychology, Oklahoma State University, Stillwater, OK

ARTURO OLIVAREZ, JR., Associate Professor of Educational Psychology, Texas Tech University, Lubbock, TX

D. JOE OLMI, Associate Professor and Clinic Director, School Psychology Program, Department of Psychology, The University of Southern Mississippi, Hattiesburg, MS

DENIZ S. ONES, Hellervik Professor of Industrial Psychology, University of Minnesota, Minneapolis, MN

DONALD P. OSWALD, Associate Professor of Psychiatry and Psychology, Virginia Commonwealth University, Richmond, VA

SANDYE M. OUZTS, Graduate Student in Psychology, North Carolina State University, Raleigh, NC

GRETCHEN OWENS, Professor of Child Study, St. Joseph's College, Patchogue, NY

NATHANIEL J. PALLONE, University Distinguished Professor (Psychology), Center of Alcohol Studies, Rutgers—The State University, New Brunswick, NJ

CAROL S. PARKE, Assistant Professor, School of Education, Duquesne University, Pittsburgh, PA

CHARLES K. PARSONS, Professor of Management, Georgia Institute of Technology, Atlanta, GA

THANOS PATELIS, Director of Secondary School Research and Computer-Based Testing, The College Board, New York, NY

JOSHUA W. PAYNE, Doctoral Student, Department of Psychology, University of North Texas, Denton, TX

CAROLYN MITCHELL PERSON, Nationally Certified and Licensed Speech Pathologist, Associate Professor, Special Education Department, and Director, Research Roundtable (Title III) and Southern University Online at Southern University and A&M College, Baton Rouge, LA

STEVEN I. PFEIFFER, Professor, Psychological Services in Education Program, Florida State University, Tallahassee, FL

JENNIFER PICCOLO, Doctoral Student of School Psychology, State University of New York at Buffalo, Buffalo, NY

DAVID J. PITTENGER, Associate Provost, Academic Administration, The University of Tennessee at Chattanooga, Chattanooga, TN

MARK L. POPE, Associate Professor, Division of Counseling and Family Therapy, University of Missouri—St. Louis, St. Louis, MO

JULIA Y. PORTER, Assistant Professor of Counseling, Mississippi State University, Meridian, MS

G. MICHAEL POTEAT, Director of Institutional Effectiveness, East Carolina University, Greenville, NC

SHAWN POWELL, Associate Professor, United States Air Force Academy, USAF Academy, CO

SHEILA PRATT, Associate Professor, Communication Science and Disorders Department, University of Pittsburgh, Pittsburgh, PA

NAMBURY S. RAJU, Distinguished Professor, Institute of Psychology, Illinois Institute of Technology, Chicago, IL

PAMILLA RAMSDEN, Senior Lecturer, Bolton Institute, Bolton, Lancashire, England

NATALIE RATHVON, Project Director, Early Reading Initiative, Center City Consortium Schools, Washington, DC

AMY M. REES, Assistant Professor of Counseling Psychology, Lewis & Clark College, Portland, OR

SEAN P. REILLEY, Assistant Professor of Psychology, Morehead State University, Morehead, KY

JUDITH A. REIN, Adjunct Assistant Professor, Department of Educational Psychology, University of Arizona, Tucson, AZ

PAUL RETZLAFF, Professor of Psychology, University of Northern Colorado, Greeley, CO

ELIZABETH KELLEY RHOADES, Associate Professor of Psychology, West Texas A&M University, Canyon, TX

BRUCE G. ROGERS, Professor Emeritus of Education, University of Northern Iowa, Cedar Falls, IA

CYNTHIA A. ROHRBECK, Associate Professor of Psychology, The George Washington University, Washington, DC

DARRELL L. SABERS, Professor and Head of Educational Psychology, University of Arizona, Tucson, AZ

VINCENT J. SAMAR, Associate Professor, Department of Research, National Technical Institute for the Deaf, Rochester Institute of Technology, Rochester, NY

ELEANOR E. SANFORD, Vice-President of Research and Development, MetaMetrics, Inc., Durham, NC

TIMOTHY SARES, Director of Testing and Psychometrics, American Registry of Diagnostic Medical Sonography (ARDMS), Rockville, MD

WILLIAM I. SAUSER, JR., Associate Dean and Professor, Business and Engineering Outreach, Auburn University, Auburn, AL

WILLIAM D. SCHAFER, Affiliated Professor (Emeritus) of Measurement, Statistics, and Evaluation, University of Maryland, College Park, MD

FRANK SCHMIDT, Professor, Tippie College of Business, University of Iowa, Iowa City, IA

W. JOEL SCHNEIDER, Assistant Professor of Psychology, Illinois State University, Normal, IL

GREGORY SCHRAW, Professor, Department of Educational Psychology, University of Nevada—Las Vegas, Las Vegas, NV

GENE SCHWARTING, Associate Professor, Education Department, Fontbonne University, St. Louis, MO

TIMOTHY SHANAHAN, Professor of Urban Education, University of Illinois at Chicago, Chicago, IL

STEVEN R. SHAW, School Psychologist, The School District of Greenville County, Greenville, SC

EUGENE P. SHEEHAN, Dean, College of Education, University of Northern Colorado, Greeley, CO

CARL J. SHEPERIS, Assistant Professor of Counselor Education, Mississippi State University, Starkville, MS

JAMES W. SHERBON, Professor Emeritus of Music, School of Music, University of North Carolina at Greensboro, Greensboro, NC

MARK D. SHRIVER, Associate Professor, Pediatric Psychology, Munroe-Meyer Institute for Genetics and Rehabilitation, University of Nebraska Medical Center, Omaha, NE

JEANNE SIMENTAL, Doctoral Student, Counseling/Clinical/School Psychology, University of California—Santa Barbara, Santa Barbara, CA

DOROTHY M. SINGLETON, Associate Professor of Education, Winston-Salem State University, Winston-Salem, NC

CHRISTOPHER A. SINK, Professor and Chair, School Counseling and Psychology, Seattle Pacific University, Seattle, WA

JANET V. SMITH, Assistant Professor, Department of Psychology and Counseling, Pittsburg State University, Pittsburg, KS

JEFFREY K. SMITH, Professor of Educational Psychology, Rutgers, the State University of New Jersey, New Brunswick, NJ

LISA F. SMITH, Associate Professor, Psychology Department, Kean University, Union, NJ

KATHARINE A. SNYDER, Assistant Professor of Psychology, Methodist College, Fayetteville, NC

LOUISE M. SOARES, Professor of Educational Psychology, University of New Haven, West Haven, CT

ALICIA SOLIZ, Doctoral Student, Counseling/Clinical/School Psychology, University of California—Santa Barbara, Santa Barbara, CA

C. RUTH SOLOMON SCHERZER, Associate Professor, Département de psychologie, Université de Montréal, Montreal, Quebec, Canada

MICHAEL SPANGLER, Dean of Business & Technology, Highland Community College, Freeport, IL

LORAINE J. SPENCINER, Professor of Special Education, University of Maine at Farmington, Farmington, ME

RAYNE A. SPERLING, Assistant Professor of Educational Psychology, The Pennsylvania State University, University Park, PA

JACLYN B. SPITZER, Professor, Clinical Professor of Clinical Audiology and Speech Pathology in Otolaryngology/Head and Neck Surgery, Columbia University College of Physicians and Surgeons, New York, NY

STEPHANIE STEIN, Professor of Psychology, Central Washington University, Ellensburg, WA

WENDY J. STEINBERG, Assistant Professor of Psychology, Eastern University, St. Davids, PA

GABRIELLE STUTMAN, Private Practice, Westchester and Manhattan, NY

HOI K. SUEN, Professor of Educational Psychology, Pennsylvania State University, University Park, PA

CAROLYN H. SUPPA, Associate Professor of Counseling, Marshall University, South Charleston, WV

ROSEMARY E. SUTTON, Professor, Department of Curriculum and Foundations, Cleveland State University, Cleveland, OH

SUSAN M. SWEARER, Associate Professor of School Psychology, University of Nebraska–Lincoln, Lincoln, NE

MARK E. SWERDLIK, Professor of Psychology, Illinois State University, Normal, IL

WENDI L. TAI, Doctoral Student, Counseling Psychology, Indiana University, Bloomington, IN

XUAN TAN, Research Associate, Department of Educational Psychology, University of Alberta, Edmonton, Alberta, Canada

BRUCE THOMPSON, Professor and Distinguished Research Fellow, Texas A&M University, College Station, TX, and Adjunct Professor of Family and Community Medicine, Baylor College of Medicine (Houston), Houston, TX

DONALD L. THOMPSON, Professor of Counseling and Psychology (Adjunct), Troy University—Montgomery, Montgomery, AL

NORA M. THOMPSON, Private Practice, Mountlake Terrace, WA

ROBERT M. THORNDIKE, Professor of Psychology, Western Washington University, Bellingham, WA

ROGER L. TOWNE, Associate Professor and Head, Department of Communication Disorders, Northern Michigan University, Marquette, MI

MICHAEL S. TREVISAN, Associate Professor, Department of Educational Leadership and Counseling Psychology, Washington State University, Pullman, WA

STEPHEN E. TROTTER, Associate Professor, Department of Psychology, Tennessee State University, Nashville, TN

SUSANA URBINA, Professor of Psychology, University of North Florida, Jacksonville, FL

JOHN J. VACCA, Assistant Professor of Individual and Family Studies, Developmental School Psychologist, University of Delaware, Middletown, DE

WILFRED G. VAN GORP, Professor of Clinical Psychology and Director, Neuropsychology, Columbia University College of Physicians & Surgeons, Department of Psychiatry, New York, NY

GABRIELLE VAN LINGEN, Visiting Associate Professor in School Psychology, University of the Virgin Islands, U.S. Virgin Islands

JOHN J. VENN, Professor, College of Education and Human Services, University of North Florida, Jacksonville, FL

DOLORES KLUPPEL VETTER, Professor Emeritus, University of Wisconsin—Madison, Madison, WI

CHOCKALINGAM VISWESVARAN, Associate Professor of Psychology, Florida International University, Miami, FL

METTA K. VOLKER-FRY, Graduate Student, School Psychology Department, University of Nebraska at Omaha, Omaha, NE

DELORES D. WALCOTT, Associate Professor, Counseling and Testing Center, Western Michigan University, Kalamazoo, MI

CINDY M. WALKER, Associate Professor of Educational Psychology, University of Wisconsin—Milwaukee, Milwaukee, WI

ANNITA MARIE WARD, Associate Professor of Education and TESL, Salem International University, Salem, WV

SANDRA A. WARD, Professor of Education, The College of William & Mary, Williamsburg, VA

T. STEUART WATSON, Professor and Chair of Educational Psychology, Miami University, Oxford, OH

SUSAN C. WHISTON, Professor, Counseling Psychology, Indiana University, Bloomington, IN

KEITH F. WIDAMAN, Professor of Psychology, University of California, Davis, CA

WILLIAM K. WILKINSON, Consulting Educational Psychologist, Boleybeg, Barna, Co. Galway, Republic of Ireland

JOHN T. WILLSE, Assistant Professor of Educational Research Methodology, University of North Carolina at Greensboro, Greensboro, NC

GREGORY C. WOCHOS, Doctoral Student in School Psychology, Programs in School Psychology, University of Northern Colorado, Greeley, CO

CLAUDIA R. WRIGHT, Professor, Educational Psychology, California State University, Long Beach, CA

GEORGETTE YETTER, Postgraduate Researcher, Gevirtz Graduate School of Education, Center for School-Based Youth Development, University of California—Santa Barbara, Santa Barbara, CA

JOHN W. YOUNG, Associate Professor of Educational Statistics and Measurement, Rutgers University, New Brunswick, NJ

SUZANNE YOUNG, Associate Professor of Educational Research, University of Wyoming, Laramie, WY

JAMES E. YSSELDYKE, Associate Dean for Research, College of Education and Human Development, University of Minnesota—Twin Cities, Minneapolis, MN

PETER ZACHAR, Associate Professor of Psychology, Auburn University—Montgomery, Montgomery, AL

BO ZHANG, Assistant Professor of Educational Psychology, University of Wisconsin—Milwaukee, Milwaukee, WI

INDEX OF TITLES

This title index lists all the tests included in The Sixteenth Mental Measurements Yearbook. *Citations are to test entry numbers, not to pages (e.g., 54 refers to test 54 and not page 54). Test numbers along with test titles are indicated in the running heads at the top of each page, whereas page numbers, used only in the Table of Contents but not in the indexes, appear at the bottom of each page. Superseded titles are listed with cross references to current titles, and alternative titles are also cross referenced.*

Some tests in this volume were previously listed in Tests in Print VI *(2002). An* (N) *appearing immediately after a test number indicates that the test is a new, recently published test, and/or that it has not appeared before in any Buros Institute publication other than* Tests in Print VI. *An* (R) *indicates that the test has been revised or supplemented since last included in a Buros publication.*

INDEX OF ACRONYMS

This Index of Acronyms refers the reader to the appropriate test in The Sixteenth Mental Measurements Yearbook. *In some cases tests are better known by their acronyms than by their full titles, and this index can be of substantial help to the person who knows the former but not the latter. Acronyms are only listed if the author or publisher has made substantial use of the acronym in referring to the test, or if the test is widely known by the acronym. A few acronyms are registered trademarks (e.g., SAT); where this is known to us, only the test with the registered trademarks is referenced. There is some danger in the overuse of acronyms. However, this index, like all other indexes in this work, is provided to make the task of identifying a test as easy as possible. All numbers refer to test numbers, not page numbers.*

ABAS-Second Edition: Adaptive Behavior Assessment System,—Second Edition, 4
ACE 6–11: Assessment of Comprehension and Expression 6–11, 16
ACES: Academic Competence Evaluation Scales, 1
ADAS: Adolescent American Drug and Alcohol Survey with Prevention Planning Survey, 6
ADCQ: Alzheimer's Disease Caregiver's Questionnaire, 10
AMAS-A AMAS-C AMAS-E: The Adult Manifest Anxiety Scale, 7
APAT: Auditory Processing Abilities Test, 17
APSD: Antisocial Process Screening Device, 13
APT: Arabic Proficiency Test, 14
AQT: Alzheimer's Quick Test: Assessment of Parietal Function, 11
ARIZONA-3: Arizona Articulation Proficiency Scale, Third Revision, 15
ASEBA: Achenbach System of Empirically Based Assessment, 3CBCL/1 1/2-5
ASQ: Ages and Stages Questionnaires: A Parent-Completed, Child-Monitoring System, Second Edition, 8
ASQ-SE: Ages & Stages Questionnaires: Social-Emotional: A Parent-Completed, Child-Monitoring System for Social-Emotional Behaviors, 9

BAB, Form M: Ball Aptitude Battery, Form M, 19
BarOn EQ-i:S: BarOn Emotional Quotient Inventory: Short Development Edition, 20
BAS II: British Ability Scales: Second Edition, 37

BASLCUS: Customer Service Skills Test, 68
BDI-FastScreen: BDI-FastScreen for Medical Patients, 25
BDIS-2: Behavior Disorders Identification Scale—Second Edition, 26
BEAR: Basic Early Assessment of Reading, 23
Bender-Gestalt II: Bender Visual-Motor Gestalt Test, Second Edition, 30
BERS-2: Behavioral and Emotional Rating Scale, Second Edition, 29
BESI: Barrier to Employment Success Inventory, Second Edition, 22
BMCT: Bennett Mechanical Comprehension Test, Second Edition, 31
Boehm-3: Boehm Test of Basic Concepts—Third Edition, 34
BPVS-II: The British Picture Vocabulary Scale, Second Edition, 38
BRIEF-P™: Behavior Rating Inventory of Executive Function—Preschool Version, 27
BRIEF-SR: Behavior Rating Inventory of Executive Function—Self-Report Version, 28
BRSD: CERAD Behavior Rating Scale for Dementia, Second Edition, 44
BSRA: Bracken School Readiness Assessment, 36
BSTS: British Spelling Test Series, 39
BTSA: The Benziger Thinking Styles Assessment, 32
BUSAN: Business Analyst Skills Evaluation [One-Hour], 40

CLASSIFIED SUBJECT INDEX

The Classified Subject Index classifies all tests included in The Mental Measurements Yearbook *into 18 major categories: Achievement, Behavior Assessment, Developmental, Education, English and Language, Fine Arts, Foreign Languages, Intelligence and General Aptitude, Mathematics, Miscellaneous, Neuropsychological, Personality, Reading, Science, Sensory-Motor, Social Studies, Speech and Hearing, and Vocations. This Classified Subject Index for the tests reviewed in* The Sixteenth Mental Measurements Yearbook *includes tests in 17 of the 18 available categories. (The category of Social Studies has no representative tests in this volume.) Each category appears in alphabetical order and tests are ordered alphabetically within each category. Each test entry includes test title, population for which the test is intended, and the test entry number in* The Sixteenth Mental Measurements Yearbook. *All numbers refer to test numbers, not to page numbers. Brief suggestions for the use of this index are presented in the introduction and definitions of the categories are provided at the beginning of this index.*

Achievement

Tests that measure acquired knowledge across school subject content areas. Included here are test batteries that measure multiple content areas and individual subject areas not having separate classification categories. (Note: Some batteries include both achievement and aptitude subtests. Such batteries may be classified under the categories of either Achievement or Intelligence and Aptitude depending upon the principal content area.)

See also Fine Arts, Intelligence and General Aptitude, Mathematics, Reading, Science, and Social Studies.

Behavior Assessment

Tests that measure general or specific behavior within educational, vocational, community, or home settings. Included here are checklists, rating scales, and surveys that measure observer's interpretations of behavior in relation to adaptive or social skills, functional skills, and appropriateness or dysfunction within settings/situations.

Developmental

Tests that are designed to assess skills or emerging skills (such as number concepts, conservation, memory, fine motor, gross motor, communication, letter recognition, social competence) of young children (0-7 years) or tests which are designed to assess such skills in severely or profoundly disabled school-aged individuals. Included here are early screeners, developmental surveys/profiles, kindergarten or school readiness tests, early learning profiles, infant development scales, tests of play behavior, social acceptance/social skills; and preschool psychoeducational batteries. Content specific screeners, such as those assessing readiness, are classified by content area (e.g., Reading).

See also Neuropsychological and Sensory-Motor.

Education

General education-related tests, including measures of instructional/school environment, effective schools/teaching, study skills and strategies, learning styles and strategies, school attitudes, educational programs/curriculae, interest inventories, and educational leadership.

Specific content area tests (i.e., science, mathematics, social studies, etc.) are listed by their content area.

English and Language

Tests that measure skills in using or understanding the English language in spoken or written form. Included here are tests of language proficiency, applied literacy, language comprehension/development/proficiency, English skills/proficiency, communication skills, listening comprehension, linguistics, and receptive/expressive vocabulary. (Tests designed to measure the mechanics of speaking or communicating are classified under the category Speech and Hearing.)

Fine Arts

Tests that measure knowledge, skills, abilities, attitudes, and interests within the various areas of fine and performing arts. Included here are tests of aptitude, achievement, creativity/talent/giftedness specific to the Fine Arts area, and tests of aesthetic judgment.

Foreign Languages

Tests that measure competencies and readiness in reading, comprehending, and speaking a language other than English.

Intelligence and General Aptitude

Tests that measure general acquired knowledge, aptitudes, or cognitive ability and those that assess specific aspects of these general categories. Included here are tests of critical thinking skills, nonverbal/verbal reasoning, cognitive abilities/processing, learning potential/aptitude/efficiency, logical reasoning, abstract thinking, creative thinking/creativity; entrance exams and academic admissions tests.

Mathematics

Tests that measure competencies and attitudes in any of the various areas of mathematics (e.g., algebra, geometry, calculus) and those related to general mathematics achievement/proficiency. (Note: Included here are tests that assess personality or affective variables related to mathematics.)

Miscellaneous

Tests that cannot be sorted into any of the current MMY categories as listed and defined above. Included here are tests of handwriting, ethics and morality, religion, driving and safety, health and physical education, environment (e.g., classroom environment, family environment), custody decisions, substance abuse, and addictions. (See also Personality.)

Neuropsychological

Tests that measure neurological functioning or brain-behavior relationships either generally or in relation to specific areas of functioning. Included here are neuropsychological test batteries, questionnaires, and screening tests. Also included are tests that measure memory impairment, various disorders or decline associated with dementia, brain/head injury, visual attention, digit recognition, finger tapping, laterality, aphasia, and behavior (associated with organic brain dysfunction or brain injury).

See also Developmental, Intelligence and General Aptitude, Sensory-Motor, and Speech and Hearing.

Personality

Tests that measure individuals' ways of thinking, behaving, and functioning within family and society. Included here are projective and apperception tests, needs inventories, anxiety/depression scales; tests assessing substance use/abuse (or propensity for abuse), risk taking behavior, general mental health, emotional intelligence, self-image/-concept/-esteem, empathy, suicidal ideation, schizophrenia, depression/hopelessness, abuse, coping skills/stress, eating disorders, grief, decision-making, racial attitudes; general motivation, attributions, perceptions; adjustment, parenting styles, and marital issues/satisfaction.

For content-specific tests, see subject area categories (e.g., math efficacy instruments are located in Mathematics). Some areas, such as substance abuse, are cross-referenced with the Personality category.

Reading

Tests that measure competencies and attitudes within the broadly defined area of reading. Included here are reading inventories, tests of reading achievement and aptitude, reading readiness/early reading ability, reading comprehension, reading decoding, and oral reading. (Note: Included here are tests that assess personality or affective variables related to reading.)

Science

Tests that measure competencies and attitudes within any of the various areas of science (e.g., biology, chemistry, physics), and those related to general science achievement/proficiency. (Note: Included here are tests that assess personality or affective variables related to science.)

Sensory-Motor

Tests that are general or specific measures of any or all of the five senses and those that assess fine or gross motor skills. Included here are tests of manual dexterity, perceptual skills, visual-motor skills, perceptual-motor skills, movement and posture, laterality preference, sensory integration, motor development, color blindness/discrimination, visual perception/organization, and visual acuity. (Note: See also the categories Neuropsychological and Speech and Hearing.)

Social Studies

Tests that measure competencies and attitudes within the broadly defined area of social studies. In cluded here are tests related to economics, sociology, history, geography, and political science, and those related to general social studies achievement/proficiency. (Note: Also included here are tests that assess personality or affective variables related to social studies.)

Speech and Hearing

Tests that measure the mechanics of speaking or hearing the spoken word. Included here are tests of articulation, voice fluency, stuttering, speech sound perception/discrimination, auditory discrimination/comprehension, audiometry, deafness, and hearing loss/impairment. (Note: See Developmental, English and Language, Neuropsychological, and Sensory-Motor.)

Vocations

Tests that measure employee skills, behaviors, attitudes, values, and perceptions relative to jobs, employment, and the work place or organizational environment. Included here are tests of management skill/style/competence, leader behavior, careers (development, exploration, attitudes); job- or work-related selection/admission/entrance tests; tests of work adjustment, team or group processes/communication/effectiveness, employability, vocational/occupational interests, employee aptitudes/competencies, and organizational climate.

See also Intelligence and General Aptitude, and Personality and also specific content area categories (e.g., Mathematics, Reading).

ACHIEVEMENT

Academic Competence Evaluation Scales; Grades K–12, Grades 6–12, 2- or 4-year college; 1

Canadian Achievement Tests, Third Edition; Grades 1.6–postsecondary; 43

Iowa Tests of Educational Development, Forms A and B; Grades 9–12; 116

Kaufman Test of Educational Achievement—Second Edition, Comprehensive Form; Ages 4.6–25; 124

Metropolitan Achievement Tests, Eighth Edition; Grades K.0–12; 146

Multiple Assessment Series for the Primary Grades; Grades 1–3; 155

Personalized Achievement Summary System; Grades 3–8; 185

Quest, Second Edition; Ages 6 to 8; 205

Stanford Achievement Test, Tenth Edition; Grades K.0–12.9; 232

TerraNova, The Second Edition; Grades K–12; 245

Wide Range Achievement Test—Expanded Edition; Grades 2–12; Ages 5–24; 272

BEHAVIOR ASSESSMENT

Achenbach System of Empirically Based Assessment; Ages 18 months to 90+ years; 3

Adaptive Behavior Assessment System,—Second Edition; Birth to 89 years; 4

Behavior Disorders Identification Scale—Second Edition; Ages 4.5-21; 26

Behavior Rating Inventory of Executive Function—Preschool Version; Ages 2-0 to 5-11; 27

Behavior Rating Inventory of Executive Function—Self-Report Version; Ages 11–18; 28

Behavioral and Emotional Rating Scale, Second Edition; Ages 5-0 to 18-11; 29

CERAD Behavior Rating Scale for Dementia, Second Edition; Adults who have, or are suspected to have, acquired cognitive deficits; 44

Child Symptom Inventory-4 [2002 Update]; Ages 5–12; 46

Clinical Assessment of Behavior; Ages 2–18; 52

College ADHD Response Evaluation; College students, Parents of college students; 57

Conduct Disorder Scale; Ages 5–22 years; 64

Conners' Adult ADHD Diagnostic Interview for DSM-IV; Age 18 and older; 66

Conners' Kiddie Continuous Performance Test; Age 4–5; 67

Devereux Early Childhood Assessment—Clinical Form; Ages 2:0–5:11; 71

Emotional and Behavior Problem Scale—Second Edition; Ages 5–18; 83

Emotional or Behavior Disorder Scale—Revised; Ages 5–18; 85

Functional Assessment and Intervention System: Improving School Behavior; Early childhood through high school; 93

DEVELOPMENTAL

EDUCATION

ENGLISH AND LANGUAGE

FINE ARTS

FOREIGN LANGUAGES

INTELLIGENCE AND GENERAL APTITUDE

MATHEMATICS

MISCELLANEOUS

NEUROPSYCHOLOGICAL

PERSONALITY

READING

Group Reading Test II (6-14); Ages 6 years to 15 years 9 months; 98

LARR Test of Emergent Literacy; Students entering school; 133

Martin and Pratt Nonword Reading Test; Ages 6–16; 139

Neale Analysis of Reading Ability: Second Revised British Edition; 6-0 to 12-11; 161

Phonics-Based Reading Test; Ages 6-0 to 12-11; 187

Process Assessment of the Learner: Test Battery for Reading and Writing; Grades K–6; 199

Reading Style Inventory 2000; Grade 1 to adults; 207

Signposts Early Assessment System; Grades K–3.5; 224

Spanish Reading Inventory; Grades 1–4+; 230

Suffolk Reading Scale 2; Ages 6.0 to 14.11; 237

Test of Silent Word Reading Fluency; Ages 6-6 to 17-11; 251

Wechsler Objective Reading Dimensions; Ages 6 to 16-11; 266

Wide Range Achievement Test—Expanded Early Reading Assessment; Ages 4.6–7.11; 271

Word Identification and Spelling Test; Ages 7.0–18.11; 276

Wordchains: A Word Reading Test for All Ages; Ages 7 and over; 278

SCIENCE

Science Assessment Series 1 and 2; Ages 5–9, Ages 8–13; 219

SENSORY MOTOR

Adolescent/Adult Sensory Profile; Ages 11–65+; 5

Bender Visual-Motor Gestalt Test, Second Edition; Ages 4–85+; 30

Developmental Test of Visual Perception—Adolescent and Adult; Ages 11-0 to 74-11 years; 70

Kent Visual Perceptual Test; Ages 5–11; 126

Motor-Free Visual Perception Test, Third Edition; Ages 4–94; 152

Sensory Profile; Birth to 36 months, Ages 3–10, Ages 5-10; 220

Spatial Reasoning; Ages 5.4–15.5; 231

Swallowing Ability and Function Evaluation; Ages 30 and over; 240

SPEECH AND HEARING

Arizona Articulation Proficiency Scale, Third Revision; Ages 1-6 through 18-11 years; 15

Auditory Processing Abilities Test; Ages 5.0–12.11; 17

Clinical Evaluation of Language Fundamentals, Fourth Edition; Ages 5–21; 53

Khan-Lewis Phonological Analysis—Second Edition; Ages 2-0 to 21-11; 127

Preschool and Primary Inventory of Phonological Awareness; Ages 3 to 6-11; 195

Receptive-Expressive Emergent Language Test, Third Edition; Ages 0–36 months; 208

SCAN-C: Test for Auditory Processing Disorders in Children—Revised; Ages 5-0 to 11-11; 217

Structured Photographic Articulation Test II Featuring Dudsberry; Ages 3-0 through 9-11 years; 236

Test of Phonological Awareness in Spanish; Ages 4-0 to 10-11; 248

Test of Phonological Awareness—Second Edition: PLUS; Ages 5–8; 249

Test of Phonological Awareness Skills; Ages 5-0 to 10-11; 250

Verbal Motor Production Assessment for Children; Speech-disordered children ages 3–12; 257

Weidner-Fensch Speech Screening Test; Grades 1–3; 269

VOCATIONS

PUBLISHERS DIRECTORY
AND INDEX

This directory and index gives the names and test entry numbers of all publishers represented in The Sixteenth Mental Measurements Yearbook. *Current addresses are listed for all publishers for which this is known. This directory and index also provides telephone and FAX numbers and e-mail and Web addresses for those publishers who responded to our request for this information. Please note that all test numbers refer to test entry numbers, not page numbers. Publishers are an important source of information about catalogs, specimen sets, price changes, test revisions, and many other matters.*

AAMR American Association on Mental Retardation
444 North Capitol Street, NW, Suite 846
Washington, DC 20001-1512
Tests: 238

Academic Therapy Publications
20 Commercial Boulevard
Novato, CA 94949-6191
Telephone: 800-422-7249
FAX: 415-883-3720
E-mail: atp@aol.com
Web: www.atpub.com
Tests: 17, 88, 152, 187, 209, 291

AdvisorTeam, Inc.
340 Brannan Street, Suite 402
San Francisco, CA 94107-1891
Tests: 125

AGS Publishing
4201 Woodland Road
Circle Pines, MN 55014-1796
Telephone: 800-328-2560
FAX: 651-287-7221
E-mail: agsmail@agsnet
Web: www.agsnet.com
Tests: 103, 123, 124, 127, 141

Karl Albrecht International
3120 Old Bridgeport Way, #100
San Diego, CA 92111
Tests: 306, 309

American Psychiatric Publishing, Inc.
1000 Wilson Blvd., Suite #1825
Arlington, VA 22209
Telephone: 800-368-5777
FAX: 703-907-1091
E-mail: appi@psych.org
Web: www.appi.org
Tests: 314

ASEBA Research Center for Children, Youth, and
    Families
1 South Prospect Street
Burlington, VT 05401-3456
Telephone: 802-656-8313
FAX: 802-656-2602
E-mail: mail@ASEBA.org
Web: www.ASEBA.org
Tests: 3

Assessment-Intervention Resources
2285 Elysium Avenue
Eugene, OR 97401-4903
Telephone: 541-338-8736
FAX: 541-338-8736
E-mail: kmerrell@oregon.uoregon.edu
Web: www.assessment-intervention.com
Tests: 107, 218

Australian Council for Educational Research Ltd.
19 Prospect Hill Road
Camberwell, Melbourne,
Victoria 3124
Australia
Telephone: +61 3 8266 5555
FAX: +61 3 9277 5500
E-mail: sales@acer.edu.au
Web: www.acer.edu.au
Tests: 109, 139

The Ball Foundation
800 Roosevelt Road
Building E, Suite 200
Glen Ellyn, IL 60137-5850
Telephone: 630-469-6270
FAX: 630-469-6279
E-mail: TESTINFO@BALLFOUNDATION.ORG
Web: www.ballfoundation.org
Tests: 19

Behavioral-Developmental Initiatives
14636 North 55th Street
Scottsdale, AZ 85254
Telephone: 800-405-2313
FAX: 602-494-2688
E-mail: BDI@TEMPERAMENT.COM
Web: www.b-di.com
Tests: 166

Brandt Management Group
OUT OF BUSINESS
Tests: 138

Brookes Publishing Co., Inc.
P.O. Box 10624
Baltimore, MD 21285-0624
Telephone: 800-638-3775
FAX: 410-337-8539
E-mail: custserv@brookespublishing.com
Web: www.brookespublishing.com
Tests: 8, 9, 60, 244, 286

Canadian Test Centre
Educational Assessment Services
85 Citizen Court, Suites 7 & 8
Markham, Ontario L6G 1A8
Canada
Tests: 43

CASAS
5151 Murphy Canyon Road, Suite 220
San Diego, CA 92123-4339
Telephone: 858-292-2900
FAX: 858-292-2910
E-mail: bwalsh@casas.org
Web: WWW.CASAS.ORG
Tests: 61

Center for Applications of Psychological Type
2815 Northwest 13th Street, Suite 401
Gainesville, FL 32609
Tests: 178, 180

Center for Applied Linguistics
4646 40th Street, NW
Washington, DC 20016-1859
Telephone: 202-362-0700
FAX: 202-363-7204
E-mail: store@cal.org
Web: www.cal.org
Tests: 14, 189

Center for Creative Leadership
One Leadership Place
P.O. Box 26300
Greensboro, NC 27438-6300
Telephone: 336-286-7210
FAX: 336-286-3999
Web: www.ccl.org
Tests: 119

CERAD Administrative Core
Box 3203
Duke University Medical Center
Durham, NC 27710
Telephone: 919-286-6406
FAX: 919-286-9219
E-mail: stric007@mc.duke.edu
Tests: 44

Change Companies
5221 Sigstrom Drive
Carson City, NV 89706
Tests: 193

Checkmate Plus, Ltd.
P.O. Box 696
Stony Brook, NY 11790-0696
Telephone: 800-779-4292
FAX: 631-360-3432
E-mail: info@checkmateplus.com
Web: www.checkmateplus.com
Tests: 46

CNS Vital Signs
1829 East Franklin Street, Bldg. 500
Chapel Hill, NC 27514
Tests: 54

Consulting Resource Group International, Inc.
#386 - 200 West Third Street
Sumas, WA 98295-8000
Tests: 134, 311

CPP, Inc.
3803 East Bayshore Road
Palo Alto, CA 94303
Telephone: 800-624-1765
FAX: 650-623-9273
E-mail: knw@cpp-db.com
Web: www.cpp-db.com
Tests: 140

Creative Learning Press, Inc.
P.O. Box 320
Mansfield Center, CT 06250
Tests: 302

CTB/McGraw-Hill
20 Ryan Ranch Road
Monterey, CA 93940-5703
Tests: 18, 92, 114, 245

Curriculum Associates, Inc.
153 Rangeway Road
North Billerica, MA 01862-0901
Telephone: 800-225-0248
FAX: 800-366-1158
E-mail: cainfo@curriculumassociates.com
Web: www.curriculumassociates.com
Tests: 288, 289

Denver Developmental Materials, Inc.
P.O. Box 371075
Denver, CO 80237-5075
Telephone: 800-419-4729
FAX: 303-355-5622
Tests: 292

EdITS/Educational and Industrial Testing Service
P.O. Box 7234
San Diego, CA 92167
Tests: 154

Educational Evaluations
Awre, Newnham,
Gloucestershire GL14 1ET
England
Telephone: 01594 510503
FAX: 01594 510503
Tests: 277

Educational Resources, Inc.
8910 West 62nd Terrace
P.O. Box 29160
Shawnee Mission, KS 66201
Telephone: 1-800-292-2273
FAX: 913-362-4627
E-mail: testing@eriworld.com
Web: www.eriworld.com
Tests: 105, 169

Educators Publishing Service, Inc.
P.O. Box 9031
Cambridge, MA 02139-9031
Telephone: 800-225-5750
FAX: 888-440-2665
E-mail: cpsbooks@epsbooks.com
Web: www.epsbooks.com
Tests: 239

English Language Institute
University of Michigan
401 East Liberty Street, Suite 350
Ann Arbor, MI 48104-2298
Telephone: 734-764-2416
FAX: 734-763-0369
E-mail: melabelium@umich.edu
Web: www.lsa.umich.edu/eli/
Tests: 148

GIA Publications, Inc.
7404 South Mason Avenue
Chicago, IL 60638
Telephone: 708-496-3800
FAX: 708-496-3828
E-mail: custserv@giamusic.com
Web: www.giamusic.com
Tests: 12, 157

Gordian Group
P.O. Box 1587
Hartsville, SC 29550
Tests: 76

Harcourt Assessment England
1 Procter Street
London WC1V 6EU
United Kingdom
Telephone: 020 7424 4262
FAX: 020 7424 4457
Web: www.tpc-international.com
Tests: 48, 79, 80, 97, 195, 196, 215, 235, 264, 265, 266,
280

Harcourt Assessment, Inc.
19500 Bulverde Road
San Antonio, TX 78259-3701
Telephone: 800-211-8378
FAX: 877-576-1816
Tests: 31, 146, 147, 149, 164, 165, 191, 198, 232

Hawthorne Educational Services, Inc.
800 Gray Oak Drive
Columbia, MO 65201
Telephone: 800-542-1673
FAX: 800-442-9509
E-mail: cs@hes-inc.com
Web: www.hes-inc.com
Tests: 26, 83, 85, 253

Hewitt Homeschooling Resources
P.O. Box 9
Washougal, WA 98684
Tests: 185

Hilson Research, Inc.
P.O. Box 150239
82-28 Abingdon Road
Kew Gardens, NY 11415-0239
Tests: 297, 298, 303

Hodder & Stoughton Educational
Hodder Headline PLC
338 Euston Road
London NW1 3BH
England
Telephone: 0207 873 6000
FAX: 0207 873 6299
E-mail: chas.knight@hodder.co.uk
Web: www.hoddertests.co.uk
Tests: 24

Hogrefe & Huber Publishers
875 Massachusetts Avenue
7th Floor
Cambridge, MA 02139
Telephone: 800-228-3749
FAX: 425-823-8324
E-mail: HH@HHPUB.COM
Web: WWW.HHPUB.COM
Tests: 117

The IDEA Center
211 South Seth Child Road
Manhattan, KS 66502-3089
Telephone: 800-255-2757
FAX: 785-532-5725
E-mail: IDEA@KSU.EDU
Web: WWW.IDEA.KSU.EDU
Tests: 299, 300

Indiana University Center for Postsecondary Research
  and Planning
1913 East 7th Street
Ashton-Aley Hall, Suite 102
Bloomington, IN 47405-7510
Telephone: 812-856-5824
FAX: 812-856-5150
E-mail: nsse@indiana.edu
Web: www.iub.edu/~cseq or www.iub.edu/~nsse
Tests: 58, 160

Inscape Publishing
6465 Wayzata Blvd., Suite 800
Minneapolis, MN 55426
Tests: 74, 75

Institute for Personality and Ability Testing, Inc. (IPAT)
P.O. Box 1188
Champaign, IL 61824-1188
Telephone: 217-352-4739
FAX: 217-352-9674
E-mail: custserv@ipat.com
Web: www.ipat.com
Tests: 84

The Institute of Conflict Analysis
Wilburton Inn
P.O. Box 468
Manchester Village, VT 05254
Tests: 65

International Personnel Management Association
1617 Duke Street
Alexandria, VA 22314
Tests: 304

Janelle Publications, Inc.
P.O. Box 811
1189 Twombley Road
DeKalb, IL 60115
Tests: 236

JIST Publishing, Inc.
8902 Otis Avenue
Indianapolis, IN 46216-1033
Telephone: 800-648-5478
FAX: 800-547-8329
E-mail: info@jist.com
Web: www.jist.com
Tests: 22, 99, 120, 172, 173, 285, 301, 307, 316

Kaplan Early Learning Company
1310 Lewisville-Clemmons Road
Lewisville, NC 27023-0609
Tests: 71, 136, 287

KBA, LLC
P.O. Box 3673
Carbondale, IL 62902
Tests: 32

Kendall/Hunt Publishing Company
4050 Westmark Drive
P.O. Box 1840
Dubuque, IA 52004-1840
Telephone: 800-228-0810
FAX: 800-772-9165
E-mail: orders@kendallhunt.com
Web: WWW.KENDALLHUNT.COM
Tests: 230

KIDS, Inc.
1156 Point Vista Road
Corinth, TX 76210
Tests: 129, 130

Maddak Inc.
6 Industrial Road
Pequannock, NJ 07440-1993
Tests: 252

Mind Garden, Inc.
1690 Woodside Road, Suite #202
Redwood City, CA 94061
Telephone: 650-261-3500
FAX: 650-261-3505
E-mail: info@mindgarden.com
Web: www.mindgarden.com
Tests: 45, 270

The Morrisby Organisation
83 High Street
Hemel Hempstead,
Hertfordshire HP1 3AH
England
Tests: 151

Multi-Health Systems, Inc.
P.O. Box 950
North Tonawanda, NY 14120-0950
Telephone: 416-424-1700
FAX: 416-424-1736
E-mail: CUSTOMERSERVICE@MHS.COM
Web: www.mhs.com
Tests: 13, 20, 21, 50, 66, 67, 90, 101, 102, 104, 110, 113, 118, 143, 144, 184, 204, 210, 227, 282, 293

National Reading Styles Institute, Inc.
P.O. Box 737
Syosset, NY 11791-0737
Tests: 207

NFER-Nelson Publishing Co., Ltd.
The Chiswick Centre/9th Floor
414 Chiswick High Road
London W4 5TF
England
Tests: 16, 37, 38, 39, 56, 78, 98, 112, 133, 137, 142, 145, 161, 167, 168, 201, 205, 219, 225, 228, 231, 237, 258, 278, 294, 296, 308, 315

Nichols & Molinder Assessments
437 Bowes Drive
Fircrest, WA 98466-7047
Tests: 153

Noel-Levitz
2101 ACT Circle
Iowa City, IA 52245-9581
Telephone: 319-337-4700
FAX: 319-337-5274
E-mail: info@noellevitz.com
Web: www.noellevitz.com
Tests: 59

Northwest Psychological Publishers, Inc.
P.O. Box 494958
Redding, CA 96049-4958
Tests: 312

Nova Media, Inc.
1724 N. State
Big Rapids, MI 49307-9073
Telephone: 231-796-4637
FAX: 231-796-4637
E-mail: trund@nov.com
Web: www.nov.com
Tests: 206

OQ Measures LLC
P.O. Box 521047
Salt Lake City, UT 84152-1047
Telephone: 1-888-647-2673
Tests: 176, 283

Ordinate Corporation
1040 Noel Drive, Suite 102
Menlo Park, CA 94025-3357
Tests: 177

Personal Strengths Publishing
P.O. Box 2605
Carlsbad, CA 92018-2605
Telephone: 800-624-7347
FAX: 760-602-0087
E-mail: mail@PersonalStrengths.com
Web: www.PersonalStrengths.com
Tests: 150, 295

Personalysis Corporation
5847 San Felipe, Suite 650
Houston, TX 77057-3008
Telephone: 713-784-4421
FAX: 713-784-9909
E-mail: info@personalysis.com
Web: www.personalysis.com
Tests: 186

PITS: Psychologische Instrumenten Tests en Services
Postbus 1084
2302 BB Leiden
The Netherlands
Tests: 261

PRO-ED
8700 Shoal Creek Blvd.
Austin, TX 78757-6897
Telephone: 800-897-3202
FAX: 512-451-8542
E-mail: proedrd2@aol.com
Web: WWW.PROEDINC.COM
Tests: 29, 62, 64, 70, 96, 132, 171, 194, 197, 208, 226,
    240, 246, 247, 248, 249, 250, 251, 255, 276

PsychCorp, A brand of Harcourt Assessment, Inc.
19500 Bulverde Road
San Antonio, TX 78259
Telephone: 800-211-8378
FAX: 800-232-1223
E-mail: customer_care@harcourt.com
Web: www.PsychCorp.com
Tests: 1, 4, 5, 11, 25, 33, 34, 35, 36, 41, 49, 53, 72, 77,
    81, 82, 93, 95, 121, 159, 162, 199, 212, 217, 220,
    257, 260, 262, 263, 267, 268

Psychological Assessment Resources, Inc.
16204 N. Florida Avenue
Lutz, FL 33549-8119
Telephone: 800-331-8378
FAX: 800-727-9329
E-mail: custsupp@parinc.com
Web: www.parinc.com
Tests: 10, 27, 28, 47, 52, 57, 87, 108, 126, 156, 163,
    211, 213, 214, 243, 271, 272, 273, 274

Psychological Publications, Inc.
P.O. Box 3577
Thousand Oaks, CA 91359-0577
Telephone: 800-345-8378
FAX: 805-527-9266
E-mail: TJTA@aol.com
Web: www.TJTA.com
Tests: 241

Psychological Services, Inc.
100 West Broadway, Suite #1100
Glendale, CA 91210
Telephone: 818-244-0033
FAX: 818-247-7223
Web: www.psionline.com
Tests: 259

Psychometric Affiliates
P.O. Box 807
Murfreesboro, TN 37133-0807
Telephone: 615-890-6296
FAX: 615-890-6296
E-mail: jheritage@a1.mtsu.edu
Tests: 269

Psychometrics Canada Ltd.
7125 - 77 Avenue
Edmonton, Alberta T6B 0B5
Canada
Telephone: 1-800-661-5158
FAX: 780-469-2283
E-mail: info@psychometrics.com
Web: www.psychometrics.com
Tests: 111, 279

Renaissance Learning, Inc.
P.O. Box 8036
Wisconsin Rapids, WI 54495-8036
Telephone: 866-846-7323
FAX: 877-279-7642
E-mail: answers@renlearn.com
Web: www.renlearn.com
Tests: 234

Riverside Publishing
425 Spring Lake Drive
Itasca, IL 60143-2079
Telephone: 800-323-9540
FAX: 630-467-7192
Web: www.riversidepublishing.com
Tests: 23, 30, 55, 94, 115, 116, 155, 233, 275

Rocky Mountain Behavioral Science Institute, Inc.
419 Canyon Avenue, Suite 316
Fort Collins, CO 80521
Tests: 6

Rose Wolfe Family Partnership LLP
c/o Walden Personnel Performance, Inc.
4115 Sherbrooke, W — #100
Montreal, Quebec H3Z 1K9
Canada
Telephone: 514-989-9555
FAX: 514-989-9934
E-mail: tests@waldentesting.com
Web: www.waldentesting.com
Tests: 317

Scholastic Testing Service, Inc.
480 Meyer Road
Bensenville, IL 60106-1617
Telephone: 1-800-642-6787
FAX: 630-766-8054
E-mail: stesting@email.com
Web: www.ststesting.com
Tests: 128, 179

Sigma Assessment Systems, Inc.
511 Fort Street, Suite 435
P.O. Box 610984
Port Huron, MI 48061-0984
Telephone: 800-265-1285
FAX: 800-361-9411
E-mail: SIGMA@sigmaassessmentsystems.com
Web: www.sigmaassessmentsystems.com
Tests: 86, 135, 221, 222, 223

Silverwood Enterprises, LLC
P.O. Box 363
Sharon Center, OH 44273
Telephone: 330-239-1646
FAX: 330-239-0250
E-mail: silverasoc@aol.com
Tests: 106

Sopris West
4093 Specialty Place
Longmont, CO 80504-5400
Telephone: 800-547-6747
FAX: 303-776-5934
E-mail: WWW.SOPRISWEST.COM
Tests: 73

Stoelting Co.
620 Wheat Lane
Wood Dale, IL 60191
Telephone: 630-860-9700
FAX: 630-860-9775
E-mail: psychtests@stoeltingco.com
Web: www.stoeltingco.com/tests
Tests: 131, 229

Sue Teele & Associates
P.O. Box 7302
Redlands, CA 92373
Tests: 242

The Test Agency Limited
Cray House
Woodlands Road
Henley-on-Thames
Oxfordshire RG9 4AE
England
Telephone: 01491 413413
FAX: 01491 572249
E-mail: info@testagency.com
Web: www.testagency.com
Tests: 192

Touchstone Applied Science Associates (TASA), Inc.
4 Hardscrabble Heights
P.O. Box 382
Brewster, NY 10509-0382
Web: WWW.TASA.COM
Tests: 69, 224

U.S. Department of Labor
Division Chief for Evaluation and Skill Assessment
Office of Policy and Research
200 Constitution Avenue, NW
Washington, DC 20210
Tests: 174, 175

Valpar International Corporation
P.O. Box 5767
Tucson, AZ 85703-5767
Tests: 256

Variety Child Learning Center
47 Humphrey Drive
Syosset, NY 11791-4098
Telephone: 516-921-7171
FAX: 516-921-8130
E-mail: jfriedman@vclc.org
Web: www.vclc.org
Tests: 91

Walden Personnel Performance, Inc.
4115 Sherbrooke W, Suite #100
Montreal, Quebec H3Z 1K9
Canada
Telephone: 514-989-9555
FAX: 514-989-9934
E-mail: tests@waldentesting.com
Web: www.waldentesting.com
Tests: 2, 40, 42, 51, 63, 68, 170, 200, 202, 216, 284, 290, 305, 310, 313, 318

Western Psychological Services
12031 Wilshire Blvd.
Los Angeles, CA 90025-1251
Telephone: 310-478-2061
FAX: 310-478-7838
Web: www.wpspublish.com
Tests: 7, 15, 89, 122, 158, 182, 183, 188, 190, 203, 254

Wonderlic, Inc.
1795 N. Butterfield Road
Libertyville, IL 60048-1238
Tests: 181

World of Work, Inc.
410 West 1st Street, Suite #103
Tempe, AZ 85281-2574
Tests: 281

INDEX OF NAMES

This index indicates whether a citation refers to authorship of a test, a test review, or a reviewer's reference for a specific test. Numbers refer to test entries, not to pages. The abbreviations and numbers following the names may be interpreted as follows: "test, 73" indicates authorship of test 73; "rev, 86" indicates authorship of a review of test 86; "ref, 45" indicates a reference in one of the "Reviewer's References" sections for test 45. Reviewer names mentioned in cross references are also indexed.

Hajcak, G.: ref, 49
Haladyna, T. M.: rev, 232
Hall, C. W.: rev, 241
Hall, L. E.: ref, 84
Hall, L. G.: test, 100
Hall, P. K.: rev, 15
Halle, P. M.: ref, 254
Haller, R. M.: rev, 15
Halstead, W. C.: ref, 54
Hambleton, R. K.: rev, 1, 31, 146, 263; ref, 146, 209, 262
Hambrecht, M.: ref, 117
Hamilton, E. E.: ref, 186
Hamilton, S.: test, 176
Hamlett, C.: test, 77
Hammer, A. L.: test, 178
Hammill, D.: ref, 195
Hammill, D. D.: test, 152, 251; ref, 64, 70, 197, 248
Hancock, T. E.: rev, 207, 266
Hand, L.: ref, 15
Handley, R.: test, 21
Hanes, K. R.: rev, 54
Hanna, B.: ref, 190
Hanna, G. S.: rev, 69; ref, 69
Hanna, L. A.: rev, 116
Hanna, P. R.: rev, 232
Hansen, J. C.: ref, 103
Hanson, G.: rev, 191
Hanson, W. E.: rev, 176
Harcourt Assessment, Inc.: test, 232
Harcourt Educational Measurement: test, 147; ref, 34, 77
Harding, R. E.: rev, 32, 173
Hardman, M. L.: ref, 93
Hare, R.: ref, 282
Hare, R. D.: test, 13, 101, 102; ref, 13, 101
Hargrove, D. S.: rev, 140
Harmon, C.: test, 176
Harmon, L.: ref, 40
Harrington, T. F.: test, 103; ref, 103
Harris, D.: ref, 6
Harris, D. B.: test, 188
Harris, G. T.: ref, 50
Harris, W. G.: ref, 221
Harrison, K.: ref, 87
Harrison, P. L.: test, 4; rev, 85; ref, 85, 91
Harrison, W.: ref, 214
Harsh, C. M.: rev, 31
Hart, B.: ref, 247
Hartell, C. E. J.: ref, 143
Harwell, M.: ref, 147
Harwell, M. R.: rev, 146
Hasbrouck, J. E.: test, 248; ref, 237
Hassenstab, J.: rev, 163, 214
Hastings, J. T.: rev, 232
Hatfield, D.: test, 176
Hathaway, S. R.: ref, 122, 154, 184
Hattie, J.: rev, 43, 52, 283

Havighurst, R. J.: ref, 122
Hawkins, J.: rev, 196
Haworth, M. R.: rev, 233
Haxby, J. V.: ref, 11
Hayden, D.: test, 257
Hayek, J. C.: test, 160
Hayes, T. L.: rev, 42, 210; ref, 210
Haynes, S. D.: rev, 184, 273
Haynes, W. O.: rev, 197
Hazler, R. I.: ref, 270
Healthcare Testing, Inc.: test, 106
Heaton, R. K.: ref, 252
Hegarty, M.: ref, 31
Hegedus, A. M.: ref, 76
Heinsman, D. T.: ref, 199
Helmes, E.: ref, 241
Helwig, A. A.: ref, 120
Henderson, A.: test, 205
Henley, G. A.: ref, 182
Henly, G. A.: ref, 173, 175
Hennen, M. E.: rev, 222
Hennessey, J. J.: rev, 6, 25
Henning-Stout, M.: rev, 134; ref, 134
Heppner, P. P.: ref, 227
Herman, D. O.: rev, 253; ref, 253
Hermelin, B.: ref, 161
Hermon, D. A.: ref, 270
Herold, E. S.: rev, 229
Herrick, V. E.: rev, 232
Herron, S. R.: test, 62
Hersen, M.: ref, 282
Hertzig, M.: ref, 166
Herzberg, D. S.: test, 188
Hesketh, A.: test, 16
Hess, A. K.: rev, 117, 242
Hesse, K.: test, 24
Hewitt Research Foundation: test, 185
Hibbard, K. M.: test, 214
Hicks, J. S.: test, 91
Hieronymus, A. N.: ref, 77
Hill, N. L.: ref, 13
Hiltonsmith, R. W.: rev, 37, 93
Hoag, M. J.: test, 283
Hodgson, J. M.: rev, 70
Hoff, K. E.: rev, 46, 70
Hoffman, J. V.: ref, 92
Hoffmann, N. G.: test, 193; ref, 193
Hogan, T. P.: rev, 59, 224
Hoge, R. D.: test, 282
Hoien, T.: ref, 195
Holcom, M. L.: test, 259
Holland, J.: ref, 172, 174
Holland, J. L.: ref, 103, 274
Holland, P. W.: ref, 233, 262
Holligan, C.: ref, 133
Holmes, J. M.: ref, 32
Hooper, S. R.: test, 239; rev, 218; ref, 147

SCORE INDEX

This Score Index lists all the scores, in alphabetical order, for all the tests included in The Sixteenth Mental Measurements Yearbook. Because test scores can be regarded as operational definitions of the variable measured, sometimes the scores provide better leads to what a test actually measures than the test title or other available information. The Score Index is very detailed, and the reader should keep in mind that a given variable (or concept) of interest may be defined in several different ways. Thus the reader should look up these several possible alternative definitions before drawing final conclusions about whether tests measuring a particular variable of interest can be located in this volume. If the kind of score sought is located in a particular test or tests, the reader should then read the test descriptive information carefully to determine whether the test(s) in which the score is found is (are) consistent with reader purpose. Used wisely, the Score Index can be another useful resource in locating the right score in the right test. As usual, all numbers in the index are test numbers, not page numbers.

Abilities: 100, 103
Abstract Thinking: 181
Abstractions: 281
Abuse: 214
Academic: 105, 169
Academic Ability: 95
Academic Assistance: 59
Academic Behavior: 218
Academic Confidence: 59
Academic Enablers: 1
Academic Motivation: 59
Academic Performance: 3
Academic Progress: 85
Academic Skills: 1
Acceptance of Authority: 128
Accommodate: 106
Accommodating: 171
Accuracy: 86, 161
Achievement: 173, 175, 279
Achievement and Motivation: 222
Achievement/Motivation: 135
Achievement Scales: 37
Achievement Striving: 181
Across-List Intrusions: 41
Act: 186
Active and Collaborative Learning: 160

Active-Social vs. Quiet: 241
Activities: 3
Activities of Daily living: 214
Activity: 166
AD/HD Combined: 46
AD/HD Hyper-Impulsive: 46
AD/HD Inattentive: 46
Adapt: 186
Adaptability: 20, 21, 166
Adaptable to Performing Under Specific Instructions: 281
Adaptable to Repetitive Work: 281
Adaptation to Fairy Tale Content: 90
Adaptive: 118
Adaptive Behaviors: 52
Adaptive Functioning: 9
Addition: 62, 205
Additional Questions: 58
Adjustment: 183, 279
Adult Motivated: 207
Advanced Calculations: 62
Adventurous: 184
Aesthetics-Arts: 100
Affect: 9
Affective: 101, 102
Affective Problems: 3
Affective Strength: 29